How to use your Connected Casebook

Step 1: Go to **www.CasebookConnect.com** and redeem your access code to get started.

Access Code:  CHEM66568173883

Step 2: Go to your **BOOKSHELF** and select your Connected Casebook to start reading, highlighting, and taking notes in the margins of your e-book.

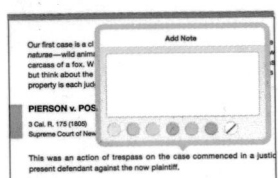

Step 3: Select the **STUDY** tab in your toolbar to access a variety of practice materials designed to help you master the course material. These materials may include explanations, videos, multiple-choice questions, flashcards, short answer, essays, and issue spotting.

Step 4: Select the **OUTLINE** tab in your toolbar to access chapter outlines that automatically incorporate your highlights and annotations from the e-book. Use the My Notes area for copying, pasting, and editing your book notes or creating new notes.

Step 5: If your professor has enrolled your class, you can select the **CLASS INSIGHTS** tab and compare your own study center results against the average of your classmates.

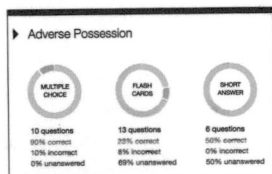

Is this a used casebook? Access code already scratched off?

You can purchase the Digital Version and still access all of the powerful tools listed above. Please visit CasebookConnect.com and select Catalog to learn more.

CRIMINAL PROCEDURE

ASPEN CASEBOOK SERIES

CRIMINAL PROCEDURE
Third Edition

Erwin Chemerinsky
Dean and Professor of Law
University of California, Berkeley School of Law

Laurie L. Levenson
Professor of Law, William M. Rains Fellow
and David W. Burcham Chair in Ethical Advocacy
Loyola Law School

Wolters Kluwer

Published by Wolters Kluwer in New York.

Wolters Kluwer Legal & Regulatory U.S. serves customers worldwide with CCH, Aspen Publishers, and Kluwer Law International products. (www.WKLegaledu.com)

To contact Customer Service, e-mail customer.service@wolterskluwer.com, call 1-800-234-1660, fax 1-800-901-9075, or mail correspondence to:

    Wolters Kluwer
    Attn: Order Department
    PO Box 990
    Frederick, MD 21705

Printed in the United States of America.

2 3 4 5 6 7 8 9 0

ISBN 978-1-4548-7665-6

Library of Congress Cataloging-in-Publication Data
Names: Chemerinsky, Erwin, author. | Levenson, Laurie L., 1956- author.
Title: Criminal procedure / Erwin Chemerinsky, Dean and Professor of Law,
   University of California, Berkeley School of Law; Laurie L. Levenson,
   Professor of Law, William M. Rains Fellow and David W. Burcham, Chair in
   Ethical Advocacy, Loyola Law School.
Description: Third edition. | New York : Wolters Kluwer Legal & Regulatory
   U.S., [2018] | Series: Aspen casebook series | Includes index.
Identifiers: LCCN 2017048930 | ISBN 9781454876656
Subjects: LCSH: Criminal procedure—United States. | Due process of
   law—United States. | LCGFT: Casebooks.
Classification: LCC KF9619 .C48 2018 | DDC 345.73/05—dc23
LC record available at https://lccn.loc.gov/2017048930

Certified Chain of Custody
Promoting Sustainable Forestry

www.sfiprogram.org
SFI-01681

SFI label applies to the text stock

About Wolters Kluwer Legal & Regulatory U.S.

Wolters Kluwer Legal & Regulatory U.S. delivers expert content and solutions in the areas of law, corporate compliance, health compliance, reimbursement, and legal education. Its practical solutions help customers successfully navigate the demands of a changing environment to drive their daily activities, enhance decision quality and inspire confident outcomes.

Serving customers worldwide, its legal and regulatory portfolio includes products under the Aspen Publishers, CCH Incorporated, Kluwer Law International, ftwilliam.com and MediRegs names. They are regarded as exceptional and trusted resources for general legal and practice-specific knowledge, compliance and risk management, dynamic workflow solutions, and expert commentary.

CHECK IN RECEIPT
0965 Suffolk University Store
12/16/2022 12:52:27 PM
09650000002230217947IN

ITEM	QTY	FEE

CRIMINAL PROCEDURE
P/9781454876656   [SURPLUS]
CHECKED IN   1   0.00

	QTY	TOTAL
TOTAL:	1	0.00

Patron Name: HANNAH CASEY
Patron ID: 14141419

Associate: 137875
Transaction Date: 12/16/2022

STORE COPY

For our families and for our students

SUMMARY OF CONTENTS

CONTENTS

xi

CHAPTER 3

THE EXCLUSIONARY RULE 451

CHAPTER 4

POLICE INTERROGATION AND THE PRIVILEGE AGAINST SELF-INCRIMINATION   547

CHAPTER 5

IDENTIFICATION PROCEDURES 751

CHAPTER 6

INITIATING PROSECUTION   801

CHAPTER 10

SPEEDY TRIAL RIGHTS   951

CHAPTER 11

CHAPTER 12

CHAPTER 13

SENTENCING   1149

CHAPTER 14

DOUBLE JEOPARDY   **1267**

CHAPTER 15

HABEAS CORPUS   **1305**

PREFACE

Our goal is to write the most student-friendly book we can to help teach students about the fascinating area of criminal procedure. Between us, we have over 50 years of experience in teaching in law schools. We have used many different casebooks in teaching criminal procedure and other subjects. We have consistently seen that students strongly prefer a casebook that presents the material in a clear and well-organized fashion and that does not hide the law. That is our goal for this book.

In aspiring to provide such a book, we have made several choices. First, the book focuses on the key cases regarding each issue of criminal procedure. To help students in understanding these cases and provide a context for understanding them, we include brief comments before and after the cases. We recognize that professors have different ways in which they like to discuss these cases. Therefore, rather than providing lengthy notes and questions after each case, we provide suggested discussion questions in our teacher's manual. This method has the benefit of not limiting professors in how they approach the discussion. Also, our experience is that students often find notes filled with rhetorical questions frustrating, and only occasionally do they reflect the questions that the instructor wants to raise.

Second, there are no long passages excerpting the scholarly literature. There is a rich scholarly literature concerning almost every aspect of criminal procedure. At many places, we provide brief essays that describe and cite to this literature. But we have eschewed providing long block quotes of this material and make no pretense of being comprehensive in summarizing the literature. Our goal is to provide a casebook, not a reference tool.

Third, we decided to include "practical" materials in a supplement rather than in the casebook. For example, we think it is useful for students in studying the Fourth Amendment to see a search warrant or in learning about the Fifth Amendment to see an indictment. We considered including these in the casebook but decided for reasons of length to place them in a separate supplement. We recognize that instructors vary as to how they wish to use this material, and having the materials in a supplement was the best solution. We also provide material using other media, such as PowerPoint slides, for professors who wish to use them.

Fourth, the major cases are presented in slightly longer form, with a bit less editing than in many other books. Criminal procedure, of course, is an area of constitutional law, and the law is very much the product of the Supreme Court's decisions. Lawyers practicing criminal law base their arguments on these decisions, and thus we believe that it is desirable to expose students to the cases in their fuller form. Space constraints required more editing than we would have liked, but we have done our best to present the cases in as accurate and full a form as possible.

We do not indicate deletions of material in the cases by ellipses. Our experience is that the necessary frequent use of ellipses is distracting and does not provide useful information to the students. On the other hand, any addition, however small, is indicated by brackets.

Finally, our goal is to be comprehensive on criminal procedure. We cover everything from investigation through habeas corpus. We have organized the book roughly along the chronology of a criminal case. Chapter 1 is an introduction and includes an overview of the stages of the criminal justice system. Subsequent chapters examine each step of criminal proceedings, beginning in Chapter 2 with search and seizure and concluding in Chapter 15 with habeas corpus. We were careful in writing the book to be sure that each chapter is independent so that professors can cover the material in any order and use those chapters that fit their curriculum.

Criminal procedure, of course, is an area in which there are constantly new developments. We are grateful to all who sent us comments on the first edition. We plan to provide an annual supplement and write new editions of this book about every four years. We, of course, continue to welcome comments and suggestions from faculty and students who use it. Our goal is to provide the best possible teaching tool for criminal procedure, and we very much would appreciate any ideas for how to better accomplish this objective.

Erwin Chemerinsky
Laurie L. Levenson

November 2017

ACKNOWLEDGMENTS

This book is the product of our having taught this material for many years. We are very grateful to our students, who have constantly challenged us to think about this material in new ways. It is to them that we dedicate this book. We also dedicate this book to our families, whose patience, support, and love made this book — and everything else we do — possible.

We are also very grateful to Marcy Strauss for her detailed comments on the first edition and to many users who sent us valuable suggestions. In addition, we thank the following sources for permission to reprint portions of their work:

Inmate Convicted of Indecent Exposure. Used with permission of The Associated Press. © 2007.

Judge Dismisses Molestation Case — Again. Copyright © 2008 The New Mexican, Inc. Reprinted with permission. All rights reserved.

Lawyer Disbarred over Lacrosse Rape Case. Used with permission of The Associated Press. © 2007.

Mandatory 55-Year Sentence "Extreme"? Reprinted with permission of the Salt Lake Tribune.

Right to a Speedy Trial? Justice Delayed. The Atlanta Journal-Constitution, Copyright © 2007.

State Loses Appeal in Child-Rape Case. Copyright © The Albuquerque Journal, Mountain View Telegraph. Reprinted with permission. Permission does not imply endorsement.

THE CONSTITUTION OF THE UNITED STATES

We the People of the United States, in Order to form a more perfect Union, establish Justice, insure domestic Tranquility, provide for the common defense, promote the general Welfare, and secure the Blessings of Liberty to ourselves and our Posterity, do ordain and establish this Constitution for the United States of America.

ARTICLE I

Section 1. All legislative Powers herein granted shall be vested in a Congress of the United States, which shall consist of a Senate and House of Representatives.

Section 2. [1] The House of Representatives shall be composed of Members chosen every second Year by the People of the several States, and the Electors in each State shall have the Qualifications requisite for Electors of the most numerous Branch of the State Legislature.

[2] No Person shall be a Representative who shall not have attained to the Age of twenty five Years, and been seven Years a Citizen of the United States, and who shall not, when elected, be an Inhabitant of that State in which he shall be chosen.

[3] Representatives and direct Taxes shall be apportioned among the several States which may be included within this Union, according to their respective Numbers, which shall be determined by adding to the whole Number of free Persons, including those bound to Service for a Term of Years, and excluding Indians not taxed, three fifths of all other Persons. The actual Enumeration shall be made within three Years after the first Meeting of the Congress of the United States, and within every subsequent Term of ten Years, in such Manner as they shall by Law direct. The Number of Representatives shall not exceed one for every thirty Thousand, but each State shall have at Least one Representative; and until such enumeration shall be made, the State of New Hampshire shall be entitled to chuse three, Massachusetts eight, Rhode Island and Providence Plantations one, Connecticut five, New York six, New Jersey four, Pennsylvania eight, Delaware one, Maryland six, Virginia ten, North Carolina five, South Carolina five, and Georgia three.

[4] When vacancies happen in the Representation from any State, the Executive Authority thereof shall issue Writs of Election to fill such Vacancies.

[5] The House of Representatives shall chuse their Speaker and other Officers; and shall have the sole Power of Impeachment.

Section 3. [1] The Senate of the United States shall be composed of two Senators from each State, chosen by the Legislature thereof, for six Years; and each Senator shall have one Vote.

[2] Immediately after they shall be assembled in Consequence of the first Election, they shall be divided as equally as may be into three Classes. The Seats of the Senators of the first Class shall be vacated at the Expiration of the second Year, of the second Class at the Expiration of the fourth Year, and of the third Class at the Expiration of the sixth Year, so that one third may be chosen every second Year; and if Vacancies happen by Resignation, or otherwise, during the Recess of the Legislature of any State, the Executive thereof may make temporary Appointments until the next Meeting of the Legislature, which shall then fill such Vacancies.

[3] No Person shall be a Senator who shall not have attained to the Age of thirty Years, and been nine Years a Citizen of the United States, and who shall not, when elected, be an Inhabitant of that State for which he shall be chosen.

[4] The Vice President of the United States shall be President of the Senate, but shall have no Vote, unless they be equally divided.

[5] The Senate shall chuse their other Officers, and also a President pro tempore, in the absence of the Vice President, or when he shall exercise the Office of President of the United States.

[6] The Senate shall have the sole Power to try all Impeachments. When sitting for that Purpose, they shall be on Oath or Affirmation. When the President of the United States is tried, the Chief Justice shall preside: And no Person shall be convicted without the Concurrence of two thirds of the Members present.

[7] Judgment in Cases of Impeachment shall not extend further than to removal from Office, and disqualification to hold and enjoy any Office of honor, Trust or Profit under the United States: but the Party convicted shall nevertheless be liable and subject to Indictment, Trial, Judgment and Punishment, according to Law.

Section 4. [1] The Times, Places and Manner of holding Elections for Senators and Representatives, shall be prescribed in each State by the Legislature thereof; but the Congress may at any time by Law make or alter such Regulations, except as to the Places of chusing Senators.

[2] The Congress shall assemble at least once in every Year, and such Meeting shall be on the first Monday in December, unless they shall by Law appoint a different Day.

Section 5. [1] Each House shall be the Judge of the Elections, Returns and Qualifications of its own Members, and a Majority of each shall constitute a Quorum to do Business; but a smaller Number may adjourn from day to day, and may be authorized to compel the Attendance of absent Members, in such Manner, and under such Penalties as each House may provide.

[2] Each House may determine the Rules of its Proceedings, punish its Members for disorderly Behaviour, and, with the Concurrence of two thirds, expel a Member.

[3] Each House shall keep a Journal of its Proceedings, and from time to time publish the same, excepting such Parts as may in their Judgment require Secrecy; and the Yeas and Nays of the Members of either House on any question shall, at the Desire of one fifth of those Present, be entered on the Journal.

[4] Neither House, during the Session of Congress, shall, without the Consent of the other, adjourn for more than three days, nor to any other Place than that in which the two Houses shall be sitting.

Section 6. [1] The Senators and Representatives shall receive a Compensation for their Services, to be ascertained by Law, and paid out of the Treasury of the United States. They shall in all Cases, except Treason, Felony and Breach of the Peace, be privileged from Arrest during their Attendance at the Session of their respective Houses, and in going to and returning from the same; and for any Speech or Debate in either House, they shall not be questioned in any other Place.

[2] No Senator or Representative shall, during the Time for which he was elected, be appointed to any civil Office under the Authority of the United States, which shall have been created, or the Emoluments whereof shall have been increased during such time; and no Person holding any Office under the United States, shall be a Member of either House during his Continuance in Office.

Section 7. [1] All Bills for raising Revenue shall originate in the House of Representatives; but the Senate may propose or concur with Amendments as on other Bills.

[2] Every Bill which shall have passed the House of Representatives and the Senate, shall, before it become a Law, be presented to the President of the United States; If he approve he shall sign it, but if not he shall return it, with his Objections to that House in which it shall have originated, who shall enter the Objections at large on their Journal, and proceed to reconsider it. If after such Reconsideration two thirds of that House shall agree to pass the Bill, it shall be sent, together with the Objections, to the other House, by which it shall likewise be reconsidered, and if approved by two thirds of that House, it shall become a Law. But in all such Cases the Votes of both Houses shall be determined by Yeas and Nays, and the Names of the Persons voting for and against the Bill shall be entered on the Journal of each House respectively. If any Bill shall not be returned by the President within ten Days (Sundays excepted) after it shall have been presented to him, the Same shall be a Law, in like Manner as if he had signed it, unless the Congress by their Adjournment prevent its Return, in which Case it shall not be a Law.

[3] Every Order, Resolution, or Vote to which the Concurrence of the Senate and House of Representatives may be necessary (except on a question of Adjournment) shall be presented to the President of the United States; and before the Same shall take Effect, shall be approved by him, or being disapproved by him, shall be repassed by two thirds of the Senate and House of Representatives, according to the Rules and Limitations prescribed in the Case of a Bill.

Section 8. [1] The Congress shall have Power To lay and collect Taxes, Duties, Imposts and Excises, to pay the Debts and provide for the common Defence and general Welfare of the United States; but all Duties, Imposts and Excises shall be uniform throughout the United States;

[2] To borrow money on the credit of the United States;

[3] To regulate Commerce with foreign Nations, and among the several States, and with the Indian Tribes;

[4] To establish an uniform Rule of Naturalization, and uniform Laws on the subject of Bankruptcies throughout the United States;

[5] To coin Money, regulate the Value thereof, and of foreign Coin, and fix the Standard of Weights and Measures;

[6] To provide for the Punishment of counterfeiting the Securities and current Coin of the United States;

[7] To establish Post Offices and post Roads;

[8] To promote the Progress of Science and useful Arts, by securing for limited Times to Authors and Inventors the exclusive Right to their respective Writings and Discoveries;

[9] To constitute Tribunals inferior to the supreme Court;

[10] To define and punish Piracies and Felonies committed on the high Seas, and Offences against the Law of Nations;

[11] To declare War, grant Letters of Marque and Reprisal, and make Rules concerning Captures on Land and Water;

[12] To raise and support Armies, but no Appropriation of Money to that Use shall be for a longer Term than two Years;

[13] To provide and maintain a Navy;

[14] To make Rules for the Government and Regulation of the land and naval Forces;

[15] To provide for calling forth the Militia to execute the Laws of the Union, suppress Insurrections and repel Invasions;

[16] To provide for organizing, arming, and disciplining, the Militia, and for governing such Part of them as may be employed in the Service of the United States, reserving to the States respectively, the Appointment of the Officers, and the Authority of training the Militia according to the discipline prescribed by Congress;

[17] To exercise exclusive Legislation in all Cases whatsoever, over such District (not exceeding ten Miles square) as may, by Cession of particular States, and the Acceptance of Congress, become the Seat of the Government of the United States, and to exercise like Authority over all Places purchased by the Consent of the Legislature of the State in which the Same shall be, for

the Erection of Forts, Magazines, Arsenals, dock-Yards, and other needful Buildings; — And

[18] To make all Laws which shall be necessary and proper for carrying into Execution the foregoing Powers, and all other Powers vested by this Constitution in the Government of the United States, or in any Department or Officer thereof.

Section 9. [1] The Migration or Importation of such Persons as any of the States now existing shall think proper to admit, shall not be prohibited by the Congress prior to the Year one thousand eight hundred and eight, but a Tax or duty may be imposed on such Importation, not exceeding ten dollars for each Person.

[2] The Privilege of the Writ of Habeas Corpus shall not be suspended, unless when in Cases of Rebellion or Invasion the public Safety may require it.

[3] No Bill of Attainder or ex post facto Law shall be passed.

[4] No Capitation, or other direct, Tax shall be laid, unless in Proportion to the Census or Enumeration herein before directed to be taken.

[5] No Tax or Duty shall be laid on Articles exported from any State.

[6] No Preference shall be given by any Regulation of Commerce or Revenue to the Ports of one State over those of another: nor shall Vessels bound to, or from, one State, be obliged to enter, clear, or pay Duties in another.

[7] No Money shall be drawn from the Treasury, but in Consequence of Appropriations made by Law; and a regular Statement and Account of the Receipts and Expenditures of all public Money shall be published from time to time.

[8] No Title of Nobility shall be granted by the United States: And no Person holding any Office of Profit or Trust under them, shall, without the Consent of the Congress, accept of any present, Emolument, Office, or Title, of any kind whatever, from any King, Prince, or foreign State.

Section 10. [1] No State shall enter into any Treaty, Alliance, or Confederation; grant Letters of Marque and Reprisal; coin Money; emit Bills of Credit; make any Thing but gold and silver Coin a Tender in Payment of Debts; pass any Bill of Attainder, ex post facto Law, or Law impairing the Obligation of Contracts, or grant any Title of Nobility.

[2] No State shall, without the Consent of the Congress, lay any Imposts or Duties on Imports or Exports, except what may be absolutely necessary for executing its inspection Laws: and the net Produce of all Duties and Imposts, laid by any State on Imports or Exports, shall be for the Use of the Treasury of the United States; and all such Laws shall be subject to the Revision and Controul of the Congress.

[3] No State shall, without the Consent of Congress, lay any Duty of Tonnage, keep Troops, or Ships of War in time of Peace, enter into any Agreement or Compact with another State, or with a foreign Power, or engage in War, unless actually invaded, or in such imminent Danger as will not admit of delay.

ARTICLE II

Section 1. [1] The executive Power shall be vested in a President of the United States of America. He shall hold his Office during the Term of four Years, and, together with the Vice President, chosen for the same Term, be elected, as follows:

[2] Each State shall appoint, in such Manner as the Legislature thereof may direct, a Number of Electors, equal to the whole Number of Senators and Representatives to which the State may be entitled in the Congress: but no Senator or Representative, or Person holding an Office of Trust or Profit under the United States, shall be appointed an Elector.

[3] The Electors shall meet in their respective States, and vote by Ballot for two Persons, of whom one at least shall not be an Inhabitant of the same State with themselves. And they shall make a List of all the Persons voted for, and of the Number of Votes for each; which List they shall sign and certify, and transmit sealed to the Seat of the Government of the United States, directed to the President of the Senate. The President of the Senate shall, in the Presence of the Senate and House of Representatives, open all the Certificates, and the Votes shall then be counted. The Person having the greatest Number of Votes shall be the President, if such Number be a Majority of the whole Number of Electors appointed; and if there be more than one who have such Majority, and have an equal Number of Votes, then the House of Representatives shall immediately chuse by Ballot one of them for President; and if no Person have a Majority, then from the five highest on the List the said House shall in like Manner chuse the President. But in chusing the President, the Votes shall be taken by States, the Representation from each State having one Vote; a quorum for this Purpose shall consist of a Member or Members from two thirds of the States, and a Majority of all the States shall be necessary to a Choice. In every Case, after the Choice of the President, the Person having the greatest Number of Votes of the Electors shall be the Vice President. But if there should remain two or more who have equal Votes, the Senate shall chuse from them by Ballot the Vice President.

[4] The Congress may determine the Time of chusing the Electors, and the Day on which they shall give their Votes; which Day shall be the same throughout the United States.

[5] No Person except a natural born Citizen, or a Citizen of the United States, at the time of the Adoption of this Constitution, shall be eligible to the Office of President; neither shall any Person be eligible to that Office who shall not have attained to the Age of thirty five Years, and been fourteen Years a Resident within the United States.

[6] In Case of the Removal of the President from Office, or of his Death, Resignation, or Inability to discharge the Powers and Duties of the said Office, the Same shall devolve on the Vice President, and the Congress may by Law provide for the Case of Removal, Death, Resignation or Inability, both of the President and Vice President, declaring what Officer shall then

act as President, and such Officer shall act accordingly, until the Disability be removed, or a President shall be elected.

[7] The President shall, at stated Times, receive for his Services, a Compensation, which shall neither be increased nor diminished during the Period for which he shall have been elected, and he shall not receive within that Period any other Emolument from the United States, or any of them.

[8] Before he enter on the Execution of his Office, he shall take the following Oath or Affirmation: "I do solemnly swear (or affirm) that I will faithfully execute the Office of President of the United States, and will to the best of my Ability, preserve, protect and defend the Constitution of the United States."

Section 2. [1] The President shall be Commander in Chief of the Army and Navy of the United States, and of the Militia of the several States, when called into the actual Service of the United States; he may require the Opinion, in writing, of the principal Officer in each of the executive Departments, upon any subject relating to the Duties of their respective Offices, and he shall have Power to grant Reprieves and Pardons for Offences against the United States, except in Cases of Impeachment.

[2] He shall have Power, by and with the Advice and Consent of the Senate, to make Treaties, provided two thirds of the Senators present concur; and he shall nominate, and by and with the Advice and Consent of the Senate, shall appoint Ambassadors, other public Ministers and Consuls, Judges of the supreme Court, and all other Officers of the United States, whose Appointments are not herein otherwise provided for, and which shall be established by Law: but the Congress may by Law vest the Appointment of such inferior Officers, as they think proper, in the President alone, in the Courts of Law, or in the Heads of Departments.

[3] The President shall have Power to fill up all Vacancies that may happen during the Recess of the Senate, by granting Commissions which shall expire at the End of their next Session.

Section 3. He shall from time to time give to the Congress Information of the State of the Union, and recommend to their Consideration such Measures as he shall judge necessary and expedient; he may, on extraordinary Occasions, convene both Houses, or either of them, and in Case of Disagreement between them, with Respect to the Time of Adjournment, he may adjourn them to such Time as he shall think proper; he shall receive Ambassadors and other public Ministers; he shall take Care that the Laws be faithfully executed, and shall Commission all the Officers of the United States.

Section 4. The President, Vice President and all civil Officers of the United States, shall be removed from Office on Impeachment for, and Conviction of, Treason, Bribery, or other high Crimes and Misdemeanors.

ARTICLE III

Section 1. The judicial Power of the United States shall be vested in one supreme Court, and in such inferior Courts as the Congress may from time to time ordain and establish. The Judges, both of the supreme and inferior Courts, shall hold their Offices during good Behaviour, and shall, at stated Times, receive for their Services a Compensation, which shall not be diminished during their Continuance in Office.

Section 2. [1] The Judicial Power shall extend to all Cases, in Law and Equity, arising under this Constitution, the Laws of the United States, and Treaties made, or which shall be made, under their Authority; — to all Cases affecting Ambassadors, other public Ministers and Consuls; — to all Cases of admiralty and maritime Jurisdiction; — to Controversies to which the United States shall be a Party; — to Controversies between two or more States; — between a State and Citizens of another State; — between Citizens of different States; — between Citizens of the same State claiming Lands under Grants of different States, and between a State, or the Citizens thereof, and foreign States, Citizens or Subjects.

[2] In all Cases affecting Ambassadors, other public Ministers and Consuls, and those in which a State shall be Party, the supreme Court shall have original Jurisdiction. In all the other Cases before mentioned, the supreme Court shall have appellate Jurisdiction, both as to Law and Fact, with such Exceptions, and under such Regulations as the Congress shall make.

[3] The Trial of all Crimes, except in Cases of Impeachment, shall be by Jury; and such Trial shall be held in the State where the said Crimes shall have been committed; but when not committed within any State, the Trial shall be at such Place or Places as the Congress may by Law have directed.

Section 3. [1] Treason against the United States, shall consist only in levying War against them, or in adhering to their Enemies, giving them Aid and Comfort. No Person shall be convicted of Treason unless on the Testimony of two Witnesses to the same overt Act, or on Confession in open Court.

[2] The Congress shall have Power to declare the Punishment of Treason, but no Attainder of Treason shall work Corruption of Blood, or Forfeiture except during the Life of the Person attainted.

ARTICLE IV

Section 1. Full Faith and Credit shall be given in each State to the public Acts, Records, and judicial Proceedings of every other State. And the Congress may by general Laws prescribe the Manner in which such Acts, Records and Proceedings shall be proved, and the Effect thereof.

Section 2. [1] The Citizens of each State shall be entitled to all Privileges and Immunities of Citizens in the several States.

[2] A Person charged in any State with Treason, Felony, or other Crime, who shall flee from Justice, and be found in another State, shall on demand of the executive Authority of the State from which he fled, be delivered up, to be removed to the State having Jurisdiction of the Crime.

[3] No Person held to Service or Labour in one State, under the Laws thereof, escaping into another, shall, in Consequence of any Law or

Regulation therein, be discharged from such Service or Labour, but shall be delivered up on Claim of the Party to whom such Service or Labour may be due.

Section 3. [1] New States may be admitted by the Congress into this Union; but no new State shall be formed or erected within the Jurisdiction of any other State; nor any State be formed by the Junction of two or more States, or Parts of States, without the Consent of the Legislatures of the States concerned as well as of the Congress.

[2] The Congress shall have Power to dispose of and make all needful Rules and Regulations respecting the Territory or other Property belonging to the United States; and nothing in this Constitution shall be so construed as to Prejudice any Claims of the United States, or of any particular State.

Section 4. The United States shall guarantee to every State in this Union a Republican Form of Government, and shall protect each of them against Invasion; and on Application of the Legislature, or of the Executive (when the Legislature cannot be convened) against domestic Violence.

ARTICLE V

The Congress, whenever two thirds of both Houses shall deem it necessary, shall propose Amendments to this Constitution, or, on the Application of the Legislatures of two thirds of the several States, shall call a Convention for proposing Amendments, which, in either Case, shall be valid to all Intents and Purposes, as Part of this Constitution, when ratified by the Legislatures of three fourths of the several States, or by Conventions in three fourths thereof, as the one or the other Mode of Ratification may be proposed by the Congress; Provided that no Amendment which may be made prior to the Year One thousand eight hundred and eight shall in any Manner affect the first and fourth Clauses in the Ninth Section of the first Article; and that no State, without its Consent, shall be deprived of its equal Suffrage in the Senate.

ARTICLE VI

[1] All Debts contracted and Engagements entered into, before the Adoption of this Constitution, shall be as valid against the United States under this Constitution, as under the Confederation.

[2] This Constitution, and the Laws of the United States which shall be made in Pursuance thereof; and all Treaties made, or which shall be made, under the Authority of the United States, shall be the supreme Law of the Land; and the Judges in every State shall be bound thereby, any Thing in the Constitution or Laws of any State to the Contrary notwithstanding.

[3] The Senators and Representatives before mentioned, and the Members of the several State Legislatures, and all executive and judicial Officers, both of the United States and of the several States, shall be bound by Oath or

Affirmation, to support this Constitution; but no religious Test shall ever be required as a Qualification to any Office or public Trust under the United States.

ARTICLE VII

The Ratification of the Conventions of nine States, shall be sufficient for the Establishment of this Constitution between the States so ratifying the Same.

Done in Convention by the Unanimous Consent of the States present the Seventeenth Day of September in the Year of our Lord one thousand seven hundred and Eighty seven and of the Independence of the United States of America the Twelfth.

ARTICLES IN ADDITION TO, AND AMENDMENT OF THE CONSTI-TUTION OF THE UNITED STATES OF AMERICA, PROPOSED BY CON-GRESS, AND RATIFIED BY THE LEGISLATURES OF THE SEVERAL STATES, PURSUANT TO THE FIFTH ARTICLE OF THE ORIGINAL CONSTITUTION.

AMENDMENT I [1791]

Congress shall make no law respecting an establishment of religion, or prohibiting the free exercise thereof; or abridging the freedom of speech, or of the press; or the right of the people peaceably to assemble, and to petition the Government for a redress of grievances.

AMENDMENT II [1791]

A well regulated Militia, being necessary to the security of a free State, the right of the people to keep and bear Arms, shall not be infringed.

AMENDMENT III [1791]

No Soldier shall, in time of peace be quartered in any house, without the consent of the Owner, nor in time of war, but in a manner to be pre-scribed by law.

AMENDMENT IV [1791]

The right of the people to be secure in their persons, houses, papers, and effects, against unreasonable searches and seizures, shall not be violated, and no Warrants shall issue, but upon probable cause, supported by Oath or affirmation, and particularly describing the place to be searched, and the persons or things to be seized.

AMENDMENT V [1791]

No person shall be held to answer for a capital, or otherwise infamous crime, unless on a presentment or indictment of a Grand Jury, except in cases arising in the land or naval forces, or in the Militia, when in actual service in time of War or public danger; nor shall any person be subject for the same offence to be twice put in jeopardy of life or limb; nor shall be compelled in any criminal case to be a witness against himself, nor be deprived of life, liberty, or property, without due process of law; nor shall private property be taken for public use, without just compensation.

AMENDMENT VI [1791]

In all criminal prosecutions, the accused shall enjoy the right to a speedy and public trial, by an impartial jury of the State and district wherein the crime shall have been committed, which district shall have been previously ascertained by law, and to be informed of the nature and cause of the accusation; to be confronted with the witnesses against him; to have compulsory process for obtaining witnesses in his favor, and to have the Assistance of Counsel for his defence.

AMENDMENT VII [1791]

In Suits at common law, where the value in controversy shall exceed twenty dollars, the right of trial by jury shall be preserved, and no fact tried by a jury, shall be otherwise reexamined in any Court of the United States, than according to the rules of the common law.

AMENDMENT VIII [1791]

Excessive bail shall not be required, nor excessive fines imposed, nor cruel and unusual punishments inflicted.

AMENDMENT IX [1791]

The enumeration in the Constitution, of certain rights, shall not be construed to deny or disparage others retained by the people.

AMENDMENT X [1791]

The powers not delegated to the United States by the Constitution, nor prohibited by it to the States, are reserved to the States respectively, or to the people.

AMENDMENT XI [1798]

The Judicial power of the United States shall not be construed to extend to any suit in law or equity, commenced or prosecuted against one of the United States by Citizens of another State, or by Citizens or Subjects of any Foreign State.

AMENDMENT XII [1804]

The Electors shall meet in their respective states and vote by ballot for President and Vice-President, one of whom, at least, shall not be an inhabitant of the same state with themselves; they shall name in their ballots the person voted for as President, and in distinct ballots the person voted for as Vice-President, and they shall make distinct lists of all persons voted for as President, and of all persons voted for as Vice-President, and of the number of votes for each, which lists they shall sign and certify, and transmit sealed to the seat of the government of the United States, directed to the President of the Senate; — The President of the Senate shall, in the presence of the Senate and House of Representatives, open all the certificates and the votes shall then be counted; — The person having the greatest number of votes for President, shall be the President, if such number be a majority of the whole number of Electors appointed; and if no person have such majority, then from the persons having the highest numbers not exceeding three on the list of those voted for as President, the House of Representatives shall choose immediately, by ballot, the President. But in choosing the President, the votes shall be taken by states, the representation from each state having one vote; a quorum for this purpose shall consist of a member or members from two-thirds of the states, and a majority of all the states shall be necessary to a choice. And if the House of Representatives shall not choose a President whenever the right of choice shall devolve upon them, before the fourth day of March next following, then the Vice-President shall act as President, as in case of the death or other constitutional disability of the President. — The person having the greatest number of votes as Vice-President, shall be the Vice-President, if such number be a majority of the whole number of Electors appointed, and if no person have a majority, then from the two highest numbers on the list, the Senate shall choose the Vice-President; a quorum for the purpose shall consist of two-thirds of the whole number of Senators, and a majority of the whole number shall be necessary to a choice. But no person constitutionally ineligible to the office of President shall be eligible to that of Vice-President of the United States.

AMENDMENT XIII [1865]

Section 1. Neither slavery nor involuntary servitude, except as a punishment for crime whereof the party shall have been duly convicted, shall exist within the United States, or any place subject to their jurisdiction.

Section 2. Congress shall have power to enforce this article by appropriate legislation.

AMENDMENT XIV [1868]

Section 1. All persons born or naturalized in the United States, and subject to the jurisdiction thereof, are citizens of the United States and of the State wherein they reside. No State shall make or enforce any law which shall abridge the privileges or immunities of citizens of the United States; nor shall any State deprive any person of life, liberty, or property, without due process of law; nor deny to any person within its jurisdiction the equal protection of the laws.

Section 2. Representatives shall be apportioned among the several States according to their respective numbers, counting the whole number of persons in each State, excluding Indians not taxed. But when the right to vote at any election for the choice of electors for President and Vice-President of the United States, Representatives in Congress, the Executive and Judicial officers of a State, or the members of the Legislature thereof, is denied to any of the male inhabitants of such State, being twenty-one years of age, and citizens of the United States, or in any way abridged, except for participation in rebellion, or other crime, the basis of representation therein shall be reduced in the proportion which the number of such male citizens shall bear to the whole number of male citizens twenty-one years of age in such State.

Section 3. No person shall be a Senator or Representative in Congress, or elector of President and Vice-President, or hold any office, civil or military, under the United States, or under any State, who, having previously taken an oath, as a member of Congress, or as an officer of the United States, or as a member of any State legislature, or as an executive or judicial officer of any State, to support the Constitution of the United States, shall have engaged in insurrection or rebellion against the same, or given aid or comfort to the enemies thereof. But Congress may by a vote of two-thirds of each House, remove such disability.

Section 4. The validity of the public debt of the United States, authorized by law, including debts incurred for payment of pensions and bounties for services in suppressing insurrection or rebellion, shall not be questioned.

But neither the United States nor any State shall assume or pay any debt or obligation incurred in aid of insurrection or rebellion against the United States, or any claim for the loss or emancipation of any slave; but all such debts, obligations and claims shall be held illegal and void.

Section 5. The Congress shall have the power to enforce, by appropriate legislation, the provisions of this article.

AMENDMENT XV [1870]

Section 1. The right of citizens of the United States to vote shall not be denied or abridged by the United States or by any State on account of race, color, or previous condition of servitude.

Section 2. The Congress shall have the power to enforce this article by appropriate legislation.

AMENDMENT XVI [1913]

The Congress shall have power to lay and collect taxes on incomes, from whatever source derived, without apportionment among the several States, and without regard to any census or enumeration.

AMENDMENT XVII [1913]

[1] The Senate of the United States shall be composed of two Senators from each State, elected by the people thereof, for six years; and each Senator shall have one vote. The electors in each State shall have the qualifications requisite for electors of the most numerous branch of the State legislatures.

[2] When vacancies happen in the representation of any State in the Senate, the executive authority of such State shall issue writs of election to fill such vacancies: *Provided,* That the legislature of any State may empower the executive thereof to make temporary appointments until the people fill the vacancies by election as the legislature may direct.

[3] This amendment shall not be so construed as to affect the election or term of any Senator chosen before it becomes valid as part of the Constitution.

AMENDMENT XVIII [1919]

Section 1. After one year from the ratification of this article the manufacture, sale, or transportation of intoxicating liquors within, the importation thereof into, or the exportation thereof from the United States and all territory subject to the jurisdiction thereof for beverage purposes is hereby prohibited.

Section 2. The Congress and the several States shall have concurrent power to enforce this article by appropriate legislation.

Section 3. This article shall be inoperative unless it shall have been ratified as an amendment to the Constitution by the legislatures of the several States, as provided in the Constitution, within seven years from the date of the submission hereof to the States by the Congress.

AMENDMENT XIX [1920]

[1] The right of citizens of the United States to vote shall not be denied or abridged by the United States or by any State on account of sex.

[2] Congress shall have power to enforce this article by appropriate legislation.

AMENDMENT XX [1933]

Section 1. The terms of the President and the Vice President shall end at noon on the 20th day of January, and the terms of Senators and Representatives at noon on the 3d day of January, of the years in which such terms would have ended if this article had not been ratified; and the terms of their successors shall then begin.

Section 2. The Congress shall assemble at least once in every year, and such meeting shall begin at noon on the 3d day of January, unless they shall by law appoint a different day.

Section 3. If, at the time fixed for the beginning of the term of the President, the President elect shall have died, the Vice President elect shall become President. If a President shall not have been chosen before the time fixed for the beginning of his term, or if the President elect shall have failed to qualify, then the Vice President elect shall act as President until a President shall have qualified; and the Congress may by law provide for the case wherein neither a President elect nor a Vice President shall have qualified, declaring who shall then act as President, or the manner in which one who is to act shall be selected, and such person shall act accordingly until a President or Vice President shall have qualified.

Section 4. The Congress may by law provide for the case of the death of any of the persons from whom the House of Representatives may chuse a President whenever the right of choice shall have devolved upon them, and for the case of the death of any of the persons from whom the Senate may choose a Vice President whenever the right of choice shall have devolved upon them.

Section 5. Sections 1 and 2 shall take effect on the 15th day of October following the ratification of this article.

Section 6. This article shall be inoperative unless it shall have been ratified as an amendment to the Constitution by the legislatures of three-fourths of the several States within seven years from the date of its submission.

AMENDMENT XXI [1933]

Section 1. The eighteenth article of amendment to the Constitution of the United States is hereby repealed.

Section 2. The transportation or importation into any State, Territory, or Possession of the United States for delivery or use therein of intoxicating liquors, in violation of the laws thereof, is hereby prohibited.

Section 3. This article shall be inoperative unless it shall have been ratified as an amendment to the Constitution by conventions in the several States, as provided in the Constitution, within seven years from the date of the submission hereof to the States by the Congress.

AMENDMENT XXII [1951]

Section 1. No person shall be elected to the office of the President more than twice, and no person who has held the office of President, or acted as President, for more than two years of a term to which some other person was elected President shall be elected to the office of President more than once. But this Article shall not apply to any person holding the office of President when this Article was proposed by Congress, and shall not prevent any person who may be holding the office of President, or acting as President, during the term within which this Article becomes operative from holding the office of President or acting as President during the remainder of such term.

Section 2. This article shall be inoperative unless it shall have been ratified as an amendment to the Constitution by the legislatures of three-fourths of the several States within seven years from the date of its submission to the States by the Congress.

AMENDMENT XXIII [1961]

Section 1. The District constituting the seat of Government of the United States shall appoint in such manner as Congress may direct: A number of electors of President and Vice President equal to the whole number of Senators and Representatives in Congress to which the District would be entitled if it were a State, but in no event more than the least populous State; they shall be in addition to those appointed by the States, but they shall be considered, for the purposes of the election of President and Vice President, to be electors appointed by a State; and they shall meet in the District and perform such duties as provided by the twelfth article of amendment.

Section 2. The Congress shall have power to enforce this article by appropriate legislation.

AMENDMENT XXIV [1964]

Section 1. The right of citizens of the United States to vote in any primary or other election for President or Vice President, for electors for President or Vice President, or for Senator or Representative in Congress, shall not be denied or abridged by the United States or any State by reason of failure to pay poll tax or other tax.

Section 2. The Congress shall have power to enforce this article by appropriate legislation.

AMENDMENT XXV [1967]

Section 1. In case of the removal of the President from office or of his death or resignation, the Vice President shall become President.

Section 2. Whenever there is a vacancy in the office of the Vice President, the President shall nominate a Vice President who shall take office upon confirmation by a majority vote of both Houses of Congress.

Section 3. Whenever the President transmits to the President pro tempore of the Senate and the Speaker of the House of Representatives his written declaration that he is unable to discharge the powers and duties of his office, and until he transmits to them a written declaration to the contrary, such powers and duties shall be discharged by the Vice President as Acting President.

Section 4. Whenever the Vice President and a majority of either the principal officers of the executive departments or of such other body as Congress may by law provide, transmit to the President pro tempore of the Senate and the Speaker of the House of Representatives their written declaration that the President is unable to discharge the powers and duties of his office, the Vice President shall immediately assume the powers and duties of the office as Acting President.

Thereafter, when the President transmits to the President pro tempore of the Senate and the Speaker of the House of Representatives his written declaration that no inability exists, he shall resume the powers and duties of his office unless the Vice President and a majority of either the principal officers of the executive department or of such other body as Congress may by law provide, transmit within four days to the President pro tempore of the Senate and the Speaker of the House of Representatives their written declaration that the President is unable to discharge the powers and duties of his office. Thereupon Congress shall decide the issue, assembling within forty-eight hours for that purpose if not in session. If the Congress, within twenty-one days after receipt of the latter written declaration, or, if Congress is not in session, within twenty-one days after Congress is required to assemble, determines by two-thirds vote of both Houses that the President is unable to discharge the powers and duties of his office, the Vice President shall continue to discharge the same as Acting President; otherwise, the President shall resume the powers and duties of his office.

AMENDMENT XXVI [1971]

Section 1. The right of citizens of the United States, who are eighteen years of age or older, to vote shall not be denied or abridged by the United States or by any State on account of age.

Section 2. The Congress shall have power to enforce this article by appropriate legislation.

AMENDMENT XXVII [1992]

No law, varying the compensation for the services of the Senators and Representatives, shall take effect, until an election of representatives shall have intervened.

CHAPTER 1

INTRODUCTION TO CRIMINAL PROCEDURE

Criminal procedure covers the rules and practices that govern the investigation and prosecution of criminal cases. "Investigatory criminal procedure" generally refers to the rules governing police conduct in investigating a case. These rules derive from the Fourth, Fifth, and Sixth Amendments to the United States Constitution. "Accusatory criminal procedure" generally refers to the rights of a defendant as a case proceeds through the criminal justice system. The rules governing this stage of the criminal process generally derive from the Fifth and Fourteenth Amendment rights to due process, the Sixth Amendment right to counsel and a speedy and public trial, the Eighth Amendment prohibition of excessive bail and double jeopardy, and the rules of procedure enacted by Congress or the states. Although federal constitutional rules govern these areas of criminal procedure, there are other laws that may control, including federal statutory laws, state constitutions, state laws, court rules of procedure, and ethical codes.

Section A of this introduction reviews the roles of the various participants in the criminal justice process. Section B provides an overview of how a case progresses through the criminal justice system. Section C then discusses why procedural rules are important, and section D sets forth the governing constitutional principles. Finally, section E discusses the applicability of constitutional rights to the states through the Incorporation Doctrine, with section F addressing the test for determining when new procedural rules are to be applied retroactively.

A. THE PARTICIPANTS IN THE CRIMINAL JUSTICE SYSTEM

Many types of individuals play a role in the criminal justice system. The rules of procedure constantly attempt to address the needs of each of these participants while also respecting the rights and interests of the others.

1

1. *Defendants*

All defendants have an interest in ensuring that their constitutional rights are respected, and that they have an opportunity to zealously contest the charges brought against them. To ensure that they receive fair trials, defendants will ordinarily be represented by defense counsel — either retained or appointed by the court (see Chapter 11). Moreover, although some refer to the adversarial system as a "search for the truth," criminal defendants' main interest and goal is to avoid conviction.

2. *Defense Counsel*

Defense counsel represents defendants in criminal actions. Unlike prosecutors, who must serve the "interests of justice" regardless of whether doing so entails convicting or acquitting a defendant, "[t]he basic duty defense counsel owe[] to the administration of justice and as . . . officer[s] of the court is to serve as [defendants'] counselor[s] and advocate[s] with courage and devotion and to render effective, quality representation." ABA Standards Relating to the Administration of Criminal Justice, Defense Standard 4-1.2(b).

Many defendants cannot afford a lawyer, yet a lawyer is critical to having a fair adversarial process. Accordingly, the Supreme Court has recognized a right to the assistance of counsel in all cases in which the defendant faces incarceration. The right to counsel and the standards for effective assistance of counsel are discussed in Chapters 5 and 11.

3. *Prosecutors*

Currently, prosecutors file over 10 million criminal cases annually in the United States.[1] Prosecutors represent the community in criminal actions. Federal prosecutors represent the United States and are assigned by either the local U.S. Attorney's Office or the Department of Justice. City attorneys, district attorneys, and county prosecutors represent local jurisdictions; the state attorney general represents the state at large. Unlike U.S. Attorneys, most states' prosecutors are elected officials.

The prosecutor has a unique role in the criminal justice system. "The prosecutor is an administrator of justice, an advocate, and an officer of the court. . . . The duty of the prosecutor is to seek justice, not merely to convict." ABA Standards Relating to the Administration of Criminal Justice, Prosecution Standard 3-1.2(b)–(c).

---

1. For more information regarding criminal caseloads in state courts, *see* National Center for State Courts, *Examining the Work of State Courts: An Overview of 2015 State Court Caseloads*, http://www.courtstatistics.org/~/media/microsites/files/csp/ewsc%202015.ashx.

Prosecutors enjoy great discretion in the exercise of their duties. As discussed in Chapter 6, prosecutors can decide which cases and defendants to charge, what charges to bring, and how serious a sentence to seek.

If a case goes to trial, the prosecutor has a duty to represent the government in those prosecutions. Moreover, during the investigative phase of trial, a prosecutor may also be responsible for supervising the work of police and investigators. This duty may require the prosecutor to prepare search warrants, issue subpoenas, and supervise grand jury proceedings.

4.   Victims

Victims' interests are represented in criminal cases by the prosecutor. Prosecutors, not victims, decide which cases to charge, whether to plea bargain, trial strategies, and even sentencing recommendations. Criminal victims' roles are circumscribed. Some states have passed laws, or even constitutional amendments, that provide victims a limited right to observe criminal proceedings, *see, e.g.*, Ariz. Const. art. II, §2.1(3), and to speak at sentencing, *see, e.g.*, N.Y. Crim. Proc. Law §380.50(2) (McKinney 2007). However, because a crime is considered to be an offense against the entire community and not just individual victims, victims do not control the handling of criminal cases.

5.   Police and Other Law Enforcement Officers

Police officers are on the front line of the criminal justice system. They serve several purposes, from ensuring the public's safety to investigating allegations of crimes to apprehending individuals responsible for those crimes. Police officers, like prosecutors, wield an enormous amount of discretion. They make the initial decision of whether to investigate a case, and whether to arrest and charge an individual with an offense. Police officers make these decisions even though they are not ordinarily lawyers.

The focus of police officers is on the safety of the community. Although they may be aware of defendants' constitutional rights, the pressure on police officers to ensure community safety and their eagerness to secure convictions may lead to violation of these rights.

Investigative criminal procedure focuses on what procedures police may use when apprehending and investigating defendants. Specifically, it addresses the rules for searches, seizures, and interrogations of defendants.

There are many different types of law enforcement officers in the United States. Each jurisdiction is likely to have its own police force. Currently, there are over 18,000 law enforcement agencies in the United States, with over 15,000 of them consisting of municipal police departments. The primary federal law enforcement agencies include the Federal Bureau of Investigation (FBI), the Secret Service, the Drug Enforcement Administration (DEA), the Bureau of Alcohol, Tobacco and Firearms (ATF), the Bureau of Customs and Borders Prosecution (CBP), Immigration and Customs Enforcement (ICE), and the Securities and Exchange Commission (SEC).

6. Magistrates and Judges

Magistrates and judges are the neutral decision makers in the criminal justice system. One crucial aspect of their role is to ensure that defendants' constitutional rights are respected. Thus, in federal courts, magistrates determine whether search or arrest warrants should issue, whether there is sufficient evidence to hold an arrested defendant, and even whether bail should be granted. Both magistrates and judges may review police conduct to determine if evidence should be suppressed because of constitutional violations. Judges have the additional responsibility of supervising criminal trials. Magistrates and judges must perform their responsibilities both efficiently and fairly, and are often faced with huge dockets of cases to process through their courts.

The method of selecting judges and holding them accountable varies. In federal court, federal district court and federal court of appeals judges are appointed by the president and must be confirmed by the Senate; once confirmed, they serve for life unless they resign or are impeached and removed from office. Federal magistrate judges are appointed by the district courts and sit for eight-year terms. Many states elect their state court judges through many different types of election systems, and other states have appointed judges.

7. Jurors

There are two types of jurors in the criminal justice system: grand jurors and trial jurors. Grand jurors (discussed in Chapter 6) oversee investigations of cases and decide whether to return indictments against individuals for specific crimes. Trial jurors (discussed in Chapter 12), by contrast, are the fact-finders in most criminal trials. After listening to all of the evidence, they decide whether there is sufficient evidence to convict a defendant. To make this decision, trial jurors ordinarily have to make key credibility decisions in the case by deciding which side's witnesses to believe.

8. Corrections Officials

Once defendants are convicted, corrections officials have the responsibility of supervising defendants' incarceration or release on parole or probation.

Like police officers and prosecutors, corrections officials often have huge caseloads. In 2015, there were close to 5 million individuals on probation or parole in the United States.[2]

9. Public

The general public also has an interest in the criminal justice system. Indeed, one of the primary concerns for members of the public is their safety.[3] The public also has a financial interest in ensuring that cases are efficiently processed, and that government officials respect the constitutional rights of citizens. In a criminal prosecution, the prosecutor has the responsibility of representing the interests of the public. However, the legislature also represents the public by enacting the laws that, to a large extent, govern the prosecutor's and judge's authority.

10. Media

Finally, the media have an interest in covering criminal cases and serving as a check on government powers. However, the First Amendment rights and interests of the media easily come into conflict with a defendant's Sixth Amendment right to a fair trial. As discussed in Chapter 11, judges must ensure, to the greatest extent possible, that both the media's and defendants' constitutional rights are respected.

B.   STAGES OF THE CRIMINAL JUSTICE PROCESS

Before embarking on a detailed discussion of the rules governing criminal procedure, it is helpful to understand how a case proceeds through the criminal justice system. Although there may be slight variations in the process depending on the nature of a particular case and the jurisdiction in which it is adjudicated,[4] the typical route for criminal cases is as follows:

---

2. Bureau of Justice Statistics, *Probation and Parole in the United States, 2015, February 2017*, https://www.bjs.gov/content/pub/pdf/ppus15.pdf.

3. In 2016, 53 percent of Americans said that they worry a great deal about crime and violence. Source: "In U.S., Concern About Crime Climbs to 15-Year High," Alyssa Davis, April 6, 2016, http://www.gallup.com/poll/190475/americans-concern-crime-climbs-year-high.aspx?g_source=worry+about+crime&g_medium=search&g_campaign=tiles.

4. There are 52 different jurisdictions (each state, the District of Columbia, and federal prosecutions), each having its own rules of procedure.

1. Step 1: Pre-Arrest Investigation[5]

If a crime occurs, the police may have little time to investigate the case. When time is of the essence, police officers may have to make their own observations, or use the accounts of others at the scene, to gather the minimal amount of information necessary to execute an arrest. For these on-the-scene arrests, the majority of the investigation will occur after the suspect is already in custody. Such investigations may include witness and victim interviews, interrogations of the suspect, identification procedures, undercover follow-up investigations, searches, and issuance of evidence subpoenas. Close to 50 percent of all criminal cases are handled in this manner. Thus, police officers will often have only a few minutes to decide whether to arrest a suspect, and their ability to conduct a pre-arrest investigation will be greatly limited.

In the remainder of cases, however, a lengthy investigation will typically occur before a suspect is arrested. Police will use their investigative tools, such as search warrants, interviews, informants, and evidence collection, to seek formal charges against the suspect before they execute an arrest. A magistrate may then issue an arrest warrant, together with a formal complaint filed by the prosecution, or the prosecution will obtain an arrest warrant in conjunction with a grand jury indictment. When there has been a grand jury indictment, months or years of pre-arrest investigation may have occurred, including witnesses testifying before the grand jury.

2. Step 2: Arrest[6]

Police have enormous discretion to decide whether to arrest a suspect. When an arrest occurs, it may be with or without a warrant. Once a suspect is taken into custody, he begins his journey through the criminal justice process. If the police did not use an arrest warrant, they must file an affidavit with the court setting forth the probable cause for the arrest and getting a complaint to hold the defendant for further proceedings. Even if the police did use an arrest warrant, the defendant has the right to appear before a judge, be informed of his constitutional rights, be advised of the charges against him, and be assigned counsel.

For some minor offenses, a suspect may merely receive a citation and will not be formally arrested. A citation or summons requires that the suspect appear at a later date to answer the charges against him. Likewise, if a suspect is not a flight risk, an indictment may be issued along with a summons for the suspect to appear instead of an authorization for an arrest warrant.

If a suspect is arrested, he is taken to the police station for booking. Once his picture and background information is taken, the suspect is placed into a

---

5. For a detailed discussion of the rules governing pretrial investigations, see Chapters 2 through 5.

6. See Chapter 3.

holding facility. Depending on the offense, the suspect may be able to post bail based on an approved bail schedule. If the suspect posts bail, he will be ordered to appear in court on a specific date for further proceedings. If the suspect does not post bail, he will be held in jail until he is released by the court.

3. Step 3: Filing the Complaint[7]

For police to be able to hold a suspect after arrest, the prosecution must file charges. Once the prosecution does so, it takes over the decision-making process from the police, and has discretion as to which charges to file. If the suspect has not been indicted, the prosecutor will use a complaint to file initial charges against the suspect. The complaint must be supported by a showing of probable cause based on a sworn affidavit by law enforcement officers.

4. Step 4: Gerstein Review[8]

The magistrate judge must review the prosecution's complaint and supporting affidavit to determine whether there is probable cause supporting the initial charges against the defendant. This review is called a "*Gerstein* review" because it was first prescribed by the Supreme Court in Gerstein v. Pugh, 420 U.S. 103 (1975). The magistrate's review for probable cause is done ex parte and is based on the filings alone — no evidentiary hearing is required. Often, the court will conduct a *Gerstein* review at the time of the defendant's first appearance, as long as that first appearance occurs within 48 hours of the defendant's arrest, as required by the Supreme Court in County of Riverside v. McLaughlin, 500 U.S. 44 (1991).

5. Step 5: First Appearance/Arraignment on Complaint[9]

Once the prosecution files a complaint, the defendant is also entitled to appear before the court to be advised of the charges against him, have an opportunity to seek bail, and be advised of his right to retain counsel or to have counsel assigned. For example, Rule 5 of the Federal Rules of Criminal Procedure requires that arresting officers bring the accused before a magistrate judge "without unnecessary delay." Ordinarily, the first appearance, sometimes called an "initial arraignment" or "preliminary arraignment," depending on the jurisdiction, will occur within 48 hours of the defendant's arrest. This proceeding is usually a brief one and is merely a minimal check to ensure that a basis for the defendant's arrest exists.

---

7. See Chapter 6.
8. See Chapter 3.
9. See Chapter 3.

6. *Step 6: Grand Jury or Preliminary Hearing*[10]

Before a defendant is required to stand trial, there must be another screening of the cases that establishes the charges the defendant will face at trial. The Fifth Amendment promises that for all federal felonies, a defendant is entitled to grand jury indictment. With ancient roots in British common law, the grand jury serves as a screening process to formalize charges for trial. It serves as a minimum check on the prosecutor's decision to bring charges.

A federal grand jury consists of 23 members of the community who listen to evidence presented by the prosecution and decide whether there is probable cause to prosecute the defendant. There is no judge in the grand jury, nor is the defendant or defense counsel entitled to be present.

The prosecutor generally directs the grand jury operations. If there is probable cause, the grand jury issues an indictment, or "true bill." The indictment sets forth the charges the defendant will face at trial. If the grand jury does not want to indict, it issues a "no bill." Grand juries also have the power to investigate cases by calling witnesses or issuing subpoenas.

Although some states choose to use grand juries in felony prosecutions, they are not bound to do so by the Fifth Amendment. In addition, they need not use the same procedures as federal grand juries. Thus, unlike federal grand juries, some states may limit the type of evidence that grand juries may hear or give the defense a greater opportunity to present evidence to the grand jury. A detailed analysis of grand jury procedures is set forth in Chapter 6.

Another mechanism to screen cases before trial is the preliminary hearing. The Constitution does not require preliminary hearings, but a majority of jurisdictions use them to decide whether there is enough evidence to hold a defendant for trial and to settle on which charges the prosecution will bring. A preliminary hearing is very different from a grand jury proceeding. No jury is present during a preliminary hearing. The judge presiding over the hearing decides whether there is probable cause to "bind the case over" for trial. Although procedures can differ by jurisdiction, both sides are generally given an opportunity to present evidence during the preliminary hearing. In some jurisdictions, hearsay evidence can be used to establish probable cause. As an adversarial process, both sides have an opportunity to cross-examine witnesses. The preliminary hearing gives the defendant a preview of the prosecution's case. If the prosecution does not establish probable cause for a particular charge, the court can reject that charge. If all charges are rejected, the court may order the case dismissed. If the defendant is bound over for trial, however, the court will replace the complaint with a formal information charging the defendant with the offenses he will face at trial. Preliminary hearings are also discussed in Chapter 6.

---

10. See Chapter 6.

7. Step 7: Arraignment on Indictment or Information

Once an indictment or information is filed, the defendant will appear for arraignment on those charges. At the arraignment, the defendant will typically be asked to enter a plea of guilty or not guilty, be advised of the charges against him, and be assigned counsel if counsel has not yet been assigned. The court will then assign a trial date. The trial date must comply with constitutional standards for a speedy trial (see Chapter 10) and any applicable Speedy Trial Acts.

8. Step 8: Discovery[11]

To prepare for trial, the parties will engage in discovery. Discovery is the process by which the parties seek to examine the evidence that the other party is likely to use at trial. Statutes and procedural rules often govern discovery. However, defendants also have a due process right to exculpatory evidence and evidence that may impeach the prosecution's witnesses (see Chapter 8).

In the federal system, discovery of witness statements is covered by separate statutes. In state courts, comprehensive discovery statutes often cover both inculpatory and exculpatory evidence, including witness statements.

9. Step 9: Pretrial Motions

Frequently, the parties will file pretrial motions regarding a variety of issues. The defense will seek to suppress evidence illegally obtained by the prosecution, move to change venue, and seek dismissal for speedy trial violations or problems with the charges. The prosecution will also have an opportunity to file pretrial motions. For example, the prosecution may file pretrial motions *in limine* to get pretrial rulings on key evidentiary issues in the case. Pretrial motions help the parties define the scope of their own cases, and to assess the relative strength of the other side's case.

10. Step 10: Plea Bargaining and Guilty Pleas[12]

More than 90 percent of all criminal cases never go to trial. Rather, the vast majority of cases — 97 percent in federal court and 94 percent in state courts — end with a guilty or *nolo contendere* (no contest) plea. During the plea bargaining process, prosecutors may choose to reduce the charges or sentence exposure for a defendant in exchange for the defendant's guilty

---

11. See Chapter 8.
12. See Chapter 9.

plea, and oftentimes, the defendant's cooperation. Anticipating that plea bargaining will occur, it is not unusual for prosecutors to load up charges against the defendant so that there is room to compromise during plea bargaining.

If a defendant decides to plead guilty, a formal hearing is held for the defendant to enter his plea. A guilty plea is both an admission that the defendant committed the crime, and a waiver of all of the rights the defendant would have had if he proceeded to trial. Thus, at a guilty plea hearing, the defendant will be advised of his right to counsel, right to confront witnesses, right to present evidence, right to a jury, and privilege against self-incrimination. If the defendant waives these rights, the court will ask for a factual basis for the plea. Either the prosecutor or the defense may provide the recitation necessary to establish that there is a basis for the plea. The court will also determine whether the plea is voluntary, and the nature of any inducements for the plea. Finally, the court will advise the defendant of the consequences of pleading guilty. If the defendant's guilty plea is knowing and voluntary, the court will accept the plea. The guilty plea obviates the need for a trial.

A defendant may also enter a *nolo contendere* plea. A *nolo contendere* plea has the same effect in the criminal case as a guilty plea. The defendant can receive the same criminal punishment as a defendant who enters a guilty plea. However, unlike a guilty plea, which serves as an admission for a civil case that the defendant is responsible, a *nolo contendere* plea has no impact on any companion civil case. Both guilty pleas and *nolo contendere* pleas are examined in Chapter 9.

11.   Step 11: Trial[13]

If a defendant does not plead guilty, the case proceeds to trial. A trial may be a court ("bench") trial or jury trial. If the case is going to be decided by a judge alone, both sides must agree to waive the right to jury trial. The judge will then hear the evidence adduced at trial, and decide whether there is proof beyond reasonable doubt for each of the charges.

The right to jury trial is guaranteed by the Sixth Amendment for all serious offenses, which the Supreme Court has defined as offenses that carry a possible sentence of more than six months in custody. Although there is a popular notion that 12 persons must sit on a jury, the Supreme Court has held to the contrary. States may choose to have juries as small as six persons for noncapital felony cases. Moreover, there is no constitutional requirement that the jurors' verdict be unanimous. Depending on the size of the jury, a nonunanimous jury may be sufficient.

___

13. See Chapter 11.

The jury selection process begins with a panel of jurors (called the "venire") being summoned for jury selection. Potential jurors are questioned in a process called "voir dire" to reveal their backgrounds, attitudes, and any possible biases they may hold. The parties can excuse jurors from the jury by using challenges for cause, or by exercising peremptory challenges. Challenges for cause are allegations that specific jurors cannot be fair. Each side has an unlimited number of challenges for cause. By contrast, each party will have a limited number of peremptory challenges. Peremptory challenges need not be supported by a showing of actual bias by the juror. Each side has wide discretion in exercising peremptory challenges, although it is improper to use them in a discriminatory manner. Once jurors are finally chosen to sit on a case, they are referred to as the "petit" jury.

It is the jury's job to listen to all of the evidence, consider the court's jury instructions, and decide whether the defendant is guilty beyond a reasonable doubt. If the jury is not able to reach a decision, it constitutes a hung jury, and the court will declare a mistrial. In general, the prosecution can retry a defendant following a hung jury.

12.   Step 12: Sentencing[14]

If the defendant is convicted, he will be sentenced by the court, ordinarily at a separate sentencing hearing. Before deciding on a sentence, the court will receive reports by the probation officer and input from the parties. At the sentencing hearing, the defendant has an opportunity to address the court. Sentencing systems vary greatly in the United States. In some jurisdictions, judges have broad discretion in imposing a sentence. In other jurisdictions, sentencing guidelines and mandatory sentences control a judge's sentence. If the judge's sentence must be based on specific factual findings other than a defendant's prior criminal record, the trier of fact must find the existence of those facts beyond a reasonable doubt if they will increase the defendant's sentence beyond the presumptive sentence for that crime.

13.   Step 13: Appeals and Habeas Corpus[15]

Finally, a defendant is entitled to challenge his conviction on direct appeal or through collateral proceedings known as habeas corpus proceedings. On direct appeal, the defendant may challenge errors by the court or prosecution at trial. A defendant has the right to an initial appeal to an intermediate court. Unless otherwise provided by statute, a defendant does not have the right to review by the state's high court. On appeal, the burden shifts to the

14. See Chapter 12.
15. See Chapter 15.

defendant to demonstrate why he did not receive a fair trial, or that there was insufficient evidence to support the jury's verdict.

After all direct appeals are completed, a defendant also may challenge constitutional violations in his case through a habeas corpus petition. These are sometimes called forms of "collateral review." Habeas corpus petitions are suits that allege that the defendant is being held unconstitutionally. Both state and federal courts have procedures for collateral review; in federal court it is via a petition for a writ of habeas corpus. One of the primary grounds for habeas corpus petitions is ineffective assistance of counsel. Fourth Amendment search and seizure issues are not sufficient bases for habeas corpus challenges. In a habeas corpus petition, the court may hold an evidentiary hearing to determine whether there has been a constitutional violation. However, most habeas petitions are decided without a hearing. Because habeas corpus petitions are considered civil proceedings, defendants are not constitutionally entitled to the assistance of counsel. Habeas corpus is discussed in Chapter 15.

If a defendant succeeds on appeal or with a habeas corpus petition, the ordinary remedy is a retrial. However, if the appellate court finds that there was insufficient evidence to support the verdict, the defendant may not be retried because of double jeopardy principles.

C. THE PURPOSE OF PROCEDURAL RULES

To understand why procedural rules are important, it is helpful to consider situations in which fair procedures are not afforded to defendants. In the infamous "Scottsboro trial," nine young black men were accused of raping two white women on a train from Chattanooga to Memphis, Tennessee. The train was intercepted as it traveled through Alabama, and the boys were captured and nearly lynched. There, they faced trial. Newspapers decried them as guilty, and all of the ugly traits of racism in the South in 1931 took hold. The defendants were brought to trial six days after they were indicted. The newspapers proclaimed them guilty of their "atrocious crime" even before the trial began. The judge perfunctorily appointed the entire local bar to represent the boys, although none of them investigated the case or assumed the role of zealous representatives of the defendants. The defendants were convicted and sentenced to death after a one-day trial before an all-white jury. During the trial, the credibility of the alleged victims was seriously impeached. Even though the victims, Victoria Price and Ruby Bates, were known prostitutes and transients, and Bates later recanted her testimony, it took years before the defendants' sentences were finally vacated.

As you read the Supreme Court's decision in their appeal, consider the importance of the rights to a fair trial, effective counsel, discovery, and due process. Consider also the role that race and economic status play in the criminal justice system.

POWELL v. ALABAMA
287 U.S. 45 (1932)

Justice SUTHERLAND delivered the opinion of the Court.

The petitioners, hereinafter referred to as defendants, are negroes charged with the crime of rape, committed upon the persons of two white girls. The crime is said to have been committed on March 25, 1931. The indictment was returned in a state court of first instance on March 31, and the record recites that on the same day the defendants were arraigned and entered pleas of not guilty. There is a further recital to the effect that upon the arraignment they were represented by counsel. But no counsel had been employed, and aside from a statement made by the trial judge several days later during a colloquy immediately preceding the trial, the record does not disclose when, or under what circumstances, an appointment of counsel was made, or who was appointed.

Each of the three trials was completed within a single day. Under the Alabama statute the punishment for rape is to be fixed by the jury, and in its discretion may be from ten years imprisonment to death. The juries found defendants guilty and imposed the death penalty upon all.

In this court the judgments are assailed upon the grounds that the defendants, and each of them, were denied due process of law and the equal protection of the laws, in contravention of the Fourteenth Amendment, specifically as follows: (1) they were not given a fair, impartial and deliberate trial; (2) they were denied the right of counsel, with the accustomed incidents of consultation and opportunity of preparation for trial; and (3) they were tried before juries from which qualified members of their own race were systematically excluded.

The only one of the assignments which we shall consider is the second, in respect of the denial of counsel; and it becomes unnecessary to discuss the facts of the case or the circumstances surrounding the prosecution except in so far as they reflect light upon that question.

The record shows that on the day when the offense is said to have been committed, these defendants, together with a number of other negroes, were upon a freight train on its way through Alabama. On the same train were seven white boys and the two white girls. A fight took place between the negroes and the white boys, in the course of which the white boys, with the exception of one named Gilley, were thrown off the train. A message was sent ahead, reporting the fight and asking that every negro be gotten off the train. The participants in the fight, and the two girls, were in an open gondola car. The two girls testified that each of them was assaulted by six different negroes in turn, and they identified the seven defendants as having been among the number. None of the white boys was called to testify, with the exception of Gilley, who was called in rebuttal.

Before the train reached Scottsboro, Alabama, a sheriff's posse seized the defendants and two other negroes. Both girls and the negroes then were taken to Scottsboro, the county seat. Word of their coming and of the alleged assault had preceded them, and they were met at Scottsboro by a large crowd. The sheriff thought it necessary to call for the militia to assist in safeguarding the prisoners. It is perfectly apparent that the proceedings, from beginning to end, took place in an atmosphere of tense, hostile and excited public sentiment. [T]he record clearly indicates that most, if not all, of them were youthful, and they are constantly referred to as "the boys." They were ignorant and illiterate. All of them were residents of other states, where alone members of their families or friends resided.

However guilty defendants, upon due inquiry, might prove to have been, they were, until convicted, presumed to be innocent. It was the duty of the court having their cases in charge to see that they were denied no necessary incident of a fair trial. With any error of the state court involving alleged contravention of the state statutes or constitution we, of course, have nothing to do. The sole inquiry which we are permitted to make is whether the federal Constitution was contravened and as to that, we confine our-selves, as already suggested, to the inquiry whether the defendants were in substance denied the right of counsel, and if so, whether such denial infringes the due process clause of the Fourteenth Amendment.

First. The record shows that immediately upon the return of the indict-ment defendants were arraigned and pleaded not guilty. Apparently they were not asked whether they had, or were able to employ, counsel, or wished to have counsel appointed; or whether they had friends or relatives who might assist in that regard if communicated with. "They were nonresidents," he said, "and had little time or opportunity to get in touch with their families and friends who were scattered throughout two other states, and time has demonstrated that they could or would have been represented by able counsel had a better opportunity been given by a reasonable delay in the trial of the cases. . . ."

April 6, six days after indictment, the trials began. When the first case was called, the court inquired whether the parties were ready for trial. The state's attorney replied that he was ready to proceed. No one answered for the defendants or appeared to represent or defend them. Mr. Roddy, a Tennes-see lawyer not a member of the local bar, addressed the court, saying that he had not been employed, but that people who were interested had spoken to him about the case. He was asked by the court whether he intended to appear for the defendants, and answered that he would like to appear along with counsel that the court might appoint. The record then proceeds:

Mr. Roddy: Your Honor has appointed counsel, is that correct?

The Court: I appointed all the members of the bar for the purpose of arraigning the defendants and then of course I anticipated them to continue to help them if no counsel appears.

Mr. Roddy: Then I don't appear then as counsel but I do want to stay in and not be ruled out in this case.

I merely came down here as a friend of the people who are interested and not as paid counsel I am merely here at the solicitation of people who have become interested in this case without any payment of fee and without any preparation for trial and I think the boys would be better off if I step entirely out of the case according to my way of looking at it and according to my lack of preparation of it and not being familiar with the procedure in Alabama, . . .

The Court: All right.

It thus will be seen that until the very morning of the trial no lawyer had been named or definitely designated to represent the defendants. Prior to that time, the trial judge had "appointed all the members of the bar" for the limited "purpose of arraigning the defendants."

That this action of the trial judge in respect of appointment of counsel was little more than an expansive gesture, imposing no substantial or definite obligation upon any one, is borne out by the fact that prior to the calling of the case for trial on April 6, a leading member of the local bar accepted employment on the side of the prosecution and actively participated in the trial. [T]he circumstance lends emphasis to the conclusion that during perhaps the most critical period of the proceedings against these defendants, that is to say, from the time of their arraignment until the beginning of their trial, when consultation, thoroughgoing investigation and preparation were vitally important, the defendants did not have the aid of counsel in any real sense. . . .

Under the circumstances disclosed, we hold that defendants were not accorded the right of counsel in any substantial sense. To decide otherwise, would simply be to ignore actualities.

In the light of the facts outlined in the forepart of this opinion — the ignorance and illiteracy of the defendants, their youth, the circumstances of public hostility, the imprisonment and the close surveillance of the defendants by the military forces, the fact that their friends and families were all in other states and communication with them necessarily difficult, and above all that they stood in deadly peril of their lives — we think the failure of the trial court to give them reasonable time and opportunity to secure counsel was a clear denial of due process.

Judgments reversed.

———————————

Why are procedures so important? As *Powell* demonstrates, without fair procedures and respect for constitutional rights, there is a strong likelihood that the defendants will not be treated fairly, and that persons will be held accountable for crimes they did not commit. Procedural rules thus play a crucial role in ensuring the fair and efficient processing of cases, as well as the perception of the public and defendants that the criminal justice system has acted in a reliable and fair manner.

Even today, there are numerous obstacles to the fair handling of criminal investigations and prosecutions. Many defendants are poor and do not receive effective representation in asserting their rights. A large percentage of defendants are uneducated, unemployed, and have a substance abuse problem. Law enforcement officials are often overworked and undertrained. Racial stereotypes permeate society, including the criminal justice system. There can also be political pressure on prosecutors to secure convictions. All of these factors may impact how effectively our laws are implemented.

Moreover, it is not just the courts who must abide by fair procedures. Much of criminal procedure is devoted to ensuring that law enforcement officers respect the rights of defendants during the investigative phase of cases. Consider how police conduct affects the likelihood of reaching a correct and fair result in a case.

PATTERSON v. FORMER CHICAGO POLICE LT. JON BURGE

328 F. Supp. 2d 878 (N.D. Ill. 2004)

Opinion by Joan B. GOTTSCHALL:

After being convicted for the 1986 murders of Rafaela and Vincent Sanchez and spending 13 years on death row, plaintiff Aaron Patterson was pardoned by Illinois Governor George Ryan on January 10, 2003. Patterson filed this civil action in June of 2003, asserting that defendants, individually and in conspiracy, violated his rights under the United States Constitution when they knowingly filed false charges and framed him for the Sanchez murders, tortured and beat him at Chicago Police Department's Area 2 headquarters, fabricated his "confession" and falsified inculpatory evidence, coerced witnesses to testify against him, gave perjured testimony, published defamatory statements regarding his guilt, and obstructed justice and suppressed exculpatory evidence throughout his suppression hearing, trial, and post-conviction proceedings.

I. BACKGROUND

On April 19, 1986, Chicago Police Department officers discovered the dead bodies of Rafaela and Vincent Sanchez in their apartment at 8849 South Burley. Officers and defendants Lt. Jon Burge, Sgt. John Byrne, Detectives James Pienta, William Marley, Daniel McWeeny, Joseph Danzl (collectively, "Area 2 defendants"), and other Area 2 detectives were assigned to investigate the Sanchez murders. On April 21, Danzl allegedly coerced and intimidated 16 year-old Marva Hall, whose uncle was a suspect in the murders, into falsely implicating Patterson. On April 22, Burge and another Area 2 detective took a different suspect, Michael Arbuckle, into custody at Area 2 headquarters. Burge allegedly told Arbuckle that they "really wanted to get Aaron Patterson" and wanted Arbuckle to say that Patterson was involved in the murders. When Arbuckle refused to implicate Patterson and asked for his lawyer, Burge threatened him with electrocution and lethal injection and told him that they would get Arbuckle to "cooperate one way or another." Still, Arbuckle denied his and Patterson's involvement.

On or about April 23, McWeeny, Byrne, and other Area 2 detectives on the case were informed by several persons that Willie Washington and his brother killed Rafaela and Vincent Sanchez. Nevertheless, for the next week, Byrne, McWeeny, and other Area 2 detectives searched unsuccessfully for Patterson. On April 30, Patterson was arrested on an outstanding warrant by Chicago Police Department officers from the Fourth District. Defendants Pienta, Marley, and Pedersen were called to transport Patterson from the Fourth District police station to Area 2. During the ride, Pienta allegedly told Patterson that if he had arrested him, he would have killed him.

At Area 2 Patterson was placed in an interview room, handcuffed to the wall, and questioned by Area 2 detectives about the Sanchez murders for about an hour. Patterson denied any involvement. He was then taken to 11th and State before being returned to the interview room at Area 2. After brief questioning, Pienta told Patterson that he was "tired of this bullshit," left the room, and came back with a grey typewriter cover. When Patterson refused to implicate himself in the murders, the Area 2 defendants, including Pienta, Marley, and Pedersen, handcuffed him behind his back, turned out the lights, and repeatedly beat him in the chest and suffocated him by holding the typewriter cover over his face and ears for at least a minute. Pienta continued to urge Patterson to "cooperate," and when he refused, the Area 2 defendants again turned out the lights and suffocated Patterson with the plastic cover. The second time, the "bagging" and beating lasted for over two minutes. Patterson found the abuse unbearable and told the detectives he would "say anything you say" if they would stop the suffocation and beating.

After Patterson agreed to cooperate, the Area 2 defendants left the room to get a state's attorney from the felony review division to take his statement. While alone in the room, Patterson used a paper clip to scratch into the interview room bench that he was "suffocated with plastic" and that his statement to the police was false. Defendant Burge returned with an Assistant State's Attorney ("ASA") who said that Burge told him Patterson wanted to make a statement. After Burge left the room at Patterson's request, Patterson told the ASA that he had nothing to say. The ASA left and told Burge that Patterson refused to confess. Burge then returned to the room, told Patterson "you're fucking up," placed his handgun on the table in front of Patterson, and said "we told you if you don't do what we tell you to, you're going to get something worse than before — it will have been a snap compared to what you will get." He also told Patterson that if he revealed the torture, "it's your word against ours and who are they going to believe, you or us." Burge then told Patterson that they could do anything they wanted to him.

Next, defendant Peter Troy, an ASA with the State's Attorney's Office ("SAO"), entered the interview room with Area 2 defendant Madigan. Initially, Patterson agreed to make a statement in exchange for phone privileges, but he refused to sign the statement Troy had written out after the Area 2 defendants terminated his calls. In an attempt to make Patterson sign the statement, Troy and Madigan physically attacked Patterson. McWeeny entered the room at this time, professing not to be involved in the prior beatings and suffocation, and urged Patterson to cooperate because the other defendants "could do something serious to him if he didn't." As a result of this coercion and under threat of continued torture, Patterson said he would agree with whatever the Area 2 defendants and Troy said had happened.

Around the same time, defendant Pienta arrested Eric Caine, Patterson's co-defendant in the Sanchez murder prosecution. Caine was interrogated and beaten and told that if he did not make a statement he would get the same treatment as Patterson. Caine initially gave a statement, but when he tried to repudiate it Madigan hit Caine with his open hand over his ear and cheekbone, causing a loud pop and rupturing his ear drum. Caine screamed in pain; he later gave and signed a court-reported statement prepared by the Area 2 defendants which falsely implicated Patterson in the murders.

The Area 2 defendants, together with SAO defendants Troy and William Lacy, allegedly fabricated oral admissions and reduced these "admissions" to false reports implicating Patterson and Caine in the Sanchez murders. Defendants communicated these false reports to the prosecuting attorneys, who used them at Patterson's suppression hearing and at trial. Defendants also testified falsely about the fabricated admissions and the torture and abuse which produced them throughout Patterson's prosecution. No physical evidence linking Patterson to the murders was ever discovered, though a bloody fingerprint that was not Patterson's was found at the scene and not introduced at trial. Patterson was convicted for the Sanchez murders on the basis of his false confession and the testimony of Marva Hall and defendants. Patterson was sentenced to death, and after his conviction was affirmed on appeal, spent over 13 years incarcerated on death row until his pardon in January of 2003.

In a televised interview in December of 1999 defendant Byrne made defamatory statements concerning Patterson's protestations of his innocence and claims of torture at Area 2, including that Patterson was "without a doubt" "guilty of the [Sanchez] murders" and that "the detectives who worked with him would not" and did not torture suspects. On January 10, 2003, then Governor of Illinois George Ryan granted Patterson and three other death row victims allegedly tortured by Burge and other Area 2 detectives pardons on the basis of innocence. In granting the pardons Governor Ryan announced that "the category of horrors was hard to believe," and the evidence showed that the four men — Patterson, Madison Hobley, Leroy Orange, and Stanley Howard — had been "beaten and tortured and convicted on the basis of confessions they allegedly provided." In response, State's Attorney Devine publicly condemned the pardons of the four men, whom he referred to as "evil" and "convicted murderers," as "outrageous" and "unconscionable."

As *Patterson* illustrates, constitutional rights are not just formalities. They are critical to ensuring that police respect people's rights and that the right people are held responsible for criminal actions.

D. KEY PROVISIONS OF THE BILL OF RIGHTS

The Bill of Rights protects individuals against the power of the State. Fundamental rights ensured by a number of the first ten amendments have been made applicable to the states under the Fourteenth Amendment's Due Process Clause. The following key constitutional provisions are covered in this book.

AMENDMENT IV

The right of the people to be secure in their persons, houses, papers, and effects, against unreasonable searches and seizures, shall not be violated, and no Warrants shall issue but upon probable cause, supported by Oath or affirmation, and particularly describing the place to be searched, and the persons or things to be seized.

The Fourth Amendment is the key constitutional provision governing police conduct during searches and arrest. As discussed in Chapter 2, the amendment has been interpreted as generally requiring a warrant based on probable cause for a search or arrest. However, there are numerous exceptions that allow for warrantless searches and stops as long as they are "reasonable."

AMENDMENT V

No person shall be held to answer for a capital, or otherwise infamous crime, unless on a presentment or indictment of a Grand Jury . . . ; nor shall any person be subject for the same offense to be twice put in jeopardy of life or limb; nor shall be compelled in any criminal case to be a witness against himself, nor be deprived of life, liberty, or property, without due process of law.

There are several aspects to the Fifth Amendment. It sets forth the right in federal cases to indictment by a grand jury (see Chapter 6). It also provides for the right against double jeopardy (see Chapter 14), the privilege against self-incrimination (see Chapter 4), and the general right of due process in criminal cases.

AMENDMENT VI

In all criminal prosecutions, the accused shall enjoy the right to a speedy and public trial, by an impartial jury of the State and district wherein the crime shall have been committed, which district shall have been previously ascertained by law; and to be informed of the nature and cause of the accusation; to be confronted with the witnesses against him; to have compulsory process for obtaining witnesses in his favor, and to have the Assistance of Counsel for his defense.

The Sixth Amendment guarantees a defendant the right to a speedy and public jury trial. (See Chapter 12.) It also requires that the defendant be given an opportunity to confront the witnesses against him and to call his own witnesses. However, the most important right that the defendant enjoys under the Sixth Amendment is the right to assistance of counsel. (See Chapter 11.) Through counsel's diligent efforts, a defendant can preserve his other rights.

> **AMENDMENT VIII**
> Excessive bail shall not be required, nor excessive fines imposed, nor cruel and unusual punishment inflicted.

The Eighth Amendment prohibits cruel and unusual punishment. (See Chapter 13.) The standard for "cruel and unusual punishment" evolves. Generally, the term "cruel and unusual punishment" relates to the proportionality of the sentence, not just the manner in which the sentence is imposed.

E. THE APPLICATION OF THE BILL OF RIGHTS TO THE STATES

1. *The Provisions of the Bill of Rights and the Idea of "Incorporation"*

There are a few criminal procedure protections in the first seven articles of the Constitution, such as the prohibition on Congress suspending the writ of habeas corpus found in Article I, section 9, and the assurance of trial by jury in Article III. But the key protections of criminal procedure examined through this book are found in the Fourth, Fifth, Sixth, and Eighth Amendments.

In understanding the material in this book, it is important to know that these provisions of the Bill of Rights did not apply to state governments until the twentieth century and generally not until the second half of the twentieth century. Initially, it was thought that the Bill of Rights was meant just to limit the federal government; state constitutions were deemed adequate to protect people from abuses by state and local governments.

In Barron v. Mayor & City of Baltimore, 32 U.S. (7 Pet.) 243 (1833), the Supreme Court held that the Bill of Rights did not apply to the states. The specific issue was whether the states had to comply with the Fifth Amendment's prohibition of the taking of private property without just compensation. The Court, in an opinion by Chief Justice John Marshall, declared, "The question thus presented is, we think, of great importance, but not of much difficulty. The constitution was ordained and established by the people of the United States for themselves, for their own government, and not for the government of the individual states." The Court held that the Bill of Rights simply did not apply to the States: "If these propositions be correct, the fifth amendment must be understood as restraining the power of the general government, not as applicable to the states. In their several constitutions, they have imposed such restrictions on their respective governments, as their own wisdom suggested; such as they deemed most proper for themselves."

In the late nineteenth century, the Supreme Court suggested an alternate approach: finding that at least some of the Bill of the Rights provisions are part of the liberty protected from state interference by the Due Process Clause of the Fourteenth Amendment. In other words, the Court indicated that the Due Process Clause of the Fourteenth Amendment, which applies to state and local governments, incorporates and protects at least some of the Bill of Rights.

In 1897, in Chicago, Burlington & Quincy Railroad Co. v. City of Chicago, 166 U.S. 226 (1897), the Supreme Court ruled that the Due Process Clause of the Fourteenth Amendment prevents states from taking property without just compensation. Although the Court did not speak explicitly of the Fourteenth Amendment incorporating the Takings Clause, that was the practical effect of the decision.

In Twining v. New Jersey, 211 U.S. 78 (1908), the Supreme Court first expressly discussed applying the Bill of Rights to the states through the process of incorporation. The specific issue was whether a jury in state court could draw an adverse inference against a criminal defendant for failing to testify. Although the Court held that this does not apply to the states (a conclusion that the Court later would reverse in Griffin v. California, 380 U.S. 609 (1965)), it stated, "[I]t is possible that some of the personal rights safeguarded by the first eight Amendments against national action may also be safeguarded against state action, because a denial of them would be a denial of due process of law. If this is so, it is not because those rights are enumerated in the first eight Amendments, but because they are of such a nature that they are included in the conception of due process of law."

Twining expressly opened the door to the Supreme Court applying provisions of the Bill of Rights to the states by finding them to be included — incorporated — into the Due Process Clause of the Fourteenth Amendment. Soon the Court began to use this door. In Gitlow v. New York, 268 U.S. 652 (1925), the Court for the first time said that the First Amendment's protection of freedom of speech applies to the states through its incorporation into the Due Process Clause of the Fourteenth Amendment. The Court declared, "For present purposes we may and do assume that freedom of speech and of the press — which are protected by the First Amendment from abridgment by Congress — are among the fundamental personal rights and liberties protected by the due process clause of the Fourteenth Amendment from impairment by the States." In *Gitlow*, the Court actually rejected the constitutional challenge to a state law that made it a crime to advocate the violent overthrow of government by force or violence. Two years later, in Fiske v. Kansas, 274 U.S. 380 (1927), the Court for the first time found that a state law regulating speech violated the Due Process Clause of the Fourteenth Amendment.

In 1933, in Powell v. Alabama, 287 U.S. 45 (1932), which is presented above, the Court found that a state's denial of counsel in a capital case denied due process, thereby in essence applying the Sixth Amendment to the states in capital cases. The infamous Scottsboro trial involved two African American men who were convicted of rape without the assistance of an

attorney at trial and with a jury from which all blacks had been excluded. The Supreme Court concluded that the Due Process Clause of the Fourteenth Amendment protects fundamental rights from state interference and that this can include Bill of Rights provisions. But the Court said that "[i]f this is so, it is not because those rights are enumerated in the first eight Amendments, but because they are of such a nature that they are included in the 'conception of due process of law.'" The Court held that in a capital case, "it [is] clear that the right to the aid of counsel is of this fundamental character."

2. The Debate over Incorporation

Once the Court found that the Due Process Clause of the Fourteenth Amendment protected fundamental rights from state infringement, there was a major debate over which liberties are safeguarded. For many years, this debate raged among Justices and commentators. On the one side, there were the total incorporationists who believed that all of the Bill of Rights should be deemed to be included in the Due Process Clause of the Fourteenth Amendment. Justices Black and Douglas were the foremost advocates of this position.[16]

On the other side, there were the selective incorporationists who believed that only some of the Bill of Rights were sufficiently fundamental to apply to state and local governments. Justice Cardozo, for example, wrote that "[t]he process of absorption . . . [applied to rights where] neither liberty nor justice would exist if they were sacrificed."[17] Justice Cardozo said that the Due Process Clause included "principles of justice so rooted in the tradition and conscience of our people as to be ranked as fundamental" and that were therefore "implicit in the concept of ordered liberty."[18] Justice Frankfurter said that due process precludes those practices that "offend those canons of decency and fairness which express the notions of justice of English-speaking peoples."[19]

The debate between total and selective incorporation was extremely important because it determined the reach of the Bill of Rights and the extent to which individuals could turn to the federal courts for protection from state and local governments.

For example, in Palko v. Connecticut, 302 U.S. 319 (1937), the Court held the prohibition of double jeopardy, which keeps states from appealing acquittals in criminal cases, does not apply to the states. Justice Cardozo, writing for the Court, stated, "Is [allowing the State to appeal the] kind of double jeopardy to which the statute has subjected him a hardship so acute

---

16. *See, e.g.*, Adamson v. California, 332 U.S. 46, 71-72 (1947) (Black, J., dissenting).
17. 302 U.S. 319, 326 (1937).
18. *Id.* at 325.
19. Adamson v. California, 332 U.S. 46, 67 (1947) (Frankfurter, J., concurring).

and shocking that our policy will not endure it? Does it violate those 'fundamental principles of liberty and justice which lie at the base of all our civil and political institutions'? The answer surely must be 'no.' There is here no seismic innovation. The edifice of justice stands."

Similarly, in Adamson v. California, 332 U.S. 46 (1947), the Court held that states were not obligated to follow the Fifth Amendment's prohibition on a prosecutor's commenting on a criminal defendant's failure to take the witness stand. Justice Black wrote a famous dissent. He declared:

> The first 10 amendments were proposed and adopted largely because of fear that Government might unduly interfere with prized individual liberties. . . . My study of the historical events that culminated in the Fourteenth Amendment, and the expressions of those who sponsored and favored, as well as those who opposed its submission and passage, persuades me that one of the chief objects that the provisions of the Amendment's first section, separately, and as a whole, were intended to accomplish was to make the Bill of Rights applicable to the states. With full knowledge of the import of the *Barron* decision, the framers and backers of the Fourteenth Amendment proclaimed its purpose to be to overturn the constitutional rule that case had announced. This historical purpose has never received full consideration or exposition in any opinion of this Court interpreting the Amendment.[20]

The debate over incorporation primarily was centered on three issues.[21] First, the debate was over history and whether the framers of the Fourteenth Amendment intended for it to apply the Bill of Rights to the states. Both sides of the debate claimed that history supported their view.

Second, the incorporation debate was over federalism. Applying the Bill of Rights to the states imposes a substantial set of restrictions on state and local governments. Not surprisingly, opponents of total incorporation argued based on federalism: the desirability of preserving state and local governing autonomy by freeing them from the application of the Bill of Rights. Defenders of total incorporation responded that federalism is not a sufficient reason for tolerating violations of fundamental liberties.

Third, the debate was over the appropriate judicial role. Advocates of total incorporation, such as Justice Black, claimed that allowing the Court to pick and choose which rights to incorporate left too much to the subjective preference of the justices. In contrast, advocates of selective incorporation denied this and maintained that total incorporation would mean more judicial oversight of state and local actions and thus less room for democracy to operate.

---

20. In Griffin v. California, 380 U.S. 609 (1965), the Supreme Court overruled *Adamson* and held that the Due Process Clause of the Fourteenth Amendment was violated by a prosecutor's comments on a defendant's silence.

21. For a detailed description of the debate and the issues, *see* Jerold Israel, *Selective Incorporation Revisited*, 71 Geo. L.J. 253, 336-338 (1982).

3.   The Current Law as to What's Incorporated

The selective incorporationists prevailed in this debate in that the Supreme Court never has accepted the total incorporationist approach. However, from a practical perspective, the total incorporationists largely succeeded in their objective because, one by one, the Supreme Court found almost all of the provisions to be incorporated. This is reflected in the following case, Duncan v. Louisiana, which summarizes the many decisions, particularly of the Warren Court during the 1950s and 1960s, finding almost all of the Bill of Rights to be incorporated.

DUNCAN v. LOUISIANA
391 U.S. 145 (1968)

Justice WHITE delivered the opinion of the Court.

Appellant, Gary Duncan, was convicted of simple battery in the Twenty-fifth Judicial District Court of Louisiana. Under Louisiana law simple battery is a misdemeanor, punishable by a maximum of two years' imprisonment and a $300 fine. Appellant sought trial by jury, but because the Louisiana Constitution grants jury trials only in cases in which capital punishment or imprisonment at hard labor may be imposed, the trial judge denied the request. Appellant was convicted and sentenced to serve 60 days in the parish prison and pay a fine of $150.

The Fourteenth Amendment denies the States the power to "deprive any person of life, liberty, or property, without due process of law." In resolving conflicting claims concerning the meaning of this spacious language, the Court has looked increasingly to the Bill of Rights for guidance; many of the rights guaranteed by the first eight Amendments to the Constitution have been held to be protected against state action by the Due Process Clause of the Fourteenth Amendment. That clause now protects the right to compensation for property taken by the State, Chicago, B. & Q.R. Co. v. City of Chicago (1897); the rights of speech, press, and religion covered by the First Amendment, see, e.g., Fiske v. State of Kansas (1927); the Fourth Amendment rights to be free from unreasonable searches and seizures and to have excluded from criminal trials any evidence illegally seized, Mapp v. State of Ohio (1961); the right guaranteed by the Fifth Amendment to be free of compelled self-incrimination, Malloy v. Hogan (1964); and the Sixth Amendment rights to counsel, Gideon v. Wainwright (1963); to a speedy, Klopfer v. State of North Carolina (1967) and public trial, In re Oliver (1948); to confrontation of opposing witnesses, Pointer v. State of Texas (1965); and to compulsory process for obtaining witnesses, Washington v. State of Texas (1967).

The test for determining whether a right extended by the Fifth and Sixth Amendments with respect to federal criminal proceedings is also protected against state action by the Fourteenth Amendment has been phrased in a variety of ways in the opinions of this Court. The question has been asked whether a right is among those "fundamental principles of liberty and justice which lie at the base of all our civil and political institutions," Powell v. State of Alabama, (1932); whether it is "basic in our system of jurisprudence," In re Oliver (1948); and whether it is "a fundamental right, essential to a fair trial," Gideon v. Wainwright (1963).

The claim before us is that the right to trial by jury guaranteed by the Sixth Amendment meets these tests. The position of Louisiana, on the other hand, is that the Constitution imposes upon the States no duty to give a jury trial in any criminal case, regardless of the seriousness of the crime or the size of the punishment which may be imposed. Because we believe that trial by jury in criminal cases is fundamental to the American scheme of justice, we hold that the Fourteenth Amendment guarantees a right of jury trial in all criminal cases which—were they to be tried in a federal court—would come within the Sixth Amendment's guarantee.

The guarantees of jury trial in the Federal and State Constitutions reflect a profound judgment about the way in which law should be enforced and justice administered. A right to jury trial is granted to criminal defendants in order to prevent oppression by the Government. Those who wrote our constitutions knew from history and experience that it was necessary to protect against unfounded criminal charges brought to eliminate enemies and against judges too responsive to the voice of higher authority. The framers of the constitutions strove to create an independent judiciary but insisted upon further protection against arbitrary action. Providing an accused with the right to be tried by a jury of his peers gave him an inestimable safeguard against the corrupt or overzealous prosecutor and against the compliant, biased, or eccentric judge. If the defendant preferred the common-sense judgment of a jury to the more tutored but perhaps less sympathetic reaction of the single judge, he was to have it. Beyond this, the jury trial provisions in the Federal and State Constitutions reflect a fundamental decision about the exercise of official power—a reluctance to entrust plenary powers over the life and liberty of the citizen to one judge or to a group of judges. Fear of unchecked power, so typical of our State and Federal Governments in other respects, found expression in the criminal law in this insistence upon community participation in the determination of guilt or innocence. The deep commitment of the Nation to the right of jury trial in serious criminal cases as a defense against arbitrary law enforcement qualifies for protection under the Due Process Clause of the Fourteenth Amendment, and must therefore be respected by the States.

Justice BLACK, with whom Justice DOUGLAS joins, concurring.

The Court today holds that the right to trial by jury guaranteed defendants in criminal cases in federal courts by Art. III of the United States Constitution and by the Sixth Amendment is also guaranteed by the Fourteenth

Amendment to defendants tried in state courts. With this holding I agree for reasons given by the Court.

I am very happy to support this selective process through which our Court has since the *Adamson* case held most of the specific Bill of Rights' protections applicable to the States to the same extent they are applicable to the Federal Government. All of these holdings making Bill of Rights' provisions applicable as such to the States mark, of course, a departure from the *Twining* doctrine holding that none of those provisions were enforceable as such against the States.

My view has been and is that the Fourteenth Amendment, as a whole, makes the Bill of Rights applicable to the States. This would certainly include the language of the Privileges and Immunities Clause, as well as the Due Process Clause. I can say only that the words "No State shall make or enforce any law which shall abridge the privileges or immunities of citizens of the United States" seem to me an eminently reasonable way of expressing the idea that henceforth the Bill of Rights shall apply to the States. What more precious "privilege" of American citizenship could there be than that privilege to claim the protections of our great Bill of Rights? I suggest that any reading of "privileges or immunities of citizens of the United States" which excludes the Bill of Rights' safeguards renders the words of this section of the Fourteenth Amendment meaningless. Senator Howard, who introduced the Fourteenth Amendment for passage in the Senate, certainly read the words this way.

Finally I want to add that I am not bothered by the argument that applying the Bill of Rights to the States "according to the same standards that protect those personal rights against federal encroachment," interferes with our concept of federalism in that it may prevent States from trying novel social and economic experiments. I have never believed that under the guise of federalism the States should be able to experiment with the protections afforded our citizens through the Bill of Rights.

In closing I want to emphasize that I believe as strongly as ever that the Fourteenth Amendment was intended to make the Bill of Rights applicable to the States. I have been willing to support the selective incorporation doctrine, however, as an alternative, although perhaps less historically supportable than complete incorporation. The selective incorporation process, if used properly, does limit the Supreme Court in the Fourteenth Amendment field to specific Bill of Rights' protections only and keeps judges from roaming at will in their own notions of what policies outside the Bill of Rights are desirable and what are not. And, most importantly for me, the selective incorporation process has the virtue of having already worked to make most of the Bill of Rights' protections applicable to the States.

There are still four provisions of the Bill of Rights that never have been incorporated and do not apply to state and local governments. First, the Third Amendment right to not have soldiers quartered in a person's home never has been deemed incorporated. The reason almost certainly is that a Third Amendment case presenting the incorporation question never has reached the Supreme Court. If ever such a case would arise, the Supreme Court surely would find this provision applies to the states.[22]

Second, the Court has held that the Fifth Amendment's right to a grand jury indictment in criminal cases is not incorporated.[23] Thus, states need not use grand juries and can choose alternatives such as preliminary hearings and prosecutorial information.

Third, the Court has ruled that the Seventh Amendment right to jury trial in civil cases is not incorporated.[24] States therefore can eliminate juries in some or even all civil suits without violating the United States Constitution.

Finally, the Court never has ruled as to whether the prohibition of excessive fines in the Eighth Amendment is incorporated.[25]

All of the rest of the Bill of Rights, as detailed above, have been deemed incorporated. Technically, the Bill of Rights still applies directly only to the federal government; Barron v. Mayor & City Council of Baltimore never has been expressly overruled. Therefore, whenever a case involves a state or local violation of a Bill of Rights provision, to be precise, it involves that provision as applied to the states through the Due Process Clause of the Fourteenth Amendment.

4. The Content of Incorporated Rights

If a provision of the Bill of Rights applies to the states, is its content identical as to when it is applied to the federal government? Or as it is sometimes phrased, does the Bill of Rights provision apply "jot for jot"?[26]

The Supreme Court has not consistently answered these questions. In some cases, the Court has expressly stated that the Bill of Rights provision applied in exactly the same manner whether it is a federal or a state government action. For example, the Supreme Court has declared that it is "firmly embedded in our constitutional jurisprudence . . . that the several States have no greater power to restrain the individual freedoms protected by the First Amendment than does the Congress of the United States."[27] Similarly, the Court has said that "the guarantees of the First Amendment, the prohibition of unreasonable searches and seizures of the Fourth Amendment, and the right to counsel guaranteed by the Sixth Amendment, are all

---

22. *See* Engblom v. Carey, 677 F.2d 957 (2d Cir. 1982) (finding that the Third Amendment is incorporated).

23. Hutardo v. California, 110 U.S. 516 (1884).

24. Minneapolis & St. Louis Railroad Co. v. Bombolis, 241 U.S. 211 (1916).

25. Browning-Ferris Industries of Vt., Inc. v. Kelco Disposal, Inc., 492 U.S. 257, 262, 276 n.2 (1989).

26. *See* Duncan v. Louisiana, 391 U.S. at 181 (Harlan, J., dissenting) (using the "jot-for-jot" language).

27. Wallace v. Jaffree, 472 U.S. 38, 48-49 (1985).

to be enforced against the States under the Fourteenth Amendment according to the same standards that protect those personal rights against federal encroachment."[28] The Court said that it "rejected the notion that the Fourteenth Amendment applies to the states only a watered-down, subjective version of the individual guarantees of the Bill of Rights."[29]

However, in other instances, the Court has ruled that some Bill of Rights provisions apply differently to the states than to the federal government. In Williams v. Florida, 399 U.S. 78 (1970), the Supreme Court held that states need not use 12-person juries in criminal cases, even though that is required by the Sixth Amendment for federal trials. The Court upheld the constitutionality of six-person juries in state criminal trials and explained that the jury of 12 was "a historical accident, unnecessary to effect the purposes of the jury system."

In Apodaca v. Oregon, 406 U.S. 404 (1972), and Johnson v. Louisiana, 406 U.S. 356 (1972), the Supreme Court held that states may allow nonunanimous jury verdicts in criminal cases. Although the Sixth Amendment has been interpreted to require unanimous juries in federal criminal trials, the Supreme Court ruled that states may allow convictions based on 11-1 or 10-2 jury votes. However, the Court has ruled that conviction by a nonunanimous six-person jury violates due process.[30]

From a practical perspective, except for the requirements of a 12-person jury and a unanimous verdict, the Bill of Rights provisions that have been incorporated apply to the states exactly as they apply to the federal government. This might be criticized on federalism grounds as unduly limiting the states. But rights such as freedom of speech are fundamental liberties and there is no reason why their content should vary depending on the level of government.

Of course, apart from the Bill of Rights, there are many differences between criminal procedure in federal and state courts. The Federal Rules of Criminal Procedure, mentioned at many points throughout this book, are sometimes different than the rules followed in many states. Also, the Supreme Court often articulates requirements as part of its supervisory role over federal courts in areas where states are free to follow their own procedures. For example, the contempt powers of a federal court, as defined by the Supreme Court, may be different than those in a state court.

Although the debate over incorporation raged among justices and scholars during the 1940s, 1950s, and 1960s, now the issue seems settled. Except for the few provisions mentioned above, the Bill of Rights do apply to state and local governments and, in almost all instances, with the same content regardless of whether it is a challenge to federal, state, or local actions.

28. Malloy v. Hogan, 378 U.S. at 10.
29. *Id.* at 10-11 (citations omitted).
30. Burch v. Louisiana, 441 U.S. 130 (1979).

F.   RETROACTIVITY

In reading the cases throughout this book, it is important to keep in mind that generally criminal procedure decisions apply only in that case and in future ones; they do not apply retroactively to already decided cases. Actually, to be more precise, a Supreme Court decision recognizing a right of criminal procedure generally applies to that case, to any cases pending at the time (in a trial court or on appeal, but not to those pending on habeas corpus), and to future cases. Generally, Supreme Court criminal procedure rulings do not apply retroactively to cases where the appeals have already been completed.

It is easy to understand the reason for this. If Supreme Court decisions recognizing new criminal procedure rights applied retroactively, hundreds or thousands of convicted criminals would seek to reopen their cases to take advantage of the new right. The burden on the courts, depending on the new right, would be enormous. In many instances, the government simply could not retry the person because witnesses would no longer be available. But there is a serious cost to not applying Supreme Court decisions retroactively: People remain in prison, or even are executed, in violation of the Constitution. An accident of timing is determinative; those whose appeals are pending get the benefit of the new right, which could lead to the reversal of their conviction, but those whose appeal is over are out of luck in taking advantage of the new right.

Occasionally, though rarely, the Supreme Court will apply a criminal procedure protection retroactively. The Court has identified two situations in which this will occur. One situation is where a Supreme Court decision places a matter beyond the reach of the criminal law; that is, the Court holds that certain behavior cannot be criminally punished. For instance, in Lawrence v. Texas, 539 U.S. 558 (2003), the Court held that states may not punish private consensual homosexual activity between adults. This obviously puts such conduct beyond the reach of the criminal law and thus the decision would apply retroactively.

In its most recent case concerning retroactivity, Montgomery v. Louisiana, 136 S. Ct. 718 (2016), the Court said that the key question is whether the prior Supreme Court decision is *substantive,* in which case it applies retroactively, or whether it is *procedural,* in which case it does not apply retroactively. Justice Kennedy, writing for the Court, explained: "This Court's precedents addressing the nature of substantive rules, their differences from procedural rules, and their history of retroactive application establish that the Constitution requires substantive rules to have retroactive effect regardless of when a conviction became final."

Second, the Supreme Court has said that a "watershed" rule of criminal procedure would apply retroactively. Rarely, though, has the Supreme Court found any decision to constitute a watershed rule of criminal procedure.

In Whorton v. Bocking, 549 U.S. 406 (2007), the Supreme Court elaborated that it must be a "'watershed rul[e] of criminal procedure' implicating the fundamental fairness and accuracy of the criminal proceeding."[31] The Court said that "[t]his exception is 'extremely narrow.'" Justice Alito, writing for a unanimous Court, stated, "In order to qualify as watershed, a new rule must meet two requirements. First, the rule must be necessary to prevent an 'impermissibly large risk' of an inaccurate conviction. Second, the rule must 'alter our understanding of the bedrock procedural elements essential to the fairness of a proceeding.'"

In theory, it is possible that a criminal procedure decision would apply retroactively. Gideon v. Wainwright, 372 U.S. 335 (1963), which held that criminal defendants have a right to counsel at trial in any case where the sentence potentially includes imprisonment, is often mentioned as the classic example of a decision that would apply retroactively. Without counsel there is an impermissibly large risk of a wrongful conviction and *Gideon* altered the basic understanding "of the bedrock procedural elements essential to the fairness of a proceeding." But this is the exception; in reality, almost always, criminal procedure rulings, such as those in this book, apply only prospectively.

---

31. Whorton v. Bocking involved whether a major Supreme Court decision concerning the Confrontation Clause of the Sixth Amendment applies retroactively. Crawford v. Washington, 541 U.S. 36 (2004), held that a prosecutor could not use "testimonial" statements against a criminal defendant that had been made by a witness who was unavailable at trial on the grounds that they were reliable. In *Whorton*, the Court unanimously held that *Crawford* does not apply retroactively to those whose convictions were final before it was decided.

CHAPTER
2

SEARCHES AND SEIZURES

A. INTRODUCTION

The Fourth Amendment states:

> The right of the people to be secure in their persons, houses, papers, and effects against unreasonable searches and seizures, shall not be violated, and no Warrants shall issue, but upon probable cause, supported by Oath or affirmation, and particularly describing the place to be searched, and the persons or things to be seized.

No technique of law enforcement is more important than the ability of the police to search for evidence and the ability of the police to seize what they find and to arrest individuals suspected of criminal activity. No aspect of criminal procedure has produced more Supreme Court decisions or arises more frequently in the lower courts.

In England and in the American colonies, general warrants were issued where entire neighborhoods could be searched. The Fourth Amendment was a reaction to such practices and embodies a requirement for individualized suspicion: Generally, a person can be searched only if there is reason to believe that person committed a crime or has evidence of one.

There are many interrelated aspects of the Fourth Amendment. There is the prohibition of "unreasonable searches and seizures." The Supreme Court often has emphasized that "its 'central requirement' is one of reasonableness." Illinois v. McArthur, 531 U.S. 326 (2001). Of course, the key is deciding what is reasonable. The amendment also says that warrants must be based on probable cause. But when is a warrant required? What is sufficient for probable cause?

All of this is the focus of this chapter. The next chapter considers the remedies for violation of the Fourth Amendment, especially the exclusionary rule. This chapter, in considering the requirements of the Fourth Amendment, considers a number of key issues. Section B looks at what a "search" is. Section C focuses on the requirement for "probable cause." The warrant requirement and the execution of search warrants are discussed in section D. Next, section E looks at the many exceptions to the warrant requirement. Section F examines seizures and arrests. Section G looks at "stop and frisk." Finally, section H considers electronic eavesdropping.

A consistent theme throughout this material is how to balance the privacy interests protected by the Fourth Amendment with the government's need for effective law enforcement techniques. In reading the many cases below, it is important to consider whether the Court has struck the right balance between these competing interests.

In reading this material it is important to remember that the Fourth Amendment applies to actions by government officials (or those acting in concert with the government), but that like all of the Bill of Rights it does not apply to purely private conduct. Also, it is important to note that the Supreme Court has said that the initial words of the Fourth Amendment — "The right of the people to be secure" — means that it applies only within the United States. In United States v. Verdugo-Urquidez, 494 U.S. 259 (1990), the Court held that the Fourth Amendment did not apply to a search by United States law enforcement officials in Mexico. The Court said that the emphasis in the amendment on protecting "the people" means that it does not apply even to actions of United States law enforcement personnel when operating in a foreign country.

B.   WHAT IS A SEARCH?

In Olmstead v. United States, 277 U.S. 438 (1928), the Supreme Court held that electronic eavesdropping without a physical trespass was not a search within the meaning of the Fourth Amendment. This very limited view of a "search" was overruled and rejected in the landmark case of Katz v. United States.

KATZ v. UNITED STATES
389 U.S. 347 (1967)

Justice STEWART delivered the opinion of the Court.

The petitioner was convicted in the District Court for the Southern District of California under an eight-count indictment charging him with transmitting wagering information by telephone from Los Angeles to Miami and Boston in violation of a federal statute. At trial the Government was permitted, over the petitioner's objection, to introduce evidence of the petitioner's end of telephone conversations, overheard by FBI agents who had attached an electronic listening and recording device to the outside of the public telephone booth from which he had placed his calls. In affirming his conviction, the Court of Appeals rejected the contention that the recordings had been obtained in violation of the Fourth Amendment, because "[t]here was no physical entrance into the area occupied by, [the petitioner]."

We decline to adopt this formulation of the issues. In the first place the correct solution of Fourth Amendment problems is not necessarily promoted by incantation of the phrase "constitutionally protected area." Secondly, the Fourth Amendment cannot be translated into a general constitutional "right to privacy." That Amendment protects individual privacy against certain kinds of governmental intrusion, but its protections go further, and often have nothing to do with privacy at all. Other provisions of the Constitution protect personal privacy from other forms of governmental invasion. But the protection of a person's general right to privacy — his right to be let alone by other people — is, like the protection of his property and of his very life, left largely to the law of the individual States.

Because of the misleading way the issues have been formulated, the parties have attached great significance to the characterization of the telephone booth from which the petitioner placed his calls. The petitioner has strenuously argued that the booth was a "constitutionally protected area." The Government has maintained with equal vigor that it was not. But this effort to decide whether or not a given "area," viewed in the abstract, is "constitutionally protected" deflects attention from the problem presented by this case. For the Fourth Amendment protects people, not places. What a person knowingly exposes to the public, even in his own home or office, is not a subject of Fourth Amendment protection. But what he seeks to preserve as private, even in an area accessible to the public, may be constitutionally protected.

The Government stresses the fact that the telephone booth from which the petitioner made his calls was constructed partly of glass, so that he was as visible after he entered it as he would have been if he had remained outside. But what he sought to exclude when he entered the booth was not the intruding eye — it was the uninvited ear. He did not shed his right to do so simply because he made his calls from a place where he might be seen. No less than an individual in a business office, in a friend's apartment, or in a taxicab, a person in a telephone booth may rely upon the protection of the Fourth Amendment. One who occupies it, shuts the door behind him, and pays the toll that permits him to place a call is surely entitled to assume that the words he utters into the mouthpiece will not be broadcast to the world. To read the Constitution more narrowly is to ignore the vital role that the public telephone has come to play in private communication.

The Government contends, however, that the activities of its agents in this case should not be tested by Fourth Amendment requirements, for the surveillance technique they employed involved no physical penetration of the telephone booth from which the petitioner placed his calls. It is true that the absence of such penetration was at one time thought to foreclose further Fourth Amendment inquiry, Olmstead v. United States, for that Amendment was thought to limit only searches and seizures of tangible property. But "[t]he premise that property interests control the right of the Government to search and seize has been discredited." Thus, although a closely divided Court supposed in *Olmstead* that surveillance without any trespass and without the seizure of any material object fell outside the ambit of the Constitution, we have since departed from the narrow view on which that decision rested. Indeed, we have expressly held that the Fourth Amendment governs not only the seizure of tangible items, but extends as well to the recording of oral statements overheard without any "technical trespass under local property law." Once this much is acknowledged, and once it is recognized that the Fourth Amendment protects people — and not simply "areas" — against unreasonable searches and seizures it becomes clear that the reach of that Amendment cannot turn upon the presence or absence of a physical intrusion into any given enclosure.

We conclude that the underpinnings of *Olmstead* have been so eroded by our subsequent decisions that the "trespass" doctrine there enunciated can no longer be regarded as controlling. The Government's activities in electronically listening to and recording the petitioner's words violated the privacy upon which he justifiably relied while using the telephone booth and thus constituted a "search and seizure" within the meaning of the Fourth Amendment. The fact that the electronic device employed to achieve that end did not happen to penetrate the wall of the booth can have no constitutional significance.

The question remaining for decision, then, is whether the search and seizure conducted in this case complied with constitutional standards. In that regard, the Government's position is that its agents acted in an entirely defensible manner: They did not begin their electronic surveillance until investigation of the petitioner's activities had established a strong probability that he was using the telephone in question to transmit gambling information to persons in other States, in violation of federal law. Moreover, the surveillance was limited, both in scope and in duration, to the specific purpose of establishing the contents of the petitioner's unlawful telephonic communications. The agents confined their surveillance to the brief periods during which he used the telephone booth, and they took great care to overhear only the conversations of the petitioner himself.

Accepting this account of the Government's actions as accurate, it is clear that this surveillance was so narrowly circumscribed that a duly authorized magistrate, properly notified of the need for such investigation, specifically informed of the basis on which it was to proceed, and clearly apprised of the precise intrusion it would entail, could constitutionally have authorized, with appropriate safeguards, the very limited search and seizure that the Government asserts in fact took place. Here, too, a similar judicial order could have accommodated "the legitimate needs of law enforcement" by authorizing the carefully limited use of electronic surveillance.

The Government urges that, because its agents relied upon the decision in *Olmstead* and [other cases], and because they did no more here than they might properly have done with prior judicial sanction, we should retroactively validate their conduct. That we cannot do. It is apparent that the agents in this case acted with restraint. Yet the inescapable fact is that this restraint was imposed by the agents themselves, not by a judicial officer. They were not required, before commencing the search, to present their estimate of probable cause for detached scrutiny by a neutral magistrate. They were not compelled, during the conduct of the search itself, to observe precise limits established in advance by a specific court order. Nor were they directed, after the search had been completed, to notify the authorizing magistrate in detail of all that had been seized. In the absence of such safeguards, this Court has never sustained a search upon the sole ground that officers reasonably expected to find evidence of a particular crime and voluntarily confined their activities to the least intrusive means consistent with that end. Searches conducted without warrants have been held unlawful "notwithstanding facts unquestionably showing probable cause," for the Constitution requires "that the deliberate, impartial judgment of a judicial officer . . . be interposed between the citizen and the police." Over and again this Court has emphasized that the mandate of the [Fourth] Amendment requires adherence to judicial processes, and that searches conducted outside the judicial process, without prior approval by judge or magistrate, are per se unreasonable under the Fourth Amendment — subject only to a few specifically established and well-delineated exceptions.

It is difficult to imagine how any of those exceptions could ever apply to the sort of search and seizure involved in this case. Even electronic surveillance substantially contemporaneous with an individual's arrest could hardly be deemed an "incident" of that arrest. Nor could the use of electronic surveillance without prior authorization be justified on grounds of "hot pursuit." And, of course, the very nature of electronic surveillance precludes its use pursuant to the suspect's consent.

These considerations do not vanish when the search in question is transferred from the setting of a home, an office, or a hotel room to that of a telephone booth. Wherever a man may be, he is entitled to know that he will remain free from unreasonable searches and seizures. The government agents here ignored "the procedure of antecedent justification . . . that is central to the Fourth Amendment," a procedure that we hold to be a constitutional precondition of the kind of electronic surveillance involved in this case. Because the surveillance here failed to meet that condition, and because it led to the petitioner's conviction, the judgment must be reversed.

Justice DOUGLAS, with whom Justice BRENNAN joins, concurring.

While I join the opinion of the Court, I feel compelled to reply to the separate concurring opinion of my Brother White, which I view as a wholly unwarranted green light for the Executive Branch to resort to electronic eavesdropping without a warrant in cases which the Executive Branch itself labels "national security" matters.

Neither the President nor the Attorney General is a magistrate. In matters where they believe national security may be involved they are not detached, disinterested, and neutral as a court or magistrate must be. Under the separation of powers created by the Constitution, the Executive Branch is not supposed to be neutral and disinterested. Rather it should vigorously investigate and prevent breaches of national security and prosecute those who violate the pertinent federal laws. The President and Attorney General are properly interested parties, cast in the role of adversary, in national security cases. They may even be the intended victims of subversive action. Since spies and saboteurs are as entitled to the protection of the Fourth Amendment as suspected gamblers like petitioner, I cannot agree that where spies and saboteurs are involved adequate protection of Fourth Amendment rights is assured when the President and Attorney General assume both the position of adversary-and-prosecutor and disinterested, neutral magistrate.

Justice HARLAN, concurring.

I join the opinion of the Court, which I read to hold only (a) that an enclosed telephone booth is an area where, like a home, and unlike a field, a person has a constitutionally protected reasonable expectation of privacy; (b) that electronic as well as physical intrusion into a place that is in this sense private may constitute a violation of the Fourth Amendment; and (c) that the invasion of a constitutionally protected area by federal authorities is, as the Court has long held, presumptively unreasonable in the absence of a search warrant.

As the Court's opinion states, "the Fourth Amendment protects people, not places." The question, however, is what protection it affords to those people. Generally, as here, the answer to that question requires reference to a "place." My understanding of the rule that has emerged from prior decisions is that there is a twofold requirement, first that a person have exhibited an actual (subjective) expectation of privacy and, second, that the expectation be one that society is prepared to recognize as "reasonable." Thus a man's home is, for most purposes, a place where he expects privacy, but objects, activities, or statements that he exposes to the "plain view" of outsiders are not "protected" because no intention to keep them to himself has been exhibited. On the other hand, conversations in the open would not be protected against being overheard, for the expectation of privacy under the circumstances would be unreasonable.

The critical fact in this case is that "[o]ne who occupies it [a telephone booth], shuts the door behind him, and pays the toll that permits him to place a call is surely entitled to assume" that his conversation is not being intercepted. The point is not that the booth is "accessible to the public" at other times, but that it is a temporarily private place whose momentary occupants' expectations of freedom from intrusion are recognized as reasonable.

Finally, I do not read the Court's opinion to declare that no interception of a conversation one-half of which occurs in a public telephone booth can be reasonable in the absence of a warrant. As elsewhere under the Fourth Amendment, warrants are the general rule, to which the legitimate needs of law enforcement may demand specific exceptions. It will be time enough to consider any such exceptions when an appropriate occasion presents itself, and I agree with the Court that this is not one.

Justice WHITE, concurring.

I agree that the official surveillance of petitioner's telephone conversations in a public booth must be subjected to the test of reasonableness under the Fourth Amendment and that on the record now before us the particular surveillance undertaken was unreasonable absent a warrant properly authorizing it. This application of the Fourth Amendment need not interfere with legitimate needs of law enforcement.

In joining the Court's opinion, I note the Court's acknowledgment that there are circumstance in which it is reasonable to search without a warrant. Wiretapping to protect the security of the Nation has been authorized by successive Presidents. The present Administration would apparently save national security cases from restrictions against wiretapping. We should not require the warrant procedure and the magistrate's judgment if the President of the United States or his chief legal officer, the Attorney General, has considered the requirements of national security and authorized electronic surveillance as reasonable.

Justice BLACK, dissenting.

If I could agree with the Court that eavesdropping carried on by electronic means (equivalent to wiretapping) constitutes a "search" or "seizure," I would be happy to join the Court's opinion.

My basic objection is twofold: (1) I do not believe that the words of the Amendment will bear the meaning given them by today's decision, and (2) I do not believe that it is the proper role of this Court to rewrite the Amendment in order "to bring it into harmony with the times" and thus reach a result that many people believe to be desirable.

While I realize that an argument based on the meaning of words lacks the scope, and no doubt the appeal, of broad policy discussions and philosophical discourses on such nebulous subjects as privacy, for me the language of the Amendment is the crucial place to look in construing a written document such as our Constitution.

The first clause protects "persons, houses, papers, and effects, against unreasonable searches and seizures." These words connote the idea of tangible things with size, form, and weight, things capable of being searched, seized, or both. The second clause of the Amendment still further establishes its Framers' purpose to limit its protection to tangible things by providing that no warrants shall issue but those "particularly describing the place to be searched, and the persons or things to be seized." A conversation overheard by eavesdropping, whether by plain snooping or wiretapping, is not tangible and, under the normally accepted meanings of the words, can neither be searched nor seized. In addition the language of the second clause indicates that the Amendment refers not only to something tangible so it can be seized but to something already in existence so it can be described. Yet the Court's interpretation would have the Amendment apply to overhearing future conversations which by their very nature are nonexistent until they take place. How can one "describe" a future conversation, and, if one cannot, how can a magistrate issue a warrant to eavesdrop one in the future?

Tapping telephone wires, of course, was an unknown possibility at the time the Fourth Amendment was adopted. But eavesdropping (and wiretapping is nothing more than eavesdropping by telephone) was "an ancient practice which at common law was condemned as a nuisance." There can be no doubt that the Framers were aware of this practice, and if they had desired to outlaw or restrict the use of evidence obtained by eavesdropping, I believe that they would have used the appropriate language to do so in the Fourth Amendment. They certainly would not have left such a task to the ingenuity of language-stretching judges.

Katz indicates that a trespass is neither necessary nor sufficient for the existence of a search. But in a recent case, involving whether placing a GPS device on a car and tracking its movements is a search, the majority held that a trespass is sufficient for a search. United States v. Jones is a major decision about when government monitoring of public behavior — driving on public streets — is a search within the meaning of the Fourth Amendment. In reading *Jones*, it is important to contrast the approaches of the justices and how their views will apply when monitoring of a person's movements is done via a satellite or drone or cellular technology as opposed to a GPS device.

UNITED STATES v. JONES
565 U.S. 400 (2012)

Justice SCALIA delivered the opinion of the Court.

We decide whether the attachment of a Global Positioning System (GPS) tracking device to an individual's vehicle, and subsequent use of that device to monitor the vehicle's movements on public streets, constitutes a search or seizure within the meaning of the Fourth Amendment.

I

In 2004 respondent Antoine Jones, owner and operator of a nightclub in the District of Columbia, came under suspicion of trafficking in narcotics and was made the target of an investigation by a joint FBI and Metropolitan Police Department task force. Officers employed various investigative techniques, including visual surveillance of the nightclub, installation of a camera focused on the front door of the club, and a pen register and wiretap covering Jones's cellular phone.

Based in part on information gathered from these sources, in 2005 the Government applied to the United States District Court for the District of Columbia for a warrant authorizing the use of an electronic tracking device on the Jeep Grand Cherokee registered to Jones's wife. A warrant issued, authorizing installation of the device in the District of Columbia and within 10 days.

On the 11th day, and not in the District of Columbia but in Maryland,[1] agents installed a GPS tracking device on the undercarriage of the Jeep while it was parked in a public parking lot. Over the next 28 days, the Government used the device to track the vehicle's movements, and once had to replace the device's battery when the vehicle was parked in a different public lot in Maryland. By means of signals from multiple satellites, the device established the vehicle's location within 50 to 100 feet, and communicated that location by cellular phone to a Government computer. It relayed more than 2,000 pages of data over the 4-week period.

The Government ultimately obtained a multiple-count indictment charging Jones and several alleged co-conspirators with, as relevant here, conspiracy to distribute and possess with intent to distribute five kilograms or more of cocaine and 50 grams or more of cocaine base. Before trial, Jones filed a motion to suppress evidence obtained through the GPS device. The District Court granted the motion only in part, suppressing the data obtained while the vehicle was parked in the garage adjoining Jones's residence. It held the remaining data admissible, because "'[a] person traveling in an automobile on public thoroughfares has no reasonable expectation of privacy in his movements from one place to another.'" Jones's trial in October 2006 produced a hung jury on the conspiracy count.

In March 2007, a grand jury returned another indictment, charging Jones and others with the same conspiracy. The Government introduced at trial the same GPS-derived locational data admitted in the first trial, which connected Jones to the alleged conspirators' stash house that contained $850,000 in cash, 97 kilograms of cocaine, and 1 kilogram of cocaine base. The jury returned a guilty verdict, and the District Court sentenced Jones to life imprisonment.

The United States Court of Appeals for the District of Columbia Circuit reversed the conviction because of admission of the evidence obtained by warrantless use of the GPS device which, it said, violated the Fourth Amendment.

II

A

We hold that the Government's installation of a GPS device on a target's vehicle and its use of that device to monitor the vehicle's movements,

---

1. In this litigation, the Government has conceded noncompliance with the warrant and has argued only that a warrant was not required. [Footnote by the Court.]

constitutes a "search." It is important to be clear about what occurred in this case: The Government physically occupied private property for the purpose of obtaining information. We have no doubt that such a physical intrusion would have been considered a "search" within the meaning of the Fourth Amendment when it was adopted. *Entick v. Carrington*, 95 Eng. Rep. 807 (C.P. 1765), is a "case we have described as a 'monument of English freedom undoubtedly familiar' to 'every American statesman' at the time the Constitution was adopted, and considered to be 'the true and ultimate expression of constitutional law'" with regard to search and seizure. In that case, Lord Camden expressed in plain terms the significance of property rights in search-and-seizure analysis: "[O]ur law holds the property of every man so sacred, that no man can set his foot upon his neighbour's close without his leave; if he does he is a trespasser, though he does no damage at all; if he will tread upon his neighbour's ground, he must justify it by law."

The text of the Fourth Amendment reflects its close connection to property, since otherwise it would have referred simply to "the right of the people to be secure against unreasonable searches and seizures"; the phrase "in their persons, houses, papers, and effects" would have been superfluous.

Consistent with this understanding, our Fourth Amendment jurisprudence was tied to common-law trespass, at least until the latter half of the 20th century. Our later cases, of course, have deviated from that exclusively property-based approach. In *Katz v. United States* (1967), we said that "the Fourth Amendment protects people, not places," and found a violation in attachment of an eavesdropping device to a public telephone booth. Our later cases have applied the analysis of Justice Harlan's concurrence in that case, which said that a violation occurs when government officers violate a person's "reasonable expectation of privacy."

The Government contends that the Harlan standard shows that no search occurred here, since Jones had no "reasonable expectation of privacy" in the area of the Jeep accessed by Government agents (its underbody) and in the locations of the Jeep on the public roads, which were visible to all. But we need not address the Government's contentions, because Jones's Fourth Amendment rights do not rise or fall with the *Katz* formulation. At bottom, we must "assur[e] preservation of that degree of privacy against government that existed when the Fourth Amendment was adopted." As explained, for most of our history the Fourth Amendment was understood to embody a particular concern for government trespass upon the areas ("persons, houses, papers, and effects") it enumerates. *Katz* did not repudiate that understanding.

Related to this, and similarly irrelevant, is the concurrence's point that, if analyzed separately, neither the installation of the device nor its use would constitute a Fourth Amendment search. Of course not. A trespass on "houses" or "effects," or a *Katz* invasion of privacy, is not alone a search unless it is done to obtain information; and the obtaining of information is not alone a search unless it is achieved by such a trespass or invasion of privacy.

The Government contends that several of our post-*Katz* cases foreclose the conclusion that what occurred here constituted a search. It relies principally on two cases in which we rejected Fourth Amendment challenges to "beepers," electronic tracking devices that represent another form of electronic monitoring. The first case, *Knotts* upheld against Fourth Amendment challenge the use of a "beeper" that had been placed in a container of chloroform, allowing law enforcement to monitor the location of the container. We said that there had been no infringement of Knotts' reasonable expectation of privacy since the information obtained — the location of the automobile carrying the container on public roads, and the location of the off-loaded container in open fields near Knotts' cabin — had been voluntarily conveyed to the public. But as we have discussed, the *Katz* reasonable-expectation-of-privacy test has been *added to*, not *substituted for*, the common-law trespassory test. The holding in *Knotts* addressed only the former, since the latter was not at issue. The beeper had been placed in the container before it came into Knotts' possession, with the consent of the then-owner. Knotts did not challenge that installation, and we specifically declined to consider its effect on the Fourth Amendment analysis. *Knotts* would be relevant, perhaps, if the Government were making the argument that what would otherwise be an unconstitutional search is not such where it produces only public information. The Government does not make that argument, and we know of no case that would support it.

The second "beeper" case, *United States v. Karo* (1984), does not suggest a different conclusion. There we addressed the question left open by *Knotts*, whether the installation of a beeper in a container amounted to a search or seizure. As in *Knotts* at the time the beeper was installed the container belonged to a third party, and it did not come into possession of the defendant until later. Thus, the specific question we considered was whether the installation "*with the consent of the original owner* constitute[d] a search or seizure . . . when the container is delivered to a buyer having no knowledge of the presence of the beeper." We held not. The Government, we said, came into physical contact with the container only before it belonged to the defendant Karo; and the transfer of the container with the unmonitored beeper inside did not convey any information and thus did not invade Karo's privacy. That conclusion is perfectly consistent with the one we reach here. Karo accepted the container as it came to him, beeper and all, and was therefore not entitled to object to the beeper's presence, even though it was used to monitor the container's location.

B

The concurrence begins by accusing us of applying "18th-century tort law." That is a distortion. What we apply is an 18th-century guarantee against unreasonable searches, which we believe must provide *at a minimum* the degree of protection it afforded when it was adopted. The concurrence does not share that belief. It would apply *exclusively Katz's* reasonable-expectation-of-privacy test, even when that eliminates rights that previously existed.

The concurrence faults our approach for "present[ing] particularly vexing problems" in cases that do not involve physical contact, such as those that involve the transmission of electronic signals. We entirely fail to understand that point. For unlike the concurrence, which would make *Katz* the *exclusive* test, we do not make trespass the exclusive test. Situations involving merely the transmission of electronic signals without trespass would *remain* subject to *Katz* analysis.

In fact, it is the concurrence's insistence on the exclusivity of the *Katz* test that needlessly leads us into "particularly vexing problems" in the present case. This Court has to date not deviated from the understanding that mere visual observation does not constitute a search. We accordingly held in *Knotts* that "[a] person traveling in an automobile on public thoroughfares has no reasonable expectation of privacy in his movements from one place to another." Thus, even assuming that the concurrence is correct to say that "[t]raditional surveillance" of Jones for a 4-week period "would have required a large team of agents, multiple vehicles, and perhaps aerial assistance," our cases suggest that such visual observation is constitutionally permissible. It may be that achieving the same result through electronic means, without an accompanying trespass, is an unconstitutional invasion of privacy, but the present case does not require us to answer that question.

And answering it affirmatively leads us needlessly into additional thorny problems. The concurrence posits that "relatively short-term monitoring of a person's movements on public streets" is okay, but that "the use of longer term GPS monitoring in investigations *of most offenses*" is no good. That introduces yet another novelty into our jurisprudence. There is no precedent for the proposition that whether a search has occurred depends on the nature of the crime being investigated. And even accepting that novelty, it remains unexplained why a 4-week investigation is "surely" too long and why a drug-trafficking conspiracy involving substantial amounts of cash and narcotics is not an "extraordinary offens[e]" which may permit longer observation. What of a 2-day monitoring of a suspected purveyor of stolen electronics? Or of a 6-month monitoring of a suspected terrorist? We may have to grapple with these "vexing problems" in some future case where a classic trespassory search is not involved and resort must be had to *Katz* analysis; but there is no reason for rushing forward to resolve them here.

Justice SOTOMAYOR, concurring.

I join the Court's opinion because I agree that a search within the meaning of the Fourth Amendment occurs, at a minimum, "[w]here, as here, the Government obtains information by physically intruding on a constitutionally protected area." In this case, the Government installed a Global Positioning System (GPS) tracking device on respondent Antoine Jones' Jeep without a valid warrant and without Jones' consent, then used that device to monitor the Jeep's movements over the course of four weeks. The Government usurped Jones' property for the purpose of conducting surveillance on him, thereby invading privacy interests long afforded, and undoubtedly entitled to, Fourth Amendment protection. Justice Alito's approach, which discounts altogether the constitutional relevance of the Government's physical intrusion on Jones' Jeep, erodes that longstanding protection for privacy expectations inherent in items of property that people possess or control. By contrast, the trespassory test applied in the majority's opinion reflects an irreducible constitutional minimum: When the Government physically invades personal property to gather information, a search occurs. The reaffirmation of that principle suffices to decide this case.

Nonetheless, as Justice Alito notes, physical intrusion is now unnecessary to many forms of surveillance. With increasing regularity, the Government will be capable of duplicating the monitoring undertaken in this case by enlisting factory- or owner-installed vehicle tracking devices or GPS-enabled smartphones. In cases of electronic or other novel modes of surveillance that do not depend upon a physical invasion on property, the majority opinion's trespassory test may provide little guidance. As Justice Alito incisively observes, the same technological advances that have made possible nontrespassory surveillance techniques will also affect the *Katz* test by shaping the evolution of societal privacy expectations. Under that rubric, I agree with Justice Alito that, at the very least, "longer term GPS monitoring in investigations of most offenses impinges on expectations of privacy."

In cases involving even short-term monitoring, some unique attributes of GPS surveillance relevant to the *Katz* analysis will require particular attention. GPS monitoring generates a precise, comprehensive record of a person's public movements that reflects a wealth of detail about her familial, political, professional, religious, and sexual associations. The Government can store such records and efficiently mine them for information years into the future. And because GPS monitoring is cheap in comparison to conventional surveillance techniques and, by design, proceeds surreptitiously, it evades the ordinary checks that constrain abusive law enforcement practices: "limited police resources and community hostility."

Awareness that the Government may be watching chills associational and expressive freedoms. And the Government's unrestrained power to assemble data that reveal private aspects of identity is susceptible to abuse. The net result is that GPS monitoring — by making available at a relatively low cost such a substantial quantum of intimate information about any person whom the Government, in its unfettered discretion, chooses to track — may "alter the relationship between citizen and government in a way that is inimical to democratic society."

I would take these attributes of GPS monitoring into account when considering the existence of a reasonable societal expectation of privacy in the sum of one's public movements. I would ask whether people reasonably expect that their movements will be recorded and aggregated in a manner that enables the Government to ascertain, more or less at will, their political and religious beliefs, sexual habits, and so on. I do not regard as dispositive the fact that the Government might obtain the fruits of GPS monitoring through lawful conventional surveillance techniques. I would also consider the appropriateness of entrusting to the Executive, in the absence of any oversight from a coordinate branch, a tool so amenable to misuse, especially in light of the Fourth Amendment's goal to curb arbitrary exercises of police power to and prevent "a too permeating police surveillance."

More fundamentally, it may be necessary to reconsider the premise that an individual has no reasonable expectation of privacy in information voluntarily disclosed to third parties. This approach is ill suited to the digital age, in which people reveal a great deal of information about themselves to third parties in the course of carrying out mundane tasks. People disclose the phone numbers that they dial or text to their cellular providers; the URLs that they visit and the e-mail addresses with which they correspond to their Internet service providers; and the books, groceries, and medications they purchase to online retailers. Perhaps, as Justice Alito notes, some people may find the "tradeoff" of privacy for convenience "worthwhile," or come to accept this "diminution of privacy" as "inevitable," and perhaps not. I for one doubt that people would accept without complaint the warrantless disclosure to the Government of a list of every Web site they had visited in the last week, or month, or year. But whatever the societal expectations, they can attain constitutionally protected status only if our Fourth Amendment jurisprudence ceases to treat secrecy as a prerequisite for privacy. I would not assume that all information voluntarily disclosed to some member of the public for a limited purpose is, for that reason alone, disentitled to Fourth Amendment protection. Resolution of these difficult questions in this case is unnecessary, however, because the Government's physical intrusion on Jones' Jeep supplies a narrower basis for decision. I therefore join the majority's opinion.

Justice ALITO, with whom Justice GINSBURG, Justice BREYER, and Justice KAGAN join, concurring in the judgment.

This case requires us to apply the Fourth Amendment's prohibition of unreasonable searches and seizures to a 21st-century surveillance technique, the use of a Global Positioning System (GPS) device to monitor a vehicle's movements for an extended period of time. Ironically, the Court has chosen to decide this case based on 18th-century tort law. By attaching a small GPS device to the underside of the vehicle that respondent drove, the law enforcement officers in this case engaged in conduct that might have provided grounds in 1791 for a suit for trespass to chattels. And for this reason, the Court concludes, the installation and use of the GPS device constituted a search.

This holding, in my judgment, is unwise. It strains the language of the Fourth Amendment; it has little if any support in current Fourth Amendment case law; and it is highly artificial. I would analyze the question presented in this case by asking whether respondent's reasonable expectations of privacy were violated by the long-term monitoring of the movements of the vehicle he drove.

I

The Fourth Amendment prohibits "unreasonable searches and seizures," and the Court makes very little effort to explain how the attachment or use of the GPS device fits within these terms. The Court does not contend that there was a seizure. A seizure of property occurs when there is "some meaningful interference with an individual's possessory interests in that property," and here there was none. Indeed, the success of the surveillance technique that the officers employed was dependent on the fact that the GPS did not interfere in any way with the operation of the vehicle, for if any such interference had been detected, the device might have been discovered.

The Court does claim that the installation and use of the GPS constituted a search, but this conclusion is dependent on the questionable proposition that these two procedures cannot be separated for purposes of Fourth Amendment analysis. If these two procedures are analyzed separately, it is not at all clear from the Court's opinion why either should be regarded as a search. It is clear that the attachment of the GPS device was not itself a search; if the device had not functioned or if the officers had not used it, no information would have been obtained. And the Court does not contend that the use of the device constituted a search either. On the contrary, the Court accepts the holding in *United States v. Knotts* (1983), that the use of a surreptitiously planted electronic device to monitor a vehicle's movements on public roads did not amount to a search.

The Court argues — and I agree — that "we must 'assur[e] preservation of that degree of privacy against government that existed when the Fourth Amendment was adopted.'" But it is almost impossible to think of late-18th-century situations that are analogous to what took place in this case. The Court's theory seems to be that the concept of a search, as originally understood, comprehended any technical trespass that led to the gathering of evidence, but we know that this is incorrect.

The Court's reasoning in this case is very similar to that in the Court's early decisions involving wiretapping and electronic eavesdropping, namely, that a technical trespass followed by the gathering of evidence constitutes a search. In the early electronic surveillance cases, the Court concluded that a Fourth Amendment search occurred when private conversations were monitored as a result of an "unauthorized physical penetration into the premises occupied" by the defendant. By contrast, in cases in which there was no trespass, it was held that there was no search.

This trespass-based rule was repeatedly criticized. *Katz v. United States* (1967), finally did away with the old approach, holding that a trespass was not required for a Fourth Amendment violation. What mattered, the Court now held, was whether the conduct at issue "violated the privacy upon which [the defendant] justifiably relied while using the telephone booth." Under this approach, as the Court later put it when addressing the relevance of a technical trespass, "an actual trespass is neither necessary *nor sufficient* to establish a constitutional violation."

[II]

Disharmony with a substantial body of existing case law is only one of the problems with the Court's approach in this case.

I will briefly note four others. First, the Court's reasoning largely disregards what is really important (the *use* of a GPS for the purpose of long-term tracking) and instead attaches great significance to something that most would view as relatively minor (attaching to the bottom of a car a small, light object that does not interfere in any way with the car's operation). Attaching such an object is generally regarded as so trivial that it does not provide a basis for recovery under modern tort law. But under the Court's reasoning, this conduct may violate the Fourth Amendment. By contrast, if long-term monitoring can be accomplished without committing a technical trespass — suppose, for example, that the Federal Government required or persuaded auto manufacturers to include a GPS tracking device in every car — the Court's theory would provide no protection.

Second, the Court's approach leads to incongruous results. If the police attach a GPS device to a car and use the device to follow the car for even a brief time, under the Court's theory, the Fourth Amendment applies. But if the police follow the same car for a much longer period using unmarked cars and aerial assistance, this tracking is not subject to any Fourth Amendment constraints.

Third, under the Court's theory, the coverage of the Fourth Amendment may vary from State to State. If the events at issue here had occurred in a community property State or a State that has adopted the Uniform Marital Property Act, respondent would likely be an owner of the vehicle, and it would not matter whether the GPS was installed before or after his wife turned over the keys. In non-community-property States, on the other hand, the registration of the vehicle in the name of respondent's wife would generally be regarded as presumptive evidence that she was the sole owner.

Fourth, the Court's reliance on the law of trespass will present particularly vexing problems in cases involving surveillance that is carried out by making electronic, as opposed to physical, contact with the item to be tracked. For example, suppose that the officers in the present case had followed respondent by surreptitiously activating a stolen vehicle detection system that came with the car when it was purchased. Would the sending of a radio signal to activate this system constitute a trespass to chattels? Trespass to chattels has traditionally required a physical touching of the property.

[III]

The *Katz* expectation-of-privacy test avoids the problems and complications noted above, but it is not without its own difficulties. It involves a degree of circularity, and judges are apt to confuse their own expectations of privacy with those of the hypothetical reasonable person to which the *Katz* test looks. In addition, the *Katz* test rests on the assumption that this hypothetical reasonable person has a well-developed and stable set of privacy expectations. But technology can change those expectations. Dramatic technological change may lead to periods in which popular expectations are in flux and may ultimately produce significant changes in popular attitudes. New technology may provide increased convenience or security at the expense of privacy, and many people may find the tradeoff worthwhile. And even if the public does not welcome the diminution of privacy that new technology entails, they may eventually reconcile themselves to this development as inevitable.

On the other hand, concern about new intrusions on privacy may spur the enactment of legislation to protect against these intrusions. This is what ultimately happened with respect to wiretapping. After *Katz*, Congress did not leave it to the courts to develop a body of Fourth Amendment case law governing that complex subject. Instead, Congress promptly enacted a comprehensive statute and since that time, the regulation of wiretapping has been governed primarily by statute and not by case law.

B

Recent years have seen the emergence of many new devices that permit the monitoring of a person's movements. In some locales, closed-circuit television video monitoring is becoming ubiquitous. On toll roads, automatic toll collection systems create a precise record of the movements of motorists who choose to make use of that convenience. Many motorists purchase cars that are equipped with devices that permit a central station to ascertain the car's location at any time so that roadside assistance may be provided if needed and the car may be found if it is stolen.

Perhaps most significant, cell phones and other wireless devices now permit wireless carriers to track and record the location of users — and as of June 2011, it has been reported, there were more than 322 million wireless devices in use in the United States. For older phones, the accuracy of the location information depends on the density of the tower network, but new "smart phones," which are equipped with a GPS device, permit more precise tracking. Similarly, phone-location-tracking services are offered as "social" tools, allowing consumers to find (or to avoid) others who enroll in these services. The availability and use of these and other new devices will continue to shape the average person's expectations about the privacy of his or her daily movements.

[IV]

In the pre-computer age, the greatest protections of privacy were neither constitutional nor statutory, but practical. Traditional surveillance for any extended period of time was difficult and costly and therefore rarely undertaken. The surveillance at issue in this case — constant monitoring of the location of a vehicle for four weeks — would have required a large team of agents, multiple vehicles, and perhaps aerial assistance. Only an investigation of unusual importance could have justified such an expenditure of law enforcement resources. Devices like the one used in the present case, however, make long-term monitoring relatively easy and cheap. In circumstances involving dramatic technological change, the best solution to privacy concerns may be legislative. A legislative body is well situated to gauge changing public attitudes, to draw detailed lines, and to balance privacy and public safety in a comprehensive way.

To date, however, Congress and most States have not enacted statutes regulating the use of GPS tracking technology for law enforcement purposes. The best that we can do in this case is to apply existing Fourth Amendment doctrine and to ask whether the use of GPS tracking in a particular case involved a degree of intrusion that a reasonable person would not have anticipated.

Under this approach, relatively short-term monitoring of a person's movements on public streets accords with expectations of privacy that our society has recognized as reasonable. But the use of longer term GPS monitoring in investigations of most offenses impinges on expectations of privacy. For such offenses, society's expectation has been that law enforcement agents and others would not — and indeed, in the main, simply could not — secretly monitor and catalogue every single movement of an individual's car for a very long period. In this case, for four weeks, law enforcement agents tracked every movement that respondent made in the vehicle he was driving. We need not identify with precision the point at which the tracking of this vehicle became a search, for the line was surely crossed before the 4-week mark. Other cases may present more difficult questions. But where uncertainty exists with respect to whether a certain period of GPS surveillance is long enough to constitute a Fourth Amendment search, the police may always seek a warrant. We also need not consider whether prolonged GPS monitoring in the context of investigations involving extraordinary offenses would similarly intrude on a constitutionally protected sphere of privacy. In such cases, long-term tracking might have been mounted using previously available techniques.

For these reasons, I conclude that the lengthy monitoring that occurred in this case constituted a search under the Fourth Amendment. I therefore agree with the majority that the decision of the Court of Appeals must be affirmed.

The crucial question after *Katz* is in defining when a person has a "reasonable expectation of privacy." On the one hand, the test has the advantage that, as the Court says, it focuses on persons and not property; it puts a central aspect of the Fourth Amendment, protecting privacy, at the core of analysis as to whether there has been a search. On other hand, "reasonable expectation of privacy" is inherently vague and there is the concern that the government could undermine it just by making clear that people should not expect privacy in certain circumstances.

The Court has considered the application of this test in a number of specific contexts. For example, the Court has considered whether the following violate a reasonable expectation of privacy: searches in open fields; aerial searches; use of thermal imaging devices directed at homes; searches of a person's trash; observation and monitoring of public behavior; and use of dogs to sniff for contraband. Each is discussed below. These are important areas where the Court has applied the "reasonable expectation of privacy" standard, but these are by no means the only areas where the issue arises. In considering these cases, it is important to consider whether they follow a sensible approach to determining what is a search and to effectuating the Fourth Amendment, or whether they are an inconsistent body of decisions that shows the problems with a vague standard like "reasonable expectation of privacy."

1.   Open Fields

A half century before *Katz*, in Hester v. United States, 265 U.S. 57 (1924), the Supreme Court held that "[t]he special protection accorded by the Fourth Amendment to the person in their 'persons, houses, papers, and effects' is not extended to the open fields. The distinction between the latter and the house is as old as the common law." A distinction thus developed between police actions in open fields, where the Fourth Amendment does not apply, and searches of a person's home and the areas immediately adjacent to it (the "curtilage"), where the Fourth Amendment applies. Oliver v. United States is an important case, decided after *Katz*, which reaffirms the "open fields" doctrine.

OLIVER v. UNITED STATES
466 U.S. 170 (1984)

Justice POWELL delivered the opinion of the Court.

The "open fields" doctrine, first enunciated by this Court in Hester v. United States (1924), permits police officers to enter and search a field without a warrant. We granted certiorari in these cases to clarify confusion that has arisen as to the continued vitality of the doctrine.

I

Acting on reports that marihuana was being raised on the farm of petitioner Oliver, two narcotics agents of the Kentucky State Police went to the farm to investigate.[2] Arriving at the farm, they drove past petitioner's house to a locked gate with a "No Trespassing" sign. A footpath led around one side of the gate. The agents walked around the gate and along the road for several hundred yards, passing a barn and a parked camper. At that point, someone

---

2. It is conceded that the police did not have a warrant authorizing the search, that there was no probable cause for the search, and that no exception to the warrant requirement is applicable. [Footnote by the Court.]

standing in front of the camper shouted: "No hunting is allowed, come back up here." The officers shouted back that they were Kentucky State Police officers, but found no one when they returned to the camper. The officers resumed their investigation of the farm and found a field of marihuana over a mile from petitioner's home.

Petitioner was arrested and indicted for "manufactur[ing]" a "controlled substance." After a pretrial hearing, the District Court suppressed evidence of the discovery of the marihuana field. Applying Katz v. United States (1967), the court found that petitioner had a reasonable expectation that the field would remain private because petitioner "had done all that could be expected of him to assert his privacy in the area of farm that was searched." He had posted "No Trespassing" signs at regular intervals and had locked the gate at the entrance to the center of the farm. Further, the court noted that the field itself is highly secluded: it is bounded on all sides by woods, fences, and embankments and cannot be seen from any point of public access. The court concluded that this was not an "open" field that invited casual intrusion.

The Court of Appeals for the Sixth Circuit, sitting en banc, reversed the District Court. The court concluded that *Katz*, upon which the District Court relied, had not impaired the vitality of the open fields doctrine of *Hester*.

II

The rule announced in Hester v. United States was founded upon the explicit language of the Fourth Amendment. That Amendment indicates with some precision the places and things encompassed by its protections. As Justice Holmes explained for the Court in his characteristically laconic style: "[T]he special protection accorded by the Fourth Amendment to the people in their 'persons, houses, papers, and effects,' is not extended to the open fields."

Nor are the open fields "effects" within the meaning of the Fourth Amendment. In this respect, it is suggestive that James Madison's proposed draft of what became the Fourth Amendment preserves "[t]he rights of the people to be secured in their persons, their houses, their papers, and their other property, from all unreasonable searches and seizures. . . ." Although Congress' revisions of Madison's proposal broadened the scope of the Amendment in some respects, the term "effects" is less inclusive than "property" and cannot be said to encompass open fields. We conclude, as did the Court in deciding Hester v. United States, that the government's intrusion upon the open fields is not one of those "unreasonable searches" proscribed by the text of the Fourth Amendment.

III

This interpretation of the Fourth Amendment's language is consistent with the understanding of the right to privacy expressed in our Fourth

Amendment jurisprudence. Since Katz v. United States (1967), the touchstone of Amendment analysis has been the question whether a person has a "constitutionally protected reasonable expectation of privacy." The Amendment does not protect the merely subjective expectation of privacy, but only those "expectation[s] that society is prepared to recognize as 'reasonable.'"

No single factor determines whether an individual legitimately may claim under the Fourth Amendment that a place should be free of government intrusion not authorized by warrant. In assessing the degree to which a search infringes upon individual privacy, the Court has given weight to such factors as the intention of the Framers of the Fourth Amendment, the uses to which the individual has put a location, and our societal understanding that certain areas deserve the most scrupulous protection from government invasion. These factors are equally relevant to determining whether the government's intrusion upon open fields without a warrant or probable cause violates reasonable expectations of privacy and is therefore a search proscribed by the Amendment.

In this light, the rule of Hester v. United States that we reaffirm today, may be understood as providing that an individual may not legitimately demand privacy for activities conducted out of doors in fields, except in the area immediately surrounding the home. This rule is true to the conception of the right to privacy embodied in the Fourth Amendment. The Amendment reflects the recognition of the Framers that certain enclaves should be free from arbitrary government interference. For example, the Court since the enactment of the Fourth Amendment has stressed "the overriding respect for the sanctity of the home that has been embedded in our traditions since the origins of the Republic."

In contrast, open fields do not provide the setting for those intimate activities that the Amendment is intended to shelter from government interference or surveillance. There is no societal interest in protecting the privacy of those activities, such as the cultivation of crops, that occur in open fields. Moreover, as a practical matter these lands usually are accessible to the public and the police in ways that a home, an office, or commercial structure would not be. It is not generally true that fences or "No Trespassing" signs effectively bar the public from viewing open fields in rural areas. [P]etitioner Oliver concede[s] that the public and police lawfully may survey lands from the air. For these reasons, the asserted expectation of privacy in open fields is not an expectation that "society recognizes as reasonable."

Nor is the government's intrusion upon an open field a "search" in the constitutional sense because that intrusion is a trespass at common law. The existence of a property right is but one element in determining whether expectations of privacy are legitimate. "The premise that property interests control the right of the Government to search and seize has been discredited." "[E]ven a property interest in premises may not be sufficient to establish a legitimate expectation of privacy with respect to particular items located on the premises or activity conducted thereon."

The common law may guide consideration of what areas are protected by the Fourth Amendment by defining areas whose invasion by others is wrongful. The law of trespass, however, forbids intrusions upon land that the Fourth Amendment would not proscribe. For trespass law extends to instances where the exercise of the right to exclude vindicates no legitimate privacy interest. Thus, in the case of open fields, the general rights of property protected by the common law of trespass have little or no relevance to the applicability of the Fourth Amendment.

Justice MARSHALL, with whom Justice BRENNAN and Justice STEVENS join, dissenting.

[P]olice officers, ignoring clearly visible "No Trespassing" signs, entered upon private land in search of evidence of a crime. At a spot that could not be seen from any vantage point accessible to the public, the police discovered contraband, which was subsequently used to incriminate the owner of the land. In neither case did the police have a warrant authorizing their activities.

The Court holds that police conduct of this sort does not constitute an "unreasonable search" within the meaning of the Fourth Amendment. The Court reaches that startling conclusion by two independent analytical routes. First, the Court argues that, because the Fourth Amendment by its terms renders people secure in their "persons, houses, papers, and effects," it is inapplicable to trespasses upon land not lying within the curtilage of a dwelling. Second, the Court contends that "an individual may not legitimately demand privacy for activities conducted out of doors in fields, except in the area immediately surrounding the home." Because I cannot agree with either of these propositions, I dissent.

[I]

The second ground for the Court's decision is its contention that any interest a landowner might have in the privacy of his woods and fields is not one that "society is prepared to recognize as 'reasonable.'" But the Court's conclusion cannot withstand scrutiny.

As the Court acknowledges, we have traditionally looked to a variety of factors in determining whether an expectation of privacy asserted in a physical space is "reasonable." Though those factors do not lend themselves to precise taxonomy, they may be roughly grouped into three categories. First, we consider whether the expectation at issue is rooted in entitlements defined by positive law. Second, we consider the nature of the uses to which spaces of the sort in question can be put. Third, we consider whether the person claiming a privacy interest manifested that interest to the public in a way that most people would understand and respect. When the expectations of privacy asserted by petitioner Oliver [is] examined through these lenses, it becomes clear that those expectations are entitled to constitutional protection.

We have frequently acknowledged that privacy interests are not coterminous with property rights. However, because "property rights reflect society's explicit recognition of a person's authority to act as he wishes in certain areas, [they] should be considered in determining whether an individual's expectations of privacy are reasonable." Indeed, the Court has suggested that, insofar as "[o]ne of the main rights attaching to property is the right to exclude others, . . . one who owns or lawfully possesses or controls property will in all likelihood have a legitimate expectation of privacy by virtue of this right to exclude."

It is undisputed that Oliver owned the land into which the police intruded. That fact alone provides considerable support for their assertion of legitimate privacy interests in their woods and fields. But even more telling is the nature of the sanctions that Oliver could invoke, under local law, for violation of [his] property rights. In Kentucky, a knowing entry upon fenced or otherwise enclosed land, or upon unenclosed land conspicuously posted with signs excluding the public, constitutes criminal trespass. Thus, positive law not only recognizes the legitimacy of Oliver's fixed insistence that strangers keep off [his] land, but subjects those who refuse to respect their wishes to the most severe of penalties — criminal liability. Under these circumstances, it is hard to credit the Court's assertion that Oliver's expectations of privacy were not of a sort that society is prepared to recognize as reasonable.

The uses to which a place is put are highly relevant to the assessment of a privacy interest asserted therein. If, in light of our shared sensibilities, those activities are of a kind in which people should be able to engage without fear of intrusion by private persons or government officials, we extend the protection of the Fourth Amendment to the space in question, even in the absence of any entitlement derived from positive law.

Privately owned woods and fields that are not exposed to public view regularly are employed in a variety of ways that society acknowledges deserve privacy. Many landowners like to take solitary walks on their property, confident that they will not be confronted in their rambles by strangers or policemen. Others conduct agricultural businesses on their property. Some landowners use their secluded spaces to meet lovers, others to gather together with fellow worshippers, still others to engage in sustained creative endeavor. Private land is sometimes used as a refuge for wildlife, where flora and fauna are protected from human intervention of any kind. Our respect for the freedom of landowners to use their posted "open fields" in ways such as these partially explains the seriousness with which the positive law regards deliberate invasions of such spaces, and substantially reinforces the landowners' contention that their expectations of privacy are "reasonable."

Whether a person "took normal precautions to maintain his privacy" in a given space affects whether his interest is one protected by the Fourth Amendment. The reason why such precautions are relevant is that we do not insist that a person who has a right to exclude others exercise that right. A claim to privacy is therefore strengthened by the fact that the claimant somehow manifested to other people his desire that they keep their distance.

Certain spaces are so presumptively private that signals of this sort are unnecessary; a homeowner need not post a "Do Not Enter" sign on his door in order to deny entrance to uninvited guests. Privacy interests in other spaces are more ambiguous, and the taking of precautions is consequently more important; placing a lock on one's footlocker strengthens one's claim that an examination of its contents is impermissible. Still other spaces are, by positive law and social convention, presumed accessible to members of the public unless the owner manifests his intention to exclude them.

Undeveloped land falls into the last-mentioned category. If a person has not marked the boundaries of his fields or woods in a way that informs passersby that they are not welcome, he cannot object if members of the public enter onto the property. There is no reason why he should have any greater rights as against government officials. Accordingly, we have held that an official may, without a warrant, enter private land from which the public is not excluded and make observations from that vantage point.

A very different case is presented when the owner of undeveloped land has taken precautions to exclude the public. As indicated above, a deliberate entry by a private citizen onto private property marked with "No Trespassing" signs will expose him to criminal liability. I see no reason why a government official should not be obliged to respect such unequivocal and universally understood manifestations of a landowner's desire for privacy.

In sum, examination of the three principal criteria we have traditionally used for assessing the reasonableness of a person's expectation that a given space would remain private indicates that interests of the sort asserted by Oliver are entitled to constitutional protection. An owner's right to insist that others stay off his posted land is firmly grounded in positive law. Many of the uses to which such land may be put deserve privacy. And, by marking the boundaries of the land with warnings that the public should not intrude, the owner has dispelled any ambiguity as to his desires.

[II]

A clear, easily administrable rule emerges from the analysis set forth above: Private land marked in a fashion sufficient to render entry thereon a criminal trespass under the law of the State in which the land lies is protected by the Fourth Amendment's proscription of unreasonable searches and seizures. One of the advantages of the foregoing rule is that it draws upon a doctrine already familiar to both citizens and government officials.

By contrast, the doctrine announced by the Court today is incapable of determinate application. Police officers, making warrantless entries upon private land, will be obliged in the future to make on-the-spot judgments as to how far the curtilage extends, and to stay outside that zone. In addition, we may expect to see a spate of litigation over the question of how much improvement is necessary to remove private land from the category of "unoccupied or undeveloped area" to which the "open fields exception" is now deemed applicable.

The Court's holding not only ill serves the need to make constitutional doctrine "workable for application by rank-and-file, trained police officers," it withdraws the shield of the Fourth Amendment from privacy interests that clearly deserve protection. By exempting from the coverage of the Amendment large areas of private land, the Court opens the way to investigative activities we would all find repugnant.

The Fourth Amendment, properly construed, embodies and gives effect to our collective sense of the degree to which men and women, in civilized society, are entitled "to be let alone" by their governments. The Court's opinion bespeaks and will help to promote an impoverished vision of that fundamental right.

The Court in *Oliver* says that the Fourth Amendment applies if police search a person's home or the "curtilage" immediately adjacent to the home, but not if the police are searching in an open field. The distinction between curtilage and open fields is thus crucial in determining whether the Fourth Amendment applies at all. In United States v. Dunn, the Court attempted to clarify this distinction.

UNITED STATES v. DUNN
480 U.S. 294 (1987)

Justice WHITE delivered the opinion of the Court.

We granted the Government's petition for certiorari to decide whether the area near a barn, located approximately 50 yards from a fence surrounding a ranch house, is, for Fourth Amendment purposes, within the curtilage of the house. We conclude that the barn and the area around it lay outside the curtilage of the house.

I

Respondent Ronald Dale Dunn and a codefendant, Robert Lyle Carpenter, were convicted by a jury of conspiring to manufacture phenylacetone and amphetamine, and to possess amphetamine with intent to distribute, in violation of 21 U.S.C. §846. Respondent was also convicted of manufacturing these two controlled substances and possessing amphetamine with intent to distribute. The events giving rise to respondent's apprehension and conviction began in 1980 when agents from the Drug Enforcement Administration (DEA) discovered that Carpenter had purchased large quantities of chemicals and equipment used in the manufacture of amphetamine and phenylacetone. DEA agents obtained warrants from a Texas state judge authorizing installation of miniature electronic transmitter tracking devices, or "beepers," in an electric hot plate stirrer, a drum of acetic anhydride, and a container holding phenylacetic acid, a precursor to phenylacetone. All of these items had been ordered by Carpenter. On September 3, 1980, Carpenter took possession of the electric hot plate stirrer, but the agents lost the signal from the "beeper" a few days later. The agents were able to track the "beeper" in the container of chemicals, however, from October 27, 1980, until November 5, 1980, on which date Carpenter's pickup truck, which was carrying the container, arrived at respondent's ranch. Aerial photographs of the ranch property showed Carpenter's truck backed up to a barn behind the ranch house. The agents also began receiving transmission signals from the "beeper" in the hot plate stirrer that they had lost in early September and determined that the stirrer was on respondent's ranch property.

Respondent's ranch comprised approximately 198 acres and was completely encircled by a perimeter fence. The property also contained several interior fences, constructed mainly of posts and multiple strands of barbed wire. The ranch residence was situated $1/2$ mile from a public road. A fence encircled the residence and a nearby small greenhouse. Two barns were located approximately 50 yards from this fence. The front of the larger of the two barns was enclosed by a wooden fence and had an open overhang. Locked, waist-high gates barred entry into the barn proper, and netting material stretched from the ceiling to the top of the wooden gates.

On the evening of November 5, 1980, law enforcement officials made a warrantless entry onto respondent's ranch property. A DEA agent accompanied by an officer from the Houston Police Department crossed over the perimeter fence and one interior fence. Standing approximately midway between the residence and the barns, the DEA agent smelled what he believed to be phenylacetic acid, the odor coming from the direction of the barns. The officers approached the smaller of the barns — crossing over a barbed wire fence — and, looking into the barn, observed only empty boxes. The officers then proceeded to the larger barn, crossing another barbed wire fence as well as a wooden fence that enclosed the front portion of the barn. The officers walked under the barn's overhang to the locked wooden gates and, shining a flashlight through the netting on top of the gates, peered into the barn. They observed what the DEA agent thought to be a phenylacetone laboratory. The officers did not enter the barn. At this point the officers departed from respondent's property, but entered it twice more on November 6 to confirm the presence of the phenylacetone laboratory.

On November 6, 1980, at 8:30 P.M., a Federal Magistrate issued a warrant authorizing a search of respondent's ranch. DEA agents and state law enforcement officials executed the warrant on November 8, 1980. The officers arrested respondent and seized chemicals and equipment, as well as bags of amphetamines they discovered in a closet in the ranch house.

II

The curtilage concept originated at common law to extend to the area immediately surrounding a dwelling house the same protection under the law of burglary as was afforded the house itself. The concept plays a part, however, in interpreting the reach of the Fourth Amendment. Hester v. United States (1924), held that the Fourth Amendment's protection accorded "persons, houses, papers, and effects" did not extend to the open fields, the Court observing that the distinction between a person's house and open fields "is as old as the common law."

[W]e believe that curtilage questions should be resolved with particular reference to four factors: the proximity of the area claimed to be curtilage to the home, whether the area is included within an enclosure surrounding the home, the nature of the uses to which the area is put, and the steps taken by the resident to protect the area from observation by people passing by. We do not suggest that combining these factors produces a finely tuned formula that, when mechanically applied, yields a "correct" answer to all extent-of-curtilage questions. Rather, these factors are useful analytical tools only to the degree that, in any given case, they bear upon the centrally relevant consideration — whether the area in question is so intimately tied to the home itself that it should be placed under the home's "umbrella" of Fourth Amendment protection. Applying these factors to respondent's barn and to the area immediately surrounding it, we have little difficulty in concluding that this area lay outside the curtilage of the ranch house.

First. The record discloses that the barn was located 50 yards from the fence surrounding the house and 60 yards from the house itself. Standing in isolation, this substantial distance supports no inference that the barn should be treated as an adjunct of the house.

Second. It is also significant that respondent's barn did not lie within the area surrounding the house that was enclosed by a fence. Viewing the physical layout of respondent's ranch in its entirety, it is plain that the fence surrounding the residence serves to demark a specific area of land immediately adjacent to the house that is readily identifiable as part and parcel of the house. Conversely, the barn — the front portion itself enclosed by a fence — and the area immediately surrounding it, stands out as a distinct portion of respondent's ranch, quite separate from the residence.

Third. It is especially significant that the law enforcement officials possessed objective data indicating that the barn was not being used for intimate activities of the home.

Fourth. Respondent did little to protect the barn area from observation by those standing in the open fields. Nothing in the record suggests that the various interior fences on respondent's property had any function other

than that of the typical ranch fence; the fences were designed and constructed to corral livestock, not to prevent persons from observing what
lay inside the enclosed areas.

Justice BRENNAN, with whom Justice MARSHALL joins, dissenting.

The Government agents' intrusions upon Ronald Dunn's privacy and
property violated the Fourth Amendment for two reasons. First, the
barnyard invaded by the agents lay within the protected curtilage of
Dunn's farmhouse. Second, the agents infringed upon Dunn's reasonable
expectation of privacy in the barn and its contents. Our society is not so
exclusively urban that it is unable to perceive or unwilling to preserve the
expectation of farmers and ranchers that barns and their contents are protected from (literally) unwarranted government intrusion.

Thus, case law demonstrates that a barn is an integral part of a farm home
and therefore lies within the curtilage. The Court's opinion provides no
justification for its indifference to the weight of state and federal precedent.

First, the distance between the house and the barn does not militate
against the barn or barnyard's presence in the curtilage. Many of the
cases cited involve a barn separated from a residence by a distance in excess
of 60 yards. Second, the cases make evident that the configuration of fences
is not determinative of the status of an outbuilding. Here, where the barn
was connected to the house by a "well walked" and a "well driven" and was
clustered with the farmhouse and other outbuildings in a clearing surrounded by woods, the presence of intervening fences fades into
irrelevance.

The third factor in the test — the nature of the uses to which the area
is put — has been badly misunderstood and misapplied by the Court.
The Court reasons that, because the barn and barnyard were not actually
in domestic use, they were not within the curtilage. This reveals a misunderstanding of the level of generality at which the constitutional
inquiry must proceed and is flatly inconsistent with the Court's analysis
in *Oliver*.

Finally, neither the smell of the chemicals nor the sound of the motor
running would remove the protection of the Fourth Amendment from an
otherwise protected structure. A barn, like a home, may simultaneously be
put to domestic and nondomestic uses, even the manufacture of drugs. Dual
use does not strip a home or any building within the curtilage of Fourth
Amendment protection. What the evidence cited by the Court might suggest
is that the DEA agents had probable cause to enter the barn or barnyard
before they made any unconstitutional intrusion. If so — and I do not concede it — they should have obtained a warrant.

With regard to the fourth factor of the curtilage test, I find astounding the
Court's conclusion that "[r]espondent did little to protect the barn area
from observation by those standing in the open fields." Initially, I note
that the fenced area immediately adjacent to the barn in this case is not
part of the open fields, but is instead part of the curtilage and an area in

which Dunn had a reasonable expectation of privacy. Second, Dunn, in fact, took elaborate measures to ensure his privacy. He locked his driveway, fenced in his barn, and covered its open end with a locked gate and fish-netting. The Fourth Amendment does not require the posting of a 24-hour guard to preserve an expectation of privacy.

Even if Dunn's barn were not within the curtilage of his farmhouse, his reasonable expectation of privacy in the barnyard would bring the Fourth Amendment into play. It is well established that the Fourth Amendment protects a privacy interest in commercial premises.

The Fourth Amendment prohibits police activity which, if left unrestricted, would jeopardize individuals' sense of security or would too heavily burden those who wished to guard their privacy. In this case, in order to look inside respondent's barn, the DEA agents traveled a one-half mile off a public road over respondent's fenced-in property, crossed over three additional wooden and barbed wire fences, stepped under the eaves of the barn, and then used a flashlight to peer through otherwise opaque fishnetting. For the police habitually to engage in such surveillance — without a warrant — is constitutionally intolerable. Because I believe that farmers' and ranchers' expectations of privacy in their barns and other outbuildings are expectations society would regard as reasonable, and because I believe that sanctioning the police behavior at issue here does violence to the purpose and promise of the Fourth Amendment, I dissent.

2. Aerial Searches

What if the police observe behavior in a person's home and curtilage by use of low flying airplanes? Does this violate a person's reasonable expectation of privacy? The Court has found that such police conduct is not a search within the meaning of the Fourth Amendment and thus need not comply with the Fourth Amendment's requirements. In reading these cases, consider how they would apply if police are using drones for their surveillance. In light of these cases, is it possible to argue that the police must comply with the requirement of the Fourth Amendment in using drones?

CALIFORNIA v. CIRAOLO
476 U.S. 207 (1986)

Chief Justice BURGER delivered the opinion of the Court.

We granted certiorari to determine whether the Fourth Amendment is violated by aerial observation without a warrant from an altitude of 1,000 feet of a fenced-in backyard within the curtilage of a home.

I

On September 2, 1982, Santa Clara Police received an anonymous telephone tip that marijuana was growing in respondent's backyard. Police were unable to observe the contents of respondent's yard from ground level because of a 6-foot outer fence and a 10-foot inner fence completely enclosing the yard. Later that day, Officer Shutz, who was assigned to investigate, secured a private plane and flew over respondent's house at an altitude of 1,000 feet, within navigable airspace; he was accompanied by Officer Rodriguez. Both officers were trained in marijuana identification. From the overflight, the officers readily identified marijuana plants 8 feet to 10 feet in height growing in a 15- by 25-foot plot in respondent's yard; they photographed the area with a standard 35mm camera.

On September 8, 1982, Officer Shutz obtained a search warrant on the basis of an affidavit describing the anonymous tip and their observations; a photograph depicting respondent's house, the backyard, and neighboring homes was attached to the affidavit as an exhibit. The warrant was executed the next day and 73 plants were seized; it is not disputed that these were marijuana.

II

The touchstone of Fourth Amendment analysis is whether a person has a "constitutionally protected reasonable expectation of privacy." Katz v. United States (1967). *Katz* posits a two-part inquiry: first, has the individual manifested a subjective expectation of privacy in the object of the challenged search? Second, is society willing to recognize that expectation as reasonable?

Clearly — and understandably — respondent has met the test of manifesting his own subjective intent and desire to maintain privacy as to his unlawful agricultural pursuits. However, we need not address that issue, for the State has not challenged the finding of the California Court of Appeal that respondent had such an expectation. It can reasonably be assumed that the 10-foot fence was placed to conceal the marijuana crop from at least street-level views. So far as the normal sidewalk traffic was concerned, this fence served that purpose, because respondent "took normal precautions to maintain his privacy."

Yet a 10-foot fence might not shield these plants from the eyes of a citizen or a policeman perched on the top of a truck or a two-level bus. Whether respondent therefore manifested a subjective expectation of privacy from all observations of his backyard, or whether instead he manifested merely a hope that no one would observe his unlawful gardening pursuits, is not entirely clear in these circumstances. Respondent appears to challenge the authority of government to observe his activity from any vantage point or place if the viewing is motivated by a law enforcement purpose, and not the result of a casual, accidental observation.

We turn, therefore, to the second inquiry under *Katz*, i.e., whether that expectation is reasonable. In pursuing this inquiry, we must keep in mind that "[t]he test of legitimacy is not whether the individual chooses to conceal assertedly 'private' activity," but instead "whether the government's intrusion infringes upon the personal and societal values protected by the Fourth Amendment." Respondent argues that because his yard was in the curtilage of his home, no governmental aerial observation is permissible under the Fourth Amendment without a warrant.

The history and genesis of the curtilage doctrine are instructive. "At common law, the curtilage is the area to which extends the intimate activity associated with the 'sanctity of a man's home and the privacies of life.'" The protection afforded the curtilage is essentially a protection of families and personal privacy in an area intimately linked to the home, both physically and psychologically, where privacy expectations are most heightened. The claimed area here was immediately adjacent to a suburban home, surrounded by high double fences. This close nexus to the home would appear to encompass this small area within the curtilage. Accepting, as the State does, that this yard and its crop fall within the curtilage, the question remains whether naked-eye observation of the curtilage by police from an aircraft lawfully operating at an altitude of 1,000 feet violates an expectation of privacy that is reasonable.

That the area is within the curtilage does not itself bar all police observation. The Fourth Amendment protection of the home has never been extended to require law enforcement officers to shield their eyes when passing by a home on public thoroughfares. Nor does the mere fact that an individual has taken measures to restrict some views of his activities preclude an officer's observations from a public vantage point where he has a right to be and which renders the activities clearly visible. "What a person knowingly exposes to the public, even in his own home or office, is not a subject of Fourth Amendment protection."

The observations by Officers Shutz and Rodriguez in this case took place within public navigable airspace, see 49 U.S.C. App. §1304, in a physically nonintrusive manner; from this point they were able to observe plants readily discernible to the naked eye as marijuana. That the observation from aircraft was directed at identifying the plants and the officers were trained to recognize marijuana is irrelevant. Such observation is precisely what a judicial officer needs to provide a basis for a warrant. Any member of the public flying in this airspace who glanced down could have seen everything that these officers observed. On this record, we readily conclude that respondent's expectation that his garden was protected from such observation is unreasonable and is not an expectation that society is prepared to honor.

Justice POWELL, with whom Justice BRENNAN, Justice MARSHALL, and Justice BLACKMUN join, dissenting.

Concurring in Katz v. United States (1967), Justice Harlan warned that any decision to construe the Fourth Amendment as proscribing only physical intrusions by police onto private property "is, in the present day, bad physics as well as bad law, for reasonable expectations of privacy may be defeated by electronic as well as physical invasion." Because the Court today ignores that warning in an opinion that departs significantly from the standard developed in *Katz* for deciding when a Fourth Amendment violation has occurred, I dissent.

The Fourth Amendment protects "[t]he right of the people to be secure in their persons, houses, papers, and effects, against unreasonable searches and seizures." While the familiar history of the Amendment need not be recounted here, we should remember that it reflects a choice that our society should be one in which citizens "dwell in reasonable security and freedom from surveillance."

This case involves surveillance of a home, for as we stated in Oliver v. United States, the curtilage "has been considered part of the home itself for Fourth Amendment purposes."

The Court begins its analysis of the Fourth Amendment issue posed here by deciding that respondent had an expectation of privacy in his backyard. I agree with that conclusion because of the close proximity of the yard to the house, the nature of some of the activities respondent conducted there, and because he had taken steps to shield those activities from the view of passersby.

The Court concludes, nevertheless, that Shutz could use an airplane — a product of modern technology — to intrude visually into respondent's yard. The Court argues that respondent had no reasonable expectation of privacy from aerial observation. It then relies on the fact that the surveillance was not accompanied by a physical invasion of the curtilage. Reliance on the manner of surveillance is directly contrary to the standard of *Katz*, which identifies a constitutionally protected privacy right by focusing on the interests of the individual and of a free society. Since *Katz*, we have consistently held that the presence or absence of physical trespass by police is constitutionally irrelevant to the question whether society is prepared to recognize an asserted privacy interest as reasonable.

The Court's holding, therefore, must rest solely on the fact that members of the public fly in planes and may look down at homes as they fly over them. The Court does not explain why it finds this fact to be significant. One may assume that the Court believes that citizens bear the risk that air travelers will observe activities occurring within backyards that are open to the sun and air. This risk, the Court appears to hold, nullifies expectations of privacy in those yards even as to purposeful police surveillance from the air.

This line of reasoning is flawed. First, the actual risk to privacy from commercial or pleasure aircraft is virtually nonexistent. Travelers on commercial flights, as well as private planes used for business or personal reasons, normally obtain at most a fleeting, anonymous, and nondiscriminating glimpse of the landscape and buildings over which they pass. The risk that a passenger on such a plane might observe private activities, and might connect those activities with particular people, is simply too trivial to protect against. It is no accident that, as a matter of common experience, many people build fences around their residential areas, but few build roofs over their backyards. Therefore, contrary to the Court's suggestion, people do not "knowingly expos[e]" their residential yards "to the public" merely by failing to build barriers that prevent aerial surveillance.

Comings and goings on public streets are public matters, and the Constitution does not disable police from observing what every member of the public can see. The activity in this case, by contrast, took place within the private area immediately adjacent to a home. Yet the Court approves purposeful police surveillance of that activity and area similar to that approved with respect to public activities and areas. The only possible basis for this holding is a judgment that the risk to privacy posed by the remote possibility that a private airplane passenger will notice outdoor activities is equivalent to the risk of official aerial surveillance. But the Court fails to acknowledge the qualitative difference between police surveillance and other uses made of the airspace.

Since respondent had a reasonable expectation of privacy in his yard, aerial surveillance undertaken by the police for the purpose of discovering evidence of crime constituted a "search" within the meaning of the Fourth Amendment.

In *Ciraolo*, the Court stressed that the plane was flying lawfully at a level of 1,000 feet. In another case, decided the same day, Dow Chemical v. United States, 476 U.S. 227 (1986), the Court considered whether aerial surveillance and photography of an industrial plant was a search. Although the factory had implemented elaborate security precautions to protect its activities from scrutiny, the Court concluded that "the taking of aerial photographs of an industrial plant complex from navigable airspace is not a search prohibited by the Fourth Amendment."

Florida v. Riley, below, involved aerial surveillance from a helicopter at 400 feet. In reading the case, it is important to note that there was no majority opinion and the distinctly different approaches taken by Justice White's plurality opinion, Justice O'Connor's opinion concurring in the judgment, and the dissents of Justice Brennan and Justice Blackmun. These differing approaches would lead to very different results as to many other questions of what is a search.

FLORIDA v. RILEY

488 U.S. 445 (1989)

Justice WHITE announced the judgment of the Court and delivered an opinion, in which THE CHIEF JUSTICE, Justice SCALIA, and Justice KENNEDY join.

On certification to it by a lower state court, the Florida Supreme Court addressed the following question: "Whether surveillance of the interior of a partially covered greenhouse in a residential backyard from the vantage point of a helicopter located 400 feet above the greenhouse constitutes a 'search' for which a warrant is required under the Fourth Amendment and Article I, §12 of the Florida Constitution." The court answered the question in the affirmative.

Respondent Riley lived in a mobile home located on five acres of rural property. A greenhouse was located 10 to 20 feet behind the mobile home. Two sides of the greenhouse were enclosed. The other two sides were not enclosed but the contents of the greenhouse were obscured from view from surrounding property by trees, shrubs, and the mobile home. The greenhouse was covered by corrugated roofing panels, some translucent and some opaque. At the time relevant to this case, two of the panels, amounting to approximately 10% of the roof area, were missing. A wire fence surrounded the mobile home and the greenhouse, and the property was posted with a "DO NOT ENTER" sign.

This case originated with an anonymous tip to the Pasco County Sheriff's office that marijuana was being grown on respondent's property. When an investigating officer discovered that he could not see the contents of the greenhouse from the road, he circled twice over respondent's property in a helicopter at the height of 400 feet. With his naked eye, he was able to see through the openings in the roof and one or more of the open sides of the greenhouse and to identify what he thought was marijuana growing in the structure. A warrant was obtained based on these observations, and the ensuing search revealed marijuana growing in the greenhouse. Respondent was charged with possession of marijuana under Florida law.

We agree with the State's submission that our decision in California v. Ciraolo (1986), controls this case.

We arrive at the same conclusion in the present case. In this case, as in *Ciraolo*, the property surveyed was within the curtilage of respondent's home. Riley no doubt intended and expected that his greenhouse would not be open to public inspection, and the precautions he took protected against ground-level observation. Because the sides and roof of his greenhouse were left partially open, however, what was growing in the greenhouse was subject to viewing from the air. Under the holding in *Ciraolo*, Riley could not reasonably have expected the contents of his greenhouse to be immune from examination by an officer seated in a fixed-wing aircraft flying in navigable airspace at an altitude of 1,000 feet or, as the Florida Supreme Court seemed to recognize, at an altitude of 500 feet, the lower limit of the navigable airspace for such an aircraft. Here, the inspection was made from a helicopter, but as is the case with fixed-wing planes, "private and commercial flight [by helicopter] in the public airways is routine" in this country, and there is no indication that such flights are unheard of in Pasco County, Florida. Riley could not reasonably have expected that his greenhouse was protected from public or official observation from a helicopter had it been flying within the navigable air-space for fixed-wing aircraft.

Nor on the facts before us, does it make a difference for Fourth Amendment purposes that the helicopter was flying at 400 feet when the officer saw what was growing in the greenhouse through the partially open roof and sides of the structure. We would have a different case if flying at that altitude had been contrary to law or regulation. But helicopters are not bound by the lower limits of the navigable airspace allowed to other aircraft. Any member of the public could legally have been flying over Riley's property in a helicopter at the altitude of 400 feet and could have observed Riley's greenhouse. The police officer did no more. This is not to say that an inspection of the curtilage of a house from an aircraft will always pass muster under the Fourth Amendment simply because the plane is within the navigable airspace specified by law. But it is of obvious importance that the helicopter in this case was not violating the law, and there is nothing in the record or before us to suggest that helicopters flying at 400 feet are sufficiently rare in this country to lend substance to respondent's claim that he reasonably anticipated that his greenhouse would not be subject to observation from that altitude. Neither is there any intimation here that the helicopter interfered with respondent's normal use of the greenhouse or of other parts of the curtilage. As far as this record reveals, no intimate details connected with the use of the home or curtilage were observed, and there was no undue noise, and no wind, dust, or threat of injury. In these circumstances, there was no violation of the Fourth Amendment.

Justice O'CONNOR, concurring in the judgment.

I concur in the judgment reversing the Supreme Court of Florida because I agree that police observation of the greenhouse in Riley's curtilage from a helicopter passing at an altitude of 400 feet did not violate an expectation of privacy "that society is prepared to recognize as 'reasonable.'" I write separately, however, to clarify the standard I believe follows from California v. Ciraolo (1986). In my view, the plurality's approach rests the scope of Fourth Amendment protection too heavily on compliance with FAA regulations whose purpose is to promote air safety, not to protect "[t]he right of the people to be secure in their persons, houses, papers, and effects, against unreasonable searches and seizures."

Observations of curtilage from helicopters at very low altitudes are not perfectly analogous to ground-level observations from public roads or sidewalks. While in both cases the police may have a legal right to occupy the physical space from which their observations are made, the two situations are not necessarily comparable in terms of whether expectations of privacy from such vantage points should be considered reasonable. Public roads, even those less traveled by, are clearly demarked public thoroughfares. Individuals who seek privacy can take precautions, tailored to the location of the road, to avoid disclosing private activities to those who pass by. They can build a tall fence, for example, and thus ensure private enjoyment of the curtilage without risking public observation from the road or sidewalk. If they do not take such precautions, they cannot reasonably expect privacy from public observation. In contrast, even individuals who have taken effective precautions to ensure against ground-level observations cannot block off all conceivable aerial views of their outdoor patios and yards without entirely giving up their enjoyment of those areas. To require individuals to completely cover and enclose their curtilage is to demand more than the "precautions customarily taken by those seeking privacy." The fact that a helicopter could conceivably observe the curtilage at virtually any altitude or angle, without violating FAA regulations, does not in itself mean that an individual has no reasonable expectation of privacy from such observation.

In determining whether Riley had a reasonable expectation of privacy from aerial observation, the relevant inquiry after *Ciraolo* is not whether the helicopter was where it had a right to be under FAA regulations. Rather, consistent with *Katz*, we must ask whether the helicopter was in the public airways at an altitude at which members of the public travel with sufficient regularity that Riley's expectation of privacy from aerial observation was not "one that society is prepared to recognize as 'reasonable.'" Thus, in determining "whether the government's intrusion infringes upon the personal and societal values protected by the Fourth Amendment," it is not conclusive to observe, as the plurality does, that "[a]ny member of the public could legally have been flying over Riley's property in a helicopter at the altitude of 400 feet and could have observed Riley's greenhouse." Nor is it conclusive that police helicopters may often fly at 400 feet. If the public rarely, if ever, travels overhead at such altitudes, the observation cannot be said to be from a vantage point generally used by the public and Riley cannot be said to have "knowingly expose[d]" his greenhouse to public view. However, if the public can generally be expected to travel over residential backyards at an altitude of 400 feet, Riley cannot reasonably expect his curtilage to be free from such aerial observation.

In my view, the defendant must bear the burden of proving that his expectation of privacy was a reasonable one, and thus that a "search" within the meaning of the Fourth Amendment even took place. Because there is reason to believe that there is considerable public use of airspace at altitudes of 400 feet and above, and because Riley introduced no evidence to the contrary before the Florida courts, I conclude that Riley's expectation that his curtilage was protected from naked-eye aerial observation from that altitude was not a reasonable one. However, public use of altitudes lower than that — particularly public observations from helicopters circling over the curtilage of a home — may be sufficiently rare that police surveillance from such altitudes would violate reasonable expectations of privacy, despite compliance with FAA air safety regulations.

Justice BRENNAN, with whom Justice MARSHALL, and Justice STEVENS, join, dissenting.

The Court holds today that police officers need not obtain a warrant based on probable cause before circling in a helicopter 400 feet above a home in order to investigate what is taking place behind the walls of the curtilage. I cannot agree that the Fourth Amendment to the Constitution tolerates such an intrusion on privacy and personal security.

The opinion for a plurality of the Court reads almost as if Katz v. United States (1967) had never been decided. Notwithstanding the disclaimers of its final paragraph, the opinion relies almost exclusively on the fact that the police officer conducted his surveillance from a vantage point where, under applicable Federal Aviation Administration regulations, he had a legal right to be. *Katz* teaches, however, that the relevant inquiry is whether the police surveillance "violated the privacy upon which [the defendant] justifiably relied," — or, as Justice Harlan put it, whether the police violated an "expectation of privacy . . . that society is prepared to recognize as 'reasonable.'"

The plurality undertakes no inquiry into whether low-level helicopter surveillance by the police of activities in an enclosed backyard is consistent with the "aims of a free and open society." Instead, it summarily concludes that Riley's expectation of privacy was unreasonable because "[a]ny member of the public could legally have been flying over Riley's property in a helicopter at the altitude of 400 feet and could have observed Riley's greenhouse." This observation is, in turn, based solely on the fact that the police helicopter was within the airspace within which such craft are allowed by federal safety regulations to fly.

I agree, of course, that "[w]hat a person knowingly exposes to the public . . . is not a subject of Fourth Amendment protection." But I cannot agree that one "knowingly exposes [an area] to the public" solely because a helicopter may legally fly above it. Under the plurality's exceedingly grudging Fourth Amendment theory, the expectation of privacy is defeated if a single member of the public could conceivably position herself to see into the area in question without doing anything illegal. It is defeated whatever the difficulty a person would have in so positioning herself, and however infrequently anyone would in fact do so. In taking this view the plurality ignores the very essence of *Katz.* The reason why there is no reasonable expectation of privacy in an area that is exposed to the public is that little diminution in "the amount of privacy and freedom remaining to citizens" will result from police surveillance of something that any passerby readily sees. To pretend, as the plurality opinion does, that the same is true when the police use a helicopter to peer over high fences is, at best, disingenuous. Notwithstanding the plurality's statistics about the number of helicopters registered in this country, can it seriously be questioned that Riley enjoyed virtually complete privacy in his backyard greenhouse, and that that privacy was invaded solely by police helicopter surveillance? Is the theoretical possibility that any member of the public (with sufficient means) could also have hired a helicopter and looked over Riley's fence of any relevance at all in determining whether Riley suffered a serious loss of privacy and personal security through the police action?

The police officer positioned 400 feet above Riley's backyard was not, however, standing on a public road. The vantage point he enjoyed was not one any citizen could readily share. His ability to see over Riley's fence depended on his use of a very expensive and sophisticated piece of machinery to which few ordinary citizens have access. In such circumstances it makes no more sense to rely on the legality of the officer's position in the skies than it would to judge the constitutionality of the wiretap in *Katz* by the legality of the officer's position outside the telephone booth. The simple inquiry whether the police officer had the legal right to be in the position from which he made his observations cannot suffice, for we cannot assume that Riley's curtilage was so open to the observations of passersby in the skies that he retained little privacy or personal security to be lost to police surveillance. The question before us must be not whether the police were where they had a right to be, but whether public observation of Riley's curtilage was so commonplace that Riley's expectation of privacy in his backyard could not be considered reasonable. To say that an invasion of Riley's privacy from the skies was not impossible is most emphatically not the same as saying that his expectation of privacy within his enclosed curtilage was not "one that society is prepared to recognize as 'reasonable.'"

Equally disconcerting is the lack of any meaningful limit to the plurality's holding. It is worth reiterating that the FAA regulations the plurality relies on as establishing that the officer was where he had a right to be set no minimum flight altitude for helicopters. It is difficult, therefore, to see what, if any, helicopter surveillance would run afoul of the plurality's rule that there exists no reasonable expectation of privacy as long as the helicopter is where it has a right to be.

If indeed the purpose of the restraints imposed by the Fourth Amendment is to "safeguard the privacy and security of individuals," then it is puzzling why it should be the helicopter's noise, wind, and dust that provides the measure of whether this constitutional safeguard has been infringed. Imagine a helicopter capable of hovering just above an enclosed courtyard or patio without generating any noise, wind, or dust at all—and, for good measure, without posing any threat of injury. Suppose the police employed this miraculous tool to discover not only what crops people were growing in their greenhouses, but also what books they were reading and who their dinner guests were. Suppose, finally, that the FAA regulations remained unchanged, so that the police were undeniably "where they had a right to be." Would today's plurality continue to assert that "[t]he right of the people to be secure in their persons, houses, papers, and effects, against unreasonable searches and seizures" was not infringed by such surveillance? Yet that is the logical consequence of the plurality's rule that, so long as the police are where they have a right to be under air traffic regulations, the Fourth Amendment is offended only if the aerial surveillance interferes with the use of the backyard as a garden spot. Nor is there anything in the plurality's opinion to suggest that any different rule would apply were the police looking from their helicopter, not into the open curtilage, but through an open window into a room viewable only from the air.

Perhaps the most remarkable passage in the plurality opinion is its suggestion that the case might be a different one had any "intimate details connected with the use of the home or curtilage [been] observed." What, one wonders, is meant by "intimate details"? If the police had observed Riley embracing his wife in the backyard greenhouse, would we then say that his reasonable expectation of privacy had been infringed? Where in the Fourth Amendment or in our cases is there any warrant for imposing a requirement that the activity observed must be "intimate" in order to be protected by the Constitution?

It is difficult to avoid the conclusion that the plurality has allowed its analysis of Riley's expectation of privacy to be colored by its distaste for the activity in which he was engaged. It is indeed easy to forget, especially in view of current concern over drug trafficking, that the scope of the Fourth Amendment's protection does not turn on whether the activity disclosed by a search is illegal or innocuous. But we dismiss this as a "drug case" only at the peril of our own liberties. Justice Frankfurter once noted that "[i]t is a fair summary of history to say that the safeguards of liberty have frequently been forged in controversies involving not very nice people," and nowhere is this observation more apt than in the area of the Fourth Amendment, whose words have necessarily been given meaning largely through decisions suppressing evidence of criminal activity. The principle enunciated in this case determines what limits the Fourth Amendment imposes on aerial surveillance of any person, for any reason. If the Constitution does not protect Riley's marijuana garden against such surveillance, it is hard to see how it will prohibit the government from aerial spying on the activities of a law-abiding citizen on her fully enclosed outdoor patio. As Professor Amsterdam has eloquently written: "The question is not whether you or I must draw the blinds before we commit a crime. It is whether you and I must discipline ourselves to draw the blinds every time we enter a room, under pain of surveillance if we do not."

Justice BLACKMUN, dissenting.

The question before the Court is whether the helicopter surveillance over Riley's property constituted a "search" within the meaning of the Fourth Amendment. I believe that answering this question depends upon whether Riley has a "reasonable expectation of privacy" that no such surveillance would occur, and does not depend upon the fact that the helicopter was flying at a lawful altitude under FAA regulations. A majority of this Court thus agrees to at least this much.

Thus, because I believe that private helicopters rarely fly over curtilages at an altitude of 400 feet, I would impose upon the prosecution the burden of proving contrary facts necessary to show that Riley lacked a reasonable expectation of privacy. Indeed, I would establish this burden of proof for any helicopter surveillance case in which the flight occurred below 1,000 feet—in other words, for any aerial surveillance case not governed by the Court's decision in California v. Ciraolo (1986).

In this case, the prosecution did not meet this burden of proof. This failure should compel a finding that a Fourth Amendment search occurred. But because our prior cases gave the parties little guidance on the burden of proof issue, I would remand this case to allow the prosecution an opportunity to meet this burden.

3. *Thermal Imaging of Homes*

Justice Brennan's dissent in Florida v. Riley raises many hypotheticals as to what types of government surveillance might be allowed. In Kyllo v. United States, the Court considered whether police use of a device to take a "thermal image" of a home is a search. In examining the Court's opinion and its conclusion that there is a search, it is important to consider whether there is a meaningful difference between surveillance from a low-flying helicopter and via a thermal imaging device. The Court says that the former is not a search, but the latter is and must comply with the Fourth Amendment. *Kyllo* is based, in part, on the special place of homes in the Fourth Amendment, though the aerial surveillance cases above also involved people's homes. The Court in *Kyllo* also stressed that the technology is "not in general public use." It is worth considering whether this should matter and whether it distinguishes aerial surveillance.

KYLLO v. UNITED STATES

533 U.S. 27 (2001)

Justice SCALIA delivered the opinion of the Court.

This case presents the question whether the use of a thermal-imaging device aimed at a private home from a public street to detect relative amounts of heat within the home constitutes a "search" within the meaning of the Fourth Amendment.

I

In 1991 Agent William Elliott of the United States Department of the Interior came to suspect that marijuana was being grown in the home belonging to petitioner Danny Kyllo, part of a triplex on Rhododendron Drive in Florence, Oregon. Indoor marijuana growth typically requires high-intensity lamps. In order to determine whether an amount of heat was emanating from petitioner's home consistent with the use of such lamps, at 3:20 A.M. on January 16, 1992, Agent Elliott and Dan Haas used an Agema Thermovision 210 thermal imager to scan the triplex. Thermal imagers detect infrared radiation, which virtually all objects emit but which is not visible to the naked eye. The imager converts radiation into images based on relative warmth — black is cool, white is hot, shades of gray connote relative differences; in that respect, it operates somewhat like a video camera showing heat images. The scan of Kyllo's home took only a few minutes and was performed from the passenger seat of Agent Elliott's vehicle across the street from the front of the house and also from the street in back of the house. The scan showed that the roof over the garage and a side wall of petitioner's home were relatively hot compared to the rest of the home and substantially warmer than neighboring homes in the triplex. Agent Elliott concluded that petitioner was using halide lights to grow marijuana in his house, which indeed he was. Based on tips from informants, utility bills, and the thermal imaging, a Federal Magistrate Judge issued a warrant authorizing a search of petitioner's home, and the agents found an indoor growing operation involving more than 100 plants. Petitioner was indicted on one count of manufacturing marijuana, in violation of 21 U.S.C. §841(a)(1). He unsuccessfully moved to suppress the evidence seized from his home and then entered a conditional guilty plea.

II

At the very core of the Fourth Amendment stands the right of a man to retreat into his own home and there be free from unreasonable governmental intrusion. With few exceptions, the question whether a warrantless search of a home is reasonable and hence constitutional must be answered no.

On the other hand, the antecedent question whether or not a Fourth Amendment "search" has occurred is not so simple under our precedent. The permissibility of ordinary visual surveillance of a home used to be clear because, well into the 20th century, our Fourth Amendment jurisprudence was tied to common-law trespass. Visual surveillance was unquestionably lawful because "'the eye cannot by the laws of England be guilty of a trespass.'" We have since decoupled violation of a person's Fourth Amendment rights from trespassory violation of his property, but the lawfulness of warrantless visual surveillance of a home has still been preserved. As we observed in California v. Ciraolo (1986), "[t]he Fourth Amendment protection of the home has never been extended to require law enforcement officers to shield their eyes when passing by a home on public thoroughfares."

One might think that the new validating rationale would be that examining the portion of a house that is in plain public view, while it is a "search" despite the absence of trespass, is not an "unreasonable" one under the Fourth Amendment. But in fact we have held that visual observation is no "search" at all — perhaps in order to preserve somewhat more intact our doctrine that warrantless searches are presumptively unconstitutional. In assessing when a search is not a search, we have applied somewhat in reverse the principle first enunciated in Katz v. United States (1967). As Justice

Harlan's oft-quoted concurrence described it, a Fourth Amendment search occurs when the government violates a subjective expectation of privacy that society recognizes as reasonable.

The present case involves officers on a public street engaged in more than naked-eye surveillance of a home. We have previously reserved judgment as to how much technological enhancement of ordinary perception from such a vantage point, if any, is too much.

III

It would be foolish to contend that the degree of privacy secured to citizens by the Fourth Amendment has been entirely unaffected by the advance of technology. The question we confront today is what limits there are upon this power of technology to shrink the realm of guaranteed privacy.

The *Katz* test — whether the individual has an expectation of privacy that society is prepared to recognize as reasonable — has often been criticized as circular, and hence subjective and unpredictable. While it may be difficult to refine *Katz* when the search of areas such as telephone booths, automobiles, or even the curtilage and uncovered portions of residences is at issue, in the case of the search of the interior of homes — the prototypical and hence most commonly litigated area of protected privacy — there is a ready criterion, with roots deep in the common law, of the minimal expectation of privacy that exists, and that is acknowledged to be reasonable. To withdraw protection of this minimum expectation would be to permit police technology to erode the privacy guaranteed by the Fourth Amendment. We think that obtaining by sense-enhancing technology any information regarding the interior of the home that could not otherwise have been obtained without physical "intrusion into a constitutionally protected area," constitutes a search — at least where (as here) the technology in question is not in general public use. This assures preservation of that degree of privacy against government that existed when the Fourth Amendment was adopted. On the basis of this criterion, the information obtained by the thermal imager in this case was the product of a search.[3]

The Government maintains, however, that the thermal imaging must be upheld because it detected "only heat radiating from the external surface of

3. The dissent's repeated assertion that the thermal imaging did not obtain information regarding the interior of the home, is simply inaccurate. A thermal imager reveals the relative heat of various rooms in the home. The dissent may not find that information particularly private or important, but there is no basis for saying it is not information regarding the interior of the home. The dissent's comparison of the thermal imaging to various circumstances in which outside observers might be able to perceive, without technology, the heat of the home — for example, by observing snowmelt on the roof, is quite irrelevant. The fact that equivalent information could sometimes be obtained by other means does not make lawful the use of means that violate the Fourth Amendment. The police might, for example, learn how many people are in a particular house by setting up year-round surveillance; but that does not make breaking and entering to find out the same information lawful. In any event, on the night of January 16, 1992, no outside observer could have discerned the relative heat of Kyllo's home without thermal imaging. [Footnote by the Court.]

the house." The dissent makes this its leading point, contending that there is a fundamental difference between what it calls "off-the-wall" observations and "through-the-wall surveillance." But just as a thermal imager captures only heat emanating from a house, so also a powerful directional microphone picks up only sound emanating from a house — and a satellite capable of scanning from many miles away would pick up only visible light emanating from a house. We rejected such a mechanical interpretation of the Fourth Amendment in *Katz,* where the eavesdropping device picked up only sound waves that reached the exterior of the phone booth. Reversing that approach would leave the homeowner at the mercy of advancing technology — including imaging technology that could discern all human activity in the home. While the technology used in the present case was relatively crude, the rule we adopt must take account of more sophisticated systems that are already in use or in development. The dissent's reliance on the distinction between "off-the-wall" and "through-the-wall" observation is entirely incompatible with the dissent's belief, which we discuss below, that thermal-imaging observations of the intimate details of a home are impermissible. The most sophisticated thermal-imaging devices continue to measure heat "off-the-wall" rather than "through-the-wall"; the dissent's disapproval of those more sophisticated thermal-imaging devices, is an acknowledgement that there is no substance to this distinction. As for the dissent's extraordinary assertion that anything learned through "an inference" cannot be a search, that would validate even the "through-the-wall" technologies that the dissent purports to disapprove. Surely the dissent does not believe that the through-the-wall radar or ultrasound technology produces an 8-by-10 Kodak glossy that needs no analysis (i.e., the making of inferences).

The Government also contends that the thermal imaging was constitutional because it did not "detect private activities occurring in private areas." The Fourth Amendment's protection of the home has never been tied to measurement of the quality or quantity of information obtained. In the home, our cases show, all details are intimate details, because the entire area is held safe from prying government eyes. Limiting the prohibition of thermal imaging to "intimate details" would not only be wrong in principle; it would be impractical in application. To begin with, there is no necessary connection between the sophistication of the surveillance equipment and the "intimacy" of the details that it observes — which means that one cannot say (and the police cannot be assured) that use of the relatively crude equipment at issue here will always be lawful. The Agema Thermovision 210 might disclose, for example, at what hour each night the lady of the house takes her daily sauna and bath — a detail that many would consider "intimate"; and a much more sophisticated system might detect nothing more intimate than the fact that someone left a closet light on. We could not, in other words, develop a rule approving only that through-the-wall surveillance which identifies objects no smaller than 36 by 36 inches, but would have to develop a jurisprudence specifying which home activities are "intimate" and which are not. And even when (if ever) that jurisprudence were fully developed, no police officer would be able to know in advance whether his through-the-wall surveillance picks up "intimate" details — and thus would be unable to know in advance whether it is constitutional.

We have said that the Fourth Amendment draws "a firm line at the entrance to the house." That line, we think, must be not only firm but also bright — which requires clear specification of those methods of surveillance that require a warrant. While it is certainly possible to conclude from the videotape of the thermal imaging that occurred in this case that no "significant" compromise of the homeowner's privacy has occurred, we must take the long view, from the original meaning of the Fourth Amendment forward.

Where, as here, the Government uses a device that is not in general public use, to explore details of the home that would previously have been unknowable without physical intrusion, the surveillance is a "search" and is presumptively unreasonable without a warrant.

Since we hold the Thermovision imaging to have been an unlawful search, it will remain for the District Court to determine whether, without the evidence it provided, the search warrant issued in this case was supported by probable cause — and if not, whether there is any other basis for supporting admission of the evidence that the search pursuant to the warrant produced.

Justice STEVENS, with whom THE CHIEF JUSTICE, Justice O'CONNOR, and Justice KENNEDY join, dissenting.

There is, in my judgment, a distinction of constitutional magnitude between "through-the-wall surveillance" that gives the observer or listener direct access to information in a private area, on the one hand, and the thought processes used to draw inferences from information in the public domain, on the other hand. The Court has crafted a rule that purports to deal with direct observations of the inside of the home, but the case before us merely involves indirect deductions from "off-the-wall" surveillance, that is, observations of the exterior of the home. Those observations were made with a fairly primitive thermal imager that gathered data exposed on the outside of petitioner's home but did not invade any constitutionally protected interest in privacy. Moreover, I believe that the supposedly "bright-line" rule the Court has created in response to its concerns about future technological developments is unnecessary, unwise, and inconsistent with the Fourth Amendment.

I

There is no need for the Court to craft a new rule to decide this case, as it is controlled by established principles from our Fourth Amendment jurisprudence. One of those core principles, of course, is that "searches and seizures inside a home without a warrant are presumptively unreasonable." But it is equally well settled that searches and seizures of property in plain view are presumptively reasonable. Whether that property is residential or commercial, the basic principle is the same: "'What a person knowingly exposes to the public, even in his own home or office, is not a subject of Fourth Amendment protection.'" That is the principle implicated here.

While the Court "take[s] the long view" and decides this case based largely on the potential of yet-to-be-developed technology that might allow "through-the-wall surveillance," this case involves nothing more than off-the-wall surveillance by law enforcement officers to gather information exposed to the general public from the outside of petitioner's home. All that the infrared camera did in this case was passively measure heat emitted from the exterior surfaces of petitioner's home; all that those measurements showed were relative differences in emission levels, vaguely indicating that some areas of the roof and outside walls were warmer than others. As still images from the infrared scans show, no details regarding the interior of petitioner's home were revealed. Unlike an x-ray scan, or other possible "through-the-wall" techniques, the detection of infrared radiation emanating from the home did not accomplish "an unauthorized physical penetration into the premises," nor did it "obtain information that it could not have obtained by observation from outside the curtilage of the house."

Indeed, the ordinary use of the senses might enable a neighbor or passerby to notice the heat emanating from a building, particularly if it is vented, as was the case here. Additionally, any member of the public might notice that one part of a house is warmer than another part or a nearby building if, for example, rainwater evaporates or snow melts at different rates across its surfaces. Such use of the senses would not convert into an unreasonable search if, instead, an adjoining neighbor allowed an officer onto her property to verify her perceptions with a sensitive thermometer. Nor, in my view, does such observation become an unreasonable search if made from a distance with the aid of a device that merely discloses that the exterior of one house, or one area of the house, is much warmer than another. Nothing more occurred in this case.

Thus, the notion that heat emissions from the outside of a dwelling are a private matter implicating the protections of the Fourth Amendment is not only unprecedented but also quite difficult to take seriously. Heat waves, like aromas that are generated in a kitchen, or in a laboratory or opium den, enter the public domain if and when they leave a building. A subjective expectation that they would remain private is not only implausible but also surely not "one that society is prepared to recognize as 'reasonable.'"

To be sure, the homeowner has a reasonable expectation of privacy concerning what takes place within the home, and the Fourth Amendment's protection against physical invasions of the home should apply to their functional equivalent. But the equipment in this case did not penetrate the walls of petitioner's home, and while it did pick up "details of the home" that were exposed to the public, it did not obtain "any information regarding the interior of the home." In the Court's own words, based on what the thermal imager "showed" regarding the outside of petitioner's home, the officers "concluded" that petitioner was engaging in illegal activity inside the home. It would be quite absurd to characterize their thought processes as "searches," regardless of whether they inferred (rightly) that petitioner was growing marijuana in his house, or (wrongly) that "the lady of the house [was taking] her daily sauna and bath." For the first time in its history, the Court assumes that an inference can amount to a Fourth Amendment violation.

Notwithstanding the implications of today's decision, there is a strong public interest in avoiding constitutional litigation over the monitoring of emissions from homes, and over the inferences drawn from such monitoring. Just as "the police cannot reasonably be expected to avert their eyes from evidence of criminal activity that could have been observed by any member of the public," so too public officials should not have to avert their senses or their equipment from detecting emissions in the public domain such as excessive heat, traces of smoke, suspicious odors, odorless gases, airborne particulates, or radioactive emissions, any of which could identify hazards to the community. In my judgment, monitoring such emissions with "sense-enhancing technology," and drawing useful conclusions from such monitoring, is an entirely reasonable public service.

On the other hand, the countervailing privacy interest is at best trivial. After all, homes generally are insulated to keep heat in, rather than to prevent the detection of heat going out, and it does not seem to me that society will suffer from a rule requiring the rare homeowner who both intends to engage in uncommon activities that produce extraordinary amounts of heat, and wishes to conceal that production from outsiders, to make sure that the surrounding area is well insulated. The interest in concealing the heat escaping from one's house pales in significance to "the chief evil against which the wording of the Fourth Amendment is directed," the "physical entry of the home," and it is hard to believe that it is an interest the Framers sought to protect in our Constitution.

Since what was involved in this case was nothing more than drawing inferences from off-the-wall surveillance, rather than any "through-the-wall" surveillance, the officers' conduct did not amount to a search and was perfectly reasonable.

II

Instead of trying to answer the question whether the use of the thermal imager in this case was even arguably unreasonable, the Court has fashioned a rule that is intended to provide essential guidance for the day when "more sophisticated systems" gain the "ability to 'see' through walls and other opaque barriers." The newly minted rule encompasses "obtaining [1] by sense-enhancing technology [2] any information regarding the interior of the home [3] that could not otherwise have been obtained without physical intrusion into a constitutionally protected area . . . [4] at least where (as here) the technology in question is not in general public use." In my judgment, the Court's new rule is at once too broad and too narrow, and is not justified by the Court's explanation for its adoption. As I have suggested, I would not erect a constitutional impediment to the use of sense-enhancing technology unless it provides its user with the functional equivalent of actual presence in the area being searched.

Despite the Court's attempt to draw a line that is "not only firm but also bright," the contours of its new rule are uncertain because its protection apparently dissipates as soon as the relevant technology is "in general public use." Yet how much use is general public use is not even hinted at by the Court's opinion, which makes the somewhat doubtful assumption that the thermal imager used in this case does not satisfy that criterion. In any event, putting aside its lack of clarity, this criterion is somewhat perverse because it seems likely that the threat to privacy will grow, rather than recede, as the use of intrusive equipment becomes more readily available.

III

Although the Court is properly and commendably concerned about the threats to privacy that may flow from advances in the technology available to the law enforcement profession, it has unfortunately failed to heed the tried and true counsel of judicial restraint. Instead of concentrating on the rather mundane issue that is actually presented by the case before it, the Court has endeavored to craft an all-encompassing rule for the future. It would be far wiser to give legislators an unimpeded opportunity to grapple with these emerging issues rather than to shackle them with prematurely devised constitutional constraints.

4. Searches of Trash

Does a person have a reasonable expectation of privacy in his trash? If police go through a person's garbage, do the officers need to follow the Fourth Amendment's requirements? In California v. Greenwood, the Court considered this and found no reasonable expectation of privacy in what a person chooses to discard.

CALIFORNIA v. GREENWOOD

486 U.S. 35 (1988)

Justice WHITE delivered the opinion of the Court.

The issue here is whether the Fourth Amendment prohibits the warrantless search and seizure of garbage left for collection outside the curtilage of a home. We conclude, in accordance with the vast majority of lower courts that have addressed the issue, that it does not.

I

In early 1984, Investigator Jenny Stracner of the Laguna Beach Police Department received information indicating that respondent Greenwood might be engaged in narcotics trafficking. Stracner learned that a criminal suspect had informed a federal drug enforcement agent in February 1984 that a truck filled with illegal drugs was en route to the Laguna Beach address at which Greenwood resided. In addition, a neighbor complained of heavy vehicular traffic late at night in front of Greenwood's single-family home. The neighbor reported that the vehicles remained at Greenwood's house for only a few minutes.

Stracner sought to investigate this information by conducting a surveillance of Greenwood's home. She observed several vehicles make brief stops at the house during the late-night and early morning hours, and she followed a truck from the house to a residence that had previously been under investigation as a narcotics-trafficking location.

On April 6, 1984, Stracner asked the neighborhood's regular trash collector to pick up the plastic garbage bags that Greenwood had left on the curb in front of his house and to turn the bags over to her without mixing their contents with garbage from other houses. The trash collector cleaned his truck bin of other refuse, collected the garbage bags from the street in front of Greenwood's house, and turned the bags over to Stracner. The officer searched through the rubbish and found items indicative of narcotics use. She recited the information that she had gleaned from the trash search in an affidavit in support of a warrant to search Greenwood's home.

Police officers encountered both respondents at the house later that day when they arrived to execute the warrant. The police discovered quantities of cocaine and hashish during their search of the house. Respondents were arrested on felony narcotics charges. They subsequently posted bail.

The police continued to receive reports of many late-night visitors to the Greenwood house. On May 4, Investigator Robert Rahaeuser obtained Greenwood's garbage from the regular trash collector in the same manner as had Stracner. The garbage again contained evidence of narcotics use.

Rahaeuser secured another search warrant for Greenwood's home based on the information from the second trash search. The police found more narcotics and evidence of narcotics trafficking when they executed the warrant. Greenwood was again arrested.

II

The warrantless search and seizure of the garbage bags left at the curb outside the Greenwood house would violate the Fourth Amendment only if respondents manifested a subjective expectation of privacy in their garbage that society accepts as objectively reasonable. Respondents do not disagree with this standard.

They assert, however, that they had, and exhibited, an expectation of privacy with respect to the trash that was searched by the police: The trash, which was placed on the street for collection at a fixed time, was contained in opaque plastic bags, which the garbage collector was expected to pick up, mingle with the trash of others, and deposit at the garbage dump. The trash was only temporarily on the street, and there was little likelihood that it would be inspected by anyone.

It may well be that respondents did not expect that the contents of their garbage bags would become known to the police or other members of the public. An expectation of privacy does not give rise to Fourth Amendment protection, however, unless society is prepared to accept that expectation as objectively reasonable.

Here, we conclude that respondents exposed their garbage to the public sufficiently to defeat their claim to Fourth Amendment protection. It is common knowledge that plastic garbage bags left on or at the side of a public street are readily accessible to animals, children, scavengers, snoops, and other members of the public. Moreover, respondents placed their refuse at the curb for the express purpose of conveying it to a third party, the trash collector, who might himself have sorted through respondents' trash or permitted others, such as the police, to do so. Accordingly, having deposited their garbage "in an area particularly suited for public inspection and, in a manner of speaking, public consumption, for the express purpose of having strangers take it," respondents could have had no reasonable expectation of privacy in the inculpatory items that they discarded.

Furthermore, as we have held, the police cannot reasonably be expected to avert their eyes from evidence of criminal activity that could have been observed by any member of the public.

Justice BRENNAN, with whom Justice MARSHALL joins, dissenting.

Every week for two months, and at least once more a month later, the Laguna Beach police clawed through the trash that respondent Greenwood left in opaque, sealed bags on the curb outside his home. Complete strangers minutely scrutinized their bounty, undoubtedly dredging up intimate details of Greenwood's private life and habits. The intrusions proceeded without a warrant, and no court before or since has concluded that the police acted on probable cause to believe Greenwood was engaged in any criminal activity.

Scrutiny of another's trash is contrary to commonly accepted notions of civilized behavior. I suspect, therefore, that members of our society will be shocked to learn that the Court, the ultimate guarantor of liberty, deems unreasonable our expectation that the aspects of our private lives that are concealed safely in a trash bag will not become public.

"A container which can support a reasonable expectation of privacy may not be searched, even on probable cause, without a warrant." United States v. Jacobsen (1984). Thus, as the Court observes, if Greenwood had a reasonable expectation that the contents of the bags that he placed on the curb would remain private, the warrantless search of those bags violated the Fourth Amendment.

Respondents deserve no less protection just because Greenwood used the bags to discard rather than to transport his personal effects. Their contents are not inherently any less private, and Greenwood's decision to discard them, at least in the manner in which he did, does not diminish his expectation of privacy.

A trash bag, like any of the above-mentioned containers, "is a common repository for one's personal effects" and, even more than many of them, is "therefore . . . inevitably associated with the expectation of privacy." A single bag of trash testifies eloquently to the eating, reading, and recreational habits of the person who produced it. A search of trash, like a search of the bedroom, can relate intimate details about sexual practices, health, and personal hygiene. Like rifling through desk drawers or intercepting phone calls, rummaging through trash can divulge the target's financial and professional status, political affiliations and inclinations, private thoughts, personal relationships, and romantic interests. It cannot be doubted that a sealed trash bag harbors telling evidence of the "intimate activity associated with the 'sanctity of a man's home and the privacies of life,'" which the Fourth Amendment is designed to protect.

Had Greenwood flaunted his intimate activity by strewing his trash all over the curb for all to see, or had some nongovernmental intruder invaded his privacy and done the same, I could accept the Court's conclusion that an expectation of privacy would have been unreasonable. Similarly, had police searching the city dump run across incriminating evidence that, despite commingling with the trash of others, still retained its identity as Greenwood's, we would have a different case. But all that Greenwood "exposed . . . to the public," were the exteriors of several opaque, sealed containers. Until the bags were opened by police, they hid their contents from the public's view every bit as much as did Chadwick's double-locked footlocker and Robbins' green, plastic wrapping. Faithful application of the warrant requirement does not require police to "avert their eyes from evidence of criminal activity that could have been observed by any member of the public." Rather, it only requires them to adhere to norms of privacy that members of the public plainly acknowledge.

The mere possibility that unwelcome meddlers might open and rummage through the containers does not negate the expectation of privacy in their contents any more than the possibility of a burglary negates an expectation of privacy in the home; or the possibility of a private intrusion negates an expectation of privacy in an unopened package; or the possibility that an operator will listen in on a telephone conversation negates an expectation of privacy in the words spoken on the telephone. "What a person . . . seeks to preserve as private, even in an area accessible to the public, may be constitutionally protected."

Nor is it dispositive that "respondents placed their refuse at the curb for the express purpose of conveying it to a third party, . . . who might himself have sorted through respondents' trash or permitted others, such as the police, to do so." In the first place, Greenwood can hardly be faulted for leaving trash on his curb when a county ordinance commanded him to do so.

Unlike in other circumstances where privacy is compromised, Greenwood could not "avoid exposing personal belongings . . . by simply leaving them at home." More importantly, even the voluntary relinquishment of possession or control over an effect does not necessarily amount to a relinquishment of a privacy expectation in it. Were it otherwise, a letter or package would lose all Fourth Amendment protection when placed in a mailbox or other depository with the "express purpose" of entrusting it to the postal officer or a private carrier; those bailees are just as likely as trash collectors (and certainly have greater incentive) to "sor[t] through" the personal effects entrusted to them, "or permi[t] others, such as police to do so." Yet, it has been clear for at least 110 years that the possibility of such an intrusion does not justify a warrantless search by police in the first instance.

In holding that the warrantless search of Greenwood's trash was consistent with the Fourth Amendment, the Court paints a grim picture of our society. It depicts a society in which local authorities may command their citizens to dispose of their personal effects in the manner least protective of the "sanctity of [the] home and the privacies of life," and then monitor them arbitrarily and without judicial oversight—a society that is not prepared to recognize as reasonable an individual's expectation of privacy in the most private of personal effects sealed in an opaque container and disposed of in a manner designed to commingle it imminently and inextricably with the trash of others. The American society with which I am familiar "chooses to dwell in reasonable security and freedom from surveillance," and is more dedicated to individual liberty and more sensitive to intrusions on the sanctity of the home than the Court is willing to acknowledge.

5.   Observation and Monitoring of Public Behavior

As indicated above, the Supreme Court frequently has stated, "What a person knowingly exposes to the public, even in his own home or office, is not a subject of Fourth Amendment protection." California v. Ciraolo (1986) (quoting Katz v. United States (1967)). But what is considered public behavior? The Court has considered this in a number of contexts. For instance, in United States v. Knotts, the Court considered whether the police putting a radio-transmitter in a container is a search. In considering *Knotts*, recall United States v. Jones, above, and consider whether there is a meaningful distinction between these decisions.

UNITED STATES v. KNOTTS
460 U.S. 276 (1983)

Justice REHNQUIST announced the opinion of the Court.

A beeper is a radio transmitter, usually battery operated, which emits periodic signals that can be picked up by a radio receiver. In this case, a beeper was placed in a five gallon drum containing chloroform purchased by one of respondent's codefendants. By monitoring the progress of a car carrying the chloroform Minnesota law enforcement agents were able to trace the can of chloroform from its place of purchase in Minneapolis, Minnesota to respondent's secluded cabin near Shell Lake, Wisconsin. The issue presented by the case is whether such use of a beeper violated respondent's rights secured by the Fourth Amendment to the United States Constitution.

Respondent and two codefendants were charged in the United States District Court for the District of Minnesota with conspiracy to manufacture controlled substances, including but not limited to methamphetamine, in violation of 21 U.S.C. §846 (1976). One of the codefendants, Darryl Petschen, was tried jointly with respondent; the other codefendant, Tristan Armstrong, pleaded guilty and testified for the government at trial.

Suspicion attached to this trio when the 3M Company, which manufactures chemicals in St. Paul, notified a narcotics investigator for the Minnesota Bureau of Criminal Apprehension that Armstrong, a former 3M employee, had been stealing chemicals which could be used in manufacturing illicit drugs. Visual surveillance of Armstrong revealed that after leaving the employ of 3M Company, he had been purchasing similar chemicals from the Hawkins Chemical Company in Minneapolis. The Minnesota narcotics officers observed that after Armstrong had made a purchase, he would deliver the chemicals to codefendant Petschen.

With the consent of the Hawkins Chemical Company, officers installed a beeper inside a five gallon container of chloroform, one of the so-called "precursor" chemicals used to manufacture illicit drugs. Hawkins agreed that when Armstrong next purchased chloroform, the chloroform would be placed in this particular container. When Armstrong made the purchase, officers followed the car in which the chloroform had been placed, maintaining contact by using both visual surveillance and a monitor which received the signals sent from the beeper.

Armstrong proceeded to Petschen's house, where the container was transferred to Petschen's automobile. Officers then followed that vehicle eastward towards the state line, across the St. Croix River, and into Wisconsin. During the latter part of this journey, Petschen began making evasive maneuvers, and the pursuing agents ended their visual surveillance. At about the same time officers lost the signal from the beeper, but with the assistance of a monitoring device located in a helicopter the approximate location of the signal was picked up again about one hour later. The signal now was stationary and the location identified was a cabin occupied by respondent near Shell Lake, Wisconsin. The record before us does not reveal that the beeper was used after the location in the area of the cabin had been initially determined.

Relying on the location of the chloroform derived through the use of the beeper and additional information obtained during three days of intermittent visual surveillance of respondent's cabin, officers secured a search warrant. During execution of the warrant, officers discovered a fully operable, clandestine drug laboratory in the cabin. In the laboratory area officers found formulas for amphetamine and methamphetamine, over $10,000 worth of laboratory equipment, and chemicals in quantities sufficient to produce 14 pounds of pure amphetamine. Under a barrel outside the cabin, officers located the five gallon container of chloroform.

After his motion to suppress evidence based on the warrantless monitoring of the beeper was denied, respondent was convicted for conspiring to manufacture controlled substances in violation of 21 U.S.C. §846 (1976). He was sentenced to five years imprisonment.

II

The governmental surveillance conducted by means of the beeper in this case amounted principally to the following of an automobile on public streets and highways. We have commented more than once on the diminished expectation of privacy in an automobile: "One has a lesser expectation of privacy in a motor vehicle because its function is transportation and it seldom serves as one's residence or as the repository of personal effects. A car has little capacity for escaping public scrutiny. It travels public thoroughfares where both its occupants and its contents are in plain view." Cardwell v. Lewis (1974).

A person travelling in an automobile on public thoroughfares has no reasonable expectation of privacy in his movements from one place to another. When Petschen travelled over the public streets he voluntarily conveyed to anyone who wanted to look the fact that he was travelling over particular roads in a particular direction, the fact of whatever stops he made, and the fact of his final destination when he exited from public roads onto private property.

Respondent Knotts, as the owner of the cabin and surrounding premises to which Petschen drove, undoubtedly had the traditional expectation of privacy within a dwelling place insofar as the cabin was concerned. But no such expectation of privacy extended to the visual observation of Petschen's automobile arriving on his premises after leaving a public highway, nor to movements of objects such as the drum of chloroform outside the cabin in the "open fields." Visual surveillance from public places along Petschen's route or adjoining Knotts' premises would have sufficed to reveal all of these facts to the police. The fact that the officers in this case relied not only on visual surveillance, but on the use of the beeper to signal the presence of Petschen's automobile to the police receiver, does not alter the situation. Nothing in the Fourth Amendment prohibited the police from augmenting the sensory faculties bestowed upon them at birth with such enhancement as science and technology afforded them in this case.

We thus return to the question posed at the beginning of our inquiry: did monitoring the beeper signals complained of by respondent invade any legitimate expectation of privacy on his part? For the reasons previously stated, we hold they did not. Since they did not, there was neither a "search" nor a "seizure" within the contemplation of the Fourth Amendment.

Justice STEVENS, with whom Justice BRENNAN and Justice MARSHALL join, concurring in the judgment.

Since the respondent in this case has never questioned the installation of the radio transmitter in the chloroform drum, I agree that it was entirely reasonable for the police officers to make use of the information received over the airwaves when they were trying to ascertain the ultimate destination of the chloroform. I do not join the Court's opinion, however, because it contains two unnecessarily broad dicta: One distorts the record in this case, and both may prove confusing to courts that must apply this decision in the future.

First, the Court implies that the chloroform drum was parading in "open fields" outside of the cabin, in a manner tantamount to its public display on the highways. The record does not support that implication. [T]his case does not pose any "open fields" issue.

Second, the Court suggests that the Fourth Amendment does not inhibit "the police from augmenting the sensory facilities bestowed upon them at birth with such enhancement as science and technology afforded them." But the Court held to the contrary in Katz v. United States (1967). Although the augmentation in this case was unobjectionable, it by no means follows that the use of electronic detection techniques does not implicate especially sensitive concerns.

Interestingly, in United States v. Karo, 468 U.S. 705 (1984), the Court found that the placement of an unmonitored beeper in a container of chemicals was not a search, but that if the beeper was used to obtain information that could not be procured through visual surveillance, it did constitute a search subject to Fourth Amendment protections. More importantly, as explained above, in United States v. Jones, in 2012, the Court held that placing a device on a person's car and tracking the car's movements for 28 days was a search within the meaning of the Fourth Amendment. The majority opinion by Justice Scalia focused on the placing of the device on the car being a trespass and thus constituting a search.

The issue of what is sufficiently "public behavior" arises in other contexts as well. For example, in United States v. White, 401 U.S. 745 (1971), the Court considered whether there was a search when a government informer carrying a radio transmitter engaged in a conversation with a suspect. The Court held that the listening to this conversation by another agent, in possession of a radio receiver, was not a search. Justice White wrote for a plurality of four and concluded that the suspect had no reasonable expectation of privacy in the conversation. He wrote:

Concededly a police agent who conceals his police connections may write down for official use his conversations with a defendant and testify concerning them, without a warrant authorizing his encounters with the defendant and without otherwise violating the latter's Fourth Amendment rights. For constitutional purposes, no different result is required if the agent instead of immediately reporting and transcribing his conversations with defendant, either (1) simultaneously records them with electronic equipment which he is carrying on his person; (2) or carries radio equipment which simultaneously transmits the conversations either to recording equipment located elsewhere or to other agents monitoring the transmitting frequency. If the conduct and revelations of an agent operating without electronic equipment do not invade the defendant's constitutionally justifiable expectations of privacy, neither does a simultaneous recording of the same conversations made by the agent or by others from transmissions received from the agent to whom the defendant is talking and whose trustworthiness the defendant necessarily risks.

The Court has similarly found that inspection of bank records are not searches under the Fourth Amendment because banks are parties to any transactions and thus have knowledge of them. California Bankers Assn. v. Schultz, 416 U.S. 21 (1974). The case involved a federal law, the Bank Secrecy Act of 1970, which required that banks file reports with the federal government of certain types of transactions. A Fourth Amendment challenge was rejected by the Court on the grounds that people have no reasonable expectation of privacy as to this information because it is known by others, the banks that process the transactions. In other words, because some others in the government will see the bank records, the Court concluded that there is no privacy expectation in them.

The Court has gone even further and found that people have no reasonable expectation of privacy in the phone numbers they dial or receive calls from. The specific issue was whether police use of "pen registers" — sometimes called "trap" and "trace" equipment — to monitor calls is a search.

SMITH v. MARYLAND

442 U.S. 735 (1979)

Justice BLACKMUN delivered the opinion of the Court.

This case presents the question whether the installation and use of a pen register constitutes a "search" within the meaning of the Fourth Amendment.[4] A pen register is "usually installed at a central telephone facility [and] records on a paper tape all numbers dialed from [the] line" to which it is attached.

---

4. A pen register is a mechanical device that records the numbers dialed on a telephone by monitoring the electrical impulses caused when the dial on the telephone is released. It does not overhear oral communications and does not indicate whether calls are actually completed. [Footnote by the Court.]

I

On March 5, 1976, in Baltimore, Md., Patricia McDonough was robbed. She gave the police a description of the robber and of a 1975 Monte Carlo automobile she had observed near the scene of the crime. After the robbery, McDonough began receiving threatening and obscene phone calls from a man identifying himself as the robber. On one occasion, the caller asked that she step out on her front porch; she did so, and saw the 1975 Monte Carlo she had earlier described to police moving slowly past her home. On March 16, police spotted a man who met McDonough's description driving a 1975 Monte Carlo in her neighborhood. By tracing the license plate number, police learned that the car was registered in the name of petitioner, Michael Lee Smith.

The next day, the telephone company, at police request, installed a pen register at its central offices to record the numbers dialed from the telephone at petitioner's home. The police did not get a warrant or court order before having the pen register installed. The register revealed that on March 17 a call was placed from petitioner's home to McDonough's phone. On the basis of this and other evidence, the police obtained a warrant to search petitioner's residence. The search revealed that a page in petitioner's phone book was turned down to the name and number of Patricia McDonough; the phone book was seized. Petitioner was arrested, and a six-man lineup was held on March 19. McDonough identified petitioner as the man who had robbed her.

II

In determining whether a particular form of government-initiated electronic surveillance is a "search" within the meaning of the Fourth Amendment, our lodestar is Katz v. United States (1967). Consistently with *Katz*, this Court uniformly has held that the application of the Fourth Amendment depends on whether the person invoking its protection can claim a "justifiable," a "reasonable," or a "legitimate expectation of privacy" that has been invaded by government action. This inquiry, as Justice Harlan aptly noted in his *Katz* concurrence, normally embraces two discrete questions. The first is whether the individual, by his conduct, has "exhibited an actual (subjective) expectation of privacy," — whether, in the words of the *Katz* majority, the individual has shown that "he seeks to preserve [something] as private." The second question is whether the individual's subjective expectation of privacy is "one that society is prepared to recognize as 'reasonable,'" — whether, in the words of the *Katz* majority, the individual's expectation, viewed objectively, is "justifiable" under the circumstances.

In applying the *Katz* analysis to this case, it is important to begin by specifying precisely the nature of the state activity that is challenged. The activity here took the form of installing and using a pen register. Since the pen register was installed on telephone company property at the telephone company's central offices, petitioner obviously cannot claim that his "property" was invaded or that police intruded into a "constitutionally protected area." Petitioner's claim, rather, is that, notwithstanding the absence of a trespass, the State, as did the Government in *Katz*, infringed a "legitimate expectation of privacy" that petitioner held. Yet a pen register differs significantly from the listening device employed in *Katz*, for pen registers do not acquire the contents of communications.

Given a pen register's limited capabilities, therefore, petitioner's argument that its installation and use constituted a "search" necessarily rests upon a claim that he had a "legitimate expectation of privacy" regarding the numbers he dialed on his phone.

This claim must be rejected. First, we doubt that people in general entertain any actual expectation of privacy in the numbers they dial. All telephone users realize that they must "convey" phone numbers to the telephone company, since it is through telephone company switching equipment that their calls are completed. All subscribers realize, moreover, that the phone company has facilities for making permanent records of the numbers they dial, for they see a list of their long-distance (toll) calls on their monthly bills. In fact, pen registers and similar devices are routinely used by telephone companies "for the purposes of checking billing operations, detecting fraud and preventing violations of law." Electronic equipment is used not only to keep billing records of toll calls, but also "to keep a record of all calls dialed from a telephone which is subject to a special rate structure." Pen registers are regularly employed "to determine whether a home phone is being used to conduct a business, to check for a defective dial, or to check for overbilling." Although most people may be oblivious to a pen register's esoteric functions, they presumably have some awareness of one common use: to aid in the identification of persons making annoying or obscene calls. Telephone users, in sum, typically know that they must convey numerical information to the phone company; that the phone company has facilities for recording this information; and that the phone company does in fact record this information for a variety of legitimate business purposes. Although subjective expectations cannot be scientifically gauged, it is too much to believe that telephone subscribers, under these circumstances, harbor any general expectation that the numbers they dial will remain secret.

Petitioner argues, however, that, whatever the expectations of telephone users in general, he demonstrated an expectation of privacy by his own conduct here, since he "us[ed] the telephone in his house to the exclusion of all others." But the site of the call is immaterial for purposes of analysis in this case. Although petitioner's conduct may have been calculated to keep the contents of his conversation private, his conduct was not and could not have been calculated to preserve the privacy of the number he dialed. Regardless of his location, petitioner had to convey that number to the telephone company in precisely the same way if he wished to complete his call. The fact that he dialed the number on his home phone rather than on some other phone could make no conceivable difference, nor could any subscriber rationally think that it would.

Second, even if petitioner did harbor some subjective expectation that the phone numbers he dialed would remain private, this expectation is not "one that society is prepared to recognize as 'reasonable.'" This Court consistently has held that a person has no legitimate expectation of privacy in information he voluntarily turns over to third parties.

This analysis dictates that petitioner can claim no legitimate expectation of privacy here. When he used his phone, petitioner voluntarily conveyed numerical information to the telephone company and "exposed" that information to its equipment in the ordinary course of business. In so doing, petitioner assumed the risk that the company would reveal to police the numbers he dialed. The switching equipment that processed those numbers is merely the modern counterpart of the operator who, in an earlier day, personally completed calls for the subscriber.

Justice STEWART, with whom Justice BRENNAN joins, dissenting.

I am not persuaded that the numbers dialed from a private telephone fall outside the constitutional protection of the Fourth and Fourteenth Amendments. In Katz v. United States, the Court acknowledged the "vital role that the public telephone has come to play in private communication[s]." The role played by a private telephone is even more vital, and since *Katz* it has been abundantly clear that telephone conversations carried on by people in their homes or offices are fully protected by the Fourth and Fourteenth Amendments.

Nevertheless, the Court today says that those safeguards do not extend to the numbers dialed from a private telephone, apparently because when a caller dials a number the digits may be recorded by the telephone company for billing purposes. But that observation no more than describes the basic nature of telephone calls. A telephone call simply cannot be made without the use of telephone company property and without payment to the company for the service. The telephone conversation itself must be electronically transmitted by telephone company equipment, and may be recorded or overheard by the use of other company equipment. Yet we have squarely held that the user of even a public telephone is entitled "to assume that the words he utters into the mouthpiece will not be broadcast to the world."

The central question in this case is whether a person who makes telephone calls from his home is entitled to make a similar assumption about the numbers he dials. What the telephone company does or might do with those numbers is no more relevant to this inquiry than it would be in a case involving the conversation itself. It is simply not enough to say, after *Katz*, that there is no legitimate expectation of privacy in the numbers dialed because the caller assumes the risk that the telephone company will disclose them to the police.

I think that the numbers dialed from a private telephone — like the conversations that occur during a call — are within the constitutional protection recognized in *Katz*. It seems clear to me that information obtained by pen register surveillance of a private telephone is information in which the telephone subscriber has a legitimate expectation of privacy. The information captured by such surveillance emanates from private conduct within a person's home or office — locations that without question are entitled to Fourth and Fourteenth Amendment protection. Further, that information is an integral part of the telephonic communication that under *Katz* is entitled to constitutional protection, whether or not it is captured by a trespass into such an area.

The numbers dialed from a private telephone — although certainly more prosaic than the conversation itself — are not without "content." Most private telephone subscribers may have their own numbers listed in a publicly distributed directory, but I doubt there are any who would be happy to have broadcast to the world a list of the local or long distance numbers they have called. This is not because such a list might in some sense be incriminating, but because it easily could reveal the identities of the persons and the places called, and thus reveal the most intimate details of a person's life.

In 1986, Congress enacted a statute that prohibits the installation or use of pen registers, except relating to the "operation, maintenance, and testing of a wire or electronic communication service or to the protection of the rights or property of such a provider" without a court order. 18 U.S.C. §2131. A federal court may issue such an order for a 60-day period upon application of a United States Attorney or a state law enforcement officer, if the federal or state attorney "has certified to the court that the relevant information is likely to be obtained by such installation and [its] use is relevant to an ongoing criminal investigation." 18 U.S.C. §3132(a)(1) and (2). The law also provides that a pen register may be installed without a court order for a period of 48 hours if there is an emergency involving "immediate death or serious bodily injury."

The USA Patriot Act allows the Attorney General to obtain authority for a pen register from the Foreign Intelligence Surveillance Court "for any investigation to obtain foreign intelligence information not concerning a United States person or to protect against international terrorism or clandestine intelligence activities, provided that such investigation of a United States person is not conducted solely upon the basis of activities protected by the First Amendment to the Constitution." 50 U.S.C. §1842(a)(1).

In light of *Smith,* should it be considered a search within the meaning of the Fourth Amendment when the National Security Agency obtains from service providers (like Verizon and Sprint) the records of whom people call or receive calls from and for how long? What about when police use cellular tower information to determine a person's whereabouts?

6. Use of Dogs to Sniff for Contraband

Is it a search if the police use drug-sniffing dogs? There is no overall answer to this question yet from the Supreme Court. But the Supreme Court has found the use of such dogs is not a search in a couple of contexts. In United States v. Place, 462 U.S. 696 (1983), the Court held that a canine sniff of closed luggage is not a search. Place aroused police suspicions when he was flying out of the Miami Airport to LaGuardia. Police were waiting for Place there. Justice O'Connor, who wrote the Court's opinion, stated the facts:

> The agents then took the bags to Kennedy Airport, where they subjected the bags to a "sniff test" by a trained narcotics detection dog. The dog reacted positively to the smaller of the two bags but ambiguously to the larger bag. Approximately 90 minutes had elapsed since the seizure of respondent's luggage. Because it was late on a Friday afternoon, the agents retained the luggage until Monday morning, when they secured a search warrant from a magistrate for the smaller bag. Upon opening that bag, the agents discovered 1,125 grams of cocaine.

The Court held that the dog sniff was not a search within the meaning of the Fourth Amendment:

> The purpose for which respondent's luggage was seized, of course, was to arrange its exposure to a narcotics detection dog. Obviously, if this investigative procedure is itself a search requiring probable cause, the initial seizure of respondent's luggage for the purpose of subjecting it to the sniff test — no matter how brief — could not be justified on less than probable cause.
>
> The Fourth Amendment "protects people from unreasonable government intrusions into their legitimate expectations of privacy." We have affirmed that a person possesses a privacy interest in the contents of personal luggage that is protected by the Fourth Amendment. A "canine sniff" by a well-trained narcotics detection dog, however, does not require opening the luggage. It does not expose noncontraband items that otherwise would remain hidden from public view, as does, for example, an officer's rummaging through the contents of the luggage. Thus, the manner in which information is obtained through this investigative technique is much less intrusive than a typical search. Moreover, the sniff discloses only the presence or absence of narcotics, a contraband item. Thus, despite the fact that the sniff tells the authorities something about the contents of the luggage, the information obtained is limited. This limited disclosure also ensures that the owner of the property is not subjected to the embarrassment and inconvenience entailed in less discriminate and more intrusive investigative methods.
>
> In these respects, the canine sniff is sui generis. We are aware of no other investigative procedure that is so limited both in the manner in which the information is obtained and in the content of the information revealed by the procedure. Therefore, we conclude that the particular course of investigation that the agents intended to pursue here — exposure of respondent's luggage, which was located in a public place, to a trained canine — did not constitute a "search" within the meaning of the Fourth Amendment.

In its more recent decision, Illinois v. Caballes, the Court considered dog sniffs in another context: a traffic stop. Again, the Court found that there was not a search. In light of *Place* and *Caballes*, it is worth thinking of other situations where dogs might be used and whether these uses should be regarded as searches.

ILLINOIS v. CABALLES

543 U.S. 405 (2005)

Justice STEVENS delivered the opinion of the Court.

Illinois State Trooper Daniel Gillette stopped respondent for speeding on an interstate highway. When Gillette radioed the police dispatcher to report the stop, a second trooper, Craig Graham, a member of the Illinois State Police Drug Interdiction Team, overheard the transmission and immediately headed for the scene with his narcotics-detection dog. When they arrived, respondent's car was on the shoulder of the road and respondent was in Gillette's vehicle. While Gillette was in the process of writing a warning ticket, Graham walked his dog around respondent's car. The dog alerted at the trunk. Based on that alert, the officers searched the trunk, found marijuana, and arrested respondent. The entire incident lasted less than 10 minutes.

Respondent was convicted of a narcotics offense and sentenced to 12 years' imprisonment and a $256,136 fine. The trial judge denied his motion to suppress the seized evidence and to quash his arrest. He held that the officers had not unnecessarily prolonged the stop and that the dog alert was sufficiently reliable to provide probable cause to conduct the search. Although the Appellate Court affirmed, the Illinois Supreme Court reversed, concluding that because the canine sniff was performed without any "specific and articulable facts" to suggest drug activity, the use of the dog "unjustifiably enlarg[ed] the scope of a routine traffic stop into a drug investigation."

The question on which we granted certiorari is narrow: "Whether the Fourth Amendment requires reasonable, articulable suspicion to justify using a drug-detection dog to sniff a vehicle during a legitimate traffic stop." Thus, we proceed on the assumption that the officer conducting the dog sniff had no information about respondent except that he had been stopped for speeding; accordingly, we have omitted any reference to facts about respondent that might have triggered a modicum of suspicion.

Here, the initial seizure of respondent when he was stopped on the highway was based on probable cause and was concededly lawful. It is nevertheless clear that a seizure that is lawful at its inception can violate the Fourth Amendment if its manner of execution unreasonably infringes interests protected by the Constitution. A seizure that is justified solely by the interest in issuing a warning ticket to the driver can become unlawful if it is prolonged beyond the time reasonably required to complete that mission.

Official conduct that does not "compromise any legitimate interest in privacy" is not a search subject to the Fourth Amendment. We have held that any interest in possessing contraband cannot be deemed "legitimate," and thus, governmental conduct that only reveals the possession of contraband "compromises no legitimate privacy interest." This is because the expectation "that certain facts will not come to the attention of the authorities" is not the same as an interest in "privacy that society is prepared to consider reasonable." In United States v. Place, we treated a canine sniff by a well-trained narcotics-detection dog as "sui generis" because it "discloses only the presence or absence of narcotics, a contraband item." Respondent likewise concedes that "drug sniffs are designed, and if properly conducted are generally likely, to reveal only the presence of contraband." Although respondent argues that the error rates, particularly the existence of false positives, call into question the premise that drug-detection dogs alert only to contraband, the record contains no evidence or findings that support his argument. Moreover, respondent does not suggest that an erroneous alert, in and of itself, reveals any legitimate private information, and, in this case, the trial judge found that the dog sniff was sufficiently reliable to establish probable cause to conduct a full-blown search of the trunk.

Accordingly, the use of a well-trained narcotics-detection dog—one that "does not expose noncontraband items that otherwise would remain hidden from public view," —during a lawful traffic stop, generally does not implicate legitimate privacy interests. In this case, the dog sniff was performed on the exterior of respondent's car while he was lawfully seized for a traffic violation. Any intrusion on respondent's privacy expectations does not rise to the level of a constitutionally cognizable infringement.

This conclusion is entirely consistent with our recent decision that the use of a thermal-imaging device to detect the growth of marijuana in a home constituted an unlawful search. Kyllo v. United States (2001). Critical to that decision was the fact that the device was capable of detecting lawful activity—in that case, intimate details in a home, such as "at what hour each night the lady of the house takes her daily sauna and bath." The legitimate expectation that information about perfectly lawful activity will remain private is categorically distinguishable from respondent's hopes or expectations concerning the nondetection of contraband in the trunk of his car. A dog sniff conducted during a concededly lawful traffic stop that reveals no information other than the location of a substance that no individual has any right to possess does not violate the Fourth Amendment.

Justice SOUTER, dissenting.

I would hold that using the dog for the purposes of determining the presence of marijuana in the car's trunk was a search unauthorized as an incident of the speeding stop and unjustified on any other ground.

In United States v. Place (1983), we categorized the sniff of the narcotics-seeking dog as "sui generis" under the Fourth Amendment and held it was not a search. The classification rests not only upon the limited nature of the intrusion, but on a further premise that experience has shown to be untenable, the assumption that trained sniffing dogs do not err. What we have learned about the fallibility of dogs in the years since *Place* was decided would itself be reason to call for reconsidering *Place*'s decision against treating the intentional use of a trained dog as a search. The portent of this very case, however, adds insistence to the call, for an uncritical adherence to *Place* would render the Fourth Amendment indifferent to suspicionless and indiscriminate sweeps of cars in parking garages and pedestrians on sidewalks; if a sniff is not preceded by a seizure subject to Fourth Amendment notice, it escapes Fourth Amendment review entirely unless it is treated as a search. We should not wait for these developments to occur before rethinking *Place*'s analysis, which invites such untoward consequences.

At the heart both of *Place* and the Court's opinion today is the proposition that sniffs by a trained dog are sui generis because a reaction by the dog in going alert is a response to nothing but the presence of contraband. Hence, the argument goes, because the sniff can only reveal the presence of items devoid of any legal use, the sniff "does not implicate legitimate privacy interests" and is not to be treated as a search.

The infallible dog, however, is a creature of legal fiction. Although the Supreme Court of Illinois did not get into the sniffing averages of drug dogs, their supposed infallibility is belied by judicial opinions describing well-trained animals sniffing and alerting with less than perfect accuracy, whether owing to errors by their handlers, the limitations of the dogs themselves, or even the pervasive contamination of currency by cocaine. Indeed, a study cited by Illinois in this case for the proposition that dog sniffs are "generally reliable" shows that dogs in artificial testing situations return false positives anywhere from 12.5% to 60% of the time, depending on the length of the search. In practical terms, the evidence is clear that the dog that alerts hundreds of times will be wrong dozens of times.

Once the dog's fallibility is recognized, however, that ends the justification claimed in *Place* for treating the sniff as sui generis under the Fourth Amendment: The sniff alert does not necessarily signal hidden contraband, and opening the container or enclosed space whose emanations the dog has sensed will not necessarily reveal contraband or any other evidence of crime.

It makes sense, then, to treat a sniff as the search that it amounts to in practice, and to rely on the body of our Fourth Amendment cases, including *Kyllo*, in deciding whether such a search is reasonable. As a general proposition, using a dog to sniff for drugs is subject to the rule that the object of enforcing criminal laws does not, without more, justify suspicionless Fourth Amendment intrusions.

Justice GINSBURG, with whom Justice SOUTER joins, dissenting.

Illinois State Police Trooper Daniel Gillette stopped Roy Caballes for driving 71 miles per hour in a zone with a posted speed limit of 65 miles per hour. Trooper Craig Graham of the Drug Interdiction Team heard on the radio that Trooper Gillette was making a traffic stop. Although Gillette requested no aid, Graham decided to come to the scene to conduct a dog sniff.

It is hardly dispositive that the dog sniff in this case may not have lengthened the duration of the stop. *Terry*, it merits repetition, instructs that any investigation must be "reasonably related in scope to the circumstances which justified the interference in the first place." The unwarranted and nonconsensual expansion of the seizure here from a routine traffic stop to a drug investigation broadened the scope of the investigation in a manner that, in my judgment, runs afoul of the Fourth Amendment.

In Illinois v. Caballes, the Supreme Court held that it does not violate the Fourth Amendment for police to have a dog sniff for drugs during a routine traffic stop. But in United States v. Rodriguez, the Court imposed an important limit: Police cannot extend the duration of a stop beyond what is needed to carry out the traffic stop in order to facilitate a dog sniff.

RODRIGUEZ v. UNITED STATES

135 S. Ct. 1609 (2015)

Justice GINSBURG delivered the opinion of the Court.

In Illinois v. Caballes (2005), this Court held that a dog sniff conducted during a lawful traffic stop does not violate the Fourth Amendment's proscription of unreasonable seizures. This case presents the question whether the Fourth Amendment tolerates a dog sniff conducted after completion of a traffic stop. We hold that a police stop exceeding the time needed to handle the matter for which the stop was made violates the Constitution's shield against unreasonable seizures. A seizure justified only by a police-observed traffic violation, therefore, "become[s] unlawful if it is prolonged beyond the time reasonably required to complete th[e] mission" of issuing a ticket for the violation. The Court so recognized in *Caballes,* and we adhere to the line drawn in that decision.

I

Just after midnight on March 27, 2012, police officer Morgan Struble observed a Mercury Mountaineer veer slowly onto the shoulder of Nebraska State Highway 275 for one or two seconds and then jerk back onto the road. Nebraska law prohibits driving on highway shoulders, and on that basis, Struble pulled the Mountaineer over at 12:06 A.M. Struble is a K-9 officer with the Valley Police Department in Nebraska, and his dog Floyd was in his patrol car that night. Two men were in the Mountaineer: the driver, Dennys Rodriguez, and a front-seat passenger, Scott Pollman.

Struble approached the Mountaineer on the passenger's side. After Rodriguez identified himself, Struble asked him why he had driven onto the shoulder. Rodriguez replied that he had swerved to avoid a pothole. Struble then gathered Rodriguez's license, registration, and proof of insurance, and asked Rodriguez to accompany him to the patrol car. Rodriguez asked if he was required to do so, and Struble answered that he was not. Rodriguez decided to wait in his own vehicle.

After running a records check on Rodriguez, Struble returned to the Mountaineer. Struble asked passenger Pollman for his driver's license and began to question him about where the two men were coming from and where they were going. Pollman replied that they had traveled to Omaha, Nebraska, to look at a Ford Mustang that was for sale and that they were returning to Norfolk, Nebraska. Struble returned again to his patrol car, where he completed a records check on Pollman, and called for a second officer. Struble then began writing a warning ticket for Rodriguez for driving on the shoulder of the road.

Struble returned to Rodriguez's vehicle a third time to issue the written warning. By 12:27 or 12:28 A.M., Struble had finished explaining the warning to Rodriguez, and had given back to Rodriguez and Pollman the documents obtained from them. As Struble later testified, at that point, Rodriguez and Pollman "had all their documents back and a copy of the written warning. I got all the reason[s] for the stop out of the way[,] . . . took care of all the business."

Nevertheless, Struble did not consider Rodriguez "free to leave." Although justification for the traffic stop was "out of the way," Struble asked for permission to walk his dog around Rodriguez's vehicle. Rodriguez said no. Struble then instructed Rodriguez to turn off the ignition, exit the vehicle, and stand in front of the patrol car to wait for the second officer. Rodriguez complied. At 12:33 A.M., a deputy sheriff arrived. Struble retrieved his dog and led him twice around the Mountaineer. The dog alerted to the presence of drugs halfway through Struble's second pass. All told, seven or eight minutes had elapsed from the time Struble issued the written warning until the dog indicated the presence of drugs. A search of the vehicle revealed a large bag of methamphetamine.

II

A seizure for a traffic violation justifies a police investigation of that violation. "[A] relatively brief encounter," a routine traffic stop is "more analogous to a so-called '*Terry* stop' . . . than to a formal arrest." Like a *Terry* stop, the tolerable duration of police inquiries in the traffic-stop context is determined by the seizure's "mission" — to address the traffic violation that warranted the stop, and attend to related safety concerns. Because addressing the infraction is the purpose of the stop, it may "last no longer than is necessary to effectuate th[at] purpose." Authority for the seizure thus ends when tasks tied to the traffic infraction are — or reasonably should have been — completed.

In *Caballes*, however, we cautioned that a traffic stop "can become unlawful if it is prolonged beyond the time reasonably required to complete th[e] mission" of issuing a warning ticket. An officer, in other words, may conduct certain unrelated checks during an otherwise lawful traffic stop. But he may not do so in a way that prolongs the stop, absent the reasonable suspicion ordinarily demanded to justify detaining an individual.

Beyond determining whether to issue a traffic ticket, an officer's mission includes "ordinary inquiries incident to [the traffic] stop." Typically such inquiries involve checking the driver's license, determining whether there are outstanding warrants against the driver, and inspecting the automobile's registration and proof of insurance. These checks serve the same objective as enforcement of the traffic code: ensuring that vehicles on the road are operated safely and responsibly.

A dog sniff, by contrast, is a measure aimed at "detect[ing] evidence of ordinary criminal wrongdoing." Lacking the same close connection to roadway safety as the ordinary inquiries, a dog sniff is not fairly characterized as part of the officer's traffic mission.

Justice THOMAS, with whom Justice ALITO joins, and with whom Justice KENNEDY joins as to all but Part III, dissenting.

Ten years ago, we explained that "conducting a dog sniff [does] not change the character of a traffic stop that is lawful at its inception and otherwise executed in a reasonable manner." The only question here is whether an officer executed a stop in a reasonable manner when he waited to conduct a dog sniff until after he had given the driver a written warning and a backup unit had arrived, bringing the overall duration of the stop to 29 minutes. Because the stop was reasonably executed, no Fourth Amendment violation occurred. The Court's holding to the contrary cannot be reconciled with our decision in *Caballes* or a number of common police practices. It was also unnecessary, as the officer possessed reasonable suspicion to continue to hold the driver to conduct the dog sniff. I respectfully dissent.

I

Because Rodriguez does not dispute that Officer Struble had probable cause to stop him, the only question is whether the stop was otherwise executed in a reasonable manner. I easily conclude that it was. Approximately 29 minutes passed from the time Officer Struble stopped Rodriguez until his narcotics-detection dog alerted to the presence of drugs. That amount of time is hardly out of the ordinary for a traffic stop by a single officer of a vehicle containing multiple occupants even when no dog sniff is involved. During that time, Officer Struble conducted the ordinary activities of a traffic stop—he approached the vehicle, questioned Rodriguez about the observed violation, asked Pollman about their travel plans, ran serial warrant checks on Rodriguez and Pollman, and issued a written warning to Rodriguez. And when he decided to conduct a dog sniff, he took the precaution of calling for backup out of concern for his safety.

As *Caballes* makes clear, the fact that Officer Struble waited until after he gave Rodriguez the warning to conduct the dog sniff does not alter this analysis. Because "the use of a well-trained narcotics-detection dog . . . generally does not implicate legitimate privacy interests," "conducting a dog sniff would not change the character of a traffic stop that is lawful at its inception and otherwise executed in a reasonable manner." The stop here was "lawful at its inception and otherwise executed in a reasonable manner." As in *Caballes,* "conducting a dog sniff [did] not change the character of [the] traffic stop," *ibid.,* and thus no Fourth Amendment violation occurred.

II

Rather than adhere to the reasonableness requirement that we have repeatedly characterized as the "touchstone of the Fourth Amendment," the majority constructed a test of its own that is inconsistent with our precedents.

The majority's rule requires a traffic stop to "en[d] when tasks tied to the traffic infraction are — or reasonably should have been — completed." "If an officer can complete traffic-based inquiries expeditiously, then that is the amount of time reasonably required to complete the stop's mission" and he may hold the individual no longer. The majority's rule thus imposes a one-way ratchet for constitutional protection linked to the characteristics of the individual officer conducting the stop: If a driver is stopped by a particularly efficient officer, then he will be entitled to be released from the traffic stop after a shorter period of time than a driver stopped by a less efficient officer. Similarly, if a driver is stopped by an officer with access to technology that can shorten a records check, then he will be entitled to be released from the stop after a shorter period of time than an individual stopped by an officer without access to such technology.

I "cannot accept that the search and seizure protections of the Fourth Amendment are so variable and can be made to turn upon such trivialities." We have repeatedly explained that the reasonableness inquiry must not hinge on the characteristics of the individual officer conducting the seizure.

The majority's logic would produce similarly arbitrary results. Under its reasoning, a traffic stop made by a rookie could be executed in a reasonable manner, whereas the same traffic stop made by a knowledgeable, veteran officer *in precisely the same circumstances* might not, if in fact his knowledge and experience made him capable of completing the stop faster. We have long rejected interpretations of the Fourth Amendment that would produce such haphazard results, and I see no reason to depart from our consistent practice today.

III

Today's revision of our Fourth Amendment jurisprudence was also entirely unnecessary. Rodriguez suffered no Fourth Amendment violation here for an entirely independent reason: Officer Struble had reasonable suspicion to continue to hold him for investigative purposes. Our precedents make clear that the Fourth Amendment permits an officer to conduct an investigative traffic stop when that officer has "a particularized and objective basis for suspecting the particular person stopped of criminal activity."

Officer Struble testified that he first became suspicious that Rodriguez was engaged in criminal activity for a number of reasons. When he approached the vehicle, he smelled an "overwhelming odor of air freshener coming from the vehicle," which is, in his experience, "a common attempt to conceal an odor that [people] don't want . . . to be smelled by the police." He also observed, upon approaching the front window on the passenger side of the vehicle, that Rodriguez's passenger, Scott Pollman, appeared nervous. Pollman pulled his hat down low, puffed nervously on a cigarette, and refused to make eye contact with him. The officer thought he was "more nervous than your typical passenger" who "do[esn't] have anything to worry about because [t]hey didn't commit a [traffic] violation."

Officer Struble's interactions with the vehicle's occupants only increased his suspicions. When he asked Rodriguez why he had driven onto the shoulder, Rodriguez claimed that he swerved to avoid a pothole. But that story could not be squared with Officer Struble's observation of the vehicle slowly driving off the road before being jerked back onto it. And when Officer Struble asked Pollman where they were coming from and where they were going, Pollman told him they were traveling from Omaha, Nebraska, back to Norfolk, Nebraska, after looking at a vehicle they were considering purchasing. Pollman told the officer that he had neither seen pictures of the vehicle nor confirmed title before the trip. As Officer Struble explained, it "seemed suspicious" to him "to drive . . . approximately two hours . . . late at night to see a vehicle sight unseen to possibly buy it," and to go from Norfolk to Omaha to look at it because "[u]sually people leave Omaha to go get vehicles, not the other way around" due to higher Omaha taxes.

These facts, taken together, easily meet our standard for reasonable suspicion. Taking into account all the relevant facts, Officer Struble possessed reasonable suspicion of criminal activity to conduct the dog sniff.

Justice ALITO, dissenting.

This is an unnecessary, impractical, and arbitrary decision. It addresses a purely hypothetical question: whether the traffic stop in this case *would be* unreasonable if the police officer, prior to leading a drug-sniffing dog around the exterior of petitioner's car, did not already have reasonable suspicion that the car contained drugs. In fact, however, the police officer *did have* reasonable suspicion, and, as a result, the officer was justified in detaining the occupants for the short period of time (seven or eight minutes) that is at issue.

Not only does the Court reach out to decide a question not really presented by the facts in this case, but the Court's answer to that question is arbitrary. The Court refuses to address the real Fourth Amendment question: whether the stop was unreasonably prolonged. Instead, the Court latches onto the fact that Officer Struble delivered the warning prior to the dog sniff and proclaims that the authority to detain based on a traffic stop ends when a citation or warning is handed over to the driver. The Court thus holds that the Fourth Amendment was violated, not because of the length of the stop, but simply because of the sequence in which Officer Struble chose to perform his tasks.

This holding is not only arbitrary; it is perverse since Officer Struble chose that sequence for the purpose of protecting his own safety and possibly the safety of others. Without prolonging the stop, Officer Struble could have conducted the dog sniff while one of the tasks that the Court regards as properly part of the traffic stop was still in progress, but that sequence would have entailed unnecessary risk.

The Court's holding therefore makes no practical sense. And nothing in the Fourth Amendment, which speaks of *reasonableness,* compels this arbitrary line.

The rule that the Court adopts will do little good going forward. It is unlikely to have any appreciable effect on the length of future traffic stops. Most officers will learn the prescribed sequence of events even if they cannot fathom the reason for that requirement. (I would love to be the proverbial fly on the wall when police instructors teach this rule to officers who make traffic stops.)

The Court has decided two other recent cases concerning the use of drug-sniffing dogs. In Florida v. Jardines, the Court held that bringing a drug-sniffing dog on to someone's property was a search within the meaning of the Fourth Amendment. As in United States v. Jones, above, the Court (in an opinion by Justice Scalia) found that this was a trespass and that was sufficient for a search. In Florida v. Harris, the Court held that there are no special burdens on prosecutors and police in showing the reliability of a drug-sniffing dog as the basis for probable cause for a search.

FLORIDA v. JARDINES
133 S. Ct. 1409 (2013)

Justice SCALIA delivered the opinion of the Court.

We consider whether using a drug-sniffing dog on a homeowner's porch to investigate the contents of the home is a "search" within the meaning of the Fourth Amendment.

I

In 2006, Detective William Pedraja of the Miami-Dade Police Department received an unverified tip that marijuana was being grown in the home of respondent Joelis Jardines. One month later, the Department and the Drug Enforcement Administration sent a joint surveillance team to Jardines' home. Detective Pedraja was part of that team. He watched the home for fifteen minutes and saw no vehicles in the driveway or activity around the home, and could not see inside because the blinds were drawn. Detective

Pedraja then approached Jardines' home accompanied by Detective Douglas Bartelt, a trained canine handler who had just arrived at the scene with his drug-sniffing dog. The dog was trained to detect the scent of marijuana, cocaine, heroin, and several other drugs, indicating the presence of any of these substances through particular behavioral changes recognizable by his handler.

Detective Bartelt had the dog on a six-foot leash, owing in part to the dog's "wild" nature and tendency to dart around erratically while searching. As the dog approached Jardines' front porch, he apparently sensed one of the odors he had been trained to detect, and began energetically exploring the area for the strongest point source of that odor. As Detective Bartelt explained, the dog "began tracking that airborne odor by . . . tracking back and forth," engaging in what is called "bracketing," "back and forth, back and forth." Detective Bartelt gave the dog "the full six feet of the leash plus whatever safe distance [he could] give him" to do this—he testified that he needed to give the dog "as much distance as I can." And Detective Pedraja stood back while this was occurring, so that he would not "get knocked over" when the dog was "spinning around trying to find" the source.

After sniffing the base of the front door, the dog sat, which is the trained behavior upon discovering the odor's strongest point. Detective Bartelt then pulled the dog away from the door and returned to his vehicle. He left the scene after informing Detective Pedraja that there had been a positive alert for narcotics.

On the basis of what he had learned at the home, Detective Pedraja applied for and received a warrant to search the residence. When the warrant was executed later that day, Jardines attempted to flee and was arrested; the search revealed marijuana plants, and he was charged with trafficking in cannabis.

We granted certiorari, limited to the question of whether the officers' behavior was a search within the meaning of the Fourth Amendment.

II

The [Fourth] Amendment establishes a simple baseline, one that for much of our history formed the exclusive basis for its protections: When "the Government obtains information by physically intruding" on persons, houses, papers, or effects, "a 'search' within the original meaning of the Fourth Amendment" has "undoubtedly occurred." United States v. Jones (2012). By reason of our decision in Katz v. United States (1967), property rights "are not the sole measure of Fourth Amendment violations," but though *Katz* may add to the baseline, it does not subtract anything from the Amendment's protections "when the Government *does* engage in [a] physical intrusion of a constitutionally protected area."

That principle renders this case a straightforward one. The officers were gathering information in an area belonging to Jardines and immediately surrounding his house — in the curtilage of the house, which we have held enjoys protection as part of the home itself. And they gathered that information by physically entering and occupying the area to engage in conduct not explicitly or implicitly permitted by the homeowner.

A

The Fourth Amendment "indicates with some precision the places and things encompassed by its protections": persons, houses, papers, and effects. The Fourth Amendment does not, therefore, prevent all investigations conducted on private property; for example, an officer may (subject to *Katz*) gather information in what we have called "open fields" — even if those fields are privately owned — because such fields are not enumerated in the Amendment's text.

But when it comes to the Fourth Amendment, the home is first among equals. At the Amendment's "very core" stands "the right of a man to retreat into his own home and there be free from unreasonable governmental intrusion." This right would be of little practical value if the State's agents could stand in a home's porch or side garden and trawl for evidence with impunity; the right to retreat would be significantly diminished if the police could enter a man's property to observe his repose from just outside the front window.

We therefore regard the area "immediately surrounding and associated with the home" — what our cases call the curtilage — as "part of the home itself for Fourth Amendment purposes." That principle has ancient and durable roots. This area around the home is "intimately linked to the home, both physically and psychologically," and is where "privacy expectations are most heightened."

While the boundaries of the curtilage are generally "clearly marked," the "conception defining the curtilage" is at any rate familiar enough that it is "easily understood from our daily experience." Here there is no doubt that the officers entered it: The front porch is the classic exemplar of an area adjacent to the home and "to which the activity of home life extends."

B

Since the officers' investigation took place in a constitutionally protected area, we turn to the question of whether it was accomplished through an unlicensed physical intrusion. Entick v. Carrington (K.B. 1765), a case "undoubtedly familiar" to "every American statesman" at the time of the Founding, states the general rule clearly: "[O]ur law holds the property of every man so sacred, that no man can set his foot upon his neighbour's close without his leave." As it is undisputed that the detectives had all four of their feet and all four of their companion's firmly planted on the constitutionally protected extension of Jardines' home, the only question is whether he had given his leave (even implicitly) for them to do so. He had not.

"A license may be implied from the habits of the country," notwithstanding the "strict rule of the English common law as to entry upon a close." We have accordingly recognized that "the knocker on the front door is treated as an invitation or license to attempt an entry, justifying ingress to the home by solicitors, hawkers and peddlers of all kinds." This implicit license typically permits the visitor to approach the home by the front path, knock promptly, wait briefly to be received, and then (absent invitation to linger longer) leave. Complying with the terms of that traditional invitation does not require fine-grained legal knowledge; it is generally managed without incident by the Nation's Girl Scouts and trick-or-treaters. Thus, a police officer not armed with a warrant may approach a home and knock, precisely because that is "no more than any private citizen might do."

But introducing a trained police dog to explore the area around the home in hopes of discovering incriminating evidence is something else. There is no customary invitation to do *that*. An invitation to engage in canine forensic investigation assuredly does not inhere in the very act of hanging a knocker. To find a visitor knocking on the door is routine (even if sometimes unwelcome); to spot that same visitor exploring the front path with a metal detector, or marching his bloodhound into the garden before saying hello and asking permission, would inspire most of us to — well, call the police. The scope of a license — express or implied — is limited not only to a particular area but also to a specific purpose. Consent at a traffic stop to an officer's checking out an anonymous tip that there is a body in the trunk does not permit the officer to rummage through the trunk for narcotics. Here, the background social norms that invite a visitor to the front door do not invite him there to conduct a search.

III

The State argues that investigation by a forensic narcotics dog by definition cannot implicate any legitimate privacy interest. [W]e need not decide whether the officers' investigation of Jardines' home violated his expectation of privacy under *Katz*. One virtue of the Fourth Amendment's property-rights baseline is that it keeps easy cases easy. That the officers learned what they learned only by physically intruding on Jardines' property to gather evidence is enough to establish that a search occurred.

The government's use of trained police dogs to investigate the home and its immediate surroundings is a "search" within the meaning of the Fourth Amendment.

Justice KAGAN, with whom Justice GINSBURG and Justice SOTOMAYOR join, concurring.

For me, a simple analogy clinches this case — and does so on privacy as well as property grounds. A stranger comes to the front door of your home carrying super-high-powered binoculars. He doesn't knock or say hello. Instead, he stands on the porch and uses the binoculars to peer through your windows, into your home's furthest corners. It doesn't take long (the binoculars are really very fine): In just a couple of minutes, his uncommon behavior allows him to learn details of your life you disclose to no one. Has your "visitor" trespassed on your property, exceeding the license you have granted to members of the public to, say, drop off the mail or distribute campaign flyers? Yes, he has. And has he also invaded your "reasonable expectation of privacy," by nosing into intimacies you sensibly thought protected from disclosure? Yes, of course, he has done that too.

That case is this case in every way that matters. Here, police officers came to Joelis Jardines' door with a super-sensitive instrument, which they deployed to detect things inside that they could not perceive unassisted. The equipment they used was animal, not mineral. But contra the dissent, that is of no significance in determining whether a search occurred. Detective Bartelt's dog was not your neighbor's pet, come to your porch on a leisurely stroll. They are to the poodle down the street as high-powered binoculars are to a piece of plain glass. Like the binoculars, a drug-detection dog is a specialized device for discovering objects not in plain view (or plain smell). And as in the hypothetical above, that device was aimed here at a home — the most private and inviolate (or so we expect) of all the places and things the Fourth Amendment protects. Was this activity a trespass? Yes, as the Court holds today. Was it also an invasion of privacy? Yes, that as well.

The Court today treats this case under a property rubric; I write separately to note that I could just as happily have decided it by looking to Jardines' privacy interests. I can think of only one divergence: If we had decided this case on privacy grounds, we would have realized that Kyllo v. United States (2001), already resolved it. The *Kyllo* Court held that police officers conducted a search when they used a thermal-imaging device to detect heat emanating from a private home, even though they committed no trespass.

With these further thoughts, suggesting that a focus on Jardines' privacy interests would make an "easy cas[e] easy" twice over, I join the Court's opinion in full.

Justice ALITO, with whom THE CHIEF JUSTICE, Justice KENNEDY, and Justice BREYER join, dissenting.

The Court's decision in this important Fourth Amendment case is based on a putative rule of trespass law that is nowhere to be found in the annals of Anglo-American jurisprudence.

The law of trespass generally gives members of the public a license to use a walkway to approach the front door of a house and to remain there for a brief time. This license is not limited to persons who intend to speak to an occupant or who actually do so. (Mail carriers and persons delivering packages and flyers are examples of individuals who may lawfully approach a front door without intending to converse.) Nor is the license restricted to categories of visitors whom an occupant of the dwelling is likely to welcome; as the Court acknowledges, this license applies even to "solicitors, hawkers and peddlers of all kinds." And the license even extends to police officers who wish to gather evidence against an occupant (by asking potentially incriminating questions).

According to the Court, however, the police officer in this case, Detective Bartelt, committed a trespass because he was accompanied during his otherwise lawful visit to the front door of respondent's house by his dog, Franky. Where is the authority evidencing such a rule? Dogs have been domesticated for about 12,000 years; they were ubiquitous in both this country and Britain at the time of the adoption of the Fourth Amendment; and their acute sense of smell has been used in law enforcement for centuries. Yet the Court has been unable to find a single case — from the United States or any other common-law nation — that supports the rule on which its decision is based. Thus, trespass law provides no support for the Court's holding today.

The Court's decision is also inconsistent with the reasonable-expectations-of-privacy test that the Court adopted in 1967. A reasonable person understands that odors emanating from a house may be detected from locations that are open to the public, and a reasonable person will not count on the strength of those odors remaining within the range that, while detectible by a dog, cannot be smelled by a human.

For these reasons, I would hold that no search within the meaning of the Fourth Amendment took place in this case, and I would reverse the decision below.

The conduct of the police officer in this case did not constitute a trespass and did not violate respondent's reasonable expectations of privacy. I would hold that this conduct was not a search, and I therefore respectfully dissent.

FLORIDA v. HARRIS

133 S. Ct. 1050 (2013)

Justice KAGAN delivered the opinion of the Court.

In this case, we consider how a court should determine if the "alert" of a drug-detection dog during a traffic stop provides probable cause to search a vehicle. The Florida Supreme Court held that the State must in every case present an exhaustive set of records, including a log of the dog's performance in the field, to establish the dog's reliability. We think that demand inconsistent with the "flexible, common-sense standard" of probable cause.

I

William Wheetley is a K-9 Officer in the Liberty County, Florida Sheriff's Office. On June 24, 2006, he was on a routine patrol with Aldo, a German shepherd trained to detect certain narcotics (methamphetamine, marijuana, cocaine, heroin, and ecstasy). Wheetley pulled over respondent Clayton Harris's truck because it had an expired license plate. On approaching the driver's-side door, Wheetley saw that Harris was "visibly nervous," unable to sit still, shaking, and breathing rapidly. Wheetley also noticed an open can of beer in the truck's cup holder. Wheetley asked Harris for consent to search the truck, but Harris refused. At that point, Wheetley retrieved Aldo from the patrol car and walked him around Harris's truck for a "free air sniff." Aldo alerted at the driver's-side door handle — signaling, through a distinctive set of behaviors, that he smelled drugs there.

Wheetley concluded, based principally on Aldo's alert, that he had probable cause to search the truck. His search did not turn up any of the drugs Aldo was trained to detect. But it did reveal 200 loose pseudoephedrine pills, 8,000 matches, a bottle of hydrochloric acid, two containers of antifreeze, and a coffee filter full of iodine crystals — all ingredients for making methamphetamine. Wheetley accordingly arrested Harris, who admitted after proper *Miranda* warnings that he routinely "cooked" methamphetamine at his house and could not go "more than a few days without using" it. The State charged Harris with possessing pseudoephedrine for use in manufacturing methamphetamine.

While out on bail, Harris had another run-in with Wheetley and Aldo. This time, Wheetley pulled Harris over for a broken brake light. Aldo again sniffed the truck's exterior, and again alerted at the driver's-side door handle. Wheetley once more searched the truck, but on this occasion discovered nothing of interest.

Harris moved to suppress the evidence found in his truck on the ground that Aldo's alert had not given Wheetley probable cause for a search. At the hearing on that motion, Wheetley testified about both his and Aldo's training in drug detection. In 2004, Wheetley (and a different dog) completed a 160-hour course in narcotics detection offered by the Dothan, Alabama Police Department, while Aldo (and a different handler) completed a similar, 120-hour course given by the Apopka, Florida Police Department. That same year, Aldo received a one-year certification from Drug Beat, a private company that specializes in testing and certifying K-9 dogs. Wheetley and Aldo teamed up in 2005 and went through another, 40-hour refresher course in Dothan together. They also did four hours of training exercises each week to maintain their skills. Wheetley would hide drugs in certain vehicles or buildings while leaving others "blank" to determine whether Aldo alerted at the right places. According to Wheetley, Aldo's performance in those exercises was "really good." The State introduced "Monthly Canine Detection Training Logs" consistent with that testimony: They showed that Aldo always found hidden drugs and that he performed "satisfactorily" (the higher of two possible assessments) on each day of training.

On cross-examination, Harris's attorney chose not to contest the quality of Aldo's or Wheetley's training. She focused instead on Aldo's certification and his performance in the field, particularly the two stops of Harris's truck. Wheetley conceded that the certification (which, he noted, Florida law did not require) had expired the year before he pulled Harris over. Wheetley also acknowledged that he did not keep complete records of Aldo's performance in traffic stops or other field work; instead, he maintained records only of alerts resulting in arrests. But Wheetley defended Aldo's two alerts to Harris's seemingly narcotics-free truck: According to Wheetley, Harris probably transferred the odor of methamphetamine to the door handle, and Aldo responded to that "residual odor."

The trial court concluded that Wheetley had probable cause to search Harris's truck and so denied the motion to suppress. Harris then entered a no-contest plea while reserving the right to appeal the trial court's ruling. An intermediate state court summarily affirmed.

The Florida Supreme Court reversed, holding that Wheetley lacked probable cause to search Harris's vehicle under the Fourth Amendment. "[W]hen a dog alerts," the court wrote, "the fact that the dog has been trained and certified is simply not enough to establish probable cause." To demonstrate a dog's reliability, the State needed to produce a wider array of evidence:

"[T]he State must present . . . the dog's training and certification records, an explanation of the meaning of the particular training and certification, field performance records (including any unverified alerts), and evidence concerning the experience and training of the officer handling the dog, as well as any other objective evidence known to the officer about the dog's reliability."

The court particularly stressed the need for "evidence of the dog's performance history," including records showing "how often the dog has alerted in the field without illegal contraband having been found." That data, the court stated, could help to expose such problems as a handler's tendency (conscious or not) to "cue [a] dog to alert" and "a dog's inability to distinguish between residual odors and actual drugs." Accordingly, an officer like Wheetley who did not keep full records of his dog's field performance could never have the requisite cause to think "that the dog is a reliable indicator of drugs."

II

A police officer has probable cause to conduct a search when "the facts available to [him] would 'warrant a [person] of reasonable caution in the belief'" that contraband or evidence of a crime is present. The test for probable cause is not reducible to "precise definition or quantification." "Finely tuned standards such as proof beyond a reasonable doubt or by a preponderance of the evidence . . . have no place in the [probable-cause] decision." All we have required is the kind of "fair probability" on which "reasonable and prudent [people,] not legal technicians, act."

In evaluating whether the State has met this practical and common-sensical standard, we have consistently looked to the totality of the circumstances. We have rejected rigid rules, bright-line tests, and mechanistic inquiries in favor of a more flexible, all-things-considered approach.

The Florida Supreme Court flouted this established approach to determining probable cause. To assess the reliability of a drug-detection dog, the court created a strict evidentiary checklist, whose every item the State must tick off. Most prominently, an alert cannot establish probable cause under the Florida court's decision unless the State introduces comprehensive documentation of the dog's prior "hits" and "misses" in the field. (One wonders how the court would apply its test to a rookie dog.) No matter how much other proof the State offers of the dog's reliability, the absent field performance records will preclude a finding of probable cause. That is the antithesis of a totality-of-the-circumstances analysis.

Making matters worse, the decision below treats records of a dog's field performance as the gold standard in evidence, when in most cases they have relatively limited import. Errors may abound in such records. If a dog on patrol fails to alert to a car containing drugs, the mistake usually will go undetected because the officer will not initiate a search. Field data thus may not capture a dog's false negatives. Conversely (and more relevant here), if the dog alerts to a car in which the officer finds no narcotics, the dog may not have made a mistake at all. The dog may have detected substances that were too well hidden or present in quantities too small for the officer to locate. Or the dog may have smelled the residual odor of drugs previously in the vehicle or on the driver's person. Field data thus may markedly overstate a dog's real false positives. By contrast, those inaccuracies — in either direction — do not taint records of a dog's performance in standard training and certification settings. There, the designers of an assessment know where drugs are hidden and where they are not — and so where a dog should alert and where he should not. The better measure of a dog's reliability thus comes away from the field, in controlled testing environments.

For that reason, evidence of a dog's satisfactory performance in a certification or training program can itself provide sufficient reason to trust his alert. If a bona fide organization has certified a dog after testing his reliability in a controlled setting, a court can presume (subject to any conflicting evidence offered) that the dog's alert provides probable cause to search. The same is true, even in the absence of formal certification, if the dog has recently and successfully completed a training program that evaluated his proficiency in locating drugs. After all, law enforcement units have their own strong incentive to use effective training and certification programs, because only accurate drug-detection dogs enable officers to locate contraband without incurring unnecessary risks or wasting limited time and resources.

A defendant, however, must have an opportunity to challenge such evidence of a dog's reliability, whether by cross-examining the testifying officer or by introducing his own fact or expert witnesses. The defendant, for example, may contest the adequacy of a certification or training program, perhaps asserting that its standards are too lax or its methods faulty. So too, the defendant may examine how the dog (or handler) performed in the assessments made in those settings. Indeed, evidence of the dog's (or handler's) history in the field, although susceptible to the kind of misinterpretation we have discussed, may sometimes be relevant. And even assuming a dog is generally reliable, circumstances surrounding a particular alert may undermine the case for probable cause — if, say, the officer cued the dog (consciously or not), or if the team was working under unfamiliar conditions.

In short, a probable-cause hearing focusing on a dog's alert should proceed much like any other. The court should allow the parties to make their best case, consistent with the usual rules of criminal procedure. And the court should then evaluate the proffered evidence to decide what all the circumstances demonstrate. If the State has produced proof from controlled settings that a dog performs reliably in detecting drugs, and the defendant has not contested that showing, then the court should find probable cause. If, in contrast, the defendant has challenged the State's case (by disputing the reliability of the dog overall or of a particular alert), then the court should weigh the competing evidence. In all events, the court should not prescribe, as the Florida Supreme Court did, an inflexible set of evidentiary requirements. The question — similar to every inquiry into probable cause — is whether all the facts surrounding a dog's alert, viewed through the lens of common sense, would make a reasonably prudent person think that a search would reveal contraband or evidence of a crime. A sniff is up to snuff when it meets that test.

III

And here, Aldo's did. The record in this case amply supported the trial court's determination that Aldo's alert gave Wheetley probable cause to search Harris's truck.

The State, as earlier described, introduced substantial evidence of Aldo's training and his proficiency in finding drugs.

Because training records established Aldo's reliability in detecting drugs and Harris failed to undermine that showing, we agree with the trial court that Wheetley had probable cause to search Harris's truck.

———————————

Although cases like United States v. Place and Illinois v. Caballes rejected the idea that the dog sniff violated the Fourth Amendment and Florida v. Harris rejected the claim that prosecutors have a special duty to demonstrate the reliability of a drug sniffing dog, the Court has limited what police can do to effectuate a drug sniff by a dog. United States v. Rodriguez says that the police cannot extend the time of a traffic stop to effectuate a drug sniff by a dog. Florida v. Jardines holds that the police cannot trespass on private property to conduct a dog sniff. Thus, the cases seem to be less concerned about the dog's drug sniff and more focused on how it is effectuated.

C. THE REQUIREMENT FOR PROBABLE CAUSE

A core requirement of the Fourth Amendment is the requirement for probable cause. Generally, a judge may issue a search or arrest warrant only if there is probable cause. If it is a circumstance where a warrant is not required (and these are discussed below in section E), a police officer generally can search or arrest only if there is probable cause. There are exceptions. For example, in some situations searches are allowed with less than probable cause. As discussed below, in schools, searches of students' purses require only the lesser standard of "reasonable suspicion," not the usual requirement of probable cause. New Jersey v. T.L.O., 469 U.S. 325 (1986). Sometimes searches are even allowed without any individualized suspicion, such as when the Court has approved random drug testing (also discussed below). *See, e.g.*, Vernonia School Dist. 47J v. Acton, 515 U.S. 646 (1995) (upholding random drug testing for student athletes).

But the Supreme Court has been clear that probable cause is the "traditional standard" of the Fourth Amendment. Arizona v. Hicks, 480 U.S. 321 (1987). There is no precise definition of probable cause. The classic definition of probable cause, often cited by the Supreme Court, was articulated in Stacey v. Emery, 97 U.S. 642 (1878). The Supreme Court said that the question is whether "the facts and circumstances before the officer are such to warrant a man of prudence and caution in believing that the offense had been committed."

Three questions are particularly important in understanding probable cause. First, what is sufficient belief to meet the standard for probable cause? Second, is it an objective or a subjective standard? Third, what if the police make a reasonable mistake as to the law?

1. What Is Sufficient Belief to Meet the Standard for Probable Cause?

The Supreme Court has said that "in dealing with probable cause . . . we deal with probabilities." Brinegar v. United States, 338 U.S. 160 (1949). But the Court did not attempt to define what probabilities are sufficient. The Court simply said that "more than bare suspicion," but "less than evidence which would justify conviction."

The Supreme Court has confronted this question of what is sufficient for probable cause in determining whether information from informants was sufficient to constitute probable cause. Initially, the Court addressed this in two cases in the 1960s: Aguilar v. Texas, 378 U.S. 108 (1964), and Spinelli v. United States, 393 U.S. 410 (1969). These cases gave rise to the

Aguilar-Spinelli two-part test. First, was the informant credible — was it likely that he or she was telling the truth? Second, was the informant reliable — was it likely that the informant had knowledge? If an informant did not meet these requirements, there was not probable cause and the fruits of the search had to be excluded.

In Illinois v. Gates, below, the Court departed from the *Aguilar-Spinelli* approach and emphasized the need to consider the "totality of the circumstances." This is the general approach used in determining whether there is probable cause, even beyond the issue of determining whether an informant is reliable.

ILLINOIS v. GATES
462 U.S. 213 (1983)

Justice REHNQUIST delivered the opinion of the Court.

Respondents Lance and Susan Gates were indicted for violation of state drug laws after police officers, executing a search warrant, discovered marijuana and other contraband in their automobile and home. Prior to trial the Gateses moved to suppress evidence seized during this search. The Illinois Supreme Court affirmed the decisions of lower state courts, granting the motion. It held that the affidavit submitted in support of the State's application for a warrant to search the Gateses' property was inadequate under this Court's decisions in Aguilar v. Texas (1964) and Spinelli v. United States (1969).

[I]

We turn to the question presented in the State's original petition for certiorari, which requires us to decide whether respondents' rights under the Fourth and Fourteenth Amendments were violated by the search of their car and house. A chronological statement of events usefully introduces the issues at stake. Bloomingdale, Ill., is a suburb of Chicago located in DuPage County. On May 3, 1978, the Bloomingdale Police Department received by mail an anonymous handwritten letter which read as follows:

> This letter is to inform you that you have a couple in your town who strictly make their living on selling drugs. They are Sue and Lance Gates, they live on Greenway, off Bloomingdale Rd. in the condominiums. Most of their buys are done in Florida. Sue his wife drives their car to Florida, where she leaves it to be loaded up with drugs, then Lance flys down and drives it back. Sue flys back after she drops the car off in Florida. May 3 she is driving down there again and Lance will be flying down in a few days to drive it back. At the time Lance drives the car back he has the trunk loaded with over $100,000.00 in drugs. Presently they have over $100,000.00 worth of drugs in their basement.
>
> They brag about the fact they never have to work, and make their entire living on pushers.

> I guarantee if you watch them carefully you will make a big catch. They are
> friends with some big drug dealers, who visit their house often.

The letter was referred by the Chief of Police of the Bloomingdale Police Department to Detective Mader, who decided to pursue the tip. Mader learned, from the office of the Illinois Secretary of State, that an Illinois driver's license had been issued to one Lance Gates, residing at a stated address in Bloomingdale. He contacted a confidential informant, whose examination of certain financial records revealed a more recent address for the Gateses, and he also learned from a police officer assigned to O'Hare Airport that "L. Gates" had made a reservation on Eastern Airlines flight 245 to West Palm Beach, Fla., scheduled to depart from Chicago on May 5 at 4:15 P.M.

Mader then made arrangements with an agent of the Drug Enforcement Administration for surveillance of the May 5 Eastern Airlines flight. The agent later reported to Mader that Gates had boarded the flight, and that federal agents in Florida had observed him arrive in West Palm Beach and take a taxi to the nearby Holiday Inn. They also reported that Gates went to a room registered to one Susan Gates and that, at 7:00 A.M. the next morning, Gates and an unidentified woman left the motel in a Mercury bearing Illinois license plates and drove northbound on an interstate frequently used by travelers to the Chicago area. In addition, the DEA agent informed Mader that the license plate number on the Mercury registered to a Hornet station wagon owned by Gates. The agent also advised Mader that the driving time between West Palm Beach and Bloomingdale was approximately 22 to 24 hours.

Mader signed an affidavit setting forth the foregoing facts, and submitted it to a judge of the Circuit Court of DuPage County, together with a copy of the anonymous letter. The judge of that court thereupon issued a search warrant for the Gateses' residence and for their automobile. The judge, in deciding to issue the warrant, could have determined that the modus operandi of the Gateses had been substantially corroborated. As the anonymous letter predicted, Lance Gates had flown from Chicago to West Palm Beach late in the afternoon of May 5th, had checked into a hotel room registered in the name of his wife, and, at 7:00 A.M. the following morning, had headed north, accompanied by an unidentified woman, out of West Palm Beach on an interstate highway used by travelers from South Florida to Chicago in an automobile bearing a license plate issued to him.

At 5:15 A.M. on March 7th, only 36 hours after he had flown out of Chicago, Lance Gates, and his wife, returned to their home in Bloomingdale, driving the car in which they had left West Palm Beach some 22 hours earlier. The Bloomingdale police were awaiting them, searched the trunk of the Mercury, and uncovered approximately 350 pounds of marijuana. A search of the Gateses' home revealed marijuana, weapons, and other contraband. The Illinois Circuit Court ordered suppression of all these items, on the ground that the affidavit submitted to the Circuit Judge failed to support the necessary determination of probable cause to believe that the Gateses' automobile and home contained the contraband in question. This decision was affirmed in turn by the Illinois Appellate Court and by a divided vote of the Supreme Court of Illinois.

The Illinois Supreme Court concluded — and we are inclined to agree — that, standing alone, the anonymous letter sent to the Bloomingdale Police Department would not provide the basis for a magistrate's determination that there was probable cause to believe contraband would be found in the Gateses' car and home. The letter provides virtually nothing from which one might conclude that its author is either honest or his information reliable; likewise, the letter gives absolutely no indication of the basis for the writer's predictions regarding the Gateses' criminal activities. Something more was required, then, before a magistrate could conclude that there was probable cause to believe that contraband would be found in the Gateses' home and car.

The Illinois Supreme Court also properly recognized that Detective Mader's affidavit might be capable of supplementing the anonymous letter with information sufficient to permit a determination of probable cause. In holding that the affidavit in fact did not contain sufficient additional information to sustain a determination of probable cause, the Illinois court applied a "two-pronged test," derived from our decision in Spinelli v. United States (1969).

We agree with the Illinois Supreme Court that an informant's "veracity," "reliability" and "basis of knowledge" are all highly relevant in determining the value of his report. We do not agree, however, that these elements should be understood as entirely separate and independent requirements to be rigidly exacted in every case, which the opinion of the Supreme Court of Illinois would imply. Rather, as detailed below, they should be understood simply as closely intertwined issues that may usefully illuminate the common-sense, practical question whether there is "probable cause" to believe that contraband or evidence is located in a particular place.

[II]

This totality-of-the-circumstances approach is far more consistent with our prior treatment of probable cause than is any rigid demand that specific "tests" be satisfied by every informant's tip. Perhaps the central teaching of our decisions bearing on the probable cause standard is that it is a "practical, nontechnical conception." "In dealing with probable cause, . . . as the very name implies, we deal with probabilities. These are not technical; they are the factual and practical considerations of everyday life on which reasonable and prudent men, not legal technicians, act."

As our language indicates, we intended neither a rigid compartmentalization of the inquiries into an informant's "veracity," "reliability" and "basis of knowledge," nor that these inquiries be elaborate exegeses of an informant's tip. Rather, we required only that some facts bearing on two particular issues be provided to the magistrate.

The process does not deal with hard certainties, but with probabilities. Long before the law of probabilities was articulated as such, practical people formulated certain common-sense conclusions about human behavior; jurors as factfinders are permitted to do the same — and so are law enforcement officers. Finally, the evidence thus collected must be seen and weighed not in terms of library analysis by scholars, but as understood by those versed in the field of law enforcement.

As these comments illustrate, probable cause is a fluid concept — turning on the assessment of probabilities in particular factual contexts — not readily, or even usefully, reduced to a neat set of legal rules. Informants' tips doubtless come in many shapes and sizes from many different types of persons.

Moreover, the "two-pronged test" directs analysis into two largely independent channels — the informant's "veracity" or "reliability" and his "basis of knowledge." There are persuasive arguments against according these two elements such independent status. Instead, they are better understood as relevant considerations in the totality-of-the-circumstances analysis that traditionally has guided probable cause determinations: a deficiency in one may be compensated for, in determining the overall reliability of a tip, by a strong showing as to the other, or by some other indicia of reliability.

If, for example, a particular informant is known for the unusual reliability of his predictions of certain types of criminal activities in a locality, his failure, in a particular case, to thoroughly set forth the basis of his knowledge surely should not serve as an absolute bar to a finding of probable cause based on his tip. Likewise, if an unquestionably honest citizen comes forward with a report of criminal activity — which if fabricated would subject him to criminal liability — we have found rigorous scrutiny of the basis of his knowledge unnecessary. Conversely, even if we entertain some doubt as to an informant's motives, his explicit and detailed description of alleged wrongdoing, along with a statement that the event was observed first-hand, entitles his tip to greater weight than might otherwise be the case. Unlike a totality-of-the-circumstances analysis, which permits a balanced assessment of the relative weights of all the various indicia of reliability (and unreliability) attending an informant's tip, the "two-pronged test" has encouraged an excessively technical dissection of informants' tips, with undue attention being focused on isolated issues that cannot sensibly be divorced from the other facts presented to the magistrate.

Finally, the direction taken by decisions following *Spinelli* poorly serves "the most basic function of any government": "to provide for the security of the individual and of his property." The strictures that inevitably accompany the "two-pronged test" cannot avoid seriously impeding the task of law enforcement. If, as the Illinois Supreme Court apparently thought, that test must be rigorously applied in every case, anonymous tips seldom would be of greatly diminished value in police work. Ordinary citizens, like ordinary witnesses, generally do not provide extensive recitations of the basis of their everyday observations. Likewise, as the Illinois Supreme Court observed in this case, the veracity of persons supplying anonymous tips is by hypothesis largely unknown, and unknowable. As a result, anonymous tips seldom could survive a rigorous application of either of the *Spinelli* prongs. Yet, such tips, particularly when supplemented by independent police investigation, frequently contribute to the solution of otherwise "perfect crimes." While a conscientious assessment of the basis for crediting such tips is required by the Fourth Amendment, a standard that leaves virtually no place for anonymous citizen informants is not.

For all these reasons, we conclude that it is wiser to abandon the "two-pronged test" established by our decisions in *Aguilar* and *Spinelli*. In its place we reaffirm the totality-of-the-circumstances analysis that traditionally has informed probable cause determinations. The task of the issuing magistrate is simply to make a practical, common-sense decision whether, given all the circumstances set forth in the affidavit before him, including the "veracity" and "basis of knowledge" of persons supplying hearsay information, there is a fair probability that contraband or evidence of a crime will be found in a particular place. And the duty of a reviewing court is simply to ensure that the magistrate had a "substantial basis for . . . conclud[ing]" that probable cause existed. We are convinced that this flexible, easily applied standard will better achieve the accommodation of public and private interests that the Fourth Amendment requires than does the approach that has developed from *Aguilar* and *Spinelli*.

Our earlier cases illustrate the limits beyond which a magistrate may not venture in issuing a warrant. A sworn statement of an affiant that "he has cause to suspect and does believe that" liquor illegally brought into the United States is located on certain premises will not do. An affidavit must provide the magistrate with a substantial basis for determining the existence of probable cause, and [a] wholly conclusory statement fail[s] to meet this requirement. An officer's statement that "affiants have received reliable information from a credible person and believe" that heroin is stored in a home, is likewise inadequate. [T]his is a mere conclusory statement that gives the magistrate virtually no basis at all for making a judgment regarding probable cause. Sufficient information must be presented to the magistrate to allow that official to determine probable cause; his action cannot be a mere ratification of the bare conclusions of others. In order to ensure that such an abdication of the magistrate's duty does not occur, courts must continue to conscientiously review the sufficiency of affidavits on which warrants are issued. But when we move beyond the "bare bones" affidavits, this area simply does not lend itself to a prescribed set of rules. Instead, the flexible, common-sense standard articulated better serves the purposes of the Fourth Amendment's probable cause requirement.

[III]

Our decisions applying the totality-of-the-circumstances analysis outlined above have consistently recognized the value of corroboration of details of an informant's tip by independent police work. Likewise, we recognized the probative value of corroborative efforts of police officials.

In addition, the magistrate could rely on the anonymous letter, which had been corroborated in major part by Mader's efforts. The corroboration of the letter's predictions that the Gateses' car would be in Florida, that Lance Gates would fly to Florida in the next day or so, and that he would drive the car north toward Bloomingdale all indicated, albeit not with certainty, that the informant's other assertions also were true. "Because an informant is right about some things, he is more probably right about other facts," including the claim regarding the Gateses' illegal activity. This may well not be the type of "reliability" or "veracity" necessary to satisfy some views of the "veracity prong" of *Spinelli,* but we think it suffices for the practical, common-sense judgment called for in making a probable cause determination. It is enough, for purposes of assessing probable cause, that "corroboration through other sources of information reduced the chances of a reckless or prevaricating tale," thus providing "a substantial basis for crediting the hearsay."

This is perfectly reasonable. As discussed previously, probable cause requires only a probability or substantial chance of criminal activity, not an actual showing of such activity. By hypothesis, therefore, innocent behavior frequently will provide the basis for a showing of probable cause; to require otherwise would be to sub silentio impose a drastically more rigorous definition of probable cause than the security of our citizens demands. We think the Illinois court attempted a too rigid classification of the types of conduct that may be relied upon in seeking to demonstrate probable cause. In making a determination of probable cause the relevant inquiry is not whether particular conduct is "innocent" or "guilty," but the degree of suspicion that attaches to particular types of non-criminal acts.

Finally, the anonymous letter contained a range of details relating not just to easily obtained facts and conditions existing at the time of the tip, but to future actions of third parties ordinarily not easily predicted. The letter writer's accurate information as to the travel plans of each of the Gateses was of a character likely obtained only from the Gateses themselves, or from someone familiar with their not entirely ordinary travel plans. If the informant had access to accurate information of this type a magistrate could properly conclude that it was not unlikely that he also had access to reliable information of the Gateses' alleged illegal activities. Of course, the Gateses' travel plans might have been learned from a talkative neighbor or travel agent; under the "two-pronged test" developed from *Spinelli,* the character of the details in the anonymous letter might well not permit a sufficiently clear inference regarding the letter writer's "basis of knowledge." But, as discussed previously, probable cause does not demand the certainty we associate with formal trials. It is enough that there was a fair probability that the writer of the anonymous letter had obtained his entire story either from the Gates[es] or someone they trusted. And corroboration of major portions of the letter's predictions provides just this probability. It is apparent, therefore, that the judge issuing the warrant had a "substantial basis for . . . conclud[ing]" that probable cause to search the Gateses' home and car existed.

Justice BRENNAN, with whom Justice MARSHALL joins, dissenting.

Although I join Justice Stevens' dissenting opinion and agree with him that the warrant is invalid even under the Court's newly announced "totality of the circumstances" test, I write separately to dissent from the Court's unjustified and ill-advised rejection of the two-prong test for evaluating the validity of a warrant based on hearsay announced in Aguilar v. Texas (1964), and refined in Spinelli v. United States (1969).

I

In recognition of the judiciary's role as the only effective guardian of Fourth Amendment rights, this Court has developed over the last half century a set of coherent rules governing a magistrate's consideration of a warrant application and the showings that are necessary to support a finding of probable cause. We start with the proposition that a neutral and detached magistrate, and not the police, should determine whether there is probable cause to support the issuance of a warrant. In order to emphasize the magistrate's role as an independent arbiter of probable cause and to insure that searches or seizures are not effected on less than probable cause, the Court has insisted that police officers provide magistrates with the underlying facts and circumstances that support the officers' conclusions. The Court stated that "[u]nder the Fourth Amendment, an officer may not properly issue a warrant to search a private dwelling unless he can find probable cause therefor from facts or circumstances presented to him under oath or affirmation. Mere affirmance of belief or suspicion is not enough."

The *Aguilar* standard was refined in Spinelli v. United States (1969). In *Spinelli*, the Court reviewed a search warrant based on an affidavit that was "more ample," than the one in *Aguilar*. The affidavit in *Spinelli* contained not only a tip from an informant, but also a report of an independent police investigation that allegedly corroborated the informant's tip. Under these circumstances, the Court stated that it was "required to delineate the manner in which *Aguilar*'s two-pronged test should be applied. . . ."

The Court held that the *Aguilar* test should be applied to the tip, and approved two additional ways of satisfying that test. First, the Court suggested that if the tip contained sufficient detail describing the accused's criminal activity it might satisfy *Aguilar*'s basis of knowledge prong. Such detail might assure the magistrate that he is "relying on something more substantial than a casual rumor circulating in the underworld or an accusation based merely on an individual's general reputation." "A magistrate, when confronted with such detail, could reasonably infer that the informant had gained his information in a reliable way."

Second, the Court stated that police corroboration of the details of a tip could provide a basis for satisfying *Aguilar*.

I find this reasoning persuasive. Properly understood, therefore, *Spinelli* stands for the proposition that corroboration of certain details in a tip may be sufficient to satisfy the veracity, but not the basis of knowledge, prong of *Aguilar*. As noted, *Spinelli* also suggests that in some limited circumstances considerable detail in an informant's tip may be adequate to satisfy the basis of knowledge prong of *Aguilar*.

Although the rules drawn from the cases discussed above are cast in procedural terms, they advance an important underlying substantive value: Findings of probable cause, and attendant intrusions, should not be authorized unless there is some assurance that the information on which they are based has been obtained in a reliable way by an honest or credible person. As applied to police officers, the rules focus on the way in which the information was acquired. As applied to informants, the rules focus both on the honesty or credibility of the informant and on the reliability of the way in which the information was acquired. Insofar as it is more complicated, an evaluation of affidavits based on hearsay involves a more difficult inquiry. This suggests a need to structure the inquiry in an effort to insure greater accuracy. The standards announced in *Aguilar*, as refined by *Spinelli*, fulfill that need. The standards inform the police of what information they have to provide and magistrates of what information they should demand. The standards also inform magistrates of the subsidiary findings they must make in order to arrive at an ultimate finding of probable cause. *Spinelli*, properly understood, directs the magistrate's attention to the possibility that the presence of self-verifying detail might satisfy *Aguilar*'s basis of knowledge prong and that corroboration of the details of a tip might satisfy *Aguilar*'s veracity prong. By requiring police to provide certain crucial information to magistrates and by structuring magistrates' probable cause inquiries, *Aguilar* and *Spinelli* assure the magistrate's role as an independent arbiter of probable cause, insure greater accuracy in probable cause determinations, and advance the substantive value identified above.

In light of the important purposes served by *Aguilar* and *Spinelli*, I would not reject the standards they establish. If anything, I simply would make more clear that *Spinelli*, properly understood, does not depart in any fundamental way from the test established by *Aguilar*. For reasons I shall next state, I do not find persuasive the Court's justifications for rejecting the test established by *Aguilar* and refined by *Spinelli*.

II

In rejecting the *Aguilar-Spinelli* standards, the Court suggests that a "totality-of-the-circumstances approach is far more consistent with our prior treatment of probable cause than is any rigid demand that specific 'tests' be satisfied by every informant's tip."

The Court also insists that the *Aguilar-Spinelli* standards must be abandoned because they are inconsistent with the fact that non-lawyers frequently serve as magistrates. To the contrary, the standards help to structure probable cause inquiries and, properly interpreted, may actually help a non-lawyer magistrate in making a probable cause determination. Moreover, the *Aguilar* and *Spinelli* tests are not inconsistent with deference to magistrates' determinations of probable cause. *Aguilar* expressly acknowledged that reviewing courts "will pay substantial deference to judicial determinations of probable cause. . . ."

At the heart of the Court's decision to abandon *Aguilar* and *Spinelli* appears to be its belief that "the direction taken by decisions following *Spinelli* poorly serves 'the most basic function of any government: to provide for the security of the individual and of his property.'" This conclusion rests on the judgment that *Aguilar* and *Spinelli* "seriously imped[e] the task of law enforcement," and render anonymous tips valueless in police work. Surely, the Court overstates its case. But of particular concern to all Americans must be that the Court gives virtually no consideration to the value of insuring that findings of probable cause are based on information that a magistrate can reasonably say has been obtained in a reliable way by an honest or credible person.

———————

Gates remains one of the Supreme Court's most important decisions concerning the standard for probable cause. Yet there is an inherent uncertainty as to what is enough. Probable cause is more than the lesser standard of "reasonable suspicion," and it is thought to be less than preponderance of the evidence. Another case that raised this question was Maryland v. Pringle. If a police officer knows that someone within the car is responsible for contraband, is there probable cause to arrest all of those within the car? More generally, it is worth considering whether probable cause can be expressed as a probability; if there is a 25 percent chance that a person has committed a crime or has evidence of a crime, is that enough, or should it be 30 percent or 40 percent or 50 percent? Of course, there is the question of whether any such numbers are simply invented and therefore not helpful in deciding whether there is probable cause.

MARYLAND v. PRINGLE

540 U.S. 366 (2003)

Chief Justice REHNQUIST delivered the opinion of the Court.

In the early morning hours a passenger car occupied by three men was stopped for speeding by a police officer. The officer, upon searching the car, seized $763 of rolled-up cash from the glove compartment and five glassine baggies of cocaine from between the back-seat armrest and the back seat. After all three men denied ownership of the cocaine and money, the officer arrested each of them. We hold that the officer had probable cause to arrest Pringle — one of the three men.

At 3:16 A.M. on August 7, 1999, a Baltimore County Police officer stopped a Nissan Maxima for speeding. There were three occupants in the car: Donte

Partlow, the driver and owner, respondent Pringle, the front-seat passenger, and Otis Smith, the back-seat passenger. The officer asked Partlow for his license and registration. When Partlow opened the glove compartment to retrieve the vehicle registration, the officer observed a large amount of rolled-up money in the glove compartment. The officer returned to his patrol car with Partlow's license and registration to check the computer system for outstanding violations. The computer check did not reveal any violations. The officer returned to the stopped car, had Partlow get out, and issued him an oral warning.

After a second patrol car arrived, the officer asked Partlow if he had any weapons or narcotics in the vehicle. Partlow indicated that he did not. Partlow then consented to a search of the vehicle. The search yielded $763 from the glove compartment and five plastic glassine baggies containing cocaine from behind the back-seat armrest. When the officer began the search the armrest was in the upright position flat against the rear seat. The officer pulled down the armrest and found the drugs, which had been placed between the armrest and the back seat of the car.

The officer questioned all three men about the ownership of the drugs and money, and told them that if no one admitted to ownership of the drugs he was going to arrest them all. The men offered no information regarding the ownership of the drugs or money. All three were placed under arrest and transported to the police station.

Later that morning, Pringle waived his rights under Miranda v. Arizona (1966), and gave an oral and written confession in which he acknowledged that the cocaine belonged to him, that he and his friends were going to a party, and that he intended to sell the cocaine or "[u]se it for sex." Pringle maintained that the other occupants of the car did not know about the drugs, and they were released.

The trial court denied Pringle's motion to suppress his confession as the fruit of an illegal arrest, holding that the officer had probable cause to arrest Pringle. A jury convicted Pringle of possession with intent to distribute cocaine and possession of cocaine. He was sentenced to 10 years' incarceration without the possibility of parole. The Court of Special Appeals of Maryland affirmed. The Court of Appeals of Maryland, by divided vote, reversed, holding that, absent specific facts tending to show Pringle's knowledge and dominion or control over the drugs, "the mere finding of cocaine in the back armrest when [Pringle] was a front seat passenger in a car being driven by its owner is insufficient to establish probable cause for an arrest for possession."

It is uncontested in the present case that the officer, upon recovering the five plastic glassine baggies containing suspected cocaine, had probable cause to believe a felony had been committed. The sole question is whether the officer had probable cause to believe that Pringle committed that crime.

The long-prevailing standard of probable cause protects "citizens from rash and unreasonable interferences with privacy and from unfounded charges of crime," while giving "fair leeway for enforcing the law in the community's protection."

The probable-cause standard is incapable of precise definition or quantification into percentages because it deals with probabilities and depends on the totality of the circumstances. We have stated, however, that "[t]he substance of all the definitions of probable cause is a reasonable ground for belief of guilt," and that the belief of guilt must be particularized with respect to the person to be searched or seized.

To determine whether an officer had probable cause to arrest an individual, we examine the events leading up to the arrest, and then decide "whether these historical facts, viewed from the standpoint of an objectively reasonable police officer, amount to" probable cause. In this case, Pringle was one of three men riding in a Nissan Maxima at 3:16 A.M. There was $763 of rolled-up cash in the glove compartment directly in front of Pringle. Five plastic glassine baggies of cocaine were behind the back-seat armrest and accessible to all three men. Upon questioning, the three men failed to offer any information with respect to the ownership of the cocaine or the money.

We think it an entirely reasonable inference from these facts that any or all three of the occupants had knowledge of, and exercised dominion and control over, the cocaine. Thus, a reasonable officer could conclude that there was probable cause to believe Pringle committed the crime of possession of cocaine, either solely or jointly.

"[A] person's mere propinquity to others independently suspected of criminal activity does not, without more, give rise to probable cause to search that person. Where the standard is probable cause, a search or seizure of a person must be supported by probable cause particularized with respect to that person. This requirement cannot be undercut or avoided by simply pointing to the fact that coincidentally there exists probable cause to search or seize another or to search the premises where the person may happen to be."

We hold that the officer had probable cause to believe that Pringle had committed the crime of possession of a controlled substance. Pringle's arrest therefore did not contravene the Fourth and Fourteenth Amendments.

2.   Is It an Objective or a Subjective Standard?

Often, a crucial question is whether probable cause focuses on the subjective knowledge and intent of the particular officer, or whether it is an objective standard focusing on what the reasonable officer in the circumstances would do. A subjective standard provides a basis for challenging officers who act in bad faith or for impermissible purposes. But the problem is that subjective standards are far harder to administer because of the difficulty of ever knowing the officers' subjective intention. The objective standard focuses on what the reasonable officer could have done in the circumstances.

The Court has expressly held that the test for probable cause is an objective one. Whren v. United States is a key case adopting and elaborating the objective standard.

WHREN v. UNITED STATES

517 U.S. 806 (1996)

Justice SCALIA delivered the opinion of the Court.

In this case we decide whether the temporary detention of a motorist who the police have probable cause to believe has committed a civil traffic violation is inconsistent with the Fourth Amendment's prohibition against unreasonable seizures unless a reasonable officer would have been motivated to stop the car by a desire to enforce the traffic laws.

I

On the evening of June 10, 1993, plainclothes vice-squad officers of the District of Columbia Metropolitan Police Department were patrolling a "high drug area" of the city in an unmarked car. Their suspicions were aroused when they passed a dark Pathfinder truck with temporary license plates and youthful occupants waiting at a stop sign, the driver looking down into the lap of the passenger at his right. The truck remained stopped at the intersection for what seemed an unusually long time — more than 20 seconds. When the police car executed a U-turn in order to head back toward the truck, the Pathfinder turned suddenly to its right, without signaling, and sped off at an "unreasonable" speed. The policemen followed, and in a short while overtook the Pathfinder when it stopped behind other traffic at a red light. They pulled up alongside, and Officer Ephraim Soto stepped out and approached the driver's door, identifying himself as a police officer and directing the driver, petitioner Brown, to put the vehicle in park. When Soto drew up to the driver's window, he immediately observed two large plastic bags of what appeared to be crack cocaine in petitioner Whren's hands. Petitioners were arrested, and quantities of several types of illegal drugs were retrieved from the vehicle.

Petitioners were charged in a four-count indictment with violating various federal drug laws, including 21 U.S.C. §§844(a) and 860(a). At a pretrial suppression hearing, they challenged the legality of the stop and the resulting seizure of the drugs. They argued that the stop had not been justified by probable cause to believe, or even reasonable suspicion, that petitioners were engaged in illegal drug-dealing activity; and that Officer Soto's asserted ground for approaching the vehicle — to give the driver a warning concerning traffic violations — was pretextual. The District Court denied the suppression motion, concluding that "the facts of the stop were not controverted," and "[t]here was nothing to really demonstrate that the actions of the officers were contrary to a normal traffic stop."

Petitioners were convicted of the counts at issue here. The Court of Appeals affirmed the convictions, holding with respect to the suppression issue that, "regardless of whether a police officer subjectively believes that the occupants of an automobile may be engaging in some other illegal behavior, a traffic stop is permissible as long as a reasonable officer in the same circumstances could have stopped the car for the suspected traffic violation."

II

Temporary detention of individuals during the stop of an automobile by the police, even if only for a brief period and for a limited purpose, constitutes a "seizure" of "persons" within the meaning of this provision. An automobile stop is thus subject to the constitutional imperative that it not be "unreasonable" under the circumstances. As a general matter, the decision to stop an automobile is reasonable where the police have probable cause to believe that a traffic violation has occurred.

Petitioners accept that Officer Soto had probable cause to believe that various provisions of the District of Columbia traffic code had been violated. They argue, however, that "in the unique context of civil traffic regulations" probable cause is not enough. Since, they contend, the use of automobiles is so heavily and minutely regulated that total compliance with traffic and safety rules is nearly impossible, a police officer will almost invariably be able to catch any given motorist in a technical violation. This creates the temptation to use traffic stops as a means of investigating other law violations, as to which no probable cause or even articulable suspicion exists. Petitioners, who are both black, further contend that police officers might decide which motorists to stop based on decidedly impermissible factors, such as the race of the car's occupants. To avoid this danger, they say, the Fourth Amendment test for traffic stops should be, not the normal one (applied by the Court of Appeals) of whether probable cause existed to justify the stop; but rather, whether a police officer, acting reasonably, would have made the stop for the reason given.

A

Petitioners contend that the standard they propose is consistent with our past cases' disapproval of police attempts to use valid bases of action against citizens as pretexts for pursuing other investigatory agendas.

We think [our earlier] cases foreclose any argument that the constitutional reasonableness of traffic stops depends on the actual motivations of the individual officers involved. We of course agree with petitioners that the Constitution prohibits selective enforcement of the law based on considerations such as race. But the constitutional basis for objecting to intentionally discriminatory application of laws is the Equal Protection Clause, not the Fourth Amendment. Subjective intentions play no role in ordinary, probable-cause Fourth Amendment analysis.

B

Recognizing that we have been unwilling to entertain Fourth Amendment challenges based on the actual motivations of individual officers, petitioners disavow any intention to make the individual officer's subjective good faith the touchstone of "reasonableness." They insist that the standard they have put forward—whether the officer's conduct deviated materially from usual police practices, so that a reasonable officer in the same circumstances would not have made the stop for the reasons given—is an "objective" one.

But although framed in empirical terms, this approach is plainly and indisputably driven by subjective considerations. Its whole purpose is to prevent the police from doing under the guise of enforcing the traffic code what they would like to do for different reasons. Petitioners' proposed standard may not use the word "pretext," but it is designed to combat nothing other than the perceived "danger" of the pretextual stop, albeit only indirectly and over the run of cases. Instead of asking whether the individual officer had the proper state of mind, the petitioners would have us ask, in effect, whether (based on general police practices) it is plausible to believe that the officer had the proper state of mind.

Why one would frame a test designed to combat pretext in such fashion that the court cannot take into account actual and admitted pretext is a curiosity that can only be explained by the fact that our cases have foreclosed the more sensible option. If those cases were based only upon the evidentiary difficulty of establishing subjective intent, petitioners' attempt to root out subjective vices through objective means might make sense. But they were not based only upon that, or indeed even principally upon that. Their principal basis— which applies equally to attempts to reach subjective intent through ostensibly objective means—is simply that the Fourth Amendment's concern with "reasonableness" allows certain actions to be taken in certain circumstances, whatever the subjective intent. But even if our concern had been only an evidentiary one, petitioners' proposal would by no means assuage it. Indeed, it seems to us somewhat easier to figure out the intent of an individual officer than to plumb the collective consciousness of law enforcement in order to determine whether a "reasonable officer" would have been moved to act upon the traffic violation. While police manuals and standard procedures may sometimes provide objective assistance, ordinarily one would be reduced to speculating about the hypothetical reaction of a hypothetical constable— an exercise that might be called virtual subjectivity.

Moreover, police enforcement practices, even if they could be practicably assessed by a judge, vary from place to place and from time to time. We cannot accept that the search and seizure protections of the Fourth Amendment are so variable, and can be made to turn upon such trivialities. The difficulty is illustrated by petitioners' arguments in this case. Their claim that a reasonable officer would not have made this stop is based largely on District of Columbia police regulations which permit plainclothes officers in unmarked vehicles to enforce traffic laws "only in the case of a violation that is so grave as to pose an immediate threat to the safety of others." This basis of invalidation would not apply in jurisdictions that had a different practice. And it would not have applied even in the District of Columbia, if Officer Soto had been wearing a uniform or patrolling in a marked police cruiser.

III

In what would appear to be an elaboration on the "reasonable officer" test, petitioners argue that the balancing inherent in any Fourth Amendment inquiry requires us to weigh the governmental and individual interests implicated in a traffic stop such as we have here.

It is of course true that in principle every Fourth Amendment case, since it turns upon a "reasonableness" determination, involves a balancing of all relevant factors. With rare exceptions not applicable here, however, the result of that balancing is not in doubt where the search or seizure is based upon probable cause.

Where probable cause has existed, the only cases in which we have found it necessary actually to perform the "balancing" analysis involved searches or seizures conducted in an extraordinary manner, unusually harmful to an individual's privacy or even physical interests — such as, for example, seizure by means of deadly force, unannounced entry into a home, entry into a home without a warrant, or physical penetration of the body. The making of a traffic stop out of uniform does not remotely qualify as such an extreme practice, and so is governed by the usual rule that probable cause to believe the law has been broken "outbalances" private interest in avoiding police contact.

For the run-of-the-mill case, which this surely is, we think there is no realistic alternative to the traditional common-law rule that probable cause justifies a search and seizure.

———————————

On many occasions since *Whren*, the Supreme Court has reaffirmed that the test for probable cause is objective and focuses on whether the reasonable officer could have found probable cause under the circumstances; the subjective intent of that officer does not matter. For example, in Devenpeck v. Alford, 543 U.S. 146 (2004), Jerome Alford was arrested for recording without permission a conversation with the police officer who stopped him for allegedly impersonating a police officer. The arresting officer believed, wrongly it turned out, that it violated the State of Washington's privacy law to record a conversation without permission of both parties.

Alford sued the officer, Devenpeck, for violating his Fourth Amendment rights. The Supreme Court ruled against Alford and made clear that the test for probable cause is objective, not subjective. Justice Scalia, writing for the Court, declared:

> Our cases make clear that an arresting officer's state of mind (except for the facts that he knows) is irrelevant to the existence of probable cause. That is to say, his subjective reason for making the arrest need not be the criminal offense as to which the known facts provide probable cause. As we have repeatedly explained, the fact that the officer does not have the state of mind which is hypothecated by

the reasons which provide the legal justification for the officer's action does not invalidate the action taken as long as the circumstances, viewed objectively, justify that action.

The Court held that the arrest did not violate the Fourth Amendment because there was probable cause that Alford violated other state laws (such as the prohibition of impersonating an officer), even though the grounds given for the arrest were wrong. The Court stated, "Subjective intent of the arresting officer, however it is determined (and of course subjective intent is always determined by objective means), is simply no basis for invalidating an arrest. Those are lawfully arrested whom the facts known to the arresting officers give probable cause to arrest."

3. What if the Police Make a Mistake as to the Law?

Is it different if officers make a mistake as to the law as opposed to the facts? In Heien v. North Carolina, the Court held that a stop that results from a police officer's mistake as to the law does not violate the Fourth Amendment.

HEIEN v. NORTH CAROLINA
135 S. Ct. 530 (2014)

Chief Justice ROBERTS delivered the opinion of the Court.

The Fourth Amendment prohibits "unreasonable searches and seizures." Under this standard, a search or seizure may be permissible even though the justification for the action includes a reasonable factual mistake. An officer might, for example, stop a motorist for traveling alone in a high-occupancy vehicle lane, only to discover upon approaching the car that two children are slumped over asleep in the back seat. The driver has not violated the law, but neither has the officer violated the Fourth Amendment.

But what if the police officer's reasonable mistake is not one of fact but of law? In this case, an officer stopped a vehicle because one of its two brake lights was out, but a court later determined that a single working brake light was all the law required. The question presented is whether such a mistake of law can nonetheless give rise to the reasonable suspicion necessary to uphold the seizure under the Fourth Amendment. We hold that it can. Because the officer's mistake about the brake-light law was reasonable, the stop in this case was lawful under the Fourth Amendment.

I

On the morning of April 29, 2009, Sergeant Matt Darisse of the Surry County Sheriff's Department sat in his patrol car near Dobson, North Carolina, observing northbound traffic on Interstate 77. Shortly before 8 A.M., a

Ford Escort passed by. Darisse thought the driver looked "very stiff and nervous," so he pulled onto the interstate and began following the Escort. A few miles down the road, the Escort braked as it approached a slower vehicle, but only the left brake light came on. Noting the faulty right brake light, Darisse activated his vehicle's lights and pulled the Escort over.

Two men were in the car: Maynor Javier Vasquez sat behind the wheel, and petitioner Nicholas Brady Heien lay across the rear seat. Sergeant Darisse explained to Vasquez that as long as his license and registration checked out, he would receive only a warning ticket for the broken brake light. A records check revealed no problems with the documents, and Darisse gave Vasquez the warning ticket. But Darisse had become suspicious during the course of the stop — Vasquez appeared nervous, Heien remained lying down the entire time, and the two gave inconsistent answers about their destination. Darisse asked Vasquez if he would be willing to answer some questions. Vasquez assented, and Darisse asked whether the men were transporting various types of contraband. Told no, Darisse asked whether he could search the Escort. Vasquez said he had no objection, but told Darisse he should ask Heien, because Heien owned the car. Heien gave his consent, and Darisse, aided by a fellow officer who had since arrived, began a thorough search of the vehicle. In the side compartment of a duffle bag, Darisse found a sandwich bag containing cocaine. The officers arrested both men.

The State charged Heien with attempted trafficking in cocaine. Heien moved to suppress the evidence seized from the car, contending that the stop and search had violated the Fourth Amendment of the United States Constitution. After a hearing at which both officers testified and the State played a video recording of the stop, the trial court denied the suppression motion, concluding that the faulty brake light had given Sergeant Darisse reasonable suspicion to initiate the stop, and that Heien's subsequent consent to the search was valid. Heien pleaded guilty but reserved his right to appeal the suppression decision.

The North Carolina Court of Appeals reversed. The initial stop was not valid, the court held, because driving with only one working brake light was not actually a violation of North Carolina law. The relevant provision of the vehicle code provides that a car must be "equipped with a stop lamp on the rear of the vehicle. The stop lamp shall display a red or amber light visible from a distance of not less than 100 feet to the rear in normal sunlight, and shall be actuated upon application of the service (foot) brake. The stop lamp may be incorporated into a unit with one or more other rear lamps."

The State appealed, and the North Carolina Supreme Court reversed.

II

A traffic stop for a suspected violation of law is a "seizure" of the occupants of the vehicle and therefore must be conducted in accordance with the Fourth Amendment. All parties agree that to justify this type of seizure, officers need only "reasonable suspicion" — that is, "a particularized and objective basis for suspecting the particular person stopped" of breaking the law. The question here is whether reasonable suspicion can rest on a mistaken understanding of the scope of a legal prohibition. We hold that it can.

As the text indicates and we have repeatedly affirmed, "the ultimate touchstone of the Fourth Amendment is 'reasonableness.'" To be reasonable is not to be perfect, and so the Fourth Amendment allows for some mistakes on the part of government officials, giving them "fair leeway for enforcing the law in the community's protection." We have recognized that searches and seizures based on mistakes of fact can be reasonable. The warrantless search of a home, for instance, is reasonable if undertaken with the consent of a resident, and remains lawful when officers obtain the consent of someone who reasonably appears to be but is not in fact a resident. By the same token, if officers with probable cause to arrest a suspect mistakenly arrest an individual matching the suspect's description, neither the seizure nor an accompanying search of the arrestee would be unlawful. The limit is that "the mistakes must be those of reasonable men."

But reasonable men make mistakes of law, too, and such mistakes are no less compatible with the concept of reasonable suspicion. Reasonable suspicion arises from the combination of an officer's understanding of the facts and his understanding of the relevant law. The officer may be reasonably mistaken on either ground. Whether the facts turn out to be not what was thought, or the law turns out to be not what was thought, the result is the same: the facts are outside the scope of the law. There is no reason, under the text of the Fourth Amendment or our precedents, why this same result should be acceptable when reached by way of a reasonable mistake of fact, but not when reached by way of a similarly reasonable mistake of law.

Contrary to the suggestion of Heien and *amici,* our decision does not discourage officers from learning the law. The Fourth Amendment tolerates only *reasonable* mistakes, and those mistakes — whether of fact or of law — must be *objectively* reasonable. We do not examine the subjective understanding of the particular officer involved. And the inquiry is not as forgiving as the one employed in the distinct context of deciding whether an officer is entitled to qualified immunity for a constitutional or statutory violation. Thus, an officer can gain no Fourth Amendment advantage through a sloppy study of the laws he is duty-bound to enforce.

Finally, Heien and *amici* point to the well-known maxim, "Ignorance of the law is no excuse," and contend that it is fundamentally unfair to let police officers get away with mistakes of law when the citizenry is accorded no such leeway. Though this argument has a certain rhetorical appeal, it misconceives the implication of the maxim. The true symmetry is this: Just as an individual generally cannot escape criminal liability based on a mistaken understanding of the law, so too the government cannot impose criminal liability based on a mistaken understanding of the law. If the law required two working brake lights, Heien could not escape a ticket by claiming he reasonably thought he needed only one; if the law required only one, Sergeant Darisse could not issue a valid ticket by claiming he reasonably thought drivers needed two. But just because mistakes of law cannot justify either the imposition or the avoidance of criminal liability, it does not follow that they cannot justify an investigatory stop. And Heien is not appealing a brake-light ticket; he is appealing a cocaine-trafficking conviction as to which there is no asserted mistake of fact or law.

III

Here we have little difficulty concluding that the officer's error of law was reasonable. Although the North Carolina statute at issue refers to "*a* stop lamp," suggesting the need for only a single working brake light, it also provides that "[t]he stop lamp may be incorporated into a unit with one or more *other* rear lamps." The use of "other" suggests to the everyday reader of English that a "stop lamp" is a type of "rear lamp." And another subsection of the same provision requires that vehicles "have all originally equipped rear lamps or the equivalent in good working order," arguably indicating that if a vehicle has multiple "stop lamp[s]," all must be functional.

This "stop lamp" provision, moreover, had never been previously construed by North Carolina's appellate courts. It was thus objectively reasonable for an officer in Sergeant Darisse's position to think that Heien's faulty right brake light was a violation of North Carolina law. And because the mistake of law was reasonable, there was reasonable suspicion justifying the stop.

Justice KAGAN, with whom Justice GINSBURG joins, concurring.

I concur in full in the Court's opinion, which explains why certain mistakes of law can support the reasonable suspicion needed to stop a vehicle under the Fourth Amendment. In doing so, the Court correctly emphasizes that the "Fourth Amendment tolerates only . . . *objectively* reasonable" mistakes of law. And the Court makes clear that the inquiry into whether an officer's mistake of law counts as objectively reasonable "is not as forgiving as the one employed in the distinct context of deciding whether an officer is entitled to qualified immunity." I write separately to elaborate briefly on those important limitations.

First, an officer's "subjective understanding" is irrelevant: As the Court notes, "[w]e do not examine" it at all. That means the government cannot defend an officer's mistaken legal interpretation on the ground that the officer was unaware of or untrained in the law. And it means that, contrary to the dissenting opinion in the court below, an officer's reliance on "an incorrect memo or training program from the police department" makes no difference to the analysis. Those considerations pertain to the officer's subjective understanding of the law and thus cannot help to justify a seizure.

Second, the inquiry the Court permits today is more demanding than the one courts undertake before awarding qualified immunity. Our modern qualified immunity doctrine protects "all but the plainly incompetent or those who knowingly violate the law."

A court tasked with deciding whether an officer's mistake of law can support a seizure thus faces a straightforward question of statutory construction. If the statute is genuinely ambiguous, such that overturning the officer's judgment requires hard interpretive work, then the officer has made a reasonable mistake. But if not, not. As the Solicitor General made the point at oral argument, the statute must pose a "really difficult" or "very hard question of statutory interpretation." And indeed, both North Carolina and the Solicitor General agreed that such cases will be "exceedingly rare."

Justice SOTOMAYOR, dissenting.

The Court is, of course, correct that "the ultimate touchstone of the Fourth Amendment is 'reasonableness.'" But this broad statement simply sets the standard a court is to apply when it conducts its inquiry into whether the Fourth Amendment has been violated. It does not define the categories of inputs that courts are to consider when assessing the reasonableness of a search or seizure, each of which must be independently justified. What this case requires us to decide is whether a police officer's understanding of the law is an input into the reasonableness inquiry, or whether this inquiry instead takes the law as a given and assesses an officer's understanding of the facts against a fixed legal yardstick.

I would hold that determining whether a search or seizure is reasonable requires evaluating an officer's understanding of the facts against the actual state of the law.

Both our enunciation of the reasonableness inquiry and our justification for it thus have always turned on an officer's factual conclusions and an officer's expertise with respect to those factual conclusions. Neither has hinted at taking into account an officer's understanding of the law, reasonable or otherwise.

Departing from this tradition means further eroding the Fourth Amendment's protection of civil liberties in a context where that protection has already been worn down. Traffic stops like those at issue here can be "annoying, frightening, and perhaps humiliating." We have nevertheless held that an officer's subjective motivations do not render a traffic stop unlawful. Whren v. United States (1996). But we assumed in *Whren* that when an officer acts on pretext, at least that pretext would be the violation of an actual law. Giving officers license to effect seizures so long as they can attach to their reasonable view of the facts some reasonable legal interpretation (or misinterpretation) that suggests a law has been violated significantly expands this authority. One wonders how a citizen seeking to be law-abiding and to structure his or her behavior to avoid these invasive, frightening, and humiliating encounters could do so.

In addition to these human consequences — including those for communities and for their relationships with the police — permitting mistakes of law to justify seizures has the perverse effect of preventing or delaying the clarification of the law. Under such an approach, courts need not interpret statutory language but can instead simply decide whether an officer's interpretation was reasonable.

Of course, if the law enforcement system could not function without permitting mistakes of law to justify seizures, one could at least argue that permitting as much is a necessary evil. But I have not seen any persuasive argument that law enforcement will be unduly hampered by a rule that precludes consideration of mistakes of law in the reasonableness inquiry. After all, there is no indication that excluding an officer's mistake of law from the reasonableness inquiry has created a problem for law enforcement in the overwhelming number of Circuits which have adopted that approach. If an officer makes a stop in good faith but it turns out that, as in this case, the officer was wrong about what the law proscribed or required, I know of no penalty that the officer would suffer.

In short, there is nothing in our case law requiring us to hold that a reasonable mistake of law can justify a seizure under the Fourth Amendment, and quite a bit suggesting just the opposite. I also see nothing to be gained from such a holding, and much to be lost.

While I appreciate that the Court has endeavored to set some bounds on the types of mistakes of law that it thinks will qualify as reasonable, and while I think that the set of reasonable mistakes of law ought to be narrowly circumscribed if they are to be countenanced at all, I am not at all convinced that the Court has done so in a clear way. It seems to me that the difference between qualified immunity's reasonableness standard — which the Court insists without elaboration does not apply here — and the Court's conception of reasonableness in this context — which remains undefined — will prove murky in application. I fear the Court's unwillingness to sketch a fuller view of what makes a mistake of law reasonable only presages the likely difficulty that courts will have applying the Court's decision in this case.

To my mind, the more administrable approach — and the one more consistent with our precedents and principles — would be to hold that an officer's mistake of law, no matter how reasonable, cannot support the individualized suspicion necessary to justify a seizure under the Fourth Amendment. I respectfully dissent.

D. THE WARRANT REQUIREMENT

The Fourth Amendment states that "no Warrants shall issue, but upon probable cause, supported by Oath or affirmation, and particularly describing the place to be searched, and the persons or things to be seized." There is no doubt that the warrant requirement is a crucial aspect of the Fourth Amendment. It functions as a check on the police; a search or arrest must be approved by a neutral judge. Also, the warrant limits the police conduct by restricting the scope of the search or the seizure; that which is to be searched or seized must be described with specificity in the warrant.

Yet there is even dispute among the justices, and some inconsistency in the Court's opinion, as to whether there actually is a warrant requirement or whether the Fourth Amendment requires only that searches and seizures be reasonable and a warrant is part of that analysis. Justice Thomas, in a recent dissenting opinion, summarized this when he stated:

> The precise relationship between the Amendment's Warrant Clause and Unreasonableness Clause is unclear. But neither Clause explicitly requires a warrant. While it is of course textually possible to consider [a warrant requirement] implicit within the requirement of reasonableness, the text of the Fourth Amendment certainly does not mandate this result. Nor does the Amendment's history, which is clear as to the Amendment's principal target (general warrants), but not as clear with respect to when warrants were required, if ever. Indeed, because of the very different nature and scope of federal authority and ability to conduct searches and arrests at the founding, it is possible that neither the history of the Fourth Amendment nor the common law provides much guidance.
>
>   As a result, the Court has vacillated between imposing a categorical warrant requirement and applying a general reasonableness standard. The Court has most frequently held that warrantless searches are presumptively unreasonable, but has also found a plethora of exceptions to presumptive unreasonableness. That is, our cases stand for the illuminating proposition that warrantless searches are per se unreasonable, except, of course, when they are not.

Groh v. Ramirez, 540 U.S. 551 (2004) (Thomas, J., dissenting). To say that the search is presumptively reasonable means that the defendant has the burden of challenging the legality of the search, whereas if conduct is presumptively unreasonable the burden is on the government to demonstrate its legality.

There are four important issues to be considered with regard to the warrant. First, what must be included in the application for a warrant? Second, what form must the warrant take in order to be valid? Third, what are the requirements police must follow in executing the warrant? These questions are discussed in subsections 1-3 below.

Fourth and finally, when is a warrant required? A warrant is often required, but not always. The Supreme Court has created many exceptions to the warrant requirement and, at times, has declared that a search or seizure is allowed as long as it is "reasonable." The exceptions to the warrant requirement, and thus the issue of when a warrant is needed, are discussed in section E below.

1. What Information Must Be Included in the Application for a Warrant?

Warrants are used both for searches and for arrests. For example, the Federal Rules of Criminal Procedure provide that a warrant may be sought for evidence of a crime; contraband, fruits of a crime, or other items illegally possessed; property designed for use, intended for use, or used in committing a crime; or a person to be arrested or a person who is unlawfully restrained. Federal Rule of Criminal Procedure 41.

The Fourth Amendment requires that the warrant be based on probable cause and "supported by oath or affirmation, and particularly describing the place to be searched, and the persons or things to be seized." The affidavit supporting the request for a warrant must include the information that provides a basis for concluding that there is probable cause. The affidavit may be based on hearsay. Federal Rule of Criminal Procedure 41. Often prosecutors and police present their request for warrants in person to the court, but the rules also allow for requesting a warrant by telephone. Federal Rule of Criminal Procedure 41.

The warrant will specify the time period for its execution. For instance, Rule 41 of the Federal Rules of Criminal Procedure provides that the warrant shall command the officer to "execute the warrant within a specified time not longer than 14 days." It also provides that a warrant for a "tracking device" must "specify a reasonable length of time that the device may be used. This time must not exceed 45 days from the date the warrant was issued."

The Supreme Court has held that the warrant must be issued by a "neutral and detached magistrate." Coolidge v. New Hampshire, 403 U.S. 443 (1971). In *Coolidge*, the Court ruled that allowing the state attorney general to issue warrants violated the Fourth Amendment. The key, the Court has said, is that the magistrate be "neutral and detached" and "capable of determining whether probable cause exists." Shadwick v. City of Tampa, 407 U.S. 345 (1972) (holding that a clerk of court could issue warrants consistent with the Fourth Amendment). For example, in Lo-Ji Sales, Inc. v. New York, 442 U.S. 319 (1979), the Court held that the requirement for a neutral and detached magistrate was violated when the judge who issued the warrant essentially became the "leader of the search party which was essentially a police operation."

2. What Form Must the Warrant Take?

The warrant must detail with specificity that which is to be searched or seized. Andresen v. Maryland addresses this requirement.

ANDRESEN v. MARYLAND
427 U.S. 463 (1976)

Justice BLACKMUN delivered the opinion of the Court.

We must determine whether the particular searches and seizures here were "unreasonable" and thus violated the prohibition of the Fourth Amendment.

I

In early 1972, a Bi-County Fraud Unit, acting under the joint auspices of the State's Attorneys' Offices of Montgomery and Prince George's Counties,

Md., began an investigation of real estate settlement activities in the Washington, D.C., area. At the time, petitioner Andresen was an attorney who, as a sole practitioner, specialized in real estate settlements in Montgomery County. During the Fraud Unit's investigation, his activities came under scrutiny, particularly in connection with a transaction involving Lot 13T in the Potomac Woods subdivision of Montgomery County. The investigation, which included interviews with the purchaser, the mortgage holder, and other lienholders of Lot 13T, as well as an examination of county land records, disclosed that petitioner, acting as settlement attorney, had defrauded Standard-Young Associates, the purchaser of Lot 13T. Petitioner had represented that the property was free of liens and that, accordingly, no title insurance was necessary, when in fact, he knew that there were two outstanding liens on the property. In addition, investigators learned that the lienholders, by threatening to foreclose their liens, had forced a halt to the purchaser's construction on the property. When Standard-Young had confronted petitioner with this information, he responded by issuing, as an agent of a title insurance company, a title policy guaranteeing clear title to the property. By this action, petitioner also defrauded that insurance company by requiring it to pay the outstanding liens.

The investigators, concluding that there was probable cause to believe that petitioner had committed the state crime of false pretenses against Standard-Young, applied for warrants to search petitioner's law office and the separate office of Mount Vernon Development Corporation, of which petitioner was incorporator, sole shareholder, resident agent, and director. The application sought permission to search for specified documents pertaining to the sale and conveyance of Lot 13T. A judge of the Sixth Judicial Circuit of Montgomery County concluded that there was probable cause and issued the warrants.

The searches of the two offices were conducted simultaneously during daylight hours on October 31, 1972. Petitioner was present during the search of his law office and was free to move about. Counsel for him was present during the latter half of the search. Between 2% and 3% of the files in the office were seized. A single investigator, in the presence of a police officer, conducted the search of Mount Vernon Development Corporation. This search, taking about four hours, resulted in the seizure of less than 5% of the corporation's files.

Petitioner eventually was charged with the crime of false pretenses, based on his misrepresentation to Standard-Young concerning Lot 13T, and with fraudulent misappropriation by a fiduciary, based on similar false claims made to three home purchasers. Before trial began, petitioner moved to suppress the seized documents.

At trial, the State proved its case primarily by public land records and by records provided by the complaining purchasers, lienholders, and the title insurance company. It did introduce into evidence, however, a number of the seized items. Three documents from the "Potomac Woods General" file, seized during the search of petitioner's corporation, were admitted. These were notes in the handwriting of an employee who used them to prepare abstracts in the course of his duties as a title searcher and law clerk. The notes concerned deeds of trust affecting the Potomac Woods subdivision and related to the transaction involving Lot 13T. Five items seized from petitioner's law office were also admitted. One contained information relating to the transactions with one of the defrauded home buyers. The second was a file partially devoted to the Lot 13T transaction; among the documents were settlement statements, the deed conveying the property to Standard-Young Associates, and the original and a copy of a notice to the buyer about releases of liens. The third item was a file devoted exclusively to Lot 13T. The fourth item consisted of a copy of a deed of trust, dated March 27, 1972, from the seller of certain lots in the Potomac Woods subdivision to a lienholder. The fifth item contained drafts of documents and memoranda written in petitioner's handwriting.

After a trial by jury, petitioner was found guilty upon five counts of false pretenses and three counts of fraudulent misappropriation by a fiduciary. He was sentenced to eight concurrent two-year prison terms.

We turn to petitioner's contention that rights guaranteed him by the Fourth Amendment were violated because the descriptive terms of the search warrants were so broad as to make them impermissible "general" warrants.

The specificity of the search warrants. Although petitioner concedes that the warrants for the most part were models of particularity, he contends that they were rendered fatally "general" by the addition, in each warrant, to the exhaustive list of particularly described documents, of the phrase "together with other fruits, instrumentalities and evidence of crime at this (time) unknown." The quoted language, it is argued, must be read in isolation and without reference to the rest of the long sentence at the end of which it appears. When read "properly," petitioner contends, it permits the search for and seizure of any evidence of any crime.

General warrants of course, are prohibited by the Fourth Amendment. "[T]he problem (posed by the general warrant) is not that of intrusion Per se, but of a general, exploratory rummaging in a person's belongings. . . . [The Fourth Amendment addresses the problem] by requiring a 'particular description' of the things to be seized." This requirement "makes general searches . . . impossible and prevents the seizure of one thing under a warrant describing another. As to what is to be taken, nothing is left to the discretion of the officer executing the warrant."

In this case we agree with the determination of the Court of Special Appeals of Maryland that the challenged phrase must be read as authorizing only the search for and seizure of evidence relating to "the crime of false pretenses with respect to Lot 13T." The challenged phrase is not a separate sentence. Instead, it appears in each warrant at the end of a sentence containing a lengthy list of specified and particular items to be seized, all pertaining to Lot 13T. We think it clear from the context that the term "crime" in the warrants refers only to the crime of false pretenses with respect to the sale of Lot 13T. The "other fruits" clause is one of a series that follows the colon after the word "Maryland." All clauses in the series are limited by what precedes that colon, namely, "items pertaining to . . . lot 13, block T." The warrants, accordingly, did not authorize the executing officers to conduct a search for evidence of other crimes but only to search for and seize evidence relevant to the crime of false pretenses and Lot 13T.

Petitioner also suggests that the specific list of the documents to be seized constitutes a "general" warrant. We disagree. Under investigation was a complex real estate scheme whose existence could be proved only by piecing together many bits of evidence. Like a jigsaw puzzle, the whole "picture" of petitioner's false-pretense scheme with respect to Lot 13T could be shown only by placing in the proper place the many pieces of evidence that, taken singly, would show comparatively little. The complexity of an illegal scheme may not be used as a shield to avoid detection when the State has demonstrated probable cause to believe that a crime has been committed and probable cause to believe that evidence of this crime is in the suspect's possession.

We recognize that there are grave dangers inherent in executing a warrant authorizing a search and seizure of a person's papers that are not necessarily present in executing a warrant to search for physical objects whose relevance is more easily ascertainable. In searches for papers, it is certain that some innocuous documents will be examined, at least cursorily, in order to determine whether they are, in fact, among those papers authorized to be seized. Similar dangers, of course, are present in executing a warrant for the "seizure" of telephone conversations. In both kinds of searches, responsible officials, including judicial officials, must take care to assure that they are conducted in a manner that minimizes unwarranted intrusions upon privacy.

Justice BRENNAN, dissenting.

I believe that the warrants under which petitioner's papers were seized were impermissibly general. I therefore dissent.

General warrants are specially prohibited by the Fourth Amendment. The problem to be avoided is "not that of intrusion Per se, but of a general, exploratory rummaging in a person's belongings." Thus the requirement plainly appearing on the face of the Fourth Amendment that a warrant specify with particularity the place to be searched and the things to be seized is imposed to the end that "unauthorized invasions of 'the sanctity of a man's home and the privacies of life'" be prevented. "As to what is to be taken, nothing is left to the discretion of the officer executing the warrant."

The Court recites these requirements, but their application in this case renders their limitation on unlawful governmental conduct an empty promise. After a lengthy and admittedly detailed listing of items to be seized, the warrants in this case further authorized the seizure of "other fruits, instrumentalities and evidence of crime at this (time) unknown." The Court construes this sweeping authorization to be limited to evidence pertaining to the crime of false pretenses with respect to the sale of Lot 13T. However, neither this Court's construction of the warrants nor the similar construction by the Court of Special Appeals of Maryland was available to the investigators at the time they executed the warrants. The question is not how those warrants are to be viewed in hindsight, but how they were in fact viewed by those executing them. The overwhelming quantity of seized material that was either suppressed or returned to petitioner is irrefutable testimony to the unlawful generality of the warrants. The Court's attempt to cure this defect by Post hoc judicial construction evades principles settled in this Court's Fourth Amendment decisions. "The scheme of the Fourth Amendment becomes meaningful only when it is assured that at some point the conduct of those charged with enforcing the laws can be subjected to the more detached, neutral scrutiny of a judge. . . ." Terry v. Ohio (1968). It is not the function of a detached and neutral review to give effect to warrants whose terms unassailably authorize the far-reaching search and seizure of a person's papers especially where that has in fact been the result of executing those warrants.

The Supreme Court subsequently considered the requirement for particularity in the warrant in the context of a situation where the affidavit in support of the warrant contained the necessary particularity, but the warrant itself did not list specifically what was to be searched for or seized. The Court found that this warrant violated the Fourth Amendment. In reading the case, it is important to note the different ways that the majority and the dissent interpret the Fourth Amendment's warrant clause. Justice Stevens's majority opinion sees it as an independent requirement and the failure to comply makes the search illegal. By contrast, Justice Thomas's dissent argues that even if the warrant is defective, there is no Fourth Amendment violation as long as the search is reasonable.

GROH v. RAMIREZ

540 U.S. 551 (2004)

Justice STEVENS delivered the opinion of the Court.

Petitioner conducted a search of respondents' home pursuant to a warrant that failed to describe the "persons or things to be seized." The question presented [is] whether the search violated the Fourth Amendment.[5]

---

5. There also was an issue of whether the officers could be held civilly liable for relying on such a warrant. The specific question was whether they violated clearly established law that the reasonable officer should know. This issue is omitted from the opinion. [Footnote by casebook authors.]

I

Respondents, Joseph Ramirez and members of his family, live on a large ranch in Butte-Silver Bow County, Montana. Petitioner, Jeff Groh, has been a Special Agent for the Bureau of Alcohol, Tobacco and Firearms (ATF) since 1989. In February 1997, a concerned citizen informed petitioner that on a number of visits to respondents' ranch the visitor had seen a large stock of weaponry, including an automatic rifle, grenades, a grenade launcher, and a rocket launcher. Based on that information, petitioner prepared and signed an application for a warrant to search the ranch. The application stated that the search was for "any automatic firearms or parts to automatic weapons, destructive devices to include but not limited to grenades, grenade launchers, rocket launchers, and any and all receipts pertaining to the purchase or manufacture of automatic weapons or explosive devices or launchers." Petitioner supported the application with a detailed affidavit, which he also prepared and executed, that set forth the basis for his belief that the listed items were concealed on the ranch. Petitioner then presented these documents to a Magistrate, along with a warrant form that petitioner also had completed. The Magistrate signed the warrant form.

Although the application particularly described the place to be searched and the contraband petitioner expected to find, the warrant itself was less specific; it failed to identify any of the items that petitioner intended to seize. In the portion of the form that called for a description of the "person or property" to be seized, petitioner typed a description of respondents' two-story blue house rather than the alleged stockpile of firearms. The warrant did not incorporate by reference the itemized list contained in the application. It did, however, recite that the Magistrate was satisfied the affidavit established probable cause to believe that contraband was concealed on the premises, and that sufficient grounds existed for the warrant's issuance.

Respondents sued petitioner and the other officers. The District Court entered summary judgment for all defendants. The court found no Fourth Amendment violation.

II

The warrant was plainly invalid. The Fourth Amendment states unambiguously that "no Warrants shall issue, but upon probable cause, supported by Oath or affirmation, and particularly describing the place to be searched, and the persons or things to be seized." The warrant in this case complied with the first three of these requirements: It was based on probable cause and supported by a sworn affidavit, and it described particularly the place of the search. On the fourth requirement, however, the warrant failed altogether. Indeed, petitioner concedes that "the warrant . . . was deficient in particularity because it provided no description of the type of evidence sought."

The fact that the application adequately described the "things to be seized" does not save the warrant from its facial invalidity. The Fourth Amendment by its terms requires particularity in the warrant, not in the supporting documents. And for good reason: "The presence of a search warrant serves a high function," and that high function is not necessarily vindicated when some other document, somewhere, says something about the objects of the search, but the contents of that document are neither known to the person whose home is being searched nor available for her inspection. We do not say that the Fourth Amendment prohibits a warrant from cross-referencing other documents. Indeed, most Courts of Appeals have held that a court may construe a warrant with reference to a supporting application or affidavit if the warrant uses appropriate words of incorporation, and if the supporting document accompanies the warrant. But in this case the warrant did not incorporate other documents by reference, nor did either the affidavit or the application (which had been placed under seal) accompany the warrant. Hence, we need not further explore the matter of incorporation.

Petitioner argues that even though the warrant was invalid, the search nevertheless was "reasonable" within the meaning of the Fourth Amendment. He notes that a Magistrate authorized the search on the basis of adequate evidence of probable cause, that petitioner orally described to respondents the items to be seized, and that the search did not exceed the limits intended by the Magistrate and described by petitioner. Thus, petitioner maintains, his search of respondents' ranch was functionally equivalent to a search authorized by a valid warrant.

We disagree. This warrant did not simply omit a few items from a list of many to be seized, or misdescribe a few of several items. Nor did it make what fairly could be characterized as a mere technical mistake or typographical error. Rather, in the space set aside for a description of the items to be seized, the warrant stated that the items consisted of a "single dwelling residence . . . blue in color." In other words, the warrant did not describe the items to be seized at all. In this respect the warrant was so obviously deficient that we must regard the search as "warrantless" within the meaning of our case law. "We are not dealing with formalities." Because "'the right of a man to retreat into his own home and there be free from unreasonable governmental intrusion'" stands "'[a]t the very core' of the Fourth Amendment," our cases have firmly established the "'basic principle of Fourth Amendment law' that searches and seizures inside a home without a warrant are presumptively unreasonable."

We have clearly stated that the presumptive rule against warrantless searches applies with equal force to searches whose only defect is a lack of particularity in the warrant. Petitioner asks us to hold that a search conducted pursuant to a warrant lacking particularity should be exempt from the presumption of unreasonableness if the goals served by the particularity requirement are otherwise satisfied. He maintains that the search in this case satisfied those goals—which he says are "to prevent general searches, to prevent the seizure of one thing under a warrant describing another, and to prevent warrants from being issued on vague or dubious information," — because the scope of the search did not exceed the limits set forth in the application. But unless the particular items described in the affidavit are also set forth in the warrant itself (or at least incorporated by reference, and the affidavit present at the search), there can be no written assurance that the Magistrate actually found probable cause to search for, and to seize, every item mentioned in the affidavit. In this case, for example, it is at least theoretically possible that the Magistrate was satisfied that the search for weapons and explosives was justified by the showing in the affidavit, but not convinced that any evidentiary basis existed for rummaging through respondents' files and papers for receipts pertaining to the purchase or manufacture of such items. Or, conceivably, the Magistrate might have believed that some of the weapons mentioned in the affidavit could have been lawfully possessed and therefore should not be seized. The mere fact that the Magistrate issued a warrant does not necessarily establish that he agreed that the scope of the search should be as broad as the affiant's request. Even though petitioner acted with restraint in conducting the search, "the inescapable fact is that this restraint was imposed by the agents themselves, not by a judicial officer."

We have long held, moreover, that the purpose of the particularity requirement is not limited to the prevention of general searches. A particular warrant also "assures the individual whose property is searched or seized of the lawful authority of the executing officer, his need to search, and the limits of his power to search."

It is incumbent on the officer executing a search warrant to ensure the search is lawfully authorized and lawfully conducted. Because petitioner did not have in his possession a warrant particularly describing the things he intended to seize, proceeding with the search was clearly "unreasonable" under the Fourth Amendment. The Court of Appeals correctly held that the search was unconstitutional.

Justice THOMAS, with whom Justice SCALIA joins, dissenting.

Today the Court holds that the warrant in this case was "so obviously deficient" that the ensuing search must be regarded as a warrantless search and thus presumptively unreasonable. However, the text of the Fourth Amendment, its history, and the sheer number of exceptions to the Court's categorical warrant requirement seriously undermine the bases upon which the Court today rests its holding. Instead of adding to this confusing jurisprudence, as the Court has done, I would turn to first principles in order to determine the relationship between the Warrant Clause and the Unreasonableness Clause. But even within the Court's current framework, a search conducted pursuant to a defective warrant is constitutionally different from a "warrantless search." Consequently, despite the defective warrant, I would still ask whether this search was unreasonable and would conclude that it was not. For these reasons, I respectfully dissent.

"[A]ny Fourth Amendment case may present two separate questions: whether the search was conducted pursuant to a warrant issued in accordance with the second Clause, and, if not, whether it was nevertheless 'reasonable' within the meaning of the first." By categorizing the search here to be a "warrantless" one, the Court declines to perform a reasonableness inquiry and ignores the fact that this search is quite different from searches that the Court has considered to be "warrantless" in the past. Our cases involving "warrantless" searches do not generally involve situations in which an officer has obtained a warrant that is later determined to be facially defective, but rather involve situations in which the officers neither sought nor obtained a warrant. By simply treating this case as if no warrant had even been sought or issued, the Court glosses over what should be the key inquiry: whether it is always appropriate to treat a search made pursuant to a warrant that fails to describe particularly the things to be seized as presumptively unreasonable.

The Court also rejects the argument that the details of the warrant application and affidavit save the warrant, because "[t]he presence of a search warrant serves a high function." But it is not only the physical existence of the warrant and its typewritten contents that serve this high function. The Warrant Clause's principal protection lies in the fact that the "'Fourth Amendment has interposed a magistrate between the citizen and the police . . . so that an objective mind might weigh the need to invade [the searchee's] privacy in order to enforce the law.'"

But the actual contents of the warrant are simply manifestations of this protection. Hence, in contrast to the case of a truly warrantless search, where a warrant (due to a mistake) does not specify on its face the particular items to be seized but the warrant application passed on by the magistrate judge contains such details, a searchee still has the benefit of a determination by a neutral magistrate that there is probable cause to search a particular place and to seize particular items. In such a circumstance, the principal justification for applying a rule of presumptive unreasonableness falls away.

In the instant case, the items to be seized were clearly specified in the warrant application and set forth in the affidavit, both of which were given to the Judge (Magistrate). The Magistrate reviewed all of the documents and signed the warrant application and made no adjustment or correction to this application. It is clear that respondents here received the protection of the Warrant Clause. I would not hold that any ensuing search constitutes a presumptively unreasonable warrantless search. Instead, I would determine whether, despite the invalid warrant, the resulting search was reasonable and hence constitutional.

Because the search was not unreasonable, I would conclude that it was constitutional. Prior to execution of the warrant, petitioner briefed the search team and provided a copy of the search warrant application, the supporting affidavit, and the warrant for the officers to review. Petitioner orally reviewed the terms of the warrant with the officers, including the specific items for which the officers were authorized to search. Petitioner and his search team then conducted the search entirely within the scope of the warrant application and warrant; that is, within the scope of what the Magistrate had authorized. Finding no illegal weapons or explosives, the search team seized nothing. When petitioner left, he gave respondents a copy of the search warrant. Upon request the next day, petitioner faxed respondents a copy of the more detailed warrant application. Indeed, putting aside the technical defect in the warrant, it is hard to imagine how the actual search could have been carried out any more reasonably.

An interesting issue that subsequently arose concerning the content of warrants is whether anticipatory warrants are allowed. An anticipatory warrant is based on an affidavit for a search warrant that states that the search will occur only if certain events take place. In United States v. Grubbs, 547 U.S. 90 (2006), "[f]ederal law enforcement officers obtained a search warrant for respondent's house on the basis of an affidavit explaining that the warrant would be executed only after a controlled delivery of contraband to that location."

The Court held that anticipatory warrants are permissible. Justice Scalia, writing for the Court, explained:

> Anticipatory warrants are, therefore, no different in principle from ordinary warrants. They require the magistrate to determine (1) that it is now probable that (2) contraband, evidence of a crime, or a fugitive will be on the described premises (3) when the warrant is executed. It should be noted, however, that where the anticipatory warrant places a condition (other than the mere passage of time) upon its execution, the first of these determinations goes not merely to what will probably be found if the condition is met. (If that were the extent of the probability determination, an anticipatory warrant could be issued for every house in the country, authorizing search and seizure if contraband should be delivered—though for any single location there is no likelihood that contraband will be delivered.) Rather, the probability determination for a conditioned anticipatory warrant looks also to the likelihood that the condition will occur, and thus that a proper object of seizure will be on the described premises. In other words, for a conditioned anticipatory warrant to comply with the Fourth Amendment's requirement of probable cause, two prerequisites of probability must be satisfied. It must be true not only that if the triggering condition occurs "there is a fair probability that contraband or evidence of a crime will be found in a particular place," but also that there is probable cause to believe the triggering condition will occur. The supporting affidavit must provide the magistrate with sufficient information to evaluate both aspects of the probable-cause determination.

3. What Are the Requirements in Executing Warrants?

Rule 41 of the Federal Rules of Criminal Procedure provides that the warrant must command the officer to "execute the warrant during the daytime, unless the judge for good cause expressly authorizes execution at another time." The Rule defines daytime to be the hours from 6:00 A.M. to 10:00 P.M. (Rule 41(a)(2)(B).) However, there is a federal statute that provides that there does not have to be a special showing of need for searches of narcotics. (21 U.S.C. §879.)

There also is a federal statute limiting searches of newsrooms. In Zurcher v. Stanford Daily, 436 U.S. 547 (1978), the Supreme Court rejected any special protections for newsrooms. The police had obtained a warrant to search the newsroom of a college newspaper, the Stanford Daily, for negatives of photographs that had been taken of demonstrators attacking police officers. The Court upheld the search and said, "Under existing law, valid warrants may be issued to search *any* property, whether or not occupied by a third party, at which there is probable cause to believe that fruits, instrumentalities, or evidence of a crime will be found." The Court expressly rejected any special First Amendment protection for newsrooms.

However, Congress reacted by adopting the Privacy Protection Act of 1990, 42 U.S.C. §2000a, to protect the press from searches of newsrooms. The law prohibits law enforcement from searches of those reasonably believed to be engaged in disseminating information to the public unless there is probable cause to believe that the person committed a crime or that giving notice by subpoena likely would result in the loss of evidence.

Several issues have arisen concerning the requirements when executing a warrant. First, how may police treat those who are present when the warrant is being executed; may they be searched or detained? Second, do the police have to knock and announce their presence before executing a warrant to search a dwelling? Third, what happens if there are unforeseen circumstances or if mistakes are made in executing a warrant?

a.   How May Police Treat Those Who Are Present When a Warrant Is Being Executed?

The Supreme Court has held that a person who happens to be present in premises that are subject to a search cannot be searched just by virtue of being there. Ybarra v. Illinois, 444 U.S. 85 (1979). The Court explained that a search "must be supported by probable cause particularized with respect to that person."

However, in Michigan v. Summers, 452 U.S. 692 (1981), the Supreme Court has held that when there is a search of a residence, those present at the time of the search may be detained. The Court explained that allowing such detentions serves many purposes: preventing flight by the individual in case incriminating evidence is found, minimizing the risk of harm to the police, and helping the police complete the search in the event that questions arise. The Court applied this in the recent case of Muehler v. Mena.

MUEHLER v. MENA
544 U.S. 93 (2005)

Chief Justice REHNQUIST delivered the opinion of the Court.

Respondent Iris Mena was detained in handcuffs during a search of the premises that she and several others occupied. Petitioners were lead members of a police detachment executing a search warrant of these premises. She sued the officers under 42 U.S.C. §1983, and the District Court found in her favor. The Court of Appeals affirmed the judgment, holding that the use of handcuffs to detain Mena during the search violated the Fourth Amendment and that the officers' questioning of Mena about her immigration status during the detention constituted an independent Fourth Amendment violation. We hold that Mena's detention in handcuffs for the length of the search was consistent with our opinion in Michigan v. Summers (1981), and that the officers' questioning during that detention did not violate her Fourth Amendment rights.

Based on information gleaned from the investigation of a gang-related, driveby shooting, petitioners Muehler and Brill had reason to believe at least one member of a gang—the West Side Locos—lived at 1363 Patricia Avenue. They also suspected that the individual was armed and dangerous, since he had recently been involved in the driveby shooting. As a result, Muehler obtained a search warrant for 1363 Patricia Avenue that authorized a broad search of the house and premises for, among other things, deadly weapons and evidence of gang membership. In light of the high degree of risk involved in searching a house suspected of housing at least one, and perhaps multiple, armed gang members, a Special Weapons and Tactics (SWAT) team was used to secure the residence and grounds before the search.

At 7 A.M. on February 3, 1998, petitioners, along with the SWAT team and other officers, executed the warrant. Mena was asleep in her bed when the SWAT team, clad in helmets and black vests adorned with badges and the word "POLICE," entered her bedroom and placed her in handcuffs at gunpoint. The SWAT team also handcuffed three other individuals found on the property. The SWAT team then took those individuals and Mena into a converted garage, which contained several beds and some other bedroom furniture. While the search proceeded, one or two officers guarded the four detainees, who were allowed to move around the garage but remained in handcuffs.

Aware that the West Side Locos gang was composed primarily of illegal immigrants, the officers had notified the Immigration and Naturalization Service (INS) that they would be conducting the search, and an INS officer accompanied the officers executing the warrant. During their detention in the garage, an officer asked for each detainee's name, date of birth, place of birth, and immigration status. The INS officer later asked the detainees for their immigration documentation. Mena's status as a permanent resident was confirmed by her papers.

The search of the premises yielded a .22 caliber handgun with .22 caliber ammunition, a box of .25 caliber ammunition, several baseball bats with gang writing, various additional gang paraphernalia, and a bag of marijuana. Before the officers left the area, Mena was released.

In her §1983 suit against the officers she alleged that she was detained "for an unreasonable time and in an unreasonable manner" in violation of the Fourth Amendment. In addition, she claimed that the warrant and its execution were overbroad, that the officers failed to comply with the "knock and announce" rule, and that the officers had needlessly destroyed property during the search. After a trial, a jury, pursuant to a special verdict form, found that Officers Muehler and Brill violated Mena's Fourth Amendment right to be free from unreasonable seizures by detaining her both with force greater than that which was reasonable and for a longer period than that which was reasonable. The jury awarded Mena $10,000 in actual damages and $20,000 in punitive damages against each petitioner for a total of $60,000.

The Court of Appeals affirmed the judgment on two grounds. [I]t first held that the officers' detention of Mena violated the Fourth Amendment because it was objectively unreasonable to confine her in the converted garage and keep her in handcuffs during the search. In the Court of Appeals' view, the officers should have released Mena as soon as it became clear that she posed no immediate threat. The court additionally held that the questioning of Mena about her immigration status constituted an independent Fourth Amendment violation. *Id.*, at 1264-1266.

In Michigan v. Summers (1981), we held that officers executing a search warrant for contraband have the authority "to detain the occupants of the premises while a proper search is conducted." Such detentions are appropriate, we explained, because the character of the additional intrusion caused by detention is slight and because the justifications for detention are substantial. We made clear that the detention of an occupant is "surely less intrusive than the search itself," and the presence of a warrant assures that a neutral magistrate has determined that probable cause exists to search the home. Against this incremental intrusion, we posited three legitimate law enforcement interests that provide substantial justification for detaining an occupant: "preventing flight in the event that incriminating evidence is found"; "minimizing the risk of harm to the officers"; and facilitating "the orderly completion of the search," as detainees' "self-interest may induce them to open locked doors or locked containers to avoid the use of force."

Mena's detention was, under *Summers*, plainly permissible. An officer's authority to detain incident to a search is categorical; it does not depend on the "quantum of proof justifying detention or the extent of the intrusion to be imposed by the seizure." Thus, Mena's detention for the duration of the search was reasonable under *Summers* because a warrant existed to search

1363 Patricia Avenue and she was an occupant of that address at the time of the search.

Inherent in *Summers*' authorization to detain an occupant of the place to be searched is the authority to use reasonable force to effectuate the detention. Indeed, *Summers* itself stressed that the risk of harm to officers and occupants is minimized "if the officers routinely exercise unquestioned command of the situation."

The officers' use of force in the form of handcuffs to effectuate Mena's detention in the garage, as well as the detention of the three other occupants, was reasonable because the governmental interests outweigh the marginal intrusion. The imposition of correctly applied handcuffs on Mena, who was already being lawfully detained during a search of the house, was undoubtedly a separate intrusion in addition to detention in the converted garage. The detention was thus more intrusive than that which we upheld in *Summers*.

But this was no ordinary search. The governmental interests in not only detaining, but using handcuffs, are at their maximum when, as here, a warrant authorizes a search for weapons and a wanted gang member resides on the premises. In such inherently dangerous situations, the use of handcuffs minimizes the risk of harm to both officers and occupants. Though this safety risk inherent in executing a search warrant for weapons was sufficient to justify the use of handcuffs, the need to detain multiple occupants made the use of handcuffs all the more reasonable.

Mena argues that, even if the use of handcuffs to detain her in the garage was reasonable as an initial matter, the duration of the use of handcuffs made the detention unreasonable. The duration of a detention can, of course, affect the balance of interests. However, the 2- to 3-hour detention in handcuffs in this case does not outweigh the government's continuing safety interests. As we have noted, this case involved the detention of four detainees by two officers during a search of a gang house for dangerous weapons. We conclude that the detention of Mena in handcuffs during the search was reasonable.

The Court of Appeals also determined that the officers violated Mena's Fourth Amendment rights by questioning her about her immigration status during the detention. This holding, it appears, was premised on the assumption that the officers were required to have independent reasonable suspicion in order to question Mena concerning her immigration status because the questioning constituted a discrete Fourth Amendment event. But the premise is faulty. We have "held repeatedly that mere police questioning does not constitute a seizure." "[E]ven when officers have no basis for suspecting a particular individual, they may generally ask questions of that individual; ask to examine the individual's identification; and request consent to search his or her luggage." As the Court of Appeals did not hold that the detention was prolonged by the questioning, there was no additional seizure within the meaning of the Fourth Amendment. Hence, the officers did not need reasonable suspicion to ask Mena for her name, date and place of birth, or immigration status.

In summary, the officers' detention of Mena in handcuffs during the execution of the search warrant was reasonable and did not violate the Fourth Amendment. Additionally, the officers' questioning of Mena did not constitute an independent Fourth Amendment violation. Mena has advanced in this Court, as she did before the Court of Appeals, an alternative argument for affirming the judgment below. She asserts that her detention extended beyond the time the police completed the tasks incident to the search. Because the Court of Appeals did not address this contention, we too decline to address it.

In Michigan v. Summers and Muehler v. Mena, the Supreme Court held that the police may detain an individual while a search is being conducted of the person's home. What, though, if the person is arrested a short distance from the home while the search is being conducted? That was the issue in United States v. Bailey, 133 S. Ct. 1031 (2013). The Court said: "The issue to be resolved is whether the seizure of the person was reasonable when he was stopped and detained at some distance away from the premises to be searched when the only justification for the detention was to ensure the safety and efficacy of the search."

The Court distinguished *Summers* and explained:

> In sum, of the three law enforcement interests identified to justify the detention in *Summers*, none applies with the same or similar force to the detention of recent occupants beyond the immediate vicinity of the premises to be searched. Any of the individual interests is also insufficient, on its own, to justify an expansion of the rule in *Summers* to permit the detention of a former occupant, wherever he may be found away from the scene of the search. This would give officers too much discretion. The categorical authority to detain incident to the execution of a search warrant must be limited to the immediate vicinity of the premises to be searched.

The Court concluded:

> A spatial constraint defined by the immediate vicinity of the premises to be searched is therefore required for detentions incident to the execution of a search warrant. The police action permitted here — the search of a residence — has a spatial dimension, and so a spatial or geographical boundary can be used to determine the area within which both the search and detention incident to that search may occur. Limiting the rule in *Summers* to the area in which an occupant poses a real threat to the safe and efficient execution of a search warrant ensures that the scope of the detention incident to a search is confined to its underlying justification. Once an occupant is beyond the immediate vicinity of the premises to be searched, the search-related law enforcement interests are diminished and the intrusiveness of the detention is more severe. . . . Confining an officer's authority to detain under *Summers* to the immediate vicinity of a premises to be searched is a proper limit because it accords with the rationale of the rule.

Detentions incident to the execution of a search warrant are reasonable under the Fourth Amendment because the limited intrusion on personal liberty is outweighed by the special law enforcement interests at stake. Once an individual has left the immediate vicinity of a premises to be searched, however, detentions must be justified by some other rationale. In this respect it must be noted that the District Court, as an alternative ruling, held that stopping petitioner was lawful under *Terry*. This opinion expresses no view on that issue. It will be open, on remand, for the Court of Appeals to address the matter and to determine whether, assuming the *Terry* stop was valid, it yielded information that justified the detention the officers then imposed.

b.   Do Police Have to Knock and Announce Before Searching a Dwelling?

The Supreme Court has held that absent exigent circumstances, the police must knock and announce their presence before entering a residence to execute a search warrant. This was initially articulated as a requirement in Wilson v. Arkansas.

WILSON v. ARKANSAS

514 U.S. 927 (1995)

Justice THOMAS delivered the opinion of the Court.

At the time of the framing, the common law of search and seizure recognized a law enforcement officer's authority to break open the doors of a dwelling, but generally indicated that he first ought to announce his presence and authority. In this case, we hold that this common-law "knock and announce" principle forms a part of the reasonableness inquiry under the Fourth Amendment.

I

During November and December 1992, petitioner Sharlene Wilson made a series of narcotics sales to an informant acting at the direction of the Arkansas State Police. In late November, the informant purchased marijuana and methamphetamine at the home that petitioner shared with Bryson Jacobs. On December 30, the informant telephoned petitioner at her home and arranged to meet her at a local store to buy some marijuana. According to testimony presented below, petitioner produced a semiautomatic pistol at this meeting and waved it in the informant's face, threatening to kill her if she turned out to be working for the police. Petitioner then sold the informant a bag of marijuana.

The next day, police officers applied for and obtained warrants to search petitioner's home and to arrest both petitioner and Jacobs. Affidavits filed in support of the warrants set forth the details of the narcotics transactions and stated that Jacobs had previously been convicted of arson and firebombing. The search was conducted later that afternoon. Police officers found the main door to petitioner's home open. While opening an unlocked screen door and entering the residence, they identified themselves as police officers and stated that they had a warrant. Once inside the home, the officers seized marijuana, methamphetamine, valium, narcotics paraphernalia, a gun, and ammunition. They also found petitioner in the bathroom, flushing marijuana down the toilet. Petitioner and Jacobs were arrested and charged with delivery of marijuana, delivery of methamphetamine, possession of drug paraphernalia, and possession of marijuana.

Before trial, petitioner filed a motion to suppress the evidence seized during the search. Petitioner asserted that the search was invalid on various grounds, including that the officers had failed to "knock and announce" before entering her home. The trial court summarily denied the suppression motion. After a jury trial, petitioner was convicted of all charges and sentenced to 32 years in prison. The Arkansas Supreme Court affirmed petitioner's conviction on appeal.

We granted certiorari to resolve the conflict among the lower courts as to whether the common-law knock and announce principle forms a part of the Fourth Amendment reasonableness inquiry. We hold that it does, and accordingly reverse and remand.

II

The Fourth Amendment to the Constitution protects "[t]he right of the people to be secure in their persons, houses, papers, and effects, against unreasonable searches and seizures." In evaluating the scope of this right, we have looked to the traditional protections against unreasonable searches and seizures afforded by the common law at the time of the framing. "Although the underlying command of the Fourth Amendment is always that searches and seizures be reasonable," our effort to give content to this term may be guided by the meaning ascribed to it by the Framers of the Amendment. An examination of the common law of search and seizure leaves no doubt that the reasonableness of a search of a dwelling may depend in part on whether law enforcement officers announced their presence and authority prior to entering.

Although the common law generally protected a man's house as "his castle of defense and asylum," 3 W. Blackstone, Commentaries, common-law courts long have held that "when the King is party, the sheriff (if the doors be not open) may break the party's house, either to arrest him, or to do other execution of the K[ing]'s process, if otherwise he cannot enter." *Semayne's Case* (K.B.1603). To this rule, however, common-law courts appended an important qualification: "But before he breaks it, he ought to signify the cause of his coming, and to make request to open doors . . . , for the law without a default in the owner abhors the destruction or breaking of any house (which is for the habitation and safety of man) by which great damage and inconvenience might ensue to the party, when no default is in him; for perhaps he did not know of the process, of which, if he had notice, it is to be presumed that he would obey it. . . ."

Several prominent founding-era commentators agreed on this basic principle. According to Sir Matthew Hale, the "constant practice" at common law was that "the officer may break open the door, if he be sure the offender is there, if after acquainting them of the business, and demanding the prisoner, he refuses to open the door." Sir William Blackstone stated simply that the sheriff may "justify breaking open doors, if the possession be not quietly delivered."

The common-law knock and announce principle was woven quickly into the fabric of early American law. Most of the States that ratified the Fourth Amendment had enacted constitutional provisions or statutes generally incorporating English common law.

Our own cases have acknowledged that the common-law principle of announcement is "embedded in Anglo-American law," but we have never squarely held that this principle is an element of the reasonableness inquiry under the Fourth Amendment. We now so hold. Given the long-standing common-law endorsement of the practice of announcement, we have little doubt that the Framers of the Fourth Amendment thought that the method of an officer's entry into a dwelling was among the factors to be considered in assessing the reasonableness of a search or seizure. Contrary to the decision below, we hold that in some circumstances an officer's unannounced entry into a home might be unreasonable under the Fourth Amendment.

This is not to say, of course, that every entry must be preceded by an announcement. The Fourth Amendment's flexible requirement of reasonableness should not be read to mandate a rigid rule of announcement that ignores countervailing law enforcement interests. As even petitioner concedes, the common-law principle of announcement was never stated as an inflexible rule requiring announcement under all circumstances.

Indeed, at the time of the framing, the common-law admonition that an officer "ought to signify the cause of his coming," had not been extended conclusively to the context of felony arrests. Thus, because the common-law rule was justified in part by the belief that announcement generally would avoid "the destruction or breaking of any house . . . by which great damage and inconvenience might ensue," courts acknowledged that the presumption in favor of announcement would yield under circumstances presenting a threat of physical violence. Similarly, courts held that an officer may dispense with announcement in cases where a prisoner escapes from him and retreats to his dwelling. Proof of "demand and refusal" was deemed unnecessary in such cases because it would be a "senseless ceremony" to require an officer in pursuit of a recently escaped arrestee to make an announcement prior to breaking the door to retake him. Finally, courts have indicated that unannounced entry may be justified where police officers have reason to believe that evidence would likely be destroyed if advance notice were given.

We need not attempt a comprehensive catalog of the relevant countervailing factors here. For now, we leave to the lower courts the task of determining the circumstances under which an unannounced entry is reasonable under the Fourth Amendment. We simply hold that although a search or seizure of a dwelling might be constitutionally defective if police officers enter without prior announcement, law enforcement interests may also establish the reasonableness of an unannounced entry.

————————

Soon after Wilson v. Arkansas, the Supreme Court faced the question of whether there are inherently exigent circumstances in drug cases that justify a categorical exception to the knock and announce requirement.

RICHARDS v. WISCONSIN
520 U.S. 385 (1997)

Justice STEVENS delivered the opinion of the Court.

In Wilson v. Arkansas (1995), we held that the Fourth Amendment incorporates the common law requirement that police officers entering a dwelling must knock on the door and announce their identity and purpose before attempting forcible entry. At the same time, we recognized that the "flexible requirement of reasonableness should not be read to mandate a rigid rule of announcement that ignores countervailing law enforcement interests," and left "to the lower courts the task of determining the circumstances under which an unannounced entry is reasonable under the Fourth Amendment."

In this case, the Wisconsin Supreme Court concluded that police officers are never required to knock and announce their presence when executing a search warrant in a felony drug investigation. We disagree with the court's conclusion that the Fourth Amendment permits a blanket exception to the knock-and-announce requirement for this entire category of criminal activity. But because the evidence presented to support the officers' actions in this case establishes that the decision not to knock and announce was a reasonable one under the circumstances, we affirm the judgment of the Wisconsin court.

I

On December 31, 1991, police officers in Madison, Wisconsin, obtained a warrant to search Steiney Richards' motel room for drugs and related paraphernalia. The search warrant was the culmination of an investigation that had uncovered substantial evidence that Richards was one of several individuals dealing drugs out of motel rooms in Madison. The police requested a warrant that would have given advance authorization for a "no-knock" entry into the motel room, but the Magistrate explicitly deleted those portions of the warrant.

The officers arrived at the motel room at 3:40 A.M. Officer Pharo, dressed as a maintenance man, led the team. With him were several plainclothes officers and at least one man in uniform. Officer Pharo knocked on Richards' door and, responding to the query from inside the room, stated that he was a maintenance man. With the chain still on the door, Richards cracked it open. Although there is some dispute as to what occurred next, Richards acknowledges that when he opened the door he saw the man in uniform standing behind Officer Pharo. He quickly slammed the door closed and, after waiting two or three seconds, the officers began kicking and ramming the door to gain entry to the locked room. At trial, the officers testified that they identified themselves as police while they were kicking the door in. When they finally did break into the room, the officers caught Richards trying to escape through the window. They also found cash and cocaine hidden in plastic bags above the bathroom ceiling tiles.

Richards sought to have the evidence from his motel room suppressed on the ground that the officers had failed to knock and announce their presence prior to forcing entry into the room. The trial court denied the motion, concluding that the officers could gather from Richards' strange behavior when they first sought entry that he knew they were police officers and that he might try to destroy evidence or to escape. The judge emphasized that the easily disposable nature of the drugs the police were searching for further justified their decision to identify themselves as they crossed the threshold instead of announcing their presence before seeking entry. Richards appealed the decision to the Wisconsin Supreme Court and that court affirmed.

II

We recognized in *Wilson* that the knock-and-announce requirement could give way "under circumstances presenting a threat of physical violence," or "where police officers have reason to believe that evidence would likely be destroyed if advance notice were given." It is indisputable that felony drug investigations may frequently involve both of these circumstances. The question we must resolve is whether this fact justifies dispensing with case-by-case evaluation of the manner in which a search was executed.

The Wisconsin court explained its blanket exception as necessitated by the special circumstances of today's drug culture, and the State asserted at oral argument that the blanket exception was reasonable in "felony drug cases because of the convergence in a violent and dangerous form of commerce of weapons and the destruction of drugs." But creating exceptions to the knock-and-announce rule based on the "culture" surrounding a general category of criminal behavior presents at least two serious concerns.

First, the exception contains considerable overgeneralization. For example, while drug investigation frequently does pose special risks to officer safety and the preservation of evidence, not every drug investigation will pose these risks to a substantial degree. For example, a search could be conducted at a time when the only individuals present in a residence have no

connection with the drug activity and thus will be unlikely to threaten officers or destroy evidence. Or the police could know that the drugs being
searched for were of a type or in a location that made them impossible to
destroy quickly. In those situations, the asserted governmental interests in
preserving evidence and maintaining safety may not outweigh the individual
privacy interests intruded upon by a no-knock entry. Wisconsin's blanket
rule impermissibly insulates these cases from judicial review.

Additionally, when police enter a residence without announcing their presence, the residents are not given any opportunity to prepare themselves for
such an entry. The State pointed out at oral argument that, in Wisconsin, most
search warrants are executed during the late night and early morning hours.
The brief interlude between announcement and entry with a warrant may be
the opportunity that an individual has to pull on clothes or get out of bed.

A second difficulty with permitting a criminal-category exception to the
knock-and-announce requirement is that the reasons for creating an exception in one category can, relatively easily, be applied to others. Armed bank
robbers, for example, are, by definition, likely to have weapons, and the
fruits of their crime may be destroyed without too much difficulty. If a per
se exception were allowed for each category of criminal investigation that
included a considerable — albeit hypothetical — risk of danger to officers or
destruction of evidence, the knock-and-announce element of the Fourth
Amendment's reasonableness requirement would be meaningless.

Thus, the fact that felony drug investigations may frequently present circumstances warranting a no-knock entry cannot remove from the neutral
scrutiny of a reviewing court the reasonableness of the police decision not to
knock and announce in a particular case. Instead, in each case, it is the duty
of a court confronted with the question to determine whether the facts and
circumstances of the particular entry justified dispensing with the knock-
and-announce requirement.

In order to justify a "no-knock" entry, the police must have a reasonable
suspicion that knocking and announcing their presence, under the
particular circumstances, would be dangerous or futile, or that it would
inhibit the effective investigation of the crime by, for example, allowing
the destruction of evidence. This standard — as opposed to a probable-
cause requirement — strikes the appropriate balance between the legitimate
law enforcement concerns at issue in the execution of search warrants and
the individual privacy interests affected by no-knock entries. This showing is
not high, but the police should be required to make it whenever the reasonableness of a no-knock entry is challenged.

III

Although we reject the Wisconsin court's blanket exception to the knock-
and-announce requirement, we conclude that the officers' no-knock entry
into Richards' motel room did not violate the Fourth Amendment. We agree
with the trial court that the circumstances in this case show that the officers

had a reasonable suspicion that Richards might destroy evidence if given further opportunity to do so.

In arguing that the officers' entry was unreasonable, Richards places great emphasis on the fact that the Magistrate who signed the search warrant for his motel room deleted the portions of the proposed warrant that would have given the officers permission to execute a no-knock entry. But this fact does not alter the reasonableness of the officers' decision, which must be evaluated as of the time they entered the motel room. At the time the officers obtained the warrant, they did not have evidence sufficient, in the judgment of the Magistrate, to justify a no-knock warrant. Of course, the Magistrate could not have anticipated in every particular the circumstances that would confront the officers when they arrived at Richards' motel room. These actual circumstances—petitioner's apparent recognition of the officers combined with the easily disposable nature of the drugs—justified the officers' ultimate decision to enter without first announcing their presence and authority.

The practice of allowing magistrates to issue no-knock warrants seems entirely reasonable when sufficient cause to do so can be demonstrated ahead of time. But, as the facts of this case demonstrate, a magistrate's decision not to authorize a no-knock entry should not be interpreted to remove the officers' authority to exercise independent judgment concerning the wisdom of a no-knock entry at the time the warrant is being executed.

In its most recent cases concerning the knock and announce requirement, the Court has been deferential to law enforcement. In United States v. Banks, 540 U.S. 31 (2004), the Court held that the police did not violate the Fourth Amendment when they waited only 15-20 seconds if they had reason to believe that waiting longer would provide the opportunity for the suspects to destroy contraband.

More dramatically and more importantly, in Hudson v. Michigan, 126 S. Ct. 2159 (2006), the Court held that the exclusionary rule does not apply to evidence gained after police violate the knock and announce requirement. *Hudson* is presented in the next chapter, Chapter 3, which considers the exclusionary rule. A crucial question will be whether police have sufficient incentives to comply with the knock and announce requirement since violations do not result in the suppression of evidence.

c.   What If There Are Unforeseen Circumstances or Mistakes While Executing a Warrant?

If a mistake is made in executing a warrant, the search is permissible as long as the police action is reasonable. Maryland v. Garrison illustrates this point.

MARYLAND v. GARRISON

480 U.S. 79 (1987)

Justice STEVENS delivered the opinion of the Court.

Baltimore police officers obtained and executed a warrant to search the person of Lawrence McWebb and "the premises known as 2036 Park Avenue third floor apartment." When the police applied for the warrant and when they conducted the search pursuant to the warrant, they reasonably believed that there was only one apartment on the premises described in the warrant. In fact, the third floor was divided into two apartments, one occupied by McWebb and one by respondent Garrison. Before the officers executing the warrant became aware that they were in a separate apartment occupied by respondent, they had discovered the contraband that provided the basis for respondent's conviction for violating Maryland's Controlled Substances Act. The question presented is whether the seizure of that contraband was prohibited by the Fourth Amendment.

There is no question that the warrant was valid and was supported by probable cause. The trial court found, and the two appellate courts did not dispute, that after making a reasonable investigation, including a verification of information obtained from a reliable informant, an exterior examination of the three-story building at 2036 Park Avenue, and an inquiry of the utility company, the officer who obtained the warrant reasonably concluded that there was only one apartment on the third floor and that it was occupied by McWebb. When six Baltimore police officers executed the warrant, they fortuitously encountered McWebb in front of the building and used his key to gain admittance to the first-floor hallway and to the locked door at the top of the stairs to the third floor. As they entered the vestibule on the third floor, they encountered respondent, who was standing in the hallway area. The police could see into the interior of both McWebb's apartment to the left and respondent's to the right, for the doors to both were open. Only after respondent's apartment had been entered and heroin, cash, and drug paraphernalia had been found did any of the officers realize that the third floor contained two apartments. As soon as they became aware of that fact, the search was discontinued. All of the officers reasonably believed that they were searching McWebb's apartment. No further search of respondent's apartment was made.

In our view, the case presents two separate constitutional issues, one concerning the validity of the warrant and the other concerning the reasonableness of the manner in which it was executed. We shall discuss the questions separately.

I

The Warrant Clause of the Fourth Amendment categorically prohibits the issuance of any warrant except one "particularly describing the place to be searched and the persons or things to be seized." The manifest purpose of this particularity requirement was to prevent general searches. By limiting the authorization to search to the specific areas and things for which there is probable cause to search, the requirement ensures that the search will be carefully tailored to its justifications, and will not take on the character of the wide-ranging exploratory searches the Framers intended to prohibit. Thus, the scope of a lawful search is "defined by the object of the search and the places in which there is probable cause to believe that it may be found. Just as probable cause to believe that a stolen lawnmower may be found in a garage will not support a warrant to search an upstairs bedroom, probable cause to believe that undocumented aliens are being transported in a van will not justify a warrantless search of a suitcase."

In this case there is no claim that the "persons or things to be seized" were inadequately described or that there was no probable cause to believe that those things might be found in "the place to be searched" as it was described in the warrant. With the benefit of hindsight, however, we now know that the description of that place was broader than appropriate because it was based on the mistaken belief that there was only one apartment on the third floor of the building at 2036 Park Avenue. The question is whether that factual mistake invalidated a warrant that undoubtedly would have been valid if it had reflected a completely accurate understanding of the building's floor plan.

Plainly, if the officers had known, or even if they should have known, that there were two separate dwelling units on the third floor of 2036 Park Avenue, they would have been obligated to exclude respondent's apartment from the scope of the requested warrant. But we must judge the constitutionality of their conduct in light of the information available to them at the time they acted. Those items of evidence that emerge after the warrant is issued have no bearing on whether or not a warrant was validly issued. Just as the discovery of contraband cannot validate a warrant invalid when issued, so is it equally clear that the discovery of facts demonstrating that a valid warrant was unnecessarily broad does not retroactively invalidate the warrant. The validity of the warrant must be assessed on the basis of the information that the officers disclosed, or had a duty to discover and to disclose, to the issuing Magistrate. On the basis of that information, we agree with the conclusion of all three Maryland courts that the warrant, insofar as it authorized a search that turned out to be ambiguous in scope, was valid when it issued.

II

The question whether the execution of the warrant violated respondent's constitutional right to be secure in his home is somewhat less clear. We have no difficulty concluding that the officers' entry into the third-floor common area was legal; they carried a warrant for those premises, and they were accompanied by McWebb, who provided the key that they used to open the door giving access to the third-floor common area. If the officers had known, or should have known, that the third floor contained two apartments before they entered the living quarters on the third floor, and thus had been aware of the error in the warrant, they would have been obligated to limit their search to McWebb's apartment. Moreover, as the officers recognized, they were required to discontinue the search of respondent's apartment as soon as they discovered that there were two separate units on the third floor and therefore were put on notice of the risk that they might be in a unit erroneously included within the terms of the warrant. The officers' conduct and the limits of the search were based on the information available as the search proceeded. While the purposes justifying a police search strictly limit the permissible extent of the search, the Court has also recognized the need to allow some latitude for honest mistakes that are made by officers in the dangerous and difficult process of making arrests and executing search warrants.

[T]he validity of the search of respondent's apartment pursuant to a warrant authorizing the search of the entire third floor depends on whether the officers' failure to realize the overbreadth of the warrant was objectively understandable and reasonable. Here it unquestionably was. The objective facts available to the officers at the time suggested no distinction between McWebb's apartment and the third-floor premises.

For that reason, the officers properly responded to the command contained in a valid warrant even if the warrant is interpreted as authorizing a search limited to McWebb's apartment rather than the entire third floor. Prior to the officers' discovery of the factual mistake, they perceived McWebb's apartment and the third-floor premises as one and the same; therefore their execution of the warrant reasonably included the entire third floor. Under either interpretation of the warrant, the officers' conduct was consistent with a reasonable effort to ascertain and identify the place intended to be searched within the meaning of the Fourth Amendment.

Justice BLACKMUN, with whom Justice BRENNAN and Justice MARSHALL join, dissenting.

Under this Court's precedents, the search of respondent Garrison's apartment violated the Fourth Amendment. While executing a warrant specifically limited to McWebb's residence, the officers expanded their search to include respondent's adjacent apartment, an expansion made without a warrant and in the absence of exigent circumstances. In my view, Maryland's highest court correctly concluded that the trial judge should have granted respondent's motion to suppress the evidence seized as a result of this warrantless search of his apartment. Moreover, even if I were to accept the majority's analysis of this case as one involving a mistake on the part of the police officers, I would find that the officers' error, either in obtaining or in executing the warrant, was not reasonable under the circumstances.

In applying [the Fourth Amendment's] requirement to searches aimed at residences within multiunit buildings, such as the search in the present case, courts have declared invalid those warrants that fail to describe the targeted unit with enough specificity to prevent a search of all the units. Courts have used different criteria to determine whether a warrant has identified a unit with sufficient particularity.

Applying the above principles to this case, I conclude that the search of respondent's apartment was improper. The words of the warrant were plain and distinctive: the warrant directed the officers to seize marijuana and drug paraphernalia on the person of McWebb and in McWebb's apartment, i.e., "on the premises known as 2036 Park Avenue third floor apartment." As the Court of Appeals observed, this warrant specifically authorized a search only of McWebb's—not respondent's—residence. In its interpretation of the warrant, the majority suggests that the language of this document, as well as that in the supporting affidavit, permitted a search of the entire third floor. It escapes me why the language in question, "third floor apartment," when used with reference to a single unit in a multiple-occupancy building and in the context of one person's residence, plainly has the meaning the majority discerns, rather than its apparent and, indeed, obvious significa-tion—one apartment located on the third floor. Accordingly, if, as appears to be the case, the warrant was limited in its description to the third floor apartment of McWebb, then the search of an additional apartment— respondent's—was warrantless and is presumed unreasonable "in the absence of some one of a number of well defined 'exigent circumstances.'" Because the State has not advanced any such exception to the warrant requirement, the evidence obtained as a result of this search should have been excluded.

The willingness of the Court to excuse mistakes in executing warrants is illustrated by a case with egregious facts.

LOS ANGELES COUNTY, CALIFORNIA v. RETTELE

550 U.S. 609 (2007)

PER CURIAM.

Deputies of the Los Angeles County Sheriff's Department obtained a valid warrant to search a house, but they were unaware that the suspects being sought had moved out three months earlier. When the deputies searched the house, they found in a bedroom two residents who were of a different race than the suspects. The deputies ordered these innocent residents, who had been sleeping unclothed, out of bed. The deputies required them to stand for a few minutes before allowing them to dress.

The residents brought suit under 42 U.S.C. §1983, naming the deputies and other parties and accusing them of violating the Fourth Amendment right to be free from unreasonable searches and seizures. The District Court granted summary judgment to all named defendants. The Court of Appeals for the Ninth Circuit reversed, concluding both that the deputies violated the Fourth Amendment and that they were not entitled to qualified immunity because a reasonable deputy would have stopped the search upon discovering that respondents were of a different race than the suspects and because a reasonable deputy would not have ordered respondents from their bed. We grant the petition for certiorari and reverse the judgment of the Court of Appeals by this summary disposition.

I

From September to December 2001, Los Angeles County Sheriff's Department Deputy Dennis Watters investigated a fraud and identity-theft crime ring. There were four suspects of the investigation. One had registered a 9-millimeter Glock handgun. The four suspects were known to be African-Americans.

On December 11, Watters obtained a search warrant for two houses in Lancaster, California, where he believed he could find the suspects. The warrant authorized him to search the homes and three of the suspects for documents and computer files. In support of the search warrant an affidavit cited various sources showing the suspects resided at respondents' home. The sources included Department of Motor Vehicles reports, mailing address listings, an outstanding warrant, and an Internet telephone directory. In this Court respondents do not dispute the validity of the warrant or the means by which it was obtained.

What Watters did not know was that one of the houses (the first to be searched) had been sold in September to a Max Rettele. He had purchased the home and moved into it three months earlier with his girlfriend Judy Sadler and Sadler's 17-year-old son Chase Hall. All three, respondents here, are Caucasians.

On the morning of December 19, Watters briefed six other deputies in preparation for the search of the houses. Watters informed them they would be searching for three African-American suspects, one of whom owned a registered handgun. The possibility a suspect would be armed caused the deputies concern for their own safety. Watters had not obtained special permission for a night search, so he could not execute the warrant until 7 A.M. Around 7:15 Watters and six other deputies knocked on the door and announced their presence. Chase Hall answered. The deputies entered the house after ordering Hall to lie face down on the ground.

The deputies' announcement awoke Rettele and Sadler. The deputies entered their bedroom with guns drawn and ordered them to get out of their bed and to show their hands. They protested that they were not wearing clothes. Rettele stood up and attempted to put on a pair of sweatpants, but deputies told him not to move. Sadler also stood up and attempted, without success, to cover herself with a sheet. Rettele and Sadler were held at gunpoint for one to two minutes before Rettele was allowed to retrieve a robe for

Sadler. He was then permitted to dress. Rettele and Sadler left the bedroom within three to four minutes to sit on the couch in the living room.

By that time the deputies realized they had made a mistake. They apologized to Rettele and Sadler, thanked them for not becoming upset, and left within five minutes. They proceeded to the other house the warrant authorized them to search, where they found three suspects. Those suspects were arrested and convicted.

Rettele and Sadler, individually and as guardians ad litem for Hall, filed this §1983 suit against Los Angeles County, the Los Angeles County Sheriff's Department, Deputy Watters, and other members of the sheriff's department. Respondents alleged petitioners violated their Fourth Amendment rights by obtaining a warrant in reckless fashion and conducting an unreasonable search and detention. The District Court held that the warrant was obtained by proper procedures and the search was reasonable. A divided panel of the Court of Appeals for the Ninth Circuit reversed in an unpublished opinion.

II

Because respondents were of a different race than the suspects the deputies were seeking, the Court of Appeals held that "[a]fter taking one look at [respondents], the deputies should have realized that [respondents] were not the subjects of the search warrant and did not pose a threat to the deputies' safety." We need not pause long in rejecting this unsound proposition. When the deputies ordered respondents from their bed, they had no way of knowing whether the African-American suspects were elsewhere in the house. The presence of some Caucasians in the residence did not eliminate the possibility that the suspects lived there as well. As the deputies stated in their affidavits, it is not uncommon in our society for people of different races to live together. Just as people of different races live and work together, so too might they engage in joint criminal activity. The deputies, who were searching a house where they believed a suspect might be armed, possessed authority to secure the premises before deciding whether to continue with the search.

In Michigan v. Summers (1981), this Court held that officers executing a search warrant for contraband may "detain the occupants of the premises while a proper search is conducted." In executing a search warrant officers may take reasonable action to secure the premises and to ensure their own safety and the efficacy of the search. The test of reasonableness under the Fourth Amendment is an objective one. Unreasonable actions include the use of excessive force or restraints that cause unnecessary pain or are imposed for a prolonged and unnecessary period of time.

The orders by the police to the occupants, in the context of this lawful search, were permissible, and perhaps necessary, to protect the safety of the deputies. Blankets and bedding can conceal a weapon, and one of the suspects was known to own a firearm, factors which underscore this point. The

Constitution does not require an officer to ignore the possibility that an armed suspect may sleep with a weapon within reach. The reports are replete with accounts of suspects sleeping close to weapons.

The deputies needed a moment to secure the room and ensure that other persons were not close by or did not present a danger. Deputies were not required to turn their backs to allow Rettele and Sadler to retrieve clothing or to cover themselves with the sheets. Rather, "[t]he risk of harm to both the police and the occupants is minimized if the officers routinely exercise unquestioned command of the situation."

This is not to say, of course, that the deputies were free to force Rettele and Sadler to remain motionless and standing for any longer than necessary. We have recognized that "special circumstances, or possibly a prolonged detention" might render a search unreasonable. There is no accusation that the detention here was prolonged. The deputies left the home less than 15 minutes after arriving. The detention was shorter and less restrictive than the 2- to 3-hour handcuff detention upheld in *Mena*. And there is no allegation that the deputies prevented Sadler and Rettele from dressing longer than necessary to protect their safety. Sadler was unclothed for no more than two minutes, and Rettele for only slightly more time than that. Sadler testified that once the police were satisfied that no immediate threat was presented, "they wanted us to get dressed and they were pressing us really fast to hurry up and get some clothes on."

The Fourth Amendment allows warrants to issue on probable cause, a standard well short of absolute certainty. Valid warrants will issue to search the innocent, and people like Rettele and Sadler unfortunately bear the cost. Officers executing search warrants on occasion enter a house when residents are engaged in private activity; and the resulting frustration, embarrassment, and humiliation may be real, as was true here. When officers execute a valid warrant and act in a reasonable manner to protect themselves from harm, however, the Fourth Amendment is not violated.

E. EXCEPTIONS TO THE WARRANT REQUIREMENT

The Supreme Court often has said that there is a warrant requirement within the Fourth Amendment and that a warrantless search is presumptively unreasonable. But many Justices have disputed this and have said that the Fourth Amendment does not require a warrant, but rather that the search be reasonable.

The Court has recognized many exceptions where searches or seizures are permissible without a warrant. As mentioned earlier, Justice Thomas said that the case law "stand[s] for the illuminating proposition that warrantless searches are per se unreasonable, except, of course, when they are not." Groh v. Ramirez, 540 U.S. 551 (2004) (Thomas, J., dissenting).

The exceptions to the warrant requirement include exigent circumstances, searches of things in plain view, automobile searches, searches incident to arrest, inventory searches, protective sweeps, searches with consent, searches when there are special needs, and searches of those on probation and parole. Each of these has produced its own body of law. Each is reviewed below.

These exceptions, of course, are not mutually exclusive; more than one can apply in a situation. For example, screening at airports, such as through metal detectors and even physical examinations, can be justified because a person consents by entering and also because there is a special need in protecting safety.

In creating the exceptions to the warrant requirement, the Court has balanced the privacy interests involved against the extent to which adhering to the warrant requirement would unduly hamper effective law enforcement. In evaluating the exceptions, it is important to consider whether the Court has struck the proper balance.

1.   *Exigent Circumstances*

In an emergency, the police can search without a warrant if there is probable cause. This situation is often referred to as exigent circumstances. For this exception to apply, it must be an emergency situation justifying warrantless activity, and there must be probable cause.

The Court generally has been reluctant to find exigent circumstances. For example, in Mincey v. Arizona, 437 U.S. 385 (1978), the Court rejected a claim that there should be a blanket exception to the warrant requirement for all murder scenes. But the Court has found exigent circumstances in a number of situations: hot pursuit of a felon, protecting safety, and preventing destruction of evidence.

a.   Hot Pursuit

The Supreme Court has been most insistent on a warrant requirement when there are searches of a home, even going so far as to say that warrantless searches and seizures in homes are presumptively invalid. But the Court has recognized an exception to this when the police enter a home in "hot pursuit" of a suspected felon.

WARDEN, MARYLAND PENITENTIARY v. HAYDEN
387 U.S. 294 (1967)

About 8 A.M. on March 17, 1962, an armed robber entered the business premises of the Diamond Cab Company in Baltimore, Maryland. He took some $363 and ran. Two cab drivers in the vicinity, attracted by shouts of

"Holdup," followed the man to 2111 Cocoa Lane. One driver notified the company dispatcher by radio that the man was a Negro about 5'8" tall, wearing a light cap and dark jacket, and that he had entered the house on Cocoa Lane. The dispatcher relayed the information to police who were proceeding to the scene of the robbery. Within minutes, police arrived at the house in a number of patrol cars. An officer knocked and announced their presence. Mrs. Hayden answered, and the officers told her they believed that a robber had entered the house, and asked to search the house. She offered no objection.

The officers spread out through the first and second floors and the cellar in search of the robber. Hayden was found in an upstairs bedroom feigning sleep. He was arrested when the officers on the first floor and in the cellar reported that no other man was in the house. Meanwhile an officer was attracted to an adjoining bathroom by the noise of running water, and discovered a shotgun and a pistol in a flush tank; another officer who, according to the District Court, "was searching the cellar for a man or the money" found in a washing machine a jacket and trousers of the type the fleeing man was said to have worn. A clip of ammunition for the pistol and a cap were found under the mattress of Hayden's bed, and ammunition for the shotgun was found in a bureau drawer in Hayden's room. All these items of evidence were introduced against respondent at his trial.

We agree with the Court of Appeals that neither the entry without warrant to search for the robber, nor the search for him without warrant was invalid. Under the circumstances of this case, the exigencies of the situation made that course imperative. The police were informed that an armed robbery had taken place, and that the suspect had entered 2111 Cocoa Lane less than five minutes before they reached it. They acted reasonably when they entered the house and began to search for a man of the description they had been given and for weapons which he had used in the robbery or might use against them. The Fourth Amendment does not require police officers to delay in the course of an investigation if to do so would gravely endanger their lives or the lives of others. Speed here was essential, and only a thorough search of the house for persons and weapons could have insured that Hayden was the only man present and that the police had control of all weapons which could be used against them or to effect an escape.

Here, the seizures occurred prior to or immediately contemporaneous with Hayden's arrest, as part of an effort to find a suspected felon, armed, within the house into which he had run only minutes before the police arrived. The permissible scope of search must, therefore, at the least, be as broad as may reasonably be necessary to prevent the dangers that the suspect at large in the house may resist or escape.

But Payton v. New York is important in making clear that police cannot enter a home without a warrant to make a routine arrest.

PAYTON v. NEW YORK
445 U.S. 573 (1980)

Justice STEVENS delivered the opinion of the Court.

These appeals challenge the constitutionality of New York statutes that authorize police officers to enter a private residence without a warrant and with force, if necessary, to make a routine felony arrest.

We hold that the Fourth Amendment to the United States Constitution prohibits the police from making a warrantless and nonconsensual entry into a suspect's home in order to make a routine felony arrest.

On January 14, 1970, after two days of intensive investigation, New York detectives had assembled evidence sufficient to establish probable cause to believe that Theodore Payton had murdered the manager of a gas station two days earlier. At about 7:30 A.M. on January 15, six officers went to Payton's apartment in the Bronx, intending to arrest him. They had not obtained a warrant. Although light and music emanated from the apartment, there was no response to their knock on the metal door. They summoned emergency assistance and, about 30 minutes later, used crowbars to break open the door and enter the apartment. No one was there. In plain view, however, was a .30-caliber shell casing that was seized and later admitted into evidence at Payton's murder trial. In due course Payton surrendered to the police, was indicted for murder, and moved to suppress the evidence taken from his apartment.

It is familiar history that indiscriminate searches and seizures conducted under the authority of "general warrants" were the immediate evils that motivated the framing and adoption of the Fourth Amendment. It is perfectly clear that the evil the Amendment was designed to prevent was broader than the abuse of a general warrant. Unreasonable searches or seizures conducted without any warrant at all are condemned by the plain language of the first clause of the Amendment. The simple language of the Amendment applies equally to seizures of persons and to seizures of property. As the Court reiterated just a few years ago, the "physical entry of the home is the chief evil against which the wording of the Fourth Amendment is directed." And we have long adhered to the view that the warrant procedure minimizes the danger of needless intrusions of that sort.

It is a "basic principle of Fourth Amendment law" that searches and seizures inside a home without a warrant are presumptively unreasonable.

The Fourth Amendment protects the individual's privacy in a variety of settings. In none is the zone of privacy more clearly defined than when bounded by the unambiguous physical dimensions of an individual's home — a zone that finds its roots in clear and specific constitutional terms: "The right of the people to be secure in their . . . houses . . . shall not be violated." That language unequivocally establishes the proposition that "[a]t the very core [of the Fourth Amendment] stands the right of a man to retreat into his own home and there be free from unreasonable governmental intrusion." In terms that apply equally to seizures of property and to seizures of persons, the Fourth Amendment has drawn a firm line at the entrance to the house. Absent exigent circumstances, that threshold may not reasonably be crossed without a warrant.

Justice WHITE, with whom THE CHIEF JUSTICE and Justice REHNQUIST join, dissenting.

The Court today holds that absent exigent circumstances officers may never enter a home during the daytime to arrest for a dangerous felony unless they have first obtained a warrant. This hard-and-fast rule, founded on erroneous assumptions concerning the intrusiveness of home arrest entries, finds little or no support in the common law or in the text and history of the Fourth Amendment. I respectfully dissent.

As the Court notes, the common law of searches and seizures, as evolved in England, as transported to the Colonies, and as developed among the States, is highly relevant to the present scope of the Fourth Amendment. Today's decision virtually ignores these centuries of common-law development, and distorts the historical meaning of the Fourth Amendment, by proclaiming for the first time a rigid warrant requirement for all nonexigent home arrest entries.

The history of the Fourth Amendment does not support the rule announced today. At the time that Amendment was adopted the constable possessed broad inherent powers to arrest. The limitations on those powers derived, not from a warrant "requirement," but from the generally ministerial nature of the constable's office at common law. Far from restricting the constable's arrest power, the institution of the warrant was used to expand that authority by giving the constable delegated powers of a superior officer such as a justice of the peace. Hence at the time of the Bill of Rights, the warrant functioned as a powerful tool of law enforcement rather than as a protection for the rights of criminal suspects.

In fact, it was the abusive use of the warrant power, rather than any excessive zeal in the discharge of peace officers' inherent authority, that precipitated the Fourth Amendment. That Amendment grew out of colonial opposition to the infamous general warrants known as writs of assistance, which empowered customs officers to search at will, and to break open receptacles or packages, wherever they suspected uncustomed goods to be. The writs did not specify where searches could occur and they remained effective throughout the sovereign's lifetime. In effect, the writs placed complete discretion in the hands of executing officials.

That the Fourth Amendment was directed toward safeguarding the rights at common law, and restricting the warrant practice which gave officers vast new powers beyond their inherent authority, is evident from the legislative history of that provision. As originally drafted by James Madison, it was directed only at warrants; so deeply ingrained was the basic common-law premise that it was not even expressed: "The rights of the people to be secured in their persons[,] their houses, their papers, and their other property, from all unreasonable searches and seizures, shall not be violated by warrants issued without probable cause, supported by oath or affirmation, or not particularly describing the places to be searched, or the persons or things to be seized."

In sum, the background, text, and legislative history of the Fourth Amendment demonstrate that the purpose was to restrict the abuses that had developed with respect to warrants; the Amendment preserved common-law rules of arrest. Because it was not considered generally unreasonable at common law for officers to break doors to effect a warrantless felony arrest, I do not believe that the Fourth Amendment was intended to outlaw the types of police conduct at issue in the present cases.

While exaggerating the invasion of personal privacy involved in home arrests, the Court fails to account for the danger that its rule will "severely hamper effective law enforcement." The policeman on his beat must now make subtle discriminations that perplex even judges in their chambers. Further, police officers will often face the difficult task of deciding whether the circumstances are sufficiently exigent to justify their entry to arrest without a warrant. This is a decision that must be made quickly in the most trying of circumstances. If the officers mistakenly decide that the circumstances are exigent, the arrest will be invalid and any evidence seized incident to the arrest or in plain view will be excluded at trial. On the other hand, if the officers mistakenly determine that exigent circumstances are lacking, they may refrain from making the arrest, thus creating the possibility that a dangerous criminal will escape into the community. The police could reduce the likelihood of escape by staking out all possible exits until the circumstances become clearly exigent or a warrant is obtained. But the costs of such a stakeout seem excessive in an era of rising crime and scarce police resources.

The uncertainty inherent in the exigent-circumstances determination burdens the judicial system as well. In the case of searches, exigent circumstances are sufficiently unusual that this Court has determined that the benefits of a warrant outweigh the burdens imposed, including the burdens on the judicial system. In contrast, arrests recurringly involve exigent circumstances, and this Court has heretofore held that a warrant can be dispensed with without undue sacrifice in Fourth Amendment values. The situation should be no different with respect to arrests in the home. Under today's decision, whenever the police have made a warrantless home arrest there will be the possibility of "endless litigation with respect to the existence of exigent circumstances, whether it was practicable to get a warrant, whether the suspect was about to flee, and the like."

Our cases establish that the ultimate test under the Fourth Amendment is one of "reasonableness." I cannot join the Court in declaring unreasonable a practice which has been thought entirely reasonable by so many for so long. It would be far preferable to adopt a clear and simple rule: After knocking and announcing their presence, police may enter the home to make a daytime arrest without a warrant when there is probable cause to believe that the person to be arrested committed a felony and is present in the house. This rule would best comport with the common-law background, with the traditional practice in the States, and with the history and policies of the Fourth Amendment. Accordingly, I respectfully dissent.

b. Safety

The police may enter without a warrant if there is a reasonable basis to believe that an occupant of the home would be endangered were they to wait to obtain a warrant before entering. This was made clear in Brigham City, Utah v. Stuart.

BRIGHAM CITY, UTAH v. STUART

547 U.S. 398 (2006)

Chief Justice ROBERTS delivered the opinion of the Court.

In this case we consider whether police may enter a home without a warrant when they have an objectively reasonable basis for believing that an occupant is seriously injured or imminently threatened with such injury. We conclude that they may.

I

This case arises out of a melee that occurred in a Brigham City, Utah, home in the early morning hours of July 23, 2000. At about 3 A.M., four police officers responded to a call regarding a loud party at a residence. Upon arriving at the house, they heard shouting from inside, and proceeded down the driveway to investigate. There, they observed two juveniles drinking beer in the backyard. They entered the backyard, and saw — through a screen door and windows — an altercation taking place in the kitchen of the home. According to the testimony of one of the officers, four adults were attempting, with some difficulty, to restrain a juvenile. The juvenile eventually "broke free, swung a fist and struck one of the adults in the face." The officer testified that he observed the victim of the blow spitting blood into a nearby sink. The other adults continued to try to restrain the juvenile, pressing him up against a refrigerator with such force that the refrigerator began moving across the floor. At this point, an officer opened the screen door and announced the officers' presence. Amid the tumult, nobody noticed. The officer entered the kitchen and again cried out, and as the occupants slowly became aware that the police were on the scene, the altercation ceased.

The officers subsequently arrested respondents and charged them with contributing to the delinquency of a minor, disorderly conduct, and intoxication. In the trial court, respondents filed a motion to suppress all evidence obtained after the officers entered the home, arguing that the warrantless entry violated the Fourth Amendment. The court granted the motion, and the Utah Court of Appeals affirmed.

II

It is a "basic principle of Fourth Amendment law that searches and seizures inside a home without a warrant are presumptively unreasonable." Nevertheless, because the ultimate touchstone of the Fourth Amendment is "reasonableness," the warrant requirement is subject to certain exceptions.

One exigency obviating the requirement of a warrant is the need to assist persons who are seriously injured or threatened with such injury. "The need to protect or preserve life or avoid serious injury is justification for what would be otherwise illegal absent an exigency or emergency." Accordingly, law enforcement officers may enter a home without a warrant to render emergency assistance to an injured occupant or to protect an occupant from imminent injury.

Respondents do not take issue with these principles, but instead advance two reasons why the officers' entry here was unreasonable. First, they argue that the officers were more interested in making arrests than quelling violence. They urge us to consider, in assessing the reasonableness of the entry, whether the officers were "indeed motivated primarily by a desire to save lives and property." *subjective*

Our cases have repeatedly rejected this approach. An action is "reasonable" under the Fourth Amendment, regardless of the individual officer's state of mind, "as long as the circumstances, viewed objectively, justify [the] action." The officer's subjective motivation is irrelevant.

We think the officers' entry here was plainly reasonable under the circumstances. The officers were responding, at 3 o'clock in the morning, to complaints about a loud party. As they approached the house, they could hear from within "an altercation occurring, some kind of a fight." "It was loud and it was tumultuous." The officers heard "thumping and crashing" and people yelling "stop, stop" and "get off me." As the trial court found, "it was obvious that . . . knocking on the front door" would have been futile. The noise seemed to be coming from the back of the house; after looking in the front window and seeing nothing, the officers proceeded around back to investigate further. They found two juveniles drinking beer in the backyard. From there, they could see that a fracas was taking place inside the kitchen. A juvenile, fists clenched, was being held back by several adults. As the officers watch, he breaks free and strikes one of the adults in the face, sending the adult to the sink spitting blood.

In these circumstances, the officers had an objectively reasonable basis for believing both that the injured adult might need help and that the violence in the kitchen was just beginning. Nothing in the Fourth Amendment required them to wait until another blow rendered someone "unconscious" or "semi-conscious" or worse before entering. The role of a peace officer includes preventing violence and restoring order, not simply rendering first aid to casualties; an officer is not like a boxing (or hockey) referee, poised to stop a bout only if it becomes too one-sided.

The manner of the officers' entry was also reasonable. After witnessing the punch, one of the officers opened the screen door and "yelled in police." When nobody heard him, he stepped into the kitchen and announced himself again. Only then did the tumult subside. The officer's announcement of his presence was at least equivalent to a knock on the screen door. Indeed, it was probably the only option that had even a chance of rising above the din. Under these circumstances, there was no violation of the Fourth Amendment's knock-and-announce rule. Furthermore, once the announcement was made, the officers were free to enter; it would serve no purpose to require them to stand dumbly at the door awaiting a response while those within brawled on, oblivious to their presence.

---

c. Preventing Destruction of Evidence

In Kentucky v. King, the Court returned to the exigent circumstances exception and considered when police conduct itself can be the basis for exigent circumstances. In reading Kentucky v. King, it is important to focus on when police can enter a home without a warrant based on the sounds they hear that might mean the destruction of evidence.

KENTUCKY v. KING

563 U.S. 452 (2011)

Justice ALITO delivered the opinion of the Court.

It is well established that "exigent circumstances," including the need to prevent the destruction of evidence, permit police officers to conduct an otherwise permissible search without first obtaining a warrant. In this case, we consider whether this rule applies when police, by knocking on the door of a residence and announcing their presence, cause the occupants to attempt to destroy evidence. The Kentucky Supreme Court held that the exigent circumstances rule does not apply in the case at hand because the police should have foreseen that their conduct would prompt the occupants to attempt to destroy evidence. We reject this interpretation of the exigent circumstances rule. The conduct of the police prior to their entry into the apartment was entirely lawful. They did not violate the Fourth Amendment or threaten to do so. In such a situation, the exigent circumstances rule applies.

I

This case concerns the search of an apartment in Lexington, Kentucky. Police officers set up a controlled buy of crack cocaine outside an apartment complex. Undercover Officer Gibbons watched the deal take place from an unmarked car in a nearby parking lot. After the deal occurred, Gibbons radioed uniformed officers to move in on the suspect. He told the officers that the suspect was moving quickly toward the breezeway of an apartment building, and he urged them to "hurry up and get there" before the suspect entered an apartment.

In response to the radio alert, the uniformed officers drove into the nearby parking lot, left their vehicles, and ran to the breezeway. Just as they entered the breezeway, they heard a door shut and detected a very strong odor of burnt marijuana. At the end of the breezeway, the officers saw two apartments, one on the left and one on the right, and they did not know which apartment the suspect had entered. Gibbons had radioed that the suspect was running into the apartment on the right, but the officers did not hear this statement because they had already left their vehicles. Because they smelled marijuana smoke emanating from the apartment on the left, they approached the door of that apartment.

Officer Steven Cobb, one of the uniformed officers who approached the door, testified that the officers banged on the left apartment door "as loud as [they] could" and announced, "'This is the police'" or "'Police, police, police.'" Cobb said that "[a]s soon as [the officers] started banging on the door," they "could hear people inside moving," and "[i]t sounded as [though] things were being moved inside the apartment." These noises, Cobb testified, led the officers to believe that drug-related evidence was about to be destroyed.

At that point, the officers announced that they "were going to make entry inside the apartment." Cobb then kicked in the door, the officers entered the apartment, and they found three people in the front room: respondent Hollis King, respondent's girlfriend, and a guest who was smoking marijuana. The officers performed a protective sweep of the apartment during which they saw marijuana and powder cocaine in plain view. In a subsequent search, they also discovered crack cocaine, cash, and drug paraphernalia. Police eventually entered the apartment on the right. Inside, they found the suspected drug dealer who was the initial target of their investigation.

II

Although the text of the Fourth Amendment does not specify when a search warrant must be obtained, this Court has inferred that a warrant must generally be secured. "It is a 'basic principle of Fourth Amendment law,'" we have often said, "'that searches and seizures inside a home without a warrant are presumptively unreasonable.'" But we have also recognized that this presumption may be overcome in some circumstances because "[t]he ultimate touchstone of the Fourth Amendment is 'reasonableness.'" Accordingly, the warrant requirement is subject to certain reasonable exceptions.

One well-recognized exception applies when "'the exigencies of the situation' make the needs of law enforcement so compelling that [a] warrantless search is objectively reasonable under the Fourth Amendment." This Court has identified several exigencies that may justify a warrantless search of a home. Under the "emergency aid" exception, for example, "officers may enter a home without a warrant to render emergency assistance to an injured occupant or to protect an occupant from imminent injury." Police officers may enter premises without a warrant when they are in hot pursuit of a fleeing suspect. And — what is relevant here — the need "to prevent the imminent destruction of evidence" has long been recognized as a sufficient justification for a warrantless search.

Over the years, lower courts have developed an exception to the exigent circumstances rule, the so-called "police-created exigency" doctrine. Under this doctrine, police may not rely on the need to prevent destruction of evidence when that exigency was "created" or "manufactured" by the conduct of the police.

In applying this exception for the "creation" or "manufacturing" of an exigency by the police, courts require something more than mere proof that fear of detection by the police caused the destruction of evidence. An additional showing is obviously needed because, as the Eighth Circuit has recognized, "in some sense the police always create the exigent circumstances." That is to say, in the vast majority of cases in which evidence is destroyed by persons who are engaged in illegal conduct, the reason for the destruction is fear that the evidence will fall into the hands of law enforcement. Destruction of evidence issues probably occur most frequently in drug cases because drugs may be easily destroyed by flushing them down a toilet or rinsing them down a drain. Persons in possession of valuable drugs are unlikely to destroy them unless they fear discovery by the police. Consequently, a rule that precludes the police from making a warrantless entry to prevent the destruction of evidence whenever their conduct causes the exigency would unreasonably shrink the reach of this well-established exception to the warrant requirement.

Presumably for the purpose of avoiding such a result, the lower courts have held that the police-created exigency doctrine requires more than simple causation, but the lower courts have not agreed on the test to be applied.

III

Despite the welter of tests devised by the lower courts, the answer to the question presented in this case follows directly and clearly from the principle that permits warrantless searches in the first place. As previously noted, warrantless searches are allowed when the circumstances make it reasonable, within the meaning of the Fourth Amendment, to dispense with the warrant requirement. Therefore, the answer to the question before us is that the exigent circumstances rule justifies a warrantless search when the conduct of the police preceding the exigency is reasonable in the same sense. Where, as here, the police did not create the exigency by engaging or threatening to engage in conduct that violates the Fourth Amendment, warrantless entry to prevent the destruction of evidence is reasonable and thus allowed.

Some lower courts have adopted a rule that is similar to the one that we recognize today. But others, including the Kentucky Supreme Court, have imposed additional requirements that are unsound and that we now reject.

Bad faith. Some courts, including the Kentucky Supreme Court, ask whether law enforcement officers "'deliberately created the exigent circumstances with the bad faith intent to avoid the warrant requirement.'" This approach is fundamentally inconsistent with our Fourth Amendment jurisprudence. "Our cases have repeatedly rejected" a subjective approach, asking only whether "the circumstances, viewed *objectively*, justify the action." Indeed, we have never held, outside limited contexts such as an "inventory search or administrative inspection . . . , that an officer's motive invalidates objectively justifiable behavior under the Fourth Amendment."

The reasons for looking to objective factors, rather than subjective intent, are clear. Legal tests based on reasonableness are generally objective, and this Court has long taken the view that "evenhanded law enforcement is best achieved by the application of objective standards of conduct, rather than standards that depend upon the subjective state of mind of the officer."

Reasonable foreseeability. Some courts, again including the Kentucky Supreme Court, hold that police may not rely on an exigency if "'it was reasonably foreseeable that the investigative tactics employed by the police would create the exigent circumstances.'" Courts applying this test have invalidated warrantless home searches on the ground that it was reasonably foreseeable that police officers, by knocking on the door and announcing their presence, would lead a drug suspect to destroy evidence. Contrary to this reasoning, however, we have rejected the notion that police may seize evidence without a warrant only when they come across the evidence by happenstance.

Adoption of a reasonable foreseeability test would also introduce an unacceptable degree of unpredictability. For example, whenever law enforcement officers knock on the door of premises occupied by a person who may be involved in the drug trade, there is *some* possibility that the occupants may possess drugs and may seek to destroy them. Under a reasonable foreseeability test, it would be necessary to quantify the degree of predictability that must be reached before the police-created exigency doctrine comes into play.

A simple example illustrates the difficulties that such an approach would produce. Suppose that the officers in the present case did not smell marijuana smoke and thus knew only that there was a 50% chance that the fleeing suspect had entered the apartment on the left rather than the apartment on the right. Under those circumstances, would it have been reasonably foreseeable that the occupants of the apartment on the left would seek to destroy evidence upon learning that the police were at the door? Or suppose that the officers knew only that the suspect had disappeared into one of the apartments on a floor with 3, 5, 10, or even 20 units? If the police chose a door at random and knocked for the purpose of asking the occupants if they knew a person who fit the description of the suspect, would it have been reasonably foreseeable that the occupants would seek to destroy evidence?

We have noted that "[t]he calculus of reasonableness must embody allowance for the fact that police officers are often forced to make split-second judgments — in circumstances that are tense, uncertain, and rapidly evolving." The reasonable foreseeability test would create unacceptable and unwarranted difficulties for law enforcement officers who must make quick decisions in the field, as well as for judges who would be required to determine after the fact whether the destruction of evidence in response to a knock on the door was reasonably foreseeable based on what the officers knew at the time.

Probable cause and time to secure a warrant. Some courts, in applying the police-created exigency doctrine, fault law enforcement officers if, after acquiring evidence that is sufficient to establish probable cause to search particular premises, the officers do not seek a warrant but instead knock on the door and seek either to speak with an occupant or to obtain consent to search.

This approach unjustifiably interferes with legitimate law enforcement strategies. There are many entirely proper reasons why police may not want to seek a search warrant as soon as the bare minimum of evidence needed to establish probable cause is acquired.

Standard or good investigative tactics. Finally, some lower court cases suggest that law enforcement officers may be found to have created or manufactured an exigency if the court concludes that the course of their investigation was "contrary to standard or good law enforcement practices (or to the policies or practices of their jurisdictions)." This approach fails to provide clear guidance for law enforcement officers and authorizes courts to make judgments on matters that are the province of those who are responsible for federal and state law enforcement agencies.

For these reasons, we conclude that the exigent circumstances rule applies when the police do not gain entry to premises by means of an actual or threatened violation of the Fourth Amendment. This holding provides ample protection for the privacy rights that the Amendment protects.

When law enforcement officers who are not armed with a warrant knock on a door, they do no more than any private citizen might do. And whether the person who knocks on the door and requests the opportunity to speak is a police officer or a private citizen, the occupant has no obligation to open the door or to speak. When the police knock on a door but the occupants choose not to respond or to speak, "the investigation will have reached a conspicuously low point," and the occupants "will have the kind of warning that even the most elaborate security system cannot provide." And even if an occupant chooses to open the door and speak with the officers, the occupant need not allow the officers to enter the premises and may refuse to answer any questions at any time.

Occupants who choose not to stand on their constitutional rights but instead elect to attempt to destroy evidence have only themselves to blame for the warrantless exigent-circumstances search that may ensue.

IV

We now apply our interpretation of the police-created exigency doctrine to the facts of this case.

We need not decide whether exigent circumstances existed in this case. Any warrantless entry based on exigent circumstances must, of course, be supported by a genuine exigency. The trial court and the Kentucky Court of Appeals found that there was a real exigency in this case, but the Kentucky Supreme Court expressed doubt on this issue, observing that there was "certainly some question as to whether the sound of persons moving [inside the apartment] was sufficient to establish that evidence was being destroyed." The Kentucky Supreme Court "assum[ed] for the purpose of argument that exigent circumstances existed," and it held that the police had impermissibly manufactured the exigency.

We, too, assume for purposes of argument that an exigency existed. We decide only the question on which the Kentucky Supreme Court ruled and on which we granted certiorari: Under what circumstances do police impermissibly create an exigency? Any question about whether an exigency actually existed is better addressed by the Kentucky Supreme Court on remand.

In this case, we see no evidence that the officers either violated the Fourth Amendment or threatened to do so prior to the point when they entered the apartment. This conduct was entirely consistent with the Fourth Amendment, and we are aware of no other evidence that might show that the officers either violated the Fourth Amendment or threatened to do so (for example, by announcing that they would break down the door if the occupants did not open the door voluntarily).

Like the court below, we assume for purposes of argument that an exigency existed. Because the officers in this case did not violate or threaten to violate the Fourth Amendment prior to the exigency, we hold that the exigency justified the warrantless search of the apartment.

Justice GINSBURG, dissenting.

The Court today arms the police with a way routinely to dishonor the Fourth Amendment's warrant requirement in drug cases. In lieu of presenting their evidence to a neutral magistrate, police officers may now knock, listen, then break the door down, nevermind that they had ample time to obtain a warrant. I dissent from the Court's reduction of the Fourth Amendment's force.

The Fourth Amendment guarantees to the people "[t]he right . . . to be secure in their . . . houses . . . against unreasonable searches and seizures." Warrants to search, the Amendment further instructs, shall issue only upon a showing of "probable cause" to believe criminal activity is afoot. These complementary provisions are designed to ensure that police will seek the authorization of a neutral magistrate before undertaking a search or seizure. Exceptions to the warrant requirement, this Court has explained, must be "few in number and carefully delineated," if the main rule is to remain hardy.

This case involves a principal exception to the warrant requirement, the exception applicable in "exigent circumstances." "[C]arefully delineated," the exception should govern only in genuine emergency situations. Circumstances qualify as "exigent" when there is an imminent risk of death or serious injury, or danger that evidence will be immediately destroyed, or that a suspect will escape. The question presented: May police, who could pause to gain the approval of a neutral magistrate, dispense with the need to get a warrant by themselves creating exigent circumstances? I would answer no, as did the Kentucky Supreme Court. The urgency must exist, I would rule, when the police come on the scene, not subsequent to their arrival, prompted by their own conduct.

That heavy burden has not been carried here. There was little risk that drug-related evidence would have been destroyed had the police delayed the search pending a magistrate's authorization. As the Court recognizes, "[p]ersons in possession of valuable drugs are unlikely to destroy them unless they fear discovery by the police." Nothing in the record shows that, prior to the knock at the apartment door, the occupants were apprehensive about police proximity.

In no quarter does the Fourth Amendment apply with greater force than in our homes, our most private space which, for centuries, has been regarded as "'entitled to special protection.'" Home intrusions, the Court has said, are indeed "the chief evil against which . . . the Fourth Amendment is directed." How "secure" do our homes remain if police, armed with no warrant, can pound on doors at will and, on hearing sounds indicative of things moving, forcibly enter and search for evidence of unlawful activity?

As above noted, to justify the police activity in this case, Kentucky invoked the once-guarded exception for emergencies "in which the delay necessary to obtain a warrant . . . threaten[s] 'the destruction of evidence.'" To fit within this exception, "police action literally must be [taken] 'now or never' to preserve the evidence of the crime."

Under an appropriately reined-in "emergency" or "exigent circumstances" exception, the result in this case should not be in doubt. The target of the investigation's entry into the building, and the smell of marijuana seeping under the apartment door into the hallway, the Kentucky Supreme Court rightly determined, gave the police "probable cause . . . sufficient . . . to obtain a warrant to search the . . . apartment." As that court observed, nothing made it impracticable for the police to post officers on the premises while proceeding to obtain a warrant authorizing their entry.

"If the officers in this case were excused from the constitutional duty of presenting their evidence to a magistrate, it is difficult to think of [any] case in which [a warrant] should be required." I agree, and would not allow an expedient knock to override the warrant requirement. Instead, I would accord that core requirement of the Fourth Amendment full respect. When possible, "a warrant must generally be secured," the Court acknowledges. There is every reason to conclude that securing a warrant was entirely feasible in this case, and no reason to contract the Fourth Amendment's dominion.

d.   Limits on Exigent Circumstances

But the Court has made clear that "exigent circumstances" requires a serious enough offense to justify a warrantless entry. In Welsh v. Wisconsin, 466 U.S. 740 (1984), the Court said that a warrantless arrest was not permissible to arrest a person for a nonjailable traffic offense. The Court, in an opinion by Justice Brennan, explained:

> "Even if one were to conclude that urgent circumstances might justify a forced entry without a warrant, no such emergency was present in this case. This method of law enforcement displays a shocking lack of all sense of proportion. Whether there is reasonable necessity for a search without waiting to obtain a warrant certainly depends somewhat upon the gravity of the offense thought to be in progress as well as the hazards of the method of attempting to reach it. . . . It is to me a shocking proposition that private homes, even quarters in a tenement, may be indiscriminately invaded at the discretion of any suspicious police officer engaged in following up offenses that involve no violence or threats of it. While I should be human enough to apply the letter of the law with some indulgence to officers acting to deal with threats or crimes of violence which endanger life or security, it is notable that few of the searches found by this Court to be unlawful dealt with that category of crime. . . . While the enterprise of parting fools from their money by the 'numbers' lottery is one that ought to be suppressed, I do not think its suppression is more important to society than the security of the people against unreasonable searches and seizures. When an officer undertakes to act as his own magistrate, he ought to be in a position to justify it by pointing to some real immediate and serious consequences if he postponed action to get a warrant."

We therefore conclude that the common-sense approach utilized by most lower courts is required by the Fourth Amendment prohibition on "unreasonable searches and seizures," and hold that an important factor to be considered when determining whether any exigency exists is the gravity of the underlying offense for which the arrest is being made. Moreover, although no exigency is created simply because there is probable cause to believe that a serious crime has been committed, application of the exigent-circumstances exception in the context of a home entry should rarely be sanctioned when there is probable cause to believe that only a minor offense, such as the kind at issue in this case, has been committed.

Over the last decade, the Court has dealt with the question of exigent circumstances in driving under the influence cases and whether there are inherently exigent circumstances because the body fairly quickly metabolizes alcohol. In Missouri v. McNeely, the Court rejected this argument. In reading this decision, compare how Justice Sotomayor and Chief Justice Roberts differ in how to determine if there are exigent circumstances.

MISSOURI v. McNEELY
133 S. Ct. 1552 (2013)

Justice Sotomayor announced the judgment of the Court and delivered the opinion of the Court with respect to Parts I, II-A, II-B, and IV, and an opinion with respect to Parts II-C and III, in which Justice Scalia, Justice Ginsburg, and Justice Kagan join.

In (1966), this Court upheld a warrantless blood test of an individual arrested for driving under the influence of alcohol because the officer "might reasonably have believed that he was confronted with an emergency, in which the delay necessary to obtain a warrant, under the circumstances, threatened the destruction of evidence." The question presented here is whether the natural metabolization of alcohol in the bloodstream presents a *per se* exigency that justifies an exception to the Fourth Amendment's warrant requirement for nonconsensual blood testing in all drunk-driving cases. We conclude that it does not, and we hold, consistent with general Fourth Amendment principles, that exigency in this context must be determined case by case based on the totality of the circumstances.

I

While on highway patrol at approximately 2:08 A.M., a Missouri police officer stopped Tyler McNeely's truck after observing it exceed the posted speed limit and repeatedly cross the centerline. The officer noticed several signs that McNeely was intoxicated, including McNeely's bloodshot eyes, his slurred speech, and the smell of alcohol on his breath. McNeely acknowledged to the officer that he had consumed "a couple of beers" at a bar, and he appeared unsteady on his feet when he exited the truck. After McNeely performed poorly on a battery of field-sobriety tests and declined to use a portable breath-test device to measure his blood alcohol concentration (BAC), the officer placed him under arrest.

The officer began to transport McNeely to the station house. But when McNeely indicated that he would again refuse to provide a breath sample, the officer changed course and took McNeely to a nearby hospital for blood testing. The officer did not attempt to secure a warrant. Upon arrival at the hospital, the officer asked McNeely whether he would consent to a blood test. Reading from a standard implied consent form, the officer explained to McNeely that under state law refusal to submit voluntarily to the test would lead to the immediate revocation of his driver's license for one year and could be used against him in a future prosecution. McNeely nonetheless refused. The officer then directed a hospital lab technician to take a blood sample, and the sample was secured at approximately 2:35 A.M. Subsequent laboratory testing measured McNeely's BAC at 0.154 percent, which was well above the legal limit of 0.08 percent.

McNeely was charged with driving while intoxicated (DWI). He moved to suppress the results of the blood test, arguing in relevant part that, under the circumstances, taking his blood for chemical testing without first obtaining a search warrant violated his rights under the Fourth Amendment. The trial court agreed. The Missouri Supreme Court affirmed.

II

A

Our cases have held that a warrantless search of the person is reasonable only if it falls within a recognized exception. That principle applies to the type of search at issue in this case, which involved a compelled physical intrusion beneath McNeely's skin and into his veins to obtain a sample of his blood for use as evidence in a criminal investigation. Such an invasion of bodily integrity implicates an individual's "most personal and deep-rooted expectations of privacy."

We first considered the Fourth Amendment restrictions on such searches in Schmerber v. California (1966), . . . where, as in this case, a blood sample was drawn from a defendant suspected of driving while under the influence of alcohol. Noting that "[s]earch warrants are ordinarily required for searches of dwellings," we reasoned that "absent an emergency, no less could be required where intrusions into the human body are concerned," even when the search was conducted following a lawful arrest.

As noted, the warrant requirement is subject to exceptions. "One well-recognized exception," and the one at issue in this case, "applies when the exigencies of the situation make the needs of law enforcement so compelling that a warrantless search is objectively reasonable under the Fourth Amendment."

To determine whether a law enforcement officer faced an emergency that justified acting without a warrant, this Court looks to the totality of circumstances.

Our decision in *Schmerber* applied this totality of the circumstances approach. In that case, the petitioner had suffered injuries in an automobile accident and was taken to the hospital. While he was there receiving treatment, a police officer arrested the petitioner for driving while under the influence of alcohol and ordered a blood test over his objection. After explaining that the warrant requirement applied generally to searches that intrude into the human body, we concluded that the warrantless blood test "in the present case" was nonetheless permissible because the officer "might reasonably have believed that he was confronted with an emergency, in which the delay necessary to obtain a warrant, under the circumstances, threatened 'the destruction of evidence.'"

B

The State properly recognizes that the reasonableness of a warrantless search under the exigency exception to the warrant requirement must be evaluated based on the totality of the circumstances. But the State nevertheless seeks a *per se* rule for blood testing in drunk-driving cases. The State contends that whenever an officer has probable cause to believe an individual has been driving under the influence of alcohol, exigent circumstances will necessarily exist because BAC evidence is inherently evanescent. As a result, the State claims that so long as the officer has probable cause and the blood test is conducted in a reasonable manner, it is categorically reasonable for law enforcement to obtain the blood sample without a warrant.

It is true that as a result of the human body's natural metabolic processes, the alcohol level in a person's blood begins to dissipate once the alcohol is fully absorbed and continues to decline until the alcohol is eliminated. Testimony before the trial court in this case indicated that the percentage of alcohol in an individual's blood typically decreases by approximately 0.015 percent to 0.02 percent per hour once the alcohol has been fully absorbed. Regardless of the exact elimination rate, it is sufficient for our purposes to note that because an individual's alcohol level gradually declines soon after he stops drinking, a significant delay in testing will negatively affect the probative value of the results. This fact was essential to our holding in *Schmerber*, as we recognized that, under the circumstances, further delay in order to secure a warrant after the time spent investigating the scene of the accident and transporting the injured suspect to the hospital to receive treatment would have threatened the destruction of evidence.

But it does not follow that we should depart from careful case-by-case assessment of exigency and adopt the categorical rule proposed by the State and its *amici*. In those drunk-driving investigations where police officers can reasonably obtain a warrant before a blood sample can be drawn without significantly undermining the efficacy of the search, the Fourth Amendment mandates that they do so. We do not doubt that some circumstances will make obtaining a warrant impractical such that the dissipation of alcohol from the bloodstream will support an exigency justifying a properly conducted warrantless blood test. That, however, is a reason to decide each case on its facts, as we did in *Schmerber*, not to accept the "considerable overgeneralization" that a *per se* rule would reflect.

The context of blood testing is different in critical respects from other destruction-of-evidence cases in which the police are truly confronted with a "'now or never'" situation. In contrast to, for example, circumstances in which the suspect has control over easily disposable evidence, BAC evidence from a drunk-driving suspect naturally dissipates over time in a gradual and relatively predictable manner. Moreover, because a police officer must typically transport a drunk-driving suspect to a medical facility and obtain the assistance of someone with appropriate medical training before conducting a blood test, some delay between the time of the arrest or accident and the time of the test is inevitable regardless of whether police officers are required to obtain a warrant.

The State's proposed *per se* rule also fails to account for advances in the 47 years since *Schmerber* was decided that allow for the more expeditious processing of warrant applications, particularly in contexts like drunk-driving investigations where the evidence offered to establish probable cause is simple. The Federal Rules of Criminal Procedure were amended in 1977 to permit federal magistrate judges to issue a warrant based on sworn testimony communicated by telephone. As amended, the law now allows a federal magistrate judge to consider "information communicated by telephone or other reliable electronic means." States have also innovated. Well over a majority of States allow police officers or prosecutors to apply for search warrants remotely through various means, including telephonic or radio communication, electronic communication such as e-mail, and video conferencing. And in addition to technology-based developments, jurisdictions have found other ways to streamline the warrant process, such as by using standard-form warrant applications for drunk-driving investigations.

We by no means claim that telecommunications innovations have, will, or should eliminate all delay from the warrant-application process. Warrants inevitably take some time for police officers or prosecutors to complete and for magistrate judges to review. Telephonic and electronic warrants may still require officers to follow time-consuming formalities designed to create an adequate record, such as preparing a duplicate warrant before calling the magistrate judge. See Fed. Rule Crim. Proc. 4.1(b)(3). And improvements in communications technology do not guarantee that a magistrate judge will be available when an officer needs a warrant after making a late-night arrest. But technological developments that enable police officers to secure warrants more quickly, and do so without undermining the neutral magistrate judge's essential role as a check on police discretion, are relevant to an assessment of exigency. That is particularly so in this context, where BAC evidence is lost gradually and relatively predictably.

Of course, there are important countervailing concerns. While experts can work backwards from the BAC at the time the sample was taken to determine the BAC at the time of the alleged offense, longer intervals may raise questions about the accuracy of the calculation. For that reason, exigent circumstances justifying a warrantless blood sample may arise in the regular course of law enforcement due to delays from the warrant application process. But adopting the State's *per se* approach would improperly ignore the current and future technological developments in warrant procedures, and might well diminish the incentive for jurisdictions "to pursue progressive approaches to warrant acquisition that preserve the protections afforded by the warrant while meeting the legitimate interests of law enforcement."

In short, while the natural dissipation of alcohol in the blood may support a finding of exigency in a specific case, as it did in *Schmerber*, it does not do so categorically. Whether a warrantless blood test of a drunk-driving suspect is reasonable must be determined case by case based on the totality of the circumstances.

C

In an opinion concurring in part and dissenting in part, The Chief Justice agrees that the State's proposed *per se* rule is overbroad because "[f]or exigent circumstances to justify a warrantless search . . . there must . . . be 'no time to secure a warrant.'" But The Chief Justice then goes on to suggest his own categorical rule under which a warrantless blood draw is permissible if the officer could not secure a warrant (or reasonably believed he could not secure a warrant) in the time it takes to transport the suspect to a hospital or similar facility and obtain medical assistance. Although we agree that delay inherent to the blood-testing process is relevant to evaluating exigency, we decline to substitute The Chief Justice's modified *per se* rule for our traditional totality of the circumstances analysis.

For one thing, making exigency completely dependent on the window of time between an arrest and a blood test produces odd consequences. Under The Chief Justice's rule, if a police officer serendipitously stops a suspect near an emergency room, the officer may conduct a nonconsensual warrantless blood draw even if all agree that a warrant could be obtained with very little delay under the circumstances (perhaps with far less delay than an average ride to the hospital in the jurisdiction). The rule would also distort law enforcement incentives. As with the State's *per se* rule, The Chief Justice's rule might discourage efforts to expedite the warrant process because it categorically authorizes warrantless blood draws so long as it takes more time to secure a warrant than to obtain medical assistance. On the flip side, making the requirement of independent judicial oversight turn exclusively on the amount of time that elapses between an arrest and BAC testing could induce police departments and individual officers to minimize testing delay to the detriment of other values.

III

The remaining arguments advanced in support of a *per se* exigency rule are unpersuasive.

The State and several of its *amici*, including the United States, express concern that a case-by-case approach to exigency will not provide adequate guidance to law enforcement officers deciding whether to conduct a blood test of a drunk-driving suspect without a warrant. The Chief Justice and the dissent also raise this concern. While the desire for a bright-line rule is understandable, the Fourth Amendment will not tolerate adoption of an overly broad categorical approach that would dilute the warrant requirement in a context where significant privacy interests are at stake. Moreover, a case-by-case approach is hardly unique within our Fourth Amendment jurisprudence. Numerous police actions are judged based on fact-intensive, totality-of-the-circumstances analyses rather than according to categorical rules, including in situations that are more likely to require police officers to make difficult split-second judgments.

"No one can seriously dispute the magnitude of the drunken driving problem or the States' interest in eradicating it." Certainly we do not. While some progress has been made, drunk driving continues to exact a terrible toll on our society. *See* NHTSA, Traffic Safety Facts, 2011 Data 1 (No. 811700, Dec. 2012) (reporting that 9,878 people were killed in alcohol-impaired driving crashes in 2011, an average of one fatality every 53 minutes).

But the general importance of the government's interest in this area does not justify departing from the warrant requirement without showing exigent circumstances that make securing a warrant impractical in a particular case. To the extent that the State and its *amici* contend that applying the traditional Fourth Amendment totality-of-the-circumstances analysis to determine whether an exigency justified a warrantless search will undermine the governmental interest in preventing and prosecuting drunk-driving offenses, we are not convinced.

As an initial matter, States have a broad range of legal tools to enforce their drunk-driving laws and to secure BAC evidence without undertaking warrantless nonconsensual blood draws. For example, all 50 States have adopted implied consent laws that require motorists, as a condition of operating a motor vehicle within the State, to consent to BAC testing if they are arrested or otherwise detained on suspicion of a drunk-driving offense. Such laws impose significant consequences when a motorist withdraws consent; typically the motorist's driver's license is immediately suspended or revoked, and most States allow the motorist's refusal to take a BAC test to be used as evidence against him in a subsequent criminal prosecution.

IV

The State argued before this Court that the fact that alcohol is naturally metabolized by the human body creates an exigent circumstance in every case. The State did not argue that there were exigent circumstances in this particular case because a warrant could not have been obtained within a reasonable amount of time. In his testimony before the trial court, the arresting officer did not identify any other factors that would suggest he faced an emergency or unusual delay in securing a warrant.

Here and in its own courts the State based its case on an insistence that a driver who declines to submit to testing after being arrested for driving under the influence of alcohol is always subject to a nonconsensual blood test without any precondition for a warrant. That is incorrect.

Because this case was argued on the broad proposition that drunk-driving cases present a *per se* exigency, the arguments and the record do not provide the Court with an adequate analytic framework for a detailed discussion of all the relevant factors that can be taken into account in determining the reasonableness of acting without a warrant. It suffices to say that the metabolization of alcohol in the bloodstream and the ensuing loss of evidence are among the factors that must be considered in deciding whether a warrant is required. No doubt, given the large number of arrests for this offense in different jurisdictions nationwide, cases will arise when anticipated delays in obtaining a warrant will justify a blood test without judicial authorization, for in every case the law must be concerned that evidence is being destroyed. But that inquiry ought not to be pursued here where the question is not properly before this Court.

We hold that in drunk-driving investigations, the natural dissipation of alcohol in the bloodstream does not constitute an exigency in every case sufficient to justify conducting a blood test without a warrant.

Chief Justice ROBERTS, with whom Justice BREYER and Justice ALITO join, concurring in part and dissenting in part.

A police officer reading this Court's opinion would have no idea — no idea — what the Fourth Amendment requires of him, once he decides to obtain a blood sample from a drunk driving suspect who has refused a breathalyzer test. I have no quarrel with the Court's "totality of the circumstances" approach as a general matter; that is what our cases require. But the circumstances in drunk driving cases are often typical, and the Court should be able to offer guidance on how police should handle cases like the one before us.

In my view, the proper rule is straightforward. Our cases establish that there is an exigent circumstances exception to the warrant requirement. That exception applies when there is a compelling need to prevent the imminent destruction of important evidence, and there is no time to obtain a warrant. The natural dissipation of alcohol in the bloodstream constitutes not only the imminent but ongoing destruction of critical evidence. That would qualify as an exigent circumstance, except that there may be time to secure a warrant before blood can be drawn. If there is, an officer must seek a warrant. If an officer could reasonably conclude that there is not, the exigent circumstances exception applies by its terms, and the blood may be drawn without a warrant.

The reasonable belief that critical evidence is being destroyed gives rise to a compelling need for blood draws in cases like this one. Here, in fact, there is not simply a belief that any alcohol in the bloodstream will be destroyed; it is a biological certainty. Alcohol dissipates from the bloodstream at a rate of 0.01 percent to 0.025 percent per hour. Evidence is literally disappearing by the minute. That certainty makes this case an even stronger one than usual for application of the exigent circumstances exception.

And that evidence is important. A serious and deadly crime is at issue. According to the Department of Transportation, in 2011, one person died every 53 minutes due to drinking and driving. No surprise then that drinking and driving is punished severely, including with jail time. McNeely, for instance, faces up to four years in prison.

Evidence of a driver's blood alcohol concentration (BAC) is crucial to obtain convictions for such crimes. All 50 States and the District of Columbia have laws providing that it is *per se* illegal to drive with a BAC of 0.08 percent or higher. Most States also have laws establishing additional penalties for drivers who drive with a "high BAC," often defined as 0.15 percent or above. BAC evidence clearly matters. And when drivers refuse breathalyzers, as McNeely did here, a blood draw becomes necessary to obtain that evidence.

The need to prevent the imminent destruction of BAC evidence is no less compelling because the incriminating alcohol dissipates over a limited period of time, rather than all at once. As noted, the concentration of alcohol can make a difference not only between guilt and innocence, but between different crimes and different degrees of punishment. The officer is unlikely to know precisely when the suspect consumed alcohol or how much; all he knows is that critical evidence is being steadily lost. Fire can spread gradually, but that does not lessen the need and right of the officers to respond immediately.

McNeely contends that there is no compelling need for a warrantless blood draw, because if there is some alcohol left in the blood by the time a warrant is obtained, the State can use math and science to work backwards and identify a defendant's BAC at the time he was driving. But that's not good enough. We have indicated that exigent circumstances justify warrantless entry when drugs are about to be flushed down the toilet. We have not said that, because there could well be drug paraphernalia elsewhere in the home, or because a defendant's co-conspirator might testify to the amount of drugs involved, the drugs themselves are not crucial and there is no compelling need for warrantless entry.

The same approach should govern here. There is a compelling need to search because alcohol — the nearly conclusive evidence of a serious crime — is dissipating from the bloodstream. The need is no less compelling because the police might be able to acquire second-best evidence some other way.

For exigent circumstances to justify a warrantless search, however, there must also be "no time to secure a warrant." As noted, the fact that alcohol dissipates gradually from the bloodstream does not diminish the compelling need for a search — critical evidence is still disappearing. But the fact that the dissipation persists for some time means that the police — although they may not be able to do anything about it right away—may still be able to respond to the ongoing destruction of evidence later on.

There might, therefore, be time to obtain a warrant in many cases. As the Court explains, police can often request warrants rather quickly these days. At least 30 States provide for electronic warrant applications. In many States, a police officer can call a judge, convey the necessary information, and be authorized to affix the judge's signature to a warrant.

In a case such as this, applying the exigent circumstances exception to the general warrant requirement of the Fourth Amendment seems straightforward: If there is time to secure a warrant before blood can be drawn, the police must seek one. If an officer could reasonably conclude that there is not sufficient time to seek and receive a warrant, or he applies for one but does not receive a response before blood can be drawn, a warrantless blood draw may ensue.

Justice THOMAS, dissenting.

This case requires the Court to decide whether the Fourth Amendment prohibits an officer from obtaining a blood sample without a warrant when there is probable cause to believe that a suspect has been driving under the influence of alcohol. Because the body's natural metabolization of alcohol inevitably destroys evidence of the crime, it constitutes an exigent circumstance. As a result, I would hold that a warrantless blood draw does not violate the Fourth Amendment.

Once police arrest a suspect for drunk driving, each passing minute eliminates probative evidence of the crime. The human liver eliminates alcohol from the bloodstream at a rate of approximately 0.015 percent to 0.020 percent per hour, with some heavy drinkers as high as 0.022 percent per hour, depending on, among other things, a person's sex, weight, body type, and drinking history.

The rapid destruction of evidence acknowledged by the parties, the majority, and *Schmerber*'s exigency determination occurs in *every* situation where police have probable cause to arrest a drunk driver. In turn, that destruction of evidence implicates the exigent-circumstances doctrine.

A hypothetical involving classic exigent circumstances further illustrates the point. Officers are watching a warehouse and observe a worker carrying bundles from the warehouse to a large bonfire and throwing them into the blaze. The officers have probable cause to believe the bundles contain marijuana. Because there is only one person carrying the bundles, the officers believe it will take hours to completely destroy the drugs. During that time the officers likely could obtain a warrant. But it is clear that the officers need not sit idly by and watch the destruction of evidence while they wait for a warrant. The fact that it will take time for the evidence to be destroyed and that *some* evidence may remain by the time the officers secure a warrant are not relevant to the exigency. However, the ever-diminishing quantity of drugs may have an impact on the severity of the crime and the length of the sentence. Conducting a warrantless search of the warehouse in this situation would be entirely reasonable.

The same obtains in the drunk-driving context. Just because it will take time for the evidence to be completely destroyed does not mean there is no exigency.

In light of Missouri v. McNeely, may a state make it a crime for a person to refuse to consent to a blood or breath test? The Court held that it is permissible for the state to require a person to submit to a breath test, but not a blood test.

BIRCHFIELD v. NORTH DAKOTA
136 S. Ct. 2160 (2016)

Justice ALITO delivered the opinion of the Court.

Drunk drivers take a grisly toll on the Nation's roads, claiming thousands of lives, injuring many more victims, and inflicting billions of dollars in property damage every year. To fight this problem, all States have laws that prohibit motorists from driving with a blood alcohol concentration (BAC) that exceeds a specified level. But determining whether a driver's BAC is over the legal limit requires a test, and many drivers stopped on suspicion of drunk driving would not submit to testing if given the option. So every State also has long had what are termed "implied consent laws." These laws impose penalties on motorists who refuse to undergo testing when there is sufficient reason to believe they are violating the State's drunk-driving laws.

In the past, the typical penalty for noncompliance was suspension or revocation of the motorist's license. The cases now before us involve laws that go beyond that and make it a crime for a motorist to refuse to be tested after being lawfully arrested for driving while impaired. The question presented is whether such laws violate the Fourth Amendment's prohibition against unreasonable searches.

I

The most common and economical method of calculating BAC is by means of a machine that measures the amount of alcohol in a person's breath. Today, such devices can detect the presence of alcohol more quickly and accurately than before, typically using infrared technology rather than a chemical reaction. And in practice all breath testing machines used for evidentiary purposes must be approved by the National Highway Traffic Safety Administration. These machines are generally regarded as very reliable because the federal standards require that the devices produce accurate and reproducible test results at a variety of BAC levels, from the very low to the very high.

Measurement of BAC based on a breath test requires the cooperation of the person being tested. The subject must take a deep breath and exhale through a mouthpiece that connects to the machine. Typically the test subject must blow air into the device "'for a period of several seconds'" to produce an adequate breath sample, and the process is sometimes repeated so that analysts can compare multiple samples to ensure the device's accuracy. Modern breath test machines are designed to capture so-called "deep lung" or alveolar air. Air from the alveolar region of the lungs provides the best basis for determining the test subject's BAC, for it is in that part of the lungs that alcohol vapor and other gases are exchanged between blood and breath.

When a standard infrared device is used, the whole process takes only a few minutes from start to finish. Most evidentiary breath tests do not occur next to the vehicle, at the side of the road, but in a police station, where the controlled environment is especially conducive to reliable testing, or in some cases in the officer's patrol vehicle or in special mobile testing facilities.

Because the cooperation of the test subject is necessary when a breath test is administered and highly preferable when a blood sample is taken, the enactment of laws defining intoxication based on BAC made it necessary for States to find a way of securing such cooperation. So-called "implied consent" laws were enacted to achieve this result. They provided that cooperation with BAC testing was a condition of the privilege of driving on state roads and that the privilege would be rescinded if a suspected drunk driver refused to honor that condition. Suspension or revocation of the motorist's driver's license remains the standard legal consequence of refusal. In addition, evidence of the motorist's refusal is admitted as evidence of likely intoxication in a drunk-driving prosecution.

In recent decades, the States and the Federal Government have toughened drunk-driving laws, and those efforts have corresponded to a dramatic decrease in alcohol-related fatalities. As of the early 1980's, the number of annual fatalities averaged 25,000; by 2014, the most recent year for which statistics are available, the number had fallen to below 10,000. One legal change has been further lowering the BAC standard from 0.10% to 0.08%. In addition, many States now impose increased penalties for recidivists and for drivers with a BAC level that exceeds a higher threshold.

Many other States have taken a similar approach, but this new structure threatened to undermine the effectiveness of implied consent laws. If the penalty for driving with a greatly elevated BAC or for repeat violations exceeds the penalty for refusing to submit to testing, motorists who fear conviction for the more severely punished offenses have an incentive to reject testing. And in some States, the refusal rate is high. On average, over one-fifth of all drivers asked to submit to BAC testing in 2011 refused to do so.

To combat the problem of test refusal, some States have begun to enact laws making it a crime to refuse to undergo testing.

II

Petitioner Danny Birchfield accidentally drove his car off a North Dakota highway on October 10, 2013. A state trooper arrived and watched as Birchfield unsuccessfully tried to drive back out of the ditch in which his car was stuck. The trooper approached, caught a strong whiff of alcohol, and saw that Birchfield's eyes were bloodshot and watery. Birchfield spoke in slurred speech and struggled to stay steady on his feet. At the trooper's request, Birchfield agreed to take several field sobriety tests and performed poorly on each. He had trouble reciting sections of the alphabet and counting backwards in compliance with the trooper's directions.

The state trooper arrested Birchfield for driving while impaired, gave the usual *Miranda* warnings, again advised him of his obligation under North Dakota law to undergo BAC testing, and informed him, as state law requires that refusing to take the test would expose him to criminal penalties. Although faced with the prospect of prosecution under this law, Birchfield refused to let his blood be drawn.

On August 5, 2012, Minnesota police received a report of a problem at a South St. Paul boat launch. Three apparently intoxicated men had gotten their truck stuck in the river while attempting to pull their boat out of the water. When police arrived, witnesses informed them that a man in underwear had been driving the truck. That man proved to be William Robert Bernard, Jr., petitioner in the second of these cases. Bernard admitted that he had been drinking but denied driving the truck (though he was holding its keys) and refused to perform any field sobriety tests. After noting that Bernard's breath smelled of alcohol and that his eyes were bloodshot and watery, officers arrested Bernard for driving while impaired.

Back at the police station, officers read Bernard Minnesota's implied consent advisory, which like North Dakota's informs motorists that it is a crime under state law to refuse to submit to a legally required BAC test. The officers asked Bernard to take a breath test. After he refused, prosecutors charged him with test refusal in the first degree because he had four prior impaired-driving convictions.

A police officer spotted our third petitioner, Steve Michael Beylund, driving the streets of Bowman, North Dakota, on the night of August 10, 2013. The officer saw Beylund try unsuccessfully to turn into a driveway. In the process, Beylund's car nearly hit a stop sign before coming to a stop still partly on the public road. The officer walked up to the car and saw that Beylund had an empty wine glass in the center console next to him. Noticing that Beylund also smelled of alcohol, the officer asked him to step out of the car. As Beylund did so, he struggled to keep his balance. The officer arrested Beylund for driving while impaired and took him to a nearby hospital. There he read Beylund North Dakota's implied consent advisory, informing him that test refusal in these circumstances is itself a crime. Unlike the other two petitioners in these cases, Beylund agreed to have his blood drawn and analyzed. A nurse took a blood sample, which revealed a blood alcohol concentration of 0.250%, more than three times the legal limit.

Given the test results, Beylund's driver's license was suspended for two years after an administrative hearing. Beylund appealed the hearing officer's decision to a North Dakota District Court, principally arguing that his consent to the blood test was coerced by the officer's warning that refusing to consent would itself be a crime.

III

As our summary of the facts and proceedings in these three cases reveals, the cases differ in some respects. Petitioners Birchfield and Beylund were told that they were obligated to submit to a blood test, whereas petitioner Bernard was informed that a breath test was required.

Despite these differences, success for all three petitioners depends on the proposition that the criminal law ordinarily may not compel a motorist to submit to the taking of a blood sample or to a breath test unless a warrant authorizing such testing is issued by a magistrate. If, on the other hand, such warrantless searches comport with the Fourth Amendment, it follows that a State may criminalize the refusal to comply with a demand to submit to the required testing, just as a State may make it a crime for a person to obstruct the execution of a valid search warrant.

IV

The [Fourth] Amendment prohibits "unreasonable searches," and our cases establish that the taking of a blood sample or the administration of a breath test is a search. The question, then, is whether the warrantless searches at issue here were reasonable.

In the three cases now before us, the drivers were searched or told that they were required to submit to a search after being placed under arrest for drunk driving. We therefore consider how the search-incident-to-arrest doctrine applies to breath and blood tests incident to such arrests.

V

We begin by considering the impact of breath and blood tests on individual privacy interests, and we will discuss each type of test in turn.

1

Years ago we said that breath tests do not "implicat[e] significant privacy concerns." That remains so today. First, the physical intrusion is almost negligible. Breath tests "do not require piercing the skin" and entail "a minimum of inconvenience." As Minnesota describes its version of the breath test, the process requires the arrestee to blow continuously for 4 to 15 seconds into a straw-like mouthpiece that is connected by a tube to the test machine. The effort is no more demanding than blowing up a party balloon.

Petitioner Bernard argues, however, that the process is nevertheless a significant intrusion because the arrestee must insert the mouthpiece of the machine into his or her mouth. But there is nothing painful or strange about this requirement. The use of a straw to drink beverages is a common practice and one to which few object. Nor, contrary to Bernard, is the test a significant intrusion because it does not capture an ordinary exhalation of the kind that routinely is exposed to the public but instead requires a sample of alveolar (deep lung) air. Humans have never been known to assert a possessory interest in or any emotional attachment to *any* of the air in their lungs. The air that humans exhale is not part of their bodies. Exhalation is a natural process — indeed, one that is necessary for life. Humans cannot hold their breath for more than a few minutes, and all the air that is breathed into a breath analyzing machine, including deep lung air, sooner or later would be exhaled even without the test.

Second, breath tests are capable of revealing only one bit of information, the amount of alcohol in the subject's breath. A breath test results in a BAC reading on a machine, nothing more. No sample of anything is left in the possession of the police.

Finally, participation in a breath test is not an experience that is likely to cause any great enhancement in the embarrassment that is inherent in any arrest. The act of blowing into a straw is not inherently embarrassing, nor are evidentiary breath tests administered in a manner that causes embarrassment. Again, such tests are normally administered in private at a police station, in a patrol car, or in a mobile testing facility, out of public view. Moreover, once placed under arrest, the individual's expectation of privacy is necessarily diminished.

For all these reasons, a breath test does not "implicat[e] significant privacy concerns."

2

Blood tests are a different matter. They "require piercing the skin" and extract a part of the subject's body. And while humans exhale air from their lungs many times per minute, humans do not continually shed blood. It is true, of course, that people voluntarily submit to the taking of blood samples as part of a physical examination, and the process involves little pain or risk. Nevertheless, for many, the process is not one they relish. It is significantly more intrusive than blowing into a tube. In addition, a blood test, unlike a breath test, places in the hands of law enforcement authorities a sample that can be preserved and from which it is possible to extract information beyond a simple BAC reading. Even if the law enforcement agency is precluded from testing the blood for any purpose other than to measure BAC, the potential remains and may result in anxiety for the person tested.

c

Having assessed the impact of breath and blood testing on privacy interests, we now look to the States' asserted need to obtain BAC readings for persons arrested for drunk driving. The States and the Federal Government have a "paramount interest . . . in preserving the safety of . . . public highways." Although the number of deaths and injuries caused by motor vehicle accidents has declined over the years, the statistics are still staggering. Alcohol consumption is a leading cause of traffic fatalities and injuries. During the past decade, annual fatalities in drunk-driving accidents ranged from 13,582 deaths in 2005 to 9,865 deaths in 2011. The most recent data report a total of 9,967 such fatalities in 2014—on average, one death every 53 minutes.

Justice Sotomayor's partial dissent suggests that States' interests in fighting drunk driving are satisfied once suspected drunk drivers are arrested, since such arrests take intoxicated drivers off the roads where they might do harm. But of course States are not solely concerned with neutralizing the threat posed by a drunk driver who has already gotten behind the wheel. They also have a compelling interest in creating effective "deterrent[s] to drunken driving" so such individuals make responsible decisions and do not become a threat to others in the first place.

Petitioners and Justice Sotomayor next suggest that requiring a warrant for BAC testing in every case in which a motorist is arrested for drunk driving would not impose any great burden on the police or the courts. But of course the same argument could be made about searching through objects found on the arrestee's possession, which our cases permit even in the absence of a warrant. What about the cigarette package in *Robinson*? What if a motorist arrested for drunk driving has a flask in his pocket? What if a motorist arrested for driving while under the influence of marijuana has what appears to be a marijuana cigarette on his person? What about an unmarked bottle of pills?

If a search warrant were required for every search incident to arrest that does not involve exigent circumstances, the courts would be swamped. And even if we arbitrarily singled out BAC tests incident to arrest for this special treatment, as it appears the dissent would do, the impact on the courts would be considerable. The number of arrests every year for driving under the influence is enormous—more than 1.1 million in 2014. Particularly in sparsely populated areas, it would be no small task for courts to field a large new influx of warrant applications that could come on any day of the year and at any hour. In many jurisdictions, judicial officers have the authority to issue warrants only within their own districts, and in rural areas, some districts may have only a small number of judicial officers.

Having assessed the effect of BAC tests on privacy interests and the need for such tests, we conclude that the Fourth Amendment permits warrantless breath tests incident to arrests for drunk driving. The impact of breath tests on privacy is slight, and the need for BAC testing is great.

We reach a different conclusion with respect to blood tests. Blood tests are significantly more intrusive, and their reasonableness must be judged in light of the availability of the less invasive alternative of a breath test. Respondents have offered no satisfactory justification for demanding the more intrusive alternative without a warrant.

Neither respondents nor their *amici* dispute the effectiveness of breath tests in measuring BAC. Breath tests have been in common use for many years. Their results are admissible in court and are widely credited by juries, and respondents do not dispute their accuracy or utility. What, then, is the justification for warrantless blood tests?

One advantage of blood tests is their ability to detect not just alcohol but also other substances that can impair a driver's ability to operate a car safely. A breath test cannot do this, but police have other measures at their disposal when they have reason to believe that a motorist may be under the influence of some other substance (for example, if a breath test indicates that a clearly impaired motorist has little if any alcohol in his blood). Nothing prevents the police from seeking a warrant for a blood test when there is sufficient time to do so in the particular circumstances or from relying on the exigent circumstances exception to the warrant requirement when there is not.

A blood test also requires less driver participation than a breath test. In order for a technician to take a blood sample, all that is needed is for the subject to remain still, either voluntarily or by being immobilized. Thus, it is possible to extract a blood sample from a subject who forcibly resists, but many States reasonably prefer not to take this step.

It is true that a blood test, unlike a breath test, may be administered to a person who is unconscious (perhaps as a result of a crash) or who is unable to do what is needed to take a breath test due to profound intoxication or injuries. But we have no reason to believe that such situations are common in drunk-driving arrests, and when they arise, the police may apply for a warrant if need be.

A breath test may also be ineffective if an arrestee deliberately attempts to prevent an accurate reading by failing to blow into the tube for the requisite length of time or with the necessary force. But courts have held that such conduct qualifies as a refusal to undergo testing, and it may be prosecuted as such. And again, a warrant for a blood test may be sought.

Because breath tests are significantly less intrusive than blood tests and in most cases amply serve law enforcement interests, we conclude that a breath test, but not a blood test, may be administered as a search incident to a lawful arrest for drunk driving. As in all cases involving reasonable searches incident to arrest, a warrant is not needed in this situation.

Justice SOTOMAYOR, with whom Justice GINSBURG joins, concurring in part and dissenting in part.

The Court today considers three consolidated cases. I join the majority's disposition of Birchfield v. North Dakota, and Beylund v. Levi in which the Court holds that the search-incident-to-arrest exception to the Fourth Amendment's warrant requirement does not permit warrantless blood tests. But I dissent from the Court's disposition of Bernard v. Minnesota, in which the Court holds that the same exception permits warrantless breath tests. Because no governmental interest categorically makes it impractical for an officer to obtain a warrant before measuring a driver's alcohol level, the Fourth Amendment prohibits such searches without a warrant, unless exigent circumstances exist in a particular case.

The States do not challenge *McNeely*'s holding that a categorical exigency exception is not necessary to accommodate the governmental interests associated with the dissipation of blood alcohol after drunk-driving arrests. They instead seek to exempt breath tests from the warrant requirement categorically under the search-incident-to-arrest doctrine. The majority agrees. Both are wrong.

As discussed above, regardless of the exception a State requests, the Court's traditional framework asks whether, in light of the privacy interest at stake, a legitimate governmental interest ever requires conducting breath searches without a warrant — and, if so, whether that governmental interest is adequately addressed by a case-by-case exception or requires a categorical exception to the warrant requirement. That framework directs the conclusion that a categorical search-incident-to-arrest rule for breath tests is unnecessary to address the States' governmental interests in combating drunk driving.

Beginning with the governmental interests, there can be no dispute that States must have tools to combat drunk driving. But neither the States nor the Court has demonstrated that "obtaining a warrant" in cases not already covered by the exigent circumstances exception "is likely to frustrate the governmental purpose[s] behind [this] search."

First, the Court cites the governmental interest in protecting the public from drunk drivers. But it is critical to note that once a person is stopped for drunk driving and arrested, he no longer poses an immediate threat to the public. Because the person is already in custody prior to the administration of the breath test, there can be no serious claim that the time it takes to obtain a warrant would increase the danger that drunk driver poses to fellow citizens.

Second, the Court cites the governmental interest in preventing the destruction or loss of evidence. But neither the Court nor the States identify any practical reasons why obtaining a warrant after making an arrest and before conducting a breath test compromises the quality of the evidence obtained. To the contrary, the delays inherent in administering reliable breath tests generally provide ample time to obtain a warrant.

There is a common misconception that breath tests are conducted roadside, immediately after a driver is arrested. While some preliminary testing is conducted roadside, reliability concerns with roadside tests confine their use in most circumstances to establishing probable cause for an arrest. The standard evidentiary breath test is conducted after a motorist is arrested and transported to a police station, governmental building, or mobile testing facility where officers can access reliable, evidence-grade breath testing machinery. Transporting the motorist to the equipment site is not the only potential delay in the process, however. Officers must also observe the subject for 15 to 20 minutes to ensure that "residual mouth alcohol," which can inflate results and expose the test to an evidentiary challenge at trial, has dissipated and that the subject has not inserted any food or drink into his mouth. In many States, including Minnesota, officers must then give the motorist a window of time within which to contact an attorney before administering a test. Finally, if a breath test machine is not already active, the police officer must set it up. North Dakota's Intoxilyzer 8000 machine can take as long as 30 minutes to "warm-up."

Because of these necessary steps, the standard breath test is conducted well after an arrest is effectuated. The Minnesota Court of Appeals has explained that nearly all breath tests "involve a time lag of 45 minutes to two hours." Both North Dakota and Minnesota give police a 2-hour period from the time the motorist was pulled over within which to administer a breath test.

During this built-in window, police can seek warrants. That is particularly true in light of "advances" in technology that now permit "the more expeditious processing of warrant applications." Moreover, counsel for North Dakota explained at oral argument that the State uses a typical "on-call" system in which some judges are available even during off-duty times.

Where "an officer can . . . secure a warrant while" the motorist is being transported and the test is being prepared, this Court has said that "there would be no plausible justification for an exception to the warrant requirement." Neither the Court nor the States provide any evidence to suggest that, in the normal course of affairs, obtaining a warrant and conducting a breath test will exceed the allotted 2-hour window.

Third, the Court and the States cite a governmental interest in minimizing the costs of gathering evidence of drunk driving. But neither has demonstrated that requiring police to obtain warrants for breath tests would impose a sufficiently significant burden on state resources to justify the elimination of the Fourth Amendment's warrant requirement.

Assuming that North Dakota police officers do not obtain warrants for any drunk-driving arrests today, and assuming that they would need to obtain a warrant for every drunk-driving arrest tomorrow, each of the State's 82 judges and magistrate judges would need to issue fewer than two extra warrants per week. Minnesota has nearly the same ratio of judges to drunk-driving arrests, and so would face roughly the same burden. These back-of-the-envelope numbers suggest that the burden of obtaining a warrant before conducting a breath test would be small in both States.

But even these numbers *overstate* the burden by a significant degree. States only need to obtain warrants for drivers who refuse testing and a significant majority of drivers voluntarily consent to breath tests, even in States without criminal penalties for refusal. In North Dakota, only 21% of people refuse breath tests and in Minnesota, only 12% refuse. Each of their judges and magistrate judges would need to issue fewer than one extra warrant a week. That bears repeating: The Court finds a categorical exception to the warrant requirement because each of a State's judges and magistrate judges would need to issue less than one extra warrant a week.

Fourth, the Court alludes to the need to collect evidence conveniently. But mere convenience in investigating drunk driving cannot itself justify an exception to the warrant requirement. This Court has never said that mere convenience in gathering evidence justifies an exception to the warrant requirement.

After evaluating the governmental and privacy interests at stake here, the final step is to determine whether any situations in which warrants would interfere with the States' legitimate governmental interests should be accommodated through a case-by-case or categorical exception to the warrant requirement.

As shown, because there are so many circumstances in which obtaining a warrant will not delay the administration of a breath test or otherwise compromise any governmental interest cited by the States, it should be clear that allowing a categorical exception to the warrant requirement is a "considerable overgeneralization" here.

Here, the Court lacks even the pretense of attempting to situate breath searches within the narrow and weighty law enforcement needs that have historically justified the limited use of warrantless searches. I fear that if the Court continues down this road, the Fourth Amendment's warrant requirement will become nothing more than a suggestion.

Justice THOMAS, concurring in judgment in part and dissenting in part.

The compromise the Court reaches today is not a good one. By deciding that some (but not all) warrantless tests revealing the blood alcohol concentration (BAC) of an arrested driver are constitutional, the Court contorts the search-incident-to-arrest exception to the Fourth Amendment's warrant requirement. The far simpler answer to the question presented is the one rejected in (2013). Here, the tests revealing the BAC of a driver suspected of driving drunk are constitutional under the exigent-circumstances exception to the warrant requirement.

I

Today's decision chips away at a well-established exception to the warrant requirement. Until recently, we have admonished that "[a] police officer's determination as to how and where to search the person of a suspect whom he has arrested is necessarily a quick *ad hoc* judgment which the Fourth Amendment does not require to be broken down in each instance into an analysis of each step in the search." Under our precedents, a search incident to lawful arrest "require[d] no additional justification."

The Court justifies its result — an arbitrary line in the sand between blood and breath tests — by balancing the invasiveness of the particular type of search against the government's reasons for the search. Such case-by-case balancing is bad for the People, who "through ratification, have already weighed the policy tradeoffs that constitutional rights entail." It is also bad for law enforcement officers, who depend on predictable rules to do their job, as Members of this Court have exhorted in the past.

Today's application of the search-incident-to-arrest exception is bound to cause confusion in the lower courts. The Court's choice to allow some (but not all) BAC searches is undeniably appealing, for it both reins in the pernicious problem of drunk driving and also purports to preserve some Fourth Amendment protections. But that compromise has little support under this Court's existing precedents.

The better (and far simpler) way to resolve these cases is by applying the *per se* rule that I proposed in *McNeely*. Under that approach, both warrantless breath and blood tests are constitutional because "the natural metabolization of [BAC] creates an exigency once police have probable cause to believe the driver is drunk. It naturally follows that police may conduct a search in these circumstances."

The Court in *McNeely* rejected that bright-line rule and instead adopted a totality-of-the-circumstances test examining whether the facts of a particular case presented exigent circumstances justifying a warrantless search. The Court ruled that "the natural dissipation of alcohol in the blood" could not "categorically" create an "exigency" in every case. The destruction of "BAC evidence from a drunk-driving suspect" that "naturally dissipates over time in a gradual and relatively predictable manner," according to the Court, was qualitatively different from the destruction of evidence in "circumstances in which the suspect has control over easily disposable evidence."

The Court was wrong in *McNeely*, and today's compromise is perhaps an inevitable consequence of that error. Both searches contemplated by the state laws at issue in these cases would be constitutional under the exigent-circumstances exception to the warrant requirement. I respectfully concur in the judgment in part and dissent in part.

2.   Plain View

If officers are lawfully present in a place, they may use all of their senses. For example, imagine that an officer has a warrant to search a home for child pornography. After lawfully entering the home, the officer sees illegal drugs on a table. They may be seized and used as evidence. In fact, the same is true if the officer is lawfully in the place for any reason.

Coolidge v. New Hampshire provides the classic articulation of the plain view exception to the warrant requirement.

Justice Stewart wrote for the Court.

COOLIDGE v. NEW HAMPSHIRE, 403 U.S. 443 (1971): It is well established that under certain circumstances the police may seize evidence in plain view without a warrant. But it is important to keep in mind that, in the vast majority of cases, any evidence seized by the police will be in plain view, at least at the moment of seizure. The problem with the "plain view" doctrine has been to identify the circumstances in which plain view has legal significance rather than being simply the normal concomitant of any search, legal or illegal.

An example of the applicability of the "plain view" doctrine is the situation in which the police have a warrant to search a given area for specified objects, and in the course of the search come across some other article of incriminating character. Where the initial intrusion that brings the police within plain view of such an article is supported, not by a warrant, but by one of the recognized exceptions to the warrant requirement, the seizure is also legitimate. Thus the police may inadvertently come across evidence while in "hot pursuit" of a fleeing suspect. And an object that comes into view during a search incident to arrest that is appropriately limited in scope under existing law may be seized without a warrant. Finally, the "plain view" doctrine has been applied where a police officer is not searching for evidence against the accused, but nonetheless inadvertently comes across an incriminating object.

What the "plain view" cases have in common is that the police officer in each of them had a prior justification for an intrusion in the course of which he came inadvertently across a piece of evidence incriminating the accused. The doctrine serves to supplement the prior justification—whether it be a warrant for another object, hot pursuit, search incident to lawful arrest, or some other legitimate reason for being present unconnected with a search directed against the accused—and permits the warrantless seizure. Of course, the extension of the original justification is legitimate only where it is immediately apparent to the police that they have evidence before them; the "plain view" doctrine may not be used to extend a general exploratory search from one object to another until something incriminating at last emerges.

The rationale for the "plain view" exception is evident if we keep in mind the two distinct constitutional protections served by the warrant requirement. First, the magistrate's scrutiny is intended to eliminate altogether searches not based on probable cause. The premise here is that any intrusion in the way of search or seizure is an evil, so that no intrusion at all is justified without a careful prior determination of necessity. The second, distinct objective is that those searches deemed necessary should be as limited as possible. Here, the specific evil is the "general warrant" abhorred by the colonists, and the problem is not that of intrusion per se, but of a general, exploratory rummaging in a person's belongings. The warrant accomplishes this second objective by requiring a "particular description" of the things to be seized.

The "plain view" doctrine is not in conflict with the first objective because plain view does not occur until a search is in progress. In each case, this initial intrusion is justified by a warrant or by an exception such as "hot pursuit" or search incident to a lawful arrest, or by an extraneous valid reason for the officer's presence. And, given the initial intrusion, the seizure of an object in plain view is consistent with the second objective, since it does not convert the search into a general or exploratory one. As against the minor peril to Fourth Amendment protections, there is a major gain in effective law enforcement. Where, once an otherwise lawful search is in progress, the police inadvertently come upon a piece of evidence, it would often be a needless inconvenience, and sometimes dangerous — to the evidence or to the police themselves — to require them to ignore it until they have obtained a warrant particularly describing it.

The limits on the doctrine are implicit in the statement of its rationale. The first of these is that plain view alone is never enough to justify the warrantless seizure of evidence. This is simply a corollary of the familiar principle discussed above, that no amount of probable cause can justify a warrantless search or seizure absent "exigent circumstances." Incontrovertible testimony of the senses that an incriminating object is on premises belonging to a criminal suspect may establish the fullest possible measure of probable cause. But even where the object is contraband, this Court has repeatedly stated and enforced the basic rule that the police may not enter and make a warrantless seizure.

In Horton v. California, 496 U.S. 128 (1990), the Court said that "even though inadvertence is a characteristic of most legitimate 'plain-view' seizures, it is not a necessary condition."

However, it must be immediately apparent that the seized item is illegal. For example, in Arizona v. Hicks, 480 U.S. 321 (1987), police entered an apartment without a warrant to investigate shots that had been fired and saw stereo equipment that they thought might be stolen merchandise. They did not have probable cause to support this. An officer moved the equipment, found a product identification number, and radioed it in to headquarters. It was found that the merchandise was stolen.

The Supreme Court held that the plain view doctrine did not apply here. The Court found that moving the stereo equipment was a search:

> Officer Nelson's moving of the equipment, however, did constitute a "search" separate and apart from the search for the shooter, victims, and weapons that was the lawful objective of his entry into the apartment. Merely inspecting those parts of the turntable that came into view during the latter search would not have constituted an independent search, because it would have produced no additional invasion of respondent's privacy interest. But taking action, unrelated to the objectives of the authorized intrusion, which exposed to view concealed portions of the apartment or its contents, did produce a new invasion of respondent's privacy unjustified by the exigent circumstance that validated the entry. This is why the distinction between "looking" at a suspicious object in plain view and "moving" it even a few inches is much more than trivial for purposes of the Fourth Amendment. It matters not that the search uncovered nothing of any great personal value

to respondent—serial numbers rather than (what might conceivably have been hidden behind or under the equipment) letters or photographs. A search is a search, even if it happens to disclose nothing but the bottom of a turntable.

The Court explained that since it was not apparent that the item was contraband, the officers needed to have probable cause for their search. The Court stated:

> We now hold that probable cause is required. To say otherwise would be to cut the "plain view" doctrine loose from its theoretical and practical moorings. The theory of that doctrine consists of extending to nonpublic places such as the home, where searches and seizures without a warrant are presumptively unreasonable, the police's longstanding authority to make warrantless seizures in public places of such objects as weapons and contraband. And the practical justification for that extension is the desirability of sparing police, whose viewing of the object in the course of a lawful search is as legitimate as it would have been in a public place, the inconvenience and the risk—to themselves or to preservation of the evidence—of going to obtain a warrant. Dispensing with the need for a warrant is worlds apart from permitting a lesser standard of cause for the seizure than a warrant would require, i.e., the standard of probable cause. No reason is apparent why an object should routinely be seizable on lesser grounds, during an unrelated search and seizure, than would have been needed to obtain a warrant for that same object if it had been known to be on the premises.

It must be remembered that the police are allowed to use all of their senses when they are lawfully present. Usually, sight is the most important, but it could be "plain smell" or "plain touch" that is used by the officer. Minnesota v. Dickerson involved the latter.

MINNESOTA v. DICKERSON
508 U.S. 366 (1993)

Justice WHITE delivered the opinion of the Court.

In this case, we consider whether the Fourth Amendment permits the seizure of contraband detected through a police officer's sense of touch during a protective patdown search.

I

On the evening of November 9, 1989, two Minneapolis police officers were patrolling an area on the city's north side in a marked squad car. At about 8:15 P.M., one of the officers observed respondent leaving a 12-unit apartment building on Morgan Avenue North. The officer, having previously responded to complaints of drug sales in the building's hallways and having executed several search warrants on the premises, considered the building to be a notorious "crack house." According to testimony credited by the trial court, respondent began walking toward the police but, upon spotting the squad car and making eye contact with one of the officers, abruptly halted and began walking in the opposite direction. His suspicion aroused, this officer watched as respondent turned and entered an alley on the other side of the apartment building. Based upon respondent's seemingly evasive actions and the fact that he had just left a building known for cocaine traffic, the officers decided to stop respondent and investigate further.

The officers pulled their squad car into the alley and ordered respondent to stop and submit to a patdown search. The search revealed no weapons, but the officer conducting the search did take an interest in a small lump in respondent's nylon jacket. The officer later testified: "[A]s I pat-searched the front of his body, I felt a lump, a small lump, in the front pocket. I examined it with my fingers and it slid and it felt to be a lump of crack cocaine in cellophane."

The officer then reached into respondent's pocket and retrieved a small plastic bag containing one fifth of one gram of crack cocaine. Respondent was arrested and charged in Hennepin County District Court with possession of a controlled substance.

Before trial, respondent moved to suppress the cocaine. The trial court first concluded that the officers were justified under Terry v. Ohio (1968),[6] in stopping respondent to investigate whether he might be engaged in criminal activity. The court further found that the officers were justified in frisking respondent to ensure that he was not carrying a weapon. Finally, analogizing to the "plain-view" doctrine, under which officers may make a warrantless seizure of contraband found in plain view during a lawful search for other items, the trial court ruled that the officers' seizure of the cocaine did not violate the Fourth Amendment.

His suppression motion having failed, respondent proceeded to trial and was found guilty. On appeal, the Minnesota Court of Appeals reversed. The court concluded, however, that the officers had overstepped the bounds allowed by seizing the cocaine. In doing so, the Court of Appeals "decline[d] to adopt the plain feel exception" to the warrant requirement. The Minnesota Supreme Court affirmed.

The question presented today is whether police officers may seize non-threatening contraband detected during a protective patdown search. We think the answer is clearly that they may.

We have already held that police officers, at least under certain circumstances, may seize contraband detected during the lawful execution of a search.

Under [the plain view] doctrine, if police are lawfully in a position from which they view an object, if its incriminating character is immediately apparent, and if the officers have a lawful right of access to the object, they may seize it without a warrant.

We think that this doctrine has an obvious application by analogy to cases in which an officer discovers contraband through the sense of touch during

6. Terry v. Ohio is discussed in section G of this chapter and authorizes the police to "stop and frisk" individuals if there is a reasonable suspicion. [Footnote by casebook authors.]

an otherwise lawful search. The rationale of the plain-view doctrine is that if contraband is left in open view and is observed by a police officer from a lawful vantage point, there has been no invasion of a legitimate expectation of privacy and thus no "search" within the meaning of the Fourth Amendment — or at least no search independent of the initial intrusion that gave the officers their vantage point. The warrantless seizure of contraband that presents itself in this manner is deemed justified by the realization that resort to a neutral magistrate under such circumstances would often be impracticable and would do little to promote the objectives of the Fourth Amendment. The same can be said of tactile discoveries of contraband. If a police officer lawfully pats down a suspect's outer clothing and feels an object whose contour or mass makes its identity immediately apparent, there has been no invasion of the suspect's privacy beyond that already authorized by the officer's search for weapons; if the object is contraband, its warrantless seizure would be justified by the same practical considerations that inhere in the plain-view context.

It remains to apply these principles to the facts of this case. Respondent has not challenged the finding made by the trial court and affirmed by both the Court of Appeals and the State Supreme Court that the police were justified under *Terry* in stopping him and frisking him for weapons. Thus, the dispositive question before this Court is whether the officer who conducted the search was acting within the lawful bounds at the time he gained probable cause to believe that the lump in respondent's jacket was contraband.

Under the State Supreme Court's interpretation of the record before it, it is clear that the court was correct in holding that the police officer in this case overstepped the bounds of the "strictly circumscribed" search for weapons allowed under *Terry*. Where, as here, "an officer who is executing a valid search for one item seizes a different item," this Court rightly "has been sensitive to the danger . . . that officers will enlarge a specific authorization, furnished by a warrant or an exigency, into the equivalent of a general warrant to rummage and seize at will." Here, the officer's continued exploration of respondent's pocket after having concluded that it contained no weapon was unrelated to "[t]he sole justification of the search [under *Terry*] . . . the protection of the police officer and others nearby." It therefore amounted to the sort of evidentiary search that *Terry* expressly refused to authorize and that we have condemned in subsequent cases.

3. The Automobile Exception

One of the most important exceptions to the warrant requirement is for automobiles; cars and other movable vehicles can be searched without a warrant if there is probable cause. In presenting the automobile exception, first, the basic cases articulating and explaining the exception are presented. Second, the question is examined of whether police can search containers found in automobiles. Finally, the issue of the ability of the police to search automobiles after the arrest of the driver is discussed.

a. The Exception and Its Rationale

The Court first articulated an automobile exception to the Fourth Amendment in Carroll v. United States, 267 U.S. 132 (1925). Agents of the federal Treasury Department, during the Prohibition era, had probable cause that Carroll was transporting alcoholic beverages in his car in violation of the law. They searched his vehicle without a warrant. The Court held that the search did not violate the Fourth Amendment and stressed that a warrant was not needed to search the car. Chief Justice Taft, writing for the Court, declared:

> On reason and authority the true rule is that if the search and seizure without a warrant are made upon probable cause, that is, upon a belief, reasonably arising out of circumstances known to the seizing officer, that an automobile or other vehicle contains that which by law is subject to seizure and destruction, the search and seizure are valid. The Fourth Amendment is to be construed in the light of what was deemed an unreasonable search and seizure when it was adopted, and in a manner which will conserve public interests as well as the interests and rights of individual citizens.
>
> [T]he guaranty of freedom from unreasonable searches and seizures by the Fourth Amendment has been construed, practically since the beginning of the government, as recognizing a necessary difference between a search of a store, dwelling house, or other structure in respect of which a proper official warrant readily may be obtained and a search of a ship, motor boat, wagon, or automobile for contraband goods, where it is not practicable to secure a warrant, because the vehicle can be quickly moved out of the locality or jurisdiction in which the warrant must be sought.

The Court reaffirmed and explained the automobile exception to the Fourth Amendment in California v. Carney.

CALIFORNIA v. CARNEY

471 U.S. 386 (1985)

Chief Justice BURGER delivered the opinion of the Court.

We granted certiorari to decide whether law enforcement agents violated the Fourth Amendment when they conducted a warrantless search, based on probable cause, of a fully mobile "motor home" located in a public place.

I

On May 31, 1979, Drug Enforcement Agency Agent Robert Williams watched respondent, Charles Carney, approach a youth in downtown San Diego. The youth accompanied Carney to a Dodge Mini Motor Home parked in a nearby lot. Carney and the youth closed the window shades in the motor home, including one across the front window. Agent Williams had previously received uncorroborated information that the same motor home was used by another person who was exchanging marijuana for sex. Williams, with assistance from other agents, kept the motor home under surveillance for the entire one and one-quarter hours that Carney and the youth remained inside. When the youth left the motor home, the agents followed and stopped him. The youth told the agents that he had received marijuana in return for allowing Carney sexual contacts.

At the agents' request, the youth returned to the motor home and knocked on its door; Carney stepped out. The agents identified themselves as law enforcement officers. Without a warrant or consent, one agent entered the motor home and observed marijuana, plastic bags, and a scale of the kind used in weighing drugs on a table. Agent Williams took Carney into custody and took possession of the motor home. A subsequent search of the motor home at the police station revealed additional marijuana in the cupboards and refrigerator.

Respondent was charged with possession of marijuana for sale. Respondent [presented] his suppression motion in the Superior Court. The Superior Court also rejected the claim, holding that there was probable cause to arrest respondent, that the search of the motor home was authorized under the automobile exception to the Fourth Amendment's warrant requirement, and that the motor home itself could be seized without a warrant as an instrumentality of the crime. Respondent then pleaded nolo contendere to the charges against him, and was placed on probation for three years. The California Supreme Court reversed the conviction.

II

[The] fundamental right [protected by the Fourth Amendment] is preserved by a requirement that searches be conducted pursuant to a warrant issued by an independent judicial officer. There are, of course, exceptions to the general rule that a warrant must be secured before a search is undertaken; one is the so-called "automobile exception" at issue in this case. This exception to the warrant requirement was first set forth by the Court 60 years ago in Carroll v. United States (1925). There, the Court recognized that the privacy interests in an automobile are constitutionally protected; however, it held that the ready mobility of the automobile justifies a lesser degree of protection of those interests. However, although ready mobility alone was perhaps the original justification for the vehicle exception, our later cases have made clear that ready mobility is not the only basis for the exception. The reasons for the vehicle exception, we have said, are twofold. "Besides the element of mobility, less rigorous warrant requirements govern because the expectation of privacy with respect to one's automobile is significantly less than that relating to one's home or office."

reasons why

Even in cases where an automobile was not immediately mobile, the lesser expectation of privacy resulting from its use as a readily mobile vehicle justified application of the vehicular exception. In some cases, the configuration of the vehicle contributed to the lower expectations of privacy; for example, we [have] said that, because the passenger compartment of a standard automobile is relatively open to plain view, there are lesser expectations of privacy. But even when enclosed "repository" areas have been involved, we have concluded that the lesser expectations of privacy warrant application of the exception. We have applied the exception in the context of a locked car trunk, a sealed package in a car trunk.

These reduced expectations of privacy derive not from the fact that the area to be searched is in plain view, but from the pervasive regulation of vehicles capable of traveling on the public highways. As we explained in South Dakota v. Opperman, an inventory search case: "Automobiles, unlike homes, are subjected to pervasive and continuing governmental regulation and controls, including periodic inspection and licensing requirements. As an everyday occurrence, police stop and examine vehicles when license plates or inspection stickers have expired, or if other violations, such as exhaust fumes or excessive noise, are noted, or if headlights or other safety equipment are not in proper working order."

The public is fully aware that it is accorded less privacy in its automobiles because of this compelling governmental need for regulation. Historically, "individuals always [have] been on notice that movable vessels may be stopped and searched on facts giving rise to probable cause that the vehicle contains contraband, without the protection afforded by a magistrate's prior evaluation of those facts." In short, the pervasive schemes of regulation, which necessarily lead to reduced expectations of privacy, and the exigencies attendant to ready mobility justify searches without prior recourse to the authority of a magistrate so long as the overriding standard of probable cause is met.

When a vehicle is being used on the highways, or if it is readily capable of such use and is found stationary in a place not regularly used for residential purposes — temporary or otherwise — the two justifications for the vehicle exception come into play. First, the vehicle is obviously readily mobile by the turn of an ignition key, if not actually moving. Second, there is a reduced expectation of privacy stemming from its use as a licensed motor vehicle subject to a range of police regulation inapplicable to a fixed dwelling. At least in these circumstances, the overriding societal interests in effective law enforcement justify an immediate search before the vehicle and its occupants become unavailable.

While it is true that respondent's vehicle possessed some, if not many of the attributes of a home, it is equally clear that the vehicle falls clearly within the scope of the exception laid down in *Carroll* and applied in succeeding cases. Like the automobile in *Carroll*, respondent's motor home was readily mobile. Absent the prompt search and seizure, it could readily have been moved beyond the reach of the police. Furthermore, the vehicle was licensed to "operate on public streets; [was] serviced in public places; . . . and [was] subject to extensive regulation and inspection." And the vehicle was so situated that an objective observer would conclude that it was being used not as a residence, but as a vehicle.

Respondent urges us to distinguish his vehicle from other vehicles within the exception because it was capable of functioning as a home. In our increasingly mobile society, many vehicles used for transportation can be and are being used not only for transportation but for shelter, i.e., as a "home" or "residence." To distinguish between respondent's motor home and an ordinary sedan for purposes of the vehicle exception would require that we apply the exception depending upon the size of the vehicle and the quality of its appointments. Moreover, to fail to apply the exception to vehicles such as a motor home ignores the fact that a motor home lends itself easily to use as an instrument of illicit drug traffic and other illegal activity.[7]

However, in Chambers v. Maroney, 399 U.S. 42 (1970), the Court went even further and held that even if the automobile had been taken to the police station, and thus was not movable, the automobile exception still applies. Justice White, writing for the Court, explained:

> The principal question in this case concerns the admissibility of evidence seized from an automobile, in which petitioner was riding at the time of his arrest, after the automobile was taken to a police station and was there thoroughly searched without a warrant.
>
> [T]he search that produced the incriminating evidence was made at the police station some time after the arrest and cannot be justified as a search incident to an arrest. In terms of the circumstances justifying a warrantless search, the Court has long distinguished between an automobile and a home or office.
>
> Having thus established that contraband goods concealed and illegally transported in an automobile or other vehicle may be searched for without a warrant, we come now to consider under what circumstances such search may be made. . . . In enforcing the Fourth Amendment's prohibition against unreasonable searches and seizures, the Court has insisted upon probable cause as a minimum requirement for a reasonable search permitted by the Constitution. As a general rule, it has also required the judgment of a magistrate on the probable-cause issue and the issuance of a warrant before a search is made. Only in exigent circumstances will the judgment of the police as to probable cause serve as a sufficient authorization for a search. Carroll holds a search warrant unnecessary where there is probable cause to search an automobile stopped on the highway; the car is movable, the

----

7. We need not pass on the application of the vehicle exception to a motor home that is situated in a way or place that objectively indicates that it is being used as a residence. Among the factors that might be relevant in determining whether a warrant would be required in such a circumstance is its location, whether the vehicle is readily mobile or instead, for instance, elevated on blocks, whether the vehicle is licensed, whether it is connected to utilities, and whether it has convenient access to a public road. [Footnote by the Court].

occupants are alerted, and the car's contents may never be found again if a warrant must be obtained. Hence an immediate search is constitutionally permissible.

Arguably, because of the preference for a magistrate's judgment, only the immobilization of the car should be permitted until a search warrant is obtained; arguably, only the "lesser" intrusion is permissible until the magistrate authorizes the "greater." But which is the "greater" and which the "lesser" intrusion is itself a debatable question and the answer may depend on a variety of circumstances. For constitutional purposes, we see no difference between on the one hand seizing and holding a car before presenting the probable cause issue to a magistrate and on the other hand carrying out an immediate search without a warrant. Given probable cause to search, either course is reasonable under the Fourth Amendment.

b.   Searches of Containers in Automobiles

Does the automobile exception extend to allowing warrantless searches of containers within the car? California v. Acevedo addressed this.

CALIFORNIA v. ACEVEDO
500 U.S. 565 (1991)

Justice BLACKMUN delivered the opinion of the Court.

This case requires us once again to consider the so-called "automobile exception" to the warrant requirement of the Fourth Amendment and its application to the search of a closed container in the trunk of a car.

I

On October 28, 1987, Officer Coleman of the Santa Ana, Cal., Police Department received a telephone call from a federal drug enforcement agent in Hawaii. The agent informed Coleman that he had seized a package containing marijuana which was to have been delivered to the Federal Express Office in Santa Ana and which was addressed to J.R. Daza at 805 West Stevens Avenue in that city. The agent arranged to send the package to Coleman instead. Coleman then was to take the package to the Federal Express office and arrest the person who arrived to claim it.

Coleman received the package on October 29, verified its contents, and took it to the Senior Operations Manager at the Federal Express office. At about 10:30 A.M. on October 30, a man, who identified himself as Jamie Daza, arrived to claim the package. He accepted it and drove to his apartment on West Stevens. He carried the package into the apartment.

At 11:45 A.M., officers observed Daza leave the apartment and drop the box and paper that had contained the marijuana into a trash bin. Coleman at that point left the scene to get a search warrant. About 12:05 P.M., the officers saw Richard St. George leave the apartment carrying a blue knapsack which appeared to be half full. The officers stopped him as he was driving off, searched the knapsack, and found 1½ pounds of marijuana.

At 12:30 P.M., respondent Charles Steven Acevedo arrived. He entered Daza's apartment, stayed for about 10 minutes, and reappeared carrying a brown paper bag that looked full. The officers noticed that the bag was the size of one of the wrapped marijuana packages sent from Hawaii. Acevedo walked to a silver Honda in the parking lot. He placed the bag in the trunk of the car and started to drive away. Fearing the loss of evidence, officers in a marked police car stopped him. They opened the trunk and the bag, and found marijuana.

II

Contemporaneously with the adoption of the Fourth Amendment, the First Congress, and, later, the Second and Fourth Congresses, distinguished between the need for a warrant to search for contraband concealed in "a dwelling house or similar place" and the need for a warrant to search for contraband concealed in a movable vessel. In *Carroll*, this Court established an exception to the warrant requirement for moving vehicles, for it recognized "a necessary difference between a search of a store, dwelling house or other structure in respect of which a proper official warrant readily may be obtained, and a search of a ship, motor boat, wagon or automobile, for contraband goods, where it is not practicable to secure a warrant because the vehicle can be quickly moved out of the locality or jurisdiction in which the warrant must be sought."

It therefore held that a warrantless search of an automobile, based upon probable cause to believe that the vehicle contained evidence of crime in the light of an exigency arising out of the likely disappearance of the vehicle, did not contravene the Warrant Clause of the Fourth Amendment.

In United States v. Ross, decided in 1982, we held that a warrantless search of an automobile under the *Carroll* doctrine could include a search of a container or package found inside the car when such a search was supported by probable cause. The warrantless search of Ross' car occurred after an informant told the police that he had seen Ross complete a drug transaction using drugs stored in the trunk of his car. The police stopped the car, searched it, and discovered in the trunk a brown paper bag containing drugs. We decided that the search of Ross' car was not unreasonable under the Fourth Amendment: "The scope of a warrantless search based on probable cause is no narrower—and no broader—than the scope of a search authorized by a warrant supported by probable cause." Thus, "[i]f probable cause justifies the search of a lawfully stopped vehicle, it justifies the search of every part of the vehicle and its contents that may conceal the object of the search." In *Ross*, therefore, we clarified the scope of the *Carroll* doctrine as properly including a "probing search" of compartments and containers within the automobile so long as the search is supported by probable cause.

The facts in this case closely resemble the facts in *Ross*. In *Ross*, the police had probable cause to believe that drugs were stored in the trunk of a particular car. Here, the California Court of Appeal concluded that the police had probable cause to believe that respondent was carrying marijuana in a bag in his car's trunk. Furthermore, for what it is worth, in *Ross*, as here, the drugs in the trunk were contained in a brown paper bag.

We now must decide the question deferred in *Ross:* whether the Fourth Amendment requires the police to obtain a warrant to open the sack in a movable vehicle simply because they lack probable cause to search the entire car. We conclude that it does not.

[III]

We now agree that a container found after a general search of the automobile and a container found in a car after a limited search for the container are equally easy for the police to store and for the suspect to hide or destroy. In fact, we see no principled distinction in terms of either the privacy expectation or the exigent circumstances between the paper bag found by the police in *Ross* and the paper bag found by the police here. Furthermore, by attempting to distinguish between a container for which the police are specifically searching and a container which they come across in a car, we have provided only minimal protection for privacy and have impeded effective law enforcement.

The line between probable cause to search a vehicle and probable cause to search a package in that vehicle is not always clear, and separate rules that govern the two objects to be searched may enable the police to broaden their power to make warrantless searches and disserve privacy interests. We noted this in *Ross* in the context of a search of an entire vehicle. Recognizing that under *Carroll*, the "entire vehicle itself . . . could be searched without a warrant," we concluded that "prohibiting police from opening immediately a container in which the object of the search is most likely to be found and instead forcing them first to comb the entire vehicle would actually exacerbate the intrusion on privacy interests." At the moment when officers stop an automobile, it may be less than clear whether they suspect with a high degree of certainty that the vehicle contains drugs in a bag or simply contains drugs. If the police know that they may open a bag only if they are actually searching the entire car, they may search more extensively than they otherwise would in order to establish the general probable cause required by *Ross*.

Finally, the search of a paper bag intrudes far less on individual privacy than does the incursion sanctioned long ago in *Carroll*. In that case, prohibition agents slashed the upholstery of the automobile. This Court nonetheless found their search to be reasonable under the Fourth Amendment. If destroying the interior of an automobile is not unreasonable, we cannot conclude that looking inside a closed container is. [W]e now hold that the Fourth Amendment does not compel separate treatment for an automobile search that extends only to a container within the vehicle. The interpretation of the *Carroll* doctrine set forth in *Ross* now applies to all searches of containers found in an automobile. In other words, the police may search without a warrant if their search is supported by probable cause.

Justice STEVENS, with whom Justice MARSHALL joins, dissenting.

It is "a cardinal principle that searches conducted outside the judicial process, without prior approval by judge or magistrate, are per se unreasonable under the Fourth Amendment — subject only to a few specifically established and well-delineated exceptions." Relying on arguments that conservative judges have repeatedly rejected in past cases, the Court today — despite its disclaimer to the contrary, — enlarges the scope of the automobile exception to this "cardinal principle," which undergirded our Fourth Amendment jurisprudence prior.

Our decisions have always acknowledged that the warrant requirement imposes a burden on law enforcement. And our cases have not questioned that trained professionals normally make reliable assessments of the existence of probable cause to conduct a search. We have repeatedly held, however, that these factors are outweighed by the individual interest in privacy that is protected by advance judicial approval. The Fourth Amendment dictates that the privacy interest is paramount, no matter how marginal the risk of error might be if the legality of warrantless searches were judged only after the fact.

In its opinion today, the Court recognizes that the police did not have probable cause to search respondent's vehicle and that a search of anything but the paper bag that respondent had carried from Daza's apartment and placed in the trunk of his car would have been unconstitutional. Moreover, as I read the opinion, the Court assumes that the police could not have made a warrantless inspection of the bag before it was placed in the car. Finally, the Court also does not question the fact that, under our prior cases, it would have been lawful for the police to seize the container and detain it (and respondent) until they obtained a search warrant.

The Court does not attempt to identify any exigent circumstances that would justify its refusal to apply the general rule against warrantless searches.

Every citizen clearly has an interest in the privacy of the contents of his or her luggage, briefcase, handbag or any other container that conceals private papers and effects from public scrutiny. That privacy interest has been recognized repeatedly in cases spanning more than a century. Under the Court's holding today, the privacy interest that protects the contents of a suitcase or a briefcase from a warrantless search when it is in public view simply vanishes when its owner climbs into a taxicab. Unquestionably today's decision will result in a significant loss of individual privacy.

The Court's suggestion that [prior decisions create a] significant burden on effective law enforcement is unsupported, inaccurate, and, in any event, an insufficient reason for creating a new exception to the warrant requirement. Even if the warrant requirement does inconvenience the police to some extent, that fact does not distinguish this constitutional requirement from any other procedural protection secured by the Bill of Rights. It is merely a part of the price that our society must pay in order to preserve its freedom.

It is too early to know how much freedom America has lost today. The magnitude of the loss is, however, not nearly as significant as the Court's willingness to inflict it without even a colorable basis for its rejection of prior law.

Does the ability to search packages include the packages of the occupants of the car? Earlier, in United States v. Di Re, 332 U.S. 581 (1948), the Court held that passengers could not be searched without probable cause simply because the automobile was lawfully stopped by police. However, in Wyoming v. Houghton, 526 U.S. 295 (1999), the Court held that police do not violate the Fourth Amendment when they search a passenger's personal belongings inside an automobile that they have probable cause to believe contains contraband.

Justice Scalia, writing for the majority, stated the facts of the case:

> In the early morning hours of July 23, 1995, a Wyoming Highway Patrol officer stopped an automobile for speeding and driving with a faulty brake light. There were three passengers in the front seat of the car: David Young (the driver), his girlfriend, and respondent. While questioning Young, the officer noticed a hypodermic syringe in Young's shirt pocket. He left the occupants under the supervision of two backup officers as he went to get gloves from his patrol car. Upon his return, he instructed Young to step out of the car and place the syringe on the hood. The officer then asked Young why he had a syringe; with refreshing candor, Young replied that he used it to take drugs.
>
> At this point, the backup officers ordered the two female passengers out of the car and asked them for identification. Respondent falsely identified herself as "Sandra James" and stated that she did not have any identification. Meanwhile, in light of Young's admission, the officer searched the passenger compartment of the car for contraband. On the back seat, he found a purse, which respondent claimed as hers. He removed from the purse a wallet containing respondent's driver's license, identifying her properly as Sandra K. Houghton. When the officer asked her why she had lied about her name, she replied: "In case things went bad."
>
> Continuing his search of the purse, the officer found a brown pouch and a black wallet-type container. Respondent denied that the former was hers, and claimed ignorance of how it came to be there; it was found to contain drug paraphernalia and a syringe with 60 ccs of methamphetamine. Respondent admitted ownership of the black container, which was also found to contain drug paraphernalia, and a syringe (which respondent acknowledged was hers) with 10 ccs of methamphetamine — an amount insufficient to support the felony conviction at issue in this case. The officer also found fresh needle-track marks on respondent's arms. He placed her under arrest.

The Court held that the search of the purse did not violate the Fourth Amendment. The Court said that there was no basis for a distinction among packages or containers based on ownership. When there is probable cause to search for contraband in a car, it is reasonable for police officers—like customs officials in the founding era—to examine packages and containers without a showing of individualized probable cause for each one. A passenger's personal belongings, just like the driver's belongings or containers attached to the car like a glove compartment, are "in" the car, and the officer has probable cause to search for contraband in the car.

Justice Stevens dissented, joined by Justices Souter and Ginsburg. He stated:

> In all of our prior cases applying the automobile exception to the Fourth Amendment's warrant requirement, either the defendant was the operator of the vehicle and in custody of the object of the search, or no question was raised as to the defendant's ownership or custody. In the only automobile case confronting the search of a passenger defendant—United States v. Di Re (1948)—the Court held that the exception to the warrant requirement did not apply.
>
> Nor am I persuaded that the mere spatial association between a passenger and a driver provides an acceptable basis for presuming that they are partners in crime or for ignoring privacy interests in a purse. Whether or not the Fourth Amendment required a warrant to search Houghton's purse, at the very least the trooper in this case had to have probable cause to believe that her purse contained contraband. The Wyoming Supreme Court concluded that he did not.

c. Searching Automobiles Incident to Arrest

When the police lawfully stop a vehicle, they may order the driver and the passengers to exit. Pennsylvania v. Mimms, 496 U.S. 582 (1977) (driver); Maryland v. Wilson, 519 U.S. 408 (1997) (passengers). If the police arrest the driver, may they then search the vehicle as part of a search incident to arrest? This is discussed below in connection with the more general exception to the Fourth Amendment for searches incident to arrests.

4. *Searches Incident to Arrest*

Whereas the above are exceptions to the warrant requirement, an exception to the requirement for both a warrant and probable cause for a search is the ability of police to search a person at the time of a lawful arrest.

CHIMEL v. CALIFORNIA
395 U.S. 752 (1969)

Justice STEWART delivered the opinion of the Court.

This case raises basic questions concerning the permissible scope under the Fourth Amendment of a search incident to a lawful arrest.

The relevant facts are essentially undisputed. Late in the afternoon of September 13, 1965, three police officers arrived at the Santa Ana, California, home of the petitioner with a warrant authorizing his arrest for the burglary of a coin shop. The officers knocked on the door, identified themselves to the petitioner's wife, and asked if they might come inside. She ushered them into the house, where they waited 10 or 15 minutes until the petitioner returned home from work. When the petitioner entered the house, one of the officers handed him the arrest warrant and asked for permission to "look around." The petitioner objected, but was advised that "on the basis of the lawful arrest," the officers would nonetheless conduct a search. No search warrant had been issued.

Accompanied by the petitioner's wife, the officers then looked through the entire three-bedroom house, including the attic, the garage, and a small workshop. In some rooms the search was relatively cursory. In the master bedroom and sewing room, however, the officers directed the petitioner's wife to open drawers and "to physically move contents of the drawers from side to side so that [they] might view any items that would have come from [the] burglary." After completing the search, they seized numerous items — primarily coins, but also several medals, tokens, and a few other objects. The entire search took between 45 minutes and an hour.

At the petitioner's subsequent state trial on two charges of burglary, the items taken from his house were admitted into evidence against him, over his objection that they had been unconstitutionally seized. He was convicted, and the judgments of conviction were affirmed by both the California Court of Appeal and the California Supreme Court.

Without deciding the question, we proceed on the hypothesis that the California courts were correct in holding that the arrest of the petitioner was valid under the Constitution. This brings us directly to the question whether the warrantless search of the petitioner's entire house can be constitutionally justified as incident to that arrest. The decisions of this Court bearing upon that question have been far from consistent, as even the most cursory review makes evident.

The presence of a search warrant serves a high function. Absent some grave emergency, the Fourth Amendment has interposed a magistrate between the citizen and the police. This was done not to shield criminals nor to make the home a safe haven for illegal activities. It was done so that an objective mind might weigh the need to invade that privacy in order to enforce the law. The right of privacy was deemed too precious to entrust to the discretion of those whose job is the detection of crime and the arrest of criminals. And so the Constitution requires a magistrate to pass on the desires of the police before they violate the privacy of the home. We cannot be true to that constitutional requirement and excuse the absence of a search warrant without a showing by those who seek exemption from the constitutional mandate that the exigencies of the situation made that course imperative.

When an arrest is made, it is reasonable for the arresting officer to search the person arrested in order to remove any weapons that the latter might seek to use in order to resist arrest or effect his escape. Otherwise, the officer's safety might well be endangered, and the arrest itself frustrated.

In addition, it is entirely reasonable for the arresting officer to search for and seize any evidence on the arrestee's person in order to prevent its concealment or destruction. And the area into which an arrestee might reach in order to grab a weapon or evidentiary items must, of course, be governed by a like rule. A gun on a table or in a drawer in front of one who is arrested can be as dangerous to the arresting officer as one concealed in the clothing of the person arrested. There is ample justification, therefore, for a search of the arrestee's person and the area "within his immediate control" — construing that phrase to mean the area from within which he might gain possession of a weapon or destructible evidence.

There is no comparable justification, however, for routinely searching any room other than that in which an arrest occurs — or, for that matter, for searching through all the desk drawers or other closed or concealed areas in that room itself. Such searches, in the absence of well-recognized exceptions, may be made only under the authority of a search warrant. The "adherence to judicial processes" mandated by the Fourth Amendment requires no less.

It is argued in the present case that it is "reasonable" to search a man's house when he is arrested in it. But that argument is founded on little more than a subjective view regarding the acceptability of certain sorts of police conduct, and not on consideration relevant to Fourth Amendment interests. Under such an unconfined analysis, Fourth Amendment protection in this area would approach the evaporation point. It is not easy to explain why, for instance, it is less subjectively "reasonable" to search a man's house when he is arrested on his front lawn — or just down the street — than it is when he happens to be in the house at the time of arrest.

Application of sound Fourth Amendment principles to the facts of this case produces a clear result. The search here went far beyond the petitioner's person and the area from within which he might have obtained either a weapon or something that could have been used as evidence against him. There was no constitutional justification, in the absence of a search warrant, for extending the search beyond that area. The scope of the search was, therefore, "unreasonable" under the Fourth and Fourteenth Amendments and the petitioner's conviction cannot stand.

Justice WHITE, with whom Justice BLACK joins, dissenting.

The rule which has prevailed, but for very brief or doubtful periods of aberration, is that a search incident to an arrest may extend to those areas under the control of the defendant and where items subject to constitutional seizure may be found. The justification for this rule must, under the language of the Fourth Amendment, lie in the reasonableness of the rule.

In terms, then, the Court must decide whether a given search is reasonable. The Amendment does not proscribe "warrantless searches" but instead it proscribes "unreasonable searches" and this Court has never held nor does the majority today assert that warrantless searches are necessarily unreasonable.

Applying this reasonableness test to the area of searches incident to arrests, one thing is clear at the outset. Search of an arrested man and of the items within his immediate reach must in almost every case be reasonable. There is always a danger that the suspect will try to escape, seizing concealed weapons with which to overpower and injure the arresting officers, and there is a danger that he may destroy evidence vital to the prosecution. Circumstances in which these justifications would not apply are sufficiently rare that inquiry is not made into searches of this scope, which have been considered reasonable throughout.

The justifications which make such a search reasonable obviously do not apply to the search of areas to which the accused does not have ready physical access. This is not enough, however, to prove such searches unconstitutional. The Court has always held, and does not today deny, that when there is probable cause to search and it is "impracticable" for one reason or another to get a search warrant, then a warrantless search may be reasonable.

An arrested man, by definition conscious of the police interest in him, and provided almost immediately with a lawyer and a judge, is in an excellent position to dispute the reasonableness of his arrest and contemporaneous search in a full adversary proceeding. I would uphold the constitutionality of this search contemporaneous with an arrest since there were probable cause both for the search and for the arrest, exigent circumstances involving the removal or destruction of evidence, and satisfactory opportunity to dispute the issues of probable cause shortly thereafter. In this case, the search was reasonable.

———————

In United States v. Robinson, 414 U.S. 218 (1973), the Supreme Court held that police may search a person incident to arrest regardless of the crime that led to the arrest. Robinson was stopped by police officers for driving with an expired driver's license. When Robinson got out of the car, the officer told him that he was "under arrest for 'operating after revocation and obtaining a permit by misrepresentation.' [T]he [officer then] effected a full custody arrest." The officer searched Robinson, and heroin was found.

Justice Rehnquist, writing for the Court, upheld the constitutionality of the search. He began by stating the law: "It is well settled that a search incident to a lawful arrest is a traditional exception to the warrant requirement of the Fourth Amendment. This general exception has historically been formulated into two distinct propositions. The first is that a search may be made of the person of the arrestee by virtue of the lawful arrest. The second is that a search may be made of the area within the control of the arrestee."

The Court rejected the claim that only a frisk for weapons was appropriate when a person was arrested for a traffic violation and concluded that a search incident to arrest is permissible even if there is no reason to believe that the individual has weapons. Justice Rehnquist stated:

> The authority to search the person incident to a lawful custodial arrest, while based upon the need to disarm and to discover evidence, does not depend on what a court may later decide was the probability in a particular arrest situation that weapons or evidence would in fact be found upon the person of the suspect. A custodial arrest of a suspect based on probable cause is a reasonable intrusion under the Fourth Amendment; that intrusion being lawful, a search incident to the arrest requires no additional justification. It is the fact of the lawful arrest which establishes the authority to search, and we hold that in the case of a lawful custodial arrest a full search of the person is not only an exception to the warrant requirement of the Fourth Amendment, but is also a "reasonable" search under that Amendment.

However, in order for there to be a search incident to arrest, there must actually be an arrest. This was the point of Knowles v. Iowa.

KNOWLES v. IOWA
525 U.S. 113 (1998)

Chief Justice REHNQUIST delivered the opinion of the Court.

An Iowa police officer stopped petitioner Knowles for speeding, but issued him a citation rather than arresting him. The question presented is whether such a procedure authorizes the officer, consistently with the Fourth Amendment, to conduct a full search of the car. We answer this question "no."

Knowles was stopped in Newton, Iowa, after having been clocked driving 43 miles per hour on a road where the speed limit was 25 miles per hour. The police officer issued a citation to Knowles, although under Iowa law he might have arrested him. The officer then conducted a full search of the car, and under the driver's seat he found a bag of marijuana and a "pot pipe." Knowles was then arrested and charged with violation of state laws dealing with controlled substances.

Before trial, Knowles moved to suppress the evidence so obtained. He argued that the search could not be sustained under the "search incident to arrest" exception recognized in United States v. Robinson (1973), because he had not been placed under arrest. At the hearing on the motion to suppress, the police officer conceded that he had neither Knowles' consent nor probable cause to conduct the search. He relied on Iowa law dealing with such searches. Iowa Code Ann. §321.485(1)(a) provides that Iowa peace officers having cause to believe that a person has violated any traffic or motor vehicle equipment law may arrest the person and immediately take the person before a magistrate. Iowa law also authorizes the far more usual practice of issuing a citation in lieu of arrest or in lieu of continued custody after an initial arrest. Section 805.1(4) provides that the issuance of a citation in lieu of an arrest "does not affect the officer's authority to conduct an otherwise lawful search." The Iowa Supreme Court has interpreted this provision as providing authority to officers to conduct a full-blown search of an automobile and driver in those cases where police elect not to make a custodial arrest and instead issue a citation—that is, a search incident to citation.

In *Robinson,* we noted the two historical rationales for the "search incident to arrest" exception: (1) the need to disarm the suspect in order to take him into custody, and (2) the need to preserve evidence for later use at trial. But neither of these underlying rationales for the search incident to arrest exception is sufficient to justify the search in the present case.

We have recognized that the first rationale—officer safety—is "'both legitimate and weighty.'" The threat to officer safety from issuing a traffic citation, however, is a good deal less than in the case of a custodial arrest. In *Robinson,* we stated that a custodial arrest involves "danger to an officer" because of "the extended exposure which follows the taking of a suspect into custody and transporting him to the police station." A routine traffic stop, on the other hand, is a relatively brief encounter and "is more analogous to a so-called '*Terry* stop' . . . than to a formal arrest." This is not to say that the concern for officer safety is absent in the case of a routine traffic stop. It plainly is not. But while the concern for officer safety in this context may justify the "minimal" additional intrusion of ordering a driver and passengers out of the car, it does not by itself justify the often considerably greater intrusion attending a full field-type search. Even without the search authority Iowa urges, officers have other, independent bases to search for weapons and protect themselves from danger. For example, they may order out of a vehicle both the driver, and any passengers; perform a "patdown" of a driver and any passengers upon reasonable suspicion that they may be armed and dangerous; conduct a patdown of the passenger compartment of a vehicle upon reasonable suspicion that an occupant is dangerous and may gain immediate control of a weapon, and even conduct a full search of the passenger compartment, including any containers therein, pursuant to a custodial arrest.

Nor has Iowa shown the second justification for the authority to search incident to arrest—the need to discover and preserve evidence. Once Knowles was stopped for speeding and issued a citation, all the evidence necessary to prosecute that offense had been obtained. No further evidence of excessive speed was going to be found either on the person of the offender or in the passenger compartment of the car.

Iowa nevertheless argues that a "search incident to citation" is justified because a suspect who is subject to a routine traffic stop may attempt to hide or destroy evidence related to his identity (e.g., a driver's license or vehicle registration), or destroy evidence of another, as yet undetected crime. As for the destruction of evidence relating to identity, if a police officer is not satisfied with the identification furnished by the driver, this may be a basis for arresting him rather than merely issuing a citation. As for destroying evidence of other crimes, the possibility that an officer would stumble onto evidence wholly unrelated to the speeding offense seems remote.

In *Robinson*, we held that the authority to conduct a full field search as incident to an arrest was a "bright-line rule," which was based on the concern for officer safety and destruction or loss of evidence, but which did not depend in every case upon the existence of either concern. Here we are asked to extend that "bright-line rule" to a situation where the concern for officer safety is not present to the same extent and the concern for destruction or loss of evidence is not present at all. We decline to do so.

The Court recently decided one of its most important questions concerning the scope of searches incident to arrest: May the police look at the contents of a cell phone that a person is carrying at the time of the arrest? In saying that police generally cannot do so, the Court emphatically spoke of the privacy interest that people have in the contents of their cell phones.

RILEY v. CALIFORNIA
134 S. Ct. 2473 (2014)

Chief Justice ROBERTS delivered the opinion of the Court.

These two cases raise a common question: whether the police may, without a warrant, search digital information on a cell phone seized from an individual who has been arrested.

I

In the first case, petitioner David Riley was stopped by a police officer for driving with expired registration tags. In the course of the stop, the officer also learned that Riley's license had been suspended. The officer impounded Riley's car, pursuant to department policy, and another officer conducted an inventory search of the car. Riley was arrested for possession of concealed and loaded firearms when that search turned up two handguns under the car's hood.

An officer searched Riley incident to the arrest and found items associated with the "Bloods" street gang. He also seized a cell phone from Riley's pants pocket. According to Riley's uncontradicted assertion, the phone was a "smart phone," a cell phone with a broad range of other functions based on advanced computing capability, large storage capacity, and Internet connectivity. The officer accessed information on the phone and noticed that some words (presumably in text messages or a contacts list) were preceded by the letters "CK"—a label that, he believed, stood for "Crip Killers," a slang term for members of the Bloods gang.

At the police station about two hours after the arrest, a detective specializing in gangs further examined the contents of the phone. The detective testified that he "went through" Riley's phone "looking for evidence, because . . . gang members will often video themselves with guns or take pictures of themselves with the guns." Although there was "a lot of stuff" on the phone, particular files that "caught [the detective's] eye" included videos of young men sparring while someone yelled encouragement using the moniker "Blood." The police also found photographs of Riley standing in front of a car they suspected had been involved in a shooting a few weeks earlier.

Prior to trial, Riley moved to suppress all evidence that the police had obtained from his cell phone. The trial court rejected that argument.

In the second case, a police officer performing routine surveillance observed respondent Brima Wurie make an apparent drug sale from a car. Officers subsequently arrested Wurie and took him to the police station. At the station, the officers seized two cell phones from Wurie's person. The one at issue here was a "flip phone," a kind of phone that is flipped open for use and that generally has a smaller range of features than a smart phone. Five to ten minutes after arriving at the station, the officers noticed that the phone was repeatedly receiving calls from a source identified as "my house" on the phone's external screen. A few minutes later, they opened the phone and saw a photograph of a woman and a baby set as the phone's wallpaper. They pressed one button on the phone to access its call log, then another button to determine the phone number associated with the "my house" label. They next used an online phone directory to trace that phone number to an apartment building.

When the officers went to the building, they saw Wurie's name on a mailbox and observed through a window a woman who resembled the woman in the photograph on Wurie's phone. They secured the apartment while obtaining a search warrant and, upon later executing the warrant, found and seized 215 grams of crack cocaine, marijuana, drug paraphernalia, a firearm and ammunition, and cash.

He moved to suppress the evidence obtained from the search of the apartment, arguing that it was the fruit of an unconstitutional search of his cell phone. The District Court denied the motion. A divided panel of the First Circuit reversed the denial of Wurie's motion to suppress and vacated Wurie's convictions for possession with intent to distribute and possession of a firearm as a felon.

II

As the text [of the Fourth Amendment] makes clear, "the ultimate touchstone of the Fourth Amendment is 'reasonableness.'" Our cases have determined that "[w]here a search is undertaken by law enforcement officials to discover evidence of criminal wrongdoing, ... reasonableness generally requires the obtaining of a judicial warrant." Such a warrant ensures that the inferences to support a search are "drawn by a neutral and detached magistrate instead of being judged by the officer engaged in the often competitive enterprise of ferreting out crime." In the absence of a warrant, a search is reasonable only if it falls within a specific exception to the warrant requirement.

The two cases before us concern the reasonableness of a warrantless search incident to a lawful arrest. In 1914, this Court first acknowledged in dictum "the right on the part of the Government, always recognized under English and American law, to search the person of the accused when legally arrested to discover and seize the fruits or evidences of crime." Since that time, it has been well accepted that such a search constitutes an exception to the warrant requirement. Indeed, the label "exception" is something of a misnomer in this context, as warrantless searches incident to arrest occur with far greater frequency than searches conducted pursuant to a warrant.

III

These cases require us to decide how the search incident to arrest doctrine applies to modern cell phones, which are now such a pervasive and insistent part of daily life that the proverbial visitor from Mars might conclude they were an important feature of human anatomy. A smart phone of the sort taken from Riley was unheard of ten years ago; a significant majority of American adults now own such phones. Even less sophisticated phones like Wurie's, which have already faded in popularity since Wurie was arrested in 2007, have been around for less than 15 years. Both phones are based on technology nearly inconceivable just a few decades ago, when *Chimel* and *Robinson* were decided.

Absent more precise guidance from the founding era, we generally determine whether to exempt a given type of search from the warrant requirement "by assessing, on the one hand, the degree to which it intrudes upon an individual's privacy and, on the other, the degree to which it is needed for the promotion of legitimate governmental interests."

But while *Robinson*'s categorical rule strikes the appropriate balance in the context of physical objects, neither of its rationales has much force with respect to digital content on cell phones. On the government interest side, *Robinson* concluded that the two risks identified in *Chimel*—harm to officers and destruction of evidence—are present in all custodial arrests. There are no comparable risks when the search is of digital data. In addition, *Robinson* regarded any privacy interests retained by an individual after arrest as significantly diminished by the fact of the arrest itself. Cell phones, however, place vast quantities of personal information literally in the hands of individuals. A search of the information on a cell phone bears little resemblance to the type of brief physical search considered in *Robinson*.

We therefore decline to extend *Robinson* to searches of data on cell phones, and hold instead that officers must generally secure a warrant before conducting such a search.

A

We first consider each *Chimel* concern in turn.

Digital data stored on a cell phone cannot itself be used as a weapon to harm an arresting officer or to effectuate the arrestee's escape. Law enforcement officers remain free to examine the physical aspects of a phone to ensure that it will not be used as a weapon — say, to determine whether there is a razor blade hidden between the phone and its case. Once an officer has secured a phone and eliminated any potential physical threats, however, data on the phone can endanger no one.

Perhaps the same might have been said of the cigarette pack seized from Robinson's pocket. Once an officer gained control of the pack, it was unlikely that Robinson could have accessed the pack's contents. But unknown physical objects may always pose risks, no matter how slight, during the tense atmosphere of a custodial arrest. The officer in *Robinson* testified that he could not identify the objects in the cigarette pack but knew they were not cigarettes. Given that, a further search was a reasonable protective measure. No such unknowns exist with respect to digital data.

The United States and California both suggest that a search of cell phone data might help ensure officer safety in more indirect ways, for example by alerting officers that confederates of the arrestee are headed to the scene. There is undoubtedly a strong government interest in warning officers about such possibilities, but neither the United States nor California offers evidence to suggest that their concerns are based on actual experience. The proposed consideration would also represent a broadening of *Chimel*'s concern that an *arrestee himself* might grab a weapon and use it against an officer "to resist arrest or effect his escape." And any such threats from outside the arrest scene do not "lurk[ ] in all custodial arrests." Accordingly, the interest in protecting officer safety does not justify dispensing with the warrant requirement across the board.

The United States and California focus primarily on the second *Chimel* rationale: preventing the destruction of evidence.

Both Riley and Wurie concede that officers could have seized and secured their cell phones to prevent destruction of evidence while seeking a warrant. And once law enforcement officers have secured a cell phone, there is no longer any risk that the arrestee himself will be able to delete incriminating data from the phone.

The United States and California argue that information on a cell phone may nevertheless be vulnerable to two types of evidence destruction unique to digital data-remote wiping and data encryption. Remote wiping occurs when a phone, connected to a wireless network, receives a signal that erases stored data. This can happen when a third party sends a remote signal or when a phone is preprogrammed to delete data upon entering or leaving certain geographic areas (so-called "geofencing"). Encryption is a security feature that some modern cell phones use in addition to password protection. When such phones lock, data becomes protected by sophisticated encryption that renders a phone all but "unbreakable" unless police know the password.

As an initial matter, these broader concerns about the loss of evidence are distinct from *Chimel*'s focus on a defendant who responds to arrest by trying to conceal or destroy evidence within his reach. With respect to remote wiping, the Government's primary concern turns on the actions of third parties who are not present at the scene of arrest. And data encryption is even further afield. There, the Government focuses on the ordinary operation of a phone's security features, apart from *any* active attempt by a defendant or his associates to conceal or destroy evidence upon arrest.

We have also been given little reason to believe that either problem is prevalent. The briefing reveals only a couple of anecdotal examples of remote wiping triggered by an arrest. Similarly, the opportunities for officers to search a password-protected phone before data becomes encrypted are quite limited. Law enforcement officers are very unlikely to come upon such a phone in an unlocked state because most phones lock at the touch of a button or, as a default, after some very short period of inactivity. This may explain why the encryption argument was not made until the merits stage in this Court, and has never been considered by the Courts of Appeals.

Moreover, in situations in which an arrest might trigger a remote-wipe attempt or an officer discovers an unlocked phone, it is not clear that the ability to conduct a warrantless search would make much of a difference. The need to effect the arrest, secure the scene, and tend to other pressing matters means that law enforcement officers may well not be able to turn their attention to a cell phone right away. Cell phone data would be vulnerable to remote wiping from the time an individual anticipates arrest to the time any eventual search of the phone is completed, which might be at the station house hours later. Likewise, an officer who seizes a phone in an unlocked state might not be able to begin his search in the short time remaining before the phone locks and data becomes encrypted.

In any event, as to remote wiping, law enforcement is not without specific means to address the threat. Remote wiping can be fully prevented by disconnecting a phone from the network. There are at least two simple ways to do this: First, law enforcement officers can turn the phone off or remove its battery. Second, if they are concerned about encryption or other potential problems, they can leave a phone powered on and place it in an enclosure that isolates the phone from radio waves. They are essentially sandwich bags made of aluminum foil: cheap, lightweight, and easy to use. They may not be a complete answer to the problem, but at least for now they provide a reasonable response.

B

The United States asserts that a search of all data stored on a cell phone is "materially indistinguishable" from searches of physical items. That is like saying a ride on horseback is materially indistinguishable from a flight to the moon. Both are ways of getting from point A to point B, but little else justifies lumping them together. Modern cell phones, as a category, implicate privacy concerns far beyond those implicated by the search of a cigarette pack, a wallet, or a purse.

Cell phones differ in both a quantitative and a qualitative sense from other objects that might be kept on an arrestee's person. The term "cell phone" is itself misleading shorthand; many of these devices are in fact minicomputers that also happen to have the capacity to be used as a telephone. They could just as easily be called cameras, video players, rolodexes, calendars, tape recorders, libraries, diaries, albums, televisions, maps, or newspapers.

One of the most notable distinguishing features of modern cell phones is their immense storage capacity. Before cell phones, a search of a person was limited by physical realities and tended as a general matter to constitute only a narrow intrusion on privacy. Most people cannot lug around every piece of mail they have received for the past several months, every picture they have taken, or every book or article they have read—nor would they have any reason to attempt to do so. And if they did, they would have to drag behind them a trunk of the sort held to require a search warrant in *Chadwick*, rather than a container the size of the cigarette package in *Robinson*.

But the possible intrusion on privacy is not physically limited in the same way when it comes to cell phones. The current top-selling smart phone has a standard capacity of 16 gigabytes (and is available with up to 64 gigabytes). Sixteen gigabytes translates to millions of pages of text, thousands of pictures, or hundreds of videos. Cell phones couple that capacity with the ability to store many different types of information: Even the most basic phones that sell for less than $20 might hold photographs, picture messages, text messages, Internet browsing history, a calendar, a thousand-entry phone book, and so on. We expect that the gulf between physical practicability and digital capacity will only continue to widen in the future.

The storage capacity of cell phones has several interrelated consequences for privacy. First, a cell phone collects in one place many distinct types of information—an address, a note, a prescription, a bank statement, a video—that reveal much more in combination than any isolated record. Second, a cell phone's capacity allows even just one type of information to convey far more than previously possible. The sum of an individual's private life can be reconstructed through a thousand photographs labeled with dates, locations, and descriptions; the same cannot be said of a photograph or two of loved ones tucked into a wallet. Third, the data on a phone can date back to the purchase of the phone, or even earlier. A person might carry in his pocket a slip of paper reminding him to call Mr. Jones; he would not carry a record of all his communications with Mr. Jones for the past several months, as would routinely be kept on a phone.

Finally, there is an element of pervasiveness that characterizes cell phones but not physical records. Prior to the digital age, people did not typically carry a cache of sensitive personal information with them as they went about their day. Now it is the person who is not carrying a cell phone, with all that it contains, who is the exception. According to one poll, nearly three-quarters of smart phone users report being within five feet of their phones most of the time, with 12% admitting that they even use their phones in the shower. A decade ago police officers searching an arrestee might have occasionally stumbled across a highly personal item such as a diary. But those discoveries were likely to be few and far between. Today, by contrast, it is no exaggeration to say that many of the more than 90% of American adults who own a cell phone keep on their person a digital record of nearly every aspect of their lives — from the mundane to the intimate. Allowing the police to scrutinize such records on a routine basis is quite different from allowing them to search a personal item or two in the occasional case.

Although the data stored on a cell phone is distinguished from physical records by quantity alone, certain types of data are also qualitatively different. An Internet search and browsing history, for example, can be found on an Internet-enabled phone and could reveal an individual's private interests or concerns — perhaps a search for certain symptoms of disease, coupled with frequent visits to WebMD. Data on a cell phone can also reveal where a person has been. Historic location information is a standard feature on many smart phones and can reconstruct someone's specific movements down to the minute, not only around town but also within a particular building.

Mobile application software on a cell phone, or "apps," offer a range of tools for managing detailed information about all aspects of a person's life. There are apps for Democratic Party news and Republican Party news; apps for alcohol, drug, and gambling addictions; apps for sharing prayer requests; apps for tracking pregnancy symptoms; apps for planning your budget; apps for every conceivable hobby or pastime; apps for improving your romantic life. There are popular apps for buying or selling just about anything, and the records of such transactions may be accessible on the phone indefinitely. There are over a million apps available in each of the two major app stores; the phrase "there's an app for that" is now part of the popular lexicon. The average smart phone user has installed 33 apps, which together can form a revealing montage of the user's life.

To further complicate the scope of the privacy interests at stake, the data a user views on many modern cell phones may not in fact be stored on the device itself. Treating a cell phone as a container whose contents may be searched incident to an arrest is a bit strained as an initial matter. But the analogy crumbles entirely when a cell phone is used to access data located elsewhere, at the tap of a screen. That is what cell phones, with increasing frequency, are designed to do by taking advantage of "cloud computing." Cloud computing is the capacity of Internet-connected devices to display data stored on remote servers rather than on the device itself. Cell phone users often may not know whether particular information is stored on the device or in the cloud, and it generally makes little difference. Moreover, the same type of data may be stored locally on the device for one user and in the cloud for another.

The United States concedes that the search incident to arrest exception may not be stretched to cover a search of files accessed remotely — that is, a search of files stored in the cloud. Such a search would be like finding a key in a suspect's pocket and arguing that it allowed law enforcement to unlock and search a house. But officers searching a phone's data would not typically know whether the information they are viewing was stored locally at the time of the arrest or has been pulled from the cloud.

Although the Government recognizes the problem, its proposed solutions are unclear. It suggests that officers could disconnect a phone from the network before searching the device — the very solution whose feasibility it contested with respect to the threat of remote wiping. Alternatively, the Government proposes that law enforcement agencies "develop protocols to address" concerns raised by cloud computing. Probably a good idea, but the Founders did not fight a revolution to gain the right to government agency protocols. The possibility that a search might extend well beyond papers and effects in the physical proximity of an arrestee is yet another reason that the privacy interests here dwarf those in *Robinson*.

C

Apart from their arguments for a direct extension of *Robinson*, the United States and California offer various fallback options for permitting warrantless cell phone searches under certain circumstances. Each of the proposals is flawed and contravenes our general preference to provide clear guidance to law enforcement through categorical rules.

The United States first proposes that the *Gant* standard be imported from the vehicle context, allowing a warrantless search of an arrestee's cell phone whenever it is reasonable to believe that the phone contains evidence of the crime of arrest. But *Gant* relied on "circumstances unique to the vehicle context" to endorse a search solely for the purpose of gathering evidence. [T]hose unique circumstances are "a reduced expectation of privacy" and "heightened law enforcement needs" when it comes to motor vehicles. For reasons that we have explained, cell phone searches bear neither of those characteristics.

At any rate, a *Gant* standard would prove no practical limit at all when it comes to cell phone searches. In the vehicle context, *Gant* generally protects against searches for evidence of past crimes. In the cell phone context, however, it is reasonable to expect that incriminating information will be found on a phone regardless of when the crime occurred.

We also reject the United States' final suggestion that officers should always be able to search a phone's call log, as they did in Wurie's case. The Government relies on Smith v. Maryland (1979), which held that no warrant was required to use a pen register at telephone company premises to identify numbers dialed by a particular caller. The Court in that case, however, concluded that the use of a pen register was not a "search" at all under the Fourth Amendment. There is no dispute here that the officers engaged in a search of Wurie's cell phone. Moreover, call logs typically contain more than just phone numbers; they include any identifying information that an individual might add, such as the label "my house" in Wurie's case.

Finally, at oral argument California suggested a different limiting principle, under which officers could search cell phone data if they could have obtained the same information from a pre-digital counterpart. But the fact that a search in the pre-digital era could have turned up a photograph or two in a wallet does not justify a search of thousands of photos in a digital gallery. The fact that someone could have tucked a paper bank statement in a pocket does not justify a search of every bank statement from the last five years. And to make matters worse, such an analogue test would allow law enforcement to search a range of items contained on a phone, even though people would be unlikely to carry such a variety of information in physical form.

IV

We cannot deny that our decision today will have an impact on the ability of law enforcement to combat crime. Cell phones have become important tools in facilitating coordination and communication among members of criminal enterprises, and can provide valuable incriminating information about dangerous criminals. Privacy comes at a cost.

Our holding, of course, is not that the information on a cell phone is immune from search; it is instead that a warrant is generally required before such a search, even when a cell phone is seized incident to arrest. Our cases have historically recognized that the warrant requirement is "an important working part of our machinery of government," not merely "an inconvenience to be somehow 'weighed' against the claims of police efficiency." Recent technological advances similar to those discussed here have, in addition, made the process of obtaining a warrant itself more efficient.

Moreover, even though the search incident to arrest exception does not apply to cell phones, other case-specific exceptions may still justify a warrantless search of a particular phone. "One well-recognized exception applies when '"the exigencies of the situation" make the needs of law enforcement so compelling that [a] warrantless search is objectively reasonable under the Fourth Amendment.'" Such exigencies could include the need to prevent the imminent destruction of evidence in individual cases, to pursue a fleeing suspect, and to assist persons who are seriously injured or are threatened with imminent injury.

In light of the availability of the exigent circumstances exception, there is no reason to believe that law enforcement officers will not be able to address some of the more extreme hypotheticals that have been suggested: a suspect texting an accomplice who, it is feared, is preparing to detonate a bomb, or a child abductor who may have information about the child's location on his cell phone.

Modern cell phones are not just another technological convenience. With all they contain and all they may reveal, they hold for many Americans "the privacies of life," The fact that technology now allows an individual to carry such information in his hand does not make the information any less worthy of the protection for which the Founders fought. Our answer to the question of what police must do before searching a cell phone seized incident to an arrest is accordingly simple — get a warrant.

Justice ALITO, concurring in part and concurring in the judgment.

I agree with the Court that law enforcement officers, in conducting a lawful search incident to arrest, must generally obtain a warrant before searching information stored or accessible on a cell phone. I write separately to address two points.

First, I am not convinced at this time that the ancient rule on searches incident to arrest is based exclusively (or even primarily) on the need to protect the safety of arresting officers and the need to prevent the destruction of evidence.

This brings me to my second point. While I agree with the holding of the Court, I would reconsider the question presented here if either Congress or state legislatures, after assessing the legitimate needs of law enforcement and the privacy interests of cell phone owners, enact legislation that draws reasonable distinctions based on categories of information or perhaps other variables.

Modern cell phones are of great value for both lawful and unlawful purposes. They can be used in committing many serious crimes, and they present new and difficult law enforcement problems. At the same time, because of the role that these devices have come to play in contemporary life, searching their contents implicates very sensitive privacy interests that this Court is poorly positioned to understand and evaluate.

In light of these developments, it would be very unfortunate if privacy protection in the 21st century were left primarily to the federal courts using the blunt instrument of the Fourth Amendment. Legislatures, elected by the people, are in a better position than we are to assess and respond to the changes that have already occurred and those that almost certainly will take place in the future.

———————————

The Court has specifically focused on how searches incident to arrests apply in terms of the ability of police to search a car when a person has been lawfully arrested after his or her vehicle has been pulled over. In New York v. Belton, 453 U.S. 454 (1981), the Court held that when the police pulled over a car and ordered the occupants out of the car, "the police may also examine the contents of any containers found within the passenger compartment, for if the passenger compartment is within reach of the arrestee, so also will containers in it be within his reach. Such a container may, of course, be searched whether it is open or closed, since the justification for the search is not that the arrestee has no privacy interest in the container, but that the lawful custodial arrest justifies the infringement of any privacy interest the arrestee may have." The Court said that "'Container' here denotes any object capable of holding another object. It thus includes closed or open glove compartments, consoles, or other receptacles located anywhere within the passenger compartment, as well as luggage, boxes, bags, clothing, and the like. Our holding encompasses only the interior of the passenger compartment of an automobile and does not encompass the trunk."

In Thornton v. United States, 541 U.S. 615 (2004), the Court extended *Belton* to a situation in which the car was already stopped and the driver had exited and then the arrest was made. The Court said that *Belton* applied even though the driver was under arrest in the squad car when the search was done. Some of the justices urge a reconsideration of *Belton*.

In Arizona v. Gant, the Court reconsidered *Belton*. The Court held that if the suspect is not near the car, then there is no need for the exception created in *Belton*. However, *Belton* would still apply if the suspect was near the car. Also, the Court said that even in situations where the driver and passengers are restrained and do not have access to the car, the police may search the interior of the car only if they reasonably believe that evidence of the crime that led to the arrest might be found.

ARIZONA v. GANT

556 U.S. 332 (2009)

Justice STEVENS delivered the opinion of the Court.

After Rodney Gant was arrested for driving with a suspended license, handcuffed, and locked in the back of a patrol car, police officers searched his car and discovered cocaine in the pocket of a jacket on the backseat. Because Gant could not have accessed his car to retrieve weapons or evidence at the time of the search, the Arizona Supreme Court held that the search-incident-to-arrest exception to the Fourth Amendment's warrant requirement, as defined in *Chimel v. California* (1969), and applied to vehicle searches in *New York v. Belton* (1981), did not justify the search in this case. We agree with that conclusion.

Under *Chimel*, police may search incident to arrest only the space within an arrestee's "immediate control," meaning "the area from within which he might gain possession of a weapon or destructible evidence." The safety and evidentiary justifications underlying *Chimel*'s reaching-distance rule determine *Belton*'s scope. Accordingly, we hold that *Belton* does not authorize a vehicle search incident to a recent occupant's arrest after the arrestee has been secured and cannot access the interior of the vehicle. Consistent with the holding in *Thornton v. United States* (2004), we also conclude that circumstances unique to the automobile context justify a search incident to arrest when it is reasonable to believe that evidence of the offense of arrest might be found in the vehicle.

I

On August 25, 1999, acting on an anonymous tip that the residence at 2524 North Walnut Avenue was being used to sell drugs, Tucson police officers Griffith and Reed knocked on the front door and asked to speak to the owner. Gant answered the door and, after identifying himself, stated that he expected the owner to return later. The officers left the residence and conducted a records check, which revealed that Gant's driver's license had been suspended and there was an outstanding warrant for his arrest for driving with a suspended license.

When the officers returned to the house that evening, they found a man near the back of the house and a woman in a car parked in front of it. After a third officer arrived, they arrested the man for providing a false name and the woman for possessing drug paraphernalia. Both arrestees were handcuffed and secured in separate patrol cars when Gant arrived. The officers recognized his car as it entered the driveway, and Officer Griffith confirmed that Gant was the driver by shining a flashlight into the car as it drove by him. Gant parked at the end of the driveway, got out of his car, and shut the door. Griffith, who was about 30 feet away, called to Gant, and they approached each other, meeting 10 to 12 feet from Gant's car. Griffith immediately arrested Gant and handcuffed him.

Because the other arrestees were secured in the only patrol cars at the scene, Griffith called for backup. When two more officers arrived, they locked Gant in the backseat of their vehicle. After Gant had been handcuffed and placed in the back of a patrol car, two officers searched his car: One of them found a gun, and the other discovered a bag of cocaine in the pocket of a jacket on the backseat.

Gant was charged with two offenses — possession of a narcotic drug for sale and possession of drug paraphernalia (*i.e.*, the plastic bag in which the cocaine was found). He moved to suppress the evidence seized from his car on the ground that the warrantless search violated the Fourth Amendment. Among other things, Gant argued that *Belton* did not authorize the search of his vehicle because he posed no threat to the officers after he was handcuffed in the patrol car and because he was arrested for a traffic offense for which no evidence could be found in his vehicle. When asked at the suppression hearing why the search was conducted, Officer Griffith responded: "Because the law says we can do it." The trial court rejected the State's contention that the officers had probable cause to search Gant's car for contraband when the search began, but it denied the motion to suppress. Relying on the fact that the police saw

Gant commit the crime of driving without a license and apprehended him only shortly after he exited his car, the court held that the search was permissible as a search incident to arrest. A jury found Gant guilty on both drug counts, and he was sentenced to a 3-year term of imprisonment.

After protracted state-court proceedings, the Arizona Supreme Court concluded that the search of Gant's car was unreasonable within the meaning of the Fourth Amendment. The court's opinion discussed at length our decision in *Belton*, which held that police may search the passenger compartment of a vehicle and any containers therein as a contemporaneous incident of an arrest of the vehicle's recent occupant. The court distinguished *Belton* as a case concerning the permissible scope of a vehicle search incident to arrest and concluded that it did not answer "the threshold question whether the police may conduct a search incident to arrest at all once the scene is secure." When "the justifications underlying *Chimel* no longer exist because the scene is secure and the arrestee is handcuffed, secured in the back of a patrol car, and under the supervision of an officer," the court concluded, a "warrantless search of the arrestee's car cannot be justified as necessary to protect the officers at the scene or prevent the destruction of evidence." Accordingly, the court held that the search of Gant's car was unreasonable.

II

Consistent with our precedent, our analysis begins, as it should in every case addressing the reasonableness of a warrantless search, with the basic rule that "searches conducted outside the judicial process, without prior approval by judge or magistrate, are *per se* unreasonable under the Fourth Amendment — subject only to a few specifically established and well-delineated exceptions." Among the exceptions to the warrant requirement is a search incident to a lawful arrest. The exception derives from interests in officer safety and evidence preservation that are typically implicated in arrest situations.

In *Chimel*, we held that a search incident to arrest may only include "the arrestee's person and the area 'within his immediate control' — construing that phrase to mean the area from within which he might gain possession of a weapon or destructible evidence." That limitation, which continues to define the boundaries of the exception, ensures that the scope of a search incident to arrest is commensurate with its purposes of protecting arresting officers and safeguarding any evidence of the offense of arrest that an arrestee might conceal or destroy. If there is no possibility that an arrestee could reach into the area that law enforcement officers seek to search, both justifications for the search-incident-to-arrest exception are absent and the rule does not apply.

In *Belton*, we considered *Chimel*'s application to the automobile context. A lone police officer in that case stopped a speeding car in which Belton was one of four occupants. While asking for the driver's license and registration, the officer smelled burnt marijuana and observed an envelope on the car floor marked "Supergold" — a name he associated with marijuana. Thus having probable cause to believe the occupants had committed a drug offense, the officer ordered them out of the vehicle, placed them under arrest, and patted them down. Without handcuffing the arrestees, the officer "'split them up into four separate areas of the Thruway . . . so they would not be in physical touching area of each other'" and searched the vehicle, including the pocket of a jacket on the backseat, in which he found cocaine.

After considering these arguments, we held that when an officer lawfully arrests "the occupant of an automobile, he may, as a contemporaneous incident of that arrest, search the passenger compartment of the automobile" and any containers therein. That holding was based in large part on our assumption "that articles inside the relatively narrow compass of the passenger compartment of an automobile are in fact generally, even if not inevitably, within 'the area into which an arrestee might reach.'"

III

Despite the textual and evidentiary support for the Arizona Supreme Court's reading of *Belton*, our opinion has been widely understood to allow a vehicle search incident to the arrest of a recent occupant even if there is no possibility the arrestee could gain access to the vehicle at the time of the search. Under this broad reading of *Belton*, a vehicle search would be authorized incident to every arrest of a recent occupant notwithstanding that in most cases the vehicle's passenger compartment will not be within the arrestee's reach at the time of the search. To read *Belton* as authorizing a vehicle search incident to every recent occupant's arrest would thus untether the rule from the justifications underlying the *Chimel* exception—a result clearly incompatible with our statement in *Belton* that it "in no way alters the fundamental principles established in the *Chimel* case regarding the basic scope of searches incident to lawful custodial arrests." Accordingly, we reject this reading of *Belton* and hold that the *Chimel* rationale authorizes police to search a vehicle incident to a recent occupant's arrest only when the arrestee is unsecured and within reaching distance of the passenger compartment at the time of the search.

Although it does not follow from *Chimel*, we also conclude that circumstances unique to the vehicle context justify a search incident to a lawful arrest when it is "reasonable to believe evidence relevant to the crime of arrest might be found in the vehicle." In many cases, as when a recent occupant is arrested for a traffic violation, there will be no reasonable basis to believe the vehicle contains relevant evidence. But in others, including *Belton* and *Thornton*, the offense of arrest will supply a basis for searching the passenger compartment of an arrestee's vehicle and any containers therein.

Neither the possibility of access nor the likelihood of discovering offense-related evidence authorized the search in this case. Unlike in *Belton*, which involved a single officer confronted with four unsecured arrestees, the five officers in this case outnumbered the three arrestees, all of whom had been handcuffed and secured in separate patrol cars before the officers searched

Gant's car. Under those circumstances, Gant clearly was not within reaching distance of his car at the time of the search. An evidentiary basis for the search was also lacking in this case. Whereas Belton and Thornton were arrested for drug offenses, Gant was arrested for driving with a suspended license — an offense for which police could not expect to find evidence in the passenger compartment of Gant's car. Because police could not reasonably have believed either that Gant could have accessed his car at the time of the search or that evidence of the offense for which he was arrested might have been found therein, the search in this case was unreasonable.

IV

The State does not seriously disagree with the Arizona Supreme Court's conclusion that Gant could not have accessed his vehicle at the time of the search, but it nevertheless asks us to uphold the search of his vehicle under the broad reading of *Belton* discussed above. The State argues that *Belton* searches are reasonable regardless of the possibility of access in a given case because that expansive rule correctly balances law enforcement interests, including the interest in a bright-line rule, with an arrestee's limited privacy interest in his vehicle.

For several reasons, we reject the State's argument. First, the State seriously undervalues the privacy interests at stake. Although we have recognized that a motorist's privacy interest in his vehicle is less substantial than in his home, the former interest is nevertheless important and deserving of constitutional protection. It is particularly significant that *Belton* searches authorize police officers to search not just the passenger compartment but every purse, briefcase, or other container within that space. A rule that gives police the power to conduct such a search whenever an individual is caught committing a traffic offense, when there is no basis for believing evidence of the offense might be found in the vehicle, creates a serious and recurring threat to the privacy of countless individuals. Indeed, the character of that threat implicates the central concern underlying the Fourth Amendment — the concern about giving police officers unbridled discretion to rummage at will among a person's private effects.

At the same time as it undervalues these privacy concerns, the State exaggerates the clarity that its reading of *Belton* provides. Courts that have read *Belton* expansively are at odds regarding how close in time to the arrest and how proximate to the arrestee's vehicle an officer's first contact with the arrestee must be to bring the encounter within *Belton*'s purview and whether a search is reasonable when it commences or continues after the arrestee has been removed from the scene. The rule has thus generated a great deal of uncertainty, particularly for a rule touted as providing a "bright line."

Contrary to the State's suggestion, a broad reading of *Belton* is also unnecessary to protect law enforcement safety and evidentiary interests. Under our view, *Belton* and *Thornton* permit an officer to conduct a vehicle search when an arrestee is within reaching distance of the vehicle or it is reasonable to believe the vehicle contains evidence of the offense of arrest. Other established exceptions to the warrant requirement authorize a vehicle search under additional circumstances when safety or evidentiary concerns demand.

These exceptions together ensure that officers may search a vehicle when genuine safety or evidentiary concerns encountered during the arrest of a vehicle's recent occupant justify a search. Construing *Belton* broadly to allow vehicle searches incident to any arrest would serve no purpose except to provide a police entitlement, and it is anathema to the Fourth Amendment to permit a warrantless search on that basis. For these reasons, we are unpersuaded by the State's arguments that a broad reading of *Belton* would meaningfully further law enforcement interests and justify a substantial intrusion on individuals' privacy.

V

Our dissenting colleagues argue that the doctrine of *stare decisis* requires adherence to a broad reading of *Belton* even though the justifications for searching a vehicle incident to arrest are in most cases absent. The doctrine of *stare decisis* is of course "essential to the respect accorded to the judgments of the Court and to the stability of the law," but it does not compel us to follow a past decision when its rationale no longer withstands "careful analysis."

We have never relied on *stare decisis* to justify the continuance of an unconstitutional police practice. And we would be particularly loath to uphold an unconstitutional result in a case that is so easily distinguished from the decisions that arguably compel it. The safety and evidentiary interests that supported the search in *Belton* simply are not present in this case. Indeed, it is hard to imagine two cases that are factually more distinct, as *Belton* involved one officer confronted by four unsecured arrestees suspected of committing a drug offense and this case involves several officers confronted with a securely detained arrestee apprehended for driving with a suspended license. This case is also distinguishable from *Thornton*, in which the petitioner was arrested for a drug offense. It is thus unsurprising that Members of this Court who concurred in the judgments in *Belton* and *Thornton* also concur in the decision in this case.

VI

Police may search a vehicle incident to a recent occupant's arrest only if the arrestee is within reaching distance of the passenger compartment at the time of the search or it is reasonable to believe the vehicle contains evidence of the offense of arrest. When these justifications are absent, a search of an arrestee's vehicle will be unreasonable unless police obtain a warrant or show that another exception to the warrant requirement applies.

Justice SCALIA, concurring.

To determine what is an "unreasonable" search within the meaning of the Fourth Amendment, we look first to the historical practices the Framers sought to preserve; if those provide inadequate guidance, we apply traditional standards of reasonableness. Since the historical scope of officers' authority to search vehicles incident to arrest is uncertain, traditional standards of reasonableness govern. It is abundantly clear that those standards do not justify what I take to be the rule set forth in *New York v. Belton* (1981), that arresting officers may always search an arrestee's vehicle in order to protect themselves from hidden weapons. When an arrest is made in connection with a roadside stop, police virtually always have a less intrusive and more effective means of ensuring their safety—and a means that is virtually always employed: ordering the arrestee away from the vehicle, patting him down in the open, handcuffing him, and placing him in the squad car.

Law enforcement officers face a risk of being shot whenever they pull a car over. But that risk is at its height at the time of the initial confrontation; and it is *not at all* reduced by allowing a search of the stopped vehicle after the driver has been arrested and placed in the squad car. I observed in *Thornton* that the government had failed to provide a single instance in which a formerly restrained arrestee escaped to retrieve a weapon from his own vehicle; Arizona and its *amici* have not remedied that significant deficiency in the present case.

It must be borne in mind that we are speaking here only of a rule automatically permitting a search when the driver or an occupant is arrested. Where no arrest is made, we have held that officers may search the car if they reasonably believe "the suspect is dangerous and . . . may gain immediate control of weapons." In the no-arrest case, the possibility of access to weapons in the vehicle always exists, since the driver or passenger will be allowed to return to the vehicle when the interrogation is completed. The rule of *Michigan v. Long* is not at issue here.

Justice Stevens acknowledges that an officer-safety rationale cannot justify all vehicle searches incident to arrest, but asserts that that is not the rule *Belton* and *Thornton* adopted. Justice Stevens would therefore retain the application of *Chimel v. California* (1969), in the car-search context but would apply in the future what he believes our cases held in the past: that officers making a roadside stop may search the vehicle so long as the "arrestee is within reaching distance of the passenger compartment at the time of the search." I believe that this standard fails to provide the needed guidance to arresting officers and also leaves much room for manipulation, inviting officers to leave the scene unsecured (at least where dangerous suspects are not involved) in order to conduct a vehicle search. In my view we should simply abandon the *Belton-Thornton* charade of officer safety and overrule those cases. I would hold that a vehicle search incident to arrest is *ipso facto* "reasonable" only when the object of the search is evidence of the crime for which the arrest was made, or of another crime that the officer has probable cause to believe occurred. Because respondent was arrested for driving without a license (a crime for which no evidence could be expected to be found in the vehicle), I would hold in the present case that the search was unlawful.

Justice Alito insists that the Court must demand a good reason for abandoning prior precedent. That is true enough, but it seems to me ample reason that the precedent was badly reasoned and produces erroneous (in this case unconstitutional) results.

No other Justice, however, shares my view that application of *Chimel* in this context should be entirely abandoned. It seems to me unacceptable for the Court to come forth with a 4-to-1-to-4 opinion that leaves the governing rule uncertain. I am therefore confronted with the choice of either leaving the current understanding of *Belton* and *Thornton* in effect, or acceding to what seems to me the artificial narrowing of those cases adopted by Justice Stevens. The latter, as I have said, does not provide the degree of certainty I think desirable in this field; but the former opens the field to what I think are plainly unconstitutional searches — which is the greater evil. I therefore join the opinion of the Court.

Justice ALITO, with whom THE CHIEF JUSTICE and Justice KENNEDY join, and with whom Justice BREYER joins except as to Part II-E, dissenting.

Twenty-eight years ago, in *New York v. Belton* (1981), this Court held that "when a policeman has made a lawful custodial arrest of the occupant of an automobile, he may, as a contemporaneous incident of that arrest, search the passenger compartment of that automobile." Five years ago, in *Thornton v. United States* (2004) — a case involving a situation not materially distinguishable from the situation here — the Court not only reaffirmed but extended the holding of *Belton*, making it applicable to recent occupants. Today's decision effectively overrules those important decisions, even though respondent Gant has not asked us to do so.

To take the place of the overruled precedents, the Court adopts a new two-part rule under which a police officer who arrests a vehicle occupant or recent occupant may search the passenger compartment if (1) the arrestee is within reaching distance of the vehicle at the time of the search or (2) the officer has reason to believe that the vehicle contains evidence of the offense of arrest. The first part of this new rule may endanger arresting officers and is truly endorsed by only four Justices; Justice Scalia joins solely for the purpose of avoiding a "4-to-1-to-4 opinion." The second part of the new rule is taken from Justice Scalia's separate opinion in *Thornton* without any independent explanation of its origin or justification and is virtually certain to confuse law enforcement officers and judges for some time to come. The Court's decision will cause the suppression of evidence gathered in many searches carried out in good-faith reliance on well-settled case law, and although the Court purports to base its analysis on the landmark decision in *Chimel v. California* (1969), the Court's reasoning undermines *Chimel*. I would follow *Belton*, and I therefore respectfully dissent.

I

Although the Court refuses to acknowledge that it is overruling *Belton* and *Thornton*, there can be no doubt that it does so. The precise holding in *Belton* could not be clearer. The Court stated unequivocally: "[W]e hold that when a policeman has made a lawful custodial arrest of the occupant of an automobile, he may, as a contemporaneous incident of that arrest, search the passenger compartment of that automobile."

Despite this explicit statement, the opinion of the Court in the present case curiously suggests that *Belton* may reasonably be read as adopting a holding that is narrower than the one explicitly set out in the *Belton* opinion, namely, that an officer arresting a vehicle occupant may search the passenger compartment "*when* the passenger compartment is within an arrestee's reaching distance."

II

Because the Court has substantially overruled *Belton* and *Thornton*, the Court must explain why its departure from the usual rule of *stare decisis* is justified. I recognize that stare decisis is not an "inexorable command," and applies less rigidly in constitutional cases. But the Court has said that a constitutional precedent should be followed unless there is a "special justification" for its abandonment. Relevant factors identified in prior cases include whether the precedent has engendered reliance, whether there has been an important change in circumstances in the outside world, whether the precedent has proved to be unworkable, whether the precedent has been undermined by later decisions, and whether the decision was badly reasoned. These factors weigh in favor of retaining the rule established in *Belton*.

A

Reliance. While reliance is most important in "cases involving property and contract rights," the Court has recognized that reliance by law enforcement officers is also entitled to weight. [T]here certainly is substantial reliance here. The *Belton* rule has been taught to police officers for more than a quarter century. Many searches—almost certainly including more than a few that figure in cases now on appeal—were conducted in scrupulous reliance on that precedent. It is likely that, on the very day when this opinion is announced, numerous vehicle searches will be conducted in good faith by police officers who were taught the *Belton* rule.

B

Changed circumstances. Abandonment of the *Belton* rule cannot be justified on the ground that the dangers surrounding the arrest of a vehicle occupant are different today than they were 28 years ago.

C

Workability. The *Belton* rule has not proved to be unworkable. On the contrary, the rule was adopted for the express purpose of providing a test that would be relatively easy for police officers and judges to apply. The Court correctly notes that even the *Belton* rule is not perfectly clear in all situations. Specifically, it is sometimes debatable whether a search is or is not contemporaneous with an arrest, but that problem is small in comparison with the problems that the Court's new two-part rule will produce.

D

Consistency with later cases. The *Belton* bright-line rule has not been undermined by subsequent cases. On the contrary, that rule was reaffirmed and extended just five years ago in *Thornton.*

E

Bad reasoning. The Court is harshly critical of *Belton*'s reasoning, but the problem that the Court perceives cannot be remedied simply by overruling *Belton. Belton* represented only a modest — and quite defensible — extension of *Chimel,* as I understand that decision.

F

The Court, however, does not reexamine *Chimel* and thus leaves the law relating to searches incident to arrest in a confused and unstable state. The first part of the Court's new two-part rule — which permits an arresting officer to search the area within an arrestee's reach at the time of the search — applies, at least for now, only to vehicle occupants and recent occupants, but there is no logical reason why the same rule should not apply to all arrestees.

The second part of the Court's new rule, which the Court takes uncritically from Justice Scalia's separate opinion in *Thornton,* raises doctrinal and practical problems that the Court makes no effort to address. Why, for example, is the standard for this type of evidence-gathering search "reason to believe" rather than probable cause? And why is this type of search restricted to evidence of the offense of arrest? It is true that an arrestee's vehicle is probably more likely to contain evidence of the crime of arrest than of some other crime, but if reason-to-believe is the governing standard for an evidence-gathering search incident to arrest, it is not easy to see why an officer should not be able to search when the officer has reason to believe that the vehicle in question possesses evidence of a crime other than the crime of arrest.

Nor is it easy to see why an evidence-gathering search incident to arrest should be restricted to the passenger compartment. The *Belton* rule was limited in this way because the passenger compartment was considered to be the area that vehicle occupants can generally reach but since the second part of the new rule is not based on officer safety or the preservation of evidence, the ground for this limitation is obscure.

III

Respondent in this case has not asked us to overrule *Belton*, much less *Chimel*. Respondent's argument rests entirely on an interpretation of *Belton* that is plainly incorrect, an interpretation that disregards *Belton*'s explicit delineation of its holding. I would therefore leave any reexamination of our prior precedents for another day, if such a reexamination is to be undertaken at all. In this case, I would simply apply *Belton* and reverse the judgment below.

5.   Inventory Searches

Another exception to the warrant requirement is for inventory searches. If property is lawfully in the possession of the police, they may inventory the contents to protect the owner's property while it is in police possession. In South Dakota v. Opperman, the Court considered the ability of the police to inventory the contents of a car that had been impounded for a parking violation.

SOUTH DAKOTA v. OPPERMAN
428 U.S. 364 (1976)

Chief Justice BURGER delivered the opinion of the Court.

We review the judgment of the Supreme Court of South Dakota, holding that local police violated the Fourth Amendment to the Federal Constitution, as applicable to the States under the Fourteenth Amendment, when they conducted a routine inventory search of an automobile lawfully impounded by police for violations of municipal parking ordinances.

Local ordinances prohibit parking in certain areas of downtown Vermillion, S.D., between the hours of 2 A.M. and 6 A.M. During the early morning hours of December 10, 1973, a Vermillion police officer observed respondent's unoccupied vehicle illegally parked in the restricted zone. At approximately 3 A.M., the officer issued an overtime parking ticket and placed it on the car's windshield. The citation warned: "Vehicles in violation of any parking ordinance may be towed from the area."

At approximately 10 o'clock on the same morning, another officer issued a second ticket for an overtime parking violation. These circumstances were routinely reported to police headquarters, and after the vehicle was inspected, the car was towed to the city impound lot.

From outside the car at the impound lot, a police officer observed a watch on the dashboard and other items of personal property located on the back seat and back floorboard. At the officer's direction, the car door was then unlocked and, using a standard inventory form pursuant to standard police procedures, the officer inventoried the contents of the car, including the contents of the glove compartment which was unlocked. There he found marihuana contained in a plastic bag. All items, including the contraband, were removed to the police department for safekeeping. During the late afternoon of December 10, respondent appeared at the police department to claim his property. The marihuana was retained by police.

Respondent was subsequently arrested on charges of possession of marihuana. His motion to suppress the evidence yielded by the inventory search was denied; he was convicted after a jury trial and sentenced to a fine of $100 and 14 days' incarceration in the county jail. On appeal, the Supreme Court of South Dakota reversed the conviction. The court concluded that the evidence had been obtained in violation of the Fourth Amendment prohibition against unreasonable searches and seizures. We granted certiorari and we reverse.

This Court has traditionally drawn a distinction between automobiles and homes or offices in relation to the Fourth Amendment. Although automobiles are "effects" and thus within the reach of the Fourth Amendment, warrantless examinations of automobiles have been upheld in circumstances in which a search of a home or office would not. [T]he inherent mobility of automobiles creates circumstances of such exigency that, as a practical necessity, rigorous enforcement of the warrant requirement is impossible. Automobiles, unlike homes, are subjected to pervasive and continuing governmental regulation and controls, including periodic inspection and licensing requirements. As an everyday occurrence, police stop and examine vehicles when license plates or inspection stickers have expired, or if other violations, such as exhaust fumes or excessive noise, are noted, or if headlights or other safety equipment are not in proper working order. The expectation of privacy as to automobiles is further diminished by the obviously public nature of automobile travel.

In the interests of public safety and as part of what the Court has called "community caretaking functions," automobiles are frequently taken into police custody. Vehicle accidents present one such occasion. To permit the uninterrupted flow of traffic and in some circumstances to preserve evidence, disabled or damaged vehicles will often be removed from the highways or streets at the behest of police engaged solely in caretaking and traffic-control activities. Police will also frequently remove and impound automobiles which violate parking ordinances and which thereby jeopardize both the public safety and the efficient movement of vehicular traffic. The authority of police to seize and remove from the streets vehicles impeding traffic or threatening public safety and convenience is beyond challenge.

When vehicles are impounded, local police departments generally follow a routine practice of securing and inventorying the automobiles' contents. These procedures developed in response to three distinct needs: the protection of the owner's property while it remains in police custody; the protection of the police against claims or disputes over lost or stolen property; and the protection of the police from potential danger. The practice has been viewed as essential to respond to incidents of theft or vandalism. In addition, police frequently attempt to determine whether a vehicle has been stolen and thereafter abandoned.

In view of the noncriminal context of inventory searches, and the inapplicability in such a setting of the requirement of probable cause, courts have held and quite correctly that search warrants are not required, linked as the warrant requirement textually is to the probable-cause concept. We have frequently observed that the warrant requirement assures that legal inferences and conclusions as to probable cause will be drawn by a neutral magistrate unrelated to the criminal investigative-enforcement process. With respect to noninvestigative police inventories of automobiles lawfully within governmental custody, however, the policies underlying the warrant requirement are inapplicable.

The decisions of this Court point unmistakably to the conclusion reached by both federal and state courts that inventories pursuant to standard police procedures are reasonable. In applying the reasonableness standard adopted by the Framers, this Court has consistently sustained police intrusions into automobiles impounded or otherwise in lawful police custody where the process is aimed at securing or protecting the car and its contents. [I]n Cady v. Dombrowski (1973), [t]he Court upheld a warrantless search of an automobile towed to a private garage even though no probable cause existed to believe that the vehicle contained fruits of a crime. The sole justification for the warrantless incursion was that it was incident to the caretaking function of the local police to protect the community's safety. Indeed, the protective search was instituted solely because the local police "were under the impression" that the incapacitated driver, a Chicago police officer, was required to carry his service revolver at all times; the police had reasonable grounds to believe a weapon might be in the car, and thus available to vandals. The Court carefully noted that the protective search was carried out in accordance with standard procedures in the local police department, a factor tending to ensure that the intrusion would be limited in scope to the extent necessary to carry out the caretaking function.

On this record we conclude that in following standard police procedures, prevailing throughout the country and approved by the overwhelming majority of courts, the conduct of the police was not "unreasonable" under the Fourth Amendment.

Justice MARSHALL, with whom Justice BRENNAN and Justice STEWART join, dissenting.

The Court today holds that the Fourth Amendment permits a routine police inventory search of the closed glove compartment of a locked automobile impounded for ordinary traffic violations. Under the Court's holding, such a search may be made without attempting to secure the consent of the owner and without any particular reason to believe the impounded automobile contains contraband, evidence, or valuables, or presents any danger to its custodians or the public.[8] Because I believe this holding to be contrary to sound elaboration of established Fourth Amendment principles, I dissent.

[T]he requirement of a warrant aside, resolution of the question whether an inventory search of closed compartments inside a locked automobile can ever be justified as a constitutionally "reasonable" search depends upon a reconciliation of the owner's constitutionally protected privacy interests against governmental intrusion, and legitimate governmental interests furthered by securing the car and its contents. The Court fails clearly to articulate the reasons for its reconciliation of these interests in this case, but it is at least clear to me that the considerations alluded to by the Court are insufficient to justify the Court's result in this case.

Contrary to the Court's assertion, however, the search of respondent's car was not in any way "prompted by the presence in plain view of a number of valuables inside the car." In fact, the record plainly states that every vehicle taken to the city impound lot was inventoried, and that as a matter of "standard procedure," "every inventory search" would involve entry into the car's closed glove compartment.

The Court's opinion appears to suggest that its result may in any event be justified because the inventory search procedure is a "reasonable" response to "three distinct needs: the protection of the owner's property while it remains in police custody . . . ; the protection of the police against claims or disputes over lost or stolen property . . . ; and the protection of the police from potential danger." This suggestion is flagrantly misleading, however, because the record of this case explicitly belies any relevance of the last two concerns. In any event it is my view that none of these "needs," separately or together, can suffice to justify the inventory search procedure approved by the Court.

First, this search cannot be justified in any way as a safety measure, for though the Court ignores it the sole purpose given by the State for the Vermillion police's inventory procedure was to secure valuables. Nor is there any indication that the officer's search in this case was tailored in any way to safety concerns, or that ordinarily it is so circumscribed. Even aside from the actual basis for the police practice in this case, however, I do not believe that any blanket safety argument could justify a program of routine searches of the scope permitted here.

The Court suggests a further "crucial" justification for the search in this case: "protection of the Public from vandals who might find a firearm, or as here, contraband drugs." This rationale, too, is absolutely without support in this record. There is simply no indication the police were looking for dangerous items. Indeed, even though the police found shotgun shells in the interior of the car, they never opened the trunk to determine whether it might contain a shotgun. Aside from this, the suggestion is simply untenable as a matter of law. If this asserted rationale justifies search of all impounded

---

8. The Court does not consider, however, whether the police might open and search the glove compartment if it is locked, or whether the police might search a locked trunk or other compartment. [Footnote by the Court.]

automobiles, it must logically also justify the search of all automobiles, whether impounded or not, located in a similar area, for the argument is not based upon the custodial role of the police. But this Court has never permitted the search of any car or home on the mere undifferentiated assumption that it might be vandalized and the vandals might find dangerous weapons or substances.

Second, the Court suggests that the search for valuables in the closed glove compartment might be justified as a measure to protect the police against lost property claims. Again, this suggestion is belied by the record, since although the Court declines to discuss it, the South Dakota Supreme Court's interpretation of state law explicitly absolves the police, as "gratuitous depositors," from any obligation beyond inventorying objects in plain view and locking the car.

Finally, the Court suggests that the public interest in protecting valuables that may be found inside a closed compartment of an impounded car may justify the inventory procedure. I recognize the genuineness of this governmental interest in protecting property from pilferage. But even if I assume that the posting of a guard would be fiscally impossible as an alternative means to the same protective end, I cannot agree with the Court's conclusion. The Court's result authorizes, indeed it appears to require, the routine search of nearly every car impounded. In my view, the Constitution does not permit such searches as a matter of routine; absent specific consent, such a search is permissible only in exceptional circumstances of particular necessity.

———————————

South Dakota v. Opperman involves an inventory search of a car. Illinois v. Lafayette applies this to a person's possessions.

ILLINOIS v. LAFAYETTE
462 U.S. 640 (1983)

Chief Justice BURGER delivered the opinion of the Court.

The question presented is whether, at the time an arrested person arrives at a police station, the police may, without obtaining a warrant, search a shoulder bag carried by that person.

On September 1, 1980, at about 10 P.M., Officer Maurice Mietzner of the Kankakee City Police arrived at the Town Cinema in Kankakee, Illinois, in response to a call about a disturbance. There he found respondent involved in an altercation with the theatre manager. He arrested respondent for disturbing the peace, handcuffed him, and took him to the police station. Respondent carried a purse-type shoulder bag on the trip to the station.

At the police station respondent was taken to the booking room; there, Officer Mietzner removed the handcuffs from respondent and ordered him to empty his pockets and place the contents on the counter. After doing so, respondent took a package of cigarettes from his shoulder bag and placed the bag on the counter. Mietzner then removed the contents of the bag, and found ten amphetamine pills inside a cigarette case package.

Respondent was subsequently charged with violating the Illinois Controlled Substances Act on the basis of the controlled substances found in his shoulder bag.

The question here is whether, consistent with the Fourth Amendment, it is reasonable for police to search the personal effects of a person under lawful arrest as part of the routine administrative procedure at a police stationhouse incident to booking and jailing the suspect. The justification for such searches does not rest on probable cause, and hence the absence of a warrant is immaterial to the reasonableness of the search. Indeed, we have previously established that the inventory search constitutes a well-defined exception to the warrant requirement. *See* South Dakota v. Opperman.

A so-called inventory search is not an independent legal concept but rather an incidental administrative step following arrest and preceding incarceration. To determine whether the search of respondent's shoulder bag was unreasonable we must "balanc[e] its intrusion on the individual's Fourth Amendment interests against its promotion of legitimate governmental interests." Delaware v. Prouse (1979).

In order to see an inventory search in proper perspective, it is necessary to study the evolution of interests along the continuum from arrest to incarceration. We have held that immediately upon arrest an officer may lawfully search the person of an arrestee; he may also search the area within the arrestee's immediate control.

An arrested person is not invariably taken to a police station or confined; if an arrestee is taken to the police station, that is no more than a continuation of the custody inherent in the arrest status. Nonetheless, the factors justifying a search of the person and personal effects of an arrestee upon reaching a police station but prior to being placed in confinement are somewhat different from the factors justifying an immediate search at the time and place of arrest.

The governmental interests underlying a stationhouse search of the arrestee's person and possessions may in some circumstances be even greater than those supporting a search immediately following arrest. Consequently, the scope of a stationhouse search will often vary from that made at the time of arrest. Police conduct that would be impractical or unreasonable — or embarrassingly intrusive — on the street can more readily — and privately — be performed at the station. For example, the interests supporting a search incident to arrest would hardly justify disrobing an arrestee on the street, but the practical necessities of routine jail administration may even justify taking a prisoner's clothes before confining him, although that step would be rare.

At the stationhouse, it is entirely proper for police to remove and list or inventory property found on the person or in the possession of an arrested person who is to be jailed. A range of governmental interests support an inventory process. It is not unheard of for persons employed in police activities to steal property taken from arrested persons; similarly, arrested persons have been known to make false claims regarding what was taken from their possession at the stationhouse. A standardized procedure for making a list or inventory as soon as reasonable after reaching the stationhouse not only deters false claims but also inhibits theft or careless handling of articles taken from the arrested person. Arrested persons have also been known to injure themselves—or others—with belts, knives, drugs or other items on their person while being detained. Dangerous instrumentalities—such as razor blades, bombs, or weapons—can be concealed in innocent-looking articles taken from the arrestee's possession. The bare recital of these mundane realities justifies reasonable measures by police to limit these risks—either while the items are in police possession or at the time they are returned to the arrestee upon his release. Examining all the items removed from the arrestee's person or possession and listing or inventorying them is an entirely reasonable administrative procedure. It is immaterial whether the police actually fear any particular package or container; the need to protect against such risks arises independent of a particular officer's subjective concerns. Finally, inspection of an arrestee's personal property may assist the police in ascertaining or verifying his identity. In short, every consideration of orderly police administration benefiting both police and the public points toward the appropriateness of the examination of respondent's shoulder bag prior to his incarceration.

The reasonableness of any particular governmental activity does not necessarily or invariably turn on the existence of alternative "less intrusive" means. We are hardly in a position to second-guess police departments as to what practical administrative method will best deter theft by and false claims against its employees and preserve the security of the stationhouse. It is evident that a stationhouse search of every item carried on or by a person who has lawfully been taken into custody by the police will amply serve the important and legitimate governmental interests involved.

Even if less intrusive means existed of protecting some particular types of property, it would be unreasonable to expect police officers in the everyday course of business to make fine and subtle distinctions in deciding which containers or items may be searched and which must be sealed as a unit. Applying these principles, we hold that it is not "unreasonable" for police, as part of the routine procedure incident to incarcerating an arrested person, to search any container or article in his possession, in accordance with established inventory procedures.

6. Protective Sweeps

Similarly, the Court has held that when the police arrest a person, they may conduct a protective sweep of the premises if they have reasonable suspicion that a person might be there who poses a threat to them. In Maryland v. Buie,

494 U.S. 325 (1990), the Court said upheld such protective sweeps but said that such a sweep "may extend only to a cursory inspection of those places where a person may be found."

MARYLAND v. BUIE

494 U.S. 325 (1990)

Justice WHITE delivered the opinion of the Court.

A "protective sweep" is a quick and limited search of premises, incident to an arrest and conducted to protect the safety of police officers or others. It is narrowly confined to a cursory visual inspection of those places in which a person might be hiding. In this case we must decide what level of justification is required by the Fourth and Fourteenth Amendments before police officers, while effecting the arrest of a suspect in his home pursuant to an arrest warrant, may conduct a warrantless protective sweep of all or part of the premises. The Court of Appeals of Maryland held that a running suit seized in plain view during such a protective sweep should have been suppressed at respondent's armed robbery trial because the officer who conducted the sweep did not have probable cause to believe that a serious and demonstrable potentiality for danger existed. We conclude that the Fourth Amendment would permit the protective sweep undertaken here if the searching officer "possesse[d] a reasonable belief based on 'specific and articulable facts which, taken together with the rational inferences from those facts, reasonably warrant[ed]' the officer in believing" that the area swept harbored an individual posing a danger to the officer or others.

I

On February 3, 1986, two men committed an armed robbery of a Godfather's Pizza restaurant in Prince George's County, Maryland. One of the robbers was wearing a red running suit. That same day, Prince George's County police obtained arrest warrants for respondent Jerome Edward Buie and his suspected accomplice in the robbery, Lloyd Allen. Buie's house was placed under police surveillance.

On February 5, the police executed the arrest warrant for Buie. They first had a police department secretary telephone Buie's house to verify that he was home. The secretary spoke to a female first, then to Buie himself. Six or seven officers proceeded to Buie's house. Once inside, the officers fanned out through the first and second floors. Corporal James Rozar announced that he would "freeze" the basement so that no one could come up and surprise the officers. With his service revolver drawn, Rozar twice shouted into the basement, ordering anyone down there to come out. When a voice asked who was calling, Rozar announced three times: "this is the police, show me your hands." Eventually, a pair of hands appeared around the bottom of the stairwell and Buie emerged from the basement. He was arrested, searched, and handcuffed by Rozar. Thereafter, Detective Joseph Frolich entered the basement "in case there was someone else" down there. He noticed a red running suit lying in plain view on a stack of clothing and seized it.

The trial court denied Buie's motion to suppress the running suit, stating in part: "The man comes out from a basement, the police don't know how many other people are down there. He is charged with a serious offense." The State introduced the running suit into evidence at Buie's trial. A jury convicted Buie of robbery with a deadly weapon and using a handgun in the commission of a felony.

The Court of Special Appeals of Maryland affirmed the trial court's denial of the suppression motion. The court stated that Detective Frolich did not go into the basement to search for evidence, but to look for the suspected accomplice or anyone else who might pose a threat to the officers on the scene. The Court of Appeals of Maryland reversed by a 4-to-3 vote. The court, however, stated that when the sanctity of the home is involved, the exceptions to the warrant requirement are few, and held: "[T]o justify a protective sweep of a home, the government must show that there is probable cause to believe that "'a serious and demonstrable potentiality for danger'" exists."

II

It is not disputed that until the point of Buie's arrest the police had the right, based on the authority of the arrest warrant, to search anywhere in the house that Buie might have been found, including the basement. "If there is sufficient evidence of a citizen's participation in a felony to persuade a judicial officer that his arrest is justified, it is constitutionally reasonable to require him to open his doors to the officers of the law." There is also no dispute that if Detective Frolich's entry into the basement was lawful, the seizure of the red running suit, which was in plain view and which the officer had probable cause to believe was evidence of a crime, was also lawful under the Fourth Amendment. The issue in this case is what level of justification the Fourth Amendment required before Detective Frolich could legally enter the basement to see if someone else was there.

III

Possessing an arrest warrant and probable cause to believe Buie was in his home, the officers were entitled to enter and to search anywhere in the house in which Buie might be found. Once he was found, however, the search for him was over, and there was no longer that particular justification for entering any rooms that had not yet been searched.

That Buie had an expectation of privacy in those remaining areas of his house, however, does not mean such rooms were immune from entry. In the instant case, there is an analogous interest of the officers in taking steps to assure themselves that the house in which a suspect is being, or has just been, arrested is not harboring other persons who are dangerous and who could unexpectedly launch an attack. The risk of danger in the context of an arrest in the home is as great as, if not greater than, it is in an on-the-street or roadside investigatory encounter. A protective sweep, in contrast, occurs as an adjunct to the serious step of taking a person into custody for the purpose of prosecuting him for a crime. Moreover, unlike an encounter on the street or along a highway, an in-home arrest puts the officer at the disadvantage of being on his adversary's "turf." An ambush in a confined setting of unknown configuration is more to be feared than it is in open, more familiar surroundings.

We agree with the State, as did the court below, that a warrant was not required. We also hold that as an incident to the arrest the officers could, as a precautionary matter and without probable cause or reasonable suspicion, look in closets and other spaces immediately adjoining the place of arrest from which an attack could be immediately launched. Beyond that, however, we hold that there must be articulable facts which, taken together with the rational inferences from those facts, would warrant a reasonably prudent officer in believing that the area to be swept harbors an individual posing a danger to those on the arrest scene. This is no more and no less than was required in *Terry* and *Long,* and as in those cases, we think this balance is the proper one.

We should emphasize that such a protective sweep, aimed at protecting the arresting officers, if justified by the circumstances, is nevertheless not a full search of the premises, but may extend only to a cursory inspection of those spaces where a person may be found. The sweep lasts no longer than is necessary to dispel the reasonable suspicion of danger and in any event no longer than it takes to complete the arrest and depart the premises.

We conclude that by requiring a protective sweep to be justified by probable cause to believe that a serious and demonstrable potentiality for danger existed, the Court of Appeals of Maryland applied an unnecessarily strict Fourth Amendment standard. The Fourth Amendment permits a properly limited protective sweep in conjunction with an in-home arrest when the searching officer possesses a reasonable belief based on specific and articulable facts that the area to be swept harbors an individual posing a danger to those on the arrest scene.

Justice BRENNAN, with whom Justice MARSHALL joins, dissenting.

Today the Court for the first time extends *Terry v. Ohio* (1968), into the home, dispensing with the Fourth Amendment's general requirements of a warrant and probable cause and carving a "reasonable suspicion" exception for protective sweeps in private dwellings. In *Terry,* the Court held that a police officer may briefly detain a suspect based on a reasonable suspicion of criminal activity and may conduct a limited "frisk" of the suspect for concealed weapons in order to protect herself from personal danger. The Court deemed such a frisk "reasonable" under the Fourth Amendment in light of the special "need for law enforcement officers to protect themselves and other prospective victims of violence" during investigative detentions, and the "brief, though far from inconsiderable, intrusion upon the sanctity of the person."

The Court today holds that *Terry*'s "reasonable suspicion" standard "strikes the proper balance between officer safety and citizen privacy" for protective sweeps in private dwellings. I agree with the majority that officers executing an arrest warrant within a private dwelling have an interest in protecting themselves against potential ambush by third parties, but the majority offers no support for its assumption that the danger of ambush during planned home arrests approaches the danger of unavoidable "on-the-beat" confrontations in "the myriad daily situations in which policemen and citizens confront each other on the street." In any event, the Court's implicit judgment that a protective sweep constitutes a "minimally intrusive" search akin to that involved in *Terry* markedly undervalues the nature and scope of the privacy interests involved.

While the Fourth Amendment protects a person's privacy interests in a variety of settings, "physical entry of the home is the chief evil against which the wording of the Fourth Amendment is directed." The Court discounts the nature of the intrusion because it believes that the scope of the intrusion is limited. The Court explains that a protective sweep's scope is "narrowly confined to a cursory visual inspection of those places in which a person might be hiding," and confined in duration to a period "no longer than is necessary to dispel the reasonable suspicion of danger and in any event no longer than it takes to complete the arrest and depart the premises." But these spatial and temporal restrictions are not particularly limiting. A protective sweep would bring within police purview virtually all personal possessions within the house not hidden from view in a small enclosed space. Police officers searching for potential ambushers might enter every room including basements and attics; open up closets, lockers, chests, wardrobes, and cars; and peer under beds and behind furniture. The officers will view letters, documents, and personal effects that are on tables or desks or are visible inside open drawers; books, records, tapes, and pictures on shelves; and clothing, medicines, toiletries and other paraphernalia not carefully stored in dresser drawers or bathroom cupboards. While perhaps not a "full-blown" or "top-to-bottom" search, a protective sweep is much closer to it than to a "limited patdown for weapons" or a "'frisk' of an automobile."

In light of the special sanctity of a private residence and the highly intrusive nature of a protective sweep, I firmly believe that police officers must have probable cause to fear that their personal safety is threatened by a hidden confederate of an arrestee before they may sweep through the entire home. Given the state-court determination that the officers searching Buie's home lacked probable cause to perceive such a danger and therefore were not lawfully present in the basement, I would affirm the state court's decision to suppress the incriminating evidence. I respectfully dissent.

7. *Consent*

A search is permissible without a warrant or even probable cause if there is voluntary consent. The standard for voluntariness was initially articulated in Schneckloth v. Bustamonte.

SCHNECKLOTH v. BUSTAMONTE

412 U.S. 218 (1973)

Justice STEWART delivered the opinion of the Court.

It is well settled under the Fourth and Fourteenth Amendments that a search conducted without a warrant issued upon probable cause is "per se unreasonable . . . subject only to a few specifically established and well-delineated exceptions." It is equally well settled that one of the specifically established exceptions to the requirements of both a warrant and probable cause is a search that is conducted pursuant to consent. The constitutional question in the present case concerns the definition of "consent" in this Fourth and Fourteenth Amendment context.

I

The respondent was brought to trial in a California court upon a charge of possessing a check with intent to defraud. He moved to suppress the introduction of certain material as evidence against him on the ground that the material had been acquired through an unconstitutional search and seizure. In response to the motion, the trial judge conducted an evidentiary hearing where it was established that the material in question had been acquired by the State under the following circumstances:

While on routine patrol in Sunnyvale, California, at approximately 2:40 in the morning, Police Officer James Rand stopped an automobile when he observed that one headlight and its license plate light were burned out. Six men were in the vehicle. Joe Alcala and the respondent, Robert Bustamonte, were in the front seat with Joe Gonzales, the driver. Three older men were seated in the rear. When, in response to the policeman's question, Gonzales could not produce a driver's license, Officer Rand asked if any of the other five had any evidence of identification. Only Alcala produced a license, and he explained that the car was his brother's. After the six occupants had stepped out of the car at the officer's request and after two additional policemen had arrived, Officer Rand asked Alcala if he could search the car. Alcala replied, "Sure, go ahead." Prior to the search no one was threatened with arrest and, according to Officer Rand's uncontradicted testimony, it "was all very congenial at this time." Gonzales testified that Alcala actually helped in the search of the car, by opening the trunk and glove compartment. In Gonzales' words: "[T]he police officer asked Joe [Alcala], he goes, 'Does the trunk open?' And Joe said, 'Yes.' He went to the car and got the keys and opened up the trunk." Wadded up under the left rear seat, the police officers found three checks that had previously been stolen from a car wash.

The trial judge denied the motion to suppress, and the checks in question were admitted in evidence at Bustamonte's trial. On the basis of this and other evidence he was convicted.

II

It is important to make it clear at the outset what is not involved in this case. The respondent concedes that a search conducted pursuant to a valid consent is constitutionally permissible. And similarly the State concedes that when a prosecutor seeks to rely upon consent to justify the lawfulness of a search, he has the burden of proving that the consent was, in fact, freely and voluntarily given.

The precise question in this case, then, is what must the prosecution prove to demonstrate that a consent was "voluntarily" given.

The most extensive judicial exposition of the meaning of "voluntariness" has been developed in those cases in which the Court has had to determine the "voluntariness" of a defendant's confession for purposes of the Fourteenth Amendment.[9] In determining whether a defendant's will was overborne in a particular case, the Court has assessed the totality of all the surrounding circumstances — both the characteristics of the accused and the details of the interrogation.

Similar considerations lead us to [conclude] that the question whether a consent to a search was in fact "voluntary" or was the product of duress or coercion, express or implied, is a question of fact to be determined from the totality of all the circumstances. While knowledge of the right to refuse consent is one factor to be taken into account, the government need not establish such knowledge as the sine qua non of an effective consent. As with police questioning, two competing concerns must be accommodated in determining the meaning of a "voluntary" consent — the legitimate need for such searches and the equally important requirement of assuring the absence of coercion.

In situations where the police have some evidence of illicit activity, but lack probable cause to arrest or search, a search authorized by a valid consent may be the only means of obtaining important and reliable evidence. In the present case, for example, while the police had reason to stop the car for traffic violations, the State does not contend that there was probable cause to search the vehicle or that the search was incident to a valid arrest of any of the occupants. Yet, the search yielded tangible evidence that served as a basis for a prosecution, and provided some assurance that others, wholly innocent of the crime, were not mistakenly brought to trial. And in those cases where

9. These cases are discussed in Chapter 4. [Footnote by casebook authors.]

there is probable cause to arrest or search, but where the police lack a warrant, a consent search may still be valuable. If the search is conducted and proves fruitless, that in itself may convince the police that an arrest with its possible stigma and embarrassment is unnecessary, or that a far more extensive search pursuant to a warrant is not justified. In short, a search pursuant to consent may result in considerably less inconvenience for the subject of the search, and, properly conducted, is a constitutionally permissible and wholly legitimate aspect of effective police activity.

But the Fourth and Fourteenth Amendments require that a consent not be coerced, by explicit or implicit means, by implied threat or covert force. For, no matter how subtly the coercion was applied, the resulting "consent" would be no more than a pretext for the unjustified police intrusion against which the Fourth Amendment is directed.

The problem of reconciling the recognized legitimacy of consent searches with the requirement that they be free from any aspect of official coercion cannot be resolved by any infallible touchstone. To approve such searches without the most careful scrutiny would sanction the possibility of official coercion; to place artificial restrictions upon such searches would jeopardize their basic validity. Just as was true with confessions, the requirement of a "voluntary" consent reflects a fair accommodation of the constitutional requirements involved. In examining all the surrounding circumstances to determine if in fact the consent to search was coerced, account must be taken of subtly coercive police questions, as well as the possibly vulnerable subjective state of the person who consents. Those searches that are the product of police coercion can thus be filtered out without undermining the continuing validity of consent searches. In sum, there is no reason for us to depart in the area of consent searches, from the traditional definition of "voluntariness."

The approach of the Court of Appeals for the Ninth Circuit finds no support in any of our decisions that have attempted to define the meaning of "voluntariness." Its ruling, that the State must affirmatively prove that the subject of the search knew that he had a right to refuse consent, would, in practice, create serious doubt whether consent searches could continue to be conducted. There might be rare cases where it could be proved from the record that a person in fact affirmatively knew of his right to refuse — such as a case where he announced to the police that if he didn't sign the consent form, "you [police] are going to get a search warrant"; or a case where by prior experience and training a person had clearly and convincingly demonstrated such knowledge. But more commonly where there was no evidence of any coercion, explicit or implicit, the prosecution would nevertheless be unable to demonstrate that the subject of the search in fact had known of his right to refuse consent.

The very object of the inquiry — the nature of a person's subjective understanding — underlines the difficulty of the prosecution's burden under the rule applied by the Court of Appeals in this case. Any defendant who was the subject of a search authorized solely by his consent could effectively frustrate the introduction into evidence of the fruits of that search by simply failing to testify that he in fact knew he could refuse to consent. And the near impossibility of meeting this prosecutorial burden suggests why this Court has never accepted any such litmus-paper test of voluntariness.

One alternative that would go far toward proving that the subject of a search did know he had a right to refuse consent would be to advise him of that right before eliciting his consent. That, however, is a suggestion that has been almost universally repudiated by both federal and state courts, and, we think, rightly so. For it would be thoroughly impractical to impose on the normal consent search the detailed requirements of an effective warning. Consent searches are part of the standard investigatory techniques of law enforcement agencies. They normally occur on the highway, or in a person's home or office, and under informal and unstructured conditions. The circumstances that prompt the initial request to search may develop quickly or be a logical extension of investigative police questioning. The police may seek to investigate further suspicious circumstances or to follow up leads developed in questioning persons at the scene of a crime. These situations are a far cry from the structured atmosphere of a trial where, assisted by counsel if he chooses, a defendant is informed of his trial rights. And, while surely a closer question, these situations are still immeasurably, far removed from "custodial interrogation" where, in Miranda v. Arizona we found that the Constitution required certain now familiar warnings as a prerequisite to police interrogation. Indeed, in language applicable to the typical consent search, we refused to extend the need for warnings.

Consequently, we cannot accept the position of the Court of Appeals in this case that proof of knowledge of the right to refuse consent is a necessary prerequisite to demonstrating a "voluntary" consent. Rather it is only by analyzing all the circumstances of an individual consent that it can be ascertained whether in fact it was voluntary or coerced. It is this careful sifting of the unique facts and circumstances of each case that is evidenced in our prior decisions involving consent searches.

It is said, however, that a "consent" is a "waiver" of a person's rights under the Fourth and Fourteenth Amendments. The argument is that by allowing the police to conduct a search, a person "waives" whatever right he had to prevent the police from searching. It is argued that under the doctrine of Johnson v. Zerbst to establish such a "waiver" the State must demonstrate "an intentional relinquishment or abandonment of a known right or privilege."

But these standards were enunciated in *Johnson* in the context of the safeguards of a fair criminal trial. Our cases do not reflect an uncritical demand for a knowing and intelligent waiver in every situation where a person has failed to invoke a constitutional protection. The requirement of a "knowing" and "intelligent" waiver was articulated in a case involving the validity of a defendant's decision to forego a right constitutionally guaranteed to protect a fair trial and the reliability of the truth-determining process. Johnson v. Zerbst dealt with the denial of counsel in a federal criminal trial.

Almost without exception, the requirement of a knowing and intelligent waiver has been applied only to those rights which the Constitution guarantees to a criminal defendant in order to preserve a fair trial. Hence, and hardly surprisingly in view of the facts of *Johnson* itself, the standard of a knowing and intelligent waiver has most often been applied to test the validity of a waiver of counsel, either at trial, or upon a guilty plea.

Our cases concerning the validity of guilty pleas underscore the fact that the question whether a person has acted "voluntarily" is quite distinct from the question whether he has "waived" a trial right.

There is a vast difference between those rights that protect a fair criminal trial and the rights guaranteed under the Fourth Amendment. Nothing, either in the purposes behind requiring a "knowing" and "intelligent" waiver of trial rights, or in the practical application of such a requirement suggests that it ought to be extended to the constitutional guarantee against unreasonable searches and seizures.

In short, there is nothing in the purposes or application of the waiver requirements of Johnson v. Zerbst that justifies, much less compels, the easy equation of a knowing waiver with a consent search. To make such an equation is to generalize from the broad rhetoric of some of our decisions, and to ignore the substance of the differing constitutional guarantees.

Much of what has already been said disposes of the argument that the Court's decision in the *Miranda* case requires the conclusion that knowledge of a right to refuse is an indispensable element of a valid consent. The considerations that informed the Court's holding in *Miranda* are simply inapplicable in the present case. In this case, there is no evidence of any inherently coercive tactics — either from the nature of the police questioning or the environment in which it took place. Indeed, since consent searches will normally occur on a person's own familiar territory, the specter of incommunicado police interrogation in some remote station house is simply inapposite. There is no reason to believe, under circumstances such as are present here, that the response to a policeman's question is presumptively coerced; and there is, therefore, no reason to reject the traditional test for determining the voluntariness of a person's response.

Our decision today is a narrow one. We hold only that when the subject of a search is not in custody and the State attempts to justify a search on the basis of his consent, the Fourth and Fourteenth Amendments require that it demonstrate that the consent was in fact voluntarily given, and not the result of duress or coercion, express or implied. Voluntariness is a question of fact to be determined from all the circumstances, and while the subject's knowledge of a right to refuse is a factor to be taken into account, the prosecution is not required to demonstrate such knowledge as a prerequisite to establishing a voluntary consent.

Justice BRENNAN, dissenting.

The Court holds today that an individual can effectively waive this right even though he is totally ignorant of the fact that, in the absence of his consent, such invasions of his privacy would be constitutionally prohibited. It wholly escapes me how our citizens can meaningfully be said to have waived something as precious as a constitutional guarantee without ever being aware of its existence. In my view, the Court's conclusion is supported neither by "linguistics," nor by "epistemology," nor, indeed, by "common sense." I respectfully dissent.

Justice MARSHALL, dissenting.

I would have thought that the capacity to choose necessarily depends upon knowledge that there is a choice to be made. But today the Court reaches the curious result that one can choose to relinquish a constitutional right—the right to be free of unreasonable searches—without knowing that he has the alternative of refusing to accede to a police request to search. I cannot agree, and therefore dissent.

I believe that the Court misstates the true issue in this case. That issue is not, as the Court suggests, whether the police overbore Alcala's will in eliciting his consent, but rather, whether a simple statement of assent to search, without more, should be sufficient to permit the police to search and thus act as a relinquishment of Alcala's constitutional right to exclude the police. This Court has always scrutinized with great care claims that a person has forgone the opportunity to assert constitutional rights. I see no reason to give the claim that a person consented to a search any less rigorous scrutiny. Every case in this Court involving this kind of search has heretofore spoken of consent as a waiver.

To begin, it is important to understand that the opinion of the Court is misleading in its treatment of the issue here in three ways. First, it derives its criterion for determining when a verbal statement of assent to search operates as a relinquishment of a person's right to preclude entry from a justification of consent searches that is inconsistent with our treatment in earlier cases of exceptions to the requirements of the Fourth Amendment, and that is not responsive to the unique nature of the consent-search exception. Second, it applies a standard of voluntariness that was developed in a very different context, where the standard was based on policies different from those involved in this case. Third, it mischaracterizes our prior cases involving consent searches.

My approach to the case is straight-forward and, to me, obviously required by the notion of consent as a relinquishment of Fourth Amendment rights. I am at a loss to understand why consent "cannot be taken literally to mean a 'knowing' choice." In fact, I have difficulty in comprehending how a decision made without knowledge of available alternatives can be treated as a choice at all.

The Supreme Court has consistently reaffirmed Schneckloth v. Busta-monte. For example, in Ohio v. Robinette, 519 U.S. 33 (1996), the Court held that a person lawfully stopped by the police, but free to leave, does not need to be informed by the police of his or her ability to leave.

In the more recent case, United States v. Drayton, 536 U.S. 194 (2002), the Court reaffirmed that the test for consent is whether it is voluntary under the totality of the circumstances. Three police officers boarded a bus as part of a routine drug enforcement effort. One officer sat in the driver's seat and the other two went and asked passengers "about their travel plans and sought to match passengers with luggage in the overhead racks. To avoid blocking the aisle, [Officer] Lang stood next to or just behind each passenger with whom he spoke. According to Lang's testimony, passengers who declined to cooperate with him or who chose to exit the bus at any time would have been allowed to do so without argument. In Lang's experience, however, most people are willing to cooperate."

The Court described what happened next:

> Lang approached respondents from the rear and leaned over Drayton's shoulder. He held up his badge long enough for respondents to identify him as a police officer. With his face 12 to 18 inches away from Drayton's, Lang spoke in a voice just loud enough for respondents to hear: "I'm Investigator Lang with the Tallahassee Police Department. We're conducting bus interdiction [sic], attempting to deter drugs and illegal weapons being transported on the bus. Do you have any bags on the bus?"
>
> Both respondents pointed to a single green bag in the overhead luggage rack. Lang asked, "Do you mind if I check it?," and Brown responded, "Go ahead." Lang handed the bag to Officer Blackburn to check. The bag contained no contraband.
>
> Officer Lang noticed that both respondents were wearing heavy jackets and baggy pants despite the warm weather. In Lang's experience drug traffickers often use baggy clothing to conceal weapons or narcotics. The officer thus asked Brown if he had any weapons or drugs in his possession. And he asked Brown: "Do you mind if I check your person?" Brown answered, "Sure," and cooperated by leaning up in his seat, pulling a cell phone out of his pocket, and opening up his jacket. Lang reached across Drayton and patted down Brown's jacket and pockets, including his waist area, sides, and upper thighs. In both thigh areas, Lang detected hard objects similar to drug packages detected on other occasions. Lang arrested and handcuffed Brown.

The issue was whether there was voluntary consent under these circumstances. The Court concluded:

> There were ample grounds for the District Court to conclude that "everything that took place between Officer Lang and [respondents] suggests that it was cooperative" and that there "was nothing coercive [or] confrontational" about the encounter. There was no application of force, no intimidating movement, no overwhelming show of force, no brandishing of weapons, no blocking of exits, no threat, no command, not even an authoritative tone of voice. It is beyond question that had this encounter occurred on the street, it would be constitutional. The fact that an encounter takes place on a bus does not on its own transform standard police questioning of citizens into an illegal seizure. Indeed, because many fellow passengers are present to witness officers' conduct, a reasonable person may feel

even more secure in his or her decision not to cooperate with police on a bus than in other circumstances.

The Court thus concluded that "respondents' consent to the search of their luggage and their persons was voluntary."

An issue sometimes arises as to who may give consent. In United States v. Matlock, 415 U.S. 164 (1974), the Court held that one occupant of a residence may give consent if the other is not present. But what if both occupants are present and one consents and the other, the target of the search, refuses? This was the question in Georgia v. Randolph.

GEORGIA v. RANDOLPH

547 U.S. 103 (2006)

Justice SOUTER delivered the opinion of the Court.

The Fourth Amendment recognizes a valid warrantless entry and search of premises when police obtain the voluntary consent of an occupant who shares, or is reasonably believed to share, authority over the area in common with a co-occupant who later objects to the use of evidence so obtained. The question here is whether such an evidentiary seizure is likewise lawful with the permission of one occupant when the other, who later seeks to suppress the evidence, is present at the scene and expressly refuses to consent. We hold that, in the circumstances here at issue, a physically present co-occupant's stated refusal to permit entry prevails, rendering the warrantless search unreasonable and invalid as to him.

I

Respondent Scott Randolph and his wife, Janet, separated in late May 2001, when she left the marital residence in Americus, Georgia, and went to stay with her parents in Canada, taking their son and some belongings. In July, she returned to the Americus house with the child, though the record does not reveal whether her object was reconciliation or retrieval of remaining possessions.

On the morning of July 6, she complained to the police that after a domestic dispute her husband took their son away, and when officers reached the house she told them that her husband was a cocaine user whose habit had caused financial troubles. She mentioned the marital problems and said that she and their son had only recently returned after a stay of several weeks with her parents. Shortly after the police arrived, Scott Randolph returned and explained that he had removed the child to a neighbor's house out of concern that his wife might take the boy out of the country again; he denied cocaine use, and countered that it was in fact his wife who abused drugs and alcohol.

One of the officers, Sergeant Murray, went with Janet Randolph to reclaim the child, and when they returned she not only renewed her complaints about her husband's drug use, but also volunteered that there were "items of drug evidence" in the house. Sergeant Murray asked Scott Randolph for permission to search the house, which he unequivocally refused.

The sergeant turned to Janet Randolph for consent to search, which she readily gave. She led the officer upstairs to a bedroom that she identified as Scott's, where the sergeant noticed a section of a drinking straw with a powdery residue he suspected was cocaine. He then left the house to get an evidence bag from his car and to call the district attorney's office, which instructed him to stop the search and apply for a warrant. When Sergeant Murray returned to the house, Janet Randolph withdrew her consent. The police took the straw to the police station, along with the Randolphs. After getting a search warrant, they returned to the house and seized further evidence of drug use, on the basis of which Scott Randolph was indicted for possession of cocaine.

He moved to suppress the evidence, as products of a warrantless search of his house unauthorized by his wife's consent over his express refusal. The trial court denied the motion, ruling that Janet Randolph had common authority to consent to the search.

II

To the Fourth Amendment rule ordinarily prohibiting the warrantless entry of a person's house as unreasonable per se, one "jealously and carefully drawn" exception, recognizes the validity of searches with the voluntary consent of an individual possessing authority. That person might be the householder against whom evidence is sought, or a fellow occupant who shares common authority over property, when the suspect is absent, and the exception for consent extends even to entries and searches with the permission of a co-occupant whom the police reasonably, but erroneously, believe to possess shared authority as an occupant. None of our co-occupant consent-to-search cases, however, has presented the further fact of a second occupant physically present and refusing permission to search, and later moving to suppress evidence so obtained. The significance of such a refusal turns on the underpinnings of the co-occupant consent rule, as recognized since *Matlock*.

The constant element in assessing Fourth Amendment reasonableness in the consent cases, then, is the great significance given to widely shared social expectations, which are naturally enough influenced by the law of property, but not controlled by its rules. *Matlock* accordingly not only holds that a solitary co-inhabitant may sometimes consent to a search of shared premises, but stands for the proposition that the reasonableness of such a search is in significant part a function of commonly held understanding about the authority that co-inhabitants may exercise in ways that affect each other's interests.

To begin with, it is fair to say that a caller standing at the door of shared premises would have no confidence that one occupant's invitation was a sufficiently good reason to enter when a fellow tenant stood there saying, "stay out." Without some very good reason, no sensible person would go inside under those conditions. Fear for the safety of the occupant issuing the invitation, or of someone else inside, would be thought to justify entry, but the justification then would be the personal risk, the threats to life or limb, not the disputed invitation. The visitor's reticence without some such good reason would show not timidity but a realization that when people living together disagree over the use of their common quarters, a resolution must come through voluntary accommodation, not by appeals to authority. Unless the people living together fall within some recognized hierarchy, like a household of parent and child or barracks housing military personnel of different grades, there is no societal understanding of superior and inferior, a fact reflected in a standard formulation of domestic property law, that "[e]ach cotenant . . . has the right to use and enjoy the entire property as if he or she were the sole owner, limited only by the same right in the other cotenants." The want of any recognized superior authority among disagreeing tenants is also reflected in the law's response when the disagreements cannot be resolved. The law does not ask who has the better side of the conflict; it simply provides a right to any co-tenant, even the most unreasonable, to obtain a decree partitioning the property (when the relationship is one of co-ownership) and terminating the relationship. In sum, there is no common understanding that one co-tenant generally has a right or authority to prevail over the express wishes of another, whether the issue is the color of the curtains or invitations to outsiders.

Since the co-tenant wishing to open the door to a third party has no recognized authority in law or social practice to prevail over a present and objecting co-tenant, his disputed invitation, without more, gives a police officer no better claim to reasonableness in entering than the officer would have in the absence of any consent at all. Accordingly, in the balancing of competing individual and governmental interests entailed by the bar to unreasonable searches, the cooperative occupant's invitation adds nothing to the government's side to counter the force of an objecting individual's claim to security against the government's intrusion into his dwelling place.

Disputed permission is thus no match for this central value of the Fourth Amendment, and the State's other countervailing claims do not add up to outweigh it. Yes, we recognize the consenting tenant's interest as a citizen in bringing criminal activity to light. But society can often have the benefit of these interests without relying on a theory of consent that ignores an inhabitant's refusal to allow a warrantless search. The co-tenant acting on his own initiative may be able to deliver evidence to the police, and can tell the police what he knows, for use before a magistrate in getting a warrant. Additional exigent circumstances might justify warrantless searches.

This case invites a straightforward application of the rule that a physically present inhabitant's express refusal of consent to a police search is dispositive as to him, regardless of the consent of a fellow occupant. Scott

Randolph's refusal is clear, and nothing in the record justifies the search on grounds independent of Janet Randolph's consent. The State does not argue that she gave any indication to the police of a need for protection inside the house that might have justified entry into the portion of the premises where the police found the powdery straw (which, if lawfully seized, could have been used when attempting to establish probable cause for the warrant issued later). Nor does the State claim that the entry and search should be upheld under the rubric of exigent circumstances, owing to some apprehension by the police officers that Scott Randolph would destroy evidence of drug use before any warrant could be obtained.

Chief Justice ROBERTS, with whom Justice SCALIA joins, dissenting.

The Court creates constitutional law by surmising what is typical when a social guest encounters an entirely atypical situation. The rule the majority fashions does not implement the high office of the Fourth Amendment to protect privacy, but instead provides protection on a random and happenstance basis, protecting, for example, a co-occupant who happens to be at the front door when the other occupant consents to a search, but not one napping or watching television in the next room. And the cost of affording such random protection is great, as demonstrated by the recurring cases in which abused spouses seek to authorize police entry into a home they share with a nonconsenting abuser.

The correct approach to the question presented is clearly mapped out in our precedents: The Fourth Amendment protects privacy. If an individual shares information, papers, or places with another, he assumes the risk that the other person will in turn share access to that information or those papers or places with the government. And just as an individual who has shared illegal plans or incriminating documents with another cannot interpose an objection when that other person turns the information over to the government, just because the individual happens to be present at the time, so too someone who shares a place with another cannot interpose an objection when that person decides to grant access to the police, simply because the objecting individual happens to be present.

A warrantless search is reasonable if police obtain the voluntary consent of a person authorized to give it. Co-occupants have "assumed the risk that one of their number might permit [a] common area to be searched." Just as Mrs. Randolph could walk upstairs, come down, and turn her husband's cocaine straw over to the police, she can consent to police entry and search of what is, after all, her home, too.

After Georgia v. Randolph, the obvious question is what if the police wait until the non-consenting occupant is no longer present; can the police then get valid consent from the other occupant? That was the issue in Fernandez v. California.

FERNANDEZ v. CALIFORNIA

134 S. Ct. 1126 (2014)

Justice ALITO delivered the opinion of the Court.

Our cases firmly establish that police officers may search jointly occupied premises if one of the occupants consents. In Georgia v. Randolph (2006), we recognized a narrow exception to this rule, holding that the consent of one occupant is insufficient when another occupant is present and objects to the search. In this case, we consider whether *Randolph* applies if the objecting occupant is absent when another occupant consents. Our opinion in *Randolph* took great pains to emphasize that its holding was limited to situations in which the objecting occupant is physically present. We therefore refuse to extend *Randolph* to the very different situation in this case, where consent was provided by an abused woman well after her male partner had been removed from the apartment they shared.

I

The events involved in this case occurred in Los Angeles in October 2009. After observing Abel Lopez cash a check, petitioner Walter Fernandez approached Lopez and asked about the neighborhood in which he lived. When Lopez responded that he was from Mexico, Fernandez laughed and told Lopez that he was in territory ruled by the "D.F.S.," i.e., the "Drifters" gang. Petitioner then pulled out a knife and pointed it at Lopez' chest. Lopez raised his hand in self-defense, and petitioner cut him on the wrist.

Lopez ran from the scene and called 911 for help, but petitioner whistled, and four men emerged from a nearby apartment building and attacked Lopez. After knocking him to the ground, they hit and kicked him and took his cell phone and his wallet, which contained $400 in cash.

A police dispatch reported the incident and mentioned the possibility of gang involvement, and two Los Angeles police officers, Detective Clark and Officer Cirrito, drove to an alley frequented by members of the Drifters. A man who appeared scared walked by the officers and said: "'[T]he guy is in the apartment.'" The officers then observed a man run through the alley and into the building to which the man was pointing. A minute or two later, the officers heard sounds of screaming and fighting coming from that building.

After backup arrived, the officers knocked on the door of the apartment unit from which the screams had been heard. Roxanne Rojas answered the door. She was holding a baby and appeared to be crying. Her face was red, and she had a large bump on her nose. The officers also saw blood on her shirt and hand from what appeared to be a fresh injury. Rojas told the police that she had been in a fight. Officer Cirrito asked if anyone else was in the apartment, and Rojas said that her 4-year-old son was the only other person present.

After Officer Cirrito asked Rojas to step out of the apartment so that he could conduct a protective sweep, petitioner appeared at the door wearing only boxer shorts. Apparently agitated, petitioner stepped forward and said, "'You don't have any right to come in here. I know my rights.'" Suspecting that petitioner had assaulted Rojas, the officers removed him from the apartment and then placed him under arrest. Lopez identified petitioner as his initial attacker, and petitioner was taken to the police station for booking.

Approximately one hour after petitioner's arrest, Detective Clark returned to the apartment and informed Rojas that petitioner had been arrested. Detective Clark requested and received both oral and written consent from Rojas to search the premises. In the apartment, the police found Drifters gang paraphernalia, a butterfly knife, clothing worn by the robbery suspect, and ammunition. Rojas' young son also showed the officers where petitioner had hidden a sawed-off shotgun.

II

The Fourth Amendment prohibits unreasonable searches and seizures and provides that a warrant may not be issued without probable cause, but "the text of the Fourth Amendment does not specify when a search warrant must be obtained." Our cases establish that a warrant is generally required for a search of a home, but "the ultimate touchstone of the Fourth Amendment is 'reasonableness.'" And certain categories of permissible warrantless searches have long been recognized.

Consent searches occupy one of these categories. "Consent searches are part of the standard investigatory techniques of law enforcement agencies" and are "a constitutionally permissible and wholly legitimate aspect of effective police activity." It would be unreasonable — indeed, absurd — to require police officers to obtain a warrant when the sole owner or occupant of a house or apartment voluntarily consents to a search. The owner of a home has a right to allow others to enter and examine the premises, and there is no reason why the owner should not be permitted to extend this same privilege to police officers if that is the owner's choice. Where the owner believes that he or she is under suspicion, the owner may want the police to search the premises so that their suspicions are dispelled. This may be particularly important where the owner has a strong interest in the apprehension of the perpetrator of a crime and believes that the suspicions of the police are deflecting the course of their investigation. An owner may want the police to search even where they lack probable cause, and if a warrant were always required, this could not be done. And even where the police could establish probable cause, requiring a warrant despite the owner's consent would needlessly inconvenience everyone involved — not only the officers and the magistrate but also the occupant of the premises, who would generally either be compelled or would feel a need to stay until the search was completed.

While it is clear that a warrantless search is reasonable when the sole occupant of a house or apartment consents, what happens when there are two or more occupants? Must they all consent? Must they all be asked? Is consent by one occupant enough? The Court faced that problem 40 years ago in United States v. Matlock (1974). In that case, Matlock and a woman named Graff were living together in a house that was also occupied by several of Graff's siblings and by her mother, who had rented the house. While in the front yard of the house, Matlock was arrested for bank robbery and was placed in a squad car. Although the police could have easily asked him for consent to search the room that he and Graff shared, they did not do so. Instead, they knocked on the door and obtained Graff's permission to search. The search yielded incriminating evidence, which the defendant sought to suppress, but this Court held that Graff's consent justified the warrantless search. As the Court put it, "the consent of one who possesses common authority over premises or effects is valid as against the absent, nonconsenting person with whom that authority is shared."

While consent by one resident of jointly occupied premises is generally sufficient to justify a warrantless search, we recognized a narrow exception to this rule in Georgia v. Randolph (2006). In that case, police officers responded to the Randolphs' home after receiving a report of a domestic dispute. When the officers arrived, Janet Randolph informed the officers that her estranged husband, Scott Randolph, was a cocaine user and that there were "items of drug evidence" in the house. The officers first asked Scott for consent to search, but he "unequivocally refused." The officers then turned to Janet, and she consented to the search, which produced evidence that was later used to convict Scott for possession of cocaine.

Without questioning the prior holdings in *Matlock* and *Rodriguez*, this Court held that Janet Randolph's consent was insufficient under the circumstances to justify the warrantless search. The Court reiterated the proposition that a person who shares a residence with others assumes the risk that "any one of them may admit visitors, with the consequence that a guest obnoxious to one may nevertheless be admitted in his absence by another." But the Court held that "*a physically present inhabitant's* express refusal of consent to a police search [of his home] is dispositive as to him, regardless of the consent of a fellow occupant."

The Court's opinion went to great lengths to make clear that its holding was limited to situations in which the objecting occupant is present. Again and again, the opinion of the Court stressed this controlling factor.

III

In this case, petitioner was not present when Rojas consented, but petitioner still contends that *Randolph* is controlling. He advances two main arguments. First, he claims that his absence should not matter since he was absent only because the police had taken him away. Second, he maintains that it was sufficient that he objected to the search while he was still present. Such an objection, he says, should remain in effect until the objecting party "no longer wishes to keep the police out of his home." Neither of these arguments is sound.

We first consider the argument that the presence of the objecting occupant is not necessary when the police are responsible for his absence. In *Randolph*, the Court suggested in dictum that consent by one occupant might not be sufficient if "there is evidence that the police have removed the potentially objecting tenant from the entrance for the sake of avoiding a possible objection." We do not believe the statement should be read to suggest that improper motive may invalidate objectively justified removal. Hence, it does not govern here.

The *Randolph* dictum is best understood not to require an inquiry into the subjective intent of officers who detain or arrest a potential objector but instead to refer to situations in which the removal of the potential objector is not objectively reasonable. As petitioner acknowledges, our Fourth Amendment cases "have repeatedly rejected" a subjective approach.

Petitioner does not claim that the *Randolph* Court meant to break from this consistent practice, and we do not think that it did. And once it is recognized that the test is one of objective reasonableness, petitioner's argument collapses. He does not contest the fact that the police had reasonable grounds for removing him from the apartment so that they could speak with Rojas, an apparent victim of domestic violence, outside of petitioner's potentially intimidating presence. In fact, he does not even contest the existence of probable cause to place him under arrest. We therefore hold that an occupant who is absent due to a lawful detention or arrest stands in the same shoes as an occupant who is absent for any other reason.

This conclusion does not "make a mockery of *Randolph*, "as petitioner protests. It simply accepts *Randolph* on its own terms. The *Randolph* holding unequivocally requires the presence of the objecting occupant in every situation other than the one mentioned in the dictum discussed above.

This brings us to petitioner's second argument, that his objection, made at the threshold of the premises that the police wanted to search, remained effective until he changed his mind and withdrew his objection. This argument is inconsistent with *Randolph*'s reasoning in at least two important ways. First, the argument cannot be squared with the "widely shared social expectations" or "customary social usage" upon which the *Randolph* holding was based. When the objecting occupant is standing at the threshold saying "stay out," a friend or visitor invited to enter by another occupant can expect at best an uncomfortable scene and at worst violence if he or she tries to brush past the objector. But when the objector is not on the scene (and especially when it is known that the objector will not return during the course of the visit), the friend or visitor is much more likely to accept the invitation to enter. Thus, petitioner's argument is inconsistent with *Randolph*'s reasoning.

Second, petitioner's argument would create the very sort of practical complications that *Randolph* sought to avoid. The rule that petitioner would have us adopt would produce a plethora of practical problems. For one thing, there is the question of duration. Petitioner argues that an objection, once made, should last until it is withdrawn by the objector, but such a rule would be unreasonable. Suppose that a husband and wife owned a house as joint tenants and that the husband, after objecting to a search of the house, was convicted and sentenced to a 15-year prison term. Under petitioner's proposed rule, the wife would be unable to consent to a search of the house 10 years after the date on which her husband objected. We refuse to stretch *Randolph* to such strange lengths.

Nor are we persuaded to hold that an objection lasts for a "reasonable" time. "[I]t is certainly unusual for this Court to set forth precise time limits governing police action," and what interval of time would be reasonable in this context? A week? A month? A year? Ten years?

Petitioner's rule would also require the police and ultimately the courts to determine whether, after the passage of time, an objector still had "common authority" over the premises, and this would often be a tricky question. Suppose that an incarcerated objector and a consenting co-occupant were joint tenants on a lease. If the objector, after incarceration, stopped paying rent, would he still have "common authority," and would his objection retain its force? Would it be enough that his name remained on the lease? Would the result be different if the objecting and consenting lessees had an oral month-to-month tenancy?

Another problem concerns the procedure needed to register a continuing objection. Would it be necessary for an occupant to object while police officers are at the door? If presence at the time of consent is not needed, would an occupant have to be present at the premises when the objection was made? Could an objection be made pre-emptively? Could a person like Scott Randolph, suspecting that his estranged wife might invite the police to view his drug stash and paraphernalia, register an objection in advance? Could this be done by posting a sign in front of the house? Could a standing objection be registered by serving notice on the chief of police?

Finally, there is the question of the particular law enforcement officers who would be bound by an objection. Would this set include just the officers who were present when the objection was made? Would it also apply to other officers working on the same investigation? Would it extend to officers who were unaware of the objection? How about officers assigned to different but arguably related cases? Would it be limited by law enforcement agency?

If *Randolph* is taken at its word — that it applies only when the objector is standing in the door saying "stay out" when officers propose to make a consent search — all of these problems disappear.

Petitioner argues strenuously that his expansive interpretation of *Randolph* would not hamper law enforcement because in most cases where officers have probable cause to arrest a physically present objector they also have probable cause to search the premises that the objector does not want them to enter, but this argument misunderstands the constitutional status of consent searches. A warrantless consent search is reasonable and thus consistent with the Fourth Amendment irrespective of the availability of a warrant. Even with modern technological advances, the warrant procedure imposes burdens on the officers who wish to search, the magistrate who must review the warrant application, and the party willing to give consent. When a warrantless search is justified, requiring the police to obtain a warrant may "unjustifiably interfer[e] with legitimate law enforcement strategies." Such a requirement may also impose an unmerited burden on the person who consents to an immediate search, since the warrant application procedure entails delay. Putting the exception the Court adopted in *Randolph* to one side, the lawful occupant of a house or apartment should have the right to invite the police to enter the dwelling and conduct a search. Any other rule would trample on the rights of the occupant who is willing to consent.

Denying someone in Rojas' position the right to allow the police to enter *her* home would also show disrespect for her independence. Having beaten Rojas, petitioner would bar her from controlling access to her own home until such time as he chose to relent. The Fourth Amendment does not give him that power.

Justice SCALIA, concurring.

Like Justice Thomas, I believe Georgia v. Randolph was wrongly decided. I nonetheless join the Court's opinion because it is a faithful application of *Randolph.* I write separately to address the argument that the search of petitioner's shared apartment violated the Fourth Amendment because he had a right under property law to exclude the police.

I would therefore find this a more difficult case if it were established that property law did not give petitioner's cotenant the right to admit visitors over petitioner's objection. That difficulty does not arise, however, because the authorities cited by the *amicus* association fail to establish that a guest would commit a trespass if one of two joint tenants invited the guest to enter and the other tenant forbade the guest to do so. Indeed, what limited authority there is on the subject points to the opposite conclusion. There accordingly is no basis for us to conclude that the police infringed on any property right of petitioner's when they entered the premises with his cotenant's consent.

Justice THOMAS, concurring.

I join the opinion of the Court, which faithfully applies Georgia v. Randolph. I write separately to make clear the extent of my disagreement with *Randolph.*

I dissented in *Randolph* because the facts of that case did not implicate a Fourth Amendment search and never should have been analyzed as such.

Justice GINSBURG, with whom Justice SOTOMAYOR and Justice KAGAN join, dissenting.

Instead of adhering to the warrant requirement, today's decision tells the police they may dodge it, never mind ample time to secure the approval of a neutral magistrate. Suppressing the warrant requirement, the Court shrinks to petite size our holding in Georgia v. Randolph, that "a physically present inhabitant's express refusal of consent to a police search [of his home] is dispositive as to him, regardless of the consent of a fellow occupant."

I

This case calls for a straightforward application of *Randolph*. The police officers in *Randolph* were confronted with a scenario closely resembling the situation presented here. After Walter Fernandez, while physically present at his home, rebuffed the officers' request to come in, the police removed him from the premises and then arrested him, albeit with cause to believe he had assaulted his cohabitant, Roxanne Rojas. At the time of the arrest, Rojas said nothing to contradict Fernandez' refusal. About an hour later, however, and with no attempt to obtain a search warrant, the police returned to the apartment and prevailed upon Rojas to sign a consent form authorizing search of the premises.

The circumstances triggering "the Fourth Amendment's traditional hostility to police entry into a home without a warrant," are at least as salient here as they were in *Randolph*. In both cases, "[t]he search at issue was a search solely for evidence"; "[t]he objecting party," while on the premises, "made his objection [to police entry] known clearly and directly to the officers seeking to enter the [residence]"; and "the officers might easily have secured the premises and sought a warrant permitting them to enter." Here, moreover, with the objector in custody, there was scant danger to persons on the premises, or risk that evidence might be destroyed or concealed, pending request for, and receipt of, a warrant.

Despite these marked similarities, the Court removes this case from *Randolph*'s ambit. The Court does so principally by seizing on the fact that Fernandez, unlike Scott Randolph, was no longer present and objecting when the police obtained the co-occupant's consent. But Fernandez *was* present when he stated his objection to the would-be searchers in no uncertain terms. The officers could scarcely have forgotten, one hour later, that Fernandez refused consent while physically present. That express, on-premises objection should have been "dispositive as to him."

Next, the Court cautions, applying *Randolph* to these facts would pose "a plethora of practical problems." For instance, the Court asks, must a cotenant's objection, once registered, be respected indefinitely? Yet it blinks reality to suppose that Fernandez, by withholding consent, could stop police in their tracks eternally. To mount the prosecution eventuating in a conviction, of course, the State would first need to obtain incriminating evidence, and could get it easily simply by applying for a warrant. Warrant in police hands, the Court's practical problems disappear.

Indeed, as the Court acknowledges, reading *Randolph* to require continuous physical presence poses administrative difficulties of its own. Does an occupant's refusal to consent lose force as soon as she absents herself from the doorstep, even if only for a moment? Are the police free to enter the instant after the objector leaves the door to retire for a nap, answer the phone, use the bathroom, or speak to another officer outside? Hypothesized practical considerations, in short, provide no cause for today's drastic reduction of *Randolph*'s holding and attendant disregard for the warrant requirement.

II

In its zeal to diminish *Randolph,* today's decision overlooks the warrant requirement's venerable role as the "bulwark of Fourth Amendment protection." Reducing *Randolph* to a "narrow exception," the Court declares the main rule to be that "consent by one resident of jointly occupied premises is generally sufficient to justify a warrantless search." That declaration has it backwards, for consent searches themselves are a "'jealously and carefully drawn' exception" to "the Fourth Amendment rule ordinarily prohibiting the warrantless entry of a person's house as unreasonable *per se.*"

In this case, the police could readily have obtained a warrant to search the shared residence. The Court does not dispute this, but instead disparages the warrant requirement as inconvenient, burdensome, entailing delay "[e]ven with modern technological advances." Shut from the Court's sight is the ease and speed with which search warrants nowadays can be obtained.

Although the police have probable cause and could obtain a warrant with dispatch, if they can gain the consent of someone other than the suspect, why should the law insist on the formality of a warrant? Because the Framers saw the neutral magistrate as an essential part of the criminal process shielding all of us, good or bad, saint or sinner, from unchecked police activity.

A final word is in order about the Court's reference to Rojas' autonomy, which, in its view, is best served by allowing her consent to trump an abusive cohabitant's objection. Rojas' situation is not distinguishable from Janet Randolph's in this regard. If a person's health and safety are threatened by a domestic abuser, exigent circumstances would justify immediate removal of the abuser from the premises, as happened here. As the Court understood in *Randolph,* however, the specter of domestic abuse hardly necessitates the diminution of the Fourth Amendment rights at stake here.

For the reasons stated, I would honor the Fourth Amendment's warrant requirement and hold that Fernandez' objection to the search did not become null upon his arrest and removal from the scene.

8. *Searches When There Are "Special Needs"*

The Supreme Court has said that there is a category of searches where there are "special needs," where warrants do not need to be obtained and often where less than probable cause is required. There is no precise definition of the category of "special needs." Some of the examples above, such as checkpoints and border searches, could be regarded as "special needs" situations.

The Court also has considered this in the context of administrative inspections and also drug testing. These are considered below. The special needs category often, though not always, involves searches for reasons other than criminal law enforcement. In fact, Ferguson v. City of Charleston, presented later in this subsection, stresses that "special needs" must be more than the special need to have more effective law enforcement. Most recently, the Court has considered "special needs" in terms of the ability of police to take DNA from a suspect to see if it matches DNA from an unsolved crime.

a.   Administrative Searches

CAMARA v. MUNICIPAL COURT OF CITY AND COUNTY OF SAN FRANCISCO

387 U.S. 523 (1967)

Justice WHITE delivered the opinion of the Court.

In Frank v. State of Maryland [1959], this Court upheld, by a five-to-four vote, a state court conviction of a homeowner who refused to permit a municipal health inspector to enter and inspect his premises without a search warrant. Since [that] closely divided decision, more intensive efforts at all levels of government to contain and eliminate urban blight have led to increasing use of such inspection techniques, while numerous decisions of this Court have more fully defined the Fourth Amendment's effect on state and municipal action. In view of the growing nationwide importance of the problem, we noted probable jurisdiction in this case and in See v. City of Seattle to re-examine whether administrative inspection programs, as presently authorized and conducted, violate Fourth Amendment rights as those rights are enforced against the States through the Fourteenth Amendment.

On November 6, 1963, an inspector of the Division of Housing Inspection of the San Francisco Department of Public Health entered an apartment building to make a routine annual inspection for possible violations of the city's Housing Code. The building's manager informed the inspector that appellant, lessee of the ground floor, was using the rear of his leasehold as a personal residence. Claiming that the building's occupancy permit did not allow residential use of the ground floor, the inspector confronted appellant and demanded that he permit an inspection of the premises. Appellant refused to allow the inspection because the inspector lacked a search warrant.

The inspector returned on November 8, again without a warrant, and appellant again refused to allow an inspection. A citation was then mailed ordering appellant to appear at the district attorney's office. When appellant failed to appear, two inspectors returned to his apartment on November 22. They informed appellant that he was required by law to permit an inspection under §503 of the Housing Code. Appellant nevertheless refused the inspectors access to his apartment without a search warrant. Thereafter, a complaint was filed charging him with refusing to permit a lawful inspection. Appellant was arrested on December 2 and released on bail.

I

The basic purpose of [the Fourth] Amendment, as recognized in countless decisions of this Court, is to safeguard the privacy and security of individuals against arbitrary invasions by governmental officials. Though there has been general agreement as to the fundamental purpose of the Fourth Amendment, translation of the abstract prohibition against "unreasonable searches and seizures" into workable guidelines for the decision of particular cases is a difficult task which has for many years divided the members of this Court. Nevertheless, one governing principle, justified by history and by current experience, has consistently been followed: except in certain carefully defined classes of cases, a search of private property without proper consent is "unreasonable" unless it has been authorized by a valid search warrant.

We may agree that a routine inspection of the physical condition of private property is a less hostile intrusion than the typical policeman's search for the fruits and instrumentalities of crime. But we cannot agree that the Fourth Amendment interests at stake in these inspection cases are merely "peripheral." It is surely anomalous to say that the individual and his private property are fully protected by the Fourth Amendment only when the individual is suspected of criminal behavior. For instance, even the most law-abiding citizen has a very tangible interest in limiting the circumstances under which the sanctity of his home may be broken by official authority, for the possibility of criminal entry under the guise of official sanction is a serious threat to personal and family security. And inspections of the kind we are here considering do in fact jeopardize "self-protection" interests of the property owner. Like most regulatory laws, fire, health, and housing codes are enforced by criminal processes. In some cities, discovery of a violation by the inspector leads to a criminal complaint. Even in cities where discovery of a violation produces only an administrative compliance order, refusal to comply is a criminal offense, and the fact of compliance is verified by a second inspection, again without a warrant. Finally, as this case demonstrates, refusal to permit an inspection is itself a crime, punishable by fine or even by jail sentence.

[T]wo other justifications for permitting administrative health and safety inspections without a warrant [are urged]. First, it is argued that these inspections are "designed to make the least possible demand on the individual occupant." The ordinances authorizing inspections are hedged with safeguards, and at any rate the argument proceeds, the warrant process could not function effectively in this field. The decision to inspect an entire municipal area is based upon legislative or administrative assessment of broad factors such as the area's age and condition. Unless the magistrate is to review such policy matters, he must issue a "rubber stamp" warrant which provides no protection at all to the property owner.

In our opinion, these arguments unduly discount the purposes behind the warrant machinery contemplated by the Fourth Amendment. Under the present system, when the inspector demands entry, the occupant has no way of knowing whether enforcement of the municipal code involved requires inspection of his premises, no way of knowing the lawful limits of the inspector's power to search, and no way of knowing whether the inspector himself is acting under proper authorization. These are questions which may be reviewed by a neutral magistrate without any reassessment of the basic agency decision to canvass an area. Yet, only by refusing entry and risking a criminal conviction can the occupant at present challenge the inspector's decision to search. And even if the occupant possesses sufficient fortitude to take this risk, as appellant did here, he may never learn any more about the reason for the inspection than that the law generally allows housing inspectors to gain entry. The practical effect of this system is to leave the occupant subject to the discretion of the official in the field. This is precisely the discretion to invade private property which we have consistently circumscribed by a requirement that a disinterested party warrant the need to search. We simply cannot say that the protections provided by the warrant procedure are not needed in this context; broad statutory safeguards are no substitute for individualized review, particularly when those safeguards may only be invoked at the risk of a criminal penalty.

The final justification suggested for warrantless administrative searches is that the public interest demands such a rule: it is vigorously argued that the health and safety of entire urban populations is dependent upon enforcement of minimum fire, housing, and sanitation standards, and that the only effective means of enforcing such codes is by routine systematized inspection of all physical structures. Of course, in applying any reasonableness standard, including one of constitutional dimension, an argument that the public interest demands a particular rule must receive careful consideration. But we think this argument misses the mark. The question is not, at this stage at least, whether these inspections may be made, but whether they may be made without a warrant. For example, to say that gambling raids may not be made at the discretion of the police without a warrant is not necessarily to say that gambling raids may never be made. In assessing whether the public interest demands creation of a general exception to the Fourth Amendment's warrant requirement, the question is not whether the public interest justifies the type of search in question, but whether the authority to search should be evidenced by a warrant, which in turn depends in part upon whether the burden of obtaining a warrant is likely to frustrate the governmental purpose behind the search. It has nowhere been urged that fire, health, and housing code inspection programs could not achieve their goals within the confines of a reasonable search warrant requirement. Thus, we do not find the public need argument dispositive.

In summary, we hold that administrative searches of the kind at issue here are significant intrusions upon the interests protected by the Fourth Amendment, that such searches when authorized and conducted without a warrant procedure lack the traditional safeguards which the Fourth Amendment guarantees to the individual, and that the reasons put forth for upholding these warrantless searches are insufficient to justify so substantial a weakening of the Fourth Amendment's protections. Because of the nature of the municipal programs under consideration, however, these conclusions must be the beginning, not the end, of our inquiry.

II

Borrowing from more typical Fourth Amendment cases, appellant argues not only that code enforcement inspection programs must be circumscribed by a warrant procedure, but also that warrants should issue only when the inspector possesses probable cause to believe that a particular dwelling contains violations of the minimum standards prescribed by the code being enforced. We disagree.

In cases in which the Fourth Amendment requires that a warrant to search be obtained, "probable cause" is the standard by which a particular decision to search is tested against the constitutional mandate of reasonableness. To apply this standard, it is obviously necessary first to focus upon the governmental interest which allegedly justifies official intrusion upon the constitutionally protected interests of the private citizen. For example, in a criminal investigation, the police may undertake to recover specific stolen or contraband goods. But that public interest would hardly justify a sweeping search of an entire city conducted in the hope that these goods might be found. Consequently, a search for these goods, even with a warrant, is "reasonable" only when there is "probable cause" to believe that they will be uncovered in a particular dwelling.

Unlike the search pursuant to a criminal investigation, the inspection programs at issue here are aimed at securing city-wide compliance with minimum physical standards for private property. The primary governmental interest at stake is to prevent even the unintentional development of conditions which are hazardous to public health and safety. Because fires and epidemics may ravage large urban areas, because unsightly conditions adversely affect the economic values of neighboring structures, numerous courts have upheld the police power of municipalities to impose and enforce such minimum standards even upon existing structures. In determining whether a particular inspection is reasonable — and thus in determining whether there is probable cause to issue a warrant for that inspection — the need for the inspection must be weighed in terms of these reasonable goals of code enforcement.

There is unanimous agreement among those most familiar with this field that the only effective way to seek universal compliance with the minimum standards required by municipal codes is through routine periodic inspections of all structures. It is here that the probable cause debate is focused, for the agency's decision to conduct an area inspection is unavoidably based on its appraisal of conditions in the area as a whole, not on its knowledge of conditions in each particular building. Appellee contends that, if the probable cause standard urged by appellant is adopted, the area inspection will be eliminated as a means of seeking compliance with code standards and the reasonable goals of code enforcement will be dealt a crushing blow.

[W]e think that a number of persuasive factors combine to support the reasonableness of area code-enforcement inspections. First, such programs have a long history of judicial and public acceptance. Second, the public interest demands that all dangerous conditions be prevented or abated, yet it is doubtful that any other canvassing technique would achieve acceptable results. Many such conditions — faulty wiring is an obvious example — are not observable from outside the building and indeed may not be apparent to the inexpert occupant himself. Finally, because the inspections are neither personal in nature nor aimed at the discovery of evidence of crime, they involve a relatively limited invasion of the urban citizen's privacy.

Having concluded that the area inspection is a "reasonable" search of private property within the meaning of the Fourth Amendment, it is obvious that "probable cause" to issue a warrant to inspect must exist if reasonable legislative or administrative standards for conducting an area inspection are satisfied with respect to a particular dwelling. Such standards, which will vary with the municipal program being enforced, may be based upon the passage of time, the nature of the building (e.g., a multifamily apartment house), or the condition of the entire area, but they will not necessarily depend upon specific knowledge of the condition of the particular dwelling. It has been suggested that so to vary the probable cause test from the standard applied in criminal cases would be to authorize a "synthetic search warrant" and thereby to lessen the overall protections of the Fourth Amendment. But we do not agree. The warrant procedure is designed to guarantee that a decision to search private property is justified by a reasonable governmental interest. But reasonableness is still the ultimate standard. If a valid public interest justifies the intrusion contemplated, then there is probable cause to issue a suitably restricted search warrant. Such an approach neither endangers time-honored doctrines applicable to criminal investigations nor makes a nullity of the probable cause requirement in this area. It merely gives full recognition to the competing public and private interests here at stake and, in so doing, best fulfills the historic purpose behind the constitutional right to be free from unreasonable government invasions of privacy.

III

Since our holding emphasizes the controlling standard of reasonableness, nothing we say today is intended to foreclose prompt inspections, even without a warrant, that the law has traditionally upheld in emergency situations. On the other hand, in the case of most routine area inspections, there is no compelling urgency to inspect at a particular time or on a particular day. Moreover, most citizens allow inspections of their property without a warrant. Thus, as a practical matter and in light of the Fourth Amendment's requirement that a warrant specify the property to be searched, it seems likely that warrants should normally be sought only after entry is refused unless there has been a citizen complaint or there is other satisfactory reason for securing immediate entry. Similarly, the requirement of a warrant procedure does not suggest any change in what seems to be the prevailing local policy, in most situations, of authorizing entry, but not entry by force, to inspect.

In the companion case, See v. City of Seattle, 387 U.S. 541 (1967), the Court applied *Camara* to nonresidential commercial property. The Court, though, said that its decision did "not in any way imply that business premises may not reasonably be inspected in many more situations than private homes." The Court returned to the issue of administrative searches of business premises in New York v. Burger.

NEW YORK v. BURGER
482 U.S. 691 (1987)

Justice BLACKMUN delivered the opinion of the Court.

This case presents the question whether the warrantless search of an automobile junkyard, conducted pursuant to a statute authorizing such a search, falls within the exception to the warrant requirement for administrative inspections of pervasively regulated industries. The case also presents the question whether an otherwise proper administrative inspection is unconstitutional because the ultimate purpose of the regulatory statute pursuant to which the search is done — the deterrence of criminal behavior — is the same as that of penal laws, with the result that the inspection may disclose violations not only of the regulatory statute but also of the penal statutes.

I

Respondent Joseph Burger is the owner of a junkyard in Brooklyn, N.Y. His business consists, in part, of the dismantling of automobiles and the selling of their parts. His junkyard is an open lot with no buildings. A high metal fence surrounds it, wherein are located, among other things, vehicles and parts of vehicles. At approximately noon on November 17, 1982, Officer Joseph Vega and four other plainclothes officers, all members of the Auto Crimes Division of the New York City Police Department, entered respondent's junkyard to conduct an inspection pursuant to [New York law]. On any given day, the Division conducts from 5 to 10 inspections of vehicle dismantlers, automobile junkyards, and related businesses.

Upon entering the junkyard, the officers asked to see Burger's license and his "police book" — the record of the automobiles and parts in his possession. Burger replied that he had neither a license nor a police book. The officers then announced their intention to conduct an inspection. Burger did not object. In accordance with their practice, the officers copied down the Vehicle Identification Numbers (VINs) of several vehicles and parts of vehicles that were in the junkyard. After checking these numbers against a police computer, the officers determined that respondent was in possession of stolen vehicles and parts. Accordingly, Burger was arrested and charged with five counts of possession of stolen property and one count of unregistered operation as a vehicle dismantler.

II

The Court long has recognized that the Fourth Amendment's prohibition on unreasonable searches and seizures is applicable to commercial premises, as well as to private homes. An owner or operator of a business thus has an expectation of privacy in commercial property, which society is prepared to consider to be reasonable. This expectation exists not only with respect to traditional police searches conducted for the gathering of criminal evidence but also with respect to administrative inspections designed to enforce regulatory statutes. An expectation of privacy in commercial premises, however, is different from, and indeed less than, a similar expectation in an individual's home. This expectation is particularly attenuated in commercial property employed in "closely regulated" industries. The Court observed: "Certain industries have such a history of government oversight that no reasonable expectation of privacy could exist for a proprietor over the stock of such an enterprise."

Because the owner or operator of commercial premises in a "closely regulated" industry has a reduced expectation of privacy, the warrant and probable-cause requirements, which fulfill the traditional Fourth Amendment standard of reasonableness for a government search, have lessened application in this context. Rather, we conclude that, as in other situations of "special need," where the privacy interests of the owner are weakened and the government interests in regulating particular businesses are concomitantly heightened, a warrantless inspection of commercial premises may well be reasonable within the meaning of the Fourth Amendment.

This warrantless inspection, however, even in the context of a pervasively regulated business, will be deemed to be reasonable only so long as three criteria are met. First, there must be a "substantial" government interest that informs the regulatory scheme pursuant to which the inspection is made. Second, the warrantless inspections must be "necessary to further [the] regulatory scheme." Finally, "the statute's inspection program, in terms of the certainty and regularity of its application, [must] provid[e] a constitutionally adequate substitute for a warrant." In other words, the regulatory statute must perform the two basic functions of a warrant: it must advise the owner of the commercial premises that the search is being made pursuant to the law and has a properly defined scope, and it must limit the discretion of the inspecting officers. To perform this first function, the statute must be "sufficiently comprehensive and defined that the owner of commercial property cannot help but be aware that his property will be subject to periodic inspections undertaken for specific purposes." In addition, in defining how a statute limits the discretion of the inspectors, we have observed that it must be "carefully limited in time, place, and scope."

III

Searches made pursuant to [the New York law], in our view, clearly fall within this established exception to the warrant requirement for administrative inspections in "closely regulated" businesses. First, the nature of the regulatory statute reveals that the operation of a junkyard, part of which is devoted to vehicle dismantling, is a "closely regulated" business in the State of New York. The provisions regulating the activity of vehicle dismantling are extensive. An operator cannot engage in this industry without first obtaining a license, which means that he must meet the registration requirements and must pay a fee. [T]he operator must maintain a police book recording the acquisition and disposition of motor vehicles and vehicle parts, and make such records and inventory available for inspection by the police or any agent of the Department of Motor Vehicles. The operator also must display his registration number prominently at his place of business, on business documentation, and on vehicles and parts that pass through his business. Moreover, the person engaged in this activity is subject to criminal penalties, as well as to loss of license or civil fines, for failure to comply with these provisions. That other States besides New York have imposed similarly extensive regulations on automobile junkyards further supports the "closely regulated" status of this industry.

Accordingly, in light of the regulatory framework governing his business and the history of regulation of related industries, an operator of a junkyard engaging in vehicle dismantling has a reduced expectation of privacy in this "closely regulated" business.

The New York regulatory scheme satisfies the three criteria necessary to make reasonable warrantless inspections. First, the State has a substantial interest in regulating the vehicle-dismantling and automobile-junkyard industry because motor vehicle theft has increased in the State and because the problem of theft is associated with this industry. In this day, automobile theft has become a significant social problem, placing enormous economic and personal burdens upon the citizens of different States.

Second, regulation of the vehicle-dismantling industry reasonably serves the State's substantial interest in eradicating automobile theft. It is well established that the theft problem can be addressed effectively by controlling the receiver of, or market in, stolen property. Moreover, the warrantless administrative inspections "are necessary to further [the] regulatory scheme."

Third, [the New York statute] provides a "constitutionally adequate substitute for a warrant." The statute informs the operator of a vehicle dismantling business that inspections will be made on a regular basis. Thus, the vehicle dismantler knows that the inspections to which he is subject do not constitute discretionary acts by a government official but are conducted pursuant to statute. [The law] also sets forth the scope of the inspection and, accordingly, places the operator on notice as to how to comply with the statute. In addition, it notifies the operator as to who is authorized to conduct an inspection. Finally, the "time, place, and scope" of the inspection is limited, to place appropriate restraints upon the discretion of the inspecting officers.

Justice BRENNAN, with whom Justice MARSHALL and Justice O'CONNOR join, dissenting.

Warrantless inspections of pervasively regulated businesses are valid if necessary to further an urgent state interest, and if authorized by a statute that carefully limits their time, place, and scope. I have no objection to this general rule. Today, however, the Court finds pervasive regulation in the barest of administrative schemes. Burger's vehicle-dismantling business is not closely regulated (unless most New York City businesses are), and an administrative warrant therefore was required to search it. The Court also perceives careful guidance and control of police discretion in a statute that is patently insufficient to eliminate the need for a warrant. Finally, the Court characterizes as administrative a search for evidence of only criminal wrongdoing. As a result, the Court renders virtually meaningless the general rule that a warrant is required for administrative searches of commercial property.

The provisions governing vehicle dismantling in New York simply are not extensive. A vehicle dismantler must register and pay a fee, display the registration in various circumstances, maintain a police book, and allow inspections. Of course, the inspections themselves cannot be cited as proof of pervasive regulation justifying elimination of the warrant requirement; that would be obvious bootstrapping. Nor can registration and recordkeeping requirements be characterized as close regulation. New York City, like many States and municipalities, imposes similar, and often more stringent licensing, recordkeeping, and other regulatory requirements on a myriad of trades and businesses. Few substantive qualifications are required of an aspiring vehicle dismantler; no regulation governs the condition of the premises, the method of operation, the hours of operation, the equipment utilized, etc.

Even if vehicle dismantling were a closely regulated industry, I would nonetheless conclude that this search violated the Fourth Amendment.

The warrant requirement protects the owner of a business from the "unbridled discretion [of] executive and administrative officers," by ensuring that "reasonable legislative or administrative standards for conducting an . . . inspection are satisfied with respect to a particular [business]." In order to serve as the equivalent of a warrant, an administrative statute must create "a predictable and guided [governmental] presence." [The New York law] does not approach the level of "certainty and regularity of . . . application" necessary to provide "a constitutionally adequate substitute for a warrant." The statute does not inform the operator of a vehicle-dismantling business that inspections will be made on a regular basis; in fact, there is no assurance that any inspections at all will occur. There is neither an upper nor a lower limit on the number of searches that may be conducted at any given operator's establishment in any given time period. Neither the statute, nor any regulations, nor any regulatory body, provides limits or guidance on the selection of vehicle dismantlers for inspection. In fact, the State could not explain why Burger's operation was selected for inspection.

The implications of the Court's opinion, if realized, will virtually eliminate Fourth Amendment protection of commercial entities in the context of administrative searches. No State may require, as a condition of doing business, a blanket submission to warrantless searches for any purpose. I respectfully dissent.

––––––––––––

In City of Los Angeles v. Patel, the Court considered the administrative search doctrine in the context of the constitutionality of a city's ordinance that allowed police to examine the registers of hotels and motels at any time. The Court declared the law facially unconstitutional, emphasizing the need for some neutral review before hotel or motel operators could be punished for not allowing police examinations.

CITY OF LOS ANGELES v. PATEL
135 S. Ct. 2443 (2015)

Justice SOTOMAYOR delivered the opinion of the Court.

Respondents brought a Fourth Amendment challenge to a provision of the Los Angeles Municipal Code that compels "[e]very operator of a hotel to keep a record" containing specified information concerning guests and to make this record "available to any officer of the Los Angeles Police Department for inspection" on demand. The questions presented are whether facial challenges to statutes can be brought under the Fourth Amendment and, if so, whether this provision of the Los Angeles Municipal Code is facially invalid. We hold facial challenges can be brought under the Fourth Amendment. We further hold that the provision of the Los Angeles

Municipal Code that requires hotel operators to make their registries available to the police on demand is facially unconstitutional because it penalizes them for declining to turn over their records without affording them any opportunity for precompliance review.

I

Los Angeles Municipal Code (LAMC) §41.49 requires hotel operators to record information about their guests, including: the guest's name and address; the number of people in each guest's party; the make, model, and license plate number of any guest's vehicle parked on hotel property; the guest's date and time of arrival and scheduled departure date; the room number assigned to the guest; the rate charged and amount collected for the room; and the method of payment. Guests without reservations, those who pay for their rooms with cash, and any guests who rent a room for less than 12 hours must present photographic identification at the time of check-in, and hotel operators are required to record the number and expiration date of that document. For those guests who check in using an electronic kiosk, the hotel's records must also contain the guest's credit card information. This information can be maintained in either electronic or paper form, but it must be "kept on the hotel premises in the guest reception or guest check-in area or in an office adjacent" thereto for a period of 90 days.

Section 41.49(3)(a) — the only provision at issue here — states, in pertinent part, that hotel guest records "shall be made available to any officer of the Los Angeles Police Department for inspection," provided that "[w]henever possible, the inspection shall be conducted at a time and in a manner that minimizes any interference with the operation of the business." A hotel operator's failure to make his or her guest records available for police inspection is a misdemeanor punishable by up to six months in jail and a $1,000 fine.

II

We first clarify that facial challenges under the Fourth Amendment are not categorically barred or especially disfavored. A facial challenge is an attack on a statute itself as opposed to a particular application. While such challenges are "the most difficult . . . to mount successfully," the Court has never held that these claims cannot be brought under any otherwise enforceable provision of the Constitution. Instead, the Court has allowed such challenges to proceed under a diverse array of constitutional provisions.

Fourth Amendment challenges to statutes authorizing warrantless searches are no exception. Petitioner principally contends that facial challenges to statutes authorizing warrantless searches must fail because such searches will never be unconstitutional in all applications. In particular, the City points to situations where police are responding to an emergency, where the subject of the search consents to the intrusion, and where police are acting under a court-ordered warrant. While petitioner frames this argument as an objection to respondents' challenge in this case, its logic would preclude facial relief in every Fourth Amendment challenge to a statute authorizing warrantless searches. For this reason alone, the City's argument must fail: The Court's precedents demonstrate not only that facial challenges to statutes authorizing warrantless searches can be brought, but also that they can succeed.

Moreover, the City's argument misunderstands how courts analyze facial challenges. Under the most exacting standard the Court has prescribed for facial challenges, a plaintiff must establish that a "law is unconstitutional in all of its applications." But when assessing whether a statute meets this standard, the Court has considered only applications of the statute in which it actually authorizes or prohibits conduct.

Similarly, when addressing a facial challenge to a statute authorizing warrantless searches, the proper focus of the constitutional inquiry is searches that the law actually authorizes, not those for which it is irrelevant. If exigency or a warrant justifies an officer's search, the subject of the search must permit it to proceed irrespective of whether it is authorized by statute. Statutes authorizing warrantless searches also do not work where the subject of a search has consented. Accordingly, the constitutional "applications" that petitioner claims prevent facial relief here are irrelevant to our analysis because they do not involve actual applications of the statute.

III

Turning to the merits of the particular claim before us, we hold that §41.49(3)(a) is facially unconstitutional because it fails to provide hotel operators with an opportunity for precompliance review.

[T]he Court has repeatedly held that "'searches conducted outside the judicial process, without prior approval by [a] judge or [a] magistrate [judge], are *per se* unreasonable . . . subject only to a few specifically established and well-delineated exceptions.'" This rule "applies to commercial premises as well as to homes." Search regimes where no warrant is ever required may be reasonable where "'special needs . . . make the warrant and probable-cause requirement impracticable,'" and where the "primary purpose" of the searches is "[d]istinguishable from the general interest in crime control." Here, we assume that the searches authorized by §41.49 serve a "special need" other than conducting criminal investigations: They ensure compliance with the recordkeeping requirement, which in turn deters criminals from operating on the hotels' premises. The Court has referred to this kind of search as an "administrative searc[h]." Thus, we consider whether §41.49 falls within the administrative search exception to the warrant requirement.

The Court has held that absent consent, exigent circumstances, or the like, in order for an administrative search to be constitutional, the subject of the search must be afforded an opportunity to obtain precompliance review before a neutral decisionmaker. And, we see no reason why this minimal requirement is inapplicable here. While the Court has never attempted to prescribe the exact form an opportunity for precompliance review must take, the City does not even attempt to argue that §41.49(3)(a) affords hotel operators any opportunity whatsoever. Section 41.49(3)(a) is, therefore, facially invalid.

A hotel owner who refuses to give an officer access to his or her registry can be arrested on the spot. The Court has held that business owners cannot reasonably be put to this kind of choice.

Absent an opportunity for precompliance review, the ordinance creates an intolerable risk that searches authorized by it will exceed statutory limits, or be used as a pretext to harass hotel operators and their guests. Even if a hotel has been searched 10 times a day, every day, for three months, without any violation being found, the operator can only refuse to comply with an officer's demand to turn over the registry at his or her own peril.

To be clear, we hold only that a hotel owner must be afforded an *opportunity* to have a neutral decisionmaker review an officer's demand to search the registry before he or she faces penalties for failing to comply. Actual review need only occur in those rare instances where a hotel operator objects to turning over the registry. Moreover, this opportunity can be provided without imposing onerous burdens on those charged with an administrative scheme's enforcement. For instance, respondents accept that the searches authorized by §41.49(3)(a) would be constitutional if they were performed pursuant to an administrative subpoena. These subpoenas, which are typically a simple form, can be issued by the individual seeking the record — here, officers in the field — without probable cause that a regulation is being infringed. Issuing a subpoena will usually be the full extent of an officer's burden because "the great majority of businessmen can be expected in normal course to consent to inspection without warrant." Indeed, the City has cited no evidence suggesting that without an ordinance authorizing on-demand searches, hotel operators would regularly refuse to cooperate with the police.

Finally, we underscore the narrow nature of our holding. Respondents have not challenged and nothing in our opinion calls into question those parts of §41.49 that require hotel operators to maintain guest registries containing certain information. And, even absent legislative action to create a procedure along the lines discussed above, police will not be prevented from obtaining access to these documents. As they often do, hotel operators remain free to consent to searches of their registries and police can compel them to turn them over if they have a proper administrative warrant — including one that was issued *ex parte* — or if some other exception to the warrant requirement applies, including exigent circumstances.

Rather than arguing that §41.49(3)(a) is constitutional under the general administrative search doctrine, the City and Justice Scalia contend that hotels are "closely regulated," and that the ordinance is facially valid under the more relaxed standard that applies to searches of this category of businesses. They are wrong on both counts.

Over the past 45 years, the Court has identified only four industries that "have such a history of government oversight that no reasonable expectation of privacy . . . could exist for a proprietor over the stock of such an enterprise." Simply listing these industries refutes petitioner's argument that hotels should be counted among them. Unlike liquor sales, firearms dealing, mining, or running an automobile junkyard, nothing inherent in the operation of hotels poses a clear and significant risk to the public welfare.

To classify hotels as pervasively regulated would permit what has always been a narrow exception to swallow the rule.

Justice Scalia, with whom the Chief Justice and Justice Thomas join, dissenting.

The city of Los Angeles, like many jurisdictions across the country, has a law that requires motels, hotels, and other places of overnight accommodation (hereinafter motels) to keep a register containing specified information about their guests. The purpose of this recordkeeping requirement is to deter criminal conduct, on the theory that criminals will be unwilling to carry on illicit activities in motel rooms if they must provide identifying information at check-in. Because this deterrent effect will only be accomplished if motels actually do require guests to provide the required information, the ordinance also authorizes police to conduct random spot checks of motels' guest registers to ensure that they are properly maintained. The ordinance limits these spot checks to the four corners of the register, and does not authorize police to enter any nonpublic area of the motel. To the extent possible, police must conduct these spot checks at times that will minimize any disruption to a motel's business.

The parties do not dispute the governmental interests at stake. Motels not only provide housing to vulnerable transient populations, they are also a particularly attractive site for criminal activity ranging from drug dealing and prostitution to human trafficking. Offering privacy and anonymity on the cheap, they have been employed as prisons for migrants smuggled across the border and held for ransom, and rendezvous sites where child sex workers meet their clients on threat of violence from their procurers.

Nevertheless, the Court today concludes that Los Angeles's ordinance is "unreasonable" inasmuch as it permits police to flip through a guest register to ensure it is being filled out without first providing an opportunity for the motel operator to seek judicial review. Because I believe that such a limited inspection of a guest register is eminently reasonable under the circumstances presented, I dissent.

I assume that respondents may bring a facial challenge to the City's ordinance under the Fourth Amendment. Even so, their claim must fail because, as discussed *infra*, the law is constitutional in most, if not all, of its applications.

One exception to normal warrant requirements applies to searches of closely regulated businesses. "[W]hen an entrepreneur embarks upon such a business, he has voluntarily chosen to subject himself to a full arsenal of governmental regulation," and so a warrantless search to enforce those regulations is not unreasonable. Recognizing that warrantless searches of closely regulated businesses may nevertheless *become* unreasonable if arbitrarily conducted, we have required laws authorizing such searches to satisfy three criteria: (1) There must be a "'substantial' government interest that informs the regulatory scheme pursuant to which the inspection is made"; (2) "the warrantless inspections must be 'necessary to further [the] regulatory scheme'"; and (3) "'the statute's inspection program, in terms of the certainty and regularity of its application, [must] provid[e] a constitutionally adequate substitute for a warrant.'" Los Angeles's ordinance easily meets these standards.

In determining whether a business is closely regulated, this Court has looked to factors including the duration of the regulatory tradition; the comprehensiveness of the regulatory regime; and the imposition of similar regulations by other jurisdictions. These factors are not talismans, but shed light on the expectation of privacy the owner of a business may reasonably have, which in turn affects the reasonableness of a warrantless search.

Reflecting the unique public role of motels and their commercial forebears, governments have long subjected these businesses to unique public duties, and have established inspection regimes to ensure compliance. As Blackstone observed, "Inns, in particular, being intended for the lodging and receipt of travellers, may be indicted, suppressed, and the inn-keepers fined, if they refuse to entertain a traveller without a very sufficient cause: for thus to frustrate the end of their institution is held to be disorderly behavior." 4 W. Blackstone, Commentaries on the Laws of England 168 (1765). Justice Story similarly recognized "[t]he soundness of the public policy of subjecting particular classes of persons to extraordinary responsibility, in cases where an extraordinary confidence is necessarily reposed in them, and there is an extraordinary temptation to fraud, or danger of plunder." J. Story, Commentaries on the Law of Bailments §464, pp. 487-488 (5th ed. 1851).

Finally, this ordinance is not an outlier. The City has pointed us to more than 100 similar register-inspection laws in cities and counties across the country, and that is far from exhaustive. In all, municipalities in at least 41 States have laws similar to Los Angeles's, and at least 8 States have their own laws authorizing register inspections.

The City's ordinance easily satisfies the remaining requirements: It furthers a substantial governmental interest, it is necessary to achieving that interest, and it provides an adequate substitute for a search warrant.

Neither respondents nor the Court question the substantial interest of the City in deterring criminal activity. The private pain and public costs imposed by drug dealing, prostitution, and human trafficking are beyond contention, and motels provide an obvious haven for those who trade in human misery.

Warrantless inspections are also necessary to advance this interest. Although the Court acknowledges that law enforcement can enter a motel room without a warrant when exigent circumstances exist, the whole reason criminals use motel rooms in the first place is that they offer privacy and secrecy, so that police will never come to discover these exigencies. The recordkeeping requirement, which all parties admit is permissible, therefore operates by *deterring* crime. Criminals, who depend on the anonymity that motels offer, will balk when confronted with a motel's demand that they produce identification. And a motel's evasion of the recordkeeping requirement fosters crime.

Respondents and the Court acknowledge that *inspections* are necessary to achieve the purposes of the recordkeeping regime, but insist that *warrantless* inspections are not. They have to acknowledge, however, that the motel operators who conspire with drug dealers and procurers may demand pre-compliance judicial review simply as a pretext to buy time for making fraudulent entries in their guest registers. The Court therefore must resort to arguing that warrantless inspections are not "necessary" because other alternatives exist.

The Court suggests that police could obtain an administrative subpoena to search a guest register and, if a motel moves to quash, the police could "guar[d] the registry pending a hearing" on the motion. This proposal is equal parts 1984 and Alice in Wonderland. It protects motels from government inspection of their registers by authorizing government agents to seize the registers (if "guarding" entails forbidding the register to be moved) or to upset guests by a prolonged police presence at the motel. The Court also notes that police can obtain an *ex parte* warrant before conducting a register inspection. Presumably such warrants could issue without probable cause of wrongdoing by a particular motel; otherwise, this would be no alternative at all. Even so, under this regime police would have to obtain an *ex parte* warrant before *every* inspection. That is because law enforcement would have no way of knowing ahead of time which motels would refuse consent to a search upon request; and if they wait to obtain a warrant until consent is refused, motels will have the opportunity to falsify their guest registers while the police jump through the procedural hoops required to obtain a warrant. It is quite plausible that the costs of this always-get-a-warrant "alternative" would be prohibitive for a police force in one of America's largest cities, juggling numerous law-enforcement priorities, and confronting more than 2,000 motels within its jurisdiction.

But all that discussion is in any case irrelevant. The administrative search need only be reasonable. It is not the burden of Los Angeles to show that there are no less restrictive means of achieving the City's purposes.

The Court reaches its wrongheaded conclusion not simply by misapplying our precedent, but by mistaking our precedent for the Fourth Amendment itself. Rather than bother with the text of that Amendment, the Court relies exclusively on our administrative-search cases. But the Constitution predates 1967, and it remains the supreme law of the land today. Because I believe that the limited warrantless searches authorized by Los Angeles's ordinance are reasonable under the circumstances, I respectfully dissent.

Justice ALITO with whom Justice THOMAS joins, dissenting.

After today, the city of Los Angeles can never, under any circumstances, enforce its 116-year-old requirement that hotels make their registers available to police officers. That is because the Court holds that §41.49(3)(a) of the Los Angeles Municipal Code (2015) is *facially* unconstitutional. Before entering a judgment with such serious safety and federalism implications, the Court must conclude that every application of this law is unconstitutional—i.e., that "'no set of circumstances exists under which the [law] would be valid.'" I have doubts about the Court's approach to administrative searches and closely regulated industries. But even if the Court were 100% correct, it still should uphold §41.49(3)(a) because many other applications of this law are constitutional. Here are five examples.

Example One. The police have probable cause to believe that a register contains evidence of a crime. They go to a judge and get a search warrant. The hotel operator, however, refuses to surrender the register, but instead stashes it away. Officers could tear the hotel apart looking for it. Or they could simply order the operator to produce it. The Fourth Amendment does not create a right to defy a warrant. Hence §41.49(3)(a) could be constitutionally applied in this scenario. Indeed, the Court concedes that it is proper to apply a California obstruction of justice law in such a case. How could applying a city law with a similar effect be different? And a specific law gives more notice than a general law.

Example Two. A murderer has kidnapped a woman with the intent to rape and kill her and there is reason to believe he is holed up in a certain motel. The Fourth Amendment's reasonableness standard accounts for exigent circumstances. When the police arrive, the motel operator folds her arms and says the register is locked in a safe. Invoking §41.49(3)(a), the police order the operator to turn over the register. She refuses. The Fourth Amendment does not protect her from arrest.

Example Three. A neighborhood of "pay by the hour" motels is a notorious gathering spot for child-sex traffickers. Police officers drive through the neighborhood late one night and see unusual amounts of activity at a particular motel. The officers stop and ask the motel operator for the names of those who paid with cash to rent rooms for less than three hours. The operator refuses to provide the information. Requesting to see the register—and arresting the operator for failing to provide it—would be reasonable under the "totality of the circumstances."

Example Four. A motel is operated by a dishonest employee. He has been charging more for rooms than he records, all the while pocketing the difference. The owner finds out and eagerly consents to a police inspection of the register. But when officers arrive and ask to see the register, the operator hides it. The Fourth Amendment does not allow the operator's refusal to defeat the owner's consent.

Example Five. A "mom and pop" motel always keeps its old-fashioned guest register open on the front desk. Anyone who wants to can walk up and leaf through it. (Such motels are not as common as they used to be, but Los Angeles is a big place.) The motel has no reasonable expectation of privacy in the register, and no one doubts that police officers — like anyone else — can enter into the lobby. But when an officer starts looking at the register, as others do, the motel operator at the desk snatches it away and will not give it back. Arresting that person would not violate the Fourth Amendment.

These are just five examples. There are many more. The Court rushes past examples like these by suggesting that §41.49(3)(a) does no "work" in such scenarios. That is not true. Under threat of legal sanction, this law orders hotel operators to do things they do not want to do.

There are serious arguments that the Fourth Amendment's application to warrantless searches and seizures is inherently inconsistent with facial challenges. But assuming such facial challenges ever make sense conceptually, this particular one fails under basic principles of facial invalidation. The Court's contrary holding is befuddling. I respectfully dissent.

b.   Border Crossing

The Supreme Court has made clear that the government has broad authority to conduct warrantless searches of people, vehicles, and mail entering the border. In United States v. Montoya de Hernandez, 473 U.S 531 (1985), the Court explained, "At the border, customs officials have more than merely an investigative law enforcement role. They are also charged, along with immigration officials, with protecting this Nation from entrants who may bring anything harmful into this country, whether that be communicable diseases, narcotics, or explosives."

The government has the ability to stop all cars at the border and to conduct warrantless searches. In 2004, the Court considered whether this includes the ability to take apart a car's gas tank without a warrant, probable cause, or even reasonable suspicion.

UNITED STATES v. FLORES-MONTANO

541 U.S. 149 (2004)

Chief Justice Rehnquist delivered the opinion of the Court.

Customs officials seized 37 kilograms — a little more than 81 pounds — of marijuana from respondent Manuel Flores-Montano's gas tank at the international border. The Court of Appeals for the Ninth Circuit held that the Fourth Amendment forbade the fuel tank search absent reasonable suspicion. We hold that the search in question did not require reasonable suspicion.

Respondent, driving a 1987 Ford Taurus station wagon, attempted to enter the United States at the Otay Mesa Port of Entry in southern California. A customs inspector conducted an inspection of the station wagon, and requested respondent to leave the vehicle. The vehicle was then taken to a secondary inspection station.

At the secondary station, a second customs inspector inspected the gas tank by tapping it, and noted that the tank sounded solid. Subsequently, the inspector requested a mechanic under contract with Customs to come to the border station to remove the tank. Within 20 to 30 minutes, the mechanic arrived. He raised the car on a hydraulic lift, loosened the straps and unscrewed the bolts holding the gas tank to the undercarriage of the vehicle, and then disconnected some hoses and electrical connections. After the gas tank was removed, the inspector hammered off bondo (a putty-like hardening substance that is used to seal openings) from the top of the gas tank. The inspector opened an access plate underneath the bondo and found 37 kilograms of marijuana bricks. The process took 15 to 25 minutes.

A grand jury for the Southern District of California indicted respondent on one count of unlawfully importing marijuana, in violation of 21 U.S.C. §952, and one count of possession of marijuana with intent to distribute, in violation of §841(a)(1). [R]espondent filed a motion to suppress the marijuana recovered from the gas tank. The Government advised the District Court that it was not relying on reasonable suspicion as a basis for denying respondent's suppression motion. The District Court held that reasonable suspicion was required to justify the search and, accordingly, granted respondent's motion to suppress. The Court of Appeals summarily affirmed and we now reverse.

The Government's interest in preventing the entry of unwanted persons and effects is at its zenith at the international border. Time and again, we have stated that "searches made at the border, pursuant to the longstanding right of the sovereign to protect itself by stopping and examining persons and property crossing into this country, are reasonable simply by virtue of the fact that they occur at the border." United States v. Ramsey (1977). Congress, since the beginning of our Government, "has granted the Executive plenary authority to conduct routine searches and seizures at the border, without probable cause or a warrant, in order to regulate the collection of duties and to prevent the introduction of contraband into this country." It is axiomatic that the United States, as sovereign, has the inherent authority to protect, and a paramount interest in protecting, its territorial integrity.

That interest in protecting the borders is illustrated in this case by the evidence that smugglers frequently attempt to penetrate our borders with contraband secreted in their automobiles' fuel tank. Over the past 5½ fiscal years, there have been 18,788 vehicle drug seizures at the southern California ports of entry. Of those 18,788, gas tank drug seizures have accounted for 4,619 of the vehicle drug seizures, or approximately 25%. In addition, instances of persons smuggled in and around gas tank compartments are discovered at the ports of entry of San Ysidro and Otay Mesa at a rate averaging 1 approximately every 10 days.

Respondent asserts two main arguments with respect to his Fourth Amendment interests. First, he urges that he has a privacy interest in his fuel tank, and that the suspicionless disassembly of his tank is an invasion of his privacy. But on many occasions, we have noted that the expectation of privacy is less at the border than it is in the interior. We have long recognized that automobiles seeking entry into this country may be searched. It is difficult to imagine how the search of a gas tank, which should be solely a repository for fuel, could be more of an invasion of privacy than the search of the automobile's passenger compartment.

Second, respondent argues that the Fourth Amendment "protects property as well as privacy," and that the disassembly and reassembly of his gas tank is a significant deprivation of his property interest because it may damage the vehicle. He does not, and on the record cannot, truly contend that the procedure of removal, disassembly, and reassembly of the fuel tank in this case or any other has resulted in serious damage to, or destruction of, the property. According to the Government, for example, in fiscal year 2003, 348 gas tank searches conducted along the southern border were negative (i.e., no contraband was found), the gas tanks were reassembled, and the vehicles continued their entry into the United States without incident.

Respondent cites not a single accident involving the vehicle or motorist in the many thousands of gas tank disassemblies that have occurred at the border. A gas tank search involves a brief procedure that can be reversed without damaging the safety or operation of the vehicle. If damage to a vehicle were to occur, the motorist might be entitled to recovery. While the interference with a motorist's possessory interest is not insignificant when the Government removes, disassembles, and reassembles his gas tank, it nevertheless is justified by the Government's paramount interest in protecting the border.

The procedure in this case took about an hour (including the wait for the mechanic). At oral argument, the Government advised us that, depending on the type of car, a search involving the disassembly and reassembly of a gas tank may take one to two hours. We think it clear that delays of one to two hours at international borders are to be expected.

For the reasons stated, we conclude that the Government's authority to conduct suspicionless inspections at the border includes the authority to remove, disassemble, and reassemble a vehicle's fuel tank. While it may be true that some searches of property are so destructive as to require a different result, this was not one of them.

———————————

The Court has said that the ability of the government to monitor the borders includes the ability to have a fixed checkpoint near the border where cars are stopped to ensure that all are lawfully in the United States. In United States v. Martinez-Fuerte, 428 U.S. 543 (1976), the Court stated:

These cases involve criminal prosecutions for offenses relating to the transportation of illegal Mexican aliens. Each defendant was arrested at a permanent checkpoint operated by the Border Patrol away from the international border with Mexico, and each sought the exclusion of certain evidence on the ground that the operation of the checkpoint was incompatible with the Fourth Amendment. In each instance whether the Fourth Amendment was violated turns primarily on whether a vehicle may be stopped at a fixed checkpoint for brief questioning of its occupants even though there is no reason to believe the particular vehicle contains illegal aliens. We hold today that such stops are consistent with the Fourth Amendment. We also hold that the operation of a fixed checkpoint need not be authorized in advance by a judicial warrant.

The Court has extended this beyond automobiles and has held that mail entering the country can be inspected without a warrant.

UNITED STATES v. RAMSEY

431 U.S. 606 (1977)

Justice REHNQUIST delivered the opinion of the Court.

Customs officials, acting with "reasonable cause to suspect" a violation of customs laws, opened for inspection incoming international letter-class mail without first obtaining a search warrant.

Charles W. Ramsey and James W. Kelly jointly commenced a heroin-by-mail enterprise in the Washington, D.C., area. The process involved their procuring of heroin, which was mailed in letters from Bangkok, Thailand, and sent to various locations in the District of Columbia area for collection. Two of their suppliers, Sylvia Bailey and William Ward, who were located in West Germany, were engaged in international narcotics trafficking during the latter part of 1973 and the early part of 1974. West German agents, pursuant to court-authorized electronic surveillance, intercepted several trans-Atlantic conversations between Bailey and Ramsey during which their narcotics operation was discussed. By late January 1974, Bailey and Ward had gone to Thailand. Thai officials, alerted to their presence by West German authorities, placed them under surveillance. Ward was observed mailing letter-sized envelopes in six different mail boxes; five of these envelopes were recovered; and one of the addresses in Washington, D.C., was later linked to respondents. Bailey and Ward were arrested by Thai officials on February 2, 1974; among the items seized were eleven heroin-filed envelopes addressed to the Washington, D.C., area, and later connected with respondents.

Two days after this arrest of Bailey and Ward, Inspector George Kall-nischkies, a United States customs officer in New York City, without any knowledge of the foregoing events, inspecting a sack of incoming international mail from Thailand, spotted eight envelopes that were bulky and which he believed might contain merchandise. The envelopes, all of which appeared to him to have been typed on the same typewriter, were addressed to four different locations in the Washington, D.C., area.

Inspector Kallnischkies, based on the fact that the letters were from Thailand, a known source of narcotics, and were "rather bulky," suspected that the envelopes might contain merchandise or contraband rather than correspondence. He took the letters to an examining area in the post office, and felt one of the letters: It "felt like there was something in there, in the envelope. It was not just plain paper that the envelope is supposed to contain." He weighed one of the envelopes, and found it weighed 42 grams, some three to six times the normal weight of an airmail letter. Inspector Kallnischkies then opened that envelope.

The envelopes were then sent to Washington in a locked pouch where agents of the Drug Enforcement Administration, after obtaining a search warrant, opened the envelopes again and removed most of the heroin. The envelopes were then resealed, and six of them were delivered under surveillance. After Kelly collected the envelopes from the three different addressees, rendezvoused with Ramsey, and gave Ramsey a brown paper bag, federal agents arrested both of them. The bag contained the six envelopes with heroin, $1,100 in cash, and "cutting" material for the heroin.

Congress and the applicable postal regulations authorized the actions undertaken in this case. Title 19 U.S.C. §482 explicitly deals with the search of an "envelope": "Any of the officers or persons authorized to board or search vessels may . . . search any trunk or envelope, wherever found, in which he may have a reasonable cause to suspect there is merchandise which was imported contrary to law. . . ." This provision authorizes customs officials to inspect, under the circumstances therein stated, incoming international mail. The "reasonable cause to suspect" test adopted by the statute is, we think, a practical test which imposes a less stringent requirement than that of "probable cause" imposed by the Fourth Amendment as a requirement for the issuance of warrants. Inspector Kallnischkies, at the time he opened the letters, knew that they were from Thailand, were bulky, were many times the weight of a normal airmail letter, and "felt like there was something in there." Under these circumstances, we have no doubt that he had reasonable "cause to suspect" that there was merchandise or contraband in the envelopes. The search, therefore, was plainly authorized by the statute.

Since the search in this case was authorized by statute, we are left simply with the question of whether the search nevertheless violated the Constitution. That searches made at the border, pursuant to the long-standing right of the sovereign to protect itself by stopping and examining persons and property crossing into this country, are reasonable simply by virtue of the fact that they occur at the border, should, by now, require no extended demonstration. Border searches, then, from before the adoption of the Fourth Amendment, have been considered to be "reasonable" by the single fact that the person or item in question had entered into our country from outside. There has never been any additional requirement that the reasonableness of a border search depended on the existence of probable cause. This long-standing recognition that searches at our borders without probable cause and without a warrant are nonetheless "reasonable" has a history as old as the Fourth Amendment itself. We reaffirm it now.

The border-search exception is grounded in the recognized right of the sovereign to control, subject to substantive limitations imposed by the Constitution, who and what may enter the country. It is clear that there is nothing in the rationale behind the border-search exception which suggests that the mode of entry will be critical. It was conceded at oral argument that customs officials could search, without probable cause and without a warrant, envelopes carried by an entering traveler, whether in his luggage or on his person. Surely no different constitutional standard should apply simply because the envelopes were mailed not carried. The critical fact is that the envelopes cross the border and enter this country, not that they are brought in by one mode of transportation rather than another. It is their entry into this country from without it that makes a resulting search "reasonable."

We therefore conclude that the Fourth Amendment does not interdict the actions taken by Inspector Kallnischkies in opening and searching the eight envelopes.

Justice STEVENS, with whom Justice BRENNAN and Justice MARSHALL join, dissenting.

[The dissent disputed that the statute authorizes such warrantless searches of mail entering the country.] If the Government is allowed to exercise the power it claims, the door will be open to the wholesale, secret examination of all incoming international letter mail. No notice would be necessary either before or after the search. Until Congress has made an unambiguous policy decision that such an unprecedented intrusion upon a vital method of personal communication is in the Nation's interest, this Court should not address the serious constitutional question it decides today.

Individuals, of course, can be stopped at the border to ensure that they are lawfully entering the country. But more intrusive searches, such as body cavity searches or detentions, require at least reasonable suspicion. United States v. Montoya-Hernandez raises the question of whether people crossing the border can be detained based on reasonable suspicion to see if they are trying to smuggle drugs in their alimentary canal.

UNITED STATES v. MONTOYA-HERNANDEZ

473 U.S. 531 (1985)

Justice REHNQUIST delivered the opinion of the Court.

Respondent Rosa Elvira Montoya de Hernandez was detained by customs officials upon her arrival at the Los Angeles Airport on a flight from Bogota, Colombia. She was found to be smuggling 88 cocaine-filled balloons in her alimentary canal, and was convicted after a bench trial of various federal narcotics offenses. A divided panel of the United States Court of Appeals for the Ninth Circuit reversed her convictions, holding that her detention violated the Fourth Amendment to the United States Constitution because the customs inspectors did not have a "clear indication" of alimentary canal smuggling at the time she was detained. We now reverse.

Respondent arrived at Los Angeles International Airport shortly after midnight, March 5, 1983, on Avianca Flight 080, a direct 10-hour flight from Bogota, Colombia. Her visa was in order so she was passed through Immigration and proceeded to the customs desk. At the customs desk she encountered Customs Inspector Talamantes, who reviewed her documents and noticed from her passport that she had made at least eight recent trips to either Miami or Los Angeles. Talamantes referred respondent to a secondary customs desk for further questioning. At this desk Talamantes and another inspector asked respondent general questions concerning herself and the purpose of her trip. Respondent revealed that she spoke no English and had no family or friends in the United States. She explained in Spanish that she had come to the United States to purchase goods for her husband's store in Bogota. The customs inspectors recognized Bogota as a "source city" for narcotics. Respondent possessed $5,000 in cash, mostly $50 bills, but had no billfold. She indicated to the inspectors that she had no appointments with merchandise vendors, but planned to ride around Los Angeles in taxi-cabs visiting retail stores such as J.C. Penney and K-Mart in order to buy goods for her husband's store with the $5,000.

Respondent admitted that she had no hotel reservations, but stated that she planned to stay at a Holiday Inn. Respondent could not recall how her airline ticket was purchased. When the inspectors opened respondent's one small valise they found about four changes of "cold weather" clothing. Respondent had no shoes other than the high-heeled pair she was wearing. Although respondent possessed no checks, waybills, credit cards, or letters of credit, she did produce a Colombian business card and a number of old receipts, waybills, and fabric swatches displayed in a photo album.

At this point Talamantes and the other inspector suspected that respondent was a "balloon swallower," one who attempts to smuggle narcotics into this country hidden in her alimentary canal. Over the years Inspector Talamantes had apprehended dozens of alimentary canal smugglers arriving on Avianca Flight 080.

The inspectors requested a female customs inspector to take respondent to a private area and conduct a patdown and strip search. During the search the female inspector felt respondent's abdomen area and noticed a firm fullness, as if respondent were wearing a girdle. The search revealed no contraband, but the inspector noticed that respondent was wearing two pairs of elastic underpants with a paper towel lining the crotch area.

When respondent returned to the customs area and the female inspector reported her discoveries, the inspector in charge told respondent that he suspected she was smuggling drugs in her alimentary canal. Respondent agreed to the inspector's request that she be x-rayed at a hospital but in answer to the inspector's query stated that she was pregnant. She agreed to a pregnancy test before the x ray. Respondent withdrew the consent for an x ray when she learned that she would have to be handcuffed en route to the hospital. The inspector then gave respondent the option of returning to Colombia on the next available flight, agreeing to an x ray, or remaining in detention until she produced a monitored bowel movement that would confirm or rebut the inspectors' suspicions. Respondent chose the first option and was placed in a customs office under observation. She was told that if she went to the toilet she would have to use a wastebasket in the women's restroom, in order that female customs inspectors could inspect her stool for balloons or capsules carrying narcotics. The inspectors refused respondent's request to place a telephone call.

Respondent sat in the customs office, under observation, for the remainder of the night. During the night customs officials attempted to place respondent on a Mexican airline that was flying to Bogota via Mexico City in the morning. The airline refused to transport respondent because she lacked a Mexican visa necessary to land in Mexico City. Respondent was not permitted to leave, and was informed that she would be detained until she agreed to an x ray or her bowels moved. She remained detained in the customs office under observation, for most of the time curled up in a chair leaning to one side. She refused all offers of food and drink, and refused to use the toilet facilities.

At the shift change at 4 o'clock the next afternoon, almost 16 hours after her flight had landed, respondent still had not defecated or urinated or partaken of food or drink. At that time customs officials sought a court order authorizing a pregnancy test, an x ray, and a rectal examination. The Federal Magistrate issued an order just before midnight that evening, which authorized a rectal examination and involuntary x ray, provided that the physician in charge considered respondent's claim of pregnancy. Respondent was taken to a hospital and given a pregnancy test, which later turned out to be negative. Before the results of the pregnancy test were known, a physician conducted a rectal examination and removed from respondent's rectum a balloon containing a foreign substance. Respondent was then placed formally under arrest. By 4:10 A.M. respondent had passed 6 similar balloons; over the next four days she passed 88 balloons containing a total of 528 grams of 80% pure cocaine hydrochloride.

The Fourth Amendment commands that searches and seizures be reasonable. What is reasonable depends upon all of the circumstances surrounding the search or seizure and the nature of the search or seizure itself. The permissibility of a particular law enforcement practice is judged by "balancing its intrusion on the individual's Fourth Amendment interests against its promotion of legitimate governmental interests."

Here the seizure of respondent took place at the international border. Since the founding of our Republic, Congress has granted the Executive plenary authority to conduct routine searches and seizures at the border, without probable cause or a warrant, in order to regulate the collection of duties and to prevent the introduction of contraband into this country.

Consistently, therefore, with Congress' power to protect the Nation by stopping and examining persons entering this country, the Fourth Amendment's balance of reasonableness is qualitatively different at the international border than in the interior.

Balanced against the sovereign's interests at the border are the Fourth Amendment rights of respondent. Having presented herself at the border for admission, and having subjected herself to the criminal enforcement powers of the Federal Government, respondent was entitled to be free from unreasonable search and seizure. But not only is the expectation of privacy less at the border than in the interior, the Fourth Amendment balance between the interests of the Government and the privacy right of the individual is also struck much more favorably to the Government at the border.

We have not previously decided what level of suspicion would justify a seizure of an incoming traveler for purposes other than a routine border search.

We hold that the detention of a traveler at the border, beyond the scope of a routine customs search and inspection, is justified at its inception if customs agents, considering all the facts surrounding the traveler and her trip, reasonably suspect that the traveler is smuggling contraband in her alimentary canal.

The "reasonable suspicion" standard has been applied in a number of contexts and effects a needed balance between private and public interests when law enforcement officials must make a limited intrusion on less than probable cause. It thus fits well into the situations involving alimentary canal smuggling at the border: this type of smuggling gives no external signs and inspectors will rarely possess probable cause to arrest or search, yet governmental interests in stopping smuggling at the border are high indeed. Under this standard officials at the border must have a "particularized and objective basis for suspecting the particular person" of alimentary canal smuggling.

The facts, and their rational inferences, known to customs inspectors in this case clearly supported a reasonable suspicion that respondent was an alimentary canal smuggler. We need not belabor the facts, including respondent's implausible story, that supported this suspicion. The trained customs inspectors had encountered many alimentary canal smugglers and certainly had more than an "inchoate and unparticularized suspicion or 'hunch,'" that respondent was smuggling narcotics in her alimentary canal. The inspectors' suspicion was a "'common-sense conclusio[n] about human behavior' upon which 'practical people,' including government officials, are entitled to rely."

Under these circumstances, we conclude that the detention in this case was not unreasonably long. It occurred at the international border, where the Fourth Amendment balance of interests leans heavily to the Government. At the border, customs officials have more than merely an investigative law enforcement role. They are also charged, along with immigration officials, with protecting this Nation from entrants who may bring anything harmful into this country, whether that be communicable diseases, narcotics, or explosives. In this regard the detention of a suspected alimentary canal smuggler at the border is analogous to the detention of a suspected tuberculosis carrier at the border: both are detained until their bodily processes dispel the suspicion that they will introduce a harmful agent into this country.

Respondent's detention was long, uncomfortable, indeed, humiliating; but both its length and its discomfort resulted solely from the method by which she chose to smuggle illicit drugs into this country. Here, by analogy, in the presence of articulable suspicion of smuggling in her alimentary canal, the customs officers were not required by the Fourth Amendment to pass respondent and her 88 cocaine-filled balloons into the interior. Her detention for the period of time necessary to either verify or dispel the suspicion was not unreasonable.

Justice BRENNAN, with whom Justice MARSHALL joins, dissenting.

We confront a "disgusting and saddening episode" at our Nation's border. Shortly after midnight on March 5, 1983, the respondent Rosa Elvira Montoya De Hernandez was detained by customs officers because she fit the profile of an "alimentary canal smuggler." This profile did not of course give the officers probable cause to believe that De Hernandez was smuggling drugs into the country, but at most a "reasonable suspicion" that she might be engaged in such an attempt. After a thorough strip search failed to uncover any contraband, De Hernandez agreed to go to a local hospital for an abdominal x ray to resolve the matter.

Stymied in their efforts, the officers decided on an alternative course: they would simply lock De Hernandez away in an adjacent manifest room "until her peristaltic functions produced a monitored bowel movement." The officers explained to De Hernandez that she could not leave until she had excreted by squatting over a wastebasket pursuant to the watchful eyes of two attending matrons. De Hernandez responded: "I will not submit to your degradation and I'd rather die." She was locked away with the matrons.

De Hernandez remained locked up in the room for almost 24 hours. Three shifts of matrons came and went during this time. The room had no bed or couch on which she could lie, but only hard chairs and a table. The matrons told her that if she wished to sleep she could lie down on the hard, uncarpeted floor. De Hernandez instead "sat in her chair clutching her purse," "occasionally putting her head down on the table to nap." Most of the time she simply wept and pleaded "to go home." She repeatedly begged for permission "to call my husband and tell him what you are doing to me." Permission was denied. Sobbing, she insisted that she had to "make a phone call home so that she could talk to her children and to let them know that everything was all right." Permission again was denied. In fact, the matrons considered it highly "unusual" that "each time someone entered the search room, she would take out two small pictures of her children and show them to the person." De Hernandez also demanded that her attorney be contacted. Once again, permission was denied. As far as the outside world knew, Rosa De Hernandez had simply vanished. And although she already had been stripped and searched and probed, the customs officers decided about halfway through her ordeal to repeat that process — "to ensure the safety of the surveilling officers. The result was again negative."

After almost 24 hours had passed, someone finally had the presence of mind to consult a Magistrate and to obtain a court order for an x ray and a body-cavity search. De Hernandez, "very agitated," was handcuffed and led away to the hospital. A rectal examination disclosed the presence of a cocaine-filled balloon. At approximately 3:15 on the morning of March 6, almost 27 hours after her initial detention, De Hernandez was formally placed under arrest and advised of her Miranda rights. Over the course of the next four days she excreted a total of 88 balloons.

The standards we fashion to govern the ferreting out of the guilty apply equally to the detention of the innocent, and "may be exercised by the most unfit and ruthless officers as well as by the fit and responsible." Nor is the issue whether there is a "veritable national crisis in law enforcement caused by smuggling of illicit narcotics." There is, and "[s]tern enforcement of the criminal law is the hallmark of a healthy and self-confident society." "But in our democracy such enforcement presupposes a moral atmosphere and a reliance upon intelligence whereby the effective administration of justice can be achieved with due regard for those civilized standards in the use of the criminal law which are formulated in our Bill of Rights."

The issue, instead, is simply this: Does the Fourth Amendment permit an international traveler, citizen or alien, to be subjected to the sort of treatment that occurred in this case without the sanction of a judicial officer and based on nothing more than the "reasonable suspicion" of low-ranking investigative officers that something might be amiss? The Court today concludes that the Fourth Amendment grants such sweeping and unmonitored authority to customs officials.

I dissent. Indefinite involuntary incommunicado detentions "for investigation" are the hallmark of a police state, not a free society. In my opinion, Government officials may no more confine a person at the border under such circumstances for purposes of criminal investigation than they may within the interior of the country. The nature and duration of the detention here may well have been tolerable for spoiled meat or diseased animals, but not for human beings held on simple suspicion of criminal activity. I believe such indefinite detentions can be "reasonable" under the Fourth Amendment only with the approval of a magistrate. I also believe that such approval can be given only upon a showing of probable cause.

In my opinion, allowing the Government to hold someone in indefinite, involuntary, incommunicado isolation without probable cause and a judicial warrant violates our constitutional charter whether the purpose is to extract ransom or to investigate suspected criminal activity. Nothing in the Fourth

Amendment permits an exception for such actions at the Nation's border. It is tempting, of course, to look the other way in a case that so graphically illustrates the "veritable national crisis" caused by narcotics trafficking. But if there is one enduring lesson in the long struggle to balance individual rights against society's need to defend itself against lawlessness, it is that "[i]t is easy to make light of insistence on scrupulous regard for the safeguards of civil liberties when invoked on behalf of the unworthy. It is too easy. History bears testimony that by such disregard are the rights of liberty extinguished, heedlessly at first, then stealthily, and brazenly in the end."

c. Checkpoints

Of course, the police may stop a vehicle if they observe a traffic violation and may demand to see the driver's license and the vehicle's registration. But what about a checkpoint where cars are stopped for a brief period, such as to see if the driver is intoxicated? In Michigan Department of State Police v. Sitz, the Court upheld the constitutionality of such sobriety checkpoints.

MICHIGAN DEPARTMENT OF STATE POLICE v. SITZ
496 U.S. 444 (1990)

Chief Justice REHNQUIST delivered the opinion of the Court.

This case poses the question whether a State's use of highway sobriety checkpoints violates the Fourth and Fourteenth Amendments to the United States Constitution. We hold that it does not.

Petitioners, the Michigan Department of State Police and its director, established a sobriety checkpoint pilot program in early 1986. The director appointed a Sobriety Checkpoint Advisory Committee comprising representatives of the State Police force, local police forces, state prosecutors, and the University of Michigan Transportation Research Institute. Pursuant to its charge, the advisory committee created guidelines setting forth procedures governing checkpoint operations, site selection, and publicity.

Under the guidelines, checkpoints would be set up at selected sites along state roads. All vehicles passing through a checkpoint would be stopped and their drivers briefly examined for signs of intoxication. In cases where a checkpoint officer detected signs of intoxication, the motorist would be directed to a location out of the traffic flow where an officer would check the motorist's driver's license and car registration and, if warranted, conduct further sobriety tests. Should the field tests and the officer's observations suggest that the driver was intoxicated, an arrest would be made. All other drivers would be permitted to resume their journey immediately.

The first — and to date the only — sobriety checkpoint operated under the program was conducted in Saginaw County with the assistance of the

Saginaw County Sheriff's Department. During the 75-minute duration of the checkpoint's operation, 126 vehicles passed through the checkpoint. The average delay for each vehicle was approximately 25 seconds. Two drivers were detained for field sobriety testing, and one of the two was arrested for driving under the influence of alcohol. A third driver who drove through without stopping was pulled over by an officer in an observation vehicle and arrested for driving under the influence.

On the day before the operation of the Saginaw County checkpoint, respondents filed a complaint in the Circuit Court of Wayne County seeking declaratory and injunctive relief from potential subjection to the checkpoints. Each of the respondents "is a licensed driver in the State of Michigan . . . who regularly travels throughout the State in his automobile."

Petitioners concede, correctly in our view, that a Fourth Amendment "seizure" occurs when a vehicle is stopped at a checkpoint. Fourth Amendment seizure occurs "when there is a governmental termination of freedom of movement through means intentionally applied." The question thus becomes whether such seizures are "reasonable" under the Fourth Amendment.

We address only the initial stop of each motorist passing through a checkpoint and the associated preliminary questioning and observation by checkpoint officers. Detention of particular motorists for more extensive field sobriety testing may require satisfaction of an individualized suspicion standard.

No one can seriously dispute the magnitude of the drunken driving problem or the States' interest in eradicating it. Media reports of alcohol-related death and mutilation on the Nation's roads are legion. The anecdotal is confirmed by the statistical. "Drunk drivers cause an annual death toll of over 25,000 and in the same time span cause nearly one million personal injuries and more than five billion dollars in property damage." For decades, this Court has "repeatedly lamented the tragedy."

Conversely, the weight bearing on the other scale — the measure of the intrusion on motorists stopped briefly at sobriety checkpoints — is slight.

"[T]he circumstances surrounding a checkpoint stop and search are far less intrusive than those attending a roving-patrol stop. Roving patrols often operate at night on seldom-traveled roads, and their approach may frighten motorists. At traffic checkpoints the motorist can see that other vehicles are being stopped, he can see visible signs of the officers' authority, and he is much less likely to be frightened or annoyed by the intrusion."

Here, checkpoints are selected pursuant to the guidelines, and uniformed police officers stop every approaching vehicle. In sum, the balance of the State's interest in preventing drunken driving, the extent to which this system can reasonably be said to advance that interest, and the degree of intrusion upon individual motorists who are briefly stopped, weighs in favor of the state program. We therefore hold that it is consistent with the Fourth Amendment.

Justice STEVENS, with whom Justice BRENNAN and Justice MARSHALL join, dissenting.

A sobriety checkpoint is usually operated at night at an unannounced location. Surprise is crucial to its method. The test operation conducted by the Michigan State Police and the Saginaw County Sheriff's Department began shortly after midnight and lasted until about 1 A.M. During that period, the 19 officers participating in the operation made two arrests and stopped and questioned 124 other unsuspecting and innocent drivers. It is, of course, not known how many arrests would have been made during that period if those officers had been engaged in normal patrol activities. However, the findings of the trial court, based on an extensive record and affirmed by the Michigan Court of Appeals, indicate that the net effect of sobriety checkpoints on traffic safety is infinitesimal and possibly negative.

Indeed, the record in this case makes clear that a decision holding these suspicionless seizures unconstitutional would not impede the law enforcement community's remarkable progress in reducing the death toll on our highways. Because the Michigan program was patterned after an older program in Maryland, the trial judge gave special attention to that State's experience. Over a period of several years, Maryland operated 125 checkpoints; of the 41,000 motorists passing through those checkpoints, only 143 persons (0.3%) were arrested. The number of man-hours devoted to these operations is not in the record, but it seems inconceivable that a higher arrest rate could not have been achieved by more conventional means. Yet, even if the 143 checkpoint arrests were assumed to involve a net increase in the number of drunken driving arrests per year, the figure would still be insignificant by comparison to the 71,000 such arrests made by Michigan State Police without checkpoints in 1984 alone. Any relationship between sobriety checkpoints and an actual reduction in highway fatalities is even less substantial than the minimal impact on arrest rates.

In light of these considerations, it seems evident that the Court today misapplies the balancing test. The Court overvalues the law enforcement interest in using sobriety checkpoints, undervalues the citizen's interest in freedom from random, unannounced investigatory seizures, and mistakenly assumes that there is "virtually no difference" between a routine stop at a permanent, fixed checkpoint and a surprise stop at a sobriety checkpoint. I believe this case is controlled by our several precedents condemning suspicionless random stops of motorists for investigatory purposes.

What if the checkpoint is not for purposes of stopping intoxicated drivers, but exists for officers to look into the cars to see whether there are visible illegal drugs in the car? In City of Indianapolis v. Edmond, the Court found this unconstitutional. In reading the decision, it is important to consider whether the distinction of *Sitz* is persuasive.

CITY OF INDIANAPOLIS v. EDMOND

531 U.S. 32 (2000)

Justice O'CONNOR delivered the opinion of the Court.

In Michigan Dept. of State Police v. Sitz (1990), and United States v. Martinez-Fuerte (1976), we held that brief, suspicionless seizures at highway checkpoints for the purposes of combating drunk driving and intercepting illegal immigrants were constitutional. We now consider the constitutionality of a highway checkpoint program whose primary purpose is the discovery and interdiction of illegal narcotics.

I

In August 1998, the city of Indianapolis began to operate vehicle checkpoints on Indianapolis roads in an effort to interdict unlawful drugs. The city conducted six such roadblocks between August and November that year, stopping 1,161 vehicles and arresting 104 motorists. Fifty-five arrests were for drug-related crimes, while 49 were for offenses unrelated to drugs. The overall "hit rate" of the program was thus approximately nine percent.

The parties stipulated to the facts concerning the operation of the checkpoints by the Indianapolis Police Department (IPD) for purposes of the preliminary injunction proceedings instituted below. At each checkpoint location, the police stop a predetermined number of vehicles. Approximately 30 officers are stationed at the checkpoint. Pursuant to written directives issued by the chief of police, at least one officer approaches the vehicle, advises the driver that he or she is being stopped briefly at a drug checkpoint, and asks the driver to produce a license and registration. The officer also looks for signs of impairment and conducts an open-view examination of the vehicle from the outside. A narcotics-detection dog walks around the outside of each stopped vehicle.

The directives instruct the officers that they may conduct a search only by consent or based on the appropriate quantum of particularized suspicion. The officers must conduct each stop in the same manner until particularized suspicion develops, and the officers have no discretion to stop any vehicle out of sequence. The city agreed in the stipulation to operate the checkpoints in such a way as to ensure that the total duration of each stop, absent reasonable suspicion or probable cause, would be five minutes or less.

Respondents James Edmond and Joell Palmer were each stopped at a narcotics checkpoint in late September 1998. Respondents then filed a lawsuit on behalf of themselves and the class of all motorists who had been stopped or were subject to being stopped in the future at the Indianapolis drug checkpoints. Respondents claimed that the roadblocks violated the Fourth Amendment of the United States Constitution and the search and seizure provision of the Indiana Constitution. Respondents requested declaratory and injunctive relief for the class, as well as damages and attorney's fees for themselves.

II

The Fourth Amendment requires that searches and seizures be reasonable. A search or seizure is ordinarily unreasonable in the absence of individualized suspicion of wrongdoing. While such suspicion is not an "irreducible" component of reasonableness, we have recognized only limited circumstances in which the usual rule does not apply.

It is well established that a vehicle stop at a highway checkpoint effectuates a seizure within the meaning of the Fourth Amendment. The fact that officers walk a narcotics-detection dog around the exterior of each car at the Indianapolis checkpoints does not transform the seizure into a search. *See* United States v. Place (1983). Just as in *Place*, an exterior sniff of an automobile does not require entry into the car and is not designed to disclose any information other than the presence or absence of narcotics. Like the dog sniff in *Place*, a sniff by a dog that simply walks around a car is "much less intrusive than a typical search." Rather, what principally distinguishes these checkpoints from those we have previously approved is their primary purpose.

As petitioners concede, the Indianapolis checkpoint program unquestionably has the primary purpose of interdicting illegal narcotics. In their stipulation of facts, the parties repeatedly refer to the checkpoints as "drug checkpoints" and describe them as "being operated by the City of Indianapolis in an effort to interdict unlawful drugs in Indianapolis."

We have never approved a checkpoint program whose primary purpose was to detect evidence of ordinary criminal wrongdoing. Rather, our checkpoint cases have recognized only limited exceptions to the general rule that a seizure must be accompanied by some measure of individualized suspicion. [E]ach of the checkpoint programs that we have approved was designed primarily to serve purposes closely related to the problems of policing the border or the necessity of ensuring roadway safety. Because the primary purpose of the Indianapolis narcotics checkpoint program is to uncover evidence of ordinary criminal wrongdoing, the program contravenes the Fourth Amendment.

The primary purpose of the Indianapolis narcotics checkpoints is in the end to advance "the general interest in crime control." We decline to suspend the usual requirement of individualized suspicion where the police seek to employ a checkpoint primarily for the ordinary enterprise of investigating crimes. We cannot sanction stops justified only by the generalized and ever-present possibility that interrogation and inspection may reveal that any given motorist has committed some crime.

Of course, there are circumstances that may justify a law enforcement checkpoint where the primary purpose would otherwise, but for some emergency, relate to ordinary crime control. For example, as the Court of Appeals

noted, the Fourth Amendment would almost certainly permit an appropriately tailored roadblock set up to thwart an imminent terrorist attack or to
catch a dangerous criminal who is likely to flee by way of a particular route.
The exigencies created by these scenarios are far removed from the circumstances under which authorities might simply stop cars as a matter of course
to see if there just happens to be a felon leaving the jurisdiction. While we do
not limit the purposes that may justify a checkpoint program to any rigid set
of categories, we decline to approve a program whose primary purpose is
ultimately indistinguishable from the general interest in crime control.

Petitioners argue that the Indianapolis checkpoint program is justified by
its lawful secondary purposes of keeping impaired motorists off the road and
verifying licenses and registrations. If this were the case, however, law
enforcement authorities would be able to establish checkpoints for virtually
any purpose so long as they also included a license or sobriety check. For this
reason, we examine the available evidence to determine the primary purpose
of the checkpoint program. While we recognize the challenges inherent in a
purpose inquiry, courts routinely engage in this enterprise in many areas of
constitutional jurisprudence as a means of sifting abusive governmental conduct from that which is lawful. As a result, a program driven by an impermissible purpose may be proscribed while a program impelled by licit
purposes is permitted, even though the challenged conduct may be out-
wardly similar. While reasonableness under the Fourth Amendment is pre-
dominantly an objective inquiry, our special needs and administrative search
cases demonstrate that purpose is often relevant when suspicionless intrusions pursuant to a general scheme are at issue. When law enforcement
authorities pursue primarily general crime control purposes at checkpoints
such as here, however, stops can only be justified by some quantum of individualized suspicion.

Because the primary purpose of the Indianapolis checkpoint program is
ultimately indistinguishable from the general interest in crime control, the
checkpoints violate the Fourth Amendment.

Chief Justice REHNQUIST, with whom Justice THOMAS joins, and with whom
Justice SCALIA joins as to Part I, dissenting.

The State's use of a drug-sniffing dog, according to the Court's holding,
annuls what is otherwise plainly constitutional under our Fourth Amendment jurisprudence: brief, standardized, discretionless, roadblock seizures
of automobiles, seizures which effectively serve a weighty state interest with
only minimal intrusion on the privacy of their occupants. Because these
seizures serve the State's accepted and significant interests of preventing
drunken driving and checking for driver's licenses and vehicle registrations,
and because there is nothing in the record to indicate that the addition of
the dog sniff lengthens these otherwise legitimate seizures, I dissent.

As it is nowhere to be found in the Court's opinion, I begin with blackletter
roadblock seizure law. Roadblock seizures are consistent with the Fourth
Amendment if they are "carried out pursuant to a plan embodying explicit,

neutral limitations on the conduct of individual officers." Specifically, the constitutionality of a seizure turns upon "a weighing of the gravity of the public concerns served by the seizure, the degree to which the seizure advances the public interest, and the severity of the interference with individual liberty."

Petitioners acknowledge that the "primary purpose" of these roadblocks is to interdict illegal drugs, but this fact should not be controlling. [T]he question whether a law enforcement purpose could support a roadblock seizure is not presented in this case. The District Court found that another "purpose of the checkpoints is to check driver's licenses and vehicle registrations," and the written directives state that the police officers are to "[l]ook for signs of impairment." That the roadblocks serve these legitimate state interests cannot be seriously disputed, as the 49 people arrested for offenses unrelated to drugs can attest.

Because of the valid reasons for conducting these roadblock seizures, it is constitutionally irrelevant that petitioners also hoped to interdict drugs. In Whren v. United States (1996), we held that an officer's subjective intent would not invalidate an otherwise objectively justifiable stop of an automobile. The reasonableness of an officer's discretionary decision to stop an automobile, at issue in *Whren*, turns on whether there is probable cause to believe that a traffic violation has occurred. The reasonableness of highway checkpoints, at issue here, turns on whether they effectively serve a significant state interest with minimal intrusion on motorists. The stop in *Whren* was objectively reasonable because the police officers had witnessed traffic violations; so too the roadblocks here are objectively reasonable because they serve the substantial interests of preventing drunken driving and checking for driver's licenses and vehicle registrations with minimal intrusion on motorists.

Once the constitutional requirements for a particular seizure are satisfied, the subjective expectations of those responsible for it, be they police officers or members of a city council, are irrelevant. It is the objective effect of the State's actions on the privacy of the individual that animates the Fourth Amendment.

These stops effectively serve the State's legitimate interests; they are executed in a regularized and neutral manner; and they only minimally intrude upon the privacy of the motorists. They should therefore be constitutional.

———————————

There has thus far been one other Supreme Court decision concerning checkpoints: Illinois v. Lidster, 540 U.S. 419 (2004). Justice Breyer, writing for the Court, began his opinion by stating that the case concerned "a highway checkpoint where police stopped motorists to ask them for information about a recent hit-and-run accident. We hold that the police stops were reasonable, hence, constitutional."

A hit-and-run accident killed a man on a bicycle. The Court described the checkpoint that was created:

> About one week later at about the same time of night and at about the same place, local police set up a highway checkpoint designed to obtain more information about the accident from the motoring public. Police cars with flashing lights partially blocked the eastbound lanes of the highway. The blockage forced traffic to slow down, leading to lines of up to 15 cars in each lane. As each vehicle drew up to the checkpoint, an officer would stop it for 10 to 15 seconds, ask the occupants whether they had seen anything happen there the previous weekend, and hand each driver a flyer. The flyer said "ALERT . . . FATAL HIT & RUN ACCIDENT" and requested "ASSISTANCE IN IDENTIFYING THE VEHICLE AND DRIVER INVOLVED IN THIS ACCIDENT WHICH KILLED A 70 YEAR OLD BICYCLIST."
>
> Robert Lidster, the respondent, drove a minivan toward the checkpoint. As he approached the checkpoint, his van swerved, nearly hitting one of the officers. The officer smelled alcohol on Lidster's breath. He directed Lidster to a side street where another officer administered a sobriety test and then arrested Lidster. Lidster was tried and convicted in Illinois state court of driving under the influence of alcohol.

The issue was whether the checkpoint violated the Fourth Amendment. The Court distinguished *Edmond*:

> The checkpoint stop here differs significantly from that in *Edmond*. The stop's primary law enforcement purpose was not to determine whether a vehicle's occupants were committing a crime, but to ask vehicle occupants, as members of the public, for their help in providing information about a crime in all likelihood committed by others. The police expected the information elicited to help them apprehend, not the vehicle's occupants, but other individuals.
>
> Neither do we believe, *Edmond* aside, that the Fourth Amendment would have us apply an *Edmond*-type rule of automatic unconstitutionality to brief, information-seeking highway stops of the kind now before us. For one thing, the fact that such stops normally lack individualized suspicion cannot by itself determine the constitutional outcome. As in *Edmond*, the stop here at issue involves a motorist. The Fourth Amendment does not treat a motorist's car as his castle. And special law enforcement concerns will sometimes justify highway stops without individualized suspicion. Moreover, unlike *Edmond*, the context here (seeking information from the public) is one in which, by definition, the concept of individualized suspicion has little role to play. Like certain other forms of police activity, say, crowd control or public safety, an information-seeking stop is not the kind of event that involves suspicion, or lack of suspicion, of the relevant individual.
>
> For another thing, information-seeking highway stops are less likely to provoke anxiety or to prove intrusive. The stops are likely brief. The police are not likely to ask questions designed to elicit self-incriminating information. And citizens will often react positively when police simply ask for their help as "responsible citizen[s]" to "give whatever information they may have to aid in law enforcement."
>
> Further, the law ordinarily permits police to seek the voluntary cooperation of members of the public in the investigation of a crime. "[L]aw enforcement officers do not violate the Fourth Amendment by merely approaching an individual on the street or in another public place, by asking him if he is willing to answer some questions, [or] by putting questions to him if the person is willing to listen."
>
> Finally, we do not believe that an *Edmond*-type rule is needed to prevent an unreasonable proliferation of police checkpoints. Practical considerations—namely,

limited police resources and community hostility to related traffic tieups —
seem likely to inhibit any such proliferation. And, of course, the Fourth Amendment's normal insistence that the stop be reasonable in context will still provide
an important legal limitation on police use of this kind of information-seeking
checkpoint.

These considerations, taken together, convince us that an *Edmond*-type presumptive rule of unconstitutionality does not apply here. That does not mean the stop is
automatically, or even presumptively, constitutional. It simply means that we must
judge its reasonableness, hence, its constitutionality, on the basis of the individual
circumstances.

The Court concluded that this checkpoint was reasonable as the police were
investigating a death and had been stymied in obtaining other sources of
information. The Court said that the intrusion was minimal and justified by
the importance of the investigation.

d. Schools

In New Jersey v. T.L.O., 469 U.S. 325 (1985), the Court held that school
officials could search a student's purse based on reasonable suspicion; there
did not need to be a warrant or probable cause. The Court said that "the
Fourth Amendment [is] applicable to the activities of civil as well as criminal
authorities."

But the Court said that it was sufficient under the Fourth Amendment that
there be "reasonable grounds for suspecting that the search will turn up
evidence that the student has violated or is violating either the law or the
rules of the school." The Court came to this conclusion by balancing the
diminished expectation of privacy of students in schools and the need for
schools to maintain discipline and order. The Court stressed that the search
must be reasonable in scope. It explained that "the measures adopted are
reasonably related to the objectives of the search and not excessively
intrusive in light of the age and sex of the student and the nature of the
infraction."

The Court applied this in Safford Unified School District v. Redding,
where the Court considered the circumstances under which a student
may be subjected to a strip search.

SAFFORD UNIFIED SCHOOL DISTRICT #1 v. REDDING

557 U.S. 364 (2009)

Justice SOUTER delivered the opinion of the Court.

The issue here is whether a 13-year-old student's Fourth Amendment right
was violated when she was subjected to a search of her bra and underpants by
school officials acting on reasonable suspicion that she had brought forbidden prescription and over-the-counter drugs to school. Because there were

no reasons to suspect the drugs presented a danger or were concealed in her underwear, we hold that the search did violate the Constitution, but because there is reason to question the clarity with which the right was established, the official who ordered the unconstitutional search is entitled to qualified immunity from liability.

I

The events immediately prior to the search in question began in 13-year-old Savana Redding's math class at Safford Middle School one October day in 2003. The assistant principal of the school, Kerry Wilson, came into the room and asked Savana to go to his office. There, he showed her a day planner, unzipped and open flat on his desk, in which there were several knives, lighters, a permanent marker, and a cigarette. Wilson asked Savana whether the planner was hers; she said it was, but that a few days before she had lent it to her friend, Marissa Glines. Savana stated that none of the items in the planner belonged to her.

Wilson then showed Savana four white prescription-strength ibuprofen 400-mg pills, and one over-the-counter blue naproxen 200-mg pill, all used for pain and inflammation but banned under school rules without advance permission. He asked Savana if she knew anything about the pills. Savana answered that she did not. Wilson then told Savana that he had received a report that she was giving these pills to fellow students; Savana denied it and agreed to let Wilson search her belongings. Helen Romero, an administrative assistant, came into the office, and together with Wilson they searched Savana's backpack, finding nothing.

At that point, Wilson instructed Romero to take Savana to the school nurse's office to search her clothes for pills. Romero and the nurse, Peggy Schwallier, asked Savana to remove her jacket, socks, and shoes, leaving her in stretch pants and a T-shirt (both without pockets), which she was then asked to remove. Finally, Savana was told to pull her bra out and to the side and shake it, and to pull out the elastic on her underpants, thus exposing her breasts and pelvic area to some degree. No pills were found.

Savana's mother filed suit against Safford Unified School District #1, Wilson, Romero, and Schwallier for conducting a strip search in violation of Savana's Fourth Amendment rights. The individuals (hereinafter petitioners) moved for summary judgment, raising a defense of qualified immunity.

II

In [*New Jersey v.*] *T.L.O.*, we recognized that the school setting "requires some modification of the level of suspicion of illicit activity needed to justify a search," and held that for searches by school officials "a careful balancing of governmental and private interests suggests that the public interest is best served by a Fourth Amendment standard of reasonableness that stops short of probable cause." We have thus applied a standard of reasonable suspicion to determine the legality of a school administrator's search of a student, and have held that a school search "will be permissible in its scope when the measures adopted are reasonably related to the objectives of the search and not excessively intrusive in light of the age and sex of the student and the nature of the infraction."

III

A

In this case, the school's policies strictly prohibit the nonmedical use, possession, or sale of any drug on school grounds, including "'[a]ny prescription or over-the-counter drug, except those for which permission to use in school has been granted pursuant to Board policy.'" A week before Savana was searched, another student, Jordan Romero (no relation of the school's administrative assistant), told the principal and Assistant Principal Wilson that "certain students were bringing drugs and weapons on campus," and that he had been sick after taking some pills that "he got from a classmate." On the morning of October 8, the same boy handed Wilson a white pill that he said Marissa Glines had given him. He told Wilson that students were planning to take the pills at lunch.

Wilson learned from Peggy Schwallier, the school nurse, that the pill was Ibuprofen 400 mg, available only by prescription. Wilson then called Marissa out of class. Outside the classroom, Marissa's teacher handed Wilson the day planner, found within Marissa's reach, containing various contraband items. Wilson escorted Marissa back to his office.

In the presence of Helen Romero, Wilson requested Marissa to turn out her pockets and open her wallet. Marissa produced a blue pill, several white ones, and a razor blade. Wilson asked where the blue pill came from, and Marissa answered, "'I guess it slipped in when *she* gave me the IBU 400s.'" When Wilson asked whom she meant, Marissa replied, "'Savana Redding.'" Wilson then enquired about the day planner and its contents; Marissa denied knowing anything about them. Wilson did not ask Marissa any followup questions to determine whether there was any likelihood that Savana presently had pills: neither asking when Marissa received the pills from Savana nor where Savana might be hiding them.

Schwallier did not immediately recognize the blue pill, but information provided through a poison control hotline indicated that the pill was a 200-mg dose of an anti-inflammatory drug, generically called naproxen, available over the counter. At Wilson's direction, Marissa was then subjected to a search of her bra and underpants by Romero and Schwallier, as Savana was later on. The search revealed no additional pills.

It was at this juncture that Wilson called Savana into his office and showed her the day planner. Their conversation established that Savana and Marissa were on friendly terms: while she denied knowledge of the contraband,

Savana admitted that the day planner was hers and that she had lent it to Marissa. Wilson had other reports of their friendship from staff members, who had identified Savana and Marissa as part of an unusually rowdy group at the school's opening dance in August, during which alcohol and cigarettes were found in the girls' bathroom. Wilson had reason to connect the girls with this contraband, for Wilson knew that Jordan Romero had told the principal that before the dance, he had been at a party at Savana's house where alcohol was served. Marissa's statement that the pills came from Savana was thus sufficiently plausible to warrant suspicion that Savana was involved in pill distribution.

This suspicion of Wilson's was enough to justify a search of Savana's backpack and outer clothing. If a student is reasonably suspected of giving out contraband pills, she is reasonably suspected of carrying them on her person and in the carryall that has become an item of student uniform in most places today. If Wilson's reasonable suspicion of pill distribution were not understood to support searches of outer clothes and backpack, it would not justify any search worth making. And the look into Savana's bag, in her presence and in the relative privacy of Wilson's office, was not excessively intrusive, any more than Romero's subsequent search of her outer clothing.

B

Here it is that the parties part company, with Savana's claim that extending the search at Wilson's behest to the point of making her pull out her under-wear was constitutionally unreasonable. The exact label for this final step in the intrusion is not important, though strip search is a fair way to speak of it. Romero and Schwallier directed Savana to remove her clothes down to her underwear, and then "pull out" her bra and the elastic band on her under-pants. Although Romero and Schwallier stated that they did not see anything when Savana followed their instructions, we would not define strip search and its Fourth Amendment consequences in a way that would guarantee litigation about who was looking and how much was seen. The very fact of Savana's pulling her underwear away from her body in the presence of the two officials who were able to see her necessarily exposed her breasts and pelvic area to some degree, and both subjective and reasonable societal expectations of personal privacy support the treatment of such a search as categorically distinct, requiring distinct elements of justification on the part of school authorities for going beyond a search of outer clothing and belongings.

Savana's subjective expectation of privacy against such a search is inherent in her account of it as embarrassing, frightening, and humiliating. The rea-sonableness of her expectation (required by the Fourth Amendment standard) is indicated by the consistent experiences of other young people similarly searched, whose adolescent vulnerability intensifies the patent intrusiveness of the exposure. The common reaction of these adolescents simply registers the obviously different meaning of a search exposing the body from the experience of nakedness or near undress in other school circumstances. Changing for gym is getting ready for play; exposing for a search is responding to an accusation reserved for suspected wrongdoers and fairly understood as so degrading that a number of communities have decided that strip searches in schools are never reasonable and have banned them no matter what the facts may be.

The indignity of the search does not, of course, outlaw it, but it does implicate the rule of reasonableness as stated in *T.L.O.*, that "the search as actually conducted [be] reasonably related in scope to the circumstances which justified the interference in the first place." The scope will be permissible, that is, when it is "not excessively intrusive in light of the age and sex of the student and the nature of the infraction."

Here, the content of the suspicion failed to match the degree of intrusion. Wilson knew beforehand that the pills were prescription-strength ibuprofen and over-the-counter naproxen, common pain relievers equivalent to two Advil, or one Aleve. He must have been aware of the nature and limited threat of the specific drugs he was searching for, and while just about anything can be taken in quantities that will do real harm, Wilson had no reason to suspect that large amounts of the drugs were being passed around, or that individual students were receiving great numbers of pills.

Nor could Wilson have suspected that Savana was hiding common painkillers in her underwear. Petitioners suggest, as a truth universally acknowledged, that "students . . . hid[e] contraband in or under their clothing," and cite a smattering of cases of students with contraband in their underwear. But when the categorically extreme intrusiveness of a search down to the body of an adolescent requires some justification in suspected facts, general background possibilities fall short; a reasonable search that extensive calls for suspicion that it will pay off. But nondangerous school contraband does not raise the specter of stashes in intimate places, and there is no evidence in the record of any general practice among Safford Middle School students of hiding that sort of thing in underwear; neither Jordan nor Marissa suggested to Wilson that Savana was doing that, and the preceding search of Marissa that Wilson ordered yielded nothing. Wilson never even determined when Marissa had received the pills from Savana; if it had been a few days before, that would weigh heavily against any reasonable conclusion that Savana presently had the pills on her person, much less in her underwear.

In sum, what was missing from the suspected facts that pointed to Savana was any indication of danger to the students from the power of the drugs or their quantity, and any reason to suppose that Savana was carrying pills in her underwear. We think that the combination of these deficiencies was fatal to finding the search reasonable.

In so holding, we mean to cast no ill reflection on the assistant principal, for the record raises no doubt that his motive throughout was to eliminate drugs from his school and protect students from what Jordan Romero had gone through. Parents are known to overreact to protect their children from danger, and a school official with responsibility for safety may tend to do the same. The difference is that the Fourth Amendment places limits on the official, even with the high degree of deference that courts must pay to the educator's professional judgment.

We do mean, though, to make it clear that the *T.L.O.* concern to limit a school search to reasonable scope requires the support of reasonable suspicion of danger or of resort to underwear for hiding evidence of wrong-doing before a search can reasonably make the quantum leap from outer clothes and backpacks to exposure of intimate parts. The meaning of such a search, and the degradation its subject may reasonably feel, place a search that intrusive in a category of its own demanding its own specific suspicions.

IV

[The Court then held that the school officials could not be held liable for money damages because they were protected by qualified immunity; that is, they did not violate clearly established law that the reasonable officer should know. The Court remanded the case to determine if the school district could be held liable for a policy that violated the Fourth Amendment.]

Justice THOMAS, concurring in the judgment in part and dissenting in part.

I agree with the Court that the judgment against the school officials with respect to qualified immunity should be reversed. Unlike the majority, however, I would hold that the search of Savana Redding did not violate the Fourth Amendment. The majority imposes a vague and amorphous standard on school administrators. It also grants judges sweeping authority to second-guess the measures that these officials take to maintain discipline in their schools and ensure the health and safety of the students in their charge. This deep intrusion into the administration of public schools exemplifies why the Court should return to the common-law doctrine of *in loco parentis* under which "the judiciary was reluctant to interfere in the routine business of school administration, allowing schools and teachers to set and enforce rules and to maintain order." But even under the prevailing Fourth Amendment test established by *New Jersey v. T.L.O.* (1985), all petitioners, including the school district, are entitled to judgment as a matter of law in their favor.

I

"Although the underlying command of the Fourth Amendment is always that searches and seizures be reasonable, what is reasonable depends on the context within which a search takes place." Thus, although public school students retain Fourth Amendment rights under this Court's precedent, those rights "are different . . . than elsewhere; the 'reasonableness' inquiry cannot disregard the schools' custodial and tutelary responsibility for children." For nearly 25 years this Court has understood that "[m]aintaining order in the classroom has never been easy, but in more recent years, school disorder has often taken particularly ugly forms: drug use and violent crime in the schools have become major social problems." In schools, "[e]vents calling for discipline are frequent occurrences and sometimes require immediate, effective action."

For this reason, school officials retain broad authority to protect students and preserve "order and a proper educational environment" under the Fourth Amendment. This authority requires that school officials be able to engage in the "close supervision of schoolchildren, as well as . . . enforc[e] rules against conduct that would be perfectly permissible if undertaken by an adult." Seeking to reconcile the Fourth Amendment with this unique public school setting, the Court in *T.L.O.* held that a school search is "reasonable" if it is "'justified at its inception'" and "'reasonably related in scope to the circumstances which justified the interference in the first place.'" The search under review easily meets this standard.

A

A "search of a student by a teacher or other school official will be 'justified at its inception' when there are reasonable grounds for suspecting that the search will turn up evidence that the student has violated or is violating either the law or the rules of the school." As the majority rightly concedes, this search was justified at its inception because there were reasonable grounds to suspect that Redding possessed medication that violated school rules.

B

The remaining question is whether the search was reasonable in scope. Under *T.L.O.*, "a search will be permissible in its scope when the measures adopted are reasonably related to the objectives of the search and not excessively intrusive in light of the age and sex of the student and the nature of the infraction." The majority concludes that the school officials' search of Redding's underwear was not "reasonably related in scope to the circumstances which justified the interference in the first place," notwithstanding the officials' reasonable suspicion that Redding "was involved in pill distribution." According to the majority, to be reasonable, this school search required a showing of "danger to the students from the power of the drugs or their quantity" or a "reason to suppose that [Redding] was carrying pills in her underwear." Each of these additional requirements is an unjustifiable departure from bedrock Fourth Amendment law in the school setting, where this Court has heretofore read the Fourth Amendment to grant considerable leeway to school officials. Because the school officials searched in a location where the pills could have been hidden, the search was reasonable in scope under *T.L.O.*

1

The majority finds that "subjective and reasonable societal expectations of personal privacy support . . . treat[ing]" this type of search, which it labels a "strip search," as "categorically distinct, requiring distinct elements of justification on the part of school authorities for going beyond a search of clothing and belongings." Thus, in the majority's view, although the school officials had reasonable suspicion to believe that Redding had the pills on her person, they needed some greater level of particularized suspicion to conduct this "strip search." There is no support for this contortion of the Fourth Amendment.

The Court has generally held that the reasonableness of a search's scope depends only on whether it is limited to the area that is capable of concealing the object of the search. In keeping with this longstanding rule, the "nature of the infraction" referenced in *T.L.O.* delineates the proper scope of a search of students in a way that is identical to that permitted for searches outside the school — *i.e.*, the search must be limited to the areas where the object of that infraction could be concealed. A search of a student therefore is permissible in scope under *T.L.O.* so long as it is objectively reasonable to believe that the area searched could conceal the contraband.

The analysis of whether the scope of the search here was permissible under that standard is straightforward. Indeed, the majority does not dispute that "general background possibilities" establish that students conceal "contraband in their underwear." It acknowledges that school officials had reasonable suspicion to look in Redding's backpack and outer clothing because if "Wilson's reasonable suspicion of pill distribution were not understood to support searches of outer clothes and backpack, it would not justify any search worth making." The majority nevertheless concludes that proceeding any further with the search was unreasonable. But there is no support for this conclusion. The reasonable suspicion that Redding possessed the pills for distribution purposes did not dissipate simply because the search of her backpack turned up nothing. It was eminently reasonable to conclude that the backpack was empty because Redding was secreting the pills in a place she thought no one would look. Redding would not have been the first person to conceal pills in her undergarments.

2

The majority's decision in this regard also departs from another basic principle of the Fourth Amendment: that law enforcement officials can enforce with the same vigor all rules and regulations irrespective of the perceived importance of any of those rules. "In a long line of cases, we have said that when an officer has probable cause to believe a person committed even a minor crime in his presence, the balancing of private and public interests is not in doubt. The arrest is constitutionally reasonable." The Fourth Amendment rule for searches is the same: Police officers are entitled to search regardless of the perceived triviality of the underlying law. As we have explained, requiring police to make "sensitive, case-by-case determinations of government need," for a particular prohibition before conducting a search would "place police in an almost impossible spot."

The majority has placed school officials in this "impossible spot" by questioning whether possession of Ibuprofen and Naproxen causes a severe enough threat to warrant investigation. Had the suspected infraction involved a street drug, the majority implies that it would have approved the scope of the search. In effect, then, the majority has replaced a school rule that draws no distinction among drugs with a new one that does. As a result, a full search of a student's person for prohibited drugs will be permitted only if the Court agrees that the drug in question was sufficiently dangerous. Such a test is unworkable and unsound. School officials cannot be expected to halt searches based on the possibility that a court might later find that the particular infraction at issue is not severe enough to warrant an intrusive investigation.

A rule promulgated by a school board represents the judgment of school officials that the rule is needed to maintain "school order" and "a proper educational environment." Teachers, administrators, and the local school board are called upon both to "protect the . . . safety of students and school personnel" and "maintain an environment conducive to learning." They are tasked with "watch[ing] over a large number of students" who "are inclined to test the outer boundaries of acceptable conduct and to imitate the misbehavior of a peer if that misbehavior is not dealt with quickly." In such an environment, something as simple as a "water pistol or peashooter can wreak [havoc] until it is taken away." The danger posed by unchecked distribution and consumption of prescription pills by students certainly needs no elaboration.

Judges are not qualified to second-guess the best manner for maintaining quiet and order in the school environment. Such institutional judgments, like those concerning the selection of the best methods for "restrain[ing students] from assaulting one another, abusing drugs and alcohol, and committing other crimes," "involve a host of policy choices that must be made by locally elected representatives, rather than by federal judges interpreting the basic charter of Government for the entire country."

3

Even if this Court were authorized to second-guess the importance of school rules, the Court's assessment of the importance of this district's policy is flawed. It is a crime to possess or use prescription-strength Ibuprofen without a prescription. By prohibiting unauthorized prescription drugs on school grounds — and conducting a search to ensure students abide by that prohibition — the school rule here was consistent with a routine provision of the state criminal code. It hardly seems unreasonable for school officials to enforce a rule that, in effect, proscribes conduct that amounts to a crime. Moreover, school districts have valid reasons for punishing the unauthorized possession of prescription drugs on school property as severely as the possession of street drugs; "[t]eenage abuse of over-the-counter and prescription drugs poses an increasingly alarming national crisis." As one study noted, "more young people ages 12-17 abuse prescription drugs than any illicit drug except marijuana — more than cocaine, heroin, and methamphetamine combined."

In determining whether the search's scope was reasonable under the Fourth Amendment, it is therefore irrelevant whether officials suspected

Redding of possessing prescription-strength Ibuprofen, nonprescription-strength Naproxen, or some harder street drug. Safford prohibited its possession on school property. Reasonable suspicion that Redding was in possession of drugs in violation of these policies, therefore, justified a search extending to any area where small pills could be concealed. The search did not violate the Fourth Amendment.

II

By declaring the search unreasonable in this case, the majority has "surrender[ed] control of the American public school system to public school students" by invalidating school policies that treat all drugs equally and by second-guessing swift disciplinary decisions made by school officials. The Court's interference in these matters of great concern to teachers, parents, and students illustrates why the most constitutionally sound approach to the question of applying the Fourth Amendment in local public schools would in fact be the complete restoration of the common-law doctrine of *in loco parentis.*

"[T]he nationwide drug epidemic makes the war against drugs a pressing concern in every school." And yet the Court has limited the authority of school officials to conduct searches for the drugs that the officials believe pose a serious safety risk to their students. By doing so, the majority has confirmed that a return to the doctrine of *in loco parentis* is required to keep the judiciary from essentially seizing control of public schools. Only then will teachers again be able to "govern the[ir] pupils, quicken the slothful, spur the indolent, restrain the impetuous, and control the stubborn" by making "rules, giv[ing] commands, and punish[ing] disobedience" without interference from judges. By deciding that it is better equipped to decide what behavior should be permitted in schools, the Court has undercut student safety and undermined the authority of school administrators and local officials. Even more troubling, it has done so in a case in which the underlying response by school administrators was reasonable and justified. I cannot join this regrettable decision.

e. The Government Employment Context

In City of Ontario v. Quon, the Supreme Court considered the application of the Fourth Amendment in the context of government employment.

CITY OF ONTARIO v. QUON
560 U.S. 746 (2010)

Justice KENNEDY delivered the opinion of the Court.

This case involves the assertion by a government employer of the right, in circumstances to be described, to read text messages sent and received on a pager the employer owned and issued to an employee. The employee contends that the privacy of the messages is protected by the ban on "unreasonable searches and seizures" found in the Fourth Amendment to the United States Constitution, made applicable to the States by the Due Process Clause of the Fourteenth Amendment. Though the case touches issues of far reaching significance, the Court concludes it can be resolved by settled principles determining when a search is reasonable.

I

The City of Ontario (City) is a political subdivision of the State of California. The case arose out of incidents in 2001 and 2002 when respondent Jeff Quon was employed by the Ontario Police Department (OPD). He was a police sergeant and member of OPD's Special Weapons and Tactics (SWAT) Team. As will be discussed, two respondents share the last name Quon. In this opinion "Quon" refers to Jeff Quon, for the relevant events mostly revolve around him.

In October 2001, the City acquired 20 alphanumeric pagers capable of sending and receiving text messages. Arch Wireless Operating Company provided wireless service for the pagers. Under the City's service contract with Arch Wireless, each pager was allotted a limited number of characters sent or received each month. Usage in excess of that amount would result in an additional fee. The City issued pagers to Quon and other SWAT Team members in order to help the SWAT Team mobilize and respond to emergency situations.

Before acquiring the pagers, the City announced a "Computer Usage, Internet and E-Mail Policy" (Computer Policy) that applied to all employees. Among other provisions, it specified that the City "reserves the right to monitor and log all network activity including e-mail and Internet use, with or without notice. Users should have no expectation of privacy or confidentiality when using these resources." In March 2000, Quon signed a statement acknowledging that he had read and understood the Computer Policy.

The Computer Policy did not apply, on its face, to text messaging. Although the Computer Policy did not cover text messages by its explicit terms, the City made clear to employees, including Quon, that the City would treat text messages the same way as it treated e-mails. At an April 18, 2002, staff meeting at which Quon was present, Lieutenant Steven Duke, the OPD officer responsible for the City's contract with Arch Wireless, told officers that messages sent on the pagers "are considered e-mail messages. This means that [text] messages would fall under the City's policy as public information and [would be] eligible for auditing." Duke's comments were put in writing in a memorandum sent on April 29, 2002, by Chief Scharf to Quon and other City personnel.

Within the first or second billing cycle after the pagers were distributed, Quon exceeded his monthly text message character allotment. Duke told Quon about the overage, and reminded him that messages sent on the pagers were "considered e-mail and could be audited." Duke said, however, that "it was not his intent to audit [an] employee's text messages to see if the overage [was] due to work related transmissions." Duke suggested that Quon could reimburse the City for the overage fee rather than have Duke audit the messages. Quon wrote a check to the City for the overage. Duke offered the same arrangement to other employees who incurred overage fees.

Over the next few months, Quon exceeded his character limit three or four times. Each time he reimbursed the City. Quon and another officer again incurred overage fees for their pager usage in August 2002. At a meeting in October, Duke told Scharf that he had become "'tired of being a bill collector.'" Scharf decided to determine whether the existing character limit was too low — that is, whether officers such as Quon were having to pay fees for sending work-related messages — or if the overages were for personal messages. Scharf told Duke to request transcripts of text messages sent in August and September by Quon and the other employee who had exceeded the character allowance.

At Duke's request, an administrative assistant employed by OPD contacted Arch Wireless. After verifying that the City was the subscriber on the accounts, Arch Wireless provided the desired transcripts. Duke reviewed the transcripts and discovered that many of the messages sent and received on Quon's pager were not work related, and some were sexually explicit. Duke reported his findings to Scharf, who, along with Quon's immediate supervisor, reviewed the transcripts himself. After his review, Scharf referred the matter to OPD's internal affairs division for an investigation into whether Quon was violating OPD rules by pursuing personal matters while on duty.

The officer in charge of the internal affairs review was Sergeant Patrick McMahon. Before conducting a review, McMahon used Quon's work schedule to redact the transcripts in order to eliminate any messages Quon sent while off duty. He then reviewed the content of the messages Quon sent during work hours. McMahon's report noted that Quon sent or received 456 messages during work hours in the month of August 2002, of which no more than 57 were work related; he sent as many as 80 messages during a single day at work; and on an average workday, Quon sent or received 28 messages, of which only 3 were related to police business. The report concluded that Quon had violated OPD rules. Quon was allegedly disciplined.

Quon filed suit against petitioners in the United States District Court for the Central District of California. Arch Wireless and an individual not relevant here were also named as defendants. Quon was joined in his suit by another plaintiff who is not a party before this Court and by the other respondents, each of whom exchanged text messages with Quon during August and September 2002: Jerilyn Quon, Jeff Quon's then-wife, from whom he was separated; April Florio, an OPD employee with whom Jeff Quon was romantically involved; and Steve Trujillo, another member of the OPD SWAT Team. Among the allegations in the complaint was that petitioners violated respondents' Fourth Amendment rights and the SCA by obtaining and reviewing the transcript of Jeff Quon's pager messages and that Arch Wireless had violated the SCA by turning over the transcript to the City.

II

It is well settled that the Fourth Amendment's protection extends beyond the sphere of criminal investigations. "The Amendment guarantees the privacy, dignity, and security of persons against certain arbitrary and invasive acts by officers of the Government," without regard to whether the government actor is investigating crime or performing another function. The Fourth Amendment applies as well when the Government acts in its capacity as an employer.

The Court discussed this principle in *O'Connor* [*v. Ortega*]. There a physician employed by a state hospital alleged that hospital officials investigating workplace misconduct had violated his Fourth Amendment rights by searching his office and seizing personal items from his desk and filing cabinet. All Members of the Court agreed with the general principle that "[i]ndividuals do not lose Fourth Amendment rights merely because they work for the government instead of a private employer." A majority of the Court further agreed that "'special needs, beyond the normal need for law enforcement,'" make the warrant and probable-cause requirement impracticable for government employers.

The *O'Connor* Court did disagree on the proper analytical framework for Fourth Amendment claims against government employers. A four-Justice plurality concluded that the correct analysis has two steps. First, because "some government offices may be so open to fellow employees or the public that no expectation of privacy is reasonable," a court must consider "[t]he operational realities of the workplace" in order to determine whether an employee's Fourth Amendment rights are implicated. On this view, "the question whether an employee has a reasonable expectation of privacy must be addressed on a case-by-case basis." Next, where an employee has a legitimate privacy expectation, an employer's intrusion on that expectation "for noninvestigatory, work-related purposes, as well as for investigations of work-related misconduct, should be judged by the standard of reasonableness under all the circumstances."

In the two decades since *O'Connor*, however, the threshold test for determining the scope of an employee's Fourth Amendment rights has not been clarified further. Here, though they disagree on whether Quon had a reasonable expectation of privacy, both petitioners and respondents start from the premise that the *O'Connor* plurality controls. It is not necessary to resolve whether that premise is correct. The case can be decided by determining that the search was reasonable even assuming Quon had a reasonable expectation of privacy.

III

Before turning to the reasonableness of the search, it is instructive to note the parties' disagreement over whether Quon had a reasonable expectation of privacy. The Court must proceed with care when considering the whole concept of privacy expectations in communications made on electronic equipment owned by a government employer. The judiciary risks error by elaborating too fully on the Fourth Amendment implications of emerging technology before its role in society has become clear. Prudence counsels caution before the facts in the instant case are used to establish far-reaching premises that define the existence, and extent, of privacy expectations enjoyed by employees when using employer-provided communication devices.

Rapid changes in the dynamics of communication and information transmission are evident not just in the technology itself but in what society accepts as proper behavior. Even if the Court were certain that the *O'Connor* plurality's approach were the right one, the Court would have difficulty predicting how employees' privacy expectations will be shaped by those changes or the degree to which society will be prepared to recognize those expectations as reasonable. Cell phone and text message communications are so pervasive that some persons may consider them to be essential means or necessary instruments for self-expression, even self-identification. That might strengthen the case for an expectation of privacy. On the other hand, the ubiquity of those devices has made them generally affordable, so one could counter that employees who need cell phones or similar devices for personal matters can purchase and pay for their own. And employer policies concerning communications will of course shape the reasonable expectations of their employees, especially to the extent that such policies are clearly communicated.

A broad holding concerning employees' privacy expectations vis-à-vis employer-provided technological equipment might have implications for future cases that cannot be predicted. It is preferable to dispose of this case on narrower grounds. For present purposes we assume several propositions *arguendo:* First, Quon had a reasonable expectation of privacy in the text messages sent on the pager provided to him by the City; second, petitioners' review of the transcript constituted a search within the meaning of the Fourth Amendment; and third, the principles applicable to a government employer's search of an employee's physical office apply with at least the same force when the employer intrudes on the employee's privacy in the electronic sphere.

Even if Quon had a reasonable expectation of privacy in his text messages, petitioners did not necessarily violate the Fourth Amendment by obtaining and reviewing the transcripts. Although as a general matter, warrantless searches "are *per se* unreasonable under the Fourth Amendment," there are "a few specifically established and well-delineated exceptions" to that general rule. The Court has held that the "'special needs'" of the workplace justify one such exception.

Under the approach of the *O'Connor* plurality, when conducted for a "noninvestigatory, work-related purpos[e]" or for the "investigatio[n] of work-related misconduct," a government employer's warrantless search is reasonable if it is "'justified at its inception'" and if "'the measures adopted are reasonably related to the objectives of the search and not excessively intrusive in light of'" the circumstances giving rise to the search.

The search was justified at its inception because there were "reasonable grounds for suspecting that the search [was] necessary for a noninvestigatory work-related purpose." As a jury found, Chief Scharf ordered the search in order to determine whether the character limit on the City's contract with Arch Wireless was sufficient to meet the City's needs. This was, as the Ninth Circuit noted, a "legitimate work-related rationale." The City and OPD had a legitimate interest in ensuring that employees were not being forced to pay out of their own pockets for work-related expenses, or on the other hand that the City was not paying for extensive personal communications.

As for the scope of the search, reviewing the transcripts was reasonable because it was an efficient and expedient way to determine whether Quon's overages were the result of work-related messaging or personal use. The review was also not "'excessively intrusive.'" Although Quon had gone over his monthly allotment a number of times, OPD requested transcripts for only the months of August and September 2002. While it may have been reasonable as well for OPD to review transcripts of all the months in which Quon exceeded his allowance, it was certainly reasonable for OPD to review messages for just two months in order to obtain a large enough sample to decide whether the character limits were efficacious. And it is worth noting that during his internal affairs investigation, McMahon redacted all messages Quon sent while off duty, a measure which reduced the intrusiveness of any further review of the transcripts.

Furthermore, and again on the assumption that Quon had a reasonable expectation of privacy in the contents of his messages, the extent of an expectation is relevant to assessing whether the search was too intrusive. Even if he could assume some level of privacy would inhere in his messages, it would not have been reasonable for Quon to conclude that his messages were in all circumstances immune from scrutiny. Quon was told that his messages were subject to auditing. As a law enforcement officer, he would or should have known that his actions were likely to come under legal scrutiny, and that this might entail an analysis of his on-the-job communications. Under the circumstances, a reasonable employee would be aware that sound management principles might require the audit of messages to determine whether the pager was being appropriately used. Given that the City issued the pagers to Quon and other SWAT Team members in order to help them more quickly respond to crises—and given that Quon had received no assurances of privacy—Quon could have anticipated that it might be necessary for the City to audit pager messages to assess the SWAT Team's performance in particular emergency situations.

From OPD's perspective, the fact that Quon likely had only a limited privacy expectation, with boundaries that we need not here explore, lessened the risk that the review would intrude on highly private details of Quon's life. OPD's audit of messages on Quon's employer-provided pager was not nearly as intrusive as a search of his personal e-mail account or pager, or a wiretap on his home phone line, would have been. That the search did reveal intimate details of Quon's life does not make it unreasonable, for under the circumstances a reasonable employer would not expect that such a review would intrude on such matters. The search was permissible in its scope.

Because the search was motivated by a legitimate work-related purpose, and because it was not excessive in scope, the search was reasonable under the approach of the *O'Connor* plurality. The search was reasonable, and the Court of Appeals erred by holding to the contrary. Petitioners did not violate Quon's Fourth Amendment rights.

Finally, the Court must consider whether the search violated the Fourth Amendment rights of Jerilyn Quon, Florio, and Trujillo, the respondents who sent text messages to Jeff Quon. Petitioners and respondents disagree whether a sender of a text message can have a reasonable expectation of privacy in a message he knowingly sends to someone's employer-provided pager. It is not necessary to resolve this question in order to dispose of the case, however. Respondents argue that because "the search was unreasonable as to Sergeant Quon, it was also unreasonable as to his correspondents." They make no corollary argument that the search, if reasonable as to Quon, could nonetheless be unreasonable as to Quon's correspondents. In light of this litigating position and the Court's conclusion that the search was reasonable as to Jeff Quon, it necessarily follows that these other respondents cannot prevail.

Because the search was reasonable, petitioners did not violate respondents' Fourth Amendment rights, and the court below erred by concluding otherwise.

Justice SCALIA, concurring in part and concurring in the judgment.

I continue to believe that the "operational realities" rubric for determining the Fourth Amendment's application to public employees invented by the plurality in *O'Connor v. Ortega* (1987), is standardless and unsupported. In this case, the proper threshold inquiry should be not whether the Fourth Amendment applies to messages on *public* employees' employer-issued pagers, but whether it applies *in general* to such messages on employer-issued pagers.

Here, however, there is no need to answer that threshold question. Even accepting at face value Quon's and his co-plaintiffs' claims that the Fourth Amendment applies to their messages, the city's search was reasonable, and thus did not violate the Amendment. Since it is unnecessary to decide whether the Fourth Amendment applies, it is unnecessary to resolve which approach in *O'Connor* controls: the plurality's or mine. That should end the matter.

Applying the Fourth Amendment to new technologies may sometimes be difficult, but when it is necessary to decide a case we have no choice. The Court's implication that where electronic privacy is concerned we should decide less than we otherwise would (that is, less than the principle of law necessary to resolve the case and guide private action) — or that we should hedge our bets by concocting case-specific standards or issuing opaque opinions — is in my view indefensible. The-times-they-are-a-changin' is a feeble excuse for disregard of duty.

f. Drug Testing

When may the government require drug testing without a warrant and even without any individualized suspicion? There is no single answer to this question. To this point, the Court has considered drug testing in three contexts: employment, schools, and hospitals. It has arrived at different conclusions in each.

First, in the area of employment, in Skinner v. Railway Executives' Assn., 489 U.S. 602 (1989), the Court upheld Federal Railroad Administration regulations requiring drug testing of railroad workers involved in accidents. The Fourth Amendment applied because it was a federal government requirement for testing by private railroads of their employees. The Court stressed the "special needs": the need to ensure the safety of the traveling public. The Court said that the privacy expectations of the employees were diminished by their working in "an industry that is regulated pervasively to ensure safety." The Court explained that there was virtually no discretion in the requirement so that there was nothing for a neutral magistrate to evaluate and further that drugs or alcohol could dissipate from an employee's body before a warrant could be obtained.

In National Treasury Employees Union v. Von Raab, 489 U.S. 656 (1989), the Court upheld the United States Customs Service program requiring drug testing through urinalysis for customs workers upon their transfer or promotion to positions having a direct involvement in drug interdiction or requiring the carrying of firearms. The Court struck down the requirement as applied to those who would be handling classified documents.

Unlike *Skinner*, results could not be turned over to law enforcement authorities for criminal prosecutions. The Court stressed the "Government's compelling interests in preventing the promotions of drug users to positions where they might endanger the integrity of our Nation's borders or the life of the citizenry." The Court stressed the special need to ensure that those handling weapons or involved in drug interdiction themselves be free of drugs.

But not all drug testing in the employment context is allowed. In Chandler v. Miller, 520 U.S. 305 (1997), the Court struck down a Georgia statute requiring that candidates for state office pass a drug test. The law required that candidates for office submit to drug testing within 30 days of qualifying for nomination or election. A candidate who refused or tested positive for illegal drugs could not be placed on the ballot. The Court found that this "did not fit within the closely guarded category of constitutionally permissible suspicionless searches." The Court stressed that "Georgia asserts no evidence of a drug problem among the State's elected officials, those officials do not typically perform high-risk, safety-sensitive tasks, and the required certification immediately aids to interdiction effort. The need revealed, in short, is symbolic, not 'special' as that term draws meaning from our caselaw."

A second area where the Court considered and approved drug testing is in schools, for student athletes and for students participating in extracurricular activities. In reading these cases, it is important to note that the Court generally has relaxed the usual Fourth Amendment requirements for searches of students in schools. As explained above, in New Jersey v. T.L.O., 469 U.S. 325 (1985), the Court held that school officials could search a student's purse based on reasonable suspicion; there did not need to be a warrant or probable cause.

In Vernonia School Dist. 47J v. Acton, the Court upheld random drug testing for students participating in athletic events, and in Board of Education of Independent School District No. 92 of Pottawatomie County v. Earls, the Court upheld random drug testing for students participating in extracurricular activities. In reading these cases, it is worth considering whether there are any limits on the ability of schools to require random drug testing. Could a school require drug testing of all students?

VERNONIA SCHOOL DISTRICT 47J v. ACTON

515 U.S. 646 (1995)

Justice SCALIA delivered the opinion of the Court.

The Student Athlete Drug Policy adopted by School District 47J in the town of Vernonia, Oregon, authorizes random urinalysis drug testing of students who participate in the District's school athletics programs. We granted certiorari to decide whether this violates the Fourth and Fourteenth Amendments to the United States Constitution.

I

Petitioner Vernonia School District 47J (District) operates one high school and three grade schools in the logging community of Vernonia, Oregon. As elsewhere in small-town America, school sports play a prominent role in the town's life, and student athletes are admired in their schools and in the community.

Drugs had not been a major problem in Vernonia schools. In the mid-to-late 1980's, however, teachers and administrators observed a sharp increase in drug use. Students began to speak out about their attraction to the drug culture, and to boast that there was nothing the school could do about it. Along with more drugs came more disciplinary problems. Between 1988 and 1989 the number of disciplinary referrals in Vernonia schools rose to more than twice the number reported in the early 1980's, and several students were suspended. Students became increasingly rude during class; outbursts of profane language became common.

Not only were student athletes included among the drug users but, as the District Court found, athletes were the leaders of the drug culture. This caused the District's administrators particular concern, since drug use increases the risk of sports-related injury. Expert testimony at the trial confirmed the deleterious effects of drugs on motivation, memory, judgment, reaction, coordination, and performance. The high school football and wrestling coach witnessed a severe sternum injury suffered by a wrestler, and various omissions of safety procedures and misexecutions by football players, all attributable in his belief to the effects of drug use.

Initially, the District responded to the drug problem by offering special classes, speakers, and presentations designed to deter drug use. It even brought in a specially trained dog to detect drugs, but the drug problem persisted. At that point, District officials began considering a drug-testing program. They held a parent "input night" to discuss the proposed Student Athlete Drug Policy (Policy), and the parents in attendance gave their unanimous approval. The school board approved the Policy for implementation in the fall of 1989. Its expressed purpose is to prevent student athletes from using drugs, to protect their health and safety, and to provide drug users with assistance programs.

The Policy applies to all students participating in interscholastic athletics. Students wishing to play sports must sign a form consenting to the testing and must obtain the written consent of their parents. Athletes are tested at the beginning of the season for their sport. In addition, once each week of the season the names of the athletes are placed in a "pool" from which a student, with the supervision of two adults, blindly draws the names of 10% of the athletes for random testing. Those selected are notified and tested that same day, if possible.

The student to be tested completes a specimen control form which bears an assigned number. Prescription medications that the student is taking must be identified by providing a copy of the prescription or a doctor's authorization. The student then enters an empty locker room accompanied by an adult monitor of the same sex. Each boy selected produces a sample at a urinal, remaining fully clothed with his back to the monitor, who stands approximately 12 to 15 feet behind the student. Monitors may (though do not always) watch the student while he produces the sample, and they listen for normal sounds of urination. Girls produce samples in an enclosed bathroom stall, so that they can be heard but not observed. After the sample is produced, it is given to the monitor, who checks it for temperature and tampering and then transfers it to a vial.

The samples are sent to an independent laboratory, which routinely tests them for amphetamines, cocaine, and marijuana. Other drugs, such as LSD, may be screened at the request of the District, but the identity of a particular student does not determine which drugs will be tested. The laboratory's procedures are 99.94% accurate. The District follows strict procedures regarding the chain of custody and access to test results. The laboratory does not know the identity of the students whose samples it tests. It is authorized to mail written test reports only to the superintendent and to provide test results to District personnel by telephone only after the requesting official recites a code confirming his authority. Only the superintendent, principals, vice-principals, and athletic directors have access to test results, and the results are not kept for more than one year.

If a sample tests positive, a second test is administered as soon as possible to confirm the result. If the second test is negative, no further action is taken. If the second test is positive, the athlete's parents are notified, and the school principal convenes a meeting with the student and his parents, at which the student is given the option of (1) participating for six weeks in an assistance program that includes weekly urinalysis, or (2) suffering suspension from athletics for the remainder of the current season and the next athletic season. The student is then retested prior to the start of the next athletic season for which he or she is eligible. The Policy states that a second offense results in automatic imposition of option (2); a third offense in suspension for the remainder of the current season and the next two athletic seasons.

In the fall of 1991, respondent James Acton, then a seventh grader, signed up to play football at one of the District's grade schools. He was denied participation, however, because he and his parents refused to sign the testing consent forms. The Actons filed suit, seeking declaratory and injunctive relief from enforcement of the Policy on the grounds that it violated the Fourth and Fourteenth Amendments to the United States Constitution and Article I, §9, of the Oregon Constitution.

II

As the text of the Fourth Amendment indicates, the ultimate measure of the constitutionality of a governmental search is "reasonableness." At least in a case such as this, where there was no clear practice, either approving or disapproving the type of search at issue, at the time the constitutional provision was enacted, whether a particular search meets the reasonableness standard "'is judged by balancing its intrusion on the individual's Fourth Amendment interests against its promotion of legitimate governmental interests.'" Where a search is undertaken by law enforcement officials to discover evidence of criminal wrongdoing, this Court has said that reasonableness generally requires the obtaining of a judicial warrant, Warrants cannot be issued, of course, without the showing of probable cause required by the Warrant Clause. But a warrant is not required to establish the reasonableness of all government searches; and when a warrant is not required (and the Warrant

Clause therefore not applicable), probable cause is not invariably required either. A search unsupported by probable cause can be constitutional, we have said, "when special needs, beyond the normal need for law enforcement, make the warrant and probable-cause requirement impracticable."

We have found such "special needs" to exist in the public school context. There, the warrant requirement "would unduly interfere with the maintenance of the swift and informal disciplinary procedures [that are] needed," and "strict adherence to the requirement that searches be based upon probable cause" would undercut "the substantial need of teachers and administrators for freedom to maintain order in the schools." New Jersey v. T.L.O.

III

The first factor to be considered is the nature of the privacy interest upon which the search here at issue intrudes.

Fourth Amendment rights, no less than First and Fourteenth Amendment rights, are different in public schools than elsewhere; the "reasonableness" inquiry cannot disregard the schools' custodial and tutelary responsibility for children. For their own good and that of their classmates, public school children are routinely required to submit to various physical examinations, and to be vaccinated against various diseases. Particularly with regard to medical examinations and procedures, therefore, "students within the school environment have a lesser expectation of privacy than members of the population generally."

Legitimate privacy expectations are even less with regard to student athletes. School sports are not for the bashful. They require "suiting up" before each practice or event, and showering and changing afterwards. Public school locker rooms, the usual sites for these activities, are not notable for the privacy they afford. The locker rooms in Vernonia are typical: No individual dressing rooms are provided; shower heads are lined up along a wall, unseparated by any sort of partition or curtain; not even all the toilet stalls have doors.

There is an additional respect in which school athletes have a reduced expectation of privacy. By choosing to "go out for the team," they voluntarily subject themselves to a degree of regulation even higher than that imposed on students generally. In Vernonia's public schools, they must submit to a preseason physical exam (James testified that his included the giving of a urine sample), they must acquire adequate insurance coverage or sign an insurance waiver, maintain a minimum grade point average, and comply with any "rules of conduct, dress, training hours and related matters as may be established for each sport by the head coach and athletic director with the principal's approval." Somewhat like adults who choose to participate in a "closely regulated industry," students who voluntarily participate in school athletics have reason to expect intrusions upon normal rights and privileges, including privacy.

IV

Having considered the scope of the legitimate expectation of privacy at issue here, we turn next to the character of the intrusion that is complained of. We recognized in *Skinner* that collecting the samples for urinalysis intrudes upon "an excretory function traditionally shielded by great privacy." We noted, however, that the degree of intrusion depends upon the manner in which production of the urine sample is monitored. Under the District's Policy, male students produce samples at a urinal along a wall. They remain fully clothed and are only observed from behind, if at all. Female students produce samples in an enclosed stall, with a female monitor standing outside listening only for sounds of tampering. These conditions are nearly identical to those typically encountered in public restrooms, which men, women, and especially school-children use daily. Under such conditions, the privacy interests compromised by the process of obtaining the urine sample are in our view negligible.

The other privacy-invasive aspect of urinalysis is, of course, the information it discloses concerning the state of the subject's body, and the materials he has ingested. In this regard it is significant that the tests at issue here look only for drugs, and not for whether the student is, for example, epileptic, pregnant, or diabetic. Moreover, the drugs for which the samples are screened are standard, and do not vary according to the identity of the student. And finally, the results of the tests are disclosed only to a limited class of school personnel who have a need to know; and they are not turned over to law enforcement authorities or used for any internal disciplinary function.

V

Finally, we turn to consider the nature and immediacy of the governmental concern at issue here, and the efficacy of this means for meeting it. In both *Skinner* and *Von Raab*, we characterized the government interest motivating the search as "compelling." It is a mistake, however, to think that the phrase "compelling state interest," in the Fourth Amendment context, describes a fixed, minimum quantum of governmental concern, so that one can dispose of a case by answering in isolation the question: Is there a compelling state interest here? Rather, the phrase describes an interest that appears impor-tant enough to justify the particular search at hand, in light of other factors that show the search to be relatively intrusive upon a genuine expectation of privacy. Whether that relatively high degree of government concern is necessary in this case or not, we think it is met.

That the nature of the concern is important—indeed, perhaps compel-ling—can hardly be doubted. Deterring drug use by our Nation's school-children is at least as important as enhancing efficient enforcement of the Nation's laws against the importation of drugs, which was the governmental concern in *Von Raab*, or deterring drug use by engineers and trainmen, which was the governmental concern in *Skinner*. School years are the time when the physical, psychological, and addictive effects of drugs are most severe. "Maturing nervous systems are more critically impaired by intoxicants than mature ones are; childhood losses in learning are lifelong and profound"; "children grow chemically dependent more quickly than adults, and their record of recovery is depressingly poor." And of course the effects of a drug-infested school are visited not just upon the users, but upon the entire student body and faculty, as the educational process is disrupted. In the present case, moreover, the necessity for the State to act is magnified by the fact that this evil is being visited not just upon individuals at large, but upon children for whom it has undertaken a special responsibility of care and direction. Finally, it must not be lost sight of that this program is directed more narrowly to drug use by school athletes, where the risk of immediate physical harm to the drug user or those with whom he is playing his sport is particularly high. Apart from psychological effects, which include impairment of judgment, slow reaction time, and a lessening of the perception of pain, the particular drugs screened by the District's Policy have been demonstrated to pose substantial physical risks to athletes.

As for the immediacy of the District's concerns: We are not inclined to question — indeed, we could not possibly find clearly erroneous — the District Court's conclusion that "a large segment of the student body, particularly those involved in interscholastic athletics, was in a state of rebellion," that "[d]isciplinary actions had reached 'epidemic proportions,'" and that "the rebellion was being fueled by alcohol and drug abuse as well as by the student's misperceptions about the drug culture." That is an immediate crisis of greater proportions than existed in *Skinner*, where we upheld the Government's drug-testing program based on findings of drug use by railroad employees nationwide, without proof that a problem existed on the particular railroads whose employees were subject to the test. And of much greater proportions than existed in *Von Raab*, where there was no documented history of drug use by any customs officials.

As to the efficacy of this means for addressing the problem: It seems to us self-evident that a drug problem largely fueled by the "role model" effect of athletes' drug use, and of particular danger to athletes, is effectively addressed by making sure that athletes do not use drugs. Respondents argue that a "less intrusive means to the same end" was available, namely, "drug testing on suspicion of drug use." We have repeatedly refused to declare that only the "least intrusive" search practicable can be reasonable under the Fourth Amendment. Respondents' alternative entails substantial difficulties — if it is indeed practicable at all. It may be impracticable, for one thing, simply because the parents who are willing to accept random drug testing for athletes are not willing to accept accusatory drug testing for all students, which transforms the process into a badge of shame. Respondents' proposal brings the risk that teachers will impose testing arbitrarily upon troublesome but not drug-likely students. It generates the expense of defending lawsuits that charge such arbitrary imposition, or that simply demand greater process before accusatory drug testing is imposed. And not least of all, it adds to the ever-expanding diversionary duties of schoolteachers the new function of spotting and bringing to account drug abuse, a task for which they are ill prepared, and which is not readily compatible with their vocation.

VI

Taking into account all the factors we have considered above — the decreased expectation of privacy, the relative unobtrusiveness of the search, and the severity of the need met by the search — we conclude Vernonia's Policy is reasonable and hence constitutional.

We caution against the assumption that suspicionless drug testing will readily pass constitutional muster in other contexts. The most significant element in this case is the first we discussed: that the Policy was undertaken in furtherance of the government's responsibilities, under a public school system, as guardian and tutor of children entrusted to its care. Just as when the government conducts a search in its capacity as employer (a warrantless search of an absent employee's desk to obtain an urgently needed file, for example), the relevant question is whether that intrusion upon privacy is one that a reasonable employer might engage in; so also when the government acts as guardian and tutor the relevant question is whether the search is one that a reasonable guardian and tutor might undertake. Given the findings of need made by the District Court, we conclude that in the present case it is.

Justice O'CONNOR, with whom Justice STEVENS and Justice SOUTER join, dissenting.

The population of our Nation's public schools, grades 7 through 12, numbers around 18 million. By the reasoning of today's decision, the millions of these students who participate in interscholastic sports, an overwhelming majority of whom have given school officials no reason whatsoever to suspect they use drugs at school, are open to an intrusive bodily search.

In justifying this result, the Court dispenses with a requirement of individualized suspicion on considered policy grounds. First, it explains that precisely because every student athlete is being tested, there is no concern that school officials might act arbitrarily in choosing whom to test. Second, a broad-based search regime, the Court reasons, dilutes the accusatory nature of the search. In making these policy arguments, of course, the Court sidesteps powerful, countervailing privacy concerns. Blanket searches, because they can involve "thousands or millions" of searches, "pos[e] a greater threat to liberty" than do suspicion-based ones, which "affec[t] one person at a time." Searches based on individualized suspicion also afford potential targets considerable control over whether they will, in fact, be searched because a person can avoid such a search by not acting in an objectively suspicious way. And given that the surest way to avoid acting suspiciously is to avoid the underlying wrongdoing, the costs of such a regime, one would think, are minimal.

But whether a blanket search is "better" than a regime based on individualized suspicion is not a debate in which we should engage. In my view, it is not open to judges or government officials to decide on policy grounds which is better and which is worse. For most of our constitutional history, mass, suspicionless searches have been generally considered per se unreasonable within the meaning of the Fourth Amendment. And we have allowed exceptions in recent years only where it has been clear that a suspicion-based regime would be ineffectual. Because that is not the case here, I dissent.

One searches today's majority opinion in vain for recognition that history and precedent establish that individualized suspicion is "usually required" under the Fourth Amendment (regardless of whether a warrant and probable cause are also required) and that, in the area of intrusive personal searches, the only recognized exception is for situations in which a suspicion-based scheme would be likely ineffectual. Far from acknowledging anything special about individualized suspicion, the Court treats a suspicion-based regime as if it were just any run-of-the-mill, less intrusive alternative — that is, an alternative that officials may bypass if the lesser intrusion, in their reasonable estimation, is outweighed by policy concerns unrelated to practicability.

In addition to overstating its concerns with a suspicion-based program, the District seems to have understated the extent to which such a program is less intrusive of students' privacy. By invading the privacy of a few students rather than many (nationwide, of thousands rather than millions), and by giving potential search targets substantial control over whether they will, in fact, be searched, a suspicion-based scheme is significantly less intrusive.

In any event, whether the Court is right that the District reasonably weighed the lesser intrusion of a suspicion-based scheme against its policy concerns is beside the point. As stated, a suspicion-based search regime is not just any less intrusive alternative; the individualized suspicion requirement has a legal pedigree as old as the Fourth Amendment itself, and it may not be easily cast aside in the name of policy concerns. It may only be forsaken, our cases in the personal search context have established, if a suspicion-based regime would likely be ineffectual.

But having misconstrued the fundamental role of the individualized suspicion requirement in Fourth Amendment analysis, the Court never seriously engages the practicality of such a requirement in the instant case. And that failure is crucial because nowhere is it less clear that an individualized suspicion requirement would be ineffectual than in the school context. In most schools, the entire pool of potential search targets — students — is under constant supervision by teachers and administrators and coaches, be it in classrooms, hallways, or locker rooms.

I recognize that a suspicion-based scheme, even where reasonably effective in controlling in-school drug use, may not be as effective as a mass, suspicionless testing regime. In one sense, that is obviously true, just as it is obviously true that suspicion-based law enforcement is not as effective as mass, suspicionless enforcement might be. "But there is nothing new in the realization" that Fourth Amendment protections come with a price. Indeed, the price we pay is higher in the criminal context, given that police do not closely observe the entire class of potential search targets (all citizens in the area) and must ordinarily adhere to the rigid requirements of a warrant and probable cause.

The principal counterargument to all this, central to the Court's opinion, is that the Fourth Amendment is more lenient with respect to school searches. That is no doubt correct, for, as the Court explains, schools have traditionally had special guardian-like responsibilities for children that necessitate a degree of constitutional leeway. This principle explains the considerable Fourth Amendment leeway we gave school officials in *T.L.O.* In that case, we held that children at school do not enjoy two of the Fourth Amendment's traditional categorical protections against unreasonable searches and seizures: the warrant requirement and the probable cause requirement. And this was true even though the same children enjoy such protections "in a nonschool setting."

The instant case, however, asks whether the Fourth Amendment is even more lenient than that, i.e., whether it is so lenient that students may be deprived of the Fourth Amendment's only remaining, and most basic, categorical protection: its strong preference for an individualized suspicion requirement, with its accompanying antipathy toward personally intrusive, blanket searches of mostly innocent people. Thus, if we are to mean what we often proclaim — that students do not "shed their constitutional rights . . . at the schoolhouse gate," — the answer must plainly be no.

It cannot be too often stated that the greatest threats to our constitutional freedoms come in times of crisis. But we must also stay mindful that not all government responses to such times are hysterical overreactions; some crises are quite real, and when they are, they serve precisely as the compelling state interest that we have said may justify a measured intrusion on constitutional rights. The only way for judges to mediate these conflicting impulses is to do what they should do anyway: stay close to the record in each case that appears before them, and make their judgments based on that alone. Having reviewed the record here, I cannot avoid the conclusion that the District's suspicionless policy of testing all student athletes sweeps too broadly, and too imprecisely, to be reasonable under the Fourth Amendment.

What, though, if the school has no evidence of a drug problem and the program applies not just to athletes but to all students participating in extracurricular activities?

BOARD OF EDUCATION OF INDEPENDENT SCHOOL DISTRICT NO. 92 OF POTTAWATOMIE COUNTY v. EARLS

536 U.S. 822 (2002)

Justice THOMAS delivered the opinion of the Court.

The Student Activities Drug Testing Policy implemented by the Board of Education of Independent School District No. 92 of Pottawatomie County

(School District) requires all students who participate in competitive extracurricular activities to submit to drug testing. Because this Policy reasonably serves the School District's important interest in detecting and preventing drug use among its students, we hold that it is constitutional.

I

The city of Tecumseh, Oklahoma, is a rural community located approximately 40 miles southeast of Oklahoma City. The School District administers all Tecumseh public schools. In the fall of 1998, the School District adopted the Student Activities Drug Testing Policy (Policy), which requires all middle and high school students to consent to drug testing in order to participate in any extracurricular activity. In practice, the Policy has been applied only to competitive extracurricular activities sanctioned by the Oklahoma Secondary Schools Activities Association, such as the Academic Team, Future Farmers of America, Future Homemakers of America, band, choir, pom-pom, cheerleading, and athletics. Under the Policy, students are required to take a drug test before participating in an extracurricular activity, must submit to random drug testing while participating in that activity, and must agree to be tested at any time upon reasonable suspicion. The urinalysis tests are designed to detect only the use of illegal drugs, including amphetamines, marijuana, cocaine, opiates, and barbituates, not medical conditions or the presence of authorized prescription medications.

At the time of their suit, both respondents attended Tecumseh High School. Respondent Lindsay Earls was a member of the show choir, the marching band, the Academic Team, and the National Honor Society. Respondent Daniel James sought to participate in the Academic Team. Together with their parents, Earls and James brought a 42 U.S.C. §1983, action against the School District, challenging the Policy both on its face and as applied to their participation in extracurricular activities. They alleged that the Policy violates the Fourth Amendment as incorporated by the Fourteenth Amendment and requested injunctive and declarative relief. They also argued that the School District failed to identify a special need for testing students who participate in extracurricular activities, and that the "Drug Testing Policy neither addresses a proven problem nor promises to bring any benefit to students or the school."

II

Searches by public school officials, such as the collection of urine samples, implicate Fourth Amendment interests. We must therefore review the School District's Policy for "reasonableness," which is the touchstone of the constitutionality of a governmental search.

In the criminal context, reasonableness usually requires a showing of probable cause. The probable-cause standard, however, "is peculiarly related to criminal investigations" and may be unsuited to determining the reasonableness of administrative searches where the "Government seeks to prevent the development of hazardous conditions." The Court has also held that a warrant and finding of probable cause are unnecessary in the public school context because such requirements "would unduly interfere with the maintenance of the swift and informal disciplinary procedures [that are] needed."

Given that the School District's Policy is not in any way related to the conduct of criminal investigations, respondents do not contend that the School District requires probable cause before testing students for drug use. Respondents instead argue that drug testing must be based at least on some level of individualized suspicion. It is true that we generally determine the reasonableness of a search by balancing the nature of the intrusion on the individual's privacy against the promotion of legitimate governmental interests. But we have long held that "the Fourth Amendment imposes no irreducible requirement of [individualized] suspicion." "[I]n certain limited circumstances, the Government's need to discover such latent or hidden conditions, or to prevent their development, is sufficiently compelling to justify the intrusion on privacy entailed by conducting such searches without any measure of individualized suspicion." Therefore, in the context of safety and administrative regulations, a search unsupported by probable cause may be reasonable "when 'special needs, beyond the normal need for law enforcement, make the warrant and probable-cause requirement impracticable.'"

Significantly, this Court has previously held that "special needs" inhere in the public school context. While schoolchildren do not shed their constitutional rights when they enter the schoolhouse, "Fourth Amendment rights . . . are different in public schools than elsewhere; the 'reasonableness' inquiry cannot disregard the schools' custodial and tutelary responsibility for children." In particular, a finding of individualized suspicion may not be necessary when a school conducts drug testing.

We first consider the nature of the privacy interest allegedly compromised by the drug testing. As in *Vernonia*, the context of the public school environment serves as the backdrop for the analysis of the privacy interest at stake and the reasonableness of the drug testing policy in general. A student's privacy interest is limited in a public school environment where the State is responsible for maintaining discipline, health, and safety. Schoolchildren are routinely required to submit to physical examinations and vaccinations against disease. Securing order in the school environment sometimes requires that students be subjected to greater controls than those appropriate for adults.

Respondents argue that because children participating in nonathletic extracurricular activities are not subject to regular physicals and communal undress, they have a stronger expectation of privacy than the athletes tested in *Vernonia*. This distinction, however, was not essential to our decision in *Vernonia*, which depended primarily upon the school's custodial responsibility and authority.

In any event, students who participate in competitive extracurricular activities voluntarily subject themselves to many of the same intrusions on their privacy as do athletes. Some of these clubs and activities require occasional off-campus travel and communal undress. All of them have their own rules and requirements for participating students that do not apply to the student body as a whole.

Next, we consider the character of the intrusion imposed by the Policy. Urination is "an excretory function traditionally shielded by great privacy." But the "degree of intrusion" on one's privacy caused by collecting a urine sample "depends upon the manner in which production of the urine sample is monitored." Under the Policy, a faculty monitor waits outside the closed restroom stall for the student to produce a sample and must "listen for the normal sounds of urination in order to guard against tampered specimens and to insure an accurate chain of custody." The monitor then pours the sample into two bottles that are sealed and placed into a mailing pouch along with a consent form signed by the student. This procedure is virtually identical to that reviewed in *Vernonia*, except that it additionally protects privacy by allowing male students to produce their samples behind a closed stall. Given that we considered the method of collection in *Vernonia* a "negligible" intrusion, the method here is even less problematic. In addition, the Policy clearly requires that the test results be kept in confidential files separate from a student's other educational records and released to school personnel only on a "need to know" basis.

Moreover, the test results are not turned over to any law enforcement authority. Nor do the test results here lead to the imposition of discipline or have any academic consequences. Rather, the only consequence of a failed drug test is to limit the student's privilege of participating in extracurricular activities. Indeed, a student may test positive for drugs twice and still be allowed to participate in extracurricular activities. After the first positive test, the school contacts the student's parent or guardian for a meeting. The student may continue to participate in the activity if within five days of the meeting the student shows proof of receiving drug counseling and submits to a second drug test in two weeks. For the second positive test, the student is suspended from participation in all extracurricular activities for 14 days, must complete four hours of substance abuse counseling, and must submit to monthly drug tests. Only after a third positive test will the student be suspended from participating in any extracurricular activity for the remainder of the school year, or 88 school days, whichever is longer.

Given the minimally intrusive nature of the sample collection and the limited uses to which the test results are put, we conclude that the invasion of students' privacy is not significant.

Finally, this Court must consider the nature and immediacy of the government's concerns and the efficacy of the Policy in meeting them. This Court has already articulated in detail the importance of the governmental concern in preventing drug use by schoolchildren. The drug abuse problem among our Nation's youth has hardly abated since *Vernonia* was decided in 1995. In fact, evidence suggests that it has only grown worse. As in *Vernonia*, "the necessity for the State to act is magnified by the fact that this evil is being visited not just upon individuals at large, but upon children for whom it has undertaken a special responsibility of care and direction." The health and safety risks identified in *Vernonia* apply with equal force to Tecumseh's children. Indeed, the nationwide drug epidemic makes the war against drugs a pressing concern in every school.

Additionally, the School District in this case has presented specific evidence of drug use at Tecumseh schools. Teachers testified that they had seen students who appeared to be under the influence of drugs and that they had heard students speaking openly about using drugs. A drug dog found marijuana cigarettes near the school parking lot. Police officers once found drugs or drug paraphernalia in a car driven by a Future Farmers of America member. And the school board president reported that people in the community were calling the board to discuss the "drug situation." We decline to second-guess the finding of the District Court that "[v]iewing the evidence as a whole, it cannot be reasonably disputed that the [School District] was faced with a 'drug problem' when it adopted the Policy."

Respondents consider the proffered evidence insufficient and argue that there is no "real and immediate interest" to justify a policy of drug testing nonathletes. We have recognized, however, that "[a] demonstrated problem of drug abuse . . . [is] not in all cases necessary to the validity of a testing regime," but that some showing does "shore up an assertion of special need for a suspicionless general search program." The School District has provided sufficient evidence to shore up the need for its drug testing program. Furthermore, this Court has not required a particularized or pervasive drug problem before allowing the government to conduct suspicionless drug testing.

Given the nationwide epidemic of drug use, and the evidence of increased drug use in Tecumseh schools, it was entirely reasonable for the School District to enact this particular drug testing policy.

Respondents also argue that the testing of nonathletes does not implicate any safety concerns, and that safety is a "crucial factor" in applying the special needs framework. They contend that there must be "surpassing safety interests," or "extraordinary safety and national security hazards," in order to override the usual protections of the Fourth Amendment. Respondents are correct that safety factors into the special needs analysis, but the safety interest furthered by drug testing is undoubtedly substantial for all children, athletes and nonathletes alike. We know all too well that drug use carries a variety of health risks for children, including death from overdose.

We also reject respondents' argument that drug testing must presumptively be based upon an individualized reasonable suspicion of wrongdoing because such a testing regime would be less intrusive. In this context, the Fourth Amendment does not require a finding of individualized suspicion, and we decline to impose such a requirement on schools attempting to prevent and detect drug use by students. Moreover, we question whether testing based on individualized suspicion in fact would be less intrusive. Such a regime would place an additional burden on public school teachers who are already tasked with the difficult job of maintaining order and discipline. A program of individualized suspicion might unfairly target members of unpopular groups. The fear of lawsuits resulting from such targeted searches may chill enforcement of the program, rendering it ineffective in combating drug use. In any case, this Court has repeatedly stated that reasonableness under the Fourth Amendment does not require employing the least intrusive means, because "[t]he logic of such elaborate less-restrictive-alternative arguments could raise insuperable barriers to the exercise of virtually all search-and-seizure powers."

Finally, we find that testing students who participate in extracurricular activities is a reasonably effective means of addressing the School District's legitimate concerns in preventing, deterring, and detecting drug use. While in *Vernonia* there might have been a closer fit between the testing of athletes and the trial court's finding that the drug problem was "fueled by the 'role model' effect of athletes' drug use," such a finding was not essential to the holding. *Vernonia* did not require the school to test the group of students most likely to use drugs, but rather considered the constitutionality of the program in the context of the public school's custodial responsibilities. Evaluating the Policy in this context, we conclude that the drug testing of Tecumseh students who participate in extracurricular activities effectively serves the School District's interest in protecting the safety and health of its students.

III

Within the limits of the Fourth Amendment, local school boards must assess the desirability of drug testing schoolchildren. In upholding the constitutionality of the Policy, we express no opinion as to its wisdom. Rather, we hold only that Tecumseh's Policy is a reasonable means of furthering the School District's important interest in preventing and deterring drug use among its schoolchildren.

Justice BREYER, concurring.

I agree with the Court that Vernonia School Dist. 47J v. Acton (1995) governs this case and requires reversal of the Tenth Circuit's decision. The school's drug testing program addresses a serious national problem by focusing upon demand, avoiding the use of criminal or disciplinary sanctions, and relying upon professional counseling and treatment. In my view, this program does not violate the Fourth Amendment's prohibition of "unreasonable searches and seizures." I reach this conclusion primarily for the reasons given by the Court, but I would emphasize several underlying considerations, which I understand to be consistent with the Court's opinion.

I

In respect to the school's need for the drug testing program, I would emphasize the following: First, the drug problem in our Nation's schools is serious in terms of size, the kinds of drugs being used, and the consequences of that use both for our children and the rest of us.

Second, the government's emphasis upon supply side interdiction apparently has not reduced teenage use in recent years.

Third, public school systems must find effective ways to deal with this problem. Today's public expects its schools not simply to teach the fundamentals, but "to shoulder the burden of feeding students breakfast and lunch, offering before and after school child care services, and providing medical and psychological services," all in a school environment that is safe and encourages learning.

Fourth, the program at issue here seeks to discourage demand for drugs by changing the school's environment in order to combat the single most important factor leading schoolchildren to take drugs, namely, peer pressure. It offers the adolescent a nonthreatening reason to decline his friend's drug-use invitations, namely, that he intends to play baseball, participate in debate, join the band, or engage in any one of half a dozen useful, interesting, and important activities.

II

In respect to the privacy-related burden that the drug testing program imposes upon students, I would emphasize the following: First, not everyone would agree with this Court's characterization of the privacy-related significance of urine sampling as "negligible." Some find the procedure no more intrusive than a routine medical examination, but others are seriously embarrassed by the need to provide a urine sample with someone listening "outside the closed restroom stall." When trying to resolve this kind of close question involving the interpretation of constitutional values, I believe it important that the school board provided an opportunity for the airing of these differences at public meetings designed to give the entire community "the opportunity to be able to participate" in developing the drug policy.

Second, the testing program avoids subjecting the entire school to testing. And it preserves an option for a conscientious objector. He can refuse testing while paying a price (nonparticipation) that is serious, but less severe than expulsion from the school.

Third, a contrary reading of the Constitution, as requiring "individualized suspicion" in this public school context, could well lead schools to push the boundaries of "individualized suspicion" to its outer limits, using subjective criteria that may "unfairly target members of unpopular groups," or leave those whose behavior is slightly abnormal stigmatized in the minds of others. If so, direct application of the Fourth Amendment's prohibition against "unreasonable searches and seizures" will further that Amendment's liberty-protecting objectives at least to the same extent as application of the mediating "individualized suspicion" test, where, as here, the testing program is neither criminal nor disciplinary in nature.

I cannot know whether the school's drug testing program will work. But, in my view, the Constitution does not prohibit the effort. Emphasizing the considerations I have mentioned, along with others to which the Court refers, I conclude that the school's drug testing program, constitutionally speaking, is not "unreasonable." And I join the Court's opinion.

Justice GINSBURG, with whom Justice STEVENS, Justice O'CONNOR, and Justice SOUTER join, dissenting.

Seven years ago, in Vernonia School Dist. 47J v. Acton (1995), this Court determined that a school district's policy of randomly testing the urine of its student athletes for illicit drugs did not violate the Fourth Amendment. In so ruling, the Court emphasized that drug use "increase[d] the risk of sports-related injury" and that Vernonia's athletes were the "leaders" of an aggressive local "drug culture" that had reached "'epidemic proportions.'" Today, the Court relies upon *Vernonia* to permit a school district with a drug problem its superintendent repeatedly described as "not . . . major," to test the urine of an academic team member solely by reason of her participation in a nonathletic, competitive extracurricular activity — participation associated with neither special dangers from, nor particular predilections for, drug use.

Although "special needs inhere in the public school context," those needs are not so expansive or malleable as to render reasonable any program of student drug testing a school district elects to install. The particular testing program upheld today is not reasonable; it is capricious, even perverse: Petitioners' policy targets for testing a student population least likely to be at risk from illicit drugs and their damaging effects. I therefore dissent.

It is a sad irony that the petitioning School District seeks to justify its edict here by trumpeting "the schools' custodial and tutelary responsibility for children." In regulating an athletic program or endeavoring to combat an exploding drug epidemic, a school's custodial obligations may permit searches that would otherwise unacceptably abridge students' rights. When custodial duties are not ascendant, however, schools' tutelary obligations to their students require them to "teach by example" by avoiding symbolic measures that diminish constitutional protections. "That [schools] are educating the young for citizenship is reason for scrupulous protection of Constitutional freedoms of the individual, if we are not to strangle the free mind at its source and teach youth to discount important principles of our government as mere platitudes." West Virginia Bd. of Ed. v. Barnette (1943).

———————————

The Court has considered drug testing in a third context besides employees and students: hospitals. Specifically, in Ferguson v. City of Charleston, the Court considered whether a city could require drug testing of pregnant women, with results to be used for law enforcement purposes. The Court held that this does not fit within the "special needs" exception.

FERGUSON v. CITY OF CHARLESTON

532 U.S. 67 (2001)

Justice STEVENS delivered the opinion of the Court.

In this case, we must decide whether a state hospital's performance of a diagnostic test to obtain evidence of a patient's criminal conduct for law enforcement purposes is an unreasonable search if the patient has not consented to the procedure. More narrowly, the question is whether the interest in using the threat of criminal sanctions to deter pregnant women from using cocaine can justify a departure from the general rule that an official nonconsensual search is unconstitutional if not authorized by a valid warrant.

I

In the fall of 1988, staff members at the public hospital operated in the city of Charleston by the Medical University of South Carolina (MUSC) became concerned about an apparent increase in the use of cocaine by patients who were receiving prenatal treatment. In response to this perceived increase, as of April 1989, MUSC began to order drug screens to be performed on urine samples from maternity patients who were suspected of using cocaine. If a patient tested positive, she was then referred by MUSC staff to the county substance abuse commission for counseling and treatment. However, despite the referrals, the incidence of cocaine use among the patients at MUSC did not appear to change.

Some four months later, Nurse Shirley Brown, the case manager for the MUSC obstetrics department, heard a news broadcast reporting that the police in Greenville, South Carolina, were arresting pregnant users of cocaine on the theory that such use harmed the fetus and was therefore child abuse. Nurse Brown discussed the story with MUSC's general counsel, Joseph C. Good, Jr., who then contacted Charleston Solicitor Charles Condon in order to offer MUSC's cooperation in prosecuting mothers whose children tested positive for drugs at birth.[10]

II

Petitioners are 10 women who received obstetrical care at MUSC and who were arrested after testing positive for cocaine. Four of them were arrested during the initial implementation of the policy; they were not offered the opportunity to receive drug treatment as an alternative to arrest. The others were arrested after the policy was modified in 1990; they either failed to

---

10. Under South Carolina law, a viable fetus has historically been regarded as a person; in 1995, the South Carolina Supreme Court held that the ingestion of cocaine during the third trimester of pregnancy constitutes criminal child neglect. [Footnote by the Court.]

comply with the terms of the drug treatment program or tested positive for a second time.

Petitioners' complaint challenged the validity of the policy under various theories, including the claim that warrantless and nonconsensual drug tests conducted for criminal investigatory purposes were unconstitutional searches.

[III]

Because MUSC is a state hospital, the members of its staff are government actors, subject to the strictures of the Fourth Amendment. Moreover, the urine tests conducted by those staff members were indisputably searches within the meaning of the Fourth Amendment. Neither the District Court nor the Court of Appeals concluded that any of the nine criteria used to identify the women to be searched provided either probable cause to believe that they were using cocaine, or even the basis for a reasonable suspicion of such use. Rather, the District Court and the Court of Appeals viewed the case as one involving MUSC's right to conduct searches without warrants or probable cause. Furthermore, given the posture in which the case comes to us, we must assume for purposes of our decision that the tests were performed without the informed consent of the patients.

Because the hospital seeks to justify its authority to conduct drug tests and to turn the results over to law enforcement agents without the knowledge or consent of the patients, this case differs from the four previous cases in which we have considered whether comparable drug tests "fit within the closely guarded category of constitutionally permissible suspicionless searches."

In each of those cases, we employed a balancing test that weighed the intrusion on the individual's interest in privacy against the "special needs" that supported the program. As an initial matter, we note that the invasion of privacy in this case is far more substantial than in those cases. In the previous four cases, there was no misunderstanding about the purpose of the test or the potential use of the test results, and there were protections against the dissemination of the results to third parties. The use of an adverse test result to disqualify one from eligibility for a particular benefit, such as a promotion or an opportunity to participate in an extracurricular activity, involves a less serious intrusion on privacy than the unauthorized dissemination of such results to third parties. The reasonable expectation of privacy enjoyed by the typical patient undergoing diagnostic tests in a hospital is that the results of those tests will not be shared with nonmedical personnel without her consent. In none of our prior cases was there any intrusion upon that kind of expectation.

The critical difference between those four drug-testing cases and this one, however, lies in the nature of the "special need" asserted as justification for the warrantless searches. In each of those earlier cases, the "special need" that was advanced as a justification for the absence of a warrant or individualized suspicion was one divorced from the State's general interest in law enforcement. In this case, however, the central and indispensable feature of the policy from its inception was the use of law enforcement to coerce the patients into substance abuse treatment. This fact distinguishes this case from circumstances in which physicians or psychologists, in the course of ordinary medical procedures aimed at helping the patient herself, come across information that under rules of law or ethics is subject to reporting requirements, which no one has challenged here.

Respondents argue in essence that their ultimate purpose — namely, protecting the health of both mother and child — is a beneficent one. In this case, a review of the M-7 policy plainly reveals that the purpose actually served by the MUSC searches "is ultimately indistinguishable from the general interest in crime control." In looking to the programmatic purpose, we consider all the available evidence in order to determine the relevant primary purpose. Tellingly, the document codifying the policy incorporates the police's operational guidelines. It devotes its attention to the chain of custody, the range of possible criminal charges, and the logistics of police notification and arrests. Nowhere, however, does the document discuss different courses of medical treatment for either mother or infant, aside from treatment for the mother's addiction.

Moreover, throughout the development and application of the policy, the Charleston prosecutors and police were extensively involved in the day-to-day administration of the policy. Police and prosecutors decided who would receive the reports of positive drug screens and what information would be included with those reports. Law enforcement officials also helped determine the procedures to be followed when performing the screens. Police took pains to coordinate the timing and circumstances of the arrests with MUSC staff, and, in particular, Nurse Brown.

While the ultimate goal of the program may well have been to get the women in question into substance abuse treatment and off of drugs, the immediate objective of the searches was to generate evidence for law enforcement purposes in order to reach that goal. The threat of law enforcement may ultimately have been intended as a means to an end, but the direct and primary purpose of MUSC's policy was to ensure the use of those means. In our opinion, this distinction is critical. Because law enforcement involvement always serves some broader social purpose or objective, under respondents' view, virtually any nonconsensual suspicionless search could be immunized under the special needs doctrine by defining the search solely in terms of its ultimate, rather than immediate, purpose. Such an approach is inconsistent with the Fourth Amendment. Given the primary purpose of the Charleston program, which was to use the threat of arrest and prosecution in order to force women into treatment, and given the extensive involvement of law enforcement officials at every stage of the policy, this case simply does not fit within the closely guarded category of "special needs."

Justice SCALIA, with whom THE CHIEF JUSTICE and Justice THOMAS join, dissenting.

There is always an unappealing aspect to the use of doctors and nurses, ministers of mercy, to obtain incriminating evidence against the supposed objects of their ministration — although here, it is correctly pointed out, the doctors and nurses were ministering not just to the mothers but also to the children whom their cooperation with the police was meant to protect. But whatever may be the correct social judgment concerning the desirability of what occurred here, that is not the issue in the present case. The Constitution does not resolve all difficult social questions, but leaves the vast majority of them to resolution by debate and the democratic process — which would produce a decision by the citizens of Charleston, through their elected representatives, to forbid or permit the police action at issue here. The question before us is a narrower one: whether, whatever the desirability of this police conduct, it violates the Fourth Amendment's prohibition of unreasonable searches and seizures. In my view, it plainly does not.

The first step in Fourth Amendment analysis is to identify the search or seizure at issue. What petitioners, the Court, and to a lesser extent the concurrence really object to is not the urine testing, but the hospital's reporting of positive drug-test results to police. But the latter is obviously not a search. At most it may be a "derivative use of the product of a past unlawful search," which, of course, "work[s] no new Fourth Amendment wrong" and "presents a question, not of rights, but of remedies." There is only one act that could conceivably be regarded as a search of petitioners in the present case: the taking of the urine sample. I suppose the testing of that urine for traces of unlawful drugs could be considered a search of sorts, but the Fourth Amendment protects only against searches of citizens' "persons, houses, papers, and effects"; and it is entirely unrealistic to regard urine as one of the "effects" (i.e., part of the property) of the person who has passed and abandoned it. Some would argue, I suppose, that testing of the urine is prohibited by some generalized privacy right "emanating" from the "penumbras" of the Constitution (a question that is not before us); but it is not even arguable that the testing of urine that has been lawfully obtained is a Fourth Amendment search. (I may add that, even if it were, the factors legitimizing the taking of the sample, which I discuss below, would likewise legitimize the testing of it.)

It is rudimentary Fourth Amendment law that a search which has been consented to is not unreasonable. There is no contention in the present case that the urine samples were extracted forcibly. The only conceivable bases for saying that they were obtained without consent are the contentions (1) that the consent was coerced by the patients' need for medical treatment, (2) that the consent was uninformed because the patients were not told that the tests would include testing for drugs, and (3) that the consent was uninformed because the patients were not told that the results of the tests would be provided to the police.

Until today, we have never held — or even suggested — that material which a person voluntarily entrusts to someone else cannot be given by that person to the police, and used for whatever evidence it may contain.

Without so much as discussing the point, the Court today opens a hole in our Fourth Amendment jurisprudence, the size and shape of which is entirely indeterminate. I would adhere to our established law, which says that information obtained through violation of a relationship of trust is obtained consensually, and is hence not a search.

I think it clear, therefore, that there is no basis for saying that obtaining of the urine sample was unconstitutional. The special-needs doctrine is thus quite irrelevant, since it operates only to validate searches and seizures that are otherwise unlawful. In the ensuing discussion, however, I shall assume (contrary to legal precedent) that the taking of the urine sample was (either because of the patients' necessitous circumstances, or because of failure to disclose that the urine would be tested for drugs, or because of failure to disclose that the results of the test would be given to the police) coerced. Indeed, I shall even assume (contrary to common sense) that the testing of the urine constituted an unconsented search of the patients' effects. On those assumptions, the special-needs doctrine would become relevant; and, properly applied, would validate what was done here.

The conclusion of the Court that the special-needs doctrine is inapplicable rests upon its contention that respondents "undert[ook] to obtain [drug] evidence from their patients" not for any medical purpose, but "for the specific purpose of incriminating those patients." In other words, the purported medical rationale was merely a pretext; there was no special need. This contention contradicts the District Court's finding of fact that the goal of the testing policy "was not to arrest patients but to facilitate their treatment and protect both the mother and unborn child." This finding is binding upon us unless clearly erroneous. Not only do I find it supportable; I think any other finding would have to be overturned.

In sum, there can be no basis for the Court's purported ability to "distinguis[h] this case from circumstances in which physicians or psychologists, in the course of ordinary medical procedures aimed at helping the patient herself, come across information that . . . is subject to reporting requirements," unless it is this: That the addition of a law-enforcement-related purpose to a legitimate medical purpose destroys applicability of the "special-needs" doctrine. But that is quite impossible, since the special-needs doctrine was developed, and is ordinarily employed, precisely to enable searches by law enforcement officials who, of course, ordinarily have a law enforcement objective.

As I indicated at the outset, it is not the function of this Court — at least not in Fourth Amendment cases — to weigh petitioners' privacy interest against the State's interest in meeting the crisis of "crack babies" that developed in the late 1980's. I cannot refrain from observing, however, that the outcome of a wise weighing of those interests is by no means clear. The initial goal of the doctors and nurses who conducted cocaine testing in this case was to refer pregnant drug addicts to treatment centers, and to prepare for necessary treatment of their possibly affected children. When the doctors and nurses agreed to the program providing test results to the police, they did so because (in addition to the fact that child abuse was required by law to be reported) they wanted to use the sanction of arrest as a strong incentive for their addicted patients to undertake drug-addiction treatment. And the police themselves used it for that benign purpose, as is shown by the fact that only 30 of 253 women testing positive for cocaine were ever arrested, and only 2 of those prosecuted. It would not be unreasonable to conclude that today's judgment, authorizing the assessment of damages against the county solicitor and individual doctors and nurses who participated in the program, proves once again that no good deed goes unpunished.

But as far as the Fourth Amendment is concerned: There was no unconsented search in this case. And if there was, it would have been validated by the special-needs doctrine. For these reasons, I respectfully dissent.

g.   Searches in Jails and Prisons

The issue in Florence v. Board of Chosen Freeholders is whether a strip search in a jail requires reasonable suspicion.

FLORENCE v. BOARD OF CHOSEN FREEHOLDERS OF THE COUNTY OF BURLINGTON

566 U.S. 318 (2012)

Justice KENNEDY delivered the opinion of the Court, except as to Part IV.[11]

Correctional officials have a legitimate interest, indeed a responsibility, to ensure that jails are not made less secure by reason of what new detainees may carry in on their bodies. Facility personnel, other inmates, and the new detainee himself or herself may be in danger if these threats are introduced into the jail population. This case presents the question of what rules, or limitations, the Constitution imposes on searches of arrested persons who are to be held in jail while their cases are being processed. The term "jail" is used here in a broad sense to include prisons and other detention facilities. The specific measures being challenged will be described in more detail; but, in broad terms, the controversy concerns whether every detainee who will be admitted to the general population may be required to undergo a close visual inspection while undressed.

The case turns in part on the extent to which this Court has sufficient expertise and information in the record to mandate, under the Constitution, the specific restrictions and limitations sought by those who challenge the visual search procedures at issue. In addressing this type of constitutional claim courts must defer to the judgment of correctional officials unless the record contains substantial evidence showing their policies are an

---

11. Justice Thomas joins all but Part IV of this opinion. [Footnote by the Court.]

unnecessary or unjustified response to problems of jail security. That necessary showing has not been made in this case.

I

In 1998, seven years before the incidents at issue, petitioner Albert Florence was arrested after fleeing from police officers in Essex County, New Jersey. He was charged with obstruction of justice and use of a deadly weapon. Petitioner entered a plea of guilty to two lesser offenses and was sentenced to pay a fine in monthly installments. In 2003, after he fell behind on his payments and failed to appear at an enforcement hearing, a bench warrant was issued for his arrest. He paid the outstanding balance less than a week later; but, for some unexplained reason, the warrant remained in a statewide computer database.

Two years later, in Burlington County, New Jersey, petitioner and his wife were stopped in their automobile by a state trooper. Based on the outstanding warrant in the computer system, the officer arrested petitioner and took him to the Burlington County Detention Center. He was held there for six days and then was transferred to the Essex County Correctional Facility. It is not the arrest or confinement but the search process at each jail that gives rise to the claims before the Court.

Burlington County jail procedures required every arrestee to shower with a delousing agent. Officers would check arrestees for scars, marks, gang tattoos, and contraband as they disrobed. Petitioner claims he was also instructed to open his mouth, lift his tongue, hold out his arms, turn around, and lift his genitals. Petitioner shared a cell with at least one other person and interacted with other inmates following his admission to the jail.

The Essex County Correctional Facility, where petitioner was taken after six days, is the largest county jail in New Jersey. It admits more than 25,000 inmates each year and houses about 1,000 gang members at any given time. When petitioner was transferred there, all arriving detainees passed through a metal detector and waited in a group holding cell for a more thorough search. When they left the holding cell, they were instructed to remove their clothing while an officer looked for body markings, wounds, and contraband. Apparently without touching the detainees, an officer looked at their ears, nose, mouth, hair, scalp, fingers, hands, arms, armpits, and other body openings. This policy applied regardless of the circumstances of the arrest, the suspected offense, or the detainee's behavior, demeanor, or criminal history. Petitioner alleges he was required to lift his genitals, turn around, and cough in a squatting position as part of the process. After a mandatory shower, during which his clothes were inspected, petitioner was admitted to the facility. He was released the next day, when the charges against him were dismissed.

Petitioner sued the governmental entities that operated the jails, one of the wardens, and certain other defendants. Seeking relief for violations of his Fourth and Fourteenth Amendment rights, petitioner maintained that persons arrested for a minor offense could not be required to remove their clothing and expose the most private areas of their bodies to close visual inspection as a routine part of the intake process. Rather, he contended, officials could conduct this kind of search only if they had reason to suspect a particular inmate of concealing a weapon, drugs, or other contraband.

II

The difficulties of operating a detention center must not be underestimated by the courts. Jails (in the stricter sense of the term, excluding prison facilities) admit more than 13 million inmates a year. The largest facilities process hundreds of people every day; smaller jails may be crowded on weekend nights, after a large police operation, or because of detainees arriving from other jurisdictions. Maintaining safety and order at these institutions requires the expertise of correctional officials, who must have substantial discretion to devise reasonable solutions to the problems they face. The Court has confirmed the importance of deference to correctional officials and explained that a regulation impinging on an inmate's constitutional rights must be upheld "if it is reasonably related to legitimate penological interests."

The Court has recognized that deterring the possession of contraband depends in part on the ability to conduct searches without predictable exceptions. Inmates would adapt to any pattern or loopholes they discovered in the search protocol and then undermine the security of the institution.

These cases establish that correctional officials must be permitted to devise reasonable search policies to detect and deter the possession of contraband in their facilities. The task of determining whether a policy is reasonably related to legitimate security interests is "peculiarly within the province and professional expertise of corrections officials." This Court has repeated the admonition that, "'in the absence of substantial evidence in the record to indicate that the officials have exaggerated their response to these considerations courts should ordinarily defer to their expert judgment in such matters.'"

In many jails officials seek to improve security by requiring some kind of strip search of everyone who is to be detained. Persons arrested for minor offenses may be among the detainees processed at these facilities.

III

The question here is whether undoubted security imperatives involved in jail supervision override the assertion that some detainees must be exempt from the more invasive search procedures at issue absent reasonable suspicion of a concealed weapon or other contraband. The Court has held that deference must be given to the officials in charge of the jail unless there is "substantial evidence" demonstrating their response to the situation is exaggerated. Petitioner has not met this standard, and the record provides full justifications for the procedures used.

Correctional officials have a significant interest in conducting a thorough search as a standard part of the intake process. The admission of inmates creates numerous risks for facility staff, for the existing detainee population, and for a new detainee himself or herself. The danger of introducing lice or contagious infections, for example, is well documented. Persons just arrested may have wounds or other injuries requiring immediate medical attention. It may be difficult to identify and treat these problems until detainees remove their clothes for a visual inspection.

Jails and prisons also face grave threats posed by the increasing number of gang members who go through the intake process. "Gang rivalries spawn a climate of tension, violence, and coercion." The groups recruit new members by force, engage in assaults against staff, and give other inmates a reason to arm themselves. Fights among feuding gangs can be deadly, and the officers who must maintain order are put in harm's way. These considerations provide a reasonable basis to justify a visual inspection for certain tattoos and other signs of gang affiliation as part of the intake process. The identification and isolation of gang members before they are admitted protects everyone in the facility.

Detecting contraband concealed by new detainees, furthermore, is a most serious responsibility. Weapons, drugs, and alcohol all disrupt the safe operation of a jail. Correctional officers have had to confront arrestees concealing knives, scissors, razor blades, glass shards, and other prohibited items on their person, including in their body cavities. They have also found crack, heroin, and marijuana. Everyday items can undermine security if introduced into a detention facility: "Lighters and matches are fire and arson risks or potential weapons. Cell phones are used to orchestrate violence and criminality both within and without jailhouse walls. Pills and medications enhance suicide risks. Chewing gum can block locking devices; hairpins can open handcuffs; wigs can conceal drugs and weapons." Something as simple as an overlooked pen can pose a significant danger. Inmates commit more than 10,000 assaults on correctional staff every year and many more among themselves.

[I]nmates, who might be thought to pose the least risk, have been caught smuggling prohibited items into jail. Concealing contraband often takes little time and effort. It might be done as an officer approaches a suspect's car or during a brief commotion in a group holding cell. Something small might be tucked or taped under an armpit, behind an ear, between the buttocks, in the instep of a foot, or inside the mouth or some other body cavity.

It is not surprising that correctional officials have sought to perform thorough searches at intake for disease, gang affiliation, and contraband. Jails are often crowded, unsanitary, and dangerous places. There is a substantial interest in preventing any new inmate, either of his own will or as a result of coercion, from putting all who live or work at these institutions at even greater risk when he is admitted to the general population.

Petitioner acknowledges that correctional officials must be allowed to conduct an effective search during the intake process and that this will require at least some detainees to lift their genitals or cough in a squatting position. These procedures are designed to uncover contraband that can go undetected by a patdown, metal detector, and other less invasive searches. Petitioner maintains there is little benefit to conducting these more invasive steps on a new detainee who has not been arrested for a serious crime or for any offense involving a weapon or drugs. In his view these detainees should be exempt from this process unless they give officers a particular reason to suspect them of hiding contraband. It is reasonable, however, for correctional officials to conclude this standard would be unworkable. The record provides evidence that the seriousness of an offense is a poor predictor of who has contraband and that it would be difficult in practice to determine whether individual detainees fall within the proposed exemption.

People detained for minor offenses can turn out to be the most devious and dangerous criminals. Experience shows that people arrested for minor offenses have tried to smuggle prohibited items into jail, sometimes by using their rectal cavities or genitals for the concealment. They may have some of the same incentives as a serious criminal to hide contraband. A detainee might risk carrying cash, cigarettes, or a penknife to survive in jail. Others may make a quick decision to hide unlawful substances to avoid getting in more trouble at the time of their arrest. Even if people arrested for a minor offense do not themselves wish to introduce contraband into a jail, they may be coerced into doing so by others. Exempting people arrested for minor offenses from a standard search protocol thus may put them at greater risk and result in more contraband being brought into the detention facility. This is a substantial reason not to mandate the exception petitioner seeks as a matter of constitutional law.

It also may be difficult, as a practical matter, to classify inmates by their current and prior offenses before the intake search. Jails can be even more dangerous than prisons because officials there know so little about the people they admit at the outset. An arrestee may be carrying a false ID or lie about his identity. The officers who conduct an initial search often do not have access to criminal history records.

IV

This case does not require the Court to rule on the types of searches that would be reasonable in instances where, for example, a detainee will be held without assignment to the general jail population and without substantial contact with other detainees. Petitioner's *amici* raise concerns about instances of officers engaging in intentional humiliation and other abusive practices. There also may be legitimate concerns about the invasiveness of searches that involve the touching of detainees. These issues are not implicated on the facts of this case, however, and it is unnecessary to consider them here.

V

Even assuming all the facts in favor of petitioner, the search procedures at the Burlington County Detention Center and the Essex County Correctional

Facility struck a reasonable balance between inmate privacy and the needs of the institutions. The Fourth and Fourteenth Amendments do not require adoption of the framework of rules petitioner proposes.

Chief Justice ROBERTS, concurring.

I join the opinion of the Court. As with Justice Alito, however, it is important for me that the Court does not foreclose the possibility of an exception to the rule it announces. Justice Kennedy explains that the circumstances before it do not afford an opportunity to consider that possibility. Those circumstances include the facts that Florence was detained not for a minor traffic offense but instead pursuant to a warrant for his arrest, and that there was apparently no alternative, if Florence were to be detained, to holding him in the general jail population.

The Court makes a persuasive case for the general applicability of the rule it announces. The Court is nonetheless wise to leave open the possibility of exceptions, to ensure that we "not embarrass the future."

Justice ALITO, concurring.

I join the opinion of the Court but emphasize the limits of today's holding. The Court holds that jail administrators may require all arrestees *who are committed to the general population of a jail* to undergo visual strip searches not involving physical contact by corrections officers. To perform the searches, officers may direct the arrestees to disrobe, shower, and submit to a visual inspection. As part of the inspection, the arrestees may be required to manipulate their bodies.

Undergoing such an inspection is undoubtedly humiliating and deeply offensive to many, but there are reasonable grounds for strip searching arrestees before they are admitted to the general population of a jail.

It is important to note, however, that the Court does not hold that it is *always* reasonable to conduct a full strip search of an arrestee whose detention has not been reviewed by a judicial officer and who could be held in available facilities apart from the general population. Most of those arrested for minor offenses are not dangerous, and most are released from custody prior to or at the time of their initial appearance before a magistrate. In some cases, the charges are dropped. In others, arrestees are released either on their own recognizance or on minimal bail. In the end, few are sentenced to incarceration. For these persons, admission to the general jail population, with the concomitant humiliation of a strip search, may not be reasonable, particularly if an alternative procedure is feasible. For example, the Federal Bureau of Prisons (BOP) and possibly even some local jails appear to segregate temporary detainees who are minor offenders from the general population.

The Court does not address whether it is always reasonable, without regard to the offense or the reason for detention, to strip search an arrestee before the arrestee's detention has been reviewed by a judicial officer. The lead opinion explicitly reserves judgment on that question. In light of that limitation, I join the opinion of the Court in full.

Justice BREYER, with whom Justice GINSBURG, Justice SOTOMAYOR, and Justice KAGAN join dissenting.

The petition for certiorari asks us to decide "[w]hether the Fourth Amendment permits a . . . suspicionless strip search of every individual arrested for any minor offense. . . ." This question is phrased more broadly than what is at issue. The case is limited to strip searches of those arrestees entering a jail's general population. And the kind of strip search in question involves more than undressing and taking a shower (even if guards monitor the shower area for threatened disorder). Rather, the searches here involve close observation of the private areas of a person's body and for that reason constitute a far more serious invasion of that person's privacy.

The visually invasive kind of strip search at issue here is not unique. [It involves:]

> a visual inspection of the inmate's naked body. This should include the inmate opening his mouth and moving his tongue up and down and from side to side, removing any dentures, running his hands through his hair, allowing his ears to be visually examined, lifting his arms to expose his arm pits, lifting his feet to examine the sole, spreading and/or lifting his testicles to expose the area behind them and bending over and/or spreading the cheeks of his buttocks to expose his anus. For females, the procedures are similar except females must in addition, squat to expose the vagina.

In my view, such a search of an individual arrested for a minor offense that does not involve drugs or violence — say a traffic offense, a regulatory offense, an essentially civil matter, or any other such misdemeanor — is an "unreasonable searc[h]" forbidden by the Fourth Amendment, unless prison authorities have reasonable suspicion to believe that the individual possesses drugs or other contraband. And I dissent from the Court's contrary determination.

[I]

A strip search that involves a stranger peering without consent at a naked individual, and in particular at the most private portions of that person's body, is a serious invasion of privacy. Even when carried out in a respectful manner, and even absent any physical touching, such searches are inherently harmful, humiliating, and degrading. And the harm to privacy interests would seem particularly acute where the person searched may well have no expectation of being subject to such a search, say, because she had simply received a traffic ticket for failing to buckle a seatbelt, because he had not previously paid a civil fine, or because she had been arrested for a minor trespass.

I doubt that we seriously disagree about the nature of the strip search or about the serious affront to human dignity and to individual privacy that it presents. The basic question before us is whether such a search is nonetheless justified when an individual arrested for a minor offense is involuntarily placed in the general jail or prison population.

III

The majority, like the respondents, argues that strip searches are needed (1) to detect injuries or diseases, such as lice, that might spread in confinement, (2) to identify gang tattoos, which might reflect a need for special housing to avoid violence, and (3) to detect contraband, including drugs, guns, knives, and even pens or chewing gum, which might prove harmful or dangerous in prison. In evaluating this argument, I, like the majority, recognize: that managing a jail or prison is an "inordinately difficult undertaking," that prison regulations that interfere with important constitutional interests are generally valid as long as they are "reasonably related to legitimate penological interests," that finding injuries and preventing the spread of disease, minimizing the threat of gang violence, and detecting contraband are "legitimate penological interests," and that we normally defer to the expertise of jail and prison administrators in such matters.

Nonetheless, the "particular" invasion of interests, must be "'reasonably related'" to the justifying "penological interest" and the need must not be "'exaggerated.'" It is at this point that I must part company with the majority. I have found no convincing reason indicating that, in the absence of reasonable suspicion, involuntary strip searches of those arrested for minor offenses are necessary in order to further the penal interests mentioned. And there are strong reasons to believe they are not justified.

The lack of justification is fairly obvious with respect to the first two penological interests advanced. The searches already employed at Essex and Burlington include: (a) pat-frisking all inmates; (b) making inmates go through metal detectors (including the Body Orifice Screening System (BOSS) chair used at Essex County Correctional Facility that identifies metal hidden within the body); (c) making inmates shower and use particular delousing agents or bathing supplies; and (d) searching inmates' clothing. In addition, petitioner concedes that detainees could be lawfully subject to being viewed in their undergarments by jail officers or during showering (for security purposes). No one here has offered any reason, example, or empirical evidence suggesting the inadequacy of such practices for detecting injuries, diseases, or tattoos. In particular, there is no connection between the genital lift and the "squat and cough" that Florence was allegedly subjected to and health or gang concerns.

The lack of justification for such a strip search is less obvious but no less real in respect to the third interest, namely that of detecting contraband. The information demonstrating the lack of justification is of three kinds. First, there are empirically based conclusions reached in specific cases. The New York Federal District Court, to which I have referred, conducted a study of 23,000 persons admitted to the Orange County correctional facility between 1999 and 2003. These 23,000 persons underwent a strip search of the kind described. Of these 23,000 persons, the court wrote, "the County encountered three incidents of drugs recovered from an inmate's anal cavity and two incidents of drugs falling from an inmate's underwear during the course of a strip search." The court added that in four of these five instances there may have been "reasonable suspicion" to search, leaving only one instance in 23,000 in which the strip search policy "arguably" detected additional contraband.

Second, there is the plethora of recommendations of professional bodies, such as correctional associations, that have studied and thoughtfully considered the matter. The American Correctional Association (ACA) — an association that informs our view of "what is obtainable and what is acceptable in corrections philosophy," — has promulgated a standard that forbids suspicionless strip searches. Moreover, many correctional facilities apply a reasonable suspicion standard before strip searching inmates entering the general jail population, including the U.S. Marshals Service, the Immigration and Customs Service, and the Bureau of Indian Affairs.

Third, there is general experience in areas where the law has forbidden here-relevant suspicionless searches. Laws in at least 10 States prohibit suspicionless strip searches. At the same time at least seven Courts of Appeals have considered the question and have required reasonable suspicion that an arrestee is concealing weapons or contraband before a strip search of one arrested for a minor offense can take place.

Indeed, neither the majority's opinion nor the briefs set forth any clear example of an instance in which contraband was smuggled into the general jail population during intake that could not have been discovered if the jail was employing a reasonable suspicion standard. Nor do I find the majority's lack of examples surprising. After all, those arrested for minor offenses are often stopped and arrested unexpectedly. And they consequently will have had little opportunity to hide things in their body cavities. Thus, the widespread advocacy by prison experts and the widespread application in many States and federal circuits of "reasonable suspicion" requirements indicates an ability to apply such standards in practice without unduly interfering with the legitimate penal interest in preventing the smuggling of contraband.

For the reasons set forth, I cannot find justification for the strip search policy at issue here — a policy that would subject those arrested for minor offenses to serious invasions of their personal privacy. I consequently dissent.

h.   DNA Testing of Those Arrested

The Court's most recent case about special needs focuses on an important question concerning laws that exist at the federal level and virtually every state: May the police take DNA from those arrested for purposes of investigating crimes other than the one for which the person was arrested?

MARYLAND v. KING

133 S. Ct. 1958 (2013)

Justice KENNEDY delivered the opinion of the Court.

In 2003 a man concealing his face and armed with a gun broke into a woman's home in Salisbury, Maryland. He raped her. The police were unable to identify or apprehend the assailant based on any detailed description or other evidence they then had, but they did obtain from the victim a sample of the perpetrator's DNA.

In 2009 Alonzo King was arrested in Wicomico County, Maryland, and charged with first- and second-degree assault for menacing a group of people with a shotgun. As part of a routine booking procedure for serious offenses, his DNA sample was taken by applying a cotton swab or filter paper — known as a buccal swab — to the inside of his cheeks. The DNA was found to match the DNA taken from the Salisbury rape victim. King was tried and convicted for the rape. Additional DNA samples were taken from him and used in the rape trial, but there seems to be no doubt that it was the DNA from the cheek sample taken at the time he was booked in 2009 that led to his first having been linked to the rape and charged with its commission.

The Court of Appeals of Maryland, on review of King's rape conviction, ruled that the DNA taken when King was booked for the 2009 charge was an unlawful seizure because obtaining and using the cheek swab was an unreasonable search of the person. It set the rape conviction aside. This Court granted certiorari and now reverses the judgment of the Maryland court.

I

When King was arrested on April 10, 2009, for menacing a group of people with a shotgun and charged in state court with both first- and second-degree assault, he was processed for detention in custody at the Wicomico County Central Booking facility. Booking personnel used a cheek swab to take the DNA sample from him pursuant to provisions of the Maryland DNA Collection Act (or Act).

On July 13, 2009, King's DNA record was uploaded to the Maryland DNA database, and three weeks later, on August 4, 2009, his DNA profile was matched to the DNA sample collected in the unsolved 2003 rape case. Once the DNA was matched to King, detectives presented the forensic evidence to a grand jury, which indicted him for the rape. Detectives obtained a search warrant and took a second sample of DNA from King, which again matched the evidence from the rape.

II

The advent of DNA technology is one of the most significant scientific advancements of our era. The full potential for use of genetic markers in medicine and science is still being explored, but the utility of DNA identification in the criminal justice system is already undisputed. Since the first use of forensic DNA analysis to catch a rapist and murderer in England in 1986, see J. Butler, Fundamentals of Forensic DNA Typing 5 (2009) (hereinafter Butler), law enforcement, the defense bar, and the courts have acknowledged DNA testing's "unparalleled ability both to exonerate the wrongly convicted and to identify the guilty. It has the potential to significantly improve both the criminal justice system and police investigative practices."

The current standard for forensic DNA testing relies on an analysis of the chromosomes located within the nucleus of all human cells. "The DNA material in chromosomes is composed of 'coding' and 'noncoding' regions. The coding regions are known as *genes* and contain the information necessary for a cell to make proteins. . . . Non-protein-coding regions . . . are not related directly to making proteins, [and] have been referred to as 'junk' DNA." The adjective "junk" may mislead the layperson, for in fact this is the DNA region used with near certainty to identify a person. The term apparently is intended to indicate that this particular noncoding region, while useful and even dispositive for purposes like identity, does not show more far-reaching and complex characteristics like genetic traits.

Many of the patterns found in DNA are shared among all people, so forensic analysis focuses on "repeated DNA sequences scattered throughout the human genome," known as "short tandem repeats" (STRs). The alternative possibilities for the size and frequency of these STRs at any given point along a strand of DNA are known as "alleles," *id.*, at 25; and multiple alleles are analyzed in order to ensure that a DNA profile matches only one individual. Future refinements may improve present technology, but even now STR analysis makes it "possible to determine whether a biological tissue matches a suspect with near certainty."

The Act authorizes Maryland law enforcement authorities to collect DNA samples from "an individual who is charged with . . . a crime of violence or an attempt to commit a crime of violence; or . . . burglary or an attempt to commit burglary." Maryland law defines a crime of violence to include murder, rape, first-degree assault, kidnaping, arson, sexual assault, and a variety of other serious crimes. Once taken, a DNA sample may not be processed or placed in a database before the individual is arraigned (unless the individual consents). It is at this point that a judicial officer ensures that there is probable cause to detain the arrestee on a qualifying serious offense. If "all qualifying criminal charges are determined to be unsupported by probable cause . . . the DNA sample shall be immediately destroyed." DNA samples are also destroyed if "a criminal action begun against the individual . . . does not result in a conviction," "the conviction is finally reversed or vacated and no new trial is permitted," or "the individual is granted an unconditional pardon."

The Act also limits the information added to a DNA database and how it may be used. Specifically, "[o]nly DNA records that directly relate to the identification of individuals shall be collected and stored." No purpose other than identification is permissible: "A person may not willfully test a DNA sample for information that does not relate to the identification of individuals as specified in this subtitle." Tests for familial matches are also prohibited.

Respondent's DNA was collected in this case using a common procedure known as a "buccal swab." "Buccal cell collection involves wiping a small piece of filter paper or a cotton swab similar to a Q-tip against the inside cheek of an individual's mouth to collect some skin cells." The procedure is quick and painless. The swab touches inside an arrestee's mouth, but it requires no "surgical intrusio[n] beneath the skin," and it poses no "threa[t] to the health or safety" of arrestees.

B

Respondent's identification as the rapist resulted in part through the operation of a national project to standardize collection and storage of DNA profiles. Authorized by Congress and supervised by the Federal Bureau of Investigation, the Combined DNA Index System (CODIS) connects DNA laboratories at the local, state, and national level. Since its authorization in 1994, the CODIS system has grown to include all 50 States and a number of federal agencies. CODIS collects DNA profiles provided by local laboratories taken from arrestees, convicted offenders, and forensic evidence found at crime scenes.

All 50 States require the collection of DNA from felony convicts, and respondent does not dispute the validity of that practice. Twenty-eight States and the Federal Government have adopted laws similar to the Maryland Act authorizing the collection of DNA from some or all arrestees. Although those statutes vary in their particulars, such as what charges require a DNA sample, their similarity means that this case implicates more than the specific Maryland law. At issue is a standard, expanding technology already in widespread use throughout the Nation.

III

A

Although the DNA swab procedure used here presents a question the Court has not yet addressed, the framework for deciding the issue is well established. It can be agreed that using a buccal swab on the inner tissues of a person's cheek in order to obtain DNA samples is a search. Virtually any "intrusio[n] into the human body," Schmerber v. California (1966), will work an invasion of "'cherished personal security' that is subject to constitutional scrutiny."

A buccal swab is a far more gentle process than a venipuncture to draw blood. It involves but a light touch on the inside of the cheek; and although it can be deemed a search within the body of the arrestee, it requires no "surgical intrusions beneath the skin." The fact than an intrusion is negligible is of central relevance to determining reasonableness, although it is still a search as the law defines that term.

B

To say that the Fourth Amendment applies here is the beginning point, not the end of the analysis. "[T]he Fourth Amendment's proper function is to constrain, not against all intrusions as such, but against intrusions which are not justified in the circumstances, or which are made in an improper manner." "As the text of the Fourth Amendment indicates, the ultimate measure of the constitutionality of a governmental search is 'reasonableness.'" In giving content to the inquiry whether an intrusion is reasonable, the Court has preferred "some quantum of individualized suspicion . . . [as] a prerequisite to a constitutional search or seizure. But the Fourth Amendment imposes no irreducible requirement of such suspicion."

The Maryland DNA Collection Act provides that, in order to obtain a DNA sample, all arrestees charged with serious crimes must furnish the sample on a buccal swab applied, as noted, to the inside of the cheeks. The arrestee is already in valid police custody for a serious offense supported by probable cause. The DNA collection is not subject to the judgment of officers whose perspective might be "colored by their primary involvement in 'the often competitive enterprise of ferreting out crime.'" Here, the search effected by the buccal swab of respondent falls within the category of cases this Court has analyzed by reference to the proposition that the "touchstone of the Fourth Amendment is reasonableness, not individualized suspicion."

Even if a warrant is not required, a search is not beyond Fourth Amendment scrutiny; for it must be reasonable in its scope and manner of execution. Urgent government interests are not a license for indiscriminate police behavior. To say that no warrant is required is merely to acknowledge that "rather than employing a *per se* rule of unreasonableness, we balance the privacy-related and law enforcement-related concerns to determine if the intrusion was reasonable." This application of "traditional standards of reasonableness" requires a court to weigh "the promotion of legitimate governmental interests" against "the degree to which [the search] intrudes upon an individual's privacy." An assessment of reasonableness to determine the lawfulness of requiring this class of arrestees to provide a DNA sample is central to the instant case.

IV

A

The legitimate government interest served by the Maryland DNA Collection Act is one that is well established: the need for law enforcement officers in a safe and accurate way to process and identify the persons and possessions they must take into custody. It is beyond dispute that "probable cause provides legal justification for arresting a person suspected of crime, and for a brief period of detention to take the administrative steps incident to arrest." Also uncontested is the "right on the part of the Government, always recognized under English and American law, to search the person of the accused when legally arrested."

The "routine administrative procedure[s] at a police station house incident to booking and jailing the suspect" derive from different origins and have different constitutional justifications than, say, the search of a place; for the search of a place not incident to an arrest depends on the "fair probability that contraband or evidence of a crime will be found in a particular place." The interests are further different when an individual is formally processed into police custody. Then "the law is in the act of subjecting the body of the accused to its physical dominion." When probable cause exists to remove an individual from the normal channels of society and hold him in legal custody, DNA identification plays a critical role in serving those interests.

First, "[i]n every criminal case, it is known and must be known who has been arrested and who is being tried." An individual's identity is more than just his name or Social Security number, and the government's interest in identification goes beyond ensuring that the proper name is typed on the indictment. Identity has never been considered limited to the name on the arrestee's birth certificate. In fact, a name is of little value compared to the real interest in identification at stake when an individual is brought into custody. "It is a well recognized aspect of criminal conduct that the perpetrator will take unusual steps to conceal not only his conduct, but also his identity. Disguises used while committing a crime may be supplemented or replaced by changed names, and even changed physical features."

A suspect's criminal history is a critical part of his identity that officers should know when processing him for detention. Police already seek this crucial identifying information. They use routine and accepted means as varied as comparing the suspect's booking photograph to sketch artists' depictions of persons of interest, showing his mugshot to potential witnesses, and of course making a computerized comparison of the arrestee's fingerprints against electronic databases of known criminals and unsolved crimes. In this respect the only difference between DNA analysis and the accepted use of fingerprint databases is the unparalleled accuracy DNA provides.

The task of identification necessarily entails searching public and police records based on the identifying information provided by the arrestee to see what is already known about him. The DNA collected from arrestees is an irrefutable identification of the person from whom it was taken. Like a fingerprint, the 13 CODIS loci are not themselves evidence of any particular crime, in the way that a drug test can by itself be evidence of illegal narcotics use. A DNA profile is useful to the police because it gives them a form of identification to search the records already in their valid possession. In this respect the use of DNA for identification is no different than matching an arrestee's face to a wanted poster of a previously unidentified suspect; or matching tattoos to known gang symbols to reveal a criminal affiliation; or matching the arrestee's fingerprints to those recovered from a crime scene. DNA is another metric of identification used to connect the arrestee with his or her public persona, as reflected in records of his or her actions that are available to the police. Those records may be linked to the arrestee by a variety of relevant forms of identification, including name, alias, date and time of previous convictions and the name then used, photograph, Social Security number, or CODIS profile. These data, found in official records, are checked as a routine matter to produce a more comprehensive record of the suspect's complete identity. Finding occurrences of the arrestee's CODIS profile in outstanding cases is consistent with this common practice. It uses a different form of identification than a name or fingerprint, but its function is the same.

Second, law enforcement officers bear a responsibility for ensuring that the custody of an arrestee does not create inordinate "risks for facility staff, for the existing detainee population, and for a new detainee." DNA identification can provide untainted information to those charged with detaining suspects and detaining the property of any felon. For these purposes officers must know the type of person whom they are detaining, and DNA allows them to make critical choices about how to proceed.

Third, looking forward to future stages of criminal prosecution, "the Government has a substantial interest in ensuring that persons accused of crimes are available for trials." A person who is arrested for one offense but knows that he has yet to answer for some past crime may be more inclined to flee the instant charges, lest continued contact with the criminal justice system expose one or more other serious offenses. For example, a defendant who had committed a prior sexual assault might be inclined to flee on a burglary charge, knowing that in every State a DNA sample would be taken from him after his conviction on the burglary charge that would tie him to the more serious charge of rape. In addition to subverting the administration of justice with respect to the crime of arrest, this ties back to the interest in safety; for a detainee who absconds from custody presents a risk to law enforcement officers, other detainees, victims of previous crimes, witnesses, and society at large.

Fourth, an arrestee's past conduct is essential to an assessment of the danger he poses to the public, and this will inform a court's determination whether the individual should be released on bail. DNA identification of a suspect in a violent crime provides critical information to the police and judicial officials in making a determination of the arrestee's future dangerousness.

Finally, in the interests of justice, the identification of an arrestee as the perpetrator of some heinous crime may have the salutary effect of freeing a person wrongfully imprisoned for the same offense. "[P]rompt [DNA] testing . . . would speed up apprehension of criminals before they commit additional crimes, and prevent the grotesque detention of . . . innocent people." J. Dwyer, P. Neufeld, & B. Scheck, Actual Innocence 245 (2000).

B

DNA identification represents an important advance in the techniques used by law enforcement to serve legitimate police concerns for as long as there have been arrests, concerns the courts have acknowledged and approved for more than a century. Law enforcement agencies routinely have used scientific advancements in their standard procedures for the identification of arrestees.

Perhaps the most direct historical analogue to the DNA technology used to identify respondent is the familiar practice of fingerprinting arrestees. From the advent of this technique, courts had no trouble determining that fingerprinting was a natural part of "the administrative steps incident to arrest."

DNA identification is an advanced technique superior to fingerprinting in many ways, so much so that to insist on fingerprints as the norm would make little sense to either the forensic expert or a layperson. The additional intrusion upon the arrestee's privacy beyond that associated with fingerprinting is not significant, and DNA is a markedly more accurate form of identifying arrestees. A suspect who has changed his facial features to evade photographic identification or even one who has undertaken the more arduous task of altering his fingerprints cannot escape the revealing power of his DNA.

In sum, there can be little reason to question "the legitimate interest of the government in knowing for an absolute certainty the identity of the person arrested, in knowing whether he is wanted elsewhere, and in ensuring his identification in the event he flees prosecution." In the balance of reasonableness required by the Fourth Amendment, therefore, the Court must give great weight both to the significant government interest at stake in the identification of arrestees and to the unmatched potential of DNA identification to serve that interest.

V

By comparison to this substantial government interest and the unique effectiveness of DNA identification, the intrusion of a cheek swab to obtain a DNA sample is a minimal one. True, a significant government interest does not alone suffice to justify a search. The government interest must outweigh the degree to which the search invades an individual's legitimate expectations of privacy. In considering those expectations in this case, however, the necessary predicate of a valid arrest for a serious offense is fundamental.

In this critical respect, the search here at issue differs from the sort of programmatic searches of either the public at large or a particular class of regulated but otherwise law-abiding citizens that the Court has previously labeled as "'special needs'" searches. Once an individual has been arrested on probable cause for a dangerous offense that may require detention before trial, however, his or her expectations of privacy and freedom from police scrutiny are reduced. DNA identification like that at issue here thus does not require consideration of any unique needs that would be required to justify searching the average citizen. The special needs cases, though in full accord with the result reached here, do not have a direct bearing on the issues presented in this case, because unlike the search of a citizen who has not been suspected of a wrong, a detainee has a reduced expectation of privacy.

In addition the processing of respondent's DNA sample's 13 CODIS loci did not intrude on respondent's privacy in a way that would make his DNA identification unconstitutional.

First, as already noted, the CODIS loci come from noncoding parts of the DNA that do not reveal the genetic traits of the arrestee. While science can always progress further, and those progressions may have Fourth Amendment consequences, alleles at the CODIS loci "are not at present revealing information beyond identification." The argument that the testing at issue in this case reveals any private medical information at all is open to dispute.

And even if non-coding alleles could provide some information, they are not in fact tested for that end. It is undisputed that law enforcement officers analyze DNA for the sole purpose of generating a unique identifying number against which future samples may be matched. This parallels a similar safeguard based on actual practice in the school drug-testing context, where the Court deemed it "significant that the tests at issue here look only for drugs, and not for whether the student is, for example, epileptic, pregnant, or diabetic." If in the future police analyze samples to determine, for instance, an arrestee's predisposition for a particular disease or other hereditary factors not relevant to identity, that case would present additional privacy concerns not present here.

Finally, the Act provides statutory protections that guard against further invasion of privacy. As noted above, the Act requires that "[o]nly DNA records that directly relate to the identification of individuals shall be collected and stored." No purpose other than identification is permissible.

In light of the context of a valid arrest supported by probable cause, respondent's expectations of privacy were not offended by the minor intrusion of a brief swab of his cheeks. By contrast, that same context of arrest gives rise to significant state interests in identifying respondent not only so that the proper name can be attached to his charges but also so that the criminal justice system can make informed decisions concerning pretrial custody. Upon these considerations the Court concludes that DNA identification of arrestees is a reasonable search that can be considered part of a routine booking procedure. When officers make an arrest supported by probable cause to hold for a serious offense and they bring the suspect to the station to be detained in custody, taking and analyzing a cheek swab of the arrestee's DNA is, like fingerprinting and photographing, a legitimate police booking procedure that is reasonable under the Fourth Amendment.

Justice SCALIA, with whom Justice GINSBURG, Justice SOTOMAYOR, and Justice KAGAN join, dissenting.

The Fourth Amendment forbids searching a person for evidence of a crime when there is no basis for believing the person is guilty of the crime or is in possession of incriminating evidence. That prohibition is categorical and without exception; it lies at the very heart of the Fourth Amendment. Whenever this Court has allowed a suspicionless search, it has insisted upon a justifying motive apart from the investigation of crime.

It is obvious that no such noninvestigative motive exists in this case. The Court's assertion that DNA is being taken, not to solve crimes, but to *identify* those in the State's custody, taxes the credulity of the credulous. And the Court's comparison of Maryland's DNA searches to other techniques, such as fingerprinting, can seem apt only to those who know no more than today's opinion has chosen to tell them about how those DNA searches actually work.

I

At the time of the Founding, Americans despised the British use of so-called "general warrants" — warrants not grounded upon a sworn oath of a specific infraction by a particular individual, and thus not limited in scope and application.

Although there is a "closely guarded category of constitutionally permissible suspicionless searches," that has never included searches designed to serve "the normal need for law enforcement." Even the common name for suspicionless searches — "special needs" searches — itself reflects that they must be justified, *always*, by concerns "other than crime detection."

So while the Court is correct to note that there are instances in which we have permitted searches without individualized suspicion, "[i]n none of these cases . . . did we indicate approval of a [search] whose primary purpose was to detect evidence of ordinary criminal wrongdoing." That limitation is crucial. It is only when a governmental purpose aside from crime-solving is at stake that we engage in the free-form "reasonableness" inquiry that the Court indulges at length today. To put it another way, both the legitimacy of the Court's method and the correctness of its outcome hinge entirely on the truth of a single proposition: that the primary purpose of these DNA searches is something other than simply discovering evidence of criminal wrongdoing. As I detail below, that proposition is wrong.

The Court alludes at several points to the fact that King was an arrestee, and arrestees may be validly searched incident to their arrest. But the Court does not really *rest* on this principle, and for good reason: The objects of a search incident to arrest must be either (1) weapons or evidence that might easily be destroyed, or (2) evidence relevant to the crime of arrest. Neither is the object of the search at issue here.

At any rate, all this discussion is beside the point. No matter the degree of invasiveness, suspicionless searches are *never* allowed if their principal end is ordinary crime-solving. A search incident to arrest either serves other ends (such as officer safety, in a search for weapons) or is not suspicionless (as when there is reason to believe the arrestee possesses evidence relevant to the crime of arrest).

Sensing (correctly) that it needs more, the Court elaborates at length the ways that the search here served the special purpose of "identifying" King. But that seems to me quite wrong — unless what one means by "identifying" someone is "searching for evidence that he has committed crimes unrelated to the crime of his arrest." If identifying someone means finding out what unsolved crimes he has committed, then identification is indistinguishable from the ordinary law-enforcement aims that have never been thought to justify a suspicionless search. Searching every lawfully stopped car, for example, might turn up information about unsolved crimes the driver had committed, but no one would say that such a search was aimed at "identifying" him, and no court would hold such a search lawful.

The portion of the Court's opinion that explains the identification rationale is strangely silent on the actual workings of the DNA search at issue here. To know those facts is to be instantly disabused of the notion that what happened had anything to do with identifying King.

King was arrested on April 10, 2009, on charges unrelated to the case before us. That same day, April 10, the police searched him and seized the DNA evidence at issue here. What happened next? Reading the Court's opinion, particularly its insistence that the search was necessary to know "who [had] been arrested," one might guess that King's DNA was swiftly processed and his identity thereby confirmed — perhaps against some master database of known DNA profiles, as is done for fingerprints. After all, was not the suspicionless search here crucial to avoid "inordinate risks for facility staff" or to "existing detainee population"? Surely, then — *surely* — the State of Maryland got cracking on those grave risks immediately, by rushing to identify King with his DNA as soon as possible.

Nothing could be further from the truth. Maryland officials did not even begin the process of testing King's DNA that day. Or, actually, the next day. Or the day after that. And that was for a simple reason: Maryland law forbids them to do so. A "DNA sample collected from an individual charged with a crime . . . *may not* be tested or placed in the statewide DNA data base system prior to the first scheduled arraignment date." And King's first appearance in court was not until three days after his arrest. (I suspect, though, that they did not wait three days to ask his name or take his fingerprints.)

It gets worse. King's DNA sample was not received by the Maryland State Police's Forensic Sciences Division until April 23, 2009 — two weeks after his arrest. It sat in that office, ripening in a storage area, until the custodians got around to mailing it to a lab for testing on June 25, 2009 — two months after it was received, and nearly *three* since King's arrest. After it was mailed, the data from the lab tests were not available for several more weeks, until July 13, 2009, which is when the test results were entered into Maryland's DNA database, *together with information identifying the person from whom the sample was taken.* Meanwhile, bail had been set, King had engaged in discovery, and he had requested a speedy trial—presumably not a trial of John Doe. It was not until August 4, 2009—four months after King's arrest—that the forwarded sample transmitted (*without* identifying information) from the Maryland DNA database to the Federal Bureau of Investigation's national database was matched with a sample taken from the scene of an unrelated crime years earlier.

In fact, if anything was "identified" at the moment that the DNA database returned a match, it was not King—his identity was already known. (The docket for the original criminal charges lists his full name, his race, his sex, his height, his weight, his date of birth, and his address.) Rather, what the August 4 match "identified" was *the previously-taken sample from the earlier crime.* That sample was genuinely mysterious to Maryland; the State knew that it had probably been left by the victim's attacker, but nothing else. King was not identified by his association with the sample; rather, the sample was identified by its association with King. The Court effectively destroys its own "identification" theory when it acknowledges that the object of this search was "to see what [was] already known about [King]." King was who he was, and volumes of his biography could not make him any more or any less King. No minimally competent speaker of English would say, upon noticing a known arrestee's similarity "to a wanted poster of a previously unidentified suspect," that the *arrestee* had thereby been identified. It was the previously unidentified suspect who had been identified—just as, here, it was the previously unidentified rapist.

So, to review: DNA testing does not even begin until after arraignment and bail decisions are already made. The samples sit in storage for months, and take weeks to test. When they are tested, they are checked against the Unsolved Crimes Collection—rather than the Convict and Arrestee Collection, which could be used to identify them. The Act forbids the Court's purpose (identification), but prescribes as its purpose what our suspicionless-search cases forbid ("official investigation into a crime"). Against all of that, it is safe to say that if the Court's identification theory is not wrong, there is no such thing as error.

II

The Court also attempts to bolster its identification theory with a series of inapposite analogies. Is not taking DNA samples the same, asks the Court, as taking a person's photograph? No—because that is not a Fourth Amendment search at all. It does not involve a physical intrusion onto the person, and we have never held that merely taking a person's photograph invades any recognized "expectation of privacy."

But is not the practice of DNA searches, the Court asks, the same as taking "Bertillon" measurements—noting an arrestee's height, shoe size, and so on, on the back of a photograph? No, because that system was not, in the ordinary case, used to solve unsolved crimes. It is possible, I suppose, to imagine situations in which such measurements might be useful to generate leads. (If witnesses described a very tall burglar, all the "tall man" cards could then be pulled.) But the obvious primary purpose of such measurements, as the Court's description of them makes clear, was to verify that, for example, the person arrested today is the same person that was arrested a year ago. Which is to say, Bertillon measurements were *actually* used as a system of identification, and drew their primary usefulness from that task.

It is on the fingerprinting of arrestees, however, that the Court relies most heavily. The Court does not actually say whether it believes that taking a person's fingerprints is a Fourth Amendment search, and our cases provide no ready answer to that question. Even assuming so, however, law enforcement's post-arrest use of fingerprints could not be more different from its post-arrest use of DNA. Fingerprints of arrestees are taken primarily to identify them (though that process sometimes solves crimes); the DNA of arrestees is taken to solve crimes (and nothing else).

The Court asserts that the taking of fingerprints was "constitutional for generations prior to the introduction" of the FBI's rapid computer-matching system. *Ante*, at 1977. This bold statement is bereft of citation to authority because there is none for it. The "great expansion in fingerprinting came before the modern era of Fourth Amendment jurisprudence," and so we were never asked to decide the legitimacy of the practice.

Today, it can fairly be said that fingerprints really are used to identify people — so well, in fact, that there would be no need for the expense of a separate, wholly redundant DNA confirmation of the same information. What DNA adds — what makes it a valuable weapon in the law-enforcement arsenal — is the ability to solve unsolved crimes, by matching old crime-scene evidence against the profiles of people whose identities are already known. That is what was going on when King's DNA was taken, and we should not disguise the fact. Solving unsolved crimes is a noble objective, but it occupies a lower place in the American pantheon of noble objectives than the protection of our people from suspicionless law-enforcement searches. The Fourth Amendment must prevail.

The Court disguises the vast (and scary) scope of its holding by promising a limitation it cannot deliver. The Court repeatedly says that DNA testing, and entry into a national DNA registry, will not befall thee and me, dear reader, but only those arrested for "serious offense[s]." I cannot imagine what principle could possibly justify this limitation, and the Court does not attempt to suggest any. If one believes that DNA will "identify" someone arrested for assault, he must believe that it will "identify" someone arrested for a traffic offense. This Court does not base its judgments on senseless distinctions. At the end of the day, *logic will out*. When there comes before us the taking of DNA from an arrestee for a traffic violation, the Court will predictably (and quite rightly) say, "We can find no significant difference between this case and *King*." Make no mistake about it: As an entirely predictable consequence of today's decision, your DNA can be taken and entered into a national DNA database if you are ever arrested, rightly or wrongly, and for whatever reason.

The most regrettable aspect of the suspicionless search that occurred here is that it proved to be quite unnecessary. All parties concede that it would have been entirely permissible, as far as the Fourth Amendment is concerned, for Maryland to take a sample of King's DNA as a consequence of his conviction for second-degree assault. So the ironic result of the Court's error is this: The only arrestees to whom the outcome here will ever make a difference are those who *have been acquitted* of the crime of arrest (so that their DNA could not have been taken upon conviction). In other words, this Act manages to burden uniquely the sole group for whom the Fourth Amendment's protections ought to be most jealously guarded: people who are innocent of the State's accusations.

Today's judgment will, to be sure, have the beneficial effect of solving more crimes; then again, so would the taking of DNA samples from anyone who flies on an airplane (surely the Transportation Security Administration needs to know the "identity" of the flying public), applies for a driver's license, or attends a public school. Perhaps the construction of such a genetic panopticon is wise. But I doubt that the proud men who wrote the charter of our liberties would have been so eager to open their mouths for royal inspection.

I therefore dissent, and hope that today's incursion upon the Fourth Amendment, like an earlier one, will some day be repudiated.

9.   Searches of Those on Probation and Parole

The Supreme Court has upheld warrantless, suspicionless searches for those on parole, but requires reasonable suspicion for those on probation. In part, the Court has stressed that individuals on probation and parole often consent to such searches as a condition for release. But the Court also has emphasized the diminished expectation of privacy for such individuals and the government's interest in preventing recidivism.

UNITED STATES v. KNIGHTS
534 U.S. 112 (2001)

Chief Justice Rehnquist delivered the opinion of the Court.

A California court sentenced respondent Mark James Knights to summary probation for a drug offense. The probation order included the following condition: that Knights would "[s]ubmit his . . . person, property, place of residence, vehicle, personal effects, to search at any time, with or without a search warrant, warrant of arrest or reasonable cause by any probation officer or law enforcement officer." Knights signed the probation order, which stated immediately above his signature that "I HAVE RECEIVED A COPY, READ AND UNDERSTAND THE ABOVE TERMS AND CONDITIONS OF PROBATION AND AGREE TO ABIDE BY SAME." In this case, we decide whether a search pursuant to this probation condition, and supported by reasonable suspicion, satisfied the Fourth Amendment.

Three days after Knights was placed on probation, a Pacific Gas & Electric (PG & E) power transformer and adjacent Pacific Bell telecommunications vault near the Napa County Airport were pried open and set on fire, causing an estimated $1.5 million in damage. Brass padlocks had been removed and a gasoline accelerant had been used to ignite the fire. This incident was the latest in more than 30 recent acts of vandalism against PG & E facilities in Napa County. Suspicion for these acts had long focused on Knights and his friend, Steven Simoneau. The incidents began after PG & E had filed a theft-of-services complaint against Knights and discontinued his electrical service for failure to pay his bill. Detective Todd Hancock of the Napa County Sheriff's Department had noticed that the acts of vandalism coincided with Knights' court appearance dates concerning the theft of PG & E services. And just a week before the arson, a sheriff's deputy had stopped Knights and Simoneau near a PG & E gas line and observed pipes and gasoline in Simoneau's pickup truck.

After the PG & E arson, a sheriff's deputy drove by Knights' residence, where he saw Simoneau's truck parked in front. The deputy felt the hood of the truck. It was warm. Detective Hancock decided to set up surveillance of Knights' apartment. At about 3:10 the next morning, Simoneau exited the apartment carrying three cylindrical items. Detective Hancock believed the items were pipe bombs. Simoneau walked across the street to the bank of the Napa River, and Hancock heard three splashes. Simoneau returned without the cylinders and drove away in his truck. Simoneau then stopped in a driveway, parked, and left the area. Detective Hancock entered the driveway and observed a number of suspicious objects in the truck: a Molotov cocktail and explosive materials, a gasoline can, and two brass padlocks that fit the description of those removed from the PG & E transformer vault.

After viewing the objects in Simoneau's truck, Detective Hancock decided to conduct a search of Knights' apartment. Detective Hancock was aware of the search condition in Knights' probation order and thus believed that a warrant was not necessary. The search revealed a detonation cord, ammunition, liquid chemicals, instruction manuals on chemistry and electrical circuitry, bolt cutters, telephone pole-climbing spurs, drug paraphernalia, and a brass padlock stamped "PG & E."

Knights was arrested, and a federal grand jury subsequently indicted him for conspiracy to commit arson, for possession of an unregistered destructive device, and for being a felon in possession of ammunition. Knights moved to suppress the evidence obtained during the search of his apartment. The District Court held that Detective Hancock had "reasonable suspicion" to believe that Knights was involved with incendiary materials. The District

Court nonetheless granted the motion to suppress on the ground that the search was for "investigatory" rather than "probationary" purposes. The Court of Appeals for the Ninth Circuit affirmed.

Certainly nothing in the condition of probation suggests that it was confined to searches bearing upon probationary status and nothing more. The search condition provides that Knights will submit to a search "by any probation officer or law enforcement officer" and does not mention anything about purpose. The question then is whether the Fourth Amendment limits searches pursuant to this probation condition to those with a "probationary" purpose.

We need not decide whether Knights' acceptance of the search condition constituted consent in the sense of a complete waiver of his Fourth Amendment rights, however, because we conclude that the search of Knights was reasonable under our general Fourth Amendment approach of "examining the totality of the circumstances," with the probation search condition being a salient circumstance.

The touchstone of the Fourth Amendment is reasonableness, and the reasonableness of a search is determined "by assessing, on the one hand, the degree to which it intrudes upon an individual's privacy and, on the other, the degree to which it is needed for the promotion of legitimate governmental interests." Knights' status as a probationer subject to a search condition informs both sides of that balance. "Probation, like incarceration, is 'a form of criminal sanction imposed by a court upon an offender after verdict, finding, or plea of guilty.'" Just as other punishments for criminal convictions curtail an offender's freedoms, a court granting probation may impose reasonable conditions that deprive the offender of some freedoms enjoyed by law-abiding citizens.

The judge who sentenced Knights to probation determined that it was necessary to condition the probation on Knights' acceptance of the search provision. It was reasonable to conclude that the search condition would further the two primary goals of probation — rehabilitation and protecting society from future criminal violations. The probation order clearly expressed the search condition and Knights was unambiguously informed of it. The probation condition thus significantly diminished Knights' reasonable expectation of privacy.

In assessing the governmental interest side of the balance, it must be remembered that "the very assumption of the institution of probation" is that the probationer "is more likely than the ordinary citizen to violate the law." The recidivism rate of probationers is significantly higher than the general crime rate. And probationers have even more of an incentive to conceal their criminal activities and quickly dispose of incriminating evidence than the ordinary criminal because probationers are aware that they may be subject to supervision and face revocation of probation, and possible incarceration, in proceedings in which the trial rights of a jury and proof beyond a reasonable doubt, among other things, do not apply.

The State has a dual concern with a probationer. On the one hand is the hope that he will successfully complete probation and be integrated back into the community. On the other is the concern, quite justified, that he will be more likely to engage in criminal conduct than an ordinary member of the community. The view of the Court of Appeals in this case would require the State to shut its eyes to the latter concern and concentrate only on the former. But we hold that the Fourth Amendment does not put the State to such a choice. Its interest in apprehending violators of the criminal law, thereby protecting potential victims of criminal enterprise, may therefore justifiably focus on probationers in a way that it does not on the ordinary citizen.

We hold that the balance of these considerations requires no more than reasonable suspicion to conduct a search of this probationer's house. The degree of individualized suspicion required of a search is a determination of when there is a sufficiently high probability that criminal conduct is occurring to make the intrusion on the individual's privacy interest reasonable. Although the Fourth Amendment ordinarily requires the degree of probability embodied in the term "probable cause," a lesser degree satisfies the Constitution when the balance of governmental and private interests makes such a standard reasonable. Those interests warrant a lesser than probable-cause standard here. When an officer has reasonable suspicion that a probationer subject to a search condition is engaged in criminal activity, there is enough likelihood that criminal conduct is occurring that an intrusion on the probationer's significantly diminished privacy interests is reasonable. The same circumstances that lead us to conclude that reasonable suspicion is constitutionally sufficient also render a warrant requirement unnecessary.

SAMSON v. CALIFORNIA

547 U.S. 843 (2006)

Justice THOMAS delivered the opinion of the Court.

California law provides that every prisoner eligible for release on state parole "shall agree in writing to be subject to search or seizure by a parole officer or other peace officer at any time of the day or night, with or without a search warrant and with or without cause." We granted certiorari to decide whether a suspicionless search, conducted under the authority of this statute, violates the Constitution. We hold that it does not.

I

In September 2002, petitioner Donald Curtis Samson was on state parole in California, following a conviction for being a felon in possession of a firearm. On September 6, 2002, Officer Alex Rohleder of the San Bruno Police

Department observed petitioner walking down a street with a woman and a child. Based on a prior contact with petitioner, Officer Rohleder was aware that petitioner was on parole and believed that he was facing an at large warrant. Accordingly, Officer Rohleder stopped petitioner and asked him whether he had an outstanding parole warrant. Petitioner responded that there was no outstanding warrant and that he "was in good standing with his parole agent." Officer Rohleder confirmed, by radio dispatch, that petitioner was on parole and that he did not have an outstanding warrant. Nevertheless, based solely on petitioner's status as a parolee, Officer Rohleder searched petitioner. During the search, Officer Rohleder found a cigarette box in petitioner's left breast pocket. Inside the box he found a plastic baggie containing methamphetamine.

The State charged petitioner with possession of methamphetamine. The trial court denied petitioner's motion to suppress the methamphetamine evidence. A jury convicted petitioner of the possession charge and the trial court sentenced him to seven years' imprisonment.

We granted certiorari, to answer a variation of the question this Court left open in United States v. Knights (2001) — whether a condition of release can so diminish or eliminate a released prisoner's reasonable expectation of privacy that a suspicionless search by a law enforcement officer would not offend the Fourth Amendment.

"[U]nder our general Fourth Amendment approach" we "examin[e] the totality of the circumstances" to determine whether a search is reasonable within the meaning of the Fourth Amendment. Whether a search is reasonable "is determined by assessing, on the one hand, the degree to which it intrudes upon an individual's privacy and, on the other, the degree to which it is needed for the promotion of legitimate governmental interests."

As we noted in *Knights*, parolees are on the "continuum" of state-imposed punishments. On this continuum, parolees have fewer expectations of privacy than probationers, because parole is more akin to imprisonment than probation is to imprisonment. California's system of parole is consistent with these observations: A California inmate may serve his parole period either in physical custody, or elect to complete his sentence out of physical custody and subject to certain conditions. Under the latter option, an inmate-turned-parolee remains in the legal custody of the California Department of Corrections through the remainder of his term, and must comply with all of the terms and conditions of parole, including mandatory drug tests, restrictions on association with felons or gang members, and mandatory meetings with parole officers.

Additionally, as we found "salient" in *Knights* with respect to the probation search condition, the parole search condition under California law requiring inmates who opt for parole to submit to suspicionless searches by a parole officer or other peace officer "at any time," was "clearly expressed" to petitioner. He signed an order submitting to the condition and thus was "unambiguously" aware of it. In *Knights*, we found that acceptance of a clear and unambiguous search condition "significantly diminished Knights' reasonable expectation of privacy."

The State's interests, by contrast, are substantial. This Court has repeatedly acknowledged that a State has an "overwhelming interest" in supervising parolees because "parolees . . . are more likely to commit future criminal offenses." Similarly, this Court has repeatedly acknowledged that a State's interests in reducing recidivism and thereby promoting reintegration and positive citizenship among probationers and parolees warrant privacy intrusions that would not otherwise be tolerated under the Fourth Amendment.

Thus, we conclude that the Fourth Amendment does not prohibit a police officer from conducting a suspicionless search of a parolee. Accordingly, we affirm the judgment of the California Court of Appeal.

Justice STEVENS, with whom Justice SOUTER and Justice BREYER join, dissenting.

Our prior cases have consistently assumed that the Fourth Amendment provides some degree of protection for probationers and parolees. The protection is not as robust as that afforded to ordinary citizens; we have held that probationers' lowered expectation of privacy may justify their warrantless search upon reasonable suspicion of wrongdoing. We have also recognized that the supervisory responsibilities of probation officers, who are required to provide "individualized counseling" and to monitor their charges' progress, and who are in a unique position to judge "how close a supervision the probationer requires," may give rise to special needs justifying departures from Fourth Amendment strictures. But [prior cases do not] support a regime of suspicionless searches, conducted pursuant to a blanket grant of discretion untethered by any procedural safeguards, by law enforcement personnel who have no special interest in the welfare of the parolee or probationer.

What the Court sanctions today is an unprecedented curtailment of liberty. Combining faulty syllogism with circular reasoning, the Court concludes that parolees have no more legitimate an expectation of privacy in their persons than do prisoners. However superficially appealing that parity in treatment may seem, it runs roughshod over our precedent. It also rests on an intuition that fares poorly under scrutiny. And once one acknowledges that parolees do have legitimate expectations of privacy beyond those of prisoners, our Fourth Amendment jurisprudence does not permit the conclusion, reached by the Court here for the first time, that a search supported by neither individualized suspicion nor "special needs" is nonetheless "reasonable."

The suspicionless search is the very evil the Fourth Amendment was intended to stamp out. Not surprisingly, the majority does not seek to justify the search of petitioner on "special needs" grounds. Although the Court has in the past relied on special needs to uphold warrantless searches of probationers, it has never gone so far as to hold that a probationer or parolee may be subjected to full search at the whim of any law enforcement officer he happens to encounter, whether or not the officer has reason to suspect him of wrongdoing.

Ignoring just how "closely guarded" is that "category of constitutionally permissible suspicionless searches," the Court for the first time upholds an entirely suspicionless search unsupported by any special need. And it goes further: In special needs cases we have at least insisted upon programmatic safeguards designed to ensure evenhandedness in application; if individualized suspicion is to be jettisoned, it must be replaced with measures to protect against the state actor's unfettered discretion.

The Court seems to acknowledge that unreasonable searches "inflic[t] dignitary harms that arouse strong resentment in parolees and undermine their ability to reintegrate into productive society." It is satisfied, however, that the California courts' prohibition against "arbitrary, capricious or harassing" searches suffices to avert those harms—which are of course counterproductive to the State's purported aim of rehabilitating former prisoners and reintegrating them into society. I am unpersuaded. The requirement of individualized suspicion, in all its iterations, is the shield the Framers selected to guard against the evils of arbitrary action, caprice, and harassment. To say that those evils may be averted without that shield is, I fear, to pay lipservice to the end while withdrawing the means.

F.   SEIZURES AND ARRESTS

The Fourth Amendment, of course, applies to seizures, whether of a person or of his or her property. Arrests must be based on probable cause, though as discussed in section G, a person may be stopped by the police with just reasonable suspicion. Both arrests and stops are seizures within the meaning of the Fourth Amendment. Also, an illegal arrest or stop generally requires the exclusion of the evidence gained as its result. (The exclusionary rule is discussed in Chapter 3.)

Three questions seem particularly important with regard to seizures. First, is a warrant needed for arrests? Second, when does a seizure occur? Finally, is an arrest permissible for a minor offense that does not carry with it the possibility of a prison term? Each of these is discussed in turn.

1.   Is a Warrant Needed for Arrests?

Although the Court has expressed a preference for warrants, it also has been clear that a warrant is not required for an arrest as long as there is probable cause.

UNITED STATES v. WATSON

423 U.S. 411 (1976)

Justice WHITE delivered the opinion of the Court.

This case presents questions under the Fourth Amendment as to the legality of a warrantless arrest and of an ensuing search of the arrestee's automobile carried out with his purported consent.

I

The relevant events began on August 17, 1972, when an informant, one Khoury, telephoned a postal inspector informing him that respondent Watson was in possession of a stolen credit card and had asked Khoury to cooperate in using the card to their mutual advantage. On five to 10 previous occasions Khoury had provided the inspector with reliable information on postal inspection matters, some involving Watson. Later that day Khoury delivered the card to the inspector. On learning that Watson had agreed to furnish additional cards, the inspector asked Khoury to arrange to meet with Watson. Khoury did so, a meeting being scheduled for August 22. Watson canceled that engagement, but at noon on August 23, Khoury met with Watson at a restaurant designated by the latter. Khoury had been instructed that if Watson had additional stolen credit cards, Khoury was to give a designated signal. The signal was given, the officers closed in, and Watson was forthwith arrested. He was removed from the restaurant to the street where he was given the warnings required by Miranda v. Arizona (1966). A search having revealed that Watson had no credit cards on his person, the inspector asked if he could look inside Watson's car, which was standing within view. Watson said, "Go ahead," and repeated these words when the inspector cautioned that "[i]f I find anything, it is going to go against you." Using keys furnished by Watson, the inspector entered the car and found under the floor mat an envelope containing two credit cards in the names of other persons. These cards were the basis for two counts of a four-count indictment charging Watson with possessing stolen mail.

Prior to trial, Watson moved to suppress the cards, claiming that his arrest was illegal for want of probable cause and an arrest warrant and that his consent to search the car was involuntary and ineffective because he had not been told that he could withhold consent. The motion was denied, and Watson was convicted of illegally possessing the two cards seized from his car.

II

Contrary to the Court of Appeals' view, Watson's arrest was not invalid because executed without a warrant. Title 18 U.S.C. §3061(a)(3) expressly empowers the Board of Governors of the Postal Service to authorize Postal

Service officers and employees "performing duties related to the inspection of postal matters" to "make arrests without warrant for felonies cognizable under the laws of the United States if they have reasonable grounds to believe that the person to be arrested has committed or is committing such a felony." Because there was probable cause in this case to believe that Watson had violated §1708, the inspector and his subordinates, in arresting Watson, were acting strictly in accordance with the governing statute and regulations.

Section 3061 represents a judgment by Congress that it is not unreasonable under the Fourth Amendment for postal inspectors to arrest without a warrant provided they have probable cause to do so. This was not an isolated or quixotic judgment of the legislative branch. Other federal law enforcement officers have been expressly authorized by statute for many years to make felony arrests on probable cause but without a warrant. This is true of United States marshals, and of agents of the Federal Bureau of Investigation, the Drug Enforcement Administration, the Secret Service, and the Customs Service.

Because there is a "strong presumption of constitutionality due to an Act of Congress, especially when it turns on what is 'reasonable,'" "[o]bviously the Court should be reluctant to decide that a search thus authorized by Congress was unreasonable and that the Act was therefore unconstitutional." Moreover, there is nothing in the Court's prior cases indicating that under the Fourth Amendment a warrant is required to make a valid arrest for a felony. Indeed, the relevant prior decisions are uniformly to the contrary.

"The usual rule is that a police officer may arrest without warrant one believed by the officer upon reasonable cause to have been guilty of a felony. . . ." The cases construing the Fourth Amendment thus reflect the ancient common-law rule that a peace officer was permitted to arrest without a warrant for a misdemeanor or felony committed in his presence as well as for a felony not committed in his presence if there was reasonable ground for making the arrest. This has also been the prevailing rule under state constitutions and statutes. "The rule of the common law, that a peace officer or a private citizen may arrest a felon without a warrant, has been generally held by the courts of the several States to be in force in cases of felony punishable by the civil tribunals." Kurtz v. Moffitt (1885).

Watson's arrest did not violate the Fourth Amendment, and the Court of Appeals erred in holding to the contrary. Because our judgment is that Watson's arrest comported with the Fourth Amendment, Watson's consent to the search of his car was not the product of an illegal arrest.

Justice MARSHALL, with whom Justice BRENNAN joins, dissenting.

By granting police broad powers to make warrantless arrests, the Court today sharply reverses the course of our modern decisions construing the Warrant Clause of the Fourth Amendment.

I

Before addressing what the Court does today, I note what it does not do. It does not decide this case on the narrow question that is presented. That is unfortunate for this is, fundamentally, a simple case.

On the afternoon of August 23, 1972, Awad Khoury, an informant of proved reliability, met with respondent Watson at a public restaurant under the surveillance of two postal inspectors. Khoury was under instructions to light a cigarette as a signal to the watching agents if Watson was in possession of stolen credit cards. Khoury lit a cigarette, and the postal inspectors moved in, made the arrest, and, ultimately, discovered under the floor mat of Watson's automobile the stolen credit cards that formed the basis of Watson's conviction and this appeal.

The signal of the reliable informant that Watson was in possession of stolen credit cards gave the postal inspectors probable cause to make the arrest. This probable cause was separate and distinct from the probable cause relating to the offense six days earlier, and provided an adequate independent basis for the arrest. Whether or not a warrant ordinarily is required prior to making an arrest, no warrant is required when exigent circumstances are present. When law enforcement officers have probable cause to believe that an offense is taking place in their presence and that the suspect is at that moment in possession of the evidence, exigent circumstances exist. Delay could cause the escape of the suspect or the destruction of the evidence. Accordingly, Watson's warrantless arrest was valid under the recognized exigent-circumstances exception to the warrant requirement, and the Court has no occasion to consider whether a warrant would otherwise be necessary.

This conclusion should properly dispose of the case before us.

Since, for reasons it leaves unexpressed, the Court does not take this traditional course, I am constrained to express my views on the issues it unnecessarily decides. The Court reaches its conclusion that a warrant is not necessary for a police officer to make an arrest in a public place, so long as he has probable cause to believe a felony has been committed, on the basis of its views of precedent and history. [A]n examination of the history relied on by the Court shows that it does not support the conclusion laid upon it.

There is no doubt that by the reference to the seizure of persons, the Fourth Amendment was intended to apply to arrests. Indeed, we have often considered whether arrests were made in conformity with the Fourth Amendment. Admittedly, as the Court observes, some of our decisions make passing reference to the common-law rule on arrests. However, none of the cases cited by the Court, nor any other warrantless arrest case in this Court, mandates the decision announced today. Frequently exigent circumstances were present, so that the warrantless arrest was proper even if a warrant ordinarily may be required. Many cases have invalidated arrests as not based on probable cause, thereby bypassing the need to reach the warrant question. Elsewhere the Court has simply assumed the propriety of the arrest and resolved the case before it on other grounds.

The Court next turns to history. It relies on the English common-law rule of arrest and the many state and federal statutes following it. There are two serious flaws in this approach. First, as a matter of factual analysis, the substance of the ancient common-law rule provides no support for the far-reaching modern rule that the Court fashions on its model. Second, as a matter of doctrine, the longstanding existence of a Government practice does not immunize the practice from scrutiny under the mandate of our Constitution.

In sum, the Court's opinion is without foundation. It relies on precedents that are not precedents. It relies on history that offers no clear rule to impose, but only conflicting interests to balance. It relies on statutes that constitute, at best, no more than an aid to construction. The Court never grapples with the warrant requirement of the Fourth Amendment and the cases construing it. It simply announces, by ipse dixit, a rule squarely rejecting the warrant requirement we have favored for so long.

The Court has typically engaged in a two-part analysis in deciding whether the presumption favoring a warrant should be given effect in situations where a warrant has not previously been clearly required. Utilizing that approach we must now consider (1) whether the privacy of our citizens will be better protected by ordinarily requiring a warrant to be issued before they may be arrested; and (2) whether a warrant requirement would unduly burden legitimate governmental interests.

The first question is easily answered. Of course, the privacy of our citizens will be better protected by a warrant requirement. We have recognized that "the Fourth Amendment protects people, not places." Indeed, the privacy guaranteed by the Fourth Amendment is quintessentially personal. Thus a warrant is required in search situations not because of some high regard for property, but because of our regard for the individual, and his interest in his possessions and person.

Not only is the Fourth Amendment directly addressed to the privacy of our citizens, but it speaks in indistinguishable terms about the freedom of both persons and property from unreasonable seizures. A warrant is required in the search situation to protect the privacy of the individual, but there can be no less invasion of privacy when the individual himself, rather than his property, is searched and seized. Indeed, an unjustified arrest that forces the individual temporarily to forfeit his right to control his person and movements and interrupts the course of his daily business may be more intrusive than an unjustified search.

A warrant requirement for arrests would, of course, minimize the possibility that such an intrusion into the individual's sacred sphere of personal privacy would occur on less than probable cause. Primarily for this reason, a warrant is required for searches. Surely there is no reason to place greater trust in the partisan assessment of a police officer that there is probable cause for an arrest than in his determination that probable cause exists for a search.

We come then to the second part of the warrant test: whether a warrant requirement would unduly burden legitimate law enforcement interests. I believe, however, that the suggested concerns are wholly illusory. Indeed, the argument that a warrant requirement for arrests would be an onerous chore for the police seems somewhat anomalous in light of the Government's concession that "it is the standard practice of the Federal Bureau of Investigation (FBI) to present its evidence to the United States Attorney, and to obtain a warrant, before making an arrest." In the past, the practice and experience of the FBI have been taken as a substantial indication that no intolerable burden would be presented by a proposed rule of procedure. Miranda v. Arizona (1966). There is no reason to accord less deference to the FBI practice here.

The Government's assertion that a warrant requirement would impose an intolerable burden stems, in large part, from the specious supposition that procurement of an arrest warrant would be necessary as soon as probable cause ripens. There is no requirement that a search warrant be obtained the moment police have probable cause to search. The rule is only that present probable cause be shown and a warrant obtained before a search is undertaken. The same rule should obtain for arrest warrants, where it may even make more sense. Certainly, there is less need for prompt procurement of a warrant in the arrest situation. Unlike probable cause to search, probable cause to arrest, once formed will continue to exist for the indefinite future, at least if no intervening exculpatory facts come to light.

This sensible approach obviates most of the difficulties that have been suggested with an arrest warrant rule. Police would not have to cut their investigation short the moment they obtain probable cause to arrest, nor would undercover agents be forced suddenly to terminate their work and forfeit their covers. Moreover, if in the course of the continued police investigation exigent circumstances develop that demand an immediate arrest, the arrest may be made without fear of unconstitutionality, so long as the exigency was unanticipated and not used to avoid the arrest warrant requirement. Likewise, if in the course of the continued investigation police uncover evidence tying the suspect to another crime, they may immediately arrest him for that crime if exigency demands it, and still be in full conformity with the warrant rule. This is why the arrest in this case was not improper. Other than where police attempt to evade the warrant requirement, the rule would invalidate an arrest only in the obvious situation: where police, with probable cause but without exigent circumstances, set out to arrest a suspect. Such an arrest must be void, even if exigency develops in the course of the arrest that would ordinarily validate it; otherwise the warrant requirement would be reduced to a toothless prescription.

2.   *When Is a Person Seized?*

What constitutes a seizure for purposes of the Fourth Amendment? If a person is arrested, then there are significant consequences for both the police and the individual. For example, if there is an arrest, as explained above, police may conduct a search incident to the arrest.

In some instances, it is obvious when a person has been arrested, such as when the police tell a person, "You are under arrest," and put on the handcuffs. A seizure also can occur if a person is stopped pursuant to a "stop and frisk," which is discussed in the next section. The Supreme Court has held, such as in United States v. Mendenhall, that a person is seized if a reasonable person under the circumstances would believe that he or she was not free to leave.

UNITED STATES v. MENDENHALL

446 U.S. 544 (1980)

Justice STEWART announced the judgment of the Court.

The respondent was brought to trial in the United States District Court for the Eastern District of Michigan on a charge of possessing heroin with intent to distribute it. She moved to suppress the introduction at trial of the heroin as evidence against her on the ground that it had been acquired from her through an unconstitutional search and seizure by agents of the Drug Enforcement Administration (DEA). The District Court denied the respondent's motion, and she was convicted after a trial upon stipulated facts. The Court of Appeals reversed, finding the search of the respondent's person to have been unlawful.

I

At the hearing in the trial court on the respondent's motion to suppress, it was established how the heroin she was charged with possessing had been obtained from her. The respondent arrived at the Detroit Metropolitan Airport on a commercial airline flight from Los Angeles early in the morning on February 10, 1976. As she disembarked from the airplane, she was observed by two agents of the DEA, who were present at the airport for the purpose of detecting unlawful traffic in narcotics. After observing the respondent's conduct, which appeared to the agents to be characteristic of persons unlawfully carrying narcotics, the agents approached her as she was walking through the concourse, identified themselves as federal agents, and asked to see her identification and airline ticket. The respondent produced her driver's license, which was in the name of Sylvia Mendenhall, and, in answer to a question of one of the agents, stated that she resided at the address appearing on the license. The airline ticket was issued in the

different Name

name of "Annette Ford." When asked why the ticket bore a name different from her own, the respondent stated that she "just felt like using that name." In response to a further question, the respondent indicated that she had been in California only two days. Agent Anderson then specifically identified himself as a federal narcotics agent and, according to his testimony, the respondent "became quite shaken, extremely nervous. She had a hard time speaking."

After returning the airline ticket and driver's license to her, Agent Anderson asked the respondent if she would accompany him to the airport DEA office for further questions. She did so, although the record does not indicate a verbal response to the request. The office, which was located up one flight of stairs about 50 feet from where the respondent had first been approached, consisted of a reception area adjoined by three other rooms. At the office the agent asked the respondent if she would allow a search of her person and handbag and told her that she had the right to decline the search if she desired. She responded: "Go ahead." She then handed Agent Anderson her purse, which contained a receipt for an airline ticket that had been issued to "F. Bush" three days earlier for a flight from Pittsburgh through Chicago to Los Angeles. The agent asked whether this was the ticket that she had used for her flight to California, and the respondent stated that it was.

another Name

A female police officer then arrived to conduct the search of the respondent's person. She asked the agents if the respondent had consented to be searched. The agents said that she had, and the respondent followed the policewoman into a private room. There the policewoman again asked the respondent if she consented to the search, and the respondent replied that she did. The policewoman explained that the search would require that the respondent remove her clothing. The respondent stated that she had a plane to catch and was assured by the policewoman that if she were carrying no narcotics, there would be no problem. The respondent then began to disrobe without further comment. As the respondent removed her clothing, she took from her undergarments two small packages, one of which appeared to contain heroin, and handed both to the policewoman. The agents then arrested the respondent for possessing heroin.

It was on the basis of this evidence that the District Court denied the respondent's motion to suppress. The court concluded that the agents' conduct in initially approaching the respondent and asking to see her ticket and identification was a permissible investigative stop, finding that this conduct was based on specific and articulable facts that justified a suspicion of criminal activity. The court also found that the respondent had not been placed under arrest or otherwise detained when she was asked to accompany the agents to the DEA office, but had accompanied the agents "voluntarily in a spirit of apparent cooperation." It was the court's view that no arrest occurred until after the heroin had been found. Finally, the trial court found that the respondent "gave her consent to the search [in the DEA office] and . . . such consent was freely and voluntarily given."

II

Here the Government concedes that its agents had neither a warrant nor probable cause to believe that the respondent was carrying narcotics when the agents conducted a search of the respondent's person. It is the Government's position, however, that the search was conducted pursuant to the respondent's consent, and thus was excepted from the requirements of both a warrant and probable cause.

A

The Fourth Amendment's requirement that searches and seizures be founded upon an objective justification, governs all seizures of the person, including seizures that involve only a brief detention short of traditional arrest. Accordingly, if the respondent was "seized" when the DEA agents approached her on the concourse and asked questions of her, the agents' conduct in doing so was constitutional only if they reasonably suspected the respondent of wrongdoing. But "[o]bviously, not all personal intercourse between policemen and citizens involves 'seizures' of persons. Only when the officer, by means of physical force or show of authority, has in some way restrained the liberty of a citizen may we conclude that a 'seizure' has occurred."

We adhere to the view that a person is "seized" only when, by means of physical force or a show of authority, his freedom of movement is restrained. Only when such restraint is imposed is there any foundation whatever for invoking constitutional safeguards. The purpose of the Fourth Amendment is not to eliminate all contact between the police and the citizenry, but "to prevent arbitrary and oppressive interference by enforcement officials with the privacy and personal security of individuals." As long as the person to whom questions are put remains free to disregard the questions and walk away, there has been no intrusion upon that person's liberty or privacy as would under the Constitution require some particularized and objective justification.

Moreover, characterizing every street encounter between a citizen and the police as a "seizure," while not enhancing any interest secured by the Fourth Amendment, would impose wholly unrealistic restrictions upon a wide variety of legitimate law enforcement practices. The Court has on other occasions referred to the acknowledged need for police questioning as a tool in the effective enforcement of the criminal laws. Without such investigation, those who were innocent might be falsely accused, those who were guilty might wholly escape prosecution, and many crimes would go unsolved. In short, the security of all would be diminished.

We conclude that a person has been "seized" within the meaning of the Fourth Amendment only if, in view of all of the circumstances surrounding the incident, a reasonable person would have believed that he was not free to leave. Examples of circumstances that might indicate a seizure, even where the person did not attempt to leave, would be the threatening presence of several officers, the display of a weapon by an officer, some physical touching of the person of the citizen, or the use of language or tone of voice indicating that compliance with the officer's request might be compelled. In the absence of some such evidence, otherwise inoffensive contact between a member of the public and the police cannot, as a matter of law, amount to a seizure of that person.

On the facts of this case, no "seizure" of the respondent occurred. The events took place in the public concourse. The agents wore no uniforms and displayed no weapons. They did not summon the respondent to their presence, but instead approached her and identified themselves as federal agents. They requested, but did not demand to see the respondent's identification and ticket. Such conduct without more, did not amount to an intrusion upon any constitutionally protected interest. The respondent was not seized simply by reason of the fact that the agents approached her, asked her if she would show them her ticket and identification, and posed to her a few questions. Nor was it enough to establish a seizure that the person asking the questions was a law enforcement official. In short, nothing in the record suggests that the respondent had any objective reason to believe that she was not free to end the conversation in the concourse and proceed on her way, and for that reason we conclude that the agents' initial approach to her was not a seizure.

Our conclusion that no seizure occurred is not affected by the fact that the respondent was not expressly told by the agents that she was free to decline to cooperate with their inquiry, for the voluntariness of her responses does not depend upon her having been so informed. We also reject the argument that the only inference to be drawn from the fact that the respondent acted in a manner so contrary to her self-interest is that she was compelled to answer the agents' questions. It may happen that a person makes statements to law enforcement officials that he later regrets, but the issue in such cases is not whether the statement was self-protective, but rather whether it was made voluntarily.

B

Although we have concluded that the initial encounter between the DEA agents and the respondent on the concourse at the Detroit Airport did not constitute an unlawful seizure, it is still arguable that the respondent's Fourth Amendment protections were violated when she went from the concourse to the DEA office. Such a violation might in turn infect the subsequent search of the respondent's person.

The District Court specifically found that the respondent accompanied the agents to the office "'voluntarily in a spirit of apparent cooperation.'" The question whether the respondent's consent to accompany the agents was in fact voluntary or was the product of duress or coercion, express or implied, is to be determined by the totality of all the circumstances and is a matter which the Government has the burden of proving.

On the other hand, it is argued that the incident would reasonably have appeared coercive to the respondent, who was 22 years old and had not been graduated from high school. It is additionally suggested that the respondent, a female and a Negro, may have felt unusually threatened by the officers, who were white males. While these factors were not irrelevant, neither were they decisive, and the totality of the evidence in this case was plainly adequate to support the District Court's finding that the respondent voluntarily consented to accompany the officers to the DEA office.

C

Because the search of the respondent's person was not preceded by an impermissible seizure of her person, it cannot be contended that her apparent consent to the subsequent search was infected by an unlawful detention. We conclude that the District Court's determination that the respondent consented to the search of her person "freely and voluntarily" was sustained by the evidence and that the Court of Appeals was, therefore, in error in setting it aside.

Justice WHITE, with whom Justice BRENNAN, Justice MARSHALL, and Justice STEVENS join, dissenting.

The Court today concludes that agents of the Drug Enforcement Administration (DEA) acted lawfully in stopping a traveler changing planes in an airport terminal and escorting her to a DEA office for a strip-search of her person. The Court then concludes, based on the absence of evidence that Ms. Mendenhall resisted her detention, that she voluntarily consented to being taken to the DEA office, even though she in fact had no choice in the matter. This conclusion is inconsistent with our recognition that consent cannot be presumed from a showing of acquiescence to authority.

Beginning with Terry v. Ohio (1968), the Court has recognized repeatedly that the Fourth Amendment's proscription of unreasonable "seizures" protects individuals during encounters with police that do not give rise to an arrest.

Throughout the lower court proceedings in this case, the Government never questioned that the initial stop of Ms. Mendenhall was a "seizure" that required reasonable suspicion. Rather, the Government sought to justify the stop by arguing that Ms. Mendenhall's behavior had given rise to reasonable suspicion because it was consistent with portions of the so-called "drug courier profile," an informal amalgam of characteristics thought to be associated with persons carrying illegal drugs. Having failed to convince the Court of Appeals that the DEA agents had reasonable suspicion for the stop, the Government seeks reversal here by arguing for the first time that no "seizure" occurred, an argument that Justice Stewart now accepts, thereby pretermitting the question whether there was reasonable suspicion to stop Ms. Mendenhall. Justice Stewart's opinion not only is inconsistent with our usual refusal to reverse judgments on grounds not raised below, but it also addresses a fact-bound question with a totality-of-circumstances assessment that is best left in the first instance to the trial court, particularly since the question was not litigated below and hence we cannot be sure is adequately addressed by the record before us.

Justice Stewart believes that a "seizure" within the meaning of the Fourth Amendment occurs when an individual's freedom of movement is restrained by means of physical force or a show of authority. Although it is undisputed that Ms. Mendenhall was not free to leave after the DEA agents stopped her and inspected her identification, Justice Stewart concludes that she was not "seized" because he finds that, under the totality of the circumstances, a reasonable person would have believed that she was free to leave. While basing this finding on an alleged absence from the record of objective evidence indicating that Ms. Mendenhall was not free to ignore the officer's inquiries and continue on her way, Justice Stewart's opinion brushes off the fact that this asserted evidentiary deficiency may be largely attributable to the fact that the "seizure" question was never raised below. In assessing what the record does reveal, the opinion discounts certain objective factors that would tend to support a "seizure" finding, while relying on contrary factors inconclusive even under its own illustrations of how a "seizure" may be established. Moreover, although Justice Stewart's opinion purports to make its "seizure" finding turn on objective factors known to the person accosted, in distinguishing prior decisions holding that investigatory stops constitute "seizures," it does not rely on differences in the extent to which persons accosted could reasonably believe that they were free to leave.

II

Assuming, as we should, that Ms. Mendenhall was "seized" within the meaning of the Fourth Amendment when she was stopped by the DEA agents, the legality of that stop turns on whether there were reasonable grounds for suspecting her of criminal activity at the time of the stop. To establish that there was reasonable suspicion for the stop, it was necessary for the police at least to "be able to point to specific and articulable facts which, taken together with rational inferences from those facts, reasonably warrant that intrusion."

At the time they stopped Ms. Mendenhall, the DEA agents' suspicion that she was engaged in criminal activity was based solely on their brief observations of her conduct at the airport. The officers had no advance information that Ms. Mendenhall, or anyone on her flight, would be carrying drugs. What the agents observed Ms. Mendenhall do in the airport was not "unusual conduct" which would lead an experienced officer reasonably to conclude that criminal activity was afoot, but rather the kind of behavior that could reasonably be expected of anyone changing planes in an airport terminal.

None of the aspects of Ms. Mendenhall's conduct, either alone or in combination, were sufficient to provide reasonable suspicion that she was engaged in criminal activity. The fact that Ms. Mendenhall was the last person to alight from a flight originating in Los Angeles was plainly insufficient to provide a basis for stopping her. Nor was the fact that her flight originated from a "major source city," for the mere proximity of a person to areas with a high incidence of drug activity or to persons known to be drug addicts, does not provide the necessary reasonable suspicion for an investigatory stop.

III

Whatever doubt there may be concerning whether Ms. Mendenhall's Fourth Amendment interests were implicated during the initial stages of her confrontation with the DEA agents, she undoubtedly was "seized" within the meaning of the Fourth Amendment when the agents escorted her from the public area of the terminal to the DEA office for questioning and a strip-search of her person. Although Ms. Mendenhall was not told that she was under arrest, she in fact was not free to refuse to go to the DEA office and was not told that she was. Furthermore, once inside the office, Ms. Mendenhall would not have been permitted to leave without submitting to a strip-search.

Because Ms. Mendenhall was being illegally detained at the time of the search of her person, her suppression motion should have been granted in the absence of evidence to dissipate the taint.

———

On many subsequent occasions, the Supreme Court reaffirmed and applied the *Mendenhall* definition of a seizure. In Florida v. Bostick, 501 U.S. 429 (1991), the Court considered whether there was a seizure when police boarded a bus and asked passengers for permission to search their luggage. Passengers on the bus are generally not "free to leave" when this happens. The police officers asked Terrance Bostick for permission to search his luggage. Bostick consented, and cocaine was found.

The Court said that the test was not whether a reasonable person in his situation would have felt free to leave but whether a person would "feel free to decline the officers' requests or otherwise terminate the encounter." The Court remanded the case to determine whether there was a seizure under that standard.

As explained above, in the subsequent case, United States v. Drayton, 536 U.S. 194 (2002), the Court found that there was not a seizure when three police officers boarded a bus and asked the passengers permission to search their bags. One officer sat in the driver's seat, and the other two went down the aisle, though the Court stressed that the aisle was not blocked, and no one told the passengers that they were required to remain. The Court said, "If a reasonable person would feel free to terminate the encounter, then he or she has not been seized. The reasonable person test is objective and presupposes an innocent person."

Most recently, in Brendlin v. California, 551 U.S. 249 (2007), the Supreme Court expressly applied *Mendenhall* and concluded that passengers are seized when they are riding in a car stopped by police officers. Justice Souter, writing for a unanimous Court, stated, "When a police officer makes a traffic stop, the driver of the car is seized within the meaning of the Fourth Amendment. The question in this case is whether the same is true of a passenger. We hold that a passenger is seized as well and so may challenge the constitutionality of the stop." *Brendlin* is presented in detail in Chapter 3, which focuses on the exclusionary rule, because the effect of finding a seizure is that the passenger can invoke the exclusionary rule by arguing that the police acted illegally.

Under this test, is there a seizure if police officers chase someone? At what point does that become a seizure? That was the issue addressed by the Court in California v. Hodari D.

CALIFORNIA v. HODARI D.
499 U.S. 621 (1991)

Justice SCALIA delivered the opinion of the Court.

Late one evening in April 1988, Officers Brian McColgin and Jerry Pertoso were on patrol in a high-crime area of Oakland, California. They were dressed in street clothes but wearing jackets with "Police" embossed on both front and back. Their unmarked car proceeded west on Foothill Boulevard, and turned south onto 63rd Avenue. As they rounded the corner, they saw four or five youths huddled around a small red car parked at the curb. When the youths saw the officers' car approaching they apparently panicked, and took flight. The respondent here, Hodari D., and one companion ran west through an alley; the others fled south. The red car also headed south, at a high rate of speed.

The officers were suspicious and gave chase. McColgin remained in the car and continued south on 63rd Avenue; Pertoso left the car, ran back north along 63rd, then west on Foothill Boulevard, and turned south on 62nd Avenue. Hodari, meanwhile, emerged from the alley onto 62nd and ran north. Looking behind as he ran, he did not turn and see Pertoso until the officer was almost upon him, whereupon he tossed away what appeared to be a small rock. A moment later, Pertoso tackled Hodari, handcuffed him, and radioed for assistance. Hodari was found to be carrying $130 in cash and a pager; and the rock he had discarded was found to be crack cocaine.

In the juvenile proceeding brought against him, Hodari moved to suppress the evidence relating to the cocaine. The court denied the motion without opinion. The California Court of Appeal reversed, holding that Hodari had been "seized" when he saw Officer Pertoso running towards him, that this seizure was unreasonable under the Fourth Amendment, and that the evidence of cocaine had to be suppressed as the fruit of that illegal seizure. As this case comes to us, the only issue presented is whether, at the time he dropped the drugs, Hodari had been "seized" within the meaning of the Fourth Amendment. If so, respondent argues, the drugs were the fruit of that seizure and the evidence concerning them was properly excluded. If not, the drugs were abandoned by Hodari and lawfully recovered by the police, and the evidence should have been admitted. (In addition, of course, Pertoso's seeing the rock of cocaine, at least if he recognized it as such, would provide reasonable suspicion for the unquestioned seizure that occurred when he tackled Hodari.)

We have long understood that the Fourth Amendment's protection against "unreasonable . . . seizures" includes seizure of the person. From the time of the founding to the present, the word "seizure" has meant a "taking possession." For most purposes at common law, the word connoted not merely grasping, or applying physical force to, the animate or inanimate object in question, but actually bringing it within physical control. A ship still fleeing, even though under attack, would not be considered to have been seized as a war prize. A res capable of manual delivery was not seized until "tak[en] into custody." To constitute an arrest, however—the quintessential "seizure of the person" under our Fourth Amendment jurisprudence—the mere grasping or application of physical force with lawful authority, whether or not it succeeded in subduing the arrestee, was sufficient.

To say that an arrest is effected by the slightest application of physical force, despite the arrestee's escape, is not to say that for Fourth Amendment purposes there is a continuing arrest during the period of fugitivity. If, for example, Pertoso had laid his hands upon Hodari to arrest him, but Hodari had broken away and had then cast away the cocaine, it would hardly be realistic to say that that disclosure had been made during the course of an arrest. The present case, however, is even one step further removed. It does not involve the application of any physical force; Hodari was untouched by Officer Pertoso at the time he discarded the cocaine. His defense relies instead upon the proposition that a seizure occurs "when the officer, by means of physical force or show of authority, has in some way restrained the liberty of a citizen." Hodari contends (and we accept as true for purposes of this decision) that Pertoso's pursuit qualified as a "show of authority" calling upon Hodari to halt. The narrow question before us is whether, with respect to a show of authority as with respect to application of physical force, a seizure occurs even though the subject does not yield. We hold that it does not.

The language of the Fourth Amendment, of course, cannot sustain respondent's contention. The word "seizure" readily bears the meaning of a laying on of hands or application of physical force to restrain movement, even when it is ultimately unsuccessful. ("She seized the purse-snatcher, but he broke out of her grasp.") It does not remotely apply, however, to the prospect of a policeman yelling "Stop, in the name of the law!" at a fleeing form that continues to flee. That is no seizure. Nor can the result respondent wishes to achieve be produced—indirectly, as it were—by suggesting that Pertoso's uncomplied-with show of authority was a common-law arrest, and then appealing to the principle that all common-law arrests are seizures. An arrest requires either physical force (as described above) or, where that is absent, submission to the assertion of authority.

We do not think it desirable, even as a policy matter, to stretch the Fourth Amendment beyond its words and beyond the meaning of arrest, as respondent urges. Street pursuits always place the public at some risk, and compliance with police orders to stop should therefore be encouraged. Only a few of those orders, we must presume, will be without adequate basis, and since the addressee has no ready means of identifying the deficient ones it almost invariably is the responsible course to comply. Unlawful orders will not be deterred, moreover, by sanctioning through the exclusionary rule those of them that are not obeyed. Since policemen do not command "Stop!" expecting to be ignored, or give chase hoping to be outrun, it fully suffices to apply the deterrent to their genuine, successful seizures.

Respondent contends that his position is sustained by the so-called *Mendenhall* test: "[A] person has been 'seized' within the meaning of the Fourth Amendment only if, in view of all the circumstances surrounding the incident, a reasonable person would have believed that he was not free to leave." In seeking to rely upon that test here, respondent fails to read it carefully. It says that a person has been seized "only if," not that he has been seized "whenever"; it states a necessary, but not a sufficient, condition for seizure — or, more precisely, for seizure effected through a "show of authority." *Mendenhall* establishes that the test for existence of a "show of authority" is an objective one: not whether the citizen perceived that he was being ordered to restrict his movement, but whether the officer's words and actions would have conveyed that to a reasonable person.

In sum, assuming that Pertoso's pursuit in the present case constituted a "show of authority" enjoining Hodari to halt, since Hodari did not comply with that injunction he was not seized until he was tackled. The cocaine abandoned while he was running was in this case not the fruit of a seizure, and his motion to exclude evidence of it was properly denied.

Justice STEVENS, with whom Justice MARSHALL joins, dissenting.

The Court's narrow construction of the word "seizure" represents a significant, and in my view, unfortunate, departure from prior case law construing the Fourth Amendment. Almost a quarter of a century ago, in two landmark cases — one broadening the protection of individual privacy, and the other broadening the powers of law enforcement officers — we rejected the method of Fourth Amendment analysis that today's majority endorses. In particular, the Court now adopts a definition of "seizure" that is unfaithful to a long line of Fourth Amendment cases. Even if the Court were defining seizure for the first time, which it is not, the definition that it chooses today is profoundly unwise. In its decision, the Court assumes, without acknowledging, that a police officer may now fire his weapon at an innocent citizen and not implicate the Fourth Amendment — as long as he misses his target.

In *United States v. Mendenhall* (1980), the Court "adhere[d] to the view that a person is 'seized' only when, by means of physical force or a show of authority, his freedom of movement is restrained." The Court looked to whether the citizen who is questioned "remains free to disregard the questions and walk away," and if he or she is able to do so, then "there has been no intrusion upon that person's liberty or privacy" that would require some "particularized and objective justification" under the Constitution. The test for a "seizure," as formulated by the Court in *Mendenhall,* was whether, "in view of all of the circumstances surrounding the incident, a reasonable person would have believed that he was not free to leave." Examples of seizures include "the threatening presence of several officers, the display of a weapon by an officer, some physical touching of the person of the citizen, or the use of language or tone of voice indicating that compliance with the officer's request might be compelled." The Court's unwillingness today to adhere to the "reasonable person" standard, as formulated by Justice Stewart in *Mendenhall,* marks an unnecessary departure from Fourth Amendment case law.

The Court today draws the novel conclusion that even though no seizure can occur unless the *Mendenhall* reasonable person standard is met, the fact that the standard has been met does not necessarily mean that a seizure has occurred.

Even though momentary, a seizure occurs whenever an objective evaluation of a police officer's show of force conveys the message that the citizen is not entirely free to leave — in other words, that his or her liberty is being restrained in a significant way. [T]he Court understood the *Mendenhall* definition as both necessary and sufficient to describe a Fourth Amendment seizure.

Whatever else one may think of today's decision, it unquestionably represents a departure from earlier Fourth Amendment case law. The notion that our prior cases contemplated a distinction between seizures effected by a touching on the one hand, and those effected by a show of force on the other hand, and that all of our repeated descriptions of the *Mendenhall* test stated only a necessary, but not a sufficient, condition for finding seizures in the latter category, is nothing if not creative lawmaking. Moreover, by narrowing the definition of the term seizure, instead of enlarging the scope of reasonable justifications for seizures, the Court has significantly limited the protection provided to the ordinary citizen by the Fourth Amendment.

In this case the officer's show of force — taking the form of a head-on chase — adequately conveyed the message that respondent was not free to leave. Whereas in *Mendenhall,* there was "nothing in the record [to] sugges[t] that the respondent had any objective reason to believe that she was not free to end the conversation in the concourse and proceed on her way," here, respondent attempted to end "the conversation" before it began and soon found himself literally "not free to leave" when confronted by an officer running toward him head-on who eventually tackled him to the ground. There was an interval of time between the moment that respondent saw the officer fast approaching and the moment when he was tackled, and thus brought under the control of the officer. The question is whether the Fourth Amendment was implicated at the earlier or the later moment.

It is too early to know the consequences of the Court's holding. If carried to its logical conclusion, it will encourage unlawful displays of force that will frighten countless innocent citizens into surrendering whatever privacy rights they may still have. The message that today's literal-minded majority conveys is that the common law, rather than our understanding of the Fourth Amendment as it has developed over the last quarter of a century, defines, and limits, the scope of a seizure. The Court today defines a seizure as commencing, not with egregious police conduct, but rather with submission by the citizen. Thus, it both delays the point at which "the Fourth Amendment becomes relevant" to an encounter and limits the range of encounters that will come under the heading of "seizure." Today's qualification of the Fourth Amendment means that innocent citizens may remain "secure in their persons . . . against unreasonable searches and seizures" only at the discretion of the police.

3. For What Crimes May a Person Be Arrested?

May the police arrest a person for a crime that has no possibility of a prison sentence? The Court said yes in Atwater v. City of Lago Vista, a case that produced a vehement dissent and attracted a great deal of media attention.

ATWATER v. CITY OF LAGO VISTA

532 U.S. 318 (2001)

Justice SOUTER delivered the opinion of the Court.

The question is whether the Fourth Amendment forbids a warrantless arrest for a minor criminal offense, such as a misdemeanor seatbelt violation punishable only by a fine. We hold that it does not.

I

In Texas, if a car is equipped with safety belts, a front-seat passenger must wear one, and the driver must secure any small child riding in front. Violation of either provision is "a misdemeanor punishable by a fine not less than $25 or more than $50." Texas law expressly authorizes "[a]ny peace officer [to] arrest without warrant a person found committing a violation" of these seatbelt laws, although it permits police to issue citations in lieu of arrest.

In March 1997, petitioner Gail Atwater was driving her pickup truck in Lago Vista, Texas, with her 3-year-old son and 5-year-old daughter in the front seat. None of them was wearing a seatbelt. Respondent Bart Turek, a

Lago Vista police officer at the time, observed the seatbelt violations and pulled Atwater over. According to Atwater's complaint (the allegations of which we assume to be true for present purposes), Turek approached the truck and "yell[ed]" something to the effect of "[w]e've met before" and "[y]ou're going to jail." He then called for backup and asked to see Atwater's driver's license and insurance documentation, which state law required her to carry. When Atwater told Turek that she did not have the papers because her purse had been stolen the day before, Turek said that he had "heard that story two-hundred times."

Atwater asked to take her "frightened, upset, and crying" children to a friend's house nearby, but Turek told her, "[y]ou're not going anywhere." As it turned out, Atwater's friend learned what was going on and soon arrived to take charge of the children. Turek then handcuffed Atwater, placed her in his squad car, and drove her to the local police station, where booking officers had her remove her shoes, jewelry, and eyeglasses, and empty her pockets. Officers took Atwater's "mug shot" and placed her, alone, in a jail cell for about one hour, after which she was taken before a magistrate and released on $310 bond.

Atwater was charged with driving without her seatbelt fastened, failing to secure her children in seatbelts, driving without a license, and failing to provide proof of insurance. She ultimately pleaded no contest to the misdemeanor seatbelt offenses and paid a $50 fine; the other charges were dismissed.

Atwater and her husband, petitioner Michael Haas, filed suit in a Texas state court under 42 U.S.C. §1983 against Turek and respondents City of Lago Vista and Chief of Police Frank Miller. So far as concerns us, petitioners (whom we will simply call Atwater) alleged that respondents (for simplicity, the City) had violated Atwater's Fourth Amendment "right to be free from unreasonable seizure," and sought compensatory and punitive damages.

II

In reading the [Fourth] Amendment, we are guided by "the traditional protections against unreasonable searches and seizures afforded by the common law at the time of the framing," since "[a]n examination of the common-law understanding of an officer's authority to arrest sheds light on the obviously relevant, if not entirely dispositive, consideration of what the Framers of the Amendment might have thought to be reasonable." Thus, the first step here is to assess Atwater's claim that peace officers' authority to make warrantless arrests for misdemeanors was restricted at common law (whether "common law" is understood strictly as law judicially derived or, instead, as the whole body of law extant at the time of the framing). Atwater's specific contention is that "founding-era common-law rules" forbade peace officers to make warrantless misdemeanor arrests except in cases of "breach of the peace," a category she claims was then understood narrowly as covering only those nonfelony offenses "involving or tending toward violence."

Although her historical argument is by no means insubstantial, it ultimately fails. We begin with the state of pre-founding English common law and find that, even after making some allowance for variations in the common-law usage of the term "breach of the peace," the "founding-era common-law rules" were not nearly as clear as Atwater claims; on the contrary, the common-law commentators (as well as the sparsely reported cases) reached divergent conclusions with respect to officers' warrantless misdemeanor arrest power. Moreover, in the years leading up to American independence, Parliament repeatedly extended express warrantless arrest authority to cover misdemeanor-level offenses not amounting to or involving any violent breach of the peace. [The Court reviewed in detail English common law decisions.] We find disagreement, not unanimity, among both the common-law jurists and the text writers who sought to pull the cases together and summarize accepted practice. Having reviewed the relevant English decisions, as well as English and colonial American legal treatises, legal dictionaries, and procedure manuals, we simply are not convinced that Atwater's is the correct, or even necessarily the better, reading of the common-law history.

A second, and equally serious, problem for Atwater's historical argument is posed by the "divers Statutes," enacted by Parliament well before this Republic's founding that authorized warrantless misdemeanor arrests without reference to violence or turmoil.

An examination of specifically American evidence is to the same effect. Neither the history of the framing era nor subsequent legal development indicates that the Fourth Amendment was originally understood, or has traditionally been read, to embrace Atwater's position.

To begin with, Atwater has cited no particular evidence that those who framed and ratified the Fourth Amendment sought to limit peace officers' warrantless misdemeanor arrest authority to instances of actual breach of the peace, and our own review of the recent and respected compilations of framing-era documentary history has likewise failed to reveal any such design. Nor have we found in any of the modern historical accounts of the Fourth Amendment's adoption any substantial indication that the Framers intended such a restriction. Indeed, to the extent these modern histories address the issue, their conclusions are to the contrary.

The evidence of actual practice also counsels against Atwater's position. During the period leading up to and surrounding the framing of the Bill of Rights, colonial and state legislatures, like Parliament before them, regularly authorized local peace officers to make warrantless misdemeanor arrests without conditioning statutory authority on breach of the peace.

Nor does Atwater's argument from tradition pick up any steam from the historical record as it has unfolded since the framing, there being no indication that her claimed rule has ever become "woven . . . into the fabric" of American law. The story, on the contrary, is of two centuries of uninterrupted (and largely unchallenged) state and federal practice permitting warrantless arrests for misdemeanors not amounting to or involving breach of the peace.

Small wonder, then, that today statutes in all 50 States and the District of Columbia permit warrantless misdemeanor arrests by at least some (if not all) peace officers without requiring any breach of the peace, as do a host of congressional enactments.

III

While it is true here that history, if not unequivocal, has expressed a decided, majority view that the police need not obtain an arrest warrant merely because a misdemeanor stopped short of violence or a threat of it, Atwater does not wager all on history. Instead, she asks us to mint a new rule of constitutional law on the understanding that when historical practice fails to speak conclusively to a claim grounded on the Fourth Amendment, courts are left to strike a current balance between individual and societal interests by subjecting particular contemporary circumstances to traditional standards of reasonableness. Atwater accordingly argues for a modern arrest rule, one not necessarily requiring violent breach of the peace, but nonetheless forbidding custodial arrest, even upon probable cause, when conviction could not ultimately carry any jail time and when the government shows no compelling need for immediate detention.

If we were to derive a rule exclusively to address the uncontested facts of this case, Atwater might well prevail. She was a known and established resident of Lago Vista with no place to hide and no incentive to flee, and common sense says she would almost certainly have buckled up as a condition of driving off with a citation. In her case, the physical incidents of arrest were merely gratuitous humiliations imposed by a police officer who was (at best) exercising extremely poor judgment. Atwater's claim to live free of pointless indignity and confinement clearly outweighs anything the City can raise against it specific to her case.

But we have traditionally recognized that a responsible Fourth Amendment balance is not well served by standards requiring sensitive, case-by-case determinations of government need, lest every discretionary judgment in the field be converted into an occasion for constitutional review. Often enough, the Fourth Amendment has to be applied on the spur (and in the heat) of the moment, and the object in implementing its command of reasonableness is to draw standards sufficiently clear and simple to be applied with a fair prospect of surviving judicial second-guessing months and years after an arrest or search is made. Courts attempting to strike a reasonable Fourth Amendment balance thus credit the government's side with an essential interest in readily administrable rules.

At first glance, Atwater's argument may seem to respect the values of clarity and simplicity, so far as she claims that the Fourth Amendment generally forbids warrantless arrests for minor crimes not accompanied by violence or some demonstrable threat of it (whether "minor crime" be defined as a fine-only traffic offense, a fine-only offense more generally, or a misdemeanor). But the claim is not ultimately so simple, nor could it be, for complications arise the moment we begin to think about the possible applications of the several criteria Atwater proposes for drawing a line between minor crimes with limited arrest authority and others not so restricted.

One line, she suggests, might be between "jailable" and "fine-only" offenses, between those for which conviction could result in commitment and those for which it could not. The trouble with this distinction, of course, is that an officer on the street might not be able to tell. It is not merely that we cannot expect every police officer to know the details of frequently complex penalty schemes, but that penalties for ostensibly identical conduct can vary on account of facts difficult (if not impossible) to know at the scene of an arrest. Is this the first offense or is the suspect a repeat offender? Is the weight of the marijuana a gram above or a gram below the fine-only line? Where conduct could implicate more than one criminal prohibition, which one will the district attorney ultimately decide to charge? And so on.

But Atwater's refinements would not end there. She represents that if the line were drawn at nonjailable traffic offenses, her proposed limitation should be qualified by a proviso authorizing warrantless arrests where "necessary for enforcement of the traffic laws or when [an] offense would otherwise continue and pose a danger to others on the road." (Were the line drawn at misdemeanors generally, a comparable qualification would presumably apply.) The proviso only compounds the difficulties. Would, for instance, either exception apply to speeding? But is it not fair to expect that the chronic speeder will speed again despite a citation in his pocket, and should that not qualify as showing that the "offense would . . . continue" under Atwater's rule? And why, as a constitutional matter, should we assume that only reckless driving will "pose a danger to others on the road" while speeding will not?

There is no need for more examples to show that Atwater's general rule and limiting proviso promise very little in the way of administrability. It is no answer that the police routinely make judgments on grounds like risk of immediate repetition; they surely do and should. But there is a world of difference between making that judgment in choosing between the discretionary leniency of a summons in place of a clearly lawful arrest, and making the same judgment when the question is the lawfulness of the warrantless arrest itself. It is the difference between no basis for legal action challenging the discretionary judgment, on the one hand, and the prospect of evidentiary exclusion or (as here) personal §1983 liability for the misapplication of a constitutional standard, on the other. Atwater's rule therefore would not only place police in an almost impossible spot but would guarantee increased litigation over many of the arrests that would occur. For all these reasons, Atwater's various distinctions between permissible and impermissible arrests for minor crimes strike us as "very unsatisfactory line[s]" to require police officers to draw on a moment's notice.

Accordingly, we confirm today what our prior cases have intimated: the standard of probable cause "applie[s] to all arrests, without the need to 'balance' the interests and circumstances involved in particular situations." If an officer has probable cause to believe that an individual has committed even a very minor criminal offense in his presence, he may, without violating the Fourth Amendment, arrest the offender.

Atwater's arrest satisfied constitutional requirements. There is no dispute that Officer Turek had probable cause to believe that Atwater had committed a crime in his presence. She admits that neither she nor her children were wearing seatbelts, as required. Turek was accordingly authorized (not required, but authorized) to make a custodial arrest without balancing costs and benefits or determining whether or not Atwater's arrest was in some sense necessary.

Justice O'CONNOR, with whom Justice STEVENS, Justice GINSBURG, and Justice BREYER join, dissenting.

The Fourth Amendment guarantees the right to be free from "unreasonable searches and seizures." The Court recognizes that the arrest of Gail Atwater was a "pointless indignity" that served no discernible state interest, and yet holds that her arrest was constitutionally permissible. Because the Court's position is inconsistent with the explicit guarantee of the Fourth Amendment, I dissent.

I

A full custodial arrest, such as the one to which Ms. Atwater was subjected, is the quintessential seizure. When a full custodial arrest is effected without a warrant, the plain language of the Fourth Amendment requires that the arrest be reasonable. It is beyond cavil that "[t]he touchstone of our analysis under the Fourth Amendment is always 'the reasonableness in all the circumstances of the particular governmental invasion of a citizen's personal security.'"

We have "often looked to the common law in evaluating the reasonableness, for Fourth Amendment purposes, of police activity." But history is just one of the tools we use in conducting the reasonableness inquiry. And when history is inconclusive, as the majority amply demonstrates it is in this case, we will "evaluate the search or seizure under traditional standards of reasonableness by assessing, on the one hand, the degree to which it intrudes upon an individual's privacy and, on the other, the degree to which it is needed for the promotion of legitimate governmental interests."

The majority gives a brief nod to this bedrock principle of our Fourth Amendment jurisprudence, and even acknowledges that "Atwater's claim to live free of pointless indignity and confinement clearly outweighs anything the City can raise against it specific to her case." But instead of remedying this imbalance, the majority allows itself to be swayed by the worry that "every discretionary judgment in the field [will] be converted into an occasion for constitutional review." It therefore mints a new rule that "[i]f an officer has probable cause to believe that an individual has committed even a very minor criminal offense in his presence, he may, without violating the Fourth Amendment, arrest the offender." This rule is not only unsupported by our precedent, but runs contrary to the principles that lie at the core of the Fourth Amendment.

As the majority tacitly acknowledges, we have never considered the precise question presented here, namely, the constitutionality of a warrantless arrest for an offense punishable only by fine. Indeed, on the rare occasions that Members of this Court have contemplated such an arrest, they have indicated disapproval.

A custodial arrest exacts an obvious toll on an individual's liberty and privacy, even when the period of custody is relatively brief. The arrestee is subject to a full search of her person and confiscation of her possessions. If the arrestee is the occupant of a car, the entire passenger compartment of the car, including packages therein, is subject to search as well. The arrestee may be detained for up to 48 hours without having a magistrate determine whether there in fact was probable cause for the arrest. See County of Riverside v. McLaughlin (1991). Because people arrested for all types of violent and nonviolent offenses may be housed together awaiting such review, this detention period is potentially dangerous. And once the period of custody is over, the fact of the arrest is a permanent part of the public record.

We have said that "the penalty that may attach to any particular offense seems to provide the clearest and most consistent indication of the State's interest in arresting individuals suspected of committing that offense." If the State has decided that a fine, and not imprisonment, is the appropriate punishment for an offense, the State's interest in taking a person suspected of committing that offense into custody is surely limited, at best. This is not to say that the State will never have such an interest. A full custodial arrest may on occasion vindicate legitimate state interests, even if the crime is punishable only by fine. Arrest is the surest way to abate criminal conduct. It may also allow the police to verify the offender's identity and, if the offender poses a flight risk, to ensure her appearance at trial. But when such considerations are not present, a citation or summons may serve the State's remaining law enforcement interests every bit as effectively as an arrest.

Because a full custodial arrest is such a severe intrusion on an individual's liberty, its reasonableness hinges on "the degree to which it is needed for the promotion of legitimate governmental interests." In light of the availability of citations to promote a State's interests when a fine-only offense has been committed, I cannot concur in a rule which deems a full custodial arrest to be reasonable in every circumstance. Giving police officers constitutional carte blanche to effect an arrest whenever there is probable cause to believe a fine-only misdemeanor has been committed is irreconcilable with the Fourth Amendment's command that seizures be reasonable. Instead, I would require that when there is probable cause to believe that a fine-only offense has been committed, the police officer should issue a citation unless the officer is "able to point to specific and articulable facts which, taken together with rational inferences from those facts, reasonably warrant [the additional] intrusion" of a full custodial arrest.

The record in this case makes it abundantly clear that Ms. Atwater's arrest was constitutionally unreasonable. While Turek was justified in stopping Atwater, neither law nor reason supports his decision to arrest her instead of simply giving her a citation. The officer's actions cannot sensibly be viewed as a permissible means of balancing Atwater's Fourth Amendment interests with the State's own legitimate interests.

There is no question that Officer Turek's actions severely infringed on Atwater's liberty and privacy. Turek was loud and accusatory from the moment he approached Atwater's car. Atwater's young children were terrified and hysterical. Yet when Atwater asked Turek to lower his voice because he was scaring the children, he responded by jabbing his finger in Atwater's face and saying, "You're going to jail." Having made the decision to arrest, Turek did not inform Atwater of her right to remain silent. He instead asked for her license and insurance information.

Atwater asked if she could at least take her children to a friend's house down the street before going to the police station. But Turek—who had just castigated Atwater for not caring for her children—refused and said he would take the children into custody as well. Only the intervention of neighborhood children who had witnessed the scene and summoned one of Atwater's friends saved the children from being hauled to jail with their mother.

With the children gone, Officer Turek handcuffed Ms. Atwater with her hands behind her back, placed her in the police car, and drove her to the police station. Ironically, Turek did not secure Atwater in a seatbelt for the drive. At the station, Atwater was forced to remove her shoes, relinquish her possessions, and wait in a holding cell for about an hour. A judge finally informed Atwater of her rights and the charges against her, and released her when she posted bond. Atwater returned to the scene of the arrest, only to find that her car had been towed.

Ms. Atwater ultimately pleaded no contest to violating the seatbelt law and was fined $50. The city's justifications fall far short of rationalizing the extraordinary intrusion on Gail Atwater and her children. Measuring "the degree to which [Atwater's custodial arrest was] needed for the promotion of legitimate governmental interests," against "the degree to which it intrud[ed] upon [her] privacy," it can hardly be doubted that Turek's actions were disproportionate to Atwater's crime. The majority's assessment that "Atwater's claim to live free of pointless indignity and confinement clearly outweighs anything the City can raise against it specific to her case," is quite correct. In my view, the Fourth Amendment inquiry ends there.

The Court's error, however, does not merely affect the disposition of this case. The per se rule that the Court creates has potentially serious consequences for the everyday lives of Americans. A broad range of conduct falls into the category of fine-only misdemeanors. In Texas alone, for example, disobeying any sort of traffic warning sign is a misdemeanor punishable only by fine, as is failing to pay a highway toll, and driving with expired license plates. Nor are fine-only crimes limited to the traffic context. In several States, for example, littering is a criminal offense punishable only by fine.

To be sure, such laws are valid and wise exercises of the States' power to protect the public health and welfare. My concern lies not with the decision to enact or enforce these laws, but rather with the manner in which they may be enforced. Under today's holding, when a police officer has probable cause to believe that a fine-only misdemeanor offense has occurred, that officer may stop the suspect, issue a citation, and let the person continue on her way. Or, if a traffic violation, the officer may stop the car, arrest the driver, search the driver, search the entire passenger compartment of the car including any purse or package inside, and impound the car and inventory all of its contents.

Although the Fourth Amendment expressly requires that the latter course be a reasonable and proportional response to the circumstances of the offense, the majority gives officers unfettered discretion to choose that course without articulating a single reason why such action is appropriate. Such unbounded discretion carries with it grave potential for abuse. After today, the arsenal available to any officer extends to a full arrest and the searches permissible concomitant to that arrest. The Court neglects the Fourth Amendment's express command in the name of administrative ease. In so doing, it cloaks the pointless indignity that Gail Atwater suffered with the mantle of reasonableness.

An issue left open in *Atwater* is whether such arrests are permissible if the arrest violates *state* law. In Virginia v. Moore, 533 U.S. 164 (2008), the Court said that it was considering "whether a police officer violates the Fourth Amendment by making an arrest based on probable cause but prohibited by state law." The Court said that a state law prohibiting an arrest is irrelevant; so long as there is probable cause an arrest is permissible. Justice Scalia wrote:

> Even if we thought that state law changed the nature of the Commonwealth's interests for purposes of the Fourth Amendment, we would adhere to the probable-cause standard. In determining what is reasonable under the Fourth Amendment, we have given great weight to the "essential interest in readily administrable rules." In Atwater [v. City of Lago Vista (2001)], we acknowledged that nuanced judgments about the need for warrantless arrest were desirable, but we nonetheless declined to limit to felonies and disturbances of the peace the Fourth Amendment rule allowing arrest based on probable cause to believe a law has been broken in the presence of the arresting officer. The rule extends even to minor

misdemeanors, we concluded, because of the need for a bright-line constitutional standard. If the constitutionality of arrest for minor offenses turned in part on inquiries as to risk of flight and danger of repetition, officers might be deterred from making legitimate arrests. We found little to justify this cost, because there was no "epidemic of unnecessary minor-offense arrests," and hence "a dearth of horribles demanding redress."

Incorporating state-law arrest limitations into the Constitution would produce a constitutional regime no less vague and unpredictable than the one we rejected in Atwater. The constitutional standard would be only as easy to apply as the underlying state law, and state law can be complicated indeed. The Virginia statute in this case, for example, calls on law enforcement officers to weigh just the sort of case-specific factors that Atwater said would deter legitimate arrests if made part of the constitutional inquiry. It would authorize arrest if a misdemeanor suspect fails or refuses to discontinue the unlawful act, or if the officer believes the suspect to be likely to disregard a summons. Atwater specifically noted the "extremely poor judgment" displayed in arresting a local resident who would "almost certainly" have discontinued the offense and who had "no place to hide and no incentive to flee." It nonetheless declined to make those considerations part of the constitutional calculus. Atwater differs from this case in only one significant respect: It considered (and rejected) federal constitutional remedies for all minor-misdemeanor arrests; Moore seeks them in only that subset of minor-misdemeanor arrests in which there is the least to be gained — that is, where the State has already acted to constrain officers' discretion and prevent abuse. Here we confront fewer horribles than in Atwater, and less of a need for redress.

Finally, linking Fourth Amendment protections to state law would cause them to "vary from place to place and from time to time." Even at the same place and time, the Fourth Amendment's protections might vary if federal officers were not subject to the same statutory constraints as state officers.

We conclude that warrantless arrests for crimes committed in the presence of an arresting officer are reasonable under the Constitution, and that while States are free to regulate such arrests however they desire, state restrictions do not alter the Fourth Amendment's protections.

G.   STOP AND FRISK

The previous section discusses seizures under the Fourth Amendment, whether in an arrest or in a police stop. There is, though, an important difference between arrests and stops under the Fourth Amendment. For example, for an arrest there must be probable cause, but for a stop there has to be only reasonable suspicion. If a person is arrested, police can do a search incident to the arrest. But if a person is stopped, there can be a frisk only if there is reasonable suspicion that the person is armed and dangerous.

This section examines the topic of stops and frisks. First, the authority for police stops and frisks is presented. Second, the distinction between stops and arrests is considered. Third, there is discussion of what police may do when they stop an individual. Finally, the important question of what is sufficient for reasonable suspicion is examined.

1. The Authority for Police to Stop and Frisk

The seminal case granting police the power to stop and frisk individuals based on reasonable suspicion (as opposed to probable cause) is Terry v. Ohio.

TERRY v. OHIO
392 U.S. 1 (1968)

Chief Justice WARREN delivered the opinion of the Court.

This case presents serious questions concerning the role of the Fourth Amendment in the confrontation on the street between the citizen and the policeman investigating suspicious circumstances.

Petitioner Terry was convicted of carrying a concealed weapon and sentenced to the statutorily prescribed term of one to three years in the penitentiary. Following the denial of a pretrial motion to suppress, the prosecution introduced in evidence two revolvers and a number of bullets seized from Terry and a codefendant, Richard Chilton, by Cleveland Police Detective Martin McFadden. At the hearing on the motion to suppress this evidence, Officer McFadden testified that while he was patrolling in plain clothes in downtown Cleveland at approximately 2:30 in the afternoon of October 31, 1963, his attention was attracted by two men, Chilton and Terry, standing on the corner of Huron Road and Euclid Avenue. He had never seen the two men before, and he was unable to say precisely what first drew his eye to them. However, he testified that he had been a policeman for 39 years and a detective for 35 and that he had been assigned to patrol this vicinity of downtown Cleveland for shoplifters and pickpockets for 30 years. He explained that he had developed routine habits of observation over the years and that he would "stand and watch people or walk and watch people at many intervals of the day." He added: "Now, in this case when I looked over they didn't look right to me at the time."

His interest aroused, Officer McFadden took up a post of observation in the entrance to a store 300 to 400 feet away from the two men. "I get more purpose to watch them when I see their movements," he testified. He saw one of the men leave the other one and walk southwest on Huron Road, past some stores. The man paused for a moment and looked in a store window, then walked on a short distance, turned around and walked back toward the corner, pausing once again to look in the same store window. He rejoined his companion at the corner, and the two conferred briefly. Then the second man went through the same series of motions, strolling down Huron Road, looking in the same window, walking on a short distance, turning back, peering in the store window again, and returning to confer with the first man at the corner. The two men repeated this ritual alternately between five and six times apiece—in all, roughly a dozen trips. At one point, while the two were standing together on the corner, a third man approached them and engaged them briefly in conversation. This man then left the two others and walked west on Euclid Avenue. Chilton and Terry resumed their measured pacing, peering and conferring. After this had gone on for 10 to 12 minutes, the two men walked off together, heading west on Euclid Avenue, following the path taken earlier by the third man.

By this time Officer McFadden had become thoroughly suspicious. He testified that after observing their elaborately casual and oft-repeated reconnaissance of the store window on Huron Road, he suspected the two men of "casing a job, a stick-up," and that he considered it his duty as a police officer to investigate further. He added that he feared "they may have a gun." Thus, Officer McFadden followed Chilton and Terry and saw them stop in front of Zucker's store to talk to the same man who had conferred with them earlier on the street corner. Deciding that the situation was ripe for direct action, Officer McFadden approached the three men, identified himself as a police officer and asked for their names. At this point his knowledge was confined to what he had observed. He was not acquainted with any of the three men by name or by sight, and he had received no information concerning them from any other source. When the men "mumbled something" in response to his inquiries, Officer McFadden grabbed petitioner Terry, spun him around so that they were facing the other two, with Terry between McFadden and the others, and patted down the outside of his clothing. In the left breast pocket of Terry's overcoat Officer McFadden felt a pistol. He reached inside the overcoat pocket, but was unable to remove the gun. At this point, keeping Terry between himself and the others, the officer ordered all three men to enter Zucker's store. As they went in, he removed Terry's overcoat completely, removed a .38-caliber revolver from the pocket and ordered all three men to face the wall with their hands raised. Officer McFadden proceeded to pat down the outer clothing of Chilton and the third man, Katz. He discovered another revolver in the outer pocket of Chilton's overcoat, but no weapons were found on Katz. The officer testified that he only patted the men down to see whether they had weapons, and that he did not put his hands beneath the outer garments of either Terry or Chilton until he felt their guns. So far as appears from the record, he never placed his hands beneath Katz' outer garments. Officer McFadden seized Chilton's gun, asked the proprietor of the store to call a police wagon, and took all three men to the station, where Chilton and Terry were formally charged with carrying concealed weapons.

On the motion to suppress the guns the prosecution took the position that they had been seized following a search incident to a lawful arrest. The trial court rejected this theory, stating that it "would be stretching the facts beyond reasonable comprehension" to find that Officer McFadden had had probable cause to arrest the men before he patted them down for

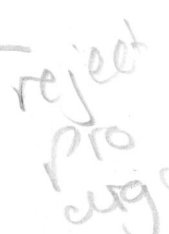

weapons. However, the court denied the defendants' motion on the ground that Officer McFadden, on the basis of his experience, "had reasonable cause to believe that the defendants were conducting themselves suspiciously, and some interrogation should be made of their action." Purely for his own protection, the court held, the officer had the right to pat down the outer clothing of these men, who he had reasonable cause to believe might be armed. The court distinguished between an investigatory "stop" and an arrest, and between a "frisk" of the outer clothing for weapons and a full-blown search for evidence of crime. The frisk, it held, was essential to the proper performance of the officer's investigatory duties, for without it "the answer to the police officer may be a bullet, and a loaded pistol discovered during the frisk is admissible." After the court denied their motion to suppress, Chilton and Terry waived jury trial and pleaded not guilty. The court adjudged them guilty, and the Court of Appeals for the Eighth Judicial District, Cuyahoga County, affirmed. We affirm the conviction.

I

The Fourth Amendment provides that "the right of the people to be secure in their persons, houses, papers, and effects, against unreasonable searches and seizures, shall not be violated." This inestimable right of personal security belongs as much to the citizen on the streets of our cities as to the homeowner closeted in his study to dispose of his secret affairs.

We would be less than candid if we did not acknowledge that this question thrusts to the fore difficult and troublesome issues regarding a sensitive area of police activity—issues which have never before been squarely presented to this Court. Reflective of the tensions involved are the practical and constitutional arguments pressed with great vigor on both sides of the public debate over the power of the police to "stop and frisk"—as it is sometimes euphemistically termed—suspicious persons.

On the one hand, it is frequently argued that in dealing with the rapidly unfolding and often dangerous situations on city streets the police are in need of an escalating set of flexible responses, graduated in relation to the amount of information they possess. For this purpose it is urged that distinctions should be made between a "stop" and an "arrest" (or a "seizure" of a person), and between a "frisk" and a "search." Thus, it is argued, the police should be allowed to "stop" a person and detain him briefly for questioning upon suspicion that he may be connected with criminal activity. Upon suspicion that the person may be armed, the police should have the power to "frisk" him for weapons. If the "stop" and the "frisk" give rise to probable cause to believe that the suspect has committed a crime, then the police should be empowered to make a formal "arrest," and a full incident "search" of the person. This scheme is justified in part upon the notion that a "stop" and a "frisk" amount to a mere "minor inconvenience and petty indignity," which can properly be imposed upon the citizen in the interest of effective law enforcement on the basis of a police officer's suspicion.

On the other side the argument is made that the authority of the police must be strictly circumscribed by the law of arrest and search as it has developed to date in the traditional jurisprudence of the Fourth Amendment. It is contended with some force that there is not — and cannot be — a variety of police activity which does not depend solely upon the voluntary cooperation of the citizen and yet which stops short of an arrest based upon probable cause to make such an arrest. The heart of the Fourth Amendment, the argument runs, is a severe requirement of specific justification for any intrusion upon protected personal security, coupled with a highly developed system of judicial controls to enforce upon the agents of the State the commands of the Constitution. Acquiescence by the courts in the compulsion inherent in the field interrogation practices at issue here, it is urged, would constitute an abdication of judicial control over, and indeed an encouragement of, substantial interference with liberty and personal security by police officers whose judgment is necessarily colored by their primary involvement in "the often competitive enterprise of ferreting out crime." This, it is argued, can only serve to exacerbate police-community tensions in the crowded centers of our Nation's cities.

Having thus roughly sketched the perimeters of the constitutional debate over the limits on police investigative conduct in general and the background against which this case presents itself, we turn our attention to the quite narrow question posed by the facts before us: whether it is always unreasonable for a policeman to seize a person and subject him to a limited search for weapons unless there is probable cause for an arrest. Given the narrowness of this question, we have no occasion to canvass in detail the constitutional limitations upon the scope of a policeman's power when he confronts a citizen without probable cause to arrest him.

II

Our first task is to establish at what point in this encounter the Fourth Amendment becomes relevant. That is, we must decide whether and when Officer McFadden "seized" Terry and whether and when he conducted a "search." There is some suggestion in the use of such terms as "stop" and "frisk" that such police conduct is outside the purview of the Fourth Amendment because neither action rises to the level of a "search" or "seizure" within the meaning of the Constitution. We emphatically reject this notion. It is quite plain that the Fourth Amendment governs "seizures" of the person which do not eventuate in a trip to the station house and prosecution for crime — "arrests" in traditional terminology. It must be recognized that whenever a police officer accosts an individual and restrains his freedom to walk away, he has "seized" that person. And it is nothing less than sheer torture of the English language to suggest that a careful exploration of the outer surfaces of a person's clothing all over his or her body in an attempt to find weapons is not a "search." Moreover, it is simply fantastic to urge that such a procedure performed in public by a policeman while the citizen stands helpless, perhaps facing a wall with his hands raised, is a "petty indignity." It is a serious intrusion upon the sanctity of the person, which may inflict great indignity and arouse strong resentment, and it is not to be undertaken lightly.

We have noted that the abusive practices which play a major, though by no means exclusive, role in creating this friction are not susceptible of control by means of the exclusionary rule, and cannot properly dictate our decision with respect to the powers of the police in genuine investigative and preventive situations. However, the degree of community resentment aroused by particular practices is clearly revelant to an assessment of the quality of the intrusion upon reasonable expectations of personal security caused by those practices.

The danger in the logic which proceeds upon distinctions between a "stop" and an "arrest," or "seizure" of the person, and between a "frisk" and a "search" is twofold. It seeks to isolate from constitutional scrutiny the initial stages of the contact between the policeman and the citizen. And by suggesting a rigid all-or-nothing model of justification and regulation under the Amendment, it obscures the utility of limitations upon the scope, as well as the initiation, of police action as a means of constitutional regulation. The scope of the search must be "strictly tied to and justified by" the circumstances which rendered its initiation permissible.

In our view the sounder course is to recognize that the Fourth Amendment governs all intrusions by agents of the public upon personal security, and to make the scope of the particular intrusion, in light of all the exigencies of the case, a central element in the analysis of reasonableness. This seems preferable to an approach which attributes too much significance to an overly technical definition of "search," and which turns in part upon a judge-made hierarchy of legislative enactments in the criminal sphere. Focusing the inquiry squarely on the dangers and demands of the particular situation also seems more likely to produce rules which are intelligible to the police and the public alike than requiring the officer in the heat of an unfolding encounter on the street to make a judgment as to which laws are "of limited public consequence."

The distinctions of classical "stop-and-frisk" theory thus serve to divert attention from the central inquiry under the Fourth Amendment — the reasonableness in all the circumstances of the particular governmental invasion of a citizen's personal security. "Search" and "seizure" are not talismans. We therefore reject the notions that the Fourth Amendment does not come into play at all as a limitation upon police conduct if the officers stop short of something called a "technical arrest" or a "full-blown search."

In this case there can be no question, then, that Officer McFadden "seized" petitioner and subjected him to a "search" when he took hold of him and patted down the outer surfaces of his clothing. We must decide whether at that point it was reasonable for Officer McFadden to have interfered with petitioner's personal security as he did. And in determining whether the seizure and search were "unreasonable" our inquiry is a dual one — whether the officer's action was justified at its inception, and whether it was reasonably related in scope to the circumstances which justified the interference in the first place. *2 inquiries*

III

If this case involved police conduct subject to the Warrant Clause of the Fourth Amendment, we would have to ascertain whether "probable cause" existed to justify the search and seizure which took place. However, that is not the case. We do not retreat from our holdings that the police must, whenever practicable, obtain advance judicial approval of searches and seizures through the warrant procedure, or that in most instances failure to comply with the warrant requirement can only be excused by exigent circumstances. But we deal here with an entire rubric of police conduct — necessarily swift action predicated upon the on-the-spot observations of the officer on the beat — which historically has not been, and as a practical matter could not be, subjected to the warrant procedure. Instead, the conduct involved in this case must be tested by the Fourth Amendment's general proscription against unreasonable searches and seizures.

Nonetheless, the notions which underlie both the warrant procedure and the requirement of probable cause remain fully relevant in this context. In order to assess the reasonableness of Officer McFadden's conduct as a general proposition, it is necessary "first to focus upon the governmental interest which allegedly justifies official intrusion upon the constitutionally protected interests of the private citizen," for there is "no ready test for determining reasonableness other than by balancing the need to search (or seize) against the invasion which the search (or seizure) entails." And in justifying the particular intrusion the police officer must be able to point to specific and articulable facts which, taken together with rational inferences from those facts, reasonably warrant that intrusion. The scheme of the Fourth Amendment becomes meaningful only when it is assured that at some point the conduct of those charged with enforcing the laws can be subjected to the more detached, neutral scrutiny of a judge who must evaluate the reasonableness of a particular search or seizure in light of the particular circumstances. And in making that assessment it is imperative that the facts be judged against an objective standard: would the facts available to the officer at the moment of the seizure or the search "warrant a man of reasonable caution in the belief" that the action taken was appropriate? Anything less would invite intrusions upon constitutionally guaranteed rights based on nothing more substantial than inarticulate hunches, a result this Court has consistently refused to sanction. And simple "good faith on the part of the arresting officer is not enough." If subjective good faith alone were the test, the protections of the

Fourth Amendment would evaporate, and the people would be "secure in their persons, houses, papers and effects," only in the discretion of the police.

Applying these principles to this case, we consider first the nature and extent of the governmental interests involved. One general interest is of course that of effective crime prevention and detection; it is this interest which underlies the recognition that a police officer may in appropriate circumstances and in an appropriate manner approach a person for purposes of investigating possibly criminal behavior even though there is no probable cause to make an arrest. It was this legitimate investigative function Officer McFadden was discharging when he decided to approach petitioner and his companions. He had observed Terry, Chilton, and Katz go through a series of acts, each of them perhaps innocent in itself, but which taken together warranted further investigation. There is nothing unusual in two men standing together on a street corner, perhaps waiting for someone. Nor is there anything suspicious about people in such circumstances strolling up and down the street, singly or in pairs. Store windows, moreover, are made to be looked in. But the story is quite different where, as here, two men hover about a street corner for an extended period of time, at the end of which it becomes apparent that they are not waiting for anyone or anything; where these men pace alternately along an identical route, pausing to stare in the same store window roughly 24 times; where each completion of this route is followed immediately by a conference between the two men on the corner; where they are joined in one of these conferences by a third man who leaves swiftly; and where the two men finally follow the third and rejoin him a couple of blocks away. It would have been poor police work indeed for an officer of 30 years' experience in the detection of thievery from stores in this same neighborhood to have failed to investigate this behavior further.

The crux of this case, however, is not the propriety of Officer McFadden's taking steps to investigate petitioner's suspicious behavior, but rather, whether there was justification for McFadden's invasion of Terry's personal security by searching him for weapons in the course of that investigation. We are now concerned with more than the governmental interest in investigating crime; in addition, there is the more immediate interest of the police officer in taking steps to assure himself that the person with whom he is dealing is not armed with a weapon that could unexpectedly and fatally be used against him. Certainly it would be unreasonable to require that police officers take unnecessary risks in the performance of their duties. American criminals have a long tradition of armed violence, and every year in this country many law enforcement officers are killed in the line of duty, and thousands more are wounded. Virtually all of these deaths and a substantial portion of the injuries are inflicted with guns and knives.

The easy availability of firearms to potential criminals in this country is well known and has provoked much debate. Whatever the merits of gun-control proposals, this fact is relevant to an assessment of the need for some form of self-protective search power.

In view of these facts, we cannot blind ourselves to the need for law enforcement officers to protect themselves and other prospective victims of violence in situations where they may lack probable cause for an arrest. When an officer is justified in believing that the individual whose suspicious behavior he is investigating at close range is armed and presently dangerous to the officer or to others, it would appear to be clearly unreasonable to deny the officer the power to take necessary measures to determine whether the person is in fact carrying a weapon and to neutralize the threat of physical harm.

We must still consider, however, the nature and quality of the intrusion on individual rights which must be accepted if police officers are to be conceded the right to search for weapons in situations where probable cause to arrest for crime is lacking. Even a limited search of the outer clothing for weapons constitutes a severe, though brief, intrusion upon cherished personal security, and it must surely be an annoying, frightening, and perhaps humiliating experience. Petitioner contends that such an intrusion is permissible only incident to a lawful arrest, either for a crime involving the possession of weapons or for a crime the commission of which led the officer to investigate in the first place.

Our evaluation of the proper balance that has to be struck in this type of case leads us to conclude that there must be a narrowly drawn authority to permit a reasonable search for weapons for the protection of the police officer, where he has reason to believe that he is dealing with an armed and dangerous individual, regardless of whether he has probable cause to arrest the individual for a crime. The officer need not be absolutely certain that the individual is armed; the issue is whether a reasonably prudent man in the circumstances would be warranted in the belief that his safety or that of others was in danger. And in determining whether the officer acted reasonably in such circumstances, due weight must be given, not to his inchoate and unparticularized suspicion or "hunch," but to the specific reasonable inferences which he is entitled to draw from the facts in light of his experience.

We need not develop at length in this case, however, the limitations which the Fourth Amendment places upon a protective seizure and search for weapons. These limitations will have to be developed in the concrete factual circumstances of individual cases. Suffice it to note that such a search, unlike a search without a warrant incident to a lawful arrest, is not justified by any need to prevent the disappearance or destruction of evidence of crime. The sole justification of the search in the present situation is the protection of the police officer and others nearby, and it must therefore be confined in scope to an intrusion reasonably designed to discover guns, knives, clubs, or other hidden instruments for the assault of the police officer.

The scope of the search in this case presents no serious problem in light of these standards. Officer McFadden patted down the outer clothing of petitioner and his two companions. He did not place his hands in their pockets or under the outer surface of their garments until he had felt weapons, and then he merely reached for and removed the guns. He never did invade Katz' person beyond the outer surfaces of his clothes, since he discovered nothing in his patdown which might have been a weapon. Officer McFadden confined his search strictly to what was minimally necessary to learn whether the men were armed and to disarm them once he discovered the weapons. He did not conduct a general exploratory search for whatever evidence of criminal activity he might find.

V

We conclude that the revolver seized from Terry was properly admitted in evidence against him. At the time he seized petitioner and searched him for weapons, Officer McFadden had reasonable grounds to believe that petitioner was armed and dangerous, and it was necessary for the protection of himself and others to take swift measures to discover the true facts and neutralize the threat of harm if it materialized. The policeman carefully restricted his search to what was appropriate to the discovery of the particular items which he sought. Each case of this sort will, of course, have to be decided on its own facts. We merely hold today that where a police officer observes unusual conduct which leads him reasonably to conclude in light of his experience that criminal activity may be afoot and that the persons with whom he is dealing may be armed and presently dangerous, where in the course of investigating this behavior he identifies himself as a policeman and makes reasonable inquiries, and where nothing in the initial stages of the encounter serves to dispel his reasonable fear for his own or others' safety, he is entitled for the protection of himself and others in the area to conduct a carefully limited search of the outer clothing of such persons in an attempt to discover weapons which might be used to assault him. Such a search is a reasonable search under the Fourth Amendment, and any weapons seized may properly be introduced in evidence against the person from whom they were taken.

Justice DOUGLAS, dissenting.

I agree that petitioner was "seized" within the meaning of the Fourth Amendment. I also agree that frisking petitioner and his companions for guns was a "search." But it is a mystery how that "search" and that "seizure" can be constitutional by Fourth Amendment standards, unless there was "probable cause" to believe that (1) a crime had been committed or (2) a crime was in the process of being committed or (3) a crime was about to be committed.

The opinion of the Court disclaims the existence of "probable cause." If loitering were in issue and that was the offense charged, there would be "probable cause" shown. But the crime here is carrying concealed weapons; and there is no basis for concluding that the officer had "probable cause" for believing that that crime was being committed. Had a warrant been sought, a magistrate would, therefore, have been unauthorized to issue one, for he can act only if there is a showing of "probable cause." We hold today that the police have greater authority to make a "seizure" and conduct a "search" than a judge has to authorize such action. We have said precisely the opposite over and over again.

[P]olice officers up to today have been permitted to effect arrests or searches without warrants only when the facts within their personal knowledge would satisfy the constitutional standard of probable cause. At the time of their "seizure" without a warrant they must possess facts concerning the person arrested that would have satisfied a magistrate that "probable cause" was indeed present. The term "probable cause" rings a bell of certainty that is not sounded by phrases such as "reasonable suspicion." Moreover, the meaning of "probable cause" is deeply imbedded in our constitutional history.

To give the police greater power than a magistrate is to take a long step down the totalitarian path. Perhaps such a step is desirable to cope with modern forms of lawlessness. But if it is taken, it should be the deliberate choice of the people through a constitutional amendment. Until the Fourth Amendment, which is closely allied with the Fifth, is rewritten, the person and the effects of the individual are beyond the reach of all government agencies until there are reasonable grounds to believe (probable cause) that a criminal venture has been launched or is about to be launched.

There have been powerful hydraulic pressures throughout our history that bear heavily on the Court to water down constitutional guarantees and give the police the upper hand. That hydraulic pressure has probably never been greater than it is today.

Yet if the individual is no longer to be sovereign, if the police can pick him up whenever they do not like the cut of his jib, if they can "seize" and "search" him in their discretion, we enter a new regime. The decision to enter it should be made only after a full debate by the people of this country.

———————

In assessing *Terry*, it is important to consider a key problem that Chief Justice Warren's majority opinion acknowledged: the likelihood that police may use race as a factor in stopping individuals. African Americans and Latinos frequently describe being stopped by police solely for "driving while black" or "driving while brown." There have been widely reported incidents of famous athletes and actors being stopped seemingly solely for driving a nice car in a predominately white area. Many studies have documented racial disparities in the frequency of stops. Although the Supreme Court has not yet decided a case dealing directly with "racial profiling," some cities and states have attempted to outlaw it. It is important to consider whether *Terry* exacerbated the problem of racial profiling and if limits, constitutional or statutory, are possible.

2. *The Distinction Between Stops and Arrests*

Under Terry v. Ohio, both stops and arrests are seizures within the meaning of the Fourth Amendment. Arrests, though, must be based on probable cause, while stops require only reasonable suspicion. There is often not a bright line to distinguish when a stop becomes an arrest.

The Court has made clear that if a person is detained for sustained interrogation that is an arrest within the meaning of the Fourth Amendment. For example, an arrest has occurred if police officers take a suspect to the station house for questioning. In Dunaway v. New York, 442 U.S. 200 (1979), the Court stated, "[D]etention for custodial interrogation — regardless of its label — intrudes so severely on interests protected by the Fourth Amendment as necessarily to trigger the traditional safeguards against illegal arrest." The Court said that "any exception that could cover a seizure as intrusive as that in this case would threaten to swallow the general rule that the Fourth Amendment seizures are reasonable only if based upon probable cause."

In Florida v. Royer, 460 U.S. 491 (1983), the Court held that taking a suspect from the public area of an airport into a small room constituted an arrest. Justice White, writing for the plurality, clarified the distinction between stops and arrests:

> The scope of the intrusion permitted will vary to some extent with the particular facts and circumstances of each case. This much, however, is clear: an investigative detention must be temporary and last no longer than is necessary to effectuate the purpose of the stop. Similarly, the investigative methods employed should be the least intrusive means reasonably available to verify or dispel the officer's suspicion in a short period of time. It is the State's burden to demonstrate that the seizure it seeks to justify on the basis of a reasonable suspicion was sufficiently limited in scope and duration to satisfy the conditions of an investigative seizure.

Similarly, in Hayes v. Florida, 470 U.S. 811 (1985), the Court held that taking a suspect to the police station house for fingerprinting was an arrest and had to be based on probable cause. Earlier, in Davis v. Mississippi, 394 U.S. 21 (1969), the Court found that the Fourth Amendment was violated when police fingerprinted and questioned 25 African American men to match fingerprints found at a rape scene. Neither of these cases, though, hold that fingerprinting, if done in the field as part of a brief encounter, always constitute an arrest.

The duration of the detention also matters in determining whether there has been a stop or an arrest. In United States v. Place, 462 U.S. 696 (1983), the Court found that detaining a person's luggage for 90 minutes was a seizure under the Fourth Amendment. The Court explained that the "limitations applicable to investigative detentions of the person should define the permissible scope of the person's luggage on less than probable cause." The Court noted that it had "never approved a seizure of the person for the prolonged 90 minute period involved here."

But the Court has not imposed rigid time limits in determining when a stop becomes an arrest. In United States v. Sharpe, 470 U.S. 675 (1985), a police officer detained the suspects between 30 and 40 minutes while waiting for the arrival of a drug enforcement agent. The Court ruled that this was a stop, not an arrest. The Court said that "if an investigative stop continues indefinitely, at some point it can no longer be justified as an investigative stop." But the Court said that there is no "hard-and-fast time limit." The Court emphasized that there was no delay "unnecessary to the legitimate investigation of the law enforcement officers." The Court acknowledged the "difficult linedrawing problems in distinguishing an investigative stop from a de facto arrest."

3.   What May Police Do When They Stop an Individual?

Terry v. Ohio says that police may frisk an individual if there is reasonable suspicion to believe that the suspect is armed and dangerous. In Michigan v. Long, 463 U.S. 1032 (1983), the Court said that the police may conduct a cursory "frisk" of a car if there is reason to believe that there is a weapon in the car and that the person may gain access to that weapon.

When the police frisk a person, they may seize any evidence that is apparent to their experienced "plain feel." Minnesota v. Dickerson, 508 U.S. 366 (1993), which is presented above, drew a distinction between "plain touch," which is allowed, and the police manipulating the lining of a person's clothes to look for evidence, which is not permitted.

The Supreme Court recently confronted the question of whether the police may require that a person identify himself or herself when stopped.

HIIBEL v. SIXTH JUDICIAL DISTRICT COURT OF NEVADA
542 U.S. 177 (2004)

Justice KENNEDY delivered the opinion of the Court.

The petitioner was arrested and convicted for refusing to identify himself during a stop allowed by Terry v. Ohio (1968). He challenges his conviction under the Fourth and Fifth Amendments to the United States Constitution, applicable to the States through the Fourteenth Amendment.

I

The sheriff's department in Humboldt County, Nevada, received an afternoon telephone call reporting an assault. The caller reported seeing a man assault a woman in a red and silver GMC truck on Grass Valley Road. Deputy Sheriff Lee Dove was dispatched to investigate. When the officer arrived at the scene, he found the truck parked on the side of the road. A man was standing by the truck, and a young woman was sitting inside it.

The officer observed skid marks in the gravel behind the vehicle, leading him to believe it had come to a sudden stop.

The officer approached the man and explained that he was investigating a report of a fight. The man appeared to be intoxicated. The officer asked him if he had "any identification on [him]," which we understand as a request to produce a driver's license or some other form of written identification. The man refused and asked why the officer wanted to see identification. The officer responded that he was conducting an investigation and needed to see some identification. The unidentified man became agitated and insisted he had done nothing wrong. The officer explained that he wanted to find out who the man was and what he was doing there. After continued refusals to comply with the officer's request for identification, the man began to taunt the officer by placing his hands behind his back and telling the officer to arrest him and take him to jail. This routine kept up for several minutes: The officer asked for identification 11 times and was refused each time. After warning the man that he would be arrested if he continued to refuse to comply, the officer placed him under arrest.

We now know that the man arrested on Grass Valley Road is Larry Dudley Hiibel. Hiibel was charged with "willfully resist[ing], delay[ing] or obstruct[ing] a public officer in discharging or attempting to discharge any legal duty of his office" in violation of Nev. Rev. Stat. (NRS) §199.280 (2003). The government reasoned that Hiibel had obstructed the officer in carrying out his duties under §171.123, a Nevada statute that defines the legal rights and duties of a police officer in the context of an investigative stop. Section 171.123 provides in relevant part:

> 1. Any peace officer may detain any person whom the officer encounters under circumstances which reasonably indicate that the person has committed, is committing or is about to commit a crime.
> 3. The officer may detain the person pursuant to this section only to ascertain his identity and the suspicious circumstances surrounding his presence abroad. Any person so detained shall identify himself, but may not be compelled to answer any other inquiry of any peace officer.

Hiibel was tried in the Justice Court of Union Township. The court agreed that Hiibel's refusal to identify himself as required by §171.123 "obstructed and delayed Dove as a public officer in attempting to discharge his duty" in violation of §199.280. Hiibel was convicted and fined $250.

II

NRS §171.123(3) is an enactment sometimes referred to as a "stop and identify" statute.

Stop and identify statutes often combine elements of traditional vagrancy laws with provisions intended to regulate police behavior in the course of investigatory stops. The statutes vary from State to State, but all permit an officer to ask or require a suspect to disclose his identity. A few States model their statutes on the Uniform Arrest Act, a model code that permits an officer to stop a person reasonably suspected of committing a crime and "demand of him his name, address, business abroad and whither he is going." In some States, a suspect's refusal to identify himself is a misdemeanor offense or civil violation; in others, it is a factor to be considered in whether the suspect has violated loitering laws. In other States, a suspect may decline to identify himself without penalty.

The present case begins where our prior cases left off. Here there is no question that the initial stop was based on reasonable suspicion, satisfying the Fourth Amendment requirements. Further, the petitioner has not alleged that the statute is unconstitutionally vague. [T]he Nevada Supreme Court has interpreted NRS §171.123(3) to require only that a suspect disclose his name. As we understand it, the statute does not require a suspect to give the officer a driver's license or any other document. Provided that the suspect either states his name or communicates it to the officer by other means — a choice, we assume, that the suspect may make — the statute is satisfied and no violation occurs.

III

Hiibel argues that his conviction cannot stand because the officer's conduct violated his Fourth Amendment rights. We disagree.

Asking questions is an essential part of police investigations. In the ordinary course a police officer is free to ask a person for identification without implicating the Fourth Amendment. "[I]nterrogation relating to one's identity or a request for identification by the police does not, by itself, constitute a Fourth Amendment seizure." Beginning with Terry v. Ohio (1968), the Court has recognized that a law enforcement officer's reasonable suspicion that a person may be involved in criminal activity permits the officer to stop the person for a brief time and take additional steps to investigate further. To ensure that the resulting seizure is constitutionally reasonable, a *Terry* stop must be limited. The officer's action must be "'justified at its inception, and . . . reasonably related in scope to the circumstances which justified the interference in the first place.'" For example, the seizure can not continue for an excessive period of time, or resemble a traditional arrest.

Our decisions make clear that questions concerning a suspect's identity are a routine and accepted part of many *Terry* stops.

Obtaining a suspect's name in the course of a *Terry* stop serves important government interests. Knowledge of identity may inform an officer that a suspect is wanted for another offense, or has a record of violence or mental disorder. On the other hand, knowing identity may help clear a suspect and allow the police to concentrate their efforts elsewhere. Identity may prove particularly important in cases such as this, where the police are investigating what appears to be a domestic assault. Officers called to investigate domestic disputes need to know whom they are dealing with in order to assess the situation, the threat to their own safety, and possible danger to the potential victim.

Although it is well established that an officer may ask a suspect to identify himself in the course of a *Terry* stop, it has been an open question whether the suspect can be arrested and prosecuted for refusal to answer.

The principles of *Terry* permit a State to require a suspect to disclose his name in the course of a *Terry* stop. The reasonableness of a seizure under the Fourth Amendment is determined "by balancing its intrusion on the individual's Fourth Amendment interests against its promotion of legitimate government interests." The Nevada statute satisfies that standard. The request for identity has an immediate relation to the purpose, rationale, and practical demands of a *Terry* stop. The threat of criminal sanction helps ensure that the request for identity does not become a legal nullity. On the other hand, the Nevada statute does not alter the nature of the stop itself: it does not change its duration or its location. A state law requiring a suspect to disclose his name in the course of a valid *Terry* stop is consistent with Fourth Amendment prohibitions against unreasonable searches and seizures.

Petitioner argues that the Nevada statute circumvents the probable-cause requirement, in effect allowing an officer to arrest a person for being suspicious. According to petitioner, this creates a risk of arbitrary police conduct that the Fourth Amendment does not permit. These are familiar concerns. Petitioner's concerns are met by the requirement that a *Terry* stop must be justified at its inception and "reasonably related in scope to the circumstances which justified" the initial stop. Under these principles, an officer may not arrest a suspect for failure to identify himself if the request for identification is not reasonably related to the circumstances justifying the stop.

It is clear in this case that the request for identification was "reasonably related in scope to the circumstances which justified" the stop. The officer's request was a commonsense inquiry, not an effort to obtain an arrest for failure to identify after a *Terry* stop yielded insufficient evidence. The stop, the request, and the State's requirement of a response did not contravene the guarantees of the Fourth Amendment.

[The Court then rejected the argument that requiring a person to identify him- or herself in such circumstances violates the Fifth Amendment privilege against self-incrimination.]

[Justice Stevens dissented on the grounds that there was a Fifth Amendment violation.]

Justice BREYER, with whom Justice SOUTER and Justice GINSBURG join, dissenting.

[T]his Court's Fourth Amendment precedents make clear that police may conduct a *Terry* stop only within circumscribed limits. And one of those limits invalidates laws that compel responses to police questioning.

There is no good reason now to reject this generation-old statement of the law. There are sound reasons rooted in Fifth Amendment considerations for adhering to this Fourth Amendment legal condition circumscribing police authority to stop an individual against his will. Administrative considerations also militate against change. Can a State, in addition to requiring a stopped individual to answer "What's your name?" also require an answer to "What's your license number?" or "Where do you live?" Can a police officer, who must know how to make a *Terry* stop, keep track of the constitutional answers? After all, answers to any of these questions may, or may not, incriminate, depending upon the circumstances.

The majority presents no evidence that the rule which for nearly a generation has set forth a settled *Terry* stop condition, has significantly interfered with law enforcement. Nor has the majority presented any other convincing justification for change. I would not begin to erode a clear rule with special exceptions.

4.   What Is Sufficient for Reasonable Suspicion?

Terry v. Ohio draws a distinction between reasonable suspicion and probable cause. This, of course, is a distinction that appears elsewhere in the law of the Fourth Amendment. For example, as explained earlier, in New Jersey v. T.L.O., 469 U.S. 325 (1969), the Court held that school officials may search a student's purse based on reasonable suspicion.

But such phrases as "reasonable suspicion" and "probable cause" do not lend themselves to precise definitions. There is no bright-line rule for determining what is sufficient for reasonable suspicion. But the Supreme Court has considered this question in a number of contexts. A few of these are presented below: reasonable suspicion for stopping cars, reasonable suspicion based on informants' tips, reasonable suspicion based on a person's trying to avoid a police officer, and reasonable suspicions based on profiles. This, of course, is not an exhaustive list, but these are some of the key situations so far in which the Court has confronted the question of what is enough for reasonable suspicion.

a.   Reasonable Suspicion: General Principles

Can many facts, which themselves are not evidence of any crime, be taken together to create reasonable suspicion to stop a car?

UNITED STATES v. ARVIZU

534 U.S. 266 (2002)

Chief Justice Rehnquist delivered the opinion of the Court.

Respondent Ralph Arvizu was stopped by a border patrol agent while driving on an unpaved road in a remote area of southeastern Arizona. A search of his vehicle turned up more than 100 pounds of marijuana. The District Court for the District of Arizona denied respondent's motion to suppress, but the Court of Appeals for the Ninth Circuit reversed. In the course of its opinion, it categorized certain factors relied upon by the District Court as simply out of bounds in deciding whether there was "reasonable suspicion" for the stop. We hold that the Court of Appeals' methodology was contrary to our prior decisions and that it reached the wrong result in this case.

On an afternoon in January 1998, Agent Clinton Stoddard was working at a border patrol checkpoint along U.S. Highway 191 approximately 30 miles north of Douglas, Arizona. Douglas has a population of about 13,000 and is situated on the United States-Mexico border in the southeastern part of the State. Only two highways lead north from Douglas. Highway 191 leads north to Interstate 10, which passes through Tucson and Phoenix. State Highway 80 heads northeast through less populated areas toward New Mexico, skirting south and east of the portion of the Coronado National Forest that lies approximately 20 miles northeast of Douglas.

The checkpoint is located at the intersection of 191 and Rucker Canyon Road, an unpaved east-west road that connects 191 and the Coronado National Forest. When the checkpoint is operational, border patrol agents stop the traffic on 191 as part of a coordinated effort to stem the flow of illegal immigration and smuggling across the international border. Agents use roving patrols to apprehend smugglers trying to circumvent the checkpoint by taking the backroads, including those roads through the sparsely populated area between Douglas and the national forest. Magnetic sensors, or "intrusion devices," facilitate agents' efforts in patrolling these areas. Directionally sensitive, the sensors signal the passage of traffic that would be consistent with smuggling activities.

Around 2:15 p.m., Stoddard received a report via Douglas radio that a Leslie Canyon Road sensor had been triggered. This was significant to Stoddard for two reasons. First, it suggested to him that a vehicle might be trying to circumvent the checkpoint. Second, the timing coincided with the point when agents begin heading back to the checkpoint for a shift change, which leaves the area unpatrolled. Stoddard knew that alien smugglers did extensive scouting and seemed to be most active when agents were en route back to the checkpoint. Another border patrol agent told Stoddard that the same sensor had gone off several weeks before and that he had apprehended a minivan using the same route and witnessed the occupants throwing bundles of marijuana out the door.

Stoddard drove eastbound on Rucker Canyon Road to investigate. As he did so, he received another radio report of sensor activity. It indicated that the vehicle that had triggered the first sensor was heading westbound on Rucker Canyon Road. He saw the dust trail of an approaching vehicle about a half mile away. Stoddard had not seen any other vehicles and, based on the timing, believed that this was the one that had tripped the sensors. He pulled off to the side of the road at a slight slant so he could get a good look at the oncoming vehicle as it passed by.

It was a minivan, a type of automobile that Stoddard knew smugglers used. As it approached, it slowed dramatically, from about 50-55 to 25-30 miles per hour. He saw five occupants inside. An adult man was driving, an adult woman sat in the front passenger seat, and three children were in the back. The driver appeared stiff and his posture very rigid. He did not look at Stoddard and seemed to be trying to pretend that Stoddard was not there. Stoddard thought this suspicious because in his experience on patrol most persons look over and see what is going on, and in that area most drivers give border patrol agents a friendly wave. Stoddard noticed that the knees of the two children sitting in the very back seat were unusually high, as if their feet were propped up on some cargo on the floor.

At that point, Stoddard decided to get a closer look, so he began to follow the vehicle as it continued westbound on Rucker Canyon Road toward Kuykendall Cutoff Road. Shortly thereafter, all of the children, though still facing forward, put their hands up at the same time and began to wave at Stoddard in an abnormal pattern. It looked to Stoddard as if the children were being instructed. Their odd waving continued on and off for about four to five minutes.

Several hundred feet before the Kuykendall Cutoff Road intersection, the driver signaled that he would turn. At one point, the driver turned the signal off, but just as he approached the intersection he put it back on and abruptly turned north onto Kuykendall. The turn was significant to Stoddard because it was made at the last place that would have allowed the minivan to avoid the checkpoint. Also, Kuykendall, though passable by a sedan or van, is rougher than either Rucker Canyon or Leslie Canyon Roads, and the normal traffic is four-wheel-drive vehicles. Stoddard did not recognize the minivan as part of the local traffic agents encounter on patrol and he did not think it likely that the minivan was going to or coming from a picnic outing. He was not aware of any picnic grounds on Turkey Creek, which could be reached by following Kuykendall Cutoff all the way up.

Stoddard radioed for a registration check and learned that the minivan was registered to an address in Douglas that was four blocks north of the border in an area notorious for alien and narcotics smuggling. After receiving the information, Stoddard decided to make a vehicle stop. He approached the driver and learned that his name was Ralph Arvizu. Stoddard asked if respondent would mind if he looked inside and searched the vehicle. Respondent agreed, and Stoddard discovered marijuana in a black duffel bag under the feet of the two children in the back seat. Another bag containing marijuana was behind the rear seat. *Id.*, at 46. In all, the van contained 128.85 pounds of marijuana, worth an estimated $99,080.

Respondent was charged with possession with intent to distribute marijuana. He moved to suppress the marijuana, arguing among other things that Stoddard did not have reasonable suspicion to stop the vehicle as required by the Fourth Amendment.

The Fourth Amendment prohibits "unreasonable searches and seizures" by the Government, and its protections extend to brief investigatory stops of persons or vehicles that fall short of traditional arrest. Because the "balance between the public interest and the individual's right to personal security," tilts in favor of a standard less than probable cause in such cases, the Fourth

Amendment is satisfied if the officer's action is supported by reasonable suspicion to believe that criminal activity "may be afoot."

When discussing how reviewing courts should make reasonable-suspicion determinations, we have said repeatedly that they must look at the "totality of the circumstances" of each case to see whether the detaining officer has a "particularized and objective basis" for suspecting legal wrongdoing. This process allows officers to draw on their own experience and specialized training to make inferences from and deductions about the cumulative information available to them that "might well elude an untrained person." Although an officer's reliance on a mere "hunch" is insufficient to justify a stop, the likelihood of criminal activity need not rise to the level required for probable cause, and it falls considerably short of satisfying a preponderance of the evidence standard.

Our cases have recognized that the concept of reasonable suspicion is somewhat abstract. But we have deliberately avoided reducing it to "a neat set of legal rules."

We think that the approach taken by the Court of Appeals here departs sharply from the teachings of these cases. The court's evaluation and rejection of seven of the listed factors in isolation from each other does not take into account the "totality of the circumstances," as our cases have understood that phrase. The court appeared to believe that each observation by Stoddard that was by itself readily susceptible to an innocent explanation was entitled to "no weight." *Terry*, however, precludes this sort of divide-and-conquer analysis. The officer in *Terry* observed the petitioner and his companions repeatedly walk back and forth, look into a store window, and confer with one another. Although each of the series of acts was "perhaps innocent in itself," we held that, taken together, they "warranted further investigation."

Having considered the totality of the circumstances and given due weight to the factual inferences drawn by the law enforcement officer and District Court Judge, we hold that Stoddard had reasonable suspicion to believe that respondent was engaged in illegal activity. It was reasonable for Stoddard to infer from his observations, his registration check, and his experience as a border patrol agent that respondent had set out from Douglas along a little-traveled route used by smugglers to avoid the 191 checkpoint. Stoddard's knowledge further supported a commonsense inference that respondent intended to pass through the area at a time when officers would be leaving their backroads patrols to change shifts. The likelihood that respondent and his family were on a picnic outing was diminished by the fact that the minivan had turned away from the known recreational areas accessible to the east on Rucker Canyon Road. Corroborating this inference was the fact that recreational areas farther to the north would have been easier to reach by taking 191, as opposed to the 40-to-50-mile trip on unpaved and primitive roads. The children's elevated knees suggested the existence of concealed cargo in the passenger compartment. Finally, for the reasons we have given, Stoddard's assessment of respondent's reactions upon seeing him and the children's mechanical-like waving, which continued for a full four to five minutes, were entitled to some weight.

Respondent argues that we must rule in his favor because the facts suggested a family in a minivan on a holiday outing. A determination that reasonable suspicion exists, however, need not rule out the possibility of innocent conduct. Undoubtedly, each of these factors alone is susceptible of innocent explanation, and some factors are more probative than others. Taken together, we believe they sufficed to form a particularized and objective basis for Stoddard's stopping the vehicle, making the stop reasonable within the meaning of the Fourth Amendment.

b. Reasonable Suspicion Based on Informants' Tips

In Illinois v. Gates, 462 U.S. 213 (1983), presented above, the Court considered when an informant's tip is sufficient for probable cause. What is a sufficient tip to meet the standard of reasonable suspicion? In assessing this, compare the following two cases, Alabama v. White and Florida v. J.L.

ALABAMA v. WHITE
496 U.S. 325 (1990)

Justice WHITE delivered the opinion of the Court.

Based on an anonymous telephone tip, police stopped respondent's vehicle. A consensual search of the car revealed drugs. The issue is whether the tip, as corroborated by independent police work, exhibited sufficient indicia of reliability to provide reasonable suspicion to make the investigatory stop. We hold that it did.

On April 22, 1987, at approximately 3 P.M., Corporal B. H. Davis of the Montgomery Police Department received a telephone call from an anonymous person, stating that Vanessa White would be leaving 235-C Lynwood Terrace Apartments at a particular time in a brown Plymouth station wagon with the right taillight lens broken, that she would be going to Dobey's Motel, and that she would be in possession of about an ounce of cocaine inside a brown attaché case.

Corporal Davis and his partner, Corporal P. A. Reynolds, proceeded to the Lynwood Terrace Apartments. The officers saw a brown Plymouth station wagon with a broken right taillight in the parking lot in front of the 235 building. The officers observed respondent leave the 235 building, carrying nothing in her hands, and enter the station wagon. They followed the vehicle as it drove the most direct route to Dobey's Motel. When the vehicle reached the Mobile Highway, on which Dobey's Motel is located, Corporal Reynolds requested a patrol unit to stop the vehicle. The vehicle was stopped at approximately 4:18 P.M., just short of Dobey's Motel. Corporal Davis asked respondent to step to the rear of her car, where he informed her that she had been stopped because she was suspected of carrying cocaine in the vehicle. He asked if they could look for cocaine, and respondent said they could look. The officers found a locked brown attaché case in the car, and, upon request, respondent provided the combination to the lock. The officers found marijuana in the attaché case and placed respondent under arrest. During processing at the station, the officers found three milligrams of cocaine in respondent's purse.

Respondent was charged in Montgomery County Court with possession of marijuana and possession of cocaine. The trial court denied respondent's motion to suppress, and she pleaded guilty to the charges, reserving the right to appeal the denial of her suppression motion. The Court of Criminal Appeals of Alabama held that the officers did not have the reasonable suspicion necessary under Terry v. Ohio (1968) to justify the investigatory stop of respondent's car, and that the marijuana and cocaine were fruits of respondent's unconstitutional detention.

Adams v. Williams (1972) sustained a *Terry* stop and frisk undertaken on the basis of a tip given in person by a known informant who had provided information in the past. We concluded that, while the unverified tip may have been insufficient to support an arrest or search warrant, the information carried sufficient "indicia of reliability" to justify a forcible stop. We did not address the issue of anonymous tips in *Adams*, except to say that "[t]his is a stronger case than obtains in the case of an anonymous telephone tip."

Illinois v. Gates (1983), dealt with an anonymous tip in the probable-cause context. The Court there abandoned the "two-pronged test" of Aguilar v. Texas (1964), and Spinelli v. United States (1969), in favor of a "totality of the circumstances" approach to determining whether an informant's tip establishes probable cause. *Gates* made clear, however, that those factors that had been considered critical under *Aguilar* and *Spinelli* — an informant's "veracity," "reliability," and "basis of knowledge" — remain "highly relevant in determining the value of his report." These factors are also relevant in the reasonable-suspicion context, although allowance must be made in applying them for the lesser showing required to meet that standard.

The opinion in *Gates* recognized that an anonymous tip alone seldom demonstrates the informant's basis of knowledge or veracity inasmuch as ordinary citizens generally do not provide extensive recitations of the basis of their everyday observations and given that the veracity of persons supplying anonymous tips is "by hypothesis largely unknown, and unknowable." This is not to say that an anonymous caller could never provide the reasonable suspicion necessary for a *Terry* stop.

Simply put, a tip such as this one, standing alone, would not "'warrant a man of reasonable caution in the belief' that [a stop] was appropriate." As there was in *Gates*, however, in this case there is more than the tip itself. The tip was not as detailed, and the corroboration was not as complete, as in

Gates, but the required degree of suspicion was likewise not as high. Reasonable suspicion is a less demanding standard than probable cause not only in the sense that reasonable suspicion can be established with information that is different in quantity or content than that required to establish probable cause, but also in the sense that reasonable suspicion can arise from information that is less reliable than that required to show probable cause. Adams v. Williams demonstrates as much. We there assumed that the unverified tip from the known informant might not have been reliable enough to establish probable cause, but nevertheless found it sufficiently reliable to justify a *Terry* stop. Reasonable suspicion, like probable cause, is dependent upon both the content of information possessed by police and its degree of reliability. Both factors—quantity and quality—are considered in the "totality of the circumstances—the whole picture," that must be taken into account when evaluating whether there is reasonable suspicion. Thus, if a tip has a relatively low degree of reliability, more information will be required to establish the requisite quantum of suspicion than would be required if the tip were more reliable. The *Gates* Court applied its totality-of-the-circumstances approach in this manner, taking into account the facts known to the officers from personal observation, and giving the anonymous tip the weight it deserved in light of its indicia of reliability as established through independent police work. The same approach applies in the reasonable-suspicion context, the only difference being the level of suspicion that must be established.

Contrary to the court below, we conclude that when the officers stopped respondent, the anonymous tip had been sufficiently corroborated to furnish reasonable suspicion that respondent was engaged in criminal activity and that the investigative stop therefore did not violate the Fourth Amendment.

We think it also important that, as in *Gates*, "the anonymous [tip] contained a range of details relating not just to easily obtained facts and conditions existing at the time of the tip, but to future actions of third parties ordinarily not easily predicted." The fact that the officers found a car precisely matching the caller's description in front of the 235 building is an example of the former. Anyone could have "predicted" that fact because it was a condition presumably existing at the time of the call. What was important was the caller's ability to predict respondent's future behavior, because it demonstrated inside information—a special familiarity with respondent's affairs. The general public would have had no way of knowing that respondent would shortly leave the building, get in the described car, and drive the most direct route to Dobey's Motel. Because only a small number of people are generally privy to an individual's itinerary, it is reasonable for police to believe that a person with access to such information is likely to also have access to reliable information about that individual's illegal activities. When significant aspects of the caller's predictions were verified, there was reason to believe not only that the caller was honest but also that he was well informed, at least well enough to justify the stop.

Although it is a close case, we conclude that under the totality of the circumstances the anonymous tip, as corroborated, exhibited sufficient indicia of reliability to justify the investigatory stop of respondent's car.

Justice STEVENS, with whom Justice BRENNAN and Justice MARSHALL join, dissenting.

Millions of people leave their apartments at about the same time every day carrying an attaché case and heading for a destination known to their neighbors. Usually, however, the neighbors do not know what the briefcase contains. An anonymous neighbor's prediction about somebody's time of departure and probable destination is anything but a reliable basis for assuming that the commuter is in possession of an illegal substance — particularly when the person is not even carrying the attaché case described by the tipster.

The record in this case does not tell us how often respondent drove from the Lynwood Terrace Apartments to Dobey's Motel; for all we know, she may have been a room clerk or telephone operator working the evening shift. It does not tell us whether Officer Davis made any effort to ascertain the informer's identity, his reason for calling, or the basis of his prediction about respondent's destination. Indeed, for all that this record tells us, the tipster may well have been another police officer who had a "hunch" that respondent might have cocaine in her attaché case.

Anybody with enough knowledge about a given person to make her the target of a prank, or to harbor a grudge against her, will certainly be able to formulate a tip about her like the one predicting Vanessa White's excursion. In addition, under the Court's holding, every citizen is subject to being seized and questioned by any officer who is prepared to testify that the warrantless stop was based on an anonymous tip predicting whatever conduct the officer just observed. Fortunately, the vast majority of those in our law enforcement community would not adopt such a practice. But the Fourth Amendment was intended to protect the citizen from the overzealous and unscrupulous officer as well as from those who are conscientious and truthful. This decision makes a mockery of that protection.

FLORIDA v. J.L.
529 U.S. 266 (2000)

Justice GINSBURG delivered the opinion of the Court.

The question presented in this case is whether an anonymous tip that a person is carrying a gun is, without more, sufficient to justify a police officer's stop and frisk of that person. We hold that it is not.

I

On October 13, 1995, an anonymous caller reported to the Miami-Dade Police that a young black male standing at a particular bus stop and wearing a plaid shirt was carrying a gun. So far as the record reveals, there is no audio recording of the tip, and nothing is known about the informant. Sometime after the police received the tip — the record does not say how long — two officers were instructed to respond. They arrived at the bus stop about six minutes later and saw three black males "just hanging out [there]." One of the three, respondent J.L., was wearing a plaid shirt. Apart from the tip, the officers had no reason to suspect any of the three of illegal conduct. The officers did not see a firearm, and J.L. made no threatening or otherwise unusual movements.

One of the officers approached J.L., told him to put his hands up on the bus stop, frisked him, and seized a gun from J.L.'s pocket. The second officer frisked the other two individuals, against whom no allegations had been made, and found nothing.

J.L., who was at the time of the frisk "10 days shy of his 16th birth[day]," was charged under state law with carrying a concealed firearm without a license and possessing a firearm while under the age of 18. He moved to suppress the gun as the fruit of an unlawful search, and the trial court granted his motion. The intermediate appellate court reversed, but the Supreme Court of Florida quashed that decision and held the search invalid under the Fourth Amendment.

II

In the instant case, the officers' suspicion that J.L. was carrying a weapon arose not from any observations of their own but solely from a call made from an unknown location by an unknown caller. Unlike a tip from a known informant whose reputation can be assessed and who can be held responsible if her allegations turn out to be fabricated, *see* Adams v. Williams (1972), "an anonymous tip alone seldom demonstrates the informant's basis of knowledge or veracity." As we have recognized, however, there are situations in which an anonymous tip, suitably corroborated, exhibits "sufficient indicia of reliability to provide reasonable suspicion to make the investigatory stop." The question we here confront is whether the tip pointing to J.L. had those indicia of reliability.

The tip in the instant case lacked the moderate indicia of reliability present in *White* and essential to the Court's decision in that case. The anonymous call concerning J.L. provided no predictive information and therefore left the police without means to test the informant's knowledge or credibility. That the allegation about the gun turned out to be correct does not suggest that the officers, prior to the frisks, had a reasonable basis for suspecting J.L. of engaging in unlawful conduct: The reasonableness of official suspicion must be measured by what the officers knew before they conducted their search. All the police had to go on in this case was the bare report of an unknown, unaccountable informant who neither explained how he knew about the gun nor supplied any basis for believing he had inside information about J.L. If *White* was a close case on the reliability of anonymous tips, this one surely falls on the other side of the line.

Florida contends that the tip was reliable because its description of the suspect's visible attributes proved accurate: There really was a young black male wearing a plaid shirt at the bus stop. These contentions misapprehend the reliability needed for a tip to justify a *Terry* stop.

An accurate description of a subject's readily observable location and appearance is of course reliable in this limited sense: It will help the police correctly identify the person whom the tipster means to accuse. Such a tip, however, does not show that the tipster has knowledge of concealed criminal activity. The reasonable suspicion here at issue requires that a tip be reliable in its assertion of illegality, not just in its tendency to identify a determinate person.

A second major argument advanced by Florida and the United States as amicus is, in essence, that the standard *Terry* analysis should be modified to license a "firearm exception." Under such an exception, a tip alleging an illegal gun would justify a stop and frisk even if the accusation would fail standard pre-search reliability testing. We decline to adopt this position.

Firearms are dangerous, and extraordinary dangers sometimes justify unusual precautions. Our decisions recognize the serious threat that armed criminals pose to public safety; *Terry*'s rule, which permits protective police searches on the basis of reasonable suspicion rather than demanding that officers meet the higher standard of probable cause, responds to this very concern. But an automatic firearm exception to our established reliability analysis would rove too far. Such an exception would enable any person seeking to harass another to set in motion an intrusive, embarrassing police search of the targeted person simply by placing an anonymous call falsely reporting the target's unlawful carriage of a gun. Nor could one securely confine such an exception to allegations involving firearms. If police officers may properly conduct *Terry* frisks on the basis of bare-boned tips about guns, it would be reasonable to maintain that the police should similarly have discretion to frisk based on bare-boned tips about narcotics.

The facts of this case do not require us to speculate about the circumstances under which the danger alleged in an anonymous tip might be so great as to justify a search even without a showing of reliability. We do not say, for example, that a report of a person carrying a bomb need bear the indicia of reliability we demand for a report of a person carrying a firearm before the police can constitutionally conduct a frisk. Nor do we hold that public safety officials in quarters where the reasonable expectation of Fourth Amendment privacy is diminished, such as airports and schools, cannot conduct protective searches on the basis of information insufficient to justify searches elsewhere.

Finally, the requirement that an anonymous tip bear standard indicia of reliability in order to justify a stop in no way diminishes a police officer's prerogative, in accord with *Terry*, to conduct a protective search of a person who has already been legitimately stopped. We speak in today's decision only of cases in which the officer's authority to make the initial stop is at issue. In that context, we hold that an anonymous tip lacking indicia of reliability of the kind contemplated in *Adams* and *White* does not justify a stop and frisk whenever and however it alleges the illegal possession of a firearm.

What if police pull over a car based on an anonymous tip that the driver was driving erratically? That is the issue in Navarette v. California and the Court holds, 5-4, that an anonymous tip is sufficient for a stop in this context. In light of the prior cases, should this be sufficient?

NAVARETTE v. CALIFORNIA
134 S. Ct. 1683 (2014)

Justice THOMAS delivered the opinion of the Court.

After a 911 caller reported that a vehicle had run her off the road, a police officer located the vehicle she identified during the call and executed a traffic stop. We hold that the stop complied with the Fourth Amendment because, under the totality of the circumstances, the officer had reasonable suspicion that the driver was intoxicated.

I

On August 23, 2008, a Mendocino County 911 dispatch team for the California Highway Patrol (CHP) received a call from another CHP dispatcher in neighboring Humboldt County. The Humboldt County dispatcher relayed a tip from a 911 caller, which the Mendocino County team recorded as follows: "'Showing southbound Highway 1 at mile marker 88, Silver Ford 150 pickup. Plate of 8-David-94925. Ran the reporting party off the roadway and was last seen approximately five [minutes] ago.'" The Mendocino County team then broadcast that information to CHP officers at 3:47 P.M.

A CHP officer heading northbound toward the reported vehicle responded to the broadcast. At 4:00 P.M., the officer passed the truck near mile marker 69. At about 4:05 P.M., after making a U-turn, he pulled the truck over. A second officer, who had separately responded to the broadcast, also arrived on the scene. As the two officers approached the truck, they smelled marijuana. A search of the truck bed revealed 30 pounds of marijuana. The officers arrested the driver, petitioner Lorenzo Prado Navarette, and the passenger, petitioner José Prado Navarette.

II

The Fourth Amendment permits brief investigative stops — such as the traffic stop in this case — when a law enforcement officer has "a particularized and objective basis for suspecting the particular person stopped of criminal activity." The "reasonable suspicion" necessary to justify such a stop "is dependent upon both the content of information possessed by police and its degree of reliability." The standard takes into account "the totality of the circumstances — the whole picture." Although a mere "'hunch'" does not create reasonable suspicion, the level of suspicion the standard requires is "considerably less than proof of wrongdoing by a preponderance of the evidence," and "obviously less" than is necessary for probable cause.

These principles apply with full force to investigative stops based on information from anonymous tips. We have firmly rejected the argument "that reasonable cause for a[n investigative stop] can only be based on the officer's personal observation, rather than on information supplied by another person." Of course, "an anonymous tip *alone* seldom demonstrates the informant's basis of knowledge or veracity." That is because "ordinary citizens generally do not provide extensive recitations of the basis of their everyday observations," and an anonymous tipster's veracity is "'by hypothesis largely unknown, and unknowable.'" But under appropriate circumstances, an anonymous tip can demonstrate "sufficient indicia of reliability to provide reasonable suspicion to make [an] investigatory stop."

Our decisions in Alabama v. White (1990), and Florida v. J. L. (2000), are useful guides. In *White,* an anonymous tipster told the police that a woman would drive from a particular apartment building to a particular motel in a brown Plymouth station wagon with a broken right tail light. The tipster further asserted that the woman would be transporting cocaine. After confirming the innocent details, officers stopped the station wagon as it neared the motel and found cocaine in the vehicle. We held that the officers' corroboration of certain details made the anonymous tip sufficiently reliable to create reasonable suspicion of criminal activity. By accurately predicting future behavior, the tipster demonstrated "a special familiarity with respondent's affairs," which in turn implied that the tipster had "access to reliable information about that individual's illegal activities."

In *J. L.,* by contrast, we determined that no reasonable suspicion arose from a bare-bones tip that a young black male in a plaid shirt standing at a bus stop was carrying a gun. The tipster did not explain how he knew about the gun, nor did he suggest that he had any special familiarity with the young man's affairs. As a result, police had no basis for believing "that the tipster ha[d] knowledge of concealed criminal activity." Furthermore, the tip included no predictions of future behavior that could be corroborated to assess the tipster's credibility. We accordingly concluded that the tip was insufficiently reliable to justify a stop and frisk.

The initial question in this case is whether the 911 call was sufficiently reliable to credit the allegation that petitioners' truck "ran the [caller] off the roadway." Even assuming for present purposes that the 911 call was anonymous, we conclude that the call bore adequate indicia of reliability for the officer to credit the caller's account. The officer was therefore justified in proceeding from the premise that the truck had, in fact, caused the caller's car to be dangerously diverted from the highway.

By reporting that she had been run off the road by a specific vehicle — a silver Ford F-150 pickup, license plate 8D94925 — the caller necessarily claimed eyewitness knowledge of the alleged dangerous driving. That basis of knowledge lends significant support to the tip's reliability. A driver's claim that another vehicle ran her off the road, however, necessarily implies that the informant knows the other car was driven dangerously.

There is also reason to think that the 911 caller in this case was telling the truth. Police confirmed the truck's location near mile marker 69 (roughly 19 highway miles south of the location reported in the 911 call) at 4:00 P.M. (roughly 18 minutes after the 911 call). That timeline of events suggests that the caller reported the incident soon after she was run off the road. That sort of contemporaneous report has long been treated as especially reliable. In evidence law, we generally credit the proposition that statements about an event and made soon after perceiving that event are especially trustworthy because "substantial contemporaneity of event and statement negate the likelihood of deliberate or conscious misrepresentation."

As this case illustrates, 911 calls can be recorded, which provides victims with an opportunity to identify the false tipster's voice and subject him to prosecution. The 911 system also permits law enforcement to verify important information about the caller. None of this is to suggest that tips in 911 calls are *per se* reliable. Given the foregoing technological and regulatory developments, however, a reasonable officer could conclude that a false tipster would think twice before using such a system. The caller's use of the 911 system is therefore one of the relevant circumstances that, taken together, justified the officer's reliance on the information reported in the 911 call.

Even a reliable tip will justify an investigative stop only if it creates reasonable suspicion that "criminal activity may be afoot." We must therefore determine whether the 911 caller's report of being run off the roadway created reasonable suspicion of an ongoing crime such as drunk driving as opposed to an isolated episode of past recklessness. We conclude that the behavior alleged by the 911 caller, "viewed from the standpoint of an objectively reasonable police officer, amount[s] to reasonable suspicion" of drunk driving. The stop was therefore proper.

Reasonable suspicion depends on "the factual and practical considerations of everyday life on which reasonable and prudent men, not legal technicians, act." Under that commonsense approach, we can appropriately recognize certain driving behaviors as sound indicia of drunk driving. Indeed, the accumulated experience of thousands of officers suggests that these sorts of erratic behaviors are strongly correlated with drunk driving. Of course, not all traffic infractions imply intoxication. Unconfirmed reports of driving without a seatbelt or slightly over the speed limit, for example, are so tenuously connected to drunk driving that a stop on those grounds alone would be constitutionally suspect. But a reliable tip alleging the dangerous behaviors discussed above generally would justify a traffic stop on suspicion of drunk driving.

The 911 caller in this case reported more than a minor traffic infraction and more than a conclusory allegation of drunk or reckless driving. Instead, she alleged a specific and dangerous result of the driver's conduct: running another car off the highway. That conduct bears too great a resemblance to paradigmatic manifestations of drunk driving to be dismissed as an isolated example of recklessness. Running another vehicle off the road suggests lane-positioning problems, decreased vigilance, impaired judgment, or some combination of those recognized drunk driving cues. And the experience of many officers suggests that a driver who almost strikes a vehicle or another object — the exact scenario that ordinarily causes "running [another vehicle] off the roadway" — is likely intoxicated. As a result, we cannot say that the officer acted unreasonably under these circumstances in stopping a driver whose alleged conduct was a significant indicator of drunk driving.

Petitioners' attempts to second-guess the officer's reasonable suspicion of drunk driving are unavailing. It is true that the reported behavior might also be explained by, for example, a driver responding to "an unruly child or other distraction." But we have consistently recognized that reasonable suspicion "need not rule out the possibility of innocent conduct."

Nor did the absence of additional suspicious conduct, after the vehicle was first spotted by an officer, dispel the reasonable suspicion of drunk driving. It is hardly surprising that the appearance of a marked police car would inspire more careful driving for a time. Extended observation of an allegedly drunk driver might eventually dispel a reasonable suspicion of intoxication, but the 5-minute period in this case hardly sufficed in that regard. Of course, an officer who already has such a reasonable suspicion need not surveil a vehicle at length in order to personally observe suspicious driving. This would be a particularly inappropriate context to depart from that settled rule, because allowing a drunk driver a second chance for dangerous conduct could have disastrous consequences.

III

Like *White*, this is a "close case." Under the totality of the circumstances, we find the indicia of reliability in this case sufficient to provide the officer with reasonable suspicion that the driver of the reported vehicle had run another vehicle off the road. That made it reasonable under the circumstances for the officer to execute a traffic stop. We accordingly affirm.

Justice SCALIA, with whom Justice GINSBURG, Justice SOTOMAYOR, and Justice KAGAN join, dissenting.

Today's opinion does not explicitly adopt a departure from our normal Fourth Amendment requirement that anonymous tips must be corroborated; it purports to adhere to our prior cases. Be not deceived.

Law enforcement agencies follow closely our judgments on matters such as this, and they will identify at once our new rule: So long as the caller identifies where the car is, anonymous claims of a single instance of possibly careless or reckless driving, called in to 911, will support a traffic stop. This is not my concept, and I am sure would not be the Framers', of a people secure from unreasonable searches and seizures.

I

The California Highway Patrol in this case knew nothing about the tipster on whose word — and that alone — they seized Lorenzo and José Prado Navarette. They did not know her name. They did not know her phone number or address. They did not even know where she called from (she may have dialed in from a neighboring county).

The tipster said the truck had "[run her] off the roadway," but the police had no reason to credit that charge and many reasons to doubt it, beginning with the peculiar fact that the accusation was anonymous. "[E]liminating accountability . . . is ordinarily the very purpose of anonymity." The unnamed tipster "can lie with impunity." Anonymity is especially suspicious with respect to the call that is the subject of the present case. When does a victim complain to the police about an arguably criminal act (running the victim off the road) without giving his identity, so that he can accuse and testify when the culprit is caught?

The question before us, the Court agrees, is whether the "content of information possessed by police and its degree of reliability," gave the officers reasonable suspicion that the driver of the truck (Lorenzo) was committing an ongoing crime. When the only source of the government's information is an informant's tip, we ask whether the tip bears sufficient "indicia of reliability," to establish "a particularized and objective basis for suspecting the particular person stopped of criminal activity."

Here the Court makes a big deal of the fact that the tipster was dead right about the fact that a silver Ford F-150 truck (license plate 8D94925) was traveling south on Highway 1 somewhere near mile marker 88. But everyone in the world who saw the car would have that knowledge, and anyone who wanted the car stopped would have to provide that information.

The Court says, that "[b]y reporting that she had been run off the road by a specific vehicle . . . the caller necessarily claimed eyewitness knowledge." So what? The issue is not how she claimed to know, but whether what she claimed to know was true. The claim to "eyewitness knowledge" of being run off the road supports *not at all* its veracity; nor does the amazing, mystifying prediction (so far short of what existed in *White*) that the petitioners' truck *would be heading south on Highway 1.*

The Court finds "reason to think" that the informant "was telling the truth" in the fact that police observation confirmed that the truck had been driving near the spot at which, and at the approximate time at which, the tipster alleged she had been run off the road. So, the Court says, we can fairly suppose that the accusation was true.

No, we cannot. [T]he Court says that another "indicator of veracity" is the anonymous tipster's mere "use of the 911 emergency system," Because, you see, recent "technological and regulatory developments" suggest that the identities of unnamed 911 callers are increasingly less likely to remain unknown. Indeed, the systems are able to identify "the caller's geographic location with increasing specificity." *Amici* disagree with this, see Brief for National Association of Criminal Defense Lawyers and the present case surely suggests that *amici* are right — since we know neither the identity of the tipster nor even the county from which the call was made. But assuming the Court is right about the ease of identifying 911 callers, it proves absolutely nothing in the present case unless the anonymous caller was *aware* of that fact. "It is the tipster's *belief* in anonymity, not its *reality*, that will control his behavior." There is no reason to believe that your average anonymous 911 tipster is aware that 911 callers are readily identifiable.

II

All that has been said up to now assumes that the anonymous caller made, at least in effect, an accusation of drunken driving. But in fact she did not. She said that the petitioners' truck "'[r]an [me] off the roadway.'" That neither asserts that the driver was drunk nor even raises the *likelihood* that the driver was drunk. The most it conveys is that the truck did some apparently non-typical thing that forced the tipster off the roadway, whether partly or fully, temporarily or permanently. Who really knows what (if anything) happened? The truck might have swerved to avoid an animal, a pothole, or a jaywalking pedestrian.

But let us assume the worst of the many possibilities: that it was a careless, reckless, or even intentional maneuver that forced the tipster off the road. Lorenzo might have been distracted by his use of a hands-free cell phone, or distracted by an intense sports argument with Jose, Or, indeed, he might have intentionally forced the tipster off the road because of some personal animus, or hostility to her "Make Love, Not War" bumper sticker. I fail to see how reasonable suspicion of a *discrete instance* of irregular or hazardous driving generates a reasonable suspicion of *ongoing intoxicated driving.* What proportion of the hundreds of thousands — perhaps millions — of careless, reckless, or intentional traffic violations committed each day is attributable to drunken drivers? I say 0.1 percent. I have no basis for that except my own guesswork. But unless the Court has some basis in reality to believe that the proportion is many orders of magnitude above that — say 1 in 10 or at least 1 in 20 — it has no grounds for its unsupported assertion that the tipster's report in this case gave rise to a *reasonable suspicion* of drunken driving.

Bear in mind that that is the only basis for the stop that has been asserted in this litigation. The stop required suspicion of an ongoing crime, not merely suspicion of having run someone off the road earlier. And driving while being a careless or reckless person, unlike driving while being a drunk person, is not an ongoing crime. In other words, in order to stop the petitioners the officers here not only had to assume without basis the accuracy of the anonymous accusation but also had to posit an unlikely reason (drunkenness) for the accused behavior.

In sum, at the moment the police spotted the truck, it was more than merely "*possib[le]*" that the petitioners were not committing an ongoing traffic crime. It was overwhelmingly likely that they were not.

III

It gets worse. Not only, it turns out, did the police have no good reason *at first* to believe that Lorenzo was driving drunk, they had very good reason *at last* to know that he was not. The Court concludes that the tip, plus confirmation of the truck's location, produced reasonable suspicion that the truck not only had been *but still was* barreling dangerously and drunkenly down Highway 1. In fact, alas, it was not, and the officers knew it. They followed the truck for five minutes, presumably to see if it was being operated recklessly. And *that* was good police work. While the anonymous tip was not enough to support a stop for drunken driving under Terry v. Ohio (1968), it was surely enough to counsel observation of the truck to see if it was driven by a drunken driver. But the pesky little detail left out of the Court's reasonable-suspicion equation is that, for the five minutes that the truck was being followed (five minutes is a *long* time), Lorenzo's driving was irreproachable. Had the officers witnessed the petitioners violate a single traffic law, they would have had cause to stop the truck, and this case would not be before us. And not only was the driving *irreproachable,* but the State offers no evidence to suggest that the petitioners even did anything *suspicious,* such as suddenly slowing down, pulling off to the side of the road, or turning somewhere to see whether they were being followed. Consequently, the tip's suggestion of ongoing drunken driving (if it could be deemed to suggest that) not only went uncorroborated; it was affirmatively undermined.

Similarly, here, the crime supposedly suggested by the tip was ongoing intoxicated driving, the hallmarks of which are many, readily identifiable, and difficult to conceal. That the officers witnessed nary a minor traffic violation nor any other "sound indici[um] of drunk driving," strongly suggests that the suspected crime was *not* occurring after all. The tip's implication of continuing criminality, already weak, grew even weaker.

Resisting this line of reasoning, the Court curiously asserts that, since drunk drivers who see marked squad cars in their rearview mirrors may evade detection simply by driving "more careful[ly]," the "absence of additional suspicious conduct" is "hardly surprising" and thus largely irrelevant. Whether a drunk driver drives drunkenly, the Court seems to think, is up to him. That is not how I understand the influence of alcohol. I subscribe to the more traditional view that the dangers of intoxicated driving are the intoxicant's impairing effects on the body—effects that no mere act of the will can resist. Consistent with this view, I take it as a fundamental premise of our intoxicated-driving laws that a driver soused enough to swerve once can be expected to swerve again — and soon. If he does not, and if the only evidence of his first episode of irregular driving is a mere inference from an uncorroborated, vague, and nameless tip, then the Fourth Amendment requires that he be left alone.

The Court's opinion serves up a freedom-destroying cocktail consisting of two parts patent falsity: (1) that anonymous 911 reports of traffic violations are reliable so long as they correctly identify a car and its location, and (2) that a single instance of careless or reckless driving necessarily supports a reasonable suspicion of drunkenness. All the malevolent 911 caller need do is assert a traffic violation, and the targeted car will be stopped, forcibly if necessary, by the police. If the driver turns out not to be drunk (which will almost always be the case), the caller need fear no consequences, even if 911 knows his identity. After all, he never alleged drunkenness, but merely called in a traffic violation — and on that point his word is as good as his victim's.

Drunken driving is a serious matter, but so is the loss of our freedom to come and go as we please without police interference. To prevent and detect murder we do not allow searches without probable cause or targeted *Terry* stops without reasonable suspicion. We should not do so for drunken driving either. After today's opinion all of us on the road, and not just drug dealers, are at risk of having our freedom of movement curtailed on suspicion of drunkenness, based upon a phone tip, true or false, of a single instance of careless driving. I respectfully dissent.

c. Reasonable Suspicion Based on a Person's Trying to Avoid a Police Officer

Is it sufficient to create reasonable suspicion that a person sees a police officer and then walks in the opposite direction to avoid contact or even passing the officer?

ILLINOIS v. WARDLOW
528 U.S. 119 (2000)

Chief Justice Rehnquist delivered the opinion of the Court.

Respondent Wardlow fled upon seeing police officers patrolling an area known for heavy narcotics trafficking. Two of the officers caught up with him, stopped him and conducted a protective patdown search for weapons. Discovering a .38-caliber handgun, the officers arrested Wardlow. We hold that the officers' stop did not violate the Fourth Amendment to the United States Constitution.

On September 9, 1995, Officers Nolan and Harvey were working as uniformed officers in the special operations section of the Chicago Police

Department. The officers were driving the last car of a four-car caravan converging on an area known for heavy narcotics trafficking in order to investigate drug transactions. The officers were traveling together because they expected to find a crowd of people in the area, including lookouts and customers.

As the caravan passed 4035 West Van Buren, Officer Nolan observed respondent Wardlow standing next to the building holding an opaque bag. Respondent looked in the direction of the officers and fled. Nolan and Harvey turned their car southbound, watched him as he ran through the gangway and an alley, and eventually cornered him on the street. Nolan then exited his car and stopped respondent. He immediately conducted a protective patdown search for weapons because in his experience it was common for there to be weapons in the near vicinity of narcotics transactions. During the frisk, Officer Nolan squeezed the bag respondent was carrying and felt a heavy, hard object similar to the shape of a gun. The officer then opened the bag and discovered a .38-caliber handgun with five live rounds of ammunition. The officers arrested Wardlow.

The Illinois trial court denied respondent's motion to suppress, finding the gun was recovered during a lawful stop and frisk. Following a stipulated bench trial, Wardlow was convicted of unlawful use of a weapon by a felon. The Illinois Appellate Court reversed Wardlow's conviction, concluding that the gun should have been suppressed because Officer Nolan did not have reasonable suspicion sufficient to justify an investigative stop pursuant to Terry v. Ohio (1968). The Illinois Supreme Court agreed.

This case, involving a brief encounter between a citizen and a police officer on a public street, is governed by the analysis we first applied in Terry. In Terry, we held that an officer may, consistent with the Fourth Amendment, conduct a brief, investigatory stop when the officer has a reasonable, articulable suspicion that criminal activity is afoot.[12] While "reasonable suspicion" is a less demanding standard than probable cause and requires a showing considerably less than preponderance of the evidence, the Fourth Amendment requires at least a minimal level of objective justification for making the stop. The officer must be able to articulate more than an "inchoate and unparticularized suspicion or 'hunch'" of criminal activity.

Nolan and Harvey were among eight officers in a four-car caravan that was converging on an area known for heavy narcotics trafficking, and the officers anticipated encountering a large number of people in the area, including drug customers and individuals serving as lookouts. It was in this context that Officer Nolan decided to investigate Wardlow after observing him flee. An individual's presence in an area of expected criminal activity, standing alone, is not enough to support a reasonable, particularized suspicion that the person is committing a crime. But officers are not required to ignore the

---

12. We granted certiorari solely on the question whether the initial stop was supported by reasonable suspicion. Therefore, we express no opinion as to the lawfulness of the frisk independently of the stop. [Footnote by the Court.]

relevant characteristics of a location in determining whether the circumstances are sufficiently suspicious to warrant further investigation. Accordingly, we have previously noted the fact that the stop occurred in a "high crime area" among the relevant contextual considerations in a *Terry* analysis.

In this case, moreover, it was not merely respondent's presence in an area of heavy narcotics trafficking that aroused the officers' suspicion, but his unprovoked flight upon noticing the police. Our cases have also recognized that nervous, evasive behavior is a pertinent factor in determining reasonable suspicion. Headlong flight — wherever it occurs — is the consummate act of evasion: It is not necessarily indicative of wrongdoing, but it is certainly suggestive of such. In reviewing the propriety of an officer's conduct, courts do not have available empirical studies dealing with inferences drawn from suspicious behavior, and we cannot reasonably demand scientific certainty from judges or law enforcement officers where none exists. Thus, the determination of reasonable suspicion must be based on commonsense judgments and inferences about human behavior. We conclude Officer Nolan was justified in suspecting that Wardlow was involved in criminal activity, and, therefore, in investigating further.

Respondent and amici also argue that there are innocent reasons for flight from police and that, therefore, flight is not necessarily indicative of ongoing criminal activity. This fact is undoubtedly true, but does not establish a violation of the Fourth Amendment. Even in *Terry*, the conduct justifying the stop was ambiguous and susceptible of an innocent explanation. The officer observed two individuals pacing back and forth in front of a store, peering into the window and periodically conferring. All of this conduct was by itself lawful, but it also suggested that the individuals were casing the store for a planned robbery. *Terry* recognized that the officers could detain the individuals to resolve the ambiguity.

In allowing such detentions, *Terry* accepts the risk that officers may stop innocent people. Indeed, the Fourth Amendment accepts that risk in connection with more drastic police action; persons arrested and detained on probable cause to believe they have committed a crime may turn out to be innocent. The *Terry* stop is a far more minimal intrusion, simply allowing the officer to briefly investigate further. If the officer does not learn facts rising to the level of probable cause, the individual must be allowed to go on his way. But in this case the officers found respondent in possession of a handgun, and arrested him for violation of an Illinois firearms statute. No question of the propriety of the arrest itself is before us.

Justice STEVENS, with whom Justice SOUTER, Justice GINSBURG, and Justice BREYER join, concurring in part and dissenting in part.

The State of Illinois asks this Court to announce a "bright-line rule" authorizing the temporary detention of anyone who flees at the mere sight of a police officer. Respondent counters by asking us to adopt the opposite per se rule — that the fact that a person flees upon seeing the police can never, by itself, be sufficient to justify a temporary investigative stop of the kind authorized by Terry v. Ohio.

I

The Court today wisely endorses neither per se rule. Instead, it rejects the proposition that "flight is . . . necessarily indicative of ongoing criminal activity," adhering to the view that "[t]he concept of reasonable suspicion . . . is not readily, or even usefully, reduced to a neat set of legal rules," but must be determined by looking to "the totality of the circumstances — the whole picture." Abiding by this framework, the Court concludes that "Officer Nolan was justified in suspecting that Wardlow was involved in criminal activity."

Although I agree with the Court's rejection of the per se rules proffered by the parties, unlike the Court, I am persuaded that in this case the brief testimony of the officer who seized respondent does not justify the conclusion that he had reasonable suspicion to make the stop.

The question in this case concerns "the degree of suspicion that attaches to" a person's flight — or, more precisely, what "commonsense conclusions" can be drawn respecting the motives behind that flight. A pedestrian may break into a run for a variety of reasons — to catch up with a friend a block or two away, to seek shelter from an impending storm, to arrive at a bus stop before the bus leaves, to get home in time for dinner, to resume jogging after a pause for rest, to avoid contact with a bore or a bully, or simply to answer the call of nature — any of which might coincide with the arrival of an officer in the vicinity. A pedestrian might also run because he or she has just sighted one or more police officers. In the latter instance, the State properly points out "that the fleeing person may be (1) an escapee from jail; (2) wanted on a warrant; (3) in possession of contraband (i.e. drugs, weapons, stolen goods, etc.); or (4) someone who has just committed another type of crime." In short, there are unquestionably circumstances in which a person's flight is suspicious, and undeniably instances in which a person runs for entirely innocent reasons.

Given the diversity and frequency of possible motivations for flight, it would be profoundly unwise to endorse either per se rule. The inference we can reasonably draw about the motivation for a person's flight, rather, will depend on a number of different circumstances. Factors such as the time of day, the number of people in the area, the character of the neighborhood, whether the officer was in uniform, the way the runner was dressed, the direction and speed of the flight, and whether the person's behavior was otherwise unusual might be relevant in specific cases. This number of variables is surely sufficient to preclude either a bright-line rule that always justifies, or that never justifies, an investigative stop based on the sole fact that flight began after a police officer appeared nearby.

Among some citizens, particularly minorities and those residing in high crime areas, there is also the possibility that the fleeing person is entirely innocent, but, with or without justification, believes that contact with the police can itself be dangerous, apart from any criminal activity associated with the officer's sudden presence. For such a person, unprovoked flight is neither "aberrant" nor "abnormal." Moreover, these concerns and fears are known to the police officers themselves, and are validated by law enforcement investigations into their own practices.

"Unprovoked flight," in short, describes a category of activity too broad and varied to permit a per se reasonable inference regarding the motivation for the activity. While the innocent explanations surely do not establish that the Fourth Amendment is always violated whenever someone is stopped solely on the basis of an unprovoked flight, neither do the suspicious motivations establish that the Fourth Amendment is never violated when a *Terry* stop is predicated on that fact alone. For these reasons, the Court is surely correct in refusing to embrace either per se rule advocated by the parties. The totality of the circumstances, as always, must dictate the result.

II

Guided by that totality-of-the-circumstances test, the Court concludes that Officer Nolan had reasonable suspicion to stop respondent. In this respect, my view differs from the Court's. The entire justification for the stop is articulated in the brief testimony of Officer Nolan. Some facts are perfectly clear; others are not. This factual insufficiency leads me to conclude that the Court's judgment is mistaken.

Officer Nolan and his partner were in the last of the four patrol cars that "were all caravaning eastbound down Van Buren." Nolan first observed respondent "in front of 4035 West Van Buren." Wardlow "looked in our direction and began fleeing." Nolan then "began driving southbound down the street observing [respondent] running through the gangway and the alley southbound," and observed that Wardlow was carrying a white, opaque bag under his arm. After the car turned south and intercepted respondent as he "ran right towards us," Officer Nolan stopped him and conducted a "protective search," which revealed that the bag under respondent's arm contained a loaded handgun.

This terse testimony is most noticeable for what it fails to reveal. Though asked whether he was in a marked or unmarked car, Officer Nolan could not recall the answer. He was not asked whether any of the other three cars in the caravan were marked, or whether any of the other seven officers were in uniform. Though he explained that the size of the caravan was because "[n]ormally in these different areas there's an enormous amount of people, sometimes lookouts, customers," Officer Nolan did not testify as to whether anyone besides Wardlow was nearby 4035 West Van Buren. Nor is it clear that that address was the intended destination of the caravan. As the Appellate Court of Illinois interpreted the record, "it appears that the officers were simply driving by, on their way to some unidentified location, when they noticed defendant standing at 4035 West Van Buren." Officer Nolan's testimony also does not reveal how fast the officers were driving. It does not indicate whether he saw respondent notice the other patrol cars. And it does not say whether the caravan, or any part of it, had already passed Wardlow by before he began to run.

Indeed, the Appellate Court thought the record was even "too vague to support the inference that . . . defendant's flight was related to his expectation of police focus on him." Presumably, respondent did not react to the first three cars, and we cannot even be sure that he recognized the occupants of the fourth as police officers. The adverse inference is based entirely on the officer's statement: "He looked in our direction and began fleeing."

No other factors sufficiently support a finding of reasonable suspicion. Though respondent was carrying a white, opaque bag under his arm, there is nothing at all suspicious about that. Certainly the time of day—shortly after noon—does not support Illinois' argument. Nor were the officers "responding to any call or report of suspicious activity in the area." Officer Nolan did testify that he expected to find "an enormous amount of people," including drug customers or lookouts, and the Court points out that "[i]t was in this context that Officer Nolan decided to investigate Wardlow after observing him flee." This observation, in my view, lends insufficient weight to the reasonable suspicion analysis; indeed, in light of the absence of testimony that anyone else was nearby when respondent began to run, this observation points in the opposite direction.

The State, along with the majority of the Court, relies as well on the assumption that this flight occurred in a high crime area. Even if that assumption is accurate, it is insufficient because even in a high crime neighborhood unprovoked flight does not invariably lead to reasonable suspicion. On the contrary, because many factors providing innocent motivations for unprovoked flight are concentrated in high crime areas, the character of the neighborhood arguably makes an inference of guilt less appropriate, rather than more so. Like unprovoked flight itself, presence in a high crime neighborhood is a fact too generic and susceptible to innocent explanation to satisfy the reasonable suspicion inquiry.

It is the State's burden to articulate facts sufficient to support reasonable suspicion. In my judgment, Illinois has failed to discharge that burden. I am not persuaded that the mere fact that someone standing on a sidewalk looked in the direction of a passing car before starting to run is sufficient to justify a forcible stop and frisk.

d. Reasonable Suspicion Based on Profiles

Can the use of profiles by the police be sufficient for reasonable suspicion? In United States v. Sokolow, the Court found that the use of factors within a drug courier profile in an airport provided reasonable suspicion for a stop under Terry v. Ohio.

UNITED STATES v. SOKOLOW

490 U.S. 1 (1989)

Chief Justice REHNQUIST delivered the opinion of the Court.

Respondent Andrew Sokolow was stopped by Drug Enforcement Administration (DEA) agents upon his arrival at Honolulu International Airport. The agents found 1,063 grams of cocaine in his carry-on luggage. When respondent was stopped, the agents knew that (1) he paid $2,100 for two airplane tickets from a roll of $20 bills; (2) he traveled under a name that did not match the name under which his telephone number was listed; (3) his original destination was Miami, a source city for illicit drugs; (4) he stayed in Miami for only 48 hours, even though a round-trip flight from Honolulu to Miami takes 20 hours; (5) he appeared nervous during his trip; and (6) he checked none of his luggage. A divided panel of the United States Court of Appeals for the Ninth Circuit held that the DEA agents did not have a reasonable suspicion to stop respondent, as required by the Fourth Amendment. We take the contrary view.

This case involves a typical attempt to smuggle drugs through one of the Nation's airports. On a Sunday in July 1984, respondent went to the United Airlines ticket counter at Honolulu Airport, where he purchased two round-trip tickets for a flight to Miami leaving later that day. The tickets were purchased in the names of "Andrew Kray" and "Janet Norian" and had open return dates. Respondent paid $2,100 for the tickets from a large roll of $20 bills, which appeared to contain a total of $4,000. He also gave the ticket agent his home telephone number. The ticket agent noticed that respondent seemed nervous; he was about 25 years old; he was dressed in a black jumpsuit and wore gold jewelry; and he was accompanied by a woman, who turned out to be Janet Norian. Neither respondent nor his companion checked any of their four pieces of luggage.

After the couple left for their flight, the ticket agent informed Officer John McCarthy of the Honolulu Police Department of respondent's cash purchase of tickets to Miami. Officer McCarthy determined that the telephone number respondent gave to the ticket agent was subscribed to a "Karl Herman," who resided at 348-A Royal Hawaiian Avenue in Honolulu. Unbeknownst to McCarthy (and later to the DEA agents), respondent was Herman's roommate. The ticket agent identified respondent's voice on the answering machine at Herman's number. Officer McCarthy was unable to find any listing under the name "Andrew Kray" in Hawaii. McCarthy subsequently learned that return reservations from Miami to Honolulu had been made in the names of Kray and Norian, with their arrival scheduled for July 25, three days after respondent and his companion had left. He also learned that Kray and Norian were scheduled to make stopovers in Denver and Los Angeles.

On July 25, during the stopover in Los Angeles, DEA agents identified respondent. He "appeared to be very nervous and was looking all around the waiting area." Later that day, at 6:30 P.M., respondent and Norian arrived in Honolulu. As before, they had not checked their luggage. Respondent was still wearing a black jumpsuit and gold jewelry. The couple proceeded directly to the street and tried to hail a cab, where Agent Richard Kempshall and three other DEA agents approached them. Kempshall displayed his credentials, grabbed respondent by the arm, and moved him back onto the sidewalk. Kempshall asked respondent for his airline ticket and identification; respondent said that he had neither. He told the agents that his name was "Sokolow," but that he was traveling under his mother's maiden name, "Kray."

Respondent and Norian were escorted to the DEA office at the airport. There, the couple's luggage was examined by "Donker," a narcotics detector dog, which alerted on respondent's brown shoulder bag. The agents arrested respondent. He was advised of his constitutional rights and declined to make any statements. The agents obtained a warrant to search the shoulder bag. They found no illicit drugs, but the bag did contain several suspicious documents indicating respondent's involvement in drug trafficking. The agents had Donker reexamine the remaining luggage, and this time the dog alerted on a medium-sized Louis Vuitton bag. By now, it was 9:30 P.M., too late for the agents to obtain a second warrant. They allowed respondent to leave for the night, but kept his luggage. The next morning, after a second dog confirmed Donker's alert, the agents obtained a warrant and found 1,063 grams of cocaine inside the bag.

Respondent was indicted for possession with the intent to distribute cocaine in violation of 21 U.S.C. §841(a)(1). The United States District Court for Hawaii denied his motion to suppress the cocaine and other evidence seized from his luggage, finding that the DEA agents had a reasonable suspicion that he was involved in drug trafficking when they stopped him at the airport. Respondent then entered a conditional plea of guilty to the offense charged.

The United States Court of Appeals for the Ninth Circuit reversed respondent's conviction by a divided vote, holding that the DEA agents did not have a reasonable suspicion to justify the stop.

The Court of Appeals held that the DEA agents seized respondent when they grabbed him by the arm and moved him back onto the sidewalk. The Government does not challenge that conclusion, and we assume — without deciding — that a stop occurred here. Our decision, then, turns on whether the agents had a reasonable suspicion that respondent was engaged in wrongdoing when they encountered him on the sidewalk. In Terry v. Ohio (1968), we held that the police can stop and briefly detain a person for investigative purposes if the officer has a reasonable suspicion supported by articulable facts that criminal activity "may be afoot," even if the officer lacks probable cause.

The officer, of course, must be able to articulate something more than an "inchoate and unparticularized suspicion or 'hunch.'" The Fourth Amendment requires "some minimal level of objective justification" for making the stop. That level of suspicion is considerably less than proof of wrongdoing by a preponderance of the evidence. We have held that probable cause means "a fair probability that contraband or evidence of a crime will be found," and the level of suspicion required for a *Terry* stop is obviously less demanding than that for probable cause.

The concept of reasonable suspicion, like probable cause, is not "readily, or even usefully, reduced to a neat set of legal rules."

Paying $2,100 in cash for two airplane tickets is out of the ordinary, and it is even more out of the ordinary to pay that sum from a roll of $20 bills containing nearly twice that amount of cash. Most business travelers, we feel confident, purchase airline tickets by credit card or check so as to have a record for tax or business purposes, and few vacationers carry with them thousands of dollars in $20 bills. We also think the agents had a reasonable ground to believe that respondent was traveling under an alias; the evidence was by no means conclusive, but it was sufficient to warrant consideration. While a trip from Honolulu to Miami, standing alone, is not a cause for any sort of suspicion, here there was more: surely few residents of Honolulu travel from that city for 20 hours to spend 48 hours in Miami during the month of July.

Any one of these factors is not by itself proof of any illegal conduct and is quite consistent with innocent travel. But we think taken together they amount to reasonable suspicion. Indeed, *Terry* itself involved "a series of acts, each of them perhaps innocent" if viewed separately, "but which taken together warranted further investigation." We noted in *Gates* that "innocent behavior will frequently provide the basis for a showing of probable cause," and that "[i]n making a determination of probable cause the relevant inquiry is not whether particular conduct is 'innocent' or 'guilty,' but the degree of suspicion that attaches to particular types of noncriminal acts." That principle applies equally well to the reasonable suspicion inquiry.

We do not agree with respondent that our analysis is somehow changed by the agents' belief that his behavior was consistent with one of the DEA's "drug courier profiles." A court sitting to determine the existence of reasonable suspicion must require the agent to articulate the factors leading to that conclusion, but the fact that these factors may be set forth in a "profile" does not somehow detract from their evidentiary significance as seen by a trained agent.

Respondent also contends that the agents were obligated to use the least intrusive means available to verify or dispel their suspicions that he was smuggling narcotics. In respondent's view, the agents should have simply approached and spoken with him, rather than forcibly detaining him. The reasonableness of the officer's decision to stop a suspect does not turn on the availability of less intrusive investigatory techniques. Such a rule would unduly hamper the police's ability to make swift, on-the-spot decisions — here, respondent was about to get into a taxicab — and it would require courts to "indulge in 'unrealistic second-guessing.'"

We hold that the agents had a reasonable basis to suspect that respondent was transporting illegal drugs on these facts.

Justice MARSHALL, with whom Justice BRENNAN joins, dissenting.

Because the strongest advocates of Fourth Amendment rights are frequently criminals, it is easy to forget that our interpretations of such rights apply to the innocent and the guilty alike. In the present case, the chain of events set in motion when respondent Andrew Sokolow was stopped by Drug Enforcement Administration (DEA) agents at Honolulu International Airport led to the discovery of cocaine and, ultimately, to Sokolow's conviction for drug trafficking. But in sustaining this conviction on the ground that the agents reasonably suspected Sokolow of ongoing criminal activity, the Court diminishes the rights of all citizens "to be secure in their persons," as they traverse the Nation's airports. Finding this result constitutionally impermissible, I dissent.

[T]he facts about Andrew Sokolow known to the DEA agents at the time they stopped him fall short of reasonably indicating that he was engaged at the time in criminal activity. It is highly significant that the DEA agents stopped Sokolow because he matched one of the DEA's "profiles" of a paradigmatic drug courier. In my view, a law enforcement officer's mechanistic application of a formula of personal and behavioral traits in deciding whom to detain can only dull the officer's ability and determination to make sensitive and fact-specific inferences "in light of his experience," particularly in ambiguous or borderline cases. Reflexive reliance on a profile of drug courier characteristics runs a far greater risk than does ordinary, case-by-case police work of subjecting innocent individuals to unwarranted police harassment and detention. This risk is enhanced by the profile's "chameleon-like way of adapting to any particular set of observations." In asserting that it is not "somehow" relevant that the agents who stopped Sokolow did so in reliance on a prefabricated profile of criminal characteristics, the majority thus ducks serious issues relating to a questionable law enforcement practice, to address the validity of which we granted certiorari in this case.

The remaining circumstantial facts known about Sokolow, considered either singly or together, are scarcely indicative of criminal activity. [T]he fact that Sokolow took a brief trip to a resort city for which he brought only carry-on luggage also "describe[s] a very large category of presumably innocent travelers." That Sokolow embarked from Miami, "a source city for illicit drugs," is no more suggestive of illegality; thousands of innocent persons travel from "source cities" every day and, judging from the DEA's testimony in past cases, nearly every major city in the country may be characterized as a source or distribution city. That Sokolow had his phone listed in another person's name also does not support the majority's assertion that the DEA agents reasonably believed Sokolow was using an alias; it is commonplace to have one's phone registered in the name of a roommate, which, it later turned out, was precisely what Sokolow had done. That

Sokolow was dressed in a black jumpsuit and wore gold jewelry also provides no grounds for suspecting wrongdoing, the majority's repeated and unexplained allusions to Sokolow's style of dress notwithstanding. For law enforcement officers to base a search, even in part, on a "pop" guess that persons dressed in a particular fashion are likely to commit crimes not only stretches the concept of reasonable suspicion beyond recognition, but also is inimical to the self-expression which the choice of wardrobe may provide.

Finally, that Sokolow paid for his tickets in cash indicates no imminent or ongoing criminal activity. The majority "feel[s] confident" that "[m]ost business travelers . . . purchase airline tickets by credit card or check." Why the majority confines its focus only to "business travelers" I do not know, but I would not so lightly infer ongoing crime from the use of legal tender. Making major cash purchases, while surely less common today, may simply reflect the traveler's aversion to, or inability to obtain, plastic money. Moreover, it is unreasonable to suggest that, had Sokolow left the airport, he would have been gone forever and thus immune from subsequent investigation. Sokolow, after all, had given the airline his phone number, and the DEA, having ascertained that it was indeed Sokolow's voice on the answering machine at that number, could have learned from that information where Sokolow resided.

The fact is that, unlike the taking of patently evasive action, the use of an alias, the casing of a store, or the provision of a reliable report from an informant that wrongdoing is imminent, nothing about the characteristics shown by airport traveler Sokolow reasonably suggests that criminal activity is afoot. The majority's hasty conclusion to the contrary serves only to indicate its willingness, when drug crimes or antidrug policies are at issue, to give short shrift to constitutional rights.

H. ELECTRONIC SURVEILLANCE

It is now clearly established that electronic surveillance, such as wiretapping and interception of electronic communications, is a search and is governed by Fourth Amendment principles. It is a bit different than other aspects of the Fourth Amendment because electronic surveillance by law enforcement officials is governed by specific statutes that define the procedures to be used. The result is that electronic surveillance is less likely than other forms of searches to lead to litigation and decisions under the Fourth Amendment, but there have been many decisions interpreting the statutes.

Subsection 1 briefly describes how the Supreme Court initially rejected viewing surveillance as a search but then changed course and applied the Fourth Amendment. Subsection 2 describes the statutes governing electronic eavesdropping by federal officials. Finally, subsection 3 considers whether the president has the power to authorize warrantless wiretapping for national security purposes.

1.   Is Electronic Eavesdropping a Search?

In Olmstead v. United States, 277 U.S. 438 (1928), the Supreme Court held that wiretapping was not a search because the wires were tapped outside the suspect's property, and thus there was not a physical trespass. The Court explained, "The insertions were made without trespass upon any property of the defendants. They were made in the basement of the large office building. The taps from house lines were made in the streets near the houses." Chief Justice Taft, writing for the Court, said, "The language of the amendment cannot be extended and expanded to include telephone wires, reaching to the whole world from the defendant's house or office. The intervening wires are not part of his house or office, any more than are the highways along which they are stretched."

The Court concluded:

> Congress may, of course, protect the secrecy of telephone messages by making them, when intercepted, inadmissible in evidence in federal criminal trials, by direct legislation, and thus depart from the common law of evidence. But the courts may not adopt such a policy by attributing an enlarged and unusual meaning to the Fourth Amendment. The reasonable view is that one who installs in his house a telephone instrument with connecting wires intends to project his voice to those quite outside, and that the wires beyond his house, and messages while passing over them, are not within the protection of the Fourth Amendment. Here those who intercepted the projected voices were not in the house of either party to the conversation.

Justice Brandeis dissented and wrote an opinion that remains influential for articulating the right to privacy as a core of the Fourth Amendment. He stated:

> The makers of our Constitution undertook to secure conditions favorable to the pursuit of happiness. They recognized the significance of man's spiritual nature, of his feelings and of his intellect. They knew that only a part of the pain, pleasure and satisfactions of life are to be found in material things. They sought to protect Americans in their beliefs, their thoughts, their emotions and their sensations. They conferred, as against the government, the right to be let alone — the most comprehensive of rights and the right most valued by civilized men. To protect that right, every unjustifiable intrusion by the government upon the privacy of the individual, whatever the means employed, must be deemed a violation of the Fourth Amendment.

In words that seem particularly apt today, Justice Brandeis declared:

> It is, of course, immaterial where the physical connection with the telephone wires leading into the defendants' premises was made. And it is also immaterial that the intrusion was in aid of law enforcement. Experience should teach us to be most on our guard to protect liberty when the government's purposes are beneficent. Men born to freedom are naturally alert to repel invasion of their liberty by evil-minded rulers. The greatest dangers to liberty lurk in insidious encroachment by men of zeal, well-meaning but without understanding.

For several decades, the Supreme Court adhered to the *Olmstead* view that electronic eavesdropping is not a search as long as there is no physical trespass. For example, in Goldman v. United States, 316 U.S. 129 (1942), the Court held that there was not a search when police placed a listening device against an office wall because they had not entered the premises of the office. By contrast, in Silverman v. United States, 365 U.S. 505 (1961), the Court found that there was a Fourth Amendment violation when police inserted an electric device (a "spike mike") into the shared wall of a person's apartment.

In 1967, the Court abandoned the *Olmstead* approach and said that the Fourth Amendment is about protecting a reasonable expectation of privacy, not simply stopping trespassing by law enforcement. In Berger v. United States, 388 U.S. 41 (1967), the Court found that the New York procedures for electronic eavesdropping lacked sufficient procedural protections to comply with the Fourth Amendment. The Court explained:

> The Fourth Amendment commands that a warrant issue not only upon probable cause supported by oath or affirmation, but also "particularly describing the place to be searched, and the persons or things to be seized." New York's statute lacks this particularization. It merely says that a warrant may issue on reasonable ground to believe that evidence of crime may be obtained by the eavesdrop. It lays down no requirement for particularity in the warrant as to what specific crime has been or is being committed, nor "the place to be searched," or "the persons or things to be seized" as specifically required by the Fourth Amendment. The need for particularity and evidence of reliability in the showing required when judicial authorization of a search is sought is especially great in the case of eavesdropping. By its very nature eavesdropping involves an intrusion on privacy that is broad in scope.
>
> First, as we have mentioned, eavesdropping is authorized without requiring belief that any particular offense has been or is being committed; nor that the "property" sought, the conversations, be particularly described. The purpose of the probable cause requirement of the Fourth Amendment, to keep the state out of constitutionally protected areas until it has reason to believe that a specific crime has been or is being committed, is thereby wholly aborted. Likewise the statute's failure to describe with particularity the conversations sought gives the officer a roving commission to "seize" any and all conversations. It is true that the statute requires the naming of "the person or persons whose communications, conversations or discussions are to be overheard or recorded." But this does no more than identify the person whose constitutionally protected area is to be invaded rather than "particularly describing" the communications, conversations, or discussions to be seized. As with general warrants this leaves too much to the discretion of the officer executing the order. Secondly, authorization of eavesdropping for a two-month period is the equivalent of a series of intrusions, searches, and seizures pursuant to a single showing of probable cause. Prompt execution is also avoided. During such a long and continuous (24 hours a day) period the conversations of any and all persons coming into the area covered by the device will be seized indiscriminately and without regard to their connection with the crime under investigation. Moreover, the statute permits, and there were authorized here, extensions of the original two-month period — presumably for two months each — on a mere showing that such extension is "in the public interest." Apparently the original grounds on which the eavesdrop order was initially issued also form the basis of the renewal. This we believe insufficient without a showing of present

probable cause for the continuance of the eavesdrop. Third, the statute places no termination date on the eavesdrop once the conversation sought is seized. This is left entirely in the discretion of the officer. Finally, the statute's procedure, necessarily because its success depends on secrecy, has no requirement for notice as do conventional warrants, nor does it overcome this defect by requiring some showing of special facts. On the contrary, it permits uncontested entry without any showing of exigent circumstances. Such a showing of exigency, in order to avoid notice would appear more important in eavesdropping, with its inherent dangers, than that required when conventional procedures of search and seizure are utilized. Nor does the statute provide for a return on the warran[t,] thereby leaving full discretion in the officer as to the use of seized conversations of innocent as well as guilty parties. In short, the statute's blanket grant of permission to eavesdrop is without adequate judicial supervision or protective procedures.

It is said with fervor that electronic eavesdropping is a most important technique of law enforcement and that outlawing it will severely cripple crime detection. In any event we cannot forgive the requirements of the Fourth Amendment in the name of law enforcement. This is no formality that we require today but a fundamental rule that has long been recognized as basic to the privacy of every home in America. Few threats to liberty exist which are greater than that posed by the use of eavesdropping devices. Some may claim that without the use of such devices crime detection in certain areas may suffer some delays since eavesdropping is quicker, easier, and more certain. However, techniques and practices may well be developed that will operate just as speedily and certainly and—what is more important—without attending illegality.

A few months after *Berger*, the Supreme Court expressly repudiated the trespass test of *Olmstead*. In United States v. Katz, presented at the beginning of this chapter, the Court held that the Fourth Amendment was violated by the warrantless wiretapping of a phone booth. The Court held that the Fourth Amendment protects reasonable expectations of privacy and that electronic eavesdropping is a search. The Court said that the amendment governs "not only the seizure of tangible items, but extends as well to the recording of oral statements . . . without any technical trespass under . . . local property law."

2.   *Statutory Requirements*

The year after *Katz* and *Berger*, Congress adopted Title III of the Omnibus Crime Control and Safe Streets Act of 1968 to regulate electronic eavesdropping. 18 U.S.C. §§2510, *et seq.* The statute addresses the procedural requirements that the Court articulated in *Berger*. The law was adopted under Congress' Commerce Clause power and regulates eavesdropping by government officials at all levels (federal, state, and local) and also private actors. In other words, the law is significantly broader than the Fourth Amendment in its regulating private behavior where the Constitution does not apply. The law was amended by the Electronic Communications Privacy Act of 1964 and the Digital Telephone Act of 1994. As amended, Title III covers the intentional interception by any means of wire, oral, and electronic communications. The act defines interception as "the aural acquisition or other acquisition of the contents of any wire, electronic, or oral communication through the use of any electronic, mechanical, or other device."

The statute provides that no information gained in violation of statute, and no evidence derived as a result, may be admitted in any court proceeding. 18 U.S.C. §2515. The statute provides that a court order may be obtained authorizing interception for any one of a long list of specified crimes. The application for a warrant must state with particularity the basis for probable cause, a description of the type of communications sought to be intercepted, the identity of the person (if known) whose communications are to be intercepted, whether other investigative techniques have been used, and the period of time during which interception will occur.

The statute provides that the court may issue an order authorizing interception if it finds that (a) there is probable cause to believe that an individual is committing, has committed, or is about to commit an enumerated offense; (b) there is probable cause to believe that the communications concerning that offense will be obtained through the interception; and (c) "normal investigative procedures have been tried and failed or reasonably appear to be unlikely to succeed if tried or to be too dangerous." The court order must enumerate this and be specific as to whose communications may be intercepted, by what specific agency, and for what period of time. Generally, the court order must specify which specific communications media are to be monitored (such as what phone number), but the act now allows "roving wiretaps," in which all communication devices used by a person will be subject to surveillance, if there is a showing that a stationary wiretap will not be sufficient.

The act is specific that the order cannot authorize interception "for any period longer than necessary to achieve the objective of the authorization, nor in any event longer than 30 days." Extensions may be granted but only upon applications demonstrating necessity.

Title III requires that interception "shall be conducted in a way as to minimize the interception of communications." "Minimization" requires that law enforcement stop monitoring a communication when it becomes apparent that it is not about criminal activity. For example, if police obtain a court order to wiretap a phone for evidence of illegal drug transactions, they must stop listening when they realize that the conversation involves the suspect's child talking with a friend about unrelated matters.

The act allows interception without a court order in emergency situations. Specifically, the act provides that for a period not to exceed 48 hours, there can be interception if a specifically designated law enforcement official determines that "(a) an emergency situation exists that involves (i) immediate danger of death or serious physical injury to any person, (ii) conspiratorial activities threatening the national security interest, or (iii) conspiratorial activities characteristic of organized crime, that require a wire, oral, or electronic communication to be intercepted before an order authorizing such interception with due diligence can be obtained, and (b) there are grounds upon which an order can be entered." Also, Title III says that it does not limit the power of the president to obtain foreign intelligence information that is essential to the security of the United States.

The act requires that a person whose communications were intercepted be notified in a reasonable period, not to exceed 90 days. The court may make available for inspection "such portions of the intercepted communications, applications and orders as the judge determines to be in the interests of justice."

As mentioned above, Title III provides for the exclusion of evidence obtained in violation of its provisions. It also provides criminal and civil penalties against those who violate it, although good faith reliance on a court order or legislative authorization is a complete defense to criminal or civil liability.

In 1978, Congress adopted the Foreign Intelligence Surveillance Act (FISA), 50 U.S.C. §§1801, *et seq.* FISA creates a special court comprising 11 federal district court judges, chosen by the chief justice, to hear requests for eavesdropping under it. The FISA court operates in secret. Appeals are heard by a panel of federal court of appeals judges designated by the chief justice.

FISA, as amended, applies if a significant purpose of the interception is the gathering of foreign intelligence information. As originally adopted, FISA applied only to electronic interceptions, but later was amended to include physical searches. The government, to obtain a FISA warrant, need not show probable cause that a crime has been or will be committed. Rather, the government must show that "the target of the electronic surveillance is a foreign power or an agent of a foreign power." Unlike interceptions pursuant to Title III, the government never is required to notify the target if the Attorney General determines that it is in the interests of national security to keep this secret. The government can engage in interceptions without a court order in exigent circumstances for up to 72 hours.

The USA Patriot Act, adopted soon after the attacks of September 11, 2001, amended provisions of FISA in several important ways. Previously, the law applied only if the purpose was foreign intelligence gathering and not if it was for purposes of a criminal prosecution. But under the Patriot Act, FISA procedures can be used as long as a significant purpose is foreign intelligence gathering. The Patriot Act also provides for the sharing of information gained for intelligence purposes with law enforcement officials. Such sharing of information is allowed if it will "assist the official who is to receive that information in the performance of his duties." The act authorizes "roving wiretaps," in which all phones used by a person can be monitored.

The Patriot Act also modifies provisions of Title III. For example, it authorizes so-called sneak and peak warrants where the government may engage in searches or interceptions without notifying the target if there is reason to believe that giving notice will create an "adverse result" in the form of danger to persons or evidence. The act allows for nationwide warrants for searching of stored electronic communications and for pen registers to monitor from whom a person is calling or receiving calls or sending or receiving e-mail communication.

3. Warrantless Eavesdropping

The Foreign Intelligence Surveillance Act provides that all interception by law enforcement officials must be done in compliance either with Title III or FISA. The exclusivity provision states that Title III and FISA "shall be the exclusive means by which electronic surveillance, as defined in section 101 of [FISA], and the interception of domestic wire, oral, and electronic communications may be conducted." 18 U.S.C. §2511(2)(f). But does the president have the inherent power to authorize electronic surveillance for security purposes? There is just one Supreme Court decision concerning this, and it held that there is no such authority for eavesdropping for *domestic* security purposes. The Court expressly said that it was not considering the president's authority when *foreign* threats were involved.

UNITED STATES v. UNITED STATES DISTRICT COURT FOR THE EASTERN DISTRICT OF MICHIGAN

407 U.S. 297 (1972)

Justice POWELL delivered the opinion of the Court.

The issue before us is an important one for the people of our country and their Government. It involves the delicate question of the President's power, acting through the Attorney General, to authorize electronic surveillance in internal security matters without prior judicial approval. Successive Presidents for more than one-quarter of a century have authorized such surveillance in varying degrees, without guidance from the Congress or a definitive decision of this Court. This case brings the issue here for the first time. Its resolution is a matter of national concern, requiring sensitivity both to the Government's right to protect itself from unlawful subversion and attack and to the citizen's right to be secure in his privacy against unreasonable Government intrusion.

This case arises from a criminal proceeding in the United States District Court for the Eastern District of Michigan, in which the United States charged three defendants with conspiracy to destroy Government property in violation of 18 U.S.C. §371. One of the defendants, Plamondon, was charged with the dynamite bombing of an office of the Central Intelligence Agency in Ann Arbor, Michigan.

During pretrial proceedings, the defendants moved to compel the United States to disclose certain electronic surveillance information and to conduct a hearing to determine whether this information "tainted" the evidence on which the indictment was based or which the Government intended to offer at trial. In response, the Government filed an affidavit of the Attorney General, acknowledging that its agents had overheard conversations in which Plamondon had participated. On the basis of the Attorney General's affidavit and the sealed exhibit, the Government asserted that the surveillance was lawful, though conducted without prior judicial approval, as a reasonable exercise of the President's power (exercised through the Attorney General) to protect the national security. The District Court held that the surveillance violated the Fourth Amendment, and ordered the Government to make full disclosure to Plamondon of his overheard conversations.

Title III of the Omnibus Crime Control and Safe Streets Act authorizes the use of electronic surveillance for classes of crimes carefully specified. Such surveillance is subject to prior court order. The Act represents a comprehensive attempt by Congress to promote more effective control of crime while protecting the privacy of individual thought and expression. Much of Title III was drawn to meet the constitutional requirements for electronic surveillance enunciated by this Court in Berger v. New York (1967), and Katz v. United States (1967).

Together with the elaborate surveillance requirements in Title III, there is the following proviso: "Nothing contained in this chapter or in section 605 of the Communications Act of 1934 shall limit the constitutional power of the President to take such measures as he deems necessary to protect the Nation against actual or potential attack or other hostile acts of a foreign power, to obtain foreign intelligence information deemed essential to the security of the United States, or to protect national security information against foreign intelligence activities. Nor shall anything contained in this chapter be deemed to limit the constitutional power of the President to take such measures as he deems necessary to protect the United States against the overthrow of the Government by force or other unlawful means, or against any other clear and present danger to the structure or existence of the Government. The contents of any wire or oral communication intercepted by authority of the President in the exercise of the foregoing powers may be received in evidence in any trial hearing, or other proceeding only where such interception was reasonable, and shall not be otherwise used or disclosed except as is necessary to implement that power."

The Government argues that in excepting national security surveillances from the Act's warrant requirement Congress recognized the President's authority to conduct such surveillances without prior judicial approval. We think the language of 2511(3), as well as the legislative history of the statute, refutes this interpretation. The relevant language is that: "Nothing contained in this chapter . . . shall limit the constitutional power of the President to take such measures as he deems necessary to protect . . ." against the dangers specified. At most, this is an implicit recognition that the President does have certain powers in the specified areas. Few would doubt this, as the section refers — among other things — to protection "against actual or potential attack or other hostile acts of a foreign power." But so far as the use of the President's electronic surveillance power is concerned, the language is essentially neutral.

Section 2511(3) certainly confers no power, as the language is wholly inappropriate for such a purpose. It merely provides that the Act shall not be interpreted to limit or disturb such power as the President may have under the Constitution. In short, Congress simply left presidential powers where it found them.

In view of these and other interrelated provisions delineating permissible interceptions of particular criminal activity upon carefully specified conditions, it would have been incongruous for Congress to have legislated with respect to the important and complex area of national security in a single brief and nebulous paragraph. This would not comport with the sensitivity of the problem involved or with the extraordinary care Congress exercised in drafting other sections of the Act. We therefore think the conclusion inescapable that Congress only intended to make clear that the Act simply did not legislate with respect to national security surveillances.

It is important at the outset to emphasize the limited nature of the question before the Court. This case raises no constitutional challenge to electronic surveillance as specifically authorized by Title III of the Omnibus Crime Control and Safe Streets Act of 1968. Nor is there any question or doubt as to the necessity of obtaining a warrant in the surveillance of crimes unrelated to the national security interest. Further, the instant case requires no judgment on the scope of the President's surveillance power with respect to the activities of foreign powers, within or without this country. The Attorney General's affidavit in this case states that the surveillances were "deemed necessary to protect the nation from attempts of domestic organizations to attack and subvert the existing structure of Government." There is no evidence of any involvement, directly or indirectly, of a foreign power.

We begin the inquiry by noting that the President of the United States has the fundamental duty, under Art. II, §1, of the Constitution, to "preserve, protect and defend the Constitution of the United States." Implicit in that duty is the power to protect our Government against those who would subvert or overthrow it by unlawful means. In the discharge of this duty, the President — through the Attorney General — may find it necessary to employ electronic surveillance to obtain intelligence information on the plans of those who plot unlawful acts against the Government. The use of such surveillance in internal security cases has been sanctioned more or less continuously by various Presidents and Attorneys General since July 1946.

Though the Government and respondents debate their seriousness and magnitude, threats and acts of sabotage against the Government exist in sufficient number to justify investigative powers with respect to them. The covertness and complexity of potential unlawful conduct against the Government and the necessary dependency of many conspirators upon the telephone make electronic surveillance an effective investigatory instrument in certain circumstances. The marked acceleration in technological developments and sophistication in their use have resulted in new techniques for the planning, commission, and concealment of criminal activities. It would be contrary to the public interest for Government to deny to itself the prudent and lawful employment of those very techniques which are employed against the Government and its law-abiding citizens.

But a recognition of these elementary truths does not make the employment by Government of electronic surveillance a welcome development — even when employed with restraint and under judicial supervision. There is, understandably, a deep-seated uneasiness and apprehension that this capability will be used to intrude upon cherished privacy of law-abiding citizens. We look to the Bill of Rights to safeguard this privacy. Though physical entry of the home is the chief evil against which the wording of the Fourth Amendment is directed, its broader spirit now shields private speech from unreasonable surveillance.

National security cases, moreover, often reflect a convergence of First and Fourth Amendment values not present in cases of "ordinary" crime. Though the investigative duty of the executive may be stronger in such cases, so also is there greater jeopardy to constitutionally protected speech. Fourth Amendment protections become the more necessary when the targets of official surveillance may be those suspected of unorthodoxy in their political beliefs. The danger to political dissent is acute where the Government attempts to act under so vague a concept as the power to protect "domestic security." Given the difficulty of defining the domestic security interest, the danger of abuse in acting to protect that interest becomes apparent.

The price of lawful public dissent must not be a dread of subjection to an unchecked surveillance power. Nor must the fear of unauthorized official eavesdropping deter vigorous citizen dissent and discussion of Government action in private conversation. For private dissent, no less than open public discourse, is essential to our free society.

As the Fourth Amendment is not absolute in its terms, our task is to examine and balance the basic values at stake in this case: the duty of Government to protect the domestic security, and the potential danger posed by unreasonable surveillance to individual privacy and free expression. If the legitimate need of Government to safeguard domestic security requires the use of electronic surveillance, the question is whether the needs of citizens for privacy and the free expression may not be better protected by requiring a warrant before such surveillance is undertaken. We must also ask whether a warrant requirement would unduly frustrate the efforts of Government to protect itself from acts of subversion and overthrow directed against it.

Though the Fourth Amendment speaks broadly of "unreasonable searches and seizures," the definition of "reasonableness" turns, at least in part, on the more specific commands of the warrant clause. Some have argued that "[t]he relevant test is not whether it is reasonable to procure a search warrant, but whether the search was reasonable." This view, however, overlooks the second clause of the Amendment. The warrant clause of the Fourth Amendment is not dead language. Rather, it has been "a valued part of our constitutional law for decades, and it has determined the result in scores and scores of cases in courts all over this country. It is not an inconvenience to be somehow 'weighed' against the claims of police efficiency. It is, or should be, an important working part of our machinery of government, operating as a matter of course to check the 'well-intentioned but mistakenly over-zealous executive officers' who are a party of any system of law enforcement."

These Fourth Amendment freedoms cannot properly be guaranteed if domestic security surveillances may be conducted solely within the discretion of the Executive Branch. The Fourth Amendment does not contemplate the executive officers of Government as neutral and disinterested magistrates. Their duty and responsibility are to enforce the laws, to investigate, and to prosecute. But those charged with this investigative and prosecutorial duty should not be the sole judges of when to utilize constitutionally sensitive means in pursuing their tasks. The historical judgment, which the Fourth Amendment accepts, is that unreviewed executive discretion may yield too readily to pressures to obtain incriminating evidence and overlook potential invasions of privacy and protected speech.

It may well be that, in the instant case, the Government's surveillance of Plamondon's conversations was a reasonable one which readily would have gained prior judicial approval. But this Court "has never sustained a search upon the sole ground that officers reasonably expected to find evidence of a particular crime and voluntarily confined their activities to the least intrusive means consistent with that end." The Fourth Amendment contemplates a prior judicial judgment, not the risk that executive discretion may be reasonably exercised. This judicial role accords with our basic constitutional doctrine that individual freedoms will best be preserved through a separation of powers and division of functions among the different branches and levels of Government. The independent check upon executive discretion is not satisfied, as the Government argues, by "extremely limited" post-surveillance judicial review. Indeed, post-surveillance review would never reach the surveillances which failed to result in prosecutions. Prior review by a neutral and detached magistrate is the time-tested means of effectuating Fourth Amendment rights.

It is true that there have been some exceptions to the warrant requirement. But those exceptions are few in number and carefully delineated; in general, they serve the legitimate needs of law enforcement officers to protect their own well-being and preserve evidence from destruction. Even while carving out those exceptions, the Court has reaffirmed the principle that the "police must, whenever practicable, obtain advance judicial approval of searches and seizures through the warrant procedure."

The Government argues that the special circumstances applicable to domestic security surveillances necessitate a further exception to the warrant requirement. It is urged that the requirement of prior judicial review would obstruct the President in the discharge of his constitutional duty to protect domestic security. We are told further that these surveillances are directed primarily to the collecting and maintaining of intelligence with respect to subversive forces, and are not an attempt to gather evidence for specific criminal prosecutions. It is said that this type of surveillance should not be subject to traditional warrant requirements which were established to govern investigation of criminal activity, not ongoing intelligence gathering.

The Government further insists that courts "as a practical matter would have neither the knowledge nor the techniques necessary to determine whether there was probable cause to believe that surveillance was necessary to protect national security." These security problems, the Government contends, involve "a large number of complex and subtle factors" beyond the competence of courts to evaluate.

As a final reason for exemption from a warrant requirement, the Government believes that disclosure to a magistrate of all or even a significant portion of the information involved in domestic security surveillances "would create serious potential dangers to the national security and to the lives of informants and agents. . . . Secrecy is the essential ingredient in intelligence gathering; requiring prior judicial authorization would create a greater 'danger of leaks . . . , because in addition to the judge, you have the clerk, the stenographer and some other officer like a law assistant or bailiff who may be apprised of the nature' of the surveillance."

These contentions on behalf of a complete exemption from the warrant requirement, when urged on behalf of the President and the national security in its domestic implications, merit the most careful consideration. We certainly do not reject them lightly, especially at a time of worldwide ferment and when civil disorders in this country are more prevalent than in the less turbulent periods of our history. There is, no doubt, pragmatic force to the Government's position.

But we do not think a case has been made for the requested departure from Fourth Amendment standards. The circumstances described do not justify complete exemption of domestic security surveillance from prior judicial scrutiny. Official surveillance, whether its purpose be criminal investigation or ongoing intelligence gathering, risks infringement of constitutionally protected privacy of speech. Security surveillances are especially sensitive because of the inherent vagueness of the domestic security concept, the necessarily broad and continuing nature of intelligence gathering, and the temptation to utilize such surveillances to oversee political dissent. We recognize, as we have before, the constitutional basis of the President's domestic security role, but we think it must be exercised in a manner compatible with the Fourth Amendment. In this case we hold that this requires an appropriate prior warrant procedure.

We cannot accept the Government's argument that internal security matters are too subtle and complex for judicial evaluation. Courts regularly deal with the most difficult issues of our society. There is no reason to believe that federal judges will be insensitive to or uncomprehending of the issues involved in domestic security cases. Certainly courts can recognize that domestic security surveillance involves different considerations from the surveillance of "ordinary crime." If the threat is too subtle or complex for our senior law enforcement officers to convey its significance to a court, one may question whether there is probable cause for surveillance.

Nor do we believe prior judicial approval will fracture the secrecy essential to official intelligence gathering. The investigation of criminal activity has long involved imparting sensitive information to judicial officers who have respected the confidentialities involved. Judges may be counted upon to be especially conscious of security requirements in national security cases. Title III of the Omnibus Crime Control and Safe Streets Act already has imposed this responsibility on the judiciary in connection with such crimes as espionage, sabotage, and treason, each of which may involve domestic as well as foreign security threats. Moreover, a warrant application involves no public or adversary proceedings: it is an ex parte request before a magistrate or judge. Whatever security dangers clerical and secretarial personnel may pose can be minimized by proper administrative measures, possibly to the point of allowing the Government itself to provide the necessary clerical assistance.

Thus, we conclude that the Government's concerns do not justify departure in this case from the customary Fourth Amendment requirement of judicial approval prior to initiation of a search or surveillance. Although some added burden will be imposed upon the Attorney General, this inconvenience is justified in a free society to protect constitutional values. Nor do we think the Government's domestic surveillance powers will be impaired to any significant degree. A prior warrant establishes presumptive validity of the surveillance and will minimize the burden of justification in post-surveillance judicial review. By no means of least importance will be the reassurance of the public generally that indiscriminate wiretapping and bugging of law-abiding citizens cannot occur.

We emphasize, before concluding this opinion, the scope of our decision. As stated at the outset, this case involves only the domestic aspects of national security. We have not addressed and express no opinion as to the issues which may be involved with respect to activities of foreign powers or their agents. Moreover, we do not hold that the same type of standards and procedures prescribed by Title III are necessarily applicable to this case. We recognize that domestic security surveillance may involve different policy and practical considerations from the surveillance of "ordinary crime." The gathering of security intelligence is often long range and involves the interrelation of various sources and types of information. The exact targets of such surveillance may be more difficult to identify than in surveillance operations against many types of crime specified in Title III. Often, too, the emphasis of domestic intelligence gathering is on the prevention of unlawful activity or the enhancement of the Government's preparedness for some possible future crisis or emergency. Thus, the focus of domestic surveillance may be less precise than that directed against more conventional types of crime.

Given those potential distinctions between Title III criminal surveillances and those involving the domestic security, Congress may wish to consider protective standards for the latter which differ from those already prescribed for specified crimes in Title III. Different standards may be compatible with the Fourth Amendment if they are reasonable both in relation to the legitimate need of Government for intelligence information and the protected rights of our citizens. For the warrant application may vary according to the governmental interest to be enforced and the nature of citizen rights deserving protection.

We do not attempt to detail the precise standards for domestic security warrants any more than our decision in *Katz* sought to set the refined requirements for the specified criminal surveillances which now constitute Title III. We do hold, however, that prior judicial approval is required for the type of domestic security surveillance involved in this case and that such approval may be made in accordance with such reasonable standards as the Congress may prescribe.

The Court was clear that it was not discussing whether the president has the power to authorize warrantless wiretapping directed at foreign threats to national security. The issue has arisen in recent years in connection with the Bush administration's authorization for the National Security Agency to engage in warrantless electronic eavesdropping. In December 2005, the New York Times reported that since 2002, the National Security Agency had engaged in a Terrorist Surveillance Program that included data mining and warrantless interception of telephone and e-mail communications in which one party to the communication was located outside the United States and the NSA had reasonable basis to conclude that one party to the communication was connected to al Qaeda. James Risen and Eric Lichthlau, *Bush Lets U.S. Spy on Callers Without Courts*, N.Y. Times, Dec. 16, 2005. The day after this story appeared, President George W. Bush confirmed the existence of a "terrorist surveillance program" in his weekly radio address: "In the weeks following the [September 11, 2001] terrorist attacks on our Nation, I authorized the National Security Agency, consistent with U.S. law and the Constitution, to intercept the international communications of people with known links to Al Qaeda and related terrorist organizations. Before we intercept these communications, the Government must have information that establishes a clear link to these terrorist networks."

The American Civil Liberties Union filed a lawsuit on behalf of journalists, academics, and lawyers who regularly communicate with individuals located overseas, who the plaintiffs believe are the types of people the NSA suspects of being al Qaeda terrorists, affiliates, or supporters, and are therefore likely to be monitored under the TSP. The United States District Court for the Eastern District of Michigan ruled that the plaintiffs had standing and that the warrantless electronic eavesdropping violated the Constitution and the FISA statute. American Civil Liberties Union v. National Sec. Agency, 438 F. Supp. 2d 754 (E.D. Mich. 2006). The United States Court of Appeals for the Sixth Circuit, in a 2-1 decision, reversed. American Civil Liberties Union v. National Sec. Agency, 493 F.3d 644 (6th Cir. 2007). The court concluded that the plaintiffs lacked standing because they could not demonstrate that their conversations had been intercepted. The court stated, "Notably, the plaintiffs do not allege as injury that they personally, either as individuals or associations, anticipate or fear any form of direct reprisal by the government (e.g., the NSA, the Justice Department, the Department of Homeland Security, etc.), such as criminal prosecution, deportation, administrative inquiry, civil litigation, or even public exposure." The court concluded, "Based on the evidence in the record, as applied in the foregoing analysis, none of the plaintiffs in the present case is able to establish standing for any of the asserted claims."

The Supreme Court denied certiorari. 552 U.S. 1179 (2008). Although the case was resolved based on whether the plaintiffs have standing to sue, the underlying issue is of enormous importance: Does the president have the power to authorize warrantless interception of electronic communication to protect against foreign threats to national security? The Bush administration claimed that this is inherent power to protect the nation that Congress cannot constitutionally limit. Critics argued that the Fourth Amendment is based on the need for judicial approval of all searches and that warrantless searches are unnecessary and undesirable because there is no protection of privacy.

The issue returned in Clapper v. Amnesty International, 133 S. Ct. 1138 (2013). *Clapper* involved a challenge to a law enacted in 2008 to amend the Foreign Intelligence Surveillance Act to allow the gathering of foreign intelligence information by intercepting communications between persons in the United States and those in foreign countries. A lawsuit was brought by lawyers, journalists, and business people who said that their speech was chilled by the fear that their communications might be intercepted. The Court rejected this injury as being sufficient for standing and stated: "Because '[a]llegations of a subjective "chill" are not an adequate substitute for a claim of specific present objective harm or a threat of specific future harm,' the plaintiffs in *Laird*—and respondents here—lack standing." Thus, the constitutionality of the law and the government's practice remain unresolved.

CHAPTER
3

THE EXCLUSIONARY RULE

What are the consequences if the police violate the Fourth Amendment requirements for searches and seizures described in Chapter 2? Similarly, what are the consequences if the police violate other constitutional limits in investigations, such as interrogations that violate the privilege against self-incrimination (discussed in Chapter 4) or identification procedures that violate due process (discussed in Chapter 5)? The most important enforcement mechanism is the exclusionary rule. This rule states that material obtained in violation of the Constitution cannot be introduced at trial against a criminal defendant.

This chapter focuses primarily on the exclusionary rule in Fourth Amendment cases. Its application to other investigative techniques, such as interrogations and identification procedures, is discussed in the following chapters. Section A considers whether the exclusionary rule is a desirable remedy for unconstitutional police behavior. Section B examines the cases that created the exclusionary rule and applied it to the states. Section C discusses when the exclusionary rule applies. Section D examines who can object to the introduction of illegal evidence and raise the exclusionary rule. Section E considers the exceptions to the exclusionary rule. Finally, section F discusses the primary mechanism for raising the exclusionary rule: suppression hearings.

A. IS THE EXCLUSIONARY RULE A DESIRABLE REMEDY FOR UNCONSTITUTIONAL POLICE BEHAVIOR?

The exclusionary rule is defended as a key way of deterring police misconduct. Officers know that if they violate the Constitution, the fruits of their efforts will be excluded. Officers, who obviously desire that their work will lead to convictions, will thus refrain from violating the Constitution. The Supreme Court often has expressed deterrence as a key purpose of the exclusionary rule. For example, the Court has declared that the exclusionary rule is "a judicially created remedy designed to safeguard Fourth Amendment rights through its deterrence effect." United States v. Calandra, 428 U.S. 465 (1976).

The exclusionary rule also is justified based on concerns for judicial integrity. The view is that courts are tainted if they convict people based on illegally obtained evidence. In some areas, the concern is that illegally obtained evidence is unreliable and could lead to the conviction of innocent people. For example, involuntary confessions or suggestive police lineups are excluded, in part, for fear that the results are not trustworthy. On the other hand, this concern is not present when tangible evidence is gained as a result of an illegal search.

There also is a notion that the exclusionary rule sends a powerful message that the government cannot and will not benefit from wrongdoing by its officers. Justice Brennan argued that application of the exclusionary rule "assures the people—all potential victims of unlawful government conduct—that the government [will] not profit from its lawless behavior, thus minimizing the risk of seriously undermining public trust in the government." United States v. Calandra, 414 U.S. 338 (1974) (Brennan, J., dissenting).

Critics of the exclusionary rule primarily focus on its cost in letting potentially guilty people go free. Justice Cardozo captured this in his famous lament that under the exclusionary rule, "[t]he criminal is to go free because the constable has blundered." People v. Defore, 242 N.Y. 13, 21, 150 N.E. 585, 587 (1926). Indeed, the existence of the exclusionary rule may make judges less likely to find a Fourth Amendment violation since they know that the outcome of the case might be determined by the loss of key evidence.

Critics also argue that the exclusionary rule is unnecessary. In a recent majority opinion, Justice Scalia advanced these criticisms. The case, Hudson v. Michigan, 547 U.S. 586 (2006),[1] involved the question of whether evidence must be excluded when police violate the requirement for "knocking" and "announcing" before executing a warrant to search a residence. The Court held that the exclusionary rule does not apply. In defending this conclusion, Justice Scalia's majority opinion presents many of the traditional arguments against the exclusionary rule.

HUDSON v. MICHIGAN

547 U.S. 586 (2006)

Justice SCALIA delivered the opinion of the Court.

Suppression of evidence, however, has always been our last resort, not our first impulse. The exclusionary rule generates "substantial social costs," which sometimes include setting the guilty free and the dangerous at large. We have therefore been "cautio[us] against expanding" it, and "have repeatedly emphasized that the rule's 'costly toll' upon truth-seeking and law

---

1. *Hudson* is discussed in more detail in section E below, which considers the exceptions to the exclusionary rule and *Hudson*'s holding that the exclusionary rule does not apply if the police violate the requirements for knocking and announcing before searching a dwelling.

enforcement objectives presents a high obstacle for those urging [its] application." We have rejected "[i]ndiscriminate application" of the rule, and have held it to be applicable only "where its remedial objectives are thought most efficaciously served," — that is, "where its deterrence benefits outweigh its 'substantial social costs.'" The exclusionary rule has never been applied except "where its deterrence benefits outweigh its 'substantial social costs.'" The costs here are considerable. In addition to the grave adverse consequence that exclusion of relevant incriminating evidence always entails (viz., the risk of releasing dangerous criminals into society), imposing that massive remedy for a knock-and-announce violation would generate a constant flood of alleged failures to observe the rule. The cost of entering this lottery would be small, but the jackpot enormous: suppression of all evidence, amounting in many cases to a get-out-of-jail-free card. Courts would experience as never before the reality that "[t]he exclusionary rule frequently requires extensive litigation to determine whether particular evidence must be excluded."

Another consequence of the incongruent remedy Hudson proposes would be police officers' refraining from timely entry after knocking and announcing. As we have observed, the amount of time they must wait is necessarily uncertain. If the consequences of running afoul of the rule were so massive, officers would be inclined to wait longer than the law requires — producing preventable violence against officers in some cases, and the destruction of evidence in many others. We deemed these consequences severe enough to produce our unanimous agreement that a mere "reasonable suspicion" that knocking and announcing "under the particular circumstances, would be dangerous or futile, or that it would inhibit the effective investigation of the crime," will cause the requirement to yield.

Next to these "substantial social costs" we must consider the deterrence benefits, existence of which is a necessary condition for exclusion. (It is not, of course, a sufficient condition: "[I]t does not follow that the Fourth Amendment requires adoption of every proposal that might deter police misconduct.") To begin with, the value of deterrence depends upon the strength of the incentive to commit the forbidden act. Viewed from this perspective, deterrence of knock-and-announce violations is not worth a lot. Violation of the warrant requirement sometimes produces incriminating evidence that could not otherwise be obtained. But ignoring knock-and-announce can realistically be expected to achieve absolutely nothing except the prevention of destruction of evidence and the avoidance of life-threatening resistance by occupants of the premises — dangers which, if there is even "reasonable suspicion" of their existence, suspend the knock-and-announce requirement anyway. Massive deterrence is hardly required.

It seems to us not even true, as Hudson contends, that without suppression there will be no deterrence of knock-and-announce violations at all. Of course even if this assertion were accurate, it would not necessarily justify suppression. Assuming (as the assertion must) that civil suit is not an effective deterrent, one can think of many forms of police misconduct that are similarly "undeterred." When, for example, a confessed suspect in the killing of a police officer, arrested (along with incriminating evidence) in a lawful warranted search, is subjected to physical abuse at the station house, would it seriously be suggested that the evidence must be excluded, since that is the only "effective deterrent"? And what, other than civil suit, is the "effective deterrent" of police violation of an already-confessed suspect's Sixth Amendment rights by denying him prompt access to counsel? Many would regard these violated rights as more significant than the right not to be intruded upon in one's nightclothes—and yet nothing but "ineffective" civil suit is available as a deterrent. And the police incentive for those violations is arguably greater than the incentive for disregarding the knock-and-announce rule.

We cannot assume that exclusion in this context is necessary deterrence simply because we found that it was necessary deterrence in different contexts and long ago. That would be forcing the public today to pay for the sins and inadequacies of a legal regime that existed almost half a century ago. Dollree Mapp could not turn to 42 U.S.C. §1983 for meaningful relief; Monroe v. Pape (1961), which began the slow but steady expansion of that remedy, was decided the same Term as *Mapp*. It would be another 17 years before the §1983 remedy was extended to reach the deep pocket of municipalities, Monell v. New York City Dept. of Social Servs., (1978). Citizens whose Fourth Amendment rights were violated by federal officers could not bring suit until 10 years after *Mapp*, with this Court's decision in Bivens v. Six Unknown Fed. Narcotics Agents (1971).

Hudson complains that "it would be very hard to find a lawyer to take a case such as this," but 42 U.S.C. §1988(b) answers this objection. Since some civil-rights violations would yield damages too small to justify the expense of litigation, Congress has authorized attorney's fees for civil-rights plaintiffs. This remedy was unavailable in the heydays of our exclusionary-rule jurisprudence, because it is tied to the availability of a cause of action. For years after *Mapp*, "very few lawyers would even consider representation of persons who had civil rights claims against the police," but now "much has changed. Citizens and lawyers are much more willing to seek relief in the courts for police misconduct." M. Avery, D. Rudovsky, & K. Blum, Police Misconduct: Law and Litigation, p. v (3d ed. 2005); see generally N. Aron, Liberty and Justice for All: Public Interest Law in the 1980s and Beyond (1989) (describing the growth of public-interest law). The number of public-interest law firms and lawyers who specialize in civil-rights grievances has greatly expanded.

Hudson points out that few published decisions to date announce huge awards for knock-and-announce violations. But this is an unhelpful statistic. Even if we thought that only large damages would deter police misconduct (and that police somehow are deterred by "damages" but indifferent to the prospect of large §1988 attorney's fees), we do not know how many claims have been settled, or indeed how many violations have occurred that produced anything more than nominal injury. It is clear, at least, that the lower courts are allowing colorable knock-and-announce suits to go forward, unimpeded by assertions of qualified immunity. As far as we know, civil liability is an effective deterrent here, as we have assumed it is in other contexts.

Another development over the past half-century that deters civil-rights violations is the increasing professionalism of police forces, including a new emphasis on internal police discipline. Even as long ago as 1980 we felt it proper to "assume" that unlawful police behavior would "be dealt with appropriately" by the authorities, but we now have increasing evidence that police forces across the United States take the constitutional rights of citizens seriously. There have been "wide-ranging reforms in the education, training, and supervision of police officers." Numerous sources are now available to teach officers and their supervisors what is required of them under this Court's cases, how to respect constitutional guarantees in various situations, and how to craft an effective regime for internal discipline. Moreover, modern police forces are staffed with professionals; it is not credible to assert that internal discipline, which can limit successful careers, will not have a deterrent effect. There is also evidence that the increasing use of various forms of citizen review can enhance police accountability.

In sum, the social costs of applying the exclusionary rule to knock-and-announce violations are considerable; the incentive to such violations is minimal to begin with, and the extant deterrences against them are substantial — incomparably greater than the factors deterring warrantless entries when *Mapp* was decided. Resort to the massive remedy of suppressing evidence of guilt is unjustified.

It is striking that Justice Scalia's arguments are not simply reasons for an exception to the exclusionary rule for knock and announce violations; they are arguments against the existence of the exclusionary rule. They prompted Justice Kennedy, who concurred in Justice Scalia's opinion, to declare, "[T]he continued operation of the exclusionary rule, as settled and defined by our precedents, is not in doubt." Yet *Hudson* suggests that there may be four votes on the current Court — Chief Justice Roberts and Justices Scalia, Thomas, and Alito — to eliminate the exclusionary rule and that it will continue to exist, and exceptions will be created, to the extent Justice Kennedy wishes.

Justice Scalia's majority opinion in *Hudson* argues that the costs of the exclusionary rule outweigh its benefits. The primary cost, of course, is allowing guilty people to go free. He argues that deterring police misconduct, the central benefit of the exclusionary rule, does not warrant its existence. He says that civil suits for damages against the police who violate the Fourth Amendment are an adequate deterrent. He also maintains that increased professionalization of police forces makes the exclusionary rule unnecessary.

There long has been a debate over whether money damages against police officers for Fourth Amendment violations are a sufficient deterrent. Those who take this view, like Justice Scalia in *Hudson*, argue that the ability to sue police officers makes the exclusionary rule unnecessary.[2]

Others argue that such suits have so little chance of success that there will be little deterrence without the exclusionary rule.[3] Juries are unlikely to find against the police in favor of convicted criminals and if they did, any damages would be nominal. Justice Breyer, in dissent in *Hudson*, makes these points in response to the majority opinion:

> What reason is there to believe that those remedies (such as private damages actions under 42 U.S.C. §1983), which the Court found inadequate in *Mapp*, can adequately deter unconstitutional police behavior here?
>
> The cases reporting knock-and-announce violations are legion. Indeed, these cases of reported violations seem sufficiently frequent and serious as to indicate "a widespread pattern." Yet the majority, like Michigan and the United States, has failed to cite a single reported case in which a plaintiff has collected more than nominal damages solely as a result of a knock-and-announce violation. Even Michigan concedes that, "in cases like the present one . . . , damages may be virtually non-existent." And Michigan's amici further concede that civil immunities prevent tort law from being an effective substitute for the exclusionary rule at this time.
>
> As Justice Stewart, the author of a number of significant Fourth Amendment opinions, explained, the deterrent effect of damage actions "can hardly be said to be great," as such actions are "expensive, time-consuming, not readily available, and rarely successful." The upshot is that the need for deterrence — the critical factor driving this Court's Fourth Amendment cases for close to a century — argues with at least comparable strength for evidentiary exclusion here.
>
> There may be instances in the law where text or history or tradition leaves room for a judicial decision that rests upon little more than an unvarnished judicial instinct. But this is not one of them. Rather, our Fourth Amendment traditions place high value upon protecting privacy in the home. They emphasize the need to assure that its constitutional protections are effective, lest the Amendment "sound the word of promise to the ear but break it to the hope." They include an exclusionary principle, which since *Weeks* has formed the centerpiece of the criminal law's effort to ensure the practical reality of those promises. That is why the Court should assure itself that any departure from that principle is firmly grounded in logic, in history, in precedent, and in empirical fact. It has not done so. That is why, with respect, I dissent.

B. THE ORIGINS OF THE EXCLUSIONARY RULE

The Court first invoked the exclusionary rule as a remedy for Fourth Amendment violations in Weeks v. United States in 1914.

---

2. *See, e.g.*, Christopher Slobogin, *Why Liberals Should Chuck the Exclusionary Rule*, 1999 Univ. Ill. L. Rev. 363.

3. *See, e.g.*, Yale Kamisar, *In Defense of the Search and Seizure Exclusionary Rule*, 26 Harv. J.L. & Pub. Pol'y 119, 126-129 (2003) (arguing that "five decades of post-*Weeks* 'freedom' from the inhibiting effect of the federal exclusionary rule failed to produce any meaningful alternative to the exclusionary rule in any jurisdiction" and that there is no evidence that "times have changed" post-*Mapp*).

WEEKS v. UNITED STATES

232 U.S. 383 (1914)

Justice DAY delivered the opinion of the Court:

An indictment was returned against the defendant in the district court of the United States for the western district of Missouri, containing nine counts. The seventh count, upon which a conviction was had, charged the use of the mails for the purpose of transporting certain coupons or tickets representing chances or shares in a lottery or gift enterprise, in violation of §213 of the Criminal Code. Sentence of fine and imprisonment was imposed.

The defendant was arrested by a police officer, so far as the record shows, without warrant, at the Union Station in Kansas City, Missouri, where he was employed by an express company. Other police officers had gone to the house of the defendant, and being told by a neighbor where the key was kept, found it and entered the house. They searched the defendant's room and took possession of various papers and articles found there, which were afterwards turned over to the United States marshal. Later in the same day police officers returned with the marshal, who thought he might find additional evidence, and, being admitted by someone in the house, probably a boarder, in response to a rap, the marshal searched the defendant's room and carried away certain letters and envelopes found in the drawer of a chiffonier. Neither the marshal nor the police officer had a search warrant.

After the jury had been sworn and before any evidence had been given, the defendant urged his petition for the return of his property, which was denied by the court. Upon the introduction of such papers during the trial, the defendant objected on the ground that the papers had been obtained without a search warrant, and by breaking open his home, in violation of the 4th and 5th Amendments to the Constitution of the United States, which objection was overruled by the court. Among the papers retained and put in evidence were a number of lottery tickets and statements with reference to the lottery, taken at the first visit of the police to the defendant's room, and a number of letters written to the defendant in respect to the lottery, taken by the marshal upon his search of defendant's room.

The defendant assigns error, among other things, in the court's refusal to grant his petition for the return of his property, and in permitting the papers to be used at the trial.

It is thus apparent that the question presented involves the determination of the duty of the court with reference to the motion made by the defendant for the return of certain letters, as well as other papers, taken from his room by the United States marshal, who, without authority of process, if any such could have been legally issued, visited the room of the defendant for the declared purpose of obtaining additional testimony to support the charge against the accused, and, having gained admission to the house, took from the drawer of a chiffonier there found certain letters written to the defendant, tending to show his guilt. These letters were placed in the control of the district attorney, and were subsequently produced by him and offered in evidence against the accused at the trial. The defendant contends that such appropriation of his private correspondence was in violation of rights secured to him by the 4th and 5th Amendments to the Constitution of the United States. We shall deal with the 4th Amendment.

The effect of the 4th Amendment is to put the courts of the United States and Federal officials, in the exercise of their power and authority, under limitations and restraints as to the exercise of such power and authority, and to forever secure the people, their persons, houses, papers, and effects, against all unreasonable searches and seizures under the guise of law. This protection reaches all alike, whether accused of crime or not, and the duty of giving to it force and effect is obligatory upon all intrusted under our Federal system with the enforcement of the laws. The tendency of those who execute the criminal laws of the country to obtain conviction by means of unlawful seizures and enforced confessions, the latter often obtained after subjecting accused persons to unwarranted practices destructive of rights secured by the Federal Constitution, should find no sanction in the judgments of the courts, which are charged at all times with the support of the Constitution, and to which people of all conditions have a right to appeal for the maintenance of such fundamental rights.

If letters and private documents can thus be seized and held and used in evidence against a citizen accused of an offense, the protection of the 4th Amendment, declaring his right to be secure against such searches and seizures, is of no value, and, so far as those thus placed are concerned, might as well be stricken from the Constitution. The efforts of the courts and their officials to bring the guilty to punishment, praiseworthy as they are, are not to be aided by the sacrifice of those great principles established by years of endeavor and suffering which have resulted in their embodiment in the fundamental law of the land. The United States marshal could only have invaded the house of the accused when armed with a warrant issued as required by the Constitution, upon sworn information, and describing with reasonable particularity the thing for which the search was to be made. Instead, he acted without sanction of law, doubtless prompted by the desire to bring further proof to the aid of the government, and under color of his office undertook to make a seizure of private papers in direct violation of the constitutional prohibition against such action. Under such circumstances, without sworn information and particular description, not even an order of court would have justified such procedure; much less was it within the authority of the United States marshal to thus invade the house and privacy of the accused.

The court before which the application was made in this case recognized the illegal character of the seizure, and ordered the return of property not in its judgment competent to be offered at the trial, but refused the application of the accused to turn over the letters, which were afterwards put in evidence on behalf of the government.

We therefore reach the conclusion that the letters in question were taken from the house of the accused by an official of the United States, acting under color of his office, in direct violation of the constitutional rights of the defendant; that having made a seasonable application for their return, which was heard and passed upon by the court, there was involved in the order refusing the application a denial of the constitutional rights of the accused, and that the court should have restored these letters to the accused. In holding them and permitting their use upon the trial, we think prejudicial error was committed. As to the papers and property seized by the policemen, it does not appear that they acted under any claim of Federal authority such as would make the amendment applicable to such unauthorized seizures. The record shows that what they did by way of arrest and search and seizure was done before the finding of the indictment in the Federal court; under what supposed right or authority does not appear. What remedies the defendant may have against them we need not inquire, as the 4th Amendment is not directed to individual misconduct of such officials. Its limitations reach the Federal government and its agencies.

Weeks involves the application of the exclusionary rule to the federal government. The Court initially considered and rejected the application of the exclusionary rule to the states in Wolf v. Colorado, 338 U.S. 25 (1949). Although the Court in *Wolf* said that "[t]he security of one's privacy against arbitrary intrusion by the police . . . is . . . implicit in 'the concept of ordered liberty' and as such enforceable against the States through the Due Process Clause," the Court held that the exclusionary rule is not enforceable against the States as "an essential ingredient of the right." The Court concluded, "We hold, therefore, that in a prosecution in a State court for a State crime the Fourteenth Amendment does not forbid the admission of evidence obtained by an unreasonable search and seizure." *Wolf* was decided at a time when there was intense debate over whether the Bill of Rights should be applied to the states and when a majority of the Court was generally reluctant to apply Bill of Rights provisions to the states.

This changed with the Warren Court, which found almost all of the Bill of Rights to be incorporated and to apply to the states. In 1961, the Supreme Court overruled *Wolf* and held that the exclusionary rule applies to the states in the landmark decision of Mapp v. Ohio.

MAPP v. OHIO

367 U.S. 643 (1961)

Justice CLARK delivered the opinion of the Court.

Appellant stands convicted of knowingly having had in her possession and under her control certain lewd and lascivious books, pictures, and photographs in violation of §2905.34 of Ohio's Revised Code. As officially stated in the syllabus to its opinion, the Supreme Court of Ohio found that her conviction was valid though "based primarily upon the introduction in evidence of lewd and lascivious books and pictures unlawfully seized during an unlawful search of defendant's home."

On May 23, 1957, three Cleveland police officers arrived at appellant's residence in that city pursuant to information that "a person [was] hiding out in the home, who was wanted for questioning in connection with a recent bombing, and that there was a large amount of policy paraphernalia being hidden in the home." Miss Mapp and her daughter by a former marriage lived on the top floor of the two-family dwelling. Upon their arrival at that house, the officers knocked on the door and demanded entrance but appellant, after telephoning her attorney, refused to admit them without a search warrant. They advised their headquarters of the situation and undertook a surveillance of the house.

The officers again sought entrance some three hours later when four or more additional officers arrived on the scene. When Miss Mapp did not come to the door immediately, at least one of the several doors to the house was forcibly opened and the policemen gained admittance. Meanwhile Miss Mapp's attorney arrived, but the officers, having secured their own entry, and continuing in their defiance of the law, would permit him neither to see Miss Mapp nor to enter the house. It appears that Miss Mapp was halfway down the stairs from the upper floor to the front door when the officers, in this highhanded manner, broke into the hall. She demanded to see the search warrant. A paper, claimed to be a warrant, was held up by one of the officers. She grabbed the "warrant" and placed it in her bosom. A struggle ensued in which the officers recovered the piece of paper and as a result of which they handcuffed appellant because she had been "belligerent" in resisting their official rescue of the "warrant" from her person. Running roughshod over appellant, a policeman "grabbed" her, "twisted [her] hand," and she "yelled [and] pleaded with him" because "it was hurting." Appellant, in handcuffs, was then forcibly taken upstairs to her bedroom where the officers searched a dresser, a chest of drawers, a closet and some suitcases. They also looked into a photo album and through personal papers belonging to the appellant. The search spread to the rest of the second floor including the child's bedroom, the living room, the kitchen and a dinette. The basement of the building and a trunk found therein were also searched. The obscene materials for possession of which she was ultimately convicted were discovered in the course of that widespread search.

At the trial no search warrant was produced by the prosecution, nor was the failure to produce one explained or accounted for. At best, "There is, in the record, considerable doubt as to whether there ever was any warrant for the search of defendant's home."

The State says that even if the search were made without authority, or otherwise unreasonably, it is not prevented from using the unconstitutionally seized evidence at trial, citing Wolf v. People of State of Colorado (1949).

There are in the cases of this Court some passing references to the *Weeks* rule as being one of evidence. But the plain and unequivocal language of *Weeks*—and its later paraphrase in *Wolf*—to the effect that the *Weeks* rule is of constitutional origin, remains entirely undisturbed.

Since the Fourth Amendment's right of privacy has been declared enforceable against the States through the Due Process Clause of the Fourteenth, it is enforceable against them by the same sanction of exclusion as is used against the Federal Government. Were it otherwise, then just as without the *Weeks* rule the assurance against unreasonable federal searches and seizures would be "a form of words," valueless and undeserving of mention in a perpetual charter of inestimable human liberties, so too, without that rule the freedom from state invasions of privacy would be so ephemeral and so neatly severed from its conceptual nexus with the freedom from all brutish means of coercing evidence as not to merit this Court's high regard as a freedom "implicit in 'the concept of ordered liberty.'" At the time that the Court held in *Wolf* that the Amendment was applicable to the States through the Due Process Clause, the cases of this Court had steadfastly held that as to federal officers the Fourth Amendment included the exclusion of the evidence seized in violation of its provisions. Even *Wolf* "stoutly adhered" to that proposition. The right to privacy, when conceded operatively enforceable against the States, was not susceptible of destruction by avulsion of the sanction upon which its protection and enjoyment had always been deemed dependent. Therefore, in extending the substantive protections of due process to all constitutionally unreasonable searches — state or federal—it was logically and constitutionally necessary that the exclusion doctrine—an essential part of the right to privacy—be also insisted upon as an essential ingredient of the right newly recognized by the *Wolf* case. In short, the admission of the new constitutional right by *Wolf* could not consistently tolerate denial of its most important constitutional privilege, namely, the exclusion of the evidence which an accused had been forced to give by reason of the unlawful seizure. To hold otherwise is to grant the right but in reality to withhold its privilege and enjoyment. Only last year the Court itself recognized that the purpose of the exclusionary rule "is to deter—to compel respect for the constitutional guaranty in the only effectively available way—by removing the incentive to disregard it."

Indeed, we are aware of no restraint, similar to that rejected today, conditioning the enforcement of any other basic constitutional right. The right to privacy, no less important than any other right carefully and particularly reserved to the people, would stand in marked contrast to all other rights declared as "basic to a free society." This Court has not hesitated to enforce as strictly against the States as it does against the Federal Government the rights of free speech and of a free press, the rights to notice and to a fair, public trial, including, as it does, the right not to be convicted by use of a coerced confession, however logically relevant it be, and without regard to its reliability. And nothing could be more certain than that when a coerced confession is involved, "the relevant rules of evidence" are overridden without regard to "the incidence of such conduct by the police," slight or frequent. Why should not the same rule apply to what is tantamount to coerced testimony by way of unconstitutional seizure of goods, papers, effect, documents, etc.? We find that, as to the Federal Government, the Fourth and Fifth Amendments and, as to the States, the freedom from unconscionable invasions of privacy and the freedom from convictions based upon coerced confessions do enjoy an "intimate relation" in their perpetuation of "principles of humanity and civil liberty (secured) . . . only after years of struggle." They express "supplementing phases of the same constitutional purpose — to maintain inviolate large areas of personal privacy." The philosophy of each Amendment and of each freedom is complementary to, although not dependent upon, that of the other in its sphere of influence — the very least that together they assure in either sphere is that no man is to be convicted on unconstitutional evidence.

Moreover, our holding that the exclusionary rule is an essential part of both the Fourth and Fourteenth Amendments is not only the logical dictate of prior cases, but it also makes very good sense. There is no war between the Constitution and common sense. Presently, a federal prosecutor may make no use of evidence illegally seized, but a State's attorney across the street may, although he supposedly is operating under the enforceable prohibitions of the same Amendment. Thus the State, by admitting evidence unlawfully seized, serves to encourage disobedience to the Federal Constitution which it is bound to uphold.

In non-exclusionary States, federal officers, being human, were by it invited to and did, as our cases indicate, step across the street to the State's attorney with their unconstitutionally seized evidence. Prosecution on the basis of that evidence was then had in a state court in utter disregard of the enforceable Fourth Amendment. If the fruits of an unconstitutional search had been inadmissible in both state and federal courts, this inducement to evasion would have been sooner eliminated. There would be no need to reconcile such cases as *Rea* and *Schnettler*, each pointing up the hazardous uncertainties of our heretofore ambivalent approach.

Federal-state cooperation in the solution of crime under constitutional standards will be promoted, if only by recognition of their now mutual obligation to respect the same fundamental criteria in their approaches. "However much in a particular case insistence upon such rules may appear as a technicality that inures to the benefit of a guilty person, the history of the criminal law proves that tolerance of shortcut methods in law enforcement impairs its enduring effectiveness." Denying shortcuts to only one of two cooperating law enforcement agencies tends naturally to breed legitimate suspicion of "working arrangements" whose results are equally tainted.

There are those who say, as did Justice (then Judge) Cardozo, that under our constitutional exclusionary doctrine "[t]he criminal is to go free because the constable has blundered." In some cases this will undoubtedly be the result. But, "there is another consideration — the imperative of judicial integrity." The criminal goes free, if he must, but it is the law that sets him free. Nothing can destroy a government more quickly than its failure to observe its own laws, or worse, its disregard of the charter of its own existence. As Mr. Justice Brandeis, dissenting, said in Olmstead v. United States, 1928: "Our government is the potent, the omnipresent teacher. For good or for ill, it teaches the whole people by its example. . . . If the government becomes a lawbreaker, it breeds contempt for law; it invites every man to become a law unto himself; it invites anarchy."

Nor can it lightly be assumed that, as a practical matter, adoption of the exclusionary rule fetters law enforcement. Only last year this Court expressly considered that contention and found that "pragmatic evidence of a sort" to the contrary was not wanting.

The ignoble shortcut to conviction left open to the State tends to destroy the entire system of constitutional restraints on which the liberties of the people rest. Having once recognized that the right to privacy embodied in the Fourth Amendment is enforceable against the States, and that the right to be secure against rude invasions of privacy by state officers is, therefore, constitutional in origin, we can no longer permit that right to remain an empty promise. Because it is enforceable in the same manner and to like effect as other basic rights secured by the Due Process Clause, we can no longer permit it to be revocable at the whim of any police officer who, in the name of law enforcement itself, chooses to suspend its enjoyment. Our decision, founded on reason and truth, gives to the individual no more than that which the Constitution guarantees him, to the police officer no less than that to which honest law enforcement is entitled, and, to the courts, that judicial integrity so necessary in the true administration of justice.

Justice HARLAN, whom Justice FRANKFURTER and Justice WHITTAKER join, dissenting.

In overruling the *Wolf* case the Court, in my opinion, has forgotten the sense of judicial restraint which, with due regard for stare decisis, is one element that should enter into deciding whether a past decision of this Court should be overruled. Apart from that I also believe that the *Wolf* rule represents sounder Constitutional doctrine than the new rule which now replaces it.

Essential to the majority's argument against *Wolf* is the proposition that the rule of Weeks v. United States excluding in federal criminal trials the use of evidence obtained in violation of the Fourth Amendment, derives not from the "supervisory power" of this Court over the federal judicial system, but from Constitutional requirement. This is so because no one, I suppose, would suggest that this Court possesses any general supervisory power over the state courts. Although I entertain considerable doubt as to the soundness of this foundational proposition of the majority, I shall assume, for present purposes, that the *Weeks* rule "is of constitutional origin."

At the heart of the majority's opinion in this case is the following syllogism: (1) the rule excluding in federal criminal trials evidence which is the product of all illegal search and seizure is a "part and parcel" of the Fourth Amendment; (2) *Wolf* held that the "privacy" assured against federal action by the Fourth Amendment is also protected against state action by the Fourteenth Amendment; and (3) it is therefore "logically and constitutionally necessary" that the *Weeks* exclusionary rule should also be enforced against the States.

This reasoning ultimately rests on the unsound premise that because *Wolf* carried into the States, as part of "the concept of ordered liberty" embodied in the Fourteenth Amendment, the principle of "privacy" underlying the Fourth Amendment, it must follow that whatever configurations of the Fourth Amendment have been developed in the particularizing federal precedents are likewise to be deemed a part of "ordered liberty," and as such are enforceable against the States. For me, this does not follow at all.

It cannot be too much emphasized that what was recognized in *Wolf* was not that the Fourth Amendment as such is enforceable against the States as a facet of due process, a view of the Fourteenth Amendment which, as *Wolf* itself pointed out, has long since been discredited, but the principle of privacy "which is at the core of the Fourth Amendment." It would not be proper to expect or impose any precise equivalence, either as regards the scope of the right or the means of its implementation, between the requirements of the Fourth and Fourteenth Amendments.

Thus, even in a case which presented simply the question of whether a particular search and seizure was constitutionally "unreasonable" — say in a tort action against state officers — we would not be true to the Fourteenth Amendment were we merely to stretch the general principle of individual privacy on a Procrustean bed of federal precedents under the Fourth Amendment. But in this instance more than that is involved, for here we are reviewing not a determination that what the state police did was Constitutionally permissible (since the state court quite evidently assumed that it was not), but a determination that appellant was properly found guilty of conduct which, for present purposes, it is to be assumed the State could Constitutionally punish. Since there is not the slightest suggestion that Ohio's policy is "affirmatively to sanction . . . police incursion into privacy" what the Court is now doing is to impose upon the States not only federal substantive standards of "search and seizure" but also the basic federal remedy for violation of those standards. For I think it entirely clear that the *Weeks* exclusionary rule is but a remedy which, by penalizing past official misconduct, is aimed at deterring such conduct in the future.

I would not impose upon the States this federal exclusionary remedy. The reasons given by the majority for now suddenly turning its back on *Wolf* seem to me notably unconvincing. The preservation of a proper balance between state and federal responsibility in the administration of criminal justice demands patience on the part of those who might like to see things move faster among the States in this respect. Problems of criminal law enforcement vary widely from State to State. One State, in considering the totality of its legal picture, may conclude that the need for embracing the *Weeks* rule is pressing because other remedies are unavailable or inadequate to secure compliance with the substantive Constitutional principle involved. Another, though equally solicitous of Constitutional rights, may choose to pursue one purpose at a time, allowing all evidence relevant to guilt to be brought into a criminal trial, and dealing with Constitutional infractions by other means. Still another may consider the exclusionary rule too rough-and-ready a remedy, in that it reaches only unconstitutional intrusions which eventuate in criminal prosecution of the victims. Further, a State after experimenting with the *Weeks* rule for a time may, because of unsatisfactory experience with it, decide to revert to a non-exclusionary rule.

A state conviction comes to us as the complete product of a sovereign judicial system. Typically a case will have been tried in a trial court, tested in some final appellate court, and will go no further. In the comparatively rare instance when a conviction is reviewed by us on due process grounds we deal then with a finished product in the creation of which we are allowed no hand, and our task, far from being one of over-all supervision, is, speaking generally, restricted to a determination of whether the prosecution was Constitutionally fair. The specifics of trial procedure, which in every mature legal system will vary greatly in detail, are within the sole competence of the States. I do not see how it can be said that a trial becomes unfair simply because a State determines that evidence may be considered by the trier of fact, regardless of how it was obtained, if it is relevant to the one issue with which the trial is concerned, the guilt or innocence of the accused. Of course, a court may use its procedures as an incidental means of pursuing other ends than the correct resolution of the controversies before it. Such indeed is the *Weeks* rule, but if a State does not choose to use its courts in this way, I do not believe that this Court is empowered to impose this much-debated procedure on local courts, however efficacious we may consider the *Weeks* rule to be as a means of securing Constitutional rights.

I regret that I find so unwise in principle and so inexpedient in policy a decision motivated by the high purpose of increasing respect for Constitutional rights. But in the last analysis I think this Court can increase respect for the Constitution only if it rigidly respects the limitations which the Constitution places upon it, and respects as well the principles inherent in its own processes. In the present case I think we exceed both, and that our voice becomes only a voice of power, not of reason.

C.   WHEN DOES THE EXCLUSIONARY RULE APPLY?

In Herring v. United States, the Supreme Court imposed substantial limits on the application of the exclusionary rule. The Court held that the exclusionary rule applies only to deliberate or reckless violations of the Fourth Amendment or those that are the result of systematic government policies. The exclusionary rule does not apply to negligent or good faith violations of the Fourth Amendment. The Court emphasized that the sole purpose of the exclusionary rule is to deter police misconduct. It is notable that, as in Hudson v. Michigan, *Herring* is a 5-4 decision with the same justices in the majority—Roberts, Scalia, Kennedy, Thomas, and Alito.

HERRING v. UNITED STATES

555 U.S. 135 (2009)

Chief Justice ROBERTS delivered the opinion of the Court.

The Fourth Amendment forbids "unreasonable searches and seizures," and this usually requires the police to have probable cause or a warrant before making an arrest. What if an officer reasonably believes there is an outstanding arrest warrant, but that belief turns out to be wrong because of a negligent bookkeeping error by another police employee? The parties here agree that the ensuing arrest is still a violation of the Fourth Amendment, but dispute whether contraband found during a search incident to that arrest must be excluded in a later prosecution.

Our cases establish that such suppression is not an automatic consequence of a Fourth Amendment violation. Instead, the question turns on the culpability of the police and the potential of exclusion to deter wrongful police conduct. Here the error was the result of isolated negligence attenuated from the arrest. We hold that in these circumstances the jury should not be barred from considering all the evidence.

I

On July 7, 2004, Investigator Mark Anderson learned that Bennie Dean Herring had driven to the Coffee County Sheriff's Department to retrieve something from his impounded truck. Herring was no stranger to law enforcement, and Anderson asked the county's warrant clerk, Sandy Pope, to check for any outstanding warrants for Herring's arrest. When she found none, Anderson asked Pope to check with Sharon Morgan, her counterpart in neighboring Dale County. After checking Dale County's computer database, Morgan replied that there was an active arrest warrant for Herring's failure to appear on a felony charge. Pope relayed the information to Anderson and asked Morgan to fax over a copy of the warrant as confirmation. Anderson and a deputy followed Herring as he left the impound lot, pulled him over, and arrested him. A search incident to the arrest revealed methamphetamine in Herring's pocket, and a pistol (which as a felon he could not possess) in his vehicle.

There had, however, been a mistake about the warrant. The Dale County sheriff's computer records are supposed to correspond to actual arrest warrants, which the office also maintains. But when Morgan went to the files to retrieve the actual warrant to fax to Pope, Morgan was unable to find it. She called a court clerk and learned that the warrant had been recalled five months earlier. Normally when a warrant is recalled the court clerk's office or a judge's chambers calls Morgan, who enters the information in the sheriff's computer database and disposes of the physical copy. For whatever reason, the information about the recall of the warrant for Herring did not appear in the database. Morgan immediately called Pope to alert her to the mixup, and Pope contacted Anderson over a secure radio. This all unfolded in 10 to 15 minutes, but Herring had already been arrested and found with the gun and drugs, just a few hundred yards from the sheriff's office.

Herring was indicted in the District Court for the Middle District of Alabama for illegally possessing the gun and drugs, violations of 18 U.S.C. §922(g)(1) and 21 U.S.C. §844(a). He moved to suppress the evidence on the ground that his initial arrest had been illegal because the warrant had been rescinded.

II

When a probable-cause determination was based on reasonable but mistaken assumptions, the person subjected to a search or seizure has not necessarily been the victim of a constitutional violation. The very phrase "probable cause" confirms that the Fourth Amendment does not demand all possible precision. And whether the error can be traced to a mistake by a state actor or some other source may bear on the analysis. For purposes of deciding this case, however, we accept the parties' assumption that there was a Fourth Amendment violation. The issue is whether the exclusionary rule should be applied.

A

The Fourth Amendment protects "[t]he right of the people to be secure in their persons, houses, papers, and effects, against unreasonable searches and seizures," but "contains no provision expressly precluding the use of evidence obtained in violation of its commands," *Arizona v. Evans* (1995). Nonetheless, our decisions establish an exclusionary rule that, when applicable, forbids the use of improperly obtained evidence at trial. We have stated that this judicially created rule is "designed to safeguard Fourth Amendment rights generally through its deterrent effect."

In analyzing the applicability of the rule, we must consider the actions of all the police officers involved. The Coffee County officers did nothing improper. Indeed, the error was noticed so quickly because Coffee County requested a faxed confirmation of the warrant.

The Eleventh Circuit concluded, however, that somebody in Dale County should have updated the computer database to reflect the recall of the arrest warrant. The court also concluded that this error was negligent, but did not find it to be reckless or deliberate. That fact is crucial to our holding that this error is not enough by itself to require "the extreme sanction of exclusion."

B

1. The fact that a Fourth Amendment violation occurred — *i.e.*, that a search or arrest was unreasonable — does not necessarily mean that the exclusionary rule applies. Indeed, exclusion "has always been our last resort, not our first impulse," *Hudson v. Michigan*, (2006), and our precedents establish important principles that constrain application of the exclusionary rule.

First, the exclusionary rule is not an individual right and applies only where it "'result[s] in appreciable deterrence.'" We have repeatedly rejected the argument that exclusion is a necessary consequence of a Fourth Amendment violation. Instead we have focused on the efficacy of the rule in deterring Fourth Amendment violations in the future.

In addition, the benefits of deterrence must outweigh the costs. "We have never suggested that the exclusionary rule must apply in every circumstance in which it might provide marginal deterrence." "[T]o the extent that application of the exclusionary rule could provide some incremental deterrent, that possible benefit must be weighed against [its] substantial social costs." The principal cost of applying the rule is, of course, letting guilty and possibly dangerous defendants go free — something that "offends basic concepts of the criminal justice system." "[T]he rule's costly toll upon truth-seeking and law enforcement objectives presents a high obstacle for those urging [its] application."

These principles are reflected in the holding of *Leon*: When police act under a warrant that is invalid for lack of probable cause, the exclusionary rule does not apply if the police acted "in objectively reasonable reliance" on the subsequently invalidated search warrant. We (perhaps confusingly) called this objectively reasonable reliance "good faith."

Shortly thereafter we extended these holdings to warrantless administrative searches performed in good-faith reliance on a statute later declared unconstitutional. Finally, we applied this good-faith rule to police who reasonably relied on mistaken information in a court's database that an arrest warrant was outstanding. We held that a mistake made by a judicial employee could not give rise to exclusion for three reasons: The exclusionary rule was crafted to curb police rather than judicial misconduct; court employees were unlikely to try to subvert the Fourth Amendment; and "most important, there [was] no basis for believing that application of the exclusionary rule in [those] circumstances" would have any significant effect in deterring the errors. [*Arizona v.*] *Evans* left unresolved "whether the evidence should be suppressed if police personnel were responsible for the error," an issue not argued by the State in that case, but one that we now confront.

2. Anticipating the good-faith exception to the exclusionary rule, Judge Friendly wrote that "[t]he beneficent aim of the exclusionary rule to deter police misconduct can be sufficiently accomplished by a practice . . . outlawing evidence obtained by flagrant or deliberate violation of rights." The Bill of Rights as a Code of Criminal Procedure, 53 Calif. L.Rev. 929, 953 (1965). Indeed, the abuses that gave rise to the exclusionary rule featured intentional conduct that was patently unconstitutional.

3. To trigger the exclusionary rule, police conduct must be sufficiently deliberate that exclusion can meaningfully deter it, and sufficiently culpable that such deterrence is worth the price paid by the justice system. As laid out in our cases, the exclusionary rule serves to deter deliberate, reckless, or grossly negligent conduct, or in some circumstances recurring or systemic negligence. The error in this case does not rise to that level.[4]

The pertinent analysis of deterrence and culpability is objective, not an "inquiry into the subjective awareness of arresting officers." We have already held that "our good-faith inquiry is confined to the objectively ascertainable question whether a reasonably well trained officer would have known that the search was illegal" in light of "all of the circumstances." These circumstances frequently include a particular officer's knowledge and experience, but that does not make the test any more subjective than the one for probable cause, which looks to an officer's knowledge and experience, but not his subjective intent.

4. We do not suggest that all recordkeeping errors by the police are immune from the exclusionary rule. In this case, however, the conduct at issue was not so objectively culpable as to require exclusion. In *Leon* we held that "the marginal or nonexistent benefits produced by suppressing evidence obtained in objectively reasonable reliance on a subsequently invalidated search warrant cannot justify the substantial costs of exclusion." The same is true when evidence is obtained in objectively reasonable reliance on a subsequently recalled warrant.

If the police have been shown to be reckless in maintaining a warrant system, or to have knowingly made false entries to lay the groundwork for future false arrests, exclusion would certainly be justified under our cases should such misconduct cause a Fourth Amendment violation. Petitioner's fears that our decision will cause police departments to deliberately keep their officers ignorant are thus unfounded. The dissent also adverts to the possible unreliability of a number of databases not relevant to this case. In a case where systemic errors were demonstrated, it might be reckless for officers to rely on an unreliable warrant system. But there is no evidence that errors in Dale County's system are routine or widespread.

Petitioner's claim that police negligence automatically triggers suppression cannot be squared with the principles underlying the exclusionary rule, as they have been explained in our cases. In light of our repeated holdings that the deterrent effect of suppression must be substantial and outweigh any harm to the justice system, we conclude that when police mistakes are the result of negligence such as that described here, rather than systemic error or reckless disregard of constitutional requirements, any marginal deterrence does not "pay its way." In such a case, the criminal should not

---

4. We do not quarrel with Justice Ginsburg's claim that "liability for negligence . . . creates an incentive to act with greater care," and we do not suggest that the exclusion of this evidence could have *no* deterrent effect. But our cases require any deterrence to "be weighed against the 'substantial social costs exacted by the exclusionary rule,'" and here exclusion is not worth the cost. [Footnote by the Court.]

"go free because the constable has blundered." *People v. Defore*, (1926) (opinion of the Court by Cardozo, J.).

Justice GINSBURG, with whom Justice STEVENS, Justice SOUTER, and Justice BREYER join, dissenting.

Petitioner Bennie Dean Herring was arrested, and subjected to a search incident to his arrest, although no warrant was outstanding against him, and the police lacked probable cause to believe he was engaged in criminal activity. The arrest and ensuing search therefore violated Herring's Fourth Amendment right "to be secure . . . against unreasonable searches and seizures." The Court of Appeals so determined, and the Government does not contend otherwise. The exclusionary rule provides redress for Fourth Amendment violations by placing the government in the position it would have been in had there been no unconstitutional arrest and search. The rule thus strongly encourages police compliance with the Fourth Amendment in the future. The Court, however, holds the rule inapplicable because careless recordkeeping by the police — not flagrant or deliberate misconduct — accounts for Herring's arrest.

I would not so constrict the domain of the exclusionary rule and would hold the rule dispositive of this case: "[I]f courts are to have any power to discourage [police] error of [the kind here at issue], it must be through the application of the exclusionary rule." The unlawful search in this case was contested in court because the police found methamphetamine in Herring's pocket and a pistol in his truck. But the "most serious impact" of the Court's holding will be on innocent persons "wrongfully arrested based on erroneous information [carelessly maintained] in a computer data base."

I

A

The Court states that the exclusionary rule is not a defendant's right, rather, it is simply a remedy applicable only when suppression would result in appreciable deterrence that outweighs the cost to the justice system. The Court's discussion invokes a view of the exclusionary rule famously held by renowned jurists Henry J. Friendly and Benjamin Nathan Cardozo. Over 80 years ago, Cardozo, then seated on the New York Court of Appeals, commented critically on the federal exclusionary rule, which had not yet been applied to the States. He suggested that in at least some cases the rule exacted too high a price from the criminal justice system. See *People v. Defore*, (1926). In words often quoted, Cardozo questioned whether the criminal should "go free because the constable has blundered." Judge Friendly later elaborated on Cardozo's query. "The sole reason for exclusion," Friendly wrote, "is that experience has demonstrated this to be the only effective method for deterring the police from violating the Constitution." He thought it excessive, in light of the rule's aim to deter police conduct, to require exclusion when the constable had merely "blundered"—when a police officer committed a technical error in an on-the-spot judgment, or made a "slight and unintentional miscalculation."

B

Others have described "a more majestic conception" of the Fourth Amendment and its adjunct, the exclusionary rule. Protective of the fundamental "right of the people to be secure in their persons, houses, papers, and effects," the Amendment "is a constraint on the power of the sovereign, not merely on some of its agents." I share that vision of the Amendment.

The exclusionary rule is "a remedy necessary to ensure that" the Fourth Amendment's prohibitions "are observed in fact." The rule's service as an essential auxiliary to the Amendment earlier inclined the Court to hold the two inseparable.

Beyond doubt, a main objective of the rule "is to deter—to compel respect for the constitutional guaranty in the only effectively available way—by removing the incentive to disregard it." But the rule also serves other important purposes: It "enabl[es] the judiciary to avoid the taint of partnership in official lawlessness," and it "assur[es] the people—all potential victims of unlawful government conduct—that the government would not profit from its lawless behavior, thus minimizing the risk of seriously undermining popular trust in government."

The exclusionary rule, it bears emphasis, is often the only remedy effective to redress a Fourth Amendment violation. Civil liability will not lie for "the vast majority of [F]ourth [A]mendment violations—the frequent infringements motivated by commendable zeal, not condemnable malice." Criminal prosecutions or administrative sanctions against the offending officers and injunctive relief against widespread violations are an even farther cry.

II

The Court maintains that Herring's case is one in which the exclusionary rule could have scant deterrent effect and therefore would not "pay its way." I disagree.

A

The exclusionary rule, the Court suggests, is capable of only marginal deterrence when the misconduct at issue is merely careless, not intentional or reckless. The suggestion runs counter to a foundational premise of tort law—that liability for negligence, *i.e.*, lack of due care, creates an incentive to act with greater care.

That the mistake here involved the failure to make a computer entry hardly means that application of the exclusionary rule would have minimal value. "Just as the risk of *respondeat superior* liability encourages employers to supervise . . . their employees' conduct [more carefully], so the risk of exclusion of evidence encourages policymakers and systems managers to monitor the performance of the systems they install and the personnel employed to operate those systems."

Consider the potential impact of a decision applying the exclusionary rule in this case. As earlier observed, the record indicates that there is no electronic connection between the warrant database of the Dale County Sheriff's Department and that of the County Circuit Clerk's office, which is located in the basement of the same building. When a warrant is recalled, one of the "many different people that have access to th[e] warrants," must find the hard copy of the warrant in the "two or three different places" where the department houses warrants, return it to the Clerk's office, and manually update the Department's database. The record reflects no routine practice of checking the database for accuracy, and the failure to remove the entry for Herring's warrant was not discovered until Investigator Anderson sought to pursue Herring five months later. Is it not altogether obvious that the Department could take further precautions to ensure the integrity of its database? The Sheriff's Department "is in a position to remedy the situation and might well do so if the exclusionary rule is there to remove the incentive to do otherwise."

B

Is the potential deterrence here worth the costs it imposes? In light of the paramount importance of accurate recordkeeping in law enforcement, I would answer yes, and next explain why, as I see it, Herring's motion presents a particularly strong case for suppression.

Electronic databases form the nervous system of contemporary criminal justice operations. In recent years, their breadth and influence have dramatically expanded. Police today can access databases that include not only the updated National Crime Information Center (NCIC), but also terrorist watchlists, the Federal Government's employee eligibility system, and various commercial databases. Moreover, States are actively expanding information sharing between jurisdictions. As a result, law enforcement has an increasing supply of information within its easy electronic reach.

The risk of error stemming from these databases is not slim. Herring's *amici* warn that law enforcement databases are insufficiently monitored and often out of date. Government reports describe, for example, flaws in NCIC databases, terrorist watchlist databases, and databases associated with the Federal Government's employment eligibility verification system.

Inaccuracies in expansive, interconnected collections of electronic information raise grave concerns for individual liberty. "The offense to the dignity of the citizen who is arrested, handcuffed, and searched on a public street simply because some bureaucrat has failed to maintain an accurate computer data base" is evocative of the use of general warrants that so outraged the authors of our Bill of Rights.

C

The Court assures that "exclusion would certainly be justified" if "the police have been shown to be reckless in maintaining a warrant system, or to have knowingly made false entries to lay the groundwork for future false arrests." This concession provides little comfort.

First, by restricting suppression to bookkeeping errors that are deliberate or reckless, the majority leaves Herring, and others like him, with no remedy for violations of their constitutional rights.

Second, I doubt that police forces already possess sufficient incentives to maintain up-to-date records. The Government argues that police have no desire to send officers out on arrests unnecessarily, because arrests consume resources and place officers in danger. The facts of this case do not fit that description of police motivation. Here the officer wanted to arrest Herring and consulted the Department's records to legitimate his predisposition.

Third, even when deliberate or reckless conduct is afoot, the Court's assurance will often be an empty promise: How is an impecunious defendant to make the required showing? If the answer is that a defendant is entitled to discovery (and if necessary, an audit of police databases), then the Court has imposed a considerable administrative burden on courts and law enforcement.[5]

IV

Negligent recordkeeping errors by law enforcement threaten individual liberty, are susceptible to deterrence by the exclusionary rule, and cannot be remedied effectively through other means. Such errors present no occasion to further erode the exclusionary rule. The rule "is needed to make the Fourth Amendment something real; a guarantee that does not carry with it the exclusion of evidence obtained by its violation is a chimera." In keeping with the rule's "core concerns," suppression should have attended the unconstitutional search in this case.

Justice BREYER, with whom Justice SOUTER joins, dissenting.

I agree with Justice Ginsburg and join her dissent. I write separately to note one additional supporting factor that I believe important. In *Arizona v. Evans* (1995), we held that recordkeeping errors made by a court clerk do not trigger the exclusionary rule, so long as the police reasonably relied upon the court clerk's recordkeeping. The rationale for our decision was premised on a distinction between judicial errors and police errors, and we gave several reasons for recognizing that distinction.

First, we noted that "the exclusionary rule was historically designed as a means of deterring *police* misconduct, not mistakes by court employees."

---

5. It is not clear how the Court squares its focus on deliberate conduct with its recognition that application of the exclusionary rule does not require inquiry into the mental state of the police. [Footnote by the Court.]

Second, we found "no evidence that court employees are inclined to ignore or subvert the Fourth Amendment or that lawlessness among these actors requires application of the extreme sanction of exclusion." *Third,* we recognized that there was "no basis for believing that application of the exclusionary rule . . . [would] have a significant effect on court employees responsible for informing the police that a warrant has been quashed. Because court clerks are not adjuncts to the law enforcement team engaged in the often competitive enterprise of ferreting out crime, they have no stake in the outcome of particular criminal prosecutions." Taken together, these reasons explain why police recordkeeping errors should be treated differently than judicial ones.

Other cases applying the "good faith" exception to the exclusionary rule have similarly recognized the distinction between police errors and errors made by others, such as judicial officers or legislatures.

Distinguishing between police recordkeeping errors and judicial ones not only is consistent with our precedent, but also is far easier for courts to administer than The Chief Justice's case-by-case, multifactored inquiry into the degree of police culpability. I therefore would apply the exclusionary rule when police personnel are responsible for a recordkeeping error that results in a Fourth Amendment violation.

The need for a clear line, and the recognition of such a line in our precedent, are further reasons in support of the outcome that Justice Ginsburg's dissent would reach.

———————————

In Davis v. United States (2011), the Court reaffirmed that the exclusionary rule exists solely to deter violations of the Fourth Amendment and thus concluded that it does not apply when police follow the law as it existed as of the time of the search, even though the law was changed while the case was pending on appeal.

DAVIS v. UNITED STATES
564 U.S. 229 (2011)

Justice ALITO delivered the opinion of the Court.

The Fourth Amendment protects the right to be free from "unreasonable searches and seizures," but it is silent about how this right is to be enforced. To supplement the bare text, this Court created the exclusionary rule, a deterrent sanction that bars the prosecution from introducing evidence obtained by way of a Fourth Amendment violation. The question here is whether to apply this sanction when the police conduct a search in compliance with binding precedent that is later overruled. Because suppression would do nothing to deter police misconduct in these circumstances, and because it would come at a high cost to both the truth and the public safety, we hold that searches conducted in objectively reasonable reliance on binding appellate precedent are not subject to the exclusionary rule.

I

The question presented arises in this case as a result of a shift in our Fourth Amendment jurisprudence on searches of automobiles incident to arrests of recent occupants.

Under this Court's decision in *Chimel v. California* (1969), a police officer who makes a lawful arrest may conduct a warrantless search of the arrestee's person and the area "within his immediate control." This rule "may be stated clearly enough," but in the early going after *Chimel* it proved difficult to apply, particularly in cases that involved searches "inside [of] automobile[s] after the arrestees [we]re no longer in [them]." In *New York v. Belton* (1981), this Court announced "that when a policeman has made a lawful custodial arrest of the occupant of an automobile, he may, as a contemporaneous incident of that arrest, search the passenger compartment of that automobile."

In *Arizona v. Gant* (2009), the Court adopted a new, two-part rule under which an automobile search incident to a recent occupant's arrest is constitutional (1) if the arrestee is within reaching distance of the vehicle during the search, or (2) if the police have reason to believe that the vehicle contains "evidence relevant to the crime of arrest."

The search at issue in this case took place a full two years before this Court announced its new rule in *Gant*. On an April evening in 2007, police officers in Greenville, Alabama, conducted a routine traffic stop that eventually resulted in the arrests of driver Stella Owens (for driving while intoxicated) and passenger Willie Davis (for giving a false name to police). The police handcuffed both Owens and Davis, and they placed the arrestees in the back of separate patrol cars. The police then searched the passenger compartment of Owens's vehicle and found a revolver inside Davis's jacket pocket.

While Davis's appeal was pending, this Court decided *Gant*. The Eleventh Circuit, in the opinion below, applied *Gant*'s new rule and held that the vehicle search incident to Davis's arrest "violated [his] Fourth Amendment rights." As for whether this constitutional violation warranted suppression, the Eleventh Circuit viewed that as a separate issue that turned on "the potential of exclusion to deter wrongful police conduct." The court concluded that "penalizing the [arresting] officer" for following binding appellate precedent would do nothing to "dete[r] . . . Fourth Amendment violations." It therefore declined to apply the exclusionary rule and affirmed Davis's conviction.

II

The Fourth Amendment protects the "right of the people to be secure in their persons, houses, papers, and effects, against unreasonable searches and seizures." The Amendment says nothing about suppressing evidence obtained in violation of this command. That rule — the exclusionary rule — is a "prudential" doctrine, Exclusion is "not a personal constitutional right," nor is it designed to "redress the injury" occasioned by an unconstitutional search. The rule's sole purpose, we have repeatedly held, is to deter future Fourth Amendment violations. Where suppression fails to yield "appreciable deterrence," exclusion is "clearly . . . unwarranted."

Real deterrent value is a "necessary condition for exclusion," but it is not "a sufficient" one. The analysis must also account for the "substantial social costs" generated by the rule. Exclusion exacts a heavy toll on both the judicial system and society at large. It almost always requires courts to ignore reliable, trustworthy evidence bearing on guilt or innocence. And its bottom-line effect, in many cases, is to suppress the truth and set the criminal loose in the community without punishment. Our cases hold that society must swallow this bitter pill when necessary, but only as a "last resort." For exclusion to be appropriate, the deterrence benefits of suppression must outweigh its heavy costs. Admittedly, there was a time when our exclusionary-rule cases were not nearly so discriminating in their approach to the doctrine. "Expansive dicta" in several decisions, suggested that the rule was a self-executing mandate implicit in the Fourth Amendment itself. In time, however, we came to acknowledge the exclusionary rule for what it undoubtedly is — a "judicially created remedy" of this Court's own making. We abandoned the old, "reflexive" application of the doctrine, and imposed a more rigorous weighing of its costs and deterrence benefits. In a line of cases beginning with *United States v. Leon* we also recalibrated our cost-benefit analysis in exclusion cases to focus the inquiry on the "flagrancy of the police misconduct" at issue.

The basic insight of the *Leon* line of cases is that the deterrence benefits of exclusion "var[y] with the culpability of the law enforcement conduct" at issue. When the police exhibit "deliberate," "reckless," or "grossly negligent" disregard for Fourth Amendment rights, the deterrent value of exclusion is strong and tends to outweigh the resulting costs. But when the police act with an objectively "reasonable good-faith belief" that their conduct is lawful, or when their conduct involves only simple, "isolated" negligence, the "'deterrence rationale loses much of its force,'" and exclusion cannot "pay its way." The Court has over time applied this "good-faith" exception across a range of cases.

III

The question in this case is whether to apply the exclusionary rule when the police conduct a search in objectively reasonable reliance on binding judicial precedent. At the time of the search at issue here, we had not yet decided *Arizona v. Gant,* and the Eleventh Circuit had interpreted our decision in *New York v. Belton,* to establish a bright-line rule authorizing the search of a vehicle's passenger compartment incident to a recent occupant's arrest.

Under our exclusionary-rule precedents, this acknowledged absence of police culpability dooms Davis's claim. Police practices trigger the harsh sanction of exclusion only when they are deliberate enough to yield "meaningfu[l]" deterrence, and culpable enough to be "worth the price paid by the justice system." The conduct of the officers here was neither of these things. The officers who conducted the search did not violate Davis's Fourth Amendment rights deliberately, recklessly, or with gross negligence. Nor does this case involve any "recurring or systemic negligence" on the part of law enforcement. The police acted in strict compliance with binding precedent, and their behavior was not wrongful. Unless the exclusionary rule is to become a strict-liability regime, it can have no application in this case.

Indeed, in 27 years of practice under *Leon*'s good-faith exception, we have "never applied" the exclusionary rule to suppress evidence obtained as a result of nonculpable, innocent police conduct. About all that exclusion would deter in this case is conscientious police work. Responsible law-enforcement officers will take care to learn "what is required of them" under Fourth Amendment precedent and will conform their conduct to these rules. But by the same token, when binding appellate precedent specifically *authorizes* a particular police practice, well-trained officers will and should use that tool to fulfill their crime-detection and public-safety responsibilities. An officer who conducts a search in reliance on binding appellate precedent does no more than "'ac[t] as a reasonable officer would and should act'" under the circumstances. The deterrent effect of exclusion in such a case can only be to discourage the officer from "'do[ing] his duty.'"

That is not the kind of deterrence the exclusionary rule seeks to foster. We have stated before, and we reaffirm today, that the harsh sanction of exclusion "should not be applied to deter objectively reasonable law enforcement activity." Evidence obtained during a search conducted in reasonable reliance on binding precedent is not subject to the exclusionary rule.

It is one thing for the criminal "to go free because the constable has blundered." It is quite another to set the criminal free because the constable has scrupulously adhered to governing law. Excluding evidence in such cases deters no police misconduct and imposes substantial social costs. We therefore hold that when the police conduct a search in objectively reasonable reliance on binding appellate precedent, the exclusionary rule does not apply.

Justice BREYER, with whom Justice GINSBURG joins, dissenting.

In 2009, this Court held that a police search of an automobile without a warrant violates the Fourth Amendment if the police have previously removed the automobile's occupants and placed them securely in a squad car. The present case involves these same circumstances, and it was pending on appeal when this Court decided *Gant*. Because *Gant* represents a "shift" in the Court's Fourth Amendment jurisprudence, we must decide *whether* and *how Gant*'s new rule applies here.

I

I agree with the Court about *whether Gant's* new rule applies. It does apply.

"[A] new rule for the conduct of criminal prosecutions is to be applied retroactively to all cases, state or federal, pending on direct review or not yet final, with no exception for cases in which the new rule constitutes a 'clear break' with the past."

II

The Court goes on, however, to decide *how Gant's* new rule will apply. And here it adds a fatal twist. While conceding that, like the search in *Gant*, this search violated the Fourth Amendment, it holds that, unlike Gant, this defendant is not entitled to a remedy. That is because the Court finds a new "good faith" exception which prevents application of the normal remedy for a Fourth Amendment violation, namely, suppression of the illegally seized evidence. Leaving Davis with a right but not a remedy, the Court "keep[s] the word of promise to our ear" but "break[s] it to our hope."

At this point I can no longer agree with the Court. A new "good faith" exception and this Court's retroactivity decisions are incompatible. For one thing, the Court's distinction between (1) retroactive application of a new rule and (2) availability of a remedy is highly artificial and runs counter to precedent. To determine that a new rule is retroactive *is* to determine that, at least in the normal case, there is a remedy. As we have previously said, the "source of a 'new rule' is the Constitution itself, not any judicial power to create new rules of law"; hence, "[w]hat we are actually determining when we assess the 'retroactivity' of a new rule is not the temporal scope of a newly announced right, but whether a violation of the right that occurred prior to the announcement of the new rule will entitle a criminal defendant to the relief sought." The Court's "good faith" exception (unlike, say, inevitable discovery, a remedial doctrine that applies only upon occasion) creates "a categorical bar to obtaining redress" in *every* case pending when a precedent is overturned.

Another such problem concerns fairness. It treats the defendant in a case announcing a new rule one way while treating similarly situated defendants whose cases are pending on appeal in a different way.

Of course, the Court may, as it suggests, avoid this unfairness by refusing to apply the exclusionary rule even to the defendant in the very case in which it announces a "new rule." But that approach would make matters worse. What would then happen in the lower courts? How would courts of appeals, for example, come to reconsider their prior decisions when other circuits' cases lead them to believe those decisions may be wrong? Why would a defendant seek to overturn any such decision? After all, if the (incorrect) circuit precedent is clear, then even if the defendant wins (on the constitutional question), he loses (on relief). To what extent then could this Court rely upon lower courts to work out Fourth Amendment differences among themselves — through circuit reconsideration of a precedent that other circuits have criticized?

Perhaps more important, the Court's rationale for creating its new "good faith" exception threatens to undermine well-settled Fourth Amendment law. The Court correctly says that pre-*Gant* Eleventh Circuit precedent had held that a *Gant*-type search was constitutional; hence the police conduct in this case, consistent with that precedent, was "innocent." But the Court then finds this fact sufficient to create a new "good faith" exception to the exclusionary rule. It reasons that the "sole purpose" of the exclusionary rule "is to deter future Fourth Amendment violations."

If the Court means what it says, what will happen to the exclusionary rule, a rule that the Court adopted nearly a century ago for federal courts, and made applicable to state courts a half century ago through the Fourteenth Amendment? The Court has thought of that rule not as punishment for the individual officer or as reparation for the individual defendant but more generally as an effective way to secure enforcement of the Fourth Amendment's commands.

The fact that such exceptions are few and far between is understandable. Defendants frequently move to suppress evidence on Fourth Amendment grounds. In many, perhaps most, of these instances the police, uncertain of how the Fourth Amendment applied to the particular factual circumstances they faced, will have acted in objective good faith. Yet, in a significant percentage of these instances, courts will find that the police were wrong. And, unless the police conduct falls into one of the exceptions previously noted, courts have required the suppression of the evidence seized.

But an officer who conducts a search that he believes complies with the Constitution but which, it ultimately turns out, falls just outside the Fourth Amendment's bounds is no more culpable than an officer who follows erroneous "binding precedent." Nor is an officer more culpable where circuit precedent is simply suggestive rather than "binding," where it only describes how to treat roughly analogous instances, or where it just does not exist. Thus, if the Court means what it now says, if it would place determinative weight upon the culpability of an individual officer's conduct, and if it would apply the exclusionary rule only where a Fourth Amendment violation was "deliberate, reckless, or grossly negligent," then the "good faith" exception will swallow the exclusionary rule. Indeed, our broad dicta in *Herring* — dicta the Court repeats and expands upon today — may already be leading lower courts in this direction.

Any such change (which may already be underway) would affect not "an exceedingly small set of cases," but a very large number of cases, potentially many thousands each year. And since the exclusionary rule is often the only sanction available for a Fourth Amendment violation, the Fourth Amendment would no longer protect ordinary Americans from "unreasonable searches and seizures." It would become a watered-down Fourth Amendment, offering its protection against only those searches and seizures that are *egregiously* unreasonable.

D.   WHO CAN OBJECT TO THE INTRODUCTION OF EVIDENCE AND RAISE THE EXCLUSIONARY RULE?

In Jones v. United States, 362 U.S. 257 (1960), the Supreme Court took a broad view of who could object to the introduction of evidence and raise the exclusionary rule. The Court said that a person who "was aggrieved by an unlawful search or seizure" had standing to challenge it. The Court said that "[i]n order to qualify as a 'person aggrieved by an unlawful search and seizure' one must have been a victim of a search or seizure, one against whom the search was directed, as distinguished from one who claims prejudice only through the use of evidence gathered as a consequence of a search or seizure directed at someone else." The Court concluded that "anyone legitimately on premises where a search occurs may challenge its legality by way of a motion to suppress, when its fruits are proposed to be used against him."

In Rakas v. Illinois, below, the Court changed the approach to determining who may raise the exclusionary rule. The Court held that only those whose Fourth Amendment rights were violated may raise the exclusionary rule. In other words, a person cannot raise the exclusionary rule just because he or she is "aggrieved" by an illegal search; to raise the exclusionary rule a person must show a violation of his or her Fourth Amendment rights.

RAKAS v. ILLINOIS
439 U.S. 128 (1978)

Justice REHNQUIST delivered the opinion of the Court.

Petitioners were convicted of armed robbery in the Circuit Court of Kankakee County, Ill., and their convictions were affirmed on appeal. At their trial, the prosecution offered into evidence a sawed-off rifle and rifle shells that had been seized by police during a search of an automobile in which petitioners had been passengers. Neither petitioner is the owner of the automobile and neither has ever asserted that he owned the rifle or shells seized. The Illinois Appellate Court held that petitioners lacked standing to object to the allegedly unlawful search and seizure and denied their motion to suppress the evidence.

I

Because we are not here concerned with the issue of probable cause, a brief description of the events leading to the search of the automobile will suffice. A police officer on a routine patrol received a radio call notifying him of a robbery of a clothing store in Bourbonnais, Ill., and describing the getaway car. Shortly thereafter, the officer spotted an automobile which he thought might be the getaway car. After following the car for some time and after the arrival of assistance, he and several other officers stopped the vehicle. The occupants of the automobile, petitioners and two female companions, were ordered out of the car and, after the occupants had left the car, two officers searched the interior of the vehicle. They discovered a box of rifle shells in the glove compartment, which had been locked, and a sawed-off rifle under the front passenger seat. After discovering the rifle and the shells, the officers took petitioners to the station and placed them under arrest.

Before trial petitioners moved to suppress the rifle and shells seized from the car on the ground that the search violated the Fourth and Fourteenth Amendments. They conceded that they did not own the automobile and were simply passengers; the owner of the car had been the driver of the vehicle at the time of the search. Nor did they assert that they owned the rifle or the shells seized. The prosecutor challenged petitioners' standing to object to the lawfulness of the search of the car because neither the car, the shells nor the rifle belonged to them. The trial court agreed that petitioners lacked standing and denied the motion to suppress the evidence. In view of this holding, the court did not determine whether there was probable cause for the search and seizure. On appeal after petitioners' conviction, the Appellate Court of Illinois, Third Judicial District, affirmed the trial court's denial of petitioners' motion to suppress because it held that "without a proprietary or other similar interest in an automobile, a mere passenger therein lacks standing to challenge the legality of the search of the vehicle."

We reject petitioners' suggestion. The proponent of a motion to suppress has the burden of establishing that his own Fourth Amendment rights were violated by the challenged search or seizure. The prosecutor argued that petitioners lacked standing to challenge the search because they did not own the rifle, the shells or the automobile. Petitioners did not contest the factual predicates of the prosecutor's argument and instead, simply stated that they were not required to prove ownership to object to the search. The prosecutor's argument gave petitioners notice that they were to be put to their proof on any issue as to which they had the burden, and because of their failure to assert ownership, we must assume, for purposes of our review, that petitioners do not own the rifle or the shells.

II

Petitioners first urge us to relax or broaden the rule of standing enunciated in Jones v. United States (1960), so that any criminal defendant at whom a search was "directed" would have standing to contest the legality of that search and object to the admission at trial of evidence obtained as a result of the search. Alternatively, petitioners argue that they have standing to object to the search under *Jones* because they were "legitimately on [the] premises" at the time of the search.

The concept of standing discussed in *Jones* focuses on whether the person seeking to challenge the legality of a search as a basis for suppressing evidence was himself the "victim" of the search or seizure. Adoption of the so-called "target" theory advanced by petitioners would in effect permit a defendant to assert that a violation of the Fourth Amendment rights of a third party entitled him to have evidence suppressed at his trial. If we reject petitioners' request for a broadened rule of standing such as this, and reaffirm the holding of *Jones* and other cases that Fourth Amendment rights are personal rights that may not be asserted vicariously, we will have occasion to re-examine the "standing" terminology emphasized in *Jones*. For we are not at all sure that the determination of a motion to suppress is materially aided by labeling the inquiry identified in *Jones* as one of standing, rather than simply recognizing it as one involving the substantive question of whether or not the proponent of the motion to suppress has had his own Fourth Amendment rights infringed by the search and seizure which he seeks to challenge.

A

We decline to extend the rule of standing in Fourth Amendment cases in the manner suggested by petitioners. As we stated in Alderman v. United States (1969), "Fourth Amendment rights are personal rights which, like some other constitutional rights, may not be vicariously asserted." A person who is aggrieved by an illegal search and seizure only through the introduction of damaging evidence secured by a search of a third person's premises or property has not had any of his Fourth Amendment rights infringed. And since the exclusionary rule is an attempt to effectuate the guarantees of the Fourth Amendment, it is proper to permit only defendants whose Fourth Amendment rights have been violated to benefit from the rule's protections. There is no reason to think that a party whose rights have been infringed will not, if evidence is used against him, have ample motivation to move to suppress it. Even if such a person is not a defendant in the action, he may be able to recover damages for the violation of his Fourth Amendment rights, or seek redress under state law for invasion of privacy or trespass.

Conferring standing to raise vicarious Fourth Amendment claims would necessarily mean a more widespread invocation of the exclusionary rule during criminal trials. The Court's opinion in *Alderman* counseled against such an extension of the exclusionary rule. Each time the exclusionary rule is applied it exacts a substantial social cost for the vindication of Fourth Amendment rights. Relevant and reliable evidence is kept from the trier of fact and the search for truth at trial is deflected. Since our cases generally have held that one whose Fourth Amendment rights are violated may successfully suppress evidence obtained in the course of an illegal search and seizure, misgivings as to the benefit of enlarging the class of persons who may invoke that rule are properly considered when deciding whether to expand standing to assert Fourth Amendment violations.

B

Had we accepted petitioners' request to allow persons other than those whose own Fourth Amendment rights were violated by a challenged search and seizure to suppress evidence obtained in the course of such police activity, it would be appropriate to retain *Jones'* use of standing in Fourth Amendment analysis. Under petitioners' target theory, a court could determine that a defendant had standing to invoke the exclusionary rule without having to inquire into the substantive question of whether the challenged search or seizure violated the Fourth Amendment rights of that particular defendant. However, having rejected petitioners' target theory and reaffirmed the principle that the "rights assured by the Fourth Amendment are personal rights, [which] . . . may be enforced by exclusion of evidence only at the instance of one whose own protection was infringed by the search and seizure," the question necessarily arises whether it serves any useful analytical purpose to consider this principle a matter of standing, distinct from the merits of a defendant's Fourth Amendment claim. We can think of no decided cases of this Court that would have come out differently had we concluded, as we do now, that the type of standing requirement discussed in *Jones* and reaffirmed today is more properly subsumed under substantive Fourth Amendment doctrine. Rigorous application of the principle that the rights secured by this Amendment are personal, in place of a notion of "standing," will produce no additional situations in which evidence must be excluded. The inquiry under either approach is the same. But we think the better analysis forthrightly focuses on the extent of a particular defendant's rights under the Fourth Amendment, rather than on any theoretically separate, but invariably intertwined concept of standing.

Analyzed in these terms, the question is whether the challenged search or seizure violated the Fourth Amendment rights of a criminal defendant who seeks to exclude the evidence obtained during it. That inquiry in turn requires a determination of whether the disputed search and seizure has infringed an interest of the defendant which the Fourth Amendment was designed to protect. We are under no illusion that by dispensing with the rubric of standing used in *Jones* we have rendered any simpler the determination of whether the proponent of a motion to suppress is entitled to contest the legality of a search and seizure. But by frankly recognizing that this aspect of the analysis belongs more properly under the heading of substantive Fourth Amendment doctrine than under the heading of standing, we think the decision of this issue will rest on sounder logical footing.

C

Judged by the foregoing analysis, petitioners' claims must fail. They asserted neither a property nor a possessory interest in the automobile, nor an interest in the property seized. And as we have previously indicated, the fact that they were "legitimately on [the] premises" in the sense that they were in the car with the permission of its owner is not determinative of whether they had a legitimate expectation of privacy in the particular areas of the automobile searched. It is unnecessary for us to decide here whether the same expectations of privacy are warranted in a car as would be justified in a dwelling place in analogous circumstances. We have on numerous occasions pointed out that cars are not to be treated identically with houses or apartments for Fourth Amendment purposes. But here petitioners' claim is one which would fail even in an analogous situation in a dwelling place, since they made no showing that they had any legitimate expectation of privacy in the glove compartment or area under the seat of the car in which they were merely passengers. Like the trunk of an automobile, these are areas in which a passenger qua passenger simply would not normally have a legitimate expectation of privacy.

Justice WHITE, with whom Justice BRENNAN, Justice MARSHALL, and Justice STEVENS join, dissenting.

The Court today holds that the Fourth Amendment protects property, not people, and specifically that a legitimate occupant of an automobile may not invoke the exclusionary rule and challenge a search of that vehicle unless he happens to own or have a possessory interest in it. Though professing to acknowledge that the primary purpose of the Fourth Amendment's prohibition of unreasonable searches is the protection of privacy — not property — the Court nonetheless effectively ties the application of the Fourth Amendment and the exclusionary rule in this situation to property law concepts. Insofar as passengers are concerned, the Court's opinion today declares an "open season" on automobiles. However unlawful stopping and searching a car may be, absent a possessory or ownership interest, no "mere" passenger may object, regardless of his relationship to the owner. Because the majority's conclusion has no support in the Court's controlling decisions, in the logic of the Fourth Amendment, or in common sense, I must respectfully dissent. If the Court is troubled by the practical impact of the exclusionary rule, it should face the issue of that rule's continued validity squarely instead of distorting other doctrines in an attempt to reach what are perceived as the correct results in specific cases.

Two intersecting doctrines long established in this Court's opinions control here. The first is the recognition of some cognizable level of privacy in the interior of an automobile. Though the reasonableness of the expectation of privacy in a vehicle may be somewhat weaker than that in a home, "[a] search even of an automobile, is a substantial invasion of privacy. To protect that privacy from official arbitrariness, the Court always has regarded probable cause as the minimum requirement for a lawful search."

The second tenet is that when a person is legitimately present in a private place, his right to privacy is protected from unreasonable governmental interference even if he does not own the premises.

These two fundamental aspects of Fourth Amendment law demand that petitioners be permitted to challenge the search and seizure of the automobile in this case. It is of no significance that a car is different for Fourth Amendment purposes from a house, for if there is some protection for the privacy of an automobile then the only relevant analogy is between a person legitimately in someone else's vehicle and a person legitimately in someone else's home. If both strands of the Fourth Amendment doctrine adumbrated above are valid, the Court must reach a different result. Instead, it chooses to eviscerate the *Jones* principle, an action in which I am unwilling to participate.

It is true that the Court asserts that it is not limiting the Fourth Amendment bar against unreasonable searches to the protection of property rights, but in reality it is doing exactly that. Petitioners were in a private place with the permission of the owner, but the Court states that that is not sufficient to establish entitlement to a legitimate expectation of privacy. But if that is not sufficient, what would be? We are not told, and it is hard to imagine anything short of a property interest that would satisfy the majority. Insofar as the Court's rationale is concerned, no passenger in an automobile, without an ownership or possessory interest and regardless of his relationship to the owner, may claim Fourth Amendment protection against illegal stops and searches of the automobile in which he is rightfully present.

More importantly, how is the Court able to avoid answering the question why presence in a private place with the owner's permission is insufficient? If it is "tautological to fall back on the notion that those expectations of privacy which are legitimate depend primarily on cases deciding exclusionary rule issues in criminal cases," then it surely must be tautological to decide that issue simply by unadorned fiat.

As a control on governmental power, the Fourth Amendment assures that some expectations of privacy are justified and will be protected from official intrusion. That should be true in this instance, for if protected zones of privacy can only be purchased or obtained by possession of property, then much of our daily lives will be unshielded from unreasonable governmental prying, and the reach of the Fourth Amendment will have been narrowed to protect chiefly those with possessory interests in real or personal property.

At most, one could say that perhaps the Constitution provides some degree less protection for the personal freedom from unreasonable governmental intrusion when one does not have a possessory interest in the invaded private place. But that would only change the extent of the protection; it would not free police to do the unreasonable, as does the decision today. And since the accused should be entitled to litigate the application of the Fourth Amendment where his privacy interest is merely arguable, the failure to allow such litigation here is the more incomprehensible.

The Court's holding is contrary not only to our past decisions and the logic of the Fourth Amendment but also to the everyday expectations of privacy that we all share. Because of that, it is unworkable in all the various situations that arise in real life. If the owner of the car had not only invited petitioners to join her but had said to them, "I give you a temporary possessory interest in my vehicle so that you will share the right to privacy that the Supreme Court says that I own," then apparently the majority would reverse. But people seldom say such things, though they may mean their invitation to encompass them if only they had thought of the problem. If the nonowner were the spouse or child of the owner, would the Court recognize a sufficient interest? If so, would distant relatives somehow have more of an expectation of privacy than close friends? What if the nonowner were driving with the owner's permission? Would nonowning drivers have more of an expectation of privacy than mere passengers? What about a passenger in a taxicab? *Katz* expressly recognized protection for such passengers. Why should Fourth Amendment rights be present when one pays a cabdriver for a ride but be absent when one is given a ride by a friend?

The distinctions the Court would draw are based on relationships between private parties, but the Fourth Amendment is concerned with the relationship of one of those parties to the government. Divorced as it is from the purpose of the Fourth Amendment, the Court's essentially property-based rationale can satisfactorily answer none of the questions posed above. That is reason enough to reject it. The *Jones* rule is relatively easily applied by police and courts; the rule announced today will not provide law enforcement officials with a bright line between the protected and the unprotected. Only rarely will police know whether one private party has or has not been granted a sufficient possessory or other interest by another private party. Surely in this case the officers had no such knowledge. The Court's rule will ensnare defendants and police in needless litigation over factors that should not be determinative of Fourth Amendment rights.

More importantly, the ruling today undercuts the force of the exclusionary rule in the one area in which its use is most certainly justified — the deterrence of bad-faith violations of the Fourth Amendment. This decision invites police to engage in patently unreasonable searches every time an automobile contains more than one occupant. Should something be found, only the owner of the vehicle, or of the item, will have standing to seek suppression, and the evidence will presumably be usable against the other occupants. The danger of such bad faith is especially high in cases such as this one where the officers are only after the passengers and can usually infer accurately that the driver is the owner. The suppression remedy for those owners in whose vehicles something is found and who are charged with crime is small consolation for all those owners and occupants whose privacy will be needlessly invaded by officers following mistaken hunches not rising to the level of probable cause but operated on in the knowledge that someone in a crowded car will probably be unprotected if contraband or incriminating evidence happens to be found. After this decision, police will have little to lose by unreasonably searching vehicles occupied by more than one person.

Of course, most police officers will decline the Court's invitation and will continue to do their jobs as best they can in accord with the Fourth Amendment. But the very purpose of the Bill of Rights was to answer the justified fear that governmental agents cannot be left totally to their own devices, and the Bill of Rights is enforceable in the courts because human experience teaches that not all such officials will otherwise adhere to the stated precepts. Some policemen simply do act in bad faith, even if for understandable ends, and some deterrent is needed. In the rush to limit the applicability of the exclusionary rule somewhere, anywhere, the Court ignores precedent, logic, and common sense to exclude the rule's operation from situations in which, paradoxically, it is justified and needed.

Rakas, then, disavows the use of the term "standing" and says instead that the focus in determining who can raise the exclusionary rule is on whether a person's Fourth Amendment rights were violated, which generally turns on whether a person has a reasonable expectation of privacy. For example, in Rawlings v. Kentucky, 448 U.S. 98 (1980), the Court held that a man could not raise the exclusionary rule when contraband belonging to him was found inside a woman's purse when he and the woman were visiting premises that were searched. The Court concluded that the man had no reasonable expectation of privacy under the circumstances and thus could not raise the exclusionary rule.

The Court has considered the application of *Rakas* in two situations that repeatedly occur: When can visitors in a person's home raise the exclusionary rule? When can passengers in a person's car raise the exclusionary rule? Minnesota v. Carter addresses the former question, and the recent decision in Brendlin v. California concerns the latter.

MINNESOTA v. CARTER
525 U.S. 83 (1998)

Chief Justice REHNQUIST delivered the opinion of the Court.

Respondents and the lessee of an apartment were sitting in one of its rooms, bagging cocaine. While so engaged they were observed by a police officer, who looked through a drawn window blind. The Supreme Court of Minnesota held that the officer's viewing was a search that violated respondents' Fourth Amendment rights. We hold that no such violation occurred.

James Thielen, a police officer in the Twin Cities' suburb of Eagan, Minnesota, went to an apartment building to investigate a tip from a confidential informant. The informant said that he had walked by the window of a ground-floor apartment and had seen people putting a white powder into bags. The officer looked in the same window through a gap in the closed blind and observed the bagging operation for several minutes. He then notified headquarters, which began preparing affidavits for a search warrant while he returned to the apartment building. When two men left the building in a previously identified Cadillac, the police stopped the car. Inside were respondents Carter and Johns. As the police opened the door of the car to let Johns out, they observed a black, zippered pouch and a handgun, later determined to be loaded, on the vehicle's floor. Carter and Johns were arrested, and a later police search of the vehicle the next day discovered pagers, a scale, and 47 grams of cocaine in plastic sandwich bags.

After seizing the car, the police returned to Apartment 103 and arrested the occupant, Kimberly Thompson, who is not a party to this appeal. A search of the apartment pursuant to a warrant revealed cocaine residue on the kitchen table and plastic baggies similar to those found in the Cadillac. Thielen identified Carter, Johns, and Thompson as the three people he had observed placing the powder into baggies. The police later learned that while Thompson was the lessee of the apartment, Carter and Johns lived in Chicago and had come to the apartment for the sole purpose of packaging the cocaine. Carter and Johns had never been to the apartment before and were only in the apartment for approximately 2½ hours. In return for the use of the apartment, Carter and Johns had given Thompson one-eighth of an ounce of the cocaine.

Carter and Johns were charged with conspiracy to commit a controlled substance crime in the first degree and aiding and abetting in a controlled substance crime in the first degree, in violation of Minn. Stat. §§152.021. They moved to suppress all evidence obtained from the apartment and the Cadillac, as well as to suppress several postarrest incriminating statements they had made. They argued that Thielen's initial observation of their drug packaging activities was an unreasonable search in violation of the Fourth Amendment and that all evidence obtained as a result of this unreasonable search was inadmissible as fruit of the poisonous tree.

The Minnesota courts analyzed whether respondents had a legitimate expectation of privacy under the rubric of "standing" doctrine, an analysis that this Court expressly rejected 20 years ago in *Rakas*. The [Fourth] Amendment protects persons against unreasonable searches of "their persons [and] houses" and thus indicates that the Fourth Amendment is a personal right that must be invoked by an individual. *See* Katz v. United States (1967) ("[T]he Fourth Amendment protects people, not places"). But the extent to which the Fourth Amendment protects people may depend upon where those people are. We have held that "capacity to claim the protection of the Fourth Amendment depends . . . upon whether the person who claims the protection of the Amendment has a legitimate expectation of privacy in the invaded place."

The text of the Amendment suggests that its protections extend only to people in "their" houses. But we have held that in some circumstances a person may have a legitimate expectation of privacy in the house of someone else. In Minnesota v. Olson (1990), for example, we decided that an overnight guest in a house had the sort of expectation of privacy that the Fourth Amendment protects.

In Jones v. United States (1960), the defendant seeking to exclude evidence resulting from a search of an apartment had been given the use of the apartment by a friend. He had clothing in the apartment, had slept there "maybe a night," and at the time was the sole occupant of the apartment. But while the holding of *Jones*—that a search of the apartment violated the defendant's Fourth Amendment rights—is still valid, its statement that "anyone legitimately on the premises where a search occurs may challenge its legality," was expressly repudiated in Rakas v. Illinois (1978). Thus, an overnight guest in a home may claim the protection of the Fourth Amendment, but one who is merely present with the consent of the house-holder may not.

Respondents here were obviously not overnight guests, but were essentially present for a business transaction and were only in the home a matter of hours. There is no suggestion that they had a previous relationship with Thompson, or that there was any other purpose to their visit. Nor was there anything similar to the overnight guest relationship in *Olson* to suggest a degree of acceptance into the household. While the apartment was a dwelling place for Thompson, it was for these respondents simply a place to do business.

Property used for commercial purposes is treated differently for Fourth Amendment purposes from residential property. "An expectation of privacy in commercial premises, however, is different from, and indeed less than, a similar expectation in an individual's home." New York v. Burger (1987). And while it was a "home" in which respondents were present, it was not their home.

If we regard the overnight guest in Minnesota v. Olson as typifying those who may claim the protection of the Fourth Amendment in the home of another, and one merely "legitimately on the premises" as typifying those who may not do so, the present case is obviously somewhere in between. But the purely commercial nature of the transaction engaged in here, the relatively short period of time on the premises, and the lack of any previous connection between respondents and the householder, all lead us to conclude that respondents' situation is closer to that of one simply permitted on the premises. We therefore hold that any search which may have occurred did not violate their Fourth Amendment rights.

Because we conclude that respondents had no legitimate expectation of privacy in the apartment, we need not decide whether the police officer's observation constituted a "search."

Justice KENNEDY, concurring.

I join the Court's opinion, for its reasoning is consistent with my view that almost all social guests have a legitimate expectation of privacy, and hence protection against unreasonable searches, in their host's home.

The Fourth Amendment protects "[t]he right of the people to be secure in their . . . houses," and it is beyond dispute that the home is entitled to special protection as the center of the private lives of our people. Security of the home must be guarded by the law in a world where privacy is diminished by enhanced surveillance and sophisticated communication systems. As is well established, however, Fourth Amendment protection, though dependent upon spatial definition, is in essence a personal right. Thus, as the Court held in Rakas v. Illinois (1978), there are limits on who may assert it.

In this case respondents have established nothing more than a fleeting and insubstantial connection with Thompson's home. For all that appears in the record, respondents used Thompson's house simply as a convenient processing station, their purpose involving nothing more than the mechanical act of chopping and packing a substance for distribution. There is no suggestion that respondents engaged in confidential communications with Thompson about their transaction. Respondents had not been to Thompson's apartment before, and they left it even before their arrest.

If respondents here had been visiting 20 homes, each for a minute or two, to drop off a bag of cocaine and were apprehended by a policeman wrongfully present in the 19th home; or if they had left the goods at a home where they were not staying and the police had seized the goods in their absence, we would have said that *Rakas* compels rejection of any privacy interest respondents might assert. So it does here, given that respondents have established no meaningful tie or connection to the owner, the owner's home, or the owner's expectation of privacy.

We cannot remain faithful to the underlying principle in *Rakas* without reversing in this case, and I am not persuaded that we need depart from it to protect the homeowner's own privacy interests. Respondents have made no persuasive argument that we need to fashion a per se rule of home protection, with an automatic right for all in the home to invoke the exclusionary rule, in order to protect homeowners and their guests from unlawful police intrusion. With these observations, I join the Court's opinion.

Justice GINSBURG, with whom Justice STEVENS and Justice SOUTER join, dissenting.

The Court's decision undermines not only the security of short-term guests, but also the security of the home resident herself. In my view, when a homeowner or lessee personally invites a guest into her home to share in a common endeavor, whether it be for conversation, to engage in leisure activities, or for business purposes licit or illicit, that guest should share his host's shelter against unreasonable searches and seizures.

I do not here propose restoration of the "legitimately on the premises" criterion stated in Jones v. United States (1960), for the Court rejected that formulation in Rakas v. Illinois (1978), as it did the "automatic standing rule." First, the disposition I would reach in this case responds to the unique importance of the home — the most essential bastion of privacy recognized by the law. Further, I would here decide only the case of the homeowner who chooses to share the privacy of her home and her company with a guest, and would not reach classroom hypotheticals like the milkman or pizza deliverer.

My concern centers on an individual's choice to share her home and her associations there with persons she selects. Our decisions indicate that people have a reasonable expectation of privacy in their homes in part because they have the prerogative to exclude others. The power to exclude implies the power to include. Our Fourth Amendment decisions should reflect these complementary prerogatives.

A homedweller places her own privacy at risk, the Court's approach indicates, when she opens her home to others, uncertain whether the duration of their stay, their purpose, and their "acceptance into the household" will earn protection. It remains textbook law that "[s]earches and seizures inside a home without a warrant are presumptively unreasonable absent exigent circumstances." The law in practice is less secure. Human frailty suggests that today's decision will tempt police to pry into private dwellings without warrant, to find evidence incriminating guests who do not rest there through the night.

Through the host's invitation, the guest gains a reasonable expectation of privacy in the home. Minnesota v. Olson (1990), so held with respect to an overnight guest. The logic of that decision extends to shorter term guests as well. One need not remain overnight to anticipate privacy in another's home, "a place where [the guest] and his possessions will not be disturbed by anyone but his host and those his host allows inside." In sum, when a homeowner chooses to share the privacy of her home and her company with a short-term guest, the twofold requirement "emerg[ing] from prior decisions" has been satisfied: Both host and guest "have exhibited an actual (subjective) expectation of privacy"; that "expectation [is] one [our] society is prepared to recognize as 'reasonable.'"

BRENDLIN v. CALIFORNIA
551 U.S. 249 (2007)

Justice SOUTER delivered the opinion of the Court.

When a police officer makes a traffic stop, the driver of the car is seized within the meaning of the Fourth Amendment. The question in this case is whether the same is true of a passenger. We hold that a passenger is seized as well and so may challenge the constitutionality of the stop.

I

Early in the morning of November 27, 2001, Deputy Sheriff Robert Brokenbrough and his partner saw a parked Buick with expired registration tags. In his ensuing conversation with the police dispatcher, Brokenbrough learned that an application for renewal of registration was being processed. The officers saw the car again on the road, and this time Brokenbrough noticed its display of a temporary operating permit with the number "11," indicating it was legal to drive the car through November. The officers decided to pull the Buick over to verify that the permit matched the vehicle, even though, as Brokenbrough admitted later, there was nothing unusual about the permit or the way it was affixed. Brokenbrough asked the driver, Karen Simeroth, for her license and saw a passenger in the front seat, petitioner Bruce Brendlin, whom he recognized as "one of the Brendlin brothers." He recalled that either Scott or Bruce Brendlin had dropped out of parole supervision and asked Brendlin to identify himself. Brokenbrough returned to his cruiser, called for backup, and verified that Brendlin was a parole violator with an outstanding no-bail warrant for his arrest. While he was in the patrol car, Brokenbrough saw Brendlin briefly open and then close the passenger door of the Buick. Once reinforcements arrived, Brokenbrough went to the passenger side of the Buick, ordered him out of the car at gunpoint, and declared him under arrest. When the police searched Brendlin incident to arrest, they found an orange syringe cap on his person. A patdown search of Simeroth revealed syringes and a plastic bag of a green leafy substance, and she was also formally arrested. Officers then searched the car and found tubing, a scale, and other things used to produce methamphetamine.

Brendlin was charged with possession and manufacture of methamphetamine, and he moved to suppress the evidence obtained in the searches of his person and the car as fruits of an unconstitutional seizure, arguing that the officers lacked probable cause or reasonable suspicion to make the traffic stop. He did not assert that his Fourth Amendment rights were violated by the search of Simeroth's vehicle, *cf.* Rakas v. Illinois (1978), but claimed only that the traffic stop was an unlawful seizure of his person. The trial court denied the suppression motion after finding that the stop was lawful and Brendlin was not seized until Brokenbrough ordered him out of the car and formally arrested him. Brendlin pleaded guilty, subject to appeal on the suppression issue, and was sentenced to four years in prison.

We granted certiorari to decide whether a traffic stop subjects a passenger, as well as the driver, to Fourth Amendment seizure.

II

A

A person is seized by the police and thus entitled to challenge the government's action under the Fourth Amendment when the officer, "by means of physical force or show of authority," terminates or restrains his freedom of movement, "through means intentionally applied." Thus, an "unintended person . . . [may be] the object of the detention," so long as the detention is "willful" and not merely the consequence of "an unknowing act." A police officer may make a seizure by a show of authority and without the use of physical force, but there is no seizure without actual submission; otherwise, there is at most an attempted seizure, so far as the Fourth Amendment is concerned.

When the actions of the police do not show an unambiguous intent to restrain or when an individual's submission to a show of governmental authority takes the form of passive acquiescence, there needs to be some test for telling when a seizure occurs in response to authority, and when it does not. The test was devised by Justice Stewart in United States v. Mendenhall (1980), who wrote that a seizure occurs if "in view of all of the circumstances surrounding the incident, a reasonable person would have believed that he was not free to leave." Later on, the Court adopted Justice Stewart's touchstone, but added that when a person "has no desire to leave" for reasons unrelated to the police presence, the "coercive effect of the encounter" can be measured better by asking whether "a reasonable person would feel free to decline the officers' requests or otherwise terminate the encounter."

The law is settled that in Fourth Amendment terms a traffic stop entails a seizure of the driver "even though the purpose of the stop is limited and the resulting detention quite brief." Delaware v. Prouse (1979). And although we have not, until today, squarely answered the question whether a passenger is also seized, we have said over and over in dicta that during a traffic stop an officer seizes everyone in the vehicle, not just the driver.

B

The State concedes that the police had no adequate justification to pull the car over, but argues that the passenger was not seized and thus cannot claim that the evidence was tainted by an unconstitutional stop. We resolve this question by asking whether a reasonable person in Brendlin's position when the car stopped would have believed himself free to "terminate the encounter" between the police and himself. We think that in these circumstances any reasonable passenger would have understood the police officers to be exercising control to the point that no one in the car was free to depart without police permission.

A traffic stop necessarily curtails the travel a passenger has chosen just as much as it halts the driver, diverting both from the stream of traffic to the side of the road, and the police activity that normally amounts to intrusion on "privacy and personal security" does not normally (and did not here) distinguish between passenger and driver. An officer who orders one particular car to pull over acts with an implicit claim of right based on fault of some sort, and a sensible person would not expect a police officer to allow people to come and go freely from the physical focal point of an investigation into faulty behavior or wrongdoing. If the likely wrongdoing is not the driving, the passenger will reasonably feel subject to suspicion owing to close association; but even when the wrongdoing is only bad driving, the passenger will expect to be subject to some scrutiny, and his attempt to leave the scene would be so obviously likely to prompt an objection from the officer that no passenger would feel free to leave in the first place.

It is also reasonable for passengers to expect that a police officer at the scene of a crime, arrest, or investigation will not let people move around in ways that could jeopardize his safety.

C

The contrary conclusion drawn by the Supreme Court of California, that seizure came only with formal arrest, reflects three premises as to which we respectfully disagree. First, the State Supreme Court reasoned that Brendlin was not seized by the stop because Deputy Sheriff Brokenbrough only intended to investigate Simeroth and did not direct a show of authority toward Brendlin. The court saw Brokenbrough's "flashing lights [as] directed at the driver," and pointed to the lack of record evidence that Brokenbrough "was even aware [Brendlin] was in the car prior to the vehicle stop." But that view of the facts ignores the objective *Mendenhall* test of what a reasonable passenger would understand. To the extent that there is anything ambiguous in the show of force (was it fairly seen as directed only at the driver or at the car and its occupants?), the test resolves the ambiguity, and here it leads to the intuitive conclusion that all the occupants were subject to like control by the successful display of authority. The State Supreme Court's approach, on the contrary, shifts the issue from the intent of the police as objectively manifested to the motive of the police for taking the intentional action to stop the car, and we have repeatedly rejected attempts to introduce this kind of subjectivity into Fourth Amendment analysis.

Second, the Supreme Court of California assumed that Brendlin, "as the passenger, had no ability to submit to the deputy's show of authority" because only the driver was in control of the moving vehicle. But what may amount to submission depends on what a person was doing before the show of authority: a fleeing man is not seized until he is physically overpowered, but one sitting in a chair may submit to authority by not getting up to run away. Here, Brendlin had no effective way to signal submission while the car was still moving on the roadway, but once it came to a stop he could, and apparently did, submit by staying inside.

Third, the State Supreme Court shied away from the rule we apply today for fear that it "would encompass even those motorists following the vehicle subject to the traffic stop who, by virtue of the original detention, are forced to slow down and perhaps even come to a halt in order to accommodate that vehicle's submission to police authority." But an occupant of a car who knows that he is stuck in traffic because another car has been pulled over (like the motorist who can't even make out why the road is suddenly clogged) would not perceive a show of authority as directed at him or his car. Such incidental restrictions on freedom of movement would not tend to affect an individual's "sense of security and privacy in traveling in an automobile." Nor would the consequential blockage call for a precautionary rule to avoid the kind of "arbitrary and oppressive interference by [law] enforcement officials with the privacy and personal security of individuals" that the Fourth Amendment was intended to limit.[6]

_____

6. California claims that, under today's rule, "all taxi cab and bus passengers would be 'seized' under the Fourth Amendment when the cab or bus driver is pulled over by the police for running a red light." But the relationship between driver and passenger is not the same in a common carrier as it is in a private vehicle, and the expectations of police officers and passengers differ accordingly. In those cases, as here, the crucial question would be whether a reasonable person in the passenger's position would feel free to take steps to terminate the encounter. [Footnote by the Court.]

Indeed, the consequence to worry about would not flow from our conclusion, but from the rule that almost all courts have rejected. Holding that the passenger in a private car is not (without more) seized in a traffic stop would invite police officers to stop cars with passengers regardless of probable cause or reasonable suspicion of anything illegal. The fact that evidence uncovered as a result of an arbitrary traffic stop would still be admissible against any passengers would be a powerful incentive to run the kind of "roving patrols" that would still violate the driver's Fourth Amendment right.

Brendlin was seized from the moment Simeroth's car came to a halt on the side of the road, and it was error to deny his suppression motion on the ground that seizure occurred only at the formal arrest.

E.   EXCEPTIONS TO THE EXCLUSIONARY RULE

There are several situations in which the Supreme Court has said that even though there is a Fourth Amendment violation, the exclusionary rule does not apply. In examining these exceptions, it is important to consider whether they are justified or whether they unduly undercut the ability to achieve the purposes of the exclusionary rule.

1.   Independent Source

Even if police obtain evidence in violation of the Fourth Amendment, it is still admissible if it is also obtained through a source independent of the police misconduct and untainted by the illegal actions of the police. In a footnote, in his dissenting opinion in Murray v. United States, below, Justice Marshall gives a clear illustration:

> The clearest case for the application of the independent source exception is when a wholly separate line of investigation, shielded from information gathered in an illegal search, turns up the same evidence through a separate, lawful search. Under these circumstances, there is little doubt that the lawful search was not connected to the constitutional violation. The exclusion of such evidence would not significantly add to the deterrence facing the law enforcement officers conducting the illegal search, because they would have little reason to anticipate the separate investigation leading to the same evidence.

For example, in Segura v. United States, 468 U.S. 796 (1984), agents unlawfully entered the defendant's apartment and remained there until a search warrant was obtained. But the Court held that the evidence found for the first time during the execution of the valid and untainted search warrant was admissible because it was discovered pursuant to an "independent source."

Murray v. United States is one of the Supreme Court's most detailed examinations of the independent source exception to the exclusionary rule.

MURRAY v. UNITED STATES

487 U.S. 533 (1988)

Justice SCALIA delivered the opinion of the Court.

In Segura v. United States (1984), we held that police officers' illegal entry upon private premises did not require suppression of evidence subsequently discovered at those premises when executing a search warrant obtained on the basis of information wholly unconnected with the initial entry. In these consolidated cases we are faced with the question whether, again assuming evidence obtained pursuant to an independently obtained search warrant, the portion of such evidence that had been observed in plain view at the time of a prior illegal entry must be suppressed.

I

Both cases arise out of the conviction of petitioner Michael F. Murray, petitioner James D. Carter, and others for conspiracy to possess and distribute illegal drugs. Insofar as relevant for our purposes, the facts are as follows: Based on information received from informants, federal law enforcement agents had been surveilling petitioner Murray and several of his co-conspirators. At about 1:45 P.M. on April 6, 1983, they observed Murray drive a truck and Carter drive a green camper into a warehouse in South Boston. When the petitioners drove the vehicles out about 20 minutes later, the surveilling agents saw within the warehouse two individuals and a tractor-trailer rig bearing a long, dark container. Murray and Carter later turned over the truck and camper to other drivers, who were in turn followed and ultimately arrested, and the vehicles lawfully seized. Both vehicles were found to contain marijuana.

After receiving this information, several of the agents converged on the South Boston warehouse and forced entry. They found the warehouse unoccupied, but observed in plain view numerous burlap-wrapped bales that were later found to contain marijuana. They left without disturbing the bales, kept the warehouse under surveillance, and did not reenter it until they had a search warrant. In applying for the warrant, the agents did not mention the prior entry, and did not rely on any observations made during that entry. When the warrant was issued — at 10:40 P.M., approximately eight hours after the initial entry — the agents immediately reentered the warehouse and seized 270 bales of marijuana and notebooks listing customers for whom the bales were destined.

Before trial, petitioners moved to suppress the evidence found in the warehouse. The District Court denied the motion, rejecting petitioners' arguments that the warrant was invalid because the agents did not inform the Magistrate about their prior warrantless entry, and that the warrant was tainted by that entry. The First Circuit affirmed, assuming for purposes of its decision that the first entry into the warehouse was unlawful.

II

The exclusionary rule prohibits introduction into evidence of tangible materials seized during an unlawful search, and of testimony concerning knowledge acquired during an unlawful search. Beyond that, the exclusionary rule also prohibits the introduction of derivative evidence, both tangible and testimonial, that is the product of the primary evidence, or that is otherwise acquired as an indirect result of the unlawful search, up to the point at which the connection with the unlawful search becomes "so attenuated as to dissipate the taint."

Almost simultaneously with our development of the exclusionary rule, in the first quarter of this century, we also announced what has come to be known as the "independent source" doctrine. See Silverthorne Lumber Co. v. United States (1920). That doctrine, which has been applied to evidence acquired not only through Fourth Amendment violations but also through Fifth and Sixth Amendment violations, has recently been described as follows: "[T]he interest of society in deterring unlawful police conduct and the public interest in having juries receive all probative evidence of a crime are properly balanced by putting the police in the same, not a worse, position that they would have been in if no police error or misconduct had occurred. . . . When the challenged evidence has an independent source, exclusion of such evidence would put the police in a worse position than they would have been in absent any error or violation." Nix v. Williams (1984).

The dispute here is over the scope of this doctrine. Petitioners contend that it applies only to evidence obtained for the first time during an independent lawful search. The Government argues that it applies also to evidence initially discovered during, or as a consequence of, an unlawful search, but later obtained independently from activities untainted by the initial illegality. We think the Government's view has better support in both precedent and policy.

Our cases have used the concept of "independent source" in a more general and a more specific sense. The more general sense identifies all evidence acquired in a fashion untainted by the illegal evidence-gathering activity. Thus, where an unlawful entry has given investigators knowledge of facts x and y, but fact z has been learned by other means, fact z can be said to be admissible because derived from an "independent source." This is how we used the term in Segura v. United States (1984).

The original use of the term, however, and its more important use for purposes of these cases, was more specific. It was originally applied in the exclusionary rule context, by Justice Holmes, with reference to that particular category of evidence acquired by an untainted search which is identical to the evidence unlawfully acquired — that is, in the example just given, to knowledge of facts x and y derived from an independent source:

> The essence of a provision forbidding the acquisition of evidence in a certain way is
> that not merely evidence so acquired shall not be used before the Court but that it

shall not be used at all. Of course this does not mean that the facts thus obtained become sacred and inaccessible. If knowledge of them is gained from an independent source they may be proved like any others.

Petitioners' asserted policy basis for excluding evidence which is initially discovered during an illegal search, but is subsequently acquired through an independent and lawful source, is that a contrary rule will remove all deterrence to, and indeed positively encourage, unlawful police searches. As petitioners see the incentives, law enforcement officers will routinely enter without a warrant to make sure that what they expect to be on the premises is in fact there. If it is not, they will have spared themselves the time and trouble of getting a warrant; if it is, they can get the warrant and use the evidence despite the unlawful entry. We see the incentives differently. An officer with probable cause sufficient to obtain a search warrant would be foolish to enter the premises first in an unlawful manner. By doing so, he would risk suppression of all evidence on the premises, both seen and unseen, since his action would add to the normal burden of convincing a magistrate that there is probable cause the much more onerous burden of convincing a trial court that no information gained from the illegal entry affected either the law enforcement officers' decision to seek a warrant or the magistrate's decision to grant it. Nor would the officer without sufficient probable cause to obtain a search warrant have any added incentive to conduct an unlawful entry, since whatever he finds cannot be used to establish probable cause before a magistrate.

III

To apply what we have said to the present cases: Knowledge that the marijuana was in the warehouse was assuredly acquired at the time of the unlawful entry. But it was also acquired at the time of entry pursuant to the warrant, and if that later acquisition was not the result of the earlier entry there is no reason why the independent source doctrine should not apply. Invoking the exclusionary rule would put the police (and society) not in the same position they would have occupied if no violation occurred, but in a worse one.

The ultimate question, therefore, is whether the search pursuant to warrant was in fact a genuinely independent source of the information and tangible evidence at issue here. This would not have been the case if the agents' decision to seek the warrant was prompted by what they had seen during the initial entry, or if information obtained during that entry was presented to the Magistrate and affected his decision to issue the warrant. On this point the Court of Appeals said the following: "[W]e can be absolutely certain that the warrantless entry in no way contributed in the slightest either to the issuance of a warrant or to the discovery of the evidence during the lawful search that occurred pursuant to the warrant."

Although these statements can be read to provide emphatic support for the Government's position, it is the function of the District Court rather than the

Court of Appeals to determine the facts, and we do not think the Court of Appeals' conclusions are supported by adequate findings. The District Court found that the agents did not reveal their warrantless entry to the Magistrate, and that they did not include in their application for a warrant any recitation of their observations in the warehouse. It did not, however, explicitly find that the agents would have sought a warrant if they had not earlier entered the warehouse. The Government concedes this in its brief. To be sure, the District Court did determine that the purpose of the warrantless entry was in part "to guard against the destruction of possibly critical evidence," and one could perhaps infer from this that the agents who made the entry already planned to obtain that "critical evidence" through a warrant-authorized search. That inference is not, however, clear enough to justify the conclusion that the District Court's findings amounted to a determination of independent source.

Accordingly, we vacate the judgment and remand these cases to the Court of Appeals with instructions that it remand to the District Court for determination whether the warrant-authorized search of the warehouse was an independent source of the challenged evidence in the sense we have described.

Justice MARSHALL, with whom Justice STEVENS and Justice O'CONNOR join, dissenting.

The Court today holds that the "independent source" exception to the exclusionary rule may justify admitting evidence discovered during an illegal warrantless search that is later "rediscovered" by the same team of investigators during a search pursuant to a warrant obtained immediately after the illegal search. I believe the Court's decision, by failing to provide sufficient guarantees that the subsequent search was, in fact, independent of the illegal search, emasculates the Warrant Clause and undermines the deterrence function of the exclusionary rule. I therefore dissent.

This Court has stated frequently that the exclusionary rule is principally designed to deter violations of the Fourth Amendment. By excluding evidence discovered in violation of the Fourth Amendment, the rule "compel[s] respect for the constitutional guaranty in the only effectively available way, by removing the incentive to disregard it." The Court has crafted exceptions to the exclusionary rule when the purposes of the rule are not furthered by the exclusion. As the Court today recognizes, the independent source exception to the exclusionary rule "allows admission of evidence that has been discovered by means wholly independent of any constitutional violation." The independent source exception, like the inevitable discovery exception, is primarily based on a practical view that under certain circumstances the beneficial deterrent effect that exclusion will have on future constitutional violations is too slight to justify the social cost of excluding probative evidence from a criminal trial. When the seizure of the evidence at issue is "wholly independent of" the constitutional violation, then exclusion arguably will have no effect on a law enforcement officer's incentive to commit an unlawful search.

Under the circumstances of these cases, the admission of the evidence "reseized" during the second search severely undermines the deterrence function of the exclusionary rule. Indeed, admission in these cases affirmatively encourages illegal searches. The incentives for such illegal conduct are clear. Obtaining a warrant is inconvenient and time consuming. Even when officers have probable cause to support a warrant application, therefore, they have an incentive first to determine whether it is worthwhile to obtain a warrant. Probable cause is much less than certainty, and many "confirmatory" searches will result in the discovery that no evidence is present, thus saving the police the time and trouble of getting a warrant. If contraband is discovered, however, the officers may later seek a warrant to shield the evidence from the taint of the illegal search. The police thus know in advance that they have little to lose and much to gain by forgoing the bother of obtaining a warrant and undertaking an illegal search.

The Court, however, "see[s] the incentives differently." Under the Court's view, today's decision does not provide an incentive for unlawful searches, because the officer undertaking the search would know that "his action would add to the normal burden of convincing a magistrate that there is probable cause the much more onerous burden of convincing a trial court that no information gained from the illegal entry affected either the law enforcement officers' decision to seek a warrant or the magistrate's decision to grant it." The Court, however, provides no hint of why this risk would actually seem significant to the officers. Under the circumstances of these cases, the officers committing the illegal search have both knowledge and control of the factors central to the trial court's determination.

The strong Fourth Amendment interest in eliminating these incentives for illegal entry should cause this Court to scrutinize closely the application of the independent source exception to evidence obtained under the circumstances of the instant cases; respect for the constitutional guarantee requires a rule that does not undermine the deterrence function of the exclusionary rule. When, as here, the same team of investigators is involved in both the first and second search, there is a significant danger that the "independence" of the source will in fact be illusory, and that the initial search will have affected the decision to obtain a warrant notwithstanding the officers' subsequent assertions to the contrary. It is therefore crucial that the factual premise of the exception—complete independence—be clearly established before the exception can justify admission of the evidence. I believe the Court's reliance on the intent of the law enforcement officers who conducted the warrantless search provides insufficient guarantees that the subsequent legal search was unaffected by the prior illegal search.

To ensure that the source of the evidence is genuinely independent, the basis for a finding that a search was untainted by a prior illegal search must focus, as with the inevitable discovery doctrine, on "demonstrated historical facts capable of ready verification or impeachment." In the instant cases, there are no "demonstrated historical facts" capable of supporting a finding that the subsequent warrant search was wholly unaffected by the prior illegal search. The same team of investigators was involved in both searches. The warrant was obtained immediately after the illegal search, and no effort was made to obtain a warrant prior to the discovery of the marijuana during the illegal search. The only evidence available that the warrant search was wholly independent is the testimony of the agents who conducted the illegal search. Under these circumstances, the threat that the subsequent search was tainted by the illegal search is too great to allow for the application of the independent source exception. The Court's contrary holding lends itself to easy abuse, and offers an incentive to bypass the constitutional requirement that probable cause be assessed by a neutral and detached magistrate before the police invade an individual's privacy.

In sum, under circumstances as are presented in these cases, when the very law enforcement officers who participate in an illegal search immediately thereafter obtain a warrant to search the same premises, I believe the evidence discovered during the initial illegal entry must be suppressed. Any other result emasculates the Warrant Clause and provides an intolerable incentive for warrantless searches. I respectfully dissent.

2. Inevitable Discovery

Closely related to the "independent source" exception is the "inevitable discovery" exception. If the police can demonstrate that they inevitably would have discovered the evidence, without a violation of the Fourth Amendment, the exclusionary rule does not apply and the evidence is admissible. Nix v. Williams is the key case recognizing an "inevitable discovery" exception to the exclusionary rule.

NIX v. WILLIAMS
467 U.S. 431 (1984)

Chief Justice BURGER delivered the opinion of the Court.

We granted certiorari to consider whether, at respondent Williams' second murder trial in state court, evidence pertaining to the discovery and condition of the victim's body was properly admitted on the ground that it would ultimately or inevitably have been discovered even if no violation of any constitutional or statutory provision had taken place.

I

A

On December 24, 1968, 10-year-old Pamela Powers disappeared from a YMCA building in Des Moines, Iowa, where she had accompanied her parents to watch an athletic contest. Shortly after she disappeared, Williams was seen leaving the YMCA carrying a large bundle wrapped in a blanket; a 14-year-old boy who had helped Williams open his car door reported that he had seen "two legs in it and they were skinny and white."

Williams' car was found the next day 160 miles east of Des Moines in Davenport, Iowa. Later several items of clothing belonging to the child, some of Williams' clothing, and an army blanket like the one used to wrap the bundle that Williams carried out of the YMCA were found at a rest stop on Interstate 80 near Grinnell, between Des Moines and Davenport. A warrant was issued for Williams' arrest.

Police surmised that Williams had left Pamela Powers or her body somewhere between Des Moines and the Grinnell rest stop where some of the young girl's clothing had been found. On December 26, the Iowa Bureau of Criminal Investigation initiated a large-scale search. Two hundred volunteers divided into teams began the search 21 miles east of Grinnell, covering an area several miles to the north and south of Interstate 80. They moved westward from Poweshiek County, in which Grinnell was located, into Jasper County. Searchers were instructed to check all roads, abandoned farm buildings, ditches, culverts, and any other place in which the body of a small child could be hidden.

Meanwhile, Williams surrendered to local police in Davenport, where he was promptly arraigned. Williams contacted a Des Moines attorney who arranged for an attorney in Davenport to meet Williams at the Davenport police station. Des Moines police informed counsel they would pick Williams up in Davenport and return him to Des Moines without questioning him. Two Des Moines detectives then drove to Davenport, took Williams into custody, and proceeded to drive him back to Des Moines.

During the return trip, one of the policemen, Detective Leaming, began a conversation with Williams, saying: "I want to give you something to think about while we're traveling down the road. . . . They are predicting several inches of snow for tonight, and I feel that you yourself are the only person that knows where this little girl's body is . . . and if you get a snow on top of it you yourself may be unable to find it. And since we will be going right past the area [where the body is] on the way into Des Moines, I feel that we could stop and locate the body, that the parents of this little girl should be entitled to a Christian burial for the little girl who was snatched away from them on Christmas [E]ve and murdered. . . . [A]fter a snow storm [we may not be] able to find it at all."

Leaming told Williams he knew the body was in the area of Mitchellville — a town they would be passing on the way to Des Moines. He concluded the conversation by saying "I do not want you to answer me. . . . Just think about it. . . ." Later, as the police car approached Grinnell, Williams asked Leaming whether the police had found the young girl's shoes. After Leaming replied that he was unsure, Williams directed the police to a point near a service station where he said he had left the shoes; they were not found. As they continued to drive to Des Moines, Williams asked whether the blanket had been found and then directed the officers to a rest area in

Grinnell where he said he had disposed of the blanket; they did not find the blanket. At this point Leaming and his party were joined by the officers in charge of the search. As they approached Mitchellville, Williams, without any further conversation, agreed to direct the officers to the child's body.

The officers directing the search had called off the search at 3 P.M., when they left the Grinnell Police Department to join Leaming at the rest area. At that time, one search team near the Jasper County-Polk County line was only two and one-half miles from where Williams soon guided Leaming and his party to the body. The child's body was found next to a culvert in a ditch beside a gravel road in Polk County, about two miles south of Interstate 80, and essentially within the area to be searched.

B

First Trial

In February 1969 Williams was indicted for first-degree murder. Before trial in the Iowa court, his counsel moved to suppress evidence of the body and all related evidence including the condition of the body as shown by the autopsy. The ground for the motion was that such evidence was the "fruit" or product of Williams' statements made during the automobile ride from Davenport to Des Moines and prompted by Leaming's statements. The motion to suppress was denied.

The jury found Williams guilty of first-degree murder; the judgment of conviction was affirmed by the Iowa Supreme Court. Williams then sought release on habeas corpus in the United States District Court for the Southern District of Iowa. That court concluded that the evidence in question had been wrongly admitted at Williams' trial; a divided panel of the Court of Appeals for the Eighth Circuit agreed.

We granted certiorari, and a divided Court affirmed, holding that Detective Leaming had obtained incriminating statements from Williams by what was viewed as interrogation in violation of his right to counsel.

Second Trial

At Williams' second trial in 1977 in the Iowa court, the prosecution did not offer Williams' statements into evidence, nor did it seek to show that Williams had directed the police to the child's body. However, evidence of the condition of her body as it was found, articles and photographs of her clothing, and the results of post mortem medical and chemical tests on the body were admitted. The trial court concluded that the State had proved by a preponderance of the evidence that, if the search had not been suspended and Williams had not led the police to the victim, her body would have been discovered "within a short time" in essentially the same condition as it was actually found. The trial court also ruled that if the police had not located the body, "the search would clearly have been taken up again where it left off, given the extreme circumstances of this case and the body would [have] been found in short order."

In finding that the body would have been discovered in essentially the same condition as it was actually found, the court noted that freezing temperatures had prevailed and tissue deterioration would have been suspended. The challenged evidence was admitted and the jury again found Williams guilty of first-degree murder; he was sentenced to life in prison.

II

A

The Iowa Supreme Court correctly stated that the "vast majority" of all courts, both state and federal, recognize an inevitable discovery exception to the exclusionary rule. We are now urged to adopt and apply the so-called ultimate or inevitable discovery exception to the exclusionary rule.

Williams contends that evidence of the body's location and condition is "fruit of the poisonous tree," i.e., the "fruit" or product of Detective Leaming's plea to help the child's parents give her "a Christian burial," which this Court had already held equated to interrogation. He contends that admitting the challenged evidence violated the Sixth Amendment whether it would have been inevitably discovered or not. Williams also contends that, if the inevitable discovery doctrine is constitutionally permissible, it must include a threshold showing of police good faith.

B

The doctrine requiring courts to suppress evidence as the tainted "fruit" of unlawful governmental conduct had its genesis in Silverthorne Lumber Co. v. United States (1920); there, the Court held that the exclusionary rule applies not only to the illegally obtained evidence itself, but also to other incriminating evidence derived from the primary evidence.

The core rationale consistently advanced by this Court for extending the exclusionary rule to evidence that is the fruit of unlawful police conduct has been that this admittedly drastic and socially costly course is needed to deter police from violations of constitutional and statutory protections. This Court has accepted the argument that the way to ensure such protections is to exclude evidence seized as a result of such violations notwithstanding the high social cost of letting persons obviously guilty go unpunished for their crimes. On this rationale, the prosecution is not to be put in a better position than it would have been in if no illegality had transpired.

By contrast, the derivative evidence analysis ensures that the prosecution is not put in a worse position simply because of some earlier police error or misconduct. The independent source doctrine allows admission of evidence that has been discovered by means wholly independent of any constitutional violation. That doctrine, although closely related to the inevitable discovery doctrine, does not apply here; Williams' statements to Leaming indeed led police to the child's body, but that is not the whole story. The independent source doctrine teaches us that the interest of society in deterring unlawful police conduct and the public interest in having juries receive all probative evidence of a crime are properly balanced by putting the police in the same, not a worse, position than they would have been in if no police error or misconduct had occurred. When the challenged evidence has an independent source, exclusion of such evidence would put the police in a worse position than they would have been in absent any error or violation. There is a functional similarity between these two doctrines in that exclusion of evidence that would inevitably have been discovered would also put the government in a worse position, because the police would have obtained that evidence if no misconduct had taken place. Thus, while the independent source exception would not justify admission of evidence in this case, its rationale is wholly consistent with and justifies our adoption of the ultimate or inevitable discovery exception to the exclusionary rule.

If the prosecution can establish by a preponderance of the evidence that the information ultimately or inevitably would have been discovered by lawful means — here the volunteers' search — then the deterrence rationale has so little basis that the evidence should be received. Anything less would reject logic, experience, and common sense.

The requirement that the prosecution must prove the absence of bad faith, imposed here by the Court of Appeals, would place courts in the position of withholding from juries relevant and undoubted truth that would have been available to police absent any unlawful police activity. Of course, that view would put the police in a worse position than they would have been in if no unlawful conduct had transpired. And, of equal importance, it wholly fails to take into account the enormous societal cost of excluding truth in the search for truth in the administration of justice. Nothing in this Court's prior holdings supports any such formalistic, pointless, and punitive approach.

The Court of Appeals concluded, without analysis, that if an absence-of-bad-faith requirement were not imposed, "the temptation to risk deliberate violations of the Sixth Amendment would be too great, and the deterrent effect of the Exclusionary Rule reduced too far." We reject that view. A police officer who is faced with the opportunity to obtain evidence illegally will rarely, if ever, be in a position to calculate whether the evidence sought would inevitably be discovered.

On the other hand, when an officer is aware that the evidence will inevitably be discovered, he will try to avoid engaging in any questionable practice. In that situation, there will be little to gain from taking any dubious "shortcuts" to obtain the evidence. Significant disincentives to obtaining evidence illegally — including the possibility of departmental discipline and civil liability — also lessen the likelihood that the ultimate or inevitable discovery exception will promote police misconduct. In these circumstances, the societal costs of the exclusionary rule far outweigh any possible benefits to deterrence that a good-faith requirement might produce.

The Court of Appeals did not find it necessary to consider whether the record fairly supported the finding that the volunteer search party would ultimately or inevitably have discovered the victim's body. However, three courts independently reviewing the evidence have found that the body of the child inevitably would have been found by the searchers.

Justice STEVENS, concurring in the judgment.

This litigation is exceptional for at least three reasons. The facts are unusually tragic; it involves an unusually clear violation of constitutional rights; and it graphically illustrates the societal costs that may be incurred when police officers decide to dispense with the requirements of law. Because the Court does not adequately discuss any of these aspects of the case, I am unable to join its opinion.

The constitutional violation that gave rise to the decision in *Williams I* is neither acknowledged nor fairly explained in the Court's opinion. Yet the propriety of admitting evidence relating to the victim's body can only be evaluated if that constitutional violation is properly identified.

Before he was taken into custody, Williams, as a recent escapee from a mental hospital who had just abducted and murdered a small child, posed a special threat to public safety. Acting on his lawyer's advice, Williams surrendered to the Davenport police. The lawyer notified the Des Moines police of Williams' imminent surrender, and police officials, in the presence of Detective Leaming, agreed that Williams would not be questioned while being brought back from Davenport. Williams was advised of this agreement by his attorney. After he was arraigned in Davenport, Williams conferred with another lawyer who was acting as local counsel. This lawyer reminded Williams that he would not be questioned. When Detective Leaming arrived in Davenport, local counsel stressed that the agreement was to be carried out and that Williams was not to be questioned. Detective Leaming then took custody of respondent, and denied counsel's request to ride to Des Moines in the police car with Williams. The "Christian burial speech" occurred during the ensuing trip. As Justice Powell succinctly observed, this was a case "in which the police deliberately took advantage of an inherently coercive setting in the absence of counsel, contrary to their express agreement."

The Sixth Amendment guarantees that the conviction of the accused will be the product of an adversarial process, rather than the ex parte investigation and determination by the prosecutor.

Once the constitutional violation is properly identified, the answers to the questions presented in this case follow readily. Admission of the victim's body, if it would have been discovered anyway, means that the trial in this case was not the product of an inquisitorial process; that process was untainted by illegality. The good or bad faith of Detective Leaming is therefore simply irrelevant. If the trial process was not tainted as a result of his conduct, this defendant received the type of trial that the Sixth Amendment envisions. Generalizations about the exclusionary rule employed by the majority simply do not address the primary question in the case.

The majority is correct to insist that any rule of exclusion not provide the authorities with an incentive to commit violations of the Constitution. If the inevitable discovery rule provided such an incentive by permitting the prosecution to avoid the uncertainties inherent in its search for evidence, it would undermine the constitutional guarantee itself, and therefore be inconsistent with the deterrent purposes of the exclusionary rule. But when the burden of proof on the inevitable discovery question is placed on the prosecution, it must bear the risk of error in the determination made necessary by its constitutional violation. The uncertainty as to whether the body would have been discovered can be resolved in its favor here only because, as the Court explains, petitioner adduced evidence demonstrating that at the time of the constitutional violation an investigation was already under way which, in the natural and probable course of events, would have soon discovered the body. This is not a case in which the prosecution can escape responsibility for a constitutional violation through speculation; to the extent uncertainty was created by the constitutional violation the prosecution was required to resolve that uncertainty through proof. Even if Detective Leaming acted in bad faith in the sense that he deliberately violated the Constitution in order to avoid the possibility that the body would not be discovered, the prosecution ultimately does not avoid that risk; its burden of proof forces it to assume the risk. The need to adduce proof sufficient to discharge its burden, and the difficulty in predicting whether such proof will be available or sufficient, means that the inevitable discovery rule does not permit state officials to avoid the uncertainty they would have faced but for the constitutional violation.

Justice BRENNAN, with whom Justice MARSHALL joins, dissenting.

To the extent that today's decision adopts this "inevitable discovery" exception to the exclusionary rule, it simply acknowledges a doctrine that is akin to the "independent source" exception recognized by the Court. In particular, the Court concludes that unconstitutionally obtained evidence may be admitted at trial if it inevitably would have been discovered in the same condition by an independent line of investigation that was already being pursued when the constitutional violation occurred. As has every Federal Court of Appeals previously addressing this issue, I agree that in these circumstances the "inevitable discovery" exception to the exclusionary rule is consistent with the requirements of the Constitution.

In its zealous efforts to emasculate the exclusionary rule, however, the Court loses sight of the crucial difference between the "inevitable discovery" doctrine and the "independent source" exception from which it is derived. When properly applied, the "independent source" exception allows the prosecution to use evidence only if it was, in fact, obtained by fully lawful means. It therefore does no violence to the constitutional protections that the exclusionary rule is meant to enforce. The "inevitable discovery" exception is likewise compatible with the Constitution, though it differs in one key respect from its next of kin: specifically, the evidence sought to be introduced at trial has not actually been obtained from an independent source, but rather would have been discovered as a matter of course if independent investigations were allowed to proceed.

In my view, this distinction should require that the government satisfy a heightened burden of proof before it is allowed to use such evidence. The inevitable discovery exception necessarily implicates a hypothetical finding that differs in kind from the factual finding that precedes application of the independent source rule. To ensure that this hypothetical finding is narrowly confined to circumstances that are functionally equivalent to an independent source, and to protect fully the fundamental rights served by the exclusionary rule, I would require clear and convincing evidence before concluding that the government had met its burden of proof on this issue. Increasing the burden of proof serves to impress the factfinder with the importance of the decision and thereby reduces the risk that illegally obtained evidence will be admitted. Because the lower courts did not impose such a requirement, I would remand this case for application of this heightened burden of proof by the lower courts in the first instance. I am therefore unable to join either the Court's opinion or its judgment.

3. Inadequate Causal Connection — Attenuation of the Taint

The exclusionary rule applies if there is a substantial causal connection between the illegal police behavior and the evidence. Indeed, the Supreme Court has made clear that all evidence that is the product of the illegal police activity — the "fruit of the poisonous tree" — must be excluded. If, however, the link between the illegal police act and the evidence is attenuated, then the evidence is admissible.

Wong Sun v. United States, 371 U.S. 471 (1963), illustrates this. Police illegally broke into Wong Sun's laundry and adjacent apartment. The police handcuffed Wong Sun and held him at gunpoint. Wong Sun made incriminating statements. Wong Sun was arrested, charged, and released on his own recognizance. Subsequently, he was questioned by an agent who informed Wong Sun of his right to remain silent and to consult with counsel. Wong Sun again gave incriminating statements.

The Supreme Court held that Wong Sun's statements to the police at the time of his arrest had to be excluded as the fruits of his unlawful arrest. By contrast, though, the Court said that Wong Sun's later confession was admissible because the connection with the earlier illegal police activity "became so attenuated as to dissipate the taint."

Brown v. Illinois, below, is one of the most widely cited cases with regard to this exception to the exclusionary rule. It is followed by a very recent case, Utah v. Strieff, that applies this exception.

BROWN v. ILLINOIS

422 U.S. 590 (1975)

Justice BLACKMUN delivered the opinion of the Court.

This case lies at the crossroads of the Fourth and the Fifth Amendments. Petitioner was arrested without probable cause and without a warrant. He was given, in full, the warnings prescribed by Miranda v. Arizona (1966). Thereafter, while in custody, he made two inculpatory statements. The issue is whether evidence of those statements was properly admitted, or should have been excluded, in petitioner's subsequent trial for murder in state court. Expressed another way, the issue is whether the statements were to be excluded as the fruit of the illegal arrest, or were admissible because the giving of the *Miranda* warnings sufficiently attenuated the taint of the arrest. *See* Wong Sun v. United States (1963).

I

As petitioner Richard Brown was climbing the last of the stairs leading to the rear entrance of his Chicago apartment in the early evening of May 13, 1968, he happened to glance at the window near the door. He saw, pointed at him through the window, a revolver held by a stranger who was inside the apartment. The man said: "Don't move, you are under arrest." Another man, also with a gun, came up behind Brown and repeated the statement that he was under arrest. It was about 7:45 P.M. The two men turned out to be Detectives William Nolan and William Lenz of the Chicago police force. It is not clear from the record exactly when they advised Brown of their identity, but it is not disputed that they broke into his apartment, searched it, and then arrested Brown, all without probable cause and without any warrant, when he arrived. They later testified that they made the arrest for the purpose of questioning Brown as part of their investigation of the murder of a man named Roger Corpus.

Corpus was murdered one week earlier, on May 6, with a .38-caliber revolver in his Chicago West Side second-floor apartment. Shortly thereafter, Detective Lenz obtained petitioners' name, among others, from Corpus' brother. Petitioner and the others were identified as acquaintances of the victim, not as suspects.

On the day of petitioner's arrest, Detectives Lenz and Nolan, armed with a photograph of Brown, and another officer arrived at petitioner's apartment about 5 P.M. While the third officer covered the front entrance downstairs, the two detectives broke into Brown's apartment and searched it. Lenz then positioned himself near the rear door and watched through the adjacent window which opened onto the back porch. Nolan sat near the front door.

As both officers held him at gunpoint, the three entered the apartment. Brown was ordered to stand against the wall and was searched. No weapon was found. He was asked his name. When he denied being Richard Brown,

Detective Lenz showed him the photograph, informed him that he was under arrest for the murder of Roger Corpus, handcuffed him, and escorted him to the squad car. The two detectives took petitioner to the Maxwell Street police station. During the 20-minute drive Nolan again asked Brown, who then was sitting with him in the back seat of the car, whether his name was Richard Brown and whether he owned a 1966 Oldsmobile. Brown alternately evaded these questions or answered them falsely. Upon arrival at the station house Brown was placed in the second-floor central interrogation room. The room was bare, except for a table and four chairs. He was left alone, apparently without handcuffs, for some minutes while the officers obtained the file on the Corpus homicide. They returned with the file, sat down at the table, one across from Brown and the other to his left, and spread the file on the table in front of him.

The officers warned Brown of his rights under *Miranda.* They then informed him that they knew of an incident that had occurred in a poolroom on May 5, when Brown, angry at having been cheated at dice, fired a shot from a revolver into the ceiling. Brown answered: "Oh, you know about that." Lenz informed him that a bullet had been obtained from the ceiling of the poolroom and had been taken to the crime laboratory to be compared with bullets taken from Corpus' body. Brown responded: "Oh, you know that, too." At this point — it was about 8:45 P.M. — Lenz asked Brown whether he wanted to talk about the Corpus homicide. Petitioner answered that he did. For the next 20 to 25 minutes Brown answered questions put to him by Nolan, as Lenz typed.

This questioning produced a two-page statement in which Brown acknowledged that he and a man named Jimmy Claggett visited Corpus on the evening of May 5; that the three for some time sat drinking and smoking marihuana; that Claggett ordered him at gunpoint to bind Corpus' hands and feet with cord from the headphone of a stereo set; and that Claggett, using a .38-caliber revolver sold to him by Brown, shot Corpus three times through a pillow. The statement was signed by Brown.

About 9:30 P.M. the two detectives and Brown left the station house to look for Claggett in an area of Chicago Brown knew him to frequent. They made a tour of that area but did not locate their quarry. They then went to police headquarters where they endeavored, without success, to obtain a photograph of Claggett. They resumed their search — it was now about 11 P.M. — and they finally observed Claggett crossing at an intersection. Lenz and Nolan arrested him. All four, the two detectives and the two arrested men, returned to the Maxwell Street station about 12:15 A.M.

Brown was again placed in the interrogation room. He was given coffee and was left alone, for the most part, until 2 A.M. when Assistant State's Attorney Crilly arrived.

Crilly, too, informed Brown of his *Miranda* rights. After a half hour's conversation, a court reporter appeared. Once again the *Miranda* warnings were given. Brown gave a second statement, providing a factual account of the murder substantially in accord with his first statement, but containing factual inaccuracies with respect to his personal background. When the statement was completed, at about 3 A.M., Brown refused to sign it. An hour later he made a phone call to his mother. At 9:30 that morning, about 14 hours after his arrest, he was taken before a magistrate.

On June 20 Brown and Claggett were jointly indicted by a Cook County grand jury for Corpus' murder. Prior to trial, petitioner moved to suppress the two statements he had made. He alleged that his arrest and detention had been illegal and that the statements were taken from him in violation of his constitutional rights. After a hearing, the motion was denied.

The case proceeded to trial. The State introduced evidence of both statements. The jury found petitioner guilty of murder. He was sentenced to imprisonment for not less than 15 years nor more than 30 years. On appeal, the Supreme Court of Illinois affirmed the judgment of conviction.

II

In *Wong Sun*, the Court pronounced the principles to be applied where the issue is whether statements and other evidence obtained after an illegal arrest or search should be excluded. [We stated,] "We need not hold that all evidence is 'fruit of the poisonous tree' simply because it would not have come to light but for the illegal actions of the police. Rather, the more apt question in such a case is 'whether, granting establishment of the primary illegality, the evidence to which instant objection is made has been come at by exploitation of that illegality or instead by means sufficiently distinguishable to be purged of the primary taint.'"

The exclusionary rule thus was applied in *Wong Sun* primarily to protect Fourth Amendment rights. Protection of the Fifth Amendment right against self-incrimination was not the Court's paramount concern there. To the extent that the question whether [defendant] Toy's statement was voluntary was considered, it was only to judge whether it "was sufficiently an act of free will to purge the primary taint of the unlawful invasion."

III

The Illinois courts refrained from resolving the question, as apt here as it was in *Wong Sun*, whether Brown's statements were obtained by exploitation of the illegality of his arrest. They assumed that the *Miranda* warnings, by themselves, assured that the statements (verbal acts, as contrasted with physical evidence) were of sufficient free will as to purge the primary taint of the unlawful arrest. *Wong Sun*, of course, preceded *Miranda*.

Although, almost 90 years ago, the Court observed that the Fifth Amendment is in "intimate relation" with the Fourth, the *Miranda* warnings thus far have not been regarded as a means either of remedying or deterring violations of Fourth Amendment rights. Frequently, as here, rights under the two Amendments may appear to coalesce since "the unreasonable searches and seizures condemned in the Fourth Amendment are almost always made for the purpose of compelling a man to give evidence against himself, which in criminal cases is condemned in the Fifth Amendment." The exclusionary rule, however, when utilized to effectuate the Fourth Amendment, serves interests and policies that are distinct from those it serves under the Fifth. It is directed at all unlawful searches and seizures, and not merely those that happen to produce incriminating material or testimony as fruits. In short, exclusion of a confession made without *Miranda* warnings might be regarded as necessary to effectuate the Fifth Amendment, but it would not be sufficient fully to protect the Fourth. *Miranda* warnings, and the exclusion of a confession made without them, do not alone sufficiently deter a Fourth Amendment violation.

Thus, even if the statements in this case were found to be voluntary under the Fifth Amendment, the Fourth Amendment issue remains. In order for the causal chain, between the illegal arrest and the statements made subsequent thereto, to be broken, *Wong Sun* requires not merely that the statement meet the Fifth Amendment standard of voluntariness but that it be "sufficiently an act of free will to purge the primary taint." *Wong Sun* thus mandates consideration of a statement's admissibility in light of the distinct policies and interests of the Fourth Amendment.

If *Miranda* warnings, by themselves, were held to attenuate the taint of an unconstitutional arrest, regardless of how wanton and purposeful the Fourth Amendment violation, the effect of the exclusionary rule would be substantially diluted. Arrests made without warrant or without probable cause, for questioning or "investigation," would be encouraged by the knowledge that evidence derived therefrom could well be made admissible at trial by the simple expedient of giving *Miranda* warnings. Any incentive to avoid Fourth Amendment violations would be eviscerated by making the warnings, in effect, a "cure-all," and the constitutional guarantee against unlawful searches and seizures could be said to be reduced to "a form of words."

It is entirely possible, of course, as the State here argues, that persons arrested illegally frequently may decide to confess, as an act of free will unaffected by the initial illegality. But the *Miranda* warnings, alone and per se, cannot always make the act sufficiently a product of free will to break, for Fourth Amendment purposes, the causal connection between the illegality and the confession. They cannot assure in every case that the Fourth Amendment violation has not been unduly exploited.

While we therefore reject the per se rule which the Illinois courts appear to have accepted, we also decline to adopt any alternative per se or "but for" rule. The petitioner himself professes not to demand so much. The question whether a confession is the product of a free will under *Wong Sun* must be answered on the facts of each case. No single fact is dispositive. The workings of the human mind are too complex, and the possibilities of misconduct too diverse, to permit protection of the Fourth Amendment to turn on such a talismanic test. The *Miranda* warnings are an important factor, to be sure, in determining whether the confession is obtained by exploitation of an illegal arrest. But they are not the only factor to be considered. The temporal proximity of the arrest and the confession, the presence of intervening circumstances, and, particularly, the purpose and flagrancy of the official misconduct are all relevant. The voluntariness of the statement is a threshold requirement. And the burden of showing admissibility rests, of course, on the prosecution.

IV

Although the Illinois courts failed to undertake the inquiry mandated by *Wong Sun* to evaluate the circumstances of this case in the light of the policy served by the exclusionary rule, the trial resulted in a record of amply sufficient detail and depth from which the determination may be made. We conclude that the State failed to sustain the burden of showing that the evidence in question was admissible under *Wong Sun*.

Brown's first statement was separated from his illegal arrest by less than two hours, and there was no intervening event of significance whatsoever. In its essentials, his situation is remarkably like that of James Wah Toy in *Wong Sun*. We could hold Brown's first statement admissible only if we overrule *Wong Sun*. We decline to do so. And the second statement was clearly the result and the fruit of the first.

The illegality here, moreover, had a quality of purposefulness. The impropriety of the arrest was obvious; awareness of that fact was virtually conceded by the two detectives when they repeatedly acknowledged, in their testimony, that the purpose of their action was "for investigation" or for "questioning." The arrest, both in design and in execution, was investigatory. The detectives embarked upon this expedition for evidence in the hope that something might turn up. The manner in which Brown's arrest was affected gives the appearance of having been calculated to cause surprise, fright, and confusion.

We emphasize that our holding is a limited one. We decide only that the Illinois courts were in error in assuming that the *Miranda* warnings, by themselves, under *Wong Sun* always purge the taint of an illegal arrest.

Justice POWELL, with whom Justice REHNQUIST joins, concurring in part.

I join the Court insofar as it holds that the per se rule adopted by the Illinois Supreme Court for determining the admissibility of petitioner's two statements inadequately accommodates the diverse interests underlying the Fourth Amendment exclusionary rule. I would, however, remand the case for reconsideration under the general standards articulated in the Court's opinion and elaborated herein.

On this record, I cannot conclude as readily as the Court that admission of the statements here at issue would constitute an effective overruling of *Wong Sun*.

The notion of the "dissipation of the taint" attempts to mark the point at which the detrimental consequences of illegal police action become so attenuated that the deterrent effect of the exclusionary rule no longer justifies its cost. Application of the *Wong Sun* doctrine will generate fact-specific cases bearing distinct differences as well as similarities, and the question of attenuation inevitably is largely a matter of degree. The Court today identifies the general factors that the trial court must consider in making this determination. I think it appropriate, however, to attempt to articulate the possible relationships to those factors in particular, broad categories of cases.

All Fourth Amendment violations are, by constitutional definition, "unreasonable." There are, however, significant practical differences that distinguish among violations, differences that measurably assist in identifying the kinds of cases in which disqualifying the evidence is likely to serve the deterrent purposes of the exclusionary rule. In my view, the point at which the taint can be said to have dissipated should be related, in the absence of other controlling circumstances, to the nature of that taint.

Bearing these considerations in mind, and recognizing that the deterrent value of the Fourth Amendment exclusionary rule is limited to certain kinds of police conduct, the following general categories can be identified. Those most readily identifiable are on the extremes: the flagrantly abusive violation of Fourth Amendment rights, on the one hand, and "technical" Fourth Amendment violations, on the other. In my view, these extremes call for significantly different judicial responses.

I would require the clearest indication of attenuation in cases in which official conduct was flagrantly abusive of Fourth Amendment rights. If, for example, the factors relied on by the police in determining to make the arrest were so lacking in indicia of probable cause as to render official belief in its existence entirely unreasonable, or if the evidence clearly suggested that the arrest was effectuated as a pretext for collateral objectives, or the physical circumstances of the arrest unnecessarily intrusive on personal privacy, I would consider the equalizing potential of *Miranda* warnings rarely sufficient to dissipate the taint. In such cases the deterrent value of the exclusionary rule is most likely to be effective, and the corresponding mandate to preserve judicial integrity, most clearly demands that the fruits of official misconduct be denied. I thus would require some demonstrably effective break in the chain of events leading from the illegal arrest to the statement, such as actual consultation with counsel or the accused's presentation before a magistrate for a determination of probable cause, before the taint can be deemed removed.

At the opposite end of the spectrum lie "technical" violations of Fourth Amendment rights where, for example, officers in good faith arrest an individual in reliance on a warrant later invalidated or pursuant to a statute that subsequently is declared unconstitutional. Absent aggravating circumstances, I would consider a statement given at the station house after one has been advised of *Miranda* rights to be sufficiently removed from the immediate circumstances of the illegal arrest to justify its admission at trial.

Between these extremes lies a wide range of situations that defy ready categorization, and I will not attempt to embellish on the factors set forth in the Court's opinion other than to emphasize that the *Wong Sun* inquiry always should be conducted with the deterrent purpose of the Fourth Amendment exclusionary rule sharply in focus. And, in view of the inevitably fact-specific nature of the inquiry, we must place primary reliance on the "learning, good sense, fairness and courage" of judges who must make the determination in the first instance.

On the facts of record as I view them, it is possible that the police may have believed reasonably that there was probable cause for petitioner's arrest. I am not able to conclude on this record that the officers arrested petitioner solely for the purpose of questioning. To be sure, there is evidence suggesting, as the Court notes, an investigatory arrest. But the evidence is conflicting.

I would leave the question of admissibility of this statement to the lower Illinois courts. In any event, the question whether there was sufficient attenuation between the first and second statements to render the second admissible in spite of the inadmissibility of the first presents a factual issue which, like the factual issue underlying the possible admissibility of the first statement, has not been passed on by the state courts.

If the police illegally stop an individual and then learn that there is an outstanding warrant, must evidence gained from a search incident to the arrest be excluded? The Court says generally the evidence does not need to be excluded. Does that create an incentive for the police to engage in illegal stops knowing that if they discover an outstanding warrant they can do a search incident to an arrest?

UTAH v. STRIEFF

136 S. Ct. 2056 (2016)

Justice THOMAS delivered the opinion of the Court.

To enforce the Fourth Amendment's prohibition against "unreasonable searches and seizures," this Court has at times required courts to exclude evidence obtained by unconstitutional police conduct. But the Court has also held that, even when there is a Fourth Amendment violation, this exclusionary rule does not apply when the costs of exclusion outweigh its deterrent benefits. In some cases, for example, the link between the unconstitutional conduct and the discovery of the evidence is too attenuated to justify suppression. The question in this case is whether this attenuation doctrine applies when an officer makes an unconstitutional investigatory stop; learns during that stop that the suspect is subject to a valid arrest warrant; and proceeds to arrest the suspect and seize incriminating evidence during a search incident to that arrest. We hold that the evidence the officer seized as part of the search incident to arrest is admissible because the officer's discovery of the arrest warrant attenuated the connection between the unlawful stop and the evidence seized incident to arrest.

I

This case began with an anonymous tip. In December 2006, someone called the South Salt Lake City police's drug-tip line to report "narcotics activity" at a particular residence. Narcotics detective Douglas Fackrell investigated the tip. Over the course of about a week, Officer Fackrell conducted intermittent surveillance of the home. He observed visitors who left a few minutes after arriving at the house. These visits were sufficiently frequent to raise his suspicion that the occupants were dealing drugs.

One of those visitors was respondent Edward Strieff. Officer Fackrell observed Strieff exit the house and walk toward a nearby convenience store. In the store's parking lot, Officer Fackrell detained Strieff, identified himself, and asked Strieff what he was doing at the residence.

As part of the stop, Officer Fackrell requested Strieff's identification, and Strieff produced his Utah identification card. Officer Fackrell relayed Strieff's information to a police dispatcher, who reported that Strieff had an outstanding arrest warrant for a traffic violation. Officer Fackrell then arrested Strieff pursuant to that warrant. When Officer Fackrell searched Strieff incident to the arrest, he discovered a baggie of methamphetamine and drug paraphernalia.

The State charged Strieff with unlawful possession of methamphetamine and drug paraphernalia. Strieff moved to suppress the evidence, arguing that the evidence was inadmissible because it was derived from an unlawful investigatory stop. At the suppression hearing, the prosecutor conceded that Officer Fackrell lacked reasonable suspicion for the stop but argued that the evidence should not be suppressed because the existence of a valid arrest warrant attenuated the connection between the unlawful stop and the discovery of the contraband.

II

In the 20th century, however, the exclusionary rule — the rule that often requires trial courts to exclude unlawfully seized evidence in a criminal trial — became the principal judicial remedy to deter Fourth Amendment violations.

Under the Court's precedents, the exclusionary rule encompasses both the "primary evidence obtained as a direct result of an illegal search or seizure" and, relevant here, "evidence later discovered and found to be derivative of an illegality," the so-called "'fruit of the poisonous tree.'" But the significant costs of this rule have led us to deem it "applicable only . . . where its deterrence benefits outweigh its substantial social costs." "Suppression of evidence . . . has always been our last resort, not our first impulse."

We have accordingly recognized several exceptions to the rule. Three of these exceptions involve the causal relationship between the unconstitutional act and the discovery of evidence. First, the independent source doctrine allows trial courts to admit evidence obtained in an unlawful search if officers independently acquired it from a separate, independent source. Second, the inevitable discovery doctrine allows for the admission of evidence that would have been discovered even without the unconstitutional source. Third, and at issue here, is the attenuation doctrine: Evidence is admissible when the connection between unconstitutional police conduct and the evidence is remote or has been interrupted by some intervening circumstance, so that "the interest protected by the constitutional guarantee that has been violated would not be served by suppression of the evidence obtained."

Turning to the application of the attenuation doctrine to this case, we first address a threshold question: whether this doctrine applies at all to a case like this, where the intervening circumstance that the State relies on is the discovery of a valid, pre-existing, and untainted arrest warrant. The three factors articulated in Brown v. Illinois (1975), guide our analysis. First, we look to the "temporal proximity" between the unconstitutional conduct and the discovery of evidence to determine how closely the discovery of evidence followed the unconstitutional search. Second, we consider "the presence of intervening circumstances." Third, and "particularly" significant, we examine "the purpose and flagrancy of the official misconduct." In evaluating these factors, we assume without deciding (because the State conceded the point) that Officer Fackrell lacked reasonable suspicion to initially stop Strieff.

The first factor, temporal proximity between the initially unlawful stop and the search, favors suppressing the evidence. Our precedents have declined to find that this factor favors attenuation unless "substantial time" elapses between an unlawful act and when the evidence is obtained. Here, however, Officer Fackrell discovered drug contraband on Strieff's person only minutes after the illegal stop.

In contrast, the second factor, the presence of intervening circumstances, strongly favors the State. In this case, the warrant was valid, it predated Officer Fackrell's investigation, and it was entirely unconnected with the stop. And once Officer Fackrell discovered the warrant, he had an obligation to arrest Strieff. "A warrant is a judicial mandate to an officer to conduct a search or make an arrest, and the officer has a sworn duty to carry out its provisions." United States v. Leon (1984). Officer Fackrell's arrest of Strieff thus was a ministerial act that was independently compelled by the pre-existing warrant. And once Officer Fackrell was authorized to arrest Strieff, it was undisputedly lawful to search Strieff as an incident of his arrest to protect Officer Fackrell's safety.

Finally, the third factor, "the purpose and flagrancy of the official misconduct," also strongly favors the State. The exclusionary rule exists to deter police misconduct. The third factor of the attenuation doctrine reflects that rationale by favoring exclusion only when the police misconduct is most in need of deterrence — that is, when it is purposeful or flagrant.

Officer Fackrell was at most negligent. In stopping Strieff, Officer Fackrell made two good-faith mistakes. First, he had not observed what time Strieff entered the suspected drug house, so he did not know how long Strieff had been there. Officer Fackrell thus lacked a sufficient basis to conclude that Strieff was a short-term visitor who may have been consummating a drug transaction. Second, because he lacked confirmation that Strieff was a short-term visitor, Officer Fackrell should have asked Strieff whether he would speak with him, instead of demanding that Strieff do so. Officer Fackrell's stated purpose was to "find out what was going on [in] the house." Nothing prevented him from approaching Strieff simply to ask. But these errors in judgment hardly rise to a purposeful or flagrant violation of Strieff's Fourth Amendment rights.

While Officer Fackrell's decision to initiate the stop was mistaken, his conduct thereafter was lawful. The officer's decision to run the warrant check was a "negligibly burdensome precautio[n]" for officer safety. And Officer Fackrell's actual search of Strieff was a lawful search incident to arrest. Moreover, there is no indication that this unlawful stop was part of any systemic or recurrent police misconduct. To the contrary, all the evidence suggests that the stop was an isolated instance of negligence that occurred in connection with a bona fide investigation of a suspected drug house. Officer Fackrell saw Strieff leave a suspected drug house. And his suspicion about the house was based on an anonymous tip and his personal observations.

Applying these factors, we hold that the evidence discovered on Strieff's person was admissible because the unlawful stop was sufficiently attenuated by the pre-existing arrest warrant. Although the illegal stop was close in time to Strieff's arrest, that consideration is outweighed by two factors supporting the State. The outstanding arrest warrant for Strieff's arrest is a critical intervening circumstance that is wholly independent of the illegal stop. The discovery of that warrant broke the causal chain between the unconstitutional stop and the discovery of evidence by compelling Officer Fackrell to arrest Strieff. And, it is especially significant that there is no evidence that Officer Fackrell's illegal stop reflected flagrantly unlawful police misconduct.

We hold that the evidence Officer Fackrell seized as part of his search incident to arrest is admissible because his discovery of the arrest warrant attenuated the connection between the unlawful stop and the evidence seized from Strieff incident to arrest. The judgment of the Utah Supreme Court, accordingly, is reversed.

JUSTICE SOTOMAYOR, with whom JUSTICE GINSBURG joins as to Parts I, II, and III, dissenting.

The Court today holds that the discovery of a warrant for an unpaid parking ticket will forgive a police officer's violation of your Fourth Amendment rights. Do not be soothed by the opinion's technical language: This case allows the police to stop you on the street, demand your identification, and check it for outstanding traffic warrants — even if you are doing nothing wrong. If the officer discovers a warrant for a fine you forgot to pay, courts will now excuse his illegal stop and will admit into evidence anything he happens to find by searching you after arresting you on the warrant. Because the Fourth Amendment should prohibit, not permit, such misconduct, I dissent.

I

Minutes after Edward Strieff walked out of a South Salt Lake City home, an officer stopped him, questioned him, and took his identification to run it through a police database. The officer did not suspect that Strieff had done anything wrong. Strieff just happened to be the first person to leave a house that the officer thought might contain "drug activity."

As the State of Utah concedes, this stop was illegal. The Fourth Amendment protects people from "unreasonable searches and seizures." An officer breaches that protection when he detains a pedestrian to check his license without any evidence that the person is engaged in a crime. The officer deepens the breach when he prolongs the detention just to fish further for evidence of wrongdoing. In his search for lawbreaking, the officer in this case himself broke the law.

II

It is tempting in a case like this, where illegal conduct by an officer uncovers illegal conduct by a civilian, to forgive the officer. After all, his instincts, although unconstitutional, were correct. But a basic principle lies at the heart of the Fourth Amendment: Two wrongs don't make a right. When "lawless police conduct" uncovers evidence of lawless civilian conduct, this Court has long required later criminal trials to exclude the illegally obtained evidence.

This "exclusionary rule" removes an incentive for officers to search us without proper justification. It also keeps courts from being "made party to lawless invasions of the constitutional rights of citizens by permitting unhindered governmental use of the fruits of such invasions." When courts admit only lawfully obtained evidence, they encourage "those who formulate law enforcement polices, and the officers who implement them, to incorporate Fourth Amendment ideals into their value system." But when courts admit illegally obtained evidence as well, they reward "manifest neglect if not an open defiance of the prohibitions of the Constitution."

These factors confirm that the officer in this case discovered Strieff's drugs by exploiting his own illegal conduct. The officer did not ask Strieff to volunteer his name only to find out, days later, that Strieff had a warrant against him. The officer illegally stopped Strieff and immediately ran a warrant check. The officer's discovery of a warrant was not some intervening surprise that he could not have anticipated. Utah lists over 180,000 misdemeanor warrants in its database, and at the time of the arrest, Salt Lake County had a "backlog of outstanding warrants" so large that it faced the "potential for civil liability." The officer's violation was also calculated to procure evidence. His sole reason for stopping Strieff, he acknowledged, was investigative — he wanted to discover whether drug activity was going on in the house Strieff had just exited.

The warrant check, in other words, was not an "intervening circumstance" separating the stop from the search for drugs. It was part and parcel of the officer's illegal "expedition for evidence in the hope that something might turn up." Under our precedents, because the officer found Strieff's drugs by exploiting his own constitutional violation, the drugs should be excluded.

III

The Court sees things differently. To the Court, the fact that a warrant gives an officer cause to arrest a person severs the connection between illegal policing and the resulting discovery of evidence. This is a remarkable proposition: The mere existence of a warrant not only gives an officer legal cause to arrest and search a person, it also forgives an officer who, with no knowledge of the warrant at all, unlawfully stops that person on a whim or hunch.

The majority misses the point when it calls the warrant check here a "'negligibly burdensome recaution[n]'" taken for the officer's "safety." Remember, the officer stopped Strieff without suspecting him of committing any crime. By his own account, the officer did not fear Strieff. The majority also posits that the officer could not have exploited his illegal conduct because he did not violate the Fourth Amendment on purpose. Rather, he made "good-faith mistakes." Never mind that the officer's sole purpose was to fish for evidence. The majority casts his unconstitutional actions as "negligent" and therefore incapable of being deterred by the exclusionary rule.

But the Fourth Amendment does not tolerate an officer's unreasonable searches and seizures just because he did not know any better. Even officers prone to negligence can learn from courts that exclude illegally obtained evidence. Indeed, they are perhaps the most in need of the education, whether by the judge's opinion, the prosecutor's future guidance, or an updated manual on criminal procedure. If the officers are in doubt about what the law requires, exclusion gives them an "incentive to err on the side of constitutional behavior."

Most striking about the Court's opinion is its insistence that the event here was "isolated," with "no indication that this unlawful stop was part of any systemic or recurrent police misconduct." Respectfully, nothing about this case is isolated.

Outstanding warrants are surprisingly common. When a person with a traffic ticket misses a fine payment or court appearance, a court will issue a warrant. When a person on probation drinks alcohol or breaks curfew, a court will issue a warrant. The States and Federal Government maintain databases with over 7.8 million outstanding warrants, the vast majority of which appear to be for minor offenses. Even these sources may not track the "staggering" numbers of warrants, "'drawers and drawers'" full, that many cities issue for traffic violations and ordinance infractions. The Department of Justice recently reported that in the town of Ferguson, Missouri, with a population of 21,000, 16,000 people had outstanding warrants against them. In Newark, New Jersey, officers stopped 52,235 pedestrians within a 4-year period and ran warrant checks on 39,308 of them. The Justice Department analyzed these warrant-checked stops and reported that "approximately 93% of the stops would have been considered unsupported by articulated reasonable suspicion."

I do not doubt that most officers act in "good faith" and do not set out to break the law. That does not mean these stops are "isolated instance[s] of negligence," however. Many are the product of institutionalized training procedures. The New York City Police Department long trained officers to, in the words of a District Judge, "stop and question first, develop reasonable suspicion later."

The majority does not suggest what makes this case "isolated" from these and countless other examples. Nor does it offer guidance for how a defendant can prove that his arrest was the result of "widespread" misconduct. Surely it should not take a federal investigation of Salt Lake County before the Court would protect someone in Strieff's position.

IV

Writing only for myself, and drawing on my professional experiences, I would add that unlawful "stops" have severe consequences much greater than the inconvenience suggested by the name. This Court has given officers an array of instruments to probe and examine you. When we condone officers' use of these devices without adequate cause, we give them reason to target pedestrians in an arbitrary manner. We also risk treating members of our communities as second-class citizens.

Although many Americans have been stopped for speeding or jaywalking, few may realize how degrading a stop can be when the officer is looking for more. This Court has allowed an officer to stop you for whatever reason he wants — so long as he can point to a pretextual justification after the fact. Whren v. United States (1996). The indignity of the stop is not limited to an officer telling you that you look like a criminal. The officer may next ask for your "consent" to inspect your bag or purse without telling you that you can decline. Regardless of your answer, he may order you to stand "helpless, perhaps facing a wall with [your] hands raised." If the officer thinks you might be dangerous, he may then "frisk" you for weapons. This involves more than just a pat down. As onlookers pass by, the officer may "'feel with sensitive fingers every portion of [your] body. A thorough search [may] be made of [your] arms and armpits, waistline and back, the groin and area about the testicles, and entire surface of the legs down to the feet.'"

The officer's control over you does not end with the stop. If the officer chooses, he may handcuff you and take you to jail for doing nothing more than speeding, jaywalking, or "driving [your] pickup truck . . . with [your]

3-year-old son and 5-year-old daughter . . . without [your] seatbelt fastened."
Atwater v. Lago Vista (2001). At the jail, he can fingerprint you, swab
DNA from the inside of your mouth, and force you to "shower with a delousing agent" while you "lift [your] tongue, hold out [your] arms, turn around,
and lift [your] genitals." Florence v. Board of Chosen Freeholders of County
of Burlington (2012); Maryland v. King (2013). Even if you are innocent, you
will now join the 65 million Americans with an arrest record and experience
the "civil death" of discrimination by employers, landlords, and whoever else
conducts a background check. And, of course, if you fail to pay bail or appear
for court, a judge will issue a warrant to render you "arrestable on sight" in
the future.

This case involves a *suspicionless* stop, one in which the officer initiated this
chain of events without justification. As the Justice Department notes, many
innocent people are subjected to the humiliations of these unconstitutional
searches. The white defendant in this case shows that anyone's dignity can be
violated in this manner. But it is no secret that people of color are disproportionate victims of this type of scrutiny. See M. Alexander, The New Jim
Crow 95-136 (2010). For generations, black and brown parents have given
their children "the talk" — instructing them never to run down the street;
always keep your hands where they can be seen; do not even think of talking
back to a stranger — all out of fear of how an officer with a gun will react to
them. See, e.g.,W.E.B. Du Bois, The Souls of Black Folk (1903); J. Baldwin,
The Fire Next Time (1963); T. Coates, Between the World and Me (2015).

By legitimizing the conduct that produces this double consciousness, this case
tells everyone, white and black, guilty and innocent, that an officer can verify
your legal status at any time. It says that your body is subject to invasion while
courts excuse the violation of your rights. It implies that you are not a citizen of a
democracy but the subject of a carceral state, just waiting to be cataloged.

We must not pretend that the countless people who are routinely targeted
by police are "isolated." They are the canaries in the coal mine whose deaths,
civil and literal, warn us that no one can breathe in this atmosphere. See L.
Guinier & G. Torres, The Miner's Canary 274-283 (2002). They are the ones
who recognize that unlawful police stops corrode all our civil liberties and
threaten all our lives. Until their voices matter too, our justice system will
continue to be anything but.

Justice KAGAN, with whom Justice GINSBURG joins, dissenting.
If a police officer stops a person on the street without reasonable
suspicion, that seizure violates the Fourth Amendment. And if the officer
pats down the unlawfully detained individual and finds drugs in his pocket,
the State may not use the contraband as evidence in a criminal prosecution.
That much is beyond dispute. The question here is whether the prohibition
on admitting evidence dissolves if the officer discovers, after making the stop
but before finding the drugs, that the person has an outstanding arrest
warrant. Because that added wrinkle makes no difference under the
Constitution, I respectfully dissent.

Since Brown v. Illinois (1975), three factors have guided that analysis. First, the closer the "temporal proximity" between the unlawful act and the discovery of evidence, the greater the deterrent value of suppression. Second, the more "purpose[ful]" or "flagran[t]" the police illegality, the clearer the necessity, and better the chance, of preventing similar misbehavior. And third, the presence (or absence) of "intervening circumstances" makes a difference: The stronger the causal chain between the misconduct and the evidence, the more exclusion will curb future constitutional violations. Here, as shown below, each of those considerations points toward suppression: Nothing in Fackrell's discovery of an outstanding warrant so attenuated the connection between his wrongful behavior and his detection of drugs as to diminish the exclusionary rule's deterrent benefits.

Start where the majority does: The temporal proximity factor, it forthrightly admits, "favors suppressing the evidence." After all, Fackrell's discovery of drugs came just minutes after the unconstitutional stop. And in prior decisions, this Court has made clear that only the lapse of "substantial time" between the two could favor admission. So the State, by all accounts, takes strike one.

Move on to the purposefulness of Fackrell's conduct, where the majority is less willing to see a problem for what it is. The majority chalks up Fackrell's Fourth Amendment violation to a couple of innocent "mistakes." But far from a Barney Fife-type mishap, Fackrell's seizure of Strieff was a calculated decision, taken with so little justification that the State has never tried to defend its legality. In *Brown,* the Court held those facts to support suppression — and they do here as well. Swing and a miss for strike two.

Finally, consider whether any intervening circumstance "br[oke] the causal chain" between the stop and the evidence. Fackrell's discovery of an arrest warrant — the only event the majority thinks intervened — was an eminently foreseeable consequence of stopping Strieff. As Fackrell testified, checking for outstanding warrants during a stop is the "normal" practice of South Salt Lake City police. In other words, the department's standard detention procedures — stop, ask for identification, run a check — are partly designed to find outstanding warrants. And find them they will, given the staggering number of such warrants on the books.

To take just a few examples: The State of California has 2.5 million outstanding arrest warrants (a number corresponding to about 9% of its adult population); Pennsylvania (with a population of about 12.8 million) contributes 1.4 million more; and New York City (population 8.4 million) adds another 1.2 million. So outstanding warrants do not appear as bolts from the blue. They are the run-of-the-mill results of police stops — what officers look for when they run a routine check of a person's identification and what they know will turn up with fair regularity. In short, they are nothing like what intervening circumstances are supposed to be. Strike three.

The majority's misapplication of *Brown*'s three-part inquiry creates unfortunate incentives for the police — indeed, practically invites them to do what Fackrell did here. Consider an officer who, like Fackrell, wishes to stop someone for investigative reasons, but does not have what a court would view as reasonable suspicion. If the officer believes that any evidence he discovers will be inadmissible, he is likely to think the unlawful stop not worth making—precisely the deterrence the exclusionary rule is meant to achieve. But when he is told of today's decision? Now the officer knows that the stop may well yield admissible evidence: So long as the target is one of the many millions of people in this country with an outstanding arrest warrant, anything the officer finds in a search is fair game for use in a criminal prosecution. The officer's incentive to violate the Constitution thus increases: From here on, he sees potential advantage in stopping individuals without reasonable suspicion—exactly the temptation the exclusionary rule is supposed to remove. Because the majority thus places Fourth Amendment protections at risk, I respectfully dissent.

In other cases, the Supreme Court found that statements obtained after a Fourth Amendment violation did not have to be excluded because the taint was sufficiently attenuated. For example, in Rawlings v. Kentucky, 448 U.S. 98 (1980), the defendant was illegally detained in his home while the police went to obtain a search warrant. Rawlings made incriminating statements during this time, and the issue was whether they had to be excluded. The Court, in an opinion by Justice Rehnquist, said that the taint was sufficiently attenuated so as to allow the statements to be admitted. The Court pointed to the lack of flagrant misconduct by the police, the lack of a coercive atmosphere, and the fact that the statements were a spontaneous result of the discovery of evidence.

Similarly, in New York v. Harris, 495 U.S. 14 (1990), the Court found that a statement made by a suspect at the police station house was admissible, even though it followed an illegal search of the suspect's home. The Court explained that evidence from the warrantless home search would need to be excluded, but the subsequent statement to the police—at a different place and time from the search—was admissible.

These cases focus on when statements must be excluded when they follow a violation of the Fourth Amendment. The distinct, though obviously related, question of whether statements must be excluded when they follow illegal questioning is discussed in Chapter 4, which considers interrogations.[7]

4.   The Good Faith Exception to the Exclusionary Rule

In United States v. Leon, below, the Court held that the exclusionary rule does not apply if police reasonably rely on an invalid warrant to conduct a

----

7. Also discussed in Chapter 4 is the related question of whether physical evidence must be suppressed if it is the result of questioning without *Miranda* warnings in violation of the Fifth Amendment. In United States v. Patane, 542 U.S. 630 (2004), presented in Chapter 4, the Court held (5-4) that physical evidence gained in such circumstances need not be excluded.

search or seizure. This is the most hotly disputed of the exceptions to the exclusionary rule, and not surprisingly, *Leon* provided the occasion for an important debate among the justices as to the purposes of the exclusionary rule. In reading this case, it is important to keep in mind that subsequently, in Herring v. United States (2009), presented above, the Court held that the exclusionary rule does not apply to negligent or good faith violations of the Fourth Amendment.

UNITED STATES v. LEON

468 U.S. 897 (1984)

good Faith

Justice WHITE delivered the opinion of the Court.

This case presents the question whether the Fourth Amendment exclusionary rule should be modified so as not to bar the use in the prosecution's case in chief of evidence obtained by officers acting in reasonable reliance on a search warrant issued by a detached and neutral magistrate but ultimately found to be unsupported by probable cause. To resolve this question, we must consider once again the tension between the sometimes competing goals of, on the one hand, deterring official misconduct and removing inducements to unreasonable invasions of privacy and, on the other, establishing procedures under which criminal defendants are "acquitted or convicted on the basis of all the evidence which exposes the truth."

I

In August 1981, a confidential informant of unproven reliability informed an officer of the Burbank Police Department that two persons known to him as "Armando" and "Patsy" were selling large quantities of cocaine and methaqualone from their residence at 620 Price Drive in Burbank, Cal. The informant also indicated that he had witnessed a sale of methaqualone by "Patsy" at the residence approximately five months earlier and had observed at that time a shoebox containing a large amount of cash that belonged to "Patsy." He further declared that "Armando" and "Patsy" generally kept only small quantities of drugs at their residence and stored the remainder at another location in Burbank.

On the basis of this information, the Burbank police initiated an extensive investigation focusing first on the Price Drive residence and later on two other residences as well. Cars parked at the Price Drive residence were determined to belong to respondents Armando Sanchez, who had previously been arrested for possession of marihuana, and Patsy Stewart, who had no criminal record. During the course of the investigation, officers observed an automobile belonging to respondent Ricardo Del Castillo, who had previously been arrested for possession of 50 pounds of marihuana, arrive at the Price Drive residence. The driver of that car entered the house, exited shortly thereafter carrying a small paper sack, and drove away. A check of

Del Castillo's probation records led the officers to respondent Alberto Leon, whose telephone number Del Castillo had listed as his employer's. Leon had been arrested in 1980 on drug charges, and a companion had informed the police at that time that Leon was heavily involved in the importation of drugs into this country. Before the current investigation began, the Burbank officers had learned that an informant had told a Glendale police officer that Leon stored a large quantity of methaqualone at his residence in Glendale. During the course of this investigation, the Burbank officers learned that Leon was living at 716 South Sunset Canyon in Burbank.

Subsequently, the officers observed several persons, at least one of whom had prior drug involvement, arriving at the Price Drive residence and leaving with small packages; observed a variety of other material activity at the two residences as well as at a condominium at 7902 Via Magdalena; and witnessed a variety of relevant activity involving respondents' automobiles. The officers also observed respondents Sanchez and Stewart board separate flights for Miami. The pair later returned to Los Angeles together, consented to a search of their luggage that revealed only a small amount of marihuana, and left the airport. Based on these and other observations summarized in the affidavit, Officer Cyril Rombach of the Burbank Police Department, an experienced and well-trained narcotics investigator, prepared an application for a warrant to search 620 Price Drive, 716 South Sunset Canyon, 7902 Via Magdalena, and automobiles registered to each of the respondents for an extensive list of items believed to be related to respondents' drug-trafficking activities. Officer Rombach's extensive application was reviewed by several Deputy District Attorneys.

A facially valid search warrant was issued in September 1981 by a State Superior Court Judge. The ensuing searches produced large quantities of drugs at the Via Magdalena and Sunset Canyon addresses and a small quantity at the Price Drive residence. Other evidence was discovered at each of the residences and in Stewart's and Del Castillo's automobiles. Respondents were indicted by a grand jury in the District Court for the Central District of California and charged with conspiracy to possess and distribute cocaine and a variety of substantive counts.

The respondents then filed motions to suppress the evidence seized pursuant to the warrant. The District Court held an evidentiary hearing and, while recognizing that the case was a close one, granted the motions to suppress in part. It concluded that the affidavit was insufficient to establish probable cause, but did not suppress all of the evidence as to all of the respondents because none of the respondents had standing to challenge all of the searches. In response to a request from the Government, the court made clear that Officer Rombach had acted in good faith, but it rejected the Government's suggestion that the Fourth Amendment exclusionary rule should not apply where evidence is seized in reasonable, good-faith reliance on a search warrant.

The Government's petition for certiorari expressly declined to seek review of the lower courts' determinations that the search warrant was unsupported by probable cause and presented only the question "[w]hether the Fourth Amendment exclusionary rule should be modified so as not to bar the admission of evidence seized in reasonable, good-faith reliance on a search warrant that is subsequently held to be defective." We granted certiorari to consider the propriety of such a modification. We have concluded that, in the Fourth Amendment context, the exclusionary rule can be modified somewhat without jeopardizing its ability to perform its intended functions.

II

Language in opinions of this Court and of individual Justices has sometimes implied that the exclusionary rule is a necessary corollary of the Fourth Amendment, or that the rule is required by the conjunction of the Fourth and Fifth Amendments. These implications need not detain us long. The Fifth Amendment theory has not withstood critical analysis or the test of time, and the Fourth Amendment "has never been interpreted to proscribe the introduction of illegally seized evidence in all proceedings or against all persons."

A

The Fourth Amendment contains no provision expressly precluding the use of evidence obtained in violation of its commands, and an examination of its origin and purposes makes clear that the use of fruits of a past unlawful search or seizure "work[s] no new Fourth Amendment wrong." The wrong condemned by the Amendment is "fully accomplished" by the unlawful search or seizure itself, *ibid.*, and the exclusionary rule is neither intended nor able to "cure the invasion of the defendant's rights which he has already suffered." The rule thus operates as "a judicially created remedy designed to safeguard Fourth Amendment rights generally through its deterrent effect, rather than a personal constitutional right of the party aggrieved."

Whether the exclusionary sanction is appropriately imposed in a particular case, our decisions make clear, is "an issue separate from the question whether the Fourth Amendment rights of the party seeking to invoke the rule were violated by police conduct." Only the former question is currently before us, and it must be resolved by weighing the costs and benefits of preventing the use in the prosecution's case in chief of inherently trustworthy tangible evidence obtained in reliance on a search warrant issued by a detached and neutral magistrate that ultimately is found to be defective.

The substantial social costs exacted by the exclusionary rule for the vindication of Fourth Amendment rights have long been a source of concern. "Our cases have consistently recognized that unbending application of the exclusionary sanction to enforce ideals of governmental rectitude would impede unacceptably the truth-finding functions of judge and jury." An objectionable collateral consequence of this interference with the criminal justice system's truth-finding function is that some guilty defendants may go free or receive reduced sentences as a result of favorable plea bargains.[8] Particularly when law enforcement officers have acted in objective good faith or their transgressions have been minor, the magnitude of the benefit conferred on such guilty defendants offends basic concepts of the criminal justice system. Indiscriminate application of the exclusionary rule, therefore, may well "generat[e] disrespect for the law and administration of justice." Accordingly, "[a]s with any remedial device, the application of the rule has been restricted to those areas where its remedial objectives are thought most efficaciously served."

Many of these researchers have concluded that the impact of the exclusionary rule is insubstantial, but the small percentages with which they deal mask a large absolute number of felons who are released because the cases against them were based in part on illegal searches or seizures. "[A]ny rule of evidence that denies the jury access to clearly probative and reliable evidence must bear a heavy burden of justification, and must be carefully limited to the circumstances in which it will pay its way by deterring official unlawlessness." Because we find that the rule can have no substantial deterrent effect in the sorts of situations under consideration in this case, we conclude that it cannot pay its way in those situations.

B

Close attention to those remedial objectives has characterized our recent decisions concerning the scope of the Fourth Amendment exclusionary rule. The Court has, to be sure, not seriously questioned, "in the absence of a more efficacious sanction, the continued application of the rule to suppress evidence from the [prosecution's] case where a Fourth Amendment violation has been substantial and deliberate. . . ." Nevertheless, the balancing approach that has evolved in various contexts — including criminal trials — "forcefully suggest[s] that the exclusionary rule be more generally modified to permit the introduction of evidence obtained in the reasonable good-faith belief that a search or seizure was in accord with the Fourth Amendment."

As cases considering the use of unlawfully obtained evidence in criminal trials themselves make clear, it does not follow from the emphasis on the exclusionary rule's deterrent value that "anything which deters

8. Researchers have only recently begun to study extensively the effects of the exclusionary rule on the disposition of felony arrests. One study suggests that the rule results in the nonprosecution or nonconviction of between 0.6% and 2.35% of individuals arrested for felonies. Davies, A Hard Look at What We Know (and Still Need to Learn) About the "Costs" of the Exclusionary Rule: The NIJ Study and Other Studies of "Lost" Arrests, 1983 A.B.F.Res.J. 611, 621. The estimates are higher for particular crimes the prosecution of which depends heavily on physical evidence. Thus, the cumulative loss due to nonprosecution or nonconviction of individuals arrested on felony drug charges is probably in the range of 2.8% to 7.1%. Davies' analysis of California data suggests that screening by police and prosecutors results in the release because of illegal searches or seizures of as many as 1.4% of all felony arrestees, id., at 650, that 0.9% of felony arrestees are released, because of illegal searches or seizures, at the preliminary hearing or after trial, id., at 653, and that roughly 0.5% of all felony arrestees benefit from reversals on appeal because of illegal searches. [Footnote by the Court.]

illegal searches is thereby commanded by the Fourth Amendment." In determining whether persons aggrieved solely by the introduction of damaging evidence unlawfully obtained from their co-conspirators or co-defendants could seek suppression, for example, we found that the additional benefits of such an extension of the exclusionary rule would not outweigh its costs. Standing to invoke the rule has thus been limited to cases in which the prosecution seeks to use the fruits of an illegal search or seizure against the victim of police misconduct. Rakas v. Illinois (1978).

Even defendants with standing to challenge the introduction in their criminal trials of unlawfully obtained evidence cannot prevent every conceivable use of such evidence. Evidence obtained in violation of the Fourth Amendment and inadmissible in the prosecution's case in chief may be used to impeach a defendant's direct testimony. Walder v. United States (1954). A similar assessment of the "incremental furthering" of the ends of the exclusionary rule led us to conclude in United States v. Havens (1980), that evidence inadmissible in the prosecution's case in chief or otherwise as substantive evidence of guilt may be used to impeach statements made by a defendant in response to "proper cross-examination reasonably suggested by the defendant's direct examination."

When considering the use of evidence obtained in violation of the Fourth Amendment in the prosecution's case in chief, moreover, we have declined to adopt a per se or "but for" rule that would render inadmissible any evidence that came to light through a chain of causation that began with an illegal arrest. We also have held that a witness' testimony may be admitted even when his identity was discovered in an unconstitutional search. United States v. Ceccolini (1978). The perception underlying these decisions — that the connection between police misconduct and evidence of crime may be sufficiently attenuated to permit the use of that evidence at trial — is a product of considerations relating to the exclusionary rule and the constitutional principles it is designed to protect. In short, the "dissipation of the taint" concept that the Court has applied in deciding whether exclusion is appropriate in a particular case "attempts to mark the point at which the detrimental consequences of illegal police action become so attenuated that the deterrent effect of the exclusionary rule no longer justifies its cost." Not surprisingly in view of this purpose, an assessment of the flagrancy of the police misconduct constitutes an important step in the calculus.

As yet, we have not recognized any form of good-faith exception to the Fourth Amendment exclusionary rule. But the balancing approach that has evolved during the years of experience with the rule provides strong support for the modification currently urged upon us. As we discuss below, our evaluation of the costs and benefits of suppressing reliable physical evidence seized by officers reasonably relying on a warrant issued by a detached and neutral magistrate leads to the conclusion that such evidence should be admissible in the prosecution's case in chief.

III

A

Because a search warrant "provides the detached scrutiny of a neutral magistrate, which is a more reliable safeguard against improper searches than the hurried judgment of a law enforcement officer 'engaged in the often competitive enterprise of ferreting out crime,'" we have expressed a strong preference for warrants and declared that "in a doubtful or marginal case a search under a warrant may be sustainable where without one it would fall." Reasonable minds frequently may differ on the question whether a particular affidavit establishes probable cause, and we have thus concluded that the preference for warrants is most appropriately effectuated by according "great deference" to a magistrate's determination.

Deference to the magistrate, however, is not boundless. It is clear, first, that the deference accorded to a magistrate's finding of probable cause does not preclude inquiry into the knowing or reckless falsity of the affidavit on which that determination was based. Second, the courts must also insist that the magistrate purport to "perform his 'neutral and detached' function and not serve merely as a rubber stamp for the police." A magistrate failing to "manifest that neutrality and detachment demanded of a judicial officer when presented with a warrant application" and who acts instead as "an adjunct law enforcement officer" cannot provide valid authorization for an otherwise unconstitutional search.

Third, reviewing courts will not defer to a warrant based on an affidavit that does not "provide the magistrate with a substantial basis for determining the existence of probable cause." "Sufficient information must be presented to the magistrate to allow that official to determine probable cause; his action cannot be a mere ratification of the bare conclusions of others." Even if the warrant application was supported by more than a "bare bones" affidavit, a reviewing court may properly conclude that, notwithstanding the deference that magistrates deserve, the warrant was invalid because the magistrate's probable-cause determination reflected an improper analysis of the totality of the circumstances, or because the form of the warrant was improper in some respect.

We adhere to this view and emphasize that nothing in this opinion is intended to suggest a lowering of the probable-cause standard. On the contrary, we deal here only with the remedy to be applied to a concededly unconstitutional search.

Only in the first of these three situations, however, has the Court set forth a rationale for suppressing evidence obtained pursuant to a search warrant; in the other areas, it has simply excluded such evidence without considering whether Fourth Amendment interests will be advanced. To the extent that proponents of exclusion rely on its behavioral effects on judges and magistrates in these areas, their reliance is misplaced. First, the exclusionary rule is designed to deter police misconduct rather than to punish the errors of judges and magistrates. Second, there exists no evidence suggesting that judges and magistrates are inclined to ignore or subvert the Fourth Amendment or that lawlessness among these actors requires application of the extreme sanction of exclusion.

Third, and most important, we discern no basis, and are offered none, for believing that exclusion of evidence seized pursuant to a warrant will have a significant deterrent effect on the issuing judge or magistrate. Many of the factors that indicate that the exclusionary rule cannot provide an effective "special" or "general" deterrent for individual offending law enforcement officers apply as well to judges or magistrates. And, to the extent that the rule is thought to operate as a "systemic" deterrent on a wider audience, it clearly can have no such effect on individuals empowered to issue search warrants. Judges and magistrates are not adjuncts to the law enforcement team; as neutral judicial officers, they have no stake in the outcome of particular criminal prosecutions. The threat of exclusion thus cannot be expected significantly to deter them. Imposition of the exclusionary sanction is not necessary meaningfully to inform judicial officers of their errors, and we cannot conclude that admitting evidence obtained pursuant to a warrant while at the same time declaring that the warrant was somehow defective will in any way reduce judicial officers' professional incentives to comply with the Fourth Amendment, encourage them to repeat their mistakes, or lead to the granting of all colorable warrant requests.

B

If exclusion of evidence obtained pursuant to a subsequently invalidated warrant is to have any deterrent effect, therefore, it must alter the behavior of individual law enforcement officers or the policies of their departments. One could argue that applying the exclusionary rule in cases where the police failed to demonstrate probable cause in the warrant application deters future inadequate presentations or "magistrate shopping" and thus promotes the ends of the Fourth Amendment. Suppressing evidence obtained pursuant to a technically defective warrant supported by probable cause also might encourage officers to scrutinize more closely the form of the warrant and to point out suspected judicial errors. We find such arguments speculative and conclude that suppression of evidence obtained pursuant to a warrant should be ordered only on a case-by-case basis and only in those unusual cases in which exclusion will further the purposes of the exclusionary rule.

We have frequently questioned whether the exclusionary rule can have any deterrent effect when the offending officers acted in the objectively reasonable belief that their conduct did not violate the Fourth Amendment. "No empirical researcher, proponent or opponent of the rule, has yet been able to establish with any assurance whether the rule has a deterrent effect. . . ." But even assuming that the rule effectively deters some police misconduct and provides incentives for the law enforcement profession as a whole to conduct itself in accord with the Fourth Amendment, it cannot be expected, and should not be applied, to deter objectively reasonable law enforcement activity. In short, where the officer's conduct is objectively reasonable,[9] "excluding the evidence will not further the ends of the exclusionary rule in any appreciable way; for it is painfully apparent that . . . the officer is acting as a reasonable officer would and should act in similar circumstances. Excluding the evidence can in no way affect his future conduct unless it is to make him less willing to do his duty."

This is particularly true, we believe, when an officer acting with objective good faith has obtained a search warrant from a judge or magistrate and acted within its scope. In most such cases, there is no police illegality and thus nothing to deter. It is the magistrate's responsibility to determine whether the officer's allegations establish probable cause and, if so, to issue a warrant comporting in form with the requirements of the Fourth Amendment. In the ordinary case, an officer cannot be expected to question the magistrate's probable-cause determination or his judgment that the form of the warrant is technically sufficient. "[O]nce the warrant issues, there is literally nothing more the policeman can do in seeking to comply with the law." Penalizing the officer for the magistrate's error, rather than his own, cannot logically contribute to the deterrence of Fourth Amendment violations.

C

We conclude that the marginal or nonexistent benefits produced by suppressing evidence obtained in objectively reasonable reliance on a subsequently invalidated search warrant cannot justify the substantial costs of exclusion. We do not suggest, however, that exclusion is always inappropriate in cases where an officer has obtained a warrant and abided by its terms. "[S]earches pursuant to a warrant will rarely require any deep inquiry into reasonableness," for "a warrant issued by a magistrate normally suffices to establish" that a law enforcement officer has "acted in good faith in conducting the search." Nevertheless, the officer's reliance on the magistrate's probable-cause determination and on the technical sufficiency of the warrant he issues must be objectively reasonable, and it is clear that in some circumstances the officer will have no reasonable grounds for believing that the warrant was properly issued.

Suppression therefore remains an appropriate remedy if the magistrate or judge in issuing a warrant was misled by information in an affidavit that the affiant knew was false or would have known was false except for his reckless disregard of the truth. The exception we recognize today will also not apply in cases where the issuing magistrate wholly abandoned his judicial role; in

9. We emphasize that the standard of reasonableness we adopt is an objective one. Many objections to a good-faith exception assume that the exception will turn on the subjective good faith of individual officers. "Grounding the modification in objective reasonableness, however, retains the value of the exclusionary rule as an incentive for the law enforcement profession as a whole to conduct themselves in accord with the Fourth Amendment." The objective standard we adopt, moreover, requires officers to have a reasonable knowledge of what the law prohibits. [Footnote by the Court.]

such circumstances, no reasonably well trained officer should rely on the warrant. Nor would an officer manifest objective good faith in relying on a warrant based on an affidavit "so lacking in indicia of probable cause as to render official belief in its existence entirely unreasonable." Finally, depending on the circumstances of the particular case, a warrant may be so facially deficient—i.e., in failing to particularize the place to be searched or the things to be seized—that the executing officers cannot reasonably presume it to be valid.

In so limiting the suppression remedy, we leave untouched the probable-cause standard and the various requirements for a valid warrant. The good-faith exception for searches conducted pursuant to warrants is not intended to signal our unwillingness strictly to enforce the requirements of the Fourth Amendment, and we do not believe that it will have this effect. As we have already suggested, the good-faith exception, turning as it does on objective reasonableness, should not be difficult to apply in practice. When officers have acted pursuant to a warrant, the prosecution should ordinarily be able to establish objective good faith without a substantial expenditure of judicial time.

IV

When the principles we have enunciated today are applied to the facts of this case, it is apparent that the judgment of the Court of Appeals cannot stand. The Court of Appeals applied the prevailing legal standards to Officer Rombach's warrant application and concluded that the application could not support the magistrate's probable-cause determination. Having determined that the warrant should not have issued, the Court of Appeals understandably declined to adopt a modification of the Fourth Amendment exclusionary rule that this Court had not previously sanctioned. Although the modification finds strong support in our previous cases, the Court of Appeals' commendable self-restraint is not to be criticized. We have now reexamined the purposes of the exclusionary rule and the propriety of its application in cases where officers have relied on a subsequently invalidated search warrant. Our conclusion is that the rule's purposes will only rarely be served by applying it in such circumstances.

In the absence of an allegation that the magistrate abandoned his detached and neutral role, suppression is appropriate only if the officers were dishonest or reckless in preparing their affidavit or could not have harbored an objectively reasonable belief in the existence of probable cause. Under these circumstances, the officers' reliance on the magistrate's determination of probable cause was objectively reasonable, and application of the extreme sanction of exclusion is inappropriate.

Justice BRENNAN, with whom Justice MARSHALL joins, dissenting.

Ten years ago, I expressed the fear that the Court's decision "may signal that a majority of my colleagues have positioned themselves to reopen the door [to evidence secured by official lawlessness] still further and abandon altogether the exclusionary rule in search-and-seizure cases." Since then, in case after case, I have witnessed the Court's gradual but determined strangulation of the rule. It now appears that the Court's victory over the Fourth Amendment is complete. That today's decisions represent the pièce de résistance of the Court's past efforts cannot be doubted, for today the Court sanctions the use in the prosecution's case in chief of illegally obtained evidence against the individual whose rights have been violated—a result that had previously been thought to be foreclosed.

The Court seeks to justify this result on the ground that the "costs" of adhering to the exclusionary rule in cases like those before us exceed the "benefits." But the language of deterrence and of cost/benefit analysis, if used indiscriminately, can have a narcotic effect. It creates an illusion of technical precision and ineluctability. It suggests that not only constitutional principle but also empirical data support the majority's result. When the Court's analysis is examined carefully, however, it is clear that we have not been treated to an honest assessment of the merits of the exclusionary rule, but have instead been drawn into a curious world where the "costs" of excluding illegally obtained evidence loom to exaggerated heights and where the "benefits" of such exclusion are made to disappear with a mere wave of the hand.

The majority ignores the fundamental constitutional importance of what is at stake here. While the machinery of law enforcement and indeed the nature of crime itself have changed dramatically since the Fourth Amendment became part of the Nation's fundamental law in 1791, what the Framers understood then remains true today—that the task of combating crime and convicting the guilty will in every era seem of such critical and pressing concern that we may be lured by the temptations of expediency into forsaking our commitment to protecting individual liberty and privacy. It was for that very reason that the Framers of the Bill of Rights insisted that law enforcement efforts be permanently and unambiguously restricted in order to preserve personal freedoms. In the constitutional scheme they ordained, the sometimes unpopular task of ensuring that the government's enforcement efforts remain within the strict boundaries fixed by the Fourth Amendment was entrusted to the courts.

A proper understanding of the broad purposes sought to be served by the Fourth Amendment demonstrates that the principles embodied in the exclusionary rule rest upon a far firmer constitutional foundation than the shifting sands of the Court's deterrence rationale. But even if I were to accept the Court's chosen method of analyzing the question posed by these cases, I would still conclude that the Court's decision cannot be justified.

I

The Court holds that physical evidence seized by police officers reasonably relying upon a warrant issued by a detached and neutral magistrate is admissible in the prosecution's case in chief, even though a reviewing court has subsequently determined either that the warrant was defective, or that those officers failed to demonstrate when applying for the warrant that there was probable cause to conduct the search. I have no doubt that these decisions will prove in time to have been a grave mistake. But, as troubling and important as today's new doctrine may be for the administration of criminal justice in this country, the mode of analysis used to generate that doctrine also requires critical examination, for it may prove in the long run to pose the greater threat to our civil liberties.

At bottom, the Court's decision turns on the proposition that the exclusionary rule is merely a "'judicially created remedy designed to safeguard Fourth Amendment rights generally through its deterrent effect, rather than a personal constitutional right.'" The essence of this view, as expressed initially in the *Calandra* opinion and as reiterated today, is that the sole "purpose of the Fourth Amendment is to prevent unreasonable governmental intrusions into the privacy of one's person, house, papers, or effects. The wrong condemned is the unjustified governmental invasion of these areas of an individual's life. That wrong . . . is fully accomplished by the original search without probable cause." This reading of the Amendment implies that its proscriptions are directed solely at those government agents who may actually invade an individual's constitutionally protected privacy. The courts are not subject to any direct constitutional duty to exclude illegally obtained evidence, because the question of the admissibility of such evidence is not addressed by the Amendment. This view of the scope of the Amendment relegates the judiciary to the periphery. Because the only constitutionally cognizable injury has already been "fully accomplished" by the police by the time a case comes before the courts, the Constitution is not itself violated if the judge decides to admit the tainted evidence. Indeed, the most the judge can do is wring his hands and hope that perhaps by excluding such evidence he can deter future transgressions by the police.

Such a reading appears plausible, because, as critics of the exclusionary rule never tire of repeating, the Fourth Amendment makes no express provision for the exclusion of evidence secured in violation of its commands. A short answer to this claim, of course, is that many of the Constitution's most vital imperatives are stated in general terms and the task of giving meaning to these precepts is therefore left to subsequent judicial decision-making in the context of concrete cases.

A more direct answer may be supplied by recognizing that the Amendment, like other provisions of the Bill of Rights, restrains the power of the government as a whole; it does not specify only a particular agency and exempt all others. The judiciary is responsible, no less than the executive, for ensuring that constitutional rights are respected.

When that fact is kept in mind, the role of the courts and their possible involvement in the concerns of the Fourth Amendment comes into sharper focus. Because seizures are executed principally to secure evidence, and because such evidence generally has utility in our legal system only in the context of a trial supervised by a judge, it is apparent that the admission of illegally obtained evidence implicates the same constitutional concerns as the initial seizure of that evidence. Indeed, by admitting unlawfully seized evidence, the judiciary becomes a part of what is in fact a single governmental action prohibited by the terms of the Amendment. Once that connection between the evidence-gathering role of the police and the evidence-admitting function of the courts is acknowledged, the plausibility of the Court's interpretation becomes more suspect. Certainly nothing in the language or history of the Fourth Amendment suggests that a recognition of this evidentiary link between the police and the courts was meant to be foreclosed. It is difficult to give any meaning at all to the limitations imposed by the Amendment if they are read to proscribe only certain conduct by the police but to allow other agents of the same government to take advantage of evidence secured by the police in violation of its requirements. The Amendment therefore must be read to condemn not only the initial unconstitutional invasion of privacy — which is done, after all, for the purpose of securing evidence — but also the subsequent use of any evidence so obtained.

The Court evades this principle by drawing an artificial line between the constitutional rights and responsibilities that are engaged by actions of the police and those that are engaged when a defendant appears before the courts. According to the Court, the substantive protections of the Fourth Amendment are wholly exhausted at the moment when police unlawfully invade an individual's privacy and thus no substantive force remains to those protections at the time of trial when the government seeks to use evidence obtained by the police.

I submit that such a crabbed reading of the Fourth Amendment casts aside the teaching of those Justices who first formulated the exclusionary rule, and rests ultimately on an impoverished understanding of judicial responsibility in our constitutional scheme. For my part, "[t]he right of the people to be secure in their persons, houses, papers, and effects, against unreasonable searches and seizures" comprises a personal right to exclude all evidence secured by means of unreasonable searches and seizures. The right to be free from the initial invasion of privacy and the right of exclusion are coordinate components of the central embracing right to be free from unreasonable searches and seizures.

From the foregoing, it is clear why the question whether the exclusion of evidence would deter future police misconduct was never considered a relevant concern in the early cases from *Weeks* to *Olmstead.* In those formative decisions, the Court plainly understood that the exclusion of illegally obtained evidence was compelled not by judicially fashioned remedial purposes, but rather by a direct constitutional command.

Despite this clear pronouncement, however, the Court has gradually pressed the deterrence rationale for the rule back to center stage. The various arguments advanced by the Court in this campaign have only strengthened my conviction that the deterrence theory is both misguided and unworkable. First, the Court has frequently bewailed the "cost" of excluding reliable evidence. In large part, this criticism rests upon a refusal to acknowledge the function of the Fourth Amendment itself. If nothing else, the Amendment plainly operates to disable the government from gathering information and securing evidence in certain ways. In practical terms, of course, this restriction of official power means that some incriminating evidence inevitably will go undetected if the government obeys these constitutional restraints. It is the loss of that evidence that is the "price" our society pays for enjoying the freedom and privacy safeguarded by the Fourth Amendment. Thus, some criminals will go free not, in Justice (then Judge) Cardozo's misleading epigram, "because the constable has blundered," but rather because official compliance with Fourth Amendment requirements makes it more difficult to catch criminals. Understood in this way, the Amendment directly contemplates that some reliable and incriminating evidence will be lost to the government; therefore, it is not the exclusionary rule, but the Amendment itself that has imposed this cost.

In addition, the Court's decisions over the past decade have made plain that the entire enterprise of attempting to assess the benefits and costs of the exclusionary rule in various contexts is a virtually impossible task for the judiciary to perform honestly or accurately. Although the Court's language in those cases suggests that some specific empirical basis may support its analyses, the reality is that the Court's opinions represent inherently unstable compounds of intuition, hunches, and occasional pieces of partial and often inconclusive data. To the extent empirical data are available regarding the general costs and benefits of the exclusionary rule, such data have shown, on the one hand, as the Court acknowledges today, that the costs are not as substantial as critics have asserted in the past, and, on the other hand, that while the exclusionary rule may well have certain deterrent effects, it is extremely difficult to determine with any degree of precision whether the incidence of unlawful conduct by police is now lower than it was prior to *Mapp*. The Court has sought to turn this uncertainty to its advantage by casting the burden of proof upon proponents of the rule. "Obviously," however, "the assignment of the burden of proof on an issue where evidence does not exist and cannot be obtained is outcome determinative. [The] assignment of the burden is merely a way of announcing a predetermined conclusion." By remaining within its redoubt of empiricism and by basing the rule solely on the deterrence rationale, the Court has robbed the rule of legitimacy. A doctrine that is explained as if it were an empirical proposition but for which there is only limited empirical support is both inherently unstable and an easy mark for critics. The extent of this Court's fidelity to Fourth Amendment requirements, however, should not turn on such statistical uncertainties.

What the Framers of the Bill of Rights sought to accomplish through the express requirements of the Fourth Amendment was to define precisely the conditions under which government agents could search private property so that citizens would not have to depend solely upon the discretion and restraint of those agents for the protection of their privacy. Although the self-restraint and care exhibited by the officers in this case is commendable, that alone can never be a sufficient protection for constitutional liberties. I am convinced that it is not too much to ask that an attentive magistrate take those minimum steps necessary to ensure that every warrant he issues describes with particularity the things that his independent review of the warrant application convinces him are likely to be found in the premises. And I am equally convinced that it is not too much to ask that well-trained and experienced police officers take a moment to check that the warrant they have been issued at least describes those things for which they have sought leave to search. These convictions spring not from my own view of sound criminal law enforcement policy, but are instead compelled by the language of the Fourth Amendment and the history that led to its adoption.

III

Even if I were to accept the Court's general approach to the exclusionary rule, I could not agree with today's result. There is no question that in the hands of the present Court the deterrence rationale has proved to be a powerful tool for confining the scope of the rule.

Thus, in this bit of judicial stagecraft, while the sets sometimes change, the actors always have the same lines. Given this well-rehearsed pattern, one might have predicted with some assurance how the present case would unfold. First there is the ritual incantation of the "substantial social costs" exacted by the exclusionary rule, followed by the virtually foreordained conclusion that, given the marginal benefits, application of the rule in the circumstances of these cases is not warranted. Upon analysis, however, such a result cannot be justified even on the Court's own terms.

At the outset, the Court suggests that society has been asked to pay a high price — in terms either of setting guilty persons free or of impeding the proper functioning of trials — as a result of excluding relevant physical evidence in cases where the police, in conducting searches and seizing evidence, have made only an "objectively reasonable" mistake concerning the constitutionality of their actions. But what evidence is there to support such a claim?

Significantly, the Court points to none, and, indeed, as the Court acknowledges, recent studies have demonstrated that the "costs" of the exclusionary rule — calculated in terms of dropped prosecutions and lost convictions — are quite low. Contrary to the claims of the rule's critics that exclusion leads to "the release of countless guilty criminals," these studies have demonstrated that federal and state prosecutors very rarely drop cases because of potential search and seizure problems. For example, a 1979 study prepared at the request of Congress by the General Accounting Office reported that only 0.4% of all cases actually declined for prosecution by federal prosecutors were declined primarily because of illegal search problems. If the GAO data are restated as a percentage of all arrests, the study shows that only 0.2% of all felony arrests are declined for prosecution because of potential exclusionary rule problems. Of course, these data describe only the costs attributable to the exclusion of evidence in all cases; the costs due to the exclusion of evidence in the narrower category of cases where police have made objectively reasonable mistakes must necessarily be even smaller. The Court, however, ignores this distinction and mistakenly weighs the aggregated costs of exclusion in all cases, irrespective of the circumstances that led to exclusion, against the potential benefits associated with only those cases in which evidence is excluded because police reasonably but mistakenly believe that their conduct does not violate the Fourth Amendment. When such faulty scales are used, it is little wonder that the balance tips in favor of restricting the application of the rule.

What then supports the Court's insistence that this evidence be admitted? Apparently, the Court's only answer is that even though the costs of exclusion are not very substantial, the potential deterrent effect in these circumstances is so marginal that exclusion cannot be justified. The key to the Court's conclusion in this respect is its belief that the prospective deterrent effect of the exclusionary rule operates only in those situations in which police officers, when deciding whether to go forward with some particular search, have reason to know that their planned conduct will violate the requirements of the Fourth Amendment. If these officers in fact understand (or reasonably should understand because the law is well settled) that their proposed conduct will offend the Fourth Amendment and that, consequently, any evidence they seize will be suppressed in court, they will refrain from conducting the planned search. In those circumstances, the incentive system created by the exclusionary rule will have the hoped-for deterrent effect. But in situations where police officers reasonably (but mistakenly) believe that their planned conduct satisfies Fourth Amendment requirements — presumably either (a) because they are acting on the basis of an apparently valid warrant, or (b) because their conduct is only later determined to be invalid as a result of a subsequent change in the law or the resolution of an unsettled question of law — then such officers will have no reason to refrain from conducting the search and the exclusionary rule will have no effect.

At first blush, there is some logic to this position. Undoubtedly, in the situation hypothesized by the Court, the existence of the exclusionary rule cannot be expected to have any deterrent effect on the particular officers at the moment they are deciding whether to go forward with the search. Indeed, the subsequent exclusion of any evidence seized under such circumstances appears somehow "unfair" to the particular officers involved. As the Court suggests, these officers have acted in what they thought was an appropriate and constitutionally authorized manner, but then the fruit of their efforts is nullified by the application of the exclusionary rule.

The flaw in the Court's argument, however, is that its logic captures only one comparatively minor element of the generally acknowledged deterrent purposes of the exclusionary rule. To be sure, the rule operates to some extent

to deter future misconduct by individual officers who have had evidence suppressed in their own cases. But what the Court overlooks is that the deterrence
rationale for the rule is not designed to be, nor should it be thought of as, a
form of "punishment" of individual police officers for their failures to obey
the restraints imposed by the Fourth Amendment. Instead, the chief deterrent
function of the rule is its tendency to promote institutional compliance with
Fourth Amendment requirements on the part of law enforcement agencies
generally. Thus, as the Court has previously recognized, "over the long term,
[the] demonstration [provided by the exclusionary rule] that our society
attaches serious consequences to violation of constitutional rights is thought
to encourage those who formulate law enforcement policies, and the officers
who implement them, to incorporate Fourth Amendment ideals into their
value system." It is only through such an institutionwide mechanism that
information concerning Fourth Amendment standards can be effectively
communicated to rank-and-file officers.

If the overall educational effect of the exclusionary rule is considered,
application of the rule to even those situations in which individual police
officers have acted on the basis of a reasonable but mistaken belief that their
conduct was authorized can still be expected to have a considerable long-
term deterrent effect. If evidence is consistently excluded in these circumstances, police departments will surely be prompted to instruct their officers
to devote greater care and attention to providing sufficient information to
establish probable cause when applying for a warrant, and to review with
some attention the form of the warrant that they have been issued, rather
than automatically assuming that whatever document the magistrate has
signed will necessarily comport with Fourth Amendment requirements.

After today's decisions, however, that institutional incentive will be lost.
Indeed, the Court's "reasonable mistake" exception to the exclusionary rule
will tend to put a premium on police ignorance of the law. Armed with the
assurance provided by today's decisions that evidence will always be admissible whenever an officer has "reasonably" relied upon a warrant, police
departments will be encouraged to train officers that if a warrant has simply
been signed, it is reasonable, without more, to rely on it. Since in close cases
there will no longer be any incentive to err on the side of constitutional
behavior, police would have every reason to adopt a "let's-wait-until-it's-
decided" approach in situations in which there is a question about a
warrant's validity or the basis for its issuance.

Although the Court brushes these concerns aside, a host of grave
consequences can be expected to result from its decision to carve this
new exception out of the exclusionary rule. A chief consequence of today's
decisions will be to convey a clear and unambiguous message to magistrates that their decisions to issue warrants are now insulated from
subsequent judicial review. Creation of this new exception for good-faith
reliance upon a warrant implicitly tells magistrates that they need not take
much care in reviewing warrant applications, since their mistakes will from
now on have virtually no consequence: If their decision to issue a

warrant was correct, the evidence will be admitted; if their decision was incorrect but the police relied in good faith on the warrant, the evidence will also be admitted. Inevitably, the care and attention devoted to such an inconsequential chore will dwindle. Although the Court is correct to note that magistrates do not share the same stake in the outcome of a criminal case as the police, they nevertheless need to appreciate that their role is of some moment in order to continue performing the important task of carefully reviewing warrant applications. Today's decisions effectively remove that incentive.

After today's decisions, there will be little reason for reviewing courts to conduct such a conscientious review; rather, these courts will be more likely to focus simply on the question of police good faith. Despite the Court's confident prediction that such review will continue to be conducted, it is difficult to believe that busy courts faced with heavy dockets will take the time to render essentially advisory opinions concerning the constitutionality of the magistrate's decision before considering the officer's good faith.

Moreover, the good-faith exception will encourage police to provide only the bare minimum of information in future warrant applications. The police will now know that if they can secure a warrant, so long as the circumstances of its issuance are not "entirely unreasonable," all police conduct pursuant to that warrant will be protected from further judicial review. The clear incentive that operated in the past to establish probable cause adequately because reviewing courts would examine the magistrate's judgment carefully, has now been so completely vitiated that the police need only show that it was not "entirely unreasonable" under the circumstances of a particular case for them to believe that the warrant they were issued was valid. The long-run effect unquestionably will be to undermine the integrity of the warrant process.

The same day it decided United States v. Leon, the Court also handed down Massachusetts v. Sheppard, 468 U.S. 961 (1984). Police investigating a murder obtained a warrant to search Sheppard's residence. The officers used a preprinted warrant form which listed "controlled substances" as the items to be seized. The judge said that he would make changes in the warrant, but the final version continued to list controlled substances as the items to be searched for and seized. Sheppard moved to suppress the evidence. The Supreme Court, however, said that the evidence did not need to be excluded because the officers reasonably relied on the warrant.[10]

---

10. The Court did not deny that there was a Fourth Amendment violation. In fact, in a subsequent case, Groh v. Ramirez, 540 U.S. 551 (2004), the Court held that the Fourth Amendment is violated if the warrant fails to list the specifics of what is to searched for and seized, even if that information is in an affidavit supporting the warrant. *Groh*, though, was a civil suit for money damages for violation of the Fourth Amendment and not an attempt to exclude evidence from use in a criminal prosecution.

Justice White, writing for the Court, said:

> Having already decided that the exclusionary rule should not be applied when the officer conducting the search acted in objectively reasonable reliance on a warrant issued by a detached and neutral magistrate that subsequently is determined to be invalid, the sole issue before us in this case is whether the officers reasonably believed that the search they conducted was authorized by a valid warrant. There is no dispute that the officers believed that the warrant authorized the search that they conducted. Thus, the only question is whether there was an objectively reasonable basis for the officers' mistaken belief. Both the trial court, and a majority of the Supreme Judicial Court, concluded that there was. We agree.

Ultimately, the disagreement over whether there should be a good faith exception is about whether there should be an exclusionary rule, what purposes the exclusionary rule serves, and what is the best way to achieve them.

5. The Exception for Violations of the Requirement for "Knocking and Announcing"

As explained in Chapter 2, the Supreme Court has held that absent exigent circumstances, the police must knock and announce their presence before searching a residence. In Hudson v. Michigan, 547 U.S. 586 (2006), the Court held that the exclusionary rule does not apply if police violate this Fourth Amendment requirement. As explained at the beginning of this chapter, Justice Scalia's majority opinion in the 5-4 decision stressed the costs of the exclusionary rule as compared with its benefits. He also discussed the problems with applying the exclusionary rule to the knock and announce context:

> The costs here are considerable. In addition to the grave adverse consequence that exclusion of relevant incriminating evidence always entails (viz., the risk of releasing dangerous criminals into society), imposing that massive remedy for a knock-and-announce violation would generate a constant flood of alleged failures to observe the rule, and claims that any asserted *Richards* justification for a no-knock entry, had inadequate support. The cost of entering this lottery would be small, but the jackpot enormous: suppression of all evidence, amounting in many cases to a get-out-of-jail-free card. Courts would experience as never before the reality that "[t]he exclusionary rule frequently requires extensive litigation to determine whether particular evidence must be excluded." Unlike the warrant or *Miranda* requirements, compliance with which is readily determined (either there was or was not a warrant; either the *Miranda* warning was given, or it was not), what constituted a "reasonable wait time" in a particular case (or, for that matter, how many seconds the police in fact waited), or whether there was "reasonable suspicion" of the sort that would invoke the exceptions, is difficult for the trial court to determine and even more difficult for an appellate court to review.
>
> Another consequence of the incongruent remedy Hudson proposes would be police officers' refraining from timely entry after knocking and announcing. As we have observed, the amount of time they must wait is necessarily uncertain. If

the consequences of running afoul of the rule were so massive, officers would be inclined to wait longer than the law requires — producing preventable violence against officers in some cases, and the destruction of evidence in many others. We deemed these consequences severe enough to produce our unanimous agreement that a mere "reasonable suspicion" that knocking and announcing "under the particular circumstances, would be dangerous or futile, or that it would inhibit the effective investigation of the crime," will cause the requirement to yield.

Next to these "substantial social costs" we must consider the deterrence benefits, existence of which is a necessary condition for exclusion. (It is not, of course, a sufficient condition: "[I]t does not follow that the Fourth Amendment requires adoption of every proposal that might deter police misconduct.") To begin with, the value of deterrence depends upon the strength of the incentive to commit the forbidden act. Viewed from this perspective, deterrence of knock-and-announce violations is not worth a lot. Violation of the warrant requirement sometimes produces incriminating evidence that could not otherwise be obtained. But ignoring knock-and-announce can realistically be expected to achieve absolutely nothing except the prevention of destruction of evidence and the avoidance of life-threatening resistance by occupants of the premises — dangers which, if there is even "reasonable suspicion" of their existence, suspend the knock-and-announce requirement anyway. Massive deterrence is hardly required.

Justice Breyer, writing for the four dissenters, began his opinion by stating:

In Wilson v. Arkansas (1995), a unanimous Court held that the Fourth Amendment normally requires law enforcement officers to knock and announce their presence before entering a dwelling. Today's opinion holds that evidence seized from a home following a violation of this requirement need not be suppressed.

As a result, the Court destroys the strongest legal incentive to comply with the Constitution's knock-and-announce requirement. And the Court does so without significant support in precedent. At least I can find no such support in the many Fourth Amendment cases the Court has decided in the near century since it first set forth the exclusionary principle in Weeks v. United States (1914).

Today's opinion is thus doubly troubling. It represents a significant departure from the Court's precedents. And it weakens, perhaps destroys, much of the practical value of the Constitution's knock-and-announce protection.

The question after *Hudson* is whether police will have a sufficient incentive to comply with the knock-and-announce requirement knowing that evidence gained will not be excluded and, if not, whether this exception is justified by the benefits of the evidence being introduced. This, of course, is the same underlying question as to whether there should be an exclusionary rule and, if so, which exceptions should be created.

F. SUPPRESSION HEARINGS

The primary mechanism for raising the exclusionary rule is via a "suppression hearing." Generally, these occur before trial and it is the occasion for the trial court's hearing the defendant's motion that evidence was illegally obtained and should be excluded.[11] In fact, many jurisdictions require that such motions be made before trial and bar a defendant from doing so later unless there is good cause for the failure to do so.[12]

A defendant seeking to challenge the truthfulness of statements made in warrant applications must make a showing that the officers who prepared the warrant engaged in deliberate falsification or reckless disregard for the truth. In Franks v. Delaware, 438 U.S. 154 (1978), the Court stated:

> There is, of course, a presumption of validity with respect to the affidavit supporting the search warrant. To mandate an evidentiary hearing, the challenger's attack must be more than conclusory and must be supported by more than a mere desire to cross-examine. There must be allegations of deliberate falsehood or of reckless disregard for the truth, and those allegations must be accompanied by an offer of proof. They should point out specifically the portion of the warrant affidavit that is claimed to be false; and they should be accompanied by a statement of supporting reasons. Affidavits or sworn or otherwise reliable statements of witnesses should be furnished, or their absence satisfactorily explained. Allegations of negligence or innocent mistake are insufficient. The deliberate falsity or reckless disregard whose impeachment is permitted today is only that of the affiant, not of any nongovernmental informant.

The Court in *Franks* went on to emphasize that even if these requirements are met, no hearing is required if there is sufficient other content in the warrant application to support its issuance. The Court explained:

> Finally, if these requirements are met, and if, when material that is the subject of the alleged falsity or reckless disregard is set to one side, there remains sufficient content in the warrant affidavit to support a finding of probable cause, no hearing is required. On the other hand, if the remaining content is insufficient, the defendant is entitled, under the Fourth and Fourteenth Amendments, to his hearing. Whether he will prevail at that hearing is, of course, another issue.

The suppression motion occurs outside the presence of the jury. The ordinary rules of evidence do not apply at suppression hearings. In United States v. Matlock, 415 U.S. 164 (1974), the Court held that judges can rely on hearsay evidence at suppression hearings. The Court declared, "[I]n proceedings where the judge himself is considering the admissibility of evidence, the exclusionary rules, aside from rules of privilege, should not be applicable, and the judge should receive the evidence and give it such weight as his judgment and experience counsel."

Many have raised concerns that police officers sometimes do not tell the truth at suppression hearings, instead saying what is necessary to make their conduct seem lawful and to gain use of the illegally obtained evidence. *See* Christopher Slobogin, *Testilying: Police Perjury and What to Do About It*, 67 Colo.

---

11. Defendants also can raise Fourth Amendment violations by bringing a motion for the return of illegally obtained evidence.

12. For example, Federal Rule of Criminal Procedure 12(h)(3)(c) provides that motions to suppress must be made before trial unless there is good cause.

L. Rev. 1037 (1996); Donald Dripps, *The Case for the Contingent Exclusionary Rule*, 38 Am. Crim. L. Rev. 1 (2001). Often the only witnesses to the police violation are the defendant and the officers, and the concern is that officers sometimes lie to avoid the exclusionary rule. When it is the officer's word against a criminal defendant caught with contraband, courts tend to believe the officer. The concern is that officers violate the Fourth Amendment and then lie in court to ensure that the fruit of their illegal search is admitted. There is, of course, no agreement as to how often this occurs or, if it is a problem, what to do about it.

CHAPTER

4

POLICE INTERROGATION AND THE PRIVILEGE AGAINST SELF-INCRIMINATION

The Fifth Amendment provides, in part, "No person . . . shall be compelled in any criminal case to be a witness against himself." This is referred to as the privilege against self-incrimination and is a crucial protection provided to suspects and criminal defendants in the criminal justice system.

The privilege against self-incrimination arises in many contexts, including during police interrogation. Police questioning of suspects is a crucial investigative tool. The problem, though, is that police questioning can be coercive, physically or psychologically, and false confessions can result. One study estimated that there are over 6,000 false confessions each year in the United States.[1] A study of cases where there were false confessions found that often these lead to conviction of innocent people. Obviously, a confession is very powerful evidence at trial. Professors Drizin and Leo explained, "[C]onfession evidence is inherently prejudicial and highly damaging to a defendant, even if it is the product of coercive interrogation, even if it is supported by no other evidence, and even if it is proven false beyond any reasonable doubt."[2]

The Supreme Court has dealt with issues of police interrogation for over a century. In examining the law in this area, this chapter is divided into three parts. First, section A examines the requirement under the Due Process Clause that any statement introduced against a criminal defendant be "voluntary." Whether the interrogation by the police is in-custody or not, a statement that is deemed "involuntary" will be excluded from being used against a criminal defendant as being a violation of due process of law. Second, section B examines the protections accorded to suspects during in-custodial interrogation under Miranda v. Arizona, 384 U.S. 436 (1966). A large body of case law has developed concerning when *Miranda* applies,

---

1. Jerome H. Skolnick & James J. Frye, Above the Law: The Police and the Excessive Use of Force 63 (1987).
2. Steven A. Drizen & Richard A. Leo, *The Problem of False Confessions in the Post-DNA World*, 82 N.C. L. Rev. 891 (2004).

when it is waived, and remedies for its violation. All of these issues are examined in section B. Section C then considers the Sixth Amendment right to counsel, which also provides protection during some police interrogations. Finally, section D looks at the privilege against self-incrimination in other contexts besides police interrogation.

A. DUE PROCESS AND THE REQUIREMENT FOR VOLUNTARINESS

1. The Requirement for Voluntariness

The Supreme Court first discussed limits on the admissibility of confessions in Hopt v. People of Territory of Utah, 110 U.S. 574 (1884). The Court said that "a confession . . . should not go to the jury unless it appears to the court to have been voluntary." The Court based its decision on English common law and not the Constitution, but it made clear that involuntary confessions are unreliable and should not be admissible as evidence:

> But the presumption upon which weight is given to such evidence, namely, that one who is innocent will not imperil his safety or prejudice his interests by an untrue statement, ceases when the confession appears to have been made either in consequence of inducements of a temporal nature, held out by one in authority, touching the charge preferred, or because of a threat or promise by or in the presence of such person, which, operating upon the fears or hopes of the accused, in reference to the charge, deprive him of that freedom of will or self-control essential to make his confession voluntary within the meaning of the law.

In Bram v. United States, 168 U.S. 532 (1897), the Supreme Court first found that involuntary confessions violate the privilege against self-incrimination under the Fifth Amendment. The Court stated:

> In criminal trials, in the courts of the United States, wherever a question arises whether a confession is incompetent because not voluntary, the issue is controlled by that portion of the fifth amendment to the constitution of the United States commanding that no person "shall be compelled in any criminal case to be a witness against himself." The legal principle by which the admissibility of the confession of an accused person is to be determined is expressed in the text-books. [I]t is stated as follows: "But a confession, in order to be admissible, must be free and voluntary; that is, must not be extracted by any sort of threats or violence, nor obtained by any direct or implied promises, however slight, nor by the exertion of any improper influence. . . . A confession can never be received in evidence where the prisoner has been influenced by any threat or promise; for the law cannot measure the force of the influence used, or decide upon its effect upon the mind of the prisoner, and therefore excludes the declaration if any degree of influence has been exerted."

Brown v. Mississippi is a crucial case holding that confessions gained involuntarily are inadmissible as violating due process of law.

BROWN v. MISSISSIPPI

297 U.S. 278 (1936)

Chief Justice HUGHES delivered the opinion of the Court.

The question in this case is whether convictions, which rest solely upon confessions shown to have been extorted by officers of the state by brutality and violence, are consistent with the due process of law required by the Fourteenth Amendment of the Constitution of the United States.

Petitioners were indicted for the murder of one Raymond Stewart, whose death occurred on March 30, 1934. They were indicted on April 4, 1934, and were then arraigned and pleaded not guilty. Counsel were appointed by the court to defend them. Trial was begun the next morning and was concluded on the following day, when they were found guilty and sentenced to death.

Aside from the confessions, there was no evidence sufficient to warrant the submission of the case to the jury. After a preliminary inquiry, testimony as to the confessions was received over the objection of defendants' counsel. Defendants then testified that the confessions were false and had been procured by physical torture.

There is no dispute as to the facts upon this point, and as they are clearly and adequately stated in the dissenting opinion of Judge Griffith showing both the extreme brutality of the measures to extort the confessions and the participation of the state authorities, we quote this part of his opinion in full, as follows: "The crime with which these defendants, all ignorant negroes, are charged, was discovered about 1 o'clock P.M. on Friday, March 30, 1934. On that night one Dial, a deputy sheriff, accompanied by others, came to the home of Ellington, one of the defendants, and requested him to accompany them to the house of the deceased, and there a number of white men were gathered, who began to accuse the defendant of the crime. Upon his denial they seized him, and with the participation of the deputy they hanged him by a rope to the limb of a tree, and, having let him down, they hung him again, and when he was let down the second time, and he still protested his innocence, he was tied to a tree and whipped, and, still declining to accede to the demands that he confess, he was finally released, and he returned with some difficulty to his home, suffering intense pain and agony. The record of the testimony shows that the signs of the rope on his neck were plainly visible during the so-called trial. A day or two thereafter the said deputy, accompanied by another, returned to the home of the said defendant and arrested him, and departed with the prisoner towards the jail in an adjoining county, but went by a route which led into the state of Alabama; and while on the way, in that state, the deputy stopped and again severely whipped the defendant, declaring that he would continue the whipping until he confessed, and the defendant then agreed to confess to such a statement as the deputy would dictate, and he did so, after which he was delivered to jail.

The other two defendants, Ed Brown and Henry Shields, were also arrested and taken to the same jail. On Sunday night, April 1, 1934, the same deputy, accompanied by a number of white men, one of whom was also an officer, and by the jailer, came to the jail, and the two last named defendants were made to strip and they were laid over chairs and their backs were cut to pieces with a leather strap with buckles on it, and they were likewise made by the said deputy definitely to understand that the whipping would be continued unless and until they confessed, and not only confessed, but confessed in every matter of detail as demanded by those present; and in this manner the defendants confessed the crime, and, as the whippings progressed and were repeated, they changed or adjusted their confession in all particulars of detail so as to conform to the demands of their torturers. *confessed* When the confessions had been obtained in the exact form and contents as desired by the mob, they left with the parting admonition and warning that, if the defendants changed their story at any time in any respect from that last stated, the perpetrators of the outrage would administer the same or equally effective treatment."

The state is free to regulate the procedure of its courts in accordance with its own conceptions of policy, unless in so doing it "offends some principle of justice so rooted in the traditions and conscience of our people as to be ranked as fundamental." But the freedom of the state in establishing its policy is the freedom of constitutional government and is limited by the requirement of due process of law. Because a state may dispense with a jury trial, it does not follow that it may substitute trial by ordeal. The rack and torture chamber may not be substituted for the witness stand. The state may not permit an accused to be hurried to conviction under mob domination — where the whole proceeding is but a mask — without supplying corrective process. The state may not deny to the accused the aid of counsel. Nor may a state, through the action of its officers, contrive a conviction through the pretense of a trial which in truth is "but used as a means of depriving a defendant of liberty through a deliberate deception of court and jury by the presentation of testimony known to be perjured." And the trial equally is a mere pretense where the state authorities have contrived a conviction resting solely upon confessions obtained by violence. The due process clause requires "that state action, whether through one agency or another, shall be consistent with the fundamental principles of liberty and justice which lie at the base of all our civil and political institutions." It would be difficult to conceive of methods more revolting to the sense of justice than those taken to procure the confessions of these petitioners, and the use of the confessions thus obtained as the basis for conviction and sentence was a clear denial of due process. *No due process*

Over 30 years, between when *Brown* was decided in 1936 and when Miranda v. Arizona was decided in 1966, the Supreme Court decided a large number of cases concerning when confessions are voluntary. As discussed below in section B, after *Miranda*, there is a presumption of the admissibility of confessions if police follow *Miranda*'s dictates. But even after *Miranda*, due process requires that any confession be voluntary in order to be admissible as evidence. For example, as explained below, *Miranda* applies only to interrogations while a person is in police custody. The key protection for questioning that occurs when a person is not in police custody is that any confession must be voluntary. Also, a person can waive his or her rights under *Miranda*, but even if there is a waiver, a confession is not admissible unless it is voluntary.

2. Determining Whether a Confession Is Voluntary

The Supreme Court has held that the prosecution has the burden of proving that a confession is voluntary in order to admit it into evidence. Jackson v. Denno, 378 U.S. 368 (1964). Of course, even if the judge deems the confession to be voluntary and it is admitted, a defendant still can argue to the jury that the confession was obtained under circumstances and conditions that make it unreliable. Crane v. Kentucky, 476 U.S. 683 (1986). Ultimately, the Court has been clear that voluntariness is to be determined by the "totality of the circumstances."

The Court has considered a number of factors in assessing the voluntariness of confessions based on the totality of the circumstances.

a. The Length of the Interrogation and Whether the Defendant Was Deprived of Basic Bodily Needs

If an interrogation went on over a very long period of time, it is more likely to be deemed involuntary, especially where a suspect has been denied sleep, food, water, and/or access to a restroom. For example, in Ashcraft v. Tennessee, 322 U.S. 143 (1944), a confession was deemed involuntary when a suspect was not permitted to sleep for the 36 hours during which the interrogation occurred. In Payne v. Arkansas, 356 U.S. 560 (1958), the fact that the suspect was given no food for 24 hours was important to the Court's conclusion that the confession was involuntary.

b. The Use of Force and Threats of Force

A confession obtained after a defendant is physically coerced, as in Brown v. Mississippi, or threatened with physical force, is not voluntary. In *Payne*, the suspect was told that a mob of 30 to 40 people were waiting outside the station to get him unless he confessed. Arizona v. Fulminante is an important, relatively recent case in which a confession was deemed involuntary because of the threat of force against a criminal suspect.

ARIZONA v. FULMINANTE

499 U.S. 279 (1991)

Justice WHITE delivered an opinion, Parts I and II, which are the opinion of the Court.[3]

The Arizona Supreme Court ruled in this case that respondent Oreste Fulminante's confession, received in evidence at his trial for murder, had been coerced and that its use against him was barred by the Fifth and Fourteenth Amendments to the United States Constitution.

I

Early in the morning of September 14, 1982, Fulminante called the Mesa, Arizona, Police Department to report that his 11-year-old stepdaughter, Jeneane Michelle Hunt, was missing. He had been caring for Jeneane while his wife, Jeneane's mother, was in the hospital. Two days later, Jeneane's body was found in the desert east of Mesa. She had been shot twice in the head at close range with a large caliber weapon, and a ligature was around her neck. Because of the decomposed condition of the body, it was impossible to tell whether she had been sexually assaulted.

Fulminante's statements to police concerning Jeneane's disappearance and his relationship with her contained a number of inconsistencies, and he became a suspect in her killing. When no charges were filed against him, Fulminante left Arizona for New Jersey. Fulminante was later convicted in New Jersey on federal charges of possession of a firearm by a felon.

Fulminante was incarcerated in the Ray Brook Federal Correctional Institution in New York. There he became friends with another inmate, Anthony Sarivola, then serving a 60-day sentence for extortion. The two men came to spend several hours a day together. Sarivola, a former police officer, had been involved in loansharking for organized crime but then became a paid informant for the Federal Bureau of Investigation. While at Ray Brook, he masqueraded as an organized crime figure. After becoming friends with Fulminante, Sarivola heard a rumor that Fulminante was suspected of killing a child in Arizona. Sarivola then raised the subject with Fulminante in several conversations, but Fulminante repeatedly denied any involvement in Jeneane's death. During one conversation, he told Sarivola that Jeneane had been killed by bikers looking for drugs; on another occasion, he said he did not know what had happened. Sarivola passed this information on to an agent of the Federal Bureau of Investigation, who instructed Sarivola to find out more.

---

3. Justices Brennan, Marshall, Stevens, and Scalia joined Parts I and II of the opinion, which are included here. The remainder of the opinion, which is not included, concerns whether harmless error analysis should apply to confessions that are deemed involuntary. [Footnote by casebook authors.]

Sarivola learned more one evening in October 1983, as he and Fulminante walked together around the prison track. Sarivola said that he knew Fulminante was "starting to get some tough treatment and whatnot" from other inmates because of the rumor. Sarivola offered to protect Fulminante from his fellow inmates, but told him, "'You have to tell me about it,' you know. I mean, in other words, 'For me to give you any help.'" *Ibid.* Fulminante then admitted to Sarivola that he had driven Jeneane to the desert on his motorcycle, where he choked her, sexually assaulted her, and made her beg for her life, before shooting her twice in the head. *Confess to get protection*

Sarivola was released from prison in November 1983. Fulminante was released the following May, only to be arrested the next month for another weapons violation. On September 4, 1984, Fulminante was indicted in Arizona for the first-degree murder of Jeneane.

Prior to trial, Fulminante moved to suppress the statement he had given Sarivola in prison, as well as a second confession he had given to Donna Sarivola, then Anthony Sarivola's fiancée and later his wife, following his May 1984 release from prison. He asserted that the confession to Sarivola was coerced, and that the second confession was the "fruit" of the first. Following the hearing, the trial court denied the motion to suppress, specifically finding that, based on the stipulated facts, the confessions were voluntary. The State introduced both confessions as evidence at trial, and on December 19, 1985, Fulminante was convicted of Jeneane's murder. He was subsequently sentenced to death. *Death sentence*

Fulminante appealed, arguing, among other things, that his confession to Sarivola was the product of coercion and that its admission at trial violated his rights to due process under the Fifth and Fourteenth Amendments to the United States Constitution. After considering the evidence at trial as well as the stipulated facts before the trial court on the motion to suppress, the Arizona Supreme Court held that the confession was coerced, but initially determined that the admission of the confession at trial was harmless error, because of the overwhelming nature of the evidence against Fulminante. Upon Fulminante's motion for reconsideration, however, the court ruled that this Court's precedent precluded the use of the harmless-error analysis in the case of a coerced confession. The court therefore reversed the conviction and ordered that Fulminante be retried without the use of the confession to Sarivola.

II

We deal first with the State's contention that the court below erred in holding Fulminante's confession to have been coerced. We normally give great deference to the factual findings of the state court. Nevertheless, "the ultimate issue of 'voluntariness' is a legal question requiring independent federal determination."

Although the question is a close one, we agree with the Arizona Supreme Court's conclusion that Fulminante's confession was coerced. The Arizona

Supreme Court found a credible threat of physical violence unless Fulminante confessed. Our cases have made clear that a finding of coercion need not depend upon actual violence by a government agent; a credible threat is sufficient. As we have said, "coercion can be mental as well as physical, and . . . the blood of the accused is not the only hallmark of an unconstitutional inquisition." Blackburn v. Alabama (1960). As in *Payne*, where the Court found that a confession was coerced because the interrogating police officer had promised that if the accused confessed, the officer would protect the accused from an angry mob outside the jailhouse door, so too here, the Arizona Supreme Court found that it was fear of physical violence, absent protection from his friend (and Government agent) Sarivola, which motivated Fulminante to confess. Accepting the Arizona court's finding, permissible on this record, that there was a credible threat of physical violence, we agree with its conclusion that Fulminante's will was overborne in such a way as to render his confession the product of coercion.

Chief Justice REHNQUIST, with whom Justices O'CONNOR, KENNEDY, and SOUTER join, dissenting.

The Court today properly concludes that the admission of an "involuntary" confession at trial is subject to harmless error analysis. Nonetheless, the independent review of the record which we are required to make shows that respondent Fulminante's confession was not in fact involuntary.

The admissibility of a confession such as that made by respondent Fulminante depends upon whether it was voluntarily made. "The ultimate test remains that which has been the only clearly established test in Anglo-American courts for two hundred years: the test of voluntariness. Is the confession the product of an essentially free and unconstrained choice by its maker? If it is, if he has willed to confess, it may be used against him. If it is not, if his will has been overborne and his capacity for self-determination critically impaired, the use of his confession offends due process." *Culombe v. Connecticut*, 367 U.S. 568 (1961).

Exercising our responsibility to make the independent examination of the record necessary to decide this federal question, I am at a loss to see how the Supreme Court of Arizona reached the conclusion that it did. Fulminante offered no evidence that he believed that his life was in danger or that he in fact confessed to Sarivola in order to obtain the proffered protection. Indeed, he had stipulated that "[a]t no time did the defendant indicate he was in fear of other inmates nor did he ever seek Mr. Sarivola's 'protection.'" Sarivola's testimony that he told Fulminante that "if [he] would tell the truth, he could be protected," adds little if anything to the substance of the parties' stipulation. The decision of the Supreme Court of Arizona rests on an assumption that is squarely contrary to this stipulation, and one that is not supported by any testimony of Fulminante.

The facts of record in the present case are quite different from those present in cases where we have found confessions to be coerced and involuntary. Since Fulminante was unaware that Sarivola was an FBI informant, there existed none of "the danger of coercion result[ing] from the interaction of custody and official interrogation." The fact that Sarivola was a Government informant does not by itself render Fulminante's confession involuntary, since we have consistently accepted the use of informants in the discovery of evidence of a crime as a legitimate investigatory procedure consistent with the Constitution. The conversations between Sarivola and Fulminante were not lengthy, and the defendant was free at all times to leave Sarivola's company. Sarivola at no time threatened him or demanded that he confess; he simply requested that he speak the truth about the matter. Fulminante was an experienced habitue of prisons, and presumably able to fend for himself. In concluding on these facts that Fulminante's confession was involuntary, the Court today embraces a more expansive definition of that term than is warranted by any of our decided cases.

c. Psychological Pressure Tactics

Coercion obviously can be psychological as well as physical. It is difficult, though, to define when psychological pressure is sufficient to rise to the level of coercion. The most famous Supreme Court case on this is Spano v. New York.

SPANO v. NEW YORK

360 U.S. 315 (1959)

Chief Justice WARREN delivered the opinion of the Court.

This is another in the long line of cases presenting the question whether a confession was properly admitted into evidence under the Fourteenth Amendment. As in all such cases, we are forced to resolve a conflict between two fundamental interests of society; its interest in prompt and efficient law enforcement, and its interest in preventing the rights of its individual members from being abridged by unconstitutional methods of law enforcement. Because of the delicate nature of the constitutional determination which we must make, we cannot escape the responsibility of making our own examination of the record.

The State's evidence reveals the following: Petitioner Vincent Joseph Spano is a derivative citizen of this country, having been born in Messina, Italy. He was 25 years old at the time of the shooting in question and had graduated from junior high school. He had a record of regular employment. The shooting took place on January 22, 1957.

On that day, petitioner was drinking in a bar. The decedent, a former professional boxer weighing almost 200 pounds who had fought in Madison Square Garden, took some of petitioner's money from the bar. Petitioner followed him out of the bar to recover it. A fight ensued, with the decedent knocking petitioner down and then kicking him in the head three or four times. Shock from the force of these blows caused petitioner to vomit. After the bartender applied some ice to his head, petitioner left the bar, walked to his apartment, secured a gun, and walked eight or nine blocks to a candy store where the decedent was frequently to be found. He entered the store in which decedent, three friends of decedent, at least two of whom were ex-convicts, and a boy who was supervising the store were present. He fired five shots, two of which entered the decedent's body, causing his death. The boy was the only eyewitness; the three friends of decedent did not see the person who fired the shot. Petitioner then disappeared for the next week or so.

On February 1, 1957, the Bronx County Grand Jury returned an indictment for first-degree murder against petitioner. Accordingly, a bench warrant was issued for his arrest. On February 3, 1957, petitioner called one Gaspar Bruno, a close friend of 8 or 10 years' standing who had attended school with him. Bruno was a fledgling police officer, having at that time not yet finished attending police academy. According to Bruno's testimony, petitioner told him "that he took a terrific beating, that the deceased hurt him real bad and he dropped him a couple of times and he was dazed; he didn't know what he was doing and that he went and shot at him." Petitioner told Bruno that he intended to get a lawyer and give himself up. Bruno relayed this information to his superiors.

The following day, February 4, at 7:10 P.M., petitioner, accompanied by counsel, surrendered himself to the authorities in front of the Bronx County Building, where both the office of the Assistant District Attorney who ultimately prosecuted his case and the court-room in which he was ultimately tried were located. His attorney had cautioned him to answer no questions, and left him in the custody of the officers. He was promptly taken to the office of the Assistant District Attorney and at 7:15 P.M. the questioning began, being conducted by Assistant District Attorney Goldsmith, Lt. Gannon, Detectives Farrell, Lehrer and Motta, and Sgt. Clarke. The record reveals that the questioning was both persistent and continuous. Petitioner, in accordance with his attorney's instructions, steadfastly refused to answer. Detective Motta testified: "He refused to talk to me." "He just looked up to the ceiling and refused to talk to me."

At 12:15 A.M. on the morning of February 5, after five hours of questioning in which it became evident that petitioner was following his attorney's instructions, on the Assistant District Attorney's orders petitioner was transferred to the 46th Squad, Ryer Avenue Police Station. The Assistant District Attorney also went to the police station and to some extent continued to participate in the interrogation. Petitioner arrived at 12:30 and questioning was resumed at 12:40. But petitioner persisted in his refusal to answer, and again requested permission to see his attorney, this time from Detective Lehrer. His request was again denied.

It was then that those in charge of the investigation decided that petitioner's close friend, Bruno, could be of use. He had been called out on the case around 10 or 11 P.M., although he was not connected with the 46th

Squad or Precinct in any way. Although, in fact, his job was in no way threatened, Bruno was told to tell petitioner that petitioner's telephone call had gotten him "in a lot of trouble," and that he should seek to extract sympathy from petitioner for Bruno's pregnant wife and three children. Bruno developed this theme with petitioner without success, and petitioner, also without success, again sought to see his attorney, a request which Bruno relayed unavailingly to his superiors. After this first session with petitioner, Bruno was again directed by Lt. Gannon to play on petitioner's sympathies, but again no confession was forthcoming. But the Lieutenant a third time ordered Bruno falsely to importune his friend to confess but again petitioner clung to his attorney's advice. Inevitably, in the fourth such session directed by the Lieutenant, lasting a full hour, petitioner succumbed to his friend's prevarications and agreed to make a statement. Accordingly, at 3:25 A.M. the Assistant District Attorney, a stenographer, and several other law enforcement officials entered the room where petitioner was being questioned, and took his statement in question and answer form with the Assistant District Attorney asking the questions. The statement was completed at 4:05 A.M.

But this was not the end. At 4:30 A.M. three detectives took petitioner to Police Headquarters in Manhattan. On the way they attempted to find the bridge from which petitioner said he had thrown the murder weapon. They crossed the Triborough Bridge into Manhattan, arriving at Police Headquarters at 5 A.M., and left Manhattan for the Bronx at 5:40 A.M. via the Willis Avenue Bridge. When petitioner recognized neither bridge as the one from which he had thrown the weapon, they re-entered Manhattan via the Third Avenue Bridge, which petitioner stated was the right one, and then returned to the Bronx well after 6 A.M. During that trip the officers also elicited a statement from petitioner that the deceased was always "on [his] back," "always pushing" him and that he was "not sorry" he had shot the deceased. All three detectives testified to that statement at the trial. Court opened at 10 A.M. that morning, and petitioner was arraigned at 10:15.

At the trial, the confession was introduced in evidence over appropriate objections. The jury was instructed that it could rely on it only if it was found to be voluntary. The jury returned a guilty verdict and petitioner was sentenced to death.

We find use of the confession obtained here inconsistent with the Fourteenth Amendment under traditional principles. The abhorrence of society to the use of involuntary confessions does not turn alone on their inherent untrustworthiness. It also turns on the deep-rooted feeling that the police must obey the law while enforcing the law; that in the end life and liberty can be as much endangered from illegal methods used to convict those thought to be criminals as from the actual criminals themselves. Accordingly, the actions of police in obtaining confessions have come under scrutiny in a long series of cases. Those cases suggest that in recent years law enforcement officials have become increasingly aware of the burden which they share, along with our courts, in protecting fundamental rights of our citizenry, including that portion of our citizenry suspected of crime. The facts of no case recently in this Court have quite approached the brutal beatings in Brown v. State of Mississippi (1936), or the 36 consecutive hours of questioning present in Ashcraft v. State of Tennessee (1944). But as law enforcement officers become more responsible, and the methods used to extract confessions more sophisticated, our duty to enforce federal constitutional protections does not cease. It only becomes more difficult because of the more delicate judgments to be made. Our judgment here is that, on all the facts, this conviction cannot stand.

Petitioner was a foreign-born young man of 25 with no past history of law violation or of subjection to official interrogation, at least insofar as the record shows. He had progressed only one-half year into high school and the record indicates that he had a history of emotional instability. He did not make a narrative statement, but was subject to the leading questions of a skillful prosecutor in a question and answer confession. He was subjected to questioning not by a few men, but by many. They included Assistant District Attorney Goldsmith, one Hyland of the District Attorney's Office, Deputy Inspector Halks, Lieutenant Gannon, Detective Ciccone, Detective Motta, Detective Lehrer, Detective Marshal, Detective Farrell, Detective Leira, Detective Murphy, Detective Murtha, Sergeant Clarke, Patrolman Bruno and Stenographer Baldwin. All played some part, and the effect of such massive official interrogation must have been felt. Petitioner was questioned for virtually eight straight hours before he confessed, with his only respite being a transfer to an arena presumably considered more appropriate by the police for the task at hand. Nor was the questioning conducted during normal business hours, but began in early evening, continued into the night, and did not bear fruition until the not-too-early morning. The drama was not played out, with the final admissions obtained, until almost sunrise. In such circumstances slowly mounting fatigue does, and is calculated to, play its part. The questioners persisted in the face of his repeated refusals to answer on the advice of his attorney, and they ignored his reasonable requests to contact the local attorney whom he had already retained and who had personally delivered him into the custody of these officers in obedience to the bench warrant.

The use of Bruno, characterized in this Court by counsel for the State as a "childhood friend" of petitioner's, is another factor which deserves mention in the totality of the situation. Bruno's was the one face visible to petitioner in which he could put some trust. There was a bond of friendship between them going back a decade into adolescence. It was with this material that the officers felt that they could overcome petitioner's will. They instructed Bruno falsely to state that petitioner's telephone call had gotten him into trouble, that his job was in jeopardy, and that loss of his job would be disastrous to his three children, his wife and his unborn child. And Bruno played this part of a worried father, harried by his superiors, in not one, but four different acts, the final one lasting an hour. Petitioner was apparently unaware of John Gay's famous couplet: "An open foe may prove a curse, But a pretended friend is worse," and he yielded to his false friend's entreaties.

We conclude that petitioner's will was overborne by official pressure, fatigue and sympathy falsely aroused after considering all the facts in their post-indictment setting.

d. Deception

In Lynumn v. Illinois, 372 U.S. 528 (1963), a suspect was told that if she cooperated and answered the questions from the police officers, she would not be prosecuted for participating in a marijuana sale. But she was told that if she did not cooperate, she would face ten years in prison and have her children taken away from her. She told the police that she would say whatever they wanted. They told her to admit the marijuana sale, and she did. The Court held that it is "clear that a confession made under such circumstances must not be deemed voluntary."

Although deception can make a confession involuntary, the Court has been tolerant of many police techniques. For example, in Leyra v. Dennis, 347 U.S. 556 (1954), the Court found that a confession was voluntary, even though the police lied to the suspect and told a suspect that his accomplice had already confessed. In Frazier v. Cupp, 394 U.S. 731 (1969), the Court found that an officer acting as a friend to a suspect and expressing sympathy for his or her plight is not deception requiring suppression of a confession.

e. The Age, Level of Education, and Mental Condition of a Suspect

For example, in Payne v. Arkansas, the Court, in finding a confession involuntary, stressed that the suspect had a fifth-grade education. In *Spano*, above, the Court focused on the defendant's level of education as a factor in determining his confession to be involuntary. In Culombe v. Connecticut, 367 U.S. 568 (1961), the Court emphasized that the suspect was illiterate and of low intelligence. By contrast, in finding a confession to be voluntary in Crooker v. California, 357 U.S. 433 (1958), the Court noted that the suspect had completed a year of law school.

However, in Colorado v. Connelly, below, the Court imposed a major limit on consideration of a defendant's mental condition in determining whether a confession is voluntary. The Court held that a confession is to be deemed involuntary, regardless of the defendant's mental condition, only if it is the product of police misconduct. The contrast between Chief Justice Rehnquist's majority opinion and Justice Brennan's dissent is important in illuminating different views about the voluntariness requirement and the privilege against self-incrimination.

COLORADO v. CONNELLY

479 U.S. 157 (1986)

Chief Justice REHNQUIST delivered the opinion of the Court.

In this case, the Supreme Court of Colorado held that the United States Constitution requires a court to suppress a confession when the mental state of the defendant, at the time he made the confession, interfered with his "rational intellect" and his "free will." We conclude that the admissibility of this kind of statement is governed by state rules of evidence, rather than by our previous decisions regarding coerced confessions and *Miranda* waivers. We therefore reverse.

I

On August 18, 1983, Officer Patrick Anderson of the Denver Police Department was in uniform, working in an off-duty capacity in downtown Denver. Respondent Francis Connelly approached Officer Anderson and, without any prompting, stated that he had murdered someone and wanted to talk about it. Anderson immediately advised respondent that he had the right to remain silent, that anything he said could be used against him in court, and that he had the right to an attorney prior to any police questioning. *See* Miranda v. Arizona (1966). Respondent stated that he understood these rights but he still wanted to talk about the murder. Understandably bewildered by this confession, Officer Anderson asked respondent several questions. Connelly denied that he had been drinking, denied that he had been taking any drugs, and stated that, in the past, he had been a patient in several mental hospitals. Officer Anderson again told Connelly that he was under no obligation to say anything. Connelly replied that it was "all right," and that he would talk to Officer Anderson because his conscience had been bothering him. To Officer Anderson, respondent appeared to understand fully the nature of his acts.

Shortly thereafter, Homicide Detective Stephen Antuna arrived. Respondent was again advised of his rights, and Detective Antuna asked him "what he had on his mind." Respondent answered that he had come all the way from Boston to confess to the murder of Mary Ann Junta, a young girl whom he had killed in Denver sometime during November 1982. Respondent was taken to police headquarters, and a search of police records revealed that the body of an unidentified female had been found in April 1983. Respondent openly detailed his story to Detective Antuna and Sergeant Thomas Haney, and readily agreed to take the officers to the scene of the killing. Under Connelly's sole direction, the two officers and respondent proceeded in a police vehicle to the location of the crime. Respondent pointed out the exact location of the murder. Throughout this episode, Detective Antuna perceived no indication whatsoever that respondent was suffering from any kind of mental illness.

Respondent was held overnight. During an interview with the public defender's office the following morning, he became visibly disoriented. He began giving confused answers to questions, and for the first time, stated that "voices" had told him to come to Denver and that he had followed the directions of these voices in confessing. Respondent was sent to a state hospital for evaluation. He was initially found incompetent to assist in his own defense. By March 1984, however, the doctors evaluating respondent determined that he was competent to proceed to trial.

At a preliminary hearing, respondent moved to suppress all of his statements. Dr. Jeffrey Metzner, a psychiatrist employed by the state hospital, testified that respondent was suffering from chronic schizophrenia and was in a psychotic state at least as of August 17, 1983, the day before he confessed. Metzner's interviews with respondent revealed that respondent was following the "voice of God." This voice instructed respondent to withdraw money from the bank, to buy an airplane ticket, and to fly from Boston to Denver. When respondent arrived from Boston, God's voice became stronger and told respondent either to confess to the killing or to commit suicide. Reluctantly following the command of the voices, respondent approached Officer Anderson and confessed. Dr. Metzner testified that, in his expert opinion, respondent was experiencing "command hallucinations." This condition interfered with respondent's "volitional abilities; that is, his ability to make free and rational choices." Dr. Metzner further testified that Connelly's illness did not significantly impair his cognitive abilities. Thus, respondent understood the rights he had when Officer Anderson and Detective Antuna advised him that he need not speak. Dr. Metzner admitted that the "voices" could in reality be Connelly's interpretation of his own guilt, but explained that in his opinion, Connelly's psychosis motivated his confession. On the basis of this evidence the Colorado trial court decided that respondent's statements must be suppressed because they were "involuntary." The Colorado Supreme Court affirmed.

II

The Due Process Clause of the Fourteenth Amendment provides that no State shall "deprive any person of life, liberty, or property, without due process of law."[W]e have held that by virtue of the Due Process Clause "certain interrogation techniques, either in isolation or as applied to the unique characteristics of a particular suspect, are so offensive to a civilized system of justice that they must be condemned." Indeed, coercive government misconduct was the catalyst for this Court's seminal confession case, Brown v. Mississippi (1936).

Thus the cases considered by this Court over the 50 years since Brown v. Mississippi have focused upon the crucial element of police overreaching. While each confession case has turned on its own set of factors justifying the conclusion that police conduct was oppressive, all have contained a substantial element of coercive police conduct. Absent police conduct causally related to the confession, there is simply no basis for concluding that any state actor has deprived a criminal defendant of due process of law. Respondent correctly notes that as interrogators have turned to more subtle forms of psychological persuasion, courts have found the mental condition of the defendant a more significant factor in the "voluntariness" calculus. *See* Spano v. New York (1959). But this fact does not justify a conclusion that a defendant's mental condition, by itself and apart from its relation to official coercion, should ever dispose of the inquiry into constitutional "voluntariness."

Our "involuntary confession" jurisprudence is entirely consistent with the settled law requiring some sort of "state action" to support a claim of violation of the Due Process Clause of the Fourteenth Amendment. The Colorado trial court, of course, found that the police committed no wrongful acts, and that finding has been neither challenged by respondent nor disturbed by the Supreme Court of Colorado.

The difficulty with the approach of the Supreme Court of Colorado is that it fails to recognize the essential link between coercive activity of the State, on the one hand, and a resulting confession by a defendant, on the other. The flaw in respondent's constitutional argument is that it would expand our previous line of "voluntariness" cases into a far-ranging requirement that courts must divine a defendant's motivation for speaking or acting as he did even though there be no claim that governmental conduct coerced his decision.

The most outrageous behavior by a private party seeking to secure evidence against a defendant does not make that evidence inadmissible under the Due Process Clause. We have also observed that "[j]urists and scholars uniformly have recognized that the exclusionary rule imposes a substantial cost on the societal interest in law enforcement by its proscription of what concededly is relevant evidence." Moreover, suppressing respondent's statements would serve absolutely no purpose in enforcing constitutional guarantees. The purpose of excluding evidence seized in violation of the Constitution is to substantially deter future violations of the Constitution. Only if we were to establish a brand new constitutional right—the right of a criminal defendant to confess to his crime only when totally rational and properly motivated—could respondent's present claim be sustained.

We have previously cautioned against expanding "currently applicable exclusionary rules by erecting additional barriers to placing truthful and probative evidence before state juries. . . ." We abide by that counsel now. "[T]he central purpose of a criminal trial is to decide the factual question of the defendant's guilt or innocence," and while we have previously held that exclusion of evidence may be necessary to protect constitutional guarantees, both the necessity for the collateral inquiry and the exclusion of evidence deflect a criminal trial from its basic purpose. Respondent would now have us require sweeping inquiries into the state of mind of a criminal defendant who has confessed, inquiries quite divorced from any coercion brought to bear on the defendant by the State. We think the Constitution rightly leaves this sort of inquiry to be resolved by state laws governing the admission of evidence and erects no standard of its own in this area. A statement rendered by one in the condition of respondent might be proved to be quite unreliable, but this is a matter to be governed by the evidentiary laws of the forum, and not by the Due Process Clause of the Fourteenth Amendment. "The aim of the requirement of due process is not to exclude presumptively false evidence, but to prevent fundamental unfairness in the use of evidence, whether true or false."

We hold that coercive police activity is a necessary predicate to the finding that a confession is not "voluntary" within the meaning of the Due Process Clause of the Fourteenth Amendment. We also conclude that the taking of respondent's statements, and their admission into evidence, constitute no violation of that Clause.

Justice BRENNAN, with whom Justice MARSHALL joins, dissenting.

Today the Court denies Mr. Connelly his fundamental right to make a vital choice with a sane mind, involving a determination that could allow the State to deprive him of liberty or even life. This holding is unprecedented: "Surely in the present stage of our civilization a most basic sense of justice is affronted by the spectacle of incarcerating a human being upon the basis of a statement he made while insane. . . ." Blackburn v. Alabama (1960). Because I believe that the use of a mentally ill person's involuntary confession is antithetical to the notion of fundamental fairness embodied in the Due Process Clause, I dissent.

I

The respondent's seriously impaired mental condition is clear on the record of this case. At the time of his confession, Mr. Connelly suffered from a "longstanding severe mental disorder," diagnosed as chronic paranoid schizophrenia. He had been hospitalized for psychiatric reasons five times prior to his confession; his longest hospitalization lasted for seven months. Mr. Connelly heard imaginary voices and saw nonexistent objects. He believed that his father was God, and that he was a reincarnation of Jesus.

At the time of his confession, Mr. Connelly's mental problems included "grandiose and delusional thinking." He had a known history of "thought withdrawal and insertion." Although physicians had treated Mr. Connelly "with a wide variety of medications in the past including antipsychotic medications," he had not taken any antipsychotic medications for at least six months prior to his confession. Following his arrest, Mr. Connelly initially was found incompetent to stand trial because the court-appointed psychiatrist, Dr. Metzner, "wasn't very confident that he could consistently relate accurate information." Dr. Metzner testified that Mr. Connelly was unable "to make free and rational choices" due to auditory hallucinations: "[W]hen he was read his *Miranda* rights, he probably had the capacity to know that he was being read his *Miranda* rights [but] he wasn't able to use that information because of the command hallucinations that he had experienced." He achieved competency to stand trial only after six months of hospitalization and treatment with antipsychotic and sedative medications.

The state trial court found that the "overwhelming evidence presented by the Defense" indicated that the prosecution did not meet its burden of demonstrating by a preponderance of the evidence that the initial statement to Officer Anderson was voluntary.

II

The absence of police wrongdoing should not, by itself, determine the voluntariness of a confession by a mentally ill person. The requirement that a confession be voluntary reflects a recognition of the importance of free will and of reliability in determining the admissibility of a confession, and thus demands an inquiry into the totality of the circumstances surrounding the confession.

Today's decision restricts the application of the term "involuntary" to those confessions obtained by police coercion. Confessions by mentally ill individuals or by persons coerced by parties other than police officers are now considered "voluntary." The Court's failure to recognize all forms of involuntariness or coercion as antithetical to due process reflects a refusal to acknowledge free will as a value of constitutional consequence. But due process derives much of its meaning from a conception of fundamental fairness that emphasizes the right to make vital choices voluntarily: "The Fourteenth Amendment secures against state invasion . . . the right of a person to remain silent unless he chooses to speak in the unfettered exercise of his own will. . . ." Malloy v. Hogan (1964). This right requires vigilant protection if we are to safeguard the values of private conscience and human dignity.

This Court's assertion that we would be required "to establish a brand new constitutional right" to recognize the respondent's claim, ignores 200 years of constitutional jurisprudence.

A true commitment to fundamental fairness requires that the inquiry be "not whether the conduct of state officers in obtaining the confession is shocking, but whether the confession was 'free and voluntary.'. . ." Malloy v. Hogan.

We have never confined our focus to police coercion, because the value of freedom of will has demanded a broader inquiry. While it is true that police overreaching has been an element of every confession case to date, it is also true that in every case the Court has made clear that ensuring that a confession is a product of free will is an independent concern. The fact that involuntary confessions have always been excluded in part because of police overreaching signifies only that this is a case of first impression. Until today, we have never upheld the admission of a confession that does not reflect the exercise of free will.

Since the Court redefines voluntary confessions to include confessions by mentally ill individuals, the reliability of these confessions becomes a central concern. A concern for reliability is inherent in our criminal justice system, which relies upon accusatorial rather than inquisitorial practices. While an inquisitorial system prefers obtaining confessions from criminal defendants, an accusatorial system must place its faith in determinations of "guilt by evidence independently and freely secured."

Our distrust for reliance on confessions is due, in part, to their decisive impact upon the adversarial process. Triers of fact accord confessions such heavy weight in their determinations that "the introduction of a confession makes the other aspects of a trial in court superfluous, and the real trial, for all practical purposes, occurs when the confession is obtained." No other class of evidence is so profoundly prejudicial.

Because the admission of a confession so strongly tips the balance against the defendant in the adversarial process, we must be especially careful about a confession's reliability. We have to date not required a finding of reliability for involuntary confessions only because all such confessions have been excluded upon a finding of involuntariness, regardless of reliability. The Court's adoption today of a restrictive definition of an "involuntary" confession will require heightened scrutiny of a confession's reliability.

Minimum standards of due process should require that the trial court find substantial indicia of reliability, on the basis of evidence extrinsic to the confession itself, before admitting the confession of a mentally ill person into evidence. I would require the trial court to make such a finding on remand. To hold otherwise allows the State to imprison and possibly to execute a mentally ill defendant based solely upon an inherently unreliable confession.

3. Is the Voluntariness Test Desirable?

The voluntariness test has the advantage that it focuses on the totality of the circumstances in deciding whether a confession should be admitted into evidence. Underlying the voluntariness test, and often expressed by the Supreme Court, is a concern for the reliability of a confession. Obviously, a confession gained through violence and threats of violence, or when a person has been deprived sleep and food for over a day, is unreliable. But the Court is explicit, in cases such as *Spano*, above, that reliability is not the only concern; certain police techniques are repugnant and override free will and thus are not to be tolerated.

On the other hand, the voluntariness test provides relatively little in the way of clear guidance to police officers as to what they can and cannot do in questioning a suspect. Judges inherently have great discretion under a "totality of the circumstances" test. Critics argue that police, who question suspects literally every day, need more instructions than a voluntariness test can provide. In fact, some police organizations have come to support the requirements imposed under Miranda v. Arizona because they provide clear and simple requirements for police to follow with the knowledge that if they do so, there is a presumption that any confession obtained will be deemed voluntary.

4. Coercive Questioning, Torture, and the War on Terrorism

The issue of coercive questioning techniques has arisen as part of the war on terror. In a famous memorandum, since repudiated, high-level legal advisors within the Bush administration urged that the president has the authority to override treaties and statutes prohibiting torture and that the definition of torture should be limited to pain and suffering causing failure of bodily organs or similar to that suffered when there is the failure of major bodily organs. The Bush administration, in response to great pressure, repudiated that but continued to argue that while torture is prohibited, coercive questioning is allowed and necessary in fighting terrorism.

The Military Commission Act of 2006, Pub. L. No. 109-366, 120 Stat. 2600 (2006), follows this distinction. The act provides for military commissions to try noncitizens accused of terrorism and prohibits the admissibility of statements gained through torture. The act provides that in determining whether a statement is admissible before a military commission, the tribunal should consider whether under the totality of the circumstances the statement should be deemed reliable, whether the interests of justice would be served by admission of the statement, and whether the methods used to gain the statement amount to "cruel, inhuman, or degrading treatment."

As a constitutional matter, there is the question of whether due process applies to noncitizens held and questioned outside the United States. As a practical matter, there is the issue of whether statements made after coercive questioning ever can be sufficiently reliable to justify the practice. As an ethical matter, there is the question of whether coercive questioning is ever acceptable.

B. FIFTH AMENDMENT LIMITS ON IN-CUSTODIAL INTERROGATION: MIRANDA v. ARIZONA

1. Miranda v. Arizona and Its Affirmation by the Supreme Court

Probably the most famous Supreme Court case dealing with criminal procedure, and one of the most famous Supreme Court decisions of all time, is Miranda v. Arizona. The Court spoke of the inherently coercive nature of in-custodial interrogation and as a solution required that every suspect questioned by the police be given certain warnings. A key difference between the majority and the dissent is whether more than a voluntariness test is needed to protect criminal suspects: The majority believes that more than a voluntariness test is essential; the dissent argues that the voluntariness test is sufficient.

In reading the decision, it also is important to note that the majority opinion was written by Chief Justice Earl Warren. He had been a district attorney, the attorney general of California, and the governor of California before becoming chief justice. This may have been important in providing additional credibility for a particularly controversial decision.

MIRANDA v. ARIZONA
384 U.S. 436 (1966)

Chief Justice WARREN delivered the opinion of the Court.

The cases before us raise questions which go to the roots of our concepts of American criminal jurisprudence: the restraints society must observe consistent with the Federal Constitution in prosecuting individuals for crime. More specifically, we deal with the admissibility of statements obtained from an individual who is subjected to custodial police interrogation and the necessity for procedures which assure that the individual is accorded his privilege under the Fifth Amendment to the Constitution not to be compelled to incriminate himself.

We dealt with certain phases of this problem recently in Escobedo v. State of Illinois (1964). There, as in the four cases before us, law enforcement officials took the defendant into custody and interrogated him in a police station for the purpose of obtaining a confession. The police did not effectively advise him of his right to remain silent or of his right to consult with his attorney. Rather, they confronted him with an alleged accomplice who accused him of having perpetrated a murder. When the defendant denied the accusation and said "I didn't shoot Manuel, you did it," they handcuffed him and took him to an interrogation room. There, while handcuffed and standing, he was questioned for four hours until he confessed. During this interrogation, the police denied his request to speak to his attorney, and they prevented his retained attorney, who had come to the police station, from consulting with him. At his trial, the State, over his objection, introduced the confession against him. We held that the statements thus made were constitutionally inadmissible.

This case has been the subject of judicial interpretation and spirited legal debate since it was decided two years ago.

We start here, as we did in *Escobedo*, with the premise that our holding is not an innovation in our jurisprudence, but is an application of principles long recognized and applied in other settings. We have undertaken a thorough re-examination of the *Escobedo* decision and the principles it announced, and we reaffirm it. That case was but an explication of basic rights that are enshrined in our Constitution — that "No person . . . shall be compelled in any criminal case to be a witness against himself," and that "the accused shall . . . have the Assistance of Counsel" — rights which were put in jeopardy in that case through official overbearing. These precious rights were fixed in our Constitution only after centuries of persecution and struggle.

Our holding will be spelled out with some specificity in the pages which follow but briefly stated it is this: the prosecution may not use statements, whether exculpatory or inculpatory, stemming from custodial interrogation of the defendant unless it demonstrates the use of procedural safeguards effective to secure the privilege against self-incrimination. By custodial interrogation, we mean questioning initiated by law enforcement officers after a person has been taken into custody or otherwise deprived of his freedom of action in any significant way. As for the procedural safeguards to be employed, unless other fully effective means are devised to inform accused persons of their right of silence and to assure a continuous opportunity to exercise it, the following measures are required. Prior to any questioning, the person must be warned that he has a right to remain silent, that any statement he does make may be used as evidence against him, and that he has a right to the presence of an attorney, either retained or appointed. The defendant may waive effectuation of these rights, provided the waiver is made voluntarily, knowingly and intelligently. If, however, he indicates in any manner and at any stage of the process that he wishes to consult with an attorney before speaking there can be no questioning. Likewise, if the individual is alone and indicates in any manner that he does not wish to be interrogated, the police may not question him. The mere fact that he may have answered some questions or volunteered some statements on his own does not deprive him of the right to refrain from answering any further inquiries until he has consulted with an attorney and thereafter consents to be questioned.

I

The constitutional issue we decide in each of these cases is the admissibility of statements obtained from a defendant questioned while in custody or otherwise deprived of his freedom of action in any significant way. In each, the defendant was questioned by police officers, detectives, or a prosecuting attorney in a room in which he was cut off from the outside world. In none of these cases was the defendant given a full and effective warning of his rights at the outset of the interrogation process. In all the cases, the questioning elicited oral admissions, and in three of them, signed statements as well which were admitted at their trials. They all thus share salient features — incommunicado interrogation of individuals in a police-dominated atmosphere, resulting in self-incriminating statements without full warnings of constitutional rights.

An understanding of the nature and setting of this in-custody interrogation is essential to our decisions today. The difficulty in depicting what transpires at such interrogations stems from the fact that in this country they have largely taken place incommunicado. From extensive factual studies undertaken in the early 1930's, including the famous Wickersham Report to Congress by a Presidential Commission, it is clear that police violence and the "third degree" flourished at that time. In a series of cases decided by this Court long after these studies, the police resorted to physical brutality—beatings, hanging, whipping—and to sustained and protracted questioning incommunicado in order to extort confessions. The use of physical brutality and violence is not, unfortunately, relegated to the past or to any part of the country. Only recently in Kings County, New York, the police brutally beat, kicked and placed lighted cigarette butts on the back of a potential witness under interrogation for the purpose of securing a statement incriminating a third party.

The examples given above are undoubtedly the exception now, but they are sufficiently widespread to be the object of concern. Unless a proper limitation upon custodial interrogation is achieved—such as these decisions will advance—there can be no assurance that practices of this nature will be eradicated in the foreseeable future.

Again we stress that the modern practice of in-custody interrogation is psychologically rather than physically oriented. As we have stated before, this Court has recognized that coercion can be mental as well as physical, and that the blood of the accused is not the only hallmark of an unconstitutional inquisition. Interrogation still takes place in privacy. Privacy results in secrecy and this in turn results in a gap in our knowledge as to what in fact goes on in the interrogation rooms. A valuable source of information about present police practices, however, may be found in various police manuals and texts which document procedures employed with success in the past, and which recommend various other effective tactics. These texts are used by law enforcement agencies themselves as guides. It should be noted that these texts professedly present the most enlightened and effective means presently used to obtain statements through custodial interrogation. By considering these texts and other data, it is possible to describe procedures observed and noted around the country.

The officers are told by the manuals that the "principal psychological factor contributing to a successful interrogation is privacy—being alone with the person under interrogation." To highlight the isolation and unfamiliar surroundings, the manuals instruct the police to display an air of confidence in the suspect's guilt and from outward appearance to maintain only an interest in confirming certain details. The guilt of the subject is to be posited as a fact. The interrogator should direct his comments toward the reasons why the subject committed the act, rather than court failure by asking the subject whether he did it. Like other men, perhaps the subject has had a bad family life, had an unhappy childhood, had too much to drink, had an unrequited desire for women. The officers are instructed to minimize the moral seriousness of the offense, to cast blame on the victim or on society. These tactics are designed to put the subject in a psychological state where his story is but an elaboration of what the police purport to know already — that he is guilty. Explanations to the contrary are dismissed and discouraged. The texts thus stress that the major qualities an interrogator should possess are patience and perseverance.

When the techniques described above prove unavailing, the texts recommend they be alternated with a show of some hostility. One ploy often used has been termed the "friendly-unfriendly" or the "Mutt and Jeff" act.

The interrogators sometimes are instructed to induce a confession out of trickery. The technique here is quite effective in crimes which require identification or which run in series. In the identification situation, the interrogator may take a break in his questioning to place the subject among a group of men in a line-up. "The witness or complainant (previously coached, if necessary) studies the line-up and confidently points out the subject as the guilty party." Then the questioning resumes "as though there were now no doubt about the guilt of the subject."

The manuals also contain instructions for police on how to handle the individual who refuses to discuss the matter entirely, or who asks for an attorney or relatives. The examiner is to concede him the right to remain silent. "This usually has a very undermining effect. First of all, he is disappointed in his expectation of an unfavorable reaction on the part of the interrogator. Secondly, a concession of this right to remain silent impresses the subject with the apparent fairness of his interrogator." After this psychological conditioning, however, the officer is told to point out the incriminating significance of the suspect's refusal to talk. Few will persist in their initial refusal to talk, it is said, if this monologue is employed correctly.

From these representative samples of interrogation techniques, the setting prescribed by the manuals and observed in practice becomes clear. In essence, it is this: To be alone with the subject is essential to prevent distraction and to deprive him of any outside support. The aura of confidence in his guilt undermines his will to resist. He merely confirms the preconceived story the police seek to have him describe. Patience and persistence, at times relentless questioning, are employed. To obtain a confession, the interrogator must "patiently maneuver himself or his quarry into a position from which the desired objective may be attained." When normal procedures fail to produce the needed result, the police may resort to deceptive stratagems such as giving false legal advice. It is important to keep the subject off balance, for example, by trading on his insecurity about himself or his surroundings. The police then persuade, trick, or cajole him out of exercising his constitutional rights.

Even without employing brutality, the "third degree" or the specific stratagems described above, the very fact of custodial interrogation exacts a heavy toll on individual liberty and trades on the weakness of individuals.

In the cases before us today, given this background, we concern ourselves primarily with this interrogation atmosphere and the evils it can bring. In No. 759, Miranda v. Arizona, the police arrested the defendant and took him to a special interrogation room where they secured a confession. In No. 760,

Vignera v. New York, the defendant made oral admissions to the police after interrogation in the afternoon, and then signed an inculpatory statement upon being questioned by an assistant district attorney later the same evening. In No. 761, Westover v. United States, the defendant was handed over to the Federal Bureau of Investigation by local authorities after they had detained and interrogated him for a lengthy period, both at night and the following morning. After some two hours of questioning, the federal officers had obtained signed statements from the defendant. Lastly, in No. 584, California v. Stewart, the local police held the defendant five days in the station and interrogated him on nine separate occasions before they secured his inculpatory statement.

In these cases, we might not find the defendants' statements to have been involuntary in traditional terms. Our concern for adequate safeguards to protect precious Fifth Amendment rights is, of course, not lessened in the slightest. In each of the cases, the defendant was thrust into an unfamiliar atmosphere and run through menacing police interrogation procedures. The potentiality for compulsion is forcefully apparent, for example, in *Miranda*, where the indigent Mexican defendant was a seriously disturbed individual with pronounced sexual fantasies, and in *Stewart*, in which the defendant was an indigent Los Angeles Negro who had dropped out of school in the sixth grade. To be sure, the records do not evince overt physical coercion or patent psychological ploys. The fact remains that in none of these cases did the officers undertake to afford appropriate safeguards at the outset of the interrogation to insure that the statements were truly the product of free choice.

It is obvious that such an interrogation environment is created for no purpose other than to subjugate the individual to the will of his examiner. This atmosphere carries its own badge of intimidation. To be sure, this is not physical intimidation, but it is equally destructive of human dignity. The current practice of incommunicado interrogation is at odds with one of our Nation's most cherished principles — that the individual may not be compelled to incriminate himself. Unless adequate protective devices are employed to dispel the compulsion inherent in custodial surroundings, no statement obtained from the defendant can truly be the product of his free choice.

II

We sometimes forget how long it has taken to establish the privilege against self-incrimination, the sources from which it came and the fervor with which it was defended. Its roots go back into ancient times. [W]e may view the historical development of the privilege as one which groped for the proper scope of governmental power over the citizen.

The question in these cases is whether the privilege is fully applicable during a period of custodial interrogation. We are satisfied that all the principles embodied in the privilege apply to informal compulsion exerted by law-enforcement officers during in-custody questioning. An individual swept from familiar surroundings into police custody, surrounded by antagonistic forces, and subjected to the techniques of persuasion described above cannot be otherwise than under compulsion to speak. As a practical matter, the compulsion to speak in the isolated setting of the police station may well be greater than in courts or other official investigations, where there are often impartial observers to guard against intimidation or trickery.

III

Today, then, there can be no doubt that the Fifth Amendment privilege is available outside of criminal court proceedings and serves to protect persons in all settings in which their freedom of action is curtailed in any significant way from being compelled to incriminate themselves. We have concluded that without proper safeguards the process of in-custody interrogation of persons suspected or accused of crime contains inherently compelling pressures which work to undermine the individual's will to resist and to compel him to speak where he would not otherwise do so freely. In order to combat these pressures and to permit a full opportunity to exercise the privilege against self-incrimination, the accused must be adequately and effectively apprised of his rights and the exercise of those rights must be fully honored.

It is impossible for us to foresee the potential alternatives for protecting the privilege which might be devised by Congress or the States in the exercise of their creative rule-making capacities. Therefore we cannot say that the Constitution necessarily requires adherence to any particular solution for the inherent compulsions of the interrogation process as it is presently conducted. Our decision in no way creates a constitutional straitjacket which will handicap sound efforts at reform, nor is it intended to have this effect. We encourage Congress and the States to continue their laudable search for increasingly effective ways of protecting the rights of the individual while promoting efficient enforcement of our criminal laws. However, unless we are shown other procedures which are at least as effective in apprising accused persons of their right of silence and in assuring a continuous opportunity to exercise it, the following safeguards must be observed.

At the outset, if a person in custody is to be subjected to interrogation, he must first be informed in clear and unequivocal terms that he has the right to remain silent. For those unaware of the privilege, the warning is needed simply to make them aware of it — the threshold requirement for an intelligent decision as to its exercise. More important, such a warning is an absolute prerequisite in overcoming the inherent pressures of the interrogation atmosphere. It is not just the subnormal or woefully ignorant who succumb to an interrogator's imprecations, whether implied or expressly stated, that the interrogation will continue until a confession is obtained or that silence in the face of accusation is itself damning and will bode ill when presented to a jury. Further, the warning will show the individual that his interrogators are prepared to recognize his privilege should he choose to exercise it.

In accord with our decision today, it is impermissible to penalize an individual for exercising his Fifth Amendment privilege when he is under police custodial interrogation. The prosecution may not, therefore, use at trial the fact that he stood mute or claimed his privilege in the face of accusation. *Can't use against*

The Fifth Amendment privilege is so fundamental to our system of constitutional rule and the expedient of giving an adequate warning as to the availability of the privilege so simple, we will not pause to inquire in individual cases whether the defendant was aware of his rights without a warning being given. Assessments of the knowledge the defendant possessed, based on information as to his age, education, intelligence, or prior contact with authorities, can never be more than speculation; a warning is a clearcut fact. More important, whatever the background of the person interrogated, a warning at the time of the interrogation is indispensable to overcome its pressures and to insure that the individual knows he is free to exercise the privilege at that point in time.

The warning of the right to remain silent must be accompanied by the explanation that anything said can and will be used against the individual in court. This warning is needed in order to make him aware not only of the privilege, but also of the consequences of forgoing it. It is only through an awareness of these consequences that there can be any assurance of real understanding and intelligent exercise of the privilege. Moreover, this warning may serve to make the individual more acutely aware that he is faced with a phase of the adversary system — that he is not in the presence of persons acting solely in his interest.

The circumstances surrounding in-custody interrogation can operate very quickly to overbear the will of one merely made aware of his privilege by his interrogators. Therefore, the right to have counsel present at the interrogation is indispensable to the protection of the Fifth Amendment privilege under the system we delineate today. Our aim is to assure that the individual's right to choose between silence and speech remains unfettered throughout the interrogation process. A once-stated warning, delivered by those who will conduct the interrogation, cannot itself suffice to that end among those who most require knowledge of their rights. A mere warning given by the interrogators is not alone sufficient to accomplish that end. Prosecutors themselves claim that the admonishment of the right to remain silent without more "will benefit only the recidivist and the professional." Thus, the need for counsel to protect the Fifth Amendment privilege comprehends not merely a right to consult with counsel prior to questioning, but also to have counsel present during any questioning if the defendant so desires.

The presence of counsel at the interrogation may serve several significant subsidiary functions as well. If the accused decides to talk to his interrogators, the assistance of counsel can mitigate the dangers of untrustworthiness. With a lawyer present the likelihood that the police will practice coercion is reduced, and if coercion is nevertheless exercised the lawyer can testify to it in court. The presence of a lawyer can also help to guarantee that the accused gives a fully accurate statement to the police and that the statement is rightly reported by the prosecution at trial.

An individual need not make a pre-interrogation request for a lawyer. While such request affirmatively secures his right to have one, his failure to ask for a lawyer does not constitute a waiver. No effective waiver of the right to counsel during interrogation can be recognized unless specifically made after the warnings we here delineate have been given. The accused who does not know his rights and therefore does not make a request may be the person who most needs counsel.

Accordingly we hold that an individual held for interrogation must be clearly informed that he has the right to consult with a lawyer and to have the lawyer with him during interrogation under the system for protecting the privilege we delineate today. As with the warnings of the right to remain silent and that anything stated can be used in evidence against him, this warning is an absolute prerequisite to interrogation. No amount of circumstantial evidence that the person may have been aware of this right will suffice to stand in its stead. Only through such a warning is there ascertainable assurance that the accused was aware of this right.

If an individual indicates that he wishes the assistance of counsel before any interrogation occurs, the authorities cannot rationally ignore or deny his request on the basis that the individual does not have or cannot afford a retained attorney. The financial ability of the individual has no relationship to the scope of the rights involved here. The privilege against self-incrimination secured by the Constitution applies to all individuals. The need for counsel in order to protect the privilege exists for the indigent as well as the affluent. In fact, were we to limit these constitutional rights to those who can retain an attorney, our decisions today would be of little significance. The cases before us as well as the vast majority of confession cases with which we have dealt in the past involve those unable to retain counsel. While authorities are not required to relieve the accused of his poverty, they have the obligation not to take advantage of indigence in the administration of justice. Denial of counsel to the indigent at the time of interrogation while allowing an attorney to those who can afford one would be no more supportable by reason or logic than the similar situation at trial and on appeal struck down in Gideon v. Wainwright (1963) and Douglas v. People of State of California (1963).

In order fully to apprise a person interrogated of the extent of his rights under this system then, it is necessary to warn him not only that he has the right to consult with an attorney, but also that if he is indigent a lawyer will be appointed to represent him. Without this additional warning, the admonition of the right to consult with counsel would often be understood as meaning only that he can consult with a lawyer if he has one or has the funds to obtain one. The warning of a right to counsel would be hollow if not couched in terms that would convey to the indigent — the person most often subjected to interrogation — the knowledge that he too has a right to have counsel present. As with the warnings of the right to remain silent and of the general right to counsel, only by effective and express explanation to the indigent of this right can there be assurance that he was truly in a position to exercise it.

Once warnings have been given, the subsequent procedure is clear. If the individual indicates in any manner, at any time prior to or during questioning, that he wishes to remain silent, the interrogation must cease. At this point he has shown that he intends to exercise his Fifth Amendment privilege; any statement taken after the person invokes his privilege cannot be other than the product of compulsion, subtle or otherwise. Without the right to cut off questioning, the setting of in-custody interrogation operates on the individual to overcome free choice in producing a statement after the privilege has been once invoked. If the individual states that he wants an attorney, the interrogation must cease until an attorney is present. At that time, the individual must have an opportunity to confer with the attorney and to have him present during any subsequent questioning. If the individual cannot obtain an attorney and he indicates that he wants one before speaking to police, they must respect his decision to remain silent.

This does not mean, as some have suggested, that each police station must have a "station house lawyer" present at all times to advise prisoners. It does mean, however, that if police propose to interrogate a person they must make known to him that he is entitled to a lawyer and that if he cannot afford one, a lawyer will be provided for him prior to any interrogation. If authorities conclude that they will not provide counsel during a reasonable period of time in which investigation in the field is carried out, they may refrain from doing so without violating the person's Fifth Amendment privilege so long as they do not question him during that time.

If the interrogation continues without the presence of an attorney and a statement is taken, a heavy burden rests on the government to demonstrate that the defendant knowingly and intelligently waived his privilege against self-incrimination and his right to retained or appointed counsel. This Court has always set high standards of proof for the waiver of constitutional rights, and we reassert these standards as applied to in-custody interrogation. Since the State is responsible for establishing the isolated circumstances under which the interrogation takes place and has the only means of making available corroborated evidence of warnings given during incommunicado interrogation, the burden is rightly on its shoulders.

An express statement that the individual is willing to make a statement and does not want an attorney followed closely by a statement could constitute a waiver. But a valid waiver will not be presumed simply from the silence of the accused after warnings are given or simply from the fact that a confession was in fact eventually obtained.

Whatever the testimony of the authorities as to waiver of rights by an accused, the fact of lengthy interrogation or incommunicado incarceration before a statement is made is strong evidence that the accused did not validly waive his rights. In these circumstances the fact that the individual eventually made a statement is consistent with the conclusion that the compelling influence of the interrogation finally forced him to do so. It is inconsistent with any notion of a voluntary relinquishment of the privilege. Moreover, any evidence that the accused was threatened, tricked, or cajoled into a waiver will, of course, show that the defendant did not voluntarily waive his privilege. The requirement of warnings and waiver of rights is a fundamental with respect to the Fifth Amendment privilege and not simply a preliminary ritual to existing methods of interrogation.

The principles announced today deal with the protection which must be given to the privilege against self-incrimination when the individual is first subjected to police interrogation while in custody at the station or otherwise deprived of his freedom of action in any significant way. It is at this point that our adversary system of criminal proceedings commences, distinguishing itself at the outset from the inquisitorial system recognized in some countries. Under the system of warnings we delineate today or under any other system which may be devised and found effective, the safeguards to be erected about the privilege must come into play at this point.

Our decision is not intended to hamper the traditional function of police officers in investigating crime. When an individual is in custody on probable cause, the police may, of course, seek out evidence in the field to be used at trial against him. Such investigation may include inquiry of persons not under restraint. General on-the-scene questioning as to facts surrounding a crime or other general questioning of citizens in the fact-finding process is not affected by our holding. It is an act of responsible citizenship for individuals to give whatever information they may have to aid in law enforcement. In such situations the compelling atmosphere inherent in the process of in-custody interrogation is not necessarily present.

In dealing with statements obtained through interrogation, we do not purport to find all confessions inadmissible. Confessions remain a proper element in law enforcement. Any statement given freely and voluntarily without any compelling influences is, of course, admissible in evidence. The fundamental import of the privilege while an individual is in custody is not whether he is allowed to talk to the police without the benefit of warnings and counsel, but whether he can be interrogated. There is no requirement that police stop a person who enters a police station and states that he wishes to confess to a crime, or a person who calls the police to offer a confession or any other statement he desires to make. Volunteered statements of any kind are not barred by the Fifth Amendment and their admissibility is not affected by our holding today.

To summarize, we hold that when an individual is taken into custody or otherwise deprived of his freedom by the authorities in any significant way and is subjected to questioning, the privilege against self-incrimination is jeopardized. Procedural safeguards must be employed to protect the privilege and unless other fully effective means are adopted to notify the person of his right of silence and to assure that the exercise of the right will be scrupulously honored, the following measures are required. He must be warned prior to any questioning that he has the right to remain silent, that anything he says can be used against him in a court of law, that he has the right to the presence of an attorney, and that if he cannot afford an attorney one will be appointed for him prior to any questioning if he so desires. Opportunity to exercise these rights must be afforded to him throughout the interrogation. After such warnings have been given, and such opportunity afforded him, the individual may knowingly and intelligently waive these rights and agree to answer questions or make a statement. But unless and until such warnings and waiver are demonstrated by the prosecution at trial, no evidence obtained as a result of interrogation can be used against him.

IV

A recurrent argument made in these cases is that society's need for interrogation outweighs the privilege. This argument is not unfamiliar to this Court. The whole thrust of our foregoing discussion demonstrates that the Constitution has prescribed the rights of the individual when confronted with the power of government when it provided in the Fifth Amendment that an individual cannot be compelled to be a witness against himself. That right cannot be abridged. In this connection, one of our country's distinguished jurists has pointed out: "The quality of a nation's civilization can be largely measured by the methods it uses in the enforcement of its criminal law."

In announcing these principles, we are not unmindful of the burdens which law enforcement officials must bear, often under trying circumstances. We also fully recognize the obligation of all citizens to aid in enforcing the criminal laws. This Court, while protecting individual rights, has always given ample latitude to law enforcement agencies in the legitimate exercise of their duties. The limits we have placed on the interrogation process should not constitute an undue interference with a proper system of law enforcement. As we have noted, our decision does not in any way preclude police from carrying out their traditional investigatory functions. Although confessions may play an important role in some convictions, the cases before us present graphic examples of the overstatement of the "need" for confessions. In each case authorities conducted interrogations ranging up to five days in duration despite the presence, through standard investigating practices, of considerable evidence against each defendant.

Over the years the Federal Bureau of Investigation has compiled an exemplary record of effective law enforcement while advising any suspect or arrested person, at the outset of an interview, that he is not required to make a statement, that any statement may be used against him in court, that the individual may obtain the services of an attorney of his own choice and, more recently, that he has a right to free counsel if he is unable to pay. The practice of the FBI can readily be emulated by state and local

enforcement agencies. The argument that the FBI deals with different crimes than are dealt with by state authorities does not mitigate the significance of the FBI experience.

The experience in some other countries also suggests that the danger to law enforcement in curbs on interrogation is overplayed. The English procedure since 1912 under the Judges' Rules is significant. As recently strengthened, the Rules require that a cautionary warning be given an accused by a police officer as soon as he has evidence that affords reasonable grounds for suspicion; they also require that any statement made be given by the accused without questioning by police. The right of the individual to consult with an attorney during this period is expressly recognized.

The safeguards present under Scottish law may be even greater than in England. Scottish judicial decisions bar use in evidence of most confessions obtained through police interrogation. In India, confessions made to police not in the presence of a magistrate have been excluded by rule of evidence since 1872, at a time when it operated under British law. Identical provisions appear in the Evidence Ordinance of Ceylon, enacted in 1895.

Justice CLARK, dissenting.

I would continue to follow th[e] rule [that the use of involuntary confessions as evidence violates due process]. Under the "totality of circumstances" rule, I would consider in each case whether the police officer prior to custodial interrogation added the warning that the suspect might have counsel present at the interrogation and, further, that a court would appoint one at his request if he was too poor to employ counsel. In the absence of warnings, the burden would be on the State to prove that counsel was knowingly and intelligently waived or that in the totality of the circumstances, including the failure to give the necessary warnings, the confession was clearly voluntary.

Rather than employing the arbitrary Fifth Amendment rule which the Court lays down I would follow the more pliable dictates of the Due Process Clauses of the Fifth and Fourteenth Amendments which we are accustomed to administering and which we know from our cases are effective instruments in protecting persons in police custody. In this way we would not be acting in the dark nor in one full sweep changing the traditional rules of custodial interrogation which this Court has for so long recognized as a justifiable and proper tool in balancing individual rights against the rights of society. It will be soon enough to go further when we are able to appraise with somewhat better accuracy the effect of such a holding.

Justice HARLAN, whom Justice STEWART and Justice WHITE join, dissenting.

I believe the decision of the Court represents poor constitutional law and entails harmful consequences for the country at large. How serious these consequences may prove to be only time can tell. But the basic flaws in the Court's justification seem to me readily apparent now once all sides of the problem are considered.

I. INTRODUCTION

At the outset, it is well to note exactly what is required by the Court's new constitutional code of rules for confessions. The foremost requirement, upon which later admissibility of a confession depends, is that a fourfold warning be given to a person in custody before he is questioned, namely, that he has a right to remain silent, that anything he says may be used against him, that he has a right to have present an attorney during the questioning, and that if indigent he has a right to a lawyer without charge. To forgo these rights, some affirmative statement of rejection is seemingly required, and threats, tricks, or cajolings to obtain this waiver are forbidden. If before or during questioning the suspect seeks to invoke his right to remain silent, interrogation must be forgone or cease; a request for counsel brings about the same result until a lawyer is procured. Finally, there are a miscellany of minor directives, for example, the burden of proof of waiver is on the State, admissions and exculpatory statements are treated just like confessions, withdrawal of a waiver is always permitted, and so forth.

While the fine points of this scheme are far less clear than the Court admits, the tenor is quite apparent. The new rules are not designed to guard against police brutality or other unmistakably banned forms of coercion. Those who use third-degree tactics and deny them in court are equally able and destined to lie as skillfully about warnings and waivers. Rather, the thrust of the new rules is to negate all pressures, to reinforce the nervous or ignorant suspect, and ultimately to discourage any confession at all. The aim in short is toward "voluntariness" in a utopian sense, or to view it from a different angle, voluntariness with a vengeance.

To incorporate this notion into the Constitution requires a strained reading of history and precedent and a disregard of the very pragmatic concerns that alone may on occasion justify such strains. I believe that reasoned examination will show that the Due Process Clauses provide an adequate tool for coping with confessions and that, even if the Fifth Amendment privilege against self-incrimination be invoked, its precedents taken as a whole do not sustain the present rules. Viewed as a choice based on pure policy, these new rules prove to be a highly debatable, if not one-sided, appraisal of the competing interests, imposed over widespread objection, at the very time when judicial restraint is most called for by the circumstances.

II. POLICY CONSIDERATIONS

Examined as an expression of public policy, the Court's new regime proves so dubious that there can be no due compensation for its weakness in constitutional law. The foregoing discussion has shown, I think, how mistaken is the Court in implying that the Constitution has struck the balance in favor of the approach the Court takes. Rather, precedent reveals that the Fourteenth Amendment in practice has been construed to strike a different balance, that the Fifth Amendment gives the Court little solid support in this context, and that the Sixth Amendment should have no bearing at all. Legal history has been stretched before to satisfy deep needs of society. In this instance, however, the Court has not and cannot make the powerful showing that its new rules are plainly desirable in the context of our society, something which is surely demanded before those rules are engrafted onto the Constitution and imposed on every State and county in the land.

Without at all subscribing to the generally black picture of police conduct painted by the Court, I think it must be frankly recognized at the outset that police questioning allowable under due process precedents may inherently entail some pressure on the suspect and may seek advantage in his ignorance or weaknesses. The atmosphere and questioning techniques, proper and fair though they be, can in themselves exert a tug on the suspect to confess. The Court's new rules aim to offset these minor pressures and disadvantages intrinsic to any kind of police interrogation. The rules do not serve due process interests in preventing blatant coercion since, as I noted earlier, they do nothing to contain the policeman who is prepared to lie from the start. The rules work for reliability in confessions almost only in the Pickwickian sense that they can prevent some from being given at all. In short, the benefit of this new regime is simply to lessen or wipe out the inherent compulsion and inequalities to which the Court devotes some nine pages of description.

What the Court largely ignores is that its rules impair, if they will not eventually serve wholly to frustrate, an instrument of law enforcement that has long and quite reasonably been thought worth the price paid for it. There can be little doubt that the Court's new code would markedly decrease the number of confessions. To warn the suspect that he may remain silent and remind him that his confession may be used in court are minor obstructions. To require also an express waiver by the suspect and an end to questioning whenever he demurs must heavily handicap questioning. And to suggest or provide counsel for the suspect simply invites the end of the interrogation.

How much harm this decision will inflict on law enforcement cannot fairly be predicted with accuracy. Evidence on the role of confessions is notoriously incomplete, and little is added by the Court's reference to the FBI experience and the resources believed wasted in interrogation. We do know that some crimes cannot be solved without confessions, that ample expert testimony attests to their importance in crime control, and that the Court is taking a real risk with society's welfare in imposing its new regime on the country. The social costs of crime are too great to call the new rules anything but a hazardous experimentation.

In conclusion: Nothing in the letter or the spirit of the Constitution or in the precedents squares with the heavy-handed and one-sided action that is so precipitously taken by the Court in the name of fulfilling its constitutional responsibilities. The foray which the Court makes today brings to mind the wise and farsighted words of Justice Jackson: "This Court is forever adding new stories to the temples of constitutional law, and the temples have a way of collapsing when one story too many is added."

Miranda v. Arizona was enormously controversial when it was decided. The arguments for and against *Miranda* are described below. In 2000, the Supreme Court had the occasion to reconsider the decision and in a 7-2 decision emphatically reaffirmed it. United States v. Dickerson arose in an unusual procedural context. In 1968, two years after *Miranda*, Congress adopted a statute that provided that confessions shall be admissible as evidence in federal court, notwithstanding the failure to properly administer warnings, as long as the confession was voluntary. 18 U.S.C. §3501. From the Nixon administration through the Clinton presidency, every Justice Department, whether under a Democratic or a Republican president, refused to invoke this statute because of a belief that it was unconstitutional.

In *Dickerson*, a confession was excluded by the federal district court for failure to properly administer *Miranda* warnings. The government appealed. The United States Court of Appeals for the Fourth Circuit, on its own, raised §3501, asked for briefing as to its constitutionality, upheld the law, and held the confession was admissible because it was voluntary. The Supreme Court granted certiorari and reconsidered *Miranda* and its constitutional status.

DICKERSON v. UNITED STATES
530 U.S. 428 (2000)

Chief Justice REHNQUIST delivered the opinion of the Court.

In Miranda v. Arizona (1966), we held that certain warnings must be given before a suspect's statement made during custodial interrogation could be admitted in evidence. In the wake of that decision, Congress enacted 18 U.S.C. §3501, which in essence laid down a rule that the admissibility of such statements should turn only on whether or not they were voluntarily made. We hold that *Miranda*, being a constitutional decision of this Court, may not be in effect overruled by an Act of Congress, and we decline to overrule *Miranda* ourselves. We therefore hold that *Miranda* and its progeny in this Court govern the admissibility of statements made during custodial interrogation in both state and federal courts.

Given §3501's express designation of voluntariness as the touchstone of admissibility, its omission of any warning requirement, and the instruction for trial courts to consider a nonexclusive list of factors relevant to the circumstances of a confession, we agree with the Court of Appeals that Congress intended by its enactment to overrule *Miranda*. Because of the obvious conflict between our decision in *Miranda* and §3501, we must address whether Congress has constitutional authority to thus supersede *Miranda*

If Congress has such authority, §3501's totality-of-the-circumstances approach must prevail over *Miranda*'s requirement of warnings; if not, that section must yield to *Miranda*'s more specific requirements.

The law in this area is clear. This Court has supervisory authority over the federal courts, and we may use that authority to prescribe rules of evidence and procedure that are binding in those tribunals. However, the power to judicially create and enforce nonconstitutional "rules of procedure and evidence for the federal courts exists only in the absence of a relevant Act of Congress." Congress retains the ultimate authority to modify or set aside any judicially created rules of evidence and procedure that are not required by the Constitution.

But Congress may not legislatively supersede our decisions interpreting and applying the Constitution. This case therefore turns on whether the *Miranda* Court announced a constitutional rule or merely exercised its supervisory authority to regulate evidence in the absence of congressional direction.

[T]he Court of Appeals concluded that the protections announced in *Miranda* are not constitutionally required. We disagree with the Court of Appeals' conclusion, although we concede that there is language in some of our opinions that supports the view taken by that court. But first and foremost of the factors on the other side — that *Miranda* is a constitutional decision — is that both *Miranda* and two of its companion cases applied the rule to proceedings in state courts. Since that time, we have consistently applied *Miranda*'s rule to prosecutions arising in state courts. It is beyond dispute that we do not hold a supervisory power over the courts of the several States.

Additional support for our conclusion that *Miranda* is constitutionally based is found in the *Miranda* Court's invitation for legislative action to protect the constitutional right against coerced self-incrimination. However, the Court emphasized that it could not foresee "the potential alternatives for protecting the privilege which might be devised by Congress or the States," and it accordingly opined that the Constitution would not preclude legislative solutions that differed from the prescribed *Miranda* warnings but which were "at least as effective in apprising accused persons of their right of silence and in assuring a continuous opportunity to exercise it."

Miranda requires procedures that will warn a suspect in custody of his right to remain silent and which will assure the suspect that the exercise of that right will be honored. As discussed above, §3501 explicitly eschews a requirement of preinterrogation warnings in favor of an approach that looks to the administration of such warnings as only one factor in determining the voluntariness of a suspect's confession.

The dissent argues that it is judicial overreaching for this Court to hold §3501 unconstitutional unless we hold that the *Miranda* warnings are required by the Constitution, in the sense that nothing else will suffice to satisfy constitutional requirements. But we need not go further than *Miranda* to decide this case. In *Miranda*, the Court noted that reliance on the traditional totality-of-the-circumstances test raised a risk of overlooking an involuntary custodial confession, a risk that the Court found unacceptably great when the confession is offered in the case in chief to prove guilt. The Court therefore concluded that something more than the totality test was necessary. As discussed above, §3501 reinstates the totality test as sufficient. Section 3501 therefore cannot be sustained if *Miranda* is to remain the law.

Whether or not we would agree with *Miranda*'s reasoning and its resulting rule, were we addressing the issue in the first instance, the principles of stare decisis weigh heavily against overruling it now. While "'stare decisis is not an inexorable command,'" particularly when we are interpreting the Constitution, "even in constitutional cases, the doctrine carries such persuasive force that we have always required a departure from precedent to be supported by some 'special justification.'"

We do not think there is such justification for overruling *Miranda*. *Miranda* has become embedded in routine police practice to the point where the warnings have become part of our national culture. While we have overruled our precedents when subsequent cases have undermined their doctrinal underpinnings, we do not believe that this has happened to the *Miranda* decision. If anything, our subsequent cases have reduced the impact of the *Miranda* rule on legitimate law enforcement while reaffirming the decision's core ruling that unwarned statements may not be used as evidence in the prosecution's case in chief.

The disadvantage of the *Miranda* rule is that statements which may be by no means involuntary, made by a defendant who is aware of his "rights," may nonetheless be excluded and a guilty defendant go free as a result. But experience suggests that the totality-of-the-circumstances test which §3501 seeks to revive is more difficult than *Miranda* for law enforcement officers to conform to, and for courts to apply in a consistent manner.

In sum, we conclude that *Miranda* announced a constitutional rule that Congress may not supersede legislatively. Following the rule of stare decisis, we decline to overrule *Miranda* ourselves.

Justice SCALIA, with whom Justice THOMAS joins, dissenting.

Those to whom judicial decisions are an unconnected series of judgments that produce either favored or disfavored results will doubtless greet today's decision as a paragon of moderation, since it declines to overrule Miranda v. Arizona (1966). Those who understand the judicial process will appreciate that today's decision is not a reaffirmation of *Miranda*, but a radical revision of the most significant element of *Miranda* (as of all cases): the rationale that gives it a permanent place in our jurisprudence.

Marbury v. Madison (1803) held that an Act of Congress will not be enforced by the courts if what it prescribes violates the Constitution of the United States. That was the basis on which *Miranda* was decided. One will search today's opinion in vain, however, for a statement (surely simple enough to make) that what 18 U.S.C. §3501 prescribes — the use at trial of a voluntary confession, even when a *Miranda* warning or its equivalent has failed to be given — violates the Constitution. The reason the statement does not appear is not only (and perhaps not so much) that it would be absurd, inasmuch as §3501 excludes from trial precisely what the Constitution excludes from trial, viz., compelled confessions; but also that Justices whose votes are needed to compose today's majority are on record as believing that a violation of *Miranda* is not a violation of the Constitution.

And so, to justify today's agreed-upon result, the Court must adopt a significant new, if not entirely comprehensible, principle of constitutional law. As the Court chooses to describe that principle, statutes of Congress can be disregarded, not only when what they prescribe violates the Constitution, but when what they prescribe contradicts a decision of this Court that "announced a constitutional rule."[T]he only thing that can possibly mean in the context of this case is that this Court has the power, not merely to apply the Constitution but to expand it, imposing what it regards as useful "prophylactic" restrictions upon Congress and the States. That is an immense and frightening antidemocratic power, and it does not exist.

It takes only a small step to bring today's opinion out of the realm of power-judging and into the mainstream of legal reasoning: The Court need only go beyond its carefully couched iterations that "*Miranda* is a constitutional decision," that "*Miranda* is constitutionally based," that *Miranda* has "constitutional underpinnings," and come out and say quite clearly: "We reaffirm today that custodial interrogation that is not preceded by *Miranda* warnings or their equivalent violates the Constitution of the United States." It cannot say that, because a majority of the Court does not believe it. The Court therefore acts in plain violation of the Constitution when it denies effect to this Act of Congress.

I dissent from today's decision, and, until §3501 is repealed, will continue to apply it in all cases where there has been a sustainable finding that the defendant's confession was voluntary.

Despite the reaffirmation of *Miranda* in *Dickerson*, there remained an unanswered constitutional question. Is *Miranda* simply a rule of evidence that has no application until and unless a prosecutor seeks to admit a confession into evidence? Or is it a rule concerning police behavior under the Fifth Amendment? The Court confronted that question in deciding whether an individual could sue police officers for damages for a violation of *Miranda*. In Chavez v. Martinez, 538 U.S. 760 (2003), four justices took the former view of *Miranda*, but five rejected that position. Nonetheless, the Court held that there cannot be civil suits for violation of *Miranda*'s requirements. The case involved a man who was shot by the police and was questioned without *Miranda* warnings while being rushed to the hospital and in the emergency room. He sued for excessive force, which was handled separately, and also for the questioning without proper administration of *Miranda* warnings.

Justice Thomas, writing for a plurality of four (joined by Chief Justice Rehnquist and Justices O'Connor and Scalia), stated that the Fifth Amendment applied only if there is a criminal case and that

> [i]n our view, a "criminal case" at the very least requires the initiation of legal proceedings. We need not decide today the precise moment when a "criminal case" commences; it is enough to say that police questioning does not constitute a "case" any more than a private investigator's precomplaint activities constitute a "civil case." Statements compelled by police interrogations of course may not be used against a defendant at trial, but it is not until their use in a criminal case that a violation of the Self-Incrimination Clause occurs. The text of the Self-Incrimination Clause simply cannot support the view that the mere use of compulsive questioning, without more, violates the Constitution.

Justices Souter and Breyer disagreed with this conclusion but said that money damages are not necessary to enforce *Miranda*; the exclusionary rule is a sufficient enforcement mechanism. Justice Souter wrote:

> I do not, however, believe that Martinez can make the "powerful showing," subject to a realistic assessment of costs and risks, necessary to expand protection of the privilege against compelled self-incrimination to the point of the civil liability he asks us to recognize here. The most obvious drawback inherent in Martinez's purely Fifth Amendment claim to damages is its risk of global application in every instance of interrogation producing a statement inadmissible under Fifth and Fourteenth Amendment principles, or violating one of the complementary rules we have accepted in aid of the privilege against evidentiary use. If obtaining Martinez's statement is to be treated as a stand-alone violation of the privilege subject to compensation, why should the same not be true whenever the police obtain any involuntary self-incriminating statement, or whenever the government so much as threatens a penalty in derogation of the right to immunity, or whenever the police fail to honor *Miranda*? Martinez offers no limiting principle or reason to foresee a stopping place short of liability in all such cases.

Justices Stevens, Kennedy, and Ginsburg dissented. They also believed that the Fifth Amendment privilege against self-incrimination applies even if no statement is used as evidence against a defendant, and they believed that a damage remedy should be allowed for violations of the Fifth Amendment's requirements by the police. Justice Stevens wrote, "As a matter of fact, the interrogation of respondent was the functional equivalent of an attempt to obtain an involuntary confession from a prisoner by torturous methods. As a matter of law, that type of brutal police conduct constitutes an immediate deprivation of the prisoner's constitutionally protected interest in liberty. Because these propositions are so clear [Martinez should be entitled to damages for violation of his Fifth Amendment rights]." Justice Kennedy stated, "A constitutional right is traduced the moment torture or its close equivalents are brought to bear. Constitutional protection for a tortured suspect is not held in abeyance until some later criminal proceeding takes place." Justice Ginsburg declared, "I would hold that the Self-Incrimination Clause applies at the time and place police use severe compulsion to extract a statement from a suspect."

The issue of whether the privilege against self-incrimination applies only as a rule of evidence at trial is of great importance. For instance, may a person invoke the privilege against self-incrimination in a civil deposition or before a grand jury? The law is clear that the privilege can be invoked in these contexts. But under Justice Thomas's view, the privilege would not apply then and could not be invoked until and unless the prosecutor attempted to use the statements at trial against the defendant.

Given the importance of the issue and the closeness of the vote in Chavez v. Martinez, it is likely that the Court will return to the question in the years ahead.

2. *Is* Miranda *Desirable?*

The debate over *Miranda* began when it was decided and continues to this day. Three very different criticisms have been advanced. First, some argue that *Miranda* is ineffective; it does not succeed in curing the inherently coercive nature of in-custodial interrogation. Some studies seem to confirm this criticism. For example, a study was done by Yale law students of the impact of *Miranda* in New Haven, Connecticut, soon after the decision.[4] The study found that administering the warnings caused a person to stop the questioning in only 8 of 81 cases. Another study found that *Miranda* had little impact because virtually the same percentage of people talked to the police after receiving warnings as did without warnings.[5] Perhaps the lack of effect is because of the ability of police to undermine the warnings or perhaps it is just that in-custodial interrogation is inherently coercive and having the police read warnings cannot lessen that.

A second criticism of *Miranda* is exactly the opposite: *Miranda* prevents police from gaining confessions, and it allows guilty people to go free. Law professor and former federal district court judge Paul Cassell is the leading advocate of this view. Cassell reexamined the data and concluded that *Miranda* resulted in the loss of confessions in 3.8 percent of cases involving serious crimes and has led to guilty people escaping punishment.[6]

A third criticism of *Miranda* is based on constitutional interpretation and the role of the judiciary. Critics, including the dissenters in *Miranda* and *Dickerson*, argue that neither the text nor the history of the Fifth Amendment support the Court's requiring warnings be administered or a right to counsel during interrogation.[7]

---

4. Michael Wald et al., *Interrogations in New Haven: The Impact of Miranda*, 76 Yale L.J. 1519 (1967).

5. Richard J. Medalie, *Custodial Police Interrogation in Our Nation's Capital: The Attempt to Implement Miranda*, 66 Mich. L. Rev. 1347 (1968) (44 percent who received warnings talked to the police, whereas 42 percent who did not receive warnings talked to the police).

6. Paul G. Cassell, *Miranda's Social Costs: An Empirical Reassessment*, 90 Nw. L. Rev. 387 (1996).

7. *See, e.g.*, Joseph Grano, Confessions, Truth, and the Law 106 (1993).

On the other hand, *Miranda* has its defenders. They dispute that *Miranda* has had a significant effect in hampering law enforcement. Professor Stephen Schulhofer has responded at length to Judge Cassell, criticized his methodology, and concluded that "*Miranda*'s empirically detectable net damage to law enforcement is zero."[8] Professor Schulhofer also argues that *Miranda* is consistent with the original purpose of the Self-Incrimination Clause of the Fifth Amendment. He explains that the "privilege was intended primarily to bar pretrial examination by magistrates, the only form of pretrial interrogation known at the time."[9]

Defenders of *Miranda* argue that it provides clear guidance to police: Administer the simple warnings and follow the procedures outlines and there is a presumption that any confession is admissible. The Supreme Court has declared:

> *Miranda*'s holding has the virtue of informing police and prosecutors with speci-
> ficity as to what they may do in conducting custodial interrogation, and of inform-
> ing courts under what circumstances statements obtained during such inter-
> rogation are not admissible. This gain in specificity, which benefits the accused
> and the State alike, has been thought to outweigh the burdens that the decision
> in *Miranda* imposes on law enforcement agencies and the courts by requiring
> the suppression of trustworthy and highly probative evidence even though the
> confession might be voluntary under traditional Fifth Amendment analysis.

Fare v. Michael C., 442 U.S. 707 (1979).

Professor Richard Leo has argued that *Miranda* has had a significant effect in increasing professional behavior by police officers and enhancing the public's awareness of constitutional rights.[10] As Chief Justice Rehnquist stated in *Dickerson*, "*Miranda* has become embedded in routine police practice to the point where the warnings have become part of our national culture."

What, if anything, needs to be done obviously depends on one's views of this debate. Critics who believe that *Miranda* hampers law enforcement would like to see it overruled. Critics who think that *Miranda* has not done enough to protect suspects would like to see additional protections, such as a requirement that all in-custodial interrogations be videotaped. Ultimately, the underlying issue is the same as in examining all police investigative techniques: how to balance the need for effective law enforcement tools with the desire to prevent police abuse, protect the dignity of the individual, and lessen the likelihood that innocent people will be convicted.

---

8. Stephen Schulhofer, *Miranda's Practical Effect: "Substantial Benefits and Surprisingly Small Costs,"* 90 Nw. U. L. Rev. 500 (1996).

9. Stephen Schulhofer, *Reconsidering Miranda and the Fifth Amendment,* in The Bill of Rights: Original Meaning and Original Understanding 289 (Eugene W. Hickok, Jr. ed., 1991).

10. Richard A. Leo, *The Impact of Miranda Revisited,* 86 J. Crim. L. & Criminology 621 (1996).

3.   *What Are the Requirements for* Miranda *to Apply?*

Miranda requires that during in-custodial interrogation police administer the prescribed warnings, make counsel available, and behave as described in the decision. Therefore, three key questions arise in applying *Miranda*: (1) When is a person "in custody"? (2) What is interrogation? (3) What police actions are sufficient to meet the requirements of *Miranda*?

a.   **When Is a Person "in Custody"?**

The Supreme Court in *Miranda* focused on the coercion inherent to in-custodial interrogation. The Court repeatedly has reaffirmed that this is a requirement in order for *Miranda* to apply. For example, soon after *Miranda*, in Orozco v. Texas, 394 U.S. 324 (1969), the Court found that a person who has been arrested is in custody and that *Miranda* warnings must be given, even if the questioning occurs in a person's home. In *Orozco*, a man was a suspect in a murder. Justice Black describes what happened:

> At about 4 A.M. four police officers arrived at petitioner's boardinghouse, were admitted by an unidentified woman, and were told that petitioner was asleep in the bedroom. All four officers entered the bedroom and began to question petitioner. From the moment he gave his name, according to the testimony of one of the officers, petitioner was not free to go where he pleased but was "under arrest." The officers asked him if he had been to the El Farleto restaurant that night and when he answered "yes" he was asked if he owned a pistol. Petitioner admitted owning one. After being asked a second time where the pistol was located, he admitted that it was in the washing machine in a backroom of the boardinghouse. Ballistics tests indicated that the gun found in the washing machine was the gun that fired the fatal shot. The trial testimony clearly shows that the officers questioned petitioner about incriminating facts without first informing him of his right to remain silent, his right to have the advice of a lawyer before making any statement, and his right to have a lawyer appointed to assist him if he could not afford to hire one.

The Court concluded, "[W]e hold that the use of these admissions obtained in the absence of the required warnings was a flat violation of the Self-Incrimination Clause of the Fifth Amendment as construed in *Miranda*." The Court explained:

> The State has argued here that since petitioner was interrogated on his own bed, in familiar surroundings, our *Miranda* holding should not apply. It is true that the Court did say in *Miranda* that "compulsion to speak in the isolated setting of the police station may well be greater than in courts or other official investigations, where there are often impartial observers to guard against intimidation or trickery." But the opinion iterated and reiterated the absolute necessity for officers interrogating people "in custody" to give the described warnings. According to the officer's testimony, petitioner was under arrest and not free to leave when he was questioned in his bedroom in the early hours of the morning. The *Miranda*

opinion declared that the warnings were required when the person being interrogated was "in custody at the station or otherwise deprived of his freedom of action in any significant way." We do not, as the dissent implies, expand or extend to the slightest extent our *Miranda* decision. We do adhere to our well-considered holding in that case and therefore reverse the conviction below.

By contrast, a person who is free to leave is not in custody and no *Miranda* warnings are required. Oregon v. Mathiason expresses this.

OREGON v. MATHIASON

429 U.S. 492 (1977)

PER CURIAM.

Respondent Carl Mathiason was convicted of first-degree burglary after a bench trial in which his confession was critical to the State's case. At trial he moved to suppress the confession as the fruit of questioning by the police not preceded by the warnings required in Miranda v. Arizona (1966).

The Supreme Court of Oregon described the factual situation surrounding the confession as follows: "An officer of the State Police investigated a theft at a residence near Pendleton. He asked the lady of the house which had been burglarized if she suspected anyone. She replied that the defendant was the only one she could think of. The defendant was a parolee and a 'close associate' of her son. The officer tried to contact defendant on three or four occasions with no success. Finally, about 25 days after the burglary, the officer left his card at defendant's apartment with a note asking him to call because 'I'd like to discuss something with you.' The next afternoon the defendant did call. The officer asked where it would be convenient to meet. The defendant had no preference; so the officer asked if the defendant could meet him at the state patrol office in about an hour and a half, about 5:00 P.M. The patrol office was about two blocks from defendant's apartment. The building housed several state agencies.

"The officer met defendant in the hallway, shook hands and took him into an office. The defendant was told he was not under arrest. The door was closed. The two sat across a desk. The police radio in another room could be heard. The officer told defendant he wanted to talk to him about a burglary and that his truthfulness would possibly be considered by the district attorney or judge. The officer further advised that the police believed defendant was involved in the burglary and [falsely stated that] defendant's fingerprints were found at the scene. The defendant sat for a few minutes and then said he had taken the property. This occurred within five minutes after defendant had come to the office. The officer then advised defendant of his *Miranda* rights and took a taped confession.

"At the end of the taped conversation the officer told defendant he was not arresting him at this time; he was released to go about his job and return to his family. The officer said he was referring the case to the district attorney for him to determine whether criminal charges would be brought. It was 5:30 P.M. when the defendant left the office."

Our decision in *Miranda* set forth rules of police procedure applicable to "custodial interrogation." "By custodial interrogation, we mean questioning initiated by law enforcement officers after a person has been taken into custody or otherwise deprived of his freedom of action in any significant way." Subsequently we have found the *Miranda* principle applicable to questioning which takes place in a prison setting during a suspect's term of imprisonment on a separate offense, Mathis v. United States (1968), and to questioning taking place in a suspect's home, after he has been arrested and is no longer free to go where he pleases, Orozco v. Texas (1969).

In the present case, however, there is no indication that the questioning took place in a context where respondent's freedom to depart was restricted in any way. He came voluntarily to the police station, where he was immediately informed that he was not under arrest. At the close of a 1/2-hour interview respondent did in fact leave the police station without hindrance. It is clear from these facts that Mathiason was not in custody "or otherwise deprived of his freedom of action in any significant way."

Such a noncustodial situation is not converted to one in which *Miranda* applies simply because a reviewing court concludes that, even in the absence of any formal arrest or restraint on freedom of movement, the questioning took place in a "coercive environment." Any interview of one suspected of a crime by a police officer will have coercive aspects to it, simply by virtue of the fact that the police officer is part of a law enforcement system which may ultimately cause the suspect to be charged with a crime. But police officers are not required to administer *Miranda* warnings to everyone whom they question. Nor is the requirement of warnings to be imposed simply because the questioning takes place in the station house, or because the questioned person is one whom the police suspect. *Miranda* warnings are required only where there has been such a restriction on a person's freedom as to render him "in custody." It was that sort of coercive environment to which *Miranda* by its terms was made applicable, and to which it is limited.

Justice MARSHALL, dissenting.

The respondent in this case was interrogated behind closed doors at police headquarters in connection with a burglary investigation. He had been named by the victim of the burglary as a suspect, and was told by the police that they believed he was involved. He was falsely informed that his fingerprints had been found at the scene, and in effect was advised that by cooperating with the police he could help himself. Not until after he had confessed was he given the warnings set forth in Miranda v. Arizona (1966).

The Court today holds that for constitutional purposes all this is irrelevant because respondent had not "'been taken into custody or otherwise deprived of his freedom of action in any significant way.'" I do not believe that such a determination is possible on the record before us. It is true that respondent was not formally placed under arrest, but surely formalities alone cannot control. At the very least, if respondent entertained an objectively reasonable belief that he was not free to leave during the questioning, then he was "deprived of his freedom of action in a significant way." Plainly the respondent could have so believed, after being told by the police that they thought he was involved in a burglary and that his fingerprints had been found at the scene.

In my view, even if respondent were not in custody, the coercive elements in the instant case were so pervasive as to require *Miranda*-type warnings. Respondent was interrogated in "privacy" and in "unfamiliar surroundings," factors on which *Miranda* places great stress. The investigation had focused on respondent. And respondent was subjected to some of the "deceptive stratagems," which called forth the *Miranda* decision. I therefore agree with the Oregon Supreme Court that to excuse the absence of warnings given these facts is "contrary to the rationale expressed in *Miranda*."

Similarly, in Beckwith v. United States, 425 U.S. 341 (1976), the Court held that a special agent of the Internal Revenue Service, investigating potential criminal income tax violations, in an interview with a taxpayer, not in custody, is not required to give the warnings called for in Miranda v. Arizona. The Court explained, "An interview with Government agents in a situation such as the one shown by this record simply does not present the elements which the *Miranda* Court found so inherently coercive as to require its holding. Although the 'focus' of an investigation may indeed have been on Beckwith at the time of the interview in the sense that it was his tax liability which was under scrutiny, he hardly found himself in the custodial situation described by the *Miranda* Court as the basis for its holding." Likewise, in Minnesota v. Murphy, 465 U.S. 420 (1984), the Court held that statements made in a meeting with a person's probation officer were not uttered in a custodial context and no *Miranda* warnings were required. Although a person on probation is deemed to be in custody for some purposes, the Court explained that "[u]nder the narrower standard appropriate in the *Miranda* context, it is clear that Murphy was not 'in custody' for purposes of receiving *Miranda* protection since there was no 'formal arrest or restraint on freedom of movement' of the degree associated with a formal arrest."

The Supreme Court has emphasized that the determination of whether a person is in custody is an objective one, not a subjective one focusing on the individual's or the officer's state of mind. For example, in Stansbury v. California, 511 U.S. 318 (1994), the Court held that "an officer's subjective and undisclosed view concerning whether the person being interrogated is a suspect is irrelevant to the assessment whether the person is in custody." The Court said that "[o]ur decisions make clear that the initial determination of custody depends on the objective circumstances of the interrogation, not on the subjective views harbored by either the interrogating officers or the person being questioned."

The Court considered the "objective" determination of custody in J.D.B. v. North Carolina in deciding whether the age of a suspect is relevant in determining whether he or she is in custody.

J.D.B. v. NORTH CAROLINA
564 U.S. 261 (2011)

Justice SOTOMAYOR delivered the opinion of the Court.

This case presents the question whether the age of a child subjected to police questioning is relevant to the custody analysis of *Miranda v. Arizona* (1966). It is beyond dispute that children will often feel bound to submit to police questioning when an adult in the same circumstances would feel free to leave. Seeing no reason for police officers or courts to blind themselves to that commonsense reality, we hold that a child's age properly informs the *Miranda* custody analysis.

I

Petitioner J.D.B. was a 13-year-old, seventh-grade student attending class at Smith Middle School in Chapel Hill, North Carolina when he was removed from his classroom by a uniformed police officer, escorted to a closed-door conference room, and questioned by police for at least half an hour.

This was the second time that police questioned J.D.B. in the span of a week. Five days earlier, two home break-ins occurred, and various items were stolen. Police stopped and questioned J.D.B. after he was seen behind a residence in the neighborhood where the crimes occurred. That same day, police also spoke to J.D.B.'s grandmother — his legal guardian — as well as his aunt.

Police later learned that a digital camera matching the description of one of the stolen items had been found at J.D.B.'s middle school and seen in J.D.B.'s possession. Investigator DiCostanzo, the juvenile investigator with the local police force who had been assigned to the case, went to the school to question J.D.B. Upon arrival, DiCostanzo informed the uniformed police officer on detail to the school (a so-called school resource officer), the assistant principal, and an administrative intern that he was there to question J.D.B. about the break-ins. Although DiCostanzo asked the school administrators to verify J.D.B.'s date of birth, address, and parent contact information from school records, neither the police officers nor the school administrators contacted J.D.B.'s grandmother.

The uniformed officer interrupted J.D.B.'s afternoon social studies class, removed J.D.B. from the classroom, and escorted him to a school conference room. There, J.D.B. was met by DiCostanzo, the assistant principal, and the administrative intern. The door to the conference room was closed. With the two police officers and the two administrators present, J.D.B. was questioned for the next 30 to 45 minutes. Prior to the commencement of questioning, J.D.B. was given neither *Miranda* warnings nor the opportunity to speak to his grandmother. Nor was he informed that he was free to leave the room.

Questioning began with small talk — discussion of sports and J.D.B.'s family life. DiCostanzo asked, and J.D.B. agreed, to discuss the events of the prior weekend. Denying any wrongdoing, J.D.B. explained that he had been in the neighborhood where the crimes occurred because he was seeking work mowing lawns. DiCostanzo pressed J.D.B. for additional detail about his efforts to obtain work; asked J.D.B. to explain a prior incident, when one of the victims returned home to find J.D.B. behind her house; and confronted J.D.B. with the stolen camera. The assistant principal urged J.D.B. to "do the right thing," warning J.D.B. that "the truth always comes out in the end."

Eventually, J.D.B. asked whether he would "still be in trouble" if he returned the "stuff." In response, DiCostanzo explained that return of the stolen items would be helpful, but "this thing is going to court" regardless. DiCostanzo then warned that he may need to seek a secure custody order if he believed that J.D.B. would continue to break into other homes. When J.D.B. asked what a secure custody order was, DiCostanzo explained that "it's where you get sent to juvenile detention before court."

After learning of the prospect of juvenile detention, J.D.B. confessed that he and a friend were responsible for the break-ins. DiCostanzo only then informed J.D.B. that he could refuse to answer the investigator's questions and that he was free to leave. Asked whether he understood, J.D.B. nodded and provided further detail, including information about the location of the stolen items. Eventually J.D.B. wrote a statement, at DiCostanzo's request. When the bell rang indicating the end of the schoolday, J.D.B. was allowed to leave to catch the bus home.

Two juvenile petitions were filed against J.D.B., each alleging one count of breaking and entering and one count of larceny. J.D.B.'s public defender moved to suppress his statements and the evidence derived therefrom, arguing that suppression was necessary because J.D.B. had been "interrogated by police in a custodial setting without being afforded *Miranda* warning[s]," and because his statements were involuntary under the totality of the circumstances test. After a suppression hearing at which DiCostanzo and J.D.B. testified, the trial court denied the motion, deciding that J.D.B. was not in custody at the time of the schoolhouse interrogation and that his statements were voluntary.

II

Any police interview of an individual suspected of a crime has "coercive aspects to it." Only those interrogations that occur while a suspect is in police custody, however, "heighte[n] the risk" that statements obtained are not the product of the suspect's free choice.

By its very nature, custodial police interrogation entails "inherently compelling pressures." Even for an adult, the physical and psychological isolation of custodial interrogation can "undermine the individual's will to resist and . . . compel him to speak where he would not otherwise do so freely." Indeed, the pressure of custodial interrogation is so immense that it "can induce a frighteningly high percentage of people to confess to crimes they never committed." That risk is all the more troubling — and recent studies suggest, all the more acute — when the subject of custodial interrogation is a juvenile.

Recognizing that the inherently coercive nature of custodial interrogation "blurs the line between voluntary and involuntary statements," this Court in *Miranda* adopted a set of prophylactic measures designed to safeguard the constitutional guarantee against self-incrimination.

Because these measures protect the individual against the coercive nature of custodial interrogation, they are required "'only where there has been such a restriction on a person's freedom as to render him "in custody."'" As we have repeatedly emphasized, whether a suspect is "in custody" is an objective inquiry.

The benefit of the objective custody analysis is that it is "designed to give clear guidance to the police."

The State and its *amici* contend that a child's age has no place in the custody analysis, no matter how young the child subjected to police questioning. We cannot agree. In some circumstances, a child's age "would have affected how a reasonable person" in the suspect's position "would perceive his or her freedom to leave." That is, a reasonable child subjected to police questioning will sometimes feel pressured to submit when a reasonable adult would feel free to go. We think it clear that courts can account for that reality without doing any damage to the objective nature of the custody analysis.

A child's age is far "more than a chronological fact." It is a fact that "generates commonsense conclusions about behavior and perception." Such conclusions apply broadly to children as a class. And, they are self-evident to anyone who was a child once himself, including any police officer or judge.

Time and again, this Court has drawn these commonsense conclusions for itself. We have observed that children "generally are less mature and responsible than adults"; that they "often lack the experience, perspective, and judgment to recognize and avoid choices that could be detrimental to them"; that they "are more vulnerable or susceptible to . . . outside pressures" than adults; and so on. Addressing the specific context of police interrogation, we have observed that events that "would leave a man cold and unimpressed can overawe and overwhelm a lad in his early teens." Describing no one child in particular, these observations restate what "any parent knows" — indeed, what any person knows — about children generally.

Our various statements to this effect are far from unique. The law has historically reflected the same assumption that children characteristically lack the capacity to exercise mature judgment and possess only an incomplete ability to understand the world around them. Indeed, even where a "reasonable person" standard otherwise applies, the common law has reflected the reality that children are not adults. In negligence suits, for instance, where liability turns on what an objectively reasonable person would do in the circumstances, "[a]ll American jurisdictions accept the idea that a person's childhood is a relevant circumstance" to be considered.

As this discussion establishes, "[o]ur history is replete with laws and judicial recognition" that children cannot be viewed simply as miniature adults. We see no justification for taking a different course here. So long as the child's age was known to the officer at the time of the interview, or would have been objectively apparent to any reasonable officer, including age as part of the custody analysis requires officers neither to consider circumstances "unknowable" to them, nor to "anticipat[e] the frailties or idiosyncrasies" of the particular suspect whom they question. The same "wide basis of community experience" that makes it possible, as an objective matter, "to determine what is to be expected" of children in other contexts, likewise makes it possible to know what to expect of children subjected to police questioning.

In fact, in many cases involving juvenile suspects, the custody analysis would be nonsensical absent some consideration of the suspect's age. This case is a prime example. Were the court precluded from taking J.D.B.'s youth into account, it would be forced to evaluate the circumstances present here through the eyes of a reasonable person of average years. In other words, how would a reasonable adult understand his situation, after being removed from a seventh-grade social studies class by a uniformed school resource officer; being encouraged by his assistant principal to "do the right thing"; and being warned by a police investigator of the prospect of juvenile detention and separation from his guardian and primary caretaker? To describe such an inquiry is to demonstrate its absurdity. Neither officers nor courts can reasonably evaluate the effect of objective circumstances that, by their nature, are specific to children without accounting for the age of the child subjected to those circumstances.

Indeed, although the dissent suggests that concerns "regarding the application of the *Miranda* custody rule to minors can be accommodated by considering the unique circumstances present when minors are questioned in school," the effect of the schoolhouse setting cannot be disentangled from the identity of the person questioned. A student—whose presence at school is compulsory and whose disobedience at school is cause for disciplinary action—is in a far different position than, say, a parent volunteer on school grounds to chaperone an event, or an adult from the community on school grounds to attend a basketball game. Without asking whether the person "questioned in school" is a "minor," the coercive effect of the schoolhouse setting is unknowable.

Reviewing the question *de novo* today, we hold that so long as the child's age was known to the officer at the time of police questioning, or would have been objectively apparent to a reasonable officer, its inclusion in the custody analysis is consistent with the objective nature of that test. This is not to say that a child's age will be a determinative, or even a significant, factor in every case. It is, however, a reality that courts cannot simply ignore.

The question remains whether J.D.B. was in custody when police interrogated him. We remand for the state courts to address that question, this time taking account of all of the relevant circumstances of the interrogation, including J.D.B.'s age at the time.

Justice ALITO, with whom THE CHIEF JUSTICE, Justice SCALIA, and Justice THOMAS join, dissenting.

The Court's decision in this case may seem on first consideration to be modest and sensible, but in truth it is neither. It is fundamentally inconsistent with one of the main justifications for the *Miranda* rule: the perceived need for a clear rule that can be easily applied in all cases. And today's holding is not needed to protect the constitutional rights of minors who are questioned by the police.

Miranda's prophylactic regime places a high value on clarity and certainty. Dissatisfied with the highly fact-specific constitutional rule against the admission of involuntary confessions, the *Miranda* Court set down rigid standards that often require courts to ignore personal characteristics that may be highly relevant to a particular suspect's actual susceptibility to police pressure. This rigidity, however, has brought with it one of *Miranda*'s principal strengths — "the ease and clarity of its application" by law enforcement officials and courts. A key contributor to this clarity, at least up until now, has been *Miranda*'s objective reasonable-person test for determining custody.

Miranda's custody requirement is based on the proposition that the risk of unconstitutional coercion is heightened when a suspect is placed under formal arrest or is subjected to some functionally equivalent limitation on freedom of movement. When this custodial threshold is reached, *Miranda* warnings must precede police questioning. But in the interest of simplicity, the custody analysis considers only whether, under the circumstances, a hypothetical reasonable person would consider himself to be confined.

Many suspects, of course, will differ from this hypothetical reasonable person. Some, including those who have been hardened by past interrogations, may have no need for *Miranda* warnings at all. And for other suspects — those who are unusually sensitive to the pressures of police questioning — *Miranda* warnings may come too late to be of any use. That is a necessary consequence of *Miranda*'s rigid standards, but it does not mean that the constitutional rights of these especially sensitive suspects are left unprotected. A vulnerable defendant can still turn to the constitutional rule against *actual* coercion and contend that that his confession was extracted against his will.

Today's decision shifts the *Miranda* custody determination from a one-size-fits-all reasonable-person test into an inquiry that must account for at least one individualized characteristic — age — that is thought to correlate with susceptibility to coercive pressures. Age, however, is in no way the only personal characteristic that may correlate with pliability, and in future cases the Court will be forced to choose between two unpalatable alternatives. It may choose to limit today's decision by arbitrarily distinguishing a suspect's age from other personal characteristics — such as intelligence, education, occupation, or prior experience with law enforcement — that may also correlate with susceptibility to coercive pressures. Or, if the Court is unwilling to draw these arbitrary lines, it will be forced to effect a fundamental transformation of the *Miranda* custody test — from a clear, easily applied prophylactic rule into a highly fact-intensive standard resembling the voluntariness test that the *Miranda* Court found to be unsatisfactory.

For at least three reasons, there is no need to go down this road. First, many minors subjected to police interrogation are near the age of majority, and for these suspects the one-size-fits-all *Miranda* custody rule may not be a bad fit. Second, many of the difficulties in applying the *Miranda* custody rule to minors arise because of the unique circumstances present when the police conduct interrogations at school. The *Miranda* custody rule has always taken into account the setting in which questioning occurs, and accounting for the school setting in such cases will address many of these problems. Third, in cases like the one now before us, where the suspect is especially young, courts applying the constitutional voluntariness standard can take special care to ensure that incriminating statements were not obtained through coercion.

Safeguarding the constitutional rights of minors does not require the extreme makeover of *Miranda* that today's decision may portend.

The Court rests its decision to inject personal characteristics into the *Miranda* custody inquiry on the principle that judges applying *Miranda* cannot "blind themselves to . . . commonsense reality." But the Court's shift is fundamentally at odds with the clear prophylactic rules that *Miranda* has long enforced. *Miranda* frequently requires judges to blind themselves to the reality that many un-Mirandized custodial confessions are "by no means involuntary" or coerced. It also requires police to provide a rote recitation of *Miranda* warnings that many suspects already know and could likely recite from memory. Under today's new, "reality"-based approach to the doctrine, perhaps these and other principles of our *Miranda* jurisprudence will, like the custody standard, now be ripe for modification. Then, bit by bit, *Miranda* will lose the clarity and ease of application that has long been viewed as one of its chief justifications.

The cases thus establish that a person is in custody if, from an objective perspective, the person is under arrest. What if the person is not under arrest but would not feel free to leave. In other words, what about questioning during a traffic stop? Is the person in custody in that situation for purposes of *Miranda*?

BERKEMER v. McCARTY

468 U.S. 420 (1984)

Justice MARSHALL delivered the opinion of the Court.

This case presents two related questions: First, does our decision in Miranda v. Arizona (1966), govern the admissibility of statements made during custodial interrogation by a suspect accused of a misdemeanor traffic offense? Second, does the roadside questioning of a motorist detained pursuant to a traffic stop constitute custodial interrogation for the purposes of the doctrine enunciated in *Miranda?*

I

The parties have stipulated to the essential facts. On the evening of March 31, 1980, Trooper Williams of the Ohio State Highway Patrol observed respondent's car weaving in and out of a lane on Interstate Highway 270. After following the car for two miles, Williams forced respondent to stop and asked him to get out of the vehicle. When respondent complied, Williams noticed that he was having difficulty standing. At that point, "Williams concluded that [respondent] would be charged with a traffic offense and, therefore, his freedom to leave the scene was terminated." However, respondent was not told that he would be taken into custody. Williams then asked respondent to perform a field sobriety test, commonly known as a "balancing test." Respondent could not do so without falling.

While still at the scene of the traffic stop, Williams asked respondent whether he had been using intoxicants. Respondent replied that "he had consumed two beers and had smoked several joints of marijuana a short time before." Respondent's speech was slurred, and Williams had difficulty understanding him. Williams thereupon formally placed respondent under arrest and transported him in the patrol car to the Franklin County Jail.

At the jail, respondent was given an intoxilyzer test to determine the concentration of alcohol in his blood. The test did not detect any alcohol whatsoever in respondent's system. Williams then resumed questioning respondent in order to obtain information for inclusion in the State Highway Patrol Alcohol Influence Report. Respondent answered affirmatively a question whether he had been drinking. When then asked if he was under the influence of alcohol, he said, "I guess, barely." Williams next asked respondent to indicate on the form whether the marijuana he had smoked had been treated with any chemicals. In the section of the report headed "Remarks," respondent wrote, "No ang[el] dust or PCP in the pot. Rick McCarty."

At no point in this sequence of events did Williams or anyone else tell respondent that he had a right to remain silent, to consult with an attorney, and to have an attorney appointed for him if he could not afford one.

Respondent was charged with operating a motor vehicle while under the influence of alcohol and/or drugs in violation of Ohio Rev. Code Ann.

§4511.19. Under Ohio law, that offense is a first-degree misdemeanor and is punishable by fine or imprisonment for up to six months.

Respondent moved to exclude the various incriminating statements he had made to Trooper Williams on the ground that introduction into evidence of those statements would violate the Fifth Amendment insofar as he had not been informed of his constitutional rights prior to his interrogation. When the trial court denied the motion, respondent pleaded "no contest" and was found guilty. He was sentenced to 90 days in jail, 80 of which were suspended, and was fined $300, $100 of which were suspended.

II

In the years since the decision in *Miranda*, we have frequently reaffirmed the central principle established by that case: if the police take a suspect into custody and then ask him questions without informing him of the rights enumerated above, his responses cannot be introduced into evidence to establish his guilt. Petitioner asks us to carve an exception out of the foregoing principle. When the police arrest a person for allegedly committing a misdemeanor traffic offense and then ask him questions without telling him his constitutional rights, petitioner argues, his responses should be admissible against him. We cannot agree.

One of the principal advantages of the doctrine that suspects must be given warnings before being interrogated while in custody is the clarity of that rule. The exception to *Miranda* proposed by petitioner would substantially undermine this crucial advantage of the doctrine. The police often are unaware when they arrest a person whether he may have committed a misdemeanor or a felony.

It might be argued that the police would not need to make such guesses; whenever in doubt, they could ensure compliance with the law by giving the full *Miranda* warnings. It cannot be doubted, however, that in some cases a desire to induce a suspect to reveal information he might withhold if informed of his rights would induce the police not to take the cautious course.

Equally importantly, the doctrinal complexities that would confront the courts if we accepted petitioner's proposal would be Byzantine. Difficult questions quickly spring to mind: For instance, investigations into seemingly minor offenses sometimes escalate gradually into investigations into more serious matters; at what point in the evolution of an affair of this sort would the police be obliged to give *Miranda* warnings to a suspect in custody? What evidence would be necessary to establish that an arrest for a misdemeanor offense was merely a pretext to enable the police to interrogate the suspect (in hopes of obtaining information about a felony) without providing him the safeguards prescribed by *Miranda*? The litigation necessary to resolve such matters would be time-consuming and disruptive of law enforcement. And the end result would be an elaborate set of rules, interlaced with exceptions and subtle distinctions, discriminating between different kinds of custodial interrogations. Neither the police nor criminal defendants would benefit from such a development.

We do not suggest that there is any reason to think improper efforts were made in this case to induce respondent to make damaging admissions. More generally, we have no doubt that, in conducting most custodial interrogations of persons arrested for misdemeanor traffic offenses, the police behave responsibly and do not deliberately exert pressures upon the suspect to confess against his will. But the same might be said of custodial interrogations of persons arrested for felonies. The purposes of the safeguards prescribed by *Miranda* are to ensure that the police do not coerce or trick captive suspects into confessing, to relieve the "'inherently compelling pressures'" generated by the custodial setting itself, "which work to undermine the individual's will to resist," and as much as possible to free courts from the task of scrutinizing individual cases to try to determine, after the fact, whether particular confessions were voluntary. Those purposes are implicated as much by in-custody questioning of persons suspected of misdemeanors as they are by questioning of persons suspected of felonies.

Petitioner's second argument is that law enforcement would be more expeditious and effective in the absence of a requirement that persons arrested for traffic offenses be informed of their rights. Again, we are unpersuaded. The occasions on which the police arrest and then interrogate someone suspected only of a misdemeanor traffic offense are rare. The police are already well accustomed to giving *Miranda* warnings to persons taken into custody. Adherence to the principle that all suspects must be given such warnings will not significantly hamper the efforts of the police to investigate crimes.

We hold therefore that a person subjected to custodial interrogation is entitled to the benefit of the procedural safeguards enunciated in *Miranda*, regardless of the nature or severity of the offense of which he is suspected or for which he was arrested.

III

To assess the admissibility of the self-incriminating statements made by respondent prior to his formal arrest, we are obliged to address a second issue concerning the scope of our decision in *Miranda*: whether the roadside questioning of a motorist detained pursuant to a routine traffic stop should be considered "custodial interrogation." Respondent urges that it should, on the ground that *Miranda* by its terms applies whenever "a person has been taken into custody or otherwise deprived of his freedom of action in any significant way." Petitioner contends that a holding that every detained motorist must be advised of his rights before being questioned would constitute an unwarranted extension of the *Miranda* doctrine.

It must be acknowledged at the outset that a traffic stop significantly curtails the "freedom of action" of the driver and the passengers, if any, of the detained vehicle. Under the law of most States, it is a crime either to ignore a policeman's signal to stop one's car or, once having stopped, to drive away without permission. Certainly few motorists would feel free either to disobey a directive to pull over or to leave the scene of a traffic stop without being told they might do so. Partly for these reasons, we have long acknowledged that "stopping an automobile and detaining its occupants constitute a 'seizure' within the meaning of [the Fourth] Amendmen[t], even though the purpose of the stop is limited and the resulting detention quite brief."

However, we decline to accord talismanic power to the phrase in the *Miranda* opinion emphasized by respondent. Fidelity to the doctrine announced in *Miranda* requires that it be enforced strictly, but only in those types of situations in which the concerns that powered the decision are implicated. Thus, we must decide whether a traffic stop exerts upon a detained person pressures that sufficiently impair his free exercise of his privilege against self-incrimination to require that he be warned of his constitutional rights.

Two features of an ordinary traffic stop mitigate the danger that a person questioned will be induced "to speak where he would not otherwise do so freely," Miranda v. Arizona. First, detention of a motorist pursuant to a traffic stop is presumptively temporary and brief. The vast majority of roadside detentions last only a few minutes.

Second, circumstances associated with the typical traffic stop are not such that the motorist feels completely at the mercy of the police. To be sure, the aura of authority surrounding an armed, uniformed officer and the knowledge that the officer has some discretion in deciding whether to issue a citation, in combination, exert some pressure on the detainee to respond to questions. But other aspects of the situation substantially offset these forces. Perhaps most importantly, the typical traffic stop is public, at least to some degree. Passersby, on foot or in other cars, witness the interaction of officer and motorist. This exposure to public view both reduces the ability of an unscrupulous policeman to use illegitimate means to elicit self-incriminating statements and diminishes the motorist's fear that, if he does not cooperate, he will be subjected to abuse. The fact that the detained motorist typically is confronted by only one or at most two policemen further mutes his sense of vulnerability. In short, the atmosphere surrounding an ordinary traffic stop is substantially less "police dominated" than that surrounding the kinds of interrogation at issue in *Miranda* itself, and in the subsequent cases in which we have applied *Miranda*.

In both of these respects, the usual traffic stop is more analogous to a so-called "*Terry* stop," *see* Terry v. Ohio (1968), than to a formal arrest. Under the Fourth Amendment, we have held, a policeman who lacks probable cause but whose "observations lead him reasonably to suspect" that a particular person has committed, is committing, or is about to commit a crime, may detain that person briefly in order to "investigate the circumstances that provoke suspicion." "[T]he stop and inquiry must be 'reasonably related in scope to the justification for their initiation.'" Typically, this means that the officer may ask the detainee a moderate number of questions to determine his identity and to try to obtain information confirming or dispelling the officer's suspicions. But the detainee is not obliged to respond. And, unless the detainee's answers provide the officer with probable cause to arrest him, he must then be released. The comparatively non-threatening character of detentions of this sort explains the absence of any suggestion in our opinions that *Terry* stops are subject to the dictates of *Miranda*. The similarly noncoercive aspect of ordinary traffic stops prompts us to hold that persons temporarily detained pursuant to such stops are not "in custody" for the purposes of *Miranda*.

b. What Is an "Interrogation"?

Miranda applies only if the police engage in interrogation. This, of course, is not an issue in the vast majority of cases. If police are questioning a person, that is an interrogation; if a person blurts out something to the police without being questioned, that is not an interrogation. Sometimes, though, the question of whether there is an interrogation is crucial in determining whether a confession is to be admitted. Rhode Island v. Innis is the leading case in defining an interrogation.

RHODE ISLAND v. INNIS

446 U.S. 291 (1980)

Justice STEWART delivered the opinion of the Court.

In Miranda v. Arizona (1966), the Court held that, once a defendant in custody asks to speak with a lawyer, all interrogation must cease until a lawyer is present. The issue in this case is whether the respondent was "interrogated" in violation of the standards promulgated in the *Miranda* opinion.

I

On the night of January 12, 1975, John Mulvaney, a Providence, R.I., taxicab driver, disappeared after being dispatched to pick up a customer. His body was discovered four days later buried in a shallow grave in Coventry, R.I. He had died from a shotgun blast aimed at the back of his head.

On January 17, 1975, shortly after midnight, the Providence police received a telephone call from Gerald Aubin, also a taxicab driver, who reported that he had just been robbed by a man wielding a sawed-off shotgun. Aubin further reported that he had dropped off his assailant near Rhode Island College in a section of Providence known as Mount Pleasant. While at the Providence police station waiting to give a statement, Aubin noticed a picture of his assailant on a bulletin board. Aubin so informed one of the police officers present. The officer prepared a photo array, and again Aubin identified a picture of the same person. That person was the respondent. Shortly thereafter, the Providence police began a search of the Mount Pleasant area.

At approximately 4:30 A.M. on the same date, Patrolman Lovell, while cruising the streets of Mount Pleasant in a patrol car, spotted the respondent standing in the street facing him. When Patrolman Lovell stopped his car, the respondent walked towards it. Patrolman Lovell then arrested the respondent, who was unarmed, and advised him of his so-called *Miranda* rights. While the two men waited in the patrol car for other police officers to arrive, Patrolman Lovell did not converse with the respondent other than to respond to the latter's request for a cigarette.

Within minutes, Sergeant Sears arrived at the scene of the arrest, and he also gave the respondent the *Miranda* warnings. Immediately thereafter, Captain Leyden and other police officers arrived. Captain Leyden advised the respondent of his *Miranda* rights. The respondent stated that he understood those rights and wanted to speak with a lawyer. Captain Leyden then directed that the respondent be placed in a "caged wagon," a four-door police car with a wire screen mesh between the front and rear seats, and be driven to the central police station. Three officers, Patrolmen Gleckman, Williams, and McKenna, were assigned to accompany the respondent to the central station. They placed the respondent in the vehicle and shut the doors. Captain Leyden then instructed the officers not to question the respondent or intimidate or coerce him in any way. The three officers then entered the vehicle, and it departed.

While en route to the central station, Patrolman Gleckman initiated a conversation with Patrolman McKenna concerning the missing shotgun. As Patrolman Gleckman later testified:

A. At this point, I was talking back and forth with Patrolman McKenna stating that I frequent this area while on patrol and [that because a school for handicapped children is located nearby,] there's a lot of handicapped children running around in this area, and God forbid one of them might find a weapon with shells and they might hurt themselves.

Patrolman McKenna apparently shared his fellow officer's concern:

A. I more or less concurred with him [Gleckman] that it was a safety factor and that we should, you know, continue to search for the weapon and try to find it.

While Patrolman Williams said nothing, he overheard the conversation between the two officers:

A. He [Gleckman] said it would be too bad if the little — I believe he said a girl — would pick up the gun, maybe kill herself.

The respondent then interrupted the conversation, stating that the officers should turn the car around so he could show them where the gun was located. At this point, Patrolman McKenna radioed back to Captain Leyden that they were returning to the scene of the arrest and that the respondent would inform them of the location of the gun. At the time the respondent indicated that the officers should turn back, they had traveled no more than a mile, a trip encompassing only a few minutes.

The police vehicle then returned to the scene of the arrest where a search for the shotgun was in progress. There, Captain Leyden again advised the respondent of his *Miranda* rights. The respondent replied that he understood those rights but that he "wanted to get the gun out of the way because of the kids in the area in the school." The respondent then led the police to a nearby field, where he pointed out the shotgun under some rocks by the side of the road.

On March 20, 1975, a grand jury returned an indictment charging the respondent with the kidnaping, robbery, and murder of John Mulvaney. Before trial, the respondent moved to suppress the shotgun and the statements he had made to the police regarding it. After an evidentiary hearing at which the respondent elected not to testify, the trial judge found that the respondent had been "repeatedly and completely advised of his *Miranda* rights." He further found that it was "entirely understandable that [the officers in the police vehicle] would voice their concern [for the safety of the handicapped children] to each other." Thus, without passing on whether the police officers had in fact "interrogated" the respondent, the trial court sustained the admissibility of the shotgun and testimony related to its discovery. That evidence was later introduced at the respondent's trial, and the jury returned a verdict of guilty on all counts.

On appeal, the Rhode Island Supreme Court, in a 3-2 decision, set aside the respondent's conviction. [T]he court concluded that the respondent had invoked his *Miranda* right to counsel and that, contrary to *Miranda*'s mandate that, in the absence of counsel, all custodial interrogation then cease, the police officers in the vehicle had "interrogated" the respondent without a valid waiver of his right to counsel. We granted certiorari to address for the first time the meaning of "interrogation" under Miranda v. Arizona.

II

In its *Miranda* opinion, the Court concluded that in the context of "custodial interrogation" certain procedural safeguards are necessary to protect a defendant's Fifth and Fourteenth Amendment privilege against compulsory self-incrimination. In the present case, the parties are in agreement that the respondent was fully informed of his *Miranda* rights and that he invoked his *Miranda* right to counsel when he told Captain Leyden that he wished to consult with a lawyer. It is also uncontested that the respondent was "in custody" while being transported to the police station. The issue, therefore, is whether the respondent was "interrogated" by the police officers in violation of the respondent's undisputed right under *Miranda* to remain silent until he had consulted with a lawyer. In resolving this issue, we first define the term "interrogation" under *Miranda* before turning to a consideration of the facts of this case.

The starting point for defining "interrogation" in this context is, of course, the Court's *Miranda* opinion. There the Court observed that "[b]y custodial interrogation, we mean questioning initiated by law enforcement officers after a person has been taken into custody or otherwise deprived of his freedom of action in any significant way." This passage and other references throughout the opinion to "questioning" might suggest that the *Miranda* rules were to apply only to those police interrogation practices that involve express questioning of a defendant while in custody.

We do not, however, construe the *Miranda* opinion so narrowly. The concern of the Court in *Miranda* was that the "interrogation environment" created by the interplay of interrogation and custody would "subjugate the individual to the will of his examiner" and thereby undermine the privilege against compulsory self-incrimination. The police practices that evoked this concern included several that did not involve express questioning. For example, one of the practices discussed in *Miranda* was the use of line-ups in which a coached witness would pick the defendant as the perpetrator. This was designed to establish that the defendant was in fact guilty as a predicate for further interrogation. The Court in *Miranda* also included in its survey of interrogation practices the use of psychological ploys, such as to "posi[t]" "the guilt of the subject," to "minimize the moral seriousness of the offense," and "to cast blame on the victim or on society." It is clear that these techniques of persuasion, no less than express questioning, were thought, in a custodial setting, to amount to interrogation.

This is not to say, however, that all statements obtained by the police after a person has been taken into custody are to be considered the product of interrogation. As the Court in *Miranda* noted: "Confessions remain a proper element in law enforcement. Any statement given freely and voluntarily without any compelling influences is, of course, admissible in evidence. The fundamental import of the privilege while an individual is in custody is not whether he is allowed to talk to the police without the benefit of warnings and counsel, but whether he can be interrogated. . . . Volunteered statements of any kind are not barred by the Fifth Amendment and their admissibility is not affected by our holding today."

It is clear therefore that the special procedural safeguards outlined in *Miranda* are required not where a suspect is simply taken into custody, but rather where a suspect in custody is subjected to interrogation. "Interrogation," as conceptualized in the *Miranda* opinion, must reflect a measure of compulsion above and beyond that inherent in custody itself.

We conclude that the *Miranda* safeguards come into play whenever a person in custody is subjected to either express questioning or its functional equivalent. That is to say, the term "interrogation" under *Miranda* refers not only to express questioning, but also to any words or actions on the part of the police (other than those normally attendant to arrest and custody) that the police should know are reasonably likely to elicit an incriminating response from the suspect. The latter portion of this definition focuses primarily upon the perceptions of the suspect, rather than the intent of the police. This focus reflects the fact that the *Miranda* safeguards were designed to vest a suspect in custody with an added measure of protection against coercive police practices, without regard to objective proof of the underlying intent of the police. A practice that the police should know is reasonably likely to evoke an incriminating response from a suspect thus amounts to interrogation. But, since the police surely cannot be held accountable for the unforeseeable results of their words or actions, the definition of interrogation can extend only to words or actions on the part of police officers that they should have known were reasonably likely to elicit an incriminating response.

Turning to the facts of the present case, we conclude that the respondent was not "interrogated" within the meaning of *Miranda*. It is undisputed that the first prong of the definition of "interrogation" was not satisfied, for the conversation between Patrolmen Gleckman and McKenna included no express questioning of the respondent. Rather, that conversation was, at least in form, nothing more than a dialogue between the two officers to which no response from the respondent was invited.

Moreover, it cannot be fairly concluded that the respondent was subjected to the "functional equivalent" of questioning. It cannot be said, in short, that Patrolmen Gleckman and McKenna should have known that their conversation was reasonably likely to elicit an incriminating response from the respondent. There is nothing in the record to suggest that the officers were aware that the respondent was peculiarly susceptible to an appeal to his conscience concerning the safety of handicapped children. Nor is there anything in the record to suggest that the police knew that the respondent was unusually disoriented or upset at the time of his arrest.

The case thus boils down to whether, in the context of a brief conversation, the officers should have known that the respondent would suddenly be moved to make a self-incriminating response. Given the fact that the entire conversation appears to have consisted of no more than a few off hand remarks, we cannot say that the officers should have known that it was reasonably likely that Innis would so respond. This is not a case where the police carried on a lengthy harangue in the presence of the suspect. Nor does the record support the respondent's contention that, under the circumstances, the officers' comments were particularly "evocative." It is our view, therefore, that the respondent was not subjected by the police to words or actions that the police should have known were reasonably likely to elicit an incriminating response from him.

Justice MARSHALL, with whom Justice BRENNAN joins, dissenting.

I am substantially in agreement with the Court's definition of "interrogation" within the meaning of Miranda v. Arizona (1966). In my view, the *Miranda* safeguards apply whenever police conduct is intended or likely to produce a response from a suspect in custody. As I read the Court's opinion, its definition of "interrogation" for *Miranda* purposes is equivalent, for practical purposes, to my formulation, since it contemplates that "where a police practice is designed to elicit an incriminating response from the accused, it is unlikely that the practice will not also be one which the police should have known was reasonably likely to have that effect." Thus, the Court requires an objective inquiry into the likely effect of police conduct on a typical individual, taking into account any special susceptibility of the suspect to certain kinds of pressure of which the police know or have reason to know.

I am utterly at a loss, however, to understand how this objective standard as applied to the facts before us can rationally lead to the conclusion that there was no interrogation. Innis was arrested at 4:30 A.M., handcuffed, searched, advised of his rights, and placed in the back seat of a patrol car. Within a short time he had been twice more advised of his rights and driven away in a four-door sedan with three police officers. Two officers sat in the front seat and one sat beside Innis in the back seat. Since the car traveled no more than a mile before Innis agreed to point out the location of the murder weapon, Officer Gleckman must have begun almost immediately to talk about the search for the shotgun.

The Court attempts to characterize Gleckman's statements as "no more than a few off hand remarks" which could not reasonably have been expected to elicit a response. If the statements had been addressed to respondent, it would be impossible to draw such a conclusion. The simple message of the "talking back and forth" between Gleckman and McKenna was that they had to find the shotgun to avert a child's death.

One can scarcely imagine a stronger appeal to the conscience of a suspect — any suspect — than the assertion that if the weapon is not found an innocent person will be hurt or killed. And not just any innocent person, but an innocent child — a little girl — a helpless, handicapped little girl on her way to school. The notion that such an appeal could not be expected to have any effect unless the suspect were known to have some special interest in handicapped children verges on the ludicrous. As a matter of fact, the appeal to a suspect to confess for the sake of others, to "display some evidence of decency and honor," is a classic interrogation technique.

Gleckman's remarks would obviously have constituted interrogation if they had been explicitly directed to respondent, and the result should not be different because they were nominally addressed to McKenna. This is not a case where police officers speaking among themselves are accidentally overheard by a suspect. These officers were "talking back and forth" in close quarters with the handcuffed suspect, traveling past the very place where they believed the weapon was located. They knew respondent would hear and attend to their conversation, and they are chargeable with knowledge of and responsibility for the pressures to speak which they created.

I firmly believe that this case is simply an aberration, and that in future cases the Court will apply the standard adopted today in accordance with its plain meaning.

Justice STEVENS, dissenting.

In my opinion the state court's conclusion that there was interrogation rests on a proper interpretation of both the facts and the law; thus, its determination that the products of the interrogation were inadmissible at trial should be affirmed.

In short, in order to give full protection to a suspect's right to be free from any interrogation at all, the definition of "interrogation" must include any police statement or conduct that has the same purpose or effect as a direct question. Statements that appear to call for a response from the suspect, as well as those that are designed to do so, should be considered interrogation. By prohibiting only those relatively few statements or actions that a police officer should know are likely to elicit an incriminating response, the Court today accords a suspect considerably less protection. Indeed, since I suppose most suspects are unlikely to incriminate themselves even when questioned directly, this new definition will almost certainly exclude every statement that is not punctuated with a question mark from the concept of "interrogation."

In subsequent cases, the Supreme Court continued to adhere to the narrow view of what constitutes interrogation that it used in Rhode Island v. Innis. For example, in Arizona v. Mauro, 481 U.S. 520 (1987), an individual was in police custody and indicated that he did not wish to answer any questions until a lawyer was present. The question was whether the officers interrogated the individual in violation of the Fifth and Fourteenth Amendments when they allowed him to speak with his wife in the presence of a police officer.

Justice Powell, writing for the Court in a 5-4 decision, held that there was not an interrogation. He stated:

> The sole issue, then, is whether the officers' subsequent actions rose to the level of interrogation — that is, in the language of *Innis*, whether they were the "functional equivalent" of police interrogation. We think it is clear under both *Miranda* and *Innis* that Mauro was not interrogated. The tape recording of the conversation between Mauro and his wife shows that Detective Manson asked Mauro no questions about the crime or his conduct. Nor is it suggested — or supported by any evidence — that Sergeant Allen's decision to allow Mauro's wife to see him was the kind of psychological ploy that properly could be treated as the functional equivalent of interrogation.

Justice Powell stressed that the purposes of *Miranda* did not call for finding this to be interrogation:

> In deciding whether particular police conduct is interrogation, we must remember the purpose behind our decisions: preventing government officials from using the coercive nature of confinement to extract confessions that would not be given in an unrestrained environment. The government actions in this case do not

implicate this purpose in any way. Police departments need not adopt inflexible rules barring suspects from speaking with their spouses, nor must they ignore legitimate security concerns by allowing spouses to meet in private. In this situation, the Federal Constitution does not forbid use of Mauro's subsequent statements at his criminal trial.

Justice Stevens, writing for the four dissenters, took a very different view of what had transpired:

> The record indicates, however, that the police employed a powerful psychological ploy; they failed to give respondent any advance warning that Mrs. Mauro was coming to talk to him, that a police officer would accompany her, or that their conversation would be recorded. As the transcript of the conversation reveals, respondent would not have freely chosen to speak with her. These facts compel the conclusion that the police took advantage of Mrs. Mauro's request to visit her husband, setting up a confrontation between them at a time when he manifestly desired to remain silent. Because they allowed respondent's conversation with his wife to commence at a time when they knew it was reasonably likely to produce an incriminating statement, the police interrogated him. The Court's opposite conclusion removes an important brick from the wall of protection against police overreaching that surrounds the Fifth Amendment rights of suspects in custody.

The issue of what is interrogation also arises in the context when the police use an informant who speaks to a person who is in custody. When, if at all, should this be regarded as "interrogation"?

ILLINOIS v. PERKINS

496 U.S. 292 (1990)

Justice KENNEDY delivered the opinion of the Court.

An undercover government agent was placed in the cell of respondent Perkins, who was incarcerated on charges unrelated to the subject of the agent's investigation. Respondent made statements that implicated him in the crime that the agent sought to solve. Respondent claims that the statements should be inadmissible because he had not been given *Miranda* warnings by the agent. We hold that the statements are admissible. *Miranda* warnings are not required when the suspect is unaware that he is speaking to a law enforcement officer and gives a voluntary statement.

I

In November 1984, Richard Stephenson was murdered in a suburb of East St. Louis, Illinois. The murder remained unsolved until March 1986, when one Donald Charlton told police that he had learned about a homicide from a fellow inmate at the Graham Correctional Facility, where Charlton had been serving a sentence for burglary. The fellow inmate was Lloyd Perkins, who is the respondent here. Charlton told police that, while at Graham, he had befriended respondent, who told him in detail about a murder that respondent had committed in East St. Louis. On hearing Charlton's account, the police recognized details of the Stephenson murder that were not well known, and so they treated Charlton's story as a credible one.

By the time the police heard Charlton's account, respondent had been released from Graham, but police traced him to a jail in Montgomery County, Illinois, where he was being held pending trial on a charge of aggravated battery, unrelated to the Stephenson murder. The police wanted to investigate further respondent's connection to the Stephenson murder, but feared that the use of an eavesdropping device would prove impracticable and unsafe. They decided instead to place an undercover agent in the cell-block with respondent and Charlton. The plan was for Charlton and undercover agent John Parisi to pose as escapees from a work release program who had been arrested in the course of a burglary. Parisi and Charlton were instructed to engage respondent in casual conversation and report anything he said about the Stephenson murder.

Parisi, using the alias "Vito Bianco," and Charlton, both clothed in jail garb, were placed in the cellblock with respondent at the Montgomery County jail. The cellblock consisted of 12 separate cells that opened onto a common room. Respondent greeted Charlton who, after a brief conversation with respondent, introduced Parisi by his alias. Parisi told respondent that he "wasn't going to do any more time" and suggested that the three of them escape. Respondent replied that the Montgomery County jail was "rinky-dink" and that they could "break out." The trio met in respondent's cell later that evening, after the other inmates were asleep, to refine their plan. Respondent said that his girlfriend could smuggle in a pistol. Charlton said: "Hey, I'm not a murderer, I'm a burglar. That's your guys' profession." After telling Charlton that he would be responsible for any murder that occurred, Parisi asked respondent if he had ever "done" anybody. Respondent said that he had and proceeded to describe at length the events of the Stephenson murder. Parisi and respondent then engaged in some casual conversation before respondent went to sleep. Parisi did not give respondent *Miranda* warnings before the conversations.

Respondent was charged with the Stephenson murder. Before trial, he moved to suppress the statements made to Parisi in the jail. The trial court granted the motion to suppress, and the State appealed. The Appellate Court of Illinois affirmed. We granted certiorari to decide whether an undercover law enforcement officer must give *Miranda* warnings to an incarcerated suspect before asking him questions that may elicit an incriminating response. We now reverse.

II

Conversations between suspects and undercover agents do not implicate the concerns underlying *Miranda.* The essential ingredients of a "police-dominated atmosphere" and compulsion are not present when an incarcerated person speaks freely to someone whom he believes to be a fellow inmate. Coercion is determined from the perspective of the suspect. When a suspect considers himself in the company of cellmates and not officers, the coercive atmosphere is lacking. There is no empirical basis for the assumption that a suspect speaking to those whom he assumes are not officers will feel compelled to speak by the fear of reprisal for remaining silent or in the hope of more lenient treatment should he confess.

It is the premise of *Miranda* that the danger of coercion results from the interaction of custody and official interrogation. We reject the argument that *Miranda* warnings are required whenever a suspect is in custody in a technical sense and converses with someone who happens to be a government agent. Questioning by captors, who appear to control the suspect's fate, may create mutually reinforcing pressures that the Court has assumed will weaken the suspect's will, but where a suspect does not know that he is conversing with a government agent, these pressures do not exist. The state court here mistakenly assumed that because the suspect was in custody, no undercover questioning could take place. When the suspect has no reason to think that the listeners have official power over him, it should not be assumed that his words are motivated by the reaction he expects from his listeners. "[W]hen the agent carries neither badge nor gun and wears not 'police blue,' but the same prison gray" as the suspect, there is no "interplay between police interrogation and police custody."

Miranda forbids coercion, not mere strategic deception by taking advantage of a suspect's misplaced trust in one he supposes to be a fellow prisoner. As we recognized in *Miranda*: "[C]onfessions remain a proper element in law enforcement. Any statement given freely and voluntarily without any compelling influences is, of course, admissible in evidence." Ploys to mislead a suspect or lull him into a false sense of security that do not rise to the level of compulsion or coercion to speak are not within *Miranda*'s concerns.

Miranda was not meant to protect suspects from boasting about their criminal activities in front of persons whom they believe to be their cellmates. This case is illustrative. Respondent had no reason to feel that undercover agent Parisi had any legal authority to force him to answer questions or that Parisi could affect respondent's future treatment. Respondent viewed the cellmate-agent as an equal and showed no hint of being intimidated by the atmosphere of the jail. In recounting the details of the Stephenson murder, respondent was motivated solely by the desire to impress his fellow inmates. He spoke at his own peril.

The tactic employed here to elicit a voluntary confession from a suspect does not violate the Self-Incrimination Clause. We held in Hoffa v. United States (1966), that placing an undercover agent near a suspect in order to gather incriminating information was permissible under the Fifth Amendment.

We hold that an undercover law enforcement officer posing as a fellow inmate need not give *Miranda* warnings to an incarcerated suspect before asking questions that may elicit an incriminating response. The statements at issue in this case were voluntary, and there is no federal obstacle to their admissibility at trial.

Justice MARSHALL, dissenting.

This Court clearly and simply stated its holding in Miranda v. Arizona (1966): "[T]he prosecution may not use statements, whether exculpatory or inculpatory, stemming from custodial interrogation of the defendant unless it demonstrates the use of procedural safeguards effective to secure the privilege against self-incrimination." The conditions that require the police to apprise a defendant of his constitutional rights—custodial interrogation conducted by an agent of the police—were present in this case. Because Lloyd Perkins received no *Miranda* warnings before he was subjected to custodial interrogation, his confession was not admissible.

The Court reaches the contrary conclusion by fashioning an exception to the *Miranda* rule that applies whenever "an undercover law enforcement officer posing as a fellow inmate . . . ask[s] questions that may elicit an incriminating response" from an incarcerated suspect. This exception is inconsistent with the rationale supporting *Miranda* and allows police officers intentionally to take advantage of suspects unaware of their constitutional rights. I therefore dissent.

The Court does not dispute that the police officer here conducted a custodial interrogation of a criminal suspect. Perkins was incarcerated in county jail during the questioning at issue here; under these circumstances, he was in custody as that term is defined in *Miranda.*

While Perkins was confined, an undercover police officer, with the help of a police informant, questioned him about a serious crime. Although the Court does not dispute that Perkins was interrogated, it downplays the nature of the 35-minute questioning by disingenuously referring to it as a "conversatio[n]." The officer's narration of the "conversation" at Perkins' suppression hearing however, reveals that it clearly was an interrogation.

The police officer continued the inquiry, asking a series of questions designed to elicit specific information about the victim, the crime scene, the weapon, Perkins' motive, and his actions during and after the shooting. This interaction was not a "conversation"; Perkins, the officer, and the informant were not equal participants in a free-ranging discussion, with each man offering his views on different topics. Rather, it was an interrogation: Perkins was subjected to express questioning likely to evoke an incriminating response.

Because Perkins was interrogated by police while he was in custody, *Miranda* required that the officer inform him of his rights. In rejecting that conclusion, the Court finds that "conversations" between undercover agents and suspects are devoid of the coercion inherent in station house interrogations conducted by law enforcement officials who openly represent the State. *Miranda* was not, however, concerned solely with police coercion. It dealt with any police tactics that may operate to compel a suspect in custody to make incriminating statements without full awareness of his constitutional rights. Thus, when a law enforcement agent structures a custodial interrogation so that a suspect feels compelled to reveal incriminating information, he must inform the suspect of his constitutional rights and give him an opportunity to decide whether or not to talk. The compulsion proscribed by *Miranda* includes deception by the police.

Even if *Miranda*, as interpreted by the Court, would not permit such obviously compelled confessions, the ramifications of today's opinion are still disturbing. The exception carved out of the *Miranda* doctrine today may well result in a proliferation of departmental policies to encourage police officers to conduct interrogations of confined suspects through undercover agents, thereby circumventing the need to administer *Miranda* warnings. Indeed, if *Miranda* now requires a police officer to issue warnings only in those situations in which the suspect might feel compelled "to speak by the fear of reprisal for remaining silent or in the hope of more lenient treatment should he confess," presumably it allows custodial interrogation by an undercover officer posing as a member of the clergy or a suspect's defense attorney. Although such abhorrent tricks would play on a suspect's need to confide in a trusted adviser, neither would cause the suspect to "think that the listeners have official power over him." The Court's adoption of the "undercover agent" exception to the *Miranda* rule thus is necessarily also the adoption of a substantial loophole in our jurisprudence protecting suspects' Fifth Amendment rights.

c. What Is Required of the Police?

As explained above, *Miranda* has been defended, in part, based on the argument that it is clear in terms of what is required of the police: They must administer the prescribed warnings; they must provide an attorney if one is requested; they must stop questioning a suspect who is in custody if the suspect requests an attorney or says that he does not wish to answer further questions. But what deviations from this are allowed without their being deemed to be a violation of the Fifth Amendment? The following two decisions, California v. Prysock and Duckworth v. Eagan, address that question.

CALIFORNIA v. PRYSOCK
453 U.S. 355 (1981)

PER CURIAM.

This case presents the question whether the warnings given to respondent prior to a recorded conversation with a police officer satisfied the requirements of Miranda v. Arizona (1966). Although ordinarily this Court would not be inclined to review a case involving application of that precedent to a particular set of facts, the opinion of the California Court of Appeal essentially laid down a flat rule requiring that the content of *Miranda* warnings be a virtual incantation of the precise language contained in the *Miranda* opinion. Because such a rigid rule was not mandated by *Miranda* or any other decision of this Court, and is not required to serve the purposes of *Miranda*, we reverse.

On January 30, 1978, Mrs. Donna Iris Erickson was brutally murdered. Later that evening respondent and a codefendant were apprehended for commission of the offense. Respondent was brought to a substation of the Tulare County Sheriff's Department and advised of his *Miranda* rights. He declined to talk and, since he was a minor, his parents were notified. Respondent's parents arrived and after meeting with them respondent decided to answer police questions. An officer questioned respondent, on tape, with respondent's parents present. The tape reflects that the following warnings were given prior to any questioning:

Sgt. Byrd. . . . Mr. Randall James Prysock, earlier today I advised you of your legal rights and at that time you advised me you did not wish to talk to me, is that correct?

Randall P. Yeh.

Sgt. Byrd. And, uh, during, at the first interview your folks were not present, they are now present. I want to go through your legal rights again with you and after each legal right I would like for you to answer whether you understand it or not. . . . Your legal rights, Mr. Prysock, is [sic] follows: Number One, you have the right to remain silent. This means you don't have to talk to me at all unless you so desire. Do you understand this?

Randall P. Yeh.

Sgt. Byrd. If you give up your right to remain silent, anything you say can and will be used as evidence against you in a court of law. Do you understand this?

Randall P. Yes.

Sgt. Byrd. You have the right to talk to a lawyer before you are questioned, have him present with you while you are being questioned, and all during the questioning. Do you understand this?

Randall P. Yes.

Sgt. Byrd. You also, being a juvenile, you have the right to have your parents present, which they are. Do you understand this?

Randall P. Yes.

Sgt. Byrd. Even if they weren't here, you'd have this right. Do you understand this?

Randall P. Yes.

Sgt. Byrd. You all, uh, — if, — you have the right to have a lawyer appointed to represent you at no cost to yourself. Do you understand this?

Randall P. Yes.

Sgt. Byrd. Now, having all these legal rights in mind, do you wish to talk to me at this time?

Randall P. Yes.

At this point, at the request of Mrs. Prysock, a conversation took place with the tape recorder turned off. According to Sgt. Byrd, Mrs. Prysock asked if respondent could still have an attorney at a later time if he gave a statement now without one. Sgt. Byrd assured Mrs. Prysock that respondent would have an attorney when he went to court and that "he could have one at this time if he wished one."

At trial in the Superior Court of Tulare County the court denied respondent's motion to suppress the taped statement. Respondent was convicted by a jury of first-degree murder with two special circumstances—torture and robbery. The Court of Appeal for the Fifth Appellate District reversed respondent's convictions and ordered a new trial because of what it thought to be error under *Miranda*. The Court of Appeal ruled that respondent's recorded incriminating statements, given with his parents present, had to be excluded from consideration by the jury because respondent was not properly advised of his right to the services of a free attorney before and during interrogation. Although respondent was indisputably informed that he had "the right to talk to a lawyer before you are questioned, have him present with you while you are being questioned, and all during the questioning," and further informed that he had "the right to have a lawyer appointed to represent you at no cost to yourself," the Court of Appeal ruled that these warnings were inadequate because respondent was not explicitly informed of his right to have an attorney appointed before further questioning. The Court of Appeal stated that "[o]ne of [*Miranda*'s] virtues is its precise requirements which are so easily met," and that "'the rigidity of the *Miranda* rules and the way in which they are to be applied was conceived of and continues to be recognized as the decision's greatest strength.'"

This Court has never indicated that the "rigidity" of *Miranda* extends to the precise formulation of the warnings given a criminal defendant. This Court and others have stressed as one virtue of *Miranda* the fact that the giving of the warnings obviates the need for a case-by-case inquiry into the actual voluntariness of the admissions of the accused. Nothing in these observations suggests any desirable rigidity in the form of the required warnings. Quite the contrary, *Miranda* itself indicated that no talismanic incantation was required to satisfy its strictures.

[N]othing in the warnings given respondent suggested any limitation on the right to the presence of appointed counsel different from the clearly conveyed rights to a lawyer in general, including the right "to a lawyer before you are questioned, . . . while you are being questioned, and all during the questioning."

It is clear that the police in this case fully conveyed to respondent his rights as required by *Miranda*. He was told of his right to have a lawyer present prior to and during interrogation, and his right to have a lawyer appointed at no cost if he could not afford one. These warnings conveyed to respondent his right to have a lawyer appointed if he could not afford one prior to and during interrogation. The Court of Appeal erred in holding that the warnings were inadequate simply because of the order in which they were given.

Justice Stevens, with whom Justice Brennan and Justice Marshall join, dissenting.

A juvenile informed by police that he has a right to counsel may understand that right to include one or more of three options: (1) that he has a right to have a lawyer represent him if he or his parents are able and willing to hire one; (2) that, if he cannot afford to hire an attorney, he has a right to have a lawyer represent him without charge at trial, even if his parents are unwilling to spend money on his behalf; or (3) that, if he is unable to afford an attorney, he has a right to consult a lawyer without charge before he decides whether to talk to the police, even if his parents decline to pay for such legal representation. All three of these options are encompassed within the right to counsel possessed by a juvenile charged with a crime. In this case, the first two options were explained to respondent, but the third was not.

The California Court of Appeal in this case analyzed the warning given respondent, and concluded that he had not been adequately informed of this crucial right. The police sergeant informed respondent that he had the right to have counsel present during questioning and, after a brief interlude, informed him that he had the right to appointed counsel. The Court of Appeal concluded that this warning was constitutionally inadequate, not because it deviated from the precise language of *Miranda*, but because "[u]nfortunately, the minor was not given the crucial information that the services of the free attorney were available prior to the impending questioning."

There can be no question that *Miranda* requires, as a matter of federal constitutional law, that an accused effectively be provided with this "crucial information" in some form. The Court's demonstration that the Constitution does not require that the precise language of *Miranda* be recited to an accused simply fails to come to terms with the express finding of the California Court of Appeal that respondent was not given this information. The warning recited by the police sergeant is sufficiently ambiguous on its face to provide adequate support for the California court's finding. That court's conclusion is at least reasonable, and is clearly not so patently erroneous as to warrant summary reversal.

DUCKWORTH v. EAGAN

492 U.S. 195 (1989)

Chief Justice REHNQUIST delivered the opinion of the Court.

Respondent confessed to stabbing a woman nine times after she refused to have sexual relations with him, and he was convicted of attempted murder. Before confessing, respondent was given warnings by the police, which included the advice that a lawyer would be appointed "if and when you go to court." The United States Court of Appeals for the Seventh Circuit held that such advice did not comply with the requirements of Miranda v. Arizona (1966). We disagree and reverse.

Late on May 16, 1982, respondent contacted a Chicago police officer he knew to report that he had seen the naked body of a dead woman lying on a Lake Michigan beach. Respondent denied any involvement in criminal activity. He then took several Chicago police officers to the beach, where the woman was crying for help. When she saw respondent, the woman exclaimed: "Why did you stab me? Why did you stab me?" Respondent told the officers that he had been with the woman earlier that night, but that they had been attacked by several men who abducted the woman in a van.

The next morning, after realizing that the crime had been committed in Indiana, the Chicago police turned the investigation over to the Hammond, Indiana, Police Department. Respondent repeated to the Hammond police officers his story that he had been attacked on the lakefront, and that the woman had been abducted by several men. After he filled out a battery complaint at a local police station, respondent agreed to go to the Hammond police headquarters for further questioning.

At about 11 A.M., the Hammond police questioned respondent. Before doing so, the police read to respondent a waiver form, entitled "Voluntary Appearance; Advice of Rights," and they asked him to sign it. The form provided: "Before we ask you any questions, you must understand your rights. You have the right to remain silent. Anything you say can be used against you in court. You have a right to talk to a lawyer for advice before we ask you any questions, and to have him with you during questioning. You have this right to the advice and presence of a lawyer even if you cannot afford to hire one. We have no way of giving you a lawyer, but one will be appointed for you, if you wish, if and when you go to court. If you wish to answer questions now without a lawyer present, you have the right to stop answering questions at any time. You also have the right to stop answering at any time until you've talked to a lawyer." Respondent signed the form and repeated his exculpatory explanation for his activities of the previous evening.

Respondent was then placed in the "lock up" at the Hammond police headquarters. Some 29 hours later, at about 4 P.M. on May 18, the police again interviewed respondent. Before this questioning, one of the officers read the following waiver form to respondent:

> 1. Before making this statement, I was advised that I have the right to remain silent and that anything I might say may or will be used against me in a court of law.
> 2. That I have the right to consult with an attorney of my own choice before saying anything, and that an attorney may be present while I am making any statement or throughout the course of any conversation with any police officer if I so choose.
> 3. That I can stop and request an attorney at any time during the course of the taking of any statement or during the course of any such conversation.
> 4. That in the course of any conversation I can refuse to answer any further questions and remain silent, thereby terminating the conversation.
> 5. That if I do not hire an attorney, one will be provided for me.

Respondent read the form back to the officers and signed it. He proceeded to confess to stabbing the woman. The next morning, respondent led the officers to the Lake Michigan beach where they recovered the knife he had used in the stabbing and several items of clothing.

At trial, over respondent's objection, the state court admitted his confession, his first statement denying any involvement in the crime, the knife, and the clothing. The jury found respondent guilty of attempted murder, but acquitted him of rape. He was sentenced to 35 years' imprisonment. The conviction was upheld on appeal.

Respondent sought a writ of habeas corpus in the United States District Court for the Northern District of Indiana, claiming, inter alia, that his confession was inadmissible because the first waiver form did not comply with *Miranda*. The District Court denied the petition. A divided United States Court of Appeals for the Seventh Circuit reversed. The majority held that the advice that counsel would be appointed "if and when you go to court," which was included in the first warnings given to respondent, was "constitutionally defective because it denies an accused indigent a clear and unequivocal warning of the right to appointed counsel before any interrogation," and "link[s] an indigent's right to counsel before interrogation with a future event."

In Miranda v. Arizona (1966), the Court established certain procedural safeguards that require police to advise criminal suspects of their rights under the Fifth and Fourteenth Amendments before commencing custodial interrogation. We have never insisted that *Miranda* warnings be given in the exact form described in that decision. In *Miranda* itself, the Court said that "[t]he warnings required and the waiver necessary in accordance with our opinion today are, in the absence of a fully effective equivalent, prerequisites to the admissibility of any statement made by a defendant." Reviewing courts therefore need not examine *Miranda* warnings as if construing a will or defining the terms of an easement. The inquiry is simply whether the warnings reasonably "conve[y] to [a suspect] his rights as required by *Miranda*."

We think the initial warnings given to respondent touched all of the bases required by *Miranda*. The police told respondent that he had the right to remain silent, that anything he said could be used against him in court, that he had the right to speak to an attorney before and during questioning, that he had "this right to the advice and presence of a lawyer even if [he could] not afford to hire one," and that he had the "right to stop answering at any time until [he] talked to a lawyer." As noted, the police also added that they could not provide respondent with a lawyer, but that one would be appointed "if and when you go to court." The Court of Appeals thought this "if and when you go to court" language suggested that "only those accused who can afford an attorney have the right to have one present before answering any questions," and "implie[d] that if the accused does not 'go to court,' i.e.[,] the government does not file charges, the accused is not entitled to [counsel] at all."

In our view, the Court of Appeals misapprehended the effect of the inclusion of "if and when you go to court" language in *Miranda* warnings. First, this instruction accurately described the procedure for the appointment of counsel in Indiana. Under Indiana law, counsel is appointed at the defendant's initial appearance in court, and formal charges must be filed at or before that hearing. We think it must be relatively commonplace for a suspect, after receiving *Miranda* warnings, to ask when he will obtain counsel. The "if and when you go to court" advice simply anticipates that question. Second, *Miranda* does not require that attorneys be producible on call, but only that the suspect be informed, as here, that he has the right to an attorney before and during questioning, and that an attorney would be appointed for him if he could not afford one. The Court in *Miranda* emphasized that it was not suggesting that "each police station must have a 'station house lawyer' present at all times to advise prisoners." If the police cannot provide appointed counsel, *Miranda* requires only that the police not question a suspect unless he waives his right to counsel. Here, respondent did just that.

Justice MARSHALL, with whom Justice BRENNAN joins, and with whom Justice BLACKMUN and Justice STEVENS join, dissenting.

The majority holds today that a police warning advising a suspect that he is entitled to an appointed lawyer only "if and when he goes to court" satisfies the requirements of *Miranda v. Arizona* (1966). The majority reaches this result by seriously mischaracterizing that decision. Under *Miranda*, a police warning must "clearly infor[m]" a suspect taken into custody "that if he cannot afford an attorney one will be appointed for him prior to any questioning if he so desires." A warning qualified by an "if and when you go to court" caveat does nothing of the kind; instead, it leads the suspect to believe that a lawyer will not be provided until some indeterminate time in the future after questioning. I refuse to acquiesce in the continuing debasement of this historic precedent and therefore dissent.

Miranda mandated no specific verbal formulation that police must use, but the Court, speaking through Chief Justice Warren, emphasized repeatedly that the offer of appointed counsel must be "effective and express." In concluding that the first warning given to respondent Eagan, satisfies the dictates of *Miranda*, the majority makes a mockery of that decision. Eagan was initially advised that he had the right to the presence of counsel before and during questioning. But in the very next breath, the police informed Eagan that, if he could not afford a lawyer, one would be appointed to represent him only "if and when" he went to court. As the Court of Appeals found, Eagan could easily have concluded from the "if and when" caveat that only "those accused who can afford an attorney have the right to have one present before answering any questions; those who are not so fortunate must wait." Eagan was, after all, never told that questioning would be delayed until a lawyer was appointed "if and when" Eagan did, in fact, go to court. Thus, the "if and when" caveat may well have had the effect of negating the initial promise that counsel could be present. At best, a suspect like Eagan "would not know . . . whether or not he had a right to the services of a lawyer."

In lawyerlike fashion, the Chief Justice parses the initial warnings given Eagan and finds that the most plausible interpretation is that Eagan would not be questioned until a lawyer was appointed when he later appeared in court. What goes wholly overlooked in the Chief Justice's analysis is that the recipients of police warnings are often frightened suspects unlettered in the law, not lawyers or judges or others schooled in interpreting legal or semantic nuance. Such suspects can hardly be expected to interpret, in as facile a manner as the Chief Justice, "the pretzel-like warnings here — intertwining, contradictory, and ambiguous as they are."

Even if the typical suspect could draw the inference the majority does — that questioning will not commence until a lawyer is provided at a later court appearance — a warning qualified by an "if and when" caveat still fails to give a suspect any indication of when he will be taken to court. Upon hearing the warnings given in this case, a suspect would likely conclude that no lawyer would be provided until trial. In common parlance, "going to court" is synonymous with "going to trial." Furthermore, the negative implication of the caveat is that, if the suspect is never taken to court, he "is not entitled to an attorney at all." An unwitting suspect harboring uncertainty on this score is precisely the sort of person who may feel compelled to talk "voluntarily" to the police, without the presence of counsel, in an effort to extricate himself from his predicament.

It poses no great burden on law enforcement officers to eradicate the confusion stemming from the "if and when" caveat. Deleting the sentence containing the offending language is all that needs to be done. Purged of this language, the warning tells the suspect in a straightforward fashion that he has the right to the presence of a lawyer before and during questioning, and that a lawyer will be appointed if he cannot afford one. The suspect is given no reason to believe that the appointment of an attorney may come after interrogation.

4. What Are the Consequences of a Violation of Miranda?

Miranda is clear that a confession obtained in violation of its requirements, as well as a confession deemed involuntary, must be excluded from evidence. The more difficult question concerns the extent to which the police may use the knowledge that they gain from questioning in violation of Miranda or whether the use of such information must be suppressed as the "fruit of the poisonous tree."

The Supreme Court first addressed this in Michigan v. Tucker, 417 U.S. 433 (1974). The police questioned a suspect without properly administering Miranda warnings and during this interrogation learned the identity of a key witness. The issue was whether the prosecutor could use this witness at trial. The Court stressed that the interrogation occurred prior to its decision in Miranda v. Arizona, but it nonetheless addressed the broader issue as to the consequences of violations of Miranda's requirements.

Justice Rehnquist, writing for the Court, said that in deciding what should be excluded courts must consider the underlying purpose of the exclusionary rule. He wrote:

> The deterrent purpose of the exclusionary rule necessarily assumes that the police have engaged in willful, or at the very least negligent, conduct which has deprived the defendant of some right. By refusing to admit evidence gained as a result of such conduct, the courts hope to instill in those particular investigating officers, or in their future counterparts, a greater degree of care toward the rights of an accused. Where the official action was pursued in complete good faith, however, the deterrence rationale loses much of its force.

Justice Rehnquist said that balancing the competing interests warranted allowing the use of the witness at trial:

> In summary, we do not think that any single reason supporting exclusion of this witness' testimony, or all of them together, are very persuasive. By contrast, we find the arguments in favor of admitting the testimony quite strong. For, when balancing the interests involved, we must weigh the strong interest under any system of justice of making available to the trier of fact all concededly relevant and trustworthy evidence which either party seeks to adduce. In this particular case we also "must consider society's interest in the effective prosecution of criminals in light of the protection our pre-*Miranda* standards afford criminal defendants." These interests may be outweighed by the need to provide an effective sanction to a constitutional right, but they must in any event be valued. Here respondent's own statement, which might have helped the prosecution show respondent's guilty conscience at trial, had already been excised from the prosecution's case pursuant to this Court's *Johnson* decision. To extend the excision further under the circumstances of this case and exclude relevant testimony of a third-party witness would require far more persuasive arguments than those advanced by respondent.

Justice Brennan, in dissent, criticized the Court for reaching the question as to remedy at all since this case involved questioning that occurred prior to *Miranda*. He wrote:

> The Court finds it unnecessary to decide "the broad question" of whether the fruits of "statements taken in violation of the *Miranda* rules must be excluded regardless of when the interrogation took place," since respondent's interrogation occurred prior to our decision in Miranda v. Arizona (1966). In my view, however, it is unnecessary, too, for the Court to address the narrower question of whether the principles of *Miranda* require that fruits be excluded when obtained as a result of a pre-*Miranda* interrogation without the requisite prior warnings.

Until the decisions in two recent cases, Oregon v. Elstad was the leading decision concerning the admissibility of evidence gained as the "fruits" of a *Miranda* violation.

OREGON v. ELSTAD

470 U.S. 298 (1985)

Justice O'CONNOR delivered the opinion of the Court.

This case requires us to decide whether an initial failure of law enforcement officers to administer the warnings required by Miranda v. Arizona (1966), without more, "taints" subsequent admissions made after a suspect has been fully advised of and has waived his *Miranda* rights. Respondent, Michael James Elstad, was convicted of burglary by an Oregon trial court. The Oregon Court of Appeals reversed, holding that respondent's signed confession, although voluntary, was rendered inadmissible by a prior remark made in response to questioning without benefit of *Miranda* warnings.

I

In December 1981, the home of Mr. and Mrs. Gilbert Gross, in the town of Salem, Polk County, Ore., was burglarized. Missing were art objects and furnishings valued at $150,000. A witness to the burglary contacted the Polk County Sheriff's office, implicating respondent Michael Elstad, an 18-year-old neighbor and friend of the Grosses' teenage son. Thereupon, Officers Burke and McAllister went to the home of respondent Elstad, with a warrant for his arrest. Elstad's mother answered the door. She led the officers to her son's room where he lay on his bed, clad in shorts and listening to his stereo. The officers asked him to get dressed and to accompany them into the living room. Officer McAllister asked respondent's mother to step into the kitchen, where he explained that they had a warrant for her son's arrest for the burglary of a neighbor's residence. Officer Burke remained with Elstad in the living room. He later testified: "I sat down with Mr. Elstad and I asked him if he was aware of why Detective McAllister and myself were there to talk with him. He stated no, he had no idea why we were there. I then asked him if he knew a person by the name of Gross, and he said yes, he did, and also added that he heard that there was a robbery at the Gross house. And at that point I told Mr. Elstad that I felt he was involved in that, and he looked at me and stated, 'Yes, I was there.'"

Elstad was transported to the Sheriff's headquarters and approximately one hour later, Officers Burke and McAllister joined him in McAllister's office. McAllister then advised respondent for the first time of his *Miranda* rights, reading from a standard card. Respondent indicated he understood his rights, and, having these rights in mind, wished to speak with the officers. Elstad gave a full statement, explaining that he had known that the Gross family was out of town and had been paid to lead several acquaintances to the Gross residence and show them how to gain entry through a defective sliding glass door. The statement was typed, reviewed by respondent, read back to him for correction, initialed and signed by Elstad and both officers. As an afterthought, Elstad added and initialed the sentence, "After leaving the house Robby & I went back to [the] van & Robby handed me a small bag of grass." Respondent concedes that the officers made no threats or promises either at his residence or at the Sheriff's office.

Respondent was charged with first-degree burglary. Respondent moved at once to suppress his oral statement and signed confession. He contended that the statement he made in response to questioning at his house "let the cat out of the bag," and tainted the subsequent confession as "fruit of the poisonous tree." The judge ruled that the statement, "I was there," had to be excluded because the defendant had not been advised of his *Miranda* rights. The written confession taken after Elstad's arrival at the Sheriff's office, however, was admitted in evidence.

II

The arguments advanced in favor of suppression of respondent's written confession rely heavily on metaphor. One metaphor, familiar from the Fourth Amendment context, would require that respondent's confession, regardless of its integrity, voluntariness, and probative value, be suppressed as the "tainted fruit of the poisonous tree" of the *Miranda* violation. A second metaphor questions whether a confession can be truly voluntary once the "cat is out of the bag." Taken out of context, each of these metaphors can be misleading. They should not be used to obscure fundamental differences between the role of the Fourth Amendment exclusionary rule and the function of *Miranda* in guarding against the prosecutorial use of compelled statements as prohibited by the Fifth Amendment. The Oregon court assumed and respondent here contends that a failure to administer *Miranda* warnings necessarily breeds the same consequences as police infringement of a constitutional right, so that evidence uncovered following an unwarned statement must be suppressed as "fruit of the poisonous tree." We believe this view misconstrues the nature of the protections afforded by *Miranda* warnings and therefore misreads the consequences of police failure to supply them.

A

Respondent's contention that his confession was tainted by the earlier failure of the police to provide *Miranda* warnings and must be excluded as "fruit of the poisonous tree" assumes the existence of a constitutional violation. This figure of speech is drawn from Wong Sun v. United States (1963), in which the Court held that evidence and witnesses discovered as a result of a search in violation of the Fourth Amendment must be excluded from evidence. The *Wong Sun* doctrine applies as well when the fruit of the Fourth Amendment violation is a confession.

But a procedural *Miranda* violation differs in significant respects from violations of the Fourth Amendment, which have traditionally mandated a broad application of the "fruits" doctrine. The purpose of the Fourth Amendment exclusionary rule is to deter unreasonable searches, no matter how probative their fruits.

The *Miranda* exclusionary rule, however, serves the Fifth Amendment and sweeps more broadly than the Fifth Amendment itself. It may be triggered even in the absence of a Fifth Amendment violation. The Fifth Amendment prohibits use by the prosecution in its case in chief only of compelled testimony. Failure to administer *Miranda* warnings creates a presumption of compulsion. Consequently, unwarned statements that are otherwise voluntary within the meaning of the Fifth Amendment must nevertheless be excluded from evidence under *Miranda*. Thus, in the individual case, *Miranda*'s preventive medicine provides a remedy even to the defendant who has suffered no identifiable constitutional harm.

But the *Miranda* presumption, though irrebuttable for purposes of the prosecution's case in chief, does not require that the statements and their fruits be discarded as inherently tainted. Despite the fact that patently voluntary statements taken in violation of *Miranda* must be excluded from the prosecution's case, the presumption of coercion does not bar their use for impeachment purposes on cross-examination. Harris v. New York (1971).

In Michigan v. Tucker, the Court was asked to extend the *Wong Sun* fruits doctrine to suppress the testimony of a witness for the prosecution whose identity was discovered as the result of a statement taken from the accused without benefit of full *Miranda* warnings. The Court concluded that the unwarned questioning "did not abridge respondent's constitutional privilege . . . but departed only from the prophylactic standards later laid down by this Court in *Miranda* to safeguard that privilege." Since there was no actual infringement of the suspect's constitutional rights, the case was not controlled by the doctrine expressed in *Wong Sun* that fruits of a constitutional violation must be suppressed. In deciding "how sweeping the judicially imposed consequences" of a failure to administer *Miranda* warnings should be, the *Tucker* Court noted that neither the general goal of deterring improper police conduct nor the Fifth Amendment goal of assuring trustworthy evidence would be served by suppression of the witness' testimony.

We believe that this reasoning applies with equal force when the alleged "fruit" of a noncoercive *Miranda* violation is neither a witness nor an article of evidence but the accused's own voluntary testimony. As in *Tucker*, the absence of any coercion or improper tactics undercuts the twin rationales — trustworthiness and deterrence — for a broader rule. Once warned, the suspect is free to exercise his own volition in deciding whether or not to make a statement to the authorities.

Because *Miranda* warnings may inhibit persons from giving information, this Court has determined that they need be administered only after the person is taken into "custody" or his freedom has otherwise been significantly restrained. Unfortunately, the task of defining "custody" is a slippery one, and "policemen investigating serious crimes [cannot realistically be expected to] make no errors whatsoever." If errors are made by law enforcement officers in administering the prophylactic *Miranda* procedures, they should not breed the same irremediable consequences as police infringement of the Fifth Amendment itself. It is an unwarranted extension of

Miranda to hold that a simple failure to administer the warnings, unaccompanied by any actual coercion or other circumstances calculated to undermine the suspect's ability to exercise his free will, so taints the investigatory process that a subsequent voluntary and informed waiver is ineffective for some indeterminate period. Though *Miranda* requires that the unwarned admission must be suppressed, the admissibility of any subsequent statement should turn in these circumstances solely on whether it is knowingly and voluntarily made.

B

The Oregon court, however, believed that the unwarned remark compromised the voluntariness of respondent's later confession. It was the court's view that the prior answer and not the unwarned questioning impaired respondent's ability to give a valid waiver and that only lapse of time and change of place could dissipate what it termed the "coercive impact" of the inadmissible statement. When a prior statement is actually coerced, the time that passes between confessions, the change in place of interrogations, and the change in identity of the interrogators all bear on whether that coercion has carried over into the second confession.

The Oregon court nevertheless identified a subtle form of lingering compulsion, the psychological impact of the suspect's conviction that he has let the cat out of the bag and, in so doing, has sealed his own fate. But endowing the psychological effects of voluntary unwarned admissions with constitutional implications would, practically speaking, disable the police from obtaining the suspect's informed cooperation even when the official coercion proscribed by the Fifth Amendment played no part in either his warned or unwarned confessions.

This Court has never held that the psychological impact of voluntary disclosure of a guilty secret qualifies as state compulsion or compromises the voluntariness of a subsequent informed waiver. The Oregon court, by adopting this expansive view of Fifth Amendment compulsion, effectively immunizes a suspect who responds to pre-*Miranda* warning questions from the consequences of his subsequent informed waiver of the privilege of remaining silent. This immunity comes at a high cost to legitimate law enforcement activity, while adding little desirable protection to the individual's interest in not being compelled to testify against himself. When neither the initial nor the subsequent admission is coerced, little justification exists for permitting the highly probative evidence of a voluntary confession to be irretrievably lost to the factfinder.

We must conclude that, absent deliberately coercive or improper tactics in obtaining the initial statement, the mere fact that a suspect has made an unwarned admission does not warrant a presumption of compulsion. A subsequent administration of *Miranda* warnings to a suspect who has given a voluntary but unwarned statement ordinarily should suffice to remove the conditions that precluded admission of the earlier statement. In such circumstances, the finder of fact may reasonably conclude that the suspect made a rational and intelligent choice whether to waive or invoke his rights.

Justice BRENNAN, with whom Justice MARSHALL joins, dissenting.

The Self-Incrimination Clause of the Fifth Amendment guarantees every individual that, if taken into official custody, he shall be informed of important constitutional rights and be given the opportunity knowingly and voluntarily to waive those rights before being interrogated about suspected wrongdoing. Miranda v. Arizona. This guarantee embodies our society's conviction that "no system of criminal justice can, or should, survive if it comes to depend for its continued effectiveness on the citizens' abdication through unawareness of their constitutional rights." Escobedo v. Illinois (1964).

Even while purporting to reaffirm these constitutional guarantees, the Court has engaged of late in a studied campaign to strip the *Miranda* decision piecemeal and to undermine the rights *Miranda* sought to secure. Today's decision not only extends this effort a further step, but delivers a potentially crippling blow to *Miranda* and the ability of courts to safeguard the rights of persons accused of crime. For at least with respect to successive confessions, the Court today appears to strip remedies for *Miranda* violations of the "fruit of the poisonous tree" doctrine prohibiting the use of evidence presumptively derived from official illegality.

Two major premises undergird the Court's decision. The Court rejects as nothing more than "speculative" the long-recognized presumption that an illegally extracted confession causes the accused to confess again out of the mistaken belief that he already has sealed his fate, and it condemns as "extravagant" the requirement that the prosecution affirmatively rebut the presumption before the subsequent confession may be admitted. The Court instead adopts a new rule that, so long as the accused is given the usual *Miranda* warnings before further interrogation, the taint of a previous confession obtained in violation of *Miranda* "ordinarily" must be viewed as automatically dissipated.

In the alternative, the Court asserts that neither the Fifth Amendment itself nor the judicial policy of deterring illegal police conduct requires the suppression of the "fruits" of a confession obtained in violation of *Miranda*, reasoning that to do otherwise would interfere with "legitimate law enforcement activity." As the Court surely understands, however, "[t]o forbid the direct use of methods . . . but to put no curb on their full indirect use would only invite the very methods deemed 'inconsistent with ethical standards and destructive of personal liberty.'" If violations of constitutional rights may not be remedied through the well-established rules respecting derivative evidence, as the Court has held today, there is a critical danger that the rights will be rendered nothing more than a mere "form of words."

The Court's decision says much about the way the Court currently goes about implementing its agenda. In imposing its new rule, for example, the

Court mischaracterizes our precedents, obfuscates the central issues, and altogether ignores the practical realities of custodial interrogation that have led nearly every lower court to reject its simplistic reasoning. Moreover, the Court adopts startling and unprecedented methods of construing constitutional guarantees. Finally the Court reaches out once again to address issues not before us. For example, although the State of Oregon has conceded that the arresting officers broke the law in this case, the Court goes out of its way to suggest that they may have been objectively justified in doing so.

Today's decision, in short, threatens disastrous consequences far beyond the outcome in this case. The threshold question is this: What effect should an admission or confession of guilt obtained in violation of an accused's *Miranda* rights be presumed to have upon the voluntariness of subsequent confessions that are preceded by *Miranda* warnings? The correct approach, administered for almost 20 years by most courts with no untoward results, is to presume that an admission or confession obtained in violation of *Miranda* taints a subsequent confession unless the prosecution can show that the taint is so attenuated as to justify admission of the subsequent confession. Until today the Court has recognized that the dissipation inquiry requires the prosecution to demonstrate that the official illegality did not taint the challenged confession, and we have rejected the simplistic view that abstract notions of "free will" are alone sufficient to dissipate the challenged taint.

———

The Supreme Court returned to the issue of when information gained in violation of *Miranda* can be used as evidence in two decisions in 2004. In one, Missouri v. Seibert, the Court held that subsequent statements must be excluded, even if *Miranda* warnings were given before the statements were repeated. But in United States v. Patane, the Court said that tangible evidence could be introduced even if it resulted from violations of *Miranda*. In reading these cases, it is important to consider whether there is a meaningful distinction between these two cases. Interestingly, eight of the nine justices saw no difference; only Justice Kennedy was in the majority in both decisions. Four justices—Chief Justice Rehnquist and Justices O'Connor, Scalia, and Thomas—would have allowed both the statement in *Seibert* and the gun in *Patane* to be admitted notwithstanding the failure to properly administer *Miranda* warnings. On the other hand, there also were four justices—Justices Stevens, Souter, Ginsburg, and Breyer—who would have excluded both as the fruits of violations of *Miranda*. Justice Kennedy, though, determined the outcome of both cases by voting for the exclusion of the subsequent statement in *Seibert* but not the gun in *Patane*. Also, in considering Missouri v. Seibert, it is important to consider whether there is a meaningful distinction between it and the earlier decision in Oregon v. Elstad.

MISSOURI v. SEIBERT
542 U.S. 600 (2004)

Justice SOUTER announced the judgment of the Court and delivered an opinion, in which Justice STEVENS, Justice GINSBURG, and Justice BREYER join.

This case tests a police protocol for custodial interrogation that calls for giving no warnings of the rights to silence and counsel until interrogation has produced a confession. Although such a statement is generally inadmissible, since taken in violation of Miranda v. Arizona (1966), the interrogating officer follows it with *Miranda* warnings and then leads the suspect to cover the same ground a second time. The question here is the admissibility of the repeated statement. Because this midstream recitation of warnings after interrogation and unwarned confession could not effectively comply with *Miranda*'s constitutional requirement, we hold that a statement repeated after a warning in such circumstances is inadmissible.

I

Respondent Patrice Seibert's 12-year-old son Jonathan had cerebral palsy, and when he died in his sleep she feared charges of neglect because of bedsores on his body. In her presence, two of her teenage sons and two of their friends devised a plan to conceal the facts surrounding Jonathan's death by incinerating his body in the course of burning the family's mobile home, in which they planned to leave Donald Rector, a mentally ill teenager living with the family, to avoid any appearance that Jonathan had been unattended. Seibert's son Darian and a friend set the fire, and Donald died.

Five days later, the police awakened Seibert at 3 A.M. at a hospital where Darian was being treated for burns. In arresting her, Officer Kevin Clinton followed instructions from Rolla, Missouri, Officer Richard Hanrahan that he refrain from giving *Miranda* warnings. After Seibert had been taken to the police station and left alone in an interview room for 15 to 20 minutes, Officer Hanrahan questioned her without *Miranda* warnings for 30 to 40 minutes, squeezing her arm and repeating "Donald was also to die in his sleep." After Seibert finally admitted she knew Donald was meant to die in the fire, she was given a 20-minute coffee and cigarette break. Officer Hanrahan then turned on a tape recorder, gave Seibert the *Miranda* warnings, and obtained a signed waiver of rights from her. He resumed the questioning with "OK, Trice, we've been talking for a little while about what happened on Wednesday the twelfth, haven't we?" and confronted her with her prewarning statements:

Hanrahan.   Now, in discussion you told us, you told us that there was a[n] understanding about Donald.
Seibert.   Yes.
Hanrahan.   Did that take place earlier that morning?
Seibert.   Yes.

Hanrahan. And what was the understanding about Donald?
Seibert. If they could get him out of the trailer, to take him out of the trailer.
Hanrahan. And if they couldn't?
Seibert. I, I never even thought about it. I just figured they would.
Hanrahan. Trice, didn't you tell me that he was supposed to die in his sleep?
Seibert. If that would happen, 'cause he was on that new medicine, you know. . . .
Hanrahan. The Prozac? And it makes him sleepy. So he was supposed to die in his sleep?
Seibert. Yes.

After being charged with first-degree murder for her role in Donald's death, Seibert sought to exclude both her prewarning and postwarning statements. At the suppression hearing, Officer Hanrahan testified that he made a "conscious decision" to withhold *Miranda* warnings, thus resorting to an interrogation technique he had been taught: question first, then give the warnings, and then repeat the question "until I get the answer that she's already provided once." He acknowledged that Seibert's ultimate statement was "largely a repeat of information . . . obtained" prior to the warning.

The trial court suppressed the prewarning statement but admitted the responses given after the *Miranda* recitation. A jury convicted Seibert of second-degree murder. On appeal, the Missouri Court of Appeals affirmed, treating this case as indistinguishable from Oregon v. Elstad (1985). The Supreme Court of Missouri reversed, holding that "[i]n the circumstances here, where the interrogation was nearly continuous, . . . the second statement, clearly the product of the invalid first statement, should have been suppressed."

II

The technique of interrogating in successive, unwarned and warned phases raises a new challenge to *Miranda*. Although we have no statistics on the frequency of this practice, it is not confined to Rolla, Missouri. An officer of that police department testified that the strategy of withholding *Miranda* warnings until after interrogating and drawing out a confession was promoted not only by his own department, but by a national police training organization and other departments in which he had worked. Consistently with the officer's testimony, the Police Law Institute, for example, instructs that "officers may conduct a two-stage interrogation. . . . At any point during the pre-*Miranda* interrogation, usually after arrestees have confessed, officers may then read the *Miranda* warnings and ask for a waiver. If the arrestees waive their *Miranda* rights, officers will be able to repeat any subsequent incriminating statements later in court."

The object of question-first is to render *Miranda* warnings ineffective by waiting for a particularly opportune time to give them, after the suspect has already confessed. Just as "no talismanic incantation [is] required to satisfy [*Miranda*'s] strictures," California v. Prysock (1981), it would be absurd to think that mere recitation of the litany suffices to satisfy *Miranda* in every conceivable circumstance. The threshold issue when interrogators question first and warn later is thus whether it would be reasonable to find that in these circumstances the warnings could function "effectively" as *Miranda* requires. Could the warnings effectively advise the suspect that he had a real choice about giving an admissible statement at that juncture? Could they reasonably convey that he could choose to stop talking even if he had talked earlier? For unless the warnings could place a suspect who has just been interrogated in a position to make such an informed choice, there is no practical justification for accepting the formal warnings as compliance with *Miranda*, or for treating the second stage of interrogation as distinct from the first, unwarned and inadmissible segment.

There is no doubt about the answer that proponents of question-first give to this question about the effectiveness of warnings given only after successful interrogation, and we think their answer is correct. By any objective measure, applied to circumstances exemplified here, it is likely that if the interrogators employ the technique of withholding warnings until after interrogation succeeds in eliciting a confession, the warnings will be ineffective in preparing the suspect for successive interrogation, close in time and similar in content. After all, the reason that question-first is catching on is as obvious as its manifest purpose, which is to get a confession the suspect would not make if he understood his rights at the outset; the sensible underlying assumption is that with one confession in hand before the warnings, the interrogator can count on getting its duplicate, with trifling additional trouble. Upon hearing warnings only in the aftermath of interrogation and just after making a confession, a suspect would hardly think he had a genuine right to remain silent, let alone persist in so believing once the police began to lead him over the same ground again. A more likely reaction on a suspect's part would be perplexity about the reason for discussing rights at that point, bewilderment being an unpromising frame of mind for knowledgeable decision. What is worse, telling a suspect that "anything you say can and will be used against you," without expressly excepting the statement just given, could lead to an entirely reasonable inference that what he has just said will be used, with subsequent silence being of no avail. Thus, when *Miranda* warnings are inserted in the midst of coordinated and continuing interrogation, they are likely to mislead and "depriv[e] a defendant of knowledge essential to his ability to understand the nature of his rights and the consequences of abandoning them." By the same token, it would ordinarily be unrealistic to treat two spates of integrated and proximately conducted questioning as independent interrogations subject to independent evaluation simply because *Miranda* warnings formally punctuate them in the middle.

Missouri argues that a confession repeated at the end of an interrogation sequence envisioned in a question-first strategy is admissible on the authority of Oregon v. Elstad (1985), but the argument disfigures that case. In *Elstad*, the police went to the young suspect's house to take him into custody on a charge of burglary. Before the arrest, one officer spoke with the suspect's mother, while the other one joined the suspect in a "brief stop in the living room," where the officer said he "felt" the young man was involved in a burglary. The suspect acknowledged he had been at the scene. This Court noted that the pause in the living room "was not to interrogate the suspect but to notify his mother of the reason for his arrest," and described the incident as having "none of the earmarks of coercion." The Court, indeed, took care to mention that the officer's initial failure to warn was an "oversight" that "may have been the result of confusion as to whether the brief exchange qualified as 'custodial interrogation' or . . . may simply have reflected . . . reluctance to initiate an alarming police procedure before [an officer] had spoken with respondent's mother." At the outset of a later and systematic station house interrogation going well beyond the scope of the laconic prior admission, the suspect was given *Miranda* warnings and made a full confession. In holding the second statement admissible and voluntary, *Elstad* rejected the "cat out of the bag" theory that any short, earlier admission, obtained in arguably innocent neglect of *Miranda*, determined the character of the later, warned confession; on the facts of that case, the Court thought any causal connection between the first and second responses to the police was "speculative and attenuated." Although the *Elstad* Court expressed no explicit conclusion about either officer's state of mind, it is fair to read *Elstad* as treating the living room conversation as a good-faith *Miranda* mistake, not only open to correction by careful warnings before systematic questioning in that particular case, but posing no threat to warn-first practice generally.

The contrast between *Elstad* and this case reveals a series of relevant facts that bear on whether *Miranda* warnings delivered midstream could be effective enough to accomplish their object: the completeness and detail of the questions and answers in the first round of interrogation, the overlapping content of the two statements, the timing and setting of the first and the second, the continuity of police personnel, and the degree to which the interrogator's questions treated the second round as continuous with the first. In *Elstad*, it was not unreasonable to see the occasion for questioning at the station house as presenting a markedly different experience from the short conversation at home; since a reasonable person in the suspect's shoes could have seen the station house questioning as a new and distinct experience, the *Miranda* warnings could have made sense as presenting a genuine choice whether to follow up on the earlier admission.

At the opposite extreme are the facts here, which by any objective measure reveal a police strategy adapted to undermine the *Miranda* warnings. The unwarned interrogation was conducted in the station house, and the questioning was systematic, exhaustive, and managed with psychological skill. When the police were finished there was little, if anything, of incriminating potential left unsaid. The warned phase of questioning proceeded after a pause of only 15 to 20 minutes, in the same place as the unwarned segment. When the same officer who had conducted the first phase recited the *Miranda* warnings, he said nothing to counter the probable misimpression that the advice that anything Seibert said could be used against her also applied to the details of the inculpatory statement previously elicited. In particular, the police did not advise that her prior statement could not be used. Nothing was said or done to dispel the oddity of warning about legal rights to silence and counsel right after the police had led her through a systematic interrogation, and any uncertainty on her part about a right to stop talking about matters previously discussed would only have been aggravated by the way Officer Hanrahan set the scene by saying "we've been talking for a little while about what happened on Wednesday the twelfth, haven't we?" The impression that the further questioning was a mere continuation of the earlier questions and responses was fostered by references back to the confession already given. It would have been reasonable to regard the two sessions as parts of a continuum, in which it would have been unnatural to refuse to repeat at the second stage what had been said before. These circumstances must be seen as challenging the comprehensibility and efficacy of the *Miranda* warnings to the point that a reasonable person in the suspect's shoes would not have understood them to convey a message that she retained a choice about continuing to talk.

Strategists dedicated to draining the substance out of *Miranda* cannot accomplish by training instructions what *Dickerson* held Congress could not do by statute. Because the question-first tactic effectively threatens to thwart *Miranda*'s purpose of reducing the risk that a coerced confession would be admitted, and because the facts here do not reasonably support a conclusion that the warnings given could have served their purpose, Seibert's postwarning statements are inadmissible.

Justice BREYER, concurring.

In my view, the following simple rule should apply to the two-stage interrogation technique: Courts should exclude the "fruits" of the initial unwarned questioning unless the failure to warn was in good faith. I believe this is a sound and workable approach to the problem this case presents. Prosecutors and judges have long understood how to apply the "fruits" approach, which they use in other areas of law. And in the workaday world of criminal law enforcement the administrative simplicity of the familiar has significant advantages over a more complex exclusionary rule.

Justice KENNEDY, concurring in the judgment.

The interrogation technique used in this case is designed to circumvent Miranda v. Arizona (1966). It undermines the *Miranda* warning and obscures its meaning. The plurality opinion is correct to conclude that statements obtained through the use of this technique are inadmissible. Although I agree with much in the careful and convincing opinion for the plurality, my approach does differ in some respects, requiring this separate statement.

In my view, *Elstad* was correct in its reasoning and its result. *Elstad* reflects a balanced and pragmatic approach to enforcement of the *Miranda* warning. An officer may not realize that a suspect is in custody and warnings are required. The officer may not plan to question the suspect or may be waiting for a more appropriate time. Skilled investigators often interview suspects multiple times, and good police work may involve referring to prior statements to test their veracity or to refresh recollection. In light of these realities it would be extravagant to treat the presence of one statement that cannot be admitted under *Miranda* as sufficient reason to prohibit subsequent statements preceded by a proper warning.

This case presents different considerations. The police used a two-step questioning technique based on a deliberate violation of *Miranda*. The *Miranda* warning was withheld to obscure both the practical and legal significance of the admonition when finally given. The strategy is based on the assumption that *Miranda* warnings will tend to mean less when recited mid-interrogation, after inculpatory statements have already been obtained. This tactic relies on an intentional misrepresentation of the protection that *Miranda* offers and does not serve any legitimate objectives that might otherwise justify its use.

Further, the interrogating officer here relied on the defendant's prewarning statement to obtain the postwarning statement used against her at trial. The postwarning interview resembled a cross-examination. The officer confronted the defendant with her inadmissible prewarning statements and pushed her to acknowledge them. This shows the temptations for abuse inherent in the two-step technique. Reference to the prewarning statement was an implicit suggestion that the mere repetition of the earlier statement was not independently incriminating. The implicit suggestion was false.

The technique used in this case distorts the meaning of *Miranda* and furthers no legitimate countervailing interest. The *Miranda* rule would be frustrated were we to allow police to undermine its meaning and effect. The technique simply creates too high a risk that postwarning statements will be obtained when a suspect was deprived of "knowledge essential to his ability to understand the nature of his rights and the consequences of abandoning them." When an interrogator uses this deliberate, two-step strategy, predicated upon violating *Miranda* during an extended interview, postwarning statements that are related to the substance of prewarning statements must be excluded absent specific, curative steps.

The plurality concludes that whenever a two-stage interview occurs, admissibility of the postwarning statement should depend on "whether [the] *Miranda* warnings delivered midstream could have been effective enough to accomplish their object" given the specific facts of the case. This test envisions an objective inquiry from the perspective of the suspect, and applies in the case of both intentional and unintentional two-stage interrogations. In my view, this test cuts too broadly. *Miranda*'s clarity is one of its strengths, and a multifactor test that applies to every two-stage interrogation may serve to undermine that clarity. I would apply a narrower test applicable only in the infrequent case, such as we have here, in which the two-step interrogation technique was used in a calculated way to undermine the *Miranda* warning.

The admissibility of postwarning statements should continue to be governed by the principles of *Elstad* unless the deliberate two-step strategy was employed. If the deliberate two-step strategy has been used, postwarning statements that are related to the substance of prewarning statements must be excluded unless curative measures are taken before the postwarning statement is made. Curative measures should be designed to ensure that a reasonable person in the suspect's situation would understand the import and effect of the *Miranda* warning and of the *Miranda* waiver. For example, a substantial break in time and circumstances between the prewarning statement and the *Miranda* warning may suffice in most circumstances, as it allows the accused to distinguish the two contexts and appreciate that the interrogation has taken a new turn. Alternatively, an additional warning that explains the likely inadmissibility of the prewarning custodial statement may be sufficient. No curative steps were taken in this case, however, so the postwarning statements are inadmissible and the conviction cannot stand.

Justice O'CONNOR, with whom THE CHIEF JUSTICE, Justice SCALIA, and Justice THOMAS join, dissenting.

The plurality devours Oregon v. Elstad (1985), even as it accuses petitioner's argument of "disfigur[ing]" that decision. I believe that we are bound by *Elstad* to reach a different result.

I believe that the approach espoused by Justice Kennedy is ill advised. Justice Kennedy would extend *Miranda*'s exclusionary rule to any case in which the use of the "two-step interrogation technique" was "deliberate" or "calculated." This approach untethers the analysis from facts knowable to, and therefore having any potential directly to affect, the suspect. Far from promoting "clarity," the approach will add a third step to the suppression inquiry. In virtually every two-stage interrogation case, in addition to addressing the standard *Miranda* and voluntariness questions, courts will be forced to conduct the kind of difficult, state-of-mind inquiry that we normally take pains to avoid.

UNITED STATES v. PATANE

542 U.S. 630 (2004)

Justice THOMAS announced the judgment of the Court and delivered an opinion, in which THE CHIEF JUSTICE and Justice SCALIA join.

In this case we must decide whether a failure to give a suspect the warnings prescribed by Miranda v. Arizona (1966), requires suppression of the physical fruits of the suspect's unwarned but voluntary statements. Because the *Miranda* rule protects against violations of the Self-Incrimination Clause, which, in turn, is not implicated by the introduction at trial of physical evidence resulting from voluntary statements, we answer the question presented in the negative.

I

In June 2001, respondent, Samuel Francis Patane, was arrested for harassing his ex-girlfriend, Linda O'Donnell. He was released on bond, subject to a temporary restraining order that prohibited him from contacting O'Donnell. Respondent apparently violated the restraining order by attempting to telephone O'Donnell. On June 6, 2001, Officer Tracy Fox of the Colorado Springs Police Department began to investigate the matter. On the same day, a county probation officer informed an agent of the Bureau of Alcohol, Tobacco and Firearms (ATF), that respondent, a convicted felon, illegally possessed a .40 Glock pistol. The ATF relayed this information to Detective Josh Benner, who worked closely with the ATF. Together, Detective Benner and Officer Fox proceeded to respondent's residence.

After reaching the residence and inquiring into respondent's attempts to contact O'Donnell, Officer Fox arrested respondent for violating the restraining order. Detective Benner attempted to advise respondent of his *Miranda* rights but got no further than the right to remain silent. At that point, respondent interrupted, asserting that he knew his rights, and neither officer attempted to complete the warning.[11]

Detective Benner then asked respondent about the Glock. Respondent was initially reluctant to discuss the matter, stating: "I am not sure I should tell you anything about the Glock because I don't want you to take it away from me." Detective Benner persisted, and respondent told him that the pistol was in his bedroom. Respondent then gave Detective Benner permission to retrieve the pistol. Detective Benner found the pistol and seized it.

A grand jury indicted respondent for possession of a firearm by a convicted felon, in violation of 18 U.S.C. §922(g)(1). The District Court granted respondent's motion to suppress the firearm, reasoning that the officers lacked probable cause to arrest respondent for violating the restraining order. It therefore declined to rule on respondent's alternative argument that the gun should be suppressed as the fruit of an unwarned statement.

The Court of Appeals reversed the District Court's ruling with respect to probable cause but affirmed the suppression order on respondent's alternative theory.

As we explain below, the *Miranda* rule is a prophylactic employed to protect against violations of the Self-Incrimination Clause. The Self-Incrimination Clause, however, is not implicated by the admission into evidence of the physical fruit of a voluntary statement. Accordingly, there is no justification for extending the *Miranda* rule to this context. And just as the Self-Incrimination Clause primarily focuses on the criminal trial, so too

11. The Government concedes that respondent's answers to subsequent on-the-scene questioning are inadmissible at trial under Miranda v. Arizona despite the partial warning and respondent's assertions that he knew his rights. [Footnote by the Court.]

does the *Miranda* rule. The *Miranda* rule is not a code of police conduct, and police do not violate the Constitution (or even the *Miranda* rule, for that matter) by mere failures to warn. For this reason, the exclusionary rule articulated in cases such as *Wong Sun* does not apply.

II

The Self-Incrimination Clause provides: "No person . . . shall be compelled in any criminal case to be a witness against himself." We need not decide here the precise boundaries of the Clause's protection. For present purposes, it suffices to note that the core protection afforded by the Self-Incrimination Clause is a prohibition on compelling a criminal defendant to testify against himself at trial. To be sure, the Court has recognized and applied several prophylactic rules designed to protect the core privilege against self-incrimination. For example, although the text of the Self-Incrimination Clause at least suggests that "its coverage [is limited to] compelled testimony that is used against the defendant in the trial itself," potential suspects may, at times, assert the privilege in proceedings in which answers might be used to incriminate them in a subsequent criminal case.

Similarly, in *Miranda,* the Court concluded that the possibility of coercion inherent in custodial interrogations unacceptably raises the risk that a suspect's privilege against self-incrimination might be violated. To protect against this danger, the *Miranda* rule creates a presumption of coercion, in the absence of specific warnings, that is generally irrebuttable for purposes of the prosecution's case in chief.

But because these prophylactic rules (including the *Miranda* rule) necessarily sweep beyond the actual protections of the Self-Incrimination Clause, any further extension of these rules must be justified by its necessity for the protection of the actual right against compelled self-incrimination.

Our cases also make clear the related point that a mere failure to give *Miranda* warnings does not, by itself, violate a suspect's constitutional rights or even the *Miranda* rule. It follows that police do not violate a suspect's constitutional rights (or the *Miranda* rule) by negligent or even deliberate failures to provide the suspect with the full panoply of warnings prescribed by *Miranda.* Potential violations occur, if at all, only upon the admission of unwarned statements into evidence at trial. And, at that point, "[t]he exclusion of unwarned statements . . . is a complete and sufficient remedy" for any perceived *Miranda* violation.

Thus, unlike unreasonable searches under the Fourth Amendment or actual violations of the Due Process Clause or the Self-Incrimination Clause, there is, with respect to mere failures to warn, nothing to deter. There is therefore no reason to apply the "fruit of the poisonous tree" doctrine. It is not for this Court to impose its preferred police practices on either federal law enforcement officials or their state counterparts.

The Court of Appeals ascribed significance to the fact that, in this case, there might be "little [practical] difference between [respondent's] confessional statement" and the actual physical evidence. But, putting policy aside, we have held that "[t]he word 'witness' in the constitutional text limits the" scope of the Self-Incrimination Clause to testimonial evidence. The Constitution itself makes the distinction. And although it is true that the Court requires the exclusion of the physical fruit of actually coerced statements, it must be remembered that statements taken without sufficient *Miranda* warnings are presumed to have been coerced only for certain purposes and then only when necessary to protect the privilege against self-incrimination. For the reasons discussed above, we decline to extend that presumption further.

Justice KENNEDY, with whom Justice O'CONNOR joins, concurring in the judgment.

In Oregon v. Elstad (1984) and Harris v. New York (1971), evidence obtained following an unwarned interrogation was held admissible. This result was based in large part on our recognition that the concerns underlying the Miranda v. Arizona (1966), rule must be accommodated to other objectives of the criminal justice system. Here, it is sufficient to note that the Government presents an even stronger case for admitting the evidence obtained as the result of Patane's unwarned statement. Admission of non-testimonial physical fruits (the Glock in this case), even more so than the postwarning statements to the police in *Elstad* and Michigan v. Tucker (1974), does not run the risk of admitting into trial an accused's coerced incriminating statements against himself. In light of the important probative value of reliable physical evidence, it is doubtful that exclusion can be justified by a deterrence rationale sensitive to both law enforcement interests and a suspect's rights during an in-custody interrogation. Unlike the plurality, however, I find it unnecessary to decide whether the detective's failure to give Patane the full *Miranda* warnings should be characterized as a violation of the *Miranda* rule itself, or whether there is "[any]thing to deter" so long as the unwarned statements are not later introduced at trial.

Justice SOUTER, with whom Justice STEVENS and Justice GINSBURG join, dissenting.

The plurality repeatedly says that the Fifth Amendment does not address the admissibility of nontestimonial evidence, an overstatement that is beside the point. The issue actually presented today is whether courts should apply the fruit of the poisonous tree doctrine lest we create an incentive for the police to omit *Miranda* warnings, before custodial interrogation. In closing their eyes to the consequences of giving an evidentiary advantage to those who ignore *Miranda*, the plurality adds an important inducement for interrogators to ignore the rule in that case.

Miranda rested on insight into the inherently coercive character of custodial interrogation and the inherently difficult exercise of assessing the voluntariness of any confession resulting from it. Unless the police give the prescribed warnings meant to counter the coercive atmosphere, a custodial confession is inadmissible, there being no need for the previous time-consuming and difficult enquiry into voluntariness. That inducement to forestall involuntary statements and troublesome issues of fact can only atrophy if we turn around and recognize an evidentiary benefit when an unwarned statement leads investigators to tangible evidence. There is, of course, a price for excluding evidence, but the Fifth Amendment is worth a price, and in the absence of a very good reason, the logic of *Miranda* should be followed: a *Miranda* violation raises a presumption of coercion, and the Fifth Amendment privilege against compelled self-incrimination extends to the exclusion of derivative evidence. That should be the end of this case.

There is no way to read this case except as an unjustifiable invitation to law enforcement officers to flout *Miranda* when there may be physical evidence to be gained. The incentive is an odd one, coming from the Court on the same day it decides Missouri v. Seibert.

Justice BREYER, dissenting.

For reasons similar to those set forth in Justice Souter's dissent and in my concurring opinion in Missouri v. Seibert, I would extend to this context the "fruit of the poisonous tree" approach, which I believe the Court has come close to adopting in *Seibert*. Under that approach, courts would exclude physical evidence derived from unwarned questioning unless the failure to provide Miranda v. Arizona warnings was in good faith.

5. *Waiver of* Miranda *Rights*

In *Miranda*, the Court recognized that individuals may waive their right to remain silent and their right to counsel. However, the Court said that the government would have a "heavy burden" of demonstrating "that the defendant knowingly and intelligently waived his privilege against self-incrimination and his right to retained or appointed counsel." The Court said that "a valid waiver will not be presumed from the silence of the accused after warnings are given or simply from the fact that a confession was in fact eventually obtained." Yet in subsequent cases, such as Berghuis v. Thompkins, the Court seems to be taking a much more lenient approach to finding permissible waivers.

a.   What Is Sufficient to Constitute a Waiver?

Must a waiver be express or are implied waivers permissible? The Court resolved this in North Carolina v. Butler by holding that implied waivers are allowed.

NORTH CAROLINA v. BUTLER

441 U.S. 369 (1979)

Justice STEWART delivered the opinion of the Court.

In evident conflict with the present view of every other court that has considered the issue, the North Carolina Supreme Court has held that Miranda v. Arizona requires that no statement of a person under custodial interrogation may be admitted in evidence against him unless, at the time the statement was made, he explicitly waived the right to the presence of a lawyer.

The respondent was convicted in a North Carolina trial court of kidnaping, armed robbery, and felonious assault. The evidence at his trial showed that he and a man named Elmer Lee had robbed a gas station in Goldsboro, N.C., in December 1976, and had shot the station attendant as he was attempting to escape. The attendant was paralyzed, but survived to testify against the respondent. The prosecution also produced evidence of incriminating statements made by the respondent shortly after his arrest by Federal Bureau of Investigation agents in the Bronx, N.Y., on the basis of a North Carolina fugitive warrant. Outside the presence of the jury, FBI Agent Martinez testified that at the time of the arrest he fully advised the respondent of the rights delineated in the *Miranda* case. According to the uncontroverted testimony of Martinez, the agents then took the respondent to the FBI office in nearby New Rochelle, N.Y. There, after the agents determined that the respondent had an 11th grade education and was literate, he was given the Bureau's "Advice of Rights" form which he read. When asked if he understood his rights, he replied that he did. The respondent refused to sign the waiver at the bottom of the form. He was told that he need neither speak nor sign the form, but that the agents would like him to talk to them. The respondent replied: "I will talk to you but I am not signing any form." He then made inculpatory statements. Agent Martinez testified that the respondent said nothing when advised of his right to the assistance of a lawyer. At no time did the respondent request counsel or attempt to terminate the agents' questioning.

At the conclusion of this testimony the respondent moved to suppress the evidence of his incriminating statements on the ground that he had not waived his right to the assistance of counsel at the time the statements were made. On appeal, the North Carolina Supreme Court reversed the convictions and ordered a new trial. It found that the statements had been admitted in violation of the requirements of the *Miranda* decision, noting that the respondent had refused to waive in writing his right to have counsel present and that there had not been a specific oral waiver.

We conclude that the North Carolina Supreme Court erred in its reading of the *Miranda* opinion. An express written or oral statement of waiver of the right to remain silent or of the right to counsel is usually strong proof of the validity of that waiver, but is not inevitably either necessary or sufficient to establish waiver. The question is not one of form, but rather whether the defendant in fact knowingly and voluntarily waived the rights delineated in the *Miranda* case. As was unequivocally said in *Miranda*, mere silence is not enough. That does not mean that the defendant's silence, coupled with an understanding of his rights and a course of conduct indicating waiver, may never support a conclusion that a defendant has waived his rights. The courts must presume that a defendant did not waive his rights; the prosecution's burden is great; but in at least some cases waiver can be clearly inferred from the actions and words of the person interrogated.

The per se rule that the North Carolina Supreme Court has found in *Miranda* does not speak to these concerns. There is no doubt that this respondent was adequately and effectively apprised of his rights. The only question is whether he waived the exercise of one of those rights, the right to the presence of a lawyer. Neither the state court nor the respondent has offered any reason why there must be a negative answer to that question in the absence of an express waiver.

Justice BRENNAN, with whom Justice MARSHALL and Justice STEVENS join, dissenting.

There is no allegation of an affirmative waiver in this case. As the Court concedes, the respondent here refused to sign the waiver form, and "said nothing when advised of his right to the assistance of a lawyer." In the absence of an "affirmative waiver" in the form of an express written or oral statement, the Supreme Court of North Carolina correctly granted a new trial. I would, therefore, affirm its decision.

The rule announced by the Court today allows a finding of waiver based upon "infer[ence] from the actions and words of the person interrogated." The Court thus shrouds in half-light the question of waiver, allowing courts to construct inferences from ambiguous words and gestures. But the very premise of *Miranda* requires that ambiguity be interpreted against the interrogator. That premise is the recognition of the "compulsion inherent in custodial" interrogation, and of its purpose "to subjugate the individual to the will of [his] examiner." Under such conditions, only the most explicit waivers of rights can be considered knowingly and freely given.

The Supreme Court has ruled that whether there was a waiver is to be determined from the totality of the circumstances. In Fare v. Michael C., 442 U.S. 507 (1979), the Court said that the "totality of the circumstances approach is adequate to determine whether there has been a waiver even when interrogation of juveniles is involved." This includes considering the "juvenile's age, experience, education, background, and intelligence, and into whether he has the capacity to understand the warnings given him, the nature of his Fifth Amendment rights, and the consequences of waiving those rights."

However, the Court has stressed that these factors are relevant only as they relate to determining whether there was impermissible police behavior in obtaining incriminating statements. In Colorado v. Connelly, which is presented at the beginning of this chapter, the Court rejected the argument that a waiver of *Miranda* rights was invalid because the defendant was suffering from psychosis that prevented him from making free and voluntary choices. The Court explained that "*Miranda* protects defendants from government coercion, [but] goes no further than that." The Court said that "voluntariness of a waiver has always depended on the absence of police overreaching, not on 'free choice' in any broader sense of the word."

Can there be a knowing and voluntary waiver if police withhold from a suspect the information that an attorney sought to consult with him? This knowledge and the resulting consultation might well have prevented the incriminating statements. In Moran v. Burbine, 475 U.S. 412 (1986), the Court resolved this issue in favor of the police. A suspect in a murder case waived his *Miranda* rights, including his right to counsel, and confessed. The suspect's sister had hired an attorney who telephoned the police station and was told that no interrogation would occur until the next day. At no point was the suspect told that there was an attorney who had been retained and wanted to see him. The Court found no constitutional violation and said that "events occurring outside of the presence of the suspect and entirely unknown to him can have no bearing on the capacity to comprehend and knowingly relinquish a constitutional right." Although the Court criticized the police conduct as "inimical to the Fifth Amendment['s] values," it nonetheless found no constitutional violation.

Similarly, in Spring v. Colorado, 479 U.S. 564 (1987), the Court ruled that the police had no duty to inform a suspect of the nature of the crime for which he or she is under suspicion. The Court explained that "the additional information could affect only the wisdom of a *Miranda* waiver, not its essentially voluntary and knowing nature."

A subsequent decision, Berghuis v. Thompkins, goes the furthest in allowing a waiver to be inferred and requiring an explicit invocation of the right to remain silent.

BERGHUIS v. THOMPKINS

560 U.S. 370 (2010)

Justice KENNEDY delivered the opinion of the Court.

I

On January 10, 2000, a shooting occurred outside a mall in Southfield, Michigan. Among the victims was Samuel Morris, who died from multiple gunshot wounds. The other victim, Frederick France, recovered from his injuries and later testified. Thompkins, who was a suspect, fled. About one year later he was found in Ohio and arrested there.

Two Southfield police officers traveled to Ohio to interrogate Thompkins, then awaiting transfer to Michigan. The interrogation began around 1:30 P.M. and lasted about three hours. The interrogation was conducted in a room that was 8 by 10 feet, and Thompkins sat in a chair that resembled a school desk (it had an arm on it that swings around to provide a surface to write on). At the beginning of the interrogation, one of the officers, Detective Helgert, presented Thompkins with a form derived from the *Miranda* rule.

Helgert then read the other *Miranda* warnings out loud and asked Thompkins to sign the form to demonstrate that he understood his rights. Thompkins declined to sign the form. The record contains conflicting evidence about whether Thompkins then verbally confirmed that he understood the rights listed on the form.

Officers began an interrogation. At no point during the interrogation did Thompkins say that he wanted to remain silent, that he did not want to talk with the police, or that he wanted an attorney. Thompkins was "[l]argely" silent during the interrogation, which lasted about three hours. He did give a few limited verbal responses, however, such as "yeah," "no," or "I don't know." And on occasion he communicated by nodding his head. Thompkins also said that he "didn't want a peppermint" that was offered to him by the police and that the chair he was "sitting in was hard."

About 2 hours and 45 minutes into the interrogation, Helgert asked Thompkins, "Do you believe in God?" Thompkins made eye contact with Helgert and said "Yes," as his eyes "well[ed] up with tears." Helgert asked, "Do you pray to God?" Thompkins said "Yes." Helgert asked, "Do you pray to God to forgive you for shooting that boy down?" Thompkins answered "Yes" and looked away. Thompkins refused to make a written confession, and the interrogation ended about 15 minutes later.

Thompkins was charged with first-degree murder, assault with intent to commit murder, and certain firearms-related offenses. He moved to suppress the statements made during the interrogation. He argued that he had invoked his Fifth Amendment right to remain silent, requiring police to end the interrogation at once, that he had not waived his right to remain silent, and that his inculpatory statements were involuntary. The trial court denied the motion.

The jury found Thompkins guilty on all counts. He was sentenced to life in prison without parole.

II

The *Miranda* Court formulated a warning that must be given to suspects before they can be subjected to custodial interrogation. All concede that the warning given in this case was in full compliance with these requirements. The dispute centers on the response — or nonresponse — from the suspect.

A

Thompkins makes various arguments that his answers to questions from the detectives were inadmissible. He first contends that he "invoke[d] his privilege" to remain silent by not saying anything for a sufficient period of time, so the interrogation should have "cease[d]" before he made his inculpatory statements.

This argument is unpersuasive. In the context of invoking the *Miranda* right to counsel, the Court in *Davis v. United States* (1994), held that a suspect must do so "unambiguously." If an accused makes a statement concerning the right to counsel "that is ambiguous or equivocal" or makes no statement, the police are not required to end the interrogation, or ask questions to clarify whether the accused wants to invoke his or her *Miranda* rights.

The Court has not yet stated whether an invocation of the right to remain silent can be ambiguous or equivocal, but there is no principled reason to adopt different standards for determining when an accused has invoked the *Miranda* right to remain silent and the *Miranda* right to counsel at issue in *Davis*. Both protect the privilege against compulsory self-incrimination, by requiring an interrogation to cease when either right is invoked.

There is good reason to require an accused who wants to invoke his or her right to remain silent to do so unambiguously. A requirement of an unambiguous invocation of *Miranda* rights results in an objective inquiry that "avoid[s] difficulties of proof and . . . provide[s] guidance to officers" on how to proceed in the face of ambiguity. If an ambiguous act, omission, or statement could require police to end the interrogation, police would be required to make difficult decisions about an accused's unclear intent and face the consequence of suppression "if they guess wrong." Suppression of a voluntary confession in these circumstances would place a significant burden on society's interest in prosecuting criminal activity. Treating an ambiguous or equivocal act, omission, or statement as an invocation of *Miranda* rights "might add marginally to *Miranda*'s goal of dispelling the compulsion inherent in custodial interrogation." But "as *Miranda* holds, full comprehension of the rights to remain silent and request an attorney are sufficient to dispel whatever coercion is inherent in the interrogation process."

Thompkins did not say that he wanted to remain silent or that he did not want to talk with the police. Had he made either of these simple, unambiguous statements, he would have invoked his "'right to cut off questioning.'" Here he did neither, so he did not invoke his right to remain silent.

B

We next consider whether Thompkins waived his right to remain silent. Even absent the accused's invocation of the right to remain silent, the accused's statement during a custodial interrogation is inadmissible at trial unless the prosecution can establish that the accused "in fact knowingly and voluntarily waived [*Miranda*] rights" when making the statement. The waiver inquiry "has two distinct dimensions": waiver must be "voluntary in the sense that it was the product of a free and deliberate choice rather than intimidation, coercion, or deception," and "made with a full awareness of both the nature of the right being abandoned and the consequences of the decision to abandon it."

Some language in *Miranda* could be read to indicate that waivers are difficult to establish absent an explicit written waiver or a formal, express oral statement. The course of decisions since *Miranda*, informed by the application of *Miranda* warnings in the whole course of law enforcement, demonstrates that waivers can be established even absent formal or express statements of waiver that would be expected in, say, a judicial hearing to determine if a guilty plea has been properly entered. The main purpose of *Miranda* is to ensure that an accused is advised of and understands the right to remain silent and the right to counsel. Thus, "[i]f anything, our subsequent cases have reduced the impact of the *Miranda* rule on legitimate law enforcement while reaffirming the decision's core ruling that unwarned statements may not be used as evidence in the prosecution's case in chief."

The prosecution therefore does not need to show that a waiver of *Miranda* rights was express. An "implicit waiver" of the "right to remain silent" is sufficient to admit a suspect's statement into evidence. If the State establishes that a *Miranda* warning was given and the accused made an uncoerced statement, this showing, standing alone, is insufficient to demonstrate "a valid waiver" of *Miranda* rights. The prosecution must make the additional showing that the accused understood these rights. Where the prosecution shows that a *Miranda* warning was given and that it was understood by the accused, an accused's uncoerced statement establishes an implied waiver of the right to remain silent.

Although *Miranda* imposes on the police a rule that is both formalistic and practical when it prevents them from interrogating suspects without first providing them with a *Miranda* warning, it does not impose a formalistic waiver procedure that a suspect must follow to relinquish those rights. As a general proposition, the law can presume that an individual who, with a full understanding of his or her rights, acts in a manner inconsistent with their exercise has made a deliberate choice to relinquish the protection those rights afford.

The record in this case shows that Thompkins waived his right to remain silent. There is no basis in this case to conclude that he did not understand his rights; and on these facts it follows that he chose not to invoke or rely on those rights when he did speak. First, there is no contention that Thompkins did not understand his rights; and from this it follows that he knew what he gave up when he spoke. There was more than enough evidence in the record to conclude that Thompkins understood his *Miranda* rights. Thompkins received a written copy of the *Miranda* warnings; Detective Helgert determined that Thompkins could read and understand English; and Thompkins was given time to read the warnings. Thompkins, furthermore, read aloud the fifth warning, which stated that "you have the right to decide at any time before or during questioning to use your right to remain silent and your right to talk with a lawyer while you are being questioned." He was thus aware that his right to remain silent would not dissipate after a certain amount of time and that police would have to honor his right to be silent and his right to counsel during the whole course of interrogation.

Second, Thompkins's answer to Detective Helgert's question about whether Thompkins prayed to God for forgiveness for shooting the victim is a "course of conduct indicating waiver" of the right to remain silent. If Thompkins wanted to remain silent, he could have said nothing in response to Helgert's questions, or he could have unambiguously invoked his *Miranda* rights and ended the interrogation. The fact that Thompkins made a statement about three hours after receiving a *Miranda* warning does not overcome the fact that he engaged in a course of conduct indicating waiver. Police are not required to rewarn suspects from time to time. Thompkins's answer to Helgert's question about praying to God for forgiveness for shooting the victim was sufficient to show a course of conduct indicating waiver. This is confirmed by the fact that before then Thompkins had given sporadic answers to questions throughout the interrogation.

Third, there is no evidence that Thompkins's statement was coerced. Thompkins does not claim that police threatened or injured him during the interrogation or that he was in any way fearful. The interrogation was conducted in a standard-sized room in the middle of the afternoon. It is true that apparently he was in a straight-backed chair for three hours, but there is no authority for the proposition that an interrogation of this length is inherently coercive. Indeed, even where interrogations of greater duration were held to be improper, they were accompanied, as this one was not, by other facts indicating coercion, such as an incapacitated and sedated suspect, sleep and food deprivation, and threats.

In sum, a suspect who has received and understood the *Miranda* warnings, and has not invoked his *Miranda* rights, waives the right to remain silent by making an uncoerced statement to the police. Thompkins did not invoke his right to remain silent and stop the questioning. Understanding his rights in full, he waived his right to remain silent by making a voluntary statement to the police. The police, moreover, were not required to obtain a waiver of Thompkins's right to remain silent before interrogating him. The state court's decision rejecting Thompkins's *Miranda* claim was thus correct under *de novo* review and therefore necessarily reasonable under the more deferential AEDPA standard of review, 28 U.S.C. §2254(d).

Justice SOTOMAYOR, with whom Justice STEVENS, Justice GINSBURG, and Justice BREYER join, dissenting.

The Court concludes today that a criminal suspect waives his right to remain silent if, after sitting tacit and uncommunicative through nearly three hours of police interrogation, he utters a few one-word responses. The Court also concludes that a suspect who wishes to guard his right to remain silent against such a finding of "waiver" must, counterintuitively, speak — and must do so with sufficient precision to satisfy a clear-statement rule that construes ambiguity in favor of the police. Both propositions mark a substantial retreat from the protection against compelled self-incrimination that *Miranda v. Arizona* (1966), has long provided during custodial interrogation.

I

The strength of Thompkins' *Miranda* claims depends in large part on the circumstances of the 3-hour interrogation, at the end of which he made inculpatory statements later introduced at trial. The Court's opinion downplays record evidence that Thompkins remained almost completely silent and unresponsive throughout that session. One of the interrogating officers, Detective Helgert, testified that although Thompkins was administered *Miranda* warnings, the last of which he read aloud, Thompkins expressly declined to sign a written acknowledgment that he had been advised of and understood his rights. There is conflicting evidence in the record about whether Thompkins ever verbally confirmed understanding his rights. The record contains no indication that the officers sought or obtained an express waiver.

As to the interrogation itself, Helgert candidly characterized it as "very, very one-sided" and "nearly a monologue." Thompkins was "[p]eculiar," "[s]ullen," and "[g]enerally quiet." Helgert and his partner "did most of the talking," as Thompkins was "not verbally communicative" and "[l]argely" remained silent. To the extent Thompkins gave any response, his answers consisted of "a word or two. A 'yeah,' or a 'no,' or 'I don't know.' . . . And sometimes . . . he simply sat down . . . with [his] head in [his] hands looking down. Sometimes . . . he would look up and make eye-contact would be the only response." After proceeding in this fashion for approximately 2 hours and 45 minutes, Helgert asked Thompkins three questions relating to his faith in God. The prosecution relied at trial on Thompkins' one-word answers of "yes."

Miranda prescribed the now-familiar warnings that police must administer prior to questioning. *Miranda* and our subsequent cases also require police to "respect the accused's decision to exercise the rights outlined in the warnings." "If [an] individual indicates in any manner, at any time prior to or during questioning, that he wishes to remain silent" or if he "states that he wants an attorney," the interrogation "must cease."

Even when warnings have been administered and a suspect has not affirmatively invoked his rights, statements made in custodial interrogation may not be admitted as part of the prosecution's case in chief "unless and until" the prosecution demonstrates that an individual "knowingly and intelligently waive [d] [his] rights." "[A] heavy burden rests on the government to demonstrate that the defendant knowingly and intelligently waived his privilege against self-incrimination and his right to retained or appointed counsel."

The question whether a suspect has validly waived his right is "entirely distinct" as a matter of law from whether he invoked that right. The questions are related, however, in terms of the practical effect on the exercise of a suspect's rights. A suspect may at any time revoke his prior waiver of rights — or, closer to the facts of this case, guard against the possibility of a future finding that he implicitly waived his rights — by invoking the rights and thereby requiring the police to cease questioning.

II

Like the Sixth Circuit, I begin with the question whether Thompkins waived his right to remain silent. Even if Thompkins did not invoke that right, he is entitled to relief because Michigan did not satisfy its burden of establishing waiver.

Miranda's discussion of the prosecution's burden in proving waiver speaks with particular clarity to the facts of this case and therefore merits reproducing at length:

> If [an] interrogation continues without the presence of an attorney and a statement is taken, a heavy burden rests on the government to demonstrate that the defendant knowingly and intelligently waived his privilege against self-incrimination and his right to retained or appointed counsel. . . . Since the State is responsible for establishing the isolated circumstances under which [an] interrogation takes place and has the only means of making available corroborated evidence of warnings given during incommunicado interrogation, the burden is rightly on its shoulders.
>
> An express statement that the individual is willing to make a statement and does not want an attorney followed closely by a statement could constitute a waiver. But a valid waiver will not be presumed simply from the silence of the accused after warnings are given or simply from the fact that a confession was in fact eventually obtained.

This Court's decisions subsequent to *Miranda* have emphasized the prosecution's "heavy burden" in proving waiver. We have also reaffirmed that a court may not presume waiver from a suspect's silence or from the mere fact that a confession was eventually obtained.

It is undisputed here that Thompkins never expressly waived his right to remain silent. His refusal to sign even an acknowledgment that he understood his *Miranda* rights evinces, if anything, an intent not to waive those rights. That Thompkins did not make the inculpatory statements at issue until after approximately 2 hours and 45 minutes of interrogation serves as "strong evidence" against waiver. *Miranda* and *Butler* expressly preclude the possibility that the inculpatory statements themselves are sufficient to establish waiver.

In these circumstances, Thompkins' "actions and words" preceding the inculpatory statements simply do not evidence a "course of conduct indicating waiver" sufficient to carry the prosecution's burden. I believe it is objectively unreasonable under our clearly established precedents to conclude the prosecution met its "heavy burden" of proof on a record consisting of three one-word answers, following 2 hours and 45 minutes of silence punctuated by a few largely nonverbal responses to unidentified questions.

The Court concludes that when *Miranda* warnings have been given and understood, "an accused's uncoerced statement establishes an implied waiver of the right to remain silent." More broadly still, the Court states that, "[a]s a general proposition, the law can presume that an individual who, with a full understanding of his or her rights, acts in a manner inconsistent with their exercise has made a deliberate choice to relinquish the protection those rights afford."

These principles flatly contradict our longstanding views that "a valid waiver will not be presumed . . . simply from the fact that a confession was in fact eventually obtained," and that "[t]he courts must presume that a defendant did not waive his rights." At best, the Court today creates an unworkable and conflicting set of presumptions that will undermine *Miranda*'s goal of providing "concrete constitutional guidelines for law enforcement agencies and courts to follow." At worst, it overrules *sub silentio* an essential aspect of the protections *Miranda* has long provided for the constitutional guarantee against self-incrimination.

Today's dilution of the prosecution's burden of proof to the bare fact that a suspect made inculpatory statements after *Miranda* warnings were given and understood takes an unprecedented step away from the "high standards of proof for the waiver of constitutional rights" this Court has long demanded. When waiver is to be inferred during a custodial interrogation, there are sound reasons to require evidence beyond inculpatory statements themselves. *Miranda* and our subsequent cases are premised on the idea that custodial interrogation is inherently coercive.

Today's decision thus ignores the important interests *Miranda* safeguards. The underlying constitutional guarantee against self-incrimination reflects "many of our fundamental values and most noble aspirations," our society's "preference for an accusatorial rather than an inquisitorial system of criminal justice"; a "fear that self-incriminating statements will be elicited by inhumane treatment and abuses" and a resulting "distrust of self-deprecatory statements"; and a realization that while the privilege is "sometimes a shelter to the guilty, [it] is often a protection to the innocent." For these reasons, we have observed, a criminal law system "which comes to depend on the 'confession' will, in the long run, be less reliable and more subject to abuses than a system relying on independent investigation."

III

Thompkins separately argues that his conduct during the interrogation invoked his right to remain silent, requiring police to terminate questioning. Like the Sixth Circuit, I would not reach this question because Thompkins is in any case entitled to relief as to waiver. But even if Thompkins would not prevail on his invocation claim under AEDPA's deferential standard of review, I cannot agree with the Court's much broader ruling that a suspect must clearly invoke his right to silence by speaking. Taken together with the Court's reformulation of the prosecution's burden of proof as to waiver, today's novel clear-statement rule for invocation invites police to question a suspect at length—notwithstanding his persistent refusal to answer questions—in the hope of eventually obtaining a single inculpatory response which will suffice to prove waiver of rights. Such a result bears little semblance to the "fully effective" prophylaxis that *Miranda* requires.

The Court asserts in passing that treating ambiguous statements or acts as an invocation of the right to silence will only "'marginally'" serve *Miranda*'s goals. Experience suggests the contrary. In the 16 years since *Davis* was decided, ample evidence has accrued that criminal suspects often use equivocal or colloquial language in attempting to invoke their right to silence. A number of lower courts that have (erroneously, in my view) imposed a clear-statement requirement for invocation of the right to silence have rejected as ambiguous an array of statements whose meaning might otherwise be thought plain. At a minimum, these decisions suggest that differentiating "clear" from "ambiguous" statements is often a subjective inquiry. Even if some of the cited decisions are themselves in tension with *Davis*' admonition that a suspect need not "'speak with the discrimination of an Oxford don'" to invoke his rights, they demonstrate that today's decision will significantly burden the exercise of the right to silence. Notably, when a suspect "understands his (expressed) wishes to have been ignored . . . in contravention of the 'rights' just read to him by his interrogator, he may well see further objection as futile and confession (true or not) as the only way to end his interrogation."

For these reasons, I believe a precautionary requirement that police "scrupulously hono[r]" a suspect's right to cut off questioning is a more faithful application of our precedents than the Court's awkward and needless extension of *Davis*.

Today's decision turns *Miranda* upside down. Criminal suspects must now unambiguously invoke their right to remain silent—which, counterintuitively, requires them to speak. At the same time, suspects will be legally presumed to have waived their rights even if they have given no clear expression of their intent to do so. Those results, in my view, find no basis in *Miranda* or our subsequent cases and are inconsistent with the fair-trial principles on which those precedents are grounded. Today's broad new rules are all the more unfortunate because they are unnecessary to the disposition of the case before us. I respectfully dissent.

In Berguis v. Thompkins, the Court held that the right to remain silent must be expressly invoked. Berguis v. Thompkins was after a person was arrested and *Miranda* warnings were given. What about *before* a person is taken into custody, arrested, and given *Miranda* warnings?

SALINAS v. TEXAS

133 S. Ct. 2174 (2013)

Justice ALITO announced the judgment of the Court and delivered an opinion in which THE CHIEF JUSTICE and Justice KENNEDY join.

Without being placed in custody or receiving *Miranda* warnings, petitioner voluntarily answered the questions of a police officer who was investigating a murder. But petitioner balked when the officer asked whether a ballistics test would show that the shell casings found at the crime scene would match petitioner's shotgun. Petitioner was subsequently charged with murder, and at trial prosecutors argued that his reaction to the officer's question suggested that he was guilty. Petitioner claims that this argument violated the Fifth Amendment, which guarantees that "[n]o person . . . shall be compelled in any criminal case to be a witness against himself."

Petitioner's Fifth Amendment claim fails because he did not expressly invoke the privilege against self-incrimination in response to the officer's question. It has long been settled that the privilege "generally is not self-executing" and that a witness who desires its protection "'must claim it.'" Although "no ritualistic formula is necessary in order to invoke the privilege," a witness does not do so by simply standing mute.

I

On the morning of December 18, 1992, two brothers were shot and killed in their Houston home. There were no witnesses to the murders, but a neighbor who heard gunshots saw someone run out of the house and speed away in a dark-colored car. Police recovered six shotgun shell casings at the scene. The investigation led police to petitioner, who had been a guest at a party the victims hosted the night before they were killed. Police visited petitioner at his home, where they saw a dark blue car in the driveway. He agreed to hand over his shotgun for ballistics testing and to accompany police to the station for questioning.

Petitioner's interview with the police lasted approximately one hour. All agree that the interview was noncustodial, and the parties litigated this case on the assumption that he was not read *Miranda* warnings. For most of the interview, petitioner answered the officer's questions. But when asked whether his shotgun "would match the shells recovered at the scene of the murder," petitioner declined to answer. Instead, petitioner "[l]ooked down at the floor, shuffled his feet, bit his bottom lip, cl[e]nched his hands in his lap, [and] began to tighten up." After a few moments of silence, the officer asked additional questions, which petitioner answered.

Petitioner did not testify at trial. Over his objection, prosecutors used his reaction to the officer's question during the 1993 interview as evidence of his guilt. The jury found petitioner guilty, and he received a 20-year sentence.

We granted certiorari, to resolve a division of authority in the lower courts over whether the prosecution may use a defendant's assertion of the privilege against self-incrimination during a noncustodial police interview as part of its case in chief. But because petitioner did not invoke the privilege during his interview, we find it unnecessary to reach that question.

II

The privilege against self-incrimination "is an exception to the general principle that the Government has the right to everyone's testimony." To prevent the privilege from shielding information not properly within its scope, we have long held that a witness who "'desires the protection of the privilege . . . must claim it'" at the time he relies on it.

That requirement ensures that the Government is put on notice when a witness intends to rely on the privilege so that it may either argue that the testimony sought could not be self-incriminating, or cure any potential self-incrimination through a grant of immunity. The express invocation requirement also gives courts tasked with evaluating a Fifth Amendment claim a contemporaneous record establishing the witness' reasons for refusing to answer. In these ways, insisting that witnesses expressly invoke the privilege "assures that the Government obtains all the information to which it is entitled."

We have previously recognized two exceptions to the requirement that witnesses invoke the privilege, but neither applies here. First, we held in Griffin v. California (1965), that a criminal defendant need not take the stand and assert the privilege at his own trial. That exception reflects the fact that a criminal defendant has an "absolute right not to testify." Because petitioner had no comparable unqualified right during his interview with police, his silence falls outside the *Griffin* exception.

Second, we have held that a witness' failure to invoke the privilege must be excused where governmental coercion makes his forfeiture of the privilege involuntary. Thus, in *Miranda*, we said that a suspect who is subjected to the "inherently compelling pressures" of an unwarned custodial interrogation need not invoke the privilege. Due to the uniquely coercive nature of custodial interrogation, a suspect in custody cannot be said to have voluntarily forgone the privilege "unless [he] fails to claim [it] after being suitably warned."

Petitioner cannot benefit from that principle because it is undisputed that his interview with police was voluntary. As petitioner himself acknowledges, he agreed to accompany the officers to the station and "was free to leave at any time during the interview." That places petitioner's situation outside the scope of *Miranda* and other cases in which we have held that various forms of governmental coercion prevented defendants from voluntarily invoking the privilege. The critical question is whether, under the "circumstances" of this case, petitioner was deprived of the ability to voluntarily invoke the Fifth Amendment. He was not. We have before us no allegation that petitioner's failure to assert the privilege was involuntary, and it would have been a simple matter for him to say that he was not answering the officer's question on Fifth Amendment grounds. Because he failed to do so, the prosecution's use of his noncustodial silence did not violate the Fifth Amendment.

B

Petitioner urges us to adopt a third exception to the invocation requirement for cases in which a witness stands mute and thereby declines to give an answer that officials suspect would be incriminating. Our cases all but foreclose such an exception, which would needlessly burden the Government's interests in obtaining testimony and prosecuting criminal activity. We therefore decline petitioner's invitation to craft a new exception to the "general rule" that a witness must assert the privilege to subsequently benefit from it.

Our cases establish that a defendant normally does not invoke the privilege by remaining silent. We have also repeatedly held that the express invocation requirement applies even when an official has reason to suspect that the answer to his question would incriminate the witness.

Petitioner's proposed exception would also be very difficult to reconcile with Berghuis v. Thompkins (2010). There, we held in the closely related context of post-*Miranda* silence that a defendant failed to invoke the privilege when he refused to respond to police questioning for 2 hours and 45 minutes. If the extended custodial silence in that case did not invoke the privilege, then surely the momentary silence in this case did not do so either.

At oral argument, counsel for petitioner suggested that it would be unfair to require a suspect unschooled in the particulars of legal doctrine to do anything more than remain silent in order to invoke his "right to remain silent." But popular misconceptions notwithstanding, the Fifth Amendment guarantees that no one may be "compelled in any criminal case to be a witness against himself"; it does not establish an unqualified "right to remain silent." A witness' constitutional right to refuse to answer questions depends on his reasons for doing so, and courts need to know those reasons to evaluate the merits of a Fifth Amendment claim.

C

Finally, we are not persuaded by petitioner's arguments that applying the usual express invocation requirement where a witness is silent during a noncustodial police interview will prove unworkable in practice. We also reject petitioner's argument that an express invocation requirement will encourage police officers to "'unfairly "tric[k]"'" suspects into cooperating. Petitioner worries that officers could unduly pressure suspects into talking by telling them that their silence could be used in a future prosecution. But as petitioner himself concedes, police officers "have done nothing wrong" when they "accurately stat[e] the law." So long as police do not deprive a witness of the ability to voluntarily invoke the privilege, there is no Fifth Amendment violation.

Before petitioner could rely on the privilege against self-incrimination, he was required to invoke it. Because he failed to do so, the judgment of the Texas Court of Criminal Appeals is affirmed.

Justice THOMAS, with whom Justice SCALIA joins, concurring in the judgment.

We granted certiorari to decide whether the Fifth Amendment privilege against compulsory self-incrimination prohibits a prosecutor from using a defendant's pre-custodial silence as evidence of his guilt. The plurality avoids reaching that question and instead concludes that Salinas' Fifth Amendment claim fails because he did not expressly invoke the privilege. I think there is a simpler way to resolve this case. In my view, Salinas' claim would fail even if he had invoked the privilege because the prosecutor's comments regarding his precustodial silence did not compel him to give self-incriminating testimony.

In Griffin v. California (1965), this Court held that the Fifth Amendment prohibits a prosecutor or judge from commenting on a defendant's failure to testify. The Court reasoned that such comments, and any adverse inferences drawn from them, are a "penalty" imposed on the defendant's exercise of his Fifth Amendment privilege. *Ibid.* Salinas argues that we should extend *Griffin*'s no-adverse-inference rule to a defendant's silence during a precustodial interview. I have previously explained that the Court's decision in *Griffin* "lacks foundation in the Constitution's text, history, or logic" and should not be extended. I adhere to that view today.

Griffin is impossible to square with the text of the Fifth Amendment, which provides that "[n]o person . . . shall be compelled in any criminal case to be a witness against himself." A defendant is not "compelled . . . to be a witness against himself" simply because a jury has been told that it may draw an adverse inference from his silence.

Nor does the history of the Fifth Amendment support *Griffin*. At the time of the founding, English and American courts strongly encouraged defendants to give unsworn statements and drew adverse inferences when they failed to do so. Given *Griffin*'s indefensible foundation, I would not extend it to a defendant's silence during a precustodial interview. I agree with the plurality that Salinas' Fifth Amendment claim fails and, therefore, concur in the judgment.

Justice BREYER, with whom Justice GINSBURG, Justice SOTOMAYOR, and Justice KAGAN join, dissenting.

In my view the Fifth Amendment here prohibits the prosecution from commenting on the petitioner's silence in response to police questioning. And I dissent from the Court's contrary conclusion.

The question before us is whether the Fifth Amendment prohibits the prosecutor from eliciting and commenting upon the evidence about Salinas' silence. The plurality believes that the Amendment does not bar the evidence and comments because Salinas "did not expressly invoke the privilege against self-incrimination" when he fell silent during the questioning at the police station. But, in my view, that conclusion is inconsistent with this Court's case law and its underlying practical rationale.

The Fifth Amendment prohibits prosecutors from commenting on an individual's silence where that silence amounts to an effort to avoid becoming "a witness against himself." This Court has specified that "a rule of evidence" permitting "commen[t] . . . by counsel" in a criminal case upon a defendant's failure to testify "violates the Fifth Amendment." And, since "it is impermissible to penalize an individual for exercising his Fifth Amendment privilege when he is under police custodial interrogation," the "prosecution may not . . . use at trial *the fact that he stood mute* or claimed his privilege in the face of accusation."

Particularly in the context of police interrogation, a contrary rule would undermine the basic protection that the Fifth Amendment provides. To permit a prosecutor to comment on a defendant's constitutionally protected silence would put that defendant in an impossible predicament. He must either answer the question or remain silent. If he answers the question, he may well reveal, for example, prejudicial facts, disreputable associates, or suspicious circumstances—even if he is innocent. If he remains silent, the prosecutor may well use that silence to suggest a consciousness of guilt. And if the defendant then takes the witness stand in order to explain either his speech or his silence, the prosecution may introduce, say for impeachment purposes, a prior conviction that the law would otherwise make inadmissible. Thus, where the Fifth Amendment is at issue, to allow comment on silence directly or indirectly can compel an individual to act as "a witness against himself"—very much what the Fifth Amendment forbids. And that is similarly so whether the questioned individual, as part of his decision to remain silent, invokes the Fifth Amendment explicitly or implicitly, through words, through deeds, or through reference to surrounding circumstances.

It is consequently not surprising that this Court, more than half a century ago, explained that "no ritualistic formula is necessary in order to invoke the privilege." Thus, a prosecutor may not comment on a defendant's failure to testify at trial—even if neither the defendant nor anyone else ever mentions a Fifth Amendment right not to do so. Circumstances, not a defendant's statement, tie the defendant's silence to the right. Similarly, a prosecutor may not comment on the fact that a defendant in custody, *after* receiving *Miranda* warnings, "stood mute"—regardless of whether he "claimed his privilege" in so many words. Again, it is not any explicit statement but, instead, the defendant's deeds (silence) and circumstances (receipt of the warnings) that tie together silence and constitutional right.

Applying these principles to the present case, I would hold that Salinas need not have expressly invoked the Fifth Amendment. The context was that of a criminal investigation. Police told Salinas that and made clear that he was a suspect. His interrogation took place at the police station. Salinas was not represented by counsel. The relevant question—about whether the shotgun from Salinas' home would incriminate him — amounted to a switch in subject matter. And it was obvious that the new question sought to ferret out whether Salinas was guilty of murder.

These circumstances give rise to a reasonable inference that Salinas' silence derived from an exercise of his Fifth Amendment rights. This Court has recognized repeatedly that many, indeed most, Americans are aware that they have a constitutional right not to incriminate themselves by answering questions posed by the police during an interrogation conducted in order to figure out the perpetrator of a crime. The nature of the surroundings, the switch of topic, the particular question — all suggested that the right we have and generally *know* we have was at issue at the critical moment here. Salinas, not being represented by counsel, would not likely have used the precise words "Fifth Amendment" to invoke his rights because he would not likely have been aware of technical legal requirements, such as a need to identify the Fifth Amendment by name.

At the same time, the need to categorize Salinas' silence as based on the Fifth Amendment is supported here by the presence, in full force, of the predicament I discussed earlier, namely that of not forcing Salinas to choose between incrimination through speech and incrimination through silence.

I recognize that other cases may arise where facts and circumstances surrounding an individual's silence present a closer question. The critical question — whether those circumstances give rise to a fair inference that the silence rests on the Fifth Amendment — will not always prove easy to administer. But that consideration does not support the plurality's rule-based approach here, for the administrative problems accompanying the plurality's approach are even worse.

Far better, in my view, to pose the relevant question directly: Can one fairly infer from an individual's silence and surrounding circumstances an exercise of the Fifth Amendment's privilege? The need for simplicity, the constitutional importance of applying the Fifth Amendment to those who seek its protection, and this Court's case law all suggest that this is the right question to ask here. And the answer to that question in the circumstances of today's case is clearly: yes.

For these reasons, I believe that the Fifth Amendment prohibits a prosecutor from commenting on Salinas's silence.

b. How Is a Waiver After the Assertion of Rights Treated?

If a suspect asserts his or her rights under *Miranda*, how is a subsequent waiver handled? The Court here has drawn a distinction between the two key rights specified in *Miranda*: the right to remain silent and the right to counsel. As for the former, the Court has been willing to find waivers in these situations where the defendant speaks to police after initially invoking the right to remain silent. Michigan v. Mosley is the key case.

MICHIGAN v. MOSLEY
423 U.S. 96 (1975)

Justice STEWART delivered the opinion of the Court.

The respondent, Richard Bert Mosley, was arrested in Detroit, Mich., in the early afternoon of April 8, 1971, in connection with robberies that had recently occurred at the Blue Goose Bar and the White Tower Restaurant on that city's lower east side. The arresting officer, Detective James Cowie of the Armed Robbery Section of the Detroit Police Department, was acting on a tip implicating Mosley and three other men in the robberies. After effecting the arrest, Detective Cowie brought Mosley to the Robbery, Breaking and Entering Bureau of the Police Department, located on the fourth floor of the departmental headquarters building. The officer advised Mosley of his rights under this Court's decision in Miranda v. Arizona and had him read and sign the department's constitutional rights notification certificate. After filling out the necessary arrest papers, Cowie began questioning Mosley about the robbery of the White Tower Restaurant. When Mosley said he did not want to answer any questions about the robberies, Cowie promptly ceased the interrogation. The completion of the arrest papers and the questioning of Mosley together took approximately 20 minutes. At no time during the questioning did Mosley indicate a desire to consult with a lawyer, and there is no claim that the procedures followed to this point did not fully comply with the strictures of the *Miranda* opinion. Mosley was then taken to a ninth-floor cell block.

Shortly after 6 P.M., Detective Hill of the Detroit Police Department Homicide Bureau brought Mosley from the cell block to the fifth-floor office of the Homicide Bureau for questioning about the fatal shooting of a man named Leroy Williams. Williams had been killed on January 9, 1971, during a holdup attempt outside the 101 Ranch Bar in Detroit. Mosley had not been arrested on this charge or interrogated about it by Detective Cowie. Before questioning Mosley about this homicide, Detective Hill carefully advised him of his "*Miranda* rights." Mosley read the notification form both silently and aloud, and Detective Hill then read and explained the warnings to him and had him sign the form. Mosley at first denied any involvement in the Williams murder, but after the officer told him that Anthony Smith had confessed to participating in the slaying and had named him as the "shooter," Mosley made a statement implicating himself in the homicide. The interrogation by Detective Hill lasted approximately 15 minutes, and at no time during its course did Mosley ask to consult with a lawyer or indicate that he did not want to discuss the homicide. In short, there is no claim that the procedures followed during Detective Hill's interrogation of Mosley, standing alone, did not fully comply with the strictures of the *Miranda* opinion.

Mosley was subsequently charged in a one-count information with first-degree murder. Before the trial he moved to suppress his incriminating statement on a number of grounds, among them the claim that under the doctrine of the *Miranda* case it was constitutionally impermissible for Detective Hill to question him about the Williams murder after he had told Detective Cowie that he did not want to answer any questions about the robberies. The trial court denied the motion to suppress after an evidentiary hearing, and the incriminating statement was subsequently introduced in evidence against Mosley at his trial. The jury convicted Mosley of first-degree murder, and the court imposed a mandatory sentence of life imprisonment.

The issue in this case, rather, is whether the conduct of the Detroit police that led to Mosley's incriminating statement did in fact violate the *Miranda* "guidelines," so as to render the statement inadmissible in evidence against Mosley at his trial.

[*Miranda*] states that "the interrogation must cease" when the person in custody indicates that "he wishes to remain silent." It does not state under what circumstances, if any, a resumption of questioning is permissible. The passage could be literally read to mean that a person who has invoked his "right to silence" can never again be subjected to custodial interrogation by any police officer at any time or place on any subject. Another possible construction of the passage would characterize "any statement taken after the person invokes his privilege" as "the product of compulsion" and would therefore mandate its exclusion from evidence, even if it were volunteered by the person in custody without any further interrogation whatever. Or the passage could be interpreted to require only the immediate cessation of questioning, and to permit a resumption of interrogation after a momentary respite.

It is evident that any of these possible literal interpretations would lead to absurd and unintended results. To permit the continuation of custodial interrogation after a momentary cessation would clearly frustrate the purposes of *Miranda* by allowing repeated rounds of questioning to undermine the will of the person being questioned. At the other extreme, a blanket prohibition against the taking of voluntary statements or a permanent immunity from further interrogation, regardless of the circumstances, would transform the *Miranda* safeguards into wholly irrational obstacles to legitimate police investigative activity, and deprive suspects of an opportunity to make informed and intelligent assessments of their interests. Clearly, therefore, neither this passage nor any other passage in the *Miranda* opinion can sensibly be read to create a per se proscription of indefinite duration upon any further questioning by any police officer on any subject, once the person in custody has indicated a desire to remain silent.

A reasonable and faithful interpretation of the *Miranda* opinion must rest on the intention of the Court in that case to adopt "fully effective means . . . to notify the person of his right of silence and to assure that the exercise of the right will be scrupulously honored. . . ." The critical safeguard identified in the passage at issue is a person's "right to cut off questioning." Through the exercise of his option to terminate questioning he can control the time at which questioning occurs, the subjects discussed, and the duration of the interrogation. The requirement that law enforcement authorities must respect a person's exercise of that option counteracts the coercive pressures of the custodial setting. We therefore conclude that the admissibility of statements obtained after the person in custody has decided to remain silent depends under *Miranda* on whether his "right to cut off questioning" was "scrupulously honored."

This is not a case, therefore, where the police failed to honor a decision of a person in custody to cut off questioning, either by refusing to discontinue the interrogation upon request or by persisting in repeated efforts to wear down his resistance and make him change his mind. In contrast to such practices, the police here immediately ceased the interrogation, resumed questioning only after the passage of a significant period of time and the provision of a fresh set of warnings, and restricted the second interrogation to a crime that had not been a subject of the earlier interrogation.

For these reasons, we conclude that the admission in evidence of Mosley's incriminating statement did not violate the principles of Miranda v. Arizona.

Justice BRENNAN, with whom Justice MARSHALL joins, dissenting.

In formulating its procedural safeguard, the Court skirts the problem of compulsion and thereby fails to join issue with the dictates of *Miranda*. The language which the Court finds controlling in this case teaches that renewed questioning itself is part of the process which invariably operates to overcome the will of a suspect. That teaching is embodied in the form of a proscription on any further questioning once the suspect has exercised his right to remain silent. Today's decision uncritically abandons that teaching. The Court assumes, contrary to the controlling language, that "scrupulously honoring" an initial exercise of the right to remain silent preserves the efficaciousness of initial and future warnings despite the fact that the suspect has once been subjected to interrogation and then has been detained for a lengthy period of time.

Observing that the suspect can control the circumstances of interrogation "[t]hrough the exercise of his option to terminate questioning," the Court concludes "that the admissibility of statements obtained after the person in custody has decided to remain silent depends . . . on whether his 'right to cut off questioning' was 'scrupulously honored.'" But scrupulously honoring exercises of the right to cut off questioning is only meaningful insofar as the suspect's will to exercise that right remains wholly unfettered. The Court's formulation thus assumes the very matter at issue here: whether renewed questioning following a lengthy period of detention acts to overbear the suspect's will, irrespective of giving the *Miranda* warnings a second time (and scrupulously honoring them), thereby rendering inconsequential any failure to exercise the right to remain silent. For the Court it is enough conclusorily to assert that "[t]he subsequent questioning did not undercut Mosley's previous decision not to answer Detective Cowie's inquiries." Under *Miranda*, however, Mosley's failure to exercise the right upon renewed questioning is presumptively the consequence of an overbearing in which detention and that subsequent questioning played central roles.

I agree that *Miranda* is not to be read, on the one hand, to impose an absolute ban on resumption of questioning "at any time or place on any subject," or on the other hand, "to permit a resumption of interrogation after a momentary respite." But this surely cannot justify adoption of a vague and ineffective procedural standard that falls somewhere between those absurd extremes, for *Miranda* in flat and unambiguous terms requires that questioning "cease" when a suspect exercises the right to remain silent. *Miranda*'s terms, however, are not so uncompromising as to preclude the fashioning of guidelines to govern this case. Those guidelines must, of course, necessarily be sensitive to the reality that "[a]s a practical matter, the compulsion to speak in the isolated setting of the police station may well be greater than in courts or other official investigations, where there are often impartial observers to guard against intimidation or trickery."

However, the Court has treated a defendant's invocation of the right to counsel differently. If a defendant invokes the right to counsel, then the police cannot initiate further interrogation unless the suspect initiates the communications. Edwards v. Arizona, an especially important decision in this area, articulated the rule here.

EDWARDS v. ARIZONA
451 U.S. 477 (1981)

Justice WHITE delivered the opinion of the Court.

We granted certiorari in this case, limited to whether the Fifth, Sixth, and Fourteenth Amendments require suppression of a post-arrest confession, which was obtained after Edwards had invoked his right to consult counsel before further interrogation.

I

On January 19, 1976, a sworn complaint was filed against Edwards in Arizona state court charging him with robbery, burglary, and first-degree murder. An arrest warrant was issued pursuant to the complaint, and Edwards was arrested at his home later that same day. At the police station, he was informed of his rights as required by Miranda v. Arizona. Petitioner stated that he understood his rights, and was willing to submit to questioning. After being told that another suspect already in custody had implicated him in the crime, Edwards denied involvement and gave a taped statement presenting an alibi defense. He then sought to "make a deal." The interrogating officer told him that he wanted a statement, but that he did not have the authority to negotiate a deal. The officer provided Edwards with the telephone number of a county attorney. Petitioner made the call, but hung up after a few moments. Edwards then said: "I want an attorney before making a deal." At that point, questioning ceased and Edwards was taken to county jail.

At 9:15 the next morning, two detectives, colleagues of the officer who had interrogated Edwards the previous night, came to the jail and asked to see Edwards. When the detention officer informed Edwards that the detectives wished to speak with him, he replied that he did not want to talk to anyone. The guard told him that "he had" to talk and then took him to meet with the detectives. The officers identified themselves, stated they wanted to talk to him, and informed him of his *Miranda* rights. Edwards was willing to talk, but he first wanted to hear the taped statement of the alleged accomplice who had implicated him. After listening to the tape for several minutes, petitioner said that he would make a statement so long as it was not tape-recorded. The detectives informed him that the recording was irrelevant since they could testify in court concerning whatever he said. Edwards replied: "I'll tell you anything you want to know, but I don't want it on tape." He thereupon implicated himself in the crime.

Prior to trial, Edwards moved to suppress his confession on the ground that his *Miranda* rights had been violated when the officers returned to question him after he had invoked his right to counsel.

II

Edwards insists that having exercised his right on the 19th to have counsel present during interrogation, he did not validly waive that right on the 20th. For the following reasons, we agree.

First, the Arizona Supreme Court applied an erroneous standard for determining waiver where the accused has specifically invoked his right to counsel. It is reasonably clear under our cases that waivers of counsel must not only be voluntary, but must also constitute a knowing and intelligent relinquishment or abandonment of a known right or privilege, a matter which depends in each case "upon the particular facts and circumstances surrounding that case, including the background, experience, and conduct of the accused."

Considering the proceedings in the state courts in the light of this standard, we note that in denying petitioner's motion to suppress, the trial court found the admission to have been "voluntary," without separately focusing on whether Edwards had knowingly and intelligently relinquished his right to counsel. Here, however sound the conclusion of the state courts as to the voluntariness of Edwards' admission may be, neither the trial court nor the Arizona Supreme Court undertook to focus on whether Edwards understood his right to counsel and intelligently and knowingly relinquished it. It is thus apparent that the decision below misunderstood the requirement for finding a valid waiver of the right to counsel, once invoked.

Second, although we have held that after initially being advised of his *Miranda* rights, the accused may himself validly waive his rights and respond to interrogation, see North Carolina v. Butler, the Court has strongly indicated that additional safeguards are necessary when the accused asks for counsel; and we now hold that when an accused has invoked his right to have counsel present during custodial interrogation, a valid waiver of that right cannot be established by showing only that he responded to further police-initiated custodial interrogation even if he has been advised of his rights. We further hold that an accused, such as Edwards, having expressed his desire to deal with the police only through counsel, is not subject to further interrogation by the authorities until counsel has been made available to him, unless the accused himself initiates further communication, exchanges, or conversations with the police.

Miranda itself indicated that the assertion of the right to counsel was a significant event and that once exercised by the accused, "the interrogation must cease until an attorney is present." Our later cases have not abandoned that view.

Justice POWELL, with whom Justice REHNQUIST joins, concurring in the result.

Although I agree that the judgment of the Arizona Supreme Court must be reversed, I do not join the Court's opinion because I am not sure what it means. I have thought it settled law, as these cases tell us, that one accused of crime may waive any of the constitutional safeguards—including the right to remain silent, to jury trial, to call witnesses, to cross-examine one's accusers, to testify in one's own behalf, and—of course—to have counsel. Whatever the right, the standard for waiver is whether the actor fully understands the right in question and voluntarily intends to relinquish it.

In its opinion today, however, the Court—after reiterating the familiar principles of waiver—goes on to say: "We further hold that an accused, such as Edwards, having expressed his desire to deal with the police only through counsel, is not subject to further interrogation by the authorities until counsel has been made available to him, unless the accused [has] himself initiate[d] further communication, exchanges, or conversations with the police."

In view of the emphasis placed on "initiation," I find the Court's opinion unclear. If read to create a new per se rule, requiring a threshold inquiry as to precisely who opened any conversation between an accused and state officials, I cannot agree. I would not superimpose a new element of proof on the established doctrine of waiver of counsel.

In sum, once warnings have been given and the right to counsel has been invoked, the relevant inquiry—whether the suspect now desires to talk to police without counsel—is a question of fact to be determined in light of all of the circumstances. Who "initiated" a conversation may be relevant to the question of waiver, but it is not the sine qua non to the inquiry. The ultimate question is whether there was a free and knowing waiver of counsel before interrogation commenced.

The Court often has reaffirmed and applied the holding of *Edwards*. In Michigan v. Jackson, 475 U.S. 625 (1986), the Court ruled that "if the police initiate interrogation after a defendant's assertion, at arraignment or similar proceeding, of the right to counsel, any waiver of the defendant's right to counsel for that police-initiated interrogation is invalid." Minnick v. Mississippi is a particularly important affirmation and application of *Edwards*.

MINNICK v. MISSISSIPPI
498 U.S. 146 (1990)

Justice KENNEDY delivered the opinion of the Court.

To protect the privilege against self-incrimination guaranteed by the Fifth Amendment, we have held that the police must terminate interrogation of an accused in custody if the accused requests the assistance of counsel. Miranda v. Arizona (1966). We reinforced the protections of *Miranda* in Edwards v. Arizona (1981), which held that once the accused requests counsel, officials may not reinitiate questioning "until counsel has been made available" to him. The issue in the case before us is whether *Edwards'* protection ceases once the suspect has consulted with an attorney.

Petitioner Robert Minnick and fellow prisoner James Dyess escaped from a county jail in Mississippi and, a day later, broke into a mobile home in search of weapons. In the course of the burglary they were interrupted by the arrival of the trailer's owner, Ellis Thomas, accompanied by Lamar Lafferty and Lafferty's infant son. Dyess and Minnick used the stolen weapons to kill Thomas and the senior Lafferty. Minnick's story is that Dyess murdered one victim and forced Minnick to shoot the other. Before the escapees could get away, two young women arrived at the mobile home. They were held at gunpoint, then bound hand and foot. Dyess and Minnick fled in Thomas' truck, abandoning the vehicle in New Orleans. The fugitives continued to Mexico, where they fought, and Minnick then proceeded alone to California. Minnick was arrested in Lemon Grove, California, on a Mississippi warrant, some four months after the murders.

The confession at issue here resulted from the last interrogation of Minnick while he was held in the San Diego jail, but we first recount the events which preceded it. Minnick was arrested on Friday, August 22, 1986. Petitioner testified that he was mistreated by local police during and after the arrest. The day following the arrest, Saturday, two Federal Bureau of Investigation (FBI) agents came to the jail to interview him. Petitioner testified that he refused to go to the interview, but was told he would "have to go down or else." The FBI report indicates that the agents read petitioner his *Miranda* warnings, and that he acknowledged he understood his rights. He refused to sign a rights waiver form, however, and said he would not answer "very many" questions. Minnick told the agents about the jailbreak and the flight, and described how Dyess threatened and beat him. Early in the interview, he sobbed "[i]t was my life or theirs," but otherwise he hesitated to tell what happened at the trailer. The agents reminded him he did not have to answer questions without a lawyer present. According to the report, "Minnick stated 'Come back Monday when I have a lawyer,' and stated that he would make a more complete statement then with his lawyer present." The FBI interview ended.

After the FBI interview, an appointed attorney met with petitioner. Petitioner spoke with the lawyer on two or three occasions, though it is not clear from the record whether all of these conferences were in person.

On Monday, August 25, Deputy Sheriff J.C. Denham of Clarke County, Mississippi, came to the San Diego jail to question Minnick. Minnick testified that his jailers again told him he would "have to talk" to Denham and that he "could not refuse." Denham advised petitioner of his rights, and petitioner again declined to sign a rights waiver form. Petitioner told Denham about the escape and then proceeded to describe the events at the mobile home. According to petitioner, Dyess jumped out of the mobile home and shot the first of the two victims, once in the back with a shotgun and once in the head with a pistol. Dyess then handed the pistol to petitioner and ordered him to shoot the other victim, holding the shotgun on petitioner until he did so. Petitioner also said that when the two girls arrived, he talked Dyess out of raping or otherwise hurting them.

Minnick was tried for murder in Mississippi. He moved to suppress all statements given to the FBI or other police officers, including Denham. The trial court denied the motion with respect to petitioner's statements to Denham, but suppressed his other statements. Petitioner was convicted on two counts of capital murder and sentenced to death.

Edwards is "designed to prevent police from badgering a defendant into waiving his previously asserted *Miranda* rights." The rule ensures that any statement made in subsequent interrogation is not the result of coercive pressures. *Edwards* conserves judicial resources which would otherwise be expended in making difficult determinations of voluntariness, and implements the protections of *Miranda* in practical and straightforward terms.

The merit of the *Edwards* decision lies in the clarity of its command and the certainty of its application. We have confirmed that the *Edwards* rule provides "'clear and unequivocal' guidelines to the law enforcement profession."

We do not interpret [*Edwards*] to mean, as the Mississippi court thought, that the protection of *Edwards* terminates once counsel has consulted with the suspect. In context, the requirement that counsel be "made available" to the accused refers to more than an opportunity to consult with an attorney outside the interrogation room.

In *Edwards*, we focused on *Miranda*'s instruction that when the accused invokes his right to counsel, "the interrogation must cease until an attorney is present," agreeing with Edwards' contention that he had not waived his right "to have counsel present during custodial interrogation."

Our emphasis on counsel's presence at interrogation is not unique to *Edwards*. It derives from *Miranda*, where we said that in the cases before us "[t]he presence of counsel . . . would be the adequate protective device necessary to make the process of police interrogation conform to the dictates of the [Fifth Amendment] privilege. His presence would insure that statements made in the government-established atmosphere are not the product of compulsion." In our view, a fair reading of *Edwards* and subsequent cases demonstrates that we have interpreted the rule to bar police-initiated interrogation unless the accused has counsel with him at the time of questioning. Whatever the ambiguities of our earlier cases on this point, we now hold that when counsel is requested, interrogation must cease, and officials may not reinitiate interrogation without counsel present, whether or not the accused has consulted with his attorney.

We consider our ruling to be an appropriate and necessary application of the *Edwards* rule. A single consultation with an attorney does not remove the suspect from persistent attempts by officials to persuade him to waive his rights, or from the coercive pressures that accompany custody and that may increase as custody is prolonged.

The case before us well illustrates the pressures, and abuses, that may be concomitants of custody. Petitioner testified that though he resisted, he was required to submit to both the FBI and the Denham interviews. In the latter instance, the compulsion to submit to interrogation followed petitioner's unequivocal request during the FBI interview that questioning cease until counsel was present. The case illustrates also that consultation is not always effective in instructing the suspect of his rights. One plausible interpretation of the record is that petitioner thought he could keep his admissions out of evidence by refusing to sign a formal waiver of rights. If the authorities had complied with Minnick's request to have counsel present during interrogation, the attorney could have corrected Minnick's misunderstanding, or indeed counseled him that he need not make a statement at all. We decline to remove protection from police-initiated questioning based on isolated consultations with counsel who is absent when the interrogation resumes.

Edwards does not foreclose finding a waiver of Fifth Amendment protections after counsel has been requested, provided the accused has initiated the conversation or discussions with the authorities; but that is not the case before us. There can be no doubt that the interrogation in question was initiated by the police; it was a formal interview which petitioner was compelled to attend. Since petitioner made a specific request for counsel before the interview, the police-initiated interrogation was impermissible. Petitioner's statement to Denham was not admissible at trial.

Justice SCALIA, with whom THE CHIEF JUSTICE joins, dissenting.

The Court today establishes an irrebuttable presumption that a criminal suspect, after invoking his *Miranda* right to counsel, can never validly waive that right during any police-initiated encounter, even after the suspect has been provided multiple *Miranda* warnings and has actually consulted his attorney. Because I see no justification for applying the *Edwards* irrebuttable presumption when a criminal suspect has actually consulted with his attorney, I respectfully dissent.

In this case, of course, we have not been called upon to reconsider *Edwards*, but simply to determine whether its irrebuttable presumption should continue after a suspect has actually consulted with his attorney. Whatever justifications might support *Edwards* are even less convincing in this context.

Most of the Court's discussion of *Edwards*—which stresses repeatedly, in various formulations, the case's emphasis upon the "right 'to have counsel present during custodial interrogation,'"—is beside the point. The existence and the importance of the *Miranda*-created right "to have counsel present" are unquestioned here. What is questioned is why a State should not be given the opportunity to prove that the right was voluntarily waived by a suspect who, after having been read his *Miranda* rights twice and having consulted with counsel at least twice, chose to speak to a police officer (and to admit his involvement in two murders) without counsel present.

Edwards did not assert the principle that no waiver of the *Miranda* right "to have counsel present" is possible. It simply adopted the presumption that no waiver is voluntary in certain circumstances, and the issue before us today is how broadly those circumstances are to be defined. They should not, in my view, extend beyond the circumstances present in *Edwards* itself—where the suspect in custody asked to consult an attorney and was interrogated before that attorney had ever been provided. In those circumstances, the *Edwards* rule rests upon an assumption similar to that of *Miranda* itself: that when a suspect in police custody is first questioned he is likely to be ignorant of his rights and to feel isolated in a hostile environment. This likelihood is thought to justify special protection against unknowing or coerced waiver of rights. After a suspect has seen his request for an attorney honored, however, and has actually spoken with that attorney, the probabilities change. The suspect then knows that he has an advocate on his side, and that the police will permit him to consult that advocate. He almost certainly also has a heightened awareness (above what the *Miranda* warning itself will provide) of his right to remain silent—since at the earliest opportunity "any lawyer worth his salt will tell the suspect in no uncertain terms to make no statement to the police under any circumstances."

Under these circumstances, an irrebuttable presumption that any police-prompted confession is the result of ignorance of rights, or of coercion, has no genuine basis in fact.

One should not underestimate the extent to which the Court's expansion of *Edwards* constricts law enforcement. Today's ruling, that the invocation of a right to counsel permanently prevents a police-initiated waiver, makes it largely impossible for the police to urge a prisoner who has initially declined to confess to change his mind — or indeed, even to ask whether he has changed his mind. Many persons in custody will invoke the *Miranda* right to counsel during the first interrogation, so that the permanent prohibition will attach at once. Those who do not do so will almost certainly request or obtain counsel at arraignment.

Today's extension of the *Edwards* prohibition is the latest stage of prophylaxis built upon prophylaxis, producing a veritable fairyland castle of imagined constitutional restriction upon law enforcement. It seems obvious to me that, even in *Edwards* itself but surely in today's decision, we have gone far beyond any genuine concern about suspects who do not know their right to remain silent, or who have been coerced to abandon it. Both holdings are explicable, in my view, only as an effort to protect suspects against what is regarded as their own folly. The sharp-witted criminal would know better than to confess; why should the dull-witted suffer for his lack of mental endowment? Providing him an attorney at every stage where he might be induced or persuaded (though not coerced) to incriminate himself will even the odds. Apart from the fact that this protective enterprise is beyond our authority under the Fifth Amendment or any other provision of the Constitution, it is unwise. The procedural protections of the Constitution protect the guilty as well as the innocent, but it is not their objective to set the guilty free. That some clever criminals may employ those protections to their advantage is poor reason to allow criminals who have not done so to escape justice.

Thus, even if I were to concede that an honest confession is a foolish mistake, I would welcome rather than reject it; a rule that foolish mistakes do not count would leave most offenders not only unconvicted but undetected. More fundamentally, however, it is wrong, and subtly corrosive of our criminal justice system, to regard an honest confession as a "mistake." While every person is entitled to stand silent, it is more virtuous for the wrongdoer to admit his offense and accept the punishment he deserves. Not only for society, but for the wrongdoer himself, "admissio[n] of guilt, . . . if not coerced, [is] inherently desirable" because it advances the goals of both "justice and rehabilitation." We should, then, rejoice at an honest confession, rather than pity the "poor fool" who has made it; and we should regret the attempted retraction of that good act, rather than seek to facilitate and encourage it. To design our laws on premises contrary to these is to abandon belief in either personal responsibility or the moral claim of just government to obedience. Today's decision is misguided.

Yet there is the question of how long will *Edwards* preclude questioning after a suspect invokes his or her right to counsel under *Miranda*. In Maryland v. Shatzer, the Court held that this expires after 14 days. In reading this decision, it is important to consider whether this is an arbitrary line drawn by the Court or a desirable approach to balancing competing interests.

MARYLAND v. SHATZER

559 U.S. 98 (2010)

Justice SCALIA delivered the opinion of the Court.

We consider whether a break in custody ends the presumption of involuntariness established in *Edwards v. Arizona* (1981).

I

In August 2003, a social worker assigned to the Child Advocacy Center in the Criminal Investigation Division of the Hagerstown Police Department referred to the department allegations that respondent Michael Shatzer, Sr., had sexually abused his 3-year-old son. At that time, Shatzer was incarcerated at the Maryland Correctional Institution—Hagerstown, serving a sentence for an unrelated child-sexual-abuse offense. Detective Shane Blankenship was assigned to the investigation and interviewed Shatzer at the correctional institution on August 7, 2003. Before asking any questions, Blankenship reviewed Shatzer's *Miranda* rights with him, and obtained a written waiver of those rights. When Blankenship explained that he was there to question Shatzer about sexually abusing his son, Shatzer expressed confusion—he had thought Blankenship was an attorney there to discuss the prior crime for which he was incarcerated. Blankenship clarified the purpose of his visit, and Shatzer declined to speak without an attorney. Accordingly, Blankenship ended the interview, and Shatzer was released back into the general prison population. Shortly thereafter, Blankenship closed the investigation.

Two years and six months later, the same social worker referred more specific allegations to the department about the same incident involving Shatzer. Detective Paul Hoover, from the same division, was assigned to the investigation. He and the social worker interviewed the victim, then eight years old, who described the incident in more detail. With this new information in hand, on March 2, 2006, they went to the Roxbury Correctional Institute, to which Shatzer had since been transferred, and interviewed Shatzer in a maintenance room outfitted with a desk and three chairs. Hoover explained that he wanted to ask Shatzer about the alleged incident involving Shatzer's son. Shatzer was surprised because he thought that the investigation had been closed, but Hoover explained they had opened a new file. Hoover then read Shatzer his *Miranda* rights and obtained a written waiver on a standard department form.

Hoover interrogated Shatzer about the incident for approximately 30 minutes. Before the interview ended, Shatzer agreed to Hoover's request that he submit to a polygraph examination. At no point during the interrogation did Shatzer request to speak with an attorney or refer to his prior refusal to answer questions without one.

Five days later, on March 7, 2006, Hoover and another detective met with Shatzer at the correctional facility to administer the polygraph examination. After reading Shatzer his *Miranda* rights and obtaining a written waiver, the other detective administered the test and concluded that Shatzer had failed. When the detectives then questioned Shatzer, he became upset, started to cry, and incriminated himself. After making this inculpatory statement, Shatzer requested an attorney, and Hoover promptly ended the interrogation.

II

In *Miranda v. Arizona* (1966), the Court adopted a set of prophylactic measures to protect a suspect's Fifth Amendment right from the "inherently compelling pressures" of custodial interrogation.

In *Edwards*, the Court determined that [the] traditional standard for waiver was not sufficient to protect a suspect's right to have counsel present at a subsequent interrogation if he had previously requested counsel; "additional safeguards" were necessary. The Court therefore superimposed a "second layer of prophylaxis." *Edwards* held:

> [W]hen an accused has invoked his right to have counsel present during custodial interrogation, a valid waiver of that right cannot be established by showing only that he responded to further police-initiated custodial interrogation even if he has been advised of his rights. . . . [He] is not subject to further interrogation by the authorities until counsel has been made available to him, unless the accused himself initiates further communication, exchanges, or conversations with the police.

The rationale of *Edwards* is that once a suspect indicates that "he is not capable of undergoing [custodial] questioning without advice of counsel," "any subsequent waiver that has come at the authorities' behest, and not at the suspect's own instigation, is itself the product of the 'inherently compelling pressures' and not the purely voluntary choice of the suspect." Under this rule, a voluntary *Miranda* waiver is sufficient at the time of an initial attempted interrogation to protect a suspect's right to have counsel present, but it is not sufficient at the time of subsequent attempts if the suspect initially requested the presence of counsel. The implicit assumption, of course, is that the subsequent requests for interrogation pose a significantly greater risk of coercion. That increased risk results not only from the police's persistence in trying to get the suspect to talk, but also from the continued pressure that begins when the individual is taken into custody as a suspect and sought to be interrogated—pressure likely to "increase as custody is prolonged." The *Edwards* presumption of involuntariness ensures that police will not take advantage of the mounting coercive pressures of "prolonged police custody," by repeatedly attempting to question a suspect who previously requested counsel until the suspect is "badgered into submission."

We have frequently emphasized that the *Edwards* rule is not a constitutional mandate, but judicially prescribed prophylaxis. Because *Edwards* is "our rule, not a constitutional command," "it is our obligation to justify its expansion."

A judicially crafted rule is "justified only by reference to its prophylactic purpose," and applies only where its benefits outweigh its costs. We begin with the benefits. *Edwards'* presumption of involuntariness has the incidental effect of "conserv[ing] judicial resources which would otherwise be expended in making difficult determinations of voluntariness." Its fundamental purpose, however, is to "[p]reserv[e] the integrity of an accused's choice to communicate with police only through counsel," by "prevent[ing] police from badgering a defendant into waiving his previously asserted *Miranda* rights." Thus, the benefits of the rule are measured by the number of coerced confessions it suppresses that otherwise would have been admitted.

It is easy to believe that a suspect may be coerced or badgered into abandoning his earlier refusal to be questioned without counsel in the paradigm *Edwards* case. That is a case in which the suspect has been arrested for a particular crime and is held in uninterrupted pretrial custody while that crime is being actively investigated. After the initial interrogation, and up to and including the second one, he remains cut off from his normal life and companions, "thrust into" and isolated in an "unfamiliar," "police-dominated atmosphere," where his captors "appear to control [his] fate."

When, unlike what happened in these three cases, a suspect has been released from his pretrial custody and has returned to his normal life for some time before the later attempted interrogation, there is little reason to think that his change of heart regarding interrogation without counsel has been coerced. He has no longer been isolated. He has likely been able to seek advice from an attorney, family members, and friends. And he knows from his earlier experience that he need only demand counsel to bring the interrogation to a halt; and that investigative custody does not last indefinitely. In these circumstances, it is far fetched to think that a police officer's asking the suspect whether he would like to waive his *Miranda* rights will any more "wear down the accused," than did the first such request at the original attempted interrogation—which is of course not deemed coercive. His change of heart is less likely attributable to "badgering" than it is to the fact that further deliberation in familiar surroundings has caused him to believe (rightly or wrongly) that cooperating with the investigation is in his interest. Uncritical extension of *Edwards* to this situation would not significantly increase the number of genuinely coerced confessions excluded. The "justification for a conclusive presumption disappears when application of the presumption will not reach the correct result most of the time."

At the same time that extending the *Edwards* rule yields diminished benefits, extending the rule also increases its costs: the in-fact voluntary confessions it excludes from trial, and the voluntary confessions it deters law enforcement officers from even trying to obtain. Voluntary confessions are not merely "a proper element in law enforcement," they are an "unmitigated good," "'essential to society's compelling interest in finding, convicting, and punishing those who violate the law.'"

The only logical endpoint of *Edwards* disability is termination of *Miranda* custody and any of its lingering effects. Without that limitation — and barring some purely arbitrary time-limit — every *Edwards* prohibition of custodial interrogation of a particular suspect would be eternal. The prohibition applies, of course, when the subsequent interrogation pertains to a different crime, *Roberson, supra*, when it is conducted by a different law enforcement authority, and even when the suspect has met with an attorney after the first interrogation. And it not only prevents questioning *ex ante*; it would render invalid *ex post*, confessions invited and obtained from suspects who (unbeknownst to the interrogators) have acquired *Edwards* immunity previously in connection with any offense in any jurisdiction. In a country that harbors a large number of repeat offenders, this consequence is disastrous.

We conclude that such an extension of *Edwards* is not justified; we have opened its "protective umbrella," far enough. The protections offered by *Miranda*, which we have deemed sufficient to ensure that the police respect the suspect's desire to have an attorney present the first time police interrogate him, adequately ensure that result when a suspect who initially requested counsel is reinterrogated after a break in custody that is of sufficient duration to dissipate its coercive effects.

If Shatzer's return to the general prison population qualified as a break in custody, there is no doubt that it lasted long enough (2½ years) to meet that durational requirement. But what about a break that has lasted only one year? Or only one week? It is impractical to leave the answer to that question for clarification in future case-by-case adjudication; law enforcement officers need to know, with certainty and beforehand, when renewed interrogation is lawful. And while it is certainly unusual for this Court to set forth precise time limits governing police action, it is not unheard-of. In *County of Riverside v. McLaughlin* (1991), we specified 48 hours as the time within which the police must comply with the requirement that a person arrested without a warrant be brought before a magistrate to establish probable cause for continued detention.

Like *McLaughlin*, this is a case in which the requisite police action (there, presentation to a magistrate; here, abstention from further interrogation) has not been prescribed by statute but has been established by opinion of this Court. We think it appropriate to specify a period of time to avoid the consequence that continuation of the *Edwards* presumption "will not reach the correct result most of the time." It seems to us that period is 14 days. That provides plenty of time for the suspect to get reacclimated to his normal life, to consult with friends and counsel, and to shake off any residual coercive effects of his prior custody.

The 14-day limitation meets Shatzer's concern that a break-in-custody rule lends itself to police abuse. He envisions that once a suspect invokes his *Miranda* right to counsel, the police will release the suspect briefly (to end the *Edwards* presumption) and then promptly bring him back into custody for reinterrogation. But once the suspect has been out of custody long enough (14 days) to eliminate its coercive effect, there will be nothing to gain by such gamesmanship—nothing, that is, except the entirely appropriate gain of being able to interrogate a suspect who has made a valid waiver of his *Miranda* rights.

III

The facts of this case present an additional issue. No one questions that Shatzer was in custody for *Miranda* purposes during the interviews with Detective Blankenship in 2003 and Detective Hoover in 2006. After the 2003 interview, Shatzer was released back into the general prison population where he was serving an unrelated sentence. The issue is whether that constitutes a break in *Miranda* custody.

Here, we are addressing the interim period during which a suspect was not interrogated, but was subject to a baseline set of restraints imposed pursuant to a prior conviction. Without minimizing the harsh realities of incarceration, we think lawful imprisonment imposed upon conviction of a crime does not create the coercive pressures identified in *Miranda*.

Interrogated suspects who have previously been convicted of crime live in prison. When they are released back into the general prison population, they return to their accustomed surroundings and daily routine—they regain the degree of control they had over their lives prior to the interrogation. Sentenced prisoners, in contrast to the *Miranda* paradigm, are not isolated with their accusers. They live among other inmates, guards, and workers, and often can receive visitors and communicate with people on the outside by mail or telephone.

Their detention, moreover, is relatively disconnected from their prior unwillingness to cooperate in an investigation. The former interrogator has no power to increase the duration of incarceration, which was determined at sentencing. And even where the possibility of parole exists, the former interrogator has no apparent power to decrease the time served.

Because Shatzer experienced a break in *Miranda* custody lasting more than two weeks between the first and second attempts at interrogation, *Edwards* does not mandate suppression of his March 2006 statements.

Justice STEVENS, concurring in the judgment.

While I agree that the presumption from *Edwards v. Arizona* (1981), is not "eternal," and does not mandate suppression of Shatzer's statement made after a 2½-year break in custody, I do not agree with the Court's newly announced rule: that *Edwards always* ceases to apply when there is a 14-day break in custody.

I

The most troubling aspect of the Court's time-based rule is that it disregards the compulsion caused by a second (or third, or fourth) interrogation of an indigent suspect who was told that if he requests a lawyer, one will be provided for him. When police tell an indigent suspect that he has the right to an attorney, that he is not required to speak without an attorney present, and that an attorney will be provided to him at no cost before questioning, the police have made a significant promise. If they cease questioning and then reinterrogate the suspect 14 days later without providing him with a lawyer, the suspect is likely to feel that the police lied to him and that he really does not have any right to a lawyer.

When officers informed Shatzer of his rights during the first interrogation, they presumably informed him that if he requested an attorney, one would be appointed for him before he was asked any further questions. But if an indigent suspect requests a lawyer, "any further interrogation" (even 14 days later) "without counsel having been provided will surely exacerbate whatever compulsion to speak the suspect may be feeling." When police have not honored an earlier commitment to provide a detainee with a lawyer, the detainee likely will "understan[d] his (expressed) wishes to have been ignored" and "may well see further objection as futile and confession (true or not) as the only way to end his interrogation."

II

The Court never explains why its rule cannot depend on, in addition to a break in custody and passage of time, a concrete event or state of affairs, such as the police having honored their commitment to provide counsel. Instead, the Court simply decides to create a time-based rule, and in so doing, disregards much of the analysis upon which *Edwards* and subsequent decisions were based. However, as discussed above, the Court ignores the effects not of badgering but of reinterrogating a suspect who took the police at their word that he need not answer questions without an attorney present. The Court, moreover, ignores that when a suspect asks for counsel, until his request is answered, there are still the same "inherently compelling" pressures of custodial interrogation on which the *Miranda* line of cases is based, and that the concern about compulsion is especially serious for a detainee who has requested a lawyer, an act that signals his "inability to cope with the pressures of custodial interrogation."

Instead of deferring to these well-settled understandings of the *Edwards* rule, the Court engages in its own speculation that a 14-day break in custody eliminates the compulsion that animated *Edwards*. But its opinion gives no strong basis for believing that this is the case. A 14-day break in custody does not eliminate the rationale for the initial *Edwards* rule: The detainee has been told that he may remain silent and speak only through a lawyer and that if he cannot afford an attorney, one will be provided for him. He has asked for a lawyer. He does not have one. He is in custody. And police are still questioning him. A 14-day break in custody does not change the fact that custodial interrogation is inherently compelling. It is unlikely to change the fact that a detainee "considers himself unable to deal with the pressures of custodial interrogation without legal assistance." And in some instances, a 14-day break in custody may make matters worse "[w]hen a suspect understands his (expressed) wishes to have been ignored" and thus "may well see further objection as futile and confession (true or not) as the only way to end his interrogation."

The many problems with the Court's new rule are exacerbated in the very situation in this case: a suspect who is in prison. Even if, as the Court assumes, a trip to one's home significantly changes the *Edwards* calculus, a trip to one's prison cell is not the same. A prisoner's freedom is severely limited, and his entire life remains subject to government control. Such an environment is not conducive to "shak[ing] off any residual coercive effects of his prior custody." Nor can a prisoner easily "seek advice from an attorney, family members, and friends," especially not within 14 days; prisoners are frequently subject to restrictions on communications. Nor, in most cases, can he live comfortably knowing that he cannot be badgered by police; prison is not like a normal situation in which a suspect "is in control, and need only shut his door or walk away to avoid police badgering." Indeed, for a person whose every move is controlled by the State, it is likely that "his sense of dependence on, and trust in, counsel as the guardian of his interests in dealing with government officials intensified." Moreover, even if it is true as a factual matter that a prisoner's fate is not controlled by the police who come to interrogate him, how is the prisoner supposed to know that? As the Court itself admits, compulsion is likely when a suspect's "captors appear to control [his] fate," But when a guard informs a suspect that he must go speak with police, it will "appear" to the prisoner that the guard and police are not independent. "Questioning by captors, who *appear* to control the suspect's fate, may create mutually reinforcing pressures that the Court has assumed will weaken the suspect's will."

III

Because, at the very least, we do not know whether Shatzer could obtain a lawyer, and thus would have felt that police had lied about providing one, I cannot join the Court's opinion. I concur in today's judgment, however, on another ground: Even if Shatzer could not consult a lawyer and the police never provided him one, the $2^{1}/_{2}$-year break in custody is a basis for treating the second interrogation as no more coercive than the first. Neither a break in custody nor the passage of time has an inherent, curative power. But certain things change over time. An indigent suspect who took police at their word that they would provide an attorney probably will feel that he has "been denied the counsel he has clearly requested," when police begin to question him, without a lawyer, only 14 days later. But, when a suspect has been left alone for a significant period of time, he is not as likely to draw such conclusions when the police interrogate him again. It is concededly "impossible to determine with precision" where to draw such a line. In the case before us, however, the suspect was returned to the general prison population for 2½ years. I am convinced that this period of time is sufficient. I therefore concur in the judgment.

———

What, though, of the situation where a suspect's request for counsel is equivocal or unclear? Do the police in such situations have the obligation to stop questioning or at least clarify the suspect's desires? In Davis v. United States, the Court resolved this in favor of the police and held that "the suspect must unambiguously request counsel." Recall that above, in Berghuis v. Thompkins, the Court relied on *Davis* and that the invocation of the right to remain silent must be unambiguous.

DAVIS v. UNITED STATES
512 U.S. 452 (1994)

Justice O'CONNOR delivered the opinion of the Court.

In Edwards v. Arizona (1981), we held that law enforcement officers must immediately cease questioning a suspect who has clearly asserted his right to have counsel present during custodial interrogation. In this case we decide how law enforcement officers should respond when a suspect makes a reference to counsel that is insufficiently clear to invoke the *Edwards* prohibition on further questioning.

I

Pool brought trouble — not to River City, but to the Charleston Naval Base. Petitioner, a member of the United States Navy, spent the evening of October 2, 1988, shooting pool at a club on the base. Another sailor, Keith Shackleton, lost a game and a $30 wager to petitioner, but Shackleton refused to pay. After the club closed, Shackleton was beaten to death with a pool cue on a loading dock behind the commissary. The body was found early the next morning.

The investigation by the Naval Investigative Service (NIS) gradually focused on petitioner. Investigative agents determined that petitioner was at the club that evening, and that he was absent without authorization from his duty station the next morning. The agents also learned that only privately owned pool cues could be removed from the club premises, and that petitioner owned two cues—one of which had a bloodstain on it. The agents were told by various people that petitioner either had admitted committing the crime or had recounted details that clearly indicated his involvement in the killing.

On November 4, 1988, petitioner was interviewed at the NIS office. As required by military law, the agents advised petitioner that he was a suspect in the killing, that he was not required to make a statement, that any statement could be used against him at a trial by court-martial, and that he was entitled to speak with an attorney and have an attorney present during questioning. Petitioner waived his rights to remain silent and to counsel, both orally and in writing.

About an hour and a half into the interview, petitioner said, "Maybe I should talk to a lawyer." According to the uncontradicted testimony of one of the interviewing agents, the interview then proceeded as follows: "[We m]ade it very clear that we're not here to violate his rights, that if he wants a lawyer, then we will stop any kind of questioning with him, that we weren't going to pursue the matter unless we have it clarified is he asking for a lawyer or is he just making a comment about a lawyer, and he said, [']No, I'm not asking for a lawyer,' and then he continued on, and said, 'No, I don't want a lawyer.'"

After a short break, the agents reminded petitioner of his rights to remain silent and to counsel. The interview then continued for another hour, until petitioner said, "I think I want a lawyer before I say anything else." At that point, questioning ceased.

At his general court-martial, petitioner moved to suppress statements made during the November 4 interview. The Military Judge denied the motion, holding that "the mention of a lawyer by [petitioner] during the course of the interrogation [was] not in the form of a request for counsel and . . . the agents properly determined that [petitioner] was not indicating a desire for or invoking his right to counsel." Petitioner was convicted on one specification of unpremeditated murder. He was sentenced to confinement for life, a dishonorable discharge, forfeiture of all pay and allowances, and a reduction to the lowest pay grade. The convening authority approved the findings and sentence. The Navy-Marine Corps Court of Military Review affirmed.

II

The Sixth Amendment right to counsel attaches only at the initiation of adversary criminal proceedings and before proceedings are initiated a suspect in a criminal investigation has no constitutional right to the assistance of counsel. Nevertheless, we held in Miranda v. Arizona (1966), that a suspect subject to custodial interrogation has the right to consult with an attorney and to have counsel present during questioning, and that the police must explain this right to him before questioning begins. The right to counsel recognized in *Miranda* is sufficiently important to suspects in criminal investigations, we have held, that it "requir[es] the special protection of the knowing and intelligent waiver standard." Edwards v. Arizona. If the suspect effectively waives his right to counsel after receiving the *Miranda* warnings, law enforcement officers are free to question him. But if a suspect requests counsel at any time during the interview, he is not subject to further questioning until a lawyer has been made available or the suspect himself reinitiates conversation. This "second layer of prophylaxis for the *Miranda* right to counsel," is "designed to prevent police from badgering a defendant into waiving his previously asserted *Miranda* rights." To that end, we have held that a suspect who has invoked the right to counsel cannot be questioned regarding any offense unless an attorney is actually present.

The applicability of the "'rigid' prophylactic rule" of *Edwards* requires courts to "determine whether the accused actually invoked his right to counsel." To avoid difficulties of proof and to provide guidance to officers conducting interrogations, this is an objective inquiry. Invocation of the *Miranda* right to counsel "requires, at a minimum, some statement that can reasonably be construed to be an expression of a desire for the assistance of an attorney." But if a suspect makes a reference to an attorney that is ambiguous or equivocal in that a reasonable officer in light of the circumstances would have understood only that the suspect might be invoking the right to counsel, our precedents do not require the cessation of questioning.

Rather, the suspect must unambiguously request counsel. As we have observed, "a statement either is such an assertion of the right to counsel or it is not." Although a suspect need not "speak with the discrimination of an Oxford don," he must articulate his desire to have counsel present sufficiently clearly that a reasonable police officer in the circumstances would understand the statement to be a request for an attorney. If the statement fails to meet the requisite level of clarity, *Edwards* does not require that the officers stop questioning the suspect.

We decline petitioner's invitation to extend *Edwards* and require law enforcement officers to cease questioning immediately upon the making of an ambiguous or equivocal reference to an attorney. The rationale underlying *Edwards* is that the police must respect a suspect's wishes regarding his right to have an attorney present during custodial interrogation. But when the officers conducting the questioning reasonably do not know whether or not the suspect wants a lawyer, a rule requiring the immediate cessation of questioning "would transform the *Miranda* safeguards into wholly irrational obstacles to legitimate police investigative activity," because it would needlessly prevent the police from questioning a suspect in the absence of counsel even if the suspect did not wish to have a lawyer present. Nothing in *Edwards* requires the provision of counsel to a suspect who consents to answer questions without the assistance of a lawyer. In *Miranda* itself, we expressly rejected the suggestion "that each police station must have a 'station house lawyer' present at all times to advise prisoners," and held instead that a suspect must be told of his right to have an attorney present and that he may not be questioned after invoking his right to counsel. We also noted that if a suspect is "indecisive in his request for counsel," the officers need not always cease questioning.

We recognize that requiring a clear assertion of the right to counsel might disadvantage some suspects who — because of fear, intimidation, lack of linguistic skills, or a variety of other reasons — will not clearly articulate their right to counsel although they actually want to have a lawyer present. But the primary protection afforded suspects subject to custodial interrogation is the *Miranda* warnings themselves. "[F]ull comprehension of the rights to remain silent and request an attorney [is] sufficient to dispel whatever coercion is inherent in the interrogation process." A suspect who knowingly and voluntarily waives his right to counsel after having that right explained to him has indicated his willingness to deal with the police unassisted. Although *Edwards* provides an additional protection — if a suspect subsequently requests an attorney, questioning must cease — it is one that must be affirmatively invoked by the suspect.

In considering how a suspect must invoke the right to counsel, we must consider the other side of the *Miranda* equation: the need for effective law enforcement. Although the courts ensure compliance with the *Miranda* requirements through the exclusionary rule, it is police officers who must actually decide whether or not they can question a suspect. The *Edwards* rule — questioning must cease if the suspect asks for a lawyer — provides a bright line that can be applied by officers in the real world of investigation and interrogation without unduly hampering the gathering of information. But if we were to require questioning to cease if a suspect makes a statement that might be a request for an attorney, this clarity and ease of application would be lost. Police officers would be forced to make difficult judgment calls about whether the suspect in fact wants a lawyer even though he has not said so, with the threat of suppression if they guess wrong. We therefore hold that, after a knowing and voluntary waiver of the *Miranda* rights, law enforcement officers may continue questioning until and unless the suspect clearly requests an attorney.

Of course, when a suspect makes an ambiguous or equivocal statement it will often be good police practice for the interviewing officers to clarify whether or not he actually wants an attorney. That was the procedure followed by the NIS agents in this case. Clarifying questions help protect the rights of the suspect by ensuring that he gets an attorney if he wants one, and will minimize the chance of a confession being suppressed due to subsequent judicial second-guessing as to the meaning of the suspect's statement regarding counsel. But we decline to adopt a rule requiring officers to ask clarifying questions. If the suspect's statement is not an unambiguous or unequivocal request for counsel, the officers have no obligation to stop questioning him.

To recapitulate: We held in *Miranda* that a suspect is entitled to the assistance of counsel during custodial interrogation even though the

Constitution does not provide for such assistance. We held in *Edwards* that if the suspect invokes the right to counsel at any time, the police must immediately cease questioning him until an attorney is present. But we are unwilling to create a third layer of prophylaxis to prevent police questioning when the suspect might want a lawyer. Unless the suspect actually requests an attorney, questioning may continue.

Justice SOUTER, with whom Justice BLACKMUN, Justice STEVENS, and Justice GINSBURG join, concurring in the judgment.

In the midst of his questioning by naval investigators, petitioner said "Maybe I should talk to a lawyer." The investigators promptly stopped questioning Davis about the killing of Keith Shackleton and instead undertook to determine whether he meant to invoke his right to counsel. According to testimony accepted by the courts below, Davis answered the investigators' questions on that point by saying, "I'm not asking for a lawyer," and "No, I don't want to talk to a lawyer." Only then did the interrogation resume (stopping for good when petitioner said, "I think I want a lawyer before I say anything else").

I agree with the majority that the Constitution does not forbid law enforcement officers to pose questions (like those directed at Davis) aimed solely at clarifying whether a suspect's ambiguous reference to counsel was meant to assert his Fifth Amendment right. Accordingly I concur in the judgment affirming Davis's conviction, resting partly on evidence of statements given after agents ascertained that he did not wish to deal with them through counsel. I cannot, however, join in my colleagues' further conclusion that if the investigators here had been so inclined, they were at liberty to disregard Davis's reference to a lawyer entirely, in accordance with a general rule that interrogators have no legal obligation to discover what a custodial subject meant by an ambiguous statement that could reasonably be understood to express a desire to consult a lawyer. Our own precedent, the reasonable judgments of the majority of the many courts already to have addressed the issue before us, and the advocacy of a considerable body of law enforcement officials are to the contrary. All argue against the Court's approach today, which draws a sharp line between interrogated suspects who "clearly" assert their right to counsel and those who say something that may, but may not, express a desire for counsel's presence, the former suspects being assured that questioning will not resume without counsel present, the latter being left to fend for themselves. The concerns of fairness and practicality that have long anchored our *Miranda* case law point to a different response: when law enforcement officials "reasonably do not know whether or not the suspect wants a lawyer," they should stop their interrogation and ask him to make his choice clear.

6. What Are the Exceptions to Miranda?

Under what circumstances can a statement from a criminal defendant be used against him or her at trial despite the failure to properly administer *Miranda* warnings where they are required? There are three major exceptions:

1. If the statements are used for impeachment purposes
2. If the statements were obtained in an emergency situation
3. If the statements were made at the time of booking the suspect in response to routine questions by the police

a. Impeachment

In Harris v. New York, the Court held that statements gained from a criminal defendant are admissible for impeachment purposes if the defendant chooses to testify at trial. In reading *Harris*, it is important to consider the competing views of *Miranda* and the exclusionary rule. Chief Justice Burger's majority opinion emphasizes the need to protect the integrity of trials by allowing prior statements to the police to be used to impeach a criminal defendant who takes the stand and does not tell the truth. Justice Brennan's dissent, by contrast, focuses especially on the concern that allowing impermissibly obtained statements to be used for impeachment will give police an incentive to ignore *Miranda*, knowing that the statements they obtain still can be used for impeachment.[12]

HARRIS v. NEW YORK
401 U.S. 222 (1971)

Chief Justice BURGER delivered the opinion of the Court.

We granted the writ in this case to consider petitioner's claim that a statement made by him to police under circumstances rendering it inadmissible to establish the prosecution's case in chief under Miranda v. Arizona (1966), may not be used to impeach his credibility.

The State of New York charged petitioner in a two-count indictment with twice selling heroin to an undercover police officer. At a subsequent jury trial the officer was the State's chief witness, and he testified as to details of the two sales. A second officer verified collateral details of the sales, and a third offered testimony about the chemical analysis of the heroin.

Petitioner took the stand in his own defense. He admitted knowing the undercover police officer but denied a sale on January 4, 1966. He admitted making a sale of contents of a glassine bag to the officer on January 6

---

12. For an excellent discussion of police intentionally questioning "outside *Miranda*," *see* Charles Weisselberg, *Saving Miranda*, 84 Cornell L. Rev. 109 (1998) (collecting California training materials encouraging questioning "outside *Miranda*").

but claimed it was baking powder and part of a scheme to defraud the purchaser.

On cross-examination petitioner was asked seriatim whether he had made specified statements to the police immediately following his arrest on January 7 — statements that partially contradicted petitioner's direct testimony at trial. In response to the cross-examination, petitioner testified that he could not remember virtually any of the questions or answers recited by the prosecutor. At the request of petitioner's counsel the written statement from which the prosecutor had read questions and answers in his impeaching process was placed in the record for possible use on appeal; the statement was not shown to the jury.

The trial judge instructed the jury that the statements attributted to petitioner by the prosecution could be considered only in passing on petitioner's credibility and not as evidence of guilt. In closing summations both counsel argued the substance of the impeaching statements. The jury then found petitioner guilty on the second count of the indictment. The New York Court of Appeals affirmed in a per curiam opinion.

At trial the prosecution made no effort in its case in chief to use the statements allegedly made by petitioner, conceding that they were inadmissible under Miranda v. Arizona (1966). The transcript of the interrogation used in the impeachment, but not given to the jury, shows that no warning of a right to appointed counsel was given before questions were put to petitioner when he was taken into custody. Petitioner makes no claim that the statements made to the police were coerced or involuntary.

Some comments in the *Miranda* opinion can indeed be read as indicating a bar to use of an uncounseled statement for any purpose, but discussion of that issue was not at all necessary to the Court's holding and cannot be regarded as controlling. *Miranda* barred the prosecution from making its case with statements of an accused made while in custody prior to having or effectively waiving counsel. It does not follow from *Miranda* that evidence inadmissible against an accused in the prosecution's case in chief is barred for all purposes, provided of course that the trustworthiness of the evidence satisfies legal standards.

Petitioner's testimony in his own behalf concerning the events of January 7 contrasted sharply with what he told the police shortly after his arrest. The impeachment process here undoubtedly provided valuable aid to the jury in assessing petitioner's credibility, and the benefits of this process should not be lost, in our view, because of the speculative possibility that impermissible police conduct will be encouraged thereby. Assuming that the exclusionary rule has a deterrent effect on proscribed police conduct, sufficient deterrence flows when the evidence in question is made unavailable to the prosecution in its case in chief.

Every criminal defendant is privileged to testify in his own defense, or to refuse to do so. But that privilege cannot be construed to include the right to commit perjury. Having voluntarily taken the stand, petitioner was under an obligation to speak truthfully and accurately, and the prosecution here did no more than utilize the traditional truth-testing devices of the adversary process. Had inconsistent statements been made by the accused to some third person, it could hardly be contended that the conflict could not be laid before the jury by way of cross-examination and impeachment.

The shield provided by *Miranda* cannot be perverted into a license to use perjury by way of a defense, free from the risk of confrontation with prior inconsistent utterances. We hold, therefore, that petitioner's credibility was appropriately impeached by use of his earlier conflicting statements.

Justice BRENNAN, with whom Justice DOUGLAS and Justice MARSHALL join, dissenting.

It is conceded that the question-and-answer statement used to impeach petitioner's direct testimony was, under Miranda v. Arizona (1966), constitutionally inadmissible as part of the State's direct case against petitioner. I think that the Constitution also denied the State the use of the statement on cross-examination to impeach the credibility of petitioner's testimony given in his own defense.

The prosecution's use of the tainted statement cuts down on the privilege by making its assertion costly. Thus, the accused is denied an "unfettered" choice when the decision whether to take the stand is burdened by the risk that an illegally obtained prior statement may be introduced to impeach his direct testimony denying complicity in the crime charged against him. We settled this proposition in *Miranda* where we said:

> An incriminating statement is as incriminating when used to impeach credibility as it is when used as direct proof of guilt and no constitutional distinction can legitimately be drawn. The objective of deterring improper police conduct is only part of the larger objective of safeguarding the integrity of our adversary system. The "essential mainstay" of that system, is the privilege against self-incrimination, which for that reason has occupied a central place in our jurisprudence since before the Nation's birth. Moreover, "we may view the historical development of the privilege as one which groped for the proper scope of governmental power over the citizen. . . . All these policies point to one overriding thought: the constitutional foundation underlying the privilege is the respect a government . . . must accord to the dignity and integrity of its citizens.

These values are plainly jeopardized if an exception against admission of tainted statements is made for those used for impeachment purposes. Moreover, it is monstrous that courts should aid or abet the law-breaking police officer. It is abiding truth that "[N]othing can destroy a government more quickly than its failure to observe its own laws, or worse, its disregard of the charter of its own existence." Mapp v. Ohio (1961). Thus even to the extent that *Miranda* was aimed at deterring police practices in disregard of the Constitution, I fear that today's holding will seriously undermine the achievement of that objective. The Court today tells the police that they may freely interrogate an accused incommunicado and without counsel and know that although any statement they obtain in violation of *Miranda* cannot be used on the State's direct case, it may be introduced if the defendant has the temerity to testify in his own defense. This goes far toward undoing much of the progress made in conforming police methods to the Constitution.

b. Emergencies

In New York v. Quarles, the Supreme Court held that statements obtained by police from suspects during emergency situations could be used against a criminal defendant even if *Miranda* warnings were not properly administered. In assessing *Quarles*, it is important to consider whether there should be such an exception and, if so, what is sufficient to constitute such an emergency.

NEW YORK v. QUARLES
467 U.S. 649 (1984)

Justice REHNQUIST delivered the opinion of the Court.

Respondent Benjamin Quarles was charged in the New York trial court with criminal possession of a weapon. The trial court suppressed the gun in question, and a statement made by respondent, because the statement was obtained by police before they read respondent his "*Miranda* rights." That ruling was affirmed on appeal through the New York Court of Appeals. We granted certiorari and we now reverse. We conclude that under the circumstances involved in this case, overriding considerations of public safety justify the officer's failure to provide *Miranda* warnings before he asked questions devoted to locating the abandoned weapon.

On September 11, 1980, at approximately 12:30 A.M., Officer Frank Kraft and Officer Sal Scarring were on road patrol in Queens, N.Y., when a young woman approached their car. She told them that she had just been raped by a black male, approximately six feet tall, who was wearing a black jacket with the name "Big Ben" printed in yellow letters on the back. She told the officers that the man had just entered an A & P supermarket located nearby and that the man was carrying a gun.

The officers drove the woman to the supermarket, and Officer Kraft entered the store while Officer Scarring radioed for assistance. Officer Kraft quickly spotted respondent, who matched the description given by the woman, approaching a checkout counter. Apparently upon seeing the officer, respondent turned and ran toward the rear of the store, and Officer Kraft pursued him with a drawn gun. When respondent turned the corner at the end of an aisle, Officer Kraft lost sight of him for several seconds, and upon regaining sight of respondent, ordered him to stop and put his hands over his head.

Although more than three other officers had arrived on the scene by that time, Officer Kraft was the first to reach respondent. He frisked him and discovered that he was wearing a shoulder holster which was then empty. After handcuffing him, Officer Kraft asked him where the gun was. Respondent nodded in the direction of some empty cartons and responded, "the gun is over there." Officer Kraft thereafter retrieved a loaded .38-caliber revolver from one of the cartons, formally placed respondent under arrest, and read him his *Miranda* rights from a printed card. Respondent indicated that he would be willing to answer questions without an attorney present. Officer Kraft then asked respondent if he owned the gun and where he had purchased it. Respondent answered that he did own it and that he had purchased it in Miami, Fla.

In the subsequent prosecution of respondent for criminal possession of a weapon, the judge excluded the statement, "the gun is over there," and the gun because the officer had not given respondent the warnings required by our decision in Miranda v. Arizona (1966), before asking him where the gun was located. The judge excluded the other statements about respondent's ownership of the gun and the place of purchase, as evidence tainted by the prior *Miranda* violation.

In this case we have before us no claim that respondent's statements were actually compelled by police conduct which overcame his will to resist. Thus the only issue before us is whether Officer Kraft was justified in failing to make available to respondent the procedural safeguards associated with the privilege against compulsory self-incrimination since *Miranda*.[13]

The New York Court of Appeals was undoubtedly correct in deciding that the facts of this case come within the ambit of the *Miranda* decision as we have subsequently interpreted it. We agree that respondent was in police custody because we have noted that "the ultimate inquiry is simply whether there is a 'formal arrest or restraint on freedom of movement' of the degree associated with a formal arrest." Here Quarles was surrounded by at least four police officers and was handcuffed when the questioning at issue took place.

We hold that on these facts there is a "public safety" exception to the requirement that *Miranda* warnings be given before a suspect's answers may be admitted into evidence, and that the availability of that exception does not depend upon the motivation of the individual officers involved. In a kaleidoscopic situation such as the one confronting these officers, where spontaneity rather than adherence to a police manual is necessarily the

---

13. The dissent curiously takes us to task for "endors[ing] the introduction of coerced self-incriminating statements in criminal prosecutions," and for "sanction[ing] sub silentio criminal prosecutions based on compelled self-incriminating statements." Of course our decision today does nothing of the kind. As the *Miranda* Court itself recognized, the failure to provide *Miranda* warnings in and of itself does not render a confession involuntary, and respondent is certainly free on remand to argue that his statement was coerced under traditional due process standards. Today we merely reject the only argument that respondent has raised to support the exclusion of his statement, that the statement must be presumed compelled because of Officer Kraft's failure to read him his *Miranda* warnings. [Footnote by the Court.]

order of the day, the application of the exception which we recognize today should not be made to depend on post hoc findings at a suppression hearing concerning the subjective motivation of the arresting officer. Undoubtedly most police officers, if placed in Officer Kraft's position, would act out of a host of different, instinctive, and largely unverifiable motives — their own safety, the safety of others, and perhaps as well the desire to obtain incriminating evidence from the suspect.

Whatever the motivation of individual officers in such a situation, we do not believe that the doctrinal underpinnings of *Miranda* require that it be applied in all its rigor to a situation in which police officers ask questions reasonably prompted by a concern for the public safety. The *Miranda* decision was based in large part on this Court's view that the warnings which it required police to give to suspects in custody would reduce the likelihood that the suspects would fall victim to constitutionally impermissible practices of police interrogation in the presumptively coercive environment of the station house.

The police in this case, in the very act of apprehending a suspect, were confronted with the immediate necessity of ascertaining the whereabouts of a gun which they had every reason to believe the suspect had just removed from his empty holster and discarded in the supermarket. So long as the gun was concealed somewhere in the supermarket, with its actual whereabouts unknown, it obviously posed more than one danger to the public safety: an accomplice might make use of it, a customer or employee might later come upon it.

In such a situation, if the police are required to recite the familiar *Miranda* warnings before asking the whereabouts of the gun, suspects in Quarles' position might well be deterred from responding. Procedural safeguards which deter a suspect from responding were deemed acceptable in *Miranda* in order to protect the Fifth Amendment privilege; when the primary social cost of those added protections is the possibility of fewer convictions, the *Miranda* majority was willing to bear that cost. Here, had *Miranda* warnings deterred Quarles from responding to Officer Kraft's question about the whereabouts of the gun, the cost would have been something more than merely the failure to obtain evidence useful in convicting Quarles. Officer Kraft needed an answer to his question not simply to make his case against Quarles but to insure that further danger to the public did not result from the concealment of the gun in a public area.

We conclude that the need for answers to questions in a situation posing a threat to the public safety outweighs the need for the prophylactic rule protecting the Fifth Amendment's privilege against self-incrimination. We decline to place officers such as Officer Kraft in the untenable position of having to consider, often in a matter of seconds, whether it best serves society for them to ask the necessary questions without the *Miranda* warnings and render whatever probative evidence they uncover inadmissible, or for them to give the warnings in order to preserve the admissibility of evidence they might uncover but possibly damage or destroy their ability to obtain that evidence and neutralize the volatile situation confronting them.[14]

As we have in other contexts, we recognize here the importance of a workable rule "to guide police officers, who have only limited time and expertise to reflect on and balance the social and individual interests involved in the specific circumstances they confront." But as we have pointed out, we believe that the exception which we recognize today lessens the necessity of that on-the-scene balancing process. The exception will not be difficult for police officers to apply because in each case it will be circumscribed by the exigency which justifies it. We think police officers can and will distinguish almost instinctively between questions necessary to secure their own safety or the safety of the public and questions designed solely to elicit testimonial evidence from a suspect.

We hold that the Court of Appeals in this case erred in excluding the statement, "the gun is over there," and the gun because of the officer's failure to read respondent his *Miranda* rights before attempting to locate the weapon. Accordingly we hold that it also erred in excluding the subsequent statements as illegal fruits of a *Miranda* violation.

Justice O'CONNOR, concurring in the judgment in part and dissenting in part.

In Miranda v. Arizona (1966), the Court held unconstitutional, because inherently compelled, the admission of statements derived from in-custody questioning not preceded by an explanation of the privilege against self-incrimination and the consequences of forgoing it. Today, the Court concludes that overriding considerations of public safety justify the admission of evidence — oral statements and a gun — secured without the benefit of such warnings. In so holding, the Court acknowledges that it is departing from prior precedent, and that it is "lessen[ing] the desirable clarity of [the *Miranda*] rule." Were the Court writing from a clean slate, I could agree with its holding. But *Miranda* is now the law and, in my view, the Court has not provided sufficient justification for departing from it or for blurring its now clear strictures. Accordingly, I would require suppression of the initial statement taken from respondent in this case. On the other hand, nothing in *Miranda* or the privilege itself requires exclusion of nontestimonial evidence derived from informal custodial interrogation, and I therefore agree with the Court that admission of the gun in evidence is proper.

In my view, a "public safety" exception unnecessarily blurs the edges of the clear line heretofore established and makes *Miranda*'s requirements more difficult to understand. In some cases, police will benefit because a reviewing

---

14. The dissent argues that a public safety exception to *Miranda* is unnecessary because in every case an officer can simply ask the necessary questions to protect himself or the public, and then the prosecution can decline to introduce any incriminating responses at a subsequent trial. But absent actual coercion by the officer, there is no constitutional imperative requiring the exclusion of the evidence that results from police inquiry of this kind; and we do not believe that the doctrinal underpinnings of *Miranda* require us to exclude the evidence, thus penalizing officers for asking the very questions which are the most crucial to their efforts to protect themselves and the public. [Footnote by the Court.]

court will find that an exigency excused their failure to administer the required warnings. But in other cases, police will suffer because, though they thought an exigency excused their noncompliance, a reviewing court will view the "objective" circumstances differently and require exclusion of admissions thereby obtained. The end result will be a finespun new doctrine on public safety exigencies incident to custodial interrogation, complete with the hair-splitting distinctions that currently plague our Fourth Amendment jurisprudence. "While the rigidity of the prophylactic rules was a principal weakness in the view of dissenters and critics outside the Court, . . . that rigidity [has also been called a] strength of the decision. It [has] afforded police and courts clear guidance on the manner in which to conduct a custodial investigation: if it was rigid, it was also precise. . . . [T]his core virtue of *Miranda* would be eviscerated if the prophylactic rules were freely [ignored] by . . . courts under the guise of [reinterpreting] *Miranda*. . . ."

The justification the Court provides for upsetting the equilibrium that has finally been achieved — that police cannot and should not balance considerations of public safety against the individual's interest in avoiding compulsory testimonial self-incrimination — really misses the critical question to be decided. *Miranda* has never been read to prohibit the police from asking questions to secure the public safety. Rather, the critical question *Miranda* addresses is who shall bear the cost of securing the public safety when such questions are asked and answered: the defendant or the State. *Miranda*, for better or worse, found the resolution of that question implicit in the prohibition against compulsory self-incrimination and placed the burden on the State. When police ask custodial questions without administering the required warnings, *Miranda* quite clearly requires that the answers received be presumed compelled and that they be excluded from evidence at trial.

The Court concedes, as it must, both that respondent was in "custody" and subject to "interrogation" and that his statement "the gun is over there" was compelled within the meaning of our precedent. In my view, since there is nothing about an exigency that makes custodial interrogation any less compelling, a principled application of *Miranda* requires that respondent's statement be suppressed.

The court below assumed, without discussion, that the privilege against self-incrimination required that the gun derived from respondent's statement also be suppressed, whether or not the State could independently link it to him. That conclusion was, in my view, incorrect.

The gun respondent was compelled to supply is clearly evidence of the "real or physical" sort. What makes the question of its admissibility difficult is the fact that, in asking respondent to produce the gun, the police also "compelled" him, in the *Miranda* sense, to create an incriminating testimonial response. In other words, the case is problematic because police compelled respondent not only to provide the gun but also to admit that he knew where it was and that it was his.

To be sure, admission of nontestimonial evidence secured through informal custodial interrogation will reduce the incentives to enforce the *Miranda* code. But that fact simply begs the question of how much enforcement is appropriate. There are some situations, as the Court's struggle to accommodate a "public safety" exception demonstrates, in which the societal cost of administering the *Miranda* warnings is very high indeed. The *Miranda* decision quite practically does not express any societal interest in having those warnings administered for their own sake. Rather, the warnings and waiver are only required to ensure that "testimony" used against the accused at trial is voluntarily given. Therefore, if the testimonial aspects of the accused's custodial communications are suppressed, the failure to administer the *Miranda* warnings should cease to be of concern. The harm caused by failure to administer *Miranda* warnings relates only to admission of testimonial self-incriminations, and the suppression of such incriminations should by itself produce the optimal enforcement of the *Miranda* rule.

Justice MARSHALL, with whom Justice BRENNAN and Justice STEVENS join, dissenting.

The police in this case arrested a man suspected of possessing a firearm in violation of New York law. Once the suspect was in custody and found to be unarmed, the arresting officer initiated an interrogation. Without being advised of his right not to respond, the suspect incriminated himself by locating the gun. The majority concludes that the State may rely on this incriminating statement to convict the suspect of possessing a weapon. I disagree. The arresting officers had no legitimate reason to interrogate the suspect without advising him of his rights to remain silent and to obtain assistance of counsel. By finding on these facts justification for unconsented interrogation, the majority abandons the clear guidelines enunciated in Miranda v. Arizona (1966), and condemns the American judiciary to a new era of post hoc inquiry into the propriety of custodial interrogations. More significantly and in direct conflict with this Court's longstanding interpretation of the Fifth Amendment, the majority has endorsed the introduction of coerced self-incriminating statements in criminal prosecutions. I dissent.

The majority contends that the law, as it currently stands, places police officers in a dilemma whenever they interrogate a suspect who appears to know of some threat to the public's safety. If the police interrogate the suspect without advising him of his rights, the suspect may reveal information that the authorities can use to defuse the threat, but the suspect's statements will be inadmissible at trial. If, on the other hand, the police advise the suspect of his rights, the suspect may be deterred from responding to the police's questions, and the risk to the public may continue unabated. According to the majority, the police must now choose between establishing the suspect's guilt and safeguarding the public from danger.

The majority proposes to eliminate this dilemma by creating an exception to Miranda v. Arizona for custodial interrogations concerning matters of public safety. Under the majority's exception, police would be permitted to interrogate suspects about such matters before the suspects have been advised of their constitutional rights. Without being "deterred" by the knowledge that they have a constitutional right not to respond, these suspects will be likely to answer the questions. Should the answers also be incriminating, the State would be free to introduce them as evidence in a criminal prosecution. Through this "narrow exception to the *Miranda* rule," the majority proposes to protect the public's safety without jeopardizing the prosecution of criminal defendants. I find in this reasoning an unwise and unprincipled departure from our Fifth Amendment precedents.

Before today's opinion, the procedures established in Miranda v. Arizona had "the virtue of informing police and prosecutors with specificity as to what they may do in conducting custodial interrogation, and of informing courts under what circumstances statements obtained during such interrogation are not admissible." In a chimerical quest for public safety, the majority has abandoned the rule that brought 18 years of doctrinal tranquility to the field of custodial interrogations. As the majority candidly concedes, a public-safety exception destroys forever the clarity of *Miranda* for both law enforcement officers and members of the judiciary. The Court's candor cannot mask what a serious loss the administration of justice has incurred.

This case is illustrative of the chaos the "public-safety" exception will unlease. The circumstances of Quarles' arrest have never been in dispute. After the benefit of briefing and oral argument, the New York Court of Appeals, as previously noted, concluded that there was "no evidence in the record before us that there were exigent circumstances posing a risk to the public safety." Upon reviewing the same facts and hearing the same arguments, a majority of this Court has come to precisely the opposite conclusion: "So long as the gun was concealed somewhere in the supermarket, with its actual whereabouts unknown, it obviously posed more than one danger to the public safety. . . ."

If after plenary review two appellate courts so fundamentally differ over the threat to public safety presented by the simple and uncontested facts of this case, one must seriously question how law enforcement officers will respond to the majority's new rule in the confusion and haste of the real world.

Though unfortunate, the difficulty of administering the "public-safety" exception is not the most profound flaw in the majority's decision. The majority has lost sight of the fact Miranda v. Arizona and our earlier custodial-interrogation cases all implemented a constitutional privilege against self-incrimination. The rules established in these cases were designed to protect criminal defendants against prosecutions based on coerced self-incriminating statements. The majority today turns its back on these constitutional considerations, and invites the government to prosecute through the use of what necessarily are coerced statements.

The "public-safety" exception is efficacious precisely because it permits police officers to coerce criminal defendants into making involuntary statements. Indeed, in the efficacy of the "public-safety" exception lies a fundamental and constitutional defect. Until today, this Court could truthfully state that the Fifth Amendment is given "broad scope" "[w]here there has been genuine compulsion of testimony." Coerced confessions were simply inadmissible in criminal prosecutions. The "public-safety" exception departs from this principle by expressly inviting police officers to coerce defendants into making incriminating statements, and then permitting prosecutors to introduce those statements at trial. Though the majority's opinion is cloaked in the beguiling language of utilitarianism, the Court has sanctioned sub silentio criminal prosecutions based on compelled self-incriminating statements. I find this result in direct conflict with the Fifth Amendment's dictate that "[n]o person . . . shall be compelled in any criminal case to be a witness against himself."

The irony of the majority's decision is that the public's safety can be perfectly well protected without abridging the Fifth Amendment. If a bomb is about to explode or the public is otherwise imminently imperiled, the police are free to interrogate suspects without advising them of their constitutional rights. Such unconsented questioning may take place not only when police officers act on instinct but also when higher faculties lead them to believe that advising a suspect of his constitutional rights might decrease the likelihood that the suspect would reveal life-saving information. If trickery is necessary to protect the public, then the police may trick a suspect into confessing. While the Fourteenth Amendment sets limits on such behavior, nothing in the Fifth Amendment or our decision in Miranda v. Arizona proscribes this sort of emergency questioning. All the Fifth Amendment forbids is the introduction of coerced statements at trial.

Having determined that the Fifth Amendment renders inadmissible Quarles' response to Officer Kraft's questioning, I have no doubt that our precedents require that the gun discovered as a direct result of Quarles' statement must be presumed inadmissible as well. The gun was the direct product of a coercive custodial interrogation. In Silverthorne Lumber Co. v. United States (1920), and Wong Sun v. United States (1963), this Court held that the Government may not introduce incriminating evidence derived from an illegally obtained source.

c. Booking Exception

The Supreme Court has held that the police can ask a person questions that are needed in the booking process, such as name, address, date of birth, height, and weight, when taking a him or her into custody. The Court has said that the answers to these questions are admissible, even without administration of *Miranda* warnings. In Pennsylvania v. Muniz, 496 U.S. 583 (1990), the Court considered whether "various incriminating utterances of a drunken-driving suspect, made while performing a series of sobriety tests, constitute testimonial responses to custodial interrogation for purposes of the Self-Incrimination Clause of the Fifth Amendment." The suspect was taken to the booking station and "was not at this time (nor had he been previously) advised of his rights under Miranda v. Arizona." The officer asked Muniz "his name, address, height, weight, eye color, date of birth, and current age. He responded to each of these questions, stumbling over his address and age. The officer then asked Muniz, 'Do you know what the date was of your sixth birthday?' After Muniz offered an inaudible reply, the officer repeated, 'When you turned six years old, do you remember what the date was?' Muniz responded, 'No, I don't.'"

The Court held that the slurred speech that was evident on the videotape did not violate the privilege against self-incrimination because it was not testimonial. As explained below, in section D of this chapter, the privilege against self-incrimination applies only if a person is compelled to make statements; physical evidence or observation of physical characteristics are not testimonial. As to the questions asking him for identifying information, the Court held that these fell within the "booking exception" to *Miranda*. Justice Brennan, writing for the Court, stated:

> Muniz's answers to these first seven questions are nonetheless admissible because the questions fall within a "routine booking question" exception which exempts from *Miranda*'s coverage questions to secure the biographical data necessary to complete booking or pretrial services. The state court found that the first seven questions were "requested for record-keeping purposes only," and therefore the questions appear reasonably related to the police's administrative concerns. In this context, therefore, the first seven questions asked at the booking center fall outside the protections of *Miranda* and the answers thereto need not be suppressed.

The Court, however, found that asking the suspect the date of his sixth birthday did not fit within the booking exception and had to be suppressed.

C. THE SIXTH AMENDMENT RIGHT TO COUNSEL AND POLICE INTERROGATIONS

The right to counsel in interrogations required under Miranda v. Arizona, discussed above, is based on the Fifth Amendment's privilege against self-incrimination and is regarded as a key protector of that right. In addition, the Sixth Amendment provides that "in all criminal prosecutions, the accused shall enjoy the right . . . to have the Assistance of Counsel for his defense." Of course, one of the most important aspects of the Sixth Amendment is ensuring counsel at trial for those accused of crimes involving possible imprisonment. This topic is discussed in detail in Chapter 11.

Further, the Sixth Amendment right to counsel applies to police interrogations that occur after adversarial proceedings have begun; that is, the Court has said that the Sixth Amendment applies when judicial proceedings have been initiated against the accused "whether by way of formal charge, preliminary hearing, indictment, information, or arraignment."

There is obvious overlap between the Fifth Amendment and the Sixth Amendment rights to counsel: Both have been interpreted to require the provision of counsel to in-custodial interrogation of a criminal suspect after formal judicial proceedings have begun. But there are differences as well.

The Fifth Amendment right to counsel under Miranda v. Arizona applies only to in-custodial interrogations; the Sixth Amendment right to counsel applies to all efforts by the police to deliberately elicit statements from a person after formal criminal proceedings have been initiated.

Subsection 1 looks at the origin of this rule in Massiah v. United States, Escobedo v. Illinois, and Brewer v. Williams. Subsection 2 focuses on the fact that this right is offense-specific; the right only applies to those crimes for which adversarial proceedings have begun and does not prevent questioning without counsel as to other crimes. Subsection 3 examines what is sufficient for a waiver of this right. Finally, subsection 4 considers what is impermissible police eliciting of statements when someone is represented by counsel; specifically, does the use of undercover agents violate this right in that it involves communication through police agents without counsel after questioning without counsel is not allowed?

1. The Sixth Amendment Right to Counsel During Interrogations

The initial key case in this area is Massiah v. United States. It continues to be the basis for the Sixth Amendment right to counsel during interrogations.

MASSIAH v. UNITED STATES
377 U.S. 201 (1964)

Justice STEWART delivered the opinion of the Court.

The petitioner was indicted for violating the federal narcotics laws. He retained a lawyer, pleaded not guilty, and was released on bail. While he was free on bail a federal agent succeeded by surreptitious means in listening to incriminating statements made by him. Evidence of these statements was introduced against the petitioner at his trial over his objection. He was convicted, and the Court of Appeals affirmed. We granted certiorari to consider whether, under the circumstances here presented, the prosecution's use at the trial of evidence of the petitioner's own incriminating statements deprived him of any right secured to him under the Federal Constitution.

The petitioner, a merchant seaman, was in 1958 a member of the crew of the S. S. Santa Maria. In April of that year federal customs officials in New York received information that he was going to transport a quantity of narcotics aboard that ship from South America to the United States. As a result of this and other information, the agents searched the Santa Maria upon its arrival in New York and found in the afterpeak of the vessel five packages containing about three and a half pounds of cocaine. They also learned of circumstances, not here relevant, tending to connect the petitioner with the cocaine. He was arrested, promptly arraigned, and subsequently indicted for possession of narcotics aboard a United States vessel. In July a superseding indictment was returned, charging the petitioner and a man named Colson with the same substantive offense, and in separate counts charging the petitioner, Colson, and others with having conspired to possess narcotics aboard a United States vessel, and to import, conceal, and facilitate the sale of narcotics. The petitioner, who had retained a lawyer, pleaded not guilty and was released on bail, along with Colson.

A few days later, and quite without the petitioner's knowledge, Colson decided to cooperate with the government agents in their continuing investigation of the narcotics activities in which the petitioner, Colson, and others had allegedly been engaged. Colson permitted an agent named Murphy to install a Schmidt radio transmitter under the front seat of Colson's automobile, by means of which Murphy, equipped with an appropriate receiving device, could overhear from some distance away conversations carried on in Colson's car.

On the evening of November 19, 1959, Colson and the petitioner held a lengthy conversation while sitting in Colson's automobile, parked on a New York street. By prearrangement with Colson, and totally unbeknownst to the petitioner, the agent Murphy sat in a car parked out of sight down the street and listened over the radio to the entire conversation. The petitioner made several incriminating statements during the course of this conversation. At the petitioner's trial these incriminating statements were brought before the jury through Murphy's testimony, despite the insistent objection of defense counsel. The jury convicted the petitioner of several related narcotics offenses, and the convictions were affirmed by the Court of Appeals.

The petitioner argues that it was an error of constitutional dimensions to permit the agent Murphy at the trial to testify to the petitioner's incriminating statements which Murphy had overheard under the circumstances disclosed by this record. [I]t is said that the petitioner's Fifth and Sixth Amendment rights were violated by the use in evidence against him of incriminating statements which government agents had deliberately elicited from him after he had been indicted and in the absence of his retained counsel.

[A] constitutional principle established as long ago as Powell v. Alabama [1933], [is that] "during perhaps the most critical period of the proceedings . . . that is to say, from the time of their arraignment until the beginning of their trial, when consultation, thorough-going investigation and preparation [are] vitally important, the defendants . . . [are] as much entitled to such aid [of counsel] during that period as at the trial itself."

Here we deal not with a state court conviction, but with a federal case, where the specific guarantee of the Sixth Amendment directly applies. We hold that the petitioner was denied the basic protections of that guarantee when there was used against him at his trial evidence of his own incriminating words, which federal agents had deliberately elicited from him after he had been indicted and in the absence of his counsel.

The Solicitor General, in his brief and oral argument, has strenuously contended that the federal law enforcement agents had the right, if not indeed the duty, to continue their investigation of the petitioner and his alleged criminal associates even though the petitioner had been indicted. He points out that the Government was continuing its investigation in order to uncover not only the source of narcotics found on the S. S. Santa Maria, but also their intended buyer. He says that the quantity of narcotics involved was such as to suggest that the petitioner was part of a large and well-organized ring, and indeed that the continuing investigation confirmed this suspicion, since it resulted in criminal charges against many defendants. Under these circumstances the Solicitor General concludes that the Government agents were completely "justified in making use of Colson's cooperation by having Colson continue his normal associations and by surveilling them."

We do not question that in this case, as in many cases, it was entirely proper to continue an investigation of the suspected criminal activities of the defendant and his alleged confederates, even though the defendant had already been indicted. All that we hold is that the defendant's own incriminating statements, obtained by federal agents under the circumstances here disclosed, could not constitutionally be used by the prosecution as evidence against him at his trial.

Justice WHITE, with whom Justice CLARK and Justice HARLAN join, dissenting.

The current incidence of serious violations of the law represents not only an appalling waste of the potentially happy and useful lives of those who engage in such conduct but also an overhanging, dangerous threat to those unidentified and innocent people who will be the victims of crime today and tomorrow. This is a festering problem for which no adequate cures have yet been devised. At the very least there is much room for discontent with remedial measures so far undertaken. And admittedly there remains much to be settled concerning the disposition to be made of those who violate the law.

But dissatisfaction with preventive programs aimed at eliminating crime and profound dispute about whether we should punish, deter, rehabilitate or cure cannot excuse concealing one of our most menacing problems until the millennium has arrived. In my view, a civilized society must maintain its capacity to discover transgressions of the law and to identify those who flout it. This much is necessary even to know the scope of the problem, much less to formulate intelligent counter-measures. It will just not do to sweep these disagreeable matters under the rug or to pretend they are not there at all.

It is therefore a rather portentous occasion when a constitutional rule is established barring the use of evidence which is relevant, reliable and highly probative of the issue which the trial court has before it—whether the accused committed the act with which he is charged. Without the evidence, the quest for truth may be seriously impeded and in many cases the trial court, although aware of proof showing defendant's guilt, must nevertheless release him because the crucial evidence is deemed inadmissible. This result is entirely justified in some circumstances because exclusion serves other policies of overriding importance, as where evidence seized in an illegal search is excluded, not because of the quality of the proof, but to secure meaningful enforcement of the Fourth Amendment. But this only emphasizes that the soundest of reasons is necessary to warrant the exclusion of evidence otherwise admissible and the creation of another area of privileged testimony. With all due deference, I am not at all convinced that the additional barriers to the pursuit of truth which the Court today erects rest on anything like the solid foundations which decisions of this gravity should require.

The importance of the matter should not be underestimated, for today's rule promises to have wide application well beyond the facts of this case. The reason given for the result here — the admissions were obtained in the absence of counsel — would seem equally pertinent to statements obtained at any time after the right to counsel attaches, whether there has been an indictment or not; to admissions made prior to arraignment, at least where the defendant has counsel or asks for it; to the fruits of admissions improperly obtained under the new rule; to criminal proceedings in state courts; and to defendants long since convicted upon evidence including such admissions. The new rule will immediately do service in a great many cases.

Whatever the content or scope of the rule may prove to be, I am unable to see how this case presents an unconstitutional interference with Massiah's right to counsel. Massiah was not prevented from consulting with counsel as often as he wished. No meetings with counsel were disturbed or spied upon. Preparation for trial was in no way obstructed. It is only a sterile syllogism — an unsound one, besides — to say that because Massiah had a right to counsel's aid before and during the trial, his out-of-court conversations and admissions must be excluded if obtained without counsel's consent or presence. The right to counsel has never meant as much before, and its extension in this case requires some further explanation, so far unarticulated by the Court.

Since the new rule would exclude all admissions made to the police, no matter how voluntary and reliable, the requirement of counsel's presence or approval would seem to rest upon the probability that counsel would foreclose any admissions at all. This is nothing more than a thinly disguised constitutional policy of minimizing or entirely prohibiting the use in evidence of voluntary out-of-court admissions and confessions made by the accused. Carried as far as blind logic may compel some to go, the notion that statements from the mouth of the defendant should not be used in evidence would have a severe and unfortunate impact upon the great bulk of criminal cases.

Viewed in this light, the Court's newly fashioned exclusionary principle goes far beyond the constitutional privilege against self-incrimination, which neither requires nor suggests the barring of voluntary pretrial admissions. The Court presents no facts, no objective evidence, no reasons to warrant scrapping the voluntary-involuntary test for admissibility in this area. Without such evidence I would retain it in its present form.

Applying the new exclusionary rule is peculiarly inappropriate in this case. At the time of the conversation in question, petitioner was not in custody but free on bail. He was not questioned in what anyone could call an atmosphere of official coercion. What he said was said to his partner in crime who had also been indicted. There was no suggestion or any possibility of coercion.

Meanwhile, of course, the public will again be the loser and law enforcement will be presented with another serious dilemma. The general issue lurking in the background of the Court's opinion is the legitimacy of penetrating or obtaining confederates in criminal organizations. For the law enforcement agency, the answer for the time being can only be in the form of a prediction about the future application of today's new constitutional doctrine. More narrowly, and posed by the precise situation involved here, the question is this: when the police have arrested and released on bail one member of a criminal ring and another member, a confederate, is cooperating with the police, can the confederate be allowed to continue his association with the ring or must he somehow be withdrawn to avoid challenge to trial evidence on the ground that it was acquired after rather than before the arrest, after rather than before the indictment?

Massiah and those like him receive ample protection from the long line of precedents in this Court holding that confessions may not be introduced unless they are voluntary. In making these determinations the courts must consider the absence of counsel as one of several factors by which voluntariness is to be judged. This is a wiser rule than the automatic rule announced by the Court, which requires courts and juries to disregard voluntary admissions which they might well find to be the best possible evidence in discharging their responsibility for ascertaining truth.

The same year, in Escobedo v. Illinois, 378 U.S. 478 (1964), the Court extended the Sixth Amendment right to counsel to those who were questioned by the police but had not yet been formally charged. Escobedo had been arrested on suspicion of murder, but he had not been formally charged. During the police questioning, he several times requested a lawyer. Even though his mother had retained an attorney for him, the police refused to allow Escobedo to meet with the lawyer. The police obtained incriminating statements from Escobedo, and the question was whether they had to be excluded.

The Supreme Court, in an opinion by Justice Goldberg, found that the police behavior violated the Sixth Amendment right to counsel. He stressed that the police had shifted from a "general investigation of an unsolved crime" to accusations directed at Escobedo. Although Escobedo had not been indicted, the Court found this distinction irrelevant. The Court said that *Massiah* was applicable because "no meaningful distinction can be drawn between interrogation of an accused before and after formal indictment."

Escobedo was very controversial at the time it was decided, but its holding has little lasting significance. Two years later, in Miranda v. Arizona, the Supreme Court found a right to counsel under the Fifth Amendment's privilege against self-incrimination for in-custodial police interrogation. This made it unnecessary to rely on the Sixth Amendment and *Escobedo* for police interrogations. Also, subsequent cases have made clear that the Sixth Amendment right to counsel applies only after the initiation of formal adversarial proceedings. For example, in Kirby v. Illinois, 406 U.S. 682 (1972), the Court held that the Sixth Amendment right to counsel at police identification procedures (such as lineups) applies only "at or after the initiation of adversary judicial criminal proceedings—whether by way of formal charge, preliminary hearing, indictment, information, or arraignment." (*Kirby* and the law concerning identification procedures are discussed in detail in Chapter 5.)

But *Massiah* remains an important case in holding that there is a Sixth Amendment right to counsel that applies whenever a person is questioned after adversarial proceedings have begun. Brewer v. Williams is a significant elaboration and application of this principle.

BREWER v. WILLIAMS

430 U.S. 387 (1977)

Justice STEWART delivered the opinion of the Court.

I

On the afternoon of December 24, 1968, a 10-year-old girl named Pamela Powers went with her family to the YMCA in Des Moines, Iowa, to watch a wrestling tournament in which her brother was participating. When she failed to return from a trip to the washroom, a search for her began. The search was unsuccessful.

Robert Williams, who had recently escaped from a mental hospital, was a resident of the YMCA. Soon after the girl's disappearance Williams was seen in the YMCA lobby carrying some clothing and a large bundle wrapped in a blanket. He obtained help from a 14-year-old boy in opening the street door of the YMCA and the door to his automobile parked outside. When Williams placed the bundle in the front seat of his car the boy "saw two legs in it and they were skinny and white." Before anyone could see what was in the bundle Williams drove away. His abandoned car was found the following day in Davenport, Iowa, roughly 160 miles east of Des Moines. A warrant was then issued in Des Moines for his arrest on a charge of abduction.

On the morning of December 26, a Des Moines lawyer named Henry McKnight went to the Des Moines police station and informed the officers present that he had just received a long-distance call from Williams, and that he had advised Williams to turn himself in to the Davenport police. Williams did surrender that morning to the police in Davenport, and they booked him on the charge specified in the arrest warrant and gave him the warnings required by Miranda v. Arizona. The Davenport police then telephoned their counterparts in Des Moines to inform them that Williams had surrendered. McKnight, the lawyer, was still at the Des Moines police headquarters, and Williams conversed with McKnight on the telephone. In the presence of the Des Moines chief of police and a police detective named Leaming, McKnight advised Williams that Des Moines police officers would be driving to Davenport to pick him up, that the officers would not interrogate him or mistreat him, and that Williams was not to talk to the officers about Pamela Powers until after consulting with McKnight upon his return to Des Moines. As a result of these conversations, it was agreed between McKnight and the Des Moines police officials that Detective Leaming and a fellow officer would drive to Davenport to pick up Williams, that they would bring him directly back to Des Moines, and that they would not question him during the trip.

In the meantime Williams was arraigned before a judge in Davenport on the outstanding arrest warrant. The judge advised him of his *Miranda* rights and committed him to jail. Before leaving the courtroom, Williams conferred with a lawyer named Kelly, who advised him not to make any statements until consulting with McKnight back in Des Moines.

Detective Leaming and his fellow officer arrived in Davenport about noon to pick up Williams and return him to Des Moines. Soon after their arrival they met with Williams and Kelly, who, they understood, was acting as Williams' lawyer. Detective Leaming repeated the *Miranda* warnings.

Williams then conferred again with Kelly alone, and after this conference Kelly reiterated to Detective Leaming that Williams was not to be questioned about the disappearance of Pamela Powers until after he had consulted with McKnight back in Des Moines. When Leaming expressed some reservations, Kelly firmly stated that the agreement with McKnight was to be carried out that there was to be no interrogation of Williams during the automobile journey to Des Moines. Kelly was denied permission to ride in the police car back to Des Moines with Williams and the two officers.

The two detectives, with Williams in their charge, then set out on the 160-mile drive. At no time during the trip did Williams express a willingness to be interrogated in the absence of an attorney. Instead, he stated several times that "[w]hen I get to Des Moines and see Mr. McKnight, I am going to tell you the whole story." Detective Leaming knew that Williams was a former mental patient, and knew also that he was deeply religious.

The detective and his prisoner soon embarked on a wide-ranging conversation covering a variety of topics, including the subject of religion. Then, not long after leaving Davenport and reaching the interstate highway, Detective Leaming delivered what has been referred to in the briefs and oral arguments as the "Christian burial speech." Addressing Williams as "Reverend," the detective said: "I want to give you something to think about while we're traveling down the road. . . . Number one, I want you to observe the weather conditions, it's raining, it's sleeting, it's freezing, driving is very treacherous, visibility is poor, it's going to be dark early this evening. They are predicting several inches of snow for tonight, and I feel that you yourself are the only person that knows where this little girl's body is, that you yourself have only been there once, and if you get a snow on top of it you yourself may be unable to find it. And, since we will be going right past the area on the way into Des Moines, I feel that we could stop and locate the body, that the parents of this little girl should be entitled to a Christian burial for the little girl who was snatched away from them on Christmas [E]ve and murdered. And I feel we should stop and locate it on the way in rather than waiting until morning and trying to come back out after a snow storm and possibly not being able to find it at all."

Williams asked Detective Leaming why he thought their route to Des Moines would be taking them past the girl's body, and Leaming responded that he knew the body was in the area of Mitchellville[,] a town they would be passing on the way to Des Moines. Leaming then stated: "I do not want you to answer me. I don't want to discuss it any further. Just think about it as we're riding down the road."

As the car approached Grinnell, a town approximately 100 miles west of Davenport, Williams asked whether the police had found the victim's shoes. When Detective Leaming replied that he was unsure, Williams directed the officers to a service station where he said he had left the shoes; a search for them proved unsuccessful. As they continued towards Des Moines, Williams asked whether the police had found the blanket, and directed the officers to a rest area where he said he had disposed of the blanket. Nothing was found. The car continued towards Des Moines, and as it approached Mitchellville, Williams said that he would show the officers where the body was. He then directed the police to the body of Pamela Powers.

Williams was indicted for first-degree murder. Before trial, his counsel moved to suppress all evidence relating to or resulting from any statements Williams had made during the automobile ride from Davenport to Des Moines. The evidence in question was introduced over counsel's continuing objection at the subsequent trial. The jury found Williams guilty of murder, and the judgment of conviction was affirmed by the Iowa Supreme Court.

II

[T]here is no need to review in this case the doctrine of Miranda v. Arizona, a doctrine designed to secure the constitutional privilege against compulsory self-incrimination. For it is clear that the [conviction] in any event be [reversed] upon the ground that Williams was deprived of a different constitutional right: the right to the assistance of counsel.

This right, guaranteed by the Sixth and Fourteenth Amendments, is indispensable to the fair administration of our adversary system of criminal justice. Its vital need at the pretrial stage has perhaps nowhere been more succinctly explained than in Justice Sutherland's memorable words for the

Court 44 years ago in Powell v. Alabama: "[D]uring perhaps the most critical period of the proceedings against these defendants, that is to say, from the time of their arraignment until the beginning of their trial, when consultation, thorough-going investigation and preparation were vitally important, the defendants did not have the aid of counsel in any real sense, although they were as much entitled to such aid during that period as at the trial itself."

There has occasionally been a difference of opinion within the Court as to the peripheral scope of this constitutional right. But its basic contours, which are identical in state and federal contexts, are too well established to require extensive elaboration here. Whatever else it may mean, the right to counsel granted by the Sixth and Fourteenth Amendments means at least that a person is entitled to the help of a lawyer at or after the time that judicial proceedings have been initiated against him "whether by way of formal charge, preliminary hearing, indictment, information, or arraignment."

There can be no doubt in the present case that judicial proceedings had been initiated against Williams before the start of the automobile ride from Davenport to Des Moines. A warrant had been issued for his arrest, he had been arraigned on that warrant before a judge in a Davenport courtroom, and he had been committed by the court to confinement in jail. The State does not contend otherwise.

There can be no serious doubt, either, that Detective Leaming deliberately and designedly set out to elicit information from Williams just as surely as and perhaps more effectively than if he had formally interrogated him. Detective Leaming was fully aware before departing for Des Moines that Williams was being represented in Davenport by Kelly and in Des Moines by McKnight. Yet he purposely sought during Williams' isolation from his lawyers to obtain as much incriminating information as possible. Indeed, Detective Leaming conceded as much when he testified at Williams' trial.

The state courts clearly proceeded upon the hypothesis that Detective Leaming's "Christian burial speech" had been tantamount to interrogation. Both courts recognized that Williams had been entitled to the assistance of counsel at the time he made the incriminating statements. Yet no such constitutional protection would have come into play if there had been no interrogation.

The circumstances of this case are thus constitutionally indistinguishable from those presented in Massiah v. United States. That the incriminating statements were elicited surreptitiously in the *Massiah* case, and otherwise here, is constitutionally irrelevant. Rather, the clear rule of *Massiah* is that once adversary proceedings have commenced against an individual, he has a right to legal representation when the government interrogates him. It thus requires no wooden or technical application of the *Massiah* doctrine to conclude that Williams was entitled to the assistance of counsel guaranteed to him by the Sixth and Fourteenth Amendments.

The District Court and the Court of Appeals were also correct in their understanding of the proper standard to be applied in determining the question of waiver as a matter of federal constitutional law — that it was incumbent upon the State to prove "an intentional relinquishment or abandonment of a known right or privilege." That standard has been reiterated in many cases. We have said that the right to counsel does not depend upon a request by the defendant and that courts indulge in every reasonable presumption against waiver. This strict standard applies equally to an alleged waiver of the right to counsel whether at trial or at a critical stage of pretrial proceedings.

Despite Williams' express and implicit assertions of his right to counsel, Detective Leaming proceeded to elicit incriminating statements from Williams. Leaming did not preface this effort by telling Williams that he had a right to the presence of a lawyer, and made no effort at all to ascertain whether Williams wished to relinquish that right. The circumstances of record in this case thus provide no reasonable basis for finding that Williams waived his right to the assistance of counsel.

The crime of which Williams was convicted was senseless and brutal, calling for swift and energetic action by the police to apprehend the perpetrator and gather evidence with which he could be convicted. No mission of law enforcement officials is more important. Yet "[d]isinterested zeal for the public good does not assure either wisdom or right in the methods it pursues." Although we do not lightly affirm the issuance of a writ of habeas corpus in this case, so clear a violation of the Sixth and Fourteenth Amendments as here occurred cannot be condoned. The pressures on state executive and judicial officers charged with the administration of the criminal law are great, especially when the crime is murder and the victim a small child. But it is precisely the predictability of those pressures that makes imperative a resolute loyalty to the guarantees that the Constitution extends to us all.

Chief Justice BURGER, dissenting.

The result in this case ought to be intolerable in any society which purports to call itself an organized society. It continues the Court by the narrowest margin on the much-criticized course of punishing the public for the mistakes and misdeeds of law enforcement officers, instead of punishing the officer directly, if in fact he is guilty of wrongdoing. It mechanically and blindly keeps reliable evidence from juries whether the claimed constitutional violation involves gross police misconduct or honest human error.

Williams is guilty of the savage murder of a small child; no member of the Court contends he is not. While in custody, and after no fewer than five warnings of his rights to silence and to counsel, he led police to the concealed body of his victim. The Court concedes Williams was not threatened or coerced and that he spoke and acted voluntarily and with full awareness of his constitutional rights. In the face of all this, the Court now holds that because Williams was prompted by the detective's statement—not interrogation but a statement—the jury must not be told how the police found the body.

Today's holding fulfills Judge (later Mr. Justice) Cardozo's grim prophecy that someday some court might carry the exclusionary rule to the absurd extent that its operative effect would exclude evidence relating to the body of a murder victim because of the means by which it was found. In so ruling the Court regresses to playing a grisly game of "hide and seek," once more exalting the sporting theory of criminal justice which has been experiencing a decline in our jurisprudence. I categorically reject the remarkable notion that the police in this case were guilty of unconstitutional misconduct, or any conduct justifying the bizarre result reached by the Court. Apart from a brief comment on the merits, however, I wish to focus on the irrationality of applying the increasingly discredited exclusionary rule to this case.

The evidence is uncontradicted that Williams had abundant knowledge of his right to have counsel present and of his right to silence. Since the Court does not question his mental competence, it boggles the mind to suggest that Williams could not understand that leading police to the child's body would have other than the most serious consequences. All of the elements necessary to make out a valid waiver are shown by the record and acknowledged by the Court; we thus are left to guess how the Court reached its holding.

Justice WHITE, with whom Justice BLACKMUN and Justice REHNQUIST join, dissenting.

The respondent in this case killed a 10-year-old child, holding that certain statements of unquestioned reliability were unconstitutionally obtained from him, and under the circumstances probably makes it impossible to retry him. Because there is nothing in the Constitution or in our previous cases which requires the Court's action, I dissent.

Respondent relinquished his right not to talk to the police about his crime when the car approached the place where he had hidden the victim's clothes. Men usually intend to do what they do, and there is nothing in the record to support the proposition that respondent's decision to talk was anything but an exercise of his own free will. Apparently, without any prodding from the officers, respondent—who had earlier said that he would tell the whole story when he arrived in Des Moines—spontaneously changed his mind about the timing of his disclosures when the car approached the places where he had hidden the evidence. However, even if his statements were influenced by Detective Leaming's above-quoted statement, respondent's decision to talk in the absence of counsel can hardly be viewed as the product of an overborne will. The statement by Leaming was not coercive; it was accompanied by a request that respondent not respond to it; and it was delivered hours before respondent decided to make any statement. Respondent's waiver was thus knowing and intentional.

The majority's contrary conclusion seems to rest on the fact that respondent "asserted" his right to counsel by retaining and consulting with one lawyer and by consulting with another. How this supports the conclusion that respondent's later relinquishment of his right not to talk in the absence of counsel was unintentional is a mystery. The fact that respondent consulted with counsel on the question whether he should talk to the police in counsel's absence makes his later decision to talk in counsel's absence better informed and, if anything, more intelligent.

The consequence of the majority's decision is, as the majority recognizes, extremely serious. A mentally disturbed killer whose guilt is not in question may be released. Why? Apparently the answer is that the majority believes that the law enforcement officers acted in a way which involves some risk of injury to society and that such conduct should be deterred. However, the officers' conduct did not, and was not likely to, jeopardize the fairness of respondent's trial or in any way risk the conviction of an innocent man[,] the risk against which the Sixth Amendment guarantee of assistance of counsel is designed to protect. The police did nothing "wrong," let alone anything "unconstitutional." To anyone not lost in the intricacies of the prophylactic rules of Miranda v. Arizona, the result in this case seems utterly senseless; the statements made by respondent were properly admitted. In light of these considerations, the majority's protest that the result in this case is justified by a "clear violation" of the Sixth and Fourteenth Amendments has a distressing hollow ring. I respectfully dissent.

Subsequently, the Court applied *Massiah* and *Brewer* in Fellers v. United States, 540 U.S. 519 (2004). Fellers was indicted for conspiracy to distribute methamphetamines. Police came to his house to arrest him, and Fellers made several incriminating statements. The Supreme Court held that the statements had to be excluded. Justice O'Connor, writing for the Court, said that "there is no question that the officers in this case 'deliberately elicited' information from petitioner. Indeed, the officers, upon arriving at petitioner's house, informed him that their purpose was to discuss his involvement in the distribution of methamphetamines and his association with certain charged co-conspirators." The Court concluded that "[b]ecause the ensuing discussion took place after petitioner had been indicted, outside the presence of counsel, and in the absence of any waiver of petitioner's Sixth Amendment rights," the statements made to the police had to be excluded.

2. *The Sixth Amendment Right to Counsel Is Offense Specific*

A key distinction between the Fifth Amendment right to counsel and the Sixth Amendment right to counsel is that the latter is offense-specific. Under the Fifth Amendment right to counsel, police cannot initiate questioning about any crime after a suspect has invoked the right to counsel. But under the Sixth Amendment the police are limited only in questioning the suspect about the specific crimes for which formal judicial proceedings have been initiated.

This was initially the holding in McNeil v. Wisconsin, 501 U.S. 171 (1991). McNeil was formally charged with armed robbery and asserted his right to counsel at a court appearance. Subsequently, police questioned McNeil about a murder and armed robbery in another part of the state. McNeil was given his *Miranda* warnings and confessed. The question was whether his earlier invocation of the right to counsel made the questioning about the other offenses impermissible.

In a 6-3 decision, the Court found no violation of the Sixth Amendment. In an opinion by Justice Scalia, the Court concluded that "just as the right is offense-specific," so is the effect of asserting the right to counsel "in police-initiated interviews offense-specific." The Court said that a contrary rule would interfere with effective law enforcement because then "most people in pretrial custody for serious offenses would be unapproachable by police officers suspecting them of involvement in other crimes, even though they have never expressed any unwillingness to be questioned."

The Court reaffirmed and clarified this in Texas v. Cobb.

TEXAS v. COBB

532 U.S. 162 (2001)

Chief Justice Rehnquist delivered the opinion of the Court.

The Texas Court of Criminal Appeals held that a criminal defendant's Sixth Amendment right to counsel attaches not only to the offense with which he is charged, but to other offenses "closely related factually" to the charged offense. We hold that our decision in McNeil v. Wisconsin (1991), meant what it said, and that the Sixth Amendment right is "offense-specific."

In December 1993, Lindsey Owings reported to the Walker County, Texas, Sheriff's Office that the home he shared with his wife, Margaret, and their 16-month-old daughter, Kori Rae, had been burglarized. He also informed police that his wife and daughter were missing. Respondent Raymond Levi Cobb lived across the street from the Owings. Acting on an anonymous tip that respondent was involved in the burglary, Walker County investigators questioned him about the events. He denied involvement. In July 1994, while under arrest for an unrelated offense, respondent was again questioned about the incident. Respondent then gave a written statement confessing to the burglary, but he denied knowledge relating to the disappearances. Respondent was subsequently indicted for the burglary, and Hal Ridley was appointed in August 1994 to represent respondent on that charge.

Shortly after Ridley's appointment, investigators asked and received his permission to question respondent about the disappearances. Respondent continued to deny involvement. Investigators repeated this process in September 1995, again with Ridley's permission and again with the same result.

In November 1995, respondent, free on bond in the burglary case, was living with his father in Odessa, Texas. At that time, respondent's father contacted the Walker County Sheriff's Office to report that respondent had confessed to him that he killed Margaret Owings in the course of the burglary. Walker County investigators directed respondent's father to the Odessa police station, where he gave a statement. Odessa police then faxed the statement to Walker County, where investigators secured a warrant for respondent's arrest and faxed it back to Odessa. Shortly thereafter, Odessa police took respondent into custody and administered warnings pursuant to Miranda v. Arizona. Respondent waived these rights.

After a short time, respondent confessed to murdering both Margaret and Kori Rae. Respondent explained that when Margaret confronted him as he was attempting to remove the Owings' stereo, he stabbed her in the stomach with a knife he was carrying. Respondent told police that he dragged her body to a wooded area a few hundred yards from the house. Respondent later led police to the location where he had buried the victims' bodies.

Respondent was convicted of capital murder for murdering more than one person in the course of a single criminal transaction. He was sentenced to death.

In McNeil v. Wisconsin (1991), we explained: "The Sixth Amendment right [to counsel] . . . is offense-specific. It cannot be invoked once for all future prosecutions, for it does not attach until a prosecution is commenced, that is, at or after the initiation of adversary judicial criminal proceedings—whether by way of formal charge, preliminary hearing, indictment, information, or arraignment." Accordingly, we held that a defendant's statements regarding offenses for which he had not been charged were admissible notwithstanding the attachment of his Sixth Amendment right to counsel on other charged offenses.

Some state courts and Federal Courts of Appeals, however, have read into McNeil's offense-specific definition an exception for crimes that are "factually related" to a charged offense. We decline to do so.

Respondent predicts that the offense-specific rule will prove "disastrous" to suspects' constitutional rights and will "permit law enforcement officers almost complete and total license to conduct unwanted and uncounseled interrogations." Besides offering no evidence that such a parade of horribles has occurred in those jurisdictions that have not enlarged upon McNeil, he fails to appreciate the significance of two critical considerations. First, there can be no doubt that a suspect must be apprised of his rights against compulsory self-incrimination and to consult with an attorney before authorities may conduct custodial interrogation. In the present case, police scrupulously followed Miranda's dictates when questioning respondent. Second, it is critical to recognize that the Constitution does not negate society's interest in the ability of police to talk to witnesses and suspects, even those who have been charged with other offenses.

It is also worth noting that, contrary to the dissent's suggestion, there is no "background principle" of our Sixth Amendment jurisprudence establishing that there may be no contact between a defendant and police without counsel present. The dissent would expand the Sixth Amendment right to the assistance of counsel in a criminal prosecution into a rule which "exists to prevent lawyers from taking advantage of uncounseled laypersons and to preserve the integrity of the lawyer-client relationship." The Sixth Amendment right to counsel is personal to the defendant and specific to the offense.

Although it is clear that the Sixth Amendment right to counsel attaches only to charged offenses, we have recognized in other contexts that the definition of an "offense" is not necessarily limited to the four corners of a charging instrument. In Blockburger v. United States (1932), we explained that "where the same act or transaction constitutes a violation of two distinct statutory provisions, the test to be applied to determine whether there are two offenses or only one, is whether each provision requires proof of a fact which the other does not." We have since applied the *Blockburger* test to delineate the scope of the Fifth Amendment's Double Jeopardy Clause, which prevents multiple or successive prosecutions for the "same offence." We see no constitutional difference between the meaning of the term "offense" in the contexts of double jeopardy and of the right to counsel. Accordingly, we hold that when the Sixth Amendment right to counsel attaches, it does encompass offenses that, even if not formally charged, would be considered the same offense under the *Blockburger* test.

It remains only to apply these principles to the facts at hand. At the time he confessed to Odessa police, respondent had been indicted for burglary of the Owings residence, but he had not been charged in the murders of Margaret and Kori Rae. As defined by Texas law, burglary and capital murder are not the same offense under *Blockburger*. Accordingly, the Sixth Amendment right to counsel did not bar police from interrogating respondent regarding the murders, and respondent's confession was therefore admissible.

Justice BREYER, with whom Justice STEVENS, Justice SOUTER, and Justice GINSBURG join, dissenting.

This case focuses upon the meaning of a single word, "offense," when it arises in the context of the Sixth Amendment. Several basic background principles define that context.

First, the Sixth Amendment right to counsel plays a central role in ensuring the fairness of criminal proceedings in our system of justice. Second, the right attaches when adversary proceedings, triggered by the government's formal accusation of a crime, begin. Third, once this right attaches, law enforcement officials are required, in most circumstances, to deal with the defendant through counsel rather than directly, even if the defendant has waived his Fifth Amendment rights.

Fourth, the particular aspect of the right here at issue — the rule that the police ordinarily must communicate with the defendant through counsel — has important limits. In particular, recognizing the need for law enforcement officials to investigate "new or additional crimes" not the subject of current proceedings, this Court has made clear that the right to counsel does not attach to any and every crime that an accused may commit or have committed. The right "cannot be invoked once for all future prosecutions," and it does not forbid "interrogation unrelated to the charge." In a word, as this Court previously noted, the right is "offense-specific."

This case focuses upon the last-mentioned principle, in particular upon the meaning of the words "offense specific." These words appear in this Court's Sixth Amendment case law, not in the Sixth Amendment's text. The definition of these words is not self-evident. Sometimes the term "offense" may refer to words that are written in a criminal statute; sometimes it may refer generally to a course of conduct in the world, aspects of which constitute the elements of one or more crimes; and sometimes it may refer, narrowly and technically, just to the conceptually severable aspects of the latter. This case requires us to determine whether an "offense" — for Sixth Amendment purposes — includes factually related aspects of a single course of conduct other than those few acts that make up the essential elements of the crime charged.

We should answer this question in light of the Sixth Amendment's basic objectives as set forth in this Court's case law. At the very least, we should answer it in a way that does not undermine those objectives. But the Court today decides that "offense" means the crime set forth within "the four corners of a charging instrument," along with other crimes that "would be considered the same offense" under the test established by Blockburger v. United States (1932). In my view, this unnecessarily technical definition undermines Sixth Amendment protections while doing nothing to further effective law enforcement.

For one thing, the majority's rule, while leaving the Fifth Amendment's protections in place, threatens to diminish severely the additional protection that, under this Court's rulings, the Sixth Amendment provides when it grants the right to counsel to defendants who have been charged with a crime and insists that law enforcement officers thereafter communicate with them through that counsel.

For these reasons, the Sixth Amendment right at issue is independent of the Fifth Amendment's protections; and the importance of this Sixth Amendment right has been repeatedly recognized in our cases. The majority's rule permits law enforcement officials to question those charged with a crime without first approaching counsel, through the simple device of asking questions about any other related crime not actually charged in the indictment. Thus, the police could ask the individual charged with robbery about, say, the assault of the cashier not yet charged, or about any other uncharged offense (unless under Blockburger's definition it counts as the "same crime"), all without notifying counsel. Indeed, the majority's rule would permit law enforcement officials to question anyone charged with any crime in any one of the examples just given about his or her conduct on the single relevant occasion without notifying counsel unless the prosecutor has charged every possible crime arising out of that same brief course of conduct. What Sixth Amendment sense — what common sense — does such a rule make? What is left of the "communicate through counsel" rule? The majority's approach is inconsistent with any common understanding of the scope of counsel's representation. It will undermine the lawyer's role as "'medium'" between the defendant and the government. And it will, on a random basis, remove a significant portion of the protection that this Court has found inherent in the Sixth Amendment.

[T]he simple-sounding *Blockburger* test has proved extraordinarily difficult to administer in practice. Judges, lawyers, and law professors often disagree about how to apply it. Yet the Court now asks, not the lawyers and judges who ordinarily work with double jeopardy law, but police officers in the field, to navigate *Blockburger* when they question suspects. Some will apply the test successfully; some will not. Legal challenges are inevitable. The result, I believe, will resemble not so much the Sargasso Sea as the criminal law equivalent of Milton's "Serbonian Bog . . . Where Armies whole have sunk."

There is, of course, an alternative. We can, and should, define "offense" in terms of the conduct that constitutes the crime that the offender committed on a particular occasion, including criminal acts that are "closely related to" or "inextricably intertwined with" the particular crime set forth in the charging instrument. This alternative is not perfect. The language used lacks the precision for which police officers may hope; and it requires lower courts to specify its meaning further as they apply it in individual cases. Yet virtually every lower court in the United States to consider the issue has defined "offense" in the Sixth Amendment context to encompass such closely related acts.

One cannot say in favor of this commonly followed approach that it is perfectly clear — only that, because it comports with common sense, it is far easier to apply than that of the majority. And, most importantly, the "closely related" test furthers, rather than undermines, the Sixth Amendment's "right to counsel," a right so necessary to the realization in practice of that most "noble ideal," a fair trial.

3.   Waivers

The Sixth Amendment right to counsel, like the Fifth Amendment right to counsel under the privilege against self-incrimination, can be waived. Here, too, the Supreme Court has stressed that it must be a knowing and intelligent waiver. In Michigan v. Jackson, 475 U.S. 625 (1986), the Supreme Court held that once the Sixth Amendment right to counsel has been invoked, there is not a valid waiver if it was made in response to government-initiated interrogation. But in Montejo v. Louisiana, the Court overruled Jackson v.

Michigan. The Court stressed, though, that if the right to counsel is invoked under the Fifth Amendment, Edwards v. Arizona still precludes police from eliciting incriminating statements without the presence of counsel.

MONTEJO v. LOUISIANA
556 U.S. 778 (2009)

Justice SCALIA delivered the opinion of the Court.

We consider in this case the scope and continued viability of the rule announced by this Court in *Michigan v. Jackson* (1986), forbidding police to initiate interrogation of a criminal defendant once he has requested counsel at an arraignment or similar proceeding.

I

Petitioner Jesse Montejo was arrested on September 6, 2002, in connection with the robbery and murder of Lewis Ferrari, who had been found dead in his own home one day earlier. Suspicion quickly focused on Jerry Moore, a disgruntled former employee of Ferrari's dry cleaning business. Police sought to question Montejo, who was a known associate of Moore.

Montejo waived his rights under *Miranda v. Arizona* (1966), and was interrogated at the sheriff's office by police detectives through the late afternoon and evening of September 6 and the early morning of September 7. During the interrogation, Montejo repeatedly changed his account of the crime, at first claiming that he had only driven Moore to the victim's home, and ultimately admitting that he had shot and killed Ferrari in the course of a botched burglary. These police interrogations were videotaped.

On September 10, Montejo was brought before a judge for what is known in Louisiana as a "72-hour hearing" — a preliminary hearing required under state law. Although the proceedings were not transcribed, the minute record indicates what transpired: "The defendant being charged with First Degree Murder, Court ordered N[o] Bond set in this matter. Further, Court ordered the Office of Indigent Defender be appointed to represent the defendant."

Later that same day, two police detectives visited Montejo back at the prison and requested that he accompany them on an excursion to locate the murder weapon (which Montejo had earlier indicated he had thrown into a lake). After some back-and-forth, the substance of which remains in dispute, Montejo was again read his *Miranda* rights and agreed to go along; during the excursion, he wrote an inculpatory letter of apology to the victim's widow. Only upon their return did Montejo finally meet his court-appointed attorney, who was quite upset that the detectives had interrogated his client in his absence.

   At trial, the letter of apology was admitted over defense objection. The jury convicted Montejo of first-degree murder, and he was sentenced to death.

   The Louisiana Supreme Court affirmed the conviction and sentence. As relevant here, the court rejected Montejo's argument that under the rule of *Jackson*, the letter should have been suppressed. *Jackson* held that "if police initiate interrogation after a defendant's assertion, at an arraignment or similar proceeding, of his right to counsel, any waiver of the defendant's right to counsel for that police-initiated interrogation is invalid."

II

Montejo's solution is untenable as a theoretical and doctrinal matter. Under his approach, once a defendant is *represented* by counsel, police may not initiate any further interrogation. Such a rule would be entirely untethered from the original rationale of *Jackson*.

A

It is worth emphasizing first what is *not* in dispute or at stake here. Under our precedents, once the adversary judicial process has been initiated, the Sixth Amendment guarantees a defendant the right to have counsel present at all "critical" stages of the criminal proceedings. Interrogation by the State is such a stage.

   Our precedents also place beyond doubt that the Sixth Amendment right to counsel may be waived by a defendant, so long as relinquishment of the right is voluntary, knowing, and intelligent. The defendant may waive the right whether or not he is already represented by counsel; the decision to waive need not itself be counseled. And when a defendant is read his *Miranda* rights (which include the right to have counsel present during interrogation) and agrees to waive those rights, that typically does the trick, even though the *Miranda* rights purportedly have their source in the *Fifth* Amendment.

   The *only* question raised by this case, and the only one addressed by the *Jackson* rule, is whether courts must *presume* that such a waiver is invalid under certain circumstances. We created such a presumption in *Jackson* by analogy to a similar prophylactic rule established to protect the Fifth Amendment based *Miranda* right to have counsel present at any custodial interrogation. *Edwards v. Arizona* (1981), decided that once "an accused has invoked his right to have counsel present during custodial interrogation . . . [he] is not subject to further interrogation by the authorities until counsel has been made available," unless he initiates the contact.

   The *Edwards* rule is "designed to prevent police from badgering a defendant into waiving his previously asserted *Miranda* rights." It does this by presuming his postassertion statements to be involuntary, "even where the suspect executes a waiver and his statements would be considered voluntary under traditional standards." This prophylactic rule thus "protect[s] a suspect's voluntary choice not to speak outside his lawyer's presence."

Jackson represented a "wholesale importation of the *Edwards* rule into the Sixth Amendment." The *Jackson* Court decided that a request for counsel at an arraignment should be treated as an invocation of the Sixth Amendment right to counsel "at every critical stage of the prosecution," despite doubt that defendants "actually inten[d] their request for counsel to encompass representation during any further questioning," because doubts must be "resolved in favor of protecting the constitutional claim." Citing *Edwards*, the Court held that any subsequent waiver would thus be "insufficient to justify police-initiated interrogation." In other words, we presume such waivers involuntary "based on the supposition that suspects who assert their right to counsel are unlikely to waive that right voluntarily" in subsequent interactions with police.

The dissent presents us with a revisionist view of *Jackson*. The defendants' *request* for counsel, it contends, was important only because it proved that counsel *had been appointed*. Such a non sequitur (nowhere alluded to in the case) hardly needs rebuttal. Proceeding from this fanciful premise, the dissent claims that the decision actually established "a rule designed to safeguard a defendant's right to rely on the assistance of counsel," not one "designed to prevent police badgering." To safeguard the right to assistance of counsel from *what?* From a knowing and voluntary waiver by the defendant himself? Unless the dissent seeks to prevent a defendant altogether from waiving his Sixth Amendment rights, *i.e.*, to "imprison a man in his privileges and call it the Constitution," — a view with zero support in reason, history or case law — the answer must be: from police pressure, *i.e.*, badgering. The antibadgering rationale is the only way to make sense of *Jackson*'s repeated citations of *Edwards*, and the only way to reconcile the opinion with our waiver jurisprudence.

B

With this understanding of what *Jackson* stands for and whence it came, it should be clear that Montejo's interpretation of that decision — that no *represented* defendant can ever be approached by the State and asked to consent to interrogation — is off the mark. When a court appoints counsel for an indigent defendant in the absence of any request on his part, there is no basis for a presumption that any subsequent waiver of the right to counsel will be involuntary. There is no "*initial* election" to exercise the right, that must be preserved through a prophylactic rule against later waivers. No reason exists to assume that a defendant like Montejo, who has done *nothing at all* to express his intentions with respect to his Sixth Amendment rights, would not be perfectly amenable to speaking with the police without having counsel present. And no reason exists to prohibit the police from inquiring. *Edwards* and *Jackson* are meant to prevent police from badgering defendants into changing their minds about their rights, but a defendant who never asked for counsel has not yet made up his mind in the first instance.

The dissent's argument to the contrary rests on a flawed *a fortiori*: "If a defendant is entitled to protection from police-initiated interrogation under the Sixth Amendment when he merely *requests* a lawyer, he is even more obviously entitled to such protection when he has *secured* a lawyer." The question in *Jackson*, however, was not whether respondents were entitled to counsel (they unquestionably were), but "whether respondents validly waived their right to counsel," and even if it is reasonable to presume from a defendant's *request* for counsel that any subsequent waiver of the right was coerced, no such presumption can seriously be entertained when a lawyer was merely "secured" on the defendant's behalf, by the State itself, as a matter of course. Of course, reading the dissent's analysis, one would have no idea that Montejo executed any waiver at all.

In practice, Montejo's rule would prevent police-initiated interrogation entirely once the Sixth Amendment right attaches, at least in those States that appoint counsel promptly without request from the defendant. As the dissent in *Jackson* pointed out, with no expressed disagreement from the majority, the opinion "most assuredly [did] *not* hold that the *Edwards per se* rule prohibiting all police-initiated interrogations applies from the moment the defendant's Sixth Amendment right to counsel attaches, with or without a request for counsel by the defendant." That would have constituted a "shockingly dramatic restructuring of the balance this Court has traditionally struck between the rights of the defendant and those of the larger society."

Montejo's rule appears to have its theoretical roots in codes of legal ethics, not the Sixth Amendment. The American Bar Association's Model Rules of Professional Conduct (which nearly all States have adopted into law in whole or in part) mandate that "a lawyer shall not communicate about the subject of [a] representation with a party the lawyer knows to be represented by another lawyer in the matter, unless the lawyer has the consent of the other lawyer or is authorized to do so by law or a court order." Model Rule 4.2 (2008). But the Constitution does not codify the ABA's Model Rules, and does not make investigating police officers lawyers. Montejo's proposed rule is both broader and narrower than the Model Rule. Broader, because Montejo would apply it to all agents of the State, including the detectives who interrogated him, while the ethical rule governs only lawyers. And narrower, because he agrees that if a defendant initiates contact with the police, they may talk freely — whereas a lawyer could be sanctioned for interviewing a represented party even if that party "initiates" the communication and consents to the interview.

The upshot is that even on *Jackson*'s own terms, it would be completely unjustified to presume that a defendant's consent to police-initiated interrogation was involuntary or coerced simply because he had previously been appointed a lawyer.

III

We do not think that *stare decisis* requires us to expand significantly the holding of a prior decision — fundamentally revising its theoretical basis in the process — in order to cure its practical deficiencies. To the contrary, the fact that a decision has proved "unworkable" is a traditional ground for overruling it. Accordingly, we called for supplemental briefing addressed to the question whether *Michigan v. Jackson* should be overruled.

Beyond workability, the relevant factors in deciding whether to adhere to the principle of *stare decisis* include the antiquity of the precedent, the reliance interests at stake, and of course whether the decision was well reasoned. The first two cut in favor of abandoning *Jackson*: the opinion is only two decades old, and eliminating it would not upset expectations. Any criminal defendant learned enough to order his affairs based on the rule announced in *Jackson* would also be perfectly capable of interacting with the police on his own. Of course it is likely true that police and prosecutors have been trained to comply with *Jackson*, but that is hardly a basis for retaining it as a constitutional requirement. If a State *wishes* to abstain from requesting interviews with represented defendants when counsel is not present, it obviously may continue to do so.

Which brings us to the strength of *Jackson*'s reasoning. When this Court creates a prophylactic rule in order to protect a constitutional right, the relevant "reasoning" is the weighing of the rule's benefits against its costs. "The value of any prophylactic rule . . . must be assessed not only on the basis of what is gained, but also on the basis of what is lost." We think that the marginal benefits of *Jackson* (viz., the number of confessions obtained coercively that are suppressed by its bright-line rule and would otherwise have been admitted) are dwarfed by its substantial costs (viz., hindering "society's compelling interest in finding, convicting, and punishing those who violate the law.")

What does the *Jackson* rule actually achieve by way of preventing unconstitutional conduct? Recall that the purpose of the rule is to preclude the State from badgering defendants into waiving their previously asserted rights. The effect of this badgering might be to coerce a waiver, which would render the subsequent interrogation a violation of the Sixth Amendment. Even though involuntary waivers are invalid even apart from *Jackson* . . . mistakes are of course possible when courts conduct case-by-case voluntariness review. A bright-line rule like that adopted in *Jackson* ensures that no fruits of interrogations made possible by badgering-induced involuntary waivers are ever erroneously admitted at trial.

But without *Jackson*, how many would be? The answer is few if any. The principal reason is that the Court has already taken substantial other, overlapping measures toward the same end. Under *Miranda*'s prophylactic protection of the right against compelled self-incrimination, any suspect subject to custodial interrogation has the right to have a lawyer present if he so requests, and to be advised of that right. Under *Edwards*' prophylactic protection of the *Miranda* right, once such a defendant "has invoked his right to have counsel present," interrogation must stop. And under *Minnick*'s prophylactic protection of the *Edwards* right, no subsequent interrogation may take place until counsel is present, "whether or not the accused has consulted with his attorney."

These three layers of prophylaxis are sufficient. Under the *Miranda-Edwards-Minnick* line of cases (which is not in doubt), a defendant who does not want to speak to the police without counsel present need only say as much when he is first approached and given the *Miranda* warnings. At that point, not only must the immediate contact end, but "badgering" by later requests is prohibited. If that regime suffices to protect the integrity of "a suspect's voluntary choice not to speak outside his lawyer's presence" before his arraignment, it is hard to see why it would not also suffice to protect that same choice after arraignment, when Sixth Amendment rights have attached. And if so, then *Jackson* is simply superfluous.

It is true, as Montejo points out in his supplemental brief, that the doctrine established by *Miranda* and *Edwards* is designed to protect Fifth Amendment, not Sixth Amendment, rights. But that is irrelevant. What matters is that these cases, like *Jackson*, protect the right to have counsel during custodial interrogation—which right happens to be guaranteed (once the adversary judicial process has begun) by *two* sources of law. Since the right under both sources is waived using the same procedure, doctrines ensuring voluntariness of the Fifth Amendment waiver simultaneously ensure the voluntariness of the Sixth Amendment waiver.

Montejo also correctly observes that the *Miranda-Edwards* regime is narrower than *Jackson* in one respect: The former applies only in the context of custodial interrogation. If the defendant is not in custody then those decisions do not apply; nor do they govern other, noninterrogative types of interactions between the defendant and the State (like pretrial lineups). However, those uncovered situations are the *least* likely to pose a risk of coerced waivers. When a defendant is not in custody, he is in control, and need only shut his door or walk away to avoid police badgering. And noninterrogative interactions with the State do not involve the "inherently compelling pressures," that one might reasonably fear could lead to involuntary waivers.

Jackson was policy driven, and if that policy is being adequately served through other means, there is no reason to retain its rule. *Miranda* and the cases that elaborate upon it already guarantee not simply noncoercion in the traditional sense, but what Justice *Harlan* referred to as "voluntariness with a vengeance." There is no need to take *Jackson*'s further step of requiring voluntariness on stilts.

On the other side of the equation are the costs of adding the bright-line *Jackson* rule on top of *Edwards* and other extant protections. The principal cost of applying any exclusionary rule "is, of course, letting guilty and possibly dangerous criminals go free. . . ." *Jackson* not only "operates to invalidate a confession given by the free choice of suspects who have received proper advice of their *Miranda* rights but waived them nonetheless," but also deters law enforcement officers from even trying to obtain voluntary confessions. The "ready ability to obtain uncoerced confessions is not an evil but an unmitigated good." Without these confessions, crimes go unsolved and criminals unpunished. These are not negligible costs, and in our view the *Jackson* Court gave them too short shrift.

In sum, when the marginal benefits of the *Jackson* rule are weighed against its substantial costs to the truth-seeking process and the criminal justice system, we readily conclude that the rule does not "pay its way." *Michigan v. Jackson* should be and now is overruled.

Justice STEVENS, with whom Justice SOUTER and Justice GINSBURG join, and with whom Justice BREYER joins, dissenting.

Today the Court properly concludes that the Louisiana Supreme Court's parsimonious reading of our decision in *Michigan v. Jackson* (1986) is indefensible. Yet the Court does not reverse. Rather, on its own initiative and without any evidence that the longstanding Sixth Amendment protections established in *Jackson* have caused any harm to the workings of the criminal justice system, the Court rejects *Jackson* outright on the ground that it is "untenable as a theoretical and doctrinal matter." That conclusion rests on a misinterpretation of *Jackson*'s rationale and a gross undervaluation of the rule of *stare decisis.* The police interrogation in this case clearly violated petitioner's Sixth Amendment right to counsel.

I

The Sixth Amendment provides that "[i]n all criminal prosecutions, the accused shall enjoy the right . . . to have the Assistance of Counsel for his defence." The right to counsel attaches during "the initiation of adversary judicial criminal proceedings," and it guarantees the assistance of counsel not only during in-court proceedings but during all critical stages, including postarraignment interviews with law enforcement officers.

In *Jackson*, this Court considered whether the Sixth Amendment bars police from interrogating defendants who have requested the appointment of counsel at arraignment. Applying the presumption that such a request constitutes an invocation of the right to counsel "at every critical stage of the prosecution," we held that "a defendant who has been formally charged with a crime and who has requested appointment of counsel at his arraignment" cannot be subject to uncounseled interrogation unless he initiates "exchanges or conversations with the police."

II

Today the Court correctly concludes that the Louisiana Supreme Court's holding is "troublesome," "impractical," and "unsound." Instead of reversing the decision of the state court by simply answering the question on which we granted certiorari in a unanimous opinion, however, the majority has decided to change the law. Acting on its own initiative, the majority overrules *Jackson* to correct a "theoretical and doctrinal" problem of its own imagining. A more careful reading of *Jackson* and the Sixth Amendment cases upon which it relied reveals that the rule announced in *Jackson* protects a fundamental right that the Court now dishonors.

The majority's decision to overrule *Jackson* rests on its assumption that *Jackson*'s protective rule was intended to "prevent police from badgering defendants into changing their minds about their rights," just as the rule adopted in *Edwards v. Arizona* (1981), was designed to prevent police from coercing unindicted suspects into revoking their requests for counsel at interrogation. Operating on that limited understanding of the purpose behind *Jackson*'s protective rule, the Court concludes that *Jackson* provides no safeguard not already secured by this Court's Fifth Amendment jurisprudence.

The majority's analysis flagrantly misrepresents *Jackson*'s underlying rationale and the constitutional interests the decision sought to protect. While it is true that the rule adopted in *Jackson* was patterned after the rule in *Edwards*, the *Jackson* opinion does not even mention the anti-badgering considerations that provide the basis for the Court's decision today. Instead, *Jackson* relied primarily on cases discussing the broad protections guaranteed by the Sixth Amendment right to counsel — not its Fifth Amendment counterpart. *Jackson* emphasized that the purpose of the Sixth Amendment is to "protec[t] the unaided layman at critical confrontations with his adversary," by giving him "the right to rely on counsel as a 'medium' between him[self] and the State." Underscoring that the commencement of criminal proceedings is a decisive event that transforms a suspect into an accused within the meaning of the Sixth Amendment, we concluded that arraigned defendants are entitled to "at least as much protection" during interrogation as the Fifth Amendment affords unindicted suspects. Thus, although the rules adopted in *Edwards* and *Jackson* are similar, *Jackson* did not rely on the reasoning of *Edwards* but remained firmly rooted in the unique protections afforded to the attorney-client relationship by the Sixth Amendment.

Once *Jackson* is placed in its proper Sixth Amendment context, the majority's justifications for overruling the decision crumble. Ordinarily, this Court is hesitant to disturb past precedent and will do so only when a rule has proven "outdated, ill-founded, unworkable, or otherwise legitimately vulnerable to serious reconsideration." While *stare decisis* is not "an inexorable command," we adhere to it as "the preferred course because it promotes the evenhanded, predictable, and consistent development of legal principles, fosters reliance on judicial decisions, and contributes to the actual and perceived integrity of the judicial process."

Paying lip service to the rule of *stare decisis*, the majority acknowledges that the Court must consider many factors before taking the dramatic step of overruling a past decision. Specifically, the majority focuses on four considerations: the reasoning of the decision, the workability of the rule, the reliance interests at stake, and the antiquity of the precedent. The Court exaggerates the considerations favoring reversal, however, and gives short shrift to the valid considerations favoring retention of the *Jackson* rule.

First, and most central to the Court's decision to overrule *Jackson*, is its assertion that *Jackson*'s "'reasoning'" — which the Court defines as "the weighing of the [protective] rule's benefits against its costs," does not justify continued application of the rule it created. The balancing test the Court performs, however, depends entirely on its misunderstanding of *Jackson* as a rule designed to prevent police badgering, rather than a rule designed to safeguard a defendant's right to rely on the assistance of counsel.

Next, in order to reach the conclusion that the *Jackson* rule is unworkable, the Court reframes the relevant inquiry, asking not whether the *Jackson* rule as applied for the past quarter century has proved easily administrable, but instead whether the Louisiana Supreme Court's cramped interpretation of that rule is practically workable. The answer to that question, of course, is no. When framed more broadly, however, the evidence is overwhelming that *Jackson*'s simple, bright-line rule has done more to advance effective law enforcement than to undermine it.

In a supplemental brief submitted by lawyers and judges with extensive experience in law enforcement and prosecution, *amici* Larry D. Thompson et al. argue persuasively that *Jackson*'s bright-line rule has provided law enforcement officers with clear guidance, allowed prosecutors to quickly and easily assess whether confessions will be admissible in court, and assisted judges in determining whether a defendant's Sixth Amendment rights have been violated by police interrogation. See generally Thompson. While *amici* acknowledge that "*Jackson* reduces opportunities to interrogate defendants" and "may require exclusion of evidence that could support a criminal conviction," they maintain that "it is a rare case where this rule lets a guilty defendant go free." In short, there is substantial evidence suggesting that *Jackson*'s rule is not only workable, but also desirable from the perspective of law enforcement.

Turning to the reliance interests at stake in the case, the Court rejects the interests of criminal defendants with the flippant observation that any who are knowledgeable enough to rely on *Jackson* are too savvy to need its protections, and casts aside the reliance interests of law enforcement on the ground that police and prosecutors remain free to employ the *Jackson* rule if it suits them. Again as a result of its mistaken understanding of the purpose behind *Jackson*'s protective rule, the Court fails to identify the real reliance interest at issue in this case: the public's interest in knowing that counsel, once secured, may be reasonably relied upon as a medium between the accused and the power of the State. That interest lies at the heart of the Sixth Amendment's guarantee, and is surely worthy of greater consideration than it is given by today's decision.

Finally, although the Court acknowledges that "antiquity" is a factor that counsels in favor of retaining precedent, it concludes that the fact *Jackson* is "only two decades old" cuts "in favor of abandoning" the rule it established.

I would have thought that the 23-year existence of a simple bright-line rule would be a factor that cuts in the other direction.

Despite the fact that the rule established in *Jackson* remains relevant, well grounded in constitutional precedent, and easily administrable, the Court today rejects it *sua sponte*. Such a decision can only diminish the public's confidence in the reliability and fairness of our system of justice.

III

Even if *Jackson* had never been decided, it would be clear that Montejo's Sixth Amendment rights were violated. Today's decision eliminates the rule that "any waiver of Sixth Amendment rights given in a discussion initiated by police is presumed invalid" once a defendant has invoked his right to counsel. Nevertheless, under the undisputed facts of this case, there is no sound basis for concluding that Montejo made a knowing and valid waiver of his Sixth Amendment right to counsel before acquiescing in police interrogation following his 72-hour hearing. Because police questioned Montejo without notice to, and outside the presence of, his lawyer, the interrogation violated Montejo's right to counsel even under pre-*Jackson* precedent.

IV

The Court's decision to overrule *Jackson* is unwarranted. Not only does it rest on a flawed doctrinal premise, but the dubious benefits it hopes to achieve are far outweighed by the damage it does to the rule of law and the integrity of the Sixth Amendment right to counsel. Moreover, even apart from the protections afforded by *Jackson*, the police interrogation in this case violated Jesse Montejo's Sixth Amendment right to counsel.

4.   What Is Impermissible Police Eliciting of Statements?

The Supreme Court has held that the Sixth Amendment prevents the police from doing anything to elicit statements from an accused once formal adversary proceedings have been initiated unless the defendant waives the right to counsel. The Court has said that once a person is represented by counsel, the "Sixth Amendment guarantees the accused, at least after the initiation of formal charges, the right to rely on counsel as a 'medium' between him and the State." Maine v. Moulton, 474 U.S. 159 (1985). In that case, the Court found a violation of the Sixth Amendment when the police put a wire on a codefendant to record conversations with the accused. The Court held that the defendant's statements relating to the crimes for which he had been indicted were not admissible under the Sixth Amendment.

This raises a difficult question: When is there deliberate elicitation when the police use informants to gain statements from an accused after the initiation of judicial proceedings? The Supreme Court has decided two major cases on this — United States v. Henry and Kuhlmann v. Wilson. In reading them, it is important to focus on whether they can be reconciled and when use of informers is allowed and when it is impermissible eliciting of statements.

UNITED STATES v. HENRY

447 U.S. 264 (1980)

Chief Justice BURGER delivered the opinion of the Court.

We granted certiorari to consider whether respondent's Sixth Amendment right to the assistance of counsel was violated by the admission at trial of incriminating statements made by respondent to his cellmate, an undisclosed Government informant, after indictment and while in custody.

I

The Janaf Branch of the United Virginia Bank/Seaboard National in Norfolk, Va., was robbed in August 1972. Witnesses saw two men wearing masks and carrying guns enter the bank while a third man waited in the car. No witnesses were able to identify respondent Henry as one of the participants. About an hour after the robbery, the getaway car was discovered. Inside was found a rent receipt signed by one "Allen R. Norris" and a lease, also signed by Norris, for a house in Norfolk. Two men, who were subsequently convicted of participating in the robbery, were arrested at the rented house. Discovered with them were the proceeds of the robbery and the guns and masks used by the gunman. Government agents traced the rent receipt to Henry; on the basis of this information, Henry was arrested in Atlanta, Ga., in November 1972. Two weeks later he was indicted for armed robbery. He was held pending trial in the Norfolk city jail. Counsel was appointed on November 27.

On November 21, 1972, shortly after Henry was incarcerated, Government agents working on the Janaf robbery contacted one Nichols, an inmate at the Norfolk city jail, who for some time prior to this meeting had been engaged to provide confidential information to the Federal Bureau of Investigation as a paid informant. Nichols was then serving a sentence on local forgery charges. The record does not disclose whether the agent contacted Nichols specifically to acquire information about Henry or the Janaf robbery.

Nichols informed the agent that he was housed in the same cellblock with several federal prisoners awaiting trial, including Henry. The agent told him to be alert to any statements made by the federal prisoners, but not to initiate any conversation with or question Henry regarding the bank robbery. In early December, after Nichols had been released from jail, the agent again contacted Nichols, who reported that he and Henry had engaged in conversation and that Henry had told him about the robbery of the Janaf bank. Nichols was paid for furnishing the information.

When Henry was tried in March 1973, an agent of the Federal Bureau of Investigation testified concerning the events surrounding the discovery of the rental slip and the evidence uncovered at the rented house. Other witnesses also connected Henry to the rented house, including the rental agent who positively identified Henry as the "Allen R. Norris" who had rented the house and had taken the rental receipt described earlier. A neighbor testified that prior to the robbery she saw Henry at the rented house with John Luck, one of the two men who had by the time of Henry's trial been convicted for the robbery. In addition, palm prints found on the lease agreement matched those of Henry.

Nichols testified at trial that he had "an opportunity to have some conversations with Mr. Henry while he was in the jail," and that Henry told him that on several occasions he had gone to the Janaf Branch to see which employees opened the vault. Nichols also testified that Henry described to him the details of the robbery and stated that the only evidence connecting him to the robbery was the rental receipt. The jury was not informed that Nichols was a paid Government informant.

On the basis of this testimony, Henry was convicted of bank robbery and sentenced to a term of imprisonment of 25 years. On appeal he raised no Sixth Amendment claims.

On August 28, 1975, Henry moved to vacate his sentence pursuant to 28 U.S.C. §2255. At this stage, he stated that he had just learned that Nichols was a paid Government informant and alleged that he had been intentionally placed in the same cell with Nichols so that Nichols could secure information about the robbery. Thus, Henry contended that the introduction of Nichols' testimony violated his Sixth Amendment right to the assistance of counsel. The District Court denied the motion without a hearing.

II

This Court has scrutinized postindictment confrontations between Government agents and the accused to determine whether they are "critical stages" of the prosecution at which the Sixth Amendment right to the assistance of counsel attaches. The present case involves incriminating statements made by the accused to an undisclosed and undercover Government informant while in custody and after indictment. The Government characterizes Henry's incriminating statements as voluntary and not the result of any affirmative conduct on the part of Government agents to elicit evidence. From this, the Government argues that Henry's rights were not violated, even assuming the Sixth Amendment applies to such surreptitious confrontations; in short, it is contended that the Government has not interfered with Henry's right to counsel.

The question here is whether under the facts of this case a Government agent "deliberately elicited" incriminating statements from Henry within the meaning of *Massiah*. Three factors are important. First, Nichols was acting under instructions as a paid informant for the Government; second, Nichols was ostensibly no more than a fellow inmate of Henry; and third, Henry was in custody and under indictment at the time he was engaged in conversation by Nichols.

The Court of Appeals viewed the record as showing that Nichols deliberately used his position to secure incriminating information from Henry when counsel was not present and held that conduct attributable to the Government. Nichols had been a paid Government informant for more than a year; moreover, the FBI agent was aware that Nichols had access to Henry and would be able to engage him in conversations without arousing Henry's suspicion. The arrangement between Nichols and the agent was on a contingent-fee basis; Nichols was to be paid only if he produced useful information. This combination of circumstances is sufficient to support the Court of Appeals' determination. Even if the agent's statement that he did not intend that Nichols would take affirmative steps to secure incriminating information is accepted, he must have known that such propinquity likely would lead to that result.

The Government argues that the federal agents instructed Nichols not to question Henry about the robbery. Yet according to his own testimony, Nichols was not a passive listener; rather, he had "some conversations with Mr. Henry" while he was in jail and Henry's incriminatory statements were "the product of this conversation." In *Massiah*, no inquiry was made as to whether Massiah or his codefendant first raised the subject of the crime under investigation.

It is quite a different matter when the Government uses undercover agents to obtain incriminating statements from persons not in custody but suspected of criminal activity prior to the time charges are filed. In Hoffa v. United States (1966), for example, this Court held that "no interest legitimately protected by the Fourth Amendment is involved" because "the Fourth Amendment [does not protect] a wrongdoer's misplaced belief that a person to whom he voluntarily confides his wrongdoing will not reveal it." Similarly, the Fifth Amendment has been held not to be implicated by the use of undercover Government agents before charges are filed because of the absence of the potential for compulsion. But the Fourth and Fifth Amendment claims made in those cases are not relevant to the inquiry under the Sixth Amendment here — whether the Government has interfered with the right to counsel of the accused by "deliberately eliciting" incriminating statements. Our holding today does not modify *White* or *Hoffa*.

When the accused is in the company of a fellow inmate who is acting by prearrangement as a Government agent, the same cannot be said. Conversation stimulated in such circumstances may elicit information that an accused would not intentionally reveal to persons known to be Government agents. Indeed, the *Massiah* Court noted that if the Sixth Amendment "is to have any efficacy it must apply to indirect and surreptitious interrogations as well as those conducted in the jailhouse."

Finally Henry's incarceration at the time he was engaged in conversation by Nichols is also a relevant factor. As a ground for imposing the prophylactic requirements in Miranda v. Arizona, this Court noted the powerful psychological inducements to reach for aid when a person is in confinement. While the concern in *Miranda* was limited to custodial police interrogation, the mere fact of custody imposes pressures on the accused; confinement may bring into play subtle influences that will make him particularly susceptible to the ploys of undercover Government agents. The Court of Appeals determined that on this record the incriminating conversations between Henry and Nichols were facilitated by Nichols' conduct and apparent status as a person sharing a common plight. That Nichols had managed to gain the confidence of Henry, as the Court of Appeals determined, is confirmed by Henry's request that Nichols assist him in his escape plans when Nichols was released from confinement.

Under the strictures of the Court's holdings on the exclusion of evidence, we conclude that the Court of Appeals did not err in holding that Henry's statements to Nichols should not have been admitted at trial. By intentionally creating a situation likely to induce Henry to make incriminating statements without the assistance of counsel, the Government violated Henry's Sixth Amendment right to counsel. This is not a case where, in Justice Cardozo's words, "the constable . . . blundered"; rather, it is one where the "constable" planned an impermissible interference with the right to the assistance of counsel.

Justice BLACKMUN, with whom Justice WHITE joins, dissenting.

In this case the Court, I fear, cuts loose from the moorings of Massiah v. United States and overlooks or misapplies significant facts to reach a result that is not required by the Sixth Amendment, by established precedent, or by sound policy.

Massiah mandates exclusion only if a federal agent "deliberately elicited" statements from the accused in the absence of counsel. The word "deliberately" denotes intent. *Massiah* ties this intent to the act of elicitation, that is, to conduct that draws forth a response. Thus *Massiah*, by its own terms, covers only action undertaken with the specific intent to evoke an inculpatory disclosure. Faced with Agent Coughlin's unequivocal expression of an intent not to elicit statements from respondent Henry, but merely passively to receive them, the Court, in its decision to affirm the judgment of the Court of Appeals, has no choice but to depart from the natural meaning of the *Massiah* formulation.

The Court deems it critical that informant Nichols had been a paid informant; that Agent Coughlin was aware that Nichols "had access" to Henry and "would be able to engage him in conversations without arousing Henry's suspicion"; and that payment to Nichols was on a contingent-fee basis. Thus, it is said, even if Coughlin's "statement is accepted . . . he must have known that such propinquity likely would lead to that result" (that is, that Nichols would take "affirmative steps to secure incriminating information"). Later, the Court goes even further, characterizing this as a case of "intentionally creating a situation likely to induce Henry to make incriminating statements." This determination, coupled with the statement that Nichols "prompted" respondent Henry's remarks, leads the Court to find a *Massiah* violation.

Thus, while claiming to retain the "deliberately elicited" test, the Court really forges a new test that saps the word "deliberately" of all significance. The Court's extension of *Massiah* would cover even a "negligent" triggering of events resulting in reception of disclosures. This approach, in my view, is unsupported and unwise.

KUHLMANN v. WILSON
477 U.S. 436 (1986)

Justice POWELL delivered the opinion of the Court.

This case requires us to define the circumstances under which federal courts should entertain a state prisoner's petition for writ of habeas corpus that raises claims rejected on a prior petition for the same relief.

In the early morning of July 4, 1970, respondent and two confederates robbed the Star Taxicab Garage in the Bronx, New York, and fatally shot the night dispatcher. Shortly before, employees of the garage had observed respondent, a former employee there, on the premises conversing with two other men. They also witnessed respondent fleeing after the robbery, carrying loose money in his arms. After eluding the police for four days, respondent turned himself in. Respondent admitted that he had been present when the crimes took place, claimed that he had witnessed the robbery, gave the police a description of the robbers, but denied knowing them. Respondent also denied any involvement in the robbery or murder, claiming that he had fled because he was afraid of being blamed for the crimes.

After his arraignment, respondent was confined in the Bronx House of Detention, where he was placed in a cell with a prisoner named Benny Lee. Unknown to respondent, Lee had agreed to act as a police informant. Respondent made incriminating statements that Lee reported to the police. Prior to trial, respondent moved to suppress the statements on the ground that they were obtained in violation of his right to counsel. The trial court held an evidentiary hearing on the suppression motion, which revealed that the statements were made under the following circumstances.

Before respondent arrived in the jail, Lee had entered into an arrangement with Detective Cullen, according to which Lee agreed to listen to respondent's conversations and report his remarks to Cullen. Since the police had positive evidence of respondent's participation, the purpose of placing Lee in the cell was to determine the identities of respondent's confederates. Cullen instructed Lee not to ask respondent any questions, but simply to "keep his ears open" for the names of the other perpetrators. Respondent first spoke to Lee about the crimes after he looked out the cellblock window at the Star Taxicab Garage, where the crimes had occurred. Respondent said, "someone's messing with me," and began talking to Lee about the robbery, narrating the same story that he had given the police at the time of his arrest. Lee advised respondent that this explanation "didn't sound too good," but respondent did not alter his story. Over the next few days, however, respondent changed details of his original account. Respondent then received a visit from his brother, who mentioned that members of his family were upset because they believed that respondent had murdered the dispatcher. After the visit, respondent again described the crimes to Lee. Respondent now admitted that he and two other men, whom he never identified, had planned and carried out the robbery, and had murdered the dispatcher. Lee informed Cullen of respondent's statements and furnished Cullen with notes that he had written surreptitiously while sharing the cell with respondent.

After hearing the testimony of Cullen and Lee, the trial court found that Cullen had instructed Lee "to ask no questions of [respondent] about the crime but merely to listen as to what [respondent] might say in his presence." The court determined that Lee obeyed these instructions, that he "at no time asked any questions with respect to the crime," and that he "only listened to [respondent] and made notes regarding what [respondent] had to say." The trial court also found that respondent's statements to Lee were "spontaneous" and "unsolicited." Under state precedent, a defendant's volunteered statements to a police agent were admissible in evidence because the police were not required to prevent talkative defendants from making incriminating statements. The trial court accordingly denied the suppression motion. The jury convicted respondent of common-law murder and felonious possession of a weapon. On May 18, 1972, the trial court sentenced him to a term of 20 years to life on the murder count and to a concurrent term of up to 7 years on the weapons count.

Following this Court's decision in United States v. Henry (1980), which applied the *Massiah* test to suppress statements made to a paid jailhouse informant, respondent decided to relitigate his Sixth Amendment claim.

Even if the Court of Appeals had correctly decided to entertain this successive habeas petition, we conclude that it erred in holding that respondent was entitled to relief under United States v. Henry (1980). As the District Court observed, *Henry* left open the question whether the Sixth Amendment forbids admission in evidence of an accused's statements to a jailhouse informant who was "placed in close proximity but [made] no effort to stimulate conversations about the crime charged."

As our recent examination of the Sixth Amendment makes clear, the primary concern of the *Massiah* line of decisions is secret interrogation by investigatory techniques that are the equivalent of direct police interrogation. Since "the Sixth Amendment is not violated whenever — by luck or happenstance — the State obtains incriminating statements from the accused after the right to counsel has attached," a defendant does not make out a violation of that right simply by showing that an informant, either through prior arrangement or voluntarily, reported his incriminating statements to the police. Rather, the defendant must demonstrate that the police and their informant took some action, beyond merely listening, that was designed deliberately to elicit incriminating remarks.

It is thus apparent that the Court of Appeals erred in concluding that respondent's right to counsel was violated under the circumstances of this case. The state court found that Officer Cullen had instructed Lee only to listen to respondent for the purpose of determining the identities of the other participants in the robbery and murder. The police already had solid evidence of respondent's participation. The court further found that Lee followed those instructions, that he "at no time asked any questions" of respondent concerning the pending charges, and that he "only listened" to respondent's "spontaneous" and "unsolicited" statements.

Justice BRENNAN, with whom Justice MARSHALL joins, dissenting.

The Court holds that the Court of Appeals erred with respect to the merits of respondent's habeas petition. According to the Court, the Court of Appeals failed to accord §2254(d)'s presumption of correctness to the state trial court's findings that respondent's cellmate, Lee, "at no time asked any questions" of respondent concerning the pending charges, and that Lee only listened to respondent's "spontaneous" and "unsolicited" statements. As a result, the Court concludes, the Court of Appeals failed to recognize that this case presents the question, reserved in *Henry*, whether the Sixth Amendment forbids the admission into evidence of an accused's statements to a jailhouse informant who was "placed in close proximity but [made] no effort to stimulate conversations about the crime charged." I disagree with the Court's characterization of the Court of Appeals' treatment of the state court's findings and, consequently, I disagree with the Court that the instant case presents the "listening post" question.

The Sixth Amendment guarantees an accused, at least after the initiation of formal charges, the right to rely on counsel as the "medium" between himself and the State. Accordingly, the Sixth Amendment "imposes on the State an affirmative obligation to respect and preserve the accused's choice to seek [the assistance of counsel]," and therefore "[t]he determination whether particular action by state agents violates the accused's right to . . . counsel must be made in light of this obligation." To be sure, the Sixth Amendment is not violated whenever, "by luck or happenstance," the State obtains incriminating statements from the accused after the right to counsel has attached. It is violated, however, when "the State obtains incriminating statements by knowingly circumventing the accused's right to have counsel present in a confrontation between the accused and a state agent." As we explained in *Henry*, where the accused has not waived his right to counsel, the government knowingly circumvents the defendant's right to counsel where it "deliberately elicit[s]" inculpatory admissions, that is, "intentionally creat[es] a situation likely to induce [the accused] to make incriminating statements without the assistance of counsel."

In the instant case, as in *Henry*, the accused was incarcerated and therefore was "susceptible to the ploys of undercover Government agents." Like Nichols, Lee was a secret informant, usually received consideration for the services he rendered the police, and therefore had an incentive to produce the information which he knew the police hoped to obtain. Just as Nichols had done, Lee obeyed instructions not to question respondent and to report to the police any statements made by the respondent in Lee's presence about the crime in question. And, like Nichols, Lee encouraged respondent to talk about his crime by conversing with him on the subject over the course of several days and by telling respondent that his exculpatory story would not convince anyone without more work. However, unlike the situation in *Henry*, a disturbing visit from respondent's brother, rather than a conversation with the informant, seems to have been the immediate catalyst for respondent's confession to Lee. While it might appear from this sequence of events that Lee's comment regarding respondent's story and his general willingness to converse with respondent about the crime were not the immediate causes of respondent's admission, I think that the deliberate-elicitation standard requires consideration of the entire course of government behavior.

The State intentionally created a situation in which it was foreseeable that respondent would make incriminating statements without the assistance of counsel — it assigned respondent to a cell overlooking the scene of the crime and designated a secret informant to be respondent's cellmate. The informant, while avoiding direct questions, nonetheless developed a relationship of cellmate camaraderie with respondent and encouraged him to talk about his crime. While the coup de grace was delivered by respondent's brother, the groundwork for respondent's confession was laid by the State. Clearly the State's actions had a sufficient nexus with respondent's admission of guilt to constitute deliberate elicitation within the meaning of *Henry*.

The use of prison informants is thus an area where the Fifth Amendment privilege against self-incrimination is different from the Sixth Amendment right to counsel. The former does not apply because there is not an interrogation. On the other hand, once formal adjudicatory proceedings have been initiated, the Sixth Amendment is violated by government-initiated communications to elicit statements from an individual represented by counsel.

Also, there is the issue of whether the statements obtained in violation of the Sixth Amendment purposes may be used for other purposes even if they are not admissible. In Kansas v. Ventris, 556 U.S. 586 (2009), the Court held that statements obtained in violation of the Sixth Amendment right to counsel may be used for impeachment purposes. Donnie Ray Ventris was charged with murder and other crimes. The police placed an informant in his cell with the hope of obtaining incriminating statements, in violation of his Sixth Amendment rights. Ventris made incriminating statements.

At trial, Ventris testified and said that his girlfriend was responsible for the murders. The prosecutor used the cellmate as a witness to impeach Ventris's testimony. The Supreme Court held that the statements could be introduced for impeachment purposes even though they were obtained in violation of the Sixth Amendment. Justice Souter, writing for the Court in a 7-2 decision, stated, "Our precedents make clear that the game of excluding tainted evidence for impeachment purposes is not worth the candle. The interests safeguarded by such exclusion are 'outweighed by the need to prevent perjury and to assure the integrity of the trial process.'" The Court said that excluding the statements would add little deterrent effect but would interfere with the ability of courts to ensure the accuracy of testimony. The Court concluded, "We hold that the informant's testimony, concededly elicited in violation of the Sixth Amendment, was admissible to challenge Ventris's inconsistent testimony at trial."

D. THE PRIVILEGE AGAINST SELF-INCRIMINATION IN OTHER CONTEXTS

Although the focus of this chapter has been on the privilege against self-incrimination in the interrogation context, obviously it is a privilege that applies through all of the stages of criminal proceedings. Indeed, a person has the right to refuse to incriminate himself or herself in giving testimony in civil or administrative proceedings as well.

In examining the privilege against self-incrimination in this broader context, there are three especially important questions: First, what are the requirements for the privilege against self-incrimination to apply? Second, does the privilege against self-incrimination apply to protect people from having to produce documents or other things? Third, can the government overcome the privilege against self-incrimination by according the individual immunity?

1. *What Are the Requirements for the Privilege Against Self-Incrimination to Apply?*

The Supreme Court has declared that "[t]o qualify for the Fifth Amendment privilege, a communication must be testimonial, incriminating, and compelled." Hiibel v. Sixth Judicial Dist. Court of Nevada, Humboldt County, 542 U.S. 177 (2004). For the privilege against self-incrimination to apply, an individual, not an entity, must assert it; what is sought from the individual must be "testimonial"; there must be "compulsion"; and there must be the possibility of incrimination. Consider each of these requirements.

a.   Only Individuals May Invoke the Privilege

Only individuals may invoke the privilege against self-incrimination. It has been long established that entities such as corporations or unions are not entitled to invoke this privilege. Hale v. Henkel, 201 U.S. 43 (1906). The Court has explained that, in part, this is because the privilege exists to protect the privacy and dignity of the individual. The Court has said that the privilege exists to protect that "private enclave where [a person] may lead a private life." Bellis v. United States, 417 U.S. 85 (1974). The Court has also explained that extending the privilege to entities would interfere with needed government regulation. The Court stated, "The greater portion of evidence of wrongdoing by an organization or its representatives is usually to be found in the official records and documents of that organization. Were the cloak of the privilege to be thrown around these impersonal records and documents, effective enforcement of many federal and state laws would be impossible."

b.   The Privilege Applies Only to That Which Is Testimonial

Second, the privilege applies only if what is being sought is *testimonial.* A person cannot be required to give testimony that would be incriminating, but this does not prevent a person from giving physical evidence that would be incriminating. Schmerber v. California is a key case holding and illustrating this.

SCHMERBER v. CALIFORNIA

384 U.S. 757 (1966)

Justice BRENNAN delivered the opinion of the Court.

Petitioner was convicted in Los Angeles Municipal Court of the criminal offense of driving an automobile while under the influence of intoxicating liquor. He had been arrested at a hospital while receiving treatment for injuries suffered in an accident involving the automobile that he had apparently been driving. At the direction of a police officer, a blood sample was then withdrawn from petitioner's body by a physician at the hospital. The chemical analysis of this sample revealed a percent by weight of alcohol in his blood at the time of the offense which indicated intoxication, and the report of this analysis was admitted in evidence at the trial. Petitioner objected to receipt of this evidence of the analysis on the ground that the blood had been withdrawn despite his refusal, on the advice of his counsel, to consent to the test. He contended that in that circumstance the withdrawal of the blood and the admission of the analysis in evidence [violated his constitutional rights, including] his privilege against self-incrimination under the Fifth Amendment.

We hold that the privilege protects an accused only from being compelled to testify against himself, or otherwise provide the State with evidence of a testimonial or communicative nature, and that the withdrawal of blood and use of the analysis in question in this case did not involve compulsion to these ends.

It could not be denied that in requiring petitioner to submit to the withdrawal and chemical analysis of his blood the State compelled him to submit to an attempt to discover evidence that might be used to prosecute him for a criminal offense. He submitted only after the police officer rejected his objection and directed the physician to proceed. The officer's direction to the physician to administer the test over petitioner's objection constituted compulsion for the purposes of the privilege. The critical question, then, is whether petitioner was thus compelled "to be a witness against himself."

If the scope of the privilege coincided with the complex of values it helps to protect, we might be obliged to conclude that the privilege was violated. The withdrawal of blood necessarily involves puncturing the skin for extraction, and the percent by weight of alcohol in that blood, as established by chemical analysis, is evidence of criminal guilt. Compelled submission fails on one view to respect the "inviolability of the human personality." Moreover, since it enables the State to rely on evidence forced from the accused, the compulsion violates at least one meaning of the requirement that the State procure the evidence against an accused "by its own independent labors."

[H]owever, the privilege has never been given the full scope which the values it helps to protect suggest. History and a long line of authorities in lower courts have consistently limited its protection to situations in which the State seeks to submerge those values by obtaining the evidence against an accused through "the cruel, simple expedient of compelling it from his own mouth. In sum, the privilege is fulfilled only when the person is guaranteed the right 'to remain silent unless he chooses to speak in the unfettered exercise of his own will.'"

[B]oth federal and state courts have usually held that it offers no protection against compulsion to submit to fingerprinting, photographing, or measurements, to write or speak for identification, to appear in court, to stand, to assume a stance, to walk, or to make a particular gesture. The distinction which has emerged, often expressed in different ways, is that the privilege is a bar against compelling "communications" or "testimony," but that compulsion which makes a suspect or accused the source of "real or physical evidence" does not violate it.

Although we agree that this distinction is a helpful framework for analysis, we are not to be understood to agree with past applications in all instances.

There will be many cases in which such a distinction is not readily drawn. Some tests seemingly directed to obtain "physical evidence," for example, lie detector tests measuring changes in body function during interrogation, may actually be directed to eliciting responses which are essentially testimonial. To compel a person to submit to testing in which an effort will be made to determine his guilt or innocence on the basis of physiological responses, whether willed or not, is to evoke the spirit and history of the Fifth Amendment. Such situations call to mind the principle that the protection of the privilege "is as broad as the mischief against which it seeks to guard."

In the present case, however, no such problem of application is presented. Not even a shadow of testimonial compulsion upon or enforced communication by the accused was involved either in the extraction or in the chemical analysis. Petitioner's testimonial capacities were in no way implicated; indeed, his participation, except as a donor, was irrelevant to the results of the test, which depend on chemical analysis and on that alone. Since the blood test evidence, although an incriminating product of compulsion, was neither petitioner's testimony nor evidence relating to some communicative act or writing by the petitioner, it was not inadmissible on privilege grounds.

[The Court also rejected other constitutional objections based on the Fourth Amendment, due process, and the right to counsel.]

Justice BLACK, with whom Justice DOUGLAS joins, dissenting.

I disagree with the Court's holding that California did not violate petitioner's constitutional right against self-incrimination when it compelled him, against his will, to allow a doctor to puncture his blood vessels in order to extract a sample of blood and analyze it for alcoholic content, and then used that analysis as evidence to convict petitioner of a crime.

The Court admits that "the State compelled [petitioner] to submit to an attempt to discover evidence (in his blood) that might be (and was) used to prosecute him for a criminal offense." To reach the conclusion that compelling a person to give his blood to help the State convict him is not equivalent to compelling him to be a witness against himself strikes me as quite an extraordinary feat. The Court, however, overcomes what had seemed to me to be an insuperable obstacle to its conclusion by holding that the privilege protects an accused only from being compelled to testify against himself, or otherwise provide the State with evidence of a testimonial or communicative nature, and that the withdrawal of blood and use of the analysis in question in this case did not involve compulsion to these ends.

I cannot agree that this distinction and reasoning of the Court justify denying petitioner his Bill of Rights' guarantee that he must not be compelled to be a witness against himself.

In the first place it seems to me that the compulsory extraction of petitioner's blood for analysis so that the person who analyzed it could give evidence to convict him had both a "testimonial" and a "communicative nature." The sole purpose of this project which proved to be successful was to obtain "testimony" from some person to prove that petitioner had alcohol in his blood at the time he was arrested. And the purpose of the project was certainly "communicative" in that the analysis of the blood was to supply information to enable a witness to communicate to the court and jury that petitioner was more or less drunk.

I think it unfortunate that the Court rests so heavily for its very restrictive reading of the Fifth Amendment's privilege against self-incrimination on the words "testimonial" and "communicative." These words are not models of clarity and precision as the Court's rather labored explication shows. Nor can the Court, so far as I know, find precedent in the former opinions of this Court for using these particular words to limit the scope of the Fifth Amendment's protection.

How can it reasonably be doubted that the blood test evidence was not in all respects the actual equivalent of "testimony" taken from petitioner when the result of the test was offered as testimony, was considered by the jury as testimony, and the jury's verdict of guilt rests in part on that testimony? The refined, subtle reasoning and balancing process used here to narrow the scope of the Bill of Rights' safeguard against self-incrimination provides a handy instrument for further narrowing of that constitutional protection, as well as others, in the future. Believing with the Framers that these constitutional safeguards broadly construed by independent tribunals of justice provide our best hope for keeping our people free from governmental oppression, I deeply regret the Court's holding.

———————

The Supreme Court on many occasions has reaffirmed that the privilege against self-incrimination applies only to preventing a person from having to give testimony against himself or herself. For example, in United States v. Wade, 388 U.S. 218 (1967), the Supreme Court held that requiring a suspect to participate in a police lineup does not violate the privilege against self-incrimination because it is not testimonial. The Court explained, "We have no doubt that compelling the accused merely to exhibit his person for observation by a prosecution witness prior to trial involves no compulsion of the accused to give evidence of testimonial significance. It is compulsion of the accused to exhibit his physical characteristics, not compulsion to disclose any knowledge he might have." (Issues concerning lineups and identification procedures are discussed in Chapter 5.)

Similarly, in Doe v. United States, 487 U.S. 201 (1988), the Court held that compelling a person's signature on a bank form was not testimonial. A court ordered an individual to sign a form authorizing a bank outside the United States to release records. It was stipulated that the person, by signing, was not admitting the existence of any account. The Court said that this was not testimonial because it did not "convey information or assert facts."

c. There Must Be Compulsion

The privilege against self-incrimination protects a person from being compelled to give testimony against himself or herself. Voluntary statements made to the police, of course, do not violate the privilege even if they are highly incriminating. Miranda v. Arizona, above, is based on the Court's judgment of the inherently coercive nature of in-custodial interrogation.

However, the Court has held that no adverse inference can be drawn by a jury in a criminal case from the defendant's invocation of the privilege against self-incrimination. In Griffin v. California, 380 U.S. 609 (1965), the Court explained that this would be "a penalty for exercising a constitutional privilege." Typically, juries are therefore instructed that they can draw no adverse inference from the failure of a criminal defendant to testify. In Mitchell v. United States, 526 U.S. 314 (1996), the Court likewise held that no adverse inference can be drawn in imposing punishment from a defendant's failure to testify during sentencing proceedings.

However, the fact that a person faces a hard choice has not been deemed sufficient to cross the line and constitute compulsion. For example, in Ohio Adult Parole Authority v. Woodward, 523 U.S. 272 (1998), the Court found that there was not a violation of the privilege against self-incrimination when a person applying for clemency had to answer questions that could include incriminating information. Chief Justice Rehnquist, writing for a unanimous Court, stated:

> It is difficult to see how a voluntary interview could "compel" respondent to speak. He merely faces a choice quite similar to the sorts of choices that a criminal defendant must make in the course of criminal proceedings, none of which has ever been held to violate the Fifth Amendment. Here respondent has the same choice of providing information to the Authority — at the risk of damaging his case for clemency or for postconviction relief — or of remaining silent. But this pressure to speak in the hope of improving his chance of being granted clemency does not make the interview compelled. We therefore hold that the Ohio clemency interview does not violate the Fifth Amendment privilege against compelled self-incrimination.

Similarly, in McKune v. Lile, 536 U.S. 24 (2002), the Court held that it did not violate the privilege against self-incrimination to require a prisoner seeking admission to a sex offender rehabilitation program to "admit having committed the crime for which he is being treated and other past offenses." Although the treatment program meant substantially more freedom for the inmate, the Court found that the pressure to admit to crimes that could lead to further criminal liability did not violate the Fifth Amendment. Justice Kennedy, writing for the Court in a 5-4 decision, said, "Determining what constitutes unconstitutional compulsion involves a question of judgment: Courts must determine whether the consequences of an inmate's choice to remain silent are closer to the physical torture against which the Constitution protects or the *de minimus* harms which it does not." The Court said that the prison had an important interest in the rehabilitation program, which required admission of past sex crimes.

d. There Must Be the Possibility of Incrimination

For the privilege against self-incrimination to apply, there must be the opportunity that the statements could lead to a person's criminal liability. In Ullman v. United States, 350 U.S. 422 (1956), the Supreme Court made clear that the fact that a statement could lead to civil liability and even social stigma was not enough to trigger the privilege unless there also was the possibility of criminal liability.

The Supreme Court subsequently confronted the question of whether a law requiring a person to identify himself or herself violated the privilege against self-incrimination. In Hiibel v. Sixth Judicial Dist. Court of Nevada, 542 U.S. 177 (2004), the police were investigating an anonymous tip of an assault. Hiibel fit the description of the assailant. The police stopped him and asked him to identify himself. Hiibel refused; 11 times the officer asked, and 11 times Hiibel refused. He was convicted under a Nevada law that provides, "The officer may detain the person pursuant to this section only to ascertain his identity and the suspicious circumstances surrounding his presence abroad. Any person so detained shall identify himself, but may not be compelled to answer any other inquiry of any peace officer."

Hiibel was convicted of violating the law and challenged it as infringing both the Fourth and Fifth Amendments.[15] The Supreme Court, 5-4, ruled against him. As to the self-incrimination claim, Justice Kennedy, writing for the majority, stated:

> Respondents urge us to hold that the statements NRS §171.123(3) requires are nontestimonial, and so outside the Clause's scope. We decline to resolve the case on that basis. "[T]o be testimonial, an accused's communication must itself, explicitly or implicitly, relate a factual assertion or disclose information." Doe v. United States (1988). Stating one's name may qualify as an assertion of fact relating to identity. Production of identity documents might meet the definition as well. Even if these required actions are testimonial, however, petitioner's challenge must fail because in this case disclosure of his name presented no reasonable danger of incrimination.
>
> The Fifth Amendment prohibits only compelled testimony that is incriminating. As we stated in Kastigar v. United States (1972), the Fifth Amendment privilege against compulsory self-incrimination "protects against any disclosures that the witness reasonably believes could be used in a criminal prosecution or could lead to other evidence that might be so used." Suspects who have been granted immunity from prosecution may, therefore, be compelled to answer; with the threat of prosecution removed, there can be no reasonable belief that the evidence will be used against them.

15. Whether this violates the Fourth Amendment is discussed in Chapter 2.

In this case petitioner's refusal to disclose his name was not based on any articulated real and appreciable fear that his name would be used to incriminate him, or that it "would furnish a link in the chain of evidence needed to prosecute" him. As best we can tell, petitioner refused to identify himself only because he thought his name was none of the officer's business. Even today, petitioner does not explain how the disclosure of his name could have been used against him in a criminal case. While we recognize petitioner's strong belief that he should not have to disclose his identity, the Fifth Amendment does not override the Nevada Legislature's judgment to the contrary absent a reasonable belief that the disclosure would tend to incriminate him.

The narrow scope of the disclosure requirement is also important. One's identity is, by definition, unique; yet it is, in another sense, a universal characteristic. Answering a request to disclose a name is likely to be so insignificant in the scheme of things as to be incriminating only in unusual circumstances. Even witnesses who plan to invoke the Fifth Amendment privilege answer when their names are called to take the stand. Still, a case may arise where there is a substantial allegation that furnishing identity at the time of a stop would have given the police a link in the chain of evidence needed to convict the individual of a separate offense. In that case, the court can then consider whether the privilege applies, and, if the Fifth Amendment has been violated, what remedy must follow. We need not resolve those questions here.

Justice Stevens, in a dissenting opinion, disagreed:

"[T]here can be no doubt that the Fifth Amendment privilege is available outside of criminal court proceedings and serves to protect persons in all settings in which their freedom of action is curtailed in any significant way from being compelled to incriminate themselves." Miranda v. Arizona (1966). It is a "settled principle" that "the police have the right to request citizens to answer voluntarily questions concerning unsolved crimes," but "they have no right to compel them to answer." The protections of the Fifth Amendment are directed squarely toward those who are the focus of the government's investigative and prosecutorial powers. In a criminal trial, the indicted defendant has an unqualified right to refuse to testify and may not be punished for invoking that right. The unindicted target of a grand jury investigation enjoys the same constitutional protection even if he has been served with a subpoena. So does an arrested suspect during custodial interrogation in a police station.

There is no reason why the subject of police interrogation based on mere suspicion, rather than probable cause, should have any lesser protection. Indeed, we have said that the Fifth Amendment's protections apply with equal force in the context of *Terry* stops where an officer's inquiry "must be 'reasonably related in scope to the justification for [the stop's] initiation.'" "Typically, this means that the officer may ask the detainee a moderate number of questions to determine his identity and to try to obtain information confirming or dispelling the officer's suspicions. But the detainee is not obliged to respond." Given our statements to the effect that citizens are not required to respond to police officers' questions during a *Terry* stop, it is no surprise that petitioner assumed, as have we, that he had a right not to disclose his identity.

The Court correctly observes that a communication does not enjoy the Fifth Amendment privilege unless it is testimonial. Although the Court declines to resolve this question, I think it clear that this case concerns a testimonial communication. [T]he compelled statement at issue in this case is clearly testimonial. It is significant that the communication must be made in response to a question posed by a police officer. As we recently explained, albeit in the different context of the Sixth Amendment's Confrontation Clause, "[w]hatever else the term ['testimonial'] covers, it applies at a minimum . . . to police interrogations." Surely police questioning during a *Terry* stop qualifies as an interrogation, and it follows that responses to such questions are testimonial in nature.

Rather than determining whether the communication at issue is testimonial, the Court instead concludes that the State can compel the disclosure of one's identity because it is not "incriminating." But our cases have afforded Fifth Amendment protection to statements that are "incriminating" in a much broader sense than the Court suggests. It has "long been settled that [the Fifth Amendment's] protection encompasses compelled statements that lead to the discovery of incriminating evidence even though the statements themselves are not incriminating and are not introduced into evidence." By "incriminating" we have meant disclosures that "could be used in a criminal prosecution or could lead to other evidence that might be so used," — communications, in other words, that "would furnish a link in the chain of evidence needed to prosecute the claimant for a federal crime." Thus, "[c]ompelled testimony that communicates information that may 'lead to incriminating evidence' is privileged even if the information itself is not inculpatory."

Given a proper understanding of the category of "incriminating" communications that fall within the Fifth Amendment privilege, it is clear that the disclosure of petitioner's identity is protected. The Court reasons that we should not assume that the disclosure of petitioner's "name would be used to incriminate him, or that it would furnish a link in [a] chain of evidence needed to prosecute him." But why else would an officer ask for it? And why else would the Nevada Legislature require its disclosure only when circumstances "reasonably indicate that the person has committed, is committing or is about to commit a crime"? If the Court is correct, then petitioner's refusal to cooperate did not impede the police investigation. Indeed, if we accept the predicate for the Court's holding, the statute requires nothing more than a useless invasion of privacy. I think that, on the contrary, the Nevada Legislature intended to provide its police officers with a useful law enforcement tool, and that the very existence of the statute demonstrates the value of the information it demands.

A person's identity obviously bears informational and incriminating worth, "even if the [name] itself is not inculpatory." A name can provide the key to a broad array of information about the person, particularly in the hands of a police officer with access to a range of law enforcement databases. And that information, in turn, can be tremendously useful in a criminal prosecution. It is therefore quite wrong to suggest that a person's identity provides a link in the chain to incriminating evidence "only in unusual circumstances."

The officer in this case told petitioner, in the Court's words, that "he was conducting an investigation and needed to see some identification." As the target of that investigation, petitioner, in my view, acted well within his rights when he opted to stand mute.

2. When May the Government Require the Production of Documents and Other Things?

The Supreme Court has held that a person can be forced to produce documents, even documents containing highly incriminating information, unless the very act of production would be incriminating. Required production of a preexisting document does not violate the privilege against self-incrimination because it is not demanding testimony from a person. Fisher v. United States is the key case here.

FISHER v. UNITED STATES
425 U.S. 391 (1976)

Justice WHITE delivered the opinion of the Court.

In these two cases we are called upon to decide whether a summons directing an attorney to produce documents delivered to him by his client in connection with the attorney-client relationship is enforceable over claims that the documents were constitutionally immune from summons in the hands of the client and retained that immunity in the hands of the attorney.

I

In each case, an Internal Revenue agent visited the taxpayer or taxpayers and interviewed them in connection with an investigation of possible civil or criminal liability under the federal income tax laws. Shortly after the interviews, the taxpayers obtained from their respective accountants certain documents relating to the preparation by the accountants of their tax returns. Shortly after obtaining the documents, the taxpayers transferred the documents to their lawyers respondent Kasmir and petitioner Fisher, respectively each of whom was retained to assist the taxpayer in connection with the investigation.

Upon learning of the whereabouts of the documents, the Internal Revenue Service served summonses on the attorneys directing them to produce documents listed therein. In each case the summons was ordered enforced by the District Court and its order was stayed pending appeal. [I]n our view the documents were not privileged either in the hands of the lawyers or of their clients.

II

All of the parties in these cases have concurred in the proposition that if the Fifth Amendment would have excused a Taxpayer from turning over the accountant's papers had he possessed them, the Attorney to whom they are delivered for the purpose of obtaining legal advice should also be immune from subpoena. Although we agree with this proposition, we are convinced that it is not the taxpayer's Fifth Amendment privilege that would excuse the Attorney from production.

The taxpayer's privilege under this Amendment is not violated by enforcement of the summonses involved in these cases because enforcement against a taxpayer's lawyer would not "compel" the taxpayer to do anything and certainly would not compel him to be a "witness" against himself. The Court has held repeatedly that the Fifth Amendment is limited to prohibiting the use of "physical or moral compulsion" exerted on the person asserting the privilege. In Couch v. United States [1973], we recently ruled that the Fifth Amendment rights of a taxpayer were not violated by the enforcement of a documentary summons directed to her accountant and requiring production of the taxpayer's own records in the possession of the accountant. We did so on the ground that in such a case "the ingredient of personal compulsion against an accused is lacking."

Here, the taxpayers are compelled to do no more than was the taxpayer in *Couch.* The taxpayers' Fifth Amendment privilege is therefore not violated by enforcement of the summonses directed toward their attorneys. This is true whether or not the Amendment would have barred a subpoena directing the taxpayer to produce the documents while they were in his hands.

The fact that the attorneys are agents of the taxpayers does not change this result. *Couch* held as much, since the accountant there was also the taxpayer's agent, and in this respect reflected a longstanding view.

Nor is this one of those situations where constructive possession is so clear or relinquishment of possession so temporary and insignificant as to leave the personal compulsion upon the taxpayer substantially intact.

[It is argued] that if the summons was enforced, the taxpayers' Fifth Amendment privilege would be, but should not be, lost solely because they gave their documents to their lawyers in order to obtain legal advice. But this misconceives the nature of the constitutional privilege. The Amendment protects a person from being compelled to be a witness against himself. Here, the taxpayers retained any privilege they ever had not to be compelled to testify against themselves and not to be compelled themselves to produce private papers in their possession. This personal privilege was in no way decreased by the transfer. It is simply that by reason of the transfer of the documents to the attorneys, those papers may be subpoenaed without compulsion on the taxpayer. The protection of the Fifth Amendment is therefore not available.

The proposition that the Fifth Amendment protects private information obtained without compelling self-incriminating testimony is contrary to the clear statements of this Court that under appropriate safeguards private incriminating statements of an accused may be overheard and used in evidence, if they are not compelled at the time they were uttered, and that disclosure of private information may be compelled if immunity removes the risk of incrimination. If the Fifth Amendment protected generally against the obtaining of private information from a man's mouth or pen or house, its protections would presumably not be lifted by probable cause and a warrant or by immunity. The privacy invasion is not mitigated by immunity; and the Fifth Amendment's strictures, unlike the Fourth's, are not removed by showing reasonableness. First Amendment values are also plainly not implicated in these cases.

Justice BRENNAN, concurring in the judgment.

I concur in the judgment. Given the prior access by accountants retained by the taxpayers to the papers involved in these cases and the wholly business rather than personal nature of the papers, I agree that the privilege against compelled self-incrimination did not in either of these cases protect the papers from production in response to the summonses. I do not join the Court's opinion, however, because of the portent of much of what is said of a serious crippling of the protection secured by the privilege against compelled production of one's private books and papers. Although as phrased in the Fifth Amendment "nor shall [any person] be compelled in any criminal case to be a witness against himself" the privilege makes no express reference, as does the Fourth Amendment, to "papers, and effects," private papers have long been held to have the protection of the privilege, designed as it is "to maintain inviolate large areas of personal privacy."

Expressions are legion in opinions of this Court that the protection of personal privacy is a central purpose of the privilege against compelled self-incrimination. "[I]t is the invasion of [a person's] indefeasible right of personal security, personal liberty and private property" that "constitutes the essence of the offence" that violates the privilege. The privilege reflects "our respect for the inviolability of the human personality and of the right of each individual 'to a private enclave where he may lead a private life.'" "It respects a private inner sanctum of individual feeling and thought and proscribes state intrusion to extract self-condemnation." "The Fifth Amendment in its Self-Incrimination Clause enables the citizen to create a zone of privacy which government may not force him to surrender to his detriment."

The Court pays lip service to this bedrock premise of privacy in the statement that "[w]ithin the limits imposed by the language of the Fifth Amendment, which we necessarily observe, the privilege truly serves privacy interests." But this only makes explicit what elsewhere highlights the opinion, namely, the view that protection of personal privacy is merely a by product and not, as our precedents and history teach, a factor controlling in part the determination of the scope of the privilege. This cart-before-the-horse approach is fundamentally at odds with the settled principle that the scope of the privilege is not constrained by the limits of the wording of the Fifth Amendment but has the reach necessary to protect the cherished value of privacy which it safeguards. The "Court has always construed provisions of the Constitution having regard to the principles upon which it was established. The direct operation or literal meaning of the words used do not measure the purpose or scope of its provisions. . . ."

That the privilege does not protect against the production of private information where there is no compulsion, or where immunity is granted, or where there is no threat of incrimination in nowise supports the Court's argument demeaning the privilege's protection of privacy. The unavailability of the privilege in those cases only evidences that, as is the case with the First and Fourth Amendments, the protection of privacy afforded by the privilege is not absolute. The critical question then is the definition of the scope of privacy that is sheltered by the privilege.

History and principle teach that the privacy protected by the Fifth Amendment extends not just to the individual's immediate declarations, oral or written, but also to his testimonial materials in the form of books and papers.

The common-law and constitutional extension of the privilege to testimonial materials, such as books and papers, was inevitable. An individual's books and papers are generally little more than an extension of his person. They reveal no less than he could reveal upon being questioned directly. Many of the matters within an individual's knowledge may as easily be retained within his head as set down on a scrap of paper. I perceive no principle which does not permit compelling one to disclose the contents of one's mind but does permit compelling the disclosure of the contents of that scrap of paper by compelling its production. Under a contrary view, the constitutional protection would turn on fortuity, and persons would, at their peril, record their thoughts and the events of their lives. The ability to think private thoughts, facilitated as it is by pen and paper, and the ability to preserve intimate memories would be curtailed through fear that those thoughts or events of those memories would become the subjects of criminal sanctions however invalidly imposed. Indeed, it was the very reality of those fears that helped provide the historical impetus for the privilege.

The Court's treatment of the privilege falls far short of giving it the scope required by history and our precedents. It is, of course, true "that the Fifth Amendment protects against 'compelled self-incrimination, not the disclosure of private information,'" but it is also true that governmental compulsion to produce private information that might incriminate violates the protection of the privilege. Similarly, although it is necessary that the papers "contain no testimonial declarations by [the taxpayer]" in order for the privilege not to operate as a bar to production, it does not follow that papers are not "testimonial" and thus producible because they contain no declarations. And while it may be that the unavailability of the privilege depends on a showing that "the preparation of all of the papers sought in these cases was wholly voluntary," again it does not follow that the protection is necessarily unavailable if the papers were prepared voluntarily, for it is the compelled production of testimonial evidence, not just the compelled creation of such evidence, against which the privilege protects.

Though recognizing that a subpoena served on a taxpayer involves substantial compulsion, the Court concludes that since the subpoena does not compel oral testimony or require the taxpayer to restate, repeat, or affirm the truth of the contents of the documents sought, compelled production of the documents by the taxpayer would not violate the privilege, even though the documents might incriminate the taxpayer. This analysis is patently incomplete: the threshold inquiry is whether the taxpayer is compelled to produce incriminating papers. That inquiry is not answered in favor of production merely because the subpoena requires neither oral testimony from nor affirmation of the papers' contents by the taxpayer. To be sure, the Court correctly observes that "[t]he taxpayer cannot avoid compliance with the subpoena merely by asserting that the item of evidence which he is required to produce contains incriminating writing, whether his own or that of someone else." For it is not enough that the production of a writing, or books and papers, is compelled. Unless those materials are such as to come within the zone of privacy recognized by the Amendment, the privilege against compulsory self-incrimination does not protect against their production.

We are not without guideposts for determining what books, papers, and writings come within the zone of privacy recognized by the Amendment. A precise cataloguing of private papers within the ambit of the privacy protected by the privilege is probably impossible. Some papers, however, do lend themselves to classification. Production of documentary materials created or authenticated by a State or the Federal Government, such as automobile registrations or property deeds, would seem ordinarily to fall outside the protection of the privilege. They hardly reflect an extension of the person.

Economic and business records may present difficulty in particular cases. The records of business entities generally fall without the scope of the privilege. But, as noted, the Court has recognized that the privilege extends to the business records of the sole proprietor or practitioner. Such records are at least an extension of an aspect of a person's activities, though concededly not the more intimate aspects of one's life. Where the privilege would have protected one's mental notes of his business affairs in a less complicated day and age, it would seem that that protection should not fall away because the complexities of another time compel one to keep business records. Nonbusiness economic records in the possession of an individual, such as canceled checks or tax records, would also seem to be protected. They may provide clear insights into a person's total lifestyle. They are, however, like business records and the papers involved in these cases, frequently, though not always, disclosed to other parties; and disclosure, in proper cases, may foreclose reliance upon the privilege. Personal letters constitute an integral aspect of a person's private enclave. And while letters, being necessarily interpersonal, are not wholly private, their peculiarly private nature and the generally narrow extent of their disclosure would seem to render them within the scope of the privilege. Papers in the nature of a personal diary are a fortiori protected under the privilege.

The Court's treatment in the instant cases of the question whether the evidence involved here is within the protection of the privilege is, with all respect, most inadequate. The gaping hole is in the omission of any reference to the taxpayer's privacy interests and to whether the subpoenas impermissibly invade those interests.

Fisher involved the question of whether the government may compel production of documents, but its rationale applies to anything that a person might be required to produce. For example, in Baltimore City Department of Social Services v. Bouknight, 493 U.S. 549 (1990), the Court held that a court could order a parent to produce a child over whom she had custody. A court gave the Department of Social Services custody over a child as being a "child in need of assistance." The child was returned to his mother with certain conditions. She did not comply with the conditions and the Court authorized the department to remove the child. The mother did not relinquish the child and the department was concerned that the child might no longer be alive. The court ordered the mother to produce the child and she invoked the Fifth Amendment privilege against self-incrimination.

The Court, in an opinion by Justice O'Connor, ruled against Bouknight. The Court stated, "The possibility that a production order will compel testimonial assertions that may prove incriminating does not, in all contexts, justify invoking the privilege to resist production. Even assuming that this limited testimonial assertion is sufficiently incriminating and 'sufficiently testimonial for purposes of the privilege,' Bouknight may not invoke the privilege to resist the production order because she has assumed custodial duties related to production and because production is required as part of a noncriminal regulatory scheme."

The Court concluded, "Finally, production in the vast majority of cases will embody no incriminating testimony, even if in particular cases the act of production may incriminate the custodian through an assertion of possession or the existence, or the identity, of the child. These orders to produce children cannot be characterized as efforts to gain some testimonial component of the act of production. In these circumstances, Bouknight cannot invoke the privilege to resist the order to produce Maurice."

3. May the Government Require Testimony If It Provides Immunity?

As explained above, the privilege against self-incrimination applies only if the statements could lead to a person's criminal liability. If a person is granted immunity and is promised that the statements will not be used for criminal prosecutions, there is no danger of self-incrimination.

There are two types of immunity. "Transactional immunity" promises the person that he or she will not be prosecuted for offenses related to the compelled testimony. "Use and derivative use immunity" promises the person that the government will not use the statements gained under immunity, or anything derived from those statements, in a criminal prosecution. Use and derivative use immunity is more common than transactional immunity and is specifically provided for by federal statute. 18 U.S.C. §§601, *et seq.* If a person makes statements after a promise of immunity, they can be used against the person only in a perjury prosecution.

Kastigar v. United States is an important case upholding the constitutionality of use immunity and clarifying the burden on prosecutors to prove that information gained was not the product of statements gained through immunity.

KASTIGAR v. UNITED STATES
406 U.S. 441 (1972)

Justice POWELL delivered the opinion of the Court.

This case presents the question whether the United States Government may compel testimony from an unwilling witness, who invokes the Fifth Amendment privilege against compulsory self-incrimination, by conferring on the witness immunity from use of the compelled testimony in subsequent criminal proceedings, as well as immunity from use of evidence derived from the testimony.

Petitioners were subpoenaed to appear before a United States grand jury in the Central District of California on February 4, 1971. The Government believed that petitioners were likely to assert their Fifth Amendment privilege. Prior to the scheduled appearances, the Government applied to the District Court for an order directing petitioners to answer questions and produce evidence before the grand jury under a grant of immunity conferred pursuant to 18 U.S.C. §§6002, 6003. Petitioners opposed issuance of the order, contending primarily that the scope of the immunity provided by the statute was not coextensive with the scope of the privilege against self-incrimination, and therefore was not sufficient to supplant the privilege and compel their testimony. The District Court rejected this contention, and ordered petitioners to appear before the grand jury and answer its questions under the grant of immunity.

Petitioners appeared but refused to answer questions, asserting their privilege against compulsory self-incrimination. They were brought before the District Court, and each persisted in his refusal to answer the grand jury's questions, notwithstanding the grant of immunity. The court found both in contempt, and committed them to the custody of the Attorney General until either they answered the grand jury's questions or the term of the grand jury expired. This Court granted certiorari to resolve the important question whether testimony may be compelled by granting immunity from the use of compelled testimony and evidence derived therefrom ("use and derivative use" immunity), or whether it is necessary to grant immunity from prosecution for offenses to which compelled testimony relates ("transactional" immunity).

I

The power of government to compel persons to testify in court or before grand juries and other governmental agencies is firmly established in Anglo-American jurisprudence. But the power to compel testimony is not absolute.

There are a number of exemptions from the testimonial duty, the most important of which is the Fifth Amendment privilege against compulsory self-incrimination.

Immunity statutes, which have historical roots deep in Anglo-American jurisprudence, are not incompatible with these values. Rather, they seek a rational accommodation between the imperatives of the privilege and the legitimate demands of government to compel citizens to testify. The existence of these statutes reflects the importance of testimony, and the fact that many offenses are of such a character that the only persons capable of giving useful testimony are those implicated in the crime. Indeed, their origins were in the context of such offenses, and their primary use has been to investigate such offenses. Congress included immunity statutes in many of the regulatory measures adopted in the first half of this century. Indeed, prior to the enactment of the statute under consideration in this case, there were in force over 50 federal immunity statutes. In addition, every State in the Union, as well as the District of Columbia and Puerto Rico, has one or more such statutes. The commentators, and this Court on several occasions, have characterized immunity statutes as essential to the effective enforcement of various criminal statutes.

II

Petitioners contend, first, that the Fifth Amendment's privilege against compulsory self-incrimination, deprives Congress of power to enact laws that compel self-incrimination, even if complete immunity from prosecution is granted prior to the compulsion of the incriminatory testimony. In other words, petitioners assert that no immunity statute, however drawn, can afford a lawful basis for compelling incriminatory testimony. We find no merit to this contention.

III

Petitioners' second contention is that the scope of immunity provided by the federal witness immunity statute, 18 U.S.C. §6002, is not coextensive with the scope of the Fifth Amendment privilege against compulsory self-incrimination, and therefore is not sufficient to supplant the privilege and compel testimony over a claim of the privilege. The statute provides that when a witness is compelled by district court order to testify over a claim of the privilege: "the witness may not refuse to comply with the order on the basis of his privilege against self-incrimination; but no testimony or other information compelled under the order (or any information directly or indirectly derived from such testimony or other information) may be used against the witness in any criminal case, except a prosecution for perjury, giving a false statement, or otherwise failing to comply with the order."

The constitutional inquiry, rooted in logic and history, as well as in the decisions of this Court, is whether the immunity granted under this statute is coextensive with the scope of the privilege. If so, petitioners' refusals to answer based on the privilege were unjustified, and the judgments of contempt were proper, for the grant of immunity has removed the dangers against which the privilege protects. If, on the other hand, the immunity granted is not as comprehensive as the protection afforded by the privilege, petitioners were justified in refusing to answer, and the judgments of contempt must be vacated.

Petitioners draw a distinction between statutes that provide transactional immunity and those that provide, as does the statute before us, immunity from use and derivative use. They contend that a statute must at a minimum grant full transactional immunity in order to be coextensive with the scope of the privilege.

The statute's explicit proscription of the use in any criminal case of "testimony or other information compelled under the order (or any information directly or indirectly derived from such testimony or other information)" is consonant with Fifth Amendment standards. We hold that such immunity from use and derivative use is coextensive with the scope of the privilege against self-incrimination, and therefore is sufficient to compel testimony over a claim of the privilege. While a grant of immunity must afford protection commensurate with that afforded by the privilege, it need not be broader. Transactional immunity, which accords full immunity from prosecution for the offense to which the compelled testimony relates, affords the witness considerably broader protection than does the Fifth Amendment privilege. The privilege has never been construed to mean that one who invokes it cannot subsequently be prosecuted. Its sole concern is to afford protection against being "forced to give testimony leading to the infliction of penalties affixed to . . . criminal acts." Immunity from the use of compelled testimony, as well as evidence derived directly and indirectly therefrom, affords this protection. It prohibits the prosecutorial authorities from using the compelled testimony in any respect, and it therefore insures that the testimony cannot lead to the infliction of criminal penalties on the witness.

Petitioners argue that use and derivative-use immunity will not adequately protect a witness from various possible incriminating uses of the compelled testimony: for example, the prosecutor or other law enforcement officials may obtain leads, names of witnesses, or other information not otherwise available that might result in a prosecution. It will be difficult and perhaps impossible, the argument goes, to identify, by testimony or cross-examination, the subtle ways in which the compelled testimony may disadvantage a witness, especially in the jurisdiction granting the immunity.

This argument presupposes that the statute's prohibition will prove impossible to enforce. The statute provides a sweeping proscription of any use, direct or indirect, of the compelled testimony and any information derived therefrom. A person accorded this immunity and subsequently prosecuted, is not dependent for the preservation of his rights upon the integrity and good faith of the prosecuting authorities.

This burden of proof, which we reaffirm as appropriate, is not limited to a negation of taint; rather, it imposes on the prosecution the affirmative duty to prove that the evidence it proposes to use is derived from a legitimate source wholly independent of the compelled testimony. This is very substantial protection, commensurate with that resulting from invoking the privilege itself. The privilege assures that a citizen is not compelled to incriminate himself by his own testimony. It usually operates to allow a citizen to remain silent when asked a question requiring an incriminatory answer. This statute, which operates after a witness has given incriminatory testimony, affords the same protection by assuring that the compelled testimony can in no way lead to the infliction of criminal penalties. The statute, like the Fifth Amendment, grants neither pardon nor amnesty. Both the statute and the Fifth Amendment allow the government to prosecute using evidence from legitimate independent sources.

There can be no justification in reason or policy for holding that the Constitution requires an amnesty grant where, acting pursuant to statute and accompanying safeguards, testimony is compelled in exchange for immunity from use and derivative use when no such amnesty is required where the government, acting without colorable right, coerces a defendant into incriminating himself.

We conclude that the immunity provided by 18 U.S.C. §6002 leaves the witness and the prosecutorial authorities in substantially the same position as if the witness had claimed the Fifth Amendment privilege. The immunity therefore is coextensive with the privilege and suffices to supplant it.

Justice DOUGLAS, dissenting.

The Self-Incrimination Clause says: "No person . . . shall be compelled in any criminal case to be a witness against himself." I see no answer to the proposition that he is such a witness when only "use" immunity is granted. If, as some have thought, the Bill of Rights contained only "counsels of moderation" from which courts and legislatures could deviate according to their conscience or discretion, then today's contraction of the Self-Incrimination Clause of the Fifth Amendment would be understandable. But that has not been true, starting with Chief Justice Marshall's opinion in United States v. Burr, where he ruled that the reach of the Fifth Amendment was so broad as to make the privilege applicable when there was a mere possibility of a criminal charge being made.

When we allow the prosecution to offer only "use" immunity we allow it to grant far less than it has taken away. For while the precise testimony that is compelled may not be used, leads from that testimony may be pursued and used to convict the witness. My view is that the framers put it beyond the power of Congress to compel anyone to confess his crimes. The Self-Incrimination Clause creates, as I have said before, "the federally protected right of silence," making it unconstitutional to use a law "to pry open one's lips and make him a witness against himself." That is indeed one of the chief procedural guarantees in our accusatorial system. Government acts in an ignoble way when it stoops to the end which we authorize today.

It is also possible that use immunity might actually have an adverse impact on the administration of justice rather than promote law enforcement. A witness might believe, with good reason, that his "immunized" testimony will inevitably lead to a felony conviction. Under such circumstances, rather than testify and aid the investigation, the witness might decide he would be better off remaining silent even if he is jailed for contempt.

Justice MARSHALL, dissenting.

Today the Court holds that the United States may compel a witness to give incriminating testimony, and subsequently prosecute him for crimes to which that testimony relates. I cannot believe the Fifth Amendment permits that result. The Fifth Amendment gives a witness an absolute right to resist interrogation, if the testimony sought would tend to incriminate him. A grant of immunity may strip the witness of the right to refuse to testify, but only if it is broad enough to eliminate all possibility that the testimony will in fact operate to incriminate him. It must put him in precisely the same position, vis-à-vis the government that has compelled his testimony, as he would have been in had he remained silent in reliance on the privilege.

United States v. Hubbell is a subsequent Supreme Court case clarifying when production is incriminating and also what the effects of a grant of immunity are.

UNITED STATES v. HUBBELL

530 U.S. 27 (2000)

Justice STEVENS delivered the opinion of the Court.

The two questions presented concern the scope of a witness' protection against compelled self-incrimination: (1) whether the Fifth Amendment privilege protects a witness from being compelled to disclose the existence of incriminating documents that the Government is unable to describe with reasonable particularity; and (2) if the witness produces such documents pursuant to a grant of immunity, whether 18 U.S.C. §6002 prevents the Government from using them to prepare criminal charges against him.

I

This proceeding arises out of the second prosecution of respondent, Webster Hubbell, commenced by the Independent Counsel appointed in

August 1994 to investigate possible violations of federal law relating to the Whitewater Development Corporation. The first prosecution was terminated pursuant to a plea bargain. In December 1994, respondent pleaded guilty to charges of mail fraud and tax evasion arising out of his billing practices as a member of an Arkansas law firm from 1989 to 1992, and was sentenced to 21 months in prison. In the plea agreement, respondent promised to provide the Independent Counsel with "full, complete, accurate, and truthful information" about matters relating to the Whitewater investigation.

The second prosecution resulted from the Independent Counsel's attempt to determine whether respondent had violated that promise. In October 1996, while respondent was incarcerated, the Independent Counsel served him with a subpoena duces tecum calling for the production of 11 categories of documents before a grand jury sitting in Little Rock, Arkansas. On November 19, he appeared before the grand jury and invoked his Fifth Amendment privilege against self-incrimination. In response to questioning by the prosecutor, respondent initially refused "to state whether there are documents within my possession, custody, or control responsive to the Subpoena." Thereafter, the prosecutor produced an order, which had previously been obtained from the District Court pursuant to 18 U.S.C. §6003(a), directing him to respond to the subpoena and granting him immunity "to the extent allowed by law." Respondent then produced 13,120 pages of documents and records and responded to a series of questions that established that those were all of the documents in his custody or control that were responsive to the commands in the subpoena, with the exception of a few documents he claimed were shielded by the attorney-client and attorney work-product privileges.

The contents of the documents produced by respondent provided the Independent Counsel with the information that led to this second prosecution. On April 30, 1998, a grand jury in the District of Columbia returned a 10-count indictment charging respondent with various tax-related crimes and mail and wire fraud. The District Court dismissed the indictment relying, in part, on the ground that the Independent Counsel's use of the subpoenaed documents violated §6002 because all of the evidence he would offer against respondent at trial derived either directly or indirectly from the testimonial aspects of respondent's immunized act of producing those documents. The Court of Appeals vacated the judgment and remanded for further proceedings.

II

[It is a] settled proposition that a person may be required to produce specific documents even though they contain incriminating assertions of fact or belief because the creation of those documents was not "compelled" within the meaning of the privilege. On the other hand, we have also made it clear that the act of producing documents in response to a subpoena may have a compelled testimonial aspect. We have held that "the act of production" itself may implicitly communicate "statements of fact." By "producing documents in compliance with a subpoena, the witness would admit that the papers existed, were in his possession or control, and were authentic." Moreover, as was true in this case, when the custodian of documents responds to a subpoena, he may be compelled to take the witness stand and answer questions designed to determine whether he has produced everything demanded by the subpoena. The answers to those questions, as well as the act of production itself, may certainly communicate information about the existence, custody, and authenticity of the documents. Whether the constitutional privilege protects the answers to such questions, or protects the act of production itself, is a question that is distinct from the question whether the unprotected contents of the documents themselves are incriminating.

III

Acting pursuant to 18 U.S.C. §6002, the District Court entered an order compelling respondent to produce "any and all documents" described in the grand jury subpoena and granting him "immunity to the extent allowed by law." The "compelled testimony" that is relevant in this case is not to be found in the contents of the documents produced in response to the subpoena. It is, rather, the testimony inherent in the act of producing those documents. The disagreement between the parties focuses entirely on the significance of that testimonial aspect.

IV

The Government correctly emphasizes that the testimonial aspect of a response to a subpoena duces tecum does nothing more than establish the existence, authenticity, and custody of items that are produced. We assume that the Government is also entirely correct in its submission that it would not have to advert to respondent's act of production in order to prove the existence, authenticity, or custody of any documents that it might offer in evidence at a criminal trial; indeed, the Government disclaims any need to introduce any of the documents produced by respondent into evidence in order to prove the charges against him. It follows, according to the Government, that it has no intention of making improper "use" of respondent's compelled testimony.

The question, however, is not whether the response to the subpoena may be introduced into evidence at his criminal trial. That would surely be a prohibited "use" of the immunized act of production. But the fact that the Government intends no such use of the act of production leaves open the separate question whether it has already made "derivative use" of the testimonial aspect of that act in obtaining the indictment against respondent and in preparing its case for trial. It clearly has.

It is apparent from the text of the subpoena itself that the prosecutor needed respondent's assistance both to identify potential sources of information and to produce those sources. Given the breadth of the description of the 11 categories of documents called for by the subpoena, the collection and production of the materials demanded was tantamount to answering a series of interrogatories asking a witness to disclose the existence and location of particular documents fitting certain broad descriptions. The assembly of literally hundreds of pages of material in response to a request for "any and all documents reflecting, referring, or relating to any direct or indirect sources of money or other things of value received by or provided to" an individual or members of his family during a 3-year period, is the functional equivalent of the preparation of an answer to either a detailed written interrogatory or a series of oral questions at a discovery deposition. Entirely apart from the contents of the 13,120 pages of materials that respondent produced in this case, it is undeniable that providing a catalog of existing documents fitting within any of the 11 broadly worded subpoena categories could provide a prosecutor with a "lead to incriminating evidence," or "a link in the chain of evidence needed to prosecute."

Indeed, the record makes it clear that that is what happened in this case. The documents were produced before a grand jury sitting in the Eastern District of Arkansas in aid of the Independent Counsel's attempt to determine whether respondent had violated a commitment in his first plea agreement. The use of those sources of information eventually led to the return of an indictment by a grand jury sitting in the District of Columbia for offenses that apparently are unrelated to that plea agreement. What the District Court characterized as a "fishing expedition" did produce a fish, but not the one that the Independent Counsel expected to hook. It is abundantly clear that the testimonial aspect of respondent's act of producing subpoenaed documents was the first step in a chain of evidence that led to this prosecution. The documents did not magically appear in the prosecutor's office like "manna from heaven." They arrived there only after respondent asserted his constitutional privilege, received a grant of immunity, and — under the compulsion of the District Court's order — took the mental and physical steps necessary to provide the prosecutor with an accurate inventory of the many sources of potentially incriminating evidence sought by the subpoena. It was only through respondent's truthful reply to the subpoena that the Government received the incriminating documents of which it made "substantial use . . . in the investigation that led to the indictment."

For these reasons, we cannot accept the Government's submission that respondent's immunity did not preclude its derivative use of the produced documents because its "possession of the documents [was] the fruit only of a simple physical act — the act of producing the documents." It was unquestionably necessary for respondent to make extensive use of "the contents of his own mind" in identifying the hundreds of documents responsive to the requests in the subpoena. The assembly of those documents was like telling an inquisitor the combination to a wall safe, not like being forced to surrender the key to a strongbox. The Government's anemic view of respondent's act of production as a mere physical act that is principally nontestimonial in character and can be entirely divorced from its "implicit" testimonial aspect so as to constitute a "legitimate, wholly independent source" (as required by *Kastigar*) for the documents produced simply fails to account for these realities.

In sum, we have no doubt that the constitutional privilege against self-incrimination protects the target of a grand jury investigation from being compelled to answer questions designed to elicit information about the existence of sources of potentially incriminating evidence. That constitutional privilege has the same application to the testimonial aspect of a response to a subpoena seeking discovery of those sources.

Given our conclusion that respondent's act of production had a testimonial aspect, at least with respect to the existence and location of the documents sought by the Government's subpoena, respondent could not be compelled to produce those documents without first receiving a grant of immunity under §6003. As we construed §6002 in *Kastigar*, such immunity is coextensive with the constitutional privilege. *Kastigar* requires that respondent's motion to dismiss the indictment on immunity grounds be granted unless the Government proves that the evidence it used in obtaining the indictment and proposed to use at trial was derived from legitimate sources "wholly independent" of the testimonial aspect of respondent's immunized conduct in assembling and producing the documents described in the subpoena. The Government, however, does not claim that it could make such a showing. Rather, it contends that its prosecution of respondent must be considered proper unless someone — presumably respondent — shows that "there is some substantial relation between the compelled testimonial communications implicit in the act of production (as opposed to the act of production standing alone) and some aspect of the information used in the investigation or the evidence presented at trial." We could not accept this submission without repudiating the basis for our conclusion in *Kastigar* that the statutory guarantee of use and derivative-use immunity is as broad as the constitutional privilege itself. This we are not prepared to do.

Accordingly, the indictment against respondent must be dismissed.

Justice THOMAS, with whom Justice SCALIA joins, concurring.

Our decision today involves the application of the act-of-production doctrine, which provides that persons compelled to turn over incriminating papers or other physical evidence pursuant to a subpoena duces tecum or a summons may invoke the Fifth Amendment privilege against self-incrimination as a bar to production only where the act of producing the evidence would contain "testimonial" features. I join the opinion of the Court because it properly applies this doctrine, but I write separately to note that this doctrine may be inconsistent with the original meaning of the Fifth Amendment's Self-Incrimination Clause. A substantial body of evidence suggests that the Fifth Amendment privilege protects against the compelled production not just of incriminating testimony, but of any incriminating evidence. In a future case, I would be willing to reconsider the scope and meaning of the Self-Incrimination Clause.

CHAPTER
5

IDENTIFICATION PROCEDURES

Eyewitness identification is enormously powerful evidence. A witness telling a jury that he or she saw the defendant commit the crime is often sufficient by itself to lead to a conviction. The problem is that there is a large body of social science research indicating that eyewitnesses are often mistaken.[1] Events happen so quickly and often under great stress; people tend to see what they expect; memories are faulty. Cross-racial identifications, in which a person is identifying someone of a different race, are particularly inaccurate. There are many instances in which innocent individuals have been convicted of crimes, including capital crimes, based on flawed eyewitness testimony. The challenge for the law in this area is to preserve this often crucial type of evidence while increasing the likelihood of its accuracy.

In a recent dissenting opinion, Justice Sotomayor made this point: "The empirical evidence demonstrates that eyewitness misidentification is 'the single greatest cause of wrongful convictions in this country.' Researchers have found that a staggering 76% of the first 250 convictions overturned due to DNA evidence since 1989 involved eyewitness misidentification. Study after study demonstrates that eyewitness recollections are highly susceptible to distortion by postevent information or social cues; that jurors routinely overestimate the accuracy of eyewitness identifications; that jurors place the greatest weight on eyewitness confidence in assessing identifications even though confidence is a poor gauge of accuracy; and that suggestiveness can stem from sources beyond police-orchestrated procedures."[2]

There are two primary forms of identification procedures used during police investigations. First, lineups and showups occur when the police ask the witness, often the victim of the crime, to identify a particular person. In a lineup, police present a group of individuals and ask the witness if he or she can identify the person who committed the crime. In a showup, the witness is shown just one person, not a group, and asked if that is the person who committed the crime.

---

1. *See* Brian L. Cutler & Steven D. Penrod, *Mistaken Identification: The Eyewitness, Psychology and the Law* (1995); Elizabeth Loftus, *Eyewitness Testimony* (1979).

2. Perry v. New Hampshire, 132 S. Ct. 716, 738-739 (2012) (Sotomayor, J., dissenting).

Second are photo spreads, in which police ask witnesses to look through a series of photographs and see if they can identify the person who they saw commit the crime. Sometimes this involves the witness being shown anywhere from five to ten photographs — essentially a photo lineup — and sometimes it involves the witness being given a book of photographs to examine.

A key danger with both of these investigative techniques is police suggestiveness. For example, police can construct lineups in a way that increases the likelihood that a particular person will be identified. If the witness says that the perpetrator is very tall, a suggestive lineup would include one tall person and four short ones. Also, police can make comments during identification procedures that make a witness more inclined to identify a particular suspect.

The Supreme Court has developed two constitutional protections in this area for suspects of crime. First, the Court has recognized a right to counsel in some identification situations, most notably for lineups that occur after indictments. The hope is that the presence of a lawyer for the suspect will reduce the likelihood of suggestiveness by the police. However, as discussed below, the Supreme Court has not recognized a right to counsel for lineups before indictments or for photo identification procedures. Second, the Court has held that unnecessarily suggestive identification procedures *by police* that lead to unreliable identifications violate due process.

Each of these lines of cases is discussed below. In reading these cases, it is important to consider whether the Court has done enough to protect suspects from false identifications and what other steps might be taken in this regard.

A.   THE RIGHT TO COUNSEL

1.   *The Right to Counsel in Lineups*

The right to counsel for criminal suspects during identification procedures comes largely from two Supreme Court cases decided the same day: United States v. Wade and Gilbert v. California.

UNITED STATES v. WADE
388 U.S. 218 (1967)

Justice BRENNAN delivered the opinion of the Court.

The question here is whether courtroom identifications of an accused at trial are to be excluded from evidence because the accused was exhibited to the witnesses before trial at a post-indictment lineup conducted for identification purposes without notice to and in the absence of the accused's appointed counsel.

The federally insured bank in Eustace, Texas, was robbed on September 21, 1964. A man with a small strip of tape on each side of his face entered the bank, pointed a pistol at the female cashier and the vice president, the only persons in the bank at the time, and forced them to fill a pillowcase with the bank's money. The man then drove away with an accomplice who had been waiting in a stolen car outside the bank. On March 23, 1965, an indictment was returned against respondent, Wade, and two others for conspiring to rob the bank, and against Wade and the accomplice for the robbery itself. Wade was arrested on April 2, and counsel was appointed to represent him on April 26. Fifteen days later an FBI agent, without notice to Wade's lawyer, arranged to have the two bank employees observe a lineup made up of Wade and five or six other prisoners and conducted in a courtroom of the local county courthouse. Each person in the line wore strips of tape such as allegedly worn by the robber and upon direction each said something like "put the money in the bag," the words allegedly uttered by the robber. Both bank employees identified Wade in the lineup as the bank robber.

At trial, the two employees, when asked on direct examination if the robber was in the courtroom, pointed to Wade. The prior lineup identification was then elicited from both employees on cross-examination. At the close of testimony, Wade's counsel moved for a judgment of acquittal or, alternatively, to strike the bank officials' courtroom identifications on the ground that conduct of the lineup, without notice to and in the absence of his appointed counsel, violated his Fifth Amendment privilege against self-incrimination and his Sixth Amendment right to the assistance of counsel. The motion was denied, and Wade was convicted.

I

Neither the lineup itself nor anything shown by this record that Wade was required to do in the lineup violated his privilege against self-incrimination. We have only recently reaffirmed that the privilege "protects an accused only from being compelled to testify against himself, or otherwise provide the State with evidence of a testimonial or communicative nature."

We have no doubt that compelling the accused merely to exhibit his person for observation by a prosecution witness prior to trial involves no compulsion of the accused to give evidence having testimonial significance. It is compulsion of the accused to exhibit his physical characteristics, not compulsion to disclose any knowledge he might have. [C]ompelling Wade to speak within hearing distance of the witnesses, even to utter words purportedly uttered by the robber, was not compulsion to utter statements of a "testimonial" nature; he was required to use his voice as an identifying physical characteristic, not to speak his guilt.

II

The fact that the lineup involved no violation of Wade's privilege against self-incrimination does not, however, dispose of his contention that the courtroom identifications should have been excluded because the lineup was conducted without notice to and in the absence of his counsel. [I]n this case it is urged that the assistance of counsel at the lineup was indispensable to protect Wade's most basic right as a criminal defendant — his right to a fair trial at which the witnesses against him might be meaningfully cross-examined.

The Framers of the Bill of Rights envisaged a broader role for counsel than under the practice then prevailing in England of merely advising his client in "matters of law," and eschewing any responsibility for "matters of fact." The constitutions in at least 11 of the 13 States expressly or impliedly abolished this distinction. This background is reflected in the scope given by our decisions to the Sixth Amendment's guarantee to an accused of the assistance of counsel for his defense. When the Bill of Rights was adopted, there were no organized police forces as we know them today. The accused confronted the prosecutor and the witnesses against him, and the evidence was marshalled, largely at the trial itself. In contrast, today's law enforcement machinery involves critical confrontations of the accused by the prosecution at pretrial proceedings where the results might well settle the accused's fate and reduce the trial itself to a mere formality. In recognition of these realities of modern criminal prosecution, our cases have construed the Sixth Amendment guarantee to apply to "critical" stages of the proceedings. The guarantee reads: "In all criminal prosecutions, the accused shall enjoy the right . . . to have the Assistance of Counsel for his defence." The plain wording of this guarantee thus encompasses counsel's assistance whenever necessary to assure a meaningful "defence."

It is central to that principle that in addition to counsel's presence at trial, the accused is guaranteed that he need not stand alone against the State at any stage of the prosecution, formal or informal, in court or out, where counsel's absence might derogate from the accused's right to a fair trial. The security of that right is as much the aim of the right to counsel as it is of the other guarantees of the Sixth Amendment — the right of the accused to a speedy and public trial by an impartial jury, his right to be informed of the nature and cause of the accusation, and his right to be confronted with the witnesses against him and to have compulsory process for obtaining witnesses in his favor. The presence of counsel at such critical confrontations, as at the trial itself, operates to assure that the accused's interests will be protected consistently with our adversary theory of criminal prosecution.

In sum, the principle of Powell v. Alabama (1932) and succeeding cases requires that we scrutinize any pretrial confrontation of the accused to determine whether the presence of his counsel is necessary to preserve the defendant's basic right to a fair trial as affected by his right meaningfully to cross-examine the witnesses against him and to have effective assistance of counsel at the trial itself. It calls upon us to analyze whether potential substantial prejudice to defendant's rights inheres in the particular confrontation and the ability of counsel to help avoid that prejudice.

III

The Government characterizes the lineup as a mere preparatory step in the gathering of the prosecution's evidence, not different — for Sixth Amendment purposes — from various other preparatory steps, such as systematized or scientific analyzing of the accused's fingerprints, blood sample, clothing, hair, and the like. We think there are differences which preclude such stages being characterized as critical stages at which the accused has the right to the presence of his counsel. Knowledge of the techniques of science and technology is sufficiently available, and the variables in techniques few enough, that the accused has the opportunity for a meaningful confrontation of the Government's case at trial through the ordinary processes of cross-examination of the Government's expert witnesses and the presentation of the evidence of his own experts. The denial of a right to have his counsel present at such analyses does not therefore violate the Sixth Amendment; they are not critical stages since there is minimal risk that his counsel's absence at such stages might derogate from his right to a fair trial.

IV

But the confrontation compelled by the State between the accused and the victim or witnesses to a crime to elicit identification evidence is peculiarly riddled with innumerable dangers and variable factors which might seriously, even crucially, derogate from a fair trial. The vagaries of eyewitness identification are well-known; the annals of criminal law are rife with instances of mistaken identification. Mr. Justice Frankfurter once said: "What is the worth of identification testimony even when uncontradicted? The identification of strangers is proverbially untrustworthy. The hazards of such testimony are established by a formidable number of instances in the records of English and American trials. These instances are recent — not due to the brutalities of ancient criminal procedure." The Case of Sacco and Vanzetti 30 (1927). A major factor contributing to the high incidence of miscarriage of justice from mistaken identification has been the degree of suggestion inherent in the manner in which the prosecution presents the suspect to witnesses for pretrial identification. A commentator has observed that "[t]he influence of improper suggestion upon identifying witnesses probably accounts for more miscarriages of justice than any other single factor — perhaps it is responsible for more such errors than all other factors combined." Wall, Eye-Witness Identification in Criminal Cases 26. Suggestion can be created intentionally or unintentionally in many subtle ways. And the dangers for the suspect are particularly grave when the witness' opportunity for observation was insubstantial, and thus his susceptibility to suggestion the greatest.

Moreover, it is a matter of common experience that, once a witness has picked out the accused at the lineup, he is not likely to go back on his word later on, so that in practice the issue of identity may (in the absence of other relevant evidence) for all practical purposes be determined there and then, before the trial.

The pretrial confrontation for purpose of identification may take the form of a lineup, also known as an "identification parade" or "showup," as in the present case, or presentation of the suspect alone to the witness, as in Stovall v. Denno (1967). It is obvious that risks of suggestion attend either form of confrontation and increase the dangers inhering in eyewitness identification. But as is the case with secret interrogations, there is serious difficulty in depicting what transpires at lineups and other forms of identification confrontations. "Privacy results in secrecy and this in turn results in a gap in our knowledge as to what in fact goes on." Miranda v. State of Arizona (1966). For the same reasons, the defense can seldom reconstruct the manner and mode of lineup identification for judge or jury at trial. Those participating in a lineup with the accused may often be police officers; in any event, the participants' names are rarely recorded or divulged at trial.

The impediments to an objective observation are increased when the victim is the witness. Lineups are prevalent in rape and robbery prosecutions and present a particular hazard that a victim's understandable outrage may excite vengeful or spiteful motives. In any event, neither witnesses nor lineup participants are apt to be alert for conditions prejudicial to the suspect. And if they were, it would likely be of scant benefit to the suspect since neither witnesses nor lineup participants are likely to be schooled in the detection of suggestive influences. Improper influences may go undetected by a suspect, guilty or not, who experiences the emotional tension which we might expect in one being confronted with potential accusers. Even when he does observe abuse, if he has a criminal record he may be reluctant to take the stand and open up the admission of prior convictions. Moreover any protestations by the suspect of the fairness of the lineup made at trial are likely to be in vain; the jury's choice is between the accused's unsupported version and that of the police officers present. In short, the accused's inability effectively to reconstruct at trial any unfairness that occurred at the lineup may deprive him of his only opportunity meaningfully to attack the credibility of the witness' courtroom identification.

The potential for improper influence is illustrated by the circumstances, insofar as they appear, surrounding the prior identifications in the three cases we decide today. In the present case, the testimony of the identifying witnesses elicited on cross-examination revealed that those witnesses were taken to the courthouse and seated in the courtroom to await assembly of the lineup. The courtroom faced on a hallway observable to the witnesses through an open door. The cashier testified that she saw Wade "standing in the hall" within sight of an FBI agent. Five or six other prisoners later appeared in the hall. The vice president testified that he saw a person in the hall in the custody of the agent who "resembled the person that we identified as the one that had entered the bank."

The lineup in *Gilbert* [*v. California*] was conducted in an auditorium in which some 100 witnesses to several alleged state and federal robberies charged to Gilbert made wholesale identifications of Gilbert as the robber in each other's presence, a procedure said to be fraught with dangers of suggestion. And the vice of suggestion created by the identification in *Stovall* [*v. Denno*] was the presentation to the witness of the suspect alone handcuffed to police officers. It is hard to imagine a situation more clearly conveying the suggestion to the witness that the one presented is believed guilty by the police. See Frankfurter, The Case of Sacco and Vanzetti 31-32.

The few cases that have surfaced therefore reveal the existence of a process attended with hazards of serious unfairness to the criminal accused and strongly suggest the plight of the more numerous defendants who are unable to ferret out suggestive influences in the secrecy of the confrontation. We do not assume that these risks are the result of police procedures intentionally designed to prejudice an accused. Rather we assume they derive from the dangers inherent in eyewitness identification and the suggestibility inherent in the context of the pretrial identification.

Insofar as the accused's conviction may rest on a courtroom identification in fact the fruit of a suspect pretrial identification which the accused is helpless to subject to effective scrutiny at trial, the accused is deprived of that right of cross-examination which is an essential safeguard to his right to confront the witnesses against him. And even though cross-examination is a precious safeguard to a fair trial, it cannot be viewed as an absolute assurance of accuracy and reliability. Thus in the present context, where so many variables and pitfalls exist, the first line of defense must be the prevention of unfairness and the lessening of the hazards of eyewitness identification at the lineup itself. The trial which might determine the accused's fate may well not be that in the courtroom but that at the pretrial confrontation, with the State aligned against the accused, the witness the sole jury, and the accused unprotected against the overreaching, intentional or unintentional, and with little or no effective appeal from the judgment there rendered by the witness— "that's the man."

Since it appears that there is grave potential for prejudice, intentional or not, in the pretrial lineup, which may not be capable of reconstruction at trial, and since presence of counsel itself can often avert prejudice and assure a meaningful confrontation at trial, there can be little doubt that for Wade the postindictment lineup was a critical stage of the prosecution at which he was "as much entitled to such aid (of counsel) as at the trial itself." Thus both Wade and his counsel should have been notified of the impending lineup, and counsel's presence should have been a requisite to conduct of the lineup, absent an "intelligent waiver."

No substantial countervailing policy considerations have been advanced against the requirement of the presence of counsel. Concern is expressed that the requirement will forestall prompt identifications and result in obstruction of the confrontations. As for the first, we note that in the two cases in which the right to counsel is today held to apply, counsel had already been appointed and no argument is made in either case that notice to counsel would have prejudicially delayed the confrontations. Moreover, we leave open the question whether the presence of substitute counsel might not suffice where notification and presence of the suspect's own counsel would result in prejudicial delay. And to refuse to recognize the right to counsel for fear that counsel will obstruct the course of justice is contrary to the basic assumptions upon which this Court has operated in Sixth Amendment cases. We rejected similar logic in Miranda v. State of Arizona, concerning presence of counsel during custodial interrogation.

In our view counsel can hardly impede legitimate law enforcement; on the contrary, for the reasons expressed, law enforcement may be assisted by preventing the infiltration of taint in the prosecution's identification evidence. That result cannot help the guilty avoid conviction but can only help assure that the right man has been brought to justice.

V

We come now to the question whether the denial of Wade's motion to strike the courtroom identification by the bank witnesses at trial because of the absence of his counsel at the lineup required, as the Court of Appeals held, the grant of a new trial at which such evidence is to be excluded. We do not think this disposition can be justified without first giving the Government the opportunity to establish by clear and convincing evidence that the in-court identifications were based upon observations of the suspect other than the lineup identification. Where, as here, the admissibility of evidence of the lineup identification itself is not involved, a per se rule of exclusion of courtroom identification would be unjustified. A rule limited solely to the exclusion of testimony concerning identification at the lineup itself, without regard to admissibility of the courtroom identification, would render the right to counsel an empty one. The lineup is most often used, as in the present case, to crystallize the witnesses' identification of the defendant for future reference. We have already noted that the lineup identification will have that effect. The State may then rest upon the witnesses' unequivocal courtroom identifications, and not mention the pretrial identification as part of the State's case at trial. Counsel is then in the predicament in which Wade's counsel found himself — realizing that possible unfairness at the lineup may be the sole means of attack upon the unequivocal courtroom identification, and having to probe in the dark in an attempt to discover and reveal unfairness, while bolstering the government witness' courtroom identification by bringing out and dwelling upon his prior identification. Since counsel's presence at the lineup would equip him to attack not only the lineup identification but the courtroom identification as well, limiting the impact of violation of the right to counsel to exclusion of evidence only of identification at the lineup itself disregards a critical element of that right.

We think it follows that the proper test to be applied in these situations is that quoted in Wong Sun v. United States [1963]: "[W]hether, granting establishment of the primary illegality, the evidence to which instant objection is made has been come at by exploitation of that illegality or instead by means sufficiently distinguishable to be purged of the primary taint." Application of this test in the present context requires consideration of various factors; for example, the prior opportunity to observe the alleged criminal act, the existence of any discrepancy between any pre-lineup description and the defendant's actual description, any identification prior to lineup of another person, the identification by picture of the defendant prior to the lineup, failure to identify the defendant on a prior occasion, and the lapse of time between the alleged act and the lineup identification. It is also relevant to consider those facts which, despite the absence of counsel, are disclosed concerning the conduct of the lineup.

On the record now before us we cannot make the determination whether the in-court identifications had an independent origin. This was not an issue at trial, although there is some evidence relevant to a determination. That inquiry is most properly made in the District Court. We therefore think the appropriate procedure to be followed is to vacate the conviction pending a hearing to determine whether the in-court identifications had an independent source, or whether, in any event, the introduction of the evidence was harmless error, and for the District Court to reinstate the conviction or order a new trial, as may be proper.

[Chief Justice WARREN and Justices DOUGLAS, BLACK, and FORTAS dissented from Part I of the Court's opinion, which found that there was not a violation of the Fifth Amendment privilege against self-incrimination. Justice BLACK also dissented from the remand of the case to the district court. He wrote, "[T]he Court remands the case to the District Court to consider whether the courtroom identification of Wade was the fruit of the illegal lineup, and, if it was, to grant him a new trial unless the court concludes that the courtroom identification was harmless error. I would reverse the Court of Appeals' reversal of Wade's conviction, but I would not remand for further proceedings since the prosecution not having used the out-of-court lineup identification against Wade at his trial, I believe the conviction should be affirmed."]

[Justice WHITE, joined by Justices HARLAN and STEWART, dissented from the portions of the Court's opinion requiring an attorney at post-indictment lineups.]

The Court has again propounded a broad constitutional rule barring the use of a wide spectrum of relevant and probative evidence, solely because a step in its ascertainment or discovery occurs outside the presence of defense counsel. This was the approach of the Court in Miranda v. State of Arizona (1966). I objected then to what I thought was an uncritical and doctrinaire approach without satisfactory factual foundation.

The Court's opinion is far-reaching. It proceeds first by creating a new per se rule of constitutional law: a criminal suspect cannot be subjected to a pretrial identification process in the absence of his counsel without violating the Sixth Amendment. If he is, the State may not buttress a later courtroom identification of the witness by any reference to the previous identification. Furthermore, the courtroom identification is not admissible at all unless the State can establish by clear and convincing proof that the testimony is not the fruit of the earlier identification made in the absence of defendant's counsel — admittedly a heavy burden for the State and probably an impossible one. To all intents and purposes, courtroom identifications are barred if pretrial identifications have occurred without counsel being present.

The rule applies to any lineup, to any other techniques employed to produce an identification and a fortiori to a face-to-face encounter between the witness and the suspect alone, regardless of when the identification occurs, in time or place, and whether before or after indictment or information. It matters not how well the witness knows the suspect, whether the witness is the suspect's mother, brother, or long-time associate, and no matter how long or well the witness observed the perpetrator at the scene of the crime. The kidnap victim who has lived for days with his abductor is in the same category as the witness who has had only a fleeting glimpse of the criminal. Neither may identify the suspect without defendant's counsel being present. The same strictures apply regardless of the number of other witnesses who positively identify the defendant and regardless of the corroborative evidence showing that it was the defendant who had committed the crime.

The premise for the Court's rule is not the general unreliability of eyewitness identifications nor the difficulties inherent in observation, recall, and recognition. The Court assumes a narrower evil as the basis for its rule — improper police suggestion which contributes to erroneous identifications. The Court apparently believes that improper police procedures are so widespread that a broad prophylactic rule must be laid down, requiring the presence of counsel at all pretrial identifications, in order to detect recurring instances of police misconduct. I do not share this pervasive distrust of all official investigations. None of the materials the Court relies upon supports it. Certainly, I would bow to solid fact, but the Court quite obviously does not have before it any reliable, comprehensive survey of current police practices on which to base its new rule. Until it does, the Court should avoid excluding relevant evidence from state criminal trials.

The Court goes beyond assuming that a great majority of the country's police departments are following improper practices at pretrial identifications. To find the lineup a "critical" stage of the proceeding and to exclude identifications made in the absence of counsel, the Court must also assume that police "suggestion," if it occurs at all, leads to erroneous rather than accurate identifications and that reprehensible police conduct will have an unavoidable and largely undiscoverable impact on the trial. This in turn assumes that there is now no adequate source from which defense counsel can learn about the circumstances of the pretrial identification in order to place before the jury all of the considerations which should enter into an appraisal of courtroom identification evidence. But these are treacherous and unsupported assumptions resting as they do on the notion that the defendant will not be aware, that the police and the witnesses will forget or prevaricate, that defense counsel will be unable to bring out the truth and that neither jury, judge, nor appellate court is a sufficient safeguard against unacceptable police conduct occurring at a pretrial identification procedure. I am unable to share the Court's view of the willingness of the police and the ordinary citizen witness to dissemble, either with respect to the identification of the defendant or with respect to the circumstances surrounding a pretrial identification.

I share the Court's view that the criminal trial, at the very least, should aim at truthful factfinding, including accurate eyewitness identifications. I doubt, however, on the basis of our present information, that the tragic mistakes which have occurred in criminal trials are as much the product of improper police conduct as they are the consequence of the difficulties inherent in eyewitness testimony and in resolving evidentiary conflicts by court or jury. I doubt that the Court's new rule will obviate these difficulties, or that the situation will be measurably improved by inserting defense counsel into the investigative processes of police departments everywhere.

But, it may be asked, what possible state interest militates against requiring the presence of defense counsel at lineups? After all, the argument goes, he may do some good, he may upgrade the quality of identification evidence in state courts and he can scarcely do any harm. Even if true, this is a feeble foundation for fastening an ironclad constitutional rule upon state criminal procedures. Absent some reliably established constitutional violation, the processes by which the States enforce their criminal laws are their own prerogative. The States do have an interest in conducting their own affairs, an interest which cannot be displaced simply by saying that there are no valid arguments with respect to the merits of a federal rule emanating from this Court.

Beyond this, however, requiring counsel at pretrial identifications as an invariable rule trenches on other valid state interests. One of them is its concern with the prompt and efficient enforcement of its criminal laws. Identifications frequently take place after arrest but before an indictment is returned or an information is filed. The police may have arrested a suspect on probable cause but may still have the wrong man. Both the suspect and the State have every interest in a prompt identification at that stage, the suspect in order to secure his immediate release and the State because prompt and early identification enhances accurate identification and because it must know whether it is on the right investigative track. Unavoidably, however, the absolute rule requiring the presence of counsel will cause significant delay and it may very well result in no pretrial identification at all. Counsel must be appointed and a time arranged convenient for him and the witnesses. Meanwhile, it may be necessary to file charges against the suspect who may then be released on bail, in the federal system very often on his own recognizance, with neither the State nor the defendant having the benefit of a properly conducted identification procedure.

Nor do I think the witnesses themselves can be ignored. They will now be required to be present at the convenience of counsel rather than their own.

Many may be much less willing to participate if the identification stage is transformed into an adversary proceeding not under the control of a judge. Others may fear for their own safety if their identity is known at an early date, especially when there is no way of knowing until the lineup occurs whether or not the police really have the right man.

Finally, I think the Court's new rule is vulnerable in terms of its own unimpeachable purpose of increasing the reliability of identification testimony. I would not extend this system, at least as it presently operates, to police investigations and would not require counsel's presence at pretrial identification procedures. Counsel's interest is in not having his client placed at the scene of the crime, regardless of his whereabouts. Some counsel may advise their clients to refuse to make any movements or to speak any words in a lineup or even to appear in one. To that extent the impact on truthful factfinding is quite obvious. Others will not only observe what occurs and develop [the] possibility for later cross-examination, but will hover over witnesses and begin their cross-examination then, menacing truthful factfinding as thoroughly as the Court fears the police now do. Certainly there is an implicit invitation to counsel to suggest rules for the lineup and to manage and produce it as best he can. I therefore doubt that the Court's new rule, at least absent some clearly defined limits on counsel's role, will measurably contribute to more reliable pretrial identifications. My fears are that it will have precisely the opposite result. It may well produce fewer convictions, but that is hardly a proper measure of its long-run acceptability. In my view, the State is entitled to investigate and develop its case outside the presence of defense counsel. This includes the right to have private conversations with identification witnesses, just as defense counsel may have his own consultations with these and other witnesses without having the prosecutor present.

————————————

In *Wade*, the witness identified the defendant in court, but the prosecutor did not attempt to introduce the identification from the lineup as evidence. By contrast, in another case decided the same day, Gilbert v. California, 388 U.S. 263 (1967), the prosecutor had used the lineup identification as evidence at trial.

Justice Brennan again wrote the opinion for the Court and stated:

> The admission of the in-court identifications without first determining that they were not tainted by the illegal lineup but were of independent origin was constitutional error. We there held that a post-indictment pretrial lineup at which the accused is exhibited to identifying witnesses is a critical stage of the criminal prosecution; that police conduct of such a lineup without notice to and in the absence of his counsel denies the accused his Sixth Amendment right to counsel and calls in question the admissibility at trial of the in-court identifications of the accused by witnesses who attended the lineup. However, as in *Wade*, the record does not permit an informed judgment whether the in-court identifications

at the two stages of the trial had an independent source. Gilbert is therefore entitled only to a vacation of his conviction pending the holding of such proceedings as the California Supreme Court may deem appropriate to afford the State the opportunity to establish that the in-court identifications had an independent source, or that their introduction in evidence was in any event harmless error.

Quite different considerations are involved as to the admission of the testimony of the manager of the apartment house at the guilt phase and of the eight witnesses at the penalty stage that they identified Gilbert at the lineup. That testimony is the direct result of the illegal lineup "come at by exploitation of [the primary] illegality." The State is therefore not entitled to an opportunity to show that that testimony had an independent source. Only a per se exclusionary rule as to such testimony can be an effective sanction to assure that law enforcement authorities will respect the accused's constitutional right to the presence of his counsel at the critical lineup. In the absence of legislative regulations adequate to avoid the hazards to a fair trial which inhere in lineups as presently conducted, the desirability of deterring the constitutionally objectionable practice must prevail over the undesirability of excluding relevant evidence. That conclusion is buttressed by the consideration that the witness' testimony of his lineup identification will enhance the impact of his in-court identification on the jury and seriously aggravate whatever derogation exists of the accused's right to a fair trial. Therefore, unless the California Supreme Court is "able to declare a belief that it was harmless beyond a reasonable doubt," Gilbert will be entitled on remand to a new trial or, if no prejudicial error is found on the guilt stage but only in the penalty stage, to whatever relief California law affords where the penalty stage must be set aside.

Justices White, Harlan, and Stewart dissented for the reasons they stated in United States v. Wade.

2. Limits on the Right to Counsel in Identification Procedures

Within a few years of *Wade* and *Gilbert*, the Supreme Court imposed significant limits on the right to counsel in identification situations. First, in Kirby v. Illinois, the Court held that *Wade* applies only to post-indictment lineups; there is no right to counsel in lineups before indictments. Many lineups, of course, occur at this stage. Also, of course, if police want to avoid the presence of an attorney at the lineup, they can do so by holding the lineup before indictment. Second, in United States v. Ash, the Court held that defendants have no right to counsel at photographic identifications.

The key question in evaluating these cases is whether the distinctions they draw with *Wade* are desirable and whether this leaves adequate protection for suspects during identification procedures.

KIRBY v. ILLINOIS
406 U.S. 682 (1972)

Justice STEWART announced the judgment of the Court and an opinion in which Chief Justice [BURGER], Justice BLACKMUN, and Justice REHNQUIST join.

In United States v. Wade and Gilbert v. California, this Court held "that a post-indictment pretrial lineup at which the accused is exhibited to identifying witnesses is a critical stage of the criminal prosecution; that police conduct of such a lineup without notice to and in the absence of his counsel denies the accused his Sixth (and Fourteenth) Amendment right to counsel and calls in question the admissibility at trial of the in-court identifications of the accused by witnesses who attended the lineup." Those cases further held that no in-court identifications are admissible in evidence if their source is a lineup conducted in violation of this constitutional standard. "Only a per se exclusionary rule as to such testimony can be an effective sanction, the Court said, to assure that law enforcement authorities will respect the accused's constitutional right to the presence of his counsel at the critical lineup." In the present case we are asked to extend the *Wade-Gilbert* per se exclusionary rule to identification testimony based upon a police station showup that took place before the defendant had been indicted or otherwise formally charged with any criminal offense.

On February 21, 1968, a man named Willie Shard reported to the Chicago police that the previous day two men had robbed him on a Chicago street of a wallet containing, among other things, traveler's checks and a Social Security card. On February 22, two police officers stopped the petitioner and a companion, Ralph Bean, on West Madison Street in Chicago. When asked for identification, the petitioner produced a wallet that contained three traveler's checks and a Social Security card, all bearing the name of Willie Shard. Papers with Shard's name on them were also found in Bean's possession. When asked to explain his possession of Shard's property, the petitioner first said that the traveler's checks were "play money," and then told the officers that he had won them in a crap game. The officers then arrested the petitioner and Bean and took them to a police station.

Only after arriving at the police station, and checking the records there, did the arresting officers learn of the Shard robbery. A police car was then dispatched to Shard's place of employment, where it picked up Shard and brought him to the police station. Immediately upon entering the room in the police station where the petitioner and Bean were seated at a table, Shard positively identified them as the men who had robbed him two days earlier. No lawyer was present in the room, and neither the petitioner nor Bean had asked for legal assistance, or been advised of any right to the presence of counsel.

More than six weeks later, the petitioner and Bean were indicted for the robbery of Willie Shard. Upon arraignment, counsel was appointed to represent them, and they pleaded not guilty. A pretrial motion to suppress Shard's identification testimony was denied, and at the trial Shard testified as a witness for the prosecution. In his testimony he described his identification of the two men at the police station on February 22, and identified them again in the courtroom as the men who had robbed him on February 20. He was cross-examined at length regarding the circumstances of his identification of the two defendants. The jury found both defendants guilty, and the petitioner's conviction was affirmed on appeal.

In a line of constitutional cases in this Court stemming back to the Court's landmark opinion in Powell v. Alabama [1932], it has been firmly established that a person's Sixth and Fourteenth Amendment right to counsel attaches only at or after the time that adversary judicial proceedings have been initiated against him. This is not to say that a defendant in a criminal case has a constitutional right to counsel only at the trial itself. The *Powell* case makes clear that the right attaches at the time of arraignment, and the Court has recently held that it exists also at the time of a preliminary hearing. But the point is that, while members of the Court have differed as to existence of the right to counsel in the contexts of some of the above cases, all of those cases have involved points of time at or after the initiation of adversary judicial criminal proceedings — whether by way of formal charge, preliminary hearing, indictment, information, or arraignment.

The initiation of judicial criminal proceedings is far from a mere formalism. It is the starting point of our whole system of adversary criminal justice. For it is only then that the government has committed itself to prosecute, and only then that the adverse positions of government and defendant have solidified. It is then that a defendant finds himself faced with the prosecutorial forces of organized society, and immersed in the intricacies of substantive and procedural criminal law. It is this point, therefore, that marks the commencement of the "criminal prosecutions" to which alone the explicit guarantees of the Sixth Amendment are applicable.

In this case we are asked to import into a routine police investigation an absolute constitutional guarantee historically and rationally applicable only after the onset of formal prosecutorial proceedings. We decline to do so.

What has been said is not to suggest that there may not be occasions during the course of a criminal investigation when the police do abuse identification procedures. Such abuses are not beyond the reach of the Constitution. As the Court pointed out in *Wade* itself, it is always necessary to "scrutinize any pretrial confrontation." The Due Process Clause of the Fifth and Fourteenth Amendments forbids a lineup that is unnecessarily suggestive and conducive to irreparable mistaken identification. Stovall v. Denno (1967).

Justice POWELL, concurring in the result.

As I would not extend the *Wade-Gilbert* per se exclusionary rule, I concur in the result reached by the Court.[3]

Justice BRENNAN, with whom Justice DOUGLAS and Justice MARSHALL join, dissenting.

[T]he Court's formulation of the controlling principle for pretrial confrontations is that "the principle of Powell v. Alabama and succeeding cases requires that we scrutinize any pretrial confrontation of the accused to determine whether the presence of his counsel is necessary to preserve the defendant's basic right to a fair trial as affected by his right meaningfully to

---

3. This is the entirety of Justice Powell's opinion. [Footnote by casebook authors.]

cross-examine the witnesses against him and to have effective assistance of counsel at the trial itself. It calls upon us to analyze whether potential substantial prejudice to defendant's rights inheres in the particular confrontation and the ability of counsel to help avoid that prejudice."

It was that constitutional principle that the Court applied in *Wade* to pretrial confrontations for identification purposes. The Court first met the Government's contention that a confrontation for identification is "a mere preparatory step in the gathering of the prosecution's evidence," much like the scientific examination of fingerprints and blood samples. The Court responded that in the latter instances "the accused has the opportunity for a meaningful confrontation of the Government's case at trial through the ordinary processes of cross-examination of the Government's expert witnesses and the presentation of the evidence of his own experts." The accused thus has no right to have counsel present at such examinations: "they are not critical stages since there is minimal risk that his counsel's absence at such stages might derogate from his right to a fair trial."

In contrast, the Court said, "the confrontation compelled by the State between the accused and the victim or witnesses to a crime to elicit identification evidence is peculiarly riddled with innumerable dangers and variable factors which might seriously, even crucially, derogate from a fair trial." Most importantly, "the accused's inability effectively to reconstruct at trial any unfairness that occurred at the lineup may deprive him of his only opportunity meaningfully to attack the credibility of the witness' courtroom identification."

While it should go without saying, it appears necessary, in view of the plurality opinion today, to re-emphasize that *Wade* did not require the presence of counsel at pretrial confrontations for identification purposes simply on the basis of an abstract consideration of the words "criminal prosecutions" in the Sixth Amendment. Counsel is required at those confrontations because "the dangers inherent in eyewitness identification and the suggestibility inherent in the context of the pretrial identification," mean that protection must be afforded to the "most basic right [of] a criminal defendant — his right to a fair trial at which the witnesses against him might be meaningfully cross-examined."

In view of *Wade*, it is plain, and the plurality today does not attempt to dispute it, that there inhere in a confrontation for identification conducted after arrest the identical hazards to a fair trial that inhere in such a confrontation conducted "after the onset of formal prosecutional proceedings." The plurality apparently considers an arrest, which for present purposes we must assume to be based upon probable cause, to be nothing more than part of "a routine police investigation," and thus not "the starting point of our whole system of adversary criminal justice." An arrest, according to the plurality, does not face the accused "with the prosecutorial forces of organized society," nor immerse him "in the intricacies of substantive and procedural criminal law." Those consequences ensue, says the plurality, only with "[t]he initiation of judicial criminal proceedings," "[f]or it is only then that the government has committed itself to prosecute, and only then that the adverse positions of government and defendant have solidified."

If these propositions do not amount to "mere formalism," it is difficult to know how to characterize them. An arrest evidences the belief of the police that the perpetrator of a crime has been caught. A post-arrest confrontation for identification is not "a mere preparatory step in the gathering of the prosecution's evidence." A primary, and frequently sole, purpose of the confrontation for identification at that stage is to accumulate proof to buttress the conclusion of the police that they have the offender in hand. The plurality offers no reason, and I can think of none, for concluding that a post-arrest confrontation for identification, unlike a post-charge confrontation, is not among those "critical confrontations of the accused by the prosecution at pretrial proceedings where the results might well settle the accused's fate and reduce the trial itself to a mere formality."

The highly suggestive form of confrontation employed in this case underscores the point. This showup was particularly fraught with the peril of mistaken identification. In the setting of a police station squad room where all present except petitioner and Bean were police officers, the danger was quite real that Shard's understandable resentment might lead him too readily to agree with the police that the pair under arrest, and the only persons exhibited to him, were indeed the robbers. It is hard to imagine a situation more clearly conveying the suggestion to the witness that the one presented is believed guilty by the police.

The State had no case without Shard's identification testimony, and safeguards against that consequence were therefore of critical importance. Shard's testimony itself demonstrates the necessity for such safeguards. On direct examination, Shard identified petitioner and Bean not as the alleged robbers on trial in the courtroom, but as the pair he saw at the police station. His testimony thus lends strong support to the observation, quoted by the Court in *Wade*, that "[i]t is a matter of common experience that, once a witness has picked out the accused at the line-up, he is not likely to go back on his word later on, so that in practice the issue of identity may (in the absence of other relevant evidence) for all practical purposes be determined there and then, before the trial."

The confrontation of a lineup cannot have a constitutional distinction based upon the lodging of a formal charge. Every reason set forth by the Supreme Court in *Wade* for the assistance of counsel post-indictment has equal or more impact when projected against a pre-indictment atmosphere.

Justice WHITE, dissenting.[4]

United States v. Wade (1967), and Gilbert v. California (1967), govern this case and compel reversal of the judgment below.

---

4. This is the entirety of Justice White's dissent. [Footnote by casebook authors.]

UNITED STATES v. ASH

413 U.S. 300 (1973)

Justice BLACKMUN delivered the opinion of the Court.

In this case the Court is called upon to decide whether the Sixth Amendment grants an accused the right to have counsel present whenever the Government conducts a post-indictment photographic display, containing a picture of the accused, for the purpose of allowing a witness to attempt an identification of the offender.

I

On the morning of August 26, 1965, a man with a stocking mask entered a bank in Washington, D.C., and began waving a pistol. He ordered an employee to hang up the telephone and instructed all others present not to move. Seconds later a second man, also wearing a stocking mask, entered the bank, scooped up money from tellers' drawers into a bag, and left. The gunman followed, and both men escaped through an alley. The robbery lasted three or four minutes.

A Government informer, Clarence McFarland, told authorities that he had discussed the robbery with Charles J. Ash, Jr., the respondent here. Acting on this information, an FBI agent, in February 1966, showed five black-and-white mug shots of Negro males of generally the same age, height, and weight, one of which was of Ash, to four witnesses. All four made uncertain identifications of Ash's picture. At this time Ash was not in custody and had not been charged. On April 1, 1966, an indictment was returned charging Ash and a codefendant, John L. Bailey, in five counts related to this bank robbery.

Trial was finally set for May 1968, almost three years after the crime. In preparing for trial, the prosecutor decided to use a photographic display to determine whether the witnesses he planned to call would be able to make in-court identifications. Shortly before the trial, an FBI agent and the prosecutor showed five color photographs to the four witnesses who previously had tentatively identified the black-and-white photograph of Ash. Three of the witnesses selected the picture of Ash, but one was unable to make any selection. None of the witnesses selected the picture of Bailey which was in the group. This post-indictment identification provides the basis for respondent Ash's claim that he was denied the right to counsel at a "critical stage" of the prosecution.[5]

---

5. Respondent Ash does not assert a right to counsel at the black-and-white photographic display in February 1966 because he recognizes that Kirby v. Illinois (1972) forecloses application of the Sixth Amendment to events before the initiation of adversary criminal proceedings. [Footnote by the Court.]

II

[T]he core purpose of the counsel guarantee was to assure "Assistance" at trial, when the accused was confronted with both the intricacies of the law and the advocacy of the public prosecutor. Later developments have led this Court to recognize that "Assistance" would be less than meaningful if it were limited to the formal trial itself.

This extension of the right to counsel to events before trial has resulted from changing patterns of criminal procedure and investigation that have tended to generate pretrial events that might appropriately be considered to be parts of the trial itself. At these newly emerging and significant events, the accused was confronted, just as at trial, by the procedural system, or by his expert adversary, or by both. In *Wade*, the Court explained the process of expanding the counsel guarantee to these confrontations: "When the Bill of Rights was adopted, there were no organized police forces as we know them today. The accused confronted the prosecutor and the witnesses against him, and the evidence was marshalled, largely at the trial itself. In contrast, today's law enforcement machinery involves critical confrontations of the accused by the prosecution at pretrial proceedings where the results might well settle the accused's fate and reduce the trial itself to a mere formality. In recognition of these realities of modern criminal prosecution, our cases have construed the Sixth Amendment guarantee to apply to 'critical' stages of the proceedings." The Court consistently has applied a historical interpretation of the guarantee, and has expanded the constitutional right to counsel only when new contexts appear presenting the same dangers that gave birth initially to the right itself.

Throughout this expansion of the counsel guarantee to trial-like confrontations, the function of the lawyer has remained essentially the same as his function at trial. In all cases considered by the Court, counsel has continued to act as a spokesman for, or advisor to, the accused. The accused's right to the "Assistance of Counsel" has meant just that, namely, the right of the accused to have counsel acting as his assistant.

The function of counsel in rendering "Assistance" continued at the lineup under consideration in *Wade* and its companion cases. Although the accused was not confronted there with legal questions, the lineup offered opportunities for prosecuting authorities to take advantage of the accused. Counsel was seen by the Court as being more sensitive to, and aware of, suggestive influences than the accused himself, and as better able to reconstruct the events at trial. Counsel present at lineup would be able to remove disabilities of the accused in precisely the same fashion that counsel compensated for the disabilities of the layman at trial. Thus, the Court mentioned that the accused's memory might be dimmed by "emotional tension," that the accused's credibility at trial would be diminished by his status as defendant, and that the accused might be unable to present his version effectively without giving up his privilege against compulsory self-incrimination. It was in order to compensate for these deficiencies that the Court found the need for the assistance of counsel.

This review of the history and expansion of the Sixth Amendment counsel guarantee demonstrates that the test utilized by the Court has called for examination of the event in order to determine whether the accused required aid in coping with legal problems or assistance in meeting his adversary.

III

We conclude that the dangers of mistaken identification, mentioned in *Wade*, [are not applicable in the context of photo identifications.] Although *Wade* did discuss possibilities for suggestion and the difficulty for reconstructing suggestivity, this discussion occurred only after the Court had concluded that the lineup constituted a trial-like confrontation, requiring the "Assistance of Counsel" to preserve the adversary process by compensating for advantages of the prosecuting authorities.

The structure of *Wade*, viewed in light of the careful limitation of the Court's language to "confrontations," makes it clear that lack of scientific precision and inability to reconstruct an event are not the tests for requiring counsel in the first instance. These are, instead, the tests to determine whether confrontation with counsel at trial can serve as a substitute for counsel at the pretrial confrontation. If accurate reconstruction is possible, the risks inherent in any confrontation still remain, but the opportunity to cure defects at trial causes the confrontation to cease to be "critical." The opinion of the Court even indicated that changes in procedure might cause a lineup to cease to be a "critical" confrontation.

IV

A substantial departure from the historical test would be necessary if the Sixth Amendment were interpreted to give Ash a right to counsel at the photographic identification in this case. Since the accused himself is not present at the time of the photographic display, and asserts no right to be present, no possibility arises that the accused might be misled by his lack of familiarity with the law or overpowered by his professional adversary. Similarly, the counsel guarantee would not be used to produce equality in a trial-like adversary confrontation. Rather, the guarantee was used by the Court of Appeals to produce confrontation at an event that previously was not analogous to an adversary trial.

Even if we were willing to view the counsel guarantee in broad terms as a generalized protection of the adversary process, we would be unwilling to go so far as to extend the right to a portion of the prosecutor's trial-preparation interviews with witnesses. Although photography is relatively new, the interviewing of witnesses before trial is a procedure that predates the Sixth Amendment. In England in the 16th and 17th centuries counsel regularly interviewed witnesses before trial. The traditional counterbalance in the American adversary system for these interviews arises from the equal ability of defense counsel to seek and interview witnesses himself.

That adversary mechanism remains as effective for a photographic display as for other parts of pretrial interviews. No greater limitations are placed on defense counsel in constructing displays, seeking witnesses, and conducting photographic identifications than those applicable to the prosecution. Selection of the picture of a person other than the accused, or the inability of a witness to make any selection, will be useful to the defense in precisely the same manner that the selection of a picture of the defendant would be useful to the prosecution. Although we do not suggest that equality of access to photographs removes all potential for abuse, it does remove any inequality in the adversary process itself and thereby fully satisfies the historical spirit of the Sixth Amendment's counsel guarantee.

The argument has been advanced that requiring counsel might compel the police to observe more scientific procedures or might encourage them to utilize corporeal rather than photographic displays. This Court has recognized that improved procedures can minimize the dangers of suggestion. Commentators have also proposed more accurate techniques.

Pretrial photographic identifications, however, are hardly unique in offering possibilities for the actions of the prosecutor unfairly to prejudice the accused. Evidence favorable to the accused may be withheld; testimony of witnesses may be manipulated; the results of laboratory tests may be contrived. In many ways the prosecutor, by accident or by design, may improperly subvert the trial. The primary safeguard against abuses of this kind is the ethical responsibility of the prosecutor, who, as so often has been said, may "strike hard blows" but not "foul ones." If that safeguard fails, review remains available under due process standards. These same safeguards apply to misuse of photographs.

We are not persuaded that the risks inherent in the use of photographic displays are so pernicious that an extraordinary system of safeguards is required. We hold, then, that the Sixth Amendment does not grant the right to counsel at photographic displays conducted by the Government for the purpose of allowing a witness to attempt an identification of the offender.

Justice STEWART, concurring in the judgment.

A photographic identification is quite different from a lineup, for there are substantially fewer possibilities of impermissible suggestion when photographs are used, and those unfair influences can be readily reconstructed at trial. It is true that the defendant's photograph may be markedly different from the others displayed, but this unfairness can be demonstrated at trial from an actual comparison of the photographs used or from the witness' description of the display. Similarly, it is possible that the photographs could be arranged in a suggestive manner, or that by comment or gesture the prosecuting authorities might single out the defendant's picture. But these are the kinds of overt influence that a witness can easily recount and that would serve to impeach the identification testimony. In short, there are few possibilities for unfair suggestiveness — and those rather blatant and easily reconstructed. Accordingly, an accused would not be foreclosed from an effective cross-examination of an identification witness simply because his counsel was not present at the photographic display. For this reason, a photographic display cannot fairly be considered a "critical stage" of the prosecution.

Justice BRENNAN, with whom Justice DOUGLAS and Justice MARSHALL join, dissenting.

The Court holds today that a pretrial display of photographs to the witnesses of a crime for the purpose of identifying the accused, unlike a lineup, does not constitute a "critical stage" of the prosecution at which the accused is constitutionally entitled to the presence of counsel. In my view, today's decision is wholly unsupportable in terms of such considerations as logic, consistency, and, indeed, fairness. As a result, I must reluctantly conclude that today's decision marks simply another step towards the complete evisceration of the fundamental constitutional principles established by this Court, only six years ago, in United States v. Wade (1967); Gilbert v. California (1967); and Stovall v. Denno (1967). I dissent.

In June 1967, this Court decided a trilogy of "lineup" cases which brought into sharp focus the problems of pretrial identification. In essence, those decisions held (1) that a pretrial lineup is a "critical stage" in the criminal process at which the accused is constitutionally entitled to the presence of counsel; (2) that evidence of an identification of the accused at such an uncounseled lineup is per se inadmissible; and (3) that evidence of a subsequent in-court identification of the accused is likewise inadmissible unless the Government can demonstrate by clear and convincing evidence that the in-court identification was based upon observations of the accused independent of the prior uncounseled lineup identification. The considerations relied upon by the Court in reaching these conclusions are clearly applicable to photographic as well as corporeal identifications.

As the Court of Appeals recognized, "the dangers of mistaken identification . . . set forth in *Wade* are applicable in large measure to photographic as well as corporeal identifications." To the extent that misidentification may be attributable to a witness' faulty memory or perception, or inadequate opportunity for detailed observation during the crime, the risks are obviously as great at a photographic display as at a lineup. Indeed, noting "the hazards of initial identification by photograph," we have expressly recognized that "a corporeal identification . . . is normally more accurate" than a photographic identification. Simmons v. United States (1968). Thus, in this sense at least, the dangers of misidentification are even greater at a photographic display than at a lineup.

Moreover, as in the lineup situation, the possibilities for impermissible suggestion in the context of a photographic display are manifold. Such suggestion, intentional or unintentional, may derive from three possible sources. First, the photographs themselves might tend to suggest which of the pictures is that of the suspect. For example, differences in age, pose, or other physical characteristics of the persons represented, and variations in the mounting, background, lighting, or markings of the photographs all might have the effect of singling out the accused.

Second, impermissible suggestion may inhere in the manner in which the photographs are displayed to the witness. The danger of misidentification is, of course, increased if the police display to the witness . . . the pictures of several persons among which the photograph of a single such individual recurs or is in some way emphasized. And, if the photographs are arranged in an asymmetrical pattern, or if they are displayed in a time sequence that tends to emphasize a particular photograph, any identification of the photograph which stands out from the rest is no more reliable than an identification of a single photograph, exhibited alone.

Third, gestures or comments of the prosecutor at the time of the display may lead an otherwise uncertain witness to select the "correct" photograph. For example, the prosecutor might "indicate to the witness that [he has] other evidence that one of the persons pictured committed the crime," and might even point to a particular photograph and ask whether the person pictured "looks familiar." More subtly, the prosecutor's inflection, facial expressions, physical motions, and myriad other almost imperceptible means of communication might tend, intentionally or unintentionally, to compromise the witness' objectivity. Thus, as is the case with lineups, "[i]mproper photographic identification procedures, . . . by exerting a suggestive influence upon the witnesses, can often lead to an erroneous identification. . . ." And "[r]egardless of how the initial misidentification comes about, the witness thereafter is apt to retain in his memory the image of the photograph rather than of the person actually seen. . . ." As a result, "the issue of identity may (in the absence of other relevant evidence) for all practical purposes be determined there and then, before the trial."

Moreover, as with lineups, the defense can "seldom reconstruct" at trial the mode and manner of photographic identification. For, although retention of the photographs may mitigate the dangers of misidentification due to the suggestiveness of the photographs themselves, it cannot in any sense reveal to defense counsel the more subtle, and therefore more dangerous, suggestiveness that might derive from the manner in which the photographs were displayed or any accompanying comments or gestures. Moreover, the accused cannot rely upon the witnesses themselves to expose these latter sources of suggestion, for the witnesses are not apt to be alert for conditions prejudicial to the suspect. And if they were, it would likely be of scant benefit to the suspect since the witnesses are hardly likely to be schooled in the detection of suggestive influences.

Finally, and unlike the lineup situation, the accused himself is not even present at the photographic identification, thereby reducing the likelihood that irregularities in the procedures will ever come to light.

Thus, the difficulties of reconstructing at trial an uncounseled photographic display are at least equal to, and possibly greater than, those involved in reconstructing an uncounseled lineup.

Ironically, the Court does not seriously challenge the proposition that presence of counsel at a pretrial photographic display is essential to preserve the accused's right to a fair trial on the issue of identification. Rather, in what I can only characterize a triumph of form over substance, the Court seeks to justify its result by engrafting a wholly unprecedented — and wholly unsupportable — limitation on the Sixth Amendment right of "the accused . . . to have the Assistance of Counsel for his defence." Although apparently conceding that the right to counsel attaches, not only at the trial itself, but at all "critical stages" of the prosecution, the Court holds today that, in order to be deemed "critical," the particular "stage of the prosecution" under consideration must, at the very least, involve the physical "presence of the accused," at a "trial-like confrontation" with the Government, at which the accused requires the "guiding hand of counsel." According to the Court a pretrial photographic identification does not, of course, meet these criteria.

But, contrary to the Court's assumption, this is merely one facet of the Sixth Amendment guarantee, and the decisions relied upon by the Court represent, not the boundaries of the right to counsel, but mere applications of a far broader and more reasoned understanding of the Sixth Amendment than that espoused today.

The fundamental premise underlying all of this Court's decisions holding the right to counsel applicable at "critical" pretrial proceedings, is that a "stage" of the prosecution must be deemed "critical" for the purposes of the Sixth Amendment if it is one at which the presence of counsel is necessary "to protect the fairness of the trial itself." This established conception of the Sixth Amendment guarantee is, of course, in no sense dependent upon the physical "presence of the accused," at a "trial-like confrontation" with the Government, at which the accused requires the "guiding hand of counsel."

There is something ironic about the Court's conclusion today that a pretrial lineup identification is a "critical stage" of the prosecution because counsel's presence can help to compensate for the accused's deficiencies as an observer, but that a pretrial photographic identification is not a "critical stage" of the prosecution because the accused is not able to observe at all. In my view, there simply is no meaningful difference, in terms of the need for attendance of counsel, between corporeal and photographic identifications. And applying established and well-reasoned Sixth Amendment principles, I can only conclude that a pretrial photographic display, like a pretrial lineup, is a "critical stage" of the prosecution at which the accused is constitutionally entitled to the presence of counsel.

B. DUE PROCESS PROTECTION FOR IDENTIFICATION PROCEDURES

1. *Unnecessarily Suggestive Identification Procedures by Police Violate Due Process*

The other protection for criminal defendants with regard to identification is that the Supreme Court has held that unnecessarily suggestive identification procedures violate due process. This was initially the holding in Stovall v. Denno, 388 U.S. 293 (1967). It was the third case decided on the same day as United States v. Wade (1967) and California v. Gilbert (1967). The specific issue in *Stovall* was whether *Wade* and *Gilbert* were to be applied retroactively to individuals who were convicted prior to these decisions. The Supreme Court held that *Wade* and *Gilbert* do not apply retroactively, that unnecessarily suggestive identification procedures violate due process, but that the identification procedure in this case was necessary under the circumstances.

Justice Brennan, writing for the Court, described the identification procedure:

> Dr. Paul Behrendt was stabbed to death in the kitchen of his home in Garden City, Long Island, about midnight August 23, 1961. Dr. Behrendt's wife, also a physician, had followed her husband to the kitchen and jumped at the assailant. He knocked her to the floor and stabbed her 11 times. The police found a shirt on the kitchen floor and keys in a pocket which they traced to petitioner. They arrested him on the afternoon of August 24. An arraignment was promptly held but was postponed until petitioner could retain counsel.
>
> Mrs. Behrendt was hospitalized for major surgery to save her life. The police, without affording petitioner time to retain counsel, arranged with her surgeon to permit them to bring petitioner to her hospital room about noon of August 25, the day after the surgery. Petitioner was handcuffed to one of five police officers who, with two members of the staff of the District Attorney, brought him to the hospital room. Petitioner was the only Negro in the room. Mrs. Behrendt identified him from her hospital bed after being asked by an officer whether he "was the man" and after petitioner repeated at the direction of an officer a "few words for voice identification." None of the witnesses could recall the words that were used. Mrs. Behrendt and the officers testified at the trial to her identification of the petitioner in the hospital room, and she also made an in-court identification of petitioner in the courtroom. Petitioner was convicted and sentenced to death.

Nonetheless, the Court affirmed the conviction and the sentence. The Court stated, "We hold that *Wade* and *Gilbert* affect only those cases and all future cases which involve confrontations for identification purposes conducted in the absence of counsel after this date. The rulings of *Wade* and *Gilbert* are therefore inapplicable in the present case. We think also that on the facts of this case petitioner was not deprived of due process of law in violation of the Fourteenth Amendment."

After holding that *Wade* and *Gilbert* do not apply retroactively, the Court said that apart from the right to counsel, unnecessarily suggestive identification procedures violate due process. The Court stated:

> We turn now to the question whether petitioner, although not entitled to the application of *Wade* and *Gilbert* to his case, is entitled to relief on his claim that in any event the confrontation conducted in this case was so unnecessarily suggestive and conducive to irreparable mistaken identification that he was denied due process of law. This is a recognized ground of attack upon a conviction independent of any right to counsel claim. The practice of showing suspects singly to persons for the purpose of identification, and not as part of a lineup, has been widely condemned. However, a claimed violation of due process of law in the conduct of a confrontation depends on the totality of the circumstances surrounding it, and the record in the present case reveals that the showing of Stovall to Mrs. Behrendt in an immediate hospital confrontation was imperative.
>
> Here was the only person in the world who could possibly exonerate Stovall. Her words, and only her words, "He is not the man" could have resulted in freedom for Stovall. The hospital was not far distant from the courthouse and jail. No one knew how long Mrs. Behrendt might live. Faced with the responsibility of identifying the attacker, with the need for immediate action and with the knowledge that Mrs. Behrendt could not visit the jail, the police followed the only feasible procedure and took Stovall to the hospital room. Under these circumstances, the usual police station line-up, which Stovall now argues he should have had, was out of the question.[6]

Although the Court has said since *Stovall* that unnecessarily suggestive identifications violate due process, there is only one Supreme Court decision that has overturned a conviction on this basis.

FOSTER v. CALIFORNIA
394 U.S. 440 (1969)

Justice FORTAS delivered the opinion of the Court.

Petitioner was charged by information with the armed robbery of a Western Union office in violation of California Penal Code. The day after the robbery one of the robbers, Clay, surrendered to the police and implicated Foster and Grice. Allegedly, Foster and Clay had entered the office while Grice waited in a car. Foster and Grice were tried together. Grice was

---

6. Justice Douglas dissented on the grounds that *Wade* and *Gilbert* should be applied retroactively. Justice Fortas dissented on the ground that the identification process violated due process. Justice Black dissented from the conclusion that unnecessarily suggestive identification procedures violate due process. He wrote:

> But even if the Due Process Clause could possibly be construed as giving such latitudinarian powers to the Court, I would still think the Court goes too far in holding that the courts can look at the particular circumstances or each identification lineup to determine at large whether they are too "suggestive and conducive to irreparable mistaken identification" to be constitutional. That result is to freeze as constitutional or as unconstitutional the circumstances of each case, giving the States and the Federal Government no permanent constitutional standards.

acquitted. Foster was convicted. We granted certiorari, limited to the question whether the conduct of the police lineup resulted in a violation of petitioner's constitutional rights.

Except for the robbers themselves, the only witness to the crime was Joseph David, the late-night manager of the Western Union office. After Foster had been arrested, David was called to the police station to view a lineup. There were three men in the lineup. One was petitioner. He is a tall man — close to six feet in height. The other two men were short — five feet, five or six inches. Petitioner wore a leather jacket which David said was similar to the one he had seen underneath the coveralls worn by the robber. After seeing this lineup, David could not positively identify petitioner as the robber. He "thought" he was the man, but he was not sure. David then asked to speak to petitioner, and petitioner was brought into an office and sat across from David at a table. Except for prosecuting officials there was no one else in the room. Even after this one-to-one confrontation David still was uncertain whether petitioner was one of the robbers: "truthfully — I was not sure," he testified at trial. A week or 10 days later, the police arranged for David to view a second lineup. There were five men in that lineup. Petitioner was the only person in the second lineup who had appeared in the first lineup. This time David was "convinced" petitioner was the man.

At trial, David testified to his identification of petitioner in the lineups, as summarized above. He also repeated his identification of petitioner in the courtroom. The only other evidence against petitioner which concerned the particular robbery with which he was charged was the testimony of the alleged accomplice Clay.[7]

In United States v. Wade (1967), and Gilbert v. California (1967), this Court held that because of the possibility of unfairness to the accused in the way a lineup is conducted, a lineup is a "critical stage" in the prosecution, at which the accused must be given the opportunity to be represented by counsel. That holding does not, however, apply to petitioner's case, for the lineups in which he appeared occurred before June 12, 1967. Stovall v. Denno (1967). But in declaring the rule of *Wade* and *Gilbert* to be applicable only to lineups conducted after those cases were decided, we recognized that, judged by the "totality of the circumstances," the conduct of identification procedures may be "so unnecessarily suggestive and conducive to irreparable mistaken identification" as to be a denial of due process of law.

Judged by that standard, this case presents a compelling example of unfair lineup procedures. In the first lineup arranged by the police, petitioner stood out from the other two men by the contrast of his height and by the fact that he was wearing a leather jacket similar to that worn by the robber. When this did not lead to positive identification, the police permitted a one-to-one confrontation between petitioner and the witness. This

---

7. California law requires that an accomplice's testimony be corroborated. California Penal Code §1111. There was also evidence that Foster had been convicted for a similar robbery committed six years before. [Footnote by the Court.]

Court pointed out in *Stovall* that "[t]he practice of showing suspects singly to persons for the purpose of identification, and not as part of a lineup, has been widely condemned." Even after this the witness' identification of petitioner was tentative. So some days later another lineup was arranged. Petitioner was the only person in this lineup who had also participated in the first lineup. This finally produced a definite identification.

The suggestive elements in this identification procedure made it all but inevitable that David would identify petitioner whether or not he was in fact "the man." In effect, the police repeatedly said to the witness, "This is the man." This procedure so undermined the reliability of the eyewitness identification as to violate due process.

Justice BLACK, dissenting.

[M]y objection [is] to the Court's basic holding that evidence can be ruled constitutionally inadmissible whenever it results from identification procedures that the Court considers to be "unnecessarily suggestive and conducive to irreparable mistaken identification." One of the proudest achievements of this country's Founders was that they had eternally guaranteed a trial by jury in criminal cases, at least until the Constitution they wrote had been amended in the manner they prescribed. Of course it is an incontestable fact in our judicial history that the jury is the sole tribunal to weigh and determine facts. That means that the jury must, if we keep faith with the Constitution, be allowed to hear eyewitnesses and decide for itself whether it can recognize the truth and whether they are telling the truth. It means that the jury must be allowed to decide for itself whether the darkness of the night, the weakness of a witness' eyesight, or any other factor impaired the witness' ability to make an accurate identification. To take that power away from the jury is to rob it of the responsibility to perform the precise functions the Founders most wanted it to perform. And certainly a Constitution written to preserve this indispensable, unerodible core of our system for trying criminal cases would not have included, hidden among its provisions, a slumbering sleeper granting the judges license to destroy trial by jury in whole or in part.

This brings me to the constitutional theory relied upon by the Court to justify its invading the constitutional right of jury trial. The Court here holds that: "[J]udged by the 'totality of the circumstances,' the conduct of identification procedures may be 'so unnecessarily suggestive and conducive to irreparable mistaken identification' as to be a denial of due process of law." The Constitution sets up its own standards of unfairness in criminal trials in the Fourth, Fifth, and Sixth Amendments, among other provisions of the Constitution. Many of these provisions relate to evidence and its use in criminal cases.

It has become fashionable to talk of the Court's power to hold governmental laws and practices unconstitutional whenever this Court believes them to be "unfair," contrary to basic standards of decency, implicit in ordered liberty, or offensive to "those canons of decency and fairness which express the notions of justice of English-speaking peoples." All of these different general and indefinable words or phrases are the fruit of the same, what I consider to be poisonous, tree, namely, the doctrine that this Court has power to make its own ideas of fairness, decency, and so forth, enforceable as though they were constitutional precepts.

2. Limits on the Ability of Courts to Find That Identification Procedures Violate Due Process

As mentioned above, *Foster* is the only case in which the Supreme Court has found that an identification procedure violates due process. The Court has rejected due process challenges to identification procedures on three major grounds. First, the Court has found that highly suggestive procedures did not violate due process because they were necessary. In *Stovall*, above, the Court affirmed a conviction based on an identification in which the suspect was brought to the victim in her hospital room and the suspect was hand-cuffed to a police officer and was the only African American man in the room. The Court explained that the victim was critically injured, and there was not time to arrange a lineup. Necessity also played a key role in Simmons v. United States, below.

Second, the Supreme Court has been willing to allow convictions based on suggestive identifications if the witness has an "independent source for the identification," such as other contacts with the suspect besides the police identification procedure. Neil v. Biggers, below, allowed a suggestive identification procedure on this basis.

Finally, and most importantly, the Court has rejected due process challenges to suggestive identification procedures if it concludes that there are sufficient indications of reliability. This is certainly expressed in Simmons v. United States and Neil v. Biggers, but it is most clearly expressed in the final case below, Manson v. Brathwaite.

In reading these three cases, it is important to see that these factors taken together make it difficult to challenge an identification on due process grounds. Again, the crucial question is whether this is appropriate deference to a necessary police procedure or whether it fails to provide adequate protection against a police procedure that often leads to the conviction of innocent people.

SIMMONS v. UNITED STATES
390 U.S. 377 (1968)

Justice HARLAN delivered the opinion of the Court.

This case presents issues arising out of the petitioners' trial and conviction in the United States District Court for the Northern District of Illinois for the armed robbery of a federally insured savings and loan association.

The evidence at trial showed that at about 1:45 P.M. on February 27, 1964, two men entered a Chicago savings and loan association. One of them pointed a gun at a teller and ordered her to put money into a sack which the gunman supplied. The men remained in the bank about five minutes. After they left, a bank employee rushed to the street and saw one of the men sitting on the passenger side of a departing white 1960 Thunderbird automobile with a large scrape on the right door. Within an hour police located in the vicinity a car matching this description. They discovered that it belonged to a Mrs. Rey, sister-in-law of petitioner Simmons. She told the police that she had loaned the car for the afternoon to her brother, William Andrews.

At about 5:15 P.M. the same day, two FBI agents came to the house of Mrs. Mahon, Andrews' mother, about half a block from the place where the car was then parked. The agents had no warrant, and at trial it was disputed whether Mrs. Mahon gave them permission to search the house. They did search, and in the basement they found two suitcases, of which Mrs. Mahon disclaimed any knowledge. One suitcase contained, among other items, a gun holster, a sack similar to the one used in the robbery, and several coin cards and bill wrappers from the bank which had been robbed.

The following morning the FBI obtained from another of Andrews' sisters some snapshots of Andrews and of petitioner Simmons, who was said by the sister to have been with Andrews the previous afternoon. These snapshots were shown to the five bank employees who had witnessed the robbery. Each witness identified pictures of Simmons as representing one of the robbers. A week or two later, three of these employees identified photographs of petitioner Garrett as depicting the other robber, the other two witnesses stating that they did not have a clear view of the second robber.

During the trial, all five bank employee witnesses identified Simmons as one of the robbers. Three of them identified Garrett as the second robber, the other two testifying that they did not get a good look at the second robber. The jury found Simmons and Garrett, as well as Andrews, guilty as charged.

The facts as to the identification claim are these. As has been noted previously, FBI agents on the day following the robbery obtained from Andrews' sister a number of snapshots of Andrews and Simmons. There seem to have been at least six of these pictures, consisting mostly of group photographs of Andrews, Simmons, and others. Later the same day, these were shown to the five bank employees who had witnessed the robbery at their place of work, the photographs being exhibited to each employee separately. Each of the five employees identified Simmons from the photographs. At later dates, some of these witnesses were again interviewed by the FBI and shown indeterminate numbers of pictures. Again, all identified Simmons. At trial, the Government did not introduce any of the photographs, but relied upon in-court identification by the five eyewitnesses, each of whom swore that Simmons was one of the robbers.

Simmons, however, does not contend that he was entitled to counsel at the time the pictures were shown to the witnesses. Rather, he asserts simply that in the circumstances the identification procedure was so unduly prejudicial as fatally to taint his conviction. This is a claim which must be evaluated in light of the totality of surrounding circumstances. See Stovall v. Denno (1967). Viewed in that context, we find the claim untenable.

It must be recognized that improper employment of photographs by police may sometimes cause witnesses to err in identifying criminals. A witness may have obtained only a brief glimpse of a criminal, or may have seen him under poor conditions. Even if the police subsequently follow the most correct photographic identification procedures and show him the pictures of a number of individuals without indicating whom they suspect, there is some danger that the witness may make an incorrect identification. This danger will be increased if the police display to the witness only the picture of a single individual who generally resembles the person he saw, or if they show him the pictures of several persons among which the photograph of a single such individual recurs or is in some way emphasized. The chance of misidentification is also heightened if the police indicate to the witness that they have other evidence that one of the persons pictured committed the crime. Regardless of how the initial misidentification comes about, the witness thereafter is apt to retain in his memory the image of the photograph rather than of the person actually seen, reducing the trustworthiness of subsequent lineup or courtroom identification.

Despite the hazards of initial identification by photograph, this procedure has been used widely and effectively in criminal law enforcement, from the standpoint both of apprehending offenders and of sparing innocent suspects the ignominy of arrest by allowing eyewitnesses to exonerate them through scrutiny of photographs. The danger that use of the technique may result in convictions based on misidentification may be substantially lessened by a course of cross-examination at trial which exposes to the jury the method's potential for error. We are unwilling to prohibit its employment, either in the exercise of our supervisory power or, still less, as a matter of constitutional requirement. Instead, we hold that each case must be considered on its own facts, and that convictions based on eyewitness identification at trial following a pretrial identification by photograph will be set aside on that ground only if the photographic identification procedure was so impermissibly suggestive as to give rise to a very substantial likelihood of irreparable misidentification.

Applying the standard to this case, we conclude that petitioner Simmons' claim on this score must fail. In the first place, it is not suggested that it was unnecessary for the FBI to resort to photographic identification in this instance. A serious felony had been committed. The perpetrators were still at large. The inconclusive clues which law enforcement officials possessed led to Andrews and Simmons. It was essential for the FBI agents swiftly to determine whether they were on the right track, so that they could properly deploy their forces in Chicago and, if necessary, alert officials in other cities. The justification for this method of procedure was hardly less compelling than that which we found to justify the "one-man lineup" in Stovall v. Denno.

In the second place, there was in the circumstances of this case little chance that the procedure utilized led to misidentification of Simmons. The robbery took place in the afternoon in a well-lighted bank. The robbers wore no masks. Five bank employees had been able to see the robber later identified as Simmons for periods ranging up to five minutes. Those witnesses were shown the photographs only a day later, while their memories were still fresh. At least six photographs were displayed to each witness. Apparently, these consisted primarily of group photographs, with Simmons and Andrews each appearing several times in the series. Each witness was alone when he or she saw the photographs. There is no evidence to indicate that the witnesses were told anything about the progress of the investigation, or that the FBI agents in any other way suggested which persons in the pictures were under suspicion.

Under these conditions, all five eyewitnesses identified Simmons as one of the robbers. None identified Andrews, who apparently was as prominent in the photographs as Simmons. These initial identifications were confirmed by all five witnesses in subsequent viewings of photographs and at trial, where each witness identified Simmons in person. Notwithstanding cross-examination, none of the witnesses displayed any doubt about their respective identifications of Simmons. Taken together, these circumstances leave little room for doubt that the identification of Simmons was correct, even though the identification procedure employed may have in some respects fallen short of the ideal. We hold that in the factual surroundings of this case the identification procedure used was not such as to deny Simmons due process of law or to call for reversal under our supervisory authority.

NEIL v. BIGGERS
409 U.S. 188 (1972)

Justice POWELL delivered the opinion of the Court.

In 1965, after a jury trial in a Tennessee court, respondent was convicted of rape and was sentenced to 20 years' imprisonment. The State's evidence consisted in part of testimony concerning a station-house identification of respondent by the victim.

We proceed, then, to consider respondent's due process claim. As the claim turns upon the facts, we must first review the relevant testimony at the jury trial and at the habeas corpus hearing regarding the rape and the identification. The victim testified at trial that on the evening of January 22, 1965, a youth with a butcher knife grabbed her in the doorway to her kitchen:

A. [H]e grabbed me from behind, and grappled-twisted me on the floor. Threw me down on the floor.
Q. And there was no light in that kitchen?

A.   Not in the kitchen.
Q.   So you couldn't have seen him then?
A.   Yes, I could see him, when I looked up in his face.
Q.   In the dark?
A.   He was right in the doorway—it was enough light from the bedroom shining through. Yes, I could see who he was.
Q.   You could see? No light? And you could see him and know him then?
A.   Yes.

When the victim screamed, her 12-year-old daughter came out of her bedroom and also began to scream. The assailant directed the victim to "tell her (the daughter) to shut up, or I'll kill you both." She did so, and was then walked at knifepoint about two blocks along a railroad track, taken into a woods, and raped there. She testified that "the moon was shining brightly, full moon." After the rape, the assailant ran off, and she returned home, the whole incident having taken between 15 minutes and half an hour.

She then gave the police what the Federal District Court characterized as "only a very general description," describing him as "being fat and flabby with smooth skin, bushy hair and a youthful voice." Additionally, though not mentioned by the District Court, she testified at the habeas corpus hearing that she had described her assailant as being between 16 and 18 years old and between five feet ten inches and six feet tall, as weighing between 180 and 200 pounds, and as having a dark brown complexion. This testimony was substantially corroborated by that of a police officer who was testifying from his notes.

On several occasions over the course of the next seven months, she viewed suspects in her home or at the police station, some in lineups and others in showups, and was shown between 30 and 40 photographs. She told the police that a man pictured in one of the photographs had features similar to those of her assailant, but identified none of the suspects. On August 17, the police called her to the station to view respondent, who was being detained on another charge. In an effort to construct a suitable lineup, the police checked the city jail and the city juvenile home. Finding no one at either place fitting respondent's unusual physical description, they conducted a showup instead.

The showup itself consisted of two detectives walking respondent past the victim. At the victim's request, the police directed respondent to say "shut up or I'll kill you." The testimony at trial was not altogether clear as to whether the victim first identified him and then asked that he repeat the words or made her identification after he had spoken. In any event, the victim testified that she had "no doubt" about her identification. At the habeas corpus hearing, she elaborated in response to questioning.

We must decide whether, as the courts below held, this identification and the circumstances surrounding it failed to comport with due process requirements. Some general guidelines emerge from [the prior] cases as to the relationship between suggestiveness and misidentification. It is, first of all, apparent that the primary evil to be avoided is "a very substantial likelihood of irreparable misidentification." While the phrase was coined as a standard for determining whether an in-court identification would be admissible in the wake of a suggestive out-of-court identification, with the deletion of "irreparable" it serves equally well as a standard for the admissibility of testimony concerning the out-of-court identification itself. It is the likelihood of misidentification which violates a defendant's right to due process, and it is this which was the basis of the exclusion of evidence in *Foster*. Suggestive confrontations are disapproved because they increase the likelihood of misidentification, and unnecessarily suggestive ones are condemned for the further reason that the increased chance of misidentification is gratuitous. But as *Stovall* makes clear, the admission of evidence of a showup without more does not violate due process.

We turn, then, to the central question, whether under the "totality of the circumstances" the identification was reliable even though the confrontation procedure was suggestive. As indicated by our cases, the factors to be considered in evaluating the likelihood of misidentification include the opportunity of the witness to view the criminal at the time of the crime, the witness' degree of attention, the accuracy of the witness' prior description of the criminal, the level of certainty demonstrated by the witness at the confrontation, and the length of time between the crime and the confrontation. Applying these factors, we disagree with the District Court's conclusion [overturning the conviction].

In part, we think the District Court focused unduly on the relative reliability of a lineup as opposed to a showup, the issue on which expert testimony was taken at the evidentiary hearing. It must be kept in mind also that the trial was conducted before *Stovall* and that therefore the incentive was lacking for the parties to make a record at trial of facts corroborating or undermining the identification. The testimony was addressed to the jury, and the jury apparently found the identification reliable.

We find that the District Court's conclusions on the critical facts are unsupported by the record and clearly erroneous. The victim spent a considerable period of time with her assailant, up to half an hour. She was with him under adequate artificial light in her house and under a full moon outdoors, and at least twice, once in the house and later in the woods, faced him directly and intimately. She was no casual observer, but rather the victim of one of the most personally humiliating of all crimes. Her description to the police, which included the assailant's approximate age, height, weight, complexion, skin texture, build, and voice, might not have satisfied Proust but was more than ordinarily thorough. She had "no doubt" that respondent was the person who raped her. In the nature of the crime, there are rarely witnesses to a rape other than the victim, who often has a limited opportunity of observation. The victim here, a practical nurse by profession, had an unusual opportunity to observe and identify her assailant. She testified at the habeas corpus hearing that there was something about his face "I don't think I could ever forget."

There was, to be sure, a lapse of seven months between the rape and the confrontation. This would be a seriously negative factor in most cases. Here, however, the testimony is undisputed that the victim made no previous identification at any of the showups, lineups, or photographic showings. Her record for reliability was thus a good one, as she had previously resisted whatever suggestiveness inheres in a showup. Weighing all the factors, we find no substantial likelihood of misidentification. The evidence was properly allowed to go to the jury.

Justice BRENNAN, with whom Justice DOUGLAS and Justice STEWART join, dissenting in part.

Regrettably, the Court addresses the merits and delves into the factual background of the case to reverse the District Court's finding, upheld by the Court of Appeals, that under the "totality of the circumstances," the pre-*Stovall* showup was so impermissibly suggestive as to give rise to a substantial likelihood of misidentification. This is an unjustified departure from our long-established practice not to reverse findings of fact concurred in by two lower courts unless shown to be clearly erroneous.

As the Court recognizes, a pre-*Stovall* identification obtained as a result of an unnecessarily suggestive showup may still be introduced in evidence if, under the "totality of the circumstances," the identification retains strong indicia of reliability. After an extensive hearing and careful review of the state court record, however, the District Court found that, under the circumstances of this case, there existed an intolerable risk of misidentification. Moreover, in making this determination, the court specifically found that "the complaining witness did not get an opportunity to obtain a good view of the suspect during the commission of the crime," "the show-up confrontation was not conducted near the time of the alleged crime, but, rather, some seven months after its commission," and the complaining witness was unable to give "a good physical description of her assailant" to the police. The Court of Appeals, which conducted its own review of the record, upheld the District Court's findings in their entirety.

The Court argues further, however, that the rule is irrelevant here because, in its view, "the dispute between the parties is not so much over the elemental facts as over the constitutional significance to be attached to them." I cannot agree. Even a cursory examination of the Court's opinion reveals that its concern is not limited solely to the proper application of legal principles but, rather, extends to an essentially de novo inquiry into such "elemental facts" as the nature of the victim's opportunity to observe the assailant and the type of description the victim gave the police at the time of the crime. And although we might reasonably disagree with the lower courts' findings as to such matters, the "two-court" rule wisely inhibits us from cavalierly substituting our own view of the facts simply because we might adopt a different construction of the evidence or resolve the ambiguities differently. On the contrary, these findings are "final here in the absence of very exceptional showing of error." The record before us is simply not susceptible of such a showing and, indeed, the petitioner does not argue otherwise.

MANSON v. BRATHWAITE
432 U.S. 98 (1977)

Justice BLACKMUN delivered the opinion of the Court.

This case presents the issue as to whether the Due Process Clause of the Fourteenth Amendment compels the exclusion, in a state criminal trial, apart from any consideration of reliability, of pretrial identification evidence obtained by a police procedure that was both suggestive and unnecessary.

I

Jimmy D. Glover, a full-time trooper of the Connecticut State Police, in 1970 was assigned to the Narcotics Division in an undercover capacity. On May 5 of that year, about 7:45 P.M., e.d.t., and while there was still daylight, Glover and Henry Alton Brown, an informant, went to an apartment building at 201 Westland, in Hartford, for the purpose of purchasing narcotics from "Dickie Boy" Cicero, a known narcotics dealer. Cicero, it was thought, lived on the third floor of that apartment building. Glover and Brown entered the building, observed by back-up Officers D'Onofrio and Gaffey, and proceeded by stairs to the third floor. Glover knocked at the door of one of the two apartments served by the stairway. The area was illuminated by natural light from a window in the third floor hallway. The door was opened 12 to 18 inches in response to the knock. Glover observed a man standing at the door and, behind him, a woman. Brown identified himself. Glover then asked for "two things" of narcotics. The man at the door held out his hand, and Glover gave him two $10 bills. The door closed. Soon the man returned and handed Glover two glassine bags. While the door was open, Glover stood within two feet of the person from whom he made the purchase and observed his face. Five to seven minutes elapsed from the time the door first opened until it closed the second time.

Glover and Brown then left the building. This was about eight minutes after their arrival. Glover drove to headquarters where he described the seller to D'Onofrio and Gaffey. Glover at that time did not know the identity of the seller. He described him as being "a colored man, approximately five feet eleven inches tall, dark complexion, black hair, short Afro style, and having high cheekbones, and of heavy build. He was wearing at the time blue pants and a plaid shirt." D'Onofrio, suspecting from this description that respondent might be the seller, obtained a photograph of respondent from the Records Division of the Hartford Police Department. He left it at Glover's office. D'Onofrio was not acquainted with respondent personally but did know him by sight and had seen him "[s]everal times" prior to May 5.

Glover, when alone, viewed the photograph for the first time upon his return to headquarters on May 7; he identified the person shown as the one from whom he had purchased the narcotics.

The toxicological report on the contents of the glassine bags revealed the presence of heroin. The report was dated July 16, 1970.

Respondent was arrested on July 27 while visiting at the apartment of a Mrs. Ramsey on the third floor of 201 Westland. This was the apartment at which the narcotics sale had taken place on May 5.

Respondent was charged, in a two-count information, with possession and sale of heroin, in violation of Conn.Gen.Stat. At his trial in January 1971, the photograph from which Glover had identified respondent was received in evidence without objection on the part of the defense. Glover also testified that, although he had not seen respondent in the eight months that had elapsed since the sale, "there [was] no doubt whatsoever" in his mind that the person shown on the photograph was respondent. Glover also made a positive in-court identification without objection. No explanation was offered by the prosecution for the failure to utilize a photographic array or to conduct a lineup.

The jury found respondent guilty on both counts of the information. He received a sentence of not less than six nor more than nine years.

[II]

In the present case the District Court observed that the "sole evidence tying Brathwaite to the possession and sale of the heroin consisted in his identifications by the police undercover agent, Jimmy Glover." On the constitutional issue, the court stated that the first inquiry was whether the police used an impermissibly suggestive procedure in obtaining the out-of-court identification. If so, the second inquiry is whether, under all the circumstances, that suggestive procedure gave rise to a substantial likelihood of irreparable misidentification.

Petitioner at the outset acknowledges that "the procedure in the instant case was suggestive (because only one photograph was used) and unnecessary" (because there was no emergency or exigent circumstance). The respondent, in agreement with the Court of Appeals, proposes a per se rule of exclusion that he claims is dictated by the demands of the Fourteenth Amendment's guarantee of due process. He rightly observes that this is the first case in which this Court has had occasion to rule upon strictly post-*Stovall* out-of-court identification evidence of the challenged kind.

There are, of course, several interests to be considered and taken into account. The driving force behind United States v. Wade (1967), Gilbert v. California (1967), and Stovall, all decided on the same day, was the Court's concern with the problems of eyewitness identification. Usually the witness must testify about an encounter with a total stranger under circumstances of emergency or emotional stress. The witness' recollection of the stranger can be distorted easily by the circumstances or by later actions of the police. Thus, *Wade* and its companion cases reflect the concern that the jury not hear eyewitness testimony unless that evidence has aspects of reliability. It must be observed that both approaches before us are responsive to this concern. The per se rule, however, goes too far since its application automatically and peremptorily, and without consideration of alleviating factors, keeps evidence from the jury that is reliable and relevant.

The second factor is deterrence. Although the per se approach has the more significant deterrent effect, the totality approach also has an influence on police behavior. The police will guard against unnecessarily suggestive procedures under the totality rule, as well as the per se one, for fear that their actions will lead to the exclusion of identifications as unreliable.

The third factor is the effect on the administration of justice. Here the per se approach suffers serious drawbacks. Since it denies the trier reliable evidence, it may result, on occasion, in the guilty going free. Also, because of its rigidity, the per se approach may make error by the trial judge more likely than the totality approach. And in those cases in which the admission of identification evidence is error under the per se approach but not under the totality approach — cases in which the identification is reliable despite an unnecessarily suggestive identification — procedure reversal is a Draconian sanction. Certainly, inflexible rules of exclusion that may frustrate rather than promote justice have not been viewed recently by this Court with unlimited enthusiasm.

The standard, after all, is that of fairness as required by the Due Process Clause of the Fourteenth Amendment. *Stovall,* with its reference to "the totality of the circumstances," and *Biggers,* with its continuing stress on the same totality, did not, singly or together, establish a strict exclusionary rule or new standard of due process.

We therefore conclude that reliability is the linchpin in determining the admissibility of identification testimony for both pre- and post-*Stovall* confrontations. The factors to be considered are set out in *Biggers.* These include the opportunity of the witness to view the criminal at the time of the crime, the witness' degree of attention, the accuracy of his prior description of the criminal, the level of certainty demonstrated at the confrontation, and the time between the crime and the confrontation. Against these factors is to be weighed the corrupting effect of the suggestive identification itself.

[III]

We turn, then, to the facts of this case and apply the analysis:

1. The opportunity to view. Glover testified that for two to three minutes he stood at the apartment door, within two feet of the respondent. The door opened twice, and each time the man stood at the door. The moments passed, the conversation took place, and payment was made. Glover looked directly at his vendor. It was near sunset, to be sure, but the sun had not yet set, so it was not dark or even dusk or twilight. Natural light from outside

entered the hallway through a window. There was natural light, as well, from inside the apartment.

2. The degree of attention. Glover was not a casual or passing observer, as is so often the case with eyewitness identification. Trooper Glover was a trained police officer on duty and specialized and dangerous duty when he called at the third floor of 201 Westland in Hartford on May 5, 1970. Glover himself was a Negro and unlikely to perceive only general features of "hundreds of Hartford black males." It is true that Glover's duty was that of ferreting out narcotics offenders and that he would be expected in his work to produce results. But it is also true that, as a specially trained, assigned, and experienced officer, he could be expected to pay scrupulous attention to detail, for he knew that subsequently he would have to find and arrest his vendor. In addition, he knew that his claimed observations would be subject later to close scrutiny and examination at any trial.

3. The accuracy of the description. Glover's description was given to D'Onofrio within minutes after the transaction. It included the vendor's race, his height, his build, the color and style of his hair, and the high cheekbone facial feature. It also included clothing the vendor wore. No claim has been made that respondent did not possess the physical characteristics so described. D'Onofrio reacted positively at once. Two days later, when Glover was alone, he viewed the photograph D'Onofrio produced and identified its subject as the narcotics seller.

4. The witness' level of certainty. There is no dispute that the photograph in question was that of respondent. Glover, in response to a question whether the photograph was that of the person from whom he made the purchase, testified: "There is no question whatsoever." This positive assurance was repeated.

5. The time between the crime and the confrontation. Glover's description of his vendor was given to D'Onofrio within minutes of the crime. The photographic identification took place only two days later. We do not have here the passage of weeks or months between the crime and the viewing of the photograph.

These indicators of Glover's ability to make an accurate identification are hardly outweighed by the corrupting effect of the challenged identification itself. Although identifications arising from single-photograph displays may be viewed in general with suspicion, we find in the instant case little pressure on the witness to acquiesce in the suggestion that such a display entails. D'Onofrio had left the photograph at Glover's office and was not present when Glover first viewed it two days after the event. There thus was little urgency and Glover could view the photograph at his leisure. And since Glover examined the photograph alone, there was no coercive pressure to make an identification arising from the presence of another. The identification was made in circumstances allowing care and reflection.

Although it plays no part in our analysis, all this assurance as to the reliability of the identification is hardly undermined by the facts that respondent was arrested in the very apartment where the sale had taken place, and that he acknowledged his frequent visits to that apartment.

Surely, we cannot say that under all the circumstances of this case there is "a very substantial likelihood of irreparable misidentification." Short of that point, such evidence is for the jury to weigh. We are content to rely upon the good sense and judgment of American juries, for evidence with some element of untrustworthiness is customary grist for the jury mill. Juries are not so susceptible that they cannot measure intelligently the weight of identification testimony that has some questionable feature.

Of course, it would have been better had D'Onofrio presented Glover with a photographic array including "so far as practicable . . . a reasonable number of persons similar to any person then suspected whose likeness is included in the array." The use of that procedure would have enhanced the force of the identification at trial and would have avoided the risk that the evidence would be excluded as unreliable. But we are not disposed to view D'Onofrio's failure as one of constitutional dimension to be enforced by a rigorous and unbending exclusionary rule. The defect, if there be one, goes to weight and not to substance.

Justice MARSHALL, with whom Justice BRENNAN joins, dissenting.

Today's decision can come as no surprise to those who have been watching the Court dismantle the protections against mistaken eyewitness testimony erected a decade ago in United States v. Wade (1967); Gilbert v. California (1967); and Stovall v. Denno (1967). But it is still distressing to see the Court virtually ignore the teaching of experience embodied in those decisions and blindly uphold the conviction of a defendant who may well be innocent.

Apparently, the Court does not consider [Neil v.] *Biggers* controlling in this case. I entirely agree, since I believe that *Biggers* was wrongly decided. The Court, however, concludes that *Biggers* is distinguishable because it, like the identification decisions that preceded it, involved a pre-*Stovall* confrontation, and because a paragraph in *Biggers* itself seems to distinguish between pre- and post-*Stovall* confrontations. Accordingly, in determining the admissibility of the post-*Stovall* identification in this case, the Court considers two alternatives, a per se exclusionary rule and a totality-of-the-circumstances approach. The Court weighs three factors in deciding that the totality approach, which is essentially the test used in *Biggers*, should be applied. In my view, the Court wrongly evaluates the impact of these factors.

First, the Court acknowledges that one of the factors, deterrence of police use of unnecessarily suggestive identification procedures, favors the per se rule. Indeed, it does so heavily, for such a rule would make it unquestionably clear to the police they must never use a suggestive procedure when a fairer alternative is available. I have no doubt that conduct would quickly conform to the rule.

Second, the Court gives passing consideration to the dangers of eyewitness identification recognized in the *Wade* trilogy. It concludes, however, that the grave risk of error does not justify adoption of the per se approach because that would too often result in exclusion of relevant evidence. In my view, this conclusion totally ignores the lessons of *Wade*. The dangers of mistaken identification are simply too great to permit unnecessarily suggestive identifications.

Finally, the Court errs in its assessment of the relative impact of the two approaches on the administration of justice. The Court relies most heavily on this factor, finding that "reversal is a Draconian sanction" in cases where the identification is reliable despite an unnecessarily suggestive procedure used to obtain it. Relying on little more than a strong distaste for "inflexible rules of exclusion," the Court rejects the per se test. In so doing, the Court disregards two significant distinctions between the per se rule advocated in this case and the exclusionary remedies for certain other constitutional violations.

First, the per se rule here is not "inflexible." Where evidence is suppressed, for example, as the fruit of an unlawful search, it may well be forever lost to the prosecution. Identification evidence, however, can by its very nature be readily and effectively reproduced. The in-court identification, permitted under *Wade* and *Simmons* if it has a source independent of an uncounseled or suggestive procedure, is one example. Similarly, when a prosecuting attorney learns that there has been a suggestive confrontation, he can easily arrange another lineup conducted under scrupulously fair conditions. Since the same factors are evaluated in applying both the Court's totality test and the *Wade-Simmons* independent-source inquiry, any identification which is "reliable" under the Court's test will support admission of evidence concerning such a fairly conducted lineup. The evidence of an additional, properly conducted confrontation will be more persuasive to a jury, thereby increasing the chance of a justified conviction where a reliable identification was tainted by a suggestive confrontation. At the same time, however, the effect of an unnecessarily suggestive identification which has no value whatsoever in the law enforcement process will be completely eliminated.

Second, other exclusionary rules have been criticized for preventing jury consideration of relevant and usually reliable evidence in order to serve interest unrelated to guilt or innocence, such as discouraging illegal searches or denial of counsel. Suggestively obtained eyewitness testimony is excluded, in contrast, precisely because of its unreliability and concomitant irrelevance. Its exclusion both protects the integrity of the truth-seeking function of the trial and discourages police use of needlessly inaccurate and ineffective investigatory methods. Indeed, impermissibly suggestive identifications are not merely worthless law enforcement tools. They pose a grave threat to society at large in a more direct way than most governmental disobedience of the law. For if the police and the public erroneously conclude, on the basis of an unnecessarily suggestive confrontation, that the right man has been caught and convicted, the real outlaw must still remain at large. Law enforcement has failed in its primary function and has left society unprotected from the depredations of an active criminal.

For these reasons, I conclude that adoption of the per se rule would enhance, rather than detract from, the effective administration of justice. In my view, the Court's totality test will allow seriously unreliable and misleading evidence to be put before juries. Equally important, it will allow dangerous criminals to remain on the streets while citizens assume that police action has given them protection. According to my calculus, all three of the factors upon which the Court relies point to acceptance of the per se approach.

Even more disturbing than the Court's reliance on the totality test, however, is the analysis it uses, which suggests a reinterpretation of the concept of due process of law in criminal cases. The decision suggests that due process violations in identification procedures may not be measured by whether the government employed procedures violating standards of fundamental fairness. By relying on the probable accuracy of a challenged identification, instead of the necessity for its use, the Court seems to be ascertaining whether the defendant was probably guilty. Until today, I had thought that "equal justice under law" meant that the existence of constitutional violations did not depend on the race, sex, religion, nationality, or likely guilt of the accused. The Due Process Clause requires adherence to the same high standard of fundamental fairness in dealing with every criminal defendant, whatever his personal characteristics and irrespective of the strength of the State's case against him. Strong evidence that the defendant is guilty should be relevant only to the determination whether an error of constitutional magnitude was nevertheless harmless beyond a reasonable doubt. By importing the question of guilt into the initial determination of whether there was a constitutional violation, the apparent effect of the Court's decision is to undermine the protection afforded by the Due Process Clause. "It is therefore important to note that the state courts remain free, in interpreting state constitutions, to guard against the evil clearly identified by this case."

The use of a single picture (or the display of a single live suspect, for that matter) is a grave error, of course, because it dramatically suggests to the witness that the person shown must be the culprit. Why else would the police choose the person? And it is deeply ingrained in human nature to agree with the expressed opinions of others[,] particularly others who should be more knowledgeable when making a difficult decision. In this case, moreover, the pressure was not limited to that inherent in the display of a single photograph. Glover, the identifying witness, was a state police officer on special assignment. He knew that D'Onofrio, an experienced Hartford narcotics detective, presumably familiar with local drug operations, believed respondent to be the seller. There was at work, then, both loyalty to another police officer and deference to a better-informed colleague. Finally, of course, there was Glover's knowledge that without an identification and arrest, government funds used to buy heroin had been wasted.

The Court discounts this overwhelming evidence of suggestiveness, however. It reasons that because D'Onofrio was not present when Glover viewed the photograph, there was "little pressure on the witness to acquiesce in the suggestion." That conclusion blinks psychological reality. There is no doubt in my mind that even in D'Onofrio's absence, a clear and powerful message was telegraphed to Glover as he looked at respondent's photograph. He was emphatically told that "this is the man," and he responded by identifying respondent then and at trial "whether or not he was in fact 'the man.'"

I must conclude that this record presents compelling evidence that there was "a very substantial likelihood of misidentification" of respondent Brathwaite. The suggestive display of respondent's photograph to the witness Glover likely erased any independent memory that Glover had retained of the seller from his barely adequate opportunity to observe the criminal.

3. Requirement That Police Be Involved in Creating the Suggestive Identification Procedure

In Perry v. New Hampshire, the Supreme Court, for the first time in decades, returned to the question of when suggestive identification violates due process. The Court, in an 8-1 decision, held that due process is violated only if the *police* are involved in creating the suggestive identification procedure.

PERRY v. NEW HAMPSHIRE

565 U.S. 228 (2012)

Justice GINSBURG delivered the opinion of the Court.

In our system of justice, fair trial for persons charged with criminal offenses is secured by the Sixth Amendment, which guarantees to defendants the right to counsel, compulsory process to obtain defense witnesses, and the opportunity to cross-examine witnesses for the prosecution. Those safeguards apart, admission of evidence in state trials is ordinarily governed by state law, and the reliability of relevant testimony typically falls within the province of the jury to determine. This Court has recognized, in addition, a due process check on the admission of eyewitness identification, applicable when the police have arranged suggestive circumstances leading the witness to identify a particular person as the perpetrator of a crime.

An identification infected by improper police influence, our case law holds, is not automatically excluded. Instead, the trial judge must screen the evidence for reliability pretrial. If there is "a very substantial likelihood of irreparable misidentification," the judge must disallow presentation of the evidence at trial. But if the indicia of reliability are strong enough to outweigh the corrupting effect of the police-arranged suggestive circumstances, the identification evidence ordinarily will be admitted, and the jury will ultimately determine its worth.

We have not extended pretrial screening for reliability to cases in which the suggestive circumstances were not arranged by law enforcement officers. Petitioner requests that we do so because of the grave risk that mistaken identification will yield a miscarriage of justice. Our decisions, however, turn on the presence of state action and aim to deter police from rigging identification procedures, for example, at a lineup, showup, or photograph array. When no improper law enforcement activity is involved, we hold, it suffices to test reliability through the rights and opportunities generally designed for that purpose, notably, the presence of counsel at postindictment lineups, vigorous cross-examination, protective rules of evidence, and jury instructions on both the fallibility of eyewitness identification and the requirement that guilt be proved beyond a reasonable doubt.

I

Around 3 A.M. on August 15, 2008, Joffre Ullon called the Nashua, New Hampshire, Police Department and reported that an African-American male was trying to break into cars parked in the lot of Ullon's apartment building. Officer Nicole Clay responded to the call. Upon arriving at the parking lot, Clay heard what "sounded like a metal bat hitting the ground." She then saw petitioner Barion Perry standing between two cars. Perry walked toward Clay, holding two car-stereo amplifiers in his hands. A metal bat lay on the ground behind him. Clay asked Perry where the amplifiers came from. "[I] found them on the ground," Perry responded.

Meanwhile, Ullon's wife, Nubia Blandon, woke her neighbor, Alex Clavijo, and told him she had just seen someone break into his car. Clavijo immediately went downstairs to the parking lot to inspect the car. He first observed that one of the rear windows had been shattered. On further inspection, he discovered that the speakers and amplifiers from his car stereo were missing, as were his bat and wrench. Clavijo then approached Clay and told her about Blandon's alert and his own subsequent observations.

By this time, another officer had arrived at the scene. Clay asked Perry to stay in the parking lot with that officer, while she and Clavijo went to talk to Blandon. Clay and Clavijo then entered the apartment building and took the stairs to the fourth floor, where Blandon's and Clavijo's apartments were located. They met Blandon in the hallway just outside the open door to her apartment.

Asked to describe what she had seen, Blandon stated that, around 2:30 A.M., she saw from her kitchen window a tall, African-American man roaming the parking lot and looking into cars. Eventually, the man circled Clavijo's car, opened the trunk, and removed a large box.

Clay asked Blandon for a more specific description of the man. Blandon pointed to her kitchen window and said the person she saw breaking into Clavijo's car was standing in the parking lot, next to the police officer. Perry's arrest followed this identification.

About a month later, the police showed Blandon a photographic array that included a picture of Perry and asked her to point out the man who had broken into Clavijo's car. Blandon was unable to identify Perry.

Perry was charged in New Hampshire state court with one count of theft by unauthorized taking and one count of criminal mischief. Before trial, he moved to suppress Blandon's identification on the ground that admitting it at trial would violate due process. Blandon witnessed what amounted to a one-person showup in the parking lot, Perry asserted, which all but guaranteed that she would identify him as the culprit.

The New Hampshire Superior Court denied the motion. At the ensuing trial, Blandon and Clay testified to Blandon's out-of-court identification. The jury found Perry guilty of theft and not guilty of criminal mischief. The New Hampshire Supreme Court rejected Perry's argument and affirmed his conviction.

II

The Constitution, our decisions indicate, protects a defendant against a conviction based on evidence of questionable reliability, not by prohibiting introduction of the evidence, but by affording the defendant means to persuade the jury that the evidence should be discounted as unworthy of credit. Constitutional safeguards available to defendants to counter the State's evidence include the Sixth Amendment rights to counsel; compulsory process; and confrontation plus cross-examination of witnesses. Apart from these guarantees, we have recognized, state and federal statutes and rules ordinarily govern the admissibility of evidence, and juries are assigned the task of determining the reliability of the evidence presented at trial.

Contending that the Due Process Clause is implicated here, Perry relies on a series of decisions involving police-arranged identification procedures.

A primary aim of excluding identification evidence obtained under unnecessarily suggestive circumstances, the Court said, is to deter law enforcement use of improper lineups, showups, and photo arrays in the first place. Alerted to the prospect that identification evidence improperly obtained may be excluded, the Court reasoned, police officers will "guard against unnecessarily suggestive procedures." This deterrence rationale is inapposite in cases, like Perry's, in which the police engaged in no improper conduct.

Coleman v. Alabama (1970) similarly shows that the Court has linked the due process check, not to suspicion of eyewitness testimony generally, but only to improper police arrangement of the circumstances surrounding an identification.

Perry's position would open the door to judicial preview, under the banner of due process, of most, if not all, eyewitness identifications. External suggestion is hardly the only factor that casts doubt on the trustworthiness of an eyewitness' testimony. As one of Perry's *amici* points out, many other factors bear on "the likelihood of misidentification," — for example, the passage of time between exposure to and identification of the defendant, whether the witness was under stress when he first encountered the suspect, how much time the witness had to observe the suspect, how far the witness was from the suspect, whether the suspect carried a weapon, and the race of the suspect and the witness. Brief for American Psychological Association as *Amicus Curiae* 9-12. There is no reason why an identification made by an eyewitness with poor vision, for example, or one who harbors a grudge against the defendant, should be regarded as inherently more reliable, less of a "threat to the fairness of trial," than the identification Blandon made in this case. To embrace Perry's view would thus entail a vast enlargement of the reach of due process as a constraint on the admission of evidence.

Perry maintains that the Court can limit the due process check he proposes to identifications made under "suggestive circumstances." Even if we could rationally distinguish suggestiveness from other factors bearing on the reliability of eyewitness evidence, Perry's limitation would still involve trial courts, routinely, in preliminary examinations. Most eyewitness identifications involve some element of suggestion. Indeed, all in-court identifications do. Out-of-court identifications volunteered by witnesses are also likely to involve suggestive circumstances. For example, suppose a witness identifies the defendant to police officers after seeing a photograph of the defendant in the press captioned "theft suspect," or hearing a radio report implicating the defendant in the crime. Or suppose the witness knew that the defendant ran with the wrong crowd and saw him on the day and in the vicinity of the crime. Any of these circumstances might have "suggested" to the witness that the defendant was the person the witness observed committing the crime.

In urging a broadly applicable due process check on eyewitness identifications, Perry maintains that eyewitness identifications are a uniquely unreliable form of evidence. See Brief for Petitioner 17-22 (citing studies showing that eyewitness misidentifications are the leading cause of wrongful convictions); Brief for American Psychological Association as *Amicus Curiae* 14-17 (describing research indicating that as many as one in three eyewitness identifications is inaccurate). We do not doubt either the importance or the fallibility of eyewitness identifications. Indeed, in recognizing that defendants have a constitutional right to counsel at postindictment police lineups, we observed that "the annals of criminal law are rife with instances of mistaken identification."

We have concluded in other contexts, however, that the potential unreliability of a type of evidence does not alone render its introduction at the defendant's trial fundamentally unfair. We reach a similar conclusion here: The fallibility of eyewitness evidence does not, without the taint of improper state conduct, warrant a due process rule requiring a trial court to screen such evidence for reliability before allowing the jury to assess its creditworthiness.

Our unwillingness to enlarge the domain of due process as Perry and the dissent urge rests, in large part, on our recognition that the jury, not the judge, traditionally determines the reliability of evidence. We also take account of other safeguards built into our adversary system that caution juries against placing undue weight on eyewitness testimony of questionable reliability. These protections include the defendant's Sixth Amendment right to confront the eyewitness. Another is the defendant's right to the effective assistance of an attorney, who can expose the flaws in the eyewitness' testimony during cross-examination and focus the jury's attention on the fallibility of such testimony during opening and closing arguments. Eyewitness-specific jury instructions, which many federal and state courts have adopted, likewise warn the jury to take care in appraising identification evidence. The constitutional requirement that the government prove the defendant's guilt beyond a reasonable doubt also impedes convictions based on dubious identification evidence.

For the foregoing reasons, we agree with the New Hampshire courts' appraisal of our decisions. Finding no convincing reason to alter our precedent, we hold that the Due Process Clause does not require a preliminary judicial inquiry into the reliability of an eyewitness identification when the identification was not procured under unnecessarily suggestive circumstances arranged by law enforcement.

Justice SOTOMAYOR dissenting.

This Court has long recognized that eyewitness identifications' unique confluence of features — their unreliability, susceptibility to suggestion, powerful impact on the jury, and resistance to the ordinary tests of the adversarial process — can undermine the fairness of a trial. Our cases thus establish a clear rule: The admission at trial of out-of-court eyewitness identifications derived from impermissibly suggestive circumstances that pose a very substantial likelihood of misidentification violates due process. The Court today announces that that rule does not even "com[e] into play" unless the suggestive circumstances are improperly "police-arranged."

Our due process concern, however, arises not from the act of suggestion, but rather from the corrosive effects of suggestion on the reliability of the resulting identification. By rendering protection contingent on improper police arrangement of the suggestive circumstances, the Court effectively grafts a *mens rea* inquiry onto our rule. The Court's holding enshrines a murky distinction — between suggestive confrontations intentionally orchestrated by the police and, as here, those inadvertently caused by police actions — that will sow confusion. It ignores our precedents' acute sensitivity to the hazards of intentional and unintentional suggestion alike and unmoors our rule from the very interest it protects, inviting arbitrary results. And it recasts the driving force of our decisions as an interest in police deterrence, rather than reliability. Because I see no warrant for declining to assess the circumstances of this case under our ordinary approach, I respectfully dissent.

I

We have warned of the "vagaries" and "'proverbially untrustworthy'" nature of eyewitness identifications. And we have singled out a "major factor contributing" to that proverbial unreliability: "the suggestibility inherent in the context of the pretrial identification." Our precedents make no distinction between intentional and unintentional suggestion. To the contrary, they explicitly state that "[s]uggestion can be created intentionally or unintentionally in many subtle ways." Rather than equate suggestive conduct with misconduct, we specifically have disavowed the assumption that suggestive influences may only be "the result of police procedures intentionally designed to prejudice an accused."

More generally, our precedents focus not on the act of suggestion, but on suggestion's "corrupting effect" on reliability. Eyewitness evidence derived from suggestive circumstances, we have explained, is uniquely resistant to the ordinary tests of the adversary process. An eyewitness who has made an identification often becomes convinced of its accuracy. "*Regardless of how the initial misidentification comes about,* the witness thereafter is apt to retain in his memory the image of the photograph rather than of the person actually seen, reducing the trustworthiness of subsequent . . . courtroom identification." Suggestion bolsters that confidence.

At trial, an eyewitness' artificially inflated confidence in an identification's accuracy complicates the jury's task of assessing witness credibility and reliability. It also impairs the defendant's ability to attack the eyewitness' credibility. That in turn jeopardizes the defendant's basic right to subject his accuser to meaningful cross-examination.

II

The majority today creates a novel and significant limitation on our long-standing rule: Eyewitness identifications so impermissibly suggestive that they pose a very substantial likelihood of an unreliable identification will be deemed inadmissible at trial *only* if the suggestive circumstances were "police-arranged." I cannot agree.

The majority does not simply hold that an eyewitness identification must be the product of police action to trigger our ordinary two-step inquiry. Rather, the majority maintains that the suggestive circumstances giving rise to the identification must be "police-arranged," "police rigg[ed]," "police-designed," or "police-organized." Those terms connote a degree of intentional orchestration or manipulation. The majority categorically exempts all eyewitness identifications derived from suggestive circumstances that were not police-manipulated — however suggestive, and however unreliable — from our due process check. The majority thus appears to graft a *mens rea* requirement onto our existing rule.

It would be one thing if the passage of time had cast doubt on the empirical premises of our precedents. But just the opposite has happened. A vast body of scientific literature has reinforced every concern our precedents articulated nearly a half-century ago, though it merits barely a parenthetical mention in the majority opinion. Over the past three decades, more than two thousand studies related to eyewitness identification have been published. One state supreme court recently appointed a special master to conduct an exhaustive survey of the current state of the scientific evidence and concluded that "[t]he research . . . is not only extensive," but "it represents the 'gold standard in terms of the applicability of social science research to law.'"

The empirical evidence demonstrates that eyewitness misidentification is "'the single greatest cause of wrongful convictions in this country.'" Researchers have found that a staggering 76% of the first 250 convictions overturned due to DNA evidence since 1989 involved eyewitness misidentification. Study after study demonstrates that eyewitness recollections are highly susceptible to distortion by postevent information or social cues; that jurors routinely overestimate the accuracy of eyewitness identifications; that jurors place the greatest weight on eyewitness confidence in assessing identifications even though confidence is a poor gauge of accuracy; and that suggestiveness can stem from sources beyond police-orchestrated procedures. The majority today nevertheless adopts an artificially narrow conception of the dangers of suggestive identifications at a time when our concerns should have deepened.

CHAPTER

6

INITIATING PROSECUTION

This chapter focuses on mechanisms used to charge defendants with offenses. Initially, police officers will use their discretion to decide when to arrest a suspect. In most jurisdictions, initial charges are filed in a complaint or information. The complaint must be supported by an affidavit that sets forth the evidence supporting the charges. Based on this ex parte showing, the suspect may be held until more formal charges are filed through indictment (for a felony) or information.

Once initial charges are filed, a defendant has the right to have a judge assess whether there is probable cause for the charges. As discussed in Chapter 3, if the defendant has not been arrested with a warrant, this probable cause review must ordinarily be done within 48 hours of a defendant's arrest. *See* Gerstein v. Pugh, 420 U.S. 103 (1975) (defendant arrested without a warrant is entitled to "prompt" post-arrest assessment of probable cause by a magistrate); County of Riverside v. McLaughlin, 500 U.S. 44 (1991) (probable cause review should be conducted within 48 hours of arrest).

Assuming that there is probable cause, prosecutors have enormous discretion in deciding what charges to bring and against whom.[1] As long as there is probable cause to support the charges, prosecutors can decide how many counts to bring, the severity of the crime to charge, and which suspects to use as witnesses and which to charge as defendants. United States v. Batchelder, 442 U.S. 114 (1979) (prosecutors are not required to use the most lenient statute in charging a defendant).

Because of separation of powers, if judges disagree with a prosecutor's charging decision, they can decide to dismiss charges, but they cannot order prosecutors to bring other charges. As Judge Posner has stated, "A judge in our system does not have the authority to tell prosecutors which crimes to prosecute or when to prosecute them. Prosecutorial discretion resides in the executive, not in the judicial branch."[2] Although prosecutors have broad discretion in deciding what to charge, their decisions are not

---

1. *See generally* Wayne R. LaFave, *The Prosecutor's Discretion in the United States*, 18 Am. J. Comp. L. 532, 533-539 (1970).
2. United States v. Giannattasio, 979 F.2d 98 (7th Cir. 1992).

necessarily easy ones. Section A of this chapter discusses the complexities of the prosecutor's decision to file charges.

Section B then details the constitutional, statutory, and ethical limits on prosecutorial discretion. In particular, it focuses on the doctrines of selective and vindictive prosecution. Although prosecutors have broad discretion in charging cases, they cannot bring charges based on impermissible criteria, such as race or religion. They also cannot retaliate against the defendant for the exercise of a constitutional right. Prosecutors must abide by statutory, ethical, and administrative standards in making their charging decisions.

Once a decision has been made to charge a defendant, there are two primary procedures to screen which cases should be formally charged — the grand jury and the preliminary hearing. These procedures are discussed in section C. The Fifth Amendment provides a right to grand jury indictment for federal felonies. However, because this portion of the Fifth Amendment has not been incorporated under the Fourteenth Amendment, states are not required to use grand juries. Instead, many states use another mechanism — the preliminary hearing — to screen cases. Defendants have the right to waive preliminary hearing and frequently do so when they reach an early plea bargain in the case or are not yet prepared to contest the prosecution's case or do not want to disclose their likely defenses.

In addition, there are fairness considerations that may impact how a defendant is charged. Section D discusses the issues of severance and joinder. Courtroom efficiencies may favor the joinder of defendants or offenses for trial, but these benefits must be weighed against the concern of unduly prejudicing a defendant's right to a fair trial.

Finally, this chapter ends with a brief word on how charges can be corrected if mistakes are found before trial. Amendments and variances are addressed in section E of the chapter.

A. THE CHARGING DECISION

By some estimates, less than 2 percent of all crimes are actually prosecuted in the United States.[3] That means that throughout the criminal justice process, both the police and prosecutors are using their discretion to decide which cases warrant prosecution. Prosecutors have this broad discretion even though they have relatively little accountability to the public. They are often guided by abstract standards like "seeking justice" or being "fair" or "neutral." In reality, these terms are just "proxies for a constellation of other, sometimes equally vague, normative expectations about how prosecutors should make decisions." Bruce A. Green & Fred C. Zacharias, *Prosecutorial Neutrality*, 2004 Wis. L. Rev. 837, 902-903.

---

3. *See* Sara Sun Beale, *Essay: The Many Faces of Overcriminalization*, 54 Am. U. L. Rev. 747, 757 (2005).

Several factors influence the decision of whether to prosecute a case. First, there are the economic realities. There are not enough prosecutors, police, or courts to prosecute all of the crimes that are committed. For most prosecution offices, there is only one prosecutor for every 4,000 people in their district. Many prosecution offices have small operating budgets.[4] There are only 800,000 full-time sworn law enforcement officers in the United States for a population of over 300 million people. Thus, prosecutors and police must select very carefully the cases they want to prosecute.

Second, prosecutors must assess which prosecutions are likely to bring the greatest benefit to the community. Depending on community interests, prosecutors will set the priorities for their jurisdictions. In the 1980s, prosecutors launched the "war on drugs." Today, prosecutorial priorities are also focusing on terrorism crimes and Internet violations. According to government statistics, approximately one-quarter of all felony defendants are charged with violent offenses. Those charged with murder (0.8 percent) and rape (1.3 percent) account for a small percentage of defendants overall.[5] That means that three-quarters of defendants were charged with a nonviolent felony, with a majority of these being narcotics-related offenses. Nonviolent crimes can range from multimillion dollar fraud schemes to shoplifting offenses. Prosecution priorities may be influenced by political decisions of both the legislature and individual government officials. These individuals generally don't want to be viewed as "soft on crime," especially since most District Attorneys are elected officials.

Third, prosecutors must evaluate the merits and strengths of each individual case. Prosecutors only need probable cause to charge a defendant. However, they need proof beyond a reasonable doubt to succeed at trial. Typically, prosecutorial offices enjoy a conviction rate of over 90 percent because they can pick and choose the cases they prosecute. In doing so, they must consider the impact of a trial on prosecution witnesses, the strength of their evidence, the deterrence value of the case, and the harm caused by the crime.

It is not unusual for prosecutors to tack on additional charges so as to create an incentive for the defendant to cooperate and/or to plead guilty. "If the prosecutor charges five offenses instead of two, he may get the defendant to agree to plead guilty to three charges in exchange for his agreement to dismiss two, even if he would have a difficult time proving the two charges before a judge or jury."[6]

Prosecutors will also evaluate the background of individual defendants before deciding whether to prosecute a case. More than one-third of the

4. Bureau of Justice Statistics, *Prosecutors in State Courts, 2007 — Statistical Tables*, December 2011, http://bjs.gov/content/pub/pdf/psc07st.pdf (reporting that more than half of prosecution offices had a total budget of $526,000 or less).

5. *See* Department of Justice, Bureau of Justice Statistics, *Felony Defendants in Large Urban Counties,* 2009-2013 Statistical Tables, December 2013, https://www.bjs.gov/content/pub/pdf/fdluc09.pdf. Any type of violent crime accounted for only 24.9 percent of all felonies. *Id.*

6. Angela J. Davis, Arbitrary Justice: The Power of the American Prosecution (Oxford University Press 2007).

defendants prosecuted already have an active criminal justice status at the time of the new charged offense.[7] Of course, with the power to individually evaluate each case comes the danger that prosecutors will use improper factors in making their decisions. Currently, one out of every three young African American males is a defendant in the criminal justice system.[8] Based on current rates of incarceration, an estimated 32 percent of black males will enter state or federal prison during their lifetime, compared to 17 percent of Hispanic males and 5.9 percent of white males.[9] These statistics prompt important questions about conscious and unconscious racial bias in policing and charging decisions.[10] The Supreme Court has repeatedly stated that "prosecutorial discretion cannot be exercised on the basis of race," McClesky v. Kemp, 481 U.S. 279 (1987), yet statistical studies have shown that race has an impact on how a defendant is treated by the criminal justice system. For example, according to the Baldus study cited in McClesky v. Kemp, "prosecutors seek the death penalty for 70% of black defendants with white victims, but for only 15% of black defendants with black victims, and only 19% of white defendants with black victims." As the dissent in that case noted, "racial and other forms of discrimination still remain a fact of life, in the administration of justice as in our society as a whole." *Id.* at 332 (Brennan, J., dissenting).

Finally, prosecutors should factor in the overall impact of their decision to prosecute or drop a case. This includes the impact on the victims, their families, law enforcement, and all members of the broader community. There are more than enough criminal codes to prosecute defendants, but prosecutors must consider whether it is in the public interest to bring a charge. Consider the following prosecutions and whether they were a prudent exercise of prosecutorial discretion and what alternatives, if any, there might be for prosecutors in dealing with these cases.

PEOPLE v. ROBERT DENNY

NO. LACV 13-4326-JVS (LAL)

Robert Denny is a fifty year old man with a long history of mental illness and drug addiction. Not able to find mental health services, he enters an adult bookstore and falls asleep in one of the private booths in the back. Two men approach Denny and ask him to step outside. As a paranoid schizophrenic, Denny cries out to the store clerk to call him a taxi or the police.

---

7. *Id.*

8. *See* Marc Mauer & Tracy Huling, Young Black Americans and the Criminal Justice System (Oct. 1995). A black male born in 2011 has a 32 percent chance of spending time in prison at some point in his life. http://www.sentencingproject.org/publications/reducing-racial-disparity-in-the-criminal-justice-system-a-manual-for-practitioners-and-policymakers/.

9. Twenty-eight percent of all arrests and 31.1 percent of juvenile arrests in 2010 were of black suspects. *See* Department of Justice, Bureau of Justice Statistics, *Sourcebook of Criminal Justice Statistics Online*, Table 4.10.2010, http://www.albany.edu/sourcebook/pdf/t4102010.pdf.

10. *See* Angela J. Davis, *Prosecution and Race: The Power and Privilege of Discretion*, 67 Fordham L. Rev. 13 (1998).

As Denny is crying out, the two men put $20 bill on the counter for an item behind the glass. When the bill falls from the counter, Denny reaches for it. There is a three-second interaction as all three men go for the bill. When it is over, Denny is charged with attempted robbery and, based on two prior convictions more than twenty years old, he is sentenced to forty years in prison.

INMATE CONVICTED OF INDECENT EXPOSURE

Associated Press, July 25, 2007

Terry Lee Alexander thought he was having a private moment in his jail cell. But a deputy jailer thought otherwise. Alexander, 20, was sitting on his bunk alone in his cell masturbating when a female deputy, monitoring his cell by video camera from a nearby control room, took offense. Today he's scheduled to go to trial to fight a misdemeanor indecent exposure charge.

Taxpayers have been footing the bill — $91.29 a day — to keep Alexander in the main jail. The grand total for Alexander's incarceration in that case is nearly $21,000. On top of that, the public will pay $1,150 for his attorney.

Critics are appalled at what they call a deputy's "moral crusade" and question the value of prosecuting such cases. "I would think [taxpayers] would be upset that this is how their money is being spent," said Betsy Benson, a Broward assistant public defender.[11]

Prosecutorial charging discretion can also give prosecutors considerable power to influence sentencing. Consider the next example and how the prosecutor's power to charge controlled the judge's sentencing decision.

MANDATORY 55-YEAR SENTENCE "EXTREME"?

Salt Lake Tribune, Dec. 4, 2007

Lawyers for a Utah record producer serving 55 years in prison for carrying a firearm while dealing pot filed a request Monday for a resentencing, saying the punishment is "extreme" and unconstitutional.

"As a result of three sales of small amounts of marijuana to a paid informant and the suspect charging decisions by federal prosecutors, Angelos received a 55-year sentence that highlights the most unjust and arbitrary

---

11. In deciding whether the prosecutor used good judgment in bringing the charges, consider that all of the prospective jurors had to be asked about their attitudes toward masturbation and whether they engaged in it. *See* Robert Santiago, *Jury Panel Queried in Masturbation Trial*, Miami Herald, July 24, 2007.

aspects of the federal criminal justice system and mandatory minimum sentencing provisions," the motion for resentencing says.

The motion was filed in U.S. District Court in Salt Lake City, where Judge Paul Cassell reluctantly imposed the mandatory term almost four years ago. Cassell described the sentence as "unjust, cruel and irrational," but said he had no choice under the law but to impose it.

Angelos was accused of selling eight ounces of marijuana for $350 in each sale. At one sale, he had a gun strapped to his ankle and there were firearms in the vicinity during the other drug buys, according to court records.

Monday's motion — filed by a team of lawyers that recently stepped into the case — says recent statistics show that the vast majority of all felony marijuana trafficking convictions result in a prison term of less than one year.

Angelos' sentencing sparked a national debate on mandatory sentences and prompted dozens of former judges and prosecutors to join in friend-of-the-court briefs to the 10th Circuit and the U.S. Supreme Court seeking reversal of the punishment.

The charging decision is one of the most important determinations a prosecutor makes. Whereas police officers must decide on the spot whether to arrest someone, the prosecutor has the time and ability to do a closer evaluation of a case to determine whether charges are warranted. A decision to charge an individual means, at minimum, that individual will confront the expense and stress of facing trial. Because of the high rate of guilty pleas, the charging decision frequently predetermines the outcome of a criminal case. It vests enormous power in the hands of the prosecutor.

In addition to deciding when and whom to charge, prosecutors have the power to decide *not* to charge a case. Generally, judges do not have the power to second-guess decisions by the prosecution not to charge a case.

INMATES OF ATTICA CORRECTIONAL FACILITY v. ROCKEFELLER
477 F.2d 375 (2d Cir. 1973)

Circuit Judge MANSFIELD delivered the opinion of the court.

This appeal raises the question of whether the federal judiciary should, at the instance of victims, compel federal and state officials to investigate and prosecute persons who allegedly have violated certain federal and state criminal statutes. Plaintiffs are certain present and former inmates of New York State's Attica Correctional Facility [and] the mother of an inmate who was killed when Attica was retaken after the inmate uprising in September 1971. They appeal from an order of the district court dismissing their complaint. We affirm.

[F]ederal courts have traditionally and, to our knowledge, uniformly refrained from overturning, at the instance of a private person, discretionary decisions of federal prosecuting authorities not to prosecute persons regarding whom a complaint of criminal conduct is made.

The primary ground upon which this traditional judicial aversion to compelling prosecutions has been based is the separation of powers doctrine.

> Although as a member of the bar, the attorney for the United States is an officer of the court, he is nevertheless an executive official of the Government, and it is as an officer of the executive department that he exercises discretion as to whether or not there shall be a prosecution in a particular case. It follows, as an incident of the constitutional separation of powers, that the courts are not to interfere with the free exercise of the discretionary powers of the attorneys of the United States in their control over criminal prosecutions.

Nor is it clear what the judiciary's role of supervision should be were it to undertake such a review. At what point would the prosecutor be entitled to call a halt to further investigation as unlikely to be productive? What evidentiary standard would be used to decide whether prosecution should be compelled? How much judgment would the United States Attorney be allowed? What collateral factors would be permissible bases for a decision not to prosecute, e.g., the pendency of another criminal proceeding elsewhere against the same parties? With limited personnel and facilities at his disposal, what priority would the prosecutor be required to give to cases in which investigation or prosecution was directed by the court?

These difficult questions engender serious doubts as to the judiciary's capacity to review and as to the problem of arbitrariness inherent in any judicial decision to order prosecution. On balance, we believe that substitution of a court's decision to compel prosecution for the U.S. Attorney's decision not to prosecute, even upon an abuse of discretion standard of review and even if limited to directing that a prosecution be undertaken in good faith would be unwise.

Generally, prosecutors have both the responsibility and discretion to file criminal charges. In some jurisdictions, private citizens can file misdemeanor complaints (with judicial approval), but the most significant charging decisions rest in the hands of prosecutors.

B.   LIMITS ON PROSECUTORIAL DISCRETION

Although prosecutors enjoy broad discretion in charging cases, there are statutory, administrative, ethical, and constitutional limits on prosecutorial discretion.

1. Statutory and Administrative Limits

Prosecutors can only charge conduct that the legislature has designated as a crime. Each jurisdiction has governing statutes for its criminal offenses. Federal prosecutions are brought by the United States Attorney's Office or the Department of Justice. Criminal offenses are listed in the United States Code. Generally, prosecutors will have numerous charges to choose from in deciding which charges to bring. As long as the charges are supported by probable cause, it is within the prosecutor's discretion to decide whether to bring a charge with a greater or lesser potential punishment.

Local offenses are charged by state district attorneys, city attorneys, and state attorneys general. The offenses they can charge are listed in the penal codes for those jurisdictions. In some cases, a crime may be charged by state prosecutors, federal prosecutors, or both. As discussed in Chapter 13, federal double jeopardy law does not bar separate sovereigns from charging the same offense. Thus, unless a state provides greater double jeopardy protection, both state and federal officials may charge a violation of law if there are applicable statutes.

Even prosecution of criminal contempt cases arising out of private disputes should be handled by public prosecutors. In Young v. United States ex rel. Vuitton et Fils S.A., 481 U.S. 787 (1987), the Court held that Federal Rule of Criminal Procedure 42(b) allows for the prosecution of criminal contempt, but it does not allow the victim to be the prosecutor.

> The prosecutor is appointed solely to pursue the public interest in vindication of the court's authority. A private attorney appointed to prosecute a criminal contempt therefore certainly should be as disinterested as a public prosecutor who undertakes such a prosecution. . . . A prosecutor exercises considerable discretion in [determining] which persons should be targets of investigation, what methods of investigation should be used, what information will be sought as evidence, which persons should be charged with what offenses, which persons should be utilized as witnesses, whether to enter into plea bargains and the terms on which they will be established, and whether any individuals should be granted immunity. These decisions, critical to the conduct of a prosecution, [require a disinterested prosecutor].

Id. at 804-805.

Prosecutors may adopt guidelines for their decisions to prosecute. For example, federal prosecutors have the U.S. Attorney's Manual, which guides their prosecutorial decisions. These guidelines typically leave a great deal of discretion for the prosecutor's decision, although they may require approval by superiors before certain types of cases are brought. However, violation of these internal guidelines does not afford the defendant grounds to contest the charges. As internal guidelines, they do not create independent rights for the defendant.

2. Ethical Limits

Prosecutors are also governed by ethical rules. The Supreme Court has repeatedly recognized that prosecutors have special ethical responsibilities because of the power they wield:

> The United States Attorney is the representative not of an ordinary party to a controversy, but of a sovereignty whose obligation to govern impartially is as compelling as its obligation to govern at all; and whose interest, therefore, in a criminal prosecution is not that it shall win a case, but that justice shall be done. As such, he is in a peculiar and very definite sense the servant of the law, the twofold aim of which is that guilt shall not escape nor innocence suffer.

Berger v. United States, 295 U.S. 78, 88 (1935).

The unique responsibilities of prosecutors are expressed in Ethical Consideration (EC) 7-13 of Canon 7 of the American Bar Association (ABA) Model Code of Professional Responsibility (1982): "The responsibility of a public prosecutor differs from that of the usual advocate; his duty is to seek justice, not merely to convict."

For charging decisions, ABA Standards for Criminal Justice: The Prosecution Function, Standard 3-3.9 (Discretion in the Charging Decision) provides:

> (a) A prosecutor should not institute, or cause to be instituted, or permit the continued pendency of criminal charges when the prosecutor knows that the charges are not supported by probable cause. A prosecutor should not institute, cause to be instituted, or permit the continued pendency of criminal charges in the absence of sufficient admissible evidence to support conviction.
>
> (b) The prosecutor is not obliged to present all charges which the evidence might support. The prosecutor may in some circumstances and for good cause consistent with the public interest decline to prosecute, notwithstanding that sufficient evidence may exist which would support a conviction. Illustrative of the factors which the prosecutor may properly consider in exercising his or her discretion are:
>> (i) the prosecutor's reasonable doubt that the accused is in fact guilty;
>> (ii) the extent of the harm caused by the offense;
>> (iii) the disproportion of the authorized punishment in relation to the particular offense or the offender;
>> (iv) possible improper motives of a complainant;
>> (v) reluctance of the victim to testify;
>> (vi) cooperation of the accused in the apprehension or conviction of others;
>> (vii) availability and likelihood of prosecution by another jurisdiction.
>
> (c) A prosecutor should not be compelled by his or her supervisor to prosecute a case in which he or she has a reasonable doubt about the guilt of the accused.
>
> (d) In making the decision to prosecute, the prosecutor should give no weight to the personal or political advantages which might be involved or to a desire to enhance his or her record of conviction.
>
> (e) In cases which involve a serious threat to the community, the prosecutor should not be deterred from prosecution by the fact that in the jurisdiction

juries have tended to acquit persons accused of the particular criminal act in question.

(f) The prosecutor should not bring or seek charges greater in number or degree than can be supported with evidence at trial or than are necessary to fairly reflect the gravity of the offense.

Prosecutors who do not honor these ethical obligations risk causing a grave injustice to others and professional consequences to themselves. One particularly notorious case involved rape charges filed against three Duke University lacrosse players by a politically ambitious prosecutor. The prosecutor, Michael Nifong, aggressively pursued charges against the players as he ran for office. Nifong was aware of serious problems with the case. Nonetheless, he portrayed himself as the crusader for minorities and continued with the prosecution. After the defendants' reputations were tarnished, and millions of dollars were spent on their defense, North Carolina's attorney general found that there was no evidence to support the charges and dismissed them. Michael Nifong ended up being disbarred. Nifong's case, although relatively rare, offers important lessons about the role of ethics in prosecutors' charging decisions.

LAWYER DISBARRED OVER LACROSSE RAPE CASE

Associated Press, June 18, 2007

Raleigh, North Carolina: A disgraced North Carolina lawyer has been disbarred for his "selfish" rape prosecution of three lacrosse players at a top U.S. university, bringing to an end an American saga about race and class that sparked a bitter national debate.

Hours after he was found guilty of ethics violations in his prosecution of three white Duke University lacrosse players falsely accused of raping a black stripper at an off-campus house party in March last year, Durham County District Attorney Michael Nifong at the weekend surrendered his law license to the state bar and said he would waive his right to appeal.

A three-person North Carolina State Bar disciplinary panel, on the fifth day of an ethics hearing, said the evidence showed that Mr. Nifong had withheld crucial information from the students' defence lawyers and engaged in "dishonesty, fraud, deceit or misrepresentation" during his prosecution of the case.

It is the first time a sitting district attorney has been disbarred in North Carolina.

"This matter has been a fiasco. There's no doubt about it," said F. Lane Williamson, chair of the disciplinary committee. The committee said Mr. Nifong manipulated the investigation to boost his chances of winning his first election for Durham County district attorney.

Mr. Williamson specifically cited Mr. Nifong's comments in the early days of the case, which included a confident proclamation that he would not allow Durham to become known for "a bunch of lacrosse players from Duke raping a black girl." He also called the Duke lacrosse team "a bunch of hooligans."

Appointed district attorney in 2005, Mr. Nifong was in a tight race for the office when a stripper told police she had been raped at the party. "At the time he was facing a primary, and yes, he was politically naive," Mr. Williamson said.

"But we can draw no other conclusion than [that] those initial statements he made were to further his political ambitions."

The case stirred furious debate over race, class and the privileged status of college athletes, and heightened longstanding tensions in Durham between its large working-class black population and the mostly white, mostly affluent students at the private, elite university.

During the ethics trial, Mr. Nifong acknowledged he knew there was no DNA evidence connecting Duke students Reade Seligmann and Collin Finnerty to the 28-year-old accuser when he indicted them on charges of rape, sexual offence and kidnapping. Mr. Nifong later charged Dave Evans with the same crimes.

But months later, state prosecutors concluded the players were innocent and in a blistering assessment of the case Attorney-General Roy Cooper dropped all charges in April.

"This case shows the enormous consequences of overreaching by a prosecutor," he said. "In the rush to condemn, a community and a state lost the ability to see clearly."

By most accounts, what happened to the prosecutor in the Nifong case was highly unusual. Prosecutors are rarely disciplined for improper charging of cases. The ABA ethical rules are only aspirational, and prosecutors are rarely called on to justify their charging decisions.

3. *Constitutional Limits*[12]

Although prosecutorial discretion is broad, it is not unlimited. Prosecutors cannot use unconstitutional motives to charge a defendant. A defendant

---

12. This chapter focuses on due process and equal protection limits on prosecutorial discretion. In addition, Article I, section 9, clause 3 of the Constitution prohibits bills of attainder and ex post facto laws. "A *bill of attainder* is a legislative act which inflicts punishment without judicial trial and includes any legislative act which takes away the life, liberty or property of a particular named or easily ascertainable person or group of persons because the legislature thinks them guilty of conduct which deserves punishment." Cummings v. Missouri, 71 U.S. 277 (1867) (emphasis added). An *ex post facto law* is a law that punishes acts that were legal at the time they were committed. *See generally* Calder v. Bull, 3 Dall. 386 (1798). The prohibition on ex post facto laws also bars laws that increase the punishment of an act after it was committed or retroactively extend the statute of limitations so that a defendant can be charged with a crime. *See* Stogner v. California, 539 U.S. 607

who is prosecuted because of his race, religion, or other classification, in violation of the Fourteenth Amendment's Equal Protection Clause, can move to dismiss for selective or discriminatory enforcement. A defendant who is prosecuted in retaliation for the defendant's exercise of a constitutional right, such as the First Amendment right to free speech, can move to dismiss for vindictive prosecution.

a. Selective or Discriminatory Enforcement

There is a general presumption that prosecutors will exercise their discretion in good faith. However, if a defendant can show that the prosecution used an impermissible motive to prosecute, such as prosecuting a defendant because of his race or exercise of his First Amendment rights, then the prosecution can be dismissed. As the next two cases — Wayte v. United States and United States v. Armstrong — illustrate, not only has the Supreme Court set a high standard for defendants claiming selective prosecution, but it has imposed a significant burden on defendants seeking discovery to support a claim of discriminatory prosecution.

WAYTE v. UNITED STATES
470 U.S. 598 (1985)

Justice POWELL delivered the opinion of the Court.

[David Wayte was a war protestor. When he refused to register for the Selective Service System, he was warned that he could be prosecuted for violating the Military Selective Service Act. Nonetheless, Wayte continued to protest the war and refused to register. In a letter to the Selective Service System and president, Wayte stated, "I decided to obey my conscience rather than your law. I did not register for your draft. I will never register for your draft. Nor will I ever cooperate with yours or any other military system, despite the laws I might break or the consequences which may befall me." Ultimately, he was indicted. He then moved for dismissal, contending that he was "selectively prosecuted" for resisting the system. The district court granted the motion. The respondent government appealed, asserting that the petitioner did not prove a prima facie case of discrimination.]

The question presented is whether a passive enforcement policy under which the Government prosecutes only those who report themselves as having violated the law, or who are reported by others, violates the First and Fifth Amendments.

(2003) (state law that sought to resurrect prosecution of child molestation cases that were otherwise time-barred violated the Ex Post Facto Clause). However, the rule does not bar the retroactive application of registration laws, such as laws requiring sex offenders to register their whereabouts. *See* Smith v. Doe, 538 U.S. 84 (2003). The prohibition on bills of attainder and ex post facto laws applies to the states pursuant to Article I, section 10, clause 1 of the federal Constitution.

Petitioner moved to dismiss the indictment on the ground of selective prosecution. He contended that he and the other [13] indicted nonregistrants were "vocal" opponents of the registration program who had been impermissibly targeted (out of an estimated 674,000 nonregistrants) for prosecution on the basis of their exercise of First Amendment rights.

In our criminal justice system, the Government retains "broad discretion" as to whom to prosecute. "[So] long as the prosecutor has probable cause to believe that the accused committed an offense defined by statute, the decision whether or not to prosecute, and what charge to file or bring before a grand jury, generally rests entirely in his discretion." This broad discretion rests largely on the recognition that the decision to prosecute is particularly ill-suited to judicial review. Such factors as the strength of the case, the prosecution's general deterrence value, the Government's enforcement priorities, and the case's relationship to the Government's overall enforcement plan are not readily susceptible to the kind of analysis the courts are competent to undertake. Judicial supervision in this area, moreover, entails systemic costs of particular concern. Examining the basis of a prosecution delays the criminal proceeding, threatens to chill law enforcement by subjecting the prosecutor's motives and decisionmaking to outside inquiry, and may undermine prosecutorial effectiveness by revealing the Government's enforcement policy. All these are substantial concerns that make the courts properly hesitant to examine the decision whether to prosecute.

As we have noted in a slightly different context, however, although prosecutorial discretion is broad, it is not "'unfettered.' Selectivity in the enforcement of criminal laws is . . . subject to constitutional constraints." In particular, the decision to prosecute may not be "'deliberately based upon an unjustifiable standard such as race, religion, or other arbitrary classification,'" including the exercise of protected statutory and constitutional rights.

It is appropriate to judge selective prosecution claims according to ordinary equal protection standards. Under our prior cases, these standards require petitioner to show both that the passive enforcement system had a discriminatory effect and that it was motivated by a discriminatory purpose.[13] All petitioner has shown here is that those eventually prosecuted, along with many not prosecuted, reported themselves as having violated the law. He has not shown that the enforcement policy selected nonregistrants for prosecution on the basis of their speech. Indeed, he could not have done so given the way the "beg" policy[14] was carried out. The Government did not prosecute

13. A showing of discriminatory intent is not necessary when the equal protection claim is based on an overtly discriminatory classification. *See* Strauder v. West Virginia, (1880). [No such claim was presented by Wayte.] [Footnote by the Court.]

14. Pursuant to the Department of Justice "beg" policy, those referred were not immediately prosecuted. Instead, the appropriate United States Attorney was required to notify identified nonregistrants by registered mail that, unless they registered within a specified time, prosecution would be considered. In addition, an FBI agent was usually sent to interview the nonregistrant before prosecution was instituted. This effort to persuade nonregistrants to change their minds became known as the "beg" policy. [Footnote by casebook authors.]

those who reported themselves but later registered. Nor did it prosecute those who protested registration but did not report themselves or were not reported by others. In fact, the Government did not even investigate those who wrote letters to Selective Service criticizing registration unless their letters stated affirmatively that they had refused to comply with the law. The Government, on the other hand, did prosecute people who reported themselves or were reported by others but who did not publicly protest. These facts demonstrate that the Government treated all reported nonregistrants similarly. It did not subject vocal nonregistrants to any special burden. Indeed, those prosecuted in effect selected themselves for prosecution by refusing to register after being reported and warned by the Government.

Even if the passive policy had a discriminatory effect, petitioner has not shown that the Government intended such a result. The evidence he presented demonstrated only that the Government was aware that the passive enforcement policy would result in prosecution of vocal objectors and that they would probably make selective prosecution claims. As we have noted, however: "'Discriminatory purpose' . . . implies more than . . . intent as awareness of consequences. It implies that the decisionmaker . . . selected or reaffirmed a particular course of action at least in part 'because of,' not merely 'in spite of,' its adverse effects upon an identifiable group." In the present case, petitioner has not shown that the Government prosecuted him because of his protest activities. Absent such a showing, his claim of selective prosecution fails.[15]

Justice MARSHALL, with whom Justice BRENNAN joins, dissenting.

The Court decides today that petitioner "has not shown that the Government prosecuted him because of his protest activities," and it remands to permit his prosecution to go forward. However interesting the question decided by the Court may be, it is not necessary to the disposition of this case. Instead, the issue this Court must grapple with is far less momentous but no less deserving of thoughtful treatment. What it must decide is whether Wayte has earned the right to discover Government documents relevant to his claim of selective prosecution.

The District Court ordered such discovery, the Government refused to comply, and the District Court dismissed the indictment. The Court of Appeals reversed on the grounds that Wayte had failed to prevail on the merits of his selective prosecution claim, and that the discovery order was improper. If Wayte is entitled to obtain evidence currently in the Government's possession, the Court cannot dismiss his claim on the basis of only the evidence now in the record. To prevail here, then, all that Wayte needs to

---

15. Wayte also challenged his prosecution directly on First Amendment grounds. However, this claim also failed because the incidental restriction on his speech was essential to further the government's legitimate interest in having people comply with the registration laws. [Footnote by casebook authors.]

show is that the District Court applied the correct legal standard and did not abuse its discretion in determining that he had made a nonfrivolous showing of selective prosecution entitling him to discovery.

There can be no doubt that Wayte has sustained his burden. Therefore, his claim cannot properly be dismissed at this stage in the litigation. I respectfully dissent from this Court's decision to do so.

———————————

The discovery issue that Justice Marshall raised in his dissent came before the Court in United States v. Armstrong. There the Court dealt with an issue much more common in selective prosecution cases: When do racial disparities in prosecutions constitute selective/discriminatory prosecution?

UNITED STATES v. ARMSTRONG
517 U.S. 456 (1996)

Chief Justice REHNQUIST delivered the opinion of the Court.

In this case, we consider the showing necessary for a defendant to be entitled to discovery on a claim that the prosecuting attorney singled him out for prosecution on the basis of his race. We conclude that respondents failed to satisfy the threshold showing: They failed to show that the Government declined to prosecute similarly situated suspects of other races.

In April 1992, respondents were indicted on charges of conspiring to possess with intent to distribute more than 50 grams of cocaine base (crack) and conspiring to distribute the same and federal firearms offenses. In response to the indictment, respondents filed a motion for discovery or for dismissal of the indictment, alleging that they were selected for federal prosecution because they are black. In support of their motion, they offered only an affidavit by a "Paralegal Specialist," employed by the Office of the Federal Public Defender representing one of the respondents. The only allegation in the affidavit was that, in every one of the 24 [narcotics] cases closed by the office during 1991, the defendant was black. Accompanying the affidavit was a "study" listing the 24 defendants, their race, whether they were prosecuted for dealing cocaine as well as crack, and the status of each case.

The Government opposed the discovery motion, arguing, among other things, that there was no evidence or allegation "that the Government has acted unfairly or has prosecuted non-black defendants or failed to prosecute them."

A selective-prosecution claim is not a defense on the merits to the criminal charge itself, but an independent assertion that the prosecutor has brought the charge for reasons forbidden by the Constitution. Our cases delineating the necessary elements to prove a claim of selective prosecution have taken great pains to explain that the standard is a demanding one.

A selective-prosecution claim asks a court to exercise judicial power over a "special province" of the Executive. The Attorney General and United States Attorneys retain "broad discretion" to enforce the Nation's criminal laws. Wayte v. United States (1985). They have this latitude because they are designated by statute as the President's delegates to help him discharge his constitutional responsibility to "take Care that the Laws be faithfully executed." U.S. Const., Art. II, §3. As a result, "the presumption of regularity supports" their prosecutorial decisions and, "in the absence of clear evidence to the contrary, courts presume that they have properly discharged their official duties." "[S]o long as the prosecutor has probable cause to believe that the accused committed an offense defined by statute, the decision whether or not to prosecute, and what charge to file or bring before a grand jury, generally rests entirely in his discretion." Bordenkircher v. Hayes (1978).

Of course, a prosecutor's discretion is "subject to constitutional constraints." One of these constraints, imposed by the equal protection component of the Due Process Clause of the Fifth Amendment is that the decision whether to prosecute may not be based on "an unjustifiable standard such as race, religion, or other arbitrary classification." A defendant may demonstrate that the administration of a criminal law is "directed so exclusively against a particular class of persons . . . with a mind so unequal and oppressive" that the system of prosecution amounts to "a practical denial" of equal protection of the law. Yick Wo v. Hopkins (1886).

In order to dispel the presumption that a prosecutor has not violated equal protection, a criminal defendant must present "clear evidence to the contrary." The requirements for a selective-prosecution claim draw on "ordinary equal protection standards." The claimant must demonstrate that the federal prosecutorial policy "had a discriminatory effect and that it was motivated by a discriminatory purpose." To establish a discriminatory effect in a race case, the claimant must show that similarly situated individuals of a different race were not prosecuted.

The similarly situated requirement does not make a selective-prosecution claim impossible to prove. In *Hunter*, we invalidated a state law disenfranchising persons convicted of crimes involving moral turpitude. Our holding was consistent with ordinary equal protection principles, including the similarly situated requirement. There was convincing direct evidence that the State had enacted the provision for the purpose of disenfranchising blacks and indisputable evidence that the state law had a discriminatory effect on blacks as compared to similarly situated whites: Blacks were "by even the most modest estimates at least 1.7 times as likely as whites to suffer disfranchisement under" the law in question.

Having reviewed the requirements to prove a selective-prosecution claim, we turn to the showing necessary to obtain discovery in support of such a claim. If discovery is ordered, the Government must assemble from its own files documents which might corroborate or refute the defendant's claim. Discovery thus imposes many of the costs present when the Government must respond to a prima facie case of selective prosecution. It will divert prosecutors' resources and may disclose the Government's prosecutorial strategy. The justifications for a rigorous standard for the elements of a selective-prosecution claim thus require a correspondingly rigorous standard for discovery in aid of such a claim.

The parties, and the Courts of Appeals which have considered the requisite showing to establish entitlement to discovery, describe this showing with a variety of phrases, like "colorable basis," "substantial threshold showing," "substantial and concrete basis," or "reasonable likelihood." However, the many labels for this showing conceal the degree of consensus about the evidence necessary to meet it. The Courts of Appeals "require some evidence tending to show the existence of the essential elements of the defense," discriminatory effect and discriminatory intent.

In this case we consider what evidence constitutes "some evidence tending to show the existence" of the discriminatory effect element. The Court of Appeals held that a defendant may establish a colorable basis for discriminatory effect without evidence that the Government has failed to prosecute others who are similarly situated to the defendant. We think it was mistaken in this view. The Court of Appeals reached its decision in part because it started "with the presumption that people of all races commit all types of crimes — not with the premise that any type of crime is the exclusive province of any particular racial or ethnic group." It cited no authority for this proposition, which seems contradicted by the most recent statistics of the United States Sentencing Commission. Those statistics show: More than 90% of the persons sentenced in 1994 for crack cocaine trafficking were black, 93.4% of convicted LSD dealers were white, and 91% of those convicted for pornography or prostitution were white. Presumptions at war with presumably reliable statistics have no proper place in the analysis of this issue.

The Court of Appeals also expressed concern about the "evidentiary obstacles defendants face." But all of its sister Circuits that have confronted the issue have required that defendants produce some evidence of differential treatment of similarly situated members of other races or protected classes. In the present case, if the claim of selective prosecution were well founded, it should not have been an insuperable task to prove that persons of other races were being treated differently than respondents. For instance, respondents could have investigated whether similarly situated persons of other races were prosecuted by the State of California and were known to federal law enforcement officers, but were not prosecuted in federal court. We think the required threshold — a credible showing of different treatment of similarly situated persons — adequately balances the Government's interest in vigorous prosecution and the defendant's interest in avoiding selective prosecution.

In the case before us, respondents' "study" did not constitute "some evidence tending to show the existence of the essential elements of" a selective-prosecution claim. The study failed to identify individuals who were not black and could have been prosecuted for the offenses for which respondents were charged, but were not so prosecuted. The newspaper article, which discussed the discriminatory effect of federal drug sentencing laws, was not relevant to an allegation of discrimination in decisions to prosecute. Respondents' affidavits, which recounted one attorney's conversation with a drug treatment center employee and the experience of another attorney defending drug prosecutions in state court, recounted hearsay and reported personal conclusions based on anecdotal evidence. The judgment of the Court of Appeals is therefore reversed, and the case is remanded for proceedings consistent with this opinion.

Justice STEVENS, dissenting.

Federal prosecutors are respected members of a respected profession. Despite an occasional misstep, the excellence of their work abundantly justifies the presumption that "they have properly discharged their official duties." Nevertheless, the possibility that political or racial animosity may infect a decision to institute criminal proceedings cannot be ignored. For that reason, it has long been settled that the prosecutor's broad discretion to determine when criminal charges should be filed is not completely unbridled.

The United States Attorney is a member and an officer of the bar of that District Court. As such, she has a duty to the judges of that Court to maintain the standards of the profession in the performance of her official functions. If a District Judge has reason to suspect that she, or a member of her staff, has singled out particular defendants for prosecution on the basis of their race, it is surely appropriate for the judge to determine whether there is a factual basis for such a concern. I agree with the Court that Rule 16 of the Federal Rules of Criminal Procedure is not the source of the District Court's power to make the necessary inquiry. I disagree, however, with its implicit assumption that a different, relatively rigid rule needs to be crafted to regulate the use of this seldom-exercised inherent judicial power.

The District Judge's order should be evaluated in light of three circumstances that underscore the need for judicial vigilance over certain types of drug prosecutions. First, the Anti-Drug Abuse Act of 1986 and subsequent legislation established a regime of extremely high penalties for the possession and distribution of so-called "crack" cocaine. Those provisions treat one gram of crack as the equivalent of 100 grams of powder cocaine.

Second, the disparity between the treatment of crack cocaine and powder cocaine is matched by the disparity between the severity of the punishment imposed by federal law and that imposed by state law for the same conduct. For a variety of reasons, often including the absence of mandatory minimums, the existence of parole, and lower baseline penalties, terms of imprisonment for drug offenses tend to be substantially lower in state systems than in the federal system. The difference is especially marked in the case of crack offenses. The majority of States draw no distinction between types of cocaine in their penalty schemes; of those that do, none has established as stark a differential as the Federal Government.

Finally, it is undisputed that the brunt of the elevated federal penalties falls heavily on blacks. While 65% of the persons who have used crack are white, in 1993 they represented only 4% of the federal offenders convicted of trafficking in crack. Eighty-eight percent of such defendants were black. Those figures represent a major threat to the integrity of federal sentencing reform, whose main purpose was the elimination of disparity (especially racial) in sentencing.[16]

The extraordinary severity of the imposed penalties and the troubling racial patterns of enforcement give rise to a special concern about the fairness of charging practices for crack offenses. In my view, the District Judge, who has sat on both the federal and the state benches in Los Angeles, acted well within her discretion to call for the development of facts that would demonstrate what standards, if any, governed the choice of forum where similarly situated offenders are prosecuted.

The problem of racial disparity in prosecutions continues to be significant. While the legal standard requires that defendants show intentional discrimination, critics charge that unintentional discrimination poses significant challenges. Every day, prosecutors may make decisions that unintentionally discriminate. "This discriminatory impact may occur because of unconscious racism — a phenomenon that plays a powerful role in so many discretionary decisions in the criminal process — and because the lack of power and disadvantaged circumstances of so many African-American defendants and victims make it more likely that prosecutors will treat them less well than whites."[17] Nonetheless, under the Court's equal protection standards, only the most egregious situations of discrimination are likely to meet legal standards for selective prosecution motions.

b.   Vindictive Prosecution

A prosecutor's decision to increase the number or severity of charges against a defendant may also be challenged as violating due process if it penalizes a defendant's exercise of constitutional or statutory rights. The mere increase in charges does not satisfy the standard. Rather, a defendant must show actual vindictiveness.

---

16. It took many years to reform the laws applicable to crack and powder cocaine offenses. In 2007, the Congress and the U.S. Sentencing Commission finally amended the crack cocaine guidelines. The Fair Sentencing Act of 2010 reduced from 100:1 to 18:1 the ratio used to punish crack cocaine offenders more harshly than those violating laws with commensurate amounts of powder cocaine. *See* http://www.justice.gov/oip/docs/fair-sentencing-act-memo.pdf. [Footnote by casebook authors.]

17. *See* Angela J. Davis, *Prosecution and Race: The Power and Privilege of Discretion*, 67 Fordham L. Rev. 13 (1998).

Pretrial decisions by prosecutors are generally not considered to be vindictive. For example, there is no presumption of vindictiveness when a prosecutor threatens to increase charges if a defendant does not accept a plea offer. *See* Bordenkircher v. Hayes, 434 U.S. 357 (1978). Such threats are accepted as part of the plea bargaining process. Likewise, there is no presumption of vindictiveness when additional charges are added after a defendant requests a jury trial. *See* United States v. Goodwin, 457 U.S. 368 (1982).

However, there are certain situations, especially when a defendant is reindicted, in which the court is willing to presume vindictiveness. The Court discussed the issue of vindictive prosecution in Blackledge v. Perry.

BLACKLEDGE v. PERRY
417 U.S. 21 (1974)

Justice STEWART delivered the opinion of the Court.

[Perry was an inmate in a North Carolina prison where he got into a fight with another inmate. Perry was charged with misdemeanor assault with a deadly weapon. After he was convicted by a lower trial court, he exercised his statutory right to appeal his conviction and seek a trial de novo before a higher court. While that appeal was pending, the prosecutor obtained an indictment charging Perry with felony assault with intent to kill. Perry claimed vindictive prosecution.]

[Perry] urges that the indictment on the felony charge constituted a penalty for his exercising his statutory right to appeal, and thus contravened the Due Process Clause of the Fourteenth Amendment. Perry's due process arguments are derived substantially from North Carolina v. Pearce and its progeny. In *Pearce*, the Court considered the constitutional problems presented when, following a successful appeal and reconviction, a criminal defendant was subjected to a greater punishment than that imposed at the first trial. While we concluded that such a harsher sentence was not absolutely precluded by either the Double Jeopardy or Due Process Clause, we emphasized that "imposition of a penalty upon the defendant for having successfully pursued a statutory right of appeal or collateral remedy would be . . . a violation of due process of law." Because "vindictiveness against a defendant for having successfully attacked his first conviction must play no part in the sentence he receives after a new trial," we held that an increased sentence could not be imposed upon retrial unless the sentencing judge placed certain specified findings on the record.

[T]he Due Process Clause is not offended by all possibilities of increased punishment upon retrial after appeal, but only by those that pose a realistic likelihood of "vindictiveness." The question is whether the opportunities for vindictiveness in this situation are such as to impel the conclusion that due process of law requires a rule analogous to that of the *Pearce* case. We conclude that the answer must be in the affirmative.

A prosecutor clearly has a considerable stake in discouraging convicted misdemeanants from appealing and thus obtaining a trial de novo in the Superior Court, since such an appeal will clearly require increased expenditures of prosecutorial resources before the defendant's conviction becomes final, and may even result in a formerly convicted defendant's going free. And, if the prosecutor has the means readily at hand to discourage such appeals—by "upping the ante" through a felony indictment whenever a convicted misdemeanant pursues his statutory appellate remedy—the State can insure that only the most hardy defendants will brave the hazards of a de novo trial.

There is, of course, no evidence that the prosecutor in this case acted in bad faith or maliciously in seeking a felony indictment against Perry. The rationale of our judgment in the *Pearce* case, however, was not grounded upon the proposition that actual retaliatory motivation must inevitably exist. Rather, we emphasized that "since the fear of such vindictiveness may unconstitutionally deter a defendant's exercise of the right to appeal or collaterally attack his first conviction, due process also requires that a defendant be freed of apprehension of such a retaliatory motivation on the part of the sentencing judge." We think it clear that the same considerations apply here. A person convicted of an offense is entitled to pursue his statutory right to a trial de novo, without apprehension that the State will retaliate by substituting a more serious charge for the original one, thus subjecting him to a significantly increased potential period of incarceration.

Due process of law requires that such a potential for vindictiveness must not enter into North Carolina's two-tiered appellate process. We hold, therefore, that it was not constitutionally permissible for the State to respond to Perry's invocation of his statutory right to appeal by bringing a more serious charge against him prior to the trial de novo.[18]

It is rare for a vindictive trial motion to be granted. Most cases are not like *Blackledge*, and judges do not assume that the prosecutor had an impermissible motive for enhancing charges. Rather, judges generally give wide latitude to prosecutors to reevaluate their charging decisions. Thus, in United States v. Goodwin, 457 U.S. 368 (1982), the Court held that there is no presumption of vindictiveness if the prosecution increases charges pretrial because they have the right to reevaluate their case as they prepare for trial.

---

18. In its decision, the Court noted that a claim of prosecutorial vindictiveness would be overcome if the state could show "that it was impossible to proceed on the more serious charge at the outset" because, for example, the victim did not die until after the initial charges were brought. *See* Diaz v. United States, 223 U.S. 442 (1912). However, the prosecution in *Blackledge* had made no attempt to rebut the claim of vindictiveness. [Footnote by casebook authors.]

Accordingly, there is also no violation of a defendant's rights when a prosecutor threatens to add more charges during plea bargain negotiations. Moreover, even in the post-trial context, a claim of vindictiveness is easily rebutted if prosecutors can show that new evidence or a reevaluation of the case justified the imposition of the new charges. Lower courts continue to limit the impact of *Blackledge* by finding that it does not apply when a prosecutor escalates charges following a mistrial or files additional charges after an acquittal.[19]

C. FORMAL CHARGING MECHANISMS

American courts rely on two different mechanisms to screen cases before they are set for trial and to formalize the charges the defendant will face. Both the grand jury and preliminary hearing are designed to protect citizens from unjust prosecutions, but they use very different procedures to accomplish this goal.

1. *The Grand Jury*

The modern grand jury descends from the English grand jury used more than 800 years ago.[20] The grand jury consisted of a group of citizens who would act as a buffer between the Crown and the accused. Acting in secrecy, the grand jury would decide when individuals should be charged with crimes. American colonists adopted the grand jury as part of the common law system. In the famous Zenger case, a grand jury refused to indict newspaper publisher John Peter Zenger for libel after he criticized the governor of New York, although the grand jurors themselves were threatened with incarceration.

The right to a grand jury was incorporated into the Fifth Amendment. It provides that, except in military cases, "no person shall be held to answer for a capital, or otherwise infamous crime, unless on a presentment or indictment of a grand jury." Presentments, which were charges initiated by the grand jury, are no longer used. However, grand jury indictments are still the primary mechanism for bringing federal charges.

The right to an indictment only applies to "infamous crimes." A crime is "infamous" if it can result in imprisonment in a penitentiary or hard labor. Ex parte Wilson, 114 U.S. 417 (1885). Thus, federal felony charges are

---

19. For a discussion of cases limiting the doctrine of vindictive prosecution, *see* C. Peter Erlinder & David C. Thomas, *Prohibiting Prosecutorial Vindictiveness While Protecting Prosecutorial Discretion: Toward a Principled Resolution of a Due Process Dilemma*, 76 J. Crim. L. & C. 341 (1985); Barbara A. Schwartz, *The Limits of Prosecutorial Vindictiveness*, 69 Iowa L. Rev. 127 (1983).

20. For a summary of the history and purpose of the grand jury, *see* United States v. Navarro-Vargas, 408 F.3d 1184 (9th Cir. 2005).

brought by way of indictment. Misdemeanor charges can be filed directly by the prosecutor by information.

The right to a grand jury indictment only applies to federal prosecutions. In Hurtado v. California, 110 U.S. 516 (1884), the Supreme Court held that the right to a grand jury is not incorporated under the Fourteenth Amendment. Thus, states are free to bring charges for serious crimes without using a grand jury or by using a grand jury that has different procedures from a federal grand jury. Only about one-third of the states have grand juries, and some states use their grand juries primarily to conduct civil investigations of government agencies.

While the primary function of a grand jury is to screen cases and decide which should be indicted, the grand jury also performs an important investigative role. The grand jury has the power to subpoena witnesses and documents. It is an effective tool for prosecutors because they can conduct their investigations in secret without the defense being present.

Pursuant to Federal Rule of Criminal Procedure 6(a), 23 citizens sit on a grand jury. They are selected from a cross-section of the community. Grand jurors typically serve for 6 months, but their service can extend for as long as 18 months. If a grand jury refuses to issue an indictment, prosecutors can represent the same case to another grand jury.

Although the grand jury is considered to be an independent screening body, the reality is that the grand jury is directed in its operations by the prosecutor. Prosecutors suggest what cases the grand jury should investigate, prepare the subpoenas for their signature, draft the indictments, and advise the grand jurors of the law. It is therefore extremely rare for a grand jury to refuse to issue an indictment requested by a prosecutor. If the grand jury refuses to indict, it issues a "no bill." However, many people perceive the modern grand jury as nothing more than a "rubber stamp" for prosecutors.

Grand jurors do not have the power to bring charges without the agreement of the prosecutor. If the grand jury returns an indictment, and the prosecution disagrees with its decision, it may refuse to sign the indictment or issue a *nolle prosequi*, which dismisses the charges. There have been situations of "runaway" grand juries, but courts have held that grand jurors do not have independent power to bring a prosecution.[21]

A defendant can waive grand jury indictment and opt to have the prosecution file formal charges by information. Fed. R. Crim. P. 7(b). Waiver of indictment often signals that a defendant is cooperating in the government's investigation.

---

21. The most infamous case of a runaway grand jury involved an investigation of Rockwell International for operating its Rocky Flats nuclear-weapons plant in a manner that included dumping nuclear waste into the environment. The prosecutor declined to sign a grand jury indictment against Rockwell, instead reaching a financial settlement with the company. Incensed by the prosecutor's refusal, the grand jurors tried to bring charges on their own, but the court refused to intervene in the prosecutor's decision. *See* Jim Hughes, *Grand Jurors Hope to Go Public and Ask Congress to Decide in Rocky Flats Case*, Denver Post, March 14, 2004, B-04.

a. Operation of the Grand Jury

Grand jury operations are an ex parte process. Only the prosecutor is represented in grand jury proceedings. During the typical grand jury proceeding, the prosecutor calls and examines witnesses before the grand jury. Then, if the prosecutor wants to secure an indictment, the prosecutor presents a typed indictment to the grand jury, instructs them on the applicable law, and steps out when the grand jurors are asked to deliberate to determine whether there is probable cause to support the charges.

Neither the defendant nor his counsel has the right to be present in the grand jury. There is also no judge present for grand jury proceedings. The grand jury is considered to be an independent body that investigates and screens cases.

Individuals who are the focus of a grand jury investigation are typically referred to as "targets" of the grand jury. It is rare, although not prohibited, for the target of a grand jury to be called as a witness in the grand jury because an individual has the Fifth Amendment right to refuse to testify before the grand jury.

Some prosecutors also refer to "subjects" of a grand jury investigation. A subject is also a person who may be charged with a crime, but is not as likely to be indicted as the identified "target" of the investigation. Prosecutors are not required to tell individuals that they are the target or suspect of a grand jury investigation. Moreover, because of secrecy rules, Department of Justice guidelines advise prosecutors not to confirm an ongoing grand jury investigation.

Grand jury transcripts remain secret until ordered released by the court. In federal court, the testimony of a grand jury witness is not discoverable unless that witness testifies at trial or the requesting party shows a particularized need for release of the transcript. Fed. R. Crim. P. 6(e). Some states routinely release grand jury transcripts to the public once a case has been indicted.

Violations of grand jury procedures generally become moot once the defendant is convicted. For example, in United States v. Mechanik, 475 U.S. 66 (1986), the prosecution arguably violated Federal Rule of Criminal Procedure 6(d) by having two witnesses testify at once before the grand jury. The Supreme Court held that while such a procedural error could influence a grand jury to indict the defendant, once the petit jury returned a guilty verdict, there was proof beyond a reasonable doubt that such charges were warranted. Thus, any error in the grand jury proceeding was harmless.

Moreover, even if a defendant raises a claim of grand jury error before a case is tried, grand jury violations are not grounds for dismissing an indictment absent a showing of prejudice. Thus, in Bank of Nova Scotia v. United States, 487 U.S. 250 (1988), the district court found a variety of alleged violations of grand jury procedures, including unauthorized disclosures of grand jury materials to civil government employees and improper disclosure of the targets of the grand jury. Nonetheless, the Supreme Court held that dismissal is still not a proper remedy unless the defendant can demonstrate prejudice from the violations. Writing for the majority, Justice Kennedy stated, "We conclude that the District Court had no authority to dismiss the indictment on the basis of prosecutorial misconduct absent a finding that petitioners were prejudiced by such misconduct. The prejudicial inquiry must focus on whether any violations had an effect on the grand jury's decision to indict."

b. Screening Function of the Grand Jury

The role of the grand jury is to screen cases before defendants are required to stand trial. Yet it is not bound by the same rules of evidence and procedure that will govern the trial jury's decision. In light of the next two cases, how effectively do you believe the grand jury screens cases before trial?

COSTELLO v. UNITED STATES
350 U.S. 359 (1956)

Justice BLACK delivered the opinion of the Court.

We granted certiorari in this case to consider a single question: "May a defendant be required to stand trial and a conviction be sustained where only hearsay evidence was presented to the grand jury which indicted him?"

Petitioner, Frank Costello, was indicted for willfully attempting to evade payment of income taxes. Petitioner promptly filed a motion for inspection of the minutes of the grand jury and for a dismissal of the indictment. His motion was based on an affidavit stating that he was firmly convinced there could have been no legal or competent evidence before the grand jury which indicted him since he had reported all his income and paid all taxes due. The motion was denied. At the trial which followed the Government offered evidence designed to show increases in Costello's net worth in an attempt to prove that he had received more income during the years in question than he had reported. To establish its case the Government called and examined 144 witnesses and introduced 368 exhibits. All of the testimony and documents related to business transactions and expenditures by petitioner and his wife. The prosecution concluded its case by calling three government agents. Their investigations had produced the evidence used against petitioner at the trial. They were allowed to summarize the vast amount of evidence already heard and to introduce computations showing, if correct, that petitioner and his wife had received far greater income than they had reported. We have held such summarizations admissible in a "net worth" case like this.

Counsel for petitioner asked each government witness at the trial whether he had appeared before the grand jury which returned the indictment. This cross-examination developed the fact that the three investigating officers had been the only witnesses before the grand jury. After the Government concluded its case, petitioner again moved to dismiss the indictment on the ground that the only evidence before the grand jury was "hearsay," since the three officers had no firsthand knowledge of the transactions upon which their computations were based. Nevertheless the trial court again refused to dismiss the indictment, and petitioner was convicted. The Court of Appeals affirmed, holding that the indictment was valid even though the sole evidence before the grand jury was hearsay. Petitioner here urges: (1) that an indictment based solely on hearsay evidence violates that part of the Fifth Amendment providing that "No person shall be held to answer for a capital, or otherwise infamous crime, unless on a presentment or indictment of a Grand Jury . . ." and (2) that if the Fifth Amendment does not invalidate an indictment based solely on hearsay we should now lay down such a rule for the guidance of federal courts.

The Fifth Amendment provides that federal prosecutions for capital or otherwise infamous crimes must be instituted by presentments or indictments of grand juries. But neither the Fifth Amendment nor any other constitutional provision prescribes the kind of evidence upon which grand juries must act. The grand jury is an English institution, brought to this country by the early colonists and incorporated in the Constitution by the Founders. There is every reason to believe that our constitutional grand jury was intended to operate substantially like its English progenitor. The basic purpose of the English grand jury was to provide a fair method for instituting criminal proceedings against persons believed to have committed crimes. Grand jurors were selected from the body of the people and their work was not hampered by rigid procedural or evidential rules. In fact, grand jurors could act on their own knowledge and were free to make their presentments or indictments on such information as they deemed satisfactory. Despite its broad power to institute criminal proceedings the grand jury grew in popular favor with the years. It acquired an independence in England free from control by the Crown or judges. Its adoption in our Constitution as the sole method for preferring charges in serious criminal cases shows the high place it held as an instrument of justice. And in this country as in England of old the grand jury has convened as a body of laymen, free from technical rules, acting in secret, pledged to indict no one because of prejudice and to free no one because of special favor.

In Holt v. United States, this Court had to decide whether an indictment should be quashed because supported in part by incompetent evidence. The Court refused to hold that such an indictment should be quashed. If indictments were to be held open to challenge on the ground that there was inadequate or incompetent evidence before the grand jury, the resulting delay would be great indeed. The result of such a rule would be that before trial on the merits a defendant could always insist on a kind of preliminary trial to determine the competency and adequacy of the evidence before the grand jury. This is not required by the Fifth Amendment. An indictment returned by a legally constituted and unbiased grand jury, like an information drawn by the prosecutor, if valid on its face, is enough to call for trial of the charge on the merits. The Fifth Amendment requires nothing more.

Petitioner urges that this Court should exercise its power to supervise the administration of justice in federal courts and establish a rule permitting defendants to challenge indictments on the ground that they are not supported by adequate or competent evidence. No persuasive reasons are advanced for establishing such a rule. It would run counter to the whole history of the grand jury institution, in which laymen conduct their inquiries unfettered by technical rules. Neither justice nor the concept of a fair trial requires such a change. In a trial on the merits, defendants are entitled to a strict observance of all the rules designed to bring about a fair verdict. Defendants are not entitled, however, to a rule which would result in interminable delay but add nothing to the assurance of a fair trial.

In order for grand juries to be more exacting in their screening of cases, states can mandate that only admissible evidence may be presented to the grand jury to establish grounds for an indictment. *See, e.g.*, Cal. Penal Code §939.6(b). Yet, as *Costello* discussed, there is no constitutional bar to having a grand jury consider hearsay evidence in deciding whether to indict. Moreover, grand jurors can also hear evidence that would be excludable by a motion to suppress. In United States v. Calandra, 414 U.S. 338 (1974), the Supreme Court held that illegally seized evidence can also be used in a grand jury proceeding.

Not only is the grand jury not required to consider only admissible evidence; it is not, as the next case demonstrates, required to consider defense evidence that could be presented at trial. The grand jury is not an adversarial proceeding. It is a modest screening mechanism to ensure that cases that do proceed to trial are supported by probable cause.

UNITED STATES v. WILLIAMS
504 U.S. 36 (1992)

Justice SCALIA delivered the opinion of the Court.

The question presented in this case is whether a district court may dismiss an otherwise valid indictment because the Government failed to disclose to the grand jury "substantial exculpatory evidence" in its possession.

Respondent does not contend that the Fifth Amendment itself obliges the prosecutor to disclose substantial exculpatory evidence in his possession to the grand jury. Instead, building on our statement that the federal courts "may, within limits, formulate procedural rules not specifically required by the Constitution or the Congress," he argues that imposition of [a] disclosure rule is supported by the courts' "supervisory power." We think not.

Bank of Nova Scotia v. United States (1988) makes clear that the supervisory power can be used to dismiss an indictment because of misconduct before the grand jury, at least where that misconduct amounts to a violation of one of those "few, clear rules which were carefully drafted and approved by this Court and by Congress to ensure the integrity of the grand jury's functions."[22] We did not hold in *Bank of Nova Scotia,* however, that the courts' supervisory power could be used, not merely as a means of enforcing or vindicating legally compelled standards of prosecutorial conduct before the grand jury, but as a means of prescribing those standards of prosecutorial conduct in the first instance — just as it may be used as a means of establishing standards of prosecutorial conduct before the courts themselves.

"Rooted in long centuries of Anglo-American history," the grand jury is mentioned in the Bill of Rights, but not in the body of the Constitution. It has not been textually assigned, therefore, to any of the branches described in the first three Articles. It "is a constitutional fixture in its own right." In fact the whole theory of its function is that it belongs to no branch of the institutional Government, serving as a kind of buffer or referee between the Government and the people. Although the grand jury normally operates, of course, in the courthouse and under judicial auspices, its institutional relationship with the Judicial Branch has traditionally been, so to speak, at arm's length. Judges' direct involvement in the functioning of the grand jury has generally been confined to the constitutive one of calling the grand jurors together and administering their oaths of office.

The grand jury's functional independence from the Judicial Branch is evident both in the scope of its power to investigate criminal wrongdoing and in the manner in which that power is exercised. "Unlike [a] court, whose jurisdiction is predicated upon a specific case or controversy, the grand jury 'can investigate merely on suspicion that the law is being violated, or even because it wants assurance that it is not.'" It need not identify the offender it suspects, or even "the precise nature of the offense" it is investigating. The grand jury requires no authorization from its constituting court to initiate an investigation, nor does the prosecutor require leave of court to seek a grand jury indictment. And in its day-to-day functioning, the grand jury generally operates without the interference of a presiding judge.

We have insisted that the grand jury remain "free to pursue its investigations unhindered by external influence or supervision so long as it does not trench upon the legitimate rights of any witness called before it." Recognizing this tradition of independence, we have said that the Fifth Amendment's "constitutional guarantee presupposes an investigative body 'acting independently of either prosecuting attorney or judge.' . . ."

We have twice suggested, though not held, that the Sixth Amendment right to counsel does not attach when an individual is summoned to appear

---

22. These rules are set forth in Federal Rule of Criminal Procedure 6 in the Statutory Supplement, including rules on grand jury secrecy and the persons who may be present during grand jury deliberations. [Footnote by casebook authors.]

before a grand jury, even if he is the subject of the investigation. And although "the grand jury may not force a witness to answer questions in violation of [the Fifth Amendment's] constitutional guarantee" against self-incrimination, our cases suggest that an indictment obtained through the use of evidence previously obtained in violation of the privilege against self-incrimination "is nevertheless valid."

Given the grand jury's operational separateness from its constituting court, it should come as no surprise that we have been reluctant to invoke the judicial supervisory power as a basis for prescribing modes of grand jury procedure.

Respondent makes a generalized appeal to functional notions: Judicial supervision of the quantity and quality of the evidence relied upon by the grand jury plainly facilitates, he says, the grand jury's performance of its twin historical responsibilities, i.e., bringing to trial those who may be justly accused and shielding the innocent from unfounded accusation and prosecution. We do not agree. The rule would neither preserve nor enhance the traditional functioning of the institution that the Fifth Amendment demands. To the contrary, requiring the prosecutor to present exculpatory as well as inculpatory evidence would alter the grand jury's historical role, transforming it from an accusatory to an adjudicatory body.

It is axiomatic that the grand jury sits not to determine guilt or innocence, but to assess whether there is adequate basis for bringing a criminal charge. As a consequence, neither in this country nor in England has the suspect under investigation by the grand jury ever been thought to have a right to testify or to have exculpatory evidence presented.

Imposing upon the prosecutor a legal obligation to present exculpatory evidence in his possession would be incompatible with this system. If a "balanced" assessment of the entire matter is the objective, surely the first thing to be done — rather than requiring the prosecutor to say what he knows in defense of the target of the investigation — is to entitle the target to tender his own defense. To require the former while denying (as we do) the latter would be quite absurd. It would also be quite pointless, since it would merely invite the target to circumnavigate the system by delivering his exculpatory evidence to the prosecutor, whereupon it would have to be passed on to the grand jury — unless the prosecutor is willing to take the chance that a court will not deem the evidence important enough to qualify for mandatory disclosure.

Respondent acknowledges (as he must) that the "common law" of the grand jury is not violated if the grand jury itself chooses to hear no more evidence than that which suffices to convince it an indictment is proper. Respondent insists, however, that courts must require the modern prosecutor to alert the grand jury to the nature and extent of the available exculpatory evidence, because otherwise the grand jury "merely functions as an arm of the prosecution." We reject the attempt to convert a non-existent duty of the grand jury itself into an obligation of the prosecutor.

[I]n Costello v. United States, we held that "it would run counter to the whole history of the grand jury institution" to permit an indictment to be challenged "on the ground that there was inadequate or incompetent evidence before the grand jury." It would make little sense, we think, to abstain from reviewing the evidentiary support for the grand jury's judgment while scrutinizing the sufficiency of the prosecutor's presentation. A complaint about the quality or adequacy of the evidence can always be recast as a complaint that the prosecutor's presentation was "incomplete" or "misleading." Our words in *Costello* bear repeating: Review of facially valid indictments on such grounds "would run counter to the whole history of the grand jury institution[,] [and] neither justice nor the concept of a fair trial requires [it]."

[R]espondent argues that a rule requiring the prosecutor to disclose exculpatory evidence to the grand jury would, by removing from the docket unjustified prosecutions, save valuable judicial time. That depends, we suppose, upon what the ratio would turn out to be between unjustified prosecutions eliminated and grand jury indictments challenged — for the latter as well as the former consume "valuable judicial time." We need not pursue the matter; if there is an advantage to the proposal, Congress is free to prescribe it. For the reasons set forth above, however, we conclude that courts have no authority to prescribe such a duty pursuant to their inherent supervisory authority over their own proceedings.

Justice STEVENS, with whom Justice BLACKMUN and Justice O'CONNOR join, and with whom Justice THOMAS joins in part, dissenting.

Like the Hydra slain by Hercules, prosecutorial misconduct has many heads. [T]he prosecutor has [a] duty to refrain from improper methods calculated to produce a wrongful indictment. Indeed, the prosecutor's duty to protect the fundamental fairness of judicial proceedings assumes special importance when he is presenting evidence to a grand jury. "The costs of continued unchecked prosecutorial misconduct" before the grand jury are particularly substantial because there:

> the prosecutor operates without the check of a judge or a trained legal adversary, and virtually immune from public scrutiny. The prosecutor's abuse of his special relationship to the grand jury poses an enormous risk to defendants as well. For while in theory a trial provides the defendant with a full opportunity to contest and disprove the charges against him, in practice, the handing up of an indictment will often have a devastating personal and professional impact that a later dismissal or acquittal can never undo. Where the potential for abuse is so great, and the consequences of a mistaken indictment so serious, the ethical responsibilities of the prosecutor, and the obligation of the judiciary to protect against even the appearance of unfairness, are correspondingly heightened.
>
> The ex parte character of grand jury proceedings makes it peculiarly important for a federal prosecutor to remember that, in the familiar phrase, the interest of the United States "in a criminal prosecution is not that it shall win a case, but that justice shall be done."

We do not protect the integrity and independence of the grand jury by closing our eyes to the countless forms of prosecutorial misconduct that may occur inside the secrecy of the grand jury room. After all, the grand jury is not merely an investigatory body; it also serves as a "protector of citizens against arbitrary and oppressive governmental action."

It blinks reality to say that the grand jury can adequately perform this important historic role if it is intentionally misled by the prosecutor—on whose knowledge of the law and facts of the underlying criminal investigation the jurors will, of necessity, rely.

Unlike the Court, I am unwilling to hold that countless forms of prosecutorial misconduct must be tolerated—no matter how prejudicial they may be, or how seriously they may distort the legitimate function of the grand jury—simply because they are not proscribed by Rule 6 of the Federal Rules of Criminal Procedure or a statute that is applicable in grand jury proceedings. Such a sharp break with the traditional role of the federal judiciary is unprecedented, unwarranted, and unwise. Unrestrained prosecutorial misconduct in grand jury proceedings is inconsistent with the administration of justice in the federal courts and should be redressed in appropriate cases by the dismissal of indictments obtained by improper methods.

c. Grand Jury Reform

There continue to be calls for grand jury reform, but these generally go unheeded by Congress and the Supreme Court. The ABA Criminal Justice Section Committee on the Grand Jury has proposed the following reforms:

1. Witnesses before the grand jury be afforded the right to be accompanied by counsel in the grand jury room;
2. Prosecutors be required to advise the grand jury of any known exculpatory information;
3. Prosecutors not be permitted to present to the grand jury evidence that would be inadmissible at trial;
4. Targets of a grand jury investigation be given the right to testify;
5. Grand jury witnesses be provided with transcripts of their own testimony; and
6. Grand juries not name persons in an indictment as an unindicted co-conspirator.

Thus far, these reforms have not been adopted in federal court; the Supreme Court's holding in United States v. Mandujano, 425 U.S. 564 (1976)—that a grand jury witness has no constitutional right to have counsel present during grand jury proceedings—remains in effect.

2. Preliminary Hearing

Another mechanism available to screen cases is the preliminary hearing. In federal court, preliminary hearings are governed by Federal Rule of

Criminal Procedure 5.1 and are only used to hold a defendant until an indictment can be obtained.

However, states routinely rely on preliminary hearings in lieu of or in addition to grand jury proceedings. Approximately two-thirds of the states permit felony prosecutions to be initiated by information or indictment. Once the magistrate or judge finds probable cause, the defendant is "bound over" for trial on charges filed by the prosecutor in an information.

A preliminary hearing is fundamentally different from a grand jury proceeding. Preliminary hearings are more akin to "mini-trials." A judge presides over the preliminary hearing; it is an adversarial process. The defendant has the right to be present and to be represented by counsel. Coleman v. Alabama, 399 U.S. 1 (1970). Preliminary hearings are generally open to the public. The prosecution bears the burden at a preliminary hearing to present probable cause supporting the charges.

Different states use different evidentiary standards for preliminary hearings, depending on how exacting they want the case screening procedure to be. If a state wants a screening process that will authorize charges only when there is a strong chance of conviction at trial, it requires that the evidence at the preliminary hearing meet the same evidentiary standards it will have to meet for trial. Hearsay evidence is not allowed. However, many states view the preliminary hearing as a more modest check on prosecutorial discretion. In those venues, hearsay evidence may be presented at the preliminary hearing and the defense has a more limited opportunity to cross-examine the prosecution's witnesses. *See also* Fed. R. Evid. 1101(d)(3) (rules of evidence do not apply to federal preliminary hearings).

Following a preliminary hearing, the court's decision to bind a defendant over for trial generally triggers a more intense effort at plea negotiations. Having seen a preview of the prosecution's case, defense counsel is in a better position to assess a defendant's case than counsel might be if the defendant were indicted in secret by the grand jury.

If a magistrate refuses to bind over a defendant for trial, prosecutors may present their case to the grand jury or move to dismiss it and refile before a different judge. Any errors at the preliminary hearing are generally considered harmless once the defendant is tried and convicted.

In addition to screening cases for trial, a preliminary hearing is also crucial to preserving evidence for trial. In Crawford v. Washington, 541 U.S. 36 (2004), the Supreme Court held that testimonial hearsay statements cannot be presented at trial unless the declarant is unavailable and the defendant has had the opportunity to cross-examine the declarant before the statement is introduced. Thus, if a witness provides a formal statement before trial but then does not appear to testify, that statement cannot be used as evidence unless the defendant had an opportunity to cross-examine the victim regarding the statement. A preliminary hearing can provide the means to preserve that witness's testimony for trial by giving the defendant a pretrial opportunity to cross-examine the witness. Although the Supreme Court has held that the Sixth Amendment Confrontation Clause is a trial right and does not apply to the preliminary hearing (*see* Goldsby v. United States, 160 U.S. 70 (1895)), states now provide defendants the right to cross-examine pursuant to local or state rule.

D. SEVERANCE AND JOINDER

One of the decisions a prosecutor must make in deciding how to charge a case is whether to join charges and defendants for trial. Prosecutors generally favor trying defendants together. As Justice Scalia wrote in Richardson v. Marsh, 481 U.S. 200 (1987), there are advantages in joining defendants:

> Joint trials play a vital role in the criminal justice system. It would impair both the efficiency and the fairness of the criminal justice system to require . . . that prosecutors bring separate proceedings, presenting the same evidence again and again, requiring victims and witnesses to repeat the inconvenience (and sometimes trauma) of testifying, and randomly favoring the last-tried defendants who have the advantage of knowing the prosecution's case beforehand. Joint trials generally serve the interests of justice by avoiding inconsistent verdicts and enabling more accurate assessment of relative culpability — advantages which sometimes operate to the defendant's benefit. Even apart from these tactical considerations, joint trials generally serve the interests of justice by avoiding the scandal and inequity of inconsistent verdicts.

Yet there are also downsides to trying defendants together. Defendants may be tainted by the evidence against their codefendants. The mere fact that the defendants are charged together, or are facing multiple counts, can suggest to the jury that each defendant was part of a larger criminal scheme.

1. Federal Rules of Criminal Procedure 8 and 14

Federal Rules of Criminal Procedure 8 and 14 govern the issues of joinder and severance of criminal cases in federal court. Rule 8(a) permits the joinder of offenses that "are of the same or similar character, or are based on the same act or transaction, or are connected with or constitute parts of a common scheme or plan." Rule 8(b) permits two or more defendants to be charged together if they have participated in the same act or transaction, or in the same series of acts or transactions. The defendants may be charged in one or more counts together. All defendants need not be charged in each count.

Rule 14 provides relief from prejudicial joinder. "If the joinder of offenses or defendants in an indictment, or information, or a consolidation for trial, appears to prejudice a defendant or the government, the court may order separate trials of counts, sever the defendants' trials, or provide any other relief that justice requires."

2. *Irreconcilable Conflicts and* Bruton *Problems*

Two common grounds are offered in support of a defendant's motion to sever defendants who have been joined for trial: (1) finger-pointing at trial by one defendant against another and (2) introduction of confessions that implicate codefendants in a manner that violates the codefendant's right of confrontation. Generally, courts will not sever a case unless the conflict between defendants is irreconcilable.

a. Conflicting Defenses

ZAFIRO v. UNITED STATES
506 U.S. 534 (1993)

Justice O'CONNOR delivered the opinion of the Court.

Rule 8(b) of the Federal Rules of Criminal Procedure provides that defendants may be charged together "if they are alleged to have participated in the same act or transaction or in the same series of acts or transactions constituting an offense or offenses." Rule 14 of the Rules, in turn, permits a district court to grant a severance of defendants if "it appears that a defendant or the government is prejudiced by a joinder." In this case, we consider whether Rule 14 requires severance as a matter of law when codefendants present "mutually antagonistic defenses."

Gloria Zafiro, Jose Martinez, Salvador Garcia, and Alfonso Soto were accused of distributing illegal drugs in the Chicago area, operating primarily out of Soto's bungalow in Chicago and Zafiro's apartment in Cicero, a nearby suburb. One day, Government agents observed Garcia and Soto place a large box in Soto's car and drive from Soto's bungalow to Zafiro's apartment. The agents followed the two as they carried the box up the stairs. When the agents identified themselves, Garcia and Soto dropped the box and ran into the apartment. The agents entered the apartment in pursuit and found the four petitioners in the living room. The dropped box contained 55 pounds of cocaine.

The four petitioners were indicted and brought to trial together. At various points during the proceeding, Garcia and Soto moved for severance, arguing that their defenses were mutually antagonistic. Soto testified that he knew nothing about the drug conspiracy. He claimed that Garcia had asked him for a box, which he gave Garcia, and that he (Soto) did not know its contents until they were arrested. Garcia did not testify, but his lawyer argued that Garcia was innocent: The box belonged to Soto and Garcia was ignorant of its contents.

Zafiro and Martinez also repeatedly moved for severance on the ground that their defenses were mutually antagonistic. Zafiro testified that she was merely Martinez's girlfriend and knew nothing of the conspiracy. She claimed that Martinez stayed in her apartment occasionally, kept some clothes there, and gave her small amounts of money. Although she allowed Martinez to store a suitcase in her closet, she testified, she had no idea that the suitcase contained illegal drugs. Like Garcia, Martinez did not testify. But his lawyer argued that Martinez was only visiting his girlfriend and had no idea that she was involved in distributing drugs.

The District Court denied the motions for severance. The jury convicted all four petitioners of conspiring to possess cocaine, heroin, and marijuana with the intent to distribute. Petitioners appealed their convictions.

Rule 8(b) states that "two or more defendants may be charged in the same indictment or information if they are alleged to have participated in the same act or transaction or in the same series of acts or transactions constituting an offense or offenses." There is a preference in the federal system for joint trials of defendants who are indicted together. Joint trials "play a vital role in the criminal justice system." Richardson v. Marsh (1987). They promote efficiency and "serve the interests of justice by avoiding the scandal and inequity of inconsistent verdicts." For these reasons, we repeatedly have approved of joint trials. But Rule 14 recognizes that joinder, even when proper under Rule 8(b), may prejudice either a defendant or the Government. Thus, the Rule provides: "If it appears that a defendant or the government is prejudiced by a joinder of . . . defendants . . . for trial together, the court may order an election or separate trials of counts, grant a severance of defendants or provide whatever other relief justice requires."

In interpreting Rule 14, the Courts of Appeals frequently have expressed the view that "mutually antagonistic" or "irreconcilable" defenses may be so prejudicial in some circumstances as to mandate severance. Notwithstanding such assertions, the courts have reversed relatively few convictions for failure to grant a severance on grounds of mutually antagonistic or irreconcilable defenses. The low rate of reversal may reflect the inability of defendants to prove a risk of prejudice in most cases involving conflicting defenses.

Nevertheless, petitioners urge us to adopt a bright-line rule, mandating severance whenever codefendants have conflicting defenses. We decline to do so. Mutually antagonistic defenses are not prejudicial per se. Moreover, Rule 14 does not require severance even if prejudice is shown; rather, it leaves the tailoring of the relief to be granted, if any, to the district court's sound discretion.

We believe that, when defendants properly have been joined under Rule 8(b), a district court should grant a severance under Rule 14 only if there is a serious risk that a joint trial would compromise a specific trial right of one of the defendants, or prevent the jury from making a reliable judgment about guilt or innocence. [For example,] evidence that is probative of a defendant's guilt but technically admissible only against a codefendant also might present a risk of prejudice. See Bruton v. United States (1968). The risk of prejudice will vary with the facts in each case, and district courts may find prejudice in situations not discussed here. When the risk of prejudice is high, a district court is more likely to determine that separate trials are necessary, but, less drastic measures, such as limiting instructions, often will suffice to cure any risk of prejudice.

Turning to the facts of this case, we note that petitioners do not articulate any specific instances of prejudice. Instead they contend that the very nature of their defenses, without more, prejudiced them. Their theory is that when two defendants both claim they are innocent and each accuses the other of the crime, a jury will conclude (1) that both defendants are lying and convict them both on that basis, or (2) that at least one of the two must be guilty without regard to whether the Government has proved its case beyond a reasonable doubt.

As to the first contention, it is well settled that defendants are not entitled to severance merely because they may have a better chance of acquittal in separate trials. As to the second contention, the short answer is that petitioners' scenario simply did not occur here. The Government argued that all four petitioners were guilty and offered sufficient evidence as to all four petitioners; the jury in turn found all four petitioners guilty of various offenses. Moreover, even if there were some risk of prejudice, here it is of the type that can be cured with proper instructions, and "juries are presumed to follow their instructions."

Rule 14 leaves the determination of risk of prejudice and any remedy that may be necessary to the sound discretion of the district courts. Because petitioners have not shown that their joint trial subjected them to any legally cognizable prejudice, we conclude that the District Court did not abuse its discretion in denying petitioners' motions to sever.

Justice STEVENS, concurring in the judgment.

When two people are apprehended in possession of a container filled with narcotics, it is probable that they both know what is inside. The inference of knowledge is heightened when, as in this case, both people flee when confronted by police officers, or both people occupy the premises in which the container is found. At the same time, however, it remains entirely possible that one person did not have such knowledge. That, of course, is the argument made by each of the defendants in this case: that he or she did not know what was in the crucial box or suitcase.

Most important here, it is also possible that both persons lacked knowledge of the contents of the relevant container. Moreover, that hypothesis is compatible with individual defenses of lack of knowledge. There is no logical inconsistency between a version of events in which one person is ignorant, and a version in which the other is ignorant; unlikely as it may seem, it is at least theoretically possible that both versions are true, in that both persons are ignorant. In other words, dual ignorance defenses do not necessarily translate into "mutually antagonistic" defenses, as that term is used in reviewing severance motions, because acceptance of one defense does not necessarily preclude acceptance of the other and acquittal of the codefendant.

I agree with the Court that a "bright-line rule, mandating severance whenever codefendants have conflicting defenses" is unwarranted. [But]

I think district courts must retain their traditional discretion to consider severance whenever mutually antagonistic defenses are presented. Accordingly, I would refrain from announcing a preference for joint trials, or any general rule that might be construed as a limit on that discretion.

b. *Bruton* Problems

As noted in *Zafiro*, there are situations in which the introduction of a confession by one defendant may implicate a codefendant and poses a Confrontation Clause problem because the codefendant has not had an opportunity to cross-examine the defendant on his confession. This is known as a *Bruton* problem. While the confessing defendant's statement may be admissible against the defendant who confessed, introducing the statement would violate the codefendant's right of confrontation because he has never had an opportunity to cross-examine the defendant who implicated him. In such situations, either the prosecution must redact the statement so that it does not implicate any codefendants or bring two separate trials.

BRUTON v. UNITED STATES

391 U.S. 123 (1968)

Justice BRENNAN delivered the opinion of the Court.

This case presents the question whether the conviction of a defendant at a joint trial should be set aside although the jury was instructed that a codefendant's confession inculpating the defendant had to be disregarded in determining his guilt or innocence.

A joint trial of petitioner and one Evans resulted in the conviction of both by a jury on a federal charge of armed postal robbery. A postal inspector testified that Evans orally confessed to him that Evans and petitioner committed the armed robbery. We hold that, because of the substantial risk that the jury, despite instructions to the contrary, looked to the incriminating extrajudicial statements in determining petitioner's guilt, admission of Evans' confession in this joint trial violated petitioner's right of cross-examination secured by the Confrontation Clause of the Sixth Amendment. We therefore overrule [our prior decision in] *Delli Paoli* and reverse.

The basic premise of *Delli Paoli* was that it is "reasonably possible for the jury to follow" sufficiently clear instructions to disregard the confessor's extrajudicial statement that his codefendant participated with him in committing the crime. If it were true that the jury disregarded the reference to the codefendant, no question would arise under the Confrontation Clause. But since *Delli Paoli* was decided this Court has effectively repudiated its basic premise. "It is impossible realistically to suppose that when the twelve good men and women [have a defendant's confession in the privacy of the jury room, they will not use it to implicate the codefendant]."

Those who have defended reliance on the limiting instruction in this area have cited several reasons in support. Judge Learned Hand, a particularly severe critic of the proposition that juries could be counted on to disregard inadmissible hearsay, . . . [called the] limiting instruction, . . . a "recommendation to the jury of a mental gymnastic which is beyond, not only their powers, but anybody's else." Judge Hand referred to the instruction as a "placebo," medically defined as "a medicinal lie." Judge Jerome Frank suggested that its legal equivalent "is a kind of 'judicial lie.'"

Another reason cited in defense of *Delli Paoli* is the justification for joint trials in general, the argument being that the benefits of joint proceedings should not have to be sacrificed by requiring separate trials in order to use the confession against the declarant. Joint trials do conserve state funds, diminish inconvenience to witnesses and public authorities, and avoid delays in bringing those accused of crime to trial. But the answer to this argument was cogently stated by Judge Lehman in People v. Fisher:

> We still adhere to the rule that an accused is entitled to confrontation of the witnesses against him and the right to cross-examine them. . . . We destroy the age-old rule which in the past has been regarded as a fundamental principle of our jurisprudence by a legalistic formula, required of the judge, that the jury may not consider any admissions against any party who did not join in them. We secure greater speed, economy and convenience in the administration of the law at the price of fundamental principles of constitutional liberty. That price is too high.

Despite the concededly clear instructions to the jury to disregard Evans' inadmissible hearsay evidence inculpating petitioner, in the context of a joint trial we cannot accept limiting instructions as an adequate substitute for petitioner's constitutional right of cross-examination.

Justice WHITE, dissenting.

I dissent from this excessively rigid rule. There is nothing in this record to suggest that the jury did not follow the trial judge's instructions. There has been no new learning since *Delli Paoli* indicating that juries are less reliable than they were considered in that case to be. There is nothing in the prior decisions of this Court which supports this new constitutional rule.

The Court concedes that there are many instances in which reliance on limiting instructions is justified, The Court asserts, however, that the hazards to the defendant of permitting the jury to hear a codefendant's confession implicating him are so severe that we must assume the jury's inability to heed a limiting instruction. There are good reasons, however, for distinguishing the codefendant's confession from that of the defendant himself and for trusting in the jury's ability to disregard the former when instructed to do so.

First, the defendant's own confession is probably the most probative and damaging evidence that can be admitted against him. Though itself an out-of-court statement, it is admitted as reliable evidence because it is an admission of guilt by the defendant and constitutes direct evidence of the facts to which it relates. Even the testimony of an eyewitness may be less reliable than the defendant's own confession.

The rule which the Court announces today will severely limit the circumstances in which defendants may be tried together for a crime which they are both charged with committing. Unquestionably, joint trials are more economical and minimize the burden on witnesses, prosecutors, and courts. They also avoid delays in bringing those accused of crime to trial. This much the Court concedes. It is also worth saying that separate trials are apt to have varying consequences for legally indistinguishable defendants. The unfairness of this is confirmed by the common prosecutorial experience of seeing codefendants who are tried separately strenuously jockeying for position with regard to who should be the first to be tried.

In view of the practical difficulties of separate trials and their potential unfairness, I am disappointed that the Court has not spelled out how the federal courts might conduct their business consistent with today's opinion. I would suppose that it will be necessary to exclude all extrajudicial confessions unless all portions of them which implicate defendants other than the declarant are effectively deleted. Effective deletion will probably require not only omission of all direct and indirect inculpations of codefendants but also of any statement that could be employed against those defendants once their identity is otherwise established. Of course, the deletion must not be such that it will distort the statements to the substantial prejudice of either the declarant or the Government. If deletion is not feasible, then the Government will have to choose either not to use the confession at all or to try the defendants separately. To save time, money, and effort, the Government might best seek a ruling at the earliest possible stage of the trial proceedings as to whether the confession is admissible once offending portions are deleted. Oral statements, such as that involved in the present case, will present special problems, for there is a risk that the witness in testifying will inadvertently exceed permissible limits. Except for recommending that caution be used with regard to such oral statements, it is difficult to anticipate the issues which will arise in concrete factual situations.

As Justice White predicted, courts have had to fashion other alternatives to the *Bruton* problem. Prosecutors have a few options:

1.   They can agree to separate trials for the defendants.
2.   They can try the defendants jointly but forgo use of the confession.
3.   They can redact the confession to remove all references to the existence of a non-confessing defendant.

In redacting the confession, prosecutors must be careful to ensure that a non-testifying codefendant's confession still cannot be construed as implicating the defendant. In the next two cases, Richardson v. Marsh, 481 U.S. 200 (1987) and Gray v. Maryland, 523 U.S. 185 (1998), the Court provided guidance as to what kinds of redacted confessions interfere with a codefendant's Sixth Amendment confrontation rights.

RICHARDSON v. MARSH

481 U.S. 200 (1987)

Justice SCALIA delivered the opinion of the Court.

In Bruton v. United States (1968), we held that a defendant is deprived of his rights under the Confrontation Clause when his nontestifying codefendant's confession naming him as a participant in the crime is introduced at their joint trial, even if the jury is instructed to consider that confession only against the codefendant. Today we consider whether *Bruton* requires the same result when the codefendant's confession is redacted to omit any reference to the defendant, but the defendant is nonetheless linked to the confession by evidence properly admitted against him at trial.

I

Respondent Clarissa Marsh, Benjamin Williams, and Kareem Martin were charged with assaulting Cynthia Knighton and murdering her 4-year-old son, Koran, and her aunt, Ollie Scott. Respondent and Williams were tried jointly, over her objection. (Martin was a fugitive at the time of trial.) At the trial, Knighton testified as follows: On the evening of October 29, 1978, she and her son were at Scott's home when respondent and her boyfriend Martin visited. After a brief conversation in the living room, respondent announced that she had come to "pick up something" from Scott and rose from the couch. Martin then pulled out a gun, pointed it at Scott and the Knightons, and said that "someone had gotten killed and [Scott] knew something about it." Respondent immediately walked to the front door and peered out the peephole. The doorbell rang, respondent opened the door, and Williams walked in, carrying a gun. As Williams passed respondent, he asked, "Where's the money?" Martin forced Scott upstairs, and Williams went into the kitchen, leaving respondent alone with the Knightons. Knighton and her son attempted to flee, but respondent grabbed Knighton and held her until Williams returned. Williams ordered the Knightons to lie on the floor and then went upstairs to assist Martin. Respondent, again left alone with the Knightons, stood by the front door and occasionally peered out the peephole. A few minutes later, Martin, Williams, and Scott came down the stairs, and Martin handed a paper grocery bag to respondent. Martin and Williams then forced Scott and the Knightons into the basement, where Martin shot them. Only Cynthia Knighton survived.

In addition to Knighton's testimony, the State introduced (over respondent's objection) a confession given by Williams to the police shortly after his arrest. The confession was redacted to omit all reference to respondent — indeed, to omit all indication that anyone other than Martin and Williams participated in the crime. At the time the confession was admitted, the jury was admonished not to use it in any way against respondent. Williams did not testify.

During his closing argument, the prosecutor admonished the jury not to use Williams' confession against respondent. After closing arguments, the judge again instructed the jury that Williams' confession was not to be considered against respondent. The jury convicted respondent of two counts of felony murder in the perpetration of an armed robbery and one count of assault with intent to commit murder.

Respondent then filed a petition for a writ of habeas corpus. She alleged that introduction of Williams' confession at the joint trial had violated her rights under the Confrontation Clause.

II

The Confrontation Clause of the Sixth Amendment, extended against the States by the Fourteenth Amendment, guarantees the right of a criminal defendant "to be confronted with the witnesses against him." The right of confrontation includes the right to cross-examine witnesses. Therefore, where two defendants are tried jointly, the pretrial confession of one cannot be admitted against the other unless the confessing defendant takes the stand.

Ordinarily, a witness whose testimony is introduced at a joint trial is not considered to be a witness "against" a defendant if the jury is instructed to consider that testimony only against a codefendant. This accords with the almost invariable assumption of the law that jurors follow their instructions which we have applied in many varying contexts. In *Bruton*, however, we recognized a narrow exception to this principle: We held that a defendant is deprived of his Sixth Amendment right of confrontation when the facially incriminating confession of a nontestifying codefendant is introduced at their joint trial, even if the jury is instructed to consider the confession only against the codefendant.

There is an important distinction between this case and *Bruton*, which causes it to fall outside the narrow exception we have created. In *Bruton*, the codefendant's confession "expressly implicat[ed]" the defendant as his accomplice. Thus, at the time that confession was introduced there was not the slightest doubt that it would prove "powerfully incriminating." By contrast, in this case the confession was not incriminating on its face, and became so only when linked with evidence introduced later at trial (the defendant's own testimony).

The rule that juries are presumed to follow their instructions is a pragmatic one, rooted less in the absolute certitude that the presumption is true than in the belief that it represents a reasonable practical accommodation of the interests of the state and the defendant in the criminal justice process. On the precise facts of *Bruton*, involving a facially incriminating confession, we found that accommodation inadequate. As our discussion above shows, the calculus changes when confessions that do not name the defendant are at issue. While we continue to apply *Bruton* where we have found that its rationale validly applies, we decline to extend it further. We hold that the Confrontation Clause is not violated by the admission of a nontestifying codefendant's confession with a proper limiting instruction when, as here, the confession is redacted to eliminate not only the defendant's name, but any reference to his or her existence.

Compare the type of redacted confession approved by the Supreme Court in Richardson v. Marsh with the redacted confession rejected by the Court in the next case of Gray v. Maryland.

GRAY v. MARYLAND
523 U.S. 185 (1998)

Justice BREYER delivered the opinion of the Court.

The issue in this case concerns the application of Bruton v. United States (1968). The case before us differs from *Bruton* in that the prosecution here redacted the codefendant's confession by substituting for the defendant's name in the confession a blank space or the word "deleted." We must decide whether these substitutions make a significant legal difference. We hold that they do not and that *Bruton*'s protective rule applies.

I

In 1993, Stacy Williams died after a severe beating. Anthony Bell gave a confession, to the Baltimore City police, in which he said that he (Bell), Kevin Gray, and Jacquin "Tank" Vanlandingham had participated in the beating that resulted in Williams' death. Vanlandingham later died. A Maryland grand jury indicted Bell and Gray for murder. The State of Maryland tried them jointly.

The trial judge, after denying Gray's motion for a separate trial, permitted the State to introduce Bell's confession into evidence at trial. But the judge ordered the confession redacted. Consequently, the police detective who read the confession into evidence said the word "deleted" or "deletion" whenever Gray's name or Vanlandingham's name appeared. Immediately after the police detective read the redacted confession to the jury, the prosecutor asked, "after he gave you that information, you subsequently were able to arrest Mr. Kevin Gray; is that correct?" The officer responded, "That's correct."

When instructing the jury, the trial judge specified that the confession was evidence only against Bell; the instructions said that the jury should not use the confession as evidence against Gray. The jury convicted both Bell and Gray. Gray appealed.

We granted certiorari in order to consider *Bruton*'s application to a redaction that replaces a name with an obvious blank space or symbol or word such as "deleted."

II

In deciding whether *Bruton*'s protective rule applies to the redacted confession before us, we must consider both *Bruton*, and a later case, Richardson v. Marsh (1987), which limited *Bruton*'s scope.

Bruton, as we have said, involved two defendants — Evans and Bruton — tried jointly for robbery. Evans did not testify, but the Government introduced into evidence Evans' confession, which stated that both he (Evans) and Bruton together had committed the robbery. The trial judge told the jury it could consider the confession as evidence only against Evans, not against Bruton.

This Court held that, despite the limiting instruction, the introduction of Evans' out-of-court confession at Bruton's trial had violated Bruton's right, protected by the Sixth Amendment, to cross-examine witnesses. [The Court said that]

> there are some contexts in which the risk that the jury will not, or cannot, follow instructions is so great, and the consequences of failure so vital to the defendant, that the practical and human limitations of the jury system cannot be ignored. Such a context is presented here, where the powerfully incriminating extrajudicial statements of a codefendant, who stands accused side-by-side with the defendant, are deliberately spread before the jury in a joint trial.

In *Richardson v. Marsh*, the Court considered a redacted confession. The case involved a joint murder trial of Marsh and Williams. The State had redacted the confession of one defendant, Williams, so as to "omit all reference" to his codefendant, Marsh — "indeed, to omit all indication that anyone other than . . . Williams" and a third person had "participated in the crime." The trial court also instructed the jury not to consider the confession against Marsh. As redacted, the confession indicated that Williams and the third person had discussed the murder in the front seat of a car while they traveled to the victim's house. The redacted confession contained no indication that Marsh — or any other person — was in the car.

The Court held that this redacted confession fell outside *Bruton*'s scope and was admissible (with appropriate limiting instructions) at the joint trial.

The Court added: "We express no opinion on the admissibility of a confession in which the defendant's name has been replaced with a symbol or neutral pronoun."

III

[U]nlike *Richardson*'s redacted confession, this confession refers directly to the "existence" of the nonconfessing defendant. The State has simply replaced the nonconfessing defendant's name with a kind of symbol, namely the word "deleted" or a blank space set off by commas. We therefore must decide a question that *Richardson* left open, namely whether redaction that replaces a defendant's name with an obvious indication of deletion, such as a blank space, the word "deleted," or a similar symbol, still falls within *Bruton*'s protective rule. We hold that it does.

Redactions that simply replace a name with an obvious blank space or a word such as "deleted" or a symbol or other similarly obvious indications of alteration, however, leave statements that, considered as a class, so closely resemble *Bruton*'s unredacted statements that, in our view, the law must require the same result.

For one thing, a jury will often react similarly to an unredacted confession and a confession redacted in this way, for the jury will often realize that the confession refers specifically to the defendant. This is true even when the State does not blatantly link the defendant to the deleted name, as it did in this case by asking whether Gray was arrested on the basis of information in Bell's confession as soon as the officer had finished reading the redacted statement. Consider a simplified but typical example, a confession that reads "I, Bob Smith, along with Sam Jones, robbed the bank." To replace the words "Sam Jones" with an obvious blank will not likely fool anyone. A juror somewhat familiar with criminal law would know immediately that the blank, in the phrase "I, Bob Smith, along with _____, robbed the bank," refers to defendant Jones. A juror who does not know the law and who therefore wonders to whom the blank might refer need only lift his eyes to Jones, sitting at counsel table, to find what will seem the obvious answer, at least if the juror hears the judge's instruction not to consider the confession as evidence against Jones, for that instruction will provide an obvious reason for the blank. A more sophisticated juror, wondering if the blank refers to someone else, might also wonder how, if it did, the prosecutor could argue the confession is reliable, for the prosecutor, after all, has been arguing that Jones, not someone else, helped Smith commit the crime.

IV

For these reasons, we hold that the confession here at issue, which substituted blanks and the word "delete" for the respondent's proper name, falls within the class of statements to which *Bruton*'s protections apply.

Justice SCALIA, with whom Chief Justice REHNQUIST, Justice KENNEDY and Justice THOMAS join, dissenting.

We declined in *Richardson* . . . to extend *Bruton* to confessions that incriminate only by inference from other evidence. When incrimination is inferential, "it is a less valid generalization that the jury will not likely obey the instruction to disregard the evidence." Today the Court struggles to decide whether a confession redacted to omit the defendant's name is incriminating on its face or by inference. The Court should have stopped with its concession: the statement "Me, deleted, deleted, and a few other guys" does not facially incriminate anyone but the speaker.

The Court's extension of *Bruton* to name-redacted confessions "as a class" will seriously compromise "society's compelling interest in finding, convicting, and punishing those who violate the law."

The United States Constitution guarantees, not a perfect system of criminal justice (as to which there can be considerable disagreement), but a minimum standard of fairness.

E. AMENDMENTS AND VARIANCES

Not all mistakes in the charges against a defendant will result in dismissal of a case. Federal Rule of Criminal Procedure 7(c) does not require that formal, legal language be used in an indictment. Rather, an indictment is sufficient if it is "a plain, concise, and definite written statement of the essential facts constituting the offense charged." The indictment or information need only inform a defendant of the charge the defendant must defend and provide sufficient detail that the defendant can raise a double jeopardy objection to a future prosecution for the same offense. *See* Hamling v. United States, 418 U.S. 87 (1974).

A defendant may request a *bill of particulars* to ascertain more details regarding the charged offense. The court has discretion pursuant to Federal Rule of Criminal Procedure 7(e) to grant a bill of particulars. Alternatively, the prosecution may provide such information through discovery. See Chapter 8.

Defendants may challenge indictments on *duplicity* grounds if they charge two or more distinct offenses in a single count of the indictment. Generally, duplicity is not fatal to an indictment. The government can correct the problem by selecting a single basis on which it will try the case.

Defendants may also challenge an indictment because a single offense is charged in multiple counts of an indictment. The simple solution to the problem of *multiplicity* is for the court to order the government to elect which count it will use and dismiss the remaining counts.

If there is a defect in an indictment, the prosecutor may seek to re-present the case to the grand jury for a *superseding indictment.* There is no limit on the number of times a prosecutor can return to the grand jury for a superseding indictment. If the original grand jury is no longer available, the prosecutor can re-present the case in summary fashion to a new grand jury. Superseding indictments are typically used to add new defendants or charges to an indictment or to correct errors before trial.

Indictments can also be *amended* to correct obvious clerical errors or delete surplusage from the indictment. However, it is improper to substantively amend an indictment because a defendant in federal court has a Fifth Amendment right to be tried only for those offenses charged by the grand jury. *See* Stirone v. United States, 361 U.S. 212 (1960).

A *variance* occurs when the evidence at trial proves facts other than those alleged in the indictment. For example, there may be a variance in the time of the crime charged or the number of conspiracies. If a defendant can demonstrate prejudice from a variance, the conviction cannot stand.

CHAPTER
7

BAIL AND PRETRIAL RELEASE

A. INTRODUCTION

After a suspect is arrested and booked on charges, he or she will typically seek release by posting bail. Defendants want bail for many reasons. First and foremost, no one wants to be incarcerated. The conditions in many jails are deplorable and the very loss of liberty is demoralizing, especially for a defendant who has not yet been convicted of a crime. Second, it is much more difficult to prepare for trial when a defendant is incarcerated. Behind bars the defendant is limited in how much he can assist his lawyer and it is much more cumbersome for defense counsel to meet with the client when the client is incarcerated. Third, defendants who remain in pretrial custody face the loss of income, social consequences, and even the loss of support by their families. Finally, there are the intangible effects of a defendant remaining in pretrial custody. A defendant can become demoralized and fear that he will be incarcerated for a long period of time.

On the other side of the ledger, there may be legitimate reasons that the prosecution wants the defendant to remain in pretrial custody. The defendant may pose a threat to society or prosecutors may worry that the defendant is a flight risk if not kept incarcerated before trial.

In general, unfairness in the bail system and its impact on poor defendants is one of the significant issues facing the criminal justice system today.[1] However, very little guidance is given in the Constitution regarding bail. The Eighth Amendment simply states that "[e]xcessive bail shall not be required." This does not provide answers as to the types of cases where bail is allowed or what is considered to be excessive. In Stack v. Boyle, 342 U.S. 1 (1951), the Supreme Court held that the Eighth Amendment did not guarantee the right to bail in all cases. Rather, it said that the Eighth

---

1. *See* Paul Heaton, Sandra Mayson & Megan Stevenson, *The Downstream Consequences of Misdemeanor Pretrial Detention*, 69 Stan. L. Rev. 711 (2017); Judge Lisa Foster, *Injustice Under Law: Perpetuating and Criminalizing Poverty Through the Courts*, 33 Ga. St. U. L. Rev. 695 (2017). Bail reform efforts have focused on addressing the problem of inequities in the criminal justice system; namely, the ability of defendants with more money to post bail and avoid jail time. *See* Richard A. Oppel, Jr., *Defendants Can't be Jailed Solely Because of Inability to Post Bail, Judge Says*, N.Y. Times (July 17, 2017).

Amendment provides that where bail is permitted, it cannot be excessive. It also noted that bail need not be allowed in capital offense cases.

In addition, the Supreme Court has never held that the "no excessive bail" clause of the Eighth Amendment applies to state prosecutions. Rather, it has been left to statutes and lower court decisions to sort out when bail is permitted and what factors may be considered in deciding to grant, or not grant, bail. The current standard directs the court to evaluate whether the defendant is a flight risk or a danger to the community.

Bail in the federal system is governed by the Bail Reform Act of 1984, 18 U.S.C. §§3142 and 3144. States have their own statutes governing the granting of bail. In most jurisdictions, the police have a *bail schedule* that they can use to release a suspect on bail even before the defendant has made a court appearance. However, in more serious cases, the court will determine whether there will be bail and, if so, what will be the amount.

There are many types of bail.[2] *Own recognizance (OR)* or *personal recognizance (PR)* release permits a defendant to be released upon a mere promise to appear in court. Under *conditions of pretrial release* a defendant may be subject to supervision, or perhaps a rehabilitation program, before trial. Failure to comply with the terms of supervision, including failure to report to probation officers or to have drug testing, can result in the defendant's reincarceration.

A *financial bond* requires a defendant to post money with the court. The posting of a bond may be handled by a bail bondsman, a third party, or the defendant. There are two basic types of bonds: a *secured bond*, usually secured by a deed to property, and an *unsecured bond*, which is based on a cash deposit and a promise to pay the remainder if the defendant fails to appear. If a bail bondsman posts bond for a defendant, the bondsman will typically take 10 percent of the amount of the bond to be posted with the court as his fee. If a defendant or family member posts bond for the defendant, and the defendant satisfies all of the conditions for pretrial release (including appearing for trial), the cash deposit is refunded by the court.[3]

Judges can take steps to prevent defendants from posting money or property derived from illegal proceeds. The court has the right to reject illegally derived funds as bail. To determine whether the proceeds being posted as bond are from an illegal source, the court may hold a special hearing referred to as a *Nebbia hearing*. In United States v. Nebbia, 357 F.2d 303 (2d Cir. 1966), the court held that a court does not need to accept a cash bond if it was illegally obtained because that is not the type of bail that is likely to secure a defendant's presence.

A court can impose many different types of conditions on a defendant posting bond. They may include drug testing, restrictions on travel, surrender of passport, counseling, lack of contact with witnesses and victims,

---

2. *See generally* Mary A. Tuborg, *Pretrial Release: A National Evaluation of Practices and Outcomes* (National Institute of Justice, 1981), 7, 9.

3. Sample bail schedules and 10 percent bail plans are set forth in the supplemental materials for this book.

home confinement, and other similar measures. Sometimes, individuals are placed under house arrest and a monitoring device is placed on their body to monitor their presence. Effective defense lawyers try to fashion a bail package that imposes those conditions that will assure the court that it is in the court's and defendant's best interest to grant bail.

If a defendant fails to comply with the terms of bail, such as not appearing at trial, bail may be forfeited. Forfeiture is governed by Federal Rule of Criminal Procedure 46(f).[4]

B. PREVENTIVE DETENTION

1. Pretrial Detention

The issue of bail pending trial raises the basic question of whether it is fair to hold a defendant in custody before he has been adjudged guilty of a crime. Prior to the Bail Reform Act of 1984,[5] the sole factor that courts were to consider was whether the defendant was a flight risk. However, in the 1984 Act, Congress added a second factor—danger to the community.

Prior to the Bail Reform Act, prosecutors would include concerns over dangerousness by claiming that a person who is dangerous to the community is a person who is unlikely to follow the laws and therefore unlikely to appear for trial. Following the 1984 Bail Reform Act, danger to the community became an express factor for denying bail. Given that the defendant has not been convicted, does it violate the presumption of innocence and due process to use danger to the community as a factor to deny or raise the amount of bail? The Supreme Court answered that question in United States v. Salerno.

UNITED STATES v. SALERNO

481 U.S. 739 (1987)

Chief Justice REHNQUIST delivered the opinion of the Court.

The Bail Reform Act of 1984 (Act) allows a federal court to detain an arrestee pending trial if the Government demonstrates by clear and convincing evidence after an adversary hearing that no release conditions "will reasonably assure . . . the safety of any other person and the community." The United States Court of Appeals for the Second Circuit struck down this provision of the Act as facially unconstitutional, because, in that court's words, this type of pretrial detention violates "substantive due process." We granted certiorari because of a conflict among the Courts. We hold

---

4. Federal Rule of Criminal Procedure 46 is set forth in the Statutory Supplement.
5. The Bail Reform Act of 1984, 18 U.S.C. §3141, is set forth in the Statutory Supplement.

that, as against the facial attack mounted by these respondents, the Act fully comports with constitutional requirements. We therefore reverse.

Responding to "the alarming problem of crimes committed by persons on release," Congress formulated the Bail Reform Act of 1984, 18 U.S.C. §3141 et seq., as the solution to a bail crisis in the federal courts. The Act represents the National Legislature's considered response to numerous perceived deficiencies in the federal bail process. By providing for sweeping changes in both the way federal courts consider bail applications and the circumstances under which bail is granted, Congress hoped to "give the courts adequate authority to make release decisions that give appropriate recognition to the danger a person may pose to others if released."

To this end, §3141(a) of the Act requires a judicial officer to determine whether an arrestee shall be detained. Section 3142(e) provides that "if, after a hearing pursuant to the provisions of subsection (f), the judicial officer finds that no condition or combination of conditions will reasonably assure the appearance of the person as required and the safety of any other person and the community, he shall order the detention of the person prior to trial." Section 3142(f) provides the arrestee with a number of procedural safeguards. He may request the presence of counsel at the detention hearing, he may testify and present witnesses in his behalf, as well as proffer evidence, and he may cross-examine other witnesses appearing at the hearing. If the judicial officer finds that no conditions of pretrial release can reasonably assure the safety of other persons and the community, he must state his findings of fact in writing, §3142(i), and support his conclusion with "clear and convincing evidence," §3142(f).

The judicial officer is not given unbridled discretion in making the detention determination. Congress has specified the considerations relevant to that decision. These factors include the nature and seriousness of the charges, the substantiality of the Government's evidence against the arrestee, the arrestee's background and characteristics, and the nature and seriousness of the danger posed by the suspect's release. §3142(g). Should a judicial officer order detention, the detainee is entitled to expedited appellate review of the detention order. §§3145(b), (c).

Respondents Anthony Salerno and Vincent Cafaro were arrested on March 21, 1986, after being charged in a 29-count indictment alleging various Racketeer Influenced and Corrupt Organizations Act (RICO) violations, mail and wire fraud offenses, extortion, and various criminal gambling violations. The RICO counts alleged 35 acts of racketeering activity, including fraud, extortion, gambling, and conspiracy to commit murder. At respondents' arraignment, the Government moved to have Salerno and Cafaro detained pursuant to §3142(e), on the ground that no condition of release would assure the safety of the community or any person. The District Court held a hearing at which the Government made a detailed proffer of evidence. The Government's case showed that Salerno was the "boss" of the Genovese crime family of La Cosa Nostra and that Cafaro was a "captain" in the Genovese family. According to the Government's proffer, based in large part on conversations intercepted by a court-ordered wiretap, the two respondents had participated in wide-ranging conspiracies to aid their illegitimate enterprises through violent means. The Government also offered the testimony of two of its trial witnesses, who would assert that Salerno personally participated in two murder conspiracies. Salerno opposed the motion for detention, challenging the credibility of the Government's witnesses. He offered the testimony of several character witnesses as well as a letter from his doctor stating that he was suffering from a serious medical condition. Cafaro presented no evidence at the hearing, but instead characterized the wiretap conversations as merely "tough talk."

The District Court granted the Government's detention motion, concluding that the Government had established by clear and convincing evidence that no condition or combination of conditions of release would ensure the safety of the community or any person: "The activities of a criminal organization such as the Genovese Family do not cease with the arrest of its principals and their release on even the most stringent of bail conditions. The illegal businesses, in place for many years, require constant attention and protection, or they will fail. Under these circumstances, this court recognizes a strong incentive on the part of its leadership to continue business as usual. When business as usual involves threats, beatings, and murder, the present danger such people pose in the community is self-evident."

Respondents appealed, contending that to the extent that the Bail Reform Act permits pretrial detention on the ground that the arrestee is likely to commit future crimes, it is unconstitutional on its face. Over a dissent, the United States Court of Appeals for the Second Circuit agreed.

The court concluded that the Government could not, consistent with due process, detain persons who had not been accused of any crime merely because they were thought to present a danger to the community. It reasoned that our criminal law system holds persons accountable for past actions, not anticipated future actions. Although a court could detain an arrestee who threatened to flee before trial, such detention would be permissible because it would serve the basic objective of a criminal system — bringing the accused to trial.

Respondents present two grounds for invalidating the Bail Reform Act's provisions permitting pretrial detention on the basis of future dangerousness. First, they rely upon . . . the Due Process Clause of the Fifth Amendment. Second, they contend that the Act contravenes the Eighth Amendment's proscription against excessive bail. We treat these contentions in turn.

A

The Due Process Clause of the Fifth Amendment provides that "No person shall . . . be deprived of life, liberty, or property, without due process of law. . . ." This Court has held that the Due Process Clause protects individuals against two types of government action. So-called "substantive due process" prevents the government from engaging in conduct that "shocks the conscience." When government action depriving a person of life, liberty, or property survives substantive due process scrutiny, it must still be implemented in a fair manner. This requirement has traditionally been referred to as "procedural" due process.

Respondents first argue that the Act violates substantive due process because the pretrial detention it authorizes constitutes impermissible punishment before trial. The Government, however, has never argued that pretrial detention could be upheld if it were "punishment." The Court of Appeals assumed that pretrial detention under the Bail Reform Act is regulatory, not penal, and we agree that it is.

As an initial matter, the mere fact that a person is detained does not inexorably lead to the conclusion that the government has imposed punishment. To determine whether a restriction on liberty constitutes impermissible punishment or permissible regulation, we first look to legislative intent. Unless Congress expressly intended to impose punitive restrictions, the punitive/regulatory distinction turns on "whether an alternative purpose to which [the restriction] may rationally be connected is assignable for it, and whether it appears excessive in relation to the alternative purpose assigned [to it]."

We conclude that the detention imposed by the Act falls on the regulatory side of the dichotomy. The legislative history of the Bail Reform Act clearly indicates that Congress did not formulate the pretrial detention provisions as punishment for dangerous individuals. Congress instead perceived pretrial detention as a potential solution to a pressing societal problem. There is no doubt that preventing danger to the community is a legitimate regulatory goal.

Moreover, the conditions of confinement envisioned by the Act "appear to reflect the regulatory purposes relied upon by the" Government. The statute at issue here requires that detainees be housed in a "facility separate, to the extent practicable, from persons awaiting or serving sentences or being held in custody pending appeal." 18 U.S.C. §3142(i)(2). We conclude, therefore, that the pretrial detention contemplated by the Bail Reform Act is regulatory in nature, and does not constitute punishment before trial in violation of the Due Process Clause.

We have repeatedly held that the Government's regulatory interest in community safety can, in appropriate circumstances, outweigh an individual's liberty interest. For example, in times of war or insurrection, when society's interest is at its peak, the Government may detain individuals whom the Government believes to be dangerous. Even outside the exigencies of war, we have found that sufficiently compelling governmental interests can justify detention of dangerous persons. Thus, we have found no absolute constitutional barrier to detention of potentially dangerous resident aliens pending deportation proceedings. We have also held that the government may detain mentally unstable individuals who present a danger to the public. We have approved of post-arrest regulatory detention of juveniles when they present a continuing danger to the community. Even competent adults may face substantial liberty restrictions as a result of the operation of our criminal justice system. If the police suspect an individual of a crime, they may arrest and hold him until a neutral magistrate determines whether probable cause exists.

The government's interest in preventing crime by arrestees is both legitimate and compelling. The Government must first of all demonstrate probable cause to believe that the charged crime has been committed by the arrestee, but that is not enough. In a full-blown adversary hearing, the Government must convince a neutral decisionmaker by clear and convincing evidence that no conditions of release can reasonably assure the safety of the community or any person.

On the other side of the scale, of course, is the individual's strong interest in liberty. We do not minimize the importance and fundamental nature of this right. But, as our cases hold, this right may, in circumstances where the government's interest is sufficiently weighty, be subordinated to the greater needs of society. When the Government proves by clear and convincing evidence that an arrestee presents an identified and articulable threat to an individual or the community, we believe that, consistent with the Due Process Clause, a court may disable the arrestee from executing that threat.

Under the Bail Reform Act, the procedures by which a judicial officer evaluates the likelihood of future dangerousness are specifically designed to further the accuracy of that determination. Detainees have a right to counsel at the detention hearing. They may testify in their own behalf, present information by proffer or otherwise, and cross-examine witnesses who appear at the hearing. The Government must prove its case by clear and convincing evidence. Finally, the judicial officer must include written findings of fact and a written statement of reasons for a decision to detain. The Act's review provisions provide for immediate appellate review of the detention decision.

We think these extensive safeguards suffice to repel a facial challenge. Given the legitimate and compelling regulatory purpose of the Act and the procedural protections it offers, we conclude that the Act is not facially invalid under the Due Process Clause of the Fifth Amendment.

B

Respondents also contend that the Bail Reform Act violates the Excessive Bail Clause of the Eighth Amendment. We think that the Act survives a challenge founded upon the Eighth Amendment.

The Eighth Amendment addresses pretrial release by providing merely that "excessive bail shall not be required." This Clause, of course, says nothing about whether bail shall be available at all. Respondents nevertheless contend that this Clause grants them a right to bail calculated solely upon considerations of flight. They rely on Stack v. Boyle (1951), in which the Court stated that "bail set at a figure higher than an amount reasonably calculated [to ensure the defendant's presence at trial] is 'excessive' under the Eighth Amendment." Respondents concede that the right to bail they have discovered in the Eighth Amendment is not absolute. A court may, for example, refuse bail in capital cases.

While we agree that a primary function of bail is to safeguard the courts' role in adjudicating the guilt or innocence of defendants, we reject the proposition that the Eighth Amendment categorically prohibits the government from pursuing other admittedly compelling interests through regulation of pretrial release. The above-quoted dictum in Stack v. Boyle is far too slender a reed on which to rest this argument. The Court in *Stack* had no occasion to consider whether the Excessive Bail Clause requires courts to admit all defendants to bail, because the statute before the Court in that case in fact allowed the defendants to be bailed.

III

In our society liberty is the norm, and detention prior to trial or without trial is the carefully limited exception. We hold that the provisions for pretrial detention in the Bail Reform Act of 1984 fall within that carefully limited exception. The Act authorizes the detention prior to trial of arrestees charged with serious felonies who are found after an adversary hearing to pose a threat to the safety of individuals or to the community which no condition of release can dispel. The numerous procedural safeguards detailed above must attend this adversary hearing. We are unwilling to say that this congressional determination, based as it is upon that primary concern of every government — a concern for the safety and indeed the lives of its citizens — on its face violates either the Due Process Clause of the Fifth Amendment or the Excessive Bail Clause of the Eighth Amendment.

Justice MARSHALL, dissenting.

This case brings before the Court for the first time a statute in which Congress declares that a person innocent of any crime may be jailed indefinitely, pending the trial of allegations which are legally presumed to be untrue, if the Government shows to the satisfaction of a judge that the accused is likely to commit crimes, unrelated to the pending charges, at any time in the future. Such statutes, consistent with the usages of tyranny and the excesses of what bitter experience teaches us to call the police state, have long been thought incompatible with the fundamental human rights protected by our Constitution. Today a majority of this Court holds otherwise. Its decision disregards basic principles of justice established centuries ago and enshrined beyond the reach of governmental interference in the Bill of Rights.

The essence of this case may be found, ironically enough, in a provision of the Act to which the majority does not refer. Title 18 U.S.C. §3142(j) provides that "nothing in this section shall be construed as modifying or limiting the presumption of innocence." But the very pith and purpose of this statute is an abhorrent limitation of the presumption of innocence. The majority's untenable conclusion that the present Act is constitutional arises from a specious denial of the role of the Bail Clause and the Due Process Clause in protecting the invaluable guarantee afforded by the presumption of innocence.

"The principle that there is a presumption of innocence in favor of the accused is the undoubted law, axiomatic and elementary, and its enforcement lies at the foundation of the administration of our criminal law." The statute now before us declares that persons who have been indicted may be detained if a judicial officer finds clear and convincing evidence that they pose a danger to individuals or to the community.

As Chief Justice Vinson wrote for the Court in Stack v. Boyle: "Unless th[e] right to bail before trial is preserved, the presumption of innocence, secured only after centuries of struggle, would lose its meaning."

Throughout the world today there are men, women, and children interned indefinitely, awaiting trials which may never come or which may be a mockery of the word, because their governments believe them to be "dangerous." Our Constitution, whose construction began two centuries ago, can shelter us forever from the evils of such unchecked power. Over 200 years it has slowly, through our efforts, grown more durable, more expansive, and more just. But it cannot protect us if we lack the courage, and the self-restraint, to protect ourselves. Today a majority of the Court applies itself to an ominous exercise in demolition. Theirs is truly a decision which will go forth without authority, and come back without respect.

Salerno cleared the way for courts to consider both a defendant's *flight risk* and *future danger to the community* in deciding bail. Some crimes, such as violent offenses and drug trafficking, may even carry a rebuttable presumption that detention is warranted.

In general, courts will consider several factors in determining whether the defendant should be granted bail and the amount of that bail:

1. The seriousness of the offense
2. The punishment the defendant faces
3. Defendant's prior criminal record
4. Defendant's ties to the community
5. Defendant's character
6. Defendant's financial status
7. Any other information relevant to its determination of whether defendant is a flight risk or poses a future risk to the community

Bail pending appeal does not pose the same issues as bail before trial because the defendant no longer enjoys a presumption of innocence. Thus, under the Bail Reform Act of 1984, the burden shifts to the defendant to show why he should be released pending appeal. Under the Bail Reform Act, a defendant may only be released pending appeal if the court finds "by clear and convincing evidence that the person is not likely to flee or pose a danger to the safety of another person or the community" and "the appeal is not for purposes of delay and raises a substantial question of law or fact likely to result in reversal or an order for a new trial."

With such a high standard, it is extremely difficult for defendants to secure pending appeal. A good example is the case of former presidential advisor I. Lewis Libby, who was convicted of lying to a grand jury regarding its probe into persons leaking information regarding CIA operative Valerie Plame. *See* United States v. Libby, 498 F. Supp. 2d 1 (D.D.C. 2007). In denying Libby's motion for bail pending appeal, the court held that even though Libby was not a flight risk, the burden had shifted to the defendant to show why he should be released pending appeal. The court rejected Libby's challenge to the appointment of Special Prosecutor Patrick Fitzgerald, finding that the appellate issue raised by Libby did not present a "substantial question of law or fact likely to result in . . . reversal."

2. *Other Types of Preventive Detention*

Salerno had a dramatic impact on courts' attitudes toward preventive detention. Not only may defendants now be detained because they pose a risk of future danger to the community, but persons who are not being held on criminal charges may also be detained. This may include preventative detention of material witnesses, sexual predators, psychiatric patients, persons subject to deportation and removal proceedings, and individuals designated as enemy combatants. Each of these situations requires a balancing of the detainee's liberty interests with the government's reasons for seeking detention.

a. **Detention of Material Witnesses**

Pursuant to 18 U.S.C. §3144, persons designated as "material witnesses" may be detained pretrial. A material witness is an individual who has information regarding a criminal proceeding whose appearance "may become impracticable to secure . . . by subpoena." These individuals are not themselves accused of any crime; however, they are kept in custody because they may have information regarding a crime that was committed and their appearance at trial cannot otherwise be secured. After the terrorist attacks of September 11, 2001, the government increased its use of the material witness statute and sought to use it for both trial and grand jury witnesses. This led to additional challenges to the use of preventive detention. Not surprisingly, the balance in these cases fell in favor of the government, especially when the court was convinced that the statute provided sufficient procedural protections for the detainee before the detention was ordered. In the next case, the court discussed why it would permit preventive detention of material witnesses in grand jury proceedings.

UNITED STATES v. AWADALLAH

349 F.3d 42 (2d Cir. 2003)

JACOBS, Circuit Judge:

This appeal, which arises from the government's investigation of the September 11, 2001 terrorist attacks, presents questions about the scope of the federal material witness statute and the government's powers of arrest and detention thereunder. *See* 18 U.S.C. §3144. The district court ruled that the statute cannot be applied constitutionally to a grand jury witness such as the defendant-appellee, Osama Awadallah, and dismissed the perjury indictment against him as fruit of an illegal detention.

We conclude that these rulings must be reversed and the indictment reinstated.

BACKGROUND

In the days immediately following September 11, 2001, the United States Attorney for the Southern District of New York initiated a grand jury investigation into the terrorist attacks. Investigators quickly identified Nawaf Al-Hazmi and Khalid Al-Mihdhar as two of the hijackers on American Airlines Flight 77, which crashed into the Pentagon. The Justice Department released the identities of all nineteen hijackers on Friday, September 14, 2001, and news media around the country publicized their names and photographs the following day.

A search of the car Al-Hazmi abandoned at Dulles Airport in Virginia produced a piece of paper with the notation, "Osama 589-5316." Federal agents tracked this number to a San Diego address at which the defendant, Osama Awadallah, had lived approximately eighteen months earlier. Al-Hazmi and Al-Mihdhar also had lived in the San Diego vicinity around that time.

On the morning of September 20, 2001, federal agents went to Awadallah's current residence in San Diego. When the agents arrived at the apartment, Awadallah was attending a course in English as a second language at nearby Grossmont College, where he was enrolled. The agents interviewed Awadallah's roommate in their apartment for several hours.

When Awadallah came home at around 2:00 P.M. that afternoon, several agents approached him as he entered the parking lot and got out of his car (a gray Honda). They questioned him in the parking lot for a few minutes and then told him that he had to accompany them to the FBI office for questioning. Awadallah insisted on returning to his apartment first to observe the afternoon Muslim prayer, which he did as the agents watched. When Awadallah went into the bathroom, the agents insisted that the bathroom door be left open.

Before leaving for the FBI office, an agent asked Awadallah to sign a consent form allowing them to search his apartment and car. Otherwise, the agent told him, they would get a warrant and "tear up" his home. Believing he had no choice, Awadallah signed the form without reading it. The agents then put him in their car and drove him to the FBI office. Awadallah told them that he had to return in time for a 6:00 P.M. computer class; they told him that would be no problem.

At the FBI office, agents offered Awadallah a drink, but he declined because he was fasting. They asked him to sign another consent form for the search of his second car, an inoperative white Honda in the parking lot of his apartment building. This time, Awadallah read the form and learned that he had a right to refuse consent; and though he signed the consent form for his second car, he explicitly revoked his consent for the search of the first car. An agent tried to reach the agents at the apartment building by cell phone, but did not reach them until fifteen minutes later, after the search of the first car had been completed. The agents at the scene then searched the apartment and the second car. The search of Awadallah's home produced several computer-generated photographs of Osama bin Laden; the searches of his cars produced two videotapes on Bosnia and one on Islam and a retractable razor which could be described as a box-cutter or a carpet knife.

Awadallah was alone in a locked interview room for a while, until agents arrived to question him. They did not advise him of his rights or tell him that he could leave. They asked him about the September 11 hijackers and about his life and acquaintances. He told the agents that he knew Al-Hazmi, and that he had frequently seen another man with him, whose name he did not know.

The district court found that Awadallah was "cooperative" throughout this questioning. When 6:00 P.M. approached, the agents told Awadallah that they had called his school and that it was alright for him to miss class. They told him he would "have to stay" with them until they were finished. The entire interview lasted approximately six hours, ending at nearly 11:00 P.M. Before allowing Awadallah to leave, the agents scheduled a polygraph examination for the next morning.

At 6:30 A.M. the following day, September 21, 2001, Awadallah called the FBI and refused to come in for the polygraph test until he had a lawyer. The agent told him they would get an arrest warrant. Believing he had no choice, Awadallah went with two agents who picked him up at his apartment at 7:00 A.M.

At the FBI office, agents advised Awadallah of his rights and he signed an advice-of-rights acknowledgment form. The polygraph exam lasted one-and-a-half to two hours. Afterward, the agents told Awadallah that the polygraph registered lies in response to two questions: whether he had advance knowledge of the September 11 attacks and whether he had participated in them in any way. It is unclear whether these were in fact the results. The conversation became heated as the agents accused Awadallah of being a terrorist. They refused Awadallah's requests to call a lawyer and his brother, and did not release him in time for Friday prayer.

Throughout the questioning that day, the FBI agents in San Diego had been in contact with an Assistant United States Attorney ("AUSA") in New York. At approximately 2:00 P.M. Eastern time, the AUSA instructed the agents to arrest Awadallah as a material witness. The agents handcuffed Awadallah and took him to the San Diego correctional center for booking.

During the period of his detention, Awadallah spent time in four prisons as he was transferred to the New York correctional center by way of Oklahoma City. He alleges that he received harsh and improper treatment during this period. Awadallah spent most of his time in solitary confinement; at times lacked access to his family, his lawyer, or a phone; and was repeatedly strip-searched. The government did not dispute that, by October 4, 2001, "Awadallah had bruises on his upper arms," and an agent's report indicated several other injuries on his shoulder, ankles, hand, and face. Awadallah sometimes refrained from eating because the meals provided did not comply with his religious dietary restrictions.

On October 10, 2001, twenty days after his arrest as a material witness, Awadallah testified before the grand jury in the Southern District of New York. The prosecutor questioned him for most of the day. In the course of his testimony, Awadallah denied knowing anyone named Khalid Al-Mihdhar or Khalid. The government then showed him an examination booklet he had written in September, which the government obtained from his English teacher in San Diego. The booklet contained the following handwritten sentence: "One of the quietest people I have met is Nawaf. Another one his name Khalid. They have stayed in S.D. [San Diego] for 6 months." Awadallah acknowledged that it was his examination booklet, and that most of the writing in it was his own, but he denied that the name Khalid and a few other words on the page were written in his handwriting. On October 15, 2001, when Awadallah again appeared before the grand jury, he stated that his recollection of Khalid's name had been refreshed by his October 10 testimony and that the disputed writing in the exam booklet was in fact his own. However, he did not admit to making false statements in his first grand jury appearance.

The United States Attorney for the Southern District of New York filed charges against Awadallah on two counts of making false statements to the grand jury in violation of 18 U.S.C. §1623: falsely denying that he knew Khalid Al-Mihdhar; and falsely denying that the handwriting in the exam booklet was his own.

On November 27, 2001, the district court (Scheindlin, J.) granted Awadallah's bail application. He satisfied the bail conditions and was released approximately two weeks later.

In December 2001, Awadallah moved to dismiss the indictment. The court ruled that the federal material witness statute, 18 U.S.C. §3144, did not apply to grand jury witnesses. Judge Scheindlin ruled that Awadallah's perjured grand jury testimony had to be suppressed as fruit of this illegal arrest and detention. The government filed a timely notice of appeal.

DISCUSSION

APPLICABILITY OF 18 U.S.C. §3144

The first issue presented is whether the federal material witness statute, 18 U.S.C. §3144, allows the arrest and detention of grand jury witnesses. As discussed at oral argument, we might evade this issue by holding that Awadallah's allegedly false testimony should not have been suppressed as fruit of the poisonous tree even if his detention under §3144 was improper, and that the indictment therefore should not have been dismissed. We reach the issue, however, because the present split within our Circuit on the scope of §3144 affects the liberty interests of persons identified as material witnesses, the security and law enforcement interests of the government, and the ability of courts to make prompt and fair rulings on present and future detentions.

Section 3144, titled "release or detention of a material witness," provides in its entirety:

> If it appears from an affidavit filed by a party that the testimony of a person is material in a criminal proceeding, and if it is shown that it may become impracticable to secure the presence of the person by subpoena, a judicial officer may order the arrest of the person and treat the person in accordance with the provisions of section 3142 of this title. No material witness may be detained because of inability to comply with any condition of release if the testimony of such witness can adequately be secured by deposition, and if further detention is not necessary to prevent a failure of justice. Release of a material witness may be delayed for a reasonable period of time until the deposition of the witness can be taken pursuant to the Federal Rules of Criminal Procedure.

The statute is cast in terms of a material witness in "a criminal proceeding." The decisive question here is whether that term encompasses proceedings before a grand jury.

Given the broad language of the statute, its legislative history . . . , the substantial body of case law indicating that there is no constitutional impediment to detention of grand jury witnesses, and the unquestioned application of the statute to grand jury witnesses over a period of decades before Awadallah, to perceive a Congressional intention that grand jury witnesses be excluded from the reach of section 3144 is to perceive something that is not there. [W]e conclude that the district court's ruling in this case must be reversed.

[Section] 3144 applies to witnesses whose testimony is material in "a criminal proceeding." "Criminal proceeding" is a broad and capacious term, and there is good reason to conclude that it includes a grand jury proceeding. [T]he term "criminal proceeding" has been construed in other statutes to encompass grand jury proceedings. Notwithstanding this support for the general view that "criminal proceedings" encompass grand jury proceedings, however, we cannot say that the statutory wording alone compels that conclusion. Black's Law Dictionary defines a "criminal proceeding" as "[a] proceeding instituted to determine a person's guilt or innocence or to set a convicted person's punishment; a criminal hearing or trial." Defined this way, a grand jury proceeding is not a "proceeding instituted to determine a person's guilt or innocence or to set a convicted person's punishment," but rather a proceeding to "decide whether to issue indictments." For these reasons, we must look beyond the text of §3144 to discern the meaning of "criminal proceeding."

In surveying legislative history we have repeatedly stated that the authoritative source for finding the Legislature's intent lies in the Committee Reports on the bill. . . . Here, the Senate committee report states in so many words the intent to include grand jury proceedings within the ambit of the statute — an intent that is consistent with the statute's language, even if not compelled by it.

The Fourth Amendment prohibits "unreasonable searches and seizures." Determining the reasonableness of a seizure involves a balancing of competing interests: "The essential purpose of the proscriptions in the Fourth Amendment is to impose a standard of 'reasonableness' upon the exercise of discretion by government officials, including law enforcement agents, in order 'to safeguard the privacy and security of individuals against arbitrary invasions. . . .' Thus, the permissibility of a particular law enforcement practice is judged by balancing its intrusion on the individual's Fourth Amendment interests against its promotion of legitimate governmental interests."

In its balancing analysis, the district court found that "the only legitimate reason to detain a grand jury witness is to aid in 'an ex parte investigation to determine whether a crime has been committed and whether criminal proceedings should be instituted against any person.'" This is no small interest. The grand jury is an integral part of our constitutional heritage which was brought to this country with the common law. Indispensable to the exercise of its power is the authority to compel the attendance and the testimony of witnesses.

The district court noted (and we agree) that it would be improper for the government to use §3144 for other ends, such as the detention of persons suspected of criminal activity for which probable cause has not yet been established. However, the district court made no finding (and we see no evidence to suggest) that the government arrested Awadallah for any purpose other than to secure information material to a grand jury investigation. Moreover, that grand jury was investigating the September 11 terrorist attacks. The particular governmental interests at stake therefore were the indictment and successful prosecution of terrorists whose attack, if committed by a sovereign, would have been tantamount to war, and the discovery of the conspirators' means, contacts, and operations in order to forestall future attacks.

On the other side of the balance, the district court found in essence that §3144 was not calibrated to minimize the intrusion on the liberty of a grand jury witness. We agree with the district court, of course, that arrest and detention are significant infringements on liberty, but we conclude that §3144 sufficiently limits that infringement and reasonably balances it against the government's countervailing interests. [Given the procedural safeguards of §3144 that provide that] "no material witness may be detained because of inability to comply with any condition of release if the testimony of such witness can adequately be secured by deposition," and that detention must be necessary to prevent a failure of justice, [we disagree with the district court's balancing of interests].

Postscript

Osama Awadallah was ultimately tried on charges of lying to a grand jury investigating the terrorist attacks. His first trial ended in a hung jury, 11-1 for conviction. However, after a retrial, he was acquitted of all charges.

b. Preventive Detention of Sexual Predators

The concept of preventive detention is also used to incarcerate other types of individuals who do not face criminal charges but continue to pose a danger to society. In response to the growing number of sexual offenders, states have passed "sexual predator" laws that allow the ongoing detention of defendants after they have completed their sentences for sexual offenses. The Supreme Court upheld the constitutionality of this type of preventive detention in Kansas v. Hendricks by once again, in its substantive due process analysis, balancing the need for detention against the defendant's liberty interests.

KANSAS v. HENDRICKS

521 U.S. 346 (1996)

Justice THOMAS delivered the opinion of the Court.

In 1994, Kansas enacted the Sexually Violent Predator Act, which establishes procedures for the civil commitment of persons who, due to a "mental abnormality" or a "personality disorder," are likely to engage in "predatory acts of sexual violence." The State invoked the Act for the first time to commit Leroy Hendricks, an inmate who had a long history of sexually molesting children, and who was scheduled for release from prison shortly after the Act became law. Hendricks challenged his commitment on, inter alia, "substantive" due process, double jeopardy, and ex post facto grounds. The Kansas Supreme Court invalidated the Act, holding that its pre-commitment condition of a "mental abnormality" did not satisfy what the court perceived to be the "substantive" due process requirement that involuntary civil commitment must be predicated on a finding of "mental illness." The State of Kansas petitioned for certiorari. We now reverse the judgment below.

I

The Kansas Legislature enacted the Sexually Violent Predator Act (Act) in 1994 to grapple with the problem of managing repeat sexual offenders. Although Kansas already had a statute addressing the involuntary commitment of those defined as "mentally ill," the legislature determined that existing civil commitment procedures were inadequate to confront the risks presented by "sexually violent predators." In the Act's preamble, the legislature explained: "[A] small but extremely dangerous group of sexually violent predators exist who do not have a mental disease or defect that renders them appropriate for involuntary treatment pursuant to the [general involuntary civil commitment statute]. . . . In contrast to persons appropriate for civil commitment under the [general involuntary civil commitment statute], sexually violent predators generally have anti-social personality features which are unamenable to existing mental illness treatment modalities and those features render them likely to engage in sexually violent behavior."

As a result, the Legislature found it necessary to establish "a civil commitment procedure for the long-term care and treatment of the sexually violent predator." The Act's civil commitment procedures pertained to: (1) a presently confined person who, like Hendricks, "has been convicted of a sexually violent offense" and is scheduled for release; (2) a person who has been "charged with a sexually violent offense" but has been found incompetent to stand trial; (3) a person who has been found "not guilty by reason of insanity of a sexually violent offense"; and (4) a person found "not guilty" of a sexually violent offense because of a mental disease or defect. [The Act] was designed to initiate a specific series of procedures. The custodial agency was required to notify the local prosecutor 60 days before the anticipated release of a person who might have met the Act's criteria. The prosecutor was then obligated, within 45 days, to decide whether to file a petition in state court seeking the person's involuntary commitment. If such a petition were filed, the court was to determine whether "probable cause" existed to support a finding that the person was a "sexually violent predator" and thus eligible for civil commitment. Upon such a determination, transfer of the individual to a secure facility for professional evaluation would occur. After that evaluation, a trial would be held to determine beyond a reasonable doubt whether the individual was a sexually violent predator. If that determination were made, the person would then be transferred to the custody of the Secretary of Social and Rehabilitation Services (Secretary) for "control, care and treatment until such time as the person's mental abnormality or personality disorder has so changed that the person is safe to be at large."

Once an individual was confined, confined persons were afforded three different avenues of review, [including an annual review] to determine whether continued detention was warranted.

B

In 1984, Hendricks was convicted of taking "indecent liberties" with two 13-year-old boys. After serving nearly 10 years of his sentence, he was slated for release to a halfway house. Shortly before his scheduled release, however, the State filed a petition in state court seeking Hendricks' civil confinement as a sexually violent predator.

Hendricks subsequently requested a jury trial to determine whether he qualified as a sexually violent predator. During that trial, Hendricks' own testimony revealed a chilling history of repeated child sexual molestation and abuse, beginning in 1955 when he exposed his genitals to two young girls. At that time, he pleaded guilty to indecent exposure. Then, in 1957, he was convicted of lewdness involving a young girl and received a brief jail sentence. In 1960, he molested two young boys while he worked for a carnival. After serving two years in prison for that offense, he was paroled, only to be rearrested for molesting a 7-year-old girl. Attempts were made to treat him for his sexual deviance, and in 1965 he was considered "safe to be at large," and was discharged from a state psychiatric hospital.

Shortly thereafter, however, Hendricks sexually assaulted another young boy and girl — he performed oral sex on the 8-year-old girl and fondled the 11-year-old boy. He was again imprisoned in 1967, but refused to participate in a sex offender treatment program, and thus remained incarcerated until his parole in 1972. Diagnosed as a pedophile, Hendricks entered into, but then abandoned, a treatment program. He testified that despite having received professional help for his pedophilia, he continued to harbor sexual desires for children. Indeed, soon after his 1972 parole, Hendricks began to abuse his own stepdaughter and stepson. He forced the children to engage in sexual activity with him over a period of approximately four years. Then, as noted above, Hendricks was convicted of "taking indecent liberties" with two adolescent boys after he attempted to fondle them. As a result of that conviction, he was once again imprisoned, and was serving that sentence when he reached his conditional release date in September 1994.

The jury unanimously found beyond a reasonable doubt that Hendricks was a sexually violent predator. The trial court subsequently determined, as a matter of state law, that pedophilia qualifies as a "mental abnormality" as defined by the Act, and thus ordered Hendricks committed to the Secretary's custody.

Hendricks appealed, claiming, among other things, that application of the Act to him violated the Federal Constitution's Due Process clause. The Kansas Supreme Court accepted Hendricks' due process claim.

II

A

Kansas argues that the Act's definition of "mental abnormality" satisfies "substantive" due process requirements. We agree. Although freedom from physical restraint "has always been at the core of the liberty protected by the Due Process Clause from arbitrary governmental action," that liberty interest is not absolute. The Court has recognized that an individual's constitutionally protected interest in avoiding physical restraint may be overridden even in the civil context:

> The liberty secured by the Constitution of the United States to every person within its jurisdiction does not import an absolute right in each person to be, at all times

and in all circumstances, wholly free from restraint. There are manifold restraints to which every person is necessarily subject for the common good. On any other basis organized society could not exist with safety to its members.

Accordingly, States have in certain narrow circumstances provided for the forcible civil detainment of people who are unable to control their behavior and who thereby pose a danger to the public health and safety. We have consistently upheld such involuntary commitment statutes provided the confinement takes place pursuant to proper procedures and evidentiary standards. It thus cannot be said that the involuntary civil confinement of a limited subclass of dangerous persons is contrary to our understanding of ordered liberty.

The challenged Act unambiguously requires a finding of dangerousness either to one's self or to others as a prerequisite to involuntary confinement. Commitment proceedings can be initiated only when a person "has been convicted of or charged with a sexually violent offense," and "suffers from a mental abnormality or personality disorder which makes the person likely to engage in the predatory acts of sexual violence." The statute thus requires proof of more than a mere predisposition to violence; rather, it requires evidence of past sexually violent behavior and a present mental condition that creates a likelihood of such conduct in the future if the person is not incapacitated. These added statutory requirements serve to limit involuntary civil confinement to those who suffer from a volitional impairment rendering them dangerous beyond their control. The Kansas Act is plainly of a kind with these other civil commitment statutes: It requires a finding of future dangerousness, and then links that finding to the existence of a "mental abnormality" or "personality disorder" that makes it difficult, if not impossible, for the person to control his dangerous behavior. The pre-commitment requirement of a "mental abnormality" or "personality disorder" is consistent with the requirements of these other statutes that we have upheld in that it narrows the class of persons eligible for confinement to those who are unable to control their dangerousness.

B

We granted Hendricks' cross-petition to determine whether the Act violates the Constitution's double jeopardy prohibition or its ban on ex post facto lawmaking. The thrust of Hendricks' argument is that the Act establishes criminal proceedings; hence confinement under it necessarily constitutes punishment. He contends that where, as here, newly enacted "punishment" is predicated upon past conduct for which he has already been convicted and forced to serve a prison sentence, the Constitution's Double Jeopardy and Ex Post Facto Clauses are violated. We are unpersuaded by Hendricks' argument that Kansas has established criminal proceedings.

The categorization of a particular proceeding as civil or criminal "is first of all a question of statutory construction." Here, Kansas' objective to create a civil proceeding is evidenced by its placement of the Sexually Violent

Predator Act within the Kansas probate code, instead of the criminal code, as well as its description of the Act as creating a "civil commitment procedure." Nothing on the face of the statute suggests that the legislature sought to create anything other than a civil commitment scheme designed to protect the public from harm.

Although we recognize that a "civil label is not always dispositive," we will reject the legislature's manifest intent only where a party challenging the statute provides "the clearest proof" that "the statutory scheme [is] so punitive either in purpose or effect as to negate [the State's] intention" to deem it "civil." In those limited circumstances, we will consider the statute to have established criminal proceedings for constitutional purposes. Hendricks, however, has failed to satisfy this heavy burden.

As a threshold matter, commitment under the Act does not implicate either of the two primary objectives of criminal punishment: retribution or deterrence. The Act's purpose is not retributive because it does not affix culpability for prior criminal conduct. In addition, the Kansas Act does not make a criminal conviction a prerequisite for commitment—persons absolved of criminal responsibility may nonetheless be subject to confinement under the Act. An absence of the necessary criminal responsibility suggests that the State is not seeking retribution for a past misdeed. Thus, the fact that the Act may be "tied to criminal activity" is "insufficient to render the statute punitive."

Although the civil commitment scheme at issue here does involve an affirmative restraint, "the mere fact that a person is detained does not inexorably lead to the conclusion that the government has imposed punishment." United States v. Salerno (1987). The State may take measures to restrict the freedom of the dangerously mentally ill. This is a legitimate non-punitive governmental objective and has been historically so regarded. If detention for the purpose of protecting the community from harm necessarily constituted punishment, then all involuntary civil commitments would have to be considered punishment. But we have never so held.

[A claim] that treatment is not possible for this category of individuals does not obligate us to adopt its legal conclusions. We have already observed that, under the appropriate circumstances and when accompanied by proper procedures, incapacitation may be a legitimate end of the civil law. Accordingly, the Kansas court's determination that the Act's "overriding concern" was the continued "segregation of sexually violent offenders" is consistent with our conclusion that the Act establishes civil proceedings. Accord Compagnie Francaise de Navigation a Vapeur v. Louisiana Bd. of Health (1902) (permitting involuntary quarantine of persons suffering from communicable diseases). What is significant, however, is that Hendricks was placed under the supervision of the Kansas Department of Health and Social and Rehabilitative Services, housed in a unit segregated from the general prison population and operated not by employees of the Department of Corrections, but by other trained individuals.

Where the State has "disavowed any punitive intent"; limited confinement to a small segment of particularly dangerous individuals; provided strict procedural safeguards; directed that confined persons be segregated from the general prison population and afforded the same status as others who have been civilly committed; recommended treatment if such is possible; and permitted immediate release upon a showing that the individual is no longer dangerous or mentally impaired, we cannot say that it acted with punitive intent. We therefore hold that the Act does not establish criminal proceedings and that involuntary confinement pursuant to the Act is not punitive. Our conclusion that the Act is nonpunitive thus removes an essential prerequisite for both Hendricks' double jeopardy and ex post facto claims.

The Double Jeopardy Clause provides: "Nor shall any person be subject for the same offence to be twice put in jeopardy of life or limb." Because we have determined that the Kansas Act is civil in nature, initiation of its commitment proceedings does not constitute a second prosecution.

Hendricks' ex post facto claim is similarly flawed. The Ex Post Facto Clause, which "forbids the application of any new punitive measure to a crime already consummated," has been interpreted to pertain exclusively to penal statutes. As we have previously determined, the Act does not impose punishment; thus, its application does not raise ex post facto concerns.

We hold that the Kansas Sexually Violent Predator Act comports with due process requirements and neither runs afoul of double jeopardy principles nor constitutes an exercise in impermissible ex post facto lawmaking. Accordingly, the judgment of the Kansas Supreme Court is reversed.

Justice KENNEDY, concurring.

I join the opinion of the Court in full and add these additional comments. My brief, further comment is to caution against dangers inherent when a civil confinement law is used in conjunction with the criminal process, whether or not the law is given retroactive application.

Notwithstanding its civil attributes, the practical effect of the Kansas law may be to impose confinement for life. A common response to this may be, "A life term is exactly what the sentence should have been anyway," or, in the words of a Kansas task force member, "So be it." The point, however, is not how long Hendricks and others like him should serve a criminal sentence. With his criminal record, after all, a life term may well have been the only sentence appropriate to protect society and vindicate the wrong. The concern instead is whether it is the criminal system or the civil system which should make the decision in the first place. If the civil system is used simply to impose punishment after the State makes an improvident plea bargain on the criminal side, then it is not performing its proper function. These concerns persist whether the civil confinement statute is put on the books before or after the offense. We should bear in mind that while incapacitation is a goal common to both the criminal and civil systems of confinement, retribution and general deterrence are reserved for the criminal system alone.

c. Preventive Detention for Immigration Detainees

Immigrants illegally in the United States may also be detained by the government even if they have not been convicted of or charged with a specific crime. For example, in Zadvydas v. Davis, 533 U.S. 678 (2001), the Supreme Court addressed a statute that provides for the detention of aliens who have been ordered removed but cannot be deported because there is no receiving country. The statute permitted the aliens to be detained whenever they are "determined by the Attorney General to be a risk to the community or unlikely to comply with the order of removal." Aliens complained that, under the statute, they could be held indefinitely. Using a due process analysis, the Supreme Court held that civil confinement may be justified by the government's regulatory needs, but that indefinite detention without court review would violate due process. Thus, it held that an alien not removed within the 90-day period of the statute could file a habeas corpus action to determine if his continued detention was unreasonable.

Zadvydas was decided before September 11, 2001. In 2003, the Supreme Court decided Denmore v. Kim, 538 U.S. 510 (2003). Kim, a citizen of South Korea, challenged an immigration law that provides that an alien subject to removal must be detained pending removal proceedings. Kim had been convicted of burglary and petty theft and was therefore subject to removal. He complained that the immigration law violated due process because there had never been a determination that he posed a danger to society or flight risk. The Supreme Court rejected his challenge. Noting the ongoing need by the government to detain deportable aliens for a limited period because more than 20 percent of them fail to appear for their removal hearings, the Court held that detention was permissible. "[D]etention necessarily serves the purpose of preventing deportable criminal aliens from fleeing prior to or during their removal proceedings, thus increasing the chance that, if ordered removed, the aliens will be successfully removed."

d. Enemy Combatants

The doctrine of preventative detention most dramatically affects individuals who are not charged in the criminal justice system or protected by immigration procedures. It allows for the ongoing detention of individuals, including American citizens, suspected of terrorism whom the president designates to be enemy combatants.

In Rasul v. Bush, 542 U.S. 466 (2004), the Supreme Court held that foreign nationals detained at the military base in Guantanamo Bay, Cuba, have the right to challenge the legality of their long-term detention. The Court did not, however, establish what constitutional limits there would be on their continued detention.

In Hamdi v. Rumsfeld, 542 U.S. 507 (2004), the Court held that it had jurisdiction to review the legality of a citizen's designation and detention as an enemy combatant. It held that "due process demands that a citizen held in the United States as an enemy combatant be given a meaningful opportunity to contest the factual basis for that detention before a neutral decision maker." Once again, the Court left open what kind of process was required for enemy combatants.

The Court again examined the rights of detainees in Hamdan v. Rumsfeld, 126 S. Ct. 2749 (2006). It held that the military commissions convened to try enemy combatants violated the Uniform Code of Military Justice and the Geneva Convention. However, it did not identify exactly what procedures would satisfy due process concerns in the indefinite detention of enemy combatants and left that decision to future cases. Meanwhile, Congress passed the Military Commission Act of 2006, setting forth new procedural protections for enemy combatants but depriving the courts of jurisdiction to hear challenges by the detainees. In Boumediene v. Bush, 553 U.S. 723 (2008), the Court ruled that the Military Commission Act of 2006 violated the detainee's rights by unconstitutionally suspending the right of habeas corpus. A full discussion of that case is in Chapter 15 ("Habeas Corpus"). Thus, although detainees now have some access to the courts, judges are still extremely deferential to the executive branch's decision to detain enemy combatants.

CHAPTER
8

DISCOVERY

A. INTRODUCTION

Imagine trying to play a baseball game blindfolded. Faced with such a scenario, the crowd would quickly cry, "Not fair!" There is much more at stake in a criminal trial than in a sporting event, and a fundamental principle of fairness is that there should not be trial by ambush.

Discovery in criminal cases serves many important purposes. First, it gives the prosecution and defense an idea of the evidence that the other side will present at trial. This allows the parties to prepare ahead of time and to be more efficient in their presentation of trials. Second, discovery leads to pretrial settlement of cases. More than 90 percent of criminal cases are settled before trial. Discovery provides valuable information to the parties for assessing the strength of their cases, thereby facilitating the plea bargaining process. Third, discovery allows each party to contest evidence before it is presented to the court. Using pretrial *motions in limine*, the parties can bring to the court's attention evidence they want to introduce or preclude at trial. Finally, discovery creates more of a level playing field for trial.

Prosecutors have many tools they can use to obtain evidence prior to and after the filing of charges. Before trial, they can use grand jury subpoenas, search warrants, surveillance, and government investigators to investigate cases. While defense counsel can use private or court-appointed investigators, their investigative resources are more limited. Discovery gives the defense an opportunity to see the evidence that the prosecution has uncovered.

Despite these benefits, criminal cases do not have unlimited discovery. Only a few jurisdictions currently have "open-file" discovery,[1] a procedure that allows the defense access to everything in the prosecutor's files. However, most jurisdictions limit the discovery available to the defense, in part because of concerns about witness intimidation and the fabrication of

---

1. For example, in 2004 North Carolina enacted a law for open-file discovery in order to reduce the number of wrongful convictions. The law was modified in 2007 to require the sharing of witness statements, although it still has an exception for information regarding confidential informants. *See* N.C. Gen. Stat. §15A-501(6).

evidence. Conversely, concerns about interference with the defendant's Fifth Amendment privilege against self-incrimination limit the prosecutor's right to reciprocal discovery from the defense.

In learning the rules of discovery, it is helpful to think of its two primary aspects. First, some discovery rules are statutory. These rules generally cover the inculpatory evidence the prosecutor must disclose to the defense. Inculpatory evidence is evidence the prosecution will use to prove its case-in-chief at trial. Statutory discovery also covers the defense's reciprocal discovery obligations, such as the obligation to make available expert reports or physical evidence the defense will introduce in its case-in-chief at trial. In addition, there are statutory rules that govern the disclosure of witness statements that each side plans to use.

The second type of discovery is mandated by the defendant's constitutional right to a fair trial. Pursuant to the Fifth and Fourteenth Amendments, the defendant has a due process right to the discovery of exculpatory information. Exculpatory evidence is evidence that undermines the prosecution's case either by supporting the defendant's claim of innocence or by impeaching the prosecution's witnesses. Constitutional discovery applies only to the defendant because the government has no due process rights under the Constitution. Rather, the government must rely on statutes and rules to provide it a right of discovery.

Section B of this chapter begins with a review of the statutory rights to discovery of both the government and the defense. Pursuant to rules of procedure, each side may be entitled to examine certain types of evidence that the other side plans to introduce at trial.

Section C then focuses on the defendant's constitutional right to discovery. As set forth in the seminal cases of Brady v. Maryland, 373 U.S. 83 (1963), United States v. Bagley, 473 U.S. 667 (1985), and Giglio v. United States, 405 U.S. 150 (1972), the government has an obligation to disclose evidence favorable to the defense.

Section D briefly discusses what discovery rights defendants have before entering guilty pleas. Although defendants going to trial have the full panoply of constitutional discovery rights, a defendant pleading guilty has more limited rights to discovery.

Finally, section E of this chapter examines the defendant's limited right to have evidence preserved for trial. Although the Supreme Court held in California v. Trombetta, 467 U.S. 479 (1984), that the Constitution requires the government to preserve evidence "that might be expected to play a significant role in the suspect's defense," its later decision in Arizona v. Youngblood, 488 U.S. 51 (1988), clarified that a failure to preserve potentially useful evidence does not constitute a denial of due process absent a showing of bad faith by the police.

Discovery is a critical part of the criminal justice process. Unfortunately, it is also a part of the criminal justice system that is particularly prone to violations. In 2007, the failure of North Carolina District Attorney Michael Nifong to abide by his discovery obligations led to three white Duke lacrosse players being falsely charged with rape by a black exotic dancer who accused them of abusing her at an off-campus party. Nifong failed to disclose to the defendants that laboratory tests indicated that the DNA found on the alleged victim did not come from the defendants. Outrage over the incident led to Nifong's disbarment and increased public attention to the need to adhere to discovery rules.[2]

According to one study, at least 381 defendants nationally have had a homicide conviction thrown out because prosecutors concealed evidence of a defendant's innocence or knowingly presented perjured testimony.[3] The Innocence Project reports that 38 percent of all prosecutorial misconduct cases involve suppression of exculpatory evidence.[4] At least one federal judge has called Brady violations an "epidemic."[5] If prosecutors do not abide by their discovery obligations, the chances of wrongful conviction increase dramatically.

The prosecutor's violations were discovered in the Duke lacrosse case because the defendants came from affluent families who could afford expensive investigations and representation by defense counsel. However, as commentators have recognized, race and financial means can have a dramatic impact on whether defendants' rights are respected by the criminal justice system.[6]

As a result of problems with prosecutors complying with their constitutional discovery duties, the states have now adopted ethical rules requiring prosecutors to disclose exculpatory evidence to the defense. *See* ABA Model Rule of Professional Conduct 3.8(d). Typically, these rules also require that prosecutors also come forward post-conviction with "new, credible and material evidence creating a reasonable likelihood that a convicted defendant" did not commit an offense. ABA Model Rule 3.8(g).

Just as it is important that prosecutors comply with their discovery obligations, it is also critical that defense lawyers abide by their discovery requirements. While the federal constitutional right to discovery applies only to prosecutors, general policy interests in fair and expeditious proceedings also support the prosecution's right to statutory and rule discovery. Specifically, defense discovery to the prosecution can (1) prevent surprise at trial, (2) deter perjured testimony, and (3) reduce trial delay.[7]

---

2. For an excellent discussion of this incident, *see* Robert P. Mosteller, *Exculpatory Evidence, Ethics, and the Road to the Disbarment of Mike Nifong: The Critical Importance of Full Open-File Discovery*, 76 Fordham L. Rev. 1337 (2007). *Brady* violations affect a wide variety of cases, including some of the highest profile defendants. For example, the conviction of U.S. Senator Ted Stevens was reversed because of a *Brady* violation. *See* Charlie Savage, *Prosecutors Face Penalty in '08 Trial of a Senator,* N.Y. Times (May 24, 2012).

3. *See* Ken Armstrong & Steve Mills, *Death Row Justice Derailed,* Chicago Tribune, Nov. 14, 1999, 1C.

4. *See* Emily M. West, *Court Findings of Prosecutorial Misconduct Claims in Post-Conviction Appeals and Civil Suits Among the First 255 DNA Exoneration Cases,* Aug. 2010, http://www.innocenceproject.org/docs/Innocence_Project_Pros_Misconduct.pdf.

5. United States v. Olsen, 737 F.3d 625, 626 (9th Cir. 2013) (Kozinski, C.J., dissenting).

6. *See generally* Angela J. Davis, *Arbitrary Justice: The Power of the American Prosecutor* (Oxford Univ. Press 2007).

7. *See* Robert P. Mosteller, *Discovery Against the Defense: Tilting the Adversarial Balance,* 74 Cal. L. Rev. 1567, 1674 (1986) (describing "revolutionary expansion" in defense discovery obligations during the early 1970s).

B.   STATUTORY AND RULE DISCOVERY:
A TWO-WAY STREET

Unlike Constitution-based discovery, statutory rules of discovery are ordinarily two-way streets. These rules require prosecutors and defense attorneys to disclose to each other certain types of evidence that they plan to use in their respective cases-in-chief.

Every jurisdiction has rules governing discovery. For example, in federal court, Federal Rule of Criminal Procedure 16(a)[8] requires that the prosecution disclose to the defense all statements of the defendant, the defendant's prior criminal record, documents and physical objects the prosecutor will seek to introduce during trial, experts' reports, and the bases of experts' opinions. Rule 26.2, also known as the *Jencks Act*, requires that the prosecutor disclose a witness's pretrial statements after the witness testifies on direct examination so that these statements are available for impeachment. However, because defense counsel needs time to review these statements, and judges do not want mid-trial delays, it is the practice of many to make earlier disclosure of witness statements. Unlike in civil cases, depositions are rarely used by prosecutors or defense counsel in criminal prosecutions.[9]

Under the Federal Rules of Criminal Procedure, the defense also has statutory duties to disclose certain types of evidence that it plans to use at trial. Under Rule 16(b), if the defense requests discovery from the prosecution, the defense has a reciprocal duty to provide documents and tangible objects it intends to introduce in its case-in-chief, as well as access to experts' reports and the bases for their testimony. In addition, Rule 26.2 requires that the defense provide a copy of its witnesses' pretrial statements after defense witnesses testify on direct examination.

The Federal Rules of Criminal Procedure also contain notice requirements that both sides must follow. Rule 12.1 requires the defense, upon the government's request, to provide written notice of an intention to offer an alibi defense. Once the defense provides such notice, the prosecution has a duty to provide to the defense information regarding rebuttal witnesses it will use to establish the defendant's presence at the scene of the crime or to rebut the testimony of the defendant's alibi witnesses. Similarly, Rule 12.2 requires that the defendant give notice of an intention to rely on a mental defense at trial. Once the defense provides such notice, the government has an opportunity to have its expert examine the defendant so that it can prepare for the defense's case.

If there is a violation of the statutory rules of discovery, the court has broad discretion in ordering a remedy. The court may exclude the evidence, grant

---

8. Federal Rules of Criminal Procedure 12.1, 12.2, 16, and 26.2 are set forth in the Statutory Supplement.

9. The limited circumstances for depositions in criminal cases are set forth in Federal Rule of Criminal Procedure 15. The use of depositions is limited by the rule and the defendant's Sixth Amendment right of confrontation.

an appropriate continuance, or sanction counsel. Courts generally will impose the least severe sanction that will accomplish the goal of compliance with the discovery rules. However, in Taylor v. Illinois, 484 U.S. 400 (1988), the Supreme Court held that a defendant's Sixth Amendment right to compel witnesses is not violated if a court bars a defense witness from testifying because the defense has not complied with a valid court discovery order. In deciding what, if any, sanction to impose on parties that violate discovery rules, courts consider whether the violating party acted in bad faith and whether the opposing party suffered any prejudice as a result of the violation.

Defendants have been unsuccessful in attacking discovery rules that require early notification of the evidence that the defense plans to use in its case-in-chief. *See* Michigan v. Lucas, 500 U.S. 145 (1991) (upholding statute that requires disclosure of evidence defense plans to offer regarding rape victim's sexual history). Although the Fifth Amendment confers on defendants a right not to incriminate themselves, this right does not permit defendants to refuse to comply with discovery rules. Discovery rules are designed to prevent either side from being ambushed at trial.

WILLIAMS v. FLORIDA
399 U.S. 78 (1970)

Justice WHITE delivered the opinion of the Court.

[Before trial, Williams sought an order excusing him from complying with a Florida discovery rule that requires a defendant, upon written demand of the prosecuting attorney, to give pretrial notice if the defendant intends to claim an alibi, and to furnish the prosecuting attorney with information regarding the defendant's location and with the names and addresses of the alibi witnesses he intends to use. In his motion Williams openly declared his intent to claim an alibi, but objected to the further disclosure requirements on the ground that the rule "compels the Defendant in a criminal case to be a witness against himself" in violation of his Fifth and Fourteenth Amendment rights.]

We need not linger over the suggestion that the discovery permitted the State against petitioner in this case deprived him of "due process" or a "fair trial." Florida law provides for liberal discovery by the defendant against the State and the notice-of-alibi rule is itself carefully hedged with reciprocal duties requiring state disclosure to the defendant. Given the ease with which an alibi can be fabricated, the State's interest in protecting itself against an eleventh-hour defense is both obvious and legitimate. The adversary system of trial is hardly an end in itself; it is not yet a poker game in which players enjoy an absolute right always to conceal their cards until played. We find ample room in that system, at least as far as "due process" is concerned, for the instant Florida rule, which is designed to enhance the search for truth in the criminal trial by insuring both the defendant and the State ample opportunity to investigate certain facts crucial to the determination of guilt or innocence.

Petitioner's major contention is that he was "compelled . . . to be a witness against himself" contrary to the commands of the Fifth and Fourteenth Amendments because the notice-of-alibi rule required him to give the State the name and address of [his alibi witness] in advance of trial and thus to furnish the State with information useful in convicting him. We conclude, however, as has apparently every other court that has considered the issue that the privilege against self-incrimination is not violated by a requirement that the defendant give notice of an alibi defense and disclose his alibi witnesses.

The defendant in a criminal trial is frequently forced to testify himself and to call other witnesses in an effort to reduce the risk of conviction. That the defendant faces such a dilemma demanding a choice between complete silence and presenting a defense has never been thought an invasion of the privilege against compelled self-incrimination. The pressures generated by the State's evidence may be severe but they do not vitiate the defendant's choice to present an alibi defense and witnesses to prove it, even though the attempted defense ends in catastrophe for the defendant.

In the case before us, the notice-of-alibi rule by itself in no way affected petitioner's crucial decision to call alibi witnesses or added to the legitimate pressures leading to that course of action. At most, the rule only compelled petitioner to accelerate the timing of his disclosure, forcing him to divulge at an earlier date information that the petitioner from the beginning planned to divulge at trial. Nothing in the Fifth Amendment privilege entitles a defendant as a matter of constitutional right to await the end of the State's case before announcing the nature of his defense, any more than it entitles him to await the jury's verdict on the State's case-in-chief before deciding whether or not to take the stand himself.

Chief Justice BURGER, concurring.

I join fully in [the] opinion for the Court. I see an added benefit to the notice-of-alibi rule in that it will serve important functions by way of disposing of cases without trial in appropriate circumstances — a matter of considerable importance when courts, prosecution offices, and legal aid and defender agencies are vastly overworked. The prosecutor upon receiving notice will, of course, investigate prospective alibi witnesses. If he finds them reliable and unimpeachable he will doubtless re-examine his entire case and this process would very likely lead to dismissal of the charges. In turn he might be obliged to determine why false charges were instituted and where the breakdown occurred in the examination of evidence that led to a charge.

On the other hand, inquiry into a claimed alibi defense may reveal it to be contrived and fabricated and the witnesses accordingly subject to impeachment or other attack. In this situation defense counsel would be obliged to re-examine his case and, if he found his client has proposed the use of false testimony, either seek to withdraw from the case or try to persuade his client to enter a plea of guilty, possibly by plea discussions which could lead to disposition on a lesser charge.

In either case the ends of justice will have been served and the processes expedited. These are the likely consequences of an enlarged and truly reciprocal pretrial disclosure of evidence and the move away from the "sporting contest" idea of criminal justice.

Justice BLACK, with whom Justice DOUGLAS, joins, concurring in part and dissenting in part.

The Court . . . holds that a State can require a defendant in a criminal case to disclose in advance of trial the nature of his alibi defense and give the names and addresses of witnesses he will call to support that defense. This decision, in my view, is a radical and dangerous departure from the historical and constitutionally guaranteed right of a defendant in a criminal case to remain completely silent, requiring the State to prove its case without any assistance of any kind from the defendant himself.

The core of the majority's decision is an assumption that compelling a defendant to give notice of an alibi defense before a trial is no different from requiring a defendant, after the State has produced the evidence against him at trial, to plead alibi before the jury retires to consider the case.

When a defendant is required to indicate whether he might plead alibi in advance of trial, he faces a vastly different decision from that faced by one who can wait until the State has presented the case against him before making up his mind. Before trial the defendant knows only what the State's case might be. Therefore any appraisal of the desirability of pleading alibi will be beset with guesswork and gambling. . . . Any lawyer who has actually tried a case knows that, regardless of the amount of pretrial preparation, a case looks far different when it is actually being tried than when it is only being thought about.

[T]he Fifth Amendment itself clearly provides that "no person . . . shall be compelled in any criminal case to be a witness against himself." If words are to be given their plain and obvious meaning, that provision, in my opinion, states that a criminal defendant cannot be required to give evidence, testimony, or any other assistance to the State to aid it in convicting him of crime. The Florida notice-of-alibi rule in my opinion is a patent violation of that constitutional provision because it requires a defendant to disclose information to the State so that the State can use that information to destroy him.

A criminal trial is in part a search for truth. But it is also a system designed to protect "freedom" by insuring that no one is criminally punished unless the State has first succeeded in the admittedly difficult task of convincing a jury that the defendant is guilty. The Framers decided that the benefits to be derived from the kind of trial required by the Bill of Rights were well worth any loss in "efficiency" that resulted. Their decision constitutes the final word on the subject, absent some constitutional amendment. That decision should not be set aside as the Court does today.

C. CONSTITUTIONAL DISCOVERY:
A ONE-WAY STREET

In addition to statutory rights to discovery, defendants also have a constitutional right to certain types of evidence. The Bill of Rights does not refer explicitly to "the right to discovery." Rather, the Court has fashioned the right to discovery from the defendant's right of due process. Because only defendants have constitutional due process rights, constitutional discovery rights are a one-way street — the prosecutor must give evidence to the defense that may help the defendant avoid conviction, but there is no corresponding obligation for the defense to give evidence to the prosecution that may help secure a conviction.

Why does the prosecution have an obligation to help the defense by providing exculpatory evidence if we have an adversarial system? Shouldn't each side have the responsibility of finding the evidence it needs to win the case? The Supreme Court answered this question in its historic case of Brady v. Maryland.

BRADY v. MARYLAND
373 U.S. 83 (1963)

Justice DOUGLAS' opinion was announced by Justice BRENNAN.

Petitioner and a companion, Boblit, were found guilty of murder in the first degree and were sentenced to death. Their trials were separate, [Brady] being tried first. At his trial Brady took the stand and admitted his participation in the crime, but he claimed that Boblit did the actual killing. And, in his summation to the jury, Brady's counsel conceded that Brady was guilty of murder in the first degree, asking only that the jury return that verdict "without capital punishment." Prior to the trial petitioner's counsel had requested the prosecution to allow him to examine Boblit's extrajudicial statements. Several of those statements were shown to him; but one . . . in which Boblit admitted the actual homicide, was withheld by the prosecution and did not come to petitioner's notice until after he had been tried, convicted, and sentenced.

We agree with the Court of Appeals that suppression of the confession was a violation of the Due Process Clause of the Fourteenth Amendment. This ruling is an extension of Mooney v. Holohan (1935) where the court ruled [that a prosecutor could not knowingly present perjured testimony] and Napue v. Illinois (1959) [where the Court barred the State from allowing unsolicited false evidence to go uncorrected].

We now hold that the suppression by the prosecution of evidence favorable to an accused upon request violates due process where the evidence is material either to guilt or to punishment, irrespective of the good faith or bad faith of the prosecution.

The principle . . . is not punishment of society for misdeeds of a prosecutor but avoidance of an unfair trial to the accused. Society wins not only when the guilty are convicted but when criminal trials are fair; our system of the administration of justice suffers when any accused is treated unfairly. An inscription on the walls of the Department of Justice states the proposition candidly for the federal domain: "The United States wins its point whenever justice is done its citizens in the courts." A prosecution that withholds evidence on demand of an accused which, if made available, would tend to exculpate him or reduce the penalty . . . casts the prosecutor in the role of an architect of a proceeding that does not comport with standards of justice.

Brady implicitly recognizes that practical obstacles, including lack of resources and law enforcement's zeal to win, often make it difficult for defendants to discover evidence to support their cases. Yet the decision does not depend on the good or bad faith of the prosecutor in withholding discovery. What is important is what possible effect the exculpatory evidence may have had on the defendant's guilt or punishment.

Under *Brady*, the prosecutor has the responsibility of anticipating what defenses might be presented in a case. Regardless of whether the defense requests discovery, the prosecutor has the constitutional duty to provide exculpatory evidence.

Brady did not set forth a requirement that exculpatory evidence be provided at a particular time, as long as it is provided in sufficient time for the defense to use it at trial. It also did not establish how "material" the withheld evidence needs to be. That is an issue the Court would address in future cases, beginning with United States v. Bagley, *infra*.

Thus, while *Brady* was an important step toward ensuring the defendant a fair trial, its effectiveness continues to depend on the judgment and ethics of the prosecutor. Nothing in *Brady* itself prohibited prosecutors from taking their chances by withholding exculpatory evidence and later arguing that the withheld evidence would not have affected the verdict. Subsequent ethical rules have filled in that gap by directing a prosecutor to "make timely disclosure to the defense all evidence or information known to the prosecutor that tends to negate the guilt of the accused or mitigates the offense [or could impact on sentencing]." ABA Model Rule of Professional Conduct 3.8(d).

Shortly after *Brady*, the Supreme Court extended the constitutional right to discovery to not only evidence that tends to exculpate the defendant but also evidence that undermines the prosecution's case by impeaching its witnesses.

GIGLIO v. UNITED STATES

405 U.S. 150 (1972)

Chief Justice BURGER delivered the opinion of the Court.

Petitioner was convicted of passing forged money orders and sentenced to five years' imprisonment. While appeal was pending in the Court of Appeals, defense counsel discovered new evidence indicating that the Government had failed to disclose an alleged promise made to its key witness that he would not be prosecuted if he testified for the Government. We granted certiorari to determine whether the evidence not disclosed was such as to require a new trial under the due process criteria of . . . Brady v. Maryland (1963).

The controversy in this case centers around the testimony of Robert Taliento, [Giglio's alleged coconspirator and the prosecution's key witness in the case against Giglio. Taliento testified that Giglio participated in a scheme to pass forged money orders. When he was cross-examined by defense counsel, Taliento denied that he had been promised leniency in a scheme to pass forged money orders. After trial, however, the defense discovered that a prosecutor had promised Taliento that if he testified before the grand jury and at trial, he would not be prosecuted. That prosecutor ended up not trying the case and the trial prosecutor, whether purposely or inadvertently, did not reveal to the defense that Taliento had been promised immunity.]

As long ago as Mooney v. Holohan (1935), this Court made clear that deliberate deception of a court and jurors by the presentation of known false evidence is incompatible with "rudimentary demands of justice." In Napue v. Illinois (1959), we said, "the same result obtains when the State, although not soliciting false evidence, allows it to go uncorrected when it appears." Thereafter Brady v. Maryland held that suppression of material evidence justifies a new trial "irrespective of the good faith or bad faith of the prosecution." When the "reliability of a given witness may well be determinative of guilt or innocence," nondisclosure of evidence affecting credibility falls within this general rule. We do not, however, automatically require a new trial whenever "a combing of the prosecutors' files after the trial has disclosed evidence possibly useful to the defense but not likely to have changed the verdict. . . ." A finding of materiality of the evidence is required under *Brady*.

The prosecutor's office is an entity and as such it is the spokesman for the Government. A promise made by one attorney must be attributed, for these purposes, to the Government. To the extent this places a burden on the large prosecution offices, procedures and regulations can be established to carry that burden and to insure communication of all relevant information on each case to every lawyer who deals with it.

Here the Government's case depended almost entirely on Taliento's testimony; without it there could have been no indictment and no evidence to carry the case to the jury. Taliento's credibility as a witness was therefore an important issue in the case, and evidence of any understanding or agreement as to a future prosecution would be relevant to his credibility and the jury was entitled to know of it.

For these reasons, the due process requirements enunciated in *Napue* and the other cases cited earlier require a new trial.

Although the Court in *Brady* and *Giglio* established the due process right of discovery of exculpatory and impeachment evidence, it limited its holdings to "material" evidence. It took 20 years for the Court to agree on a standard for materiality. What circumstances and what types of withheld evidence trigger a defendant's right to a new trial under the Due Process Clause? The justices debated this issue and ultimately resolved it in United States v. Bagley.

UNITED STATES v. BAGLEY

473 U.S. 667 (1985)

Justice BLACKMUN delivered the opinion of the Court, except as to Part III.

In Brady v. Maryland (1963), this Court held that "the suppression by the prosecution of evidence favorable to an accused upon request violates due process where the evidence is material either to guilt or punishment." The issue in the present case concerns the standard of materiality to be applied in determining whether a conviction should be reversed because the prosecutor failed to disclose requested evidence that could have been used to impeach Government witnesses.

I

Bagley was indicted on 15 charges of violating federal narcotics and firearms statutes. [Twenty-four] days before trial, he filed a discovery motion. [He requested, among other things]: "The names and addresses of witnesses that the government intends to call at trial. Also the prior criminal records of witnesses, and any deals, promises or inducements made to witnesses in exchange for their testimony."

The Government's two principal witnesses at the trial were James F. O'Connor and Donald E. Mitchell. The Government's response to the discovery motion did not disclose that any "deals, promises or inducements" had been made to O'Connor or Mitchell. In apparent reply to a [defendant's discovery] request, the Government produced a series of affidavits that O'Connor and Mitchell had signed that concluded with the statement, "I made this statement freely and voluntarily without any threats or rewards, or promises of reward having been made to me in return for it."

Respondent waived his right to a jury trial and was tried before the court in December 1977. At the trial, O'Connor and Mitchell testified about both the firearms and the narcotics charges. [T]he court found respondent guilty on the narcotics charges, but not guilty on the firearms charges.

In mid-1980, respondent filed requests for information pursuant to the Freedom of Information Act. He received in response copies of ATF form contracts that O'Connor and Mitchell had signed on May 3, 1977. Each form was entitled "Contract for Purchase of Information and Payment of Lump Sum Therefor." The printed portion of the form stated that the vendor "will provide" information to ATF and that "upon receipt of such information . . . the United States will pay to said vendor a sum commensurate with services and information rendered." The figure "$300.00" was handwritten in each form on a line entitled "Sum to Be Paid to Vendor."

Because these contracts had not been disclosed to respondent in response to his pretrial discovery motion, [Bagley] alleged that the Government's failure to disclose the contracts, which he could have used to impeach O'Connor and Mitchell, violated his right to due process under Brady v. Maryland. [The Court of Appeals held that the failure to provide this information required automatic reversal of Bagley's conviction.]

II

The holding in Brady v. Maryland requires disclosure only of evidence that is both favorable to the accused and "material either to guilt or to punishment." The Court explained in United States v. Agurs (1976): "A fair analysis of the holding in *Brady* indicates that implicit in the requirement of materiality is a concern that the suppressed evidence might have affected the outcome of the trial."

The *Brady* rule is based on the requirement of due process. Its purpose is not to displace the adversary system as the primary means by which truth is uncovered, but to ensure that a miscarriage of justice does not occur. Thus, the prosecutor is not required to deliver his entire file to defense counsel, but only to disclose evidence favorable to the accused that, if suppressed, would deprive the defendant of a fair trial.[10]

In *Brady* and *Agurs*, the prosecutor failed to disclose exculpatory evidence. In the present case, the prosecutor failed to disclose evidence that the defense might have used to impeach the Government's witnesses by showing bias or interest. Impeachment evidence, however, as well as exculpatory evidence, falls within the *Brady* rule. See *Giglio* (1972). Such evidence is "evidence favorable to an accused," so that, if disclosed and used effectively, it may make the difference between conviction and acquittal.

The Court of Appeals treated impeachment evidence as constitutionally different from exculpatory evidence. According to that court, failure to disclose impeachment evidence is "even more egregious" than failure to

10. By requiring the prosecutor to assist the defense in making its case, the *Brady* rule represents a limited departure from a pure adversary model. The Court has recognized, however, that the prosecutor's role transcends that of an adversary: He "is the representative not of an ordinary party to a controversy, but of a sovereignty . . . whose interest . . . in a criminal prosecution is not that it shall win a case, but that justice shall be done." Berger v. United States (1935). [Footnote by the Court.]

disclose exculpatory evidence "because it threatens the defendant's right to confront adverse witnesses." Relying on Davis v. Alaska, 415 U.S. 308 (1974), the Court of Appeals held that the Government's failure to disclose requested impeachment evidence that the defense could use to conduct an effective cross-examination of important prosecution witnesses constitutes "'constitutional error of the first magnitude'" requiring automatic reversal.

This Court has rejected any such distinction between impeachment evidence and exculpatory evidence. Thus, the Court of Appeals' holding is inconsistent with our precedents.

Moreover, the court's reliance on Davis v. Alaska for its "automatic reversal" rule is misplaced. In *Davis*, the defense sought to cross-examine a crucial prosecution witness concerning his probationary status as a juvenile delinquent. Pursuant to a state rule of procedure . . . , the trial judge prohibited the defense from conducting the cross-examination. This Court reversed the defendant's conviction, ruling that the direct restriction on the scope of cross-examination denied the defendant "the right of effective cross-examination which would be constitutional error of the first magnitude and no amount of showing of want of prejudice would cure it."

The present case, in contrast, does not involve any direct restriction on the scope of cross-examination. The defense was free to cross-examine the witnesses on any relevant subject, including possible bias or interest resulting from inducements made by the Government. The constitutional error, if any, in this case was the Government's failure to assist the defense by disclosing information that might have been helpful in conducting the cross-examination. As discussed above, such suppression of evidence amounts to a constitutional violation only if it deprives the defendant of a fair trial. [A] constitutional error occurs, and the conviction must be reversed, only if the evidence is material in the sense that its suppression undermines confidence in the outcome of the trial.

III

It remains to determine the standard of materiality applicable to the non-disclosed evidence at issue in this case. Our starting point is the framework for evaluating the materiality of *Brady* evidence established in United States v. Agurs. The Court in *Agurs* distinguished three situations involving the discovery, after trial, of information favorable to the accused that had been known to the prosecution but unknown to the defense. The first situation was the prosecutor's knowing use of perjured testimony or, equivalently, the prosecutor's knowing failure to disclose that testimony used to convict the defendant was false. The Court noted the well-established rule that "a conviction obtained by the knowing use of perjured testimony is fundamentally unfair, and must be set aside if there is any reasonable likelihood that the false testimony could have affected the judgment of the jury."

At the other extreme is the situation in *Agurs* itself, where the defendant does not make a *Brady* request and the prosecutor fails to disclose certain evidence favorable to the accused. The Court rejected a harmless-error rule in that situation. The Court reasoned: "If the standard applied to the usual motion for a new trial based on newly discovered evidence were the same when the evidence was in the State's possession as when it was found in a neutral source, there would be no special significance to the prosecutor's obligation to serve the cause of justice." The standard of materiality applicable in the absence of a specific *Brady* request is therefore stricter than the harmless-error standard but more lenient to the defense than the newly-discovered-evidence standard.

The third situation identified by the Court in *Agurs* is where the defense makes a specific request and the prosecutor fails to disclose responsive evidence. The Court . . . suggested that the standard might be more lenient to the defense than in the situation in which the defense makes no request or only a general request.

The Court has relied on and reformulated the *Agurs* standard for the materiality of undisclosed evidence in two subsequent cases arising outside the *Brady* context. In [one of them], Strickland v. Washington (1984), the Court held that a new trial must be granted when evidence is not introduced because of the incompetence of counsel only if "there is a reasonable probability that, but for counsel's unprofessional errors, the result of the proceeding would have been different." The *Strickland* Court defined a "reasonable probability" as "a probability sufficient to undermine confidence in the outcome."

We find the *Strickland* formulation of the *Agurs* test for materiality sufficiently flexible to cover the "no request," "general request," and "specific request" cases of prosecutorial failure to disclose evidence favorable to the accused: The evidence is material only if there is a reasonable probability that, had the evidence been disclosed to the defense, the result of the proceeding would have been different. A "reasonable probability" is a probability sufficient to undermine confidence in the outcome.

The Government suggests that a materiality standard more favorable to the defendant reasonably might be adopted in specific request cases. The Government notes that an incomplete response to a specific request not only deprives the defense of certain evidence, but also has the effect of representing to the defense that the evidence does not exist. In reliance on this misleading representation, the defense might abandon lines of independent investigation, defenses, or trial strategies that it otherwise would have pursued.

We agree that the prosecutor's failure to respond fully to a *Brady* request may impair the adversary process in this manner. And the more specifically the defense requests certain evidence, thus putting the prosecutor on notice of its value, the more reasonable it is for the defense to assume from the nondisclosure that the evidence does not exist, and to make pretrial and trial decisions on the basis of this assumption. This possibility of impairment does not necessitate a different standard of materiality, however, for under the *Strickland* formulation the reviewing court may consider directly any adverse effect that the prosecutor's failure to respond might have had on the preparation or presentation of the defendant's case. The reviewing court should assess the possibility that such effect might have occurred in light of the totality of the circumstances and with an awareness of the difficulty of reconstructing in a post-trial proceeding the course that the defense and the trial would have taken had the defense not been misled by the prosecutor's incomplete response.

In the present case, we think that there is a significant likelihood that the prosecutor's response to respondent's discovery motion misleadingly induced defense counsel to believe that O'Connor and Mitchell could not be impeached on the basis of bias or interest arising from inducements offered by the Government.

The District Court, nonetheless, found beyond a reasonable doubt that, had the information that the Government held out the possibility of reward to its witnesses been disclosed, the result of the criminal prosecution would not have been different [because O'Connor's and Mitchell's testimony was directed at the weapons charges on which Bagley was acquitted].

[The Supreme Court reversed the Circuit Court's holding that Bagley's case should be automatically reversed for a *Brady* violation and remanded the case to the lower court to decide whether the withheld evidence was "material" under the standard it established in this opinion.]

Justice WHITE, with whom Chief Justice BURGER and Justice REHNQUIST join, concurring in part and concurring in the judgment.

I agree with the Court that respondent is not entitled to have his conviction overturned unless he can show that the evidence withheld by the Government was "material," and I therefore join Parts I and II of the Court's opinion. I also agree . . . that for purposes of this inquiry, "evidence is material only if there is a reasonable probability that, had the evidence been disclosed to the defense, the result of the proceeding would have been different." As the Justice correctly observes, this standard is "sufficiently flexible" to cover all instances of prosecutorial failure to disclose evidence favorable to the accused. Given the flexibility of the standard and the inherently fact-bound nature of the cases to which it will be applied, however, I see no reason to attempt to elaborate on the relevance to the inquiry of the specificity of the defense's request for disclosure, either generally or with respect to this case. I would hold simply that the proper standard is one of reasonable probability and that the Court of Appeals' failure to apply this standard necessitates reversal. I therefore concur in the judgment.

Justice MARSHALL, with whom Justice BRENNAN joins, dissenting.

When the Government withholds from a defendant evidence that might impeach the prosecution's only witnesses, that failure to disclose cannot be deemed harmless error. Because that is precisely the nature of the undisclosed evidence in this case, I would affirm the judgment of the Court of Appeals and would not remand for further proceedings.

The record plainly demonstrates that on the two counts for which Bagley received sentences of imprisonment, the Government's entire case hinged on the testimony of O'Connor and Mitchell.

Whenever the Government fails, in response to a request, to disclose impeachment evidence relating to the credibility of its key witnesses, the truth-finding process of trial is necessarily thrown askew. The failure to disclose evidence affecting the overall credibility of witnesses corrupts the process to some degree in all instances.

Instead of affirming, the Court today chooses to reverse and remand the case for application of its newly stated standard to the facts of this case. While I believe that the evidence at issue here, which remained undisclosed despite a particular request, undoubtedly was material under the Court's standard, I also have serious doubts whether the Court's definition of the constitutional right at issue adequately takes account of the interests this Court sought to protect in its decision in Brady v. Maryland (1963).

I begin from the fundamental premise, which hardly bears repeating, that "[the] purpose of a trial is as much the acquittal of an innocent person as it is the conviction of a guilty one." When evidence favorable to the defendant is known to exist, disclosure only enhances the quest for truth; it takes no direct toll on that inquiry. Moreover, the existence of any small piece of evidence favorable to the defense may, in a particular case, create just the doubt that prevents the jury from returning a verdict of guilty. The private whys and wherefores of jury deliberations pose an impenetrable barrier to our ability to know just which piece of information might make, or might have made, a difference.

When the state does not disclose information in its possession that might reasonably be considered favorable to the defense, it precludes the trier of fact from gaining access to such information and thereby undermines the reliability of the verdict. . . . With a minimum of effort, the state could improve the real and apparent fairness of the trial enormously, by assuring that the defendant may place before the trier of fact favorable evidence known to the government. This proposition is not new. We have long recognized that, within the limit of the state's ability to identify so-called exculpatory information, the state's concern for a fair verdict precludes it from withholding from the defense evidence favorable to the defendant's case in the prosecutor's files.

This recognition no doubt stems in part from the frequently considerable imbalance in resources between most criminal defendants and most prosecutors' offices. Many, perhaps most, criminal defendants in the United States are represented by appointed counsel, who often are paid minimal wages and operate on shoestring budgets. In addition, unlike police, defense counsel generally is not present at the scene of the crime, or at the time of arrest, but instead comes into the case late. Moreover, unlike the government, defense counsel is not in the position to make deals with witnesses to gain evidence. Thus, an inexperienced, unskilled, or unaggressive attorney often is unable to amass the factual support necessary to a reasonable defense. When favorable evidence is in the hands of the prosecutor but not disclosed, the result may well be that the defendant is deprived of a fair chance before the trier of fact, and the trier of fact is deprived of the ingredients necessary to a fair decision. This grim reality, of course, poses a direct challenge to the traditional model of the adversary criminal process, and perhaps because this reality so directly questions the fairness of our longstanding processes, change has been cautious and halting. Thus, the Court has not gone the full road and expressly required that the state provide to the defendant access to the prosecutor's complete files, or investigators who will assure that the defendant has an opportunity to discover every existing piece of helpful evidence. Instead, in acknowledgment of the fact that important interests are served when potentially favorable evidence is disclosed, the Court has fashioned a compromise, requiring that the prosecution identify and disclose to the defendant favorable material that it possesses. This requirement is but a small, albeit important, step toward equality of justice.

At the trial level, the duty of the state to effectuate *Brady* devolves into the duty of the prosecutor; the dual role that the prosecutor must play poses a serious obstacle to implementing *Brady*. The prosecutor is by trade, if not necessity, a zealous advocate. He is a trained attorney who must aggressively seek convictions in court on behalf of a victimized public. At the same time, as a representative of the state, he must place foremost in his hierarchy of interests the determination of truth. Thus, for purposes of *Brady*, the prosecutor must abandon his role as an advocate and pore through his files, as objectively as possible, to identify the material that could undermine his case. Given this obviously unharmonious role, it is not surprising that these advocates oftentimes overlook or downplay potentially favorable evidence, often in cases in which there is no doubt that the failure to disclose was a result of absolute good faith.

The prosecutor surely greets the moment at which he must turn over *Brady* material with little enthusiasm. In perusing his files, he must make the often difficult decision as to whether evidence is favorable, and must decide on which side to err when faced with doubt. In his role as advocate, the answers are clear. In his role as representative of the state, the answers should be equally clear, and often to the contrary. Evidence that is of doubtful worth in the eyes of the prosecutor could be of inestimable value to the defense, and might make the difference to the trier of fact.

Once the prosecutor suspects that certain information might have favorable implications for the defense, either because it is potentially exculpatory or relevant to credibility, I see no reason why he should not be required to disclose it. After all, favorable evidence indisputably enhances the truth-seeking process at trial. And it is the job of the defense, not the prosecution, to decide whether and in what way to use arguably favorable evidence. In addition, to require disclosure of all evidence that might reasonably be considered favorable to the defendant would have the precautionary effect of assuring that no information of potential consequence is mistakenly overlooked. By requiring full disclosure of favorable evidence in this way, courts could begin to assure that a possibly dispositive piece of information is not withheld from the trier of fact by a prosecutor who is torn between the two roles he must play. A clear rule of this kind, coupled with a presumption in favor of disclosure, also would facilitate the prosecutor's admittedly difficult task by removing a substantial amount of unguided discretion.

Under the foregoing analysis, the prosecutor's duty is quite straightforward: he must divulge all evidence that reasonably appears favorable to the defendant, erring on the side of disclosure.

The Court, however, offers a complex alternative. [T]he Court holds that due process does not require the prosecutor to turn over evidence unless the evidence is "material," and the Court states that evidence is "material" "only if there is a reasonable probability that, had the evidence been disclosed to the defense, the result of the proceeding would have been different."

The standard for disclosure that the Court articulates today enables prosecutors to avoid disclosing obviously exculpatory evidence while acting well within the bounds of their constitutional obligation.

The Court's definition poses other, serious problems. Besides legitimizing the nondisclosure of clearly favorable evidence, the standard set out by the Court also asks the prosecutor to predict what effect various pieces of evidence will have on the trial. He must evaluate his case and the case of the defendant — of which he presumably knows very little — and perform the impossible task of deciding whether a certain piece of information will have a significant impact on the trial, bearing in mind that a defendant will later shoulder the heavy burden of proving how it would have affected the outcome. At best, this standard places on the prosecutor a responsibility to speculate, at times without foundation, since the prosecutor will not normally know what strategy the defense will pursue or what evidence the defense will find useful. At worst, the standard invites a prosecutor, whose interests are conflicting, to gamble, to play the odds, and to take a chance that evidence will later turn out not to have been potentially dispositive. One Court of Appeals has recently vented its frustration at these unfortunate consequences:

> The Court's standard also encourages the prosecutor to assume the role of the jury, and to decide whether certain evidence will make a difference. In our system of justice, that decision properly and wholly belongs to the jury. The prosecutor, convinced of the guilt of the defendant and of the truthfulness of his witnesses, may all too easily view as irrelevant or unpersuasive evidence that draws his own judgments into question. Accordingly he will decide the evidence need not be disclosed. But the ideally neutral trier of fact, who approaches the case from a wholly different perspective, is by the prosecutor's decision denied the opportunity to consider the evidence.

I simply cannot agree with the Court that the due process right to favorable evidence recognized in *Brady* was intended to become entangled in prosecutorial determinations of the likelihood that particular information would affect the outcome of trial. Almost a decade of lower court practice with *Agurs* convinces me that courts and prosecutors have come to pay "too much deference to the federal common law policy of discouraging discovery in criminal cases, and too little regard to due process of law for defendants." Eager to apply the "materiality" standard at the pretrial stage, as the Court permits them to do, prosecutors lose sight of the basic principles underlying the doctrine. I would return to the original theory and promise of *Brady* and reassert the duty of the prosecutor to disclose all evidence in his files that might reasonably be considered favorable to the defendant's case. No prosecutor can know prior to trial whether such evidence will be of consequence at trial; the mere fact that it might be, however, suffices to mandate disclosure.

In so saying, I recognize that a failure to divulge favorable information should not result in reversal in all cases. It may be that a conviction should be affirmed on appeal despite the prosecutor's failure to disclose evidence that reasonably might have been deemed potentially favorable prior to trial. However, in making the determination of harmlessness, I would apply our normal constitutional error test and reverse unless it is clear beyond a reasonable doubt that the withheld evidence would not have affected the outcome of the trial.

In practical effect, it might be argued, there is little difference between the rule I propose — that a prosecutor must disclose all favorable evidence in his files, subject to harmless-error review — and the rule the Court adopts — that the prosecutor must disclose only the favorable information that might affect the outcome of the trial. According to this argument, if a constitutional right to all favorable evidence leads to reversal only when the withheld evidence might have affected the outcome of the trial, the result will be the same as with a constitutional right only to evidence that will affect the trial outcome. For several reasons, however, I disagree. First, I have faith that a prosecutor would treat a rule requiring disclosure of all information of a certain kind differently from a rule requiring disclosure only of some of that information. Second, persistent or egregious failure to comply with the constitutional duty could lead to disciplinary actions by the courts. Third, the standard of harmlessness I adopt is more protective of the defendant than that chosen by the Court, placing the burden on the prosecutor, rather than the defendant, to prove the harmlessness of his actions. It would be a foolish prosecutor who gambled too glibly with that standard of review.

[O]nly a strict appellate standard, which places on the prosecutor a burden to defend his decisions, will remove the incentive to gamble on a finding of harmlessness. Any lesser standard, and especially one in which the defendant bears the burden of proof, provides the prosecutor with ample room to withhold favorable evidence, and provides a reviewing court with a simple means to affirm whenever in its view the correct result was reached. This is especially true given the speculative nature of retrospective review.

The Court's *Brady/Bagley* standard requires judges to evaluate on a case-by-case basis whether withheld information would have had a reasonable probability of affecting the defendant's case. Ten years after *Bagley*, the Court reaffirmed this approach in Kyles v. Whitley, taking the opportunity to clarify some of the details of the materiality standard and how the *Brady/Bagley* rule should be applied. Rather than requiring that any individual piece of withheld evidence be enough to change the outcome of the defendant's case, the Court emphasized "that the favorable evidence [withheld should] be taken to put the whole case in such a different light as to undermine confidence in the verdict." Kyles v. Whitley, 514 U.S. 419, 435 (1995).

KYLES v. WHITLEY
514 U.S. 419 (1995)

Justice SOUTER delivered the opinion of the Court.

After his first trial in 1984 ended in a hung jury, petitioner Curtis Lee Kyles was tried again, convicted of first-degree murder, and sentenced to death. Because the net effect of the evidence withheld by the State in this case raises a reasonable probability that its disclosure would have produced a different result, Kyles is entitled to a new trial.

[I]

A

The record indicates that, at about 2:20 P.M. on Thursday, September 20, 1984, 60-year-old Dolores Dye left the Schwegmann Brothers' store (Schwegmann's) on Old Gentilly Road in New Orleans after doing some food shopping. As she put her grocery bags into the trunk of her red Ford LTD, a man accosted her and after a short struggle drew a revolver, fired into her left temple, and killed her. The gunman took Dye's keys and drove away in the LTD.

New Orleans police took statements from six eyewitnesses, who offered various descriptions of the gunman. They agreed that he was a black man, and four of them said that he had braided hair. The witnesses differed significantly, however, in their descriptions of height, age, weight, build, and hair length. Two reported seeing a man of 17 or 18, while another described the gunman as looking as old as 28. One witness described him as 5'4" or 5'5", medium build, 140-150 pounds; another described the man as slim and close to six feet. One witness said he had a mustache; none of the others spoke of any facial hair at all. One witness said the murderer had shoulder-length hair; another described the hair as "short."

Since the police believed the killer might have driven his own car to Schwegmann's and left it there when he drove off in Dye's LTD, they recorded the license numbers of the cars remaining in the parking lots around the store at 9:15 P.M. on the evening of the murder. Matching these numbers with registration records produced the names and addresses of the owners of the cars, with a notation of any owner's police record. Despite this list and the eyewitness descriptions, the police had no lead to the gunman until the Saturday evening after the shooting.

At 5:30 P.M., on September 22, a man identifying himself as James Joseph called the police and reported that on the day of the murder he had bought a red Thunderbird from a friend named Curtis, whom he later identified as petitioner, Curtis Kyles. He said that he had subsequently read about Dye's murder in the newspapers and feared that the car he purchased was the victim's. He agreed to meet with the police.

A few hours later, the informant met New Orleans Detective John Miller, who was wired with a hidden body microphone, through which the ensuing conversation was recorded. The informant now said his name was Joseph Banks and that he was called Beanie. His actual name was Joseph Wallace.

His story, as well as his name, had changed since his earlier call. In place of his original account of buying a Thunderbird from Kyles on Thursday, Beanie told Miller that he had not seen Kyles at all on Thursday and had bought a red LTD the previous day, Friday. Beanie led Miller to the parking lot of a nearby bar, where he had left the red LTD, later identified as Dye's.

Beanie told Miller that he lived with Kyles's brother-in-law (later identified as Johnny Burns), whom Beanie repeatedly called his "partner." Beanie described Kyles as slim, about 6-feet tall, 24 or 25 years old, with a "bush" hairstyle. When asked if Kyles ever wore his hair in plaits, Beanie said that he did but that he "had a bush" when Beanie bought the car.

During the conversation, Beanie repeatedly expressed concern that he might himself be a suspect in the murder. He explained that he had been seen driving Dye's car on Friday evening in the French Quarter, admitted that he had changed its license plates, and worried that he "could have been charged" with the murder on the basis of his possession of the LTD. He asked if he would be put in jail. Miller acknowledged that Beanie's possession of the car would have looked suspicious, but reassured him that he "didn't do anything wrong," *id.*

Beanie seemed eager to cast suspicion on Kyles, who allegedly made his living by "robbing people," and had tried to kill Beanie at some prior time. Beanie said that Kyles regularly carried two pistols, a .38 and a .32, and that if the police could "set him up good," they could "get that same gun" used to kill Dye. Beanie rode with Miller and Miller's supervisor, Sgt. James Eaton, in an unmarked squad car to Desire Street, where he pointed out the building containing Kyles's apartment.

Beanie told the officers that after he bought the car, he and his "partner" (Burns) drove Kyles to Schwegmann's about 9 P.M. on Friday evening to pick up Kyles's car, described as an orange four-door Ford.[11] When asked where Kyles's car had been parked, Beanie replied that it had been "on the same side [of the lot] where the woman was killed at." The officers later drove Beanie to Schwegmann's, where he indicated the space where he claimed Kyles's car had been parked. Beanie went on to say that when he and Burns had brought Kyles to pick up the car, Kyles had gone to some nearby bushes to retrieve a brown purse, which Kyles subsequently hid in a wardrobe at his apartment. Beanie said that Kyles had "a lot of groceries" in Schwegmann's bags and a new baby's potty "in the car." Beanie told Eaton that Kyles's garbage would go out the next day and that if Kyles was "smart" he would "put [the purse] in [the] garbage." Beanie made it clear that he expected some reward for his help, saying at one point that he was not "doing all of this for nothing." The police repeatedly assured Beanie that he would not lose the $400 he paid for the car.

After the visit to Schwegmann's, Eaton and Miller took Beanie to a police station where Miller interviewed him again on the record, which was transcribed and signed by Beanie, using his alias "Joseph Banks." This statement, Beanie's third (the telephone call being the first, then the recorded conversation), repeats some of the essentials of the second one. Portions of the third statement, however, embellished or contradicted Beanie's preceding story and were even internally inconsistent.

Although the police did not thereafter put Kyles under surveillance, they learned about events at his apartment from Beanie, who went there twice on Sunday. According to a fourth statement by Beanie, this one given to the chief prosecutor in November (between the first and second trials), he first went to the apartment about 2 P.M., after a telephone conversation with a police officer who asked whether Kyles had the gun that was used to kill Dye. Beanie stayed in Kyles's apartment. [Thereafter,] Sgt. Eaton wrote in an interoffice memorandum, he had "reason to believe the victims [sic] personal papers and the Schwegmann's bags will be in the trash."

At 10:40 A.M., Kyles was arrested as he left the apartment, which was then searched under a warrant. Behind the kitchen stove, the police found a .32-caliber revolver containing five live rounds and one spent cartridge. Ballistics tests later showed that this pistol was used to murder Dye. In a wardrobe in a hallway leading to the kitchen, the officers found a homemade shoulder holster that fit the murder weapon. In a bedroom dresser drawer, they discovered two boxes of ammunition, one containing several .32-caliber rounds of the same brand as those found in the pistol. Back in the kitchen, various cans of cat and dog food, some of them of the brands Dye typically purchased, were found in Schwegmann's sacks. No other groceries were identified as possibly being Dye's, and no potty was found. Later that

---

11. According to photographs later introduced at trial, Kyles's car was actually a Mercury and, according to trial testimony, a two-door model. [Footnote by the Court.]

afternoon at the police station, police opened the rubbish bags and found the victim's purse, identification, and other personal belongings wrapped in a Schwegmann's sack.

The gun, the LTD, the purse, and the cans of pet food were dusted for fingerprints. The gun had been wiped clean. Several prints were found on the purse and on the LTD, but none was identified as Kyles's. Dye's prints were not found on any of the cans of pet food. Kyles's prints were found, however, on a small piece of paper taken from the front passenger-side floorboard of the LTD. A second Schwegmann's receipt was found in the trunk of the LTD, but Kyles's prints were not found on it. Beanie's fingerprints were not compared to any of the fingerprints found.

The lead detective on the case, John Dillman, put together a photo lineup that included a photograph of Kyles (but not of Beanie) and showed the array to five of the six eyewitnesses who had given statements. Three of them picked the photograph of Kyles; the other two could not confidently identify Kyles as Dye's assailant.

B

Kyles was indicted for first-degree murder. Before trial, his counsel filed a lengthy motion for disclosure by the State of any exculpatory or impeachment evidence. The prosecution responded that there was "no exculpatory evidence of any nature," despite the government's knowledge of the following evidentiary items: (1) the six contemporaneous eyewitness statements taken by police following the murder; (2) records of Beanie's initial call to the police; (3) the tape recording of the Saturday conversation between Beanie and officers Eaton and Miller; (4) the typed and signed statement given by Beanie on Sunday morning; (5) the computer printout of license numbers of cars parked at Schwegmann's on the night of the murder, which did not list the number of Kyles's car; (6) the internal police memorandum calling for the seizure of the rubbish after Beanie had suggested that the purse might be found there; and (7) evidence linking Beanie to other crimes at Schwegmann's and to the unrelated murder of one Patricia Leidenheimer, committed in January before the Dye murder.

At the first trial, in November, the heart of the State's case was eyewitness testimony from four people who were at the scene of the crime. Kyles maintained his innocence, offered supporting witnesses, and supplied an alibi that he had been picking up his children from school at the time of the murder. The theory of the defense was that Kyles had been framed by Beanie, who had planted evidence in Kyles's apartment and his rubbish for the purposes of shifting suspicion away from himself, removing an impediment to romance with Pinky Burns, and obtaining reward money. Beanie did not testify as a witness for either the defense or the prosecution.

Because the State withheld evidence, its case was much stronger, and the defense case much weaker, than the full facts would have suggested. Even so, after four hours of deliberation, the jury became deadlocked on the issue of guilt, and a mistrial was declared.

After the mistrial, the chief trial prosecutor, Cliff Strider, interviewed Beanie. Strider's notes show that Beanie again changed important elements of his story. Notwithstanding the many inconsistencies and variations among Beanie's statements, neither Strider's notes nor any of the other notes and transcripts were given to the defense.

In December 1984, Kyles was tried a second time. Again, the heart of the State's case was the testimony of four eyewitnesses who positively identified Kyles in front of the jury. Once again, Beanie did not testify.

As in the first trial, the defense contended that the eyewitnesses were mistaken. Kyles's counsel called several individuals, including Kevin Black, who testified to seeing Beanie, with his hair in plaits, driving a red car similar to the victim's about an hour after the killing. Another witness testified that Beanie, with his hair in braids, had tried to sell him the car on Thursday evening, shortly after the murder. Another witness testified that Beanie, with his hair in a "Jheri curl," had attempted to sell him the car on Friday. One witness, Beanie's "partner," Burns, testified that he had seen Beanie on Sunday at Kyles's apartment, stooping down near the stove where the gun was eventually found, and the defense presented testimony that Beanie was romantically interested in Pinky Burns. To explain the pet food found in Kyles's apartment, there was testimony that Kyles's family kept a dog and cat and often fed stray animals in the neighborhood.

Finally, Kyles again took the stand. Denying any involvement in the shooting, he explained his fingerprints on the cash register receipt found in Dye's car by saying that Beanie had picked him up in a red car on Friday, September 21, and had taken him to Schwegmann's, where he purchased transmission fluid and a pack of cigarettes. He suggested that the receipt may have fallen from the bag when he removed the cigarettes.

On rebuttal, the prosecutor had Beanie brought into the courtroom. All of the testifying eyewitnesses, after viewing Beanie standing next to Kyles, reaffirmed their previous identifications of Kyles as the murderer. Kyles was convicted of first-degree murder and sentenced to death.

Following direct appeal, it was revealed in the course of state collateral review that the State had failed to disclose evidence favorable to the defense. After exhausting state remedies, Kyles sought relief on federal habeas. Although the United States District Court denied relief and the Fifth Circuit affirmed, Judge King dissented, writing that "for the first time in my fourteen years on this court . . . I have serious reservations about whether the State has sentenced to death the right man."

[II]

The prosecution's affirmative duty to disclose evidence favorable to a defendant can trace its origins to early 20th-century strictures against misrepresentation and is of course most prominently associated with this Court's decision in Brady v. Maryland (1963). *Brady* held "that the suppression by the prosecution of evidence favorable to an accused upon request violates due process where the evidence is material either to guilt or to punishment, irrespective of the good faith or bad faith of the prosecution."

[In] United States v. Bagley (1985), the Court disavowed any difference between exculpatory and impeachment evidence for *Brady* purposes, and it abandoned the distinction between the . . . "specific-request" and "general- or no-request" situations. *Bagley* held that regardless of request, favorable evidence is material, and constitutional error results from its suppression by the government, "if there is a reasonable probability that, had the evidence been disclosed to the defense, the result of the proceeding would have been different."

Four aspects of materiality under *Bagley* bear emphasis. Although the constitutional duty is triggered by the potential impact of favorable but undisclosed evidence, a showing of materiality does not require demonstration by a preponderance that disclosure of the suppressed evidence would have resulted ultimately in the defendant's acquittal. *Bagley*'s touchstone of materiality is a "reasonable probability" of a different result, and the adjective is important. The question is not whether the defendant would more likely than not have received a different verdict with the evidence, but whether in its absence he received a fair trial, understood as a trial resulting in a verdict worthy of confidence. A "reasonable probability" of a different result is accordingly shown when the government's evidentiary suppression "undermines confidence in the outcome of the trial."

The second aspect of *Bagley* materiality bearing emphasis here is that it is not a sufficiency of evidence test. A defendant need not demonstrate that after discounting the inculpatory evidence in light of the undisclosed evidence, there would not have been enough left to convict. The possibility of an acquittal on a criminal charge does not imply an insufficient evidentiary basis to convict. One does not show a *Brady* violation by demonstrating that some of the inculpatory evidence should have been excluded, but by showing that the favorable evidence could reasonably be taken to put the whole case in such a different light as to undermine confidence in the verdict.

Third, we note that, contrary to the assumption made by the Court of Appeals once a reviewing court applying *Bagley* has found constitutional error there is no need for further harmless-error review.

The fourth and final aspect of *Bagley* materiality to be stressed here is its definition in terms of suppressed evidence considered collectively, not item by item.

[III]

In this case, disclosure of the suppressed evidence to competent counsel would have made a different result reasonably probable.

As the District Court put it, "the essence of the State's case" was the testimony of eyewitnesses, who identified Kyles as Dye's killer. Disclosure of their statements would have resulted in a markedly weaker case for the prosecution and a markedly stronger one for the defense. To begin with, the value of two of those witnesses would have been substantially reduced or destroyed.

The State rated Henry Williams as its best witness, who testified that he had seen the struggle and the actual shooting by Kyles. The jury would have found it helpful to probe this conclusion in the light of Williams's contemporaneous statement, in which he told the police that the assailant was "a black male, about 19 or 20 years old, about 5'4" or 5'5", 140 to 150 pounds, medium build" and that "his hair looked like it was platted." If cross-examined on this description, Williams would have had trouble explaining how he could have described Kyles, 6-feet tall and thin, as a man more than half a foot shorter with a medium build.[12] Indeed, since Beanie was 22 years old, 5'5" tall, and 159 pounds, the defense would have had a compelling argument that Williams's description pointed to Beanie but not to Kyles.[13]

The trial testimony of a second eyewitness, Isaac Smallwood, was equally damning to Kyles. Smallwood's statement taken at the parking lot, however, was vastly different. . . . A jury would reasonably have been troubled by the adjustments to Smallwood's original story by the time of the second trial.[14]

Damage to the prosecution's case would not have been confined to evidence of the eyewitnesses, for Beanie's various statements would have raised opportunities to attack not only the probative value of crucial physical evidence and the circumstances in which it was found, but the thoroughness and even the good faith of the investigation, as well.

If the defense had called Beanie as an adverse witness, he could not have said anything of any significance without being trapped by his inconsistencies.

Even if Kyles's lawyer had followed the more conservative course of leaving Beanie off the stand, though, the defense could have examined the police to good effect on their knowledge of Beanie's statements and so have attacked the reliability of the investigation in failing even to consider Beanie's possible guilt and in tolerating (if not countenancing) serious possibilities that incriminating evidence had been planted.

By demonstrating the detectives' knowledge of Beanie's affirmatively self-incriminating statements, the defense could have laid the foundation for a vigorous argument that the police had been guilty of negligence.

---

12. The record makes numerous references to Kyles being approximately six feet tall and slender; photographs in the record tend to confirm these descriptions. The description of Beanie in the text comes from his police file. Record photographs of Beanie also depict a man possessing a medium build. [Footnote by the Court.]

13. The defense could have further underscored the possibility that Beanie was Dye's killer through cross-examination of the police on their failure to direct any investigation against Beanie. [Footnote by the Court.]

14. The implication of coaching would have been complemented by the fact that Smallwood's testimony at the second trial was much more precise and incriminating than his testimony at the first, which produced a hung jury. [Footnote by the Court.]

Exposure to Beanie's own words, even through cross-examination of the police officers, would have made the defense's case more plausible and reduced its vulnerability to credibility attack.

In assessing the significance of the evidence withheld, one must of course bear in mind that not every item of the State's case would have been directly undercut if the *Brady* evidence had been disclosed. It is significant, however, that the physical evidence remaining unscathed would, by the State's own admission, hardly have amounted to overwhelming proof that Kyles was the murderer. Ammunition and a holster were found in Kyles's apartment, but if the jury had suspected the gun had been planted the significance of these items might have been left in doubt. The fact that pet food was found in Kyles's apartment was consistent with the testimony of several defense witnesses that Kyles owned a dog and that his children fed stray cats.

Similarly undispositive is the small Schwegmann's receipt on the front passenger floorboard of the LTD, the only physical evidence that bore a fingerprint identified as Kyles's. Kyles explained that Beanie had driven him to Schwegmann's on Friday to buy cigarettes and transmission fluid, and he theorized that the slip must have fallen out of the bag when he removed the cigarettes. This explanation is consistent with the location of the slip when found and with its small size.

The inconclusiveness of the physical evidence does not, to be sure, prove Kyles's innocence. . . . But the question is not whether the State would have had a case to go to the jury if it had disclosed the favorable evidence, but whether we can be confident that the jury's verdict would have been the same. [Finding in favor of Kyles, the Court reversed the lower court's decision and remanded the case for a new trial in compliance with *Brady* and *Bagley.*]

Justice SCALIA, with whom Chief Justice REHNQUIST, Justice KENNEDY, and Justice THOMAS join, dissenting.

In any analysis of this case, the desperate implausibility of the theory that petitioner put before the jury must be kept firmly in mind. The first half of that theory — designed to neutralize the physical evidence . . . was that petitioner was the victim of a "frame-up" by the police informer and evil genius, Beanie. Now it is not unusual for a guilty person who knows that he is suspected of a crime to try to shift blame to someone else; and it is less common, but not unheard of, for a guilty person who is neither suspected nor subject to suspicion (because he has established a perfect alibi), to call attention to himself by coming forward to point the finger at an innocent person. But petitioner's theory is that the guilty Beanie, who could plausibly be accused of the crime . . . , but who was not a suspect any more than Kyles was (the police as yet had no leads), injected both Kyles and himself into the investigation in order to get the innocent Kyles convicted. If this were not stupid enough, the wicked Beanie is supposed to have suggested that the police search his victim's premises a full day before he got around to planting the incriminating evidence on the premises.

The second half of petitioner's theory was that he was the victim of a quadruple coincidence, in which four eyewitnesses to the crime mistakenly identified him as the murderer — three picking him out of a photo array without hesitation, and all four affirming their identification in open court after comparing him with Beanie. The extraordinary mistake petitioner had to persuade the jury these four witnesses made was not simply to mistake the real killer, Beanie, for the very same innocent third party (hard enough to believe), but in addition to mistake him for the very man Beanie had chosen to frame — the last and most incredible level of coincidence. However small the chance that the jury would believe any one of those improbable scenarios, the likelihood that it would believe them all together is far smaller. The Court concludes that it is "reasonably probable" the undisclosed witness interviews would have persuaded the jury of petitioner's implausible theory of mistaken eyewitness testimony, and then argues that it is "reasonably probable" the undisclosed information regarding Beanie would have persuaded the jury of petitioner's implausible theory regarding the incriminating physical evidence. I think neither of those conclusions is remotely true, but even if they were the Court would still be guilty of a fallacy in declaring victory on each implausibility in turn, and thus victory on the whole, without considering the infinitesimal probability of the jury's swallowing the entire concoction of implausibility squared.

The State presented to the jury a massive core of evidence (including four eyewitnesses) showing that petitioner was guilty of murder, and that he lied about his guilt. The effect that the *Brady* materials would have had in chipping away at the edges of the State's case can only be called immaterial. For the same reasons I reject petitioner's claim that the *Brady* materials would have created a "residual doubt" sufficient to cause the sentencing jury to withhold capital punishment.

As *Kyles* demonstrates, *Brady* inquiries are extremely fact-intensive. In deciding whether there has been a *Brady* violation, the focus should be on the collective impact of the withheld evidence and whether it undermines confidence in the verdict. The prosecutors' duty to provide exculpatory and impeachment materials includes evidence not directly in the prosecution's possession, such as evidence that the prosecutor can obtain from his or her investigating officers.

Courts tend to scrutinize cases most closely when the death sentence is imposed. For example, in Banks v. Dretke, 540 U.S. 668 (2004), the Supreme Court reversed Bank's death sentence because the prosecutor failed to disclose that its key witness, Bank's associate, was paid $200 for his testimony. Yet even in death penalty cases, the concept of "materiality" requires a judgment call that can be influenced by the gruesome nature of the case and the strength of the other evidence presented by the prosecution and defense.

BANKS v. DRETKE

540 U.S. 668 (2004)

Justice GINSBURG delivered the opinion of the Court.

Here, the State elected to call Farr as a witness. Indeed, he was a key witness at both guilt and punishment phases of Banks's capital trial. Farr's status as a paid informant was unquestionably "relevant"; similarly beyond doubt, disclosure of Farr's status would have been "helpful to [Banks's] defense." Nothing in [any] decision of this Court suggests that the State can examine an informant at trial, withholding acknowledgment of his informant status in the hope that defendant will not catch on, so will make no disclosure motion.

Banks's prosecutors represented at trial and in state postconviction proceedings that the State had held nothing back. . . . Because Banks had no criminal record, Farr's testimony about Banks's propensity to commit violent acts was crucial to the prosecution. Without that testimony, the State could not have underscored, as it did three times in the penalty phase, that Banks would use the gun fetched in Dallas to "take care" of trouble arising during the robberies. The stress placed by the prosecution on this part of Farr's testimony, uncorroborated by any other witness, belies the State's suggestion that "Farr's testimony was adequately corroborated." The prosecution's penalty-phase summation, moreover, left no doubt about the importance the State attached to Farr's testimony. What Farr told the jury, the prosecution urged, was "of the utmost significance" to show "[Banks] is a danger to friends and strangers, alike."

The jury, moreover, did not benefit from customary, truth-promoting precautions that generally accompany the testimony of informants. This Court has long recognized the "serious questions of credibility" informers pose.

At least as to the penalty phase, in sum, one can hardly be confident that Banks received a fair trial, given the jury's ignorance of Farr's true role in the investigation and trial of the case.

Justice THOMAS, with whom Justice SCALIA joins, concurring in part and dissenting in part.

Although I find it to be a very close question, I cannot conclude that the nondisclosure of Farr's informant status was prejudicial under Kyles v. Whitley (1995), and *Brady.*

To demonstrate prejudice, Banks must show that "the favorable evidence could reasonably be taken to put the whole case in such a different light as to undermine confidence in the verdict."

I do not believe that there is a reasonable probability that the jury would have altered its finding. The jury was presented with the facts of a horrible crime. Banks, after meeting the victim, Richard Whitehead, a 16-year-old boy who had the misfortune of owning a car that Banks wanted, decided "to kill the person for the hell of it" and take his car. Banks proceeded to shoot Whitehead three times, twice in the head and once in the upper back. Banks fired one of the shots only 18 to 24 inches away from Whitehead. The jury was thus presented with evidence showing that Banks, apparently on a whim, executed Whitehead simply to get his car.

The jury was also presented with evidence, in the form of Banks' own testimony, that he was willing to abet another individual in obtaining a gun, with the full knowledge that this gun would aid future armed robberies.

Accordingly, the jury was also presented with Banks' willingness to assist others in committing deadly crimes. . . . The jury also heard testimony that Banks had violently pistol-whipped and threatened to kill his brother-in-law one week before the murder.

In sum, the jury knew that Banks had murdered a 16-year-old on a whim, had violently attacked and threatened a relative shortly before the murder, and was willing to assist another individual in committing armed robberies by providing the "means and possible death weapon" for these robberies. Even if the jury were to discredit entirely Farr's testimony that Banks was planning more robberies, in all likelihood the jury still would have found "beyond a reasonable doubt" that there "[was] a probability that [Banks] would commit criminal acts of violence that would constitute a continuing threat to society." The randomness and wantonness of the murder would perhaps, standing alone, mandate such a finding. Accordingly, I cannot find that the nondisclosure of the evidence was prejudicial.

It took more than 40 years, but the Supreme Court has finally established through this series of cases the contours of the defendant's due process right to discovery. Under *Brady*, due process requires the prosecutor to disclose evidence favorable to an accused when such evidence is material to guilt or innocence. As established in *Bagley*, evidence is "material" if there is a reasonable probability that disclosure of the evidence would have changed the outcome of the proceeding. A "reasonable probability" is defined as a probability sufficient to undermine confidence in the outcome. Per *Kyle*, the focus should be on the collective impact of the withheld evidence. A defendant's due process right to discovery does not depend on whether the prosecutor acts in good faith or bad faith, or whether there is a defense request for the evidence. Both of these may be used to argue whether the evidence was material, but they are not by themselves separate threshold requirements for constitutional discovery.

Because the focus of the constitutional standard is on the "materiality" of the evidence not disclosed, there is no *Brady* violation if the prosecution fails to disclose speculative or irrelevant information, evidence that is cumulative, or information the defense already possesses or could obtain from other sources.[15]

---

15. *See, e.g.,* Turner v. United States, 137 S. Ct. 1885, 582 U.S. ___ (2017) (prosecution failed to disclose exculpatory evidence suggesting alternative perpetrator, but Court held no *Brady* violation because evidence was cumulative and did not meet materiality requirement under *Brady*).

But, as established in *Kyles*, a prosecutor's duty extends beyond disclosure of evidence already in the prosecutor's possession and includes the duty to learn of and disclose any favorable evidence possessed by government agents or police working on the case. It is also imperative for the government to disclose problems with eyewitness testimony. In Smith v. Cain, 565 U.S. 73 (2012), the Court reversed a murder conviction because the prosecutors failed to disclose notes undermining defendant's identification by the government's only eyewitness. The Court held that it was material that the witness had said the night of the crime that he "could not ID anyone because [he] couldn't see faces" and "would not know them if [he] saw them."

Late disclosure of *Brady* material, while not in the spirit of the Court's holding, will not necessarily result in a reversal unless the defendant can show that the delay denied him or her a fair trial. A defendant must show specifically how he or she was prejudiced by the late disclosure of the discovery. Additionally, there is no requirement that the prosecution disclose *Brady* material before a defendant enters a guilty plea. United States v. Ruiz, 536 U.S. 622 (2002).

Finally, the remedy for a *Brady* violation is the grant of a new trial at which the defendant will be able to use the previously undisclosed exculpatory evidence. Thus, even when a defendant has been improperly convicted because of a clear *Brady* violation, a defendant may still not be able to sue the individual prosecutor for violation of the defendant's due process rights. *See* Connick v. Thompson, 563 U.S. 51 (2011).

D.   DISCOVERY FOR GUILTY PLEAS

The focus of the *Brady* line of cases was on whether a defendant received enough information to have a fair trial or sentencing proceeding. However, these cases never addressed whether due process requires disclosure of exculpatory and impeachment materials if a defendant is willing to plead guilty and admit his guilt. That question was decided by the Court in United States v. Ruiz, 536 U.S. 622 (2002).

In *Ruiz*, immigration agents caught Angela Ruiz with 30 kilograms of marijuana. As part of the prosecution's "fast track" plea bargain program, she was offered a deal in which prosecutors would recommend a lesser sentence if she agreed to plead guilty. Under the details of the agreement, the government would provide Ruiz with information of factual innocence, but she had to waive the right to receive impeachment information. Ruiz refused to do so. The government withdrew its offer, but she pled guilty anyway. When the court refused to give her the same sentencing reduction she would have received under the plea bargain, Ruiz appealed.

Justice Breyer, writing for a unanimous Supreme Court, held that due process does not require that the government disclose impeachment evidence before a defendant's guilty plea. Disclosure of impeachment evidence is required to ensure a fair trial, but a guilty plea may be voluntary without it. "It is particularly difficult to characterize impeachment information as critical information of which the defendant must always be aware prior to pleading guilty given the random way in which such information may, or may not, help a particular defendant."

Moreover, requiring the prosecution to disclose impeachment evidence may render the prosecution less likely to engage in plea bargains, because disclosure would impose additional preparation burdens on the prosecution and put its witnesses and ongoing investigations at risk. "[A] constitutional obligation to provide impeachment information during plea bargaining, prior to entry of a guilty plea, could seriously interfere with the Government's interest in securing those guilty pleas that are factually justified, desired by defendants, and help to secure the efficient administration of justice. . . . These considerations, taken together, lead us to conclude that the Constitution does not require the Government to disclose material impeachment evidence prior to entering a plea agreement with a criminal defendant."

Although the Supreme Court held that due process does not require disclosure of material exculpatory evidence before a guilty plea, the prosecution's failure to disclose such evidence may affect whether the court finds that there was a "knowing and voluntary" guilty plea.[16] If a defendant is unaware of evidence that could support a defense, it is easier for the defendant to claim that he or she did not enter a valid guilty plea.

E. DUTY TO PRESERVE EVIDENCE

Brady and its progeny hold that the government has a duty to disclose exculpatory evidence. However, is a prosecutor obliged to preserve evidence that *may be* exculpatory? The Supreme Court addressed the extent of the prosecution's responsibility to preserve potentially exculpatory evidence in another line of cases.

First, in California v. Trombetta, 467 U.S. 479 (1984), the Supreme Court, in a unanimous decision written by Justice Marshall, held that due process did not require the police to preserve breath samples collected from drunk drivers because the preserved samples were unlikely to help the suspect's defense. In addition, the state had developed procedures to ensure that the alcohol tests that were used on the defendant were accurate.

Then, in Arizona v. Youngblood, the Court expanded on its ruling in *Trombetta*, setting forth the standard to be used when a defendant claims that the government's failure to preserve evidence has denied him the right to a fair trial.

---

16. Guilty pleas are discussed in more detail in Chapter 9.

ARIZONA v. YOUNGBLOOD

488 U.S. 51 (1988)

Chief Justice REHNQUIST delivered the opinion of the Court.

Respondent Larry Youngblood was convicted by a Pima County, Arizona, jury of child molestation, sexual assault, and kidnaping. The Arizona Court of Appeals reversed his conviction on the ground that the State had failed to preserve semen samples from the victim's body and clothing. We granted certiorari to consider the extent to which the Due Process Clause of the Fourteenth Amendment requires the State to preserve evidentiary material that might be useful to a criminal defendant.

On October 29, 1983, David L., a 10-year-old boy, attended a church service with his mother. After he left the service at about 9:30 P.M., the boy went to a carnival behind the church, where he was abducted by a middle-aged man of medium height and weight. The assailant drove the boy to a secluded area near a ravine and molested him. He then took the boy to an unidentified, sparsely furnished house where he sodomized the boy [five times]. He threatened to kill the boy if he told anyone about the attack. The entire ordeal lasted about 1½ hours.

After the boy made his way home, his mother took him to Kino Hospital. At the hospital, a physician treated the boy for rectal injuries. The physician also used a "sexual assault kit" to collect evidence of the attack. Here, the physician used the swab to collect samples from the boy's rectum and mouth. The police placed the kit in a secure refrigerator at the police station. At the hospital, the police also collected the boy's underwear and T-shirt. This clothing was not refrigerated or frozen.

Nine days after the attack, on November 7, 1983, the police asked the boy to pick out his assailant from a photographic lineup. The boy identified respondent as the assailant. Respondent was not located by the police until four weeks later; he was arrested on December 9, 1983.

On November 8, 1983, Edward Heller, a police criminologist, examined the sexual assault kit. After he determined that such contact had occurred, the criminologist did not perform any other tests, although he placed the assault kit back in the refrigerator. He testified that tests to identify blood group substances were not routinely conducted during the initial examination of an assault kit and in only about half of all cases in any event. He did not test the clothing at this time.

Respondent was indicted on charges of child molestation, sexual assault, and kidnaping. The State moved to compel respondent to provide blood and saliva samples for comparison with the material gathered through the use of the sexual assault kit, but the trial court denied the motion on the ground that the State had not obtained a sufficiently large semen sample to make a valid comparison.

In January 1985, the police criminologist examined the boy's clothing for the first time. He found one semen stain on the boy's underwear and another on the rear of his T-shirt. The criminologist tried to obtain blood group substances from both stains using the ABO technique, but was unsuccessful. He also performed a P-30 protein molecule test on the stains, which indicated that only a small quantity of semen was present on the clothing; it was inconclusive as to the assailant's identity. The Tucson Police Department had just begun using this test, which was then used in slightly more than half of the crime laboratories in the country.

Respondent's principal defense at trial was that the boy had erred in identifying him as the perpetrator of the crime. In this connection, both a criminologist for the State and an expert witness for respondent testified as to what might have been shown by tests performed on the samples shortly after they were gathered, or by later tests performed on the samples from the boy's clothing had the clothing been properly refrigerated. The court instructed the jury that if they found the State had destroyed or lost evidence, they might "infer that the true fact is against the State's interest."

The jury found respondent guilty as charged, but the Arizona Court of Appeals reversed the judgment of conviction. It stated that "when identity is an issue at trial and the police permit the destruction of evidence that could eliminate the defendant as the perpetrator, such loss is material to the defense and is a denial of due process." The Court of Appeals reached this conclusion even though it did "not imply any bad faith on the part of the State." We now reverse.

Decision of this case requires us to again consider "what might loosely be called the area of constitutionally guaranteed access to evidence." In Brady v. Maryland (1963), we held that "the suppression by the prosecution of evidence favorable to the accused upon request violates due process where the evidence is material either to guilt or to punishment, irrespective of the good faith or bad faith of the prosecution."

There is no question but that the State complied with *Brady* here. The State disclosed relevant police reports to respondent, which contained information about the existence of the swab and the clothing, and the boy's examination at the hospital. The State provided respondent's expert with the laboratory reports and notes prepared by the police criminologist, and respondent's expert had access to the swab and to the clothing.

If respondent is to prevail on federal constitutional grounds, then, it must be because of some constitutional duty over and above that imposed by cases such as *Brady*. Our most recent decision in this area of the law, California v. Trombetta (1984), arose out of a drunken driving prosecution in which the State had introduced test results indicating the concentration of alcohol in the blood of two motorists. The defendants sought to suppress the test results on the ground that the State had failed to preserve the breath samples used in the test. We rejected this argument for several reasons: first, "the officers here were acting in 'good faith and in accord with their normal practice'"; second, in the light of the procedures actually used the chances that preserved samples would have exculpated the defendants were slim;

and, third; even if the samples might have shown inaccuracy in the tests, the defendants had "alternative means of demonstrating their innocence."

Our decisions in related areas have stressed the importance for constitutional purposes of good or bad faith on the part of the Government when the claim is based on loss of evidence attributable to the Government.

The Due Process Clause of the Fourteenth Amendment, as interpreted in *Brady*, makes the good or bad faith of the State irrelevant when the State fails to disclose to the defendant material exculpatory evidence. But we think the Due Process Clause requires a different result when we deal with the failure of the State to preserve evidentiary material of which no more can be said than that it could have been subjected to tests, the results of which might have exonerated the defendant. Part of the reason for the difference in treatment is found in the observation made by the Court in *Trombetta*, that "[w]henever potentially exculpatory evidence is permanently lost, courts face the treacherous task of divining the import of materials whose contents are unknown and, very often, disputed." Part of it stems from our unwillingness to read the "fundamental fairness" requirement of the Due Process Clause, as imposing on the police an undifferentiated and absolute duty to retain and to preserve all material that might be of conceivable evidentiary significance in a particular prosecution. We think that requiring a defendant to show bad faith on the part of the police both limits the extent of the police's obligation to preserve evidence to reasonable bounds and confines it to that class of cases where the interests of justice most clearly require it, i.e., those cases in which the police themselves by their conduct indicate that the evidence could form a basis for exonerating the defendant. We therefore hold that unless a criminal defendant can show bad faith on the part of the police, failure to preserve potentially useful evidence does not constitute a denial of due process of law.

In this case, the police collected the rectal swab and clothing on the night of the crime; respondent was not taken into custody until six weeks later. The failure of the police to refrigerate the clothing and to perform tests on the semen samples can at worst be described as negligent. None of this information was concealed from respondent at trial, and the evidence — such as it was — was made available to respondent's expert who declined to perform any tests on the samples. [T]here was no suggestion of bad faith on the part of the police. It follows, therefore, from what we have said, that there was no violation of the Due Process Clause.

Justice BLACKMUN, with whom Justice BRENNAN and Justice MARSHALL join, dissenting.

The Constitution requires that criminal defendants be provided with a fair trial, not merely a "good faith" try at a fair trial. Respondent here, by what may have been nothing more than police ineptitude, was denied the opportunity to present a full defense. That ineptitude, however, deprived respondent of his guaranteed right to due process of law.

I recognize the difficulties presented by such a situation. The societal interest in seeing criminals punished rightly requires that indictments be dismissed only when the unavailability of the evidence prevents the defendant from receiving a fair trial. [I]n a situation like the present one [which is unlike *Trombetta* where there was alternative evidence available to the defense], due process requires something more. Rather than allow a State's ineptitude to saddle a defendant with an impossible burden, a court should focus on the type of evidence, the possibility it might prove exculpatory, and the existence of other evidence going to the same point of contention in determining whether the failure to preserve the evidence in question violated due process. To put it succinctly, where no comparable evidence is likely to be available to the defendant, police must preserve physical evidence of a type that they reasonably should know has the potential, if tested, to reveal immutable characteristics of the criminal, and hence to exculpate a defendant charged with the crime.

Youngblood was decided before post-conviction DNA testing became prevalent. The first DNA exoneration took place in 1989, the year after *Youngblood* was decided. Since then, DNA has exonerated defendants in 31 states, including 15 people serving time on death row. Since 2000, there have been at least 147 exonerations from DNA testing. Given this experience with DNA testing, one might question whether the Court was correct to assume in *Youngblood* that just because evidence is only "potentially" exculpatory, failure to preserve it will not deprive the defendant of a fair trial unless officers or prosecutors act out of bad faith. DNA testing has shown that evidence that is only potentially exculpatory today could be the key to overturning a wrongful conviction in the future. As a result, many states have now passed laws requiring law enforcement to preserve biological materials for future testing. *See* Cynthia E. Jones, *Evidence Destroyed, Innocence Lost: The Preservation of Biological Evidence Under Innocence Protection Statutes*, 42 Am. Crim. L. Rev. 129 (2005).[17] While most states have enacted laws authorizing post-conviction DNA testing, the Supreme Court declined to hold that due process requires such testing. *See* District Attorney's Office for the Third Judicial Dist. v. Osborne, 557 U.S. 52 (2009).

F. FINAL NOTE

Both statutes and the Supreme Court's decisions have created duties for the prosecution to provide discovery to the defense, and the defense has a responsibility to provide limited discovery to the prosecution. Nevertheless,

---

17. *See also* D. Michael Risinger, *Innocents Convicted: An Empirically Justified Factual Wrongful Conviction Rate*, 97 J. Crim. L. & Criminology 61 (2007).

most jurisdictions still have not adopted an "open-file" approach. The prevailing approach is still rooted in the adversarial system but with a recognition that a defendant has a due process right to a fair trial. The Court has not required the prosecution to disclose evidence that it will use to impeach defense witnesses (unless required under alibi discovery rules). Further, neither side is required to disclose matters covered by other privileges, such as the attorney-client privilege and the defendant's Fifth Amendment privilege against self-incrimination. Finally, neither side has the right to know the other's trial strategy.

CHAPTER
9

PLEA BARGAINING
AND GUILTY PLEAS

A. INTRODUCTION

In a criminal case, there are three types of pleas: not guilty, guilty, or *nolo contendere.* A plea of not guilty does not mean "I didn't do it." Rather, it means "Prosecutor, prove your case." A guilty plea, on the other hand, is an admission by the defendant that he committed the crime and waives his right to trial. A *nolo contendere* is a no-contest plea by the defendant: The defendant does not admit guilt to the charged offense but may be sentenced the same as if he pled guilty. Because a *nolo contendere* plea is not an admission, it does not result in an automatic judgment against the defendant in any companion civil case.

By most accounts, more than 90 percent of all criminal cases never go to trial. In federal court, 97 percent of all of the defendants who are convicted are convicted by their own no-contest or guilty pleas.[1] Nevertheless, plea bargaining remains a controversial practice. Opponents of the practice argue that plea bargaining compromises the criminal justice system by allowing defendants to escape full punishment for their crimes. Other opponents worry that plea bargaining will do exactly the opposite—pressure innocent defendants to plead guilty. Supporters of plea bargaining argue that the practice enables the criminal justice system to process a high volume of cases, while allowing disposition of cases to be tailored to the specific situations of individual defendants.

Section B of this chapter examines the role of plea bargaining in the American criminal justice system and the arguments for and against its use. It also reviews the Supreme Court's decisions upholding the constitutionality of plea bargaining. Section C analyzes the constitutional standards for a valid guilty plea. Section D provides an overview of the practical steps of entering a guilty plea, as set forth in Federal Rule of Criminal Procedure 11.

---

1. *See* Missouri v. Frye, 132 S. Ct. 1407, citing Department of Justice, Bureau of Justice Statistics, *Sourcebook of Criminal Justice Statistics Online*, Table 5.22.2009, http://www.albany.edu/sourcebook/pdf/t5222009.pdf.

Section E sets forth the consequences of breaching a plea agreement. Finally, section F discusses when and how a defendant can seek to withdraw a guilty plea.

B. PLEA BARGAINING

Plea bargaining is the process through which the defendant agrees to admit guilt in exchange for some concession from the government. There are two main types of plea bargaining: (1) bargaining that reduces the number or severity of the charges the defendant faces and (2) bargaining that reduces the defendant's sentence or the government's recommendation for a sentence.

1. History of Plea Bargaining

The practice of plea bargaining stems back to the earliest days of the common law. Generally, courts did not support the practice. Rather, judges would counsel defendants to plead not guilty and proceed to trial. At the time, there were fewer institutional pressures for a defendant to plead guilty because trials were relatively short and did not consume much of the court's time.[2] When defendants began to plead guilty, judges openly feared that innocent defendants would be forced into pleas, including guilty pleas for capital offenses.

The legal landscape for plea bargaining changed significantly in the second half of the nineteenth century. Magistrates, prosecutors, and even police officers became "fixers." For a price, they would arrange for defendants to plead guilty and receive lesser punishments. Pressure was placed on innocent defendants to plead guilty. As a result, states began to impose specific requirements for guilty pleas in order to safeguard "the protection of prisoners and of the public" in response "to serious abuses caused by [prosecutors] procuring prisoners to plead guilty when a fair trial might show they were not guilty."[3]

By the 1920s, plea bargaining had become an integral part of the judicial system. The number of prosecutions grew and the guilty plea rate in some jurisdictions jumped from 25 percent in 1839 to 90 percent of the convictions in 1920. A commission study at the time noted that the major inducement for a defendant to plead guilty was not necessarily his actual guilt but the kind of bargain the defendant could make with the state.

For the last 100 years, plea bargaining has continued to be one of the essential, yet most controversial, aspects of the American criminal justice

---

2. For an excellent discussion of the history of plea bargaining, *see* Albert W. Alschuler, *Plea Bargaining and Its History*, 13 Law & Soc'y Rev. 211 (1979).

3. *See* Douglas D. Guidorizzi, *Should We Really "Ban" Plea Bargaining?: The Core Concerns of Plea Bargaining Critics*, 47 Emory L.J. 753, 759 (1998).

system. Even though some jurisdictions have tried to ban or limit the practice,[4] the reality of growing caseloads has pretty much guaranteed that the practice will not disappear in the near future.

2.   The Pros and Cons of Plea Bargaining

a.   Support for Plea Bargaining

Plea bargaining supporters argue that plea bargaining offers crucial advantages to both the prosecution and the defense. For the prosecution, plea bargaining ensures a conviction, reduces the stress on government resources, and relieves victims of the burden of testifying in court. It allows prosecutors to concentrate their resources and efforts on more serious and high profile cases. It also provides benefits to the police, especially if there were problems in the investigation. By allowing the defendant to plead guilty pursuant to a plea bargain, law enforcement can avoid airing their mistakes in public.

Supporters argue that plea bargaining also benefits the defense. By plea bargaining, defendants and their lawyers expend fewer resources, reduce the defendant's punishment exposure, and provide greater certainty to the outcome of their cases. Defendants need not go through the anxious process of a trial. By pleading guilty, a defendant can assert more control over his or her fate. A plea bargain can help individualize the criminal justice system's response to the defendant's case.

Judges also tend to support plea bargaining. Quick disposition of cases eases court congestion and reduces the cost of providing jury trials. It also shifts the public's attention from the judge to the decisions and practices of prosecutors.

Finally, plea bargaining can benefit the victims in a case. If there is no trial, victims are spared the agony, inconvenience, and embarrassment of trial proceedings. Plea bargaining provides victims with some assurance that the defendant will be held responsible for his crime.

b.   Criticisms of Plea Bargaining

Despite these advantages, there are a number of strong arguments against plea bargaining. First, plea bargaining can pressure innocent persons to plead guilty to avoid the consequences of conviction on more serious charges. This has been the concern with plea bargaining since its earliest

---

4. *See, e.g.*, Cal. Penal Code §1192.7 (creating plea bargain limitations for serious felonies); DOJ Policy Concerning Charging Criminal Offenses, Disposition of Charges, and Sentencing (Attorney General John Ashcroft, Sept. 22, 2003) (general order to charge and pursue most serious offenses, unless limited exceptions exist).

use. Guilty pleas are one of the principal causes for wrongful convictions. One critic has written:

> Plea bargains have corrupted the justice system by creating fictional crimes in place of real ones. The practice of having people admit to what did not happen in order to avoid charges for what did happen creates a legal culture that elevates fiction over truth. By making the facts of the case malleable, plea bargains enable prosecutors to supplement weak evidence with psychological pressure. Legal scholar John Langbein compares "the modern American plea bargaining system" with "the ancient system of judicial torture." Many innocent people cop a plea just to end their ordeal. Confession and self-incrimination have replaced the jury trial. Just as Bentham wanted, torture has been resurrected as a principal method of conviction. As this legal culture now operates, it permits prosecutors to bring charges in the absence of crimes.
>
> Plea bargaining is a major cause of wrongful conviction. First, plea bargains undermine police investigative work. Because few cases go to trial, police have learned that their evidence is seldom tested in the courtroom. Carelessness creeps in. Sloppy investigations are less likely to lead to apprehension of the guilty party. Second, plea bargaining greatly increases the number of cases that can be prosecuted. Prosecutors have found that they can coerce a plea and elevate their conviction rate by raising the number and seriousness of the charges that they throw at a defendant. Counsel advises defendants that conviction at trial on even one charge can carry more severe punishment than a plea to a lesser charge. The sentencing differential alone is enough to make plea bargaining coercive.[5]

Although courts discuss plea bargains as a "contract" or "agreement" between the prosecutor and the defendant, the reality is that "the prosecutor substantially dictates the terms of plea agreements in most cases." There is often relatively little "give-and-take," as there is in settlement discussions for civil cases, because of the disparity in bargaining power between the prosecutor and defendant.[6] Prosecutors have an overwhelming bargaining advantage and can bring enormous institutional pressures on the defendant to agree to the plea bargain. Defense lawyers regularly acquiesce to the prosecutor's wishes. For example, as Professor Alschuler discussed in his classic work, *The Defense Attorney's Role in Plea Bargaining*, 84 Yale L.J. 1179 (1975), defense lawyers will plead for months with their clients to plead guilty, and if that doesn't work, they will call in family members to talk about how hard it would be to collect the defendant's body after he had been electrocuted. *See* United States ex rel. Brown v. LaValle, 424 F.2d 457 (2d Cir.), *cert. denied*, 401 U.S. 942 (1972).

Second, plea bargaining is also criticized because it frequently takes place outside the public view. Not only does it allow police to cover up mistakes and abuses, but it shields from public scrutiny the process that prosecutors use to evaluate their cases. "The sub rosa nature of plea bargaining and the lack of citizen participation reduce public confidence that justice has been done." *Gifford, supra* at 71.

---

5. Paul Craig Roberts, *The Causes of Wrongful Conviction*, 4 The Indep. Rev. No. 4 (Spring 2003).

6. *See generally* Donald G. Gifford, *Meaningful Reform of Plea Bargaining: The Control of Prosecutorial Discretion*, 1983 U. Ill. L. Rev. 37 (1983).

Third, some of the strongest arguments made against plea bargaining stem from the belief that the practice subverts the values of the criminal justice system; in essence, plea bargaining allows a defendant to escape full accountability for his actions by receiving a "discount on justice." As one critic of plea bargaining observed, "the plea bargain convinces criminals that the majesty of the law is a fraud, that the law is like a Turkish bazaar."[7] Because a defendant is not held fully responsible for his or her acts, plea bargaining reduces the deterrent effect of punishment. The not-so-subtle message of the plea deal is that the defendant can "get away" with something because it is too much trouble for the government to pursue him.

Fourth, plea bargaining can be particularly frustrating for victims. They are ordinarily not direct participants in the process and must stand by as defendants plead guilty to crimes that do not reflect the seriousness of the offense or receive sentences less severe than what the victims believe they deserved. While there are growing efforts to notify victims before plea deals are reached, the ultimate power to decide whether to accept a plea agreement rests with the prosecutor, not the victim.

Finally, plea bargaining is criticized because of the discriminatory impact it can have on defendants. Defendants who have greater resources to challenge the prosecution secure more favorable resolutions than those who cannot mount such a challenge. "[D]efendants perceive plea bargaining as a 'game' where the most important factors are money and luck." *Gifford, supra* at 73. Because judges typically are not involved in the plea negotiations, they have little way of preventing prosecutorial prejudices from influencing the plea bargaining process.[8]

c. Evaluating a Plea Bargain

Plea bargaining must be evaluated through the eyes of those it affects. Given the arguments for and against it, it is often helpful to ask how various constituents of the criminal justice system would react to a proposed plea bargain in any given case. What would the victim's reaction be? Why would the police and prosecutor support it? What concerns would the defense lawyer have? What would be the public's reaction? Should the court accept the plea bargain?

Jurisdictions differ on how much involvement the judge may have in the plea bargaining process. Federal Rule of Criminal Procedure 11(c)(1) bars the court from participating in plea discussions. Some states, however, authorize the judge to take part in the negotiations. *See* N.C. Gen. Stat. 15-1021(a). Most states neither bar nor encourage court involvement in plea negotiations.

---

7. John Kaplan, *American Merchandising and the Guilty Plea: Replacing the Bazaar with the Department Store*, 5 Am. J. Crim. L. 215, 218 (1977).

8. *See* Angela J. Davis, Arbitrary Justice: The Power of the American Prosecutor 43-59, 140-141 (Oxford Univ. Press 2007).

3. Bans on Plea Bargaining

Over time, there have been efforts to limit or eliminate plea bargaining. "District attorneys and attorneys general have instituted plea cut-off dates, bans on plea bargaining after a felony indictment, total bans on plea bargaining, as well as replacing plea bargaining with the jury waiver or the 'slow plea.'" Guidorizzi, *supra* at 772-773. In 1975, Alaska experimented with an attempt to abolish plea bargaining. The changed policy prohibited both charge- and sentence-related bargaining. Contrary to predictions, the ban did not cause significant backlogs in criminal cases or an increased dismissal rate of cases. Nonetheless, Alaska relaxed its prohibition in the 1980s when it adopted presumptive sentencing guidelines that gave prosecutors increased flexibility in deciding which charges to pursue.

Despite efforts to restrict plea bargaining in both state and federal prosecutions, the practice persists today.[9] Rather than eliminate plea bargaining, jurisdictions tend to try to regulate its use. Ultimately, it is a habit that is hard to break, especially when the parties perceive benefits in engaging in the practice.

4. The Legality of Plea Bargaining

The constitutionality of plea bargaining was not addressed by the Supreme Court until the practice was in full swing. In United States v. Jackson, 390 U.S. 570 (1968), the Court invalidated a statute that put undue pressure on a defendant to plead guilty because it made defendants eligible for the death penalty only if they were convicted in a jury trial. The Court struck down the statute because it chilled a defendant's assertion of his right to pursue a jury trial.

Yet soon thereafter, the Court refused to go the next step and invalidate all plea bargaining simply because it put pressure on a defendant to forgo his right to a jury trial.

BRADY v. UNITED STATES

397 U.S. 742 (1970)

Justice WHITE delivered the opinion of the Court.

In 1959, petitioner was charged with kidnaping in violation of 18 U.S.C. §1201(a). Since the indictment charged that the victim of the kidnaping was not liberated unharmed, petitioner faced a maximum penalty of death if the verdict of the jury should so recommend. Petitioner, represented by competent counsel throughout, first elected to plead not guilty. Apparently because the trial judge was unwilling to try the case without a jury, petitioner

---

9. *See generally* George Fisher, *Plea Bargaining's Triumph*, 109 Yale L.J. 857 (2000).

made no serious attempt to reduce the possibility of a death penalty by waiving a jury trial. Upon learning that his codefendant, who had confessed to the authorities, would plead guilty and be available to testify against him, petitioner changed his plea to guilty. His plea was accepted after the trial judge twice questioned him as to the voluntariness of his plea. Petitioner was sentenced to 50 years' imprisonment, later reduced to 30.

In 1967, petitioner sought relief under 28 U.S.C. §2255, claiming that his plea of guilty was not voluntarily given because §1201(a) operated to coerce his plea, because his counsel exerted impermissible pressure upon him, and because his plea was induced by representations with respect to reduction of sentence and clemency. It was also alleged that the trial judge had not fully complied with Rule 11 of the Federal Rules of Criminal Procedure.[10]

After a hearing, the District Court for the District of New Mexico denied relief. According to the District Court's findings, petitioner's counsel did not put impermissible pressure on petitioner to plead guilty. The court concluded that "the plea was voluntarily and knowingly made."

The Court of Appeals for the Tenth Circuit affirmed, [and the Supreme Court granted review].

[In United States v. Jackson (1968), defendants were indicted under §1201(a), the same statute charged against Brady.] The District Court dismissed the §1201(a) count of the indictment, holding the statute unconstitutional because it permitted imposition of the death sentence only upon a jury's recommendation and thereby made the risk of death the price of a jury trial. This Court held the statute valid, except for the death penalty provision. [The statute makes the death penalty] applicable only to those defendants who assert the right to contest their guilt before a jury. The inevitable effect of the provision was said to be to discourage assertion of the Fifth Amendment right not to plead guilty and to deter exercise of the Sixth Amendment right to demand a jury trial. Because the legitimate goal of limiting the death penalty to cases in which a jury recommends it could be achieved without penalizing those defendants who plead not guilty and elect a jury trial, the death penalty provision "needlessly penalize[d] the assertion of a constitutional right," and was therefore unconstitutional.

Since the "inevitable effect" of the death penalty provision of §1201(a) was said by the Court to be the needless encouragement of pleas of guilty and waivers of jury trial, Brady contends that *Jackson* requires the invalidation of every plea of guilty entered under that section, at least when the fear of death is shown to have been a factor in the plea. Petitioner, however, has read far too much into the *Jackson* opinion.

---

10. When petitioner pleaded guilty, Rule 11 read as follows: "A defendant may plead not guilty, guilty or, with the consent of the court, nolo contendere. The court may refuse to accept a plea of guilty, and shall not accept the plea without first determining that the plea is made voluntarily with understanding of the nature of the charge. If a defendant refuses to plead or if the court refuses to accept a plea of guilty or if a defendant corporation fails to appear, the court shall enter a plea of not guilty." [Footnote by the Court.]

Jackson ruled neither that all pleas of guilty encouraged by the fear of a possible death sentence are involuntary pleas nor that such encouraged pleas are invalid whether involuntary or not. *Jackson* prohibits the imposition of the death penalty under §1201(a), but that decision neither fashioned a new standard for judging the validity of guilty pleas nor mandated a new application of the test theretofore fashioned by courts and since reiterated that guilty pleas are valid if both "voluntary" and "intelligent." Boykin v. Alabama (1969).

That a guilty plea is a grave and solemn act to be accepted only with care and discernment has long been recognized. Central to the plea and the foundation for entering judgment against the defendant is the defendant's admission in open court that he committed the acts charged in the indictment. He thus stands as a witness against himself and he is shielded by the Fifth Amendment from being compelled to do so — hence the minimum requirement that his plea be the voluntary expression of his own choice. But the plea is more than an admission of past conduct; it is the defendant's consent that judgment of conviction may be entered without a trial — a waiver of his right to trial before a jury or a judge. Waivers of constitutional rights not only must be voluntary but must be knowing, intelligent acts done with sufficient awareness of the relevant circumstances and likely consequences. On neither score was Brady's plea of guilty invalid.

The voluntariness of Brady's plea can be determined only by considering all of the relevant circumstances surrounding it. One of these circumstances was the possibility of a heavier sentence following a guilty verdict after a trial. It may be that Brady, faced with a strong case against him and recognizing that his chances for acquittal were slight, preferred to plead guilty and thus limit the penalty to life imprisonment rather than to elect a jury trial which could result in a death penalty. But even if we assume that Brady would not have pleaded guilty except for the death penalty provision of §1201(a), [this] does not necessarily prove that the plea was coerced and invalid as an involuntary act.

The State to some degree encourages pleas of guilty at every important step in the criminal process. For some people, their breach of a State's law is alone sufficient reason for surrendering themselves and accepting punishment. For others, apprehension and charge, both threatening acts by the Government, jar them into admitting their guilt. In still other cases, the post-indictment accumulation of evidence may convince the defendant and his counsel that a trial is not worth the agony and expense to the defendant and his family. All these pleas of guilty are valid in spite of the State's responsibility for some of the factors motivating the pleas; the pleas are no more improperly compelled than is the decision by a defendant at the close of the State's evidence at trial that he must take the stand or face certain conviction.

Of course, the agents of the State may not produce a plea by actual or threatened physical harm or by mental coercion overbearing the will of the defendant. But nothing of the sort is claimed in this case; nor is there evidence that Brady was so gripped by fear of the death penalty or hope of leniency that he did not or could not, with the help of counsel, rationally weigh the advantages of going to trial against the advantages of pleading guilty. Brady's claim is of a different sort: that it violates the Fifth Amendment to influence or encourage a guilty plea by opportunity or promise of leniency and that a guilty plea is coerced and invalid if influenced by the fear of a possibly higher penalty for the crime charged if a conviction is obtained after the State is put to its proof.

Insofar as the voluntariness of his plea is concerned, there is little to differentiate Brady from (1) the defendant, in a jurisdiction where the judge and jury have the same range of sentencing power, who pleads guilty because his lawyer advises him that the judge will very probably be more lenient than the jury; (2) the defendant, in a jurisdiction where the judge alone has sentencing power, who is advised by counsel that the judge is normally more lenient with defendants who plead guilty than with those who go to trial; (3) the defendant who is permitted by prosecutor and judge to plead guilty to a lesser offense included in the offense charged; and (4) the defendant who pleads guilty to certain counts with the understanding that other charges will be dropped. In each of these situations, as in Brady's case, the defendant might never plead guilty absent the possibility or certainty that the plea will result in a lesser penalty than the sentence that could be imposed after a trial and a verdict of guilty. We decline to hold, however, that a guilty plea is compelled and invalid under the Fifth Amendment whenever motivated by the defendant's desire to accept the certainty or probability of a lesser penalty rather than face a wider range of possibilities extending from acquittal to conviction and a higher penalty authorized by law for the crime charged.

The issue we deal with is inherent in the criminal law and its administration because guilty pleas are not constitutionally forbidden, because the criminal law characteristically extends to judge or jury a range of choice in setting the sentence in individual cases, and because both the State and the defendant often find it advantageous to preclude the possibility of the maximum penalty authorized by law. For a defendant who sees slight possibility of acquittal, the advantages of pleading guilty and limiting the probable penalty are obvious—his exposure is reduced, the correctional processes can begin immediately, and the practical burdens of a trial are eliminated. For the State there are also advantages—the more promptly imposed punishment after an admission of guilt may more effectively attain the objectives of punishment; and with the avoidance of trial, scarce judicial and prosecutorial resources are conserved for those cases in which there is a substantial issue of the defendant's guilt or in which there is substantial doubt that the State can sustain its burden of proof. It is this mutuality of advantage that perhaps explains the fact that at present well over three-fourths of the criminal convictions in this country rest on pleas of guilty, a great many of them no doubt motivated at least in part by the hope or assurance of a lesser penalty than might be imposed if there were a guilty verdict after a trial to judge or jury.[11]

Of course, that the prevalence of guilty pleas is explainable does not necessarily validate those pleas or the system which produces them. But we cannot hold that it is unconstitutional for the State to extend a benefit to a defendant who in turn extends a substantial benefit to the State and who demonstrates by his plea that he is ready and willing to admit his crime and to enter the correctional system in a frame of mind that affords hope for success in rehabilitation over a shorter period of time than might otherwise be necessary.

A contrary holding would require the States and Federal Government to forbid guilty pleas altogether, to provide a single invariable penalty for each crime defined by the statutes, or to place the sentencing function in a separate authority having no knowledge of the manner in which the conviction in each case was obtained. In any event, it would be necessary to forbid prosecutors and judges to accept guilty pleas to selected counts, to lesser included offenses, or to reduced charges. The Fifth Amendment does not reach so far.

Brady first pleaded not guilty; prior to changing his plea to guilty he was subjected to no threats or promises in face-to-face encounters with the authorities. He had competent counsel and full opportunity to assess the advantages and disadvantages of a trial as compared with those attending a plea of guilty; there was no hazard of an impulsive and improvident response to a seeming but unreal advantage. His plea of guilty was entered in open court and before a judge obviously sensitive to the requirements of the law with respect to guilty pleas. Brady's plea . . . was voluntary.

The standard as to the voluntariness of guilty pleas must be essentially that defined by Judge Tuttle of the Court of Appeals for the Fifth Circuit:

> [A] plea of guilty entered by one fully aware of the direct consequences, including the actual value of any commitments made to him by the court, prosecutor, or his own counsel, must stand unless induced by threats (or promises to discontinue improper harassment), misrepresentation (including unfulfilled or unfulfillable promises), or perhaps by promises that are by their nature improper as having no proper relationship to the prosecutor's business (e.g. bribes).

Under this standard, a plea of guilty is not invalid merely because entered to avoid the possibility of a death penalty.

The record before us also supports the conclusion that Brady's plea was intelligently made. He was advised by competent counsel, he was made aware of the nature of the charge against him, and there was nothing to indicate that he was incompetent or otherwise not in control of his mental faculties; once his confederate had pleaded guilty and became available to testify, he chose to plead guilty, perhaps to ensure that he would face no more than life

---

11. It has been estimated that about 90 percent, and perhaps 95 percent, of all criminal convictions are by pleas of guilty; between 70 percent and 85 percent of all felony convictions are estimated to be by guilty plea. D. Newman, Conviction, The Determination of Guilt or Innocence Without Trial 3 and n. 1 (1966). [Footnote by the Court.]

imprisonment or a term of years. Brady was aware of precisely what he was doing when he admitted that he had kidnaped the victim and had not released her unharmed.

It is true that Brady's counsel advised him that §1201(a) empowered the jury to impose the death penalty and that nine years later in United States v. Jackson, the Court held that the jury had no such power as long as the judge could impose only a lesser penalty if trial was to the court or there was a plea of guilty. But these facts do not require us to set aside Brady's conviction.

Often the decision to plead guilty is heavily influenced by the defendant's appraisal of the prosecution's case against him and by the apparent likelihood of securing leniency should a guilty plea be offered and accepted. [J]udgments may be made that in the light of later events seem improvident, although they were perfectly sensible at the time. The rule that a plea must be intelligently made to be valid does not require that a plea be vulnerable to later attack if the defendant did not correctly assess every relevant factor entering into his decision. A defendant is not entitled to withdraw his plea merely because he discovers long after the plea has been accepted that his calculus misapprehended the quality of the State's case or the likely penalties attached to alternative courses of action. More particularly, absent misrepresentation or other impermissible conduct by state agents, a voluntary plea of guilty intelligently made in the light of the then applicable law does not become vulnerable because later judicial decisions indicate that the plea rested on a faulty premise.

The fact that Brady did not anticipate United States v. Jackson, does not impugn the truth or reliability of his plea. We find no requirement in the Constitution that a defendant must be permitted to disown his solemn admissions in open court that he committed the act with which he is charged simply because it later develops that the State would have had a weaker case than the defendant had thought or that the maximum penalty then assumed applicable has been held inapplicable in subsequent judicial decisions.

This is not to say that guilty plea convictions hold no hazards for the innocent or that the methods of taking guilty pleas presently employed in this country are necessarily valid in all respects. This mode of conviction is no more foolproof than full trials to the court or to the jury. Accordingly, we take great precautions against unsound results, and we should continue to do so, whether conviction is by plea or by trial. In the case before us, nothing in the record impeaches Brady's plea or suggests that his admissions in open court were anything but the truth.

Although Brady's plea of guilty may well have been motivated in part by a desire to avoid a possible death penalty, we are convinced that his plea was voluntarily and intelligently made and we have no reason to doubt that his solemn admission of guilt was truthful.

Affirmed.

After *Jackson* and *Brady*, what kind of pressure can be asserted on defendants to encourage them to accept a plea deal? The Supreme Court addressed this issue in Bordenkircher v. Hayes, 434 U.S. 357 (1978).

In *Bordenkircher*, a grand jury indicted Paul Lewis Hayes on a charge of uttering a forged instrument in the amount of $88.30, an offense then punishable by a term of two to ten years in prison. After arraignment, Hayes, his retained counsel, and the Commonwealth's Attorney met to discuss a possible plea agreement. During these conferences the prosecutor offered to recommend a sentence of five years in prison if Hayes would plead guilty to the indictment. He also said that if Hayes did not plead guilty and "save the court the inconvenience and necessity of a trial," he would return to the grand jury to seek an indictment under the Kentucky Habitual Criminal Act, which would subject Hayes to a mandatory sentence of life imprisonment by reason of his two prior felony convictions. Hayes chose not to plead guilty, and the prosecutor did obtain an indictment charging him under the Habitual Criminal Act. Hayes complained that the prosecution's plea negotiations violated his right to due process.

The Supreme Court, in a 5-4 decision, held that prosecutors have the option of either charging the defendant at the outset with the most serious crimes and then reducing those charges as part of a plea bargain or charging the defendant with lesser charges and then threatening more serious charges if the defendant refuses its plea offer. In upholding the defendant's guilty plea, Justice Stewart, writing for the majority, stated:

> To punish a person because he has done what the law plainly allows him to do is a due process violation of the most basic sort, *see* North Carolina v. Pearce (1969), and for an agent of the State to pursue a course of action whose objective is to penalize a person's reliance on his legal rights is "patently unconstitutional." But in the "give-and-take" of plea bargaining, there is no such element of punishment or retaliation so long as the accused is free to accept or reject the prosecution's offer.
>
> Plea bargaining flows from "the mutuality of advantage" to defendants and prosecutors, each with his own reasons for wanting to avoid trial. Indeed, acceptance of the basic legitimacy of plea bargaining necessarily implies rejection of any notion that a guilty plea is involuntary in a constitutional sense simply because it is the end result of the bargaining process. By hypothesis, the plea may have been induced by promises of a recommendation of a lenient sentence or a reduction of charges, and thus by fear of the possibility of a greater penalty upon conviction after a trial.
>
> While confronting a defendant with the risk of more severe punishment clearly may have a "discouraging effect on the defendant's assertion of his trial rights, the imposition of these difficult choices [is] an inevitable" — and permissible — "attribute of any legitimate system which tolerates and encourages the negotiation of pleas." It follows that, by tolerating and encouraging the negotiation of pleas, this Court has necessarily accepted as constitutionally legitimate the simple reality that the prosecutor's interest at the bargaining table is to persuade the defendant to forgo his right to plead not guilty.
>
> It is not disputed here that Hayes was properly chargeable under the recidivist statute, since he had in fact been convicted of two previous felonies. In our system,

so long as the prosecutor has probable cause to believe that the accused committed an offense defined by statute, the decision whether or not to prosecute, and what charge to file or bring before a grand jury, generally rests entirely in his discretion. "[T]he conscious exercise of some selectivity in enforcement is not in itself a federal constitutional violation" so long as "the selection was [not] deliberately based upon an unjustifiable standard such as race, religion, or other arbitrary classification." A rigid constitutional rule that would prohibit a prosecutor from acting forthrightly in his dealings with the defense could only invite unhealthy subterfuge that would drive the practice of plea bargaining back into the shadows from which it has so recently emerged.

But Justice Blackmun, joined by Justices Brennan and Marshall, dissented. They argued:

> Even if overcharging is to be sanctioned, there are strong reasons of fairness why the charge should be presented at the beginning of the charging process, rather than as a filliped thread at the end. First, it means that a prosecutor is required to reach a charging decision without any knowledge of the particular defendant's willingness to plead guilty; hence the defendant who truly believes himself to be innocent, and wishes for that reason to go to trial, is not likely to be subject to quite such a devastating gamble since the prosecutor has fixed the incentives for the average case.
>
> Second, it is healthful to keep charging practices visible to the general public, so that political bodies can judge whether the policy being followed is a fair one. Visibility is enhanced if the prosecutor is required to lay his cards on the table with an indictment of public record at the beginning of the bargaining process, rather than making use of unrecorded verbal warnings of more serious indictments yet to come.
>
> Finally, I would question whether it is fair to pressure defendants to plead guilty by threat of reindictment on an enhanced charge for the same conduct when the defendant has no way of knowing whether the prosecutor would indeed be entitled to bring him to trial on the enhanced charge.

1. requires to make decision w/o D willingness

In a separate dissent, Justice Powell acknowledged the constitutionality of plea bargaining in general, but argued that the situation in this case violated the defendant's due process rights:

> No explanation appears in the record for the prosecutor's decision to escalate the charge against respondent other than respondent's refusal to plead guilty. It seems to me that the question to be asked under the circumstances is whether the prosecutor reasonably might have charged respondent under the Habitual Criminal Act in the first place. The deference that courts properly accord the exercise of a prosecutor's discretion perhaps would foreclose judicial criticism if the prosecutor originally had sought an indictment under that Act, as unreasonable as it would have seemed. But here the prosecutor evidently made a reasonable, responsible judgment not to subject an individual to a mandatory life sentence when his only new offense had societal implications as limited as those accompanying the uttering of a single $88 forged check. I think it may be inferred that the prosecutor himself deemed it unreasonable and not in the public interest to put this defendant in jeopardy of a sentence of life imprisonment.
>
> There may be situations in which a prosecutor would be fully justified in seeking a fresh indictment for a more serious offense. Here, any inquiry into the

prosecutor's purpose is made unnecessary by his candid acknowledgment that he threatened to procure and in fact procured the habitual criminal indictment because of respondent's insistence on exercising his constitutional rights.

The plea-bargaining process, as recognized by this Court, is essential to the functioning of the criminal-justice system. It normally affords genuine benefits to defendants as well as to society. And if the system is to work effectively, prosecutors must be accorded the widest discretion, within constitutional limits, in conducting bargaining. Only in the most exceptional case should a court conclude that the scales of the bargaining are so unevenly balanced as to arouse suspicion. In this case, the prosecutor's actions denied respondent due process because their admitted purpose was to discourage and then to penalize with unique severity his exercise of constitutional rights. Implementation of a strategy calculated solely to deter the exercise of constitutional rights is not a constitutionally permissible exercise of discretion.

Given the Court's decisions, prosecutors today have considerable leverage in the plea bargaining process. They may use the threat of mandatory minimum sentences, including mandatory life sentences under "three strikes" laws, to encourage defendants to plead guilty. *See* Chris Kemmitt, *Function over Form: Reviving the Criminal Jury's Historical Role as a Sentencing Body*, 40 U. Mich. J.L. Reform 93, 138 (Fall 2006) ("Prosecutors can now afford to threaten defendants with more oppressive punishments than under earlier sentencing regimes because the jury is ignorant of the sentencing consequences faced by defendants and the judge lacks the power to rein them in. By threatening more oppressive punishment if defendants risk trial, prosecutors can coerce defendants into accepting less favorable sentencing terms through plea bargaining").

Jurisdictions vary as to what role, if any, the judge may play in the plea bargaining process. In federal courts, judges may not participate in the plea bargaining process because of a concern that the court may have undue influence on the defendant's decision to accept a plea offer. *See* Fed. R. Crim. P. 11(c). However, many states allow court participation.

Under the Federal Rules of Criminal Procedure, the court has the power to accept, reject, or defer its decision as to whether to be bound by the parties' proposed plea agreement. Fed. R. Crim. P. 11(c)(3). Ordinarily, plea agreements do not bind a court in its sentencing decision. Rather, they merely commit the prosecution to make certain sentencing recommendations. However, pursuant to Rule 11(c)(1)(C), a defendant can plead guilty contingent to the court's acceptance of a binding sentence plea agreement.

5. *Effective Assistance of Counsel for Plea Bargaining*

Although the Supreme Court has never held that there is a constitutional right to a plea bargain, it has recognized a right to effective assistance of counsel during the plea bargaining process. In the companion cases of Missouri v. Frye, 566 U.S. 134 (2012), and Lafler v. Cooper, 566 U.S. 156

(2012), the Court held that a claim of ineffective assistance of counsel can be made when defense counsel gives bad advice during the plea bargaining process.

MISSOURI v. FRYE
566 U.S. 134 (2012)

Justice KENNEDY delivered the opinion of the Court.

The *Sixth Amendment*, applicable to the States by the terms of the *Fourteenth Amendment*, provides that the accused shall have the assistance of counsel in all criminal prosecutions. The right to counsel is the right to effective assistance of counsel. See *Strickland v. Washington (1984)*. This case arises in the context of claimed ineffective assistance that led to the lapse of a prosecution offer of a plea bargain, a proposal that offered terms more lenient than the terms of the guilty plea entered later. The initial question is whether the constitutional right to counsel extends to the negotiation and consideration of plea offers that lapse or are rejected. If there is a right to effective assistance with respect to those offers, a further question is what a defendant must demonstrate in order to show that prejudice resulted from counsel's deficient performance. Other questions relating to ineffective assistance with respect to plea offers, including the question of proper remedies, are considered in a second case decided today. See *Lafler v. Cooper.*

I

In August 2007, respondent Galin Frye was charged with driving with a revoked license. Frye had been convicted for that offense on three other occasions, so the State of Missouri charged him with a class D felony, which carries a maximum term of imprisonment of four years.

On November 15, the prosecutor sent a letter to Frye's counsel offering a choice of two plea bargains. The prosecutor first offered to recommend a 3-year sentence if there was a guilty plea to the felony charge, without a recommendation regarding probation but with a recommendation that Frye serve 10 days in jail as so-called "shock" time. The second offer was to reduce the charge to a misdemeanor and, if Frye pleaded guilty to it, to recommend a 90-day sentence. The misdemeanor charge of driving with a revoked license carries a maximum term of imprisonment of one year. The letter stated both offers would expire on December 28. Frye's attorney did not advise Frye that the offers had been made. The offers expired.

Frye's preliminary hearing was scheduled for January 4, 2008. On December 30, 2007, less than a week before the hearing, Frye was again arrested for driving with a revoked license. At the January 4 hearing, Frye waived his right to a preliminary hearing on the charge arising from the August 2007 arrest. He pleaded not guilty at a subsequent arraignment but then changed his plea to guilty. There was no underlying plea agreement. The state trial court accepted Frye's guilty plea. The prosecutor recommended a 3-year sentence, made no recommendation regarding probation, and requested 10 days shock time in jail. The trial judge sentenced Frye to three years in prison.

Frye filed for postconviction relief in state court. He alleged his counsel's failure to inform him of the prosecution's plea offer denied him the effective assistance of counsel. At an evidentiary hearing, Frye testified he would have entered a guilty plea to the misdemeanor had he known about the offer.

II

A

It is well settled that the right to the effective assistance of counsel applies to . . . all "'critical" stages of the criminal proceedings. Critical stages include arraignments, postindictment interrogations, postindictment line-ups, and the entry of a guilty plea.

With respect to the right to effective counsel in plea negotiations, a proper beginning point is to discuss two cases from this Court considering the role of counsel in advising a client about a plea offer and an ensuing guilty plea: *Hill v. Lockhart* (1985); and *Padilla v. Kentucky* (2010).

Hill established that claims of ineffective assistance of counsel in the plea bargain context are governed by the two-part test set forth in *Strickland*. In *Hill*, the decision turned on the second part of the *Strickland* test. There, a defendant who had entered a guilty plea claimed his counsel had misinformed him of the amount of time he would have to serve before he became eligible for parole. But the defendant had not alleged that, even if adequate advice and assistance had been given, he would have elected to plead not guilty and proceed to trial. Thus, the Court found that no prejudice from the inadequate advice had been shown or alleged.

In *Padilla*, the Court again discussed the duties of counsel in advising a client with respect to a plea offer that leads to a guilty plea. *Padilla* held that a guilty plea, based on a plea offer, should be set aside because counsel misinformed the defendant of the immigration consequences of the conviction.

In the case now before the Court the State, as petitioner, points out that the legal question presented is different from that in *Hill* and *Padilla*. In those cases the claim was that the prisoner's plea of guilty was invalid because counsel had provided incorrect advice pertinent to the plea. In the instant case, by contrast, the guilty plea that was accepted, and the plea proceedings concerning it in court, were all based on accurate advice and information from counsel. The challenge is not to the advice pertaining to the plea that was accepted but rather to the course of legal representation that preceded it with respect to other potential pleas and plea offers.

[T]he State urges that there is no right to a plea offer or a plea bargain in any event. See *Weatherford v.* Bursey (1977). It claims Frye therefore was not deprived of any legal benefit to which he was entitled. Under this view, any wrongful or mistaken action of counsel with respect to earlier plea offers is beside the point.

The State is correct to point out that . . . [b]efore a guilty plea is entered the defendant's understanding of the plea and its consequences can be established on the record. This affords the State substantial protection against later claims that the plea was the result of inadequate advice.

When a plea offer has lapsed or been rejected, however, no formal court proceedings are involved. Indeed, discussions between client and defense counsel are privileged. So the prosecution has little or no notice if something may be amiss and perhaps no capacity to intervene in any event. And, as noted, the State insists there is no right to receive a plea offer. For all these reasons, the State contends, it is unfair to subject it to the consequences of defense counsel's inadequacies, especially when the opportunities for a full and fair trial, or, as here, for a later guilty plea albeit on less favorable terms, are preserved.

The State's contentions are neither illogical nor without some persuasive force, yet they do not suffice to overcome a simple reality. Ninety-seven percent of federal convictions and ninety-four percent of state convictions are the result of guilty pleas. The reality is that plea bargains have become so central to the administration of the criminal justice system that defense counsel have responsibilities in the plea bargain process, responsibilities that must be met to render the adequate assistance of counsel that the *Sixth Amendment* requires in the criminal process at critical stages. Because ours "is for the most part a system of pleas, not a system of trials," it is insufficient simply to point to the guarantee of a fair trial as a backstop that inoculates any errors in the pretrial process. "To a large extent . . . horse trading [between prosecutor and defense counsel] determines who goes to jail and for how long. That is what plea bargaining is. It is not some adjunct to the criminal justice system; it *is* the criminal justice system." In today's criminal justice system, therefore, the negotiation of a plea bargain, rather than the unfolding of a trial, is almost always the critical point for a defendant.

To note the prevalence of plea bargaining is not to criticize it. The potential to conserve valuable prosecutorial resources and for defendants to admit their crimes and receive more favorable terms at sentencing means that a plea agreement can benefit both parties. In order that these benefits can be realized, however, criminal defendants require effective counsel during plea negotiations. "Anything less . . . might deny a defendant 'effective representation by counsel at the only stage when legal aid and advice would help him.'"

B

The inquiry then becomes how to define the duty and responsibilities of defense counsel in the plea bargain process. This is a difficult question. Bargaining is, by its nature, defined to a substantial degree by personal style. The alternative courses and tactics in negotiation are so individual that it may be neither prudent nor practicable to try to elaborate or define detailed standards for the proper discharge of defense counsel's participation in the process.

This case presents neither the necessity nor the occasion to define the duties of defense counsel in those respects, however. Here the question is whether defense counsel has the duty to communicate the terms of a formal offer to accept a plea on terms and conditions that may result in a lesser sentence, a conviction on lesser charges, or both.

This Court now holds that, as a general rule, defense counsel has the duty to communicate formal offers from the prosecution to accept a plea on terms and conditions that may be favorable to the accused. Any exceptions to that rule need not be explored here, for the offer was a formal one with a fixed expiration date. When defense counsel allowed the offer to expire without advising the defendant or allowing him to consider it, defense counsel did not render the effective assistance the Constitution requires.

Here defense counsel did not communicate the formal offers to the defendant. As a result of that deficient performance, the offers lapsed. Under *Strickland*, the question then becomes what, if any, prejudice resulted from the breach of duty.

C

To show prejudice from ineffective assistance of counsel where a plea offer has lapsed or been rejected because of counsel's deficient performance, defendants must demonstrate a reasonable probability they would have accepted the earlier plea offer had they been afforded effective assistance of counsel. Defendants must also demonstrate a reasonable probability the plea would have been entered without the prosecution canceling it or the trial court refusing to accept it, if they had the authority to exercise that discretion under state law.

III

These standards must be applied to the instant case.

There appears to be a reasonable probability Frye would have accepted the prosecutor's original offer of a plea bargain if the offer had been communicated to him, because he pleaded guilty to a more serious charge, with no promise of a sentencing recommendation from the prosecutor.

The Court of Appeals failed, however, to require Frye to show that the first plea offer, if accepted by Frye, would have been adhered to by the prosecution and accepted by the trial court. Whether the prosecution and trial court are required to do so is a matter of state law, and it is not the place of this Court to settle those matters.

We remand for the Missouri Court of Appeals to consider these state-law questions, because they bear on the federal question of *Strickland* prejudice. If, as the Missouri court stated here, the prosecutor could have canceled the plea agreement, and if Frye fails to show a reasonable probability the prosecutor would have adhered to the agreement, there is no *Strickland* prejudice.

Justice SCALIA, with whom THE CHIEF JUSTICE, Justice THOMAS, and Justice ALITO join, dissenting.

The Court acknowledges, moreover, that Frye's conviction was untainted by attorney error: "[T]he guilty plea that was accepted, and the plea proceedings concerning it in court, were all based on accurate advice and information from counsel." Given the "ultimate focus" of our ineffective-assistance cases on "the fundamental fairness of the proceeding whose result is being challenged," that should be the end of the matter.

The plea-bargaining process is a subject worthy of regulation, since it is the means by which most criminal convictions are obtained. It happens not to be, however, a subject covered by the *Sixth Amendment*, which is concerned not with the fairness of bargaining but with the fairness of conviction.

LAFLER v. COOPER
566 U.S. 156 (2012)

Justice KENNEDY delivered the opinion of the Court.

In this case, as in *Missouri* v. *Frye*, also decided today, a criminal defendant seeks a remedy when inadequate assistance of counsel caused nonacceptance of a plea offer and further proceedings led to a less favorable outcome. In *Frye*, defense counsel did not inform the defendant of the plea offer; and after the offer lapsed the defendant still pleaded guilty, but on more severe terms. Here, the favorable plea offer was reported to the client but, on advice of counsel, was rejected. In *Frye* there was a later guilty plea. Here, after the plea offer had been rejected, there was a full and fair trial before a jury. After a guilty verdict, the defendant received a sentence harsher than that offered in the rejected plea bargain. The instant case comes to the Court with the concession that counsel's advice with respect to the plea offer fell below the standard of adequate assistance of counsel guaranteed by the *Sixth Amendment*, applicable to the States through the *Fourteenth Amendment*.

I

On the evening of March 25, 2003, respondent pointed a gun toward Kali Mundy's head and fired. [T]he shot missed and Mundy fled. Respondent followed in pursuit, firing repeatedly. Mundy was shot in her buttock, hip, and abdomen but survived the assault.

Respondent was charged under Michigan law with assault with intent to murder, possession of a firearm by a felon, possession of a firearm in the commission of a felony, misdemeanor possession of marijuana, and for being a habitual offender. On two occasions, the prosecution offered to dismiss two of the charges and to recommend a sentence of 51 to 85 months for the other two, in exchange for a guilty plea. In a communication with the court respondent admitted guilt and expressed a willingness to accept the offer. Respondent, however, later rejected the offer on both occasions, allegedly after his attorney convinced him that the prosecution would be unable to establish his intent to murder Mundy because she had been shot below the waist. After trial, respondent was convicted on all counts and received a mandatory minimum sentence of 185 to 360 months' imprisonment.

II

A

Defendants have a *Sixth Amendment* right to counsel, a right that extends to the plea-bargaining process. In this case all parties agree the performance of respondent's counsel was deficient when he advised respondent to reject the plea offer on the grounds he could not be convicted at trial. In light of this concession, it is unnecessary for this Court to explore the issue.

The question for this Court is how to apply *Strickland*'s prejudice test where ineffective assistance results in a rejection of the plea offer and the defendant is convicted at the ensuing trial.

B

To establish *Strickland* prejudice a defendant must "show that there is a reasonable probability that, but for counsel's unprofessional errors, the result of the proceeding would have been different."

In contrast to *Hill*, here the ineffective advice led not to an offer's acceptance but to its rejection. Having to stand trial, not choosing to waive it, is the prejudice alleged.

Petitioner and the Solicitor General propose a different, far more narrow, view of the *Sixth Amendment*. They contend there can be no finding of *Strickland* prejudice arising from plea bargaining if the defendant is later convicted at a fair trial. The three reasons petitioner and the Solicitor General offer for their approach are unpersuasive.

First, petitioner and the Solicitor General claim that the sole purpose of the *Sixth Amendment* is to protect the right to a fair trial. Errors before trial, they argue, are not cognizable under the *Sixth Amendment* unless they affect the fairness of the trial itself. The *Sixth Amendment*, however, is not so narrow in its reach. The *Sixth Amendment* requires effective assistance of counsel at critical stages of a criminal proceeding. The constitutional guarantee applies to pretrial critical stages that are part of the whole course of a criminal proceeding, a proceeding in which defendants cannot be presumed to make critical decisions without counsel's advice.

In the instant case respondent went to trial rather than accept a plea deal, and it is conceded this was the result of ineffective assistance during the plea negotiation process. Respondent received a more severe sentence at trial, one $3^{1}/_{2}$ times more severe than he likely would have received by pleading guilty. Far from curing the error, the trial caused the injury from the error. Even if the trial itself is free from constitutional flaw, the defendant who goes to trial instead of taking a more favorable plea may be prejudiced from either a conviction on more serious counts or the imposition of a more severe sentence.

[Second], [i]t is, of course, true that defendants have "no right to be offered a plea . . . nor a federal right that the judge accept it." In the circumstances here, that is beside the point. If no plea offer is made, or a plea deal is accepted by the defendant but rejected by the judge, the issue raised here simply does not arise. [But] "[w]hen a State opts to act in a field where its action has significant discretionary elements, it must nonetheless act in accord with the dictates of the Constitution."

Third, petitioner seeks to preserve the conviction obtained by the State by arguing that the purpose of the *Sixth Amendment* is to ensure "the reliability of [a] conviction following trial." This argument, too, fails to comprehend the full scope of the *Sixth Amendment's* protections; and it is refuted by precedent.

In the end, petitioner's three arguments amount to one general contention: A fair trial wipes clean any deficient performance by defense counsel during plea bargaining. That position ignores the reality that criminal justice today is for the most part a system of pleas, not a system of trials. Ninety-seven percent of federal convictions and ninety-four percent of state convictions are the result of guilty pleas. As explained in *Frye*, the right to adequate assistance of counsel cannot be defined or enforced without taking account of the central role plea bargaining plays in securing convictions and determining sentences.

C

Even if a defendant shows ineffective assistance of counsel has caused the rejection of a plea leading to a trial and a more severe sentence, there is the question of what constitutes an appropriate remedy. That question must now be addressed.

The specific injury suffered by defendants who decline a plea offer as a result of ineffective assistance of counsel and then receive a greater sentence as a result of trial can come in at least one of two forms. In some cases, the sole advantage a defendant would have received under the plea is a lesser sentence. In this situation the court may conduct an evidentiary hearing to determine whether the defendant has shown a reasonable probability that but for counsel's errors he would have accepted the plea. If the showing is made, the court may exercise discretion in determining whether the defendant should receive the term of imprisonment the government offered in the plea, the sentence he received at trial, or something in between. [In other situations,] the proper exercise of discretion to remedy the constitutional injury may be to require the prosecution to reoffer the plea proposal.

Justice SCALIA, with whom Justice THOMAS joins, and with whom THE CHIEF JUSTICE joins as to all but Part IV, dissenting.

Anthony Cooper received a full and fair trial, was found guilty of all charges by a unanimous jury, and was given the sentence that the law prescribed.

It is impossible to conclude discussion of today's extraordinary opinion without commenting upon the remedy it provides for the unconstitutional conviction. It is a remedy unheard-of in American jurisprudence—and, I would be willing to bet, in the jurisprudence of any other country.

The Court requires Michigan to "reoffer the plea agreement" that was rejected because of bad advice from counsel. [T]he acceptance or rejection of a plea agreement that has no status whatever under the United States Constitution.

I suspect that the Court's squeamishness in fashioning a remedy, and the incoherence of what it comes up with, is attributable to its realization, deep down, that there is no real constitutional violation here anyway. The defendant has been fairly tried, lawfully convicted, and properly sentenced, and *any* "remedy" provided for this will do nothing but undo the just results of a fair adversarial process.

In the United States, we have plea bargaining aplenty, but until today it has been regarded as a necessary evil. It presents grave risks of prosecutorial overcharging that effectively compels an innocent defendant to avoid massive risk by pleading guilty to a lesser offense; and for guilty defendants it often—perhaps usually—results in a sentence well below what the law prescribes for the actual crime. But even so, we accept plea bargaining because many believe that without it our long and expensive process of criminal trial could not sustain the burden imposed on it, and our system of criminal justice would grind to a halt.

Today, however, the Supreme Court of the United States elevates plea bargaining from a necessary evil to a constitutional entitlement. It is no longer a somewhat embarrassing adjunct to our criminal justice system; rather, as the Court announces in the companion case to this one, "'it *is* the criminal justice system.'" Thus, even though there is no doubt that the respondent here is guilty of the offense with which he was charged; even though he has received the exorbitant gold standard of American justice—a full-dress criminal trial with its innumerable constitutional and statutory limitations upon the evidence that the prosecution can bring forward, and (in Michigan as in most States) the requirement of a unanimous guilty verdict by impartial jurors—the Court says that his conviction is invalid because he was deprived of his *constitutional entitlement* to plea-bargain.

I am less saddened by the outcome of this case than I am by what it says about this Court's attitude toward criminal justice. The Court today embraces the sporting chance theory of criminal law, in which the State functions like a conscientious casino-operator, giving each player a fair chance to beat the house, that is, to serve less time than the law says he deserves. And when a player is excluded from the tables, his *constitutional rights* have been violated. I do not subscribe to that theory. No one should, least of all the Justices of the Supreme Court.

C. GUILTY PLEAS

What is a guilty plea? It is more than just a confession or a waiver of the right to a jury trial. Rather, it is a combination of both. A guilty plea is a waiver of the right to trial (and all of the rights that go with it), as well as an admission that the defendant committed the crime to which he is pleading guilty. The requirements for a constitutionally valid guilty plea were set forth by the Court in Boykin v. Alabama.

BOYKIN v. ALABAMA
395 U.S. 238 (1969)

Justice DOUGLAS delivered the opinion of the Court.

In the spring of 1966, within the period of a fortnight, a series of armed robberies occurred in Mobile, Alabama. [A] local grand jury returned five indictments against petitioner, a 27-year-old Negro, for common-law robbery — an offense punishable in Alabama by death.

Before the matter came to trial, the court determined that petitioner was indigent and appointed counsel to represent him. Three days later, at his arraignment, petitioner pleaded guilty to all five indictments. So far as the record shows, the judge asked no questions of petitioner concerning his plea, and petitioner did not address the court.

A plea of guilty is more than a confession which admits that the accused did various acts; it is itself a conviction; nothing remains but to give judgment and determine punishment. Admissibility of a confession must be based on a "reliable determination on the voluntariness issue which satisfies the constitutional rights of the defendant." The requirement that the prosecution spread on the record the prerequisites of a valid waiver is no constitutional innovation. "Presuming waiver from a silent record is impermissible. The record must show, or there must be an allegation and evidence which show, that an accused was offered counsel but intelligently and understandingly rejected the offer. Anything less is not waiver."

We think that the same standard must be applied to determining whether a guilty plea is voluntarily made. For, as we have said, a plea of guilty is more than an admission of conduct; it is a conviction. Ignorance, incomprehension, coercion, terror, inducements, subtle or blatant threats might be a perfect cover-up of unconstitutionality. The question of an effective waiver of a federal constitutional right in a proceeding is of course governed by federal standards.

Several federal constitutional rights are involved in a waiver that takes place when a plea of guilty is entered in a state criminal trial. First, is the privilege against compulsory self-incrimination guaranteed by the Fifth Amendment and applicable to the States by reason of the Fourteenth. Second, is the right to trial by jury. Third, is the right to confront one's accusers. We cannot presume a waiver of these three important federal rights from a silent record.

What is at stake for an accused facing death or imprisonment demands the utmost solicitude of which courts are capable in canvassing the matter with the accused to make sure he has a full understanding of what the plea connotes and of its consequence. When the judge discharges that function, he leaves a record adequate for any review that may be later sought and forestalls the spin-off of collateral proceedings that seek to probe murky memories.[12]

[Because the trial court failed to obtain from the defendant a full waiver of his rights, the conviction was overturned.]

Justice HARLAN, whom Justice BLACK joins, dissenting.

The Court today holds that petitioner Boykin was denied due process of law, and that his robbery convictions must be reversed outright, solely because "the record [is] inadequate to show that petitioner . . . intelligently and knowingly pleaded guilty." The Court thus in effect fastens upon the States, as a matter of federal constitutional law, the rigid prophylactic requirements of Rule 11 of the Federal Rules of Criminal Procedure. Moreover, the Court does all this at the behest of a petitioner who has never at any time alleged that his guilty plea was involuntary or made without knowledge of the consequences. I cannot possibly subscribe to so bizarre a result.

So far as one can make out from the Court's opinion, what is now in effect being held is that the prophylactic procedures of Criminal Rule 11 are substantially applicable to the States as a matter of federal constitutional due process.

I would hold that petitioner Boykin is not entitled to outright reversal of his conviction simply because of the "inadequacy" of the record pertaining to his guilty plea.

How informed must a defendant be to enter a "knowing and voluntary" guilty plea? In Henderson v. Morgan, 426 U.S. 637 (1976), the Court held that a defendant must understand the nature of the offense to which he pleads.

HENDERSON v. MORGAN
426 U.S. 637 (1976)

Justice STEVENS delivered the opinion of the Court.

The question presented is whether a defendant may enter a voluntary plea of guilty to a charge of second-degree murder without being informed that intent to cause the death of his victim was an element of the offense.

---

12. A majority of criminal convictions are obtained after a plea of guilty. If these convictions are to be insulated from attack, the trial court is best advised to conduct an on the record examination of the defendant which should include, inter alia, an attempt to satisfy itself that the defendant understands the nature of the charges, his right to a jury trial, the acts sufficient to constitute the offenses for which he is charged and the permissible range of sentences. [Footnote by the Court.]

I

On April 6, 1965, respondent killed Mrs. Ada Francisco in her home.

When he was in seventh grade, respondent was committed to the Rome State School for Mental Defectives where he was classified as "retarded." He was released to become a farm laborer and ultimately went to work on Mrs. Francisco's farm. Following an argument, she threatened to return him to state custody. He then decided to abscond. During the night he entered Mrs. Francisco's bedroom with a knife, intending to collect his earned wages before leaving; she awoke, began to scream, and he stabbed her. He took a small amount of money, fled in her car, and became involved in an accident about 80 miles away. The knife was found in the glove compartment of her car. He was promptly arrested and made a statement to the police. He was then 19 years old and substantially below average intelligence.

Respondent was indicted for first-degree murder. Defense counsel held a series of conferences with the prosecutors, with the respondent, and with members of his family. The lawyers "thought manslaughter first would satisfy the needs of justice." They therefore endeavored to have the charge reduced to manslaughter, but the prosecution would agree to nothing less than second-degree murder and a minimum sentence of 25 years. The lawyers gave respondent advice about the different sentences which could be imposed for the different offenses, but, as the District Court found, did not explain the required element of intent.

On June 8, 1965, respondent appeared in court with his attorneys and entered a plea of guilty to murder in the second degree in full satisfaction of the first-degree murder charge made in the indictment. In direct colloquy with the trial judge respondent stated that his plea was based on the advice of his attorneys, that he understood he was accused of killing Mrs. Francisco in Fulton County, that he was waiving his right to a jury trial, and that he would be sent to prison. There was no discussion of the elements of the offense of second-degree murder, no indication that the nature of the offense had ever been discussed with respondent, and no reference of any kind to the requirement of intent to cause the death of the victim.

At the sentencing hearing a week later his lawyers made a statement explaining his version of the offense, particularly noting that respondent "meant no harm to that lady" when he entered her room with the knife.[13]

---

13. The attorney described the incident, in part, in these words:

> He awakened Mrs. Francisco for the purpose of obtaining the money which was rightfully his, and which he had a right to. Of course it was an unusual hour to do it, but he had returned home late, and he had been threatened with that other thing on the part of Mrs. Francisco of returning him to the Rome School. So I assume, putting all of those factors together, the one idea in his mind was to take his money and get away as far as he could to avoid being transferred back.
>
> Now, Mrs. Francisco was awakened. Apparently he had stayed there in the house, and she had no fear of him because her bedroom was open. There was no door on it. No locks at all.

After studying the probation officer's report, the trial judge pronounced sentence.

At the evidentiary hearing [where respondent challenged his plea, he] testified that he would not have pleaded guilty if he had known that an intent to cause the death of his victim was an element of the offense of second-degree murder. The District Judge did not indicate whether or not he credited this testimony.

II

We assume, as petitioner argues, that the prosecutor had overwhelming evidence of guilt available. Nevertheless, such a plea cannot support a judgment of guilt unless it was voluntary in a constitutional sense. And clearly the plea could not be voluntary in the sense that it constituted an intelligent admission that he committed the offense unless the defendant received "real notice of the true nature of the charge against him, the first and most universally recognized requirement of due process."[14]

The charge of second-degree murder was never formally made. Had it been made, it necessarily would have included a charge that respondent's assault was "committed with a design to effect the death of the person killed." [A]n admission by respondent that he killed Mrs. Francisco does not necessarily also admit that he was guilty of second-degree murder.

There is nothing in this record that can serve as a substitute for either a finding after trial, or a voluntary admission, that respondent had the requisite intent. Defense counsel did not purport to stipulate to that fact; they did not explain to him that his plea would be an admission of that fact; and he made no factual statement or admission necessarily implying that he had such intent. In these circumstances it is impossible to conclude that his plea to the unexplained charge of second-degree murder was voluntary.[15]

So when he awakened her, instead of responding to him, she merely started to scream. Now, I assume if she had talked to him that night in a normal tone, this thing would never have happened. But the minute she screamed, of course with his uncontrollable and ungovernable temper, and the idea in mind of perhaps she may awaken the people who were living in the other apartment of the house — there was a man and his wife who were working there for Mrs. Francisco and living in the house — in order to stop the screaming and in the excitement and tension of it all, the assault occurred and as a result Mrs. Francisco met her death. [Footnote by the Court.]

14. A plea may be involuntary either because the accused does not understand the nature of the constitutional protections that he is waiving, or because he has such an incomplete understanding of the charge that his plea cannot stand as an intelligent admission of guilt. Without adequate notice of the nature of the charge against him, or proof that he in fact understood the charge, the plea cannot be voluntary in this latter sense. [Footnote by the Court.]

15. There is no need in this case to decide whether notice of the true nature, or substance, of a charge always requires a description of every element of the offense; we assume it does not. Nevertheless, intent is such a critical element of the offense of second-degree murder that notice of that element is required. [Footnote by the Court.]

Normally the record contains either an explanation of the charge by the trial judge, or at least a representation by defense counsel that the nature of the offense has been explained to the accused. Moreover, even without such an express representation, it may be appropriate to presume that in most cases defense counsel routinely explain the nature of the offense in sufficient detail to give the accused notice of what he is being asked to admit. This case is unique because the trial judge found as a fact that the element of intent was not explained to respondent. Moreover, respondent's unusually low mental capacity provides a reasonable explanation for counsel's oversight; it also forecloses the conclusion that the error was harmless beyond a reasonable doubt, for it lends at least a modicum of credibility to defense counsel's appraisal of the homicide as a manslaughter rather than a murder.

Since respondent did not receive adequate notice of the offense to which he pleaded guilty, his plea was involuntary and the judgment of conviction was entered without due process of law.

Justice REHNQUIST, with whom Chief Justice BURGER joins, dissenting.

There was no contention in the federal habeas court that respondent's guilty plea was not "voluntary" in the normal sense of that word. There was no hint of physical or psychological coercion, and respondent was represented by not one but two admittedly capable defense attorneys.

But the Court refers to "voluntary in a constitutional sense" stating that the term includes the requirement of "'real notice of the true nature of the . . .' charge." [T]he test to be applied is not whether respondent's attorneys mechanically recited to him the elements of the crime with which he was charged as those elements would have been set forth in black letter law in a criminal law hornbook, but rather it is a test based on the practices of reasonably competent attorneys experienced in the day-to-day business of representing criminal defendants in a trial court.

His attorneys were motivated by the eminently reasonable tactical judgment on their part that he should plead guilty to second-degree murder in order to avoid the possibility of conviction for first-degree murder with its more serious attendant penalties. Since the Court concedes both the competence of respondent's counsel and the wisdom of their advice, that should be the end of the inquiry.

Although the Court in *Henderson* struck down the defendant's plea, it is not always easy to get a guilty plea overturned. Even outside the plea bargaining context, a defendant must also show that he would not have pled guilty absent counsel's improper advice. Only significant errors, such as when defense counsel fails to advise the defendant of the deportation consequences of his plea, are likely to lead to reversal.

HILL v. LOCKHART

474 U.S. 52 (1985)

Justice REHNQUIST delivered the opinion of the Court.

Petitioner William Lloyd Hill pleaded guilty in the Arkansas trial court to charges of first-degree murder and theft of property. More than two years later he sought federal habeas relief on the ground that his court-appointed attorney had failed to advise him that, as a second offender, he was required to serve one-half of his sentence before becoming eligible for parole. [W]e conclude that petitioner failed to allege the kind of prejudice from the allegedly incompetent advice of counsel that would have entitled him to a hearing.

Under Arkansas law, the murder charge to which petitioner pleaded guilty carried a potential sentence of 5 to 50 years or life in prison, along with a fine of up to $15,000. Petitioner's court-appointed attorney negotiated a plea agreement pursuant to which the State, in return for petitioner's plea of guilty to both the murder and theft charges, agreed to recommend that the trial judge impose concurrent prison sentences of 35 years for the murder and 10 years for the theft. Petitioner signed a written "plea statement" indicating that he understood the charges against him and the consequences of pleading guilty, that his plea had not been induced "by any force, threat, or promise" apart from the plea agreement itself, that he realized that the trial judge was not bound by the plea agreement and retained the sole "power of sentence," and that he had discussed the plea agreement with his attorney and was satisfied with his attorney's advice. The last two lines of the "plea statement," just above petitioner's signature, read: "I am aware of everything in this document. I fully understand what my rights are, and I voluntarily plead guilty because I am guilty as charged."

Petitioner appeared before the trial judge at the plea hearing, recounted the events that gave rise to the charges against him, affirmed that he had signed and understood the written "plea statement," reiterated that no "threats or promises" had been made to him other than the plea agreement itself, and entered a plea of guilty to both charges. The trial judge accepted the guilty plea and sentenced petitioner in accordance with the State's recommendations. The trial judge also granted petitioner credit for the time he had already served in prison, and told petitioner that "[you] will be required to serve at least one-third of your time before you are eligible for parole."

More than two years later petitioner filed a federal habeas corpus petition alleging, inter alia, that his guilty plea was involuntary by reason of ineffective assistance of counsel because his attorney had misinformed him as to his parole eligibility date. According to petitioner, his attorney had told him that if he pleaded guilty he would become eligible for parole after serving one-third of his prison sentence. In fact, because petitioner previously had been convicted of a felony in Florida, he was classified under Arkansas law as a "second offender" and was required to serve one-half of his sentence before becoming eligible for parole. Petitioner asked the United States District

Court to reduce his sentence to a term of years that would result in his becoming eligible for parole in conformance with his original expectations.

The District Court denied habeas relief without a hearing. The court noted that neither Arkansas nor federal law required that petitioner be informed of his parole eligibility date prior to pleading guilty, and concluded that, even if petitioner was misled by his attorney's advice, parole eligibility "is not such a consequence of [petitioner's] guilty plea that such misinformation renders his plea involuntary." The court also held that "even if an attorney's advice concerning such eligibility is not wholly accurate, such advice does not render that attorney's performance constitutionally inadequate."

The longstanding test for determining the validity of a guilty plea is "whether the plea represents a voluntary and intelligent choice among the alternative courses of action open to the defendant." Here petitioner does not contend that his plea was "involuntary" or "unintelligent" simply because the State through its officials failed to supply him with information about his parole eligibility date. We have never held that the United States Constitution requires the State to furnish a defendant with information about parole eligibility in order for the defendant's plea of guilty to be voluntary, and indeed such a constitutional requirement would be inconsistent with the current rules of procedure governing the entry of guilty pleas in the federal courts. Instead, petitioner relies entirely on the claim that his plea was "involuntary" as a result of ineffective assistance of counsel because his attorney supplied him with information about parole eligibility that was erroneous. Where, as here, a defendant is represented by counsel during the plea process and enters his plea upon the advice of counsel, the voluntariness of the plea depends on whether counsel's advice "was within the range of competence demanded of attorneys in criminal cases."

Attorney errors come in an infinite variety and are as likely to be utterly harmless in a particular case as they are to be prejudicial. Representation is an art, and an act or omission that is unprofessional in one case may be sound or even brilliant in another. "Even if a defendant shows that particular errors of counsel were unreasonable, therefore, the defendant must show that they actually had an adverse effect on the defense."

[As stated] in United States v. Timmreck, 441 U.S. 780 (1979):

> Every inroad on the concept of finality undermines confidence in the integrity of our procedures; and, by increasing the volume of judicial work, inevitably delays and impairs the orderly administration of justice. The impact is greatest when new grounds for setting aside guilty pleas are approved because the vast majority of criminal convictions result from such pleas.

We hold, therefore, that . . . in order to satisfy the "prejudice" requirement, the defendant must show that there is a reasonable probability that, but for counsel's errors, he would not have pleaded guilty and would have insisted on going to trial.

Petitioner did not allege in his habeas petition that, had counsel correctly informed him about his parole eligibility date, he would have pleaded not guilty and insisted on going to trial. He alleged no special circumstances that might support the conclusion that he placed particular emphasis on his parole eligibility in deciding whether or not to plead guilty. Indeed, petitioner's mistaken belief that he would become eligible for parole after serving one-third of his sentence would seem to have affected not only his calculation of the time he likely would serve if sentenced pursuant to the proposed plea agreement, but also his calculation of the time he likely would serve if he went to trial and were convicted.

Because petitioner in this case failed to allege the kind of "prejudice" necessary to satisfy [his burden, his petition was properly denied].

PADILLA v. KENTUCKY

559 U.S. 356 (2010)

Justice STEVENS delivered the opinion of the Court.

Petitioner Jose Padilla, a native of Honduras, has been a lawful permanent resident of the United States for more than 40 years. Padilla served this Nation with honor as a member of the U. S. Armed Forces during the Vietnam War. He now faces deportation after pleading guilty to the transportation of a large amount of marijuana in his tractor-trailer in the Commonwealth of Kentucky.

In this postconviction proceeding, Padilla claims that his counsel not only failed to advise him of this consequence prior to his entering the plea, but also told him that he "did not have to worry about immigration status since he had been in the country so long." Padilla relied on his counsel's erroneous advice when he pleaded guilty to the drug charges that made his deportation virtually mandatory. He alleges that he would have insisted on going to trial if he had not received incorrect advice from his attorney.

Assuming the truth of his allegations, the Supreme Court of Kentucky denied Padilla postconviction relief without the benefit of an evidentiary hearing. The court held that the *Sixth Amendment's* guarantee of effective assistance of counsel does not protect a criminal defendant from erroneous advice about deportation because it is merely a "collateral" consequence of his conviction. In its view, neither counsel's failure to advise petitioner about the possibility of removal, nor counsel's incorrect advice, could provide a basis for relief.

We granted certiorari, to decide whether, as a matter of federal law, Padilla's counsel had an obligation to advise him that the offense to which he was pleading guilty would result in his removal from this country. We agree with Padilla that constitutionally competent counsel would have advised him that his conviction for drug distribution made him subject to automatic deportation. Whether he is entitled to relief depends on whether he has been prejudiced, a matter that we do not address.

I

The landscape of federal immigration law has changed dramatically over the last 90 years. While once there was only a narrow class of deportable offenses and judges wielded broad discretionary authority to prevent deportation, immigration reforms over time have expanded the class of deportable offenses and limited the authority of judges to alleviate the harsh consequences of deportation. The "drastic measure" of deportation or removal is now virtually inevitable for a vast number of noncitizens convicted of crimes.

[C]hanges to our immigration law have dramatically raised the stakes of a noncitizen's criminal conviction. The importance of accurate legal advice for noncitizens accused of crimes has never been more important. These changes confirm our view that as a matter of federal law, deportation is an integral part — indeed, sometimes the most important part — of the penalty that may be imposed on noncitizen defendants who plead guilty to specified crimes.

II

Before deciding whether to plead guilty, a defendant is entitled to "the effective assistance of competent counsel." The Supreme Court of Kentucky rejected Padilla's ineffectiveness claim on the ground that the advice he sought about the risk of deportation concerned only collateral matters, *i.e.*, those matters not within the sentencing authority of the state trial court.

We, however, have never applied a distinction between direct and collateral consequences to define the scope of constitutionally "reasonable professional assistance" required under *Strickland*. Whether that distinction is appropriate is a question we need not consider in this case because of the unique nature of deportation.

We have long recognized that deportation is a particularly severe "penalty," but it is not, in a strict sense, a criminal sanction. Although removal proceedings are civil in nature, deportation is nevertheless intimately related to the criminal process. Our law has enmeshed criminal convictions and the penalty of deportation for nearly a century. And, importantly, recent changes in our immigration law have made removal nearly an automatic result for a broad class of noncitizen offenders. Thus, we find it "most difficult" to divorce the penalty from the conviction in the deportation context.

Deportation as a consequence of a criminal conviction is, because of its close connection to the criminal process, uniquely difficult to classify as either a direct or a collateral consequence. The collateral versus direct distinction is thus ill-suited to evaluating a *Strickland* claim concerning the specific risk of deportation. We conclude that advice regarding deportation is not categorically removed from the ambit of the *Sixth Amendment* right to counsel. *Strickland* applies to Padilla's claim.

III

Under *Strickland*, we first determine whether counsel's representation "fell below an objective standard of reasonableness." Then we ask whether "there is a reasonable probability that, but for counsel's unprofessional errors, the result of the proceeding would have been different."

The weight of prevailing professional norms supports the view that counsel must advise her client regarding the risk of deportation. "[A]uthorities of every stripe — including the American Bar Association, criminal defense and public defender organizations, authoritative treatises, and state and city bar publications — universally require defense attorneys to advise as to the risk of deportation consequences for non-citizen clients. . . ."

In the instant case, the terms of the relevant immigration statute are succinct, clear, and explicit in defining the removal consequence for Padilla's conviction. Padilla's counsel could have easily determined that his plea would make him eligible for deportation simply from reading the text of the statute, which addresses not some broad classification of crimes but specifically commands removal for all controlled substances convictions except for the most trivial of marijuana possession offenses. Instead, Padilla's counsel provided him false assurance that his conviction would not result in his removal from this country. This is not a hard case in which to find deficiency: The consequences of Padilla's plea could easily be determined from reading the removal statute, his deportation was presumptively mandatory, and his counsel's advice was incorrect.

V

[W]e have little difficulty concluding that Padilla has sufficiently alleged that his counsel was constitutionally deficient. Whether Padilla is entitled to relief will depend on whether he can demonstrate prejudice. The judgment of the Supreme Court of Kentucky is reversed, and the case is remanded for further proceedings not inconsistent with this opinion.[16]

———————————

Although a defendant may claim ineffective assistance of counsel to challenge a guilty plea, the primary protection for a defendant lies not in a subsequent constitutional challenge but in reliance on statutory rules designed to protect a defendant's constitutional rights. In the federal system, Federal Rule of Criminal Procedure 11 governs the procedures required for a valid guilty plea.

———————————

16. In Chaidez v. United States, 133 S. Ct. 1103 (2013), the Court held that Padilla is not retroactive.

D. RULE 11 AND THE PROCEDURAL REQUIREMENTS FOR ENTERING GUILTY PLEAS

A guilty plea is valid only if it demonstrates on the record that the defendant has knowingly and voluntarily waived his constitutional rights. Federal Rule of Criminal Procedure 11 is designed to accomplish this goal. Rule 11(b)(1) requires that the judge address the defendant personally in open court to inform the defendant, and to determine that the defendant personally understands, that the defendant will be waiving the following rights by pleading guilty:[17]

1. The right not to plead guilty
2. The right to a jury trial
3. The right to be represented by counsel
4. The nature of the charge to which the defendant is pleading
5. Any mandatory minimum penalty
6. Any maximum possible penalty
7. The defendant's waiver of certain appeal rights
8. The government's right to use the defendant's statements in a perjury prosecution

The court must also advise the defendant of the likely consequences of pleading guilty and establish that there is a factual basis for the plea. In addition, the court must ensure that the plea is voluntary and did not result from force, threats of force, or promises other than those in a plea agreement. Finally, the plea must be entered on the record.

Ordinarily, the defendant will establish the factual basis for the guilty plea by briefly describing his criminal actions. In some courts, however, the prosecutor will set forth the factual basis for the plea. In North Carolina v. Alford, 400 U.S. 25 (1970), the Court held that as long as the record reflects a factual basis for a guilty plea, the defendant need not personally admit his guilt for the guilty plea to be valid. Alford, who was indicted for first-degree murder, chose to plead guilty to avoid the death penalty. Although Alford was not willing to admit that he committed the murder, the court was presented with testimony that strongly indicated the defendant's guilt. Alford later claimed that his plea was not voluntary because he had not admitted to the murder. Justice White, expressing the view of six members of the court, held that there was no constitutional error in accepting a guilty plea that contained a protestation of innocence when, as in Alford's case, the defendant intelligently concluded that his interests required entry of a guilty plea and the record before the judge contained strong evidence of actual guilt.

---

17. A sample guilty plea transcript is set forth in the Statutory Supplement.

A defendant must be mentally competent to plead guilty. In Godinez v. Moran, 509 U.S. 389 (1993), the Supreme Court held that the competency standard for pleading guilty is no higher than the competency standard for standing trial. That standard requires that the defendant understand the proceedings against him and be able to consult with his lawyer with a reasonable degree of rational understanding. *See generally* Dusky v. United States, 362 U.S. 402 (1960) (per curiam).

A defendant has only limited discovery rights before pleading guilty. As discussed in Chapter 8, in United States v. Ruiz, 536 U.S. 622 (2002), the Supreme Court held that the Constitution does not require prosecutors to disclose "impeachment information relating to any informants or other witnesses" before entering into a binding plea agreement with the defendant. The Supreme Court has not yet decided whether directly exculpatory evidence must be revealed, but lower courts have allowed defendants to withdraw their guilty pleas when the prosecutor failed to disclose exculpatory information prior to the defendant's guilty plea. *See, e.g.,* State v. Harris, 266 Wis. 2d 200, 667 N.W. 813 (Wis. App. 2003). Given that innocent people sometimes plead guilty,[18] it is important to consider carefully how much information a defendant should have before entering a knowing and voluntary plea.

A guilty plea ordinarily effectively ends the prosecution except for sentencing. By pleading guilty, a defendant waives the right to appeal the denial of a motion to suppress. In order to preserve this right, the defendant must enter a conditional plea.

E. REMEDIES FOR VIOLATIONS OF PLEA AGREEMENTS

Plea agreements are treated as contracts and are enforceable under contract principles. Thus, if a guilty plea is based on a plea agreement, both the prosecution and defense have the right to enforce that agreement.

SANTOBELLO v. NEW YORK

404 U.S. 257 (1971)

Chief Justice BURGER delivered the opinion of the Court.

We granted certiorari in this case to determine whether the State's failure to keep a commitment concerning the sentence recommendation on a guilty plea required a new trial.

---

18. *See generally* Andrew D. Leipold, *How the Pretrial Process Contributes to Wrongful Convictions*, 42 Am. Crim. L. Rev. 1123 (2005).

The facts are not in dispute. The State of New York indicted petitioner in 1969 on two felony counts, Promoting Gambling in the First Degree, and Possession of Gambling Records in the First Degree. Petitioner first entered a plea of not guilty to both counts. After negotiations, the Assistant District Attorney in charge of the case agreed to permit petitioner to plead guilty to a lesser-included offense, Possession of Gambling Records in the Second Degree, conviction of which would carry a maximum prison sentence of one year. The prosecutor agreed to make no recommendation as to the sentence.

On June 16, 1969, petitioner accordingly withdrew his plea of not guilty and entered a plea of guilty to the lesser charge. At [sentencing], another prosecutor had replaced the prosecutor who had negotiated the plea. The new prosecutor recommended the maximum one-year sentence. In making this recommendation, he cited petitioner's criminal record and alleged links with organized crime. Defense counsel immediately objected on the ground that the State had promised petitioner before the plea was entered that there would be no sentence recommendation by the prosecution. He sought to adjourn the sentence hearing in order to have time to prepare proof of the first prosecutor's promise. The second prosecutor, apparently ignorant of his colleague's commitment, argued that there was nothing in the record to support petitioner's claim of a promise, but the State, in subsequent proceedings, has not contested that such a promise was made.

The sentencing judge ended discussion, with the following statement, quoting extensively from the presentence report:

"[Defense Counsel], I am not at all influenced by what the District Attorney says, so that there is no need to adjourn the sentence, and there is no need to have any testimony. It doesn't make a particle of difference what the District Attorney says he will do, or what he doesn't do.

"I have here . . . a probation report. I have here a history of a long, long serious criminal record. I have here a picture of the life history of this man. . . .

"'He is unamenable to supervision in the community. He is a professional criminal.'" Under the plea, I can only send him to the New York City Correctional Institution for men for one year, which I am hereby doing."

The judge then imposed the maximum sentence of one year.

This record represents another example of an unfortunate lapse in orderly prosecutorial procedures, in part, no doubt, because of the enormous increase in the workload of the often understaffed prosecutor's offices. The heavy workload may well explain these episodes, but it does not excuse them. The disposition of criminal charges by agreement between the prosecutor and the accused, sometimes loosely called "plea bargaining," is an essential component of the administration of justice. Properly administered, it is to be encouraged. If every criminal charge were subjected to a full-scale trial, the States and the Federal Government would need to multiply by many times the number of judges and court facilities.

Disposition of charges after plea discussions is not only an essential part of the process but a highly desirable part for many reasons. It leads to prompt and largely final disposition of most criminal cases; it avoids much of the corrosive impact of enforced idleness during pretrial confinement for those who are denied release pending trial; it protects the public from those accused persons who are prone to continue criminal conduct even while on pretrial release; and, by shortening the time between charge and disposition, it enhances whatever may be the rehabilitative prospects of the guilty when they are ultimately imprisoned. *See* Brady v. United States (1970). [W]hen a plea rests in any significant degree on a promise or agreement of the prosecutor, so that it can be said to be part of the inducement or consideration, such promise must be fulfilled.

On this record, petitioner "bargained" and negotiated for a particular plea in order to secure dismissal of more serious charges, but also on condition that no sentence recommendation would be made by the prosecutor. It is now conceded that the promise to abstain from a recommendation was made, and at this stage the prosecution is not in a good position to argue that its inadvertent breach of agreement is immaterial. The staff lawyers in a prosecutor's office have the burden of "letting the left hand know what the right hand is doing" or has done. That the breach of agreement was inadvertent does not lessen its impact.

We need not reach the question whether the sentencing judge would or would not have been influenced had he known all the details of the negotiations for the plea. He stated that the prosecutor's recommendation did not influence him and we have no reason to doubt that. Nevertheless, we conclude that the interests of justice and appropriate recognition of the duties of the prosecution in relation to promises made in the negotiation of pleas of guilty will be best served by remanding the case to the state courts for further consideration. The ultimate relief to which petitioner is entitled we leave to the discretion of the state court, which is in a better position to decide whether the circumstances of this case require only that there be specific performance of the agreement on the plea, in which case petitioner should be resentenced by a different judge, or whether, in the view of the state court, the circumstances require granting the relief sought by petitioner, i.e., the opportunity to withdraw his plea of guilty. We emphasize that this is in no sense to question the fairness of the sentencing judge; the fault here rests on the prosecutor, not on the sentencing judge.

The judgment is vacated and the case is remanded for reconsideration not inconsistent with this opinion.

Justice DOUGLAS, concurring.

I join the opinion of the Court and add only a word. [There] is no excuse for the default merely because a member of the prosecutor's staff who was not a party to the "plea bargain" was in charge of the case when it came before the New York court. The staff of the prosecution is a unit and each member must be presumed to know the commitments made by any other member.

[It] is . . . clear that a prosecutor's promise may deprive a guilty plea of the "character of a voluntary act." Where the "plea bargain" is not kept by the prosecutor, the sentence must be vacated and the state court will decide in light of the circumstances of each case whether due process requires (a) that there be specific performance of the plea bargain or (b) that the defendant be given the option to go to trial on the original charges. One alternative may do justice in one case, and the other in a different case. In choosing a remedy, however, a court ought to accord a defendant's preference considerable, if not controlling, weight inasmuch as the fundamental rights flouted by a prosecutor's breach of a plea bargain are those of the defendant, not of the State.

Just as the Court found in Santobello v. New York that a defendant is entitled to have a plea agreement enforced, the Court held in Ricketts v. Adamson that the defendant can be held to his side of the bargain.

RICKETTS v. ADAMSON
483 U.S. 1 (1987)

Justice WHITE delivered the opinion of the Court.

The question for decision is whether the Double Jeopardy Clause bars the prosecution of respondent for first-degree murder following his breach of a plea agreement. The Court of Appeals for the Ninth Circuit held that the prosecution of respondent violated double jeopardy principles and directed the issuance of a writ of habeas corpus. We reverse.

In 1976, Donald Bolles, a reporter for the Arizona Republic, was fatally injured when a dynamite bomb exploded underneath his car. Respondent was arrested and charged with first-degree murder in connection with Bolles' death. Shortly after his trial had commenced, while jury selection was underway, respondent and the state prosecutor reached an agreement whereby respondent agreed to plead guilty to a charge of second-degree murder and to testify against two other individuals — Max Dunlap and James Robison — who were allegedly involved in Bolles' murder. Specifically, respondent agreed to "testify fully and completely in any Court, State or Federal, when requested by proper authorities against any and all parties involved in the murder of Don Bolles. . . ." The agreement provided that "should the defendant refuse to testify or should he at any time testify untruthfully . . . then this entire agreement is null and void and the original charge will be automatically reinstated." The parties agreed that respondent would receive a prison sentence of 48-49 years, with a total incarceration time of 20 years and 2 months. In January 1977, the state trial court accepted the plea agreement and the proposed sentence, but withheld imposition of the sentence. Thereafter, respondent testified as obligated under the agreement, and both Dunlap and Robison were convicted of the first-degree murder of Bolles. While their convictions and sentences were on appeal, the trial court, upon motion of the State, sentenced respondent. In February 1980, the Arizona Supreme Court reversed the convictions of Dunlap and Robison and remanded their cases for retrial. This event sparked the dispute now before us.

The State sought respondent's cooperation and testimony in preparation for the retrial of Dunlap and Robison. On April 3, 1980, however, respondent's counsel informed the prosecutor that respondent believed his obligation to provide testimony under the agreement had terminated when he was sentenced. Respondent would again testify against Dunlap and Robison only if certain conditions were met, including, among others, that the State release him from custody following the retrial. The State then informed respondent's attorney on April 9, 1980, that it deemed respondent to be in breach of the plea agreement. On April 18, 1980, the State called respondent to testify in pretrial proceedings. In response to questions, and upon advice of counsel, respondent invoked his Fifth Amendment privilege against self-incrimination.

On May 8, 1980, the State filed a new information charging respondent with first-degree murder. Respondent's motion to quash the information on double jeopardy grounds was denied. The court rejected respondent's double jeopardy claim, holding that the plea agreement "by its very terms waives the defense of double jeopardy if the agreement is violated."

After these rulings, respondent offered to testify at the retrials, but the State declined his offer. Respondent was then convicted of first-degree murder and sentenced to death.

Under the terms of the plea agreement, both parties bargained for and received substantial benefits. The State obtained respondent's guilty plea and his promise to testify against "any and all parties involved in the murder of Don Bolles" and in certain specified other crimes. Respondent, a direct participant in a premeditated and brutal murder, received a specified prison sentence accompanied with a guarantee that he would serve actual incarceration time of 20 years and 2 months. He further obtained the State's promise that he would not be prosecuted for his involvement in certain other crimes.

The agreement specifies in two separate paragraphs the consequences that would flow from respondent's breach of his promises. Paragraph 5 provides that if respondent refused to testify, "this entire agreement is null and void and the original charge will be automatically reinstated." Similarly, Paragraph 15 of the agreement states that "in the event this agreement becomes null and void, then the parties shall be returned to the positions they were in before this agreement." Respondent unquestionably understood the meaning of these provisions. At the plea hearing, the trial judge read the plea agreement to respondent, line by line, and pointedly asked respondent whether he understood the provisions in Paragraphs 5 and 15. Respondent replied "Yes, sir," to each question.

The State did not force the breach; respondent chose, perhaps for strategic reasons or as a gamble, to advance an interpretation of the agreement that proved erroneous. And, there is no indication that respondent did not fully understand the potential seriousness of the position he adopted. In the April 3 letter, respondent's counsel advised the prosecutor that respondent "is fully aware of the fact that your office may feel that he has not completed his obligations under the plea agreement . . . and, further, that your office may attempt to withdraw the plea agreement from him, [and] that he may be prosecuted for the killing of Donald Bolles on a first degree murder charge." This statement of respondent's awareness of the operative terms of the plea agreement only underscores that which respondent's plea hearing made evident: respondent clearly appreciated and understood the consequences were he found to be in breach of the agreement.

Finally, it is of no moment that following the Arizona Supreme Court's decision respondent offered to comply with the terms of the agreement. At this point, respondent's second-degree murder conviction had already been ordered vacated and the original charge reinstated. The parties did not agree that respondent would be relieved from the consequences of his refusal to testify if he were able to advance a colorable argument that a testimonial obligation was not owing. The parties could have struck a different bargain, but permitting the State to enforce the agreement the parties actually made does not violate the Double Jeopardy Clause.

Justice BRENNAN, with whom Justice MARSHALL, Justice BLACKMUN, and Justice STEVENS join, dissenting.

The critical question in this case is whether Adamson ever breached his plea agreement. Only by demonstrating that such a breach occurred can it plausibly be argued that Adamson waived his rights under the Double Jeopardy Clause. By simply assuming that such a breach occurred, the Court ignores the only important issue in this case.

[T]he agreement does not contain an explicit waiver of all double jeopardy protection. Adamson's interpretation of the agreement — that he was not required to testify at the retrials of Max Dunlap and James Robison — was reasonable. Nothing in the plea agreement explicitly stated that Adamson was required to provide testimony should retrials prove necessary. At the time the State demanded that Adamson testify in the retrials, Adamson had been transferred from the custody of the Pima County Sheriff. Adamson therefore could reasonably conclude that he had provided all the testimony required by the agreement, and that, as he communicated to the State by letter of April 3, 1980, the testimony demanded by the State went beyond his duties under the agreement.[19] Adamson's interpretation of the agreement was

---

19. Prior to sentencing, Adamson had provided extensive testimony for the State. He testified that he had "made 14 court appearances . . . on five separate cases consisting of approximately 31

"reasonabl[e]," and was supported by the plain language of the agreement, "logic, and common sense."

[T]he law of commercial contract may in some cases prove useful as an analogy or point of departure in construing a plea agreement, or in framing the terms of the debate. [But] the values that underlie commercial contract law, and that govern the relations between economic actors, are not coextensive with those that underlie the Due Process Clause. Unlike some commercial contracts, plea agreements must be construed in light of the rights and obligations created by the Constitution.

Even if one assumes, *arguendo*, that Adamson breached his plea agreement by offering an erroneous interpretation of that agreement, it still does not follow that the State was entitled to retry Adamson on charges of first-degree murder. [I]mmediately following the decision of the Arizona Supreme Court adopting the State's construction of the plea agreement, Adamson sent a letter to the State stating that he was ready and willing to testify. At this point, there was no obstacle to proceeding with the retrials of Dunlap and Robison; each case had been dismissed without prejudice to refiling, and only about one month's delay had resulted from the dispute over the scope of the plea agreement. Thus, what the State sought from Adamson — testimony in the Dunlap and Robison trials — was available to it.

The State decided instead to abandon the prosecution of Dunlap and Robison, and to capitalize on what it regarded as Adamson's breach by seeking the death penalty against him. No doubt it seemed easier to proceed against Adamson at that point, since the State had the benefit of his exhaustive testimony about his role in the murder of Don Bolles. But even in the world of commercial contracts it has long been settled that the party injured by a breach must nevertheless take all reasonable steps to minimize the consequent damage.

The Court's decision flouts the law of contract, due process, and double jeopardy. It reflects a world where individuals enter agreements with the State only at their peril, where the Constitution does not demand of the State the minimal good faith and responsibility that the common law imposes on commercial enterprises, and where, in blind deference to state courts and prosecutors, this Court abdicates its duty to uphold the Constitution. I dissent.

F.   WITHDRAWAL OF GUILTY PLEAS

Ordinarily, after a defendant pleads guilty, the final step in the criminal process is for the defendant to be sentenced. A guilty plea is a waiver of

---

days of testimony. . . . Of the 81 or so jurors who have heard my testimony all have returned guilty verdicts in each case resulting in seven convictions. I have been cross-examined under oath for approximately 190 hours . . . by 22 different attorneys. . . . I have cooperated in approximately 205 interrogative sessions. . . . Fifty-five of these have been formal face-to-face in-depth question and answer sessions, approximately." [Footnote by the Court.]

the defendant's right to challenge the prosecution's case, unless the defendant has entered a conditional plea reserving issues for appeal.

Occasionally, defendants want to withdraw their guilty pleas after they are entered. Federal Rule of Criminal Procedure 11 provides that, before a guilty plea is accepted, the defendant may withdraw a guilty plea for any reason. However, once a defendant has entered his plea and the court has accepted it, a guilty plea may be withdrawn only for a "fair and just" reason.

Judges have broad latitude in deciding whether to allow the withdrawal of a guilty plea after they have accepted it. In making this decision, a court must consider the need for finality in guilty pleas, the defendant's reasons for withdrawing the plea, and the prejudice to the prosecution by allowing withdrawal of the plea.

If a defendant is not allowed to withdraw a guilty plea, his only options are to appeal the court's decision or to raise a collateral challenge to the plea. Not all errors in guilty pleas will result in reversals of convictions, however. Errors that do not affect a defendant's "substantial rights" are regarded as harmless. While the reviewing court will ordinarily rely only on the transcript of a plea to determine whether the plea was properly entered, if a defendant does not object to his plea, the court can look outside the transcript.

For example, in United States v. Vonn, 535 U.S. 55 (2002), defendant Alphonso Vonn did not object when the judge took his guilty plea to a firearm charge, even though the judge failed to mention that Vonn had a right to counsel if he went to trial. Instead, Vonn raised the issue on appeal after the trial court denied Vonn's motion to withdraw his guilty plea. The Supreme Court held that because defendant did not make an objection to the trial court, it was his burden to satisfy the plain-error rule. The Supreme Court found that Vonn could not satisfy that burden because transcripts of other proceedings in his case demonstrated that Vonn had been advised on multiple occasions of his right to counsel. He was advised at his initial appearance before the magistrate judge and twice at his first arraignment. At least four times Vonn or his counsel either affirmed that Vonn had heard or read a statement of his rights and understood what they were. Because the overall record of the case demonstrated that Vonn knew he had the right to counsel, the trial court's failure to advise Vonn of this right at the guilty plea hearing did not undermine his guilty plea. As Justice Souter wrote for a unanimous Court, a defendant must be "on his toes" to ensure that the court correctly conducts the plea hearing. If a defendant is aware of a mistake in the plea procedures at the time they are conducted, he must object when the problem can still be fixed. Otherwise, the court will look to the rest of the defendant's case record to determine whether the defendant was aware of his rights at the time of the guilty plea.

CHAPTER
10

SPEEDY TRIAL RIGHTS

A. INTRODUCTION

The Sixth Amendment provides that "[i]n all criminal prosecutions, the accused shall enjoy the right to a speedy and public trial."[1] The Framers considered the right to a speedy trial to be so important that they included it as a basic guarantee in the Bill of Rights. Yet they did not spell out in the Sixth Amendment what standard should be used to determine whether a defendant's right has been violated. Rather, like other constitutional rights, it was left to the Supreme Court to determine the contours of the right to a speedy trial. In making this decision, the Court turned to the purposes served by a speedy trial right.

Section B of this chapter focuses on the policy concerns underlying the right to a speedy trial. Whose interests does it serve? Why is it so important that criminal cases be processed in an expeditious manner? These policy interests underlie the standards created by the Court for speedy trial rights.

Although we speak generally about the "right to a speedy trial," there are really two standards at issue: (1) rules governing delay during the period from the commitment of the crime until arrest or formal charging and (2) rules governing delays during the period from charging until trial. Section C examines each of these types of delay and the standards that apply.

Finally, section D discusses the remedy for a speedy trial violation, while section E addresses whether speedy trial rights apply to sentencing.

B. WHY SPEEDY TRIAL RIGHTS MATTER

To understand why speedy trial rights matter, it is useful to put oneself in the shoes of those most affected by the criminal justice process. If a crime occurs and it takes years for it to be charged or to go to trial, how are the interests of the defendant, victim, prosecutor, witnesses, and public affected? In making

---

1. The Sixth Amendment right to a speedy trial is a fundamental right that applies to states. *See* Klopfer v. North Carolina, 386 U.S. 213 (1967).

that determination, consider the speedy trial concerns raised by the following two cases.

RIGHT TO A SPEEDY TRIAL? JUSTICE DELAYED

The Atlanta Journal-Constitution, Oct. 14, 2007

With his monotone speech, robotic movements, and a plastic tube snaking from his nostrils to a battery-powered oxygen source, Edward Kramer is beginning to resemble the science-fiction characters he writes about.

He's well-known as a science-fiction author and founder of DragonCon, a sci-fi, fantasy and gaming convention that brings thousands of visitors and millions of dollars to Atlanta every year.

Yet Kramer is also known for something else: Investigators say he molested three teenage boys.

Kramer maintains his innocence.

Police first arrested Kramer on Aug. 25, 2000 — more than seven years ago — but the case has not yet gone to trial.

Legal experts say a seven-year delay is unusual and potentially damaging, as memories fade and evidence deteriorates. Former U.S. Rep. Bob Barr, a former federal prosecutor, filed court papers this year that decry "an overwhelming sense of injustice" toward Kramer.

Prosecutors say Kramer has mischaracterized his illness and orchestrated several delays to stave off a possible 60-year prison sentence.

Nevertheless, "the amount of time here raises eyebrows," said Ron Carlson, a criminal law professor at the University of Georgia.

As he waits for his day in court, Kramer lives in his two-story home in Duluth, where he's been under house arrest since early 2001.

He has shelled out more than $250,000 in legal fees, according to a Web site his supporters maintain, and he says he's running out of money.

He no longer has an active role with DragonCon — Kramer said he resigned as convention chairman in 2000 to avoid bringing the event negative publicity.

"I'm a whole lot weaker now than I was before," Kramer said in an interview this month as he sat tethered to an oxygen tank under the shade of a patio umbrella.

He said he suffers debilitating back pain, the result of spinal injuries he suffered in jail and in a subsequent car accident. The spinal injuries caused a partial paralysis of his diaphragm, which makes it difficult to breathe.

"It's like my life has essentially halted for seven years waiting for this to end," Kramer said.

The lives of two brothers also have changed. They were 13 and 15 when Kramer began dating their mother.

Kramer dazzled them with action figures, sci-fi memorabilia and celebrity connections, their mother said. The boys told police that Kramer took advantage of them during sleepovers.

Now the brothers are in their 20s and in the Army. One serves in South Korea. The other will be deployed to Iraq in February.

STATE LOSES APPEAL IN CHILD-RAPE CASE

Kate Wilson, Albuquerque Journal, Oct. 14, 2006

The New Mexico Court of Appeals has upheld a 2005 ruling by Santa Fe state District Judge Michael Vigil, who threw out a case of alleged sex abuse after he found the defendant's speedy trial rights had been violated.

Paul Stock sat in jail for nearly 3½ years while a series of overburdened public defenders failed to move the case along.

Stock had been charged with raping a preteen.

"The delay is in part attributable to the neglect of his overworked public defenders," Appeals Court Judge Lynn Pickard states in the Sept. 29 ruling.

But prosecutors were also to blame, the appeals court judge wrote.

"It is ultimately the state's burden to make sure that defendants are brought to trial in a timely manner," Pickard wrote.

"Throughout this case, the state did little or nothing to ascertain what was happening in the case or to move the case forward. . . . We think the state's inaction in this case can be characterized as "bureaucratic indifference," which we have held to weigh against the state more heavily than mere negligence."

The delays in the case started in February 2001, when Stock's defense counsel requested an extension of time so Stock's competency could be evaluated.

At [a] hearing [regarding the delay] in August 2005, Stock's series of three attorneys testified. They carried heavy case loads, often up to 300 each. They said they didn't have the resources to both pursue the issue of competency and investigate the merits of the case.

After the hearing, Vigil dismissed the case again, saying, "It is humanly impossible for lawyers to practice law under the conditions that we're asking them to practice law."

Vigil said he would continue dismissing cases that were not properly prosecuted.

JUDGE DISMISSES MOLESTATION CASE — AGAIN

Jason Auslander, Santa Fe New Mexican, Aug. 24, 2005

The girl's father said after Tuesday's hearing that the dismissal felt "like an injustice" to his daughter, whom Stock was accused of abusing beginning when she was 7, as well as the rest of his family. He said his daughter has been in therapy for five years, and is undergoing treatment at a voluntary foster-care facility. He said he placed 70 percent of the blame for the dismissal on the defense and 30 percent on the prosecution.

In the end, Vigil dismissed the case against Stock "reluctantly," saying he felt badly that the alleged victim in the case wouldn't get her day in court. He also chastised prosecutors for letting Stock sit in jail for so long, saying they had an obligation to schedule a hearing to determine the status of the case.

"The Constitution requires minimum standards be followed and this case falls way below them," Vigil said.

As these excerpts highlight, delay in the criminal justice process can detrimentally affect the defense, the prosecution, victims, witnesses, courts, and the public.

1.   Impact on the Defendant

There are many ways that a defendant can be prejudiced by pretrial delay. First, and foremost, if a defendant is in custody, he loses his liberty even though a jury has not found him guilty of any crime. While in custody, a defendant may lose his livelihood and the support of his family and community. Pretrial delay also prolongs the anxiety a defendant faces before trial. Even defendants who are not in custody suffer from this anxiety and must bear the stigma of being charged with a crime. Long-term pretrial delay is demoralizing; a defendant must live under a cloud of suspicion until his name is cleared.

Second, pretrial delay can result in the loss of evidence. Witnesses' memories tend to fade with time. Physical evidence may disappear and a defendant's own memory of what occurred may become blurred. A defendant has a due process right to present a defense, but this cannot be done if pretrial delay has made it impossible to secure the evidence needed for a defense.

2.   Impact on the Prosecution and Witnesses

Defendants, of course, are not the only ones who suffer from pretrial delay. In fact, sometimes defendants want a delay so that it will be harder for the prosecution to present its case and meet its burden of proof beyond a reasonable doubt.

By its terms, the Sixth Amendment, like other guarantees in the Bill of Rights, only affords defendants the right to a speedy trial. This does not mean, however, that the prosecution and the public don't also have strong policy interests in a speedy trial. In addition to wanting to preserve evidence and witness testimony, prosecutors must also be concerned about the emotional toll of long delays on victims and other witnesses. Victims cannot put their experiences behind them if the criminal matter is still not resolved by the court.

3. Impact on the Public

Finally, delays in pursuing cases can impact on the public's confidence in the criminal justice system. Justice delayed is frequently viewed as justice denied. The longer it takes for a case to grind through the criminal justice system, the more resources are dedicated to that case and thus unavailable for other matters. Speedy trial delay causes congestion in the courts and undermines the efficiency of the criminal justice system.

C.   DUE PROCESS AND SPEEDY TRIAL RIGHTS

There are two periods of delay that may occur in a criminal proceeding. First, there is the period of time from commitment of the crime until charges are filed. This is referred to as "pre-charging delay." Although this delay may have an impact on a defendant's right to a fair trial, it is not covered by the defendant's Sixth Amendment right to a speedy trial. Rather, for reasons explained in the next section, the Supreme Court has held that speedy trial rights are not triggered until after a defendant has been formally charged. The period of pre-charge delay is covered by statutes of limitations and the constitutional right to due process.

The second period of delay runs from the filing of charges until the time that trial begins. This period of time is covered by the Sixth Amendment right to a speedy trial. It is often covered by Speedy Trial Acts that provide statutory limits on pretrial delay.

1. Pre-Charging Delay, Due Process Rights, and Statutes of Limitations

The Sixth Amendment right to a speedy trial does not cover all delay from the time that a defendant commits a crime until the defendant is brought to trial. Rather, the time from when a defendant commits a crime until the defendant is charged is treated differently. In United States v. Marion, the Supreme Court explained when speedy trials actually begin and what, if any, constitutional protection there is for a defendant for pre-charge delay.

UNITED STATES v. MARION
404 U.S. 307 (1971)

Justice WHITE delivered the opinion of the Court.

[Appellees] claim that their rights to a speedy trial were violated by the period of approximately three years between the end of the criminal [fraud] scheme charged and the return of the indictment; it is argued that this delay is so substantial and inherently prejudicial that the Sixth Amendment required the dismissal of the indictment. In our view, however, the Sixth Amendment speedy trial provision has no application until the putative defendant in some way becomes an "accused," an event that occurred in this case only when the appellees were indicted.

The Sixth Amendment provides that "in all criminal prosecutions, the accused shall enjoy the right to a speedy and public trial. . . ." On its face, the protection of the Amendment is activated only when a criminal prosecution has begun and extends only to those persons who have been "accused" in the course of that prosecution. These provisions would seem to afford no protection to those not yet accused, nor would they seem to require the Government to discover, investigate, and accuse any person within any particular period of time. The Amendment would appear to guarantee to a criminal defendant that the Government will move with the dispatch that is appropriate to assure him an early and proper disposition of the charges against him.

The framers could hardly have selected less appropriate language if they had intended the speedy trial provision to protect against pre-accusation delay. No opinions of this Court intimate support for appellees' thesis, and the courts of appeals that have considered the question in constitutional terms have never reversed a conviction or dismissed an indictment solely on the basis of the Sixth Amendment's speedy trial provision where only pre-indictment delay was involved.

III

Invocation of the speedy trial provision thus need not await indictment, information, or other formal charge. But we decline to extend the reach of the amendment to the period prior to arrest. Until this event occurs, a citizen suffers no restraints on his liberty and is not the subject of public accusation: his situation does not compare with that of a defendant who has been arrested and held to answer. Passage of time, whether before or after arrest, may impair memories, cause evidence to be lost, deprive the defendant of witnesses, and otherwise interfere with his ability to defend himself. But this possibility of prejudice at trial is not itself sufficient reason to wrench the Sixth Amendment from its proper context.

The law has provided other mechanisms to guard against possible as distinguished from actual prejudice resulting from the passage of time between crime and arrest or charge. As we said, "the applicable statute of limitations . . . is . . . the primary guarantee against bringing overly stale criminal charges." Such statutes represent legislative assessments of relative interests of the State and the defendant in administering and receiving justice; they "are made for the repose of society and the protection of those who may [during the limitation] . . . have lost their means of defence." These statutes provide predictability by specifying a limit beyond which there is an irrebuttable presumption that a defendant's right to a fair trial would be prejudiced. As this Court observed [previously]:

> The purpose of a statute of limitations is to limit exposure to criminal prosecution to a certain fixed period of time following the occurrence of those acts the legislature has decided to punish by criminal sanctions. Such a limitation is designed to protect individuals from having to defend themselves against charges when the basic facts may have become obscured by the passage of time and to minimize the danger of official punishment because of acts in the far-distant past. Such a time limit may also have the salutary effect of encouraging law enforcement officials promptly to investigate suspected criminal activity.

There is thus no need to press the Sixth Amendment into service to guard against the mere possibility that pre-accusation delays will prejudice the defense in a criminal case since statutes of limitation already perform that function.

[T]he Government [also] concedes that the Due Process Clause of the Fifth Amendment would require dismissal of the indictment if it were shown at trial that the pre-indictment delay in this case caused substantial prejudice to appellees' rights to a fair trial and that the delay was an intentional device to gain tactical advantage over the accused. However, we need not, and could not now, determine when and in what circumstances actual prejudice resulting from pre-accusation delays requires the dismissal of the prosecution. Actual prejudice to the defense of a criminal case may result from the shortest and most necessary delay; and no one suggests that every delay-caused detriment to a defendant's case should abort a criminal prosecution. To accommodate the sound administration of justice to the rights of the defendant to a fair trial will necessarily involve a delicate judgment based on the circumstances of each case. It would be unwise at this juncture to attempt to forecast our decision in such cases.

The 38-month delay between the end of the scheme charged in the indictment and the date the defendants were indicted did not extend beyond the period of the applicable statute of limitations here. Appellees have not, of course, been able to claim undue delay pending trial, since the indictment was brought on April 21, 1970, and dismissed on June 8, 1970. Nor have appellees adequately demonstrated that the pre-indictment delay by the Government violated the Due Process Clause. No actual prejudice to the conduct of the defense is alleged or proved, and there is no showing that the Government intentionally delayed to gain some tactical advantage over appellees or to harass them. Appellees rely solely on the real possibility of prejudice inherent in any extended delay: that memories will dim, witnesses become inaccessible, and evidence be lost. In light of the applicable statute of limitations, however, these possibilities are not in themselves enough to demonstrate that appellees cannot receive a fair trial and to therefore justify the dismissal of the indictment.

Justice DOUGLAS, with whom Justice BRENNAN and Justice MARSHALL join, concurring in the result.

Much is made of the history of the Sixth Amendment as indicating that the speedy trial guarantee had no application to pre-prosecution delays.

There are two answers to that proposition. First, British courts historically did consider delay as a condition to issuance of an information. . . . Second, and more basically, the 18th century criminal prosecution at the common law was in general commenced in a completely different way from that with which we are familiar today. By the common law of England which was brought to the American colonies, the ordinary criminal prosecution was conducted by a private prosecutor, in the name of the King. In case the victim of the crime or someone interested came forward to prosecute, he retained his own counsel and had charge of the case as in the usual civil proceeding. . . . Procedurally, the criminal prosecution was commenced by the filing of a lawsuit, and thereafter the filing of an application for criminal prosecution. . . . The English common law, with which the Framers were familiar, conceived of a criminal prosecution as being commenced prior to indictment. Thus in that setting the individual charged as the defendant in a criminal proceeding could and would be an "accused" prior to formal indictment.

"The Speedy Trial Clause protects societal interests, as well as those of the accused. The public is concerned with the effective prosecution of criminal cases, both to restrain those guilty of crime and to deter those contemplating it. Just as delay may impair the ability of the accused to defend himself, so it may reduce the capacity of the government to prove its case. Moreover, while awaiting trial, an accused who is at large may become a fugitive from justice or commit other criminal acts. And the greater the lapse of time between commission of an offense and the conviction of the offender, the less the deterrent value of his conviction."

At least some of these values served by the right to a speedy trial are not unique to any particular stage of the criminal proceeding. Undue delay may be as offensive to the right to a speedy trial before as after an indictment or information. The anxiety and concern attendant on public accusation may weigh more heavily upon an individual who has not yet been formally indicted or arrested for, to him, exoneration by a jury of his peers may be only a vague possibility lurking in the distant future. Indeed, the protection underlying the right to a speedy trial may be denied when a citizen is damned by clandestine innuendo and never given the chance promptly to defend himself in a court of law. Those who are accused of crime but never tried may lose their jobs or their positions of responsibility, or become outcasts in their communities.

The impairment of the ability to defend oneself may become acute because of delays in the pre-indictment stage. Those delays may result in the loss of alibi witnesses, the destruction of material evidence, and the blurring of memories. At least when a person has been accused of a specific crime, he can devote his powers of recall to the events surrounding the alleged occurrences. When there is no formal accusation, however, the State may proceed methodically to build its case while the prospective defendant proceeds to lose his.

In the present case, two to three years elapsed between the time the District Court found that the charges could and should have been brought and the actual return of the indictment. The justifications offered were that the United States Attorney's office was "not sufficiently staffed to proceed as expeditiously" as desirable and that priority had been given to other cases. . . . They argue that there is a great likelihood that the recollection of such events will be blurred or erased by the frailties of the human memory. If this were a simpler crime, I think the British precedent which I have cited would warrant dismissal of the indictment because of the speedy trial guarantee of the Sixth Amendment. But we know from experience that the nature of the crime charged here often has vast interstate aspects, the victims are often widely scattered and hard to locate, and the reconstruction of the total scheme of the fraudulent plan takes time. . . . I think a three-year delay even in that kind of case goes to the edge of a permissible delay. But on the bare bones of this record I hesitate to say that the guarantee of a speedy trial has been violated.

As established in *Marion*, the Sixth Amendment's speedy trial right does not apply to pre-charging delay. Rather, a defendant's rights during that time period are protected by statutes of limitations and the right to due process. A charge cannot be filed outside the statute of limitations. Different jurisdictions set different statutes of limitations for crimes. The length of time selected reflects the seriousness of the crime and how long it might take to investigate it. For example, consider the following sampling of federal statute of limitations laws and why Congress set the time periods they did in each statute.

FEDERAL STATUTES OF LIMITATION

18 U.S.C. §3281. Capital offenses

An indictment for any offense punishable by death may be found at any time without limitation.

18 U.S.C. §3282. Offenses not capital

(a) In general—Except as otherwise expressly provided by law, no person shall be prosecuted, tried or punished for any offense, not capital, unless the indictment is found or the information is instituted within five years next after such offense shall have been committed.

18 U.S.C. §3283. Offenses against children

No statute of limitations that would otherwise preclude prosecution for an offense involving the sexual or physical abuse, or kidnapping, of a child under the age of 18 years shall preclude such prosecution during the life of the child, or for ten years after the offense, whichever is longer.

18 U.S.C. §3286. Extension of statute of limitation for certain terrorism offenses

(a) Eight-year limitation — Notwithstanding section 3282, no person shall be prosecuted, tried, or punished for any noncapital offense involving [certain terrorism crimes], unless the indictment is found or the information is instituted within 8 years after the offense was committed.

(b) No limitation — Notwithstanding any other law, an indictment may be found or any information instituted at any time without limitation for any [terrorism offense], if the commission of such offense resulted in, or created a foreseeable risk of, death or serious bodily injury to another person.

18 U.S.C. §3290. Fugitive from justice

No statute of limitations shall extend to any person fleeing from justice.

18 U.S.C. §3293. Financial institution offenses

No person shall be prosecuted, tried, or punished for a violation of, or a conspiracy to violate — [certain offenses affecting financial institutions] unless the indictment is returned or the information is filed within 10 years after the commission of the offense.

18 U.S.C. §3294. Theft of major artwork

No person shall be prosecuted, tried, or punished for a violation of or conspiracy [to steal major art works] unless the indictment is returned or the information is filed within 20 years after the commission of the offense.

18 U.S.C. §3297. Cases involving DNA evidence

In a case in which DNA testing implicates an identified person in the commission of a felony, no statute of limitations that would otherwise preclude prosecution of the offense shall preclude such prosecution until a period of time following the implication of the person by DNA testing has elapsed that is equal to the otherwise applicable limitation period.

Although protection from pre-charging delay lies with the statute of limitations, a defendant also has a constitutional right to argue a due process violation if the delay is too long. As the court briefly explained in *Marion*, the due process standard is a high one. Mere possibility of prejudice is insufficient. The defendant must show intentional delay to give the government a tactical advantage and actual prejudice caused by the delay.

Six years after *Marion*, the Supreme Court took a closer look at due process challenges to pre-charging delay, elaborating on why it had set the standard so high for claims of pre-charging delay.

UNITED STATES v. LOVASCO
431 U.S. 783 (1977)

Justice MARSHALL delivered the opinion of the Court.

On March 6, 1975, respondent was indicted for possessing eight firearms stolen from the United States mails, and for dealing in firearms without a license. The offenses were alleged to have occurred between July 25 and August 31, 1973, more than 18 months before the indictment was filed. Respondent moved to dismiss the indictment due to the delay.

The District Court conducted a hearing on respondent's motion at which the respondent sought to prove that the delay was unnecessary and that it had prejudiced his defense. In an effort to establish the former proposition, respondent presented a Postal Inspector's report on his investigation that was prepared one month after the crimes were committed, and a stipulation concerning the post-report progress of the probe. The report stated, in brief, that within the first month of the investigation respondent had admitted to Government agents that he had possessed and then sold five of the stolen guns, and that the agents had developed strong evidence linking respondent to the remaining three weapons. The report also stated, however, that the agents had been unable to confirm or refute respondent's claim that he had found the guns in his car when he returned to it after visiting his son, a mail handler, at work. [L]ittle additional information concerning the crimes was uncovered in the 17 months following the preparation of the Inspector's report.

To establish prejudice to the defense, respondent testified that he had lost the testimony of two material witnesses due to the delay. The first witness, Tom Stewart, died more than a year after the alleged crimes occurred. At the hearing respondent claimed that Stewart had been his source for two or three of the guns. The second witness, respondent's brother, died in April 1974, eight months after the crimes were completed. Respondent testified that his brother was present when respondent called Stewart to secure the guns, and witnessed all of respondent's sales. Respondent did not state how the witnesses would have aided the defense had they been willing to testify.

Government made no systematic effort in the District Court to explain its long delay. The Assistant United States Attorney did expressly disagree, however, with defense counsel's suggestion that the investigation had ended after the Postal Inspector's report was prepared.

II

In United States v. Marion (1971), this Court considered the significance, for constitutional purposes, of a lengthy preindictment delay. We held that as far as the Speedy Trial Clause of the Sixth Amendment is concerned, such delay is wholly irrelevant, since our analysis of the language, history, and purposes of the Clause persuaded us that only "a formal indictment or information or else the actual restraints imposed by arrest and holding to answer a criminal charge . . . engage the particular protections" of that provision. We went on to note that statutes of limitations, which provide predictable, legislatively enacted limits on prosecutorial delay, provide "the primary guarantee against bringing overly stale criminal charges." But we did acknowledge that the "statute of limitations does not fully define [defendants'] rights with respect to the events occurring prior to indictment," and that the Due Process Clause has a limited role to play in protecting against oppressive delay.

Thus *Marion* makes clear that proof of prejudice is generally a necessary but not sufficient element of a due process claim, and that the due process inquiry must consider the reasons for the delay as well as the prejudice to the accused.

The Court of Appeals found that the sole reason for the delay here was "a hope on the part of the Government that others might be discovered who may have participated in the theft. . . ." It concluded that this hope did not justify the delay, and therefore affirmed the dismissal of the indictment. But the Due Process Clause does not permit courts to abort criminal prosecutions simply because they disagree with a prosecutor's judgment as to when to seek an indictment.

It might be argued that once the Government has assembled sufficient evidence to prove guilt beyond a reasonable doubt, it should be constitutionally required to file charges promptly, even if its investigation of the entire criminal transaction is not complete. Adopting such a rule, however, would have many of the same consequences as adopting a rule requiring immediate prosecution upon probable cause.

First, compelling a prosecutor to file public charges as soon as the requisite proof has been developed against one participant on one charge would cause numerous problems in those cases in which a criminal transaction involves more than one person or more than one illegal act. In some instances, an immediate arrest or indictment would impair the prosecutor's ability to continue his investigation, thereby preventing society from bringing lawbreakers to justice. In other cases, the prosecutor would be able to obtain additional indictments despite an early prosecution, but the necessary result would be multiple trials involving a single set of facts. Such trials place needless burdens on defendants, law enforcement officials, and courts.

Second, insisting on immediate prosecution once sufficient evidence is developed to obtain a conviction would pressure prosecutors into resolving doubtful cases in favor of early — and possibly unwarranted — prosecutions.

Finally requiring the Government to make charging decisions immediately upon assembling evidence sufficient to establish guilt would preclude the Government from giving full consideration to the desirability of not prosecuting in particular cases.

In our view, investigative delay is fundamentally unlike delay undertaken by the Government solely "to gain tactical advantage over the accused," precisely because investigative delay is not so one-sided. Rather than deviating from elementary standards of "fair play and decency," a prosecutor abides by them if he refuses to seek indictments until he is completely satisfied that he should prosecute and will be able promptly to establish guilt beyond a reasonable doubt. Penalizing prosecutors who defer action for these reasons would subordinate the goal of "orderly expedition" to that of "mere speed." This the Due Process Clause does not require. We therefore hold that to prosecute a defendant following investigative delay does not deprive him of due process, even if his defense might have been somewhat prejudiced by the lapse of time.

Justice STEVENS, dissenting.

If the record presented the question which the Court decides today, I would join its well-reasoned opinion. I am unable to do so because I believe [the record does not support the majority's findings].

After a thorough hearing on the respondent's motion to dismiss the indictment for prejudicial preindictment delay—a hearing at which both sides were given every opportunity to submit evidence concerning the question—the District Court found that "[t]he Government's delay ha[d] not been explained or justified and [was] unnecessary and unreasonable."

The findings of the District Court, as approved by the Court of Appeals, establish four relevant propositions: (1) this is a routine prosecution; (2) after the Government assembled all of the evidence on which it expects to establish respondent's guilt, it waited almost 18 months to seek an indictment; (3) the delay was prejudicial to respondent's defense; and (4) no reason whatsoever explains the delay. We may reasonably infer that the prosecutor was merely busy with other matters that he considered more important than this case.

The question presented by those facts is not an easy one. Nevertheless, unless we are to conclude that the Constitution imposes no constraints on the prosecutor's power to postpone the filing of formal charges to suit his own convenience, I believe we must affirm the judgment of the Court of Appeals.

The requirement of speedy justice has been part of the Anglo-American common law tradition since the Magna Carta. It came to this country and was embodied in the early state constitutions and later in the Sixth Amendment to the United States Constitution. As applied to this case, in which respondent made numerous anxious inquiries of the Postal Inspectors concerning whether he would be indicted, in which the delay caused substantial prejudice to the respondent, and in which the Government has offered no justification for the delay, the right to speedy justice should be honored.

There are benefits and burdens of extensive pre-indictment investigation. Sometimes, additional investigation can lead to the discovery of evidence that will show that the defendant was not responsible for the alleged crime. By awaiting this additional information, the prosecution prevents faulty prosecutions and the defendant avoids prosecution.

However, lengthy investigative delay also gives the prosecution additional time to find more evidence to prove its case. Moreover, if exculpatory evidence is not found during that time, it makes it difficult for the defense to argue that the prosecution conducted a rushed and inadequate investigation.

2.   *Post-Charging Delay and Speedy Trial Rights*

The Sixth Amendment right to a speedy trial applies to the period of time from arrest or formal charging until the beginning of trial. Where the pre-charging period is governed by statutory protections in the form of statutes of limitations and the constitutional protections of due process, the period from formal charges to trial is likewise controlled by statutes and constitutional protections.

a.   Statutory Protections

Each jurisdiction has a Speedy Trial Act that commonly prescribes the time period for bringing an accused to trial. For example, under the federal Speedy Trial Act, 18 U.S.C. §3161, trial must begin within 70 days of the filing of an information or indictment or the defendant's initial appearance, unless there is excludable delay.[2] The Act then defines what constitutes "excludable delay." This may include delay due to pretrial motions (18 U.S.C. §3161(h)(1)(F)) or the unavailability of the defendant or an essential witness (18 U.S.C. §3161(h)(3)(A)). There is also a catch-all provision that allows for excludable delay when the court determines it is necessary to serve "the ends of justice" (18 U.S.C. §3161(h)(8)).

If there is a violation of the Speedy Trial Act, the judge must decide whether to dismiss with or without prejudice. In making this decision, the court must consider, among other things, "the seriousness of the offense; the facts and circumstances of the case which led to the dismissal; and the impact of reprosecution on the administration of [the Speedy Trial Act] and on the administration of justice." 18 U.S.C. §3162(a)(2).

The purpose of the Speedy Trial Act is not just to protect a defendant's right to a speedy trial; it is also designed to protect the public's interest in a speedy trial. There are many defendants, especially those on pretrial release,

---

2. The federal Speedy Trial Act is set forth in the Statutory Supplement.

who may welcome lengthy pretrial delay. However, the public continues to have an interest in the expeditious processing of cases. Because of this public interest, the Supreme Court held in Zedner v. United States, 547 U.S. 489 (2006), that a defendant cannot prospectively waive application of the Speedy Trial Act. It also held in Bloate v. United States, 559 U.S. 196 (2010), that the act's provisions for allowing excludable time should be read narrowly and do not automatically exclude time used to prepare defense pretrial motions.

b. Constitutional Protection

The Sixth Amendment provides for a speedy trial once a person has been formally accused. Thus, apart from the Speedy Trial Act, a defendant has a right to contest a lengthy post-charging delay as a violation of the defendant's right to a speedy trial. However, the language of the Sixth Amendment does not define how long a delay is too long. When does post-charge delay become a Sixth Amendment violation and what approach should be used to make this determination?

BARKER v. WINGO
407 U.S. 514 (1972)

Justice POWELL delivered the opinion of the Court.

Although a speedy trial is guaranteed the accused by the Sixth Amendment to the Constitution, this Court has dealt with that right on infrequent occasions. [I]n none of our cases have we attempted to set out the criteria by which the speedy trial right is to be judged. This case compels us to make such an attempt.

I

On July 20, 1958, in Christian County, Kentucky, an elderly couple was beaten to death by intruders wielding an iron tire tool. Two suspects, Silas Manning and Willie Barker, the petitioner, were arrested shortly thereafter. The grand jury indicted them on September 15. Counsel was appointed on September 17, and Barker's trial was set for October 21. The Commonwealth had a stronger case against Manning, and it believed that Barker could not be convicted unless Manning testified against him. Manning was naturally unwilling to incriminate himself. Accordingly, on October 23, the day Silas Manning was brought to trial, the Commonwealth sought and obtained the first of what was to be a series of 16 continuances of Barker's trial. Barker made no objection. By first convicting Manning, the Commonwealth would remove possible problems of self-incrimination and would be able to assure his testimony against Barker.

The Commonwealth encountered more than a few difficulties in its pros-ecution of Manning. The first trial ended in a hung jury. A second trial resulted in a conviction, but the Kentucky Court of Appeals reversed because of the admission of evidence obtained by an illegal search. At his third trial, Manning was again convicted, and the Court of Appeals again reversed because the trial court had not granted a change of venue. A fourth trial resulted in a hung jury. Finally, after five trials, Manning was convicted, in March 1962, of murdering one victim, and after a sixth trial, in December 1962, he was convicted of murdering the other.

The Christian County Circuit Court holds three terms each year — in February, June, and September. Barker's initial trial was to take place in the September term of 1958. The first continuance postponed it until the February 1959 term. The second continuance was granted for one month only. Every term thereafter for as long as the Manning prosecutions were in process, the Commonwealth routinely moved to continue Barker's case to the next term. When the case was continued from the June 1959 term until the following September, Barker, having spent 10 months in jail, obtained his release by posting a $5,000 bond. He thereafter remained free in the community until his trial. Barker made no objection, through his counsel, to the first 11 continuances.

When on February 12, 1962, the Commonwealth moved for the twelfth time to continue the case until the following term, Barker's counsel filed a motion to dismiss the indictment. The motion to dismiss was denied two weeks later, and the Commonwealth's motion for a continuance was granted. The Commonwealth was granted further continuances in June 1962 and September 1962, to which Barker did not object.

In February 1963, the first term of court following Manning's final con-viction, the Commonwealth moved to set Barker's trial for March 19. But on the day scheduled for trial, it again moved for a continuance until the June term. It gave as its reason the illness of the ex-sheriff who was the chief investigating officer in the case. To this continuance, Barker objected unsuccessfully.

The witness was still unable to testify in June, and the trial, which had been set for June 19, was continued again until the September term over Barker's objection. This time the court announced that the case would be dismissed for lack of prosecution if it were not tried during the next term. The final trial date was set for October 9, 1963. On that date, Barker again moved to dismiss the indictment, and this time specified that his right to a speedy trial had been violated. The motion was denied; the trial commenced with Manning as the chief prosecution witness; Barker was convicted and given a life sentence.

The right to a speedy trial is generically different from any of the other rights enshrined in the Constitution for the protection of the accused. In addition to the general concern that all accused persons be treated accord-ing to decent and fair procedures, there is a societal interest in providing a speedy trial which exists separate from, and at times in opposition to, the interests of the accused. The inability of courts to provide a prompt trial has contributed to a large backlog of cases in urban courts which, among other things, enables defendants to negotiate more effectively for pleas of guilty to lesser offenses and otherwise manipulate the system. In addition, persons released on bond for lengthy periods awaiting trial have an opportunity to commit other crimes. It must be of little comfort to the residents of Christian County, Kentucky, to know that Barker was at large on bail for over four years while accused of a vicious and brutal murder of which he was ultimately convicted. Moreover, the longer an accused is free awaiting trial, the more tempting becomes his opportunity to jump bail and escape. Finally, delay between arrest and punishment may have a detrimental effect on rehabilitation.

If an accused cannot make bail, he is generally confined, as was Barker for 10 months, in a local jail. This contributes to the overcrowding and generally deplorable state of those institutions. Lengthy exposure to these conditions "has a destructive effect on human character and makes the rehabilitation of the individual offender much more difficult." At times the result may even be violent rioting. Finally, lengthy pretrial detention is costly. . . . In addition, society loses wages which might have been earned, and it must often support families of incarcerated breadwinners.

A second difference between the right to speedy trial and the accused's other constitutional rights is that deprivation of the right may work to the accused's advantage. Delay is not an uncommon defense tactic. As the time between the commission of the crime and trial lengthens, witnesses may become unavailable or their memories may fade. If the witnesses support the prosecution, its case will be weakened, sometimes seriously so. And it is the prosecution which carries the burden of proof. Thus, unlike the right to counsel or the right to be free from compelled self-incrimination, deprivation of the right to speedy trial does not per se prejudice the accused's ability to defend himself.

Finally, and perhaps most importantly, the right to speedy trial is a more vague concept than other procedural rights. It is, for example, impossible to determine with precision when the right has been denied. We cannot definitely say how long is too long in a system where justice is supposed to be swift but deliberate. As a consequence, there is no fixed point in the criminal process when the State can put the defendant to the choice of either exercising or waiving the right to a speedy trial.

The amorphous quality of the right also leads to the unsatisfactorily severe remedy of dismissal of the indictment when the right has been deprived. This is indeed a serious consequence because it means that a defendant who may be guilty of a serious crime will go free, without having been tried. Such a remedy is more serious than an exclusionary rule or a reversal for a new trial, but it is the only possible remedy.

III

Perhaps because the speedy trial right is so slippery, two rigid approaches are urged upon us as ways of eliminating some of the uncertainty which courts experience in protecting the right. The first suggestion is that we hold that the Constitution requires a criminal defendant to be offered a trial within a specified time period. The result of such a ruling would have the virtue of clarifying when the right is infringed and of simplifying courts' application of it. Recognizing this, some legislatures have enacted laws, and some courts have adopted procedural rules which more narrowly define the right.

But such a result would require this Court to engage in legislative or rulemaking activity, rather than in the adjudicative process to which we should confine our efforts.

The second suggested alternative would restrict consideration of the right to those cases in which the accused has demanded a speedy trial. Most States have recognized what is loosely referred to as the "demand rule." It is not clear, however, precisely what is meant by that term.

Such an approach, by presuming waiver of a fundamental right from inaction, is inconsistent with this Court's pronouncements on waiver of constitutional rights. "Presuming waiver from a silent record is impermissible. The record must show, or there must be an allegation and evidence which show, that an accused was offered counsel but intelligently and understandably rejected the offer. Anything less is not waiver."

We, therefore, reject both of the inflexible approaches — the fixed-time period because it goes further than the Constitution requires; the demand-waiver rule because it is insensitive to a right which we have deemed fundamental. The approach we accept is a balancing test, in which the conduct of both the prosecution and the defendant are weighed.

IV

A balancing test necessarily compels courts to approach speedy trial cases on an ad hoc basis. We can do little more than identify some of the factors which courts should assess in determining whether a particular defendant has been deprived of his right. [W]e identify four such factors: Length of delay, the reason for the delay, the defendant's assertion of his right, and prejudice to the defendant.

The length of the delay is to some extent a triggering mechanism. Until there is some delay which is presumptively prejudicial, there is no necessity for inquiry into the other factors that go into the balance. Nevertheless, because of the imprecision of the right to speedy trial, the length of delay that will provoke such an inquiry is necessarily dependent upon the peculiar circumstances of the case.[3] To take but one example, the delay that can be tolerated for an ordinary street crime is considerably less than for a serious, complex conspiracy charge.

Closely related to length of delay is the reason the government assigns to justify the delay. Here, too, different weights should be assigned to different reasons. A deliberate attempt to delay the trial in order to hamper the

---

3. For example, the First Circuit thought a delay of nine months overly long, absent a good reason, in a case that depended on eyewitness testimony. [Footnote by the Court.]

defense should be weighted heavily against the government. A more neutral reason such as negligence or overcrowded courts should be weighted less heavily but nevertheless should be considered since the ultimate responsibility for such circumstances must rest with the government rather than with the defendant. Finally, a valid reason, such as a missing witness, should serve to justify appropriate delay.

We have already discussed the third factor, the defendant's responsibility to assert his right. Whether and how a defendant asserts his right is closely related to the other factors we have mentioned. The strength of his efforts will be affected by the length of the delay, to some extent by the reason for the delay, and most particularly by the personal prejudice, which is not always readily identifiable, that he experiences. The more serious the deprivation, the more likely a defendant is to complain. The defendant's assertion of his speedy trial right, then, is entitled to strong evidentiary weight in determining whether the defendant is being deprived of the right. We emphasize that failure to assert the right will make it difficult for a defendant to prove that he was denied a speedy trial.

A fourth factor is prejudice to the defendant. Prejudice, of course, should be assessed in the light of the interests of defendants which the speedy trial right was designed to protect. This Court has identified three such interests: (i) to prevent oppressive pretrial incarceration; (ii) to minimize anxiety and concern of the accused; and (iii) to limit the possibility that the defense will be impaired. Of these, the most serious is the last, because the inability of a defendant adequately to prepare his case skews the fairness of the entire system. If witnesses die or disappear during a delay, the prejudice is obvious. There is also prejudice if defense witnesses are unable to recall accurately events of the distant past. Loss of memory, however, is not always reflected in the record because what has been forgotten can rarely be shown.

We have discussed previously the societal disadvantages of lengthy pretrial incarceration, but obviously the disadvantages for the accused who cannot obtain his release are even more serious. The time spent in jail awaiting trial has a detrimental impact on the individual. It often means loss of a job; it disrupts family life; and it enforces idleness. Most jails offer little or no recreational or rehabilitative programs. The time spent in jail is simply dead time. Moreover, if a defendant is locked up, he is hindered in his ability to gather evidence, contact witnesses, or otherwise prepare his defense.[4] Imposing those consequences on anyone who has not yet been convicted is serious. It is especially unfortunate to impose them on those persons who are ultimately found to be innocent. Finally, even if an accused is not incarcerated prior to trial, he is still disadvantaged by restraints on his liberty and by living under a cloud of anxiety, suspicion, and often hostility.

---

4. There is statistical evidence that persons who are detained between arrest and trial are more likely to receive prison sentences than those who obtain pretrial release, although other factors bear upon this correlation. *See* Wald, *Pretrial Detention and Ultimate Freedom: A Statistical Study,* 39 N.Y.U. L. Rev. 631 (1964) [Footnote by the Court.]

We regard none of the four factors identified above as either a necessary or sufficient condition to the finding of a deprivation of the right of speedy trial. Rather, they are related factors and must be considered together with such other circumstances as may be relevant. In sum, these factors have no talismanic qualities; courts must still engage in a difficult and sensitive balancing process.

V

The difficulty of the task of balancing these factors is illustrated by this case, which we consider to be close. It is clear that the length of delay between arrest and trial—well over five years—was extraordinary. Only seven months of that period can be attributed to a strong excuse, the illness of the ex-sheriff who was in charge of the investigation.

Two counterbalancing factors, however, outweigh these deficiencies. The first is that prejudice was minimal. [T]here is no claim that any of Barker's witnesses died or otherwise became unavailable owing to the delay. The trial transcript indicates only two very minor lapses of memory—one on the part of a prosecution witness—which were in no way significant to the outcome.

More important than the absence of serious prejudice, is the fact that Barker did not want a speedy trial. [T]he record shows no action whatever taken between October 21, 1958, and February 12, 1962, that could be construed as the assertion of the speedy trial right.

The probable reason for Barker's attitude was that he was gambling on Manning's acquittal. The evidence was not very strong against Manning, as the reversals and hung juries suggest, and Barker undoubtedly thought that if Manning were acquitted, he would never be tried.

We do not hold that there may never be a situation in which an indictment may be dismissed on speedy trial grounds where the defendant has failed to object to continuances. There may be a situation in which the defendant was represented by incompetent counsel, was severely prejudiced, or even cases in which the continuances were granted ex parte. But barring extraordinary circumstances, we would be reluctant indeed to rule that a defendant was denied this constitutional right on a record that strongly indicates, as does this one, that the defendant did not want a speedy trial. We hold, therefore, that Barker was not deprived of his due process right to a speedy trial.

[The concurring opinion of Justice White and Justice Brennan is omitted.]

———————

Barker provided a four-factor test for deciding whether there has been a constitutional speedy trial violation. To decide whether there has been a Sixth Amendment speedy trial violation, courts must consider:

1. The length of the delay
2. The reason for the delay

3. Whether, when, and how the defendant asserted his right to speedy trial
4. Whether the defendant was prejudiced by the delay

The first factor — the length of the delay — is a triggering mechanism. Unless there is some significant delay, the courts will not even examine the other factors.

Barker v. Wingo was decided three years before the enactment of the federal Speedy Trial Act in 1975. However, the Speedy Trial Act did not replace the constitutional right to a speedy trial. Rather, it provided statutory direction as to when a trial must occur. Regardless of whether statutory requirements were met, a defendant may still invoke his Sixth Amendment right to a speedy trial.

In Doggett v. United States, 505 U.S. 647 (1992), the Supreme Court revisited the speedy trial issue and gave more guidance as to what kind of delay triggers a Sixth Amendment violation and whether a showing of actual prejudice was required to prove a speedy trial violation.

DOGGETT v. UNITED STATES

505 U.S. 647 (1992)

Justice SOUTER delivered the opinion of the Court.

In this case we consider whether the delay of 8½ years between petitioner's indictment and arrest violated his Sixth Amendment right to a speedy trial. We hold that it did.

I

[Doggett was indicted with conspiring to distribute cocaine. He admitted that he knew nothing about the indictment during the lengthy delay before he was arrested. Shortly after he was indicted, Doggett left the country. When he returned two years later, he passed without trouble through Customs. He lived openly under his own name for the next six years in the United States. During that time, he got married, attended college, got a job, and had no trouble with the law. Finally, six years later, the Marshal's Service ran a credit check on several thousands of people. They found the outstanding warrant on Doggett and within minutes arrested him. On September 5, 1988, nearly six years after his return to the United States and eight and one-half years after his indictment, Doggett was arrested.]

II

The Sixth Amendment guarantees that, "in all criminal prosecutions, the accused shall enjoy the right to a speedy . . . trial. . . ." On its face, the Speedy Trial Clause is written with such breadth that, taken literally, it would forbid the government to delay the trial of an "accused" for any reason at all. Our cases, however, have qualified the literal sweep of the provision by specifically recognizing the relevance of four separate enquiries: whether delay before trial was uncommonly long, whether the government or the criminal defendant is more to blame for that delay, whether, in due course, the defendant asserted his right to a speedy trial, and whether he suffered prejudice as the delay's result.

The first of these is actually a double enquiry. Simply to trigger a speedy trial analysis, an accused must allege that the interval between accusation and trial has crossed the threshold dividing ordinary from "presumptively prejudicial" delay. If the accused makes this showing, the court must then consider, as one factor among several, the extent to which the delay stretches beyond the bare minimum needed to trigger judicial examination of the claim. In this case, the extraordinary 8½-year lag between Doggett's indictment and arrest clearly suffices to trigger the speedy trial enquiry.[5]

As for *Barker*'s second criterion, the Government claims to have sought Doggett with diligence. For six years, the Government's investigators made no serious effort to test their progressively more questionable assumption that Doggett was living abroad, and, had they done so, they could have found him within minutes. While the Government's lethargy may have reflected no more than Doggett's relative unimportance in the world of drug trafficking, it was still findable negligence, and the finding stands.

The Government goes against the record again in suggesting that Doggett knew of his indictment years before he was arrested. Were this true, *Barker*'s third factor, concerning invocation of the right to a speedy trial, would be weighed heavily against him. But here again, the Government is trying to revisit the facts. [The record was unrebutted that Doggett did not know he was wanted on the indictment.]

III

The Government is left, then, with its principal contention: that Doggett fails to make out a successful speedy trial claim because he has not shown precisely how he was prejudiced by the delay between his indictment and trial.

We have observed in prior cases that unreasonable delay between formal accusation and trial threatens to produce more than one sort of harm, including "oppressive pretrial incarceration," "anxiety and concern of the accused," and "the possibility that the [accused's] defense will be impaired" by dimming memories and loss of exculpatory evidence. Of these forms of prejudice, "the most serious is the last, because the inability of a defendant adequately to prepare his case skews the fairness of the entire system." Doggett claims this kind of prejudice, and there is probably no other kind that he can claim, since he was subjected neither to pretrial

---

5. Depending on the nature of the charges, the lower courts have generally found postaccusation delay "presumptively prejudicial" at least as it approaches one year. [Footnote by the Court.]

detention nor, he has successfully contended, to awareness of unresolved charges against him.

[T]he Government claims Doggett has failed to make any affirmative showing that the delay weakened his ability to raise specific defenses, elicit specific testimony, or produce specific items of evidence. Though Doggett did indeed come up short in this respect, affirmative proof of particularized prejudice is not essential to every speedy trial claim. *Barker* explicitly recognized that impairment of one's defense is the most difficult form of speedy trial prejudice to prove because time's erosion of exculpatory evidence and testimony "can rarely be shown." Thus, we generally have to recognize that excessive delay presumptively compromises the reliability of a trial in ways that neither party can prove or, for that matter, identify.

This brings us to an enquiry into the role that presumptive prejudice should play in the disposition of Doggett's speedy trial claim. [I]n this case, if the Government had pursued Doggett with reasonable diligence from his indictment to his arrest, his speedy trial claim would fail. The Government concedes, on the other hand, that Doggett would prevail if he could show that the Government had intentionally held back in its prosecution of him to gain some impermissible advantage at trial.

Between diligent prosecution and bad-faith delay, official negligence in bringing an accused to trial occupies the middle ground. *Barker* made it clear that "different weights [are to be] assigned to different reasons" for delay. Although negligence is obviously to be weighed more lightly than a deliberate intent to harm the accused's defense, it still falls on the wrong side of the divide between acceptable and unacceptable reasons for delaying a criminal prosecution once it has begun. [O]ur toleration of such negligence varies inversely with its protractedness.

[T]he Government's egregious persistence in failing to prosecute Doggett is clearly sufficient. The lag between Doggett's indictment and arrest was 8½ years, and he would have faced trial 6 years earlier than he did but for the Government's inexcusable oversights. The portion of the delay attributable to the Government's negligence far exceeds the threshold needed to state a speedy trial claim; indeed, we have called shorter delays "extraordinary." [The Court held that Doggett was entitled to dismissal of the indictment.]

Justice THOMAS, with whom Chief Justice REHNQUIST and Justice SCALIA join, dissenting.

Just as "bad facts make bad law," so too odd facts make odd law. Doggett's 8½-year odyssey from youthful drug dealing in the tobacco country of North Carolina, through stints in a Panamanian jail and in Colombia, to life as a computer operations manager, homeowner, and registered voter in suburban Virginia is extraordinary. But even more extraordinary is the Court's conclusion that the Government denied Doggett his Sixth Amendment right to a speedy trial despite the fact that he has suffered none of the harms that the right was designed to prevent.

There is no basis for concluding that the disruption of an accused's life years after the commission of his alleged crime is an evil independently protected by the Speedy Trial Clause. Such disruption occurs regardless of whether the individual is under indictment during the period of delay. To recognize a constitutional right to repose is to recognize a right to be tried speedily after the offense. That would, of course, convert the Speedy Trial Clause into a constitutional statute of limitations—a result with no basis in the text or history of the Clause or in our precedents.

II

So engrossed is the Court in applying the multifactor balancing test set forth in *Barker* that it loses sight of the nature and purpose of the speedy trial guarantee set forth in the Sixth Amendment. *Barker* does not apply at all—when an accused is entirely unaware of a pending indictment against him.

Today's opinion, I fear, will transform the courts of the land into boards of law enforcement supervision. For the Court compels dismissal of the charges against Doggett not because he was harmed in any way by the delay between his indictment and arrest, but simply because the Government's efforts to catch him are found wanting. By divorcing the Speedy Trial Clause from all considerations of prejudice to an accused, the Court positively invites the Nation's judges to indulge in ad hoc and result-driven second-guessing of the government's investigatory efforts. Our Constitution neither contemplates nor tolerates such a role.

Many observers were surprised by the result in *Doggett*, especially given the emphasis the Supreme Court in *Barker* had placed on the requirement that there be prejudice for Barker to prove a constitutional violation. To what extent do you think that the Court was concerned about negligent police officers and their lack of professionalism during a "war on drugs"?

More recently, the Court faced another issue arising with more frequency in speedy trial challenges. Should delays by appointed defense counsel be weighed as a factor against a defendant's motion for dismissal? The Supreme Court decided the issue in Vermont v. Brillon.

VERMONT v. BRILLON
556 U.S. 81 (2009)

Justice GINSBURG delivered the opinion of the Court.

This case concerns the *Sixth Amendment* guarantee that "[i]n all criminal prosecutions, the accused shall enjoy the right to a speedy . . . trial." Michael

Brillon, defendant below, respondent here, was arrested in July 2001 on felony domestic assault and habitual offender charges. Nearly three years later, in June 2004, he was tried by jury, found guilty as charged, and sentenced to 12 to 20 years in prison. The Vermont Supreme Court vacated Brillon's conviction and held that the charges against him must be dismissed because he had been denied his right to a speedy trial.

During the time between Brillon's arrest and his trial, at least six different attorneys were appointed to represent him. Brillon "fired" the first, who served from July 2001 to February 2002. His third lawyer, who served from March 2002 until June 2002, was allowed to withdraw when he reported that Brillon had threatened his life. The Vermont Supreme Court charged against Brillon the delays associated with those periods, but charged against the State periods in which assigned counsel failed "to move the case forward."

We hold that the Vermont Supreme Court erred in ranking assigned counsel essentially as state actors in the criminal justice system. Assigned counsel, just as retained counsel, act on behalf of their clients, and delays sought by counsel are ordinarily attributable to the defendants they represent. For a total of some six months of the time that elapsed between Brillon's arrest and his trial, Brillon lacked an attorney. The State may be charged with those months if the gaps resulted from the trial court's failure to appoint replacement counsel with dispatch. Similarly, the State may bear responsibility if there is "a breakdown in the public defender system." But, as the Vermont Supreme Court acknowledged, the record does not establish any such institutional breakdown.

I

On July 27, 2001, Michael Brillon was arrested after striking his girlfriend. Three days later he was arraigned in state court in Bennington County, Vermont and charged with felony domestic assault. His alleged status as a habitual offender exposed him to a potential life sentence. The court ordered him held without bail.

Richard Ammons, from the county public defender's office, was assigned on the day of arraignment as Brillon's first counsel. In October, Ammons filed a motion to recuse the trial judge. It was denied the next month and trial was scheduled for February 2002. In mid-January, Ammons moved for a continuance, but the State objected, and the trial court denied the motion.

On February 22, four days before the jury draw, Ammons again moved for a continuance, citing his heavy workload and the need for further investigation. Ammons acknowledged that any delay would not count (presumably against the State) for speedy-trial purposes. The State opposed the motion, and at the conclusion of a hearing, the trial court denied it. Brillon, participating in the proceedings through interactive television, then announced: "You're fired, Rick." Three days later, the trial court — over the State's objection — granted Ammons' motion to withdraw as counsel, citing Brillon's termination of Ammons and Ammons' statement that he could no longer zealously represent Brillon. The trial court warned Brillon that further delay would occur while a new attorney became familiar with the case. The same day, the trial court appointed a second attorney, but he immediately withdrew based on a conflict.

On March 1, 2002, Gerard Altieri was assigned as Brillon's third counsel. On May 20, Brillon filed a motion to dismiss Altieri for, among other reasons, failure to file motions, "[v]irtually no communication whatsoever," and his lack of diligence "because of heavy case load." At a June 11 hearing, Altieri denied several of Brillon's allegations, noted his disagreement with Brillon's trial strategy, and insisted he had plenty of time to prepare. The State opposed Brillon's motion as well. Near the end of the hearing, however, Altieri moved to withdraw on the ground that Brillon had threatened his life during a break in the proceedings. The trial court granted Brillon's motion to dismiss Altieri, but warned Brillon that "this is somewhat of a dubious victory in your case because it simply prolongs the time that you will remain in jail until we can bring this matter to trial."

That same day, the trial court appointed Paul Donaldson as Brillon's fourth counsel. At an August 5 status conference, Donaldson requested additional time to conduct discovery in light of his caseload. A few weeks later, Brillon sent a letter to the court complaining about Donaldson's unresponsiveness and lack of competence. Two months later, Brillon filed a motion to dismiss Donaldson — similar to his motion to dismiss Altieri — for failure to file motions and "virtually no communication whatsoever." At a November 26 hearing, Donaldson reported that his contract with the Defender General's office had expired in June and that he had been in discussions to have Brillon's case reassigned. The trial court released Donaldson from the case "[w]ithout making any findings regarding the adequacy of [Donaldson]'s representation."

Brillon's fifth counsel, David Sleigh, was not assigned until January 15, 2003; Brillon was without counsel during the intervening two months. On February 25, Sleigh sought extensions of various discovery deadlines, noting that he had been in trial out of town. On April 10, however, Sleigh withdrew from the case, based on "modifications to [his] firm's contract with the Defender General."

Brillon was then without counsel for the next four months. On June 20, the Defender General's office notified the court that it had received "funding from the legislature" and would hire a new special felony unit defender for Brillon. On August 1, Kathleen Moore was appointed as Brillon's sixth counsel. The trial court set November 7 as the deadline for motions, but granted several extensions in accord with the parties' stipulation. On February 23, 2004, Moore filed a motion to dismiss for lack of a speedy trial. The trial court denied the motion on April 19.

The case finally went to trial on June 14, 2004. Brillon was found guilty and sentenced to 12 to 20 years in prison. The trial court denied a post-trial motion to dismiss for want of a speedy trial, concluding that the delay in Brillon's trial was "in large part the result of his own actions" and that Brillon had "failed to demonstrate prejudice as a result of [the] pre-trial delay."

II

The *Sixth Amendment* guarantees that "[i]n all criminal prosecutions, the accused shall enjoy the right to a speedy . . . trial." The speedy-trial right is "amorphous," "slippery," and "necessarily relative." In *Barker*, the Court refused to "quantif[y]" the right "into a specified number of days or months" or to hinge the right on a defendant's explicit request for a speedy trial. Rejecting such "inflexible approaches," *Barker* established a "balancing test, in which the conduct of both the prosecution and the defendant are weighed." "[S]ome of the factors" that courts should weigh include "[l]ength of delay, the reason for the delay, the defendant's assertion of his right, and prejudice to the defendant."

Primarily at issue here is the reason for the delay in Brillon's trial. Because "the attorney is the [defendant's] agent when acting, or failing to act, in furtherance of the litigation," delay caused by the defendant's counsel is also charged against the defendant. The same principle applies whether counsel is privately retained or publicly assigned, for "[o]nce a lawyer has undertaken the representation of an accused, the duties and obligations are the same whether the lawyer is privately retained, appointed, or serving in a legal aid or defender program."

III

An assigned counsel's failure "to move the case forward" does not warrant attribution of delay to the State. Contrary to the Vermont Supreme Court's analysis, assigned counsel generally are not state actors for purposes of a speedy-trial claim. While the Vermont Defender General's office is indeed "part of the criminal justice system," the individual counsel here acted only on behalf of Brillon, not the State. Most of the delay that the Vermont Supreme Court attributed to the State must therefore be attributed to Brillon as delays caused by his counsel.

A contrary conclusion could encourage appointed counsel to delay proceedings by seeking unreasonable continuances, hoping thereby to obtain a dismissal of the indictment on speedy-trial grounds. Trial courts might well respond by viewing continuance requests made by appointed counsel with skepticism, concerned that even an apparently genuine need for more time is in reality a delay tactic.

The general rule attributing to the defendant delay caused by assigned counsel is not absolute. Delay resulting from a systemic "breakdown in the public defender system," could be charged to the State. But the Vermont Supreme Court made no determination, and nothing in the record suggests, that institutional problems caused any part of the delay in Brillon's case.[6]

In sum, delays caused by defense counsel are properly attributed to the defendant, even where counsel is assigned.

c.   Other Speedy Trial Rules and Laws

In addition to constitutional protections and rights under the Speedy Trial Act, other federal statutes contain provisions to prevent post-accusation delay. For example, Federal Rule of Criminal Procedure 48(b) grants trial courts the discretion to dismiss a case if there is "unnecessary delay" in bringing a defendant to trial. The court may dismiss the case with or without prejudice. Generally, this rule is only used if a delay is not covered by other statutory provisions.

Also, the Interstate Agreement on Detainer Act, 18 U.S.C. app. §2 (2000), provides time limits for a defendant's transfer from one jurisdiction to another to commence trial. The Juvenile Delinquency and Justice Act, 18 U.S.C. §§5031-5042 (2000), establishes time limits for various pretrial proceedings in juvenile cases that take into account the special nature of those cases.

D.   REMEDIES FOR SPEEDY TRIAL VIOLATIONS

As we have seen, the remedy for violations of Speedy Trial Acts and governing federal rules is dismissal with or without prejudice. A dismissal without prejudice allows the government to refile charges. However, the remedy for a constitutional speedy trial violation is more limited. In Strunk v. United States, 412 U.S. 434 (1973), the Supreme Court held that the only remedy that makes sense for violations of the Sixth Amendment right to speedy trial is dismissal with prejudice. By definition, once the court finds there has been a violation of the defendant's constitutional right to a speedy trial, it is too late to try the defendant.

Given the extreme remedy, it is not surprising that courts are reluctant to find that there has been a violation of the constitutional right to a speedy trial. Finding a constitutional speedy trial violation means that there will never be a trial to resolve a case. Victims may continue to be frustrated because they never have had their day in court. It also can mean that a defendant who is responsible for a serious crime will be rereleased into society because the criminal justice system failed to safeguard his constitutional rights.

---

6. By contrast, in Boyer v. Louisiana, 133 S. Ct. 1702 (2013), four Justices stated in response to an order dismissing the case as improvidently granted that a State's failure to adequately fund its defense lawyers counts against the prosecution in a determination of whether there was a speedy trial violation.

The Supreme Court noted these concerns in *Strunk*, in which it rejected an argument that it should use a balancing approach to derive different remedies for a speedy trial violation. Chief Justice Burger quoted the lower court in his opinion when he recognized that "[t]he remedy for a violation of this constitutional right has traditionally been the dismissal of the indictment or the vacation of the sentence. Perhaps the severity of that remedy has caused courts to be extremely hesitant in finding a failure to afford a speedy trial." *Id.* at 438. Nonetheless, although dismissal of an indictment for denial of a speedy trial is an "unsatisfactorily severe remedy" and in practice, "it means that a defendant who may be guilty of a serious crime will go free, without having been tried[,]" such severe remedies are not unique in the application of constitutional standards. In light of the policies which underlie the right to a speedy trial, dismissal must remain, as *Barker* noted, "the only possible remedy."

E.   SPEEDY TRIAL RIGHTS AND SENTENCING

The Supreme Court held in Betterman v. Montana, 136 S. Ct. 1609 (2016), that the Sixth Amendment right to speedy trial does not apply to sentencing proceedings. Instead, defendants can raise due process challenges if there are undue delays in sentencing.

BETTERMAN v. MONTANA

136 S. Ct. 1609 (2016)

Justice GINSBURG delivered the opinion of the Court.

The Sixth Amendment to the U. S. Constitution provides that "[i]n all criminal prosecutions, the accused shall enjoy the right to a speedy and public trial, by an impartial jury. . . ." Does the Sixth Amendment's speedy trial guarantee apply to the sentencing phase of a criminal prosecution? That is the sole question this case presents. We hold that the guarantee protects the accused from arrest or indictment through trial, but does not apply once a defendant has been found guilty at trial or has pleaded guilty to criminal charges. For inordinate delay in sentencing, although the Speedy Trial Clause does not govern, a defendant may have other recourse, including, in appropriate circumstances, tailored relief under the Due Process Clauses of the Fifth and Fourteenth Amendments.

I

Ordered to appear in court on domestic assault charges, Brandon Betterman failed to show up and was therefore charged with bail jumping. After pleading guilty to the bail-jumping charge, he was jailed for over 14 months awaiting sentence on that conviction. The holdup, in large part, was due to institutional delay: the presentence report took nearly five months to complete; the trial court took several months to deny two presentence motions (one seeking dismissal of the charge on the ground of delay); and the court was slow in setting a sentencing hearing. Betterman was eventually sentenced to seven years' imprisonment, with four of those years suspended. Arguing that the 14-month gap between conviction and sentencing violated his speedy trial right, Betterman appealed.

II

Criminal proceedings generally unfold in three discrete phases. First, the State investigates to determine whether to arrest and charge a suspect. Once charged, the suspect stands accused but is presumed innocent until conviction upon trial or guilty plea. After conviction, the court imposes sentence. There are checks against delay throughout this progression, each geared to its particular phase.

In the first stage — before arrest or indictment, when the suspect remains at liberty — statutes of limitations provide the primary protection against delay, with the Due Process Clause as a safeguard against fundamentally unfair prosecutorial conduct.

The Sixth Amendment's Speedy Trial Clause homes in on the second period: from arrest or indictment through conviction. The constitutional right, our precedent holds, does not attach until this phase begins, that is, when a defendant is arrested or formally accused. Today we hold that the right detaches upon conviction, when this second stage ends.

Prior to conviction, the accused is shielded by the presumption of innocence, the "bedrock[,] axiomatic and elementary principle whose enforcement lies at the foundation of the administration of our criminal law." The Speedy Trial Clause implements that presumption by "prevent[ing] undue and oppressive incarceration prior to trial, . . . minimiz[ing] anxiety and concern accompanying public accusation[,] and . . . limit[ing] the possibilities that long delay will impair the ability of an accused to defend himself."

Reflecting the concern that a presumptively innocent person should not languish under an unresolved charge, the Speedy Trial Clause guarantees "the accused" "the right to a speedy . . . trial." U. S. Const., Amdt. 6. At the founding, "accused" described a status preceding "convicted." And "trial" meant a discrete episode after which judgment (i.e., sentencing) would follow. This understanding of the Sixth Amendment language — "accused" as distinct from "convicted," and "trial" as separate from "sentencing" — endures today.

The sole remedy for a violation of the speedy trial right — dismissal of the charges, see Strunk v. United States (1973) — fits the preconviction focus of the Clause. It would be an unjustified windfall, in most cases, to remedy sentencing delay by vacating validly obtained convictions. Betterman concedes that a dismissal remedy ordinarily would not be in order once a defendant has been convicted.

The manner in which legislatures have implemented the speedy trial guarantee matches our reading of the Clause. Congress passed the Speedy Trial Act of 1974, 18 U. S. C. §3161 et seq., "to give effect to the sixth amendment right." With certain exceptions, the Act directs — on pain of dismissal of the charges, §3162(a) — that no more than 30 days pass between arrest and indictment, §3161(b), and that no more than 70 days pass between indictment and trial, §3161(c)(1). The Act says nothing, however, about the period between conviction and sentencing, suggesting that Congress did not regard that period as falling within the Sixth Amendment's compass. Numerous state analogs similarly impose precise time limits for charging and trial; they, too, say nothing about sentencing.

Betterman asks us to take account of the prevalence of guilty pleas and the resulting scarcity of trials in today's justice system. The sentencing hearing has largely replaced the trial as the forum for dispute resolution, Betterman urges. Therefore, he maintains, the concerns supporting the right to a speedy trial now recommend a speedy sentencing hearing. The modern reality, however, does not bear on the presumption-of-innocence protection at the heart of the Speedy Trial Clause. And factual disputes, if any there be, at sentencing, do not go to the question of guilt; they are geared, instead, to ascertaining the proper sentence within boundaries set by statutory minimums and maximums.

As we have explained, at the third phase of the criminal-justice process, i.e., between conviction and sentencing, the Constitution's presumption-of-innocence-protective speedy trial right is not engaged. That does not mean, however, that defendants lack any protection against undue delay at this stage. The primary safeguard comes from statutes and rules. The federal rule on point directs the court to "impose sentence without unnecessary delay." Fed. Rule Crim. Proc. 32(b)(1). Further, as at the prearrest stage, due process serves as a backstop against exorbitant delay. After conviction, a defendant's due process right to liberty, while diminished, is still present. He retains an interest in a sentencing proceeding that is fundamentally fair. But because Betterman advanced no due process claim here, we express no opinion on how he might fare under that more pliable standard.

CHAPTER
11

RIGHT TO COUNSEL

A. INTRODUCTION

Of all the defendant's constitutional rights, none is more important than the defendant's right to counsel. With the assistance of counsel, a defendant can protect all of his other rights. From beginning to end, the defense lawyer serves as an advocate for the accused, ensuring that both law enforcement and prosecutors comply with the defendants' constitutional rights. Chapter 4 discusses the right to counsel during police interrogations, and Chapter 5 discusses the right to counsel at post-charge identifications. This chapter focuses on the right to counsel at trial and pretrial proceedings.

Before examining the scope of the right to counsel, it is worth considering the practical challenges in providing quality counsel to the accused. Nationally, there is a shortage of funds to pay the fees for indigent counsel. As a result, in some areas of the country, defense lawyers are paid as little as $50 to handle a criminal case.[1] Not surprisingly, the low pay and demanding nature of the job make it difficult to recruit experienced and qualified lawyers to handle indigent criminal cases. While there are many dedicated public defenders who work countless hours of unpaid overtime, there continues to be a shortage of capable defense counsel. As this chapter discusses, the right to counsel is a crucial right, but it involves more than just the right to appointment of a lawyer. The Sixth Amendment provides for the right to the "effective" assistance of counsel.

Section B begins with the landmark case of Gideon v. Wainwright, 372 U.S. 335 (1963). As discussed in the notes preceding *Gideon*, the right to counsel under the Sixth Amendment was not always applied to the states. Rather, representation by counsel was considered an aspect of the right to due process. It was not until *Gideon* that the Supreme Court recognized an independent right to counsel under the Sixth Amendment.

---

1. *See* Adam Gershowitz, *Raise the Proof: A Default Rule for Indigent Defense*, 40 Conn. L. Rev. 85 (2007). Defense lawyers are often outspent by a 3:1 margin. For a detailed study of public defender systems throughout the country, *see* Alissa Pollitz Worden, Andrew Lucas Blaize Davies & Elizabeth K. Brown, *A Patchwork of Policies: Justice, Due Process and Public Defense Across American States*, 74 Alb. L. Rev. 1423 (2010).

Section C then discusses when the right to counsel is triggered. The right to counsel is available for all "critical stages" of a prosecution. Critical stages begin before trial and last through the initial appeal. Not all proceedings related to criminal cases qualify as "prosecutions" for purposes of the Sixth Amendment. Specifically, the Supreme Court does not recognize a Sixth Amendment right to counsel in misdemeanor cases in which no imprisonment is imposed or in post-conviction proceedings, such as parole hearings or habeas corpus cases.

Section D discusses the standard to be used to measure whether the defendant has been afforded "effective" assistance of counsel. How good of a lawyer is a defendant entitled to under the Sixth Amendment? What resources should be available to a defense lawyer in representing his or her client? Does the right to counsel include the right to experts to assist counsel in his or her representation of the defendant?

Section E addresses the right of self-representation. Although a defendant has the Sixth Amendment right to counsel, a competent defendant can waive the right and represent himself. Finally, section F briefly discusses the situation of enemy combatants and the nature of the right to counsel.

B. APPOINTMENT OF COUNSEL

Prior to *Gideon*, many states were providing counsel to indigent defendants but only in the most serious cases, such as death penalty cases. In Powell v. Alabama, 287 U.S. 45, 64-65 (1932),[2] the Court recognized the importance of counsel. Powell and his codefendants were young, black men accused of raping two white girls in Alabama. In what was to become the infamous "Scottsboro Boys" trial, no lawyer was designated to represent the defendants until the morning of trial. With no time to prepare, and facing an ignorant and hostile community, it was no surprise that the defendants were convicted. On appeal, the Supreme Court found that the defendants' due process rights were violated. Justice Sutherland wrote, "[W]e are of the opinion that, under the circumstances [of this case], the necessity of counsel was so vital and imperative that the failure of the trial court to make an effective appointment of counsel was . . . a denial of due process within the meaning of the Fourteenth Amendment."

In Betts v. Brady, 316 U.S. 455 (1942), the Court expressly refused to find that the Fourteenth Amendment incorporated the Sixth Amendment right to counsel to the states. As a result, the Court needed to decide on a case-by-case basis whether the lack of counsel denied the defendant due process at trial. Not surprisingly, this led to a flood of cases in which each defendant claimed that denial of counsel in his or her case denied the defendant due

---

2. This case is also discussed in Chapter 1.

process. Courts were inconsistent in their rulings and the time became ripe for the Court to reexamine the issue. It did so in Gideon v. Wainwright.

GIDEON v. WAINWRIGHT
372 U.S. 335 (1963)

Justice BLACK delivered the opinion of the Court.

Petitioner was charged in a Florida state court with having broken and entered a poolroom with intent to commit a misdemeanor. This offense is a felony under Florida law. Appearing in court without funds and without a lawyer, petitioner asked the court to appoint counsel for him, whereupon the following colloquy took place:

The COURT: Mr. Gideon, I am sorry, but I cannot appoint Counsel to represent you in this case. Under the laws of the State of Florida, the only time the Court can appoint Counsel to represent a Defendant is when that person is charged with a capital offense. I am sorry, but I will have to deny your request to appoint Counsel to defend you in this case.

The DEFENDANT: The United States Supreme Court says I am entitled to be represented by Counsel.

Put to trial before a jury, Gideon conducted his defense about as well as could be expected from a layman. He made an opening statement to the jury, cross-examined the State's witnesses, presented witnesses in his own defense, declined to testify himself, and made a short argument "emphasizing his innocence to the charge contained in the Information filed in this case." The jury returned a verdict of guilty, and petitioner was sentenced to serve five years in the state prison. Later, petitioner filed in the Florida Supreme Court this habeas corpus petition attacking his conviction and sentence on the ground that the trial court's refusal to appoint counsel for him denied him rights "guaranteed by the Constitution and the Bill of Rights by the United States Government."[3] Treating the petition for habeas corpus as properly before it, the State Supreme Court, "upon consideration thereof" but without an opinion, denied all relief. Since 1942, when Betts v. Brady was decided by a divided Court, [the rule has been that there is no automatic right to counsel unless counsel is needed to ensure due process to the defendant in his particular case]. [W]e appointed counsel to represent [Gideon] and requested both sides to discuss in their briefs and oral arguments the following: "Should this Court's holding in Betts v. Brady be reconsidered?"

The Sixth Amendment provides, "In all criminal prosecutions, the accused shall enjoy the right . . . to have the Assistance of Counsel for his

---

3. The Supreme Court accepted a handwritten petition Gideon wrote for himself. He stated, "I, Clarence Earl Gideon, claim that I was denied the rights of the 4th, 5th and 14th amendments of the Bill of Rights." See original opinion, fn.2. [Footnote by casebook authors.]

defence." Betts argued that this right is extended to indigent defendants in state courts by the Fourteenth Amendment. On the basis of . . . historical data the Court concluded that "appointment of counsel is not a fundamental right, essential to a fair trial."

We accept Betts v. Brady's assumption, based as it was on our prior cases, that a provision of the Bill of Rights which is "fundamental and essential to a fair trial" is made obligatory upon the States by the Fourteenth Amendment. We think the Court in *Betts* was wrong, however, in concluding that the Sixth Amendment's guarantee of counsel is not one of these fundamental rights.

"[The assistance of counsel] is one of the safeguards of the Sixth Amendment deemed necessary to insure fundamental human rights of life and liberty. . . . The Sixth Amendment stands as a constant admonition that if the constitutional safeguards it provides be lost, justice will not 'still be done.'" Johnson v. Zerbst (1938).

The fact is that in deciding as it did — that "appointment of counsel is not a fundamental right, essential to a fair trial" — the Court in Betts v. Brady made an abrupt break with its own well-considered precedents. In returning to these old precedents, sounder we believe than the new, we but restore constitutional principles established to achieve a fair system of justice. Not only these precedents but also reason and reflection require us to recognize that in our adversary system of criminal justice, any person haled into court, who is too poor to hire a lawyer, cannot be assured a fair trial unless counsel is provided for him. This seems to us to be an obvious truth. Governments, both state and federal, quite properly spend vast sums of money to establish machinery to try defendants accused of crime. Lawyers to prosecute are everywhere deemed essential to protect the public's interest in an orderly society. Similarly, there are few defendants charged with crime, few indeed, who fail to hire the best lawyers they can get to prepare and present their defenses. That government hires lawyers to prosecute and defendants who have the money hire lawyers to defend are the strongest indications of the widespread belief that lawyers in criminal courts are necessities, not luxuries. The right of one charged with crime to counsel may not be deemed fundamental and essential to fair trials in some countries, but it is in ours. From the very beginning, our state and national constitutions and laws have laid great emphasis on procedural and substantive safeguards designed to assure fair trials before impartial tribunals in which every defendant stands equal before the law. This noble ideal cannot be realized if the poor man charged with crime has to face his accusers without a lawyer to assist him. A defendant's need for a lawyer is nowhere better stated than in the moving words of Mr. Justice Sutherland in Powell v. Alabama:

> The right to be heard would be, in many cases, of little avail if it did not comprehend the right to be heard by counsel. Even the intelligent and educated layman has small and sometimes no skill in the science of law. If charged with crime, he is incapable, generally, of determining for himself whether the indictment is good or bad. He is unfamiliar with the rules of evidence. Left without the aid of counsel he may be put on trial without a proper charge, and convicted upon incompetent

evidence, or evidence irrelevant to the issue or otherwise inadmissible. He lacks both the skill and knowledge adequately to prepare his defense, even though he have a perfect one. He requires the guiding hand of counsel at every step in the proceedings against him. Without it, though he be not guilty, he faces the danger of conviction because he does not know how to establish his innocence.

The Court in Betts v. Brady departed from the sound wisdom upon which the Court's holding in Powell v. Alabama rested. *Betts* was "an anachronism when handed down" and . . . it should now be overruled.

Gideon was afforded a new trial with counsel. Upon retrial, he was acquitted.

The right to counsel is so important that it is automatically triggered by the prosecution of the defendant and does not depend on the defendant's request for a lawyer. Brewer v. Williams, 430 U.S. 387, 404 (1977). As *Gideon* established, if a defendant cannot afford his own lawyer, the court must appoint counsel for him.

C. WHEN THE RIGHT TO COUNSEL APPLIES

The Sixth Amendment provides that "[i]n all criminal prosecutions, the accused shall enjoy the right . . . to have the Assistance of Counsel for his defense." The Court has interpreted this language to mean that the absolute right to counsel applies to all "critical stages" of a criminal prosecution after the filing of formal charges. Kirby v. Illinois, 406 U.S. 682 (1972) (plurality opinion). Critical stages may occur before trial. Defense counsel can play a critical role before trial in the investigation of a case and in plea bargaining discussions with the prosecutor.

The Court has expressly held that the right to counsel attaches at all post-indictment pretrial lineups (United States v. Wade, 388 U.S. 218 (1967)), preliminary hearings (Coleman v. Alabama, 399 U.S. 1 (1970)), post-indictment interrogations (Massiah v. United States, 377 U.S. 201 (1964)), and arraignments (Hamilton v. Alabama, 368 U.S. 52 (1961)). In Rothgery v. Gillespie County, 554 U.S. 191 (2008), the Court clarified that the Sixth Amendment right to counsel attaches at the defendant's first appearance before a judicial officer after a formal charge is made, regardless of whether a prosecutor is present.

The right to counsel applies to a defendant's first appeal of right. *See* Douglas v. California, 372 U.S. 353 (1963); Evitts v. Lucey, 469 U.S. 387 (1985). This includes the first-tier of discretionary appeals. Halbert v. Michigan, 545 U.S. 605 (2005). Even if a defendant's appeal does not have merit, the defendant is entitled to appointed counsel who will examine the record carefully to identify any nonfrivolous issues for the appellate court to review. Anders v. California, 386 U.S. 738 (1967).

By contrast, there is no right to counsel for second-tier discretionary state appeals or petitions for review to the United States Supreme Court. Ross v. Moffitt, 417 U.S. 600 (1974). The right to counsel also does not attach at parole hearings or probation revocation hearings (Gagnon v. Scarpelli, 411 U.S. 778 (1973)) or in civil matters such as habeas corpus proceedings (Pennsylvania v. Finley, 481 U.S. 551 (1987)). By the terms of the Sixth Amendment, the right to assistance of counsel does not apply in civil cases but only "[i]n all criminal prosecutions."

As for parole and probation revocation hearings, the Supreme Court refused to create a per se requirement for the appointment of counsel. Rather, using a due process case-by-case approach, the Court held that appointment of counsel was not automatically required by the Sixth Amendment. Justice Powell wrote:

> [T]he "purpose is to help individuals reintegrate into society as constructive individuals as soon as they are able. . . ." The introduction of counsel into a revocation proceeding will alter significantly the nature of the proceeding. If counsel is provided for the probationer or parolee, the State in turn will normally provide its own counsel; lawyers, by training and disposition, are advocates and bound by professional duty to present all available evidence and arguments in support of their clients' positions and to contest with vigor all adverse evidence and views. The role of the hearing body itself, aptly described as being "predictive and discretionary" as well as factfinding, may become more akin to that of a judge at a trial, and less attuned to the rehabilitative needs of the individual probationer or parolee. In the greater self-consciousness of its quasi-judicial role, the hearing body may be less tolerant of marginal deviant behavior and feel more pressure to reincarcerate than to continue nonpunitive rehabilitation. Certainly, the decisionmaking process will be prolonged, and the financial cost to the State — for appointed counsel, counsel for the State, a longer record, and the possibility of judicial review — will not be insubstantial.
>
> In some cases, these modifications in the nature of the revocation hearing must be endured and the costs borne because the probationer's or parolee's version of a disputed issue can fairly be represented only by a trained advocate. But due process is not so rigid as to require that the significant interests in informality, flexibility, and economy must always be sacrificed.
>
> In so concluding, we are of course aware that the case-by-case approach to the right to counsel in felony prosecutions adopted in Betts v. Brady (1942), was later rejected in favor of a per se rule in Gideon v. Wainwright (1963). *See also* Argersinger v. Hamlin (1972). We do not, however, draw from [these cases] the conclusion that a case-by-case approach to furnishing counsel is necessarily inadequate to protect constitutional rights: there are critical differences between criminal trials and probation or parole revocation hearings, and both society and the probationer or parolee have stakes in preserving these differences.

Gagnon v. Scarpelli, 411 U.S. at 783-791.

A defendant has a Sixth Amendment right to counsel in any felony case or in a misdemeanor case if a sentence of incarceration is actually imposed. Argersinger v. Hamlin, 407 U.S. 25, 40 (1972). This includes cases in which the defendant received a suspended sentence and was later incarcerated for a probation violation. Alabama v. Shelton, 535 U.S. 654, 674 (2002).

As detailed in Chapter 12, there is no right to a jury trial for petty offenses. *See* Blanton v. City of North Las Vegas, 489 U.S. 538, 541-542 (1989). By contrast, there is a right to counsel if the defendant is sentenced to jail. Why? Once again, the answer lies in the role defense counsel plays in a case.

ARGERSINGER v. HAMLIN
407 U.S. 25 (1972)

Justice DOUGLAS delivered the opinion of the Court.

Petitioner, an indigent, was charged in Florida with carrying a concealed weapon, an offense punishable by imprisonment up to six months, a $1,000 fine, or both. The trial was to a judge, and petitioner was unrepresented by counsel. He was sentenced to serve 90 days in jail, and brought this habeas corpus action alleging that being deprived of his right to counsel, he was unable as an indigent layman properly to raise and present to the trial court good and sufficient defenses to the charge for which he stands convicted.

While there is historical support for limiting the "deep commitment" to trial by jury to "serious criminal cases," there is no such support for a similar limitation on the right to assistance of counsel:

> Originally, in England, a person charged with treason or felony was denied the aid of counsel, except in respect of legal questions which the accused himself might suggest. At the same time parties in civil cases and persons accused of misdemeanors were entitled to the full assistance of counsel. . . .

The Sixth Amendment thus extended the right to counsel beyond its common-law dimensions. But there is nothing in the language of the Amendment, its history, or in the decisions of this Court, to indicate that it was intended to embody a retraction of the right in petty offenses wherein the common law previously did require that counsel be provided.

We reject, therefore, the premise that since prosecutions for crimes punishable by imprisonment for less than six months may be tried without a jury, they may also be tried without a lawyer.

> The assistance of counsel is often a requisite to the very existence of a fair trial.[4] In our adversary system of criminal justice, any person haled into court, who is too poor to hire a lawyer, cannot be assured a fair trial unless counsel is provided for

4. [The Sixth Amendment] embodies a realistic recognition of the obvious truth that the average defendant does not have the professional legal skill to protect himself when brought before a tribunal with power to take his life or liberty, wherein the prosecution is represented by experienced and learned counsel. That which is simple, orderly and necessary to the lawyer, to the untrained layman may appear intricate, complex and mysterious.

Johnson v. Zerbst, 304 U.S. 458, 462-463 (1938). [Footnote by the Court.]

him. This seems to us to be an obvious truth. Governments, both state and federal, quite properly spend vast sums of money to establish machinery to try defendants accused of crime. Lawyers to prosecute are everywhere deemed essential to protect the public's interest in an orderly society. Similarly, there are few defendants charged with crime, few indeed, who fail to hire the best lawyers they can get to prepare and present their defenses. That government hires lawyers to prosecute and defendants who have the money hire lawyers to defend are the strongest indications of the widespread belief that lawyers in criminal courts are necessities, not luxuries. The right of one charged with crime to counsel may not be deemed fundamental and essential to fair trials in some countries, but it is in ours.

The requirement of counsel may well be necessary for a fair trial even in a petty-offense prosecution. We are by no means convinced that legal and constitutional questions involved in a case that actually leads to imprisonment even for a brief period are any less complex than when a person can be sent off for six months or more. The trial of vagrancy cases is illustrative. While only brief sentences of imprisonment may be imposed, the cases often bristle with thorny constitutional questions.

Beyond the problem of trials and appeals is that of the guilty plea, a problem which looms large in misdemeanor as well as in felony cases. Counsel is needed so that the accused may know precisely what he is doing, so that he is fully aware of the prospect of going to jail or prison, and so that he is treated fairly by the prosecution.

In addition, the volume of misdemeanor cases, far greater in number than felony prosecutions, may create an obsession for speedy dispositions, regardless of the fairness of the result. An inevitable consequence of volume that large is the almost total preoccupation in such a court with the movement of cases. The calendar is long, speed often is substituted for care, and casually arranged out-of-court compromise too often is substituted for adjudication. Inadequate attention tends to be given to the individual defendant, whether in protecting his rights, sifting the facts at trial, deciding the social risk he presents, or determining how to deal with him after conviction. The frequent result is futility and failure. As Dean Edward Barrett recently observed:

> Wherever the visitor looks at the system, he finds great numbers of defendants being processed by harassed and overworked officials. Police have more cases than they can investigate. Prosecutors walk into courtrooms to try simple cases as they take their initial looks at the files. Defense lawyers appear having had no more than time for hasty conversations with their clients. Judges face long calendars with the certain knowledge that their calendars tomorrow and the next day will be, if anything, longer, and so there is no choice but to dispose of the cases.
>
> Suddenly it becomes clear that for most defendants in the criminal process, there is scant regard for them as individuals. They are numbers on dockets, faceless ones to be processed and sent on their way. The gap between the theory and the reality is enormous.

There is evidence of the prejudice which results to misdemeanor defendants from this "assembly-line justice." One study concluded that "misdemeanants represented by attorneys are five times as likely to emerge from police court with all charges dismissed as are defendants who face similar charges without counsel."

We must conclude, therefore, that the problems associated with misdemeanor and petty offenses often require the presence of counsel to insure the accused a fair trial.

We hold, therefore, that absent a knowing and intelligent waiver, no person may be imprisoned for any offense, whether classified as petty, misdemeanor, or felony, unless he was represented by counsel at his trial.

Despite the important role of counsel—even in misdemeanor prosecutions—the Supreme Court reaffirmed in Scott v. Illinois, 440 U.S. 567 (1979), that the right to counsel in misdemeanor cases applies only where a term of imprisonment is imposed. A court may impose a fine regardless of whether the defendant was represented by counsel. As Justice Rehnquist wrote, "[T]he central premise of *Argersinger*—that actual imprisonment is a penalty different in kind from fines or the mere threat of imprisonment—is eminently sound and warrants adoption of actual imprisonment as the line defining the constitutional right to appointment of counsel."

D. STANDARD FOR "EFFECTIVE ASSISTANCE" OF COUNSEL

Following *Gideon*, the courts struggled with the issue of how competent counsel must be to satisfy Sixth Amendment standards. Is the defendant entitled to a lawyer who makes no mistakes? What if the lawyer makes mistakes but those mistakes were unlikely to affect the outcome of the defendant's trial? What does the Sixth Amendment mean when it guarantees the right to "effective" assistance of counsel? The Court settled on its standard for effective assistance of counsel in Strickland v. Washington.

STRICKLAND v. WASHINGTON

466 U.S. 668 (1984)

Justice O'CONNOR delivered the opinion of the Court.

This case requires us to consider the proper standards for judging a criminal defendant's contention that the Constitution requires a conviction or death sentence to be set aside because counsel's assistance at the trial or sentencing was ineffective.

I

During a 10-day period in September 1976, respondent planned and committed three groups of crimes, which included three brutal stabbing murders, torture, kidnaping, severe assaults, attempted murders, attempted extortion, and theft. After his two accomplices were arrested, respondent surrendered to police and voluntarily gave a lengthy statement confessing to the third of the criminal episodes. The State of Florida indicted respondent for kidnaping and murder and appointed an experienced criminal lawyer to represent him.

Counsel actively pursued pretrial motions and discovery. He cut his efforts short, however, and he experienced a sense of hopelessness about the case, when he learned that, against his specific advice, respondent had also confessed to the first two murders. By the date set for trial, respondent was subject to indictment for three counts of first-degree murder and multiple counts of robbery, kidnaping for ransom, breaking and entering and assault, attempted murder, and conspiracy to commit robbery. Respondent waived his right to a jury trial, again acting against counsel's advice, and pleaded guilty to all charges, including the three capital murder charges.

In the plea colloquy, respondent told the trial judge that, although he had committed a string of burglaries, he had no significant prior criminal record and that at the time of his criminal spree he was under extreme stress caused by his inability to support his family. He also stated, however, that he accepted responsibility for the crimes. The trial judge told respondent that he had "a great deal of respect for people who are willing to step forward and admit their responsibility" but that he was making no statement at all about his likely sentencing decision.

Counsel advised respondent to invoke his right under Florida law to an advisory jury at his capital sentencing hearing. Respondent rejected the advice and waived the right. He chose instead to be sentenced by the trial judge without a jury recommendation.

In preparing for the sentencing hearing, counsel spoke with respondent about his background. He also spoke on the telephone with respondent's wife and mother, though he did not follow up on the one unsuccessful effort to meet with them. He did not otherwise seek out character witnesses for respondent. Nor did he request a psychiatric examination, since his conversations with his client gave no indication that respondent had psychological problems.

Counsel decided not to present and hence not to look further for evidence concerning respondent's character and emotional state. That decision reflected trial counsel's sense of hopelessness about overcoming the evidentiary effect of respondent's confessions to the gruesome crimes. It also reflected the judgment that it was advisable to rely on the plea colloquy for evidence about respondent's background and about his claim of emotional stress: the plea colloquy communicated sufficient information about these subjects, and by forgoing the opportunity to present new evidence on these subjects, counsel prevented the State from cross-examining respondent on his claim and from putting on psychiatric evidence of its own.

Counsel also excluded from the sentencing hearing other evidence he thought was potentially damaging. He successfully moved to exclude respondent's "rap sheet." Because he judged that a presentence report might prove more detrimental than helpful, as it would have included respondent's criminal history and thereby would have undermined the claim of no significant history of criminal activity, he did not request that one be prepared.

At the sentencing hearing, counsel's strategy was based primarily on the trial judge's remarks at the plea colloquy as well as on his reputation as a sentencing judge who thought it important for a convicted defendant to own up to his crime. Counsel argued that respondent's remorse and acceptance of responsibility justified sparing him from the death penalty. Counsel also argued that respondent had no history of criminal activity and that respondent committed the crimes under extreme mental or emotional disturbance, thus coming within the statutory list of mitigating circumstances. He further argued that respondent should be spared death because he had surrendered, confessed, and offered to testify against a codefendant and because respondent was fundamentally a good person who had briefly gone badly wrong in extremely stressful circumstances. The State put on evidence and witnesses largely for the purpose of describing the details of the crimes. Counsel did not cross-examine the medical experts who testified about the manner of death of respondent's victims.

The trial judge found several aggravating circumstances with respect to each of the three murders. He found that all three murders were especially heinous, atrocious, and cruel, all involving repeated stabbings. All three murders were committed in the course of at least one other dangerous and violent felony, and since all involved robbery, the murders were for pecuniary gain. All three murders were committed to avoid arrest for the accompanying crimes and to hinder law enforcement. In the course of one of the murders, respondent knowingly subjected numerous persons to a grave risk of death by deliberately stabbing and shooting the murder victim's sisters-in-law, who sustained severe — in one case, ultimately fatal — injuries.

With respect to mitigating circumstances, the trial judge made the same findings for all three capital murders. First, although there was no admitted evidence of prior convictions, respondent had stated that he had engaged in a course of stealing. In any case, even if respondent had no significant history of criminal activity, the aggravating circumstances "would still clearly far outweigh" that mitigating factor. Second, the judge found that, during all three crimes, respondent was not suffering from extreme mental or emotional disturbance and could appreciate the criminality of his acts. Third, none of the victims was a participant in, or consented to, respondent's conduct. Fourth, respondent's participation in the crimes was neither minor nor the result of duress or domination by an accomplice.

In short, the trial judge found numerous aggravating circumstances and no (or a single comparatively insignificant) mitigating circumstance. With respect to each of the three convictions for capital murder, the trial judge concluded: "A careful consideration of all matters presented to the court impels the conclusion that there are insufficient mitigating circumstances . . . to outweigh the aggravating circumstances." He therefore sentenced respondent to death on each of the three counts of murder and to prison terms for the other crimes.

Respondent subsequently sought collateral relief in state court on numerous grounds, among them that counsel had rendered ineffective assistance at the sentencing proceeding. Respondent challenged counsel's assistance in six respects. He asserted that counsel was ineffective because he failed to move for a continuance to prepare for sentencing, to request a psychiatric report, to investigate and present character witnesses, to seek a presentence investigation report, to present meaningful arguments to the sentencing judge, and to investigate the medical examiner's reports or cross-examine the medical experts. In support of the claim, respondent submitted 14 affidavits from friends, neighbors, and relatives stating that they would have testified if asked to do so. He also submitted one psychiatric report and one psychological report stating that respondent, though not under the influence of extreme mental or emotional disturbance, was "chronically frustrated and depressed because of his economic dilemma" at the time of his crimes.

The trial court denied relief.

In assessing attorney performance, all the Federal Courts of Appeals and all but a few state courts have now adopted the "reasonably effective assistance" standard in one formulation or another. Yet this Court has not had occasion squarely to decide whether that is the proper standard. [W]e granted certiorari to consider the standards by which to judge a contention that the Constitution requires that a criminal judgment be overturned because of the actual ineffective assistance of counsel.

II

In a long line of cases that includes . . . Gideon v. Wainwright (1963), this Court has recognized that the Sixth Amendment right to counsel exists, and is needed, in order to protect the fundamental right to a fair trial. The Constitution guarantees:

> In all criminal prosecutions, the accused shall enjoy the right to a speedy and public trial, by an impartial jury of the State and district wherein the crime shall have been committed, which district shall have been previously ascertained by law, and to be informed of the nature and cause of the accusation; to be confronted with the witnesses against him; to have compulsory process for obtaining witnesses in his favor, and to have the Assistance of Counsel for his defence.

Thus, a fair trial is one in which evidence subject to adversarial testing is presented to an impartial tribunal for resolution of issues defined in advance of the proceeding. The right to counsel plays a crucial role in the adversarial system embodied in the Sixth Amendment, since access to counsel's skill and knowledge is necessary to accord defendants the "ample opportunity to meet the case of the prosecution" to which they are entitled.

Because of the vital importance of counsel's assistance, this Court has held that, with certain exceptions, a person accused of a federal or state crime has the right to have counsel appointed if retained counsel cannot be obtained. *See* Argersinger v. Hamlin (1972). That a person who happens to be a lawyer is present at trial alongside the accused, however, is not enough to satisfy the constitutional command. The Sixth Amendment recognizes the right to the assistance of counsel because it envisions counsel's playing a role that is critical to the ability of the adversarial system to produce just results. An accused is entitled to be assisted by an attorney, whether retained or appointed, who plays the role necessary to ensure that the trial is fair.

For that reason, the Court has recognized that "the right to counsel is the right to the effective assistance of counsel." Government violates the right to effective assistance when it interferes in certain ways with the ability of counsel to make independent decisions about how to conduct the defense. *See, e.g.,* Geders v. United States (1976) (bar on attorney-client consultation during overnight recess). Counsel, however, can also deprive a defendant of the right to effective assistance, simply by failing to render "adequate legal assistance," Cuyler v. Sullivan (actual conflict of interest adversely affecting lawyer's performance renders assistance ineffective).

The Court has not elaborated on the meaning of the constitutional requirement of effective assistance in the latter class of cases — that is, those presenting claims of "actual ineffectiveness." In giving meaning to the requirement, however, we must take its purpose — to ensure a fair trial — as the guide. The benchmark for judging any claim of ineffectiveness must be whether counsel's conduct so undermined the proper functioning of the adversarial process that the trial cannot be relied on as having produced a just result.

The same principle applies to a capital sentencing proceeding such as that provided by Florida law. We need not consider the role of counsel in an ordinary sentencing, which may involve informal proceedings and standardless discretion in the sentencer, and hence may require a different approach to the definition of constitutionally effective assistance. A capital sentencing proceeding like the one involved in this case, however, is sufficiently like a trial in its adversarial format and in the existence of standards for decision, that counsel's role in the proceeding is comparable to counsel's role at trial — to ensure that the adversarial testing process works to produce a just result under the standards governing decision. For purposes of describing counsel's duties, therefore, Florida's capital sentencing proceeding need not be distinguished from an ordinary trial.

III

A convicted defendant's claim that counsel's assistance was so defective as to require reversal of a conviction or death sentence has two components. First, the defendant must show that counsel's performance was deficient. This requires showing that counsel made errors so serious that counsel was not functioning as the "counsel" guaranteed the defendant by the Sixth Amendment. Second, the defendant must show that the deficient performance prejudiced the defense. This requires showing that counsel's errors were so serious as to deprive the defendant of a fair trial, a trial whose result is reliable. Unless a defendant makes both showings, it cannot be said that the conviction or death sentence resulted from a breakdown in the adversary process that renders the result unreliable.

A

As all the Federal Courts of Appeals have now held, the proper standard for attorney performance is that of reasonably effective assistance. . . . When a convicted defendant complains of the ineffectiveness of counsel's assistance, the defendant must show that counsel's representation fell below an objective standard of reasonableness.

More specific guidelines are not appropriate. The Sixth Amendment refers simply to "counsel," not specifying particular requirements of effective assistance. It relies instead on the legal profession's maintenance of standards sufficient to justify the law's presumption that counsel will fulfill the role in the adversary process that the Amendment envisions. The proper measure of attorney performance remains simply reasonableness under prevailing professional norms.

Representation of a criminal defendant entails certain basic duties. Counsel's function is to assist the defendant, and hence counsel owes the client a duty of loyalty, a duty to avoid conflicts of interest. From counsel's function as assistant to the defendant derive the overarching duty to advocate the defendant's cause and the more particular duties to consult with the defendant on important decisions and to keep the defendant informed of important developments in the course of the prosecution. Counsel also has a duty to bring to bear such skill and knowledge as will render the trial a reliable adversarial testing process.

These basic duties neither exhaustively define the obligations of counsel nor form a checklist for judicial evaluation of attorney performance. In any case presenting an ineffectiveness claim, the performance inquiry must be whether counsel's assistance was reasonable considering all the circumstances. Prevailing norms of practice as reflected in American Bar Association standards and the like are guides to determining what is reasonable, but they are only guides. No particular set of detailed rules for counsel's conduct can satisfactorily take account of the variety of circumstances faced by defense counsel or the range of legitimate decisions regarding how best to represent a criminal defendant. Any such set of rules would interfere with the constitutionally protected independence of counsel and restrict the wide latitude counsel must have in making tactical decisions.

Judicial scrutiny of counsel's performance must be highly deferential. It is all too tempting for a defendant to second-guess counsel's assistance after conviction or adverse sentence, and it is all too easy for a court, examining counsel's defense after it has proved unsuccessful, to conclude that a particular act or omission of counsel was unreasonable. A fair assessment of attorney performance requires that every effort be made to eliminate the distorting effects of hindsight, to reconstruct the circumstances of counsel's challenged conduct, and to evaluate the conduct from counsel's perspective at the time. Because of the difficulties inherent in making the evaluation, a court must indulge a strong presumption that counsel's conduct falls within the wide range of reasonable professional assistance; that is, the defendant must overcome the presumption that, under the circumstances, the challenged action "might be considered sound trial strategy." There are countless ways to provide effective assistance in any given case. Even the best criminal defense attorneys would not defend a particular client in the same way.

The availability of intrusive post-trial inquiry into attorney performance or of detailed guidelines for its evaluation would encourage the proliferation of ineffectiveness challenges. Criminal trials resolved unfavorably to the defendant would increasingly come to be followed by a second trial, this one of counsel's unsuccessful defense. Counsel's performance and even willingness to serve could be adversely affected. Intensive scrutiny of counsel and rigid requirements for acceptable assistance could dampen the ardor and impair the independence of defense counsel, discourage the acceptance of assigned cases, and undermine the trust between attorney and client.

Thus, a court deciding an actual ineffectiveness claim must judge the reasonableness of counsel's challenged conduct on the facts of the particular case, viewed as of the time of counsel's conduct. A convicted defendant making a claim of ineffective assistance must identify the acts or omissions of counsel that are alleged not to have been the result of reasonable professional judgment. The court must then determine whether, in light of all the circumstances, the identified acts or omissions were outside the wide range of professionally competent assistance. In making that determination, the court should keep in mind that counsel's function, as elaborated in prevailing professional norms, is to make the adversarial testing process work in the particular case. At the same time, the court should recognize that counsel is strongly presumed to have rendered adequate assistance and made all significant decisions in the exercise of reasonable professional judgment.

These standards require no special amplification in order to define counsel's duty to investigate, the duty at issue in this case. [C]ounsel has a duty to make reasonable investigations or to make a reasonable decision that makes particular investigations unnecessary.

The reasonableness of counsel's actions may be determined or substantially influenced by the defendant's own statements or actions. Counsel's actions are usually based, quite properly, on informed strategic choices made by the defendant and on information supplied by the defendant. In particular, what investigation decisions are reasonable depends critically on such information. For example, when the facts that support a certain potential line of defense are generally known to counsel because of what the defendant has said, the need for further investigation may be considerably diminished or eliminated altogether. And when a defendant has given counsel reason to believe that pursuing certain investigations would be fruitless or even harmful, counsel's failure to pursue those investigations may not later be challenged as unreasonable. In short, inquiry into counsel's conversations with the defendant may be critical to a proper assessment of counsel's investigation decisions, just as it may be critical to a proper assessment of counsel's other litigation decisions.

B

An error by counsel, even if professionally unreasonable, does not warrant setting aside the judgment of a criminal proceeding if the error had no effect on the judgment. The purpose of the Sixth Amendment guarantee of counsel is to ensure that a defendant has the assistance necessary to justify reliance on the outcome of the proceeding. Accordingly, any deficiencies in counsel's performance must be prejudicial to the defense in order to constitute ineffective assistance under the Constitution.

In certain Sixth Amendment contexts, prejudice is presumed. Actual or constructive denial of the assistance of counsel altogether is legally presumed to result in prejudice. So are various kinds of state interference with counsel's assistance. Prejudice in these circumstances is so likely that case-by-case inquiry into prejudice is not worth the cost. Moreover, such circumstances involve impairments of the Sixth Amendment right that are easy to identify and, for that reason and because the prosecution is directly responsible, easy for the government to prevent.

One type of actual ineffectiveness claim warrants a similar, though more limited, presumption of prejudice. In Cuyler v. Sullivan, the Court held that prejudice is presumed when counsel is burdened by an actual conflict of interest. In those circumstances, counsel breaches the duty of loyalty, perhaps the most basic of counsel's duties. Moreover, it is difficult to measure the precise effect on the defense of representation corrupted by conflicting interests. Given the obligation of counsel to avoid conflicts of interest and the ability of trial courts to make early inquiry in certain situations likely to give rise to conflicts, *see, e.g.*, Fed. Rule Crim. Proc. 44(c), it is reasonable for the criminal justice system to maintain a fairly rigid rule of presumed prejudice for conflicts of interest.

Conflict of interest claims aside, actual ineffectiveness claims alleging a deficiency in attorney performance are subject to a general requirement that the defendant affirmatively prove prejudice. The government is not responsible for, and hence not able to prevent, attorney errors that will result in reversal of a conviction or sentence. Attorney errors come in an infinite variety and are as likely to be utterly harmless in a particular case as they are to be prejudicial. They cannot be classified according to likelihood of causing prejudice. Nor can they be defined with sufficient precision to inform defense attorneys correctly just what conduct to avoid. Representation is an art, and an act or omission that is unprofessional in one case may be sound or even brilliant in another. Even if a defendant shows that particular errors of counsel were unreasonable, therefore, the defendant must show that they actually had an adverse effect on the defense.

It is not enough for the defendant to show that the errors had some conceivable effect on the outcome of the proceeding. Virtually every act or omission of counsel would meet that test, and not every error that conceivably could have influenced the outcome undermines the reliability of the result of the proceeding. Respondent suggests requiring a showing that the errors "impaired the presentation of the defense." That standard, however, provides no workable principle. Since any error, if it is indeed an error, "impairs" the presentation of the defense, the proposed standard is inadequate because it provides no way of deciding what impairments are sufficiently serious to warrant setting aside the outcome of the proceeding.

On the other hand, we believe that a defendant need not show that counsel's deficient conduct more likely than not altered the outcome in the case. . . . The result of a proceeding can be rendered unreliable, and hence the proceeding itself unfair, even if the errors of counsel cannot be shown by a preponderance of the evidence to have determined the outcome.

Accordingly, the appropriate test for prejudice finds its roots in the test for materiality of exculpatory information not disclosed to the defense by the prosecution. The defendant must show that there is a reasonable probability that, but for counsel's unprofessional errors, the result of the proceeding would have been different. A reasonable probability is a probability sufficient to undermine confidence in the outcome.

When a defendant challenges a conviction, the question is whether there is a reasonable probability that, absent the errors, the factfinder would have had a reasonable doubt respecting guilt. When a defendant challenges a death sentence such as the one at issue in this case, the question is whether there is a reasonable probability that, absent the errors, the sentencer — including an appellate court, to the extent it independently reweighs the evidence — would have concluded that the balance of aggravating and mitigating circumstances did not warrant death.

In making this determination, a court hearing an ineffectiveness claim must consider the totality of the evidence before the judge or jury. Some of the factual findings will have been unaffected by the errors, and factual findings that were affected will have been affected in different ways. Some errors will have had a pervasive effect on the inferences to be drawn from the evidence, altering the entire evidentiary picture, and some will have had an isolated, trivial effect. Moreover, a verdict or conclusion only weakly supported by the record is more likely to have been affected by errors than one with overwhelming record support. Taking the unaffected findings as a given, and taking due account of the effect of the errors on the remaining findings, a court making the prejudice inquiry must ask if the defendant has met the burden of showing that the decision reached would reasonably likely have been different absent the errors.

IV

A number of practical considerations are important for the application of the standards we have outlined. Most important, in adjudicating a claim of actual ineffectiveness of counsel, a court should keep in mind that the principles we have stated do not establish mechanical rules. Although those principles should guide the process of decision, the ultimate focus of inquiry must be on the fundamental fairness of the proceeding whose result is being challenged. In every case the court should be concerned with whether, despite the strong presumption of reliability, the result of the particular proceeding is unreliable because of a breakdown in the adversarial process that our system counts on to produce just results.

Although we have discussed the performance component of an ineffectiveness claim prior to the prejudice component, there is no reason for a court deciding an ineffective assistance claim to approach the inquiry in the same order or even to address both components of the inquiry if the defendant makes an insufficient showing on one. In particular, a court need not determine whether counsel's performance was deficient before examining the prejudice suffered by the defendant as a result of the alleged deficiencies. The object of an ineffectiveness claim is not to grade counsel's performance. If it is easier to dispose of an ineffectiveness claim on the ground of lack of sufficient prejudice, which we expect will often be so, that course should be followed. Courts should strive to ensure that ineffectiveness claims not become so burdensome to defense counsel that the entire criminal justice system suffers as a result.

V

Application of the governing principles is not difficult in this case. The facts as described make clear that the conduct of respondent's counsel at and before respondent's sentencing proceeding cannot be found unreasonable. They also make clear that, even assuming the challenged conduct of counsel was unreasonable, respondent suffered insufficient prejudice to warrant setting aside his death sentence.

With respect to the performance component, the record shows that respondent's counsel made a strategic choice to argue for the extreme emotional distress mitigating circumstance and to rely as fully as possible on respondent's acceptance of responsibility for his crimes. Although counsel understandably felt hopeless about respondent's prospects, nothing in the record indicates that counsel's sense of hopelessness distorted his professional judgment. Counsel's strategy choice was well within the range of professionally reasonable judgments, and the decision not to seek more character or psychological evidence than was already in hand was likewise reasonable.

The trial judge's views on the importance of owning up to one's crimes were well known to counsel. The aggravating circumstances were utterly overwhelming. Trial counsel could reasonably surmise from his conversations with respondent that character and psychological evidence would be of little help. Respondent had already been able to mention at the plea colloquy the substance of what there was to know about his financial and emotional troubles. Restricting testimony on respondent's character to what had come in at the plea colloquy ensured that contrary character and psychological evidence and respondent's criminal history, which counsel had successfully moved to exclude, would not come in. On these facts, there can be little question, even without application of the presumption of adequate performance, that trial counsel's defense, though unsuccessful, was the result of reasonable professional judgment.

With respect to the prejudice component, the lack of merit of respondent's claim is even more stark. The evidence that respondent says his trial counsel should have offered at the sentencing hearing would barely have altered the sentencing profile presented to the sentencing judge. As the state courts and District Court found, at most this evidence shows that numerous people who knew respondent thought he was generally a good person and that a psychiatrist and a psychologist believed he was under considerable emotional stress that did not rise to the level of extreme disturbance. Given the overwhelming aggravating factors, there is no reasonable probability that the omitted evidence would have changed the conclusion that the aggravating circumstances outweighed the mitigating circumstances and, hence, the sentence imposed. Indeed, admission of the evidence respondent now offers might even have been harmful to his case: his "rap sheet" would probably have been admitted into evidence, and the psychological reports would have directly contradicted respondent's claim that the mitigating circumstance of extreme emotional disturbance applied to his case.

Failure to make the required showing of either deficient performance or sufficient prejudice defeats the ineffectiveness claim. Here there is a double failure. More generally, respondent has made no showing that the justice of his sentence was rendered unreliable by a breakdown in the adversary process caused by deficiencies in counsel's assistance. Respondent's sentencing proceeding was not fundamentally unfair.

We conclude, therefore, that the District Court properly declined to issue a writ of habeas corpus.

Justice MARSHALL, dissenting.

The Sixth and Fourteenth Amendments guarantee a person accused of a crime the right to the aid of a lawyer in preparing and presenting his defense.

It has long been settled that "the right to counsel is the right to the effective assistance of counsel."

My objection to the performance standard adopted by the Court is that it is so malleable that, in practice, it will either have no grip at all or will yield excessive variation in the manner in which the Sixth Amendment is interpreted and applied by different courts. To tell lawyers and the lower courts that counsel for a criminal defendant must behave "reasonably" and must act like "a reasonably competent attorney," is to tell them almost nothing. In essence, the majority has instructed judges called upon to assess claims of ineffective assistance of counsel to advert to their own intuitions regarding what constitutes "professional" representation, and has discouraged them from trying to develop more detailed standards governing the performance of defense counsel. In my view, the Court has thereby not only abdicated its own responsibility to interpret the Constitution, but also impaired the ability of the lower courts to exercise theirs.

I object to the prejudice standard adopted by the Court for two independent reasons. First, it is often very difficult to tell whether a defendant convicted after a trial in which he was ineffectively represented would have fared better if his lawyer had been competent. Seemingly impregnable cases can sometimes be dismantled by good defense counsel. On the basis of a cold record, it may be impossible for a reviewing court confidently to ascertain how the government's evidence and arguments would have stood up against rebuttal and cross-examination by a shrewd, well-prepared lawyer. The difficulties of estimating prejudice after the fact are exacerbated by the possibility that evidence of injury to the defendant may be missing from the record precisely because of the incompetence of defense counsel. In view of all these impediments to a fair evaluation of the probability that the outcome of a trial was affected by ineffectiveness of counsel, it seems to me senseless to impose on a defendant whose lawyer has been shown to have been incompetent the burden of demonstrating prejudice.

Second and more fundamentally, the assumption on which the Court's holding rests is that the only purpose of the constitutional guarantee of effective assistance of counsel is to reduce the chance that innocent persons will be convicted. In my view, the guarantee also functions to ensure that convictions are obtained only through fundamentally fair procedures. The majority contends that the Sixth Amendment is not violated when a manifestly guilty defendant is convicted after a trial in which he was represented by a manifestly ineffective attorney. I cannot agree. Every defendant is entitled to a trial in which his interests are vigorously and conscientiously advocated by an able lawyer. A proceeding in which the defendant does not receive meaningful assistance in meeting the forces of the State does not, in my opinion, constitute due process.

———————————

The same day that the Court issued its decision in *Strickland,* it punctuated its decision by deciding Cronic v. United States, 466 U.S. 648 (1984). In *Cronic,* a young real estate lawyer had less than 30 days to prepare for his first criminal case (a mail fraud check kiting scheme) after the government had taken four and one-half years to prepare its prosecution. The defendant argued that his lawyer's lack of preparation time and inexperience gave rise to a presumption of prejudice. Writing for the Court, Justice Stevens rejected Cronic's argument:

> Neither the period of time that the Government spent investigating the case, nor the number of documents that its agents reviewed during that investigation, is necessarily relevant to the question whether a competent lawyer could prepare to defend the case in 25 days. The Government's task of finding and assembling admissible evidence that will carry its burden of proving guilt beyond a reasonable doubt is entirely different from the defendant's task in preparing to deny or rebut a criminal charge. . . .
>
> That conclusion is not undermined by the fact that respondent's lawyer was young, that his principal practice was in real estate, or that this was his first jury trial. Every experienced criminal defense attorney once tried his first criminal case. Moreover, a lawyer's experience with real estate transactions might be more useful in preparing to try a criminal case involving financial transactions than would prior experience in handling, for example, armed robbery prosecutions. . . .
>
> This case is not one in which the surrounding circumstances make it unlikely that the defendant could have received the effective assistance of counsel. . . . [On remand, respondent] can therefore make out a claim of ineffective assistance only by pointing to specific errors made by trial counsel.

In *Cronic,* the Court identified three circumstances under which prejudice may be presumed: (1) if there has been a complete denial of counsel, (2) "if counsel entirely fails to subject the prosecution's case to meaningful adversarial testing," or (3) when there is an actual conflict of interest for counsel.

1. Conflicts of Interest

Before *Cronic,* the Supreme Court had held in Holloway v. Arkansas, 435 U.S. 475 (1978), that it violates a defendant's Sixth Amendment rights to force defense counsel to represent codefendants over counsel's timely objection. When there is a potential conflict of interest, the trial court should inquire regarding it and whether the defendant will still be able to receive effective assistance of counsel.

However, in Cuyler v. Sullivan, 446 U.S. 335 (1980), the Supreme Court held that a defendant can demonstrate a Sixth Amendment violation only by showing (1) defense counsel was actively representing conflicting interests, and (2) the conflict adversely affected counsel's performance for the defendant. In distinguishing its holding in Holloway v. Arkansas and rejecting Sullivan's claim that his privately retained counsel had a disqualify-ing conflict of interest because he represented all three defendants in their murder cases, the Court noted:

> In Holloway, a single public defender represented three defendants at the same trial. The trial court refused to consider the appointment of separate counsel despite the defense lawyer's timely and repeated assertions that the interests of his clients conflicted.
>
> Holloway requires state trial courts to investigate timely objections to multiple representation. But nothing in our precedents suggests that the Sixth Amendment requires state courts themselves to initiate inquiries into the propriety of multiple representation in every case. Defense counsel have an ethical obligation to avoid conflicting representations and to advise the court promptly when a conflict of interest arises during the course of trial.
>
> Nothing in the circumstances of this case indicates that the trial court had a duty to inquire whether there was a conflict of interest. The provision of separate trials for Sullivan and his codefendants significantly reduced the potential for a diver-gence in their interests. No participant in Sullivan's trial ever objected to the multiple representation. Counsel's opening argument for Sullivan outlined a defense compatible with the view that none of the defendants was connected with the murders. The opening argument also suggested that counsel was not afraid to call witnesses whose testimony might be needed at the trials of Sullivan's codefendants. Finally, counsel's critical decision to rest Sullivan's defense was on its face a reasonable tactical response to the weakness of the circumstantial evidence presented by the prosecutor.

As *Cuyler* makes clear, there is no per se rule of reversal when defense counsel has an actual or potential conflict of interest. Rather, the burden is on the defendant to demonstrate that defense counsel's conflicting inter-ests negatively impacted counsel's performance at trial. For example, in Mickens v. Taylor, 535 U.S. 162 (2002), the Court held that there was no automatic claim of ineffective assistance of counsel even though defense counsel in that capital murder case had previously represented the murder victim.

Likewise, in Burger v. Kemp, 483 U.S. 776 (1987), the Court refused to find that the defendant's lawyer had an actual conflict of interest simply because his law partner represented Burger's codefendant. Burger argued that his lawyer's relationship with his codefendant's counsel prejudiced his case because Burger's lawyer did not claim that he was less culpable than his codefendant, but the Supreme Court found that the claim was mere spec-ulation and that there was no actual conflict of interest that violated Burger's Sixth Amendment rights.

When there is a conflict of interest, the defendants may waive the right to conflict-free assistance of counsel if the waiver is knowing and intelligent. Holloway v. Arkansas, 435 U.S. at 483 n.5. However, the trial judge is not obliged to accept this waiver. The court still carries the responsibility of deciding whether the conflicted counsel can adequately represent the defen-dant's interests. *See* Wheat v. United States, 486 U.S. 153 (1988); *see also* Federal Rule of Criminal Procedure 44.

2. Complete Denial of Counsel

While the Court held in *Cronic* that prejudice may be presumed "if counsel entirely fails to subject the prosecution's case to meaningful adversarial testing," this exception is rarely recognized by the Court. For example, in Bell v. Cone, 535 U.S. 685 (2002), Cone argued that he was completely denied the assistance of counsel because his lawyer did not call any witnesses in mitigation of punishment at the penalty phase of his capital trial, although counsel did cross-examine some of the prosecution witnesses. The Court refused to find that counsel had "*entirely*" failed to test the prosecutor's case, and therefore, Cone needed to satisfy the prejudice standard of the *Strickland* test.

3. Strategic Decisions by Defense Counsel

Most claims of ineffective assistance of counsel are challenges to defense counsel's strategic decisions. Defense counsels have broad leeway in deciding on trial strategy. In *Strickland*, the Supreme Court cautioned against second-guessing defense counsels' decisions. Generally, it is very difficult for a defendant to succeed on a claim of ineffective assistance of counsel because an attorney's poor performance is excused if the evidence is otherwise strong in the case and the defendant, therefore, cannot satisfy the prejudice prong of *Strickland*'s ineffective assistance of counsel test. Courts have said that there is no per se rule of reversal even if defense counsel sleeps through portions of the trial. *See* Tippins v. Walker, 77 F.3d 682 (2d Cir. 1996) (in some cases, defense counsel's appearance of sleeping can be a tactical maneuver; however, in this case daily sleeping by counsel met *Cronic* standard of ineffective assistance of counsel).

However, are there any limits on the trial strategy a defense lawyer may choose without violating the Sixth Amendment? For example, what if defense counsel in a death penalty case concedes a defendant's guilt? Does that still meet *Strickland*'s standard for effective assistance of counsel?

FLORIDA v. NIXON
543 U.S. 175 (2004)

Justice GINSBURG delivered the opinion of the Court.

This capital case concerns defense counsel's strategic decision to concede, at the guilt phase of the trial, the defendant's commission of murder, and to concentrate the defense on establishing, at the penalty phase, cause for sparing the defendant's life. Any concession of that order, the Florida Supreme Court held, made without the defendant's express consent— however gruesome the crime and despite the strength of the evidence of guilt—automatically ranks as prejudicial ineffective assistance of counsel necessitating a new trial. We reverse the Florida Supreme Court's judgment.

Defense counsel undoubtedly has a duty to discuss potential strategies with the defendant. *See* Strickland v. Washington (1984). But when a defendant, informed by counsel, neither consents nor objects to the course counsel describes as the most promising means to avert a sentence of death, counsel is not automatically barred from pursuing that course. The reasonableness of counsel's performance, after consultation with the defendant yields no response, must be judged in accord with the inquiry generally applicable to ineffective-assistance-of-counsel claims: Did counsel's representation "f[a]ll below an objective standard of reasonableness"? The Florida Supreme Court erred in applying, instead, a presumption of deficient performance, as well as a presumption of prejudice; that latter presumption, we have instructed, is reserved for cases in which counsel fails meaningfully to oppose the prosecution's case. United States v. Cronic (1984). A presumption of prejudice is not in order based solely on a defendant's failure to provide express consent to a tenable strategy counsel has adequately disclosed to and discussed with the defendant.

I

On Monday, August 13, 1984, near a dirt road in the environs of Tallahassee, Florida, a passing motorist discovered Jeanne Bickner's charred body. Bickner had been tied to a tree and set on fire while still alive. Her left leg and arm, and most of her hair and skin, had been burned away. The next day, police found Bickner's car, abandoned on a Tallahassee street corner, on fire. Police arrested 23-year-old Joe Elton Nixon later that morning, after Nixon's brother informed the sheriff's office that Nixon had confessed to the murder.

Questioned by the police, Nixon described in graphic detail how he had kidnaped Bickner, then killed her. . . . The State gathered overwhelming evidence establishing that Nixon had committed the murder in the manner he described.

Nixon was indicted in Leon County, Florida, for first-degree murder, kidnaping, robbery, and arson. Assistant public defender Michael Corin, assigned to represent Nixon, filed a plea of not guilty, and deposed all of the State's potential witnesses. Corin concluded, given the strength of the evidence, that Nixon's guilt was not "subject to any reasonable dispute."[5] Corin thereupon commenced plea negotiations, hoping to persuade the prosecution to drop the death penalty in exchange for Nixon's guilty pleas to all charges. Negotiations broke down when the prosecutors indicated their unwillingness to recommend a sentence other than death.

---

5. Every court to consider this case, including the judge who presided over Nixon's trial, agreed with Corin's assessment of the evidence. [Footnote by the Court.]

Faced with the inevitability of going to trial on a capital charge, Corin turned his attention to the penalty phase, believing that the only way to save Nixon's life would be to present extensive mitigation evidence centering on Nixon's mental instability. Experienced in capital defense, . . . Corin concluded that the best strategy would be to concede guilt, thereby preserving his credibility in urging leniency during the penalty phase.

Corin attempted to explain this strategy to Nixon at least three times. Nixon was generally unresponsive during their discussions. He never verbally approved or protested Corin's proposed strategy. Overall, Nixon gave Corin very little, if any, assistance or direction in preparing the case. Corin eventually exercised his professional judgment to pursue the concession strategy.

When Nixon's trial began on July 15, 1985, his unresponsiveness deepened into disruptive and violent behavior. On the second day of jury selection, Nixon pulled off his clothing, demanded a black judge and lawyer, refused to be escorted into the courtroom, and threatened to force the guards to shoot him. When the judge examined Nixon on the record in a holding cell, Nixon stated he had no interest in the trial and threatened to misbehave if forced to attend. The judge ruled that Nixon had intelligently and voluntarily waived his right to be present at trial.

The guilt phase of the trial thus began in Nixon's absence. In his opening statement, Corin acknowledged Nixon's guilt and urged the jury to focus on the penalty phase:

> In this case, there won't be any question, none whatsoever, that my client, Joe Elton Nixon, caused Jeannie Bickner's death. . . . [T]hat fact will be proved to your satisfaction beyond any doubt.
>
> This case is about the death of Joe Elton Nixon and whether it should occur within the next few years by electrocution or maybe its natural expiration after a lifetime of confinement. . . .
>
> Now, in arriving at your verdict, in your penalty recommendation, for we will get that far, you are going to learn many facts . . . about Joe Elton Nixon. Some of those facts are going to be good. That may not seem clear to you at this time. But, and sadly, most of the things you learn of Joe Elton Nixon are not going to be good. But, I'm suggesting to you that when you have seen all the testimony, heard all the testimony and the evidence that has been shown, there are going to be reasons why you should recommend that his life be spared.

At the start of the penalty phase, Corin argued to the jury that "Joe Elton Nixon is not normal organically, intellectually, emotionally or educationally or in any other way." Corin presented the testimony of eight witnesses. Relatives and friends described Nixon's childhood emotional troubles and his erratic behavior in the days preceding the murder. A psychiatrist and a psychologist addressed Nixon's antisocial personality, his history of emotional instability and psychiatric care, his low IQ, and the possibility that at some point he suffered brain damage.

In his closing argument, Corin emphasized Nixon's youth, the psychiatric evidence, and the jury's discretion to consider any mitigating circumstances.

Corin urged that, if not sentenced to death, "Joe Elton Nixon would [n]ever be released from confinement." The death penalty, Corin maintained, was appropriate only for "intact human being[s]," and "Joe Elton Nixon is not one of those. He's never been one of those. He never will be one of those." Corin concluded: "You know, we're not around here all that long. And it's rare when we have the opportunity to give or take life. And you have that opportunity to give life. And I'm going to ask you to do that. Thank you." After deliberating for approximately three hours, the jury recommended that Nixon be sentenced to death.

We granted certiorari to resolve an important question of constitutional law, i.e., whether counsel's failure to obtain the defendant's express consent to a strategy of conceding guilt in a capital trial automatically renders counsel's performance deficient, and whether counsel's effectiveness should be evaluated under *Cronic* or *Strickland.*

II

An attorney undoubtedly has a duty to consult with the client regarding "important decisions," including questions of overarching defense strategy. That obligation, however, does not require counsel to obtain the defendant's consent to "every tactical decision." But certain decisions regarding the exercise or waiver of basic trial rights are of such moment that they cannot be made for the defendant by a surrogate. A defendant, this Court affirmed, has "the ultimate authority" to determine "whether to plead guilty, waive a jury, testify in his or her own behalf, or take an appeal." Concerning those decisions, an attorney must both consult with the defendant and obtain consent to the recommended course of action.

The Florida Supreme Court required Nixon's "affirmative, explicit acceptance" of Corin's strategy because it deemed Corin's statements to the jury "the functional equivalent of a guilty plea." We disagree with that assessment.

Corin was obliged to, and in fact several times did, explain his proposed trial strategy to Nixon. Given Nixon's constant resistance to answering inquiries put to him by counsel and court, Corin was not additionally required to gain express consent before conceding Nixon's guilt. The two evidentiary hearings conducted by the Florida trial court demonstrate beyond doubt that Corin fulfilled his duty of consultation by informing Nixon of counsel's proposed strategy and its potential benefits. Nixon's characteristic silence each time information was conveyed to him, in sum, did not suffice to render unreasonable Corin's decision to concede guilt and to home in, instead, on the life or death penalty issue.

On the record thus far developed, Corin's concession of Nixon's guilt does not rank as a "fail[ure] to function in any meaningful sense as the Government's adversary." Although such a concession in a run-of-the-mine trial might present a closer question, the gravity of the potential sentence in a capital trial and the proceeding's two-phase structure vitally affect counsel's strategic calculus. Attorneys representing capital defendants face daunting challenges in developing trial strategies, not least because the defendant's guilt is often clear. Prosecutors are more likely to seek the death penalty, and to refuse to accept a plea to a life sentence, when the evidence is overwhelming and the crime heinous. In such cases, "avoiding execution [may be] the best and only realistic result possible."

Renowned advocate Clarence Darrow, we note, famously employed a similar strategy as counsel for the youthful, cold-blooded killers Richard Loeb and Nathan Leopold. Imploring the judge to spare the boys' lives, Darrow declared: "I do not know how much salvage there is in these two boys. . . . I will be honest with this court as I have tried to be from the beginning. I know that these boys are not fit to be at large."

To summarize, in a capital case, counsel must consider in conjunction both the guilt and penalty phases in determining how best to proceed. When counsel informs the defendant of the strategy counsel believes to be in the defendant's best interest and the defendant is unresponsive, counsel's strategic choice is not impeded by any blanket rule demanding the defendant's explicit consent. Instead, if counsel's strategy, given the evidence bearing on the defendant's guilt, satisfies the *Strickland* standard, that is the end of the matter; no tenable claim of ineffective assistance would remain.

The Court has held firm to its decision not to require lawyers to follow specific guidelines in trying cases. However, in her opinion in Wiggins v. Smith, 539 U.S. 510 (2003), Justice O'Connor suggested that compliance with ABA Standards for Criminal Justice — especially those setting forth a lawyer's responsibility in investigating a case — may provide defense lawyers a safe harbor against claims of ineffective assistance of counsel. Kevin Wiggins was convicted of murder and sentenced to death. He argued that his Sixth Amendment right to counsel was violated because his lawyer failed to investigate his personal background, which would have provided mitigating evidence for his capital sentencing proceedings. If his lawyer had made the effort, he would have found that Wiggins had lived a nightmare as a child. He was abandoned by his mother, ended up in foster care where he was repeatedly raped and tortured, and ended up homeless with diminished mental capacities. In these extreme circumstances, the Supreme Court held that there was a reasonable probability that the sentencing jury would have returned a different verdict had it known of these facts.

In Rompilla v. Beard, 545 U.S. 374 (2005), the Supreme Court continued to focus on counsel's duty to adequately investigate a case before trial. It found that it was ineffective assistance of counsel in a capital case for defense counsel not to request defendant's file from prior cases that would have shown that he too suffered from mental health issues and childhood deprivations that could have been presented to the jury in mitigation of his sentence.

More recently, the Court reaffirmed the importance of having defense counsel adequately investigate a case before trial. In Porter v. McCollum, 558 U.S. 30 (2009), the Court held that it was ineffective assistance of counsel for defense counsel to fail to discover or present evidence during the penalty phase of Porter's murder trial that Porter had a long and distinguished military record, had been the victim of childhood abuse, and had impaired mental capacity. These cases emphasize that pretrial investigation is a critical aspect of defense counsel's responsibilities, especially in capital cases.

While the Court has repeatedly found that lack of investigation by defense counsel may be grounds for a Sixth Amendment challenge, the mere failure of defense counsel to comply with ABA Guidelines for the Appointment and Performance of Defense Counsel in Death Penalty Cases does not automatically establish a claim of ineffective assistance of counsel. Bobby v. Van Hook, 558 U.S. 4 (2009). After doing extensive investigation, it may be reasonable for defense counsel to decide not to seek out all possible evidence that could assist a defendant. Moreover, as Justice Alito expressed in his concurrence in Bobby v. Van Hook, some justices do not believe that the ABA guidelines have "special relevance in determining whether an attorney's performance meets the standard required by the Sixth Amendment."

Additionally, the right to counsel does not include the right to have counsel present any evidence the defendant wishes to admit. A defendant does not have the right to insist on counsel engaging in dishonest or unethical behavior for the defendant. In Nix v. Whiteside, 475 U.S. 157 (1986), the Court held that the defendant was not denied his right to counsel because he told the defendant that he would seek to withdraw if his client perjured himself on the witness stand. "[The] duty is limited to legitimate, lawful conduct compatible with the very nature of a trial as a search for truth. Although counsel must take all reasonable lawful means to attain the objectives of the client, counsel is precluded from taking steps or in any way assisting the client in presenting false evidence or otherwise violating the law." See also Disciplinary Rule 7-102(A)(4), (7).

4. Right to Retain Counsel

The right to counsel also does not entitle an indigent defendant to select his or her counsel (United States v. Allen, 789 F.2d 90 (1st Cir. 1986)), and it does not entitle a defendant to a "meaningful attorney-client relationship" (Morris v. Slappy, 461 U.S. 1 (1983)). Rather, the standards for a Sixth Amendment challenge to defense counsel are those set forth in *Strickland*.

A defendant who can afford to do so may retain counsel of his choosing. As long as that lawyer does not have an unwaivable conflict of interest or violate any of the other court rules, it is a per se error for the court to deny the defendant retained counsel of choice. United States v. Gonzales-Lopez,

548 U.S. 140 (2006).[6] Despite this right, the government may seek to forfeit illegal funds paid to retain a lawyer. "[T]here is a strong governmental interest in obtaining full recovery of all forfeitable assets, an interest that overrides any Sixth Amendment interest in permitting criminals to use assets adjudged forfeitable to pay for their defensel." Caplin & Drysdale v. United States, 491 U.S. 617 (1989). However, only tainted funds may be seized. Luis v. United States, 135 S. Ct. 1083 (2016).

5. *Right to Retain Experts*

In addition to the right to counsel, the defendant enjoys a limited due process right to the use of experts who will assist in the presentation of the defense. In Ake v. Oklahoma, 470 U.S. 68 (1985), the Supreme Court recognized an indigent defendant's right to a psychiatrist to assist with the defendant's insanity defense in a capital murder case. Justice Marshall wrote:

> This Court has long recognized that when a State brings its judicial power to bear on an indigent defendant in a criminal proceeding, it must take steps to assure that the defendant had a fair opportunity to present his defense. This elementary principle, grounded in significant part on the Fourteenth Amendment's due process guarantee of fundamental fairness, derives from the belief that justice cannot be equal where, simply as a result of his poverty, a defendant is denied the opportunity to participate meaningfully in a judicial proceeding in which his liberty is at stake.
>
> [A] criminal trial is fundamentally unfair if the State proceeds against an individual defendant without making certain that he has access to the raw materials integral to the building of an effective defense. Thus, while the Court has not held that a State must purchase for the indigent defendant all the assistance that his wealthier counterpart might buy, it has often reaffirmed that fundamental fairness entitles indigent defendants to "an equal opportunity to present their claims within the adversary system."
>
> Without the assistance of a psychiatrist . . . to help determine whether the insanity defense is viable . . . , the risk of an inaccurate resolution of sanity issues is extremely high. With such assistance, the defendant is fairly able to present at least enough information to the jury, in a meaningful manner, as to permit it to make a sensible determination.

Ake does not put defendants on equal footing with the prosecution, but it does provide a basis for requesting those "basic tools" necessary to present an effective defense, including access to investigators and expert witnesses. In 2017, the Supreme Court reaffirmed *Ake* and held in McWilliams v. Dunn, 582 U.S. —— (2017), that a defendant is entitled to a state-provided mental

---

6. Moreover, it is a Sixth Amendment violation for the government to intrude on the attorney-client relationship. *See* Weatherford v. Bursey, 429 U.S. 545 (1977). The court considers four factors in determining whether the government has interfered with the right to counsel: (1) whether the government purposely intruded into the attorney-client relationship, (2) whether the government obtained any evidence it used at trial from the intrusion, (3) whether the prosecutor obtained any details about the defense's trial strategy from the intrusion, and (4) whether the information obtained was used in any other way to the substantial detriment of the defendant.

health expert who is independent of the prosecution. Although linked to a defendant's Sixth Amendment right to counsel, the right to expert assistance is a right that actually derives (like the right to counsel once did) from the Due Process clause. However, failure by defense counsel to request additional funds to hire a competent expert can constitute ineffective assistance of counsel. Hinton v. Alabama, 134 S. Ct. 1081 (2014) (per curiam).

E.   RIGHT OF SELF-REPRESENTATION

Instead of being represented by counsel, can a defendant represent himself? The Sixth Amendment refers to the right to "assistance of counsel." Does that encompass the right of self-representation?

FARETTA v. CALIFORNIA
422 U.S. 806 (1975)

Justice STEWART delivered the opinion of the Court.

The Sixth and Fourteenth Amendments of our Constitution guarantee that a person brought to trial in any state or federal court must be afforded the right to the assistance of counsel before he can be validly convicted and punished by imprisonment. The question before us now is whether a defendant in a state criminal trial has a constitutional right to proceed without counsel when he voluntarily and intelligently elects to do so. Stated another way, the question is whether a State may constitutionally hale a person into its criminal courts and there force a lawyer upon him, even when he insists that he wants to conduct his own defense. It is not an easy question, but we have concluded that a State may not constitutionally do so.

I

Anthony Faretta was charged with grand theft. At the arraignment, the Superior Court Judge assigned to preside at the trial appointed the public defender to represent Faretta. Well before the date of trial, however, Faretta requested that he be permitted to represent himself. Questioning by the judge revealed that Faretta had once represented himself in a criminal prosecution, that he had a high school education, and that he did not want to be represented by the public defender because he believed that that office was "very loaded down with . . . a heavy case load." The judge responded that he believed Faretta was "making a mistake" and emphasized that in further proceedings Faretta would receive no special favors. Nevertheless, after establishing that Faretta wanted to represent himself and did not want a lawyer, the judge, in a "preliminary ruling," accepted Faretta's waiver of the assistance of counsel. The judge indicated, however, that he might reverse this ruling if it later appeared that Faretta was unable adequately to represent himself.

Several weeks thereafter, but still prior to trial, the judge sua sponte held a hearing to inquire into Faretta's ability to conduct his own defense, and questioned him specifically about both the hearsay rule and the state law governing the challenge of potential jurors.[7]

The California Court of Appeal affirmed the trial judge's ruling that Faretta had no federal or state constitutional right to represent himself and the California Supreme Court denied review. We granted certiorari.

---

7. The colloquy was as follows:

THE COURT: In the Faretta matter, I brought you back down here to do some reconsideration as to whether or not you should continue to represent yourself. How have you been getting along on your research?

THE DEFENDANT: Not bad, your Honor. Last night I put in the mail a 995 motion and it should be with the Clerk within the next day or two.

THE COURT: Have you been preparing yourself for the intricacies of the trial of the matter?

THE DEFENDANT: Well, your Honor, I was hoping that the case could possibly be disposed of on the 995.

   Mrs. Ayers informed me yesterday that it was the Court's policy to hear the pretrial motions at the time of trial. If possible, your Honor, I would like a date set as soon as the Court deems adequate after they receive the motion, sometime before trial.

THE COURT: Let's see how you have been doing on your research. How many exceptions are there to the hearsay rule?

THE DEFENDANT: Well, the hearsay rule would, I guess, be called the best evidence rule, your Honor. And there are several exceptions in case law, but in actual statutory law, I don't feel there is none.

THE COURT: What are the challenges to the jury for cause?

THE DEFENDANT: Well, there is twelve peremptory challenges.

THE COURT: And how many for cause?

THE DEFENDANT: Well, as many as the Court deems valid.

THE COURT: And what are they? What are the grounds for challenging a juror for cause?

THE DEFENDANT: Well, numerous grounds to challenge a witness—I mean, a juror, your Honor, one being the juror is perhaps suffered, was a victim of the same type of offense, might be prejudiced toward the defendant. Any substantial ground that might make the juror prejudice[d] toward the defendant.

THE COURT: Anything else?

THE DEFENDANT: Well, a relative perhaps of the victim.

THE COURT: Have you taken a look at that code section to see what it is?

THE DEFENDANT: Challenge a juror?

THE COURT: Yes.

THE DEFENDANT: Yes, your Honor. I have done—

THE COURT: What is the code section?

THE DEFENDANT: On voir diring a jury, your Honor?

THE COURT: Yes.

THE DEFENDANT: I am not aware of the section right offhand.

THE COURT: What code is it in?

THE DEFENDANT: Well, the research I have done on challenging would be in Witkins Jurisprudence.

THE COURT: Have you looked at any of the codes to see where these various things are taken up?

THE DEFENDANT: No, your Honor, I haven't.

THE COURT: Have you looked in any of the California Codes with reference to trial procedure?

THE DEFENDANT: Yes, your Honor.

THE COURT: What codes?

THE DEFENDANT: I have done extensive research in the Penal Code, your Honor, and the Civil Code.

THE COURT: If you have done extensive research into it, then tell me about it.

THE DEFENDANT: On empaneling a jury, your Honor?

THE COURT: Yes.

THE DEFENDANT: Well, the District Attorney and the defendant, defense counsel, has both the right to 12 peremptory challenges of a jury. These 12 challenges are undisputable. Any reason that the defense or prosecution should feel that a juror would be inadequate to try the case or to rule on a case, they may then discharge that juror.

   But if there is a valid challenge due to grounds of prejudice or some other grounds, then these aren't considered in the 12 peremptory challenges. There are numerous and the defendant, the defense and the prosecution both have the right to make any inquiry to the jury as to their feelings toward the case. [Footnote by the Court.]

II

In the federal courts, the right of self-representation has been protected by statute since the beginnings of our Nation. . . . With few exceptions, each of the several States also accords a defendant the right to represent himself in any criminal case.

III

This consensus is soundly premised. The right of self-representation finds support in the structure of the Sixth Amendment, as well as in the English and colonial jurisprudence from which the Amendment emerged.

The Sixth Amendment includes a compact statement of the rights necessary to a full defense:

> In all criminal prosecutions, the accused shall enjoy the right . . . to be informed of the nature and cause of the accusation; to be confronted with the witnesses against him; to have compulsory process for obtaining witnesses in his favor, and to have the Assistance of Counsel for his defence.

Because these rights are basic to our adversary system of criminal justice, they are part of the "due process of law" that is guaranteed by the Fourteenth Amendment to defendants in the criminal courts of the States.

The Sixth Amendment does not provide merely that a defense shall be made for the accused; it grants to the accused personally the right to make his defense. It is the accused, not counsel, who must be "informed of the nature and cause of the accusation," who must be "confronted with the witnesses against him," and who must be accorded "compulsory process for obtaining witnesses in his favor." Although not stated in the Amendment in so many words, the right to self-representation — to make one's own defense personally — is thus necessarily implied by the structure of the Amendment. The right to defend is given directly to the accused; for it is he who suffers the consequences if the defense fails.

The counsel provision supplements this design. It speaks of the "assistance" of counsel, and an assistant, however expert, is still an assistant. The language and spirit of the Sixth Amendment contemplate that counsel, like the other defense tools guaranteed by the Amendment, shall be an aid to a willing defendant — not an organ of the State interposed between an unwilling defendant and his right to defend himself personally. To thrust counsel upon the accused, against his considered wish, thus violates the logic of the Amendment. In such a case, counsel is not an assistant, but a master; and the right to make a defense is stripped of the personal character upon which the Amendment insists. . . . An unwanted counsel "represents" the defendant only through a tenuous and unacceptable legal fiction. Unless the accused has acquiesced in such representation, the defense presented is not the defense guaranteed him by the Constitution, for, in a very real sense, it is not his defense.

In the American Colonies the insistence upon a right of self-representation was, if anything, more fervent than in England.

The colonists brought with them an appreciation of the virtues of self-reliance and a traditional distrust of lawyers. When the Colonies were first settled, "the lawyer was synonymous with the cringing Attorneys-General and Solicitors-General of the Crown and the arbitrary Justices of the King's Court, all bent on the conviction of those who opposed the King's prerogatives, and twisting the law to secure convictions." This prejudice gained strength in the Colonies where "distrust of lawyers became an institution."

The right of self-representation was guaranteed in many colonial charters and declarations of rights. These early documents establish that the "right to counsel" meant to the colonists a right to choose between pleading through a lawyer and representing oneself.

[T]here is no evidence that the colonists and the Framers ever doubted the right of self-representation, or imagined that this right might be considered inferior to the right of assistance of counsel. To the contrary, the colonists and the Framers, as well as their English ancestors, always conceived of the right to counsel as an "assistance" for the accused, to be used at his option, in defending himself. The Framers selected in the Sixth Amendment a form of words that necessarily implies the right of self-representation. That conclusion is supported by centuries of consistent history.

IV

There can be no blinking the fact that the right of an accused to conduct his own defense seems to cut against the grain of this Court's decisions holding that the Constitution requires that no accused can be convicted and imprisoned unless he has been accorded the right to the assistance of counsel.

But it is one thing to hold that every defendant, rich or poor, has the right to the assistance of counsel, and quite another to say that a State may compel a defendant to accept a lawyer he does not want. The value of state-appointed counsel was not unappreciated by the Founders, yet the notion of compulsory counsel was utterly foreign to them. And whatever else may be said of those who wrote the Bill of Rights, surely there can be no doubt that they understood the inestimable worth of free choice.

It is undeniable that in most criminal prosecutions defendants could better defend with counsel's guidance than by their own unskilled efforts. But where the defendant will not voluntarily accept representation by counsel, the potential advantage of a lawyer's training and experience can be realized, if at all, only imperfectly. To force a lawyer on a defendant can only lead him to believe that the law contrives against him. Moreover, it is not inconceivable that in some rare instances, the defendant might in fact present his case more effectively by conducting his own defense. Personal liberties are not rooted in the law of averages. The right to defend is personal. The defendant, and not his lawyer or the State, will bear the personal consequences of a conviction. It is the defendant, therefore, who must be free personally to decide whether in his particular case counsel is to his advantage. And although he may conduct his own defense ultimately to his own detriment, his choice must be honored out of "that respect for the individual which is the lifeblood of the law."

V

When an accused manages his own defense, he relinquishes, as a purely factual matter, many of the traditional benefits associated with the right to counsel. For this reason, in order to represent himself, the accused must "knowingly and intelligently" forgo those relinquished benefits. Although a defendant need not himself have the skill and experience of a lawyer in order competently and intelligently to choose self-representation, he should be made aware of the dangers and disadvantages of self-representation, so that the record will establish that "he knows what he is doing and his choice is made with eyes open."

Here, weeks before trial, Faretta clearly and unequivocally declared to the trial judge that he wanted to represent himself and did not want counsel. The record affirmatively shows that Faretta was literate, competent, and understanding, and that he was voluntarily exercising his informed free will. The trial judge had warned Faretta that he thought it was a mistake not to accept the assistance of counsel, and that Faretta would be required to follow all the "ground rules" of trial procedure. We need make no assessment of how well or poorly Faretta had mastered the intricacies of the hearsay rule and the California code provisions that govern challenges of potential jurors on voir dire. For his technical legal knowledge, as such, was not relevant to an assessment of his knowing exercise of the right to defend himself.

In forcing Faretta, under these circumstances, to accept against his will a state-appointed public defender, the California courts deprived him of his constitutional right to conduct his own defense.

Chief Justice BURGER, with whom Justices BLACKMUN and REHNQUIST join, dissenting.

This case is another example of the judicial tendency to constitutionalize what is thought "good." That effort fails on its own terms here, because there is nothing desirable or useful in permitting every accused person, even the most uneducated and inexperienced, to insist upon conducting his own defense to criminal charges. Moreover, there is no constitutional basis for the Court's holding, and it can only add to the problems of an already malfunctioning criminal justice system. I therefore dissent.

I

The most striking feature of the Court's opinion is that it devotes so little discussion to the matter which it concedes is the core of the decision, that is, discerning an independent basis in the Constitution for the supposed right to represent oneself in a criminal trial. Its ultimate assertion that such a right is tucked between the lines of the Sixth Amendment is contradicted by the Amendment's language and its consistent judicial interpretation.

[T]his Court's decisions have consistently included the right to counsel as an integral part of the bundle making up the larger "right to a defense as we know it."

[It is not] accurate to suggest, as the Court seems to later in its opinion, that the quality of his representation at trial is a matter with which only the accused is legitimately concerned. Although we have adopted an adversary system of criminal justice, the prosecution is more than an ordinary litigant, and the trial judge is not simply an automaton who insures that technical rules are adhered to. Both are charged with the duty of insuring that justice, in the broadest sense of that term, is achieved in every criminal trial. That goal is ill-served, and the integrity of and public confidence in the system are undermined, when an easy conviction is obtained due to the defendant's ill-advised decision to waive counsel. . . . The system of criminal justice should not be available as an instrument of self-destruction.

In short, both the "spirit and the logic" of the Sixth Amendment are that every person accused of crime shall receive the fullest possible defense; in the vast majority of cases this command can be honored only by means of the expressly guaranteed right to counsel, and the trial judge is in the best position to determine whether the accused is capable of conducting his defense. True freedom of choice and society's interest in seeing that justice is achieved can be vindicated only if the trial court retains discretion to reject any attempted waiver of counsel and insist that the accused be tried according to the Constitution.

There is no way to reconcile the idea that the Sixth Amendment impliedly guaranteed the right of an accused to conduct his own defense with the contemporaneous action of the Congress in passing a statute explicitly giving that right. If the Sixth Amendment created a right to self-representation it was unnecessary for Congress to enact any statute on the subject at all.

IV

Society has the right to expect that, when courts find new rights implied in the Constitution, their potential effect upon the resources of our criminal justice system will be considered. However, such considerations are conspicuously absent from the Court's opinion in this case.

It hardly needs repeating that courts at all levels are already handicapped by the unsupplied demand for competent advocates, with the result that it often takes far longer to complete a given case than experienced counsel would require.

Justice BLACKMUN, with whom Chief Justice BURGER and Justice REHNQUIST join, dissenting.

Today the Court holds that the Sixth Amendment guarantees to every defendant in a state criminal trial the right to proceed without counsel whenever he elects to do so. I find no textual support for this conclusion in the language of the Sixth Amendment. I find the historical evidence relied upon by the Court to be unpersuasive, especially in light of the recent history of criminal procedure. Finally, I fear that the right to self-representation constitutionalized today frequently will cause procedural confusion without advancing any significant strategic interest of the defendant. I therefore dissent.

I

The starting point, of course, is the language of the Sixth Amendment:

> In all criminal prosecutions, the accused shall enjoy the right to a speedy and public trial, by an impartial jury of the State and district wherein the crime shall have been committed, which district shall have been previously ascertained by law, and to be informed of the nature and cause of the accusation; to be confronted with the witnesses against him; to have compulsory process for obtaining witnesses in his favor, and to have the Assistance of Counsel for his defence.

It is self-evident that the Amendment makes no direct reference to self-representation. Indeed, the Court concedes that the right to self-representation is "not stated in the Amendment in so many words."

Where then in the Sixth Amendment does one find this right to self-representation? According to the Court, it is "necessarily implied by the structure of the Amendment." Stated somewhat more succinctly, the Court reasons that because the accused has a personal right to "a defense as we know it," he necessarily has a right to make that defense personally. I disagree. Although I believe the specific guarantees of the Sixth Amendment are personal to the accused, I do not agree that the Sixth Amendment guarantees any particular procedural method of asserting those rights. If an accused has enjoyed a speedy trial by an impartial jury in which he was informed of the nature of the accusation, confronted with the witnesses against him, afforded the power of compulsory process, and represented effectively by competent counsel, I do not see that the Sixth Amendment requires more.

The Court seems to suggest that so long as the accused is willing to pay the consequences of his folly, there is no reason for not allowing a defendant the right to self-representation. That view ignores the established principle that the interest of the State in a criminal prosecution "is not that it shall win a case, but that justice shall be done." For my part, I do not believe that any amount of pro se pleading can cure the injury to society of an unjust result, but I do believe that a just result should prove to be an effective balm for almost any frustrated pro se defendant.

III

In conclusion, I note briefly the procedural problems that, I suspect, today's decision will visit upon trial courts in the future. Although the Court indicates that a pro se defendant necessarily waives any claim he might otherwise make of ineffective assistance of counsel, the opinion leaves open a host of other procedural questions. Must every defendant be advised of his right to proceed pro se? If so, when must that notice be given? Since the right to assistance of counsel and the right to self-representation are mutually exclusive, how is the waiver of each right to be measured? If a defendant has elected to exercise his right to proceed pro se, does he still have a constitutional right to assistance of standby counsel? How soon in the criminal proceeding must a defendant decide between proceeding by counsel or pro se? Must he be allowed to switch in midtrial? May a violation of the right to self-representation ever be harmless error? Must the trial court treat the pro se defendant differently than it would professional counsel? I assume that many of these questions will be answered with finality in due course. Many of them, however, such as the standards of waiver and the treatment of the pro se defendant, will haunt the trial of every defendant who elects to exercise his right to self-representation. The procedural problems spawned by an absolute right to self-representation will far outweigh whatever tactical advantage the defendant may feel he has gained by electing to represent himself.

If there is any truth to the old proverb that "one who is his own lawyer has a fool for a client," the Court by its opinion today now bestows a constitutional right on one to make a fool of himself.

In *Faretta*, the Court suggested that a court could appoint standby counsel over the defendant's objection. The Supreme Court upheld the appointment of standby counsel in McKaskle v. Wiggins, 465 U.S. 168 (1984), even though standby counsel openly argued with the defendant during trial. Most of their arguments took place outside of the presence of the jury. Ultimately, the Supreme Court upheld the appointment of standby counsel but warned that standby counsel cannot act in a manner that will "destroy the jury's perception that the defendant is representing himself." The Court further noted that there is no constitutional right to "hybrid counsel" — that is, appointment of counsel that allows the defendant to perform some of the "core functions" of the lawyer. Courts can insist that the defendant decide whether he wants to represent himself or have counsel appointed to represent him. Moreover, the defendant also does not have a right to be represented by a nonlawyer. *See* United States v. Turnbull, 888 F.2d 636 (9th Cir. 1989).

Special issues can arise when a potentially incompetent defendant seeks to represent himself. Recognizing the challenge that such cases pose for trial judges, the Supreme Court held in Indiana v. Edwards (2008) that courts may impose a heightened competency standard for a defendant who wants to represent himself at trial.

INDIANA v. EDWARDS

554 U.S. 164 (2008)

Justice BREYER delivered the opinion of the Court.

This case focuses upon a criminal defendant whom a state court found mentally competent to stand trial if represented by counsel but not mentally competent to conduct that trial himself. We must decide whether in these circumstances the Constitution forbids a State from insisting that the defendant proceed to trial with counsel, the State thereby denying the defendant the right to represent himself. We conclude that the Constitution does not forbid a State so to insist.

I

In July 1999 Ahmad Edwards, the respondent, tried to steal a pair of shoes from an Indiana department store. After he was discovered, he drew a gun, fired at a store security officer, and wounded a bystander. He was caught and then charged with attempted murder, battery with a deadly weapon, criminal recklessness, and theft. His mental condition subsequently became the subject of three competency proceedings and two self-representation requests, mostly before the same trial judge:

First Competency Hearing: August 2000. Five months after Edwards' arrest, his court-appointed counsel asked for a psychiatric evaluation. After hearing psychiatrist and neuropsychologist witnesses (in February 2000 and again in August 2000), the court found Edwards incompetent to stand trial, and committed him to Logansport State Hospital for evaluation and treatment.

Second Competency Hearing: March 2002. Seven months after his commitment, doctors found that Edwards' condition had improved to the point where he could stand trial. Several months later, however, but still before trial, Edwards' counsel asked for another psychiatric evaluation. In March 2002, the judge held a competency hearing, considered additional psychiatric evidence, and (in April) found that Edwards, while "suffer[ing] from mental illness," was "competent to assist his attorneys in his defense and stand trial for the charged crimes."

Third Competency Hearing: April 2003. Seven months later but still before trial, Edwards' counsel sought yet another psychiatric evaluation of his client. And, in April 2003, the court held yet another competency hearing. A testifying psychiatrist reported that Edwards could understand the charges against him, but he was "unable to cooperate with his attorney in his defense because of his schizophrenic illness"; "[h]is delusions and his marked difficulties in thinking make it impossible for him to cooperate with his attorney." In November 2003, the court concluded that Edwards was not then competent to stand trial and ordered his recommitment to the state hospital.

First Self-Representation Request and First Trial: June 2005. About eight months after his commitment, the hospital reported that Edwards' condition had again improved to the point that he had again become competent to stand trial. And almost one year after that Edwards' trial began. Just before trial, Edwards asked to represent himself. He also asked for a continuance, which, he said, he needed in order to proceed *pro se.* The court refused the continuance. Edwards then proceeded to trial represented by counsel. The jury convicted him of criminal recklessness and theft but failed to reach a verdict on the charges of attempted murder and battery.

Second Self-Representation Request and Second Trial: December 2005. The State decided to retry Edwards on the attempted murder and battery charges. Just before the retrial, Edwards again asked the court to permit him to represent himself. Referring to the lengthy record of psychiatric reports, the trial court noted that Edwards still suffered from schizophrenia and concluded that "[w]ith these findings, he's competent to stand trial but I'm not going to find he's competent to defend himself." The court denied Edwards' self-representation request. Edwards was represented by appointed counsel at his retrial. The jury convicted Edwards on both of the remaining counts.

II

Our examination of this Court's precedents convinces us that those precedents frame the question presented, but they do not answer it. *Dusky* defines the competency standard as including both (1) "whether" the defendant has "a rational as well as factual understanding of the proceedings against him" and (2) whether the defendant "has sufficient present ability *to consult with his lawyer* with a reasonable degree of rational understanding." [Neither *Dusky* nor any other prior case, including *Faretta*] considered the mental competency issue presented here, namely, the relation of the mental competence standard to the right of self-representation.

The sole case in which this Court considered mental competence and self-representation together, *Godinez* (1993), presents a question closer to that at issue here. The case focused upon a borderline-competent criminal defendant who had asked a state trial court to permit him to represent himself and to change his pleas from not guilty to guilty. This Court, reversing the Court of Appeals, "reject[ed] the notion that competence to plead guilty or to waive the right to counsel must be measured by a standard that is higher than (or even different from) the *Dusky* standard."

We concede that *Godinez* bears certain similarities with the present case. Both involve mental competence and self-representation. Both involve a defendant who wants to represent himself. Both involve a mental condition that falls in a gray area between *Dusky*'s minimal constitutional requirement that measures a defendant's ability to stand trial and a somewhat higher standard that measures mental fitness for another legal purpose.

We nonetheless conclude that *Godinez* does not answer the question before us now. *Godinez* defendant sought only to change his pleas to guilty, he did not seek to conduct trial proceedings, and his ability to conduct a defense at trial was expressly not at issue.

We now turn to the question presented. We assume that a criminal defendant has sufficient mental competence to stand trial (*i.e.*, the defendant meets *Dusky*'s standard) and that the defendant insists on representing himself during that trial. We ask whether the Constitution permits a State to limit that defendant's self-representation right by insisting upon representation by counsel at trial — on the ground that the defendant lacks the mental capacity to conduct his trial defense unless represented.

Several considerations taken together lead us to conclude that the answer to this question is yes. First, an instance in which a defendant who would choose to forgo counsel at trial presents a very different set of circumstances, which in our view, calls for a different standard.

Second, the nature of the problem before us cautions against the use of a single mental competency standard for deciding both (1) whether a defendant who is represented by counsel can proceed to trial and (2) whether a defendant who goes to trial must be permitted to represent himself. Mental illness itself is not a unitary concept. It varies in degree. It can vary over time. It interferes with an individual's functioning at different times in different ways. The history of this case illustrates the complexity of the problem. In certain instances an individual may well be able to satisfy *Dusky*'s mental competence standard, for he will be able to work with counsel at trial, yet at the same time he may be unable to carry out the basic tasks needed to present his own defense without the help of counsel.

Third, in our view, a right of self-representation at trial will not "affirm the dignity" of a defendant who lacks the mental capacity to conduct his defense without the assistance of counsel. To the contrary, given that defendant's uncertain mental state, the spectacle that could well result from his self-representation at trial is at least as likely to prove humiliating as ennobling. Moreover, insofar as a defendant's lack of capacity threatens an improper conviction or sentence, self-representation in that exceptional context undercuts the most basic of the Constitution's criminal law objectives, providing a fair trial.

Further, proceedings must not only be fair, they must "appear fair to all who observe them." An *amicus* brief reports one psychiatrist's reaction to having observed a patient (a patient who had satisfied *Dusky*) try to conduct his own defense: "[H]ow in the world can our legal system allow an insane man to defend himself?"

We consequently conclude that the Constitution permits judges to take realistic account of the particular defendant's mental capacities by asking whether a defendant who seeks to conduct his own defense at trial is mentally competent to do so. That is to say, the Constitution permits States to insist upon representation by counsel for those competent enough to stand trial under *Dusky* but who still suffer from severe mental illness to the point where they are not competent to conduct trial proceedings by themselves.

Indiana has also asked us to overrule *Faretta*. We decline to do so. We recognize that judges have sometimes expressed concern that *Faretta*, contrary to its intent, has led to trials that are unfair. But recent empirical research suggests that such instances are not common. *See, e.g.,* Hashimoto, *Defending the Right of Self-Representation: An Empirical Look at the Pro Se Felony Defendant*, 85 N.C. L. Rev. 423, 427, 447, 428 (2007) (noting that of the small number of defendants who chose to proceed *pro se*—"roughly 0.3% to 0.5%" of the total, state felony defendants in particular "appear to have achieved higher felony acquittal rates than their represented counterparts in that they were less likely to have been convicted of felonies").

For these reasons, the judgment of the Supreme Court of Indiana is vacated, and the case is remanded for further proceedings not inconsistent with this opinion.

Justice SCALIA, with whom Justice THOMAS joins, dissenting.

The Constitution guarantees a defendant who knowingly and voluntarily waives the right to counsel the right to proceed *pro se* at his trial. *Faretta v. California* (1975). A mentally ill defendant who knowingly and voluntarily elects to proceed *pro se* instead of through counsel receives a fair trial that comports with the Fourteenth Amendment. The Court today concludes that a State may nonetheless strip a mentally ill defendant of the right to represent himself when that would be fairer. In my view the Constitution does not permit a State to substitute its own perception of fairness for the defendant's right to make his own case before the jury—a specific right long understood as essential to a fair trial.

Over the course of what became two separate criminal trials, Edwards sought to act as his own lawyer. He filed a number of incoherent written pleadings with the judge on which the Court places emphasis, but he also filed several intelligible pleadings, such as a motion to dismiss counsel, a motion to dismiss charges under the Indiana speedy trial provision, and a motion seeking a trial transcript.

Edwards made arguments in the courtroom that were more coherent than his written pleadings. In seeking to represent himself at his first trial, Edwards complained in detail that the attorney representing him had not spent adequate time preparing and was not sharing legal materials for use in his defense. The trial judge concluded that Edwards had knowingly and voluntarily waived his right to counsel and proceeded to quiz Edwards about matters of state law. Edwards correctly answered questions about the meaning of *voir dire* and how it operated, and described the basic framework for admitting videotape evidence to trial, though he was unable to answer other questions, including questions about the topics covered by state evidentiary rules that the judge identified only by number. He persisted in his request to represent himself, but the judge denied the request because Edwards acknowledged he would need a continuance. Represented by counsel, he was convicted of criminal recklessness and theft, but the jury deadlocked on charges of attempted murder and battery.

At his second trial, Edwards again asked the judge to be allowed to proceed *pro se.* He explained that he and his attorney disagreed about which defense to present to the attempted murder charge.

The court again rejected Edwards' request to proceed *pro se*, and this time it did not have the justification that Edwards had sought a continuance. The court did not dispute that Edwards knowingly and intelligently waived his right to counsel, but stated it was "going to carve out a third exception" to the right of self-representation, and — without explaining precisely what abilities Edwards lacked — stated Edwards was "competent to stand trial but I'm not going to find he's competent to defend himself."

The Constitution guarantees to every criminal defendant the "right to proceed *without* counsel when he voluntarily and intelligently elects to do so." The right reflects "a nearly universal conviction, on the part of our people as well as our courts, that forcing a lawyer upon an unwilling defendant is contrary to his basic right to defend himself if he truly wants to do so."

When a defendant appreciates the risks of forgoing counsel and chooses to do so voluntarily, the Constitution protects his ability to present his own defense even when that harms his case. In fact waiving counsel "usually" does so. We have nonetheless said that the defendant's "choice must be honored out of 'that respect for the individual which is the lifeblood of the law.'" What the Constitution requires is not that a State's case be subject to the most rigorous adversarial testing possible — after all, it permits a defendant to eliminate *all* adversarial testing by pleading guilty. What the Constitution requires is that a defendant be given the right to challenge the State's case against him using the arguments *he* sees fit.

Although a competent defendant has a right to self-representation at trial, there is no such right on appeal. In Martinez v. Court of Appeal, 528 U.S. 152 (2000), the Court found that "the overriding state interest in the fair and efficient administration of justice" outweighed whatever interest in personal autonomy a defendant has after conviction.

F. RIGHT OF COUNSEL FOR ENEMY COMBATANTS

Since September 11, 2001, the issue has arisen as to whether detainees designated as "enemy combatants" are entitled to the right to counsel. The executive branch has taken the position that enemy combatants have no such right. However, in Hamdi v. Rumsfeld, 542 U.S. 507 (2004), the Court held that "due process demands that a citizen held in the United States as an enemy combatant be given a meaningful opportunity to test the factual basis for that detention before a neutral decisionmaker." In her opinion, Justice O'Connor noted the integral role of counsel in whatever proceedings are formulated for enemy combatants, stating that Hamdi "unquestionably had the right to access to counsel in connection with the proceedings on remand."

CHAPTER
12

TRIAL

This chapter focuses on a defendant's rights at trial. The right to a fair trial is one of the most important rights in the American criminal justice system. As Alexis de Tocqueville noted in *Democracy in America*, trial by jury is more than just a judicial institution — "it is one of the forms of sovereignty of the people." The jury trial is one of the touchstones of the criminal justice system.

Although we speak of the defendant's right to a fair trial, a defendant is entitled to many rights at the trial stage of criminal proceedings. Thus, section A of this chapter begins by discussing the role of the jury, when a defendant is entitled to a jury trial, the composition of a jury, and the number of jurors needed to convict a defendant. Section B then focuses on how jurors are selected, including the voir dire and peremptory challenge procedures. Section C discusses additional issues regarding a defendant's right to a fair trial, including rulings on venue and pretrial publicity. Section D then reviews specific rules regarding the presentation of a case during trial, including the defendant's right of confrontation and right against self-incrimination. This section also discusses constitutional limits on a prosecutor's closing argument. Section E examines a defendant's right to present a defense. Finally, section F returns to the role of the jury and analyzes the burden of proof in criminal cases and the role of jury instructions.

A. TRIAL BY JURY

1. Role of the Jury

The right to a jury trial is so fundamental that it is mentioned twice in the Constitution. First, Article III, section 2, clause 3 provides that "[t]he trial of all Crimes, except in Cases of Impeachment, shall be by Jury." The Constitution addresses the right to a jury again in the Sixth Amendment, providing that "[i]n all criminal prosecutions, the accused shall enjoy the right to a speedy and public trial, by an impartial jury of the State and district wherein the crime shall have been committed."

The focus of the federal Constitution is on the defendant's right to a fair trial. However, as part of the movement to protect victims' rights, some states now guarantee the "People" the right to a fair and speedy trial.[1] Federal law also recognizes the government's right to a jury trial. Fed. R. Crim. P. 23(a)(2).

What is it about jury trials that make them so fundamental to the criminal justice process? The Supreme Court answered that question in Duncan v. Louisiana, in which it held that the right to a jury trial is so fundamental that it applies to the states.[2]

DUNCAN v. LOUISIANA
391 U.S. 145 (1968)

Justice WHITE delivered the opinion of the Court.

Appellant, Gary Duncan, was convicted of simple battery in the Twenty-fifth Judicial District Court of Louisiana. Under Louisiana law simple battery is a misdemeanor, punishable by a maximum of two years' imprisonment and a $300 fine. Appellant sought trial by jury, but because the Louisiana Constitution grants jury trials only in cases in which capital punishment or imprisonment at hard labor may be imposed, the trial judge denied the request. Appellant was convicted and sentenced to serve 60 days in the parish prison and pay a fine of $150.

Appellant was 19 years of age when tried. While driving on Highway 23 in Plaquemines Parish on October 18, 1966, he saw two younger cousins engaged in a conversation by the side of the road with four white boys. Knowing his cousins, Negroes who had recently transferred to a formerly all-white high school, had reported the occurrence of racial incidents at the school, Duncan stopped the car, got out, and approached the six boys. At trial the white boys and a white onlooker testified, as did appellant and his cousins. The testimony was in dispute on many points, but the witnesses agreed that appellant and the white boys spoke to each other, that appellant encouraged his cousins to break off the encounter and enter his car, and that appellant was about to enter the car himself for the purpose of driving away with his cousins. The whites testified that just before getting in the car appellant slapped Herman Landry, one of the white boys, on the elbow. The Negroes testified that appellant had not slapped Landry, but had merely touched him. The trial judge concluded that the State had proved beyond a reasonable doubt that Duncan had committed simple battery, and found him guilty.

---

1. *See, e.g.*, Cal. Const., Art. I, §29 ("In a criminal case, the people of the State of California have the right to due process of law and to a speedy and public trial.").

2. Chapter 1 discusses those portions of *Duncan* that expressly discuss the incorporation doctrine.

I

The claim before us is that the right to trial by jury guaranteed by the Sixth Amendment [is so fundamental to our system of justice, that it should be incorporated under the Fourteenth Amendment Due Process Clause and apply to the states]. The position of Louisiana, on the other hand, is that the Constitution imposes upon the States no duty to give a jury trial in any criminal case, regardless of the seriousness of the crime or the size of the punishment which may be imposed. Because we believe that trial by jury in criminal cases is fundamental to the American scheme of justice, we hold that the Fourteenth Amendment guarantees a right of jury trial in all criminal cases which — were they to be tried in a federal court — would come within the Sixth Amendment's guarantee. [W]e hold that the Constitution was violated when appellant's demand for jury trial was refused.

The history of trial by jury in criminal cases has been frequently told. It is sufficient for present purposes to say that by the time our Constitution was written, jury trial in criminal cases had been in existence in England for several centuries and carried impressive credentials traced by many to Magna Carta. . . . Jury trial came to America with English colonists, and received strong support from them. Royal interference with the jury trial was deeply resented.

Jury trial continues to receive strong support. The laws of every State guarantee a right to jury trial in serious criminal cases; no State has dispensed with it; nor are there significant movements underway to do so.

The guarantees of jury trial in the Federal and State Constitutions reflect a profound judgment about the way in which law should be enforced and justice administered. A right to jury trial is granted to criminal defendants in order to prevent oppression by the Government. Those who wrote our constitutions knew from history and experience that it was necessary to protect against unfounded criminal charges brought to eliminate enemies and against judges too responsive to the voice of higher authority. The framers of the constitutions strove to create an independent judiciary but insisted upon further protection against arbitrary action. Providing an accused with the right to be tried by a jury of his peers gave him an inestimable safeguard against the corrupt or overzealous prosecutor and against the compliant, biased, or eccentric judge. If the defendant preferred the common-sense judgment of a jury to the more tutored but perhaps less sympathetic reaction of the single judge, he was to have it. Beyond this, the jury trial provisions in the Federal and State Constitutions reflect a fundamental decision about the exercise of official power — a reluctance to entrust plenary powers over the life and liberty of the citizen to one judge or to a group of judges. Fear of unchecked power, so typical of our State and Federal Governments in other respects, found expression in the criminal law in this insistence upon community participation in the determination of guilt or innocence. The deep commitment of the Nation to the right of jury trial in serious criminal cases as a defense against arbitrary law enforcement qualifies for protection under the Due Process Clause of the Fourteenth Amendment, and must therefore be respected by the States.

Of course jury trial has "its weaknesses and the potential for misuse." We are aware of the long debate, especially in this century, among those who write about the administration of justice, as to the wisdom of permitting untrained laymen to determine the facts in civil and criminal proceedings. Although the debate has been intense, with powerful voices on either side, most of the controversy has centered on the jury in civil cases. Indeed, some of the severest critics of civil juries acknowledge that the arguments for criminal juries are much stronger. In addition, at the heart of the dispute have been express or implicit assertions that juries are incapable of adequately understanding evidence or determining issues of fact, and that they are unpredictable, quixotic, and little better than a roll of dice. Yet, the most recent and exhaustive study of the jury in criminal cases concluded that juries do understand the evidence and come to sound conclusions in most of the cases presented to them and that when juries differ with the result at which the judge would have arrived, it is usually because they are serving some of the very purposes for which they were created and for which they are now employed.

The State of Louisiana urges that holding that the Fourteenth Amendment assures a right to jury trial will cast doubt on the integrity of every trial conducted without a jury. Plainly, this is not the import of our holding. Our conclusion is that in the American States, as in the federal judicial system, a general grant of jury trial for serious offenses is a fundamental right, essential for preventing miscarriages of justice and for assuring that fair trials are provided for all defendants. We would not assert, however, that every criminal trial — or any particular trial — held before a judge alone is unfair or that a defendant may never be as fairly treated by a judge as he would be by a jury. Thus we hold no constitutional doubts about the practices, common in both federal and state courts, of accepting waivers of jury trial and prosecuting petty crimes without extending a right to jury trial. However, the fact is that in most places more trials for serious crimes are to juries than to a court alone; a great many defendants prefer the judgment of a jury to that of a court. Even where defendants are satisfied with bench trials, the right to a jury trial very likely serves its intended purpose of making judicial or prosecutorial unfairness less likely.

II

Louisiana's final contention is that even if it must grant jury trials in serious criminal cases, the conviction before us is valid and constitutional because here the petitioner was tried for simple battery and was sentenced to only 60 days in the parish prison. We are not persuaded. It is doubtless true that there is a category of petty crimes or offenses which is not subject to the Sixth Amendment jury trial provision and should not be subject to the Fourteenth Amendment jury trial requirement here applied to the States. Crimes carrying possible penalties up to six months do not require a jury trial if they otherwise qualify as petty offenses. But the penalty authorized for a particular crime is of major relevance in determining whether it is serious or not and may in itself, if severe enough, subject the trial to the mandates of the Sixth Amendment. The penalty authorized by the law of the locality may be taken "as a gauge of its social and ethical judgments," of the crime in question. In the case before us the Legislature of Louisiana has made simple battery a criminal offense punishable by imprisonment for up to two years and a fine. The question, then, is whether a crime carrying such a penalty is an offense which Louisiana may insist on trying without a jury.

We think not. So-called petty offenses were tried without juries both in England and in the Colonies and have always been held to be exempt from the otherwise comprehensive language of the Sixth Amendment's jury trial provisions. Of course the boundaries of the petty offense category have always been ill-defined, if not ambulatory. In the absence of an explicit constitutional provision, the definitional task necessarily falls on the courts.

In determining whether the length of the authorized prison term or the seriousness of other punishment is enough in itself to require a jury trial, we are counseled by the existing laws and practices in the Nation. In the federal system, petty offenses are defined as those punishable by no more than six months in prison and a $500 fine. In 49 of the 50 States crimes subject to trial without a jury, which occasionally include simple battery, are punishable by no more than one year in jail. Moreover, in the late 18th century in America crimes triable without a jury were for the most part punishable by no more than a six-month prison term, although there appear to have been exceptions to this rule. We need not, however, settle in this case the exact location of the line between petty offenses and serious crimes. It is sufficient for our purposes to hold that a crime punishable by two years in prison is, based on past and contemporary standards in this country, a serious crime and not a petty offense. Consequently, appellant was entitled to a jury trial and it was error to deny it.

The essential role of the jury is to decide whether the prosecution has proven each element of a crime beyond a reasonable doubt.[3] In doing so, jurors are expected to make credibility decisions and to decide what is "reasonable" for people in their community. They are not expected to be experts in the law. While jurors have a critical role in protecting defendants from the power of the government, the Supreme Court recognized, in Singer v. United States, 380 U.S. 24 (1965), that the government also has an interest in jury trials. Quoting the Court's earlier decision in Patton v. United States,

---

3. Section F analyzes the requirement that a case be proved beyond a reasonable doubt. Chapter 13 discusses in greater detail the role of jurors in making factual findings that will be used in sentencing and during the penalty phase of a capital case.

Chief Justice Warren wrote, "Not only must the right of the accused to a trial by a constitutional jury be jealously preserved, but the maintenance of the jury as a fact finding body in criminal cases is of such importance and has such a place in our traditions, that, before any waiver can become effective, the consent of government counsel and the sanction of the court must be had, in addition to the express and intelligent consent of the defendant." Accordingly, the Supreme Court upheld Federal Rule of Criminal Procedure 23(a), which requires both sides to agree before there can be a trial without a jury.

2. When Is There a Right to a Jury Trial?

The Court explained in *Duncan* that the defendant has the right to a jury trial in all but "petty" offenses. Although the *Duncan* Court did not expressly draw the line between serious and petty offenses, it suggested that, if the possible sentence for a crime is more than six months, the legislature in that jurisdiction has implicitly indicated that the offense is sufficiently serious to require the community's input through the use of juries.

In later cases, the Supreme Court affirmed that the line for the right to a jury trial should be drawn at six months. In Baldwin v. New York, 399 U.S. 66 (1970), the Court held that defendants charged with offenses carrying a maximum possible penalty of more than six months are entitled to a jury trial. In Blanton v. City of North Las Vegas, 489 U.S. 538 (1989), the Court was asked to decide whether other penalties, such as a fine and loss of driver's license, could be serious enough to indicate that the legislature considered the charged crime to be a "serious offense." While acknowledging that such circumstances might theoretically exist, Justice Marshall wrote for a unanimous Court that the Nevada penalties of a $1,000 maximum fine, community service, loss of driver's license, and maximum of six months in jail, were not enough to deem Blanton's driving-under-the-influence charge a "serious" offense.

Four years later, in United States v. Nachtigal, 507 U.S. 1 (1993) (per curiam), the Court cited *Blanton* in rejecting the argument that a man charged with driving under the influence in a national park faced a "serious" offense because the court could impose a $5,000 fine. As the Court emphasized, "it is a rare case where a legislature packs an offense it deems serious with onerous penalties that nonetheless do not puncture the 6-month incarceration line."

Most recently, in Lewis v. United States, 518 U.S. 322 (1996), the Court held that, even if a defendant is charged with multiple petty offenses, he is still not entitled to a jury trial. In *Lewis*, the defendant was charged with two misdemeanor counts of obstructing the mails. Each carried a maximum prison term of six months. However, if the sentences were ordered to run consecutively, Lewis would face one year in jail. Writing for the Court, Justice O'Connor noted that by setting the maximum authorized prison term at six months, the legislature categorized the offense of obstructing the mail as petty. The fact that the petitioner was charged with two counts of a petty offense does not revise the legislative judgment as to the gravity of that particular offense, nor does it transform the petty offense into a serious one, to which the jury-trial right would apply.

In a concurrence, Justice Kennedy attacked this reasoning, noting that "there is no limit to the length of the sentence a judge can impose on a defendant without entitling him to a jury, so long as the prosecutor carves up the charges into segments punishable by no more than six months apiece." Kennedy was willing to uphold Lewis's conviction but only because the trial judge had indicated that he would not sentence Lewis to more than six months even if he were convicted on both counts.

Thus, a firm line seems to have been drawn. Absent extraordinary circumstances, a defendant is entitled to a jury trial only if he faces a maximum of more than six months in prison on any one charge he faces.

3. Composition of the Jury

Television shows and movies frequently show juries of 12 persons.[4] But the Constitution does not specify how many persons must sit on a jury. The Supreme Court decided in Williams v. Florida whether there is a constitutional requirement regarding the number of jurors in criminal cases.

a. Number of Jurors

WILLIAMS v. FLORIDA

399 U.S. 78 (1970)

Justice WHITE delivered the opinion of the Court.

[Williams filed a pretrial motion to impanel a 12-man jury instead of the six-man jury provided by Florida law in all but capital cases. That motion was denied. Williams was convicted of robbery and was sentenced to life imprisonment. Part I of the Court's decision addressed a question regarding the state's rule that a defendant must give notice in advance of trial if he intends to claim an alibi defense. Part II of the decision discusses the right to a jury trial.]

II

In Duncan v. Louisiana (1968), we held that the Fourteenth Amendment guarantees a right to trial by jury in all criminal cases. The question in this

---

4. Among the most famous of these is *Twelve Angry Men* (1957), starring Henry Fonda.

case then is whether the constitutional guarantee of a trial by "jury" necessarily requires trial by exactly 12 persons, rather than some lesser number — in this case six. We hold that the 12-man panel is not a necessary ingredient of "trial by jury," and that respondent's refusal to impanel more than the six members provided for by Florida law did not violate petitioner's Sixth Amendment rights as applied to the States through the Fourteenth.

We had occasion in Duncan v. Louisiana to review briefly the oft-told history of the development of trial by jury in criminal cases. That history revealed a long tradition attaching great importance to the concept of relying on a body of one's peers to determine guilt or innocence as a safeguard against arbitrary law enforcement. That same history, however, affords little insight into the considerations that gradually led the size of that body to be generally fixed at 12. Some have suggested that the number 12 was fixed upon simply because that was the number of the presentment jury from the hundred, from which the petit jury developed. Other, less circular but more fanciful reasons for the number 12 have been given, and rest on little more than mystical or superstitious insights into the significance of "12." Lord Coke's explanation that the "number of twelve is much respected in holy writ, as 12 apostles, 12 stones, 12 tribes, etc.," is typical.[5] In short, while sometime in the 14th century the size of the jury at common law came to be fixed generally at 12, that particular feature of the jury system appears to have been a historical accident, unrelated to the great purposes which gave rise to the jury in the first place. The question before us is whether this accidental feature of the jury has been immutably codified into our Constitution.

While "the intent of the Framers" is often an elusive quarry, the relevant constitutional history casts considerable doubt on the easy assumption in our past decisions that if a given feature existed in a jury at common law in 1789, then it was necessarily preserved in the Constitution. The "very scanty history [of this provision] in the records of the Constitutional Convention" sheds little light either way on the intended correlation between Article III's "jury" and the features of the jury at common law.

The version that finally emerged from the Committee was the version that ultimately became the Sixth Amendment, ensuring an accused:

> the right to a speedy and public trial, by an impartial jury of the State and district wherein the crime shall have been committed, which district shall have been previously ascertained by law. . . .

---

5. In this connection it is interesting to note the following oath, required of the early 12-man jury:

> Hear this, ye Justices! that I will speak the truth of that which ye shall ask of me on the part of the king, and I will do faithfully to the best of my endeavour. So help me God, and these holy Apostles.

W. Forsyth, Trial by Jury 197 (1852). [Footnote by the Court.]

Gone were the provisions spelling out such common-law features of the jury as "unanimity," or "the accustomed requisites." And the "vicinage" requirement[6] itself had been replaced by wording that reflected a compromise between broad and narrow definitions of that term, and that left Congress the power to determine the actual size of the "vicinage" by its creation of judicial districts.

Three significant features may be observed in this sketch of the background of the Constitution's jury trial provisions. First, even though the vicinage requirement was as much a feature of the common-law jury as was the 12-man requirement, the mere reference to "trial by jury" in Article III was not interpreted to include that feature. . . . Second, provisions that would have explicitly tied the "jury" concept to the "accustomed requisites" of the time were eliminated. . . . Finally, contemporary legislative and constitutional provisions indicate that where Congress wanted to leave no doubt that it was incorporating existing common-law features of the jury system, it knew how to use express language to that effect.

We do not pretend to be able to divine precisely what the word "jury" imported to the Framers, the First Congress, or the States in 1789. It may well be that the usual expectation was that the jury would consist of 12, and that hence, the most likely conclusion to be drawn is simply that little thought was actually given to the specific question we face today. But there is absolutely no indication in "the intent of the Framers" of an explicit decision to equate the constitutional and common-law characteristics of the jury. Nothing in this history suggests, then, that we do violence to the letter of the Constitution by turning to other than purely historical considerations to determine which features of the jury system, as it existed at common law, were preserved in the Constitution. The relevant inquiry, as we see it, must be the function that the particular feature performs and its relation to the purposes of the jury trial. Measured by this standard, the 12-man requirement cannot be regarded as an indispensable component of the Sixth Amendment.

The purpose of the jury trial, as we noted in *Duncan*, is to prevent oppression by the Government. "Providing an accused with the right to be tried by a jury of his peers gave him an inestimable safeguard against the corrupt or overzealous prosecutor and against the compliant, biased, or eccentric judge." Given this purpose, the essential feature of a jury obviously lies in the interposition between the accused and his accuser of the commonsense judgment of a group of laymen, and in the community participation and shared responsibility that results from that group's determination of guilt or innocence. The performance of this role is not a function of the particular number of the body that makes up the jury. To be sure, the number should probably be large enough to promote group deliberation, free from outside attempts at intimidation, and to provide a fair possibility for obtaining a representative cross-section of the community. But we find little reason to

---

6. Technically, "vicinage" means neighborhood, and "vicinage of the jury" meant jury of the neighborhood or, in medieval England, jury of the county. [Footnote by the Court.]

think that these goals are in any meaningful sense less likely to be achieved when the jury numbers six, than when it numbers 12—particularly if the requirement of unanimity is retained. And, certainly the reliability of the jury as a factfinder hardly seems likely to be a function of its size.

It might be suggested that the 12-man jury gives a defendant a greater advantage since he has more "chances" of finding a juror who will insist on acquittal and thus prevent conviction. But the advantage might just as easily belong to the State, which also needs only one juror out of twelve insisting on guilt to prevent acquittal. What few experiments have occurred—usually in the civil area—indicate that there is no discernible difference between the results reached by the two different-sized juries. In short, neither currently available evidence nor theory suggests that the 12-man jury is necessarily more advantageous to the defendant than a jury composed of fewer members.[7]

Similarly, while in theory the number of viewpoints represented on a randomly selected jury ought to increase as the size of the jury increases, in practice the difference between the 12-man and the six-man jury in terms of the cross-section of the community represented seems likely to be negligible. Even the 12-man jury cannot insure representation of every distinct voice in the community, particularly given the use of the peremptory challenge.

We conclude, in short, as we began: the fact that the jury at common law was composed of precisely 12 is a historical accident, unnecessary to effect the purposes of the jury system and wholly without significance "except to mystics." To read the Sixth Amendment as forever codifying a feature so incidental to the real purpose of the Amendment is to ascribe a blind formalism to the Framers which would require considerably more evidence than we have been able to discover in the history and language of the Constitution or in the reasoning of our past decisions. We do not mean to intimate that legislatures can never have good reasons for concluding that the 12-man jury is preferable to the smaller jury. Legislatures may well have their own views about the relative value of the larger and smaller juries, and may conclude that, wholly apart from the jury's primary function, it is desirable to spread the collective responsibility for the determination of guilt among the larger group. Our holding does no more than leave these considerations to Congress and the States, unrestrained by an interpretation of the Sixth Amendment that would forever dictate the precise number that can constitute a jury. Consistent with this holding, we conclude that petitioner's Sixth Amendment rights, as applied to the States through the Fourteenth

---

7. It is true, of course, that the "hung jury" might be thought to result in a minimal advantage for the defendant, who remains unconvicted and who enjoys the prospect that the prosecution will eventually be dropped if subsequent juries also "hang." Thus a 100-man jury would undoubtedly be more favorable for defendants than a 12-man jury. But when the comparison is between 12 and 6, the odds of continually "hanging" the jury seem slight, and the numerical difference in the number needed to convict seems unlikely to inure perceptibly to the advantage of either side. [Footnote by the Court.]

Amendment, were not violated by Florida's decision to provide a 6-man rather than a 12-man jury.

───────────────

Not long after *Williams*, the Supreme Court had to decide whether the Constitution requires a minimum number of jurors in criminal cases to satisfy the defendant's right to a jury trial. A divided Court rendered its opinion on that issue.

BALLEW v. GEORGIA
435 U.S. 223 (1978)

Justice BLACKMUN announced the judgment of the Court and delivered an opinion in which Justice STEVENS joined.

This case presents the issue whether a state criminal trial to a jury of only five persons deprives the accused of the right to trial by jury guaranteed to him by the Sixth and Fourteenth Amendments. Our resolution of the issue requires an application of principles enunciated in Williams v. Florida (1970), where the use of a six-person jury in a state criminal trial was upheld against similar constitutional attack.

I

In November 1973 petitioner Claude Davis Ballew was the manager of the Paris Adult Theatre at 320 Peachtree Street, Atlanta, Ga. On November 9 two investigators from the Fulton County Solicitor General's office viewed at the theater a motion picture film entitled "Behind the Green Door." [P]etitioner was charged in a two-count misdemeanor accusation with "distributing obscene materials."

Petitioner was brought to trial in the Criminal Court of Fulton County. After a jury of 5 persons had been selected and sworn, petitioner moved that the court impanel a jury of 12 persons. That court, however, tried its misdemeanor cases before juries of five. Petitioner contended that for an obscenity trial, a jury of only five was constitutionally inadequate to assess the contemporary standards of the community. He also argued that the Sixth and Fourteenth Amendments required a jury of at least six members in criminal cases.

The motion for a 12-person jury was overruled, and the trial went on to its conclusion before the 5-person jury that had been impaneled. At the conclusion of the trial, the jury deliberated for 38 minutes and returned a verdict of guilty on both counts of the accusation.

In his petition for certiorari here, petitioner raised three issues: the unconstitutionality of the five-person jury; the constitutional sufficiency of the jury instructions on scienter and constructive, rather than actual, knowledge of the contents of the film; and obscenity vel non. We granted certiorari. Because we now hold that the five member jury does not satisfy the jury trial guarantee of the Sixth Amendment, as applied to the States through the Fourteenth, we do not reach the other issues.

II

In Williams v. Florida (1970), the Court reaffirmed that the "purpose of the jury trial, as we noted in *Duncan*, is to prevent oppression by the Government. 'Providing an accused with the right to be tried by a jury of his peers gave him an inestimable safeguard against the corrupt or overzealous prosecutor and against the compliant, biased, or eccentric judge.'" This purpose is attained by the participation of the community in determinations of guilt and by the application of the common sense of laymen who, as jurors, consider the case.

Williams held that these functions and this purpose could be fulfilled by a jury of six members. Although recognizing that by 1970 little empirical research had evaluated jury performance, the Court found no evidence that the reliability of jury verdicts diminished with six-member panels. Nor did the Court anticipate significant differences in result, including the frequency of "hung" juries. Because the reduction in size did not threaten exclusion of any particular class from jury roles, concern that the representative or cross-section character of the jury would suffer with a decrease to six members seemed "an unrealistic one." As a consequence, the six-person jury was held not to violate the Sixth and Fourteenth Amendments.

III

When the Court in *Williams* permitted the reduction in jury size — or, to put it another way, when it held that a jury of six was not unconstitutional — it expressly reserved ruling on the issue whether a number smaller than six passed constitutional scrutiny. The Court refused to speculate when this so-called "slippery slope" would become too steep. We face now, however, the two-fold question whether a further reduction in the size of the state criminal trial jury does make the grade too dangerous, that is, whether it inhibits the functioning of the jury as an institution to a significant degree, and, if so, whether any state interest counterbalances and justifies the disruption so as to preserve its constitutionality.

Williams v. Florida generated a quantity of scholarly work on jury size. These writings do not draw or identify a bright line below which the number of jurors would not be able to function as required by the standards enunciated in *Williams*. On the other hand, they raise significant questions about the wisdom and constitutionality of a reduction below six. We examine these concerns:

First, recent empirical data suggest that progressively smaller juries are less likely to foster effective group deliberation. At some point, this decline leads to inaccurate factfinding and incorrect application of the common sense of the community to the facts. Generally, a positive correlation exists between group size and the quality of both group performance and group productivity. The smaller the group, the less likely are members to make critical contributions necessary for the solution of a given problem. As juries decrease in size, then, they are less likely to have members who remember each of the important pieces of evidence or argument. Furthermore, the smaller the group, the less likely it is to overcome the biases of its members to obtain an accurate result.

Second, the data now raise doubts about the accuracy of the results achieved by smaller and smaller panels. Statistical studies suggest that the risk of convicting an innocent person rises as the size of the jury diminishes.

Third, the data suggest that the verdicts of jury deliberation in criminal cases will vary as juries become smaller, and that the variance amounts to an imbalance to the detriment of one side, the defense. [T]he number of hung juries would diminish as the panels decreased in size. Both studies emphasized that juries in criminal cases generally hang with only one, or more likely two, jurors remaining unconvinced of guilt. Also, group theory suggests that a person in the minority will adhere to his position more frequently when he has at least one other person supporting his argument.

Fourth, what has just been said about the presence of minority viewpoint as juries decrease in size foretells problems not only for jury decisionmaking, but also for the representation of minority groups in the community. The Court repeatedly has held that meaningful community participation cannot be attained with the exclusion of minorities or other identifiable groups from jury service. "It is part of the established tradition in the use of juries as instruments of public justice that the jury be a body truly representative of the community." The exclusion of elements of the community from participation "contravenes the very idea of a jury . . . composed of 'the peers or equals of the person whose rights it is selected or summoned to determine.'"

Fifth, several authors have identified in jury research methodological problems tending to mask differences in the operation of smaller and larger juries. Nationwide, however, these small percentages will represent a large number of cases. And it is with respect to those cases that the jury trial right has its greatest value. When the case is close, and the guilt or innocence of the defendant is not readily apparent, a properly functioning jury system will insure evaluation by the sense of the community and will also tend to insure accurate factfinding.

IV

While we adhere to, and reaffirm our holding in Williams v. Florida, these studies, most of which have been made since *Williams* was decided in 1970, lead us to conclude that the purpose and functioning of the jury in a criminal trial is seriously impaired, and to a constitutional degree, by a reduction in size to below six members. We readily admit that we do not pretend to discern a clear line between six members and five. But the assembled data raise substantial doubt about the reliability and appropriate representation of panels smaller than six. Because of the fundamental importance of the jury trial to the American system of criminal justice, any further reduction that promotes inaccurate and possibly biased decisionmaking, that causes untoward differences in verdicts, and that prevents juries from truly representing their communities, attains constitutional significance.

V

With the reduction in the number of jurors below six creating a substantial threat to Sixth and Fourteenth Amendment guarantees, we must consider whether any interest of the State justifies the reduction. We find no significant state advantage in reducing the number of jurors from six to five.

The States utilize juries of less than 12 primarily for administrative reasons. Savings in court time and in financial costs are claimed to justify the reductions. The financial benefits of the reduction from 12 to 6 are substantial; this is mainly because fewer jurors draw daily allowances as they hear cases. On the other hand, the asserted saving in judicial time is not so clear.

Petitioner, therefore, has established that his trial on criminal charges before a five-member jury deprived him of the right to trial by jury guaranteed by the Sixth and Fourteenth Amendments.

As with other aspects of jury trials, states can choose to provide defendants with more than the minimum number of six jurors required by the Supreme Court. Federal courts and most state courts provide jurors with the right to 12 jurors in a criminal case, but following *Williams* and *Ballew*, over 30 states permit fewer than 12 jurors in misdemeanor cases, and one state (Connecticut) allows 6 jurors for all noncapital trials.[8]

b.   Unanimity

A common myth about juries is that their verdicts must be unanimous. As it did in its decisions regarding the size of juries, the Supreme Court, in deciding whether jury verdicts must be unanimous, has focused on the role of jurors and how they can perform their responsibilities.

---

8. *See* U.S. Department of Justice, Bureau of Justice Statistics, State Court Organization (2011), Table 10 (Nov. 2013).

APODACA v. OREGON
406 U.S. 404 (1972)

Justice WHITE announced the judgment of the Court and an opinion in which Chief Justice BURGER, Justice BLACKMUN, and Justice REHNQUIST joined.

[Oregon juries convicted three defendants of various serious crimes. The vote in the cases of Apodaca and Madden was 11-1, while the vote in Cooper's case was 10-2, the minimum requisite vote under Oregon law for sustaining a conviction. All three defendants claimed that a conviction rendered by a less-than-unanimous jury violates the right to trial by jury in criminal cases.]

Like the requirement that juries consist of 12 men, the requirement of unanimity arose during the Middle Ages and [became] an accepted feature of the common-law jury by the 18th century. But, as we observed in *Williams*, "the relevant constitutional history casts considerable doubt on the easy assumption . . . that if a given feature existed in a jury at common law in 1789, then it was necessarily preserved in the Constitution."

Our inquiry must focus upon the function served by the jury in contemporary society. As we said in *Duncan*, the purpose of trial by jury is to prevent oppression by the Government by providing a "safeguard against the corrupt or overzealous prosecutor and against the compliant, biased, or eccentric judge." "Given this purpose, the essential feature of a jury obviously lies in the interposition between the accused and his accuser of the commonsense judgment of a group of laymen." A requirement of unanimity, however, does not materially contribute to the exercise of this commonsense judgment. As we said in *Williams*, a jury will come to such a judgment as long as it consists of a group of laymen representative of a cross section of the community who have the duty and the opportunity to deliberate, free from outside attempts at intimidation, on the question of a defendant's guilt. In terms of this function we perceive no difference between juries required to act unanimously and those permitted to convict or acquit by votes of 10 to two or 11 to one. Requiring unanimity would obviously produce hung juries in some situations where nonunanimous juries will convict or acquit. But in either case, the interest of the defendant in having the judgment of his peers interposed between himself and the officers of the State who prosecute and judge him is equally well served.

Petitioners nevertheless argue that unanimity serves other purposes constitutionally essential to the continued operation of the jury system. Their principal contention is that a Sixth Amendment "jury trial" . . . should be held to require a unanimous jury verdict in order to give substance to the reasonable-doubt standard otherwise mandated by the Due Process Clause. *See* In re Winship (1970).

We are quite sure, however, that the Sixth Amendment itself has never been held to require proof beyond a reasonable doubt in criminal cases. The reasonable-doubt standard developed separately from both the jury trial and the unanimous verdict.[9] The reasonable-doubt argument is rooted, in effect, in due process and [is not linked to the Sixth Amendment jury requirements]. Petitioners also cite quite accurately a long line of decisions of this Court upholding the principle that the Fourteenth Amendment requires jury panels to reflect a cross section of the community. They then contend that unanimity is a necessary precondition for effective application of the cross-section requirement, because a rule permitting less than unanimous verdicts will make it possible for convictions to occur without the acquiescence of minority elements within the community.

There are two flaws in this argument. One is petitioners' assumption that every distinct voice in the community has a right to be represented on every jury and a right to prevent conviction of a defendant in any case. All that the Constitution forbids, however, is systematic exclusion of identifiable segments of the community from jury panels and from the juries ultimately drawn from those panels. No group, in short, has the right to block convictions; it has only the right to participate in the overall legal processes by which criminal guilt and innocence are determined.

We also cannot accept petitioners' second assumption — that minority groups, even when they are represented on a jury, will not adequately represent the viewpoint of those groups simply because they may be outvoted in the final result. They will be present during all deliberations, and their views will be heard. We cannot assume that the majority of the jury will refuse to weigh the evidence and reach a decision upon rational grounds, just as it must now do in order to obtain unanimous verdicts, or that a majority will deprive a man of his liberty on the basis of prejudice when a minority is presenting a reasonable argument in favor of acquittal. We simply find no proof for the notion that a majority will disregard its instructions and cast its votes for guilt or innocence based on prejudice rather than the evidence.

We accordingly [hold that nonunanimous jury verdicts are constitutional, at least as to 11-1 or 10-2 votes].

Justice BLACKMUN concurring.[10]

I join the Court's opinion and judgment in each of these cases. I add only the comment, which should be obvious and should not need saying, that in so doing I do not imply that I regard a State's split-verdict system as a wise one. My vote means only that I cannot conclude that the system is constitutionally offensive. Were I a legislator, I would disfavor it as a matter of policy. Our task here, however, is not to pursue and strike down what happens to impress us as undesirable legislative policy.

I do not hesitate to say, either, that a system employing a 7-5 standard, rather than a 9-3 or 75 percent minimum, would afford me great difficulty.

---

9. The requirement of proof beyond a reasonable doubt is discussed in section F of this chapter. [Footnote by casebook authors.]

10. The concurring and dissenting opinions were issued in the companion case of Johnson v. United States, in which the Court upheld a 9-3 verdict. [Footnote by casebook authors.]

As Mr. Justice White points out, "a substantial majority of the jury" are to be convinced. That is all that is before us in each of these cases.

Justice DOUGLAS, with whom Justice BRENNAN and Justice MARSHALL join, dissenting.

The plurality approves a procedure which diminishes the reliability of a jury. First, it eliminates the circumstances in which a minority of jurors (a) could have rationally persuaded the entire jury to acquit, or (b) while unable to persuade the majority to acquit, nonetheless could have convinced them to convict only on a lesser-included offense. Second, it permits prosecutors in Oregon and Louisiana to enjoy a conviction-acquittal ratio substantially greater than that ordinarily returned by unanimous juries.

The diminution of verdict reliability flows from the fact that nonunanimous juries need not debate and deliberate as fully as must unanimous juries. As soon as the requisite majority is attained, further consideration is not required either by Oregon or by Louisiana even though the dissident jurors might, if given the chance, be able to convince the majority.

It is said that there is no evidence that majority jurors will refuse to listen to dissenters whose votes are unneeded for conviction. Yet human experience teaches that polite and academic conversation is no substitute for the earnest and robust argument necessary to reach unanimity. [E]xperience shows that the less-than-unanimous jury overwhelmingly favors the States.

Moreover, even where an initial majority wins the dissent over to its side, the ultimate result in unanimous-jury States may nonetheless reflect the reservations of uncertain jurors. I refer to many compromise verdicts on lesser-included offenses and lesser sentences. Thus, even though a minority may not be forceful enough to carry the day, their doubts may nonetheless cause a majority to exercise caution.

The new rule also has an impact on cases in which a unanimous jury would have neither voted to acquit nor to convict, but would have deadlocked. Of these deadlocked juries, 56% contain either one, two, or three dissenters. In these latter cases, the majorities favor the prosecution 44% but the defendant only 12%. Thus, by eliminating these deadlocks, Louisiana wins 44 cases for every 12 that it loses. By eliminating the one-and-two-dissenting-juror cases, Oregon does even better, gaining 4.25 convictions for every acquittal. While the statutes on their face deceptively appear to be neutral, the use of the nonunanimous jury stacks the truth-determining process against the accused. Thus, we take one step more away from the accusatorial system that has been our proud boast.

The requirements of a unanimous jury verdict in criminal cases and proof beyond a reasonable doubt are so embedded in our constitutional law and touch so directly all the citizens and are such important barricades of liberty that if they are to be changed they should be introduced by constitutional amendment.

Suppose a jury begins with a substantial minority but then in the process of deliberation a sufficient number changes to reach the required 9:3 or 10:2

for a verdict. Is not there still a lingering doubt about that verdict? Is it not clear that the safeguard of unanimity operates in this context to make it far more likely that guilt is established beyond a reasonable doubt?

Today the Court approves a nine-to-three verdict. Would the Court relax the standard of reasonable doubt still further by resorting to eight-to-four verdicts, or even a majority rule? Is the next step the elimination of the presumption of innocence?

The vast restructuring of American law which is entailed in today's decisions is for political not for judicial action. Until the Constitution is rewritten, we have the present one to support and construe. It has served us well.

If a jury is unable to reach a verdict, it is referred to as a "hung jury." No matter how compelling the evidence might be, the trial judge may not direct a verdict of guilty. However, the judge may grant an acquittal for insufficient evidence.[11]

In the United States, jurors render "general verdicts" of "guilty" or "not guilty" of the charged offense. "Special verdicts" are verdicts that require jurors to answer specific questions regarding a case, such as which acts they found each defendant committed or whether particular property was used in a crime. They are occasionally used to guide the court in its sentencing or forfeiture decisions, but are generally disfavored as a way to guide jurors in their deliberative process.

Because jurors do not ordinarily need to explain their verdicts, jurors can engage in jury nullification and reject a case even though there appears to be sufficient evidence to support the verdict. *See* United States v. Dougherty, 473 F.2d 1113 (D.C. Cir. 1972) (recognizing jurors' power to nullify but rejecting request to instruct jurors of their right to nullify). Courts are reluctant to instruct jurors that they have the power to nullify, but some observers believe that jury nullification is a valid and important part of the right to a jury trial.

> It is not by chance that the jury has the power to issue an unreviewable general verdict of acquittal; it is a considered decision that the people should apply laws when criminal punishment is at stake to ensure that an individual does not lose her liberty unless it would be just in a particular case. . . . Trial by jury "gives protection against laws which the ordinary man may regard as harsh and oppressive" and provides "insurance that the criminal law will conform to the ordinary man's idea of what is fair and just."

Rachel E. Barkow, *Recharging the Jury: The Criminal Jury's Constitutional Role in an Era of Mandatory Sentencing*, 152 U. Pa. L. Rev. 33, 59 (2003).

Similarly, because jurors need not explain their verdicts, federal courts, as well as most state courts, accept inconsistent verdicts from the jury. It is

---

11. The circumstances in which the judge's acquittal bars retrial are discussed in Chapter 14 ("Double Jeopardy").

presumed that if jurors convict on some counts but acquit on others, their decision was the product of lenity. Dunn v. United States, 284 U.S. 390 (1932).

B. JURY COMPOSITION AND SELECTION

There is a two-step process for the selection of a jury. First, a pool of jurors, called the jury "venire," is summoned. Then, the "petit jury" is selected from the venire. The petit jury consists of those jurors who will actually hear the case.

Before the petit jury is selected, prospective jurors are questioned in a process called voir dire. Following voir dire, both the prosecution and defense have an opportunity to challenge jurors "for cause." For-cause challenges may be made on the basis that a particular juror cannot perform jury service, or has an actual bias. The parties also have an opportunity to exercise a limited number of "peremptory challenges." Unlike challenges for cause, peremptory challenges may be exercised for reasons unrelated to a juror's bias, although they may not be exercised in a discriminatory manner.

1. Selecting the Jury Venire

The Sixth Amendment guarantees an "impartial jury." The Supreme Court has repeatedly held, however, that a defendant does not have a right to a jury composed of particular groups. Rather, the Sixth Amendment prohibits the prosecution from systematically excluding certain cognizable groups in assembling the venire for jury selection.

TAYLOR v. LOUISIANA
419 U.S. 522 (1975)

Justice WHITE delivered the opinion of the Court.

When this case was tried, the Louisiana Constitution provided that a woman should not be selected for jury service unless she had previously filed a written declaration of her desire to be subject to jury service. The constitutionality of these provisions is the issue in this case.

I

Appellant, Billy J. Taylor, was indicted by the grand jury for aggravated kidnapping. On April 12, 1972, appellant moved the trial court to quash the petit jury venire. Appellant alleged that women were systematically excluded from the venire and that he would therefore be deprived of what he claimed to be his federal constitutional right to "a fair trial by jury of a representative segment of the community. . . ."

The [parties have stipulated] that 53% of the persons eligible for jury service in the parish were female, and that no more than 10% of the persons on the jury wheel were women. During the period from December 8, 1971, to November 3, 1972, 12 females were among the 1,800 persons drawn to fill petit jury venires in [that] Parish. In the present case, a venire totaling 175 persons was drawn for jury service beginning April 13, 1972. There were no females on the venire.

Appellant's motion to quash the venire was denied that same day. After being tried, convicted, and sentenced to death, appellant sought review.

II

The Louisiana jury-selection system does not disqualify women from jury service, but in operation its conceded systematic impact is that only a very few women, grossly disproportionate to the number of eligible women in the community, are called for jury service. In this case, no women were on the venire from which the petit jury was drawn. The issue we have, therefore, is whether a jury-selection system which operates to exclude from jury service an identifiable class of citizens constituting 53% of eligible jurors in the community comports with the Sixth and Fourteenth Amendments.

The State first insists that Taylor, a male, has no standing to object to the exclusion of women from his jury. But Taylor's claim is that he was constitutionally entitled to a jury drawn from a venire constituting a fair cross section of the community and that the jury that tried him was not such a jury by reason of the exclusion of women. Taylor was not a member of the excluded class; but there is no rule that claims such as Taylor presents may be made only by those defendants who are members of the group excluded from jury service.

III

The background against which this case must be decided includes our holding in Duncan v. Louisiana (1968), that the Sixth Amendment's provision for jury trial is made binding on the States by virtue of the Fourteenth Amendment. Our inquiry is whether the presence of a fair cross section of the community on venires, panels, or lists from which petit juries are drawn is essential to the fulfillment of the Sixth Amendment's guarantee of an impartial jury trial in criminal prosecutions.

The Court's prior cases are instructive. Both in the course of exercising its supervisory powers over trials in federal courts and in the constitutional context, the Court has unambiguously declared that the American concept of the jury trial contemplates a jury drawn from a fair cross section of the community. A unanimous Court stated in Smith v. Texas (1940), that "[it] is part of the established tradition in the use of juries as instruments of public justice that the jury be a body truly representative of the community." To exclude racial groups from jury service was said to be "at war with our basic concepts of a democratic society and a representative government." A state jury system that resulted in systematic exclusion of Negroes as jurors was therefore held to violate the Equal Protection Clause of the Fourteenth Amendment.

The unmistakable import of this Court's opinions is that the selection of a petit jury from a representative cross section of the community is an essential component of the Sixth Amendment right to a jury trial.

We accept the fair-cross-section requirement as fundamental to the jury trial guaranteed by the Sixth Amendment and are convinced that the requirement has solid foundation. The purpose of a jury is to guard against the exercise of arbitrary power — to make available the commonsense judgment of the community as a hedge against the overzealous or mistaken prosecutor and in preference to the professional or perhaps overconditioned or biased response of a judge. This prophylactic vehicle is not provided if the jury pool is made up of only special segments of the populace or if large, distinctive groups are excluded from the pool. Community participation in the administration of the criminal law, moreover, is not only consistent with our democratic heritage but is also critical to public confidence in the fairness of the criminal justice system. Restricting jury service to only special groups or excluding identifiable segments playing major roles in the community cannot be squared with the constitutional concept of jury trial. "Trial by jury presupposes a jury drawn from a pool broadly representative of the community as well as impartial in a specific case. . . . [The] broad representative character of the jury should be maintained, partly as assurance of a diffused impartiality and partly because sharing in the administration of justice is a phase of civic responsibility."

IV

We are also persuaded that the fair-cross-section requirement is violated by the systematic exclusion of women, who in the judicial district involved here amounted to 53% of the citizens eligible for jury service. This conclusion necessarily entails the judgment that women are sufficiently numerous and distinct from men and that if they are systematically eliminated from jury panels, the Sixth Amendment's fair-cross-section requirement cannot be satisfied. This very matter was debated in Ballard v. United States. The dissenting view that an all-male panel drawn from various groups in the community would be as truly representative as if women were included, was firmly rejected:

> The thought is that the factors which tend to influence the action of women are the same as those which influence the action of men — personality, background, economic status — and not sex. Yet it is not enough to say that women when sitting

as jurors neither act nor tend to act as a class. Men likewise do not act as a class. But, if the shoe were on the other foot, who would claim that a jury was truly representative of the community if all men were intentionally and systematically excluded from the panel? The truth is that the two sexes are not fungible; a community made up exclusively of one is different from a community composed of both; the subtle interplay of influence one on the other is among the imponderables. To insulate the courtroom from either may not in a given case make an iota of difference. Yet a flavor, a distinct quality is lost if either sex is excluded. The exclusion of one may indeed make the jury less representative of the community than would be true if an economic or racial group were excluded.

If the fair-cross-section rule is to govern the selection of juries, as we have concluded it must, women cannot be systematically excluded from jury panels from which petit juries are drawn. This conclusion is consistent with the current judgment of the country, now evidenced by legislative or constitutional provisions in every State and at the federal level qualifying women for jury service.

V

There remains the argument that women as a class serve a distinctive role in society and that jury service would so substantially interfere with that function that the State has ample justification for excluding women from service unless they volunteer, even though the result is that almost all jurors are men. The right to a proper jury cannot be overcome on merely rational grounds.[12] There must be weightier reasons if a distinctive class representing 53% of the eligible jurors is for all practical purposes to be excluded from jury service. No such basis has been tendered here.

The States are free to grant exemptions from jury service to individuals in case of special hardship or incapacity and to those engaged in particular occupations the uninterrupted performance of which is critical to the community's welfare. A system excluding all women, however, is a wholly different matter. It is untenable to suggest these days that it would be a special hardship for each and every woman to perform jury service or that society cannot spare any women from their present duties. This may be the case with many, and it may be burdensome to sort out those who should be exempted from those who should serve. But that task is performed in the case of men, and the administrative convenience in dealing with women as a class is insufficient justification for diluting the quality of community judgment represented by the jury in criminal trials.

___

12. Louisiana argued that women should be automatically exempt from jury service because they are the center of the home and family life. This argument had prevailed in the Court's prior decision in Hoyt v. Florida (1961). [Footnote by casebook authors.]

VI

Accepting as we do . . . the view that the Sixth Amendment affords the defendant in a criminal trial the opportunity to have the jury drawn from venires representative of the community, we think it is no longer tenable to hold that women as a class may be excluded or given automatic exemptions based solely on sex if the consequence is that criminal jury venires are almost totally male. If it was ever the case that women were unqualified to sit on juries or were so situated that none of them should be required to perform jury service, that time has long since passed. If at one time it could be held that Sixth Amendment juries must be drawn from a fair cross section of the community but that this requirement permitted the almost total exclusion of women, this is not the case today. Communities differ at different times and places. What is a fair cross section at one time or place is not necessarily a fair cross section at another time or a different place. Nothing persuasive has been presented to us in this case suggesting that all-male venires in the parishes involved here are fairly representative of the local population otherwise eligible for jury service.

VII

It should also be emphasized that in holding that petit juries must be drawn from a source fairly representative of the community we impose no requirement that petit juries actually chosen must mirror the community and reflect the various distinctive groups in the population. Defendants are not entitled to a jury of any particular composition, but the jury wheels, pools of names, panels, or venires from which juries are drawn must not systematically exclude distinctive groups in the community and thereby fail to be reasonably representative thereof.

Justice REHNQUIST, dissenting.

The Court's opinion reverses a conviction without a suggestion, much less a showing, that the appellant has been unfairly treated or prejudiced in any way by the manner in which his jury was selected. In so doing, the Court invalidates a jury-selection system which it approved by a substantial majority only 13 years ago. I disagree with the Court and would affirm the judgment of the Supreme Court of Louisiana.

Challenges to jury venires are governed by the Sixth Amendment and may be raised by any defendant.[13] As set forth in *Taylor*, the jury pool must be

---

13. In Berghuis v. Smith, 559 U.S. 314 (2010), the Supreme Court held that no clearly established federal law requires that a particular type of statistical method be used to determine whether there has been systematic exclusion of racial groups in the selection of jury pools.

drawn from a cross-section of the community. Cognizable groups may not be excluded unless there are compelling reasons. For example, the government may have compelling reasons to exclude convicted felons from the jury pool. However, the systematic exclusion of groups based on gender, race, and ethnicity is unconstitutional.

2. Selecting the Petit Jury

Once the jury pool is selected, the parties enter the second stage of the jury-selection process. The court or the parties will question individual jurors about their background, attitudes, experiences, and knowledge of the particular case.[14] When the defendant asks the court to inquire into potential jurors' possible racial biases, the court is required to do so if there is a reasonable possibility that racial prejudice may influence the jury. Moreover, where a defendant is charged with an interracial violent crime, the court must presume that the possibility of prejudice exists, and ask the jurors about their attitudes toward race. Mu'Min v. Virginia, 500 U.S. 415 (1991). The parties then have an opportunity to challenge individual prospective jurors.

There are two types of challenges: challenges for cause and peremptory challenges. A party may raise a challenge for cause when a juror does not meet statutory requirements for serving on a jury or has indicated that he or she cannot set aside personal opinions and render a fair verdict based on the evidence. By contrast, peremptory challenges allow the parties to excuse jurors whom they believe to be unfavorable to their side.

> The essential nature of the peremptory challenge is that it is one exercised without a reason stated, without inquiry, and without being subject to the court's control. While challenges for cause permit rejection of jurors on a narrowly specified, provable and legally cognizable basis of partiality, the peremptory permits rejection for a real or imagined partiality that is less easily designated or demonstrable.

Swain v. Alabama, 380 U.S. 202 (1965). Peremptory challenges are not constitutionally required, but they are a tradition in the American criminal justice system.

---

14. In death penalty cases, the Supreme Court has held that the jurors must be "death qualified." What that means is that jurors whose personal views on capital punishment will preclude them from voting in accordance with the court's instruction may be challenged for cause. In Witherspoon v. Witt, 391 U.S. 510, 522 (1968), the Supreme Court held that prosecutors could not use this requirement to excuse jurors because those prospective jurors have expressed some misgivings about the death penalty. Rather, as the Court subsequently held in Wainwright v. Witt, 469 U.S. 412, 423 (1985), jurors can be excused only if their views on capital punishment "would prevent or substantially impair the performance of [the juror's] duties . . . in accordance with his instructions and his oath." In Uttecht v. Brown, 551 U.S. 1 (2007), the Court further held that courts should defer to the trial court in making this decision.

How much freedom do lawyers have in exercising peremptory challenges? Can they really be exercised for any reason? What if a party wants to excuse a juror because of her race or gender?

In Swain v. Alabama, the Supreme Court held that a defendant could raise an equal protection challenge to the prosecution's use of peremptory challenges but only if the defendant could prove that the prosecution, "in case after case, whatever the circumstances," removed jurors based on their race. This proof requirement was nearly impossible to meet. Thus, the Court revisited the issue in the landmark case of Batson v. Kentucky.

BATSON v. KENTUCKY

476 U.S. 79 (1986)

Justice POWELL delivered the opinion of the Court.

This case requires us to reexamine that portion of Swain v. Alabama (1965), concerning the evidentiary burden placed on a criminal defendant who claims that he has been denied equal protection through the State's use of peremptory challenges to exclude members of his race from the petit jury.

I

Petitioner, a black man, was indicted in Kentucky on charges of second-degree burglary and receipt of stolen goods. On the first day of trial, the judge conducted voir dire examination of the venire, excused certain jurors for cause, and permitted the parties to exercise peremptory challenges. The prosecutor used his peremptory challenges to strike all four black persons on the venire, and a jury composed only of white persons was selected. Defense counsel moved to discharge the jury before it was sworn on the ground that the prosecutor's removal of the black veniremen violated petitioner's rights under the Sixth and Fourteenth Amendments to a jury drawn from a cross section of the community, and under the Fourteenth Amendment to equal protection of the laws. Counsel requested a hearing on his motion. Without expressly ruling on the request for a hearing, the trial judge observed that the parties were entitled to use their peremptory challenges to "strike anybody they want to." The judge then denied petitioner's motion, reasoning that the cross-section requirement applies only to selection of the venire and not to selection of the petit jury itself.

The jury convicted petitioner on both counts.

II

In Swain v. Alabama, this Court recognized that a "State's purposeful or deliberate denial to Negroes on account of race of participation as jurors in the administration of justice violates the Equal Protection Clause." This principle has been "consistently and repeatedly" reaffirmed in numerous decisions of this Court. We reaffirm the principle today.[15]

More than a century ago, the Court decided that the State denies a black defendant equal protection of the laws when it puts him on trial before a jury from which members of his race have been purposefully excluded. Strauder v. West Virginia (1880). That decision laid the foundation for the Court's unceasing efforts to eradicate racial discrimination in the procedures used to select the venire from which individual jurors are drawn. In Strauder, the Court explained that the central concern of the recently ratified Fourteenth Amendment was to put an end to governmental discrimination on account of race. Exclusion of black citizens from service as jurors constitutes a primary example of the evil the Fourteenth Amendment was designed to cure.

In holding that racial discrimination in jury selection offends the Equal Protection Clause, the Court in Strauder recognized, however, that a defendant has no right to a "petit jury composed in whole or in part of persons of his own race." But the defendant does have the right to be tried by a jury whose members are selected pursuant to non-discriminatory criteria. The Equal Protection Clause guarantees the defendant that the State will not exclude members of his race from the jury venire on account of race, or on the false assumption that members of his race as a group are not qualified to serve as jurors.[16]

Purposeful racial discrimination in selection of the venire violates a defendant's right to equal protection because it denies him the protection that a trial by jury is intended to secure. "The very idea of a jury is a body . . . composed of the peers or equals of the person whose rights it is selected or summoned to determine; that is, of his neighbors, fellows, associates, persons having the same legal status in society as that which he holds." The petit jury has occupied a central position in our system of justice by safeguarding a person accused of crime against the arbitrary exercise of power by prosecutor or judge.

Racial discrimination in selection of jurors harms not only the accused whose life or liberty they are summoned to try. Competence to serve as a juror ultimately depends on an assessment of individual qualifications and

---

15. In this Court, petitioner has argued that the prosecutor's conduct violated his rights under the Sixth and Fourteenth Amendments to an impartial jury and to a jury drawn from a cross section of the community. Petitioner has framed his argument in these terms in an apparent effort to avoid inviting the Court directly to reconsider one of its own precedents. On the other hand, the State has insisted that petitioner is claiming a denial of equal protection and that we must reconsider Swain to find a constitutional violation on this record. We agree with the State that resolution of petitioner's claim properly turns on application of equal protection principles and express no view on the merits of any of petitioner's Sixth Amendment arguments. [Footnote by the Court.]

16. Similarly, though the Sixth Amendment guarantees that the petit jury will be selected from a pool of names representing a cross section of the community, Taylor v. Louisiana, 419 U.S. 522 (1975), we have never held that the Sixth Amendment requires that "petit juries actually chosen must mirror the community and reflect the various distinctive groups in the population," id., at 538. Indeed, it would be impossible to apply a concept of proportional representation to the petit jury in view of the heterogeneous nature of our society. [Footnote by the Court.]

ability impartially to consider evidence presented at a trial. A person's race simply "is unrelated to his fitness as a juror."

The harm from discriminatory jury selection extends beyond that inflicted on the defendant and the excluded juror to touch the entire community. Selection procedures that purposefully exclude black persons from juries undermine public confidence in the fairness of our system of justice.

B

In *Strauder*, the Court invalidated a state statute that provided that only white men could serve as jurors. We can be confident that no State now has such a law. The Constitution requires, however, that we look beyond the face of the statute defining juror qualifications and also consider challenged selection practices to afford "protection against action of the State through its administrative officers in effecting the prohibited discrimination."

Accordingly, the component of the jury selection process at issue here, the State's privilege to strike individual jurors through peremptory challenges, is subject to the commands of the Equal Protection Clause. Although a prosecutor ordinarily is entitled to exercise permitted peremptory challenges "for any reason at all, as long as that reason is related to his view concerning the outcome" of the case to be tried, the Equal Protection Clause forbids the prosecutor to challenge potential jurors solely on account of their race or on the assumption that black jurors as a group will be unable impartially to consider the State's case against a black defendant.

III

The principles announced in *Strauder* never have been questioned in any subsequent decision of this Court. Rather, the Court has been called upon repeatedly to review the application of those principles to particular facts.[17] A recurring question in these cases, as in any case alleging a violation of the Equal Protection Clause, was whether the defendant had met his burden of proving purposeful discrimination on the part of the State. That question also was at the heart of the portion of Swain v. Alabama we reexamine today.

Swain required the Court to decide, among other issues, whether a black defendant was denied equal protection by the State's exercise of peremptory challenges to exclude members of his race from the petit jury. The record in *Swain* showed that the prosecutor had used the State's peremptory challenges to strike the six black persons included on the petit jury venire. While rejecting the defendant's claim for failure to prove purposeful discrimination, the Court nonetheless indicated that the Equal Protection Clause placed some limits on the State's exercise of peremptory challenges.

The Court sought to accommodate the prosecutor's historical privilege of peremptory challenge free of judicial control, and the constitutional

---

17. We express no views on whether the Constitution imposes any limit on the exercise of peremptory challenges by defense counsel. [Footnote by the Court.]

prohibition on exclusion of persons from jury service on account of race. While the Constitution does not confer a right to peremptory challenges, those challenges traditionally have been viewed as one means of assuring the selection of a qualified and unbiased jury. To preserve the peremptory nature of the prosecutor's challenge, the Court in *Swain* declined to scrutinize his actions in a particular case by relying on a presumption that he properly exercised the State's challenges.

The Court went on to observe, however, that a State may not exercise its challenges in contravention of the Equal Protection Clause. It was impermissible for a prosecutor to use his challenges to exclude blacks from the jury "for reasons wholly unrelated to the outcome of the particular case on trial" or to deny to blacks "the same right and opportunity to participate in the administration of justice enjoyed by the white population." Accordingly, a black defendant could make out a prima facie case of purposeful discrimination on proof that the peremptory challenge system was "being perverted" in that manner. For example, an inference of purposeful discrimination would be raised on evidence that a prosecutor, "in case after case, whatever the circumstances, whatever the crime and whoever the defendant or the victim may be, is responsible for the removal of Negroes who have been selected as qualified jurors by the jury commissioners and who have survived challenges for cause, with the result that no Negroes ever serve on petit juries." Evidence offered by the defendant in *Swain* did not meet that standard. While the defendant showed that prosecutors in the jurisdiction had exercised their strikes to exclude blacks from the jury, he offered no proof of the circumstances under which prosecutors were responsible for striking black jurors beyond the facts of his own case.

A number of lower courts following the teaching of *Swain* reasoned that proof of repeated striking of blacks over a number of cases was necessary to establish a violation of the Equal Protection Clause. Since this interpretation of *Swain* has placed on defendants a crippling burden of proof, prosecutors' peremptory challenges are now largely immune from constitutional scrutiny. For reasons that follow, we reject this evidentiary formulation as inconsistent with standards that have been developed since *Swain* for assessing a prima facie case under the Equal Protection Clause.

B

Since the decision in *Swain*, we have explained that our cases concerning selection of the venire reflect the general equal protection principle that the "invidious quality" of governmental action claimed to be racially discriminatory "must ultimately be traced to a racially discriminatory purpose." As in any equal protection case, the "burden is, of course," on the defendant who alleges discriminatory selection of the venire "to prove the existence of purposeful discrimination." In deciding if the defendant has carried his burden of persuasion, a court must undertake "a sensitive inquiry into such circumstantial and direct evidence of intent as may be available."

[S]ince *Swain*, we have recognized that a black defendant alleging that members of his race have been impermissibly excluded from the venire may make out a prima facie case of purposeful discrimination by showing that the totality of the relevant facts gives rise to an inference of discriminatory purpose. Once the defendant makes the requisite showing, the burden shifts to the State to explain adequately the racial exclusion. The State cannot meet this burden on mere general assertions that its officials did not discriminate or that they properly performed their official duties. Rather, the State must demonstrate that "permissible racially neutral selection criteria and procedures have produced the monochromatic result."[18]

The showing necessary to establish a prima facie case of purposeful discrimination in selection of the venire may be discerned in this Court's decisions. The defendant initially must show that he is a member of a racial group capable of being singled out for differential treatment. In combination with that evidence, a defendant may then make a prima facie case by proving that in the particular jurisdiction members of his race have not been summoned for jury service over an extended period of time. Proof of systematic exclusion from the venire raises an inference of purposeful discrimination because the "result bespeaks discrimination."

Since the ultimate issue is whether the State has discriminated in selecting the defendant's venire, however, the defendant may establish a prima facie case "in other ways than by evidence of long-continued unexplained absence" of members of his race "from many panels."

Thus, since the decision in *Swain*, this Court has recognized that a defendant may make a prima facie showing of purposeful racial discrimination in selection of the venire by relying solely on the facts concerning its selection in his case.

C

The standards for assessing a prima facie case in the context of discriminatory selection of the venire have been fully articulated since *Swain*. These principles support our conclusion that a defendant may establish a prima facie case of purposeful discrimination in selection of the petit jury solely on evidence concerning the prosecutor's exercise of peremptory challenges at the defendant's trial. To establish such a case, the defendant first must show that he is a member of a cognizable racial group, and that the prosecutor has exercised peremptory challenges to remove from the venire members of the defendant's race. Second, the defendant is entitled to rely on the fact, as to which there can be no dispute, that peremptory challenges constitute a jury selection practice that permits "those to discriminate who are of a mind to discriminate." Finally, the defendant must show that these facts and any other relevant circumstances raise an inference that the prosecutor used that practice to exclude the veniremen from the petit jury on account of

18. Our decisions concerning "disparate treatment" under Title VII of the Civil Rights Act of 1964 have explained the operation of prima facie burden of proof rules. [Footnote by the Court.]

their race. This combination of factors in the empaneling of the petit jury, as in the selection of the venire, raises the necessary inference of purposeful discrimination.

In deciding whether the defendant has made the requisite showing, the trial court should consider all relevant circumstances. For example, a "pattern" of strikes against black jurors included in the particular venire might give rise to an inference of discrimination. Similarly, the prosecutor's questions and statements during voir dire examination and in exercising his challenges may support or refute an inference of discriminatory purpose. These examples are merely illustrative. We have confidence that trial judges, experienced in supervising voir dire, will be able to decide if the circumstances concerning the prosecutor's use of peremptory challenges creates a prima facie case of discrimination against black jurors.

Once the defendant makes a prima facie showing, the burden shifts to the State to come forward with a neutral explanation for challenging black jurors. Though this requirement imposes a limitation in some cases on the full peremptory character of the historic challenge, we emphasize that the prosecutor's explanation need not rise to the level justifying exercise of a challenge for cause. But the prosecutor may not rebut the defendant's prima facie case of discrimination by stating merely that he challenged jurors of the defendant's race on the assumption — or his intuitive judgment — that they would be partial to the defendant because of their shared race. The core guarantee of equal protection, ensuring citizens that their State will not discriminate on account of race, would be meaningless were we to approve the exclusion of jurors on the basis of such assumptions, which arise solely from the jurors' race. Nor may the prosecutor rebut the defendant's case merely by denying that he had a discriminatory motive or "[affirming] [his] good faith in making individual selections." If these general assertions were accepted as rebutting a defendant's prima facie case, the Equal Protection Clause "would be but a vain and illusory requirement." The prosecutor therefore must articulate a neutral explanation related to the particular case to be tried. The trial court then will have the duty to determine if the defendant has established purposeful discrimination.

IV

The State contends that our holding will eviscerate the fair trial values served by the peremptory challenge. Conceding that the Constitution does not guarantee a right to peremptory challenges and that *Swain* did state that their use ultimately is subject to the strictures of equal protection, the State argues that the privilege of unfettered exercise of the challenge is of vital importance to the criminal justice system.

While we recognize, of course, that the peremptory challenge occupies an important position in our trial procedures, we do not agree that our decision today will undermine the contribution the challenge generally makes to the administration of justice. The reality of practice, amply reflected in many state- and federal-court opinions, shows that the challenge may be, and unfortunately at times has been, used to discriminate against black jurors. By requiring trial courts to be sensitive to the racially discriminatory use of peremptory challenges, our decision enforces the mandate of equal protection and furthers the ends of justice. In view of the heterogeneous population of our Nation, public respect for our criminal justice system and the rule of law will be strengthened if we ensure that no citizen is disqualified from jury service because of his race.

Nor are we persuaded by the State's suggestion that our holding will create serious administrative difficulties. In those States applying a version of the evidentiary standard we recognize today, courts have not experienced serious administrative burdens and the peremptory challenge system has survived.

V

In this case, petitioner made a timely objection to the prosecutor's removal of all black persons on the venire. Because the trial court flatly rejected the objection without requiring the prosecutor to give an explanation for his action, we remand this case for further proceedings. If the trial court decides that the facts establish, prima facie, purposeful discrimination and the prosecutor does not come forward with a neutral explanation for his action, our precedents require that petitioner's conviction be reversed.[19]

It is so ordered.

Justice WHITE, concurring.

The Court overturns the principal holding in Swain v. Alabama (1965), that the Constitution does not require in any given case an inquiry into the prosecutor's reasons for using his peremptory challenges to strike blacks from the petit jury panel in the criminal trial of a black defendant and that in such a case it will be presumed that the prosecutor is acting for legitimate trial-related reasons. The Court now rules that such use of peremptory challenges in a given case may, but does not necessarily, raise an inference, which the prosecutor carries the burden of refuting, that his strikes were based on the belief that no black citizen could be a satisfactory juror or fairly try a black defendant.

I agree that, to this extent, *Swain* should be overruled. I do so because *Swain* itself indicated that the presumption of legitimacy with respect to the striking of black venire persons could be overcome by evidence that over a period of time the prosecution had consistently excluded blacks from petit juries. This should have warned prosecutors that using peremptories to exclude blacks on the assumption that no black juror could fairly judge a black defendant would violate the Equal Protection Clause.

---

19. To the extent that anything in Swain v. Alabama, 380 U.S. 202 (1965), is contrary to the principles we articulate today, that decision is overruled. [Footnote by the Court.]

It appears, however, that the practice of peremptorily eliminating blacks from petit juries in cases with black defendants remains widespread, so much so that I agree that an opportunity to inquire should be afforded when this occurs.

The Court emphasizes that using peremptory challenges to strike blacks does not end the inquiry; it is not unconstitutional, without more, to strike one or more blacks from the jury. The judge may not require the prosecutor to respond at all. If he does, the prosecutor, who in most cases has had a chance to voir dire the prospective jurors, will have an opportunity to give trial-related reasons for his strikes — some satisfactory ground other than the belief that black jurors should not be allowed to judge a black defendant.

Much litigation will be required to spell out the contours of the Court's equal protection holding today, and the significant effect it will have on the conduct of criminal trials cannot be gainsaid. But I agree with the Court that the time has come to rule as it has, and I join its opinion and judgment.

Justice MARSHALL, concurring.

I join Justice Powell's eloquent opinion for the Court, which takes a historic step toward eliminating the shameful practice of racial discrimination in the selection of juries. The Court's opinion cogently explains the pernicious nature of the racially discriminatory use of peremptory challenges, and the repugnancy of such discrimination to the Equal Protection Clause. The Court's opinion also ably demonstrates the inadequacy of any burden of proof for racially discriminatory use of peremptories that requires that "justice . . . sit supinely by" and be flouted in case after case before a remedy is available. I nonetheless write separately to express my views. The decision today will not end the racial discrimination that peremptories inject into the jury-selection process. That goal can be accomplished only by eliminating peremptory challenges entirely.

I

A little over a century ago, this Court invalidated a state statute providing that black citizens could not serve as jurors. Strauder v. West Virginia (1880). State officials then turned to somewhat more subtle ways of keeping blacks off jury venires.

Misuse of the peremptory challenge to exclude black jurors has become both common and flagrant. Black defendants rarely have been able to compile statistics showing the extent of that practice, but the few cases setting out such figures are instructive. See United States v. Carter (CA8 1975) (in the Western District of Missouri involving black defendants, prosecutors peremptorily challenged 81% of black jurors); McKinney v. Walker (SC 1974) (in Spartansburg County, South Carolina, prosecutors peremptorily challenged 82 percent of black jurors in cases involving black defendants). In 100 felony trials in Dallas County in 1983-1984, prosecutors peremptorily struck 405 out of 467 eligible black jurors; the chance of a qualified black sitting on a jury was 1 in 10, compared to 1 in 2 for a white.[20]

II

I wholeheartedly concur in the Court's conclusion that use of the peremptory challenge to remove blacks from juries, on the basis of their race, violates the Equal Protection Clause. I would go further, however, in fashioning a remedy adequate to eliminate that discrimination. Merely allowing defendants the opportunity to challenge the racially discriminatory use of peremptory challenges in individual cases will not end the illegitimate use of the peremptory challenge.

Evidentiary analysis . . . illustrate[s] the limitations of the approach. First, defendants cannot attack the discriminatory use of peremptory challenges at all unless the challenges are so flagrant as to establish a prima facie case. This means, in those States, that where only one or two black jurors survive the challenges for cause, the prosecutor need have no compunction about striking them from the jury because of their race. Prosecutors are left free to discriminate against blacks in jury selection provided that they hold that discrimination to an "acceptable" level.

Second, when a defendant can establish a prima facie case, trial courts face the difficult burden of assessing prosecutors' motives. Any prosecutor can easily assert facially neutral reasons for striking a juror, and trial courts are ill equipped to second-guess those reasons. How is the court to treat a prosecutor's statement that he struck a juror because the juror had a son about the same age as defendant, or seemed "uncommunicative," or "never cracked a smile" and, therefore "did not possess the sensitivities necessary to realistically look at the issues and decide the facts in this case." If such easily generated explanations are sufficient to discharge the prosecutor's obligation to justify his strikes on nonracial grounds, then the protection erected by the Court today may be illusory.

Nor is outright prevarication by prosecutors the only danger here. "[It] is even possible that an attorney may lie to himself in an effort to convince himself that his motives are legal." A prosecutor's own conscious or unconscious racism may lead him easily to the conclusion that a prospective black juror is "sullen," or "distant," a characterization that would not have come to his mind if a white juror had acted identically. A judge's own conscious or unconscious racism may lead him to accept such an explanation as well supported. [P]rosecutors' peremptories are based on their "seat-of-the-pants instincts" as to how particular jurors will vote. Yet "seat-of-the-pants instincts" may often be just another term for racial prejudice. Even if

---

20. An earlier jury-selection treatise circulated in the same county instructed prosecutors: "Do not take Jews, Negroes, Dagos, Mexicans or a member of any minority race on a jury, no matter how rich or how well educated." Quoted in Dallas Morning News, Mar. 9, 1986, p. 29, col. 1. [Footnote by the Court.]

all parties approach the Court's mandate with the best of conscious intentions, that mandate requires them to confront and overcome their own
racism on all levels — a challenge I doubt all of them can meet. It is worth
remembering that "114 years after the close of the War Between the States
and nearly 100 years after *Strauder*, racial and other forms of discrimination
still remain a fact of life, in the administration of justice as in our society as a
whole."

III

The inherent potential of peremptory challenges to distort the jury process
by permitting the exclusion of jurors on racial grounds should ideally lead
the Court to ban them entirely from the criminal justice system.

   Much ink has been spilled regarding the historic importance of defendants' peremptory challenges. But this Court has also repeatedly stated that
the right of peremptory challenge is not of constitutional magnitude, and
may be withheld altogether without impairing the constitutional guarantee
of impartial jury and fair trial. The potential for racial prejudice, further,
inheres in the defendant's challenge as well. If the prosecutor's peremptory
challenge could be eliminated only at the cost of eliminating the defendant's
challenge as well, I do not think that would be too great a price to pay.

   I applaud the Court's holding that the racially discriminatory use of
peremptory challenges violates the Equal Protection Clause, and I join
the Court's opinion. However, only by banning peremptories entirely can
such discrimination be ended.

   Chief Justice BURGER, joined by Justice REHNQUIST, dissenting.
   Today the Court sets aside the peremptory challenge, a procedure which
has been part of the common law for many centuries and part of our jury
system for nearly 200 years. It does so on the basis of a constitutional argument that was rejected, without a single dissent, in Swain v. Alabama (1965).
What makes today's holding truly extraordinary is that it is based on a
constitutional argument that the petitioner has expressly declined to
raise, both in this Court and in the Supreme Court of Kentucky.

   In the Kentucky Supreme Court, petitioner disclaimed specifically any
reliance on the Equal Protection Clause of the Fourteenth Amendment,
pressing instead only a claim based on the Sixth Amendment.

   In reaching the equal protection issue despite petitioner's clear refusal to
present it, the Court departs dramatically from its normal procedure without
any explanation.

II

Because the Court nonetheless chooses to decide this case on the equal
protection grounds not presented, it may be useful to discuss this issue as
well. In *Swain*, Justice White traced the development of the peremptory

challenge from the early days of the jury trial in England. Peremptory challenges have a venerable tradition in this country as well.

Instead of even considering the history or function of the peremptory challenge, the bulk of the Court's opinion is spent recounting the well-established principle that intentional exclusion of racial groups from jury venires is a violation of the Equal Protection Clause.

The Court never applies this conventional equal protection framework to the claims at hand, perhaps to avoid acknowledging that the state interest involved here has historically been regarded by this Court as substantial, if not compelling. Peremptory challenges have long been viewed as a means to achieve an impartial jury that will be sympathetic toward neither an accused nor witnesses for the State on the basis of some shared factor of race, religion, occupation, or other characteristic.

The Court also purports to express "no views on whether the Constitution imposes any limit on the exercise of peremptory challenges by defense counsel." But the clear and inescapable import of this novel holding will inevitably be to limit the use of this valuable tool to both prosecutors and defense attorneys alike. Once the Court has held that prosecutors are limited in their use of peremptory challenges, could we rationally hold that defendants are not?

Justice Rehnquist, with whom Chief Justice Burger, dissents.

In my view, there is simply nothing "unequal" about the State's using its peremptory challenges to strike blacks from the jury in cases involving black defendants, so long as such challenges are also used to exclude whites in cases involving white defendants, Hispanics in cases involving Hispanic defendants, Asians in cases involving Asian defendants, and so on. This case-specific use of peremptory challenges by the State does not single out blacks, or members of any other race for that matter, for discriminatory treatment. Such use of peremptories is at best based upon seat-of-the-pants instincts, which are undoubtedly crudely stereotypical and may in many cases be hopelessly mistaken. But as long as they are applied across-the-board to jurors of all races and nationalities, I do not see — and the Court most certainly has not explained — how their use violates the Equal Protection Clause.

———————————

Batson established a three-step process for challenging the alleged discriminatory use of peremptory challenges. First, the objecting party must establish a prima facie case of intentional racial discrimination. Then, the burden shifts to the other party to offer a race-neutral basis for its exercise of the challenges. Third, the trial court must evaluate the sincerity of the explanation and decide whether there really was a neutral reason for the exercise of the challenges. Each of these steps is discussed in more detail in the next section of this chapter.

3. *Applying* Batson

Batson left open many questions for the Court to answer:

1. Does the defendant need to be the same race as the excluded juror to have standing to raise the equal protection challenge? *N O*
2. Does the *Batson* ruling apply to civil cases? *N o*
3. Would the prohibition on discriminatory use of peremptory challenges apply to defense counsel? *yes*
4. Does *Batson* apply to other types of discrimination, such as gender and religious discrimination? *yes - ethnicity + gender*
5. How exactly are *Batson* challenges raised and refuted, and what constitutes a neutral explanation for a peremptory challenge of a juror?

a. Standing to Raise *Batson* Challenges

The first question that the Supreme Court answered concerned standing to raise a *Batson* challenge. Five years after *Batson*, in Powers v. Ohio, 499 U.S. 400 (1991), a white defendant challenged the prosecutor's use of peremptory challenges to exclude African American jurors. The Supreme Court held that the defendant had standing to bring the excluded jurors' equal protection claim. Justice Kennedy noted that a defendant suffers a real injury when jurors are excluded because of their race:

> In the ordinary course, a litigant must assert his or her own legal rights and interests, and cannot rest a claim to relief on the legal rights or interests of third parties. . . .
>
> [However,] the discriminatory use of peremptory challenges by the prosecution causes a criminal defendant cognizable injury. . . . This is not because the individual jurors dismissed by the prosecution may have been predisposed to favor the defendant. . . . Rather, it is because racial discrimination in the selection of jurors "casts doubt on the integrity of the judicial process," and places the fairness of a criminal proceeding in doubt.

The Court recognized, moreover, that "[t]he purpose of the jury system is to impress upon the criminal defendant and the community as a whole that a verdict of conviction or acquittal is given in accordance with the law by persons who are fair. The verdict will not be accepted or understood in these terms if the jury is chosen by unlawful means at the outset." Finally, the Court recognized the defendant's standing to raise the jurors' equal protection challenge, reasoning that the jurors themselves would likely be unable to raise their own equal protection claim:

> The barriers to a suit by an excluded juror are daunting. Potential jurors are not parties to the jury selection process and have no opportunity to be heard at the time of their exclusion. . . . [I]t would be difficult for an individual juror to show a likelihood that discrimination against him at the *voir dire* stage will recur. And, there exist considerable practical barriers to suit by the excluded juror because of the small

financial stake involved and the economic burdens of litigation. The reality is that a juror dismissed because of race probably will leave the courtroom possessing little incentive to set in motion the arduous process needed to vindicate his own rights.

Following Powers v. Ohio, a litigant has third-party standing to object to the discriminatory use of peremptory challenges, even if the litigant is not the same race as the excluded juror.

b. *Batson* Challenges in Civil Cases

Immediately after Powers v. Ohio, the Supreme Court also decided whether the *Batson* rule applies to private litigants in civil cases, or is just a bar on government discrimination against jurors. In Edmonson v. Leesville Concrete Co., 500 U.S. 614 (1991), a black construction worker sued his company for negligence. When the company used two of its three peremptory challenges to remove black prospective jurors, the worker raised a *Batson* objection. The district court rejected the objection, holding that *Batson* did not apply in civil proceedings.

The Supreme Court reversed. Once again, Justice Kennedy wrote the majority opinion:

> Without the direct and indispensable participation of the judge, who beyond all question is a state actor, the peremptory challenge system would serve no purpose. By enforcing a discriminatory peremptory challenge, the court "has not only made itself a party to the [biased act], but has elected to place its power, property and prestige behind the [alleged] discrimination."

Thus, the *Batson* rule applies even in civil cases.

Chief Justice Rehnquist and Justices O'Connor and Scalia dissented. Writing for the dissent, Justice O'Connor objected that "not everything that happens in a courtroom is state action." The dissent argued that the government was not responsible for the acts of private individuals acting on behalf of private clients.

c. Discriminatory Use of Peremptory Challenges by the Defense

As you will recall, Chief Justice Burger in his dissent in *Batson* predicted that the Court's ruling would soon be applied to defense counsel. That prediction came true. In Georgia v. McCollum, 505 U.S. 42 (1992), two white defendants were charged with assaulting two black victims. The black community rallied around the victims. Before the trial, the prosecution moved to prohibit the defendants from using their peremptory challenges to strike black individuals from the jury. The state court rejected the challenge, holding that *Batson* applied only to prosecutors.

The Supreme Court reversed. Writing for the majority, Justice Blackmun identified the four issues the Court needed to decide in the case:

> In deciding whether the Constitution prohibits criminal defendants from exercising racially discriminatory peremptory challenges, we must answer four questions. First, whether a criminal defendant's exercise of peremptory challenges in a racially discriminatory manner inflicts the harms addressed by *Batson*. Second, whether the exercise of peremptory challenges by a criminal defendant constitutes state action. Third, whether prosecutors have standing to raise this constitutional challenge. And fourth, whether the constitutional rights of a criminal defendant nonetheless preclude the extension of our precedents to this case.

In addressing these issues, the Court first found that a defendant's exercise of racially discriminatory peremptory challenges does inflict the harms addressed by *Batson*: "Regardless of who invokes the discriminatory challenge, there can be no doubt that the harm is the same — in all cases, the juror is subjected to open and public racial discrimination."

Next, the Court relied on *Edmonson* to find that defense counsel's actions constitute state action: "[T]he defendant in a Georgia criminal case relies on [the state's jury selection system]. By enforcing a discriminatory peremptory challenge, the Court 'has . . . elected to place its power, property and prestige behind the [alleged] discrimination.'"

Third, the Court held that prosecutors have standing to raise an equal protection claim on behalf of the excused jurors. Relying on its decision in *Edmonson* once more, the Court stated:

> While third-party standing is a limited exception, the *Powers* Court recognized that a litigant may raise a claim on behalf of a third party if the litigant can demonstrate that he has suffered a concrete injury, that he has a close relation to the third party, and that there exists some hindrance to the third party's ability to protect its own interests. . . .
>
>   . . . The State's relation to potential jurors in this case is closer than the relationships approved in *Powers* and *Edmonson*. As the representative of all its citizens, the State is the logical and proper party to assert the invasion of the constitutional rights of the excluded jurors in a criminal trial.

Finally, the Court rejected the defendants' argument that prohibiting their exercise of peremptory challenges would deny them a fair trial and the right to effective assistance of counsel: "This Court firmly has rejected the view that assumptions of partiality based on race provide a legitimate basis for disqualifying a person as an impartial juror."

Chief Justice Rehnquist concurred in the decision, but only because he felt obliged by what he believed was the Court's erroneous decision in *Edmonson*. Similarly, Justice Thomas wrote in his concurrence that he believed that the Court's *Edmonson* opinion precluded a different result in *McCollum*, but he expressed his "general dissatisfaction with [the Court's] continuing attempts to use the Constitution to regulate peremptory challenges." He warned that the Court's decision led it down a slippery slope: "Today, we decide only that white defendants may not strike black veniremen on the basis of race. Eventually, we will have to decide whether black defendants may strike white veniremen. Next will come the question whether defendants may exercise peremptories on the basis of sex."

Justice O'Connor dissented because she did not agree that criminal defendants and their lawyers could be considered government actors. She noted:

> What really seems to bother the Court is the prospect that leaving criminal defendants and their attorneys free to make racially motivated peremptory challenges will undermine the ideal of nondiscriminatory jury selection we espoused in *Batson*. The concept that the government alone must honor constitutional dictates, however, is a fundamental tenet of our legal order, not an obstacle to be circumvented. This is particularly so in the context of criminal trials, where we have held the prosecution to uniquely high standards of conduct.

Justice Scalia also dissented. Reiterating his argument that *Edmonson* was wrongly decided, he argued that "a bad decision should not be followed logically to its illogical conclusion." He warned that, "[i]n the interest of promoting the supposedly greater good of race relations in the society as a whole (make no mistake that that is what underlies all of this), we use the Constitution to destroy the ages-old right of criminal defendants to exercise peremptory challenges as they wish, to secure a jury that they consider fair."

d. *Batson* Challenges to Other Types of Discrimination

Batson focused on the exclusion of jurors on racial grounds. Its holding has been expanded, however, to other types of discrimination. Soon after *Batson*, the Court held that discrimination on the basis of ethnicity is also prohibited. In Hernandez v. New York, 400 U.S. 352 (1991), the Court held that Hispanics have a right not to be discriminated against in jury selection based on their ethnicity. Petitioner Dionisio Hernandez challenged the prosecution's use of peremptory challenges to excuse Hispanic jurors. While the Court recognized that such a use of peremptory challenges could be unconstitutional, it held that the prosecution offered a sufficient race-neutral explanation for its peremptory challenges. What was that explanation? The prosecutor argued that he excused the jurors because, as Spanish speakers, they might not follow the translations offered by the interpreters who would testify at trial. In response, Hernandez contended that Spanish-language ability bears a close relation to ethnicity and that, as a consequence, the exercise of a peremptory challenge on the ground that a Hispanic potential juror speaks Spanish violates the Equal Protection Clause. The Court, however, did not decide the issue because the prosecution argued that the jurors' demeanor during voir dire supported its argument that the jurors would not defer to the official translation of Spanish-language testimony.

In J.E.B. v. Alabama, 511 U.S. 127 (1994), the Supreme Court extended *Batson* to prohibit peremptory challenges based on gender. In a paternity and child-support case against the putative father, the state used nine of its ten jurors to strike males from the jury. The father objected on *Batson* grounds. Justice Blackmun, joined by Justices Stevens, O'Connor, Souter, and Ginsburg, held that *Batson*'s prohibition on the discriminatory use of peremptory challenges applies to all types of discrimination that receive heightened scrutiny, such as discriminating against prospective jurors on the basis of gender, race, and ethnicity. The Court held that such peremptory-challenge discrimination does not substantially further the state's legitimate interest in achieving a fair and impartial trial. The Court noted, however, that nevertheless,

> [o]ur conclusion that litigants may not strike potential jurors solely on the basis of gender does not imply the elimination of all peremptory challenges. . . . Parties still may remove jurors who they feel might be less acceptable than others on the panel; gender simply may not serve as a proxy for bias. Parties may also exercise their peremptory challenges to remove from the venire any group or class of individuals normally subject to "rational basis" review.[21]

Following J.E.B. v. Alabama, the Supreme Court has left it to lower courts to determine what other types of discrimination are prohibited by *Batson*. The Supreme Court has never held that the heightened scrutiny standard applies to challenges on the basis of religion, although prior to *J.E.B.*, the Supreme Court declined to review State v. Davis, 504 N.W.2d 767 (1994), a Minnesota Supreme Court decision that held that *Batson* does not prevent the exclusion of prospective jurors on religious affiliation grounds. Justices Thomas and Scalia dissented from the denial of review and argued that the case should have been remanded in light of the Court's decision in *J.E.B.* Justice Thomas wrote:

> [G]iven the Court's rationale in *J.E.B.*, no principled reason immediately appears for declining to apply *Batson* to any strike based on a classification that is accorded heightened scrutiny under the Equal Protection Clause. . . . In breaking the barrier between classifications that merit strict equal protection scrutiny and those that receive what we have termed "heightened" or "intermediate" scrutiny, *J.E.B.* would seem to have extended *Batson*'s equal protection analysis to all strikes based on the latter category of classifications — a category which presumably would include classifications based on religion.

Today, many states have enacted laws prohibiting discrimination in jury selection based on race, gender, religion, ethnicity, and even sexual orientation. *See, e.g.,* Cal. Code Civ. Proc. §231.5 (West 2016) (A party may not use a

---

21. For example, challenging all persons who have had military experience would disproportionately affect men at this time, while challenging all persons employed as nurses would disproportionately affect women. Without a showing of pretext, however, these challenges may well not be unconstitutional, since they are not gender or race based. [Footnote by the Court.]

peremptory challenge to remove a prospective juror on the basis of his or her sex, race, color, religion, ancestry, national origin, sexual orientation, age, disability, marital status, medical condition, or genetic information); N.Y. Civ. Rights Law §13 (McKinney 2016) ("No citizen of the state possessing all other qualifications which are or may be required or prescribed by law, shall be disqualified to serve as a grand or petit juror in any court of this state on account of race, creed, color, national origin or sex").

e. The Mechanics of Bringing *Batson* Challenges

As set forth by the Supreme Court in *Batson*, the burden is on the challenging party to make a prima facie showing of intentional discrimination during jury selection. Ordinarily, a party may meet this burden by demonstrating a pattern of challenges against a particular group of prospective jurors. However, in Johnson v. California, 545 U.S. 162 (2005), the Court held that an initial showing of intentional discrimination during jury selection need not establish that the prosecution's peremptory challenges were "more likely than not" based on group bias. Rather, Justice Kennedy wrote, "a prima facie case of discrimination can be made out by offering a wide variety of evidence, so long as the sum of the proffered facts gives 'rise to an inference of discriminatory purpose.'"

Once a prima facie case has been demonstrated, the burden shifts to the party exercising the peremptory challenge to provide a neutral explanation for its strikes. A peremptory challenge may be based on the juror's appearance and the manner in which the juror answers voir dire questions. And, as discussed in *Hernandez, supra*, a neutral explanation for excusing a juror may include something as simple as the contention that a juror of a certain ethnicity is not as likely to follow language translations in a case. In Purkett v. Elem, 514 U.S. 765 (1995), the Court, in a per curiam opinion, emphasized the minimal nature of establishing a neutral explanation for the exercise of a challenge. James Purkett, a black defendant, was accused of robbery. He objected to the prosecutor's use of peremptory challenges to strike two black men from the jury panel. The prosecutor explained that he struck the first juror because of his unkempt hair, mustache, and beard, and the second juror because he had been the victim of a prior robbery and might assume that the robbery charged against Purkett required similar circumstances. The Eighth Circuit found the prosecution's explanation for striking the first juror to be pretextual, but the U.S. Supreme Court overturned that finding. It held that while "implausible," "fantastic," "silly," or "superstitious" reasons might be pretextual, the prosecutor's explanation in this case satisfied *Batson* standards.

Finally, in the third step, the court must decide whether the proffered neutral explanation is merely a pretext for the discriminatory use of peremptory challenges. In Miller-El v. Dretke, 545 U.S. 231 (2005), the Court demonstrated the detailed examination that it and other courts might conduct to determine whether there has been a *Batson* violation. In *Miller-El,* Justice Souter, writing for the majority, stated that "[t]he whole of the *voir dire* testimony subject to consideration casts the prosecution's reasons for striking [a black juror] in an implausible light. Comparing [the excused black juror's] strike with the treatment of panel members who expressed similar views supports a conclusion that race was significant in determining who was challenged and who was not."

In *Miller-El,* the Court conducted an exhaustive comparison of the voir dire questions and answers of black and nonblack panel members. It found that the prosecution had challenged black jurors who had given answers nearly identical to those of white jurors. The Court also found that the prosecution had skewed its questions to black jurors so as to make it more likely that they would elicit answers that would make those jurors ineligible to sit on a death penalty case. Finally, the court pointed to an historic policy in that jurisdiction of excluding blacks from juries. In the end, the Court found that "[t]he prosecutors' chosen race-neutral reasons for the strikes do not hold up and are so far at odds with the evidence that pretext is the fair conclusion, indicating the very discrimination the explanations were meant to deny."

In his concurrence in *Miller-El,* Justice Breyer came around to the opinion offered by Justice Marshall in his concurrence in *Batson*: "The complexity of [the *Batson* test] reflects the difficulty of finding a legal test that will objectively measure the inherently subjective reasons that underline use of a peremptory challenge." Reasoning that, despite *Batson,* "the use of race- and gender-based stereotypes in the jury selection process seems better organized and more systematized than ever before," Justice Breyer, "[i]n light of [all] considerations . . . believe[d] it necessary to reconsider *Batson's* test and the peremptory challenge system as a whole."

Since Miller-El v. Dretke, courts have looked to the entire record of jury selection to determine the validity of a proffered race-neutral reason for challenging a juror, as it did in Snyder v. Louisiana.

SNYDER v. LOUISIANA

552 U.S. 472 (2008)

Justice ALITO delivered the opinion of the Court.

Petitioner Allen Snyder was convicted of first-degree murder in a Louisiana court and was sentenced to death. He asks us to review a decision of the Louisiana Supreme Court rejecting his claim that the prosecution exercised some of its peremptory jury challenges based on race, in violation of *Batson v. Kentucky (1986).* We hold that the trial court committed clear error in its ruling on a *Batson* objection, and we therefore reverse.

The crime for which petitioner was convicted [of murdering his estranged wife].

Eighty-five prospective jurors were questioned as members of a panel. Thirty-six of these survived challenges for cause; 5 of the 36 were black;

and all 5 of the prospective black jurors were eliminated by the prosecution through the use of peremptory strikes. The jury found petitioner guilty of first-degree murder and determined that he should receive the death penalty.

Batson provides a three-step process for a trial court to use in adjudicating a claim that a peremptory challenge was based on race:

> First, a defendant must make a prima facie showing that a peremptory challenge has been exercised on the basis of race[; s]econd, if that showing has been made, the prosecution must offer a race-neutral basis for striking the juror in question[; and t]hird, in light of the parties' submissions, the trial court must determine whether the defendant has shown purposeful discrimination.

Miller-El v. Dretke (2005).

Petitioner centers his *Batson* claim on the prosecution's strikes of two black jurors, Jeffrey Brooks and Elaine Scott. Because we find that the trial court committed clear error in overruling petitioner's *Batson* objection with respect to Mr. Brooks, we have no need to consider petitioner's claim regarding Ms. Scott.

In *Miller-El* v. *Dretke*, the Court made it clear that in considering a *Batson* objection, or in reviewing a ruling claimed to be *Batson* error, all of the circumstances that bear upon the issue of racial animosity must be consulted. In this case, . . . the explanation given for the strike of Mr. Brooks is by itself unconvincing and suffices for the determination that there was *Batson* error.

When defense counsel made a *Batson* objection concerning the strike of Mr. Brooks, a college senior who was attempting to fulfill his student-teaching obligation, the prosecution offered two race-neutral reasons for the strike. The prosecutor explained:

> I thought about it last night. Number 1, the main reason is that he looked very nervous to me throughout the questioning. Number 2, he's one of the fellows that came up at the beginning [of *voir dire*] and said he was going to miss class. He's a student teacher. My main concern is for that reason, that being that he might, to go home quickly, come back with guilty of a lesser verdict so there wouldn't be a penalty phase. Those are my two reasons.

With respect to the first reason, deference is especially appropriate where a trial judge has made a finding that an attorney credibly relied on demeanor in exercising a strike. Here, however, the record does not show that the trial judge actually made a determination concerning Mr. Brooks' demeanor.

The second reason proffered for the strike of Mr. Brooks — his student-teaching obligation — fails even under the highly deferential standard of review that is applicable here. At the beginning of *voir dire*, when the trial court asked the members of the venire whether jury service or sequestration would pose an extreme hardship, Mr. Brooks was 1 of more than 50 members of the venire who expressed concern that jury service or sequestration would interfere with work, school, family, or other obligations.

When Mr. Brooks came forward, the following exchange took place:

MR. JEFFREY BROOKS: . . . I'm a student at Southern University, New Orleans. This is my last semester. My major requires me to student teach, and today I've already missed a half a day. That is part of my — it's required for me to graduate this semester.

[DEFENSE COUNSEL]:   Mr. Brooks, if you — how many days would you miss if you were sequestered on this jury? Do you teach every day?

MR. JEFFREY BROOKS: Five days a week.

[DEFENSE COUNSEL]:   Five days a week.

MR. JEFFREY BROOKS: And it's 8:30 through 3:00.

[DEFENSE COUNSEL]:   If you missed this week, is there any way that you could make it up this semester?

MR. JEFFREY BROOKS: Well, the first two weeks I observe, the remaining I begin teaching, so there is something I'm missing right now that will better me towards my teaching career.

[DEFENSE COUNSEL]:   Is there any way that you could make up the observed observation *[sic]* that you're missing today, at another time?

MR. JEFFREY BROOKS: It may be possible, I'm not sure.

[DEFENSE COUNSEL]:   Okay. So that —

THE COURT: Is there anyone we could call, like a Dean or anything, that we could speak to?

MR. JEFFREY BROOKS: Actually, I spoke to my Dean, Doctor Tillman, who's at the university probably right now.

THE COURT: All right.

MR. JEFFREY BROOKS: Would you like to speak to him?

THE COURT: Yeah.

MR. JEFFREY BROOKS: I don't have his card on me.

THE COURT: Why don't you give [a law clerk] his number, give [a law clerk] his name and we'll call him and we'll see what we can do.

(MR. JEFFREY BROOKS LEFT THE BENCH).

Shortly thereafter, the court again spoke with Mr. Brooks:

THE LAW CLERK: Jeffrey Brooks, the requirement for his teaching is a three hundred clock hour observation. Doctor Tillman at Southern University said that as long as it's just this week, he doesn't see that it would cause a problem with Mr. Brooks completing his observation time within this semester.

THE COURT: We talked to Doctor Tillman and he says he doesn't see a problem as long as it's just this week, you know, he'll work with you on it. Okay?

MR. JEFFREY BROOKS: Okay.

Once Mr. Brooks heard the law clerk's report about the conversation with Doctor Tillman, Mr. Brooks did not express any further concern about serving on the jury, and the prosecution did not choose to question him more deeply about this matter.

The prosecutor's second proffered reason for striking Mr. Brooks must be evaluated in light of these circumstances. The prosecutor claimed to be apprehensive that Mr. Brooks, in order to minimize the student-teaching hours missed during jury service, might have been motivated to find petitioner guilty, not of first-degree murder, but of a lesser included offense because this would obviate the need for a penalty phase proceeding. But this scenario was highly speculative. Even if Mr. Brooks had favored a quick resolution, that would not have necessarily led him to reject a finding of first-degree murder. If the majority of jurors had initially favored a finding of first-degree murder, Mr. Brooks' purported inclination might have led him to agree in order to speed the deliberations. Only if all or most of the other jurors had favored the lesser verdict would Mr. Brooks have been in a position to shorten the trial by favoring such a verdict.

The implausibility of this explanation is reinforced by the prosecutor's acceptance of white jurors who disclosed conflicting obligations that appear to have been at least as serious as Mr. Brooks'. We recognize that a retrospective comparison of jurors based on a cold appellate record may be very misleading when alleged similarities were not raised at trial. In that situation, an appellate court must be mindful that an exploration of the alleged similarities at the time of trial might have shown that the jurors in question were not really comparable. In this case, however, the shared characteristic, *i.e.*, concern about serving on the jury due to conflicting obligations, was thoroughly explored by the trial court when the relevant jurors asked to be excused for cause.

A comparison between Mr. Brooks and Roland Laws, a white juror, is particularly striking. During the initial stage of *voir dire*, Mr. Laws approached the court and offered strong reasons why serving on the sequestered jury would cause him hardship. Mr. Laws stated that he was "a self-employed general contractor," with "two houses that are nearing completion, one [with the occupants] . . . moving in this weekend." Mr. Laws also had demanding family obligations:

> [M]y wife just had a hysterectomy, so I'm running the kids back and forth to school, and we're not originally from here, so I have no family in the area, so between the two things, it's kind of bad timing for me.

Although these obligations seem substantially more pressing than Mr. Brooks', the prosecution questioned Mr. Laws and attempted to elicit assurances that he would be able to serve despite his work and family obligations. And the prosecution declined the opportunity to use a peremptory strike on Mr. Laws. If the prosecution had been sincerely concerned that Mr. Brooks would favor a lesser verdict than first-degree murder in order to shorten the trial, it is hard to see why the prosecution would not have had at least as much concern regarding Mr. Laws.

As previously noted, the question presented at the third stage of the *Batson* inquiry is "'whether the defendant has shown purposeful discrimination.'" The prosecution's proffer of this pretextual explanation naturally gives rise to an inference of discriminatory intent.

We therefore reverse the judgment.

Justice THOMAS, with whom Justice SCALIA joins, dissenting.

The Court's conclusion, however, reveals that it is only paying lip service to the pivotal role of the trial court. The Court second-guesses the trial court's determinations in this case merely because the judge did not clarify which of the prosecutor's neutral bases for striking Mr. Brooks was dispositive.

The prosecution offered two neutral bases for striking Mr. Brooks: his nervous demeanor and his stated concern about missing class. The trial court, in rejecting defendant's *Batson* challenge, stated only "All right. I'm going to allow the challenge. I'm going to allow the challenge." Given the trial court's expertise in making credibility determinations and its firsthand knowledge of the *voir dire* exchanges, it is entirely proper to defer to its judgment. Accordingly, I would affirm the judgment below.

Although the Court has opened the door for greater scrutiny of the granting of possibly discriminatory peremptory challenges, it has not held that a judge's denial of a peremptory challenge — even if it was properly raised — requires automatic reversal. In Rivera v. Illinois, 556 U.S. 148 (2009), the Supreme Court held that if a judge erroneously seats a juror who could have been properly stricken by a peremptory challenge, the defendant is not entitled to reversal of the conviction if the record demonstrates that all of the seated jurors were actually qualified and unbiased.

RIVERA v. ILLINOIS

556 U.S. 148 (2009)

Justice GINSBURG delivered the opinion of the Court.

This case concerns the consequences of a state trial court's erroneous denial of a defendant's peremptory challenge to the seating of a juror in a criminal case. If all seated jurors are qualified and unbiased, does the *Due Process Clause of the Fourteenth Amendment* nonetheless require automatic reversal of the defendant's conviction?

Following a jury trial in an Illinois state court, defendant-petitioner Michael Rivera was convicted of first-degree murder and sentenced to a prison term of 85 years. On appeal, Rivera challenged the trial court's rejection of his peremptory challenge to venire member Deloris Gomez. Gomez sat on Rivera's jury and indeed served as the jury's foreperson. It is conceded that there was no basis to challenge Gomez for cause. She met the requirements for jury service, and Rivera does not contend that she was in fact biased against him. The Supreme Court of Illinois held that the peremptory challenge should have been allowed, but further held that the error was harmless and therefore did not warrant reversal of Rivera's conviction. We affirm the judgment of the Illinois Supreme Court.

The right to exercise peremptory challenges in state court is determined by state law. This Court has "long recognized" that "peremptory challenges are not of federal constitutional dimension." States may withhold peremptory challenges "altogether without impairing the constitutional guarantee of an impartial jury and a fair trial." Just as state law controls the existence and exercise of peremptory challenges, so state law determines the consequences of an erroneous denial of such a challenge. Accordingly, we have no cause to disturb the Illinois Supreme Court's determination that, in the circumstances Rivera's case presents, the trial court's error did not warrant reversal of his conviction.

I

Rivera was charged with first-degree murder in the Circuit Court of Cook County, Illinois. The State alleged that Rivera, who is Hispanic, shot and killed Marcus Lee, a 16-year-old African-American, after mistaking Lee for a member of a rival gang.

During jury selection, Rivera's counsel questioned prospective juror Deloris Gomez, a business office supervisor at Cook County Hospital's outpatient orthopedic clinic. Gomez stated that she sometimes interacted with patients during the check-in process and acknowledged that Cook County Hospital treats many gunshot victims. She maintained, however, that her work experience would not affect her ability to be impartial. After questioning Gomez, Rivera's counsel sought to use a peremptory challenge to excuse her. At that point in the jury's selection, Rivera had already used three peremptory challenges. Two of the three were exercised against women; one of the two women thus eliminated was African-American.

Rather than dismissing Gomez, the trial judge called counsel to chambers, where he expressed concern that the defense was discriminating against Gomez. Without specifying the type of discrimination he suspected or the reasons for his concern, the judge [indicated that he thought Gomez might be African American] and he directed Rivera's counsel to state his reasons for excusing Gomez. Counsel responded, first, that Gomez saw victims of violent crime on a daily basis. Dissatisfied with counsel's proffered reasons, the judge denied the challenge to Gomez, but agreed to allow counsel to question Gomez further.

Rivera's case proceeded to trial. The jury, with Gomez as its foreperson, found Rivera guilty of first-degree murder.

We granted certiorari to resolve an apparent conflict among state high courts over whether the erroneous denial of a peremptory challenge requires automatic reversal of a defendant's conviction as a matter of federal law.

II

The *Due Process Clause of the Fourteenth Amendment,* Rivera maintains, requires reversal whenever a criminal defendant's peremptory challenge is erroneously denied.

Rivera's arguments do not withstand scrutiny. If a defendant is tried before a qualified jury composed of individuals not challengeable for cause, the loss of a peremptory challenge due to a state court's good-faith error is not a matter of federal constitutional concern. Rather, it is a matter for the State to address under its own laws.

Because peremptory challenges are within the States' province to grant or withhold, the mistaken denial of a state-provided peremptory challenge does not, without more, violate the Federal Constitution.

The trial judge's refusal to excuse juror Gomez did not deprive Rivera of his constitutional right to a fair trial before an impartial jury. . . . Rivera received precisely what due process required: a fair trial before an impartial and properly instructed jury, which found him guilty of every element of the charged offense.

Despite Batson and its progeny, the Supreme Court continues to face challenges posed by racial discrimination. The recent case of Foster v. Chatman, 136 S. Ct. 1737 (2016), serves as an important reminder of the challenges in preventing discrimination in jury selection.

> Foster was convicted of capital murder and sentenced to death in a Georgia court. During jury selection at his trial, the State exercised peremptory strikes against all four black prospective jurors qualified to serve. Foster argued that the State's use of those strikes was racially motivated, in violation of our decision in Batson v. Kentucky (1986). [The evidence of racial discrimination in jury selection included:]
>
> (1) Four copies of the jury venire list. On each copy, the names of the black prospective jurors were highlighted in bright green. A legend in the upper right corner of the lists indicated that the green highlighting "represents Blacks." The letter "B" also appeared next to each black prospective juror's name.
> (2) [According to an affidavit by the investigator assisting the prosecution in jury selection, he circulated to the prosecutors his views on jury selection:]
> "If it comes down to having to pick one of the black jurors, [this one] might be okay. This is solely my opinion. . . . Upon picking of the jury after listening to all of the jurors we had to pick, if we had to pick a black juror I recommend that [this juror] be one of the jurors."
> (3) Three handwritten notes on black prospective jurors . . . denoted those individuals as "B#1," "B#2," and "B#3," respectively.
> (4) A typed list of the qualified jurors remaining after voir dire included "Ns" next to . . . the names of all five qualified black prospective jurors.
> (5) A handwritten document titled "definite NO's," listing six names. The first five were those of the five qualified black prospective jurors.
> (6) A handwritten document titled "Church of Christ." A notation on the document read: "NO. No Black Church."
> (7) The questionnaires that had been completed by several of the black prospective jurors. On each one, the juror's response indicating his or her race had been circled.

Most cases will not have such stark facts. Instead, enforcement of *Batson* and prevention of discrimination depends on the diligence of counsel and the courts.

C. PRETRIAL PUBLICITY AND THE RIGHT TO A FAIR TRIAL

The Sixth Amendment guarantees defendants the right to a fair trial. Publicity, either before or after trial, may interfere with a defendant's right to an impartial jury. The court has the responsibility of ensuring the defendant a fair trial, but the court must also balance the defendant's rights against the First Amendment rights of the press. At what point does media coverage of a case cross the line and interfere with the defendant's right to a fair trial? What steps can the court take to ensure that the defendant will be judged by an impartial jury?

This section focuses on the standards for determining whether pretrial and trial publicity have interfered with the defendant's right to a fair trial. It then examines various mechanisms that courts have used to limit the impact of publicity on cases. These include, among other things, changes of venue, limiting access to courtroom proceedings, and gag orders. Finally, the section ends with a discussion of cameras in the courtroom.

1. *When Does Pretrial Publicity Interfere with a Defendant's Right to a Fair Trial?*

The Sixth Amendment does not guarantee a defendant the right to be tried by a jury that has heard nothing about the case. Rather, the focus is on whether the defendant has been prejudiced by pretrial publicity. The Supreme Court examined this principle in Irvin v. Dowd.

IRVIN v. DOWD
366 U.S. 717 (1961)

Justice CLARK delivered the opinion of the Court.

[The defendant brought a habeas corpus petition claiming that he did not receive a fair trial because pretrial publicity prejudiced the jurors. The defendant was convicted of murder and sentenced to death in a state trial.]

The constitutional claim arises in this way. Six murders were committed in the vicinity of Evansville, Indiana, two in December 1954, and four in March 1955. The crimes, extensively covered by news media in the locality, aroused great excitement and indignation throughout the county and an adjoining rural county of approximately 30,000 inhabitants. The petitioner was arrested on April 8, 1955. Shortly thereafter, the Prosecutor of Vanderburgh County and Evansville police officials issued press releases, which were intensively publicized, stating that the petitioner had confessed to the six murders. The Grand Jury soon indicted the petitioner for the murder which resulted in his conviction. Counsel appointed to defend petitioner immediately sought a change of venue from Vanderburgh County, which was granted, but to adjoining Gibson County. Alleging that the widespread and inflammatory publicity had also highly prejudiced the inhabitants of Gibson County against the petitioner, counsel, on October 29, 1955, sought another change of venue, from Gibson County to a county sufficiently removed from the Evansville locality that a fair trial would not be prejudiced. The motion was denied, apparently because the pertinent Indiana statute allows only a single change of venue.

During the course of the voir dire examination, which lasted some four weeks, petitioner filed two more motions for a change of venue and eight motions for continuances. All were denied.

England, from whom the Western World has largely taken its concepts of individual liberty and of the dignity and worth of every man, has bequeathed to us safeguards for their preservation, the most priceless of which is that of trial by jury. This right has become as much American as it was once the most English. In essence, the right to jury trial guarantees to the criminally accused a fair trial by a panel of impartial, "indifferent" jurors. The failure to accord an accused a fair hearing violates even the minimal standards of due process.

It is not required, however, that the jurors be totally ignorant of the facts and issues involved. In these days of swift, widespread and diverse methods of communication, an important case can be expected to arouse the interest of the public in the vicinity, and scarcely any of those best qualified to serve as jurors will not have formed some impression or opinion as to the merits of the case. This is particularly true in criminal cases. To hold that the mere existence of any preconceived notion as to the guilt or innocence of an accused, without more, is sufficient to rebut the presumption of a prospective juror's impartiality would be to establish an impossible standard. It is sufficient if the juror can lay aside his impression or opinion and render a verdict based on the evidence presented in court.

Here the build-up of prejudice is clear and convincing. An examination of the then current community pattern of thought as indicated by the popular news media is singularly revealing. For example, petitioner's first motion for a change of venue from Gibson County alleged that the awaited trial of petitioner had become the cause celebre of this small community—so much so that curbstone opinions, not only as to petitioner's guilt but even as to what punishment he should receive, were solicited and recorded on the public streets by a roving reporter, and later were broadcast over the local stations. A reading of the 46 exhibits which petitioner attached to his motion indicates that a barrage of newspaper headlines, articles, cartoons and pictures was unleashed against him during the six or seven months preceding his trial. The motion further alleged that the newspapers in which the stories appeared were delivered regularly to approximately 95% of the dwellings in Gibson County and that, in addition, the Evansville radio and TV stations, which likewise blanketed that county, also carried extensive newscasts covering the same incidents. These stories revealed the details of his background, including a reference to crimes committed when a juvenile, his convictions for arson almost 20 years previously, for burglary and by a court-martial on AWOL charges during the war. He was accused of being a parole violator. The headlines announced his police line-up identification, that he faced a lie detector test, had been placed at the scene of the crime and that the six murders were solved but petitioner refused to confess. Finally, they announced his confession to the six murders and the fact of his indictment for four of them in Indiana. They reported petitioner's offer to plead guilty if promised a 99-year sentence, but also the determination, on the other hand, of the prosecutor to secure the death penalty, and that petitioner had confessed to 24 burglaries (the modus operandi of these robberies was compared to that of the murders and the similarity noted). One story dramatically relayed the promise of a sheriff to devote his life to securing petitioner's execution by the State of Kentucky, where petitioner is alleged to have committed one of the six murders, if Indiana failed to do so. Another characterized petitioner as remorseless and without conscience but also as having been found sane by a court-appointed panel of doctors. In many of the stories petitioner was described as the "confessed slayer of six," a parole violator and fraudulent-check artist. Petitioner's court-appointed counsel was quoted as having received "much criticism over being Irvin's counsel" and it was pointed out, by way of excusing the attorney, that he would be subject to disbarment should he refuse to represent Irvin. On the day before the trial the newspapers carried the story that Irvin had orally admitted the murder of Kerr (the victim in this case) as well as "the robbery-murder of Mrs. Mary Holland; the murder of Mrs. Wilhelmina Sailer in Posey County, and the slaughter of three members of the Duncan family in Henderson County, Ky."

It cannot be gainsaid that the force of this continued adverse publicity caused a sustained excitement and fostered a strong prejudice among the people of Gibson County. In fact, on the second day devoted to the selection of the jury, the newspapers reported that "strong feelings, often bitter and angry, rumbled to the surface," and that "the extent to which the multiple murders — three in one family — have aroused feelings throughout the area was emphasized Friday when 27 of the 35 prospective jurors questioned were excused for holding biased pretrial opinions. . . ." A few days later the feeling was described as "a pattern of deep and bitter prejudice against the former pipe-fitter." Spectator comments, as printed by the newspapers, were "my mind is made up"; "I think he is guilty"; and "he should be hanged."

Finally, and with remarkable understatement, the headlines reported that "impartial jurors are hard to find." The panel consisted of 430 persons. The court itself excused 268 of those on challenges for cause as having fixed opinions as to the guilt of petitioner; 103 were excused because of conscientious objection to the imposition of the death penalty; 20, the maximum allowed, were peremptorily challenged by petitioner and 10 by the State; 12 persons and two alternates were selected as jurors and the rest were excused on personal grounds, e.g., deafness, doctor's orders, etc. An examination of the 2,783-page voir dire record shows that 370 prospective jurors or almost 90% of those examined on the point (10 members of the panel were never asked whether or not they had any opinion) entertained some opinion as to guilt — ranging in intensity from mere suspicion to absolute certainty. A number admitted that, if they were in the accused's place in the dock and he in theirs on the jury with their opinions, they would not want him on a jury.

Here the "pattern of deep and bitter prejudice" shown to be present throughout the community was clearly reflected in the sum total of the voir dire examination of a majority of the jurors finally placed in the jury box. Eight out of the 12 thought petitioner was guilty. With such an opinion permeating their minds, it would be difficult to say that each could exclude this preconception of guilt from his deliberations. The influence that lurks in an opinion once formed is so persistent that it unconsciously fights detachment from the mental processes of the average man. Where one's life is at stake — and accounting for the frailties of human nature — we can only say that in the light of the circumstances here the finding of impartiality does not meet constitutional standards. Two-thirds of the jurors had an opinion that petitioner was guilty and were familiar with the material facts and circumstances involved, including the fact that other murders were attributed to him, some going so far as to say that it would take evidence to overcome their belief. One said that he "could not . . . give the defendant the benefit of the doubt that he is innocent." Another stated that he had a "somewhat" certain fixed opinion as to petitioner's guilt. No doubt each juror was sincere when he said that he would be fair and impartial to petitioner, but the psychological impact requiring such a declaration before one's fellows is often its father. Where so many, so many times, admitted prejudice, such a statement of impartiality can be given little weight. As one of the jurors put it, "You can't forget what you hear and see." With his life at stake, it is not requiring too much that petitioner be tried in an atmosphere undisturbed by so huge a wave of public passion and by a jury other than one in which two-thirds of the members admit, before hearing any testimony, to possessing a belief in his guilt.

Petitioner's detention and sentence of death pursuant to the void judgment is in violation of the Constitution.

Justice FRANKFURTER, concurring.

Of course I agree with the Court's opinion. But this is, unfortunately, not an isolated case that happened in Evansville, Indiana, nor an atypical miscarriage of justice due to anticipatory trial by newspapers instead of trial in court before a jury.

Not a Term passes without this Court being importuned to review conviction, had in States throughout the country, in which substantial claims are made that a jury trial has been distorted because of inflammatory newspaper accounts. Indeed such extraneous influences, in violation of the decencies guaranteed by our Constitution, are sometimes so powerful that an accused is forced, as a practical matter, to forego trial by jury. For one reason or another this Court does not undertake to review all such envenomed state prosecutions. But, again and again, such disregard of fundamental fairness is so flagrant that the Court is compelled . . . to reverse a conviction in which prejudicial newspaper intrusion has poisoned the outcome. This Court has not yet decided that the fair administration of criminal justice must be subordinated to another safeguard of our constitutional system — freedom of the press, properly conceived. The Court has not yet decided that, while convictions must be reversed and miscarriages of justice result because the minds of jurors or potential jurors were poisoned, the poisoner is constitutionally protected in plying his trade.

While the Court held in *Irvin* that extreme pretrial publicity may prejudice a defendant to the point where there has been a due process violation of his right to a fair trial, the Supreme Court has limited such challenges to extreme cases. The mere flooding of the airways with information about a case, especially in this Internet age, will not necessarily constitute a Sixth Amendment violation. It is difficult for defendants in even the most high-profile cases to raise Sixth Amendment challenges to their convictions.

SKILLING v. UNITED STATES

561 U.S. 358 (2010)

Justice GINSBURG delivered the opinion of the Court.

In 2001, Enron Corporation, then the seventh highest-revenue-grossing company in America, crashed into bankruptcy. We consider in this opinion [whether pretrial publicity arising from the prosecution of Jeffrey Skilling, a long-time Enron executive, prevented] Skilling from obtaining a fair trial.

We conclude that Skilling's fair-trial argument fails; Skilling, we hold, did not establish that a presumption of juror prejudice arose or that actual bias infected the jury that tried him.

I

Founded in 1985, Enron Corporation grew from its headquarters in Houston, Texas, into one of the world's leading energy companies. Skilling launched his career there in 1990 when Kenneth Lay, the company's founder, hired him to head an Enron subsidiary. Skilling steadily rose through the corporation's ranks, serving as president and chief operating officer, and then as chief executive officer. On August 14, 2001, Skilling resigned from Enron.

Less than four months after Skilling's departure, Enron spiraled into bankruptcy. The Government's investigation uncovered an elaborate conspiracy to prop up Enron's short-run stock prices by overstating the company's financial well-being. In the years following Enron's bankruptcy, the Government prosecuted dozens of Enron employees who participated in the scheme. In time, the Government worked its way up the corporation's chain of command: On July 7, 2004, a grand jury indicted Skilling, Lay, and Richard Causey, Enron's former chief accounting officer.

In November 2004, Skilling moved to transfer the trial to another venue; he contended that hostility toward him in Houston, coupled with extensive pretrial publicity, had poisoned potential jurors. To support this assertion, Skilling, aided by media experts, submitted hundreds of news reports detailing Enron's downfall; he also presented affidavits from the experts he engaged portraying community attitudes in Houston in comparison to other potential venues.

The U.S. District Court for the Southern District of Texas . . . denied the venue-transfer motion. Despite "isolated incidents of intemperate commentary," the court observed, media coverage "ha[d] [mostly] been objective and unemotional," and the facts of the case were "neither heinous nor sensational."

In the months leading up to the trial, the District Court solicited from the parties questions the court might use to screen prospective jurors. The court converted Skilling's submission, with slight modifications, into a 77-question, 14-page document that asked prospective jurors about, *inter alia*, their sources of news and exposure to Enron-related publicity, beliefs concerning Enron and what caused its collapse, opinions regarding the defendants and their possible guilt or innocence, and relationships to the company and to anyone affected by its demise.

[During voir dire], the District Court first emphasized to the venire the importance of impartiality and explained the presumption of innocence and the Government's burden of proof. After questioning the venire as a group, the District Court brought prospective jurors one by one to the bench for individual examination. The court then permitted each side to pose follow-up questions.

Following a 4-month trial and nearly five days of deliberation, the jury found Skilling guilty of 19 counts, including the honest-services-fraud conspiracy charge, and not guilty of 9 insider-trading counts.

On appeal, Skilling raised a host of challenges to his convictions. He claimed there was a presumption of prejudice "stemming from . . . the large number of victims in Houston . . . [who] lost their jobs, and . . . saw their 401(k) accounts wiped out."

II

Pointing to "the community passion aroused by Enron's collapse and the vitriolic media treatment" aimed at him, Skilling argues that his trial "never should have proceeded in Houston." Skilling's fair-trial claim . . . raises two distinct questions. First, did the District Court err by failing to move the trial to a different venue based on a presumption of prejudice? Second, did actual prejudice contaminate Skilling's jury?

A

The Sixth Amendment secures to criminal defendants the right to trial by an impartial jury. By constitutional design, that trial occurs "in the State where the . . . Crimes . . . have been committed." Art. III, §2, cl. 3. The Constitution's place-of-trial prescriptions, however, do not impede transfer of the proceeding to a different district at the defendant's request if extraordinary local prejudice will prevent a fair trial—a "basic requirement of due process."

"The theory of our [trial] system is that the conclusions to be reached in a case will be induced only by evidence and argument in open court, and not by any outside influence, whether of private talk or public print." When does the publicity attending conduct charged as criminal dim prospects that the trier can judge a case, as due process requires, impartially, unswayed by outside influence? We begin our discussion by addressing . . . Rideau v. Louisiana (1963).

Wilbert Rideau robbed a bank in a small Louisiana town, kidnaped three bank employees, and killed one of them. Police interrogated Rideau in jail without counsel present and obtained his confession. Without informing Rideau, no less seeking his consent, the police filmed the interrogation. On three separate occasions shortly before the trial, a local television station broadcast the film to audiences ranging from 24,000 to 53,000 individuals. Rideau moved for a change of venue, arguing that he could not receive a fair trial in the parish where the crime occurred, which had a population of approximately 150,000 people. The trial court denied the motion, and a jury eventually convicted Rideau. The Supreme Court of Louisiana upheld the conviction.

We reversed. "What the people [in the community] saw on their television sets," we observed, "was Rideau, in jail, flanked by the sheriff and two state troopers, admitting in detail the commission of the robbery, kidnapping, and murder." "[T]o the tens of thousands of people who saw and heard it," we explained, the interrogation "in a very real sense *was* Rideau's trial—at which he pleaded guilty." We therefore "d[id] not hesitate to hold, without pausing to examine a particularized transcript of the *voir dire*," that "[t]he kangaroo court proceedings" trailing the televised confession violated due process.

We followed *Rideau*'s lead in two later cases in which media coverage manifestly tainted a criminal prosecution. In Estes v. Texas (1965), extensive publicity before trial swelled into excessive exposure during preliminary court proceedings as reporters and television crews overran the courtroom and "bombard[ed] . . . the community with the sights and sounds of" the pretrial hearing. The media's overzealous reporting efforts, we observed, "led to considerable disruption" and denied the "judicial serenity and calm to which [Billie Sol Estes] was entitled."

Similarly, in Sheppard v. Maxwell (1966), news reporters extensively covered the story of Sam Sheppard, who was accused of bludgeoning his pregnant wife to death. "[B]edlam reigned at the courthouse during the trial and newsmen took over practically the entire courtroom," thrusting jurors "into the role of celebrities." But Sheppard's case involved more than heated reporting pretrial: We upset the murder conviction because a "carnival atmosphere" pervaded the trial.

In each of these cases, we overturned a "conviction obtained in a trial atmosphere that [was] utterly corrupted by press coverage;" our decisions, however, "cannot be made to stand for the proposition that juror exposure to . . . news accounts of the crime . . . alone presumptively deprives the defendant of due process." Murphy v. Florida (1975). Prominence does not necessarily produce prejudice, and juror *impartiality*, we have reiterated, does not require *ignorance.* Irvin v. Dowd (1961). A presumption of prejudice, our decisions indicate, attends only the extreme case.

Relying on *Rideau, Estes,* and *Sheppard,* Skilling asserts that we need not pause to examine the screening questionnaires or the *voir dire* before declaring his jury's verdict void. We are not persuaded. Important differences separate Skilling's prosecution from those in which we have presumed juror prejudice.

First, we have emphasized in prior decisions the size and characteristics of the community in which the crime occurred. In *Rideau,* for example, we noted that the murder was committed in a parish of only 150,000 residents. Houston, in contrast, is the fourth most populous city in the Nation: At the time of Skilling's trial, more than 4.5 million individuals eligible for jury duty resided in the Houston area. Given this large, diverse pool of potential jurors, the suggestion that 12 impartial individuals could not be empaneled is hard to sustain.

Second, although news stories about Skilling were not kind, they contained no confession or other blatantly prejudicial information of the type readers or viewers could not reasonably be expected to shut from sight. Rideau's dramatically staged admission of guilt, for instance, was likely imprinted indelibly in the mind of anyone who watched it.

Third, unlike cases in which trial swiftly followed a widely reported crime, over four years elapsed between Enron's bankruptcy and Skilling's trial. Although reporters covered Enron-related news throughout this period, the decibel level of media attention diminished somewhat in the years following Enron's collapse.

Finally, and of prime significance, Skilling's jury acquitted him of nine insider-trading counts. It would be odd for an appellate court to presume prejudice in a case in which jurors' actions run counter to that presumption.

Skilling's trial, in short, shares little in common with those in which we approved a presumption of juror prejudice.

B

We next consider whether actual prejudice infected Skilling's jury. *Voir dire*, Skilling asserts, did not adequately detect and defuse juror bias. We disagree with Skilling's characterization of the *voir dire* and the jurors selected through it.

Skilling deems the *voir dire* insufficient because, he argues, jury selection lasted "just five hours," "[m]ost of the court's questions were conclusory[,] high-level, and failed adequately to probe jurors' true feelings," and the court "consistently took prospective jurors at their word once they claimed they could be fair, no matter what other indications of bias were present." Our review of the record, however, yields a different appraisal.

[T]he District Court initially screened venire members by eliciting their responses to a comprehensive questionnaire drafted in large part by Skilling. That survey helped to identify prospective jurors excusable for cause and served as a springboard for further questions put to remaining members of the array. *Voir dire* thus was, in the court's words, the "culmination of a lengthy process."

The facts of *Irvin* are worlds apart from those presented here. Leslie Irvin stood accused of a brutal murder and robbery spree in a small rural community. In the months before Irvin's trial, "a barrage" of publicity was "unleashed against him," including reports of his confessions to the slayings and robberies. "[N]ewspapers in which the[se] stories appeared were delivered regularly to 95% of the dwellings in" the county where the trial occurred, which had a population of only 30,000; "radio and TV stations, which likewise blanketed that county, also carried extensive newscasts covering the same incidents."

In this case, news stories about Enron contained nothing resembling the horrifying information rife in reports about Irvin's rampage of robberies and murders. Of key importance, Houston shares little in common with the rural community in which Irvin's trial proceeded, and circulation figures for Houston media sources were far lower than the 95% saturation level recorded in *Irvin*.

Skilling also singles out several jurors in particular and contends they were openly biased. Skilling contends that Juror 11 — the only seated juror he challenged for cause — "expressed the most obvious bias." Juror 11 stated that "greed on Enron's part" triggered the company's bankruptcy and that corporate executives, driven by avarice, "walk a line that stretches sometimes the legality of something." But, as the Fifth Circuit accurately summarized, Juror 11 "had 'no idea' whether Skilling had 'crossed that line,' and he 'didn't say that' every CEO is probably a crook. He also asserted that he could be fair and require the government to prove its case, that he did not believe everything he read in the paper, that he did not 'get into the details' of the Enron coverage, that he did not watch television, and that Enron was 'old news.'"

In sum, Skilling failed to establish that a presumption of prejudice arose or that actual bias infected the jury that tried him. We therefore affirm the Fifth Circuit's ruling that Skilling received a fair trial.

Justice SOTOMAYOR, with whom Justice STEVENS and Justice BREYER join, concurring in part and dissenting in part.

I respectfully dissent from the Court's conclusion that Jeffrey Skilling received a fair trial before an impartial jury. Under our relevant precedents, the more intense the public's antipathy toward a defendant, the more careful a court must be to prevent that sentiment from tainting the jury. In this case, passions ran extremely high. The sudden collapse of Enron directly affected thousands of people in the Houston area and shocked the entire community. The accompanying barrage of local media coverage was massive in volume and often caustic in tone. As Enron's one-time CEO, Skilling was at the center of the storm. Even if these extraordinary circumstances did not constitutionally compel a change of venue, they required the District Court to conduct a thorough *voir dire* in which prospective jurors' attitudes about the case were closely scrutinized. The District Court's inquiry lacked the necessary thoroughness and left serious doubts about whether the jury empaneled to decide Skilling's case was capable of rendering an impartial decision based solely on the evidence presented in the courtroom. Accordingly, I would grant Skilling relief on his fair-trial claim.

Any doubt that the prevailing mindset in the Houston community remained overwhelmingly negative was dispelled by prospective jurors' responses to the written questionnaires. [M]ore than one-third of the prospective jurors either knew victims of Enron's collapse or were victims themselves, and two-thirds gave responses suggesting an antidefendant bias. In many instances their contempt for Skilling was palpable.

Given the extent of the antipathy evident both in the community at large and in the responses to the written questionnaire, it was critical for the District Court to take "strong measures" to ensure the selection of "an impartial jury free from outside influences." Perhaps because it had underestimated the public's antipathy toward Skilling, the District Court's 5-hour *voir dire* was manifestly insufficient to identify and remove biased jurors.

The court also rarely asked prospective jurors to describe personal interactions they may have had about the case, or to consider whether they might have difficulty avoiding discussion of the case with family, friends, or colleagues during the course of the lengthy trial. On the few occasions when prospective jurors were asked whether they would feel pressure from the public to convict, they acknowledged that it might be difficult to return home after delivering a not-guilty verdict.

The topics that the District Court did cover were addressed in cursory fashion. Most prospective jurors were asked just a few yes/no questions about their general exposure to media coverage and a handful of additional questions concerning any responses to the written questionnaire that suggested bias. In many instances, their answers were unenlightening.

Indeed, the District Court's anemic questioning did little to dispel similar doubts about the impartiality of numerous other seated jurors and alternates. In my estimation, more than half of those seated made written and oral comments suggesting active antipathy toward the defendants.

In sum, I cannot accept the majority's conclusion that *voir dire* gave the District Court "a sturdy foundation to assess fitness for jury service." Taken together, the District Court's failure to cover certain vital subjects, its superficial coverage of other topics, and its uncritical acceptance of assurances of impartiality leave me doubtful that Skilling's jury was indeed free from the deep-seated animosity that pervaded the community at large. "[R]egardless of the heinousness of the crime charged, the apparent guilt of the offender[,] or the station in life which he occupies," our system of justice demands trials that are fair in both appearance and fact. Because I do not believe Skilling's trial met this standard, I would grant him relief.

2. Remedies for Prejudicial Pretrial Publicity

Assuming there is substantial pretrial or trial publicity, what safeguards can the trial court employ to secure a defendant's right to a fair trial? The court has many available alternatives, including continuing the trial, sequestering the jury, conducting an intensive voir dire of the jury, giving cautionary jury instructions, or even changing venue.

In his concurrence in Irvin v. Dowd, *supra*, Justice Frankfurter suggested that something more may be needed, like putting restrictions on the "poisoner" (i.e., the media). In a series of decisions, the Supreme Court decided what restrictions can be placed on the media's coverage of criminal matters.

a. Closure of Courtrooms

Initially, the Supreme Court was open to the idea of allowing trial judges to exclude the press and public from pretrial hearings, such as motions to suppress. In Gannett Co. v. DePasquale, 443 U.S. 368 (1979), the Court upheld a trial judge's decision to close a suppression hearing from the media and the public. At the suppression hearing, the court was deciding whether to suppress the defendant's alleged confession and physical evidence in the case. Justice Stewart wrote for the Court:

> Publicity concerning pretrial suppression hearings such as the one involved in the present case poses special risks of unfairness. The whole purpose of such hearings is to screen out unreliable or illegally obtained evidence and insure that this evidence does not become known to the jury. Publicity concerning the proceedings at a pretrial hearing, however, could influence public opinion against a defendant and inform potential jurors of inculpatory information wholly inadmissible at the actual trial.

The *Gannett* Court held that there is no Sixth Amendment right to attend a trial but left open the question of whether there is a First Amendment right of access. The Court did note, however, that if there is a First Amendment right, it must be balanced against the defendant's right to a fair trial.

The Supreme Court soon changed directions. In Richmond Newspapers, Inc. v. Virginia, 448 U.S. 555 (1980), the defendant had moved to close his murder trial from the public and reporters. Chief Justice Burger reversed the trial court's closure order. In a plurality decision, he wrote that "a presumption of openness inheres in the very nature of a criminal trial under our system of justice." Accordingly, the First Amendment provides a presumption that the press and public will have access to criminal trials and that this right can be compromised only if there is an overriding government interest set forth in findings by the court. Generally, courts must balance a defendant's right to a fair trial against the public's and the media's First Amendment right of access.

The issue then arose as to whether states may close courtrooms in cases involving sex offenses against minors. In Globe Newspaper Co. v. Superior Court, 457 U.S. 596 (1982), the Supreme Court struck down a Virginia statute that created a per se rule that the press and public must be excluded during the testimony of an underage victim in a sex crime case. In the majority's opinion, Justice Brennan wrote:

> The Court's recent decision in *Richmond Newspapers* firmly established for the first time that the press and general public have a constitutional right of access to criminal trials. Although there was no opinion of the Court in that case, seven Justices recognized that this right of access is embodied in the First Amendment, and applied to the States through the Fourteenth Amendment.
>
> Two features of the criminal justice system, emphasized in the various opinions in *Richmond Newspapers*, together serve to explain why a right of access to criminal trials in particular is properly afforded protection by the First Amendment. First, the criminal trial historically has been open to the press and general public. "[At] the time when our organic laws were adopted, criminal trials both here and in England had long been presumptively open." And since that time, the presumption of openness has remained secure. . . .
>
> Second, the right of access to criminal trials plays a particularly significant role in the functioning of the judicial process and the government as a whole. Public scrutiny of a criminal trial enhances the quality and safeguards the integrity of the factfinding process, with benefits to both the defendant and to society as a whole. Moreover, public access to the criminal trial fosters an appearance of fairness, thereby heightening public respect for the judicial process. And in the broadest terms, public access to criminal trials permits the public to participate in and serve as a check upon the judicial process — an essential component in our structure of self-government. In sum, the institutional value of the open criminal trial is recognized in both logic and experience.
>
> Although the right of access to criminal trials is of constitutional stature, it is not absolute. But the circumstances under which the press and public can be barred from a criminal trial are limited; the State's justification in denying access must be a weighty one. Where, as in the present case, the State attempts to deny the right of access in order to inhibit the disclosure of sensitive information, it must be shown that the denial is necessitated by a compelling governmental interest, and is narrowly tailored to serve that interest.

In rejecting the automatic closure rule, the Court noted in footnote 27 of the opinion that courts could decide on a case-by-case basis whether portions of a criminal trial should be closed:

> We emphasize that our holding is a narrow one: that a rule of mandatory closure respecting the testimony of minor sex victims is constitutionally infirm. In individual cases, and under appropriate circumstances, the First Amendment does not necessarily stand as a bar to the exclusion from the courtroom of the press and general public during the testimony of minor sex-offense victims. But a mandatory rule, requiring no particularized determinations in individual cases, is unconstitutional.

Even after *Globe*, courts continued to struggle with how to balance the defendant's right to a fair trial and the media's First Amendment right of access. In Press-Enterprise Co. v. Superior Court, 464 U.S. 501 (1984) (*Press Enterprise I*), the Court struck down an order closing jury selection from the public and media. Emphasizing that the lower court must carefully weigh the media's right of access against the defendant's right to a fair trial, Chief Justice Burger wrote:

> Of course the right of an accused to fundamental fairness in the jury selection process is a compelling interest. But the California court's conclusion that Sixth Amendment and privacy interests were sufficient to warrant prolonged closure was unsupported by findings showing that an open proceeding in fact threatened those interests; hence it is not possible to conclude that closure was warranted. Even with findings adequate to support closure, the trial court's orders denying access to voir dire testimony failed to consider whether alternatives were available to protect the interests of the prospective jurors that the trial court's orders sought to guard. Absent consideration of alternatives to closure, the trial court could not constitutionally close the voir dire.

Two years later, in Press-Enterprise Co. v. Superior Court, 478 U.S. 1 (1986) (*Press Enterprise II*), the Court again upheld the media's right of access. This time, Chief Justice Burger wrote that the First Amendment right of access to criminal proceedings applies to preliminary hearings that have traditionally been open to the public, such as preliminary hearings. Two factors were key to the Court's decision: (1) a tradition of openness to the proceeding in question must exist and (2) the proceeding must be trial-like.

Thus, both the defendant and the press have the right to an open courtroom. In Presley v. Georgia, 558 U.S. 209 (2010), the Supreme Court reaffirmed that a defendant's Sixth Amendment right to a public trial includes the right to an open voir dire process.

b.   Other Remedies

In lieu of closing proceedings, courts may look for alternative means to prevent pretrial and trial publicity from prejudicing the defendant's right to a fair trial. In Sheppard v. Maxwell, 384 U.S. 333 (1966), the Court criticized the trial judge for not considering the various means it had to control the media's coverage of Dr. Sam Sheppard's murder trial. It suggested that the

court consider a wide range of remedies, from change of venue, to sequestration, to tighter control over the courtroom, to gag orders.

SHEPPARD v. MAXWELL

384 U.S. 333 (1966)

Justice CLARK delivered the opinion of the Court.

This federal habeas corpus application involves the question whether
Sheppard was deprived of a fair trial in his state conviction for the
second-degree murder of his wife because of the trial judge's failure to protect Sheppard sufficiently from the massive, pervasive and prejudicial publicity that attended his prosecution.

Marilyn Sheppard, petitioner's pregnant wife, was bludgeoned to death in
the upstairs bedroom of their lakeshore home in Bay Village, Ohio, a suburb
of Cleveland. On the day of the tragedy, July 4, 1954, Sheppard pieced
together for several local officials the following story: He and his wife had
entertained neighborhood friends, the Aherns, on the previous evening at
their home. After dinner they watched television in the living room. Sheppard became drowsy and dozed off to sleep on a couch. Later, Marilyn partially awoke him saying that she was going to bed. The next thing he
remembered was hearing his wife cry out in the early morning hours. He
hurried upstairs and in the dim light from the hall saw a "form" standing
next to his wife's bed. As he struggled with the "form" he was struck on the
back of the neck and rendered unconscious. On regaining his senses he
found himself on the floor next to his wife's bed. He rose, looked at her,
took her pulse and "felt that she was gone."

From the outset officials focused suspicion on Sheppard. On July 7, the
day of Marilyn Sheppard's funeral, a newspaper story appeared in which
Assistant County Attorney Mahon — later the chief prosecutor of Sheppard — sharply criticized the refusal of the Sheppard family to permit his
immediate questioning. From there on headline stories repeatedly stressed
Sheppard's lack of cooperation with the police and other officials.

Throughout this period the newspapers emphasized evidence that tended
to incriminate Sheppard and pointed out discrepancies in his statements to
authorities. At the same time, Sheppard made many public statements to the
press and wrote feature articles asserting his innocence. During the inquest
on July 26, a headline in large type stated: "Kerr [Captain of the Cleveland
Police] Urges Sheppard's Arrest." In the story, Detective McArthur "disclosed that scientific tests at the Sheppard home have definitely established
that the killer washed off a trail of blood from the murder bedroom to the
downstairs section," a circumstance casting doubt on Sheppard's accounts
of the murder. No such evidence was produced at trial. The newspapers also
delved into Sheppard's personal life. Articles stressed his extramarital love
affairs as a motive for the crime.

A front-page editorial on July 30 asked: "Why Isn't Sam Sheppard in Jail?" It was later titled "Quit Stalling — Bring Him In."

That night at 10 o'clock Sheppard was arrested at his father's home on a charge of murder. He was taken to the Bay Village City Hall where hundreds of people, newscasters, photographers and reporters were awaiting his arrival. He was immediately arraigned — having been denied a temporary delay to secure the presence of counsel — and bound over to the grand jury.

The publicity then grew in intensity until his indictment on August 17. There are five volumes filled with . . . clippings from each of the three Cleveland newspapers covering the period from the murder until Sheppard's conviction in December 1954.

With this background the case came on for trial two weeks before the November general election at which the chief prosecutor was a candidate for common pleas judge and the trial judge, Judge Blythin, was a candidate to succeed himself.

The courtroom in which the trial was held measured 26 by 48 feet. A long temporary table was set up inside the bar, in back of the single counsel table. It ran the width of the courtroom, parallel to the bar railing, with one end less than three feet from the jury box. Approximately 20 representatives of newspapers and wire services were assigned seats at this table by the court. Behind the bar railing there were four rows of benches. These seats were likewise assigned by the court for the entire trial. The first row was occupied by representatives of television and radio stations, and the second and third rows by reporters from out-of-town newspapers and magazines. One side of the last row, which accommodated 14 people, was assigned to Sheppard's family and the other to Marilyn's. The public was permitted to fill vacancies in this row on special passes only. Representatives of the news media also used all the rooms on the courtroom floor, including the room where cases were ordinarily called and assigned for trial. Private telephone lines and telegraphic equipment were installed in these rooms so that reports from the trial could be speeded to the papers. Station WSRS was permitted to set up broadcasting facilities on the third floor of the courthouse next door to the jury room, where the jury rested during recesses in the trial and deliberated. Newscasts were made from this room throughout the trial, and while the jury reached its verdict.

On the sidewalk and steps in front of the courthouse, television and newsreel cameras were occasionally used to take motion pictures of the participants in the trial, including the jury and the judge. Indeed, one television broadcast carried a staged interview of the judge as he entered the courthouse. In the corridors outside the courtroom there was a host of photographers and television personnel with flash cameras, portable lights and motion picture cameras. This group photographed the prospective jurors during selection of the jury. After the trial opened, the witnesses, counsel, and jurors were photographed and televised whenever they entered or left the courtroom. Sheppard was brought to the courtroom about 10 minutes before each session began; he was surrounded by reporters and extensively photographed for the newspapers and television.

All of these arrangements with the news media and their massive coverage of the trial continued during the entire nine weeks of the trial.

The jurors themselves were constantly exposed to the news media. Every juror, except one, testified at voir dire to reading about the case in the Cleveland papers or to having heard broadcasts about it. One newspaper ran pictures of the jurors at the Sheppard home when they went there to view the scene of the murder. Another paper featured the home life of an alternate juror. The day before the verdict was rendered — while the jurors were at lunch and sequestered by two bailiffs — the jury was separated into two groups to pose for photographs which appeared in the newspapers.

We now reach the conduct of the trial. [The Court described several flagrant episodes of media coverage and the jurors' exposure to this coverage.]

In light of this background, we believe that the arrangements made by the judge with the news media caused Sheppard to be deprived of that "judicial serenity and calm to which [he] was entitled." The fact is that bedlam reigned at the courthouse during the trial and newsmen took over practically the entire courtroom, hounding most of the participants in the trial, especially Sheppard.

The court's fundamental error is compounded by the holding that it lacked power to control the publicity about the trial. From the very inception of the proceedings the judge announced that neither he nor anyone else could restrict prejudicial news accounts. Since he viewed the news media as his target, the judge never considered other means that are often utilized to reduce the appearance of prejudicial material and to protect the jury from outside influence.

The carnival atmosphere at trial could easily have been avoided since the courtroom and courthouse premises are subject to the control of the court. Bearing in mind the massive pretrial publicity, the judge should have adopted stricter rules governing the use of the courtroom by newsmen, as Sheppard's counsel requested. The number of reporters in the courtroom itself could have been limited at the first sign that their presence would disrupt the trial. They certainly should not have been placed inside the bar. Furthermore, the judge should have more closely regulated the conduct of newsmen in the courtroom.

Secondly, the court should have insulated the witnesses. All of the newspapers and radio stations apparently interviewed prospective witnesses at will, and in many instances disclosed their testimony. Although the witnesses were barred from the courtroom during the trial the full verbatim testimony was available to them in the press. This completely nullified the judge's imposition of the rule.

Thirdly, the court should have made some effort to control the release of leads, information, and gossip to the press by police officers, witnesses, and the counsel for both sides. Much of the information thus disclosed was inaccurate, leading to groundless rumors and confusion.

[The judge should have sought] to alleviate this problem by imposing control over the statements made to the news media by counsel, witnesses, and especially the Coroner and police officers. The prosecution repeatedly made evidence available to the news media which was never offered in the trial.

Effective control of these sources—concededly within the court's power—might well have prevented the divulgence of inaccurate information, rumors, and accusations that made up much of the inflammatory publicity, at least after Sheppard's indictment.

More specifically, the trial court might well have proscribed extrajudicial statements by any lawyer, party, witness, or court official which divulged prejudicial matters, such as the refusal of Sheppard to submit to interrogation or take any lie detector tests; any statement made by Sheppard to officials; the identity of prospective witnesses or their probable testimony; any belief in guilt or innocence; or like statements concerning the merits of the case. In this manner, Sheppard's right to a trial free from outside interference would have been given added protection without corresponding curtailment of the news media. Had the judge, the other officers of the court, and the police placed the interest of justice first, the news media would have soon learned to be content with the task of reporting the case as it unfolded in the courtroom—not pieced together from extrajudicial statements.

Due process requires that the accused receive a trial by an impartial jury free from outside influences. Given the pervasiveness of modern communications and the difficulty of effacing prejudicial publicity from the minds of the jurors, the trial courts must take strong measures to ensure that the balance is never weighed against the accused. Of course, there is nothing that proscribes the press from reporting events that transpire in the courtroom. But where there is a reasonable likelihood that prejudicial news prior to trial will prevent a fair trial, the judge should continue the case until the threat abates, or transfer it to another county not so permeated with publicity. In addition, sequestration of the jury was something the judge should have raised sua sponte with counsel. If publicity during the proceedings threatens the fairness of the trial, a new trial should be ordered. But we must remember that reversals are but palliatives; the cure lies in those remedial measures that will prevent the prejudice at its inception. The courts must take such steps by rule and regulation that will protect their processes from prejudicial outside interferences.

Since the state trial judge did not fulfill his duty to protect Sheppard from the inherently prejudicial publicity which saturated the community and to control disruptive influences in the courtroom, we must reverse the denial of the habeas petition.

———————————

Sheppard was such an extreme case that it led the Supreme Court to reverse the defendant's conviction because of prejudicial pretrial and trial publicity.

Nonetheless, even in that case, the Court still suggested that there are many steps a trial court can take to prevent publicity from impinging on a defendant's right to a fair trial.

In deciding what steps to take to prevent the defendant from being prejudiced by pretrial or trial publicity, it is critical that a court balance the First Amendment rights of the media against the defendant's right to a fair trial. As discussed by the Court in *Sheppard*, this balancing must be done through case-by-case analysis.

c. Ethical Limitations on Lawyers' Extrajudicial Comments

What responsibilities do lawyers have to ensure that a trial is not adversely affected by pretrial and trial publicity? To what extent do lawyers possess a First Amendment right to speak out about their clients' cases, and what limitations may be placed on that right?

The American Bar Association, like state bar authorities throughout the country, has adopted ethical rules designed to limit a lawyer's comments to the press about a case. ABA Model Rule of Professional Conduct 3.6 provides:

> (a) A lawyer who is participating or has participated in the investigation or litigation of a matter shall not make an extrajudicial statement that the lawyer knows or reasonably should know will be disseminated by means of public communication and will have a substantial likelihood of materially prejudicing an adjudicative proceeding in the matter.
>
> (b) Notwithstanding paragraph (a), a lawyer may state:
>
> (1) the claim, offense or defense involved and, except when prohibited by law, the identity of the persons involved;
>
> (2) information contained in a public record;
>
> (3) that an investigation of a matter is in progress;
>
> (4) the scheduling or result of any step in litigation;
>
> (5) a request for assistance in obtaining evidence and information necessary thereto;
>
> (6) a warning of danger concerning the behavior of a person involved, when there is reason to believe that there exists the likelihood of substantial harm to an individual or to the public interest; and
>
> (7) in a criminal case, in addition to subparagraphs (1) through (6):
>
> (i)   the identity, residence, occupation and family status of the accused;
>
> (ii) if the accused has not been apprehended, information necessary to aid in apprehension of that person;
>
> (iii) the fact, time and place of arrest; and
>
> (iv) the identity of investigating and arresting officers or agencies and the length of the investigation.
>
> (c) Notwithstanding paragraph (a), a lawyer may make a statement that a reasonable lawyer would believe is required to protect a client from the substantial undue prejudicial effect of recent publicity not initiated by the lawyer or the lawyer's client. A statement made pursuant to this paragraph shall be limited to such information as is necessary to mitigate the recent adverse publicity.

In Gentile v. State Bar of Nevada, the Supreme Court considered whether ethical restrictions on a lawyer's speech are constitutional and under what conditions they can be enforced.

GENTILE v. STATE BAR OF NEVADA
501 U.S. 1030 (1991)

Justice KENNEDY announced the judgment of the Court.

Hours after his client was indicted on criminal charges, petitioner Gentile, who is a member of the Bar of the State of Nevada, held a press conference. [Gentile made a prepared statement, which was set forth in Appendix A to the court's opinion. In that statement, he accused the police of committing the crime that had been charged against his client.[22]]

Some six months later, the criminal case was tried to a jury and the client was acquitted on all counts. The State Bar of Nevada then filed a complaint against petitioner, alleging a violation of Nevada Supreme Court Rule 177, a rule governing pretrial publicity almost identical to ABA Model Rule of Professional Conduct 3.6. Rule 177(1) prohibits an attorney from making "an extrajudicial statement that a reasonable person would expect to be disseminated by means of public communication if the lawyer knows or reasonably should know that it will have a substantial likelihood of materially prejudicing an adjudicative proceeding." Rule 177(2) lists a number of statements that are "ordinarily . . . likely" to result in material prejudice. Rule 177(3) provides a safe harbor for the attorney, listing a number of statements that can be made without fear of discipline notwithstanding the other parts of the Rule.

Following a hearing, the Southern Nevada Disciplinary Board of the State Bar found that Gentile had made the statements in question and concluded that he violated Rule 177.

Nevada's application of Rule 177 in this case violates the First Amendment. Petitioner spoke at a time and in a manner that neither in law nor in fact created any threat of real prejudice to his client's right to a fair trial or to the State's interest in the enforcement of its criminal laws. Furthermore, the Rule's safe harbor provision, Rule 177(3), appears to permit the speech in question, and Nevada's decision to discipline petitioner in spite of that provision raises concerns of vagueness and selective enforcement.

---

22. A brief excerpt from Gentile's press conference appears below. The complete statement is set forth in Appendix A of the Court's opinion.

MR. GENTILE: I want to start this off by saying in clear terms that I think that this indictment is a significant event in the history of the evolution of the sophistication of the City of Las Vegas, because things of this nature, of exactly this nature have happened in New York with the French connection case and in Miami with cases — at least two cases there — have happened in Chicago as well, but all three of those cities have been honest enough to indict the people who did it; the police department, crooked cops. [Footnote by casebook authors.]

The matter before us does not call into question the constitutionality of other States' prohibitions upon an attorney's speech that will have a "substantial likelihood of materially prejudicing an adjudicative proceeding," but is limited to Nevada's interpretation of that standard.

Model Rule 3.6's requirement of substantial likelihood of material prejudice is not necessarily flawed. Interpreted in a proper and narrow manner, for instance, to prevent an attorney of record from releasing information of grave prejudice on the eve of jury selection, the phrase substantial likelihood of material prejudice might punish only speech that creates a danger of imminent and substantial harm. A rule governing speech, even speech entitled to full constitutional protection, need not use the words "clear and present danger" in order to pass constitutional muster.

The record does not support the conclusion that petitioner knew or reasonably should have known his remarks created a substantial likelihood of material prejudice, if the Rule's terms are given any meaningful content. . . . [Gentile] did not blunder into a press conference, but acted with considerable deliberation.

An attorney's duties do not begin inside the courtroom door. He or she cannot ignore the practical implications of a legal proceeding for the client. Just as an attorney may recommend a plea bargain or civil settlement to avoid the adverse consequences of a possible loss after trial, so too an attorney may take reasonable steps to defend a client's reputation and reduce the adverse consequences of indictment, especially in the face of a prosecution deemed unjust or commenced with improper motives.

Petitioner was disciplined for statements to the effect that (1) the evidence demonstrated his client's innocence, (2) the likely thief was a police detective, Steve Scholl, and (3) the other victims were not credible, as most were drug dealers or convicted money launderers, all but one of whom had only accused Sanders in response to police pressure, in the process of "trying to work themselves out of something."

Much of the information provided by petitioner had been published in one form or another, obviating any potential for prejudice.

Petitioner's judgment that no likelihood of material prejudice would result from his comments was vindicated by events at trial.

The trial took place on schedule in August 1988, with no request by either party for a venue change or continuance. The jury was empaneled with no apparent difficulty. The trial judge questioned the jury venire about publicity. [N]ot a single juror indicated any recollection of petitioner or his press conference.

At trial, all material information disseminated during petitioner's press conference was admitted in evidence before the jury. The jury acquitted petitioner's client, and, as petitioner explained before the disciplinary board, "when the trial was over with and the man was acquitted the next week the foreman of the jury phoned me and said to me that if they would have had a verdict form before them with respect to the guilt of Steve Scholl they would have found the man proven guilty beyond a reasonable doubt."

There is no support for the conclusion that petitioner's statements created a likelihood of material prejudice, or indeed of any harm of sufficient magnitude or imminence to support a punishment for speech.

In *Gentile*, the Court upheld defense counsel's right to make his extrajudicial comments but noted that it would not violate counsel's First Amendment rights to limit speech that has a substantial likelihood of materially prejudicing a proceeding. Most remarks by counsel do not rise to that level. However, occasionally counsel will cross the line.

UNITED STATES v. CUTLER

58 F.3d 825 (2d Cir. 1995)

McLaughlin, Circuit Judge:

The underworld exploits of John Gotti and the courtroom legerdemain of his attorney, Bruce Cutler, are now the stuff of legend. Cutler's last appearance on Gotti's behalf was in the United States District Court for the Eastern District of New York (I. Leo Glasser, Judge). Notwithstanding the court's pretrial admonition and orders to comply with Local Criminal Rule 7, Cutler spoke repeatedly and heatedly to the media on the merits of the government's case against his client.

Exasperated with Cutler, Judge Glasser issued an order to show cause why he should not be held in criminal contempt. Judge Glasser then recused himself, and the matter was reassigned. After a five-day bench trial, the district court found Cutler guilty of criminal contempt.

On appeal, Cutler argues that: (1) the orders and Local Rule 7 are unconstitutional; (2) the evidence, under the heightened standard applicable in First Amendment cases, does not support his contempt conviction; and (3) several aspects of his sentence were an abuse of discretion.

Background

John Gotti was arrested on December 11, 1990, on racketeering charges. This marked the fourth time that the government tried to end Gotti's criminal career, the previous attempts having failed. The then-United States Attorney, Andrew Maloney, announced the indictment at a press conference, where he called Gotti a "murderer, not a folk hero" and boasted that this time the government's case, which included extensive wiretap evidence, was much stronger than in the prior trials.

Gotti's lawyer, Bruce Cutler, a member of the New York Bar, countered by calling the prosecutors "publicity-hungry" and on a vendetta to frame his client. He was quoted in New York's four major newspapers—the Daily

News, Newsday, the New York Post, and the New York Times. He also gave an interview on Prime Time Live, a nationally-broadcast television show, where he emphatically denied that Gotti was a mob boss.

Cutler's and Maloney's comments seemed to be in tension with Local Rule 7, to phrase it charitably. That rule provides:

> It is the duty of the lawyer or law firm not to release or authorize the release of information or opinion which a reasonable person would expect to be disseminated by means of public communication, in connection with pending or imminent criminal litigation with which a lawyer or law firm is associated, if there is a reasonable likelihood that such dissemination will interfere with a fair trial or otherwise prejudice the due administration of justice. . . .

[The court admonished Cutler repeatedly to comply with the rule.] Undeterred, Cutler held a press conference outside the courthouse. He declaimed that the government had "thrown the Constitution out the window," mocked the government's witnesses as "bums," and erroneously described the government's tape recordings of wire-tapped conversations as the same ones used in earlier prosecutions. Cutler's performance at the press conference made the local news that night and the tabloids the next morning.

After four letters of complaint from the government about Cutler's extrajudicial statements, . . . Judge Glasser made clear he wanted no more comments to the press.

In the following week, stories about Gotti adorned the front pages of New York's dailies, together with excerpts from the transcripts of the wire-tapped conversations. In addition, television news programs obtained copies of the tapes of the conversations and repeatedly broadcast portions of them, allowing potential jurors to hear Gotti describe murders and other crimes.

Cutler countered with a media barrage of his own. The piece de resistance came on August 13, 1991, a mere month before the scheduled trial date. That day, Cutler appeared on a one-hour live television show called 9 Broadcast Plaza. His performance, aptly summarized by the district court, included the following:

> wherever Gotti lives, there is no problem with drugs and crime in the neighborhood; Gotti is not a danger to any community other than federal prosecutors; Gotti has "admirable qualities[,"] including being courageous, loyal, sincere, selfless and devoted to his family; Gotti is a "good man" and an "honorable man"; Gotti is not a "ruthless man"; Gotti is one of "the most compassionate men" Cutler knows; Gotti is "deadly against drugs"[;] . . . the prosecutors "are doing everything they can to destroy John Gotti" and are "dealing in vendettas[,"] "on a witch hunt[,"] and "framing people"; the Government "threw the Constitution out the window" and is on a "vendetta" against Gotti; the prosecution is an "example of McCarthyism"; Gotti was being persecuted "because of his lifestyle" and "friends"; the prosecutors want to "destroy" Gotti "because of his popularity" and because "he's deadly against drugs"; the "evidence is phony"; the "tapes are phony"[;] . . . the Government is "creating cases against individuals they target" by "giving freedom to drug dealers and murderers if they will sing the

government's tune against the likes of John Gotti"; and . . . jurors realize that "the witnesses lie" and that "even the federal investigators lie" and that is why they vote "not guilty unabashedly."

Not surprisingly, the 9 Broadcast Plaza interview provoked yet another government letter complaining about Cutler. This time, Judge Glasser had had enough. He issued an order to show cause why Cutler should not be held in criminal contempt.

Cutler's contempt trial lasted five days. He did not contest the facts the government proffered. Moreover, he did not argue that he had no duty to comply with the orders and Local Rule 7. Instead, Cutler challenged the validity of the orders, arguing that Local Rule 7 was unconstitutional.

DISCUSSION

Cutler challenges the validity of the orders, contending that Local Rule 7 is unconstitutional. Local Rule 7 proscribes generally any statements by counsel that "a reasonable person would expect to be disseminated by means of public communication, in connection with pending or imminent criminal litigation . . . , if there is a reasonable likelihood that such dissemination will interfere with a fair trial or otherwise prejudice the due administration of justice."

Cutler vastly understates the effect defense lawyers can have on prospective jurors. As *Gentile* cautions, "lawyers' statements are likely to be received as especially authoritative" because "lawyers have special access to information through discovery and client communications." Indeed, *Gentile* affirmed the very portion of Nevada's pre-trial publicity rule that considered statements of the sort Cutler made as "ordinarily" likely to have a "substantial likelihood of materially prejudicing" a pending criminal proceeding.

We thus find that Cutler's comments were reasonably likely to prejudice the Gotti proceedings.

C. WILLFULNESS

We hold attorneys to a higher standard of conduct than we do lay persons. Cutler's persistent attempts to try Gotti's case in the media, despite Judge Glasser's repeated warnings, belie any notion that he did not intend these particular comments to prejudice the proceedings, or that he did not recklessly disregard the orders.

CONCLUSION

We have considered all of Cutler's arguments, and find them without merit. We recognize that Cutler did not singlehandedly generate the media circus that threatened the fairness of the final Gotti trial; federal prosecutors and law enforcement officials deserve their share of the blame. Moreover, we sympathize with the plight of a defense lawyer torn between his duties to act as an officer of the court and to zealously defend his client. Nonetheless, a lawyer, of all people, should know that in the face of a perceived injustice, one may not take the law into his own hands. Defendant did, and now he must pay the price.

In some quarters, doubtless, this affirmance will elicit thunderbolts that we are chilling effective advocacy. Obviously, that is neither our intention nor our result. The advocate is still entitled—indeed encouraged—to strike hard blows, but not unfair blows. Trial practice, whether criminal or civil, is not a contact sport. And, its tactics do not include eye-gouging or shin-kicking.

In this case, a conscientious trial judge tried mightily to limit the lawyers to press statements that were accurate and fair. The defendant's statements were dipped in venom and were deliberately couched to poison the well from which the jury would be selected. Such conduct goes beyond the pale, by any reasonable standard, and cannot be condoned under the rubric of "effective advocacy."

d. Prior Restraints

Although the Supreme Court has sanctioned many alternatives for controlling pretrial publicity, it has resisted authorizing prior restraints on the press except in the most extreme cases. This First Amendment limitation on the court's power to control the press was set forth in the following case.

NEBRASKA PRESS ASSOCIATION v. STUART
427 U.S. 539 (1976)

Chief Justice BURGER delivered the opinion of the Court.

The respondent State District Judge entered an order restraining the petitioners from publishing or broadcasting accounts of confessions or admissions made by the accused or facts "strongly implicative" of the accused in a widely reported murder of six persons. We granted certiorari to decide whether the entry of such an order on the showing made before the state court violated the constitutional guarantee of freedom of the press.

I

On the evening of October 18, 1975, local police found the six members of the Henry Kellie family murdered in their home in Sutherland, Neb., a town of about 850 people. Police released the description of a suspect, Erwin Charles Simants, to the reporters who had hastened to the scene of the crime. Simants was arrested and arraigned in Lincoln County Court the following morning, ending a tense night for this small rural community.

The crime immediately attracted widespread news coverage. Three days after the crime, the County Attorney and Simants' attorney joined in asking the County Court to enter a restrictive order relating to "matters that may or may not be publicly reported or disclosed to the public," because of the "mass coverage by news media" and the "reasonable likelihood of prejudicial news which would make difficult, if not impossible, the impaneling of an impartial jury and tend to prevent a fair trial." The County Court granted the prosecutor's motion for a restrictive order and entered it the next day. The order prohibited everyone in attendance from "releas[ing] or authoriz[ing] the release for public dissemination in any form or manner whatsoever any testimony given or evidence adduced."

Simants' preliminary hearing was held the same day, open to the public but subject to the order. The County Court bound over the defendant for trial to the State District Court. The charges, as amended to reflect the autopsy findings, were that Simants had committed the murders in the course of a sexual assault.

Petitioners—several press and broadcast associations, publishers, and individual reporters—[asked] that the restrictive order imposed by the County Court be vacated. The judge found "because of the nature of the crimes charged in the complaint that there is a clear and present danger that pre-trial publicity could impinge upon the defendant's right to a fair trial." The order . . . specifically prohibited petitioners from reporting five subjects, [including the contents of a confession Simants had made to law enforcement officers, which had been introduced in open court at arraignment, and testimony at the preliminary hearing.] It also prohibited reporting the exact nature of the restrictive order itself.

The Nebraska Supreme Court modified the District Court's order, [in an attempt] to accommodate the defendant's right to a fair trial and the petitioners' interest in reporting pre-trial events. The order as modified prohibited reporting of only three matters: (a) the existence and nature of any confessions or admissions made by the defendant to law enforcement officers, (b) any confessions or admissions made to any third parties, except members of the press, and (c) other facts "strongly implicative" of the accused.

We granted certiorari to address the important issues raised by the District Court order as modified by the Nebraska Supreme Court.

III

The problems presented by this case are almost as old as the Republic. Neither in the Constitution nor in contemporaneous writings do we find that the conflict between these two important rights was anticipated, yet it is inconceivable that the authors of the Constitution were unaware of the potential conflicts between the right to an unbiased jury and the guarantee of freedom of the press.

The trial of Aaron Burr in 1807 presented Mr. Chief Justice Marshall, presiding as a trial judge, with acute problems in selecting an unbiased jury. Few people in the area of Virginia from which jurors were drawn had not formed some opinions concerning Mr. Burr or the case.

The speed of communication and the pervasiveness of the modern news media have exacerbated these problems, however, as numerous appeals demonstrate. The trial of Bruno Hauptmann in a small New Jersey community for the abduction and murder of the Charles Lindberghs' infant child probably was the most widely covered trial up to that time, and the nature of the coverage produced widespread public reaction.

The excesses of press and radio and lack of responsibility of those in authority in the Hauptmann case and others of that era led to efforts to develop voluntary guidelines for courts, lawyers, press, and broadcasters.

In practice, of course, even the most ideal guidelines are subjected to powerful strains when a case such as Simants' arises, with reporters from many parts of the country on the scene.

IV

The Sixth Amendment guarantees "trial, by an impartial jury . . ." in federal criminal prosecutions.

In the overwhelming majority of criminal trials, pre-trial publicity presents few unmanageable threats to this important right. But when the case is a "sensational" one tensions develop between the right of the accused to trial by an impartial jury and the rights guaranteed others by the First Amendment.

Taken together, [prior] cases demonstrate that pre-trial publicity — even pervasive, adverse publicity — does not inevitably lead to an unfair trial. The capacity of the jury eventually impaneled to decide the case fairly is influenced by the tone and extent of the publicity. The trial judge has a major responsibility. What the judge says about a case, in or out of the courtroom, is likely to appear in newspapers and broadcasts. More important, the measures a judge takes or fails to take to mitigate the effects of pretrial publicity — the measures described in *Sheppard* — may well determine whether the defendant receives a trial consistent with the requirements of due process.

The state trial judge in the case before us acted responsibly, out of a legitimate concern, in an effort to protect the defendant's right to a fair trial. What we must decide is not simply whether the Nebraska courts erred in seeing the possibility of real danger to the defendant's rights, but whether in the circumstances of this case the means employed were foreclosed by another provision of the Constitution.

V

The First Amendment provides that "Congress shall make no law . . . abridging the freedom . . . of the press."

In Near v. Minnesota ex rel. Olson (1931), the Court held invalid a Minnesota statute providing for the abatement as a public nuisance of any "malicious, scandalous and defamatory newspaper, magazine or other periodical."

Mr. Chief Justice Hughes, writing for the Court, noted . . . "[T]he main purpose of [the First Amendment] is 'to prevent all such previous restraints upon publications as had been practiced by other governments.'"

More recently in New York Times Co. v. United States (1971), the Government sought to enjoin the publication of excerpts from a massive, classified study of this Nation's involvement in the Vietnam conflict, going back to the end of the Second World War. The dispositive opinion of the Court simply concluded that the Government had not met its heavy burden of showing justification for the prior restraint.

The thread running through all these cases is that prior restraints on speech and publication are the most serious and the least tolerable infringement on First Amendment rights.

A prior restraint . . . has an immediate and irreversible sanction. If it can be said that a threat of criminal or civil sanctions after publication "chills" speech, prior restraint "freezes" it at least for the time.

The damage can be particularly great when the prior restraint falls upon the communication of news and commentary on current events. Truthful reports of public judicial proceedings have been afforded special protection against subsequent punishment.

The authors of the Bill of Rights did not undertake to assign priorities as between First Amendment and Sixth Amendment rights, ranking one as superior to the other. In this case, the petitioners would have us declare the right of an accused subordinate to their right to publish in all circumstances. But if the authors of these guarantees, fully aware of the potential conflicts between them, were unwilling or unable to resolve the issue by assigning to one priority over the other, it is not for us to rewrite the Constitution by undertaking what they declined to do. It is unnecessary, after nearly two centuries, to establish a priority applicable in all circumstances. Yet it is nonetheless clear that the barriers to prior restraint remain high unless we are to abandon what the Court has said for nearly a quarter of our national existence and implied throughout all of it.

VI

We turn now to the record in this case to determine whether, as Learned Hand put it, "the gravity of the 'evil,' discounted by its improbability, justifies such invasion of free speech as is necessary to avoid the danger."

Our review of the pre-trial record persuades us that the trial judge was justified in concluding that there would be intense and pervasive pre-trial publicity concerning this case. He could also reasonably conclude, based on common human experience, that publicity might impair the defendant's right to a fair trial. He did not purport to say more, for he found only "a clear and present danger that pre-trial publicity could impinge upon the defendant's right to a fair trial." His conclusion as to the impact of such publicity on prospective jurors was of necessity speculative, dealing as he was with factors unknown and unknowable.

B

We find little in the record that goes to another aspect of our task, determining whether measures short of an order restraining all publication would have insured the defendant a fair trial. Although the entry of the order might be read as a judicial determination that other measures would not suffice, the trial court made no express findings to that effect.

Most of the alternatives to prior restraint of publication in these circumstances were discussed with obvious approval in Sheppard v. Maxwell: (a) change of trial venue . . . (b) postponement of the trial to allow public attention to subside; (c) searching questioning of prospective jurors . . . (d) the use of emphatic and clear instructions on the sworn duty of each juror to decide the issues only on evidence presented in open court. Sequestration of jurors is, of course, always available.

We have therefore examined this record to determine the probable efficacy of the measures short of prior restraint on the press and speech. There is no finding that alternative measures would not have protected Simants' rights, and the Nebraska Supreme Court did no more than imply that such measures might not be adequate. Moreover, the record is lacking in evidence to support such a finding.

C

The Nebraska Supreme Court narrowed the scope of the restrictive order, and its opinion reflects awareness of the tensions between the need to protect the accused as fully as possible and the need to restrict publication as little as possible. The dilemma posed underscores how difficult it is for trial judges to predict what information will in fact undermine the impartiality of jurors, and the difficulty of drafting an order that will effectively keep prejudicial information from prospective jurors. When a restrictive order is sought, a court can anticipate only part of what will develop that may injure the accused. But information not so obviously prejudicial may emerge, and what may properly be published in these "gray zone" circumstances may not violate the restrictive order and yet be prejudicial.

Finally, we note that the events disclosed by the record took place in a community of 850 people. It is reasonable to assume that, without any news accounts being printed or broadcast, rumors would travel swiftly by word of mouth. One can only speculate on the accuracy of such reports, given the generative propensities of rumors; they could well be more damaging than reasonably accurate news accounts. But plainly a whole community cannot be restrained from discussing a subject intimately affecting life within it.

Given these practical problems, it is far from clear that prior restraint on publication would have protected Simants' rights.

E

The record demonstrates, as the Nebraska courts held, that there was indeed a risk that pretrial news accounts, true or false, would have some adverse impact on the attitudes of those who might be called as jurors. But on the record now before us it is not clear that further publicity, unchecked, would so distort the views of potential jurors that 12 could not be found who would, under proper instructions, fulfill their sworn duty to render a just verdict exclusively on the evidence presented in open court. We cannot say on this record that alternatives to a prior restraint on petitioners would not have sufficiently mitigated the adverse effects of pre-trial publicity so as to make prior restraint unnecessary. Nor can we conclude that the restraining order actually entered would serve its intended purpose.

Of necessity our holding is confined to the record before us. But our conclusion is not simply a result of assessing the adequacy of the showing made in this case; it results in part from the problems inherent in meeting the heavy burden of demonstrating, in advance of trial, that without prior restraint a fair trial will be denied. In this sense, the record now before us is illustrative rather than exceptional.

Our analysis ends as it began, with a confrontation between prior restraint imposed to protect one vital constitutional guarantee and the explicit command of another that the freedom to speak and publish shall not be abridged. We reaffirm that the guarantees of freedom of expression are not an absolute prohibition under all circumstances, but the barriers to prior restraint remain high and the presumption against its use continues intact.

Justice BRENNAN, with whom Justices STEWART and MARSHALL join, concurring in the judgment.

The question presented in this case is whether, consistently with the First Amendment, a court may enjoin the press, in advance of publication, from reporting or commenting on information acquired from public court proceedings, public court records, or other sources about pending judicial proceedings. The right to a fair trial by a jury of one's peers is unquestionably one of the most precious and sacred safeguards enshrined in the Bill of Rights. I would hold, however, that resort to prior restraints on the freedom of the press is a constitutionally impermissible method for enforcing that right; judges have at their disposal a broad spectrum of devices for ensuring that fundamental fairness is accorded the accused without necessitating so drastic an incursion on the equally fundamental and salutary constitutional mandate that discussion of public affairs in a free society cannot depend on the preliminary grace of judicial censors.

The Supreme Court has not yet decided on when, if ever, gag orders can be imposed on lawyers and trial participants. Lower courts remain split on the issue. *See* David D. Smthy III, *A New Framework for Analyzing Gag Orders Against Trial Witnesses*, 56 Baylor L. Rev. 89 (2004); Symposium, *The Sound of Silence: Reflections on the Use of the Gag Order*, 17 Loy. L.A. Ent. L.J. 304 (1997). Inevitably, the decision requires a balancing of the defendant's right to a fair trial against First Amendment rights of individuals and the press.

3.   Cameras in the Courtroom

The Supreme Court has never held that there is a right to cameras in the courtroom, but it has also refused to overturn defendants' convictions merely because the proceedings were broadcast. Federal Rule of Criminal Procedure 53 provides that federal court proceedings may not be broadcast, although there have been experimental programs allowing broadcasts in some federal civil and appellate cases. By contrast, a majority of states now permit the broadcast of criminal proceedings. In these states, a trial court has discretion to determine whether and when to allow such broadcasts.[23] In deciding how to exercise this discretion, a court will consider many factors, including the nature of the case; the parties' support of or opposition to the request; the privacy rights of the participants, witnesses, victims, and jurors; the effect of the coverage on the parties' ability to select a fair and unbiased jury; any ongoing needs of law enforcement; the need to maintain an orderly proceeding; and any other factors that may affect the right to a fair trial.[24]

In Chandler v. Florida, the Supreme Court addressed whether cameras in the courtroom constitute a per se violation of a defendant's fair trial right.

CHANDLER v. FLORIDA
449 U.S. 560 (1981)

Chief Justice BURGER delivered the opinion of the Court.

The question presented on this appeal is whether, consistent with constitutional guarantees, a state may provide for radio, television, and still photographic coverage of a criminal trial for public broadcast, notwithstanding the objection of the accused.

---

23. For a state-by-state guide to cameras in the courtroom, *see* http://www.rtdna.org/article/cameras_in_the_court_a_state_by_state_guide_updated.

24. *See, e.g.*, Cal. Rules of Court, R. 1.150 (2007).

I

A

Over the past 50 years, some criminal cases characterized as "sensational" have been subjected to extensive coverage by news media, sometimes seriously interfering with the conduct of the proceedings and creating a setting wholly inappropriate for the administration of justice. Judges, lawyers, and others soon became concerned, and in 1937, after study, the American Bar Association House of Delegates adopted Judicial Canon 35, declaring that all photographic and broadcast coverage of courtroom proceedings should be prohibited. In 1952, the House of Delegates amended Canon 35 to proscribe television coverage as well. The Canon's proscription was reaffirmed in 1972 when the Code of Judicial Conduct replaced the Canons. A majority of the states, including Florida, adopted the substance of the ABA provision and its amendments.

[In 1975, Florida established a pilot program permitting electronic media to cover judicial proceedings without the consent of the proceeding's participants.]

Following [the pilot program], the Florida Supreme Court concluded "that on balance there [was] more to be gained than lost by permitting electronic media coverage of judicial proceedings subject to standards for such coverage." The Florida court was of the view that because of the significant effect of the courts on the day-to-day lives of the citizenry, it was essential that the people have confidence in the process. It felt that broadcast coverage of trials would contribute to wider public acceptance and understanding of decisions. Consequently, after revising the 1977 guidelines to reflect its evaluation of the pilot program, the Florida Supreme Court promulgated a revised Canon 3A (7). The Canon provides:

> Subject at all times to the authority of the presiding judge to (i) control the conduct of proceedings before the court, (ii) ensure decorum and prevent distractions, and (iii) ensure the fair administration of justice in the pending cause, electronic media and still photography coverage of public judicial proceedings in the appellate and trial courts of this state shall be allowed in accordance with standards of conduct and technology promulgated by the Supreme Court of Florida.

In July 1977, appellants were charged with conspiracy to commit burglary, grand larceny, and possession of burglary tools. The counts covered breaking and entering a well-known Miami Beach restaurant.

The details of the alleged criminal conduct are not relevant to the issue before us, but several aspects of the case distinguish it from a routine burglary. At the time of their arrest, appellants were Miami Beach policemen. The State's principal witness was John Sion, an amateur radio operator who, by sheer chance, had overheard and recorded conversations between the appellants over their police walkie-talkie radios during the burglary. Not surprisingly, these novel factors attracted the attention of the media.

By pretrial motion, appellants sought to have . . . Canon 3A (7) declared unconstitutional on its face and as applied. The trial court denied relief.

After several additional fruitless attempts by the appellants to prevent electronic coverage of the trial, the jury was selected. At voir dire, the appellants' counsel asked each prospective juror whether he or she would be able to be "fair and impartial" despite the presence of a television camera during some, or all, of the trial. Each juror selected responded that such coverage would not affect his or her consideration in any way. A television camera recorded the voir dire.

A defense motion to sequester the jury because of the television coverage was denied by the trial judge. However, the court instructed the jury not to watch or read anything about the case in the media and suggested that jurors "avoid the local news and watch only the national news on television."

A television camera was in place for one entire afternoon, during which the State presented the testimony of . . . its chief witness. No camera was present for the presentation of any part of the case for the defense. The camera returned to cover closing arguments. Only 2 minutes and 55 seconds of the trial below were broadcast — and those depicted only the prosecution's side of the case.

The jury returned a guilty verdict on all counts. Appellants moved for a new trial, claiming that because of the television coverage, they had been denied a fair and impartial trial. No evidence of specific prejudice was tendered.

II

At the outset, it is important to note that in promulgating the revised Canon 3A (7), the Florida Supreme Court pointedly rejected any state or federal constitutional right of access on the part of photographers or the broadcast media to televise or electronically record and thereafter disseminate court proceedings.

The Florida Supreme Court predicated the revised Canon 3A (7) upon its supervisory authority over the Florida courts, and not upon any constitutional imperative.

This Court has no supervisory jurisdiction over state courts, and, in reviewing a state-court judgment, we are confined to evaluating it in relation to the Federal Constitution.

III

Appellants rely chiefly on Estes v. Texas (1965), and Chief Justice Warren's separate concurring opinion in that case. They argue that the televising of criminal trials is inherently a denial of due process, and they read *Estes* as announcing a per se constitutional rule to that effect.

If appellants' reading of *Estes* were correct, we would be obliged to apply that holding and reverse the judgment under review. [However, the six separate opinions in *Estes*, when examined carefully, do not represent a per se constitutional rule forbidding all electronic coverage.]

[In his concurring opinion in *Estes*, Justice Harlan noted what he perceived as the inherent dangers of televised trials:]

> In the context of a trial of intense public interest, there is certainly a strong possibility that the timid or reluctant witness, for whom a court appearance even at its traditional best is a harrowing affair, will become more timid or reluctant when he finds that he will also be appearing before a "hidden audience" of unknown but large dimensions. There is certainly a strong possibility that the "cocky" witness having a thirst for the limelight will become more "cocky" under the influence of television. And who can say that the juror who is gratified by having been chosen for a front-line case, an ambitious prosecutor, a publicity-minded defense attorney, and even a conscientious judge will not stray, albeit unconsciously, from doing what "comes naturally" into pluming themselves for a satisfactory television "performance"?

[But Justice Harlan also noted that there were "countervailing factors" and that broadcasting proceedings could have an "educational and information value to the public."]

Justice Harlan's opinion, upon which analysis of the constitutional holding of *Estes* turns, must be read as defining the scope of that holding; we conclude that *Estes* is not to be read as announcing a constitutional rule barring still photographic, radio, and television coverage in all cases and under all circumstances. It does not stand as an absolute ban on state experimentation with an evolving technology, which, in terms of modes of mass communication, was in its relative infancy in 1964, and is, even now, in a state of continuing change.

IV

Since we are satisfied that *Estes* did not announce a constitutional rule that all photographic or broadcast coverage of criminal trials is inherently a denial of due process, we turn to consideration, as a matter of first impression, of the appellants' suggestion that we now promulgate such a per se rule.

A

Any criminal case that generates a great deal of publicity presents some risks that the publicity may compromise the right of the defendant to a fair trial. Trial courts must be especially vigilant to guard against any impairment of the defendant's right to a verdict based solely upon the evidence and the relevant law. Over the years, courts have developed a range of curative devices to prevent publicity about a trial from infecting jury deliberations.

An absolute constitutional ban on broadcast coverage of trials cannot be justified simply because there is a danger that, in some cases, prejudicial broadcast accounts of pretrial and trial events may impair the ability of jurors to decide the issue of guilt or innocence uninfluenced by extraneous matter.

The risk of juror prejudice in some cases does not justify an absolute ban on news coverage of trials by the printed media; so also the risk of such prejudice does not warrant an absolute constitutional ban on all broadcast coverage. A case attracts a high level of public attention because of its intrinsic interest to the public and the manner of reporting the event. The risk of juror prejudice is present in any publication of a trial, but the appropriate safeguard against such prejudice is the defendant's right to demonstrate that the media's coverage of his case—be it printed or broadcast—compromised the ability of the particular jury that heard the case to adjudicate fairly.

B

Not unimportant to the position asserted by Florida and other states is the change in television technology since 1962, when *Estes* was tried. [M]any of the negative factors found in *Estes*—cumbersome equipment, cables, distracting lighting, numerous camera technicians—are less substantial factors today than they were at that time.

It is also significant that safeguards have been built into the experimental programs in state courts, and into the Florida program, to avoid some of the most egregious problems envisioned by the six opinions in the *Estes* case. Florida admonishes its courts to take special pains to protect certain witnesses—for example, children, victims of sex crimes, some informants, and even the very timid witness or party—from the glare of publicity and the tensions of being "on camera."

Inherent in electronic coverage of a trial is the risk that the very awareness by the accused of the coverage and the contemplated broadcast may adversely affect the conduct of the participants and the fairness of the trial, yet leave no evidence of how the conduct or the trial's fairness was affected. Given this danger, it is significant that Florida requires that objections of the accused to coverage be heard and considered on the record by the trial court.

D

[A] defendant has the right on review to show that the media's coverage of his case—printed or broadcast—compromised the ability of the jury to judge him fairly. Alternatively, a defendant might show that broadcast coverage of his particular case had an adverse impact on the trial participants sufficient to constitute a denial of due process. Neither showing was made in this case.

To demonstrate prejudice in a specific case a defendant must show something more than juror awareness that the trial is such as to attract the attention of broadcasters. Murphy v. Florida (1975). No doubt the very presence of a camera in the courtroom made the jurors aware that the trial was thought to be of sufficient interest to the public to warrant coverage. Jurors, forbidden to watch all broadcasts, would have had no way of knowing that only fleeting seconds of the proceeding would be reproduced. But the appellants have not attempted to show with any specificity that the presence of cameras impaired the ability of the jurors to decide the case on only the evidence before them or that their trial was affected adversely by the impact on any of the participants of the presence of cameras and the prospect of broadcast.

[Defendants' convictions are affirmed.]

Currently, 48 out of 50 states have rules allowing, in some form or another, camera coverage of the courtroom. Forty-three of these states allow coverage at the trial level, and studies in 28 states show that television coverage in court proceedings has significant social and educational benefits. Although six federal districts and the Second and Ninth Circuit Courts of Appeals launched pilot programs in the 1990s for cameras in the courtroom, the federal courts still have not adopted such a rule opening their courts to broadcast.

The case for cameras in the courtroom suffered a setback in 1995 with the broadcast of the O.J. Simpson murder trial. Troubled by what they described as the "media circus," many judges exercised their discretion not to allow cameras in their courts. However, camera coverage of high-visibility trials has resumed and no conviction has been overturned because of the televising of a trial.

D. TRIAL RIGHTS: DUE PROCESS, RIGHT OF CONFRONTATION, AND PRIVILEGE AGAINST SELF-INCRIMINATION

At trial, the defendant enjoys the Sixth Amendment right to a fair trial. To ensure that the defendant receives a fair trial, the defendant has the right to be present at trial, the right to confront witnesses, and the right to refuse to incriminate himself.

To enjoy these rights, a defendant must be competent to stand trial. The Supreme Court has held that the Due Process Clause prohibits the criminal prosecution of a defendant who is not competent to stand trial. Drope v. Missouri, 420 U.S. 162 (1975). Under Dusky v. United States, 362 U.S. 402 (1960), a defendant is competent to stand trial when he has "sufficient present ability to consult with his lawyer with a reasonable degree of rational understanding" and has a "rational as well as factual understanding of the proceedings against him."

Under certain circumstances, a state may medicate a defendant to make him competent to stand trial. In Sell v. United States, 539 U.S. 166 (2003), the Supreme Court applied a standard it had developed in the earlier case of Riggins v. Nevada, 504 U.S. 127 (1992). In general, the government may administer antipsychotic drugs to a mentally ill defendant facing serious criminal charges in order to render the defendant competent to stand trial but only if (1) treatment is medically appropriate; (2) it is substantially unlikely to have serious side effects that will undermine the fairness of the trial; and (3) there are important government interests in having the defendant medicated, such as that he poses a danger to himself or others.

Assuming a defendant is competent to stand trial, the defendant must be afforded each of the rights discussed in this section.

1. Right of Confrontation

The Sixth Amendment right of confrontation guarantees the defendant the right to confront witnesses at trial. Implicit in this right is the right of the defendant to be present at trial. This right can be limited, however, if the defendant acts in an obstreperous manner during trial.

a. Right to Be Present at Trial

ILLINOIS v. ALLEN

397 U.S. 337 (1970)

Justice BLACK delivered the opinion of the Court.

The Confrontation Clause of the Sixth Amendment to the United States Constitution provides that: "In all criminal prosecutions, the accused shall enjoy the right . . . to be confronted with the witnesses against him. . . ." One of the most basic of the rights guaranteed by the Confrontation Clause is the accused's right to be present in the courtroom at every stage of his trial. The question presented in this case is whether an accused can claim the benefit of this constitutional right to remain in the courtroom while at the same time he engages in speech and conduct which is so noisy, disorderly, and disruptive that it is exceedingly difficult or wholly impossible to carry on the trial.

The facts surrounding Allen's expulsion from the courtroom are set out in the Court of Appeals' opinion. [Allen acted as his own lawyer. He often argued with the judge in an abusive and disrespectful manner. Refusing to allow an appointed attorney to assist him, Allen finally stated to the judge: "When I go out for lunchtime, you're [the judge] going to be a corpse here." At that point he tore the file that his attorney had and threw the papers on the floor. The trial judge warned Allen, "One more outbreak of that sort and I'll remove you from the courtroom." This warning had no effect on Allen. After more abusive remarks by Allen, the trial judge ordered the trial to proceed in Allen's absence. Allen was removed from the courtroom. Although Allen was given a second chance, the court ordered him removed again from the courtroom when Allen made further outbursts. After this second removal, Allen remained out of the courtroom during the presentation of the state's case-in-chief, except that he was brought in on several occasions for purposes of identification. During one of these latter appearances, Allen responded to one of the judge's questions with vile and abusive language. After the prosecution's case had been presented, the trial judge reiterated his promise to Allen that he could return to the courtroom whenever he agreed to conduct himself properly. Allen gave some assurances of proper conduct and was permitted to be present through the remainder of the trial, principally his defense, which was conducted by his appointed counsel.]

It is essential to the proper administration of criminal justice that dignity, order, and decorum be the hallmarks of all court proceedings in our country. The flagrant disregard in the courtroom of elementary standards of proper conduct should not and cannot be tolerated. We believe trial judges confronted with disruptive, contumacious, stubbornly defiant defendants must be given sufficient discretion to meet the circumstances of each case. No one formula for maintaining the appropriate courtroom atmosphere will be best in all situations. We think there are at least three constitutionally permissible ways for a trial judge to handle an obstreperous defendant like Allen: (1) bind and gag him, thereby keeping him present; (2) cite him for contempt; (3) take him out of the courtroom until he promises to conduct himself properly.

I

Trying a defendant for a crime while he sits bound and gagged before the judge and jury would to an extent comply with that part of the Sixth Amendment's purposes that accords the defendant an opportunity to confront the witnesses at the trial. But even to contemplate such a technique, much less see it, arouses a feeling that no person should be tried while shackled and gagged except as a last resort. Not only is it possible that the sight of shackles and gags might have a significant effect on the jury's feelings about the defendant, but the use of this technique is itself something of an affront to the very dignity and decorum of judicial proceedings that the judge is seeking to uphold. Moreover, one of the defendant's primary advantages of being present at the trial, his ability to communicate with his counsel, is greatly reduced when the defendant is in a condition of total physical restraint. It is in part because of these inherent disadvantages and limitations in this method of dealing with disorderly defendants that we decline to hold with the Court of Appeals that a defendant cannot under any possible circumstances be deprived of his right to be present at trial. However, in some situations which we need not attempt to foresee, binding and gagging might possibly be the fairest and most reasonable way to handle a defendant who acts as Allen did here.

II

[C]riminal contempt has obvious limitations as a sanction when the defendant is charged with a crime so serious that a very severe sentence such as death or life imprisonment is likely to be imposed. In such a case the defendant might not be affected by a mere contempt sentence when he ultimately faces a far more serious sanction. Nevertheless, the contempt remedy should be borne in mind by a judge in the circumstances of this case.

III

The trial court in this case decided under the circumstances to remove the defendant from the courtroom and to continue his trial in his absence until and unless he promised to conduct himself in a manner befitting an American courtroom. As we said earlier, we find nothing unconstitutional about this procedure. Allen's behavior was clearly of such an extreme and aggravated nature as to justify either his removal from the courtroom or his total physical restraint. Prior to his removal he was repeatedly warned by the trial judge that he would be removed from the courtroom if he persisted in his unruly conduct. Allen was constantly informed that he could return to the trial when he would agree to conduct himself in an orderly manner. Under these circumstances we hold that Allen lost his right guaranteed by the Sixth and Fourteenth Amendments to be present throughout his trial.

———————————

Federal Rule of Criminal Procedure 43(a) provides that a defendant has the right to be present at trial and at other crucial stages of the criminal proceedings, including arraignment, plea, jury empanelment, return of the verdict, and sentencing. However, Rule 43(c) recognizes that a defendant may be tried *in absentia* if he engages in disruptive conduct or voluntarily absents himself after the trial starts.

As discussed in Illinois v. Allen, the defendant has the right to be present at trial but not the right to engage in unruly conduct. Courts may take security measures to safeguard their courts. These security measures may include the deployment of uniformed law enforcement officials (*see* Holbrook v. Flynn, 475 U.S. 560 (1986)), but the visible shackling of defendants raises serious due process concerns.

DECK v. MISSOURI

544 U.S. 622 (2005)

Justice BREYER delivered the opinion of the Court.

We here consider whether shackling a convicted offender during the penalty phase of a capital case violates the Federal Constitution. We hold that the Constitution forbids the use of visible shackles during the penalty phase, as it forbids their use during the guilt phase, unless that use is "justified by an essential state interest" — such as the interest in courtroom security—specific to the defendant on trial. Holbrook v. Flynn (1986); see also Illinois v. Allen (1970).

I

In July 1996, petitioner Carman Deck robbed, shot, and killed an elderly couple. In 1998, the State of Missouri tried Deck for the murders and the robbery. At trial, state authorities required Deck to wear leg braces that apparently were not visible to the jury. Deck was convicted and sentenced to death. The State Supreme Court upheld Deck's conviction but set aside the sentence. The State then held a new sentencing proceeding.

From the first day of the new proceeding, Deck was shackled with leg irons, handcuffs, and a belly chain. Deck's counsel objected to the shackles. The objection was overruled.

II

We first consider whether, as a general matter, the Constitution permits a State to use visible shackles routinely in the guilt phase of a criminal trial. The answer is clear: The law has long forbidden routine use of visible shackles during the guilt phase; it permits a State to shackle a criminal defendant only in the presence of a special need.

This rule has deep roots in the common law. In the 18th century, Blackstone wrote that a defendant "must be brought to the bar without irons, or any manner of shackles or bonds; unless there be evident danger of an escape."

American courts have traditionally followed Blackstone's "ancient" English rule, while making clear that "in extreme and exceptional cases, where the safe custody of the prisoner and the peace of the tribunal imperatively demand, the manacles may be retained."

More recently, this Court has suggested that a version of this rule forms part of the Fifth and Fourteenth Amendments' due process guarantee. Thirty-five years ago, when considering the trial of an unusually obstreperous criminal defendant, the Court held that the Constitution sometimes permitted special measures, including physical restraints. *Allen* (1970).

Sixteen years later, the Court considered a special courtroom security arrangement that involved having uniformed security personnel sit in the first row of the courtroom's spectator section. The Court held that the Constitution allowed the arrangement, stating that the deployment of security personnel during trial is not "the sort of inherently prejudicial practice that, like shackling, should be permitted only where justified by an essential state interest specific to each trial." *Holbrook* (1986). *See also* Estelle v. Williams (1976) (making a defendant appear in prison garb poses such a threat to the "fairness of the factfinding process" that it must be justified by an "essential state policy").

Lower courts have disagreed about the specific procedural steps a trial court must take prior to shackling, about the amount and type of evidence needed to justify restraints, and about what forms of prejudice might warrant a new trial, but they have not questioned the basic principle. We now conclude that those statements identify a basic element of the "due process of law" protected by the Federal Constitution. Thus, the Fifth and Fourteenth Amendments prohibit the use of physical restraints visible to the jury absent a trial court determination, in the exercise of its discretion, that they are justified by a state interest specific to a particular trial. Such a determination may of course take into account the factors that courts have traditionally relied on in gauging potential security problems and the risk of escape at trial.

The considerations that militate against the routine use of visible shackles during the guilt phase of a criminal trial apply with like force to penalty proceedings in capital cases. This is obviously so in respect to the latter two considerations mentioned, securing a meaningful defense and maintaining dignified proceedings. It is less obviously so in respect to the first consideration mentioned, for the defendant's conviction means that the presumption of innocence no longer applies. Hence shackles do not undermine the jury's effort to apply that presumption.

Nonetheless, shackles at the penalty phase threaten related concerns. Although the jury is no longer deciding between guilt and innocence, it is deciding between life and death. That decision, given the "'severity'" and "'finality'" of the sanction, is no less important than the decision about guilt.

Justice THOMAS, with whom Justice SCALIA joins, dissenting.

Carman Deck was convicted of murdering and robbing an elderly couple. He stood before the sentencing jury not as an innocent man, but as a convicted double murderer and robber. Today this Court holds that Deck's due process rights were violated when he appeared at sentencing in leg irons, handcuffs, and a belly chain. The Court's holding defies common sense and all but ignores the serious security issues facing our courts. I therefore respectfully dissent.

b. Right to Confront Witnesses

The Sixth Amendment's Confrontation Clause provides to a criminal defendant the right to confront and cross-examine adverse witnesses. The Supreme Court has repeatedly recognized the importance of cross-examination. As the Court stated in Coy v. Iowa, 487 U.S. 1012, 1019 (1988), "[i]t is always more difficult to tell a lie about a person 'to his face' than 'behind his back.'"

Although defendants generally enjoy a right to face-to-face confrontation of witnesses, this right is not absolute. Unique circumstances in a case may require the court to take alternative measures to ensure the essence of the defendant's right of confrontation.

MARYLAND v. CRAIG
497 U.S. 836 (1990)

Justice O'CONNOR delivered the opinion of the Court.

This case requires us to decide whether the Confrontation Clause of the Sixth Amendment categorically prohibits a child witness in a child abuse case from testifying against a defendant at trial, outside the defendant's physical presence, by one-way closed circuit television.

I

In October 1986, a Howard County grand jury charged respondent, Sandra Ann Craig, with child abuse, first and second degree sexual offenses, perverted sexual practice, assault, and battery. The named victim in each count was a 6-year-old girl who had attended a kindergarten and prekindergarten center owned and operated by Craig.

In March 1987, before the case went to trial, the State sought to invoke a Maryland statutory procedure that permits a judge to receive, by one-way closed circuit television, the testimony of a child witness who is alleged to be a victim of child abuse. To invoke the procedure, the trial judge must first "determine that testimony by the child victim in the courtroom will result in the child suffering serious emotional distress such that the child cannot reasonably communicate." Once the procedure is invoked, the child witness, prosecutor, and defense counsel withdraw to a separate room; the judge, jury, and defendant remain in the courtroom. The child witness is then examined and cross-examined in the separate room, while a video monitor records and displays the witness' testimony to those in the courtroom. During this time the witness cannot see the defendant. The defendant remains in electronic communication with defense counsel, and objections may be made and ruled on as if the witness were testifying in the courtroom.

In support of its motion invoking the one-way closed circuit television procedure, the State presented expert testimony that the named victim, as well as a number of other children who were alleged to have been sexually abused by Craig, would suffer "serious emotional distress such that [they could not] reasonably communicate if required to testify in the courtroom."

Craig objected to the use of the procedure on Confrontation Clause grounds, but the trial court rejected that contention.

We granted certiorari to resolve the important Confrontation Clause issues raised by this case.

II

The Confrontation Clause of the Sixth Amendment, made applicable to the States through the Fourteenth Amendment, provides: "In all criminal prosecutions, the accused shall enjoy the right . . . to be confronted with the witnesses against him."

We observed in Coy v. Iowa (1988) that "the Confrontation Clause guarantees the defendant a face-to-face meeting with witnesses appearing before the trier of fact." This interpretation derives not only from the literal text of the Clause, but also from our understanding of its historical roots.

We have never held, however, that the Confrontation Clause guarantees criminal defendants the absolute right to a face-to-face meeting with witnesses against them at trial. Indeed, in Coy v. Iowa, we expressly "left for another day . . . the question whether any exceptions exist" to the "irreducible literal meaning of the Clause: 'a right to meet face to face all those who appear and give evidence at trial.'" The procedure challenged in *Coy* involved the placement of a screen that prevented two child witnesses in a child abuse case from seeing the defendant as they testified against him at trial. In holding that the use of this procedure violated the defendant's right to confront witnesses against him, we suggested that any exception to the right "would surely be allowed only when necessary to further an important public policy" — i.e., only upon a showing of something more than the generalized, "legislatively imposed presumption of trauma" underlying the statute at issue in that case. We concluded that "since there had been no individualized findings that these particular witnesses needed special protection, the judgment [in the case before us] could not be sustained by any conceivable exception." Because the trial court in this case made individualized findings that each of the child witnesses needed special protection, this case requires us to decide the question reserved in *Coy*.

The central concern of the Confrontation Clause is to ensure the reliability of the evidence against a criminal defendant by subjecting it to rigorous testing in the context of an adversary proceeding before the trier of fact.

[T]he right guaranteed by the Confrontation Clause includes not only a "personal examination," but also "(1) insures that the witness will give his statements under oath — thus impressing him with the seriousness of the matter and guarding against the lie by the possibility of a penalty for perjury; (2) forces the witness to submit to cross-examination, the 'greatest legal engine ever invented for the discovery of truth'; [and] (3) permits the jury that is to decide the defendant's fate to observe the demeanor of the witness in making his statement, thus aiding the jury in assessing his credibility."

The combined effect of these elements of confrontation — physical presence, oath, cross-examination, and observation of demeanor by the trier of fact — serves the purposes of the Confrontation Clause by ensuring that evidence admitted against an accused is reliable and subject to the rigorous adversarial testing that is the norm of Anglo-American criminal proceedings.

Although face-to-face confrontation forms "the core of the values furthered by the Confrontation Clause," we have nevertheless recognized that it is not the sine qua non of the confrontation right.

For this reason, we have never insisted on an actual face-to-face encounter at trial in every instance in which testimony is admitted against a defendant. Instead, we have repeatedly held that the Clause permits, where necessary, the admission of certain hearsay statements against a defendant despite the defendant's inability to confront the declarant at trial.

[A] literal reading of the Confrontation Clause would "abrogate virtually every hearsay exception, a result long rejected as unintended and too extreme." Given our hearsay cases, the word "confronted," as used in the Confrontation Clause, cannot simply mean face-to-face confrontation.

[O]ur precedents establish that "the Confrontation Clause reflects a preference for face-to-face confrontation at trial," a preference that "must occasionally give way to considerations of public policy and the necessities of the case."

III

Although we are mindful of the many subtle effects face-to-face confrontation may have on an adversary criminal proceeding, the presence of these other elements of confrontation — oath, cross-examination, and observation of the witness' demeanor — adequately ensures that the testimony is both reliable and subject to rigorous adversarial testing in a manner functionally equivalent to that accorded live, in-person testimony. These safeguards of reliability and adversariness render the use of such a procedure a far cry from the undisputed prohibition of the Confrontation Clause: trial by ex parte affidavit or inquisition.

We . . . conclude today that a State's interest in the physical and psychological well-being of child abuse victims may be sufficiently important to outweigh, at least in some cases, a defendant's right to face his or her accusers in court.

Justice SCALIA, with whom Justices BRENNAN, MARSHALL, and STEVENS join, dissenting.

The Sixth Amendment provides, with unmistakable clarity, that "in all criminal prosecutions, the accused shall enjoy the right . . . to be confronted with the witnesses against him." The purpose of enshrining this protection in the Constitution was to assure that none of the many policy interests from time to time pursued by statutory law could overcome a defendant's right to face his or her accusers in court.

Because the text of the Sixth Amendment is clear, and because the Constitution is meant to protect against, rather than conform to, current "widespread belief," I respectfully dissent.

[Justice Scalia discussed the problems that hearsay evidence poses to compliance with the Confrontation Clause — a subject he returned to in Crawford v. Washington (2004), discussed *infra*.]

The Court today has applied "interest-balancing" analysis where the text of the Constitution simply does not permit it. We are not free to conduct a cost-benefit analysis of clear and explicit constitutional guarantees, and then to adjust their meaning to comport with our findings. The Court has convincingly proved that the Maryland procedure serves a valid interest, and gives the defendant virtually everything the Confrontation Clause guarantees (everything, that is, except confrontation). I am persuaded, therefore, that the Maryland procedure is virtually constitutional. Since it is not, however, actually constitutional I would affirm the judgment of the Maryland Court of Appeals reversing the judgment of conviction.

As Justice Scalia previewed in his dissent in Maryland v. Craig, the Confrontation Clause has important implications with regard to the admissibility of hearsay. In Crawford v. Washington, 541 U.S. 36 (2004), the Supreme Court modified its approach to the admissibility of hearsay evidence.

CRAWFORD v. WASHINGTON
541 U.S. 36 (2004)

Justice SCALIA delivered the opinion of the Court.

Petitioner Michael Crawford stabbed a man who allegedly tried to rape his wife, Sylvia. At his trial, the State played for the jury Sylvia's tape-recorded statement to the police describing the stabbing, even though he had no opportunity for cross-examination. The Washington Supreme Court upheld petitioner's conviction after determining that Sylvia's statement was reliable. The question presented is whether this procedure complied with the Sixth Amendment's guarantee that, "[i]n all criminal prosecutions, the accused shall enjoy the right . . . to be confronted with the witnesses against him."

I

On August 5, 1999, Kenneth Lee was stabbed at his apartment. Police arrested petitioner later that night. After giving petitioner and his wife *Miranda* warnings, detectives interrogated each of them twice. Petitioner eventually confessed that he and Sylvia had gone in search of Lee because he was upset over an earlier incident in which Lee had tried to rape her. The two had found Lee at his apartment, and a fight ensued in which Lee was stabbed in the torso and petitioner's hand was cut.

Sylvia generally corroborated petitioner's story about the events leading up to the fight.

The State charged petitioner with assault and attempted murder. At trial, he claimed self-defense. Sylvia did not testify because of the state marital privilege, which generally bars a spouse from testifying without the other spouse's consent. [T]he State sought to introduce Sylvia's tape-recorded statements to the police as evidence that the stabbing was not in self-defense.

Petitioner countered that, state law notwithstanding, admitting the evidence would violate his federal constitutional right to be "confronted with the witnesses against him."

We granted certiorari to determine whether the State's use of Sylvia's statement violated the Confrontation Clause.

II

The Sixth Amendment's Confrontation Clause provides that, "[i]n all criminal prosecutions, the accused shall enjoy the right . . . to be confronted with the witnesses against him." [Ohio v. Roberts] says that an unavailable witness's out-of-court statement may be admitted so long as it has adequate indicia of reliability—i.e., falls within a "firmly rooted hearsay exception" or bears "particularized guarantees of trustworthiness." Petitioner argues that this test strays from the original meaning of the Confrontation Clause and urges us to reconsider it.

A

The Constitution's text does not alone resolve this case. We must therefore turn to the historical background of the Clause to understand its meaning.

The right to confront one's accusers is a concept that dates back to Roman times. The founding generation's immediate source of the concept, however, was the common law. English common law has long differed from continental civil law in regard to the manner in which witnesses give testimony in criminal trials. The common-law tradition is one of live testimony in court subject to adversarial testing, while the civil law condones examination in private by judicial officers.

Nonetheless, England at times adopted elements of the civil-law practice. Justices of the peace or other officials examined suspects and witnesses before trial. These examinations were sometimes read in court in lieu of live testimony.

Pretrial examinations became routine under two statutes passed during the reign of Queen Mary in the 16th century. [For bail purposes], justices of the peace [would] examine suspects and witnesses in felony cases and . . . certify the results to the court. It is doubtful that the original purpose of the examinations was to produce evidence admissible at trial. Whatever the original purpose, however, they came to be used as evidence in some cases.

The most notorious instances of civil-law examination occurred in the great political trials of the 16th and 17th centuries. One such was the 1603 trial of Sir Walter Raleigh for treason. Lord Cobham, Raleigh's alleged accomplice, had implicated him in an examination before the Privy Council and in a letter. At Raleigh's trial, these were read to the jury. Raleigh argued that Cobham had lied to save himself: "Cobham is absolutely in the King's mercy; to excuse me cannot avail him; by accusing me he may hope for favour." Suspecting that Cobham would recant, Raleigh demanded that the judges call him to appear. The judges refused and, despite Raleigh's protestations that he was being tried "by the Spanish Inquisition," the jury convicted, and Raleigh was sentenced to death.

B

Controversial examination practices were also used in the Colonies. Early in the 18th century, for example, the Virginia Council protested against the Governor for having "privately issued several commissions to examine witnesses against particular men ex parte," complaining that "the person accused is not admitted to be confronted with, or defend himself against his defamers."

Many declarations of rights adopted around the time of the Revolution guaranteed a right of confrontation.

III

This history supports two inferences about the meaning of the Sixth Amendment.

A

First, the principal evil at which the Confrontation Clause was directed was the civil-law mode of criminal procedure, and particularly its use of ex parte examinations as evidence against the accused. It was these practices that the Crown deployed in notorious treason cases like Raleigh's. The Sixth Amendment must be interpreted with this focus in mind.

The text of the Confrontation Clause . . . applies to "witnesses" against the accused—in other words, those who "bear testimony." "Testimony," in turn, is typically "[a] solemn declaration or affirmation made for the purpose of establishing or proving some fact."

Various formulations of this core class of "testimonial" statements exist: ". . . material such as affidavits, custodial examinations, prior testimony that the defendant was unable to cross-examine, or similar pretrial statements that declarants would reasonably expect to be used prosecutorially."

Statements taken by police officers in the course of interrogations are also testimonial under even a narrow standard. Police interrogations bear a striking resemblance to examinations by justices of the peace in England.

B

The historical record also supports a second proposition: that the Framers would not have allowed admission of testimonial statements of a witness who did not appear at trial unless he was unavailable to testify, and the defendant had had a prior opportunity for cross-examination. The text of the Sixth

Amendment does not suggest any open-ended exceptions from the confrontation requirement to be developed by the courts. Rather, the "right . . . to be confronted with the witnesses against him," is most naturally read as a reference to the right of confrontation at common law, admitting only those exceptions established at the time of the founding.[25]

Where testimonial statements are involved, we do not think the Framers meant to leave the Sixth Amendment's protection to the vagaries of the rules of evidence, much less to amorphous notions of "reliability." To be sure, the Clause's ultimate goal is to ensure reliability of evidence, but it is a procedural rather than a substantive guarantee. It commands, not that evidence be reliable, but that reliability be assessed in a particular manner: by testing in the crucible of cross-examination. The Clause thus reflects a judgment, not only about the desirability of reliable evidence (a point on which there could be little dissent), but about how reliability can best be determined.

C

Where testimonial evidence is at issue . . . the Sixth Amendment demands what the common law required: unavailability and a prior opportunity for cross-examination. We leave for another day any effort to spell out a comprehensive definition of "testimonial." Whatever else the term covers, it applies at a minimum to prior testimony at a preliminary hearing, before a grand jury, or at a former trial; and to police interrogations. These are the modern practices with closest kinship to the abuses at which the Confrontation Clause was directed.

In this case, the State admitted Sylvia's testimonial statement against petitioner, despite the fact that he had no opportunity to cross-examine her. That alone is sufficient to make out a violation of the Sixth Amendment. *Roberts* notwithstanding, we decline to mine the record in search of indicia of reliability. Where testimonial statements are at issue, the only indicium of reliability sufficient to satisfy constitutional demands is the one the Constitution actually prescribes: confrontation.

———————————

The Court's decision in *Crawford* rocked the world of evidence. Hearsay exceptions that were previously used routinely by trial courts could no longer be used simply because they met the prior Ohio v. Roberts standard of reliability. Many states had adopted statutes that allowed hearsay testimony for victims of sexual and domestic abuse. These statutes became unconstitutional under the new *Crawford* standard unless the victims had been subject to prior cross-examination and were unavailable at the time of trial.

Justice Scalia's opinion left it open for the lower courts to decide what constituted "testimonial" evidence subject to the new constitutional rule of

25. For example, dying declarations had become accepted hearsay exceptions by the time the Confrontation Clause was adopted. *See* fn. 6 in original opinion. [Footnote by casebook authors.]

confrontation. Would it include all statements to police officers? What about spontaneous statements by witnesses when they were not subject to interrogation? How about 911 calls for help?

In Davis v. Washington, 547 U.S. 813 (2006), the Court took the first step of trying to clarify the scope of *Crawford*. Again writing for the Court, Justice Scalia held that a 911 call identifying the defendant as the attacker was not necessarily "testimonial" if it related to an ongoing emergency. By contrast, statements made by the victim to the police at the crime scene were "testimonial" because they described past events. Courts continue to sort out whether other types of statements, such as statements to third persons (not the police) should also be subject to the new confrontation rules. *Crawford* has brought front and center the crucial nature of a defendant's Sixth Amendment right of confrontation. In Michigan v. Bryant (2010), the Court sought to clarify when statements to police officers would qualify as "testimonial hearsay" in violation of the Confrontation Clause.

MICHIGAN v. BRYANT

562 U.S. 344 (2010)

Justice SOTOMAYOR delivered the opinion of the Court.

At respondent Richard Bryant's trial, the court admitted statements that the victim, Anthony Covington, made to police officers who discovered him mortally wounded in a gas station parking lot. A jury convicted Bryant of second-degree murder. We granted the State's petition for a writ of certiorari to consider whether the Confrontation Clause barred the admission at trial of Covington's statements to the police. We hold that the circumstances of the interaction between Covington and the police objectively indicate that the "primary purpose of the interrogation" was "to enable police assistance to meet an ongoing emergency." Therefore, Covington's identification and description of the shooter and the location of the shooting were not testimonial statements, and their admission at Bryant's trial did not violate the Confrontation Clause.

I

Around 3:25 A.M. on April 29, 2001, Detroit, Michigan police officers responded to a radio dispatch indicating that a man had been shot. At the scene, they found the victim, Anthony Covington, lying on the ground next to his car in a gas station parking lot. Covington had a gunshot wound to his abdomen, appeared to be in great pain, and spoke with difficulty.

The police asked him "what had happened, who had shot him, and where the shooting had occurred." Covington stated that "Rick" shot him at around 3 A.M. He also indicated that he had a conversation with Bryant, whom he recognized based on his voice, through the back door of Bryant's house. Covington explained that when he turned to leave, he was shot through the door and then drove to the gas station, where police found him.

Covington's conversation with the police ended within 5 to 10 minutes when emergency medical services arrived. Covington was transported to a hospital and died within hours.

II

The Confrontation Clause of the Sixth Amendment states: "In all criminal prosecutions, the accused shall enjoy the right . . . to be confronted with the witnesses against him." In *Ohio v. Roberts* (1980), we explained that the confrontation right does not bar admission of statements of an unavailable witness if the statements "bea[r] adequate 'indicia of reliability.'"

Nearly a quarter century later, we decided *Crawford v. Washington.* [We] explained that "the principal evil at which the Confrontation Clause was directed was the civil-law mode of criminal procedure, and particularly its use of *ex parte* examinations as evidence against the accused." We noted that in England, pretrial examinations of suspects and witnesses by government officials "were sometimes read in court in lieu of live testimony." In light of this history, we emphasized the word "witnesses" in the Sixth Amendment, defining it as "those who 'bear testimony.'" We noted that "[a]n accuser who makes a formal statement to government officers bears testimony in a sense that a person who makes a casual remark to an acquaintance does not." We therefore limited the Confrontation Clause's reach to testimonial statements and held that in order for testimonial evidence to be admissible, the Sixth Amendment "demands what the common law required: unavailability and a prior opportunity for cross-examination." Although "leav[ing] for another day any effort to spell out a comprehensive definition of 'testimonial,'" *Crawford* noted that "at a minimum" it includes "prior testimony at a preliminary hearing, before a grand jury, or at a former trial; and . . . police interrogations."

In 2006, the Court in *Davis v. Washington* took a further step to "determine more precisely which police interrogations produce testimony" and therefore implicate a Confrontation Clause bar. We . . . made clear in *Davis* that not all those questioned by the police are witnesses and not all "interrogations by law enforcement officers," are subject to the Confrontation Clause. *Davis* and *Hammon* were both domestic violence cases. In *Davis*, Michelle McCottry made the statements at issue to a 911 operator during a domestic disturbance with Adrian Davis, her former boyfriend. McCottry told the operator, "'He's here jumpin' on me again,'" and, "'He's usin' his fists.'" In *Hammon*, decided along with *Davis*, police responded to a domestic disturbance call at the home of Amy and Hershel Hammon, where they found Amy alone on the front porch. She appeared "'somewhat frightened,'" but told them "'nothing was the matter.'" One officer remained in the kitchen with Hershel, while another officer talked to Amy in the living room about what had happened.

[W]e held that the statements at issue in *Davis* were nontestimonial and the statements in *Hammon* were testimonial. We distinguished the statements in *Davis* from the testimonial statements in *Crawford* on several grounds, including that the victim in *Davis* was "speaking about events *as they were actually happening*, rather than 'describ[ing] past events,'" that there was an ongoing emergency, that the "elicited statements were necessary to be able to *resolve* the present emergency," and that the statements were not formal. In *Hammon*, on the other hand, we held that, "[i]t is entirely clear from the circumstances that the interrogation was part of an investigation into possibly criminal past conduct." There was "no emergency in progress."

III

To determine whether the "primary purpose" of an interrogation is "to enable police assistance to meet an ongoing emergency," which would render the resulting statements nontestimonial, we objectively evaluate the circumstances in which the encounter occurs and the statements and actions of the parties.

The circumstances in which an encounter occurs — *e.g.*, at or near the scene of the crime versus at a police station, during an ongoing emergency or afterwards — are clearly matters of objective fact. The statements and actions of the parties must also be objectively evaluated. [T]he relevant inquiry is not the subjective or actual purpose of the individuals involved in a particular encounter, but rather the purpose that reasonable participants would have had, as ascertained from the individuals' statements and actions and the circumstances in which the encounter occurred.

In addition to the circumstances in which an encounter occurs, the statements and actions of both the declarant and interrogators provide objective evidence of the primary purpose of the interrogation. To give an extreme example, if the police say to a victim, "Tell us who did this to you so that we can arrest and prosecute them," the victim's response that "Rick did it," appears purely accusatory because by virtue of the phrasing of the question, the victim necessarily has prosecution in mind when she answers.

Victims are also likely to have mixed motives when they make statements to the police. A victim may want the attacker to be incapacitated temporarily. Objectively ascertaining the primary purpose of the interrogation by examining the statements and actions of all participants is also the approach most consistent with our past holdings.

IV

The existence of an emergency or the parties' perception that an emergency is ongoing is among the most important circumstances that courts must take into account in determining whether an interrogation is testimonial because statements made to assist police in addressing an ongoing emergency presumably lack the testimonial purpose that would subject them to the requirement of confrontation. As the context of this case brings into sharp relief, the existence and duration of an emergency depend on the type and scope of danger posed to the victim, the police, and the public.

[The first question by the officers to Covington was] "what happened?" The answer was either "I was shot" or "Rick shot me." The police did not know, and Covington did not tell them, whether the threat was limited to him.

An emergency does not last only for the time between when the assailant pulls the trigger and the bullet hits the victim. At no point during the questioning did either Covington or the police know the location of the shooter. In fact, Bryant was not at home by the time the police searched his house at approximately 5:30 A.M. At some point between 3 A.M. and 5:30 A.M., Bryant left his house. At bottom, there was an ongoing emergency here where an armed shooter, whose motive for and location after the shooting were unknown, had mortally wounded Covington within a few blocks and a few minutes of the location where the police found Covington.

Nothing in Covington's responses indicated to the police that, contrary to their expectation upon responding to a call reporting a shooting, there was no emergency or that a prior emergency had ended. Covington did indicate that he had been shot at another location about 25 minutes earlier, but he did not know the location of the shooter at the time the police arrived and, as far as we can tell from the record, he gave no indication that the shooter, having shot at him twice, would be satisfied that Covington was only wounded. In fact, Covington did not indicate any possible motive for the shooting, and thereby gave no reason to think that the shooter would not shoot again if he arrived on the scene.

Finally, we consider the informality of the situation and the interrogation. This situation is more similar, though not identical, to the informal, harried 911 call in *Davis* than to the structured, station-house interview in *Crawford*. The informality suggests that the interrogators' primary purpose was simply to address what they perceived to be an ongoing emergency, and the circumstances lacked any formality that would have alerted Covington to or focused him on the possible future prosecutorial use of his statements.

Because the circumstances of the encounter as well as the statements and actions of Covington and the police objectively indicate that the "primary purpose of the interrogation" was "to enable police assistance to meet an ongoing emergency," Covington's identification and description of the shooter and the location of the shooting were not testimonial hearsay. The Confrontation Clause did not bar their admission at Bryant's trial.

Justice THOMAS, concurring in the judgment.

I agree with the Court that the admission of Covington's out-of-court statements did not violate the Confrontation Clause, but I reach this conclusion because Covington's questioning by police lacked sufficient formality and solemnity for his statements to be considered "testimonial."

The police questioning was not "a formalized dialogue," did not result in "formalized testimonial materials" such as a deposition or affidavit, and bore no "indicia of solemnity."

Justice SCALIA, dissenting.

Today's tale — a story of five officers conducting successive examinations of a dying man with the primary purpose, not of obtaining and preserving his testimony regarding his killer, but of protecting him, them, and others from a murderer somewhere on the loose — is so transparently false that professing to believe it demeans this institution. Because I continue to adhere to the Confrontation Clause that the People adopted, as described in *Crawford v. Washington*, I dissent.

I

Looking to the declarant's purpose (as we should), this is an absurdly easy case. Roughly 25 minutes after Anthony Covington had been shot, Detroit police responded to a 911 call reporting that a gunshot victim had appeared at a neighborhood gas station. They quickly arrived at the scene, and in less than 10 minutes five different Detroit police officers questioned Covington about the shooting. Each asked him a similar battery of questions: "what happened" and when, "who shot the victim," and "where" did the shooting take place. After Covington would answer, they would ask follow-up questions, such as "how tall is" the shooter, "[h]ow much does he weigh," what is the exact address or physical description of the house where the shooting took place, and what chain of events led to the shooting. The battery relented when the paramedics arrived and began tending to Covington's wounds.

From Covington's perspective, his statements had little value except to ensure the arrest and eventual prosecution of Richard Bryant. He knew the "threatening situation," had ended six blocks away and 25 minutes earlier when he fled from Bryant's back porch. Even if Bryant had pursued him (unlikely), and after seeing that Covington had ended up at the gas station was unable to confront him there before the police arrived (doubly unlikely), it was entirely beyond imagination that Bryant would again open fire while Covington was surrounded by five armed police officers. And Covington knew the shooting was the work of a drug dealer, not a spree killer who might randomly threaten others.

Covington's knowledge that he had nothing to fear differs significantly from [the victim's] state of mind during her "frantic" statements to a 911 operator at issue in *Davis*. None of the officers asked Covington how he was doing, attempted more than superficially to assess the severity of his wounds, or attempted to administer first aid. They instead primarily asked questions with little, if any, relevance to Covington's dire situation. Police, paramedics, and doctors do not need to know the address where a shooting took place, the name of the shooter, or the shooter's height and weight to provide proper medical care. Underscoring that Covington understood the officers' investigative role, he interrupted their interrogation to ask "when is EMS coming?" When, in other words, would the focus shift to his medical needs rather than Bryant's crime?

The Court invents a world where an ongoing emergency exists whenever "an armed shooter, whose motive for and location after the shooting [are] unknown, . . . mortally wound[s]" one individual "within a few blocks and minutes of the location where the police" ultimately find that victim. Breathlessly, it worries that a shooter could leave the scene armed and ready to pull the trigger again. Nothing suggests the five officers in this case shared the Court's dystopian view of Detroit, where drug dealers hunt their shooting victim down and fire into a crowd of police officers to finish him off.

The Court's distorted view creates an expansive exception to the Confrontation Clause for violent crimes. This is a dangerous definition of emergency.

II

[T]oday's decision is not only a gross distortion of the facts. It is a gross distortion of the law — a revisionist narrative in which reliability continues to guide our Confrontation Clause jurisprudence, at least where emergencies and faux emergencies are concerned.

Justice GINSBURG, dissenting.

I agree with Justice Scalia that Covington's statements were testimonial and that "[t]he declarant's intent is what counts." I would add, however, . . . that in *Crawford*, this Court noted that, in the law we inherited from England, there was a well-established exception to the confrontation requirement: The cloak protecting the accused against admission of out-of-court testimonial statements was removed for dying declarations. Were the issue properly tendered here, I would take up the question whether the exception for dying declarations survives our recent Confrontation Clause decisions.

In Ohio v. Clark, 135 S. Ct. 2173 (2015), the Court reaffirmed its approach in Davis v. Washington (2006) and Michigan v. Bryant (2010). Statements are not testimonial, even if made to individuals like teachers who have a duty to report such communications, so long as the primary purpose of the statements was to deal with an ongoing emergency. Accordingly, the Confrontation Clause does not bar a teacher from testifying regarding a child's statement about suspected child abuse.

OHIO v. CLARK

135 S. Ct. 2173 (2015)

Justice ALITO delivered the opinion of the Court.

Darius Clark sent his girlfriend hundreds of miles away to engage in prostitution and agreed to care for her two young children while she was out of town. A day later, teachers discovered red marks on her 3-year-old son, and the boy identified Clark as his abuser. The question in this case is whether the Sixth Amendment's Confrontation Clause prohibited prosecutors from introducing those statements when the child was not available to be cross-examined. Because neither the child nor his teachers had the primary purpose of assisting in Clark's prosecution, the child's statements do not implicate the Confrontation Clause and therefore were admissible at trial.

I

Darius Clark, who went by the nickname "Dee," lived in Cleveland, Ohio, with his girlfriend, T. T., and her two children: L. P., a 3-year-old boy, and A. T., an 18-month-old girl. Clark was also T. T.'s pimp, and he would regularly send her on trips to Washington, D.C., to work as a prostitute. In March 2010, T. T. went on one such trip, and she left the children in Clark's care.

The next day, Clark took L. P. to preschool. In the lunchroom, one of L. P.'s teachers, Ramona Whitley, observed that L. P.'s left eye appeared blood-shot. She asked him "'[w]hat happened,'" and he initially said nothing. Eventually, however, he told the teacher that he "'fell.'" Ibid. When they moved into the brighter lights of a classroom, Whitley noticed "'[r]ed marks, like whips of some sort,'" on L. P.'s face. *Ibid.* She notified the lead teacher, Debra Jones, who asked L. P., "'Who did this? What happened to you?'" According to Jones, L. P. "'seemed kind of bewildered'" and "'said something like, Dee, Dee.'" Jones asked L. P. whether Dee is "big or little," to which L. P. responded that "Dee is big." Jones then brought L. P. to her supervisor, who lifted the boy's shirt, revealing more injuries. Whitley called a child abuse hotline to alert authorities about the suspected abuse.

When Clark later arrived at the school, he denied responsibility for the injuries and quickly left with L. P. The next day, a social worker found the children at Clark's mother's house and took them to a hospital, where a physician discovered additional injuries suggesting child abuse. L. P. had a black eye, belt marks on his back and stomach, and bruises all over his body. A. T. had two black eyes, a swollen hand, and a large burn on her cheek, and two pigtails had been ripped out at the roots of her hair.

A grand jury indicted Clark on five counts of felonious assault (four related to A. T. and one related to L. P.), two counts of endangering children (one for each child), and two counts of domestic violence (one for each child). At trial, the State introduced L. P.'s statements to his teachers as evidence of Clark's guilt, but L. P. did not testify. Under Ohio law, children younger than 10 years old are incompetent to testify if they "appear incapable of receiving just impressions of the facts and transactions respecting which they are examined, or of relating them truly." After conducting a hearing, the trial court concluded that L. P. was not competent to testify. But under Ohio Rule of Evidence 807, which allows the admission of reliable hearsay by child abuse victims, the court ruled that L. P.'s statements to his teachers bore sufficient guarantees of trustworthiness to be admitted as evidence.

Clark moved to exclude testimony about L. P.'s out-of-court statements under the Confrontation Clause. The trial court denied the motion, ruling that L. P.'s responses were not testimonial statements covered by the Sixth Amendment. The jury found Clark guilty on all counts except for one assault count related to A. T., and it sentenced him to 28 years' imprisonment. Clark appealed his conviction, and a state appellate court reversed on the ground that the introduction of L. P.'s out-of-court statements violated the Confrontation Clause.

In a 4-to-3 decision, the Supreme Court of Ohio affirmed. It held that, under this Court's Confrontation Clause decisions, L. P.'s statements qualified as testimonial because the primary purpose of the teachers' questioning "was not to deal with an existing emergency but rather to gather evidence potentially relevant to a subsequent criminal prosecution." The court noted that Ohio has a "mandatory reporting" law that requires certain professionals, including preschool teachers, to report suspected child abuse to government authorities. In the court's view, the teachers acted as agents of the State under the mandatory reporting law and "sought facts concerning past criminal activity to identify the person responsible, eliciting statements that 'are functionally identical to live, in-court testimony, doing precisely what a witness does on direct examination.'" We granted certiorari and we now reverse.

II

A

The Sixth Amendment's Confrontation Clause, which is binding on the States through the Fourteenth Amendment, provides: "In all criminal prosecutions, the accused shall enjoy the right . . . to be confronted with the witnesses against him." In Ohio v. Roberts (1980), we interpreted the Clause to permit the admission of out-of-court statements by an unavailable witness, so long as the statements bore "adequate 'indicia of reliability.'" Such indicia are present, we held, if "the evidence falls within a firmly rooted hearsay exception" or bears "particularized guarantees of trustworthiness."

In Crawford v. Washington (2004), we adopted a different approach. We explained that "witnesses," under the Confrontation Clause, are those "who bear testimony," and we defined "testimony" as "a solemn declaration or affirmation made for the purpose of establishing or proving some fact." The Sixth Amendment, we concluded, prohibits the introduction of testimonial statements by a nontestifying witness, unless the witness is "unavailable to testify, and the defendant had had a prior opportunity for cross-examination." Applying that definition to the facts in Crawford, we held that statements by a witness during police questioning at the station house were testimonial and thus could not be admitted. But our decision in Crawford did not offer an exhaustive definition of "testimonial" statements. Instead, Crawford stated that the label "applies at a minimum to prior testimony at a preliminary hearing, before a grand jury, or at a former trial; and to police interrogations."

Our more recent cases have labored to flesh out what it means for a statement to [10] be "testimonial." In Davis v. Washington and Hammon v. Indiana (2006), which we decided together, we dealt with statements given to law enforcement officers by the victims of domestic abuse. The victim in Davis made statements to a 911 emergency operator during and shortly after her boyfriend's violent attack. In *Hammon*, the victim, after being isolated from her abusive husband, made statements to police that were memorialized in a "'battery affidavit.'"

We held that the statements in *Hammon* were testimonial, while the statements in *Davis* were not. Announcing what has come to be known as the "primary purpose" test, we explained: "Statements are nontestimonial when made in the course of police interrogation under circumstances objectively indicating that the primary purpose of the interrogation is to enable police assistance to meet an ongoing emergency. They are testimonial when the circumstances objectively indicate that there is no such ongoing emergency, and that the primary purpose of the interrogation is to establish or prove past events potentially relevant to later criminal prosecution." Because the cases involved statements to law enforcement officers, we reserved the question whether similar statements to individuals other than law enforcement officers would raise similar issues under the Confrontation Clause.

In Michigan v. Bryant (2010), we further expounded on the primary purpose test. The inquiry, we emphasized, must consider "all of the relevant circumstances." And we reiterated our view in *Davis* that, when "the primary purpose of an interrogation is to respond to an 'ongoing emergency,' its purpose is not to create a record for trial and thus is not within the scope of the [Confrontation] Clause." At the same time, we noted that "there may be other circumstances, aside from ongoing emergencies, when a statement is not procured with a primary purpose of creating an out-of-court substitute for trial testimony." "[T]he existence vel non of an ongoing emergency is not the touchstone of the testimonial inquiry." Instead, "whether an ongoing emergency exists is simply one factor . . . that informs the ultimate inquiry regarding the 'primary purpose' of an interrogation."

One additional factor is "the informality of the situation and the interrogation." A "formal station-house interrogation," like the questioning in Crawford, is more likely to provoke testimonial statements, while less formal questioning is less likely to reflect a primary purpose aimed at obtaining testimonial evidence against the accused. In the end, the question is whether, in light of all the circumstances, viewed objectively, the "primary purpose" of the conversation was to "creat[e] an out-of-court substitute for trial testimony."

B

In this case, we consider statements made to preschool teachers, not the police. We are therefore presented with the question we have repeatedly reserved: whether statements to persons other than law enforcement officers are subject to the Confrontation Clause. Because at least some statements to individuals who are not law enforcement officers could conceivably raise confrontation concerns, we decline to adopt a categorical rule excluding them from the Sixth Amendment's reach. Nevertheless, such statements are much less likely to be testimonial than statements to law enforcement officers. And considering all the relevant circumstances here, L. P.'s statements clearly were not made with the primary purpose of creating evidence for Clark's prosecution. Thus, their introduction at trial did not violate the Confrontation Clause.

L. P.'s statements occurred in the context of an ongoing emergency involving suspected child abuse. When L. P.'s teachers noticed his injuries, they rightly became worried that the 3-year-old was the victim of serious violence. Because the teachers needed to know whether it was safe to release L. P. to his guardian at the end of the day, they needed to determine who might be abusing the child. Thus, the immediate concern was to protect a vulnerable child who needed help. Our holding in *Bryant* is instructive. As in *Bryant*, the emergency in this case was ongoing, and the circumstances were not entirely clear. L. P.'s teachers were not sure who had abused him or how best to secure his safety. Nor were they sure whether any other children might be at risk. As a result, their questions and L. P.'s answers were primarily aimed at identifying and ending the threat. Though not as harried, the conversation here was also similar to the 911 call in *Davis*. The teachers' questions were meant to identify the abuser in order to protect the victim from future attacks. Whether the teachers thought that this would be done by apprehending the abuser or by some other means is irrelevant. And the circumstances in this case were unlike the interrogation in *Hammon*, where the police knew the identity of the assailant and questioned the victim after shielding her from potential harm.

There is no indication that the primary purpose of the conversation was to gather evidence for Clark's prosecution. On the contrary, it is clear that the first objective was to protect L. P. At no point did the teachers inform L. P. that his answers would be used to arrest or punish his abuser. L. P. never hinted that he intended his statements to be used by the police or prosecutors. And the conversation between L. P. and his teachers was informal and spontaneous. The teachers asked L. P. about his injuries immediately upon discovering them, in the informal setting of a preschool lunchroom and classroom, and they did so precisely as any concerned citizen would talk to a child who might be the victim of abuse. This was nothing like the formalized station-house questioning in Crawford or the police interrogation and battery affidavit in Hammon.

L. P.'s age fortifies our conclusion that the statements in question were not testimonial. Statements by very young children will rarely, if ever, implicate the Confrontation Clause. Few preschool students understand the details of our criminal justice system. Rather, "[r]esearch on children's understanding of the legal system finds that" young children "have little understanding of prosecution." Thus, it is extremely unlikely that a 3-year-old child in L. P.'s position would intend his statements to be a substitute for trial testimony. On the contrary, a young child in these circumstances would simply want the abuse to end, would want to protect other victims, or would have no discernible purpose at all.

As a historical matter, moreover, there is strong evidence that statements made in circumstances similar to those facing L. P. and his teachers were admissible at common law. Neither Crawford nor any of the cases that it has produced has mounted evidence that the adoption of the Confrontation Clause was understood to require the exclusion of evidence that was regularly admitted in criminal cases at the time of the founding. Certainly, the statements in this case are nothing like the notorious use of ex parte examination in Sir Walter Raleigh's trial for treason, which we have frequently identified as "the principal evil at which the Confrontation Clause was directed."

Finally, although we decline to adopt a rule that statements to individuals who are not law enforcement officers are categorically outside the Sixth Amendment, the fact that L. P. was speaking to his teachers remains highly relevant. Courts must evaluate challenged statements in context, and part of that context is the questioner's identity. Statements made to someone who is not principally charged with uncovering and prosecuting criminal behavior are significantly less likely to be testimonial than statements given to law enforcement officers. It is common sense that the relationship between a student and his teacher is very different from that between a citizen and the police. We do not ignore that reality. In light of these circumstances, the Sixth Amendment did not prohibit the State from introducing L. P.'s statements at trial.

III

Clark's efforts to avoid this conclusion are all off-base. He emphasizes Ohio's mandatory reporting obligations, in an attempt to equate L. P.'s teachers with the police and their caring questions with official interrogations. But the comparison is inapt. The teachers' pressing concern was to protect L. P. and remove him from harm's way. Like all good teachers, they undoubtedly would have acted with the same purpose whether or not they had a state-law duty to report abuse. And mandatory reporting statutes alone cannot convert a conversation between a concerned teacher and her student into a law enforcement mission aimed primarily at gathering evidence for a prosecution.

IV

We reverse the judgment of the Supreme Court of Ohio and remand the case for further proceedings not inconsistent with this opinion.

Justice SCALIA, with whom Justice GINSBURG joins, concurring in the judgment.

I agree with the Court's holding, and with its refusal to decide two questions quite unnecessary to that holding: what effect Ohio's mandatory-reporting law has in transforming a private party into a state actor for Confrontation Clause purposes, and whether a more permissive Confrontation Clause test—one less likely to hold the statements testimonial—should apply to interrogations by private actors. The statements here would not be testimonial under the usual test applicable to informal police interrogation.

I write separately, however, to protest the Court's shoveling of fresh dirt upon the Sixth Amendment right of confrontation so recently rescued from the grave in Crawford v. Washington (2004). For several decades before that case, we had been allowing hearsay statements to be admitted against a criminal defendant if they bore "'indicia of reliability.'" Ohio v. Roberts (1980). Prosecutors, past and present, love that flabby test. Crawford sought to bring our application of the Confrontation Clause back to its original meaning, which was to exclude unconfronted statements made by witnesses—i.e., statements that were testimonial.

Crawford remains the law. But when else has the categorical overruling, the thorough repudiation, of an earlier line of cases been described as nothing more than "adopt[ing] a different approach," as though Crawford is only a matter of twiddle-dum twiddle-dee preference, and the old, pre-Crawford "approach" remains available?

The Confrontation Clause categorically entitles a defendant to be confronted with the witnesses against him; and the primary-purpose test sorts out, among the many people who interact with the police informally, who is acting as a witness and who is not. Those who fall into the former category bear testimony, and are therefore acting as "witnesses," subject to the right of confrontation. There are no other mysterious requirements that the Court declines to name.

Justice THOMAS, concurring in the judgment.

I agree with the Court that Ohio mandatory reporters are not agents of law enforcement, that statements made to private persons or by very young children will rarely implicate the Confrontation Clause, and that the admission of the statements at issue here did not implicate that constitutional provision. I nonetheless cannot join the majority's analysis. In the decade since we first sought to return to the original meaning of the Confrontation Clause, we have carefully reserved consideration of that Clause's application to statements made to private persons for a case in which it was squarely presented.

This is that case; yet the majority does not offer clear guidance on the subject, declaring only that "the primary purpose test is a necessary, but not always sufficient, condition" for a statement to fall within the scope of the Confrontation Clause. The primary purpose test, however, is just as much "an exercise in fiction . . . disconnected from history" for statements made to private persons as it is for statements made to agents of law enforcement, if not more so.

Instead, I would use the same test for statements to private persons that I have employed for statements to agents of law enforcement, assessing whether those statements bear sufficient indicia of solemnity to qualify as testimonial. I have identified several categories of extrajudicial statements that bear sufficient indicia of solemnity to fall within the original meaning of testimony.

Here, L. P.'s statements do not bear sufficient indicia of solemnity to qualify as testimonial. They were neither contained in formalized testimonial materials nor obtained as the result of a formalized dialogue initiated by police.

The Court has also been concerned about the defendant's right to confront witnesses when prosecutors seek to admit evidence through forensic expert reports or certificates of analysis. In Melendez-Diaz v. Massachusetts, 129 S. Ct. 2527 (2009), the Court held that the admission of forensic reports constituted "testimonial evidence" and was subject to the Confrontation Clause. Subsequently, in Bullcoming v. New Mexico, 564 U.S. 647 (2011), the Court prohibited the introduction of a forensic laboratory report through a witness who did not sign the certification or perform the analysis. However, the Court recently held in Williams v. Illinois, 567 U.S. 50 (2012), that experts can rely on forensic reports in reaching their opinions and refer to those reports in their testimony.

2. Privilege Against Self-Incrimination and Improper Closing Arguments

Another critical right at trial is the privilege against self-incrimination. The Fifth Amendment "protects a person . . . against being incriminated by his own compelled testimonial communications." Chapter 4 discusses how that privilege affects law enforcement's ability to obtain statements and evidence from defendants. Yet the Fifth Amendment also plays a crucial role at trial. On the most basic level, the Fifth Amendment prohibits the state from calling the defendant to the witness stand and from compelling him to be a witness against himself. But does the Fifth Amendment also prevent the prosecution from asking jurors to draw adverse inferences from the fact that the defendant chose not to testify?

GRIFFIN v. CALIFORNIA
380 U.S. 609 (1965)

Justice DOUGLAS delivered the opinion of the Court.

Petitioner was convicted of murder in the first degree after a jury trial in a California court. He did not testify at the trial on the issue of guilt, though he did testify at the separate trial on the issue of penalty. The trial court instructed the jury on the issue of guilt, stating that a defendant has a constitutional right not to testify. But it told the jury:

> As to any evidence or facts against him which the defendant can reasonably be expected to deny or explain because of facts within his knowledge, if he does not testify or if, though he does testify, he fails to deny or explain such evidence, the jury may take that failure into consideration as tending to indicate the truth of such evidence and as indicating that among the inferences that may be reasonably drawn therefrom those unfavorable to the defendant are the more probable.

Petitioner had been seen with the deceased the evening of her death, the evidence placing him with her in the alley where her body was found. The prosecutor made much of the failure of petitioner to testify:

> The defendant certainly knows whether Essie Mae had this beat up appearance at the time he left her apartment and went down the alley with her.
> What kind of a man is it that would want to have sex with a woman that beat up if she was beat up at the time he left?
> He would know that. He would know how she got down the alley. He would know how the blood got on the bottom of the concrete steps. He would know how long he was with her in that box. He would know how her wig got off. He would know whether he beat her or mistreated her. He would know whether he walked away from that place cool as a cucumber when he saw Mr. Villasenor because he was conscious of his own guilt and wanted to get away from that damaged or injured woman.
> These things he has not seen fit to take the stand and deny or explain.
> And in the whole world, if anybody would know, this defendant would know.
> Essie Mae is dead, she can't tell you her side of the story. The defendant won't.

The death penalty was imposed and the California Supreme Court affirmed. [W]e granted [certiorari] to consider whether comment on the failure to testify violated the Self-Incrimination Clause of the Fifth Amendment.

If this were a federal trial, reversible error would have been committed. Wilson v. United States so holds. It is said, however, that the *Wilson* decision rested not on the Fifth Amendment, but on an Act of Congress, now 18 U.S.C. §3481. The question remains whether, statute or not, the comment rule, approved by California, violates the Fifth Amendment.

We think it does.

It is not everyone who can safely venture on the witness stand though entirely innocent of the charge against him. "Excessive timidity, nervousness when facing others and attempting to explain transactions of a suspicious character, and offences charged against him, will often confuse and embarrass him to such a degree as to increase rather than remove prejudices against him. It is not every one, however honest, who would, therefore, willingly be placed on the witness stand. The statute, in tenderness to the weakness of those who from the causes mentioned might refuse to ask to be a witness, particularly when they may have been in some degree compromised by their association with others, declares that the failure of the defendant in a criminal action to request to be a witness shall not create any presumption against him."

If the words "Fifth Amendment" are substituted for "act" and for "statute," the spirit of the Self-Incrimination Clause is reflected. For comment on the refusal to testify is a remnant of the "inquisitorial system of criminal justice." It is a penalty imposed by courts for exercising a constitutional privilege. It cuts down on the privilege by making its assertion costly. It is said, however, that the inference of guilt for failure to testify as to facts peculiarly within the accused's knowledge is in any event natural and irresistible, and that comment on the failure does not magnify that inference into a penalty for asserting a constitutional privilege. What the jury may infer, given no help from the court, is one thing. What it may infer when the court solemnizes the silence of the accused into evidence against him is quite another.

Justice STEWART, with whom Justice WHITE joins, dissenting.

The petitioner chose not to take the witness stand at his trial upon a charge of first-degree murder in a California court. Article I, §13, of the California Constitution establishes a defendant's privilege against self-incrimination and further provides:

> In any criminal case, whether the defendant testifies or not, his failure to explain or to deny by his testimony any evidence or facts in the case against him may be commented upon by the court and by counsel, and may be considered by the court or the jury.

We must determine whether the petitioner has been "compelled . . . to be a witness against himself." Compulsion is the focus of the inquiry. Certainly, if any compulsion be detected in the California procedure, it is of a dramatically different and less palpable nature than that involved in the procedures which historically gave rise to the Fifth Amendment guarantee. When a suspect was brought before the Court of High Commission or the Star Chamber, he was commanded to answer whatever was asked of him, and subjected to a far-reaching and deeply probing inquiry in an effort to ferret out some unknown and frequently unsuspected crime. He declined to answer on pain of incarceration, banishment, or mutilation. And if he spoke falsely, he was subject to further punishment. Faced with this formidable array of alternatives, his decision to speak was unquestionably coerced.

Those were the lurid realities which lay behind enactment of the Fifth Amendment, a far cry from the subject matter of the case before us. I think that the Court in this case stretches the concept of compulsion beyond all reasonable bounds, and that whatever compulsion may exist derives from the defendant's choice not to testify, not from any comment by court or counsel.

I think the California comment rule is not a coercive device which impairs the right against self-incrimination, but rather a means of articulating and bringing into the light of rational discussion a fact inescapably impressed on the jury's consciousness.

Although a defendant's assertion of his Fifth Amendment right cannot be used against him in a criminal case, it can be used against him in a related civil proceeding. *See* Baxter v. Palmigiano, 425 U.S. 308 (1976).

The Fifth Amendment privilege against self-incrimination includes the right to remain silent during the sentencing phase. Mitchell v. United States, 526 U.S. 314, 316 (1999). If a defendant chooses to testify at trial, the defendant may not choose to answer only some questions regarding her conduct but not others. Generally, by choosing to testify, the defendant waives his Fifth Amendment right against self-incrimination as to all questions regarding the subject matter of the case. *Id.*

In addition to prohibiting prosecutors from commenting on a defendant's exercise of the Fifth Amendment privilege against self-incrimination, the Court also has limited arguments designed simply to inflame the passions of the jury. The Court addressed the prosecutor's role and boundaries of proper closing arguments in Darden v. Wainwright. While there are limits on prosecutorial advocacy, prosecutorial misconduct does not necessarily result in a new trial.

DARDEN v. WAINWRIGHT
477 U.S. 168 (1986)

Justice POWELL delivered the opinion of the Court.

Petitioner was tried and found guilty of murder, robbery, and assault with intent to kill in the Circuit Court for Citrus County, Florida, in January 1974. [He was sentenced to death.]

Petitioner contends that the prosecution's closing argument at the guilt-innocence stage of the trial rendered his conviction fundamentally unfair and deprived the sentencing determination of the reliability that the Eighth Amendment requires.

The prosecutors' comments must be evaluated in light of the defense argument that preceded it, which blamed the Polk County Sheriff's Office for a lack of evidence, alluded to the death penalty, characterized the perpetrator of the crimes as an "animal," and contained counsel's personal opinion of the strength of the State's evidence.

The prosecutors then made their closing argument. That argument deserves the condemnation it has received from every court to review it, although no court has held that the argument rendered the trial unfair.

Several comments attempted to place some of the blame for the crime on the Division of Corrections, because Darden was on weekend furlough from a prison sentence when the crime occurred. Some comments implied that the death penalty would be the only guarantee against a future similar act. Others incorporated the defense's use of the word "animal." Prosecutor McDaniel made several offensive comments reflecting an emotional reaction to the case.[26] These comments undoubtedly were improper. But . . . it "is not enough that the prosecutors' remarks were undesirable or even universally condemned." The relevant question is whether the prosecutors' comments "so infected the trial with unfairness as to make the resulting conviction a denial of due process."

Under this standard of review, we agree with the reasoning of every court to consider these comments that they did not deprive petitioner of a fair trial. The prosecutors' argument did not manipulate or misstate the evidence, nor did it implicate other specific rights of the accused such as the right to counsel or the right to remain silent. Much of the objectionable content was invited by or was responsive to the opening summation of the defense. As we explained in *United States v. Young* (1985), the idea of "invited response" is used not to excuse improper comments, but to determine their effect on the trial as a whole. The trial court instructed the jurors several times that their decision was to be made on the basis of the evidence alone, and that the arguments of counsel were not evidence. The weight of the evidence against petitioner was heavy; the "overwhelming eyewitness and circumstantial evidence to support a finding of guilt on all charges," reduced the likelihood that the jury's decision was influenced by argument. Finally, defense counsel made the tactical decision not to present any witness other than petitioner. This decision not only permitted them to give their summation prior to the prosecution's closing argument, but also gave them the opportunity to make a final rebuttal argument. Defense counsel were able to use the opportunity for rebuttal very effectively, turning much of the prosecutors' closing argument against them by placing many of the prosecutors' comments and actions in a light that was more likely to engender strong disapproval than result in inflamed passions against petitioner. For these reasons, we agree with the District Court below that "Darden's trial was not perfect — few are — but neither was it fundamentally unfair."

---

26. "He shouldn't be out of his cell unless he has a leash on him and a prison guard at the other end of that leash." *Id.,* at 16. "I wish [Mr. Turman] had had a shotgun in his hand when he walked in the back door and blown his [Darden's] face off. I wish that I could see him sitting here with no face, blown away by a shotgun." *Id.,* at 20. "I wish someone had walked in the back door and blown his head off at that point." *Ibid.* "He fired in the boy's back, number five, saving one. Didn't get a chance to use it. I wish he had used it on himself." *Id.,* at 28. "I wish he had been killed in the accident, but he wasn't. Again, we are unlucky that time." *Id.,* at 29. "[D]on't forget what he has done according to those witnesses, to make every attempt to change his appearance from September the 8th, 1973. The hair, the goatee, even the moustache and the weight. The only thing he hasn't done that I know of is cut his throat." *Id.,* at 31. [Footnote by the Court.]

Justice BLACKMUN, with whom Justice BRENNAN, Justice MARSHALL, and Justice STEVENS join, dissenting.

Although the Constitution guarantees a criminal defendant only "a fair trial [and] not a perfect one," . . . this Court has stressed repeatedly in the decade since *Gregg v. Georgia* (1976), that the Eighth Amendment requires a heightened degree of reliability in any case where a State seeks to take the defendant's life. Today's opinion, however, reveals a Court willing to tolerate not only imperfection but a level of fairness and reliability so low it should make conscientious prosecutors cringe.

I

The following brief comparison of established standards of prosecutorial conduct with the prosecutors' behavior in this case merely illustrates, but hardly exhausts, the scope of the misconduct involved:

1. "A lawyer shall not . . . state a personal opinion as to . . . the credibility of a witness . . . or the guilt or innocence of an accused." Model Rules of Professional Conduct, Rule 3.4(e) (1984). Yet one prosecutor, White, stated: "I am convinced, as convinced as I know I am standing before you today, that Willie Jasper Darden is a murderer, that he murdered Mr. Turman, that he robbed Mrs. Turman and that he shot to kill Phillip Arnold. I will be convinced of that the rest of my life."

2. "The prosecutor should refrain from argument which would divert the jury from its duty to decide the case on the evidence, by injecting issues broader than the guilt or innocence of the accused under the controlling law, or by making predictions of the consequences of the jury's verdict." ABA Standards for Criminal Justice 3-5.8(d) (2d ed. 1980). Yet McDaniel's argument was filled with references to Darden's status as a prisoner on furlough who "shouldn't be out of his cell unless he has a leash on him."

3. "The prosecutor should not use arguments calculated to inflame the passions or prejudices of the jury." ABA Standards for Criminal Justice 3-5.8(c) (2d ed. 1980). Yet McDaniel repeatedly expressed a wish "that I could see [Darden] sitting here with no face, blown away by a shotgun."

The misconduct here was not "slight or confined to a single instance, but . . . was pronounced and persistent, with a probable cumulative effect upon the jury which cannot be disregarded as inconsequential." *Berger v. United States* (1935).

E.   DEFENDANT'S RIGHT TO PRESENT A DEFENSE

In an effort to ensure that a defendant has a fair trial, the Supreme Court has held in a series of decisions that evidentiary and procedural obstacles should not impair a defendant's ability to present a defense. In Chambers v. Mississippi (1973), the Court held that due process required that the defendant be allowed to present evidence that another individual committed the murder for which he was charged, notwithstanding the fact that the proffered evidence violated applicable evidentiary rules.

CHAMBERS v. MISSISSIPPI

410 U.S. 284 (1973)

Justice POWELL delivered the opinion of the Court.

Petitioner, Leon Chambers, was tried by a jury in a Mississippi trial court and convicted of murdering a policeman. The jury assessed punishment at life imprisonment. The events that led to petitioner's prosecution for murder occurred in the small town of Woodville in southern Mississippi. On Saturday evening, June 14, 1969, two Woodville policemen, James Forman and Aaron "Sonny" Liberty, entered a local bar and pool hall to execute a warrant for the arrest of a youth named C. C. Jackson. Jackson resisted and a hostile crowd of some 50 or 60 persons gathered. The officers' first attempt to handcuff Jackson was frustrated when 20 or 25 men in the crowd intervened and wrestled him free. Three deputy sheriffs arrived shortly thereafter and the officers again attempted to make their arrest. Once more, the officers were attacked by the onlookers and during the commotion five or six pistol shots were fired. Before Liberty died, he turned around and fired both barrels of his riot gun into an alley in the area from which the shots appeared to have come. Liberty hit one of the men in the crowd in the back of the head and neck as he ran down the alley. That man was Leon Chambers. Chambers was subsequently charged with Liberty's murder. He pleaded not guilty and has asserted his innocence throughout.

The story of Leon Chambers is intertwined with the story of another man, Gable McDonald. McDonald was in the crowd on the evening of Liberty's death. [McDonald gave a sworn confession to Chambers' attorney] that he shot Officer Liberty. He also stated that he had already told a friend of his, James Williams, that he shot Liberty. He said that he used his own pistol, a nine-shot .22-caliber revolver, which he had discarded shortly after the shooting. In response to questions from Chambers' attorneys, McDonald affirmed that his confession was voluntary and that no one had compelled him to come to them. Once the confession had been transcribed, signed, and witnessed, McDonald was turned over to the local police authorities and was placed in jail.

One month later, at a preliminary hearing, McDonald repudiated his prior sworn confession. He testified that [a friend] had persuaded him to confess that he shot Liberty. He claimed that this person had promised that he would not go to jail and that he would share in the proceeds of a lawsuit that Chambers would bring against the town of Woodville.

Chambers' case came on for trial in October of the next year. At trial, he endeavored to develop two grounds of defense. He first attempted to show that he did not shoot Liberty. Petitioner's second defense was that Gable McDonald had shot Officer Liberty. He was only partially successful, however, in his efforts to bring before the jury the testimony supporting this defense. Chambers endeavored to show the jury that McDonald had repeatedly confessed to the crime. In large measure, he was thwarted in his attempt to present this portion of his defense by the strict application of certain Mississippi rules of evidence. Chambers asserts that the application of these evidentiary rules rendered his trial fundamentally unfair and deprived him of due process of law.

II

At trial, after the State failed to put McDonald on the stand, Chambers called McDonald, laid a predicate for the introduction of his sworn out-of-court confession, had it admitted into evidence, and read it to the jury. The State, upon cross-examination, elicited from McDonald the fact that he had repudiated his prior confession. At the conclusion of the State's cross-examination, Chambers renewed his motion to examine McDonald as an adverse witness. The trial court denied the motion.

Defeated in his attempt to challenge directly McDonald's renunciation of his prior confession, Chambers sought to introduce the testimony of the three witnesses to whom McDonald had admitted that he shot the officer. The State objected to the admission of this testimony on the ground that it was hearsay. The trial court sustained the objection.

III

The right of an accused in a criminal trial to due process is, in essence, the right to a fair opportunity to defend against the State's accusations. The rights to confront and cross-examine witnesses and to call witnesses in one's own behalf have long been recognized as essential to due process.

Both of these elements of a fair trial are implicated in the present case.

Chambers was denied an opportunity to subject McDonald's damning repudiation and alibi to cross-examination. He was not allowed to test the witness' recollection, to probe into the details of his alibi, or to "sift" his conscience so that the jury might judge for itself whether McDonald's testimony was worthy of belief.

We need not decide, however, whether this error alone would occasion reversal since Chambers' claimed denial of due process rests on the ultimate impact of that error when viewed in conjunction with the trial court's refusal to permit him to call other witnesses. The trial court refused to allow him to introduce the testimony of [witnesses] who would have testified to the statements purportedly made by McDonald, on three separate occasions shortly after the crime, naming himself as the murderer.

The hearsay rule, which has long been recognized and respected by virtually every State, is based on experience and grounded in the notion that untrustworthy evidence should not be presented to the triers of fact.

The hearsay statements involved in this case were originally made and subsequently offered at trial under circumstances that provided considerable assurance of their reliability. First, each of McDonald's confessions was made spontaneously to a close acquaintance shortly after the murder had occurred. Second, each one was corroborated by some other evidence in the case — McDonald's sworn confession, the testimony of an eyewitness to the shooting, the testimony that McDonald was seen with a gun immediately after the shooting, and proof of his prior ownership of a .22-caliber revolver and subsequent purchase of a new weapon. The sheer number of independent confessions provided additional corroboration for each. Third, whatever may be the parameters of the penal-interest rationale, each confession here was in a very real sense self-incriminatory and unquestionably against interest. McDonald stood to benefit nothing by disclosing his role in the shooting to any of his three friends and he must have been aware of the possibility that disclosure would lead to criminal prosecution. Finally, if there was any question about the truthfulness of the extrajudicial statements, McDonald was present in the courtroom and was under oath. He could have been cross-examined by the State, and his demeanor and responses weighed by the jury.

Few rights are more fundamental than that of an accused to present witnesses in his own defense. Although perhaps no rule of evidence has been more respected or more frequently applied in jury trials than that applicable to the exclusion of hearsay, exceptions tailored to allow the introduction of evidence which in fact is likely to be trustworthy have long existed. The testimony rejected by the trial court here bore persuasive assurances of trustworthiness and thus was well within the basic rationale of the exception for declarations against interest. That testimony also was critical to Chambers' defense. In these circumstances, where constitutional rights directly affecting the ascertainment of guilt are implicated, the hearsay rule may not be applied mechanistically to defeat the ends of justice.

We conclude that the exclusion of this critical evidence, coupled with the State's refusal to permit Chambers to cross-examine McDonald, denied him a trial in accord with traditional and fundamental standards of due process. In reaching this judgment, we establish no new principles of constitutional law.

More than 30 years later, the Supreme Court again focused on a defendant's right to present evidence that a third party was responsible for the charged offense.

HOLMES v. SOUTH CAROLINA

547 U.S. 319 (2006)

Justice ALITO delivered the opinion of the Court.

This case presents the question whether a criminal defendant's federal constitutional rights are violated by an evidence rule under which the defendant may not introduce proof of third-party guilt if the prosecution has introduced forensic evidence that, if believed, strongly supports a guilty verdict.

I

On the morning of December 31, 1989, 86-year-old Mary Stewart was beaten, raped, and robbed in her home. She later died of complications stemming from her injuries. Petitioner was convicted by a South Carolina jury of murder, first-degree criminal sexual conduct, first-degree burglary, and robbery, and he was sentenced to death. Upon state postconviction review, however, petitioner was granted a new trial.

At the second trial, the prosecution relied heavily on the following forensic evidence:

> (1) [Petitioner's] palm print was found just above the door knob on the interior side of the front door of the victim's house; (2) fibers consistent with a black sweatshirt owned by [petitioner] were found on the victim's bed sheets; (3) matching blue fibers were found on the victim's pink nightgown and on [petitioner's] blue jeans; (4) microscopically consistent fibers were found on the pink nightgown and on [petitioner's] underwear; (5) [petitioner's] underwear contained a mixture of DNA from two individuals, and 99.99% of the population other than [petitioner] and the victim were excluded as contributors to that mixture; and (6) [petitioner's] tank top was found to contain a mixture of [petitioner's] blood and the victim's blood.

In addition, the prosecution introduced evidence that petitioner had been seen near Stewart's home within an hour of the time when, according to the prosecution's evidence, the attack took place.

As a major part of his defense, petitioner attempted to undermine the State's forensic evidence by suggesting that it had been contaminated and that certain law enforcement officers had engaged in a plot to frame him. Petitioner's expert witnesses criticized the procedures used by the police in handling the fiber and DNA evidence and in collecting the fingerprint evidence. Another defense expert provided testimony that petitioner cited as supporting his claim that the palm print had been planted by the police.

Petitioner also sought to introduce proof that another man, Jimmy McCaw White, had attacked Stewart. At a pretrial hearing, petitioner proffered several witnesses who placed White in the victim's neighborhood on the morning of the assault, as well as four other witnesses who testified that White had either acknowledged that petitioner was "'innocent'" or had actually admitted to committing the crimes. One witness recounted that when he asked White about the "word . . . on the street" that White was responsible for Stewart's murder, White "put his head down and he raised his head back up and he said, well, you know I like older women." According to this witness, White added that "he did what they say he did" and that he had "no regrets about it at all." Another witness, who had been incarcerated with White, testified that White had admitted to assaulting Stewart, that a police officer had asked the witness to testify falsely against petitioner, and that employees of the prosecutor's office, while soliciting the witness' cooperation, had spoken of manufacturing evidence against petitioner. White testified at the pretrial hearing and denied making the incriminating statements. He also provided an alibi for the time of the crime, but another witness refuted his alibi.

The trial court excluded petitioner's third-party guilt evidence citing [a South Carolina case] which held that such evidence is admissible if it "'raise[s] a reasonable inference or presumption as to [the defendant's] own innocence'" but is not admissible if it merely "'cast[s] a bare suspicion upon another'" or "'raise[s] a conjectural inference as to the commission of the crime by another.'"

II

"[S]tate and federal rulemakers have broad latitude under the Constitution to establish rules excluding evidence from criminal trials." This latitude, however, has limits. "Whether rooted directly in the Due Process Clause of the Fourteenth Amendment or in the Compulsory Process or Confrontation Clauses of the Sixth Amendment, the Constitution guarantees criminal defendants 'a meaningful opportunity to present a complete defense.'" This right is abridged by evidence rules that "infring[e] upon a weighty interest of the accused" and are "'arbitrary' or 'disproportionate to the purposes they are designed to serve.'"

This Court's cases contain several illustrations of "arbitrary" rules, *i.e.,* rules that excluded important defense evidence but that did not serve any legitimate interests. In *Washington v. Texas* (1967), state statutes barred a person who had been charged as a participant in a crime from testifying in defense of another alleged participant unless the witness had been acquitted. As a result, when the defendant in *Washington* was tried for murder, he was precluded from calling as a witness a person who had been charged and previously convicted of committing the same murder.

A similar constitutional violation occurred in *Chambers v. Mississipi* (1973). A murder defendant called as a witness a man named McDonald, who had previously confessed to the murder. When McDonald repudiated the confession on the stand, the defendant was denied permission to examine McDonald as an adverse witness based on the State's "'voucher' rule," which barred parties from impeaching their own witnesses. In addition, because the state hearsay rule did not include an exception for statements against penal interest, the defendant was not permitted to introduce evidence that McDonald had made self-incriminating statements to three other persons.

Another arbitrary rule was held unconstitutional in *Crane v. Kentucky* (1986). There, the defendant was prevented from attempting to show at trial that his confession was unreliable because of the circumstances under which it was obtained.

In *Rock v. Arkansas* (1987), this Court held that a rule prohibiting hypnotically refreshed testimony was unconstitutional because "[w]holesale inadmissibility of a defendant's testimony is an arbitrary restriction on the right to testify in the absence of clear evidence by the State repudiating the validity of all post-hypnosis recollections."

While the Constitution thus prohibits the exclusion of defense evidence under rules that serve no legitimate purpose or that are disproportionate to the ends that they are asserted to promote, well-established rules of evidence permit trial judges to exclude evidence if its probative value is outweighed by certain other factors such as unfair prejudice, confusion of the issues, or potential to mislead the jury.

[The South Carolina Supreme Court had previously] adopted and applied a rule [that] "evidence offered by accused as to the commission of the crime by another person must be limited to such facts as are inconsistent with his own guilt; evidence which can have (no) other effect than to cast a bare suspicion upon another, or to raise a conjectural inference as to the commission of the crime by another, is not admissible." Under this rule, the trial judge does not focus on the probative value or the potential adverse effects of admitting the defense evidence of third-party guilt. Instead, the critical inquiry concerns the strength of the prosecution's case: If the prosecution's case is strong enough, the evidence of third-party guilt is excluded even if that evidence, if viewed independently, would have great probative value and even if it would not pose an undue risk of harassment, prejudice, or confusion of the issues.

Interpreted in this way, the rule applied by the State Supreme Court does not rationally serve the end that [it was] designed to promote, *i.e.,* to focus the trial on the central issues by excluding evidence that has only a very weak logical connection to the central issues.

[B]y evaluating the strength of only one party's evidence, no logical conclusion can be reached regarding the strength of contrary evidence offered by the other side to rebut or cast doubt. Because the rule applied by the State Supreme Court in this case did not heed this point, the rule is "arbitrary" in the sense that it does not rationally serve the end that the evidentiary rule and other similar third-party guilt rules were designed to further. It follows that the rule applied in this case by the State Supreme Court violates a criminal defendant's right to have "'a meaningful opportunity to present a complete defense.'"

Just as a defendant's right of fair trial may be violated by unfair limitations on a defendant's opportunity to present a defense, the prosecution may also violate a defendant's right to a fair trial by misconduct in its presentation. Specifically, the Court has held that prosecutors must not go beyond the bounds of zealous advocacy and make closing arguments that appeal merely to jurors' passions and not the evidence in the case. As Justice Sutherland stated in Berger v. United States (1935), prosecutors "may strike hard blows, [but they are] not at liberty to strike foul ones."

Notwithstanding this rule, the Court will not automatically reverse a conviction merely because a prosecutor uses improper language at trial. The question is whether those comments, in context and with curative actions taken by the court, deprived the defendant of a fair trial.

F. ROLE OF THE JURY AND PROOF BEYOND A REASONABLE DOUBT

The last issue to be addressed in this chapter is the role of the jury. In a criminal case, the primary role of the jury is to decide whether the government has proved every element of each crime charged beyond a reasonable doubt. This requirement is inherent in the defendant's rights to a jury trial and due process.

IN RE WINSHIP
397 U.S. 358 (1970)

Justice BRENNAN delivered the opinion of the Court.

This case presents the single, narrow question whether proof beyond a reasonable doubt is among the "essentials of due process and fair treatment" required during the adjudicatory stage when a juvenile is charged with an act which would constitute a crime if committed by an adult.

[Samuel Winship, a 12-year-old boy, was charged with stealing $112 from a woman's pocketbook. Had he been charged as an adult, the prosecution would have had to prove his guilt beyond a reasonable doubt. In the juvenile proceedings, however, the judge relied on a New York law that allowed Winship to be found to be a delinquent based on "a preponderance of the evidence."]

The requirement that guilt of a criminal charge be established by proof beyond a reasonable doubt dates at least from our early years as a Nation. The "demand for a higher degree of persuasion in criminal cases was recurrently expressed from ancient times, [though] its crystallization into the formula 'beyond a reasonable doubt' seems to have occurred as late as

1798. It is now accepted in common law jurisdictions as the measure of persuasion by which the prosecution must convince the trier of all the essential elements of guilt."

Expressions in many opinions of this Court indicate that it has long been assumed that proof of a criminal charge beyond a reasonable doubt is constitutionally required. Mr. Justice Frankfurter stated that "it is the duty of the Government to establish . . . guilt beyond a reasonable doubt. This notion — basic in our law and rightly one of the boasts of a free society — is a requirement and a safeguard of due process of law in the historic, procedural content of 'due process.'"

The reasonable-doubt standard plays a vital role in the American scheme of criminal procedure. It is a prime instrument for reducing the risk of convictions resting on factual error. The standard provides concrete substance for the presumption of innocence — that bedrock "axiomatic and elementary" principle whose "enforcement lies at the foundation of the administration of our criminal law."

The requirement of proof beyond a reasonable doubt has this vital role in our criminal procedure for cogent reasons. The accused during a criminal prosecution has at stake interests of immense importance, both because of the possibility that he may lose his liberty upon conviction and because of the certainty that he would be stigmatized by the conviction. Accordingly, a society that values the good name and freedom of every individual should not condemn a man for commission of a crime when there is reasonable doubt about his guilt. As we [have previously] said: "There is always in litigation a margin of error, representing error in factfinding, which both parties must take into account. Where one party has at stake an interest of transcending value — as a criminal defendant his liberty — this margin of error is reduced as to him by the process of placing on the other party the burden of . . . persuading the factfinder at the conclusion of the trial of his guilt beyond a reasonable doubt. Due process commands that no man shall lose his liberty unless the Government has borne the burden of . . . convincing the factfinder of his guilt." To this end, the reasonable-doubt standard is indispensable, for it "impresses on the trier of fact the necessity of reaching a subjective state of certitude of the facts in issue."

Moreover, use of the reasonable-doubt standard is indispensable to command the respect and confidence of the community in applications of the criminal law. It is critical that the moral force of the criminal law not be diluted by a standard of proof that leaves people in doubt whether innocent men are being condemned. It is also important in our free society that every individual going about his ordinary affairs have confidence that his government cannot adjudge him guilty of a criminal offense without convincing a proper factfinder of his guilt with utmost certainty.

Lest there remain any doubt about the constitutional stature of the reasonable-doubt standard, we explicitly hold that the Due Process Clause protects the accused against conviction except upon proof beyond a reasonable doubt of every fact necessary to constitute the crime with which he is charged.

II

We turn to the question whether juveniles, like adults, are constitutionally entitled to proof beyond a reasonable doubt when they are charged with violation of a criminal law. The same considerations that demand extreme caution in factfinding to protect the innocent adult apply as well to the innocent child.

Justice HARLAN, concurring.

No one, I daresay, would contend that state juvenile court trials are subject to no federal constitutional limitations. Differences have existed, however, among the members of this Court as to what constitutional protections do apply.

The present case draws in question the validity of a New York statute that permits a determination of juvenile delinquency, founded on a charge of criminal conduct, to be made on a standard of proof that is less rigorous than that which would obtain had the accused been tried for the same conduct in an ordinary criminal case. While I am in full agreement that this statutory provision offends the requirement of fundamental fairness embodied in the Due Process Clause of the Fourteenth Amendment, I am constrained to add something.

The standard of proof influences the relative frequency of these two types of erroneous outcomes. If, for example, the standard of proof for a criminal trial were a preponderance of the evidence rather than proof beyond a reasonable doubt, there would be a smaller risk of factual errors that result in freeing guilty persons, but a far greater risk of factual errors that result in convicting the innocent. Because the standard of proof affects the comparative frequency of these two types of erroneous outcomes, the choice of the standard to be applied in a particular kind of litigation should, in a rational world, reflect an assessment of the comparative social disutility of each.

When one makes such an assessment, the reason for different standards of proof in civil as opposed to criminal litigation becomes apparent. In a civil suit between two private parties for money damages, for example, we view it as no more serious in general for there to be an erroneous verdict in the defendant's favor than for there to be an erroneous verdict in the plaintiff's favor. A preponderance of the evidence standard therefore seems peculiarly appropriate for, as explained most sensibly, it simply requires the trier of fact "to believe that the existence of a fact is more probable than its nonexistence before [he] may find in favor of the party who has the burden to persuade the [judge] of the fact's existence."

In a criminal case, on the other hand, we do not view the social disutility of convicting an innocent man as equivalent to the disutility of acquitting someone who is guilty.

In this context, I view the requirement of proof beyond a reasonable doubt in a criminal case as bottomed on a fundamental value determination of our society that it is far worse to convict an innocent man than to let a guilty man go free.

Because of the requirement that each element of a crime be proved beyond a reasonable doubt,[27] it is improper for a court to instruct jurors that they must presume certain facts based on evidence they have received at trial. For example, in Sandstrom v. Montana, 442 U.S. 510, 517 (1979), the Court struck down an instruction that told jurors to presume that a person who commits an act intends the consequences of that act.[28] *See also* Leary v. United States, 395 U.S. 6, 52-53 (1969) (holding that it is improper to instruct jurors that they should presume from a defendant's possession of narcotics that the defendant knew they were illegally imported). Courts may, however, give jurors instructions that allow the jurors to make permissible presumptions, but that do not require them to do so.

Shifting the burden to the defense to prove affirmative defenses also does not violate the defendant's right of due process. For example, in Patterson v. New York, 432 U.S. 197 (1977), the Court upheld a New York law that shifted the burden to the defense to prove extreme emotional disturbance by a preponderance of the evidence once the prosecution had proved an intentional homicide. If the defense could make such a showing, a murder charge could be reduced to a manslaughter conviction. *Compare* Mullaney v. Wilbur, 421 U.S. 684 (1975) (Maine law placed burden on prosecution to prove absence of heat of passion or sudden provocation, and burden could not be shifted to the defendant).

Once the jury finds a defendant guilty beyond a reasonable doubt, reviewing courts will not second guess that decision as long as the jury verdict was based on sufficient evidence. In Virginia v. Jackson, 443 U.S. 307 (1979), the Supreme Court held that the presumption of innocence applies at the trial stage but not upon review.

> The relevant question [on review] is whether, after viewing the evidence in the light most favorable to the prosecution, any rational trier of fact could have found the essential elements of the crime beyond a reasonable doubt. This familiar standard gives full play to the responsibility of the trier of fact fairly to resolve conflicts in the testimony, to weigh the evidence, and to draw reasonable inferences from basic facts to ultimate facts. Once a defendant has been found guilty of the crime charged, the factfinder's role as weigher of the evidence is preserved

---

27. The Supreme Court has never defined "beyond a reasonable doubt," other than to state that it does not require that there be a "grave uncertainty," or that the jurors have a "moral certainty" of the defendant's guilt. *See* Cage v. Louisiana, 498 U.S. 39 (1990).

28. In *Sandstrom*, the Court invalidated a jury instruction that provided, "The acts of a person of sound mind and discretion are presumed to be the product of the person's will, but the presumption may be rebutted. A person of sound mind and discretion is presumed to intend the natural and probable consequences of his acts but his presumption may be rebutted."

through a legal conclusion that upon judicial review all of the evidence is to be considered in the light most favorable to the prosecution. The criterion thus impinges upon "jury" discretion only to the extent necessary to guarantee the fundamental protection of due process of law.

Jackson, supra at 319.

In Apprendi v. New Jersey, 530 U.S. 466 (2000), the Court addressed whether a fact that is used as a sentencing enhancement must also be proved to the jury beyond a reasonable doubt, or whether the judge can make the finding based on a lower standard at the time of sentencing. As discussed in greater detail in Chapter 13, the Court started a revolution in sentencing with its decision. *Apprendi* requires that the jury find beyond a reasonable doubt not only those facts that prove the defendant's guilt but also those facts that would enhance the defendant's sentence beyond the ordinary statutory maximum.

CHAPTER
13

SENTENCING

A. INTRODUCTION

For most defendants, sentencing is the most important part of the criminal justice process. Whether the defendant has pled guilty or the case has gone to trial, sentencing will determine the defendant's fate. Likewise, sentencing is a crucial stage for the victim, because the sentence imposed will reflect society's assessment of the amount of punishment the defendant deserves.

Sentencing serves multiple objectives. It is designed to punish the defendant for his actions, deter the defendant and others from committing future offenses, protect society from the defendant, and change the defendant's behavior. These sentencing goals are reflected in the traditional purposes of punishment: retribution, deterrence, incapacitation, and rehabilitation. But there is no magic formula that courts can use to determine whether a sentence type and length will accomplish these sentencing goals. Indeed, other factors may influence the sentence imposed in a particular case, such as the prosecution's need to secure cooperation from the defendant to prosecute codefendants.

The standard feature of sentencing schemes is the court's power to sentence defendants to particular periods of incarceration. For short sentences, a defendant may be incarcerated in local jail facilities. For longer sentences, a defendant will ordinarily serve time in a state or federal prison facility. When a defendant is released from incarceration, he may remain under the supervision of corrections officials. In states that have parole boards, a defendant may be released prior to serving the full term of incarceration and will subsequently be supervised by a parole officer for a period of time. If a defendant violates a condition of *parole*, he may be forced to return to prison. There is no parole board under the federal sentencing system. Thus, federal defendants are subject to *supervised release* after being released from prison. Like parole, supervised release ordinarily places restrictions on a defendant's activities. If the defendant violates these restrictions, he will be returned to custody.[1]

For less serious crimes, a defendant may be placed on probation in lieu of a term, or after a short period, of custody. Probation typically carries with it restrictions on the defendant's behavior. It can even carry a condition such as house arrest. If the defendant violates probation, the court may order him to serve a longer period of time in custody. Under creative sentencing schemes, judges may use probationary sentences to reform the defendant's behavior by imposing unusual conditions. For example, a court may require a defendant to visit a victim's grave or write an apology letter to the victim's family. Most courts, however, limit probation conditions to work, education, and rehabilitation requirements imposed on the defendant. Conditions that unduly impede a defendant's exercise of his First Amendment rights, such as prohibitions on the sale of a defendant's book regarding his crime, are unconstitutional.[2]

The central feature of sentencing is the court's power to incarcerate a defendant. Over the years, courts have employed various types of sentencing schemes. The two primary sentencing schemes are indeterminate sentencing and determinate sentencing. As discussed in section B, indeterminate sentencing typically affords broad discretion to judges in imposing sentences. Determinate sentencing schemes tend to limit court discretion by setting guidelines and mandatory sentences that courts must follow. In Apprendi v. New Jersey, 530 U.S. 466 (2000), the Supreme Court made dramatic changes to the manner in which determinate sentencing schemes may be implemented by state and federal judges. Accordingly, section B also addresses the "*Apprendi* revolution" and its impact on sentencing procedures.

Section C addresses the Eighth Amendment limits on sentencing. This section focuses on the Supreme Court's approach to determining when a sentence constitutes "cruel and unusual punishment." It also examines when fines imposed as part of a sentence are considered "excessive fines" under the Eighth Amendment.

Finally, there are special rules for cases that involve the ultimate sanction — the death penalty. Section D discusses death penalty cases and

---

1. In determining whether a defendant has violated probation or parole, the court must comply with due process standards and allow the defendant to challenge the alleged grounds of violation. *See* Morrissey v. Brewer, 408 U.S. 471 (1972).

2. *See* Simon & Schuster, Inc. v. Members of New York State Crime Victims Board, 502 U.S. 105 (1991) (invalidating New York's "Son of Sam" law because it was a content-based statute that prohibited defendants from engaging in particular types of expression). Although some states require that defendants pay restitution to victims, states cannot prohibit defendants from authoring works regarding their crimes.

the procedures used to determine whether capital punishment should be imposed. It also addresses the constitutionality of different methods of executing defendants, including lethal injection.

Sentencing is the responsibility of the court, but each jurisdiction has procedures to ensure that both sides have an opportunity to address the court before sentencing. Likewise, the court may receive input from probation officers, victims, and members of the public. In the end, it is the responsibility of the court to balance the interests of all parties and to impose a fair and just sentence. This goal must be accomplished within the realities of today's world — a world where prisons are already overcrowded and limited resources are available to incarcerate additional defendants.[3] Thus, like many aspects of the criminal justice system, sentencing is imperfect and constantly changing.

B. INDETERMINATE VERSUS DETERMINATE SENTENCING

The two primary models of sentencing are indeterminate and determinate sentencing, but each model may be implemented slightly differently depending on the jurisdiction.

1. Indeterminate Sentencing

In indeterminate sentencing schemes, judges typically have broad discretion in imposing sentences. The sentencing judge will impose a sentence anywhere from probation to the maximum authorized sentence. If a defendant is sentenced to incarceration, a parole board later determines when the defendant will be released. Prior to 1987 and the adoption of the Federal Sentencing Guidelines, federal courts used an indeterminate sentencing scheme. Federal judges could impose a sentence anywhere between probation to the maximum statutory sentence for a crime. As a result, indeterminate sentencing led to large disparities in sentencing. One judge

---

3. Currently, approximately 1.53 million Americans are in state or federal prison, and nearly every jurisdiction suffers from a shortage of incarceration facilities. *See* U.S. Department of Justice, Office of Justice Programs, Bureau of Justice Statistics (December 2016).

See also Bureau of Justice Statistics, *Prisoners in 2011*, December 2012, http://bjs.gov/index.cfm?ty=pbdetail&iid=4559; U.S. Department of Justice, Office of Justice Programs, Bureau of Justice Statistics Bulletin: Prisoners in 2005, at 7-8 & tables 8-9 (stating that, collectively, state prisons operated at 99 percent of their highest capacity measures since 2005).

would issue a sentence of probation for an offense while another judge might impose the maximum sentence for the same offense.

Indeterminate sentencing can give great discretion to the court to fashion a sentence. Its advantages are that it allows the judge and parole supervising authority to tailor a sentence for a particular defendant. The downsides include disparities in sentencing and less control over judges who might be too lenient or too tough in the eyes of others.

Since 1984, the trend has been away from indeterminate sentencing. Following Congress's lead in its adoption of sentencing guidelines for federal courts, state courts around the nation have moved toward determinate sentencing schemes.[4]

2. Determinate Sentencing

Determinate sentencing eliminates the role of a parole board. The sentence imposed by the court is the sentence the defendant will serve, absent time credited for a defendant's good behavior in prison. Sentences are set by the legislature and depend to a great extent on the charge brought by the prosecution. As such, determinate sentencing tends to limit judicial discretion in sentencing.

Historically, determinate sentencing has often been adopted as a way to rectify perceived disparities in sentencing. For example, the Sentencing Reform Act of 1984 established the U.S. Sentencing Commission to create a set of guidelines to limit judges' discretion in sentencing. Calculating sentences under the Federal Sentencing Guidelines is a multistep process. The court must determine the base offense level for a particular defendant's crime, consider aggravating and mitigating factors that will affect the offense level, consider the impact of multiple offenses, and examine any other relevant characteristics, such as the defendant's role in the crime and the impact on victims. Then, the court must calculate the defendant's criminal history level. Ultimately, the court will determine the indices that it will apply to the sentencing grid. The point at which these indices meet indicates the range, in months, within which the judge's sentence must fall, unless the judge engages in other findings supporting a departure from the Sentencing Guidelines.

4. *See* Blakely v. Washington, 542 U.S. 296, 323 (2004).

United StatesSentencing Guidelines Sentencing Table (Effective November 1, 2010)
(in months of imprisonment)

	Criminal History Category (Criminal History Points)					
Offense Level	I (0 or 1)	II (2 or 3)	III (4, 5, 6)	IV (7, 8, 9)	V (10, 11, 12)	VI (13 or more)
1	0-6	0-6	0-6	0-6	0-6	0-6
2	0-6	0-6	0-6	0-6	0-6	1-7
3	0-6	0-6	0-6	0-6	2-8	3-9
4	0-6	0-6	0-6	2-8	4-10	6-12
5	0-6	0-6	1-7	4-10	6-12	9-15
6	0-6	1-7	2-8	6-12	9-15	12-18
7	0-6	2-8	4-10	8-14	12-18	15-21
8	0-6	4-10	6-12	10-16	15-21	18-24
9	4-10	6-12	8-14	12-18	18-24	21-27
10	6-12	8-14	10-16	15-21	21-27	24-30
11	8-14	10-16	12-18	18-24	24-30	27-33
12	10-16	12-18	15-21	21-27	27-33	30-37
13	12-18	15-21	18-24	24-30	30-37	33-41
14	15-21	18-24	21-27	27-33	33-41	37-46
15	18-24	21-27	24-30	30-37	37-46	41-51
16	21-27	24-30	27-33	33-41	41-51	46-57
17	24-30	27-33	30-37	37-46	46-57	51-63
18	27-33	30-37	33-41	41-51	51-63	57-71
19	30-37	33-41	37-46	46-57	57-71	63-78
20	33-41	37-46	41-51	51-63	63-78	70-87
21	37-46	41-51	46-57	57-71	70-87	77-96
22	41-51	46-57	51-63	63-78	77-96	84-105
23	46-57	51-63	57-71	70-87	84-105	92-115
24	51-63	57-71	63-78	77-96	92-115	100-125
25	57-71	63-78	70-87	84-105	100-125	110-137
26	63-78	70-87	78-97	92-115	110-137	120-150
27	70-87	78-97	87-108	100-125	120-150	130-162
28	78-97	87-108	97-121	110-137	130-162	140-175
29	87-108	97-121	108-135	121-151	140-175	151-188
30	97-121	108-135	121-151	135-168	151-188	168-210
31	108-135	121-151	135-168	151-188	168-210	188-235
32	121-151	135-168	151-188	168-210	188-235	210-262
33	135-168	151-188	168-210	188-235	210-262	235-293
34	151-188	168-210	188-235	210-262	235-293	262-327
35	168-210	188-235	210-262	235-293	262-327	292-365
36	188-235	210-262	235-293	262-327	292-365	324-405
37	210-262	235-293	262-327	292-365	324-405	360-life
38	235-293	262-327	292-365	324-405	360-life	360-life
39	262-327	292-365	324-405	360-life	360-life	360-life
40	292-365	324-405	360-life	360-life	360-life	360-life
41	324-405	360-life	360-life	360-life	360-life	360-life
42	360-life	360-life	360-life	360-life	360-life	360-life
43	life	life	life	life	life	life

Zones: Zone A (levels 1-8), Zone B (levels 9-11), Zone C (levels 11-13), Zone D (levels 13-43)

Application Notes

The Offense Level (1-43) forms the vertical axis of the Sentencing Table. The Criminal History Category (I-VI) forms the horizontal axis of the Table. The intersection of the Offense Level and Criminal History Category displays the Guideline Range in months of imprisonment. "Life" means life imprisonment.

Determining the Sentence

To use the above grid, a judge must first determine the base term for a particular crime. For example, the crime of bank robbery has a base offense level of 30. The court must then examine the specific offense characteristics of defendant's crime. If, for example, a person was injured during the robbery, the offense level is increased by at least 2 levels. The defendant now faces an offense level of 32. If the loss was more than $10,000, but less than $50,000, another level is added to the offense, placing defendant's crime now at a level of 33.

Next, it is time to look at the defendant's role in the offense. If the defendant was the leader of the robbery gang, another 4 levels are added, putting the total level now at a 37. If the defendant then tries to obstruct justice by intimidating potential witnesses, another 2 levels would be added, making the new total 39. In the end, the defendant may end up with an adjusted offense level. Assuming there are not multiple counts which need to be considered, the defendant's total adjusted offense level is 39.

After the court decides on the adjusted offense level, it must examine the defendant's criminal history to determine defendant's horizontal matrix for the sentencing chart. If, for example, the defendant has at least one adult prior felony conviction in the past ten years, the defendant may be at a Level II for criminal history.

Assuming there are no other adjustments for defendant accepting responsibility for his acts, or reasons to depart from the guidelines for reasons not considered by the Sentencing Commission or assistance to the government, defendant's sentence will be listed at the intersection of an offense level of 39 and a Criminal History of Level II. As shown on the chart, defendant would face 292-365 months in prison.

Supporters of determinate sentencing argue that it provides more consistency and predictability in sentencing. Opponents, however, reject the formulaic and rigid approach of determinate sentencing, arguing that it does a poor job of actually assessing how deserving of punishment a defendant is.

From 1987 to 2005, the federal courts were required to impose sentences under the Federal Sentencing Guidelines. Many states also had sentencing protocols that limited courts' power to impose a sentence based on certain findings that were made at sentencing. For example, in California, sentencing laws provided for a presumptive mid-term sentence, but the sentencing court could impose a higher sentence if it found facts that constituted aggravating factors in the case. Likewise, the sentencing court could pick a lower term if it made the appropriate findings. Other states followed schemes that prescribed statutory maximum sentences for certain crimes that courts were required to follow, unless they found certain enhancements that would allow them to impose a higher sentence.

3.   *Mandatory Minimum Sentences*

Mandatory minimum sentences are another way in which legislatures restrict judges' discretion at sentencing. Supporters argue that mandatory minimums are necessary to reflect the gravity of a crime and to ensure that defendants who have committed certain types of crimes receive similar sentences.

Mandatory minimum sentences can apply to a variety of crimes. For example, federal law dictates mandatory minimum sentences for defendants who possess certain amounts of narcotics (21 U.S.C. §841), use a firearm during the commission of a crime (18 U.S.C. §924(c)), or distribute child pornography (18 U.S.C. §2252(b)(1)). Legislatures may also impose mandatory minimum sentences for recidivists. For example, under three strikes laws, a defendant convicted of a third qualifying offense may face a mandatory minimum sentence of 15 years of incarceration for an offense that might otherwise qualify for a minimal prison term.

Mandatory minimum sentences are controversial because, as Supreme Court Justice Stephen Breyer stated, "Statutory minimums generally deny the judge the legal power to depart downward, no matter how unusual the special circumstances that call for leniency. . . . [These statutes] tend to transfer sentencing power to prosecutors, who can determine sentences through the charges they decide to bring." Harris v. United States, 536 U.S. 545 (2002) (Breyer, J., concurring). The use of mandatory minimum sentences for drug offenses has had a particularly disproportionate impact on racial minorities.[5]

Concerned about the impact of mandatory minimum sentences, the Supreme Court is requiring that the key aspects of crimes triggering mandatory minimum sentences be treated as elements of the crime and not just sentencing factors determined by the sentencing court. *See* United States v. O'Brien, 560 U.S. 218 (2010). Additionally, the Sixth Amendment right to trial by jury requires a jury to determine facts that increase a mandatory minimum sentence. Alleyne v. United States, 133 S. Ct. 2151 (2013).

4. Apprendi *and Its Progeny*

In 2000, the Supreme Court examined the constitutionality of sentencing schemes that require sentencing judges to increase a defendant's sentence based on facts never pleaded or proved to a jury but rather found by the court. In Apprendi v. New Jersey, the Court held that such sentencing schemes violate defendants' right to due process.

APPRENDI v. NEW JERSEY
530 U.S. 466 (2000)

Justice STEVENS delivered the opinion of the Court.

[A] New Jersey statute classifies the possession of a firearm for an unlawful purpose as a "second-degree" offense. Such an offense is punishable by imprisonment for "between five years and 10 years." A separate statute, described by that State's Supreme Court as a "hate crime" law, provides for an "extended term" of imprisonment if the trial judge finds, by a preponderance of the evidence, that "the defendant in committing the crime acted with a purpose to intimidate an individual or group of individuals because of race, color, gender, handicap, religion, sexual orientation or ethnicity." The extended term authorized by the hate

---

5. U.S. Sentencing Commission's Report to Congress: Mandatory Minimum Penalties in the Federal Criminal Justice System (2011).

crime law for second-degree offenses is imprisonment for "between 10 and 20 years."

The question presented is whether the Due Process Clause of the Fourteenth Amendment requires that a factual determination authorizing an increase in the maximum prison sentence for an offense from 10 to 20 years be made by a jury on the basis of proof beyond a reasonable doubt.

I

At 2:04 A.M. on December 22, 1994, petitioner Charles C. Apprendi, Jr., fired several .22-caliber bullets into the home of an African-American family that had recently moved into a previously all-white neighborhood in Vineland, New Jersey. Apprendi was promptly arrested and, at 3:05 A.M., admitted that he was the shooter. After further questioning, at 6:04 A.M., he made a statement — which he later retracted — that even though he did not know the occupants of the house personally, "because they are black in color he does not want them in the neighborhood."

A New Jersey grand jury returned a 23-count indictment charging Apprendi with four first-degree, eight second-degree, six third-degree, and five fourth-degree offenses. The charges alleged shootings on four different dates, as well as the unlawful possession of various weapons. None of the counts referred to the hate crime statute, and none alleged that Apprendi acted with a racially biased purpose.

The parties entered into a plea agreement, pursuant to which Apprendi pleaded guilty to two counts (3 and 18) of second-degree possession of a firearm for an unlawful purpose, and one count (22) of the third-degree offense of unlawful possession of an antipersonnel bomb; the prosecutor dismissed the other 20 counts. Under state law, a second-degree offense carries a penalty range of 5 to 10 years, a third-degree offense carries a penalty range of between 3 and 5 years. As part of the plea agreement, however, the State reserved the right to request the court to impose a higher "enhanced" sentence on count 18 (which was based on the December 22 shooting) on the ground that that offense was committed with a biased purpose. Apprendi, correspondingly, reserved the right to challenge the hate crime sentence enhancement on the ground that it violates the United States Constitution.

After the trial judge accepted the three guilty pleas, the prosecutor filed a formal motion for an extended term. The trial judge thereafter held an evidentiary hearing on the issue of Apprendi's "purpose" for the shooting on December 22. Apprendi adduced evidence from a psychologist and from seven character witnesses who testified that he did not have a reputation for racial bias. He also took the stand himself, explaining that the incident was an unintended consequence of overindulgence in alcohol, denying that he was in any way biased against African-Americans, and denying that his statement to the police had been accurately described. The judge, however, found the police officer's testimony credible, and concluded that the evidence supported a finding "that the crime was motivated by racial bias." Having found "by a preponderance of the evidence" that Apprendi's actions were taken "with a purpose to intimidate" as provided by the statute, the trial judge held that the hate crime enhancement applied. Rejecting Apprendi's constitutional challenge to the statute, the judge sentenced him to a 12-year term of imprisonment on count 18, and to shorter concurrent sentences on the other two counts.

Apprendi appealed, arguing . . . that the Due Process Clause of the United States Constitution requires that the finding of bias upon which his hate crime sentence was based must be proved to a jury beyond a reasonable doubt, In re Winship (1970).

II

At stake in this case are constitutional protections of surpassing importance: the proscription of any deprivation of liberty without "due process of law," and the guarantee that "in all criminal prosecutions, the accused shall enjoy the right to a speedy and public trial, by an impartial jury." Taken together, these rights indisputably entitle a criminal defendant to "a jury determination that [he] is guilty of every element of the crime with which he is charged, beyond a reasonable doubt."

Any possible distinction between an "element" of a felony offense and a "sentencing factor" was unknown to the practice of criminal indictment, trial by jury, and judgment by court as it existed during the years surrounding our Nation's founding. As a general rule, criminal proceedings were submitted to a jury after being initiated by an indictment containing "all the facts and circumstances which constitute the offence, . . . stated with such certainty and precision, that the defendant . . . may be enabled to determine the species of offence they constitute, in order that he may prepare his defence accordingly . . . and that there may be no doubt as to the judgment which should be given, if the defendant be convicted."

The historic link between verdict and judgment and the consistent limitation on judges' discretion to operate within the limits of the legal penalties provided highlight the novelty of a legislative scheme that removes the jury from the determination of a fact that, if found, exposes the criminal defendant to a penalty exceeding the maximum he would receive if punished according to the facts reflected in the jury verdict alone.

IV

It was in McMillan v. Pennsylvania (1986), that this Court, for the first time, coined the term "sentencing factor" to refer to a fact that was not found by a jury but that could affect the sentence imposed by the judge. That case involved a challenge to the State's Mandatory Minimum Sentencing Act. According to its provisions, anyone convicted of certain felonies would be subject to a mandatory minimum penalty of five years imprisonment if the judge found, by a preponderance of the evidence, that the person "visibly possessed a firearm" in the course of committing one of the specified felonies. Articulating for the first time, and then applying, a multifactor set of criteria for determining whether the *Winship* protections applied to bar such a system, we concluded that the Pennsylvania statute did not run afoul of our previous admonitions against relieving the State of its burden of proving guilt, or tailoring the mere form of a criminal statute solely to avoid *Winship*'s strictures.

We did not, however, there budge from the position that (1) constitutional limits exist to States' authority to define away facts necessary to constitute a criminal offense, and (2) that a state scheme that keeps from the jury facts that "expose [defendants] to greater or additional punishment," may raise serious constitutional concern.

Finally, . . . Almendarez-Torres v. United States (1998), represents at best an exceptional departure from the historic practice that we have described. In that case, . . . we concluded that sentencing him to a term higher than that attached to the offense alleged in the indictment did not violate the strictures of *Winship* . . . [b]ecause Almendarez-Torres had admitted the three earlier convictions for aggravated felonies.

Even though it is arguable that *Almendarez-Torres* was incorrectly decided, Apprendi does not contest the decision's validity and we need not revisit it for purposes of our decision today to treat the case as a narrow exception to the general rule we recalled at the outset. Given its unique facts, it surely does not warrant rejection of the otherwise uniform course of decision during the entire history of our jurisprudence.

In sum, our reexamination of our cases in this area, and of the history upon which they rely, confirms the opinion that we expressed in *Jones.* Other than the fact of a prior conviction, any fact that increases the penalty for a crime beyond the prescribed statutory maximum must be submitted to a jury, and proved beyond a reasonable doubt.

V

The New Jersey statutory scheme that Apprendi asks us to invalidate allows a jury to convict a defendant of a second-degree offense based on its finding beyond a reasonable doubt that he unlawfully possessed a prohibited weapon; after a subsequent and separate proceeding, it then allows a judge to impose punishment identical to that New Jersey provides for crimes of the first degree based upon the judge's finding, by a preponderance of the evidence, that the defendant's "purpose" for unlawfully possessing the weapon was "to intimidate" his victim on the basis of a particular characteristic the victim possessed. In light of the constitutional rule explained above, and all of the cases supporting it, this practice cannot stand.

New Jersey's reliance on *Almendarez-Torres* is . . . unavailing. The reasons supporting an exception from the general rule for the statute construed in that case do not apply to the New Jersey statute. Whereas recidivism [which was the issue in *Almendarez-Torres*] "does not relate to the commission of the offense" itself, New Jersey's biased purpose inquiry goes precisely to what happened in the "commission of the offense." Moreover, there is a vast difference between accepting the validity of a prior judgment of conviction entered in a proceeding in which the defendant had the right to a jury trial and the right to require the prosecutor to prove guilt beyond a reasonable doubt, and allowing the judge to find the required fact under a lesser standard of proof.

The New Jersey procedure challenged in this case is an unacceptable departure from the jury tradition that is an indispensable part of our criminal justice system. Accordingly, the judgment of the Supreme Court of New Jersey is reversed, and the case is remanded for further proceedings not inconsistent with this opinion.

Justice SCALIA, concurring.

I feel the need to say a few words in response to Justice Breyer's dissent. It sketches an admirably fair and efficient scheme of criminal justice designed for a society that is prepared to leave criminal justice to the State. The founders of the American Republic were not prepared to leave it to the State, which is why the jury-trial guarantee was one of the least controversial provisions of the Bill of Rights. It has never been efficient; but it has always been free.

What ultimately demolishes the case for the dissenters is that they are unable to say what the right to trial by jury does guarantee if, as they assert, it does not guarantee — what it has been assumed to guarantee throughout our history — the right to have a jury determine those facts that determine the maximum sentence the law allows. They provide no coherent alternative.

Justice THOMAS, with whom Justice SCALIA joins as to Parts I and II, concurring.

I write separately to explain my view that the Constitution requires a broader rule than the Court adopts.

This case turns on the seemingly simple question of what constitutes a "crime" . . . that is, which facts are the "elements" or "ingredients" of a crime.

Sentencing enhancements may be new creatures, but the question that they create for courts is not. Courts have long had to consider which facts are elements in order to determine the sufficiency of an accusation (usually an indictment). The answer that courts have provided regarding the accusation tells us what an element is, and it is then a simple matter to apply that answer to whatever constitutional right may be at issue in a case — here, *Winship* and the right to trial by jury. A long line of essentially uniform authority addressing accusations, and stretching from the earliest reported cases after the founding until well into the 20th century, establishes that the original understanding of which facts are elements was even broader than the rule that the Court adopts today.

This authority establishes that a "crime" includes every fact that is by law a basis for imposing or increasing punishment (in contrast with a fact that mitigates punishment). Thus, if the legislature defines some core crime and then provides for increasing the punishment of that crime upon a finding of some aggravating fact—of whatever sort, including the fact of a prior conviction—the core crime and the aggravating fact together constitute an aggravated crime, just as much as grand larceny is an aggravated form of petit larceny. The aggravating fact is an element of the aggravated crime. Similarly, if the legislature, rather than creating grades of crimes, has provided for setting the punishment of a crime based on some fact— such as a fine that is proportional to the value of stolen goods—that fact is also an element.

Justice O'CONNOR, with whom Chief Justice REHNQUIST, Justice KENNEDY, and Justice BREYER join, dissenting.

Our Court has long recognized that not every fact that bears on a defendant's punishment need be charged in an indictment, submitted to a jury, and proved by the government beyond a reasonable doubt. Rather, we have held that the "legislature's definition of the elements of the offense is usually dispositive." Although we have recognized that "there are obviously constitutional limits beyond which the States may not go in this regard," and that "in certain limited circumstances *Winship*'s reasonable-doubt requirement applies to facts not formally identified as elements of the offense charged," *McMillan*, we have proceeded with caution before deciding that a certain fact must be treated as an offense element despite the legislature's choice not to characterize it as such.

In one bold stroke the Court today casts aside our traditional cautious approach and instead embraces a universal and seemingly bright-line rule limiting the power of Congress and state legislatures to define criminal offenses and the sentences that follow from convictions thereunder. The Court states: "Other than the fact of a prior conviction, any fact that increases the penalty for a crime beyond the prescribed statutory maximum must be submitted to a jury, and proved beyond a reasonable doubt."

Because I do not believe that the Court's "increase in the maximum penalty" rule is required by the Constitution, I would evaluate New Jersey's sentence-enhancement statute, by analyzing the factors we have examined in past cases. *See, e.g., Almendarez-Torres; McMillan*. First, the New Jersey statute does not shift the burden of proof on an essential ingredient of the offense by presuming that ingredient upon proof of other elements of the offense. Second, the magnitude of the New Jersey sentence enhancement, as applied in petitioner's case, is constitutionally permissible. Under New Jersey law, the weapons possession offense to which petitioner pleaded guilty carries a sentence range of 5 to 10 years' imprisonment. The fact that petitioner, in committing that offense, acted with a purpose to intimidate because of race exposed him to a higher sentence range of 10 to 20 years' imprisonment. The 10-year increase in the maximum penalty to which petitioner was exposed falls well within the range we have found permissible. *See Almendarez-Torres* (approving 18-year enhancement). Third, the New Jersey statute gives no impression of having been enacted to evade the constitutional requirements that attach when a State makes a fact an element of the charged offense. For example, New Jersey did not take what had previously been an element of the weapons possession offense and transform it into a sentencing factor. *See McMillan.*

In sum, New Jersey "simply took one factor that has always been considered by sentencing courts to bear on punishment" — a defendant's motive for committing the criminal offense — "and dictated the precise weight to be given that factor" when the motive is to intimidate a person because of race.

On the basis of our prior precedent, then, I would hold that the New Jersey sentence-enhancement statute is constitutional, and affirm the judgment of the Supreme Court of New Jersey.

Justice BREYER, with whom Chief Justice REHNQUIST, joins, dissenting.

The majority holds that the Constitution contains the following requirement: "any fact [other than recidivism] that increases the penalty for a crime beyond the prescribed statutory maximum must be submitted to a jury, and proved beyond a reasonable doubt." This rule would seem to promote a procedural ideal — that of juries, not judges, determining the existence of those facts upon which increased punishment turns. But the real world of criminal justice cannot hope to meet any such ideal. It can function only with the help of procedural compromises, particularly in respect to sentencing. And those compromises, which are themselves necessary for the fair functioning of the criminal justice system, preclude implementation of the procedural model that today's decision reflects. At the very least, the impractical nature of the requirement that the majority now recognizes supports the proposition that the Constitution was not intended to embody it.

In modern times the law has left it to the sentencing judge to find those facts which (within broad sentencing limits set by the legislature) determine the sentence of a convicted offender.

There are many manner-related differences in respect to criminal behavior. Empirical data collected by the Sentencing Commission makes clear that, before the Guidelines, judges who exercised discretion within broad legislatively determined sentencing limits (say, a range of 0 to 20 years) would impose very different sentences upon offenders engaged in the same basic criminal conduct, depending, for example, upon the amount of drugs distributed (in respect to drug crimes), the amount of money taken (in respect to robbery, theft, or fraud), the presence or use of a weapon, injury to a victim, the vulnerability of a victim, the offender's role in the offense, recidivism, and many other offense-related or offender-related factors. The majority does not deny that judges have exercised, and, constitutionally speaking, may exercise sentencing discretion in this way.

[I]t is important for present purposes to understand why judges, rather than juries, traditionally have determined the presence or absence of such sentence-affecting facts in any given case. And it is important to realize that the reason is not a theoretical one, but a practical one. There are, to put it simply, far too many potentially relevant sentencing factors to permit submission of all (or even many) of them to a jury.

A sentencing system in which judges have discretion to find sentencing-related factors is a workable system and one that has long been thought consistent with the Constitution.

Apprendi requires that all facts increasing a defendant's sentence beyond the offense's statutory maximum be pleaded and proved to a jury beyond a reasonable doubt. It preserves, however, *Almendarez-Torres*'s exception for increased sentences based on the defendant's commission of prior offenses. Two years after *Apprendi* was decided, the Court, in Harris v. United States, 536 U.S. 545 (2002), clarified that the *Apprendi* rule does not apply to facts that trigger a mandatory minimum sentence. Justice Kennedy, writing for the Court, held that a sentencing judge can find those facts necessary to trigger a mandatory minimum sentencing provision. That same year, the Court, in Ring v. Arizona, 536 U.S. 584 (2002), held that Arizona's capital sentencing statute was unconstitutional because it allowed judges to find whether factors justifying imposition of the death penalty exist.

In 2004, the Court considered how *Apprendi* affects state sentencing schemes that allow sentences to be enhanced based on judicial findings in guideline sentencing schemes. Continuing the *Apprendi* movement, the Supreme Court held that *Apprendi* applies when a factual finding triggers a sentence beyond the standard sentencing range.

BLAKELY v. WASHINGTON

542 U.S. 296 (2004)

Justice SCALIA delivered the opinion of the Court.

Petitioner Ralph Howard Blakely, Jr., pleaded guilty to the kidnaping of his estranged wife. The facts admitted in his plea, standing alone, supported a maximum sentence of 53 months. Pursuant to state law, the court imposed an "exceptional" sentence of 90 months after making a judicial determination that he had acted with "deliberate cruelty." We consider whether this violated petitioner's Sixth Amendment right to trial by jury.

I

Petitioner married his wife Yolanda in 1973. He was evidently a difficult man to live with, having been diagnosed at various times with psychological and personality disorders including paranoid schizophrenia. His wife ultimately filed for divorce. In 1998, he abducted her from their orchard home in Grant County, Washington, binding her with duct tape and forcing her at knife-point into a wooden box in the bed of his pickup truck. In the process, he implored her to dismiss the divorce suit and related trust proceedings.

When the couple's 13-year-old son Ralphy returned home from school, petitioner ordered him to follow in another car, threatening to harm Yolanda with a shotgun if he did not do so. Ralphy escaped and sought help when they stopped at a gas station, but petitioner continued on with Yolanda to a friend's house in Montana. He was finally arrested after the friend called the police.

The State charged petitioner with first-degree kidnaping. Upon reaching a plea agreement, however, it reduced the charge to second-degree kidnaping involving domestic violence and use of a firearm. Petitioner entered a guilty plea admitting the elements of second-degree kidnaping and the domestic-violence and firearm allegations, but no other relevant facts.

The case then proceeded to sentencing. In Washington, second-degree kidnaping is a class B felony. State law provides that "no person convicted of a [class B] felony shall be punished by confinement . . . exceeding . . . a term of ten years." Other provisions of state law, however, further limit the range of sentences a judge may impose. Washington's Sentencing Reform Act specifies, for petitioner's offense of second-degree kidnaping with a firearm, a "standard range" of 49 to 53 months. A judge may impose a sentence above the standard range if he finds "substantial and compelling reasons justifying an exceptional sentence." The Act lists aggravating factors that justify such a departure, which it recites to be illustrative rather than exhaustive. When a judge imposes an exceptional sentence, he must set forth findings of fact and conclusions of law supporting it.

Pursuant to the plea agreement, the State recommended a sentence within the standard range of 49 to 53 months. After hearing Yolanda's description of the kidnaping, however, the judge rejected the State's recommendation and imposed an exceptional sentence of 90 months—37 months beyond the standard maximum. He justified the sentence on the ground that petitioner had acted with "deliberate cruelty," a statutorily enumerated ground for departure in domestic-violence cases.

Faced with an unexpected increase of more than three years in his sentence, petitioner objected. The judge accordingly conducted a 3-day bench hearing featuring testimony from petitioner, Yolanda, Ralphy, a police officer, and medical experts. After the hearing, he issued 32 findings of fact, concluding:

> The defendant's motivation to commit kidnapping was complex, contributed to by his mental condition and personality disorders, the pressures of the divorce litigation, the impending trust litigation trial and anger over his troubled interpersonal relationships with his spouse and children.
>
> The defendant's methods were more homogeneous than his motive. He used stealth and surprise, and took advantage of the victim's isolation. He immediately

employed physical violence, restrained the victim with tape, and threatened her with injury and death to herself and others. He immediately coerced the victim into providing information by the threatening application of a knife. He violated a subsisting restraining order.

The judge adhered to his initial determination of deliberate cruelty. Petitioner appealed, arguing that this sentencing procedure deprived him of his federal constitutional right to have a jury determine beyond a reasonable doubt all facts legally essential to his sentence. The State Court of Appeals affirmed. The Washington Supreme Court denied discretionary review. We granted certiorari.

II

This case requires us to apply the rule we expressed in Apprendi v. New Jersey (2000): "Other than the fact of a prior conviction, any fact that increases the penalty for a crime beyond the prescribed statutory maximum must be submitted to a jury, and proved beyond a reasonable doubt." This rule reflects two longstanding tenets of common-law criminal jurisprudence: that the "truth of every accusation" against a defendant "should afterwards be confirmed by the unanimous suffrage of twelve of his equals and neighbours," 4 W. Blackstone, Commentaries on the Laws of England 343 (1769), and that "an accusation which lacks any particular fact which the law makes essential to the punishment is . . . no accusation within the requirements of the common law, and it is no accusation in reason," 1 J. Bishop, Criminal Procedure §87, p. 55 (2d ed. 1872). These principles have been acknowledged by courts and treatises since the earliest days of graduated sentencing. . . .

In this case, petitioner was sentenced to more than three years above the 53-month statutory maximum of the standard range because he had acted with "deliberate cruelty." The facts supporting that finding were neither admitted by petitioner nor found by a jury. The State nevertheless contends that there was no *Apprendi* violation because the relevant "statutory maximum" is not 53 months, but the 10-year maximum for class B felonies. It observes that no exceptional sentence may exceed that limit. Our precedents make clear, however, that the "statutory maximum" for *Apprendi* purposes is the maximum sentence a judge may impose solely on the basis of the facts reflected in the jury verdict or admitted by the defendant. In other words, the relevant "statutory maximum" is not the maximum sentence a judge may impose after finding additional facts, but the maximum he may impose without any additional findings. When a judge inflicts punishment that the jury's verdict alone does not allow, the jury has not found all the facts "which the law makes essential to the punishment," and the judge exceeds his proper authority.

The judge in this case could not have imposed the exceptional 90-month sentence solely on the basis of the facts admitted in the guilty plea. Those facts alone were insufficient. . . .

Because the State's sentencing procedure did not comply with the Sixth Amendment, petitioner's sentence is invalid.

III

Our commitment to *Apprendi* in this context reflects not just respect for longstanding precedent, but the need to give intelligible content to the right of jury trial. That right is no mere procedural formality, but a fundamental reservation of power in our constitutional structure. Just as suffrage ensures the people's ultimate control in the legislative and executive branches, jury trial is meant to ensure their control in the judiciary.

IV

By reversing the judgment below, we are not, as the State would have it, "finding determinate sentencing schemes unconstitutional." This case is not about whether determinate sentencing is constitutional, only about how it can be implemented in a way that respects the Sixth Amendment.

Ultimately, our decision cannot turn on whether or to what degree trial by jury impairs the efficiency or fairness of criminal justice. One can certainly argue that both these values would be better served by leaving justice entirely in the hands of professionals; many nations of the world, particularly those following civil-law traditions, take just that course. There is not one shred of doubt, however, about the Framers' paradigm for criminal justice: not the civil-law ideal of administrative perfection, but the common-law ideal of limited state power accomplished by strict division of authority between judge and jury. As *Apprendi* held, every defendant has the right to insist that the prosecutor prove to a jury all facts legally essential to the punishment. Under the dissenters' alternative, he has no such right. That should be the end of the matter.

Petitioner was sentenced to prison for more than three years beyond what the law allowed for the crime to which he confessed, on the basis of a disputed finding that he had acted with "deliberate cruelty." The Framers would not have thought it too much to demand that, before depriving a man of three more years of his liberty, the State should suffer the modest inconvenience of submitting its accusation to "the unanimous suffrage of twelve of his equals and neighbours," 4 Blackstone, Commentaries, at 343, rather than a lone employee of the State.

The judgment of the Washington Court of Appeals is reversed, and the case is remanded for further proceedings not inconsistent with this opinion.

Justice O'CONNOR, with whom Justice BREYER joins, and with whom Chief Justice REHNQUIST and Justice KENNEDY join as to all but Part IV-B, dissenting.

The legacy of today's opinion, whether intended or not, will be the consolidation of sentencing power in the State and Federal Judiciaries. The

Court says to Congress and state legislatures: If you want to constrain the sentencing discretion of judges and bring some uniformity to sentencing, it will cost you — dearly. Congress and States, faced with the burdens imposed by the extension of *Apprendi* to the present context, will either trim or eliminate altogether their Sentencing Guidelines schemes and, with them, 20 years of sentencing reform. The "effect" of today's decision will be greater judicial discretion and less uniformity in sentencing. Because I find it implausible that the Framers would have considered such a result to be required by the Due Process Clause or the Sixth Amendment, and because the practical consequences of today's decision may be disastrous, I respectfully dissent.

I

One need look no further than the history leading up to and following the enactment of Washington's guidelines scheme to appreciate the damage that today's decision will cause. Prior to 1981, Washington, like most other States and the Federal Government, employed an indeterminate sentencing scheme. Sentencing judges, in conjunction with parole boards, had virtually unfettered discretion to sentence defendants to prison terms falling anywhere within the statutory range, including probation — i.e., no jail sentence at all.

This system of unguided discretion inevitably resulted in severe disparities in sentences received and served by defendants committing the same offense and having similar criminal histories.

To counteract these trends, the state legislature passed the Sentencing Reform Act of 1981. The Act had the laudable purposes of "making the criminal justice system accountable to the public," and "ensur[ing] that the punishment for a criminal offense is proportionate to the seriousness of the offense . . . [and] commensurate with the punishment imposed on others committing similar offenses." The Act neither increased any of the statutory sentencing ranges for the three types of felonies, nor reclassified any substantive offenses. It merely placed meaningful constraints on discretion to sentence offenders within the statutory ranges, and eliminated parole. There is thus no evidence that the legislature was attempting to manipulate the statutory elements of criminal offenses or to circumvent the procedural protections of the Bill of Rights. Rather, lawmakers were trying to bring some much-needed uniformity, transparency, and accountability to an otherwise " 'labyrinthine' sentencing and corrections system that 'lacked any principle except unguided discretion.' "

II

Far from disregarding principles of due process and the jury trial right, as the majority today suggests, Washington's reform has served them. Before passage of the Act, a defendant charged with second degree kidnaping, like petitioner, had no idea whether he would receive a 10-year sentence or probation. The ultimate sentencing determination could turn as much on the idiosyncrasies of a particular judge as on the specifics of the defendant's crime or background. A defendant did not know what facts, if any, about his offense or his history would be considered relevant by the sentencing judge or by the parole board. After passage of the Act, a defendant charged with second degree kidnaping knows what his presumptive sentence will be; he has a good idea of the types of factors that a sentencing judge can and will consider when deciding whether to sentence him outside that range; he is guaranteed meaningful appellate review to protect against an arbitrary sentence. Criminal defendants still face the same statutory maximum sentences, but they now at least know, much more than before, the real consequences of their actions.

Washington's move to a system of guided discretion has served equal protection principles as well. Over the past 20 years, there has been a substantial reduction in racial disparity in sentencing across the State.

The majority does not, because it cannot, disagree that determinate sentencing schemes, like Washington's, serve important constitutional values. Thus, the majority says: "this case is not about whether determinate sentencing is constitutional, only about how it can be implemented in a way that respects the Sixth Amendment." But extension of *Apprendi* to the present context will impose significant costs on a legislature's determination that a particular fact, not historically an element, warrants a higher sentence. While not a constitutional prohibition on guidelines schemes, the majority's decision today exacts a substantial constitutional tax.

IV

The consequences of today's decision will be as far reaching as they are disturbing. Washington's sentencing system is by no means unique. Numerous other States have enacted guidelines systems, as has the Federal Government. Today's decision casts constitutional doubt over them all and, in so doing, threatens an untold number of criminal judgments. Every sentence imposed under such guidelines in cases currently pending on direct appeal is in jeopardy. And, despite the fact that we hold in Schriro v. Summerlin that *Ring* (and a fortiori *Apprendi*) does not apply retroactively on habeas review, all criminal sentences imposed under the federal and state guidelines since *Apprendi* was decided in 2000 arguably remain open to collateral attack.

The practical consequences for trial courts, starting today, will be equally unsettling: How are courts to mete out guidelines sentences? Do courts apply the guidelines as to mitigating factors, but not as to aggravating factors? Do they jettison the guidelines altogether? The Court ignores the havoc it is about to wreak on trial courts across the country.

What I have feared most has now come to pass: Over 20 years of sentencing reform are all but lost, and tens of thousands of criminal judgments are in jeopardy. I respectfully dissent.

Justice KENNEDY, with whom Justice BREYER joins, dissenting.

The majority opinion does considerable damage to our laws and to the administration of the criminal justice system for all the reasons well stated in Justice O'Connor's dissent, plus one more: The Court, in my respectful submission, disregards the fundamental principle under our constitutional system that different branches of government "converse with each other on matters of vital common interest."

Sentencing guidelines are a prime example of this collaborative process. Dissatisfied with the wide disparity in sentencing, participants in the criminal justice system, including judges, pressed for legislative reforms. In response, legislators drew from these participants' shared experiences and enacted measures to correct the problems.

[T]he Constitution does not prohibit the dynamic and fruitful dialogue between the judicial and legislative branches of government that has marked sentencing reform on both the state and the federal levels for more than 20 years. I dissent.

Justice BREYER, with whom Justice O'CONNOR joins, dissenting.

The majority ignores the adverse consequences inherent in its conclusion. As a result of the majority's rule, sentencing must now take one of three forms, each of which risks either impracticality, unfairness, or harm to the jury trial right the majority purports to strengthen.

A first option for legislators is to create a simple, pure or nearly pure "charge offense" or "determinate" sentencing system. In such a system, an indictment would charge a few facts which, taken together, constitute a crime, such as robbery. Robbery would carry a single sentence, say, five years' imprisonment. And every person convicted of robbery would receive that sentence — just as, centuries ago, everyone convicted of almost any serious crime was sentenced to death.

Such a system assures uniformity, but at intolerable costs. First, simple determinate sentencing systems impose identical punishments on people who committed their crimes in very different ways. When dramatically different conduct ends up being punished the same way, an injustice has taken place. Simple determinate sentencing has the virtue of treating like cases alike, but it simultaneously fails to treat different cases differently.

Second, in a world of statutorily fixed mandatory sentences for many crimes, determinate sentencing gives tremendous power to prosecutors to manipulate sentences through their choice of charges. Prosecutors can simply charge, or threaten to charge, defendants with crimes bearing higher mandatory sentences. Defendants, knowing that they will not have a chance to argue for a lower sentence in front of a judge, may plead to charges that they might otherwise contest. Considering that most criminal cases do not go to trial and resolution by plea bargaining is the norm, the rule of *Apprendi*, to the extent it results in a return to determinate sentencing, threatens serious unfairness.

A second option for legislators is to return to a system of indeterminate sentencing. Under indeterminate systems, the length of the sentence is entirely or almost entirely within the discretion of the judge or of the parole board, which typically has broad power to decide when to release a prisoner.

When such systems were in vogue, they were criticized, and rightly so, for producing unfair disparities, including race-based disparities, in the punishment of similarly situated defendants. The length of time a person spent in prison appeared to depend on "what the judge ate for breakfast" on the day of sentencing, on which judge you got, or on other factors that should not have made a difference to the length of the sentence. And under such a system, the judge could vary the sentence greatly based upon his findings about how the defendant had committed the crime — findings that might not have been made by a "preponderance of the evidence," much less "beyond a reasonable doubt."

Returning to such a system would diminish the " 'reason' " the majority claims it is trying to uphold. It also would do little to "ensure [the] control" of what the majority calls "the peopl[e,]" i.e., the jury, "in the judiciary," since "the people" would only decide the defendant's guilt, a finding with no effect on the duration of the sentence. While "the judge's authority to sentence" would formally derive from the jury's verdict, the jury would exercise little or no control over the sentence itself.

A third option is that which the Court seems to believe legislators will in fact take. That is the option of retaining structured schemes that attempt to punish similar conduct similarly and different conduct differently, but modifying them to conform to *Apprendi*'s dictates. Judges would be able to depart downward from presumptive sentences upon finding that mitigating factors were present, but would not be able to depart upward unless the prosecutor charged the aggravating fact to a jury and proved it beyond a reasonable doubt. It is therefore worth exploring how this option could work in practice, as well as the assumptions on which it depends.

This option can be implemented in one of two ways. The first way would be for legislatures to subdivide each crime into a list of complex crimes, each of which would be defined to include commonly found sentencing factors such as drug quantity, type of victim, presence of violence, degree of injury, use of gun, and so on.

This possibility is, of course, merely a highly calibrated form of the "pure charge" system . . . [a]nd it suffers from some of the same defects. The prosecutor, through control of the precise charge, controls the punishment, thereby marching the sentencing system directly away from, not toward, one important guideline goal: rough uniformity of punishment for those who engage in roughly the same real criminal conduct.

The second way to make sentencing guidelines *Apprendi*-compliant would be to require at least two juries for each defendant whenever aggravating facts are present: one jury to determine guilt of the crime charged, and an additional jury to try the disputed facts that, if found, would aggravate the sentence. Our experience with bifurcated trials in the capital punishment context suggests that requiring them for run-of-the-mill sentences would be costly, both in money and in judicial time and resources.

Efforts to tie real punishment to real conduct are not new. They are embodied in well-established pre-guidelines sentencing practices — practices under which a judge, looking at a presentence report, would seek to tailor the sentence in significant part to fit the criminal conduct in which the offender actually engaged.

In these and other ways, the two-jury system would work a radical change in pre-existing criminal law. It is not surprising that this Court has never previously suggested that the Constitution — outside the unique context of the death penalty — might require bifurcated jury-based sentencing. And it is the impediment the Court's holding poses to legislative efforts to achieve that greater systematic fairness that casts doubt on its constitutional validity.

Is there a fourth option? Perhaps. Congress and state legislatures might, for example, rewrite their criminal codes, attaching astronomically high sentences to each crime, followed by long lists of mitigating facts, which, for the most part, would consist of the absence of aggravating facts.

Taken together these three sets of considerations, concerning consequences, concerning history, concerning institutional reliance, leave me where I was in *Apprendi*, i.e., convinced that the Court is wrong. Until now, I would have thought the Court might have limited *Apprendi* so that its underlying principle would not undo sentencing reform efforts. Today's case dispels that illusion.

––––––––––––

Although the individual justices remained divided on the wisdom and applicability of *Apprendi*, the case continued to have a dramatic impact on sentencing schemes throughout the country. *Blakely* led to the invalidation and revision of state sentencing schemes. Next in the line of fire were the Federal Sentencing Guidelines.

The Sentencing Guidelines establish base sentencing levels for offenses and require courts to enhance those sentences based on facts found by the sentencing judges, not juries. In United States v. Booker, the Supreme Court examined whether the federal sentencing scheme also ran afoul of defendants' right to be sentenced only on those facts (other than a prior conviction) that have been pleaded and proved to a jury. In a deeply divided decision, Justice Stevens delivered the opinion of the Court, in part, concluding that the Sixth Amendment, as construed in *Blakely*, applies to the Federal Sentencing Guidelines. Justice Breyer delivered the opinion of the

Court regarding the appropriate remedy that should be administered given that the Sentencing Guidelines, as enacted, did not comply with *Apprendi*'s requirements. Justice Ginsburg was the only justice in the majority in both opinions. She voted with Justice Stevens's majority opinion in finding that the principles of *Apprendi* apply to the Federal Sentencing Guidelines, but she joined Justice Breyer holding that the remedy is to make the guidelines advisory and not mandatory.

UNITED STATES v. BOOKER

543 U.S. 220 (2005)

STEVENS, J., delivered the opinion of the Court in part, in which SCALIA, SOUTER, THOMAS, and GINSBURG, JJ., joined.

The question presented . . . is whether an application of the Federal Sentencing Guidelines violated the Sixth Amendment. We hold that [the lower] courts correctly concluded that the Sixth Amendment as construed in *Blakely* does apply to the Sentencing Guidelines. In a separate opinion authored by Justice Breyer, the Court concludes that in light of this holding, two provisions of the Sentencing Reform Act of 1984 (SRA) that have the effect of making the Guidelines mandatory must be invalidated in order to allow the statute to operate in a manner consistent with congressional intent.

I

Respondent Booker was charged with possession with intent to distribute at least 50 grams of cocaine base (crack). Having heard evidence that he had 92.5 grams in his duffel bag, the jury found him guilty of violating 21 U.S.C. §841(a)(1). That statute prescribes a minimum sentence of 10 years in prison and a maximum sentence of life for that offense.

Based upon Booker's criminal history and the quantity of drugs found by the jury, the Sentencing Guidelines required the District Court Judge to select a "base" sentence of not less than 210 nor more than 262 months in prison. The judge, however, held a post-trial sentencing proceeding and concluded by a preponderance of the evidence that Booker had possessed an additional 566 grams of crack and that he was guilty of obstructing justice. Those findings mandated that the judge select a sentence between 360 months and life imprisonment; the judge imposed a sentence at the low end of the range. Thus, instead of the sentence of 21 years and 10 months that the judge could have imposed on the basis of the facts proved to the jury beyond a reasonable doubt, Booker received a 30-year sentence.

[T]he Government asks us to determine whether our *Apprendi* line of cases applies to the Sentencing Guidelines, and if so, what portions of the Guidelines remain in effect.

II

It has been settled throughout our history that the Constitution protects every criminal defendant "against conviction except upon proof beyond a reasonable doubt of every fact necessary to constitute the crime with which he is charged." It is equally clear that the "Constitution gives a criminal defendant the right to demand that a jury find him guilty of all the elements of the crime with which he is charged." These basic precepts, firmly rooted in the common law, have provided the basis for recent decisions interpreting modern criminal statutes and sentencing procedures.

In Apprendi v. New Jersey (2000), [t]his Court set aside the enhanced sentence. We held: "Other than the fact of a prior conviction, any fact that increases the penalty for a crime beyond the prescribed statutory maximum must be submitted to a jury, and proved beyond a reasonable doubt." The fact that New Jersey labeled the hate crime a "sentence enhancement" rather than a separate criminal act was irrelevant for constitutional purposes.

In Blakely v. Washington (2004), we dealt with a determinate sentencing scheme similar to the Federal Sentencing Guidelines. The application of Washington's sentencing scheme violated the defendant's right to have the jury find the existence of " 'any particular fact' " that the law makes essential to his punishment. That right is implicated whenever a judge seeks to impose a sentence that is not solely based on "facts reflected in the jury verdict or admitted by the defendant."

As the dissenting opinions in *Blakely* recognized, there is no distinction of constitutional significance between the Federal Sentencing Guidelines and the Washington procedures at issue in that case. This conclusion rests on the premise, common to both systems, that the relevant sentencing rules are mandatory and impose binding requirements on all sentencing judges.

If the Guidelines as currently written could be read as merely advisory provisions that recommended, rather than required, the selection of particular sentences in response to differing sets of facts, their use would not implicate the Sixth Amendment.

The Guidelines as written, however, are not advisory; they are mandatory and binding on all judges.

The availability of a departure in specified circumstances does not avoid the constitutional issue, just as it did not in *Blakely* itself. The Guidelines permit departures from the prescribed sentencing range in cases in which the judge "finds that there exists an aggravating or mitigating circumstance of a kind, or to a degree, not adequately taken into consideration by the Sentencing Commission in formulating the guidelines that should result in a sentence different from that described." At first glance, one might believe that the ability of a district judge to depart from the Guidelines means that she is bound only by the statutory maximum. Were this the case, there would be no *Apprendi* problem. Importantly, however, departures are not available in every case, and in fact are unavailable in most. In most cases, as a matter of law, the Commission will have adequately taken all relevant factors into account, and no departure will be legally permissible. In those instances, the judge is bound to impose a sentence within the Guidelines range. It was for this reason that we rejected a similar argument in *Blakely*, holding that although the Washington statute allowed the judge to impose a sentence outside the sentencing range for " 'substantial and compelling reasons,' " that exception was not available for Blakely himself.

It is quite true that once determinate sentencing had fallen from favor, American judges commonly determined facts justifying a choice of a heavier sentence on account of the manner in which particular defendants acted. In 1986, however, our own cases first recognized a new trend in the legislative regulation of sentencing when we considered the significance of facts selected by legislatures that not only authorized, or even mandated, heavier sentences than would otherwise have been imposed, but increased the range of sentences possible for the underlying crime. Provisions for such enhancements of the permissible sentencing range reflected growing and wholly justified legislative concern about the proliferation and variety of drug crimes and their frequent identification with firearms offences.

The effect of the increasing emphasis on facts that enhanced sentencing ranges, however, was to increase the judge's power and diminish that of the jury. It became the judge, not the jury, who determined the upper limits of sentencing, and the facts determined were not required to be raised before trial or proved by more than a preponderance.

As the enhancements became greater, the jury's finding of the underlying crime became less significant. The new sentencing practice forced the Court to address the question how the right of jury trial could be preserved, in a meaningful way guaranteeing that the jury would still stand between the individual and the power of the government under the new sentencing regime.

All of the foregoing support our conclusion that our holding in *Blakely* applies to the Sentencing Guidelines. We recognize . . . that in some cases jury factfinding may impair the most expedient and efficient sentencing of defendants. But the interest in fairness and reliability protected by the right to a jury trial — a common-law right that defendants enjoyed for centuries and that is now enshrined in the Sixth Amendment — has always outweighed the interest in concluding trials swiftly.

Justice BREYER delivered the opinion of the Court in part.[6]

The first question that the Government has presented in these cases is the following: "Whether the Sixth Amendment is violated by the imposition of an enhanced sentence under the United States Sentencing Guidelines based on the sentencing judge's determination of a fact (other than a prior

---

6. The Chief Justice, Justice O'Connor, Justice Kennedy, and Justice Ginsburg join this opinion. [Footnote by the Court.]

conviction) that was not found by the jury or admitted by the defendant."
The Court, in an opinion by Justice Stevens, answers this question in the
affirmative.

We here turn to the second question presented, a question that concerns
the remedy. We answer the remedial question by looking to legislative intent.

One approach, that of Justice Stevens' dissent, would retain the Sentencing Act (and the Guidelines) as written, but would engraft onto the existing
system today's Sixth Amendment "jury trial" requirement. The addition
would change the Guidelines by preventing the sentencing court from
increasing a sentence on the basis of a fact that the jury did not find (or
that the offender did not admit).

The other approach, which we now adopt, would (through severance
and excision of two provisions) make the Guidelines system advisory
while maintaining a strong connection between the sentence imposed
and the offender's real conduct — a connection important to the increased
uniformity of sentencing that Congress intended its Guidelines system to
achieve.

Several considerations convince us that, were the Court's constitutional
requirement added onto the Sentencing Act as currently written, the
requirement would so transform the scheme that Congress created that
Congress likely would not have intended the Act as so modified to stand.

[T]he sentencing statutes, read to include the Court's Sixth Amendment
requirement, would create a system far more complex than Congress could
have intended.

Application of these criteria indicates that we must sever and excise two
specific statutory provisions: the provision that requires sentencing courts to
impose a sentence within the applicable Guidelines range (in the absence of
circumstances that justify a departure), and the provision that sets forth
standards of review on appeal, including de novo review of departures
from the applicable Guidelines range. With these two sections excised,
the remainder of the Act satisfies the Court's constitutional requirements.

The remainder of the Act "function[s] independently." Without the
"mandatory" provision, the Act nonetheless requires judges to take account
of the Guidelines together with other sentencing goals.

In our view, it is more consistent with Congress' likely intent in enacting
the Sentencing Reform Act (1) to preserve important elements of that
system while severing and excising two provisions than (2) to maintain all
provisions of the Act and engraft today's constitutional requirement onto
that statutory scheme.

Ours, of course, is not the last word: The ball now lies in Congress' court.
The National Legislature is equipped to devise and install, long term, the
sentencing system, compatible with the Constitution, that Congress judges
best for the federal system of justice.

———————————

Booker marked the end of mandatory Federal Sentencing Guidelines. Post-*Booker*, such guidelines are only advisory. The Supreme Court and lower courts continue to struggle over what it means for the Sentencing Guidelines to be advisory and not mandatory. In *Booker*, the Court held that the sentence must be "reasonable." However, the Court then slowly articulated the standards to determine whether a sentence is reasonable. In Rita v. United States, 551 U.S. 338 (2007), the Supreme Court began by holding that sentences falling within the advisory guidelines are presumptively reasonable.

Then, in Gall v. United States, 552 U.S. 38 (2007), the Supreme Court has held in an opinion authored by Justice Stevens that appellate courts must give great deference to the sentencing court's decision to impose a sentence outside the range of the guidelines. When deciding to depart from the guidelines range, a trial court need not show "extraordinary" circumstances or employ a rigid mathematical approach. Rather, after correctly calculating the applicable guidelines range, the sentencing court should base its sentence on all of the relevant factors in the case (as set forth in 18 U.S.C. §3553(a)) and determine whether it wants to deviate from the guidelines and, if so, by how much. In reviewing the sentencing court's determination for reasonableness, the appellate court must first ensure that the sentencing court made no significant procedural errors and then consider the sentence under an abuse-of-discretion standard. Using this approach, the Supreme Court held that it was reasonable for the sentencing judge to depart from a guidelines sentence of 30 to 37 months for Brian Gall to a sentence of probation. Gall was a college student who voluntarily withdrew from a conspiracy to distribute the drug ecstasy, turned his life around, and pled guilty.

In a companion case, Kimbrough v. United States, 552 U.S. 85 (2007), the Supreme Court held that a sentencing judge may depart from the Sentencing Guidelines if he or she disagrees with the guidelines' approach of imposing significantly higher sentences for the possession of crack cocaine. As Justice Ginsburg noted in her opinion, the 100-to-1 ratio imposed for the possession of crack rather than powder cocaine "fails to meet the sentencing objectives set forth by Congress." The crack/powder sentencing differential "fosters disrespect for and lack of confidence in the criminal justice system" and has had a significant impact on the sentencing of black offenders. Derrick Kimbrough was facing a guidelines sentence of 19 to 22.5 years in prison for possessing more than 50 grams of crack cocaine. Had he possessed the equivalent amount of powder cocaine, his guidelines range would have been 8 to 9 years. The trial judge found that a sentence of 15 years in prison was "clearly long enough" to accomplish the goals of sentencing set forth in §3553(a).

Federal sentencing today is governed by the sentencing judge's evaluation of a sentence under 18 U.S.C. §3553(a). It provides that a federal offender's sentence should be based on:

> (1) the nature and circumstances of the offense and the history of the defendant;

(2) the need for the sentence imposed—

(A) to reflect the seriousness of the offense, to promote respect for the law, and to provide just punishment for the offense;

(B) to afford adequate deterrence to criminal conduct;

(C) to protect the public from future crimes of the defendant;

(D) to provide the defendant with needed educational or vocational training, medical care, or other correctional treatment in the most effective manner;

(3) the kinds of sentences available;

(4) [the applicable sentencing guidelines];

(5) any pertinent policy statement . . . ;

(6) the need to avoid unwarranted sentence disparities . . . ; and

(7) the need to provide restitution to any victims of the offense.

Great deference is given to the sentencing court as long as the judge complies with the terms of 18 U.S.C. §3553a. The appellate courts can strike down a sentence for being too excessive. However, unless the government cross-appeals, the appellate court cannot increase a sentence even if it believes that it was plainly wrong. In Greenlaw v. United States, 564 U.S. 237 (2008), the Court held that it was up to the parties to frame the issues on appeal and the court will not "sally forth each day looking for wrongs to right." By reaching this result, the Supreme Court made it less risky for defendants to appeal their federal sentences.

As for state determinative sentencing laws, the Court has also made it clear that sentencing schemes that allow trial judges to impose sentences in a higher sentencing category than supported by a jury's verdict or a defendant's guilty plea are invalid under *Apprendi* and *Blakely*, regardless of how those categories are structured. For instance, in Cunningham v. California, 549 U.S. 270 (2007), the Supreme Court struck down California's determinative sentencing scheme.

In recent years, the Court limited the impact of *Apprendi* by holding that its ruling does not extend to judges deciding facts that will determine whether a defendant receives a consecutive or concurrent sentence. In Oregon v. Ice (2009), Justice Ginsburg, writing for a 5-4 majority, held that the historical practice of having judges decide whether sentences will be consecutive or concurrent does not violate the Sixth Amendment.

Yet the Court still remains very committed to *Apprendi*. In 2012, the Court held in Southern Union Co. v. United States, 567 U.S. 343 (2012), that *Apprendi* applies to the imposition of criminal fines. Except in petty offenses, a jury must find the predicate facts to support the imposition of criminal fines.

Overall, the *Apprendi* revolution has had a dramatic impact on state and federal sentencing laws. The sentencing pendulum has swung back toward indeterminate sentencing schemes that give broader discretion to sentencing judges and thus do not require jury determinations regarding the facts that the court uses to make some of its sentencing decisions.

Recently, in addition to the *Apprendi* revolution, the Supreme Court has also struck down sentences as unconstitutionally vague, in violation of defendants' due process rights. In Johnson v. United States, 135 S. Ct. 2551 (2015), the Court struck down the residual clause for the Armed Career Criminal Act, for violating Due Process. However, vague Sentencing Guidelines are not subject to the same Due Process challenge. Beckles v. United States, 580 U.S. ___, S. Ct. 886 (2017).

C.   EIGHTH AMENDMENT: WHEN DOES A SENTENCE CONSTITUTE CRUEL AND UNUSUAL PUNISHMENT?

In addition to statutory limits on sentences and the Sixth Amendment requirements of *Apprendi* and its progeny, the Eighth Amendment prohibits "cruel and unusual punishment" and "excessive fines." The standard for what constitutes cruel and unusual punishment is one of proportionality. Instead of looking at the manner in which punishment is imposed, as some justices would favor, the current approach to determining whether a sentence constitutes cruel and unusual punishment involves determining whether the sentence "fits the crime." The Supreme Court developed this standard in two cases: Rummell v. Estelle, 445 U.S. 263 (1980), and Solem v. Helm, 463 U.S. 277 (1983).

In Rummell v. Estelle, the defendant was sentenced, under the state's recidivist statute, to life imprisonment with the possibility of parole in 12 years for his third felony: obtaining $120.75 by false pretenses. Rummell's two prior felony convictions involved fraudulent use of a credit card to obtain $80 and passing a forged check in the amount of $28.36. The Supreme Court, in a decision authored by Justice Rehnquist, held that Rummell's sentence did not amount to cruel and unusual punishment.

Three years later, the Court reexamined the issue in Solem v. Helm and articulated its standard for determining whether a sentence constitutes cruel and unusual punishment.

1.   *Determining When a Sentence Is Proportional*

<u>SOLEM v. HELM</u>
463 U.S. 277 (1983)

Justice POWELL delivered the opinion of the Court.

The issue presented is whether the Eighth Amendment proscribes a life sentence without possibility of parole for a seventh nonviolent felony.

I

By 1975 the State of South Dakota had convicted respondent Jerry Helm of six nonviolent felonies. In 1964, 1966, and 1969 Helm was convicted of third-degree burglary. In 1972 he was convicted of obtaining money under false pretenses. In 1973 he was convicted of grand larceny. And in 1975 he was convicted of third-offense driving while intoxicated. The record contains no details about the circumstances of any of these offenses, except that they were all nonviolent, none was a crime against a person, and alcohol was a contributing factor in each case.

In 1979 Helm was charged with uttering a "no account" check for $100. Ordinarily the maximum punishment for uttering a "no account" check would have been five years' imprisonment in the state penitentiary and a $5,000 fine. As a result of his criminal record, however, Helm was subject to South Dakota's recidivist statute: "When a defendant has been convicted of at least three prior convictions in addition to the principal felony, the sentence for the principal felony shall be enhanced to the sentence for a Class 1 felony."

The maximum penalty for a "Class 1 felony" was life imprisonment in the state penitentiary and a $25,000 fine. The Governor is authorized to pardon prisoners, or to commute their sentences, S. D. Const., Art. IV, §3, but no other relief from sentence is available even to a rehabilitated prisoner.

Immediately after accepting Helm's guilty plea, the South Dakota Circuit Court sentenced Helm to life imprisonment. The Court of Appeals examined the nature of Helm's offenses, the nature of his sentence, and the sentence he could have received in other States for the same offense. It concluded, on the basis of this examination, that Helm's sentence was "grossly disproportionate to the nature of the offense."

We granted certiorari to consider the Eighth Amendment question presented by this case.

II

The Eighth Amendment declares: "Excessive bail shall not be required, nor excessive fines imposed, nor cruel and unusual punishments inflicted." The final clause prohibits not only barbaric punishments, but also sentences that are disproportionate to the crime committed.

A

The principle that a punishment should be proportionate to the crime is deeply rooted and frequently repeated in common-law jurisprudence. In 1215 three chapters of Magna Carta were devoted to the rule that "amercements" [fines] may not be excessive. When prison sentences became the normal criminal sanctions, the common law recognized that these, too, must be proportional.

When the Framers of the Eighth Amendment adopted the language of the English Bill of Rights, they also adopted the English principle of proportionality.

B

The constitutional principle of proportionality has been recognized explicitly in this Court for almost a century. In the leading case of Weems v. United States (1910), the defendant had been convicted of falsifying a public document and sentenced to 15 years [of] hard labor in chains and permanent civil disabilities. The Court noted that "it is a precept of justice that punishment for crime should be graduated and proportioned to offense," and held that the sentence violated the Eighth Amendment.

Most recently, the Court has applied the principle of proportionality to hold capital punishment excessive in certain circumstances. Enmund v. Florida (1982) (death penalty excessive for felony murder when defendant did not take life, attempt to take life, or intend that a life be taken or that lethal force be used).

III

A

When sentences are reviewed under the Eighth Amendment, courts should be guided by objective factors that our cases have recognized. First, we look to the gravity of the offense and the harshness of the penalty.

Second, it may be helpful to compare the sentences imposed on other criminals in the same jurisdiction. If more serious crimes are subject to the same penalty, or to less serious penalties, that is some indication that the punishment at issue may be excessive.

Third, courts may find it useful to compare the sentences imposed for commission of the same crime in other jurisdictions.

In sum, a court's proportionality analysis under the Eighth Amendment should be guided by objective criteria, including (i) the gravity of the offense and the harshness of the penalty; (ii) the sentences imposed on other criminals in the same jurisdiction; and (iii) the sentences imposed for commission of the same crime in other jurisdictions.

IV

It remains to apply the analytical framework established by our prior decisions to the case before us.

A

Helm's crime was "one of the most passive felonies a person could commit. It involved neither violence nor threat of violence to any person. The $100 face value of Helm's "no account" check was not trivial, but neither was it a large amount. One hundred dollars was less than half the amount South Dakota required for a felonious theft. It is easy to see why such a crime is viewed by society as among the less serious offenses.

Helm, of course, was not charged simply with uttering a "no account" check, but also with being a habitual offender. And a State is justified in punishing a recidivist more severely than it punishes a first offender. Helm's status, however, cannot be considered in the abstract. His prior offenses, although classified as felonies, were all relatively minor. All were nonviolent and none was a crime against a person.

Helm's present sentence is life imprisonment without possibility of parole. Barring executive clemency, Helm will spend the rest of his life in the state penitentiary. This sentence is far more severe than the life sentence we considered in Rummel v. Estelle. Rummel was likely to have been eligible for parole within 12 years of his initial confinement, a fact on which the Court relied heavily. Helm's sentence is the most severe punishment that the State could have imposed on any criminal for any crime. Only capital punishment, a penalty not authorized in South Dakota when Helm was sentenced, exceeds it.

We next consider the sentences that could be imposed on other criminals in the same jurisdiction. When Helm was sentenced, a South Dakota court was required to impose a life sentence for murder, and was authorized to impose a life sentence for treason, first-degree manslaughter, first-degree arson, and kidnaping, No other crime was punishable so severely on the first offense.

Finally, we compare the sentences imposed for commission of the same crime in other jurisdictions. The Court of Appeals found that "Helm could have received a life sentence without parole for his offense in only one other state, Nevada." At the very least, therefore, it is clear that Helm could not have received such a severe sentence in 48 of the 50 States. But even under Nevada law, a life sentence without possibility of parole is merely authorized in these circumstances. We are not advised that any defendant such as Helm, whose prior offenses were so minor, actually has received the maximum penalty in Nevada. It appears that Helm was treated more severely than he would have been in any other State.

B

The State argues that the present case is essentially the same as Rummel v. Estelle, for the possibility of parole in that case is matched by the possibility of executive clemency here. The State reasons that the Governor could commute Helm's sentence to a term of years. We conclude, however, that the South Dakota commutation system is fundamentally different from the parole system that was before us in *Rummel.*

As a matter of law, parole and commutation are different concepts, despite some surface similarities. Parole is a regular part of the rehabilitative process. Assuming good behavior, it is the normal expectation in the vast majority of cases. The law generally specifies when a prisoner will be eligible to be considered for parole, and details the standards and procedures applicable at that time. Thus it is possible to predict, at least to some extent, when parole might be granted. Commutation, on the other hand, is an ad hoc exercise of executive clemency.

The possibility of commutation is nothing more than a hope for "an ad hoc exercise of clemency." It is little different from the possibility of executive clemency that exists in every case in which a defendant challenges his sentence under the Eighth Amendment. Recognition of such a bare possibility would make judicial review under the Eighth Amendment meaningless.

V

The Constitution requires us to examine Helm's sentence to determine if it is proportionate to his crime. Applying objective criteria, we find that Helm has received the penultimate sentence for relatively minor criminal conduct. He has been treated more harshly than other criminals in the State who have committed more serious crimes. He has been treated more harshly than he would have been in any other jurisdiction, with the possible exception of a single State. We conclude that his sentence is significantly disproportionate to his crime, and is therefore prohibited by the Eighth Amendment.

Chief Justice BURGER, with whom Justice WHITE, Justice REHNQUIST, and Justice O'CONNOR join, dissenting.

The controlling law governing this case is crystal clear, but today the Court blithely discards any concept of stare decisis, trespasses gravely on the authority of the states, and distorts the concept of proportionality of punishment by tearing it from its moorings in capital cases. Only three Terms ago, we held in Rummel v. Estelle (1980), that a life sentence imposed after only a third nonviolent felony conviction did not constitute cruel and unusual punishment under the Eighth Amendment. Today, the Court ignores its recent precedent and holds that a life sentence imposed after a seventh felony conviction constitutes cruel and unusual punishment under the Eighth Amendment. Moreover, I reject the fiction that all Helm's crimes were innocuous or nonviolent. Among his felonies were three burglaries and a third conviction for drunken driving. By comparison Rummel was a relatively "model citizen." Although today's holding cannot rationally be reconciled with *Rummel*, the Court does not purport to overrule *Rummel.* I therefore dissent.

Although historians and scholars have disagreed about the Framers' original intentions, the more common view seems to be that the Framers viewed the Cruel and Unusual Punishments Clause as prohibiting the kind of torture meted out during the reign of the Stuarts. Moreover, it is clear that until 1892, over 100 years after the ratification of the Bill of Rights, not a single Justice of this Court even asserted the doctrine adopted for the first time by the Court today. The prevailing view up to now has been that the Eighth Amendment reaches only the mode of punishment and not the length of a sentence of imprisonment. In light of this history, it is disingenuous for the Court blandly to assert that "[the] constitutional principle of proportionality has been recognized explicitly in this Court for almost a century."

This Court has applied a proportionality test only in extraordinary cases, *Weems* being one example and the line of capital cases another. Today's conclusion by five Justices that they are able to say that one offense has less "gravity" than another is nothing other than a bald substitution of individual subjective moral values for those of the legislature.

By asserting the power to review sentences of imprisonment for excessiveness the Court launches into uncharted and unchartable waters. Today it holds that a sentence of life imprisonment, without the possibility of parole, is excessive punishment for a seventh allegedly "nonviolent" felony. How about the eighth "nonviolent" felony? The ninth? The twelfth? Suppose one offense was a simple assault? Or selling liquor to a minor? Or statutory rape? Or price fixing? The permutations are endless and the Court's opinion is bankrupt of realistic guiding principles.

There is a real risk that this holding will flood the appellate courts with cases in which equally arbitrary lines must be drawn.

Indeed, Chief Justice Burger was not far off the mark. Soon after Solem v. Helm, appellate courts became flooded with claims of cruel and unusual punishment. Therefore, it was not surprising when a few years later, the Supreme Court revisited the issue of proportionality review in Harmelin v. Michigan, 501 U.S. 957 (1991).

In *Harmelin*, the Court sought to limit the effects of proportionality review. Justice Scalia, joined by Chief Justice Rehnquist, would have taken the dramatic step of overturning *Solem* and holding, based on Justice Scalia's detailed review of history, that the Eighth Amendment does not require proportionality review. Justice Scalia wrote that Eighth Amendment challenges should be limited to attacks on the mode of punishment: "Throughout the 19th century, state courts interpreting state constitutional provisions with identical or more expansive wording (i.e., 'cruel or unusual') concluded that these provisions did not proscribe disproportionality but only certain modes of punishment." *Id.* at 983. Justice Scalia gave examples of cruel and unusual punishments that would be proscribed, noting in particular the "vicious punishments for treason decreed in the Bloody Assizes (drawing and quartering, burning of women felons, beheading, disembowling, etc.)." Lengthy imprisonment, however, would not be covered.

Justice Kennedy, joined by Justices O'Connor and Souter, wrote the controlling concurrence in the case. On the basis of stare decisis, Justice Kennedy held that the Supreme Court's 80-year jurisprudence of proportionality should govern the outcome of the case. He did not believe, however, that Harmelin's sentence — mandatory life imprisonment without the possibility of parole — was disproportional given the nature of his crime: possessing 672 grams of cocaine. Even though Harmelin had never been convicted for a prior offense, Justice Kennedy held that Harmelin's sentence should be upheld.

Setting forth his view of the Eighth Amendment proportionality review, Justice Kennedy identified four principles that should govern: First, deference should be given to legislatures as to the appropriate sentence for specific crimes. Second, the Eighth Amendment "does not mandate adoption of any one penological theory." Third, "marked divergences both in underlying theories of sentencing and in the length of prescribed prison terms are the inevitable, often beneficial, result of the federal structure." Finally, proportionality review "should be informed by 'objective factors to the maximum possible extent.'"

With these considerations in mind, Justice Kennedy held that a life sentence for Harmelin's offense was not disproportionate:

> Petitioner was convicted of possession of more than 650 grams (over 1.5 pounds) of cocaine. This amount of pure cocaine has a potential yield of between 32,500 and 65,000 doses. From any standpoint, this crime falls in a different category from the relatively minor, nonviolent crime at issue in *Solem*. Petitioner's suggestion that his crime was nonviolent and victimless is false to the point of absurdity. To the contrary, petitioner's crime threatened to cause grave harm to society.
>
> The severity of petitioner's crime brings his sentence within the constitutional boundaries established by our prior decisions.

Justice Kennedy also wrote that although Harmelin's sentence may have been harsh in comparison to sentences imposed by other jurisdictions for similar crimes,

> intrajurisdictional and interjurisdictional analyses are appropriate only in the rare case in which a threshold comparison of the crime committed and the sentence imposed leads to an inference of gross disproportionality. . . . In light of the gravity of petitioner's offense, a comparison of his crime with his sentence does not give rise to an inference of gross disproportionality, and comparative analysis of his sentence with others in Michigan and across the Nation need not be performed.

Finally, Justice Kennedy wrote that the mandatory nature of Harmelin's sentence did not affect its constitutionality:

> It is beyond question that the legislature "has the power to define criminal punishments without giving the courts any sentencing discretion." Since the beginning of the Republic, Congress and the States have enacted mandatory sentencing schemes. To set aside petitioner's mandatory sentence would require rejection not of the judgment of a single jurist, as in *Solem*, but rather the collective wisdom of the Michigan Legislature and, as a consequence, the Michigan citizenry.[7]

---

7. Justice Kennedy added:

> In asserting the constitutionality of this mandatory sentence, I offer no judgment on its wisdom. Mandatory sentencing schemes can be criticized for depriving judges of the power to exercise individual discretion when remorse and acknowledgment of guilt, or other extenuating facts, present what might seem a compelling case for departure from

Justices White, Blackmun, and Stevens dissented. First, they contested Justice Scalia's contention that the words "cruel and unusual punishment" apply only to the mode of punishment and do not authorize a proportionality review. They then applied the *Solem* factors and held that, notwithstanding the gravity of Harmelin's offense, his sentence was disproportionate to the offense.

2. *Proportionality and Three Strikes Laws*

The trend in many states has been to adopt "three strikes" laws that impose particularly long sentences on repeat offenders. For example, California has adopted a "Three Strikes and You're Out" law that requires the court to impose a prison term of 25 years to life on any offender convicted of any felony who has two prior "serious" or "violent" offenses. As constructed, the law has permitted a defendant who had prior felonies for burglary and drug use to be sentenced to 50 years to life for stealing children's videos worth approximately $150 from a Kmart store. *See* Lockyer v. Andrade, 538 U.S. 63 (2003).

In the next case, the Supreme Court applied the *Rummel-Solem-Harmelin* line of cases to determine whether three strikes sentences are constitutional.

EWING v. CALIFORNIA
538 U.S. 11 (2003)

Justice O'CONNOR announced the judgment of the Court and delivered an opinion in which Chief Justice REHNQUIST and Justice KENNEDY join.

In this case, we decide whether the Eighth Amendment prohibits the State of California from sentencing a repeat felon to a prison term of 25 years to life under the State's "Three Strikes and You're Out" law.

I

A

California's three strikes law reflects a shift in the State's sentencing policies toward incapacitating and deterring repeat offenders who threaten the public safety. The law was designed "to ensure longer prison sentences

---

the maximum. On the other hand, broad and unreviewed discretion exercised by sentencing judges leads to the perception that no clear standards are being applied, and that the rule of law is imperiled by sentences imposed for no discernible reason other than the subjective reactions of the sentencing judge. The debate illustrates that, as noted at the outset, arguments for and against particular sentencing schemes are for legislatures to resolve.

and greater punishment for those who commit a felony and have been previously convicted of serious and/or violent felony offenses."

Between 1993 and 1995, 24 States and the Federal Government enacted three strikes laws. Though the three strikes laws vary from State to State, they share a common goal of protecting the public safety by providing lengthy prison terms for habitual felons.

B

When a defendant is convicted of a felony, and he has previously been convicted of one or more prior felonies defined as "serious" or "violent" in Cal. Penal Code Ann. §§667.5 and 1192.7, sentencing is conducted pursuant to the three strikes law. Prior convictions must be alleged in the charging document, and the defendant has a right to a jury determination that the prosecution has proved the prior convictions beyond a reasonable doubt.

If the defendant has one prior "serious" or "violent" felony conviction, he must be sentenced to "twice the term otherwise provided as punishment for the current felony conviction." If the defendant has two or more prior "serious" or "violent" felony convictions, he must receive "an indeterminate term of life imprisonment." Defendants sentenced to life under the three strikes law become eligible for parole on a date calculated by reference to a "minimum term," which is the greater of (a) three times the term otherwise provided for the current conviction, (b) 25 years, or (c) the term determined by the court pursuant to §1170 for the underlying conviction, including any enhancements.

Under California law, certain offenses may be classified as either felonies or misdemeanors. These crimes are known as "wobblers." Some crimes that would otherwise be misdemeanors become "wobblers" because of the defendant's prior record. For example, petty theft, a misdemeanor, becomes a "wobbler" when the defendant has previously served a prison term for committing specified theft-related crimes. Other crimes, such as grand theft, are "wobblers" regardless of the defendant's prior record. Both types of "wobblers" are triggering offenses under the three strikes law only when they are treated as felonies. Under California law, a "wobbler" is presumptively a felony and "remains a felony except when the discretion is actually exercised" to make the crime a misdemeanor.

In California, prosecutors may exercise their discretion to charge a "wobbler" as either a felony or a misdemeanor. Likewise, California trial courts have discretion to reduce a "wobbler" charged as a felony to a misdemeanor either before preliminary examination or at sentencing to avoid imposing a three strikes sentence.

California trial courts can also vacate allegations of prior "serious" or "violent" felony convictions, either on motion by the prosecution or sua sponte. In ruling whether to vacate allegations of prior felony convictions, courts consider whether, "in light of the nature and circumstances of [the defendant's] present felonies and prior serious and/or violent felony convictions, and the particulars of his background, character, and prospects, the defendant may be deemed outside the [three strikes'] scheme's spirit, in whole or in part." Thus, trial courts may avoid imposing a three strikes sentence in two ways: first, by reducing "wobblers" to misdemeanors (which do not qualify as triggering offenses), and second, by vacating allegations of prior "serious" or "violent" felony convictions.

C

On parole from a 9-year prison term, petitioner Gary Ewing walked into the pro shop of the El Segundo Golf Course in Los Angeles County on March 12, 2000. He walked out with three golf clubs, priced at $399 apiece, concealed in his pants leg. A shop employee, whose suspicions were aroused when he observed Ewing limp out of the pro shop, telephoned the police. The police apprehended Ewing in the parking lot.

Ewing is no stranger to the criminal justice system. In 1984, at the age of 22, he pleaded guilty to theft. The court sentenced him to six months in jail (suspended), three years' probation, and a $300 fine. In 1988, he was convicted of felony grand theft auto and sentenced to one year in jail and three years' probation. After Ewing completed probation, however, the sentencing court reduced the crime to a misdemeanor, permitted Ewing to withdraw his guilty plea, and dismissed the case. In 1990, he was convicted of petty theft with a prior and sentenced to 60 days in the county jail and three years' probation. In 1992, Ewing was convicted of battery and sentenced to 30 days in the county jail and two years' summary probation. One month later, he was convicted of theft and sentenced to 10 days in the county jail and 12 months' probation. In January 1993, Ewing was convicted of burglary and sentenced to 60 days in the county jail and one year's summary probation. In February 1993, he was convicted of possessing drug paraphernalia and sentenced to six months in the county jail and three years' probation. In July 1993, he was convicted of appropriating lost property and sentenced to 10 days in the county jail and two years' summary probation. In September 1993, he was convicted of unlawfully possessing a firearm and trespassing and sentenced to 30 days in the county jail and one year's probation.

In October and November 1993, Ewing committed three burglaries and one robbery at a Long Beach, California, apartment complex over a 5-week period. He awakened one of his victims, asleep on her living room sofa, as he tried to disconnect her video cassette recorder from the television in that room. When she screamed, Ewing ran out the front door. On another occasion, Ewing accosted a victim in the mailroom of the apartment complex. Ewing claimed to have a gun and ordered the victim to hand over his wallet. When the victim resisted, Ewing produced a knife and forced the victim back to the apartment itself. While Ewing rifled through the bedroom, the victim fled the apartment screaming for help. Ewing absconded with the victim's money and credit cards.

On December 9, 1993, Ewing was arrested on the premises of the apartment complex for trespassing and lying to a police officer. The knife used in the robbery and a glass cocaine pipe were later found in the back seat of the patrol car used to transport Ewing to the police station. A jury convicted Ewing of first-degree robbery and three counts of residential burglary. Sentenced to nine years and eight months in prison, Ewing was paroled in 1999.

Only 10 months later, Ewing stole the golf clubs at issue in this case. He was charged with, and ultimately convicted of, one count of felony grand theft of personal property in excess of $400. As required by the three strikes law, the prosecutor formally alleged, and the trial court later found, that Ewing had been convicted previously of four serious or violent felonies for the three burglaries and the robbery in the Long Beach apartment complex.

At the sentencing hearing, Ewing asked the court to reduce the conviction for grand theft, a "wobbler" under California law, to a misdemeanor so as to avoid a three strikes sentence. Ewing also asked the trial court to exercise its discretion to dismiss the allegations of some or all of his prior serious or violent felony convictions, again for purposes of avoiding a three strikes sentence.

In the end, the trial judge determined that the grand theft should remain a felony. The court also ruled that the four prior strikes for the three burglaries and the robbery in Long Beach should stand. As a newly convicted felon with two or more "serious" or "violent" felony convictions in his past, Ewing was sentenced under the three strikes law to 25 years to life.

II

A

The Eighth Amendment, which forbids cruel and unusual punishments, contains a "narrow proportionality principle" that "applies to noncapital sentences." Harmelin v. Michigan (1991) (Kennedy, J., concurring in part and concurring in judgment). We have most recently addressed the proportionality principle as applied to terms of years in a series of cases beginning with Rummel v. Estelle. [Justice O'Connor then reviewed Rummel v. Estelle, Solem v. Helm, and Justice Kennedy's controlling opinion in *Harmelin*.]

The proportionality principles in our cases distilled in Justice Kennedy's concurrence guide our application of the Eighth Amendment in the new context that we are called upon to consider.

B

For many years, most States have had laws providing for enhanced sentencing of repeat offenders. Yet between 1993 and 1995, three strikes laws effected a sea change in criminal sentencing throughout the Nation. These laws responded to widespread public concerns about crime by targeting the class of offenders who pose the greatest threat to public safety: career criminals.

Throughout the States, legislatures enacting three strikes laws made a deliberate policy choice that individuals who have repeatedly engaged in serious or violent criminal behavior, and whose conduct has not been deterred by more conventional approaches to punishment, must be isolated from society in order to protect the public safety.

When the California Legislature enacted the three strikes law, it made a judgment that protecting the public safety requires incapacitating criminals who have already been convicted of at least one serious or violent crime. Nothing in the Eighth Amendment prohibits California from making that choice.

California's justification is no pretext. Recidivism is a serious public safety concern in California and throughout the Nation. According to a recent report, approximately 67 percent of former inmates released from state prisons were charged with at least one "serious" new crime within three years of their release.

The State's interest in deterring crime also lends some support to the three strikes law. We have long viewed both incapacitation and deterrence as rationales for recidivism statutes: "[A] recidivist statute['s] . . . primary goals are to deter repeat offenders and, at some point in the life of one who repeatedly commits criminal offenses serious enough to be punished as felonies, to segregate that person from the rest of society for an extended period of time." *Rummel.* Four years after the passage of California's three strikes law, the recidivism rate of parolees returned to prison for the commission of a new crime dropped by nearly 25 percent.

To be sure, California's three strikes law has sparked controversy. Critics have doubted the law's wisdom, cost-efficiency, and effectiveness in reaching its goals. This criticism is appropriately directed at the legislature, which has primary responsibility for making the difficult policy choices that underlie any criminal sentencing scheme. We do not sit as a "superlegislature" to second-guess these policy choices. It is enough that the State of California has a reasonable basis for believing that dramatically enhanced sentences for habitual felons "advances the goals of [its] criminal justice system in any substantial way."

III

Against this backdrop, we consider Ewing's claim that his three strikes sentence of 25 years to life is unconstitutionally disproportionate to his offense of "shoplifting three golf clubs." We first address the gravity of the offense compared to the harshness of the penalty. At the threshold, we note that Ewing incorrectly frames the issue. The gravity of his offense was not merely "shoplifting three golf clubs." Rather, Ewing was convicted of felony grand theft for stealing nearly $1,200 worth of merchandise after previously having been convicted of at least two "violent" or "serious" felonies.

In weighing the gravity of Ewing's offense, we must place on the scales not only his current felony, but also his long history of felony recidivism. Any other approach would fail to accord proper deference to the policy judgments that find expression in the legislature's choice of sanctions.

In imposing a three strikes sentence, the State's interest is not merely punishing the offense of conviction, or the "triggering" offense: "It is in addition the interest . . . in dealing in a harsher manner with those who by repeated criminal acts have shown that they are simply incapable of conforming to the norms of society as established by its criminal law."

Ewing's sentence is justified by the State's public-safety interest in incapacitating and deterring recidivist felons, and amply supported by his own long, serious criminal record.

We hold that Ewing's sentence of 25 years to life in prison, imposed for the offense of felony grand theft under the three strikes law, is not grossly disproportionate and therefore does not violate the Eighth Amendment's prohibition on cruel and unusual punishments.

Justice SCALIA, concurring in the judgment.

In my concurring opinion in Harmelin v. Michigan (1991), I concluded that the Eighth Amendment's prohibition of "cruel and unusual punishments" was aimed at excluding only certain modes of punishment, and was not a "guarantee against disproportionate sentences." Out of respect for the principle of stare decisis, I might nonetheless accept the contrary holding of Solem v. Helm that the Eighth Amendment contains a narrow proportionality principle — if I felt I could intelligently apply it. This case demonstrates why I cannot.

Proportionality — the notion that the punishment should fit the crime — is inherently a concept tied to the penological goal of retribution. "It becomes difficult even to speak intelligently of 'proportionality,' once deterrence and rehabilitation are given significant weight," — not to mention giving weight to the purpose of California's three strikes law: incapacitation. In the present case, the game is up once the plurality has acknowledged that "the Constitution does not mandate adoption of any one penological theory," and that a "sentence can have a variety of justifications, such as incapacitation, deterrence, retribution, or rehabilitation." That acknowledgment having been made, it no longer suffices merely to assess "the gravity of the offense compared to the harshness of the penalty;" that classic description of the proportionality principle (alone and in itself quite resistant to policy-free, legal analysis) now becomes merely the "first" step of the inquiry. Having completed that step (by a discussion which, in all fairness, does not convincingly establish that 25-years-to-life is a "proportionate" punishment for stealing three golf clubs), the plurality must then add an analysis to show that "Ewing's sentence is justified by the State's public-safety interest in incapacitating and deterring recidivist felons."

Which indeed it is — though why that has anything to do with the principle of proportionality is a mystery. Perhaps the plurality should revise its terminology, so that what it reads into the Eighth Amendment is not the unstated proposition that all punishment should be reasonably proportionate to the gravity of the offense, but rather the unstated proposition that all punishment should reasonably pursue the multiple purposes of the criminal law. That formulation would make it clearer than ever, of course, that the plurality is not applying law but evaluating policy.

Justice THOMAS, concurring in the judgment.

I agree with Justice Scalia's view that the proportionality test announced in Solem v. Helm is incapable of judicial application. Even were *Solem*'s test perfectly clear, however, I would not feel compelled by stare decisis to apply it. In my view, the Cruel and Unusual Punishments Clause of the Eighth Amendment contains no proportionality principle.

Justice STEVENS, with whom Justices SOUTER, GINSBURG, and BREYER join, dissenting.

"The Eighth Amendment succinctly prohibits 'excessive' sanctions." . . . The absence of a black-letter rule does not disable judges from exercising their discretion in construing the outer limits on sentencing authority that the Eighth Amendment imposes.

Throughout most of the Nation's history — before guideline sentencing became so prevalent — federal and state trial judges imposed specific sentences pursuant to grants of authority that gave them uncabined discretion within broad ranges. It was not unheard of for a statute to authorize a sentence ranging from one year to life, for example. In exercising their discretion, sentencing judges wisely employed a proportionality principle that took into account all of the justifications for punishment — namely, deterrence, incapacitation, retribution and rehabilitation. Likewise, I think it clear that the Eighth Amendment's prohibition of "cruel and unusual punishments" expresses a broad and basic proportionality principle that takes into account all of the justifications for penal sanctions. It is this broad proportionality principle that would preclude reliance on any of the justifications for punishment to support, for example, a life sentence for overtime parking.

Justice BREYER, with whom Justice STEVENS, Justice SOUTER, and Justice GINSBURG join, dissenting.

The constitutional question is whether the "three strikes" sentence imposed by California upon repeat-offender Gary Ewing is "grossly disproportionate" to his crime. The sentence amounts to a real prison term of at least 25 years. The sentence-triggering criminal conduct consists of the theft of three golf clubs priced at a total of $1,197. The offender has a criminal history that includes four felony convictions arising out of three separate burglaries (one armed). In Solem v. Helm, the Court found grossly disproportionate a somewhat longer sentence imposed on a recidivist offender for triggering criminal conduct that was somewhat less severe. In my view, the differences are not determinative, and the Court should reach the same ultimate conclusion here.

Ewing's sentence on its face imposes one of the most severe punishments available upon a recidivist who subsequently engaged in one of the less serious forms of criminal conduct. I do not deny the seriousness of shoplifting, which an amicus curiae tells us costs retailers in the range of $30 billion annually. But consider that conduct in terms of the factors that this Court mentioned in *Solem*— the "harm caused or threatened to the victim or society," the "absolute magnitude of the crime," and the offender's "culpability." In respect to all three criteria, the sentence-triggering behavior here ranks well toward the bottom of the criminal conduct scale.

———————

In a companion case to *Ewing*, Lockyer v. Andrade, 538 U.S. 63 (2003), the Supreme Court denied habeas corpus relief to a criminal defendant who received a sentence of 50 years to life in prison for stealing $153 worth of videotapes from a Kmart store. He received the sentence under California's three strikes law even though he had never committed a violent crime. The Supreme Court, in a 5-4 decision, denied habeas relief on the ground that there was not clearly established law that the sentence was disproportionate.

As *Ewing* and *Andrade* demonstrate, although it is theoretically possible for a defendant sentenced under a three strikes law to claim an Eighth Amendment violation, the task will be very difficult because of the great deference the Court gives to the legislature's determination that a recidivist must face harsh punishment.

3. *Juveniles and Sentencing*

The Eighth Amendment proportionality test is ordinarily a case-by-case analysis. However, in addressing standards for sentencing juveniles, the Court has set forth per se rules striking down certain juvenile sentences as grossly disproportionate. In recognizing that juveniles should not be judged by the same standards as adults, the Court held in Graham v. Florida, 560 U.S. 48 (2010), that it is per se unconstitutional to impose on a juvenile offender the sentence of life without the possibility of parole (LWOP) for non-homicide offenses. In Miller v. Alabama, 567 U.S. 460 (2012), the Court recognized that mandatory LWOP sentences for juveniles, even those convicted of homicide offenses, also violate the Eighth Amendment.

GRAHAM v. FLORIDA

560 U.S. 48 (2010)

Justice KENNEDY delivered the opinion of the Court.

The issue before the Court is whether the Constitution permits a juvenile offender to be sentenced to life in prison without parole for a nonhomicide crime.

I

Petitioner is Terrance Jamar Graham. He was born on January 6, 1987. Graham's parents were addicted to crack cocaine, and their drug use persisted in his early years. Graham was diagnosed with attention deficit hyperactivity disorder in elementary school. He began drinking alcohol and using tobacco at age 9 and smoked marijuana at age 13.

In July 2003, when Graham was age 16, he and three other school-age youths attempted to rob a barbeque restaurant in Jacksonville, Florida. Graham's masked accomplice twice struck the restaurant manager in the back of the head with a metal bar. The restaurant manager required stitches for his head injury. No money was taken.

Graham was arrested for the robbery attempt [and tried as an adult and pled guilty. He was sentenced to a 3-year term of probation, requiring him to spend the first 12 months of his probation in the county jail. He was released on June 25, 2004.]

Less than 6 months later, on the night of December 2, 2004, Graham again was arrested. Graham participated in a home invasion robbery. [He and his two accomplices forcibly entered the home of Carlos Rodriguez and held a pistol to Rodriguez's chest. For the next 30 minutes, the three ransacked the home searching for money.]

The State further alleged that Graham [and his cohorts] later the same evening, attempted a second robbery. When detectives interviewed Graham, he denied involvement in the crimes [and denied knowing his codefendants]. The night that Graham allegedly committed the robbery, he was 34 days short of his 18th birthday.

The trial court held a sentencing hearing. The State recommended that Graham receive 30 years on the armed burglary count and 15 years on the attempted armed robbery count.

After hearing Graham's testimony, the trial court explained the sentence it was about to pronounce:

> Mr. Graham, as I look back on your case, yours is really candidly a sad situation. You had, as far as I can tell, you have quite a family structure. You had a lot of people who wanted to try and help you get your life turned around including the court system, and you had a judge who took the step to try and give you direction through his probation order to give you a chance to get back onto track. And at the time you seemed through your letters that that is exactly what you wanted to do. And I don't know why it is that you threw your life away. I don't know why.
>
> But you did, and that is what is so sad about this today is that you have actually been given a chance to get through this, the original charge, which were very serious charges to begin with. . . . The attempted robbery with a weapon was a very serious charge. . . .
>
> [I]n a very short period of time you were back before the Court on a violation of this probation, and then here you are two years later standing before me, literally—facing a life sentence as to count 1 and up to 15 years as to count 2.
>
> And I don't understand why you would be given such a great opportunity to do something with your life and why you would throw it away. The only thing that I can

rationalize is that you decided that this is how you were going to lead your life and that there is nothing that we can do for you. And as the state pointed out, that this is an escalating pattern of criminal conduct on your part and that we can't help you any further. We can't do anything to deter you. This is the way you are going to lead your life, and I don't know why you are going to. You've made that decision. I have no idea. But, evidently, that is what you decided to do.

So then it becomes a focus, if I can't do anything to help you, if I can't do anything to get you back on the right path, then I have to start focusing on the community and trying to protect the community from your actions. And, unfortunately, that is where we are today is I don't see where I can do anything to help you any further. You've evidently decided this is the direction you're going to take in life, and it's unfortunate that you made that choice.

I have reviewed the statute. I don't see where any further juvenile sanctions would be appropriate. I don't see where any youthful offender sanctions would be appropriate. Given your escalating pattern of criminal conduct, it is apparent to the Court that you have decided that this is the way you are going to live your life and that the only thing I can do now is to try and protect the community from your actions.

The trial court . . . sentenced him to the maximum sentence authorized by law on each charge: life imprisonment for the armed burglary and 15 years for the attempted armed robbery. Because Florida has abolished its parole system, a life sentence gives a defendant no possibility of release unless he is granted executive clemency.

II

The Eighth Amendment states: "Excessive bail shall not be required, nor excessive fines imposed, nor cruel and unusual punishments inflicted." The Cruel and Unusual Punishments Clause prohibits the imposition of inherently barbaric punishments under all circumstances. "[P]unishments of torture," for example, "are forbidden."

For the most part, however, the Court's precedents consider punishments challenged not as inherently barbaric but as disproportionate to the crime. The concept of proportionality is central to the Eighth Amendment. Embodied in the Constitution's ban on cruel and unusual punishments is the "precept of justice that punishment for crime should be graduated and proportioned to [the] offense."

The Court's cases addressing the proportionality of sentences fall within two general classifications. The first involves challenges to the length of term-of-years sentences given all the circumstances in a particular case. The second comprises cases in which the Court implements the proportionality standard by certain categorical restrictions on the death penalty.

In the first classification the Court considers all of the circumstances of the case to determine whether the sentence is unconstitutionally excessive. Under this approach, the Court has held unconstitutional a life without parole sentence for the defendant's seventh nonviolent felony, the crime of passing a worthless check. Solem v. Helm (1983).

The second classification of cases has used categorical rules to define Eighth Amendment standards. With respect to the nature of the offense, the Court has concluded that capital punishment is impermissible for non-homicide crimes against individuals. In cases turning on the characteristics of the offender, the Court has adopted categorical rules prohibiting the death penalty for defendants who committed their crimes before the age of 18, Roper v. Simmons (2005), or whose intellectual functioning is in a low range, Atkins v. Virginia (2002).

III

The analysis begins with objective indicia of national consensus. Six jurisdictions do not allow life without parole sentences for any juvenile offenders. Seven jurisdictions permit life without parole for juvenile offenders, but only for homicide crimes. Thirty-seven States as well as the District of Columbia permit sentences of life without parole for a juvenile nonhomicide offender in some circumstances. Federal law also allows for the possibility of life without parole for offenders as young as 13. Relying on this metric, the State and its amici argue that there is no national consensus against the sentencing practice at issue.

This argument is incomplete and unavailing. "There are measures of consensus other than legislation." Actual sentencing practices are an important part of the Court's inquiry into consensus. [O]nly 12 jurisdictions nationwide in fact impose life without parole sentences on juvenile nonhomicide offenders — and most of those impose the sentence quite rarely — while 26 States as well as the District of Columbia do not impose them despite apparent statutory authorization.

Roper established that because juveniles have lessened culpability they are less deserving of the most severe punishments. As compared to adults, juveniles have a " 'lack of maturity and an underdeveloped sense of responsibility' " they "are more vulnerable or susceptible to negative influences and outside pressures, including peer pressure"; and their characters are "not as well formed." A juvenile is not absolved of responsibility for his actions, but his transgression "is not as morally reprehensible as that of an adult."

[A] life without parole sentence for a juvenile defendant . . . "means denial of hope; it means that good behavior and character improvement are immaterial; it means that whatever the future might hold in store for the mind and spirit of [the convict], he will remain in prison for the rest of his days."

Life without parole is an especially harsh punishment for a juvenile. Under this sentence a juvenile offender will on average serve more years and a greater percentage of his life in prison than an adult offender. A 16-year-old and a 75-year-old each sentenced to life without parole receive the same punishment in name only. This reality cannot be ignored.

The penological justifications for the sentencing practice are also relevant to the analysis. With respect to life without parole for juvenile nonhomicide offenders, none of the goals of penal sanctions that have been recognized as legitimate — retribution, deterrence, incapacitation, and rehabilitation, provides an adequate justification.

Retribution is a legitimate reason to punish, but it cannot support the sentence at issue here. Society is entitled to impose severe sanctions on a juvenile nonhomicide offender to express its condemnation of the crime and to seek restoration of the moral imbalance caused by the offense. But "[t]he heart of the retribution rationale is that a criminal sentence must be directly related to the personal culpability of the criminal offender." [R]etribution does not justify imposing the second most severe penalty on the less culpable juvenile nonhomicide offender.

Deterrence does not suffice to justify the sentence either. Roper noted that "the same characteristics that render juveniles less culpable than adults suggest . . . that juveniles will be less susceptible to deterrence." Because juveniles' "lack of maturity and underdeveloped sense of responsibility . . . often result in impetuous and ill-considered actions and decisions," they are less likely to take a possible punishment into consideration when making decisions.

Incapacitation, a third legitimate reason for imprisonment, does not justify the life without parole sentence in question here. To justify life without parole on the assumption that the juvenile offender forever will be a danger to society requires the sentencer to make a judgment that the juvenile is incorrigible. The characteristics of juveniles make that judgment questionable. "It is difficult even for expert psychologists to differentiate between the juvenile offender whose crime reflects unfortunate yet transient immaturity, and the rare juvenile offender whose crime reflects irreparable corruption."

Finally there is rehabilitation, a penological goal that forms the basis of parole systems. A sentence of life imprisonment without parole, however, cannot be justified by the goal of rehabilitation. The penalty forswears altogether the rehabilitative ideal. By denying the defendant the right to reenter the community, the State makes an irrevocable judgment about that person's value and place in society.

In sum, penological theory is not adequate to justify life without parole for juvenile nonhomicide offenders. This Court now holds that for a juvenile offender who did not commit homicide the Eighth Amendment forbids the sentence of life without parole.

A State is not required to guarantee eventual freedom to a juvenile offender convicted of a nonhomicide crime. What the State must do, however, is give defendants like Graham some meaningful opportunity to obtain release based on demonstrated maturity and rehabilitation. Those who commit truly horrifying crimes as juveniles may turn out to be irredeemable, and thus deserving of incarceration for the duration of their lives. The Eighth Amendment does not foreclose the possibility that persons convicted of nonhomicide crimes committed before adulthood will remain behind bars for life. It does forbid States from making the judgment at the outset that those offenders never will be fit to reenter society.

Terrance Graham's sentence guarantees he will die in prison without any meaningful opportunity to obtain release, no matter what he might do to demonstrate that the bad acts he committed as a teenager are not representative of his true character, even if he spends the next half century attempting to atone for his crimes and learn from his mistakes. The State has denied him any chance to later demonstrate that he is fit to rejoin society based solely on a nonhomicide crime that he committed while he was a child in the eyes of the law. This the Eighth Amendment does not permit.

There is support for our conclusion in the fact that, in continuing to impose life without parole sentences on juveniles who did not commit homicide, the United States adheres to a sentencing practice rejected the world over. The United States is the only Nation that imposes life without parole sentences on juvenile nonhomicide offenders.

The Constitution prohibits the imposition of a life without parole sentence on a juvenile offender who did not commit homicide.

Justice STEVENS, with whom Justice GINSBURG and Justice SOTOMAYOR join, concurring.

Society changes. Knowledge accumulates. We learn, sometimes, from our mistakes. Punishments that did not seem cruel and unusual at one time may, in the light of reason and experience, be found cruel and unusual at a later time; unless we are to abandon the moral commitment embodied in the Eighth Amendment, proportionality review must never become effectively obsolete.

Chief Justice ROBERTS, concurring in the judgment.

I agree with the Court that Terrance Graham's sentence of life without parole violates the Eighth Amendment's prohibition on "cruel and unusual punishments." Unlike the majority, however, I see no need to invent a new constitutional rule of dubious provenance in reaching that conclusion. Instead, my analysis is based on an application of this Court's precedents.

Graham's case arises at the intersection of two lines of Eighth Amendment precedent. The first consists of decisions holding that the Cruel and Unusual Punishments Clause embraces a "narrow proportionality principle" that we apply, on a case-by-case basis, when asked to review noncapital sentences. Today, the Court views Roper as providing the basis for a new categorical rule that juveniles may never receive a sentence of life without parole for nonhomicide crimes. I disagree. Treating juvenile life sentences as analogous to capital punishment is at odds with our longstanding view that "the death penalty is different from other punishments in kind rather than degree."

Applying the "narrow proportionality" framework to the particular facts of this case, I conclude that Graham's sentence of life without parole violates the Eighth Amendment. There is no question that the crime for which

Graham received his life sentence . . . is "a serious crime deserving serious punishment." But [his] crimes are certainly less serious than other crimes, such as murder or rape. Both intrajurisdictional and interjurisdictional comparisons of Graham's sentence confirm the threshold inference of disproportionality.

So much for Graham. But what about Milagro Cunningham, a 17-year-old who beat and raped an 8-year-old girl before leaving her to die under 197 pounds of rock in a recycling bin in a remote landfill? Or Nathan Walker and Jakaris Taylor, the Florida juveniles who together with their friends gang-raped a woman and forced her to perform oral sex on her 12-year-old son? The fact that Graham cannot be sentenced to life without parole for his conduct says nothing whatever about these offenders, or others like them who commit nonhomicide crimes far more reprehensible than the conduct at issue here. The Court uses Graham's case as a vehicle to proclaim a new constitutional rule — applicable well beyond the particular facts of Graham's case — that a sentence of life without parole imposed on any juvenile for any nonhomicide offense is unconstitutional. This categorical conclusion is as unnecessary as it is unwise.

Justice THOMAS, with whom Justice SCALIA joins, and with whom Justice ALITO joins as to Parts I and III, dissenting.

The Court holds today that it is "grossly disproportionate" and hence unconstitutional for any judge or jury to impose a sentence of life without parole on an offender less than 18 years old, unless he has committed a homicide. [T]the Court insists that the standards of American society have evolved such that the Constitution now requires its prohibition.

The news of this evolution will, I think, come as a surprise to the American people. Congress, the District of Columbia, and 37 States allow judges and juries to consider this sentencing practice in juvenile nonhomicide cases, and those judges and juries have decided to use it in the very worst cases they have encountered.

I am unwilling to assume that we, as members of this Court, are any more capable of making such moral judgments than our fellow citizens. Nothing in our training as judges qualifies us for that task, and nothing in Article III gives us that authority.

I agree with Justice Stevens that "[w]e learn, sometimes, from our mistakes." Perhaps one day the Court will learn from this one.

MILLER v. ALABAMA

567 U.S. 460 (2012)

Justice KAGAN delivered the opinion of the Court.

The two 14-year-old offenders in these cases were convicted of murder and sentenced to life imprisonment without the possibility of parole. In neither case did the sentencing authority have any discretion to impose a different punishment. State law mandated that each juvenile die in prison even if a judge or jury would have thought that his youth and its attendant characteristics, along with the nature of his crime, made a lesser sentence (for example, life *with* the possibility of parole) more appropriate. Such a scheme prevents those meting out punishment from considering a juvenile's "lessened culpability" and greater "capacity for change," Graham v. Florida (2010), and runs afoul of our cases' requirement of individualized sentencing for defendants facing the most serious penalties. We therefore hold that mandatory life without parole for those under the age of 18 at the time of their crimes violates the Eighth Amendment's prohibition on "cruel and unusual punishments."

I

A

In November 1999, petitioner Kuntrell Jackson, then 14 years old, and two other boys decided to rob a video store. En route to the store, Jackson learned that one of the boys, Derrick Shields, was carrying a sawed-off shotgun in his coat sleeve. Jackson decided to stay outside when the two other boys entered the store. Inside, Shields pointed the gun at the store clerk, Laurie Troup, and demanded that she "give up the money." Troup refused. When Troup threatened to call the police, Shields shot and killed her. The three boys fled empty-handed.

Arkansas law gives prosecutors discretion to charge 14-year-olds as adults when they are alleged to have committed certain serious offenses. The prosecutor here exercised that authority by charging Jackson with capital felony murder and aggravated robbery. A jury later convicted Jackson of both crimes. Noting that "in view of [the] verdict, there's only one possible punishment," the judge sentenced Jackson to life without parole.

B

Like Jackson, petitioner Evan Miller was 14 years old at the time of his crime. Miller had by then been in and out of foster care because his mother suffered from alcoholism and drug addiction and his stepfather abused him. Miller, too, regularly used drugs and alcohol; and he had attempted suicide four times, the first when he was six years old.

One night in 2003, Miller was at home with a friend, Colby Smith, when a neighbor, Cole Cannon, came to make a drug deal with Miller's mother. The two boys followed Cannon back to his trailer, where all three smoked marijuana and played drinking games. When Cannon passed out, Miller stole his wallet, splitting about $300 with Smith. Miller then tried to put the wallet back in Cannon's pocket, but Cannon awoke and grabbed Miller by the throat. Smith hit Cannon with a nearby baseball bat, and once released, Miller grabbed the bat and repeatedly struck Cannon with it. Miller placed a sheet over Cannon's head, told him " 'I am God, I've come to take your life,' " and delivered one more blow. The boys then retreated to Miller's trailer, but soon decided to return to Cannon's to cover up evidence of their crime. Once there, they lit two fires. Cannon eventually died from his injuries and smoke inhalation.

Alabama law . . . allowed the District Attorney to seek removal of the case to adult court. The State accordingly charged Miller as an adult with murder in the course of arson. That crime (like capital murder in Arkansas) carries a mandatory minimum punishment of life without parole.

We granted certiorari in both cases and now reverse.

II

To start with the first set of cases: *Roper* and *Graham* establish that children are constitutionally different from adults for purposes of sentencing. Because juveniles have diminished culpability and greater prospects for reform, we explained, "they are less deserving of the most severe punishments." Those cases relied on three significant gaps between juveniles and adults. First, children have a " 'lack of maturity and an underdeveloped sense of responsibility,' " leading to recklessness, impulsivity, and heedless risk-taking. Second, children "are more vulnerable . . . to negative influences and outside pressures," including from their family and peers; they have limited "contro[l] over their own environment" and lack the ability to extricate themselves from horrific, crime-producing settings. And third, a child's character is not as "well formed" as an adult's; his traits are "less fixed" and his actions less likely to be "evidence of irretrievabl[e] deprav[ity]."

Graham concluded from this analysis that life-without-parole sentences, like capital punishment, may violate the Eighth Amendment when imposed on children. To be sure, *Graham*'s flat ban on life without parole applied only to nonhomicide crimes, and the Court took care to distinguish those offenses from murder, based on both moral culpability and consequential harm. But none of what it said about children — about their distinctive (and transitory) mental traits and environmental vulnerabilities — is crime-specific.

[T]he mandatory penalty schemes at issue here prevent the sentencer from taking account of these central considerations. By removing youth from the balance — by subjecting a juvenile to the same life-without-parole sentence applicable to an adult — these laws prohibit a sentencing authority from assessing whether the law's harshest term of imprisonment proportionately punishes a juvenile offender. That contravenes *Graham*'s (and also *Roper*'s) foundational principle: that imposition of a State's most severe penalties on juvenile offenders cannot proceed as though they were not children.

Both cases before us illustrate the problem. Take Jackson's first. As noted earlier, Jackson did not fire the bullet that killed Laurie Troup. Both his mother and his grandmother had previously shot other individuals. At the least, a sentencer should look at such facts before depriving a 14-year-old of any prospect of release from prison.

That is true also in Miller's case. No one can doubt that he and Smith committed a vicious murder. But they did it when high on drugs and alcohol consumed with the adult victim. And if ever a pathological background might have contributed to a 14-year-old's commission of a crime, it is here. Miller's stepfather physically abused him; his alcoholic and drug-addicted mother neglected him; he had been in and out of foster care as a result; and he had tried to kill himself four times, the first when he should have been in kindergarten. That Miller deserved severe punishment for killing Cole Cannon is beyond question. But once again, a sentencer needed to examine all these circumstances before concluding that life without any possibility of parole was the appropriate penalty.

We therefore hold that the Eighth Amendment forbids a sentencing scheme that mandates life in prison without possibility of parole for juvenile offenders.

Chief Justice ROBERTS, with whom Justice SCALIA, Justice THOMAS, and Justice ALITO join, dissenting.

Determining the appropriate sentence for a teenager convicted of murder presents grave and challenging questions of morality and social policy. Our role, however, is to apply the law, not to answer such questions. The pertinent law here is the Eighth Amendment to the Constitution, which prohibits "cruel and unusual punishments." Today, the Court invokes that Amendment to ban a punishment that the Court does not itself characterize as unusual, and that could not plausibly be described as such. I therefore dissent.

The parties agree that nearly 2,500 prisoners are presently serving life sentences without the possibility of parole for murders they committed before the age of 18. The Court accepts that over 2,000 of those prisoners received that sentence because it was mandated by a legislature. Put simply, if a 17-year-old is convicted of deliberately murdering an innocent victim, it is not "unusual" for the murderer to receive a mandatory sentence of life without parole. That reality should preclude finding that mandatory life imprisonment for juvenile killers violates the Eighth Amendment.

In this case, there is little doubt about the direction of society's evolution: For most of the 20th century, American sentencing practices emphasized rehabilitation of the offender and the availability of parole. But by the 1980's, outcry against repeat offenders, broad disaffection with the rehabilitative model, and other factors led many legislatures to reduce or eliminate the possibility of parole, imposing longer sentences in order to punish criminals and prevent them from committing more crimes. Statutes establishing life without parole sentences in particular became more common in the past quarter century. And the parties agree that most States have changed their laws relatively recently to expose teenage murderers to mandatory life without parole.

[T]he Court's holding does not follow from *Roper* and *Graham*. Those cases undoubtedly stand for the proposition that teenagers are less mature, less responsible, and less fixed in their ways than adults — not that a Supreme Court case was needed to establish that. What they do not stand for, and do not even suggest, is that legislators — who also know that teenagers are different from adults — may not require life without parole for juveniles who commit the worst types of murder.

Justice THOMAS, with whom Justice SCALIA joins, dissenting.

As I have previously explained, "the Cruel and Unusual Punishments Clause was originally understood as prohibiting torturous *methods* of punishment — specifically methods akin to those that had been considered cruel and unusual at the time the Bill of Rights was adopted." The clause does not contain a "proportionality principle."

The legislatures of Arkansas and Alabama, like those of 27 other jurisdictions, *ante*, at 19-20, have determined that all offenders convicted of specified homicide offenses, whether juveniles or not, deserve a sentence of life in prison without the possibility of parole. Nothing in our Constitution authorizes this Court to supplant that choice.

Justice ALITO, with whom Justice SCALIA joins, dissenting.

The Court long ago abandoned the original meaning of the Eighth Amendment, holding instead that the prohibition of "cruel and unusual punishment" embodies the "evolving standards of decency that mark the progress of a maturing society." Both the provenance and philosophical basis for this standard were problematic from the start.

The two (carefully selected) cases before us concern very young defendants. But no one should be confused by the particulars of the two cases before us. The category of murderers that the Court delicately calls "children" (murderers under the age of 18) consists overwhelmingly of young men who are fast approaching the legal age of adulthood.

Seventeen-year-olds commit a significant number of murders every year, and some of these crimes are incredibly brutal. Many of these murderers are at least as mature as the average 18-year-old. Congress and the legislatures of 43 States have concluded that at least some of these murderers should be sentenced to prison without parole, and 28 States and the Federal Government have decided that for some of these offenders life without parole should be mandatory. The majority of this Court now overrules these legislative judgments.

4. *Excessive Fines and Forfeitures*

In addition to prohibiting "cruel and unusual punishment," the Eighth Amendment also bars the imposition of "excessive fines." The Court uses a proportionality approach similar to that used in cases involving cruel and unusual punishment to determine whether a fine or forfeiture is excessive.

UNITED STATES v. BAJAKAJIAN
524 U.S. 321 (1998)

Justice THOMAS delivered the opinion of the Court.

Respondent Hosep Bajakajian attempted to leave the United States without reporting, as required by federal law, that he was transporting more than $10,000 in currency. Federal law also provides that a person convicted of willfully violating this reporting requirement shall forfeit to the government "any property . . . involved in such offense." The question in this case is whether forfeiture of the entire $357,144 that respondent failed to declare would violate the Excessive Fines Clause of the Eighth Amendment. We hold that it would, because full forfeiture of respondent's currency would be grossly disproportional to the gravity of his offense.

I

On June 9, 1994, respondent, his wife, and his two daughters were waiting at Los Angeles International Airport to board a flight to Italy; their final destination was Cyprus. Using dogs trained to detect currency by its smell, customs inspectors discovered some $230,000 in cash in the Bajakajians' checked baggage. A customs inspector approached respondent and his wife and told them that they were required to report all money in excess of $10,000 in their possession or in their baggage. Respondent said that he had $8,000 and that his wife had another $7,000, but that the family had no additional currency to declare. A search of their carry-on bags, purse, and wallet revealed more cash; in all, customs inspectors found $357,144. The currency was seized and respondent was taken into custody.

A federal grand jury indicted respondent on three counts. Count One charged him with failing to report that he was transporting more than $10,000 outside the United States, and with doing so "willfully," in violation of §5322(a). Count Two charged him with making a false material statement to the United States Customs Service, in violation of 18 U.S.C. §1001. Count Three sought forfeiture of the $357,144 pursuant to 18 U.S.C. §982(a)(1), which provides:

"The court, in imposing sentence on a person convicted of an offense in violation of section . . . 5316, . . . shall order that the person forfeit to the United States any property, real or personal, involved in such offense, or any property traceable to such property." 18 U.S.C. §982(a)(1).

Respondent pleaded guilty to the failure to report in Count One; the Government agreed to dismiss the false statement charge in Count Two; and respondent elected to have a bench trial on the forfeiture in

Count Three. After the bench trial, the District Court found that the entire $357,144 was subject to forfeiture because it was "involved in" the offense.

Although §982(a)(1) directs sentencing courts to impose full forfeiture, the District Court concluded that such forfeiture would be "extraordinarily harsh" and "grossly disproportionate to the offense in question," and that it would therefore violate the Excessive Fines Clause. The court instead ordered forfeiture of $15,000, in addition to a sentence of three years of probation and a fine of $5,000 — the maximum fine under the Sentencing Guidelines — because the court believed that the maximum Guidelines fine was "too little" and that a $15,000 forfeiture would "make up for what I think a reasonable fine should be."

The United States appealed, seeking full forfeiture of respondent's currency.

II

The Eighth Amendment provides: "Excessive bail shall not be required, nor excessive fines imposed, nor cruel and unusual punishments inflicted." This Court has had little occasion to interpret, and has never actually applied, the Excessive Fines Clause. We have, however, explained that at the time the Constitution was adopted, "the word 'fine' was understood to mean a payment to a sovereign as punishment for some offense." The Excessive Fines Clause thus "limits the government's power to extract payments, whether in cash or in kind, 'as punishment for some offense.' " Forfeitures — payments in kind — are thus "fines" if they constitute punishment for an offense.

We have little trouble concluding that the forfeiture of currency ordered by §982(a)(1) constitutes punishment. The statute directs a court to order forfeiture as an additional sanction when "imposing sentence on a person convicted of" a willful violation of §5316's reporting requirement.

The United States . . . argues that the forfeiture mandated by §982(a)(1) is constitutional because it falls within a class of historic forfeitures of property tainted by crime. In so doing, the Government relies upon a series of cases involving traditional civil in rem forfeitures that are inapposite because such forfeitures were historically considered nonpunitive.

The theory behind such forfeitures was the fiction that the action was directed against "guilty property," rather than against the offender himself.[8] Historically, the conduct of the property owner was irrelevant; indeed, the owner of forfeited property could be entirely innocent of any crime.

Traditional in rem forfeitures were thus not considered punishment against the individual for an offense. Because they were viewed as

---

8. The "guilty property" theory behind in rem forfeiture can be traced to the Bible, which describes property being sacrificed to God as a means of atoning for an offense. See Exodus 21:28. In medieval Europe and at common law, this concept evolved into the law of deodand, in which offending property was condemned and confiscated by the church or the Crown in remediation for the harm it had caused. [Footnote by the Court.]

nonpunitive, such forfeitures traditionally were considered to occupy a place outside the domain of the Excessive Fines Clause. Recognizing the nonpunitive character of such proceedings, we have held that the Double Jeopardy Clause does not bar the institution of a civil, in rem forfeiture action after the criminal conviction of the defendant.

The forfeiture in this case does not bear any of the hallmarks of traditional civil in rem forfeitures. The Government has not proceeded against the currency itself, but has instead sought and obtained a criminal conviction of respondent personally. The forfeiture serves no remedial purpose, is designed to punish the offender, and cannot be imposed upon innocent owners.

III

Because the forfeiture of respondent's currency constitutes punishment and is thus a "fine" within the meaning of the Excessive Fines Clause, we now turn to the question of whether it is "excessive."

A

The touchstone of the constitutional inquiry under the Excessive Fines Clause is the principle of proportionality: The amount of the forfeiture must bear some relationship to the gravity of the offense that it is designed to punish. Until today, however, we have not articulated a standard for determining whether a punitive forfeiture is constitutionally excessive. We now hold that a punitive forfeiture violates the Excessive Fines Clause if it is grossly disproportional to the gravity of a defendant's offense.

The constitutional question that we address, however, is just how proportional to a criminal offense a fine must be, and the text of the Excessive Fines Clause does not answer it. Nor does its history.

We must therefore rely on other considerations in deriving a constitutional excessiveness standard, and there are two that we find particularly relevant. The first, which we have emphasized in our cases interpreting the Cruel and Unusual Punishments Clause, is that judgments about the appropriate punishment for an offense belong in the first instance to the legislature. The second is that any judicial determination regarding the gravity of a particular criminal offense will be inherently imprecise.

In applying this standard, the district courts in the first instance, and the courts of appeals, reviewing the proportionality determination must compare the amount of the forfeiture to the gravity of the defendant's offense. If the amount of the forfeiture is grossly disproportional to the gravity of the defendant's offense, it is unconstitutional.

B

Under this standard, the forfeiture of respondent's entire $357,144 would violate the Excessive Fines Clause. Respondent's crime was solely a reporting offense. It was permissible to transport the currency out of the country so long as he reported it. Section 982(a)(1) orders currency to be forfeited for a "willful" violation of the reporting requirement. Thus, the essence of respondent's crime is a willful failure to report the removal of currency from the United States. Furthermore, as the District Court found, respondent's violation was unrelated to any other illegal activities. The money was the proceeds of legal activity and was to be used to repay a lawful debt. Whatever his other vices, respondent does not fit into the class of persons for whom the statute was principally designed: He is not a money launderer, a drug trafficker, or a tax evader.

The harm that respondent caused was also minimal. Failure to report his currency affected only one party, the Government, and in a relatively minor way. There was no fraud on the United States, and respondent caused no loss to the public fisc. Had his crime gone undetected, the Government would have been deprived only of the information that $357,144 had left the country.

Comparing the gravity of respondent's crime with the $357,144 forfeiture the Government seeks, we conclude that such a forfeiture would be grossly disproportional to the gravity of his offense. It is larger than the $5,000 fine imposed by the District Court by many orders of magnitude, and it bears no articulable correlation to any injury suffered by the Government.

Justice KENNEDY, with whom Chief Justice REHNQUIST, Justice O'CONNOR, and Justice SCALIA join, dissenting.

For the first time in its history, the Court strikes down a fine as excessive under the Eighth Amendment. The decision is disturbing both for its specific holding and for the broader upheaval it foreshadows. At issue is a fine Congress fixed in the amount of the currency respondent sought to smuggle or to transport without reporting. If a fine calibrated with this accuracy fails the Court's test, its decision portends serious disruption of a vast range of statutory fines.

The crime of smuggling or failing to report cash is more serious than the Court is willing to acknowledge. The drug trade, money laundering, and tax evasion all depend in part on smuggled and unreported cash.

In my view, forfeiture of all the unreported currency is sustainable whenever a willful violation is proven.

D. THE DEATH PENALTY

There is one penalty that is unique in the criminal justice system: the death penalty. Currently, 32 states have laws authorizing the imposition of the death penalty, although defendants continue to challenge its use. The Supreme Court has never held that capital punishment is per se unconstitutional under the Eighth Amendment's prohibition of cruel and unusual punishment. Rather, it has focused on the fairness of the procedures used to impose the death penalty and whether those procedures ensure that the punishment is proportionate to the crime.

Subsection 1 of this section discusses the constitutionality of the death penalty under the Eighth Amendment. Subsection 2 then analyzes what standards must be used to ensure that it is not "cruel and unusual punishment" and complies with due process. Subsection 3 examines recent limitations put on the death penalty, including prohibitions on its use against mentally retarded defendants and minors. The subsection also examines the future of the death penalty and the nature of current challenges to today's primary method of execution — lethal injection.

The death penalty remains one of the most controversial issues of the criminal justice system. Public polls show support for the penalty, but this support can vary depending on how the question is presented.[9] There are also continuing concerns about the fairness of its application and whether it has a disproportionate impact on minorities and the poor.[10] Finally, with the advent of DNA science, there is growing evidence that defendants have been wrongfully convicted and executed.[11]

Concerns about the death penalty are not new. As the following cases detail, the Supreme Court's approach sought to address these and other concerns by adjudging the procedures for death penalty cases, rather than striking down capital punishment as per se unconstitutional.

1. Is the Death Penalty Unconstitutional?

In a 5-4 decision, the Supreme Court held in Furman v. Georgia that capital punishment, as then administered, violated the Eighth Amendment's prohibition of cruel and unusual punishment. However, the Court's per curiam opinion made no attempt to set forth a majority approach, and each of the justices filed separate concurring or dissenting opinions. Only two of the justices — Brennan and Marshall — concluded that all capital punishment was per se unconstitutional. The other three concurring justices — Douglas, White, and Stewart — focused their objections on the implementation of the death penalty. Justice Douglas stressed the potential for discriminatory enforcement of the death penalty. Justices White and Stewart focused on the arbitrary manner in which the punishment was imposed in the particular cases the Court was reviewing. The dissenters, in turn, challenged the majority's position as an unwarranted intrusion into the legislative process.

9. In a 2006 poll by ABC News/Washington Post, 65 percent of the American public favors the death penalty, and 32 percent oppose it. However, when asked, "Which punishment to you prefer for people who commit murder: the death penalty or life in prison without parole?" 50 percent support the death penalty, and 46 percent support life without parole. The remaining persons are undecided. A 2016 Gallup Poll showed that death penalty support has now dropped to 60 percent for all Americans, the lowest level since 1972.

10. *See* Corinna Barrett Lain, *Deciding Death*, 57 Duke L.J. 1, *3 (2007).

11. Recent estimates have been as high as one out of every seven defendants executed being wrongfully convicted. *See* Jean Coleman Blackerby, *Life After Death Row: Preventing Wrongful Capital Convictions and Restoring Innocence After Exoneration*, 56 Vand. L. Rev. 1179 (2003).

FURMAN v. GEORGIA

408 U.S. 238 (1972)

PER CURIAM.

[Petitioners were convicted of murder or rape and sentenced to death.] Certiorari was granted limited to the following question: "Does the imposition and carrying out of the death penalty in [these cases] constitute cruel and unusual punishment in violation of the Eighth and Fourteenth Amendments?" The Court holds that the imposition and carrying out of the death penalty in these cases constitute cruel and unusual punishment in violation of the Eighth and Fourteenth Amendments. The judgment in each case is therefore reversed insofar as it leaves undisturbed the death sentence imposed, and the cases are remanded for further proceedings.

Justice BRENNAN, concurring.

The question presented in these cases is whether death is today a punishment for crime that is "cruel and unusual" and consequently, by virtue of the Eighth and Fourteenth Amendments, beyond the power of the State to inflict.

I

[W]e cannot now know exactly what the Framers thought "cruel and unusual punishments" were. Certainly they intended to ban torturous punishments.... [F]or instance, the ... "punishments of torture," which the Court labeled "atrocities," were cases where the criminal "was embowelled alive, beheaded, and quartered," and cases "of public dissection ... and burning alive."

II

Ours would indeed be a simple task were we required merely to measure a challenged punishment against those that history has long condemned. [However,] we know, therefore, that the Clause "must draw its meaning from the evolving standards of decency that mark the progress of a maturing society."

The primary principle is that a punishment must not be so severe as to be degrading to the dignity of human beings. ... In determining whether a punishment comports with human dignity, we are aided ... by a ... principle inherent in the Clause — that the State must not arbitrarily inflict a severe punishment ... that it does not inflict upon others. Indeed, the very words "cruel and unusual punishments" imply condemnation of the arbitrary infliction of severe punishments.

[Also, a] severe punishment must not be unacceptable to contemporary society. Rejection by society, of course, is a strong indication that a severe punishment does not comport with human dignity.

The final principle inherent in the Clause is that a severe punishment must not be excessive.

There are, then, four principles by which we may determine whether a particular punishment is "cruel and unusual." If a punishment is unusually severe, if there is a strong probability that it is inflicted arbitrarily, if it is substantially rejected by contemporary society, and if there is no reason to believe that it serves any penal purpose more effectively than some less severe punishment, then the continued infliction of that punishment violates the command of the Clause that the State may not inflict inhuman and uncivilized punishment upon those convicted of crimes.

III

Under these principles and this test, death is today a "cruel and unusual" punishment.

Death is truly an awesome punishment. The calculated killing of a human being by the State involves, by its very nature, a denial of the executed person's humanity. . . . In comparison to all other punishments today, then, the deliberate extinguishment of human life by the State is uniquely degrading to human dignity. I therefore turn to the second principle — that the State may not arbitrarily inflict an unusually severe punishment.

There has been a steady decline in the infliction of this punishment in every decade since the 1930's, the earliest period for which accurate statistics are available. In the 1930's, executions averaged 167 per year; in the 1940's, the average was 128; in the 1950's, it was 72; and in the years 1960-1962, it was 48. There has been a total of 46 executions since then, 36 of them in 1963-1964. Yet our population and the number of capital crimes committed have increased greatly over the past four decades. The contemporary rarity of the infliction of this punishment is thus the end result of a long-continued decline.

When a country of over 200 million people inflicts an unusually severe punishment no more than 50 times a year, the inference is strong that the punishment is not being regularly and fairly applied.

When the punishment of death is inflicted in a trivial number of the cases in which it is legally available, the conclusion is virtually inescapable that it is being inflicted arbitrarily. Indeed, it smacks of little more than a lottery system.

[Third], the progressive decline in, and the current rarity of, the infliction of death demonstrate that our society seriously questions the appropriateness of this punishment today.

The final principle to be considered is that an unusually severe and degrading punishment may not be excessive in view of the purposes for which it is inflicted.

The States' primary claim is that death is a necessary punishment because it prevents the commission of capital crimes more effectively than any less severe punishment. The sufficient answer to this is that if a criminal convicted of a capital crime poses a danger to society, effective administration of the State's pardon and parole laws can delay or deny his release from prison, and techniques of isolation can eliminate or minimize the danger while he remains confined.

The more significant argument is that the threat of death prevents the commission of capital crimes because it deters potential criminals who would not be deterred by the threat of imprisonment. The argument is not based upon evidence that the threat of death is a superior deterrent.

There is, however, another aspect to the argument that the punishment of death is necessary for the protection of society. The infliction of death, the States urge, serves to manifest the community's outrage at the commission of the crime. It is, they say, a concrete public expression of moral indignation that inculcates respect for the law and helps assure a more peaceful community.

When the overwhelming number of criminals who commit capital crimes go to prison, it cannot be concluded that death serves the purpose of retribution more effectively than imprisonment. The asserted public belief that murderers and rapists deserve to die is flatly inconsistent with the execution of a random few.

In sum, the punishment of death is inconsistent with all four principles: Death is an unusually severe and degrading punishment; there is a strong probability that it is inflicted arbitrarily; its rejection by contemporary society is virtually total; and there is no reason to believe that it serves any penal purpose more effectively than the less severe punishment of imprisonment. The function of these principles is to enable a court to determine whether a punishment comports with human dignity. Death, quite simply, does not.

Justice MARSHALL, concurring.

The criminal acts with which we are confronted are ugly, vicious, reprehensible acts. Their sheer brutality cannot and should not be minimized. But, we are not called upon to condone the penalized conduct; we are asked only to examine the penalty imposed on each of the petitioners and to determine whether or not it violates the Eighth Amendment.

Perhaps the most important principle in analyzing "cruel and unusual" punishment questions is one that is reiterated again and again in the prior opinions of the Court: i.e., the cruel and unusual language "must draw its meaning from the evolving standards of decency that mark the progress of a maturing society." Thus, a penalty that was permissible at one time in our Nation's history is not necessarily permissible today.

At the present time, 41 States, the District of Columbia, and other federal jurisdictions authorize the death penalty for at least one crime. . . . The [history of the death penalty in America] demonstrates that capital punishment was carried from Europe to America but, once here, was tempered considerably. At times in our history, strong abolitionist movements have existed. But, they have never been completely successful, as no more than one-quarter of the States of the Union have, at any one time, abolished the death penalty. They have had partial success, however, especially in reducing the number of capital crimes, replacing mandatory death sentences with jury discretion, and developing more humane methods of conducting executions.

I cannot believe that at this stage in our history, the American people would ever knowingly support purposeless vengeance. I believe that the great mass of citizens would conclude on the basis of the material already considered that the death penalty is immoral and therefore unconstitutional.

I believe that the following facts would serve to convince even the most hesitant of citizens to condemn death as a sanction: capital punishment is imposed discriminatorily against certain identifiable classes of people; there is evidence that innocent people have been executed before their innocence can be proved; and the death penalty wreaks havoc with our entire criminal justice system.

"[I]t is usually the poor, the illiterate, the underprivileged, the member of the minority group — the man who, because he is without means, and is defended by a court-appointed attorney — who becomes society's sacrificial lamb. . . ." There is also overwhelming evidence that the death penalty is employed against men and not women.

Assuming knowledge of all the facts presently available regarding capital punishment, the average citizen would, in my opinion, find it shocking to his conscience and sense of justice.

At a time in our history when the streets of the Nation's cities inspire fear and despair, rather than pride and hope, it is difficult to maintain objectivity and concern for our fellow citizens. But, the measure of a country's greatness is its ability to retain compassion in time of crisis. No nation in the recorded history of man has a greater tradition of revering justice and fair treatment for all its citizens in times of turmoil, confusion, and tension than ours. This is a country which stands tallest in troubled times, a country that clings to fundamental principles, cherishes its constitutional heritage, and rejects simple solutions that compromise the values that lie at the roots of our democratic system.

In striking down capital punishment, this Court does not malign our system of government. On the contrary, it pays homage to it. Only in a free society could right triumph in difficult times, and could civilization record its magnificent advancement. In recognizing the humanity of our fellow beings, we pay ourselves the highest tribute. We achieve "a major milestone in the long road up from barbarism" and join the approximately 70 other jurisdictions in the world which celebrate their regard for civilization and humanity by shunning capital punishment.

Justice STEWART, concurring.

The penalty of death differs from all other forms of criminal punishment, not in degree but in kind. It is unique in its total irrevocability. It is unique in its rejection of rehabilitation of the convict as a basic purpose of criminal justice. And it is unique, finally, in its absolute renunciation of all that is embodied in our concept of humanity.

For these and other reasons, at least two of my Brothers have concluded that the infliction of the death penalty is constitutionally impermissible in all circumstances under the Eighth and Fourteenth Amendments. Their case is a strong one. But I find it unnecessary to reach the ultimate question they would decide.

The constitutionality of capital punishment in the abstract is not . . . before us in these cases. . . . Instead, the death sentences now before us are the product of a legal system that brings them, I believe, within the very core of the Eighth Amendment's guarantee against cruel and unusual punishments, a guarantee applicable against the States through the Fourteenth Amendment. In the first place, it is clear that these sentences are "cruel" in the sense that they excessively go beyond, not in degree but in kind, the punishments that the state legislatures have determined to be necessary. In the second place, it is equally clear that these sentences are "unusual" in the sense that the penalty of death is infrequently imposed for murder, and that its imposition for rape is extraordinarily rare.

These death sentences are cruel and unusual in the same way that being struck by lightning is cruel and unusual. For, of all the people convicted of rapes and murders in 1967 and 1968, many just as reprehensible as these, the petitioners are among a capriciously selected random handful upon whom the sentence of death has in fact been imposed. . . . I simply conclude that the Eighth and Fourteenth Amendments cannot tolerate the infliction of a sentence of death under legal systems that permit this unique penalty to be so wantonly and so freakishly imposed.

Justice DOUGLAS, concurring.

It would seem to be incontestable that the death penalty inflicted on one defendant is "unusual" if it discriminates against him by reason of his race, religion, wealth, social position, or class, or if it is imposed under a procedure that gives room for the play of such prejudices.

The words "cruel and unusual" certainly include penalties that are barbaric. But the words, at least when read in light of the English proscription against selective and irregular use of penalties, suggest that it is "cruel and unusual" to apply the death penalty—or any other penalty—selectively to minorities whose numbers are few, who are outcasts of society, and who are unpopular. . . .

There is increasing recognition of the fact that the basic theme of equal protection is implicit in "cruel and unusual" punishments. "A penalty . . . should be considered 'unusually' imposed if it is administered arbitrarily or discriminatorily." The President's Commission on Law Enforcement and Administration of Justice recently concluded: "Finally there is evidence that the imposition of the death sentence and the exercise of dispensing power by the courts and the executive follow discriminatory patterns. The death sentence is disproportionately imposed and carried out on the poor, the Negro, and the members of unpopular groups."

A study of capital cases in Texas from 1924 to 1968 reached the following conclusions:

> Application of the death penalty is unequal: most of those executed were poor, young, and ignorant.
>
> Seventy-five of the 460 cases involved co-defendants, who, under Texas law, were given separate trials. In several instances where a white and a Negro were co-defendants, the white was sentenced to life imprisonment or a term of years, and the Negro was given the death penalty.
>
> Another ethnic disparity is found in the type of sentence imposed for rape. The Negro convicted of rape is far more likely to get the death penalty than a term sentence, whereas whites and Latins are far more likely to get a term sentence than the death penalty.

Former Attorney General Ramsey Clark has said, "It is the poor, the sick, the ignorant, the powerless and the hated who are executed." One searches our chronicles in vain for the execution of any member of the affluent strata of this society. The Leopolds and Loebs are given prison terms, not sentenced to death.

Those who wrote the Eighth Amendment knew what price their forebears had paid for a system based, not on equal justice, but on discrimination. In those days the target was not the blacks or the poor, but the dissenters, those who opposed absolutism in government, who struggled for a parliamentary regime, and who opposed governments' recurring efforts to foist a particular religion on the people. But the tool of capital punishment was used with vengence against the opposition and those unpopular with the regime. One cannot read this history without realizing that the desire for equality was reflected in the ban against "cruel and unusual punishments" contained in the Eighth Amendment.

In a Nation committed to equal protection of the laws there is no permissible "caste" aspect of law enforcement. Yet we know that the discretion of judges and juries in imposing the death penalty enables the penalty to be selectively applied, feeding prejudices against the accused if he is poor and despised, and lacking political clout, or if he is a member of a suspect or unpopular minority, and saving those who by social position may be in a more protected position.

The high service rendered by the "cruel and unusual" punishment clause of the Eighth Amendment is to require legislatures to write penal laws that are evenhanded, nonselective, and nonarbitrary, and to require judges to see to it that general laws are not applied sparsely, selectively, and spottily to unpopular groups.

Justice WHITE, concurring.

In joining the Court's judgments, therefore, I do not at all intimate that the death penalty is unconstitutional per se or that there is no system of capital punishment that would comport with the Eighth Amendment.

It is . . . my judgment that this point has been reached with respect to capital punishment as it is presently administered under the statutes involved in these cases. I cannot avoid the conclusion that as the statutes before us are now administered, the penalty is so infrequently imposed that the threat of execution is too attenuated to be of substantial service to criminal justice.

Chief Justice BURGER, with whom Justices BLACKMUN, POWELL, and REHNQUIST join, dissenting.

At the outset it is important to note that only two members of the Court, Mr. Justice Brennan and Mr. Justice Marshall, have concluded that the Eighth Amendment prohibits capital punishment for all crimes and under all circumstances. Mr. Justice Douglas has also determined that the death penalty contravenes the Eighth Amendment, although I do not read his opinion as necessarily requiring final abolition of the penalty. For the reasons set forth, I conclude that the constitutional prohibition against "cruel and unusual punishments" cannot be construed to bar the imposition of the punishment of death.

If we were possessed of legislative power, I would either join with Mr. Justice Brennan and Mr. Justice Marshall or, at the very least, restrict the use of capital punishment to a small category of the most heinous crimes. Our constitutional inquiry, however, must be divorced from personal feelings as to the morality and efficacy of the death penalty, and be confined to the meaning and applicability of the uncertain language of the Eighth Amendment.

Counsel for petitioners properly concede that capital punishment was not impermissibly cruel at the time of the adoption of the Eighth Amendment. Not only do the records of the debates indicate that the Founding Fathers were limited in their concern to the prevention of torture, but it is also clear from the language of the Constitution itself that there was no thought whatever of the elimination of capital punishment.

In the 181 years since the enactment of the Eighth Amendment, not a single decision of this Court has cast the slightest shadow of a doubt on the constitutionality of capital punishment. . . . The Court's quiescence in this area can be attributed to the fact that in a democratic society legislatures, not courts, are constituted to respond to the will and consequently the moral values of the people.

There are no obvious indications that capital punishment offends the conscience of society to such a degree that our traditional deference to the legislative judgment must be abandoned. It is not a punishment such as burning at the stake that everyone would ineffably find to be repugnant to all civilized standards. Nor is it a punishment so roundly condemned that only a few aberrant legislatures have retained it on the statute books. Capital punishment is authorized by statute in 40 States, the District of Columbia, and in the federal courts for the commission of certain crimes.

One conceivable source of evidence that legislatures have abdicated their essentially barometric role with respect to community values would be public opinion polls, of which there have been many in the past decade addressed to the question of capital punishment. Without assessing the reliability of such polls, or intimating that any judicial reliance could ever be placed on them, it need only be noted that the reported results have shown nothing approximating the universal condemnation of capital punishment that might lead us to suspect that the legislatures in general have lost touch with current social values.[12]

The selectivity of juries in imposing the punishment of death is properly viewed as a refinement on, rather than a repudiation of, the statutory authorization for that penalty. The rate of imposition of death sentences falls far short of providing the requisite unambiguous evidence that the legislatures of 40 States and the Congress have turned their backs on current or evolving standards of decency in continuing to make the death penalty available.

Capital punishment has also been attacked as violative of the Eighth Amendment on the ground that it is not needed to achieve legitimate penal aims and is thus "unnecessarily cruel." As a pure policy matter, this approach has much to recommend it, but it seeks to give a dimension to the Eighth Amendment that it was never intended to have and promotes a line of inquiry that this Court has never before pursued.

Two of the several aims of punishment are generally associated with capital punishment — retribution and deterrence. It is argued that retribution can be discounted because that, after all, is what the Eighth Amendment seeks to eliminate. There is no authority suggesting that the Eighth Amendment was intended to purge the law of its retributive elements. . . . Furthermore, responsible legal thinkers of widely varying persuasions have debated the sociological and philosophical aspects of the retribution question for generations, neither side being able to convince the other.

The less esoteric but no less controversial question is whether the death penalty acts as a superior deterrent. Those favoring abolition find no evidence that it does. Those favoring retention start from the intuitive notion that capital punishment should act as the most effective deterrent and note that there is no convincing evidence that it does not. Escape from this empirical stalemate is sought by placing the burden of proof on the States and concluding that they have failed to demonstrate that capital punishment is a more effective deterrent than life imprisonment. Comparative deterrence is not a matter that lends itself to precise measurement; to shift the burden to the States is to provide an illusory solution to an enormously complex problem. If it were proper to put the States to the test of demonstrating the deterrent value of capital punishment, we could

---

12. A 1966 poll indicated that 42% of those polled favored capital punishment while 47% opposed it, and 11% had no opinion. A 1969 poll found 51% in favor, 40% opposed, and 9% with no opinion. [Footnote by the Court.]

just as well ask them to prove the need for life imprisonment or any other punishment.

Since there is no majority of the Court on the ultimate issue presented in these cases, the future of capital punishment in this country has been left in an uncertain limbo. Rather than providing a final and unambiguous answer on the basic constitutional question, the collective impact of the majority's ruling is to demand an undetermined measure of change from the various state legislatures and the Congress.

Justice BLACKMUN, dissenting.

I join the respective opinions of [the dissenters] and add only the following, somewhat personal, comments.

Cases such as these provide for me an excruciating agony of the spirit. . . . Were I a legislator, I would vote against the death penalty for the policy reasons argued by counsel for the respective petitioners and expressed and adopted in the several opinions filed by the Justices who vote to reverse these judgments.

Having lived for many years in a State[13] that does not have the death penalty, that effectively abolished it in 1911, and that carried out its last execution on February 13, 1906, capital punishment had never been a part of life for me. In my State, it just did not exist. So far as I can determine, the State, purely from a statistical deterrence point of view, was neither the worse nor the better for its abolition, for, as the concurring opinions observe, the statistics prove little, if anything.

I do not sit on these cases, however, as a legislator, responsive, at least in part, to the will of constituents. Our task here, as must so frequently be emphasized and re-emphasized, is to pass upon the constitutionality of legislation that has been enacted and that is challenged. This is the sole task for judges. We should not allow our personal preferences as to the wisdom of legislative and congressional action, or our distaste for such action, to guide our judicial decision in cases such as these.

Justice POWELL, with whom Chief Justice BURGER, Justice BLACKMUN, and Justice REHNQUIST join, dissenting.

Although the central theme of petitioners' presentations in these cases is that the imposition of the death penalty is per se unconstitutional, only two of today's opinions explicitly conclude that so sweeping a determination is mandated by the Constitution. Both Mr. Justice Brennan and Mr. Justice Marshall call for the abolition of all existing state and federal capital punishment statutes. They intimate as well that no capital statute could be devised in the future that might comport with the Eighth Amendment.

The Constitution itself poses the first obstacle to petitioners' argument that capital punishment is per se unconstitutional. The relevant provisions

13. Minn. Stat. §609.10 (1971). [Footnote by the Court.]

are the Fifth, Eighth, and Fourteenth Amendments. The first of these provides in part:

"No person shall be held to answer for a capital, or otherwise infamous crime, unless on a presentment or indictment of a Grand Jury . . . ; nor shall any person be subject for the same offence to be twice put in jeopardy of life or limb; . . . nor be deprived of life, liberty, or property, without due process of law. . . ."

The Eighth Amendment, adopted at the same time as the Fifth, proscribes "cruel and unusual" punishments. [W]hatever punishments the Framers of the Constitution may have intended to prohibit under the "cruel and unusual" language, there cannot be the slightest doubt that they intended no absolute bar on the Government's authority to impose the death penalty.

On virtually every occasion that any opinion has touched on the question of the constitutionality of the death penalty, it has been asserted affirmatively, or tacitly assumed, that the Constitution does not prohibit the penalty. No Justice of the Court, until today, has dissented from this consistent reading of the Constitution.

One must conclude, contrary to petitioners' submission, that the indicators most likely to reflect the public's view — legislative bodies, state referenda and the juries which have the actual responsibility — do not support the contention that evolving standards of decency require total abolition of capital punishment. Indeed, the weight of the evidence indicates that the public generally has not accepted either the morality or the social merit of the views so passionately advocated by the articulate spokesmen for abolition. But however one may assess the amorphous ebb and flow of public opinion generally on this volatile issue, this type of inquiry lies at the periphery — not the core — of the judicial process in constitutional cases. The assessment of popular opinion is essentially a legislative, not a judicial, function.

Petitioners seek to salvage their thesis by arguing that the infrequency and discriminatory nature of the actual resort to the ultimate penalty tend to diffuse public opposition. We are told that the penalty is imposed exclusively on uninfluential minorities — "the poor and powerless, personally ugly and socially unacceptable."

Certainly the claim is justified that this criminal sanction falls more heavily on the relatively impoverished and underprivileged elements of society. The "have-nots" in every society always have been subject to greater pressure to commit crimes and to fewer constraints than their more affluent fellow citizens. This is, indeed, a tragic byproduct of social and economic deprivation, but it is not an argument of constitutional proportions under the Eighth or Fourteenth Amendment.

2. Standards for Constitutional Implementation of the Death Penalty

Because a clear majority in *Furman* neither rejected the death penalty nor approved of its current implementation, the Court left it up to the states to adopt procedures that would satisfy the Court's concerns. State legislatures then slowly enacted legislation to create guidelines as to who would be subjected to capital punishment. By 1976, 35 states had enacted new capital punishment legislation. Some of these states adopted mandatory death penalty provisions so that capital punishment would not be imposed in an arbitrary manner. Others opted for sentencing schemes that provided for separate penalty phases in death penalty cases. In these bifurcated trials, the jury first must convict the defendant of a qualifying death-penalty offense and then consider whether specified aggravating circumstances outweigh mitigating circumstances that militate against imposing capital punishment.

In Woodson v. North Carolina, 428 U.S. 280 (1976), the Supreme Court struck down mandatory death sentences for any first-degree murders. The Court held that mandatory capital punishment is inconsistent with contemporary standards of decency and fails to provide standards to guide the jury. The Court also wrote that mandatory capital punishment undermines respect for the dignity of the individual, a requirement under the Eighth Amendment.

Accordingly, the states and Congress were left with implementing capital punishment systems that allowed jurors to weigh the aggravating circumstances of a capital defendant's case against the mitigating factors. This approach was upheld by the Supreme Court in Gregg v. Georgia, 428 U.S. 153 (1976). In its split decision in *Gregg*, the Court held that the death penalty is not disproportionate if a jury properly considers factors that make the defendant deserving of the most severe punishment.

> [C]apital punishment is an expression of society's moral outrage at particularly offensive conduct. This function may be unappealing to many, but it is essential in an ordered society that asks its citizens to rely on legal processes rather than self-help to vindicate their wrongs.

Id. at 183. After acknowledging the role of retribution in sentencing, Justice Stewart wrote:

> There is no question that death as a punishment is unique in its severity and irrevocability. When a defendant's life is at stake, the Court has been particularly sensitive to insure that every safeguard is observed. But we are concerned here only with the imposition of capital punishment for the crime of murder, and when a life has been taken deliberately by the offender, we cannot say that the punishment is invariably disproportionate to the crime. It is an extreme sanction, suitable to the most extreme of crimes. . . .
>
> *Furman* mandates that where discretion is afforded a sentencing body on a matter so grave as the determination of whether a human life should be taken or spared, that discretion must be suitably directed and limited so as to minimize the risk of wholly arbitrary and capricious action. . . .
>
> The basic concern of *Furman* centered on those defendants who were being condemned to death capriciously and arbitrarily. Under the procedures before the Court in that case, sentencing authorities were not directed to give attention to

the nature or circumstances of the crime committed or to the character or record of the defendant. Left unguided, juries imposed the death sentence in a way that could only be called freakish. The new Georgia sentencing procedures, by contrast, focus the jury's attention on the particularized nature of the crime and the particularized characteristics of the individual defendant. While the jury is permitted to consider any aggravating or mitigating circumstances, it must find and identify at least one statutory aggravating factor before it may impose a penalty of death. In this way the jury's discretion is channeled. No longer can a jury wantonly and freakishly impose the death sentence; it is always circumscribed by the legislative guidelines. In addition, the review function of the Supreme Court of Georgia affords additional assurance that the concerns that prompted our decision in *Furman* are not present to any significant degree in the Georgia procedure applied here.

Id. at 187-189.

Since 1976, the Supreme Court has sought to fine-tune administration of the death penalty. For example, in Coker v. Georgia, 433 U.S. 584 (1977), the Court held that the death penalty is "grossly disproportionate and excessive punishment for the crime of rape and is therefore forbidden by the Eighth Amendment." In 2008, the Supreme Court further held that the death penalty is disproportionate for child rapes as well. Kennedy v. Louisiana, 554 U.S. 407 (2008).

In Enmund v. Florida, 458 U.S. 782 (1982), the Court held that the death penalty must be proportionate not only to the crime committed but also to the defendant's role in that crime. Thus, while the death penalty may be imposed in certain felony-murder cases, it is disproportionate punishment to impose the death penalty on someone who "does not himself kill, attempt to kill, or intend that a killing take place or that lethal force will be employed." In Tison v. Arizona, 481 U.S. 137 (1987), the Court held that the death penalty may be imposed in felony-murder cases in which the defendant demonstrates a "reckless disregard for human life" and plays a major role in the crime.

Attacks on the death penalty have continued, but the Supreme Court has steadfastly refused to strike it down as per se unconstitutional, even when presented with statistical studies that demonstrate that it is applied disproportionately based on the race of the defendant and victim. In McCleskey v. Kemp, 481 U.S. 279 (1987), the Court rejected a claim that the death penalty is unconstitutional because a black defendant who kills a white victim is 4.3 times more likely to receive a death sentence as a defendant charged with killing blacks.

Since *Furman*, the Supreme Court has attempted to set standards that will ensure that the death penalty is administered in a fashion consistent with the Constitution. Yet its task has not been an easy one. Almost every year, the Court is faced with some type of challenge to capital punishment—with respect to its scope or application, habeas corpus review procedures, or standards for effective assistance of counsel. Because of the challenges that inhere in the construction of a constitutional system of capital punishment, one of the justices who originally agreed in *Furman* that the death penalty was not per se unconstitutional abandoned hopes of implementing it in a constitutional manner. In his dissent to the denial of certiorari in Callins v. Collins, 510 U.S. 1141 (1994), Justice Blackmun wrote:

> On February 23, 1994, at approximately 1:00 A.M., Bruce Edwin Callins will be executed by the State of Texas. Intravenous tubes attached to his arms will carry the instrument of death, a toxic fluid designed specifically for the purpose of killing human beings. The witnesses, standing a few feet away, will behold Callins, no longer a defendant, an appellant, or a petitioner, but a man, strapped to a gurney, and seconds away from extinction.
>
> Within days, or perhaps hours, the memory of Callins will begin to fade. The wheels of justice will churn again, and somewhere, another jury or another judge will have the unenviable task of determining whether some human being is to live or die. We hope, of course, that the defendant whose life is at risk will be represented by competent counsel—someone who is inspired by the awareness that a less-than-vigorous defense truly could have fatal consequences for the defendant. We hope that the attorney will investigate all aspects of the case, follow all evidentiary and procedural rules, and appear before a judge who is still committed to the protection of defendants' rights—even now, as the prospect of meaningful judicial oversight has diminished. In the same vein, we hope that the prosecution, in urging the penalty of death, will have exercised its discretion wisely, free from bias, prejudice, or political motive, and will be humbled, rather than emboldened, by the awesome authority conferred by the State.
>
> But even if we can feel confident that these actors will fulfill their roles to the best of their human ability, our collective conscience will remain uneasy. Twenty years have passed since this Court declared that the death penalty must be imposed fairly, and with reasonable consistency, or not at all, *see* Furman v. Georgia (1972), and, despite the effort of the States and courts to devise legal formulas and procedural rules to meet this daunting challenge, the death penalty remains fraught with arbitrariness, discrimination, caprice, and mistake. This is not to say that the problems with the death penalty today are identical to those that were present 20 years ago. Rather, the problems that were pursued down one hole with procedural rules and verbal formulas have come to the surface somewhere else, just as virulent and pernicious as they were in their original form. Experience has taught us that the constitutional goal of eliminating arbitrariness and discrimination from the administration of death can never be achieved without compromising an equally essential component of fundamental fairness—individualized sentencing.
>
> From this day forward, I no longer shall tinker with the machinery of death. For more than 20 years I have endeavored—indeed, I have struggled—along with a majority of this Court, to develop procedural and substantive rules that would lend more than the mere appearance of fairness to the death penalty endeavor. Rather than continue to coddle the Court's delusion that the desired level of fairness has been achieved and the need for regulation eviscerated, I feel morally and intellectually obligated simply to concede that the death penalty experiment has failed. It is virtually self-evident to me now that no combination of procedural rules or substantive regulations ever can save the death penalty from its inherent constitutional deficiencies.
>
> Perhaps one day this Court will develop procedural rules or verbal formulas that actually will provide consistency, fairness, and reliability in a capital-sentencing scheme. I am not optimistic that such a day will come. I am more

optimistic, though, that this Court eventually will conclude that the effort to eliminate arbitrariness while preserving fairness "in the infliction of [death] is so plainly doomed to failure that it—and the death penalty—must be abandoned altogether." I may not live to see that day, but I have faith that eventually it will arrive.

3. *Recent Limits on the Scope of the Death Penalty*

The Supreme Court has not held that the death penalty is unconstitutional, but in this new century, it has decided three cases that have resulted in limiting its scope. In Atkins v. Virginia, 536 U.S. 304 (2002), the Court held that the Eighth Amendment prohibits the execution of mentally retarded persons.[14] In Roper v. Simmons, 543 U.S. 551 (2005), the Court struck down death sentences imposed on persons who were younger than 18 years of age when they committed their capital crimes. In Kennedy v. Louisiana, 554 U.S. 407 (2008), the Court struck down the death penalty for non-homicide crimes such as child rape.

a. **Prohibition of the Death Penalty for Mentally Retarded Defendants**

ATKINS v. VIRGINIA
536 U.S. 304 (2002)

Justice STEVENS delivered the opinion of the Court.

Those mentally retarded persons who meet the law's requirements for criminal responsibility should be tried and punished when they commit crimes. Because of their disabilities in areas of reasoning, judgment, and control of their impulses, however, they do not act with the level of moral culpability that characterizes the most serious adult criminal conduct. Moreover, their impairments can jeopardize the reliability and fairness of capital proceedings against mentally retarded defendants. Presumably for these reasons, in the [last] 13 years, the American public, legislators, scholars, and judges have deliberated over the question whether the death penalty should ever be imposed on a mentally retarded criminal. The consensus reflected in those deliberations informs our answer to the question presented by this case: whether such executions are "cruel and unusual punishments" prohibited by the Eighth Amendment to the Federal Constitution.

---

14. Previously, in Ford v. Wainwright, 477 U.S. 399 (1986), the Supreme Court had found that the execution of persons who become insane while awaiting execution violates the Eighth Amendment.

I

Petitioner, Daryl Renard Atkins, was convicted of abduction, armed robbery, and capital murder, and sentenced to death. At approximately midnight on August 16, 1996, Atkins and William Jones, armed with a semiautomatic handgun, abducted Eric Nesbitt, robbed him of the money on his person, drove him to an automated teller machine in his pickup truck where cameras recorded their withdrawal of additional cash, then took him to an isolated location where he was shot eight times and killed.

Jones and Atkins both testified in the guilt phase of Atkins' trial.[15] Each confirmed most of the details in the other's account of the incident, with the important exception that each stated that the other had actually shot and killed Nesbitt. Jones' testimony, which was both more coherent and credible than Atkins', was obviously credited by the jury and was sufficient to establish Atkins' guilt. At the penalty phase of the trial, the State introduced victim impact evidence and proved two aggravating circumstances: future dangerousness and "vileness of the offense." To prove future dangerousness, the State relied on Atkins' prior felony convictions as well as the testimony of four victims of earlier robberies and assaults. To prove the second aggravator, the prosecution relied upon the trial record, including pictures of the deceased's body and the autopsy report.

In the penalty phase, the defense relied on one witness, Dr. Evan Nelson, a forensic psychologist who had evaluated Atkins before trial and concluded that he was "mildly mentally retarded." His conclusion was based on interviews with people who knew Atkins, a review of school and court records, and the administration of a standard intelligence test which indicated that Atkins had a full scale IQ of 59.

The jury sentenced Atkins to death, but the Virginia Supreme Court ordered a second sentencing hearing because the trial court had used a misleading verdict form. At the resentencing, Dr. Nelson again testified. The State presented an expert rebuttal witness, Dr. Stanton Samenow, who expressed the opinion that Atkins was not mentally retarded, but rather was of "average intelligence, at least," and diagnosable as having antisocial personality disorder. The jury again sentenced Atkins to death.

The Supreme Court of Virginia affirmed the imposition of the death penalty. Atkins did not argue before the Virginia Supreme Court that his sentence was disproportionate to penalties imposed for similar crimes in Virginia, but he did contend "that he is mentally retarded and thus cannot be sentenced to death." The Court was "not willing to commute Atkins' sentence of death to life imprisonment merely because of his IQ score."

---

15. Initially, both Jones and Atkins were indicted for capital murder. The prosecution ultimately permitted Jones to plead guilty to first-degree murder in exchange for his testimony against Atkins. As a result of the plea, Jones became ineligible to receive the death penalty. [Footnote by the Court.]

Justice Hassell and Justice Koontz dissented. They rejected Dr. Same-now's opinion that Atkins possesses average intelligence as "incredulous as a matter of law," and concluded that "the imposition of the sentence of death upon a criminal defendant who has the mental age of a child between the ages of 9 and 12 is excessive." In their opinion, "it is indefensible to conclude that individuals who are mentally retarded are not to some degree less culpable for their criminal acts. By definition, such individuals have substantial limitations not shared by the general population. A moral and civilized society diminishes itself if its system of justice does not afford recognition and consideration of those limitations in a meaningful way."

Because of the gravity of the concerns expressed by the dissenters, and in light of the dramatic shift in the state legislative landscape that has occurred in the past 13 years, we granted certiorari to revisit the issue that we first addressed in the *Penry* case.

II

The Eighth Amendment succinctly prohibits "excessive" sanctions. It provides: "Excessive bail shall not be required, nor excessive fines imposed, nor cruel and unusual punishments inflicted." In *Weems v. United States* (1910), we held that a punishment of 12 years jailed in irons at hard and painful labor for the crime of falsifying records was excessive. We explained "that it is a precept of justice that punishment for crime should be graduated and proportioned to the offense." We have repeatedly applied this proportionality precept in later cases interpreting the Eighth Amendment. *See Harmelin v. Michigan* (1991).

A claim that punishment is excessive is judged not by the standards that prevailed in 1685 when Lord Jeffreys presided over the "Bloody Assizes" or when the Bill of Rights was adopted, but rather by those that currently prevail.

Proportionality review under those evolving standards should be informed by "objective factors to the maximum possible extent." We have pinpointed that the "clearest and most reliable objective evidence of contemporary values is the legislation enacted by the country's legislatures." Relying in part on such legislative evidence, we have held that death is an impermissibly excessive punishment for the rape of an adult woman, *Coker v. Georgia* (1977), or for a defendant who neither took life, attempted to take life, nor intended to take life, *Enmund v. Florida* (1982).

Guided by our approach in these cases, we shall first review the judgment of legislatures that have addressed the suitability of imposing the death penalty on the mentally retarded and then consider reasons for agreeing or disagreeing with their judgment.

III

The parties have not called our attention to any state legislative consideration of the suitability of imposing the death penalty on mentally retarded offenders prior to 1986. In that year, the public reaction to the execution of a mentally retarded murderer in Georgia, apparently led to the enactment of the first state statute prohibiting such executions. In 1988, when Congress enacted legislation reinstating the federal death penalty, it expressly provided that a "sentence of death shall not be carried out upon a person who is mentally retarded." In 1989, Maryland enacted a similar prohibition. It was in that year that we decided *Penry*, and concluded that those two state enactments, "even when added to the 14 States that have rejected capital punishment completely, do not provide sufficient evidence at present of a national consensus."

Much has changed since then. Responding to the national attention received by the Bowden execution and our decision in *Penry*, state legislatures across the country began to address the issue. In 1990 Kentucky and Tennessee enacted statutes similar to those in Georgia and Maryland, as did New Mexico in 1991, and Arkansas, Colorado, Washington, Indiana, and Kansas in 1993 and 1994. In 1995, when New York reinstated its death penalty, it emulated the Federal Government by expressly exempting the mentally retarded. Nebraska followed suit in 1998. [I]n 2000 and 2001 six more States — South Dakota, Arizona, Connecticut, Florida, Missouri, and North Carolina — joined the procession. The Texas Legislature unanimously adopted a similar bill, and bills have passed at least one house in other States, including Virginia and Nevada.

It is not so much the number of these States that is significant, but the consistency of the direction of change. Given the well-known fact that anti-crime legislation is far more popular than legislation providing protections for persons guilty of violent crime, the large number of States prohibiting the execution of mentally retarded persons (and the complete absence of States passing legislation reinstating the power to conduct such executions) provides powerful evidence that today our society views mentally retarded offenders as categorically less culpable than the average criminal. The evidence carries even greater force when it is noted that the legislatures that have addressed the issue have voted overwhelmingly in favor of the prohibition. Moreover, even in those States that allow the execution of mentally retarded offenders, the practice is uncommon. And it appears that even among those States that regularly execute offenders and that have no prohibition with regard to the mentally retarded, only five have executed offenders possessing a known IQ less than 70. The practice, therefore, has become truly unusual, and it is fair to say that a national consensus has developed against it.

To the extent there is serious disagreement about the execution of mentally retarded offenders, it is in determining which offenders are in fact retarded. As was our approach in Ford v. Wainwright, with regard to insanity, "we leave to the States the task of developing appropriate ways to enforce the constitutional restriction upon its execution of sentences."

IV

This consensus unquestionably reflects widespread judgment about the relative culpability of mentally retarded offenders, and the relationship between mental retardation and the penological purposes served by the death penalty. Additionally, it suggests that some characteristics of mental retardation undermine the strength of the procedural protections that our capital jurisprudence steadfastly guards.

[There are] two reasons consistent with the legislative consensus that the mentally retarded should be categorically excluded from execution. First, there is a serious question as to whether either justification that we have recognized as a basis for the death penalty applies to mentally retarded offenders. *Gregg v. Georgia* (1976), identified "retribution and deterrence of capital crimes by prospective offenders" as the social purposes served by the death penalty. Unless the imposition of the death penalty on a mentally retarded person "measurably contributes to one or both of these goals, it 'is nothing more than the purposeless and needless imposition of pain and suffering,' and hence an unconstitutional punishment."

With respect to retribution — the interest in seeing that the offender gets his "just deserts" — the severity of the appropriate punishment necessarily depends on the culpability of the offender. If the culpability of the average murderer is insufficient to justify the most extreme sanction available to the State, the lesser culpability of the mentally retarded offender surely does not merit that form of retribution.

With respect to deterrence — the interest in preventing capital crimes by prospective offenders — "it seems likely that 'capital punishment can serve as a deterrent only when murder is the result of premeditation and deliberation.'" Exempting the mentally retarded from that punishment will not affect the "cold calculus that precedes the decision" of other potential murderers. The theory of deterrence in capital sentencing is predicated upon the notion that the increased severity of the punishment will inhibit criminal actors from carrying out murderous conduct. Yet it is the same cognitive and behavioral impairments that make these defendants less morally culpable — for example, the diminished ability to understand and process information, to learn from experience, to engage in logical reasoning, or to control impulses — that also make it less likely that they can process the information of the possibility of execution as a penalty and, as a result, control their conduct based upon that information.

The reduced capacity of mentally retarded offenders provides a second justification for a categorical rule making such offenders ineligible for the death penalty. The risk "that the death penalty will be imposed in spite of factors which may call for a less severe penalty" is enhanced, not only by the possibility of false confessions, but also by the lesser ability of mentally retarded defendants to make a persuasive showing of mitigation in the face of prosecutorial evidence of one or more aggravating factors. Mentally retarded defendants may be less able to give meaningful assistance to their counsel and are typically poor witnesses, and their demeanor may create an unwarranted impression of lack of remorse for their crimes. Mentally retarded defendants in the aggregate face a special risk of wrongful execution.

Our independent evaluation of the issue reveals no reason to disagree with the judgment of "the legislatures that have recently addressed the matter" and concluded that death is not a suitable punishment for a mentally retarded criminal. We are not persuaded that the execution of mentally retarded criminals will measurably advance the deterrent or the retributive purpose of the death penalty. Construing and applying the Eighth Amendment in the light of our "evolving standards of decency," we therefore conclude that such punishment is excessive and that the Constitution "places a substantive restriction on the State's power to take the life" of a mentally retarded offender.

Justice SCALIA, with whom Chief Justice REHNQUIST and Justice THOMAS join, dissenting.

Today's decision is the pinnacle of our Eighth Amendment death-is-different jurisprudence. Not only does it, like all of that jurisprudence, find no support in the text or history of the Eighth Amendment; it does not even have support in current social attitudes regarding the conditions that render an otherwise just death penalty inappropriate. Seldom has an opinion of this Court rested so obviously upon nothing but the personal views of its members.

I

I begin with a brief restatement of facts that are abridged by the Court but important to understanding this case. After spending the day drinking alcohol and smoking marijuana, petitioner Daryl Renard Atkins and a partner in crime drove to a convenience store, intending to rob a customer. Their victim was Eric Nesbitt, an airman from Langley Air Force Base, whom they abducted, drove to a nearby automated teller machine, and forced to withdraw $200. They then drove him to a deserted area, ignoring his pleas to leave him unharmed. According to the co-conspirator, whose testimony the jury evidently credited, Atkins ordered Nesbitt out of the vehicle and, after he had taken only a few steps, shot him one, two, three, four, five, six, seven, eight times in the thorax, chest, abdomen, arms, and legs.

The jury convicted Atkins of capital murder. At resentencing, the jury heard extensive evidence of petitioner's alleged mental retardation. A psychologist testified that petitioner was mildly mentally retarded with an IQ of 59, that he was a "slow learner," who showed a "lack of success in pretty much every domain of his life," and that he had an "impaired" capacity to appreciate the criminality of his conduct and to conform his conduct to the law, *id.* Petitioner's family members offered additional evidence in support of his mental retardation claim.

The jury also heard testimony about petitioner's 16 prior felony convictions for robbery, attempted robbery, abduction, use of a firearm, and maiming. *Id.* The victims of these offenses provided graphic depictions of petitioner's violent tendencies: The jury sentenced petitioner to death.

II

As the foregoing history demonstrates, petitioner's mental retardation was a central issue at sentencing. The jury concluded, however, that his alleged retardation was not a compelling reason to exempt him from the death penalty in light of the brutality of his crime and his long demonstrated propensity for violence.

Under our Eighth Amendment jurisprudence, a punishment is "cruel and unusual" if it falls within one of two categories: "those modes or acts of punishment that had been considered cruel and unusual at the time that the Bill of Rights was adopted," and modes of punishment that are inconsistent with modern "standards of decency," as evinced by objective indicia, the most important of which is "legislation enacted by the country's legislatures."

The Court makes no pretense that execution of the mildly mentally retarded would have been considered "cruel and unusual" in 1791.

The Court is left to argue, therefore, that execution of the mildly retarded is inconsistent with the "evolving standards of decency that mark the progress of a maturing society." Before today, our opinions consistently emphasized that Eighth Amendment judgments regarding the existence of social "standards" "should be informed by objective factors to the maximum possible extent" and "should not be, or appear to be, merely the subjective views of individual Justices."

The Court pays lipservice to these precedents as it miraculously extracts a "national consensus" forbidding execution of the mentally retarded from the fact that 18 States — less than half (47%) of the 38 States that permit capital punishment (for whom the issue exists) — have very recently enacted legislation barring execution of the mentally retarded.

How is it possible that agreement among 47% of the death penalty jurisdictions amounts to "consensus"?

Moreover, a major factor that the Court entirely disregards is that the legislation of all 18 States it relies on is still in its infancy. The oldest of the statutes is only 14 years old. It is "myopic to base sweeping constitutional principles upon the narrow experience of [a few] years."

The Court attempts to bolster its embarrassingly feeble evidence of "consensus" with the following: "It is not so much the number of these States that is significant, but the consistency of the direction of change." But in what other direction could we possibly see change? Given that 14 years ago all the death penalty statutes included the mentally retarded, any change (except precipitate undoing of what had just been done) was bound to be in the one direction the Court finds significant enough to overcome the lack of real consensus.

Even less compelling (if possible) is the Court's argument that evidence of "national consensus" is to be found in the infrequency with which retarded persons are executed in States that do not bar their execution. To begin with, what the Court takes as true is in fact quite doubtful. It is not at all clear that execution of the mentally retarded is "uncommon," ibid., as even the sources cited by the Court suggests. If, however, execution of the mentally retarded is "uncommon," then surely the explanation is that mental retardation is a constitutionally mandated mitigating factor at sentencing.

But the Prize for the Court's Most Feeble Effort to fabricate "national consensus" must go to its appeal (deservedly relegated to a footnote) to the views of assorted professional and religious organizations, members of the so-called "world community," and respondents to opinion polls. I agree with the Chief Justice that the views of professional and religious organizations and the results of opinion polls are irrelevant. Where there is not first a settled consensus among our own people, the views of other nations, however enlightened the Justices of this Court may think them to be, cannot be imposed upon Americans through the Constitution.

III

Beyond the empty talk of a "national consensus," the Court gives us a brief glimpse of what really underlies today's decision: "The Constitution," the Court says, "contemplates that in the end *our own judgment* will be brought to bear on the question of the acceptability of the death penalty under the Eighth Amendment." The arrogance of this assumption of power takes one's breath away.

The genuinely operative portion of the opinion, then, is the Court's statement of the reasons why it agrees with the contrived consensus it has found, that the "diminished capacities" of the mentally retarded render the death penalty excessive.

Proceeding from these faulty assumptions, the Court gives two reasons why the death penalty is an excessive punishment for all mentally retarded offenders. First, the "diminished capacities" of the mentally retarded raise a "serious question" whether their execution contributes to the "social purposes" of the death penalty, viz., retribution and deterrence. Retribution is not advanced, the argument goes, because the mentally retarded are no more culpable than the average murderer, whom we have already held lacks sufficient culpability to warrant the death penalty. Who says so? Is there an established correlation between mental acuity and the ability to conform one's conduct to the law in such a rudimentary matter as murder? Are the mentally retarded really more disposed (and hence more likely) to commit willfully cruel and serious crime than others? In my experience, the opposite is true: being childlike generally suggests innocence rather than brutality.

Assuming, however, that there is a direct connection between diminished intelligence and the inability to refrain from murder, what scientific analysis can possibly show that a mildly retarded individual who commits an exquisite torture-killing is "no more culpable" than the "average" murderer in a holdup-gone-wrong or a domestic dispute? Or a moderately retarded individual who commits a series of 20 exquisite torture-killings? Surely culpability, and deservedness of the most severe retribution, depends not merely (if at all) upon the mental capacity of the criminal (above the level where he is able to distinguish right from wrong) but also upon the depravity of the crime — which is precisely why this sort of question has traditionally been thought answerable not by a categorical rule of the sort the Court today imposes upon all trials, but rather by the sentencer's weighing of the circumstances (both degree of retardation and depravity of crime) in the particular case. The fact that juries continue to sentence mentally retarded offenders to death for extreme crimes shows that society's moral outrage sometimes demands execution of retarded offenders.

As for the other social purpose of the death penalty that the Court discusses, deterrence: That is not advanced, the Court tells us, because the mentally retarded are "less likely" than their non-retarded counterparts to "process the information of the possibility of execution as a penalty and . . . control their conduct based upon that information." But surely the deterrent effect of a penalty is adequately vindicated if it successfully deters many, but not all, of the target class. In other words, the supposed fact that some retarded criminals cannot fully appreciate the death penalty has nothing to do with the deterrence rationale, but is simply an echo of the arguments denying a retribution rationale, discussed and rejected above.

The Court throws one last factor into its grab bag of reasons why execution of the retarded is "excessive" in all cases: Mentally retarded offenders "face a special risk of wrongful execution" because they are less able "to make a persuasive showing of mitigation," "to give meaningful assistance to their counsel," and to be effective witnesses. "Special risk" is pretty flabby language (even flabbier than "less likely") — and I suppose a similar "special risk" could be said to exist for just plain stupid people, inarticulate people, even ugly people. If this unsupported claim has any substance to it (which I doubt) it might support a due process claim in all criminal prosecutions of the mentally retarded; but it is hard to see how it has anything to do with an Eighth Amendment claim that execution of the mentally retarded is cruel and unusual. We have never before held it to be cruel and unusual punishment to impose a sentence in violation of some other constitutional imperative.

Today's opinion adds one more to the long list of substantive and procedural requirements impeding imposition of the death penalty imposed under this Court's assumed power to invent a death-is-different jurisprudence. None of those requirements existed when the Eighth Amendment was adopted, and some of them were not even supported by current moral consensus. They include prohibition of the death penalty for "ordinary" murder, for rape of an adult woman, and for felony murder absent a showing that the defendant possessed a sufficiently culpable state of mind; prohibition of the death penalty for any person under the age of 16 at the time of the crime, prohibition of the death penalty as the mandatory punishment for any crime, requirement that the sentencer not be given unguided discretion, a requirement that the sentencer be empowered to take into account all mitigating circumstances, and a requirement that the accused receive a judicial evaluation of his claim of insanity before the sentence can be executed. There is something to be said for popular abolition of the death penalty; there is nothing to be said for its incremental abolition by this Court.

This newest invention promises to be more effective than any of the others in turning the process of capital trial into a game.

Chief Justice REHNQUIST, with whom Justices SCALIA and THOMAS join, dissenting.

I agree with Justice Scalia that the Court's assessment of the current legislative judgment regarding the execution of defendants like petitioner more resembles a post hoc rationalization for the majority's subjectively preferred result rather than any objective effort to ascertain the content of an evolving standard of decency. I write separately, however, to call attention to the defects in the Court's decision to place weight on foreign laws, the views of professional and religious organizations, and opinion polls in reaching its conclusion.

In making determinations about whether a punishment is "cruel and unusual" under the evolving standards of decency embraced by the Eighth Amendment, we have emphasized that legislation is the "clearest and most reliable objective evidence of contemporary values." The reason we ascribe primacy to legislative enactments follows from the constitutional role legislatures play in expressing policy of a State.

Our opinions have also recognized that data concerning the actions of sentencing juries, though entitled to less weight than legislative judgments, "is a significant and reliable index of contemporary values," because of the jury's intimate involvement in the case and its function of "maintaining a link between contemporary community values and the penal system."

In my view, these two sources — the work product of legislatures and sentencing jury determinations — ought to be the sole indicators by which courts ascertain the contemporary American conceptions of decency for purposes of the Eighth Amendment. They are the only objective indicia of contemporary values firmly supported by our precedents.

To further buttress its appraisal of contemporary societal values, the Court marshals public opinion poll results and evidence that several professional organizations and religious groups have adopted official positions opposing the imposition of the death penalty upon mentally retarded offenders. In my view, none should be accorded any weight on the Eight Amendment scale when the elected representatives of a State's populace have not deemed them persuasive enough to prompt legislative action.

Even if I were to accept the legitimacy of the Court's decision to reach beyond the product of legislatures and practices of sentencing juries to discern a national standard of decency, I would take issue with the blind-faith credence it accords the opinion polls brought to our attention. An extensive body of social science literature describes how methodological and other errors can affect the reliability and validity of estimates about the opinions and attitudes of a population derived from various sampling techniques.

Following *Atkins,* the Supreme Court clarified in Hall v. Florida, 134 S. Ct. 1986 (2014), that the standard to be used to determine whether the execution of a mentally disabled defendant would violate the Eighth Amendment is not determined by an IQ test alone. Rather, courts are to consider a range of evidence related to the defendant's mental disability.

b. Prohibition of the Death Penalty for Crimes Committed by Minors

Three years later, in Roper v. Simmons, the Supreme Court again took steps to limit the scope of the death penalty. This time, the Court examined whether the imposition of the death penalty on persons who were younger than 18 years of age when they committed crimes violates the Eighth Amendment.

ROPER v. SIMMONS
543 U.S. 551 (2005)

Justice KENNEDY delivered the opinion of the Court.

This case requires us to address, for the second time in a decade and a half, whether it is permissible under the Eighth and Fourteenth Amendments to the Constitution of the United States to execute a juvenile offender who was older than 15 but younger than 18 when he committed a capital crime. In Stanford v. Kentucky (1989), a divided Court rejected the proposition that the Constitution bars capital punishment for juvenile offenders in this age group. We reconsider the question.

I

At the age of 17, when he was still a junior in high school, Christopher Simmons, the respondent here, committed murder. About nine months later, after he had turned 18, he was tried and sentenced to death. There is little doubt that Simmons was the instigator of the crime. Before its commission Simmons said he wanted to murder someone. In chilling, callous terms he talked about his plan, discussing it for the most part with two friends, Charles Benjamin and John Tessmer, then aged 15 and 16 respectively. Simmons proposed to commit burglary and murder by breaking and entering, tying up a victim, and throwing the victim off a bridge. Simmons assured his friends they could "get away with it" because they were minors.

The three met at about 2 A.M. on the night of the murder, but Tessmer left before the other two set out. (The State later charged Tessmer with conspiracy, but dropped the charge in exchange for his testimony against Simmons.) Simmons and Benjamin entered the home of the victim, Shirley Crook, after reaching through an open window and unlocking the back door. Simmons turned on a hallway light. Awakened, Mrs. Crook called out, "Who's there?" In response Simmons entered Mrs. Crook's bedroom, where he recognized her from a previous car accident involving them both. Simmons later admitted this confirmed his resolve to murder her.

Using duct tape to cover her eyes and mouth and bind her hands, the two perpetrators put Mrs. Crook in her minivan and drove to a state park. They reinforced the bindings, covered her head with a towel, and walked her to a railroad trestle spanning the Meramec River. There they tied her hands and feet together with electrical wire, wrapped her whole face in duct tape and threw her from the bridge, drowning her in the waters below.

By the afternoon of September 9, Steven Crook had returned home from an overnight trip, found his bedroom in disarray, and reported his wife missing. On the same afternoon fishermen recovered the victim's body from the river. Simmons, meanwhile, was bragging about the killing, telling friends he had killed a woman "because the bitch seen my face."

The next day, after receiving information of Simmons' involvement, police arrested him at his high school and took him to the police station in Fenton, Missouri. They read him his *Miranda* rights. Simmons waived his right to an attorney and agreed to answer questions. After less than two hours of interrogation, Simmons confessed to the murder and agreed to perform a videotaped reenactment at the crime scene.

The State charged Simmons with burglary, kidnaping, stealing, and murder in the first degree. As Simmons was 17 at the time of the crime, he was outside the criminal jurisdiction of Missouri's juvenile court system. He was tried as an adult. At trial the State introduced Simmons' confession and the videotaped reenactment of the crime, along with testimony that Simmons discussed the crime in advance and bragged about it later. The defense called no witnesses in the guilt phase. The jury having returned a verdict of murder, the trial proceeded to the penalty phase.

The State sought the death penalty. As aggravating factors, the State submitted that the murder was committed for the purpose of receiving money; was committed for the purpose of avoiding, interfering with, or preventing lawful arrest of the defendant; and involved depravity of mind and was outrageously and wantonly vile, horrible, and inhuman. The State called Shirley

Crook's husband, daughter, and two sisters, who presented moving evidence of the devastation her death had brought to their lives.

In mitigation Simmons' attorneys first called an officer of the Missouri juvenile justice system, who testified that Simmons had no prior convictions and that no previous charges had been filed against him. Simmons' mother, father, two younger half brothers, a neighbor, and a friend took the stand to tell the jurors of the close relationships they had formed with Simmons and to plead for mercy on his behalf. Simmons' mother, in particular, testified to the responsibility Simmons demonstrated in taking care of his two younger half brothers and of his grandmother and to his capacity to show love for them.

During closing arguments, both the prosecutor and defense counsel addressed Simmons' age, which the trial judge had instructed the jurors they could consider as a mitigating factor. Defense counsel reminded the jurors that juveniles of Simmons' age cannot drink, serve on juries, or even see certain movies, because "the legislatures have wisely decided that individuals of a certain age aren't responsible enough." Defense counsel argued that Simmons' age should make "a huge difference to [the jurors] in deciding just exactly what sort of punishment to make." In rebuttal, the prosecutor gave the following response: "Age, he says. Think about age. Seventeen years old. Isn't that scary? Doesn't that scare you? Mitigating? Quite the contrary I submit. Quite the contrary."

The jury recommended the death penalty after finding the State had proved each of the three aggravating factors submitted to it. Accepting the jury's recommendation, the trial judge imposed the death penalty.

Simmons obtained new counsel, who moved in the trial court to set aside the conviction and sentence. One argument was that Simmons had received ineffective assistance at trial. To support this contention, the new counsel called as witnesses Simmons' trial attorney, Simmons' friends and neighbors, and clinical psychologists who had evaluated him.

Part of the submission was that Simmons was "very immature," "very impulsive," and "very susceptible to being manipulated or influenced." The experts testified about Simmons' background including a difficult home environment and dramatic changes in behavior, accompanied by poor school performance in adolescence. Simmons was absent from home for long periods, spending time using alcohol and drugs with other teenagers or young adults. The contention by Simmons' postconviction counsel was that these matters should have been established in the sentencing proceeding.

The trial court found no constitutional violation by reason of ineffective assistance of counsel and denied the motion for postconviction relief.

After these proceedings in Simmons' case had run their course, this Court held that the Eighth and Fourteenth Amendments prohibit the execution of a mentally retarded person. Atkins v. Virginia (2002). Simmons filed a new petition for state postconviction relief, arguing that the reasoning of *Atkins* established that the Constitution prohibits the execution of a juvenile who was under 18 when the crime was committed.

The Missouri Supreme Court agreed. State ex rel. Simmons v. Roper, 112 S.W.3d 397 (2003) (en banc). It held that since *Stanford*, "a national consensus has developed against the execution of juvenile offenders, as demonstrated by the fact that eighteen states now bar such executions for juveniles, that twelve other states bar executions altogether, that no state has lowered its age of execution below 18 since *Stanford*, that five states have legislatively or by case law raised or established the minimum age at 18, and that the imposition of the juvenile death penalty has become truly unusual over the last decade." On this reasoning it set aside Simmons' death sentence and resentenced him to "life imprisonment without eligibility for probation, parole, or release except by act of the Governor."

We granted certiorari and now affirm.

II

The Eighth Amendment provides: "Excessive bail shall not be required, nor excessive fines imposed, nor cruel and unusual punishments inflicted." As the Court explained in *Atkins*, the Eighth Amendment guarantees individuals the right not to be subjected to excessive sanctions. The right flows from the basic "precept of justice that punishment for crime should be graduated and proportioned to [the] offense." By protecting even those convicted of heinous crimes, the Eighth Amendment reaffirms the duty of the government to respect the dignity of all persons.

The prohibition against "cruel and unusual punishments," like other expansive language in the Constitution, must be interpreted according to its text, by considering history, tradition, and precedent, and with due regard for its purpose and function in the constitutional design. To implement this framework we have established the propriety and affirmed the necessity of referring to "the evolving standards of decency that mark the progress of a maturing society" to determine which punishments are so disproportionate as to be cruel and unusual.

In Thompson v. Oklahoma (1988), a plurality of the Court determined that our standards of decency do not permit the execution of any offender under the age of 16 at the time of the crime. The plurality opinion explained that no death penalty State that had given express consideration to a minimum age for the death penalty had set the age lower than 16. The plurality also observed that "[t]he conclusion that it would offend civilized standards of decency to execute a person who was less than 16 years old at the time of his or her offense is consistent with the views that have been expressed by respected professional organizations, by other nations that share our Anglo-American heritage, and by the leading members of the Western European community." The opinion further noted that juries imposed the death penalty on offenders under 16 with exceeding rarity;

the last execution of an offender for a crime committed under the age of 16 had been carried out in 1948, 40 years prior.

Bringing its independent judgment to bear on the permissibility of the death penalty for a 15-year-old offender, the *Thompson* plurality stressed that "[t]he reasons why juveniles are not trusted with the privileges and responsibilities of an adult also explain why their irresponsible conduct is not as morally reprehensible as that of an adult." According to the plurality, the lesser culpability of offenders under 16 made the death penalty inappropriate as a form of retribution, while the low likelihood that offenders under 16 engaged in "the kind of cost-benefit analysis that attaches any weight to the possibility of execution" made the death penalty ineffective as a means of deterrence.

The next year, in Stanford v. Kentucky (1989), the Court, over a dissenting opinion joined by four Justices, referred to contemporary standards of decency in this country and concluded the Eighth and Fourteenth Amendments did not proscribe the execution of juvenile offenders over 15 but under 18. The Court noted that 22 of the 37 death penalty States permitted the death penalty for 16-year-old offenders, and, among these 37 States, 25 permitted it for 17-year-old offenders. These numbers, in the Court's view, indicated there was no national consensus "sufficient to label a particular punishment cruel and unusual."

The same day the Court decided *Stanford,* it held that the Eighth Amendment did not mandate a categorical exemption from the death penalty for the mentally retarded. Penry v. Lynaug (1989). In reaching this conclusion it stressed that only two States had enacted laws banning the imposition of the death penalty on a mentally retarded person convicted of a capital offense.

Three Terms ago the subject was reconsidered in *Atkins.* We held that standards of decency have evolved since *Penry* and now demonstrate that the execution of the mentally retarded is cruel and unusual punishment.

Just as the *Atkins* Court reconsidered the issue decided in *Penry,* we now reconsider the issue decided in *Stanford.* The beginning point is a review of objective indicia of consensus, as expressed in particular by the enactments of legislatures that have addressed the question. These data give us essential instruction. We then must determine, in the exercise of our own independent judgment, whether the death penalty is a disproportionate punishment for juveniles.

III

A

The evidence of national consensus against the death penalty for juveniles is similar, and in some respects parallel, to the evidence *Atkins* held sufficient to demonstrate a national consensus against the death penalty for the mentally retarded. When *Atkins* was decided, 30 States prohibited the death penalty for the mentally retarded. This number comprised 12 that had abandoned the death penalty altogether, and 18 that maintained it but excluded the mentally retarded from its reach. By a similar calculation in this case, 30 States prohibit the juvenile death penalty, comprising 12 that have rejected the death penalty altogether and 18 that maintain it but, by express provision or judicial interpretation, exclude juveniles from its reach.

There is, to be sure, at least one difference between the evidence of consensus in *Atkins* and in this case. Impressive in *Atkins* was the rate of abolition of the death penalty for the mentally retarded. Sixteen States that permitted the execution of the mentally retarded at the time of *Penry* had prohibited the practice by the time we heard *Atkins.* By contrast, the rate of change in reducing the incidence of the juvenile death penalty, or in taking specific steps to abolish it, has been slower. Five States that allowed the juvenile death penalty at the time of *Stanford* have abandoned it in the intervening 15 years — four through legislative enactments and one through judicial decision.

Though less dramatic than the change from *Penry* to *Atkins* we still consider the change from *Stanford* to this case to be significant. As noted in *Atkins*, with respect to the States that had abandoned the death penalty for the mentally retarded since *Penry*, "[i]t is not so much the number of these States that is significant, but the consistency of the direction of change." The number of States that have abandoned capital punishment for juvenile offenders since *Stanford* is smaller than the number of States that abandoned capital punishment for the mentally retarded after *Penry*; yet we think the same consistency of direction of change has been demonstrated. Since *Stanford*, no State that previously prohibited capital punishment for juveniles has reinstated it. This fact, coupled with the trend toward abolition of the juvenile death penalty, carries special force in light of the general popularity of anticrime legislation. Any difference between this case and *Atkins* with respect to the pace of abolition is thus counterbalanced by the consistent direction of the change.

B

A majority of States have rejected the imposition of the death penalty on juvenile offenders under 18, and we now hold this is required by the Eighth Amendment.

Three general differences between juveniles under 18 and adults demonstrate that juvenile offenders cannot with reliability be classified among the worst offenders. First, as any parent knows and as the scientific and sociological studies respondent and his amici cite tend to confirm, "[a] lack of maturity and an underdeveloped sense of responsibility are found in youth more often than in adults and are more understandable among the young. These qualities often result in impetuous and ill-considered actions and decisions." It has been noted that "adolescents are overrepresented statistically in virtually every category of reckless behavior." In recognition of the comparative immaturity and irresponsibility of juveniles, almost every State prohibits those under 18 years of age from voting, serving on juries, or marrying without parental consent.

The second area of difference is that juveniles are more vulnerable or susceptible to negative influences and outside pressures, including peer pressure. This is explained in part by the prevailing circumstance that juveniles have less control, or less experience with control, over their own environment.

The third broad difference is that the character of a juvenile is not as well formed as that of an adult. The personality traits of juveniles are more transitory, less fixed.

These differences render suspect any conclusion that a juvenile falls among the worst offenders. From a moral standpoint it would be misguided to equate the failings of a minor with those of an adult, for a greater possibility exists that a minor's character deficiencies will be reformed.

As for deterrence, it is unclear whether the death penalty has a significant or even measurable deterrent effect on juveniles, as counsel for petitioner acknowledged at oral argument. Here, however, the absence of evidence of deterrent effect is of special concern because the same characteristics that render juveniles less culpable than adults suggest as well that juveniles will be less susceptible to deterrence. In particular, as the plurality observed in *Thompson*, "[t]he likelihood that the teenage offender has made the kind of cost-benefit analysis that attaches any weight to the possibility of execution is so remote as to be virtually nonexistent." To the extent the juvenile death penalty might have residual deterrent effect, it is worth noting that the punishment of life imprisonment without the possibility of parole is itself a severe sanction, in particular for a young person.

The differences between juvenile and adult offenders are too marked and well understood to risk allowing a youthful person to receive the death penalty despite insufficient culpability. An unacceptable likelihood exists that the brutality or cold-blooded nature of any particular crime would overpower mitigating arguments based on youth as a matter of course, even where the juvenile offender's objective immaturity, vulnerability, and lack of true depravity should require a sentence less severe than death. In some cases a defendant's youth may even be counted against him. In this very case, as we noted above, the prosecutor argued Simmons' youth was aggravating rather than mitigating.

Drawing the line at 18 years of age is subject, of course, to the objections always raised against categorical rules. The qualities that distinguish juveniles from adults do not disappear when an individual turns 18. By the same token, some under 18 have already attained a level of maturity some adults will never reach. For the reasons we have discussed, however, a line must be drawn. The age of 18 is the point where society draws the line for many purposes between childhood and adulthood. It is, we conclude, the age at which the line for death eligibility ought to rest.

IV

Our determination that the death penalty is disproportionate punishment for offenders under 18 finds confirmation in the stark reality that the United States is the only country in the world that continues to give official sanction to the juvenile death penalty. This reality does not become controlling, for the task of interpreting the Eighth Amendment remains our responsibility. Yet at least from the time of the Court's decision in *Trop*, the Court has referred to the laws of other countries and to international authorities as instructive for its interpretation of the Eighth Amendment's prohibition of "cruel and unusual punishments."

As respondent and a number of amici emphasize, Article 37 of the United Nations Convention on the Rights of the Child, which every country in the world has ratified save for the United States and Somalia, contains an express prohibition on capital punishment for crimes committed by juveniles under 18. No ratifying country has entered a reservation to the provision prohibiting the execution of juvenile offenders.

Respondent and his amici have submitted, and petitioner does not contest, that only seven countries other than the United States have executed juvenile offenders since 1990: Iran, Pakistan, Saudi Arabia, Yemen, Nigeria, the Democratic Republic of Congo, and China. Since then each of these countries has either abolished capital punishment for juveniles or made public disavowal of the practice. In sum, it is fair to say that the United States now stands alone in a world that has turned its face against the juvenile death penalty.

It is proper that we acknowledge the overwhelming weight of international opinion against the juvenile death penalty, resting in large part on the understanding that the instability and emotional imbalance of young people may often be a factor in the crime. The opinion of the world community, while not controlling our outcome, does provide respected and significant confirmation for our own conclusions.

The Eighth and Fourteenth Amendments forbid imposition of the death penalty on offenders who were under the age of 18 when their crimes were committed.

Justice O'CONNOR, dissenting.

The Court's decision today establishes a categorical rule forbidding the execution of any offender for any crime committed before his 18th birthday, no matter how deliberate, wanton, or cruel the offense. Neither the objective evidence of contemporary societal values, nor the Court's moral proportionality analysis, nor the two in tandem suffice to justify this ruling.

Although the Court finds support for its decision in the fact that a majority of the States now disallow capital punishment of 17-year-old offenders, it refrains from asserting that its holding is compelled by a genuine national consensus. Indeed, the evidence before us fails to demonstrate conclusively that any such consensus has emerged in the brief period since we upheld the constitutionality of this practice in Stanford v. Kentucky (1989).

Instead, the rule decreed by the Court rests, ultimately, on its independent moral judgment that death is a disproportionately severe punishment for any 17-year-old offender. I do not subscribe to this judgment. Adolescents as a class are undoubtedly less mature, and therefore less culpable for their misconduct, than adults. But the Court has adduced no evidence impeaching the seemingly reasonable conclusion reached by many state legislatures: that at least some 17-year-old murderers are sufficiently mature to deserve the death penalty in an appropriate case. Nor has it been shown that capital sentencing juries are incapable of accurately assessing a youthful defendant's maturity or of giving due weight to the mitigating characteristics associated with youth.

On this record—and especially in light of the fact that so little has changed since our recent decision in *Stanford*—I would not substitute our judgment about the moral propriety of capital punishment for 17-year-old murderers for the judgments of the Nation's legislatures. Rather, I would demand a clearer showing that our society truly has set its face against this practice before reading the Eighth Amendment categorically to forbid it.

Because I do not believe that a genuine national consensus against the juvenile death penalty has yet developed, and because I do not believe the Court's moral proportionality argument justifies a categorical, age-based constitutional rule, I can assign no such confirmatory role to the international consensus described by the Court. In short, the evidence of an international consensus does not alter my determination that the Eighth Amendment does not, at this time, forbid capital punishment of 17-year-old murderers in all cases.

Nevertheless, I disagree with Justice Scalia's contention that foreign and international law have no place in our Eighth Amendment jurisprudence. Over the course of nearly half a century, the Court has consistently referred to foreign and international law as relevant to its assessment of evolving standards of decency. This inquiry reflects the special character of the Eighth Amendment, which, as the Court has long held, draws its meaning directly from the maturing values of civilized society. Obviously, American law is distinctive in many respects, not least where the specific provisions of our Constitution and the history of its exposition so dictate. But this Nation's evolving understanding of human dignity certainly is neither wholly isolated from, nor inherently at odds with, the values prevailing in other countries. At least, the existence of an international consensus of this nature can serve to confirm the reasonableness of a consonant and genuine American consensus. The instant case presents no such domestic consensus, however, and the recent emergence of an otherwise global consensus does not alter that basic fact.

Justice SCALIA, with whom THE CHIEF JUSTICE and Justice THOMAS join, dissenting.

In urging approval of a constitution that gave life-tenured judges the power to nullify laws enacted by the people's representatives, Alexander

Hamilton assured the citizens of New York that there was little risk in this, since "[t]he judiciary . . . ha[s] neither FORCE nor WILL but merely judgment." But Hamilton had in mind a traditional judiciary, "bound down by strict rules and precedents which serve to define and point out their duty in every particular case that comes before them." Bound down, indeed. What a mockery today's opinion makes of Hamilton's expectation, announcing the Court's conclusion that the meaning of our Constitution has changed over the past 15 years — not, mind you, that this Court's decision 15 years ago was wrong, but that the Constitution has changed. The Court reaches this implausible result by purporting to advert, not to the original meaning of the Eighth Amendment, but to "the evolving standards of decency." It then finds, on the flimsiest of grounds, that a national consensus which could not be perceived in our people's laws barely 15 years ago now solidly exists. Worse still, the Court says in so many words that what our people's laws say about the issue does not, in the last analysis, matter: "[I]n the end our own judgment will be brought to bear on the question of the acceptability of the death penalty under the Eighth Amendment." The Court thus proclaims itself sole arbiter of our Nation's moral standards — and in the course of discharging that awesome responsibility purports to take guidance from the views of foreign courts and legislatures. Because I do not believe that the meaning of our Eighth Amendment, any more than the meaning of other provisions of our Constitution, should be determined by the subjective views of five Members of this Court and like-minded foreigners, I dissent.

Today's opinion provides a perfect example of why judges are ill equipped to make the type of legislative judgments the Court insists on making here. To support its opinion that States should be prohibited from imposing the death penalty on anyone who committed murder before age 18, the Court looks to scientific and sociological studies, picking and choosing those that support its position. It never explains why those particular studies are methodologically sound; none was ever entered into evidence or tested in an adversarial proceeding.

In other words, all the Court has done today, to borrow from another context, is to look over the heads of the crowd and pick out its friends.

Though the views of our own citizens are essentially irrelevant to the Court's decision today, the views of other countries and the so-called international community take center stage. [T]he basic premise of the Court's argument — that American law should conform to the laws of the rest of the world — ought to be rejected out of hand. In fact the Court itself does not believe it. In many significant respects the laws of most other countries differ from our law — including not only such explicit provisions of our Constitution as the right to jury trial and grand jury indictment, but even many interpretations of the Constitution prescribed by this Court itself. The Court-pronounced exclusionary rule, for example, is distinctively American.

The Court has been oblivious to the views of other countries when deciding how to interpret our Constitution's requirement that "Congress shall make no law respecting an establishment of religion. . . ." And let us not forget the Court's abortion jurisprudence, which makes us one of only six countries that allow abortion on demand until the point of viability.

Foreign sources are cited today, not to underscore our "fidelity" to the Constitution, our "pride in its origins," and "our own [American] heritage." To the contrary, they are cited to set aside the centuries-old American practice—a practice still engaged in by a large majority of the relevant States—of letting a jury of 12 citizens decide whether, in the particular case, youth should be the basis for withholding the death penalty. What these foreign sources "affirm," rather than repudiate, is the Justices' own notion of how the world ought to be, and their diktat that it shall be so henceforth in America.

The Court's reliance on foreign law in *Roper* sparked controversy over the proper role of foreign law in American criminal law. Originalists, such as Justice Scalia, maintain that reliance on foreign law is inconsistent with the unique tradition and values of American law.[16] As he stated, "We don't have the same moral and legal framework as the rest of the world, and never have." The practice of considering foreign law invites judges to cherry-pick from foreign laws so they can reach the conclusions they have already formed. As a result, they use foreign law to impose their own moral judgments on the populace.

By contrast, Justice Breyer and those who support the transnationalist approach to constitutional interpretation argue that "consideration of foreign law permits a natural process of judicial dialogue that is inescapable in the modern world."[17] They also argue that relying on foreign laws, such as those in Great Britain, makes sense given our common reliance on common law in the development of our legal practices. Given the history of American laws, transnationalists, including Justice Kennedy in *Roper*, argue that common values transcend national borders.

c. Prohibition of the Death Penalty for Non-Homicide Offenses

In Kennedy v. Louisiana, 554 U.S. 407 (2008), the Court took another step to limit the death penalty by holding that its application to a non-homicide offense, such as child rape, violates the Eighth Amendment.

---

16. *See A Conversation Between U.S. Supreme Court Justices*, 3 Intl. J. Const. L. 519, 525 (2005) (including a transcript of a debate between Justices Antonin Scalia and Stephen Breyer held at the American University Washington College of Law on January 13, 2005).

17. Daniel J. Frank, *Constitutional Interpretation Revisited: The Effects of a Delicate Supreme Court Balance on the Inclusion of Foreign Law in American Jurisprudence*, 92 Iowa L. Rev. 1037, 1046 (2007).

KENNEDY v. LOUISIANA

554 U.S. 407 (2008)

Justice KENNEDY delivered the opinion of the Court.

Patrick Kennedy, the petitioner here, seeks to set aside his death sentence under the Eighth Amendment. He was charged by the respondent, the State of Louisiana, with the aggravated rape of his then-8-year-old stepdaughter. This case presents the question whether the Constitution bars respondent from imposing the death penalty for the rape of a child where the crime did not result, and was not intended to result, in death of the victim. We hold the Eighth Amendment prohibits the death penalty for this offense. The Louisiana statute is unconstitutional.

Petitioner's crime was one that cannot be recounted in these pages in a way sufficient to capture in full the hurt and horror inflicted on his victim or to convey the revulsion society, and the jury that represents it, sought to express by sentencing petitioner to death. [The Court then described the horrific rape of the child. Kennedy was convicted of aggravated rape of the child and sentenced to death.]

The Eighth Amendment, applicable to the States through the Fourteenth Amendment, provides that "[e]xcessive bail shall not be required, nor excessive fines imposed, nor cruel and unusual punishments inflicted." The Amendment "draw[s] its meaning from the evolving standards of decency that mark the progress of a maturing society."

In 1925, 18 States, the District of Columbia, and the Federal Government had statutes that authorized the death penalty for the rape of a child or an adult. See *Coker* (1977) (plurality opinion). Between 1930 and 1964, 455 people were executed for those crimes. To our knowledge the last individual executed for the rape of a child was Ronald Wolfe in 1964.

In 1972, *Furman* invalidated most of the state statutes authorizing the death penalty for the crime of rape; and in *Furman*'s aftermath only six States reenacted their capital rape provisions. Three States — Georgia, North Carolina, and Louisiana — did so with respect to all rape offenses. Three States — Florida, Mississippi, and Tennessee — did so with respect only to child rape.

Louisiana reintroduced the death penalty for rape of a child in 1995. Five States have since followed Louisiana's lead: Georgia, Montana, Oklahoma, South Carolina, and Texas. By contrast, 44 States have not made child rape a capital offense. As for federal law, Congress in the Federal Death Penalty Act of 1994 expanded the number of federal crimes for which the death penalty is a permissible sentence, including certain nonhomicide offenses; but it did not do the same for child rape or abuse.

The evidence of a national consensus with respect to the death penalty for child rapists, as with respect to juveniles, mentally retarded offenders, and vicarious felony murderers, shows divided opinion but, on balance, an opinion against it.

Louisiana is the only State since 1964 that has sentenced an individual to death for the crime of child rape; and petitioner and Richard Davis, who was convicted and sentenced to death for the aggravated rape of a 5-year-old child by a Louisiana jury in December 2007 are the only two individuals now on death row in the United States for a nonhomicide offense.

Our concern here is limited to crimes against individual persons. We do not address, for example, crimes defining and punishing treason, espionage, terrorism, and drug kingpin activity, which are offenses against the State. As it relates to crimes against individuals, though, the death penalty should not be expanded to instances where the victim's life was not taken.

It is not at all evident that the child rape victim's hurt is lessened when the law permits the death of the perpetrator. There are . . . serious systemic concerns in prosecuting the crime of child rape that are relevant to the constitutionality of making it a capital offense. The problem of unreliable, induced, and even imagined child testimony means there is a "special risk of wrongful execution" in some child rape cases.

In addition, by in effect making the punishment for child rape and murder equivalent, a State that punishes child rape by death may remove a strong incentive for the rapist not to kill the victim.

The rule of evolving standards of decency . . . means that resort to the penalty must be reserved for the worst of crimes and limited in its instances of application. Difficulties in administering the penalty to ensure against its arbitrary and capricious application require adherence to a rule reserving its use, at this stage of evolving standards and in cases of crimes against individuals, for crimes that take the life of the victim.

Justice ALITO, with whom THE CHIEF JUSTICE, Justice SCALIA, and Justice THOMAS join, dissenting.

The Court today holds that the Eighth Amendment categorically prohibits the imposition of the death penalty for the crime of raping a child. This is so, according to the Court, no matter how young the child, no matter how many times the child is raped, no matter how many children the perpetrator rapes, no matter how sadistic the crime, no matter how much physical or psychological trauma is inflicted, and no matter how heinous the perpetrator's prior criminal record may be.

The rape of any victim inflicts great injury, and "[s]ome victims are so grievously injured physically or psychologically that life *is* beyond repair." It has been estimated that as many as 40% of 7- to 13-year-old sexual assault victims are considered "seriously disturbed." The harm that is caused to the victims and to society at large by the worst child rapists is grave. It is the judgment of the Louisiana lawmakers and those in an increasing number of other States that these harms justify the death penalty. The Court provides no cogent explanation why this legislative judgment should be overridden. Conclusory references to "decency," "moderation," "restraint," "full progress," and "moral judgment" are not enough.

d. Method of Execution

Defendants may also challenge the method of execution as violating the prohibition against cruel and unusual punishment. The prevailing method of execution today is lethal injection. Defendants have challenged the three-drug protocol as inhumane. However, in a plurality decision in 2008, the Supreme Court held that the three-drug protocol for lethal injection, if properly administered, does not violate the Eighth Amendment. In his concurrence, Justice Stevens takes the opportunity to summarize the arguments for moving beyond the question of the constitutionality of our methods of execution to whether the death penalty should be retained.

BAZE v. REES

553 U.S. 35 (2008)

Chief Justice ROBERTS announced the judgment of the Court and delivered an opinion, in which Justice KENNEDY and Justice ALITO join.

Like 35 other States and the Federal Government, Kentucky has chosen to impose capital punishment for certain crimes. As is true with respect to each of these States and the Federal Government, Kentucky has altered its method of execution over time to more humane means of carrying out the sentence. That progress has led to the use of lethal injection by every jurisdiction that imposes the death penalty.

Petitioners in this case — each convicted of double homicide — acknowledge that the lethal injection procedure, if applied as intended, will result in a humane death. They nevertheless contend that the lethal injection protocol is unconstitutional under the Eighth Amendment's ban on "cruel and unusual punishments," because of the risk that the protocol's terms might not be properly followed, resulting in significant pain.

The trial court held extensive hearings and entered detailed Findings of Fact and Conclusions of Law. It recognized that "[t]here are no methods of legal execution that are satisfactory to those who oppose the death penalty on moral, religious, or societal grounds," but concluded that Kentucky's procedure "complies with the constitutional requirements against cruel and unusual punishment." We too agree that petitioners have not carried their burden of showing that the risk of pain from maladministration of a concededly humane lethal injection protocol, and the failure to adopt untried and untested alternatives, constitute cruel and unusual punishment.

I

By the middle of the 19th century, "hanging was the 'nearly universal form of execution' in the United States." . . . New York became the first State to authorize electrocution as a form of capital punishment. By 1915, 11 other States had followed suit, motivated by the "well-grounded belief that electrocution is less painful and more humane than hanging."

Electrocution remained the predominant mode of execution for nearly a century, although several methods, including hanging, firing squad, and lethal gas were in use at one time. Following the 9-year hiatus in executions that ended with our decision in *Gregg v. Georgia* (1976), however, state legislatures began responding to public calls to reexamine electrocution as a means of assuring a humane death. In 1977, legislators in Oklahoma, after consulting with the head of the anesthesiology department at the University of Oklahoma College of Medicine, introduced the first bill proposing lethal injection as the State's method of execution. A total of 36 States have now adopted lethal injection as the exclusive or primary means of implementing the death penalty, making it by far the most prevalent method of execution in the United States. It is also the method used by the Federal Government.

Of these 36 States, at least 30 (including Kentucky) use the same combination of three drugs in their lethal injection protocols. The first drug, sodium thiopental (also known as Pentathol), is a fast-acting barbiturate sedative that induces a deep, comalike unconsciousness when given in the amounts used for lethal injection. The second drug, pancuronium bromide (also known as Pavulon), is a paralytic agent that inhibits all muscular-skeletal movements and, by paralyzing the diaphragm, stops respiration. Potassium chloride, the third drug, interferes with the electrical signals that stimulate the contractions of the heart, inducing cardiac arrest. The proper administration of the first drug ensures that the prisoner does not experience any pain associated with the paralysis and cardiac arrest caused by the second and third drugs.

Kentucky replaced electrocution with lethal injection in 1998. The Kentucky statute does not specify the drugs or categories of drugs to be used during an execution, instead mandating that "every death sentence shall be executed by continuous intravenous injection of a substance or combination of substances sufficient to cause death."

Shortly after the adoption of lethal injection, officials working for the Kentucky Department of Corrections set about developing a written protocol for execution. Kentucky's protocol called for the injection of 2 grams of sodium thiopental, 50 milligrams of pancuronium bromide, and 240 milliequivalents of potassium chloride. In 2004, as a result of this litigation, the department chose to increase the amount of sodium thiopental from 2 grams to 3 grams. Between injections, members of the execution team flush the intravenous (IV) lines with 25 milligrams of saline to prevent clogging of the lines by precipitates that may form when residual sodium thiopental comes into contact with pancuronium bromide. The protocol reserves responsibility for inserting the IV catheters to qualified personnel having at least one year of professional experience. Currently, Kentucky uses a certified phlebotomist and an emergency medical technician (EMT) to perform the venipunctures necessary for the catheters. They have up to one hour to establish both primary and secondary peripheral intravenous sites in the arm, hand, leg, or foot of the inmate. Other personnel are responsible for mixing the solutions containing the three drugs and loading them into syringes.

Kentucky's execution facilities consist of the execution chamber, a control room separated by a one-way window, and a witness room. The warden and deputy warden remain in the execution chamber with the prisoner, who is strapped to a gurney. The execution team administers the drugs remotely from the control room through five feet of IV tubing. If, as determined by the warden and deputy warden through visual inspection, the prisoner is not unconscious within 60 seconds following the delivery of the sodium thiopental to the primary IV site, a new 3-gram dose of thiopental is administered to the secondary site before injecting the pancuronium and potassium chloride. In addition to assuring that the first dose of thiopental is successfully administered, the warden and deputy warden also watch for any problems with the IV catheters and tubing.

A physician is present to assist in any effort to revive the prisoner in the event of a last-minute stay of execution. By statute, however, the physician is prohibited from participating in the "conduct of an execution," except to certify the cause of death. An electrocardiogram (EKG) verifies the death of the prisoner. Only one Kentucky prisoner, Eddie Lee Harper, has been executed since the Commonwealth adopted lethal injection. There were no reported problems at Harper's execution.

II

The Eighth Amendment to the Constitution, applicable to the States through the Due Process Clause of the Fourteenth Amendment, provides that "[e]xcessive bail shall not be required, nor excessive fines imposed, nor cruel and unusual punishments inflicted." We begin with the principle, settled by *Gregg*, that capital punishment is constitutional. It necessarily follows that there must be a means of carrying it out. Some risk of pain is inherent in any method of execution — no matter how humane — if only from the prospect of error in following the required procedure. It is clear, then, that the Constitution does not demand the avoidance of all risk of pain in carrying out executions. Petitioners do not claim that it does. Rather, they contend that the Eighth Amendment prohibits procedures that create an "unnecessary risk" of pain.

Kentucky responds that this "unnecessary risk" standard is tantamount to a requirement that States adopt the "least risk" alternative in carrying out an execution, a standard the Commonwealth contends will cast recurring constitutional doubt on any procedure adopted by the States. Instead, Kentucky urges the Court to approve the "substantial risk" test used by the courts below.

A

This Court has never invalidated a State's chosen procedure for carrying out a sentence of death as the infliction of cruel and unusual punishment. In *Wilkerson v. Utah* (1879), we upheld a sentence to death by firing squad imposed by a territorial court, rejecting the argument that such a sentence constituted cruel and unusual punishment. We noted there the difficulty of "defin[ing] with exactness the extent of the constitutional provision which provides that cruel and unusual punishments shall not be inflicted." Rather than undertake such an effort, the *Wilkerson* Court simply noted that "it is safe to affirm that punishments of torture . . . and all others in the same line of unnecessary cruelty, are forbidden" by the Eighth Amendment. By way of example, the Court cited cases from England in which "terror, pain, or disgrace were sometimes superadded" to the sentence, such as where the condemned was "embowelled alive, beheaded, and quartered," or instances of "public dissection in murder, and burning alive."

We observed that "[p]unishments are cruel when they involve torture or a lingering death; but the punishment of death is not cruel within the meaning of that word as used in the Constitution. It implies there something inhuman and barbarous, something more than the mere extinguishment of life."

B

Petitioners do not claim that lethal injection or the proper administration of the particular protocol adopted by Kentucky by themselves constitute the cruel or wanton infliction of pain. Quite the contrary, they concede that "if performed properly," an execution carried out under Kentucky's procedures would be "humane and constitutional." Instead, petitioners claim that there is a significant risk that the procedures will *not* be properly followed — in particular, that the sodium thiopental will not be properly administered to achieve its intended effect — resulting in severe pain when the other chemicals are administered.

Simply because an execution method may result in pain, either by accident or as an inescapable consequence of death, does not establish the sort of "objectively intolerable risk of harm" that qualifies as cruel and unusual. In *Louisiana ex rel. Francis v. Reswebe* (1947), a plurality of the Court upheld a second attempt at executing a prisoner by electrocution after a mechanical malfunction had interfered with the first attempt. The principal opinion noted that "[a]ccidents happen for which no man is to blame," and concluded that such "an accident, with no suggestion of malevolence."

C

Much of petitioners' case rests on the contention that they have identified a significant risk of harm that can be eliminated by adopting alternative procedures, such as a one-drug protocol that dispenses with the use of pancuronium and potassium chloride, and additional monitoring by trained personnel to ensure that the first dose of sodium thiopental has been adequately delivered. Given what our cases have said about the nature of the risk of harm that is actionable under the Eighth Amendment, a condemned prisoner cannot successfully challenge a State's method of execution merely by showing a slightly or marginally safer alternative.

Instead, the proffered alternatives must effectively address a "substantial risk of serious harm." To qualify, the alternative procedure must be feasible, readily implemented, and in fact significantly reduce a substantial risk of severe pain. If a State refuses to adopt such an alternative in the face of these documented advantages, without a legitimate penological justification for adhering to its current method of execution, then a State's refusal to change its method can be viewed as "cruel and unusual" under the Eighth Amendment.

III

In applying these standards to the facts of this case, we note at the outset that it is difficult to regard a practice as "objectively intolerable" when it is in fact widely tolerated. No State uses or has ever used the alternative one-drug protocol belatedly urged by petitioners.

We agree with the state trial court and State Supreme Court that petitioners have not shown that the risk of an inadequate dose of the first drug is substantial. And we reject the argument that the Eighth Amendment requires Kentucky to adopt the untested alternative procedures petitioners have identified.

The broad framework of the Eighth Amendment has accommodated . . . progress toward more humane methods of execution, and our approval of a particular method in the past has not precluded legislatures from taking the steps they deem appropriate, in light of new developments, to ensure humane capital punishment. There is no reason to suppose that today's decision will be any different.

The judgment below concluding that Kentucky's procedure is consistent with the Eighth Amendment is, accordingly, affirmed.

Justice ALITO, concurring.

The issue presented in this case — the constitutionality of a *method* of execution — should be kept separate from the controversial issue of the death penalty itself. If the Court wishes to reexamine the latter issue, it should do so directly, as Justice Stevens now suggests. The Court should not produce a *de facto* ban on capital punishment by adopting method-of-execution rules that lead to litigation gridlock.

Justice STEVENS, concurring in the judgment.

When we granted certiorari in this case, I assumed that our decision would bring the debate about lethal injection as a method of execution to a close. It now seems clear that it will not. The question whether a similar three-drug protocol may be used in other States remains open, and may well be answered differently in a future case on the basis of a more complete record. Instead of ending the controversy, I am now convinced that this case will generate debate not only about the constitutionality of the three-drug protocol, and specifically about the justification for the use of the paralytic agent, pancuronium bromide, but also about the justification for the death penalty itself.

I

Because it masks any outward sign of distress, pancuronium bromide creates a risk that the inmate will suffer excruciating pain before death occurs. There is a general understanding among veterinarians that the risk of pain is sufficiently serious that the use of the drug should be proscribed when an animal's life is being terminated. As a result of this understanding among knowledgeable professionals, several States — including Kentucky — have enacted legislation prohibiting use of the drug in animal euthanasia. It is unseemly — to say the least — that Kentucky may well kill petitioners using a drug that it would not permit to be used on their pets.

Use of pancuronium bromide is particularly disturbing because — as the trial court specifically found in this case — it serves "no therapeutic purpose." The drug's primary use is to prevent involuntary muscle movements, and its secondary use is to stop respiration. In my view, neither of these purposes is sufficient to justify the risk inherent in the use of the drug.

The plurality believes that preventing involuntary movement is a legitimate justification for using pancuronium bromide because "[t]he Commonwealth has an interest in preserving the dignity of the procedure, especially where convulsions or seizures could be misperceived as signs of consciousness or distress." This is a woefully inadequate justification. Whatever minimal interest there may be in ensuring that a condemned inmate dies a dignified death, and that witnesses to the execution are not made uncomfortable by an incorrect belief (which could easily be corrected) that the inmate is in pain, is vastly outweighed by the risk that the inmate is actually experiencing excruciating pain that no one can detect.

In my view, therefore, States wishing to decrease the risk that future litigation will delay executions or invalidate their protocols would do well to reconsider their continued use of pancuronium bromide.

II

The thoughtful opinions written by The Chief Justice and by Justice Ginsburg have persuaded me that current decisions by state legislatures, by the Congress of the United States, and by this Court to retain the death penalty as a part of our law are the product of habit and inattention rather than an acceptable deliberative process that weighs the costs and risks of administering that penalty against its identifiable benefits, and rest in part on a faulty assumption about the retributive force of the death penalty.

In *Gregg v. Georgia* (1976), we explained that unless a criminal sanction serves a legitimate penological function, it constitutes "gratuitous infliction of suffering" in violation of the Eighth Amendment. While incapacitation may have been a legitimate rationale in 1976, the recent rise in statutes providing for life imprisonment without the possibility of parole demonstrates that incapacitation is neither a necessary nor a sufficient justification for the death penalty. Moreover, a recent poll indicates that support for the death penalty drops significantly when life without the possibility of parole is presented as an alternative option.

The legitimacy of deterrence as an acceptable justification for the death penalty is also questionable, at best. Despite 30 years of empirical research in the area, there remains no reliable statistical evidence that capital punishment in fact deters potential offenders. In the absence of such evidence, deterrence cannot serve as a sufficient penological justification for this uniquely severe and irrevocable punishment.

We are left, then, with retribution as the primary rationale for imposing the death penalty. And indeed, it is the retribution rationale that animates much of the remaining enthusiasm for the death penalty. [O]ur society has moved away from public and painful retribution towards ever more humane forms of punishment. In an attempt to bring executions in line with our evolving standards of decency, we have adopted increasingly less painful methods of execution, and then declared previous methods barbaric and archaic. But by requiring that an execution be relatively painless, we necessarily protect the inmate from enduring any punishment that is comparable to the suffering inflicted on his victim. This trend, while appropriate and required by the Eighth Amendment's prohibition on cruel and unusual punishment, actually undermines the very premise on which public approval of the retribution rationale is based.

Full recognition of the diminishing force of the principal rationales for retaining the death penalty should lead this Court and legislatures to reexamine the question recently posed by Professor Salinas, a former Texas prosecutor and judge: "The time for a dispassionate, impartial comparison of the enormous costs that death penalty litigation imposes on society with the benefits that it produces has surely arrived."

III

Our decisions in 1976 upholding the constitutionality of the death penalty relied heavily on our belief that adequate procedures were in place that would avoid the danger of discriminatory application. Ironically, however, more recent cases have endorsed procedures that provide less protections to capital defendants than to ordinary offenders. Of special concern to me are rules that deprive the defendant of a trial by jurors representing a fair cross section of the community. Litigation involving both challenges for cause and peremptory challenges has persuaded me that the process of obtaining a "death qualified jury" is really a procedure that has the purpose and effect of obtaining a jury that is biased in favor of conviction.

Another serious concern is that the risk of error in capital cases may be greater than in other cases because the facts are often so disturbing that the interest in making sure the crime does not go unpunished may overcome residual doubt concerning the identity of the offender.

A third significant concern is the risk of discriminatory application of the death penalty. While that risk has been dramatically reduced, the Court has allowed it to continue to play an unacceptable role in capital cases.

Finally, given the real risk of error in this class of cases, the irrevocable nature of the consequences is of decisive importance to me. Whether or not any innocent defendants have actually been executed, abundant evidence accumulated in recent years has resulted in the exoneration of an unacceptable number of defendants found guilty of capital offenses. The risk of executing innocent defendants can be entirely eliminated by treating any penalty more severe than life imprisonment without the possibility of parole as constitutionally excessive.

In sum, I have relied on my own experience in reaching the conclusion that the imposition of the death penalty represents "the pointless and needless extinction of life with only marginal contributions to any discernible social or public purposes. A penalty with such negligible returns to the State [is] patently excessive and cruel and unusual punishment violative of the Eighth Amendment."

IV

The conclusion that I have reached with regard to the constitutionality of the death penalty itself makes my decision in this case particularly difficult. It does not, however, justify a refusal to respect precedents that remain a part of our law. This Court has held that the death penalty is constitutional, and has established a framework for evaluating the constitutionality of particular methods of execution. Under those precedents, I am persuaded that the evidence adduced by petitioners fails to prove that Kentucky's lethal injection protocol violates the Eighth Amendment. Accordingly, I join the Court's judgment.

Justice SCALIA, with whom Justice THOMAS joins, concurring in the judgment.

I write separately to provide what I think is needed response to Justice Stevens' separate opinion.

According to Justice Stevens, the death penalty promotes none of the purposes of criminal punishment because it neither prevents more crimes than alternative measures nor serves a retributive purpose.

These conclusions are not supported by the available data. According to a "leading national study," "each execution prevents some eighteen murders, on average." "But even if Justice Stevens' assertion about the deterrent value of the death penalty were correct, the death penalty would yet be constitutional (as he concedes) if it served the appropriate purpose of retribution. The decision that capital punishment may be the appropriate sanction in extreme cases is an expression of the community's belief that certain crimes are themselves so grievous an affront to humanity that the only adequate response may be the penalty of death.

Justice Stevens' final refuge in his cost-benefit analysis is a familiar one: There is a risk that an innocent person might be convicted and sentenced to death. That rationale, however, supports not Justice Stevens' conclusion that the death penalty is unconstitutional, but the more sweeping proposition that any conviction in a case in which facts are disturbing is suspect — including, of course, convictions resulting in life without parole in those States that do not have capital punishment.

But of all Justice Stevens' criticisms of the death penalty, the hardest to take is his bemoaning of "the enormous costs that death penalty litigation imposes on society," including the "burden on the courts and the lack of finality for victim's families." Those costs, those burdens, and that lack of finality are in large measure the creation of Justice Stevens and other Justices opposed to the death penalty.

Justice THOMAS, with whom Justice SCALIA joins, concurring in the judgment.

Although I agree that petitioners have failed to establish that Kentucky's lethal injection protocol violates the Eighth Amendment, I write separately because I cannot subscribe to the plurality opinion's formulation of the governing standard. As I understand it, that opinion would hold that a method of execution violates the Eighth Amendment if it poses a substantial risk of severe pain that could be significantly reduced by adopting readily available alternative procedures. This standard — along with petitioners' proposed "unnecessary risk" standard and the dissent's "untoward risk" standard, — finds no support in the original understanding of the Cruel and Unusual Punishments Clause. Because, in my view, a method of execution violates the Eighth Amendment only if it is deliberately designed to inflict pain, I concur only in the judgment.

Justice BREYER, concurring in the judgment.

In respect to *how* a court should review such a claim, I agree with Justice Ginsburg. She highlights the relevant question, whether the method creates an untoward, readily avoidable risk of inflicting severe and unnecessary suffering. [However], I cannot find, either in the record in this case or in the literature on the subject, sufficient evidence that Kentucky's execution method poses the "significant and unnecessary risk of inflicting severe pain" that petitioners assert.

Justice GINSBURG, with whom Justice SOUTER joins, dissenting.

The constitutionality of Kentucky's protocol therefore turns on whether inmates are adequately anesthetized by the first drug in the protocol, sodium thiopental. Kentucky's system is constitutional, the plurality states, because "petitioners have not shown that the risk of an inadequate dose of the first drug is substantial." I would not dispose of the case so swiftly given the character of the risk at stake. Kentucky's protocol lacks basic safeguards used by other States to confirm that an inmate is unconscious before injection of the second and third drugs. I would vacate and remand with instructions to consider whether Kentucky's omission of those safeguards poses an untoward, readily avoidable risk of inflicting severe and unnecessary pain.

In Glossip v. Gross, 135 S. Ct. 2726 (2015), the Court rejected a challenge to the use of midazolam in Oklahoma's three-drug execution protocol. While the key issue was whether the use of the drug met the standards set in *Baze* for execution by lethal injection, the Court discussed two requirements for defendants challenging their execution. They must show: (1) the method being used creates an unacceptable risk of severe pain; and (2) there is a known and available alternative method of execution. In his dissent, Justice Breyer called for full briefing for a complete reexamination of the constitutionality of the death penalty.

GLOSSIP v. GROSS
135 S. Ct. 2726 (2015)

Justice ALITO delivered the opinion of the Court.

Prisoners sentenced to death in the State of Oklahoma filed an action in federal court contending that the method of execution now used by the State violates the Eighth Amendment because it creates an unacceptable risk of severe pain. They argue that midazolam, the first drug employed in the State's current three-drug protocol, fails to render a person insensate to pain. After holding an evidentiary hearing, the District Court denied four prisoners' application for a preliminary injunction, finding that they had failed to prove that midazolam is ineffective. The Court of Appeals for the Tenth Circuit affirmed and accepted the District Court's finding of fact regarding midazolam's efficacy.

For two independent reasons, we also affirm. First, the prisoners failed to identify a known and available alternative method of execution that entails a lesser risk of pain, a requirement of all Eighth Amendment method-of-execution claims. Second, the District Court did not commit clear error when it found that the prisoners failed to establish that Oklahoma's use of a massive dose of midazolam in its execution protocol entails a substantial risk of severe pain.

I

A

The death penalty was an accepted punishment at the time of the adoption of the Constitution and the Bill of Rights. In that era, death sentences were usually carried out by hanging. Hanging remained the standard method of execution through much of the 19th century, but that began to change in the century's later years. In the 1880's, the Legislature of the State of New York appointed a commission to find "'the most humane and practical method known to modern science of carrying into effect the sentence of death in capital cases.'" The commission recommended electrocution, and in 1888, the Legislature enacted a law providing for this method of execution. In subsequent years, other States followed New York's lead in the "'belief that electrocution is less painful and more humane than hanging.'"

In 1921, the Nevada Legislature adopted another new method of execution, lethal gas, after concluding that this was "the most humane manner known to modern science." The Nevada Supreme Court rejected the argument that the use of lethal gas was unconstitutional, and other States followed Nevada's lead. Nevertheless, hanging and the firing squad were retained in some States, and electrocution remained the predominant method of execution until the 9-year hiatus in executions that ended with our judgment in Gregg v. Georgia (1976).

After *Gregg* reaffirmed that the death penalty does not violate the Constitution, some States once again sought a more humane way to carry out death sentences. They eventually adopted lethal injection, which today is "by far the most prevalent method of execution in the United States."

While methods of execution have changed over the years, "[t]his Court has never invalidated a State's chosen procedure for carrying out a sentence of death as the infliction of cruel and unusual punishment." In Wilkerson v. Utah (1879), the Court upheld a sentence of death by firing squad. In In re Kemmler (1890), the Court rejected a challenge to the use of the electric chair. And the Court did not retreat from that holding even when presented with a case in which a State's initial attempt to execute a prisoner by electrocution was unsuccessful. Most recently, in Baze v. Rees (2008), seven Justices agreed that the three-drug protocol just discussed does not violate the Eighth Amendment.

Our decisions in this area have been animated in part by the recognition that because it is settled that capital punishment is constitutional, "[i]t necessarily follows that there must be a [constitutional] means of carrying it out." Holding that the Eighth Amendment demands the elimination of essentially all risk of pain would effectively outlaw the death penalty altogether. — well...

B

Baze cleared any legal obstacle to use of the most common three-drug protocol that had enabled States to carry out the death penalty in a quick and painless fashion. But a practical obstacle soon emerged, as anti-death-penalty advocates pressured pharmaceutical companies to refuse to supply the drugs used to carry out death sentences. The sole American manufacturer of sodium thiopental, the first drug used in the standard three-drug protocol, was persuaded to cease production of the drug. After suspending domestic production in 2009, the company planned to resume production in Italy. Activists then pressured both the company and the Italian Government to stop the sale of sodium thiopental for use in lethal injections in this country. That effort proved successful, and in January 2011, the company announced that it would exit the sodium thiopental market entirely.

After other efforts to procure sodium thiopental proved unsuccessful, States sought an alternative, and they eventually replaced sodium thiopental with pentobarbital, another barbiturate. In December 2010, Oklahoma became the first State to execute an inmate using pentobarbital. That execution occurred without incident, and States gradually shifted to pentobarbital as their supplies of sodium thiopental ran out. Before long, however, pentobarbital also became unavailable. Oklahoma eventually became unable to acquire the drug through any means.

C

Unable to acquire either sodium thiopental or pentobarbital, some States have turned to midazolam, a sedative in the benzodiazepine family of drugs. Oklahoma has already used this three-drug protocol twice: to execute Clayton Lockett in April 2014 and Charles Warner in January 2015.

The Lockett execution caused Oklahoma to implement new safety precautions as part of its lethal injection protocol. When Oklahoma executed Lockett, its protocol called for the administration of 100 milligrams of midazolam, as compared to the 500 milligrams that are currently required. On the morning of his execution, Lockett cut himself twice at " 'the bend of the elbow.' " That evening, the execution team spent nearly an hour making at least one dozen attempts to establish intravenous (IV) access to Lockett's cardiovascular system, including at his arms and elsewhere on his body. The team eventually believed that it had established intravenous access through Lockett's right femoral vein, and it covered the injection access point with a sheet, in part to preserve Lockett's dignity during the execution. After the team administered the midazolam and a physician determined that Lockett was unconscious, the team next administered the paralytic agent and most of the potassium chloride. Lockett began to move and speak, at which point the physician lifted the sheet and determined that the IV had "infiltrated," which means that "the IV fluid, rather than entering Lockett's blood stream, had leaked into the tissue surrounding the IV access point." The execution team stopped administering the remaining potassium chloride and terminated the execution about 33 minutes after the midazolam was first injected. About 10 minutes later, Lockett was pronounced dead.

An investigation into the Lockett execution concluded that "the viability of the IV access point was the single greatest factor that contributed to the difficulty in administering the execution drugs." The investigation recommended several changes to Oklahoma's execution protocol.

II

A

In June 2014, after Oklahoma switched from pentobarbital to midazolam and executed Lockett. Oklahoma death row inmates filed an action under 42 U. S. C. §1983 challenging the State's new lethal injection protocol. The complaint alleged that Oklahoma's use of midazolam violates the Eighth Amendment's prohibition of cruel and unusual punishment.

In November 2014, four of those plaintiffs — Richard Glossip, Benjamin Cole, John Grant, and Warner — filed a motion for a preliminary injunction. All four men had been convicted of murder and sentenced to death by Oklahoma juries. Glossip hired Justin Sneed to kill his employer, Barry Van Treese. Sneed entered a room where Van Treese was sleeping and beat him to death with a baseball bat. Cole murdered his 9-month-old daughter after she would not stop crying. Cole bent her body backwards until he snapped her spine in half. After the child died, Cole played video games. Grant, while serving terms of imprisonment totaling 130 years, killed Gay Carter, a prison food service supervisor, by pulling her into a mop closet and stabbing her numerous times with a shank. Warner anally raped and murdered an 11-month-old girl. The child's injuries included two skull fractures, internal brain injuries, two fractures to her jaw, a lacerated liver, and a bruised spleen and lungs.

The Oklahoma Court of Criminal Appeals affirmed the murder conviction and death sentence of each offender. Having exhausted the avenues for challenging their convictions and sentences, they moved for a preliminary injunction against Oklahoma's lethal injection protocol.

B

In December 2014, after discovery, the District Court held a 3-day evidentiary hearing on the preliminary injunction motion. The District Court heard testimony from 17 witnesses and reviewed numerous exhibits. Dr. David Lubarsky, an anesthesiologist, and Dr. Larry Sasich, a doctor of pharmacy, provided expert testimony about midazolam for petitioners, and Dr. Roswell Evans, a doctor of pharmacy, provided expert testimony for respondents.

After reviewing the evidence, the District Court issued an oral ruling denying the motion for a preliminary injunction. The District Court then held that petitioners failed to establish a likelihood of success on the merits of their claim that the use of midazolam violates the Eighth Amendment. The court provided two independent reasons for this conclusion. First, the court held that petitioners failed to identify a known and available method of execution that presented a substantially less severe risk of pain than the method that the State proposed to use. Second, the court found that petitioners failed to prove that Oklahoma's protocol "presents a risk that is 'sure or very likely to cause serious illness and needless suffering,' amounting to 'an objectively intolerable risk of harm.'" The court emphasized that the Oklahoma protocol featured numerous safeguards, including the establishment of two IV access sites, confirmation of the viability of those sites, and monitoring of the offender's level of consciousness throughout the procedure.

The District Court supported its decision with findings of fact about midazolam. It found that a 500-milligram dose of midazolam "would make it a virtual certainty that any individual will be at a sufficient level of unconsciousness to resist the noxious stimuli which could occur from the application of the second and third drugs." Indeed, it found that a 500-milligram dose alone would likely cause death by respiratory arrest within 30 minutes or an hour.

The Court of Appeals for the Tenth Circuit affirmed. The Court of Appeals explained that our decision in *Baze* requires a plaintiff challenging a lethal injection protocol to demonstrate that the risk of severe pain presented by an execution protocol is substantial "'when compared to the known and available alternatives.'" And it agreed with the District Court that petitioners had not identified any such alternative.

III

The Eighth Amendment, made applicable to the States through the Fourteenth Amendment, prohibits the infliction of "cruel and unusual punishments." The controlling opinion in *Baze* first concluded that prisoners cannot successfully challenge a method of execution unless they establish that the method presents a risk that is "'sure or very likely to cause serious illness and needless suffering,' and give rise to 'sufficiently imminent dangers.'" To prevail on such a claim, "there must be a 'substantial risk of serious harm,' an 'objectively intolerable risk of harm' that prevents prison officials from pleading that they were 'subjectively blameless for purposes of the Eighth Amendment.'" The controlling opinion also stated that prisoners "cannot successfully challenge a State's method of execution merely by showing a slightly or marginally safer alternative." Instead, prisoners must identify an alternative that is "feasible, readily implemented, and in fact significantly reduce[s] a substantial risk of severe pain."

The challenge in *Baze* failed both because the Kentucky inmates did not show that the risks they identified were substantial and imminent, and because they did not establish the existence of a known and available alternative method of execution that would entail a significantly less severe risk. Petitioners' arguments here fail for similar reasons.

The District Court found that midazolam is capable of placing a person "at a sufficient level of unconsciousness to resist the noxious stimuli which could occur from the application of the second and third drugs." This conclusion was not clearly erroneous. Respondents' expert, Dr. Evans, testified that the proper administration of a 500-milligram dose of midazolam would make it "a virtual certainty" that any individual would be "at a sufficient level of unconsciousness to resist the noxious stimuli which could occur from application of the 2nd and 3rd drugs" used in the Oklahoma protocol. And petitioners' experts acknowledged that they had no contrary scientific proof.

Oklahoma has also adopted important safeguards to ensure that midazolam is properly administered. The District Court emphasized three requirements in particular: The execution team must secure both a primary and backup IV access site, it must confirm the viability of the IV sites, and it must continuously monitor the offender's level of consciousness. The District Court did not commit clear error in concluding that these safeguards help to minimize any risk that might occur in the event that midazolam does not operate as intended.

B

Petitioners assert that midazolam's "ceiling effect" undermines the District Court's finding about the effectiveness of the huge dose administered in the Oklahoma protocol. Petitioners argue that midazolam has a "ceiling" above which any increase in dosage produces no effect. As a result, they maintain, it is wrong to assume that a 500-milligram dose has a much greater effect than a therapeutic dose of about 5 milligrams.

Petitioners provided little probative evidence on this point, and the speculative evidence that they did present to the District Court does not come close to establishing that its factual findings were clearly erroneous. Dr. Sasich stated in his expert report that the literature "indicates" that midazolam has a ceiling effect, but he conceded that he "was unable to determine the midazolam dose for a ceiling effect on unconsciousness because there is no literature in which such testing has been done." Dr. Lubarsky's report was similar and the testimony of petitioners' experts at the hearing was no more compelling.

C

Petitioners' remaining arguments about midazolam all lack merit. First, we are not persuaded by petitioners' argument that Dr. Evans' testimony should have been rejected because of some of the sources listed in his report. Second, petitioners argue that Dr. Evans' expert report contained a mathematical error, but we find this argument insignificant. Third, petitioners argue that there is no consensus among the States regarding midazolam's efficacy because only four States (Oklahoma, Arizona, Florida, and Ohio) have used midazolam as part of an execution. But while the near-universal use of the particular protocol at issue in *Baze* supported our conclusion that this protocol did not violate the Eighth Amendment, we did not say that the converse was true, i.e., that other protocols or methods of execution are of doubtful constitutionality. That argument, if accepted, would hamper the adoption of new and potentially more humane methods of execution and would prevent States from adapting to changes in the availability of suitable drugs.

Fourth, petitioners argue that difficulties with Oklahoma's execution of Lockett and Arizona's July 2014 execution of Joseph Wood establish that midazolam is sure or very likely to cause serious pain. We are not persuaded. Aside from the Lockett execution, 12 other executions have been conducted using the three-drug protocol at issue here, and those appear to have been conducted without any significant problems.

Finally, we find it appropriate to respond to the principal dissent's groundless suggestion that our decision is tantamount to allowing prisoners to be "drawn and quartered, slowly tortured to death, or actually burned at the stake." That is simply not true, and the principal dissent's resort to this outlandish rhetoric reveals the weakness of its legal arguments.

VI

For these reasons, the judgment of the Court of Appeals for the Tenth Circuit is affirmed.

Justice SCALIA, with whom Justice THOMAS joins, concurring.

I join the opinion of the Court, and write to respond to Justice BREYER's plea for judicial abolition of the death penalty.

Welcome to Groundhog Day. The scene is familiar: Petitioners, sentenced to die for the crimes they committed (including, in the case of one petitioner since put to death, raping and murdering an 11-month-old baby), come before this Court asking us to nullify their sentences as "cruel and unusual" under the Eighth Amendment. They rely on this provision because it is the only provision they can rely on. They were charged by a sovereign State with murder. They were afforded counsel and tried before a jury of their peers — tried twice, once to determine whether they were guilty and once to determine whether death was the appropriate sentence. They were duly convicted and sentenced. They were granted the right to appeal and to seek postconviction relief, first in state and then in federal court. And now, acknowledging that their convictions are unassailable, they ask us for clemency, as though clemency were ours to give.

The response is also familiar: A vocal minority of the Court, waving over their heads a ream of the most recent abolitionist studies (a superabundant genre) as though they have discovered the lost folios of Shakespeare, insist that now, at long last, the death penalty must be abolished for good. Mind you, not once in the history of the American Republic has this Court ever suggested the death penalty is categorically impermissible. The reason is obvious: It is impossible to hold unconstitutional that which the Constitution explicitly contemplates. The Fifth Amendment provides that "[n]o person shall be held to answer for a capital . . . crime, unless on a presentment or indictment of a Grand Jury," and that no person shall be "deprived of life . . . without due process of law." Nevertheless, today Justice Breyer takes on the role of the abolitionists in this long-running drama, arguing that the text of the Constitution and two centuries of history must yield to his "20 years of experience on this Court," and inviting full briefing on the continued permissibility of capital punishment.

Even accepting Justice Breyer's rewriting of the Eighth Amendment, his argument is full of internal contradictions and (it must be said) gobbledygook. He says that the death penalty is cruel because it is unreliable; but it is convictions, not punishments, that are unreliable.

Justice Breyer next says that the death penalty is cruel because it is arbitrary. To prove this point, he points to a study of 205 cases that "measured the 'egregiousness' of the murderer's conduct" with "a system of metrics," and then "compared the egregiousness of the conduct of the 9 defendants sentenced to death with the egregiousness of the conduct of defendants in the remaining 196 cases [who were not sentenced to death]." If only Aristotle, Aquinas, and Hume knew that moral philosophy could be so neatly distilled into a pocket-sized, vade mecum "system of metrics." Of course it cannot: Egregiousness is a moral judgment susceptible of few hard-and-fast rules.

Justice Breyer's third reason that the death penalty is cruel is that it entails delay, thereby (1) subjecting inmates to long periods on death row and (2) undermining the penological justifications of the death penalty. The first point is nonsense. Life without parole is an even lengthier period than the wait on death row; and if the objection is that death row is a more confining environment, the solution should be modifying the environment rather than abolishing the death penalty. Justice Breyer further asserts that "whatever interest in retribution might be served by the death penalty as currently administered, that interest can be served almost as well by a sentence of life in prison without parole." My goodness. If he thinks the death penalty not much more harsh (and hence not much more retributive), why is he so keen to get rid of it? With all due respect, whether the death penalty and life imprisonment constitute more-or-less equivalent retribution is a question far above the judiciary's pay grade.

And finally, Justice Breyer speculates that it does not "seem likely" that the death penalty has a "significant" deterrent effect. It seems very likely to me, and there are statistical studies that say so. The suggestion that the incremental deterrent effect of capital punishment does not seem "significant" reflects, it seems to me, a let-them-eat-cake obliviousness to the needs of others. Let the People decide how much incremental deterrence is appropriate.

Justice THOMAS, with whom Justice SCALIA joins, concurring.

I agree with the Court that petitioners' Eighth Amendment claim fails. I write separately to respond to Justice BREYER's dissent questioning the constitutionality of the death penalty generally. Justice BREYER's assertion that the death penalty in this country has fallen short of the aspiration that capital punishment be reserved for the "worst of the worst" — a notion itself based on an implicit proportionality principle that has long been discredited, merits further comment.

There is a reason the choice between life and death, within legal limits, is left to the jurors and judges who sit through the trial, and not to legal elites (or law students). That reason is memorialized not once, but twice, in our Constitution: Article III guarantees that "[t]he Trial of all Crimes, except in cases of Impeachment, shall be by Jury" and that "such Trial shall be held in the State where the said Crimes shall have been committed." Art. III, §2, cl. 3. And the Sixth Amendment promises that "[i]n all criminal prosecutions, the accused shall enjoy the right to a . . . trial, by an impartial jury of the State and district wherein the crime shall have been committed." Those provisions ensure that capital defendants are given the option to be sentenced by a jury of their peers who, collectively, are better situated to make the moral judgment between life and death than are the products of contemporary American law schools.

We owe victims more than this sort of pseudoscientific assessment of their lives. It is bad enough to tell a mother that her child's murder is not "worthy" of society's ultimate expression of moral condemnation. But to do so based on cardboard stereotypes or cold mathematical calculations is beyond my comprehension.

Justice BREYER, with whom Justice GINSBURG joins, dissenting.

For the reasons stated in Justice SOTOMAYOR's opinion, I dissent from the Court's holding. But rather than try to patch up the death penalty's legal wounds one at a time, I would ask for full briefing on a more basic question: whether the death penalty violates the Constitution.

The relevant legal standard is the standard set forth in the Eighth Amendment. The Constitution there forbids the "inflict[ion]" of "cruel and unusual punishments." The Court has recognized that a "claim that punishment is excessive is judged not by the standards that prevailed in 1685 when Lord Jeffreys presided over the 'Bloody Assizes' or when the Bill of Rights was adopted, but rather by those that currently prevail." Indeed, the Constitution prohibits various gruesome punishments that were common in Blackstone's day.

Nearly 40 years ago, this Court upheld the death penalty under statutes that, in the Court's view, contained safeguards sufficient to ensure that the penalty would be applied reliably and not arbitrarily. The circumstances and the evidence of the death penalty's application have changed radically since then. Given those changes, I believe that it is now time to reopen the question.

In 1976, the Court thought that the constitutional infirmities in the death penalty could be healed; the Court in effect delegated significant responsibility to the States to develop procedures that would protect against those constitutional problems. Almost 40 years of studies, surveys, and experience strongly indicate, however, that this effort has failed. Today's administration of the death penalty involves three fundamental constitutional defects: (1) serious unreliability, (2) arbitrariness in application, and (3) unconscionably long delays that undermine the death penalty's penological purpose. Perhaps as a result, most places within the United States have abandoned its use.

I

"Cruel" — Lack of Reliability

This Court has specified that the finality of death creates a "qualitative difference" between the death penalty and other punishments (including life in prison). That "qualitative difference" creates "a corresponding difference in the need for reliability in the determination that death is the appropriate punishment in a specific case." There is increasing evidence, however, that the death penalty as now applied lacks that requisite reliability.

For one thing, despite the difficulty of investigating the circumstances surrounding an execution for a crime that took place long ago, researchers have found convincing evidence that, in the past three decades, innocent people have been executed.

For another, the evidence that the death penalty has been wrongly imposed (whether or not it was carried out), is striking. Last year, in 2014, six death row inmates were exonerated based on actual innocence. All had been imprisoned for more than 30 years (and one for almost 40 years) at the time of their exonerations.

The stories of three of the men exonerated within the last year are illustrative. DNA evidence showed that Henry Lee McCollum did not commit the rape and murder for which he had been sentenced to death. Last Term, this Court ordered that Anthony Ray Hinton, who had been convicted of murder, receive further hearings in state court; he was exonerated earlier this year because the forensic evidence used against him was flawed.

Furthermore, exonerations occur far more frequently where capital convictions, rather than ordinary criminal convictions, are at issue. Researchers have calculated that courts (or State Governors) are 130 times more likely to exonerate a defendant where a death sentence is at issue. They are nine times more likely to exonerate where a capital murder, rather than a noncapital murder, is at issue. [R]esearchers estimate that about 4% of those sentenced to death are actually innocent,

Finally, if we expand our definition of "exoneration" (which we limited to errors suggesting the defendant was actually innocent) and thereby also categorize as "erroneous" instances in which courts failed to follow legally required procedures, the numbers soar. Between 1973 and 1995, courts identified prejudicial errors in 68% of the capital cases before them.

This research and these figures are likely controversial. Full briefing would allow us to scrutinize them with more care. But, at a minimum, they suggest a serious problem of reliability. They suggest that there are too many instances in which courts sentence defendants to death without complying with the necessary procedures; and they suggest that, in a significant number of cases, the death sentence is imposed on a person who did not commit the crime.

II

"Cruel" — Arbitrariness

The arbitrary imposition of punishment is the antithesis of the rule of law.

Despite the Gregg Court's hope for fair administration of the death penalty, 40 years of further experience make it increasingly clear that the death penalty is imposed arbitrarily, i.e., without the "reasonable consistency" legally necessary to reconcile its use with the Constitution's commands.

Thorough studies of death penalty sentences support this conclusion. A recent study, for example, examined all death penalty sentences imposed between 1973 and 2007 in Connecticut, a State that abolished the death penalty in 2012. The study reviewed treatment of all homicide defendants. It found 205 instances in which Connecticut law made the defendant eligible for a death sentence. Courts imposed a death sentence in 12 of these 205 cases, of which 9 were sustained on appeal. The study then measured the "egregiousness" of the murderer's conduct in those 9 cases, developing a system of metrics designed to do so. It then compared the egregiousness of the conduct of the 9 defendants sentenced to death with the egregiousness of the conduct of defendants in the remaining 196 cases (those in which the defendant, though found guilty of a death-eligible offense, was ultimately not sentenced to death). Application of the studies' metrics made clear that only 1 of those 9 defendants was indeed the "worst of the worst" (or was, at least, within the 15% considered most "egregious"). The remaining eight were not. Their behavior was no worse than the behavior of at least 33 and as many as 170 other defendants (out of a total pool of 205) who had not been sentenced to death.

Such studies indicate that the factors that most clearly ought to affect application of the death penalty — namely, comparative egregiousness of the crime — often do not. Other studies show that circumstances that ought not to affect application of the death penalty, such as race, gender, or geography, often do.

Numerous studies, for example, have concluded that individuals accused of murdering white victims, as opposed to black or other minority victims, are more likely to receive the death penalty. Fewer, but still many, studies have found that the gender of the defendant or the gender of the victim makes a not-otherwise-warranted difference.

Geography also plays an important role in determining who is sentenced to death. And that is not simply because some States permit the death penalty while others do not. Rather within a death penalty State, the imposition of the death penalty heavily depends on the county in which a defendant is tried. Between 2004 and 2009, for example, just 29 counties (fewer than 1% of counties in the country) accounted for approximately half of all death sentences imposed nationwide.

What accounts for this county-by-county disparity? Some studies indicate that the disparity reflects the decisionmaking authority, the legal discretion, and ultimately the power of the local prosecutor. Others suggest that the availability of resources for defense counsel (or the lack thereof) helps explain geographical differences. Still others indicate that the racial composition of and distribution within a county plays an important role. Finally, some studies suggest that political pressures, including pressures on judges who must stand for election, can make a difference. Thus, whether one looks at research indicating that irrelevant or improper factors — such as race, gender, local geography, and resources — do significantly determine who receives the death penalty, or whether one looks at research indicating that proper factors — such as "egregiousness" — do not determine who receives the death penalty, the legal conclusion must be the same: The research strongly suggests that the death penalty is imposed arbitrarily.

III

"Cruel" — Excessive Delays

The problems of reliability and unfairness almost inevitably lead to a third independent constitutional problem: excessively long periods of time that individuals typically spend on death row, alive but under sentence of death.

[U]nless we abandon the procedural requirements that assure fairness and reliability, we are forced to confront the problem of increasingly lengthy delays in capital cases. Ultimately, though these legal causes may help to explain, they do not mitigate the harms caused by delay itself.

Consider first the statistics. In 2014, 35 individuals were executed. Those executions occurred, on average, nearly 18 years after a court initially pronounced its sentence of death. The length of the average delay has increased dramatically over the years. Nearly half of the 3,000 inmates now on death row have been there for more than 15 years. And, at present execution rates, it would take more than 75 years to carry out those 3,000 death sentences; thus, the average person on death row would spend an additional 37.5 years there before being executed.

These lengthy delays create two special constitutional difficulties. First, a lengthy delay in and of itself is especially cruel because it "subjects death row inmates to decades of especially severe, dehumanizing conditions of confinement." Second, lengthy delay undermines the death penalty's penological rationale.

One might ask, why can Congress or the States not deal directly with the delay problem? Why can they not take steps to shorten the time between sentence and execution, and thereby mitigate the problems just raised? The answer is that shortening delay is much more difficult than one might think.

And that is in part because efforts to do so risk causing procedural harms that also undermine the death penalty's constitutionality.

A death penalty system that seeks procedural fairness and reliability brings with it delays that severely aggravate the cruelty of capital punishment and significantly undermine the rationale for imposing a sentence of death in the first place. But a death penalty system that minimizes delays would undermine the legal system's efforts to secure reliability and procedural fairness.

IV

"Unusual" — Decline in Use of the Death Penalty

The Eighth Amendment forbids punishments that are cruel and unusual. Last year, in 2014, only seven States carried out an execution. Perhaps more importantly, in the last two decades, the imposition and implementation of the death penalty have increasingly become unusual. I can illustrate the significant decline in the use of the death penalty in several ways.

An appropriate starting point concerns the trajectory of the number of annual death sentences nationwide, from the 1970's to present day. In 1977 — just after the Supreme Court made clear that, by modifying their legislation, States could reinstate the death penalty — 137 people were sentenced to death. Many States having revised their death penalty laws to meet Furman's requirements, the number of death sentences then increased. Between 1986 and 1999, 286 persons on average were sentenced to death each year. But, approximately 15 years ago, the numbers began to decline, and they have declined rapidly ever since. In 1999, 279 persons were sentenced to death. Last year, just 73 persons were sentenced to death.

Next, one can consider state-level data. Often when deciding whether a punishment practice is, constitutionally speaking, "unusual," this Court has looked to the number of States engaging in that practice. In this respect, the number of active death penalty States has fallen dramatically. In 1972, when the Court decided Furman, the death penalty was lawful in 41 States. Nine States had abolished it. As of today, 19 States have abolished the death penalty (along with the District of Columbia), although some did so prospectively only.

Accordingly, 30 States have either formally abolished the death penalty or have not conducted an execution in more than eight years. Indeed, last year, only seven States conducted an execution. In other words, in 43 States, no one was executed. Moreover, we have said that it " 'is not so much the number of these States that is significant, but the consistency of the direction of change.' " These circumstances perhaps reflect the fact that a majority of Americans, when asked to choose between the death penalty and life in prison without parole, now choose the latter.

I rely primarily upon domestic, not foreign events, in pointing to changes and circumstances that tend to justify the claim that the death penalty, constitutionally speaking, is "unusual." I note, however, that many nations — indeed, 95 of the 193 members of the United Nations — have formally abolished the death penalty and an additional 42 have abolished it in practice.

V

I recognize a strong counterargument that favors constitutionality. We are a court. Why should we not leave the matter up to the people acting democratically through legislatures? The Constitution foresees a country that will make most important decisions democratically. Most nations that have abandoned the death penalty have done so through legislation, not judicial decision. And legislators, unlike judges, are free to take account of matters such as monetary costs, which I do not claim are relevant here.

The answer is that the matters I have discussed, such as lack of reliability, the arbitrary application of a serious and irreversible punishment, individual suffering caused by long delays, and lack of penological purpose are quintessentially judicial matters. They concern the infliction—indeed the unfair, cruel, and unusual infliction—of a serious punishment upon an individual. I recognize that in 1972 this Court, in a sense, turned to Congress and the state legislatures in its search for standards that would increase the fairness and reliability of imposing a death penalty. The legislatures responded. But, in the last four decades, considerable evidence has accumulated that those responses have not worked.

Thus we are left with a judicial responsibility. The Eighth Amendment sets forth the relevant law, and we must interpret that law. For the reasons I have set forth in this opinion, I believe it highly likely that the death penalty violates the Eighth Amendment. At the very least, the Court should call for full briefing on the basic question.

Justice SOTOMAYOR, with whom Justice GINSBURG, Justice BREYER, and Justice KAGAN join, dissenting.

Petitioners, three inmates on Oklahoma's death row, challenge the constitutionality of the State's lethal injection protocol. The State plans to execute petitioners using three drugs: midazolam, rocuronium bromide, and potassium chloride. The latter two drugs are intended to paralyze the inmate and stop his heart. But they do so in a torturous manner, causing burning, searing pain. It is thus critical that the first drug, midazolam, do what it is supposed to do, which is to render and keep the inmate unconscious. Petitioners claim that midazolam cannot be expected to perform that function, and they have presented ample evidence showing that the State's planned use of this drug poses substantial, constitutionally intolerable risks.

Nevertheless, the Court today turns aside petitioners' plea that they at least be allowed a stay of execution while they seek to prove midazolam's inadequacy. The Court achieves this result in two ways: first, by deferring to the District Court's decision to credit the scientifically unsupported and implausible testimony of a single expert witness; and second, by faulting petitioners for failing to satisfy the wholly novel requirement of proving the availability of an alternative means for their own executions. On both counts the Court errs. As a result, it leaves petitioners exposed to what may well be the chemical equivalent of being burned at the stake

CHAPTER

14

DOUBLE JEOPARDY

The Double Jeopardy Clause of the Fifth Amendment states that "[n]o person shall . . . be subject for the same offence to be twice put in jeopardy of life or limb." U.S. Const. Amend. V. In Benton v. Maryland, 395 U.S. 784 (1969), the Supreme Court held that this right applies to the states as well. The Double Jeopardy Clause provides three separate protections: "It protects against a second prosecution for the same offense after acquittal. It protects against a second prosecution for the same offense after conviction. And it protects against multiple punishment for the same offense." North Carolina v. Pearce, 395 U.S. 711, 717 (1969).

The double jeopardy rule dates back to common law. At common law, a defendant could plead *autrefois acquit, autrefois convict,* and pardon, which meant that the defendant had been previously acquitted, convicted, or pardoned for the same offense. These pleas, if upheld, would bar the defendant from being retried.

Today, there continue to be strong policy reasons supporting the Double Jeopardy Clause. As stated by the Court in Green v. United States, 355 U.S. 184, 187-188 (1957):

> The underlying idea [for the rule] is that the State with all its resources and power should not be allowed to make repeated attempts to convict an individual for an alleged offense, thereby subjecting him to embarrassment, expense and ordeal and compelling him to live in a continuing state of anxiety and insecurity, as well as enhancing the possibility that even though he is innocent, he may be found guilty.

In its simplest application, the Double Jeopardy Clause prohibits the prosecution from trying a defendant, getting an acquittal, appealing the acquittal, and then retrying the defendant. However, there are many other scenarios in which the Double Jeopardy Clause may apply. This chapter will focus on the wide range of rules that apply when a defendant claims a violation of the Double Jeopardy Clause. Section B focuses on the basics: (1) What types of proceedings does the Double Jeopardy Clause cover? (2) When is an offense the "same offense"? (3) When does jeopardy attach? Section C then focuses on the effect of an acquittal or conviction on future prosecutions if the defendant goes to trial. Section D discusses common exceptions to the double jeopardy rule, including the permissibility of retrials after mistrials and the dual sovereignty doctrine. Section E examines whether a defendant's actions may result in multiple charges and cumulative punishments. Finally, section F looks at the related doctrine of collateral estoppel and discusses how it affects future prosecutions like the Double Jeopardy Clause.

Before jumping into the basics, it is worth examining the Court's explanation of the history and policy reasons behind the double jeopardy rule.

A. INTRODUCTION

UNITED STATES v. SCOTT
437 U.S. 82 (1978)

Justice Rehnquist delivered the opinion of the Court.

On March 5, 1975, respondent, a member of the police force in Muskegon, Mich., was charged in a three-count indictment with distribution of various narcotics. Both before his trial in the United States District Court for the Western District of Michigan, and twice during the trial, respondent moved to dismiss the two counts of the indictment . . . on the ground that his defense had been prejudiced by preindictment delay. At the close of all the evidence, the court granted respondent's motion. Although the court did not explain its reasons for dismissing the second count, it explicitly concluded that respondent had "presented sufficient proof of prejudice with respect to Count I."

The Government sought to appeal the dismissals of the first two counts.

I

The problem presented by this case could not have arisen during the first century of this Court's existence. The Court has long taken the view that the United States has no right of appeal in a criminal case, absent explicit statutory authority. Such authority was not provided until the enactment of the Criminal Appeals Act, Act of Mar. 2, 1907. In 1971, however, Congress adopted the current language of the Act, permitting Government appeals from any decision dismissing an indictment, "except that no appeal shall lie where the double jeopardy clause of the United States Constitution prohibits further prosecution." 18 U.S.C. §3731.

In our first encounter with the new statute, we concluded that "Congress intended to remove all statutory barriers to Government appeals and to allow appeals whenever the Constitution would permit." United States v. Wilson (1975). Since up to that point Government appeals had been subject to statutory restrictions independent of the Double Jeopardy Clause, our previous cases construing the statute proved to be of little assistance in determining when the Double Jeopardy Clause of the Fifth Amendment would prohibit further prosecution. A detailed canvass of the history of the double jeopardy principles in English and American law led us to conclude that the Double Jeopardy Clause was primarily "directed at the threat of multiple prosecutions," and posed no bar to Government appeals "where those appeals would not require a new trial."

II

The origin and history of the Double Jeopardy Clause are hardly a matter of dispute. The constitutional provision had its origin in the three common-law pleas of *autrefois acquit, autrefois convict,* and pardon. These three pleas prevented the retrial of a person who had previously been acquitted, convicted, or pardoned for the same offense. As this Court has described the purpose underlying the prohibition against double jeopardy:

> The underlying idea, one that is deeply ingrained in at least the Anglo-American system of jurisprudence, is that the State with all its resources and power should not be allowed to make repeated attempts to convict an individual for an alleged offense, thereby subjecting him to embarrassment, expense and ordeal and compelling him to live in a continuing state of anxiety and insecurity, as well as enhancing the possibility that even though innocent he may be found guilty.

These historical purposes are necessarily general in nature, and their application has come to abound in often subtle distinctions which cannot by any means all be traced to the original three common-law pleas referred to above.

Part of the difficulty arises from the development of other protections for criminal defendants in the years since the adoption of the Bill of Rights. At the time the Fifth Amendment was adopted, its principles were easily applied, since most criminal prosecutions proceeded to final judgment, and neither the United States nor the defendant had any right to appeal an adverse verdict. The verdict in such a case was unquestionably final, and could be raised in bar against any further prosecution for the same offense. [However, today there are numerous rulings that a trial judge may make that can lead to dismissal of a case, such as motions for preindictment delay and suppression of evidence, that the prosecution may seek to appeal.]

III

Although the primary purpose of the Double Jeopardy Clause was to protect the integrity of a final judgment, the Court has also developed a body of law guarding the separate but related interest of a defendant in avoiding multiple prosecutions even where no final determination of guilt or innocence has been made.

In the present case, the District Court's dismissal of the first count of the indictment was based upon a claim of preindictment delay and not on the court's conclusion that the Government had not produced sufficient evidence to establish the guilt of the defendant.

IV

Our [earlier decisions were] based upon our perceptions of the underlying purposes of the Double Jeopardy Clause:

> The underlying idea, one that is deeply ingrained in at least the Anglo-American system of jurisprudence, is that the State with all its resources and power should not be allowed to make repeated attempts to convict an individual for an alleged offense, thereby subjecting him to embarrassment, expense and ordeal and compelling him to live in a continuing state of anxiety and insecurity. . . .

It is quite true that the Government with all its resources and power should not be allowed to make repeated attempts to convict an individual for an alleged offense. . . . But that situation is obviously a far cry from the present case, where the Government was quite willing to continue with its production of evidence to show the defendant guilty before the jury first empaneled to try him, but the defendant elected to seek termination of the trial on grounds unrelated to guilt or innocence. This is scarcely a picture of an all-powerful state relentlessly pursuing a defendant who had either been found not guilty or who had at least insisted on having the issue of guilt submitted to the first trier of fact. It is instead a picture of a defendant who chooses to avoid conviction and imprisonment, not because of his assertion that the Government has failed to make out a case against him, but because of a legal claim that the Government's case against him must fail even though it might satisfy the trier of fact that he was guilty beyond a reasonable doubt.

We have previously noted that "the trial judge's characterization of his own action cannot control the classification of the action." Rather, a defendant is acquitted only when "the ruling of the judge, whatever its label, actually represents a resolution [in the defendant's favor], correct or not, of some or all of the factual elements of the offense charged."

We think that in a case such as this the defendant, by deliberately choosing to seek termination of the proceedings against him on a basis unrelated to factual guilt or innocence of the offense of which he is accused, suffers no injury cognizable under the Double Jeopardy Clause if the Government is permitted to appeal from such a ruling of the trial court in favor of the defendant. [W]e conclude that the Double Jeopardy Clause, which guards against Government oppression, does not relieve a defendant from the consequences of his voluntary choice.

Here, "the lessons of experience" indicate that Government appeals from midtrial dismissals requested by the defendant would significantly advance the public interest in assuring that each defendant shall be subject to a just judgment on the merits of his case, without "enhancing the possibility that even though innocent he may be found guilty."

B. THE BASICS

1. *What Is a Criminal Offense?*

By its terms, the Fifth Amendment applies only to multiple prosecutions and punishments of a defendant for the same offense. However, it does not bar a defendant from facing both criminal and civil sanctions for the same act. For example, if a defendant drives recklessly and kills another person, that defendant may face both criminal prosecution and a civil suit. Similarly, in the famous murder case of O.J. Simpson, the victims' families were able to sue and win a multimillion-dollar judgment against Simpson after he was acquitted of murder because the failure to prove murder beyond a reasonable doubt in the criminal case did not bar the victims' families from proving by a preponderance of the evidence in a civil case that Simpson was liable for the wrongful deaths.

Sometimes it is not readily apparent whether a defendant is facing multiple criminal sanctions, or civil penalties that are not subject to the double jeopardy prohibition. In Hudson v. United States, the Supreme Court set forth the approach to determine whether a sanction is civil or criminal for double jeopardy purposes.

HUDSON v. UNITED STATES
522 U.S. 93 (1997)

Chief Justice Rehnquist delivered the opinion of the Court.

The Government administratively imposed monetary penalties and occupational debarment on petitioners for violation of federal banking statutes, and later criminally indicted them for essentially the same conduct. We hold that the Double Jeopardy Clause of the Fifth Amendment is not a bar to the later criminal prosecution because the administrative proceedings were civil, not criminal. Our reasons for so holding in large part disavow the method of analysis used in United States v. Halper (1989), and reaffirm the previously established rule exemplified in United States v. Ward (1980).

During the early and mid-1980's, petitioner John Hudson [and his copetitioners] used their bank positions to arrange a series of loans to third parties, in violation of various federal banking statutes and regulations. According to the Office of the Comptroller of the Currency [OCC], those loans, while nominally made to third parties, were in reality made to Hudson in order to enable him to redeem bank stock that he had pledged as collateral on defaulted loans.

[Hudson] resolved the OCC proceedings against [him] by . . . entering into a "Stipulation and Consent Order" [that] provided [he] would pay [an] assessment[] of $16,500 [and that he would agree] not to "participate in any manner" in the affairs of any banking institution without the written authorization of the OCC.

[Thereafter, Hudson was] indicted in the Western District of Oklahoma in a 22-count indictment on charges of conspiracy, misapplication of bank funds, and making false bank entries. The violations charged in the indictment rested on the same lending transactions that formed the basis for the prior administrative actions brought by OCC. [Hudson] moved to dismiss the indictment on double jeopardy grounds.

The Double Jeopardy Clause provides that no "person [shall] be subject for the same offence to be twice put in jeopardy of life or limb." We have long recognized that the Double Jeopardy Clause does not prohibit the imposition of any additional sanction that could, " 'in common parlance,' " be described as punishment. The Clause protects only against the imposition of multiple criminal punishments for the same offense.

Whether a particular punishment is criminal or civil is, at least initially, a matter of statutory construction. A court must first ask whether the legislature, "in establishing the penalizing mechanism, indicated either expressly or impliedly a preference for one label or the other." Even in those cases where the legislature "has indicated an intention to establish a civil penalty, we have inquired further whether the statutory scheme was so punitive either in purpose or effect," as to "transform what was clearly intended as a civil remedy into a criminal penalty."

In making this latter determination, the factors listed in Kennedy v. Mendoza-Martinez (1963) provide useful guideposts, including: (1) "whether the sanction involves an affirmative disability or restraint"; (2) "whether it has historically been regarded as a punishment"; (3) "whether it comes into play only on a finding of scienter"; (4) "whether its operation will promote the traditional aims of punishment — retribution and deterrence"; (5) "whether the behavior to which it applies is already a crime"; (6) "whether an alternative purpose to which it may rationally be connected is assignable for it"; and (7) "whether it appears excessive in relation to the alternative purpose assigned." It is important to note, however, that "these factors must be considered in relation to the statute on its face," and "only the clearest proof" will suffice to override legislative intent and transform what has been denominated a civil remedy into a criminal penalty, *Ward, supra,* at 249.

Our opinion in United States v. Halper marked the first time we applied the Double Jeopardy Clause to a sanction without first determining that it was criminal in nature. In that case, Irwin Halper was convicted of violating the criminal false claims statute based on his submission of 65 inflated Medicare claims each of which overcharged the Government by $9. He was sentenced to two years' imprisonment and fined $5,000. The Government then brought an action against Halper under the civil False Claims Act. The remedial provisions of the False Claims Act provided that a violation of the Act rendered one "liable to the United States Government for a civil penalty of $2,000, an amount equal to 2 times the amount of damages the Government sustains because of the act of that person, and costs of the civil action." Given Halper's 65 separate violations of the Act, he appeared to be liable for a penalty of $130,000, despite the fact he actually defrauded the Government of less than $600. However, the District Court concluded that a penalty of this magnitude would violate the Double Jeopardy Clause in light of Halper's previous criminal conviction. While explicitly recognizing that the statutory damages provision of the Act "was not itself a criminal punishment," the District Court nonetheless concluded that application of the full penalty to Halper would constitute a second "punishment" in violation of the Double Jeopardy Clause.

On direct appeal, this Court affirmed. As the *Halper* Court saw it, the imposition of "punishment" of any kind was subject to double jeopardy constraints, and whether a sanction constituted "punishment" depended primarily on whether it served the traditional "goals of punishment," namely "retribution and deterrence." Any sanction that was so "overwhelmingly disproportionate" to the injury caused that it could not "fairly be said solely to serve [the] remedial purpose" of compensating the government for its loss, was thought to be explainable only as "serving either retributive or deterrent purposes."

The analysis applied by the *Halper* Court deviated from our traditional double jeopardy doctrine in two key respects. First, the *Halper* Court bypassed the threshold question: whether the successive punishment at issue is a "criminal" punishment. Instead, it focused on whether the sanction, regardless of whether it was civil or criminal, was so grossly disproportionate to the harm caused as to constitute "punishment." In so doing, the Court elevated a single *Kennedy* factor — whether the sanction appeared excessive in relation to its nonpunitive purposes — to dispositive status. But as we emphasized in *Kennedy* itself, no one factor should be considered controlling as they "may often point in differing directions." The second significant departure in *Halper* was the Court's decision to "assess the character of the actual sanctions imposed," rather than, as *Kennedy* demanded, evaluating the "statute on its face" to determine whether it provided for what amounted to a criminal sanction.

We believe that *Halper*'s deviation from longstanding double jeopardy principles was ill considered. As subsequent cases have demonstrated, *Halper*'s test for determining whether a particular sanction is "punitive," and thus subject to the strictures of the Double Jeopardy Clause, has proved unworkable. We have since recognized that all civil penalties have some deterrent effect. If a sanction must be "solely" remedial (i.e., entirely nondeterrent) to avoid implicating the Double Jeopardy Clause, then no civil penalties are beyond the scope of the Clause. Under *Halper*'s method of analysis, a court must also look at the "sanction actually imposed" to determine whether the Double Jeopardy Clause is implicated. Thus, it will not be possible to determine whether the Double Jeopardy Clause is violated until a defendant has proceeded through a trial to judgment. But in those cases where the civil proceeding follows the criminal proceeding, this approach flies in the face of the notion that the Double Jeopardy Clause forbids the government from even "attempting a second time to punish criminally."

Finally, it should be noted that some of the ills at which *Halper* was directed are addressed by other constitutional provisions. The Due Process and Equal Protection Clauses already protect individuals from sanctions which are downright irrational. The Eighth Amendment protects against excessive civil fines, including forfeitures.

Applying traditional double jeopardy principles to the facts of this case, it is clear that the criminal prosecution of these petitioners would not violate the Double Jeopardy Clause. It is evident that Congress intended the OCC money penalties and debarment sanctions imposed to be civil in nature.

Turning to the second stage of the *Ward* test, we find that there is little evidence, much less the clearest proof that we require, suggesting that either OCC money penalties or debarment sanctions are "so punitive in form and effect as to render them criminal despite Congress' intent to the contrary." First, neither money penalties nor debarment have historically been viewed as punishment.

Second, the sanctions imposed do not involve an "affirmative disability or restraint," as that term is normally understood. While petitioners have been prohibited from further participating in the banking industry, this is "certainly nothing approaching the 'infamous punishment' of imprisonment." Third, neither sanction comes into play "only" on a finding of scienter. The provisions under which the money penalties were imposed, allow for the assessment of a penalty against any person "who violates" any of the underlying banking statutes, without regard to the violator's state of mind.

Fourth, the conduct for which OCC sanctions are imposed may also be criminal (and in this case formed the basis for petitioners' indictments). This fact is insufficient to render the money penalties and debarment sanctions criminally punitive, particularly in the double jeopardy context.

Finally, we recognize that the imposition of both money penalties and debarment sanctions will deter others from emulating petitioners' conduct, a traditional goal of criminal punishment. But the mere presence of this purpose is insufficient to render a sanction criminal, as deterrence "may serve civil as well as criminal goals."

In sum, there simply is very little showing, to say nothing of the "clearest proof" required by *Ward*, that OCC money penalties and debarment sanctions are criminal. The Double Jeopardy Clause is therefore no obstacle to their trial on the pending indictments, and it may proceed.

Affirmed.

As the Court made clear in *Hudson*, "only the clearest proof will suffice to override legislative intent and transform what has been denominated a civil remedy into a criminal penalty." Thus, there generally is no bar to a defendant facing both a criminal and civil (and even administrative) action for the same conduct. The Double Jeopardy Clause also does not apply to private proceedings, even if punitive damages are awarded, United States v. Halper, 490 U.S. 435, 451 (1989), or to disciplinary, parole, probation, or bond revocation hearings. It does apply, however, to juvenile delinquent proceedings if the defendant faces a loss of liberty. Breed v. Jones, 421 U.S. 519, 529 (1975).

2. What Is the "Same Offense"?

Assuming that the defendant is charged with two criminal offenses, the prohibition on double jeopardy applies only if the defendant is prosecuted twice for the "*same offense.*" In other words, a single criminal act can lead to multiple charges; a double jeopardy violation occurs only if the defendant is retried for the same offense.

There are two possible approaches to determining whether two charges constitute the same offense. One approach is to determine whether both charges arose from the "same conduct" by the defendant. The other approach is to determine whether both offenses require proof of the "same elements."

For most of the last 80 years, the Supreme Court has adopted the "same elements" test, which the Court established in Blockburger v. United States.

BLOCKBURGER v. UNITED STATES
284 U.S. 299 (1932)

Justice SUTHERLAND delivered the opinion of the Court.

The petitioner was charged with violating provisions of the Harrison Narcotic Act: The indictment contained five counts. The jury returned a verdict against petitioner upon the second, third and fifth counts only. Each of these counts charged a sale of morphine hydrochloride to the same purchaser. The second count charged a sale on a specified day of ten grains of the drug not in or from the original stamped package; the third count charged a sale on the following day of eight grains of the drug not in or from the original stamped package; the fifth count charged the latter sale also as having been made not in pursuance of a written order of the purchaser as required by the statute. The court sentenced petitioner to five years imprisonment and a fine of $2,000 upon each count, the terms of imprisonment to run consecutively; and this judgment was affirmed on appeal.

The principal contentions here made by petitioner are as follows: (1) that, upon the facts, the two sales charged in the second and third counts as having been made to the same person, constitute a single offense; and (2) that the sale charged in the third count as having been made not from the original stamped package, and the same sale charged in the fifth count as having been made not in pursuance of a written order of the purchaser, constitute but one offense for which only a single penalty lawfully may be imposed.

One. The sales charged in the second and third counts, although made to the same person, were distinct and separate sales made at different times. It appears from the evidence that shortly after delivery of the drug which was the subject of the first sale, the purchaser paid for an additional quantity, which was delivered the next day. But the first sale had been consummated, and the payment for the additional drug, however closely following, was the initiation of a separate and distinct sale completed by its delivery.

In the present case, the first transaction, resulting in a sale, had come to an end. The next sale was not the result of the original impulse, but of a fresh one — that is to say, of a new bargain.

Two. Section 1 of the Narcotic Act creates the offense of selling any of the forbidden drugs except in or from the original stamped package; and §2 creates the offense of selling any of such drugs not in pursuance of a written order of the person to whom the drug is sold. Thus, upon the face of the statute, two distinct offenses are created. Here there was but one sale, and the question is whether, both sections being violated by the same act, the accused committed two offenses or only one.

Each of the offenses created requires proof of a different element. The applicable rule is that where the same act or transaction constitutes a violation of two distinct statutory provisions, the test to be applied to determine whether there are two offenses or only one, is whether each provision requires proof of a fact which the other does not. "A single act may be an offense against two statutes; and if each statute requires proof of an additional fact which the other does not, an acquittal or conviction under either statute does not exempt the defendant from prosecution and punishment under the other." Applying the test, we must conclude that here, although both sections were violated by the one sale, two offenses were committed.

Judgment affirmed.

———————————

For a short period of time, the Supreme Court adopted the "same conduct" test for determining whether crimes were the same offense for double jeopardy purposes. In Grady v. Corbin, 495 U.S. 508 (1990), a five-justice majority, led by Justice Brennan, wrote that "the Double Jeopardy Clause bars a subsequent prosecution if, to establish an essential element of an offense charged in that prosecution, the government will prove conduct that constitutes an offense for which the defendant has already been prosecuted." Thus, Corbin, who had pleaded guilty to traffic tickets arising out of his arrest for drunk driving, successfully argued that he could not be reindicted for manslaughter because the government's proof for the manslaughter charges would include the evidence used to charge him with the misdemeanor drunk driving citations. Under the *Blockburger* test, Corbin would not have prevailed because the crime of manslaughter required elements not required by the drunk driving charges. Justice Brennan wrote, however, that the Double Jeopardy Clause should nonetheless bar Corbin's re-prosecution because the charges arose from the same conduct.

The holding in Grady v. Corbin did not last long. Three years later, in United States v. Dixon, 509 U.S. 688 (1993), in an opinion written by Justice Scalia, the Court returned to the *Blockburger* "same elements" test. Thus, to determine whether a defendant is not being charged with the same offense, the Court must analyze each charge to see if its elements require proof of an additional fact that the other does not. Offenses are considered separate offenses even if there is substantial overlap in the proof required for each offense. For example, drunk driving and manslaughter are two separate offenses because (1) drunk driving requires proof that the defendant was intoxicated, but manslaughter does not; and (2) manslaughter requires proof that the defendant caused a death, but drunk driving does not.

Under the *Blockburger* test, double jeopardy bars successive prosecutions for greater- and lesser-included offenses if all of the elements of the lesser offense are included in the elements for the greater offense. In that situation, the prosecution is not entitled to "two bites at the apple." For instance, if a defendant is charged with murder and is acquitted, the government cannot retry him for manslaughter because manslaughter is a lesser-included offense of murder.

3. When Does Jeopardy Attach?

The Double Jeopardy Clause bars a second prosecution for the same offense only if jeopardy attached in the original proceeding. Ex parte Lange, 85 U.S. (18 Wall.) 163, 168-169 (1873). As a general rule, jeopardy attaches when a defendant's trial begins. In a jury trial, jeopardy attaches when the jury is impaneled and sworn. In a bench trial, jeopardy attaches when the judge begins to hear evidence. It is only at these times that a defendant faces the risk of being found guilty of an offense. Crist v. Bretz, 437 U.S. 28 (1978).

Given these rules, not every dismissal of a criminal case will bar retrying the defendant. Cases that are dismissed before the trial begins may be appealed by the prosecution because jeopardy has not attached. However, once the trial has begun and jeopardy has attached, the prosecution cannot move to dismiss and then seek to retry the defendant.

C. NO RETRIAL FOLLOWING CONVICTION OR ACQUITTAL

Both acquittals and convictions may bar a defendant's retrial for the same offense. Unless the defendant seeks a retrial by, for example, moving for a mistrial or appealing a conviction, the prosecution will only have "one bite at the apple." The Double Jeopardy Clause is designed to protect a defendant not just from double convictions but from repeated prosecutions.

1.   No Retrial After Acquittal

The Double Jeopardy Clause bars retrying a defendant for an offense after the defendant has been acquitted of that offense. An acquittal can arise in several ways: (1) the jury may return a verdict of not guilty; (2) the trial judge may find, before the jury has an opportunity to decide the case, that there is insufficient evidence for a conviction; or (3) the appellate court may find that a conviction was not supported by sufficient evidence.

The clearest case of double jeopardy is when a defendant has been acquitted of an offense, even if that acquittal resulted from a trial court's erroneous interpretation of the indictment. Justice Marshall, writing for the Court in *Sanabria v. United States*, 437 U.S. 54 (1978) explained:

> The Government's real quarrel is with the judgment of acquittal. While the numbers evidence was erroneously excluded, the judgment of acquittal produced thereby is final and unreviewable. [T]he Double Jeopardy Clause [does not permit] the Government to obtain relief from all of the adverse rulings — most of which result from defense motions — that lead to the termination of a criminal trial in the defendant's favor. To hold that a defendant waives his double jeopardy protection whenever a trial court error in his favor on a midtrial motion leads to an acquittal would undercut the adversary assumption on which our system of criminal justice rests and would vitiate one of the fundamental rights established by the Fifth Amendment.

The prohibition on retrying a defendant after an acquittal also applies when the appellate court finds that there was insufficient evidence to support a conviction. The appellate court's finding of insufficient evidence is equivalent to an acquittal.

BURKS v. UNITED STATES
437 U.S. 1 (1978)

Chief Justice BURGER delivered the opinion of the Court.

We granted certiorari to resolve the question of whether an accused may be subjected to a second trial when conviction in a prior trial was reversed by an appellate court solely for lack of sufficient evidence to sustain the jury's verdict.

I

Petitioner Burks was tried in the United States District Court for the crime of robbing a federally insured bank by use of a dangerous weapon, a violation of 18 U.S.C. §2113 (d). Burks' principal defense was insanity.

Before the case was submitted to the jury, the court denied a motion for a judgment of acquittal. The jury found Burks guilty as charged. Thereafter, he filed a timely motion for a new trial, maintaining, among other things, that "[the] evidence was insufficient to support the verdict." The motion was denied by the District Court, which concluded that petitioner's challenge to the sufficiency of the evidence was "utterly without merit."[1]

On appeal petitioner narrowed the issues by admitting the affirmative factual elements of the charge against him, leaving only his claim concerning criminal responsibility to be resolved. With respect to this point, the Court of Appeals agreed with petitioner's claim that the evidence was insufficient to support the verdict and reversed his conviction. The court began by noting that "the government has the burden of proving sanity [beyond a reasonable doubt] once a prima facie defense of insanity has been raised." Petitioner had met his obligation, the court indicated, by presenting "the specific testimony of three experts with unchallenged credentials." [E]ven when viewed in the light most favorable to the Government, [the United States] did not "effectively [rebut]" petitioner's proof with respect to insanity and criminal responsibility.

At this point, the Court of Appeals, rather than terminating the case against petitioner, remanded to the District Court "for a determination of whether a directed verdict of acquittal should be entered or a new trial ordered."

[W]e are squarely presented with the question of whether a defendant may be tried a second time when a reviewing court has determined that in a prior trial the evidence was insufficient to sustain the verdict of the jury.

It is unquestionably true that the Court of Appeals' decision "[represented] a resolution, correct or not, of some or all of the factual elements of the offense charged." United States v. Martin Linen Supply Co. (1977). By deciding that the Government had failed to come forward with sufficient proof of petitioner's capacity to be responsible for criminal acts, that court was clearly saying that Burks' criminal culpability had not been established. If the District Court had so held in the first instance, as the reviewing court said it should have done, a judgment of acquittal would have been entered and, of course, petitioner could not be retried for the same offense.

The Double Jeopardy Clause forbids a second trial for the purpose of affording the prosecution another opportunity to supply evidence which it failed to muster in the first proceeding. This is central to the objective of the prohibition against successive trials. The Clause does not allow "the State . . . to make repeated attempts to convict an individual for an alleged offense," since "[the] constitutional prohibition against 'double jeopardy' was designed to protect an individual from being subjected to the hazards of trial and possible conviction more than once for an alleged offense."

---

1. Petitioner did not file a post-trial motion for judgment of acquittal, which he was entitled to do under *Fed. Rule Crim. Proc. 29 (c)*. [Footnote by the Court.]

Various rationales have been advanced to support the policy of allowing retrial to correct trial error, but in our view the most reasonable justification is: "It would be a high price indeed for society to pay were every accused granted immunity from punishment because of any defect sufficient to constitute reversible error in the proceedings leading to conviction."

In short, reversal for trial error, as distinguished from evidentiary insufficiency, does not constitute a decision to the effect that the government has failed to prove its case. As such, it implies nothing with respect to the guilt or innocence of the defendant. Rather, it is a determination that a defendant has been convicted through a judicial process which is defective in some fundamental respect, *e.g.*, incorrect receipt or rejection of evidence, incorrect instructions, or prosecutorial misconduct. When this occurs, the accused has a strong interest in obtaining a fair readjudication of his guilt free from error, just as society maintains a valid concern for insuring that the guilty are punished.

The same cannot be said when a defendant's conviction has been overturned due to a failure of proof at trial, in which case the prosecution cannot complain of prejudice, for it has been given one fair opportunity to offer whatever proof it could assemble. Moreover, such an appellate reversal means that the government's case was so lacking that it should not have even been *submitted* to the jury. Since we necessarily afford absolute finality to a jury's *verdict* of acquittal — no matter how erroneous its decision — it is difficult to conceive how society has any greater interest in retrying a defendant when, on review, it is decided as a matter of law that the jury could not properly have returned a verdict of guilty.[2]

The importance of a reversal on grounds of evidentiary insufficiency for purposes of inquiry under the Double Jeopardy Clause is underscored by the fact that a federal court's role in deciding whether a case should be considered by the jury is quite limited. Even the trial court, which has heard the testimony of witnesses firsthand, is not to weigh the evidence or assess the credibility of witnesses when it judges the merits of a motion for acquittal. The prevailing rule has long been that a district judge is to submit a case to the jury if the evidence and inferences therefrom most favorable to the prosecution would warrant the jury's finding the defendant guilty beyond a reasonable doubt. Obviously a federal appellate court applies no higher a standard; rather, it must sustain the verdict if there is substantial evidence, viewed in the light most favorable to the Government, to uphold the jury's decision. See Glasser v. United States (1942). While this is not the appropriate occasion to re-examine in detail the standards for appellate reversal on grounds of insufficient evidence, it is apparent that such a decision will be confined to cases where the prosecution's failure is clear. Given the requirements for entry of a judgment of acquittal, the purposes of the Clause

---

2. In holding the evidence insufficient to sustain guilt, an appellate court determines that the prosecution has failed to prove guilt beyond a reasonable doubt. See American Tobacco Co. v. United States (1946). [Footnote by the Court.]

would be negated were we to afford the government an opportunity for the proverbial "second bite at the apple."

The Double Jeopardy Clause bars the prosecution from appealing an acquittal even if the judge grants an acquittal because the judge incorrectly assumes that there were additional unproved elements of the charged offense. Evans v. Michigan, 133 S. Ct. 1069 (2013). A retrial is also barred when an acquittal is based on juror misconduct or jury nullification.[3] A mid-trial ruling by the court dismissing a charge for insufficient evidence is the equivalent of an acquittal unless the judge reserves the right to reconsider the ruling or state law indicates that such judgments are not final until the end of trial. Smith v. Massachusetts, 543 U.S. 462 (2005). As Justice Scalia explained in that case, a mid-trial ruling might influence a defendant's decision as to what evidence to present in the defense case, thereby making the Double Jeopardy Clause guarantee "a potential snare for those who reasonably rely upon it."

It is only when the defendant will not face another trial that the prosecution can appeal the dismissal of a case. Thus, the prosecution can appeal the pretrial dismissal of a case or the judge's acquittal of a defendant *after* the jury has returned a guilty verdict. 28 U.S.C. §3731. In the first situation, the defendant has not yet been subject to jeopardy because the case was dismissed before trial. In the second situation, if the appellate court reverses the trial court's ruling, the defendant will not be subject to a retrial, but the jury's verdict will just be reinstated. In neither case will there be a double jeopardy violation.

2.   *No Retrial After Conviction*

The Double Jeopardy Clause also bars retrying a defendant for the same offense unless (1) the defendant is granted a retrial after a successful appeal, (2) or the trial judge grants a motion for acquittal after the jury has already convicted the defendant. In the latter situation, if the appellate court disagrees with the judge's post-conviction acquittal, there will be no need for a retrial. The jury's original conviction of the defendant can simply be reinstated and the defendant will not face an actual retrial for the same offense. *See, e.g.*, United States v. Guadagna, 183 F.3d 122, 129 (2d Cir. 1999).

As for retrial following a successful appeal, if a defendant chooses to challenge the fairness of the procedures in his first trial and seek a new trial with correct procedures, he is bound by that choice and retrial is

---

3. Some commentators challenge this rule and have advocated for a change in the rules that would allow limited government appeals of acquittals. *See* Anne Bowen Poulin, *Double Jeopardy and Judicial Accountability: When Is an Acquittal Not an Acquittal?*, 27 Ariz. St. L.J. 953 (1995).

permitted. United States v. Ball, 163 U.S. 662 (1896) ("[W]here the accused successfully seeks review of a conviction, there is no double jeopardy upon a new trial").

D.   EXCEPTIONS TO THE DOUBLE JEOPARDY RULE

1.   *Retrial After Mistrials*

Just as a defendant's appeal will not bar a retrial if the appellate court reverses for unfair trial procedures, a mistrial will not necessarily bar a retrial either. The Supreme Court has held that if there is "manifest necessity" for declaring a mistrial, retrial is not prohibited. United States v. Perez, 22 U.S. (9 Wheat) 579, 580 (1824). The key question, of course, is whether something constitutes a "manifest necessity."

a.   Retrial After Mistrial for Hung Jury

In *Perez*, the Court held that granting a mistrial when a jury cannot reach a verdict constitutes "manifest necessity" and that retrying the defendant is not barred in this situation. Although the defendant has already faced one trial, if "public justice" is served by granting the mistrial, the Double Jeopardy Clause does not prohibit retrying the defendant.

UNITED STATES v. SANFORD
429 U.S. 14 (1976)

Per Curiam.

Respondents were indicted for illegal game hunting in Yellowstone National Park. A jury trial resulted in a hung jury, and the District Court declared a mistrial. Four months later, while the Government was preparing to retry them, respondents moved to dismiss the indictment. [The district court dismissed the indictment and the government appealed. The appellate court upheld the dismissal and the prosecution filed a petition for certiorari.]

In ruling against the government, the Court of Appeals stated:

> Here appellees have undergone trial. There is no question but that jeopardy has attached. That being so, and since the proceedings in the district court have ended in appellees' favor and the consequences of a reversal in favor of the Government would be that appellees must be tried again, we conclude that they would, on retrial, be placed twice in jeopardy.

We agree with the Court of Appeals that jeopardy attached at the time of the empaneling of the jury for the first trial of respondents. But we do not agree with that court's conclusion that by reason of the sequence of events in the District Court the Government would be barred by the Double Jeopardy Clause from retrying respondents. The trial of respondents on the indictment terminated, not in their favor, but in a mistrial declared, sua sponte, by the District Court. Where the trial is terminated in this manner, the classical test for determining whether the defendants may be retried without violating the Double Jeopardy Clause is stated in Mr. Justice Story's opinion for this Court in United States v. Perez (1824):

> We are of opinion, that the facts constitute no legal bar to a future trial. The prisoner has not been convicted or acquitted, and may again be put upon his defence. We think, that in all cases of this nature, the law has invested courts of justice with the authority to discharge a jury from giving any verdict, whenever, in their opinion, taking all the circumstances into consideration, there is a manifest necessity for the act, or the ends of public justice would otherwise be defeated.

The Government's right to retry the defendant, after a mistrial, in the face of his claim of double jeopardy is generally governed by the test laid down in *Perez, supra*. The situation of a hung jury presented here is precisely the situation that was presented in *Perez, supra*, and therefore the Double Jeopardy Clause does not bar retrial of these respondents on the indictment which had been returned against them.[4]

The District Court's dismissal of the indictment occurred several months after the first trial had ended in a mistrial, but before the retrial of respondents had begun. This case is, therefore, governed by United States v. Serfass in which we held that a pretrial order of the District Court dismissing an indictment charging refusal to submit to induction into the Armed Forces was appealable under 18 U.S.C. §3731. The dismissal in this case, like that in *Serfass*, was prior to a trial that the Government had a right to prosecute and that the defendant was required to defend. Since in such cases a trial following the Government's successful appeal of a dismissal is not barred by double jeopardy, an appeal from the dismissal is authorized by 18 U.S.C. §3731.

[The Court of Appeals' judgment was reversed.]

The Court further explained the rationale for the rule that a hung jury does not bar retrial in Richardson v. United States, 468 U.S. 317 (1984). Writing for the majority, Justice Rehnquist explained:

> [Richardson] asserts that if the Government failed to introduce sufficient evidence to establish his guilt beyond a reasonable doubt at his first trial, he

---

4. If the mistrial is declared at the behest of the defendant, the manifest necessity test does not apply. See United States v. Dinitz, 424 U.S. 600 (1976). [Footnote by the Court.]

may not be tried again following a declaration of a mistrial because of a hung jury. While petitioner bases this contention on Burks v. United States (1978), we do not agree that *Burks* resulted in the sweeping change in the law of double jeopardy which petitioner would have us hold. In *Burks* we held that once a defendant obtained an unreversed appellate ruling that the Government had failed to introduce sufficient evidence to convict him at trial, a second trial was barred by the Double Jeopardy Clause.

The Court in *Burks* did not deal with the situation in which a trial court declares a mistrial because of a jury's inability to agree on a verdict.

The case law dealing with the application of the prohibition against placing a defendant twice in jeopardy following a mistrial because of a hung jury has its own sources and logic. It has been established for 160 years, since the opinion of Justice Story in United States v. Perez (1824) that a failure of the jury to agree on a verdict was an instance of "manifest necessity" which permitted a trial judge to terminate the first trial and retry the defendant, because "the ends of public justice would otherwise be defeated." [W]e have constantly adhered to the rule that a retrial following a "hung jury" does not violate the Double Jeopardy Clause. Explaining our reasons for this conclusion in Arizona v. Washington (1978), we said:

> [Without] exception, the courts have held that the trial judge may discharge a genuinely deadlocked jury and require the defendant to submit to a second trial. This rule accords recognition to society's interest in giving the prosecution one complete opportunity to convict those who have violated its laws.

Thirty-five years ago we said in Wade v. Hunter (1949):

> The double-jeopardy provision of the Fifth Amendment, however, does not mean that every time a defendant is put to trial before a competent tribunal he is entitled to go free if the trial fails to end in a final judgment. Such a rule would create an insuperable obstacle to the administration of justice in many cases in which there is no semblance of the type of oppressive practices at which the double-jeopardy prohibition is aimed. There may be unforeseeable circumstances that arise during a trial making its completion impossible, such as the failure of a jury to agree on a verdict. In such event the purpose of law to protect society from those guilty of crimes frequently would be frustrated by denying courts power to put the defendant to trial again. . . . What has been said is enough to show that a defendant's valued right to have his trial completed by a particular tribunal must in some instances be subordinated to the public's interest in fair trials designed to end in just judgments.

The Government, like the defendant, is entitled to resolution of the case by verdict from the jury, and jeopardy does not terminate when the jury is discharged because it is unable to agree. Regardless of the sufficiency of the evidence at petitioner's first trial, he has no valid double jeopardy claim to prevent his retrial.

In Blueford v. Arkansas, 132 S. Ct. 2044 (2012), the Supreme Court clarified that even if the jury indicates that it would likely have acquitted on a greater offense, but could not reach a verdict on a lesser offense, retrial is allowed on the greater offense so long as no formal verdict is issued before the mistrial is ordered.

b. Retrials After Other Mistrials

Mistrials can also occur because developments during trial make it difficult, if not impossible, to afford a fair trial. Generally, if the defendant requests a mistrial, retrial is permitted unless the government has acted in bad faith. If the prosecutor or judge goads the defendant into seeking a mistrial, retrial may be barred. The same year the Court decided *Sanford, supra,* it decided another double jeopardy case that addresses whether mistrials caused by the government necessarily bar retrial. In United States v. Dinitz, the defendant was the one who sought a mistrial.

UNITED STATES v. DINITZ

424 U.S. 600 (1976)

Justice STEWART delivered the opinion of the Court.

The question in this case is whether the Double Jeopardy Clause of the Fifth Amendment was violated by the retrial of the respondent after his original trial had ended in a mistrial granted at his request.

I

The respondent, Nathan Dinitz, [was charged with narcotics offenses]. Five days before the trial was scheduled to begin, [Dinitz retained a new] lawyer, Maurice Wagner, to conduct his defense. Wagner had not been admitted to practice [in that court], but on the first day of the trial the court permitted him to appear pro hac vice.

The jury was selected and sworn, and opening statements by counsel began. The prosecutor's opening statement briefly outlined the testimony that he expected an undercover agent to give. Wagner then began his opening statement for the defense. After introducing himself and his co-counsel, Wagner turned to the case against the respondent. [In opening statements, Wagner gave improper personal opinions regarding the prosecution's key witness and case. The prosecutor objected. The judge then warned Wagner that he did not approve of his behavior and cautioned Wagner that he did not want to have to remind him again about the purpose of the opening statement.

Following this initial incident, the trial judge found it necessary twice again to remind Wagner of the purpose of the opening statement and to instruct him to relate "the facts that you expect the evidence to show, the admissible evidence." Wagner continued to make improper arguments.

The judge then asked original defense counsel if he was prepared to proceed with the trial.] The judge then set forth three alternative courses that might be followed — (1) a stay or recess pending application to the Court of Appeals to review the propriety of expelling Wagner, (2) continuation of the trial with prior counsel, or (3) a declaration of a mistrial which would permit the respondent to obtain other counsel. Following a short recess, Meldon moved for a mistrial, stating that, after "full consideration of the situation and an explanation of the alternatives before him, [the respondent] feels that he would move for a mistrial and that this would be in his best interest." The Government prosecutor did not oppose the motion. The judge thereupon declared a mistrial, expressing his belief that such a course would serve the interest of justice.

Before his second trial, the respondent[5] moved to dismiss the indictment on the ground that a retrial would violate the Double Jeopardy Clause of the Constitution. This motion was denied. The appellate court took the view that the trial judge's exclusion of Wagner and his questioning of Meldon had left the respondent no choice but to move for a mistrial. On that basis, the court concluded that the respondent's request for a mistrial should be ignored and the case should be treated as though the trial judge had declared a mistrial over the objection of the defendant. So viewing the case, the court held that the Double Jeopardy Clause barred the second trial of the respondent, because there had been no manifest necessity requiring the expulsion of Wagner. We granted certiorari.

II

The Double Jeopardy Clause of the Fifth Amendment protects a defendant in a criminal proceeding against multiple punishments or repeated prosecutions for the same offense. Underlying this constitutional safeguard is the belief that "the State with all its resources and power should not be allowed to make repeated attempts to convict an individual for an alleged offense, thereby subjecting him to embarrassment, expense and ordeal and compelling him to live in a continuing state of anxiety and insecurity, as well as enhancing the possibility that even though innocent he may be found guilty."

Since Mr. Justice Story's 1824 opinion for the Court in United States v. Perez, this Court has held that the question whether under the Double Jeopardy Clause there can be a new trial after a mistrial has been declared without the defendant's request or consent depends on whether "there is a manifest necessity for the [mistrial], or the ends of public justice would otherwise be defeated." Different considerations obtain, however, when the mistrial has been declared at the defendant's request. The reasons for the distinction were discussed in the plurality opinion in the *Jorn* case: If that right to go to a particular tribunal is valued, it is because, independent of the threat of bad-faith conduct by judge or prosecutor, the defendant has a significant interest in the decision whether or not to take the case from the jury when circumstances occur which might be thought to warrant a declaration of mistrial. Thus, where circumstances develop not attributable

_____

5. The respondent was a third-year law student at the time of his arrest. [Footnote by the Court.]

to prosecutorial or judicial overreaching, a motion by the defendant for mistrial is ordinarily assumed to remove any barrier to reprosecution, even if the defendant's motion is necessitated by prosecutorial or judicial error. In the absence of such a motion, the *Perez* doctrine of manifest necessity stands as a command to trial judges not to foreclose the defendant's option until a scrupulous exercise of judicial discretion leads to the conclusion that the ends of public justice would not be served by a continuation of the proceedings.

The distinction between mistrials declared by the court sua sponte and mistrials granted at the defendant's request or with his consent is wholly consistent with the protections of the Double Jeopardy Clause. Even when judicial or prosecutorial error prejudices a defendant's prospects of securing an acquittal, he may nonetheless desire "to go to the first jury and, perhaps, end the dispute then and there with an acquittal." Our prior decisions recognize the defendant's right to pursue this course in the absence of circumstances of manifest necessity requiring a sua sponte judicial declaration of mistrial. But it is evident that when judicial or prosecutorial error seriously prejudices a defendant, he may have little interest in completing the trial and obtaining a verdict from the first jury. The defendant may reasonably conclude that a continuation of the tainted proceeding would result in a conviction followed by a lengthy appeal and, if a reversal is secured, by a second prosecution. In such circumstances, a defendant's mistrial request has objectives not unlike the interests served by the Double Jeopardy Clause—the avoidance of the anxiety, expense, and delay occasioned by multiple prosecutions.

The Court of Appeals viewed the doctrine that permits a retrial following a mistrial sought by the defendant as resting on a waiver theory. The court concluded, therefore, that "something more substantial than a Hobson's choice" is required before a defendant can "be said to have relinquished voluntarily his right to proceed before the first jury." The court thus held that no waiver could be imputed to the respondent because the trial judge's action in excluding Wagner left the respondent with "no choice but to move for or accept a mistrial." But traditional waiver concepts have little relevance where the defendant must determine whether or not to request or consent to a mistrial in response to judicial or prosecutorial error. In such circumstances, the defendant generally does face a "Hobson's choice" between giving up his first jury and continuing a trial tainted by prejudicial judicial or prosecutorial error. The important consideration, for purposes of the Double Jeopardy Clause, is that the defendant retain[ed] primary control over the course to be followed in the event of such error.

The Double Jeopardy Clause does protect a defendant against governmental actions intended to provoke mistrial requests and thereby to subject defendants to the substantial burdens imposed by multiple prosecutions. It bars retrials where "bad-faith conduct by judge or prosecutor," threatens the "[harassment] of an accused by successive prosecutions or declaration of a mistrial so as to afford the prosecution a more favorable opportunity to convict" the defendant.

But here the trial judge's banishment of Wagner from the proceedings was not done in bad faith in order to goad the respondent into requesting a mistrial or to prejudice his prospects for an acquittal. As the Court of Appeals noted, Wagner "was guilty of improper conduct" during his opening statement which "may have justified disciplinary action." Even accepting the appellate court's conclusion that the trial judge overreacted in expelling Wagner from the courtroom, the court did not suggest, the respondent has not contended, and the record does not show that the judge's action was motivated by bad faith or undertaken to harass or prejudice the respondent.

Under these circumstances we hold that the Court of Appeals erred in finding that the retrial violated the respondent's constitutional right not to be twice put in jeopardy.

Chief Justice BURGER, concurring.

A trial judge is under a duty, in order to protect the integrity of the trial, to take prompt and affirmative action to stop such professional misconduct. Here the misconduct of the attorney, Wagner, was not only unprofessional per se but contemptuous in that he defied the court's explicit order.

Far from "overreacting" to the misconduct of Wagner, in my view, the trial judge exercised great restraint in not citing Wagner for contempt then and there.

Justice BRENNAN, with whom Justice MARSHALL joins, dissenting.

The Court's premise is that the mistrial was directed at respondent's request or with his consent. [F]or purposes of double jeopardy analysis, it was not, but rather that "the trial judge's response to the conduct of defense counsel deprived Dinitz's motion for a mistrial of its necessary consensual character." Therefore the rule that "a motion by the defendant for mistrial is ordinarily assumed to remove any barrier to reprosecution" is inapplicable.

The most likely scenario in which a mistrial will bar retrial is when the prosecution engages in misconduct. However, even prosecutorial misconduct does not guarantee that a defendant's double jeopardy rights will prohibit retrial.

OREGON v. KENNEDY
456 U.S. 667 (1982)

Justice REHNQUIST delivered the opinion of the Court.

The Oregon Court of Appeals decided that the Double Jeopardy Clause of the Fifth Amendment to the United States Constitution barred respondent's retrial after his first trial ended in a mistrial granted on his own motion. The Court of Appeals concluded that retrial was barred because the prosecutorial misconduct that occasioned the mistrial in the first instance amounted to "overreaching." Because that court took an overly expansive view of the application of the Double Jeopardy Clause following a mistrial resulting from the defendant's own motion, we reverse its judgment.

I

Respondent was charged with the theft of an oriental rug. During his first trial, the State called an expert witness on the subject of Middle Eastern rugs to testify as to the value and the identity of the rug in question. On cross-examination, respondent's attorney apparently attempted to establish bias on the part of the expert witness by asking him whether he had filed a criminal complaint against respondent. The witness eventually acknowledged this fact, but explained that no action had been taken on his complaint. On redirect examination, the prosecutor sought to elicit the reasons why the witness had filed a complaint against respondent, but the trial court sustained a series of objections to this line of inquiry. The following colloquy then ensued:

Prosecutor: Have you ever done business with the Kennedys?
Witness: No, I have not.
Prosecutor: Is that because he is a crook?

The trial court then granted respondent's motion for a mistrial.

When the State later sought to retry respondent, he moved to dismiss the charges because of double jeopardy. After a hearing at which the prosecutor testified, the trial court found as a fact that "it was not the intention of the prosecutor in this case to cause a mistrial." On the basis of this finding, the trial court held that double jeopardy principles did not bar retrial, and respondent was then tried and convicted.

Respondent then successfully appealed to the Oregon Court of Appeals, which sustained his double jeopardy claim. That court set out what it considered to be the governing principles in this kind of case:

> The general rule is said to be that the double jeopardy clause does not bar reprosecution, ". . . where circumstances develop not attributable to prosecutorial or judicial overreaching, . . . even if defendant's motion is necessitated by a prosecutorial error." United States v. Jorn (1971). However, retrial is barred where the error that prompted the mistrial is intended to provoke a mistrial or is "motivated by bad faith or undertaken to harass or prejudice" the defendant. United States v. Dinitz (1976).

The Court of Appeals accepted the trial court's finding that it was not the intent of the prosecutor to cause a mistrial. Nevertheless, the court held that retrial was barred because the prosecutor's conduct in this case constituted what it viewed as "overreaching." Although the prosecutor intended to reha-bilitate the witness, the Court of Appeals expressed the view that the question was in fact "a direct personal attack on the general character of the defendant." This personal attack left respondent with a "Hobson's choice — either to accept a necessarily prejudiced jury, or to move for a mistrial and face the process of being retried at a later time."

II

The Double Jeopardy Clause of the Fifth Amendment protects a criminal defendant from repeated prosecutions for the same offense. As a part of this protection against multiple prosecutions, the Double Jeopardy Clause affords a criminal defendant a "valued right to have his trial completed by a particular tribunal." Wade v. Hunter (1949). The Double Jeopardy Clause, however, does not offer a guarantee to the defendant that the State will vindicate its societal interest in the enforcement of the criminal laws in one proceeding. If the law were otherwise, "the purpose of law to protect society from those guilty of crimes frequently would be frustrated by denying courts power to put the defendant to trial again."

Where the trial is terminated over the objection of the defendant, the classical test for lifting the double jeopardy bar to a second trial is the "manifest necessity" standard first enunciated in United States v. Perez. *Perez* dealt with the most common form of "manifest necessity": a mistrial declared by the judge following the jury's declaration that it was unable to reach a verdict. The "manifest necessity" standard provides sufficient pro-tection to the defendant's interests in having his case finally decided by the jury first selected while at the same time maintaining "the public's interest in fair trials designed to end in just judgments."

But in the case of a mistrial declared at the behest of the defendant, quite different principles come into play. Here the defendant himself has elected to terminate the proceedings against him, and the "manifest necessity" standard has no place in the application of the Double Jeopardy Clause.

Our cases, however, have indicated that even where the defendant moves for a mistrial, there is a narrow exception to the rule that the Double Jeopardy Clause is no bar to retrial. The circumstances under which respon-dent's first trial was terminated require us to delineate the bounds of that exception more fully than we have in previous cases.

Since one of the principal threads making up the protection embodied in the Double Jeopardy Clause is the right of the defendant to have his trial completed before the first jury empaneled to try him, it may be wondered as a matter of original inquiry why the defendant's election to terminate the first trial by his own motion should not be deemed a renunciation of that right for all purposes. We have recognized, however, that there would be great difficulty in applying such a rule where the prosecutor's actions giving rise to the motion for mistrial were done "in order to goad the [defendant] into requesting a mistrial." In such a case, the defendant's valued right to complete his trial before the first jury would be a hollow shell if the inevitable motion for mistrial were held to prevent a later invocation of the bar of double jeopardy in all circumstances. But the precise phrasing of the circumstances which will allow a defendant to interpose the defense of double jeopardy to a second prosecution where the first has terminated on his own motion for a mistrial have been stated with less than crystal clarity in our cases which deal with this area of the law.

Every act on the part of a rational prosecutor during a trial is designed to "prejudice" the defendant by placing before the judge or jury evidence leading to a finding of his guilt. Given the complexity of the rules of evidence, it will be a rare trial of any complexity in which some proffered evidence by the prosecutor or by the defendant's attorney will not be found objectionable by the trial court. Most such objections are undoubtedly curable by simply refusing to allow the proffered evidence to be admitted, or in the case of a particular line of inquiry taken by counsel with a witness, by an admonition to desist from a particular line of inquiry.

More serious infractions on the part of the prosecutor may provoke a motion for mistrial on the part of the defendant, and may in the view of the trial court warrant the granting of such a motion. The "overreaching" standard applied by the court below and urged today, however, would add another classification of prosecutorial error, one requiring dismissal of the indictment, but without supplying any standard by which to assess that error.

By contrast, a standard that examines the intent of the prosecutor, though certainly not entirely free from practical difficulties, is a manageable standard to apply. It merely calls for the court to make a finding of fact. Inferring the existence or nonexistence of intent from objective facts and circumstances is a familiar process in our criminal justice system. When it is remembered that resolution of double jeopardy questions by state trial courts are reviewable not only within the state court system, but in the federal court system on habeas corpus as well, the desirability of an easily applied principle is apparent.

Prosecutorial conduct that might be viewed as harassment or overreaching, even if sufficient to justify a mistrial on defendant's motion, therefore, does not bar retrial absent intent on the part of the prosecutor to subvert the protections afforded by the Double Jeopardy Clause. Only where the governmental conduct in question is intended to "goad" the defendant into moving for a mistrial may a defendant raise the bar of double jeopardy to a second trial after having succeeded in aborting the first on his own motion.

Were we to embrace the broad and somewhat amorphous standard adopted by the Oregon Court of Appeals, we are not sure that criminal defendants as a class would be aided. Knowing that the granting of the defendant's motion for mistrial would all but inevitably bring with it an attempt to bar a second trial on grounds of double jeopardy, the judge presiding over the first trial might well be more loath to grant a defendant's motion for mistrial.

Justice POWELL, concurring.

I join the Court's opinion holding that the intention of a prosecutor determines whether his conduct, viewed by the defendant and the court as justifying a mistrial, bars a retrial of the defendant under the Double Jeopardy Clause. Because "subjective" intent often may be unknowable, I emphasize that a court — in considering a double jeopardy motion — should rely primarily upon the objective facts and circumstances of the particular case.

In the present case the mistrial arose from the prosecutor's conduct in pursuing a line of redirect examination of a key witness. The Oregon Court of Appeals identified a single question as constituting "overreaching" so serious as to bar a retrial. Yet, there are few vigorously contested lawsuits — whether criminal or civil — in which improper questions are not asked. Our system is adversarial and vigorous advocacy is encouraged.

Nevertheless, this would have been a close case for me if there had been substantial factual evidence of intent beyond the question itself. Here, however, other relevant facts and circumstances strongly support the view that prosecutorial intent to cause a mistrial was absent. First, there was no sequence of overreaching prior to the single prejudicial question. Moreover, it is evident from a colloquy between counsel and the court, out of the presence of the jury, that the prosecutor not only resisted, but also was surprised by, the defendant's motion for a mistrial. Finally, at the hearing on respondent's double jeopardy motion, the prosecutor testified — and the trial found as a fact and the appellate court agreed — that there was no " 'intention . . . to cause a mistrial.' "

In view of these circumstances, the Double Jeopardy Clause provides no bar to retrial.

2. Dual Sovereignty

The dual sovereignty doctrine is another exception to the double jeopardy rule. The doctrine allows two different sovereigns to prosecute the defendant for the same crime, because each sovereign has a separate and legitimate interest in prosecuting the defendant. Thus, for example, state and federal authorities can prosecute a defendant for the same crime. This occurred in the famous 1992 case of four white police officers who beat black motorist, Rodney King. The officers were acquitted in a state prosecution, precipitating devastating riots in Los Angeles. Soon thereafter, federal authorities charged the officers with civil rights violations based on the same beating incidents. The officers were retried in federal court, and two of them were convicted.[6]

The rationale for the dual sovereignty doctrine is set forth in the next case.

---

6. For more details regarding the state and federal prosecutions, *see* Laurie L. Levenson, *The Future of State and Federal Civil Rights Prosecutions: The Lessons of the Rodney King Trial*, 41 UCLA L. Rev. 509 (1994).

BARTKUS v. ILLINOIS
359 U.S. 121 (1959)

Justice FRANKFURTER delivered the opinion of the Court.

Petitioner was tried in the Federal District Court for the Northern District of Illinois on December 18, 1953, for robbery of a federally insured savings and loan association, the General Savings and Loan Association of Cicero, Illinois, in violation of 18 U.S.C. §2113. The case was tried to a jury and resulted in an acquittal. On January 8, 1954, an Illinois grand jury indicted Bartkus. The facts recited in the Illinois indictment were substantially identical to those contained in the prior federal indictment. The Illinois indictment charged that these facts constituted a violation of Illinois Revised Statutes, 1951, c. 38, §501, a robbery statute. Bartkus was tried and convicted in the Criminal Court of Cook County and was sentenced to life imprisonment under the Illinois Habitual Criminal Statute.

The Illinois trial court considered and rejected petitioner's plea of *autrefois acquit*. We granted certiorari because the petition raised a substantial question concerning the application of the Fourteenth Amendment.[7]

The state and federal prosecutions were separately conducted. It is true that the agent of the Federal Bureau of Investigation who had conducted the investigation on behalf of the Federal Government turned over to the Illinois prosecuting officials all the evidence he had gathered against the petitioner. Concededly, some of that evidence had been gathered after acquittal in the federal court. The only other connection between the two trials is to be found in a suggestion that the federal sentencing of the accomplices who testified against petitioner in both trials was purposely continued by the federal court until after they testified in the state trial. The record establishes that the prosecution was undertaken by state prosecuting officials within their discretionary responsibility and on the basis of evidence that conduct contrary to the penal code of Illinois had occurred within their jurisdiction. It establishes also that federal officials acted in cooperation with state authorities, as is the conventional practice between the two sets of prosecutors throughout the country. It does not support the claim that the State of Illinois in bringing its prosecution was merely a tool of the federal authorities, who thereby avoided the prohibition of the Fifth Amendment against a retrial of a federal prosecution after an acquittal. It does not sustain a conclusion that the state prosecution was a sham and a cover for a federal prosecution, and thereby in essential fact another federal prosecution.

---

7. The case was decided under the Fourteenth Amendment because the Fifth Amendment double jeopardy right had not yet been incorporated to the states. The Double Jeopardy Clause was subsequently incorporated to the states. Missouri v. Hunter, 459 U.S. 359 (1983); Benton v. Maryland, 395 U.S. 784 (1969). [Footnote by casebook authors.]

[The convictions were affirmed.]

On the same day as it decided *Bartkus*, the Supreme Court decided the companion case of Abbate v. United States, 359 U.S. 187 (1959). Whereas *Bartkus* held that states could prosecute the same crime following a federal prosecution, *Abbate* held that federal authorities could prosecute the same crime after a state prosecution. Justice Brennan wrote:

> Every citizen of the United States is also a citizen of a State or territory. He may be said to owe allegiance to two sovereigns, and may be liable to punishment for an infraction of the laws of either. The same act may be an offence or transgression of the laws of both.
>
> That either or both may (if they see fit) punish such an offender, cannot be doubted.

Id. at 195.

The dual sovereignty doctrine allows state and federal governments to try a defendant for the same offense, two different states to try a defendant for the same offense, Heath v. Alabama, 474 U.S. 82, 88 (1985), and the United States and a foreign government to try a defendant for the same offense, United States v. Villanueva, 408 F.3d 193, 201 (5th Cir. 2005). Local governments, however, are not considered to be separate sovereigns for double jeopardy purposes and cannot try a defendant for the same offense. Waller v. Florida, 397 U.S. 387, 394-395 (1970). Cities and states are not considered to be "separate sovereigns."

The dual sovereignty doctrine has two limitations. First, as suggested in *Bartkus*, if both sovereigns are working together in a way that would make a second prosecution a "sham" prosecution, the dual sovereignty doctrine does not apply. *Bartkus*, 359 U.S. 122-124. Second, the Department of Justice has an internal policy, known as the "Petite policy,"[8] that authorizes federal prosecutors to bring a successive prosecution only when there are compelling reasons to do so and there is approval from the Assistant U.S. Attorney General. The policy, however, does not confer on a defendant the right to seek dismissal of an indictment for alleged violations of the federal authorities' protocol.

Dual prosecutions of defendants by state and federal authorities have occurred in several recent high-profile cases, including the state and federal prosecutions of the officers accused of beating black motorist Rodney King, and the state and federal prosecutions of Terry Nichols, who was accused of being a coconspirator in the bombing of the Murrah Federal Building in Oklahoma City. Yet the practice is not without controversy.

---

8. *See Dual and Successive Federal Prosecution Policy*, Department of Justice Manual 9-2.031 (2005). The "Petite policy" is named after the Supreme Court's decision in Petite v. United States, 361 U.S. 529 (1960) (per curiam).

> The protection against double jeopardy, known as non bis in idem in the international context, is part of the "universal law of nations." There are at least fifty countries that provide protection from multiple prosecutions. Accordingly, the fact that the doctrine exists internationally in both the laws of foreign countries and treaties demonstrates its strong establishment in international criminal law. Because most nations view protection against multiple prosecutions as a fundamental right, double jeopardy appears as a stipulation in human rights treaties. For example, Article 14(7) of the International Covenant of Civil and Political Rights contains a general provision of double jeopardy which states "no one shall be liable to be tried or punished again for an offense for which he has already been finally convicted or acquitted in accordance with the law and penalty of each country."

Eric M. Cranman, *The Dual Sovereign Exception to Double Jeopardy: A Champion of Justice or a Violation of a Fundamental Right,* 14 Emory Int'l L. Rev. 1641, 1645-1646 (2000). With the dual sovereignty exception, defendants cannot expect the finality associated with the double jeopardy rule and it gives the prosecution the opportunity to try a case, learn from its mistakes, and try the defendant again.

States are free to reject the dual sovereignty exception and many have done so. A majority of states prohibit a state prosecution that follows a federal prosecution for the same act or transaction. *See* Adam H. Kurland, *Successive Criminal Prosecutions: The Dual Sovereignty to Double Jeopardy in State and Federal Courts* (2001).

E.   MULTIPLE CHARGES AND CUMULATIVE PUNISHMENTS

The Double Jeopardy Clause does not bar a defendant from being charged with multiple crimes arising from the same act or transaction. Because the primary purpose of the Double Jeopardy Clause is to protect against multiple trials, a legislature may constitutionally provide for multiple punishments even when the charges arise from one activity by the defendant. Missouri v. Hunter, 459 U.S. 359 (1983). The legislative intent to impose cumulative punishment must be clearly established. United States v. Universal C.I.T. Credit Corp., 344 U.S. 218, 221 (1952).

If the legislative intent does not demonstrate that the defendant may be subject to multiple punishments, or if one charge is the lesser-included offense of the other charge, the Double Jeopardy Clause bars multiple punishments.

RUTLEDGE v. UNITED STATES
517 U.S. 292 (1996)

Justice STEVENS delivered the opinion of the Court.

A jury found petitioner guilty of participating in a conspiracy to distribute controlled substances in violation of 21 U.S.C. §846, and of conducting a continuing criminal enterprise (CCE) in violation of §848. The "in concert" element of his CCE offense was based on the same agreement as the §846 conspiracy. The question presented is whether it was therefore improper for the District Court to sentence him to concurrent life sentences on the two counts.

I

Petitioner organized and supervised a criminal enterprise that distributed cocaine in Warren County, Illinois, from 1988 until December 1990, when he was arrested by federal agents. He was charged with several offenses, of which only Count One, the CCE charge, and Count Two, the conspiracy charge, are relevant to the issue before us.

Count One alleged that during the period between early 1988 and late 1990, petitioner violated §848 by engaging in a CCE that consisted of a series of unlawful acts involving the distribution of cocaine. The count alleged that these actions were undertaken "in concert with at least five (5) other persons," that petitioner supervised those other persons, and that he obtained substantial income from the continuing series of violations.

Count Two separately alleged that during the same period, petitioner violated 21 U.S.C. §846 by conspiring with four codefendants and others to engage in the unlawful distribution of cocaine.

[A] jury found petitioner guilty on all counts. The trial court entered judgment of conviction on both Count One and Count Two and imposed a sentence of life imprisonment without possible release on each count, the sentences to be served concurrently.

On appeal, petitioner contended in a pro se supplemental brief that even though the life sentences were concurrent, entering both convictions and sentences impermissibly punished him twice for the same offense. The Court of Appeals for the Seventh Circuit accepted the premise of his argument, namely, that the conspiracy charge was a lesser included offense of the CCE charge. The Court of Appeals nonetheless affirmed his convictions and sentences.

The decision of the Seventh Circuit is at odds with the practice of other Circuits. Most federal courts that have confronted the question hold that only one judgment should be entered when a defendant is found guilty on both a CCE count and a conspiracy count based on the same agreements. The Second and Third Circuits have adopted an intermediate position, allowing judgment to be entered on both counts but permitting only one sentence rather than the concurrent sentences allowed in the Seventh Circuit. We granted certiorari to resolve the conflict.

II

Courts may not "prescrib[e] greater punishment than the legislature intended." Missouri v. Hunter (1983). In accord with principles rooted in common law and constitutional jurisprudence, we presume that "where two statutory provisions proscribe the 'same offense,'" a legislature does not intend to impose two punishments for that offense.

For over half a century we have determined whether a defendant has been punished twice for the "same offense" by applying the rule set forth in Blockburger v. United States (1932). If "the same act or transaction constitutes a violation of two distinct statutory provisions, the test to be applied to determine whether there are two offenses or only one, is whether each provision requires proof of a fact which the other does not." In subsequent applications of the test, we have often concluded that two different statutes define the "same offense," typically because one is a lesser included offense of the other.

In this case it is perfectly clear that the CCE offense requires proof of a number of elements that need not be established in a conspiracy case. The *Blockburger* test requires us to consider whether the converse is also true — whether the §846 conspiracy offense requires proof of any element that is not a part of the CCE offense. That question could be answered affirmatively only by assuming that while the §846 conspiracy requires proof of an actual agreement among the parties, the "in concert" element of the CCE offense might be satisfied by something less.

[T]he Courts of Appeals have also consistently rejected the Government's interpretation of the "in concert" language of §848; they have concluded, without exception, that conspiracy is a lesser included offense of CCE. [We also] hold that this element of the CCE offense requires proof of a conspiracy that would also violate §846. Because §846 does not require proof of any fact that is not also a part of the CCE offense, a straightforward application of the *Blockburger* test leads to the conclusion that conspiracy as defined in §846 does not define a different offense from the CCE offense defined in §848. Furthermore, since the latter offense is the more serious of the two, and because only one of its elements is necessary to prove a §846 conspiracy, it is appropriate to characterize §846 as a lesser included offense of §848.

III

The Government contends that even if conspiracy is a lesser included offense of CCE, the resulting presumption against multiple punishments does not invalidate either of petitioner's convictions. The second conviction, the Government first argues, may not amount to a punishment at all.

We begin by noting that 18 U.S.C. §3013 requires a federal district court to impose a $50 special assessment for every conviction, and that such an assessment was imposed on both convictions in this case. As long as §3013 stands, a second conviction will amount to a second punishment.

[Moreover,] "[t]he second conviction, whose concomitant sentence is served concurrently, does not evaporate simply because of the concurrence of the sentence. The separate conviction, apart from the concurrent sentence, has potential adverse collateral consequences that may not be ignored. For example, the presence of two convictions on the record may delay the defendant's eligibility for parole or result in an increased sentence under a recidivist statute for a future offense. Moreover, the second conviction may be used to impeach the defendant's credibility and certainly carries the societal stigma accompanying any criminal conviction. Thus, the second conviction, even if it results in no greater sentence, is an impermissible punishment."

IV

The Government further argues that even if the second conviction amounts to punishment, the presumption against allowing multiple punishments for the same crime may be overcome if Congress clearly indicates that it intended to allow courts to impose them.

The Government finds support for its position in this Court's judgment in *Jeffers* because that judgment allowed convictions under both §§846 and 848 to stand. Those convictions, however, had been entered in separate trials and our review only addressed the conviction under §848.[9]

VI

A guilty verdict on a §848 charge necessarily includes a finding that the defendant also participated in a conspiracy violative of §846; conspiracy is therefore a lesser included offense of CCE. Because the Government's arguments have not persuaded us otherwise, we adhere to the presumption that Congress intended to authorize only one punishment. Accordingly, "one of [petitioner's] convictions, as well as its concurrent sentence, is unauthorized punishment for a separate offense" and must be vacated.

The judgment of the Court of Appeals is reversed, and the case is remanded for further proceedings consistent with this opinion.

As noted in *Rutledge*, the test to determine whether one charge is a lesser-included offense of the other is the *Blockburger* test, discussed in section B of this chapter. If a defendant is convicted of separate offenses, multiple punishments are permitted as long as the legislative intent supports a finding that cumulative punishments may be imposed.

---

9. The Government suggests that convictions are authorized for both §§846 and 848 because they are different sections of the United States Code. This does not rise to the level of the clear statement necessary for us to conclude that despite the identity of the statutory elements, Congress intended to allow multiple punishments. After all, we concluded in *Ball* that the statutes at issue did not authorize separate convictions, and they were even more distant in the Code. If anything, the proximity of §§846 and 848 indicates that Congress understood them to be directed to similar, rather than separate, evils. [Footnote by the Court.]

F.   COLLATERAL ESTOPPEL

The Double Jeopardy Clause includes within it the concept of collateral estoppel. This means that if an issue of ultimate fact has been determined by a valid and final judgment, it cannot be relitigated in a future case. Consider, for example, a defendant who is charged with robbing two victims. In trial number one, the jurors acquit the defendant of robbing victim one because there is a reasonable doubt as to whether he was the robber. The government cannot prosecute the defendant for robbery of the other victim, because there has already been a finding that he was not the robber. The Supreme Court explained this concept in the key case of Ashe v. Swenson.

ASHE v. SWENSON
397 U.S. 436 (1970)

Justice STEWART delivered the opinion of the Court.

The question in this case is whether the State of Missouri violated [the guarantee against double jeopardy] when it prosecuted the petitioner a second time for armed robbery in the circumstances here presented.

Sometime in the early hours of the morning of January 10, 1960, six men were engaged in a poker game in the basement of the home of John Gladson at Lee's Summit, Missouri. Suddenly three or four masked men, armed with a shotgun and pistols, broke into the basement and robbed each of the poker players of money and various articles of personal property. The robbers — and it has never been clear whether there were three or four of them — then fled in a car belonging to one of the victims of the robbery. Shortly thereafter the stolen car was discovered in a field, and later that morning three men were arrested by a state trooper while they were walking on a highway not far from where the abandoned car had been found. The petitioner was arrested by another officer some distance away.

The four were subsequently charged with seven separate offenses — the armed robbery of each of the six poker players and the theft of the car. In May 1960 the petitioner went to trial on the charge of robbing Donald Knight, one of the participants in the poker game. At the trial the State called Knight and three of his fellow poker players as prosecution witnesses. Each of them described the circumstances of the holdup and itemized his own individual losses. The proof that an armed robbery had occurred and that personal property had been taken from Knight as well as from each of the others was unassailable. The testimony of the four victims in this regard was consistent both internally and with that of the others. But the State's evidence that the petitioner had been one of the robbers was weak. Two of the witnesses thought that there had been only three robbers altogether, and could not identify the petitioner as one of them. Another of the victims, who was the petitioner's uncle by marriage, said that at the "patrol station" he had positively identified each of the other three men accused of the holdup, but could say only that the petitioner's voice "sounded very much like" that of one of the robbers. The fourth participant in the poker game did identify the petitioner, but only by his "size and height, and his actions."

The cross-examination of these witnesses was brief, and it was aimed primarily at exposing the weakness of their identification testimony. Defense counsel made no attempt to question their testimony regarding the holdup itself or their claims as to their losses. Knight testified without contradiction that the robbers had stolen from him his watch, $250 in cash, and about $500 in checks. His billfold, which had been found by the police in the possession of one of the three other men accused of the robbery, was admitted in evidence. The defense offered no testimony and waived final argument.

The trial judge instructed the jury that if it found that the petitioner was one of the participants in the armed robbery, the theft of "any money" from Knight would sustain a conviction. He also instructed the jury that if the petitioner was one of the robbers, he was guilty under the law even if he had not personally robbed Knight. The jury — though not instructed to elaborate upon its verdict — found the petitioner "not guilty due to insufficient evidence."

Six weeks later the petitioner was brought to trial again, this time for the robbery of another participant in the poker game, a man named Roberts. The petitioner filed a motion to dismiss, based on his previous acquittal. The motion was overruled, and the second trial began. The witnesses were for the most part the same, though this time their testimony was substantially stronger on the issue of the petitioner's identity.

The case went to the jury on instructions virtually identical to those given at the first trial. This time the jury found the petitioner guilty, and he was sentenced to a 35-year term in the state penitentiary.

The petitioner then brought the present habeas corpus proceeding . . . claiming that the second prosecution had violated his right not to be twice put in jeopardy.

The question is [whether collateral estoppel is a part of the Fifth Amendment's guarantee against double jeopardy].

"Collateral estoppel" is an awkward phrase, but it stands for an extremely important principle in our adversary system of justice. It means simply that when an issue of ultimate fact has once been determined by a valid and final judgment, that issue cannot again be litigated between the same parties in any future lawsuit.

The federal decisions have made clear that the rule of collateral estoppel in criminal cases is not to be applied with the hypertechnical and archaic approach of a 19th century pleading book, but with realism and rationality. Where a previous judgment of acquittal was based upon a general verdict, as is usually the case, this approach requires a court to "examine the record of a prior proceeding, taking into account the pleadings, evidence, charge, and other relevant matter, and conclude whether a rational jury could have grounded its verdict upon an issue other than that which the defendant seeks to foreclose from consideration." The inquiry "must be set in a practical frame and viewed with an eye to all the circumstances of the proceedings." Any test more technically restrictive would, of course, simply amount to a rejection of the rule of collateral estoppel in criminal proceedings, at least in every case where the first judgment was based upon a general verdict of acquittal.

Straightforward application of the federal rule to the present case can lead to but one conclusion. For the record is utterly devoid of any indication that the first jury could rationally have found that an armed robbery had not occurred, or that Knight had not been a victim of that robbery. The single rationally conceivable issue in dispute before the jury was whether the petitioner had been one of the robbers. And the jury by its verdict found that he had not. The federal rule of law, therefore, would make a second prosecution for the robbery of Roberts wholly impermissible.

The question is not whether Missouri could validly charge the petitioner with six separate offenses for the robbery of the six poker players. It is not whether he could have received a total of six punishments if he had been convicted in a single trial of robbing the six victims. It is simply whether, after a jury determined by its verdict that the petitioner was not one of the robbers, the State could constitutionally hale him before a new jury to litigate that issue again.

In this case the State in its brief has frankly conceded that following the petitioner's acquittal, it treated the first trial as no more than a dry run for the second prosecution: "No doubt the prosecutor felt the state had a provable case on the first charge and, when he lost, he did what every good attorney would do — he refined his presentation in light of the turn of events at the first trial." But this is precisely what the constitutional guarantee forbids.

The judgment is reversed.

Chief Justice BURGER, dissenting.

The Fifth Amendment to the Constitution of the United States provides in part: "nor shall any person be subject for the same offence to be twice put in jeopardy of life or limb. . . ." Nothing in the language or gloss previously placed on this provision of the Fifth Amendment remotely justifies the treatment that the Court today accords to the collateral-estoppel doctrine. Nothing in the purpose of the authors of the Constitution commands or even justifies what the Court decides today; this is truly a case of expanding a sound basic principle beyond the bounds — or needs — of its rational and legitimate objectives to preclude harassment of an accused.

The majority rests its holding in part on a series of cases beginning with United States v. Oppenheimer (1916), which did not involve constitutional double jeopardy but applied collateral estoppel as developed in civil litigation to federal criminal prosecutions as a matter of this Court's supervisory power over the federal court system. The Court now finds the federal collateral estoppel rule to be an "ingredient" of the Fifth Amendment guarantee against double jeopardy and applies it to the States through the Fourteenth Amendment; this is an ingredient that eluded judges and justices for nearly two centuries.

The collateral-estoppel concept—originally a product only of civil litigation—is a strange mutant as it is transformed to control this criminal case. In civil cases the doctrine was justified as conserving judicial resources as well as those of the parties to the actions and additionally as providing the finality needed to plan for the future. It ordinarily applies to parties on each side of the litigation who have the same interest as or who are identical with the parties in the initial litigation. Here the complainant in the second trial is not the same as in the first even though the State is a party in both cases. Very properly, in criminal cases, finality and conservation of private, public, and judicial resources are lesser values than in civil litigation. Also, courts that have applied the collateral-estoppel concept to criminal actions would certainly not apply it to both parties, as is true in civil cases, i.e., here, if Ashe had been convicted at the first trial, presumably no court would then hold that he was thereby foreclosed from litigating the identification issue at the second trial.

Perhaps, then, it comes as no surprise to find that the only expressed ratio- nale for the majority's decision is that Ashe has "run the gantlet" once before. This is not a doctrine of the law or legal reasoning but a colorful and graphic phrase, which, as used originally in an opinion of the Court written by Mr. Justice Black, was intended to mean something entirely different. The full phrase is "run the gantlet once on that charge. . . ." [I]t is to be found in Green v. United States (1957), where no question of multiple crimes against multiple victims was involved. Green, having been found guilty of second- degree murder on a charge of first degree, secured a new trial. This Court held nothing more than that Green, once put in jeopardy—once having "run the gantlet . . . on that charge"—of first-degree murder, could not be com- pelled to defend against that charge again on retrial.

Today's step in this area of constitutional law ought not be taken on no more basis than casual reliance on the "gantlet" phrase lifted out of the context in which it was originally used. This is decision by slogan.

In Ashe v. Swenson, the Court established that double jeopardy barred retrial of issues that were necessarily decided in a prior case. In Yeager v. United States (2009), a slim majority of justices held that an acquittal on some counts may preclude a retrial on those issues even if the initial jury did not reach a verdict on other counts.

YEAGER v. UNITED STATES

557 U.S. 110 (2009)

Justice STEVENS delivered the opinion of the Court.

The question presented in this case is whether an apparent inconsistency between a jury's verdict of acquittal on some counts and its failure to return a verdict on other counts affects the preclusive force of the acquittals under the Double Jeopardy Clause of the Fifth Amendment. We hold that it does not.

[Petitioner F. Scott Yeager served as an officer for a division of Enron Corporation (Enron). Yeager allegedly made false and misleading statements about the value of one of Enron's projects, causing the price of Enron stock to rise dramatically. The petitioner sold stock shares that he had received as part of his compensation and made $19 million in personal profit. As it happened, the project turned out to be worthless.

Yeager was charged in a 126-count Fifth Superseding Indictment with (1) conspiracy to commit securities and wire fraud, (2) securities fraud, (3) wire fraud, (4) insider trading, and (5) money laundering. The government's theory of prosecution was that petitioner—acting in concert with other Enron executives—purposefully deceived the public about the project in order to inflate the value of Enron's stock and, ultimately, enrich himself.]

The trial lasted 13 weeks. After four days of deliberations, the jury notified the court that it had reached agreement on some counts but had deadlocked on others. The jury acquitted petitioner on the fraud counts but failed to reach a verdict on the insider trading counts. The court entered judgment on the acquittals and declared a mistrial on the hung counts.

[Thereafter], the Government obtained a new indictment against petitioner. This "Eighth Superseding Indictment" recharged petitioner with some, but not all, of the insider trading counts on which the jury had previously hung. Petitioner moved to dismiss all counts in the new indictment on the ground that the acquittals on the fraud counts precluded the Government from retrying him on the insider trading counts. He argued that the jury's acquittals had necessarily decided that he did not possess material, nonpublic information about the performance of the project and its value to Enron. In petitioner's view, because reprosecution for insider trading would require the Government to prove that critical fact, the issue-preclusion component of the Double Jeopardy Clause barred a second trial of that issue and mandated dismissal of all of the insider trading counts.

The Double Jeopardy Clause of the Fifth Amendment provides: "[N]or shall any person be subject for the same offence to be twice put in jeopardy of life or limb."

Our cases have recognized that the Clause embodies two vitally important interests. The first is the "deeply ingrained" principle that "the State with all its resources and power should not be allowed to make repeated attempts to convict an individual for an alleged offense, thereby subjecting him to embarrassment, expense and ordeal and compelling him to live in a continuing state of anxiety and insecurity, as well as enhancing the possibility that even though innocent he may be found guilty." The second interest is the preservation of "the finality of judgments."

The first interest is implicated whenever the State seeks a second trial after its first attempt to obtain a conviction results in a mistrial because the jury has failed to reach a verdict. While the case before us involves a mistrial on the insider trading counts, the question presented cannot be resolved by asking whether the Government should be given one complete opportunity to convict petitioner on those charges. Rather, the case turns on the second interest at the core of the Clause. We must determine whether the interest in preserving the finality of the jury's judgment on the fraud counts, including the jury's finding that petitioner did not possess insider information, bars a retrial on the insider trading counts.

In *Ashe*, we squarely held that the Double Jeopardy Clause precludes the Government from relitigating any issue that was necessarily decided by a jury's acquittal in a prior trial. [In this case], the Court of Appeals reasoned that the hung counts must be considered to determine what issues the jury decided in the first trial. Viewed in isolation, the court explained, the acquittals on the fraud charges would preclude retrial because they appeared to support petitioner's argument that the jury decided he lacked insider information. Viewed alongside the hung counts, however, the acquittals appeared less decisive.

The Court of Appeals' issue-preclusion analysis was in error. A hung count is not a "relevant" part of the "record of [the] prior proceeding." Because a jury speaks only through its verdict, its failure to reach a verdict cannot — by negative implication — yield a piece of information that helps put together the trial puzzle. A mistried count is therefore nothing like the other forms of record material that *Ashe* suggested should be part of the preclusion inquiry. A host of reasons — sharp disagreement, confusion about the issues, exhaustion after a long trial, to name but a few — could work alone or in tandem to cause a jury to hang. To ascribe meaning to a hung count would presume an ability to identify which factor was at play in the jury room. But that is not reasoned analysis; it is guesswork.

To identify what a jury necessarily determined at trial, courts should scrutinize a jury's decisions, not its failures to decide. Thus, if the possession of insider information was a critical issue of ultimate fact in all of the charges against petitioner, a jury verdict that necessarily decided that issue in his favor protects him from prosecution for any charge for which that is an essential element.

[W]e decline to engage in a fact-intensive analysis of the voluminous record [to determine the basis for the acquittal]. If it chooses, the Court of Appeals may revisit its factual analysis in light of the Government's arguments before this Court.

CHAPTER

15

HABEAS CORPUS

A. INTRODUCTION

After a person has been convicted of a crime and exhausted all appeals, he or she may file a petition for a writ of habeas corpus in federal court. Habeas petitions are commonly filed by inmates while they are in prison. Although there are difficult procedural issues for petitioners to navigate, there is no right to counsel to assist in the filing of habeas corpus petitions. This chapter discusses in detail the procedural hurdles for habeas corpus petitions, as well as the limitation on the types of claims that may be made through habeas corpus petitions.

A person convicted in a state court proceeding generally may secure federal court review of the state court's judgments and proceedings only by first exhausting all available appeals within the state system. Federal district courts lack the authority to hear appeals from state judicial systems. Under federal law, a person who claims to be held in custody by a state government in violation of the Constitution, treaties, or laws of the United States may file a civil lawsuit in federal court seeking a writ of habeas corpus. Technically, federal court consideration of the habeas corpus petition is not considered a direct review of the state court decision; rather, the petition constitutes a separate civil suit filed in federal court and is termed *collateral relief.* If the federal court grants a writ of habeas corpus, it may order the release of a state prisoner who is held by the state in violation of federal law. Federal courts may also hear habeas petitions of federal prisoners pursuant to 28 U.S.C. §2255.

The writ of habeas corpus has its origins in English law.[1] Blackstone referred to habeas corpus as "the most celebrated writ in English law."[2] Recognizing its importance, the Framers of the Constitution provided that "[t]he Privilege of the Writ of Habeas Corpus shall not be suspended,

---

Portions of the text in this chapter are taken from Erwin Chemerinsky, *Federal Jurisdiction* Ch. 15 (6th ed. 2012).

1. For an excellent history of habeas corpus, *see* W. Duker, *A Constitutional History of Habeas Corpus* (1980).

2. 3 *Blackstone's Commentaries* 129 (1791).

unless when in Cases of Rebellion or Invasion the public Safety may require it."[3] Under the Judiciary Act of 1789, habeas corpus was available to prisoners who claimed that they were held in custody by the *federal* government in violation of the Constitution, treaties, or laws of the United States.[4] After the Civil War, at a time of great distrust in the ability and willingness of state courts to protect federal rights, Congress provided habeas corpus relief to state prisoners if they were held "in custody in violation of the Constitution or laws or treaties of the United States."[5]

The writ of habeas corpus protects individuals against arbitrary and wrongful imprisonment. It is not surprising, therefore, that habeas corpus long has been viewed as the "great writ of liberty."[6] At the same time, however, the availability of federal court relief pursuant to the writ of habeas corpus remains enormously controversial. Conservatives feel that habeas corpus is a vehicle that guilty criminals often use to escape their convictions and their sentences.[7] But liberals see the writ as an essential protection of constitutional rights — ensuring that individuals are not held in custody in violation of those rights.[8] The writ of habeas corpus also is controversial because it is a source of direct confrontation between federal district courts and state judiciaries. The power of a single federal judge to overturn a decision affirmed by an entire state court system is troubling to many.[9] A reflection of this ideological split is that in 1996, the Republican-controlled Congress enacted the Antiterrorism and Effective Death Penalty Act, which substantially changed the law of habeas corpus and, in many ways, restricted its availability.[10] Yet the controversy over habeas corpus must be put in perspective. Statistics indicate that less than 1 percent of state prisoners who file habeas corpus petitions ultimately prevail.[11]

Over the last decade and a half, there has been a major debate over whether federal courts should be able to exercise habeas corpus over those who are detained as part of the war on terrorism, especially those held in Guantánamo Bay, Cuba.[12] In Rasul v. Bush, the Supreme Court held that federal courts have jurisdiction to hear habeas petitions by those detained in Guantánamo.[13] Congress responded by enacting the Detainee

---

3. U.S. Const. art. I, §9, cl. 2.

4. Judiciary Act of 1789, ch. 20, 1 Stat. 73.

5. 28 U.S.C. §2254.

6. Duker, *supra* note 1, at 3.

7. *See, e.g.,* Henry J. Friendly, *Is Innocence Irrelevant? Collateral Attack on Criminal Judgments,* 38 U. Chi. L. Rev. 142 (1970) (arguing that habeas corpus should be available only where there is a colorable showing of a defendant's innocence).

8. *See, e.g.,* Stephen A. Saltzburg, *Habeas Corpus: The Supreme Court and the Congress,* 44 Ohio St. L.J. 367 (1983) (habeas corpus is symbolic of the ideal that no person should be convicted in violation of the fundamental law of the land).

9. *See, e.g.,* Engle v. Isaac, 456 U.S. 107, 126 (1982).

10. Pub. L. No. 104-132, April 24, 1996.

11. John Blume, *AEDPA: The "Hype" and the "Bite,"* 91 Cornell L. Rev. 259, 284 (2006).

12. This is discussed in detail in section D below.

13. 542 U.S. 466 (2004).

Treatment Act, which held that those held in Guantánamo shall not have access to federal courts via a writ of habeas corpus; they must go through military commissions and then seek review in the District of Columbia Circuit.[14] In Hamdan v. Rumsfeld, the Supreme Court held that this provision applies only prospectively, not retroactively to those petitions that already were pending in federal court at the time that the law was enacted.[15] In the fall of 2006, Congress responded by enacting the Military Commissions Act of 2006, which makes clear that the restrictions on habeas corpus in the Detainee Treatment Act apply retroactively.[16] In Boumediene v. Bush, the Supreme Court declared this unconstitutional as an impermissible suspension of the writ of habeas corpus.[17] But since then, those in Guantanamo had little success, especially in the United States Court of Appeals for the District of Columbia Circuit, and the Supreme Court has denied review in these cases.

These events reflect a deep disagreement over whether federal courts, via habeas corpus, should be available to those held as enemy combatants. The Bush administration and Congress saw habeas corpus review as inconsistent with the war on terrorism. But the Supreme Court viewed habeas corpus review as essential to make sure that no one is detained indefinitely without meaningful due process. Yet, the Court, despite many opportunities, has not taken a case from a Guantanamo detainee since Boumediene was decided in 2008.

Because of the divergence of views concerning habeas corpus for prisoners and for detainees, it is hardly surprising that the law concerning habeas corpus availability has been particularly volatile. No area of federal jurisdiction has changed more dramatically in the last 25 years than habeas corpus. As discussed below, the Court has imposed substantial new obstacles to habeas relief, including generally preventing successive habeas petitions[18] and preventing the use of habeas corpus to develop new rules of constitutional law.[19] Even more dramatically, the Antiterrorism and Effective Death Penalty Act substantially changed many aspects of the law of habeas corpus, including creating a statute of limitations for filing petitions, precluding successive petitions except in very limited circumstances and only with the approval of a United States Court of Appeals, and narrowing the scope of federal court review.[20] In addition, as mentioned above, twice Congress enacted statutes precluding habeas corpus by those held as enemy combatants.

This chapter is divided into three major sections. First, section B considers the major issues that must be addressed in order for a federal court to grant habeas corpus review. Second, section C summarizes key procedural issues

---

14. 119 Stat. 2739, codified at 10 U.S.C. §801.
15. 548 U.S. 557 (2006).
16. Pub. L. No. 109-366, 120 Stat. 2600 (2006).
17. 553 U.S. 723 (2008).
18. McCleskey v. Zant, 499 U.S. 467 (1991), discussed below.
19. Teague v. Lane, 489 U.S. 288 (1989), discussed below.
20. Antiterrorism and Effective Death Penalty Act of 1996, Pub. L. No. 104-132, 110 Stat. 1214.

in habeas corpus litigation. Finally, section D looks at habeas corpus for those held as enemy combatants as part of the war on terrorism.

B.   THE ISSUES THAT MUST BE ADDRESSED IN ORDER FOR A FEDERAL COURT TO GRANT HABEAS CORPUS RELIEF

Federal statutes and Supreme Court interpretation of them have created a number of hurdles that must be overcome in order for a federal court to grant a habeas corpus petition. Although the order of the questions is somewhat arbitrary, a federal court considering a habeas petition must address all of the following issues:

1. Is the habeas petition time barred? The Antiterrorism and Effective Death Penalty Act has created strict time limits for when a habeas petition must be filed. If the petition is untimely, it must be dismissed.
2. Is it a first habeas petition by the individual or is it a successive petition (a second, third, fourth, etc. petition)? If it is a successive petition, it must be dismissed unless the federal court of appeals approves its filing based on finding that the case meets stringent requirements for successive petitions.
3. Has there been exhaustion of state procedures for all claims presented in the habeas petition? If there has not been exhaustion for all claims, then the entire petition must be dismissed.
4. Does the petition rely on an already established rule of criminal procedure, or does it seek recognition of a new rule? If it seeks the recognition of a new rule, the petition must be dismissed unless it is an extraordinary rule that applies retroactively.
5. Is it a claim that can be heard on habeas corpus? Generally, individuals are allowed to relitigate their constitutional claims on habeas, but there is a notable exception: Fourth Amendment claims by state prisoners generally cannot be raised on habeas corpus as long as there was a full and fair hearing in state court.
6. Has there been a procedural default in the sense of a failure to follow the required procedures of the forum, state or federal, in which the person was convicted? For example, were the claims raised in the habeas petition properly raised at trial, or were they defaulted for failure to raise them? If a claim was procedurally defaulted, it must be dismissed unless there is either a showing of good cause for the failure and prejudice to not being heard on habeas or a showing of likely actual innocence.
7. If the claim is heard, can the federal court hold an evidentiary hearing, or is it limited to the record that was in the state court?
8. Can the federal court provide habeas corpus relief? For example, under the provisions of the Antiterrorism and Effective Death Penalty Act, a

federal court may grant habeas corpus relief only if the state court decision is contrary to or an unreasonable application of law clearly established by the Supreme Court.

These eight questions might be thought of as filters, with each question causing a significant number of habeas petitions to be dismissed. Relatively few make it to the last question, and even fewer are granted. This section is organized around these eight questions. These are not the only requirements for habeas corpus. Others are discussed in section C below, such as the requirement that a person be in custody. But these issues certainly are the focus of most habeas corpus litigation in the United States.

1. Is the Petition Time Barred?

Until 1996, the federal statutes concerning habeas corpus review did not prescribe any time limit within which petitions must be filed.[21] The habeas corpus rules that went into effect in 1977 provided that a petition may be dismissed if the state is prejudiced by a delay in the filing of the petition, "unless the petitioner shows that it is based on grounds of which he could not have had knowledge by the exercise of reasonable diligence before the circumstances prejudicial to the state occurred."[22]

The Antiterrorism and Effective Death Penalty Act, enacted in 1996, imposes a one-year statute of limitations on the filing of habeas petitions. Section 101 of the act provides, "A 1-year period of limitation shall apply to an application for a writ of habeas corpus by a person in custody pursuant to the judgment of a state court."[23] Section 101 also states that "[t]he time during which a properly filed application for state post-conviction or other collateral review with respect to the pertinent judgment or claim is pending shall not be counted toward any period of limitation under this subsection."[24]

The act also provides that in capital cases a six-month statute of limitations applies if it is determined that a state has established an adequate system for providing attorneys for post-conviction proceedings.[25] In Calderon v. Ashmus, the Supreme Court unanimously dismissed as nonjusticiable a

---

21. *See, e.g.*, United States v. Smith, 331 U.S. 469, 475 (1947). Indeed, prior to the act's going into effect, the Court ruled that there was no time limit on first habeas petitions, and they could be filed even on the day of execution. Lonchar v. Thomas, 517 U.S. 314 (1996).

22. 28 U.S.C. §2254, Rule 9(a).

23. 28 U.S.C. §2244.

24. *Id.*

25. The act states that the shorter statute of limitations applies "if a State establishes by statute, rules of its court of last resort, or by another agency authorized by state law, a mechanism for the appointment, compensation, and payment of reasonable litigation expenses of competent counsel in State post-conviction proceedings brought by indigent prisoners whose capital convictions and sentences have been upheld on direct appeal to the court of last resort in the State or have otherwise become final for State law purposes." 28 U.S.C. §2261.

request for a declaratory judgment by death-row inmates that California was not in compliance with the act.[26] *Calderon* means that inmates cannot seek a system-wide determination of whether a state is in compliance with the act; rather, in each case, the issue must be raised and litigated.

The crucial issue in habeas litigation frequently is whether there was tolling of the statute of limitations. One key aspect of this is whether there is tolling while a habeas petition is pending in federal court. If a state prisoner files a habeas corpus petition in federal court that is then dismissed, is the time that it was pending counted toward the statute of limitations for the habeas petition? The Supreme Court addressed this in Duncan v. Walker, 533 U.S. 167 (2001). Justice O'Connor, writing for the Court, held that the statutory language in the act provided that the statute of limitations was tolled while a prisoner was seeking collateral relief in state court under state law but not while a habeas petition was pending in federal court.[27]

Justice O'Connor wrote:

> To begin with, Congress placed the word "State" before "post-conviction or other collateral review" without specifically naming any kind of "Federal" review. The essence of respondent's position is that Congress used the phrase "other collateral review" to incorporate federal habeas petitions into the class of applications for review that toll the limitation period. But a comparison of the text of §2244(d)(2) with the language of other AEDPA provisions supplies strong evidence that, had Congress intended to include federal habeas petitions within the scope of §2244(d)(2), Congress would have mentioned "Federal" review expressly. In several other portions of AEDPA, Congress specifically used both the words "State" and "Federal" to denote state and federal proceedings. For example, 28 U.S.C. §2254(i) provides: "The ineffectiveness or incompetence of counsel during Federal or State collateral post-conviction proceedings shall not be a ground for relief in a proceeding arising under section 2254."
>
> Section 2244(d)(2), by contrast, employs the word "State," but not the word "Federal," as a modifier for "review." It is well settled that "[w]here Congress includes particular language in one section of a statute but omits it in another section of the same Act, it is generally presumed that Congress acts intentionally and purposely in the disparate inclusion or exclusion." We find no likely explanation for Congress' omission of the word "Federal" in §2244(d)(2) other than that Congress did not intend properly filed applications for federal review to toll the limitation period. It would be anomalous, to say the least, for Congress to usher in federal review under the generic rubric of "other collateral review" in a statutory provision that refers expressly to "State" review, while denominating expressly both "State" and "Federal" proceedings in other parts of the same statute. The anomaly is underscored by the fact that the words "State" and "Federal" are likely to be of no small import when Congress drafts a statute that governs federal collateral review of state court judgments.

---

26. 523 U.S. 740 (1998).

27. Also, in Lawrence v. Florida, 549 U.S. 327 (2007), the Court considered whether there is tolling — that is, whether the statute of limitations clock stops running — while a petition for a writ of certiorari is pending in the Supreme Court seeking review of a state court's denial of relief in collateral proceedings. In other words, while a state habeas corpus petition is pending, there is tolling of the statute of limitations; does that include the time while certiorari is being sought in the Supreme Court of the state court's decision? The Supreme Court, 5-4, held that there was not tolling.

Justice Stevens, in an opinion concurring and concurring in the judgment, expressed concern that the majority's holding could lead to tremendous unfairness. Imagine a state prisoner who files an immediate habeas petition in federal court after completion of the state proceedings, but the federal court waits 13 months before dismissing the petition for failure to adequately exhaust state remedies. The entire year of the statute of limitations has expired because there is no tolling while the case was pending in federal court. Justice Stevens explained:

> This possibility is not purely theoretical. A Justice Department study indicates that 63% of all habeas petitions are dismissed, and 57% of those are dismissed for failure to exhaust state remedies. And it can take courts a significant amount of time to dispose of even those petitions that are not addressed on the merits; on the average, district courts took 268 days to dismiss petitions on procedural grounds. Thus, if the words "other collateral review" do not include federal collateral review, a large group of federal habeas petitioners, seeking to return to federal court after subsequent state-court rejection of an unexhausted claim, may find their claims time barred. Moreover, because district courts vary substantially in the time they take to rule on habeas petitions, two identically situated prisoners can receive opposite results. If Prisoner A and Prisoner B file mixed petitions in different district courts six months before the federal limitations period expires, and the court takes three months to dismiss Prisoner A's petition, but seven months to dismiss Prisoner B's petition, Prisoner A will be able to return to federal court after exhausting state remedies, but Prisoner B — due to no fault of his own — may not.

Justice Stevens suggested that the solution would be to allow federal courts to use equitable tolling to preserve the ability of the habeas petitioner to have access to the federal court. He wrote:

> [N]either the Court's narrow holding, nor anything in the text or legislative history of AEDPA, precludes a federal court from deeming the limitations period tolled for such a petition as a matter of equity. The Court's opinion does not address a federal court's ability to toll the limitations period apart from §2244(d)(2). Furthermore, a federal court might very well conclude that tolling is appropriate based on the reasonable belief that Congress could not have intended to bar federal habeas review for petitioners who invoke the court's jurisdiction within the 1-year interval prescribed by AEDPA.

In Holland v. Florida, the Supreme Court held that equitable tolling, as suggested by Justice Stevens, is permissible.

HOLLAND v. FLORIDA
560 U.S. 631 (2010)

Justice BREYER delivered the opinion of the Court.

We here decide that the timeliness provision in the federal habeas corpus statute is subject to equitable tolling. See Antiterrorism and Effective Death

Penalty Act of 1996 (AEDPA). We also consider its application in this case. In the Court of Appeals' view, when a petitioner seeks to excuse a late filing on the basis of his attorney's unprofessional conduct, that conduct, even if it is "negligent" or "grossly negligent," cannot "rise to the level of egregious attorney misconduct" that would warrant equitable tolling unless the petitioner offers "proof of bad faith, dishonesty, divided loyalty, mental impairment or so forth." In our view, this standard is too rigid.

I

AEDPA states that "[a] 1-year period of limitation shall apply to an application for a writ of habeas corpus by a person in custody pursuant to the judgment of a State court." It also says that "[t]he time during which a properly filed application for State post-conviction . . . review" is "pending shall not be counted" against the 1-year period.

On January 19, 2006, Albert Holland filed a *pro se* habeas corpus petition in the Federal District Court for the Southern District of Florida. Both Holland (the petitioner) and the State of Florida (the respondent) agree that, unless equitably tolled, the statutory limitations period applicable to Holland's petition expired approximately five weeks before the petition was filed. Holland asked the District Court to toll the limitations period for equitable reasons. We shall set forth in some detail the record facts that underlie Holland's claim.

In 1997, Holland was convicted of first-degree murder and sentenced to death. The Florida Supreme Court affirmed that judgment. On *October 1, 2001*, this Court denied Holland's petition for certiorari. And on that date — the date that our denial of the petition ended further direct review of Holland's conviction — the 1-year AEDPA limitations clock began to run.

Thirty-seven days later, on *November 7, 2001*, Florida appointed attorney Bradley Collins to represent Holland in all state and federal postconviction proceedings. By *September 19, 2002* — 316 days after his appointment and 12 days before the 1-year AEDPA limitations period expired — Collins, acting on Holland's behalf, filed a motion for postconviction relief in the state trial court. That filing automatically stopped the running of the AEDPA limitations period, with, as we have said, 12 days left on the clock.

For the next three years, Holland's petition remained pending in the state courts. During that time, Holland wrote Collins letters asking him to make certain that all of his claims would be preserved for any subsequent federal habeas corpus review. Collins wrote back, stating, "I would like to reassure you that we are aware of state-time limitations and federal exhaustion requirements." He also said that he would "presen[t] . . . to the . . . federal courts" any of Holland's claims that the state courts denied.

In mid-May 2003 the state trial court denied Holland relief, and Collins appealed that denial to the Florida Supreme Court. Almost two years later, in February 2005, the Florida Supreme Court heard oral argument in the case. But during that 2-year period, relations between Collins and Holland began to break down. Indeed, between April 2003 and January 2006, Collins communicated with Holland only three times—each time by letter.

Holland, unhappy with this lack of communication, twice wrote to the Florida Supreme Court, asking it to remove Collins from his case. In the second letter, filed on June 17, 2004, he said that he and Collins had experienced "a complete breakdown in communication." The State responded that Holland could not file any *pro se* papers with the court while he was represented by counsel, including papers seeking new counsel. The Florida Supreme Court agreed and denied Holland's requests.

Collins argued Holland's appeal before the Florida Supreme Court on February 10, 2005. Shortly thereafter, Holland wrote to Collins emphasizing the importance of filing a timely petition for habeas corpus in federal court once the Florida Supreme Court issued its ruling.

Five months later, in November 2005, the Florida Supreme Court affirmed the lower court decision denying Holland relief. Three weeks after that, on *December 1, 2005*, the court issued its mandate, making its decision final. At that point, the AEDPA federal habeas clock again began to tick—with 12 days left on the 1-year meter. Twelve days later, on December 13, 2005, Holland's AEDPA time limit expired.

Four weeks after the AEDPA time limit expired, on January 9, 2006, Holland, still unaware of the Florida Supreme Court ruling issued in his case two months earlier, wrote Collins [again].

Nine days later, on January 18, 2006, Holland, working in the prison library, learned for the first time that the Florida Supreme Court had issued a final determination in his case and that its mandate had issued—five weeks prior. He immediately wrote out his own *pro se* federal habeas petition and mailed it to the Federal District Court for the Southern District of Florida the next day.

After considering the briefs, the Federal District Court held that the facts did not warrant equitable tolling and that consequently Holland's petition was untimely. On appeal, the Eleventh Circuit agreed with the District Court that Holland's habeas petition was untimely.

II

We have not decided whether AEDPA's statutory limitations period may be tolled for equitable reasons. Now, like all 11 Courts of Appeals that have considered the question, we hold that §2244(d) is subject to equitable tolling in appropriate cases.

We base our conclusion on the following considerations. First, the AEDPA "statute of limitations defense . . . is not 'jurisdictional.'" It does not set forth "an inflexible rule requiring dismissal whenever" its "clock has run." We have previously made clear that a nonjurisdictional federal statute of limitations is normally subject to a "rebuttable presumption" in *favor* "of equitable tolling."

In the case of AEDPA, the presumption's strength is reinforced by the fact that "'equitable principles'" have traditionally "'governed'" the substantive law of habeas corpus, for we will "not construe a statute to displace courts' traditional equitable authority absent the 'clearest command.' "

[F]inally, we disagree with respondent that equitable tolling undermines AEDPA's basic purposes. We recognize that AEDPA seeks to eliminate delays in the federal habeas review process. But AEDPA seeks to do so without undermining basic habeas corpus principles and while seeking to harmonize the new statute with prior law, under which a petition's timeliness was always determined under equitable principles. When Congress codified new rules governing this previously judicially managed area of law, it did so without losing sight of the fact that the "writ of habeas corpus plays a vital role in protecting constitutional rights." It did not seek to end every possible delay at all costs. The importance of the Great Writ, the only writ explicitly protected by the Constitution, Art. I, §9, cl. 2, along with congressional efforts to harmonize the new statute with prior law, counsels hesitancy before interpreting AEDPA's statutory silence as indicating a congressional intent to close courthouse doors that a strong equitable claim would ordinarily keep open.

III

We have previously made clear that a "petitioner" is "entitled to equitable tolling" only if he shows "(1) that he has been pursuing his rights diligently, and (2) that some extraordinary circumstance stood in his way" and prevented timely filing. In this case, the "extraordinary circumstances" at issue involve an attorney's failure to satisfy professional standards of care. The Court of Appeals held that, where that is so, even attorney conduct that is "grossly negligent" can never warrant tolling absent "bad faith, dishonesty, divided loyalty, mental impairment or so forth on the lawyer's part." But in our view, the Court of Appeals' standard is too rigid.

We have said that courts of equity "must be governed by rules and precedents no less than the courts of law." But we have also made clear that often the "exercise of a court's equity powers . . . must be made on a case-by-case basis." In emphasizing the need for "flexibility," for avoiding "mechanical rules," we have followed a tradition in which courts of equity have sought to "relieve hardships which, from time to time, arise from a hard and fast adherence" to more absolute legal rules, which, if strictly applied, threaten the "evils of archaic rigidity." The "flexibility" inherent in "equitable procedure" enables courts "to meet new situations [that] demand equitable intervention, and to accord all the relief necessary to correct . . . particular injustices." Taken together, these cases recognize that courts of equity can and do draw upon decisions made in other similar cases for guidance. Such courts exercise judgment in light of prior precedent, but with awareness of the fact that specific circumstances, often hard to predict in advance, could warrant special treatment in an appropriate case.

In short, no pre-existing rule of law or precedent demands a rule like the one set forth by the Eleventh Circuit in this case. That rule is difficult to reconcile with more general equitable principles in that it fails to recognize that, at least sometimes, professional misconduct that fails to meet the Eleventh Circuit's standard could nonetheless amount to egregious behavior and create an extraordinary circumstance that warrants equitable tolling. And, given the long history of judicial application of equitable tolling, courts can easily find precedents that can guide their judgments. Several lower courts have specifically held that unprofessional attorney conduct may, in certain circumstances, prove "egregious" and can be "extraordinary" even though the conduct in question may not satisfy the Eleventh Circuit's rule.

We have previously held that "a garden variety claim of excusable neglect," such as a simple "miscalculation" that leads a lawyer to miss a filing deadline, does not warrant equitable tolling. But the case before us does not involve, and we are not considering, a "garden variety claim" of attorney negligence. Rather, the facts of this case present far more serious instances of attorney misconduct. And, as we have said, although the circumstances of a case must be "extraordinary" before equitable tolling can be applied, we hold that such circumstances are not limited to those that satisfy the test that the Court of Appeals used in this case.

IV

The record facts that we have set forth in Part I of this opinion suggest that this case may well be an "extraordinary" instance in which petitioner's attorney's conduct constituted far more than "garden variety" or "excusable neglect." Here, Collins failed to file Holland's federal petition on time despite Holland's many letters that repeatedly emphasized the importance of his doing so. Collins apparently did not do the research necessary to find out the proper filing date, despite Holland's letters that went so far as to identify the applicable legal rules. Collins failed to inform Holland in a timely manner about the crucial fact that the Florida Supreme Court had decided his case, again despite Holland's many pleas for that information. And Collins failed to communicate with his client over a period of years, despite various pleas from Holland that Collins respond to his letters. And in this case, the failures seriously prejudiced a client who thereby lost what was likely his single opportunity for federal habeas review of the lawfulness of his imprisonment and of his death sentence.

We do not state our conclusion in absolute form, however, because more proceedings may be necessary. And we also recognize the prudence, when faced with an "equitable, often fact-intensive" inquiry, of allowing the lower courts "to undertake it in the first instance." Thus, because we conclude that the District Court's determination must be set aside, we leave it to the Court of Appeals to determine whether the facts in this record entitle Holland to equitable tolling, or whether further proceedings, including an evidentiary hearing, might indicate that respondent should prevail.

Justice ALITO, concurring in part and concurring in the judgment.

Although I agree that the Court of Appeals applied the *wrong* standard, I think that the majority does not do enough to explain the *right* standard.

It is of course true that equitable tolling requires "extraordinary circumstances," but that conclusory formulation does not provide much guidance to lower courts charged with reviewing the many habeas petitions filed every year. I therefore write separately to set forth my understanding of the principles governing the availability of equitable tolling in cases involving attorney misconduct.

"Generally, a litigant seeking equitable tolling bears the burden of establishing two elements: (1) that he has been pursuing his rights diligently, and (2) that some extraordinary circumstance stood in his way." The dispute in this case concerns whether and when attorney misconduct amounts to an "extraordinary circumstance" that stands in a petitioner's way and prevents the petitioner from filing a timely petition. I agree with the majority that it is not practical to attempt to provide an exhaustive compilation of the kinds of situations in which attorney misconduct may provide a basis for equitable tolling. In my view, however, it is useful to note that several broad principles may be distilled from this Court's precedents.

First, our prior cases make it abundantly clear that attorney negligence is not an extraordinary circumstance warranting equitable tolling. Second, the mere fact that a missed deadline involves "gross negligence" on the part of counsel does not by itself establish an extraordinary circumstance. [T]he principal rationale for disallowing equitable tolling based on ordinary attorney miscalculation is that the error of an attorney is constructively attributable to the client and thus is not a circumstance beyond the litigant's control. That rationale plainly applies regardless whether the attorney error in question involves ordinary or gross negligence.

Allowing equitable tolling in cases involving *gross* rather than *ordinary* attorney negligence would not only fail to make sense in light of our prior cases; it would also be impractical in the extreme. Missing the statute of limitations will generally, if not always, amount to negligence, and it has been aptly said that gross negligence is ordinary negligence with a vituperative epithet added. Therefore, if gross negligence may be enough for equitable tolling, there will be a basis for arguing that tolling is appropriate in almost every counseled case involving a missed deadline. This would not just impose a severe burden on the district courts; it would also make the availability of tolling turn on the highly artificial distinction between gross and ordinary negligence. That line would be hard to administer, would needlessly consume scarce judicial resources, and would almost certainly yield inconsistent and often unsatisfying results.

Finally, it is worth noting that a rule that distinguishes between ordinary and gross attorney negligence for purposes of the equitable tolling analysis would have demonstrably "inequitable" consequences. For example, it is hard to see why a habeas petitioner should be effectively penalized just because his counsel was negligent rather than grossly negligent, or why the State should be penalized just because petitioner's counsel was grossly negligent rather than moderately negligent. Regardless of how one characterizes counsel's deficient performance in such cases, the petitioner is not personally at fault for the untimely filing, attorney error is a but-for cause of the late filing, and the governmental interest in enforcing the statutory limitations period is the same.

Although attorney negligence, however styled, does not provide a basis for equitable tolling, the AEDPA statute of limitations may be tolled if the missed deadline results from attorney misconduct that is not constructively attributable to the petitioner. In this case, petitioner alleges facts that amount to such misconduct. In particular, he alleges that his attorney essentially "abandoned" him, as evidenced by counsel's near-total failure to communicate with petitioner or to respond to petitioner's many inquiries and requests over a period of several years.

If true, petitioner's allegations would suffice to establish extraordinary circumstances beyond his control. Common sense dictates that a litigant cannot be held constructively responsible for the conduct of an attorney who is not operating as his agent in any meaningful sense of that word. That is particularly so if the litigant's reasonable efforts to terminate the attorney's representation have been thwarted by forces wholly beyond the petitioner's control. The Court of Appeals apparently did not consider petitioner's abandonment argument or assess whether the State improperly prevented petitioner from either obtaining new representation or assuming the responsibility of representing himself. Accordingly, I agree with the majority that the appropriate disposition is to reverse and remand so that the lower courts may apply the correct standard to the facts alleged here.

Justice SCALIA, with whom Justice THOMAS joins, dissenting.

The Antiterrorism and Effective Death Penalty Act of 1996 (AEDPA), establishes a 1-year limitations period for state prisoners to seek federal habeas relief, subject to several specific exceptions. 28 U.S.C. §2244(d). In my view §2244(d) leaves no room for equitable exceptions, and Holland could not qualify even if it did.

I

If §2244(d) merely created a limitations period for federal habeas applicants, I agree that applying equitable tolling would be appropriate.

But §2244(d) does much more than that, establishing a detailed scheme regarding the filing deadline that addresses an array of contingencies.

The question, therefore, is not whether §2244(d)'s time bar is subject to tolling, but whether it is consistent with §2244(d) for federal courts to toll the time bar for *additional* reasons beyond those Congress included.

In my view it is not. It is fair enough to infer, when a statute of limitations says nothing about equitable tolling, that Congress did not displace the default rule. But when Congress has *codified* that default rule and specified the instances where it applies, we have no warrant to extend it to other cases. Unless the Court believes §2244(d) contains an implicit, across-the-board exception that subsumes (and thus renders unnecessary) §2244(d)(1)(B)-(D) and (d)(2), it must rely on the untenable assumption that when Congress enumerated the events that toll the limitations period—with no indication the list is merely illustrative—it implicitly authorized courts to add others as they see fit. We should assume the opposite: that by specifying situations in which an equitable principle applies to a specific requirement, Congress has displaced courts' discretion to develop ad hoc exceptions.

II

Even if §2244(d) left room for equitable tolling in some situations, tolling surely should not excuse the delay here. Where equitable tolling is available, we have held that a litigant is entitled to it only if he has diligently pursued his rights and—the requirement relevant here—if " 'some extraordinary circumstance stood in his way.' " Because the attorney is the litigant's agent, the attorney's acts (or failures to act) within the scope of the representation are treated as those of his client, and thus such acts (or failures to act) are necessarily not extraordinary circumstances.

To be sure, the rule that an attorney's acts and oversights are attributable to the client is relaxed where the client has a constitutional right to effective assistance of counsel. Where a State is constitutionally obliged to provide an attorney but fails to provide an effective one, the attorney's failures that fall below the standard set forth in *Strickland v. Washington* (1984), are chargeable to the State, not to the prisoner. But where the client has no right to counsel—which in habeas proceedings he does not—the rule holding him responsible for his attorney's acts applies with full force. Thus, when a state habeas petitioner's appeal is filed too late because of attorney error, the petitioner is out of luck—no less than if he had proceeded *pro se* and neglected to file the appeal himself.

Congress could, of course, have included errors by state-appointed habeas counsel as a basis for delaying the limitations period, but it did not. Nor was that an oversight: Section 2244(d)(1)(B) expressly allows tolling for state-created impediments that prevent a prisoner from filing his application, but *only if* the impediment violates the Constitution or federal law.

The Court's impulse to intervene when a litigant's lawyer has made mistakes is understandable; the temptation to tinker with technical rules to achieve what appears a just result is often strong, especially when the client faces a capital sentence. But the Constitution does not empower federal courts to rewrite, in the name of equity, rules that Congress has made. Endowing unelected judges with that power is irreconcilable with our system, for it "would literally place the whole rights and property of the community under the arbitrary will of the judge," arming him with "a despotic and sovereign authority." The danger is doubled when we disregard our own precedent, leaving only our own consciences to constrain our discretion. Because both the statute and *stare decisis* foreclose Holland's claim, I respectfully dissent.

Another mechanism for preventing injustice from the lack of tolling discussed by some of the justices in Duncan v. Walker is "stay and abeyance"—federal courts keep the case on their docket, stay the proceedings, and allow the petitioner to return to exhaust state court proceedings. When they are completed, the petitioner then can resume the federal court habeas proceedings without needing to be concerned about the statute of limitations. However, subsequent to Duncan v. Walker, in Rhines v. Weber, 544 U.S. 269 (2005), the Supreme Court held that stay and abeyance should be used only in exceptional circumstances. The Court, in an opinion by Justice O'Connor, concluded that "[d]istrict courts do ordinarily have authority to issue stays, where such a stay would be a proper exercise of discretion. AEDPA does not deprive district courts of that authority."

But the Court then went on to declare:

> [S]tay and abeyance should be available only in limited circumstances. Because granting a stay effectively excuses a petitioner's failure to present his claims first to the state courts, stay and abeyance is only appropriate when the district court determines there was good cause for the petitioner's failure to exhaust his claims first in state court. Moreover, even if a petitioner had good cause for that failure, the district court would abuse its discretion if it were to grant him a stay when his unexhausted claims are plainly meritless. Even where stay and abeyance is appropriate, the district court's discretion in structuring the stay is limited by the timeliness concerns reflected in AEDPA. A mixed petition should not be stayed indefinitely. Without time limits, petitioners could frustrate AEDPA's goal of finality by dragging out indefinitely their federal habeas review. Thus, district courts should place reasonable time limits on a petitioner's trip to state court and back. And if a petitioner engages in abusive litigation tactics or intentional delay, the district court should not grant him a stay at all.

Still, it is crucial to note that Rhines v. Weber does expressly authorize the stay and abeyance procedure. Indeed, the Court concluded its opinion by declaring:

> On the other hand, it likely would be an abuse of discretion for a district court to deny a stay and to dismiss a mixed petition if the petitioner had good cause for his failure to exhaust, his unexhausted claims are potentially meritorious, and there is no indication that the petitioner engaged in intentionally dilatory litigation tactics. In such circumstances, the district court should stay, rather than dismiss, the mixed petition.

Most recently, the Court has recognized one other exception from the statute of limitations: showing of actual innocence by the habeas petitioner.

McQUIGGIN v. PERKINS

133 S. Ct. 1924 (2013)

Justice GINSBURG delivered the opinion of the Court.

This case concerns the "actual innocence" gateway to federal habeas review applied in Schlup v. Delo (1995), and further explained in House v. Bell (2006). In those cases, a convincing showing of actual innocence enabled habeas petitioners to overcome a procedural bar to consideration of the merits of their constitutional claims. Here, the question arises in the context of 28 U.S.C. §2244(d)(1), the statute of limitations on federal habeas petitions prescribed in the Antiterrorism and Effective Death Penalty Act of 1996. Specifically, if the petitioner does not file her federal habeas petition, at the latest, within one year of "the date on which the factual predicate of the claim or claims presented could have been discovered through the exercise of due diligence," §2244(d)(1)(D), can the time bar be overcome by a convincing showing that she committed no crime?

We hold that actual innocence, if proved, serves as a gateway through which a petitioner may pass whether the impediment is a procedural bar, as it was in *Schlup* and *House,* or, as in this case, expiration of the statute of limitations. We caution, however, that tenable actual-innocence gateway pleas are rare: "[A] petitioner does not meet the threshold requirement unless he persuades the district court that, in light of the new evidence, no juror, acting reasonably, would have voted to find him guilty beyond a reasonable doubt." And in making an assessment of the kind *Schlup* envisioned, "the timing of the [petition]" is a factor bearing on the "reliability of th[e] evidence" purporting to show actual innocence.

Our opinion clarifies that a federal habeas court, faced with an actual-innocence gateway claim, should count unjustifiable delay on a habeas petitioner's part, not as an absolute barrier to relief, but as a factor in determining whether actual innocence has been reliably shown.

I

On March 4, 1993, respondent Floyd Perkins attended a party in Flint, Michigan, in the company of his friend, Rodney Henderson, and an acquaintance, Damarr Jones. The three men left the party together. Henderson was later discovered on a wooded trail, murdered by stab wounds to his head.

Perkins was charged with the murder of Henderson. At trial, Jones was the key witness for the prosecution. He testified that Perkins alone committed the murder while Jones looked on.

Chauncey Vaughn, a friend of Perkins and Henderson, testified that, prior to the murder, Perkins had told him he would kill Henderson, and that Perkins later called Vaughn, confessing to his commission of the crime. A third witness, Torriano Player, also a friend of both Perkins and Henderson, testified that Perkins told him, had he known how Player felt about Henderson, he would not have killed Henderson.

Perkins, testifying in his own defense, offered a different account of the episode. He testified that he left Henderson and Jones to purchase cigarettes at a convenience store. When he exited the store, Perkins related, Jones and Henderson were gone. Perkins said that he then visited his girlfriend. About an hour later, Perkins recalled, he saw Jones standing under a streetlight with blood on his pants, shoes, and plaid coat.

The jury convicted Perkins of first-degree murder. He was sentenced to life in prison without the possibility of parole on October 27, 1993. The Michigan Court of Appeals affirmed Perkins' conviction and sentence, and the Michigan Supreme Court denied Perkins leave to appeal on January 31, 1997. Perkins' conviction became final on May 5, 1997.

Under the Antiterrorism and Effective Death Penalty Act of 1996 (AEDPA), 110 Stat. 1214, a state prisoner ordinarily has one year to file a federal petition for habeas corpus, starting from "the date on which the judgment became final by the conclusion of direct review or the expiration of the time for seeking such review." 28 U.S.C. §2244(d)(1)(A). If the petition alleges newly discovered evidence, however, the filing deadline is one year from "the date on which the factual predicate of the claim or claims presented could have been discovered through the exercise of due diligence." §2244(d)(1)(D).

Perkins filed his federal habeas corpus petition on June 13, 2008, more than 11 years after his conviction became final. Under Sixth Circuit precedent, the District Court stated, "a habeas petitioner who demonstrates a credible claim of actual innocence based on new evidence may, in exceptional circumstances, be entitled to equitable tolling of habeas limitations." But Perkins had not established exceptional circumstances, the District Court determined. In any event, the District Court observed, equitable tolling requires diligence and Perkins "ha[d] failed utterly to demonstrate the necessary diligence in exercising his rights." Alternatively, the District Court found that Perkins had failed to meet the strict standard by which pleas of actual innocence are measured: He had not shown that, taking account of all the evidence, "it is more likely than not that no reasonable juror would have convicted him," or even that the evidence was new.

Perkins appealed the District Court's judgment. Although recognizing that AEDPA's statute of limitations had expired and that Perkins had not diligently pursued his rights, the Sixth Circuit granted a certificate of appealability limited to a single question: Is reasonable diligence a precondition to relying on actual innocence as a gateway to adjudication of a federal habeas petition on the merits?

On consideration of the certified question, the Court of Appeals reversed the District Court's judgment. Adhering to Circuit precedent, the Sixth Circuit held that Perkins' gateway actual-innocence allegations allowed him to present his ineffective-assistance-of-counsel claim as if it were filed on time. On remand, the Court of Appeals instructed, "the [D]istrict [C]ourt [should] fully consider whether Perkins assert[ed] a credible claim of actual innocence."

II

In Holland v. Florida (2010), this Court addressed the circumstances in which a federal habeas petitioner could invoke the doctrine of "equitable tolling." *Holland* held that "a [habeas] petitioner is entitled to equitable tolling only if he shows (1) that he has been pursuing his rights diligently, and (2) that some extraordinary circumstance stood in his way and prevented timely filing." As the courts below comprehended, Perkins does not qualify for equitable tolling. In possession of all three affidavits by July 2002, he waited nearly six years to seek federal postconviction relief.

Perkins, however, asserts not an excuse for filing after the statute of limitations has run. Instead, he maintains that a plea of actual innocence can overcome AEDPA's one-year statute of limitations. He thus seeks an equitable *exception* to §2244(d)(1), not an extension of the time statutorily prescribed.

Decisions of this Court support Perkins' view of the significance of a convincing actual-innocence claim. We have not resolved whether a prisoner may be entitled to habeas relief based on a freestanding claim of actual innocence. Herrera v. Collins, 506 (1993). We have recognized, however, that a prisoner "otherwise subject to defenses of abusive or successive use of the writ [of habeas corpus] may have his federal constitutional claim considered on the merits if he makes a proper showing of actual innocence." In other words, a credible showing of actual innocence may allow a prisoner to pursue his constitutional claims (here, ineffective assistance of counsel) on the merits notwithstanding the existence of a procedural bar to relief. "This rule, or fundamental miscarriage of justice exception, is grounded in the 'equitable discretion' of habeas courts to see that federal constitutional errors do not result in the incarceration of innocent persons."

We have applied the miscarriage of justice exception to overcome various procedural defaults. These include "successive" petitions asserting previously rejected claims, "abusive" petitions asserting in a second petition claims that could have been raised in a first petition, failure to develop facts in state court, and failure to observe state procedural rules, including filing deadlines.

The miscarriage of justice exception, our decisions bear out, survived AEDPA's passage. These decisions "see[k] to balance the societal interests in finality, comity, and conservation of scarce judicial resources with the individual interest in justice that arises in the extraordinary case." Sensitivity to the injustice of incarcerating an innocent individual should not abate when the impediment is AEDPA's statute of limitations.

The State ties to §2244(d)'s text its insistence that AEDPA's statute of limitations precludes courts from considering late-filed actual-innocence gateway claims. "Section 2244(d)(1)(D)," the State contends, "forecloses any argument that a habeas petitioner has unlimited time to present new evidence in support of a constitutional claim." That is so, the State maintains, because AEDPA prescribes a comprehensive system for determining when its one-year limitations period begins to run.

The State's argument in this regard bears blinders. AEDPA's time limitations apply to the typical case in which no allegation of actual innocence is made. The miscarriage of justice exception, we underscore, applies to a severely confined category: cases in which new evidence shows "it is more likely than not that no reasonable juror would have convicted [the petitioner]." Section 2244(d)(1)(D) is both modestly more stringent (because it requires diligence) and dramatically less stringent (because it requires no showing of innocence). Many petitions that could not pass through the actual-innocence gateway will be timely or not measured by §2244(d)(1)(D)'s triggering provision. That provision, in short, will hardly be rendered superfluous by recognition of the miscarriage of justice exception.

Our reading of the statute is supported by the Court's opinion in *Holland*. "[E]quitable principles have traditionally governed the substantive law of habeas corpus," *Holland* reminded, and affirmed that "we will not construe a statute to displace courts' traditional equitable authority absent the clearest command." The text of §2244(d)(1) contains no clear command countering the courts' equitable authority to invoke the miscarriage of justice exception to overcome expiration of the statute of limitations governing a first federal habeas petition.

III

While we reject the State's argument that habeas petitioners who assert convincing actual-innocence claims must prove diligence to cross a federal court's threshold, we hold that the Sixth Circuit erred to the extent that it eliminated timing as a factor relevant in evaluating the reliability of a petitioner's proof of innocence. To invoke the miscarriage of justice exception to AEDPA's statute of limitations, we repeat, a petitioner "must show that it is more likely than not that no reasonable juror would have convicted him in the light of the new evidence." Unexplained delay in presenting new evidence bears on the determination whether the petitioner has made the requisite showing. Perkins so acknowledges. As we stated in *Schlup*, "[a] court may consider how the timing of the submission and the likely credibility of [a petitioner's] affiants bear on the probable reliability of . . . evidence [of actual innocence]."

We stress once again that the *Schlup* standard is demanding. The gateway should open only when a petition presents "evidence of innocence so strong that a court cannot have confidence in the outcome of the trial unless the court is also satisfied that the trial was free of nonharmless constitutional error."

Justice SCALIA, with whom THE CHIEF JUSTICE and Justice THOMAS join, and with whom Justice ALITO joins as to Parts I, II, and III, dissenting.

The Antiterrorism and Effective Death Penalty Act of 1996 (AEDPA) provides that a "1–year period of limitation shall apply" to a state prisoner's application for a writ of habeas corpus in federal court. 28 U.S.C. §2244(d)(1). The gaping hole in today's opinion for the Court is its failure to answer the crucial question upon which all else depends: What is the source of the Court's power to fashion what it concedes is an "exception" to this clear statutory command?

That question is unanswered because there is no answer. This Court has no such power, and not one of the cases cited by the opinion says otherwise. The Constitution vests legislative power only in Congress, which never enacted the exception the Court creates today. That inconvenient truth resolves this case.

I

"Actual innocence" has, until today, been an exception only to judge-made, prudential barriers to habeas relief, or as a means of channeling judges' statutorily conferred discretion not to apply a procedural bar. Never before have we applied the exception to circumvent a categorical *statutory* bar to relief. We have not done so because we have no power to do so. Where Congress has erected a constitutionally valid barrier to habeas relief, a court *cannot* decline to give it effect.

Because we have no "equitable" power to discard statutory barriers to habeas relief, we cannot simply extend judge-made exceptions to judge-made barriers into the statutory realm. The Court's insupportable leap from judge-made procedural bars to *all* procedural bars, including *statutory* bars, does all the work in its opinion — and there is not a whit of precedential support for it.

The opinion for the Court also trots out post-AEDPA cases to prove the irrelevant point that "[t]he miscarriage of justice exception . . . survived AEDPA's passage." What it ignores, yet again, is that after AEDPA's passage, as before, the exception applied only to *nonstatutory* obstacles to relief.

There are many statutory bars to relief other than statutes of limitations, and we had never (and before today, have never) created an actual-innocence exception to *any* of them. The reason why is obvious: Judicially amending a validly enacted statute in this way is a flagrant breach of the separation of powers.

II

The Court has no qualms about transgressing such a basic principle. It does not even attempt to cloak its act of judicial legislation in the pretense that it is merely construing the statute; indeed, it freely admits that its opinion recognizes an "exception" that the statute does not contain. And it dismisses, with a series of transparent non sequiturs, Michigan's overwhelming textual argument that the statute provides no such exception and envisions none.

The key textual point is that two provisions of §2244, working in tandem, provide a comprehensive path to relief for an innocent prisoner who has newly discovered evidence that supports his constitutional claim. Section 2244(d)(1)(D) gives him a fresh year in which to file, starting on "the date on which the factual predicate of the claim or claims presented could have been discovered through the exercise of due diligence," while §2244(b)(2)(B) lifts the bar on second or successive petitions. Congress clearly anticipated the scenario of a habeas petitioner with a credible innocence claim and addressed it by crafting an exception (and an exception, by the way, more restrictive than the one that pleases the Court today). One cannot assume that Congress left room for other, judge-made applications of the actual-innocence exception, any more than one would add another gear to a Swiss watch on the theory that the watchmaker surely would have included it if he had thought of it. In both cases, the intricate craftsmanship tells us that the designer arranged things just as he wanted them.

The Court's feeble rejoinder is that its (judicially invented) version of the "actual innocence" exception applies only to a "severely confined category" of cases. Since cases qualifying for the actual-innocence exception will be rare, it explains, the statutory path for innocent petitioners will not "be rendered superfluous." That is no answer at all. That the Court's exception would not *entirely* frustrate Congress's design does not weaken the force of the State's argument that Congress addressed the issue comprehensively and chose to exclude dilatory prisoners like respondent. By the Court's logic, a statute banning littering could simply be deemed to contain an exception for cigarette butts; after all, the statute as thus amended would still cover *something.* That is not how a court respectful of the separation of powers should interpret statutes.

III

Three years ago, in Holland v. Florida (2010), we held that AEDPA's statute of limitations is subject to equitable tolling. That holding offers no support for importing a novel actual-innocence exception. Equitable tolling — extending the deadline for a filing because of an event or circumstance that deprives the filer, through no fault of his own, of the full period accorded by the statute — seeks to vindicate what might be considered the genuine intent of the statute. By contrast, suspending the statute because of a separate policy that the court believes should trump it ("actual innocence") is a blatant overruling. Moreover, the doctrine of equitable tolling is centuries old, and dates from a time when the separation of the legislative and judicial powers was incomplete.

Here, by contrast, the Court has ambushed Congress with an utterly unprecedented (and thus unforeseeable) maneuver. Congressional silence, "while permitting an inference that Congress intended to apply *ordinary* background" principles, "cannot show that it intended to apply an unusual modification of those rules." Because there is no plausible basis for inferring that Congress intended or could have anticipated this exception, its adoption here amounts to a pure judicial override of the statute Congress enacted. "It is wrong for us to reshape" AEDPA "on the very lathe of judge-made habeas jurisprudence it was designed to repair."

* * *

"It would be marvellously inspiring to be able to boast that we have a criminal-justice system in which a claim of 'actual innocence' will always be heard, no matter how late it is brought forward, and no matter how much the failure to bring it forward at the proper time is the defendant's own fault." I suspect it is this vision of perfect justice through abundant procedure that impels the Court today. Of course, "we do not have such a system, and no society unwilling to devote unlimited resources to repetitive criminal litigation ever could." Until today, a district court could dismiss an untimely petition without delving into the underlying facts. From now on, each time an untimely petitioner claims innocence — and how many prisoners asking to be let out of jail do not? — the district court will be obligated to expend limited judicial resources wading into the murky merits of the petitioner's innocence claim. The Court notes "that tenable actual-innocence gateway pleas are rare." That discouraging reality, intended as reassurance, is in truth "the condemnation of the procedure which has encouraged frivolous cases."

It has now been 60 years since Brown v. Allen, in which we struck the Faustian bargain that traded the simple elegance of the common-law writ of habeas corpus for federal-court power to probe the substantive merits of state-court convictions. Even after AEDPA's pass through the Augean stables, no one in a position to observe the functioning of our byzantine federal-habeas system can believe it an efficient device for separating the truly deserving from the multitude of prisoners pressing false claims. "[F]loods of stale, frivolous and repetitious petitions inundate the docket of the lower courts and swell our own. . . . It must prejudice the occasional meritorious applicant to be buried in a flood of worthless ones."

The "inundation" that Justice Jackson lamented in 1953 "consisted of 541" federal habeas petitions filed by state prisoners. By 1969, that number had grown to 7,359. In the year ending on September 30, 2012, 15,929 such petitions were filed. Today's decision piles yet more dead weight onto a postconviction habeas system already creaking at its rusted joints.

2. Is It a First or a Successive Habeas Corpus Petition?

One of the most important changes in habeas corpus law in the 1990s was the imposition, by both the Supreme Court and Congress, of strict bans on successive habeas corpus petitions. As originally drafted, the habeas corpus statutes did not bar individuals from filing repeated petitions presenting the same claims. In the 1948 revisions of the habeas corpus laws, a provision was added excusing a federal court from ruling on a petition when the matter contained in it already had been presented and decided in a prior petition. Specifically, §2244(a) provided that a judge need not entertain a petition for a writ of habeas corpus when the legality of the detention "has been determined by a judge or court of the United States on a prior application for a writ of habeas corpus and the petition presents no new ground not theretofore presented and determined, and the judge or court is satisfied that the ends of justice will not be served by such inquiry."

In McCleskey v. Zant, 499 U.S. 467 (1991), the Supreme Court held that an individual who has previously filed a habeas corpus petition challenging a conviction may file a subsequent petition presenting a new issue only if the individual can show cause and prejudice from the earlier omission of the issue. A criminal defendant, who had been sentenced to death, learned after the filing of his first habeas corpus petition that there had been an informant in his cell. The defendant then filed a second habeas corpus petition arguing that the government's coaching and use of the informant violated Massiah v. United States, 377 U.S. 201 (1964), which held that the government may not, in the absence of counsel, deliberately elicit statements from a person under indictment.

The Supreme Court held that the defendant could not raise the issue in the second habeas petition. The Court explained that the doctrines of abuse of the writ and procedural default implicate "nearly identical concerns flowing from the significant costs of federal habeas corpus review." Thus, the Court concluded that "[w]e have held that a procedural default will be excused only upon a showing of cause and prejudice. . . . We now hold that the same standard applies to determine if there has been an abuse of the writ through inexcusable neglect." The majority concluded that in this case, the petitioner knew enough without the wrongly withheld information that he should have pursued his *Massiah* claim in his earlier habeas petition.

Justice Marshall, joined by Justices Blackmun and Stevens, strongly criticized the decision. Justice Marshall, in dissent, wrote that "[t]oday's decision departs drastically from the norms that inform the proper judicial function. Without even the most casual admission that it is discarding long-standing legal principles, the Court radically redefines the content of the abuse of the writ doctrine." The dissent objected especially to precluding a second habeas petition that was based on information that was not available when the first was filed, precisely because the government wrongly had withheld the information from the defendant.

McCleskey never has been overruled, but from a practical perspective it has been superseded by the ever stricter restrictions on successive petitions contained in the Antiterrorism and Effective Death Penalty Act. Under AEDPA, an individual may file a successive petition only if he or she first obtains permission from the United States Court of Appeals. The act states, "Before a second or successive application permitted by the section is filed in the district court, the applicant shall move in the appropriate court of appeals for an order authorizing the district court to consider the application." 28 U.S.C. §2244(3)(A).

Moreover, the act provides that "[t]he grant or denial of an authorization by a court of appeals to file a second or successive application shall not be appealable and shall not be the subject of a petition for rehearing or for a writ of certiorari." In Felker v. Turpin, 518 U.S. 651 (1996), the Supreme Court upheld the constitutionality of this preclusion of its ability to review court of appeals decisions denying successive petitions. The Court explained that its review was not completely foreclosed because the Court retained the ability to grant habeas corpus petitions in its original jurisdiction. The Court also stressed the broad authority of Congress to control the procedures concerning habeas corpus. Chief Justice Rehnquist, writing for the Court, said, "[W]e have long recognized that the power to award the writ, by any of the courts of the United States must be found in the written law, and we have likewise recognized that judgments about the proper scope of the writ are normally for Congress to make." The Court thus rejected the claim that the restrictions on successive petitions amounted to an unconstitutional suspension of the writ of habeas corpus.

Under the act, a court of appeals may allow a successive petition only in two circumstances. First, a successive petition may be allowed if "the applicant shows that the claim relies on a new rule of constitutional law, made retroactive to cases on collateral review by the Supreme Court that was previously unavailable." Alternatively, the petition may be permitted if "the factual predicate for the claim could not have been discovered previously through the exercise of due diligence and the facts underlying the claim, if proven and viewed in light of the evidence as a whole, would be sufficient to establish by clear and convincing evidence that, but for the constitutional error, no reasonable factfinder would have found the applicant guilty of the underlying offense."

In Tyler v. Cain, below, the Court considered whether a federal court may grant a habeas petition by finding that a Supreme Court decision applies retroactively or whether it requires that the Supreme Court, itself, deem that the rule applies retroactively. In other words, under a prior Supreme Court decision, a conviction was clearly unconstitutional. But could the federal district court and court of appeals provide habeas relief by finding that it was a decision that should be applied retroactively, or did it require an express declaration by the Supreme Court that its decision applied retroactively?

TYLER v. CAIN

533 U.S. 656 (2001)

Justice Thomas delivered the opinion of the Court.

Under Cage v. Louisiana (1990), a jury instruction is unconstitutional if there is a reasonable likelihood that the jury understood the instruction to allow conviction without proof beyond a reasonable doubt. In this case, we must decide whether this rule was "made retroactive to cases on collateral review by the Supreme Court." 28 U.S.C. §2244(b)(2)(A). We hold that it was not.

I

During a fight with his estranged girlfriend in March 1975, petitioner Melvin Tyler shot and killed their 20-day-old daughter. A jury found Tyler guilty of second-degree murder, and his conviction was affirmed on appeal. After sentencing, Tyler assiduously sought postconviction relief. By 1986, he had filed five state petitions, all of which were denied. He next filed a federal habeas petition, which was unsuccessful as well. After this Court's decision in *Cage*, Tyler continued his efforts. Because the jury instruction defining reasonable doubt at Tyler's trial was substantively identical to the instruction condemned in *Cage*, Tyler filed a sixth state postconviction petition, this time raising a *Cage* claim. The State District Court denied relief, and the Louisiana Supreme Court affirmed.

In early 1997, Tyler returned to federal court. Seeking to pursue his *Cage* claim, Tyler moved the United States Court of Appeals for the Fifth Circuit for permission to file a second habeas corpus application, as required by the Antiterrorism and Effective Death Penalty Act of 1996 (AEDPA). The Court of Appeals recognized that it could not grant the motion unless Tyler made "a prima facie showing," §2244(b)(3)(C), that his "claim relies on a new rule of constitutional law, made retroactive to cases on collateral review by the Supreme Court, that was previously unavailable," §2244(b)(2)(A). Finding that Tyler had made the requisite prima facie showing, the Court of Appeals granted the motion, thereby allowing Tyler to file a habeas petition in District Court.

II

AEDPA greatly restricts the power of federal courts to award relief to state prisoners who file second or successive habeas corpus applications. If the prisoner asserts a claim that he has already presented in a previous federal habeas petition, the claim must be dismissed in all cases. §2244(b)(1). And if the prisoner asserts a claim that was not presented in a previous petition, the claim must be dismissed unless it falls within one of two narrow exceptions. One of these exceptions is for claims predicated on newly discovered facts that call into question the accuracy of a guilty verdict. §2244(b)(2)(B). The other is for certain claims relying on new rules of constitutional law. §2244(b)(2)(A).

It is the latter exception that concerns us today. Specifically, §2244(b)(2)(A) covers claims that "rel[y] on a new rule of constitutional law, made retroactive to cases on collateral review by the Supreme Court, that was previously unavailable." This provision establishes three prerequisites to obtaining relief in a second or successive petition: First, the rule on which the claim relies must be a "new rule" of constitutional law; second, the rule must have been "made retroactive to cases on collateral review by the Supreme Court"; and third, the claim must have been "previously unavailable." In this case, the parties ask us to interpret only the second requirement; respondent does not dispute that Cage created a "new rule" that was "previously unavailable." Based on the plain meaning of the text read as a whole, we conclude that "made" means "held" and, thus, the requirement is satisfied only if this Court has held that the new rule is retroactively applicable to cases on collateral review.

A

As commonly defined, "made" has several alternative meanings, none of which is entirely free from ambiguity. See, e.g., Webster's Ninth New Collegiate Dictionary 718-719 (1991) (defining "to make" as "to cause to happen," "to cause to exist, occur or appear," "to lay out and construct," and "to cause to act in a certain way"). Out of context, it may thus be unclear which meaning should apply in §2244(b)(2)(A), and how the term should be understood. We do not, however, construe the meaning of statutory terms in a vacuum. Rather, we interpret the words "in their context and with a view to their place in the overall statutory scheme." In §2244(b)(2)(A), the word "made" falls within a clause that reads as follows: "[A] new rule of constitutional law, made retroactive to cases on collateral review by the Supreme Court." Quite significantly, under this provision, the Supreme Court is the only entity that can "ma[k]e" a new rule retroactive. The new rule becomes retroactive, not by the decisions of the lower court or by the combined action of the Supreme Court and the lower courts, but simply by the action of the Supreme Court.

The only way the Supreme Court can, by itself, "lay out and construct" a rule's retroactive effect, or "cause" that effect "to exist, occur, or appear," is through a holding. The Supreme Court does not "ma[k]e" a rule retroactive when it merely establishes principles of retroactivity and leaves the application of those principles to lower courts. In such an event, any legal conclusion that is derived from the principles is developed by the lower court (or perhaps by a combination of courts), not by the Supreme Court. We thus conclude that a new rule is not "made retroactive to cases on collateral review" unless the Supreme Court holds it to be retroactive.

B

Because "made" means "held" for purposes of §2244(b)(2)(A), it is clear that the *Cage* rule has not been "made retroactive to cases on collateral review by the Supreme Court." *Cage* itself does not hold that it is retroactive. The only holding in *Cage* is that the particular jury instruction violated the Due Process Clause.

Finally, Tyler suggests that, if *Cage* has not been made retroactive to cases on collateral review, we should make it retroactive today. We disagree. Because Tyler's habeas application was his second, the District Court was required to dismiss it unless Tyler showed that this Court already had made *Cage* retroactive. §2244(b)(4) ("A district court shall dismiss any claim presented in a second or successive application that the court of appeals has authorized to be filed unless the applicant shows that the claim satisfies the requirements of this section"). We cannot decide today whether *Cage* is retroactive to cases on collateral review, because that decision would not help Tyler in this case. Any statement on *Cage*'s retroactivity would be dictum, so we decline to comment further on the issue.

Justice O'CONNOR, concurring.

I join the Court's opinion and write separately to explain more fully the circumstances in which a new rule is "made retroactive to cases on collateral review by the Supreme Court." 28 U.S.C. §2244(b)(2)(A).

It is only through the holdings of this Court, as opposed to this Court's dicta and as opposed to the decisions of any other court, that a new rule is "made retroactive . . . by the Supreme Court" within the meaning of §2244(b)(2)(A). The clearest instance, of course, in which we can be said to have "made" a new rule retroactive is where we expressly have held the new rule to be retroactive in a case on collateral review and applied the rule to that case. But, as the Court recognizes, a single case that expressly holds a rule to be retroactive is not a sine qua non for the satisfaction of this statutory provision. This Court instead may "ma[k]e" a new rule retroactive through multiple holdings that logically dictate the retroactivity of the new rule.

The relationship between the conclusion that a new rule is retroactive and the holdings that "ma[k]e" this rule retroactive, however, must be strictly logical — i.e., the holdings must dictate the conclusion and not merely provide principles from which one may conclude that the rule applies retroactively. As the Court observes, "[t]he Supreme Court does not 'ma[k]e' a rule retroactive when it merely establishes principles of retroactivity and leaves the application of those principles to lower courts." The Court instead can be said to have "made" a rule retroactive within the meaning of §2244(b)(2)(A) only where the Court's holdings logically permit no other conclusion than that the rule is retroactive.

Justice BREYER, with whom Justice STEVENS, Justice SOUTER, and Justice GINSBURG join, dissenting.

In Cage v. Louisiana (1990), this Court held that a certain jury instruction violated the Constitution because it inaccurately defined "reasonable doubt," thereby permitting a jury to convict "based on a degree of proof below that required by the Due Process Clause." Here we must decide whether this Court has "made" *Cage* "retroactive to cases on collateral review." I believe that it has.

Insofar as the majority means to suggest that a rule may be sufficiently "new" that it does not apply retroactively but not "new enough" to qualify for the watershed exception, I note only that the cases establishing this exception suggest no such requirement. Rather than focus on the "degree of newness" of a new rule, these decisions emphasize that watershed rules are those that form part of the fundamental requirements of due process.

[T]he most likely consequence of the majority's holding is further procedural complexity. After today's opinion, the only way in which this Court can make a rule such as *Cage*'s retroactive is to repeat its reasoning in a case triggered by a prisoner's filing a first habeas petition (a "second or successive" petition itself being barred by the provision here at issue) or in some other case that presents the issue in a posture that allows such language to have the status of a "holding." Then, after the Court takes the case and says that it meant what it previously said, prisoners could file "second or successive" petitions to take advantage of the now-clearly-made-applicable new rule. We will be required to restate the obvious, case by case, even when we have explicitly said, but not "held," that a new rule is retroactive.

Even this complex route will remain open only if the relevant statute of limitations is interpreted to permit its 1-year filing period to run from the time that this Court has "made" a new rule retroactive, not from the time it initially recognized that new right. See 28 U.S.C. §2244(d)(1)(C) (limitations period runs from "the date on which the constitutional right asserted was initially recognized by the Supreme Court, if the right has been newly recognized by the Supreme Court and made retroactively applicable to cases on collateral review"). Otherwise, the Court's approach will generate not only complexity, along with its attendant risk of confusion, but also serious additional unfairness.

I do not understand the basis for the Court's approach. I fear its consequences. For these reasons, with respect, I dissent.

In Panetti v. Quarterman, 551 U.S. 930 (2007), the Supreme Court considered whether a person facing execution could bring a successive habeas corpus petition on the grounds of mental incompetence to be executed. As Justice Kennedy, who wrote for the majority, explained:

> [T]he Eighth Amendment prohibits a State from carrying out a sentence of death upon a prisoner who is insane. Ford v. Wainwright (1986). The prohibition applies despite a prisoner's earlier competency to be held responsible for committing a crime and to be tried for it. Prior findings of competency do not foreclose a prisoner from proving he is incompetent to be executed because of his present mental condition. Under *Ford*, once a prisoner makes the requisite preliminary showing that his current mental state would bar his execution, the Eighth Amendment, applicable to the States under the Due Process Clause of the Fourteenth Amendment, entitles him to an adjudication to determine his condition.

The Court, by a 5-4 margin, concluded that the bar on successive habeas petitions does not apply to those challenging competence to be executed.

> We conclude, that Congress did not intend the provisions of AEDPA addressing "second or successive" petitions to govern a filing in the unusual posture presented here: a §2254 application raising a *Ford*-based incompetency claim filed as soon as that claim is ripe.
>
> Our conclusion is confirmed when we consider AEDPA's purposes. The statute's design is to "further the principles of comity, finality, and federalism." These purposes, and the practical effects of our holdings, should be considered when interpreting AEDPA. This is particularly so when petitioners "run the risk" under the proposed interpretation of "forever losing their opportunity for any federal review of their unexhausted claims." An empty formality requiring prisoners to file unripe *Ford* claims neither respects the limited legal resources available to the States nor

encourages the exhaustion of state remedies. Instructing prisoners to file premature claims, particularly when many of these claims will not be colorable even at a later date, does not conserve judicial resources, "reduc[e] piecemeal litigation," or "streamlin[e] federal habeas proceedings." And last-minute filings that are frivolous and designed to delay executions can be dismissed in the regular course. The requirement of a threshold preliminary showing, for instance, will, as a general matter, be imposed before a stay is granted or the action is allowed to proceed.

There is, in addition, no argument that petitioner's actions constituted an abuse of the writ, as that concept is explained in our cases. To the contrary, we have confirmed that claims of incompetency to be executed remain unripe at early stages of the proceedings.

In the usual case, a petition filed second in time and not otherwise permitted by the terms of §2244 will not survive AEDPA's "second or successive" bar. There are, however, exceptions. We are hesitant to construe a statute, implemented to further the principles of comity, finality, and federalism, in a manner that would require unripe (and, often, factually unsupported) claims to be raised as a mere formality, to the benefit of no party.

The statutory bar on "second or successive" applications does not apply to a *Ford* claim brought in an application filed when the claim is first ripe. Petitioner's habeas application was properly filed, and the District Court had jurisdiction to adjudicate his claim.

Justice Thomas, writing for the four dissenters, stressed that the statutory language creates no exception for successive petitions based on incompetency to be executed. He wrote:

This case should be simple. Panetti brings a claim under Ford v. Wainwright (1986), that he is incompetent to be executed. Presented for the first time in Panetti's second federal habeas application, this claim undisputedly does not meet the statutory requirements for filing a "second or successive" habeas application. As such, Panetti's habeas application must be dismissed. Ignoring this clear statutory mandate, the Court bends over backwards to allow Panetti to bring his *Ford* claim despite no evidence that his condition has worsened—or even changed—since 1995.

The Antiterrorism and Effective Death Penalty Act of 1996 (AEDPA) requires applicants to receive permission from the court of appeals prior to filing second or successive federal habeas applications. 28 U.S.C. §2244(b)(3). Even if permission is sought, AEDPA requires courts to decline such requests in all but two narrow circumstances. §2244(b)(3)(C); §2244(b)(2). Panetti raised his *Ford* claim for the first time in his second federal habeas application, but he admits that he did not seek authorization from the Court of Appeals and that his claim does not satisfy either of the statutory exceptions. Accordingly, §2244(b) requires dismissal of Panetti's second habeas corpus application.

Requiring that *Ford* claims be included in an initial habeas application would have the added benefit of putting a State on notice that a prisoner intends to challenge his or her competency to be executed. In any event, regardless of whether the Court's concern is justified, judicial economy considerations cannot override AEDPA's plain meaning. Remaining faithful to AEDPA's mandate, I would dismiss Panetti's application as second or successive.

The Court also has considered whether it was an impermissible successive petition if a prisoner prevailed on a first habeas petition, was accorded a new trial, and then sought to file a habeas petition relative to challenge the conviction or sentence from that proceeding. The Court held that this was not a successive petition, and thus the restrictive rules of AEDPA did not apply.

MAGWOOD v. PATTERSON
561 U.S. 320 (2010)

Justice THOMAS delivered the opinion of the Court.

Petitioner Billy Joe Magwood was sentenced to death for murdering a sheriff. After the Alabama courts denied relief on direct appeal and in post-conviction proceedings, Magwood filed an application for a writ of habeas corpus in Federal District Court, challenging both his conviction and his sentence. The District Court conditionally granted the writ as to the sentence, mandating that Magwood either be released or resentenced. The state trial court conducted a new sentencing hearing and again sentenced Magwood to death. Magwood filed an application for a writ of habeas corpus in federal court challenging this new sentence. The District Court once again conditionally granted the writ, finding constitutional defects in the new sentence. The Court of Appeals for the Eleventh Circuit reversed, holding in relevant part that Magwood's challenge to his new death sentence was an unreviewable "second or successive" challenge under 28 U.S.C. §2244(b) because he could have mounted the same challenge to his original death sentence. We granted certiorari, and now reverse. Because Magwood's habeas application challenges a new judgment for the first time, it is not "second or successive" under §2244(b).

I

After a conviction for a drug offense, Magwood served several years in the Coffee County Jail in Elba, Alabama, under the watch of Sheriff C.F. "Neil" Grantham. During his incarceration, Magwood, who had a long history of mental illness, became convinced that Grantham had imprisoned him without cause, and vowed to get even upon his release. Magwood followed through on his threat. On the morning of March 1, 1979, shortly after his release, he parked outside the jail and awaited the sheriff's arrival. When Grantham exited his car, Magwood shot him and fled the scene.

The prosecution asked the jury to find Magwood guilty of aggravated murder as charged in the indictment, and sought the death penalty. Magwood pleaded not guilty by reason of insanity; however, the jury found him guilty of capital murder and imposed the sentence of death based on the aggravation charged in the indictment. In accordance with Alabama law, the trial court reviewed the basis for the jury's decision. Weighing the aggravation against the mitigating factors, the court approved the sentence of death. The Alabama courts affirmed.

Eight days before his scheduled execution, Magwood filed an application for a writ of habeas corpus under 28 U.S.C. §2254, and the District Court granted a stay of execution. After briefing by the parties, the District Court upheld Magwood's conviction but vacated his sentence and conditionally granted the writ based on the trial court's failure to find statutory mitigating circumstances relating to Magwood's mental state.

In response to the conditional writ, the state trial court held a new sentencing proceeding in September 1986. This time, the judge found that Magwood's mental state, as well as his age and lack of criminal history, qualified as statutory mitigating circumstances. As before, the court found that Magwood's capital felony included sufficient aggravation to render him death eligible. The Alabama courts affirmed, and this Court denied certiorari.

In April 1997, Magwood sought leave to file a second or successive application for a writ of habeas corpus challenging his 1981 judgment of conviction. The Court of Appeals denied his request. He simultaneously filed a petition for a writ of habeas corpus challenging his new death sentence, which the District Court conditionally granted. In that petition, Magwood again argued that his sentence was unconstitutional because he did not have fair warning at the time of his offense that his conduct would be sufficient to warrant a death sentence under Alabama law, and that his attorney rendered ineffective assistance during the resentencing proceeding.

We granted certiorari to determine whether Magwood's application challenging his 1986 death sentence, imposed as part of resentencing in response to a conditional writ from the District Court, is subject to the constraints that §2244(b) imposes on the review of "second or successive" habeas applications.

II

This case turns on the meaning of the phrase "second or successive" in §2244(b). More specifically, it turns on when a claim should be deemed to arise in a "second or successive habeas corpus application." If an application is "second or successive," the petitioner must obtain leave from the Court of Appeals before filing it with the district court. The district court must dismiss any claim presented in an authorized second or successive application unless the applicant shows that the claim satisfies certain statutory requirements. Thus, if Magwood's application was "second or successive," the District Court should have dismissed it in its entirety because he failed to obtain the requisite authorization from the Court of Appeals. If, however, Magwood's application was not second or successive, it was not subject to §2244(b) at all, and his fair-warning claim was reviewable (absent procedural default).

The State contends that although §2244(b), as amended by AEDPA, applies the phrase "second or successive" to "application[s]," it "is a claim-focused statute," and "[c]laims, not applications, are barred by

§2244(b)." According to the State, the phrase should be read to reflect a principle that "a prisoner is entitled to one, but only one, full and fair opportunity to wage a collateral attack." The State asserts that under this "one opportunity" rule, Magwood's fair-warning claim was successive because he had an opportunity to raise it in his first application, but did not do so.

Magwood, in contrast, reads §2244(b) to apply only to a "second or successive" application challenging the same state-court *judgment.* According to Magwood, his 1986 resentencing led to a new judgment, and his first application challenging that new judgment cannot be "second or successive" such that §2244(b) would apply. We agree.

We begin with the text. Although Congress did not define the phrase "second or successive," as used to modify "habeas corpus application under section 2254," it is well settled that the phrase does not simply "refe[r] to all §2254 applications filed second or successively in time."

We have described the phrase "second or successive" as a "term of art." To determine its meaning, we look first to the statutory context. The limitations imposed by §2244(b) apply only to a "habeas corpus application under §2254," that is, an "application for a writ of habeas corpus on behalf of a person in custody pursuant to *the judgment* of a State court." The reference to a state-court judgment in §2254(b) is significant because the term "application" cannot be defined in a vacuum. A §2254 petitioner is applying for something: His petition "seeks *invalidation* (in whole or in part) *of the judgment* authorizing the prisoner's confinement." If his petition results in a district court's granting of the writ, "the State may seek a *new* judgment (through a new trial or a new sentencing proceeding)." Thus, both §2254(b)'s text and the relief it provides indicate that the phrase "second or successive" must be interpreted with respect to the judgment challenged.

III

Appearing to recognize that Magwood has the stronger textual argument, the State argues that we should rule based on the statutory purpose. According to the State, a "one opportunity" rule is consistent with the statutory text, and better reflects AEDPA's purpose of preventing piecemeal litigation and gamesmanship.

We are not persuaded. AEDPA uses the phrase "second or successive" to modify "application." The State reads the phrase to modify "claims." We cannot replace the actual text with speculation as to Congress' intent.

The State's reading leads to a second, more fundamental error. Under the State's "one opportunity" rule, the phrase "second or successive" would apply to any claim that the petitioner had a full and fair opportunity to raise in a prior application. And the phrase "second or successive" would *not* apply to a claim that the petitioner did *not* have a full and fair opportunity to raise previously.

This is Magwood's *first* application challenging that intervening judgment. The errors he alleges are *new.* It is obvious to us—and the State does not dispute — that his claim of ineffective assistance at resentencing turns upon new errors. But, according to the State, his fair-warning claim does not, because the state court made the same mistake before. We disagree. An error made a second time is still a new error. That is especially clear here, where the state court conducted a full resentencing and reviewed the aggravating evidence afresh.

For these reasons, we conclude that Magwood's first application challenging his new sentence under the 1986 judgment is not "second or successive" under §2244(b). The Court of Appeals erred by reading §2244(b) to bar review of the fair-warning claim Magwood presented in that application. We do not address whether the fair-warning claim is procedurally defaulted. Nor do we address Magwood's contention that the Court of Appeals erred in rejecting his ineffective-assistance claim by not addressing whether his attorney should have objected under federal law.

Justice KENNEDY, with whom the CHIEF JUSTICE, Justice GINSBURG, and Justice ALITO join, dissenting.

The Court today decides that a state prisoner who succeeds in his first federal habeas petition on a discrete sentencing claim may later file a second petition raising numerous previously unraised claims, even if that petition is an abuse of the writ of habeas corpus. The Court, in my respectful submission, reaches this conclusion by misreading precedents on the meaning of the phrase "second or successive" in the Antiterrorism and Effective Death Penalty Act of 1996 (AEDPA). The Court then rewrites AEDPA's text but refuses to grapple with the logical consequences of its own editorial judgment. The design and purpose of AEDPA is to avoid abuses of the writ of habeas corpus, in recognition of the potential for the writ's intrusive effect on state criminal justice systems. But today's opinion, with considerable irony, is not only a step back from AEDPA protection for States but also a step back even from abuse-of-the-writ principles that were in place before AEDPA. So this respectful dissent becomes necessary.

I

Absent two exceptions that are inapplicable here, the relevant statutory provision in AEDPA provides: "A claim presented in a second or successive habeas corpus application under section 2254 that was not presented in a prior application shall be dismissed. . . ."

The question before the Court is whether petitioner Billy Joe Magwood filed "a second or successive" application by raising a claim in his second habeas petition that he had available and yet failed to raise in his first petition. The term "second or successive" is a habeas "term of art." It incorporates the pre-AEDPA abuse-of-the-writ doctrine. Under that rule, to determine whether an application is "second or successive," a court must look to the substance of the claim the application raises and decide whether the petitioner had a full and fair opportunity to raise the claim in the prior application. Applying this analytical framework puts applications into one of three categories.

First, if the petitioner had a full and fair opportunity to raise the claim in the prior application, a second-in-time application that seeks to raise the same claim is barred as "second or successive." This is consistent with pre-AEDPA cases applying the abuse-of-the-writ doctrine and the bar on "second or successive" applications.

Second, if the petitioner had no fair opportunity to raise the claim in the prior application, a subsequent application raising that claim is not "second or successive," and §2244(b)(2)'s bar does not apply. This can occur where the claim was not yet ripe at the time of the first petition, or where the alleged violation occurred only after the denial of the first petition, such as the State's failure to grant the prisoner parole as required by state law. And to respond to the Court's concern, if the applicant in his second petition raises a claim that he raised in his first petition but the District Court left unaddressed at its own discretion, the second application would not be "second or successive." Reraising a previously unaddressed claim is not abusive by any definition.

Third, a "mixed petition"—raising both abusive and nonabusive claims—would be "second or successive." In that circumstance the petitioner would have to obtain authorization from the court of appeals to proceed with the nonabusive claims. After the court of appeals makes its determination, a district court may consider nonabusive claims that the petitioner had no fair opportunity to present in his first petition and dismiss the abusive claims.

The above principles apply to a situation, like the present one, where the petitioner in his first habeas proceeding succeeds in obtaining a conditional grant of relief, which allows the state court to correct an error that occurred at the original sentencing. Assume, as alleged here, that in correcting the error in a new sentencing proceeding, the state court duplicates a different mistake that also occurred at the first sentencing. The second application is "second or successive" with respect to that claim because the alleged error "could and should have" been raised in the first petition. Put another way, under abuse-of-the-writ principles, a petitioner loses his right to challenge the error by not raising a claim at the first opportunity after his claim becomes ripe. On the other hand, if the petitioner raises a claim in his second habeas petition that could not have been raised in the earlier petition—perhaps because the error occurred for the first time during resentencing—then the application raising the claim is not "second or successive" and §2244(b)(2)'s bar does not apply.

Although the above-cited authorities are adequate to show that the application in this case is "second or successive," it must be noted that no previous case from this Court has dealt with the precise sequence of events here: A petitioner attempts to bring a previously unraised claim after a second resentencing proceeding that followed a grant of federal habeas relief. The conclusion that such an application is barred as "second or successive" unless the claim was previously unavailable is consistent with the approach of every court of appeals that has considered the issue, although some of those cases highlight subtleties that are not relevant under abuse-of-the-writ principles.

In the present case the Court should conclude that Magwood has filed a "second or successive habeas corpus application." In 1983, he filed a first federal habeas petition raising nine claims, including that the trial court improperly failed to consider two mitigating factors when it imposed Magwood's death sentence. The District Court granted Magwood's petition and ordered relief only on the mitigating factor claim. The state trial court then held a new sentencing proceeding, in which it considered all of the mitigating factors and reimposed the death penalty. In 1997, Magwood brought a second habeas petition, this time raising an argument that could have been, but was not, raised in his first petition. The argument was that he was not eligible for the death penalty because he did not have fair notice that his crime rendered him death eligible. There is no reason that Magwood could not have raised the identical argument in his first habeas petition. Because Magwood had a full and fair opportunity to adjudicate his death-eligibility claim in his first petition in 1983, his 1997 petition raising this claim is barred as "second or successive."

II

The Court reaches the opposite result by creating an ill-defined exception to the "second or successive" application bar. The Court concludes that because AEDPA refers to "second or successive" applications rather than "second or successive" claims, the nature of the claims raised in the second application is irrelevant. This is incorrect. [D]eciding whether an application itself is "second or successive" requires looking to the nature of the claim that the application raises to determine whether the petitioner had a full and fair opportunity to raise that claim in his earlier petition.

Failing to consider the nature of the claim when deciding whether an application is barred as "second or successive" raises other difficulties. Consider a second-in-time habeas petition challenging an alleged violation that occurred entirely after the denial of the first petition; for example, a failure to grant a prisoner parole at the time promised him by state law or the unlawful withdrawal of good-time credits. Under the Court's rule, it would appear that a habeas application challenging those alleged violations would be barred as "second or successive" because it would be a second-in-time application challenging custody pursuant to the same judgment. That result would be inconsistent with abuse-of-the-writ principles and might work a suspension of the writ of habeas corpus.

Having unmoored the phrase "second or successive" from its textual and historical underpinnings, the Court creates a new puzzle for itself: If the nature of the claim is not what makes an application "second or successive," then to what should a court look?

The Court's approach disregards AEDPA's " 'principles of comity, finality, and federalism.' " Under the Court's newly created exception to the "second or successive" application bar, a defendant who succeeds on even the most minor and discrete issue relating to his sentencing would be able to raise 25 or 50 new sentencing claims in his second habeas petition, all based on arguments he failed to raise in his first petition. "[I]f reexamination of [a] convictio[n] in the first round of habeas offends federalism and comity, the offense increases when a State must defend its conviction in a second or subsequent habeas proceeding on grounds not even raised in the first petition."

The Court's novel exception would also allow the once-successful petitioner to reraise every argument against a sentence that was rejected by the federal courts during the first round of federal habeas review. Because traditional res judicata principles do not apply to federal habeas proceedings, this would force federal courts to address twice (or thrice, or more) the same claims of error. The State and the victims would have to bear anew the "significant costs of federal habeas corpus review," all because the petitioner previously succeeded on a wholly different, discrete, and possibly unrelated claim.

The Court's suggestion that "[i]t will not take a court long to dispose of such claims where the court has already analyzed the legal issues," misses the point. This reassurance will be cold comfort to overworked state district attorneys, who will now have to waste time and resources writing briefs analyzing dozens of claims that should be barred by abuse-of-the-writ principles. It is difficult to motivate even the most dedicated professionals to do their best work, day after day, when they have to deal with the dispiriting task of responding to previously rejected or otherwise abusive claims. But that is exactly what the Court is mandating, under a statute that was designed to require just the opposite result. If the analysis in this dissent is sound it is to be hoped that the States will document the ill effects of the Court's opinion so that its costs and deficiencies are better understood if this issue, or a related one, can again come before the Court.

The Court's new exception will apply not only to death penalty cases like the present one, where the newly raised claim appears arguably meritorious. It will apply to all federal habeas petitions following a prior successful petition, most of which will not be in death cases and where the abusive claims the Court now permits will wholly lack merit. And, in this vein, it is striking that the Court's decision means that States subject to federal habeas review henceforth receive less recognition of a finality interest than the Federal Government does on direct review of federal criminal convictions.

The Court's approach also turns AEDPA's bar against "second or successive" applications into a one-way ratchet that favors habeas petitioners. Had Magwood been unsuccessful in his first petition, all agree that claims then available, but not raised, would be barred. But because he prevailed in his attack on one part of his sentencing proceeding the first time around, the

Court rules that he is free, postsentencing, to pursue claims on federal habeas review that might have been raised earlier. The Court is mistaken in concluding that Congress, in enacting a statute aimed at placing new restrictions on successive petitions, would have intended this irrational result.

Magwood had every chance to raise his death-eligibility claim in his first habeas petition. He has abused the writ by raising this claim for the first time in his second petition. His application is therefore "second or successive." I would affirm the judgment of the Court of Appeals.

3.   Has There Been Exhaustion of All of the Claims Raised in the Habeas Petition?

An extremely important limitation on the power of federal courts to hear habeas corpus petitions is the requirement that petitioners in state custody exhaust all available state court procedures prior to seeking federal court review. One study of habeas corpus in federal courts in Massachusetts found that over half of all habeas petitions were dismissed for failure to exhaust state remedies.[28] Because the Supreme Court has made the exhaustion requirement even more stringent since this study was completed, it is quite likely that a large number of habeas petitions will continue to be dismissed for failure to exhaust state remedies. Some studies suggest that between 30 and 50 percent of habeas petitions are dismissed for failure to exhaust.[29]

The exhaustion requirement originally was created by the Supreme Court, although now it is embodied in the habeas statutes. The original statutes authorizing habeas corpus review for state prisoners did not require exhaustion of state court proceedings prior to federal habeas corpus review. However, in Ex parte Royall, 117 U.S. 241 (1886), the Court held that because of comity considerations and deference to state courts, federal courts should not entertain a claim in a habeas corpus petition until after the state courts have had an opportunity to hear the matter. Royall had been indicted under two state statutes and sought habeas corpus review to have the statutes declared unconstitutional.

The Supreme Court upheld the lower court's refusal to hear the habeas corpus petition. The Court stated that habeas corpus jurisdiction "should be exercised in light of the relations existing under our system of government, between judicial tribunals of the Union and of the States, and in recognition of the fact that the public good requires that those relations be not disturbed by unnecessary conflict between courts equally bound to guard and protect rights secured by the Constitution."

---

28. David L. Shapiro, *Federal Habeas Corpus: A Study in Massachusetts*, 87 Harv. L. Rev. 321, 333-334 (1973).

29. *See* Richard H. Fallon, Jr., Daniel J. Meltzer & David L. Shapiro, *2002 Supplement to Hart & Wechsler's The Federal Courts and the Federal System* 218 (2002).

In 1948, the habeas corpus statutes were revised and among the changes was the inclusion of specific language requiring that individuals challenging state custody exhaust state court remedies. Specifically, 28 U.S.C. §2254(b) provides:

> An application for a writ of habeas corpus on behalf of a person in custody pursuant to the judgment of a State court shall not be granted unless it appears that (A) the applicant has exhausted remedies available in the courts of the State; or (B)(i) there is an absence of available State corrective process or (ii) circumstances exist that render such process ineffective to protect the rights of the applicant.

The exhaustion requirement prevents federal courts from interfering with ongoing state criminal prosecutions. If there were no exhaustion requirement, then a person contending that he or she was being prosecuted under an unconstitutional statute could halt the state court litigation by filing a habeas corpus petition in federal court. But the Supreme Court has emphasized that considerations of equity and comity prevent federal courts from enjoining or otherwise interfering with pending state criminal proceedings.[30] Thus, the exhaustion requirement for federal court habeas corpus review allows state courts to interpret and enforce state criminal laws. Federal court review is delayed until the state has had a full chance to correct any errors in its law or procedures.

In analyzing the exhaustion requirement, three questions are crucial: What state court procedures must be used? What must be presented to state courts? When are petitions deemed sufficient to meet the exhaustion requirement? Each question is considered in turn.

First, the petitioner must pursue all available state court remedies; that is, exhaustion of state proceedings is incomplete as long as there remains an available state court proceeding that might provide the relief sought by the petitioner. This means that a habeas corpus petition may be brought if potential state remedies once existed but are no longer available. For example, exhaustion has occurred if the time limit for direct appeal has expired such that no state remedies are available at the time of the filing of the habeas petition.[31] However, the failure to use available state procedures likely will prevent federal habeas corpus relief, not because of exhaustion problems but rather, as discussed below, because state procedural defaults bar federal habeas corpus relief unless there is good "cause" for the omission and "prejudice" to the denial of review. The Supreme Court has ruled that a failure to include claims in a petition for discretionary review before a state's highest court is a procedural default that precludes raising those claims on habeas corpus.

---

30. *See, e.g.,* Younger v. Harris, 401 U.S. 37 (1971) (federal courts may not enjoin pending state court criminal prosecutions).

31. Fay v. Noia, 372 U.S. 391 (1963).

A state prisoner need not seek United States Supreme Court review of the state court's decision in order to present a federal court habeas petition.[32] Nor is habeas corpus precluded when a state prisoner seeks Supreme Court review of the state court ruling via a writ of certiorari and the Supreme Court declines to hear the case.[33] Of course, if the Supreme Court hears and decides the case, the Court's decision is determinative and must be followed in subsequent habeas corpus proceedings.

A state prisoner need not use state procedures for collateral review, such as state court habeas corpus mechanisms, as long as the issues have been presented and decided by the state courts on direct appeal. The Court explained that it "is not necessary . . . for the prisoner to ask the state for collateral relief, based on the same evidence and issues already decided by direct review."[34] However, a petitioner must use available state court collateral review procedures for issues not raised on direct appeal.[35] Conversely, a petitioner need not present a matter on direct appeal to the state courts, even if direct appeals are still available, if the issue already was raised and decided by the state court in a collateral proceeding. In other words, once an issue is raised and litigated in state court it need not be presented again even when additional state proceedings are possible.

Section 2254(b) excuses the failure to use state procedures if "circumstances render such process ineffective to protect the rights of the prisoner." The Court has interpreted this clause as creating an exception to the exhaustion requirement "only if there is no opportunity to obtain redress in state court or if the corrective process is so clearly deficient as to render futile any effort to obtain relief."[36]

A second major issue concerning exhaustion of state remedies involves what must be presented to the state courts in order for the exhaustion requirement to be deemed fulfilled. The Supreme Court has held that the "federal claim must be fairly presented to the state courts."[37] That is, the same matter raised in the federal court habeas corpus petition must have been presented to the state court or the matter will be dismissed for the failure to exhaust if state proceedings remain available where the issue can be raised. Federal courts use state court records to determine whether the petitioner raised the same issue in state court that is now presented in the habeas proceeding.

However, the exhaustion requirement is deemed to have been met when the habeas petitioner supplements the evidence presented in state court but does not raise a new issue. In Vasquez v. Hillery, 474 U.S. 254 (1986), the Supreme Court permitted a habeas corpus petitioner to present additional

---

32. Lawrence v. Florida, 127 S. Ct. 1079, 1083 (2007); Fay v. Noia, 372 U.S. 391, 435 (1963).

33. *See, e.g.,* Brown v. Allen, 344 U.S. 443, 450 (1953).

34. Brown v. Allen, 344 U.S. 443, 447 (1953); *see also* Roberts v. LaVallee, 389 U.S. 40, 42-43 (1967).

35. *See, e.g.,* Wade v. Mayo, 334 U.S. 672, 677-678 (1948).

36. Duckworth v. Serrano, 454 U.S. 1, 3 (1981).

37. Picard v. Connor, 404 U.S. 270, 275 (1971); *see also* Anderson v. Harless, 459 U.S. 4 (1982).

statistical evidence proving discrimination in the selection of the grand jury. The Court explained that it had "never held that presentation of additional facts to the district court, pursuant to that court's directions, evades the exhaustion requirement when the prisoner has presented the substance of his claim to the state courts." In other words, exhaustion will not present a problem to the defendant who is supplementing the evidence for a claim already presented to the state court and is not raising a new issue. However, there certainly will be cases in which it is a fine line between what constitutes a new issue as opposed to merely new evidence.[38]

Finally, there is the issue of what the petition must contain in order to meet the exhaustion requirement. The Supreme Court, in Rose v. Lundy, considered how a federal court should handle a habeas petition that includes some claims that have been exhausted in state court and some in which there has not been exhaustion.

ROSE v. LUNDY
455 U.S. 509 (1982)

Justice O'CONNOR delivered the opinion of the Court, except as to Part III-C.

In this case we consider whether the exhaustion rule in 28 U.S.C. §§2254(b), (c) requires a federal district court to dismiss a petition for a writ of habeas corpus containing any claims that have not been exhausted in the state courts. Because a rule requiring exhaustion of all claims furthers the purposes underlying the habeas statute, we hold that a district court must dismiss such "mixed petitions," leaving the prisoner with the choice of returning to state court to exhaust his claims or of amending or resubmitting the habeas petition to present only exhausted claims to the district court.

I

Following a jury trial, respondent Noah Lundy was convicted on charges of rape and crime against nature, and sentenced to the Tennessee State Penitentiary. After the Tennessee Court of Criminal Appeals affirmed the convictions and the Tennessee Supreme Court denied review, the respondent filed an unsuccessful petition for post-conviction relief in the Knox County Criminal Court.

The respondent subsequently filed a petition in Federal District Court for a writ of habeas corpus under 28 U.S.C. §2254, alleging four grounds for relief: (1) that he had been denied the right to confrontation because the trial court limited the defense counsel's questioning of the victim; (2) that

---

38. It should be noted that issues must be presented to the state courts even when it is clear that the state law or procedures are unconstitutional. Duckworth v. Serrano, 454 U.S. 1, 4 (1981). Thus, there is no exception to the exhaustion requirement for patently unconstitutional state statutes.

he had been denied the right to a fair trial because the prosecuting attorney stated that the respondent had a violent character; (3) that he had been denied the right to a fair trial because the prosecutor improperly remarked in his closing argument that the State's evidence was uncontradicted; and (4) that the trial judge improperly instructed the jury that every witness is presumed to swear the truth. After reviewing the state court records, however, the District Court concluded that it could not consider claims three and four "in the constitutional framework" because the respondent had not exhausted his state remedies for those grounds. The court nevertheless stated that "in assessing the atmosphere of the cause taken as a whole these items may be referred to collaterally." In short, the District Court considered several instances of prosecutorial misconduct never challenged in the state trial or appellate courts, or even raised in the respondent's habeas petition.

The Sixth Circuit affirmed the judgment of the District Court, concluding in an unreported order that the court properly found that the respondent's constitutional rights had been "seriously impaired by the improper limitation of his counsel's cross-examination of the prosecutrix and by the prosecutorial misconduct." The court specifically rejected the State's argument that the District Court should have dismissed the petition because it included both exhausted and unexhausted claims.

II

The petitioner urges this Court to apply a "total exhaustion" rule requiring district courts to dismiss every habeas corpus petition that contains both exhausted and unexhausted claims. The petitioner argues at length that such a rule furthers the policy of comity underlying the exhaustion doctrine because it gives the state courts the first opportunity to correct federal constitutional errors and minimizes federal interference and disruption of state judicial proceedings. The petitioner also believes that uniform adherence to a total exhaustion rule reduces the amount of piecemeal habeas litigation.

Under the petitioner's approach, a district court would dismiss a petition containing both exhausted and unexhausted claims, giving the prisoner the choice of returning to state court to litigate his unexhausted claims, or of proceeding with only his exhausted claims in federal court. The petitioner believes that a prisoner would be reluctant to choose the latter route since a district court could, in appropriate circumstances under Habeas Corpus Rule 9(b), dismiss subsequent federal habeas petitions as an abuse of the writ. In other words, if the prisoner amended the petition to delete the unexhausted claims or immediately refiled in federal court a petition alleging only his exhausted claims, he could lose the opportunity to litigate his presently unexhausted claims in federal court.

In order to evaluate the merits of the petitioner's arguments, we turn to the habeas statute, its legislative history, and the policies underlying the exhaustion doctrine.

III

A

The exhaustion doctrine existed long before its codification by Congress in 1948. In Ex parte Royall (1886), this Court wrote that as a matter of comity, federal courts should not consider a claim in a habeas corpus petition until after the state courts have had an opportunity to act. Subsequent cases refined the principle that state remedies must be exhausted except in unusual circumstances. None of these cases, however, specifically applied the exhaustion doctrine to habeas petitions containing both exhausted and unexhausted claims.

In 1948, Congress codified the exhaustion doctrine in 28 U.S.C. §2254. Section 2254, however, does not directly address the problem of mixed petitions. To be sure, the provision states that a remedy is not exhausted if there exists a state procedure to raise "the question presented," but we believe this phrase to be too ambiguous to sustain the conclusion that Congress intended to either permit or prohibit review of mixed petitions. Because the legislative history of §2254, as well as the pre-1948 cases, contains no reference to the problem of mixed petitions, in all likelihood Congress never thought of the problem. Consequently, we must analyze the policies underlying the statutory provision to determine its proper scope.

B

The exhaustion doctrine is principally designed to protect the state courts' role in the enforcement of federal law and prevent disruption of state judicial proceedings. Under our federal system, the federal and state "courts [are] equally bound to guard and protect rights secured by the Constitution." Because "it would be unseemly in our dual system of government for a federal district court to upset a state court conviction without an opportunity to the state courts to correct a constitutional violation," federal courts apply the doctrine of comity, which "teaches that one court should defer action on causes properly within its jurisdiction until the courts of another sovereignty with concurrent powers, and already cognizant of the litigation, have had an opportunity to pass upon the matter."

A rigorously enforced total exhaustion rule will encourage state prisoners to seek full relief first from the state courts, thus giving those courts the first opportunity to review all claims of constitutional error. As the number of prisoners who exhaust all of their federal claims increases, state courts may become increasingly familiar with and hospitable toward federal constitutional issues. Equally as important, federal claims that have been fully exhausted in state courts will more often be accompanied by a complete factual record to aid the federal courts in their review.

The facts of the present case underscore the need for a rule encouraging exhaustion of all federal claims. In his opinion, the District Court Judge wrote that "there is such mixture of violations that one cannot be separated from and considered independently of the others." Because the two unexhausted claims for relief were intertwined with the exhausted ones, the judge apparently considered all of the claims in ruling on the petition. Requiring dismissal of petitions containing both exhausted and unexhausted claims will relieve the district courts of the difficult if not impossible task of deciding when claims are related, and will reduce the temptation to consider unexhausted claims.

Rather than increasing the burden on federal courts, strict enforcement of the exhaustion requirement will encourage habeas petitioners to exhaust all of their claims in state court and to present the federal court with a single habeas petition. To the extent that the exhaustion requirement reduces piecemeal litigation, both the courts and the prisoners should benefit, for as a result the district court will be more likely to review all of the prisoner's claims in a single proceeding, thus providing for a more focused and thorough review.

C

The prisoner's principal interest, of course, is in obtaining speedy federal relief on his claims. A total exhaustion rule will not impair that interest since he can always amend the petition to delete the unexhausted claims, rather than returning to state court to exhaust all of his claims. By invoking this procedure, however, the prisoner would risk forfeiting consideration of his unexhausted claims in federal court.[39]

IV

In sum, because a total exhaustion rule promotes comity and does not unreasonably impair the prisoner's right to relief, we hold that a district court must dismiss habeas petitions containing both unexhausted and exhausted claims.

Justice BLACKMUN, concurring in the judgment.

The important issue before the Court in this case is whether the conservative "total exhaustion" rule is required by 28 U.S.C. §§2254(b) and (c), or whether a district court may review the exhausted claims of a mixed petition is the proper interpretation of the statute.

I do not dispute the value of comity when it is applicable and productive of harmony between state and federal courts, nor do I deny the principle of exhaustion that §§2254(b) and (c) so clearly embrace. What troubles me is that the "total exhaustion" rule, now adopted by this Court, can be read into the statute, as the Court concedes, only by sheer force; that it operates as a trap for the uneducated and indigent pro se prisoner-applicant; that it delays the resolution of claims that are not frivolous; and that it tends to increase,

---

39. Subsequent to Rose v. Lundy, the Antiterrorism and Effective Death Penalty Act was adopted, which greatly limits successive habeas corpus petitions. This is discussed above. [Footnote by casebook authors.]

rather than to alleviate, the caseload burdens on both state and federal courts. To use the old expression, the Court's ruling seems to me to "throw the baby out with the bath water."

Although purporting to rely on the policies upon which the exhaustion requirement is based, the Court uses that doctrine as "a blunderbuss to shatter the attempt at litigation of constitutional claims without regard to the purposes that underlie the doctrine and that called it into existence." Those purposes do not require the result the Court reaches; in fact, they support the approach taken by the Court of Appeals in this case and call for dismissal of only the unexhausted claims of a mixed habeas petition. Moreover, to the extent that the Court's ruling today has any impact whatsoever on the workings of federal habeas, it will alter, I fear, the litigation techniques of very few habeas petitioners.

The Court correctly observes that neither the language nor the legislative history of the exhaustion provisions of §§2254(b) and (c) mandates dismissal of a habeas petition containing both exhausted and unexhausted claims. Nor does precedent dictate the result reached here.

The Court fails to note, moreover, that prisoners are not compelled to utilize every available state procedure in order to satisfy the exhaustion requirement. Although this Court's precedents do not address specifically the appropriate treatment of mixed habeas petitions, they plainly suggest that state courts need not inevitably be given every opportunity to safeguard a prisoner's constitutional rights and to provide him relief before a federal court may entertain his habeas petition.

In reversing the judgment of the Sixth Circuit, the Court focuses, as it must, on the purposes the exhaustion doctrine is intended to serve. I do not dispute the importance of the exhaustion requirement or the validity of the policies on which it is based. But I cannot agree that those concerns will be sacrificed by permitting district courts to consider exhausted habeas claims.

The first interest relied on by the Court involves an offshoot of the doctrine of federal-state comity. The Court hopes to preserve the state courts' role in protecting constitutional rights, as well as to afford those courts an opportunity to correct constitutional errors and — somewhat patronizingly — to "become increasingly familiar with and hospitable toward federal constitutional issues." My proposal, however, is not inconsistent with the Court's concern for comity: indeed, the state courts have occasion to rule first on every constitutional challenge, and have ample opportunity to correct any such error, before it is considered by a federal court on habeas.

In some respects, the Court's ruling appears more destructive than solicitous of federal-state comity. Remitting a habeas petitioner to state court to exhaust a patently frivolous claim before the federal court may consider a serious, exhausted ground for relief hardly demonstrates respect for the state courts. The state judiciary's time and resources are then spent rejecting the obviously meritless unexhausted claim, which doubtless will receive little or no attention in the subsequent federal proceeding that focuses on the substantial exhausted claim. I can "conceive of no reason why the State would wish to burden its judicial calendar with a narrow issue the resolution of which is predetermined by established federal principles."

A pending state proceeding involving claims not included in the prisoner's federal habeas petition will be mooted only if the federal court grants the applicant relief. Even in those cases, though, the state courts will be saved the trouble of undertaking the useless exercise of ruling on unexhausted claims that are unnecessary to the disposition of the case.

The second set of interests relied upon by the Court involves those of federal judicial administration — ensuring that a §2254 petition is accompanied by a complete factual record to facilitate review and relieving the district courts of the responsibility for determining when exhausted and unexhausted claims are interrelated. If a prisoner has presented a particular challenge in the state courts, however, the habeas court will have before it the complete factual record relating to that claim. And the Court's Draconian approach is hardly necessary to relieve district courts of the obligation to consider exhausted grounds for relief when the prisoner also has advanced interrelated claims not yet reviewed by the state courts. When the district court believes, on the facts of the case before it, that the record is inadequate or that full consideration of the exhausted claims is impossible, it has always been free to dismiss the entire habeas petition pending resolution of unexhausted claims in the state courts. Certainly, it makes sense to commit these decisions to the discretion of the lower federal courts, which will be familiar with the specific factual context of each case.

The federal courts that have addressed the issue of interrelatedness have had no difficulty distinguishing related from unrelated habeas claims. Mixed habeas petitions have been dismissed in toto when "the issues before the federal court logically depend for their relevance upon resolution of an unexhausted issue," or when consideration of the exhausted claim "would necessarily be affected . . ." by the unexhausted claim. Thus, some of the factors to be considered in determining whether a prisoner's grounds for collateral relief are interrelated are whether the claims are based on the same constitutional right or factual issue, and whether they require an understanding of the totality of the circumstances and therefore necessitate examination of the entire record.

The Court's interest in efficient administration of the federal courts therefore does not require dismissal of mixed habeas petitions. In fact, that concern militates against the approach taken by the Court today. In order to comply with the Court's ruling, a federal court now will have to review the record in a §2254 proceeding at least summarily in order to determine whether all claims have been exhausted. In many cases a decision on the merits will involve only negligible additional effort. And in other cases the court may not realize that one of a number of claims is unexhausted until after substantial work has been done. If the district court must nevertheless dismiss the entire petition until all grounds for relief have been exhausted, the prisoner will likely return to federal court eventually, thereby necessitating duplicative examination of the record and consideration of the exhausted claims — perhaps by another district judge. Moreover, when the §2254 petition does find its way back to federal court, the record on the exhausted grounds for relief may well be state and resolution of the merits more difficult.

The interest of the prisoner and of society in "preserv[ing] the writ of habeas corpus as a 'swift and imperative remedy in all cases of illegal restraint or confinement,'" is the final policy consideration to be weighed in the balance. Compelling the habeas petitioner to repeat his journey through the entire state and federal legal process before receiving a ruling on his exhausted claims obviously entails substantial delay. And if the prisoner must choose between undergoing that delay and forfeiting unexhausted claims, society is likewise forced to sacrifice either the swiftness of habeas or its availability to remedy all unconstitutional imprisonments. Dismissing only unexhausted grounds for habeas relief, while ruling on the merits of all unrelated exhausted claims, will diminish neither the promptness nor the efficacy of the remedy and, at the same time, will serve the state and federal interests described by the Court.

I therefore would remand the case, directing that the courts below dismiss respondent's unexhausted claims and examine those that have been properly presented to the state courts in order to determine whether they are interrelated with the unexhausted grounds and, if not, whether they warrant collateral relief.

Justice BRENNAN, with whom Justice MARSHALL joins, concurring in part and dissenting in part.

I agree with the Court's holding that the exhaustion requirement of 28 U.S.C. §§2254(b), (c) obliges a federal district court to dismiss, without consideration on the merits, a habeas corpus petition from a state prisoner when that petition contains claims that have not been exhausted in the state courts, "leaving the prisoner with the choice of returning to state court to exhaust his claims or of amending or resubmitting the habeas petition to present only exhausted claims to the district court." But I disagree with the plurality's view, that a habeas petitioner must "risk forfeiting consideration of his unexhausted claims in federal court" if he "decides to proceed only with his exhausted claims and deliberately sets aside his unexhausted claims" in the face of the district court's refusal to consider his "mixed" petition.

Justice STEVENS, dissenting.

This case raises important questions about the authority of federal judges. In my opinion claims of constitutional error are not fungible. There are at least four types. The one most frequently encountered is a claim that attaches a constitutional label to a set of facts that does not disclose a violation of any constitutional right. In my opinion, each of the four claims asserted in this case falls in that category. The second class includes constitutional violations that are not of sufficient import in a particular case to justify reversal even on direct appeal, when the evidence is still fresh and a fair retrial could be promptly conducted. A third category includes errors that are important enough to require reversal on direct appeal but do not reveal the kind of fundamental unfairness to the accused that will support a collateral attack on a final judgment. The fourth category includes those errors that are so fundamental that they infect the validity of the underlying judgment itself, or the integrity of the process by which that judgment was obtained. This category cannot be defined precisely; concepts of "fundamental fairness" are not frozen in time. But the kind of error that falls in this category is best illustrated by recalling the classic grounds for the issuance of a writ of habeas corpus — that the proceeding was dominated by mob violence; that the prosecutor knowingly made use of perjured testimony; or that the conviction was based on a confession extorted from the defendant by brutal methods. Errors of this kind justify collateral relief no matter how long a judgment may have been final and even though they may not have been preserved properly in the original trial.

In this case, I think it is clear that neither the exhausted claims nor the unexhausted claims describe any error demonstrating that respondent's trial was fundamentally unfair. Since his lawyer found insufficient merit in the two unexhausted claims to object to the error at trial or to raise the claims on direct appeal, I would expect that the Tennessee courts will consider them to have been waived as a matter of state law; thereafter, they undoubtedly will not support federal relief. This case is thus destined to return to the Federal District Court and the Court of Appeals where, it is safe to predict, those courts will once again come to the conclusion that the writ should issue. The additional procedure that the Court requires before considering the merits will be totally unproductive.

If my appraisal of respondent's exhausted claims is incorrect — if the trial actually was fundamentally unfair to the respondent — postponing relief until another round of review in the state and federal judicial systems has been completed is truly outrageous. The unnecessary delay will make it more difficult for the prosecutor to obtain a conviction on retrial if respondent is in fact guilty; if he is innocent, requiring him to languish in jail because he made a pleading error is callous indeed.

There are some situations in which a district judge should refuse to entertain a mixed petition until all of the prisoner's claims have been exhausted. If the unexhausted claim appears to involve error of the most serious kind and if it is reasonably clear that the exhausted claims do not, addressing the merits of the exhausted claims will merely delay the ultimate disposition of the case. Or if an evidentiary hearing is necessary to decide the merits of both the exhausted and unexhausted claims, a procedure that enables all fact questions to be resolved in the same hearing should be followed. I therefore would allow district judges to exercise discretion to determine whether the presence of an unexhausted claim in a habeas corpus application makes it inappropriate to consider the merits of a properly pleaded exhausted claim. The inflexible, mechanical rule the Court adopts today arbitrarily denies district judges the kind of authority they need to administer their calendars effectively.

In recent years federal judges at times have lost sight of the true office of the great writ of habeas corpus. It is quite unlike the common-law writ of error that enabled a higher court to correct errors committed by a nisi prius tribunal in the trial of civil or criminal cases by ordering further proceedings whenever trial error was detected. The writ of habeas corpus is a fundamental guarantee of liberty.

Procedural regularity is a matter of fundamental importance in the administration of justice. But procedural niceties that merely complicate and delay the resolution of disputes are another matter. In my opinion the federal habeas corpus statute should be construed to protect the former and, whenever possible, to avoid the latter.

4. Does the Petition Rely on Existing Rules or Seek Recognition of a New Rule of Constitutional Law?

Teague v. Lane, below, is one of the Supreme Court's most important habeas corpus decisions in that it substantially limits the ability of federal courts to hear constitutional claims raised in habeas corpus petitions. Until *Teague*, the Supreme Court considered habeas corpus petitions alleging constitutional violations, even when they asked the Court to recognize a new constitutional right that would not be applied retroactively to other cases. When the Court articulated a new right it benefitted the habeas petitioner and future criminal defendants. The Court subsequently would decide, in another case, whether it was to be applied retroactively to others. But in *Teague*, the Supreme Court ruled that retroactivity must be determined first; federal courts may not hear habeas petitions asking the Court to recognize new rights unless such rights would be retroactively applied in all cases. Simply put, *Teague* means that a habeas petition almost always must rely only on existing rights and cannot seek the recognition of any that would be regarded as new rights.

TEAGUE v. LANE
_____

489 U.S. 288 (1989)

Justice O'CONNOR announced the judgment of the Court and delivered the opinion of the Court with respect to Parts I, II, and III, and an opinion with respect to Parts IV and V, in which THE CHIEF JUSTICE, Justice SCALIA, and Justice KENNEDY join.

In Taylor v. Louisiana (1975), this Court held that the Sixth Amendment required that the jury venire be drawn from a fair cross section of the community. The Court stated, however, that "in holding that petit juries must be drawn from a source fairly representative of the community we impose no requirement that petit juries actually chosen must mirror the community and reflect the various distinctive groups in the population. Defendants are not entitled to a jury of any particular composition." The principal question presented in this case is whether the Sixth Amendment's fair cross section requirement should now be extended to the petit jury. Because we adopt Justice Harlan's approach to retroactivity for cases on collateral review, we leave the resolution of that question for another day.

I

Petitioner, a black man, was convicted by an all-white Illinois jury of three counts of attempted murder, two counts of armed robbery, and one count of aggravated battery. During jury selection for petitioner's trial, the prosecutor used all 10 of his peremptory challenges to exclude blacks. Petitioner's counsel used one of his 10 peremptory challenges to exclude a black woman who was married to a police officer. After the prosecutor had struck six blacks, petitioner's counsel moved for a mistrial. The trial court denied the motion. When the prosecutor struck four more blacks, petitioner's counsel again moved for a mistrial, arguing that petitioner was "entitled to a jury of his peers." The prosecutor defended the challenges by stating that he was trying to achieve a balance of men and women on the jury. The trial court denied the motion, reasoning that the jury "appear[ed] to be a fair [one]."

On appeal, petitioner argued that the prosecutor's use of peremptory challenges denied him the right to be tried by a jury that was representative of the community. The Illinois Appellate Court rejected petitioner's fair cross section claim. The Illinois Supreme Court denied leave to appeal, and we denied certiorari.

Petitioner then filed a petition for a writ of habeas corpus in the United States District Court for the Northern District of Illinois. Petitioner repeated his fair cross section claim, and argued that the opinions of several Justices concurring in, or dissenting from, the denial of certiorari in McCray v. New York (1983), had invited a reexamination of Swain v. Alabama, (1965), which prohibited States from purposefully and systematically denying blacks the opportunity to serve on juries. He also argued, for the first time, that under *Swain* a prosecutor could be questioned about his use of peremptory challenges once he volunteered an explanation. The District Court, though sympathetic to petitioner's arguments, held that it was bound by *Swain* and Circuit precedent. On appeal, petitioner repeated his fair cross section claim and his *McCray* argument. A panel of the Court of Appeals agreed with petitioner that the Sixth Amendment's fair cross section requirement applied to the petit jury and held that petitioner had made out a prima facie case of discrimination. A majority of the judges on the Court of Appeals voted to rehear the case en banc, and the panel opinion was vacated. Rehearing was postponed until after our decision in Batson v. Kentucky, (1986), which overruled a portion of *Swain*. After *Batson* was decided, the Court of Appeals held that petitioner could not benefit from the rule in that case because [we] had held that *Batson* would not be applied retroactively to cases on collateral review.

II

Petitioner's first contention is that he should receive the benefit of our decision in *Batson* even though his conviction became final before *Batson* was decided. Before addressing petitioner's argument, we think it helpful to explain how *Batson* modified *Swain*. *Swain* held that a "State's purposeful or deliberate denial" to blacks of an opportunity to serve as jurors solely on account of race violates the Equal Protection Clause of the Fourteenth Amendment. In order to establish a prima facie case of discrimination under *Swain*, a defendant had to demonstrate that the peremptory challenge system had been "perverted." A defendant could raise an inference of purposeful discrimination if he showed that the prosecutor in the county where the trial was held "in case after case, whatever the circumstances, whatever the crime and whoever the defendant or the victim may be," has been responsible for the removal of qualified blacks who had survived challenges for cause, with the result that no blacks ever served on petit juries.

In *Batson*, the Court overruled that portion of *Swain* setting forth the evidentiary showing necessary to make out a prima facie case of racial discrimination under the Equal Protection Clause. The Court held that a defendant can establish a prima facie case by showing that he is a "member of a cognizable racial group," that the prosecutor exercised "peremptory challenges to remove from the venire members of the defendant's race," and that those "facts and any other relevant circumstances raise an inference that the prosecutor used that practice to exclude the veniremen from the petit jury on account of their race." Once the defendant makes out a prima facie case of discrimination, the burden shifts to the prosecutor "to come forward with a neutral explanation for challenging black jurors."

[T]he Court concluded that the rule announced in *Batson* should not be applied retroactively on collateral review of convictions that became final before *Batson* was announced. The Court defined final to mean a case " 'where the judgment of conviction was rendered, the availability of appeal exhausted, and the time for petition for certiorari had elapsed before our decision in' *Batson*. . . ."

Petitioner's conviction became final 2 1/2 years prior to *Batson*, thus depriving petitioner of any benefit from the rule announced in that case.

[III]

Petitioner's final contention is that the Sixth Amendment's fair cross section requirement applies to the petit jury. As we noted at the outset, *Taylor* expressly stated that the fair cross section requirement does not apply to the petit jury. Petitioner nevertheless contends that the ratio decidendi of

Taylor cannot be limited to the jury venire, and he urges adoption of a new rule. Because we hold that the rule urged by petitioner should not be applied retroactively to cases on collateral review, we decline to address petitioner's contention.

A

In the past, the Court has, without discussion, often applied a new constitutional rule of criminal procedure to the defendant in the case announcing the new rule, and has confronted the question of retroactivity later when a different defendant sought the benefit of that rule.

The question of retroactivity with regard to petitioner's fair cross section claim has been raised only in an amicus brief. *See* Brief for Criminal Justice Legal Foundation as Amicus Curiae. Nevertheless, that question is not foreign to the parties, who have addressed retroactivity with respect to petitioner's *Batson* claim. In our view, the question "whether a decision [announcing a new rule should] be given prospective or retroactive effect should be faced at the time of [that] decision." Retroactivity is properly treated as a threshold question, for, once a new rule is applied to the defendant in the case announcing the rule, evenhanded justice requires that it be applied retroactively to all who are similarly situated. Thus, before deciding whether the fair cross section requirement should be extended to the petit jury, we should ask whether such a rule would be applied retroactively to the case at issue. This retroactivity determination would normally entail application of the *Linkletter* standard, but we believe that our approach to retroactivity for cases on collateral review requires modification.

It is admittedly often difficult to determine when a case announces a new rule, and we do not attempt to define the spectrum of what may or may not constitute a new rule for retroactivity purposes. In general, however, a case announces a new rule when it breaks new ground or imposes a new obligation on the States or the Federal Government. To put it differently, a case announces a new rule if the result was not dictated by precedent existing at the time the defendant's conviction became final.

B

Justice Harlan believed that new rules generally should not be applied retroactively to cases on collateral review. He argued that retroactivity for cases on collateral review could "be responsibly [determined] only by focusing, in the first instance, on the nature, function, and scope of the adjudicatory process in which such cases arise. The relevant frame of reference, in other words, is not the purpose of the new rule whose benefit the [defendant] seeks, but instead the purposes for which the writ of habeas corpus is made available." With regard to the nature of habeas corpus, Justice Harlan wrote:

> Habeas corpus always has been a collateral remedy, providing an avenue for upsetting judgments that have become otherwise final. It is not designed as a substitute for direct

review. The interest in leaving concluded litigation in a state of repose, that is, reducing the controversy to a final judgment not subject to further judicial revision, may quite legitimately be found by those responsible for defining the scope of the writ to outweigh in some, many, or most instances the competing interest in readjudicating convictions according to all legal standards in effect when a habeas petition is filed.

Given the "broad scope of constitutional issues cognizable on habeas," Justice Harlan argued that it is "sounder, in adjudicating habeas petitions, generally to apply the law prevailing at the time a conviction became final than it is to seek to dispose of [habeas] cases on the basis of intervening changes in constitutional interpretation." Justice Harlan identified only two exceptions to his general rule of nonretroactivity for cases on collateral review. First, a new rule should be applied retroactively if it places "certain kinds of primary, private individual conduct beyond the power of the criminal law-making authority to proscribe." Second, a new rule should be applied retroactively if it requires the observance of "those procedures that . . . are 'implicit in the concept of ordered liberty.' "

We agree with Justice Harlan's description of the function of habeas corpus. "[T]he Court never has defined the scope of the writ simply by reference to a perceived need to assure that an individual accused of crime is afforded a trial free of constitutional error." Rather, we have recognized that interests of comity and finality must also be considered in determining the proper scope of habeas review. These underlying considerations of finality find significant and compelling parallels in the criminal context.

Application of constitutional rules not in existence at the time a conviction became final seriously undermines the principle of finality which is essential to the operation of our criminal justice system. Without finality, the criminal law is deprived of much of its deterrent effect. The fact that life and liberty are at stake in criminal prosecutions "shows only that 'conventional notions of finality' should not have as much place in criminal as in civil litigation, not that they should have none."

We find these criticisms to be persuasive, and we now adopt Justice Harlan's view of retroactivity for cases on collateral review. Unless they fall within an exception to the general rule, new constitutional rules of criminal procedure will not be applicable to those cases which have become final before the new rules are announced.

V

Petitioner's conviction became final in 1983. As a result, the rule petitioner urges would not be applicable to this case, which is on collateral review, unless it would fall within an exception.

The first exception suggested by Justice Harlan — that a new rule should be applied retroactively if it places "certain kinds of primary, private individual conduct beyond the power of the criminal law-making authority to proscribe," — is not relevant here. Application of the fair cross section requirement to the petit jury would not accord constitutional protection to any primary activity whatsoever.

The second exception suggested by Justice Harlan — that a new rule should be applied retroactively if it requires the observance of "those procedures that . . . are 'implicit in the concept of ordered liberty,' " — we apply with a modification. The language used by Justice Harlan in *Mackey* leaves no doubt that he meant the second exception to be reserved for watershed rules of criminal procedure:

> We therefore hold that, implicit in the retroactivity approach we adopt today, is the principle that habeas corpus cannot be used as a vehicle to create new constitutional rules of criminal procedure unless those rules would be applied retroactively to all defendants on collateral review through one of the two exceptions we have articulated. Because a decision extending the fair cross section requirement to the petit jury would not be applied retroactively to cases on collateral review under the approach we adopt today, we do not address petitioner's claim.

Justice STEVENS, with whom Justice BLACKMUN joins, concurring in part and concurring in the judgment.

When a criminal defendant claims that a procedural error tainted his conviction, an appellate court often decides whether error occurred before deciding whether that error requires reversal or should be classified as harmless. I would follow a parallel approach in cases raising novel questions of constitutional law on collateral review, first determining whether the trial process violated any of the petitioner's constitutional rights and then deciding whether the petitioner is entitled to relief. If error occurred, factors relating to retroactivity — most importantly, the magnitude of unfairness — should be examined before granting the petitioner relief. Proceeding in reverse, a plurality of the Court today declares that a new rule should not apply retroactively without ever deciding whether there is such a rule.

Justice BRENNAN, with whom Justice MARSHALL joins, dissenting.

Today a plurality of this Court, without benefit of briefing and oral argument, adopts a novel threshold test for federal review of state criminal convictions on habeas corpus. It does so without regard for — indeed, without even mentioning — our contrary decisions over the past 35 years delineating the broad scope of habeas relief. The plurality further appears oblivious to the importance we have consistently accorded the principle of stare decisis in nonconstitutional cases. Out of an exaggerated concern for treating similarly situated habeas petitioners the same, the plurality would for the first time preclude the federal courts from considering on collateral review a vast range of important constitutional challenges; where those challenges have merit, it would bar the vindication of personal constitutional rights and deny society a check against further violations until the same claim is presented on direct review. In my view, the plurality's "blind adherence to the principle of treating like cases alike" amounts to "letting the tail wag the dog" when it stymies the resolution of substantial and unheralded constitutional questions. Because I cannot acquiesce in this unprecedented curtailment of the reach of the Great Writ, particularly in the absence of any discussion of these momentous changes by the parties or the lower courts, I dissent.

Unfortunately, the plurality turns its back on established case law and would erect a formidable new barrier to relief. Any time a federal habeas petitioner's claim, if successful, would result in the announcement of a new rule of law, the plurality says, it may only be adjudicated if that rule would "plac[e] 'certain kinds of primary, private individual conduct beyond the power of the criminal law-making authority to proscribe.'" Equally disturbing, in my view, is the plurality's infidelity to the doctrine of stare decisis. The plurality does not so much as mention stare decisis. Indeed, from the plurality's exposition of its new rule, one might infer that its novel fabrication will work no great change in the availability of federal collateral review of state convictions. Nothing could be further from the truth. Although the plurality declines to "define the spectrum of what may or may not constitute a new rule for retroactivity purposes," it does say that generally "a case announces a new rule when it breaks new ground or imposes a new obligation on the States or the Federal Government." Otherwise phrased, "a case announces a new rule if the result was not dictated by precedent existing at the time the defendant's conviction became final." This account is extremely broad. Few decisions on appeal or collateral review are "dictated" by what came before. Most such cases involve a question of law that is at least debatable, permitting a rational judge to resolve the case in more than one way. Virtually no case that prompts a dissent on the relevant legal point, for example, could be said to be "dictated" by prior decisions. By the plurality's test, therefore, a great many cases could only be heard on habeas if the rule urged by the petitioner fell within one of the two exceptions the plurality has sketched. Those exceptions, however, are narrow. Rules that place "'certain kinds of primary, private individual conduct beyond the power of the criminal law-making authority to proscribe,'" are rare. And rules that would require "new procedures without which the likelihood of an accurate conviction is seriously diminished," are not appreciably more common. The plurality admits, in fact, that it "believe[s] it unlikely that many such components of basic due process have yet to emerge." The plurality's approach today can thus be expected to contract substantially the Great Writ's sweep.

[There are an] abundance and variety of habeas cases we have decided in recent years that could never have been adjudicated had the plurality's new rule been in effect.

Teague applies whenever the habeas petition seeks recognition of a "new right." The Court broadly defined what is a "new" right, thus limiting the constitutional claims that can be presented to a federal court on habeas corpus. The Court said that a case announces a new rule "when it breaks new ground or imposes a new obligation on the States or Federal government. . . . [A] case announces new rule if the result was not dictated by precedent existing at the time the defendant's conviction became final."

If the petitioner is seeking a new right, the question then becomes whether it would apply retroactively. Because very few criminal procedure rights have retroactive application, the effect will be to prevent habeas petitions from preventing claims except as to rights that have been previously established. The Court recognized only two situations in which rights have retroactive effect. One is where the new rules place "certain kinds of primary, private individual conduct beyond the power of the criminal law-making authority to proscribe." The other is a new rule that adopts a procedure that is "implicit in the concept of ordered liberty." The latter, the Court emphasized, is "reserved for watershed rules of criminal procedure."

The reluctance of the Court to find criminal procedure rights to be retroactive is illustrated by Schriro v. Summerlin, 542 U.S. 348 (2004). In Ring v. Arizona, 536 U.S. 584 (2002), the Supreme Court held that it is for the jury to decide whether there are sufficient aggravating circumstances to warrant the imposition of the death penalty. In other words, it was deemed unconstitutional for states to allow the judge, on his or her own, to decide whether to impose a death sentence. The issue in Schriro v. Summerlin is whether *Ring* should apply retroactively to those who were sentenced to death before it was decided. The Court, in a 5-4 decision, held that *Ring* does not apply retroactively — that it neither puts matters beyond the reach of the criminal law nor is a watershed rule of criminal procedure. The result is that individuals who were sentenced through an unconstitutional procedure could be put to death.

The Supreme Court again considered when a criminal procedure rule applies retroactively in Whorton v. Bockting, 549 U.S. 406 (2007). In Crawford v. Washington, 541 U.S. 36 (2004), the Supreme Court significantly changed the law under the Confrontation Clause of the Sixth Amendment as to when prosecutors may use statements against a criminal defendant when the declarant is unavailable. Previously, a prosecutor could use such statements as long as they were reliable. In *Crawford*, the Supreme Court held that "testimonial" statements could not be used against a criminal defendant when the declarant was unavailable even though they were deemed reliable.

The issue in Whorton v. Bockting was whether *Crawford* applies retroactively. The Supreme Court unanimously held that it does not. Justice Alito, writing for the Court, explained:

> In *Teague* and subsequent cases, we have laid out the framework to be used in determining whether a rule announced in one of our opinions should be applied retroactively to judgments in criminal cases that are already final on direct review. Under the *Teague* framework, an old rule applies both on direct and collateral review, but a new rule is generally applicable only to cases that are still on direct review.

A new rule applies retroactively in a collateral proceeding only if (1) the rule is substantive or (2) the rule is a "watershed rul[e] of criminal procedure" implicating the fundamental fairness and accuracy of the criminal proceeding.

Because *Crawford* announced a "new rule" and because it is clear and undisputed that the rule is procedural and not substantive, that rule cannot be applied in this collateral attack on respondent's conviction unless it is a "watershed rul[e] of criminal procedure" implicating the fundamental fairness and accuracy of the criminal proceeding. This exception is "extremely narrow." We have observed that it is "unlikely" that any such rules "ha[ve] yet to emerge." And in the years since *Teague*, we have rejected every claim that a new rule satisfied the requirements for watershed status.

In order to qualify as watershed, a new rule must meet two requirements. First, the rule must be necessary to prevent "an impermissibly large risk of an inaccurate conviction." Second, the rule must alter our understanding of the bedrock procedural elements essential to the fairness of a proceeding.

The *Crawford* rule does not satisfy the first requirement relating to an impermissibly large risk of an inaccurate conviction. To be sure, the *Crawford* rule reflects the Framers' preferred mechanism (cross-examination) for ensuring that inaccurate out-of-court testimonial statements are not used to convict an accused. But in order for a new rule to meet the accuracy requirement at issue here, "[i]t is . . . not enough . . . to say that [the] rule is aimed at improving the accuracy of trial," or that the rule is directed toward the enhancement of reliability and accuracy in some sense. Instead, the question is whether the new rule remedied "an impermissibly large risk" of an inaccurate conviction.

The *Crawford* rule also did not "alter our understanding of the bedrock procedural elements essential to the fairness of a proceeding." [I]n order to meet this requirement, a new rule must itself constitute a previously unrecognized bedrock procedural element that is essential to the fairness of a proceeding. In applying this requirement, we again have looked to the example of *Gideon* [v. Wainwright], and "we have not hesitated to hold that less sweeping and fundamental rules" do not qualify.

In this case, it is apparent that the rule announced in *Crawford*, while certainly important, is not in the same category with *Gideon*. *Gideon* effected a profound and "sweeping" change. The *Crawford* rule simply lacks the "primacy" and "centrality" of the *Gideon* rule, and does not qualify as a rule that "alter[ed] our understanding of the bedrock procedural elements essential to the fairness of a proceeding."

In sum, we hold that *Crawford* announced a "new rule" of criminal procedure and that this rule does not fall within the *Teague* exception for watershed rules.

Most recently, in Montgomery v. Louisiana, 136 S. Ct. 718 (2016), the Court said that the key question is whether the prior Supreme Court decision is *substantive*, in which case it applies retroactively, or *procedural*, in which case it does not apply retroactively. In Miller v. Alabama, 567 U.S. 460 (2012), the Court ruled that it is cruel and unusual punishment to impose a mandatory sentence of life in prison without parole for a homicide committed by a juvenile. In *Montgomery*, the Court said that this applies retroactively because it is a substantive change in the law. Justice Kennedy, writing for the Court, explained:

The Court now holds that when a new substantive rule of constitutional law controls the outcome of a case, the Constitution requires state collateral review courts to give retroactive effect to that rule. *Teague*'s conclusion establishing the retroactivity of new substantive rules is best understood as resting upon constitutional premises. That constitutional command is, like all federal law, binding on state courts. . . .

This Court's precedents addressing the nature of substantive rules, their differences from procedural rules, and their history of retroactive application establish that the Constitution requires substantive rules to have retroactive effect regardless of when a conviction became final.

5. Is It an Issue That Can Be Raised on Habeas Corpus?

The principles of res judicata and collateral estoppel generally preclude a party from relitigating a matter already presented to a court and decided on. Brown v. Allen, 344 U.S. 443 (1953), created an important exception to collateral estoppel and res judicata for habeas petitions. The Supreme Court, in an opinion by Justice Frankfurter, held that a constitutional claim may be raised on habeas even though it had been raised, fully litigated, and decided in state court. Justice Frankfurter observed that "even the highest State courts" had failed to give adequate protection to federal constitutional rights. Because the *Brown* Court believed that habeas corpus exists to remedy state court disregard of violations of defendant's rights, the Court established that a state prisoner should have the chance to have a hearing in federal court on federal constitutional claims.

In fact, the Warren Court so valued the importance of the opportunity to relitigate constitutional issues to ensure correct decisions that it held that a prisoner convicted by a *federal* court also may raise issues on habeas that had been presented and decided at trial.[40] The Court concluded that "[t]he provision of federal collateral remedies rests . . . fundamentally upon a recognition that adequate protection of constitutional rights . . . requires the continuing availability of a mechanism for relief."

There is one major exception to Brown v. Allen. In Stone v. Powell, the Supreme Court held that claims that a state court improperly failed to exclude evidence as being the product of an illegal search or seizure could not be relitigated on habeas corpus if the state court provided a full and fair opportunity for a hearing.

STONE v. POWELL
428 U.S. 465 (1976)

Justice POWELL delivered the opinion of the Court.

Respondents in these cases were convicted of criminal offenses in state courts, and their convictions were affirmed on appeal. The prosecution in each case relied upon evidence obtained by searches and seizures alleged by respondents to have been unlawful. Each respondent subsequently sought

---

40. Kaufman v. United States, 394 U.S. 217 (1969).

relief in a Federal District Court by filing a petition for a writ of federal habeas corpus. The question presented is whether a federal court should consider, in ruling on a petition for habeas corpus relief filed by a state prisoner, a claim that evidence obtained by an unconstitutional search or seizure was introduced at his trial, when he has previously been afforded an opportunity for full and fair litigation of his claim in the state courts. The issue is of considerable importance to the administration of criminal justice.

I

In the landmark decision in Brown v. Allen (1953), the scope of the writ was expanded. In that case and its companion case, Daniels v. Allen, prisoners applied for federal habeas corpus relief claiming that the trial courts had erred in failing to quash their indictments due to alleged discrimination in the selection of grand jurors and in ruling certain confessions admissible. In *Brown*, the highest court of the State had rejected these claims on direct appeal, and this Court had denied certiorari. Despite the apparent adequacy of the state corrective process, the Court reviewed the denial of the writ of habeas corpus and held that Brown was entitled to a full reconsideration of these constitutional claims, including, if appropriate, a hearing in the Federal District Court.

During the period in which the substantive scope of the writ was expanded, the Court did not consider whether exceptions to full review might exist with respect to particular categories of constitutional claims. Prior to the Court's decision in Kaufman v. United States (1969), however, a substantial majority of the Federal Courts of Appeals had concluded that collateral review of search-and-seizure claims was inappropriate on motions filed by federal prisoners under 28 U.S.C. §2255, the modern post conviction procedure available to federal prisoners in lieu of habeas corpus. The primary rationale advanced in support of those decisions was that Fourth Amendment violations are different in kind from denials of Fifth or Sixth Amendment rights in that claims of illegal search and seizure do not "impugn the integrity of the fact-finding process or challenge evidence as inherently unreliable; rather, the exclusion of illegally seized evidence is simply a prophylactic device intended generally to deter Fourth Amendment violations by law enforcement officers."

Kaufman rejected this rationale and held that search-and-seizure claims are cognizable in §2255 proceedings. The Court noted that "the federal habeas remedy extends to state prisoners alleging that unconstitutionally obtained evidence was admitted against them at trial."

The discussion in *Kaufman* of the scope of federal habeas corpus rests on the view that the effectuation of the Fourth Amendment, as applied to the States through the Fourteenth Amendment, requires the granting of habeas corpus relief when a prisoner has been convicted in state court on the basis of evidence obtained in an illegal search or seizure since those Amendments were held in Mapp v. Ohio (1961), to require exclusion of such evidence at trial and reversal of conviction upon direct review. Until these cases we have not had occasion fully to consider the validity of this view. Upon examination, we conclude, in light of the nature and purpose of the Fourth Amendment exclusionary rule, that this view is unjustified. We hold, therefore, that where the State has provided an opportunity for full and fair litigation of a Fourth Amendment claim, the Constitution does not require that a state prisoner be granted federal habeas corpus relief on the ground that evidence obtained in an unconstitutional search or seizure was introduced at his trial.

III

The Fourth Amendment assures the "right of the people to be secure in their persons, houses, papers, and effects, against unreasonable searches and seizures." The Amendment was primarily a reaction to the evils associated with the use of the general warrant in England and the writs of assistance in the Colonies, and was intended to protect the "sanctity of a man's home and the privacies of life" from searches under unchecked general authority.

The exclusionary rule was a judicially created means of effectuating the rights secured by the Fourth Amendment. Prior to the Court's decisions in Weeks v. United States (1914), and Gouled v. United States (1921), there existed no barrier to the introduction in criminal trials of evidence obtained in violation of the Amendment. In *Weeks*, the Court held that the defendant could petition before trial for the return of property secured through an illegal search or seizure conducted by federal authorities. In *Gouled*, the Court held broadly that such evidence could not be introduced in a federal prosecution.

Decisions prior to *Mapp* [v. Ohio (1961)] advanced two principal reasons for application of the rule in federal trials. The Court in the context of its special supervisory role over the lower federal courts, referred to the "imperative of judicial integrity," suggesting that exclusion of illegally seized evidence prevents contamination of the judicial process. The *Mapp* majority justified the application of the rule to the States on several grounds, but relied principally upon the belief that exclusion would deter future unlawful police conduct.

Although our decisions often have alluded to the "imperative of judicial integrity," they demonstrate the limited role of this justification in the determination whether to apply the rule in a particular context. Logically extended this justification would require that courts exclude unconstitutionally seized evidence despite lack of objection by the defendant, or even over his assent. It also would require abandonment of the standing limitations on who may object to the introduction of unconstitutionally seized evidence, and retreat from the proposition that judicial proceedings need not abate when the defendant's person is unconstitutionally seized. Similarly, the interest in promoting judicial integrity does not prevent the use of illegally seized evidence in grand jury proceedings. Nor does it require that the trial court exclude such evidence from use for impeachment of a defendant, even though its introduction is certain to result in conviction in some cases.

The teaching of these cases is clear. While courts, of course, must ever be concerned with preserving the integrity of the judicial process, this concern has limited force as a justification for the exclusion of highly probative evidence. The force of this justification becomes minimal where federal habeas corpus relief is sought by a prisoner who previously has been afforded the opportunity for full and fair consideration of his search-and-seizure claim at trial and on direct review.

The primary justification for the exclusionary rule then is the deterrence of police conduct that violates Fourth Amendment rights. Post-*Mapp* decisions have established that the rule is not a personal constitutional right. It is not calculated to redress the injury to the privacy of the victim of the search or seizure, for any "[r]eparation comes too late." Instead, "the rule is a judicially created remedy designed to safeguard Fourth Amendment rights generally through its deterrent effect. . . ."

IV

We turn now to the specific question presented by these cases. Respondents allege violations of Fourth Amendment rights guaranteed them through the Fourteenth Amendment. The question is whether state prisoners who have been afforded the opportunity for full and fair consideration of their reliance upon the exclusionary rule with respect to seized evidence by the state courts at trial and on direct review may invoke their claim again on federal habeas corpus review. The answer is to be found by weighing the utility of the exclusionary rule against the costs of extending it to collateral review of Fourth Amendment claims.

The costs of applying the exclusionary rule even at trial and on direct review are well known: the focus of the trial, and the attention of the participants therein, are diverted from the ultimate question of guilt or innocence that should be the central concern in a criminal proceeding. Moreover, the physical evidence sought to be excluded is typically reliable and often the most probative information bearing on the guilt or innocence of the defendant.

Application of the rule thus deflects the truthfinding process and often frees the guilty. The disparity in particular cases between the error committed by the police officer and the windfall afforded a guilty defendant by application of the rule is contrary to the idea of proportionality that is essential to the concept of justice. Thus, although the rule is thought to deter unlawful police activity in part through the nurturing of respect for Fourth Amendment values, if applied indiscriminately it may well have the opposite effect of generating disrespect for the law and administration of justice. These long-recognized costs of the rule persist when a criminal conviction is sought to be overturned on collateral review on the ground that a search-and-seizure claim was erroneously rejected by two or more tiers of state courts.

We nevertheless afford broad habeas corpus relief, recognizing the need in a free society for an additional safeguard against compelling an innocent man to suffer an unconstitutional loss of liberty. The Court in Fay v. Noia (1963), described habeas corpus as a remedy for "whatever society deems to be intolerable restraints," and recognized that those to whom the writ should be granted "are persons whom society has grievously wronged."

But in the case of a typical Fourth Amendment claim, asserted on collateral attack, a convicted defendant is usually asking society to redetermine an issue that has no bearing on the basic justice of his incarceration.

Evidence obtained by police officers in violation of the Fourth Amendment is excluded at trial in the hope that the frequency of future violations will decrease. Despite the absence of supportive empirical evidence, we have assumed that the immediate effect of exclusion will be to discourage law enforcement officials from violating the Fourth Amendment by removing the incentive to disregard it. More importantly, over the long term, this demonstration that our society attaches serious consequences to violation of constitutional rights is thought to encourage those who formulate law enforcement policies, and the officers who implement them, to incorporate Fourth Amendment ideals into their value system.

We adhere to the view that these considerations support the implementation of the exclusionary rule at trial and its enforcement on direct appeal of state-court convictions. But the additional contribution, if any, of the consideration of search-and-seizure claims of state prisoners on collateral review is small in relation to the costs. To be sure, each case in which such claim is considered may add marginally to an awareness of the values protected by the Fourth Amendment. There is no reason to believe, however, that the overall educative effect of the exclusionary rule would be appreciably diminished if search-and-seizure claims could not be raised in federal habeas corpus review of state convictions. Nor is there reason to assume that any specific disincentive already created by the risk of exclusion of evidence at trial or the reversal of convictions on direct review would be enhanced if there were the further risk that a conviction obtained in state court and affirmed on direct review might be overturned in collateral proceedings often occurring years after the incarceration of the defendant. The view that the deterrence of Fourth Amendment violations would be furthered rests on the dubious assumption that law enforcement authorities would fear that federal habeas review might reveal flaws in a search or seizure that went undetected at trial and on appeal.[41] Even if one rationally could assume that

41. The policy arguments that respondents marshal in support of the view that federal habeas corpus review is necessary to effectuate the Fourth Amendment stem from a basic mistrust of the state courts as fair and competent forums for the adjudication of federal constitutional rights. The argument is that state courts cannot be trusted to effectuate Fourth Amendment values through fair application of the rule, and the oversight jurisdiction of this Court on certiorari is an inadequate safeguard. The principal rationale for this view emphasizes the broad differences in the respective institutional settings within which federal judges and state judges operate. Despite differences in institutional environment and the unsympathetic attitude to federal constitutional claims of some state judges in years past, we are unwilling to assume that there now exists a general lack of appropriate sensitivity to constitutional rights in the trial and appellate courts of the several States. State courts, like federal courts, have a constitutional obligation to safeguard personal liberties and to uphold federal law. Moreover, the argument that federal judges are more expert in applying federal constitutional law is especially unpersuasive in the context of search-and-seizure claims, since they are dealt with on a daily basis by trial level judges in both systems. In sum, there is "no intrinsic reason why the fact that a man is a federal judge should make him more competent, or conscientious, or learned with respect to the [consideration of Fourth Amendment claims] than his neighbor in the state courthouse." [Footnote by the Court.]

some additional incremental deterrent effect would be presented in isolated cases, the resulting advance of the legitimate goal of furthering Fourth Amendment rights would be outweighed by the acknowledged costs to other values vital to a rational system of criminal justice.

In sum, we conclude that where the State has provided an opportunity for full and fair litigation of a Fourth Amendment claim, a state prisoner may not be granted federal habeas corpus relief on the ground that evidence obtained in an unconstitutional search or seizure was introduced at his trial. In this context the contribution of the exclusionary rule, if any, to the effectuation of the Fourth Amendment is minimal, and the substantial societal costs of application of the rule persist with special force.

With all respect, the hyperbole of the dissenting opinion is misdirected. Our decision today is not concerned with the scope of the habeas corpus statute as authority for litigating constitutional claims generally. We do reaffirm that the exclusionary rule is a judicially created remedy rather than a personal constitutional right, and we emphasize the minimal utility of the rule when sought to be applied to Fourth Amendment claims in a habeas corpus proceeding. In sum, we hold only that a federal court need not apply the exclusionary rule on habeas review of a Fourth Amendment claim absent a showing that the state prisoner was denied an opportunity for a full and fair litigation of that claim at trial and on direct review. Our decision does not mean that the federal court lacks jurisdiction over such a claim, but only that the application of the rule is limited to cases in which there has been both such a showing and a Fourth Amendment violation.

Justice BRENNAN, with whom Justice MARSHALL concurs, dissenting.

The Court today holds "that where the State has provided an opportunity for full and fair litigation of a Fourth Amendment claim, a state prisoner may not be granted federal habeas corpus relief on the ground that evidence obtained in an unconstitutional search or seizure was introduced at his trial." To be sure, my Brethren are hostile to the continued vitality of the exclusionary rule as part and parcel of the Fourth Amendment's prohibition of unreasonable searches and seizures. Today's holding portends substantial evisceration of federal habeas corpus jurisdiction, and I dissent.

The Court's opinion does not specify the particular basis on which it denies federal habeas jurisdiction over claims of Fourth Amendment violations brought by state prisoners.

Much of the Court's analysis implies that respondents are not entitled to habeas relief because they are not being unconstitutionally detained. Although purportedly adhering to the principle that the Fourth and Fourteenth Amendments "require exclusion" of evidence seized in violation of their commands, the Court informs us that there has merely been a "view" in our cases that "the effectuation of the Fourth Amendment . . . requires the granting of habeas corpus relief when a prisoner has been convicted in state court on the basis of evidence obtained in an illegal search or seizure. . . ." Applying a "balancing test," the Court then concludes that this "view" is unjustified and that the policies of the Fourth Amendment would not be implemented if claims to the benefits of the exclusionary rule were cognizable in collateral attacks on state-court convictions.

Understandably the Court must purport to cast its holding in constitutional terms, because that avoids a direct confrontation with the incontrovertible facts that the habeas statutes have heretofore always been construed to grant jurisdiction to entertain Fourth Amendment claims of both state and federal prisoners, that Fourth Amendment principles have been applied in decisions on the merits in numerous cases on collateral review of final convictions, and that Congress has legislatively accepted our interpretation of congressional intent as to the necessary scope and function of habeas relief. Indeed, the Court reaches its result without explicitly overruling any of our plethora of precedents inconsistent with that result or even discussing principles of stare decisis. Rather, the Court asserts, in essence, that the Justices joining those prior decisions or reaching the merits of Fourth Amendment claims simply overlooked the obvious constitutional dimension to the problem in adhering to the "view" that granting collateral relief when state courts erroneously decide Fourth Amendment issues would effectuate the principles underlying that Amendment.

But, shorn of the rhetoric of "interest balancing" used to obscure what is at stake in this case, it is evident that today's attempt to rest the decision on the Constitution must fail so long as Mapp v. Ohio remains undisturbed.

Under *Mapp*, as a matter of federal constitutional law, a state court must exclude evidence from the trial of an individual whose Fourth and Fourteenth Amendment rights were violated by a search or seizure that directly or indirectly resulted in the acquisition of that evidence. When a state court admits such evidence, it has committed a constitutional error, and unless that error is harmless under federal standards, it follows ineluctably that the defendant has been placed "in custody in violation of the Constitution" within the comprehension of 28 U.S.C. §2254. In short, it escapes me as to what logic can support the assertion that the defendant's unconstitutional confinement obtains during the process of direct review, no matter how long that process takes, but that the unconstitutionality then suddenly dissipates at the moment the claim is asserted in a collateral attack on the conviction.

The only conceivable rationale upon which the Court's "constitutional" thesis might rest is the statement that "the [exclusionary] rule is not a personal constitutional right. . . . Instead, 'the rule is a judicially created remedy designed to safeguard Fourth Amendment rights generally through its deterrent effect.'" [I]n light of contrary decisions establishing the role of the exclusionary rule, the premise that an individual has no constitutional right to have unconstitutionally seized evidence excluded from all use by the government [has no basis]. [But] I need not dispute that point here. For today's holding is not logically defensible. However, the Court reinterprets *Mapp*, and whatever the rationale now attributed to *Mapp*'s holding or the purpose ascribed to the exclusionary rule, the prevailing constitutional rule is that unconstitutionally seized evidence cannot be admitted in the criminal trial of a person whose federal constitutional rights were violated by the search or seizure. The erroneous admission of such evidence is a violation of the Federal Constitution — *Mapp* inexorably means at least this much, or there would be no basis for applying the exclusionary rule in state criminal proceedings — and an accused against whom such evidence is admitted has been convicted in derogation of rights mandated by, and is "in custody in violation," of the Constitution of the United States. Indeed, since state courts violate the strictures of the Federal Constitution by admitting such evidence, then even if federal habeas review did not directly effectuate Fourth Amendment values, a proposition I deny, that review would nevertheless serve to effectuate what is concededly a constitutional principle concerning admissibility of evidence at trial.

The Court's arguments respecting the cost/benefit analysis of applying the exclusionary rule on collateral attack also have no merit. For all of the "costs" of applying the exclusionary rule on habeas should already have been incurred at the trial or on direct review if the state court had not misapplied federal constitutional principles. As such, these "costs" were evaluated and deemed to be outweighed when the exclusionary rule was fashioned. The only proper question on habeas is whether federal courts, acting under congressional directive to have the last say as to enforcement of federal constitutional principles, are to permit the States free enjoyment of the fruits of a conviction which by definition were only obtained through violations of the Constitution as interpreted in *Mapp*. And as to the question whether any "educative" function is served by such habeas review, today's decision will certainly provide a lesson that, tragically for an individual's constitutional rights, will not be lost on state courts.

Therefore, the real ground of today's decision — a ground that is particularly troubling in light of its portent for habeas jurisdiction generally — is the Court's novel reinterpretation of the habeas statutes; this would read the statutes as requiring the district courts routinely to deny habeas relief to prisoners "in custody in violation of the Constitution or laws . . . of the United States" as a matter of judicial "discretion" — a "discretion" judicially manufactured today contrary to the express statutory language — because such claims are "different in kind" from other constitutional violations in that they "do not 'impugn the integrity of the fact-finding process,'" and because application of such constitutional strictures "often frees the guilty." Much in the Court's opinion suggests that a construction of the habeas statutes to deny relief for non-"guilt-related" constitutional violations, based on this Court's vague notions of comity and federalism, is the actual premise for today's decision, and although the Court attempts to bury its underlying premises in footnotes, those premises mark this case as a harbinger of future eviscerations of the habeas statutes that plainly does violence to congressional power to frame the statutory contours of habeas jurisdiction. For we are told that "[r]esort to habeas corpus, especially for purposes other than to assure that no innocent person suffers an unconstitutional loss of liberty, results in serious intrusions on values important to our system of government," including waste of judicial resources, lack of finality of criminal convictions, friction between the federal and state judiciaries, and incursions on "federalism." We are told that federal determination of Fourth Amendment claims merely involves "an issue that has no bearing on the basic justice of [the defendant's] incarceration," and that "the ultimate question [in the criminal process should invariably be] guilt or innocence." We are told that the "policy arguments" of respondents to the effect that federal courts must be the ultimate arbiters of federal constitutional rights, and that our certiorari jurisdiction is inadequate to perform this task, "stem from a basic mistrust of the state courts as fair and competent forums for the adjudication of federal constitutional rights"; the Court, however, finds itself "unwilling to assume that there now exists a general lack of appropriate sensitivity to constitutional rights in the trial and appellate courts of the several States," and asserts that it is "unpersuaded" by "the argument that federal judges are more expert in applying federal constitutional law" because "there is 'no intrinsic reason why the fact that a man is a federal judge should make him more competent, or conscientious, or learned with respect to the [consideration of Fourth Amendment claims] than his neighbor in the state courthouse.' " Finally, we are provided a revisionist history of the genesis and growth of federal habeas corpus jurisdiction. If today's decision were only that erroneous state-court resolution of Fourth Amendment claims did not render the defendant's resultant confinement "in violation of the Constitution," these pronouncements would have been wholly irrelevant and unnecessary. I am therefore justified in apprehending that the groundwork is being laid today for a drastic withdrawal of federal habeas jurisdiction, if not for all grounds of alleged unconstitutional detention, then at least for claims — for example, of double jeopardy, entrapment, self-incrimination, *Miranda* violations, and use of invalid identification procedures — that this Court later decides are not "guilt related."

At least since Brown v. Allen, detention emanating from judicial proceedings in which constitutional rights were denied has been deemed "contrary to fundamental law," and all constitutional claims have thus been cognizable on federal habeas corpus. There is no foundation in the language or history of the habeas statutes for discriminating between types of constitutional transgressions, and efforts to relegate certain categories of claims to the status of "second-class rights" by excluding them from that jurisdiction have been repulsed. Today's opinion, however, marks the triumph of those who have sought to establish a hierarchy of constitutional rights, and to deny for all practical purposes a federal forum for review of those rights that this Court deems less worthy or important. Without even paying the slightest deference to principles of stare decisis or acknowledging Congress' failure for two decades to alter the habeas statutes in light of our interpretation of congressional intent to render all federal constitutional contentions cognizable on habeas, the Court today rewrites Congress' jurisdictional statutes as heretofore construed and bars access to federal courts by state prisoners with constitutional claims distasteful to a majority of my Brethren. But even ignoring principles of stare decisis dictating that Congress is the appropriate vehicle for embarking on such a fundamental shift in the jurisdiction of the federal courts, I can find no adequate justification elucidated by the Court for concluding that habeas relief for all federal constitutional claims is no longer compelled under the reasoning of *Brown, Fay,* and *Kaufman.*

For a time it appeared that *Stone* might represent a first step to overruling Brown v. Allen and thus would prevent relitigation of constitutional claims on habeas corpus. After all, if the legislative history of the habeas corpus statutes is read as preventing relitigation, or if state courts are generally equal to federal courts in their protection of constitutional rights, relitigation appears unnecessary. However, the Supreme Court has not extended *Stone* to other constitutional rights or further limited the application of Brown v. Allen.

In Rose v. Mitchell, 443 U.S. 545 (1979), the Supreme Court held that habeas petitioners could challenge the racial composition of grand juries even when the claim had been litigated and rejected in the state court. Although on the merits the Court found that there was no discrimination, the Court emphasized the availability of habeas corpus review to determine the issue. The Court, in an opinion by Justice Blackmun, said that federal habeas review was "necessary to ensure that constitutional defects in the state judiciary's grand jury selection procedure are not overlooked by the very judges who operate that system." Thus the Court concluded that a claim of discrimination in grand jury selection is not rendered harmless by a subsequent determination of guilt beyond a reasonable doubt by a petit jury and that *Stone* did not apply to foreclose federal court habeas review.

Likewise, the Supreme Court held that the constitutionality of jury instructions concerning the standard of proof to be applied could be challenged on habeas corpus even though the issue had been presented and decided at trial. In Jackson v. Virginia, 443 U.S. 307 (1979), the Court held that habeas corpus review is available for a petitioner who claims that "no rational trier of fact" could have concluded that the state presented sufficient evidence to establish each element of the crime beyond a reasonable doubt. The Court expressly stated that this contention could be relitigated on habeas corpus even though it had been rejected by the state courts.

In Kimmelman v. Morrison, 477 U.S. 365 (1986), the Supreme Court held that a Sixth Amendment claim of ineffective assistance of counsel could be relitigated on habeas corpus, even where the attorney's error was a failure to raise Fourth Amendment objections to the introduction of evidence. In *Kimmelman,* the defendant was convicted of rape largely on the basis of evidence obtained in an allegedly illegal search. The defendant sought habeas corpus relief both on the grounds that illegally seized evidence was admitted and that the defense attorney's failure to object to the introduction of the evidence constituted ineffective assistance of counsel.

The Supreme Court held that although Stone v. Powell barred litigating the Fourth Amendment claim on habeas corpus, the Sixth Amendment issue of ineffective assistance of counsel could be relitigated in federal court. The Court, in an opinion by Justice Brennan, observed that "[t]he right to counsel is a fundamental right of criminal defendants; it assures the fairness, and thus the legitimacy of our adversary process." As such the Court concluded that "while respondent's defaulted Fourth Amendment claim is one element of proof of his Sixth Amendment claim, the two claims have separate identities and reflect different constitutional values."

Most recently and most importantly, in Withrow v. Williams, 507 U.S. 680 (1993), the Court refused to extend Stone v. Powell to *Miranda* claims. Justice Souter, writing for the Court, declared, "Today we hold that *Stone*'s restriction on the exercise of federal habeas jurisdiction does not extend to a state prisoner's claim that his conviction rests on statements obtained in violation of the safeguards mandated by Miranda v. Arizona (1966)."

The decision provided the occasion for the majority and dissenting justices to express very different views about *Miranda* and its constitutional status. Justice Souter, writing for the majority, stated:

> We have made it clear that *Stone*'s limitation on federal habeas relief was not jurisdictional in nature, but rested on prudential concerns counseling against the application of the Fourth Amendment exclusionary rule on collateral review. We simply concluded in *Stone* that the costs of applying the exclusionary rule on collateral review outweighed any potential advantage to be gained by applying it there.
>
> Petitioner, supported by the United States as amicus curiae, argues that *Miranda*'s safeguards are not constitutional in character, but merely "prophylactic," and that in consequence habeas review should not extend to a claim that a state conviction rests on statements obtained in the absence of those safeguards. We accept petitioner's premise for purposes of this case, but not her conclusion.
>
> The *Miranda* Court did of course caution that the Constitution requires no "particular solution for the inherent compulsions of the interrogation process," and left it open to a State to meet its burden by adopting "other procedures . . . at least as effective in apprising accused persons" of their rights. The Court indeed acknowledged that, in barring introduction of a statement obtained without the required warnings, *Miranda* might exclude a confession that we would not condemn as "involuntary in traditional terms," and for this reason we have sometimes called the *Miranda* safeguards "prophylactic" in nature. Calling the *Miranda* safeguards "prophylactic," however, is a far cry from putting *Miranda* on all fours with *Mapp*, or from rendering *Miranda* subject to *Stone*.
>
> As we explained in *Stone*, the *Mapp* rule "is not a personal constitutional right," but serves to deter future constitutional violations; although it mitigates the juridical consequences of invading the defendant's privacy, the exclusion of evidence at trial can do nothing to remedy the completed and wholly extrajudicial Fourth Amendment violation. Nor can the *Mapp* rule be thought to enhance the soundness of the criminal process by improving the reliability of evidence introduced at

trial. Quite the contrary, as we explained in *Stone*, the evidence excluded under *Mapp* "is typically reliable and often the most probative information bearing on the guilt or innocence of the defendant."

Miranda differs from *Mapp* in both respects. "Prophylactic" though it may be, in protecting a defendant's Fifth Amendment privilege against self-incrimination, *Miranda* safeguards "a fundamental trial right." The privilege embodies "principles of humanity and civil liberty, which had been secured in the mother country only after years of struggle," and reflects "many of our fundamental values and most noble aspirations: . . . our preference for an accusatorial rather than an inquisitorial system of criminal justice"; our fear that self-incriminating statements will be elicited by inhumane treatment and abuses; our sense of fair play which dictates "a fair state-individual balance by requiring the government to leave the individual alone until good cause is shown for disturbing him and by requiring the government in its contest with the individual to shoulder the entire load"; our respect for the inviolability of the human personality and of the right of each individual "to a private enclave where he may lead a private life"; our distrust of self-deprecatory statements; and our realization that the privilege, while sometimes "a shelter to the guilty," is often "a protection to the innocent."

Nor does the Fifth Amendment "trial right" protected by *Miranda* serve some value necessarily divorced from the correct ascertainment of guilt. "[A] system of criminal law enforcement which comes to depend on the confession will, in the long run, be less reliable and more subject to abuses than a system relying on independent investigation." By bracing against "the possibility of unreliable statements in every instance of in-custody interrogation," *Miranda* serves to guard against "the use of unreliable statements at trial."

Finally, and most importantly, eliminating review of *Miranda* claims would not significantly benefit the federal courts in their exercise of habeas jurisdiction, or advance the cause of federalism in any substantial way. As one amicus concedes, eliminating habeas review of *Miranda* issues would not prevent a state prisoner from simply converting his barred *Miranda* claim into a due process claim that his conviction rested on an involuntary confession. Indeed, although counsel could provide us with no empirical basis for projecting the consequence of adopting petitioner's position, it seems reasonable to suppose that virtually all *Miranda* claims would simply be recast in this way.

If that is so, the federal courts would certainly not have heard the last of *Miranda* on collateral review. Under the due process approach, as we have already seen, courts look to the totality of circumstances to determine whether a confession was voluntary. Those potential circumstances include not only the crucial element of police coercion, the length of the interrogation, its location, the defendant's maturity, education, physical condition, and mental health. They also include the failure of police to advise the defendant of his rights to remain silent and to have counsel present during custodial interrogation. We could lock the front door against *Miranda*, but not the back.

We thus fail to see how abdicating *Miranda*'s bright-line (or, at least, brighter-line) rules in favor of an exhaustive totality-of-circumstances approach on habeas would do much of anything to lighten the burdens placed on busy federal courts. We likewise fail to see how purporting to eliminate *Miranda* issues from federal habeas would go very far to relieve such tensions as *Miranda* may now raise between the two judicial systems. Relegation of habeas petitioners to straight involuntariness claims would not likely reduce the amount of litigation, and each such claim would in any event present a legal question requiring an independent federal determination on habeas.

But four justices would have extended *Stone* to *Miranda* claims. Justice O'Connor, with whom the chief justice joined, dissented and expressed a very different view of *Miranda*. She wrote:

> Today the Court permits the federal courts to overturn on habeas the conviction of a double murderer, not on the basis of an inexorable constitutional or statutory command, but because it believes the result desirable from the standpoint of equity and judicial administration. Because the principles that inform our habeas jurisprudence — finality, federalism, and fairness — counsel decisively against the result the Court reaches, I respectfully dissent from this holding.
>
> Today we face the question whether Stone v. Powell should extend to bar claims on habeas that alleged violations of the prophylactic rule of Miranda v. Arizona (1966). Continuing the tradition of caution in this area, the Court answers that question in the negative. This time I must disagree. In my view, the "prudential concerns," that inform our habeas jurisprudence counsel the exclusion of *Miranda* claims just as strongly as they did the exclusionary rule claims at issue in *Stone* itself.
>
> I continue to believe that these same considerations apply to *Miranda* claims with equal, if not greater, force. Like the suppression of the fruits of an illegal search or seizure, the exclusion of statements obtained in violation of *Miranda* is not constitutionally required. This Court repeatedly has held that *Miranda*'s warning requirement is not a dictate of the Fifth Amendment itself, but a prophylactic rule. Because *Miranda* "sweeps more broadly than the Fifth Amendment itself," it excludes some confessions even though the Constitution would not. Indeed, "in the individual case, *Miranda*'s preventive medicine [often] provides a remedy even to the defendant who has suffered no identifiable constitutional harm."
>
> *Miranda*'s overbreadth, of course, is not without justification. The exclusion of unwarned statements provides a strong incentive for the police to adopt "procedural safeguards," against the exaction of compelled or involuntary statements. It also promotes institutional respect for constitutional values. But, like the exclusionary rule for illegally seized evidence, *Miranda*'s prophylactic rule does so at a substantial cost. Unlike involuntary or compelled statements — which are of dubious reliability and are therefore inadmissible for any purpose — confessions obtained in violation of *Miranda* are not necessarily untrustworthy. In fact, because voluntary statements are "trustworthy" even when obtained without proper warnings, their suppression actually impairs the pursuit of truth by concealing probative information from the trier of fact.
>
> When the case is on direct review, that damage to the truth-seeking function is deemed an acceptable sacrifice for the deterrence and respect for constitutional values that the *Miranda* rule brings. But once a case is on collateral review, the balance between the costs and benefits shifts; the interests of federalism, finality, and fairness compel *Miranda*'s exclusion from habeas. The benefit of enforcing *Miranda* through habeas is marginal at best. To the extent *Miranda* ensures the exclusion of involuntary statements, that task can be performed more accurately by adjudicating the voluntariness question directly. And, to the extent exclusion of voluntary but unwarned confessions serves a deterrent function, "[t]he awarding of habeas relief years after conviction will often strike like lightning, and it is absurd to think that this added possibility . . . will have any appreciable effect on police training or behavior."
>
> Despite its meager benefits, the relitigation of *Miranda* claims on habeas imposes substantial costs. Just like the application of the exclusionary rule, application of

Miranda's prophylactic rule on habeas consumes scarce judicial resources on an issue unrelated to guilt or innocence. No less than the exclusionary rule, it undercuts finality. It creates tension between the state and federal courts. And it upsets the division of responsibilities that underlies our federal system. But most troubling of all, *Miranda*'s application on habeas sometimes precludes the just application of law altogether. The order excluding the statement will often be issued "years after trial, when a new trial may be a practical impossibility." Whether the Court admits it or not, the grim result of applying *Miranda* on habeas will be, time and time again, "the release of an admittedly guilty individual who may pose a continuing threat to society."

Any rule that so demonstrably renders truth and society "the loser," "bear[s] a heavy burden of justification, and must be carefully limited to the circumstances in which it will pay its way by deterring official lawlessness." That burden is heavier still on collateral review. In light of the meager deterrent benefit it brings and the tremendous costs it imposes, in my view application of *Miranda*'s prophylactic rule on habeas "falls short" of justification.

As the Court emphasizes today, *Miranda*'s prophylactic rule is now 27 years old; the police and the state courts have indeed grown accustomed to it. But it is precisely because the rule is well accepted that there is little further benefit to enforcing it on habeas. We can depend on law enforcement officials to administer warnings in the first instance and the state courts to provide a remedy when law enforcement officers err. None of the Court's asserted justifications for enforcing Miranda's prophylactic rule through habeas—neither reverence for the Fifth Amendment nor the concerns of reliability, efficiency, and federalism—counsel in favor of the Court's chosen course. Indeed, in my view they cut in precisely the opposite direction. The Court may reconsider its decision when presented with empirical data. But I see little reason for such a costly delay. Logic and experience are at our disposal now. And they amply demonstrate that applying *Miranda*'s prophylactic rule on habeas does not increase the amount of justice dispensed; it only increases the frequency with which the admittedly guilty go free. In my view, *Miranda* imposes such grave costs and produces so little benefit on habeas that its continued application is neither tolerable nor justified.

Justice Scalia also wrote a dissent, with which Justice Thomas joined, in which he said:

> In my view, both the Court and Justice O'Connor disregard the most powerful equitable consideration: that Williams has already had full and fair opportunity to litigate this claim. He had the opportunity to raise it in the Michigan trial court; he did so and lost. He had the opportunity to seek review of the trial court's judgment in the Michigan Court of Appeals; he did so and lost. Finally, he had the opportunity to seek discretionary review of that Court of Appeals judgment in both the Michigan Supreme Court and this Court; he did so and review was denied. The question at this stage is whether, given all that, a federal habeas court should now reopen the issue and adjudicate the *Miranda* claim anew. The answer seems to me obvious: it should not. That would be the course followed by a federal habeas court reviewing a federal conviction; it mocks our federal system to accord state convictions less respect.

So, at least for now, the only constitutional claims that cannot be raised on habeas corpus are Fourth Amendment exclusionary rule claims that have had a full and fair opportunity to be litigated in state court.

6. Has There Been a Procedural Default, and If So, Is There Either Cause and Prejudice or an Adequate Showing of Actual Innocence?

Criminal defendants are required to raise their constitutional claims during their trials and direct appeals. The failure to do so is deemed a procedural default. The question is whether such procedural defaults bar a convicted defendant from then raising the issue on habeas corpus.

The law has changed dramatically over the past half century concerning when a defendant may present a matter on habeas corpus that was not litigated at the trial. Under the Warren Court's decisions, a defendant was allowed to raise matters not argued in the state courts unless it could be demonstrated that the defendant deliberately chose to bypass the state court procedures. In other words, there was a strong presumption that procedural defaults would not bar federal habeas corpus review.

In Fay v. Noia, 372 U.S. 391 (1963), the Supreme Court held that an individual convicted in state court may raise on habeas issues that were not presented at trial, unless it can be demonstrated that he or she deliberately chose to bypass the state procedures. In *Fay*, three codefendants were convicted. Two of the defendants appealed and were successful in having their convictions overturned because of the manner in which their confessions were obtained. Noia, the third defendant, then tried to obtain relief in the New York state courts. The New York courts, however, denied Noia's motion to have his conviction overturned because his failure to appeal constituted a procedural default precluding review.

The United States Supreme Court rejected the argument that failure to comply with state procedures bars federal court review on habeas corpus. The Court concluded that "a forfeiture of remedies does not legitimize the unconstitutional conduct by which . . . [a] conviction was procured." In *Fay*, the Court perceived its role and the purpose of habeas corpus as preventing the detention of individuals whose conviction resulted from unconstitutional conduct. The Court said that a habeas petitioner would be foreclosed from raising an issue on the ground that it was not presented at trial only if he or she "deliberately bypassed the orderly procedure of the state courts."

In sharp contrast, the Burger and Rehnquist Courts departed from and ultimately overruled *Fay*. The Court held that a defendant could present matters on habeas corpus that were not raised at the trial only if the defendant could demonstrate either actual innocence or good "cause" for the procedural default, and either "prejudice" from the federal court's refusal to hear the matter or a showing of actual innocence. Under this approach, there is a strong presumption that procedural defaults in state court will preclude habeas corpus litigation.

Wainwright v. Sykes was the key Supreme Court case signaling a departure from Fay v. Noia and a different approach to handling procedural defaults on habeas corpus. In reading Wainwright v. Sykes, it is important to consider how it rests on different assumptions than Fay v. Noia concerning why procedural defaults happen and the fairness of precluding constitutional claims from being raised.

WAINWRIGHT v. SYKES
433 U.S. 72 (1977)

Justice Rehnquist delivered the opinion of the Court.

We granted certiorari to consider the availability of federal habeas corpus to review a state convict's claim that testimony was admitted at his trial in violation of his rights under Miranda v. Arizona (1966), a claim which the Florida courts have previously refused to consider on the merits because of noncompliance with a state contemporaneous-objection rule.

Respondent Sykes was convicted of third-degree murder after a jury trial in the Circuit Court of DeSoto County. He testified at trial that on the evening of January 8, 1972, he told his wife to summon the police because he had just shot Willie Gilbert. Other evidence indicated that when the police arrived at respondent's trailer home, they found Gilbert dead of a shotgun wound, lying a few feet from the front porch. Shortly after their arrival, respondent came from across the road and volunteered that he had shot Gilbert, and a few minutes later respondent's wife approached the police and told them the same thing. Sykes was immediately arrested and taken to the police station.

Once there, it is conceded that he was read his *Miranda* rights, and that he declined to seek the aid of counsel and indicated a desire to talk. He then made a statement, which was admitted into evidence at trial through the testimony of the two officers who heard it, to the effect that he had shot Gilbert from the front porch of his trailer home. There were several references during the trial to respondent's consumption of alcohol during the preceding day and to his apparent state of intoxication, facts which were acknowledged by the officers who arrived at the scene. At no time during the trial, however, was the admissibility of any of respondent's statements challenged by his counsel on the ground that respondent had not understood the *Miranda* warnings. Nor did the trial judge question their admissibility on his own motion or hold a factfinding hearing bearing on that issue.

Respondent appealed his conviction, but apparently did not challenge the admissibility of the inculpatory statements. He later filed in the trial court a motion to vacate the conviction and, in the State District Court of Appeals and Supreme Court, petitions for habeas corpus. These filings, apparently for the first time, challenged the statements made to police on grounds of involuntariness. In all of these efforts respondent was unsuccessful.

The simple legal question before the Court calls for a construction of the language of 28 U.S.C. §2254(a), which provides that the federal courts shall entertain an application for a writ of habeas corpus "in behalf of a person in custody pursuant to the judgment of a state court only on the ground that he is in custody in violation of the Constitution or laws or treaties of the United States." But, to put it mildly, we do not write on a clean slate in construing this statutory provision.

As to the role of adequate and independent state grounds, it is a well-established principle of federalism that a state decision resting on an adequate foundation of state substantive law is immune from review in the federal courts. The application of this principle in the context of a federal habeas proceeding has therefore excluded from consideration any questions of state substantive law, and thus effectively barred federal habeas review where questions of that sort are either the only ones raised by a petitioner or are in themselves dispositive of his case. The area of controversy which has developed has concerned the reviewability of federal claims which the state court has declined to pass on because not presented in the manner prescribed by its procedural rules.

We conclude that Florida procedure did, consistently with the United States Constitution, require that respondents' confession be challenged at trial or not at all, and thus his failure to timely object to its admission amounted to an independent and adequate state procedural ground which would have prevented direct review here. We thus come to the crux of this case. Shall the rule of Francis v. Henderson, supra, barring federal habeas review absent a showing of "cause" and "prejudice" attendant to a state procedural waiver, be applied to a waived objection to the admission of a confession at trial? We answer that question in the affirmative.

[S]ince Brown v. Allen (1953), it has been the rule that the federal habeas petitioner who claims he is detained pursuant to a final judgment of a state court in violation of the United States Constitution is entitled to have the federal habeas court make its own independent determination of his federal claim, without being bound by the determination on the merits of that claim reached in the state proceedings. This rule of Brown v. Allen is in no way changed by our holding today. Rather, we deal only with contentions of federal law which were not resolved on the merits in the state proceeding due to respondent's failure to raise them there as required by state procedure. We leave open for resolution in future decisions the precise definition of the "cause"-and-"prejudice" standard, and note here only that it is narrower than the standard set forth in dicta in Fay v. Noia, which would make federal habeas review generally available to state convicts absent a knowing and deliberate waiver of the federal constitutional contention. It is the sweeping language of Fay v. Noia, going far beyond the facts of the case eliciting it, which we today reject.

The reasons for our rejection of it are several. The contemporaneous-objection rule itself is by no means peculiar to Florida, and deserves greater respect than *Fay* gives it, both for the fact that it is employed by a coordinate jurisdiction within the federal system and for the many interests which it serves in its own right. A contemporaneous objection enables the record to be made with respect to the constitutional claim when the recollections of witnesses are freshest, not years later in a federal habeas proceeding. It enables the judge who observed the demeanor of those witnesses to make the factual determinations necessary for properly deciding the federal constitutional question.

A contemporaneous-objection rule may lead to the exclusion of the evidence objected to, thereby making a major contribution to finality in criminal litigation. Without the evidence claimed to be vulnerable on federal constitutional grounds, the jury may acquit the defendant, and that will be the end of the case; or it may nonetheless convict the defendant, and he will have one less federal constitutional claim to assert in his federal habeas petition. Subtler considerations as well militate in favor of honoring a state contemporaneous-objection rule. An objection on the spot may force the prosecution to take a hard look at its whole card, and even if the prosecutor thinks that the state trial judge will admit the evidence he must contemplate the possibility of reversal by the state appellate courts or the ultimate issuance of a federal writ of habeas corpus based on the impropriety of the state court's rejection of the federal constitutional claim.

We think that the rule of Fay v. Noia, broadly stated, may encourage "sandbagging" on the part of defense lawyers, who may take their chances on a verdict of not guilty in a state trial court with the intent to raise their constitutional claims in a federal habeas court if their initial gamble does not pay off. The refusal of federal habeas courts to honor contemporaneous-objection rules may also make state courts themselves less stringent in their enforcement. Under the rule of Fay v. Noia, state appellate courts know that a federal constitutional issue raised for the first time in the proceeding before them may well be decided in any event by a federal habeas tribunal. Thus, their choice is between addressing the issue notwithstanding the petitioner's failure to timely object, or else face the prospect that the federal habeas court will decide the question without the benefit of their views.

The failure of the federal habeas courts generally to require compliance with a contemporaneous-objection rule tends to detract from the perception of the trial of a criminal case in state court as a decisive and portentous event. A defendant has been accused of a serious crime, and this is the time and place set for him to be tried by a jury of his peers and found either guilty or not guilty by that jury. To the greatest extent possible all issues which bear on this charge should be determined in this proceeding: the accused is in the court-room, the jury is in the box, the judge is on the bench, and the witnesses, having been subpoenaed and duly sworn, await their turn to testify. Society's resources have been concentrated at that time and place in order to decide, within the limits of human fallibility, the question of guilt or innocence of one of its citizens. Any procedural rule which encourages the result that those proceedings be as free of error as possible is thoroughly desirable, and the contemporaneous-objection rule surely falls within this classification.

We believe the adoption of the [cause and prejudice] rule in this situation will have the salutary effect of making the state trial on the merits the "main event," so to speak, rather than a "tryout on the road" for what will later be the determinative federal habeas hearing. There is nothing in the Constitution or in the language of §2254 which requires that the state trial on the issue of guilt or innocence be devoted largely to the testimony of fact witnesses directed to the elements of the state crime, while only later will there occur in a federal habeas hearing a full airing of the federal constitutional claims which were not raised in the state proceedings. If a criminal defendant thinks that an action of the state trial court is about to deprive him of a federal constitutional right there is every reason for his following state procedure in making known his objection.

The "cause"-and-"prejudice" exception will afford an adequate guarantee, we think, that the rule will not prevent a federal habeas court from adjudicating for the first time the federal constitutional claim of a defendant who in the absence of such an adjudication will be the victim of a miscarriage of justice. Whatever precise content may be given those terms by later cases, we feel confident in holding without further elaboration that they do not exist here. Respondent has advanced no explanation whatever for his failure to object at trial, and, as the proceeding unfolded, the trial judge is certainly not to be faulted for failing to question the admission of the confession himself. The other evidence of guilt presented at trial, moreover, was substantial to a degree that would negate any possibility of actual prejudice resulting to the respondent from the admission of his inculpatory statement.

Justice BRENNAN, with whom Justice MARSHALL joins, dissenting.

Over the course of the last decade, the deliberate-bypass standard announced in Fay v. Noia (1963), has played a central role in efforts by the federal judiciary to accommodate the constitutional rights of the individual with the States' interests in the integrity of their judicial procedural regimes. The Court today decides that this standard should no longer apply with respect to procedural defaults occurring during the trial of a criminal defendant. In its place, the Court adopts the two-part "cause"-and-"prejudice" test. [T]oday's decision makes no effort to provide concrete guidance as to the content of those terms. More particularly, left unanswered is the thorny question that must be recognized to be central to a realistic rationalization of this area of law: How should the federal habeas court treat a procedural default in a state court that is attributable purely and simply to the error or negligence of a defendant's trial counsel? Because this key issue remains unresolved, I shall attempt in this opinion a re-examination of the policies that should inform and in *Fay* did inform the selection of the standard governing the availability of federal habeas corpus jurisdiction in the face of an intervening procedural default in the state court.

I

I begin with the threshold question: What is the meaning and import of a procedural default? If it could be assumed that a procedural default more often than not is the product of a defendant's conscious refusal to abide by the duly constituted, legitimate processes of the state courts, then I might agree that a regime of collateral review weighted in favor of a State's procedural rules would be warranted. *Fay*, however, recognized that such rarely is the case; and therein lies *Fay*'s basic unwillingness to embrace a view of habeas jurisdiction that results in "an airtight system of (procedural) forfeitures."

This, of course, is not to deny that there are times when the failure to heed a state procedural requirement stems from an intentional decision to avoid the presentation of constitutional claims to the state forum. *Fay* was not insensitive to this possibility. Indeed, the very purpose of its bypass test is to detect and enforce such intentional procedural forfeitures of outstanding constitutionally based claims. *Fay* does so through application of the long-standing rule used to test whether action or inaction on the part of a criminal defendant should be construed as a decision to surrender the assertion of rights secured by the Constitution: To be an effective waiver, there must be "an intentional relinquishment or abandonment of a known right or privilege." Johnson v. Zerbst (1938). Incorporating this standard, *Fay* recognized that if one "understandingly and knowingly forewent the privilege of seeking to vindicate his federal claims in the state courts, whether for strategic, tactical or any other reasons that can fairly be described as the deliberate by-passing of state procedures, then it is open to the federal court on habeas to deny him all relief. . . ." For this reason, the Court's assertion that it "think[s]" that the *Fay* rule encourages intentional "sandbagging" on the part of the defense lawyers is without basis; certainly the Court points to no cases or commentary arising during the past 15 years of actual use of the *Fay* test to support this criticism. Rather, a consistent reading of case law demonstrates that the bypass formula has provided a workable vehicle for protecting the integrity of state rules in those instances when such protection would be both meaningful and just.

But having created the bypass exception to the availability of collateral review, *Fay* recognized that intentional, tactical forfeitures are not the norm upon which to build a rational system of federal habeas jurisdiction. In the ordinary case, litigants simply have no incentive to slight the state tribunal, since constitutional adjudication on the state and federal levels are not mutually exclusive. Brown v. Allen (1953). Under the regime of collateral review recognized since the days of Brown v. Allen, and enforced by the *Fay* bypass test, no rational lawyer would risk the "sandbagging" feared by the Court. If a constitutional challenge is not properly raised on the state level, the explanation generally will be found elsewhere than in an intentional tactical decision.

In brief then, any realistic system of federal habeas corpus jurisdiction must be premised on the reality that the ordinary procedural default is born of the inadvertence, negligence, inexperience, or incompetence of trial counsel. *Fay*'s answer thus is plain: the bypass test simply refuses to credit what is essentially a lawyer's mistake as a forfeiture of constitutional rights.

I persist in the belief that the interests of Sykes and the State of Florida are best rationalized by adherence to this test, and by declining to react to inadvertent defaults through the creation of an "airtight system of forfeitures."

II

What are the interests that Sykes can assert in preserving the availability of federal collateral relief in the face of his inadvertent state procedural default? Two are paramount.

As is true with any federal habeas applicant, Sykes seeks access to the federal court for the determination of the validity of his federal constitutional claim. Since at least Brown v. Allen, it has been recognized that the "fair effect [of] the habeas corpus jurisdiction as enacted by Congress" entitles a state prisoner to such federal review. While some of my Brethen may feel uncomfortable with this congressional choice of policy, the Legislative Branch nonetheless remains entirely free to determine that the constitutional rights of an individual subject to state custody are best preserved by interposing the federal courts between the states and the people, as guardians of the people's federal rights.

With respect to federal habeas corpus jurisdiction, Congress explicitly chose to effectuate the federal court's primary responsibility for preserving federal rights and privileges by authorizing the litigation of constitutional claims and defenses in a district court after the State vindicates its own interest through trial of the substantive criminal offense in the state courts. This, of course, was not the only course that Congress might have followed: As an alternative, it might well have decided entirely to circumvent all state procedure through the expansion of existing federal removal statutes such as 28 U.S.C. §§1442(a)(1) and 1443, thereby authorizing the pretrial transfer of all state criminal cases to the federal courts whenever federal defenses or claims are in issue. But liberal post-trial federal review is the redress that Congress ultimately chose to allow and the consequences of a state procedural default should be evaluated in conformance with this policy choice. Certainly, we can all agree that once a state court has assumed jurisdiction of a criminal case, the integrity of its own process is a matter of legitimate concern. The *Fay* bypass test, by seeking to discover intentional abuses of the rules of the state forum, is, I believe, compatible with this state institutional interest. But whether *Fay* was correct in penalizing a litigant solely for his intentional forfeitures properly must be read in light of Congress' desired norm of widened post-trial access to the federal courts. If the standard adopted today is later construed to require that the simple mistakes of attorneys are to be treated as binding forfeitures, it would serve to subordinate the fundamental rights contained in our constitutional charter to inadvertent defaults of rules promulgated by state agencies, and would essentially leave it to the States, through the enactment of procedure and the certification of the competence of local attorneys, to determine whether a habeas applicant will be permitted the access to the federal forum that is guaranteed him by Congress.

Thus, I remain concerned that undue deference to local procedure can only serve to undermine the ready access to a federal court to which a state defendant otherwise is entitled. But federal review is not the full measure of Sykes' interest, for there is another of even greater immediacy: assuring that his constitutional claims can be addressed to some court. For the obvious consequence of barring Sykes from the federal courthouse is to insulate Florida's alleged constitutional violation from any and all judicial review because of a lawyer's mistake. From the standpoint of the habeas petitioner, it is a harsh rule indeed that denies him "any review at all where the state has granted none," particularly when he would have enjoyed both state and federal consideration had his attorney not erred.

In sum, I believe that *Fay*'s commitment to enforcing intentional but not inadvertent procedural defaults offers a realistic measure of protection for the habeas corpus petitioner seeking federal review of federal claims that were not litigated before the State. The threatened creation of a more "airtight system of forfeitures" would effectively deprive habeas petitioners of the opportunity for litigating their constitutional claims before any forum and would disparage the paramount importance of constitutional rights in our system of government. Such a restriction of habeas corpus jurisdiction should be countenanced, I submit, only if it fairly can be concluded that *Fay*'s focus on knowing and voluntary forfeitures unduly interferes with the legitimate interests of state courts or institutions. The majority offers no suggestion that actual experience has shown that *Fay*'s bypass test can be criticized on this score.

III

A regime of federal habeas corpus jurisdiction that permits the reopening of state procedural defaults does not invalidate any state procedural rule as such; Florida's courts remain entirely free to enforce their own rules as they choose, and to deny any and all state rights and remedies to a defendant who fails to comply with applicable state procedure. The relevant inquiry is whether more is required specifically, whether the fulfillment of important interests of the State necessitates that federal courts be called upon to impose additional sanctions for inadvertent noncompliance with state procedural requirements such as the contemporaneous-objection rule involved here.

Florida, of course, can point to a variety of legitimate interests in seeking allegiance to its reasonable procedural requirements, the contemporaneous-objection rule included. The question remains, however, whether any of these policies or interests are efficiently and fairly served by enforcing both intentional and inadvertent defaults pursuant to the identical stringent standard. I remain convinced that when one pierces the surface justifications for a harsher rule posited by the Court, no standard stricter than *Fay*'s deliberate-bypass test is realistically defensible.

Punishing a lawyer's unintentional errors by closing the federal court-house door to his client is both a senseless and misdirected method of deterring the slighting of state rules. It is senseless because unplanned and unintentional action of any kind generally is not subject to deterrence; and, to the extent that it is hoped that a threatened sanction addressed to the defense will induce greater care and caution on the part of trial lawyers, thereby forestalling negligent conduct or error, the potential loss of all valuable state remedies would be sufficient to this end. And it is a misdi-rected sanction because even if the penalization of incompetence or careless-ness will encourage more thorough legal training and trial preparation, the habeas applicant, as opposed to his lawyer, hardly is the proper recipient of such a penalty. Especially with fundamental constitutional rights at stake, no fictional relationship of principal-agent or the like can justify holding the criminal defendant accountable for the naked errors of his attorney. This is especially true when so many indigent defendants are without any realistic choice in selecting who ultimately represents them at trial. Indeed, if respon-sibility for error must be apportioned between the parties, it is the State, through its attorney's admissions and certification policies, that is more fairly held to blame for the fact that practicing lawyers too often are ill-prepared or ill-equipped to act carefully and knowledgeably when faced with decisions governed by state procedural requirements.

Hence, while I can well agree that the proper functioning of our system of criminal justice, both federal and state, necessarily places heavy reliance on the professionalism and judgment of trial attorneys, I cannot accept a system that ascribes the absolute forfeiture of an individual's constitutional claims to situations where his lawyer manifestly exercises no professional judgment at all where carelessness, mistake, or ignorance is the explanation for a procedural default. Of course, it is regrettable that certain errors that might have been cured earlier had trial counsel acted expeditiously must be corrected collat-erally and belatedly. I can understand the Court's wistfully wishing for the day when the trial was the sole, binding and final "event" of the adversarial process although I hesitate to agree that in the eyes of the criminal defendant it has ever ceased being the "main" one. But it should be plain that in the real world, the interest in finality is repeatedly compromised in numerous ways that arise with far greater frequency than do procedural defaults.

In short, I believe that the demands of our criminal justice system warrant visiting the mistakes of a trial attorney on the head of a habeas corpus appli-cant only when we are convinced that the lawyer actually exercised his exper-tise and judgment in his client's service, and with his client's knowing and intelligent participation where possible. This, of course, is the precise system of habeas review established by Fay v. Noia.

Although *Wainwright* and its progeny implicitly overruled *Fay*, it was not until Coleman v. Thompson, 501 U.S. 722 (1991), that *Fay* was explicitly overturned and the Court held that all procedural defaults are to be evaluated under the cause and prejudice test. Justice O'Connor, writing for the majority, declared:

> We now make it explicit: in all cases in which a state prisoner has defaulted his federal claims in state court pursuant to an independent and adequate state procedural rule, federal habeas review of the claim is barred unless the prisoner can demonstrate cause for the default and actual prejudice as a result of the alleged violation of federal law, or demonstrate that the failure to consider the claim will result in a fundamental miscarriage of justice.

In *Coleman*, a defendant in a capital case was denied appeal to the state court of appeals of his state habeas petition because he filed the notice of appeals three days late. The issue was whether the procedural error precluded federal habeas review. The Supreme Court explained that Wainwright v. Sykes effectively had overruled Fay v. Noia and that the petitioner's procedural default would preclude federal habeas review unless he could show cause and prejudice or a likelihood of actual innocence. In May 1992, Coleman was executed in Virginia despite some evidence that he was actually innocent.[42] No federal court ever heard Coleman's claim.

While the *Wainwright* decision clearly adopted the "cause" and "prejudice" test for habeas corpus review, the Court explicitly avoided defining these two terms. Subsequent cases have given content to this test. Several decisions have focused on what is sufficient "cause" to excuse a state court procedural default and permit a habeas corpus petitioner to raise matters not presented in the state courts.

Engle v. Isaac, 456 U.S. 107 (1982), indicated how difficult it is to show "cause." In *Engle*, a defendant used habeas corpus to challenge the constitutionality of the jury instructions used in his trial. In a case decided subsequent to his conviction, the Ohio Supreme Court held that the type of jury instructions given violated Ohio law and that its ruling applied retroactively to all cases in which they had been used. Nonetheless, the Supreme Court held that the issue could not be raised on habeas corpus because the defense counsel did not object at trial, even though at that time there was no reason to think that the instructions were unconstitutional. Justice O'Connor, writing for the majority, concluded, "[T]he futility of presenting an objection to the state courts cannot alone constitute cause for failure to object at trial. . . . Even a state court that has previously rejected a constitutional argument may decide, upon reflection, that the contention is valid."

The Court in *Engle* made it clear that it took a very different view of habeas corpus than had the Warren Court. Justice O'Connor expressed great reservations about the availability of habeas corpus because it imposes "significant costs" on society, including "undermin[ing] the usual principles of finality" and "cost[ing] society the right to punish admitted offenders."

---

42. *See* Jill Smolowe, *Must This Man Die?*, Time, May 18, 1992, at 40.

According to the Court, these cost considerations outweigh the value of providing relief to an individual who was convicted and incarcerated as a result of admittedly unconstitutional jury instructions.

Two years after *Engle*, in Reed v. Ross, 468 U.S. 1 (1984), the Supreme Court recognized that under limited circumstances, "where a constitutional claim is so novel that its legal basis is not reasonably available to counsel," a defendant may present matters on habeas that were not raised at trial. *Reed* was a 5-4 decision, with four of the justices who were in the majority in *Engle*—Justices Burger, Blackmun, O'Connor, and Rehnquist—dissenting. Like *Engle*, *Reed* involved a challenge to jury instructions about the burden of proof for a claim of self-defense. The majority distinguished *Reed* from *Engle* based on the time the trial occurred. The trial took place in *Engle* after the Supreme Court's 1970 decision in In re Winship, 397 U.S. 358 (1969), which required the state to prove every element of a crime beyond a reasonable doubt. Thus, the *Engle* Court concluded that in light of *Winship* and subsequent lower court cases interpreting it, the defendant's attorney should have thought to object to the jury instructions. But in *Ross*, the trial occurred in 1969, before *Winship*, and the Court decided that it would be inappropriate to require the defense attorney to anticipate a major Supreme Court decision.

In allowing the defendant to challenge the jury instruction on habeas corpus, the Supreme Court in *Reed* identified circumstances in which habeas petitioners can raise issues based on cases decided after their trial but applied retroactively. The Court's criteria indicated the breadth of the *Engle* holding and the narrowness of the *Reed* exception. Justice Brennan, writing for a plurality, said that a defendant could present claims that became apparent subsequent to the trial when there was a Supreme Court decision that explicitly overrules precedent, or when the decision overturns "a longstanding and widespread practice to which the Court has not spoken," or when the decision disapproves "a practice this Court arguably has sanctioned in prior cases." In short, even in distinguishing *Engle*, the *Reed* Court affirmed its conclusion that mere novelty of a claim is not sufficient cause for a defense counsel's failure to present it at trial. As Professor Resnik notes, "[a]lthough the *Ross* plurality found a crevice in the seeming impregnable 'cause' requirement of *Isaac*, the aperture is narrow. . . . Under *Ross*, the hurdle of 'cause' only can be surmounted in rare instances."

In a subsequent decision concerning the meaning of "cause," Lee v. Kemna, 534 U.S. 362 (2002), the Supreme Court found that there was a sufficient basis for allowing a federal habeas petition to be heard despite a state procedural default. At a murder trial in Missouri state court, a defendant asked for an overnight continuance when key witnesses were not present in the courtroom. The trial judge denied the request for a continuance, explaining that he had a daughter in the hospital and another trial scheduled to begin the next day. After the defendant was convicted, his appeal for a violation of due process was denied on the grounds that he did not follow the Missouri law requiring that requests for continuances be in writing and supported by affidavits. The federal district court denied habeas corpus based on the failure to comply with state procedures, and the United States Court of Appeals for the Eighth Circuit affirmed.

The Supreme Court reversed. Justice Ginsburg, writing for the Court, said that "[t]here are . . . exceptional cases in which exorbitant application of a generally sound rule renders the state ground inadequate." Ginsburg explained that a written motion for a continuance would not have made any difference; it would not have overcome the reasons why the judge denied the continuance. Also, the Court said that nothing in Missouri law required compliance with the procedural rules in a circumstance where there is an unexpected disappearance of a key witness. Finally, the Court emphasized that Lee had substantially complied with the state rules through his motion for a continuance and his explanation of the reasons for the request. Lee v. Kemna is important because it clearly holds that in some circumstances the failure to comply with state procedures will not preclude a subsequent habeas corpus petition.

In a subsequent decision concerning procedural default, the Court found that abandonment by a defense lawyer, as opposed to negligence, is sufficient to excuse a procedural default.

MAPLES v. THOMAS

565 U.S. 266 (2012)

Justice GINSBURG delivered the opinion of the Court.

Cory R. Maples is an Alabama capital prisoner sentenced to death in 1997 for the murder of two individuals. At trial, he was represented by two appointed lawyers, minimally paid and with scant experience in capital cases. Maples sought postconviction relief in state court, alleging ineffective assistance of counsel and several other trial infirmities. His petition, filed in August 2001, was written by two New York attorneys serving *pro bono,* both associated with the same New York-based large law firm. An Alabama attorney, designated as local counsel, moved the admission of the out-of-state counsel *pro hac vice.* As understood by New York counsel, local counsel would facilitate their appearance, but would undertake no substantive involvement in the case.

In the summer of 2002, while Maples' postconviction petition remained pending in the Alabama trial court, his New York attorneys left the law firm; their new employment disabled them from continuing to represent Maples. They did not inform Maples of their departure and consequent inability to serve as his counsel. Nor did they seek the Alabama trial court's leave to withdraw. Neither they nor anyone else moved for the substitution of counsel able to handle Maples' case.

In May 2003, the Alabama trial court denied Maples' petition. Notices of the court's order were posted to the New York attorneys at the address of the law firm with which they had been associated. Those postings were returned, unopened, to the trial court clerk, who attempted no further mailing. With no attorney of record in fact acting on Maples' behalf, the time to appeal ran out.

Thereafter, Maples petitioned for a writ of habeas corpus in federal court. The District Court and, in turn, the Eleventh Circuit, rejected his petition, pointing to the procedural default in state court, *i.e.*, Maples' failure timely to appeal the Alabama trial court's order denying him postconviction relief. Maples, it is uncontested, was blameless for the default.

The sole question this Court has taken up for review is whether, on the extraordinary facts of Maples' case, there is "cause" to excuse the default. Maples maintains that there is, for the lawyers he believed to be vigilantly representing him had abandoned the case without leave of court, without informing Maples they could no longer represent him, and without securing any recorded substitution of counsel. We agree. Abandoned by counsel, Maples was left unrepresented at a critical time for his state postconviction petition, and he lacked a clue of any need to protect himself *pro se*. In these circumstances, no just system would lay the default at Maples' death-cell door. Satisfied that the requisite cause has been shown, we reverse the Eleventh Circuit's judgment.

I

Alabama sets low eligibility requirements for lawyers appointed to represent indigent capital defendants at trial. Appointed counsel need only be a member of the Alabama bar and have "five years' prior experience in the active practice of criminal law." Experience with capital cases is not required. Nor does the State provide, or require appointed counsel to gain, any capital-case-specific professional education or training.

Appointed counsel in death penalty cases are also undercompensated. Until 1999, the State paid appointed capital defense attorneys just "$40.00 per hour for time expended in court and $20.00 per hour for time reasonably expended out of court in the preparation of [the defendant's] case." Although death penalty litigation is plainly time intensive, the State capped at $1,000 fees recoverable by capital defense attorneys for out-of-court work. Even today, court-appointed attorneys receive only $70 per hour.

Nearly alone among the States, Alabama does not guarantee representation to indigent capital defendants in postconviction proceedings. The State has elected, instead, "to rely on the efforts of typically well-funded [out-of-state] volunteers." Thus, as of 2006, 86% of the attorneys representing Alabama's death row inmates in state collateral review proceedings "either worked for the Equal Justice Initiative (headed by NYU Law professor Bryan Stevenson), out-of-state public interest groups like the Innocence Project, or an out-of-state mega-firm." On occasion, some prisoners sentenced to death receive no postconviction representation at all.

This system was in place when, in 1997, Alabama charged Maples with two counts of capital murder; the victims, Stacy Alan Terry and Barry Dewayne

Robinson II, were Maples' friends who, on the night of the murders, had been out on the town with him. Maples pleaded not guilty, and his case proceeded to trial, where he was represented by two court-appointed Alabama attorneys. Only one of them had earlier served in a capital case. Neither counsel had previously tried the penalty phase of a capital case. Compensation for each lawyer was capped at $1,000 for time spent out-of-court preparing Maples' case, and at $40 per hour for in-court services.

Finding Maples guilty on both counts, the jury recommended that he be sentenced to death. The vote was 10 to 2, the minimum number Alabama requires for a death recommendation. Accepting the jury's recommendation, the trial court sentenced Maples to death. On direct appeal, the Alabama Court of Criminal Appeals and the Alabama Supreme Court affirmed the convictions and sentence.

Two out-of-state volunteers represented Maples in postconviction proceedings: Jaasi Munanka and Clara Ingen-Housz, both associates at the New York offices of the Sullivan & Cromwell law firm. At the time, Alabama required out-of-state attorneys to associate local counsel when seeking admission to practice *pro hac vice* before an Alabama court, regardless of the nature of the proceeding. The Alabama Rule further prescribed that the local attorney's name "appear on all notices, orders, pleadings, and other documents filed in the cause," and that local counsel "accept joint and several responsibility with the foreign attorney to the client, to opposing parties and counsel, and to the court or administrative agency in all matters [relating to the case]."

Munanka and Ingen-Housz associated Huntsville, Alabama attorney John Butler as local counsel. Notwithstanding his obligations under Alabama law, Butler informed Munanka and Ingen-Housz, "at the outset," that he would serve as local counsel only for the purpose of allowing the two New York attorneys to appear *pro hac vice* on behalf of Maples. Given his lack of "resources, available time [and] experience," Butler told the Sullivan & Cromwell lawyers, he could not "deal with substantive issues in the case." The Sullivan & Cromwell attorneys accepted Butler's conditions. This arrangement between out-of-state and local attorneys, it appears, was hardly atypical.

With the aid of his *pro bono* counsel, Maples filed a petition for postconviction relief under Alabama Rule of Criminal Procedure 32. Among other claims, Maples asserted that his court-appointed attorneys provided constitutionally ineffective assistance during both guilt and penalty phases of his capital trial. He alleged, in this regard, that his inexperienced and underfunded attorneys failed to develop and raise an obvious intoxication defense, did not object to several egregious instances of prosecutorial misconduct, and woefully underprepared for the penalty phase of his trial.

[I]n the summer of 2002, both Munanka and Ingen-Housz left Sullivan & Cromwell. Munanka gained a clerkship with a federal judge; Ingen-Housz accepted a position with the European Commission in Belgium. Neither attorney told Maples of their departure from Sullivan & Cromwell or of their resulting inability to continue to represent him. In disregard of Alabama law, neither attorney sought the trial court's leave to withdraw. Compounding Munanka's and Ingen-Housz's inaction, no other Sullivan & Cromwell lawyer entered an appearance on Maples' behalf, moved to substitute counsel, or otherwise notified the court of any change in Maples' representation.

Another nine months passed. During this time period, no Sullivan & Cromwell attorneys assigned to Maples' case sought admission to the Alabama bar, entered appearances on Maples' behalf, or otherwise advised the Alabama court that Munanka and Ingen-Housz were no longer Maples' attorneys. Thus, Munanka and Ingen-Housz (along with Butler) remained Maples' listed, and only, "attorneys of record."

There things stood when, in May 2003, the trial court, without holding a hearing, entered an order denying Maples' Rule 32 petition. The clerk of the Alabama trial court mailed copies of the order to Maples' three attorneys of record. He sent Munanka's and Ingen-Housz's copies to Sullivan & Cromwell's New York address, which the pair had provided upon entering their appearances.

When those copies arrived at Sullivan & Cromwell, Munanka and Ingen-Housz had long since departed. The notices, however, were not forwarded to another Sullivan & Cromwell attorney. Instead, a mailroom employee sent the unopened envelopes back to the court. "Returned to Sender — Attempted, Unknown" was stamped on the envelope addressed to Munanka. A similar stamp appeared on the envelope addressed to Ingen-Housz, along with the handwritten notation "Return to Sender — Left Firm."

Upon receiving back the unopened envelopes he had mailed to Munanka and Ingen-Housz, the Alabama court clerk took no further action. In particular, the clerk did not contact Munanka or Ingen-Housz at the personal telephone numbers or home addresses they had provided in their *pro hac vice* applications. Nor did the clerk alert Sullivan & Cromwell or Butler. Butler received his copy of the order, but did not act on it. He assumed that Munanka and Ingen-Housz, who had been "CC'd" on the order, would take care of filing an appeal.

Meanwhile, the clock ticked on Maples' appeal. Under Alabama's Rules of Appellate Procedure, Maples had 42 days to file a notice of appeal from the trial court's May 22, 2003 order denying Maples' petition for postconviction relief. No appeal notice was filed, and the time allowed for filing expired on July 7, 2003.

A little over a month later, on August 13, 2003, Alabama Assistant Attorney General Jon Hayden, the attorney representing the State in Maples' collateral review proceedings, sent a letter directly to Maples. Hayden's letter informed Maples of the missed deadline for initiating an appeal within the State's system, and notified him that four weeks remained during which he could file a federal habeas petition. Hayden mailed the letter to Maples only, using his prison address. No copy was sent to Maples' attorneys of record, or to anyone else acting on Maples' behalf.

Upon receiving the State's letter, Maples immediately contacted his mother. She telephoned Sullivan & Cromwell to inquire about her son's case. *Ibid.* Prompted by her call, Sullivan & Cromwell attorneys Marc De Leeuw, Felice Duffy, and Kathy Brewer submitted a motion, through Butler, asking the trial court to reissue its order denying Maples' Rule 32 petition, thereby restarting the 42-day appeal period.

The trial court denied the motion. Maples next petitioned the Alabama Court of Criminal Appeals for a writ of mandamus, granting him leave to file an out-of-time appeal. Rejecting Maples' plea, the Court of Criminal Appeals determined that, although the clerk had "assumed a duty to notify the parties of the resolution of Maples's Rule 32 petition," the clerk had satisfied that obligation by sending notices to the attorneys of record at the addresses those attorneys provided.

Having exhausted his state postconviction remedies, Maples sought federal habeas corpus relief. Addressing the ineffective-assistance-of-trial-counsel claims Maples stated in his federal petition, the State urged that Maples had forever forfeited those claims. The District Court determined that Maples had defaulted his ineffective-assistance claims, and that he had not shown "cause" sufficient to overcome the default. A divided panel of the Eleventh Circuit affirmed.

II

A

As a rule, a state prisoner's habeas claims may not be entertained by a federal court "when (1) 'a state court [has] declined to address [those] claims because the prisoner had failed to meet a state procedural requirement,' and (2) 'the state judgment rests on independent and adequate state procedural grounds.' " The bar to federal review may be lifted, however, if "the prisoner can demonstrate cause for the [procedural] default [in state court] and actual prejudice as a result of the alleged violation of federal law."

Given the single issue on which we granted review, we will assume, for purposes of this decision, that the Alabama Court of Criminal Appeals' refusal to consider Maples' ineffective-assistance claims rested on an independent and adequate state procedural ground: namely, Maples' failure to satisfy Alabama's Rule requiring a notice of appeal to be filed within 42 days from the trial court's final order. Accordingly, we confine our consideration to the question whether Maples has shown cause to excuse the missed notice of appeal deadline.

Cause for a procedural default exists where "something *external* to the petitioner, something that cannot fairly be attributed to him[,] . . . 'impeded [his] efforts to comply with the State's procedural rule.' " Negligence on the part of a prisoner's postconviction attorney does not qualify as "cause." That is so because the attorney is the prisoner's agent, and under "well-settled principles of agency law," the principal bears the risk of negligent conduct on the part of his agent. Thus, when a petitioner's postconviction attorney misses a filing deadline, the petitioner is bound by the oversight and cannot rely on it to establish cause. We do not disturb that general rule.

A markedly different situation is presented, however, when an attorney abandons his client without notice, and thereby occasions the default. Having severed the principal-agent relationship, an attorney no longer acts, or fails to act, as the client's representative. His acts or omissions therefore "cannot fairly be attributed to [the client]."

We agree that, under agency principles, a client cannot be charged with the acts or omissions of an attorney who has abandoned him. Nor can a client be faulted for failing to act on his own behalf when he lacks reason to believe his attorneys of record, in fact, are not representing him. We therefore inquire whether Maples has shown that his attorneys of record abandoned him, thereby supplying the "extraordinary circumstances beyond his control," necessary to lift the state procedural bar to his federal petition.

B

From the time he filed his initial Rule 32 petition until well after time ran out for appealing the trial court's denial of that petition, Maples had only three attorneys of record: Munanka, Ingen-Housz, and Butler. Unknown to Maples, not one of these lawyers was in fact serving as his attorney during the 42 days permitted for an appeal from the trial court's order.

The State contends that Sullivan & Cromwell represented Maples throughout his state postconviction proceedings. Accordingly, the State urges, Maples cannot establish abandonment by counsel continuing through the six weeks allowed for noticing an appeal from the trial court's denial of his Rule 32 petition. We disagree. It is undisputed that Munanka and Ingen-Housz severed their agency relationship with Maples long before the default occurred. Both Munanka and Ingen-Housz left Sullivan & Cromwell's employ in the summer of 2002, at least nine months before the Alabama trial court entered its order denying Rule 32 relief. Their new employment—Munanka as a law clerk for a federal judge, Ingen-Housz as an employee of the European Commission in Belgium—disabled them from continuing to represent Maples. Hornbook agency law establishes that the attorneys' departure from Sullivan & Cromwell and their commencement of employment that prevented them from representing Maples ended their agency relationship with him.

Furthermore, the two attorneys did not observe Alabama's Rule requiring them to seek the trial court's permission to withdraw. By failing to seek permission to withdraw, Munanka and Ingen-Housz allowed the court's records to convey that they represented Maples. As listed attorneys of record, they, not Maples, would be the addressees of court orders Alabama law requires the clerk to furnish.

Maples' only other attorney of record, local counsel Butler, also left him abandoned. Indeed, Butler did not even begin to represent Maples. Butler informed Munanka and Ingen-Housz that he would serve as local counsel only for the purpose of enabling the two out-of-state attorneys to appear *pro hac vice*. Lacking the necessary "resources, available time [and] experience," Butler told the two Sullivan & Cromwell lawyers, he would not "deal with substantive issues in the case." That the minimal participation he undertook was inconsistent with Alabama law, underscores the absurdity of holding Maples barred because Butler signed on as local counsel.

In sum, the record admits of only one reading: At no time before the missed deadline was Butler serving as Maples' agent "in any meaningful sense of that word."

Not only was Maples left without any functioning attorney of record, the very listing of Munanka, Ingen-Housz, and Butler as his representatives meant that he had no right personally to receive notice. He in fact received none or any other warning that he had better fend for himself. Had counsel of record or the State's attorney informed Maples of his plight before the time to appeal ran out, he could have filed a notice of appeal himself or enlisted the aid of new volunteer attorneys. Given no reason to suspect that he lacked counsel able and willing to represent him, Maples surely was blocked from complying with the State's procedural rule.

C

"The cause and prejudice requirement," we have said, "shows due regard for States' finality and comity interests while ensuring that 'fundamental fairness [remains] the central concern of the writ of habeas corpus.' " In the unusual circumstances of this case, principles of agency law and fundamental fairness point to the same conclusion: There was indeed cause to excuse Maples' procedural default. Through no fault of his own, Maples lacked the assistance of any authorized attorney during the 42 days Alabama allows for noticing an appeal from a trial court's denial of postconviction relief. As just observed, he had no reason to suspect that, in reality, he had been reduced to *pro se* status. Maples was disarmed by extraordinary circumstances quite beyond his control. He has shown ample cause, we hold, to excuse the procedural default into which he was trapped when counsel of record abandoned him without a word of warning.

Justice Scalia, with whom Justice Thomas joins, dissenting.

Our doctrine of procedural default reflects, and furthers, the principle that errors in state criminal trials should be remedied in state court. As we have long recognized, federal habeas review for state prisoners imposes significant costs on the States, undermining not only their practical interest in the finality of their criminal judgments, but also the primacy of their courts in adjudicating the constitutional rights of defendants prosecuted under state law. We have further recognized that "[t]hese costs are particularly high . . . when a state prisoner, through a procedural default, prevents adjudication of his constitutional claims in state court." For that reason, and because permitting federal-court review of defaulted claims would "undercu[t] the State's ability to enforce its procedural rules," we have held that when a state court has relied on an adequate and independent state procedural ground in denying a prisoner's claims, the prisoner ordinarily may not obtain federal habeas relief.

To be sure, the prohibition on federal-court review of defaulted claims is not absolute. A habeas petitioner's default in state court will not bar federal habeas review if "the petitioner demonstrates cause and actual prejudice," — "cause" constituting "something *external* to the petitioner, something that cannot fairly be attributed to him," that impeded compliance with the State's procedural rule. As a general matter, an attorney's mistakes (or omissions) do not meet the standard "because the attorney is the petitioner's agent when acting, or failing to act, in furtherance of the litigation, and the petitioner must 'bear the risk of attorney error.' "

In light of the principles just set out, the Court is correct to conclude that a habeas petitioner's procedural default may be excused when it is attributable to abandonment by his attorney. I likewise agree with the Court's conclusion that Maples' two out-of-state attorneys of record, Jaasi Munanka and Clara Ingen-Housz, had abandoned Maples by the time the Alabama trial court entered its order denying his petition for postconviction relief.

It is an unjustified leap, however, to conclude that Maples was left unrepresented during the relevant window between the Alabama trial court's dismissal of his postconviction petition and expiration of the 42-day period for filing a notice of appeal. Start with Maples' own allegations: In his amended federal habeas petition, Maples alleged that, at the time he sought postconviction relief in Alabama trial court, he "was represented by Sullivan & Cromwell of New York, New York." Although the petition went on to identify Munanka and Ingen-Housz as "the two Sullivan lawyers handling the matter," its statement that Maples was "represented" by the firm itself strongly suggests that Maples viewed himself as having retained the services of the firm as a whole, a perfectly natural understanding. "When a client retains a lawyer who practices with a firm, the presumption is that both the lawyer and the firm have been retained."

In any case, even if Maples had no attorney-client relationship with the Sullivan & Cromwell firm, Munanka and Ingen-Housz were surely not the only Sullivan & Cromwell lawyers who represented Maples on an individual basis. In sum, there is every indication that when the trial court entered its order dismissing Maples' postconviction petition in May 2003, Maples continued to be represented by a team of attorneys in Sullivan & Cromwell's New York office.

But even leaving aside the question of Maples' "unadmitted" attorneys at Sullivan & Cromwell, Maples had a fully admitted attorney, who had entered an appearance, in the person of local counsel, John Butler. There is no support for the Court's conclusion that Butler "did not even begin to represent Maples." True, the affidavit Butler filed with the Alabama trial court in the proceeding seeking extension of the deadline stated that he had "no substantive involvement" with the case, and that he had "agreed to serve as local counsel only." But a disclaimer of "substantive involvement" in a case, whether or not it violates a lawyer's ethical obligations, see is not equivalent to a denial of any agency role at all. A local attorney's "nonsubstantive" involvement would surely include, *at a minimum*, keeping track of local court orders and advising "substantive" counsel of impending deadlines. Nor did Butler's explanation for his failure to act when he received a copy of the trial court's order sound in abandonment. Butler did not say, for instance, that he ignored the order because he did not consider Maples to be his client. Instead, based on "past practice" and the content of the order, Butler "assumed" that Maples' lawyers at Sullivan & Cromwell would receive a copy.

One suspects that today's decision is motivated in large part by an understandable sense of frustration with the State's refusal to waive Maples' procedural default in the interest of fairness. Indeed, that frustration may well explain the Court's lengthy indictment of Alabama's general procedures for providing representation to capital defendants, a portion of the Court's opinion that is so disconnected from the rest of its analysis as to be otherwise inexplicable.

But if the interest of fairness justifies our excusing Maples' procedural default here, it does so whenever a defendant's procedural default is caused by his attorney. That is simply not the law — and cannot be, if the states are to have an orderly system of criminal litigation conducted by counsel. Our precedents allow a State to stand on its rights and enforce a habeas petitioner's procedural default even when counsel is to blame. Because a faithful application of those precedents leads to the conclusion that Maples has not demonstrated cause to excuse his procedural default; and because the reasoning by which the Court justifies the opposite conclusion invites future evisceration of the principle that defendants are responsible for the mistakes of their attorneys; I respectfully dissent.

Beginning in two decisions decided on the same day — Murray v. Carrier, 477 U.S. 478 (1986), and Smith v. Murray, 477 U.S. 27 (1986) — the Supreme Court has held that as an alternative to demonstrating cause, a habeas petitioner may raise matters not argued in the state courts by demonstrating that he or she is probably innocent of the charges.

The issue in Murray v. Carrier was whether a habeas petitioner could show cause for a procedural default by demonstrating that the defense counsel inadvertently failed to raise an issue. The inadvertence, however, did not amount to ineffective assistance of counsel. In *Murray*, the defense attorney inadvertently omitted an important issue from the notice of appeal. Under the pertinent state law, a failure to include an issue in the notice of appeal was deemed a waiver. Hence, the state courts refused to hear or rule on the omitted issue. The Supreme Court concluded that there was not sufficient cause to permit the defendant to raise the issue in a federal court habeas proceeding.

The *Murray* Court did indicate, however, one alternative to demonstrating cause. The Court said that a state prisoner who could show that he or she is probably actually innocent should be able to secure relief regardless of the reason for the state court procedural default. Justice O'Connor explained that "in an extraordinary case, where a constitutional violation has probably resulted in the conviction of one who is actually innocent, a federal habeas court may grant the writ even in the absence of a showing of cause for the procedural default."

In two cases, below, Herrara v. Collins and House v. Bell, the Court considered when actual innocence can excuse a procedural default. In reading these cases, it is important to note that the Court was considering two different uses of "actual innocence": as a "gateway" to raise a procedurally defaulted claim and as a "freestanding" claim that would justify overturning a conviction on habeas corpus. In reading these cases, consider how the justices approach the questions of what is the standard for showing actual innocence as a gateway to raising a procedurally defaulted claim. Also, is executing an innocent person unconstitutional so as to allow "freestanding" claims of innocence? And if so, what is the standard for freestanding claims of innocence?

HERRERA v. COLLINS
506 U.S. 390 (1993)

Chief Justice REHNQUIST delivered the opinion of the Court.

Petitioner Leonel Torres Herrera was convicted of capital murder and sentenced to death in January 1982. He unsuccessfully challenged the conviction on direct appeal and state collateral proceedings in the Texas state courts, and in a federal habeas petition. In February 1992 — 10 years after his conviction — he urged in a second federal habeas petition that he was "actually innocent" of the murder for which he was sentenced to death, and that the Eighth Amendment's prohibition against cruel and unusual punishment and the Fourteenth Amendment's guarantee of due process of law therefore forbid his execution. He supported this claim with affidavits tending to show that his now-dead brother, rather than he, had been the perpetrator of the crime. Petitioner urges us to hold that this showing of innocence entitles him to relief in this federal habeas proceeding. We hold that it does not.

Shortly before 11 P.M. on an evening in late September 1981, the body of Texas Department of Public Safety Officer David Rucker was found by a passer-by on a stretch of highway about six miles east of Los Fresnos, Texas, a few miles north of Brownsville in the Rio Grande Valley. Rucker's body was lying beside his patrol car. He had been shot in the head.

At about the same time, Los Fresnos Police Officer Enrique Carrisalez observed a speeding vehicle traveling west towards Los Fresnos, away from the place where Rucker's body had been found, along the same road. Carrisalez, who was accompanied in his patrol car by Enrique Hernandez, turned on his flashing red lights and pursued the speeding vehicle. After the car had stopped briefly at a red light, it signaled that it would pull over and did so. The patrol car pulled up behind it. Carrisalez took a flashlight and walked toward the car of the speeder. The driver opened his door and exchanged a few words with Carrisalez before firing at least one shot at Carrisalez' chest. The officer died nine days later.

Petitioner Herrera was arrested a few days after the shootings and charged with the capital murder of both Carrisalez and Rucker. He was tried and found guilty of the capital murder of Carrisalez in January 1982, and sentenced to death. In July 1982, petitioner pleaded guilty to the murder of Rucker.

At petitioner's trial for the murder of Carrisalez, Hernandez, who had witnessed Carrisalez' slaying from the officer's patrol car, identified petitioner as the person who had wielded the gun. A declaration by Officer Carrisalez to the same effect, made while he was in the hospital, was also admitted. Through a license plate check, it was shown that the speeding car involved in Carrisalez' murder was registered to petitioner's "live-in" girl-friend. Petitioner was known to drive this car, and he had a set of keys to the car in his pants pocket when he was arrested. Hernandez identified the car as the vehicle from which the murderer had emerged to fire the fatal shot. He also testified that there had been only one person in the car that night.

The evidence showed that Herrera's Social Security card had been found alongside Rucker's patrol car on the night he was killed. Splatters of blood on the car identified as the vehicle involved in the shootings, and on petitioner's blue jeans and wallet were identified as type A blood — the same type which Rucker had. (Herrera has type O blood.) Similar evidence with respect to strands of hair found in the car indicated that the hair was Rucker's and not Herrera's. A handwritten letter was also found on the person of petitioner when he was arrested, which strongly implied that he had killed Rucker.

Petitioner appealed his conviction and sentence, arguing, among other things, that Hernandez' and Carrisalez' identifications were unreliable and improperly admitted. The Texas Court of Criminal Appeals affirmed, and we denied certiorari. Petitioner's application for state habeas relief was denied. Petitioner then filed a federal habeas petition, again challenging the identifications offered against him at trial. This petition was denied, and we again denied certiorari.

Petitioner next returned to state court and filed a second habeas petition, raising, among other things, a claim of "actual innocence" based on newly discovered evidence. In support of this claim petitioner presented the affidavits of Hector Villarreal, an attorney who had represented petitioner's brother, Raul Herrera, Sr., and of Juan Franco Palacious, one of Raul, Senior's former cellmates. Both individuals claimed that Raul, Senior, who died in 1984, had told them that he — and not petitioner — had killed Officers Rucker and Carrisalez. The State District Court denied this application, finding that "no evidence at trial remotely suggest[ed] that anyone other than [petitioner] committed the offense."

In February 1992, petitioner lodged the instant habeas petition—his second—in federal court, alleging, among other things, that he is innocent of the murders of Rucker and Carrisalez, and that his execution would thus violate the Eighth and Fourteenth Amendments. In addition to proffering the above affidavits, petitioner presented the affidavits of Raul Herrera, Jr., Raul Senior's son, and Jose Ybarra, Jr., a schoolmate of the Herrera brothers. Raul, Junior, averred that he had witnessed his father shoot Officers Rucker and Carrisalez and petitioner was not present. Raul, Junior, was nine years old at the time of the killings. Ybarra alleged that Raul, Senior, told him one summer night in 1983 that he had shot the two police officers. Petitioner alleged that law enforcement officials were aware of this evidence, and had withheld it in violation of Brady v. Maryland (1963).

Petitioner asserts that the Eighth and Fourteenth Amendments to the United States Constitution prohibit the execution of a person who is innocent of the crime for which he was convicted. This proposition has an elemental appeal, as would the similar proposition that the Constitution prohibits the imprisonment of one who is innocent of the crime for which he was convicted. After all, the central purpose of any system of criminal justice is to convict the guilty and free the innocent. But the evidence upon which petitioner's claim of innocence rests was not produced at his trial, but rather eight years later. In any system of criminal justice, "innocence" or "guilt" must be determined in some sort of a judicial proceeding. Petitioner's showing of innocence, and indeed his constitutional claim for relief based upon that showing, must be evaluated in the light of the previous proceedings in this case, which have stretched over a span of 10 years.

A person when first charged with a crime is entitled to a presumption of innocence, and may insist that his guilt be established beyond a reasonable doubt. In re Winship (1970). Other constitutional provisions also have the effect of ensuring against the risk of convicting an innocent person. All of these constitutional safeguards, of course, make it more difficult for the State to rebut and finally overturn the presumption of innocence which attaches to every criminal defendant. But we have also observed that "[d]ue process does not require that every conceivable step be taken, at whatever cost, to eliminate the possibility of convicting an innocent person." To conclude otherwise would all but paralyze our system for enforcement of the criminal law.

Once a defendant has been afforded a fair trial and convicted of the offense for which he was charged, the presumption of innocence disappears. Here, it is not disputed that the State met its burden of proving at trial that petitioner was guilty of the capital murder of Officer Carrisalez beyond a reasonable doubt. Thus, in the eyes of the law, petitioner does not come before the Court as one who is "innocent," but, on the contrary, as one who has been convicted by due process of law of two brutal murders.

Based on affidavits here filed, petitioner claims that evidence never presented to the trial court proves him innocent notwithstanding the verdict reached at his trial. Such a claim is not cognizable in the state courts of Texas. For to obtain a new trial based on newly discovered evidence, a defendant must file a motion within 30 days after imposition or suspension of sentence. The Texas courts have construed this 30-day time limit as jurisdictional.

Claims of actual innocence based on newly discovered evidence have never been held to state a ground for federal habeas relief absent an independent constitutional violation occurring in the underlying state criminal proceeding. This rule is grounded in the principle that federal habeas courts sit to ensure that individuals are not imprisoned in violation of the Constitution — not to correct errors of fact.

The dissent fails to articulate the relief that would be available if petitioner were to meet its "probable innocence" standard. Would it be commutation of petitioner's death sentence, new trial, or unconditional release from imprisonment? The typical relief granted in federal habeas corpus is a conditional order of release unless the State elects to retry the successful habeas petitioner, or in a capital case a similar conditional order vacating the death sentence. Were petitioner to satisfy the dissent's "probable innocence" standard, therefore, the District Court would presumably be required to grant a conditional order of relief, which would in effect require the State to retry petitioner 10 years after his first trial, not because of any constitutional violation which had occurred at the first trial, but simply because of a belief that in light of petitioner's new-found evidence a jury might find him not guilty at a second trial.

Yet there is no guarantee that the guilt or innocence determination would be any more exact. To the contrary, the passage of time only diminishes the reliability of criminal adjudications. Under the dissent's approach, the District Court would be placed in the even more difficult position of having to weigh the probative value of "hot" and "cold" evidence on petitioner's guilt or innocence.

This is not to say that our habeas jurisprudence casts a blind eye toward innocence. In a series of cases, we have held that a petitioner otherwise subject to defenses of abusive or successive use of the writ may have his federal constitutional claim considered on the merits if he makes a proper showing of actual innocence. This rule, or fundamental miscarriage of justice exception, is grounded in the "equitable discretion" of habeas courts to see that federal constitutional errors do not result in the incarceration of innocent persons. But this body of our habeas jurisprudence makes clear that a claim of "actual innocence" is not itself a constitutional claim, but instead a gateway through which a habeas petitioner must pass to have his otherwise barred constitutional claim considered on the merits.

Petitioner in this case is simply not entitled to habeas relief based on the reasoning of this line of cases. For he does not seek excusal of a procedural error so that he may bring an independent constitutional claim challenging his conviction or sentence, but rather argues that he is entitled to habeas relief because newly discovered evidence shows that his conviction is factually incorrect. The fundamental miscarriage of justice exception is available "only where the prisoner supplements his constitutional claim with a colorable showing of factual innocence." We have never held that it extends to freestanding claims of actual innocence. Therefore, the exception is inapplicable here.

Petitioner asserts that this case is different because he has been sentenced to death. But we have "refused to hold that the fact that a death sentence has been imposed requires a different standard of review on federal habeas corpus."

Alternatively, petitioner invokes the Fourteenth Amendment's guarantee of due process of law in support of his claim that his showing of actual innocence entitles him to a new trial, or at least to a vacation of his death sentence. "[B]ecause the States have considerable expertise in matters of criminal procedure and the criminal process is grounded in centuries of common-law tradition," we have "exercis[ed] substantial deference to legislative judgments in this area." Thus, we have found criminal process lacking only where it " 'offends some principle of justice so rooted in the traditions and conscience of our people as to be ranked as fundamental.' " We cannot say that Texas' refusal to entertain petitioner's newly discovered evidence eight years after his conviction transgresses a principle of fundamental fairness "rooted in the traditions and conscience of our people."

This is not to say, however, that petitioner is left without a forum to raise his actual innocence claim. For under Texas law, petitioner may file a request for executive clemency. Clemency is deeply rooted in our Anglo-American tradition of law, and is the historic remedy for preventing miscarriages of justice where judicial process has been exhausted.

Executive clemency has provided the "fail safe" in our criminal justice system. It is an unalterable fact that our judicial system, like the human beings who administer it, is fallible. But history is replete with examples of wrongfully convicted persons who have been pardoned in the wake of after-discovered evidence establishing their innocence. In his classic work, Professor Edwin Borchard compiled 65 cases in which it was later determined that individuals had been wrongfully convicted of crimes. Clemency provided the relief mechanism in 47 of these cases; the remaining cases ended in judgments of acquittals after new trials. E. Borchard, Convicting the Innocent (1932). Recent authority confirms that over the past century clemency has been exercised frequently in capital cases in which demonstrations of "actual innocence" have been made. See M. Radelet, H. Bedau, & C. Putnam, In Spite of Innocence 282-356 (1992).

As the foregoing discussion illustrates, in state criminal proceedings the trial is the paramount event for determining the guilt or innocence of the defendant. Federal habeas review of state convictions has traditionally been limited to claims of constitutional violations occurring in the course of the underlying state criminal proceedings. Our federal habeas cases have treated claims of "actual innocence," not as an independent constitutional claim, but as a basis upon which a habeas petitioner may have an independent constitutional claim considered on the merits, even though his habeas petition would otherwise be regarded as successive or abusive. History shows that the traditional remedy for claims of innocence based on new evidence, discovered too late in the day to file a new trial motion, has been executive clemency.

We may assume, for the sake of argument in deciding this case, that in a capital case a truly persuasive demonstration of "actual innocence" made after trial would render the execution of a defendant unconstitutional, and warrant federal habeas relief if there were no state avenue open to process such a claim. But because of the very disruptive effect that entertaining claims of actual innocence would have on the need for finality in capital cases, and the enormous burden that having to retry cases based on often stale evidence would place on the States, the threshold showing for such an assumed right would necessarily be extraordinarily high. The showing made by petitioner in this case falls far short of any such threshold.

The affidavits filed in this habeas proceeding were given over eight years after petitioner's trial. No satisfactory explanation has been given as to why the affiants waited until the 11th hour — and, indeed, until after the alleged perpetrator of the murders himself was dead — to make their statements. Equally troubling, no explanation has been offered as to why petitioner, by hypothesis an innocent man, pleaded guilty to the murder of Rucker. Moreover, the affidavits themselves contain inconsistencies, and therefore fail to provide a convincing account of what took place on the night Officers Rucker and Carrisalez were killed.

This is not to say that petitioner's affidavits are without probative value. Had this sort of testimony been offered at trial, it could have been weighed by the jury, along with the evidence offered by the State and petitioner, in deliberating upon its verdict. Since the statements in the affidavits contradict the evidence received at trial, the jury would have had to decide important issues of credibility. But coming 10 years after petitioner's trial, this showing of innocence falls far short of that which would have to be made in order to trigger the sort of constitutional claim which we have assumed, arguendo, to exist.

Justice O'CONNOR, with whom Justice KENNEDY joins, concurring.

I cannot disagree with the fundamental legal principle that executing the innocent is inconsistent with the Constitution. Regardless of the verbal formula employed — "contrary to contemporary standards of decency," "shocking to the conscience," or offensive to a " 'principle of justice so rooted in the traditions and conscience of our people as to be ranked as fundamental,' " — the execution of a legally and factually innocent person would be a constitutionally intolerable event. Dispositive to this case, however, is an equally fundamental fact: Petitioner is not innocent, in any sense of the word.

As the Court explains, petitioner is not innocent in the eyes of the law because, in our system of justice, "the trial is the paramount event for determining the guilt or innocence of the defendant." In petitioner's case, that paramount event occurred 10 years ago. He was tried before a jury of his peers, with the full panoply of protections that our Constitution affords criminal defendants. At the conclusion of that trial, the jury found petitioner guilty beyond a reasonable doubt. Petitioner therefore does not appear before us as an innocent man on the verge of execution. He is instead a legally guilty one who, refusing to accept the jury's verdict, demands a hearing in which to have his culpability determined once again.

Consequently, the issue before us is not whether a State can execute the innocent. It is, as the Court notes, whether a fairly convicted and therefore legally guilty person is constitutionally entitled to yet another judicial proceeding in which to adjudicate his guilt anew, 10 years after conviction, notwithstanding his failure to demonstrate that constitutional error infected his trial. In most circumstances, that question would answer itself in the negative. Our society has a high degree of confidence in its criminal trials, in no small part because the Constitution offers unparalleled protections against convicting the innocent. The question similarly would be answered in the negative today, except for the disturbing nature of the claim before us. Petitioner contends not only that the Constitution's protections "sometimes fail," but that their failure in his case will result in his execution — even though he is factually innocent and has evidence to prove it.

Exercising restraint, the Court and Justice White assume for the sake of argument that, if a prisoner were to make an exceptionally strong showing of actual innocence, the execution could not go forward. Justice Blackmun, in contrast, would expressly so hold; he would also announce the precise burden of proof. Resolving the issue is neither necessary nor advisable in this case. The question is a sensitive and, to say the least, troubling one. It implicates not just the life of a single individual, but also the State's powerful and legitimate interest in punishing the guilty, and the nature of state-federal relations. Indeed, as the Court persuasively demonstrates, throughout our history the federal courts have assumed that they should not and could not intervene to prevent an execution so long as the prisoner had been convicted after a constitutionally adequate trial. The prisoner's sole remedy was a pardon or clemency.

Nonetheless, the proper disposition of this case is neither difficult nor troubling. No matter what the Court might say about claims of actual innocence today, petitioner could not obtain relief. The record overwhelmingly demonstrates that petitioner deliberately shot and killed Officers Rucker and Carrisalez the night of September 29, 1981; petitioner's new evidence is bereft of credibility. Indeed, despite its stinging criticism of the Court's decision, not even the dissent expresses a belief that petitioner might possibly be actually innocent. Nor could it: The record makes it abundantly clear that petitioner is not somehow the future victim of "simple murder," but instead himself the established perpetrator of two brutal and tragic ones.

Ultimately, two things about this case are clear. First is what the Court does not hold. Nowhere does the Court state that the Constitution permits the execution of an actually innocent person. Instead, the Court assumes for the sake of argument that a truly persuasive demonstration of actual innocence would render any such execution unconstitutional and that federal habeas relief would be warranted if no state avenue were open to process the claim. Second is what petitioner has not demonstrated. Petitioner has failed to make a persuasive showing of actual innocence. Not one judge — no state court judge, not the District Court Judge, none of the three judges of the Court of Appeals, and none of the Justices of this Court — has expressed doubt about petitioner's guilt. Accordingly, the Court has no reason to pass on, and appropriately reserves, the question whether federal courts may entertain convincing claims of actual innocence. That difficult question remains open. If the Constitution's guarantees of fair procedure and the safeguards of clemency and pardon fulfill their historical mission, it may never require resolution at all.

Justice SCALIA, with whom Justice THOMAS joins, concurring.

We granted certiorari on the question whether it violates due process or constitutes cruel and unusual punishment for a State to execute a person who, having been convicted of murder after a full and fair trial, later alleges that newly discovered evidence shows him to be "actually innocent." I would have preferred to decide that question, particularly since, as the Court's discussion shows, it is perfectly clear what the answer is: There is no basis in text, tradition, or even in contemporary practice (if that were enough) for finding in the Constitution a right to demand judicial consideration of newly discovered evidence of innocence brought forward after conviction. In saying that such a right exists, the dissenters apply nothing but their personal opinions to invalidate the rules of more than two-thirds of the States, and a Federal Rule of Criminal Procedure for which this Court itself is responsible. If the system that has been in place for 200 years (and remains widely approved) "shock[s]" the dissenters' consciences, perhaps they should doubt the calibration of their consciences, or, better still, the usefulness of "conscience shocking" as a legal test.

I nonetheless join the entirety of the Court's opinion, including the final portion, because there is no legal error in deciding a case by assuming, arguendo, that an asserted constitutional right exists, and because I can understand, or at least am accustomed to, the reluctance of the present Court to admit publicly that Our Perfect Constitution lets stand any injustice, much less the execution of an innocent man who has received, though to no avail, all the process that our society has traditionally deemed adequate. With any luck, we shall avoid ever having to face this embarrassing question again, since it is improbable that evidence of innocence as convincing as today's opinion requires would fail to produce an executive pardon.

Justice WHITE, concurring in the judgment.

In voting to affirm, I assume that a persuasive showing of "actual innocence" made after trial, even though made after the expiration of the time provided by law for the presentation of newly discovered evidence, would render unconstitutional the execution of petitioner in this case. To be entitled to relief, however, petitioner would at the very least be required to show that based on proffered newly discovered evidence and the entire record before the jury that convicted him, "no rational trier of fact could [find] proof of guilt beyond a reasonable doubt." For the reasons stated in the Court's opinion, petitioner's showing falls far short of satisfying even that standard, and I therefore concur in the judgment.

Justice BLACKMUN, with whom Justice STEVENS and Justice SOUTER join, dissenting.

Nothing could be more contrary to contemporary standards of decency, or more shocking to the conscience, than to execute a person who is actually innocent.

I therefore must disagree with the long and general discussion that precedes the Court's disposition of this case. That discussion, of course, is dictum because the Court assumes, "for the sake of argument in deciding this case, that in a capital case a truly persuasive demonstration of 'actual innocence' made after trial would render the execution of a defendant unconstitutional." Without articulating the standard it is applying, however, the Court then decides that this petitioner has not made a sufficiently persuasive case. Because I believe that in the first instance the District Court should decide whether petitioner is entitled to a hearing and whether he is entitled to relief on the merits of his claim, I would reverse the order of the Court of Appeals and remand this case for further proceedings in the District Court.

The Court's enumeration of the constitutional rights of criminal defendants surely is entirely beside the point. These protections sometimes fail.[43] We really are being asked to decide whether the Constitution forbids the execution of a person who has been validly convicted and sentenced but who, nonetheless, can prove his innocence with newly discovered evidence. Despite the State of Texas' astonishing protestation to the contrary, I do not see how the answer can be anything but "yes."

The Eighth Amendment prohibits "cruel and unusual punishments." This proscription is not static but rather reflects evolving standards of decency. I think it is crystal clear that the execution of an innocent person is "at odds with contemporary standards of fairness and decency." Indeed, it is at odds with any standard of decency that I can imagine.

---

43. One impressive study has concluded that 23 innocent people have been executed in the United States in this century, including one as recently as 1984. Bedau & Radelet, Miscarriages of Justice in Potentially Capital Cases, 40 Stan. L. Rev. 21, 36, 173-179 (1987); Radelet, Bedau, & Putnam, In Spite of Innocence 282-356 (1992). The majority cites this study to show that clemency has been exercised frequently in capital cases when showings of actual innocence have been made. But the study also shows that requests for clemency by persons the authors believe were innocent have been refused. See, e.g., Bedau & Radelet, 40 Stan. L. Rev., at 91 (discussing James Adams who was executed in Florida on May 10, 1984); Radelet, Bedau, & Putnam, In Spite of Innocence, at 5-10 (same). [Footnote by the Court.]

This Court has ruled that punishment is excessive and unconstitutional if it is "nothing more than the purposeless and needless imposition of pain and suffering," or if it is "grossly out of proportion to the severity of the crime." It has held that death is an excessive punishment for rape, and for mere participation in a robbery during which a killing takes place. If it is violative of the Eighth Amendment to execute someone who is guilty of those crimes, then it plainly is violative of the Eighth Amendment to execute a person who is actually innocent. Executing an innocent person epitomizes "the purposeless and needless imposition of pain and suffering."

The protection of the Eighth Amendment does not end once a defendant has been validly convicted and sentenced. Respondent and the United States as amicus curiae argue that the Eighth Amendment does not apply to petitioner because he is challenging his guilt, not his punishment. Whether petitioner is viewed as challenging simply his death sentence or also his continued detention, he still is challenging the State's right to punish him. Respondent and the United States would impose a clear line between guilt and punishment, reasoning that every claim that concerns guilt necessarily does not involve punishment. Such a division is far too facile. What respondent and the United States fail to recognize is that the legitimacy of punishment is inextricably intertwined with guilt.

The Court also suggests that allowing petitioner to raise his claim of innocence would not serve society's interest in the reliable imposition of the death penalty because it might require a new trial that would be less accurate than the first. This suggestion misses the point entirely. The question is not whether a second trial would be more reliable than the first but whether, in light of new evidence, the result of the first trial is sufficiently reliable for the State to carry out a death sentence. Furthermore, it is far from clear that a State will seek to retry the rare prisoner who prevails on a claim of actual innocence. I believe a prisoner must show not just that there was probably a reasonable doubt about his guilt but that he is probably actually innocent. I find it difficult to believe that any State would choose to retry a person who meets this standard.

I believe it contrary to any standard of decency to execute someone who is actually innocent. Because the Eighth Amendment applies to questions of guilt or innocence, and to persons upon whom a valid sentence of death has been imposed, I also believe that petitioner may raise an Eighth Amendment challenge to his punishment on the ground that he is actually innocent.

Execution of the innocent is equally offensive to the Due Process Clause of the Fourteenth Amendment.

The majority's discussion of petitioner's constitutional claims is even more perverse when viewed in the light of this Court's recent habeas jurisprudence. Beginning with a trio of decisions in 1986, this Court shifted the focus of federal habeas review of successive, abusive, or defaulted claims away from the preservation of constitutional rights to a fact-based inquiry into the habeas petitioner's guilt or innocence. The Court sought to strike a balance between the State's interest in the finality of its criminal judgments and the prisoner's interest in access to a forum to test the basic justice of his sentence. In striking this balance, the Court adopted the view of Judge Friendly that there should be an exception to the concept of finality when a prisoner can make a colorable claim of actual innocence. Friendly, *Is Innocence Irrelevant? Collateral Attack on Criminal Judgments*, 38 U.Chi.L.Rev. 142, 160 (1970).

Having adopted an "actual-innocence" requirement for review of abusive, successive, or defaulted claims, however, the majority would now take the position that "a claim of 'actual innocence' is not itself a constitutional claim, but instead a gateway through which a habeas petitioner must pass to have his otherwise barred constitutional claim considered on the merits." In other words, having held that a prisoner who is incarcerated in violation of the Constitution must show he is actually innocent to obtain relief, the majority would now hold that a prisoner who is actually innocent must show a constitutional violation to obtain relief. The only principle that would appear to reconcile these two positions is the principle that habeas relief should be denied whenever possible.

The Eighth and Fourteenth Amendments, of course, are binding on the States, and one would normally expect the States to adopt procedures to consider claims of actual innocence based on newly discovered evidence. The majority's disposition of this case, however, leaves the States uncertain of their constitutional obligations.

Whatever procedures a State might adopt to hear actual-innocence claims, one thing is certain: The possibility of executive clemency is not sufficient to satisfy the requirements of the Eighth and Fourteenth Amendments. The majority correctly points out: " 'A pardon is an act of grace.' " The vindication of rights guaranteed by the Constitution has never been made to turn on the unreviewable discretion of an executive official or administrative tribunal.

Like other constitutional claims, Eighth and Fourteenth Amendment claims of actual innocence advanced on behalf of a state prisoner can and should be heard in state court. If a State provides a judicial procedure for raising such claims, the prisoner may be required to exhaust that procedure before taking his claim of actual innocence to federal court. See 28 U.S.C. §§2254(b) and (c). Furthermore, state-court determinations of factual issues relating to the claim would be entitled to a presumption of correctness in any subsequent federal habeas proceeding. See §2254(d).

Texas provides no judicial procedure for hearing petitioner's claim of actual innocence and his habeas petition was properly filed in district court under §2254. The district court is entitled to dismiss the petition summarily only if "it plainly appears from the face of the petition and any exhibits annexed to it that the petitioner is not entitled to relief." §2254 Rule 4. If, as is the case here, the petition raises factual questions and the State has failed to provide a full and fair hearing, the district court is required to hold an evidentiary hearing.

The question that remains is what showing should be required to obtain relief on the merits of an Eighth or Fourteenth Amendment claim of actual innocence. I agree with the majority that "in state criminal proceedings the trial is the paramount event for determining the guilt or innocence of the defendant." I also think that "a truly persuasive demonstration of 'actual innocence' made after trial would render the execution of a defendant unconstitutional." The question is what "a truly persuasive demonstration" entails, a question the majority's disposition of this case leaves open.

In articulating the "actual-innocence" exception in our habeas jurisprudence, this Court has adopted a standard requiring the petitioner to show a " 'fair probability that, in light of all the evidence . . . , the trier of the facts would have entertained a reasonable doubt of his guilt.' " In other words, the habeas petitioner must show that there probably would be a reasonable doubt.

I think the standard for relief on the merits of an actual-innocence claim must be higher than the threshold standard for merely reaching that claim or any other claim that has been procedurally defaulted or is successive or abusive. I would hold that, to obtain relief on a claim of actual innocence, the petitioner must show that he probably is innocent. This standard is supported by several considerations. First, new evidence of innocence may be discovered long after the defendant's conviction. Given the passage of time, it may be difficult for the State to retry a defendant who obtains relief from his conviction or sentence on an actual-innocence claim. The actual-innocence proceeding thus may constitute the final word on whether the defendant may be punished. In light of this fact, an otherwise constitutionally valid conviction or sentence should not be set aside lightly. Second, conviction after a constitutionally adequate trial strips the defendant of the presumption of innocence.

In considering whether a prisoner is entitled to relief on an actual-innocence claim, a court should take all the evidence into account, giving due regard to its reliability. Because placing the burden on the prisoner to prove innocence creates a presumption that the conviction is valid, it is not necessary or appropriate to make further presumptions about the reliability of newly discovered evidence generally. Rather, the court charged with deciding such a claim should make a case-by-case determination about the reliability of the newly discovered evidence under the circumstances. The court then should weigh the evidence in favor of the prisoner against the evidence of his guilt. Obviously, the stronger the evidence of the prisoner's guilt, the more persuasive the newly discovered evidence of innocence must be.

It should be clear that the standard I would adopt would not convert the federal courts into " 'forums in which to relitigate state trials.' " I believe that if a prisoner can show that he is probably actually innocent, in light of all the evidence, then he has made "a truly persuasive demonstration," and his execution would violate the Constitution. I would so hold.

Thus, there are two ways in which "actual innocence" might be raised: as a "gateway" to allow procedurally defaulted claims to be raised or as a "freestanding" basis for overturning a conviction. Herrera v. Collins is unclear as to whether the latter is allowed. There is only one case in which the Supreme Court ever has found a sufficient showing of actual innocence: House v. Bell. In it, the Court clarified and applied the standard for "actual innocence" as a "gateway" for raising procedurally defaulted claims and also discussed the standard for "freestanding" claims of innocence.

HOUSE v. BELL

547 U.S. 518 (2006)

Justice KENNEDY delivered the opinion of the Court.

Some 20 years ago in rural Tennessee, Carolyn Muncey was murdered. A jury convicted petitioner Paul Gregory House of the crime and sentenced him to death, but new revelations cast doubt on the jury's verdict. House, protesting his innocence, seeks access to federal court to pursue habeas corpus relief based on constitutional claims that are procedurally barred under state law. Out of respect for the finality of state-court judgments federal habeas courts, as a general rule, are closed to claims that state courts would consider defaulted. In certain exceptional cases involving a compelling claim of actual innocence, however, the state procedural default rule is not a bar to a federal habeas corpus petition. *See* Schlup v. Delo (1995). After careful review of the full record, we conclude that House has made the stringent showing required by this exception; and we hold that his federal habeas action may proceed.

I

We begin with the facts surrounding Mrs. Muncey's disappearance, the discovery of her body, and House's arrest. Around 3 P.M. on Sunday, July 14, 1985, two local residents found her body concealed amid brush and tree branches on an embankment roughly 100 yards up the road from her driveway. Mrs. Muncey had been seen last on the evening before, when, around 8 P.M., she and her two children—Lora Muncey, age 10, and Matthew Muncey, age 8—visited their neighbor, Pam Luttrell. According to Luttrell, Mrs. Muncey mentioned her husband, William Hubert Muncey, Jr., known in the community as "Little Hube" and to his family as "Bubbie." As Luttrell recounted Mrs. Muncey's comment, Mr. Muncey "had gone to dig a grave, and he hadn't come back, but that was all right, because [Mrs. Muncey] was going to make him take her fishing the next day." Mrs. Muncey returned home, and some time later, before 11:00 P.M. at the latest, Luttrell "heard a car rev its motor as it went down the road," something Mr. Muncey customarily did when he drove by on his way home. Luttrell then went to bed.

Around 1 A.M., Lora and Matthew returned to Luttrell's home, this time with their father, Mr. Muncey, who said his wife was missing. Muncey asked Luttrell to watch the children while he searched for his wife. After he left, Luttrell talked with Lora. While Lora was talking, Luttrell recalled, "Matt kept butting in, you know, on us talking, and he said — sister they said daddy had a wreck, they said daddy had a wreck."

Lora testified that after leaving Luttrell's house with her mother, she and her brother "went to bed." Later, she heard someone, or perhaps two different people, ask for her mother.

Lora did not describe hearing any struggle. Some time later, Lora and her brother left the house to look for their mother, but no one answered when they knocked at the Luttrells' home, and another neighbor, Mike Clinton, said he had not seen her. After the children returned home, according to Lora, her father came home and "fixed him a bologna sandwich and he took a bit of it and he says — sissy, where is mommy at, and I said — she ain't been here for a little while." Lora recalled that Mr. Muncey went outside and, not seeing his wife, returned to take Lora and Matthew to the Luttrells' so that he could look further.

The next afternoon Billy Ray Hensley, the victim's first cousin, heard of Mrs. Muncey's disappearance and went to look for Mr. Muncey. As he approached the Munceys' street, Hensley allegedly "saw Mr. House come out from under a bank, wiping his hands on a black rag." Just when and where Hensley saw House, and how well he could have observed him, were disputed at House's trial. Hensley admitted on cross-examination that he could not have seen House "walking up or climbing up" the embankment; rather, he saw House, in "[j]ust a glance," "appear out of nowhere," "next to the embankment." On the Munceys' street, opposite the area where Hensley said he saw House, a white Plymouth was parked near a sawmill. Another witness, Billy Hankins, whom the defense called, claimed that around the same time he saw a "boy" walking down the street away from the parked Plymouth and toward the Munceys' home. This witness, however, put the "boy" on the side of the street with the parked car and the Munceys' driveway, not the side with the embankment.

Hensley, after turning onto the Munceys' street, continued down the road and turned into their driveway. "I pulled up in the driveway where I could see up toward Little Hube's house," Hensley testified, "and I seen Little Hube's car wasn't there, and I backed out in the road, and come back [the other way]." As he traveled up the road, Hensley saw House traveling in the opposite direction in the white Plymouth. House "flagged [Hensley] down" through his windshield, and the two cars met about 300 feet up the road from the Munceys' driveway. According to Hensley, House said he had heard Mrs. Muncey was missing and was looking for her husband. Though House had only recently moved to the area, he was acquainted with the Munceys, had attended a dance with them, and had visited their home.

He later told law enforcement officials he considered both of the Munceys his friends. According to Hensley, House said he had heard that Mrs. Muncey's husband, who was an alcoholic, was elsewhere "getting drunk."

As Hensley drove off, he "got to thinking to [him]self—he's hunting Little Hube, and Little Hube drunk—what would he be doing off that bank. . . ." His suspicion aroused, Hensley later returned to the Munceys' street with a friend named Jack Adkins. The two checked different spots on the embankment, and though Hensley saw nothing where he looked, Adkins found Mrs. Muncey. Her body lay across from the sawmill near the corner where House's car had been parked, dumped in the woods a short way down the bank leading toward a creek.

Around midnight, Dr. Alex Carabia, a practicing pathologist and county medical examiner, performed an autopsy. Dr. Carabia put the time of death between 9 and 11 P.M. Mrs. Muncey had a black eye, both her hands were bloodstained up to the wrists, and she had bruises on her legs and neck. Dr. Carabia described the bruises as consistent with a "traumatic origin," i.e., a fight or a fall on hard objects. Based on the neck bruises and other injuries, he concluded Mrs. Muncey had been choked, but he ruled this out as the cause of death. The cause of death, in Dr. Carabia's view, was a severe blow to the left forehead that inflicted both a laceration penetrating to the bone and, inside the skull, a severe right-side hemorrhage, likely caused by Mrs. Muncey's brain slamming into the skull opposite the impact. Dr. Carabia described this head injury as consistent either with receiving a blow from a fist or other instrument or with striking some object.

The county sheriff, informed about Hensley's earlier encounter with House, questioned House shortly after the body was found. That evening, House answered further questions during a voluntary interview at the local jail. Special Agent Ray Presnell of the Tennessee Bureau of Investigation (TBI) prepared a statement of House's answers, which House signed. Asked to describe his whereabouts on the previous evening, House claimed—falsely, as it turned out—that he spent the entire evening with his girlfriend, Donna Turner, at her trailer. Asked whether he was wearing the same pants he had worn the night before, House replied—again, falsely—that he was. House was on probation at the time, having recently been released on parole following a sentence of five years to life for aggravated sexual assault in Utah. House had scratches on his arms and hands, and a knuckle on his right ring finger was bruised. He attributed the scratches to Turner's cats and the finger injury to recent construction work tearing down a shed. The next day House gave a similar statement to a different TBI agent, Charles Scott.

In fact House had not been at Turner's home. After initially supporting House's alibi, Turner informed authorities that House left her trailer around 10:30 or 10:45 P.M. to go for a walk. According to Turner's trial testimony, House returned later—she was not sure when—hot and panting, missing his shirt and his shoes. House, Turner testified, told her that while he was walking on the road near her home, a vehicle pulled up beside him, and somebody inside "called him some names and then they told him he didn't belong here anymore." House said he tried to ignore the taunts and keep walking, but the vehicle pulled in behind him, and "one of them got out and grabbed him by the shoulder . . . and [House] swung around with his right hand" and "hit something." According to Turner, House said "he took off down the bank and started running and he said that he — he said it seemed forever where he was running. And he said they fired two shots at him while he took off down the bank. . . ." House claimed the assailants "grabbed ahold of his shirt," which Turner remembered as "a blue tank top, trimmed in yellow," and "they tore it to where it wouldn't stay on him and he said — I just threwed it off when I was running." Turner, noticing House's bruised knuckle, asked how he hurt it, and House told her "that's where he hit." Turner testified that she "thought maybe my ex-husband had something to do with it."

Although the white Plymouth House drove the next day belonged to Turner, Turner insisted House had not used the car that night. No forensic evidence connected the car to the crime; law enforcement officials inspected a white towel covering the driver seat and concluded it was clean. Turner's trailer was located just under two miles by road, through hilly terrain, from the Muncey residence.

Law enforcement officers also questioned the victim's husband. Though Mrs. Muncey's comments to Luttrell gave no indication she knew this, Mr. Muncey had spent the evening at a weekly dance at a recreation center roughly a mile and a half from his home. In his statement to law enforcement — a statement House's trial counsel claims he never saw — Mr. Muncey admitted leaving the dance early, but said it was only for a brief trip to the package store to buy beer. He also stated that he and his wife had had sexual relations Saturday morning.

Late in the evening on Monday, July 15 — two days after the murder — law enforcement officers visited Turner's trailer. With Turner's consent, Agent Scott seized the pants House was wearing the night Mrs. Muncey disappeared. The heavily soiled pants were sitting in a laundry hamper; years later, Agent Scott recalled noticing "reddish brown stains" he "suspected" were blood. Around 4 P.M. the next day, two local law enforcement officers set out for the Federal Bureau of Investigation in Washington, D.C., with House's pants, blood samples from the autopsy, and other evidence packed together in a box. They arrived at 2:00 A.M. the next morning. On July 17, after initial FBI testing revealed human blood on the pants, House was arrested.

II

The State of Tennessee charged House with capital murder. At House's trial, the State presented testimony by Luttrell, Hensley, Adkins, Lora Muncey, Dr. Carabia, the sheriff, and other law enforcement officials. Through TBI

Agents Presnell and Scott, the jury learned of House's false statements. Central to the State's case, however, was what the FBI testing showed — that semen consistent (or so it seemed) with House's was present on Mrs. Muncey's nightgown and panties, and that small bloodstains consistent with Mrs. Muncey's blood but not House's appeared on the jeans belonging to House.

Regarding the semen, FBI Special Agent Paul Bigbee, a serologist, testified that the source was a "secretor," meaning someone who "secrete[s] the ABO blood group substances in other body fluids, such as semen and saliva" — a characteristic shared by 80 percent of the population, including House. Agent Bigbee further testified that the source of semen on the gown was blood-type A, House's own blood type. As to the semen on the panties, Agent Bigbee found only the H blood-group substance, which A and B blood-type secretors secrete along with substances A and B, and which O-type secretors secrete exclusively. Agent Bigbee explained, however — using science an amicus here sharply disputed — that House's A antigens could have "degraded" into H. Agent Bigbee thus concluded that both semen deposits could have come from House, though he acknowledged that the H antigen could have come from Mrs. Muncey herself if she was a secretor — something he "was not able to determine," — and that, while Mr. Muncey was himself blood-type A (as was his wife), Agent Bigbee was again "not able to determine his secretor status." Agent Bigbee acknowledged on cross-examination that "a saliva sample" would have sufficed to determine whether Mr. Muncey was a secretor; the State did not provide such a sample, though it did provide samples of Mr. Muncey's blood.

As for the blood, Agent Bigbee explained that "spots of blood" appeared "on the left outside leg, the right bottom cuff, on the left thigh and in the right inside pocket and on the lower pocket on the outside." Agent Bigbee determined that the blood's source was type A (the type shared by House, the victim, and Mr. Muncey). He also successfully tested for the enzyme phosphoglucomutase and the blood serum haptoglobin, both of which "are found in all humans" and carry "slight chemical differences" that vary genetically and "can be grouped to differentiate between two individuals if those types are different." Based on these chemical traces and on the A blood type, Agent Bigbee determined that only some 6.75 percent of the population carry similar blood, that the blood was "consistent" with Mrs. Muncey's (as determined by testing autopsy samples), and that it was "impossible" that the blood came from House.

A different FBI expert, Special Agent Chester Blythe, testified about fiber analysis performed on Mrs. Muncey's clothes and on House's pants. Although Agent Blythe found blue jean fibers on Mrs. Muncey's nightgown, brassier, housecoat, and panties, and in fingernail scrapings taken from her body (scrapings that also contained trace, unidentifiable amounts of blood), he acknowledged that, as the prosecutor put it in questioning the witness, "blue jean material is common material," so "this doesn't mean that the fibers that were all over the victim's clothing were necessarily from [House's] pair of blue jeans." On House's pants, though cotton garments both transfer and retain fibers readily, Agent Blythe found neither hair nor fiber consistent with the victim's hair or clothing.

As Turner informed the jury, House's shoes were found several months after the crime in a field near her home. Turner delivered them to authorities. Though the jury did not learn of this fact (and House's counsel claims he did not either), the State tested the shoes for blood and found none. House's shirt was not found.

The State's closing argument suggested that on the night of her murder, Mrs. Muncey "was deceived. . . . She had been told [her husband] had had an accident." The prosecutor emphasized the FBI's blood analysis, noting that "after running many, many, many tests," Agent Bigbee: "was able to tell you that the blood on the defendant's blue jeans was not his own blood, could not be his own blood. He told you that the blood on the blue jeans was consistent with every characteristic in every respect of the deceased's, Carolyn Muncey's, and that ninety-three (93%) percent of the white population would not have that blood type. . . . He can't tell you one hundred (100%) percent for certain that it was her blood. But folks, he can sure give you a pretty good — a pretty good indication."

In addition the government suggested the black rag Hensley said he saw in House's hands was in fact the missing blue tank top, retrieved by House from the crime scene. And the prosecution reiterated the importance of the blood. "[D]efense counsel," he said, "does not start out discussing the fact that his client had blood on his jeans on the night that Carolyn Muncey was killed. . . . He doesn't start with the fact that nothing that the defense has introduced in this case explains what blood is doing on his jeans, all over his jeans, that is scientifically, completely different from his blood." The jury found House guilty of murder in the first degree.

The trial advanced to the sentencing phase. As aggravating factors to support a capital sentence, the State sought to prove: (1) that House had previously been convicted of a felony involving the use or threat of violence; (2) that the homicide was especially heinous, atrocious, or cruel in that it involved torture or depravity of mind; and (3) that the murder was committed while House was committing, attempting to commit, or fleeing from the commission of, rape or kidnaping. After presenting evidence of House's parole status and aggravated sexual assault conviction, the State rested.

[III]

As a general rule, claims forfeited under state law may support federal habeas relief only if the prisoner demonstrates cause for the default and prejudice from the asserted error. The rule is based on the comity and respect that must be accorded to state-court judgments. The bar is not, however, unqualified. In an effort to "balance the societal interests in finality, comity, and conservation of scarce judicial resources with the individual interest in justice that arises in the extraordinary case," the Court has recognized a miscarriage-of-justice exception.

" '[I]n appropriate cases,' " the Court has said, "the principles of comity and finality that inform the concepts of cause and prejudice 'must yield to the imperative of correcting a fundamentally unjust incarceration.' "

In *Schlup*, the Court adopted a specific rule to implement this general principle. It held that prisoners asserting innocence as a gateway to defaulted claims must establish that, in light of new evidence, "it is more likely than not that no reasonable juror would have found petitioner guilty beyond a reasonable doubt." This formulation, *Schlup* explains, "ensures that petitioner's case is truly 'extraordinary,' while still providing petitioner a meaningful avenue by which to avoid a manifest injustice." In the usual case the presumed guilt of a prisoner convicted in state court counsels against federal review of defaulted claims. Yet a petition supported by a convincing *Schlup* gateway showing "raise[s] sufficient doubt about [the petitioner's] guilt to undermine confidence in the result of the trial without the assurance that that trial was untainted by constitutional error"; hence, "a review of the merits of the constitutional claims" is justified.

For purposes of this case several features of the *Schlup* standard bear emphasis. First, although "[t]o be credible" a gateway claim requires "new reliable evidence — whether it be exculpatory scientific evidence, trustworthy eyewitness accounts, or critical physical evidence — that was not presented at trial," the habeas court's analysis is not limited to such evidence. There is no dispute in this case that House has presented some new reliable evidence; the State has conceded as much. In addition, because the District Court held an evidentiary hearing in this case, and because the State does not challenge the court's decision to do so, we have no occasion to elaborate on *Schlup*'s observation that when considering an actual-innocence claim in the context of a request for an evidentiary hearing, the District Court need not "test the new evidence by a standard appropriate for deciding a motion for summary judgment," but rather may "consider how the timing of the submission and the likely credibility of the affiants bear on the probable reliability of that evidence." Our review in this case addresses the merits of the *Schlup* inquiry, based on a fully developed record, and with respect to that inquiry *Schlup* makes plain that the habeas court must consider " 'all the evidence,' " old and new, incriminating and exculpatory, without regard to whether it would necessarily be admitted under "rules of admissibility that would govern at trial." Based on this total record, the court must make "a probabilistic determination about what reasonable, properly instructed jurors would do." The court's function is not to make an independent factual determination about what likely occurred, but rather to assess the likely impact of the evidence on reasonable jurors.

Second, it bears repeating that the *Schlup* standard is demanding and permits review only in the " 'extraordinary' " case. At the same time, though, the *Schlup* standard does not require absolute certainty about the petitioner's guilt or innocence. A petitioner's burden at the gateway stage is to demonstrate that more likely than not, in light of the new evidence, no reasonable juror would find him guilty beyond a reasonable doubt — or, to remove the double negative, that more likely than not any reasonable juror would have reasonable doubt.

The State also argues that the District Court's findings in this case tie our hands, precluding a ruling in House's favor absent a showing of clear error as to the District Court's specific determinations. This view overstates the effect of the District Court's ruling. Deference is given to a trial court's assessment of evidence presented to it in the first instance. Yet the *Schlup* inquiry, we repeat, requires a holistic judgment about " 'all the evidence,' " and its likely effect on reasonable jurors applying the reasonable-doubt standard. As a general rule, the inquiry does not turn on discrete findings regarding disputed points of fact, and "[i]t is not the district court's independent judgment as to whether reasonable doubt exists that the standard addresses." Here, although the District Court attentively managed complex proceedings, carefully reviewed the extensive record, and drew certain conclusions about the evidence, the court did not clearly apply *Schlup*'s predictive standard regarding whether reasonable jurors would have reasonable doubt. As we shall explain, moreover, we are uncertain about the basis for some of the District Court's conclusions — a consideration that weakens our reliance on its determinations.

With this background in mind we turn to the evidence developed in House's federal habeas proceedings.

DNA EVIDENCE

First, in direct contradiction of evidence presented at trial, DNA testing has established that the semen on Mrs. Muncey's nightgown and panties came from her husband, Mr. Muncey, not from House. The State, though conceding this point, insists this new evidence is immaterial. At the guilt phase at least, neither sexual contact nor motive were elements of the offense, so in the State's view the evidence, or lack of evidence, of sexual assault or sexual advance is of no consequence. We disagree. In fact we consider the new disclosure of central importance.

From beginning to end the case is about who committed the crime. When identity is in question, motive is key. The point, indeed, was not lost on the prosecution, for it introduced the evidence and relied on it in the final guilt-phase closing argument. Referring to "evidence at the scene," the prosecutor suggested that House committed, or attempted to commit, some "indignity" on Mrs. Muncey that neither she "nor any mother on that road would want to do with Mr. House." Particularly in a case like this where the proof was, as the State Supreme Court observed, circumstantial, we think a jury would have given this evidence great weight. Quite apart from providing proof of motive, it was the only forensic evidence at the scene that would link House to the murder.

Law and society, as they ought to do, demand accountability when a sexual offense has been committed, so not only did this evidence link House to the crime; it likely was a factor in persuading the jury not to let him go free. At sentencing, moreover, the jury came to the unanimous conclusion, beyond a reasonable doubt, that the murder was committed in the course of a rape or kidnaping. The alleged sexual motivation relates to both those determinations. This is particularly so given that, at the sentencing phase, the jury was advised that House had a previous conviction for sexual assault.

A jury informed that fluids on Mrs. Muncey's garments could have come from House might have found that House trekked the nearly two miles to the victim's home and lured her away in order to commit a sexual offense. By contrast a jury acting without the assumption that the semen could have come from House would have found it necessary to establish some different motive, or, if the same motive, an intent far more speculative. When the only direct evidence of sexual assault drops out of the case, so, too, does a central theme in the State's narrative linking House to the crime. In that light, furthermore, House's odd evening walk and his false statements to authorities, while still potentially incriminating, might appear less suspicious.

BLOODSTAINS

The other relevant forensic evidence is the blood on House's pants, which appears in small, even minute, stains in scattered places. As the prosecutor told the jury, they were stains that, due to their small size, "you or I might not detect[,] [m]ight not see, but which the FBI lab was able to find on [House's] jeans." The stains appear inside the right pocket, outside that pocket, near the inside button, on the left thigh and outside leg, on the seat of the pants, and on the right bottom cuff, including inside the pants. Due to testing by the FBI, cuttings now appear on the pants in several places where stains evidently were found. (The cuttings were destroyed in the testing process, and defense experts were unable to replicate the tests.) At trial, the government argued "nothing that the defense has introduced in this case explains what blood is doing on his jeans, all over [House's] jeans, that is scientifically, completely different from his blood." House, though not disputing at this point that the blood is Mrs. Muncey's, now presents an alternative explanation that, if credited, would undermine the probative value of the blood evidence.

Other evidence confirms that blood did in fact spill from the vials. It appears the vials passed from Dr. Carabia, who performed the autopsy, into the hands of two local law enforcement officers, who transported it to the FBI, where Agent Bigbee performed the enzyme tests. The blood was contained in four vials, evidently with neither preservative nor a proper seal. The vials, in turn, were stored in a styrofoam box, but nothing indicates the box was kept cool. Rather, in what an evidence protocol expert at the habeas hearing described as a violation of proper procedure, the styrofoam box was packed in the same cardboard box as other evidence including House's pants (apparently in a paper bag) and other clothing (in separate bags). The cardboard box was then carried in the officers' car while they made the 10-hour journey from Tennessee to the FBI lab. Dr. Blake stated that blood vials in hot conditions (such as a car trunk in the summer) could blow open; and in fact, by the time the blood reached the FBI it had hemolyzed, or spoiled, due to heat exposure. By the time the blood passed from the FBI to a defense expert, roughly a vial and a half were empty, though Agent Bigbee testified he used at most a quarter of one vial. Blood, moreover, had seeped onto one corner of the styrofoam box and onto packing gauze inside the box below the vials.

In addition, although the pants apparently were packaged initially in a paper bag and FBI records suggest they arrived at the FBI in one, the record does not contain the paper bag but does contain a plastic bag with a label listing the pants and Agent Scott's name — and the plastic bag has blood on it. The blood appears in a forked streak roughly five inches long and two inches wide running down the bag's outside front. Though testing by House's expert confirmed the stain was blood, the expert could not determine the blood's source. Speculations about when and how the blood got there add to the confusion regarding the origins of the stains on House's pants.

Faced with these indications of, at best, poor evidence control, the State attempted to establish at the habeas hearing that all blood spillage occurred after Agent Bigbee examined the pants. Were that the case, of course, then blood would have been detected on the pants before any spill — which would tend to undermine Dr. Blake's analysis and support using the bloodstains to infer House's guilt.

In sum, considering " 'all the evidence,' " on this issue, we think the evidentiary disarray surrounding the blood, taken together with Dr. Blake's testimony and the limited rebuttal of it in the present record, would prevent reasonable jurors from placing significant reliance on the blood evidence. We now know, though the trial jury did not, that an Assistant Chief Medical Examiner believes the blood on House's jeans must have come from autopsy samples; that a vial and a quarter of autopsy blood is unaccounted for; that the blood was transported to the FBI together with the pants in conditions that could have caused vials to spill; that the blood did indeed spill at least once during its journey from Tennessee authorities through FBI hands to a defense expert; that the pants were stored in a plastic bag bearing both a large blood stain and a label with TBI Agent Scott's name; and that the styrofoam box containing the blood samples may well have been opened before it arrived at the FBI lab. Thus, whereas the bloodstains, emphasized by the prosecution, seemed strong evidence of House's guilt at trial, the record now raises substantial questions about the blood's origin.

A DIFFERENT SUSPECT

Were House's challenge to the State's case limited to the questions he has raised about the blood and semen, the other evidence favoring the prosecution might well suffice to bar relief. There is, however, more; for in the post-trial proceedings House presented troubling evidence that Mr. Muncey, the victim's husband, himself could have been the murderer.

At trial, as has been noted, the jury heard that roughly two weeks before the murder Mrs. Muncey's brother received a frightened phone call from his sister indicating that she and Mr. Muncey had been fighting, that she was scared, and that she wanted to leave him. The jury also learned that the brother once saw Mr. Muncey "smac[k]" the victim. House now has produced evidence from multiple sources suggesting that Mr. Muncey regularly abused his wife.

Of most importance is the testimony of Kathy Parker and her sister Penny Letner. They testified at the habeas hearing that, around the time of House's trial, Mr. Muncey had confessed to the crime. Parker recalled that she and "some family members and some friends [were] sitting around drinking" at Parker's trailer when Mr. Muncey "just walked in and sit down." Muncey, who had evidently been drinking heavily, began "rambling off . . . [t]alking about what happened to his wife and how it happened and he didn't mean to do it." According to Parker, Mr. Muncey "said they had been into [an] argument and he slapped her and she fell and hit her head and it killed her and he didn't mean for it to happen." Parker said she "freaked out and run him off."

Other testimony suggests Mr. Muncey had the opportunity to commit the crime. According to Dennis Wallace, a local law enforcement official who provided security at the dance on the night of the murder, Mr. Muncey left the dance "around 10:00, 10:30, 9:30 to 10:30." Although Mr. Muncey told law enforcement officials just after the murder that he left the dance only briefly and returned, Wallace could not recall seeing him back there again. Later that evening, Wallace responded to Mr. Muncey's report that his wife was missing. Muncey denied he and his wife had been "a fussing or a fighting"; he claimed his wife had been "kidnapped."

In the habeas proceedings, then, two different witnesses (Parker and Letner) described a confession by Mr. Muncey; two more (Atkins and Lawson) described suspicious behavior (a fight and an attempt to construct a false alibi) around the time of the crime; and still other witnesses described a history of abuse.

The evidence pointing to Mr. Muncey is by no means conclusive. If considered in isolation, a reasonable jury might well disregard it. In combination, however, with the challenges to the blood evidence and the lack of motive with respect to House, the evidence pointing to Mr. Muncey likely would reinforce other doubts as to House's guilt.

OTHER EVIDENCE

Certain other details were presented at the habeas hearing. First, Dr. Blake, in addition to testifying about the blood evidence and the victim's head injury, examined photographs of House's bruises and scratches and concluded, based on 35 years' experience monitoring the development and healing of bruises, that they were too old to have resulted from the crime. In addition Dr. Blake claimed that the injury on House's right knuckle was indicative of "[g]etting mashed"; it was not consistent with striking someone.

The victim's daughter, Lora Muncey (now Lora Tharp), also testified at the habeas hearing. She repeated her recollection of hearing a man with a deep voice like her grandfather's and a statement that her father had had a wreck down by the creek. She also denied seeing any signs of struggle or hearing a fight between her parents, though she also said she could not recall her parents ever fighting physically. The District Court found her credible, and this testimony certainly cuts in favor of the State.

Finally, House himself testified at the habeas proceedings. He essentially repeated the story he allegedly told Turner about getting attacked on the road. The District Court found, however, based on House's demeanor, that he "was not a credible witness."

CONCLUSION

This is not a case of conclusive exoneration. Some aspects of the State's evidence—Lora Muncey's memory of a deep voice, House's bizarre evening walk, his lie to law enforcement, his appearance near the body, and the blood on his pants—still support an inference of guilt. Yet the central forensic proof connecting House to the crime—the blood and the semen—has been called into question, and House has put forward substantial evidence pointing to a different suspect. Accordingly, and although the issue is close, we conclude that this is the rare case where—had the jury heard all the conflicting testimony—it is more likely than not that no reasonable juror viewing the record as a whole would lack reasonable doubt.

V

In addition to his gateway claim under *Schlup*, House argues that he has shown freestanding innocence and that as a result his imprisonment and planned execution are unconstitutional. In *Herrera*, decided three years before *Schlup*, the Court assumed without deciding that "in a capital case a truly persuasive demonstration of 'actual innocence' made after trial would render the execution of a defendant unconstitutional, and warrant federal habeas relief if there were no state avenue open to process such a claim." House urges the Court to answer the question left open in *Herrera* and hold not only that freestanding innocence claims are possible but also that he has established one.

We decline to resolve this issue. We conclude here, much as in *Herrera*, that whatever burden a hypothetical freestanding innocence claim would require, this petitioner has not satisfied it. To be sure, House has cast considerable doubt on his guilt—doubt sufficient to satisfy *Schlup*'s gateway standard for obtaining federal review despite a state procedural default. In *Herrera*, however, the Court described the threshold for any hypothetical freestanding innocence claim as "extraordinarily high." The sequence of the Court's decisions in *Herrera* and *Schlup*—first leaving unresolved the status of freestanding claims and then establishing the gateway standard— implies at the least that *Herrera* requires more convincing proof of innocence than *Schlup*. It follows, given the closeness of the *Schlup* question here, that House's showing falls short of the threshold implied in *Herrera*.

House has satisfied the gateway standard set forth in *Schlup* and may proceed on remand with procedurally defaulted constitutional claims.

Chief Justice ROBERTS, with whom Justice SCALIA and Justice THOMAS join, concurring in the judgment in part and dissenting in part.

To overcome the procedural hurdle that Paul House created by failing to properly present his constitutional claims to a Tennessee court, he must demonstrate that the constitutional violations he alleges "ha[ve] probably resulted in the conviction of one who is actually innocent," such that a federal court's refusal to hear the defaulted claims would be a "miscarriage of justice." Schlup v. Delo (1995). To make the requisite showing of actual innocence, House must produce "new reliable evidence" and "must show that it is more likely than not that no reasonable juror would have convicted him in the light of the new evidence." The question is not whether House was prejudiced at his trial because the jurors were not aware of the new evidence, but whether all the evidence, considered together, proves that House was actually innocent, so that no reasonable juror would vote to convict him. Considering all the evidence, and giving due regard to the District Court's findings on whether House's new evidence was reliable, I do not find it probable that no reasonable juror would vote to convict him, and accordingly I dissent.

Because I do not think that House has satisfied the actual innocence standard set forth in *Schlup*, I do not believe that he has met the higher threshold for a freestanding innocence claim, assuming such a claim exists. *See* Herrera v. Collins (1993). I therefore concur in the judgment with respect to the Court's disposition of that separate claim.

I

Critical to the Court's conclusion here that House has sufficiently demonstrated his innocence are three pieces of new evidence presented to the District Court: DNA evidence showing that the semen on Carolyn Muncey's clothing was from her husband, Hubert Muncey, not from House; testimony from new witnesses implicating Mr. Muncey in the murder; and evidence indicating that Mrs. Muncey's blood spilled from test tubes containing autopsy samples in an evidence container. To determine whether it should open its door to House's defaulted constitutional claims, the District Court considered this evidence in a comprehensive evidentiary hearing. As House presented his new evidence, and as the State rebutted it, the District Court observed the witnesses' demeanor, examined physical evidence, and made findings about whether House's new evidence was in fact reliable. This fact-finding role is familiar to a district court. "The trial judge's major role is the determination of fact, and with experience in fulfilling that role comes expertise."

The State did not contest House's new DNA evidence excluding him as the source of the semen on Mrs. Muncey's clothing, but it strongly contested the new testimony implicating Mr. Muncey, and it insisted that the blood spillage occurred after the FBI tested House's jeans and determined that they were stained with Mrs. Muncey's blood.

At the evidentiary hearing, sisters Kathy Parker and Penny Letner testified that 14 years earlier, either during or around the time of House's trial, they heard Mr. Muncey drunkenly confess to having accidentally killed his wife when he struck her in their home during an argument, causing her to fall and hit her head. *Schlup* provided guidance on how a district court should assess this type of new evidence: The court "may consider how the timing of the submission and the likely credibility of the affiants bear on the probable reliability of that evidence," and it "must assess the probative force of the newly presented evidence in connection with the evidence of guilt adduced at trial." Consistent with this guidance, the District Court concluded that the sisters' testimony was not credible. The court noted that it was "not impressed with the allegations of individuals who wait over ten years to come forward." It also considered how the new testimony fit within the larger web of evidence, observing that Mr. Muncey's alleged confession contradicted the testimony of the Munceys' "very credible" daughter, Lora Tharp, who consistently testified that she did not hear a fight in the house that night, but instead heard a man with a deep voice who lured her mother from the house by saying that Mr. Muncey had been in a wreck near the creek.

The District Court engaged in a similar reliability inquiry with regard to House's new evidence of blood spillage. At the evidentiary hearing, House conceded that FBI testing showed that his jeans were stained with Mrs. Muncey's blood, but he set out to prove that the blood spilled from test tubes containing autopsy samples, and that it did so before the jeans were tested by the FBI. The District Court summarized the testimony of the various witnesses who handled the evidence and their recollections about bloodstains and spillage; it acknowledged that House's expert, Dr. Cleland Blake, disagreed with FBI Agent Paul Bigbee about how to interpret the results of Agent Bigbee's genetic marker analysis summary; and it summarized the testimony of the State's blood spatter expert, Paulette Sutton. After reviewing all the evidence, the District Court stated: "Based upon the evidence introduced during the evidentiary hearing . . . the court concludes that the spillage occurred after the FBI crime laboratory received and tested the evidence."

Normally, an appellate court reviews a district court's factual findings only for clear error. The majority essentially disregards the District Court's role in assessing the reliability of House's new evidence. The majority's assessment of House's new evidence is precisely the summary judgment-type inquiry *Schlup* said was inappropriate. By casting aside the District Court's factual determinations made after a comprehensive evidentiary hearing, the majority has done little more than reiterate the factual disputes presented below. Witnesses do not testify in our courtroom, and it is not our role to make credibility findings and construct theories of the possible ways in which Mrs. Muncey's blood could have been spattered and wiped on House's jeans. The District Court did not painstakingly conduct an evidentiary hearing to compile a record for us to sort through transcript by transcript and photograph by photograph, assessing for ourselves the reliability of what we see. *Schlup* made abundantly clear that reliability determinations were essential, but were for the district court to make. We are to defer to the better situated District Court on reliability, unless we determine that its findings are clearly erroneous. We are not concerned with "the district court's independent judgment as to whether reasonable doubt exists," but the District Court here made basic factual findings about the reliability of House's new evidence; it did not offer its personal opinion about whether it doubted House's guilt. *Schlup* makes clear that those findings are controlling unless clearly erroneous.

I have found no clear error in the District Court's reliability findings. Not having observed Ms. Parker and Ms. Letner testify, I would defer to the District Court's determination that they are not credible, and the evidence in the record undermining the tale of an accidental killing during a fight in the Muncey home convinces me that this credibility finding is not clearly erroneous. Dr. Alex Carabia, who performed the autopsy, testified to injuries far more severe than a bump on the head: Mrs. Muncey had bruises on the front and back of her neck, on both thighs, on her lower right leg and left knee, and her hands were bloodstained up to the wrists; her injuries were consistent with a struggle and traumatic strangulation. And, of course, Lora Tharp has consistently recalled a deep-voiced visitor arriving late at night to tell Mrs. Muncey that her husband was in a wreck near the creek.

I also find abundant evidence in the record to support the District Court's finding that blood spilled within the evidence container after the FBI received and tested House's jeans. Agent Bigbee testified that there was no leakage in the items submitted to him for testing. The majority's entire analysis on this point assumes the agent flatly lied, though there was no attack on his credibility below.

It is also worth noting that the blood evidently spilled inside the evidence container when the jeans were protected inside a plastic zip lock bag, as shown by the presence of a bloodstain on the outside of that bag. House's expert tested the exterior and interior of that plastic bag for bloodstains using an "extremely sensitive" test, and only the exterior of the bag tested positive for blood. The evidence in the record indicates that the jeans were placed in the plastic bag after they arrived at the FBI: FBI records show that the jeans arrived there in a paper bag, and the plastic bag has FBI markings on it.

II

With due regard to the District Court's reliability findings, this case invites a straightforward application of the legal standard adopted in *Schlup*. A petitioner does not pass through the *Schlup* gateway if it is "more likely than not that there is any juror who, acting reasonably, would have found the petitioner guilty beyond a reasonable doubt."

The majority states that if House had presented just one of his three key pieces of evidence — or even two of the three — he would not pass through the *Schlup* gateway. According to the majority, House has picked the trifecta of evidence that places conviction outside the realm of choices any juror, acting reasonably, would make. Because the case against House remains substantially unaltered from the case presented to the jury, I disagree.

Given the District Court's reliability findings about the first two pieces of evidence, the evidence before us now is not substantially different from that considered by House's jury. I therefore find it more likely than not that in light of this new evidence, at least one juror, acting reasonably, would vote to convict House. The evidence as a whole certainly does not establish that House is actually innocent of the crime of murdering Carolyn Muncey, and accordingly I dissent.

7. May the Federal Court Hold an Evidentiary Hearing?

Assuming that all of the above hurdles have been overcome, the issue then can arise as to whether a federal court may hold an evidentiary hearing or is limited to deciding the matter based on the record from the state court. This is addressed in 28 U.S.C. §2254(e), which states:

> (1) In a proceeding instituted by an application for a writ of habeas corpus by a person in custody pursuant to the judgment of a State court, a determination of a factual issue made by a State court shall be presumed to be correct. The applicant shall have the burden of rebutting the presumption of correctness by clear and convincing evidence.
> (2) If the applicant has failed to develop the factual basis of a claim in State court proceedings, the court shall not hold an evidentiary hearing on the claim unless the applicant shows that—
> (A) the claim relies on—
> (i) a new rule of constitutional law, made retroactive to cases on collateral review by the Supreme Court, that was previously unavailable; or
> (ii) a factual predicate that could not have been previously discovered through the exercise of due diligence; and
> (B) the facts underlying the claim would be sufficient to establish by clear and convincing evidence that but for constitutional error, no reasonable fact-finder would have found the applicant guilty of the underlying offense.

In Cullen v. Pinholster, the Court gave this a restrictive interpretation, which leaves open the issue of when, if ever, there can be an evidentiary hearing in federal court on habeas corpus.

CULLEN v. PINHOLSTER
563 U.S. 170 (2011)

Justice THOMAS delivered the opinion of the Court.

Scott Lynn Pinholster and two accomplices broke into a house in the middle of the night and brutally beat and stabbed to death two men who happened to interrupt the burglary. A jury convicted Pinholster of first-degree murder, and he was sentenced to death.

After the California Supreme Court twice unanimously denied Pinholster habeas relief, a Federal District Court held an evidentiary hearing and granted Pinholster habeas relief under 28 U.S.C. §2254. The District Court concluded that Pinholster's trial counsel had been constitutionally ineffective at the penalty phase of trial. Sitting en banc, the Court of Appeals for the Ninth Circuit affirmed. Considering the new evidence adduced in the District Court hearing, the Court of Appeals held that the California Supreme Court's decision "was contrary to, or involved an unreasonable application of, clearly established Federal law."

I

On the evening of January 8, 1982, Pinholster solicited Art Corona and Paul David Brown to help him rob Michael Kumar, a local drug dealer. On the way, they stopped at Lisa Tapar's house, where Pinholster put his buck knife through her front door and scratched a swastika into her car after she refused to talk to him. The three men, who were all armed with buck knives, found no one at Kumar's house, broke in, and began ransacking the home. They came across only a small amount of marijuana before Kumar's friends, Thomas Johnson and Robert Beckett, arrived and shouted that they were calling the police.

Pinholster and his accomplices tried to escape through the rear door, but Johnson blocked their path. Pinholster backed Johnson onto the patio, demanding drugs and money and repeatedly striking him in the chest. Johnson dropped his wallet on the ground and stopped resisting. Beckett then came around the corner, and Pinholster attacked him, too, stabbing him repeatedly in the chest. Pinholster forced Beckett to the ground, took both men's wallets, and began kicking Beckett in the head. Meanwhile, Brown stabbed Johnson in the chest, " 'bury[ing] his knife to the hilt.' " Johnson and Beckett died of their wounds.

Pinholster was arrested shortly thereafter and threatened to kill Corona if he did not keep quiet about the burglary and murders. Corona later became the State's primary witness. The prosecution brought numerous charges against Pinholster, including two counts of first-degree murder.

The California trial court appointed Harry Brainard and Wilbur Dettmar to defend Pinholster on charges of first-degree murder, robbery, and burglary. Before their appointment, Pinholster had rejected other attorneys and insisted on representing himself. During that time, the State had mailed Pinholster a letter in jail informing him that the prosecution planned to offer aggravating evidence during the penalty phase of trial to support a sentence of death. The jury convicted Pinholster on both counts of first-degree murder.

Before the penalty phase, Brainard and Dettmar moved to exclude any aggravating evidence on the ground that the prosecution had failed to provide notice of the evidence to be introduced, as required. At a hearing on April 24, Dettmar argued that, in reliance on the lack of notice, he was "not presently prepared to offer anything by way of mitigation." The trial court asked whether a continuance might be helpful, but Dettmar declined, explaining that he could not think of a mitigation witness other than Pinholster's mother and that additional time would not "make a great deal of difference." Three days later, after hearing testimony, the court found that Pinholster had received notice while representing himself and denied the motion to exclude.

The penalty phase was held before the same jury that had convicted Pinholster. The prosecution produced eight witnesses, who testified about Pinholster's history of threatening and violent behavior, including resisting arrest and assaulting police officers, involvement with juvenile gangs, and a substantial prison disciplinary record. Defense counsel called only Pinholster's mother, Burnice Brashear. She gave an account of Pinholster's troubled childhood and adolescent years, discussed Pinholster's siblings, and described Pinholster as "a perfect gentleman at home." Defense counsel did not call a psychiatrist, though they had consulted Dr. John Stalberg at least six weeks earlier. Dr. Stalberg noted Pinholster's "psychopathic personality traits," diagnosed him with antisocial personality disorder, and concluded that he "was not under the influence of extreme mental or emotional disturbance" at the time of the murders.

After 2½ days of deliberation, the jury unanimously voted for death on each of the two murder counts. On mandatory appeal, the California Supreme Court affirmed the judgment.

In August 1993, Pinholster filed his first state habeas petition. Represented by new counsel, Pinholster alleged ineffective assistance of counsel at the penalty phase of his trial. He alleged that Brainard and Dettmar had failed to adequately investigate and present mitigating evidence, including evidence of mental disorders. Pinholster supported this claim with school, medical, and legal records, as well as declarations from family members, Brainard, and Dr. George Woods, a psychiatrist who diagnosed Pinholster with bipolar mood disorder and seizure disorders. Dr. Woods criticized Dr. Stalberg's report as incompetent, unreliable, and inaccurate. The California Supreme Court unanimously and summarily denied Pinholster's penalty-phase ineffective-assistance claim "on the substantive ground that it is without merit."

Pinholster filed a federal habeas petition in April 1997. He reiterated his previous allegations about penalty-phase ineffective assistance and also added new allegations that his trial counsel had failed to furnish Dr. Stalberg with adequate background materials. In support of the new allegations, Dr. - Stalberg provided a declaration stating that in 1984, Pinholster's trial counsel had provided him with only some police reports and a 1978 probation report. Dr. Stalberg explained that, had he known about the material that had since been gathered by Pinholster's habeas counsel, he would have conducted "further inquiry" before concluding that Pinholster suffered only from a personality disorder. He noted that Pinholster's school records showed evidence of "some degree of brain damage." Dr. Stalberg did not, however, retract his earlier diagnosis. The parties stipulated that this declaration had never been submitted to the California Supreme Court, and the federal petition was held in abeyance to allow Pinholster to go back to state court.

In August 1997, Pinholster filed his second state habeas petition, this time including Dr. Stalberg's declaration and requesting judicial notice of the documents previously submitted in support of his first state habeas petition. His allegations of penalty-phase ineffective assistance of counsel mirrored those in his federal habeas petition. The California Supreme Court again unanimously and summarily denied the petition "on the substantive ground that it is without merit."

Having presented Dr. Stalberg's declaration to the state court, Pinholster returned to the District Court. In November 1997, he filed an amended petition for a writ of habeas corpus. The District Court concluded that the Antiterrorism and Effective Death Penalty Act of 1996 (AEDPA), did not apply and granted an evidentiary hearing.

The District Court granted habeas relief. Applying pre-AEDPA standards, the court granted the habeas petition "for inadequacy of counsel by failure to investigate and present mitigation evidence at the penalty hearing." After *Woodford v. Garceau* (2003), clarified that AEDPA applies to cases like Pinholster's, the court amended its order but did not alter its conclusion.

II

We first consider the scope of the record for a §2254(d)(1) inquiry. The State argues that review is limited to the record that was before the state court that adjudicated the claim on the merits. Pinholster contends that evidence presented to the federal habeas court may also be considered. We agree with the State.

As amended by AEDPA, 28 U.S.C. §2254 sets several limits on the power of a federal court to grant an application for a writ of habeas corpus on behalf of a state prisoner. If an application includes a claim that has been "adjudicated on the merits in State court proceedings," §2254(d), an additional restriction applies. Under §2254(d), that application "shall not be granted with respect to [such a] claim . . . unless the adjudication of the claim": "(1) resulted in a decision that was contrary to, or involved an unreasonable application of, clearly established Federal law, as determined by the Supreme Court of the United States; or (2) resulted in a decision that was based on an unreasonable determination of the facts in light of the evidence presented in the State court proceeding." This is a "difficult to meet," and "highly deferential standard for evaluating state-court rulings, which demands that state-court decisions be given the benefit of the doubt." The petitioner carries the burden of proof.

We now hold that review under §2254(d)(1) is limited to the record that was before the state court that adjudicated the claim on the merits. Section 2254(d)(1) refers, in the past tense, to a state-court adjudication that "resulted in" a decision that was contrary to, or "involved" an unreasonable application of, established law. This backward-looking language requires an examination of the state-court decision at the time it was made. It follows that the record under review is limited to the record in existence at that same time *i.e.*, the record before the state court.

This understanding of the text is compelled by "the broader context of the statute as a whole," which demonstrates Congress' intent to channel prisoners' claims first to the state courts. "The federal habeas scheme leaves primary responsibility with the state courts. . . ."

Limiting §2254(d)(1) review to the state-court record is consistent with our precedents interpreting that statutory provision. Our cases emphasize that review under §2254(d)(1) focuses on what a state court knew and did. State-court decisions are measured against this Court's precedents as of "the time the state court renders its decision." To determine whether a particular decision is "contrary to" then-established law, a federal court must consider whether the decision "applies a rule that contradicts [such] law" and how the decision "confronts [the] set of facts" that were before the state court. If the state-court decision "identifies the correct governing legal principle" in existence at the time, a federal court must assess whether the decision "unreasonably applies that principle to the facts of the prisoner's case." It would be strange to ask federal courts to analyze whether a state court's adjudication resulted in a decision that unreasonably applied federal law to facts not before the state court.

Pinholster's contention that our holding renders §2254(e)(2) superfluous is incorrect. Section 2254(e)(2) imposes a limitation on the discretion of federal habeas courts to take new evidence in an evidentiary hearing. Like §2254(d)(1), it carries out "AEDPA's goal of promoting comity, finality, and federalism by giving state courts the first opportunity to review [a] claim, and to correct any constitutional violation in the first instance."[44]

Section 2254(e)(2) continues to have force where §2254(d)(1) does not bar federal habeas relief. For example, not all federal habeas claims by state prisoners fall within the scope of §2254(d), which applies only to claims "adjudicated on the merits in State court proceedings." At a minimum, therefore, §2254(e)(2) still restricts the discretion of federal habeas courts to consider new evidence when deciding claims that were not adjudicated on the merits in state court.

Although state prisoners may sometimes submit new evidence in federal court, AEDPA's statutory scheme is designed to strongly discourage them

---

44. Justice Sotomayor's argument that §2254(d)(1) must be read in a way that "accommodates" §2254(e)(2) rests on a fundamental misunderstanding of §2254(e)(2). The focus of that section is not on "preserving the opportunity" for hearings, but rather on *limiting* the discretion of federal district courts in holding hearings. We see no need in this case to address the proper application of §2254(e)(2). [Footnote by the Court.]

from doing so. Provisions like §§2254(d)(1) and (e)(2) ensure that "[f]ederal courts sitting in habeas are not an alternative forum for trying facts and issues which a prisoner made insufficient effort to pursue in state proceedings."

Accordingly, we conclude that the Court of Appeals erred in considering the District Court evidence in its review under §2254(d)(1). [The Court then considered and rejected Pinholster's claim of ineffective assistance of counsel.]

Justice ALITO, concurring in part and concurring in the judgment.

Although I concur in the Court's judgment, I agree with the conclusion reached in Part I of the dissent, namely, that, when an evidentiary hearing is properly held in federal court, review under 28 U.S.C. §2254(d)(1) must take into account the evidence admitted at that hearing. As the dissent points out, refusing to consider the evidence received in the hearing in federal court gives §2254(e)(2) an implausibly narrow scope and will lead either to results that Congress surely did not intend or to the distortion of other provisions of the Antiterrorism and Effective Death Penalty Act of 1996 (AEDPA), 110 Stat. 1214, and the law on "cause and prejudice."

Under AEDPA evidentiary hearings in federal court should be rare. The petitioner generally must have made a diligent effort to produce in state court the new evidence on which he seeks to rely. If that requirement is not satisfied, the petitioner may establish the factual predicate for a claim in a federal-court hearing only if, among other things, "the facts underlying the claim would be sufficient to establish by clear and convincing evidence that but for constitutional error, no reasonable factfinder would have found the applicant guilty of the underlying offense." §2254(e)(2)(B).

Even when the petitioner does satisfy the diligence standard, a hearing should not be held in federal court unless the new evidence that the petitioner seeks to introduce was not and could not have been offered in the state-court proceeding.

In this case, I would hold that the federal-court hearing should not have been held because respondent did not diligently present his new evidence to the California courts.

Justice SOTOMAYOR, dissenting.

Some habeas petitioners are unable to develop the factual basis of their claims in state court through no fault of their own. Congress recognized as much when it enacted the Antiterrorism and Effective Death Penalty Act of 1996 (AEDPA) and permitted therein the introduction of new evidence in federal habeas proceedings in certain limited circumstances. See 28 U.S.C. §2254(e)(2). Under the Court's novel interpretation of §2254(d)(1), however, federal courts must turn a blind eye to new evidence in deciding whether a petitioner has satisfied §2254(d)(1)'s threshold obstacle to federal habeas relief — even when it is clear that the petitioner would be entitled to relief in light of that evidence. In reading the statute to "compe[l]" this harsh result, the Court ignores a key textual difference between §§2254(d)(1) and 2254(d)(2) and discards the previous understanding in our precedents that new evidence can, in fact, inform the §2254(d)(1) inquiry. I therefore dissent from the Court's first holding.

The Court first holds that, in determining whether a state-court decision is an unreasonable application of Supreme Court precedent under §2254(d)(1), "review . . . is limited to the record that was before the state court that adjudicated the claim on the merits." New evidence adduced at a federal evidentiary hearing is now irrelevant to determining whether a petitioner has satisfied §2254(d)(1). This holding is unnecessary to promote AEDPA's purposes, and it is inconsistent with the provision's text, the structure of the statute, and our precedents.

To understand the significance of the majority's holding, it is important to view the issue in context. AEDPA's entire structure — which gives state courts the opportunity to decide factual and legal questions in the first instance — ensures that evidentiary hearings in federal habeas proceedings are very rare. See N. King, F. Cheesman, & B. Ostrom, Final Technical Report: Habeas Litigation in U.S. District Courts 35-36 (2007) (evidentiary hearings under AEDPA occur in 0.4 percent of noncapital cases and 9.5 percent of capital cases). Even absent the new restriction created by today's holding, AEDPA erects multiple hurdles to a state prisoner's ability to introduce new evidence in a federal habeas proceeding.

First, "[u]nder the exhaustion requirement, a habeas petitioner challenging a state conviction must first attempt to present his claim in state court." With certain narrow exceptions, federal courts cannot consider a claim at all, let alone accept new evidence relevant to the claim, if it has not been exhausted in state court. The exhaustion requirement thus reserves to state courts the first opportunity to resolve factual disputes relevant to a state prisoner's claim.

Second, the exhaustion requirement is "complement[ed]" by the standards set forth in §2254(d). Under this provision, a federal court may not grant habeas relief on any "claim that was adjudicated on the merits in State court proceedings" unless the adjudication "(1) resulted in a decision that was contrary to, or involved an unreasonable application of, clearly established Federal law, as determined by the Supreme Court of the United States; or (2) resulted in a decision that was based on an unreasonable determination of the facts in light of the evidence presented in the State court proceeding. These standards "control whether to grant habeas relief." Accordingly, we have said, if the factual allegations a petitioner seeks to prove at an evidentiary hearing would not satisfy these standards, there is no reason for a hearing. In such a case, the district court may exercise its "discretion to deny an evidentiary hearing." This approach makes eminent sense: If district courts held evidentiary hearings without first asking whether the evidence the petitioner seeks to present would satisfy AEDPA's demanding standards, they would needlessly prolong federal habeas proceedings.

Third, even when a petitioner seeks to introduce new evidence that would entitle him to relief, AEDPA prohibits him from doing so, except in a narrow range of cases, unless he "made a reasonable attempt, in light of the information available at the time, to investigate and pursue claims in state court." Thus, §2254(e)(2) provides: "If the applicant has failed to develop the factual basis of a claim in State court proceedings, the court shall not hold an evidentiary hearing on the claim unless the applicant shows that — (A) the claim relies on — (i) a new rule of constitutional law, made retroactive to cases on collateral review by the Supreme Court, that was previously unavailable; or (ii) a factual predicate that could not have been previously discovered through the exercise of due diligence; and (B) the facts underlying the claim would be sufficient to establish by clear and convincing evidence that but for constitutional error, no reasonable factfinder would have found the applicant guilty of the underlying offense."

The majority's interpretation of §2254(d)(1) finds no support in the provision's text or the statute's structure as a whole. Section 2254(d)(1) requires district courts to ask whether a state-court adjudication on the merits "resulted in a decision that was contrary to, or involved an unreasonable application of, clearly established Federal law, as determined by the Supreme Court of the United States." Because this provision uses "backward-looking language" — *i.e.*, past-tense verbs — the majority believes that it limits review to the state-court record. But both §§2254(d)(1) and 2254(d)(2) use "backward-looking language," and §2254(d)(2) — unlike §2254(d)(1) — expressly directs district courts to base their review on "the evidence presented in the State court proceeding." If use of the past tense were sufficient to indicate Congress' intent to restrict analysis to the state-court record, the phrase "in light of the evidence presented in the State court proceeding" in §2254(d)(2) would be superfluous. The majority's construction of §2254(d)(1) fails to give meaning to Congress' decision to include language referring to the evidence presented to the state court in §2254(d)(2).

Unlike my colleagues in the majority, I refuse to assume that Congress simply engaged in sloppy drafting. The inclusion of this phrase in §2254(d)(2) — coupled with its omission from §2254(d)(2)'s partner provision, §2254(d)(1) — provides strong reason to think that Congress did not intend for the §2254(d)(1) analysis to be limited categorically to "the evidence presented in the State court proceeding."

The " 'broader context of the statute as a whole,' " reinforces this conclusion. In particular, Congress' decision to include in AEDPA a provision, §2254(e)(2), that permits federal evidentiary hearings in certain circumstances provides further evidence that Congress did not intend to limit the §2254(d)(1) inquiry to the state-court record in every case.

We have long recognized that some diligent habeas petitioners are unable to develop all of the facts supporting their claims in state court. As discussed above, in enacting AEDPA, Congress generally barred evidentiary hearings for petitioners who did not "exercise diligence in pursuing their claims" in state court.

The majority charts a novel course that, so far as I am aware, no court of appeals has adopted: §2254(d)(1) continues to apply when a petitioner has additional evidence that he was unable to present to the state court, but the district court cannot consider that evidence in deciding whether the petitioner has satisfied §2254(d)(1). The problem with this approach is its potential to bar federal habeas relief for diligent habeas petitioners who cannot present new evidence to a state court.

Consider, for example, a petitioner who diligently attempted in state court to develop the factual basis of a claim that prosecutors withheld exculpatory witness statements in violation of *Brady v. Maryland* (1963). The state court denied relief on the ground that the withheld evidence then known did not rise to the level of materiality required under *Brady*. Before the time for filing a federal habeas petition has expired, however, a state court orders the State to disclose additional documents the petitioner had timely requested under the State's public records Act. The disclosed documents reveal that the State withheld other exculpatory witness statements, but state law would not permit the petitioner to present the new evidence in a successive petition.

Under our precedent, if the petitioner had not presented his *Brady* claim to the state court at all, his claim would be deemed defaulted and the petitioner could attempt to show cause and prejudice to overcome the default. If, however, the new evidence merely bolsters a *Brady* claim that was adjudicated on the merits in state court, it is unclear how the petitioner can obtain federal habeas relief after today's holding. What may have been a reasonable decision on the state-court record may no longer be reasonable in light of the new evidence. Because the state court adjudicated the petitioner's *Brady* claim on the merits, §2254(d)(1) would still apply. Yet, under the majority's interpretation of §2254(d)(1), a federal court is now prohibited from considering the new evidence in determining the reasonableness of the state-court decision.

The majority's interpretation of §2254(d)(1) thus suggests the anomalous result that petitioners with new claims based on newly obtained evidence can obtain federal habeas relief if they can show cause and prejudice for their default but petitioners with newly obtained evidence supporting a claim adjudicated on the merits in state court cannot obtain federal habeas relief if they cannot first satisfy §2254(d)(1) without the new evidence. That the majority's interpretation leads to this anomaly is good reason to conclude that its interpretation is wrong.

The majority responds to this anomaly by suggesting that my hypothetical petitioner "may well [have] a new claim." This suggestion is puzzling. New evidence does not usually give rise to a new claim; it merely provides additional proof of a claim already adjudicated on the merits.

The majority's reading of §2254(d)(1) appears ultimately to rest on its understanding that state courts must have the first opportunity to adjudicate habeas petitioners' claims. I fully agree that habeas petitioners must attempt to present evidence to state courts in the first instance. Where I disagree with the majority is in my understanding that §2254(e)(2) already accomplishes this result. By reading §2254(d)(1) to do the work of §2254(e)(2), the majority gives §2254(e)(2) an unnaturally cramped reading. As a result, the majority either has foreclosed habeas relief for diligent petitioners who, through no fault of their own, were unable to present exculpatory evidence to the state court that adjudicated their claims or has created a new set of procedural complexities for the lower courts to navigate to ensure the availability of the Great Writ for diligent petitioners.

I fear the consequences of the Court's novel interpretation of §2254(d)(1) for diligent state habeas petitioners with compelling evidence supporting their claims who were unable, through no fault of their own, to present that evidence to the state court that adjudicated their claims.

8. May the Federal Court Grant the Habeas Corpus Petition?

Assuming the habeas petitioner makes it through the previous seven hurdles, the issue then becomes whether the federal court may grant the habeas petition. The Antiterrorism and Effective Death Penalty Act imposed a significant new restriction on the ability of a federal court to grant relief to state prisoners. Section 2254(d) provides that a

> writ of habeas corpus on behalf of a person in custody pursuant to a judgment of a State court shall not be granted with respect to any claim that was adjudicated on the merits in a State court proceeding unless the adjudication of the claim:
>
>   (1) resulted in a decision that was contrary to, or involved an unreasonable application of clearly established Federal law, as determined by the Supreme Court of the United States; or
>
>   (2) resulted in a decision that was based on an unreasonable determination of the facts in light of the evidence presented in the State court proceeding.

As for the former, the most important case addressing this provision is *Williams v. Taylor*.[45] Terry Williams was convicted of murder and sentenced to death in Virginia state court. A state trial court on a motion for postconviction relief found that there was ineffective assistance of counsel, but the Virginia Supreme Court disagreed, finding that there was not sufficient prejudice. The federal district court on habeas corpus found that there was ineffective assistance of counsel, but the Fourth Circuit reversed. The Fourth Circuit found that §2254(d)(1) precluded habeas review unless the state court "decided the question by interpreting or applying the relevant precedent in a manner that reasonable jurists all would agree is unreasonable."

The Supreme Court reversed the Fourth Circuit and expressly rejected the Fourth Circuit's conclusion that a state court judgment is unreasonable only if all reasonable jurists would agree that the state court was unreasonable. The Court stated:

45. 529 U.S. 362 (2000).

But the statute says nothing about "reasonable judges," presumably because all, or virtually all, such judges occasionally commit error; they make decisions that in retrospect may be characterized as "unreasonable." Indeed, it is most unlikely that Congress would impose such a requirement of unanimity on federal judges. As Congress is acutely aware, reasonable lawyers and lawgivers regularly disagree with one another. Congress surely did not intend that the views of one such judge who might think that relief is not warranted in a particular case should always have greater weight than the contrary, considered judgment of several other judges.[46]

Justice O'Connor, writing for five justices, emphasized that "contrary to" and "unreasonable application" are independent bases for habeas relief. For a state court's decision to be reviewable because it is "contrary to" clearly established federal law the decision must be "substantially different" from the relevant Supreme Court precedent; "the word 'contrary' is commonly understood to mean 'diametrically different' or 'mutually opposed.' "[47] A state court decision is contrary to Supreme Court precedent if it contradicts that decision or reaches a different result on facts that are materially indistinguishable. As for the second phrase, in assessing whether a state court decision involves "an unreasonable application of . . . clearly established" federal law, the question is "whether the state court's application of federal law was objectively unreasonable."[48] Justice O'Connor stressed that "the most important point is that an *unreasonable* application of federal law is different from an *incorrect* application of federal law."[49]

Justice Stevens, writing for the dissenting four justices, addressed the phrases "contrary to" and "unreasonable application of" federal law. He argued that "[t]he prevailing view in the Circuits is that the former phrase requires de novo review of 'pure' questions of law and the latter requires some sort of 'reasonability' review of so-called mixed questions of law and fact."[50] Justice Stevens said, though, that these two categories are not mutually exclusive and that "there will be a variety of cases, like this one, in which both phrases may be implicated."[51]

Justice Stevens wrote for the majority in finding that Williams was entitled to habeas corpus review. The Court concluded that the Virginia Supreme Court decision was both contrary to and an unreasonable application of clearly established federal law. The Court held that the state court failed to apply controlling Supreme Court precedent that clearly establishes that ineffectiveness of counsel deprives a defendant of rights accorded by the Constitution.

The Supreme Court reaffirmed its interpretation of §2254(d)(1) in Bell v. Cone.[52] The Court held that ineffectiveness of counsel in all cases, including

---

46. 529 U.S. at 377-378.
47. *Id.* at 405.
48. *Id.* at 409.
49. *Id.* at 410.
50. *Id.* at 384 (Stevens, J., dissenting).
51. *Id.* at 385-386.
52. 535 U.S. 685 (2002).

capital cases, is to be evaluated based on Strickland v. Washington.[53] The Court restated its interpretation of §2254(d)(1):

> A federal habeas court may issue the writ under the "contrary to" clause if the state court applies a different rule from the governing law set forth in our cases, or if it decides a case differently than we have done on a materially indistinguishable set of facts. The Court may grant relief under the "unreasonable application" clause if the state court correctly identifies the governing legal principle from our decision · but unreasonably applies it to the facts of the particular case. The focus of the latter inquiry is on whether the state court's application of clearly established law is objectively unreasonable, and we stressed in *Williams* that an unreasonable application is different from an incorrect one.[54]

In Lockyer v. Andrade, the Supreme Court again repeated and applied this standard.[55] Leandro Andrade was sentenced to life imprisonment with no possibility of parole for fifty years for stealing nine videotapes from Kmart stores in San Bernardino, California. He received this sentence under California's three strikes law even though he had never committed a violent felony.

After the California courts upheld his sentence, Andrade filed a petition for habeas corpus and argued that his sentence was cruel and unusual punishment in violation of the Eighth Amendment. The U.S. Court of Appeals for the Ninth Circuit ruled in his favor, but the Supreme Court, in a five-to-four decision, reversed.

Justice O'Connor, writing for the Court, focused on the standard under §2254(d). She said that the Supreme Court's decisions concerning cruel and unusual punishment "have not been a model of clarity" and "have not established a clear or consistent path for courts to follow."[56] Justice O'Connor said that the only "clearly established" doctrine is a "gross disproportionality principle, the precise contours of which are unclear, applicable only in the 'exceedingly rare' and 'extreme case.' "[57] The Court said that there thus was not clearly established law.

The Court also rejected the argument that the state court decision was objectively unreasonable. The Court said that the Ninth Circuit used a "clear error" standard and that this was not the same as "objectively unreasonable."[58] The Court, however, did not clarify the differences between these two standards.

Nor was the Court amenable to the petitioner's argument that the state court decision was "contrary to" a Supreme Court decision. Earlier, in Solem v. Helm, the Court held that it was cruel and unusual punishment

---

53.   466 U.S. 668 (1984).

54.   535 U.S. at 694.

55.   538 U.S. 63 (2003). I discuss this case in more detail in Erwin Chemerinsky, *The Conservative Assault on the Constitution* (2010).

56.   *Id.* at 72.

57.   *Id.* at 73.

58.   *Id.* at 75.

to sentence a person to life in prison with no possibility of parole for passing a bad check worth $100.[59] But in Lockyer v. Andrade, the Court said that *Solem* was distinguishable because in that case there was no possibility of parole, but Andrade was eligible for parole in the year 2046, when he would be 87 years old.[60]

In Renico v. Lett, the Court again discussed what is an "unreasonable" application of federal law for the purposes of §2254(d).[61] The issue was whether the state court had erred in deciding that a retrial did not violate the prohibition of double jeopardy. The Court emphasized the deference to be given to state court decisions on federal habeas corpus. Chief Justice Roberts, writing for the Court, stated: "It is important at the outset to define the question before us. That question is not whether the trial judge should have declared a mistrial. It is not even whether it was an abuse of discretion for her to have done so — the applicable standard on direct review. The question under AEDPA is instead whether the determination of the Michigan Supreme Court that there was no abuse of discretion was 'an unreasonable application of . . . clearly established Federal law.' "[62] The Court concluded that the state court decision could not be said to be "unreasonable" and therefore could not be overturned on habeas corpus. Chief Justice Roberts wrote, "AEDPA prevents defendants — and federal courts — from using federal habeas corpus review as a vehicle to second-guess the reasonable decisions of state courts. Whether or not the Michigan Supreme Court's opinion reinstating Lett's conviction in this case was *correct*, it was clearly *not unreasonable.*"[63]

Most recently, in Harrington v. Richter, the Supreme Court held that the deferential standard of §2254(d) applies even if the state court does not issue an opinion explaining its decision.[64] The California Supreme Court denied a constitutional claim in a one-sentence summary order. The Court held that relief could be granted only if the requirements of §2254(d) were met. Justice Kennedy, writing for the Court, explained, "[D]etermining whether a state court's decision resulted from an unreasonable legal or factual conclusion does not require that there be an opinion from the state court explaining the state court's reasoning."[65]

The Court then went on and found that habeas corpus relief was unwarranted because the state court decision was not an unreasonable application of clearly established federal law. The Court elaborated the analysis under §2254(d): "As a condition for obtaining habeas corpus from a federal court, a state prisoner must show that the state court's ruling on the claim being

---

59. 463 U.S. 277 (1983).

60. *See also* Yarborough v. Alvarado, 541 U.S. 652 (2004) (finding that the standard under §2254(d) was not met).

61. 559 U.S. 766 (2010).

62. *Id.* at 772-773.

63. *Id.* at 779.

64. 131 S. Ct. 770 (2011).

65. *Id.* at 784.

presented in federal court was so lacking in justification that there was an error well understood and comprehended in existing law beyond any possibility for fairminded disagreement."[66] This seems to be similar to the standard that the Court rejected in Williams v. Taylor, where it rejected the Fourth Circuit's approach that habeas relief could be granted only if no reasonable jurist could come to the conclusion of the state court. Under Harrington v. Richter, relief can be granted only if it is an error where there is not the possibility for "fair-minded disagreement."

In the cases since *Harrington*, the Court has continued to adhere to this approach for defining when habeas relief is permissible under §2254(d). In White v. Woodall, the judge at the penalty phase of a capital case did not instruct the jury that it could not draw an adverse inference from the defendant's failure to testify at that stage.[67] The Sixth Circuit granted habeas relief, but the Supreme Court reversed. The Court quoted the language from Harrington v. Richter, that habeas relief can be granted only if a state prisoner "show that the state court's ruling on the claim being presented in federal court was so lacking in justification that there was an error well understood and comprehended in existing law beyond any possibility for fairminded disagreement." The Court stressed that it had never directly ruled that there is a right to such an instruction at the penalty phase and thus concluded that it could not be said that the state court decision was "beyond any possibility for fairminded disagreement."[68]

The Court has acknowledged that this standard is "difficult to meet."[69] The question is whether the Court has adopted too restrictive a view of §2254(d), even in light of Congress's desire to restrict habeas corpus in enacting AEDPA.

C. STATUTES AND RULES GOVERNING HABEAS CORPUS

Federal statutes prescribe the availability of habeas corpus relief and define the procedures to be followed in federal habeas corpus proceedings. In addition, in 1977, the Rules Governing Section 2254 Cases in the United States District Courts went into effect. The statutes and rules describe many important aspects of federal habeas corpus litigation.

First, a writ of habeas corpus may be granted by "the Supreme Court, any justice thereof, the district courts and any circuit judge within their respective jurisdictions." 28 U.S.C. §2241(a). If a petition for a writ of habeas corpus is filed with the Supreme Court, a Supreme Court justice, or a federal

---

66. *Id.* at 787.
67. 134 S. Ct. 1697 (2014).
68. *Id.* at 1703.
69. Metrish v. Lancaster, 133 S. Ct. 1781, 1786 (2013).

court of appeals judge, the petition may be transferred to the district court having jurisdiction to entertain it.

Second, habeas corpus petitions must be in writing, signed, and verified by the person for whom relief is requested or by someone acting on his or her behalf. 28 U.S.C. §2242. The petition must describe the facts concerning the "applicant's commitment or detention," including the basis for requesting the writ. Because the writ, if granted, directs the person holding the petitioner to release him or her from custody, the petition should name the custodian — such as the warden — as the respondent.

Third, the person must be in "custody" in order to bring a habeas corpus petition. Over the last half century, the Court has broadly defined "custody." The Court has held that individuals may use habeas corpus petitions to challenge any restriction of liberty, such as parole; habeas petitions may be heard even if an individual will not necessarily be released because of consecutive or concurrent sentences; and habeas petitions should not be dismissed as moot even after a person is released from prison.

Jones v. Cunningham, 371 U.S. 286 (1963), which held that a person may present a habeas corpus petition while on parole, is a crucial case liberalizing the definition of "in custody." In *Jones*, an individual filed a habeas corpus petition while in prison but was paroled while the matter was pending in federal court. The United States Court of Appeals for the Fourth Circuit dismissed the petition because the individual was no longer in custody but, in fact, free on parole. The Supreme Court reversed. In an opinion by Justice Black, the Court observed that "[h]istory, usage, and precedent can leave no doubt that, besides physical imprisonment, there are other restraints on a man's liberty." The Court catalogued the many restrictions on liberty suffered by a person on parole — ranging from limits on travel to required visits from and meetings with a parole officer. In fact, under the state's law, a person granted parole was " 'under the custody and control of the . . . Parole Board.' " The Court said that because parole imposes restraints "not shared by the public generally," a person on parole should be regarded as in custody.

Similarly, the Court held in Hensley v. Municipal Court, 411 U.S. 34 (1973), that individuals could seek habeas corpus even when they were released on bail or on their own recognizance. The court of appeals, in accord with prior Supreme Court rulings, concluded that a person could not seek habeas corpus until incarceration began. The Supreme Court reversed and emphasized that because all appeals in the state court system had been exhausted, incarceration was imminent. The Court said that there was no reason to require a person to spend "[ten] minutes in jail" in order to file a habeas corpus petition. The Court explained that the petitioner's movement was restricted because he was required to appear at the demand of any competent court and the failure to appear was itself a crime.

Although the requirement for actual incarceration has been eliminated, habeas corpus petitions still must be brought to challenge restrictions on liberty. Habeas corpus may not be used to challenge the imposition of fines or payment of restitution as part of a sentence.

Fourth, courts have authority to grant habeas corpus to individuals held in custody "within their respective jurisdictions." 28 U.S.C. §2241(a). In Padilla v. Rumsfeld, 542 U.S. 426 (2004), the Court reaffirmed that a habeas petition must be brought in the judicial district where a person is detained. Jose Padilla was apprehended in Chicago's O'Hare Airport and detained as an enemy combatant on suspicion that he was planning to build and detonate a "dirty bomb." He was initially taken to New York, where he was held as a material witness. A habeas petition was filed on his behalf from there. He was transferred to a military prison in South Carolina, but the habeas petition continued to be litigated in the Southern District of New York and then the Second Circuit, which ruled in his favor.

The Supreme Court, in a 5-4 decision, reversed and held that the habeas petition needed to be brought in the federal district court in South Carolina, where the immediate custodian over his person was located.

Federal prisoners must file petitions pursuant to §2255 with the court that imposed the sentence. Previously, federal prisoners also could file petitions with courts located in the areas where they were confined. This proved inconvenient both for the courts and the prisoners. Courts in areas where federal prisons are located were deluged with petitions, whereas courts in areas without prisons received no petitions. Also, petitioners often were confined far from the court where the trial occurred and hence were removed from the witnesses and documents they might need for their habeas petition. Consequently, federal prisoners, pursuant to 28 U.S.C. §2255, must return to the court that sentenced them and thus have less of a choice as to where to file their habeas petitions.

Fifth, the federal statutes authorize the federal court in ruling on a habeas corpus petition to "dispose of the matter as law and justice require." 28 U.S.C. §2243. Generally, the federal court in granting a habeas corpus petition either orders the release of an individual from custody or, more commonly, orders the individual released unless a new trial is held within a reasonable amount of time.

Finally, in general, the final order of a judge in a habeas proceeding is subject to review on appeal by the court of appeals in the circuit where the federal district court is located. However, a major limitation on the right to appeal is that a state prisoner whose petition for habeas corpus is denied may appeal only if the federal district court judge or a court of appeals judge issues a certificate of appealability.[70] Before the Antiterrorism and Effective Death Penalty Act this was termed a certificate of probable cause. A court can

---

70. Section 2253(c) provides:

(1) Unless a circuit justice or judge issues a certificate of appealability, an appeal may not be taken to the court of appeals from — (A) the final order in a habeas corpus proceeding in which the detention complained of arises out of process issued by a state court; or (B) the final order is a proceeding under section 2255. (2) A certificate of appealability may issue under paragraph (1) only if the applicant has made a substantial showing of the denial of a constitutional right. (3) The certificate of appealability under paragraph (1) shall indicate which specific issue or issues satisfy the showing required by paragraph (2).

issue a certificate of appealability only if "the applicant has made a sub-stantial showing of the denial of a constitutional right." In other words, absent a certification of appealability, a state prisoner may not appeal the denial of habeas corpus. Although the text of the act seems to say that district court judges cannot issue such certificates, most courts have ruled to the contrary and concluded that either a district court or a court of appeals can authorize review.

In Miller-El v. Cockrell, 537 U.S. 322 (2003), the Supreme Court held that a certificate of appealability should be granted if "reasonable jurists could debate" whether the petition should have been granted. This "does not require a showing that the appeal will succeed." Nor is there to be full consideration of the merits. But the certificate should be granted if it presents a debatable issue for the court of appeals to consider. Similarly and more recently, in Buck v. Davis, 137 S. Ct. 759 (2017), the Court declared "We reiterate what we have said before: A 'court of appeals should limit its examination [at the COA stage] to a threshold inquiry into the underlying merit of [the] claims,' and ask 'only if the District Court's decision was debatable.' "

D. HABEAS CORPUS AND THE
WAR ON TERRORISM

In recent years, there has been a major debate over whether federal courts should be able to exercise habeas corpus over those who are detained as part of the war on terrorism, especially those held in Guan-tánamo Bay, Cuba. After the United States government began to detain individuals there in January 2002, habeas corpus petitions were filed on their behalf. In Rasul v. Bush, the Supreme Court held that federal courts have jurisdiction to hear habeas petitions by those detained in Guantánamo.

RASUL v. BUSH
542 U.S. 466 (2004)

Justice STEVENS delivered the opinion of the Court.

These two cases present the narrow but important question whether United States courts lack jurisdiction to consider challenges to the legality of the detention of foreign nationals captured abroad in connection with hostilities and incarcerated at the Guantanamo Bay Naval Base, Cuba.

I

On September 11, 2001, agents of the al Qaeda terrorist network hijacked four commercial airliners and used them as missiles to attack American targets. While one of the four attacks was foiled by the heroism of the plane's passengers, the other three killed approximately 3,000 innocent civilians, destroyed hundreds of millions of dollars of property, and severely damaged the U.S. economy. In response to the attacks, Congress passed a joint resolution authorizing the President to use "all necessary and appropriate force against those nations, organizations, or persons he determines planned, authorized, committed, or aided the terrorist attacks . . . or harbored such organizations or persons." Acting pursuant to that authorization, the President sent U.S. Armed Forces into Afghanistan to wage a military campaign against al Qaeda and the Taliban regime that had supported it.

Petitioners in these cases are 2 Australian citizens and 12 Kuwaiti citizens who were captured abroad during hostilities between the United States and the Taliban. Since early 2002, the U.S. military has held them — along with, according to the Government's estimate, approximately 640 other non-Americans captured abroad — at the naval base at Guantanamo Bay. The United States occupies the base, which comprises 45 square miles of land and water along the southeast coast of Cuba, pursuant to a 1903 Lease Agreement executed with the newly independent Republic of Cuba in the aftermath of the Spanish-American War. Under the agreement, "the United States recognizes the continuance of the ultimate sovereignty of the Republic of Cuba over the [leased areas]," while "the Republic of Cuba consents that during the period of the occupation by the United States . . . the United States shall exercise complete jurisdiction and control over and within said areas." In 1934, the parties entered into a treaty providing that, absent an agreement to modify or abrogate the lease, the lease would remain in effect "[s]o long as the United States of America shall not abandon the . . . naval station of Guantanamo."

In 2002, petitioners, through relatives acting as their next friends, filed various actions in the U.S. District Court for the District of Columbia challenging the legality of their detention at the base. All alleged that none of the petitioners has ever been a combatant against the United States or has ever engaged in any terrorist acts. They also alleged that none has been charged with any wrongdoing, permitted to consult with counsel, or provided access to the courts or any other tribunal.

Construing all [these] actions as petitions for writs of habeas corpus, the District Court dismissed them for want of jurisdiction. The court held, in reliance on our opinion in Johnson v. Eisentrager (1950), that "aliens detained outside the sovereign territory of the United States [may not] invok[e] a petition for a writ of habeas corpus." The Court of Appeals affirmed.

II

Congress has granted federal district courts, "within their respective jurisdictions," the authority to hear applications for habeas corpus by any person who claims to be held "in custody in violation of the Constitution or laws or treaties of the United States." Consistent with the historic purpose of the writ, this Court has recognized the federal courts' power to review applications for habeas relief in a wide variety of cases involving executive detention, in wartime as well as in times of peace. The Court has, for example, entertained the habeas petitions of an American citizen who plotted an attack on military installations during the Civil War, Ex parte Milligan (1866), and of admitted enemy aliens convicted of war crimes during a declared war and held in the United States, Ex parte Quirin (1942), and its insular possessions, In re Yamashita (1946).

The question now before us is whether the habeas statute confers a right to judicial review of the legality of executive detention of aliens in a territory over which the United States exercises plenary and exclusive jurisdiction, but not "ultimate sovereignty."

III

Respondents' primary submission is that the answer to the jurisdictional question is controlled by our decision in *Eisentrager*. In that case, we held that a Federal District Court lacked authority to issue a writ of habeas corpus to 21 German citizens who had been captured by U.S. forces in China, tried and convicted of war crimes by an American military commission headquartered in Nanking, and incarcerated in the Landsberg Prison in occupied Germany. The Court of Appeals in *Eisentrager* had found jurisdiction, reasoning that "any person who is deprived of his liberty by officials of the United States, acting under purported authority of that Government, and who can show that his confinement is in violation of a prohibition of the Constitution, has a right to the writ." In reversing that determination, this Court summarized the six critical facts in the case: "We are here confronted with a decision whose basic premise is that these prisoners are entitled, as a constitutional right, to sue in some court of the United States for a writ of habeas corpus. To support that assumption we must hold that a prisoner of our military authorities is constitutionally entitled to the writ, even though he (a) is an enemy alien; (b) has never been or resided in the United States; (c) was captured outside of our territory and there held in military custody as a prisoner of war; (d) was tried and convicted by a Military Commission sitting outside the United States; (e) for offenses against laws of war committed outside the United States; (f) and is at all times imprisoned outside the United States." On this set of facts, the Court concluded, "no right to the writ of habeas corpus appears."

Petitioners in these cases differ from the *Eisentrager* detainees in important respects: They are not nationals of countries at war with the United States, and they deny that they have engaged in or plotted acts of aggression against the United States; they have never been afforded access to any tribunal, much less charged with and convicted of wrongdoing; and for more than two years they have been imprisoned in territory over which the United States exercises exclusive jurisdiction and control.

Not only are petitioners differently situated from the *Eisentrager* detainees, but the Court in *Eisentrager* made quite clear that all six of the facts critical to its disposition were relevant only to the question of the prisoners' constitutional entitlement to habeas corpus. The Court had far less to say on the question of the petitioners' statutory entitlement to habeas review. Its only statement on the subject was a passing reference to the absence of statutory authorization: "Nothing in the text of the Constitution extends such a right, nor does anything in our statutes."

IV

[R]espondents contend that we can discern a limit on §2241 through application of the "longstanding principle of American law" that congressional legislation is presumed not to have extraterritorial application unless such intent is clearly manifested. Whatever traction the presumption against extraterritoriality might have in other contexts, it certainly has no application to the operation of the habeas statute with respect to persons detained within "the territorial jurisdiction" of the United States. By the express terms of its agreements with Cuba, the United States exercises "complete jurisdiction and control" over the Guantanamo Bay Naval Base, and may continue to exercise such control permanently if it so chooses. Respondents themselves concede that the habeas statute would create federal-court jurisdiction over the claims of an American citizen held at the base. Considering that the statute draws no distinction between Americans and aliens held in federal custody, there is little reason to think that Congress intended the geographical coverage of the statute to vary depending on the detainee's citizenship. Aliens held at the base, no less than American citizens, are entitled to invoke the federal courts' authority under §2241.

Application of the habeas statute to persons detained at the base is consistent with the historical reach of the writ of habeas corpus. At common law, courts exercised habeas jurisdiction over the claims of aliens detained within sovereign territory of the realm, as well as the claims of persons detained in the so-called "exempt jurisdictions," where ordinary writs did not run, and all other dominions under the sovereign's control.

In the end, the answer to the question presented is clear. Petitioners contend that they are being held in federal custody in violation of the laws of the United States. No party questions the District Court's jurisdiction over petitioners' custodians. Section 2241, by its terms, requires nothing more. We therefore hold that §2241 confers on the District Court jurisdiction to hear petitioners' habeas corpus challenges to the legality of their detention at the Guantanamo Bay Naval Base.

Justice KENNEDY, concurring in the judgment.

The Court is correct, in my view, to conclude that federal courts have jurisdiction to consider challenges to the legality of the detention of foreign nationals held at the Guantanamo Bay Naval Base in Cuba. While I reach the same conclusion, my analysis follows a different course.

The decision in *Eisentrager* indicates that there is a realm of political authority over military affairs where the judicial power may not enter. The existence of this realm acknowledges the power of the President as Commander in Chief, and the joint role of the President and the Congress, in the conduct of military affairs. A faithful application of *Eisentrager*, then, requires an initial inquiry into the general circumstances of the detention to determine whether the Court has the authority to entertain the petition and to grant relief after considering all of the facts presented. A necessary corollary of *Eisentrager* is that there are circumstances in which the courts maintain the power and the responsibility to protect persons from unlawful detention even where military affairs are implicated.

The facts here are distinguishable from those in *Eisentrager* in two critical ways, leading to the conclusion that a federal court may entertain the petitions. First, Guantanamo Bay is in every practical respect a United States territory, and it is one far removed from any hostilities. The opinion of the Court well explains the history of its possession by the United States. In a formal sense, the United States leases the Bay; the 1903 lease agreement states that Cuba retains "ultimate sovereignty" over it. At the same time, this lease is no ordinary lease. Its term is indefinite and at the discretion of the United States. What matters is the unchallenged and indefinite control that the United States has long exercised over Guantanamo Bay. From a practical perspective, the indefinite lease of Guantanamo Bay has produced a place that belongs to the United States, extending the "implied protection" of the United States to it.

The second critical set of facts is that the detainees at Guantanamo Bay are being held indefinitely, and without benefit of any legal proceeding to determine their status. In *Eisentrager*, the prisoners were tried and convicted by a military commission of violating the laws of war and were sentenced to prison terms. Having already been subject to procedures establishing their status, they could not justify "a limited opening of our courts" to show that they were "of friendly personal disposition" and not enemy aliens. Indefinite detention without trial or other proceeding presents altogether different considerations. It allows friends and foes alike to remain in detention. It suggests a weaker case of military necessity and much greater alignment with the traditional function of habeas corpus. Perhaps, where detainees are taken from a zone of hostilities, detention without proceedings or trial would be justified by military necessity for a matter of weeks; but as the period of detention stretches from months to years, the case for continued detention to meet military exigencies becomes weaker.

In light of the status of Guantanamo Bay and the indefinite pretrial detention of the detainees, I would hold that federal-court jurisdiction is permitted in these cases. This approach would avoid creating automatic statutory authority to adjudicate the claims of persons located outside the United

States, and remains true to the reasoning of *Eisentrager*. For these reasons, I concur in the judgment of the Court.

Justice SCALIA, with whom THE CHIEF JUSTICE and Justice THOMAS join, dissenting.

The Court today holds that the habeas statute, 28 U.S.C. §2241, extends to aliens detained by the United States military overseas, outside the sovereign borders of the United States and beyond the territorial jurisdictions of all its courts. This is not only a novel holding; it contradicts a half-century-old precedent on which the military undoubtedly relied, Johnson v. Eisentrager (1950). This is an irresponsible overturning of settled law in a matter of extreme importance to our forces currently in the field. I would leave it to Congress to change §2241, and dissent from the Court's unprecedented holding.

Eisentrager's directly-on-point statutory holding makes it exceedingly difficult for the Court to reach the result it desires today.

In abandoning the venerable statutory line drawn in *Eisentrager,* the Court boldly extends the scope of the habeas statute to the four corners of the earth. The consequence of this holding, as applied to aliens outside the country, is breathtaking. It permits an alien captured in a foreign theater of active combat to bring a §2241 petition against the Secretary of Defense. Over the course of the last century, the United States has held millions of alien prisoners abroad. A great many of these prisoners would no doubt have complained about the circumstances of their capture and the terms of their confinement. The military is currently detaining over 600 prisoners at Guantanamo Bay alone; each detainee undoubtedly has complaints — real or contrived — about those terms and circumstances. The Court's unheralded expansion of federal-court jurisdiction is not even mitigated by a comforting assurance that the legion of ensuing claims will be easily resolved on the merits.

Today's carefree Court disregards, without a word of acknowledgment, the dire warning of a more circumspect Court in *Eisentrager:* "To grant the writ to these prisoners might mean that our army must transport them across the seas for hearing. This would require allocation for shipping space, guarding personnel, billeting and rations. It might also require transportation for whatever witnesses the prisoners desired to call as well as transportation for those necessary to defend legality of the sentence. The writ, since it is held to be a matter of right, would be equally available to enemies during active hostilities as in the present twilight between war and peace. Such trials would hamper the war effort and bring aid and comfort to the enemy. They would diminish the prestige of our commanders, not only with enemies but with wavering neutrals. It would be difficult to devise more effective fettering of a field commander than to allow the very enemies he is ordered to reduce to submission to call him to account in his own civil courts and divert his efforts and attention from the military offensive abroad to the legal defensive at home. Nor is it unlikely that the result of such enemy litigiousness would be a conflict between judicial and military opinion highly comforting to enemies of the United States."

Departure from our rule of stare decisis in statutory cases is always extraordinary; it ought to be unthinkable when the departure has a potentially harmful effect upon the Nation's conduct of a war. The Commander in Chief and his subordinates had every reason to expect that the internment of combatants at Guantanamo Bay would not have the consequence of bringing the cumbersome machinery of our domestic courts into military affairs. Congress is in session. If it wished to change federal judges' habeas jurisdiction from what this Court had previously held that to be, it could have done so. And it could have done so by intelligent revision of the statute, instead of by today's clumsy, countertextual reinterpretation that confers upon wartime prisoners greater habeas rights than domestic detainees. For this Court to create such a monstrous scheme in time of war, and in frustration of our military commanders' reliance upon clearly stated prior law, is judicial adventurism of the worst sort. I dissent.

In 2005, in response to Rasul v. Bush, Congress enacted the Detainee Treatment Act, which provided that those held in Guantánamo shall not have access to federal courts via a writ of habeas corpus; they must go through military commissions and then seek review in the District of Columbia Circuit.[71] In Hamdan v. Rumsfeld, 548 U.S. 557 (2006), the Supreme Court ruled that this provision applies only prospectively, not retroactively, to those petitions that already were pending in federal court at the time that the law was enacted.

In the fall of 2006, Congress responded by enacting the Military Commissions Act of 2006, which makes clear that the restrictions on habeas corpus in the Detainee Treatment Act apply retroactively.[72] The act provides, "No court, justice, or judge shall have jurisdiction to hear or consider an application for a writ of habeas corpus filed by or on behalf of an alien detained by the United States who has been determined by the United States to have been properly detained as an enemy combatant or is awaiting such determination."[73] The act is explicit about its retroactive application and says that it "shall apply to all cases, without exception, pending on or after the date of the enactment of this Act which relate to any aspect of the detention, transfer, treatment, trial, or conditions of detention of an alien detained by the United States since September 11, 2001."[74]

In Boumediene v. Bush, the Supreme Court declared this unconstitutional as an impermissible suspension of the writ of habeas corpus.

---

71. 119 Stat. 2739, codified at 10 U.S.C. §801.
72. Pub. L. No. 109-366, 120 Stat. 2600 (2006).
73. 28 U.S.C. §2241(e).
74. *Id.*

BOUMEDIENE v. BUSH

553 U.S. 723 (2008)

Justice KENNEDY delivered the opinion of the Court.

Petitioners are aliens designated as enemy combatants and detained at the United States Naval Station at Guantanamo Bay, Cuba. There are others detained there, also aliens, who are not parties to this suit.

Petitioners present a question not resolved by our earlier cases relating to the detention of aliens at Guantanamo: whether they have the constitutional privilege of habeas corpus, a privilege not to be withdrawn except in conformance with the Suspension Clause, Art. I, §9, cl. 2. We hold these petitioners do have the habeas corpus privilege. Congress has enacted a statute, the Detainee Treatment Act of 2005 (DTA), that provides certain procedures for review of the detainees' status. We hold that those procedures are not an adequate and effective substitute for habeas corpus. Therefore §7 of the Military Commissions Act of 2006 (MCA), operates as an unconstitutional suspension of the writ. We do not address whether the President has authority to detain these petitioners nor do we hold that the writ must issue. These and other questions regarding the legality of the detention are to be resolved in the first instance by the District Court.

I

Under the Authorization for Use of Military Force (AUMF), the President is authorized "to use all necessary and appropriate force against those nations, organizations, or persons he determines planned, authorized, committed, or aided the terrorist attacks that occurred on September 11, 2001, or harbored such organizations or persons, in order to prevent any future acts of international terrorism against the United States by such nations, organizations or persons."

In Hamdi v. Rumsfeld (2004), five Members of the Court recognized that detention of individuals who fought against the United States in Afghanistan "for the duration of the particular conflict in which they were captured, is so fundamental and accepted an incident to war as to be an exercise of the 'necessary and appropriate force' Congress has authorized the President to use." After Hamdi, the Deputy Secretary of Defense established Combatant Status Review Tribunals (CSRTs) to determine whether individuals detained at Guantanamo were "enemy combatants," as the Department defines that term. A later memorandum established procedures to implement the CSRTs. The Government maintains these procedures were designed to comply with the due process requirements identified by the plurality in Hamdi.

Interpreting the AUMF, the Department of Defense ordered the detention of these petitioners, and they were transferred to Guantanamo. Some of these individuals were apprehended on the battlefield in Afghanistan, others in places as far away from there as Bosnia and Gambia. All are foreign nationals, but none is a citizen of a nation now at war with the United States. Each denies he is a member of the al Qaeda terrorist network that carried out the September 11 attacks or of the Taliban regime that provided sanctuary for al Qaeda. Each petitioner appeared before a separate CSRT; was determined to be an enemy combatant; and has sought a writ of habeas corpus in the United States District Court for the District of Columbia.

The first actions commenced in February 2002. We granted certiorari and reversed, holding that 28 U.S.C. §2241 extended statutory habeas corpus jurisdiction to Guantanamo. See Rasul v. Bush (2004). After Rasul, petitioners' cases were consolidated and entertained in two separate proceedings. In the first set of cases, Judge Richard J. Leon granted the Government's motion to dismiss, holding that the detainees had no rights that could be vindicated in a habeas corpus action. In the second set of cases Judge Joyce Hens Green reached the opposite conclusion, holding the detainees had rights under the Due Process Clause of the Fifth Amendment.

While appeals were pending from the District Court decisions, Congress passed the DTA. Subsection (e) of §1005 of the DTA amended 28 U.S.C. §2241 to provide that "no court, justice, or judge shall have jurisdiction to hear or consider . . . an application for a writ of habeas corpus filed by or on behalf of an alien detained by the Department of Defense at Guantanamo Bay, Cuba." Section 1005 further provides that the Court of Appeals for the District of Columbia Circuit shall have "exclusive" jurisdiction to review decisions of the CSRTs. Ibid.

In Hamdan v. Rumsfeld (2006), the Court held this provision did not apply to cases (like petitioners') pending when the DTA was enacted. Congress responded by passing the MCA.

II

As a threshold matter, we must decide whether MCA §7 denies the federal courts jurisdiction to hear habeas corpus actions pending at the time of its enactment. We hold the statute does deny that jurisdiction, so that, if the statute is valid, petitioners' cases must be dismissed.

As amended by the terms of the MCA, 28 U.S.C.A. §2241(e) now provides:

> (1) No court, justice, or judge shall have jurisdiction to hear or consider an application for a writ of habeas corpus filed by or on behalf of an alien detained by the United States who has been determined by the United States to have been properly detained as an enemy combatant or is awaiting such determination.
>
> (2) Except as provided in [§§1005(e)(2) and (e)(3) of the DTA] no court, justice, or judge shall have jurisdiction to hear or consider any other action against the United States or its agents relating to any aspect of the detention, transfer, treatment, trial, or conditions of confinement of an alien who is or was detained by the United States and has been determined by the United States to have been properly detained as an enemy combatant or is awaiting such determination.

Section 7(b) of the MCA provides the effective date for the amendment of §2241(e). It states: "The amendment made by [MCA §7(a)] shall take effect on the date of the enactment of this Act, and shall apply to all cases, without exception, pending on or after the date of the enactment of this Act which relate to any aspect of the detention, transfer, treatment, trial, or conditions of detention of an alien detained by the United States since September 11, 2001."

If this ongoing dialogue between and among the branches of Government is to be respected, we cannot ignore that the MCA was a direct response to Hamdan's holding that the DTA's jurisdiction-stripping provision had no application to pending cases. The Court of Appeals was correct to take note of the legislative history when construing the statute, and we agree with its conclusion that the MCA deprives the federal courts of jurisdiction to entertain the habeas corpus actions now before us.

III

In deciding the constitutional questions now presented we must determine whether petitioners are barred from seeking the writ or invoking the protections of the Suspension Clause either because of their status, i.e., petitioners' designation by the Executive Branch as enemy combatants, or their physical location, i.e., their presence at Guantanamo Bay. The Government contends that noncitizens designated as enemy combatants and detained in territory located outside our Nation's borders have no constitutional rights and no privilege of habeas corpus. Petitioners contend they do have cognizable constitutional rights and that Congress, in seeking to eliminate recourse to habeas corpus as a means to assert those rights, acted in violation of the Suspension Clause.

A

The Framers viewed freedom from unlawful restraint as a fundamental precept of liberty, and they understood the writ of habeas corpus as a vital instrument to secure that freedom. Experience taught, however, that the common-law writ all too often had been insufficient to guard against the abuse of monarchial power. That history counseled the necessity for specific language in the Constitution to secure the writ and ensure its place in our legal system.

That the Framers considered the writ a vital instrument for the protection of individual liberty is evident from the care taken to specify the limited grounds for its suspension: "The Privilege of the Writ of Habeas Corpus shall not be suspended, unless when in Cases of Rebellion or Invasion the public Safety may require it." Art. I, §9, cl. 2. The word "privilege" was used, perhaps, to avoid mentioning some rights to the exclusion of others. (Indeed, the only mention of the term "right" in the Constitution, as ratified, is in its clause giving Congress the power to protect the rights of authors and inventors. See Art. I, §8, cl. 8.) Surviving accounts of the ratification debates provide additional evidence that the Framers deemed the writ to be an essential mechanism in the separation-of-powers scheme.

In our own system the Suspension Clause is designed to protect against these cyclical abuses. The Clause protects the rights of the detained by a means consistent with the essential design of the Constitution. It ensures that, except during periods of formal suspension, the Judiciary will have a time-tested device, the writ, to maintain the "delicate balance of governance" that is itself the surest safeguard of liberty. The Clause protects the rights of the detained by affirming the duty and authority of the Judiciary to call the jailer to account.

B

The broad historical narrative of the writ and its function is central to our analysis, but we seek guidance as well from founding-era authorities addressing the specific question before us: whether foreign nationals, apprehended and detained in distant countries during a time of serious threats to our Nation's security, may assert the privilege of the writ and seek its protection. The Court has been careful not to foreclose the possibility that the protections of the Suspension Clause have expanded along with post-1789 developments that define the present scope of the writ. But the analysis may begin with precedents as of 1789, for the Court has said that "at the absolute minimum" the Clause protects the writ as it existed when the Constitution was drafted and ratified.

To support their arguments, the parties in these cases have examined historical sources to construct a view of the common-law writ as it existed in 1789—as have amici whose expertise in legal history the Court has relied upon in the past. Diligent search by all parties reveals no certain conclusions. In none of the cases cited do we find that a common-law court would or would not have granted, or refused to hear for lack of jurisdiction, a petition for a writ of habeas corpus brought by a prisoner deemed an enemy combatant, under a standard like the one the Department of Defense has used in these cases, and when held in a territory, like Guantanamo, over which the Government has total military and civil control.

Both arguments are premised, however, upon the assumption that the historical record is complete and that the common law, if properly understood, yields a definite answer to the questions before us. There are reasons to doubt both assumptions. Recent scholarship points to the inherent shortcomings in the historical record. And given the unique status of Guantanamo Bay and the particular dangers of terrorism in the modern age, the common-law courts simply may not have confronted cases with close parallels to this one. We decline, therefore, to infer too much, one way or the other, from the lack of historical evidence on point. Cf. Brown v. Board of Education (1954) (noting evidence concerning the circumstances surrounding the adoption of the Fourteenth Amendment, discussed in the parties' briefs and uncovered through the Court's own investigation, "convince us that, although these sources cast some light, it is not enough to resolve the problem with which we are faced. At best, they are inconclusive").

IV

Drawing from its position that at common law the writ ran only to territories over which the Crown was sovereign, the Government says the Suspension Clause affords petitioners no rights because the United States does not claim sovereignty over the place of detention.

Guantanamo Bay is not formally part of the United States. And under the terms of the lease between the United States and Cuba, Cuba retains "ultimate sovereignty" over the territory while the United States exercises "complete jurisdiction and control." Under the terms of the 1934 Treaty, however, Cuba effectively has no rights as a sovereign until the parties agree to modification of the 1903 Lease Agreement or the United States abandons the base.

The United States contends, nevertheless, that Guantanamo is not within its sovereign control. This was the Government's position well before the events of September 11, 2001. And in other contexts the Court has held that questions of sovereignty are for the political branches to decide. Even if this were a treaty interpretation case that did not involve a political question, the President's construction of the lease agreement would be entitled to great respect.

We therefore do not question the Government's position that Cuba, not the United States, maintains sovereignty, in the legal and technical sense of the term, over Guantanamo Bay. But this does not end the analysis. Our cases do not hold it is improper for us to inquire into the objective degree of control the Nation asserts over foreign territory. Accordingly, for purposes of our analysis, we accept the Government's position that Cuba, and not the United States, retains de jure sovereignty over Guantanamo Bay. As we did in Rasul, however, we take notice of the obvious and uncontested fact that the United States, by virtue of its complete jurisdiction and control over the base, maintains de facto sovereignty over this territory.

Were we to hold that the present cases turn on the political question doctrine, we would be required first to accept the Government's premise that de jure sovereignty is the touchstone of habeas corpus jurisdiction. This premise, however, is unfounded. For the reasons indicated above, the history of common-law habeas corpus provides scant support for this proposition; and, for the reasons indicated below, that position would be inconsistent with our precedents and contrary to fundamental separation-of-powers principles.

A

The Court has discussed the issue of the Constitution's extraterritorial application on many occasions. These decisions undermine the Government's argument that, at least as applied to noncitizens, the Constitution necessarily stops where de jure sovereignty ends.

Practical considerations weighed heavily as well in Johnson v. Eisentrager (1950), where the Court addressed whether habeas corpus jurisdiction extended to enemy aliens who had been convicted of violating the laws of war. The prisoners were detained at Landsberg Prison in Germany during the Allied Powers' postwar occupation. The Court stressed the difficulties of ordering the Government to produce the prisoners in a habeas corpus proceeding. It "would require allocation of shipping space, guarding personnel, billeting and rations" and would damage the prestige of military commanders at a sensitive time.

True, the Court in Eisentrager denied access to the writ, and it noted the prisoners "at no relevant time were within any territory over which the United States is sovereign, and [that] the scenes of their offense, their capture, their trial and their punishment were all beyond the territorial jurisdiction of any court of the United States." The Government seizes upon this language as proof positive that the Eisentrager Court adopted a formalistic, sovereignty-based test for determining the reach of the Suspension Clause. We reject this reading for three reasons.

First, we do not accept the idea that the above-quoted passage from Eisentrager is the only authoritative language in the opinion and that all the rest is dicta. The Court's further determinations, based on practical considerations, were integral to Part II of its opinion and came before the decision announced its holding.

Second, because the United States lacked both de jure sovereignty and plenary control over Landsberg Prison, it is far from clear that the Eisentrager Court used the term sovereignty only in the narrow technical sense and not to connote the degree of control the military asserted over the facility. The Justices who decided Eisentrager would have understood sovereignty as a multifaceted concept. That the Court devoted a significant portion of Part II to a discussion of practical barriers to the running of the writ suggests that the Court was not concerned exclusively with the formal legal status of Landsberg Prison but also with the objective degree of control the United States asserted over it. Even if we assume the Eisentrager Court considered the United States' lack of formal legal sovereignty over Landsberg Prison as the decisive factor in that case, its holding is not inconsistent with a functional approach to questions of extraterritoriality. The formal legal status of a given territory affects, at least to some extent, the political branches' control over that territory. De jure sovereignty is a factor that bears upon which constitutional guarantees apply there.

Third, if the Government's reading of Eisentrager were correct, the opinion would have marked not only a change in, but a complete repudiation of, the Insular Cases' functional approach to questions of extraterritoriality. We cannot accept the Government's view. Nothing in Eisentrager says that de jure sovereignty is or has ever been the only relevant consideration in determining the geographic reach of the Constitution or of habeas corpus.

B

The Government's formal sovereignty-based test raises troubling separation-of-powers concerns as well. The political history of Guantanamo illustrates the deficiencies of this approach. The United States has maintained complete and uninterrupted control of the bay for over 100 years. Yet the Government's view is that the Constitution had no effect there, at least as to noncitizens, because the United States disclaimed sovereignty in the formal sense of the term. The necessary implication of the argument is that by surrendering formal sovereignty over any unincorporated territory to a third party, while at the same time entering into a lease that grants total control over the territory back to the United States, it would be possible for the political branches to govern without legal constraint.

Our basic charter cannot be contracted away like this. Even when the United States acts outside its borders, its powers are not "absolute and unlimited" but are subject "to such restrictions as are expressed in the Constitution." Abstaining from questions involving formal sovereignty and territorial governance is one thing. To hold the political branches have the power to switch the Constitution on or off at will is quite another. The former position reflects this Court's recognition that certain matters requiring political judgments are best left to the political branches. The latter would permit a striking anomaly in our tripartite system of government, leading to a regime in which Congress and the President, not this Court, say "what the law is." Marbury v. Madison (1803).

These concerns have particular bearing upon the Suspension Clause question in the cases now before us, for the writ of habeas corpus is itself an indispensable mechanism for monitoring the separation of powers. The test for determining the scope of this provision must not be subject to manipulation by those whose power it is designed to restrain.

C

In addition to the practical concerns discussed above, the Eisentrager Court found relevant that each petitioner:

> (a) is an enemy alien; (b) has never been or resided in the United States; (c) was captured outside of our territory and there held in military custody as a prisoner of war; (d) was tried and convicted by a Military Commission sitting outside the United States; (e) for offenses against laws of war committed outside the United States; (f) and is at all times imprisoned outside the United States.

Based on this language from Eisentrager, and the reasoning in our other extraterritoriality opinions, we conclude that at least three factors are relevant in determining the reach of the Suspension Clause: (1) the citizenship and status of the detainee and the adequacy of the process through which that status determination was made; (2) the nature of the sites where apprehension and then detention took place; and (3) the practical obstacles inherent in resolving the prisoner's entitlement to the writ.

Applying this framework, we note at the onset that the status of these detainees is a matter of dispute. The petitioners, like those in Eisentrager, are not American citizens. But the petitioners in Eisentrager did not contest, it seems, the Court's assertion that they were "enemy alien[s]." In the instant cases, by contrast, the detainees deny they are enemy combatants. They have been afforded some process in CSRT proceedings to determine their status; but, unlike in Eisentrager, there has been no trial by military commission for violations of the laws of war. The difference is not trivial. The records from the Eisentrager trials suggest that, well before the petitioners brought their case to this Court, there had been a rigorous adversarial process to test the legality of their detention. The Eisentrager petitioners were charged by a bill of particulars that made detailed factual allegations against them. To rebut the accusations, they were entitled to representation by counsel, allowed to introduce evidence on their own behalf, and permitted to cross-examine the prosecution's witnesses.

In comparison the procedural protections afforded to the detainees in the CSRT hearings are far more limited, and, we conclude, fall well short of the procedures and adversarial mechanisms that would eliminate the need for habeas corpus review. Although the detainee is assigned a "Personal Representative" to assist him during CSRT proceedings, the Secretary of the Navy's memorandum makes clear that person is not the detainee's lawyer or even his "advocate." The Government's evidence is accorded a presumption of validity. The detainee is allowed to present "reasonably available" evidence, but his ability to rebut the Government's evidence against him is limited by the circumstances of his confinement and his lack of counsel at this stage. And although the detainee can seek review of his status determination in the Court of Appeals, that review process cannot cure all defects in the earlier proceedings.

As to the second factor relevant to this analysis, the detainees here are similarly situated to the Eisentrager petitioners in that the sites of their apprehension and detention are technically outside the sovereign territory of the United States. As noted earlier, this is a factor that weighs against finding they have rights under the Suspension Clause. But there are critical differences between Landsberg Prison, circa 1950, and the United States Naval Station at Guantanamo Bay in 2008. Unlike its present control over the naval station, the United States' control over the prison in Germany was neither absolute nor indefinite. Like all parts of occupied Germany, the prison was under the jurisdiction of the combined Allied Forces. Guantanamo Bay, on the other hand, is no transient possession. In every practical sense Guantanamo is not abroad; it is within the constant jurisdiction of the United States.

As to the third factor, we recognize, as the Court did in Eisentrager, that there are costs to holding the Suspension Clause applicable in a case of military detention abroad. Habeas corpus proceedings may require expenditure of funds by the Government and may divert the attention of military personnel from other pressing tasks. While we are sensitive to these concerns, we do not find them dispositive. Compliance with any judicial process requires some incremental expenditure of resources. Yet civilian courts and the Armed Forces have functioned along side each other at various points in our history. The Government presents no credible arguments that the military mission at Guantanamo would be compromised if habeas corpus courts had jurisdiction to hear the detainees' claims. And in light of the plenary control the United States asserts over the base, none are apparent to us.

The situation in Eisentrager was far different, given the historical context and nature of the military's mission in post-War Germany. When hostilities in the European Theater came to an end, the United States became responsible for an occupation zone encompassing over 57,000 square miles with a population of 18 million. In addition to supervising massive reconstruction and aid efforts the American forces stationed in Germany faced potential security threats from a defeated enemy. In retrospect the post-War occupation may seem uneventful. But at the time Eisentrager was decided, the Court was right to be concerned about judicial interference with the military's efforts to contain "enemy elements, guerilla fighters, and 'werewolves.'"

Similar threats are not apparent here; nor does the Government argue that they are. The United States Naval Station at Guantanamo Bay consists of 45 square miles of land and water. The base has been used, at various points, to house migrants and refugees temporarily. At present, however, other than the detainees themselves, the only long-term residents are American military personnel, their families, and a small number of workers. The detainees have been deemed enemies of the United States. At present, dangerous as they may be if released, they are contained in a secure prison facility located on an isolated and heavily fortified military base.

There is no indication, furthermore, that adjudicating a habeas corpus petition would cause friction with the host government. No Cuban court has jurisdiction over American military personnel at Guantanamo or the enemy combatants detained there. While obligated to abide by the terms of the lease, the United States is, for all practical purposes, answerable to no other sovereign for its acts on the base. Were that not the case, or if the detention facility were located in an active theater of war, arguments that issuing the writ would be "impracticable or anomalous" would have more weight. Under the facts presented here, however, there are few practical barriers to the running of the writ. To the extent barriers arise, habeas corpus procedures likely can be modified to address them.

We hold that Art. I, §9, cl. 2, of the Constitution has full effect at Guantanamo Bay. If the privilege of habeas corpus is to be denied to the detainees now before us, Congress must act in accordance with the requirements of the Suspension Clause.

V

In light of this holding the question becomes whether the statute stripping jurisdiction to issue the writ avoids the Suspension Clause mandate because Congress has provided adequate substitute procedures for habeas corpus.

The gravity of the separation-of-powers issues raised by these cases and the fact that these detainees have been denied meaningful access to a judicial forum for a period of years render these cases exceptional.

Our case law does not contain extensive discussion of standards defining suspension of the writ or of circumstances under which suspension has occurred. This simply confirms the care Congress has taken throughout our Nation's history to preserve the writ and its function. Indeed, most of the major legislative enactments pertaining to habeas corpus have acted not to contract the writ's protection but to expand it or to hasten resolution of prisoners' claims.

We do not endeavor to offer a comprehensive summary of the requisites for an adequate substitute for habeas corpus. We do consider it uncontroversial, however, that the privilege of habeas corpus entitles the prisoner to a meaningful opportunity to demonstrate that he is being held pursuant to "the erroneous application or interpretation" of relevant law. And the habeas court must have the power to order the conditional release of an individual unlawfully detained — though release need not be the exclusive remedy and is not the appropriate one in every case in which the writ is granted.

Where a person is detained by executive order, rather than, say, after being tried and convicted in a court, the need for collateral review is most pressing. A criminal conviction in the usual course occurs after a judicial hearing before a tribunal disinterested in the outcome and committed to procedures designed to ensure its own independence. These dynamics are not inherent in executive detention orders or executive review procedures. In this context the need for habeas corpus is more urgent. The intended duration of the detention and the reasons for it bear upon the precise scope of the inquiry. Habeas corpus proceedings need not resemble a criminal trial, even when the detention is by executive order. But the writ must be effective. The habeas court must have sufficient authority to conduct a meaningful review of both the cause for detention and the Executive's power to detain.

To determine the necessary scope of habeas corpus review, therefore, we must assess the CSRT process, the mechanism through which petitioners' designation as enemy combatants became final. Whether one characterizes the CSRT process as direct review of the Executive's battlefield determination that the detainee is an enemy combatant — as the parties have and as we do — or as the first step in the collateral review of a battlefield determination makes no difference in a proper analysis of whether the procedures Congress put in place are an adequate substitute for habeas corpus. What matters is the sum total of procedural protections afforded to the detainee at all stages, direct and collateral.

Petitioners identify what they see as myriad deficiencies in the CSRTs. The most relevant for our purposes are the constraints upon the detainee's ability to rebut the factual basis for the Government's assertion that he is an enemy combatant. As already noted, at the CSRT stage the detainee has limited means to find or present evidence to challenge the Government's case against him. He does not have the assistance of counsel and may not be aware of the most critical allegations that the Government relied upon to order his detention. The detainee can confront witnesses that testify during the CSRT proceedings. But given that there are in effect no limits on the admission of hearsay evidence — the only requirement is that the tribunal deem the evidence "relevant and helpful," the detainee's opportunity to question witnesses is likely to be more theoretical than real.

Even if we were to assume that the CSRTs satisfy due process standards, it would not end our inquiry. Habeas corpus is a collateral process that exists, in Justice Holmes' words, to "cu[t] through all forms and g[o] to the very tissue of the structure. It comes in from the outside, not in subordination to the proceedings, and although every form may have been preserved opens the inquiry whether they have been more than an empty shell." Even when the procedures authorizing detention are structurally sound, the Suspension Clause remains applicable and the writ relevant.

Although we make no judgment as to whether the CSRTs, as currently constituted, satisfy due process standards, we agree with petitioners that, even when all the parties involved in this process act with diligence and in good faith, there is considerable risk of error in the tribunal's findings of fact. And given that the consequence of error may be detention of persons for the duration of hostilities that may last a generation or more, this is a risk too significant to ignore.

For the writ of habeas corpus, or its substitute, to function as an effective and proper remedy in this context, the court that conducts the habeas proceeding must have the means to correct errors that occurred during the CSRT proceedings. This includes some authority to assess the sufficiency of the Government's evidence against the detainee. It also must have the authority to admit and consider relevant exculpatory evidence that was not introduced during the earlier proceeding. Federal habeas petitioners long have had the means to supplement the record on review, even in the postconviction habeas setting. Here that opportunity is constitutionally required.

The extent of the showing required of the Government in these cases is a matter to be determined. We need not explore it further at this stage. We do hold that when the judicial power to issue habeas corpus properly is invoked the judicial officer must have adequate authority to make a determination in light of the relevant law and facts and to formulate and issue appropriate orders for relief, including, if necessary, an order directing the prisoner's release.

C

We now consider whether the DTA allows the Court of Appeals to conduct a proceeding meeting these standards. The DTA does not explicitly empower the Court of Appeals to order the applicant in a DTA review proceeding released should the court find that the standards and procedures used at his CSRT hearing were insufficient to justify detention. This is troubling. Yet, for present purposes, we can assume congressional silence permits a constitutionally required remedy.

The absence of a release remedy and specific language allowing AUMF challenges are not the only constitutional infirmities from which the statute potentially suffers, however. The more difficult question is whether the DTA permits the Court of Appeals to make requisite findings of fact. Assuming the DTA can be construed to allow the Court of Appeals to review or correct the CSRT's factual determinations, as opposed to merely certifying that the tribunal applied the correct standard of proof, we see no way to construe the statute to allow what is also constitutionally required in this context: an opportunity for the detainee to present relevant exculpatory evidence that was not made part of the record in the earlier proceedings.

On its face the statute allows the Court of Appeals to consider no evidence outside the CSRT record. Under the DTA the Court of Appeals has the power to review CSRT determinations by assessing the legality of standards and procedures. This implies the power to inquire into what happened at the CSRT hearing and, perhaps, to remedy certain deficiencies in that proceeding. But should the Court of Appeals determine that the CSRT followed appropriate and lawful standards and procedures, it will have reached the limits of its jurisdiction. There is no language in the DTA that can be construed to allow the Court of Appeals to admit and consider newly discovered evidence that could not have been made part of the CSRT record because it was unavailable to either the Government or the detainee when the CSRT made its findings. This evidence, however, may be critical to the detainee's argument that he is not an enemy combatant and there is no cause to detain him.

By foreclosing consideration of evidence not presented or reasonably available to the detainee at the CSRT proceedings, the DTA disadvantages the detainee by limiting the scope of collateral review to a record that may not be accurate or complete.

Although we do not hold that an adequate substitute must duplicate §2241 in all respects, it suffices that the Government has not established that the detainees' access to the statutory review provisions at issue is an adequate substitute for the writ of habeas corpus. MCA §7 thus effects an unconstitutional suspension of the writ. In view of our holding we need not discuss the reach of the writ with respect to claims of unlawful conditions of treatment or confinement.

VI

The real risks, the real threats, of terrorist attacks are constant and not likely soon to abate. The ways to disrupt our life and laws are so many and unforeseen that the Court should not attempt even some general catalogue of crises that might occur. Certain principles are apparent, however. Practical considerations and exigent circumstances inform the definition and reach of the law's writs, including habeas corpus. The cases and our tradition reflect this precept.

In cases involving foreign citizens detained abroad by the Executive, it likely would be both an impractical and unprecedented extension of judicial power to assume that habeas corpus would be available at the moment the prisoner is taken into custody. If and when habeas corpus jurisdiction applies, as it does in these cases, then proper deference can be accorded to reasonable procedures for screening and initial detention under lawful and proper conditions of confinement and treatment for a reasonable period of time. Domestic exigencies, furthermore, might also impose such onerous burdens on the Government that here, too, the Judicial Branch would be required to devise sensible rules for staying habeas corpus proceedings until the Government can comply with its requirements in a responsible way. Here, as is true with detainees apprehended abroad, a relevant consideration in determining the courts' role is whether there are suitable alternative processes in place to protect against the arbitrary exercise of governmental power.

The cases before us, however, do not involve detainees who have been held for a short period of time while awaiting their CSRT determinations. Were that the case, or were it probable that the Court of Appeals could complete a prompt review of their applications, the case for requiring temporary abstention or exhaustion of alternative remedies would be much stronger. These qualifications no longer pertain here. In some of these cases six years have elapsed without the judicial oversight that habeas corpus or an adequate substitute demands. And there has been no showing that the Executive faces such onerous burdens that it cannot respond to habeas corpus actions. To require these detainees to complete DTA review before proceeding with their habeas corpus actions would be to require additional months, if not years, of delay. The detainees in these cases are entitled to a prompt habeas corpus hearing.

Our decision today holds only that the petitioners before us are entitled to seek the writ; that the DTA review procedures are an inadequate substitute for habeas corpus; and that the petitioners in these cases need not exhaust the review procedures in the Court of Appeals before proceeding with their habeas actions in the District Court. The only law we identify as unconstitutional is MCA §7. Accordingly, both the DTA and the CSRT process remain intact. Our holding with regard to exhaustion should not be read to imply that a habeas court should intervene the moment an enemy combatant steps foot in a territory where the writ runs. The Executive is entitled to a reasonable period of time to determine a detainee's status before a court entertains that detainee's habeas corpus petition.

In considering both the procedural and substantive standards used to impose detention to prevent acts of terrorism, proper deference must be accorded to the political branches. There are further considerations, however. Security subsists, too, in fidelity to freedom's first principles. Chief among these are freedom from arbitrary and unlawful restraint and the personal liberty that is secured by adherence to the separation of powers. It is from these principles that the judicial authority to consider petitions for habeas corpus relief derives.

Our opinion does not undermine the Executive's powers as Commander in Chief. On the contrary, the exercise of those powers is vindicated, not eroded, when confirmed by the Judicial Branch. Within the Constitution's separation-of-powers structure, few exercises of judicial power are as legitimate or as necessary as the responsibility to hear challenges to the authority of the Executive to imprison a person. Some of these petitioners have been in custody for six years with no definitive judicial determination as to the legality of their detention. Their access to the writ is a necessity to determine the lawfulness of their status, even if, in the end, they do not obtain the relief they seek.

Because our Nation's past military conflicts have been of limited duration, it has been possible to leave the outer boundaries of war powers undefined. If, as some fear, terrorism continues to pose dangerous threats to us for years to come, the Court might not have this luxury. This result is not inevitable, however. The political branches, consistent with their independent obligations to interpret and uphold the Constitution, can engage in a genuine debate about how best to preserve constitutional values while protecting the Nation from terrorism.

It bears repeating that our opinion does not address the content of the law that governs petitioners' detention. That is a matter yet to be determined. We hold that petitioners may invoke the fundamental procedural protections of habeas corpus. The laws and Constitution are designed to survive, and remain in force, in extraordinary times. Liberty and security can be reconciled; and in our system they are reconciled within the framework of the law. The Framers decided that habeas corpus, a right of first importance, must be a part of that framework, a part of that law.

Justice SOUTER, with whom Justice GINSBURG and Justice BREYER join, concurring.

I join the Court's opinion in its entirety and add this afterword only to emphasize two things one might overlook after reading the dissents.

Four years ago, this Court in Rasul v. Bush (2004) held that statutory habeas jurisdiction extended to claims of foreign nationals imprisoned by the United States at Guantanamo Bay, "to determine the legality of the Executive's potentially indefinite detention" of them. Subsequent legislation eliminated the statutory habeas jurisdiction over these claims, so that now there must be constitutionally based jurisdiction or none at all. But no one who reads the Court's opinion in Rasul could seriously doubt that the jurisdictional question must be answered the same way in purely constitutional cases, given the Court's reliance on the historical background of habeas generally in answering the statutory question.

A second fact insufficiently appreciated by the dissents is the length of the disputed imprisonments, some of the prisoners represented here today having been locked up for six years. Hence the hollow ring when the dissenters suggest that the Court is somehow precipitating the judiciary into reviewing claims that the military (subject to appeal to the Court of Appeals for the District of Columbia Circuit) could handle within some reasonable period of time. These suggestions of judicial haste are all the more out of place given the Court's realistic acknowledgment that in periods of exigency the tempo of any habeas review must reflect the immediate peril facing the country. After six years of sustained executive detentions in Guantanamo, subject to habeas jurisdiction but without any actual habeas scrutiny, today's decision is no judicial victory, but an act of perseverance in trying to make habeas review, and the obligation of the courts to provide it, mean something of value both to prisoners and to the Nation.

Chief Justice ROBERTS, with whom Justice SCALIA, Justice THOMAS, and Justice ALITO join, dissenting.

Today the Court strikes down as inadequate the most generous set of procedural protections ever afforded aliens detained by this country as enemy combatants. The political branches crafted these procedures amidst an ongoing military conflict, after much careful investigation and thorough debate. The Court rejects them today out of hand, without bothering to say what due process rights the detainees possess, without explaining how the statute fails to vindicate those rights, and before a single petitioner has even attempted to avail himself of the law's operation. And to what effect? The majority merely replaces a review system designed by the people's representatives with a set of shapeless procedures to be defined by federal courts at some future date. One cannot help but think, after surveying the modest practical results of the majority's ambitious opinion, that this decision is not really about the detainees at all, but about control of federal policy regarding enemy combatants.

The majority is adamant that the Guantanamo detainees are entitled to the protections of habeas corpus — its opinion begins by deciding that question. I regard the issue as a difficult one, primarily because of the unique and unusual jurisdictional status of Guantanamo Bay. I nonetheless agree with Justice Scalia's analysis of our precedents and the pertinent history of the writ, and accordingly join his dissent. The important point for me, however, is that the Court should have resolved these cases on other grounds. Habeas is most fundamentally a procedural right, a mechanism for contesting the legality of executive detention. The critical threshold question in these cases, prior to any inquiry about the writ's scope, is whether the system the political branches designed protects whatever rights the detainees may possess. If so, there is no need for any additional process, whether called "habeas" or something else.

Congress entrusted that threshold question in the first instance to the Court of Appeals for the District of Columbia Circuit, as the Constitution surely allows Congress to do. But before the D.C. Circuit has addressed the issue, the Court cashiers the statute, and without answering this critical threshold question itself. The Court does eventually get around to asking whether review under the DTA is, as the Court frames it, an "adequate substitute" for habeas, but even then its opinion fails to determine what rights the detainees possess and whether the DTA system satisfies them. The majority instead compares the undefined DTA process to an equally undefined habeas right — one that is to be given shape only in the future by district courts on a case-by-case basis. This whole approach is misguided.

It is also fruitless. How the detainees' claims will be decided now that the DTA is gone is anybody's guess. But the habeas process the Court mandates will most likely end up looking a lot like the DTA system it replaces, as the district court judges shaping it will have to reconcile review of the prisoners' detention with the undoubted need to protect the American people from the terrorist threat — precisely the challenge Congress undertook in drafting the DTA. All that today's opinion has done is shift responsibility for those sensitive foreign policy and national security decisions from the elected branches to the Federal Judiciary.

I believe the system the political branches constructed adequately protects any constitutional rights aliens captured abroad and detained as enemy combatants may enjoy. I therefore would dismiss these cases on that ground. With all respect for the contrary views of the majority, I must dissent.

The majority's overreaching is particularly egregious given the weakness of its objections to the DTA. Simply put, the Court's opinion fails on its own terms. The majority strikes down the statute because it is not an "adequate substitute" for habeas review, but fails to show what rights the detainees have that cannot be vindicated by the DTA system.

Because the central purpose of habeas corpus is to test the legality of executive detention, the writ requires most fundamentally an Article III court able to hear the prisoner's claims and, when necessary, order release. Beyond that, the process a given prisoner is entitled to receive depends on the circumstances and the rights of the prisoner. After much hemming and hawing, the majority appears to concede that the DTA provides an Article III court competent to order release. The only issue in dispute is the process the Guantanamo prisoners are entitled to use to test the legality of their detention. Hamdi concluded that American citizens detained as enemy combatants are entitled to only limited process, and that much of that process could be supplied by a military tribunal, with review to follow in an Article III court. That is precisely the system we have here. It is adequate to vindicate whatever due process rights petitioners may have.

The Court reaches the opposite conclusion partly because it misreads the statute. The majority appears not to understand how the review system it invalidates actually works — specifically, how CSRT review and review by the D.C. Circuit fit together. After briefly acknowledging in its recitation of the facts that the Government designed the CSRTs "to comply with the due process requirements identified by the plurality in Hamdi," the Court proceeds to dismiss the tribunal proceedings as no more than a suspect method used by the Executive for determining the status of the detainees in the first instance.

The majority is equally wrong to characterize the CSRTs as part of that initial determination process. They are instead a means for detainees to challenge the Government's determination. The Executive designed the CSRTs to mirror Army Regulation 190-8, the very procedural model the plurality in Hamdi said provided the type of process an enemy combatant could expect from a habeas court. The CSRTs operate much as habeas courts would if hearing the detainee's collateral challenge for the first time: They gather evidence, call witnesses, take testimony, and render a decision on the legality of the Government's detention. If the CSRT finds a particular detainee has been improperly held, it can order release.

The majority insists that even if "the CSRTs satisf[ied] due process standards," full habeas review would still be necessary, because habeas is a collateral remedy available even to prisoners "detained pursuant to the most rigorous proceedings imaginable." This comment makes sense only if the CSRTs are incorrectly viewed as a method used by the Executive for determining the prisoners' status, and not as themselves part of the collateral review to test the validity of that determination. The majority can deprecate the importance of the CSRTs only by treating them as something they are not.

In short, the Hamdi plurality concluded that this type of review would be enough to satisfy due process, even for citizens. Congress followed the Court's lead, only to find itself the victim of a constitutional bait and switch.

Given the statutory scheme the political branches adopted, and given Hamdi, it simply will not do for the majority to dismiss the CSRT procedures as "far more limited" than those used in military trials, and therefore beneath the level of process "that would eliminate the need for habeas corpus review." The question is not how much process the CSRTs provide in comparison to other modes of adjudication. The question is whether the CSRT procedures—coupled with the judicial review specified by the DTA—provide the "basic process" Hamdi said the Constitution affords American citizens detained as enemy combatants.

To what basic process are these detainees due as habeas petitioners? We have said that "at the absolute minimum," the Suspension Clause protects the writ " 'as it existed in 1789.' " The majority admits that a number of historical authorities suggest that at the time of the Constitution's ratification, "common-law courts abstained altogether from matters involving prisoners of war." If this is accurate, the process provided prisoners under the DTA is plainly more than sufficient—it allows alleged combatants to challenge both the factual and legal bases of their detentions.

Assuming the constitutional baseline is more robust, the DTA still provides adequate process, and by the majority's own standards. The DTA - system—CSRT review of the Executive's determination followed by D.C. Circuit review for sufficiency of the evidence and the constitutionality of the CSRT process—meets these criteria.

All told, the DTA provides the prisoners held at Guantanamo Bay adequate opportunity to contest the bases of their detentions, which is all habeas corpus need allow. The DTA provides more opportunity and more process, in fact, than that afforded prisoners of war or any other alleged enemy combatants in history.

Despite these guarantees, the Court finds the DTA system an inadequate habeas substitute, for one central reason: Detainees are unable to introduce at the appeal stage exculpatory evidence discovered after the conclusion of their CSRT proceedings. The Court hints darkly that the DTA may suffer from other infirmities, but it does not bother to name them, making a response a bit difficult. As it stands, I can only assume the Court regards the supposed defect it did identify as the gravest of the lot.

If this is the most the Court can muster, the ice beneath its feet is thin indeed. As noted, the CSRT procedures provide ample opportunity for detainees to introduce exculpatory evidence—whether documentary in nature or from live witnesses—before the military tribunals. And if their ability to introduce such evidence is denied contrary to the Constitution or laws of the United States, the D.C. Circuit has the authority to say so on review.

For all its eloquence about the detainees' right to the writ, the Court makes no effort to elaborate how exactly the remedy it prescribes will differ from the procedural protections detainees enjoy under the DTA. The Court objects to the detainees' limited access to witnesses and classified material, but proposes no alternatives of its own. Indeed, it simply ignores the many difficult questions its holding presents. What, for example, will become of the CSRT process? The majority says federal courts should generally refrain from entertaining detainee challenges until after the petitioner's CSRT proceeding has finished. But to what deference, if any, is that CSRT determination entitled?

There are other problems. Take witness availability. What makes the majority think witnesses will become magically available when the review procedure is labeled "habeas"? Will the location of most of these witnesses change—will they suddenly become easily susceptible to service of process? Or will subpoenas issued by American habeas courts run to Basra? And if they did, how would they be enforced? Speaking of witnesses, will detainees be able to call active-duty military officers as witnesses? If not, why not?

The majority has no answers for these difficulties. What it does say leaves open the distinct possibility that its "habeas" remedy will, when all is said and done, end up looking a great deal like the DTA review it rejects.

The majority rests its decision on abstract and hypothetical concerns. Step back and consider what, in the real world, Congress and the Executive have actually granted aliens captured by our Armed Forces overseas and found to be enemy combatants:

- The right to hear the bases of the charges against them, including a summary of any classified evidence.

- The ability to challenge the bases of their detention before military tribunals modeled after Geneva Convention procedures. Some 38 detainees have been released as a result of this process.
- The right, before the CSRT, to testify, introduce evidence, call witnesses, question those the Government calls, and secure release, if and when appropriate.
- The right to the aid of a personal representative in arranging and presenting their cases before a CSRT.
- Before the D.C. Circuit, the right to employ counsel, challenge the factual record, contest the lower tribunal's legal determinations, ensure compliance with the Constitution and laws, and secure release, if any errors below establish their entitlement to such relief.

In sum, the DTA satisfies the majority's own criteria for assessing adequacy. This statutory scheme provides the combatants held at Guantanamo greater procedural protections than have ever been afforded alleged enemy detainees—whether citizens or aliens—in our national history.

So who has won? Not the detainees. The Court's analysis leaves them with only the prospect of further litigation to determine the content of their new habeas right, followed by further litigation to resolve their particular cases, followed by further litigation before the D.C. Circuit—where they could have started had they invoked the DTA procedure. Not Congress, whose attempt to "determine—through democratic means—how best" to balance the security of the American people with the detainees' liberty interests, has been unceremoniously brushed aside. Not the Great Writ, whose majesty is hardly enhanced by its extension to a jurisdictionally quirky outpost, with no tangible benefit to anyone. Not the rule of law, unless by that is meant the rule of lawyers, who will now arguably have a greater role than military and intelligence officials in shaping policy for alien enemy combatants. And certainly not the American people, who today lose a bit more control over the conduct of this Nation's foreign policy to unelected, politically unaccountable judges.

Justice SCALIA, with whom THE CHIEF JUSTICE, Justice THOMAS, and Justice ALITO join, dissenting.

Today, for the first time in our Nation's history, the Court confers a constitutional right to habeas corpus on alien enemies detained abroad by our military forces in the course of an ongoing war. The Chief Justice's dissent, which I join, shows that the procedures prescribed by Congress in the Detainee Treatment Act provide the essential protections that habeas corpus guarantees; there has thus been no suspension of the writ, and no basis exists for judicial intervention beyond what the Act allows. My problem with today's opinion is more fundamental still: The writ of habeas corpus does not, and never has, run in favor of aliens abroad; the Suspension Clause thus has no application, and the Court's intervention in this military matter is entirely ultra vires.

I shall devote most of what will be a lengthy opinion to the legal errors contained in the opinion of the Court. Contrary to my usual practice, however, I think it appropriate to begin with a description of the disastrous consequences of what the Court has done today.

America is at war with radical Islamists. The enemy began by killing Americans and American allies abroad: 241 at the Marine barracks in Lebanon, 19 at the Khobar Towers in Dhahran, 224 at our embassies in Dar es Salaam and Nairobi, and 17 on the USS Cole in Yemen. On September 11, 2001, the enemy brought the battle to American soil, killing 2,749 at the Twin Towers in New York City, 184 at the Pentagon in Washington, D. C., and 40 in Pennsylvania. It has threatened further attacks against our homeland; one need only walk about buttressed and barricaded Washington, or board a plane anywhere in the country, to know that the threat is a serious one. Our Armed Forces are now in the field against the enemy, in Afghanistan and Iraq. Last week, 13 of our countrymen in arms were killed.

The game of bait-and-switch that today's opinion plays upon the Nation's Commander in Chief will make the war harder on us. It will almost certainly cause more Americans to be killed. That consequence would be tolerable if necessary to preserve a time-honored legal principle vital to our constitutional Republic. But it is this Court's blatant abandonment of such a principle that produces the decision today. The President relied on our settled precedent in Johnson v. Eisentrager (1950), when he established the prison at Guantanamo Bay for enemy aliens. Citing that case, the President's Office of Legal Counsel advised him "that the great weight of legal authority indicates that a federal district court could not properly exercise habeas jurisdiction over an alien detained at [Guantanamo Bay]." Memorandum from Patrick F. Philbin and John C. Yoo, Deputy Assistant Attorneys General, Office of Legal Counsel, to William J. Haynes II, General Counsel, Dept. of Defense (Dec. 28, 2001). Had the law been otherwise, the military surely would not have transported prisoners there, but would have kept them in Afghanistan, transferred them to another of our foreign military bases, or turned them over to allies for detention. Those other facilities might well have been worse for the detainees themselves.

In the long term, then, the Court's decision today accomplishes little, except perhaps to reduce the well-being of enemy combatants that the Court ostensibly seeks to protect. In the short term, however, the decision is devastating. At least 30 of those prisoners hitherto released from Guantanamo Bay have returned to the battlefield. See S.Rep. No. 110-90, pt. 7, p. 13 (2007) (Minority Views of Sens. Kyl, Sessions, Graham, Cornyn, and Coburn) (hereinafter Minority Report). Some have been captured or killed. See also Mintz, Released Detainees Rejoining the Fight, Washington Post, Oct. 22, 2004, pp. A1, A12. But others have succeeded in carrying on their atrocities against innocent civilians. In one case, a detainee released from Guantanamo Bay masterminded the kidnapping of two Chinese dam workers, one of whom was later shot to death when used as a human shield against Pakistani commandoes. Another former detainee promptly resumed his post as a senior Taliban commander and murdered a United Nations engineer and three Afghan soldiers. Mintz, supra. Still another murdered an Afghan judge. It was reported only last month that a released detainee carried out a suicide bombing against Iraqi soldiers in Mosul, Iraq. See White, Ex-Guantanamo Detainee Joined Iraq Suicide Attack, Washington Post, May 8, 2008, p. A18.

These, mind you, were detainees whom the military had concluded were not enemy combatants. Their return to the kill illustrates the incredible difficulty of assessing who is and who is not an enemy combatant in a foreign theater of operations where the environment does not lend itself to rigorous evidence collection. Astoundingly, the Court today raises the bar, requiring military officials to appear before civilian courts and defend their decisions under procedural and evidentiary rules that go beyond what Congress has specified. As The Chief Justice's dissent makes clear, we have no idea what those procedural and evidentiary rules are, but they will be determined by civil courts and (in the Court's contemplation at least) will be more detainee-friendly than those now applied, since otherwise there would no reason to hold the congressionally prescribed procedures unconstitutional. If they impose a higher standard of proof (from foreign battlefields) than the current procedures require, the number of the enemy returned to combat will obviously increase.

But even when the military has evidence that it can bring forward, it is often foolhardy to release that evidence to the attorneys representing our enemies. And one escalation of procedures that the Court is clear about is affording the detainees increased access to witnesses (perhaps troops serving in Afghanistan?) and to classified information. During the 1995 prosecution of Omar Abdel Rahman, federal prosecutors gave the names of 200 unindicted co-conspirators to the "Blind Sheik's" defense lawyers; that information was in the hands of Osama Bin Laden within two weeks. In another case, trial testimony revealed to the enemy that the United States had been monitoring their cellular network, whereupon they promptly stopped using it, enabling more of them to evade capture and continue their atrocities.

And today it is not just the military that the Court elbows aside. A mere two Terms ago in Hamdan v. Rumsfeld (2006), when the Court held (quite amazingly) that the Detainee Treatment Act of 2005 had not stripped habeas jurisdiction over Guantanamo petitioners' claims, four Members of today's five-Justice majority joined an opinion saying the following: "Nothing prevents the President from returning to Congress to seek the authority [for trial by military commission] he believes necessary."

Turns out they were just kidding. For in response, Congress, at the President's request, quickly enacted the Military Commissions Act, emphatically reasserting that it did not want these prisoners filing habeas petitions. It is therefore clear that Congress and the Executive — both political branches — have determined that limiting the role of civilian courts in adjudicating whether prisoners captured abroad are properly detained is important to success in the war that some 190,000 of our men and women are now fighting. As the Solicitor General argued, "the Military Commissions Act and the Detainee Treatment Act . . . represent an effort by the political branches to strike an appropriate balance between the need to preserve liberty and the need to accommodate the weighty and sensitive governmental interests in ensuring that those who have in fact fought with the enemy during a war do not return to battle against the United States."

But it does not matter. The Court today decrees that no good reason to accept the judgment of the other two branches is "apparent." "The Government," it declares, "presents no credible arguments that the military mission at Guantanamo would be compromised if habeas corpus courts had jurisdiction to hear the detainees' claims." What competence does the Court have to second-guess the judgment of Congress and the President on such a point? None whatever. But the Court blunders in nonetheless. Henceforth, as today's opinion makes unnervingly clear, how to handle enemy prisoners in this war will ultimately lie with the branch that knows least about the national security concerns that the subject entails.

Today the Court warps our Constitution in a way that goes beyond the narrow issue of the reach of the Suspension Clause, invoking judicially brainstormed separation-of-powers principles to establish a manipulable "functional" test for the extraterritorial reach of habeas corpus (and, no doubt, for the extraterritorial reach of other constitutional protections as well). It blatantly misdescribes important precedents, most conspicuously Justice Jackson's opinion for the Court in Johnson v. Eisentrager. It breaks a chain of precedent as old as the common law that prohibits judicial inquiry into detentions of aliens abroad absent statutory authorization. And, most tragically, it sets our military commanders the impossible task of proving to a civilian court, under whatever standards this Court devises in the future, that evidence supports the confinement of each and every enemy prisoner.

The Nation will live to regret what the Court has done today. I dissent.

However, since *Boumediene*, the United States Court of Appeals for the District of Columbia Circuit has denied relief in every case. Following the Supreme Court's decision, federal district court judges in the District of Columbia granted relief to a number of Guantanamo detainees. But in each instance so far, the D.C. Circuit reversed, and then the Supreme Court denied review. 559 U.S. 1005.

For example, in Kiyemba v. Obama, a federal district court ordered the release of five Chinese Muslim (Uighur) detainees who had been cleared for release from Guantánamo. But the D.C. Circuit reversed, 561 F.3d 509 (D.C. Cir. 2009), and held that a federal judge lacks the power to order the transfer of Guantánamo detainees to the United States. Subsequently, in the same case, the D.C. Circuit, 605 F.3d 1046 (D.C. Cir. 2010), denied federal judges the power to regulate transfers of Guantánamo detainees to elsewhere in the world. The Supreme Court denied review. 131 S. Ct. 1631 (2011).

In Latif v. Obama, 666 F.3d 746 (D.C. Cir. 2011), the D.C. Circuit ruled that federal district judges must "presume" that government intelligence reports used to justify detention are reliable and accurate. Adnan Farhan Abdul Latif, a Yemeni man, was picked up near the border between Afghanistan and Pakistan in December 2001. The government has relied on an intelligence report prepared at the time to justify holding him ever since. The district court ordered his release saying that the report was not sufficiently reliable to warrant keeping him imprisoned. But the D.C. Circuit, while acknowledging problems with the report, said that it was entitled to "a presumption of regularity." In dissent, D.C. Circuit Judge David Tatel said that this would mean that the government would win virtually every case and that "it is hard to see what is left of the Supreme Court's command in Boumediene." The Supreme Court denied certiorari.

TABLE OF CASES

Italics indicate principal cases.

INDEX